Hornbook Series and Basic Legal Texts
Nutshell Series

and

Black Letter Series

of

WEST PUBLISHING COMPANY
P.O. Box 64526
St. Paul, Minnesota 55164–0526

Accounting

FARIS' ACCOUNTING AND LAW IN A NUT-SHELL, 377 pages, 1984. Softcover. (Text)

Administrative Law

AMAN AND MAYTON'S HORNBOOK ON AD-MINISTRATIVE LAW, Approximately 750 pages, 1993. (Text)

GELLHORN AND LEVIN'S ADMINISTRATIVE LAW AND PROCESS IN A NUTSHELL, Third Edition, 479 pages, 1990. Soft-cover. (Text)

Admiralty

MARAIST'S ADMIRALTY IN A NUTSHELL, Second Edition, 379 pages, 1988. Soft-cover. (Text)

SCHOENBAUM'S HORNBOOK ON ADMIRAL-TY AND MARITIME LAW, Student Edi-tion, 692 pages, 1987 with 1992 pocket part. (Text)

Agency—Partnership

REUSCHLEIN AND GREGORY'S HORNBOOK ON THE LAW OF AGENCY AND PARTNER-SHIP, Second Edition, 683 pages, 1990. (Text)

STEFFEN'S AGENCY-PARTNERSHIP IN A NUTSHELL, 364 pages, 1977. Softcover. (Text)

NOLAN–HALEY'S ALTERNATIVE DISPUTE RESOLUTION IN A NUTSHELL, 298 pages, 1992. Softcover. (Text)

RISKIN'S DISPUTE RESOLUTION FOR LAW-YERS VIDEO TAPES, 1992. (Available for purchase by schools and libraries.)

American Indian Law

CANBY'S AMERICAN INDIAN LAW IN A NUTSHELL, Second Edition, 336 pages, 1988. Softcover. (Text)

Antitrust—see also Regulated Indus-tries, Trade Regulation

GELLHORN'S ANTITRUST LAW AND ECO-NOMICS IN A NUTSHELL, Third Edition, 472 pages, 1986. Softcover. (Text)

HOVENKAMP'S BLACK LETTER ON ANTI-TRUST, Second Edition approximately 325 pages, April 1993 Pub. Softcover. (Review)

HOVENKAMP'S HORNBOOK ON ECONOMICS AND FEDERAL ANTITRUST LAW, Student Edition, 414 pages, 1985. (Text)

SULLIVAN'S HORNBOOK OF THE LAW OF ANTITRUST, 886 pages, 1977. (Text)

Appellate Advocacy—see Trial and Appellate Advocacy

Art Law

DUBOFF'S ART LAW IN A NUTSHELL, Sec-ond Edition, approximately 325 pages, 1993. Softcover. (Text)

Banking Law

LOVETT'S BANKING AND FINANCIAL INSTI-

Banking Law—Cont'd

TUTIONS LAW IN A NUTSHELL, Third Edition, 470 pages, 1992. Softcover. (Text)

Civil Procedure—see also Federal Jurisdiction and Procedure

CLERMONT'S BLACK LETTER ON CIVIL PROCEDURE, Third Edition, approximately 350 pages, May, 1993 Pub. Softcover. (Review)

FRIEDENTHAL, KANE AND MILLER'S HORNBOOK ON CIVIL PROCEDURE, Second Edition, approximately 1000 pages, May 1993 Pub. (Text)

KANE'S CIVIL PROCEDURE IN A NUTSHELL, Third Edition, 303 pages, 1991. Softcover. (Text)

KOFFLER AND REPPY'S HORNBOOK ON COMMON LAW PLEADING, 663 pages, 1969. (Text)

SIEGEL'S HORNBOOK ON NEW YORK PRACTICE, Second Edition, Student Edition, 1068 pages, 1991. Softcover. (Text) 1992 Supplemental Pamphlet.

SLOMANSON AND WINGATE'S CALIFORNIA CIVIL PROCEDURE IN A NUTSHELL, 230 pages, 1992. Softcover. (Text)

Commercial Law

BAILEY AND HAGEDORN'S SECURED TRANSACTIONS IN A NUTSHELL, Third Edition, 390 pages, 1988. Softcover. (Text)

HENSON'S HORNBOOK ON SECURED TRANSACTIONS UNDER THE U.C.C., Second Edition, 504 pages, 1979, with 1979 pocket part. (Text)

MEYER AND SPEIDEL'S BLACK LETTER ON SALES AND LEASES OF GOODS, Approximately 300 pages, 1993. Softcover. (Review)

NICKLES' BLACK LETTER ON COMMERCIAL PAPER, 450 pages, 1988. Softcover. (Review)

STOCKTON AND MILLER'S SALES AND LEASES OF GOODS IN A NUTSHELL, Third Edition, 441 pages, 1992. Softcover. (Text)

STONE'S UNIFORM COMMERCIAL CODE IN A NUTSHELL, Third Edition, 580 pages, 1989. Softcover. (Text)

WEBER AND SPEIDEL'S COMMERCIAL PAPER IN A NUTSHELL, Third Edition, 404 pages, 1982. Softcover. (Text)

WHITE AND SUMMERS' HORNBOOK ON THE UNIFORM COMMERCIAL CODE, Third Edition, Student Edition, 1386 pages, 1988. (Text)

Community Property

MENNELL AND BOYKOFF'S COMMUNITY PROPERTY IN A NUTSHELL, Second Edition, 432 pages, 1988. Softcover. (Text)

Comparative Law

FOLSOM, MINAN AND OTTO'S LAW AND POLITICS IN THE PEOPLE'S REPUBLIC OF CHINA IN A NUTSHELL, 451 pages, 1992. Softcover. (Text)

GLENDON, GORDON AND OSAKWE'S COMPARATIVE LEGAL TRADITIONS IN A NUTSHELL. 402 pages, 1982. Softcover. (Text)

Conflict of Laws

HAY'S BLACK LETTER ON CONFLICT OF LAWS, 330 pages, 1989. Softcover. (Review)

SCOLES AND HAY'S HORNBOOK ON CONFLICT OF LAWS, Student Edition, 1160 pages, 1992. (Text)

SIEGEL'S CONFLICTS IN A NUTSHELL, 470 pages, 1982. Softcover. (Text)

Constitutional Law—Civil Rights

BARRON AND DIENES' BLACK LETTER ON CONSTITUTIONAL LAW, Third Edition, 440 pages, 1991. Softcover. (Review)

BARRON AND DIENES' CONSTITUTIONAL LAW IN A NUTSHELL, Second Edition, 483 pages, 1991. Softcover. (Text)

ENGDAHL'S CONSTITUTIONAL FEDERALISM IN A NUTSHELL, Second Edition, 411 pages, 1987. Softcover. (Text)

MARKS AND COOPER'S STATE CONSTITUTIONAL LAW IN A NUTSHELL, 329 pages, 1988. Softcover. (Text)

Constitutional Law—Civil Rights—
Cont'd

NOWAK AND ROTUNDA'S HORNBOOK ON CONSTITUTIONAL LAW, Fourth Edition, 1357 pages, 1991. (Text)

VIEIRA'S CONSTITUTIONAL CIVIL RIGHTS IN A NUTSHELL, Second Edition, 322 pages, 1990. Softcover. (Text)

WILLIAMS' CONSTITUTIONAL ANALYSIS IN A NUTSHELL, 388 pages, 1979. Softcover. (Text)

Consumer Law—see also Commercial Law

EPSTEIN AND NICKLES' CONSUMER LAW IN A NUTSHELL, Second Edition, 418 pages, 1981. Softcover. (Text)

Contracts

CALAMARI AND PERILLO'S BLACK LETTER ON CONTRACTS, Second Edition, 462 pages, 1990. Softcover. (Review)

CALAMARI AND PERILLO'S HORNBOOK ON CONTRACTS, Third Edition, 1049 pages, 1987. (Text)

CORBIN'S TEXT ON CONTRACTS, One Volume Student Edition, 1224 pages, 1952. (Text)

FRIEDMAN'S CONTRACT REMEDIES IN A NUTSHELL, 323 pages, 1981. Softcover. (Text)

KEYES' GOVERNMENT CONTRACTS IN A NUTSHELL, Second Edition, 557 pages, 1990. Softcover. (Text)

SCHABER AND ROHWER'S CONTRACTS IN A NUTSHELL, Third Edition, 457 pages, 1990. Softcover. (Text)

Copyright—see Patent and Copyright Law

Corporations

HAMILTON'S BLACK LETTER ON CORPORATIONS, Third Edition, 732 pages, 1992. Softcover. (Review)

HAMILTON'S THE LAW OF CORPORATIONS IN A NUTSHELL, Third Edition, 518 pages, 1991. Softcover. (Text)

HENN AND ALEXANDER'S HORNBOOK ON LAWS OF CORPORATIONS, Third Edition,

Student Edition, 1371 pages, 1983, with 1986 pocket part. (Text)

Corrections

KRANTZ' THE LAW OF CORRECTIONS AND PRISONERS' RIGHTS IN A NUTSHELL, Third Edition, 407 pages, 1988. Softcover. (Text)

Creditors' Rights

EPSTEIN'S DEBTOR-CREDITOR LAW IN A NUTSHELL, Fourth Edition, 401 pages, 1991. Softcover. (Text)

EPSTEIN, NICKLES AND WHITE'S HORNBOOK ON BANKRUPTCY, Approximately 1000 pages, January, 1992 Pub. (Text)

NICKLES AND EPSTEIN'S BLACK LETTER ON CREDITORS' RIGHTS AND BANKRUPTCY, 576 pages, 1989. (Review)

Criminal Law and Criminal Procedure—
see also Corrections, Juvenile Justice

ISRAEL AND LaFAVE'S CRIMINAL PROCEDURE—CONSTITUTIONAL LIMITATIONS IN A NUTSHELL, Fourth Edition, 461 pages, 1988. Softcover. (Text)

LaFAVE AND ISRAEL'S HORNBOOK ON CRIMINAL PROCEDURE, Second Edition, 1309 pages, 1992 with 1992 pocket part. (Text)

LaFAVE AND SCOTT'S HORNBOOK ON CRIMINAL LAW, Second Edition, 918 pages, 1986. (Text)

LOEWY'S CRIMINAL LAW IN A NUTSHELL, Second Edition, 321 pages, 1987. Softcover. (Text)

LOW'S BLACK LETTER ON CRIMINAL LAW, Revised First Edition, 443 pages, 1990. Softcover. (Review)

SUBIN, MIRSKY AND WEINSTEIN'S THE CRIMINAL PROCESS: PROSECUTION AND DEFENSE FUNCTIONS, Approximately 450 pages, February, 1993 Pub. Softcover. Teacher's Manual available. (Text)

Domestic Relations

CLARK'S HORNBOOK ON DOMESTIC RELA-

Domestic Relations—Cont'd

TIONS, Second Edition, Student Edition, 1050 pages, 1988. (Text)

KRAUSE'S BLACK LETTER ON FAMILY LAW, 314 pages, 1988. Softcover. (Review)

KRAUSE'S FAMILY LAW IN A NUTSHELL, Second Edition, 444 pages, 1986. Softcover. (Text)

MALLOY'S LAW AND ECONOMICS: A COMPARATIVE APPROACH TO THEORY AND PRACTICE, 166 pages, 1990. Softcover. (Text)

Education Law

ALEXANDER AND ALEXANDER'S THE LAW OF SCHOOLS, STUDENTS AND TEACHERS IN A NUTSHELL, 409 pages, 1984. Softcover. (Text)

Employment Discrimination—see also Gender Discrimination

PLAYER'S FEDERAL LAW OF EMPLOYMENT DISCRIMINATION IN A NUTSHELL, Third Edition, 338 pages, 1992. Softcover. (Text)

PLAYER'S HORNBOOK ON EMPLOYMENT DISCRIMINATION LAW, Student Edition, 708 pages, 1988. (Text)

Energy and Natural Resources Law— see also Oil and Gas

LAITOS AND TOMAIN'S ENERGY AND NATURAL RESOURCES LAW IN A NUTSHELL, 554 pages, 1992. Softcover. (Text)

Environmental Law—see also Energy and Natural Resources Law; Sea, Law of

FINDLEY AND FARBER'S ENVIRONMENTAL LAW IN A NUTSHELL, Third Edition, 355 pages, 1992. Softcover. (Text)

RODGERS' HORNBOOK ON ENVIRONMENTAL LAW, 956 pages, 1977, with 1984 pocket part. (Text)

Equity—see Remedies

Estate Planning—see also Trusts and Estates; Taxation—Estate and Gift

LYNN'S INTRODUCTION TO ESTATE PLAN-

NING IN A NUTSHELL, Fourth Edition, 352 pages, 1992. Softcover. (Text)

Evidence

BROUN AND BLAKEY'S BLACK LETTER ON EVIDENCE, 269 pages, 1984. Softcover. (Review)

GRAHAM'S FEDERAL RULES OF EVIDENCE IN A NUTSHELL, Third Edition, 486 pages, 1992. Softcover. (Text)

LILLY'S AN INTRODUCTION TO THE LAW OF EVIDENCE, Second Edition, 585 pages, 1987. (Text)

McCORMICK'S HORNBOOK ON EVIDENCE, Fourth Edition, Student Edition, 672 pages, 1992. (Text)

ROTHSTEIN'S EVIDENCE IN A NUTSHELL: STATE AND FEDERAL RULES, Second Edition, 514 pages, 1981. Softcover. (Text)

Federal Jurisdiction and Procedure

CURRIE'S FEDERAL JURISDICTION IN A NUTSHELL, Third Edition, 242 pages, 1990. Softcover. (Text)

REDISH'S BLACK LETTER ON FEDERAL JURISDICTION, Second Edition, 234 pages, 1991. Softcover. (Review)

WRIGHT'S HORNBOOK ON FEDERAL COURTS, Fourth Edition, Student Edition, 870 pages, 1983. (Text)

First Amendment

GARVEY AND SCHAUER'S THE FIRST AMENDMENT: A READER, 527 pages, 1992. Softcover. (Reader)

Future Interests—see Trusts and Estates

Gender Discrimination—see also Employment Discrimination

THOMAS' SEX DISCRIMINATION IN A NUTSHELL, Second Edition, 395 pages, 1991. Softcover. (Text)

Health Law—see Medicine, Law and

Human Rights—see International Law

Immigration Law

WEISSBRODT'S IMMIGRATION LAW AND

Immigration Law—Cont'd

PROCEDURE IN A NUTSHELL, Third Edition, 497 pages, 1992. Softcover. (Text)

Indian Law—see American Indian Law

Insurance Law

DOBBYN'S INSURANCE LAW IN A NUTSHELL, Second Edition, 316 pages, 1989. Softcover. (Text)

KEETON AND WIDISS' INSURANCE LAW, Student Edition, 1359 pages, 1988. (Text)

International Law—see also Sea, Law of

BUERGENTHAL'S INTERNATIONAL HUMAN RIGHTS IN A NUTSHELL, 283 pages, 1988. Softcover. (Text)

BUERGENTHAL AND MAIER'S PUBLIC INTERNATIONAL LAW IN A NUTSHELL, Second Edition, 275 pages, 1990. Softcover. (Text)

FOLSOM'S EUROPEAN COMMUNITY LAW IN A NUTSHELL, 423 pages, 1992. Softcover. (Text)

FOLSOM, GORDON AND SPANOGLE'S INTERNATIONAL BUSINESS TRANSACTIONS IN A NUTSHELL, Fourth Edition, 548 pages, 1992. Softcover. (Text)

Interviewing and Counseling

SHAFFER AND ELKINS' LEGAL INTERVIEWING AND COUNSELING IN A NUTSHELL, Second Edition, 487 pages, 1987. Softcover. (Text)

Introduction to Law—see Legal Method and Legal System

Introduction to Law Study

HEGLAND'S INTRODUCTION TO THE STUDY AND PRACTICE OF LAW IN A NUTSHELL, 418 pages, 1983. Softcover. (Text)

KINYON'S INTRODUCTION TO LAW STUDY AND LAW EXAMINATIONS IN A NUTSHELL, 389 pages, 1971. Softcover. (Text)

Judicial Process—see Legal Method and Legal System

SINHA'S JURISPRUDENCE (LEGAL PHILOSO-

PHY) IN A NUTSHELL. Approximately 350 pages, 1993. Softcover. (Text)

Juvenile Justice

FOX'S JUVENILE COURTS IN A NUTSHELL, Third Edition, 291 pages, 1984. Softcover. (Text)

Labor and Employment Law—see also Employment Discrimination, Workers' Compensation

LESLIE'S LABOR LAW IN A NUTSHELL, Third Edition, 388 pages, 1992. Softcover. (Text)

NOLAN'S LABOR ARBITRATION LAW AND PRACTICE IN A NUTSHELL, 358 pages, 1979. Softcover. (Text)

Land Finance—Property Security—see Real Estate Transactions

Land Use

HAGMAN AND JUERGENSMEYER'S HORNBOOK ON URBAN PLANNING AND LAND DEVELOPMENT CONTROL LAW, Second Edition, Student Edition, 680 pages, 1986. (Text)

WRIGHT AND WRIGHT'S LAND USE IN A NUTSHELL, Second Edition, 356 pages, 1985. Softcover. (Text)

Legal Method and Legal System—see also Legal Research, Legal Writing

KEMPIN'S HISTORICAL INTRODUCTION TO ANGLO-AMERICAN LAW IN A NUTSHELL, Third Edition, 323 pages, 1990. Softcover. (Text)

REYNOLDS' JUDICIAL PROCESS IN A NUTSHELL, Second Edition, 308 pages, 1991. Softcover. (Text)

Legal Research

COHEN AND OLSON'S LEGAL RESEARCH IN A NUTSHELL, Fifth Edition, 370 pages, 1992. Softcover. (Text)

COHEN, BERRING AND OLSON'S HOW TO FIND THE LAW, Ninth Edition, 716 pages, 1989. (Text)

Legal Writing and Drafting

MELLINKOFF'S DICTIONARY OF AMERICAN

Legal Writing and Drafting—Cont'd

LEGAL USAGE, 703 pages, 1992. Softcover. (Text)

SQUIRES AND ROMBAUER'S LEGAL WRITING IN A NUTSHELL, 294 pages, 1982. Softcover. (Text)

Legislation—see also Legal Writing and Drafting

DAVIES' LEGISLATIVE LAW AND PROCESS IN A NUTSHELL, Second Edition, 346 pages, 1986. Softcover. (Text)

Local Government

MCCARTHY'S LOCAL GOVERNMENT LAW IN A NUTSHELL, Third Edition, 435 pages, 1990. Softcover. (Text)

REYNOLDS' HORNBOOK ON LOCAL GOVERNMENT LAW, 860 pages, 1982 with 1990 pocket part. (Text)

Mass Communication Law

ZUCKMAN, GAYNES, CARTER AND DEE'S MASS COMMUNICATIONS LAW IN A NUTSHELL, Third Edition, 538 pages, 1988. Softcover. (Text)

Medicine, Law and

HALL AND ELLMAN'S HEALTH CARE LAW AND ETHICS IN A NUTSHELL, 401 pages, 1990. Softcover (Text)

JARVIS, CLOSEN, HERMANN AND LEONARD'S AIDS LAW IN A NUTSHELL, 349 pages, 1991. Softcover. (Text)

KING'S THE LAW OF MEDICAL MALPRACTICE IN A NUTSHELL, Second Edition, 342 pages, 1986. Softcover. (Text)

Military Law

SHANOR AND TERRELL'S MILITARY LAW IN A NUTSHELL, 378 pages, 1980. Softcover. (Text)

Mining Law—see Energy and Natural Resources Law

Mortgages—see Real Estate Transactions

Natural Resources Law—see Energy and Natural Resources Law, Environmental Law

TEPLY'S LEGAL NEGOTIATION IN A NUTSHELL, 282 pages, 1992. Softcover. (Text)

Office Practice—see also Computers and Law, Interviewing and Counseling, Negotiation

HEGLAND'S TRIAL AND PRACTICE SKILLS IN A NUTSHELL, 346 pages, 1978. Softcover (Text)

Oil and Gas—see also Energy and Natural Resources Law

HEMINGWAY'S HORNBOOK ON THE LAW OF OIL AND GAS, Third Edition, Student Edition, 711 pages, 1992. (Text)

LOWE'S OIL AND GAS LAW IN A NUTSHELL, Second Edition, 465 pages, 1988. Softcover. (Text)

Partnership—see Agency—Partnership

Patent and Copyright Law

MILLER AND DAVIS' INTELLECTUAL PROPERTY—PATENTS, TRADEMARKS AND COPYRIGHT IN A NUTSHELL, Second Edition, 437 pages, 1990. Softcover. (Text)

Products Liability

PHILLIPS' PRODUCTS LIABILITY IN A NUTSHELL, Third Edition, 307 pages, 1988. Softcover. (Text)

Professional Responsibility

ARONSON AND WECKSTEIN'S PROFESSIONAL RESPONSIBILITY IN A NUTSHELL, Second Edition, 514 pages, 1991. Softcover. (Text)

LESNICK'S BEING A LAWYER: INDIVIDUAL CHOICE AND RESPONSIBILITY IN THE PRACTICE OF LAW, 422 pages, 1992. Softcover. Teacher's Manual available. (Coursebook)

ROTUNDA'S BLACK LETTER ON PROFESSIONAL RESPONSIBILITY, Third Edition, 492 pages, 1992. Softcover. (Review)

WOLFRAM'S HORNBOOK ON MODERN LEGAL ETHICS, Student Edition, 1120

Professional Responsibility—Cont'd
pages, 1986. (Text)

WYDICK AND PERSCHBACHER'S CALIFOR-
NIA LEGAL ETHICS, 439 pages, 1992.
Softcover. (Coursebook)

Property—see also Real Estate Transactions, Land Use, Trusts and Estates

BERNHARDT'S BLACK LETTER ON PROPER-
TY, Second Edition, 388 pages, 1991.
Softcover. (Review)

BERNHARDT'S REAL PROPERTY IN A NUT-
SHELL, Second Edition, 448 pages,
1981. Softcover. (Text)

BOYER, HOVENKAMP AND KURTZ' THE
LAW OF PROPERTY, AN INTRODUCTORY
SURVEY, Fourth Edition, 696 pages,
1991. (Text)

BURKE'S PERSONAL PROPERTY IN A NUT-
SHELL, Second Edition, approximately
400 pages, May, 1993 Pub. Softcover.
(Text)

CUNNINGHAM, STOEBUCK AND WHIT-
MAN'S HORNBOOK ON THE LAW OF PROP-
ERTY, Second Edition, approximately
900 pages, May, 1993 Pub. (Text)

HILL'S LANDLORD AND TENANT LAW IN A
NUTSHELL, Second Edition, 311 pages,
1986. Softcover. (Text)

Real Estate Transactions

BRUCE'S REAL ESTATE FINANCE IN A
NUTSHELL, Third Edition, 287 pages,
1991. Softcover. (Text)

NELSON AND WHITMAN'S BLACK LETTER
ON LAND TRANSACTIONS AND FINANCE,
Second Edition, 466 pages, 1988. Soft-
cover. (Review)

NELSON AND WHITMAN'S HORNBOOK ON
REAL ESTATE FINANCE LAW, Second
Edition, 941 pages, 1985 with 1989
pocket part. (Text)

Regulated Industries—see also Mass
Communication Law, Banking Law

GELLHORN AND PIERCE'S REGULATED IN-
DUSTRIES IN A NUTSHELL, Second Edition, 389 pages, 1987. Softcover.

Remedies

DOBBS' HORNBOOK ON REMEDIES, Second
Edition, approximately 1000 pages,
April, 1993 Pub. (Text)

DOBBYN'S INJUNCTIONS IN A NUTSHELL,
264 pages, 1974. Softcover. (Text)

FRIEDMAN'S CONTRACT REMEDIES IN A
NUTSHELL, 323 pages, 1981. Softcover.
(Text)

O'CONNELL'S REMEDIES IN A NUTSHELL,
Second Edition, 320 pages, 1985. Softcover. (Text)

Sea, Law of

SOHN AND GUSTAFSON'S THE LAW OF
THE SEA IN A NUTSHELL, 264 pages,
1984. Softcover. (Text)

Securities Regulation

HAZEN'S HORNBOOK ON THE LAW OF SE-
CURITIES REGULATION, Second Edition,
Student Edition, 1082 pages, 1990.
(Text)

RATNER'S SECURITIES REGULATION IN A
NUTSHELL, Fourth Edition, 320 pages,
1992. Softcover. (Text)

Sports Law

CHAMPION'S SPORTS LAW IN A NUT-
SHELL,. Approximately 300 pages,
January, 1993 Pub. Softcover. (Text)

SCHUBERT, SMITH AND TRENTADUE'S
SPORTS LAW, 395 pages, 1986. (Text)

Tax Practice and Procedure

MORGAN'S TAX PROCEDURE AND TAX
FRAUD IN A NUTSHELL, 400 pages, 1990.
Softcover. (Text)

Taxation—Corporate

SCHWARZ AND LATHROPE'S BLACK LET-
TER ON CORPORATE AND PARTNERSHIP
TAXATION, 537 pages, 1991. Softcover.
(Review)

WEIDENBRUCH AND BURKE'S FEDERAL IN-
COME TAXATION OF CORPORATIONS AND
STOCKHOLDERS IN A NUTSHELL, Third
Edition, 309 pages, 1989. Softcover.
(Text)

Trusts and Estates

ATKINSON'S HORNBOOK ON WILLS, Second Edition, 975 pages, 1953. (Text)

AVERILL'S UNIFORM PROBATE CODE IN A NUTSHELL, Second Edition, 454 pages, 1987. Softcover. (Text)

BOGERT'S HORNBOOK ON TRUSTS, Sixth Edition, Student Edition, 794 pages, 1987. (Text)

MCGOVERN, KURTZ AND REIN'S HORNBOOK ON WILLS, TRUSTS AND ESTATES–INCLUDING TAXATION AND FUTURE INTERESTS, 996 pages, 1988. (Text)

MENNELL'S WILLS AND TRUSTS IN A NUTSHELL, 392 pages, 1979. Softcover. (Text)

SIMES' HORNBOOK ON FUTURE INTERESTS, Second Edition, 355 pages, 1966. (Text)

TURANO AND RADIGAN'S HORNBOOK ON NEW YORK ESTATE ADMINISTRATION, 676 pages, 1986 with 1991 pocket part. (Text)

WAGGONER'S FUTURE INTERESTS IN A NUTSHELL, 361 pages, 1981. Softcover. (Text)

Water Law—see also Environmental Law

GETCHES' WATER LAW IN A NUTSHELL, Second Edition, 459 pages, 1990. Softcover. (Text)

Wills—see Trusts and Estates

Workers' Compensation

HOOD, HARDY AND LEWIS' WORKERS' COMPENSATION AND EMPLOYEE PROTECTION LAWS IN A NUTSHELL, Second Edition, 361 pages, 1990. Softcover. (Text)

*

THE LAW OF
PROPERTY

Second Edition

By

Roger A. Cunningham

James V. Campbell Professor of Law, Emeritus,
University of Michigan School of Law

William B. Stoebuck

Professor of Law, University of Washington
School of Law

Dale A. Whitman

Guy Anderson Professor of Law, Brigham Young University
School of Law

HORNBOOK SERIES

WEST PUBLISHING CO.
ST. PAUL, MINN., 1993

COPYRIGHT © 1984 WEST PUBLISHING CO.
COPYRIGHT © 1993 By WEST PUBLISHING CO.
                        610 Opperman Drive
                        P.O. Box 64526
                        St. Paul, MN 55164–0526
                        1–800–328–9352

Library of Congress Cataloging-in-Publication Data

Cunningham, Roger A.
     The law of property / by Roger A. Cunningham, William B. Stoebuck,
and Dale A. Whitman. — 2nd ed.
        p.   cm. — (Hornbook series)
     Includes index.
     ISBN 0–314–01389–X
     1. Real property—United States.   I. Stoebuck, William B.
II. Whitman, Dale A.   III. Title.   IV. Series.
KF570.C86   1993
346.7304'3—dc20
[347.30643]

                                                                    92–38188
                                                                       CIP

ISBN 0–314–01389–X

Preface

Property law, the subject of this book, is possible only because there is property. Or is it the other way around? Who can conceive of a society of any complexity that does not enforce a system of rights and duties respecting things? To be sure, the affection for property rights varies from society to society and from time to time, but history records no nation and no time in which private property has not had an honored place. The words "proper," "propriety," and "property" have a common root. So do "good" and "goods." "*Celui est homme de bien qui est homme de biens*": he is a good man who is a man of goods, say the French.

In its essence, private property is the right of a person or a defined group of persons to use a thing and to exclude others from interfering for a time long enough to extract from the thing the benefits it is capable of affording. What would be the consequences if some society attempted to abolish all such rights? No person in the society could make effective use of any thing, neither land nor goods of any kind. Such a state of affairs is so unimaginable that every political society must have a system to insure that at any given time all items of land and goods will be in the protected use of identified persons. At any instant in time, the available goods and land in one society are as much in legally protected private use and possession as are the available goods and land in other societies. Even in a nation in which the state "owns" all property, a tractor driver may not own the tractor, as does the American farmer, but he has a protected right against others to use it for a time. He may have what we call a bailment, and a series of drivers may have a series of bailments, but that is still private property and differs from what we call absolute ownership only in what is, in the larger scheme of things, a detail.

In the larger scheme, then, this book is about the details that particularly mark the American law of property. Looking centrifugally, from within the American system of law, however, the principles of property law comprise a very large subject. It is our oldest body of law, whose writ of novel disseisin began English common law in the time of Henry II. Anyone familiar with the workings of lawyers' minds and pens must know that 800 years will produce a prodigious body of law! Within one volume of handbook size, this book surveys the chief areas and more: history and basic concepts; estates in land, present, future, and concurrent; comparable interests in personalty; landlord and tenant law; rights against neighbors and other third persons; easements and profits; running covenants; governmental controls on land use; land contracts; conveyances; titles; and recording systems.

One thinks of property law as being old, unchanging. It is old, and parts of it have been resistant to change. Yet, it is surprising how many areas are undergoing current and rapid change. All the chapter on government control of land use is new law and changeful as a dancing flame, fueled by enormous public concern for the environment. Major parts of the chapters on landlord and tenant and land contracts reflect new, rapid change. These are only the larger examples of many changing areas covered here. The value of our work lies very much in its coverage of the many recent changes in the law. We know of no other book of comparable scope that brings the law of property up to date as does the one open before you.

The three of us have, naturally, divided up our writing by subjects. But each of us read and commented freely upon the other two's work. To coordinate the writing of the book by three authors separated as we are, brought some challenges and delays. On balance, however, each of us knows it has strengthened his work to have it read and criticized by two other scholars in whom he has confidence.

We wish to acknowledge publicly the help we have received, not only from each other, but from a number of others. Professor Cunningham is grateful to his research assistants, who worked on various parts of the first edition Harold Hickok, Heather Kelley, Susan Ludlow, Stephen Mikus, Dale Oesterle, Ethan Powsner, and David Swenson. Professor Stoebuck thanks two student research assistants, Karen E. Boxx and Juanita E. Holmes, for valuable help with different parts of the first edition. Professor Whitman is thankful for the aid of his research assistants Phillip Bledsoe on the first edition and Chris Washburn on the second. We all thank West Publishing Company for their help at every stage; they have been unfailingly pleasant and cooperative.

Finally, we thank our wives, Beth Cunningham, Mary Stoebuck, and Marjorie Whitman, not only for their encouragement and sometimes help with the book, but simply for putting up with us. For a fulltime law teacher, a major writing project such as this brings many hundreds of hours of "spare-time" work and occasionally a restless night. Our families share in the toll it takes. And they share in our hope that for you the reader our work will have been worthwhile. If we lead you well and truly, then we will have advanced the cause of that jealous mistress in whose service we are bound.

R.A.C.

W.B.S.

D.A.W.

May, 1993

A Note About Pronouns of Gender

In this book pronouns that refer to persons in general are usually used in the masculine form. In part this practice is due to the fact that when the first edition was being written in the early 1980's, it was much less common than when the second edition was being prepared to use forms that were gender-neutral. In revising for the second edition, it did not seem efficient to edit every pronoun. The masculine pronouns have been retained because of the poverty of the English language: there is no neutral form of pronouns. Combinations such as "he-she" or "(s)he" are awkward, and the alternating use of feminine and masculine can produce confusion.

*

Acknowledgments

A number of authors and publishers have consented to our use of short extracts from their copyrighted materials. Such materials are clearly identified, where they appear in this book, by source and date of publication. Here, we gratefully acknowledge the permissions to reprint these copyrighted materials. In some instances, we were asked to note additional information about a work or to furnish acknowledgment in a particular form, and we are happy to comply with these requests in acknowledging permission to reprint the following materials.

Babcock, The Illinois Supreme Court and Zoning: A Study in Uncertainty, 15 U.Chi.L.Rev. 87, 97 (1947). Copyright © 1947, University of Chicago. Permission granted by University of Chicago Law Review.

C. Clark, Covenants and Other Interests Which "Run with Land," p. 97 (2d ed. 1947). Reprinted with permission from C. Clark, *Real Covenants and Other Interests Which "Run with Land"* (Ch. 4, 2d ed. 1947), published by Callaghan & Co., 3201 Old Glenview Rd., Wilmette, IL 60091.

Dunham, Possibility of Reverter and Powers of Termination—Fraternal or Identical Twins?, 20 U.Chi.L.Rev. 215, 219 (1953). Copyright © 1953, University of Chicago. Permission granted by University of Chicago Law Review.

W. Hohfeld, Fundamental Legal Conceptions, pp. 96–97 (Cook ed. 1928). Copyright © 1928, The Yale University Press. Permission granted by The Yale University Press.

Krasnowiecki, Abolish Zoning, Syracuse L.Rev. 719, 747–753 (1980). Copyright © Jan. Z. Krasnowiecki. Permission granted by Syracuse Law Review.

D. Mandelker, *Land Use Law,* pp. 273, 318 (1982). Copyright © 1982, The Michie Company. Permission granted by Michie Bobbs-Merrill Company, Inc.

The American Law Institute: Restatement (Second) of Property § 11.2 Comments, and § 11.3, copyright © 1977 by The American Law Institute; Restatement (Second) of Contracts § 360, Comment e, copyright © 1981 by The American Law Institute; Model Land Development Code, Article 4 Commentary at pp. 150, 158, copyright © 1976 by The American Law Institute. All reprinted with the permission of The American Law Institute.

*

WESTLAW® Overview

Cunningham, Stoebuck & Whitman's *Law of Property* offers a detailed and comprehensive treatment of principles and issues in property law. To supplement the information in this book, you can access WESTLAW, a computer-assisted legal research service of West Publishing Company. WESTLAW contains a broad library of property law resources, including case law, the *Restatement of the Law of Property,* law reviews, texts and journals, and portions of the Practising Law Institute's Course Handbook Series on continuing legal education in real estate law.

Learning how to use these materials effectively will enhance your legal research. So that you can coordinate your book and WESTLAW research, this volume contains an appendix listing WESTLAW databases, search techniques and sample problems.

THE PUBLISHER

*

Summary of Contents

Table of Contents

C. CREATION OF THE LANDLORD–TENANT RELATIONSHIP

D. TENANT'S RIGHT OF POSSESSION AND ENJOYMENT

E. INTERFERENCE WITH TENANT'S POSSESSION

F. CONDITION OF THE PREMISES

THE LAW OF
PROPERTY
Second Edition

*

Chapter 1

INTRODUCTION

Table of Sections

---

§ 1.1 The Concept of Property and the Institution of Private Property

When a layman is asked to define "property," he is likely to say that "property" is something tangible "owned" by a natural person (or persons), a corporation, or a unit of government. But such a response is inaccurate from a lawyer's viewpoint for at least two reasons: (1) it confuses "property" with the various *subjects* of "property," and (2) it fails to recognize that even the subjects of "property" may be intangible.

For the lawyer, "property" is not a "thing" at all, although "things" are the subject of property. Rather, as Jeremy Bentham asserted,[1] property is a legally protected "expectation * * * of being able to draw such or such an advantage from the thing" in question, "according to the nature of the case." Although Bentham conceded that [2] "[t]here have been from the beginning, and there always will be, circumstances in which a man may secure himself, by his own means, in the enjoyment of certain things," Bentham correctly noted that "the catalogue of these cases is very limited" and that "a strong and permanent expectation" of being able to draw an advantage from the thing in question "can result only from law." In this book, we shall adopt Bentham's view of the nature of property more recently summarized as follows by Felix Cohen: [3] "That is property to which the following label can be attached. To the world: Keep off unless you have my permission, which I may grant or withhold. Signed: Private citizen. Endorsed: The state."

§ 1.1

1. J. Bentham, Theory of Legislation 68 (Oceana Pub.Inc.1975).

2. Id. 69.

3. F. Cohen, Dialogue on Private Property, 9 Rutgers L.Rev. 357, 374 (1954).

1

Cohen's statement, just quoted, obviously assumes that "private" property is the norm. This has certainly been the case in the United States since its founding, and in most of Western Europe from the end of the Middle Ages to the present, although the institution of "private" property—i.e., the ownership of "things" by "private" persons—has long been a subject of controversy among philosophers, political scientists, and economists. At least five theories have been advanced as justifications for the institution of "private" property: [4] (1) the "occupation" theory—that the simple fact of occupation or possession of a thing justifies legal protection of the occupier's or possessor's claim to the thing; (2) the "labor" theory—that a person has a moral right to the ownership and control of things he produces or acquires through his or her labor; (3) the "contract" theory—that "private" property is the result of a contract between individuals and the community; (4) the "natural rights" theory—that the "natural law" dictates the recognition of "private" property; and (5) the "social utility" theory—that the law should promote the maximum fulfillment of human needs and aspirations, and that legal protection of "private" property does, in fact promote such fulfillment.

The institution of "private" property has, of course, been the subject of vigorous criticism in the Western world from very early times. Such eminent philosophers as Plato [5] and Sir Thomas More [6] rejected "private" property and argued for "communal" property. More recently, Marx [7] and Engels proposed the abolition of "private" property in the "means of production" and transfer of the ownership of the "means of production" to the State.[8] Despite important modifications, the doctrines of Marx and Engels still provide the philosophical basis for the widespread transfer of ownership of the "means of production" to the State in the Soviet Union, most of Eastern Europe, China, Viet Nam, and other "Communist" nations. But even in the "Communist" nations "private" property has not been completely abolished. In the Soviet Union, e.g., "personal ownership" is permitted with respect to certain "property which is intended for the satisfaction of * * * [citizens'] material and cultural needs." [9] Thus "[each] citizen may personally own his income from work, and his savings, a house (or part of a house) and subsidiary household production, and household articles of personal use and convenience." [10] But "[p]roperty under the personal ownership of citizens may not be used to derive non-labor income." [11]

In recent years a number of American scholars have advanced an economic theory of property. Posner,[12] e.g., asserts that "the legal protection of property rights has an important economic function: to create incentives

4. For discussion of these theories, see the Rational Basis of Legal Institutions 387–400, 195–200, 167–184, 314–344 (H. Wigmore and A. Kocourek ed. 1923), reprinting excerpts from works by H. Rashdall, J. Locke, E. de Laveleye, L. Duguit, and R. Tawney; F. Cohen, Property and Sovereignty, 13 Cornell L.J. 15–16, (1927); J. Stone, The Province and Function of Law 529 (1950).

5. Plato, Republic.

6. T. More, Utopia.

7. K. Marx, Das Kapital.

8. For discussion of socialist theories of property, see 2 W. Lecky, Democracy and Lib-

erty 224–361 (1896), excerpts from which are reprinted in The Rational Basis of Legal Institutions 232–254 (H. Wigmore and A. Kocourek ed. 1923).

9. Civil Code of the Russian Soviet Federated Socialist Republic, Art. 105 (transl. W. Gray and R. Stults 1965).

10. Ibid.

11. Ibid.

12. R. Posner, Economic Analysis of Law 10–13 (1972).

to use resources efficiently," and that there are three criteria of an efficient system of property rights:

1. *Universality* —i.e., "all resources should be owned, or ownable, by someone, except resources so plentiful that everybody can consume as much of them as he wants without reducing consumption by anyone else * * *."

2. *Exclusivity*—to give owners an incentive to incur the costs required to make efficient use of resources owned by them.

3. *Transferability*—because, "[i]f a property right cannot be transferred, there is no way of shifting a resource from a less productive to a more productive use through voluntary exchange."

Posner's assertion that the legal protection of property rights performs the economic function of creating incentives to use resources efficiently is, of course, a normative proposition rather than a factual description of the way in which the rules of property law actually operate at any given time in a particular legal system. But—although neither the courts nor the legislatures have consistently been articulate on the point—it seems clear that the Anglo–American law of property has rarely lost sight of this normative proposition. Moreover, it seems likely that the future development of the Anglo–American law of property will be more explicitly based on that proposition.[13]

§ 1.2 The Elements of Property—Hohfeldian and Other Analyses

If "property" is a legally protected "expectation" of deriving certain advantages from a "thing," it follows that "property" is comprised of legal relations between persons with respect to "things." These legal relations may be of widely varying types. The analysis of property adopted in the Restatement of the Law of Property,[1] which is based on the writings of Wesley Hohfeld,[2] postulates four basic legal relations, represented by the four sets of correlative terms, "right—duty," "privilege—absence of right," "power—liability," and "immunity—disability."

"Right" is defined as "a legally enforceable claim of one person against another, that the other shall do a given act or * * * not do a given act."[3] Any person against whom the "right" exists has a correlative "duty."[4] "Privilege" is defined as "a legal freedom on the part of one person as against another to do a given act or a legal freedom not to do a given act."[5] Any person against whom the "privilege" exists has a correlative "absence of right" that the person enjoying the "privilege" shall do or not do the act in

---

13. See id. 13–39; R. Coase, The Problem of Social Cost, 3 J.Law & Econ. 1 (1960); H. Demsetz, Toward a Theory of Property Rights, 57 Am.Econ.Rev.Papers and Proceedings 347 (1967).

§ 1.2

1. Am.L.Inst., Rest.Prop. §§ 1–10 (1936). This Restatement was prepared under the sponsorship of the American Law Institute and was published in five volumes between 1936 and 1944. It is referred to in the text hereinafter as the Property Restatement.

2. W. Hohfeld, Fundamental Legal Conceptions 23–124 (1923). See also A. Corbin, Legal Analysis and Terminology, 29 Yale L.J. 163 (1919); A. Kocourek, The Hohfeld System of Fundamental Legal Concepts, 15 Ill.L.Rev. 24 (1920); Becker, Property Rights ch. 2 (1977).

3. Am.L.Inst., Rest.Prop. § 1 (1936).

4. Id. § 1, Comment a.

5. Id. § 2.

question.[6] "Power" is defined as "an ability on the part of a person to produce a change in a given legal relation by doing or not doing a given act."[7] Any person against whom a "power" exists has a correlative "liability" to have the given legal relation changed by the doing or omission of the given act.[8] "Immunity" is defined as "a freedom on the part of one person against having a given legal relation altered by a given act or omission on the part of another person."[9] Any person against whom the "immunity" exists is under a correlative "disability" to alter the given legal relation by the doing or omission of the given act.[10]

The Property Restatement, following general legal usage, uses the term "interest" to designate any single right, privilege, power, or immunity or, generically, "varying aggregates of rights, privileges, powers and immunities."[11] The Hohfeldian analysis adopted in the Property Restatement is applicable, however, to both "personal" and "property" interests. What distinguishes "property" from "personal" interests is that "property" interests (1) relate to "things"—land, chattels, and intangible "things"[12]—and (2) are usually protected by law against an indefinitely large number of persons ("the world").[13] Some "personal" interests are protected against an indefinitely large number of persons but do not relate to "things"—e.g., the interest in freedom from personal injury caused by the intentional or negligent acts of others. Other "personal" interests relate to "things" but are generally enforceable against only one or a few persons—e.g., the interest in performance of promises made by the other party to a contract.

According to the Property Restatement the totality of "interests" (i.e., rights, privileges, powers, and immunities) which it is legally possible to have with respect to a "thing," other than those "interests" which exist in a person merely because he is a member of society, constitutes "complete property" in the "thing."[14]

> This totality varies from time to time, and from place to place, either because of changes in the common law, or because of alterations by statute. * * *. At any one time and place, however, there is a maximum combination of rights, privileges, powers and immunities * * * that is legally possible, and which constitutes complete property in * * * land or [a] thing other than land.[15]

When a person has "complete property" in a "thing"—whether land or a "thing other than land"—we say that he or she is the "owner" of the thing.[16] Indeed, we describe a person as the "owner" of a "thing" whenever he or she has numerous "interests" in that "thing," even though he or she does not have the totality comprising "complete property."[17] Thus, e.g., a person who owns the totality of property interests in a tract of land, or in an automobile,—except those interests comprising a mortgage on the subject matter—is still commonly termed "owner" of the subject matter (land or

6. Id. § 2, Comment a.

7. Id. § 3.

8. Id. § 3, Comment a.

9. Id. § 4.

10. Id. § 4, Comment a.

11. Id. § 5.

12. Id., Introductory Note.

13. Id. § 5, Comment d.

14. Id. § 5, Comment e.

15. Ibid.

16. Id. § 10, Comment b.

17. Id. § 10, Comment c.

automobile). On the other hand, a person who has property interests conventionally grouped under a single descriptive term such as "mortgage," "leasehold," or "easement" may properly be said either to "own" or to "have" the particular mortgage, leasehold, or easement although he is not the "owner" of the land (or thing other than land) which is the subject of the mortgage, leasehold, or easement.[18]

All this is pretty abstract, however. The Hohfeldian analytical scheme adopted in the Property Restatement can be made more concrete by considering Hohfeld's own application of his analytical scheme to interests in land: [19]

> Suppose * * * that A is * * * owner of Blackacre. His "legal interest" or property relating to the tangible object that we call *land* consists of a complex aggregate of rights (or claims), privileges, powers, and immunities. First, A has multital legal rights [rights in rem], or claims that *others,* respectively, shall *not* enter on the land, that they shall not cause physical harm to the land, etc., such others being under respective correlative legal duties. Second, A has an indefinite number of legal privileges of entering on the land, using the land, harming the land, etc., that is, within the limits fixed by law on grounds of social and economic policy, he has privileges of doing on or to the land what he pleases; and correlative to all such legal privileges are respective legal no-rights of other persons. Third, A has the legal power to alienate his legal interest to another, i.e., to extinguish his complex aggregate of jural relations and create a new and similar aggregate in the other person; * * * also the legal power to create a privilege of entrance in any other person by giving "leave and license"; and so on indefinitely. Correlative to all such legal powers are the legal liabilities in other persons—this meaning that the latter are subject *nolens volens* to the changes of jural relations involved in the exercise of A's powers. Fourth, A has an indefinite number of legal immunities, using the term "immunity" in the very specific sense of non-liability, or non-subjection to a power on the part of another person. Thus A has the immunity that no ordinary person can alienate A's legal interest or aggregate of legal relations to another person; the immunity that no ordinary person can extinguish A's own privileges of using the land; the immunity that no ordinary person can extinguish A's right that another person, X, shall not enter on the land, or, in other words, create in X a privilege of entering on the land. Correlative to all these immunities are the respective legal disabilities of other persons in general.

Hohfeld's analysis of legal relations has been subjected to severe criticism by a number of writers.[20] Without reviewing these criticisms in detail, it may be noted that the concepts of "right," "privilege," and "power" appear to contribute more to an understanding of property law than does the concept of "immunity"; that there is an apparent overlap of the concepts of "privilege" and "power" which Hohfeld does not adequately explain; that "absence of right" is no more entitled to be deemed *the* correlative of "privilege" than is "liability"; that the correlatives "immunity" and "dis-

18. Ibid.

19. W. Hohfeld, supra, note 2, at 96–97.

20. E.g., A. Kocourek, supra note 2.

ability" are subject to the same criticism; and that a person may be under a "disability" not only because of a lack of "power" but also because of the existence of a "duty." In addition, it is awkward to speak of a person who does not have a particular Hohfeldian "right" as having a "no-right"—a term which has not, in fact, been adopted either by the courts or by other scholarly writers.

More generally, it would seem that the principal value of the Hohfeldian analysis may lie in its facilitation of an understanding of the way in which, in Anglo–American property law, "complete property" in (or "full owner-ship" of) a "thing" may be divided into smaller segments or "interests." Thus, for example, it may not be very useful to be told that if A is "owner of Blackacre" he "has an indefinite number of legal privileges of entering on the land, using the land, harming the land, etc.," but it is quite useful to know that a single privilege of use or an aggregate of several related use privileges may be transferred by A to B, in the form of an "easement" or "license." Similarly, it is not very useful to be told that if A is "owner of Blackacre" he "has the legal power to alienate his legal interest to another," but it is quite useful to know that A may create in B such a "power" not accompanied by any other legal interest, or accompanied only by a legal interest less than "full ownership," in Blackacre—e.g., a "power of sale," a "power of appointment," or a "power of attorney." The first two terms denote the legal ability to produce a change in legal relations by a sale or by the designation of a person as appointee; the last term denotes the legal ability to produce a change in legal relations by the doing of whatever acts are authorized, including the transfer of "full ownership" of, or a legal interest less than "full ownership" in, a tract of land, a chattel, or some other "thing." When the owner of the particular "thing" creates one of these kinds of "power," the legal relation between the owner and the holder of the power can be expressed by the terms "liability" and "power." But when the owner of the "thing" retains all the possible "powers" with respect to it, the Hohfeldian terms "power" and "liability" do not express any legal relation because the owner is both endowed with those "powers" and subject to all the correlative "liabilities." [21]

It should be noted that the European Civil Law views "property" as including six kinds of legally protected "expectations": (1) a right of posses-sion (*jus possidendi*); (2) a right of exclusion (*jus prohibendi*); (3) a right of disposition (*jus disponendi*); (4) a right of use (*jus utendi*); (5) a right to enjoy fruits or profits (*jus fruendi*); and (6) a right of destruction (*jus abutendi*).[22] The *jus possidendi* and the *jus prohibendi* are clearly "rights" under the Hohfeldian–Restatement analytical scheme, while the *jus utendi, jus fruendi,* and *jus abutendi* are "privileges" and the *jus disponendi* is a "power." These "rights" and "privileges," along with the "power" of disposi-tion, are all recognized and protected in Anglo–American law.

21. With respect to a "power of sale"—or, more broadly, a "power of alienation"—there is a further difficulty, whether the power is vested in the owner or another: the owner or other person can only transfer an interest in the land with the consent of the transferee, since no person can be forced to accept a transfer of property against his or her will. Thus there is no single person who has a "power," by unilateral act, to transfer any property interest to another.

22. R. Pound, The Law of Property and Recent Juristic Thought, 25 A.B.A.J. 993, 996 (1939).

It should also be noted that the European civil law adopts a basically unitary view of "property" which emphasizes "ownership" rather than the various separate legal interests that are included in "ownership." Thus, for example, the Louisiana Civil Code, which is derived from the French Code Napoleon, states: "Ownership is the right that confers on a person direct, immediate, and exclusive authority over a thing."[23] As we shall see, the Anglo–American law adopts, at least with respect to property in land, a very different view which places much greater emphasis on the various aggregates of legal interests into which "complete property" may be divided.[24]

§ 1.3   Judicial Remedies for Protection of Property and the Relativity of Property Rights at Common Law

Although "property" law determines what "expectations of being able to draw such or such an advantage" from particular "things" will be legally protected, the mode of protection is largely determined, in the Anglo–American legal system, by the historical evolution of "common law" civil remedies in England between the twelfth and the sixteenth centuries. These remedies were mainly designed to protect those in possession of land or chattels from unauthorized interference with their possession.

Common law actions for recovery of land *in specie* developed in England as early as the reign of Henry II. Ultimately, a wide variety of "real" actions became available to a plaintiff who alleged that he was entitled to possession (*seisin*) of land presently in the defendant's possession.[1] But these "real" actions, collectively, did not provide a fully satisfactory set of judicial remedies for plaintiffs who sought to recover possession of land wrongfully taken or withheld by a defendant. When the action of "ejectment" became generally available in the sixteenth century as a specific remedy for plaintiffs seeking to recover possession of land wrongfully withheld from them, the older "real" actions gradually fell into disuse and had become practically obsolete by the end of the seventeenth century.[2]

"Ejectment," which provided a relatively expeditious method for recovering possession of land and carried with it a right to jury trial, was an offshoot of the ancient action of "trespass," which was a "personal" rather than a "real action" because it resulted in a judgment—if the plaintiff was successful—for money damages rather than for restitution *in specie*.[3] The action of "trespass" originally provided a damage remedy for any direct and tortious interference with the actual possession of either land or chattels. But "trespass" produced many offshoots, including "ejectment," that became separate forms of action. Among these other offshoots were "case" (or "trespass on the case"), which provided a damage remedy for indirect or

23. La.Stat.Ann.Civ.Code art. 477 (1980).

24. See Chapters 2 through 6, and Chapter 8, post.

§ 1.3

1. S. Milsom, Historical Foundations of the Common Law 106–124 (1969); T. Plucknett, Concise History of the Common Law 335–343 (4th ed. 1948); E. Morgan, The Study of Law 83–88 (2d ed. 1948); W. Maitland, The Forms of Action at Common Law 21–48 (1936).

2. S. Milsom, supra note 1, at 127–138; T. Plucknett, supra note 1, at 354; E. Morgan, supra note 1, at 112–115; W. Maitland, supra note 1, at 56–61. For more detailed discussion, see P. Bordwell, Ejectment Takes Over, 55 Iowa L.Rev. 1089 (1970).

3. S. Milsom, supra note 1, at 244–256; T. Plucknett, supra note 1, at 349–352; E. Morgan, supra note 1, at 102–105; W. Maitland, supra note 1, at 48–50, 53–55, 65.

consequential injury to land or chattels resulting from the wrongful act (intended or negligent) of the defendant,[4] and "trover," which provided a damage remedy in cases where the defendant had "converted" the plaintiff's chattel(s) to his own use by wrongful seizure, withholding, or disposition.[5]

Money damages was the usual remedy for wrongful interference with a plaintiff's right to possession of chattels. In certain cases the plaintiff could recover possession of chattels by means of an action of "replevin"[6] or "detinue."[7] Replevin originated as a remedy for the tenant whose chattels had been wrongfully "distrained" by his landlord for nonpayment of rent or other breach of duty. In England the courts seem never to have expanded the scope of replevin to cover wrongful seizures other than seizures by way of distraint,[8] and replevin clearly did not provide a remedy for the mere wrongful withholding of possession.[9] The latter was the function of detinue, where the defendant, if found to have wrongfully withheld possession of the plaintiff's chattel(s), had the option of returning the chattel(s) or paying their value as damages.[10] If the defendant in detinue chose to pay damages, the outcome of the action was similar to the outcome of a successful trover action.

In most American jurisdictions, from an early date, the common law action of ejectment was available to plaintiffs seeking to recover possession of land.[11] The other forms of action mentioned above were also available for protection of property interests in land and chattels. In most jurisdictions the scope of replevin was broadened so that it could be used to recover chattels *in specie* in any case where the defendant was wrongfully withholding them,[12] and to recover damages in cases where the defendant had wrongfully disposed of the plaintiff's chattel(s).[13] Since a plaintiff could recover either possession or damages by means of an action of replevin or an action of trover, detinue fell into disuse in most American jurisdictions. Where chattels were damaged but not converted to the defendant's use,

4. S. Milsom, supra note 1, at 256–270; T. Plucknett, supra note 1, at 352–353; E. Morgan, supra note 1, at 105–107; W. Maitland, supra note 1, at 65–68.

5. T. Plucknett, supra note 1, 354–356; E. Morgan, supra note 1, at 111–112; W. Maitland, supra note 1, at 71. See also S. Milsom, supra note 1, at 321–332.

6. T. Plucknett, supra note 1, at 348–349; E. Morgan, supra note 1, at 88–92; W. Maitland, supra note 1, at 48, 61.

7. S. Milsom, supra note 1, at 219–223, 227–235; T. Plucknett, supra note 1, at 345–346; E. Morgan, supra note 1, at 96–99; W. Maitland, supra note 1, at 61–63.

8. S. Milsom, supra note 1, at 95 ("never much widened in England"); T. Plucknett, supra note 1, at 349; W. Maitland, supra note 1, at 61 ("A few instances of replevin used to recover goods though not taken by distress * * * occur late in the day, and are not important in relation to general theory."). But cf. J. Ames, Lectures on Legal History 69–70 (1913).

9. Mennie v. Blake, 6 E. & B. 842 (1856).

10. W. Maitland, supra note 1, at 62; E. Morgan, supra note 1, at 98. Damages for the detention (loss of use) in addition to the value were awarded.

11. In the New England states, the action for possession of realty was called a "writ of entry" but it was substantially the same as "ejectment" and was quite different from the old English "writ of entry."

12. T. Plucknett, supra note 1, at 349. But cf. E. Morgan, supra note 1, at 91 (orthodox rule in U.S. allowed replevin only where there was a wrongful taking, but Pennsylvania and Massachusetts extended replevin to all cases of wrongful detention in early cases).

13. Although the early English cases allowed recovery of damages in such cases, the American cases were in conflict in the absence of a governing statute. E. Morgan, supra note 1, at 91. Such statutes have been enacted in most jurisdictions.

trespass and case were available in all American jurisdictions to provide a damage remedy.[14] Trespass also provided the possessor of land with a damage remedy when his right to possession was invaded but he was not dispossessed;[15] and an action on the case for nuisance gave him a remedy for non-trespassory interference with the use and enjoyment of his land.[16]

The forms of action mentioned above, along with others designed to protect personal and contract rights, evolved in the English "common law" courts. But the English Court of Chancery also developed distinctive "equitable" remedies for the protection of property interests—e.g., injunctions against interference with such interests, rescission of property transactions, reformation of instruments, and removal of "clouds" on title to land.[17] In some cases, Chancery only provided a better remedy for protection of "legal" property interests; in other cases, Chancery protected property interests not recognized in the "common law" courts.[18] Although not all American jurisdictions established separate "equity" courts, "equitable" as well as "legal" remedies were generally available in America from an early date.[19]

At the present time, the "common law" forms of action have been abolished in almost all American jurisdictions, and in most of them all forms of "legal" and "equitable" relief are now available in a single form of civil action.[20] But the "common law" forms of action and the "equitable" remedies for protection of property that evolved in England continue to have a profound influence on modern property law. For example, (1) in many instances a possessor of land or chattels is entitled either to specific restitution (in the case of land) or to damages measured by the value of the property (in the case of chattels) on the basis of his prior possession alone, when he is deprived of possession by one who cannot show a better right to possession; and (2) there is still no judicial proceeding except a proceeding to register the title to land [21]—available in only a few jurisdictions—in which the ownership of land, chattels, or intangibles can be established as against "the world."

The first of the propositions just stated is a consequence of the great importance attached to possession of land and chattels during the formative period of the common law. In ejectment, the plaintiff was allowed to recover possession of land from one who had dispossessed him unless the latter could show a better right to possession;[22] similarly, in trover, the plaintiff was allowed to recover the full value of chattels from one who had dispossessed him unless the latter could show a better right to possession.[23] In neither case could the defendant defeat the action by showing that a third party had

14. Generally, see Prosser, Torts §§ 7, 14 (4th ed. 1971).

15. See post Section 7.1.

16. See post Section 7.2.

17. Generally, as to the origin of "equity" and "equitable remedies," see H. McClintock, Equity §§ 1–7 (2d ed. 1948); W. Walsh, Equity chaps. 1–83 (1930).

18. E.g., the rights of a trust beneficiary in the trust property.

19. McClintock, Equity § 5 (2d ed. 1948).

20. McClintock, Equity, § 6 (2d ed. 1948); W. Walsh, Equity § 7 (1930); C. Clark, Code Pleading §§ 6–10, 15 (2d ed. 1947); F. James and G. Hazard, Civil Procedure 18–22 (2d ed. 1977).

21. As to title registration, see post Section 11.3.

22. E.g., Tapscott v. Cobbs, 52 Va. (11 Grat.) 172 (1854).

23. E.g., Anderson v. Gouldberg, 51 Minn. 294, 53 N.W. 636 (1892).

a better right to possession than the plaintiff.[24]   In most jurisdictions, these rules are still applied in actions to recover possession of land and in actions to recover damages for conversion of chattels.   But the cases are divided as to whether prior possession alone is a sufficient basis for specific recovery of chattels in replevin [25] or for recovery of damages equal to the full reduction in value resulting from trespassory interference with land.[26]

The second proposition stated above results from the fact that actions (other than actions for title registration) available to protect interests in property are generally considered to be either "personal" or "quasi in rem," and the judgments rendered in such actions are binding only on persons who are made parties to such actions and those in privity with them.[27]   Although statutory actions to "quiet" a plaintiff's title to land are now available in most American jurisdictions,[28] such actions are not effective to establish ownership of a particular tract of land as against persons over whom the court did not acquire jurisdiction.[29]   Only in the few states where an action to register a land title is authorized by statute can the ownership of land be conclusively established as against "the whole world." [30]

The result of all this is that property rights established by judicial decision are, generally, only relative.   In many cases a mere possessor of land or chattels, as we have seen,[31] may be treated as if he were the owner for the purpose of awarding a particular form of legal or equitable relief. Thus, e.g., if B wrongfully dispossesses A and C later wrongfully dispossesses B, B may recover from C as if he were owner of the land or chattel, and A, in turn, may recover from B as if he were the owner, solely on the basis of prior possession.   In most such cases, of course, the plaintiff will seek to show that he is entitled to possession as "true owner" or because the "true owner" has conferred the right of possession on him.   But even if the court in such an action determines, on the basis of persuasive evidence, that the plaintiff is

---

24. Supra notes 22, 23.   Contra: Russell v. Hill, 125 N.C. 470, 34 S.E. 640 (1900) (identity of true owner was known).

25. See Annot. 150 A.L.R. 163, 192 (1944); B. Shipman, Common Law Pleading 126 (3d ed. 1923).   It should be noted that the traditional procedure in replevin by which a sheriff is directed to seize a chattel and deliver it to the plaintiff upon the plaintiff's giving a bond to prosecute the action and return it to the defendant if the judgment goes against him, before any hearing on the merits of the plaintiff's claim, has encountered constitutional obstacles.   See Fuentes v. Shevin, 407 U.S. 67, 92 S.Ct. 1983, 32 L.Ed.2d 556 (1972), rehearing denied 409 U.S. 902, 93 S.Ct. 177, 34 L.Ed.2d 165 (1972).

26. Compare Todd v. Jackson, 26 N.J.L. 525 (1857), and Illinois & St. Louis Railroad & Coal Co. v. Cobb, 94 Ill. 55 (1879), with Winchester v. City of Stevens Point, 58 Wis. 350, 17 N.W. 3 (1883).   Generally, see 6A Am. L.Prop. § 28.14 (1954).

27. A. Freeman, Judgments ch. VIII (5th ed. 1925).

28. See H. McClintock, Equity ch. 19 (2d ed. 1948); W. Walsh, Equity § 117 (1930).

29. See Am.L.Inst., Rest.Judgments 2d §§ 6, 30 (1982), and the Comments and Reporter's Notes thereto, indicating that such actions are "quasi in rem" rather than "in rem," and that judgments in such actions only bind "named parties."   Quiet title statutes sometimes authorize publication of notices naming "all unknown claimants," but such claimants will be bound by a quiet title judgment based on such notice only if such notice satisfies constitutional "due process" requirements.   It is not clear whether such notice does satisfy "due process" requirements.

30. As to title registration, see post Section 11.13.   An action to register title is "in rem," and binds "the whole world."   See Am.L.Inst., Rest.Judgments 2d §§ 6, 30 (1982).   Title registration statutes provide for creation of a fund to indemnify any person who had a valid interest in the registered land, if the court's registration decree extinguished that interest and the owner of the interest had no actual knowledge of the suit to register the title.

31. Supra notes 22, 23.

the "true owner" of the land or chattel, that determination is binding only as between the parties to the action.[32]

§ 1.4   Real and Personal Property

It has already been noted that the subject matter of "property" may be land, chattels, or intangible "things." In general, property in land (and things attached thereto) is classified as "real property." (By extension, the land itself, with the things attached thereto, is often termed "real estate" or "realty.") "Real property" in Anglo–American law thus corresponds substantially with "immoveable property" in the European Civil Law. Property in chattels and in intangible "things" is classified as "personal property." The term "chattel" requires no explanation. The list of intangible "things" that may form the subject matter of "personal property" is long, including claims represented by bank accounts, promissory notes, corporate and government bonds, shares of corporate stock, life insurance policies, and annuities,[1] as well as patents, copyrights, trademarks, and even the "goodwill" of business enterprises. Thus "personal property" in Anglo–American law corresponds substantially with "moveable property" in the European Civil Law.

The classification of property as "real" or "personal" makes little sense in the modern world and can only be understood by reference to the historical development of legal remedies for the protection of property in England. In the medieval period, as we have seen,[2] property interests in land were protected by the "real actions" in which possession of the *res*—the land itself—could be recovered. Property interests in chattels, however, were generally protected only by various "personal actions"—e.g., trespass, case, trover, and detinue—in which the successful plaintiff recovered a "personal" judgment for damages.[3] Hence property interests in land came to be called "real property" and interests in chattels came to be called "personal property." [4]

Classification of property interests on the basis of the actions available for their protection sometimes had anomalous results. For example, when land was leased for a definite period of time, the lessee originally had no action by which he could recover possession of the leased land from one who wrongfully took or withheld possession; only an action for damages could be brought.[5] Hence the interest of the lessee was classified as "personal property"—a classification that persisted long after the action of ejectment was developed and then, in the latter part of the fifteenth century, was extended so as to enable the lessee to recover possession of the leased premises from one who wrongfully took or withheld possession.[6] Indeed, for

---

32. See Am.L.Inst., Rest.Judgments 2d §§ 5, 6, 17, 30 (1982).

§ 1.4

1. These intangible subjects of property are often called "choses in action."

2. See ante Section 1.3 at notes 1–3.

3. See ante Section 1.3 at notes 4–10.

4. See T. Plucknett, Concise History of the Common Law 318–324 (3d ed. 1940).

5. See 1 Am.L.Prop. 175–176 (1952); T. Plucknett, supra note 4, at 334–335.

6. See R. Powell, Real Prop. ¶ 221[2] (1977). Cf. 1 Am.L.Prop. 176 (1952) (suggesting that continued classification of the lessee's interest as "personal property" may have been due more to "the fact that leases frequently were used for security purposes" rather than because the remedy was originally only an action for damages).

some purposes at least, the interest of a lessee in the leased land is classified as "personal property" even today. This continues to be important in states where the intestate succession laws still distinguish between "real property" and "personal property." [7]

As previously indicated, "real property" includes interests in things attached to land as well as land itself. Substantial structures and all natural vegetation (trees and perennial shrubs and grasses, sometimes called *fructus naturales*) are treated as "real property" for practically all purposes.[8] Interests in cultivated crops (sometimes called *emblements or fructus industriales*), however, are sometimes treated as "real property" and sometimes as "personal property," depending upon the circumstances.[9]

Chattels placed on or affixed to land or structures attached to land by the landowner for the purpose of "improving" the land are called *fixtures* and are treated as "real property" for most purposes.[10] If such a fixture is temporarily severed from the land by accident, mistake, or "act of God" without the consent of the landowner, the landowner's interest in the fixture is still considered to be "real property." [11] But life tenants and lessees are generally privileged to remove fixtures installed by them for trade, domestic, or ornamental purposes.[12] And when the vendor of a chattel which becomes a fixture retains a chattel security interest therein, the vendor is frequently privileged to remove the fixture if the purchaser fails to pay the full purchase price, as against both the purchaser and third parties such as mortgagees of the real property.[13] If a fixture is lawfully removed by a tenant or by one who has a security interest therein, it becomes and remains a chattel unless it is again affixed to land or a structure attached to land.

§ 1.5 Legal and Equitable Property

As a result of the peculiar development of English law prior to the founding of the United States, we still have separate bodies of law based, respectively, on the "common law" and "equity jurisprudence" of England, despite the procedural reforms of the nineteenth and twentieth centuries which, to some extent, effected a "merger" of "law" and "equity." [1] One consequence of the continuing distinction between "law" and "equity" is that in many cases "equitable" property interests may be recognized and protected in persons who have no "legal" property interests. "Equitable" property

---

7. See Atkinson, Wills § 14 (2d ed. 1953) (indicating that statutes in most jurisdictions now provide that the same relatives shall succeed to both realty and personalty).

8. See 5 Am.L.Prop. §§ 19.15, 19.16 (1952).

9. See id. § 19.16.

10. See id. §§ 19.1 through 19.14; 5 R. Powell, Real Prop. ¶¶ 651–660 (1979).

11. E.g., Rogers v. Gilinger, 30 Pa. 185 (1853). Contra: Buckout v. Swift, 27 Cal. 433 (1865).

12. 5 Am.L.Prop. § 19.11 (1952); 5 R. Powell, Real Prop. ¶¶ 656, 657 (1979).

13. See 5 Am.L.Prop. § 19.12 (1952); 5 R. Powell, Real Prop. ¶ 659 (1979).

§ 1.5

1. On the historical development of "common law" and "equity" jurisprudence in England, with primary emphasis on "common law," see T. Plucknett, Concise History of the Common Law (4th ed.). For a more detailed treatment of the historical development of "equity," see 1 J. Pomeroy, Equity Jurisprudence 14–117 (5th ed. S. Symons 1941); H. McClintock, Equity 1–19 (2d ed. 1948); W. Walsh, Equity 1–36 (1930). McClintock defines "equity" as follows: "In Anglo–American law, equity means the system of legal materials developed and applied by the court of chancery in England and the courts succeeding to its powers in the British Empire and the United States." H. McClintock, Equity 1 (2d ed. 1948).

interests arise, in most cases, as a result of (1) the creation of a trust or (2) the making of a specifically enforceable contract.

A "trust" is created whenever "legal" ownership of land, chattels, or intangibles is transferred to or retained by one person—the "trustee"—to be held for the benefit of another—the "cestui que trust" or beneficiary.[2] Protection of the beneficiary's interest under the trust is provided on the "equity side of the court" in accordance with "equitable" principles by virtue of which the court will compel the trustee to deal fairly with the beneficiary and to manage trust *res* or *corpus* honestly and prudently. The beneficiary of a trust is generally described as the "equitable" owner of the *res* or *corpus,* although his or her interest was historically regarded as a claim *in personam* against the trustee rather than a claim *in rem* against the world. In litigation between the beneficiary and trustee, in the absence of statutory authority, a court does not enforce the beneficiary's rights directly against the *res* (e.g., by awarding the right to possession to the beneficiary), but merely orders the trustee to perform his duties in accordance with the terms of the trust and the applicable "equitable" principles. Moreover, the trustee as "legal" owner of the *res,* is the proper party to sue third persons in order to protect the *res.* But the "equitable" interest of the trust beneficiary is protected against unauthorized transfers of trust property by the trustee except in cases where the transferee acquires a legal interest for value and without notice of the trust. A donee or a purchaser with notice of the trust will acquire the legal interest subject to all the trustee's duties to the beneficiary with respect to the trust property.

The "trust" concept has been extended to many situations where there is no real trust—e.g., where courts impose a "constructive" or "resulting" trust or an "equitable" lien on specific land, chattels, or intangibles in order to prevent "unjust enrichment" of a wrongdoer.[3] When a "constructive" or "resulting" trust is imposed, the "legal" owner will be treated like a trustee and ordered to transfer "legal" ownership to the person who is "equitably" entitled to ownership. Similar relief may be granted where a plaintiff is entitled to the "equitable" remedy of rescission or reformation of a contract or conveyance.[4] Hence a person with an "equitable" right to rescission or reformation can be described in some cases as the "equitable" owner of land, chattels, or intangibles "legally" owned by another.

Because land is generally deemed to be unique, "equity" courts will ordinarily order specific performance of an enforceable contract for the sale of land in favor of either party to the contract.[5] The purchaser's "equitable" right to specific performance is said to make him the "equitable" owner of the land in question, although the vendor remains the "legal" owner until he

---

2. The law of trusts will be considered only incidentally in this book. The principal multi-volume treatises on the law of trusts are A. Scott, Trusts (3d ed. 1967, 6 vols.); G. Bogert, Trusts and Trustees (2d ed. 1965–69, 18 vols.). The best single-volume textbook is G. & T. Bogert, Trusts (5th ed. 1973).

3. For an extended discussion, see A. Scott, Trusts §§ 404–552 (3d ed. 1967); 1 G. Palmer, Restitution 9–21, § 6.7 (1978); H. McClintock, Equity §§ 85, 120 (2d ed. 1948).

4. See H. McClintock, Equity §§ 84, 86, 94–104 (2d ed. 1948); W. Walsh, Equity §§ 106, 110, 111 (1930); 2 G. Palmer, Restitution §§ 12.6, 13.8 through 13.19, 14.25, 14.26 (1978).

5. See 4 J. Pomeroy, Equity Jurisprudence §§ 1400–1410 (5th ed. S. Symons 1941); H. McClintock, Equity §§ 53–78 (2d ed. 1948); W. Walsh, Equity §§ 58–85 (1930).

executes an effective conveyance in favor of the purchaser.[6] Like the beneficiary of a trust, the purchaser as "equitable" owner is protected against a subsequent unauthorized transfer of the land except in cases where the transferee is a bona fide purchaser for value without notice of the prior land sale contract.

Under the recording system established in all jurisdictions in the United States,[7] the recording of a written trust instrument or land sale contract will ordinarily charge any subsequent transferee of the land in question with notice of the trust or contract, as the case may be. Moreover, the American recording statutes, in force in all states, in substance prevent any unrecorded conveyance (or other instrument affecting land ownership) from transferring more than an "equitable" interest because these statutes declare the unrecorded instrument to be void as against any subsequent bona fide purchaser for value without notice of the unrecorded instrument. Hence the distinction between "legal" and "equitable" property interests in land is substantially lessened, although it is not entirely eliminated.

The making of an enforceable contract for the sale of land does more than make the purchaser the "equitable" owner of the land so that his interest under the contract is deemed to be "real" property "in equity." In most states, the contract also effects an "equitable conversion" of the vendor's "legal" ownership of the land into "personal" property for certain purposes.[8] Thus, if the vendor dies before the contract is performed, the vendor's claim to the purchase money passes to his or her next-of-kin or legatees as "personal" property; and if the purchaser dies before the contract is performed, the purchaser's claim to the land passes to his or her heirs or devisees as "real" property. The doctrine of "equitable conversion" is also applied in cases where land is devised by will to a trustee with a direction to sell it and distribute the proceeds, or where a marriage settlement directs the conversion of land into money or vice versa. But the importance of the doctrine has been much reduced by the general enactment of intestate succession laws providing that a decedent's "real" and "personal" property shall pass to the same persons.

§ 1.6 From Feudal Tenure to Land Ownership—Some English History

In Anglo–American law the most common type of property in chattels has always been "complete property" (full ownership), although it was recognized even in medieval England that lesser interests in chattels could be created. After the Norman Conquest, however, the law of property in land developed very differently from the law of property in chattels.

The Norman conquest of England resulted in the establishment of a feudal system of landholding.[1] William the Conqueror confiscated all the

6. See H. McClintock, Equity §§ 106–117 (2d ed. 1948); W. Walsh, Equity §§ 86–98 (1930). See also Section 10.13, post.

7. The recording system is considered in detail, post Section 11.9.

8. See H. McClintock, Equity § 106 (2d ed. 1948); W. Walsh, Equity § 86 (1930).

§ 1.6

1. On feudal tenures in England, see 1 American Law of Property §§ 1.2–1.4 (A. Casner ed. 1952) (hereafter cited as Am.L.Prop.); R. Megarry and H. Wade, Law of Real Property 13–39 (4th Ed.1975) (hereafter cited as Real Property); S. Milsom, Legal Framework of

land held by the Saxon nobles and then redistributed most of it among his principal Norman barons, who were called tenants in chief.[2] Most of these tenants in chief held their land by knight service, which obligated them to furnish a specified quota of knights for military service when required by the king.[3] A few tenants in chief held their land by a tenure called "serjeanty," which obligated these tenants to fill important offices in the royal household.[4] And some land was granted to religious bodies and ecclesiastical officials in frankalmoin ("free alms"), subject to purely religious duties such as saying Masses or prayers for the King or members of his family.[5]

Soon after the Norman Conquest tenants in chief who held by knight service began to subinfeudate—i.e., to grant portions of their lands to be held of them either by knight service—which would assist the tenant in chief in supplying the required quota of knights for service in the King's army [6]—or in serjeanty or frankalmoin, or in socage. Socage was a form of tenure that required the tenant either to perform fixed agricultural services on the lord's land or, more commonly, to pay a fixed rent in money or in kind.[7] Tenants in chief who held in serjeanty or in frankalmoin, as well as those who held

English Feudalism (1976) (hereafter cited as Feudalism); S. Milsom, Historical Foundations of the Common Law 88–91, 95–102 (1969) (hereafter cited as Historical Foundations); C. Moynihan, Introduction to the Law of Real Property 1–24 (2d ed. 1988) (hereafter cited as Introduction); T. Plucknett, Concise History of the Common Law 516–520, 531–545 (5th ed. 1956) (hereafter cited as Concise History); 1 F. Pollock and W. Maitland, History of English Law 229–406 (2d ed. 1898, reissued 1968) (hereafter cited as History); A. Simpson, Introduction to the History of the Land Law 1–23, 44–46 (1961) (hereafter cited as Introduction).

2. There were probably about 1500 tenants in chief by 1086 when the Domesday Survey was carried out. A. Simpson, Introduction 3. The larger baronial holdings, or "honours," were generally created out of the holdings of numerous Saxon nobles. As many as eight Saxon holdings, located in different parts of England, might be combined to compose a single "honour." The Norman settlement resulted in the compression of several thousand smaller Saxon holdings into fewer than 200 major "honours." C. Moynihan, Introduction 3. It seems unlikely, however, that the Saxon peasantry, who actually tilled the soil, were much affected by the Norman Conquest. "In general the effect of the Norman Conquest was only to substitute a new, alien lord for his Saxon predecessor. What a tenant in chief acquired by the King's grant was not the enjoyment of land so much as the enjoyment of rights over land and services due from peasants who cultivated that land; to the peasant it may not have seemed that anything very momentous had occurred. But we know very little of the immediate effect of the Conquest on the Saxon peasantry." A. Simpson, Introduction 4.

3. At an early date, the time of service was fixed at forty days each year, and the knights were only required to serve within the kingdom of England. There is some evidence that the quota of knights due from a tenant in chief was fixed in multiples of five or ten. A. Simpson, Introduction 3 at n. 5.

4. E.g., offices such as marshal, constable, chamberlain, and butler.

5. There were two types of frankalmoin tenure: (1) where the tenant had only a general obligation to pray for the souls of the donor and his ancestors, enforceable only in the ecclesiastical court; and (2) where the tenant had an obligation to furnish specified religious services—e.g., to say ten Masses a year—enforceable in the King's courts. A. Simpson, Introduction 10.

6. The smallest unit allotted to a subtenant was the *knight's fee,* given to a single knight. The term *fee* comes from the Latin *feudum* or *feodum,* which originally simply meant *holding,* perhaps normally limited to the holding of a tenant of some importance. Several variant English forms such as *feud* and *fief* were ultimately displaced by *fee.* The transaction by which a *fee* was granted was a *feoffment.* In the twelfth century the term *fee* came to be used to designate an inheritable interest in land rather than a mere life interest. A. Simpson, Introduction 3 n. 4.

7. "Socage was the great residual category of [free] tenure; and its characteristics can only be defined negatively. By the time of Littleton a miscellaneous collection of tenures, some of which had originally been regarded as quite distinct, and had represented quite diverse economic and social relationships, had been bundled together under a single classification, * * *." A. Simpson, Introduction 11.

by knight service, might create tenures in socage by subinfeudation. And subtenants might create another layer of feudal tenures by further subinfeudation.

Once the system of feudal tenure outlined above [8] was established, it could be said that all land in England except the King's demesne land was held of some lord, and ultimately of the King, in return for service of some kind.[9] Moreover, it was clear that, as a consequence of the tenurial system, two or more persons had interests of some sort in each parcel of land except the demesne land of the King.[10] But it was not accurate to say that anyone, except the King in respect to his demesne land, had full ownership of any parcel of land.[11] And this remained true as long as feudal tenure continued to play a significant role in English land law.

It seems probable that the grants made by William the Conqueror to his tenants in chief, and the grants made by his tenants in chief to subtenants, were for life only.[12] Indeed, since feudal tenure involved "a relationship of reciprocal obligations," [13] a feudal tenure would terminate upon the death of either the lord or the tenant: if the tenant died first, the land reverted to the lord; if the lord died first, the tenant's interest terminated and the land reverted to the person who succeeded the decedent as lord.[14] But tenancies limited to the joint lives of lord and tenant were not a satisfactory basis for the complex system of military tenures resulting from extensive subinfeudation. Hence it became the custom before the end of the 11th century for lords to accept the homage of a deceased tenant's eldest son and to regrant the land to him,[15] subject only to payment of a "just and lawful relief." [16]

8. The classification of free tenures used here is that adopted in C. Moynihan, Introduction 9–12. It is a simplification of the more elaborate classification of feudal tenures set out in T. Littleton, Tenures §§ 95–171 (1481), which is summarized in A. Simpson, Introduction 7–14. Cf. 1 Am.L.Prop. 8–9, which mentions only military tenure, frankalmoin tenure, and socage tenure.

9. This proposition was fully recognized in Domesday Book (1086).

10. "An obvious consequence of the tenurial system is that a number of persons have interests of some sort in the same parcel of land. At the bottom of the feudal ladder there will be a tenant who has seisin of the land and is called the tenant in demesne, and at the top there is the King; in between there may be a string of mesne [intermediate] lords, who are lords and tenants at the same time." A. Simpson, Introduction 44.

11. Medieval English lawyers rejected both of the possible ways of ascribing ownership to one of the two or more persons holding an interest in the same parcel of land: (1) to treat the free tenant in demesne as the "owner" and the interests of the lords as "rights in the land of another"; or (2) to treat the King as "owner" of all the land in England and all his tenants, immediate or remote, as having only "rights in the land of another." A. Simpson, Introduction 44–45.

12. S. Milsom, Historical Foundations 90; T. Plucknett, Concise History 523–524; A. Simpson, Introduction 46.

13. S. Milsom, Feudalism 39.

14. Thorne, English Feudalism and Estates in Land, 1959 Camb.L.J. 193, 196–197. Accord: A. Simpson, Introduction 46.

15. Thorne, supra note 14, at 197–199; S. Milsom, Historical Foundations 91. The practical advantages of regranting a military fee to the eldest son of a deceased tenant were the original basis for the scheme of inheritance based on preference for the eldest male descendant—primogeniture—that ultimately prevailed in most of England when the fee became heritable as a matter of common law. As Thorne points out, supra note 14, at 198, "no one was likely to be more readily available, or more acceptable to the men of the fief, or (in the great majority of cases) better prepared to undertake the duties required, than the deceased tenant's eldest son."

16. During the reign of William Rufus, the amount exacted from the deceased tenant's heir was sometimes so large, it seems, as to amount to a repurchase. But Henry I's Coronation Charter (1100) provided that the heirs of both tenants in chief and of other tenants should "take up" (*relevabit*) their lands "with a just and lawful relief" instead of having to repurchase them. The relief to be paid was subsequently fixed at a definite amount.

No doubt it was originally within the lord's discretion whether to grant the land formerly held by a deceased tenant to his eldest son (or other heir), but "substitution of heir for ancestor, a practice followed independently by many lords in many cases, gradually established the general rule." [17] As the custom of regranting land to the deceased tenant's heir evolved, it also became customary for the lord expressly to grant the land to the new tenant "and his heirs," and the term *feodum* or *fee,* previously applied to any feudal holding, came to mean a feudal holding created by such language and customarily regranted to a deceased tenant's heir.[18]

During the second half of the twelfth century the customary claim of a deceased tenant's heir to have the fee regranted to him crystallized into a "common law right of inheritance." [19] From that time on, a grant to a named person "and his heirs" created a property interest of potentially infinite duration that would be inheritable by the heirs of the original grantee in all succeeding generations. Inheritance was not limited to direct descendants, but if a tenant died without any direct descendant, the fee would "escheat" to the deceased tenant's lord.[20]

As already indicated, the scheme of inheritance that evolved for fees held by military tenure was characterized by a preference for the eldest male descendant of the deceased tenant—the principle of primogeniture.[21] Ultimately, this scheme came to be applied to fees held by any kind of tenure,[22] except in those parts of England where local customs continued to

---

17. Thorne, supra note 14, 198. Accord, S. Milsom, Feudalism 180.

18. See supra note 6.

19. Thorne, supra note 14, at 198–204, concludes that this change took place about 1200. Milsom believes it occurred somewhat earlier as a result of the invention of the writ of right and the assize of *mort d'ancestor*—"the former compelling a lord to do justice to one claiming to hold of him by hereditary descent, the latter ensuring that the heir should get seisin on his ancestor's death." S. Milsom, Historical Foundations 91–92. The assize of *mort d'ancestor* was based on the Assize of Northampton, c. 4 (1176), which provided:

> If anyone dies holding a free tenement, his heir shall remain in such seisin as his father had on the day that he died * * * and if the lord of the fee denies to the heir the seisin of the dead man which he claims, the king's justices shall inquire by twelve lawful men what seisin the dead man had on the day that he died, and shall restore it to the heir in accordance with what is found. * * *

For a more detailed discussion of the evolution of the heritable fee, see S. Milsom, Feudalism 154–186, especially at 164–171.

20. In the case of tenants in chief, the fee would escheat to the King; in all other cases, it would escheat to some *mesne* lord.

21. See supra note 15. Where primogeniture was the rule of inheritance, the eldest son of a deceased tenant would inherit to the exclusion of younger children; if the eldest son predeceased the tenant but left a son who survived the tenant, that son would inherit to the exclusion of younger children of the deceased tenant; but if the deceased tenant had no surviving male descendants, the tenant's nearest female descendant or descendants would inherit; if there were two or more female descendants in the same degree (e.g., daughters), they would inherit in equal shares as *co-parceners.* If no descendants of the deceased tenant survived him, his collateral relatives would inherit, with a preference for male stocks unless the lands in fact descended from a female stock. For more detailed discussions of the common rules of inheritance, see A. Simpson, Introduction 53–60; T. Plucknett, Concise History 712–722.

22. T. Plucknett, Concise History 527–528, 530; A. Simpson, Introduction 48—both stating that even after adoption of primogeniture for fees held by military tenure, equal division among sons of a deceased tenant continued to be the rule for fees held by socage and other free non-military tenures. "But by Edward I's time primogeniture had become the common law of all tenures, and exceptions to the rule were treated as anomalous customs in opposition to common right." A. Simpson, Introduction 48.

be applied by the King's courts.[23]

In the latter part of the twelfth century, when the custom that a fee should normally be regranted to the heir of a deceased tenant was crystallizing into a rule of the common law, a tenant's power to alienate was clearly subject to some restrictions. It was doubtful whether a tenant could alienate without the consent of his lord,[24] and the tenant had only a limited power to disinherit his heir by alienating during his lifetime.[25] But by the middle of the thirteenth century the power of the tenant to alienate without his lord's consent (though still object to payment of a fine for alienation) and free of any claim by his heir became settled as a matter of common law.[26] However, the lords continued thereafter to object strongly to the practice of alienating by subinfeudation, which frequently deprived them of the value of the incidents of feudal tenure such as *wardship* and *marriage*.[27]

The Statute *Quia Emptores*[28] was enacted in 1290 to settle conclusively all questions relating to alienation of fees granted to a person "and his heirs." *Quia Emptores* established (1) that such fees—then coming to be called *fees simple*[29]—were freely transferable *inter vivos* provided the transferee was substituted for the transferor and no new tenure was created;[30] (2)

23. These customs were *gavelkind,* by which the sons of a deceased tenant inherited in equal shares, and *borough English,* by which the youngest son inherited to the exclusion of older sons. *Gavelkind* applied to all land in Kent unless a contrary custom was proved, and it could also apply to land elsewhere if the custom were proved. The custom of *borough English* was recognized in certain boroughs, mainly in Sussex and Surrey. See R. Megarry & H. Wade, Real Property 20–22; A. Simpson, Introduction 20–21.

24. In Glanvil's time it is doubtful whether a tenant was entitled to alienate his holding without the consent of his lord; to be on the safe side it was wise to secure the lord's consent to a gift, but it was not perhaps essential if the gift was a reasonable one which did not seriously affect the lord's interests. A. Simpson, Introduction 51. For more detailed discussions, see 1 Pollock and Maitland, History 329–349; S. Milsom, Feudalism 103–110.

25. See Thorne, English Feudalism and Estates in Land, 1959 Camb.L.J. 198, 207–208; S. Milsom, Feudalism 121–122; T. Plucknett, Concise History 526–527 (setting out the text of Glanvil's treatise vii, 1).

26. A. Simpson, Introduction 51. It was held in D'Arundel's Case, Bracton's Notebook, case 1054, decided in 1225, that the heir could not recover from the transferee where the transferor had given a warranty on behalf of himself and his heirs, because the heir was bound by the warranty. For a detailed discussion of the operation of such warranties, see S. Milsom, Feudalism 42–44, 73–74, 108–109, 126–132. Factors other than the warranty were also important—e.g., the rule of primogeniture. See T. Plucknett, Concise History 528–529. See also Thorne, English Feudalism and Estates in Land, 1959 Camb.L.J. 207.

27. "Suppose, for example, Osbert, who holds of Robert, wishes to alienate his holding to Richard, and does so by subinfeudating. If the alienation takes place on account of a sale, then Osbert will receive the purchase price and grant the lands to Richard to hold of him at a nominal service of, say, a red rose at midsummer. Osbert will be left seised of the seignory [lordship], worth one rose annually, and it is on the value of the seignory that the amount due in incidents to Robert, his lord, will be calculated. Thus if Osbert dies and his heir, a minor, succeeds him, Robert will be entitled to the wardship over a seignory of trivial value; if Osbert commits felony, the seignory and not the land, will come to Robert by escheat." A. Simpson, Introduction 50. Subinfeudation in frankalmoin would have an even more detrimental effect on the lord, since the grantee (a religious corporation) would never die and the lord would thus never be entitled to any of the incidents of tenure that accrued on the tenant's death. S. Milsom, Historical Foundations 97.

28. Stat. 18 Edw. I (1290).

29. The terms *pure fee* or *fee simple* came into use in the latter part of the thirteenth century to designate an interest inheritable by collateral as well as lineal heirs, as distinguished from a *fee tail,* which was inheritable only by lineal heirs ("heirs of the body"). The fee tail's evolution is discussed in the following section of this book. Although the term *pure fee* was more commonly used at first, the term *fee simple* ultimately displaced it. A. Simpson, Introduction 53, n. 4.

30. The statute provided that "from henceforth it should be lawful to every freeman to sell at his own pleasure his lands ·or tene-

that no tenant of such a fee could thereafter subinfeudate—i.e., transfer his fee so as to create a new feudal tenure between himself and his transferee— unless licensed by the King to do so; [31] and (3) that fines for alienation should not be exacted except upon transfer of lands held by tenants in chief.[32]

Even after *Quia Emptores* lands held in fee simple were not devisable by will [33] except in localities where the courts recognized local customs permitting the devise of land.[34] But enforcement of "uses" in the Court of Chancery made possible the devise of "equitable" estates in fee simple as early as 1400; [35] and the enactment of the Statute of Wills in 1540 [36] made it possible to devise "legal" estates in fee simple without regard to local custom.[37] Thus the major characteristics of the fee simple estate were fully established before the middle of the sixteenth century: (1) the estate is inheritable by either lineal or collateral heirs of a deceased tenant, generation after generation, provided the estate is not transferred by the tenant by an *inter vivos* conveyance or a will to someone other than his heir; [38] and (2) the estate is freely transferable, either *inter vivos* or by will, free of any claim of the transferor's heirs.

The system of feudal tenure established in England after the Norman Conquest had begun to disintegrate even before enactment of the statute

ments or part of them, so that the feoffee shall hold the same lands or tenements of the chief lord of the same fee, by such service and customs as his feoffor held before."

31. Although the preamble of the statute recited that the practice of subinfeudation often caused lords to lose "their escheates, marriages, and wardships of lands and tenements belonging to their fees which thing seems very hard and extreme unto those lords," the statute did not expressly prohibit subinfeudation; but it was construed by the courts as having that effect. "[T]he doctrine that there cannot have been a subinfeudation since 1290 appears early in the year books * * *." S. Milsom, Introduction 100. Since the King was not expressly mentioned in *Quia Emptores,* he retained the power to create new feudal tenures by virtue of the general rule that rights of the king were not affected by a statute unless he was specifically named therein.

32. Since the statute did not affect the King's rights, he retained the right to exact fines for alienation from his tenants in chief.

33. See A. Simpson, Introduction 59.

34. Such local customs existed most frequently with respect to *gavelkind* land in Kent and land held by *burgage* tenure. See supra note 23.

35. This was possible when a tenant in fee simple transferred land so that (a) the transferee held the land "to the use of" the transferor, or (b) the transferor held the land "to the use of" the transferee. The person who had the "use" of the land could then devise the "use" (beneficial interest) by will. Al-

though the common law courts would not give effect to such a devise, the Court of Chancery would force the person who had held the land "to the use of" the other to allow the devisee to have the "use" of the land in accord with the terms of the will. See A. Simpson, Introduction 171.

36. Stat. 32 Hen. VIII, c. 1 (1540).

37. The statute was enacted to restore the power to devise after "uses" (beneficial interests) were converted into "legal" estates— which were not devisable—by the Statute of Uses, 23 Hen. VIII, c. 10 (1535). The Statute of Wills empowered a fee simple owner to devise all of his lands held by socage tenure and two-thirds of his land held by military tenure, and provided that persons taking lands by devise should be subject to feudal services as though they took by inheritance. All restrictions on the power to devise lands were removed by the Statute of Tenures, 12 Car. II, c. 24 (1660).

38. Quite early on, tenants in fee seem to have resorted to the practice of transferring land to their eldest sons in order to avoid the incidents of feudal tenure that attached when the fee passed by inheritance. The Statute of Marlborough, 52 Hen. III, c. 6 (1267), was intended to preclude this result. See T. Plucknett, Legislation of Edward I at 79–80. Later, the doctrine of "the worthier title" evolved to assure that the result of a conveyance or devise to the transferor's "heirs" would have the same result as passage of the fee by inheritance. See post Section 3.15.

Quia Emptores. The essential personal tie between lord and tenant could hardly be maintained once land held in fee simple became freely alienable and subinfeudation was prohibited by *Quia Emptores*. Moreover, it was clear that tenure by knight service was no longer an efficient basis for maintaining a royal military force.[39] Tenure by knight service would undoubtedly have disappeared fairly quickly had not some of the "incidents" of such tenure—especially "wardship" and "marriage"[40]—continued to have substantial value to the King for another three and a half centuries.[41] New frankalmoin tenures could not be created after 1290, except by the King or with his permission,[42] and frankalmoin gradually lost its importance thereafter.[43] Serjeanty tenure became functionally obsolete as it became customary to obtain personal services by payment of money wages, and serjeanty survived after the fifteenth century only in connection with a few ceremonial offices in the royal household.[44] Socage tenure, meanwhile, gradually emerged as the most desirable form of tenure because (1) it was never subject to the burdensome "incidents" of "wardship" and "marriage," and (2) the money rents fixed when socage tenures were first created became less and less burdensome as a result of the continuing decline in the value of money.[45]

When the Statute of Tenures (1660)[46] converted all military and serjeanty tenures into socage tenures and abolished most of the "incidents" of

39. In the twelfth century it became clear that a paid professional army was more effective than a feudal levy based on actual knight service. Henry II (1154–1189) encouraged his tenants in chief to make a monetary payment, called *scutage,* instead of providing knights. By the time of Edward I (1272–1307), scutage had entirely replaced knight service and, having become a fixed rate, steadily declined in value. C. Moynihan, Introduction 10; T. Plucknett, Concise History (5th ed.) 532–533.

40. When a tenant by knight service died leaving a male heir under 21 or a female heir under 14, the lord was entitled to wardship of the heir's person and lands, which meant that the lord had a right to the rents and profits of the lands until the heir, if male, reached 21 or, if female, either reached 16 or married. The lord had a duty to maintain and educate his ward, but had no duty to account for the rents and profits of the lands. Moreover, the lord had the right to arrange a suitable marriage for his ward and to pocket the value of the marriage—i.e., the amount that the prospective spouse's family was willing to pay for the match—although the ward could refuse the marriage. If the ward refused the marriage, the lord nevertheless was entitled to receive the value of the proffered marriage; and if the ward married another without the lord's consent, the lord was entitled to double the value of the marriage. As early as the thirteenth century, wardship and marriage were viewed as valuable rights to be bought and sold, and as late as the early seventeenth century they were an important source of

royal revenue. C. Moynihan, Introduction 20–21.

For discussion of the other incidents of feudal tenure—homage and fealty, relief and primer seisin, aids, fines for alienation, escheats, and forfeitures, see C. Moynihan, Introduction 15–18; A. Simpson, Introduction 15–17, 19–20.

41. 1 Pollock and Maitland, History 276.

42. That was the effect of the statute *Quia Emptores,* c. 3.

43. C. Moynihan, Introduction 12; A. Simpson, Introduction 10.

44. C. Moynihan, Introduction 11; A. Simpson, Introduction 9. As serjeanty tenure evolved, it was divided into "grand" and "petty" serjeanty. Since the latter was not subject to the "incidents" of "wardship" and "marriage," Littleton termed it "socage in effect." T. Littleton, Tenures § 160 (1481). During the fourteenth century it became settled that only tenants in chief could hold land in serjeanty, and the serjeanty tenures of subtenants thus became tenures in socage.

45. See C. Moynihan, Introduction 20; T. Plucknett, Concise History (5th ed.) 537; A. Simpson, Introduction 11–13. In some cases the rents were only nominal to begin with—e.g., one rose annually—because the tenure was created by gifts to younger children or servants or sales of land for a capital sum.

46. 12 Car. II, c. 24, which was retroactive to February 24, 1645, and confirmed a resolution of the Long Parliament passed on that date and previously confirmed under the Commonwealth in 1656.

tenure,[47] feudal tenure ceased to have substantial significance in English law. Most tenants in fee simple already held directly of the king as a result of the prohibition of subinfeudation (except by the king) in 1290 and the consequent disappearance of "mesne" lordships through escheat [48] during the intervening centuries. Rent was sometimes still payable by a tenant in fee simple after 1660, but the rent was almost always trifling in amount and the remaining incidents of socage tenure were not onerous.[49] In substance, the English tenant in fee simple had full ownership of his land after 1660.[50]

§ 1.7   Tenure and Land Ownership in the United States

When the King of England granted land in North America to individual proprietors and proprietary companies in the seventeenth and eighteenth centuries, the grants were made in fee simple, to be held of the king and his heirs "in free and common socage." Subsequent grants by the proprietors to settlers were also in fee simple. Although subinfeudation seems to have been authorized in all the colonies except Massachusetts Bay, Plymouth, Connecticut, and Rhode Island, subinfeudation seems to have been common only in Maryland, Pennsylvania, and New York. In these states it took the form of grants to settlers in fee simple subject to payment of "ground rents" or "quit rents." Elsewhere, grantees in fee simple held of the king.[1]

 • The American Revolution clearly ended any tenurial relationship between the English king and American landholders.[2] Some of the original thirteen states adopted the view that the state had succeeded to the position of the English king as "lord" and that tenure continued to exist, while other states enacted statutes or constitutional provisions declaring that land ownership should thenceforth be "allodial," or otherwise declaring that tenure was abolished.[3] Throughout the rest of the United States, it seems

47. "This ill-drafted and obscure Act seems to have been intended to convert all tenures by knight-service, serjeanty, and frankalmoin into free and common socage—that is to say, socage which was subject to no services and was free from customary peculiarities. The poor draftsmanship led, perhaps, to the preservation of frankalmoin." A. Simpson, Introduction 22–23.

48. When a tenant in fee simple died without leaving heirs, the land "escheated" to his lord. Over time, the result of the operation of the doctrine of escheat was to eliminate most of the mesne lordships created by subinfeudation prior to 1290.

49. See supra note 45 and text therewith. Since rents were usually small or nominal, the "relief" of one year's rent payable by an heir on the death of his ancestor—which was not abolished by the Statute of Tenures—was also usually small or nominal. The most valuable "incident" of tenure remaining after the Statute of Tenures was escheat.

50. It should be noted that the growing shortage of agricultural labor after England was visited by the Black Death in the fourteenth century forced most lords to commute the labor services of their villein tenants to money rents. A. Simpson, Introduction 150–151; R. Megarry and H. Wade, Real Property 26 (also attributing the change, in part to the Peasants' Revolt of 1381); C. Moynihan, Introduction 16; T. Plucknett, Concise History 32–33. Ultimately, villein tenure evolved into a new form of free tenure called "copyhold" in which the rights and obligations of the tenants were fixed by manorial custom evidenced by the manorial court rolls. A. Simpson, Introduction 150–155; R. Megarry and H. Wade, Real Property 26–28; C. Moynihan, Introduction 12–15. But the law of "copyhold" tenure does not appear to have had any significant influence on the evolution of English or American land law. "Freehold" and "copyhold" tenures remained distinct in England until 1926, when "copyhold" was converted into "free and common socage" by the Law of Property Act (1922).

§ 1.7

1. See Am.L.Prop. at 57–59.

2. Id. at 58.

3. Ibid.

clear that tenure never existed.[4] Even in the states where tenure may theoretically still exist between the state and one who owns land in fee simple, tenure would appear to have little or no practical significance.[5] For all practical purposes, one who owns land in fee simple anywhere in the United States has "complete property" in (full ownership of) the land.[6]

§ 1.8 The Estate Concept—Present and Future Interests

Had the fee simple estate been the only possessory real property interest recognized in the period after *Quia Emptores*,[1] Anglo–American law might have developed along the same lines as the civil law of continental Europe, where the property in land was viewed in essentially unitary terms. But recognition of the fee simple as an inheritable interest did not eliminate the possibility of creating life estates. Indeed, the courts not only continued to recognize life estates in land but held that a conveyance of land to a natural person without adding the words "and his heirs" or "and the heirs of his body" could only create a life estate.[2] And the courts, even before *Quia Emptores*, had recognized inheritable estates in which the right of inheritance was limited to direct descendants of the original donee.[3] These estates had their origin in the marriage gift (*maritagium*) designed to assist a newly married couple in establishing a new family.

Typically, a marriage gift was made by the bride's father, before the marriage, to the bridegroom "and the heirs of his body begotten" on the wife-to-be, or to both the bride and the bridegroom "and the heirs of their bodies begotten," or simply, if the donor was the bridegroom's father, to the bridegroom "and the heirs of his body." In the thirteenth century, as the alienability of land given to a designated person "and his heirs" gradually came to be recognized, it seems to have become increasingly common for donors to give land to a designated person "and the heirs of his [or her] body" even where no marriage occasioned the gift. But such gifts, as well as marriage gifts, came to be construed by the courts as giving the donee a fee simple on condition that he (or she) should have issue, with full power in the donee to alienate the fee simple if a child was in fact born to him (or her).[4]

---

4. Most of the land outside the original thirteen states became part of the public domain of the United States. It is clear that land grants by the United States in fee simple were "allodial" and did not create any "tenure" between the United States and the grantee.

5. 1 Am.L.Prop. 58–60. All states have statutes providing that property (including estates in fee simple absolute) shall "escheat" to the state when the owner dies intestate and with heirs. Although "escheat" existed in England as an incident of "tenure," statutory "escheat" provisions are not based on any theory of "tenure" between landowners and the state.

6. See R. Megarry and H. Wade, Real Property 38 (4th ed. 1975), stating that this is also true in England today.

§ 1.8

1. Ante Section 1.6, text at notes 28–31.

2. R. Megarry and H. Wade, Real Property 51–52, pointing out that "no other word would do in place of 'heirs': 'relatives', 'issue', 'descendants', 'assigns', 'for ever', 'in fee simple', * * * and so on were all ineffective," and that if the magic word was omitted only a life estate would be created. No words of inheritance were required to transfer a fee simple to a corporation, since a corporation could have no heirs; but it was necessary to add the words "and successors" in order to transfer a fee simple to a corporation sole, e.g., a bishop. Id. at 53–55.

3. For a more extended discussion of the evolution of such estates, see 1 Am.L.Prop. 15–18; R. Megarry and H. Wade, Real Property 82–90; T. Plucknett, Concise History 546–557; A. Simpson, Introduction 60–64, 77–82.

4. 1 Am.L.Prop. 15; R. Megarry and H. Wade, Real Property 83; T. Plucknett, Concise History 549–551; A. Simpson, Introduction 62–64.

In most instances, of course, such a construction of the gift was contrary to the intent of the donor, who usually wanted to create an inalienable estate by a gift to a designated person "and the heirs of his [or her] body." Continued protests by landholders against the "conditional fee" construction led ultimately to enactment of the Statute *De Donis Conditionalibus* (1285),[5] which provided that "the will of the donor according to the form of the deed of gift manifestly expressed shall be from henceforward observed, so that they to whom the land was given under such condition shall have no power to alien the land so given, but that it remains unto the issue of them to whom it was given after their death, or shall revert until the donor or his heirs, if issue fail."

The Statute *De Donis Conditionalibus* resulted in judicial recognition of a new kind of inheritable estate called a *fee tail*.[6] Immediately after enactment of the statute it was clear that the first tenant in tail could not, by *inter vivos* conveyance, transfer more than an interest for his own life, whether he had a child or not. In 1311 it was held that the tenant's interest was inalienable (except for his lifetime) until the third "heir of the body" had succeeded as tenant in tail;[7] and by 1410 it was settled that a fee tail would endure so long as there were "heirs of the body" in successive generations.[8] Thus the fee tail was, by the early fifteenth century, a substantially inalienable interest that might last forever. But when—and if—the line of descendants ran out, the land would either revert to the original grantor or his heir (immediate or remote) in fee simple; or, if the original grant so provided, the land would go to a specified person or his heir (immediate or remote) in fee simple.[9]

Some time before 1472, the English courts sanctioned the use of a collusive action called a "common recovery" to enable a tenant in fee tail to transfer an estate in fee simple, free from the claims of his descendants,[10] and in the sixteenth century they held that a common recovery would also bar reversioners and remaindermen who would otherwise be entitled to the

---

5. 13 Edw. I, c. 1. For a more extended discussion of the statute, see 1 Am.L.Prop. 15–16 (setting out the text of the statute in English translation); R. Megarry and H. Wade, Real Property 83–84; T. Plucknett, Concise History 551–552 (also setting out the text of the statute); A. Simpson, Introduction 77–78.

6. A *fee tail* was a fee that was carved or shaped (french, *tailler*) in a particular way; it was also frequently called simply an "estate tail" or an "entailed estate."

7. Y.B. 5 Edw. II, Selden Society, Vol. 31, p. 177, Vol. 33, p. 326. "True the statute did not say this, but [Chief Justice] Beresford [who decided the 1311 case] had a ready explanation. Chief Justice Hengham who drew the statute had done it carelessly; as he worded it the entail only lasted two degrees, but his intention was to make it last for four. This information Beresford, no doubt, derived from tradition, and there was no rule at that time to prevent him from setting aside the clear words of a statute when he had private information that the draftsman really meant something else. It is curious to observe that one of

the greatest pillars of real property law had been erected so carelessly." T. Plucknett, Concise History 553–554.

8. Y.B. 12 Hen. IV Mich., pl. 15, f. 9 (holding that a *maritagium* creates a fee tail that is inalienable in perpetuity). See also A. Simpson, Introduction 80, stating that "[i]n 1346 the indefinite continuance of the entail seems to be accepted" in cases where the fee tail was not created by a *maritagium*.

9. The fee tail, which created rights in the descendants of the original tenant which could not be prejudiced by forfeiture, "provided what many landed proprietors wanted: a means of tying their descendants to the family property, and of preserving it from forfeiture (a practical consideration in troubled times)." R. Megarry and H. Wade, Real Property 85.

10. It is often said that the use of the common recovery to "bar the entail" originated in *Taltarum's Case*, Y.B. 12 Edw. IV 19 (1472), but its use for that purpose clearly antedates *Taltarum's* Case. 3 Holdsworth, History of English Law 119 (3d Ed.1923).

land on failure of the original grantee's issue.[11] But the fee tail continued to be an important-part of English family settlements until modern times. By making the original conveyance to "A for life, remainder to the eldest son of A and the heirs of his body" and then "resettling" the land when the eldest son of each successive life tenant reached the age of twenty-one, land continued to be entailed for generation after generation.[12]

Continued judicial recognition of life estates in the thirteenth century,[13] coupled with the development after the Statute *De Donis Conditionalibus* of the fee tail as "a different sort of fee, * * * a fee which has been cut down, and which is lesser in quantum than a fee simple,"[14] ultimately led to judicial formulation of the theory that a fee simple can be divided into at least two "smaller" estates: (1) a presently possessory estate for life or in fee tail, and (2) a "future" estate, comprising the residue of the fee simple, which would become a possessory estate upon termination of the present possessory estate for life or in fee tail. If the residue of the fee simple was not expressly transferred, the grantor would retain it, and the retained interest came to be called a *reversion*.[15] If the residue of the fee simple was expressly transferred to a designated person, that person would have an interest called a *remainder*.[16] Although the English courts later came to recognize "future" interests other than remainders and reversions,[17] the doctrine of estates in land was established once the courts sanctioned the creation of presently possessory interests "smaller" than a fee simple and began to protect the "future" interests comprising the residue of the fee simple.[18]

---

11. For a good brief discussion of the operation of the common recovery to convert a fee tail into a fee simple, see 1 Am.L.Prop. § 2.2; R. Megarry and H. Wade, Real Property 83–87. The Statute of 32 Hen. VIII, c. 36 (1540), provided for "barring the entail"—i.e., barring the descendants of the first grantee—but not the rights of reversioners or remaindermen by use of an action called a "fine" ("final concord"). The effect of a "fine" was to transfer a "base fee" rather than a fee simply absolute, which could only be transferred by common recovery. See discussion of the "fine" in R. Megarry and H. Wade, Real Property 87–89.

12. For an explanation of the English "strict settlement," see G. Radcliffe, Real Property Law ch. XIV (1933), reprinted in part in W. Leach, Future Interests (2d ed. 1940); R. Megarry and H. Wade, Real Property 283–284. "Keeping the land in the family" was ultimately rendered impossible in England by the Settled Land Act of 1882 and the Settled Land Act of 1925; see R. Megarry and H. Wade, Real Property 288–358 for a detailed discussion of these statutes.

13. " * * * by Bracton's time the position of one who had been granted lands for life was fairly well settled. Like the tenant in fee, the life tenant had seisin; he achieved a position which holders for a term of years or in wardship did not achieve, through obtaining the right to bring novel disseisin * * *. Technically this was because the life tenant had a free tenement, and thus came within the very words of the writ. In consequence a life ten-

ancy, being specifically recoverable by a real action, did not become a chattel interest, but came to be regarded as an estate in land, and although Bracton does not talk of estates the substance of this development has been reached by his time." A. Simpson, Introduction 67.

14. A. Simpson, Introduction 82.

15. So called because, when the "smaller" estate terminated, the possessory fee simple estate "reverted" to the grantor or his (or her) successors in interest.

16. Apparently so called because, when the "smaller" estate terminated, the possessory fee simple estate "remained away" from the grantor or his (or her) successors in interest.

17. See post, Sections 3.4, 3.5, and 3.14 through 3.17.

18. " * * * [T]he doctrine of estates * * * involves a recognition that the sum of possible interest—the fee simple—may be cut up into slices like a cake and distributed amongst a number of people, all of whom will obtain presently existing interests in the land, though their right to actual enjoyment, to seisin in demesne, may be postponed. In Bracton's time it was recognized * * * that land might be granted in such a way that it would revert to the donor, as where a life estate was granted, and that it might also be made to remain away from the grantor. But here the notion is rather of a cake being

The English scheme of "present" and "future" estates in land was brought to the British colonies in North America in the seventeenth century, and the doctrine of estates has developed along roughly parallel lines in England and in the United States. The distinction between "present" and "future" estates is implicit in the American Law Institute's definition of the term *estate* as "an interest in land which (a) is or may become possessory and (b) is ownership measured in terms of duration." [19] It should be emphasized, however, that a "future" estate is not merely an interest that will, or may, come into existence at a future time; it is a presently existing, legally protected interest which will, or may, become a possessory interest at a future time.[20]

Although the doctrine of estates was for several centuries confined to property in land, it was later extended to property in intangibles and non-consumable chattels. At the present time, the most important uses of the doctrine of estates occur in connection with trusts in which the trust *res* (principal) typically consists mainly of intangibles such as stocks and bonds.

passed about than of one being sliced up. The change in thought occurs when lawyers start to talk of *reversions* and *remainders,* rather than of *persons to whom the land may revert* or *remain,* for this terminology involves a recognition that reversions and remainders are *existing interests* rather than rights to obtain an interest. The new approach is the direct result of the introduction of the new actions of formedon in remainder and formedon in reverter in the late fourteenth century, and the clarification of the distinction between reversions and escheats after *Quia Emptores* in 1290; since reversioners and remaindermen have real actions to protect their interest they must have an interest to protect

* * *. Since all these interests related to the same piece of land, it was natural to regard them as parts of the sum total of possible interests in that land, and the greatest possible interest known was the fee simple; their co-existence was only explicable by the fact that some estates gave a present right to seisin and others a future right to seisin, and by the notion that the greatest possible interest, the fee simple, had been cut up and parcelled out." A. Simpson, Introduction 82–83.

19. Property Restatement § 9 (1936).

20. Supra note 18.

Chapter 2

PRESENT ESTATES IN REALTY AND EQUIVALENT INTERESTS IN PERSONALTY

Table of Sections

---

§ 2.1 Present Estates in Land—In General

Present estates in land carry with them, as their single most salient characteristic, the present right to exclusive possession of a particular parcel of land.[1] Moreover, by the traditional view, this right to exclusive possession extends downward "to the center of the earth,"[2] except where a mineral estate is created by severance of ownership of the subsurface from ownership of the surface.[3] Until fairly recently, it was also said that the owner of the

§ 2.1

1. See post Section 7.1.

2. E.g., Edwards v. Sims, 232 Ky. 791, 24 S.W.2d 619 (1929). For additional discussion see post Section 7.1.

3. In Texas, e.g., a severance of the subsurface oil and gas in place from the residue of the soil may result in a division "into two tracts as if the division had been made by superficial lines, or had been severed vertical-ly by horizontal planes." Humphreys–Mexia Co. v. Gammon, 113 Tex. 247, 254 S.W. 296, 29 A.L.R. 607 (1923), In Pennsylvania, where coal mining is a major industry, ownership may be divided into three separate estates—the surface estate, the subsurface (mineral) estate, and the support estate (the right to subjacent support of the surface). See, e.g., Patton v. Republic Steel Corp., 342 Pa.Super. 101, 492 A.2d 411 (1985).

present estate had an exclusive right to possession extending indefinitely upward from the surface of the earth.[4] The invention of the airplane and the advent of extensive air travel has, of course, brought about a modification of this ancient maxim. In the United States, enactment of the Air Commerce Act of 1926 and the Civil Aeronautics Act of 1938 have been held by the United States Supreme Court to have the effect of making the air space above the prescribed minimum altitudes for flight "a public highway," i.e., making the surface owner's rights in the superadjacent air space subject to a public easement for air travel above the minimum altitudes established by the federal statutes and regulations.[5]

Ownership of a present estate in land also carries with it very substantial privileges of use and enjoyment, subject, however, to important restrictions imposed on all possessors of land by the common law [6] or by statute for the protection of other possessors of land and the public at large.[7] The owners of present estates "smaller" than a fee simple absolute—which constitutes full ownership of land—are also subject to common law rules restricting their use and enjoyment of the land in order to protect the owners of future interests in the same land.[8] And the owner of any present estate may hold it subject to "servitudes" created on a consensual basis which limit his exclusive right to possession and the usual privileges of use and enjoyment incident to a present estate in land.[9]

It is traditional to classify present estates as either "freehold" or "nonfreehold" estates. At common law, the former were created by "livery of seisin," while the latter were not; and the former were given substantial protection very early in the development of the common law, while the latter were not given substantial protection until much later.[10] The freehold estates include all varieties of the fee simple, both absolute and defeasible, the fee tail and the fee simple conditional (where one or the other can still be created), and all kinds of life estates. The nonfreehold estates include the estate for years, all kinds of periodic estates, and the estate at will.[11] Since

---

4. The old maxim was that ownership and right to possession extended "ad coelum usque ad infernos."

5. United States v. Causby, 328 U.S. 256, 66 S.Ct. 1062, 90 L.Ed. 1206 (1946); Griggs v. Allegheny County, 369 U.S. 84, 82 S.Ct. 531, 7 L.Ed.2d 585 (1962), rehearing denied 369 U.S. 857, 83 S.Ct. 931, 8 L.Ed.2d 16 (1962). These cases recognize, however, that transit of aircraft at low levels—below the prescribed minimum flight altitudes—may be tortious or, if continued for a substantial time, amount to a "taking" of private property for public use.

6. These common law restrictions include rules forbidding the use of land in such a way as to interfere unreasonably with the use of neighboring land in the possession of others (the law of "nuisance"); rules as to lateral and subjacent support of land in the possession of others; and rules as to the use of streams and lakes, the extraction of underground percolating water, and disposal of diffused surface water. See post, Sections 7.2 through 7.4, and 7.6 through 7.10.

7. See post Chapter 9.

8. See post Chapter 4.

9. See post Chapter 8.

10. The various "real actions" could be used to recover *seisin* (possession) of freehold land only; *seisin* of a freehold meant possession of land as tenant in fee simple or fee tail, or for life. 1 Am.L.Prop. 12; A. Simpson, Introduction 37 ("the tenant for years was seised but not *seised of a free tenement*, and thus he did not fall within the terms of the writ [of novel disseisin]"); R. Megarry and H. Wade, Real Property 49.

11. Many writers also add to the list something called an "estate at sufferance." A "tenant at sufferance," however, is merely a wrongful possessor who originally gained possession rightfully as tenant and remained in possession after his legal right to possession ended. Thus the "estate" of a "tenant at sufferance" is no more substantial than the interest of any other "mere possessor" of land whose possession is legally protected as

the original reasons for differentiating freehold from nonfreehold estates have been almost entirely eliminated, the distinction is no longer very important.[12]

Present estates may also be classified as either inheritable or noninheritable. All fee simple, fee tail, and fee simple conditional estates are, of course, inheritable. Estates for the life of the tenant are noninheritable, but estates *pur autre vie* (for the life of another) are inheritable until the measuring life terminates.[13] Estates for years are also inheritable if the tenant dies during the term. Estates at will, however, are always noninheritable.[14] It is not clear whether periodic estates are inheritable, although their derivation from the estate at will suggests that they may not be inheritable.

All present estates other than the fee simple absolute, which is the "largest" possible estate in land, are, by definition, "smaller." Hence one or more future estates will always be created when a present estate other than a fee simple absolute is carved out of a present fee simple absolute.[15]

At the present time, the most important "legal" estates in land are undoubtedly the fee simple absolute and the estate for years. These are the only estates that are commercially salable, although periodic estates are also a significant factor in providing housing for low-income persons. The fee tail has almost completely disappeared in the United States, having been abolished either by statute or by constitutional provision in most states.[16] The fee simple conditional could not be created in England after 1285 because it was abolished by the Statute *De Donis Conditionalibus,*[17] but— anomalous though it may seem—can still be created in a few American jurisdictions.[18] "Legal" life estates are not very common today, although "equitable" life estates in favor of trust beneficiaries are very frequently created.

Any of the present estates in land may be owned either in severalty— i.e., by a single person—or concurrently—i.e., by two or more persons, each of whom owns an "undivided" fractional interest in the estate. At common law, there were several forms of concurrent ownership—joint tenancy, tenancy by the entirety (only possible as between husband and wife), coparcenary, and tenancy in common.[19] In some American jurisdictions, one or more of these forms of concurrent ownership has been eliminated by statute or by judicial decision;[20] and in some American jurisdictions, as between husband and wife, the common law forms of concurrent ownership have been largely supplanted by a form of concurrent ownership called

---

against those who cannot show a better right to possession. See ante, Section 1.3.

12. Until well into the nineteenth century, only "freeholders" could vote in parliamentary elections, although the legal remedies provided for protection of the two types of estates had been substantially the same since the seventeenth century.

13. That this was not always so, see post Section 2.12.

14. This is because the estate can only continue so long as both landlord and tenant personally "will" it to continue. The death of either party automatically terminates an estate at will.

15. For detailed treatment of future estates in land, see post Chapter 3.

16. See post Section 2.10. Only "equitable" entailed interests can be created in England since 1925.

17. See ante Section 1.7.

18. See post Section 2.10.

19. See post, Chapter 5.

20. Ibid.

"community property." [21]　Where concurrent ownership exists, no single co-owner has the right to exclude the other co-owners, but the co-owners collectively have the right to exclude the rest of the world.

All of the present estates except the fee tail, the fee simple conditional, and the estate at will are freely alienable by *inter vivos* conveyance unless made subject to a valid restraint on alienation by an express provision in the instrument creating the estate.　With the same exceptions, plus an additional exception for estates measured by the life of the tenant, all present estates are also freely alienable by will unless made subject to a valid restraint on alienation by an express provision in the instrument creating the interest. But where a tenancy by the entirety or a joint tenancy is created, carrying with it a right of survivorship, it is obvious that an individual co-tenant cannot transfer his or her interest by will; [22] and, in the case of a tenancy by the entirety, neither co-tenant can transfer his or her interest by *inter vivos* conveyance without the joinder of the other co-tenant in the conveyance. [23]

The validity of restraints on the alienation of present estates in land imposed by express provisions in the creating instrument will be considered in connection with the more detailed discussion of each of the present estates in the ensuing sections of this chapter.

§ 2.2　The Fee Simple Absolute

An estate in fee simple absolute carries with it the largest possible aggregate of rights, privileges, powers and immunities with respect to the land in which it exists, and thus comprises full ownership of that land.　Such an estate is inheritable by either lineal or collateral heirs, generation after generation, but is freely transferable, either *inter vivos* or by will, free of any claim of the transferor's heirs; and it is not subject to any legally effective provision for defeasance (termination) upon the happening of a stated event. Hence an estate in fee simple absolute has a potentially infinite duration. But if the owner of a fee simple absolute should die intestate and without natural heirs, the estate will pass to the state by "escheat."　In states where tenure still theoretically exists, escheat may be viewed as terminating a fee simple absolute; in states where land ownership is allodial, however, the state merely takes the estate as "ultimate heir" when it escheats.

Absent any legally effective provision for defeasance upon the happening of a stated event, any language in a deed of conveyance or a will sufficient to create a fee simple will create a fee simple absolute.　Although it was settled in the early thirteenth century that the words "and his heirs" in a grant to "A and his heirs" were only words of "limitation" defining A's estate as a fee simple, not words of "purchase" creating an estate in favor of A's heirs,[1] it nevertheless became a rigid common law rule in England that a fee simple could not be created in a natural person by *inter vivos* conveyance

---

21.　See post, Section 5.8.

22.　See post, Sections 5.3, 5.4.

23.　See post, Section 5.4.

§ 2.2

1.　This was the consequence of decisions in the early thirteenth century denying the heir

any right to recover lands alienated by a tenant in fee during his lifetime. See 1 Am. L.Prop. 82; R. Megarry and H. Wade, Real Property 50, 52; T. Plucknett, Concise History 559; A. Simpson, Introduction 49.

unless the word "heirs" was used in the grant.[2] But when the Statute of Wills,[3] in 1540, made fee simple estates (as well as other interests in land) devisable by will, the courts refused to apply the rigid common law rule requiring use of the word "heirs." Instead, it was held that a will would transfer a fee simple whenever the testator's language, taken as a whole, manifested the intent to transfer a fee simple.[4]

In England, statutes now provide that "the fee simple or other the whole interest" which a grantor or testator has the power to transfer shall pass by a conveyance or will (as the case may be), unless the instrument affirmatively manifests a contrary intent.[5] Similar statutes are now in force in almost all American jurisdictions, although in a few states such statutes are limited either to wills only or to *inter vivos* conveyances only.[6]

The statute *Quia Emptores* (1290)[7] has consistently been viewed by English and American courts as based upon a strong public policy in favor of the alienability of possessory estates in fee simple. This policy has been consistently applied to invalidate almost all attempts to impose restraints upon the alienation of possessory estates in fee simple absolute by means of express provisions in a deed of conveyance or a will. Provisions purporting, without any limitation as to duration or scope, to prohibit the transfer of a present fee simple absolute—so-called "disabling restraints"—or to defeat or

2. 1 Am.L.Prop. 82–84; R. Megarry and H. Wade, Real Property 51 (pointing out that "no other word would do in place of 'heirs': 'relatives', 'issue', 'descendants', 'assign', 'forever', 'in fee simple', * * * and so on were all ineffective"). See also T. Plucknett, Concise History 559 (although the phrase "heirs and assigns" came into common use in the thirteenth century, "[b]y the fourteenth century the word 'assigns' ceases to be necessary—at least such was Maitland's opinion, adding that 'on the whole we cannot doubt that the use of this term played a large part in the obscure process which destroyed the old rules by which alienation was fettered.'"). For a relatively recent application of the common law rule requiring use of the word "heirs" to create a fee simple, see Ivey v. Peacock, 56 Fla. 440, 47 So. 481 (1908), holding that a conveyance omitting the word "heirs" but purporting to convey "in fee simple forever" created only a life estate.

Even at common law, no words of inheritance were required to transfer a fee simple to a corporation, since a corporation could have no heirs; but it was necessary to add the words "and successors" in order to transfer a fee simple to a corporation sole, such as a bishop. 1 Am.L.Prop. 92; R. Megarry and H. Wade, Real Property 53–55; 2 R. Powell, Real Property ¶ 181.

3. 32 Hen. VIII, c. 1.

4. 1 Am.L.Prop. 89–91; R. Megarry and H. Wade, Real Property 51, 56; 2 R. Powell, Real Property ¶ 183.

5. As to conveyances, this rule was established by the Law of Property Act, 1925,

§ 60(1); as to wills, this rule was established by the Wills Act, 1837, §§ 28, 34. The Conveyancing Act, 1881, had provided that in deeds executed thereafter the words "in fee simple" would suffice, without the word "heirs."

6. 1 Am.L.Prop. § 2.4; 2 R. Powell, Real Property ¶¶ 184, 185. It would appear that the common law rule is still in force as to conveyances only in Maine and South Carolina, and as to wills, only in Florida. In South Dakota, and perhaps in Pennsylvania, the rule as to conveyances is that applied to wills in England between 1540 and 1837—the intent to create a fee simple must be expressed, but words of inheritance are unnecessary. See 2 R. Powell, Real Property ¶ 185, including footnotes.

For a recent case applying the statutory rule, see Dei Cas v. Mayfield, 199 Conn. 569, 508 A.2d 435 (1986) (a fee simple was created by a devise "to my beloved wife * * * for her own proper use and benefit, forever," despite subsequent language purporting to give testator's children any of the property "remaining" at the wife's death). The Nebraska Supreme Court has had difficulty applying a statute providing that, "In construction of every instrument creating or conveying * * * any real estate * * * it shall be the duty of the courts of justice to carry into effect the true intent of the parties, so far as such intent can be collected from the whole instrument, in so far as such intent is consistent with the rules of law." See, e.g., Sterner v. Nelson, 210 Neb. 358, 314 N.W.2d 263 (1982).

7. 18 Edw. I, c. 1.

terminate what would otherwise be a present fee simple absolute upon transfer—so-called "forfeiture restraints"—are universally held void.[8] Even "disabling restraints" limited as to duration or scope are universally held void in the United States.[9] "Forfeiture restraints" thus limited are also generally void;[10] but there is some authority that they are valid.[11] Cove-

8. "Disabling restraints": E.g., Payne v. Hart, 178 Ark. 100, 9 S.W.2d 1059 (1928); Davis v. Geyer, 151 Fla. 362, 9 So.2d 727 (1942); Freeman v. Phillips, 113 Ga. 589, 38 S.E. 943 (1901); Ogle v. Burmister, 146 Iowa 33, 124 N.W. 758 (1910); Henning v. Harrison, 76 Ky. 723 (1878); Smith v. Clark, 10 Md. 186 (1856); Blackstone Bank v. Davis, 38 Mass. 42 (1838); McDowell v. Brown, 21 Mo. 57 (1855); Nashville, Chattanooga & St. Louis Railway v. Bell, 162 Tenn. 661, 39 S.W.2d 1026 (1931). However, restrictions in a trust instrument prohibiting alienation of specific property by the trustee are valid. E.g., Legge v. Canty, 176 Md. 283, 4 A.2d 465 (1939); Matter of Roe, 119 N.Y. 509, 23 N.E. 1063 (1890); Johns v. Johns, 172 Ill. 472, 50 N.E. 337 (1898).

"Forfeiture restraints": E.g., Casey v. Casey, 287 Ark. 395, 700 S.W.2d 46 (1985); Ogle v. Burmister, 146 Iowa 33, 124 N.W. 758 (1910) (dictum); Courts v. Courts' Guardian, 230 Ky. 141, 18 S.W.2d 957 (1929) (dictum); Female Orphan Society v. Young Men's Christian Association, 119 La. 278, 44 So. 15 (1907); Stansbury v. Hubner, 73 Md. 228, 20 A. 904 (1890); Cushing v. Spalding, 164 Mass. 287, 41 N.E. 297 (1895); Magie v. German Evangelical Dutch Church, 13 N.J.Eq. 77 (1860), affirmed 15 N.J.Eq. 500; Pardue v. Givens, 54 N.C. 306 (1854). However, exceptions have been recognized when property is conveyed to a charitable trust or to a branch of a beneficial association. See Pilgrim Evangelical Lutheran Church v. Lutheran Church–Missouri Synod Foundation, 661 S.W.2d 833, 839 (Mo.App. 1983) (charitable trust); National Grange of Order of Patrons of Husbandry v. O'Sullivan Grange, 35 Wn.App. 444, 667 P.2d 1105 (1983) (fraternal order).

9. E.g., Gamble v. Gamble, 200 Ala. 176, 75 So. 924 (1917); Murray v. Green, 64 Cal. 363, 28 P. 118 (1883); Stamey v. McGinnis, 145 Ga. 226, 88 S.E. 935 (1916); Little v. Bowman, 276 Ill. 125, 114 N.E. 519 (1916); Woodford v. Glass, 168 Iowa 299, 150 N.W. 69 (1914); Superior Oil Co. v. Johnson, 161 Kan. 710, 171 P.2d 658 (1946); Turner v. Hallowell Savings Institution, 76 Me. 527 (1884); Gischell v. Ballman, 131 Md. 260, 101 A. 698 (1917); Mills v. Blakelin, 307 Mass. 542, 30 N.E.2d 873 (1941); Mandlebaum v. McDonell, 29 Mich. 78, 18 Am.Rep. 61 (1874); Triplett v. Triplett, 332 Mo. 870, 60 S.W.2d 13 (1933); State Bank v. Thiessen, 137 Neb. 426, 289 N.W. 791 (1940); Wrubel Realty Corp. v. Wrubel, 138 N.J.Eq. 466, 48 A.2d 793 (1946); Lovett v. Gillender, 35 N.Y. 617 (1866); Buckner v. Hawkins, 230 N.C. 99, 52 S.E.2d 16 (1949); Anderson v. Cary, 36 Ohio St. 506 (1881);

Breinig v. Smith, 267 Pa. 207, 110 A. 285 (1920); Goffe v. Karanyianopoulos, 53 R.I. 313, 166 A. 547 (1933); Son v. Shealy, 112 S.C. 312, 99 S.E. 825 (1919); Fowlkes v. Wagoner, 46 S.W. 586 (Tenn.Ch.App.1898); Seay v. Cockrell, 102 Tex. 280, 115 S.W. 1160 (1909); Barrows v. Ezer, 668 S.W.2d 854 (Tex.App.1984); Richardson v. Danson, 44 Wn.2d 760, 270 P.2d 802 (1954); Van Osdell v. Champion, 89 Wis. 661, 62 N.W. 539 (1895).

10. E.g. Bonnell v. McLaughlin, 173 Cal. 213, 159 P. 590 (1916); Jenne v. Jenne, 271 Ill. 526, 111 N.E. 540 (1916); Douglass v. Stevens, 214 N.C. 688, 200 S.E. 366 (1939); Andrews v. Hall, 156 Neb. 817, 58 N.W.2d 201 (1953); Friswold v. United States National Bank, 122 Or. 246, 257 P. 818 (1927); Wise v. Poston, 281 S.C. 574, 316 S.E.2d 412 (1984); Barrows v. Ezer, supra n. 9; Cobb v. Moore, 90 W.Va. 63, 110 S.E. 468 (1922).

11. Valid when limited to a "reasonable time": Turner v. Lewis, 189 Ky. 837, 226 S.W. 367 (1920) (life of conveyor); Francis v. Big Sandy Co., 171 Ky. 209, 188 S.W. 345 (1916) (term of years less than 21). See also Hutchinson v. Loomis, 244 S.W.2d 751 (Ky.1951), discussing standard of "reasonableness." Dicta suggesting that some "forfeiture restraints" limited as to duration might be upheld can be found in Libby v. Winston, 207 Ala. 681, 93 So. 631 (1922); Wright v. Jenks, 124 Kan. 604, 261 P. 840 (1927); Furst v. Lacher, 149 Minn. 53, 182 N.W. 720 (1921); Russell v. Federal Land Bank, 180 Miss. 55, 176 So. 737 (1937); Lynch v. Lynch, 161 S.C. 170, 159 S.E. 26 (1931); Nashville, Chattanooga & St. Louis Railway v. Bell, 162 Tenn. 661, 39 S.W.2d 1026 (1931).

Valid when "forfeiture restraints" are limited to members of a small group: Overton v. Lea, 108 Tenn. 505, 68 S.W. 250 (1902); Blevins v. Pittman, 189 Ga. 789, 7 S.E.2d 662 (1940).

In Casey v. Casey, supra n. 8, the court said that such a restraint is valid if so qualified as to permit alienation to some though not all possible alienees and found to be reasonable under all the circumstances of the case, but void where the restraint is unreasonable because imposed for spite or malice, even though the restraint precludes alienation to only one person—citing and relying on Prop.Rest. § 405 (1944).

In Kentucky, a "forfeiture restraint" upon alienation to all but a few persons may be found "reasonable," and thus valid, if it is also limited as to duration. E.g., Francis v. Big

nants by the grantee of a possessory fee simple absolute not to alienate—so-called "promissory restraints"—appear to be void wherever a similar restraint of the "forfeiture" type would be void.[12]

In recent years many cases have dealt with the validity of "indirect" restraints upon alienation.[13] A majority of these cases have been concerned with the validity of so-called "due-on-sale" clauses in mortgages and other security instruments such as trust deeds. These clauses afford the mortgage holder the right to accelerate the mortgage debt and to foreclose if the mortgaged land is transferred without the mortgage holder's consent. Although such clauses are sometimes used to protect mortgage holders from transactions that endanger the mortgage security and increase the risk of default, their principal purpose has undoubtedly been to enable mortgage lenders to force the refinancing of below-market interest rate mortgage loans during periods of rising interest rates.[14] The problems created by state court hostility to "due-on-sale" clauses have now been substantially resolved by a United States Supreme Court decision [15] and by federal legislation [16] validating "due-on-sale" clauses.

A number of recent cases have also considered whether various kinds of pre-emptive ("first refusal") rights to purchase land are invalid as unreasonable restraints upon alienation. A pre-emptive right to purchase at the owner's asking price, at the highest bona fide third party offer, or at market value is generally held valid; [17] but the courts have generally invalidated

Sandy Co., supra this note (20 years); Price v. Virginia Iron, Coal & Coke Co., 171 Ky. 523, 188 S.W. 658 (1916) (20 years); Auxier's Executrix v. Theobald, 255 Ky. 583, 75 S.W.2d 39 (1934) (5 years).

See, generally, 6 Am.L.Prop. §§ 26.19 through 26.26 and 26.31 through 26.34; 6 Powell, Real Property ¶¶ 841, 843.

12. E.g., Fritz v. Gilbert, 8 Cal.2d 68, 63 P.2d 291 (1936); Sisters of Mercy v. Lightner, 223 Iowa 1049, 274 N.W. 86 (1937); Winsor v. Mills, 157 Mass. 362, 32 N.E. 352 (1892). See also 6 Am.L.Prop. § 26.11 at n. 14; Rest.Prop. § 406.

Ordinarily, a covenant restricting the use of land will not constitute an invalid restraint upon alienation. 4 Rest.Prop., Introductory Note to Part II (1944). However, if use restrictions affect marketability of property by unreasonably limiting the class of persons to whom the property may be transferred, such restrictions have been held invalid as unreasonable restraints upon alienation. Falls City v. Missouri Pac. R.R., 453 F.2d 771 (8th Cir. 1971); Grossman v. Hill, 384 Pa. 590, 122 A.2d 69 (1956), dist. in Central Delaware County Authority v. Greyhound Corp., 386 Pa.Super. 423, 563 A.2d 139 (1989), rev'd 527 Pa. 47, 588 A.2d 485 (1991).

13. "An indirect restraint on alienation arises when an attempt is made to accomplish some purpose other than the restraint of alienability, but with the incidental result that the instrument, if valid, would restrain

practical alienability." L. Simes & A. Smith, Future Interests § 1112 (2d ed. 1956).

14. For a comprehensive treatment of "due-on-sale" clauses, which are not within the scope of this book, see G. Nelson & D. Whitman, Real Estate Finance Law §§ 5.21–5.24 (2d ed. 1985). For an extensive listing of periodical literature on "due-on-sale" clauses, see id. § 5.21 n. 9.

15. Fidelity Federal Sav. & Loan Ass'n v. de la Cuesta, 458 U.S. 141, 102 S.Ct. 3014, 73 L.Ed.2d 664 (1982).

16. Garn–St. Germain Depository Institutions Act of 1982, § 341, 12 U.S.C.A. § 1701j–3. For a good discussion of the Act, see G. Nelson & D. Whitman, supra n. 14, § 524.

17. See cases cited in 6 Am.L.Prop. § 26.67 nn. 7, 8. See also Rest.Prop. § 406 (1944). An important recent case reaching this result is Metropolitan Transp. Authority v. Bruken Realty Corp., 67 N.Y.2d 156, 501 N.Y.S.2d 306, 492 N.E.2d 379 (1986) (pointing out that "market value" may be "fixed by an arbitrator compelled to consider the price a willing seller would accept from a willing buyer at the time of sale."). Contra: Ferrero Const. Co. v. Dennis Rourke Corp., 311 Md. 560, 536 A.2d 1137 (1988) (pre-emptive right also held to violate Rule Against Perpetuities because it was unlimited as to time; the court relied in part on Rest.Prop. § 413, which states that a pre-emptive right is not an unreasonable restraint on alienation "unless it violates the rule against perpetuities."); In re Wildenstein v. Wallis,

pre-emptive rights of unlimited duration requiring the owner to offer land to the pre-emptioner at a fixed price before selling it to anyone else,[18] although some cases hold such rights to be valid.[19]

When the statute *Quia Emptores* conclusively established the alienability of possessory estates in fee simple, the most prominent feature of the English law of inheritance was the rule of primogeniture,[20] which made the law as to inheritance of land very complicated—and quite different from the law as to distribution of intestate personal property. The Administration of Estates Act (1925)[21] vastly simplified the English law of intestate succession, however; *inter alia,* the 1925 Act abolished primogeniture and eliminated the distinction between intestate succession to real and to personal property.

In the United States, the common law of inheritance as to real property has been changed by adoption of intestate succession laws in all jurisdictions.[22] Primogeniture has been abolished everywhere, and in nearly all the states the different rules as to real and personal property have been eliminated. In a few states in which the distinction between real and personal property still continues, a surviving spouse is still excluded from intestate succession to real property, and must rely on dower or curtesy,[23] as at common law. In all other jurisdictions, as in England, a surviving spouse takes by intestate succession under the statute, and, subject to the rights of the surviving spouse, descendants of the decedent take the property to the exclusion of all ancestors and collateral relatives. Descendants in equal degree take equal shares. In the absence of descendants, and subject to the surviving spouse's share, the decedent's parents are next in line in most states, followed by the decedent's siblings, but in some states parents and siblings share the intestate property. The statutes sometimes also make express provision for aunts and uncles, nieces and nephews, and grandparents and their issue; and most statutes provide that failing takers of any previously designated class, the property shall pass to the decedent's "next of kin." Many of the statutes expressly provide for "escheat" to the state, or

---

756 F.Supp. 158 (S.D.N.Y.1991) (the court invalidated as an unreasonable restraint on alienation under New York law a pre-emptive right given to art dealer to purchase fifteen paintings whenever art collectors received an acceptable offer to purchase, "upon the same terms and conditions as those of such offer," pursuant to an agreement that was binding on the collectors and "any of their respective executors, successors, and assigns.).

18. Edgar v. Hunt, 218 Mont. 30, 706 P.2d 120 (1985) (price was fixed and was much less than market value).

19. Lawson v. Redmoor Corp., 37 Wn.App. 351, 679 P.2d 972 (1984) (pre-emptive right to purchase at fixed price was not an unreasonable restraint on alienation because restraint was promissory in nature, the restraint was limited in duration to perpetuities period, the parties both benefited from existence of the right in that it was granted for a valuable consideration and the grantee would not have purchased the initial parcel without obtaining the pre-emptive right to buy the second parcel; thus the pre-emptive right "achieved the

purpose of encouraging the sale of the original parcel"). The *Lawson* court relied on the analysis contained in Rest.Prop. § 406, which states that a pre-emptive right to purchase at a fixed price is valid if the restraint is promissory in nature, allows alienation to some possible alienees, is reasonable under the circumstances, and does not violate the Rule Against Perpetuities. See also cases cited in 6 Am. L.Prop. § 26.67 n. 3.

20. See ante, Section 1.6 at nn. 21, 22.

21. For a discussion of the Administration of Estates Act (1925), and the subsequent changes made by the Intestates' Estates Act (1952), see R. Megarry and H. Wade, Law of Real Property 523–533 (4th ed. 1975).

22. For a discussion of the modern intestate succession laws, see T. Atkinson, Wills §§ 14–26 (2d ed. 1953). For a detailed summary of the intestate succession laws of all the states, see 7 Page, Wills ch. 63 (Rev. Bowe and Parker 1963, with 1979–1980 Supp.).

23. As to dower and curtesy, see post Sections 2.14, 2.15.

make the state the "ultimate heir," if there are no takers of any previously designated class, but in some states "escheat" is provided for in a statute other than the intestate succession law.

When the United States disposed of most of its public domain during the nineteenth and early twentieth centuries, the land was almost always granted in fee simple absolute.[24] In commercial real estate transactions, the only significant estate, other than the leasehold estate, is the fee simple absolute. When a contract for the sale of land requires the vendor simply to convey described land, or to convey "title," or "good title," or "marketable title" to land, the vendor is obligated to convey a fee simple absolute in the absence of additional contract language providing that the vendor is to convey a "smaller" estate than a fee simple absolute.[25]

The fee simple estate—albeit in an unusual form—plays an important part in the "condominium," a form of shared ownership that was almost unknown in the United States until the 1960s. In a condominium, each unit (which may be only a defined interior space within a building) is separately owned in fee simple absolute by one or more persons.[26] But the exterior walls of the building, the hallways and other common areas within the building, and the exterior grounds around the building are owned by all the unit owners as tenants in common. Although condominiums could probably have been created under the common law in some jurisdictions, utilization of the condominium concept has generally proceeded on the basis of special enabling legislation. Since the enactment of the first condominium enabling statute in Puerto Rico in 1958, all fifty states have enacted such statutes. Many of the "first generation" condominium statutes were based on the Federal Housing Administration's "Model Statute for the Creation of Apartment Ownership."[27] More recently, the Commissioners on Uniform State Laws have produced two new models for states interested in enacting "second generation" condominium statutes, the Uniform Condominium Act[28] and the Uniform Common Interest Ownership Act.[29]

The essential elements of a condominium development are as follows:[30]

24. In most cases, the grant was by a "patent," signed by, or in the name of the President; in some cases, the grant was by Congressional act. In either case, the grantee obtained "all the estate of the government except what is expressly excepted." See G. Warvelle, Abstracts of Title chaps. 10, 11 (1921).

25. See post, Section 10.12.

26. The condominium concept is not new, despite its relatively recent introduction in the United States. Ownership of individual units in buildings can be traced back to ancient Babylon; it was quite common in ancient Rome and in medieval Europe. The earliest condominium statute is Article 664 of the Code Napoleon of 1804, a very brief provision which was later substantially expanded. Condominium statutes were adopted in most nations in Europe, and in Central and South America, before any were adopted in the United States.

27. This Model Statute was promulgated in 1961, and was a response to passage of Section 234 of the National Housing Act in 1960.

28. This act was promulgated in 1977, and has been adopted (with some changes) in Minnesota, Pennsylvania, and West Virginia. The text of the act may be found in 7 Uniform Laws Annotated 101–231 (Master ed. 1978).

29. This act was promulgated in 1982, and makes broad provision for establishment of communities characterized by "common interest ownership," including condominiums and planned unit developments. The text of the act may be found in 7 Uniform Laws Annotated, 1983 Supplement 61–110.

30. This summary is drawn from Note, Condominium: A Reconciliation of Competing Interests?, 18 Vand.L.Rev. 1773, 1775–76 (1965). For the most detailed treatment of condominiums, see Rohan and Reskin, Condominium Law and Practice (1974).

(1) ownership of part of the building (or interior space therein) as an interest in land;

(2) an effective restraint against the partition of the commonly-owned land and partition of the building;

(3) an effective restraint against the separation of the unit-owner's share in the commonly-owned land from the separately-owned unit;

(4) separate assessment of units for taxation; and

(5) provision for the use, management, and maintenance of the commonly-owned property.

All the condominium statutes provide (*inter alia*) for the execution of an instrument called a "declaration" by which a particular tract of land is "submitted to the provisions" of the statute, for the election of a board of directors by the property owner's association established by the statute, and for covenants, by-laws, and administrative regulations adopted by the association to "run with" each unit and to bind all successive owners thereof. We shall consider in some detail the concept of "covenants running with the land" in Chapter 8 of this book. While most condominiums involve residential apartment buildings and the surrounding grounds, many of the statutes authorize office building condominiums or so-called "townhouse" condominiums. The latter can also be constructed, in many states, under local "planned unit development" ordinances.[31]

Full ownership of chattels and intangible personal property is, in general, analogous to ownership of land in fee simple.[32] Transfer of full ownership of personal property has never required the use of words of inheritance, but it has always been necessary to indicate by express language the intent to transfer less than full ownership—e.g., a life interest or a leasehold interest. Technically, the transaction creating a leasehold interest in chattels (tangible subjects of personal property) is called a "bailment" or a "bailment lease."[33]

§ 2.3   Defeasible Fee Simple Estates—In General

Defeasible fee simple estates are those created by instruments containing language sufficient to create a fee simple, followed by a provision for defeasance when a specified state of affairs ceases or a specified event occurs.[1] Usually, though not always, it is uncertain that defeasance will occur. The principal defeasible fee simple estates recognized in Anglo–American law are (1) the fee simple determinable,[2] (2) the fee simple subject

---

31. See post Section 9.16.

32. The leading general treatise on personal property law, R. Brown, Personal Property (3d ed. Raushenbush 1975) includes no discussion of the general legal characteristics of "full ownership" of personalty.

33. For a detailed treatment of "bailments," see R. Brown, Personal Property (3d ed. Raushenbush 1975) chaps. X through XII.

§ 2.3

1. See Rest.Prop. § 16. Such estates have also been called "qualified fee simple estates." See, e.g., 1 Am.L.Prop. § 2.6.

2. Such estates have also been called "base fees," "qualified fees," "estates in fee on limitation," "estates in fee on conditional limitation," and "estates in fee simple on special limitation." The first four terms are ambiguous because they have also been applied to quite different kinds of defeasible fee simple estates. Either "fee simple determinable" or "fee simple on special limitation" is unambig-

to a condition subsequent,[3] and (3) the fee simple subject to an executory limitation.[4] The first two are defeasible in favor of the person who originally created the defeasible fee simple estate or his successors in interest. The fee simple subject to an executory limitation, on the other hand, is defeasible in favor of a person (or persons) expressly designated in the creating instrument other than the person who created the defeasible fee simple or his successors in interest. The fee simple determinable and the fee simple subject to an executory limitation will terminate "automatically" upon the happening of the designated terminating events.[5] The fee simple subject to a condition subsequent, however, will not terminate "automatically" upon the happening of the designated terminating event—i.e., a breach of the designated "condition." When that event occurs, the person who created the defeasible estate, or his (or her) successor in interest, has the power to terminate the defeasible estate, but need not do so.

In most cases a defeasible fee simple has a potentially infinite duration, like a fee simple absolute, because the event that will (or may) defeat the estate is not certain to occur. But a fee simple subject to an executory limitation may be defeasible upon the happening of an event that is certain to occur, in which case its duration is finite.[6]

Defeasible fee simple estates generally carry with them the same rights, privileges, powers, and immunities as estates in fee simple absolute. Thus the owner of a defeasible fee simple estate has the same power to alienate his entire estate or to create smaller estates as does the owner of a fee simple absolute, and his estate passes by intestate succession in the same manner as a fee simple absolute, subject, however, to the defeasibility that existed when the estate was alienated or passed by intestate succession.[7] The rules determining the validity of restraints upon alienation of a fee simple absolute also apply to restraints upon alienation of a fee simple defeasible.[8] But there are some important differences. For example—

(1) Although the owner of a fee simple defeasible has the same exclusive right to possession and privileges of use and enjoyment as the owner of a fee simple absolute, vis-a-vis third parties, unconscionable conduct by the owner

uous, but "fee simple determinable" (or "determinable fee") has the advantage of brevity; it is the term adopted in Rest.Prop. § 44.

3. Such estates have also been called "estates in fee on condition," "estates in fee on condition subsequent," "estates in simple subject to a right of entry for breach of condition" (or "condition broken"), and "estates in fee simple subject to a power of termination." All these terms, with the possible exception of the first, are unambiguous. "Fee simple subject to a condition subsequent" is the term adopted in Rest.Prop. § 45.

4. Such estates have also been called "estates in fee simple on conditional limitation" or "estates in fee simple subject to a shifting (or springing) use (or devise)." The first term is objectionable because it is also applied to estates in fee simple determinable; the second term is now practically obsolete. "Fee simple subject to an executory limitation" is the term adopted in Rest.Prop. § 46.

5. Strictly speaking, a fee simple determinable "expires" upon cessation of the state of affairs set out in the "special limitation." But that state of affairs is always terminated by the occurrence of some *event*. For the sake of brevity, the phrase "terminating event" will be used hereafter in connection with the fee simple determinable as well as the other defeasible fee simple estates.

6. E.g., A, owning Blackacre in fee simple absolute, transfers Blackacre "to B and his heirs from and after one year from the date of this instrument." This transfer leaves in A an estate in fee simple subject to an executory limitation. Rest.Prop. § 46, Illustration 2 to subsection (1). In the example given the date of termination is certain, but this need not be the case.

7. See Rest.Prop. §§ 50, 55.

8. See ante Section 2.2 at notes 7–12.

of a defeasible fee simple that substantially reduces the value of the land may be enjoined by the person who would be entitled to possession of the land if the defeasible estate should terminate, provided that there is a reasonable probability that his estate will become possessory.[9]

(2) When the owner of a defeasible fee simple dies, the interest that arises in the decedent's spouse by virtue of dower or curtesy (in jurisdictions where dower and curtesy are still recognized) is generally held to be subject to the same condition or limitation that made the decedent's estate defeasible, although there are a few cases reaching a contrary result where the decedent's estate was subject to an executory limitation.[10]

(3) The general rules as to the power of concurrent owners to compel partition, subjection of the land to the claims of creditors, and liability of the land to condemnation are the same for defeasible fee simple estates as for fee simple absolute estates, but defeasibility may substantially alter the result of application of these rules.[11]

The interest in things other than land which is analogous to a fee simple absolute in land is simply "full ownership." Forms of defeasible ownership of things other than land, substantially identical with the defeasible fee simple estates in land, are now recognized.[12] In practice, interests in things other than land analogous to the fee simple determinable and the fee simple subject to an executory limitation are more common than interests analogous to the fee simple on a condition subsequent. Most such analogous interests are created in intangibles such as stocks and bonds held in trust, so that such interests are "equitable" rather than "legal."

Whether the subject matter is real or personal property, certain kinds of special limitations, conditions subsequent, or executory limitations—otherwise effective to create present interests that are determinable, subject to a condition subsequent, or subject to an executory limitation—are generally held to be "illegal" and "void" because they are contrary to public policy. Prominent among these are conditions and limitations in restraint of marriage, encouraging divorce or separation, and penalizing will contests. Although the law relating to such conditions and limitations is too complex to be readily summarized,[13] its broad outlines may be gathered from a reading of the Property Restatement's black-letter provisions.[14]

---

9. See 1 Am.L.Prop. § 20.23 at nn. 9–12 and cases cited; 5 R. Powell, Real Prop. ¶ 694 and cases cited; Rest.Prop. §§ 49, 193.

10. See 1 Am.L.Prop. §§ 5.26–5.29, 5.63; 2 R. Powell, Real Prop. ¶ 211; Rest.Prop. § 54.

11. See 2 R. Powell, Real Prop. ¶ 190 at nn. 61–63; Rest.Prop. §§ 51–53.

12. See, e.g., Woodard v. Clark, 236 N.C. 190, 72 S.E.2d 433 (1952) and North Carolina Gen.Stat. § 39–62. Also see Simes, Future Interests § 7 (1966) ("In the United States, by the weight of authority, it is possible to create, either *inter vivos* or by will, the same varieties of future interests in chattels real and personal as are recognized in land"; it follows, of course, that the same varieties of present interests may be created in personalty).

13. An excellent and very detailed treatment of this topic may be found in 6 Am. L.Prop. §§ 27.1 through 27.23. For an earlier version of much of the same material, see Browder, Conditions and Limitations in Restraint of Marriage, 39 Mich.L.Rev. 1288 (1941); Browder, Testamentary Conditions Against Contest, 36 Mich.L.Rev. 1066 (1938); Browder, Testamentary Conditions Against Contest Re–Examined, 49 Colum.L.Rev. 320 (1949).

14. Rest.Prop. §§ 424 through 438. The Comments to these sections may be consulted for a fuller explication of the black-letter provisions. For a parallel treatment with citation of authorities, see 6 R. Powell, Real Property ¶¶ 849 through 858.

With respect to conditions and limitations in restraint of marriage or encouraging separation or divorce, the Property Restatement broadly asserts that conditions and limitations "designed to prevent the acquisition or retention of an interest in land or in things other than land in the event of *any first marriage*" are invalid "unless the dominant motive of the conveyor is to provide support until such marriage";[15] but that a similar restraint upon "*some but not all first marriages*" is valid unless "the circumstances under which a marriage is permitted are such that a permitted marriage is not likely to occur" and "the dominant motive of the conveyor" is *not* "to provide support until such marriage or in the event of such marriage."[16] Moreover, conditions and limitations "designed to prevent the acquisition or retention" of real or personal property "in the event of *remarriage*" are valid "where the person restrained is the spouse of the person imposing the restraint" or, where that is not the case, "unless it is found to be unreasonable."[17] But conditions and limitations "designed to permit the acquisition or retention of an interest in land or in things other than land only in the event of a separation or divorce" are invalid "unless the dominant motive of the conveyor is to provide support in the event of such separation or divorce."[18]

The Property Restatement further asserts that conditions and limitations "designed to prevent the acquisition or retention" of real or personal property in the event of a contest of the entire will in which the property is devised are invalid unless the contest is "based upon a claim of forgery or * * * subsequent revocation by a later will or codicil, provided there was probable cause for the making of such contest."[19] Moreover, a condition or limitation "designed to prevent the acquisition or retention of a devised interest * * * in the event of any attack upon the validity of particular provisions" in a will is valid unless "it applies to an attack which is either successful or, although unsuccessful, is brought by a person having probable cause therefor, and which asserts that the provision attacked (a) violates the social restrictions * * * [embodied in the rule against perpetuities, the rule against restraints on alienation, or the rules against restraints on marriage, etc.] or (b) violates a mortmain statute primarily designed to curb charitable ownership."[20]

In addition to the rules relating to conditions and limitations with respect to marriage, separation or divorce, and will contests, the Property Restatement also deals with conditions and limitations imposing miscellaneous restraints concerning the relation of parent and infant, religion, "bad habits," and education or occupation.[21]

It should be noted that the rules as to illegality of conditions and limitations apply to conditions precedent as well as conditions subsequent and special and executory limitations.[22] It should also be noted that they

---

15. Rest.Prop. § 428 (emphasis added).

16. Id. § 425 (emphasis added).

17. Id. § 426 (emphasis added).

18. Id. § 427.

19. Id. § 428.

20. Id. § 429. See also id. §§ 430 through 432 as to "restraints on claims," "restraints on intermeddling," and "provisions excluding extratestamentary acquisition."

21. See Rest.Prop. §§ 433 through 438.

22. The effect of valid conditions precedent is explored in subsequent sections of this book dealing with contingent remainders and executory interests.

apply to conditions and limitations attached to life interests and leasehold interests as well as fee simple estates in land and analogous interests in personalty.

§ 2.4 The Fee Simple Determinable

Estates in fee simple subject to a qualifying limitation that the estate shall last only "so long as" a designated state of affairs shall continue or only "until" the occurrence of a designated event were recognized as permissible estates at an early date in England. For example, the owner of land in fee simple could convey it to "A church so long as the land shall be used for church purposes," or to "A church until the land shall cease to be used for church purposes." Such qualified fee simple estates may still be created under modern English and American law.[1] In both of the examples above, the qualifying language is a "special limitation"[2] and the estate obtained by A church is a fee simple determinable.[3] Such an estate continues only until the designated state of affairs ceases or the designated event occurs, at which time the estate simply expires. Such expiration is not deemed to involve "divestment" or "cutting short" of the fee simple determinable.[4]

A fee simple determinable is a "smaller" estate than a fee simple absolute because the special limitation may cause the fee simple determinable to expire even though the owner of that estate has not died without heirs capable of taking by intestate succession. The residue of the fee simple absolute owned by the person who created the fee simple determinable may simply be retained by him (or his heirs, if he creates the fee simple

---

§ 2.4

1. For John Chipman Gray's argument that such qualified fee simple estates could not be created after *Quia Emptores* because that statute abolished tenure between feoffor and feoffee when land was conveyed in fee simple, and a refutation of that argument, see 1 Am.L.Prop. § 2.6, and Powell, Determinable Fees, 23 Colum.L.Rev. 207 (1923). Although there are only a few English cases recognizing such qualified fee simple estates, there are many American cases spanning the nineteenth and twentieth centuries—e.g., Dabney v. Edwards, 5 Cal.2d 1, 53 P.2d 962, 103 A.L.R. 822 (1935); McDougall v. Palo Alto Unified School District, 212 Cal.App.2d 422, 28 Cal. Rptr. 37 (1963); Carr v. Georgia Railway, 74 Ga. 73 (1884); North v. Graham, 235 Ill. 178, 85 N.E. 267, 18 L.R.A.(N.S.) 624 (1908); Brown v. Independent Baptist Church, 325 Mass. 645, 91 N.E.2d 922 (1950); Institution for Savings v. Roxbury Home for Aged Women, 244 Mass. 583, 139 N.E. 301 (1923); First Universalist Society v. Boland, 155 Mass. 171, 29 N.E. 524, 15 L.R.A. 231 (1891); Leonard v. Burr, 18 N.Y. 96 (1858); City of Charlotte v. Charlotte Park & Recreation Commission, 278 N.C. 26, 178 S.E.2d 601 (1971); Charlotte Park & Recreation Commission v. Barringer, 242 N.C. 311, 88 S.E.2d 114 (1955), certiorari denied 350 U.S. 983, 76 S.Ct. 469, 100 L.Ed. 851 (1956); Collette v. Town of Charlotte, 114 Vt. 357, 45 A.2d 203 (1946). For many additional cases,

see 1 Simes & Smith, Future Interests § 283 n. 22 (2d ed. 1956).

2. "The term 'special limitation' denotes that part of the language of a conveyance which causes the created interest automatically to expire upon the occurrence of a stated event, and thus provides for a terminability in addition to that normally characteristic of such interest." Rest.Prop. § 23. This definition was expressly approved in Williams v. Watt, 668 P.2d 620 (Wyo.1983). The terms "collateral limitation" and "conditional limitation" are sometimes used to describe such language. The term "conditional limitation" is objectionable because it is also sometimes used to describe what in this book will be called an "executory limitation." See post, Section 2.8.

3. As to use of the term "fee simple determinable" in preference to other terms sometimes employed, see ante, Section 2.3 note 2. For an excellent modern, succinct treatment of the fee simple determinable, see Student Note, 7 W.Va.L.Rev. 367 (1969).

Recent cases holding that the words "so long as" will require the court to construe the instrument as creating a fee simple determinable include Lacer v. Navajo County, 141 Ariz. 396, 687 P.2d 404 (App.1983); Edling v. Stanford Tp., 381 N.W.2d 881 (Minn.1986).

4. Simes, Future Interests § 13 (2d ed. 1966).

determinable by will), or it may be simultaneously transferred to a third person by a "gift over." [5] When the residue of the fee simple absolute is retained by the person creating the fee simple determinable (or his heirs), he is said to retain a possibility of reverter.[6] When the residue is simultaneously transferred to a third person by a "gift over," the interest obtained by the third person is an executory interest.[7]

When a fee simple determinable is created without a "gift over" to a third person, an express provision for reverter to the grantor or his heirs is often included in the creating instrument,[8] but this is not necessary for creation of a fee simple determinable if appropriate special limitation language is used;[9] if such language is used, the possibility of reverter arises by operation of law.[10] But if the creating instrument does not contain

---

5. Thus, e.g., the owner of a fee simple absolute might convey or devise the property "to A church so long as the land shall be used for church purposes, and then to B and his heirs."

6. See Rest.Prop. § 154(3) and Comment on subsection (3); 2 Simes & Smith, Future Interests § 281 (2d ed. 1956); Simes, Future Interests § 13 (2d ed. 1966); 1 Am.L.Prop. § 4.12.

In Earle v. International Paper Co., 429 So.2d 989 (Ala.1983), it was held (5–4) that an "exception and reservation" [sic] of mineral rights subject to a special limitation in a deed conveying a fee simple should be construed as a "regrant" of the mineral rights, so that the grantee received a possibility of reverter rather than an executory interest in the mineral rights. This holding was clearly based on the court's unwillingness to conclude that the grantee's interest was void under the Rule Against Perpetuities. Cf. Williams v. Watt, infra note 7. The Rule Against Perpetuities is discussed post Sections 3.17–3.23.

7. According to modern American legal terminology, a future interest in one other than a transferor or his successors in interest (heirs or next of kin) is either a remainder or an executory interest, and if it will become possessory after termination of a fee simple, it is an executory interest. See Rest.Prop. §§ 156, 158. Thus the "gift over" in the example, supra note 5, is an "executory limitation." For more on estates in fee simple determinable followed by an executory interest, see post, Section 2.9.

But see Williams v. Watt, 668 P.2d 620 (Wyo.1983), holding that where the fee simple was conveyed with an exception of the mineral rights for 20 years and for as long thereafter as oil, gas, or other minerals continued to be produced, the grantor retained a fee simple determinable in the mineral estate and the grantee received a vested remainder rather than an executory interest. The holding seems to have been based on the court's unwillingness to find the interest of the grantee void under the Rule Against Perpetuities. Cf.

Earle v. International Paper Co., 429 So.2d 989 (Ala.1983), supra note 6.

8. Thus, e.g., the owner of a fee simple absolute might convey land "to A Church so long as the land shall be used for church purposes, and if the land shall cease to be used for church purposes it shall revert to the grantor or his heirs."

9. Language appropriate to introduce a special limitation includes "so long as," "until," "while," "during the time that," or any other word or phrase suggesting a duration of time.

10. See, e.g., Staack v. Detterding, 182 Iowa 582, 161 N.W. 44, L.R.A.1918C 856 (1917); Bailey v. Eagle Mountain Telephone Co., 202 Tenn. 195, 303 S.W.2d 726 (1957); Edling v. Stanford Tp., supra note 3. The proposition stated in the text is also supported by the many cases where language of executory limitation follows the language of special limitation and the intended executory interest is held void under the rule against perpetuities; in these cases the courts have usually held that excision of the executory limitation leaves the grantee with a determinable fee and the grantor (or his successors in interest) with a possibility of reverter, although the grantor obviously did not intend to create a possibility of reverter. See, e.g., First Universalist Society v. Boland, supra note 1. In a few cases, however, courts have held that a determinable fee was not created because no express reverter clause was included in the creating instrument. See, e.g., In re Copps Chapel Methodist Episcopal Church, 120 Ohio St. 309, 166 N.E. 218 (1929). Board of County Com'rs v. Consolidated Rail Corp., 14 Ohio Misc.2d 4, 469 N.E.2d 1361 (Comm.Pl.1983), held that "reverter" language is required if "special limitation" appears only in habendum clause, but no "reverter" language is required if "special limitation" appears in granting clause.

In Harrison v. Marcus, 396 Mass. 424, 486 N.E.2d 710 (1985), it was held that a fee simple determinable was not created by use of the

appropriate special limitation language and merely states the purpose for which the conveyance or devise is made, the addition of an express reverter clause will probably lead a court to conclude that a fee simple determinable has been created.[11] Without an express reverter clause, a mere statement of the purpose for which the property is transferred will not create a fee simple determinable.[12]

When the state of affairs upon which a fee simple determinable is limited ceases to exist or the designated terminating event occurs, the fee simple determinable expires by operation of law, without the necessity of any action by the person who owns the possibility of reverter or executory interest which constitutes the residue of the fee simple absolute.[13] Hence the owner of the possibility of reverter or executory interest, as the case may be, has an immediate right to possession of the property and may immediately bring an action to recover its possession. As a further consequence, the

words "so long as" without "reverter" language in a conveyance of land in trust for charitable purposes, with power in the trustees to "determine the existence of a breach of condition and on such determination * * * convey title to the [grantor's] heirs." In substance, the trustees were held to have a power to terminate the trust for breach of condition, and that until they did so the trustees would have a fee simple on condition subsequent.

11. E.g., Williams v. Kirby School District No. 32, 207 Ark. 458, 181 S.W.2d 488 (1944) ("to be used * * * for school and church purposes and to revert to me should school and church be discontinued or moved"). Accord: North v. Graham, 235 Ill. 178, 85 N.E. 267, 18 L.R.A.(N.S.) 624 (1908); Reichard v. Chicago, Burlington & Quincy Railroad Co., 231 Iowa 563, 1 N.W.2d 721 (1942); Board of Education v. Littrell, 173 Ky. 78, 190 S.W. 465 (1917); White v. Kentling, 345 Mo. 526, 134 S.W.2d 39 (1939); Magness v. Kerr, 121 Or. 373, 254 P. 1012, 51 A.L.R. 1466 (1927); Calhoun v. Hays, 155 Pa.Super. 519, 39 A.2d 307 (1944); Mt. Gilead Church Cemetery v. Woodham, 453 So.2d 362 (Ala.1984). Contra: Hardman v. Dahlonega–Lumpkin County Chamber of Commerce, 238 Ga. 551, 233 S.E.2d 753 (1977) (the law favors fee simple subject to condition subsequent rather than fee simple determinable in order to avoid, where possible, a forfeiture). See also cases post Section 2.6 in notes 3, 5, 6, 8, holding that language of condition or covenant followed by words such as "null and void" and "revert" created fee simple subject to condition subsequent.

12. In most cases, it has been held that a fee simple absolute was created. E.g., Lynch v. Cypert, 227 Ark. 907, 302 S.W.2d 284 (1957); Light v. Third–Woodland Presbyterian Church, Inc., 311 S.W.2d 386 (Ky.1958); Rockford Trust Co. v. Moon, 370 Ill. 250, 18 N.E.2d 447 (1938); Roadcap v. County School Board, 194 Va. 201, 72 S.E.2d 250 (1952); Garrett v. Board of Education, 109 W.Va. 714, 156 S.E. 115 (1930); Wood v. Fremont County Com'rs,

759 P.2d 1250 (Wyo.1988). But sometimes the court finds that a charitable trust was created. E.g., Abel v. Girard Trust Co., 365 Pa. 34, 73 A.2d 682 (1950).

Lacer v. Navajo County, 141 Ariz. 396, 687 P.2d 404 (App.1983); Little Miami, Inc. v. Wisecup, 13 Ohio App.3d 239, 468 N.E.2d 935 (1984). See also Indigo Realty Co. v. City of Charleston, 281 S.C. 234, 314 S.E.2d 601 (1984), holding that grantor had no possibility of reverter after giving city a deed absolute on its face, under threat of condemnation, and that city's fee simple estate was not affected by abandonment of public project for which land was acquired and subsequent sale of land to private person. In U.S. Trust Co. v. State, 226 N.J.Super. 8, 543 A.2d 457 (App.Div.1988), the court said that words merely stating the purpose for which land is conveyed usually do not indicate intent to create a determinable fee, although other language in the instrument, the amount of consideration paid, and the surrounding circumstances may indicate such intent; and that the parties claiming a deed created a determinable fee had the burden of proof as to the market value of the land at time of sale in order to show consideration paid was inadequate for a conveyance in fee simple absolute.

It should be noted that a statement of purpose may lead a court to find that a deed creates an easement rather than a fee simple estate. Hawk v. Rice, 325 N.W.2d 97 (Iowa 1982). On the other hand, a fee simple determinable may be created when a land developer, pursuant to statute, dedicates land to public use; in such a case, the developer retains a possibility of reverter in fee simple absolute. Town of Moorcroft v. Lang, 779 P.2d 1180 (Wyo.1989).

13. E.g., Williams v. Kirby School District No. 32, supra note 11; Valer Oil Co. v. Souza, 182 Cal.App.2d 790, 6 Cal.Rptr. 301 (1960); Caldwell v. Brown, 553 S.W.2d 692 (Ky.1977); Brown v. Haight, 435 Pa. 12, 255 A.2d 508

applicable statute of limitations with respect to actions for recovery of possession of land begins to run in favor of the former owner of the fee simple determinable if he remains in possession of the land.[14]

At the present time, estates in fee simple determinable are almost never created in commercial transactions,[15] although they may still occasionally be created when land is given to charitable, educational, or other eleemosynary institutions.

§ 2.5 The Fee Simple Subject to a Condition Subsequent

Early in the development of the law of estates in land, the English courts recognized the validity of an express condition or proviso attached to the transfer of a fee simple estate—e.g., "to A and his heirs upon the express condition [provided, however,] that the land hereby conveyed shall be used for no other purpose than as a burying ground."[1] Such a conveyance would give A a fee simple subject to a condition subsequent,[2] and would give the grantor a right to "re-enter" the land and oust the grantee or his successors in interest if a breach of the condition should occur.[3] Upon re-entry, the owner of the fee simple subject to a condition subsequent was divested of his estate and the grantor (or his heirs) was revested with the possessory fee simple owned by the grantor when he created the fee simple subject to a condition subsequent; but a mere breach of the condition did not defeat the estate of the owner of the fee simple subject to a condition subsequent.[4]

Although a grantor often expressly reserves a right to re-enter and terminate the estate granted for breach of condition, this was not necessary in order to create a fee simple subject to a condition subsequent according to

(1969); Saletri v. Clark, 13 Wis.2d 325, 108 N.W.2d 548 (1961).

14. See Storke v. Penn Mutual Life Insurance Co., 390 Ill. 619, 61 N.E.2d 552 (1945); but see School District v. Hanson, 186 Iowa 1314, 173 N.W. 873 (1919). For further discussion of this point and comparison of the fee simple determinable with the fee simple subject to a condition subsequent, see post, Section 2.7.

15. The principal exception to this proposition is that oil and gas leases often contain special limitations creating estates in fee simple determinable. See, e.g., Humble Oil & Refining Co. v. Harrison, 146 Tex. 216, 205 S.W.2d 355 (1947).

§ 2.5

1. Recognition of estates subject to such conditions reflects the liberality of the courts in giving effect to "the form of the gift" in the thirteenth century. 2 Pollock and Maitland, History of English Law §§ 25–27 (2d ed. 1898).

For a listing of appropriate language to create a fee simple subject to a condition subsequent, see DeHart v. Ritenour Consolidated School Dist., 663 S.W.2d 332 (Mo.App.1983) ("upon condition that," "upon express condition that," "provided that," "but if," or "if it happens that"). See also Trailsend Land Co. v. Virginia Holding Corp., 228 Va. 319, 321

S.E.2d 667 (1984) (option to repurchase is a condition subsequent).

2. As to use of the term "fee simple subject to a condition subsequent" in preference to other terms sometimes employed, see ante, Section 2.3 note 3.

3. The interest retained by the grantor was called a "right of entry for breach of condition broken" or a "right of entry for breach of condition." For a discussion of the legal characteristics of this interest, see post, Section 3.5. Some American courts, unfortunately, have referred to this interest as a "possibility of reverter"; see, e.g., Rice v. Boston & Worcester Railroad Corp., 94 Mass. (12 Allen) 141 (1866).

Performance of most, if not all, "conditions subsequent" is within the power of the person who owns the fee simple subject to condition subsequent. Failure to perform a condition requiring affirmative action within a reasonable time, when no definite time is specified, constitutes a breach and authorizes the grantor to take appropriate action to terminate the estate of the grantee by "re-entering" the premises. Forsgren v. Sollie, 659 P.2d 1068 (Utah 1983).

4. These rules were well settled by the time of Littleton. See Littleton, Tenures §§ 325–331.

the English common law because the right to re-enter was held to arise by operation of law from the use of words of condition or proviso.[5] In the United States, however, courts have often held that words of condition or proviso, standing alone, are ambiguous and that the grantor who omits any express provision for re-entry, termination, or forfeiture may be found to have intended to create only a personal covenant,[6] a real covenant[7] or equitable servitude,[8] an easement,[9] an equitable charge,[10] or a trust[11] rather than a defeasible estate. Indeed, many cases state that there is a constructional preference against finding that a defeasible estate was intended by the grantor.[12] Hence, if a grantor really wishes to create a fee simple subject to a condition subsequent, the draftsman should expressly provide for re-entry and termination of the estate granted upon breach of the stated condition. When such a provision is included in the creating instrument, most American courts will find that a fee simple subject to a condition subsequent is created,[13] although a few courts have refused to find that a defeasible estate

5. See, e.g., Mary Partington's Case, 10 Co. Rep. 35b, at 42a. An express provision for re-entry on breach of the condition would, however, create an estate subject to a condition subsequent even where no other words sufficient to create a condition subsequent were employed. Thus, e.g., a conveyance "to A and his heirs, but if A or his heirs shall ever use the land for a purpose other than a burying ground, then the grantor or his heirs may re-enter and repossess the land as of his or their former estate," would give A a fee simple subject to a condition subsequent. See Sheppard's Touchstone 121 ("there are other words as *si, si contingat,* and the like, that will make an estate conditional also; but then they must have other words joined with them * * *; as that then the grantor shall re-enter, or that then the estate shall be void or the like").

6. E.g., Skinner v. Shepard, 130 Mass. 180 (1881).

7. E.g., Post v. Weil, 115 N.Y. 361, 22 N.E. 145, 5 L.R.A. 422 (1889).

8. E.g., Queen City Park Association v. Gale, 110 Vt. 110, 3 A.2d 529 (1938).

9. E.g., Boston Consolidated Gas Co. v. Oakes, 279 Mass. 230, 181 N.E. 225 (1932).

10. E.g., Selzer v. Selzer, 146 Kan. 273, 69 P.2d 708 (1937).

11. E.g., MacKenzie v. Trustees of Presbytery of Jersey City, 67 N.J.Eq. 652, 61 A. 1027, 3 L.R.A.(N.S.) 227 (Err. & App. 1905).

12. E.g., Kinney v. State, 238 Kan. 375, 710 P.2d 1290 (1985) ("an estate upon condition subsequent * * * is never favored in law, and * * * no deed will be construed to create such an estate unless the language is so clear that no room is left for any other construction"); Victoria Hospital Association v. All Persons, 169 Cal. 455, 459, 147 P. 124, 126 (1915) ("such conditions are not favored in the law because they tend to destroy estates, and * * * no provision in a deed relied on to create a condition subsequent will be so interpreted if the

language of the provision will bear any other reasonable construction"); Congregational Conference Appeal, 352 Pa. 470, 474, 43 A.2d 1, 3 (1945) ("when there is any doubt as to whether a clause in a deed restricting the enjoyment of land is a condition or merely a covenant, the latter construction is always favored"); Ayer v. Emery, 96 Mass. 67, 70 (1867) ("an estate on condition cannot be created by deed except when the terms of the grant will admit of no other reasonable interpretation"); 4 Kent, Commentaries 132 ("If it be doubtful whether a clause in a deed be a covenant or a condition, the courts will incline against the latter construction; for a covenant is far preferable to the tenant.").

But cf. Forsgren v. Sollie, 659 P.2d 1068 (Utah 1983) (constructional preference not recognized, and a deed that contained neither an express condition nor an express provision for re-entry, termination, or forfeiture was held to create a fee simple subject to condition subsequent); Menge v. Radtke, 222 Wis. 594, 269 N.W. 313 (1936) (constructional preference relaxed when conveyance is on condition that grantee shall support grantor for rest of his life). Rest.Prop. § 45 (1944), Comments j through p, sets forth rules of construction which do not include any constructional preference against finding that a defeasible estate has been created. But id. § 394, Comment c states that if the language of a conveyance may reasonably be construed either to create in the grantor a defeasible estate or an option to repurchase, the latter construction is preferred.

13. E.g., Wolf v. Hallenbeck, 109 Colo. 70, 123 P.2d 412 (1942); Lacer v. Navajo County, 141 Ariz. 396, 687 P.2d 404 (App.1983). It should be noted, however, that courts also frequently find that a fee simple subject to a condition subsequent is created by instruments qualifying the estate granted by words such as "forfeit," "revert," or "null and void"

is created even when a right to re-enter for breach of condition has been expressly reserved by the grantor.[14]

The term "right of entry for breach of condition" was appropriate to describe the interest retained by a grantor when he created a fee simple subject to a condition subsequent under the old English common law, which required an actual entry on the land after breach of the condition, in the presence of witnesses, in order to terminate the fee simple subject to a condition subsequent and revest the grantor (or his heirs) with the grantor's original fee simple estate.[15] At the present time, however, it is probable that a fee simple subject to a condition subsequent can be terminated in all American jurisdictions without an actual entry on the land. In some jurisdictions merely starting an action to recover possession of the land is sufficient; [16] in other jurisdictions the person entitled to enforce the condition must—in lieu of an actual re-entry—manifest his election to terminate in some appropriate way before starting an action to recover possession.[17]

in connection with conditional language. See post Section 2.6, notes 3 and 6. For a recent case finding that a fee simple subject to a condition subsequent was created where the instrument provided that "if the property is not used for school buildings or school purposes, or if at any future time the name should be changed, then said property shall revert to the above grantor or her heirs," see DeHart v. Ritenour Consol. School Dist., supra note 1. In such cases the language is said to be ambiguous, and the courts have applied a constructional preference for finding a fee simple subject to a condition subsequent rather than a fee simple determinable. For a fuller discussion of this point, see post Section 2.6.

14. Second Church of Christ, Scientist v. Le Prevost, 67 Ohio App. 101, 35 N.E.2d 1015 (1941); W.F. White Land Co. v. Christenson, 14 S.W.2d 369 (Tex.Civ.App.1928); Scaling v. Sutton, 167 S.W.2d 275 (Tex.Civ.App.1942), error refused. "Such results must rest either upon a judicial conviction that conveyancers use language without an awareness of its reasonable meaning, or upon a belief that the social policy hostile to forfeitures requires frustration of the conveyor's manifested intent." 2 Powell, Real Property ¶ 188.

Although the Texas Supreme Court has never expressly approved White Land Co. v. Christenson, supra, the U.S. Court of Appeals for the 5th Circuit recently applied the *Christenson* rule as "Texas law" in Humphrey v. C.G. Jung Educational Center of Houston, 714 F.2d 477 (5th Cir.1983) ("the Texas courts will construe anything less than clear, plain and unequivocal language as creating merely a restrictive covenant, despite the fact that the deed contains provisions for reverter or re-entry upon the breach of these covenants"). It would seem, however, that cases like *Le Prevost, Christenson,* and *Scaling* might be viewed as standing for the rule that legal enforcement of forfeiture provisions will be

denied when equitable enforcement of restrictive covenants will provide an adequate remedy for breach, rather than as establishing the rule that clear forfeiture language does not create a defeasible estate of some kind.

15. See 1 Cruise's Digest of the Laws of England 50 (1835); 1 Simes and Smith, Future Interests § 255 at n. 62 (2d ed. 1956).

16. E.g., Mattox v. State, 280 N.C. 471, 186 S.E.2d 378 (1972).

"In some states distinctions may be drawn between the various kinds of possessory actions, with the result that even though ejectment might be brought by the holder of the right of entry without previous election, he cannot maintain summary statutory proceedings for recovery of possession, because the estate of the grantee has not been previously terminated." 1 Simes and Smith, Future Interests § 255 at n. 68 (2d ed. 1956), citing Onondaga Hotel Corp. v. Gurney, 62 N.Y.S.2d 550 (Mun.Ct.Syracuse 1946).

17. E.g., City of New York v. Coney Island Fire Department, 285 N.Y. 535, 32 N.E.2d 827 (1941). Presumably the simplest method of manifesting the intention of the owner of the right of entry to terminate the defeasible estate is to give notice to that effect to the owner of the latter estate. This method was expressly approved in Emrick v. Bethlehem Tp., 506 Pa. 372, 485 A.2d 736 (1984) ("the power [of termination] could be exercised by a writing with or without previous, simultaneous or subsequent physical possession"). See also Higdon v. Davis, 315 N.C. 208, 337 S.E.2d 543 (1985), stating that where an easement is subject to a condition subsequent, "re-entry is not required * * * if the owner of the servient tract is already in possession," and that "if re-entry was necessary, the plaintiff's action * * * to quiet title constitutes a re-entry." In McDowell v. Blue Ridge & Atlantic Railway, 144 N.C. 721, 57 S.E. 520 (1907), the

Under either rule, the term "power of termination" is more accurately descriptive of the interest retained by a grantor when he creates a fee simple subject to a condition subsequent than is the traditional term "right of entry." [18]

It should be noted that language in a conveyance or will giving a fee simple to the first named grantee may be followed by an express condition subsequent and a gift over to a third person upon breach of the condition.[19] In such a case, the clause introduced by the condition and containing the gift over is uniformly construed as an executory limitation.[20] An executory limitation creates an executory interest in the beneficiary of the gift over, and gives the initial grantee a fee simple subject to an executory limitation rather than a fee simple subject to a condition subsequent. If the condition—which is viewed as a condition precedent with respect to the executory limitation—is satisfied, the fee simple automatically "shifts" to the holder of the executory interest; no re-entry or manifestation of intent to terminate the interest of the initial grantee is required.

At the present time, estates in fee simple subject to a condition subsequent are rarely created in commercial transactions, but they are still sometimes created when land is given to charitable, religious, educational, or other eleemosynary institutions.

§ 2.6 Distinguishing a Fee Simple Determinable From a Fee Simple Subject to a Condition Subsequent

In theory, it should be easy to determine whether an instrument creates a fee simple determinable or a fee simple subject to a condition subsequent.

court held that a notice to stop using an easement constituted a "re-entry."

After an actual "re-entry" without legal action, the grantor (or his heirs) should bring a "quiet title" action if the ousted grantee will not give the grantor (or his heirs) a quitclaim deed. See Forsgren v. Sollie, 659 P.2d 1068 (Utah 1983).

18. The Property Restatement, for which Professor Powell was the Reporter, adopted the term "power of termination," Rest.Prop. § 155, as did Professor Powell in his treatise, 2A Powell, Real Property ¶ 272. But the logical extension of substituting "fee simple subject to a power of termination" for "fee simple subject to a condition subsequent" was not adopted either in the Property Restatement or in Powell's treatise. The term "right of entry" was employed in both 1 Simes and Smith, Future Interests §§ 241 et seq., and 1 Am. L.Prop. §§ 4.6 et seq.; see also 1 Am.L.Prop. § 2.9, criticizing the Property Restatement's adoption of the term "power of termination." Courts seem generally to have continued to use the term "right of entry." But see Emrick v. Bethlehem Tp., supra note 17, where the court said: "Appellant's right of re-entry must be viewed for what it is, namely, the power to terminate the appellee's estate and restore to appellant the former estate. This

power does not depend upon a physical entry onto the property. When the land was abandoned by railroad purposes, and written notice of appellant's desire to re-enter was given * * *, the appellants took the action necessary to cause a reversion [sic]." As Emrick indicates, the right to resume physical possession may be deemed a result of the proper exercise of a power of termination of the conditional estate, rather than termination of the conditional estate being deemed a result of the resumption of physical possession by the grantor or his heirs as at common law.

19. E.g., "to A and his heirs on the express condition that the land hereby conveyed shall be used for no other purpose than as a burying ground, and if the land hereby conveyed shall be used for any other purposes during A's lifetime, then to B and his heirs."

20. In such a case, the express condition is considered to be part of the executory limitation in favor of the third person. Thus, in the example given supra, note 19, if the words "during A's lifetime" had been omitted so that the rule against perpetuities would invalidate the executory interest given to B, the interest created in A would be a fee simple absolute, not a fee simple subject to a condition subsequent, and the grantor would retain no interest in the land.

If the instrument includes a special limitation (introduced by words such as "so long as," or "until") it creates a fee simple determinable, whether or not it also includes an express reverter clause.[1] If the instrument includes an express condition or proviso ("on condition that," or "provided that") and an express right to re-enter for breach of the stated condition, it creates a fee simple subject to a condition subsequent.[2] But deeds and wills often fail to employ the appropriate words to create one of the two types of defeasible estate or the other. Instead deeds and wills often contain a confusing mixture of words appropriate for creation of both types of defeasible estate. Consider the following cases:

1. A deed provides that the grantor and grantee "covenant and agree that no saloon shall be kept and no intoxicating liquors be sold * * * on said premises herein conveyed * * *; and that in case of breach of these covenants or any of them said premises shall immediately revert to the grantors, and the * * * [grantee] shall forfeit all right, title and interest in and to said premises."[3]

2. A deed provides: "It is hereby agreed that the said above-described property is to be used for school purposes, and that, whenever it shall cease to be so used, the said property will revert to the grantor herein, his heirs and assigns."[4]

3. A deed provides: "The conditions of the above gift is that the said School Directors * * * are to erect on the said parcel of land a good and suitable house for the purpose of having taught therein a public free school * * *; the same is to be at all times used but if at any time the same shall cease to be used for said public free school purpose then the title to said * * * parcel of land is to revert back to the said Gregg, his heirs and assigns in as full and ample a manner as if this instrument had never been given."[5]

4. A deed conveying land to a Baptist church further provides that, as soon as the land ceases to be used as Baptist church ground, "this deed to be null and void."[6]

5. A deed conveying land to a Baptist church further provides: "This deed is given expressly on condition that the premises shall be used exclusively for a Baptist Church site, and whenever the same shall cease to be used for such purpose, this deed shall become null and void and the title shall revert to the grantor, his heirs and assigns."[7]

6. A deed conveying land to a land developer lists a number of "conditions and restrictions," and further provides that "failure to comply with the covenants and conditions * * * hereof will automatically cause title to all lands to revert to the [grantor] City of Ocean City."[8]

§ 2.6

1. See ante, Section 2.4 at notes 9, 10.

2. See ante, Section 2.5 at note 13.

3. Storke v. Penn Mutual Life Insurance Co., 390 Ill. 619, 61 N.E.2d 552 (1945).

4. Denver & Santa Fe Railway Co. v. School District, 14 Colo. 327, 23 P. 978 (1890).

5. Pickens v. Daugherty, 217 Tenn. 349, 397 S.W.2d 815 (1965), noted 33 Tenn.L.Rev. 546 (1966).

6. United States v. 2,086 Acres of Land, 46 F.Supp. 411 (W.D.S.C.1942).

7. Union Missionary Baptist Church v. Fyke, 179 Okl. 102, 64 P.2d 1203 (1937).

8. Oldfield v. Stoeco Homes, Inc., 26 N.J. 246, 139 A.2d 291 (1958).

What kind of defeasible estate is created in each of the examples set out above? The word "condition" is used in four cases; the phrase "null and void" is used in two cases; and the word "revert" is used in five cases—indeed, in example 6, the term "automatically revert" is used. Thus it is difficult to determine what the grantor's intent was in any of the six examples. In such cases, it is often said that the courts will apply a constructional preference in favor of a fee simple subject to a condition subsequent.[9] In the actual cases on which the six examples are based, however, although the court found that a fee simple subject to a condition subsequent was created in cases 1,[10] 3,[11] 4,[12] and 6,[13] the court, on the contrary, found that a fee simple determinable was created in cases 2[14] and 5.[15] So the constructional preference for a fee simple subject to a condition

9. This constructional preference is apparently based on the more general rule that ambiguous language in a deed is construed in favor of the grantee, plus an assumption that a fee simple subject to a condition subsequent is more favorable to the grantee than a fee simple determinable because (1) breach of the condition does not automatically terminate the estate granted and (2) defenses such as election, waiver, and estoppel are, therefore, more likely to be successful when the grantor (or his successor in interest) does not elect to terminate within a reasonable time after breach. For discussion of the constructional preference, see 1 Simes and Smith, Future Interests § 248 at n. 35 and cases cited (2d ed. 1956) (fee simple subject to a condition subsequent, "being less drastic" as to forfeiture, "is to be preferred"); 2 Powell, Real Property ¶ 188 between nn. 13 and 14, and cases cited ("An *optional* forfeiture is less objectionable than an *automatic* forfeiture. Hence, if the limitation must be construed to create either an estate in fee simple determinable or an estate in fee simple subject to a condition subsequent, the latter construction is the less objectionable of the two.")

10. Storke v. Penn Mutual Life Insurance Co., supra note 3 (the court expressly relied on the constructional preference for a fee simple subject to a condition subsequent, but the result would have been the same even if the court had found that the ambiguous language created a fee simple determinable; the grantor's heirs would have been barred a statute of limitations).

Accord: Hardman v. Dahlonega–Lumpkin County Chamber of Commerce, 238 Ga. 551, 233 S.E.2d 753 (1977); Nielsen v. Woods, 687 P.2d 486 (Colo.App.1984) (court disregarded both "so long as" language and express statement in the deed that the estate created was "a fee simple subject to a special limitation with an automatic reverter," and held that the deed should be construed as creating "a fee simple subject to a right of entry for condition broken" because "the prevailing purpose" of grantors was "to compel compliance with the condition upon penalty of forfeiture"—a holding that enabled the court to award equi-

table relief in grantors' action for a judgment declaring that grantee had received a fee simple determinable which had automatically terminated). See post Section 2.7 n. 21.

11. Pickens v. Daugherty, supra note 5 (the court did not mention the constructional preference in concluding that the deed created "an estate upon a condition subsequent," and then applied the common law rule that a right of entry is inalienable).

12. United States v. 2,086 Acres of Land, supra note 6 (constructional preference not mentioned; when U.S. took land by eminent domain and thus prevented further church use, the breach of condition was excused and the church was entitled to the entire condemnation award).

13. Oldfield v. Stoeco Homes, Inc., supra note 8 (the court relied on the constructional preference and held that a fee simple subject to a condition subsequent was created despite use of the phrase "automatically cause title to revert"); Hardman v. Dahlonega–Lumpkin County Chamber of Commerce, 238 Ga. 551, 233 S.E.2d 753 (1977).

14. Denver & Santa Fe Railway Co. v. School District, supra note 4 (the court did not mention the constructional preference in concluding that the title conveyed was "a qualified fee" and that "whenever the event might occur upon which the limitation was based, the estate of appellee would immediately cease").

15. Union Missionary Baptist Church v. Fyke, supra note 7 (the court assumed the church had a fee simple determinable, without considering any alternative; but "forfeiture" was not an issue). Johnson v. City of Hackensack, 200 N.J.Super. 185, 491 A.2d 14 (App.Div.1985), is to the same effect, but despite the "fee simple determinable" construction the court held that "substantial performance" of the "condition" restricting the land to "park uses" provided a basis for its refusal to allow a "forfeiture," although the court could enjoin "unpermitted uses" in "an appropriate proceeding." The "substantial perfor-

subsequent is not an infallible guide.[16]

As an alternative to the constructional preference for a fee simple subject to a condition subsequent, consider the following: "If the purpose is to compel compliance with a condition by the penalty of forfeiture, an estate on condition arises, but if the intent is to give land for a stated use, the estate to cease when that * * * use is ended * * * a fee on limitation results."[17] Arguably, this rule of construction would lead to the conclusions reached by the courts in cases 1, 2, 5, and 6, but would not lead to the court's conclusions in cases 3 and 4.[18] So this rule of construction, like the one previously suggested, is not infallible.

In many of the cases on which the foregoing examples are based, it apparently made no real difference whether the court construed the language of defeasance to create a fee simple determinable or a fee simple subject to a condition subsequent.[19] Perhaps the only conclusion that can be drawn from these cases is that the courts are not much concerned with the labels they attach to defeasible estates when it makes no practical difference. On the other hand, a careful examination of a much larger group of cases might reveal—as Dunham has argued—that in cases where it does make a practical difference the courts attach the label which they believe is necessary to achieve a just result.[20] If so, we need to consider carefully what differing results may follow from attaching one label rather than the other to language creating a defeasible estate in fee simple. This consideration will be found in the next Section of this book.

Even if a court decides initially that particular language in a deed or will creates either a fee simple determinable or a fee simple subject to a

mance" concept hardly seems to be consistent with the "fee simple determinable" construction under which the estate "terminates automatically upon the happening of a stated event." Compare Hardman v. Dahlonega-Lumpkin County Chamber of Commerce, supra note 10.

16. The cases discussed in the text are not necessarily an adequate basis for any definitive judgment. But see 1 Simes and Smith, Future Interests § 248 n. 35 (2d ed. 1956, 1989 Supp.), citing 12 cases as directly supporting the asserted constructional preference and 5 cases under "but see." For a recent case applying the constructional preference, see State v. Berklund, 217 Mont. 218, 704 P.2d 59 (1985).

17. 1 Am.L.Prop. § 2.6 between nn. 15 and 16. The language quoted from 1 Am.L.Prop. § 2.6 was relied upon in Nielsen v. Woods, 687 P.2d 486 (Colo.App.1984), where the court held that a "fee simple subject to a right of entry for condition broken" was created despite inclusion in the deed of the following language: "The estate hereby created is a fee simple subject to a special limitation with an automatic reverter to the grantors if said condition is not satisfied." After having refused to give effect to this explicit language, the court also held that equitable relief against forfeiture should be granted because "the party insisting

upon it [forfeiture] may be made whole otherwise." See supra note 10.

18. See supra notes 3–8 and 10–15. Examples 3 and 4 appear to be indistinguishable from examples 2 and 5, except for the fact that example 4 does not include an express reverter clause.

19. This would seem to be the case in Storke v. Penn Mutual Life Insurance Co., supra note 3; Union Missionary Baptist Church v. Fyke, supra note 7; United States v. 2,086 Acres of Land, supra note 6. In the following cases, it also seems that it really made no difference whether the court held that a fee simple determinable or a fee simple subject to a condition subsequent was created: Union Colony Co. v. Gallie, 104 Colo. 46, 88 P.2d 120 (1939); Salt Lake City v. State, 101 Utah 543, 125 P.2d 790 (1942); Wolf v. Hallenbeck, 109 Colo. 70, 123 P.2d 412 (1942).

20. See Dunham, Possibility of Reverter and Power of Termination—Fraternal or Identical Twins?, 20 U.Chi.L.Rev. 215, 216–217 (1953). It is unclear whether Professor Dunham is willing to concede that any form of language whatever can be relied upon to produce either a fee simple determinable or a fee simple subject to a condition subsequent—assuming that the grantor understands the difference and wishes to create one or the other.

condition subsequent, as the case may be, the nature and scope of the condition or limitation may not be absolutely clear. In general, at least in *inter vivos* conveyances, courts tend to construe ambiguous language in favor of the grantee in order to reduce the chance of forfeiture. For example, where land was conveyed to a church "upon the consideration * * * that said premises shall be used for church purposes only and that in case the same is abandoned, * * * the title shall be revested in" the grantor, the court held that the execution of an oil lease and the moving of the church building to another part of the premises to make way for a drilling rig did not amount to an abandonment of use "for church purposes only" and did not constitute a breach of condition entitling the grantor's heirs to re-enter.[21] But relatively slight differences in language may produce different results.[22]

The courts not only construe language in favor of the grantee but also require that occurrence of the terminating event be clearly proved before a forfeiture will be allowed, and the courts refuse to allow a forfeiture when the purpose of the special limitation or condition subsequent (as the case may be) is still being substantially achieved.[23] In addition, as previously noted, courts often recognize defenses such as election, waiver, and estoppel in cases where a grantor (or his successors) fail to terminate a fee simple

---

21. Skipper v. Davis, 59 S.W.2d 454 (Tex. Civ.App.1933) (held, that the grantor's heirs could enjoin commission of waste although not entitled to recover possession of land). It should be noted that the court construed the language quoted in the text, supra, as creating a fee simple subject to a condition subsequent, but it referred variously to the grantor's retained interest as a "right of reverter," a "reverter," and a "right to reversion." The court also said, " 'Reversion' and 'reverter' are synonymous, and denote a vested estate or right," which, of course, is nonsense.

22. E.g., Union Missionary Baptist Church v. Fyke, supra notes 7, 15, where the deed provided that the land conveyed was to be "used exclusively for church purposes" and contained an express provision for reverter if the land should cease to be used for "such purpose," the court said there was no ambiguity in the special limitation, which "clearly means that the premises are to be used exclusively as a site for the erection and maintenance of a church building." The court also said, however, that it was unnecessary to decide whether the land had ceased to be used for "such purpose" because there was no claim that the estate conveyed by the deed had been forfeited. Cf. Priddy v. School District No. 78, 92 Okl. 254, 219 P. 141 (1923), where the court construed a deed conveying land to a school district "to have and to hold as long as used for a school house site," with an express provision for reverter if the land "is ever abandoned as a school house site." The court held that the estate conveyed to the grantee was not defeated by the grantee's execution of an oil and gas lease and the subsequent operation of an oil well on the premises, so long as a school was also conducted on the land, be-

cause "the deed provides for forfeiture if the property should be abandoned as a school site, but does not provide for a forfeiture by the additional use of the property." The court also said, "The law is opposed to forfeiture of estates and will not imply a forfeiture where none is expressed by the terms of conveyance." The court apparently thought abandonment of school use would cause an automatic reverter of the land to the grantor, although the court termed the estate conveyed to the school district an estate "upon condition subsequent."

23. Johnson v. City of Hackensack, 200 N.J.Super. 185, 491 A.2d 14 (App.Div.1985) ("Where a forfeiture results from failure to use property for the purpose specified in a deed, a minor deviation from that use will not effect a forfeiture as long as the specified use is substantially carried out. * * * If plaintiff's contentions as to the four minor uses were correct * * * the most that can be said is that these unpermitted uses could be restrained in an appropriate proceeding"); Kinney v. State, 238 Kan. 375, 710 P.2d 1290 (1985) ("The deed should be construed to require only that the State in good faith maintain the property as a public forestry, fish and game facility and as a recreational state park. * * * The lake is an important factor to be considered in determining whether the State in good faith has maintained the property for the intended uses. The maintenance of the lake, however, is not the controlling consideration. Under the circumstances, we hold that * * * the State * * * had not forfeited its title to the land simply because the quantity of water contained in the lake has not been sufficient to completely fill an area of 150 acres [as specified in the deed].").

subject to a condition subsequent within a reasonable time after a breach occurs,[24] and courts may also grant equitable relief against forfeiture if the grantor (or his successor) "may be made whole otherwise" by awarding damages or an injunction.[25]

§ 2.7 Does the Distinction Matter?

Despite the difficulty of determining whether ambiguous language in a deed or will has created a fee simple determinable or a fee simple subject to a condition subsequent, it is commonly said that it is important to make the determination because, if the former is created, the defeasible estate terminates "automatically" ("expires") by virtue of the special limitation to which it is subject, whereas, if the latter is created, breach of the stated condition does not terminate the defeasible estate unless and until the grantor (or his successor in interest) exercises the right to re-enter.[1] But it is obvious that the automatic termination of a fee simple determinable by virtue of a special limitation does not automatically dispossess the former owner of the fee simple determinable and restore possession to the grantor (or his successor in interest). Indeed, unless possession is voluntarily surrendered, the person in whom the possessory fee simple has automatically vested must sue for possession. So we must consider the defenses that may be available to the defendant when the grantor (or his successor in interest) brings an action to recover possession, either after the "automatic" termination of a fee simple determinable or after a breach of a condition subsequent giving him the right to re-enter, in order to see what practical differences, if any, there are between the two types of defeasible fee simple estates.

1. *Operation of the applicable statute of limitations.* The applicable statute of limitations governing actions to recover possession of land begins to run immediately upon the occurrence or nonoccurrence of the event which automatically terminates a fee simple determinable, because the right to possession is automatically revested in the grantor (or his successor in interest) and the continued possession of the former owner of the determinable fee is therefore wrongful.[2] However, since the estate of the owner of a

---

24. See supra note 9, and post Section 2.7 at note calls 11–20.

25. See Nielsen v. Woods, supra note 17, and post Section 2.7 around note call 21.

§ 2.7

1. E.g., 1 Simes and Smith, Future Interests § 282 at n. 10, quoting from Lynch v. Bunting, 42 Del. (3 Terry) 171, 29 A.2d 155, 157 (1942) ("There is a strong analogy between the differences between a determinable fee on the one hand and a fee simple subject to a condition subsequent on the other, and the difference between what, in other branches of the law, may be shown by the terms 'void' and 'voidable.'"); Storke v. Penn Mutual Life Insurance Co., 390 Ill. 619, 61 N.E.2d 552 (1945). Also see 2 Powell, Real Property ¶¶ 187, 188; Rest.Prop. §§ 23, 24, 44, 45.

As to what constitutes a "re-entry," see ante Section 2.5 at notecalls 16, 17.

2. E.g., Storke v. Penn Mutual Life Insurance Co., supra note 1. But see School District v. Hanson, 186 Iowa 1314, 173 N.W. 873 (1919)—holding that an action to recover possession was barred by a special 10–year statute of limitations requiring the repayment of the original purchase price plus the value of improvements, but also holding that the school district's "claim of title by adverse possession" was invalid because it "never asserted a hostile claim" to the land after ceasing to use it for school purposes. The court said, "mere continuation in possession is not sufficient. There must have been notice to the owner of the reversion [sic], or the possession must have been so notorious as to raise a presumption of notice." (186 Iowa at 1319, 173 N.W. at 874.) Thus the court seems to hold that "mere continuation in possession" is sufficient to make the special 10–year statute of limitations run against one who remains in possession after his determinable fee has ex-

fee simple subject to a condition subsequent does not automatically terminate upon a breach of the stated condition, it is clear that continued possession by the owner of the defeasible estate is not wrongful unless and until the grantor (or his successor in interest) exercises his right to re-enter by giving notice or starting an action for possession. Hence, until the right of entry is effectively exercised, the statute of limitations applicable to actions for possession of land should not run. Some courts have so held,[3] thus recognizing an important difference between a fee simple determinable and a fee simple subject to a condition subsequent. But in some states, either by statute [4] or by decision,[5] the applicable statute of limitations begins to run against the owner of a right of entry as soon as a breach of the stated condition occurs. In these jurisdictions, the positions of the owners of either type of defeasible estate would seem to be identical, after either automatic termination or breach of condition, with respect to the possibility of acquiring a new estate in fee simple absolute by adverse possession of the land for the period prescribed by the applicable statute of limitations.[6]

2. *Recovery of "mesne profits."* Since continued possession by the former owner of a determinable fee after it has terminated by virtue of a special limitation is clearly wrongful, the grantor (or his successor in interest) has a cause of action for "mesne profits" (usually measured by the reasonable rental value of the land) for the period of wrongful possession after the termination.[7] The owner of a right of entry for breach of condition, however, has no right to "mesne profits" merely because a breach of condition has occurred, because the breach alone does not make continued possession by the owner of the defeasible fee simple wrongful; hence "mesne profits" are recoverable only for the period after the right of entry for breach of condition has been exercised.[8] But this difference between the two types

pired, but is not sufficient to make the general real property statute of limitations run. No reason for such a distinction is suggested in the opinion. On principle, continued possession by the former owner of the determinable fee ought to be sufficiently "notorious" and "hostile" to make the general statute of limitations run. See post, Section 10.7, for a more detailed treatment of statutes of limitation and title by adverse possession.

3. Mills v. Pennington, 213 Ark. 43, 209 S.W.2d 281 (1948); Sanford v. Sanford, 55 Ga. 527 (1875); Thompson v. Simpson, 128 N.Y. 270, 28 N.E. 627 (1891); City of New York v. Coney Island Fire Department, 285 N.Y. 535, 32 N.E.2d 827 (1941), affirming 259 App.Div. 286, 18 N.Y.S.2d 923 (1940) (delay of 41 years did not bar right of entry); Metropolitan Park District v. Rigney's Unknown Heirs, 65 Wn.2d 788, 399 P.2d 516 (1965), noted 40 Wash.L.Rev. 377 (1965).

4. E.g., Ark.Stat. § 37–104; West's Ann. Cal.Code Proc. § 320; Ill.—S.H.A. ch. 83, ¶ 3; Mass.Gen.Laws Ann. c. 260, § 23; Minn.Stat. Ann. § 500.20. See also Colo.Rev.Stat.1973, 38–41–119 (action to recover possession for violation of any "restriction" must be brought within one year). In Wolf v. Hallenbeck, 109

Colo. 70, 123 P.2d 412 (1942), it was held that the term "restrictions" includes conditions subsequent, so that the one-year limitation period will run from the date of breach.

5. E.g., Sanford v. Sims, 192 Va. 644, 66 S.E.2d 495 (1951).

6. From a policy standpoint, the rule as to when the statute of limitations begins to run should be the same for both types of defeasible estate: it should be the date when the terminating event occurs where there is a fee simple determinable, and the date of the breach of condition where there is a fee simple subject to a condition subsequent. Such a rule would not be unfair to the owner of a right of entry for breach of condition, since in most states he may bring an action for possession as soon as a breach occurs, and in other states he need only give notice before bringing an action for possession.

7. For a good general discussion of "mesne profits," see C.J.S. Ejectment §§ 128–165.

8. No cases in point have been found, but both logic and fairness point to the conclusion stated in the text. But note the anomaly of holding that the right to "mesne profits" accrues only when the right of entry is actually exercised in a state where, by statute, the

of defeasible estate may be minimized in jurisdictions which, either by statute or by decision, limit recovery of "mesne profits" or allow set-offs and credits when land is wrongfully possessed by a claimant occupying the land in good faith.[9] The former owner of a fee simple determinable who retains possession after his estate has terminated would generally qualify as an "occupying claimant in good faith" because, as Dunham has pointed out,[10]

> The difficulty of determining in advance of litigation the correct label to be attached to the limiting clause [i.e., condition subsequent or special limitation] should put practically all possessors claiming a defeasible present estate in the position of being claimants * * * in the good faith belief that possession is rightful until the formal claim is made [by the grantor or his successor in interest] or * * * there is no defeasance possible.

3. *Application of defenses such as waiver, election and estoppel.* When a fee simple is subject to a condition subsequent, it is clear that exercise of the right to re-enter for breach of condition may be barred by "waiver," "election," or "estoppel."[11] "Waiver" and "election," in such a case, appear to be different names for the same thing.[12] Neither is subject to the writing requirement of the Statute of Frauds,[13] and neither requires proof that the owner of the defeasible estate changed position in justifiable reliance upon the conduct alleged to amount to a waiver or an election.[14] Moreover, the waiver or election need not be express; the intent not to exercise a right of entry may be inferred from nonverbal conduct.[15] Some courts have said that mere silence or inaction will not bar exercise of a right of entry;[16] but other courts have held or said that mere failure of the owner of the right of entry

---

statute of limitations begins to run against the owner of the right of entry as soon as a breach of the condition subsequent occurs.

9. See, e.g., Ill.—S.H.A. ch. 45, ¶ 53 ("Occupying Claimants' Act"), which disallows any claim for "mesne profits" accruing "prior to receipt of actual notice of the adverse claim" by the defendant if he can show a record title and that he is without notice of an adverse record title. Even in the absence of an "occupying claimants' act," courts have allowed the defendant to reduce the amount of the plaintiff's recovery by showing that he held possession under color of title and in good faith. E.g., Simmons v. Holliday, 226 Ala. 630, 148 So. 327 (1933). See also Santmyer v. Clemmancs, 147 Wash. 354, 266 P. 148 (1928).

10. Dunham, Possibility of Reverter and Powers of Termination—Fraternal or Identical Twins?, 20 U.Chi.L.Rev. 215, 219 (1953). In Storke v. Penn Mutual Life Insurance Co., supra note 2, the court said that a deed "purporting to convey the entire estate [to the defendant] constituted color of title in good faith" although an earlier deed in the record chain of title clearly created only a defeasible fee simple—arguably a fee simple determinable. But the view stated by Dunham would lead to the same conclusion, since the language creating the defeasible fee simple was

ambiguous enough to invoke the constructional preference in favor of a fee simple subject to a condition subsequent.

11. Generally, see Dunham, supra note 10, at 224–229; 1 Simes and Smith, § 258 (2d ed. 1956); 1 Am.L.Prop. § 4.9.

12. Dunham asserts that "it is more proper to say that the owner of the power of termination [i.e., right of entry] has 'elected' not to terminate than to say he 'waived' his power." Dunham, supra note 10, at 225. Simes and Smith point out that the term "waiver" is often applied in cases where the owner of the right of entry indicates, *prior to any breach,* that he does not intend to exercise the right in the event of breach; they also seem to prefer "election" to describe conduct, *after a breach occurs,* indicating that the owner of the right of entry does not intend to exercise the right. 1 Simes and Smith, Future Interests § 258 (2d ed. 1956). But the courts seem to use the terms interchangeably.

13. See infra, notes 16, 17.

14. Ibid.

15. Ibid.

16. E.g., Cottle v. Tomlinson, 192 Ga. 704, 16 S.E.2d 555 (1941); Rumford Falls Power Co. v. Waishwill, 128 Me. 320, 147 A. 343 (1929); Trustees of Union College v. New York, 173

to exercise the right within a reasonable time after learning of a breach of condition will bar the grantor (or his successor in interest) from subsequently exercising the right.[17]　In any case, if the waiver of, or election not to exercise, the right of entry after breach is not express, the owner of the defeasible estate is more likely to avoid forfeiture if he can show a substantial change of position in justifiable reliance on the failure of the owner of the right of entry to exercise his right within a reasonable time after learning of the breach.[18]　When such a change of position is shown, a successful defense of estoppel can usually be made out.[19]

When the defeasible estate is labelled a fee simple determinable, the defense of estoppel should also be available to the former owner of the defeasible estate if he substantially changes his position in reliance on a representation—either express or implied—by the owner of the possibility of reverter that he does not intend to assert his rights under the special limitation after the terminating event has occurred.[20]　But, absent such a change of position, it seems unlikely that courts would allow the former owner of a fee simple determinable to assert, after the terminating event has occurred, that the owner of the possibility of reverter "waived" his rights as owner or "elected" not to exercise them.

N.Y. 38, 65 N.E. 853, 93 Am.St.Rep. 569 (1903).

17. E.g., Kampman v. Kampman, 98 Ark. 328, 135 S.W. 905 (1911); Jeffries v. State, 216 Ark. 657, 226 S.W.2d 810 (1950); Goodman v. Southern Pacific Co., 143 Cal.App.2d 424, 299 P.2d 321 (1956); Burr v. Tierney, 99 Conn. 647, 122 A. 454 (1923) ("laches"); Hale v. Elkhorn Coal Corp., 206 Ky. 629, 268 S.W. 304 (1925); Robinson v. Cannon, 346 Mo. 1126, 145 S.W.2d 146 (1940); Lehigh Coal & Navigation Co. v. Early, 162 Pa. 338, 29 A. 736 (1894); Jones v. McLain, 16 Tex.Civ.App. 305, 41 S.W. 714 (1897). What is a "reasonable time" varies with the circumstances and the court's general attitude. In Kampman v. Kampman, supra, 2 years was too long; and in Jones v. McLain, supra, 3 to 4 years was too long. But in City of New York v. Coney Island Fire Dept., supra note 3, 41 years was a reasonable time. In Jeffries v. State, supra, 18 years— "nearly three times the period of our statute of limitations"—was too long; the court cited Kampman v. Kampman, supra, with approval, and also cited Hannah v. Culpepper, 213 Ala. 319, 104 So. 751 (1925), for the rule that "the grantor's mere inaction will constitute a waiver when continued for longer than the period of limitations." The latter rule, of course, can be viewed as an indirect way of holding that the statute of limitations begins to run from the date of the breach of condition, or at least from the date when owner of the right of entry has notice of the breach.

18. See, e.g., Jeffries v. State, supra note 17, 216 Ark. at 659, 226 S.W.2d at 811 ("a waiver of forfeiture will be found more readily when the grantee has created an element of estoppel by changing his position after the grantor's failure to re-enter").

19. E.g., Storke v. Penn Mutual Life Insurance Co., supra note 1. For an extended general discussion of the sort of estoppel arising in such cases, see 31 C.J.S. Estoppel §§ 59–152; Ewart, Estoppel by Misrepresentation (1900). The terms "equitable estoppel," "estoppel in pais," "estoppel by misrepresentation," and "estoppel by conduct" appear to be used interchangeably. See 31 C.J.S. Estoppel § 59. Although the doctrine seems to have originated with courts of equity, there is no doubt that an "equitable estoppel" may be successfully asserted in actions at law. As to the relation between "waiver" and "estoppel," see 31 C.J.S. Estoppel § 61.

20. See, e.g., applying the estoppel doctrine to determinable fees, Humble Oil & Refining Co. v. Harrison, 146 Tex. 216, 205 S.W.2d 355 (1947); Mitchell v. Simms, 63 S.W.2d 371 (Tex. Com.App.1933). Generally, see 31 C.J.S. Estoppel § 150; Ewart, Estoppel by Misrepresentation 251–295 (1900).

See also Buttars v. Buttars, 631 P.2d 892 (Utah 1981), where the court found in favor of the grantee in an action by the grantor (the grantee's mother) to quiet title on the ground that the grantee had made only seven out of fourteen annual payments required by a provision in the deed and that his defaults had caused an automatic termination of his estate. The court said that there was a "special relationship" between grantor and grantee and that the grantee had performed many personal and business services for the grantor that were not required by any language in the deed. These services, the court said, provided a basis for holding that termination of the grantee's estate was barred by "waiver and satisfaction."

When a breach of condition or a terminating event occurs, it is also possible that the owner of the defeasible estate may be able to obtain equitable relief against forfeiture. Courts frequently grant such relief when the owner of a right of entry seeks to recover possession after a breach of the condition has occurred.[21] Courts have more difficulty with the idea that equitable relief is possible when a fee simple determinable has expired "naturally" by virtue of its special limitation because, in such cases, they tend to deny that any "forfeiture" is involved; but there is at least some authority in support of granting equitable relief in such cases.[22]

Whether language of defeasance is construed as a condition subsequent or a special limitation, it has been suggested that courts tend to grant some kind of relief against forfeiture (including relief based on the doctrines of waiver, election, and estoppel) if the purpose of the defeasance clause is to penalize noncompliance with a required course of conduct, and to withhold relief if the purpose of the defeasance clause is to terminate, or permit termination of, the defeasible estate when the purpose for which it was created can no longer be realized.[23]

§ 2.8   The Fee Simple Subject to an Executory Limitation

A fee simple subject to an executory limitation is a fee simple estate which, upon the happening of a designated event, will automatically pass to a designated person other than the person who created the defeasible estate or his (or her) successors in interest.[1] From the viewpoint of the owner of

21. See the extensive citation of cases in support of this proposition in 1 Simes and Smith, Future Interests § 257 nn. 77, 78, 79, 81 (2d ed. 1956). In most of the cases where equitable relief has been granted, the condition involved the payment of money and was considered by the court to be merely for the purpose of security. Some courts tend to limit relief to such cases; other courts have said that equitable relief may be granted whenever the grantor is not damaged by the breach or can be compensated in money, although cases where such relief has been granted are rare. See Simes and Smith, supra, § 257 at nn. 81, 82, and cases cited.

See also Nielsen v. Woods, 687 P.2d 486 (Colo.App.1984), where the court quieted title in fee simple absolute in a subsequent purchaser of the land, despite the grantee's failure to satisfy the "condition" within the time stipulated in the deed. The "condition" was later satisfied, and the court said: "A court of equity may grant relief against forfeiture of land for condition broken when the breach is not gross or willful, is for the performance of an act, * * * and the thing to be done may be done afterwards so as to put the party seeking forfeiture precisely in the same situation as he would have been but for the breach." (687 P.2d at 489.)

22. Browning v. Weaver, 158 Kan. 255, 146 P.2d 390 (1944). See Equitable Relief from Termination for Failure to Make Delay Rental Payment on Time, 22 Miss.L.J. 118 (1950).

A court may, of course, construe automatic reverter language as creating a "fee simple subject to right of entry for condition broken" and then grant equitable relief. See Nielsen v. Woods, supra note 21.

23. Dunham, supra note 10, at 227–228, noting that earlier writers tended to view penalizing for noncompliance as the proper purpose of a condition subsequent and termination when the purpose of the conveyance could no longer be realized as the proper purpose of a special limitation.

§ 2.8

1. For the reasons for adoption of the term "fee simple subject to an executory limitation" in preference to other terms, see ante, Section 2.3 note 4. Rest.Prop. § 46 provides as follows: "(1) * * * an estate in fee simple subject to an executory limitation exists when any limitation, in an otherwise effective conveyance of land, (a) creates an estate in fee simple in a conveyee, or leaves an estate in fee simple in the conveyor or his successor in interest; and (b) provides that the estate subject thereto, upon the occurrence of a stated event is to be divested, before the normal expiration thereof, in favor of another interest in a person other than the conveyor, or his successor in interest."

In McKinley v. Waterloo R. Co., 368 N.W.2d 131 (Iowa 1985), the court held that "a fee simple subject to an executory limitation"

the defeasible fee simple, it generally makes no difference whether the termination of his estate results in reacquisition of the fee simple by his grantor (or his grantor's successors in interest) or by some other person or persons. But prior to the enactment of the Statute of Uses in 1536 [2] the common law courts consistently held that a present fee simple estate could not be made defeasible in favor of anyone other than the grantor or his successors in interest. It was said that the law did not sanction "conditions in favor of strangers." [3] Yet even before 1536 the Chancellor enforced future "uses" which defeated present "uses" upon the happening of a designated future event, thus recognizing present equitable estates which were defeasible in favor of persons other than the grantor or his successors in interest.[4]

As an unintended consequence of the enactment of the Statute of Uses in 1536 [5] and the Statute of Wills in 1540,[6] it became possible to create legal

---

rather than a fee simple determinable was created by a conveyance containing the following language: "should the land hereby conveyed cease to be used for railway purposes the same shall revert back to the farm from which it is taken," on the ground that "this was not a reverter clause, as the land would not necessarily go to the grantor or his heirs but to the subsequent owners of the farm out of which it was carved."

2. 27 Hen. VIII, ch. 10 (1536).

3. The reason was that livery of seisin—necessary to transfer a freehold estate—could operate only *in praesenti*. Thus if O made livery of seisin "to A and his heirs" but further provided, "if A should die without leaving children him surviving, then to B and his heirs," the seisin would immediately pass to A, but it could not later pass to B without a new livery of seisin. And if O declared that his livery of seisin should be operated in favor of "A and his heirs from and after A's marriage to B," the transaction was completely ineffective because the livery of seisin could not, contrary to O's expressed intent, operate *in praesenti;* nor could it operate *in futuro* when and if A should marry B. The rule prohibiting creation of a fee simple estate that would be defeasible in favor of "strangers" thus prevented the creation of what were later called "shifting and springing executory interests." See post in text between notes 6 and 9.

4. If the legal owner of a fee simple estate, O, enfeoffed "A and his heirs, to the use of B and his heirs, but if B shall die without children him surviving, then to the use of C and his heirs," B acquired a "use" or equitable estate in fee simple, subject to a "shifting use" in favor of C in fee simple. The same result could be produced by a bargain and sale (without feoffment) from O to "A and his heirs, but if A shall die without children him surviving, then to B and his heirs," or by O's execution of a covenant (under seal) to "stand seized of the land to the use of A and his heirs [A being

related to O by blood or marriage], but if A shall die without children him surviving, then to the use of B and his heirs." If O made a bargain and sale of the land "to A and his heirs, from and after A's marriage to B," or executed a covenant to "stand seized to the use of A and his heirs from and after A's marriage to B," O retained his legal estate in fee simple, but it was subject to a "springing use" in favor of A. Although the common law courts refused to recognize that such transactions created any rights in *cestui que use,* the Chancellor began to recognize and enforce the rights of *cestui que use* early in the fifteenth century. These rights included the right to take the profits of the land and the right to have the legal owner of the fee simple take all necessary proceedings to protect or recover the land.

5. Supra note 3. Because holding a "use" or equitable estate in land enabled *cestui que use* to evade feudal burdens, to devise the "use" by will, and to curtesy and dower, it is said that by the time of the Wars of the Roses the greater part of the land in England was held in use. But the King suffered substantial losses from the evasion of feudal dues. After various manoeuvres, "the Statute of Uses was forced upon an extremely unwilling parliament by an extremely strong-willed king," Henry VIII, in 1536. Maitland, Equity 34. The purpose and major effect of the Statute of Uses was to turn "uses" or equitable estates into legal estates which would be subject to all the usual feudal burdens and to abolish the power to devise land. A by-product of the Statute was the transformation of "shifting uses" and "springing uses" into legal interests.

6. 32 Hen. VIII, ch. 1 (1540). As indicated supra, note 5, one purpose of the Statute of Uses was to abolish the power to devise land by creating a "use" in favor of A, with a direction that the legal estate should be held after A's death "to such uses as A may by his

estates in fee simple subject to an "executory limitation" in favor of persons other than the grantor (or his successors in interest) either by deed or by will—e.g., by a conveyance or devise "to A and his heirs, but if A shall die leaving no children him surviving, then to B and his heirs." The effect of such a conveyance or devise was to give A a present fee simple subject to a shifting executory limitation and to give B an executory interest in fee simple.[7]

In the example just set out, A's fee simple is said to be subject to a "shifting" executory limitation because, upon the happening of the designated event (A's death without leaving any children him surviving), the present fee simple will automatically "shift" from A to B.[8] It is also possible to create a present fee simple subject to a "springing" executory limitation— e.g., by a conveyance "to A and his heirs, from and after A's marriage to B." Such a conveyance leaves the present fee simple vested in the grantor, subject to an executory limitation which, if and when A marries B, will cause the present fee simple to "spring" out of the grantor and automatically vest in A.[9]

A fee simple subject to an executory limitation shares important characteristics with both the fee simple determinable and the fee simple subject to a condition subsequent. Like the former, defeasance is automatic when the terminating event occurs, and the owner of the executory interest acquires the fee simple without having to take any affirmative action.[10] But when the terminating event occurs the defeasible fee simple initially created by the transfer is considered to have been "divested" or "cut off," as is the case where a breach of condition subsequent results in the exercise of a right of entry that terminates a fee simple subject to a condition subsequent, rather than simply to have "expired" as is the case where a fee simple determinable is terminated by the happening of the designated terminating event.[11]

will devise and appoint." But the attempt to abolish the power to devise was so unpopular as to force enactment of the Statute of Wills in 1540. The Statute of Wills allowed a testator to devise all land held by him in socage and two-thirds of his land held by knight service. A by-product of the Statute of Wills was that legal "shifting" and "springing" interests could be created directly by will, without the necessity of creating "uses" to be turned into legal interests ("executed") by the Statute of Uses. "Shifting" and "springing" future interests created by will were called "executory devises."

7. "Although executory interests came into the law originally in the form of shifting and springing uses that were converted into legal interests by force of the Statute of Uses, it is no longer necessary to employ the machinery of the Statute of Uses in order to create executory interests. The Statute of Uses, it is true, is deemed to be in force in many of the states, and, therefore, the modern deed can be given effect as a deed of bargain and sale. * * * But even in jurisdictions where the Statute of Uses is not deemed to be in force the modern deed is capable of creating any type of future

interest which could be created by a conveyance operating under the Statute of Uses. And since in every state there is a statute authorizing the transfer of property by will, the creation of executory devises is clearly permissible." C. Moynihan, Intro. to Law of Real Property 205 (1962). The term "executory interest" is now employed to designate any future interest formerly called a "shifting use," a "springing use" or an "executory devise."

8. The "shifting" executory interest is, in substance, like the pre–1536 "shifting use" discussed supra, note 4.

9. The "springing" executory interest is, in substance, like the pre–1536 "springing use" discussed supra, note 4.

10. E.g., Proprietors of Church in Brattle Square v. Grant, 69 Mass. 142, 63 Am.Dec. 725 (1855).

11. E.g., Pearson v. Easterling, 107 S.C. 265, 92 S.E. 619, Ann.Cas.1918D 980 (1918); Bradford v. Federal Land Bank, 338 So.2d 388 (Miss.1976). See 1 Simes and Smith, Future Interests § 228 (2d ed. 1956).

The terminating event specified in an executory limitation is almost always one that is "contingent"—i.e., uncertain to occur. Thus, e.g., the specified terminating event may be the death of the first taker without surviving issue, or without surviving children,[12] or the death of the first taker with children surviving him;[13] or the death of the first taker before reaching a certain age,[14] or the marriage, or non-marriage, of the first taker;[15] or the failure of an educational institution to continue in existence.[16] Executory limitations specifying such terminating events are valid, provided they are not illegal or against public policy,[17] and provided the terminating event is not so remote as to violate the rule against perpetuities.[18] If the executory limitation is invalid, the first taker will, of course, have a fee simple absolute instead of a fee simple subject to an executory limitation.[19]

Can a grantor create a valid executory limitation specifying, as a terminating event, something that is certain to happen? Suppose, e.g., that O conveys "to A and his heirs, from and after the death of O," or "to A and his heirs, from and after the death of B." In these cases, it is clear that the estate retained by O cannot last for more than the life of O or B, as the case may be. Hence it is arguable that O should be considered to retain only a life estate, with A receiving a vested remainder in fee simple. Some cases have so held,[20] but other cases have held that O retains a fee simple subject to an executory limitation, with A receiving only an executory interest in fee simple.[21] Since O, in such a case, presumably does not intend to limit his hitherto extensive rights of use and enjoyment as owner in fee simple, it would seem reasonable to hold that he retains a defeasible fee simple and that he is not subject to legal liability for waste.[22]

12. E.g., Dickson v. Renfro, 263 Ark. 718, 569 S.W.2d 66 (1978), appeal after remand 276 Ark. 223, 634 S.W.2d 104 (1982); In re Fleck's Estate, 261 Iowa 434, 154 N.W.2d 865 (1967); Bradford v. Federal Land Bank, supra note 11; Jernigan v. Lee, 279 N.C. 341, 182 S.E.2d 351 (1971).

13. E.g., Warrington v. Chester, 294 Ill. 524, 128 N.E. 549 (1920). Such an executory limitation would normally be in favor of the first taker's children, and would be designed to prevent the first taker from devising or conveying the property in such a way as to prevent his surviving children from receiving it at his death.

14. E.g., Thomas v. Thomas, 97 Miss. 697, 53 So. 630 (1910); Bailey v. Brannon, 293 Ala. 83, 300 So.2d 344 (1974).

15. E.g., Pumroy v. Jenkins, 151 Kan. 466, 99 P.2d 752 (1940); Hinton v. Bowen, 190 Tenn. 463, 230 S.W.2d 965 (1950).

16. E.g., Lehigh University v. Hower, 159 Pa.Super. 84, 46 A.2d 516 (1946).

17. The same qualification applies, of course, to conditions subsequent and special limitations. See ante, Sections 2.4, 2.5.

18. The great case establishing the rules against perpetuities involved the validity of an executory limitation. The Duke of Norfolk's Case, 3 Ch.Cas. 1 (1682). Cases invalidating executory limitations because they violate the rule against perpetuities are legion. See post, Sections 3.20, 3.21.

19. E.g., Proprietors of Church in Brattle Square v. Grant, supra note 10.

20. E.g., Wise v. Wise, 134 Fla. 553, 184 So. 91 (1938); Scott v. Wilcox, 238 Ga. 184, 232 S.E.2d 59 (1977); Hess v. Jones, 335 Pa. 569, 7 A.2d 299 (1939); Picadura v. Humphrey, 335 S.W.2d 6 (Mo.1960).

21. E.g., Abbott v. Holway, 72 Me. 298 (1881). See also Jones v. Caird, 153 Wis. 384, 387, 141 N.W. 228, 229, Ann.Cas.1914A 88 (1913); Lemen v. McComas, 63 Md. 153 (1884).

22. Most of the cases involving limitations of the kind under discussion also contained language to the effect that the conveyance should "not take effect" or "not become absolute" until the death of the grantor, and the issue in most of these cases was not whether waste had been committed but whether the conveyance was effective at all, or was ineffective as an attempted testamentary disposition by deed. Hence it was not material to decide whether the interest retained by the grantor was a life estate.

A similar problem may arise when, e.g., O conveys "to A and his heirs, from and after five years from the date of this conveyance," or "to A and his heirs, then to B and his heirs five years from and after the date of this conveyance." In the first case, it can be argued that O's estate can only last for five years and that he therefore retains only an estate for years, not a fee simple subject to an executory limitation. In the second case, it can similarly be argued that A receives only an estate for (five) years rather than a fee simple subject to an executory limitation. In the first case, however, O presumably intended to retain his hitherto extensive rights of use and enjoyment, while in the second case there is no reason to think that he intended to confer such extensive rights upon A. Consequently, it is arguable that O should be held to retain a fee simple subject to an executory limitation in the first case, but that A should be held to receive only an estate for years in the second case.[23] The Property Restatement supports the suggested distinction between the two cases.[24]

Equitable as well as legal estates in fee simple subject to an executory limitation may be created, and interests analogous to estates in fee simple subject to an executory limitation, either legal or equitable, may be created in personal property. Indeed, at the present time, most defeasible estates or interests subject to an executory limitation are equitable, because they are beneficial interests under a trust, and the predominant subject matter of such trusts is probably personal property such as stocks and bonds.

§ 2.9 The Fee Simple Determinable With an Executory Limitation

Suppose land is transferred "to A and her heirs until A marries B, and then to B and his heirs." A clearly receives a fee simple determinable by virtue of the express special limitation—"until A marries B"—but if the special limitation becomes operative (i.e., if A marries B), there is a gift over to B which precludes any reverter to the transferor. Since the only kind of future interest that may "follow" a fee simple is an executory interest, B's interest must be an executory interest in fee simple absolute.[1] The Property

---

23. The result suggested in the first case finds support in Thompson v. Thompson, 237 Ga. 509, 228 S.E.2d 886 (1976). No cases dealing with the second case have been found.

24. Rest.Prop. § 46, Comment i. But, in the second case, "if the language indicates clearly an intention that the first taker shall have a fee simple until the executory interest vests, then it may properly be given effect." 1 Simes and Smith, Future Interests § 223 (2d ed. 1956).

§ 2.9

1. "There can be no remainder after a determinable fee * * *. Hence, if we sustain the future interest in such cases, we must call it an executory interest. Since the executory interest was essentially a type of future interest which could not exist prior to the Statute of Uses, it is quite consistent to call the future interest in these cases an executory interest."

1 Simes and Smith, Future Interests § 228 (2d ed. 1956).

But cf. Williams v. Watt, 668 P.2d 620 (Wyo. 1983), holding that the interest "following" a fee simple determinable was a vested remainder in fee simple because the event upon which the grantor's mineral estate was to terminate was certain to occur and the grantee's interest was therefore sure to become possessory. The court was clearly motivated, in so holding, by a desire to avoid application of the Rule Against Perpetuities, which would have invalidated the grantee's interest if it were deemed to be an executory interest. See 668 P.2d at 633. One judge rejected the court's reasoning but concurred in the result on the ground that the grantee acquired an executory interest which was neither contingent nor vested in the conventional sense, but should be classified as a "vested executory interest" not subject to the Rule Against Perpetuities. For more on the question whether

Restatement calls A's estate a "fee simple with an executory limitation creating an interest which takes effect at the expiration of a prior interest." [2] But this is surely too cumbersome for general use. The term "fee simple determinable with an executory limitation" would clearly be more convenient than, and as descriptive as, the term adopted by the Property Restatement.

Since the distinction between "succeeding" a prior interest after its "natural expiration" and "divesting" or "cutting off" a prior interest has little current significance, it can be said that the distinction between a fee simple subject to an executory limitation and a fee simple determinable with an executory limitation is important only where the purported executory limitation is void *ab initio* under some rule of law such as the rule against perpetuities.[3] If the transfer purports to create a fee simple subject to an executory limitation and the purported executory limitation is void, the first taker is left with a fee simple absolute;[4] but if the transfer purports to create a fee simple determinable with an executory limitation and the purported executory limitation is void, the first taker is left with a fee simple determinable—provided that the special limitation is valid, of course.[5]

§ 2.10 The Fee Tail and the Fee Simple Conditional in the United States

Although the fee tail estate was recognized in most of the American colonies prior to the American Revolution,[1] this estate was regarded with

the possibility of violating the Rule Against Perpetuities, see post Section 3.20 at note call 13.

2. Rest.Prop. § 47.

3. The rule against perpetuities will be violated, and the executory interest rendered void *ab initio,* whenever the executory limitation, by its terms might become operative at any time in the future, however remote. See, e.g., Proprietors of Church in Brattle Square v. Grant, 69 Mass. 142, 63 Am.Dec. 725 (1855); Institution for Savings in Roxbury v. Roxbury Home for Aged Women, 244 Mass. 583, 139 N.E. 301 (1923); City of Klamath Falls v. Bell, 7 Or.App. 330, 490 P.2d 515 (1971).

4. E.g., Proprietors of Church in Brattle Square v. Grant, supra note 3; Cody v. Staples, 80 Conn. 82, 67 A. 1 (1907); Nevitt v. Woodburn, 190 Ill. 283, 60 N.E. 500 (1901); Bunting v. Hromas, 104 Neb. 381, 177 N.W. 190 (1920); City of Klamath Falls v. Bell, supra note 3.

5. E.g., Institution for Savings in Roxbury v. Roxbury Home for Aged Women, supra note 3; Brown v. Independent Baptist Church, 325 Mass. 645, 91 N.E.2d 922 (1950); Jones v. Burns, 221 Miss. 833, 74 So.2d 866 (1954); Leonard v. Burr, 18 N.Y. 96 (1858). "The real difference is deemed to be this: In the case of the special limitation, that event terminates A's estate regardless of what future interest takes effect; but, in the case of the fee simple subject to the executory limitation, the mere

happening of the event does not necessarily terminate A's estate. It is ordinarily terminated only by the vesting of the executory interest. Thus, if the executory interest were void under the rule against perpetuities, the preceding fee simple estate would not terminate." 1 Simes and Smith § 228 (2d ed. 1956). This assumes, of course—as American courts have consistently held—that possibilities of reverter are not subject to the rule against perpetuities, whereas executory interests are subject thereto.

§ 2.10

1. The common law rules as to the language necessary to create a fee tail were less rigid than the rules applicable to the fee simple. A fee tail could be created by an *inter vivos* transfer either to "A and the heirs of his body" or to "A and the heirs of his body, then to B and his heirs." In the first case, the grantor retained a *reversion;* in the second case, B received a *remainder.* But a fee tail and a remainder could also be created by an *inter vivos* transfer to "A and his heirs, but if A should die without issue, then to B and his heirs." In the last example, the words "die without issue" were said to refer to an "indefinite" failure of issue—i.e., the death of a tenant in fee tail without issue, whenever that might occur—and "A and his heirs" was therefore construed to mean "A and the heirs of his body." But the word "heirs" was always necessary for creation of a fee tail by

hostility by courts and legislatures and was abolished in most of the original thirteen states soon after the Revolution. At the present time, most states have legislation that, as a practical matter, precludes the creation of a fee tail estate.[2]

The most common type of legislation converts what would have been a fee tail under the English common law into a fee simple in the first grantee or devisee named in the deed or will.[3] About half the states with statutes of this type also provide, in substance, that any "remainder" purportedly created to "follow" the fee tail shall be construed as an executory interest in fee simple to become possessory if the first taker dies without lineal descendants ("without issue").[4] Under such a statute, if O conveys "to A and the heirs of his body, remainder to B and his heirs," A acquires a fee simple subject to an executory limitation and B acquires an executory interest in fee simple absolute which will become possessory only if A dies "without issue." In those states where the statute makes no reference to purported remainders, A would acquire a fee simple absolute and B would acquire no interest.

In the next largest group of states, the legislation changes what would be a fee tail under the English common law into a life estate in the first grantee or devisee named in the deed or will, with a remainder in fee simple absolute to the lineal descendants of the first taker.[5] Under statutes of this type, a conveyance by O "to A and the heirs of his body" will give A a life estate, with a remainder in fee simple absolute to his lineal descendants. But there is a division of authority on the question whether the interests of A's lineal descendants are subject to a condition of survival—i.e., whether a child or more remote descendant of A must survive A in order to share in the fee simple estate.[6]

---

inter vivos conveyance. After 1540, however, a fee tail could be created by will if the will, as a whole, showed the intent to create a fee tail although the words "heirs" or "heirs of the body" were not used.

2. Rest.Prop. ch. 5, Introductory Note, lists the statutes. See also 1 Am.L.Prop. § 2.13; 2 R. Powell, Real Prop. ¶ 198. Article 1, § 26 of the Texas Constitution prohibits "entailments" but no Texas statute defines the consequences of this prohibition. In Merrill v. American Baptist Missionary Union, 73 N.H. 414, 62 A. 647 (1905), the court held that the fee tail was inconsistent with New Hampshire's institutions and thus was not included in the reception of English common law in New Hampshire. Rest.Prop. ch. 5, Introductory Note lists Alaska, Idaho, Louisiana, Nevada, Utah, and Washington as having no statutes or decisions recognizing, modifying, or abolishing fees tail. It seems unlikely that any of these states will ever recognize the fee tail, and practically certain that it will not be recognized in Louisiana, a civil law jurisdiction.

3. The states with legislation of this type include Alabama, Arizona, California, Georgia, Indiana, Kentucky, Maryland, Michigan, Minnesota, Mississippi, Montana, Nebraska, New Jersey, New York, North Carolina, North Dakota, Oklahoma, Pennsylvania, South Dakota, Tennessee, Vermont, Virginia, West Virginia, Wisconsin, and Wyoming.

The same result has sometimes been reached by judicial decision in Texas, where the fee tail is prohibited by the state constitution.

Generally, see Rest.Prop. ch. 5, Introductory Note; 2 R. Powell, Real Prop. ¶ 198.

4. The states with statutes so providing include California, Indiana, Kentucky, Michigan, Montana, Nebraska, New York, North Dakota, Oklahoma, South Dakota, Virginia, and West Virginia. See Rest.Prop. ch. 5, Introductory Note; 1 Am.L.Prop. § 2.13 n. 4.

5. The states with statutes so providing include Arkansas, Colorado, Florida, Georgia, Illinois, Kansas, Missouri, New Mexico, and Vermont. See Rest.Prop. ch. 5, Introductory Note; 1 Am.L.Prop. § 2.13 n. 5; 2 Powell, Real Property ¶ 198[2] n. 79.

6. See, e.g., Mitchell v. Mitchell, 208 Ark. 478, 187 S.W.2d 163 (1945) (survival required); Schee v. Boone, 295 Mo. 212, 243 S.W. 882 (1922) (same); Stearns v. Curry, 306 Ill. 94, 137 N.E. 471 (1922) (survival not required).

A third kind of statute provides that the first taker shall acquire a fee tail and that the lineal descendants of the first taker shall acquire a fee simple estate. Connecticut and Ohio have statutes of this type applicable to both deeds and wills and Rhode Island has a similar statute applicable only to wills.[7] In cases covered by such a statute, a gift "to A and the heirs of his body" gives A a fee tail for life only, and on his death his surviving descendants take a fee simple estate. A's estate has the normal characteristics of a fee tail except that he cannot transfer anything more than an estate for his own life.

Four states—Delaware, Maine, Massachusetts, and Rhode Island (only when the estate is created by deed)—recognize the fee tail substantially as it existed in England, except that a tenant in tail has the power to convey an estate in fee simple absolute by an ordinary deed of conveyance and thereby "bar the entail" and all future interests limited to take effect upon termination of the fee tail by "failure of issue."[8] In addition, a creditor of the tenant in tail (except in Delaware) can subject the debtor's estate to the satisfaction of his claims as if it were in fee simple.[9] But the tenant in tail cannot dispose of the estate by will. It is not clear whether, on the death of the tenant in tail in these jurisdictions, the estate will descend to all of his descendants in equal shares or whether the old English rule of primogeniture will still be applied.[10]

Rather surprisingly, Iowa, Nebraska, Oregon, and South Carolina all, at one time, held that an estate in fee simple conditional—which could not be created in England after 1285—would be created by language which would

---

7. Conn.Gen.Stat.Ann. § 47–3; Ohio Rev. Code § 2131.08; Rhode Island Gen.Laws 1956, § 33–6–10. From 1939 to 1949, Wyoming also had a statute like those of Connecticut and Ohio, having previously recognized the common law fee tail. In Connecticut and Ohio, the owner of a fee tail has no power to execute a disentailing conveyance, and the power of the creditors of such owner to satisfy their claims from the entailed land is correspondingly restricted. See, e.g., Cheseboro v. Palmer, 68 Conn. 207, 36 A. 42 (1896); Wolf v. Stout, 11 Weekly L.Bull. 236 (Ohio 1884). The Rhode Island statute, supra, is ambiguously worded, but was construed as allowing a fee tail created by will to endure only for the life of the first devisee in Wilcox v. Heywood, 12 R.I. 196 (1878). A tenant in tail of Rhode Island land may convert a fee tail created by will into a fee simple by a deed expressing the intent to do so. Rhode Island Gen.Laws 1956, §§ 34–4–15, 34–4–16, 34–4–17. Entailed land in Rhode Island may be sold on execution in fee simple to satisfy the claims of creditors of the tenant in tail. Rhode Island Gen.Laws 1956, § 34–4–14.

8. See Del.Code Tit. 25, § 302 (applies to both legal and equitable estates and empowers either possessory owner in fee tail or owner of future interest in fee tail to convert fee tail into fee simple); 33 Maine Rev.Stat.Ann. § 156 (seemingly applies only to legal estates; possessory owner in fee tail, or life tenant and reversioner or remainderman in fee tail acting together, may convert fee tail into fee simple); Mass.Gen.Laws Ann. c. 183, §§ 45, 46, 47 (legal or equitable estates in fee tail may be converted into fee simple estates by deed from possessory owner in fee tail, or from life tenant and reversioner or remainderman in fee tail acting together); Rhode Island Gen. Laws 1956, §§ 34–4–15, 34–4–16, 34–4–17 (same as Mass. statutes).

9. See 14 Maine Rev.Stat.Ann. § 2008 (1980); Mass.Gen.Laws Ann. c. 183, § 4 (1977); Rhode Island Gen.Laws 1956, § 34–4–14.

10. There are a few old cases indicating the survival of primogeniture with respect to fee tail estates in Delaware, Maine, and Massachusetts. See Rest.Prop. § 85, Special Note. But it seems unlikely that primogeniture would be held to apply at the present time, having long since been abolished with respect to fee simple estates on the ground that it is inconsistent with American institutions. When the owner of a fee tail dies without having conveyed the land in fee simple, survived by both a spouse and issue, the issue acquire a fee tail subject to the surviving spouse's dower or curtesy, as the case may be. Rest.Prop. §§ 84, 85. When there are no issue, dower and curtesy will be cut off if they are deemed to be derivative estates, as stated in Rest.Prop. § 84. But see Holden v. Wells, 18 R.I. 802, 31 A. 265 (1895), contra.

have created a fee tail in England after 1285.[11] The rationale, except in Oregon, was that the English statute *De Donis* was not part of the common law in these states.[12] Nebraska abolished the fee simple conditional by statute in 1941,[13] and this medieval survival currently has substantial importance only in South Carolina.[14]

As was true in England before 1285, the owner of a fee simple conditional in South Carolina cannot transfer it by will even after the birth of issue.[15] But after the birth of issue the owner has the power to convey or mortgage the land in fee simple absolute,[16] and the owner's judgment creditors can satisfy their claims by means of an execution sale of the fee simple absolute.[17] If the owner dies survived by issue before he makes an *inter vivos* transfer, the issue will take a fee simple conditional by descent.[18] This means that the condition as to birth of issue must again be satisfied before the estate can be converted into a fee simple absolute by *inter vivos* transfer.[19]

§ 2.11 The Life Estate—In General

As we have seen, in the period immediately following the Norman Conquest of England, estates granted by the King or by lesser lords to feudal tenants were for the tenant's life only.[1] After judicial recognition of the fee simple as an estate of inheritance in the twelfth century, it was still possible to create life estates—estates with a duration measured by the life of a designated person or the survivor of a group of persons. Life estates could be intentionally created either by using express language indicating that intent when land was conveyed or simply by omitting any words of limitation.[2] Since neither a fee simple nor a fee tail could be created without

11. See, e.g., Pierson v. Lane, 60 Iowa 60, 14 N.W. 90 (1882); Yates v. Yates, 104 Neb. 678, 178 N.W. 262 (1920) (dictum); Lytle v. Hulen, 128 Or. 483, 275 P. 45 (1929); Blume v. Pearcy, 204 S.C. 409, 29 S.E.2d 673 (1944). For a vigorous critique of such decisions, see 1 Am.L.Prop. § 2.11.

12. See Pierson v. Lane, supra note 11; Yates v. Yates, supra note 11; Blume v. Pearcy, supra note 11. In Lytle v. Hulen, supra note 11, the court held that the Oregon statute providing that a deed passes the entire estate of the grantor, whether or not the word "heirs" is used, impliedly repealed *De Donis* and restored the fee simple conditional.

13. Neb.Rev.Stat. § 76–110.

14. The ultimate basis for holding *De Donis* not part of the common law in South Carolina seems to have been the adoption in 1712 of a decree selecting certain English statutes as "suited to the conditions" of the South Carolina colony and excluding all other English statutes. See Cooper, Stats.S.C. 401 (1837). More than a dozen South Carolina cases recognize the existence of the fee simple conditional—called a "fee conditional" or "special fee conditional"—in that state. See 1 Am.L.Prop. § 2.11 nn. 5–11; 2 Powell, Real Property ¶ 195 nn. 33, 36–46.

15. E.g., Burriss v. Burriss, 104 S.C. 441, 89 S.E. 405 (1916).

16. E.g., Holley v. Still, 91 S.C. 487, 74 S.E. 1065 (1912) (issue need not be alive when conveyance is made); Crawford v. Masters, 98 S.C. 458, 82 S.E. 793 (1914) (issue need not be legitimate); Bonds v. Hutchison, 199 S.C. 197, 18 S.E.2d 661 (1942) (mortgage foreclosure transfers absolute fee).

17. E.g., Williams v. Gause, 83 S.C. 265, 65 S.E. 241 (1909).

18. E.g., Withers v. Jenkins, 14 S.C. 597 (1880).

19. Withers v. Jenkins, supra note 18. But see Blume v. Pearcy, supra note 11, which can be interpreted as holding that the issue take a fee simple absolute—a clear departure from prior holdings, but clearly desirable because it would eliminate all fee simple conditional estates after the existence of only one life.

§ 2.11

1. Ante Section 1.7.

2. As to the need for words of inheritance to create a fee simple, see ante Section 2.2 at note 2.

words of inheritance, a simple conveyance by O "to A" would create only an estate for A's life.

Under modern American statutes prescribing, in substance, that every conveyance shall be deemed to convey the entire estate of the grantor unless a contrary intent is manifested,[3] the owner of a fee simple estate can create a life estate only by an instrument clearly indicating the intent to create a life estate rather than to transfer the fee simple, although no particular form of words is required.[4] On the other hand, the owner of a life estate can transfer it to another without using any words of limitation, in which case the transferee becomes a tenant *pur autre vie* (i.e., for the grantor's life).

Life estates may be expressly created to last for the life of a single transferee, for the lives of two or more transferees, for the life of the transferor, until the death of the survivor of two or more persons designated as measuring lives, or until the death of the first to die of two or more designated measuring lives.[5] When the duration of a life estate is measured by the life (or lives) or a person (or persons) other than the grantee, the estate is termed an estate *pur autre vie* (for the life of another).[6] A grantor who owns a fee simple may create either an estate for the life of the grantee or an estate *pur autre vie*.

Life estates may also arise by operation of law—e.g., where estates of dower or curtesy arise out of the marital relation,[7] or where a conveyance "to A and the heirs of his body," by statute creates a life estate in the first taker with a remainder to the issue of the first taker.[8] The latter type of life estate is very rare, since grantors nowadays rarely try to create a fee tail. Dower and curtesy are still of substantial, though decreasing, importance in the United States, and will be given separate consideration in subsequent sections of this book.[9]

A life estate, however created, is an aggregate of rights, privileges, powers and immunities, together with the correlative duties, absence of rights, liabilities, and disabilities.[10] The most important right of the owner of a present life estate (hereafter called a life tenant) is the right to exclusive possession of the land, which is protected by actions at law to recover

---

3. Ante Section 2.2 at note 6.

4. Rest., Prop. §§ 18, 107, 108. As to language that will create a life estate, see id. § 107, Illust. 6, and § 108, Illust. 6–8 (indicating that a transfer to "to A" with a "gift over" to A's children or to a third party will create a life estate in A and a remainder in A's children or the third party, as the case may be.)

See also Robinson v. King, 68 N.C.App. 86, 314 S.E.2d 768 (1984), review denied 311 N.C. 762, 321 S.E.2d 144 (1984) (granting clause of quitclaim deed executed by fee simple owners purported to convey all their "right, title and interest," but habendum clause included the words "for and during the term of * * * [the grantee's] natural life"; deed was held to convey only a life estate).

5. See 2 Powell, Real Property ¶ 202[1] and [2]. The "measuring lives" may, of course, include the grantor or the grantee, or both.

6. For examples, see 2 Powell, Real Property ¶ 202[1] at n. 12, and cases cited.

7. At common law, a widow was entitled, by operation of law to a life estate in one-third of the lands of which her deceased husband was seized in fee simple or fee tail at any time during the marriage; and a widower was entitled to a life estate in all the lands of which his deceased wife was seized in fee simple or fee tail at any time during the marriage. For more on dower and curtesy, see post Sections 2.14, 2.15.

8. See ante Section 2.10.

9. See post Sections 2.14, 2.15.

10. For a summary of the Hohfeldian analysis based on these terms, see ante Section 1.2.

possession and/or damages[11]—actions available against the world at large, including the owners of future estates (reversions or remainders) expectant upon termination of the life estate. If the owner of a future estate in a particular parcel of land causes physical injury to that land, the life tenant is entitled to recover damages to the extent of his interest in the land—i.e., the difference between the value of the life estate before and its value after the injury was inflicted.[12] The weight of authority makes the same rule of damages applicable when physical injury to the land is caused by a third party (not the owner of a future interest in the land).[13] In some states, however, the life tenant is allowed to recover, as damages, the entire diminution if the value of the land—i.e., the damages that would be recoverable by a fee simple owner—in which case he is, of course, accountable to the owner of the future interest for his "share" of the damage award.[14]

A life tenant's principal privilege is that of making a beneficial use of the land or receiving the rents or profits arising from such use.[15] Except as against the owners of future interests in the land, a life tenant's privilege of beneficial use is the same as that of any other possessor of land,[16] and is subject to restrictions imposed by the common law of "nuisance," riparian rights, and rights of support, together with land use regulations imposed by local, state, and federal governments pursuant to their "police power." As against the owners of future estates in the land, however, a life tenant is subject to the common law of "waste," which imposes additional restrictions upon his privilege of beneficial use and imposes on him a duty to use the land in such a way as not to injure the future estates that will become possessory upon termination of the life estate. In addition, a life tenant has

11. For a discussion of these actions, see ante Section 1.3.

12. This is simply a corollary of the fact that a life tenant has a possessory estate in the land. See Rest.Prop. §§ 117, 118. Note, however, that the owner of a future interest in the same land has a privilege to enter upon the land during the continuance of the life estate (1) to inspect the premises for the purpose of ascertaining whether waste has been or is being committed; (2) to demand payment of rent due; (3) for the purpose of making such repairs as may be necessary to protect the future interest from damage; (4) for the purpose of removing timber or other materials which have been severed from the land under circumstances such that the owner of the future interest is entitled to the possession thereof; and (5) in order to do such acts as are necessary to protect the future estate from the effects of a breach of covenant or to prevent "conduct on the land" causing or accelerating the defeasance of the future interest. Rest. Prop. § 117, Comment c.

13. E.g., Beard v. Hicks, 163 Ala. 329, 50 So. 232 (1909); Brown v. Woodliff, 89 Ga. 413, 15 S.E. 491 (1892); Zimmerman v. Shreeve, 59 Md. 357 (1882); Lee v. Lee, 180 N.C. 86, 104 S.E. 76 (1920). Accord: Rest.Prop. § 118.

14. E.g., Cargill v. Sewall, 19 Me. 288 (1841); Austin v. Hudson River R. Co., 25 N.Y. 334 (1862)—rationale: life tenant should re-

cover "fee simple damages" because he must reimburse owner of future interest for injury inflicted by third party without life tenant's consent; Beck v. Lynch, 306 Ky. 738, 209 S.W.2d 58 (1947); Rogers v. Atlantic, Gulf & Pacific Co., 213 N.Y. 246, 107 N.E. 661 (1915)—rationale: life tenant "represents the fee" or is "trustee" for owners of future interests. In New York, the problem has been handled by legislation providing that when landownership is divided between present and future estates, the owner of the present estate can recover for injuries to future interests only if all living persons who have interests in the land are joined as parties. McKinney's Real Prop. Actions and Proceedings Law § 833.

15. E.g., Haselwood v. Moore, 100 Colo. 556, 69 P.2d 248 (1937). See also Rest.Prop. § 119.

16. This privilege may, of course, be expressly restricted by the terms of the instrument creating the life estate. E.g., Hair v. Farrell, 21 Tenn.App. 12, 103 S.W.2d 918 (1936) (conveyance "to A for support and maintenance during his life"; held, A's estate not entitled to retain income from land during A's life not used for his support and maintenance).

certain special affirmative duties with respect to payment of taxes, mortgage interest, and special assessments for the protection of such future estates. These special negative and affirmative duties of a life tenant will be considered in more detail in a later chapter of this book.[17]

Life estates in land, like estates in fee simple and in fee tail, were classified under the English common law as "freehold" estates because they were created by livery of seisin. The life tenant, unlike the tenant for years, had seisin as well as possession of his "free tenement." But, although once important, the distinction between "freehold" and "nonfreehold" estates is no longer of much practical importance.

§ 2.12   Conventional Life Estates—Constructional Problems

When a grantor or testator wishes to create an estate for the life of the grantee or devisee, he will usually make the transfer "to A to have and to hold during his natural life," "to A for his sole use and benefit during his natural life," "to A until his death," or the like. But suppose the transfer is simply "to A for life." This could be construed to create either an estate for A's life or an estate for the grantor's life. Where the grantor has an estate in fee simple (usually the case) or in fee tail, the Property Restatement declares that such a transfer gives A an estate for his own life.[1] But where the grantor has only an estate for his own life, most of the cases hold that A acquires an estate for the life of the grantor.[2] The grantor in such a case has no power to convey an estate that will last longer than his own life, of course; the real question is whether the estate given to A will terminate upon the death of A if he predeceases the grantor. The Property Restatement asserts that an ambiguity arises in such a case which should be resolved by extrinsic evidence as to the intent of the parties, such as the consideration (if any) paid by the grantee and the relative ages of the parties.[3]

The English common law rule was that "when a lease is made to have and to hold at the will of the lessee, this must also be at the will of the lessor," so that a tenancy at will is created.[4] But the prevailing rule in the United States is that a lease simply at the will of the lessee creates either a determinable fee or a determinable life estate, depending on the language used in the lease.[5] If the language indicates that the option to terminate can only be exercised by the lessee, and not by his heirs or assigns, a determinable life estate will be created.[6]

17. Post Chapter 4. See also supra note 12 as to the privilege of the owner of a future interest to enter on the land to protect his interests while the life tenant is in possession.

§ 2.12

1. Rest.Prop. § 108, Comment a.

2. E.g., Turner v. Missouri Pacific Railway Co., 130 Mo.App. 535, 109 S.W. 101 (1908); Brevoort v. Brevoort, 70 N.Y. 136 (1877). Contra: Doe ex dem. Jeff v. Robinson, 2 M. & R. 249 (Eng.1828).

3. Rest.Prop. § 108, Comment a.

4. Co.Litt. § 55a.

5. 1 Am.L.Prop. § 3.30 and cases cited.

6. Gunnison v. Evans, 136 Kan. 791, 18 P.2d 191 (1933) (lessees "may occupy * * * as long as they wish"); Thompson v. Baxter, 107 Minn. 122, 119 N.W. 797, 21 L.R.A.(N.S.) 575 (1909) (lease to tenant "so long as he shall wish to live in Albert Lea"); Garner v. Gerrish, 63 N.Y.2d 575, 483 N.Y.S.2d 973, 473 N.E.2d 223 (1984) (lessee had the "privilege of termination [sic] this agreement at a date of his own choice"). See also Rest.Prop.2d, Landlord & Tenant § 1.6, Illust. 6.

When a conveyance or devise is made "to A for the lives of A, B, and C," or "to A for the lives of B, C, and D," it is not clear whether A's estate is to last until the death of last survivor of the persons named, or only until the death of the first of them to die. The result should turn on the intent of the grantor or testator as manifested in the deed or will. In such cases, the tendency has been to find that A's estate is to be measured by the life of the surviving member of the group.

When a conveyance or devise is made "to A, and at his death to A's [7] children," "to A, and if A dies, then to B," "to A, and at A's death to B," or the like, another constructional problem may arise. If the instrument contains additional language from which an intent to give A a fee simple can be inferred, courts have held that A acquires a fee simple subject to an executory limitation.[8] Otherwise, it is generally held that A acquires only a life estate.[9] But in some cases where the transfer was by will, courts have held that A takes a fee simple estate if he survives the testator, with a substitutionary gift to A's children or to B, as the case may be, if A predeceases the testator.[10] The substitutionary gift construction has also been adopted in some cases where the will contains a gift over "at the death of A" or "when A dies" and the instrument contains additional language indicating that the gift over was included solely to avoid intestacy in case A should predecease the testator.[11]

When a conveyance or devise "to A," without express language defining A's estate, is followed by contingent limitations to take effect at A's death,[12] it is necessary to determine whether the stated contingencies exhaust all the fact situations possible at A's death. If they do,[13] the conveyance or will in substance makes a gift over "at A's death" and A will generally take a life estate.[14] Even if the stated contingencies do not exhaust all the fact

---

7. E.g., Lowery v. Madden, 308 Ky. 342, 214 S.W.2d 592 (1948); Flagg v. Badger, 58 Me. 258 (1870); Clark v. Owens, 18 N.Y. 434 (1858).

8. E.g., Hicks v. Fairbanks' Heirs, 208 Okl. 346, 256 P.2d 169 (1953) (second gift phrased so as to affect what the first taker has not disposed of); Davis v. Davis, 225 Mass. 311, 114 N.E. 309 (1916) (limitation as a whole leads to finding of fee simple).

9. E.g., Adams v. Eagle, 194 Ark. 171, 106 S.W.2d 192 (1937) (gift over "at" the death of the first taker); Ripley v. Benjamin, 111 Vt. 76, 10 A.2d 205 (1940) (gift over "after" the death of the first taker); Rowe v. Rowe, 95 N.H. 241, 61 A.2d 526 (1948) (gift over "on" the death of the first taker).

10. E.g., Mitchell v. Snyder, 402 Ill. 279, 83 N.E.2d 680 (1949); Stevenson v. Stearns, 325 Mo. 646, 29 S.W.2d 116 (1929).

Cf. Reedy v. Propst, 169 W.Va. 473, 288 S.E.2d 526 (1982), holding that devise of an undivided one-half interest in realty to A "upon the condition that a child or children are born of her body, and if no child is born" to A, then to B, should be construed as giving

A "some limited type of possessory interest in the property during her lifetime" rather than a defeasible fee simple because other language in the will stated that A might "join in the use and enjoyment of the property during her lifetime, but may not commit waste except to the extent that she is [expressly] given the privilege of joining in the sale of timber." Presumably "some limited type of possessory interest in the property during her lifetime" means "life estate." The court also said that "upon the birth of a child" to A her interest would be enlarged to a fee simple in an undivided one-half of the land. Apparently the court thought A had both a present life estate and a contingent remainder in fee simple in the property prior to the birth of a child.

11. E.g., O'Reilly v. Irving, 284 Mass. 522, 188 N.E. 253 (1933).

12. E.g., "to A, and on the death of A survived by children, to such children but on A's death not survived by children, to B."

13. This is the case in the example given supra, note 12.

14. E.g., George v. George, 283 Ky. 381, 141 S.W.2d 558 (1940).

situations possible at A's death,[15] courts will sometimes imply an alternative gift over which (together with the expressed contingencies) exhausts all possible alternatives, and A will then generally take a life estate.[16] If the alternative gift over is not implied, A will generally take a fee simple subject to an executory limitation.[17]

A special case raising the question whether a life estate should be implied arises when land is devised "to B to take effect at the death of A." If life estate is not implied in favor of A, partial intestacy results and, if B is the heir of the testator, B will get the land immediately rather than at the future time intended by the testator. Hence the English cases [18] and some American cases [19] hold that a life estate in favor of A should be implied if, and only if, B is the testator's heir.[20] Other American cases hold that a life estate in favor of A should be implied whether or not B is the testator's heir, provided the evidence as a whole indicates that the testator intended A to have a life estate.[21]

Inconsistencies between the granting and habendum clauses in a deed—e.g., where one clause, standing alone, would create a fee simple and the other, standing alone, would create a life estate—may be resolved by a mechanical application of some rule of construction such as the rule that the granting clause controls as against the habendum,[22] or the rule that a deed must be construed in favor of the grantee.[23] But the best-reasoned modern cases emphasize that the deed is to be construed as a single instrument in order to ascertain the intent of the parties, and they reject any mechanical application of a rule of construction.[24]

When language in a deed or will would otherwise be effective to create a life estate but also contains additional language creating in the transferee a power, either limited or unlimited, to dispose of the land in fee simple, the

---

15. E.g., "to A, and on the death of A survived by children, to such children."

16. E.g., Ware v. Minot, 202 Mass. 512, 88 N.E. 1091 (1909) (property was devised to A, but if B should die without leaving a will and no lineal descendants, to the nieces of the testatrix; held, that A took a life estate, with a remainder to such persons as he by will might appoint, and in default of appointment, to his descendants or, if there were no descendants, to the nieces).

17. E.g., Hill v. Terrell, 123 Ga. 49, 51 S.E. 81 (1905). This assumes, of course, that words of inheritance are unnecessary to create a fee simple.

18. E.g., In re Springfield [1894] 3 Ch. 603.

19. E.g., Matter of Keehn's Estate, 156 Misc. 259, 281 N.Y.S. 591 (1935), affirmed 248 App.Div. 697, 289 N.Y.S. 819 (1936).

20. This rule is adopted in Rest.Prop. § 116.

21. E.g., Phoenix State Bank & Trust Co. v. Johnson, 132 Conn. 259, 43 A.2d 738 (1945).

See also Edwards v. Bradley, 227 Va. 224, 315 S.E.2d 196 (1984): life estate and remainder were implied where farm was devised subject to condition that grantee should retain

ownership and keep farm free from encumbrances, with a gift over to grantee's children upon breach of the condition, although will did not expressly limit grantee to a life estate and designate children as remaindermen. *Sed quaere* why the court didn't construe the deed as creating a fee simple in grantee subject to an executory limitation in favor of the children.

22. E.g., Dickson v. Wildman, 183 Fed. 398 (5th Cir.1910) (granting clause is essential to the deed while the habendum is not).

23. E.g., Meacham v. Blaess, 141 Mich. 258, 104 N.W. 579 (1905) (dictum that "a grant of a life estate may, by the habendum, be enlarged to a fee simple").

24. E.g., Boyer v. Murphy, 202 Cal. 23, 259 P. 38 (1927) (habendum for life, cutting down fee simple language in granting clause; intent to create only life estate clear from other parts of the deed and attendant circumstances); Luther v. Patman, 200 Ark. 853, 141 S.W.2d 42 (1940); Swearingen v. McGee, 303 Ky. 825, 198 S.W.2d 805 (1946).

Robinson v. King, 68 N.C.App. 86, 314 S.E.2d 768 (1984), review denied 311 N.C. 762, 321 S.E.2d 144 (1984).

prevailing rule in the United States is that the transferee has only a life estate despite the added power. This is true whether the added power of disposition is unlimited [25] or is (a) exercisable only by deed; [26] (b) exercisable only by will; [27] (c) exercisable only with a third person's consent; [28] (d) exercisable only in favor of designated persons; [29] (e) exercisable only on a stated contingency; [30] or (f) exercisable only by way of sale (excluding gifts).[31] In four states, the courts have departed from the prevailing rule by holding that the addition of an unlimited power of disposition in fee simple will convert what would otherwise be a life estate into a fee simple; [32] but in Maine this departure has been kept fairly narrow by decision,[33] and it has been greatly narrowed by statutes in Tennessee, Virginia, and West Virginia.[34]

When a deed or will contains language that would otherwise clearly create a fee simple but contains no express language as to the duration of the estate created, and also contains language giving the transferee an unlimited power to transfer and encumber the land, the added provision does not prevent the court from finding that a fee simple is created.[35] But if the added language gives the transferee only a limited power of disposition, such language is usually held to show the transferor's intent to create only a life estate rather than a fee simple.[36]

A life estate may be made defeasible by the use of a special limitation,

25. E.g., Burlington County National Bank v. Braddock, 24 N.J.Super. 462, 94 A.2d 868 (Ch.Div.1953) (dictum: "Where a will gives an estate directly to a tenant for life by express words, even though it vests said life tenant with the uncontrolled power to dispose of the corpus, with the balance remaining to designated remaindermen"). See also Butler v. Prudden, 182 Ga. 189, 185 S.E. 102 (1936) (power to sell, borrow money, dispose of and do anything in reference thereto, without consent, control or interference from any other person, plus testamentary special power of appointment); Powers v. Wells, 244 Ill. 558, 91 N.E. 717 (1910) (power to use and dispose as testator might do if living, and to distribute to children by gift or by will); Matter of Estate of Smythe, 132 Cal.App.2d 343, 282 P.2d 141 (1955) (broad power to consume during life plus power to appoint remainder by will to designated persons); St. Joseph Hospital v. Dwertman, 268 S.W.2d 646 (Ky.1954) (broad power to use and enjoy during life and to dispose provided that life tenant could not willfully waste property, give it away, or dispose of it by will); Matter of Martindale's Estate, 423 N.E.2d 662 (Ind.App.1981) (life beneficiary of trust who had both inter vivos and testamentary power, exercised power in favor of her estate). Rest.Prop. § 111. An express power in the life tenant either to "consume" or to "appoint" real property is, of course, generally construed as a power to convey in fee simple. The power to convey in fee simple is generally held to include the lesser

power to mortgage in fee simple. E.g., Jackson v. Everett, 58 S.W. 340 (Tenn.1894).

26. E.g., In re Fahnestock's Estate, 384 Ill. 26, 50 N.E.2d 733 (1943).

27. E.g., Nelson v. Johnson, 354 Pa. 512, 47 A.2d 650 (1946).

28. E.g., Jackson v. Robinson, 195 Ark. 431, 112 S.W.2d 417 (1938).

29. E.g., Roberts v. Randleman, 352 Mo. 980, 180 S.W.2d 674 (1944).

30. E.g., Owen v. Dumas, 200 Ark. 601, 140 S.W.2d 101 (1940).

31. E.g., Patch v. Smith, 113 Colo. 186, 155 P.2d 765 (1945).

32. E.g., Bradley v. Warren, 104 Me. 423, 72 A. 173 (1908); Hair v. Caldwell, 109 Tenn. 148, 70 S.W. 610 (1902); Rolley v. Rolley's Executrix, 109 Va. 449, 63 S.E. 988 (1909); Swan v. Pople, 118 W.Va. 538, 190 S.E. 902 (1937).

33. Barry v. Austin, 118 Me. 51, 105 A. 806 (1919) (if language expressly creating life estate is used, it will not be enlarged to a fee simple by addition of unrestricted power of disposition).

34. See 2 Powell, Real Property ¶ 202[3] between nn. 73 and 76.

35. E.g., Luckey v. McCray, 125 Iowa 691, 101 N.W. 516 (1904).

36. E.g., In re McClure's Will, 136 N.Y. 238, 32 N.E. 758 (1892). See also Rest. Prop. § 108, Comment e.

condition subsequent, or executory limitation.[37] The addition of a defeasance clause may, however, cause constructional problems. If O devises Blackacre to O's spouse "during widowhood," or "so long as she shall remain a widow," or "so long as he does not remarry," the spouse will acquire a determinable life estate.[38] But suppose O devises Blackacre to O's spouse, "and on her [or his] remarriage to X." The Property Restatement asserts that the surviving spouse will take a determinable life estate unless "the language used, or the circumstances," show that O intended to give the spouse a fee simple subject to an executory limitation.[39] Recent cases suggest a trend toward holding that the surviving spouse takes a fee simple subject to an executory limitation.[40]

Estates for life may be created in two or more grantees as tenants in common or as joint tenants (if joint tenancies are still recognized in the state where the land is located). When land is conveyed to tenants in common for life, with a gift over to a third person upon the death of the surviving cotenant, cross-remainders for life may be implied so that the surviving cotenant will hold the undivided interests of all the deceased tenants in common until the remainder becomes possessory. Although implication of cross-remainders is more common when life estates are created by will, there is substantial authority for such implication when the life estate is created by deed.[41]

§ 2.13   Marital Life Estates at Common Law

From a very early date, the English common law made provision for surviving spouses out of the land in which a deceased spouse was seised of an estate of inheritance at any time during the marriage.[1] In each case, the surviving spouse was given a life estate in such lands, or part of them. The widow's life estate, called "dower," consisted of a life estate in one-third of such lands, provided the husband's estate was inheritable by the wife's issue, and provided the wife had not during the marriage released her dower.[2]

---

37. See post Section 2.15 at note call 15, Section 3.4 following note call 4, Section 3.5 around note call 7, and Section 3.7 at note call 16. For a recent case, see Edwards v. Bradley, 227 Va. 224, 315 S.E.2d 196 (1984).

38. E.g., Mouser v. Srygler, 295 Ky. 490, 174 S.W.2d 756 (1943).

39. Rest. Prop. § 108, Comment bb. (Supp. 1948).

40. E.g., Dickson v. Alexandria Hospital, 177 F.2d 876 (4th Cir.1949); Ramsey v. Holder, 291 S.W.2d 556 (Ky.1956); Anderson v. Anderson, 150 Or. 476, 46 P.2d 98 (1935); Kautz v. Kautz, 365 Pa. 450, 76 A.2d 398 (1950); In re Mattison's Estate, 122 Vt. 486, 177 A.2d 230 (1962). Contra (finding a determinable life estate): Hutchinson's Estate v. Arnt, 210 Ind. 509, 1 N.E.2d 585, 108 A.L.R. 530 (1936), rehearing denied 210 Ind. 509, 4 N.E.2d 202 (1936).

41. See 1 Am.L.Prop. § 2.15 in text between nn. 22 and 23.

§ 2.13

1. The widow's life estate was called "dower" and the widower's life estate was called "curtesy." While both spouses were alive, the husband also enjoyed the right to control and manage all of his wife's real property *jure uxoris*—"by the marital right."

2. In the twelfth century it was the prevailing practice for a bridegroom at the time of marriage to name specific lands as the dower his wife was to enjoy if she survived him. Although the amount of dower was a matter of bargain between the parties and their kinsmen, a man was not free to marry without naming a dower. By the end of the thirteenth century "named dowers" had begun to fall into disuse, and by the fifteenth century it was settled as a matter of common law that dower consisted of one-third of the lands of which the husband was seised of an estate of inheritance—i.e., a fee simple or a fee tail—at any time during the marriage. If the husband was seised in fee tail special the

During the joint lives of the spouses, the wife had a protected expectancy called "inchoate" dower, and if she survived her husband her dower became "consummate." She was then entitled to have one-third of the lands to which her inchoate dower attached set off to her by metes and bounds, at which time she acquired a present estate in the lands assigned to her.[3] Assignment of dower could be effected by agreement between the widow and the heir of the deceased spouse, or by court order.

Inchoate dower could not be defeated either by an *inter vivos* conveyance by the husband without the wife's consent or by the husband's will (after 1540) or by seizure and sale on execution to satisfy creditors' claims against the husband.[4] But inchoate dower could be barred either by an antenuptial or a postnuptial settlement after enactment of the Statute of Uses—although a postnuptial settlement did not absolutely bar dower but merely put the widow to an election between the benefits of the settlement or dower.[5] By the seventeenth century, a widow was also required to elect "in equity" between dower and her husband's testamentary provision for her if the latter was inconsistent with a claim of dower or was expressly declared to be in lieu thereof.[6]

At common law a wife was entitled to dower only in lands in which her husband had a *present* estate of inheritance, but it was not necessary that the husband should ever have been in actual possession; only an immediate right to possession or "seisin in law," not actual possession or "seisin in deed," was required.[7] The husband's estate had to be a "legal" estate, however, for one could not be "seised" of an "equitable" estate.[8] Hence, at

wife was not entitled to dower unless the issue of her marriage might, by possibility, inherit the fee tail. The wife's dower attached both to lands of which her husband was already seised at the time of marriage and land which he subsequently acquired in fee simple or fee tail. See, e.g., Wigginton v. Leech's Administratrix, 285 Ky. 787, 149 S.W.2d 531 (1941).

3. Until dower was actually set off by metes and bounds, she was not entitled to enter on the land except insofar as she had a right to remain in her husband's principal dwelling house for forty days—the right of "quarantine." See 2 Scribner, Dower 27 et seq. (2d ed. 1883); Park, Dower * 334 et seq.; 1 Roper, Husband and Wife * 387.

4. E.g., Hamm v. Piper, 105 N.H. 418, 201 A.2d 125 (1964) (widow entitled to relief against her husband's grantees where she did not join in the conveyance); Thomas v. Thomas, 245 Ala. 607, 18 So.2d 544 (1944) (dower not subject to claims of husband's creditors). A mortgage executed by the husband alone, other than a purchase money mortgage, is not effective as against the wife's dower right. Thomas v. Thomas, supra. But a purchase money mortgage given by the husband during the marriage is almost everywhere superior to the wife's dower right, whether she joins in the mortgage or not. E.g., Jones v. Tainter, 15 Minn. 512 (1870).

5. 27 Hen. VIII c. 10, §§ 6, 9 (1536). The courts construed the statute to authorize the barring of dower by a "jointure"—i.e., either a conveyance to the wife, before marriage, of an estate for her life (at least), to take effect in possession upon the husband's death, or a conveyance, before marriage, jointly to the husband and wife in fee simple, expressly in satisfaction of the wife's entire dower right. See 2 Blackstone, Commentaries * 138; 2 Scribner, Dower 394–408 (2d ed. 1883); 1 Am. L.Prop. §§ 5.39, 5.40. A post-nuptial provision in lieu of dower that was not a "legal jointure" but was effective "in equity" to put the widow to an election between such provision and her dower. 1 Roper, Husband and Wife * 488–489; 1 Am.L.Prop. § 5.40.

6. 2 Scribner, Dower 439–440 (2d ed. 1883); 1 Am.L.Prop. § 5.41.

7. Generally, see 1 Am.L.Prop. § 5.10. If the husband had acquired a fee simple or fee tail estate by inheritance or devise, but had not yet taken possession, he was said to be "seised in law," provided the land was not held by a disseisor. The old distinction between "seisin in deed" and "seisin in law" is no longer important for most purposes, either in England or the United States.

8. See generally 1 Am.L.Prop. §§ 5.10, 5.23. The rule denying dower in equitable

common law, the widow of a trust beneficiary, mortgagor, or land contract purchaser (each of whom had only an "equitable" estate) was not entitled to dower even if the husband had actual possession of the land during his lifetime.[9] On the other hand, the widow of a trustee, mortgagee, or land vendor was also denied dower because her husband was not "beneficially" seised of the land.[10]

Dower was recognized at common law only where the husband of the claimant had "sole seisin" of an estate of inheritance.[11] Where the husband was a tenant in common of an estate of inheritance, his widow was entitled to dower because he was deemed to have "sole seisin" of his separate undivided interest.[12] But where the husband was a joint tenant, his widow was not entitled to dower for two reasons: (1) because the undivided interest of a deceased joint tenant passes to the surviving joint tenant or tenants rather than to the decedent's heirs, a joint tenant has no inheritable estate; and (2) a joint tenant is not deemed to be "solely seised" of his undivided interest.[13] But the widow of the final survivor of two or more joint tenants was entitled to dower because the survivor became "solely seised" in severalty. Similarly, the widow of one to whom the undivided interest of a joint tenant was transferred had a dower right in that undivided interest because the conveyance "severed" the joint tenancy and made her husband a tenant in common.[14]

Dower is clearly a "derivative" estate. Hence it should not be capable of enduring longer than the husband's estate which is its source. But the common law decisions in England are only partly consistent with the derivative nature of dower. If the husband had a fee simple which terminated because he, or some descendant, died without heirs, the widow was nevertheless allowed dower in the land.[15] Similarly, if the husband had a fee tail estate which terminated because he "died without issue," the widow was nevertheless allowed dower in the land [16]—a result generally explained on the ground that, by the fifteenth century, so much English land was entailed that the courts thought it necessary, on policy grounds, to protect widows of tenants in tail by holding their dower rights to be superior to the rights of remaindermen and reversioners upon termination of their husbands' fee tail estates.[17] And by analogy to the rule applied when the

estates was finally changed by statute in England. 3 & 4 Wm. IV c. 105, § 2 (1833).

9. 1 Am.L.Prop. §§ 5.23, 5.24.

10. Id. § 5.11. The widow of a trustee was entitled to dower at common law, but the Court of Chancery would enjoin her from asserting her right if the husband had no beneficial interest under the trust. Noel v. Jevon, 2 Freeman 43 (Ch. 1678).

11. Littleton, Tenures § 45; 1 Scribner, Dower 269, 335–336 (2d ed. 1883).

12. As to the characteristics of tenancies in common, see post Section 5.2.

13. As to the characteristics of joint tenancies, see post Section 5.3.

14. As to severance of a joint tenancy by transfer of one joint tenant's interest, see post Section 5.3.

15. Bracton, De Legibus, fol. 297b; 1 Atkinson, Conveyancing 258 (1839); 4 Kent, Commentaries * 49; Park, Dower * 158; 1 Scribner, Dower 286–288 (2d ed. 1883). This rule meant that the widow's dower right was superior to the right of escheat of the feudal overlord in England. The same rule applied here, although the right of escheat accrues to the state in the United States. E.g., Pacific Bank v. Hannah, 90 Fed. 72 (9th Cir. 1898).

16. E.g., Y.B. 5 Edw. II (1311), Seldon Soc. Pub. 18 et seq. (1944); Butler's Co.Litt. * 241a, note; Paine's Case, 8 Co.Rep. 34a (1587). The rule was applied whether the husband literally died "without issue" or his line of descendants became extinct after his death.

17. Rest.Prop.Appendix 13; 1 Am.L.Prop. 680 at n. 19.

husband's estate was a fee tail, the courts held that a widow was entitled to dower, as against the holder of an executory interest to which her husband's fee simple estate was subject, when the divesting contingency occurred at the husband's death—typically because the husband's fee simple was subject to an executory limitation in favor of a third party upon his death "without surviving issue." [18]

The "derivative" nature of dower has, however, been given legal effect by decisions holding that, if the husband has a fee simple determinable or a fee simple subject to a condition subsequent, the wife's dower right is extinguished by the occurrence of the special limiting event or exercise of the right of entry for breach of the specified condition, as the case may be.[19] Similarly, if the husband's estate of inheritance is subject to a power of appointment, it has been held that exercise of the power will be effective to defeat the wife's dower right, even where the power is held and exercised by the husband himself.[20]

Since inchoate dower arose by operation of law from the marital relationship, it would arise only where a valid marriage existed,[21] and an annulment or absolute divorce (not possible in England without a special act of parliament until recently) would extinguish any inchoate dower interest in the lands of the former husband.[22] Moreover, an early English statute provided that, "if a wife willingly leave her husband and go away, and continue with her advouter," her dower was barred unless her husband should take her back.[23]

The English common law provided even more handsomely for a widower than it did for a widow. During the marriage, the husband had an estate "by the marital right" in all the lands in which his wife, during the marriage, owned a present legal freehold estate—i.e., a fee simple, a fee tail, or a life estate.[24] Since English law did not until comparatively recently provide for an absolute divorce, the husband's estate by the marital right was, at common law, in substance an estate for the lives of husband and wife, or, with respect to the wife's estates of inheritance, until issue was born capable of inheriting those estates. The husband's estate by the marital

---

18. The leading case is Moody v. King, 2 Bing. 447 (C.P. 1825), following the rule laid down with respect to the husband's curtesy in Buckworth v. Thirkell, reported in 3 Bos. & P. 652–654 as a note to Doe v. Hutton, id. 643 (K.B. 1804). Both decisions were made by Lord Mansfield, who stated in Moody v. King that the purpose of dower is to secure "an independent maintenance" to a widow for whom a husband may have made inadequate provision. Recall, again, that the widow was not, at common law, an "heir" of her husband. There appear to be no cases dealing with the wife's dower right when the husband's estate of inheritance is terminated by operation of an executory limitation either during his lifetime or after his death. See 1 Am.L.Prop. § 5.29 at nn. 7–9.

19. E.g., Moriarta v. McRea, 45 Hun. 564 (N.Y.1887), affirmed 120 N.Y. 659, 24 N.E. 1103 (1890) (determinable fee); Sullivan v. Sullivan, 139 Iowa 679, 117 N.W. 1086 (1908)

(fee subject to condition subsequent); Rest. Prop. § 54, and Appendix 3.

20. E.g., Ray v. Pung, 5 B. & Ald. 561 (K.B. 1822) (power exercised by husband during his lifetime); Thompson v. Vance, 58 Ky. (1 Metc.) 669 (1858) (power exercised by will).

21. 1 Am.L.Prop. §§ 5.7, 5.8.

22. Id. §§ 5.8, 5.9, 5.36.

23. Stat. 2 Westminster II, 13 Edw. I c. 34 (1285). This statute is deemed part of the common law in some American jurisdictions, and comparable legislation is fairly common in the United States. See 1 Am.L.Prop. § 3.35.

24. The best modern treatment of the husband's estate by the marital right is to be found in 1 Am.L.Prop. §§ 5.50–5.56, reprinted substantially from Haskins, The Estate by the Marital Right, 97 U.Pa.L.Rev. 345 (1949).

right gave him the right to exclusive possession of his wife's freehold lands and to their profits, as well as the power to convey or mortgage such lands for the joint lives of the spouses without any duty to account to his wife for moneys obtained by the sale or mortgage.[25] The wife's freehold lands were also subject to execution and sale to satisfy the husband's debts,[26] but if he predeceased her the lands thus sold were returned to her free from encumbrances.[27]

The husband's estate by the marital right underwent substantial modification during the sixteenth and seventeenth centuries.[28] By the beginning of the eighteenth century the Court of Chancery had established that lands conveyed to trustees, either before or after her marriage, for a woman's "sole and separate use," were free during the marriage from her husband's control and from any liability for his debts.[29] The wife could sell or mortgage her separate "equitable" estate without her husband's consent or joinder.[30]

When a child of the marriage capable of inheriting from the wife was born, the common law gave the husband an estate called "curtesy initiate" in all the lands owned by the wife in fee simple or fee tail.[31] Like inchoate dower, curtesy initiate was a protected expectancy which could not be defeated or diminished by the wife's attempt, without the husband's joinder or release, to transfer the land to which curtesy initiate had attached by deed or (after 1540) by will,[32] or to mortgage the land.[33] Nor could the wife's creditors sell such land on execution to satisfy debts incurred by the wife after marriage.[34] Unlike inchoate dower, however, the husband's curtesy initiate was a present estate for his life, defeasible if he should predecease his wife, and it gave the husband a right to the sole possession, use, and income of the lands to which it attached.[35] And curtesy initiate extended to lands in which the wife had either a legal or equitable estate of inheritance, provided either spouse, during the marriage, had acquired "seisin in deed"

25. Co.Litt. * 325b; Eaton v. Whitaker, 18 Conn. 222 (1846). Despite his power to manage and enjoy his wife's lands, the husband could not exclude her from them except by alienation. Bracton, De Legibus, fol. 166b. If the husband unlawfully excluded her, she could obtain a judgment from the ecclesiastical court which the royal courts would enforce by jailing him until he complied.

26. 2 Kent, Comm. * 131; Beale v. Knowles, 45 Me. 479 (1858); Nicholls v. O'Neill, 10 N.J.Eq. 88 (Ch. 1854).

27. Co.Litt. * 325b; Flagg v. Bean, 25 N.H. 49 (1852).

28. See 1 Am.L.Prop. §§ 5.53, 5.54.

29. See id. § 5.55. Subsequently, it was held that lands could be conveyed to the husband as trustee for his wife's "sole and separate use," or even directly to the wife herself, in which case the husband was treated as a trustee. See 2 Scott, Trusts § 146.1 (3d ed. 1967).

30. E.g., Forbes v. Lothrop, 137 Mass. 523 (1884).

31. Co.Litt. * 30a. The best modern treatment of curtesy is to be found in 1 Am.L.Prop. §§ 5.57 through 5.74, from which the discussion in this Section is largely drawn.

32. E.g., Farley v. Stacey, 177 Ky. 109, 197 S.W. 636 (1917) (deed).

33. E.g., Wright v. Pell, 90 N.J.Eq. 11, 105 A. 20 (Ch. 1918). Although no cases in point have been found, it is clear that as in analogous cases involving inchoate dower the husband's curtesy initiate would be subordinate to a purchase money mortgage or vendor's lien given by the wife.

34. E.g., Myers v. Hansbrough, 202 Mo. 495, 100 S.W. 1137 (1907). Of course, because of the general common law disability of a married woman to contract obligations, the problem seldom arose.

35. E.g., Shortall v. Hinckley, 31 Ill. 219 (1863). Moreover, the husband could convey or encumber the land—Shortall v. Hinckley, supra—and it was subject to sale on execution for his debts—e.g., Robie v. Chapman, 59 N.H. 41 (1879). After the birth of issue had given him an estate by the curtesy initiate, the husband had essentially the same rights as he had prior to birth of issue by virtue of his estate *jure uxoris*.

or, where the wife's estate was equitable, there had been receipt of income from trustees or something else equivalent to possession of the land.[36]

If the husband predeceased his wife, his curtesy initiate terminated. But if he outlived her, he acquired an estate called "curtesy consummate" in all the lands to which his curtesy initiate previously attached.[37] Curtesy consummate was a present estate for the balance of the husband's life; it prevented the wife's heirs or devisees from taking possession until after the husband's death.[38]

Where the wife's estate, although it was in fee simple or in fee tail, terminated for want of heirs, or by the operation of a special limitation, condition subsequent, or executory limitation, the rules applicable to dower were also applied to curtesy; i.e., curtesy, like dower, was not consistently treated as a mere derivative estate, and sometimes survived the termination of the estate owned by the wife during marriage.[39]

§ 2.14 Marital Life Estates in Modern America

As Professor Richard Powell observed, dower "was a reasonable product of a society in which most wealth consisted of land, and in which it was desired to provide at least a modest social security * * * for widows"[1]—a society in which the widow was not an "heir" according to the common law canons of descent. But curtesy seems never to have had any justification other than that it served the interest of males in a male-dominated society. As a constantly increasing proportion of the total social wealth in England and the United States came to consist of personal property, and as surviving spouses became statutory "heirs" under new intestate succession laws, it began to seem that neither dower nor curtesy made a great deal of sense— especially since both constituted incumbrances (often difficult to discover) that inhibited the free transfer of land.

Thus it is not surprising to find the English Parliament, in the Dower Act of 1833,[2] providing that where a marriage thereafter took place, the wife could not claim dower in any land disposed of by her husband either by deed or by will, or in any land in respect of which he had made a declaration by deed or will barring dower. And the reforms initiated by the Court of Chancery in the sixteenth and seventeenth centuries in developing and

36. Originally, seisin of a legal estate of inheritance was required. Littleton, Tenures § 52; Co.Litt. * 29a, * 31a; 2 Blackstone, Comm. * 128. The seisin had to be beneficial, not merely as trustee. Though there was still considerable uncertainty about the matter during the seventeenth century, it became settled in the eighteenth century that the husband was entitled to curtesy out of his wife's equitable estates of inheritance, including equitable estates in fee simple which she held "for her separate use" if she had not disposed of them during her life. See 1 Am.L.Prop. § 5.59 at nn. 20–26.

37. Co.Litt. * 30a. It was not essential that legitimate issue, the birth of which was necessary to create the husband's curtesy initiate, should survive for any length of time. Littleton Tenures § 35; Co.Litt. * 30a. The

condition that issue be born alive was generally satisfied by testimony that it was heard to cry. Y.B. 20–21 Edw. I (Rolls Ser. 1866); Littleton, Tenures § 35; Co.Litt. * 29a, * 30a.

38. Since the husband's curtesy consummate applied to all the wife's inheritable estates—unlike the wife's dower consummate— there was no need for any assignment of curtesy.

39. See supra in text between notes 15 and 23.

§ 2.14

1. 2 Powell, Real Property ¶ 209.

2. 3 & 4 Wm. IV c. 105 (1833). This statute also made dower subject to the husband's debts and extended dower to the husband's equitable estates.

protecting the wife's "sole and separate" equitable estate [3] were completed in the nineteenth century by the enactment of the Married Women's Property Act, which conferred on married women the same control of their real and personal property enjoyed by unmarried women. This had the effect of abolishing the husband's estate by the marital right and, also, his estate by the curtesy initiate. Finally, both dower and curtesy were completely abolished in England in 1925.[4]

In the United States, the enactment of Married Women's Property Acts also had the effect of abolishing the husband's estate by the marital right and, in most states, his estate by the curtesy initiate.[5] Ultimately, in most of the United States as well as in England, both dower and curtesy were completely eliminated by statute.[6] And even where they have not been completely eliminated, they have usually been greatly modified. Thus, in most states where they are recognized, dower and curtesy are both confined to lands owned by the deceased spouse at death.[7] In such states, curtesy has also generally been limited to the same fraction of the deceased spouse's lands as dower—e.g., either one-third, as at common law or, in some states, one-half.[8] And in some states where dower and curtesy have been retained but have been limited to the same fraction of the deceased spouse's lands, the interest given to the surviving spouse is a fee simple rather than a life estate.[9]

Statutory abolition or modification of dower and curtesy has everywhere been preceded or accompanied by revision of the intestate succession laws to make surviving spouses "heirs" entitled to a specified share of the decedent's estate in fee simple.[10] In many states, in addition, statutes have been

---

3. See ante Section 2.13 between notes 28 and 30.

4. Administration of Estates Act, 15 & 16 Geo. V c. 23 (1925).

5. See cases collected in Notes, 14 A.L.R. 355 (1921), 29 A.L.R. 1338 (1924).

Elimination of curtesy has led, in some states, to decisions that continued recognition of dower violates the Equal Protection Clause of the Fourteenth Amendment. See, e.g., Boan v. Watson, 281 S.C. 516, 316 S.E.2d 401 (1984) (dower violates both Fourteenth Amendment and state constitution).

6. See 2 R. Powell, Real Prop. ¶ 213 (incl. 1982 Supp.). It would appear that only a handful of states still recognize either dower or curtesy even in modified form; these states currently include Alaska, Arkansas, Hawaii, Kentucky, Massachusetts, Minnesota, Ohio, Pennsylvania, Rhode Island, Virginia, and West Virginia.

7. E.g., Mass.Gen.Laws Ann. c. 189, § 1. The constitutionality of this statute was sustained in Opinion of the Justices, 337 Mass. 786, 151 N.E.2d 475 (1958).

8. E.g., Mass.Gen.Laws Ann. c. 189, § 1 (each is fixed at one-third). Alabama, New Jersey, and Oregon until recently all had statutes fixing both dower and curtesy at one-half. These statutes have all been repealed by more

recent statutes abolishing dower and curtesy completely, but since the latter operate only prospectively, the older statutes will continue to govern the rights of spouses married prior to the effective date of the statutes abolishing dower and curtesy. Note that some statutes alter dower and/or curtesy by converting the marital estates into fee simple estates. See, e.g., Va.Code 1950, § 64.1–19. Such a statute simply applies the terms dower and/or curtesy to what are, in substance, intestate shares in the estate of the deceased spouse.

It appears that the shares of the spouses must be equal in order to comply with the Equal Protection Clause of the Fourteenth Amendment. See Orr v. Orr, 440 U.S. 268, 99 S.Ct. 1102, 59 L.Ed.2d 306 (1979), on remand 374 So.2d 895 (Ala.Civ.App.1979), writ denied 374 So.2d 898 (1979). See also discussion of "gender-based discrimination," infra note 13. And see Jacobs v. Meade, 227 Va. 284, 315 S.E.2d 383 (1984).

9. E.g., Minn.Stat.Ann. §§ 507.02, 525.-16(2) and (3) (one-third or, in some cases, one-half, in fee simple). Such statutes give the surviving spouse something different than an intestate share because he or she takes dower or curtesy free from the debts of the deceased spouse.

10. Atkinson, Wills § 15 (2d ed. 1953).

enacted allowing a surviving spouse to renounce the decedent's will and take a "forced share" of the decedent's estate unless the decedent's will makes a stipulated minimum provision for the surviving spouse.[11] Indeed, "forced share" statutes have been enacted in many of the states where dower and curtesy still survive. Hence it is rarely advantageous for a surviving spouse to claim dower or curtesy, since the surviving spouse's intestate share or "forced share" (where there is a will) is usually more valuable than the property that might be obtained by electing dower or curtesy. As the Massachusetts court has observed, a claim of dower or curtesy is usually disadvantageous except in two special situations: "(1) if the deceased [spouse] owned real estate but died insolvent or so nearly so that the bulk of the real estate must be sold to pay the debts and expenses; and (2) if the deceased [spouse] during his or her lifetime conveyed a considerable amount of real estate without procuring a release * * * in the deed." [12]

Where dower and curtesy still exist, a surviving spouse must elect between dower or curtesy and an intestate share if the other spouse died intestate, or between dower or curtesy and a "forced share" if the other spouse dies testate.[13] Where dower still exists, a widow does not automatically become entitled to possession of any particular portion of her deceased husband's lands, but must, as at common law, have her dower "assigned" either by agreement with the heirs or, if agreement cannot be reached, by court order.[14] If curtesy is still recognized but is limited to some fraction of

11. See, e.g., N.Y.—McKinney's Estates, Powers & Trusts Law 5–1.1(a). Where a surviving husband is allowed to elect a "forced share" in lieu of testamentary provision, the share tends to be smaller than that given to a surviving wife.

12. Opinion of the Justices, 337 Mass. 786, 793, 151 N.E.2d 475, 478 (1958), upholding the constitutionality of a statute limiting dower and curtesy to land owned by the deceased spouse at the time of his or her death. In Matter of Estate of Epperson, 284 Ark. 35, 679 S.W.2d 792 (1984), certiorari denied 471 U.S. 1017, 105 S.Ct. 2022, 85 L.Ed.2d 303 (1985), the court upheld the constitutionality of a statute precluding a surviving spouse from claiming dower or curtesy by "taking against" the will of the deceased spouse unless the surviving spouse was married to the decedent for more than one year.

13. See, e.g., Mass.Gen.Laws Ann. c. 189, § 1, requiring the surviving spouse to file an election to take dower (which includes curtesy, by definition) within six months after approval of the bond of the decedent's executor or administrator, in which case the surviving spouse waives all rights under the decedent's will (if any), as well as any "forced share" (if there is a will) or intestate share (if there is no will). In general, see 1 Am.L.Prop. § 5.42.

Recent decisions of the United States Supreme Court striking down statutes that produce "gender-based discrimination" have had an effect on statutes providing for such election. In Orr v. Orr, 440 U.S. 268, 99 S.Ct. 1102, 59 L.Ed.2d 306 (1979), on remand 374

So.2d 895 (Ala.Civ.App.1979), writ denied 374 So.2d 898 (Ala.1979), the United States Supreme Court held that "gender-based discrimination" violates the Fourteenth Amendment's Equal Protection Clause unless it bears a "substantial relationship" to an "important governmental objective." Applying this standard, statutes allowing a widow to claim dower against the will of her deceased husband but not according a widower an equivalent privilege were invalidated in Hall v. McBride, 416 So.2d 986 (Ala.1982), and Stokes v. Stokes, 271 Ark. 300, 613 S.W.2d 372 (1981), appeal after remand 275 Ark. 110, 628 S.W.2d 6 (1982). In Land v. Bowyer, 437 So.2d 524 (Ala.1983), the court reached the same result although the widow had not "dissented" from her husband's will, which made no provision for her. But in Beck v. Merritt, 280 Ark. 331, 657 S.W.2d 549 (1983), the court held that the Arkansas dower statute does not effect any unconstitutional "gender-based discrimination" where a husband dies intestate, because in such case the widow is not "claiming against" the husband's will and her dower right under the statute is the exact equivalent of the curtesy right the husband could have asserted had he survived his wife. Accord: Dent v. Rose, 281 Ark. 42, 661 S.W.2d 361 (1983).

14. See ante Section 2.13 at note 3. See also Marino v. Smith, 454 So.2d 1380 (Ala. 1984) (if widow remains in possession without an assignment of dower she cannot acquire title by adverse possession unless she repudi-

the deceased spouse's lands, a widower must likewise obtain an assignment of his curtesy. In most states where dower and curtesy still exist, the surviving spouse is entitled to have an assignment made by "metes and bounds"—i.e., by a physical division of the land—unless this is either impossible (e.g., where the property consists of a single house and lot) or inequitable, in which case the court may award the surviving spouse a gross sum of money or a share of the income produced by the land.[15]

The wife obviously has no inchoate dower interest in a tenancy by the entirety. But where, under modern law, she can release her interest as tenant by the entirety to her husband, she may acquire inchoate dower in the fee simple of which he is "solely seised" by virtue of her release.[16]

§ 2.15   Life Estates—Alienability

A life estate, once created, is freely transferable by deed unless made subject to an effective restraint upon alienation by the person who created the life estate.[1] Since life estates are, by their very nature, not very saleable, the common law rule substantially prohibiting restraints on the alienation of fee simple estates has not been strictly applied to life estates.[2] A total "forfeiture" restraint, unlimited in scope or in time, is therefore valid

ates the title of her deceased husband and gives notice of such repudiation to his heirs. Wilder v. Mixon, 442 So.2d 922 (Ala.1983); Devers v. Chateau Corp., 748 F.2d 902 (4th Cir.1984), appeal after remand 792 F.2d 1278 (1986), rehearing denied 802 F.2d 1486 (1986) (widow's action for assignment of dower barred by 15–year statute of limitations applicable to actions for possession of land).

15. See 1 Am.L.Prop. §§ 5.45–5.47.

16. Estate of Del Guercio, 206 N.J.Super. 159, 501 A.2d 1072 (L.Div.1985). In a sense, a tenancy by the entirety is a "marital estate" since it can exist only between husband and wife. It is characterized by an indestructible right of survivorship. See post Section 5.5 for discussion of tenancies by the entirety.

§ 2.15

1. See, e.g., Guilford v. Gardner, 180 Iowa 1210, 162 N.W. 261 (1917) (dictum); Daley v. Daley, 308 Mass. 293, 32 N.E.2d 286 (1941) (dictum); Hendley v. Perry, 229 N.C. 15, 47 S.E.2d 480 (1948). Dower, once it is assigned, and curtesy consummate upon the wife's death, in jurisdictions where they still arise by operation of law, are freely transferable by deed.

When a life tenant conveys the life estate to the holder of a vested remainder or reversion in fee simple in the same land, the conveyance is called a "surrender" and the life estate is said to "merge" in the fee simple. Merger was one mode of "destroying" a contingent remainder at common law. Merger and "destruction" of a contingent remainder could be effected either by "surrender" by the life tenant or by "release" of the reversion to the life

tenant. But even at common law only "legal" contingent remainders were "destructible" by merger; "equitable" contingent remainders were never "destructible." In most states today contingent remainders are "indestructible," either by merger or otherwise. See Wagner v. Maskey, 353 N.W.2d 891 (Iowa App. 1984). For more on the obsolete "destructibility" rule, see post Section 3.10.

2. "The extent to which a restraint on the alienation of an interest in land may cause undesirable results is directly dependent on the nature of the estate restrained and the likelihood that such an estate can, as a practical matter, be alienated apart from any restraint on alienation. When the estate restrained is an estate for life, there are two reasons why the social dangers are so reduced that the intention of the one imposing the restraints is permitted to take effect.

"First, an estate for life is not a marketable estate when sold separately because the purchaser would lose all he bought should the life tenant die the next day and people are not willing to part with money or other valuable consideration under those circumstances. * * *

"[Second,] the lack of permanence of an estate for life makes it relatively unimportant that a restraint on alienation interferes with * * * available types of disposition because they are used mainly for the purpose of formulating plans for the future use of the land and when the estate is one for life that is unnecessary * * *." Rest.Prop. § 409, Comment a.

when applied to a life estate.[3] Presumably a total "promissory" restraint would also be valid.[4] But a purported "disabling" restraint upon alienation of a legal life estate is ineffective unless it can be construed as a "forfeiture" or "promissory" restraint.[5] On the other hand, an effective "disabling" restraint may be imposed upon the equitable life estate of a trust beneficiary by means of "spendthrift trust" provisions. The equitable life tenant under a "spendthrift trust" cannot transfer his interest, nor may his creditors subject it to the satisfaction of their claims.[6]

If a life estate is not subject to an effective restraint upon alienation, the life tenant may sell, give, or mortgage the entire estate,[7] or create lesser estates (such as leasehold estates for years or from period to period) or nonpossessory interests (such as easements).[8] On the other hand, a life tenant obviously cannot create in a grantee or lessee an interest that will endure longer than his own life estate [9] unless he was expressly given such a power by the creator of the life estate.[10]

The tenant of an estate for his own life obviously has no power to devise his estate by will, since it terminates upon his death.[11] But the tenant of an

3. See, e.g., Edwards v. Bradley, 227 Va. 224, 315 S.E.2d 196 (1984); Luther v. Patman, 200 Ark. 853, 141 S.W.2d 42 (1940); Lewis v. Lewis, 76 Conn. 586, 57 A. 735 (1904); Brumsey v. Brumsey, 351 Ill. 414, 184 N.E. 627 (1933); Mears v. Taylor, 142 Va. 824, 128 S.E. 264 (1925) (only involuntary conveyance prohibited). Rest.Prop. § 409 adopts the rule that forfeiture restraints are valid.

4. No cases involving promissory restraints have been found. Rest.Prop. § 409 adopts the rule that promissory restraints are valid.

5. This rule is generally accepted in the United States. E.g., Randolph v. Wilkinson, 294 Ill. 508, 128 N.E. 525 (1920); McCleary v. Ellis, 54 Iowa 311, 6 N.W. 571 (1880); Wellington v. Janvrin, 60 N.H. 174 (1880); Pilley v. Sullivan, 182 N.C. 493, 109 S.E. 359 (1921); Grossman v. Hill, 384 Pa. 590, 122 A.2d 69 (1956); Wise v. Poston, 281 S.C. 574, 316 S.E.2d 412 (1984); Sternberger v. Glenn, 175 Tenn. 644, 137 S.W.2d 269 (1940); Kerns v. Carr, 82 W.Va. 78, 95 S.E. 606 (1918). Rest. Prop. § 405 adopts the rule that disabling restraints are invalid. There is some contrary authority, however. See Gray v. Gray, 300 Ky. 265, 188 S.W.2d 440 (1945) (provision allowing transfer only to cotenants valid); Trammell v. Johnston, 54 Ga. 340 (1875) (life tenant treated as trustee for remainderman); Crawford v. Solomon, 131 Miss. 792, 95 So. 686 (1923) (disabling restraint on life estate precludes court order for sale of fee simple); Drury v. Hickinbotham, 129 Neb. 499, 262 N.W. 37 (1935).

6. For a brief discussion of "spendthrift trusts," see 6 Am.L.Prop. §§ 26.94, 26.95. For a more extensive discussion, see 2 Scott, Trusts §§ 149–162 (3d ed. 1967).

7. See, recognizing the life tenant's power to mortgage, Georgia State Savings Association v. Dearing, 128 Ark. 149, 193 S.W. 512 (1917); Kenwood Trust & Savings Bank v. Palmer, 209 Ill.App. 370 (1918), affirmed 285 Ill. 552, 121 N.E. 186 (1918); Missouri Central Building & Loan Association v. Eveler, 237 Mo. 679, 141 S.W. 877 (1911). As pointed out, supra note 3, a life estate is inherently an unattractive investment for a purchaser; it is equally unattractive from the standpoint of a mortgage lender, since the life tenant, *qua* life tenant, cannot give a mortgage that will bind owners of future interests in the land.

8. This is simply part of the life tenant's general power to alienate his interest in whole or in part. Palman v. Reynolds, 310 Mich. 35, 16 N.W.2d 657 (1944) (life tenant can create estate for years).

9. This follows from the general rule that one cannot transfer a greater interest than he has. That a mortgage given by a life tenant does not bind owners of future interests in the land, see, e.g., Spearman v. Hussey, 210 Miss. 851, 50 So.2d 610 (1951); Morrow v. Person, 195 Tenn. 370, 259 S.W.2d 665 (1953); Mid-State Homes, Inc. v. Johnson, 218 Ga. 397, 128 S.E.2d 197 (1962). That a lease given by a life tenant expires when the life estate terminates, see, e.g., Busby v. Thompson, 286 Ark. 159, 689 S.W.2d 572 (1985); Scurry v. Anderson, 191 Iowa 1058, 183 N.W. 585 (1921); Shannon v. Hixson, 210 S.W.2d 410 (Mo.App. 1948) (alternative holding); Williams v. Alt, 226 N.Y. 283, 123 N.E. 499 (1919).

10. That such a power may, in most states, be added by appropriate language in an instrument purporting to create a life estate without giving the grantee a fee simple, see ante Section 2.13 at notes 7–13.

11. But the life tenant may be given the power to dispose of the fee simple by will. E.g., Powers v. Wells, 244 Ill. 558, 91 N.E. 717

estate *pur autre vie* may devise the residue of his estates if the measuring life is still in existence.[12] If the tenant of an estate *pur autre vie* does not dispose of the residue of his estate, such residue will generally pass under the intestate succession law of the jurisdiction. In most states the residue of an estate *pur autre vie* need not be classified as either real or personal property, since both kinds of property pass to the same persons, and in the same shares, when the owner dies intestate. In those states where the intestate succession laws treat real and personal property differently, the residue of an estate *pur autre vie* will usually pass as personal property to the decedent's next-of-kin.[13] In some of these states, however, it will pass as real property to the decedent's heirs, as "special occupants," if the instrument creating the estate expressly gave it to the named grantee "and his heirs." [14]

It is implicit in the prior discussion of the validity of "forfeiture" restraints on the alienation of life estates that a life estate may be made defeasible by means of a special limitation, a condition subsequent, or an executory limitation.[15] In general, the rules for determining what types of special limitations, conditions subsequent, and executory limitations are invalid because they are contrary to public policy or "illegal" are substantially the same when such limitations or conditions are attached to life estates as when they are attached to fee simple estates.[16]

§ 2.16 Life Interests in Personalty

At the present time, most life interests are beneficial interests under trusts, the corpus of which consists mainly of personal rather than real property. The primary purpose of the trust device is to permit the creation of one or more beneficial life interests which entitle the life tenants to the income produced by the corpus, to preserve the corpus of the trust for distribution to one or more remaindermen after termination of all the life interests, and to permit professional management of the trust corpus for the benefit of both life tenants and remaindermen. The corpus of the trust may include real property, but typically consists mainly of "intangible" forms of personal property such as stocks and bonds.[1]

(1910) (power to use and dispose and to distribute to children by gift or by will).

12. The Statute of Frauds, 29 Car. II, c. 3 (1677) first authorized such devise.

13. This is true, e.g., in Alabama, Kentucky, Michigan, Minnesota, New Jersey, New York, West Virginia, and Wisconsin.

14. This was the rule established in England by the Statute of Frauds (1677), and has been adopted in several American jurisdictions. Rest.Prop. § 151, Special Note, states that this is the American common law rule in the absence of an inconsistent statute, because the English statutes "merely declare a result which would have been reached in due time if the problem had been allowed to be litigated under an evolving common law."

15. See Rest.Prop. § 112, and the Illustrations thereof. Id. § 113 provides that when a limitation in a deed or will "contains language

specifically describing the estate as to duration in terms of the life or lives of one or more designated human beings, * * * then such limitation is effective to create an estate for life although it is accompanied by further language effective to create a special limitation, a condition subsequent or an executory limitation under such estate is terminable at the will of the conveyor."

16. See ante Section 2.3 at notes 15–22.

§ 2.16

1. Treatment of the law of trusts is generally beyond the scope of this book, although the peculiar characteristics of "equitable" future interests subject to a trust are to some extent considered in Chapter 4.

Where personal property is given directly to a life tenant, with remainder to another (or others), or where a trust terminates because of merger or for other reasons before the life tenant's death, it is often said that the life tenant is a "trustee" or "quasi-trustee" of the personal property for remainderman (or remaindermen).[2] Such a characterization of the life tenant results from the special problems arising from creation of a legal life interest in personalty—e.g., the fact that the law of waste does not adequately protect the interests of remaindermen because personalty is easily transportable, often perishable, and may require expert management to avoid diminution of the value of the personalty when it consists of stocks and/or bonds. These special problems, and the statutory and judicial efforts to deal with them, are discussed in more detail post in Section 4.13.

§ 2.17 Non-freehold (or Leasehold) Estates

Even in the heyday of English feudalism, it became common practice for tenants of freehold estates (i.e., in fee simple, fee tail, or for life) to "lease" land to another for a definite period of time, thus creating a "term of years" in the lessee.[1] Such leases seem originally to have been designed to avoid the ecclesiastical prohibition against usury in connection with loans.[2] The tenant of a freehold estate who borrowed money would give the lender a term of years of sufficient duration to enable him to recover the principal amount of the loan together with a substantial profit (in lieu of interest) out of the revenues from the land. But leases creating terms of years were not used only as a means of avoiding the prohibition against usury. By the late 12th century leases were made for a fixed term, at an agreed rent, to tenants who farmed the land. Such agricultural leases became increasingly common in the centuries that followed.

For reasons that are not entirely clear, a tenant for years was not considered to have a "free tenement" (freehold estate)[3] and therefore could not use the assize of novel disseisin to recover possession from one who wrongfully dispossessed him. Although other actions were developed in the thirteenth century to give the tenant for years a means to recover possession from the lessor or one claiming by feoffment from the lessor, prior to 1499 the tenant for years was limited to a damage remedy against a "stranger"

---

2. See, e.g., Farmers' Mutual Fire and Lightning Insurance Co. v. Crowley, 354 Mo. 649, 190 S.W.2d 250 (1945); Note, 137 A.L.R. 1054 (1942).

§ 2.17

1. Generally, see 1 Am.L.Prop. § 3.1; T. Plucknett, Concise History of the Common Law 570–574 (5th ed. 1956); F. Pollock & F. Maitland, History of English Law 106–117 (2d ed. 1898). Rest.Prop. § 19 defines a tenancy for years as one "the duration of which is fixed in units of a year or multiples or divisions thereof." Though there may have been an early notion that the duration of a tenancy for years was subject to some outer limit, it has long been settled that there is no limit in the absence of statute. Terms as long as 2,000 years, or of 99 years renewable forever, have

been held valid, in which case the tenant, as a practical matter, has an estate equivalent to a fee simple. See 1 Am.L.Prop. § 3.15.

2. In medieval times, the taking of any interest on a loan was considered to be "usury."

3. It has sometimes been asserted that the refusal to treat the term of years as a freehold estate was a result of its unsavory reputation as a stratagem to evade the prohibition against usury. Another explanation is that the English judges were under the influence of a Roman law concept that, had it been fully developed, would have resulted in classification of the term of years as a mere "servitude."

who wrongfully dispossessed him.[4] In 1499, however, in response to the obvious need for a possessory remedy against "strangers," the courts finally allowed the tenant for years to recover the leased land from a "stranger" in the action of trespass *de ejectione firmae,* later called ejectment.[5]

The action of ejectment, which was available to the tenant for years as against anyone who wrongfully dispossessed him, was obviously superior to the real actions available to the tenant of a freehold estate—a fact that soon led freeholders to seek and obtain the right to use ejectment in lieu of the real actions.[6] But the interest of the tenant for years had already been classified as "personal" rather than "real" property in the fourteenth century.[7] Since the term of years was clearly an interest in land and there was a "tenure" relationship between landlord and tenant, the eventual solution was to call the interest of the tenant for years a "chattel real," thus recognizing its anomalous nature.

The term of years, subject to payment of an annual rent, filled a fundamental need for a means to secure to a tenant the possession and use of land for a fixed period for agriculture, trade, or residence without the capital outlay required for purchase of a freehold estate. Although land could be "leased" to a tenant for life at an annual rent, the term of years had obvious advantages over a life estate from the tenant's viewpoint: it had a definite duration, which could be fixed by agreement of the parties; it could be created so as to commence *in futuro,* unlike a freehold estate, which could not be so created prior to 1536;[8] it could be transferred by will (since it was personal rather than real property), unlike a freehold estate, which could not be so transferred prior to 1540;[9] it would pass upon the tenant's death intestate according to the more rational rules governing succession to personal property rather than the canons of descent applicable to real property;[10] and prior to the enactment of the Statute of Frauds in 1677 it could be created by a parol agreement followed by the tenant's entry into possession, without either livery of seisin or a written deed of conveyance.[11] The last advantage was, of course, substantially eliminated by the Statute of Frauds,[12] which provided that parol leases, except those "not exceeding the term of three years from the making thereof," should create only an "estate at will."

The term of years, despite its anomalous classification as a "chattel real," has the essential characteristics of an estate in land. The tenant for

4. 1 Am.L.Prop. § 3.1 at nn. 3–5 and authorities cited.

5. Id. at n. 6 and authorities cited.

6. See ante Section 1.3 for development of the ejectment action as an all-purpose remedy for persons wrongfully dispossessed.

7. It is often said that this resulted from the fact that trespass, and its offspring, ejectment, were classified as "personal actions." 1 Am.L.Prop. § 3.1 at n. 10 suggests, however, that it was more a result of the fact that leases creating a term of years were frequently used as security for loans.

8. See ante Section 2.8 note 3 as to the reason for the rule prohibiting creation of

freehold estates to commence *in futuro.* Enactment of the Statute of Uses in 1536 abrogated this rule.

9. The Statute of Wills, 32 Hen. VIII, c. 1 (1540) authorized devise of freehold estates by will.

10. 1 Am.L.Prop. § 3.1 at p. 177.

11. Ibid.

12. 29 Car. II, c. 3 (1677). American versions of the Statute of Frauds generally contain similar provisions. For a more detailed consideration of the American Statutes of Frauds as they apply to the creation of leasehold estates, see post Section 6.15.

years has the exclusive right of possession during the term as against the whole world. Like the freehold estates we have already considered, a term of years may be made defeasible by means of an express power of termination (right of entry for breach of condition), special limitation, or executory limitation. And a term of years is freely transferable ("assignable") except to the extent that transfer is expressly subjected to a "forfeiture" or "promissory" restraint.

The term of years (or estate for years) is not the only non-freehold (or leasehold) estate recognized in Anglo–American law. Littleton, writing near the end of the fifteenth century, stated that a tenancy at will would arise whenever one person, with the consent of the freehold tenant, occupied land as tenant (not merely as servant or agent) under an express or implied agreement that the tenancy might be terminated at the will of either party.[13] And another type of non-freehold estate came to be recognized in the sixteenth century—the tenancy from year to year, which would continue indefinitely unless terminated by proper notice from one party to the other, effective at the end of some yearly period.[14] This became a common form of agricultural tenancy because it had substantial advantages, compared to a tenancy at will, from the standpoint of both landlord and tenant. It entitled the landlord to the agreed rent for at least one year, and it assured to the tenant the right of possession and use of the land for at least one year.[15] A tenant from year to year had a much more substantial interest than a tenant at will.

Other periodic tenancies were later recognized, such as tenancies from quarter to quarter, from month to month, and from week to week.[16] The distinguishing feature of these periodic tenancies is that, like a tenancy from year to year, they will continue indefinitely unless terminated by proper notice as of the end of some period.

Like tenancies for years, tenancies at will and periodic tenancies of all types are now considered to be non-freehold "estates in land," although they are also "chattels real"—i.e., personal rather than real property.

In England, prior to 1926, many persons held land by "copyhold" tenure. "Copyhold" was derived from the medieval "villein" tenure of the English peasantry. It was classified as a non-freehold tenure but, in its essential characteristics, the estate of the copyhold tenant was more like a fee simple estate than a leasehold estate. Copyhold tenure was converted to freehold tenure by the English Law of Property Act of 1922.[17] It never existed in the United States.

Many writers also recognize a non-freehold estate called a "tenancy at sufferance." But the so-called "tenancy at sufferance" is really not an estate

---

13. See post Sections 6.18, 6.19. For a more detailed discussion, see 1 Am.L.Prop. §§ 3.28 through 3.31.

14. See post Sections 6.16, 6.17. For a more detailed discussion, see 1 Am.L.Prop. §§ 3.23 through 3.27.

15. In addition, neither the landlord nor the tenant could terminate a tenancy from year to year except by giving notice at least six months prior to the end of a yearly period.

Thus both parties had ample time to arrange for a new tenancy if they desired.

16. See post Sections 6.16, 6.17. For a more detailed discussion, see 1 Am.L.Prop. §§ 3.23 through 3.27.

17. A brief discussion of the evolution and nature of copyhold tenure may be found in Moynihan, Intro. to Real Prop. 15–17 (1962).

at all; it is simply a term used to describe the status of a tenant who has "held over" wrongfully after the termination or expiration of his leasehold estate. The possessory rights of the so-called "tenant at sufferance," as against any person other than the owner of the land, are no greater than the rights of any other wrongful possessor of land. As against the owner of the land, the so-called "tenant at sufferance" has no right to possession. But the owner may elect to treat the "tenant at sufferance" as a tenant for an additional period, at least where there was originally a periodic tenancy.[18]

The tenant of any non-freehold (leasehold) estate has, in general, the same right to exclusive possession and the same privileges of use as a life tenant. The rights and duties of landlords and tenants of non-freehold estates are largely governed by express covenants in the lease, where a written lease is executed by the parties. Other duties peculiar to landlords and tenants of non-freehold estates are imposed by law, often in the form of so-called "implied covenants." The law which imposes these duties may be either judicially or legislatively created. Whatever their source, the duties of landlords and tenants of non-freehold (or leasehold) estates usually include both affirmative and negative obligations.

The characteristics of the non-freehold (or leasehold) estates, and the legal obligations of landlords and tenants, respectively, will be considered in some detail in Chapter 6 of this book.

18. See post Section 6.20.

Chapter 3

FUTURE ESTATES IN REALTY AND FUTURE INTERESTS IN PERSONALTY

Table of Sections

A. GENERAL INTRODUCTION

A. GENERAL INTRODUCTION

§ 3.1 Future Interests in Realty and Personalty—In General

A "future" estate in land is a non-possessory interest that will, or may, become a possessory estate at some future time. But it should be emphasized, once again, that a "future" estate is a presently existing, legally protected property interest. As applied to such interests, the adjective "future" refers to only one of the components of property, the right to possession, and does not mean that the "future" estate will come into existence only at some future time.[1]

When the owner of a possessory estate in land transfers the entire estate without providing for defeasance of the estate transferred on the happening of a stated event, no future estate is created.[2] But the owner of a possessory estate in land may create a future estate (or several future estates) (1) by transferring less than his entire estate, retaining the balance of it;[3] or (2) by dividing his estate into two or more "smaller" estates and transferring each of these "smaller" estates to a different person (or group of persons);[4] or (3) by transferring his entire estate subject to defeasance on the happening of a stated event.[5] In the first case, the grantor retains a future estate. In the second case, the transferees of all but the first of the "smaller" estates receive future estates. In the third case, a future estate is either retained by the transferor or created in favor of some third party—a future estate that will become possessory upon defeasance of the possessory estate transferred to the first taker.

---

§ 3.1

1. "[T]he essence of a future interest is that it (1) involves the privilege of possession or enjoyment in the future, and (2) it is looked upon as a portion of the total ownership of the land or other thing which is its subject matter." Simes, Future Interests 2 (2d ed. 1966).

A "future interest" should be carefully distinguished from a "mere possibility" such as the "expectancy" of a person who is the "heir apparent" of a living person. A "mere possibility" is not alienable "at law," although a purported transfer of a "mere possibility" may sometimes be treated as a specifically enforceable contract to transfer an interest if and when it is acquired by the person purporting to transfer the "mere possibility," provided that the purported transfer is made for a "fair consideration." See, generally, R. Powell, Real Prop. ¶¶ 382–384 (abr. ed. 1968); 1 Am. L.Prop. § 4.1 (1952).

2. Of course, if the estate transferred is less than a fee simple—e.g., a life estate or estate for years—there will already be a future interest, or interests, comprising the balance of the fee simple, vested in some person or persons.

3. E.g., the fee simple owner, O, may transfer Blackacre "to A for life." By operation of law, O will retain a future estate in fee simple called a "reversion."

4. E.g., the fee simple owner, O, may transfer Blackacre "to A for life, remainder to B." This will give B a future estate in fee simple called a "remainder."

5. E.g., the fee simple owner, O, may transfer Blackacre "to A, but if A should die without issue him surviving, then to B." This will give B a future interest in fee simple called an "executory interest."

As the preceding discussion suggests, there are two principal kinds of future estates: (1) reversionary future estates created or arising in favor of the transferor (or his successors—i.e., heirs or next-of-kin), and non-reversionary future interests created in favor of persons other than the transferor (or his successors). Reversionary future estates come in three basic models: (a) reversions,[6] (b) possibilities of reverter,[7] and (c) powers of termination (also called rights of entry for breach of condition).[8] Non-reversionary future estates come in only two basic models—(a) remainders and (b) executory interests—but each of these basic models may be further divided into several different sub-classes.[9]

The doctrine of estates, including future estates, developed as part of the English land law. But the panoply of future estates worked out by the common law courts with some assistance from Parliament was adopted, with modifications, by the English Chancellors for application to equitable interests in land.[10] Later, the scheme of future estates, legal and equitable, was applied to certain forms of personal property, i.e., property in intangibles and in non-consumable chattels.[11] At the present time, most future interests are equitable (beneficial) interests in property—typically personalty, or a mixture of personalty and realty—held and managed by a trustee.

When the law of future interests was developing in England, its major purpose was to make possible the kinds of family settlements—*inter vivos* or testamentary schemes to provide for members of the settlor's family in succeeding generations—desired by members of the English landed gentry and aristocracy.[12] At the present time, such *inter vivos* and testamentary family settlements are still the principal setting in which future interests in real and personal property, legal or equitable, are to be found. In addition, future interests are often employed to effect charitable gifts—e.g., to trans-

---

6. See supra note 3.

7. As we have previously seen, a possibility of reverter is created when, e.g., a fee simple owner, O, transfers Blackacre "to B so long as the land is not used for other than residential purposes," in which case O retains a possibility of reverter. See ante Section 2.4.

8. As we have previously seen, a possibility of reverter is created when, e.g., a fee simple owner, O, transfers Blackacre "to B, but if the land shall ever be used for other than residential purposes, O or his heirs may re-enter and repossess the land as of O's former estate." See ante Section 2.5.

9. See supra notes 4 and 5.

10. Thus, e.g., the Chancellor even prior to 1536 recognized and protected equitable future interests ("uses") analogous to legal reversions and remainders. Moreover, the Chancellor recognized and protected new types of future interests then called "shifting uses" and "springing uses." After enactment of the Statute of Uses in 1536, it was possible to create legal future interests in the nature of "shifting uses" and "springing uses" which, collectively, came to be called "executory interests." For more on executory interests, see post Sections 3.14 through 3.17.

11. In the early English common law, future interests other than those arising out of bailments were not recognized in personal property. But the English courts in the seventeenth century relaxed the rule by holding that future interests in personal property, except "consumable" property, could be created by will. In the United States, by the great weight of authority, future interests may be created in personal property, except "consumable" property, either by deed or by will; and such authority as there is tends to support the position taken in Rest. Prop. §§ 153 through 158, that all five varieties of future interests may be created in personal property. See, e.g., Johnson v. Swann, 211 Md. 207, 126 A.2d 603 (1956); Woodard v. Clark, 236 N.C. 190, 72 S.E.2d 433 (1952) (can be created by will only; but North Carolina Gen.Stat. § 39–6.2, enacted in 1952, permits creation of the same future interest by deed as by will).

12. On the family settlement in England, see Co.Litt. (19th ed. by Hargrave and Butler, 1832) part V, note to 290b; Kales, The Will of an English Gentleman of Moderate Fortune, 19 Green Bag 214 (1907); G. Radcliffe, Real Property Law ch. XIV (2d ed. 1938); 7 W. Holdsworth, History of English Law 376 (1937).

mit wealth to a charitable organization after the donor, or a relative of the donor, has enjoyed the income of a trust fund for his life, or when the income produced by the trust corpus has accumulated for a specified period of time. In using future interests as part of a family settlement or charitable gift, minimization of federal estate and state inheritance taxes is often a primary motive. Control of future land use by means of a special limitation creating a possibility of reverter or a condition subsequent creating a power to terminate for breach of condition—once very common—is comparatively rare at the present time.

Despite the fact that most future interests at the present time are equitable interests subject to a trust, the corpus of which is likely to consist entirely or principally of personal property such as stocks and bonds, the hypothetical examples used in the following sections of this book generally involve a transfer of legal estates in land, and the terminology used (such as "fee simple") is generally appropriate to legal estates in land rather than equitable interests in personalty. This has been done for the sake of convenience only.

In all of the hypothetical examples employed in the following sections of this book, the reader should assume that immediately before the transfer set out in the example the transferor, O, owned the subject matter of the transfer in fee simple absolute unless the contrary is expressly stated. Unless it would make a difference in a particular case, the generic term "transfer" is used instead of "conveyance" (*inter vivos* transfer) or "devise" (testamentary transfer). Words of inheritance formerly necessary to create an estate in fee have generally been omitted because they are no longer necessary under the nearly universal statutes providing that the transferor's entire interest in the subject matter will pass to the transferee unless a contrary intent is indicated.

§ 3.2　Vested and Non-vested Future Interests

In determining what future estates are created when a present estate in fee simple absolute is fragmented into "smaller" estates or made subject to defeasance, the fundamental rule is that the entire fee simple absolute must always be vested, in possession and in interest, in some identifiable group of persons. That is, the various present and vested future estates resulting from a particular transfer must "add up to" a fee simple absolute—no more and no less. In addition, a particular transfer may, in theory, create any number of non-vested future estates, which do not "count" when we are accounting for the fee simple absolute.

In view of the fundamental rule stated in the preceding paragraph, it is essential to be able to distinguish between "vested" and "non-vested" future estates. A future estate is "vested" if it is created in favor of a living person who is identifiable and ready to take possession of the land immediately upon the "natural" expiration of all prior estates created by the same transfer—i.e., where there is no implied or express condition precedent to the future estate's becoming possessory, except the "natural" expiration of all such prior estates.[1] A future estate is "non-vested" if it is created in

---

§ 3.2

1. "The term 'vested' doubtless originally meant that the owner of the vested estate either had the seisin or was ready to take it immediately on the termination of prior vest-

favor of an unborn or otherwise unidentifiable person and/or its ability to become possessory is subject to an express condition precedent other than the "natural" expiration of all prior estates created by the same transfer.[2]

The only future interests that can be vested are reversions and remainders. Reversions are always vested.[3] Remainders may be either vested or non-vested.[4] Possibilities of reverter, powers of termination, and executory interests are never vested.[5] Possibilities of reverter, powers of termination, and non-vested remainders are always "contingent"—i.e., it is always uncertain at the time of their creation that they will satisfy all the conditions precedent to their becoming either possessory estates or vested future estates.[6] Most executory interests are also "contingent", but it is possible to create an executory interest that is not "contingent"—e.g., where the interest is given to a living, identifiable person, subject to a condition precedent (such as the lapse of time) that is certain to be satisfied.[7]

Future interests in personalty are, in general, subject to the same system of classification as future estates in realty—i.e., they are either "vested" or "non-vested," and the present and "vested" future interests resulting from a transfer must "add up to" the equivalent of a fee simple absolute. As is the case with future interests in realty, almost all "non-vested" future interests in personalty are "contingent"; reversions are always "vested" while possibilities of reverter and powers of termination are

---

ed estates. * * * When contingent remainders and executory interests came to be recognized as interests, they were distinguished from vested estates, in that they could become vested estates only on the happening of some condition precedent or event." 1 Am.L.Prop. 408–409 (per L. Simes).

"Viewed historically, it seems probable that the common-law concept of a vested interest was one which partook of the nature of a present interest. It was a part of the doctrine of the quantum of estates; the notion that every fee simple could be carved up into life estates and remainders in tail and in fee; that all of these parts fitted together like the pieces of a jigsaw puzzle and made one complete whole. The vested estate was a part of this whole; it had present existence even though enjoyment was postponed." 1 L. Simes and A. Smith, Future Interests § 55 (2d ed. 1956).

If we accept the definition of "vested" set out in the text, the executory interest following a fee simple determinable would be "vested" if it is certain to become a possessory fee simple, even though the date when it will become possessory is uncertain. See concurring opinion in Williams v. Watt, 668 P.2d 620 (Wyo.1983). But the *Williams* court held that the future interest in such a case is a *vested remainder* in fee simple rather than an executory interest, which is always deemed to be "contingent" and therefore subject to the Rule Against Perpetuities.

2. Thus the definition of "non-vested" is exactly the opposite of the definition of "vested." Being born or being ascertained is, of course, a kind of implied condition precedent. The condition precedent need not be one that is uncertain to be satisfied, although most non-vested future interests are, in fact, subject to implied or express conditions precedent that are uncertain to be satisfied—in which case, the future interests are usually called "contingent."

3. L. Simes, Future Interests § 18 (2d ed. 1966); 1 L. Simes and A. Smith, Future Interests § 65 (2d ed. 1956). Reversions may be indefeasibly vested or vested subject to complete defeasance. L. Simes, loc. cit. supra; 1 L. Simes and A. Smith, Future Interests § 90 (2d ed. 1956).

4. When remainders are vested, they may be indefeasibly vested, vested subject to complete defeasance, or vested subject to open (i.e., subject to partial defeasance); when remainders are non-vested, they are always "contingent." L. Simes, Future Interests § 11 (2d ed. 1966).

5. L. Simes, Future Interests §§ 12 through 14 (2d ed. 1966). Rest. Prop. § 154 describes a possibility of reverter as a "reversionary interest subject to a condition precedent." Rest.Prop. § 155 uses the term "power of termination" instead of "right of entry for breach of condition."

6. L. Simes, Future Interests §§ 11, 13, 14.

7. Id. § 12. See post Sections 3.11, 3.12.

always "contingent"; remainders may be either "vested" or "contingent," while executory interests are always "non-vested" and usually, though not always, are "contingent."

The distinction between vested and non-vested future estates in land was once extremely important because legal contingent remainders (as distinguished from equitable contingent remainders) were "destructible" in various ways.[8] Moreover, non-vested interests were, at one time, generally held to be inalienable.[9] The rule of "destructibility" has now been almost entirely eliminated and, with minor exceptions, non-vested future interests are alienable if they are held by a living person.[10] But it is still necessary to determine whether a future interest is vested or non-vested in order to decide whether the interest is subject to the Rule Against Perpetuities.[11] In addition, the terms "vested," "non-vested" and "contingent" are still so universally employed by lawyers and courts as to require an understanding of their meaning on the part of those who engage in the practice of estate and trust law.

B. REVERSIONARY FUTURE INTERESTS

§ 3.3   Reversions

A reversion is the future estate left in a transferor or (if the transfer is by will) his successors in interest when he does not transfer his entire estate—i.e., when the possessory estate and all vested future estates created by the transfer add up to an estate of "smaller" quantum than the estate held by the transferor at the time of the transfer.[1] Thus, e.g., if O transfers "to A for life, then to B for life," O retains a reversion in fee simple absolute because the life estates transferred to A and B do not add up to a fee simple absolute. For the same reason, if O transfers "to A for ten years, then to B for ten years," O retains a reversion in fee simple absolute.[2] And in jurisdictions where a fee tail may still be created, a transfer by O to A in fee tail, with a remainder to B in fee tail, would leave O with a reversion in fee simple absolute.

As the foregoing examples make clear, a reversion arises from a transferor's failure to transfer his entire estate, and it is not necessary for the transferor expressly to reserve a reversion. Indeed, a reversion may arise where the expressed intent of the transferor is to transfer his entire estate but part of the attempted transfer is void—e.g., where O's will devises land

---

8. See post Section 3.10.

9. See post Sections 3.23, 3.24.

10. Supra notes 8, 9.

11. See post Sections 3.17, 3.18.

§ 3.3

1. As to reversions generally, see 1 L. Simes and A. Smith, Future Interests §§ 81 through 92 (2d ed. 1956); L. Simes, Future Interests § 10 (2d ed. 1966); 1 Am.L.Prop. §§ 4.16 through 4.24. For purposes of applying this basic rule, all fee simple estates are regarded as having the same "quantum." Thus the owner of a possessory fee simple absolute does not retain a reversion when he

transfers a fee simple determinable, a fee simple subject to a condition subsequent, a fee simple subject to an executory limitation, or a fee simple conditional (where such an estate is recognized), because the estate transferred is not "smaller" than the original estate of the transferor. All fee tail estates (where such an estate is still recognized) are also regarded as having the same "quantum."

2. Although the owner of a freehold estate who had transferred a leasehold estate was in earlier times considered to retain a present estate rather than a reversion, because he retained the seisin, at the present time the transferor is, in such case, said to retain a reversion.

"to A for life, remainder to B" and B predeceases O, in which case the devise to B is void and O retains a reversion in fee simple absolute.[3]

A reversion in fee simple may arise where a transferor creates several successive life estates, or several successive estates for years, or (where fee tail estates may still be created), several successive fee tail estates, without expressly transferring the residue of the fee simple.[4] When all such "prior" estates have expired, the person (or persons) who then owns (or own) the reversion in fee simple will be entitled to possession as a matter of law. The reversioner's right to possession accrues automatically, without the necessity of making an entry, bringing an action for possession, or giving notice of termination.[5]

In all the examples given above, O's reversion is indefeasibly vested, and either O or his successor (or successors) in interest is (are) certain to become entitled to possession at a future time. But a reversion may be vested subject to complete defeasance because the deed or will creates a possessory life estate followed by a contingent remainder or an executory interest, or contains a provision creating a power of appointment. Thus, if O transfers land "to A for life, remainder to B's surviving children," or "to A for life, and then to B one day after A's death if B survives A," or "to A for life, remainder to such of A's children as A shall appoint," O retains a reversion in fee simple subject to complete defeasance.[6]

If we change our standard assumption and assume that O has some kind of defeasible fee simple to begin with, any reversion retained by O will necessarily be subject to the same possibility of defeasance as O's original possessory estate. Division of O's possessory estate into two or more estates will not eliminate the special limitation, condition subsequent, or executory limitation to which that possessory estate was originally subject.

Even if a transferor has only a life estate or a fee tail estate to begin with, a transfer of less than his entire estate will leave him with a reversion.[7] Thus, e.g., if O has a fee tail and he transfers "to A for life, then to B for life," O will retain a reversion in fee tail; and if O has only a life estate and transfers "to A for ten years, then to B for ten years," O will retain a reversion for life because any estate for years—however long its duration—is deemed "smaller" than a life estate. It is immaterial that O

---

3. 1 L. Simes and A. Smith, Future Interests § 87 (2d ed. 1956); L. Simes, Future Interests § 10 (2d ed. 1966); 1 Am.L.Prop. § 4.18.

4. See examples in text supra between notes 1 and 2.

5. This characteristic is shared with the possibility of reverter and the executory interest. It should be contrasted with the power of termination for breach of condition, a reversionary interest retained by one who transfers his entire estate but subjects it to a condition subsequent.

6. 1 L. Simes and A. Smith, Future Interests §§ 85, 86, 90 (2d ed. 1956); 1 Am.L.Prop. § 4.18. For illustrative cases where the reversion was defeasible because the instrument created a contingent remainder, see, e.g., St. George v. Fulton Trust Co., 273 App.Div. 516,

78 N.Y.S.2d 298 (1948); Whitten v. Whitten, 203 Okl. 196, 219 P.2d 228 (1950). As to making the reversion defeasible by means of an executory limitation, see Rest.Prop. § 154, Comment a, Illust. 5; note that, in the example given in the text, the reversion will actually become a possessory estate for one day, after which it may be completely defeated by the executory limitation in favor of B. For an illustrative case where the reversion was defeasible by exercise of the power of appointment, see McCready v. Lyon, 167 Va. 103, 187 S.E. 442 (1936).

7. This is simply another application of the general rule that a transfer that does not exhaust the transferor's estate—i.e., that does not vest in one or more transferees the transferor's entire estate—leaves a reversion in the transferor.

may, in fact, die before the expiration of successive estates for years in which case O's reversion will never become a possessory estate.[8] If O has only an estate for years to begin with, a sublease for a shorter term will also leave him with a reversion.

§ 3.4   Possibilities of Reverter

A possibility of reverter is the reversionary interest left in the owner of a possessory estate who transfers by deed, or by a will that does not dispose of the residual interest, an estate of the quantum initially held by the transferor subject to a special limitation.[1] Possibilities of reverter are most often created when the owner of a fee simple absolute transfers a fee simple determinable without any "gift over."[2] But a possibility of reverter may be created by language creating a fee simple determinable followed by a valid executory interest which does not exhaust the factual possibilities,[3] or followed by an executory interest which is void in its inception.[4] Moreover,

---

8. That O would retain a reversion even though the term of years is in excess of the possible life of any human being, see Earl of Derby v. Taylor, 1 East 502 (K.B.1801). See also Co.Litt. 142b and 143a; 2 Blackstone, Comm. * 175; 1 L. Simes and A. Smith, Future Interests § 83 (2d ed 1956); 1 Am.L.Prop. § 4.18.

§ 3.4

1. Cf. the definition in Rest.Prop. § 154(3): "A possibility of reverter is any reversionary interest which is subject to a condition precedent." This definition is not very useful, since it does not, without more, distinguish a possibility of reverter from a right of entry for breach of condition. It is consistent with the Property Restatement's position that a power of termination (right of entry) for breach of entry is not a "reversionary" interest because "it is regarded as a new creation rather than as a part of the transferor's original interest left in him" (Rest.Prop. § 154, Comment a), but this book treats both the possibility of reverter and the right of entry for breach of condition as reversionary interests. Moreover, the definition in Rest.Prop. § 154(3) does not adequately differentiate the possibility of reverter from a reversion subject to complete defeasance in a case, e.g., where O transfers "to A for life, remainder to B if B survives A, but if B predeceases A, then the land shall revert to O."

2. E.g., O, the owner of Blackacre, transfers it "to A and his heirs so long as the land is used only for residential purposes."

See Emrick v. Bethlehem Tp., 506 Pa. 372, 485 A.2d 736, 739 (1984) ("interest held by the grantor in a fee simple determinable is identified as a *possibility of reverter*").

3. E.g., O, the owner of Blackacre, transfers it "to A and his heirs so long as it is used only for residential purposes, but if it shall be used for non-residential purposes during A's lifetime, then to B and his heirs." B's execu-

tory interest is valid, but it will fail if Blackacre is used only for residential purposes during A's lifetime and O will retain a possibility of reverter that may become a possessory fee simple absolute if Blackacre is used for non-residential purposes after A's death. O could, of course, create a fee simple subject to a special limitation designating one terminating event and an executory limitation designating a different terminating event. E.g., O might transfer Blackacre "to A and his heirs so long as the land is used only for residential purposes, but if A should die without issue him surviving, then to B and his heirs." In the latter case, O retains a possibility of reverter contingent on one event, and B receives an executory interest contingent upon another event. Generally, see 1 Am.L.Prop. § 4.14; Rest.Prop. § 23, Comment e.

In a state where a fee simple conditional may still be created—e.g., South Carolina—the owner of a fee simple estate who creates a fee simple conditional in a grantee is left with a possibility of reverter. In such a case, of course, the owner of the fee simple conditional has the power, after birth of issue, to convey the land in fee simple absolute and thus extinguish the possibility of reverter. E.g., McDaniel v. Connor, 206 S.C. 96, 33 S.E.2d 75 (1945).

4. E.g., if O purports to transfer Blackacre "to A and his heirs so long as the land is used only for residential purposes, and if the land is ever used for non-residential purposes, then to B and his heirs," the executory interest limited in favor of B is void under the Rule Against Perpetuities and O therefore retains a possibility of reverter, which is not subject to the Rule. In support of this proposition, see, e.g., Institution for Savings v. Roxbury Home for Aged Women, 244 Mass. 583, 139 N.E. 301 (1923); Leonard v. Burr, 18 N.Y. 96 (1858).

A possibility of reverter may also be created without the use of any express language when

if the owner of a life estate transfers it subject to a special limitation, he will retain a possibility of reverter for the balance of his life; and if a tenant for years transfers his entire leasehold estate subject to a special limitation, he will retain a possibility of reverter for the balance of the lease term.

Suppose the owner of a possessory estate transfers a "smaller" estate subject to a special limitation—e.g., the owner of a fee simple estate, O, transfers land "to A for life, so long as the land is used only for residential purposes." Clearly A receives a life estate determinable and O retains a reversion in fee simple absolute. Does O also retain a possibility of reverter? The prevailing view is that he does not because, by definition, the future estate retained by a transferor is a reversion when the quantum of all present and vested future estates expressly created by a transfer, when added together, is less than the quantum of the transferor's original estate.[5] But even if the transferor does not have a possibility of reverter in such a case, it is obviously possible that the right to possession as owner in fee simple absolute may "revert" to the transferor before the death of the life tenant.

For the reasons set out in the preceding paragraph, the future estate retained by a lessor who owns land in fee simple or for life is simply called a reversion when he leases it for a term of years subject to a special limitation, although it is obviously possible that he may again become entitled to possession as owner in fee simple or for life before the lease term expires.

Although a deed or will often contains an express provision for "reverter" to the transferor or his successors in interest upon the happening of the specially designated terminating event, the possibility of reverter arises by operation of law whenever the transferee receives an estate subject to a special limitation.[6] If the transfer is by deed, the grantor retains the possibility of reverter; if the transfer is by will and the will does not dispose of the testator's residual interest, the testator's heirs receive a possibility of reverter by intestate succession. But if the transfer is by will and the will also disposes of the testator's residual interest either by specific devise or (by the better view) by residuary devise, the devisee of the residual interest receives an executory interest rather than a possibility of reverter.[7]

a land developer makes a statutory dedication of land to a public use. Town of Moorcroft v. Lang, 779 P.2d 1180 (Wyo.1989).

5. See ante Section 3.3.

6. E.g., Elmore v. Austin, 232 N.C. 13, 59 S.E.2d 205 (1950).

7. This is true because a will only operates once, immediately upon the testator's death; it does not operate once to create a fee simple determinable, and then a second time to dispose of the residual interest of the testator. Cf. Brown v. Independent Baptist Church of Woburn, 325 Mass. 645, 91 N.E.2d 922 (1950), holding that, where a specific executory devise was void under the Rule Against Perpetuities, a residuary devise to the same beneficiaries was valid because it transferred a possibility of reverter rather than an executory interest! For telling criticism of the *Brown* decision, see Simes, Is the Rule Against Perpetuities

Doomed, 52 Mich.L.Rev. 179 n. 4 (1953) ("Of course, under orthodox doctrines, the residuary clause created a void executory interest as well as the prior gift over. For it was created by the same instrument by which the determinable fee was created. The testatrix did not first create a determinable fee and then devise it, for she did not die twice."). Cf. Leach, Perpetuities in Perspective: Ending the Reign of Terror, 65 Harv.L.Rev. 720, 743 ("Thus, it seems, a person can by will create a determinable fee without time limit and also dispose of the future interest which takes effect at the end of the fee, *provided* the disposition is made in the residuary clause, not in the clause creating the determinable fee. This particular cherry can be eaten only in two bites; public policy is affronted by the attempt to eat it in one."). For fuller discussion of the *Brown* case, see Leach, supra, at 741–745.

Since possibilities of reverter expectant upon a fee simple estate in land (or equivalent interest in personalty) are not subject to the common law Rule Against Perpetuities, their potential duration is infinite. That is, the event upon which they are to become possessory estates may be one that is not certain to occur and which might occur at any time in the future, however remote.[8] But some states have legislation limiting the period during which a fee simple estate in land (or equivalent interest in personalty) may be made defeasible by a special limitation. Legislation of this type extinguishes a possibility of reverter and makes the possessory fee simple estate (or equivalent interest in personalty) indefeasible when the statutorily prescribed maximum period has expired.[9] Another type of statute provides that special limitations and conditions subsequent shall be disregarded if they become merely nominal and are no longer of any substantial benefit to the persons otherwise entitled to enforce such special limitations or conditions subsequent. Statutes of this type extinguish a possibility of reverter when and if a court, in litigation involving the continuing effect of a special limitation giving rise to a possibility of reverter, determines that the special limitation has become "merely nominal."[10] In most cases, such a determination will be made when there is a showing that changed conditions make it difficult or impossible to achieve the purpose for which the special limitation was originally imposed—for example, where land is transferred "to A so long as the land is used only for residential purposes" and subsequently the area surrounding the land in question is wholly developed for commercial or industrial uses.

§ 3.5   Powers of Termination

As we have already seen, whenever the owner of an estate in land made an *inter vivos* conveyance of that estate subject to a stated condition subsequent, the English common law courts held that the grantor retained a right of entry for breach of that condition even though the conveyance did not contain an express provision for reentry upon breach.[1] But in the United States it is generally necessary to include an express provision giving the grantor a right of entry or power to terminate upon breach of the condition in order to create an estate on condition subsequent, since American courts are prone to hold that words of condition, standing alone, create a "real covenant," "equitable servitude," "easement," "charge," or "trust" rather than a true condition subsequent.[2]

Although the English common law term for the interest retained by the grantor after conveyance of an estate subject to a condition subsequent is "right of entry for breach of condition," it has long been recognized that no

---

8. See post Section 3.21. It has often been said that possibilities of reverter are not subject to the Rule against Perpetuities because they are "vested," but this is obviously not true. See 2 Rest. Prop. § 154(3), supra note 1. See also L. Simes, Future Interests 29 (2d ed. 1966) ("it is difficult to see how an interest described as a 'possibility' could be vested"); Leach, supra note 7, at 740–741.

9. E.g., West's Fla.Stat.Ann. § 689.18 (21 years; thereafter, use restrictions can be enforced only as covenants or equitable servi-tudes); Conn.Gen.Stat.Ann. § 45–97 (30 years unless contingency is certain to be resolved within the period allowed by the rule against perpetuities); Me.Rev.Stat.Ann. tit. 33, § 103 (same); Ill.—S.H.A. ch. 30, ¶ 37e (40 years); Mass.Gen.Laws Ann. c. 184A, § 3 (30 years).

10. E.g., Mich.Comp.Laws Ann. § 544.46.

§ 3.5

1. Ante Section 2.5 at note 5.

2. Id. at notes 6–11.

formal entry is necessary and that bringing an action of ejectment is an appropriate method of electing to terminate the possessory estate.[3] Since the term "right of entry for breach of condition" is not appropriate to designate the interest retained by the grantor when he transfers an interest in personalty subject to a condition subsequent[4] and since the grantor's retained interest, strictly speaking, is a power rather than a right,[5] the term "power of termination" rather than the term "right of entry for breach of condition" will be used in this textbook.[6]

As has previously been indicated, a power of termination may be created by a transfer creating a fee simple, life estate, or leasehold estate subject to a condition subsequent, with an express provision giving the grantor (or successors in interest) a right to re-enter or power to terminate if a breach occurs.[7] Leases typically contain a number of covenants binding the lessee and expressly providing that, upon breach of any of these covenants, the lessor may "re-enter," or "terminate the lease," or "forfeit the lease."[8] Any of these phrases, or equivalent language, will create a power of termination in the lessor. When the owner of land in fee simple creates a life estate or a leasehold estate subject to a condition subsequent, the common law rule is that the grantor retains both a reversion and a power of termination for breach of the condition. In such cases, it is good practice to provide expressly for a power of termination on breach of the condition, although it may not be absolutely necessary.

Like possibilities of reverter, powers of termination are not subject to the common law Rule Against Perpetuities.[9] But, like possibilities of reverter, they are subject in some states to statutes limiting their duration,[10] and in other states they are subject to statutes extinguishing them when the

---

3. E.g., McElvain v. Dorris, 298 Ill. 377, 131 N.E. 608 (1921); Union College v. New York, 173 N.Y. 38, 65 N.E. 853, 93 Am.St.Rep. 569 (1903). Even a suit to quiet title may be sufficient. See Ross v. Sanderson, 63 Okl. 73, 162 P. 709, L.R.A.1917C 879 (1917). Some courts have required an election—usually by giving notice to the owner of the possessory estate—before ejectment is brought. E.g., Weber v. Ford Motor Co., 245 Mich. 213, 222 N.W. 198 (1928); Mash v. Bloom, 133 Wis. 646, 114 N.W. 457, 14 L.R.A.(N.S.) 1187 (1907).

4. The term "entry" is obviously inapplicable to personalty. It is also inapplicable to equitable estates in land subject to a trust except in cases where the trust beneficiary has possession of the land.

5. See discussion of the Hohfeldian analysis of property ante Section 1.2.

6. Rest.Prop. § 155, adopts the term "power of termination." See also id. § 24, Comment b, Special Note. L. Simes, Future Interests § 14 (2d ed. 1966) also adopts the term "power of termination." But L. Simes and A. Smith, Future Interests (2d ed. 1956), retains the older term, "right of entry for breach of condition."

7. Ante Sections 2.5, 2.11, 2.18.

8. Ante Section 2.18.

9. See post Section 3.21. Exemption of powers of termination from the rule against perpetuities is, if anything, less justified than the exemption of possibilities of reverter since powers of termination are even more clear contingent interests. See ante Section 3.4, note 8.

Rest.Prop. § 394, Comment c (1944) states that if the language of a conveyance may reasonably be construed either to create (1) a possibility of reverter or (2) a power of termination or (3) an option in the grantor to repurchase, the option to repurchase construction is preferred; that the fact that the grantor must make a money payment in order to get the land back is sufficiently indicative of the grantor's intent to create a repurchase option; and that the repurchase option construction "furthers the protective policy which underlies the rule against perpetuities, and is in accord with the general constructional preference for covenants rather than conditions." Cf. Rest.Prop. § 401 (1944), which states that a transaction which is "exclusively contractual" is not subject to the Rule Against Perpetuities.

10. See ante Section 3.4, note 9, for examples of such statutes, which apply both to possibilities of reverter and to powers of termination.

conditions upon which they are limited become merely nominal and are no longer of any substantial benefit to the persons otherwise entitled to enforce them.[11]

C. NON–REVERSIONARY FUTURE INTERESTS

§ 3.6 Non-reversionary Future Interests—Remainders and Executory Interests

Future interests created in (or in favor of) transferees are classified as non-reversionary. There are two categories of non-reversionary interests: (1) remainders[1] and (2) executory interests.[2]

A non-reversionary interest is a remainder if (a) it is created simultaneously with a present estate smaller than a fee simple—the "particular estate"; and (b) it is possible for the future interest to become a present estate as soon as all the prior interests created by the transfer have expired.[3] Thus, e.g., the interest given to B in all of the following cases is a remainder:

(1) "to A for life, then to B" (or "remainder to B");

(2) "to A for life, then to B for life" (or "remainder to B for life");

(3) "to A for life, then to B for life, then to C" (or "remainder to B for life, remainder to C").[4]

By way of contrast, an executory interest (a) need not be created simultaneously with a present estate (although it is often so created); and (b), as a general rule, will become either a present or a vested future interest automatically upon the defeasance of a present estate or a vested remainder by the operation of an executory limitation.[5] Thus, e.g., B would obtain an executory interest as a result of any of the following transfers:

11. E.g., Mich.Comp.Laws Ann. § 544.46 (applicable to both possibilities of reverter and powers of termination).

§ 3.6

1. The term "remainder" is said to be derived from the Latin word "remanere," signifying that the land was to "remain out" instead of "coming back" to the transferor as it does when a reversion becomes a possessory estate. 2 Pollock and Maitland, History of English Law 21 (2d ed. 1911).

2. The term "executory interest" has reference to the effect of the Statute of Uses (1536) in converting ("executing") equitable estates ("uses") into legal estates. See ante Section 2.8 notes 4–6.

3. Another way to state this requirement is to say that a remainder must wait patiently for the expiration of all preceding interests created at the same time, and that it may not become a present interest as a result of the defeasance of some preceding interest. Compare the definition in 2 Rest.Prop. § 156.

4. As the examples in the text indicate, it is not necessary to use the word "remainder" to create a remainder, although it is common practice to do so. On the other hand, interests termed "remainders" in a deed or will may, in fact, be executory interests.

5. " * * * with the exception of the executory interest after the determinable fee and the fee simple conditional, it [an executory interest] vests in derogation of a vested freehold estate and not at the termination of a freehold estate," and "on the happening of the condition or event, it may become a present interest automatically; no entry or election being necessary." L. Simes and A. Smith, Future Interests § 222 (2d ed. 1956). The exception stated—the executory interest after a determinable fee or a fee simple conditional—has a purely historical basis: the traditional common law rule that a fee simple could not be "limited on a fee simple by way of remainder." For a modern statement of the exception, see the 2 Rest.Prop. § 156(2) (defining "remainder"). Of course, the executory interest following a fee simple determinable is considered an exception only because a fee simple determinable is deemed to "expire" by virtue of its special limitation rather than being "cut-off" prior to its normal expiration. For a good discussion of the difference between "limitational defeasance" and "conditional defeasance," see L. Waggoner, Future Interests in a Nutshell § 4.2 (1981).

(4) "to A, but if A dies without children him surviving, then to B"; [6]

(5) "to B, from and after B's marriage to A"; [7]

(6) "to A for life, then to B one year after A's death." [8]

In each of these examples, all the language following the initial language of gift to A or B is an "executory limitation."

The "particular" estate which always precedes a remainder is usually a life estate,[9] but it can be a fee tail (where still recognized) [10] or an estate for years; [11] and the particular estate can be subject to a special limitation that may cause it to terminate before it would normally expire.[12] On the other hand, the estate which is defeated by an executory limitation and displaced by an executory interest may be either (1) a present fee simple estate created in a transferee,[13] or (2) a present fee simple estate retained by the grantor,[14] (3) a reversion in fee simple retained by the grantor,[15] or (4) an estate less than a fee simple.[16] Moreover, for purely historical reasons, any non-reversionary future interest following a fee simple determinable or a fee simple conditional is classified as an executory interest.[17]

Remainders and executory interests are most often in fee simple,[18] but they can be in fee tail (where still recognized) [19] or for life.[20] Strictly

---

6. In example (4), A's death without children him surviving is a condition subsequent as to A's present fee simple and a condition precedent as to B's executory interest. If the event specified in the condition occurs, the present fee simple estate "shifts" from A to B; hence B's interest is called a "shifting" executory interest.

7. In example (5), the present fee simple remains in the transferor unless and until B marries A. B's marriage to A is a condition subsequent as to the transferor's present fee simple and a condition precedent as to B's executory interest, which is called a "springing" executory interest because it "springs out of" the transferor's estate if and when the event specified in the condition occurs.

8. In example (6), the transferor's reversion in fee simple will necessarily become a present estate when A dies, but one year later the present fee simple will pass to B, who has a "springing" executory interest.

9. See examples (1), (2) and (3) in text, supra.

10. E.g., "to A and the heirs of his body, remainder to B."

11. E.g., "to A for ten years, remainder to B." In earlier times, such a transfer would have been said to give B a "present" estate subject to a term of years in A because the seisin would pass at once to B. Today, however, B would generally be said to have a remainder. See 2 Rest.Prop. § 156, Illust. 9.

12. E.g., "to A for life or until remarriage, remainder to B."

13. See example (4) in text and note 6, supra.

14. See example (5) in text and note 7, supra.

15. See example (6) in text and note 8, supra.

16. E.g., "to A for life, but if A remarries, then to B." This gives A a life estate subject to an executory limitation and gives B a shifting executory interest in fee simple. The transferor may, of course, create both a remainder and an executory interest in B. E.g., "to A for life, remainder to B, but if A remarries, then immediately to B."

17. See supra note 5.

But see Williams v. Watt, 668 P.2d 620 (Wyo.1983) (such future interest held to be vested remainder because it was certain to become possessory, although the time when it would become possessory was uncertain—a holding obviously based on the court's unwillingness to find that the future interest was an executory interest which, under the traditional view, was void under the Rule Against Perpetuities)

18. See examples (1), (3), (4), (5), and (6) ante in text.

19. " * * * to A for life, remainder to A and the heirs of his body" (remainder in fee tail); "to A, but if B dies without children him surviving, then to B and the heirs of his body" (executory interest in fee tail).

20. E.g., "to A for life, remainder to B for life" (remainder for life); "to A, but if A dies

speaking, neither remainders nor executory interests in land may be created for a term of years only,[21] but a term of years with the essential characteristics of a remainder or an executory interest can be created.[22]

As subsequent sections of this book will develop in more detail, remainders may be either "vested" or "contingent," and "vested" remainders may be further subdivided into remainders that are "indefeasibly vested," "vested subject to complete defeasance," and "vested subject to open." [23] Executory interests, however, are never deemed to be "vested." [24] Usually they are "contingent"—i.e., subject to a condition precedent not certain to be fulfilled [25]—but an executory interest may be subject to a condition precedent which is certain to be fulfilled, in which case it is neither "vested" nor "contingent." [26]

There is no theoretical limit to the number of remainders that may be simultaneously created, so long as the particular estate and all the vested remainders do not "add up" to more than a fee simple absolute (or equivalent interest in personalty).[27] Nor is there any theoretical limit to the number of executory interests that may be simultaneously created, other than human ingenuity in devising conditions precedent upon which alternative executory interests may be made dependent.

The requirement that a particular estate and all remainders dependent thereon must be created simultaneously is satisfied if they are created by the same deed or will, or by two deeds delivered simultaneously, or by a will and a codicil thereto.[28]

Prior to 1536, remainders were the only non-reversionary future interests recognized and protected by the English common law courts.[29] But

without children him surviving, then to B for life" (executory interest for life).

21. This because a term of years, technically is personal property—a "chattel real"—and the owner of an estate for years cannot have "seisin."

22. E.g., "to A for ten years, then to B for ten years," or "to A for life, then to B for ten years." In both cases, the term of years given to B is similar to a remainder. On the other hand, if O transfers "to A for life, but if A remarries, then to B for ten years," B obtains a term of years that is similar to an executory interest.

23. See post Sections 3.8 through 3.10.

24. "Historically, the concept of 'vestedness' had application only to the future interests evolved by the common law processes as distinguished from the Chancery practice in uses * * *. Hence, for historical reasons, executory interests are not thought of as having degrees of 'vestedness,' and the classification of remainders * * * [as to the degree of vestedness] has no exact application to executory interests. Nevertheless, executory interests differ both in the certainty of ascertainment of the ultimate holder of a present interest thereunder and also in the probability that the interest will become a present interest." 2 Rest.Prop. § 158, Comment b.

25. Most executory interests, in fact, are "contingent."

26. E.g., "to A for life, and then to B one year after A's death," in which case B's springing executory interest is certain to become a present estate.

27. O might transfer "to A for life, remainder to B for life, remainder to C for life, remainder to D if D shall survive A, B and C, but if D shall not survive A, B and C, then to E." In that case, A, B, and C would all have vested remainders for life, while D and E would have alternative contingent remainders in fee simple. Since only "vested" remainders can be "counted" as "parts" of the fee simple absolute, O would retain a reversion in fee simple subject to complete defeasance. Theoretically, there can be any number of alternative contingent remainders in fee simple; but there can be only one vested remainder in fee simple.

28. The will and the codicil would become legally operative simultaneously upon the testator's death.

29. This was because limitational and conditional defeasance provisions in favor of "strangers"—i.e., persons other than the transferor and his heirs—were not valid at common law. See examples (4) through (6)

equitable executory interests (then called "uses") were recognized and protected by the Court of Chancery during the fifteenth century,[30] and they came to be recognized and protected by the common law courts after enactment of the Statute of Uses in 1536.[31] In the United States, executory interests have always been recognized and protected both "in equity" and "at law." [32]

§ 3.7 Remainders Indefeasibly Vested and Vested Subject to Complete Defeasance

An indefeasibly vested remainder is a remainder which is (1) not subject to any express or implied condition precedent, and (2) is not subject to any condition subsequent, special limitation, executory limitation, or power of appointment that may cause the remainder to be completely or partially defeated (i.e., "prematurely terminated") either before or after it becomes a present estate.[1] A remainder not subject to a condition precedent,[2] but subject to a condition subsequent, special limitation, executory limitation, or power of appointment that may cause the remainder to be completely defeated, is vested subject to complete defeasance.

In the following cases, the final limitation clearly creates an indefeasibly vested remainder in the last taker: [3]

(1) "to A for life, remainder to B."

(2) "to A for life, remainder to B for life, remainder to C."

(3) "to A for twenty-five years, remainder to B."

In earlier times B's interest in example (3) would have been classified as a present fee simple subject to a term of years if created in land, but in

ante in text at notes 6–8. In example (4), prior to 1536, the common law courts held the limitation to B void because it was repugnant to the initial limitation to A. In example (5), it was held that a present "livery of seisin," essential for transfer of a freehold estate, could not operate *in futuro*, and hence that the attempted gift to B was void. In example (6), it was held that the seisin would revert to the transferor upon A's death, and that it could not pass to B without a new "livery of seisin."

30. Ante Section 2.8 note 4.

31. Ante Section 2.8 notes 5, 6.

32. Ante Section 2.8 note 7. "Equitable" executory interests may still be created when the legal title to property is transferred to a trustee for the benefit of designated present and future beneficiaries.

§ 3.7

1. Technically, it can be argued that "premature" termination before the vested remainder becomes a present interest should be termed "divestment," and "premature" termination after it becomes a present interest should be termed "defeasance." But courts seem to use the two terms as synonyms. 2

Rest.Prop. § 157, and L. Simes and A. Smith, Future Interests § 113 (2d ed. 1956), both use the term "defeasance" to include "premature" termination either before or after the remainder becomes a present interest.

2. Contingent remainders are discussed in more detail post Sections 3.9, 3.10, and 3.13.

If the remainder is subject to a condition precedent to its becoming "vested in interest" it is "contingent," but when a remainder is limited to a living person (or persons) "at the death of" a life tenant, the words "at the death of" the life tenant refer to the time when the remainder is to become possessory rather than the time when it "vests in interest," and the remainder is immediately vested rather then being contingent upon the remainderman's surviving the life tenant. McGill v. Johnson, 799 S.W.2d 673 (Tex.1990). There is also a strong preference for construing doubtful language as creating a vested rather than a contingent remainder. *McGill,* supra. Contingent remainders are discussed in more detail post Sections 3.9, 3.10, and 3.13.

3. In each of these cases, the transfer "exhausts" the transferor's property interest because the present and vested future interests created by the transfer "add up" to a fee

modern times B's interest is generally classified as a remainder.[4]

In the following cases, the interest given to B is clearly a remainder vested subject to complete defeasance.[5]

(4) "to A for life, remainder to B, but if the land shall ever be put to non-residential use, the grantor or his heirs may re-enter and terminate the interests hereby created."

(5) "to A for life, remainder to B, so long as the land shall be put to residential use only."

(6) "to A, remainder to B, but if B shall predecease A, then to C."

(7) "to A for life, remainder as A shall appoint, and in default of appointment to B."

In examples (4) through (6), respectively, the remainders are vested subject to complete defeasance by a condition subsequent, a special limitation, and an executory limitation. In example (7), the strong constructional preference for vested interests leads courts to hold that B's remainder, though apparently subject to a condition precedent, is vested subject to complete defeasance by A's exercise of the power of appointment.[6]

The Property Restatement asserts that vested remainders "so created as to be capable of expiration before the interests including a prior right to a present interest end"—i.e., before all prior interests created by the transfer terminate—should be classified as "remainders subject to complete defeasance."[7] If this assertion is logically applied, only a remainder in fee simple absolute should be classified as indefeasibly vested;[8] vested remainders for life or in fee tail (where still recognized) would be vested subject to complete defeasance because they may "expire" before all prior interests created by the transfer terminate. Yet the Property Restatement further asserts that a remainder in fee tail (where still recognized) may be indefeasibly vested since "[t]he element of uncertainty, present because * * * the remainderman and his issue may become extinct before the preceding interests end, is nullified" by the remainderman's power to make a disentailing conveyance in fee simple absolute.[9] But a remainderman in fee tail has the power to make a disentailing conveyance only in Delaware; in Maine, Massachusetts, and Rhode Island, therefore, it appears that vested remainders in fee tail would always be subject to complete defeasance even under the rule laid down in the Property Restatement.[10]

simple absolute (or equivalent interest in personalty).

4. See discussion in L. Simes and A. Smith, Future Interests § 116 (2d ed. 1956). See also 2 Rest.Prop. § 156, Illust. 9.

5. The comment supra note 3 is equally applicable here.

6. See L. Simes and A. Smith, Future Interests § 150 (2d ed. 1956).

7. 2 Rest.Prop. § 157, Comment p. Accord: Id. § 157, Comment f; L. Simes and A. Smith, Future Interests § 113 (2d ed. 1956).

8. Under the Property Restatement's test, even a remainder in fee simple absolute could not be indefeasibly vested unless the state, taking by "escheat" upon the death of the owner intestate, is considered to take as "ultimate heir" of the decedent, since the owner of a remainder in fee simple may die intestate and without any common law "heirs" or next of kin before the termination of all prior interests created by the same instrument.

9. 2 Rest.Prop. § 157, Comment k (also asserting that a remainder in fee simple conditional may be indefeasibly vested).

10. See L. Simes and A. Smith, Future Interests § 113 n. 54, for critical comment on the Property Restatement's creation of an exception to its general classification in the case of remainders in fee tail. In any case, a

Whether vested remainders for life or in fee tail are classified as indefeasibly vested or vested subject to complete defeasance is not really of great importance.[11] It is important to note, however, that a remainder cannot be indefeasibly vested unless it is created in favor of a person or a group of persons not capable of enlargement. If a vested remainder is created in favor of a group of persons capable of enlargement, the remainder interest of any existing member of the group is subject to partial defeasance in favor of future members of the group. In such case, the remainder is said to be "vested subject to open." [12]

In modern times, vested remainders subject to conditions subsequent or to special limitations are probably still used on occasion in connection with gifts in remainder to religious, charitable, and educational institutions. Vested remainders subject to executory limitations or to powers of appointment, on the other hand continue in frequent use to control the transmission of family wealth from generation to generation.

Indefeasibly vested remainders and remainders vested subject to complete defeasance are freely alienable either by deed [13] or by will,[14] and they will pass to heirs or next-of-kin of the remainderman by intestate succession if he does not alienate by deed or by will.[15] And since all such vested remainders are alienable by deed, they are liable to seizure and sale to satisfy creditors' claims.[16] But a remainder vested subject to complete defeasance retains its character as a defeasible estate no matter how often it is transferred by deed or will or by intestate succession or by sale for the satisfaction of creditors' claims.

§ 3.8 Remainders Vested Subject to Open

A remainder is classified as vested subject to open (or subject to partial defeasance) when it is created in favor of a class that may increase in numbers and at least one member of the class has already satisfied the requirements for having a vested interest—i.e., is living and identifiable, and has an interest that is not subject to any condition precedent to its becoming a present interest other than the expiration of all prior interests created by the same transfer.[1] Thus, if O makes a transfer "to A for life, remainder to

---

vested remainder in fee simple limited after an estate in fee tail or fee simple conditional is vested subject to complete defeasance because the owner of the preceding estate has the power to convert it into a fee simple absolute by making a disentailing conveyance, thus extinguishing the remainder. L. Simes and A. Smith, Future Interests § 113 at n. 57 (2d ed. 1956).

11. Estates in fee tail or fee simple conditional, whether present or future, are recognized only in only a few states, and are rarely created even in those states. Remainders for life not subject to an express condition precedent are simply termed "vested remainders for life" by the courts, without further qualification, because it really makes no practical difference whether they are classified as indefeasibly vested or vested subject to complete defeasance.

12. For discussion of such remainders, see post Section 3.9.

13. L. Simes and A. Smith, Future Interests § 1856 (2d ed. 1956) and cases cited.

14. Id. § 1902 and cases cited.

15. Id. § 1883 and cases cited.

16. L. Simes and A. Smith, Future Interests ch. 56 (2d ed. 1956).

For a recent case, see Edwards v. Bradley, 227 Va. 224, 315 S.E.2d 196 (1984) (life estate subject to special limitation—called "conditional limitation" by the court).

§ 3.8

1. Generally, see L. Simes and A. Smith, Future Interests § 114 (2d ed. 1956); L. Simes, Future Interests 20–21 (2d ed. 1966); 2 Rest. Prop. § 157, Comments *l* and m.

the children of A," and A has one child, B, at the time of transfer, B receives a vested remainder in fee simple subject to open.[2]

Whenever an additional member of the designated class of remaindermen[3] acquires a vested interest in the remainder, the interests of all remaindermen whose interests have already vested are partially defeated—i.e., reduced in size.

In the preceding example, if a second child, C is born to A, C will obtain an undivided one-half interest in the vested remainder and B's interest would be reduced to an undivided one-half. The birth of additional children to A will correspondingly reduce the undivided interests of all children previously born. Since the remainder is in fee simple (or an equivalent interest in personalty) and the interests of A's children are not subject to any express condition that they must survive A, the interest of any child who predeceases A will not be defeated but will pass to the deceased child's heir unless he has transferred his interest by deed or by will.[4]

Since the interest of a person like B in the example given above, though vested, is subject to partial defeasance in favor of afterborn children of A, a person in B's position will want to know the duration of the period within which the designated class of remaindermen ("children of A") can increase in membership—or, as courts more frequently put it, when the membership of the designated class will "close."[5] In the example given above, the answer is easy: the time when the designated class of remaindermen will become incapable of increase is biologically determined. The class is sure to "close" at A's death or, if A is a male, within the period of gestation thereafter (since A's wife may be pregnant at A's death).[6]

Suppose, however, that O makes a transfer "to A for life, remainder to the children of B," a living person. In such a case, the courts generally apply a so-called "rule of convenience": in the absence of an expression of contrary intent by O, the class will close when any member of the class is entitled to immediate possession or enjoyment of his undivided interest in the property transferred. In the example just given, therefore, the class will close at A's death, which is the time when the children of B—if any—are entitled to possession or enjoyment of the property.[7]

2. Cases of this kind are numerous, e.g., Stearns v. Curry, 306 Ill. 94, 137 N.E. 471 (1922); Yeaton v. Roberts, 28 N.H. 459 (1854); In re Brown, 154 N.Y. 313, 48 N.E. 537 (1897); Blanchard v. Ward, 244 N.C. 142, 92 S.E.2d 776 (1956); Mullins v. Simmons, 235 Va. 194, 365 S.E.2d 771 (1988).

3. The class generally, though not always, consists of the "children" or "grandchildren" of a named person.

4. A vested remainder subject to open is inheritable and is freely transferable by deed or by will. See post Sections 3.23, 3.24.

5. Generally, see Rest.Prop. Ch. 22, Topic 3; L. Simes and A. Smith, Future Interests §§ 632–651 (2d ed. 1956); 3 Powell, Real Property ¶¶ 362–364.

6. "In the absence of indications of a contrary intent in [the deed or] will children begotten but not born at the time when the class closes will be included in the class if subsequently born. This is in accord with the doctrine generally recognized in the law that, if it is beneficial to the child, a child begotten but not born is, for most purposes, treated as in being." L. Simes and A. Smith, Future Interests § 650 (2d ed. 1956).

7. This rule is sometimes said to be a rule of construction, designed to carry out the transferor's probable intent when he fails to express any specific intent on the question. But as the term "rule of convenience" implies, the rule is also based on considerations of expediency and policy, and its application may sometimes result in defeating the transferor's probable general intent to benefit as many potential class members as possible.

The "rule of convenience" has a number of advantages: it eliminates the potential claims of persons who may be born after the time when the class closes and tends to make the property more marketable by identifying, as of that time, all the persons who may ultimately acquire present interests in the property,[8] and when personalty is transferred, the rule allows immediate distribution of at least a minimum share to those persons who are entitled to possession or enjoyment when the class closes.

Suppose that O makes a transfer "to A for life, remainder to the children of A who attain the age of 21 years," and that A dies leaving one child who is over 21 and six children who are under 21. In such a case, the rule of convenience does not require exclusion of the six children who are under 21 at A's death, since the maximum class membership is determined at A's death.[9] If the subject matter is realty, the eldest child will take a present estate in fee simple subject to partial defeasance in favor of other children of A who may later attain the age of 21 (unless the interests of children who are under 21 at A's death are classified as contingent remainders which have failed to vest prior to termination of A's life estate).[10] If the subject matter is personalty, the eldest child is immediately entitled to one-seventh of the property (if it is divisible), and each additional child to reach 21 will be entitled to an equal share. If any child of A should later die without reaching 21, the shares of all the other children would be proportionately enlarged.

When would the class of remaindermen "close" if O makes a transfer "to A for life, remainder to the children of B who attain the age of 21 years"? In such a case, the class will "close" only when two events have occurred: (1) A has died, and (2) at least one child of B has reached 21.[11] Thus no child of B will be excluded from the class if he is born (or conceived) before the occurrence of both events; any child of B will be included in the class if he is born (or conceived) either before B's death but after at least one child of B has reached 21, or after B's death but before any child of reaches 21.

In the last case considered, there is, of course, no vested remainder at all unless at least one child of B has reached the age of 21 before A's life interest terminates.[12] If no child of B has reached the age of 21 by that time, the owner of the reversion will be entitled to possession, but his present interest will be subject to complete defeasance throughout B's lifetime unless the subject matter is land and the doctrine of destructibility of contingent remainders is still in force.[13] In most jurisdictions, of course, the destructi-

---

8. Generally, see L. Simes and A. Smith, Future Interests § 640 (2d ed. 1956) (also pointing out that if B were still alive but had no children at A's death, the class would be held open until B's death, despite the inconvenience attending such a result).

9. Since the maximum class membership is determined, the minimum share of each member of the class is determined; and in the case of land, the persons who must join in a conveyance in order to convey a marketable title are determined. See L. Simes and A. Smith, Future Interests § 654 (2d ed. 1956); R. Powell, Real Property ¶ 364.

10. As to classification of the contingent interests of such children, see post Section 3.13. As to the status of the rule that contingent remainders are destroyed by failure to vest before the termination of all supporting life estates, see post Section 3.10.

11. Simes and Smith, Future Interests § 645 (2d ed. 1956); R. Powell, Real Property ¶ 363.

12. The remainder is necessarily still contingent in such a case.

13. See post Section 3.10.

bility rule has been abolished, and it is apparently not applicable to personalty in any jurisdiction.[14]

A remainder may, of course, be vested subject both to open and to complete defeasance.[15]

§ 3.9 Contingent Remainders—In General

A remainder is "contingent" if it is (a) created in favor of unborn or otherwise unidentifiable persons and/or (b) is subject to an express condition precedent—other than the expiration of all prior interests created by the same transfer—that must be satisfied before the remainder can become a present interest.[1] Thus, e.g., all the remainders created by the following transfers are clearly contingent.

(1) "to A for life, remainder to the children of A" (assuming that A has no children).

(2) "to A for life, remainder to the heirs of B."

(3) "to A for life, remainder to the heirs of A."

(4) "to A for life, remainder to B if B reaches the age of 21" (assuming that B is under 21).

(5) "to A for life, remainder to B if B survives A."

(6) "to A for life, remainder to those children of A who reach the age of 21" (assuming no child of A has yet reached 21).

(7) "to A for life, remainder to those children of A who shall survive A."

In examples (1) and (2), above, the remainders are clearly contingent because they are created in favor of unborn or otherwise unidentifiable persons.[2] The same conclusion would probably be reached as to example (3) everywhere except New York,[3] where, from an early date, a statute has provided that a remainder is vested "when there is a person in being, who

---

14. Ibid.

15. Such a remainder is termed simply "a remainder subject to complete defeasance" in 2 Rest.Prop. § 157, Comment c, on the ground that it lacks one essential element of a remainder vested subject to open—the certainty that the remainder will actually become a present interest.

§ 3.9

1. L. Simes and A. Smith, Future Interests § 111 (2d ed. 1956) at n. 46 and cases cited. Simes and Smith quote with approval Blackstone's statement that a remainder is contingent where it "is limited to take effect, either to a dubious or uncertain person, or upon a dubious and uncertain event; so that the particular estate may chance to be determined and the remainder never take effect." 2 Bl. Comm. 169 (assuming the existence of the rule that contingent remainders are destroyed if they fail to vest on or before the termination of the last prior estate). 2 Rest., Prop. § 157(d) classifies all remainders here classified as "contingent" simply as "remainders subject to a condition precedent," treating

birth and certainty of identification as implied (and necessary) conditions precedent. See id. § 157, Comments u through x.

2. In example (1), no remainderman yet exists—i.e., there is no person to be party to the relationships which constitute an interest in realty or personalty; "there is, at most, a possibility that [such] relationships will arise"; but there "is a potential interest which does have some present consequences, as, for example, the requirement that the unborn possible takers under a remainder subject to a condition precedent be 'represented' in litigation determining ownership of the affected thing." 2 Rest.Prop. § 157, Comment w.

In example (2) the remaindermen are unidentifiable because the persons who may be heirs of any person cannot be identified with certainty during his lifetime—a fact traditionally stated in the maxim, *nemo est haeres viventis.* (See 2 Bl.Comm. 208.)

3. For an extended discussion of this point, see L. Simes and A. Smith, Future Interests §§ 154–163 (2d ed. 1956).

would have an immediate right to the possession of the property, on the determination of all the intermediate or precedent estates." [4] In the famous case of Moore v. Littel,[5] the New York court held that the remainder to "the heirs of A" in a limitation like example (3) was vested in A's heirs presumptive because, "If you can point to a human being and say as to him 'that man or that woman, by virtue of a grant of a remainder, would have an immediate right to the possession of certain lands if the precedent estate of another should now cease,' then the statute says, he or she has a vested remainder." In so holding, the court ignored a further statutory provision that a remainder is contingent "while the person to whom or the event on which it is limited to take effect remains uncertain." [6] Although Moore v. Littel was vigorously criticized, no subsequent New York case has directly repudiated it. It is doubtful that the doctrine of Moore v. Littel would be applied at the present time in any other state, although several states have statutory definitions of vested and contingent remainders like those in New York.[7]

In examples (4) through (7), above, the remainders are contingent because they are subject to express conditions precedent that must be satisfied before any of these remainders can become a present estate. And in examples (6) and (7), if A has no children at the time of the transfer, the remainders are contingent for the additional reason that they are created in favor of unborn persons.

In each of the seven examples above, the only present interest created by the transfer is a life estate, and no vested future interests are expressly created. Since there must at all times be some combination of present and vested future interests that "adds up" to a fee simple absolute (or the equivalent interest in personalty), in all of these examples the transferor necessarily retains a reversion in fee simple (or an equivalent interest in personalty). But the reversion retained by the grantor in each example is subject to complete defeasance because the contingent remainder may vest either in possession or in interest—i.e., the contingency may be resolved in favor of the remaindermen.

§ 3.10 Contingent Remainders—The Obsolete Destructibility Rule

At common law in England, "legal" contingent remainders in land were held to be "destructible." Such a contingent remainder would be destroyed if it failed to vest at or before the termination of the last preceding estate created by the same instrument; i.e., if the remainderman was not ascertained and all express conditions precedent satisfied at or before the time when the remainder was intended to become possessory.[1] Thus, if land was

---

4. N.Y.Rev.Stat., pt. 2, ch. 1, tit. 2, § 13—carried forward to former N.Y.—McKinney's Real Property Law § 40, substantially revised and later transferred to N.Y.—McKinney's Estates, Powers and Trusts Law § 6–4.7.

5. 41 N.Y. 66 (1869).

6. Supra note 4.

7. These states include Arizona, California, Idaho, Michigan, Minnesota, Montana, North

Dakota, South Dakota, and Wisconsin. See L. Simes and A. Smith, Future Interests §§ 160–163.

§ 3.10

1. The destructibility doctrine was based on the medieval English practice of transferring freehold estates by "livery of seisin." Although a remainder could become a possessory estate immediately upon expiration of the

transferred "to A for life, remainder to B if B reaches 21," and B did not reach 21 at or before A's death, the remainder was destroyed.[2]

At common law in England, "legal" contingent remainders in land could also be destroyed by premature termination of the immediately preceding ("particular") estate. Premature termination might result either from forfeiture or from merger. If A, in example given in the last paragraph, failed to perform his feudal obligations to his lord, or purported to convey a fee simple estate (a "tortious feoffment"), the lord could forfeit A's life estate; and if B had not reached 21 at the time of the forfeiture, the remainder was destroyed.[3] Destruction of the remainder by merger would occur if A transferred his life estate to the owner of the reversion in fee simple or the owner of the reversion transferred it to A. In either case, the life estate would "merge" in the reversion and would thus terminate if B had not yet reached 21, and the remainder would be destroyed.[4]

Even in England, "equitable" contingent remainders in land were never "destructible." [5] Thus, if land was transferred to T in trust to pay the income to A for life, and then to convey the land to B in fee simple if B should reach 21, B's equitable contingent remainder was not destructible and T had a duty to convey the land to B whether he reached 21 before or after A's death.[6] If B had not yet reached 21 at A's death, T would hold the land on a "resulting trust" for the grantor or his successors in interest until B either reached 21 or died before attaining that age. If B died before he reached 21, T would be obligated to convey the legal title to the grantor or

particular estate because the owner of the particular estate was said to receive the seisin both for himself and for the benefit of the remainderman, there could be no "gap in the seisin." Thus, if the life tenant died while the remainder limited after the life estate was still subject to an unfulfilled condition precedent, the seisin would revest in the reversioner; and it could not thereafter pass automatically to the remainderman even though the condition precedent was later fulfilled. After the enactment of the Statute of Uses (1536) and the Statute of Wills (1540), as we have already seen, it became possible to create executory interests that were not destroyed if they failed to vest at or before the termination of the last precedent freehold estate. But the English courts refused to treat contingent remainders which failed to vest in time as executory interests. Instead, the courts held that a contingent limitation that could possibly take effect as a remainder must be deemed to create a remainder rather than an executory interest, and that the destructibility doctrine continued to apply to such contingent remainders even when they were created by a devise or by a conveyance operating under the Statute of Uses.

2. E.g., Festing v. Allen, 12 Mees & W. 279 (1843); Price v. Hall., L.R. 5 Eq. 399 (1868).

3. E.g., Archer's Case, 1 Co.Rep. 66b (1597); Chudleigh's Case, id. 138. The conveyance was "tortious" only if effected by feoffment,

fine, or common recovery—all of which have long since become obsolete both in England and the United States.

4. E.g., Thompson v. Leach, 1 Ld.Raym. 314, 2 Salk. 427 (1696); Purefoy v. Rogers, 2 Wm. Sauders 380, 2 Lev. 39 (1845); Egerton v. Massey, 3 C.B.N.S. 338 (1857).

5. E.g., Abbiss v. Burney, 17 Ch.Div. 211 (1881); Marshall v. Gingell, 21 Ch.Div. 790 (1882). "The historical reason is that the seisin is in the holder of the legal title, and therefore there can be no question where it will go on the termination of the estate of freehold preceding the contingent remainder; it simply remains in the trustee * * *." L. Simes and A. Smith, Future Interests § 200 (2d ed. 1956). Thus equitable contingent remainders were, for all practical purposes, indistinguishable from executory interests.

6. The modern trust, as in the example given, ordinarily imposes on the trustee various affirmative duties with respect to the management of the trust property. In this respect the modern trust differs from the pre–1536 arrangement whereby the "legal" estate was vested in one person to hold "to the use" of another, which did not impose any affirmative management duties on the holder of the "legal" estate and gave the holder of the "use" (equitable estate) the right to possession and control of the land.

his successors in interest.[7]

At the time when the doctrine that legal contingent remainders in land are destructible first evolved, estates in personal property were not recognized. Moreover, the concept of "seisin" as distinct from "possession" did not apply to personal property. Thus, when the courts later came to recognize present and future interests in personal property, there was no logical or historical basis for holding that legal contingent remainders in personal property were destructible.[8] It is therefore believed that courts today would almost universally hold the destructibility doctrine inapplicable to legal contingent remainders in personalty,[9] although there are a few old cases applying the doctrine to such remainders.[10]

Even with respect to legal contingent remainders in land, the destructibility doctrine has been eliminated by statute in England[11] and in many of the American states. At least twenty-one states have express statutes completely abolishing the destructibility doctrine,[12] and at least four jurisdictions have statutes that prevent destruction of contingent remainders by forfeiture or merger but do not prevent destruction if the preceding estates terminate naturally before a contingent remainder vests.[13] In at least two other states, the courts have held that the destructibility doctrine was abolished by statutes authorizing creation of freehold estates to commence *in futuro.*[14] The destructibility doctrine has been recognized in five states[15] where there is no legislation on the subject, but only two of these states have post–1900 decisions recognizing the doctrine.[16] On the other hand, four

7. The grantor or his successors in interest would be entitled to the income so long as the resulting trust continued. For discussion of the basis for a resulting trust in such a case, see 5 A. Scott, Trusts § 430 (3d ed. 1967).

8. "The rule that a particular estate is required to support contingent remainders is founded upon feudal reasons, which have no application to personal property, and no such estate is necessary to support such remainder in chattels." Price v. Price's Administrator, 23 Ala. 609, 612 (1853) (concurring opinion of Chilton, C.J.).

9. In re Rentz' Estate, 152 So.2d 480 (Fla. App.1963), so holds.

10. E.g., Price v. Price's Administrator, supra note 8 (tortious sale); Broome v. King, 10 Ala. 819 (1846). The doctrine of destructibility was later completely abolished by statute in Alabama. See infra note 12.

11. 8 & 9 Vict. c. 106, § 8 (1845), precluded the destruction of contingent remainders by forfeiture or merger. 40 & 41 Vict. c. 33, § 1 (1877), provided that contingent remainders should not fail by reason of the natural termination of the particular estate before the condition precedent was satisfied, but should, in that event, take effect as executory interests.

12. Ala.Code 1975, § 35–4–212 (contingent remainders take effect as executory interests); Ariz.Rev.Stat. § 33–228; West's Ann.Cal.Civ. Code §§ 741, 742; Ga.Code § 85–702; Idaho Code § 55–114; Ill.—S.H.A. ch. 30, ¶ 40; Iowa

Code Ann. §§ 557.7, 557.9; Ky.Rev.Stat. 381.-100, 381.110; Md.Code, Estates and Trusts, § 11–101; Mass.Gen.Laws Ann. c. 184, § 3; Mich.Comp.Laws Ann. §§ 554–32, 554–34; Minn.Stat.Ann. § 500.15; Rev.Codes Montana 1947, §§ 67–419, 67–420; Neb.Rev.Stat. § 76–116; N.Y.—McKinney's Estates, Powers & Trust Law 6–5.11; North Dak.Cent.Code 47–02–30, 47–02–32; Ohio Rev.Code §§ 2131.05, 2131.06; South Dak.Codified Laws §§ 43–3–18, 43–3–19; Va.Code 1950, §§ 55–15, 55–16; West Virginia Code, 36–1–15; Wis.Stat.Ann. 700.14.

13. Miss.Code 1972, § 89–1–17; R.I.Gen. Laws 1956, § 34–4–14; Vernon's Ann.Tex.Civ. Stat. art. 1290; D.C.Code § 45–814.

14. West's Ann.Indiana Code § 32–1–2–34; Kan.Stat.Ann. 67–205. See Rouse v. Paidrick, 221 Ind. 517, 49 N.E.2d 528 (1943); Miller v. Miller, 91 Kan. 1, 136 P. 953, L.R.A. 1915A 671 (1913).

15. Florida, Mississippi (by natural termination of life estate), Oregon, Pennsylvania, and Tennessee.

16. These states are Florida and Oregon. See Popp v. Bond, 158 Fla. 185, 28 So.2d 259 (1946); Love v. Lindstedt, 76 Or. 66, 147 P. 935, Ann.Cas. 1917A 898 (1915). See also Smith, Destructibility of Contingent Remainders in Florida, 3 U.Fla.L.Rev. 319 (1950); Smith and Keathly, Future Interests in Florida: A Plea for Judicial Supremacy, 9 id. 123 (1956); Note, 23 Ore.L.Rev. 138 (1944).

states have eliminated the destructibility rule entirely by judicial decision [17] and several other states have cases indicating that the rule would probably not be recognized.[18] As Simes and Smith have argued,[19]

> This decisive trend away from the destructibility rule, evidenced by the legislative and judicial abolition thereof, should be influential in other jurisdictions where the matter has not yet been settled by either statute or decision. It would seem that those courts would be justified in holding that the destructibility rule no longer exists, just as the Restatement of Property has taken that position. Based purely upon a conception of continuity of seisin which has no practical significance today and has had none for centuries, the rule cannot be justified today.

When most future interests were legal estates in land, the destructibility of contingent remainders made it necessary to distinguish carefully between contingent remainders and executory interests. The latter were held, in 1620, to be indestructible.[20] At the present time, with most contingent remainders indestructible either because they are equitable in character or because their subject matter is personal property or because destructibility has been completely eliminated in the particular jurisdiction, there is no substantial difference between contingent remainders and executory interests. Hence it is rarely necessary to be able to distinguish contingent remainders from executory interests. But, as we shall see, it is still necessary to distinguish between vested future interests such as reversions and some remainders, which cannot violate the Rule Against Perpetuities, and non-vested future interests such as executory interests and contingent remainders, which may violate the Rule Against Perpetuities.

§ 3.11   Shifting Executory Interests—In General

As previously noted,[1] when a present interest or a vested remainder created in a transferee is subject to complete defeasance by the operation of an executory limitation, the future interest which will displace the defeated interest is a "shifting" executory interest. Almost all executory interests created in modern times are shifting executory interests,[2] as in all the following examples:

17. These states are Hawaii, Massachusetts, New Hampshire, and New Mexico. See, e.g., Godfrey v. Rowland, 16 Hawaii 377 (1912), rehearing denied 16 Hawaii 502; Simonds v. Simonds, 199 Mass. 552, 85 N.E. 860 (1908); Hayward v. Spaulding, 75 N.H. 92, 71 A. 219 (1908); Abo Petroleum Corp. v. Amstutz, 93 N.M. 332, 600 P.2d 278 (1979); Johnson v. Amstutz, 101 N.M. 94, 678 P.2d 1169 (1984) ("doctrine has never been the law in New Mexico"). See also Whitten v. Whitten, 203 Okl. 196, 219 P.2d 228 (1950) (court rejected assertion that contingent remainder was destroyed by original grantor's second deed conveying the property to original life tenant in fee simple absolute, without any mention of the destructibility doctrine).

18. E.g., Hughes v. Neely, 332 S.W.2d 1 (Mo.1960), noted in 25 Mo.L.Rev. 435 (1960).

See also Comment, Destructibility of Contingent Remainders in Missouri, 34 U. of M. at K.C.L.Rev. 342 (1966).

19. L. Simes and A. Smith, Future Interests 209 (2d ed. 1956). See also 2 Rest.Prop. § 240 (doctrine is no longer significant in American law).

20. Pells v. Brown, Cro.Jac. 590, 79 Eng. Rep. 504 (1620).

§ 3.11

1. See ante Section 3.7 note 6.

2. "It is fair to say that more than 90 percent of all executory interests ever encountered by a lawyer consist of shifting interests so limited that they are subject to a condition precedent not certain ever to be fulfilled, and limited after a prior estate not certain ever to end." 2A R. Powell, Real Prop. ¶ 279 (1981).

(1) "to A but if A marries B, then to B";

(2) "to A, but if A dies without children him surviving, then to B";

(3) "to A, but if A uses the land for non-residential purposes during his lifetime, then to B";

(4) "to A so long as the land is used only for residential purposes, but if the land is put to non-residential use during A's lifetime, then to B";

(5) "to A for life, remainder to B, but if B does not survive A, then to C";

(6) "to A for life, remainder to B, but if B dies without children him surviving, then to B's heirs".

In examples (1), (2), and (3), A receives a present fee simple (or equivalent interest in personalty) subject to an executory limitation, and B receives a shifting executory interest in fee simple absolute (or equivalent interest in personalty). In example (4), A receives a present fee simple determinable which is also subject to an executory limitation; the transferor retains a possibility of reverter in fee simple subject to complete defeasance; and B obtains a shifting executory limitation in fee simple absolute.[3] In examples (5) and (6), A receives a present life interest; B receives a vested remainder in fee simple (or equivalent interest in personalty) subject to an executory limitation; and C or B's heirs, respectively, receive a shifting executory interest in fee simple absolute (or equivalent interest in personalty).

In example (1), above, B's executory interest will become a present interest and A's interest will be completely defeated if A marries B. In examples (2) and (3), B's executory interest will become a present interest and A's interest will be completely defeated if the stated condition precedent is fulfilled. In example (4), B's executory interest will become a present interest only if the land is put to non-residential use during A's lifetime; but the transferor's possibility of reverter will become a present interest if the land is first put to non-residential use after A's death; and in either event, the fee simple given to A will be completely defeated.[4]

In example (5), B's vested remainder will become a present estate in fee simple absolute (or equivalent interest in personalty) if B survives A, and C's executory interest will fail; but if B predeceases A, B's vested remainder will be completely defeated and C will obtain a vested remainder in fee simple absolute (or equivalent interest in personalty) which will become a present interest upon A's death.[5]

---

3. The possibility of reverter is not subject to the common law Rule Against Perpetuities and is capable of becoming a present estate in fee simple absolute whenever the land is put to non-residential use; but the executory interest is subject to the common law Rule Against Perpetuities and would be void unless so limited that it would be certain to fail or become a present estate within the "perpetuities period"—i.e., lives in being at the creation of the interest, plus a maximum period of 21 years. For more on the Rule Against Perpetuities, see post Sections 3.17 through 3.22.

4. Since A's fee simple is subject to both a special limitation and an executory limitation in example (4), it can be argued that A's estate

will be defeated by the special limitation rather than the executory limitation if the land is put to non-residential use during A's lifetime. However, although courts have traditionally distinguished between "limitational" defeasance (e.g., by virtue of a special limitation) and "conditional" defeasance (e.g., by virtue of an executory limitation), the distinction no longer appears to have any substantial significance.

5. In all the previous examples, the executory interest "vests in possession" (i.e., becomes a present interest) if and when the preceding interest is defeated, but in example (5), the executory interest only "vests in interest" if and when the preceding interest is

In example (6), B's vested remainder will be completely defeated if B predeceases A and leaves no children him surviving, and the executory interest of B's heirs (determined at his death) will become a vested remainder in fee simple absolute (or equivalent interest in personalty) which will ultimately become a present interest when A dies. If A predeceases B, B will have a present fee simple estate (or equivalent interest in personalty), but it will remain subject to complete defeasance throughout B's lifetime; and if B later dies without leaving children him surviving, B's heirs (determined at his death) will have a present fee simple absolute (or equivalent interest in personalty).

None of the shifting executory interests in examples (1) through (6) is "vested,"[6] and since all of them are subject to a condition precedent that is not certain to be fulfilled, all of them can accurately be termed "contingent."[7] In the first five examples, the executory interests are all given to living, identifiable persons; but in example (6), the executory interest is given to a class whose membership is not ascertainable during the lifetime of B, the owner of the vested remainder, although the class membership will necessarily be ascertainable immediately upon the death of B. It is clear that shifting executory interests (and some, but not all, types of springing executory interests) can be created in favor of a class of unborn or otherwise unidentifiable persons.[8]

Is it possible to create a shifting executory interest so limited as to become a present interest at the end of a fixed period of time—e.g., by a transfer "to A and his heirs, but then to B at the end of ten years"? The Property Restatement gives a negative answer, asserting that such a transfer would give A only an estate for years, despite the use of words of inheritance, and give B a vested remainder in fee simple absolute.[9] The Property Restatement's rule seems properly applicable in cases where the instrument of transfer does not include express words of inheritance or otherwise clearly indicate that the first taker is to have a fee simple.[10] In such cases, the transferor would probably want the first taker's use privileges to be limited by the common law of waste; but where the instrument of transfer clearly indicates the intent to give the first taker a fee simple, it is at least arguable that the grantor intended the first taker to hold without "impeachment" for legal waste.[11] In any case, the holder of the executory interest would be able to enjoin "unconscionable" conduct amounting to equitable waste, since the executory interest is certain to become a possessory estate.

defeated. Since an executory interest, by definition, cannot be "vested in interest," it immediately becomes a vested remainder when the preceding interest is defeated.

6. But see supra note 5.

7. This is analogous to the common classification of remainders subject to a condition precedent as "contingent." That most executory interests are "contingent" in this sense, see supra note 2.

8. See L. Simes and A. Smith, Future Interests § 227 at n. 45 (2d ed. 1956).

9. 1 Rest.Prop. § 146, comment i.

10. If the words of inheritance were omitted, the transfer to A would be qualified by the language "at the end of ten years," and would pretty clearly give A only a term of years under the statutes in most jurisdictions providing that any conveyance shall transfer the entire interest of the transferor unless a contrary intent is manifested.

11. Accord: L. Simes and A. Smith, Future Interests § 223 (2d ed. 1956). See ante Section 2.8 at note 23.

A shifting executory interest can, of course, be so limited that it may displace a prior executory interest in those cases where the instrument of transfer contains two or more alternative executory limitations.[12] And, as we have previously noted,[13] any future interest that follows a fee simple determinable or a fee simple conditional is classified as a shifting executory interest.

When a transfer creates a vested remainder subject to open, and there are members of the class of remaindermen whose interests are still contingent when the preceding life estate terminates, it will make no difference whether those interests are classified as contingent remainders or as executory interests if (1) the interests are equitable rather than legal, or (2) are personal rather than real property, or (3) the rule that legal contingent remainders are destroyed upon failure to vest before termination of all preceding life estates has been abolished.[14] But if the case is one where the destructibility rule would be applicable to legal contingent remainders, the question of classification will be important. Since the vesting of such contingent interests prior to termination of all preceding life estates involves the partial defeasance of the interests of those remaindermen whose interests are already vested, it would seem that such contingent interests should be classified as executory interests—which are, of course, indestructible. And in the leading case of *Simonds v. Simonds* the Massachusetts court so held.[15] But a leading authority nevertheless concludes that "the opening of such vested remainders to let in subsequent members of the class is a unique process, and should not be described as the vesting of either a contingent remainder or an executory interest," but "is simply a unique characteristic of remainders vested subject to open." [16]

The dispositive clauses in modern wills, even those disposing of relatively modest estates, commonly employ a series of shifting executory limitations—e.g., "To my husband for life, then to my children in equal shares, but the share of any child who shall predecease my said husband shall pass to the children of such child, and if any child shall predecease my said husband without leaving any children him or her surviving, the share of such child shall pass in equal shares to those of my other children who shall survive my said husband."

§ 3.12 Springing Executory Interests—In General

Since "springing" executory interests are rarely created in modern times, only three examples will be given here. In all of the following

12. E.g., Lee v. Oates, 171 N.C. 717, 88 S.E. 889 (1916).

13. See ante Section 3.6, note 5, and text therewith.

14. See ante Section 3.10.

15. 199 Mass. 552, 85 N.E. 860, 19 L.R.A.(N.S.) 686 (1908). The court had before it a transfer of land to the grantor's son Charles for life, with "remainder to such of the children of Charles as shall arrive at the age of twenty-one years, their heirs and assigns." When Charles died he left five chil-

dren, two of whom had reached 21 and three who had not. One of the latter having reached 21, the issue was whether she took an interest in the property. The court decided that she did, assuming that the gift to the daughter must be classified either as a contingent remainder or an executory interest, and that the gift would fail if classified as a contingent remainder because it did not vest till after termination of the life estate.

16. L. Simes and A. Smith, Future Interests § 205 (2d ed. 1956). See also id. § 114.

examples B obtains a springing executory interest in fee simple absolute or equivalent interest in personalty.

(1) "to B, from and after B's marriage to A"; [1]

(2) "to A for life, then to B one year after A's death";

(3) "to B from and after next January 1."

In examples (1) and (3), the transferor retains a present fee simple (or equivalent interest in personalty) subject to an executory limitation, and B obtains a springing executory interest in fee simple absolute (or equivalent interest in personalty). In example (2), however, A obtains a present life estate, the transferor retains a reversion in fee simple subject to an executory limitation, and B obtains a springing executory interest in fee simple absolute (or equivalent interest in personalty).[2] Example (3) involves a recognized exception to the general rule that it is impossible to create a fee simple estate (or equivalent interest in personalty) with a fixed duration. Although it is arguable that, in example (3), the transferor has by implication reduced his interest to a term of years and given B a present fee simple (or equivalent interest in personalty) subject to the term, it seems more probable that the transferor intended to retain for himself the same virtually unlimited use privileges with respect to the property that he had before the transfer.[3] Some such rationale seems to underlie the Property Restatement's assertion that, in cases like example (3), the transferor retains a fee simple subject to a springing executory interest.[4]

In all three of the examples, above, the springing executory interests are given to identifiable persons. But a springing executory interest may be created in favor of an unborn or unidentifiable person or a class of unascertainable persons if the transfer also creates a present interest in a transferee—e.g., "to A for life, and one day after A's death to A's heirs."[5] But there are cases holding that a springing executory interest cannot be created in favor of unborn or otherwise unascertainable persons by a deed that purports to create nothing more than a springing executory interest.[6] This rule would deny any legal operation to an *inter vivos* transfer "to the heirs of A (a living person) at A's death," or "to the heirs of A (a living person 21 years after A's death." There are cases holding that such transfers will create

---

§ 3.12

1. In England, until fairly recently, such transfers were commonly made in contemplation of the transferee's marriage.

2. Note that B's executory interest, in example (2), is certain to become a present interest, although the time when this will occur is uncertain.

3. Ante Section 2.8 at note 23. The suggested rationale would seem to be fully applicable only when the transfer is by deed, however. It is less clear that a testator who makes a devise like that in example (3) would be concerned to preserve fee simple use privileges for his heirs or residuary devisees during the brief period when they will be entitled to possession.

4. 1 Rest.Prop. § 46, comment i. See also L. Simes and A. Smith, Future Interests § 223 (2d ed. 1956), suggesting that the Restatement rule may rest "on the theory that the old notion that a fee simple must last forever was qualified by the * * * Statute of Uses and the possibility of creating springing executory interests."

5. L. Simes and A. Smith, Future Interests § 227 (2d ed. 1956).

6. Legout v. Price, 318 Ill. 425, 149 N.E. 427 (1925), noted in 22 Ill.L.Rev. 894 (1928) (deed to "heirs" of a living person void); Booker v. Tarwater, 138 Ind. 385, 37 N.E. 979 (1894) (same); Hall v. Leonard, 18 Mass. (1 Pick.) 27 (1822) (same); Hickel v. Starcher, 90 W.Va. 369, 110 S.E. 695, 22 A.L.R. 708 (1922) (same).

springing executory interests, however,[7] and the cases to the contrary seem to be based on the questionable "assumption that in every case of an inter vivos conveyance, whether the interest conveyed be present or future, there must be some grantee in existence at the time of the conveyance."[8]

§ 3.13 Alternative Contingent Remainders or Vested Remainder Subject to an Executory Interest?

It is sometimes difficult to classify two or more nonreversionary future interests following a simultaneously-created present interest. The general rule is that if the first future interest is a vested remainder subject to conditional defeasance, the other future interests will be executory interests; but if the first future interest is a contingent remainder, the other future interests will also be contingent remainders. Thus classification of the first future interest is the key to classification of succeeding future interests. Consider the following examples:

(1) "to A for life, remainder to B, but if B predeceases A, then to C."

(2) "to A for life, remainder to such of A's children as shall survive A, but if no child of A shall survive him, then to B."

(3) "to A for life, remainder to B, if B reaches 21, but if B dies under 21, then to C."

In example (1), the remainder given to B is vested subject to complete defeasance, since B's predeceasing A is clearly a condition subsequent rather than a condition precedent with respect to B's remainder; and C's interest is a shifting executory interest which can vest only if B's vested remainder is completely defeated by B's predeceasing A—which is a condition subsequent with respect to B's vested remainder and a condition precedent with respect to C's executory interest.[1] In example (1) the transferor does not retain a reversion because B's vested remainder in fee simple exhausts the fee simple (or equivalent interest in personalty) originally owned by the transferor.

In example (2), above, the future interest created in favor of "such of A's children as shall survive A" is clearly a contingent remainder because the identity of the remaindermen cannot be determined until after A's death.[2]

---

7. Pibus v. Mitford, 1 Ventris 372, 86 Eng. Rep. 239, sub nom. Pybus v. Mitford, 1 Freeman 351, 369, 89 Eng.Rep. 262, 275 (1673); Loats Female Orphan Asylum v. Essom, 220 Md. 11, 150 A.2d 742 (1959); Hayes v. Kershow, 1 Sandf.Ch. 258 (N.Y.1844); Inglis v. Trustees of Sailor's Snug Harbour, 28 U.S. (3 Pet.) 99, 7 L.Ed. 617 (1830).

8. See discussion in L. Simes and A. Smith, Future Interests § 227 (2d ed. 1956).

§ 3.13

1. E.g., Witcher v. Witcher, 231 Ga. 49, 200 S.E.2d 110 (1973); Baley v. Strahan, 314 Ill. 213, 145 N.E. 359 (1924); Taylor v. Stephens, 165 Ind. 200, 74 N.E. 980 (1905); Callison v. Morris, 123 Iowa 297, 98 N.W. 780 (1904); Mercantile Bank v. Ballard's Assignee, 83 Ky. 481, 4 Am.St.Rep. 160 (1885); Wilson v. Pichon, 162 Md. 199, 159 A. 766 (1932); De Ford

v. Coleman, 348 Mass. 299, 203 N.E.2d 686 (1965); Silvester v. Snow, 373 Mich. 384, 129 N.W.2d 382 (1964); Ziegler v. Love, 185 N.C. 40, 115 S.E. 887 (1923); Roome v. Phillips, 24 N.Y. 463 (1862); Gist v. Brown, 236 S.C. 31, 113 S.E.2d 75 (1960).

2. E.g., Festing v. Allen, 21 Mees & W. 279 (1843); Price v. Hall, L.R. 5 Eq. 399 (1863); Morehead v. Goellert, 160 Kan. 598, 164 P.2d 110 (1945); Saulsberry v. Second National Bank, 400 S.W.2d 506 (Ky.1966); Buchan v. Buchan, 254 Iowa 566, 118 N.W.2d 611, 100 A.L.R.2d 1063 (1962); Love v. Lindstedt, 76 Or. 66, 147 P. 935, Ann.Cas.1917A 898 (1915).

These are cases where the persons to whom the first remainder is given are so described that they "cannot be ascertained but for that description, which contains in itself a contingency." Price v. Hall, supra.

This remainder is subject to a condition precedent that A shall have at least one child who shall survive him. And the future interest given to B is an alternative contingent remainder because it is subject to the condition precedent that A shall die without leaving a surviving child.[3] The two conditions are exact opposites; if one is fulfilled, the other must necessarily fail. Although both the contingent remainders are in fee simple absolute (or equivalent interest in personalty), the transferor retains a reversion in fee simple (or equivalent interest in personalty) subject to complete defeasance because the only present or vested future interest created by the transfer is A's present life interest.[4] In a jurisdiction where the contingent remainders cannot be destroyed by merger the reversion is valueless because one contingent remainder or the other is certain to become a present interest and the reversion is certain to be completely defeated. But in a jurisdiction where legal contingent remainders in land are destructible by merger, a reversion in land has substantial value because the reversioner and the life tenant have the power to cause a merger of the life estate in the reversion and thus to destroy the contingent remainders.[5] This is clearly an undesirable result. It could be precluded either by eliminating the destructibility rule or by holding that there is no reversion in such a case. The latter, of course, would require abrogation of the principle that the entire fee simple must at all times be "vested" in some person or group of persons.

In example (3), above, most American courts would reach the same result as in example (2) because B's reaching the age of twenty-one is an express condition precedent to the vesting of B's remainder.[6] But a few American courts have reached the same result in cases like example (3) as in cases like example (1), treating the clause, "if B reaches 21," as surplusage.[7] Such a result is said to be justified by the constructional preference for vested rather than contingent remainders.[8] It should be emphasized, however that this constructional preference has not led American courts to treat an express condition precedent as surplusage where only one remainder is created—e.g., by a transfer "to A for life, remainder to B if he reaches 21."

Suppose O makes the following transfer:

3. Ibid.

4. The alternative contingent remainders do not "count" as parts of the transferor's original fee simple absolute (or equivalent interest in personalty).

5. Merger would result from transfer of the life interest to the reversioner, or transfer of the reversion to the life tenant, or transfer of both the life interest and the reversion to a third party.

6. E.g., Brown v. Andrews, 288 Ala. 111, 257 So.2d 356 (1972); Fletcher v. Hurdle, 259 Ark. 640, 536 S.W.2d 109 (1976); Murphy v. Westhoff, 386 Ill. 136, 53 N.E.2d 931 (1944); Lambertson v. Case, 245 Mich. 208, 222 N.W. 182 (1928); Guilliams v. Koonsman, 154 Tex. 401, 279 S.W.2d 579, 57 A.L.R.2d 97 (1955); In re Wehr's Trust, 36 Wis.2d 154, 152 N.W.2d 868 (1967). The leading English case, relied on in many of the American cases, is Loddington v. Kime, 1 Salk. 224 (1695).

7. E.g., Bowman v. Long, 23 Ga. 242 (1857); Cockey v. Cockey, 141 Md. 373, 118 A. 850 (1922); Seabrook v. Gregg, 2 S.C. 68 (1870); In re McLoughlin, 507 F.2d 177 (5th Cir.1975).

8. Some of the American cases rely on the old English case of Edwards v. Hammond, 3 Lev. 132 (1683). In England, a line of cases following Edwards v. Hammond, originally confined to land but later extended to personalty, has established the rule that when a remainder is given to individuals or a class, if or when they attain a specified age or survive a specified person or for a specified time, with a gift over on failure to attain that age or to so survive, the remainder is not contingent but is vested subject to complete defeasance, and the gift over creates an executory interest. This rule is known as the rule in Phipps v. Ackers, 9 Cl. & Fin. 583, 8 Eng.Rep. 539 (1842).

(4) "to A for life, remainder to B so long as B, during B's lifetime, does not use the land for any non-residential purpose; but if B should, during his lifetime, use the land for any non-residential purpose, then to C."

In example (4), B's remainder is clearly vested subject to complete defeasance, but it is defeasible by virtue of a special limitation rather than a condition subsequent. Hence, if B, during his lifetime, uses the land for any non-residential purpose, his remainder will simply terminate "normally," not prematurely. If B's remainder were for life, C's future interest would clearly be a remainder. But because B's remainder is in fee simple (or equivalent interest in personalty), and because a remainder cannot be limited to follow a vested remainder in fee simple (or equivalent interest in personalty), C's future interest in example (4) must be classified as a shifting executory interest.

Suppose O makes the following transfer:

(5) "to A for life, and if A shall die without leaving children surviving him, then to C, remainder to B."

In example (5), if we look at the form alone, C's remainder appears to be contingent, since it is subject to an express condition precedent, and B's remainder appears to be vested, since no condition precedent is expressed in connection with B's remainder. But the old English case, Loddington v. Kime,[9] contains a dictum that a vested remainder in fee simple cannot follow a contingent remainder in fee simple. Moreover, except for the order in which the two future interests are limited, example (5) is substantially identical with example (1), above; hence it is arguable that B should be held to have a vested remainder subject to complete defeasance and that C should be held to have a shifting executory interest.[10] On the other hand, it can be argued that B's future interest is subject to an implied condition precedent that A shall die leaving children surviving him, and hence that B and C obtain alternative contingent remainders in example (5). There is very little case authority on the point,[11] and legal scholars are divided, with some supporting each of the three possible views.[12]

§ 3.14 Powers of Appointment

The Property Restatement defines a power of appointment as "a power created or reserved by a person (the donor) having property subject to his disposition, enabling the donee of the power to designate, within such limits

---

9. 1 Salk. 224 (1695).

10. This result is consistent with the universally-accepted rule that a gift in default of appointment is vested subject to defeasance by an exercise of the power of appointment. See ante Section 3.7, at note 6.

11. In support of the view that C obtains a contingent remainder and B obtains a vested remainder, see Granger v. Granger, 147 Ind. 95, 44 N.E. 189, 46 N.E. 80, 36 L.R.A. 186, 190 (1896) (dictum); Ringgold v. Carvel, 196 Md. 262, 76 A.2d 327 (1950); In re Herrmann's Estate, 130 N.J.Eq. 273, 22 A.2d 262 (1941), affirmed 132 N.J.Eq. 458, 28 A.2d 517 (1942). See also, by way of analogy, Egerton v. Mas-

sey, 3 C.B.(N.S.) 338 (1857); Friedman v. Friedman, 283 Ill. 383, 119 N.E. 321 (1918).

12. In support of the view that C obtains a contingent remainder and B obtains a vested remainder, see Warren, Progress of the Law 1918–1920, 34 Harv.L.Rev. 508, 515–518 (1921); 2 Tiffany, Real Property § 333 (3d ed. 1939). See also Gray, Rule Against Perpetuities § 113.1 (4th ed. 1942). In support of the view that B obtains a vested remainder and C obtains an executory interest, see Kales, Estates and Future Interests § 95 (2d ed. 1920); 1 Preston, Estates, 84, 502 (1820). In support of the view that C and B obtain alternative contingent remainders, see 3 Rest.Prop. § 278, Comment d.

as the donor may prescribe, the transferees of the property or the shares in which it shall be received."[1] This definition excludes powers of sale, powers of attorney, powers of revocation, powers to cause a gift of income to be augmented out of the principal of a trust, discretionary trusts, and honorary trusts.

Historically, the power of appointment was associated with the doctrine of "uses" and the development of executory interests; exercise of a power of appointment was viewed as an event upon which the equitable ownership of land shifted to a transferee by virtue of the provisions of the instrument creating the power.[2] And powers of appointment provided a means of devising land by will prior to enactment of the Statute of Wills in 1540.[3]

Powers of appointment may be classified in several ways, e.g.,[4]—

(1)(a) general powers, where the donee has the power to exercise the power in favor of anyone, including himself, during his lifetime, and to dispose of it to anyone by will, and (b) special powers, where the donee may only appoint the property to or within a specified group of persons, not unreasonably large, that does not include himself;

(2)(a) powers presently exercisable, and (b) powers exercisable only at a future time;

(3)(a) powers to appoint by deed only, (b) powers to appoint by will only, and (c) powers to appoint by deed and by will;

(4)(a) powers purely collateral, where the donee has no interest in the property other than the power, and (b) powers in gross, where the donee has an interest in the property in addition to the power, but the power relates to interests he does not own; and

(5)(a) powers in trust, where the donee under some circumstances and within a designated time period has a duty to exercise the power, and (b) powers not in trust.

For most purposes the exercise of a power of appointment relates back to the creation of the power, so that the property disposition effected by the power is treated as if it had been effected by the instrument creating the power and the appointee is deemed to take title from the donor rather than the donee of the power.[5] But the courts and legislatures have often disre-

§ 3.14

1. 3 Rest.Prop. § 318. See also L. Simes, Future Interests § 55 (2d ed. 1966); L. Simes and A. Smith, Future Interests § 871 (2d ed. 1956).

A power of appointment may be created by language that does not expressly purport to create such a power. See Estate of Stewart, 325 Pa.Super. 545, 473 A.2d 572 (1984), order affirmed 506 Pa. 336, 485 A.2d 391 (1984) (provision in will that named person should "handle my estate as she sees fit" gave that person a general, presently exercisable power of appointment over residue of testator's estate).

2. L. Simes, Future Interests § 55 (2d ed. 1966); L. Simes and A. Smith, Future Interests § 872 (2d ed. 1956).

3. Ibid.

4. L. Simes, Future Interests § 56 (2d ed. 1966); L. Simes and A. Smith §§ 874–879 (2d ed. 1956).

5. E.g., In re Harbeck's Will, 161 N.Y. 211, 55 N.E. 850 (1900); Sewall v. Wilmer, 132 Mass. 131 (1883). Generally, see L. Simes, Future Interests § 57 (2d ed. 1966); L. Simes and A. Smith, Future Interests ch. 30 (2d ed. 1956).

For a recent case supporting the text, see Smith v. Bank of Clearwater, 479 So.2d 755 (Fla.App.1985) (donee of power of appointment is mere agent of donor and appointee "takes through a transfer from the donor, * * * the creator of the power, not through a transfer from the donee"; hence the property subject

garded the "relation back" doctrine where justice or policy requires it—e.g., the "relation back" doctrine is disregarded in applying the Rule Against Perpetuities to general powers of appointment,[6] and modern tax statutes tend to tax the appointment as a transfer from the donee to the appointee, at least when the power is "general" rather "special." [7]

Although a prospective appointee might well be viewed as having a property interest substantially like a contingent executory interest, the prevailing view is that a prospective appointee has a mere expectancy like that of an heir presumptive except where the power of appointment is in trust.[8] If the power is in trust, the prospective appointee may be viewed as the beneficiary of a trust, with an equitable property interest protected by law.[9]

The interest of the donee of a power, or one who has reserved a power in himself, is said, in innumerable American judicial dicta, not to be property,[10] but the term "power of ownership" is now an accepted term in English law.[11] Certainly the donee of a general power to appoint by deed and by will has an interest that comes close to full ownership.[12] And where a power is in trust, the Trusts Restatement takes the position that the power is property because, by definition, the subject matter of a trust is property.[13]

A number of recent cases deal with problems as to the exercise [14] or

to the power "does not become part of the estate of the donee of the power").

6. E.g., Appeal of Mifflin, 121 Pa. 205, 15 A. 525, 1 L.R.A. 453 (1888).

7. I.R.C. § 2041(a)(2) provides for inclusion in a decedent's gross estate of all property subject to a general power of appointment not exercised by the decedent, as well as property with respect to which the decedent has exercised a general power by a disposition such that, if it were a transfer of the decedent's property, it would be included in his gross estate. State inheritance tax laws generally make the exercise of a general power of appointment, but not the exercise of a special power, a taxable event. Contra, see Matter of Martindale's Estate, 423 N.E.2d 662 (Ind.App. 1981) (donee's partial exercise of general power was not a taxable event under state inheritance tax law). In some states no distinction is made and the exercise of either a general or a special power of appointment is a taxable event. Generally, see L. Simes and A. Smith, Future Interests § 948 (2d ed. 1956 and Supp.)

8. E.g., In re Vizard's Trusts, [1886] 1 Ch. 587; In re Keene's Estate, 221 Pa. 201, 70 A. 706 (1908).

9. Thus, if O devises property in trust for A for life, with a power in A to determine by will the shares of his children, the power will be held in trust by A, and if A fails to exercise the power, the children of A living at his death will share equally in the property. E.g., Degman v. Degman, 98 Ky. 717, 34 S.W. 523 (1896); Bridgewater v. Turner, 161 Tenn. 111, 29 S.W.2d 659 (1930); Loosing v. Loosing, 85

Neb. 66, 122 N.W. 707, 25 L.R.A.(N.S.) 920 (1909), overruled 103 Neb. 730, 174 N.W. 317.

10. E.g., Shattuck v. Burrage, 229 Mass. 448, 451, 118 N.E. 889, 890 (1918); Matter of Martindale's Estate, 423 N.E.2d 662 (Ind.App. 1981); Tax Commission of Ohio v. Oswald, 109 Ohio St. 36, 51, 141 N.E. 678, 682 (1923); Supreme Colony v. Towne, 87 Conn. 644, 648, 89 A. 264, 266 (1914).

11. Farwell, Powers 9 (3d ed. 1916); 25 Halsbury's Laws of England 510 (2d ed. 1937).

12. Sugden, Powers 396 (8th ed. 1861).

13. Rest. Trusts § 74 (1935).

14. Schwartz v. BayBank Merrimack Valley, 17 Mass.App.Ct. 169, 456 N.E.2d 1141 (1983), review denied 391 Mass. 1102, 459 N.E.2d 825 (1984) (residuary clause of donee's will did not exercise power because it did not comply with the donor's requirement that it be exercised by specific reference—a requirement that negated any presumption that the general residuary clause of donee's will exercised the power); Estate of McNeill, 463 A.2d 782 (Me.1983) (case applies "equitable exception to the general rule that a power must be exercised in the manner prescribed by the donor," where "the appointment approximates the manner of appointment prescribed by the donor" and "the appointee is a natural object of the donee's affection"); Matter of Gold, 342 N.W.2d 332 (Minn.1984) (donee could not exercise testamentary power by indicating that appointive property, in absence of specific disposition by donee's will, should be distributed as donee's intestate property).

release [15] of powers of appointment and the disposition of appointive property when the donee fails to exercise the power completely and there is no gift in default of appointment.[16]

D. RESTRICTIONS ON CREATION OF NON-REVERSIONARY FUTURE INTERESTS

§ 3.15   The Doctrine of Worthier Title

After the English courts came to recognize the validity of contingent remainders they developed a rule of law—the so-called Doctrine of Worthier Title—which precluded the creation of a contingent remainder in favor of the heirs of a grantor or testator. Thus, e.g., if O (owner of an estate in fee simple) conveyed it "to A for life, remainder to O's heirs," the attempt to create a contingent remainder in favor of O's heirs was ineffective, and O, instead of retaining a reversion in fee simple subject to complete defeasance in favor of his heirs, retained an indefeasibly vested reversion in fee simple—an interest that was both marketable and of very substantial value.[1] If O had devised the land by a will containing the same language, the Worthier Title Doctrine would simply cause O's heir to take the future interest by descent rather than by "purchase," thus creating a tenurial relation between A and O's heir that would not have arisen had O's heir taken the remainder by "purchase."[2]

The Worthier Title Doctrine was probably invented to prevent a grantor's heir from acquiring the grantor's land by "purchase"—thus depriving the grantor's feudal overlord of the valuable rights of wardship and mar-

---

The general rule and the "equitable exception" are set out in Rest.Prop.2d, Donative Transfers §§ 18.2, 18.3 (1986).

15. Matter of Estate of Shapleigh, 675 S.W.2d 408 (Mo.1984) (no particular form of release is required; inter vivos documents under seal, given for consideration, effected partial release of general testamentary power of appointment). The court relied, *inter alia*, on Rest.Prop. §§ 334, 336 (1944); 3 R. Powell, Real Prop. ¶ 393; L. Simes & A. Smith, Future Interests § 1054 (2d ed. 1956).

16. Loring v. Marshall, 396 Mass. 166, 484 N.E.2d 1315 (1985) (where donee of special power appointed only the trust income, the donor's apparent intent to keep the assets within the family was sufficient to overcome any claim that her will provided—by rather ambiguous language—for a gift in default of appointment to named charities; hence the corpus was to be distributed to the estate of the only member of the class to whom the corpus could have been appointed who survived the donee). In support of its decision as to the proper disposition of appointive property when a special power of appointment is not exercised and there is no specific gift in default of appointment, the court cited Rest. Prop. § 367(2) (1944); 1 A. Scott Trusts § 271 (1st ed. 1939); 5 Am.L.Prop. § 23.63, at 645;

Rest.Prop.2d, Donative Transfers § 24.2 (1986).

§ 3.15

1. Since O's reversion was alienable, there was, of course, no assurance that O's heirs would ultimately acquire the fee simple. Hence the term "worthier title" is not accurate as applied to the rule that a grantor could not create a remainder in favor of his own heirs; application of the rule could lead to disinheritance of O's heirs, not just their taking the fee simple by inheritance (the "worthier title") rather than by "purchase." It should be noted that, even if O's conveyance were effective to create a contingent remainder in favor of his heirs, that remainder would have been destructible by merger at common law. Thus, O's reversion, though defeasible, would have had substantial value because, in cooperation with the life tenant, A, O could have brought about a merger that would have destroyed the contingent remainder.

2. Application of the rule to devises did, in fact, assure that O's heirs would take the reversion by inheritance instead of taking a vested remainder by "purchase," but it did not change the ultimate devolution of the fee simple.

riage.[3] But this reason for the Doctrine became completely obsolete in England with the enactment of the Statute of Tenures in 1660,[4] and the Doctrine was finally abolished by statute in 1833.[5]

In the United States there never was any rational basis for the Doctrine, yet it was generally accepted as part of the American common law in the nineteenth century.[6] The Doctrine has now been completely abolished in at least nine states[7] and, as to wills only, in at least one other state.[8] It has been abolished by judicial decision in at least two jurisdictions.[9] The Doctrine survives in its original form, as a rule of law, in a few states,[10] and in modified form, as a rule of construction, in a larger number of states.[11] The metamorphosis of the Doctrine into a rule of construction was largely the consequence of Cardozo's opinion in Doctor v. Hughes,[12] holding that when a remainder is expressly given to the grantor's heirs, it should be presumed that the grantor did not intend to create a remainder unless there is additional evidence of his intent to do so. This is ironic because the New York cases prior to Doctor v. Hughes had never recognized the Doctrine.[13] The Doctrine was recently abolished by statute in New York.[14]

Despite "some indications" that the Doctrine of Worthier Title retains a "modicum of vitality" as to dispositions by will,[15] most of the recent cases apply the Doctrine only to *inter vivos* transfers (usually in trust) and the Property Restatement has also taken the position that the Doctrine now applies only to *inter vivos* transfers.[16] But the scope of the Doctrine has

---

3. See L. Simes, Future Interests § 26 (2d ed. 1966); L. Simes and A. Smith, Future Interests § 1602 (2d ed. 1956).

4. 12 Charles II c. 24 (1660).

5. 3 & 4 Wm. IV c. 106, § 3 (1833).

6. E.g., King v. Dunham, 31 Ga. 743 (1861); Harris v. McLaran, 30 Miss. 533 (1855); Robinson v. Blankinship, 116 Tenn. 394, 92 S.W. 854 (1906).

7. West's Ann.Cal.Probate Code § 109, West's Ann.Cal.Civ.Code § 1073 (added by Laws 1959, c. 122); Ill.—S.H.A. ch. 30, ¶¶ 188, 189 (added by Laws 1955, p. 498); Mass.Gen. Laws Ann. c. 184, §§ 33A, 33B (enacted 1973); Minn.Stat.Ann. § 500.14(4); Neb.Rev.Stat. §§ 76–114, 76–115; N.Y.—McKinney's Estates, Powers and Trusts Law 6–5.9; North Car.Gen.Stat. § 4–6.2 (added by Laws 1979, c. 88); Vernon's Ann.Tex.Civ.Stat. art. 1291a (added by Laws 1963, p. 542); West Virginia Code, § 36–1–14a (added by Laws 1969, c. 56).

8. Kan.Stat.Ann. § 58–506.

9. Peter v. Peter, 136 Md. 157, 110 A. 211 (1920); Hatch v. Riggs National Bank, 361 F.2d 559 (D.C.Cir.1966), noted 16 Catholic Univ.L.Rev. 239 (1966); 66 Colum.L.Rev. 1552 (1966); 41 N.Y.U.L.Rev. 1228 (1967); 42 Wash. L.Rev. 919 (1967).

10. The Georgia and Mississippi cases cited supra note 6 are quite old, and it is uncertain whether either Georgia or Mississippi would apply the Doctrine in any form today. In Tennessee the Doctrine has apparently been

changed into a rule of construction. Cochran v. Frierson, 195 Tenn. 174, 258 S.W.2d 748 (1953); but see Standard Knitting Mills, Inc. v. Allen, 221 Tenn. 90, 424 S.W.2d 796 (1967). Fairly recent decisions in Arkansas and Pennsylvania treat the doctrine as a rule of law: Wilson v. Pharris, 203 Ark. 614, 158 S.W.2d 274 (1942); In re Brolasky's Estate, 302 Pa. 439, 153 A. 739 (1931).

11. E.g., Wilcoxen v. Owen, 237 Ala. 169, 185 So. 897, 125 A.L.R. 539 (1938); Thurman v. Hudson, 280 S.W.2d 507 (Ky.1955); Norman v. Horton, 344 Mo. 290, 126 S.W.2d 187, 125 A.L.R. 531 (1939); In re Lichtenstein's Estate, 52 N.J. 553, 247 A.2d 320 (1968); Kohler v. Ichler, 116 Ohio App. 16, 186 N.E.2d 202 (1961); Dunnett v. First National Bank, 184 Okl. 82, 85 P.2d 281 (1938); Braswell v. Braswell, 195 Va. 971, 81 S.E.2d 560 (1954).

12. 225 N.Y. 305, 122 N.E. 221 (1919), noted, 4 Corn.L.Q. 83 (1919), 28 Yale L.J. 713 (1919).

13. E.g., Genet v. Hunt, 113 N.Y. 158, 21 N.E. 91 (1889).

14. Supra note 7.

15. L. Simes and A. Smith, Future Interests § 1601 at n. 8. See also Morris, The Wills Branch of the Worthier Title Doctrine, 54 Mich.L.Rev. 451 (1956).

16. 3 Rest.Prop. § 314(2). Of course, it will generally make no practical difference today whether a testator's heirs acquire a future interest by will or by descent, since

been enlarged in some states by cases applying it to personal as well as real property,[17] and to executory interests as well as to remainders.[18]

Even as a rule of construction, the Worthier Title Doctrine applies only where the dispositive instrument expressly gives a remainder or executory interest to the transferor's "heirs" or "next-of-kin," or uses equivalent language to describe the beneficiaries—e.g., "such persons as would be entitled to receive the settlor's real and personal property in case of intestacy." [19]   But the Doctrine does not apply if the future interest is given to a named person who ultimately proves to be the sole heir or next-of-kin of the transferor.[20]   Nor does the Doctrine apply when the future interest is given to the transferor's "children," even if his children ultimately prove to be his heirs or next-of-kin; [21]   or when a statute provides that the word "heirs" shall be deemed to mean "children" unless a contrary intent is expressed; [22]   or when the future interest is given to the transferor's "heirs" as determined at a date other than his death or according to the intestate succession laws of a foreign jurisdiction.[23]

Whether held to be a rule of law or a rule of construction, the Worthier Title Doctrine has been applied mainly in the following situations:

(1) Where O has conveyed property "to A for life, remainder to my heirs at law," and thereafter has purported to convey or devise his entire interest in the property to someone other than his heirs.   If the Worthier Title Doctrine applies, the subsequent grantee or devisee will take the property at

property devolves in the same manner in either case.   For possible instances where application of the Worthier Title Doctrine to wills might make a difference, with arguments against reaching different results, see 3 Rest. Prop. § 314(2), Comment j.

17. E.g., King v. Dunham, supra note 6; In re Warren's Estate, 211 Iowa 940, 234 N.W. 835 (1931); Fidelity & Columbia Trust Co. v. Williams, 268 Ky. 671, 105 S.W.2d 814 (1937); Harris v. McLaran, supra note 6; In re Lichtenstein's Estate, supra note 11; Dunnett v. First Nat. Bank, supra note 11; Bottimore v. First & Merchants National Bank, 170 Va. 221, 196 S.E. 593 (1938).   The original policy basis for the Doctrine was never applicable, of course, to personal property; hence, the rationale for applying the Doctrine to personal property must be sought elsewhere.   As is suggested infra in the text at notes 31, 32, in many cases the reason for extension probably was the court's desire to find a basis for holding that trusts of personal property were revocable by the settlor, despite his express language giving an interest to his heirs or next-of-kin.

18. At common law in England, the Doctrine seems to have been applied only to remainders to the heirs of the transferor.   But many American cases apply it to executory interests as well.   E.g., Fletcher v. Ferrill, 216 Ark. 583, 227 S.W.2d 448, 16 A.L.R.2d 1240 (1950); Coomes v. Frey, 141 Ky. 740, 133 S.W.

758 (1911); In re Brolasky's Estate, 302 Pa. 439, 153 A. 739 (1931).

19. L. Simes and A. Smith, Future Interests § 1606 (2d ed. 1956).   And see id. §§ 1604, 1610, pointing out that where the subject matter is personal property the limitation may be either to "heirs" or to "next of kin," and that there is even some authority where the subject matter is real property that a limitation to the grantor's "next of kin" will be treated as a limitation to his "heirs."   Where a grantor uses language indicating that he is referring to his "heirs" as of some time other than the time of his death, it is generally held that the Doctrine does not apply.   E.g., Gray v. Union Trust Co., 171 Cal. 637, 154 P. 306 (1916); Department of Revenue v. Kentucky Trust Co., 313 S.W.2d 401 (Ky.1958); Schoelkopf v. Marine Trust Co., infra note 20.   Contra: E.g., Dunnett v. First Nat. Bank, supra note 11.

20. E.g., Schoellkopf v. Marine Trust Co., 267 N.Y. 358, 196 N.E. 288 (1935).

21. 3 Rest.Prop. § 314.

22. For an example of such a statute, see Official Code Ga.Ann. § 85–504.

23. E.g., Robinson v. Blankinship, supra note 6; Warren–Boynton State Bank v. Wallbaum, 123 Ill.2d 429, 123 Ill.Dec. 936, 528 N.E.2d 640 (1989) (Doctrine not applicable when the word "heirs" refers to takers at a time other than the grantor's death).

A's death and O's heirs will take nothing.[24]

(2) Where O has conveyed property to a trustee, "in trust to pay the income to O for life, and to transfer the property to O's heirs after his death," without expressly reserving the power to revoke the trust. If the Worthier Title Doctrine applies, O is the only person with a beneficial interest in the trust property and he may revoke the trust at any time.[25] If the Doctrine does not apply, O generally cannot unilaterally revoke the trust and thus destroy the contingent remainder limited to his heirs; nor can he join with them to terminate the trust, since his heirs cannot be ascertained during his lifetime.[26]

(3) Where creditors of O and/or the creditors of O's heir apparent seek to reach and apply their debtor's interest in property transferred by O "to A for life, remainder to my heirs." If the Worthier Title Doctrine applies, O has a reversion that is subject to his creditors' claims[27] and the heir apparent has no interest in the property that can be subjected to his creditors' claims.[28] If the Doctrine does not apply, it would seem that a contrary result would be reached, at least in jurisdictions where contingent remainders are alienable by deed.[29]

It should also be noted that application of the Worthier Title Doctrine may produce unexpected consequences under the federal estate tax law. If O has transferred "to A for life, remainder to my heirs," application of the Doctrine will prevent defeasance of O's reversion at his death and cause the reversion to be included in O's gross estate.[30]

The Worthier Title Doctrine has been the subject of a good deal of criticism.[31] It has been defended mainly on the ground that it is a desirable way to assure that the settlor of an *inter vivos* trust can revoke the trust

---

24. E.g., Thurman v. Hudson, 280 S.W.2d 507 (Ky.1955); All Persons v. Buie, 386 So.2d 1109 (Miss.1980); Cochran v. Frierson, 195 Tenn. 174, 258 S.W.2d 748 (1953); Braswell v. Braswell, 195 Va. 971, 81 S.E.2d 560 (1954).

25. E.g., Burton v. Boren, 308 Ill. 440, 139 N.E. 868 (1923); Fidelity & Columbia Trust Co. v. Williams, 268 Ky. 671, 105 S.W.2d 814 (1937); Stephens v. Moore, 298 Mo. 215, 249 S.W. 601 (1923); Fidelity Union Trust Co. v. Parfner, 135 N.J.Eq. 133, 37 A.2d 675 (1944); Scholtz v. Central Hanover Bank & Trust Co., 295 N.Y. 488, 68 N.E.2d 503 (1946); Bottimore v. First & Mechanics National Bank, 170 Va. 221, 196 S.E. 593 (1938).

26. E.g., Sutliff v. Aydelott, 373 Ill. 633, 27 N.E.2d 529 (1940); Clark v. Judge, 84 N.J.Super. 35, 200 A.2d 801 (1964), affirmed 44 N.J. 550, 210 A.2d 415 (1965); In re Burchell's Estate, 299 N.Y. 351, 87 N.E.2d 293 (1949).

27. E.g., Gould v. Harris, 132 A. 2 (R.I. 1926); Biwer v. Martin, 294 Ill. 488, 128 N.E. 518 (1920); Seguin State Bank & Trust Co. v. Locke, 129 Tex. 524, 102 S.W.2d 1050 (1937); McKenna v. Seattle–First National Bank, 35 Wn.2d 662, 214 P.2d 664 (1950).

28. Doctor v. Hughes, 225 N.Y. 305, 122 N.E. 221 (1919).

29. Although both the contingent remainder and the reversion (which is vested subject to complete defeasance) are alienable, it would seem that only the contingent remainder should be subject to creditors' claims in such a case, since the contingent remainder is certain to become a present interest and the reversion is certain to be completely defeated (assuming that O has an heir). See post Section 3.25.

30. See I.R.C. § 2033; Beach v. Busey, 156 F.2d 496 (6th Cir.1946), certiorari denied 329 U.S. 802, 67 S.Ct. 493, 91 L.Ed. 685 (1947); Bartlett v. United States, 146 F.Supp. 719, 137 Ct.Cl. 38 (1956). Of course, even if the Doctrine is not applied and the reversion is defeated upon O's death, the value of the interest passing to the heirs as remaindermen may be included in O's gross estate under I.R.C. § 2036 or § 2037. Moreover, since the transactions that might implicate the Worthier Title Doctrine are always gratuitous, the gift of a remainder to "heirs" would be subject to the federal gift tax, in any case.

31. E.g., L. Waggoner, Future Interests in a Nutshell § 11.3 (1981); Nossaman, Gift to Heirs, Remainder or Reversion, 24 Cal.St.Bar J. 59 (1949); Note, 34 Ill.L.Rev. 835, 851 (1940); Note 17 U.Chi.L.Rev. 87 (1949).

during his lifetime, despite his failure expressly to reserve the power to revoke.[32] As a rule of construction, however, the Worthier Title Doctrine invites litigation and increases the unpredictability of litigation results—an unpredictability that has been further increased by the rejection—in the courts of New York and some other states—of Cardozo's dictum in Doctor v. Hughes [33] that only a clear expression of intent should be sufficient to rebut the presumption against intent to create a remainder in favor of the transferor's heirs. Both in New York and elsewhere, the presumption may now be rebutted if a contrary intent can be gathered from the dispositive instrument as a whole.[34] For example, in Richardson v. Richardson,[35] the New York Court of Appeals said,

> [W]e believe that the settlor evidenced her intention to give a remainder to her next of kin because she (1) made a full and formal disposition of the principal of the trust property, (2) made no reservation of a power to grant or assign an interest in the property during her lifetime, (3) surrendered all control over the trust property except the power to make testamentary disposition thereof and the right to appoint a substitute trustee, and (4) made no provision for return of any part of the principal to herself during her lifetime.

The result of the *Richardson* case and other similar cases led Professor Richard Powell to conclude that in New York "no case involving a substantial sum of money could be fairly regarded as closed until it had been carried to the Court of Appeals," and that a similar situation—necessarily resulting in "wasteful expenditures of money by helpless clients" because of "uncertainty in the law"—was to be expected in other states where the Worthier Title Doctrine is retained as a rule of construction.[36] As to dispositions of property after the recent statutory abolition of the Doctrine, the situation has been corrected in New York and several other states.[37]

On the whole, although the Worthier Title Doctrine does make property more freely alienable, its continued application seems undesirable. If legislatures or courts believe that trusts should be revocable despite the settlor's failure to reserve a power to revoke, the goal can be achieved without retaining the outmoded and litigation-breeding Worthier Title Doctrine. New York has abolished the Doctrine by statute, but has adopted legislation providing that, for trust termination purposes only, the heirs of the settlor are not to be deemed to acquire any beneficial interest in the trust property.[38] In California, the Doctrine has also been abolished by statute,[39] but legislation enacted in 1931 makes all *inter vivos* trusts revocable unless the

---

32. This may have been, at least in part, what Judge Cardozo had in mind when he said, "seldom do the living mean to forego the power of disposition during life by the direction that upon death there shall be a transfer to their heirs." Doctor v. Hughes, supra note 28, 225 N.Y. at 313, 122 N.E. at 223.

33. Supra note 28.

34. E.g., Richardson v. Richardson, 298 N.Y. 135, 81 N.E.2d 54 (1948), noted in 62 Harv.L.Rev. 313 (1948), 24 Ind.L.J. 292 (1949), and 24 N.Y.U.L.Q.Rev. 450 (1949); In re Burc-

hell's Estate, 299 N.Y. 351, 87 N.E.2d 293 (1949), noted in 49 Mich.L.Rev. 139 (1950), 2 Syracuse L.Rev. 319 (1949), 35 Va.L.Rev. 794 (1949).

35. Supra note 34.

36. 3 R. Powell, Real Property ¶ 381.

37. Supra note 7.

38. N.Y.—McKinney's Estates, Powers and Trusts Law § 7–1.9.

39. Supra note 7.

settlor expressly provides to the contrary.[40]   And in the District of Columbia it has been held that the Worthier Title Doctrine is no longer in force but that courts may appoint a guardian *ad litem* to consent to premature termination of a trust on behalf of the settlor's unascertained heirs.[41]

In jurisdictions where the Worthier Title Doctrine is still applied as a rule of law, the only way to avoid its application is to limit the remainder to persons other than the grantor's "heirs" or "next of kin." A grantor, e.g., might accomplish substantially the same disposition of his property by limiting a remainder to his "children," or "nieces and nephews," with a clear statement that the class is not intended as equivalent to "heirs"; or by limiting a remainder to named persons who are the heirs apparent, without designating them as "heirs"; or by limiting a remainder to his "heirs" to be determined as of a date other than that of the grantor's death.[42]

If the Worthier Title Doctrine is applied as a rule of construction, a limitation to the grantor's "heirs" will be legally effective, provided the grantor clearly indicates his intention to create a remainder or executory interest in their favor—e.g., by adding a clause such as the following: "it being my intention that those persons, now unascertained, who shall prove to be my heirs, shall by this instrument take a contingent remainder as purchasers." [43]

It goes without saying that the person who drafts a deed or trust instrument should ascertain the grantor's real intention before including a limitation to the grantor's "heirs"; the draftsman should not add a final limitation to the grantor's "heirs" simply because the grantor has not, in his instructions to the draftsman, provided expressly for all possibilities.

§ 3.16   The Rule in Shelley's Case

Another English common law rule relating to contingent remainders in land—the Rule in Shelley's Case [1]—is now practically as moribund as the destructibility rule. The Rule was abolished in England by the Law of Property Act of 1925,[2] and has been completely abolished by statute in at least thirty-six American jurisdictions.[3]   Four states have statutes that abolish the Rule as to wills only.[4]   In two states the courts have refused to

40. West's Ann.Cal.Civ.Code § 2280 (as amended by Laws 1931, p. 1955, § 1).

41. Hatch v. Riggs National Bank, 361 F.2d 559 (D.C.Cir.1966).

42. See L. Simes and A. Smith, Future Interests § 1613 (2d ed. 1956).

43. Ibid.

§ 3.16

1. Wolfe v. Shelley, 1 Co.Rep. 93b, 76 Eng. Rep. 206 (1581), was not the first case recognizing the Rule, which probably antedated its early application in the Provost of Beverley's Case, Y.B. 40 Ed.Ill.Hil. pl. 18 (1366).

2. Law of Property Act § 131 (1925).

3. See L. Simes and A. Smith, Future Interests § 1563 at nn. 64 through 98 (2d ed. 1956), and statutes cited; id., 1981 Supp.

§ 1563 nn. 58, 65, 87, 98, and statutes cited. The states where the Rule has been completely abrogated are Arizona, California, Connecticut, the District of Columbia, Florida, Georgia, Idaho, Illinois, Kansas, Kentucky, Maine, Maryland, Massachusetts, Michigan, Minnesota, Mississippi, Missouri, Montana, Nebraska, New Jersey, New Mexico, New York, North Dakota, Ohio, Oklahoma, Pennsylvania, Rhode Island, South Carolina, South Dakota, Tennessee, Texas, Virginia, West Virginia, and Wisconsin.

4. L. Simes and A. Smith, Future Interests § 1563 at nn. 99, 1 (2d ed. 1956), and statutes cited, id. 1981 Supp. § 1563 n. 99. These states include Alabama, Alaska, New Hampshire, and Oregon.

recognize the Rule although the Rule has not been abolished by statute,[5] and in four states there are neither statutes nor judicial decisions concerning the Rule.[6] One of the latter is Louisiana, where it seems clear that the Rule is not in force because Louisiana adheres to the civil law rather than the common law. It thus appears that the Rule is now still in force, as to both deeds and wills, in only five states.[7]

The Rule in Shelley's Case has been completely abolished by statute rather recently in several states.[8] Since these statutes apply only to instruments taking effect after the effective dates of the statutes, it is still necessary to keep in mind the possible applicability of the Rule in such states to instruments taking effect before the statutes abolishing the Rule went into effect.[9]

As developed by the English courts, the Rule in Shelley's Case prescribed that when a deed or will purported to give a remainder to the heirs, or the heirs of the body, of a person who received a prior freehold estate by the same instrument, that person also took the remainder.[10] Thus the Rule prohibited creation of a contingent remainder in favor of the heirs, or heirs of the body, of one to whom the same instrument gave a prior freehold estate. The Rule applied whether the prior freehold estate was possessory or was itself a remainder,[11] and whether or not there was an intervening estate between the prior freehold and the purported remainder to the heirs, or heirs of the body, of the person to whom the prior freehold estate was

---

5. L. Simes and A. Smith, Future Interests § 1563 nn. 60, 61 (2d ed. 1956), and cases cited. The two states are Hawaii and Vermont.

6. L. Simes and A. Smith, Future Interests § 1563 in text between nn. 62 and 64 (2d ed. 1956). The four states are Louisiana, Nevada, Utah, and Wyoming.

7. These states are Arkansas, Colorado, Delaware, Indiana, and North Carolina.

8. See L. Simes and A. Smith, Future Interests § 1563 nn. 69, 72, 81, 84 (2d ed. 1956); id. 1981 Supp. § 1563 n. 58 (Rule abolished in Texas as to conveyances made after Jan. 1, 1964).

9. See, refusing to apply the statute abolishing the Rule, City Bank & Trust Co. v. Morrissey, 118 Ill.App.3d 640, 73 Ill.Dec. 946, 454 N.E.2d 1195 (1983) (although Rule was abolished by statute in 1953, the statute did not apply retroactively to instruments executed and delivered before enactment of statute); Society Nat. Bank v. Jacobson, 54 Ohio St.3d 15, 560 N.E.2d 217 (1990), rehearing denied 55 Ohio St.3d 709, 563 N.E.2d 302 (1990) (statute not applicable to trust instrument executed ten years before the statute was enacted). The rationale for judicial refusal to apply the Rule retroactively is dubious, since application of the rule would, in all cases, enable the court to carry out the intent of the parties. The usual justification for refusal to apply a statute retroactively is that this would defeat

the intentions of the parties, which is true in some but not all cases. The necessity of considering the possible applicability of the Rule in some of these states is mitigated, however, by adoption of "marketable title acts" which bar claims based on matters appearing in the record chain of title more than a stated number of years prior to the time when the marketability of the title to a tract of land is determined. "Marketable title acts" are now in force in Florida, Illinois, Kansas, Nebraska and Ohio (*inter alia*).

10. Sir Edward Coke stated the Rule as follows: "It is a rule of law, when the ancestor by any gift or conveyance takes an estate of freehold, and in the same gift or conveyance an estate is limited either mediately or immediately to his heirs in fee or in tail; that always in such cases, 'the heirs' are words of limitation of the estate, and not words of purchase." 1 Co.Rep. 93b, at p. 104a (1581).

The Rule does not apply where a deed merely reserves a life estate in the grantor rather than creating a life estate in a third person. Warren–Boynton State Bank v. Wallbaum, 123 Ill.2d 429, 123 Ill.Dec. 936, 528 N.E.2d 640 (1988).

11. E.g., Ryan v. Ryan, 138 Ark. 362, 211 S.W. 183 (1919); Depler v. Dyer, 312 Ill. 537, 144 N.E. 212 (1924); Wright v. Jenks, 124 Kan. 604, 261 P. 840 (1927); Dukes v. Shuler, 185 S.C. 303, 194 S.E. 817 (1938).

given.[12] But the Rule was applicable only if both the prior freehold and the remainder were of the same quality—i.e., both "legal" or both "equitable" in quality.[13]

It appears that the Rule in Shelley's Case was applicable in England, prior to its abolition, whether the prior freehold estate was for life or in fee tail,[14] but the Rule has been applied in the United States only in cases where the prior freehold was a life estate.[15] The Rule has been applied both in England and in the United States where the remainder was to "the heirs of the body" of the person to whom the prior freehold was limited.[16] American statutes abolishing the fee tail estate [17] will, of course, preclude the creation of a prior freehold estate in fee tail which could bring the Rule into operation. And the operation of the Rule may be nullified by a statute providing that language which would create a fee tail at common law shall create a life estate in the first taker with a remainder in fee simple to the heirs of his body. Under such a statute, a transfer "to A for life, remainder to the heirs of his body" would first create a fee tail in A through application of the Rule in Shelley's Case and then the statute would convert the fee tail into a life estate in A and a contingent remainder in fee simple in favor of the heirs of A's body.

Although Sir Edward Coke stated the Rule in Shelley's Case [18] in a form indicating that it would apply only when the word "heirs" denotes "all the heirs (or heirs of the body) which the ancestor might have from generation to generation throughout the future," [19] and the English courts seem generally to have adhered to this definition,[20] there are many American cases rejecting it. Thus many American cases hold that the Rule applies when the word "heirs" clearly denotes a class of persons who will inherit immediately upon the death of the ancestor intestate.[21] However, "it can hardly be said that in any given jurisdiction either doctrine as to the meaning of heirs is consistently followed," [22] although it is clear that the Rule does not apply when the remainder is expressly given to the "children" of the person to whom the

---

12. E.g., Carpenter v. Hubbard, 263 Ill. 571, 105 N.E. 688 (1914); Harlan v. Manington, 152 Iowa 707, 133 N.W. 367 (1911); Hartman v. Flynn, 189 N.C. 452, 127 S.E. 517 (1925).

13. E.g., Johnson v. Shriver, 121 Colo. 397, 216 P.2d 653 (1950) (Rule not applicable where one estate was legal and the other was equitable); Elsasser v. Elsasser, 159 Fla. 696, 32 So.2d 579 (1947); Harlan v. Manington, supra note 12.

14. Goodright v. Wright, 1 P.Wms. 397 (1717) (semble). The Rule is so stated in 1 Hayes, Conveyancing 545 (5th ed. 1840); 1 Preston on Estates 313 (1820); 1 Fearne, Contingent Remainders * 165.

15. 3 Rest.Prop. § 312 states that the Rule applies only when the ancestor has a life estate.

16. See Coke's statement of the Rule, supra note 10. Where the remainder is to the "heirs of the body" of the person taking the

prior freehold, the remainder will be either in fee tail or fee simple conditional if such estates are still recognized in the jurisdiction where the land is situated. E.g., Wayne v. Lawrence, 58 Ga. 15 (1877) (fee tail); Blume v. Pearcy, 204 S.C. 409, 29 S.E.2d 673 (1944) (fee simple conditional).

17. Ante Section 2.10 at notes 2–7.

18. Supra note 10.

19. 3 R. Powell, Real Property ¶ 379.

20. Ibid.; L. Simes and A. Smith, Future Interests § 1548 (2d ed. 1956).

21. Cf., e.g., Gordon v. Cadwalader, 164 Cal. 509, 130 P. 18 (1913) (Rule inapplicable where "heirs" described persons who would take on the ancestor's death and not those taking in indefinite succession); Ratley v. Oliver, 229 N.C. 120, 47 S.E.2d 703 (1948) (contra).

22. L. Simes and A. Smith, Future Interests § 1548 at n. 63 (2d ed. 1956).

prior freehold is given [23] or where the word "heirs" is construed to mean "children." [24] Since the Rule in Shelley's Case is a rule of law rather than a rule of construction, any direction in a deed or will that the Rule shall not apply is, of course, completely ineffective.[25]

Assuming the Rule in Shelley's Case to be in force at the time of transfer, the Rule would be applicable in all of the following cases:

(1) "to A for life, remainder to A's heirs";

(2) "to A for life, remainder to B for life, remainder to B's heirs";

(3) "to A for life, remainder to B for life, remainder to A's heirs."

In examples (1) and (3), the Rule gives A a vested remainder in fee simple as well as a possessory life estate. In example (1), A's life estate will merge in his remainder, and he will have a possessory estate in fee simple absolute.[26] In example (3), however, merger is impossible because of B's intervening remainder for life; [27] but if B predeceases A, merger will occur and A will have a possessory estate in fee simple absolute.[28] In example (2), the Rule gives B a remainder in fee simple as well as a remainder for life, and merger of the latter in the former leaves B with a remainder in fee

---

23. E.g., Bowen v. Frank, 179 Ark. 1004, 18 S.W.2d 1037 (1929); Beall v. Beall, 331 Ill. 28, 162 N.E. 152 (1928).

The general rule is that when a lesser estate and a greater estate are united in the same person, the lesser estate will "merge" with the greater estate and cease to exist as a separate interest. See, e.g., Paris Bank v. Custer, 681 P.2d 71 (Okl.1984); Village of Hillside v. Illinois Commerce Com'n, 111 Ill.App.3d 25, 66 Ill.Dec. 784, 443 N.E.2d 710 (1982). Thus merger may result when a life estate is united with a vested remainder or reversion in fee simple, when a right of entry or possibility of reverter, or an executory interest is united with a defeasible fee simple, or when a leasehold estate is united with either a life estate or a fee simple. However, in some situations a court will exercise its equity power to prevent a merger because a merger was not intended or would be contrary to the interests of the party in whom the lesser and the greater interest unite. Thus where the holder of a senior mortgage fails to join a junior mortgage holder in a foreclosure action or takes a deed from the mortgagor in lieu of foreclosure, a court will usually refuse to allow a merger and "keep the senior mortgage alive" in order to preserve the senior mortgage holder's priority over junior interests.

24. E.g., Williams v. Johnson, 228 N.C. 732, 47 S.E.2d 24 (1948); Green v. Green, 210 S.C. 391, 42 S.E.2d 884 (1947).

25. The leading English case is Perrin. v. Blake, 1 Bl.W. 672, 96 Eng.Rep. 392 (1769). The Rule has generally been applied as a rule of law in the United States—e.g., Bishop v. Williams, 221 Ark. 617, 255 S.W.2d 171 (1953) (Rule applied although instrument stated that "the term heirs herein used is a term of pur-

chase and not of limitation"); Hammer v. Brantley, 244 N.C. 71, 92 S.E.2d 424 (1956) (Rule is a rule of property without regard to the grantor's intent); Sybert v. Sybert, 250 S.W.2d 271 (Tex.Civ.App.1952), affirmed 152 Tex. 106, 254 S.W.2d 999 (1953) (Rule applied despite grantor's expressed contrary intent).

26. See discussion of this point by Lord MacNaghten in his opinion in Van Grutten v. Foxwell, [1897] A.C. 658. See also, L. Simes and A. Smith, Future Interests § 1556 (2d ed. 1956); 3 R. Powell, Real Property ¶ 379.

27. E.g., Carpenter v. Hubbard, 263 Ill. 571, 105 N.E. 688 (1914); Harlan v. Manington, 152 Iowa 707, 133 N.W. 367 (1911); Hartman v. Flynn, 189 N.C. 452, 127 S.E. 517 (1925).

28. E.g., Rose v. Rose, 219 N.C. 20, 12 S.E.2d 688 (1941); Chappell v. Chappell, 260 N.C. 737, 133 S.E.2d 666 (1963); Burnham v. Baltimore Gas & Electric Co., 217 Md. 507, 144 A.2d 80 (1958). As these cases and those cited supra in note 27 demonstrate, the Rule "operates only on the remainder, and * * * whether or not the ancestor has a present fee simple estate depends on whether the remainder can merge with the life estate." L. Simes and A. Smith, Future Interests § 1556 in text following n. 21 (2d ed. 1956). Even if the remainder limited to B for life in example (3) were subject to a condition precedent, no immediate merger would occur; but if A should later convey both his life estate and his vested remainder to a third person, B's contingent remainder would be destroyed by merger in any jurisdictions where contingent remainders are still destructible. Id. in text following n. 25.

simple absolute.[29]

Suppose a remainder to which the Rule in Shelley's Case would otherwise clearly apply is subject to an express condition precedent—e.g., "to A for life, remainder to the heirs of A if A shall marry B." The Rule applies in such a case, but there is no merger so long as the condition precedent remains unsatisfied.[30] Thus the legal effect of the last example would be as follows: A receives a life estate and a contingent in fee simple absolute, and O retains a reversion in fee simple subject to complete defeasance.

Both the Rule in Shelley's Case and the doctrine of merger may apply when both the prior freehold and the remainder are subject to the same condition precedent—e.g., in a transfer "to A for life, remainder for life to the first son of A who reaches the age of 21, remainder to the heirs of such son." Assuming that no son of A has yet reached the age of twenty-one, the legal effect of this transfer would be as follows: A receives a life estate, there is a contingent remainder in fee simple absolute in favor of the first son of A to reach twenty-one, and O retains a reversion in fee simple subject to complete defeasance.[31]

The Rule in Shelley's Case also applies when both the prior freehold and the remainder are created by an executory limitation—e.g., by a transfer "to A, but if A should die without leaving issue, to B for life, remainder to B's heirs." The Rule would give B the "remainder" created by the executory limitation, and B would end up with a shifting executory interest in fee simple absolute.[32]

§ 3.17   The Rule Against Perpetuities

The Rule Against Perpetuities, the principal common law rule limiting the creation of non-reversionary future interests, was given its classic statement by John Chipman Gray, as follows: "No interest is good unless it must vest, if at all, no later than twenty-one years after some life in being at the creation of the interest." [1]

---

29. E.g., Springbitt v. Monaghan, 43 Del. (4 Terry) 501, 50 A.2d 612 (1946); Dallmeyer v. Hermann, 437 S.W.2d 367 (Tex.Civ.App.1969), noted in 22 Baylor L.Rev. 146 (1970).

30. E.g., Federal Land Bank v. Walker, 345 Pa. 185, 26 A.2d 436 (1942), noted in 16 Temple L.Q. 449 (1942); McNeal v. Sherwood, 24 R.I. 314, 53 A. 43 (1902).

31. L. Simes, Future Interests § 24 at p. 53 (2d ed. 1966).

32. Ibid.

§ 3.17

1. J. Gray, The Rule Against Perpetuities 191 (4th ed. 1942). Gray's treatise was originally published in 1886. Cf. Professor Richard Powell's view that Gray's formulation of the Rule is defective for the following reasons:

"(1) It asserts an identity between 'remoteness of vesting' and 'invalidity under the Rule' which has never existed; and

"(2) It conceals the important social policy which generated the rule and which justifies

its modern continuance, by the use of language devoid of all reference to the preservation of the alienability of property."

5 R. Powell, Real Property ¶ 767A[3]. See also id. ¶ 767A[6]: "It is preferable to adopt the description of the rule, made by the Restatement, as one which promotes the alienability of property by destroying future interests of two types: (1) those which eliminate the power of alienation for longer than the permissible period; and (2) those which create nonvested future interests that are indestructible, thus lessening the probability of alienation for longer than the permissible period. These two prohibited types of future interests inconveniently fetter property and are socially undesirable."

Preservation of the alienability of property is clearly the rationale for a large amount of legislation enacted during the nineteenth century which prohibits suspension of the "absolute power of alienation" for longer than a stated period of time. This legislation is dis-

The Rule Against Perpetuities does not require certainty with respect to the period within which a non-vested future interest will either become a present interest or lose its capacity to become a present interest. The certainty required by the Rule relates only to "vesting in interest."[2] It should be noted, however, that the language creating a non-vested future interest may assure that, if the interest "vests in interest," it will at the same time become a present interest.[3]

The common law Rule Against Perpetuities is based upon the long-established judicial policy against permitting effective restraints upon the alienation of fee simple estates in land and equivalent interests in personalty.[4] This policy also provided the basis for judicial recognition of the common recovery as a device for converting a fee tail into a fee simple ("barring the entail") and judicial refusal to enforce any provision for defeasance conditioned upon alienation by common recovery. Had the English courts held that an estate in fee simple subject to an executory limitation could be converted into a fee simple absolute by resort to an appropriate action such as a common recovery, the Rule Against Perpetuities might never have evolved.[5] But in Pells v. Brown[6] it was held that executory interests were indestructible. This provided the impetus for judicial development of a new rule to control executory interests and prevent their use in family settlements in a way that would prevent alienation of settled land for an unreasonable period of time.[7]

As the quotation from Gray's famous treatise indicates, the Rule Against Perpetuities, in form, is a rule that invalidates executory interests and contingent remainders that are not certain to vest or fail within the stated "perpetuities period" of "lives in being" plus twenty-one years. But its underlying purpose is, in large part, to prevent the restraint on alienation that may result from the creation of a series of future interests some of which might neither vest nor fail within the perpetuities period. If such future interests were held to be valid, they could be used in such a way as to

---

cussed post Section 3.21. In some states where such legislation was enacted, the common law Rule Against Perpetuities was held to remain in force. In a few states the common law Rule Against Perpetuities was adopted in statutory form.

2. E.g., Salisbury v. Salisbury, 92 Kan. 644, 141 P. 173 (1914); Camden Safe Deposit & Trust Co. v. Scott, 121 N.J.Eq. 366, 189 A. 653, 110 A.L.R. 1442 (1937); Accounting of Estate of Isganaitis, 124 Misc.2d 1, 475 N.Y.S.2d 699 (Surr.Ct.1983) (whether interest violates Rule depends on "what might have happened rather than on what actually happened" and "if under any possible chain of events the interest may not vest within the period, it will be deemed invalid"); Sherrod v. Any Child or Children Hereafter Born to Watson N. Sherrod, Jr., 65 N.C.App. 252, 308 S.E.2d 904 (1983), modified and affirmed 312 N.C. 74, 320 S.E.2d 669 (1984).

3. This is so, e.g., if O makes a transfer "to A for life, remainder to the children of A who are living at his death, but if no children of A are living at his death, then to B." B's inter-

est is a contingent executory interest which may never "vest" at all; but if no children of A are living at A's death, B's executory interest simultaneously "vests in interest" and becomes a present interest.

4. See L. Simes and A. Smith, Future Interests §§ 1202, 1212 (2d ed. 1956); Simes, Future Interests §§ 120, 121 (2d ed. 1966); 5 R. Powell, supra note 1.

5. It should be noted that the English courts at an early date struck down an attempt to make a fee tail "unbarrable" by adding a series of contingent limitations to become operative if a tenant in tail should try to "bar the entail" by a common recovery. See 1 Co.Rep. 131b (1595).

6. Cro.Jac. 590 (1620).

7. Although contingent remainders were recognized a century before Pells v. Brown, the fact that a legal contingent remainder was destructible assured that it would normally be certain either to vest or to fail within "lives in being" at the creation of the contingent remainder.

make it impossible for an unlimited period of time for anyone to own a marketable estate in fee simple absolute.[8]

As we shall see, the Rule Against Perpetuities is applicable to executory interests and contingent remainders in both realty and personalty, and to both legal and equitable interests.[9]   When the Rule is applied to legal executory interests and contingent remainders, its utility in preventing an unreasonable restraint on alienation is clear.   But application of the Rule to the equitable interests of trust beneficiaries does not have any effect on the alienability of the specific property included in the corpus of the trust in the ordinary case where the trustee has a broad power to alienate any or all of the specific property originally comprising the corpus of the trust and to replace it with other specific property.   Similarly, when the Rule is applied to non-vested future interests in shares of corporate stock, whether or not held in trust, the effect on alienability of the corporation's assets is at best minimal, since the corporate management always has broad power to alienate corporate assets.   In these cases, the application of the Rule must be justified, it seems, on the grounds suggested by Simes: that such application is necessary to limit "dead hand" control over property and to "strike a fair balance between the policy of allowing the present generation to do as it wishes with the property which it enjoys, and the policy of allowing succeeding generations to do as they wish with the property which they will enjoy." [10]

§ 3.18   Interests Subject to the Rule Against Perpetuities

As stated by Gray, the Rule Against Perpetuities would appear to apply to all non-vested future interests, both reversionary and non-reversionary— i.e., to possibilities of reverter, rights of entry for breach of condition (powers of termination), contingent remainders, and executory interests.   But American courts have consistently held that possibilities of reverter and rights of

---

8.   Although placing property in trust certainly imposes some restraint upon alienation, a trust is not necessarily void merely because it may last longer than "twenty-one years after some life in being at the creation of the" trust.   Indeed a charitable trust is valid even though it may last forever and is made indestructible by the instrument creating it.   But— although authority is scant—it is probable that in most states a private non-charitable trust cannot be made indestructible for a period in excess of lives in being plus twenty-one years and that, if the settlor by express or implied direction attempts to make it indestructible for a longer period, the courts will declare it terminable from its inception.   And a private, noncharitable trust for an unincorporated association is simply void if, by its terms, it is not terminable within lives in being plus twenty-one years.   See L. Simes & A. Smith, Future Interests §§ 1392, 1393, 1395 (2d ed. 1956, Supp.1985); L. Simes, Future Interests §§ 144, 145, 147 (2d ed. 1966). Courts sometimes seem confused as to whether the Rule Against Perpetuities, as such, applies to "trusts."   See, e.g., Cotham v. First Nat. Bank of Hot Springs, 287 Ark. 167, 697

S.W.2d 101 (1985), where the court said "the trust at issue does not violate the rule because the trust will vest within lives in being plus twenty-one years."   Apparently the court meant that the trust would necessarily terminate within the perpetuities period because it was created to last only for "lives in being." See also Accounting of Estate of Isganaitis, supra note 2, where the court said that the trust in question "must fail" if "duration of the trust would not be measured by lives in being as required by the statute."   Apparently the court was considering the possibility that the trust violated that part of the New York statutory rule against perpetuities which forbids suspension of the absolute power of alienation for a longer period than lives in being plus twenty-one years, although this is not clear.

9.   See post Section 3.18.

10.   L. Simes and A. Smith, Future Interests § 1235 (2d ed. 1956); L. Simes, Future Interests § 121 (2d ed. 1966).   See also, for a fuller development of this thesis, L. Simes, Public Policy and the Dead Hand (1955).

entry are not subject to the common law Rule Against Perpetuities.[1] The reasons for this exemption seem to be largely historical. Possibilities of reverter and rights of entry were recognized long before the Rule began to evolve; they were somewhat analogous to a feudal lord's right of escheat, which was not deemed to be an objectionable restraint upon alienation of land; and they were often created in order to assure that property given for charitable purposes would continue to be devoted to such purposes.[2] Thus the Rule applies, at common law, only to non-reversionary future interests.

When the Rule Against Perpetuities began to evolve in the late seventeenth century, it was aimed primarily at executory interests, which in Pells v. Brown (1620) were held to be indestructible.[3] Any contingent executory interest—except one limited to a charitable organization upon the defeasance or termination of a prior estate given to another charitable organization by the same instrument—is clearly subject to the Rule.[4] Since almost all executory interests are, in fact, contingent—i.e., subject to a condition precedent that is not certain to be satisfied—almost all executory interests are subject to the Rule. But it is possible to create executory interests that are neither vested nor contingent—e.g., the springing executory interest created by a conveyance "to A, from and after the expiration of 25 years from the date of this conveyance." Although there is little authority as to the applicability of the Rule Against Perpetuities to such an executory interest,[5] it would seem that the Rule should not apply.[6] In the example given, A's executory interest is substantially equivalent to a vested remainder in fee simple (or equivalent interest in personalty) following a term of twenty-five years. The executory interest can be as easily valued as a vested remainder in fee simple following a twenty-five year term, and is as readily marketable. If a court were to decide that such an executory interest is subject to the Rule Against Perpetuities, it is probable that the court would

§ 3.18

1. E.g., Fletcher v. Ferrill, 216 Ark. 583, 227 S.W.2d 448, 16 A.L.R.2d 1240 (1950) (possibility of reverter); Collins v. Church of God of Prophecy, 304 Ark. 37, 800 S.W.2d 418 (1990) (reversing trial court's holding that a possibility of reverter is subject to the Rule and hence void); Institution for Savings in Roxbury v. Roxbury Home, 244 Mass. 583, 139 N.E. 301 (1922) (same); Hinton v. Gilbert, 221 Ala. 309, 128 So. 604, 70 A.L.R. 1192 (1930) (power of termination); Strong v. Shatto, 45 Cal.App. 29, 187 P. 159 (1919) (same). See, generally, L. Simes and A. Smith §§ 1238, 1239 (2d ed. 1956).

2. L. Simes, Future Interests § 132 (2d ed. 1966).

3. Pells v. Brown, ante Section 3.17 n. 6.

4. E.g., Dickenson v. City of Anna, 310 Ill. 222, 141 N.E. 754, 30 A.L.R. 587 (1923); Carson Park Riding Club v. Friendly Home for Children, 421 S.W.2d 832 (Ky.1967); First Church in Somerville v. Attorney General, 375 Mass. 332, 376 N.E.2d 1226 (1978); Hornets Nest Girl Scout Council, Inc. v. Cannon Foundation, Inc., 79 N.C.App. 187, 339 S.E.2d 26 (1986) (generally applicable to executory interests, but "the Rule does not apply to charitable trusts"). The exception for charitable trusts is applicable only when the property is initially given to a charitable organization with a "gift over" by way of executory limitation to another charitable organization. L. Simes, Future Interests § 136 (2d ed. 1966). See, e.g., Lancaster v. Merchants Nat. Bank, 752 F.Supp. 886 (W.D.Ark.1990), reversed 961 F.2d 713 (8th Cir.1992) (charitable gift exception is not applicable where beneficiaries of initial gift and of "gift over" are not both charitable organizations).

5. See Nicol v. Morton, 332 Ill. 533, 164 N.E. 5 (1928); Mercantile Trust Co. v. Hammerstein, 380 S.W.2d 287 (Mo.1964), discussed in Eckhardt, The Rule Against Perpetuities in Missouri, 30 Mo.L.Rev. 27 (1965); Hunt v. Carroll, 157 S.W.2d 429 (Tex.Civ.App.1941), error dismissed 140 Tex. 424, 168 S.W.2d 238 (Tex.Com.App.1943).

6. L. Simes and A. Smith, Future Interests § 1236 (2d ed. 1956); L. Simes, Future Interests § 137 (2d ed. 1966); 4 Rest.Prop. § 370, Comments g and h. The Rule is said to apply to non-contingent executory interests in J. Gray, The Rule Against Perpetuities § 201 n. 3 (4th ed. 1942).

tend to construe a conveyance like that in the example given as creating a vested remainder in fee simple (or equivalent interest in personalty) rather than an executory interest in order to prevent the invalidation of the future interest by an application of the Rule.[7]

The Rule Against Perpetuities is clearly applicable to equitable contingent remainders [8] and to all contingent remainders in personalty, whether legal or equitable.[9] There is also substantial authority in support of the view that the Rule is applicable to legal contingent remainders in land.[10] In those jurisdictions where the doctrine of destructibility has been completely abolished, legal contingent remainders in land are no longer distinguishable from shifting executory interests, and they clearly should be subject to the Rule.[11] But where legal contingent remainders in land are still destructible if they fail to vest at or before termination of all prior estates created by the same instrument, the Rule would rarely invalidate such contingent remainders because the destructibility rule will assure, in most cases, that such contingent remainders will either vest or fail within the perpetuities period.[12]

In applying the Rule Against Perpetuities to class gifts, if the gift is void as to any potential member of the class because the class is capable either of increasing or decreasing in membership for longer than the perpetuities period, the general rule is that the entire gift is void.[13] But there are two recognized exceptions to this harsh rule:

7. L. Simes, Future Interests § 132 (2d ed. 1966). Cf. Williams v. Watt, 668 P.2d 620 (Wyo.1983), holding the future interest "following" a fee simple determinable to be vested remainder in fee simple rather than an executory interest because it was certain to become possessory although it was uncertain when this would occur. The court obviously adopted the vested remainder construction in order to avoid a construction that would have invalidated the interest as violative of the Rule Against Perpetuities. See ante Section 2.9 n. 1.

8. E.g., Abbiss v. Burney, 17 Ch.D. 211 (1881); Lawrence v. Smith, 163 Ill. 149, 45 N.E. 259 (1896); In re Feeney's Estate, 293 Pa. 273, 142 A. 284 (1928).

9. E.g., Bull v. Prichard, 1 Russ. 213 (1825); Michigan Trust Co. v. Baker, 226 Mich. 72, 196 N.W. 976 (1924); Norton v. Georgia R.R. Bank & Trust, 253 Ga. 596, 322 S.E.2d 870 (1984). The famous Duke of Norfolk's Case, 3 Ch.Cas. 1 (1682), in which Lord Nottingham first formulated the modern Rule Against Perpetuities, involved contingent equitable future interests in a chattel real.

10. In re Ashforth, [1905] 1 Ch. 535, 21 T.L.R. 329. See also Owsley v. Harrison, 190 Ill. 235, 60 N.E. 89 (1901); Ryan v. Beshk, 339 Ill. 45, 170 N.E. 699 (1930); Graham v. Whitridge, 99 Md. 248, 57 A. 609, 66 L.R.A. 408 (1904); Lockridge v. Mace, 109 Mo. 162, 18 S.W. 1145 (1891); Geissler v. Reading Trust Co., 257 Pa. 329, 101 A. 797 (1917).

11. L. Simes and A. Smith, Future Interests § 1237 at n. 87 (2d ed. 1956); L. Simes, Future Interests § 132 at n. 6 (2d ed. 1966).

12. Thus, e.g., if O made a transfer "to A for life, remainder to those children of A living at A's death," the contingent remainder given to A's children would necessarily either vest or fail at the end of a life in being (A's life).

13. E.g., Leake v. Robinson, 2 Mer. 363 (1817); Keefer v. McCloy, 344 Ill. 454, 176 N.E. 743 (1931); In re Wanamaker's Estate, 335 Pa. 241, 6 A.2d 852 (1939); Crockett v. Scott, 199 Tenn. 90, 284 S.W.2d 289, 56 A.L.R.2d 442 (1955), noted in 24 Tenn.L.Rev. 617 (1956); Merrill v. Wimmer, 453 N.E.2d 356 (Ind.App.1983), reversed on another ground 481 N.E.2d 1294 (Ind.1985). Cf. Sherrod v. Any Child or Children Hereafter Born to Watson N. Sherrod, Jr., 65 N.C.App. 252, 308 S.E.2d 904 (1983), modified and affirmed 312 N.C. 74, 320 S.E.2d 669 (1984) (where real property is devised in trust without any intervening life estate and the corpus is to be distributed at a later date, the class of beneficiaries is closed at the testator's death and there is no violation of the Rule). Generally, see L. Simes and A. Smith, Future Interests § 1265 (2d ed. 1956); Leach, The Rule Against Perpetuities and Gifts to Classes, 51 Harv. L.Rev. 1329 (1938); R. Powell, Real Property ¶¶ 780–782.

(1) in cases where the gift is of a stated amount to each member of the class—e.g., where a testator bequeaths $1000 apiece to each of the children of A, whenever born, who attain the age of thirty years; and

(2) in cases where the initial gift is to a class the membership of which is certain to be determined within the perpetuities period, with a gift over of the share of each class member (or the share from which each class member is given the income) to his children, issue, heirs, or the like—e.g., where a testator bequeaths his personal estate in trust to pay the income in equal shares to the children of A for their respective lives, and on the death of each child to distribute the share from which he received income to his then living issue in equal shares.

In the first excepted case, the gift to each class member is treated separately when the Rule is applied; hence the gift may be valid as to some class members and void as to others.[14] In the second excepted case, the gift over to each designated sub-class is treated separately when the rule is applied, and the gift may be valid as to some subclasses and void as to others.[15] But if the gift over is per capita rather than per stirpes there are no separate sub-classes and the second exception does not apply.[16]

It should also be noted that a class gift is not always valid under the Rule Against Perpetuities when the maximum and minimum membership in the class is certain to be determined within the perpetuities period. If the entire gift to the class is subject to a condition precedent that may not be satisfied within the perpetuities period, the entire class gift will be void.[17]

Although the Rule Against Perpetuities is a rule of property law, not a rule of contract law, an option to purchase real or personal property may be specifically enforcible and thus create a contingent equitable future interest in the property.[18] It has generally been held both in England and in the United States that an option "in gross" to purchase land—i.e., an option not appendant to a leasehold or other property interest—is subject to the Rule and is void if it can be exercised beyond the period of perpetuities.[19] And an

---

14. E.g., In re Helme's Estate, 95 N.J.Eq. 197, 123 A. 43 (1923); Storrs v. Benbow, 3 DeG.M. & G. 390 (1853).

15. E.g., Shepard v. Union & New Haven Trust Co., 106 Conn. 627, 138 A. 809 (1927); Lanier v. Lanier, 218 Ga. 137, 126 S.E.2d 776 (1962), noted in 49 Iowa L.Rev. 200 (1963), 14 Mercer L.Rev. 275 (1962); Second Bank–State Street Trust Co. v. Second Bank–State Street Trust Co., 335 Mass. 407, 140 N.E.2d 201 (1957); In re Jones' Estate, 410 Pa. 380, 190 A.2d 120 (1963); Industrial Trust Co. v. Flynn, 74 R.I. 396, 60 A.2d 851 (1948).

16. E.g., Westport Paper–Board Co. v. Staples, 127 Conn. 115, 15 A.2d 1 (1940); Landrum v. National City Bank, 210 Ga. 316, 80 S.E.2d 300 (1954); Vickery v. Maryland Trust Co., 188 Md. 178, 52 A.2d 100 (1947).

17. E.g., Sears v. Putnam, 102 Mass. 5 (1869); In re Lee's Estate, 49 Wn.2d 254, 299 P.2d 1066 (1956).

18. See, generally 6 Am.L.Prop. § 24.55 and authorities cited. But a contract governing rights of joint venturers in exploiting oil

and gas leases is a purely personal contract and is not subject to the Rule. First Nat. Bank & Trust Co. v. Sidwell Corp., 234 Kan. 867, 678 P.2d 118 (1984). And when a contract for the sale or land contains no date for performance, a "reasonable time"—which is clearly less than 21 years—will be implied; hence the equitable contingent future interest of the purchaser will not violate the Rule. Read v. GHDC, Inc., 254 Ga. 706, 334 S.E.2d 165 (1985).

19. Central Delaware County v. Greyhound, 527 Pa. 47, 588 A.2d 485 (1991), a repurchase option "in gross" exercisable by a corporation or its successors at any time when the land conveyed ceased to devoted to a public use, however remote, was held to violate the Rule. The court rejected the optionee's argument that the repurchase language should be construed as creating a fee simple subject to a condition subsequent and hence not subject to the Rule, citing Rest.Prop. § 394, Comment c (1944). The court also rejected the trial court's determination that, on

option to purchase personal property which is specifically enforcible because of the unique character of the personal property is also subject to the Rule.[20]

In England, even options to purchase realty appendant to a leasehold estate are subject to the Rule,[21] but in the United States the better view has been that such options are not subject to the Rule Against Perpetuities because alienability is not fettered and improvement of land by the lessee is promoted by the existence of an option to purchase.[22] Thus an option in a lessee to purchase the fee simple is valid even though it might be exercised at a time beyond the period of perpetuities.

Pre-emptive rights ("rights of first refusal") should be distinguished from options to purchase. An option to purchase grants to its holder the power to compel the owner of property to sell it whether or not the owner wishes to sell. A pre-emptive right merely requires the owner, when and if he decides to sell, to offer the property first to the holder of the pre-emptive right so that he may meet a third-party offer or buy at a price set out in the pre-emption agreement. If the holder of the pre-emptive right decides not to buy, the owner is free to sell to anyone he wishes. The courts are divided as to whether the Rule applies to pre-emptive rights.[23] The courts that have

public grounds, the Rule should not apply because grantors would not freely convey their land for public use if options to repurchase exercisable without any time limit were invalidated by application of the Rule. And the trial court rejected the trial court's ruling that the repurchase option was solely a contract right not subject to the Rule, pointing out that exemption of "exclusively contractual rights" under Rest.Prop. § 401 (1944) is limited to cases where the contract "concerns no specific land or thing other than land"—see Rest.Prop. § 401, Comment b (1944)—which was not the case in Central Delaware County v. Greyhound.

See also Silvicraft, Inc. v. Southwest Timber Co., 34 Ark.App. 17, 805 S.W.2d 84 (1991) (option to repurchase did not violate the Rule because there was nothing to suggest that the option extended to the heirs of the optionee or was binding beyond his lifetime); Buffalo Seminary v. McCarthy, 86 A.D.2d 435, 451 N.Y.S.2d 457 (1982), aff'd op. below 58 N.Y.2d 867, 460 N.Y.S.2d 528, 447 N.E.2d 76 (1983); Shaffer v. Reed, 437 So.2d 98 (Ala.1983), appeal after remand 456 So.2d 1082 (1984) (options in gross to buy stock violated Rule because it was uncertain whether they would be exercised within the perpetuities period; court rejected argument that options should be construed to require exercise within a "reasonable time"; options were apparently assumed to be specifically enforceable); Certified Corp. v. GTE Products Corp., 392 Mass. 821, 467 N.E.2d 1336 (1984) (option in gross for 25 years). See also Hansen v. Stroecker, 699 P.2d 871 (Alaska 1985) (option in gross not required to be exercised within perpetuities period is void at common law, but not under statutory "wait and see" rule); Milner v. Bivens, 255 Ga. 49, 335 S.E.2d 288 (1985) (perpet-

ual option to repurchase surface rights reserved by grantor who also reserved mineral rights was void under rule; court apparently treated the option as one "in gross," although it was arguably appendant to the mineral rights); Maupin v. Dunn, 678 S.W.2d 180 (Tex. App.1984) (perpetual option void under the Rule). Cf. Byke Const. Co. v. Miller, 140 Ariz. 57, 680 P.2d 193 (App.1984) (no violation of Rule because court assumed parties "intended a reasonable time period to apply" to exercise of option and a "reasonable time" is less than 21 years). Generally, see 6 Am.L.Prop. § 24.-56.

20. Generally, see 6 Am.L.Prop. § 24.56.

21. See J. Gray, Rule Against Perpetuities § 230.3 and authorities cited.

22. See 6 Am.L.Prop. § 24.57 and authorities cited. See also Lattimore v. Fisher's Food Shoppe, Inc., 313 N.C. 467, 329 S.E.2d 346 (1985) (perpetual right of renewal contained in lease does not violate Rule); Camerlo v. Howard Johnson Co., 710 F.2d 987 (3d Cir.1983) (Pennsylvania law treats both purchase and renewal options in leases as exempt from Rule). And see Milner v. Bivens, supra note 19 ("an option to purchase within a lease does not violate the rule").

23. Pre-emptive rights were held to be subject to the Rule in the following recent cases: Morrison v. Piper, 77 N.Y.2d 165, 565 N.Y.S.2d 444, 566 N.E.2d 643 (1990), appeal after remand 171 A.D.2d 958, 567 N.E.2d 903 (1991) (pre-emptive rights are subject to the Rule, but court held the challenged provision, properly construed, did not violate the Rule); Ferrero Const. Co. v. Dennis Rourke Corp., 311 Md. 560, 536 A.2d 1137 (1988) (court stated confidently that this was the majority rule,

declined to apply the Rule have generally done so on the ground that (1) the holder of the pre-emptive right has a vested property interest or (2) the holder has only a contract right rather than a property interest. Some cases hold pre-emptive rights to be similar to options in gross and therefore subject to the Rule. Commentators have suggested that the courts might better concede that pre-emptive rights may create contingent future interests ordinarily subject to the Rule, but should also recognize that their utility in many modern legal transactions may justify exempting pre-emptive rights from the Rule where, e.g., enforceability of pre-emptive rights encourages the holders of such rights to develop their own property by assuring their ability to benefit from such development.[24]

The applicability of the Rule Against Perpetuities may cause difficulties in setting up a condominium development. In order to control the ownership of condominium units without violating the common law rule against direct restraints on alienation, most condominium association by-laws provide that the association shall have a pre-emptive "right of first refusal" whenever a unit owner wishes to sell or lease his unit.[25] But if this pre-emptive right is held to be an option in gross, it will be subject to the Rule Against Perpetuities and will be void if it is exercised at a date beyond the period of perpetuities [26] unless there is a statute making the Rule inapplicable to such pre-emptive rights. However, if such pre-emptive rights are considered to be analogous to options to purchase appendant to a leasehold

citing many cases); Henderson v. Millis, 373 N.W.2d 497 (Iowa 1985) (Rule applies to pre-emptive rights, but under "wait and see" rule, discussed post Section 3.22, pre-emptive right does not violate Rule if "triggering event" occurs within perpetuities period); Estate of Johnson v. Carr, 286 Ark. 369, 691 S.W.2d 161 (1985), appeal after remand 288 Ark. 461, 706 S.W.2d 388 (1986); Barnhart v. McKinney, 235 Kan. 511, 682 P.2d 112 (1984) (pre-emptive rights are subject to Rule, but court held that the provision, properly construed, did not violate the Rule); North Bay Council, Inc. v. Grinnell, 123 N.H. 321, 461 A.2d 114 (1983); Smith v. VanVoorhis, 170 W.Va. 729, 296 S.E.2d 851 (1982). A number of older cases are cited in *Dennis Rourke Corp.*, supra, 536 A.2d at 1139–1140. Rest.Prop. § 413 (1944) states that pre-emptive rights are subject to the Rule.

Some pre-emptive rights, at least, were held *not* subject to the Rule in Metropolitan Transp. Auth. v. Bruken Realty Corp., 67 N.Y.2d 156, 501 N.Y.S.2d 306, 492 N.E.2d 379 (1986) (pre-emptive rights created in commercial and governmental transactions not subject to Rule); Cambridge Co. v. East Slope Investment Corp., 700 P.2d 537 (Colo.1985); Shiver v. Benton, 251 Ga. 284, 304 S.E.2d 903 (1983), appeal after remand 254 Ga. 107, 326 S.E.2d 756 (1985) (although "technically subject to the rule against perpetuities" even where "triggering event" is a third party offer to buy at owner's price, the Rule "should not be applied in such case, since the future interest of the pre-emptioner constitutes no impediment to transfer of the property"—citing 6 Am.L.Prop. § 26.67 (1952)); Cherokee Water Co. v. Forderhause, 641 S.W.2d 522 (Tex.1982) (pre-emptive right given to grantee of surface estate to purchase mineral estate was not subject to Rule); Robroy Land Co. v. Prather, 95 Wn.2d 66, 622 P.2d 367 (1980). These cases were said, in *Dennis Rourke Corp.*, supra, to be "the minority view," which "appears to stem from a law review article written * * * by Professor Merrill I. Schnebly" entitled Restraints Upon the Alienation of Legal Interests, Part III, published in 44 Yale L.J. 1380 (1935). Professor Schnebly was also the author of 6 Am.L.Prop. ch. III (1952), and adopted the same "minority view" in his discussion of the application of the Rule Against Perpetuities to pre-emptive rights. See id. §§ 26.64–26.67, where Professor Schnebly expressed a preference for determining the validity of pre-emptive rights by applying the rule against restraints on alienation rather than the Rule Against Perpetuities. See discussion of restraints on alienation and pre-emptive rights, ante Section 2.2 at notecalls 17–19.

24. L. Simes & A. Smith, Future Interests § 1154, at 64 (2d ed. 1956); Leach, Perpetuities: New Absurdity, Judicial and Statutory Correctives, 73 Harv.L.Rev. 1318, 1320 (1960). Compare Professor Schnebly's view as summarized supra note 23.

25. See 4B R. Powell, Real Property ¶ 233.-14[2] (Rohan rev. 1979).

26. Supra note 18; 4B R. Powell, Real Property ¶ 633.14[2] (Rohan rev. 1979).

estate, the Rule will generally be held to be inapplicable.[27] And in some states the condominium enabling acts expressly provide that the Rule Against Perpetuities and the common law rule against restraints on alienation shall not defeat any of the provisions of the act.[28] This is highly desirable, since it clearly validates pre-emptive rights of first refusal even though they are exercisable beyond the period of perpetuities—e.g., at any time during the continuance of the condominium regime.

Statutory provisions for termination of the interests of condominium unit owners in their individual units upon destruction of their building may also run afoul of the Rule Against Perpetuities.[29] If the interest of each unit owner in his individual unit is a fee simple, a statutory provision divesting the unit owner's title and vesting it in all the property owners as tenants in common after destruction of their building has the effect of creating an executory interest in the property owners. Since these statutory executory interests are contingent upon an event that is uncertain either to occur or become impossible of occurrence within lives in being plus twenty-one years, they are void ab initio unless the statutory provision for creation of such executory interests is construed as impliedly exempting them from the Rule. Such a construction of these provisions is clearly desirable. In those states where the condominium enabling acts expressly exempt condominiums from the Rule Against Perpetuities and the common law rule against restraints on alienation, the problem is, of course, obviated.[30]

§ 3.19 The Perpetuities Period

The basic element of the perpetuities period—"some life in being at the creation of the interest"—was established in 1682 in *The Duke of Norfolk's Case,*[1] where Lord Nottingham sustained a contingent future interest in a chattel real that was certain to vest or fail within a life in being at the creation of the interest. It was held in later English cases that several lives can be used to delimit the period during which contingent future interests must be certain to vest or fail and that these lives need not be those of

27. Supra note 22; 4B R. Powell, Real Property ¶ 633.14[2] (Rohan rev. 1991). Recent cases include Cambridge Co. v. East Slope Inv. Corp., 700 P.2d 537 (Colo.1985) (pre-emptive right contained in condominium declaration did not violate Rule); Anderson v. 50 East 72nd Street Condominium, 129 Misc.2d 295, 492 N.Y.S.2d 989 (1985), order affirmed 119 A.D.2d 73, 505 N.Y.S.2d 101 (1986), appeal granted 123 A.D.2d 902, 506 N.Y.S.2d 661 (1986) (Rule should not be applied to invalidate pre-emptive option on condominium unit, but the pre-emptive option should be held subject to common law rule against restraints on alienation and court should apply test of reasonableness to determine validity under the latter rule).

28. 4B R. Powell, Real Property ¶ 633.14[2] n. 10 (Rohan rev. 1991) (listing such provisions in the condominium enabling acts of Connecticut, the District of Columbia, Idaho, Illinois, Maryland, Nevada, Rhode Island, Utah, and Virginia).

The Colorado Condominium Ownership Act, West's Colo.Rev.Stat.Ann. § 38–33–101 et seq., provides that the rules against perpetuities and against restraints on alienation shall not defeat any condominium provisions relating to "the restrictions upon partition" or "the methods by which the character of the ownership * * * is changed in the event of destruction or obsolescence," but omits any reference to voluntary sale or transfer of condominium units. See Cambridge Co. v. East Slope Inv. Corp., supra note 27.

29. For a brief discussion of typical statutory provisions of this type, see 4B R. Powell, Real Property ¶ 633.12[2] (Rohan rev. 1979). For a brief discussion of the perpetuities problems arising in connection with such provisions, see id. ¶ 633.12[3].

30. Supra note 26.

§ 3.19

1. 3 Ch.Cas. 1 (1682).

persons who receive interests under the instrument creating the contingent future interest in question,[2] provided the designated "extraneous" lives are "neither so numerous nor so situated that evidence of deaths is likely to be unreasonably difficult to obtain."[3] In most cases, of course, the relevant "lives in being" are the lives of persons who receive interests under the instrument creating the contingent future interest in question, and of other persons closely connected with such persons such as spouses and children.

The additional twenty-one years included in the perpetuities period seems to have been derived from the period of an actual minority during which a fee tail estate could be made unbarrable at common law.[4] It was eventually determined, however, that a period of twenty-one years in gross could be added to "lives in being" under the Rule Against Perpetuities, whether or not an actual minority was involved.[5] It was also determined that a person was "in being" for purposes of the Rule if conceived before, though born after, the date when the instrument creating the contingent future interest became operative.[6] But it was held that a nine-month period in gross, unconnected with any actual period of gestation, could not be added to the perpetuities period.[7]

In most cases, as indicated in Gray's statement of the Rule,[8] the perpetuities period starts to run when the contingent future interest is created.[9] But where that interest is subject to a power in any person to create an absolute beneficial interest (a fee simple absolute or equivalent interest in personalty) in himself—e.g., where the settlor of a trust reserves the power to revoke the trust and recover the trust property—the perpetuities period starts to run only upon the expiration of such power.[10]

Suppose that, instead of one person having the power to create an absolute beneficial interest in himself, there are persons in being who can join together to transfer a fee simple absolute (or equivalent interest in personalty) to a third person—e.g., where land was initially transferred "to A, but if the land is ever used for non-residential purposes, then to B." In such a case, although A and B together have the power to alienate in fee simple absolute, alienability is in fact fettered. Hence courts have held B's

---

2. E.g., Low v. Burron, 3 P.Wms. 262 (1734); Thellusson v. Woodford, 11 Ves. 112 (1805); Cadell v. Palmer, 1 Cl. & F. 372 (1833); Fitchie v. Brown, 211 U.S. 321, 29 S.Ct. 106, 53 L.Ed. 202 (1908).

3. 4 Rest.Prop. § 374 (from which the statement quoted in the text is drawn). See, e.g., In re Moore, [1901] 1 Ch. 936 ("until the period of twenty-one years from the death of the last survivor of all persons who shall be living at my death" held void for indefiniteness); In re Villar, [1928] Ch. 471, [1929] 1 Ch. 243, 98 L.J.Ch. 223 ("ending at the expiration of 20 years from the day of the death of the last survivor of all the lineal descendants of Her Late Majesty Queen Victoria who shall be living at * * * my death" held valid).

4. Stephens v. Stephens, Cas.Temp.Talb. 228 (1736); Cole v. Sewell, 2 H.L.Cas. 186 at 233 (1848).

5. Cadell v. Palmer, supra note 2.

6. Long v. Blackall, 7 T.R. 100 (1797). The period could include more than one period of gestation, which might come at the end of the lives in being as well as at the beginning. See Thellusson v. Woodford, supra note 2.

7. Cadell v. Palmer, supra note 2.

8. Ante Section 3.17 at n. 1.

9. This is the date of delivery as to *inter vivos* conveyances and the date of the testator's death as to wills. E.g., Bradford v. Griffin, 40 S.C. 468, 19 S.E. 76 (1893) (deed); Safe Deposit & Trust Co. v. Sheehan, 169 Md. 93, 179 A. 536 (1935) (will).

10. E.g., Cook v. Horn, 214 Ga. 289, 104 S.E.2d 461 (1958); Manufacturers Life Insurance Co. v. Von Hamm–Young Co., 34 Hawaii 288 (1937), rehearing denied 34 Hawaii 316.

interest void under the Rule Against Perpetuities.[11]

Any power of appointment exercisable at a time beyond the perpetuities period is void under the Rule [12] unless it is a general power of appointment that can be exercised either by deed or by will within the perpetuities period.[13] When an appointment is made pursuant to a valid general power to appoint both by deed and by will, the perpetuities period with respect to contingent future interests created by the appointment will start to run only from the date when the power was exercised.[14] But when an appointment is made pursuant to a valid special power, or a valid general power to appoint only by will, the perpetuities period with respect to contingent future interests created by the appointment will run from the date when the power was created.[15]

§ 3.20   The Rule Against Perpetuities—Selected Problems

Although it is not possible to deal with the Rule Against Perpetuities in great detail in this book, the reader may find it helpful to consider the following examples in which the contingent future interest apparently created by the transfer is invalidated by the Rule.

1. "To A so long as the property is used for church purposes, then to B."

B's executory interest obviously may neither vest nor fail within the perpetuities period, and it is therefore void under the Rule.[1] A has a possessory fee simple determinable and the transferor, O, has a possibility of

11. In re Hargreaves, 43 Ch.D. 401 (1890).

12. In re Estate of Jones, 318 So.2d 231 (Fla.App.1975), cert. denied 334 So.2d 606 (Fla. 1976); Bundy v. United States Trust Co., 257 Mass. 72, 153 N.E. 337 (1926); Camden Safe Deposit & Trust Co. v. Scott, 121 N.J.Eq. 366, 189 A. 653, 110 A.L.R. 1422 (1936), noted in 36 Mich.L.Rev. 146 (1937); American Trust Co. v. Williamson, 228 N.C. 458, 46 S.E.2d 104 (1948).

13. E.g., Keville v. Hollister Co., 29 Cal. App.3d 203, 105 Cal.Rptr. 238 (1972); Robinson v. Speer, 185 So.2d 730 (Fla.App.1966), cert. denied 192 So.2d 498 (Fla.1966); In re Ransom's Estate, 89 N.J.Super. 224, 214 A.2d 521 (1965).

14. In re McMurtry's Estate, 68 Misc.2d 553, 326 N.Y.S.2d 965 (Sur.1971); Appeal of Mifflin, 121 Pa. 205, 15 A. 525, 1 L.R.A. 453 (1888). See also Keville v. Hollister, supra note 13.

Rest.Prop.2d, Donative Transfers § 1.2, Comment d, Illust. 10 (1986), asserts that where a trust beneficiary is granted a special power to appoint by will plus an unqualified lifetime power to withdraw, for his own use, any or all of the trust corpus, period of the rule with respect to non-vested interests that may be created by the exercise of his testamentary power does not begin to run until his death. Thus, as the court held in Matter of Moore, 129 Misc.2d 639, 493 N.Y.S.2d 924

(Sup.Ct.1985), even though such a beneficiary may make little use of his lifetime power of withdrawal and then exercises his testamentary power by appointing the trust property remaining at his death to further trusts containing non-vested future interests, the perpetuities period with respect to such future interests does not begin to run until the beneficiary's death.

15. E.g., In re Bird's Estate, 225 Cal. App.2d 196, 37 Cal.Rptr. 288 (1964); Second National Bank of New Haven v. Harris Trust & Saving Bank, 29 Conn.Sup. 275, 283 A.2d 226 (1971); Hopkinson v. Swaim, 284 Ill. 11, 119 N.E. 985 (1918); Graham v. Whitridge, 99 Md. 248, 57 A. 609, 66 L.R.A. 408 (1904); Hillen v. Iselin, 144 N.Y. 365, 39 N.E. 368 (1895).

§ 3.20

1. E.g., McCrory School District of Woodruff County v. Brogden, 231 Ark. 664, 333 S.W.2d 246 (1960); First Universalist Society of North Adams v. Boland, 155 Mass. 171, 29 N.E. 524, 15 L.R.A. 231 (1892); Brown v. Independent Baptist Church of Woburn, 325 Mass. 645, 91 N.E.2d 922 (1950); Jones v. Burns, 221 Miss. 833, 74 So.2d 866 (1954); Donehue v. Nilges, 364 Mo. 705, 266 S.W.2d 553, 45 A.L.R.2d 1150 (1954); Leonard v. Burr, 18 N.Y. 96 (1856); Yarbrough v. Yarbrough, 151 Tenn. 221, 269 S.W. 36 (1925).

reverter in fee simple absolute which is valid because the Rule does not apply to contingent reversionary future interests in the United States.[2] But O could have achieved his purpose to create a valid contingent future interest in B through the use of two transfers instead of one. O could first have conveyed "to A so long as the property is used for church purposes," omitting the executory limitation to B; then, in a state where possibilities of reverter are alienable, O could have conveyed the possibility of reverter to B by a separate conveyance. Alternatively, if B were willing to cooperate, O could first have transferred the property to B in fee simple absolute, and B could then have transferred a fee simple determinable to A, retaining a valid possibility of reverter.

2. "To A, but if the property should ever cease to be used for church purposes, then to B."

Again, B's executory interest is void under the Rule because it may neither vest nor fail within the perpetuities period.[3] A, by the weight of authority, has a fee simple absolute, since excission of the entire executory limitation leaves language creating a fee simple absolute in A and courts generally will not imply a re-entry clause or a special limitation that would leave A with a defeasible fee simple estate.[4] Here, again, however, the transferor could have achieved his obvious purpose—to create a valid contingent future interest in B that would become possessory if the property should ever cease to be used for church purposes—by using two transactions instead of one. O could first have transferred a fee simple determinable to A, and then, by a separate instrument, O could have transferred the possibility of reverter to B. Alternatively, if B would cooperate, O could have transferred a fee simple absolute to B, and B could then have transferred a fee simple determinable to A, retaining the possibility of reverter.

Examples 1 and 2, above, make it clear that an executory interest is always void under the Rule if the event upon which the executory interest is to become a present interest is subject to no time limit whatever. However, the ease with which the application of the Rule may be avoided through the use of two transfers strongly suggests that it makes little sense to hold—as American courts have traditionally done—that executory interests are subject to the Rule but contingent reversionary interests are not.[5]

2. Ibid.

3. E.g., McMahon v. Consistory of St. Paul's Reformed Church at Westminster, 196 Md. 125, 75 A.2d 122 (1950); Proprietors of Church in Brattle Square v. Grant, 69 Mass. (3 Gray) 142, 63 Am.Dec. 725 (1855); Betts v. Snyder, 341 Pa. 465, 19 A.2d 82 (1941); Rust v. Rust, 147 Tex. 181, 214 S.W.2d 462 (1948).

4. Ibid. "[I]t would seem that, when an executory interest following a fee simple interest in land or an analogous interest in personalty is void under the rule against perpetuities, the prior interest becomes absolute unless the language of the creating instrument makes it very clear that the prior interest is to terminate whether the executory interest takes effect or not. In other words, a special limitation to the prior interest would not arise by implication, but would have to be ex-

pressed." L. Simes and A. Smith 828 (2d ed. 1956).

If the example given in the text is changed to read as follows: "to A on condition that the premises be used only for church purposes, and upon breach of said condition, then to B," it is likely that American courts would hold that A receives a fee simple absolute subject to a promissory use restriction, in view of the propensity of American courts to construe "condition" as "covenant" in the absence of an express reservation of a right of entry or power of termination.

5. Some American legislatures have enacted statutes either making contingent reversionary interests subject to the Rule Against Perpetuities or have limited the duration of such interests to a fixed period of years. See post Section 3.22.

3. "To A for life, remainder to the first son of A whenever born who becomes a clergyman."

Assuming that the remainder is contingent because A has no son who is a clergyman when the transfer occurs, and that the contingent remainder is indestructible, the remainder may neither vest nor fail within the perpetuities period because the only usable "lives in being" are those of A and any children of A living when the transfer occurs, and it is possible that the first son of A to become a clergyman (if any does) will do so more than twenty-one years (plus an actual period of gestation) after the deaths of A and all children of A living when the transfer occurs. So the remainder is void under the Rule, and the transferor's reversion in fee simple is indefeasible. But if the remainder were destructible it would be valid, for it would then necessarily vest or fail no later than A's death.

4. "To A for life, remainder to the first son of A to reach 25."

Assuming that A has no son who has reached twenty-five when the transfer occurs and that the contingent remainder is indestructible, the remainder may neither vest nor fail within the perpetuities period, since again the only usable "lives in being" are those of A and any children of A living when the transfer occurs, and it is possible that the first son of A to reach twenty-five (if any does) may do so more than twenty-one years (plus any actual period of gestation) after the deaths of A and all children of A living when the transfer occurs. As in example 3, the contingent remainder is void under the Rule and the transferor's reversion is indefeasible. Again, however, as in example 3, if the remainder is destructible it is valid, because it must necessarily vest or fail no later than A's death.

5. "To A for life, remainder to the children of A for life, and upon the death of the last surviving child of A, to such of A's grandchildren as may be then living."

The remainder to A's children, a class including children born to A both before and after the transfer takes effect, is valid because the ultimate membership of the class will be determined at A's death (plus any actual period of gestation in the event that a child of A is conceived before A's death and is born thereafter). But the contingent remainder in favor of A's grandchildren is void under the Rule because it is uncertain to vest or fail within the perpetuities period. This is so because the only usable "lives in being" are those of A and of any children of A living when the transfer takes effect and the last surviving child of A may not die until more than twenty-one years after the deaths of A and all of A's children who were living when the transfer took effect. Since the contingent remainder in favor of A's grandchildren is void, the transferor's reversion in fee simple is indefeasible.

6. "To A for life, remainder to such of A's lineal descendants as are alive on January 1, 2010."

Assuming the transfer is effective before January 1, 1989, and that contingent remainders are indestructible, the remainder is void because it is not certain either to vest or fail within twenty-one years and the only relevant "lives in being"—the lives of A and any descendants of A living at the date of the transfer—are not related to the date for determining the identities of the remaindermen in any legally relevant manner. The transferor's reversion is indefeasible and will become a present interest at A's death.

7. "To A for life, remainder to A's widow for her life, remainder to the children of A living at his widow's death."

In this case—often referred to as "the case of the unborn widow"—the remainder to A's children is void because they must survive A's widow, who might possibly be a person unborn at the date of the transfer who will outlive A and all children of A living at the date of the transfer (if any) by more than twenty-one years.[6] The transferor's reversion is indefeasible and will become a present estate after the death of A and his widow (if any).

8. "To A for life, remainder to such of the grandchildren of A as reach the age of 21 years."

In this case the remainder to A's grandchildren is clearly void if contingent remainders are indestructible and A is capable of having additional children after the transfer is made, since the remainder is not certain to vest or fail within twenty-one years after the death of A and all children of A living at the date of the transfer, who are the only relevant "lives in being."[7] If A has additional children after the date of the transfer, they will not be "lives in being," and they may beget grandchildren of A who will not reach twenty-one within twenty-one years after the death of A and of the children of A (if any) living at the date of the transfer. Moreover, the courts have generally presumed that A is capable of having additional children regardless of age and sex.[8] In the famous "case of the fertile octogenarian" this presumption was applied even though A was an eighty year old female.[9] To apply the presumption in such a case seems ludicrous unless "grandchildren" in the example given is construed to include children of *adopted* children of A. It should be noted, however, that adoption statutes and procedures often deny adoption to persons of advanced age. A few states have eliminated the conclusive presumption of reproductive capacity,[10] for perpetuities purposes, by statute, and at least one state has eliminated the [11] conclusive presumption by judicial decision.

---

6. E.g., Re Allan's Will Trusts, [1958] 1 All E.R. 401; Dickerson v. Union National Bank of Little Rock, 268 Ark. 292, 595 S.W.2d 677 (1980); Greenwich Trust Co. v. Shively, 110 Conn. 117, 147 A. 367 (1929); Keefer v. McCloy, 344 Ill. 454, 176 N.E. 743 (1931); Chenoweth v. Bullitt, 224 Ky. 698, 6 S.W.2d 1061 (1928); Brookover v. Grimm, 118 W.Va. 227, 190 S.E. 697 (1937).

7. E.g., Jee v. Audley, 1 Cox 324 (1787); In re Dawson, 39 Ch.D. 155 (1888); First Alabama Bank of Montgomery v. Adams, 382 So.2d 1104 (Ala.1980); Connecticut Bank & Trust Co. v. Brody, 174 Conn. 616, 392 A.2d 445 (1978); Nelson v. Mercantile Trust Co., 335 S.W.2d 167 (Mo.1960); Parker v. Parker, 252 N.C. 399, 113 S.E.2d 899 (1960); Crockett v. Scott, 199 Tenn. 90, 284 S.W.2d 289, 56 A.L.R.2d 442 (1955).

8. Ibid.

9. Jee v. Audley, supra note 7.

10. Idaho Code § 55–111 (added by Laws 1957 c. 54); N.Y.—McKinney's Estates, Powers and Trusts Law 9–1.3(e) (presumption limited to males over 14 and females aged 12 to 55, and it may be rebutted by evidence); Tenn.Code Ann. § 24–516 (as amended by Laws 1965 c. 54). See also English Perpetuities and Accumulations Act, 1964 Eliz. II c. 55 § 2 (same as N.Y. statute, supra).

11. In re Bassett's Estate, 104 N.H. 504, 190 A.2d 415, 98 A.L.R.2d 1281 (1963), noted in 43 Boston U.L.Rev. 562 (1963), 62 Mich. L.Rev. 1099 (1964). See also Leach, Perpetuities: New Hampshire Defertilizes the Octogenarian, 77 Harv.L.Rev. 279 (1963). And see Exham v. Beamish, [1939] Ir.R. 336, noted in 53 Harv.L.Rev. 490 (1940) (also holding the presumption to be rebuttable).

The conclusive presumption of reproductive capacity may, in some cases, be avoided by construing language in the dispositive instrument so as to exclude children who might theoretically be born to the transferee after the instrument becomes operative. Thus, e.g., in example 8 above, if A is a female and the transferor knows that A is eighty years old at the time of transfer, it would be fair to construe "such of the grandchildren of A as reach the age of 21 years" as referring only to children of A then living, in which case the remainder would be valid. Such a construction has been adopted in a few cases,[12] despite the traditional rule that construction of language in deeds and wills should not be influenced by the court's desire to avoid invalidation of a future interest through application of the Rule Against Perpetuities.[13] Of course, if the transferor knows that A has had a hysterectomy, the suggested construction would be warranted—indeed, it should be required!

The common law Rule Against Perpetuities has been subject to vigorous criticism for more than a generation because of (a) "the glaring absurdities of the requirement of absolute certainty from the beginning" that contingent future interests will vest or fail within the perpetuities period; (b) "the fact that if an interest violates the Rule it is completely defeated instead of being remodeled to accommodate itself to the Rule"; (c) "the fact that possibilities of reverter and rights of entry for condition broken are (under American law at least) exempt from the Rule"; and (d) "the fact that vested interests are not subject to the Rule, enabling property to be effectively tied up for over a hundred years.[14] There has been substantial legislative response to most of these criticisms. The most important of these legislative responses have been the adoption of statutes providing for determination of the validity of contingent future interests on the basis of actual rather than merely possible

12. This conclusion is supported by Worcester County Trust Co. v. Marble, 316 Mass. 294, 55 N.E.2d 446 (1944); In re Wright's Estate, 284 Pa. 334, 131 A. 188 (1925).

13. In re Lattouf's Will, 87 N.J.Super. 137, 208 A.2d 411 (1965). Generally, as to the presumption of reproductive capacity, see Leach, Perpetuities in the Atomic Age: The Sperm Bank and the Fertile Decedent, 48 A.B.A.J. 942 (1962) (suggesting that it is now possible for a male to beget children after his death); Lynn, Raising the Perpetuities Question: Conception, Adoption, "Wait and See," and Cy Pres, 17 Vand.L.Rev. 1391 (1964); Sappideen, Life After Death—Sperm Banks, Wills and Perpetuities, 53 Aust.L.J. 311 (1979); Schwartz, Mr. Justice Kenison and Creative Continuity in Perpetuities Law, 48 Boston U.L.Rev. 207, 219 (1968).

On the general question whether limitations will be construed, if possible, so as to avoid violation of the Rule Against Perpetuities, there is clearly some difference between the English and American courts. In England the stated rule is that set forth in the text as the "traditional rule," subject to the qualification that if the language is "obscure or ambiguous" the court may adopt the construction that will

avoid the Rule, provided the alternative constructions are "substantially on a par, two constructions of which the clause is equally capable, two constructions which may be put with equal fairness on the clause." See 6 Am.L.Prop. § 24.44 (quoting In re Atkinson, [1916] 1 Ch. 91 at 96). In the United States, although the traditional rule is "given lip service," the courts have gone further than the English courts "in finding the instrument ambiguous and resolving the ambiguity in favor of the construction which will uphold the gifts." 6 Am.L.Prop. § 24.45 (giving examples of judicial construction of limitations so as to avoid violation of the Rule). For recent examples, see Williams v. Watt, 668 P.2d 620 (Wyo. 1983) (construing interest following determinable fee as a vested remainder in fee simple rather than an executory interest in order to avoid violation of the Rule); Chicago Title & Trust Co. v. Schwartz, 120 Ill.App.3d 324, 76 Ill.Dec. 12, 458 N.E.2d 151 (1983) ("issue" construed to mean "children" to avoid violation of Rule); Byke Const. Co., Inc. v. Miller, 140 Ariz. 57, 680 P.2d 193 (App.1984) (time period for exercise of option held to be a "reasonable time"—less than 21 years—to avoid violation of the Rule); Drach v. Ely, 237 Kan. 654, 703 P.2d 746 (1985).

14. Am.L.Prop. § 24.11 (Supp.1976, p. 855).

events—the so-called "wait and see" rule—and/or adoption of statutes providing for *cy pres* reformation of limitations creating interests that are void under the common law Rule Against Perpetuities. Both of these modifications of the common law Rule are incorporated, along with an alternative perpetuities period of 90 years in gross, in the Uniform Statutory Rule Against Perpetuities.[15]

Another response to criticisms levelled against the common law Rule Against Perpetuities is the development of "saving clauses" to be incorporated in instruments creating contingent future interests. A Standard Saving Clause designed for inclusion without change in any such instrument was drafted by the late W. Barton Leach, in cooperation with an estate planning group and counsel for several corporate fiduciaries. The Standard Saving Clause gives a corporate fiduciary the power to reform an interest challenged as violating the common law Rule "in such manner as will most closely approximate, within permissible limits, the intention of the testator, settlor or appointer" in order to avoid violation of the Rule.[16] Others have prepared other types of "saving clauses."[17] In general, "saving clauses" appear to have been upheld by the courts.[18]

§ 3.21   Early Statutory Modifications of the Common Law Rule Against Perpetuities—Suspension of the Power of Alienation Prohibited

The first significant statutory modification of the common law Rule Against Perpetuities was enacted in New York in 1830. The 1830 New York legislation[1] prohibited the creation of any future interest that would suspend the absolute power of alienation of real property or "the absolute ownership of personal property" for a period longer than "two lives in being" at the time when the future interest was created. In the case of real property, the New York statute made an exception where a contingent remainder in fee was "created on a prior remainder in fee, to take effect in the event that the persons to whom the first remainder is limited, shall die under the age of twenty-one years, or upon any other contingency, by which the estate of such persons may be determined before they attain their full age." A similar exception as to personal property was added in 1929.[2] Although this legislation expressly prohibited only suspension of the absolute power of ownership, it was held to invalidate certain contingent future

---

15. See post Section 3.22 for discussion of all these legislative modifications of the common law Rule Against Perpetuities.

16. Leach & Logan, Perpetuities: A Standard Saving Clause to Avoid Violations of the Rule, 74 Harv.L.Rev. 1141 (1961).

17. E.g., A. Casner, Estate Planning 1251–1252 (3d ed. 1961); Goldman, Drafting Trust Instruments Revisited, 36 U.Cin.L.Rev. 650, 657–658 (1967); Comment, That "Simple and Clear Rule"—The Common Law Rule Against Perpetuities in Mississippi, 34 Miss.L.J. 63, 80 (1962).

18. E.g., Norton v. Georgia R.R. Bank & Trust, 253 Ga. 596, 322 S.E.2d 870 (1984) (trial court correctly applied the saving clause and rule that the trust was to terminate 21 years

after the death of the last surviving beneficiary who was in life at the testator's death"). Earlier cases include Nelson v. Mercantile Trust Co., 335 S.W.2d 167 (Mo.1960) (court gave effect to poorly drafted saving clause); Tolman v. Reeve, 393 Ill. 272, 65 N.E.2d 815 (1946); Zweig v. Zweig, 275 S.W.2d 201 (Tex. Civ.App.1955), error refused n.r.e.; In re Lee's Estate, 49 Wn.2d 254, 299 P.2d 1066 (1956); Lux v. Lux, 109 R.I. 592, 288 A.2d 701 (1972).

§ 3.21

1. In its current form, this legislation appears as N.Y.—McKinney's Estates, Powers & Trust Law 9–1.1 through 9–1.3.

2. Laws 1929, c. 229, § 18.

interests that were not certain to vest or fail within the statutory two-life period even though they did not cause a suspension of the power of alienation or ownership for more than two lives.[3]

In 1958, 1960, 1965 and 1967 the New York legislation was amended [4] (1) to change the permissible period during which the absolute power of alienation or ownership can be suspended to "lives in being" when the transfer in question is made plus "a term of twenty-one years";[5] and (2) to enact the common law Rule Against Perpetuities.[6] Thus the same perpetuities period is now applicable to both the prohibition against suspension of the absolute power of alienation or ownership and the prohibition against creation of future interests that may vest or fail at too remote a time. In both cases, an actual period of gestation may be added to the statutory period,[7] and in both cases the statute provides that measuring lives shall not be "so designated or so numerous as to make proof of their end unreasonably difficult."[8] The current New York rules against suspension of the power of alienation and remoteness of vesting are also qualified by a cy pres provision applicable to limitations involving the attainment by a person of an age in excess of twenty-one years,[9] and by certain rules of construction that tend to avert a finding of invalidity.[10] In addition, the current New York Legislation codifies the common law rules as to the time from which the statutory perpetuities period is counted for the purposes of determining the validity of the exercise of a power of appointment.[11]

During the nineteenth century legislation based on the 1830 New York legislation discussed in the preceding paragraph was enacted in fourteen other jurisdictions.[12] In two of these jurisdictions, however, it is possible that the legislation was intended to be merely declaratory of the common law Rule Against Perpetuities.[13] In the other twelve jurisdictions, subsequent amendments modified the original legislation in various respects, but

---

3. In re Wilcox, 194 N.Y. 288, 87 N.E. 497 (1909); Walker v. Marcellus & Otisco Lake Railway Co., 226 N.Y. 347, 123 N.E. 736 (1919).

4. These amendments were codified in what is now N.Y.—McKinney's Estates, Powers & Trust Law 9–1.1 through 9–1.3.

5. N.Y.—McKinney's Estates, Powers and Trust Law 9–1(a)(2).

6. N.Y.—McKinney's Estates, Powers and Trusts Law 9–1(b).

7. N.Y.—McKinney's Estates, Powers and Trusts Law 9–1.1(a)(2) and (b).

8. Ibid.

9. Id. § 9–1.2. As to the meaning of *cy pres,* see text post Section 3.22, second paragraph.

10. Id. § 9–1.3. *Inter alia,* these rules are designed to prevent invalidation where limitations involve an "unborn widow" or a "fertile octogenarian." See text ante § 3.20.

11. Id. §§ 10–8.1 and 10–8.3. See Matter of Will of Grunebaum, 122 Misc.2d 645, 471

N.Y.S.2d 513 (Surr.Ct.1984) (exercise of power of appointment "suspended illegally the absolute power of alienation and violated the rule against perpetuities"); Accounting of Estate of Isganaitis, 124 Misc.2d 1, 475 N.Y.S.2d 699 (Surr.Ct.1983) (testamentary provision must comply with both the remoteness of vesting and the suspension of absolute power of alienation test of the statutory rule).

12. These jurisdictions were Arizona, California, the District of Columbia, Idaho, Iowa, Indiana, Kentucky, Michigan, Minnesota, Montana, North Dakota, Oklahoma, South Dakota, and Wisconsin.

13. These jurisdictions are Iowa and Kentucky. See discussion of the Iowa and Kentucky statutes in L. Simes & A. Smith, Future Interests §§ 1413, 1414 (2d ed. 1956). In both states the law was recently changed and clarified by recent legislation. Iowa Code 1983, § 558.68, and Ky.Rev.Stat. 381.215, 381.216 now codify the common law Rule Against Perpetuities as modified by the "wait and see" and *cy pres* reformation doctrines, as proposed by Restatement (Second) of Property.

the basic tenor of the legislation in these states remained very similar to that of the New York legislation until quite recently.[14]

Since the approval of the Uniform Statutory Rule Against Perpetuities by the Commissioners on Uniform State laws in 1946, some sixteen states have adopted the USRAP.[15] In a number of states adoption of the USRAP was accompanied by repeal of long-standing legislation prohibiting suspension of the power of alienation.[16] Consequently, this type of legislation is clearly still in force in only seven jurisdictions with respect to instruments becoming effective after enactment of the USRAP.[17]

§ 3.22   Recent Statutory Modifications of the Common Law Rule Against Perpetuities: "Wait and See," *Cy Pres* Reformation, and the Uniform Statutory Rule Against Perpetuities

Beginning in 1947, many states have enacted legislation modifying the common law Rule Against Perpetuities in important respects. The so-called "wait and see" legislation provides that the validity of future interests under the Rule shall be determined by a consideration of actual future events rather than possible future events. The first "wait and see" legislation, enacted in Pennsylvania in 1947,[1] provided in part that

14. Some of the New York-type statutes were amended to provide for a permissible period for suspension of the power of alienation other than two lives in being at the creation of a future estate. In a number of states, including Arizona, the District of Columbia, Iowa, Kentucky, and Wisconsin, the period was changed to lives in being plus 21 years, and in North Dakota the period was changed to lives in being and 25 years. In California, Idaho, Indiana, and Oklahoma, the period was changed to lives in being, without any limit as to the number of lives. In Wisconsin, the period was first changed to lives in being plus twenty years, and later changed to lives in being plus thirty years. The period applicable in Oklahoma was recently changed again, this time to lives in being plus twenty years. For more detail, see L. Simes & A. Smith, Future Interests §§ 1413 through 1436 (2d ed. 1956 and 1989 Pocket Part).

15. The Uniform Statutory Rule Against Perpetuities, as well as other legislation adopting either the "wait and see" of the *cy pres* reformation modification of the common law Rule Against Perpetuities, or both, are discussed post Section 3.22.

16. This is clearly the case, for example, in California, Indiana, Michigan, and North Dakota, and would appear to be desirable in all jurisdictions where the USRAP is adopted. In Minnesota, the New York-type legislation in force for many years was extensively amended in 1989; the amendment became effective on January 1, 1990. But the USRAP was also enacted in 1989, to become effective on January 1, 1992, without repealing the New–York–

type legislation. It would clearly be desirable to effect such repeal before the USRAP becomes effective. Attempts to apply both the New York-type legislation and the USRAP to the same instrument would clearly meet with considerable difficulty.

17. These jurisdictions are Arizona, the District of Columbia, Idaho, New York, Oklahoma, South Dakota, and Wisconsin. As indicated supra note 16, Minnesota, at the time of this writing, had both its New York-type statute and the USRAP in force, but will presumably repeal the former before the latter becomes effective on January 1, 1992.

§ 3.22

1. 20 Pa.Stat., §§ 301.4, 301.5 (part of the Pennsylvania Estates Act of 1947). Interests not subject to the common law Rule are excluded from the operation of the statute. Subsequently, "wait and see" legislation was adopted in many other states. Some of this legislation differed in substantial respects from the pioneering Pennsylvania "wait and see" legislation. Some of the "wait and see" legislation directs the courts to "wait and see" for the full common law period of perpetuities, and some directs the courts to "wait and see" only until expiration of all life estates created by the instrument in question. A number of the states that originally enacted "wait and see" legislation have also adopted *cy pres* reformation legislation, and some have repealed their "wait and see" statutes and enacted the Uniform Statutory Rule Against Perpetuities. See the discussion of *cy pres* reformation and the USRAP post in this Section.

[u]pon the expiration of the period allowed by the common law rule against perpetuities as measured by actual rather than possible events, any interest not then vested and any interest in members of a class the membership of which is then subject to increase shall be void.

Another kind of legislation modifies the common law Rule Against Perpetuities by authorizing or directing courts to reform instruments containing provisions that violate the common law Rule by applying the equitable doctrine of *cy pres*. Pursuant to such legislation courts may, for example, reduce a period of more than twenty-one years in gross or an age contingency of more than twenty-one years to twenty-one years so that an interest otherwise void for remoteness will either vest or fail within the common law perpetuities period.

Legislation embodying both the "wait and see" approach and the *cy pres* reformation approach is now in force in a substantial number of states,[2] and legislation embodying only one or the other of these modifications of the common law Rule is in force in a few states.[3] However, the most important recent modification of the common law Rule has resulted from the widespread adoption of the Uniform Statutory Rule Against Perpetuities, approved by the Commissioners on Uniform State Laws in 1986 and, after addition of one new subsection, incorporated in the Uniform Probate Code in 1990.[4] In its current form, the USRAP provides as follows:[5]

2. These states include Iowa, Kentucky, Ohio, Rhode Island, South Dakota, Vermont, Virginia, and Washington (applies only to interests subject to a trust). L. Simes & A. Smith, Future Interests § 1411 (1989 Pocket Part) states that at least 20 states have legislatively adopted both the "wait and see" and *cy pres* reformation modifications, but many of the states there listed have repealed the listed statutes and have replaced them with the Uniform Statutory Rule Against Perpetuities. See listing of states that have adopted the USRAP infra note 4. The Restatement 2d of Property (1983) asserts that both the "wait and see" and *cy pres* modifications are part of the American common law, although the Restatement 2d's version of "wait and see" has neither been directly adopted by any common law court nor legislative enacted by any state.

3. States with "wait and see" but not *cy pres* reformation legislation include Alaska, Kentucky, Maine, Maryland, Pennsylvania, and Rhode Island. States with *cy pres* reformation legislation but not "wait and see" legislation include Idaho, Missouri, Oklahoma, and Texas (limited to charitable gifts only). Courts in Hawaii, Mississippi, and New Hampshire have applied the *cy pres* reformation approach to validate interests otherwise void under the common law Rule without any statutory basis. For a recent case applying a "wait and see" statute, see Newick v. Mason, 581 A.2d 1269 (Me.1990).

4. The text of the USRAP, with the 1990 Amendment appears both in 8 Uniform Laws Annotated, 1991 Pocket Part pp. 160–172, as Article II, Pt. 9 of the Uniform Probate Code,

and in 8A Uniform Laws Annotated, 1991 Pocket Part pp. 171–204, as a freestanding statute—presumably to make it easier for a state which has not adopted the Uniform Probate Code to enact the USRAP. The official Comments accompanying the text in the 1991 Pocket Part for 8A U.L.A. are substantially more copious than those accompanying the text in the 1991 Pocket Part for 8 U.L.A., and the former contains a valuable Prefatory Note discussing the rationale underlying the USRAP, 1991 Pocket Part pp. 164–171, which is not included in the 1991 Pocket Part for 8 U.L.A.

The 1990 amendment added subsection (e) to § 1 of the Act as it appears in 8A U.L.A., 1990 Pocket Part p. 172, and to § 2–901 of the Act as it appears in 8 U.L.A., 1990 Pocket Part p. 162. As if usually the case when states adopt a Uniform Law, slight changes in the text of the Act were made when the USRAP was adopted in various states.

5. Sections 6–9 of the USRAP are not reproduced in the text. These sections provide that the Act is to be cited as the Uniform Statutory Rule Against Perpetuities and that "it shall be applied and construed to effectuate its general purpose to make uniform the law with respect to the subject of this [Act] among states enacting it"; and further provide for inclusion of the effective date of the Act when enacted and for supersession of the common law Rule Against Perpetuities and/or repeal of earlier statutes (to be listed) that modified the common law Rule.

As is usually the case when states adopt a Uniform Law, some changes in the official

§ 1. Statutory Rule Against Perpetuities

(a) [Validity of nonvested property interest.] A nonvested property interest is invalid unless:

(1) when the interest is created, it is certain to vest or to terminate no later than 21 years after the death of an individual then alive; or

(2) the interest either vests or terminates within 90 years after its creation.

(b) [Validity of General Power of Appointment Subject to Condition Precedent.] A general power of appointment not presently exercisable because of a condition precedent is invalid unless:

(1) when the power is created, the condition precedent is certain to be satisfied or to become impossible to satisfy no later than 21 years after the death of an individual then alive; or

(2) the condition precedent either is satisfied or becomes impossible to satisfy within 90 years after its creation.

(c) [Validity of Nongeneral or Testamentary Power of Appointment.] A nongeneral power of appointment or a general testamentary power of appointment is invalid unless:

(1) when the power is created, it is certain to be irrevocably exercised or otherwise to terminate no later than 21 years after the death of an individual then alive; or

(2) the power is irrevocably exercised or otherwise terminates within 90 years after its creation.

(d) [Possibility of Post-death Child Disregarded.] In determining whether a nonvested property interest or a power of appointment is valid under subsection (a)(1), (b)(1), or (c)(1), the possibility that a child will be born to an individual after the individual's death is disregarded.

(e) [Effect of Certain "Later-of" Type Language.] If, in measuring a period from the creation of a trust or other property arrangement, language in a governing instrument (i) seeks to disallow the vesting or termination of any interest or trust beyond, (ii) seeks to postpone the vesting or termination of any interest or trust until, or (iii) seeks to operate in any similar fashion upon, the later of (A) the expiration of a period of time not exceeding 21 years after the death of the survivor of specified lives in being at the creation of the trust or other property arrangement or (B) the expiration of a period of time that exceeds or might exceed 21 years after the death of the survivor of lives in being at the creation of the trust or other property arrangement, that language is inoperative to the extent it produces a period of time that exceeds 21 years after the death of the survivor of the specified lives.

§ 2. When Nonvested Property Interest or Power of Appointment Created

(a) Except as provided in subsections (b) and (c) and in Section 5(a), the time of creation of a nonvested property interest or a power of appointment is determined under general principles of property law.

text were made when the USRAP was adopted
in various states.

(b) For purposes of this [Act], if there is a person who alone can exercise a power created by a governing instrument to become the unqualified beneficial owner of (i) a nonvested property interest or (ii) a property interest subject to a power of appointment described in Section 1(b) or 1(c), the nonvested property interest or power of appointment is created when the power to become the unqualified beneficial owner terminates. [For purposes of this [Act], a joint power with respect to community property or to marital property under the Uniform Marital Property Act held by individuals married to each other is a power exercisable by one person alone.]

(c) For purposes of this [Act], a nonvested property interest or a power of appointment arising from a transfer of property to a previously funded trust or other existing property arrangement is created when the nonvested property interest or power of appointment in the original contribution was created.

§ 3. Reformation

Upon the petition of an interested person, a court shall reform a disposition in the manner that most closely approximates the transferor's manifested plan of distribution and is within the 90 years allowed by Section 1(a)(2), 1(b)(2), or 1(c)(2) if:

(1) a nonvested property interest or a power of appointment becomes invalid under Section 1 (statutory rule against perpetuities);

(2) a class gift is not but might become invalid under Section 1 (statutory rule against perpetuities) and the time has arrived when the share of any class member is to take effect in possession or enjoyment; or

(3) a nonvested property interest that is not validated by Section 1(a)(1) can vest but not within 90 years after its creation.

§ 4. Exclusions From Statutory Rule Against Perpetuities

Section 1 (statutory rule against perpetuities) does not apply to:

(1) a nonvested property interest or a power of appointment arising out of a nondonative transfer, except a nonvested property interest or a power of appointment arising out of (i) a premarital or postmarital agreement, (ii) a separation or divorce settlement, (iii) a spouse's election, (iv) a similar arrangement arising out of a prospective, existing, or previous marital relationship between the parties, (v) a contract to make or not to revoke a will or trust, (vi) a contract to exercise or not to exercise a power of appointment, (vii) a transfer in satisfaction of a duty of support, or (viii) a reciprocal transfer;

(2) a fiduciary's power relating to the administration or management of assets, including the power of a fiduciary to sell, lease, or mortgage property, and the power of a fiduciary to determine principal and income;

(3) a power to appoint a fiduciary;

(4) a discretionary power of a trustee to distribute principal before termination of a trust to a beneficiary having an indefeasibly vested interest in the income and principal;

(5) a nonvested property interest held by a charity, government, or governmental agency or subdivision, if the nonvested property interest is preceded by an interest held by another charity, government, or governmental agency or subdivision;

(6) a nonvested property interest in or a power of appointment with respect to a trust or other property arrangement forming part of a pension, profit-sharing, stock bonus, health, disability, death benefit, income deferral, or other current or deferred benefit plan for one or more employees, independent contractors, or their beneficiaries or spouses, to which contributions are made for the purpose of distributing to or for the benefit of the participants or their beneficiaries or spouses the property, income, or principal in the trust or other property arrangement, except a nonvested property interest or a power of appointment that is created by an election of a participant or a beneficiary or spouse; or

(7) a property interest, power of appointment, or arrangement that was not subject to the common-law rule against perpetuities or is excluded by another statute of this State.

§ 5.   Prospective Application

(a) Except as extended by subsection (b), this [Act] applies to a nonvested property interest or a power of appointment that is created on or after the effective date of this [Act].   For purposes of this section, a nonvested property interest or a power of appointment created by the exercise of a power of appointment is created when the power is irrevocably exercised or when a revocable exercise becomes irrevocable.

(b) If a nonvested property interest or a power of appointment was created before the effective date of this [Act] and is determined by a judicial proceeding, commenced on or after the effective date of this [Act], to violate this State's rule against perpetuities as that rule existed before the effective date of this [Act], a court upon the petition of an interested person may reform the disposition in the manner that most clearly approximates the transferor's manifested plan of distribution and is within the limits of the rule against perpetuities applicable when the nonvested property interest or power of appointment was created.

The Uniform Statutory Rule Against Perpetuities, which combines the "wait and see" approach, the *cy pres* reformation approach, and an alternative 90–year perpetuities period in modifying the common law Rule, is now in force in some twenty states.[6]   The pace at which the USRAP is being

---

6. The statutes are as follows: West's Ann.Cal.Probate Code §§ 21200 through 21231 (eff. Jan. 1, 1992); West's Colo.Rev.Stat. Ann. §§ 15–11–1101 through 15–11–1107 (eff. Jan. 1, 1992); Conn.Gen.Stat.Ann. § 45a–491 et seq. (eff. May 2, 1989); West's Fla.Stat.Ann. § 689.225 (eff. Oct. 1, 1988); Official Code Ga.Ann. §§ 44–6–200 through 44–6–206 (eff. May 1, 1990); Hawaii Rev.Stat. §§ 525–1 et seq. (eff. June 1992; West's Ann.Ind.Code §§ 32–1–4.1–1 through 32–1–4.1–6 (§§ 32–1–4.1–1 through 32–1–4.1–3, 32–1–4.1–5 and 32–1–4.1–6 eff. July 1, 1991; § 32–1–4.1–4 eff. May 8, 1991); Kan.Sess.Laws 1992, ch. 302 (eff. May 1992); Mass.Ann.Laws c. 184A, §§ 1 through 11 (eff. June 30, 1990); Mich.Comp.

adopted has accelerated in recent years, and it seems likely that it will ultimately be adopted in most if not all states.

The addition of an alternative 90–year perpetuities period is probably the most significant modification of the Rule Against Perpetuities in states where both the "wait and see" and the *cy pres* reformation modifications had previously been adopted. The rationale of the "90–year permissible vesting period" is explained as follows in the Prefatory Note to the USRAP: [7]

> The myriad problems associated with the actual-measuring-lives approach are swept aside by shifting away from actual measuring lives and adopting instead a 90–year permissible vesting period as representing a reasonable approximation of—a proxy for—the period of time that would, on average be produced by identifying and tracing an actual set of measuring lives and then tacking on a 21–year period following the death of the survivor. The selection of 90 years as the period of time reasonably approximating the period that would be produced, on average, by using the set of actual measuring lives identified in the Restatement (Second) or the earlier draft of the Uniform Act is based on a statistical study published in *Perpetuities: A Progress Report on the Draft Uniform Statutory Rule Against Perpetuities*, 20 U.Miami Inst. on Est.Plan. Ch. 7 (1986). This study suggests that the youngest measuring life, on average, is about 6 years old. The remaining life expectancy of a 6–year old is reported as 69.6 years in the U.S. Bureau of the Census, Statistical Abstract of the United States: 1986, Table 108, at p. 69. In the interest of arriving at an end number that is a multiple of 5, the Uniform Act utilizes 69 years as an appropriate of the remaining life expectancy of a 6–year old, which—with the 21–year tack-on period add—yields a permissible vesting period of 90 years.

> The adoption of a flat period of 90 years rather than the use of actual measuring lives is an evolutionary step in the development and refinement of the wait-and-see doctrine. The 90–year period makes wait-and-see simple, fair, and workable. *Aggregate dead-hand control will not be increased beyond that which is already possible by competent drafting under the Common-law Rule.*

> Seen as a valid approximation of the period that would be produced under the conventional survivor–of–the–measuring–lives–plus–21–years approach, and in the interest of making the law of perpetuities uniform, *jurisdictions adopting this Act are strongly urged not to adopt a period of time different from the 90–year period.*

E. CHARACTERISTICS OF FUTURE INTERESTS

§ 3.23 The Inheritability and Devisability of Future Interests

As a general rule, future interests of all types are inheritable and devisable by will in the same manner as present interests in land and in

Laws Ann. §§ 554.71 through 554.78 (eff. Dec. 24, 1988); Minn.Stat.Ann. §§ 501A.01 through 501A.07 (eff. Jan. 1, 1992); Mont.Code Ann. §§ 70–1–801 through 70–1–807 (eff. Oct. 1, 1989); Neb.Rev.Stat. §§ 76–2001 through 76–2008 (eff. August 25, 1989); Nev.Rev.Stat.Ann. 111.103 through 111.1039 (eff. Mar. 17, 1987); N.J.Stat.Ann. §§ 46:2F–1 through 46:2F–8 (eff. July 3, 1991); N.M.St.Ann. §§ 45–2–1000 through 45–2–1006 (eff. Mar. 1992); N.D.Cent. Code 47–02–27.1 through 47–02–27.5 (eff. July 1, 1991); Or.Rev.Stat. §§ 105.950 through 105.975 (eff. Jan. 1, 1990); S.C.Code §§ 27–6–10 through 27–6–80 (eff. March 12, 1987); W.Va.Code Ann. §§ 36–1A–1 through 36–1A–6 (eff. 1992).

7. 8A U.L.A., 1991 Pocket Part pp. 166–167.

personalty, except where the future interest is limited to the life of the owner or is so limited that the death of the owner makes a required survival impossible and thus terminates the interest.[1] Reversions and remainders in fee tail (where still recognized) are, of course, inheritable only by lineal descendants of the reversioner, and are not devisable by will. And contingent future interests (remainders and executory interests) limited in favor of an unborn person or persons are obviously neither inheritable nor devisable by will.[2]

Although possibilities of reverter and powers of termination are generally inheritable and devisable in the same manner as present interests in land or personalty,[3] in some states these contingent reversionary interests pass "by representation" rather than according to the usual law of intestate succession.[4] The doctrine of "representation" can be illustrated as follows: Suppose O conveys land "to A and his heirs so long as the premises are used only for residential purposes," leaving a possibility of reverter in O. Then O dies intestate, leaving his son X as his sole heir. X takes the possibility of reverter "by representation" from O, the "stock of descent," and has the power in many states to transfer it by deed. But if X does not transfer the possibility of reverter by deed and dies intestate, the possibility of reverter will pass to the person who would have been O's heir had O died when X died—a person who may not be X's heir at all—because O, not X, was the "stock of descent." This pattern of descent will continue until either the

---

§ 3.23

1. L. Simes and A. Smith, Future Interests § 1883 (2d ed. 1956), stating the rule and asserting that although the rule is the result of modern statutes of descent and distribution in the United States, "a court would be justified in reaching that result entirely independent of statute." For an extensive citation of cases in support of the rule, see id. nn. 12, 13. Although future interests in land did not pass on intestacy in the same manner as present interests according to the English common law, it was provided by Stats. 60 and 61 Vict., c. 65, §§ 1(1) and 2(3) (1897), that interests in land should pass to the decedent's administrator and be distributed in the same way as interests in personalty. Stats. 22 and 23 Car. II, c. 10 (1670), provided that in distribution of intestate personalty to the decedent's next-of-kin, kinship should be traced from the person last entitled.

2. As soon as a person answering the description in the contingent limitation is born, it becomes possible to regard the contingent interest as both inheritable and devisable.

3. E.g., Abrahams v. Abrahams, 219 Ala. 533, 122 So. 625 (1929); School District No. Six in Weld County v. Russell, 156 Colo. 75, 396 P.2d 929 (1964); noted in 41 Denver Law Center J. 396 (1964); North v. Graham, 235 Ill. 178, 85 N.E. 267, 18 L.R.A.,N.S. 624 (1908); Reichard v. Chicago, Burlington & Quincy Railway Co., 231 Iowa 563, 1 N.W.2d 721 (1942); City of Wheeling v. Zane, 154 W.Va. 34, 173 S.E.2d 158 (1970), noted in 73 W.Va. L.Rev. 91 (1971)—all involving possibilities of

reverter. As to powers of termination, see, e.g., Fayette County Board of Education v. Bryan, 263 Ky. 61, 91 S.W.2d 990 (1936); Watson v. Dalton, 146 Neb. 78, 20 N.W.2d 610 (1945). Accord: 2 Rest., Prop. § 164. Some states have legislation making all "future estates * * * descendible, devisable, and alienable in the same manner as estates in possession." E.g., N.Y.—McKinney's Estates, Powers and Trusts Law 6–5.1, formerly McKinney's Real Property Law § 59 (as amended by N.Y.Laws 1962, ch. 146). In some states there is legislation making possibilities of reverter and powers of termination devisable. E.g., Maryland Code 1957, Art. 93, § 343; Minn. Stat.Ann. § 500.16. In other states there is legislation making all future interests, or all inheritable interests, devisable. E.g., N.Y.—McKinney's Decedent Estate Law § 11. See also N.Y.—McKinney's Estates, Powers and Trusts Law 6–5.1. Both possibilities of reverter and powers of termination are made nondevisable by Ill.—S.H.A. ch. 30, ¶ 37b.

4. As to possibilities of reverter, see, e.g., Elmore v. Austin, 232 N.C. 13, 59 S.E.2d 205 (1950); Burnett v. Snoddy, 199 S.C. 399, 405, 19 S.E.2d 904, 906 (1942) (possibility of reverter following fee simple conditional). As to powers of termination, see, e.g., Methodist Protestant Church of Henderson v. Young, 130 N.C. 8, 40 S.E. 691 (1902). See also Upington v. Corrigan, 151 N.Y. 143, 45 N.E. 359, 37 L.R.A. 794 (1896) (accord), abrogated by N.Y.Laws 1962, ch. 146, now codified as N.Y.—McKinney's Estates, Powers and Trusts Law 6–5.1.

owner of the possibility of reverter makes an effective *inter vivos* transfer or the possibility of reverter becomes a present interest. Whenever the possibility of reverter is effectively transferred *inter vivos,* the transferee becomes a new "stock of descent," and the same rule as to succession "by representation" becomes applicable if the new owner of the possibility of reverter should die intestate.[5]

In those states where possibilities of reverter and powers of termination pass "by representation" when the owner of the interest dies intestate, possibilities of reverter and powers of termination are likely to be held not to be devisable by will.[6]

A remainder for the life of the transferee is obviously neither inheritable nor devisable, but a remainder *pur autre vie* is both inheritable and devisable if the owner of such a remainder predeceases the person who provides the measuring life.[7]

§ 3.24 The Alienability of Future Interests *Inter Vivos*

All vested future interests—remainders and reversions—are freely transferable *inter vivos,* whether the subject matter is land or personalty,[1] except where the future interest is subject to a valid restraint upon alienation imposed by the person creating the interest. Attempted restraints upon the alienation of vested future interests appear to be valid in the United States only to the extent that restraints upon the alienation of present interests of the same quantum are valid.[2] Thus attempted restraints upon the alienation of vested remainders in fee simple (or the equivalent interest in personalty) are generally void,[3] but forfeiture or promissory restraints upon the alienation of a vested remainder for life are generally valid.[4]

5. This illustration is drawn from L. Simes, Future Interests § 35 (2d ed. 1966). See also L. Simes and A. Smith, Future Interests § 1882 (2d ed. 1956).

6. Methodist Protestant Church of Henderson v. Young, 130 N.C. 8, 40 S.E. 691 (1902). See also Upington v. Corrigan, supra note 4. Possibilities of reverter and powers of termination, until recently, were not considered to be property interests at all, but mere possibilities of acquiring an interest at a future time. Hence it was understandable that courts would treat such "mere possibilities" as being incapable of disposition by will.

7. See ante Section 2.15 at notes 12, 13.

§ 3.24

1. Vested future interests are transferable by deed whether they are "legal" or "equitable," and whether they are indefeasibly vested or vested subject to defeasance. E.g., Edward Fox's Case, 8 Co.Rep. 93b (1546); Greer v. Parker, 209 Ark. 553, 191 S.W.2d 584 (1946); Thurston v. Buxton, 218 Ind. 585, 34 N.E.2d 549 (1941); Grant v. Nelson, 100 N.H. 220, 122 A.2d 925 (1956). In most American jurisdictions the transferability of vested future interests in land by deed is confirmed by statutes which expressly provide that "future interests," or "expectant estates"—or, more broadly, "all estates and interests"—may be transferred by deed.

2. Freeman v. Phillips, 113 Ga. 589, 38 S.E. 943 (1901) (vested remainder); Department of Public Works and Buildings v. Porter, 327 Ill. 28, 158 N.E. 366 (1927) (same); Ramey v. Ramey, 195 Ky. 673, 243 S.W. 934 (1922) (same); Latimer v. Waddell, 119 N.C. 370, 26 S.E. 122, 3 L.R.A.(N.S.) 668 (1896). See also L. Simes and A. Smith, Future Interests § 1159 (2d ed. 1956).

3. As to restraints upon alienation of present fee simple estates, see ante Section 2.2. In England, however, there is a line of cases permitting conditions in restraint of the alienation of vested future interests. E.g., Re Porter, [1892] 3 Ch. 481 (1892); In re Goulder, [1905] 2 Ch. 100. See Sweet, Restraints on Alienation, 33 L.Q.Rev. 236, 246 (1917), asserting that these decisions are difficult to justify.

4. As to restraints upon alienation of life estates, see ante Section 2.11.

The alienability *inter vivos* of contingent future interests is not so clearly established. According to the English common law contingent remainders were inalienable because they were considered to be mere possibilities of acquiring an interest at a future time.[5] When it became possible to create legal executory interests in the sixteenth century, they also seem to have been regarded as inalienable.[6] In any case, of course, a contingent remainder or executory interest limited in favor of an unborn person or persons is not alienable *inter vivos*.

At the present time, contingent remainders and executory interests limited to living, ascertained persons appear to be transferable *inter vivos* in most American jurisdictions.[7] Such transferability has been established by statute in many American jurisdictions. Some of the statutes expressly make "contingent interests" or "contingent remainders and executory interests" transferable *inter vivos*.[8] Other statutes, however, are less specific in their terms[9] or do not cover all kinds of contingent future interests.[10] Many of the statutes appear to apply only to interests in land.[11] And some of the statutes have received a narrow construction.[12]

5. See King v. Withers, Talbot 116, 123 (1735); Doe dem. Brune v. Martyn, 8 Barn. & Cress. 497, 516 (1828); Third Report of Commissioners on the Law of Real Property 26 (1832) ("a contingent remainder is not transferable at law, except by a fine * * * "). See also 7 Holdsworth, History of English Law 102 et seq. (1926); 1 Preston, Estates 76 (1820); Challis, Real Property 76 (3d ed. 1911); Roberts, Transfer of Future Interests, 30 Mich. L.Rev. 349 (1932).

6. Like contingent remainders, executory interests were, until fairly recently, deemed to be only possibilities of acquiring an interest at a future time—a view derived from the fundamental idea that only vested estates could constitute the component parts of a fee simple absolute when it was divided into present and future estates. A contingent remainder, while it remained contingent, was not part of the fee simple absolute, although it might comprise all or part of the fee simple absolute if it should vest in possession or in interest—in which case it would defeat and displace the (vested) reversion in fee simple. Similarly, a springing or shifting executory interest, so long as it remained an executory interest, was not part of the fee simple, although it might comprise all or part of the fee simple absolute if it should vest in possession or in interest—in which case it would defeat and displace a present fee simple or a vested remainder in fee simple.

7. No doubt this is due both to the enactment of the statutes considered in the text at notes 8 through 12 and to the modern tendency to view contingent remainders and executory interests as presently existing property interests rather than mere possibilities. See 2 Rest.Prop. 162, asserting that all remainders and executory interests are alienable by the ordinary deed of conveyance used in the state where the land is situated.

8. E.g., Ala.Code tit. 47, § 13; Ariz.Rev. Stat. § 71–105; Maine Rev.Stat.Ann. c. 154, § 3; Mass.G.L.A. c. 184, § 2; Mich.Comp. Laws Ann. § 554.35; Minn.Stat.Ann. § 500.- 15; N.Y.—McKinney's Real Prop.Law § 59; Ohio Rev.Code § 2131.04; Rhode Island Gen. Laws 1956, § 43–3–10; Wis.Stat.Ann. § 230.- 35.

9. Some states have statutes declaring that "future interests pass by succession, will and transfer in the same manner as present interests." E.g., West's Ann.Cal.Civ.Code § 699; Idaho Code § 55–109; North Dakota Cent. Code 47–02–18; South Dakota Comp.Laws § 43–3–20. Other states have statutes declaring that "any interest in land may be conveyed," or that "every conveyance of real estate passes all the interest of the grantor therein" unless a contrary intent is manifested. E.g., Iowa Code Ann. § 557.3; Kan.Stat. Ann. § 67–205; Kentucky Rev.Stat. 382.010; Miss.Code 1972, § 89–1–1; Vernon's Ann. Missouri Stats. § 442.020; Tenn.Code Ann. § 66– 5–101; Virginia Code 1950, § 55–6; West Virginia Code, 50–401.

10. E.g., 25 Del.Code §§ 101, 302 (estates "in possession, reversion, or remainder"); 60 Okl.Stat.1981, § 30 ("a remainder * * * may be created and transferred by that name"); 21 Penn.Stat. § 3 ("reversions and remainders"); New Mexico Stat.Ann.1978, § 75–103 ("remainder or reversion").

11. Most of the statutes cited supra notes 8–10 are contained in subdivisions devoted to real property only.

12. E.g., Mass.Gen.Laws Ann. c. 184, § 2, has been construed to mean that, though the contingent interest of an heir apparent would be alienable, that of an heir presumptive or other person whose interest is subject to an

Even in the absence of a statute which makes contingent remainders and executory interests transferable *inter vivos,* some state courts have held that such interests are thus transferable.[13] Other courts have held, in the absence of a controlling statute that, contingent remainders and executory interests are not transferable *inter vivos* [14] unless they fall within one of the three well-recognized exceptions to the English common law rule holding such interests not to be alienable *inter vivos:* (1) where the transfer is by way of release to the person whose interest would be defeated if the contingent interest should vest,[15] (2) where the doctrine of estoppel by deed is applicable to make the transfer effective if the interest later vests in the transferor,[16] or (3) where the deed is given for adequate consideration and can be treated as a specifically enforceable contract if the interest later vests in the transferor.[17] In short, the minority rule that contingent remainders and executory interests are "inalienable by deed" really makes them inalienable only if the purported transfer is made by quitclaim deed, without adequate consideration, to someone other than a person in whose favor the contingent interest could be released.[18]

In those jurisdictions where the courts have held that a future interest contingent as to "event" is alienable *inter vivos* but a future interest contingent as to "person" is not,[19] courts have sometimes strained to find

equally uncertain contingency might not. Clarke v. Fay, 205 Mass. 228, 91 N.E. 328, 27 L.R.A.(N.S.) 454 (1910).

13. E.g., McAdams v. Bailey, 169 Ind. 518, 82 N.E. 1057, 13 L.R.A.(N.S.) 1003 (1907); Rutherford v. Keith, 444 S.W.2d 546 (Ky. 1969); Granite State Electric Co. v. Gidley, 114 N.H. 226, 318 A.2d 486 (1974); Jernigan v. Lee, 279 N.C. 341, 182 S.E.2d 351 (1971); Jerman v. Nelson, 135 Or. 126, 293 P. 592 (1930); Croft v. McKie, 235 S.C. 231, 111 S.E.2d 210 (1959); Parker v. Blackmon, 553 S.W.2d 623 (Tex.1977).

14. Fletcher v. Hurdle, 259 Ark. 640, 536 S.W.2d 109 (1976); Roper v. Finney, 7 Ill.2d 487, 131 N.E.2d 106 (1956). See also Collins v. Held, 174 Ind.App. 584, 369 N.E.2d 641 (1977), citing McAdams v. Bailey, supra note 13, in support of a dictum that a contingent remainder is not alienable by quitclaim deed; In re Will of Schmidt, 256 Minn. 64, 97 N.W.2d 441 (1959), noted in 37 U. of Detroit L.J. 411 (1960), holding that the Minnesota statute, supra note 8, applies only to real property and that a future interest in chattels personal following a trust for a term of years is an executory interest which is inalienable.

15. E.g., Towns v. Walters, 225 Ga. 293, 168 S.E.2d 144 (1969); Kohl v. Montgomery, 373 Ill. 200, 25 N.E.2d 826 (1940); Nickerson v. Harding, 267 Mass. 203, 166 N.E. 703 (1929); Trustees of Calvary Presbyterian Church v. Putnam, 249 N.Y. 111, 162 N.E. 601 (1928). There is also some authority for allowing the release by a member of a class who has a contingent interest to other members of the class. E.g., Bradley Lumber Co. v. Burbridge, 213 Ark. 165, 210 S.W.2d 284 (1948);

Rembert v. Evans, 86 S.C. 445, 68 S.E. 659 (1910).

16. E.g., Phelps v. Palmer, 192 Ga. 421, 15 S.E.2d 503 (1941); Smith v. Carroll, 286 Ill. 137, 121 N.E. 254 (1918); Byrd v. Allen, 351 Mo. 99, 171 S.W.2d 691 (1942); Cain v. Belden, 93 N.J.Eq. 576, 117 A. 39 (1922); Hobson v. Hobson, 184 Tenn. 484, 201 S.W.2d 659 (1947). At common law in England, only a conveyance by common recovery or by fine would create the necessary estoppel to claim against the grantee. In the United States, a deed with a covenant of seisin, or warranty, or of quiet enjoyment, or containing some other distinct representation that the grantor has title to a particular interest, will create the necessary estoppel. See post Section 11.5.

17. E.g., McAdams v. Bailey, supra note 13; Bishop v. Horney, 177 Md. 353, 9 A.2d 597 (1939); Hobson v. Hobson, supra note 16.

18. L. Waggoner, Future Interests in a Nutshell 95 (1981).

19. In New Jersey, the statute makes interest contingent "as to the event" alienable, but interests contingent "as to the person" are declared inalienable. New Jersey Stat.Ann. § 46:3–7. In other states the same distinction is made in the case law. E.g., Bartholomew v. Murry, 61 Conn. 387, 23 A. 604, 29 Am.St.Rep. 206 (1892); Raney v. Smith, 242 Ga. 809, 251 S.E.2d 554 (1979); Du Bois v. Judy, 291 Ill. 340, 126 N.E. 104 (1920); In re Clayton's Trust Estate, 195 Md. 622, 74 A.2d 1 (1950); Thames v. Goode, 217 N.C. 639, 9 S.E.2d 485 (1940); Frank v. Frank, 153 Tenn. 215, 218, 280 S.W. 1012, 1013 (1925).

that contingencies relate to "event" rather than "person." [20]   On the other hand, at least a few courts have sustained forfeiture restraints imposed on the alienation of contingent future interests which would have been void if imposed on a present interest or vested future interest of the same quantum.[21]   The decisions of courts upholding such restraints may well be based on doubt as to the advisability of permitting the alienation of contingent remainders and executory interests.[22]

In some states there are statutes expressly providing that possibilities of reverter and powers of termination shall be freely alienable *inter vivos*.[23]   In the absence of such statutes, the cases are divided as to the transferability of a possibility of reverter *inter vivos*.[24]   Even in states where a possibility of reverter is not freely transferable *inter vivos*, however, it may be released to the owner of the present interest;[25]   and it may be transferred to other persons through an application of the estoppel by deed doctrine[26]   or by treating the deed as a specifically enforceable contract to convey.[27]   In the absence of a statute making powers of termination transferable inter vivos, the weight of authority still holds that such interests are not transferable,[28]

20. E.g., Frank v. Frank, supra note 19; Taylor v. Stewart, 18 A. 456 (N.J.Ch.1889); Prince v. Barham, 127 Va. 462, 103 S.E. 626 (1920) (remainder to the surviving children of a living person held contingent as to event rather than person). Both Simes and Powell are critical of the distinction. L. Simes and A. Smith, Future Interests § 1859 in text between nn. 71 and 75 (2d ed. 1956); 2A R. Powell, Real Prop. ¶ 283 in text around n. 18. Cf. L. Waggoner, Future Interests in a Nutshell 96–97 (1981), arguing that a future interest contingent "as to person" cannot be *truly* alienable even where the interest is "presently owned" by a person capable of making a transfer, such as an heir apparent.

21. E.g., Security–First National Bank of Los Angeles v. Rogers, 51 Cal.2d 24, 330 P.2d 811 (1958); Wohlgemuth v. Des Moines National Bank, 199 Iowa 649, 192 N.W. 248 (1923); Gordon v. Tate, 314 Mo. 508, 284 S.W. 497 (1926).

22. See L. Simes and A. Smith, Future Interests § 1159 (2d ed. 1956). Also see id. § 1852: "As a practical matter the only interests which are really marketable are the fee simple absolute, the term of years, and the reversion dependent on a term of years. Hence it is quite possible that making contingent future interests inalienable would decrease their importance by way of nuisance value, and thus it would be easier to market the fee simple in land or the absolute interest in personalty."

23. E.g., Mich.Comp.Laws Ann. § 554.111; Minn.Stat.Ann. § 500.16; North Car.Gen.Stat. § 39–6.3. In other states, there is broader legislation making all future estates, or all interests in land, alienable. E.g., Miss.Code § 89–1–1; N.Y.Estates, Powers and Trusts Law 6–5.1. Statutes of the broader type may, however be held inapplicable to powers of

termination.   Compare P C K Properties, Inc. v. City of Cuyahoga Falls, 112 Ohio App. 492, 176 N.E.2d 441 (1960), with Magness v. Kerr, 121 Or. 373, 254 P. 1012, 51 A.L.R. 1466 (1927). For a comprehensive list of statutes, see 2 Rest., Prop. § 160, Comment d.

24. E.g., Irby v. Smith, 147 Ga. 329, 93 S.E. 877 (1917); Collette v. Town of Charlotte, 114 Vt. 357, 45 A.2d 203 (1946). Contra, e.g., Pure Oil Co. v. Miller–McFarland Drilling Co., 376 Ill. 486, 34 N.E.2d 854, 135 A.L.R. 567 (1941). The Illinois rule against alienability was later codified; see Ill.—S.H.A. ch. 30, ¶ 37b.

25. E.g., Carden v. LaGrone, 225 Ga. 365, 169 S.E.2d 168 (1969); Application of Mareck, 257 Minn. 222, 100 N.W.2d 758 (1960). Ill.—S.H.A. ch. 30, ¶ 37g, expressly permits release of a possibility of reverter.

26. E.g., Pure Oil Co. v. Miller–McFarland Drilling Co., Inc., 376 Ill. 486, 34 N.E.2d 854, 135 A.L.R. 567 (1941). As to estoppel by deed, generally, see post Section 11.5.

27. Although no cases involving possibilities of reverter have been found, the "enforcible contract" exception would clearly apply to possibilities of reverter as well as powers of termination—see infra note 29—and the "mere expectancy" of a presumptive heir.

28. E.g., Strothers v. Woodcox, 143 Iowa 648, 121 N.W. 51 (1909); Piper v. Union Pacific Railway Co., 14 Kan. 574 (1875); Craig v. Inhabitants of Franklin County, 58 Me. 479 (1870); Rice v. Boston & Worcester Railroad Corp., 94 Mass. (12 Allen) 141 (1866); Helms v. Helms, 137 N.C. 206, 49 S.E. 110 (1904); Wagner v. Wallowa County, 76 Or. 453, 148 P. 1140, L.R.A.1916F 303 (1915); Purvis v. McElveen, 234 S.C. 94, 106 S.E.2d 913 (1959) (dictum); Pickens v. Daugherty, 217 Tenn. 349, 397 S.W.2d 815 (1965), noted in 33 Tenn. L.Rev. 546 (1966).

except by release to the owner of the present interest,[29] unless the power of termination is incident to a reversion and is transferred with the reversion.[30] Indeed, there is even some American authority, now much discredited, holding that an invalid attempt to transfer a power of termination *inter vivos* destroys the interest.[31]

As has previously been indicated,[32] most of the statutes expressly making future interests alienable *inter vivos* apply only to interests in land. But it is probable that, in most jurisdictions, the same rules as to alienability *inter vivos* would be applied, so far as possible, to interests in land and in personalty.[33] It should be noted, however, that there may be some differences with respect to the mode of transfer.[34] Future interests in personalty may generally be transferred by a written deed of assignment,[35] but in some states contingent future interests are not fully alienable. In such states, it would seem that contingent future interests can be released to the persons whose interests would be defeated by the vesting of the contingent interest, although no cases on the point have been found.[36] But the doctrine of estoppel by deed would not seem to be applicable to interests in personalty,[37] and it is not clear whether an assignment of a contingent future interest in personalty for consideration can be enforced as a contract to assign.[38]

§ 3.25 Subjection of Future Interests to Creditors' Claims

To what extent may future interests be subjected, by appropriate pro-

---

29. E.g., Werner v. Graham, 181 Cal. 174, 183 P. 945 (1919). Ill.—S.H.A. ch. 30, ¶ 37b, permits the release of a power of termination. *Quaere* whether, absent any applicable statute, *inter vivos* transfer on the theory of estoppel by deed or specific performance of contract would be recognized. Any transfer except by way of release is expressly barred by Ill.—S.H.A. ch. 30, ¶ 37b.

30. E.g., Trask v. Wheeler, 89 Mass. (7 Allen) 109 (1863). That a right of entry incident to a reversion may be transferred with the reversion was established beyond doubt by Stat. 32 Hen. VIII, c. 34, § 9 (1540) (also providing that the benefit of a lessee's covenants should pass with a transfer of the reversion), which is generally held to be part of the American common law as received after the American Revolution.

31. The first case so holding was Rice v. Boston & Worcester Railroad Corp., supra note 28. Accord: Wagner v. Wallowa County, supra note 28.

32. Supra note 11.

33. Price v. Price's Administrator, 23 Ala. 609 (1853); Sinclair v. Crabtree, 211 Cal. 524, 296 P. 79 (1931); Ingersoll v. Ingersoll, 77 Conn. 408, 59 A. 413 (1904); In re Dixon's Will, 280 A.2d 735 (Del.Ch.1971) (future interest which would have been a vested remainder but for Delaware rule that legal future interests in personalty are executory interests); Brown v. Robinson, 224 N.Y. 301, 120 N.E. 694 (1918), rehearing denied 225 N.Y. 638, 121

N.E. 857 (1919); Whelen v. Phillips, 151 Pa. 312, 25 A. 44 (1892); Nalley v. First National Bank of Medford, 135 Or. 40, 293 P. 721, 76 A.L.R. 625 (1930) rehearing denied 135 Or. 409, 296 P. 61, 76 A.L.R. 625 (1931); Martin & Earle v. Maxwell, 86 S.C. 1, 67 S.E. 962, 138 Am.St.Rep. 1012 (1910); Old National Bank v. Campbell, 1 Wn.App. 773, 463 P.2d 656 (1970).

34. Generally, see L. Simes and A. Smith, Future Interests §§ 444–447 (2d ed. 1956).

35. Price v. Price's Administrator, Sinclair v. Crabtree, In re Dixon's Will, Brown v. Robinson, Whelen v. Phillips, Nalley v. First National Bank of Medford, and Old National Bank v. Campbell—all supra note 33.

36. The rationale of the rule allowing release seems applicable to personalty as well as to realty.

37. It does not appear to be common practice to include in deeds of personalty title covenants of the kind frequently included in deeds of realty, and no cases have been found suggesting that the estoppel by deed doctrine applies to deeds of personalty.

38. Since personal property is not normally regarded as unique, it is doubtful that a contract to assign a contingent future interest in personalty would be specifically enforceable. Perhaps the difficulty of determining damages for breach of a contract for the sale of such an interest would justify specific enforcement.

ceedings, to the claims of creditors?[1] The general rule is that only future interests which are fully alienable *inter vivos* may be reached and applied to the claims of creditors. Reversions and vested remainders in land (whether indefeasibly vested or vested subject to defeasance) or equivalent interests in personalty are generally subject to seizure and sale to satisfy creditors' claims.[2] In addition, contingent remainders, executory interests, possibilities of reverter, and powers of termination are generally subject to the satisfaction of creditors' claims in those jurisdictions where such interests are fully alienable *inter vivos*,[3] but not in those jurisdictions where such interests are either inalienable or alienable only by release, estoppel, or by virtue of the enforceable contract theory.[4]

Even where contingent future interests are fully alienable *inter vivos,* some cases have refused to allow them to be seized and applied to the satisfaction of creditors' claims.[5] Although the language of the opinions differs, the basic rationale of these decisions is that contingent interests are not likely to bring a "fair" price when offered at forced sales, as indicated in the following passage from an opinion of the Oklahoma court:[6]

> Where the contingencies are such * * * as to render the interest in specific property a mere remote possibility, the difficulty in determining the value of the interest for sale upon execution gives strong practical and legal reasons for denial of the right to so levy. Especially so where sacrifice of the judgment debtor's expectancy is probably without substantial benefit to the judgment creditor.

In addition, if the creditor's proceeding is in equity, the courts have sometimes regulated the time and conditions of sale in such a way as to avoid

---

§ 3.25

1. For general discussion of the question, see L. Simes and A. Smith, Future Interests §§ 1922–1927 (2d ed. 1956).

2. E.g., Williams v. Spears, 235 Ala. 611, 180 So. 266 (1938) (a vested remainder subject to power of sale in life tenant is subject to sale on execution); King v. Fay, 169 F.Supp. 934 (D.D.C.1958) (reversionary interest vested subject to defeasance is subject to sale); Stombaugh v. Morey, 388 Ill. 392, 58 N.E.2d 545 (1944) (remainder vested subject to defeasance is subject to sale); Koelliker v. Denkinger, 148 Kan. 503, 83 P.2d 703, 119 A.L.R. 1 (1938), modified 149 Kan. 259, 86 P.2d 740, 119 A.L.R. 1525 (1939) (vested remainder subject to defeasance is subject to attachment); Perabo v. Gallagher, 241 Mass. 207, 135 N.E. 113 (1922) (indefeasibly vested remainder is subject to creditor's bill); First National Bank v. Pointer, 174 Tenn. 472, 126 S.W.2d 335 (1939) (reversion is subject to sale). For additional cases, see L. Simes and A. Smith, Future Interests § 1923 n. 26 (2d ed. 1956 and 1981 Pocket Part).

3. E.g., State ex rel. Cooper v. Cloyd, 461 S.W.2d 833 (Mo.1971) (execution); Jerman v. Nelson, 135 Or. 126, 293 P. 592 (1931) (same); Jonas v. Jones, 153 Kan. 108, 109 P.2d 211 (1940) (attachment); Ragan v. Looney, 377 S.W.2d 273 (Mo.1964) (same); Cashman v.

Bangs, 200 Mass. 498, 86 N.E. 932 (1909) (creditor's bill); Noonan v. State Bank of Livermore, 211 Iowa 401, 233 N.W. 487 (1930) (bankruptcy); In re Cunningham's Estate, 340 Pa. 265, 16 A.2d 712 (1940) (same).

4. E.g., National Bank of Commerce v. Ritter, 181 Ark. 439, 26 S.W.2d 113 (1930); Kenwood Trust & Savings Bank v. Palmer, 285 Ill. 552, 121 N.E. 186 (1918). The cases cited deny creditors the power to reach the contingent future interest by execution, attachment, or creditors bill. The cases are in conflict as to whether such contingent interests will vest in the trustee when the debtor is adjudicated bankrupt. Suskin & Berry v. Rumley, 37 F.2d 304, 68 A.L.R. 768 (4th Cir.1930), and In re Martin, 47 F.2d 498 (6th Cir.1931) hold that the interest will vest in the bankruptcy trustee. Contra: In re Landis, 41 F.2d 700 (7th Cir.1930), certiorari denied sub nominee Farmers Bank v. Bickenbach, 282 U.S. 872, 51 S.Ct. 77, 75 L.Ed. 770 (1930); In re Ehle, 109 F. 625 (D.Vt.1901); Kahn v. Rockhill, 132 N.J.Eq. 188, 28 A.2d 34 (1942), affirmed 133 N.J.Eq. 300, 31 A.2d 819 (1943).

5. Muller v. Cox, 98 N.J.Eq. 188, 130 A. 811 (1925); Bourne v. Farrar, 180 N.C. 135, 137, 104 S.E. 170, 172 (1920); Adams v. Dugan, 196 Okl. 156, 163 P.2d 227 (1945).

6. Adams v. Dugan, supra note 5.

undue prejudice to the debtor.[7] But courts have rarely interfered even to this extent with the creditors' right to reach and apply future interests vested subject to defeasance to the satisfaction of their claims, despite the fact that the "prevention of sacrifice" rationale seems to apply equally to the sale of such interests.[8]

Suppose a contingent interest is not fully alienable *inter vivos*, but is devisable by will. May creditors of the deceased owner of such an interest reach and apply it to the satisfaction of their claims? There seem to be no cases dealing with this question, but it can be argued that creditors should be able to reach and apply such an interest if the contingency which makes the interest inalienable *inter vivos* is resolved at the owner's death, so that the interest is thereafter fully alienable *inter vivos*. Indeed, it is arguable that the same result should be reached where the contingent interest vests after the owner's death but during the course of administration of his estate.[9]

---

7. Mudd v. Durham, 98 Ky. 454, 33 S.W. 1116 (1896); Martin v. Martin, 54 Ohio St.2d 101, 374 N.E.2d 1384 (1978).

8. See cases cited supra note 2. Contra: Mears v. Lamona, 17 Wash. 148, 49 P. 251 (1897), involving vested equitable interests, where the court merely imposed a lien on the debtor's interest, with the sale of that interest postponed until it should become vested.

9. See L. Simes and A. Smith, Future Interests § 1927 (2d ed. 1956 and 1981 Pocket Part).

Chapter 4

RELATIONS BETWEEN OWNERS OF PRESENT AND FUTURE ESTATES AND INTERESTS IN THE SAME REALTY OR PERSONALTY

Table of Sections

---

§ 4.1 In General—Waste

When the ownership of land is divided into successive present and future estates it often becomes necessary for courts to determine the extent to which the holder of a limited interest in the land should be restricted in his use and enjoyment in order to protect the holders of other interests in the same land. The rules worked out by the courts (with some legislative assistance) to assist them in making such determinations are known, collectively, as the law of "waste." [1]

§ 4.1

1. Waste is considered post in Sections 4.2 through 4.7. Generally, see 1 Am.L.Prop. §§ 2.16(e), 4.100 through 4.105, 20.1 through 20.23; 5 R. Powell, Real Property ch. 56; L. Simes and A. Smith, Future Interests ch. 47 (2d ed. 1956); L. Simes, Future Interests § 46 (2d ed. 1966); Rest.Prop. §§ 138 through 146, 187 through 199.

For a recent case discussing the general nature of "waste," see Meyer v. Hansen, 373 N.W.2d 392 (N.D.1985), where the court said that "waste" consists of an unreasonable or improper use, abuse, mismanagement or omission of duty touching real estate by one right-

fully in possession which results in substantial injury; that "waste" implies neglect or misconduct resulting in material damage to property, but does not include ordinary depreciation of property due to age and normal use; and that personal property such as furnishings, equipment and inventory may be subject to "waste" when such items are so attached and intertwined with real property as to warrant treating them as part of the realty—i.e., when such items have become "fixtures." The same definition of waste is contained in Vogel v. Pardon, 444 N.W.2 348 (N.D.1989). See also McKibben v. Mohawk Oil Co., Ltd., 667 P.2d 1223 (Alaska 1983) ("Waste occurs when the owner of a possessory estate engages

"Waste" may be either "voluntary"—i.e., a result of the deliberate affirmative acts of the possessory tenant [2]—or "permissive"—i.e., a result of the failure of the possessory tenant to perform an affirmative duty imposed upon him for the benefit of the owners of future interests in the land.[3] At one time, moreover, the possessory tenant might be liable to the owner of a future interest even though the possessory tenant was without fault. Thus, e.g., a tenant for life or for years was liable at common law to the reversioner or remainderman for permanent injury done by a trespassing stranger, although the tenant was without fault.[4] Liability for such "innocent waste" was apparently imposed on the tenant because only he could maintain an action of trespass against the tortfeasor in such cases.[5] The tenant, in fact, could recover the full damages for the reduction in the value of the realty in such cases, and if he did so he was accountable to the reversioner or remainderman for the excess over the amount necessary to compensate him for the injury to his possessory estate.[6] But even if the possessory tenant had not sued the tortfeasor, he was liable to the reversioner or remainderman for the injury to the future interest.[7]

Although the life tenant's ability to recover full damages and his resulting liability in waste for the acts of trespassing strangers survived the development of the action on the case, which permitted the reversioner or remainderman to recover directly from the tortfeasor for injury to the future interest,[8] most of the modern cases hold that the life tenant is not liable in

in unreasonable conduct that result in physical damage to land and substantial diminution in value of the estates owned by others in the same land." Id. at 1228). See further Matter of Estate of Gauch, 308 N.W.2d 88 (Iowa 1981) ("a life tenant is chargeable with the condition of the property as it came to him at the inception of the life tenancy, not with improvements he himself adds which were not merely substitutionary." Id. at 91).

2. See post Section 4.2. Coke asserted that conventional tenants for life or years were not liable for waste prior to the Statute of Marlbridge (1267) unless they had been enjoined against waste in the conveyance creating the possessory estate, but that tenants in curtesy and dower and guardians in chivalry were liable. Co.Litt. * 54b; 2 Co.Inst. * 299. Blackstone repeated Coke's assertion. 2 Bl.Comm. * 282. But Pollock and Maitland disagreed with Coke and Blackstone as to tenants for life. 2 Pollock & Maitland, History of English Law 9 (2d ed. 1989). Holdsworth and Kirchwey each took positions similar to, but slightly different from, the position taken by Pollock & Maitland. See 3 Holdsworth, History of English Law 121 (5th ed. 1942); Kirchwey, Liability for Waste, 8 Col.L.Rev. 425, 624, at 624–630 (1908). All the writers agreed, however, that tenants for years were not liable for waste at common law. The Statute of Marlbridge, 52 Hen. III, c. 23, § 2 (1267) clearly imposed liability for waste on tenants for years and any tenants for life not already liable for waste at common law.

3. Because the Statute of Marlbridge, supra note 2, and the Statute of Gloucester, 6 Edw. I, c. 5 (1278), provided only that certain kinds of tenants should not "make" waste, there was initially some doubt as liability for failure to perform affirmative duties. But it was later held that a tenant could "make" waste either by action or by failure to act. Co.Litt. * 53a.

4. 2 Co.Inst. 145.

5. 2 Co.Inst. 303. Also see 1 Am.L.Prop. § 2.16 at p. 130; 5 id. § 20.13 at p. 104. American law now allows a tenant for life or for years, as owner of a possessory estate, to bring a trespass action whether he is actually in possession or not, provided the land is not adversely possessed by another. See 6A Am. L.Prop. § 28.12 at nn. 4–6.

6. Co.Litt. *54a ("The tenant by courtesie, the tenant in dower, the tenant for life, years, etc. shall answer for the waste done by a stranger and shall take their remedy over [against the wrongdoer].")

7. In such a case, having been subjected to a judgment in favor of the reversioner or remainderman, the possessory tenant could still sue the tortfeasor for trespass and recover the full damages, thus obtaining reimbursement for what he was compelled to pay the owner of the future interest.

8. The action on the case developed during the fourteenth century, but the right of a reversioner or remainderman to recover from the tortfeasor in an action on the case was

waste for the acts of strangers unless the life tenant is at fault.[9] As a consequence, most courts now hold that the life tenant is limited, as against a trespassing stranger, to recovery of the actual loss resulting from invasion of his rights to exclusive possession and use of the realty, and that only the reversioner or remainderman can recover for the injury to the future interest.[10]

It is sometimes said that, under the early English law, a tenant for life was liable for injury to the reversion or remainder resulting from accident and without any fault on the life tenant's part,[11] but no decisions can be found to support such an assertion.[12]

In addition to the law of "waste," the courts have also developed a closely related body of law to assist them in determining how certain burdens (such as payment of property taxes and special assessments), and certain benefits (such as rents) shall be apportioned between the holders of successive interests in the same realty.[13] And the courts have also developed rules for determining when the holder of a limited interest is entitled to compel a sale of the realty in fee simple over the objections of the owners of future interests in the same realty.[14]

Similar problems with respect to personalty may arise, but most of the judicial rules dealing with these problems are part of the law of trusts because future interests in personalty are almost always equitable interests in trust property rather than legal interests.[15]

§ 4.2 Voluntary Waste

Absent a provision in the creating instrument that would absolve the tenant for life or for years from liability for waste, the English law courts held that any affirmative act of a possessory tenant for life or for years

---

apparently not established until the end of the seventeenth century. See Bedingfield v. Onslow, 3 Lev. 209, 83 Eng.Rep. 654 (1685).

9. See Rogers v. Atlantic, Gulf & Pacific Co., 213 N.Y. 246, 107 N.E. 661, L.R.A.1916A 787 (1915). Accord: Rest., Prop. 146. All the cases to the contrary are quite old and are unlikely to be followed at the present time.

10. Zimmerman v. Shreeve, 59 Md. 357 (1882); Swick & Swick v. West Virginia Coal & Coke Co., 122 W.Va. 151, 7 S.E.2d 697 (1940). See Note, 37 Ky.L.J. 440 (1949). Contra: Rogers v. Atlantic, Gulf & Pacific Co., supra note 9, holding that a life tenant may recover for the entire loss, subject to a duty to account to the reversioner or remainderman for the latter's share of the damages recovered. The *Rogers* holding has been vigorously criticized. See 5 Am.L.Prop. § 2.16 at p. 132. The *Rogers* holding has been somewhat modified by statute in New York. McKinney's Real Prop.Actions & Proceedings Law § 833, originally enacted by N.Y.Laws 1935, chs. 794, 798.

11. Kirchwey, Liability for Waste, 8 Col. L.Rev. 425, at 435–437 (1908).

12. In all the cases cited by Kirchwey, supra note 36, the tenant was apparently guilty of what would now be called negligence.

13. This body of law is considered post in Sections 4.7 through 4.12. Generally, see 1 Am.L.Prop. §§ 216, 218 through 2.25; 5 R. Powell, Real Property chs. 58, 59; L. Simes and A. Smith, Future Interests ch. 48; L. Simes, Future Interests § 48 (2d ed. 1966); Rest.Prop. §§ 129 through 152.

14. This subject is considered post Section 4.12. Generally, see 1 Am.L.Prop. §§ 4.98, 4.99; R. Powell, Real Property ¶ 292; L. Simes and A. Smith, Future Interests ch. 57 (2d ed. 1956); L. Simes, Future Interests § 53 (2d ed. 1966); Rest.Prop. § 179.

15. The trust property often includes realty as well, in which case the rules dealing with the rights and duties of the owners of successive equitable interests are also part of the law of trusts. The protection of owners of legal future interests in personalty is briefly considered post in Section 4.13.

which "injured the inheritance" constituted "voluntary" waste.[1] Although the point was often not clearly articulated, the older English cases proceeded on the assumption that any substantial alteration of the land or the structures thereon would "injure the reversion" because the reversion or remainderman in fee simple was legally entitled, at the termination of all preceding less-than-fee simple estates, to have possession of the property in substantially the condition it was in when the fee simple was divided into successive estates.[2] In many, though not all, of the decided cases, the acts of the tenant in possession reduced the value of the reversion or remainder, but reduction in value was clearly not the determining factor in the court's decision as to whether waste was committed.[3]

Most of the English cases dealing with voluntary waste involved either (1) the cutting of mature, valuable trees, (2) changing the "course of husbandry" on farm land, (3) extracting minerals, or (4) the demolition or substantial alteration of structures.

The English law as to the cutting of mature, valuable trees was complicated and very strict. In general, such cutting was waste unless the trees were needed for fuel or necessary repairs.[4] But "it was early held in the United States that * * * the cutting of timber * * * to clear up land for cultivation, consonant with good husbandry, was not waste, although such

---

§ 4.2

1. "Voluntary waste" is contrasted with "permissive waste," which essentially means failure to perform the tenant's limited duty to keep the property in repair. "Permissive waste" is considered post in Section 4.3. The "inheritance" was the reversion or remainder in fee simple resulting from division of the present fee simple into successive present and future estates. At common law, the owner of a defeasible fee simple estate could not be guilty of waste since, by definition, he owned the "inheritance." But, as we shall see, in cases where the owner of a defeasible fee simple estate has been engaged in "wantonly destructive" conduct, a court of equity will enjoin the continuation of such conduct. See post Section 4.5.

2. See 5 R. Powell, Real Property ¶ 640, also suggesting that "this is a social judgment in favor of preserving the status quo ante and a rejection of the modern concept of 'reasonable use' in the light of changing circumstances." Cf. 1 Am.L.Prop. § 2.16 at p. 135, and 5 Am.L.Prop. § 20.1 at p. 75, asserting that the general principle is based on the presumed intent of the person who divided the fee simple into successive present and future estates.

3. This is illustrated by cases of so-called "meliorating waste," where conduct was held to constitute waste although it increased the value of the property. E.g., City of London v. Greyme, Cro.Jac. 181, 79 Eng.Rep. 158 (1607); Cole v. Green, 1 Lev. 309, 83 Eng.Rep. 422 (1670); Keepers of Harrow School v. Alderton, 2 Bos. & Pul. 86, 126 Eng.Rep. 1170 (C.B.1800);

Young v. Spencer, 10 B. & C. 145, 109 Eng. Rep. 405 (K.B.1829).

4. The rule was a reasonable one in a timber-scarce agricultural society. The prohibition against cutting by a tenant for life or for years applied to oak, ash, and elm, which were "timber trees" everywhere, and to other trees which, by local custom, were classified as "timber trees." It also applied to fruit trees, ornamental trees, and to other trees "beneficial to the inheritance" such as willows protecting the banks of streams and trees "standing in defense of houses." Trees of "timber" quality but too young for use in building could be cut for the purpose of thinning, thus benefiting other "timber" trees. Dead trees, and "timber trees" past their prime ("dotards") could also be cut without liability for waste. "Timber trees" could also be cut for use as fuel or for necessary repairs, provided there were insufficient dead or inferior trees for these purposes. The privilege of cutting "timber trees" for fuel or repairs was termed the right of "estovers" or "botes." Generally, as to the English common law, see Co.Litt. * 53a and b. One author, commenting on the privilege of cutting "timber trees" for necessary repairs, points out that the rule "developed during feudal times, when tenants were usually farmers, money was scarce, there were no sawmills or lumber companies, and it was the custom for tenants to perform all of the operations involved in felling trees, making lumber of them, and using that lumber to make repairs." 5 Am.L.Prop. § 20.4 in text between nn. 3 and 5.

acts would clearly have been waste in England." [5]   Generally, in the United States, the test of "good husbandry" or, more broadly, "reasonable use," seems to have been substituted for the strict English common law rules.[6]

The English law as to changing the "course of husbandry"—i.e., the way in which agricultural land was used—was also very strict.   Any change in use—e.g., conversion of meadow land into arable land—was waste.[7]   But even in England this strict rule "was early softened down * * *, and the doctrine of meliorating waste was adopted, which, without changing the definition of waste, still allowed the tenant to change the course of husbandry upon the estate if such change be for the betterment of the estate." [8] Consequently the strict English rule was never received in the United States.

The English rule as to extraction of minerals by a tenant for life or for years was simple: if the mine was "open" when the tenancy began, the tenant was privileged to work the mine to exhaustion; if the mine was not "open" when the tenancy began, any extraction of minerals was waste.[9] Unless altered by regulatory legislation, the American law appears to apply the same simple test.[10]

5.   Melms v. Pabst Brewing Co., 104 Wis. 7, 79 N.W. 738, 46 L.R.A. 478 (1899).   Among the early cases so holding, see Ward v. Sheppard, 3 N.C. 283, 2 Am.Dec. 625 (1803); Morehouse v. Cotheal, 22 N.J.L. 521 (1850); McGregor v. Brown, 10 N.Y. 114 (1854).   "In order to make usable the forested wilderness of this country, it was necessary to clear it for the only industry then important, farming.   * * *   In addition, * * * in a land where timber was very plentiful * * * there could not be much serious objection to the cutting of trees." 5 Am. L.Prop. § 20.5, at p. 87.

6.   "The test of good husbandry implies that the tenant is not free to cut trees whenever it would appear to be to his advantage to do so.   He is limited to a reasonable use of the land, in light of the purposes for which it was conveyed, and in the case of land leased for agriculture the good-husbandry test means that the tenant can cut trees wherever necessary to the reasonable enjoyment of the land as agricultural land.   Where the land is not suitable for farming and the facts show that it was not intended to be farmed, the good-husbandry test no longer applies and the basic standard of reasonable use must rely for its content upon the uses to which the land was intended to be put.   It is consequently not surprising that in cases wherein the land was originally acquired for timber, or where it was chiefly valuable as timber land, the tenant was allowed to cut timber for profit, this being a reasonable use in light of the nature of the land." 5 Am.L.Prop. § 20.2, at p. 79.

7.   Co.Litt. * 53a.

8.   Melms v. Pabst Brewing Co., supra note 5.   See also Bewes, Waste 134 and cases cited.

9.   Co.Litt. * 53b, * 54b.   The same rule applied to removal of soil, clay, and gravel. Co.Litt. * 53b.

10.   See, e.g., holding that a tenant may work open mines to exhaustion, Neel v. Neel, 19 Pa. 323 (1852); Ward v. Carp River Iron Co., 47 Mich. 65, 10 N.W. 109 (1881); Gaines v. Green Pond Iron Mining Co., 33 N.J.Eq. 603 (1881); Findlay v. Smith, 20 Va. (6 Munf.) 134, 8 Am.Dec. 733 (1818).   See, e.g., holding that a tenant may not open a new mine, Ohio Oil Co. v. Daughetee, 240 Ill. 361, 88 N.E. 818, 36 L.R.A.(N.S.) 1108 (1909); Russell v. Tipton, 193 Ky. 305, 235 S.W. 763 (1921); Trustees v. Lehigh Valley Coal Co., 236 Pa. 350, 84 A. 820, 41 L.R.A.(N.S.) 1059 (1912) (lessee under long-term lease not allowed to open new mine).

See also McKibben v. Mohawk Oil Co., 667 P.2d 1223 (Alaska 1983), held that, where a mining lease authorized removal of ore in a "workmanlike" manner, and the defendant's "unworkmanlike bulk mining activity damaged the removed ore, thereby impairing the plaintiff's royalty interest," the defendant was guilty of "waste."

In modern times, of course, oil and gas are probably of greater importance than "hard" minerals. See McGill v. Johnson, 799 S.W.2d 673 (Tex.1990) ("open mines" doctrine rests upon the presumed intent that, when creator of life estate gave no direction as to disposition of proceeds from open mines, the life tenant was to have all the income from the open mines; this rule applies to income derived from oil and gas leases executed before life estate was created). The extraction of oil and gas in the United States is governed by extensive legislation (and administrative regulations promulgated thereunder) designed to conserve these resources and assure equitable treatment of the owners of land overlying pools of oil and gas.

4

Perhaps the most controversial English "voluntary waste" cases were those holding that demolition or substantial alteration of structures by a tenant for life or for years was waste even if the value of the realty was thereby increased—another application of the doctrine that even "meliorating waste" was always tortious.[11] This doctrine, in its strict form, was finally rejected both in England and in the United States by the end of the nineteenth century.[12] The leading American case on the point is Melms v. Pabst Brewing Co.,[13] where the court held that a life tenant has the privilege of making substantial alterations in, or even demolishing, a structure "when * * * there has occurred a complete and permanent change of surrounding conditions, which has deprived the property of its value and usefulness" and the tenant is "not bound by contract to restore the property to the same condition in which he received it." [14] In *Melms* the trial court had found that the acts alleged to constitute waste—demolition of a large house and grading the land down to street level—"substantially increased" the value of the reversion and that the reversioners were "in no way injured thereby." [15] Thus the broad statement as to the life tenant's privilege to alter or demolish structures because of changed conditions is clearly qualified by a requirement that the value of the future interests should not be diminished.

Although the American cases since *Melms* are by no means entirely harmonious, there is now substantial American authority for the view that a life tenant or a tenant for a substantial term of years is privileged to make extensive alterations in, or to demolish and replace, structures in order to enable him to make a reasonable use of the property, provided such changes to not diminish the value of the reversion or remainder.[16] But what is a

11. The rationale in all the cases where "meliorating waste" changed the physical characteristics of the property—e.g., where pasture was changed to arable land, or existing buildings were demolished, replaced, or substantially altered—was that the change "impaired the evidence of title." See, e.g., Keepers of Harrow School v. Alderton (argument of Shepherd, Serjt.) and Young v. Spencer, supra note 3.

12. The leading English case is Doherty v. Allman, 3 App.Case. 709 (H.L.1878), where the court refused to enjoin "meliorating waste" consisting of the conversion of rundown, obsolete store buildings into dwelling houses of much greater value. The court specifically rejected the old "impairment of evidence of title" rationale for treating such changes as waste, pointing out that it was no longer persuasive once land descriptions in deeds of conveyance ceased to identify the land by reference to natural monuments or the uses to which the land was put. Id. at 725–726. But see West Ham Central Charitable Bd. v. Bd. of East London Waterworks Co., [1900] 1 Ch. 624. Acts. 17 & 18 Geo. V, c. 36 (1927), provided that a lessee of business property may alter the leased premises without liability for waste if the alteration increases the value of the premises. In any case, "meliorating waste" can only result in liability for nominal damages if—as held in Doherty v. Allman, supra—Chancery will not enjoin such waste and—as

held in Doe v. Earl of Burlington, 5 B. & Ad. 507, 110 Eng.Rep. 878 (K.B.1833)—the statutory remedy of forfeiture will be denied. For a typical case awarding nominal damages, see Keepers of Harrow School v. Alderton, 2 Bos. & Pul. 86, 126 Eng.Rep. 1170 (C.B.1800) (3 farthings damages). But cf. Young v. Spencer, 10 B. & C. 145, 109 Eng.Rep. 405 (K.B.1829).

13. Supra note 5. The *Melms* case contains a good review of the changes in the law of waste in England and the United States during the 19th century.

14. 104 Wis. at 15–16, 79 N.W. at 741.

15. See 104 Wis. at 9, 79 N.W. at 738. The facts of the *Melms* case were unusual in that the house, prior to demolition, stood twenty to thirty feet above the level of the street and was surrounded by railroad tracks, factories, and other industrial buildings, with no other dwellings in the neighborhood.

16. E.g., J.B. Hill Co. v. Pinque, 179 Cal. 759, 178 P. 952 (1919); Beers v. St. John, 16 Conn. 322 (1844); Crowe v. Wilson, 65 Md. 479, 5 A. 427 (1886); Dodds v. Sixteenth Section Development Corp., 232 Miss. 524, 99 So.2d 897 (1958); Winship v. Pitts, 3 Paige 259 (N.Y.1832); Sherrill v. Connor, 107 N.C. 630, 12 S.E. 588 (1890); J.H. Bellows Co. v. Covell, 28 Ohio App. 277, 162 N.E. 621 (1927); Melms v. Pabst Brewing Co., supra note 5. Of course,

"reasonable use" is, of course, a question on which reasonable minds may differ.

The Property Restatement has adopted the following rules apparently derived in part from the *Melms* case: [17] (1) a life tenant has a duty not to diminish the market value of subsequent interests,[18] and (2) a life tenant "has a duty not to change the premises, as to which the estate for life exists, in such a manner that the owners of the estates limited after the estate for life have a reasonable ground for objection thereto." [19] A literal reading of the second rule suggests that reversioners and remaindermen may have "reasonable ground for objection" to "changes" such as alterations in or replacement of structures even though the value of "interests limited after the estate for life" are not diminished, and the commentary, by negative inference, indicates that there would be "reasonable ground for objection," *even if* the value of the reversion or remainder is not diminished, *unless* (a) "a substantial and permanent change in the conditions of the neighborhood in which the land is located has deprived the land in its existent form of reasonable productivity or usefulness; and the proposed alteration or replacement is one which the owner of an estate in fee simple normally would make; and the owners of the interests limited after the estate for life are either not subject to financial liability or are adequately protected against financial liability arising from the proposed construction operations." [20]

The Property Restatement's tests for determining the "reasonableness" of objections to proposed changes in the realty are based only in part on *Melms*.[21] They are also based in part on the facts (though not the decision) in Brokaw v. Fairchild,[22] where the court refused to allow a life tenant to demolish a large townhouse and replace it with an apartment building.[23] The facts of the *Brokaw* case provide one of the illustrations appended to the commentary.[24] But the commentary itself fails to articulate the principal reason urged by the life tenant in *Brokaw* [25] in favor of the proposed replacement of the townhouse with an apartment building, which was that the townhouse, by 1929, had become too large and too expensive to maintain to be useful as a single family residence. It would seem that this kind of change, as well as a "substantial and permanent change in the neighborhood," should be sufficient to justify substantial alteration or replacement of a structure where, as in *Brokaw,*[26] the end result would be a substantial

---

alterations may constitute waste if, although they increase the value of the property, they also increase the burdens (such as taxes) to which the property is subject. E.g., Crewe Corp. v. Feiler, 28 N.J. 316, 146 A.2d 458 (1958) (improvements constituted waste because they increased the property taxes and other burdens of ownership).

17. Supra note 5.

18. Rest.Prop. § 138.

19. Id. § 140.

20. Id. § 140, Comment f(2).

21. Supra note 5.

22. 135 Misc. 70, 237 N.Y.S. 6 (1929), affirmed without majority opinion (Finch, J., dissenting) 231 App.Div. 704, 245 N.Y.S. 402 (1930), affirmed per curiam without opinion

256 N.Y. 670, 177 N.E. 186 (1931); noted in 15 Corn.L.Q. 501 (1930), 43 Harv.L.Rev. 506 (1930), and 30 Mich.L.Rev. 784 (1931).

23. The plaintiff, the life tenant, was opposed by the owners of the two adjoining townhouses, who had contingent remainders in the subject property that would vest only if the plaintiff outlived his four-year-old daughter and then died without other issue.

24. Rest.Prop. § 140, Illust. 6.

25. Supra note 22, 135 Misc. at 72, 237 N.Y.S. at 10–11.

26. Supra note 22. Finch, J., dissenting, said:

"It is obvious that the opposition to the application of the plaintiff is not based upon

increase in the value of the future interests without making those interests financially liable for the proposed construction project.[27]

It seems clear that, in a case like *Brokaw,* where it was extremely unlikely that the owners of the future interests would, as a practical matter, wish to use the realty in question for the purposes for which it was originally designed—where, indeed, it was highly likely that they would, if they should become entitled to possession, demolish the existing structure and erect in its place a structure like that which the life tenant wanted to erect—the court should not enjoin the proposed demolition and new construction by the life tenant. Such a case clearly meets the Property Restatement tests, and should be considered to be non-actionable "meliorating waste." On the other hand, if the realty is still capable of a reasonable use by the owners of the future interests, should they become entitled to possession, and if the owners of the future interests object to the changes proposed by the life tenant, it would seem that their objection should be deemed "reasonable" even if the value of the realty would not be decreased—or would even be increased—by the proposed changes.

It should be noted that the *Melms* court said, by way of dictum, that, where a landlord "rents his premises for a short time," after fitting them for certain uses, "he is entitled to receive them back at the end of the term still fitted for those uses; and he may well say that he does not choose to have a different property returned to him from that which he leased, even if, upon the taking of testimony, it might be found of greater value by reason of the change." [28] In fact, the rules as to what constitutes waste on the part of tenants for years (and periodic tenants) are somewhat more restrictive than those applicable to life tenants. In general, "the tenant is entitled to make changes in the physical condition of the property which are reasonably necessary in order for the tenant to use the leased property in a manner that is reasonable under all the circumstances"; but, "except to the extent the parties to a lease validly agree otherwise, there is a breach of the tenant's obligation if he * * * does not, when requested by the landlord, restore, where restoration is possible, the leased property to its former condition

---

any fear of actual damage to the inheritance, but is actuated solely by ulterior motives, namely because of its effect upon the light and air of the adjoining property, and the very remote possibility of the entire plottage occupied by the aforesaid four dwellings [owned by plaintiff and defendants at the corner of Fifth Avenue and 79th Street in New York City] being developed as a unit at some future time. These considerations have no bearing upon the question presented, namely, whether the particular inheritance will be damaged by the act proposed by the plaintiff."
231 App.Div. at 705, 245 N.Y.S. at 404.

27. The *Brokaw* decision resulted in the enactment of N.Y.Laws 1937, c. 165, now McKinney's Real Prop.Actions and Proc.Law § 803, which provides that a tenant for life or years with an expectancy or unexpired term of not less than five years may alter or replace a structure on the subject land without being

liable for waste if the change (1) will not decrease the market value of the future interests in the land, (2) is of the sort which a prudent owner in fee simple would make under the circumstances, (3) and does not violate the terms of any agreement or other instrument regulating the conduct of the tenant for life or for years. The tenant must give notice of the proposed change to each owner of a future interest in the land, and must post whatever security the court requires to assure completion of the proposed alteration or replacement. It would seem that this statute, in effect, overrules the *Brokaw* decision.

A similar English statute applies only to commercial properties. See Acts 17 & 18 Geo. V, c. 36 (1927), discussed briefly in 38 Colum.L.Rev. 532, 533 (1938).

28. Supra note 5, 104 Wis. at 12, 79 N.W. at 740.

* * *." [29] The duties of the tenant for years (or periodic tenant) will be considered in more detail post in Chapter 6.

Use of land by a tenant (whether for life or for years) in a manner expressly authorized by the instrument creating the successive estates in the land obviously cannot constitute waste. Express provisions as to the permissible uses of the premises are, of course, very common in a lease creating a term of years.[30] Such provisions are much less common in an instrument creating—usually gratuitously—a life estate. But the latter may provide that the life tenant shall hold "without impeachment of waste." Such a provision has, from the earliest times in both England and the United States, been construed as protecting a tenant for life from any "legal" liability for waste.[31] But, as we shall see, courts of equity have sometimes provided a remedy for "unconscionable" conduct that injures the reversioner or remainderman even though the life tenant holds "without impeachment for waste." [32]

§ 4.3   Permissive Waste

Absent provisions to the contrary in the instrument creating the life estate, a life tenant is subject to a limited duty to make repairs on the property [1] and to pay all or part of certain carrying charges such as property taxes, mortgage interest, and special assessments for public improvements.[2] Failure to make the required repairs constitutes "permissive waste," and failure to pay carrying charges is also frequently termed "permissive waste." [3] But all such affirmative duties are subject to the important limitation that the life tenant is under no duty to expend more than the income he receives from the land or, if he personally occupies the land, the

29. Rest.Prop.2d § 12.2(1), (3). As to the time within which leased property must be restored or the annexation removed, see id. § 12.3.

30. See post Chapter 6.

31. Rest.Prop. § 141 and Comments thereto.

32. See Rest.Prop. § 141, Comment (a) and Illust. 4, which limit the privilege of a life tenant "without impeachment of waste" to acts "such as might be done in the course of a reasonable management of such land by the owner of an estate in fee simple absolute * * *, taking into account the long time utilization thereof." For a more detailed discussion, see post Section 4.5.

§ 4.3

1. E.g., Stevens v. Citizens & Southern National Bank, 233 Ga. 612, 212 S.E.2d 792 (1975); Clark v. Childs, 253 Ga. 493, 321 S.E.2d 727 (1984); Kline v. Dowling, 176 Ind. 521, 96 N.E. 579 (1911); In re Stout's Estate, 151 Or. 411, 50 P.2d 768, 101 A.L.R. 672 (1936). Compare Grimm v. Grimm, 153 Ga. 655, 113 S.E. 91 (1922) ("willful" refusal to repair was both "permissive" and "voluntary" waste resulting in forfeiture of life estate). Although the cases are in conflict, tenants for

life are apparently not now liable for "permissive" waste in England. See Kirchwey, Liability for Waste, 8 Colum.L.Rev. 425, 624, 629, 635 (1908).

2. E.g., Dormer v. Walker, 101 Colo. 20, 69 P.2d 1049 (1937) (all taxes); Asmus v. Asmus, 122 N.J.Eq. 485, 194 A. 884 (1937) (same); Sherrill v. Board of Equalization, 224 Tenn. 201, 452 S.W.2d 857 (1970) (same); Goodspeed v. Skinner, 9 Kan.App.2d 557, 682 P.2d 686 (1984) (property taxes); Garrett v. Snowden, 226 Ala. 30, 145 So. 493, 87 A.L.R. 216 (1933) (all mortgage interest); Beliveau v. Beliveau, 217 Minn. 235, 14 N.W.2d 360 (1944) (same); Thompson v. Watkins, 285 N.C. 616, 207 S.E.2d 740 (1974) (same); Appeal of Wordin, 71 Conn. 531, 42 A. 659 (1899) (life tenant liable for entire assessment where improvement would probably last longer than life estate); Troy v. Protestant Episcopal Church, 174 Ala. 380, 56 So. 982 (1911) (assessment apportioned in ratio of value of life estate to value of future estate); Morrow v. Person, 195 Tenn. 370, 259 S.W.2d 665 (1953) (same).

3. "The tendency is to treat failure to carry out these obligations in the same manner as failure to repair, and the cases are consequently discussed together." 5 Am.L.Prop. § 20.12 at p. 100.

rental value thereof, in order to discharge such duties.[4] However, the surplus income or rental value from prior years must be applied to needed current repairs and carrying charges, and surplus current income or rental value must be applied to make up any accrued deficits in making repairs or paying carrying charges.[5]

No satisfactory general definition of the life tenant's common law duty to make repairs can be found in the decided cases, which simply illustrate typical fact patterns. The cases, however, do make it clear that the life tenant need not rebuild a structure that was completely dilapidated when he became entitled to possession or to make general repairs needed at that time;[6] that he need not rebuild a structure destroyed by fire, storm, or other casualty for which he was not responsible,[7] and that he need not eliminate the results of ordinary wear and tear unless repairs are necessary to prevent further deterioration.[8] But a life tenant has a duty to repaint when exterior surfaces will otherwise be exposed to serious deterioration [9] and to keep roofs in repair,[10] or—more generally, to preserve land and structures in a reasonable state of repair.[11]

A life tenant also has a duty to pay all current general property taxes on the land in his possession during the continuance of his life estate.[12] Similarly, he has a duty to pay the entire interest periodically accruing on any mortgage or similar consensual encumbrance which constituted a lien on the entire fee simple when the life estate was created.[13] The latter duty dates from a time when mortgages were usually written for relatively short terms, with the entire principal of the mortgage debt payable in a lump sum at the end of the term—i.e., with no provision for "amortization" of the principal by periodic payments.[14] No cases have been found dealing with the duty of a life tenant with respect to periodic payments on a mortgage which provides that the principal of the mortgage debt shall be fully "amortized"

---

4. E.g., In re Stout's Estate, supra note 1 (repairs); Nation v. Green, 188 Ind. 697, 123 N.E. 163 (1919) (taxes).

5. Ibid.

6. E.g., Savings Investment & Trust Co. v. Little, 135 N.J.Eq. 546, 39 A.2d 392 (1944).

7. E.g., Savings Investment & Trust Co. v. Little, supra note 6; In re Stout's Estate, supra note 1.

8. E.g., Matter of Steele, 19 N.J.Eq. 120 (1868).

9. E.g., Woolston v. Pullen, 88 N.J.Eq. 35, 102 A. 461 (1917).

10. Ibid.

11. Rest.Prop. 139. The older authorities all state that "the tenant must keep the premises windtight and water tight," which has "a quaint sound in modern America." 5 Am. L.Prop. § 20.12 at p. 101.

12. The life tenant owes the reversioner or remainderman no duty to pay taxes which are a lien only on the life estate. E.g., Ferguson v. Quinn, 97 Tenn. 46, 36 S.W. 576, 33 L.R.A. 688 (1896). But taxes are ordinarily a lien on the fee simple, and the life tenant therefore has a duty to pay them. See the extensive list of cases in L. Simes & A. Smith, Future Interests § 1693 n. 5 (2d ed. 1956 and Pocket Part). See also Note, 45 Iowa L.Rev. 113 (1959).

13. See cases cited supra note 2. The duty does not arise if the mortgage is a lien only on the life estate.

14. Such mortgages were the rule prior to the mid-1930's, and have again come into common use in the early 1980's as a result of unprecedentedly high interest rates. If the entire principal balance of such a mortgage falls due during the life of the life tenant, he and the owner(s) of the future interest(s) must each pay their fair shares of the principal. E.g., Murphy v. May, 243 Ala. 94, 8 So.2d 442 (1942). See also cases cited in L. Simes & A. Smith, Future Interests § 1697 n. 40 (2d ed. 1956). The fair shares of the life tenant and the owner(s) of the future interest(s) are determined on the basis of the relative values of the present and future estates. E.g., Garrett v. Snowden, 226 Ala. 30, 145 So. 493, 87 A.L.R. 216 (1933). See also Thompson v. Watkins, 285 N.C. 616, 207 S.E.2d 740 (1974).

by periodic payments over the entire term of the mortgage.[15] In the latter case, each periodic mortgage payment will include principal as well as interest;[16] but there are obvious practical difficulties in arranging for payment of each periodic installment (typically payable monthly) partly by the life tenant and partly by the reversioner or remainderman. If either party pays an entire installment, he will presumably be entitled to contribution from the other party.[17]

Where the entire fee simple was subject to a mortgage before the life estate was created, the amount required to preserve the interests of both the life tenant and the reversioner or remainderman if default occurs and the holder of the mortgage elects to declare the entire principal immediately due and payable (i.e., to "accelerate") should obviously be apportioned between the life tenant and the owner of the future interest. How should this be done if the instrument creating the successive interests prescribes no method? Many cases require the life tenant to pay the amount of interest that would have been payable during the balance of life, discounted to its present value, and require the owner of the future interest to pay the balance of the total amount necessary to satisfy the mortgage.[18] In some states, a different method of apportionment is mandated by statute.[19] In any case, of course, the life tenant and the owner of the future interest may determine the method of apportionment by contract.[20]

A life tenant has a duty to pay all special assessments levied against the property by a local government unit to cover the cost (or part of the cost) of local public improvements the estimated life of which is not in excess of the probable duration of the life estate.[21] But when the estimated life of the public improvement is in excess of the probable duration of the life tenant's estate, the duty to pay the special assessment is divided between the life tenant and the owners of future estates in the land on the basis of the values of the present and future estates, respectively.[22] The value of the life estate

15. The great majority of the mortgage loans made between the mid–1930's and the late 1970's were of this type. The shift to long-term, fully-amortized mortgages was due mainly to the enactment of the Home Owners Loan Act of 1933, authorizing the federal government to charter and regulate savings and loan associations, and the National Housing Act of 1937, which established the Federal Housing Administration to insure lenders who made such long-term mortgage loans.

16. Typically, though not invariably, the amortization schedule calls for equal monthly payments, with the earlier payments comprised mainly of interest and the later payments comprised mainly of principal.

17. It would seem that the obligation to pay the mortgage principal should be apportioned on an equitable basis as between the life tenant and the owner(s) of the future interest(s). See supra note 14 as to apportionment. See also the discussion of apportionment of special assessments, post in text between notes 21 and 25.

18. E.g., Garrett v. Snowden, 226 Ala. 30, 145 So. 493 (1933); Todd's Ex'r v. First Nat.

Bank, 173 Ky. 60, 190 S.W. 468 (1917) (dictum); Stroh v. O'Hearn, 176 Mich. 164, 142 N.W. 865 (1913); Beliveau v. Beliveau, 217 Minn. 235, 14 N.W.2d 360 (1944); In re Daily's Estate, 117 Mont. 194, 159 P.2d 327 (1945); Coughlin v. Kennedy, 132 N.J.Eq. 383, 28 A.2d 417 (1942).

19. See discussion of the New York statute in 5 R. Powell ¶ 667 in text at notecalls 24–29 and ¶ 668 in text at notecalls 10–12.

20. See, e.g., Burnett v. Quell, 202 S.W.2d 97 (Mo.1947); Kruse v. Meissner, 136 N.J.Eq. 209, 40 A.2d 777 (1945).

21. E.g., Appeal of Wordin, 71 Conn. 531, 42 A. 659 (1899); Holliday v. Phillips Petroleum Co., 275 F.Supp. 686 (E.D.Ark.1967).

22. E.g., Troy v. Protestant Episcopal Church, 174 Ala. 380, 56 So. 982 (1911). But some courts have subjected the life tenant only to a duty to pay the interest on the special assessment, leaving to the owner(s) of the future interest(s) the burden of paying the entire principal amount of the assessment. E.g., Holzhauser v. Iowa State Tax Commis-

is generally held to be the cost of an annuity equal to the annual income from or rental value of the land for the probable duration of the life estate, and value of the reversion or remainder to be the difference between the value of the life estate and the value of the fee simple.[23] This formula may result in substantial injustice to the owner of the future interest in cases where the estimated life of the public local improvement is only slightly in excess of the probable duration of the life estate. In such a case, the owner of the future interest will receive a benefit from the improvement far smaller, proportionately, than the amount he must contribute on the basis of the relative values of the present and future estates as ordinarily determined. The Property Restatement's proposed method of apportioning the special assessment [24] would seem to produce a fairer result in such cases.

When land is held in trust for the benefit of a life tenant (life beneficiary), the trustee has a duty to pay both the property taxes on and all special assessments against the trust property.[25] Whenever the trustee pays a special assessment installment, he must charge the life tenant with the interest component of that installment (deducting it from the income otherwise payable to the life tenant) and charge the owners of future interests in the trust property with the principal component of that installment.[26]

Absent an express provision in the instrument creating the life estate imposing a duty on the life tenant to keep the property insured for the benefit of the reversioner or remainderman, most courts hold that the life tenant has no such duty [27] unless the entire fee simple is subject to a mortgage containing the usual clause requiring the mortgagor to keep the property insured for the benefit of the mortgagee. In the latter case, the duty to maintain insurance is allocated to the life tenant so long as the life estate continues, and the property insurance premiums are simply an additional carrying charge to be paid by the life tenant out of the income from, or the rental value of, the property.[28] And in a few states a life tenant is held to have a duty to keep the property insured for the benefit of the

---

sion, 245 Iowa 525, 62 N.W.2d 229 (1953) (dictum).

23. E.g., Troy v. Protestant Episcopal Church, supra note 22; Morrow v. Person, 195 Tenn. 370, 259 S.W.2d 665 (1953).

24. See Rest.Prop. § 133(2)(b), which provides that, where the life of the improvement is in excess of "the period during which the estate for life can be expected, reasonably, to last," the amount chargeable to the life tenant is "the fractional part of the special assessment ascertained by dividing the present value of the estate for life by the present value of an estate for life having the duration of the life of the improvement, with interest at the legal rate" from the date of payment by the owner(s) of the future interest(s). See also Rest.Prop., Tent.Draft No. 3, § 178, Special Note.

25. See 2A Scott, Trusts § 176 at n. 19 (3d ed. 1967); G. Bogert, Trusts and Trustees § 602 at n. 81 (2d ed., rev. 1980); Wordin's

Appeal, supra note 21; Orr v. St. Louis Union Trust Co., 291 Mo. 383, 236 S.W. 642 (1922).

26. E.g., Brown v. Brown, 72 N.J.Eq. 667, 65 A. 739 (1907); Chamberlin v. Gleason, 163 N.Y. 214, 57 N.E. 487 (1900) (where assessment was payable in 10 annual installments, payment of interest by life tenant and of principal by remainderman was proper where interest on the annual principal installments paid by remainderman was trivial. But see 1 Am.L.Prop. § 2.21 at p. 157: "It seems clear * * * that a correct apportionment requires the payment of such interest [on principal amounts paid by the remainderman] while the life tenant lives, or an apportionment based on the value of the estate of each * * *."

27. E.g., Converse v. Boston Safe Deposit & Trust Co., 315 Mass. 544, 53 N.E.2d 841 (1944). See also cases cited in L. Simes & A. Smith, Future Interests § 1695 n. 29 (2d ed. 1956).

28. E.g., Livesay v. Boyd, 164 Va. 528, 180 S.E. 158 (1935).

reversioner or remainderman as part of his general duty to preserve and protect future interests in the property.[29]

Like the life tenant, the tenant for years was traditionally subject to an ill-defined common law duty to make repairs in order to prevent serious deterioration of the leased premises,[30] but without any limitation of the duty based on the value of the benefits received by the tenant in the form of income or imputed rental value.[31] In recent years, however, many residential tenants have been relieved of any common law duty to make repairs as a result of the widespread recognition of judicially "implied" warranties of habitability and the enactment in many states of statutes imposing upon residential landlords the duty to keep the leased premises in habitable condition. Both the new judicially "implied" warranties of habitability and the new statutes shift the duty of making repairs from the tenant to the landlord. In many states, the duty cannot be shifted back to the tenant even by an express written agreement.[32]

A tenant for years (or periodic tenant) has no common law duty to pay property taxes on the leased premises [33] unless (1) the lease is "perpetual," or for a long term with options in the tenant and his successors in interest to renew "forever"; [34] or (2) the tenant holds without any obligation to pay rent; [35] or (3) the tenant has erected improvements on the leased premises for his own benefit.[36] And a tenant for years (or periodic tenant) generally has no common law duty to pay carrying charges such as special assessments,[37] insurance premiums,[38] or mortgage payments.[39]

29. E.g., Clark v. Leverett, 159 Ga. 487, 126 S.E. 258, 37 A.L.R. 180 (1924). But see Clark v. Childs, 253 Ga. 493, 321 S.E.2d 727 (1984) (life tenant is not bound, as matter of law, to insure the future interest but is bound to insure it only if the exercise of ordinary care—as determined by trier of fact—requires it; statements in *Leverett,* supra, that life tenant has absolute duty to insure were only dicta).

30. E.g., Vin Wormer v. Crane, 51 Mich. 363, 16 N.W. 686 (1883); Suydam v. Jackson, 54 N.Y. 450 (1873). See Co.Litt. * 53a. Tenants at will, however, were never subject to any such duty—see, e.g., Means v. Cotton, 225 Mass. 313, 114 N.E. 361 (1916)—because the landlord can protect himself simply by terminating the tenancy if the tenant allows the premises to deteriorate.

31. See 5 Am.L.Prop. § 20.12 at n. 13. In all other respects, the duty is the same as a life tenant's duty to repair. See, e.g., Earle v. Arbogast, 180 Pa. 409, 36 A. 923 (1897); Thalheimer v. Lempert, 49 Hun 606, 1 N.Y.S. 470 (Sup.1888). The tenant's duty does not extend to areas remaining in the landlord's control ("common areas"), which the landlord has a common law duty to maintain. See, e.g., Gladden v. Walker & Dunlop, 168 F.2d 321 (D.C.Cir.1948).

32. See post Sections 6.36 through 6.45.

33. E.g., Deutsch v. Frey, 36 Ohio App. 226, 173 N.E. 40 (1930).

34. In such cases the tenant is treated as "owner" for tax purposes. E.g., Ocean Grove Camp Meeting Association v. Reeves, 79 N.J.L. 334, 75 A. 782 (1910), affirmed 80 N.J.L. 464, 79 A. 1119 (1911). See Annot., 55 A.L.R. 154 (1928).

35. E.g., Kelley v. Ball, 14 Ky.Law Rep. 132, 19 S.W. 581 (1892).

36. In such cases the tenant must pay taxes on the improvements.

37. E.g., De Clercq v. Barber Asphalt Paving Co., 167 Ill. 215, 47 N.E. 367 (1897); Blake v. Metropolitan Chain Stores, 247 Mich. 73, 225 N.W. 587, 63 A.L.R. 1386 (1929).

38. E.g., Ingold v. Phoenix Assurance Co., 230 N.C. 142, 52 S.E.2d 366, 8 A.L.R.2d 1439 (1949). See Annot., 66 A.L.R. 864 (1930), 8 A.L.R.2d 1445 (1949).

39. No cases have been found suggesting that the tenant has any such duty at common law. On the other hand, the landlord's common law duty ("implied covenant") to assure the tenant's "quiet enjoyment" of the premises clearly obligates him to protect the tenant from eviction resulting from any default on an outstanding mortgage of the fee simple. E.g., Ganz v. Clark, 252 N.Y. 92, 169 N.E. 100 (1929).

Commercial and agricultural leases, especially when they are for a long term, often contain express covenants imposing on a tenant for years the duty of making all—or specified kinds of—repairs [40] and/or paying specified carrying charges such as property taxes,[41] special assessments,[42] and insurance premiums.[43] The same is likely to be true of long-term residential leases, although shifting of the burden of keeping the premise in repair may be limited or precluded by the new "implied" or statutory warranties of habitability. Problems as to the construction and application of lease covenants as to repairs and payment of carrying charges will be considered subsequently in Chapter 6.

§ 4.4 "Legal" Remedies for Waste

At least since enactment of the Statute of Marlbridge in 1267,[1] reversioners and remaindermen have been able to recover compensatory damages for either voluntary or permissive waste committed by tenants for life or for years. The Statute of Gloucester, enacted in 1278,[2] provided that the tenant's estate in the place wasted should be forfeited and that the reversioner or remainderman should recover treble damages.[3] Although it seems that these penalties were intended to apply to both voluntary and permissive waste, eventually it was held that they applied only to voluntary waste.[4] Neither the Statute of Marlbridge nor the Statute of Gloucester changed the rule that a tenant at will was not liable for permissive waste.

Although the forfeiture and treble damages remedies were abolished in England in the nineteenth century,[5] both remedies are still available in the United States.[6] Multiple damages for waste are authorized by statute in nineteen jurisdictions.[7] In Maryland, the treble damages and forfeiture remedies are available on the theory that the Statute of Gloucester is part of Maryland's common law.[8] In at least two states, the Statute of Gloucester

---

40. The tenant may, e.g., covenant "to keep the premises in repair, reasonable wear and tear excepted," or "to maintain and keep the premises in repair," or "to surrender the premises at the expiration of the lease term in as good condition as they were at the beginning of the term, reasonable wear and tear excepted."

41. The tenant may, e.g., covenant "to pay all taxes imposed on the property during the lease term," or "to pay all taxes levied on the property, extraordinary as well as ordinary." The latter covenant was held not to create any duty to pay a special assessment for local improvements in Blake v. Metropolitan Chain Stores, supra note 37.

42. The tenant may, e.g., covenant "to pay all special assessments on the leased premises imposed during the lease term," or "to pay all installments of any special assessment on the leased premises that become due and payable during the lease term."

43. The tenant may, e.g., covenant "to maintain adequate insurance on the leased premises throughout the term of the lease, the proceeds in the event of any loss covered by

the insurance to be used to restore the premises to their former condition."

§ 4.4

1. 52 Hen. III, c. 14 (1267).

2. 6 Edw. I, c. 5 (1278).

3. The Statute of Gloucester also created a new writ of waste, thus providing both a new remedy and a new procedure. Later, actions on the case for waste were permitted in lieu of actions initiated by a writ of waste. The writ of waste was abolished in England in the 19th century. See infra note 5.

4. In England it was later held that life tenants were not liable for permissive waste at all. See, e.g., In re Parry, [1900] 1 Ch. 160.

5. 3 & 4 Wm. IV, c. 27, § 36 (1833), and 42 & 43 Vict., c. 59 (1879), which abolished both the writ of waste and the harsh remedies of forfeiture and treble damages.

6. See the detailed summary of the American statutes in case law in 5 Am.L.Prop. § 20.-18.

7. 5 Am.L.Prop. § 20.18.

8. Ibid.

has expressly been held not to be part of the common law.[9] In many states there are no statutes or decisions dealing with forfeiture or multiple damages for waste. In at least ten of the states with legislation authorizing multiple damages for waste, that remedy is expressly made available only where the waste is "voluntary," "wanton," or "malicious."[10] In eight of the states with forfeiture statutes, the wrongdoer's "estate" rather than "the place wasted" is forfeited,[11] and under many of these statutes forfeiture is authorized only where the waste is "voluntary" or "wanton," or where the damages are equal to the value of the wrongdoer's unexpired interest, or where the damages awarded are not paid by the wrongdoer.[12]

At the present time, compensatory damages and, where authorized by statute, multiple damages and/or forfeiture are generally available to one who owns an indefeasibly vested reversion or remainder in fee simple, as against a tenant for life or for years who commits waste.[13] But these "legal" remedies are not generally available to the owner of a contingent remainder, a contingent executory interest, a possibility of reverter, a power of termination, or a vested remainder or reversion subject to defeasance who sues only on his own behalf, because it is not certain that his future interest will ever become a present estate.[14] There is authority, however, that damages may be awarded when the owner of a contingent remainder sues on behalf of the owners of all future interests, with the damage award being impounded by the court pending resolution of the contingencies upon which such future interests are conditioned.[15] And it would seem that the same rule should be applied when a life estate is followed by a vested remainder subject to an executory limitation, if the action of waste is brought either by the owner of the remainder or the owner of the executory interest on behalf of all the owners of future interests.[16] But if the possessory estate is a defeasible fee simple, the owner of the future interest, whether it is an executory interest, possibility of reverter, or power of termination, generally cannot recover damages or obtain other "legal" relief for conduct which would constitute

---

9. Ibid.

10. Ibid.

11. Ibid.

12. Ibid.

13. E.g., Ferguson v. Rochford, 84 Conn. 202, 79 A. 177, Ann.Cas.1912B 1212 (1911) (damages); Ussery v. Sweet, 137 Ark. 140, 208 S.W. 600 (1919) (reimbursement). See also Sections 4.1 through 4.3, ante, and cases cited.

For a recent case, see Chapman v. Chapman, 526 So.2d 131 (Fla.App.1988) (vested remainderman entitled to recover damages for waste).

14. E.g., Strickland v. Jackson, 261 N.C. 360, 134 S.E.2d 661 (1964) (contingent remainder); Abbott v. Holway, 72 Me. 298 (1881) (executory interest); Williams v. McKenzie, 203 Ky. 376, 262 S.W. 598 (1924); Sermon v. Sullivan, 640 S.W.2d 486 (Mo.App.1982). But see Pedro v. January, 261 Or. 582, 494 P.2d 868 (1972) (contingent remainderman who

sued alone obtained a damage award, which was impounded to await vesting). See Annot., 56 A.L.R.3d 677 (1974). If the contingent future interest is an executory interest that may defeat a fee simple estate, the ordinary rules of waste are not applicable; "wanton" or "unconscionable" conduct by the holder of the executory interest may be deemed "equitable" waste, but legal remedies are not available against the owner of the fee simple. See post Section 4.5.

15. E.g., Watson v. Wolff–Goldman Realty Co., 95 Ark. 18, 128 S.W. 581, Ann.Cas. 1912A 540 (1910) (suit in equity). Accord: Rest.Prop. § 189(1)(c). See also Louisville Cooperage Co. v. Rudd, 276 Ky. 721, 124 S.W.2d 1063, 144 A.L.R. 763 (1939) (damages awarded against third party tortfeasor).

16. See Rest.Prop. § 189(1)(c); 1 Am. L.Prop. §§ 4.103 at n. 9, and 4.104 at pp. 584–585. See also Sarles v. Sarles, 3 Sandf. Ch. 601 (1846) (semble; accounting granted).

waste if engaged in by a life tenant.[17] Where the fee simple is subject to an executory interest certain to become a possessory estate, however—e.g., one created by a transfer "to A from and after ten years from the date of transfer"—it is arguable that the owner of the executory interest should be entitled to damages if the conduct of the fee simple owner is so "wanton" or "unconscionable" that a court would enjoin it.[18]

The owner of a vested remainder for life has generally been denied any action for waste "at law," in the absence of a statutory right;[19] but in some jurisdictions there are statutes authorizing the award of damages for waste to a remainderman for life.[20] Since a remainderman for life is not certain to become the owner of a present estate, it would seem either that recovery of damages should be denied or, if allowed, that the damages should be impounded until the death of the owner of the present estate or the remainderman for life, whichever first occurs. Only if the remainderman for life survives the owner of the present estate should he be permitted to receive the damage award.[21]

After the death of a life tenant who has committed waste, a remainderman whose estate then becomes indefeasibly vested may recover a judgment for damages against the personal representative of the deceased life tenant,[22] although damages would have been denied so long as the remainder was contingent or vested subject to defeasance. Similarly, the owner of an executory interest or a possibility of reverter which becomes possessory by virtue of the defeasance of a present fee simple estate should then be able to recover damages for waste, provided the conduct of the fee simple owner was "wanton," "unconscionable," or "malicious."[23]

In a proper action "at law" to recover damages for commission of waste, the appropriate measure of damages is generally the diminution in market value of the property or the cost of restoring the property to its former condition, whichever is less.[24] But it was recently held that the plaintiff

17. E.g., Abbott v. Holway, supra note 14 (executory interest); Williams v. McKenzie, supra note 14.

18. See 1 Am.L.Prop. § 4.104 at p. 586.

19. Mayo v. Feaster, 2 McCord Eq. 137 (S.C.1827); Peterson v. Clark, 15 Johns. 205 (N.Y.1818); Williams v. Peabody, 8 Hun 271 (N.Y.1876). But see contrary dicta in Dickinson v. City of Baltimore, 48 Md. 583, 589, 30 Am.Rep. 492 (1878); Dennett v. Dennett, 43 N.H. 499, 502 (1862); Dozier v. Gregory, 46 N.C. 100, 106 (1853). In 2 Wm. Saunders 252, note 7 (5th Am.ed. 1833), it is stated that an action on the case will lie in favor of a remainderman for life. If the remainderman for life is allowed to sue, he should recover only for the injury to his life estate, of course.

20. E.g., Mich.Comp.Laws Ann. § 600.-2919(2)(b). See also Kan.Stat.Ann. 58–2523 (semble).

21. If the remainderman for life predeceases the owner of the present estate, the impounded damages should be paid over to the owners of the remainder or reversion.

22. See Rhoda v. County of Alameda, 134 Cal.App. 726, 26 P.2d 691 (1933), noted in 22 Calif.L.Rev. 704 (1934); Fisher's Executor v. Haney, 180 Ky. 257, 202 S.W. 495 (1918).

23. No cases on the point have been found. Cf. Rest.Prop. § 194(b), *caveat*.

24. Jowdy v. Guerin, 10 Ariz.App. 205, 457 P.2d 745 (1969); Smith v. CAP Concrete, 133 Cal.App.3d 769, 184 Cal.Rptr. 308 (1982); Duckett v. Whorton, 312 N.W.2d 561 (Iowa 1981); Meyer v. Hansen, 373 N.W.2d 392 (N.D.1985); Johnson v. Northwest Acceptance Corp., 259 Or. 1, 485 P.2d 12 (1971). In Vogel v. Pardon, 444 N.W.2d 348 (N.D.1989), the court said that "the object of an award of damages in an action for waste is to compensate without unjust enrichment"; held that "replacement cost" award for 20–year old roof was erroneous because it would unjustly enrich plaintiff; and also upheld a damage award based on "actual value" of house furnishings which were "discarded, sold or converted" by "defendant" rather than their "replacement cost."

"has the right to elect the measure of damages deemed more accurate, and if the defendant disagrees, he has the burden to prove the alternative measure is more appropriate." [25]

§ 4.5   "Equitable" Remedies for Waste

Even where a "legal" remedy for waste is available to the plaintiff, courts often provide an alternative "equitable" remedy by way of injunction. Originally it was necessary for the plaintiff to show that the available "legal" remedies were inadequate because they would necessitate a multiplicity of actions or because the defendant was insolvent.[1]   Today, however, courts rarely refuse to grant "equitable" relief on the ground that "legal" remedies are adequate, and the plaintiff's usual allegation that "legal" remedies are inadequate has become, in many jurisdictions, a mere matter of form which is rarely questioned.[2]   An injunction will not be granted, of course, unless the plaintiff can show that the tenant has not only committed waste in the past but is continuing to do so, or at least that the tenant has threatened to commit waste in the future.[3]   But once the court has determined that an injunction should issue, it will ordinarily give the plaintiff all the relief to which he is entitled; consequently, the court will not only grant the injunction but will also order an accounting for waste already committed by the tenant.[4]   Since complete relief can be obtained in the suit for an injunction, the equitable remedy has substantially superseded all "legal" remedies for waste.[5]

Although courts are traditionally reluctant to issue mandatory injunctions because of the supposed difficulty of supervision, some courts have issued mandatory injunctions to compel tenants for life or for years to fulfill their obligation to keep the property in repair or to restore the property to its former condition after commission of voluntary waste.[6]   And in some cases where a life tenant failed to make necessary repairs or to pay carrying charges, courts have appointed receivers to take possession of the property for the purpose of collecting rental income therefrom and using such income to make repairs and/or to pay carrying charges.[7]

25. Mayer v. Hansen, supra note 24, at 397.

§ 4.5

1. Generally, see 5 Am.L.Prop. § 20.20 between nn. 5 and 6.

2. E.g., Wise v. Potomac National Bank, 393 Ill. 357, 65 N.E.2d 767 (1946). Contra: Redwood Hotel Co. v. Korbien, 195 Md. 402, 73 A.2d 468 (1950) (no injunction if plaintiff fails to allege "actual lack of adequate remedy at law").

3. Burns v. Hale, 162 Ga. 336, 133 S.E. 857 (1926); Redwood Hotel Co. v. Korbien, supra note 2.

4. E.g., Kimberlin v. Hicks, 150 Kan. 449, 94 P.2d 335 (1939); Watson v. Wolff–Goldman Realty Co., 95 Ark. 18, 128 S.W. 581, Ann.Cas. 1912A 540 (1910).

5. See Palmer v. Young, 108 Ill.App. 252 (1903). Indeed, in some cases the prayer for an injunction seems to be merely formal, with the plaintiff's main objective being to recover, in the "equitable accounting," what are in substance compensatory damages for waste without having to prove the damages before a jury. But see Beacon Theatres, Inc. v. Westover, 359 U.S. 500, 79 S.Ct. 948, 3 L.Ed.2d 988 (1959), and Dairy Queen, Inc. v. Wood, 369 U.S. 469, 82 S.Ct. 894, 8 L.Ed.2d 44 (1962) (jury trial may be required in federal courts).

6. E.g., Baltimore & Philadelphia Steamboat Co. v. Starr Methodist Protestant Church, 149 Md. 163, 130 A. 46 (1925); Klie v. Von Broock, 56 N.J.Eq. 18, 37 A. 469 (1897); Sawyer v. Adams, 140 App.Div. 756, 126 N.Y.S. 128 (1910).

7. E.g., St. Paul Trust Co. v. Mintzer, 65 Minn. 124, 67 N.W. 657, 32 L.R.A. 756 (1896) (receiver appointed to make repairs and pay taxes; if income insufficient, receiver may be authorized to sell the property); Murch v. J.O.

In some cases, "equitable" relief by way of injunction is granted even though the plaintiff is not entitled to "legal" relief against waste. Thus a plaintiff who owns a contingent remainder or a defeasible reversion or remainder in fee simple may generally enjoin waste by a life tenant.[8] However, if the plaintiff is suing on his own behalf only, injunctive relief may be denied if the probability that his future interest will ever become possessory is slight.[9] If the owner of the contingent or defeasible remainder or reversion sues on behalf of all owners of future interests, however, injunctive relief will be granted and, as previously noted, the court will order an accounting for waste already committed and will impound the sum found due and paid into court by the defendant, for the benefit of those who may ultimately become entitled to possession upon termination of the present estate for life or for years.[10]

"Equitable" relief by way of injunction and accounting may also be available to the owner of an executory interest or possibility of reverter as against the owner of a present defeasible fee simple estate, provided the latter has committed "wanton," "unconscionable," or "malicious" acts which reduce the value of the fee simple, and provided also that there is a reasonable probability that the plaintiff's future interest will become possessory.[11]

Where a life tenant holds "without impeachment of waste," he is of course not liable "at law" for conduct which would otherwise constitute waste.[12] But if his conduct is found to be "wanton," "unconscionable," or "malicious" and it reduces the value of the fee simple, it may be enjoined by the owner of the reversion or remainder.[13] In such cases, as well as in cases

Smith Manufacturing Co., 47 N.J.Eq. 193, 20 A. 213 (1890) (receiver appointed to collect rents and assessments and pay taxes); Chapman v. Chapman, 526 So.2d 131 (Fla.App. 1988) (trial court should consider appointing receiver to collect rents, pay taxes, and account to remainderman). If there is no rental income because the life tenant personally occupies the property, a court will presumably be less willing to appoint a receiver. But see Smith v. Smith, 219 Ark. 304, 241 S.W.2d 113 (1951), where the court said that appointment of a receiver was proper, even though the life tenant was personally in possession.

8. E.g., Peterson v. Ferrell, 127 N.C. 169, 37 S.E. 189 (1900) (contingent remainder); Kollock v. Webb, 113 Ga. 762, 39 S.E. 339 (1901).

9. E.g., Brown v. Brown, 89 W.Va. 339, 109 S.E. 815 (1921) (contingent remainder).

10. See supra note 4.

11. E.g., Turner v. Wright, 2 DeG.F. & J. 234, 45 Eng.Rep. 612 (Ch. 1860) (executory interest); Pavkovich v. Southern Pacific Railway, 150 Cal. 39, 87 P. 1097 (1906); Elkhorn City Land Co. v. Elkhorn City, 459 S.W.2d 762 (Ky.1970). Accord: Rest.Prop. § 193, stating that the rule is also applicable to powers of termination. See also dicta in Gannon v. Peterson, 193 Ill. 372, 62 N.E. 210, 55 L.R.A. 701 (1901). See also Landers v. Landers, 151 Ky.

206, 216, 151 S.W. 386, 390–391, Ann.Cas. 1915A 223 (1912); Camden Trust Co. v. Handle, 132 N.J.Eq. 97, 106, 26 A.2d 865, 870–871 (1942); Frensley v. White, 208 Okl. 209, 254 P.2d 982 (1953), discussed in Browder, Defeasible Fees in Oklahoma—An Addendum, 6 Okl. L.Rev. 482 (1953). "Wanton," "unconscionable," or "malicious" conduct is conduct that would not be engaged in by a prudent owner of a present fee simple estate. 5 R. Powell, Real Property ¶ 694.

Cf. Union County v. Union County Fair Ass'n, 276 Ark. 132, 633 S.W.2d 17 (1982) (possibility of reverter; court said relief available if interest is "reasonably certain" to become possessory and waste will cause "serious damage").

12. E.g., Bowles' Case, 11 Coke Rep. *79b, 25 Eng.Rul.Cas. 359, 77 Eng.Rep. 1252 (undated).

13. E.g., Vane v. Lord Barnard, 2 Vern. 738, 23 Eng.Rep. 1082 (Ch.1716); Bishop of London v. Webb, 1 P.Wms. 528, 24 Eng.Rep. 501 (1718). In these early cases it was said that to allow the tenant to perform such acts would be to allow him to destroy the thing given to him for life. In early times it may be that the term "without impeachment for waste" excused the tenant from liability for treble damages and forfeiture under the Stat-

where injunctive relief is granted to the owner of an executory interest or possibility of reverter, the conduct of the owner of the present estate is characterized as "equitable waste." [14]

Where a future interest is subject to a power, presently exercisable by the owner of the present estate, to destroy the future interest—e.g., a power of appointment or a power incident to a fee tail or fee simple conditional estate—the owner of the future interest has no rights, either "at law" or "in equity," with respect to conduct that would otherwise amount to waste; [15] but if the power is conditional, or is exercisable only by will, it would seem that the owner of the future interest might have a right to enjoin waste under some circumstances. [16]

A remainderman for life may enjoin waste by the life tenant in possession, whether or not he is entitled to damages. [17]

§ 4.6   Payment of Carrying Charges—Contribution and Subrogation

When a reversioner or remainderman has paid property taxes, mortgage interest, or special assessments which the tenant for life or for years had a duty to pay, he is legally entitled to a judgment against the possessory tenant in an action for reimbursement. [1] Moreover, the owner of the future interest, in such a case, has an equitable lien upon the estate of the possessory tenant which may be foreclosed by a court ordered sale in order to assure reimbursement of the owner of the future interest. [2] In addition, the owner of the future interest, is entitled, in such a case, to the benefit of the equitable doctrine of subrogation—a doctrine which places any person who discharges the obligation of another person in order to protect an interest of the payor in the position of the obligee so that the payor may enforce any security held by the obligee for performance of the obligation. [3] Thus the owner of the future interest may enforce the tax lien, mortgage

utes of Marlbridge and Gloucester, but not from ordinary liability for waste. But in Bowles' Case, supra note 12, it was held that the term meant that the tenant should not be liable for waste at all. For a relatively modern case, see Camden Trust Co. v. Handle, supra note 11. Accord: Rest.Prop. § 141.

14. Camden Trust Co. v. Handle, supra note 11. See also 5 Am.L.Prop. § 20.14; 4 Pomeroy, Equity Jurisprudence § 1348 (5th ed. Symons 1941).

15. See West v. United States, 310 F.Supp. 1289 (N.D.Ga.1970); Magruder v. Magruder, 525 S.W.2d 400 (Mo.App.1975); Dickerson v. Keller, 521 S.W.2d 288 (Tex.Civ.App.1975). Accord: Rest.Prop. § 197. But see In re Mitchell's Will, 15 Misc.2d 651, 181 N.Y.S.2d 436 (Sup.1959).

16. See Rudisill v. Hoyle, 254 N.C. 33, 118 S.E.2d 145 (1961); Johnson v. Messer, 437 S.W.2d 643 (Tex.Civ.App.1969), refused n.r.e.

17. E.g., Kane v. Vanderburgh, 1 Johns.Ch. 11 (N.Y.1814); Williams v. Peabody, 8 Hun

271 (1876). Accord: L. Simes & A. Smith, Future Interests § 1622 (2d ed. 1956); Rest. Prop. § 192(a).

§ 4.6

1. Ussery v. Sweet, 137 Ark. 140, 208 S.W. 600 (1919). At common law, reimbursement was obtained in an action of assumpsit for money paid to the plaintiff's use.

2. Ussery v. Sweet, supra note 1. Accord: 1 Am.L.Prop. § 2.24 at n. 6; Rest.Prop. §§ 131, 132. The rights to a personal judgment and a foreclosure sale may be asserted in the same action. E.g., Waynesboro National Bank v. Smith, 151 Va. 481, 145 S.E. 302 (1928).

3. As to subrogation, generally, see 4 Pomeroy, Equity Jurisprudence §§ 1211, 1212 (5th ed. Symons 1941). The cases are divided as to whether the party entitled to subrogation can always compel an actual assignment of the security. See 4 Pomeroy, Equity Jurisprudence § 1214 (5th ed. Symons 1941).

lien, or other security interest of the obligee by foreclosure.[4] The possessory tenant may, of course, "redeem" his estate and prevent a foreclosure sale by reimbursing the owner of the future interest.[5]

When a tenant for years or for life has paid mortgage principal, special assessments, or other carrying charges which the reversioner or remainderman had a duty to pay, the possessory tenant has the same rights of reimbursement, equitable lien enforcement, and subrogation as does the reversioner or remainderman in the situation previously considered.[6]

If a life tenant fails to pay current taxes or other carrying charges which are his sole obligation and later buys in the fee simple estate at a tax or foreclosure sale, his purchase does not give him an estate in fee simple;[7] the purchase is treated simply as "payment" of the taxes or other carrying charges, leaving the title to the property unchanged.[8] On the other hand, if the possessory tenant buys in at a foreclosure sale enforcing a mortgage or special assessment where the duty of payment rested partly on the owner of the future interest, the tenant acquires a fee simple subject to the right of the former owner of the future interest to acquire that interest by contributing his proportionate share of the amount paid by the tenant within a reasonable time.[9] And if the owner of the future interest was solely obligated to pay a particular carrying charge, such as a special assessment or an installment of an outstanding mortgage debt, the life tenant would acquire the fee simple subject to the right of the former owner of the future interest to reacquire that interest by fully reimbursing the life tenant within a reasonable time.[10] On the other hand, if the duty to pay carrying charges rests either solely or partly on the owner of a future interest who fails to pay

4. E.g., Krebs v. Bezler, 338 Mo. 365, 89 S.W.2d 935, 103 A.L.R. 1177 (1936); Elmora & West End Building & Loan Association v. Dancy, 108 N.J.Eq. 542, 155 A. 796 (1931).

5. See 1 Am.L.Prop. § 2.22 at p. 158. If the possessory tenant fails to "redeem" his estate may be extinguished by foreclosure irrespective of the amount of "rents and profits" he has received or the value of his actual use and occupation.

6. E.g., Ward v. Chambless, 238 Ala. 165, 189 So. 890 (1939); Boggs v. Boggs, 63 Cal. App.2d 576, 147 P.2d 116 (1944); Randall's Estate v. McKibben, 191 N.W.2d 693 (Iowa 1971); King v. Rainbolt, 515 P.2d 228 (Okl. 1973).

7. E.g., Wheeler v. Harris, 232 Ark. 469, 339 S.W.2d 99 (1960); Richton Tie & Timber Co. v. Tillman, 233 Miss. 12, 103 So.2d 139 (1958).

8. E.g., Rushton v. McLaughlin, 213 Ala. 380, 104 So. 824 (1925); Thompson v. Watkins, 285 N.C. 616, 207 S.E.2d 740 (1974).

Similarly, if the life tenant buys from a third party who purchased at a tax sale, the life tenant's purchase is treated as an equitable redemption of the land for the benefit of the remaindermen, leaving the interests of the parties unchanged. Henderson v. Ellis, 10 Ark.App. 276, 665 S.W.2d 289 (1984).

9. E.g., Drane v. Smith, 271 Ala. 54, 122 So.2d 135 (1960) (right lost after 16 years); Fleming v. Brunner, 224 Md. 97, 166 A.2d 901 (1961) (right barred by laches); Thompson v. Watkins, supra note 8 (right lost after 19 years). Like a land contract vendor in possession after the purchaser's default or a mortgagee in possession after the mortgagor's default, the former tenant can force the former owner of the future interest to "put up or shut up" by bringing an action to quiet title or to foreclose. E.g., Rushton v. McLaughlin, supra note 8 (quiet title); Thompson v. Watkins, supra note 8 (quiet title). See also Peak v. Peak, 228 Mo. 536, 128 S.W. 981 (1910) (remainderman can "redeem").

But see Scotch v. Hurst, 437 So.2d 497 (Ala. 1983) (right of remaindermen to quiet title against life tenant was not barred by laches after life tenant's death, despite lapse of 29 years, where no "special equities" existed to require remaindermen to "remove cloud on their remainder interests" during life tenant's lifetime and life tenant never sought to obtain contribution from remaindermen, who were life tenant's children).

10. All the authorities cited supra in notes 8 and 9 state the rule so broadly as to apply even where the owner(s) of the future interest(s) had the sole duty of paying the carrying charges.

it and later purchases the land at a foreclosure sale, it would seem that he would acquire the fee simple title subject to the possessory tenant's right to reacquire his interest by paying to the owner of the future interest the amount required to reimburse him properly.[11] In either case, the party who purchases the land has a quasi-fiduciary relationship with the other party, and acquires the fee simple subject to a constructive trust in favor of the other party.[12]

§ 4.7   Rights to Insurance Proceeds

If a life tenant has no duty to maintain property insurance for the benefit of the reversioner or remainderman, only the life tenant can recover, in the event of loss, on an insurance policy procured by him that does not expressly insure the future interest.[1] Even if the policy purports to insure the entire fee simple, the life tenant is subject to the general rule that an insurance policy is enforcible only to the extent of the actual loss sustained by the insured.[2] And if the insurer fails to invoke this rule, most courts hold that the reversioner or remainderman is not entitled to any portion of the insurance proceeds paid to the life tenant, although this may result in overcompensation of the life tenant.[3] Some courts, however, hold that the life tenant in such a case is trustee for the owner of the future interest, and that the life tenant may therefore enforce the insurance policy for the full face amount thereof, subject to a duty to account to the owner of the future interest for his share.[4]

If the life tenant has no duty to insure for the benefit of the reversioner or remainderman but nevertheless does so, the owner of the future interest may ratify the life tenant's action, even after a loss occurs, and thus put himself in position to enforce the policy for his own benefit.[5]

Where land or structures are insured against damage or destruction by a policy that effectively insures the interests of both the life tenant and the reversioner or remainderman,[6] the Property Restatement asserts that, in the

---

11. See Hall v. Hall, 173 Minn. 128, 216 N.W. 798 (1927); Smith v. Kappler, 220 Ark. 10, 245 S.W.2d 809 (1952).

12. See, e.g., the authorities cited supra in notes 8 and 9, all involving life tenants who purchased at mortgage foreclosure sales. In such cases, the purchasing party acquires the legal title in fee simple subject to a constructive trust for the benefit of the other party. However, where the owner of the future interest buys in at a foreclosure sale after the possessory tenant's failure to perform a duty which is solely his, it is arguable that there is no quasi-fiduciary duty obligating the owner of the future interest to hold the title in trust for the benefit of the possessory tenant. See L. Simes and A. Smith, Future Interests § 1700 at p. 52 (2d ed. 1956).

§ 4.7

1. This is simply an application of ordinary contract principles to the insurance contract. See Carlton v. Wilson, 665 S.W.2d 356 (Mo. App.1984) (life tenant paid all insurance premiums).

2. This rule is based on the theories (1) that the policy would become a "wagering contract" and (2) that the "moral risk" would be increased if the policy could be enforced for losses in excess of the "insurable interest" of the insured. See Vance, Insurance §§ 28–30 (3d ed. 1951); 1 Richards, Insurance §§ 64–70, 152 (5th ed. 1952).

3. E.g., Converse v. Boston Safe Deposit & Trust Co., 315 Mass. 544, 53 N.E.2d 841 (1944) (dictum). Courts so holding find that there is no "trust" relationship between the life tenant and the owners of future interests. See Vance, Insurance § 132 (3d ed. 1951).

4. E.g., Crisp County Lumber Co. v. Bridges, 187 Ga. 484, 200 S.E. 777 (1939); Sampson v. Grogan, 21 R.I. 174, 42 A. 712, 44 L.R.A. 711 (1899) (dictum).

5. 1 Am.L.Prop. § 2.23 at p. 160.

6. In such case the insurance proceeds will generally be made payable to the life tenant and the owner(s) of the future interest(s) "as their interests may appear." The life tenant

event of a loss covered by the insurance policy, the life tenant has "a privilege to use, and a power to compel the use of, the proceeds from such policy for the restoration of the land or structures to its former condition, when such restoration is both practicable and reasonable," and "a privilege to have the use of such proceeds for the duration of his estate" if the proceeds are not used for restoration.[7] "Use" of the proceeds means receiving "the interest earned by such proceeds, periodically, during the continuance of such estate for life."[8] By statute in some states, however, the court may apportion the proceeds between the life tenant and the owners of future interests, so that each will receive a portion of the proceeds in a lump sum.[9]

Leases creating estates for years often include express contractual provisions as to maintenance of property insurance, payment of insurance premiums, and the utilization or apportionment of insurance proceeds in the event of loss.[10] In the absence of such provisions, it would seem that the rules applicable as between a life tenant and the owners of future interests would also apply as between a tenant for years and the owners of such interests.

§ 4.8 Apportionment of Rents

A life tenant has the privilege of leasing the property in which he holds his life estate for any use that does not amount to waste, in the absence of a contrary provision in the instrument creating the life estates; and the life tenant is exclusively entitled to all rents received from lessees to whom the property is rightfully leased.[1] Moreover, if the life estate is created subject to an existing lease, the life tenant is exclusively entitled to the lease rentals in the absence of a contrary provision in the instrument creating the life estate.[2]

As we have already seen, it is waste for a life tenant to open and exploit new mines, oil wells, or gas wells, or to cut and sell mature timber except in the course of "good husbandry."[3] Consequently, it is also waste for him to lease the property to a tenant for such uses.[4] But in cases where mines, oil

---

must, of course, pay all the premiums required to keep the policy in force. See, e.g., Hopkins v. Keazer, 89 Me. 347, 36 A. 615 (1896); Lynch v. Johnson, 196 Va. 516, 84 S.E.2d 419 (1954).

7. Rest.Prop. § 123. As to periodic payments of interest, see Cope v. Ricketts, 130 Kan. 823, 288 P. 591 (1930).

8. Id. § 123, Comment (b).

9. Ibid. But see 5 R. Powell, Real Property ¶ 669, indicating that courts have discretion to award lump sums to the parties if the life tenant asks for apportionment, even in the absence of a statute authorizing this result.

10. See post Section 6.58. Sometimes it is provided that the lessor shall insure and that the proceeds will be used to restore the property or rebuild in the event of damage or destruction. E.g., Gelino v. Swannell, 263 Ill. App. 235 (1931). Long-term leases usually provide that the lessee shall insure and that

the proceeds shall be used for restoration or rebuilding.

§ 4.8

1. As we have already seen, the life tenant's personal obligation to keep the property in repair and to pay carrying charges such as taxes is limited, in the absence of an express covenant to the contrary, to the actual rents obtained from the property or, if personally occupied by the life tenant, the fair rental value of the property.

2. E.g., Redwine v. Ansley, 32 Okl. 317, 122 P. 679 (1912). That this rule applies to rents and royalties from mines and oil wells already open and leased when the life estate was created, see, e.g., In re Blodgett's Estate, 254 Pa. 210, 98 A. 876 (1916).

3. Ante Section 4.2.

4. In Moore v. Vines, 474 S.W.2d 437 (Tex. 1971), noted in 8 Houston L.Rev. 753 (1971), 24 Baylor L.Rev. 142 (1972), it was held that,

wells, or gas wells are already open, or the land is already in use for production and sale of timber when the life estate is created, the life tenant may rightfully lease the property for such uses.[5]   And, of course, the life tenant may join with the reversioner or remainderman in making a lease that authorizes the lessee to open new mines, oil wells, or gas wells, or to cut and sell timber.   In such case, the division of rents or royalties is usually expressly provided for in the lease.   Absent an express provision on the point, the life tenant is entitled to the present value of the use of the rents or royalties, computed on the basis of the probable duration of the life estate and the rate of return established by statute for determination of the value of a life estate.[6]

An estate for years created prior to the life estate will, of course continue after the life tenant's death if the term has not then expired, and the owner of the reversion or remainder then becomes the landlord and is therefore entitled to all rents thereafter accruing under the subsisting lease. Since rent becomes due, at common law, only on the days fixed by contract for its payment, the entire amount payable on the next rent day after the life tenant's death belongs to the new landlord.[7]   But this is manifestly unjust, and the rule has been changed in England and in some American jurisdictions by statutes providing for the apportionment of rent in such cases so that the life tenant's personal representative may recover a share of the rent proportionate to that part of the rent period which preceded the life tenant's death.[8]

§ 4.9   Emblements and Fixtures

Any estate of indefinite duration, such as a life estate, carries with it a special right—called the right of "emblements"—to harvest and remove,

even though an oil and gas lease was in existence when the life estate was created, the "open mine" doctrine was inapplicable and the life tenant had no authority to make a new oil and gas lease to the same lessee.

5. Under the "open mine" doctrine the life tenant or his lessee can work the open mine or wells even to exhaustion. E.g., Ohio Oil Co. v. Daughetee, 240 Ill. 361, 88 N.E. 818, 36 L.R.A. (N.S.) 1108 (1909); Gaines v. Green Pond Iron Mining Co., 33 N.J.Eq. 603 (1881). But the "open mine" doctrine does not authorize either the life tenant or his lessee to open additional mines, veins of ore, or wells. E.g., Westmoreland Coal Co.'s Appeal, 85 Pa. 344 (1877).   In Kimbark Exploration Co. v. Von Lintel, 192 Kan. 791, 391 P.2d 55 (1964), the "open mine" doctrine was held to be applicable where execution of an oil and gas lease preceded the creation of the life estate, although production had not begun when the life estate was created.   Contra: Moore v. Vines, supra note 4.   In Clyde v. Hamilton, 414 S.W.2d 434 (Tex.1967), it was held that the life tenant was entitled to royalties from a

well opened before the life estate was opened, but not from wells opened thereafter.

6. E.g., Weekley v. Weekley, 126 W.Va. 90, 27 S.E.2d 591, 150 A.L.R. 689 (1943).   Rest. Prop. § 119, Comment (b) urges that such an apportionment should be applied to all leases or contracts for removal and sale of minerals or timber.   But see Haskell v. Wood, 256 Cal. App.2d 799, 64 Cal.Rptr. 459 (1967).   Generally, see Annot., 18 A.L.R.2d 100–179 (1951).

7. E.g., Peery v. Fletcher, 93 Or. 43, 182 P. 143 (1919); Ex parte Smyth, 1 Swanst. 337, 36 Eng.Rep. 412 (1818).

8. See Stat. 4 Wm. IV, c. 22 (1834); Stat. 2 Geo. II, c. 19, § 15 (1738); and American statutes listed in Rest.Prop. § 120, Comment (d), Special Note.   In some states the English statutes are deemed part of the common law. See e.g., Peery v. Fletcher, supra note 7; Coleman v. Edwards, 70 N.C.App. 206, 318 S.E.2d 899 (1984) (remaindermen entitled to prepaid rent in an amount reflecting the fact that life tenant died 6 days after executing lease; one-year lease was valid for balance of term following life tenant's death).

after the termination of the tenancy, any crops planted by the tenant.[1] This special right, which constitutes an exception to the general rule that annual crops are part of the realty and pass with it,[2] exists only when termination of the estate was not caused by any act or default of the tenant.[3] When a life estate expires as a result of the life tenant's death, his personal representative is privileged to harvest and remove the annual crops planted by the life tenant by virtue of the doctrine of "emblements." [4] This right of the personal representative is not affected by the life tenant's exercise of a power to appoint the property in fee simple.[5] A tenant for years, of course, has no right to remove annual crops under the doctrine of "emblements," since his estate has a definite duration,[6] but a periodic tenant or tenant at will is privileged to do so.[7]

When a tenant for life or for years annexes a chattel to the realty, whether for "trade," "agricultural," "domestic," or "ornamental" purposes, the courts have generally presumed that the tenant does not intend to make a permanent annexation and have allowed the tenant to remove the chattel—commonly called a "fixture" in such cases—at or before the end of the tenancy if removal can be effected without causing substantial injury to the realty or substantial destruction of the fixture itself.[8] If the chattel was annexed by a life tenant, his personal representative may remove it within a reasonable time after termination of the life estate by the life tenant's death.[9] If the chattel was annexed by a tenant for years, however, the

§ 4.9

1. See 1 Am.L.Prop. § 2.6 at pp. 142–144; 5 id. § 19.16 at pp. 67–68. For the origin of the doctrine, see Co.Litt. *55b. See also Leigh v. Lynch, 133 Ill.App.3d 659, 88 Ill.Dec. 733, 479 N.E.2d 346 (1985), reversed 112 Ill.2d 411, 98 Ill.Dec. 19, 493 N.E.2d 1040 (1986) (tenancy from year to year; right to remove perennial crop did not continue after first harvest season).

2. For the general rule, see, e.g., Mitchell v. Martindill, 209 Ark. 66, 189 S.W.2d 662 (1945) (crops pass on conveyance of realty by deed); In re Andersen's Estate, 83 Neb. 8, 118 N.W. 1108 (1908) (crops pass by will). However, crops may be treated as realty or personalty as the case requires. Thus, e.g., they may be sold as personalty without compliance with the Statute of Frauds requirement of a writing for the sale of interest in land; they may be levied upon as personalty under an execution or attachment; they pass as personalty to the personal representative upon the death of the landowner intestate; and a mortgage upon them is not a lien on the land where they are grown. See 5 Am.L.Prop. § 19.16 at nn. 4–8.

3. E.g., Carpenter v. Jones, 63 Ill. 517 (1872); Eckman v. Beihl, 116 N.J.L. 308, 184 A. 430 (1936); Leigh v. Lynch, supra note 1.

4. Rest.Prop. § 121. The same privilege may be exercised by life tenant's lessee when the death of the life tenant terminates the lease. E.g., Strand v. Boll, 44 S.D. 228, 183

N.W. 284, 15 A.L.R. 652 (1921). See also Rest. Prop. § 121, Comment (a), Special Note.

5. E.g., Keays v. Blinn, 234 Ill. 121, 84 N.E. 628 (1908).

6. E.g., Miller v. Gray, 136 Tex. 196, 149 S.W.2d 582 (1941).

7. E.g., Harris v. Frink, 49 N.Y. 24 (1872) (tenancy at will).

8. The modern American rule generally allows removal of tenant fixtures without categorizing them as "trade," "agricultural" or "ornamental" fixtures. See, e.g., Romich v. Kempner Brothers Realty Co., 192 Ark. 454, 92 S.W.2d 215 (1936) (automatic sprinkler system); Warrington v. Hignutt, 42 Del. 274, 31 A.2d 480 (1943) (oil heaters and outside oil tanks, including connecting copper tubing); Leslie Pontiac, Inc. v. Novak, 202 N.W.2d 114 (Iowa 1972) (steel shell structure on concrete slab, with no insulation or utilities); American Steel & Iron Co. v. Taft, 109 Vt. 469, 199 A. 261 (1938) (railroad ties and rails); Old Line Life Insurance Co. v. Hawn, 225 Wis. 627, 275 N.W. 542 (1937) (furnace and brooder houses).

9. E.g., Ray v. Young, 160 Iowa 613, 142 N.W. 393, 46 L.R.A.(N.S.) 947 (1913). The same rule applies to a tenant at will—e.g., Henderson v. Robbins, 126 Me. 284, 138 A. 68 (1927)—or the owner of a determinable fee simple—e.g., Dickerman v. Town of Pittsford, 116 Vt. 563, 80 A.2d 529 (1951).

tenant loses the privilege of removal if he does not remove it before the end of the lease term.[10]

Most of the modern cases on removal of tenants' fixtures involve tenants for years, and further discussion of these cases will be found in the chapter dealing with the law of landlord and tenant.[11]

§ 4.10   Judicial Sale of Realty Encumbered by Future Estates

The division of land ownership between the owners of present and future estates can work substantial hardship. As we have seen, a life tenant is restricted in his use of the property by the law of waste and is obligated to pay property taxes and other carrying charges to the extent these charges do not exceed the actual rental income of the property or, if the life tenant personally occupies the property, its rental value.[1] But it may be difficult to rent the property because of the uncertainty as to the duration of the life estate or the lack of suitable improvements on the land. Even if actual rental income can be obtained by the life tenant, it may be insufficient to pay property taxes and/or other carrying charges. Non-payment of taxes, mortgage interest or special assessments may result in a sale that will extinguish not only the life estate but all future interests in the land as well. Financial inability of the life tenant to keep improvements on the land in repair may result in substantial injury to owners of future interests as well as to the life tenant. In such cases, the owners of future interests may consent to a sale of the land in fee simple and investment of the proceeds in trust for the holders of all interests in the land.[2] But consent may not always be forthcoming even if all future interests are vested, and in many instances contingent future interests may be limited in favor of unborn or otherwise unascertainable persons who are incapable of consenting to a sale.

Where sale of the property in fee simple is considered necessary for preservation of all interests therein, the weight of authority is that courts with equity jurisdiction have inherent power to order a sale in fee simple, with the proceeds of sale to be held in a judicially created trust for the benefit of all persons with interests in the property.[3] But some courts refuse to order a sale in fee simple unless it is authorized by statute.[4] In at least

---

10. E.g., Stout v. Stoppel, 30 Minn. 56, 14 N.W. 268 (1882).

11. See post Sections 6.44, 6.45.

§ 4.10

1. See ante Sections 4.2 through 4.3.

2. Where the rental income or rental value is insufficient to cover the carrying charges, the owner of the future interest may pay such charges in full and then sue the life tenant for reimbursement and enforce a lien for the amount to which he is entitled; the lien will be enforced by an order for sale of the life estate. See ante Sections 4.3, 4.4, 4.6. But a sale of the entire fee simple estate may be a better solution from the viewpoint of the owners of future interests because it requires no

financial outlay by them and because life estates are not readily salable.

3. E.g., Dunn v. Sanders, 243 Ga. 684, 256 S.E.2d 366 (1979); Baker v. Weedon, 262 So.2d 641 (Miss.1972). For the theoretical basis of this judicial power, see L. Simes & A. Smith, Future Interests § 1941 (2d ed. 1956). See also Schnebly, Power of Life Tenant or Remainderman to Extinguish Other Interests by Judicial Process, 42 Harv.L.Rev. 30 (1928); Rogers, Removal of Future Interest Encumbrances—Sale of the Fee Simple Estate, 17 Vand.L.Rev. 1437 (1964); Annot., 57 A.L.R.3d 1189 (1974).

4. E.g., Losey v. Stanley, 147 N.Y. 560, 42 N.E. 8 (1895); Brown v. Brown, 83 W.Va. 415, 422, 98 S.E. 428, 431 (1919) (dictum).

one-half the states there are statutes authorizing such a sale.[5] Some of these statutes give courts very broad powers, and others grant the power to order a sale in fee simple only in narrowly defined situations.[6]

Where courts have asserted the power to order a sale in fee simple without statutory authorization, the precise scope of their power is often not clear. Some courts have held that such a sale may be ordered only where all the non-consenting owners of future interests are either minors or are unborn or otherwise unascertained.[7] Other courts have asserted the power to order a sale as against non-consenting owners of future interests who are ascertained and of full age.[8]

It is generally said that a sale should not be ordered unless the petitioner shows that a sale is "necessary for the best interest of all the parties."[9] After stating the rule in that form, the Mississippi court recently held[10] that it had the power to order a sale, even though the property "was not deteriorating" and there was "sufficient rental income to pay taxes," in order to provide "economic relief" to the aging life tenant whose income from the property was insufficient for her to "live comfortably in view of her age and the infirmities therefrom."[11] The court also held, however, that "the best interest of all the parties would not be served by a judicial sale of the entirety of the property at this time" because it appeared that the value of the land would increase from $168,500 to $336,000 within the ensuing four years.[12] The court further suggested that the life tenant would immediately be entitled to "sale of a part of the burdened land sufficient to provide for her reasonable needs from interest derived from the investment of the

5. See statutes listed in L. Simes & A. Smith, Future Interests § 1946 n. 28 (2d ed. 1956).

6. Some statutes allow sale upon petition by the owner of any present or future interest. E.g., Mass.Gen.Laws Ann. c. 183, § 49. Other statutes allow sale upon petition by the owner of any present or specified future interest. E.g., New Hampshire Rev.Stat.Ann. 259:28. And some statutes allow sale only upon petition by the owners of present interests. E.g., Ohio Rev.Code §§ 5303.21, 5303.31.

7. E.g., Bofil v. Fisher, 3 Rich.Eq. (24 S.C.Eq.) 1, 55 Am.Dec. 627 (S.C.1850).

8. E.g., Williams v. Colleran, 230 Ga. 56, 195 S.E.2d 413 (1973); Baker v. Weedon, supra note 3 (semble).

9. Baker v. Weedon, supra note 3, at 643. Accord: Gavin v. Curtin, 171 Ill. 640, 49 N.E. 523, 40 L.R.A. 776 (1898). The "necessity" need not be absolute. Cagle v. Schaefer, 115 S.C. 35, 104 S.E. 321 (1920). But a sale has been denied where, although the life estate was "unproductive," it was not shown that the remainderman would be benefited by a sale. Soules v. Silver, 118 Or. 96, 245 P. 1069 (1926).

In DeLisi v. Caito, 463 A.2d 167 (R.I.1983), the court affirmed an order for sale of the fee simple in property described as follows: "the house is vacant, uninsured, and generally not in a condition to be rented unless certain improvements are made," and subject to "an

impending tax sale because property taxes amounting to approximately $5,000 have not been paid." The life tenant was apparently incompetent, a guardian of her person and property having been appointed. The guardian who brought the action testified that the life tenant had no funds available for maintenance or to pay the costs involved in selling her life estate. The court said that it "could not think of any party who would benefit from the house's remaining in its present vacant state." The court held that legislative authorization for the sale of the fee simple could be found in a statute providing for a court-ordered sale in "actions for partition," and characterized the instant action as one "to have both the life estate and the remaindermen's interest partitioned by sale."

10. Baker v. Weedon, supra note 3.

11. Id. at 645.

12. Id. at 643. The court said that an immediate sale of all the land in fee simple "would unjustly impinge upon the vested rights of the remaindermen." The anticipated appreciation in value was due to the planned construction of a federal highway bypass through the land. A right-of-way across the land had already been acquired by the state highway department for $20,000, out of which the life tenant had received $6,500 "to construct a new home."

proceeds," provided "the parties cannot unite to hypothecate [i.e., mortgage] the land for sufficient funds for the life tenant's reasonable needs."[13]

When a court orders a sale in fee simple of land burdened with future interests, the proceeds of the sale—as indicated in the judicial language quoted in the preceding paragraph—are held in a judicially-created trust, and the investment income is paid over to the former life tenant during the balance of his or her life. When the life tenant dies, the principal is distributed to the former owners of future interests in the land.[14]

If a court has the power to order an outright sale in fee of land burdened by future interests, it would seem *a fortiori*, that the court may order that the land be mortgaged, leased, or exchanged rather than sold.

§ 4.11 Protection of Owners of Legal Future Interests in Personalty

A donor who wishes to create future interests in personalty is well-advised to make the gift in trust, particularly if the personalty consists mainly of cash, stocks, bonds, and/or similar intangible forms of property. A life beneficiary of such a trust has a right only to the net income of the trust property, which is held and managed by the trustee for the benefit of the holders of both present and future interests. The remedies of the owners of present and future interests against each other and against the trustee are governed by the law of trusts, which is outside the scope of this book.

Suppose a donor divides the ownership of personalty into present and future interests without expressly creating a trust. (This is more likely to occur when tangible personalty such as works of art or heirlooms is transferred than when intangibles are transferred.) In such a case, the owner of a present interest (a life interest or an interest analogous to a defeasible fee simple estate in realty) is entitled to possession of the property transferred, and problems like those considered previously in this chapter may arise. But personalty poses special problems that do not arise in the case of realty because personalty is movable and readily salable, and, if it consists of cash, stocks, bonds or the like, may require expert management to avoid capital loss. Since the law of waste as developed in connection with the division of ownership of realty into present and future estates does not afford the owners of future interests in personalty adequate protection against misappropriation or misuse of the property by the possessory owner, the courts have often construed ambiguous language in wills as creating a trust with the executor as trustee.[1] Since 1947, Pennsylvania has had a statute

---

13. Baker v. Weedon, supra note 3, at 644. The court also said, "By affording the options above, we do not mean to suggest that other remedies suitable to the parties which will provide economic relief to the aging life tenant are not open to them if approved by the chancellor." Ibid.

14. See Smith v. Smith, 600 S.W.2d 666 (Mo.App.1980), holding that the life tenant is not entitled to the present value of the life estate in a lump sum when the land is sold in fee simple.

§ 4.11

1. E.g., Welsch v. Belleville Savings Bank, 94 Ill. 191 (1879); White v. Massachusetts Institute of Technology, 171 Mass. 84, 50 N.E. 512 (1898). See also Mt. Freedom Presbyterian Church v. Osborne, 81 N.J.Super. 441, 195 A.2d 907 (Law Div.1963). 2 Restatement, Property § 200 (1936) states a constructional preference for finding a trust. See Backer v. Levy, 82 F.2d 270 (2d Cir.1936), containing a dictum in support of the Restatement.

providing, in substance, that a person having a present interest in personalty subject to a future interest, but not expressly subject to a trust, shall be treated as a trustee of such personalty;[2] and several other states have statutes requiring life tenants of personalty to account periodically as if they were trustees.[3]

If the instrument of transfer does not create a trust by express language or by implication and the jurisdiction has no statute creating a trust when the ownership of personalty is divided into present and future interests, courts will often protect the owners of future interests by ordering the possessory owner to give security[4] and, if the latter fails to obey the court's order, by appointing a trustee to manage the property.[5] In some states the probate court is authorized by statute to require the possessory owner to give security before personalty passing by will is delivered to him.[6] Even in the

2. The statute is Pa.Con.Stat.Ann. tit. 20, § 6113, which provides in part as follows:

> A person having a present interest in personal property * * *, which is not in trust, and which is subject to a future interest, shall be deemed to be a trustee of such property, * * * with the ordinary powers and duties of a trustee, except that he shall not be required to change the form of the investment to an investment authorized for Pennsylvania fiduciaries, nor shall he be entitled to compensation as a trustee.

3. E.g., N.Y.—McKinney's Surr.Ct.Proc. Act 2201. Under such statutes it is clear that a life tenant is entitled to all income derived from the property, but it is not always clear whether the usual trust law rules as to allocation of stock dividends and the like between principal and interest are applicable. See 51 Am.Jur.2d, Life Tenants and Remaindermen §§ 104–107, 167–168, 207–217 (1970); Restatement, Property §§ 119, 120 (1936); Notes, 129 A.L.R. 1314 (1940), 142 id. 264 (1943), 149 id. 1376 (1944), 44 A.L.R.2d 1277 (1955), 76 id. 162 (1961), 81 A.L.R.3d 876 (1977).

4. E.g., Bethea v. Bethea, 116 Ala. 265, 22 So. 561 (1896); Frye v. Community Chest, 241 Ala. 591, 4 So.2d 140 (1941); Reed v. Reed, 80 Conn. 411, 68 A. 852 (1908); Marshall v. Hewett, 156 Fla. 645, 24 So.2d 1 (1945); Barmore v. Gilbert, 151 Ga. 260, 106 S.E. 269, 14 A.L.R. 1060 (1921); Tripp v. Krauth, 340 Ill. 11, 171 N.E. 919 (1930); Quigley v. Quigley, 370 Ill. 151, 18 N.E.2d 186 (1938); In re Blakely's Estate, 115 Kan. 644, 224 P. 65 (1924); Fewell v. Fewell, 459 S.W.2d 774 (Ky.1970); Tapley v. Douglass, 113 Me. 392, 94 A. 486 (1915); Meins v. Pease, 208 Mass. 478, 94 N.E. 845 (1911); Roberts v. Stoner, 18 Mo. 481 (1852); Brown v. Wilson, 41 N.C. 558 (1850); Long v. Lea, 177 S.C. 231, 181 S.E. 6 (1935); Evans v. Adams, 180 S.C. 214, 185 S.E. 57 (1936); McDougal v. Armstrong, 25 Tenn. (6 Humph.) 428 (1846). But see Matter of Estate of Jud, 238 Kan. 268, 710 P.2d 1241 (1985) (life tenant said to be "a trustee or quasi trustee" but court would not order life tenant to give secu-

rity—though there was statutory authority to require security—or to furnish an accounting for protection of remaindermen "in the absence of a showing of danger of loss," where life tenant had a "power to dispose of or consume the corpus"). Generally, see Nemmers, The Right of the Owner of a Future Interest in Personalty to Security, 1943 Wis. L.Rev. 229; Comment, Protecting the Remainderman, 33 Chi.Kent L.Rev. 240 (1955).

5. E.g., Frye v. Community Chest, Reed v. Reed, supra note 4; Van Dusen's Appeal, 102 Pa. 224 (1883). See also Koplon v. Koplon, 274 Ala. 214, 148 So.2d 245 (1962).

6. 20 Pa.Con.Stat.Ann. § 6113, set out in part supra note 2, further provides that the possessory owner, as statutory trustee,

> unless given a power of consumption or excused from entering security by the terms of the conveyance, shall be required to enter such security for the protection of the persons entitled to future interests as the court in its discretion shall direct. If a person having a present interest shall not enter security as directed, the court shall appoint a trustee who shall enter such security as the court shall direct, and who shall exercise all the ordinary powers and duties of a trustee, except that he shall not be required to change the form of the investment to an investment authorized for Pennsylvania fiduciaries.

Conn.Gen.Stat.Ann. § 45–183 provides as follows:

> When a life estate in any personal estate is given by will to one with remainder to another, and there is no trustee named for such estate during the continuance of the life estate * * *, the court of probate * * * may order the executor to deliver such personal estate to the person having the life estate upon his giving a probate bond, * * * and if such person fails to give bond as aforesaid, such court shall appoint a trustee for such estate during the continuance of such life estate * * *.

absence of such a statute, some courts, upon petition by the owner of a future interest in personalty, will require the possessory owner to give security if the latter has expressly been given the power to alter the form of the property or has that power by implication because the personalty consists of cash, stocks, bonds, or the like.[7] In other states—perhaps a majority—security will be required of the possessory owner only upon a showing that there is substantial danger that the personalty will be misappropriated or misused.[8] If such danger is shown to exist, all courts will require the giving of security unless the possessory owner has been given an unrestricted power to consume the property or a power to appoint the property, free of all future interests, to a person other than the owner of a future interest therein.[9] If it is reasonably probable that any of the future interests for which protection is sought will become possessory, it is immaterial whether such future interest is indefeasibly vested, vested subject to open, vested subject to complete defeasance, or contingent.[10] And it is largely immaterial whether the possessory owner has a life interest or an interest analogous to a defeasible fee simple in realty.[11]

Although most courts hold that security for protection of future interests in personalty is a matter of right where danger of loss is shown,[12] courts in fact have substantial discretion in determining whether such danger exists. Courts have given weight to a variety of factors in making such a determination—e.g., whether the possessory owner is or is likely to become insolvent,[13] whether he resides outside the jurisdiction,[14] and whether he is

---

7. E.g., Barmore v. Gilbert, Tripp v. Krauth, Blakely v. Blakely, Tapley v. Douglass, supra note 4. In these cases, in all of which the possessory owner had only a life interest, the courts appeared to view the power of changing the form of the property as itself creating a danger of loss. But see Matter of Estate of Jud, supra note 4.

8. Bethea v. Bethea, Reed v. Reed, Meins v. Pease, Roberts v. Stoner, Brown v. Wilson, Long v. Lea, McDougal v. Armstrong, supra note 4. See also, Busbee v. Haley, 220 Ga. 874, 142 S.E.2d 786 (1965); Holley v. Marks, 535 S.W.2d 861 (Tenn.1976); Wise v. Hinegardner, 97 W.Va. 587, 125 S.E. 579 (1924).

There are a few cases which hold or say that security should not be required, absent a showing of danger of loss, if the transferor indicated that the life tenant was to have possession of the property. See Barmore v. Gilbert, supra note 4; Crutcher v. Elliston's Executors, 299 Ky. 613, 186 S.W.2d 644 (1945); Phipps v. Doak, 235 Mo.App. 659, 145 S.W.2d 167 (1940); In re Von Kleist's Will, 265 N.Y. 422, 193 N.E. 256 (1934); Collins v. Hartford Accident & Indemnity Co., 178 Va. 501, 17 S.E.2d 413, 137 A.L.R. 1046 (1941).

9. See cases cited supra note 4. That an unrestricted power to consume precludes a requirement that the possessory owner shall give security, see Flanagan v. Flanagan, 8 Abb.N.C. 413 (N.Y.1880); In re Hays' Estate, 358 Pa. 38, 55 A.2d 763 (1947). See also La Tourette v. La Tourette, 15 Ariz. 200, 137 P.

426 (1914); Colburn v. Burlingame, 190 Cal. 697, 214 P. 226, 27 A.L.R. 1374 (1923); Marshall v. Hewett, 156 Fla. 645, 24 So.2d 1 (1945). Contra: Abbott v. Wagner, 108 Neb. 359, 188 N.W. 113 (1922); Reed v. Reed, supra note 4. It is not, of course, always easy to decide whether a possessory owner has been given an unrestricted power to consume the property. See, e.g., In re Phillips' Estate, 247 Cal.App.2d 510, 55 Cal.Rptr. 658 (1966); Quigley v. Quigley, supra note 4; Rhodus v. Proctor, 433 S.W.2d 625 (Ky.1968); Frederick v. Frederick, 355 Mass. 662, 247 N.E.2d 361 (1969); In re Estate of Perkins, 289 Minn. 53, 182 N.W.2d 881 (1970); Morisseau v. Biesterfeldt, 345 S.W.2d 210 (Mo.1961); In re Cross' Estate, 108 N.H. 134, 229 A.2d 170 (1967).

10. E.g., Security Co. v. Hardenberg, 53 Conn. 169, 2 A. 391 (1885) (contingent remainder); Phipps v. Doak, 235 Mo.App. 659, 145 S.W.2d 167 (1940) (indefeasibly vested remainder).

11. See Meins v. Pease, supra note 4.

12. See generally, cases cited supra note 4. Contra: Quigley v. Quigley, supra note 4; Heintz v. Parsons, 233 Iowa 984, 9 N.W.2d 355 (1943).

See also Matter of Estate of Jud, supra note 4.

13. E.g., Collins v. Barksdale, 23 Ga. 602 (1857).

14. E.g., Scott v. Scott, 137 Iowa 239, 114 N.W. 881, 23 L.R.A.(N.S.) 716 (1908).

likely to remove the personalty from the jurisdiction.[15]

All the rules stated above are, of course, subject to the qualification that the transferor's expressed intention that owners of possessory interests in personalty transferred subject to future interests therein shall, or shall not, be required to give security for the protection of the owners of future interests is controlling.[16] And even if no intent one way or the other is expressed by the transferor, an intent that security shall not be required has been inferred from the fact that the possessory interest was given to the transferor's wife,[17] or to a person also named as executor of the will and expressly exempted from any requirement that he should give bond for performance of his duties as executor.[18] But there are also cases where the court has required the possessory owner to give security despite such facts.[19]

The ability of the owners of future interests in personalty not transferred in trust to compel the possessory owner to give security and/or to account for the property seems largely to have obviated the need for other remedies. But there are cases awarding damages for injuries to the property caused by the possessory owner or a third party [20] and/or enjoining threatened injuries.[21] And the owner of a future interest in personalty may also be able to prevent removal of the property from the jurisdiction by obtaining a writ of *ne exeat.*[22]

15. Reed v. Reed, supra note 4.

16. E.g., Trustees Presbyterian Church v. Mize, 181 Ky. 567, 205 S.W. 674, 2 A.L.R. 1237 (1918); McGuire v. Gallagher, 99 Me. 334, 59 A. 445 (1904); Smith v. Smith, 359 Mo. 44, 220 S.W.2d 10 (1949); Chamberlain v. Husel, 178 Mich. 1, 144 N.W. 549 (1913); Rife v. Rife, 154 Miss. 529, 122 So. 739 (1929); In re Rowland, 153 App.Div. 327, 137 N.Y.S. 1010 (1912). But see In re Sims' Estate, 225 Miss. 311, 83 So.2d 93 (1955), suggestion of error overruled 225 Miss. 311, 83 So.2d 764, holding that the court had power to protect the remaindermen against dissipation or loss of the "corpus" despite provision in will that life tenant need not give bond or other security.

17. E.g., Underwood v. Underwood, 162 Ala. 553, 50 So. 305, 136 Am.St.Rep. 61 (1909).

18. E.g., Trustees of Presbyterian Church v. Mize, McGuire v. Gallagher, Smith v. Smith, supra note 16.

19. E.g., Tripp v. Krauth, supra note 4; Scott v. Scott, supra note 14; Koplon v. Ko-
plon, supra note 5; Gahan v. Golden, 330 Ill. 624, 162 N.E. 164 (1928); In re Taylor's Estate, 149 Misc. 705, 268 N.Y.S. 70 (1933), affirmed 242 App.Div. 608, 271 N.Y.S. 1057 (1934).

20. E.g., Broome v. King, 10 Ala. 819 (1846) (damages against possessory owner); Isler v. Isler, 88 N.C. 576 (1883) (same); Wintuska v. Peart, 237 Ky. 666, 36 S.W.2d 50 (1931) (damages against third party); Wooten v. Wilmington & Weldon Railroad Co., 128 N.C. 119, 38 S.E. 298, 56 L.R.A. 615 (1901) (same).

21. E.g., Dillen v. Fancher, 193 Ark. 715, 102 S.W.2d 87 (1937); Reed v. Reed, supra note 4; Brown v. Wilson, supra note 4.

22. E.g., Riddle v. Kellum, 8 Ga. 374 (1850); Swindall v. Bradley, 56 N.C. 353 (1857). Ala. Code 1975, § 35–4–171, provides: "The tenant for life in personalty cannot remove it beyond the jurisdiction of this state without the consent of the remainderman. If he attempts to do so, the remainderman or reversioner is entitled to the writ of ne exeat to restrain him."

Chapter 5

CONCURRENT OWNERSHIP REALTY AND PERSONALTY

Table of Sections

§ 5.1   Concurrent Estates and Interests in Realty and Personalty—In General

The English common law has recognized, from an early date, that "concurrent" as well as "several" estates in land can be created. Concurrent estates exist whenever two or more persons have a concurrent and equal right to the possession and use of the same parcel of land.[1] Several forms of concurrent estate could be created at common law: joint tenancy, tenancy by the entirety, tenancy in common, tenancy in coparcenary, and tenancy in partnership. Only the first three survive in the United States. Joint tenancies may still be created in a majority of American jurisdictions, but their creation is no longer favored as it was at common law. Tenancies by the entirety have been abolished in more than half the states. Tenancies in coparcenary have been absorbed into the tenancy in common. The

---

§ 5.1

1. Generally, see 2 Am.L.Prop. §§ 6.1 through 6.26; R. Powell, Real Property chs. 49–52. These common law concurrent interests are dealt with post in Sections 5.1 through 5.13.

tenancy in partnership—a modified form of tenancy in common—has now been eliminated in all states by adoption of the Uniform Partnership Act. The surviving forms of common law concurrent ownership—the tenancy in common, and where not abolished, the joint tenancy and the tenancy by the entirety—can be created in personal property as well as in land.[2]

In addition to the common law forms of concurrent ownership, a form of concurrent ownership called "community property"—derived from the civil law rather than the common law—is recognized (and may co-exist with common law forms) in eight western and southern states.[3]

§ 5.2 Tenancy in Common

The tenancy in common is undoubtedly the most common type of concurrent estate in land at the present time. It appears to have been first recognized by the English courts in the fourteenth century.[1] At that time, the tenancy in common differed from the joint tenancy, which had been recognized by the English courts at an even earlier date, in several important respects. A joint tenancy was characterized by a right of survivorship—i.e., the surviving joint tenant became the sole owner of the property in which the joint tenancy formerly existed [2]—but there was no right of survivorship among tenants in common.[3] And a joint tenancy could exist only where the four "unities" of time, title, interest, and possession were present—i.e., where the co-tenants acquired their undivided interests at the same time and by the same instrument of transfer and where their undivided interests were identical as to fractional shares, quality, quantity, and rights of possession and enjoyment.[4] A tenancy in common, however, required only the "unity" of possession—i.e., that each co-tenant should have an equal right of possession and enjoyment with respect to the entire property.[5]

The unities of time and title were always present when a conveyance was made to two or more persons, and the unities of interest and possession were presumed when the instrument did not provide to the contrary [6]—in which case a joint tenancy would be created. But a conveyance to two or more persons would create a tenancy in common if the instrument gave each named co-tenant a specified undivided interest, whether the fractional inter-

2. In modern times the subject matter of concurrent interests in personalty is likely to be intangible property such as bank accounts and securities rather than tangible personal property.

3. Generally, see 2 Am.L.Prop. §§ 7.1 through 7.36; R. Powell ch. 53. Community property is discussed post in Section 5.14.

§ 5.2

1. See 2 Am.L.Prop. § 6.1 at p. 94.

2. E.g., Wilken v. Young, 144 Ind. 1, 41 N.E. 68 (1895); In re Peterson's Estate, 182 Wash. 29, 45 P.2d 45 (1935). See post Section 5.3 at note 4.

3. E.g., Wolfe v. Wolfe, 207 Miss. 480, 42 So.2d 438 (1949); Burns v. Nolette, 83 N.H. 489, 144 A. 848, 67 A.L.R. 1051 (1929); In re Hoermann's Estate, 234 Wis. 130, 290 N.W. 608, 128 A.L.R. 89 (1940).

4. 2 Bl.Comm. * 180. "The requirement of the four unities necessarily arose as a result of the basic concept [of joint tenancy] rather than as prerequisites to the creation of the estate." 2 Am.L.Prop. § 6.1 at n. 9.

5. 2 Bl.Comm. * 191; Freeman, Cotenancy § 86; 2 Am.L.Prop. § 6.1 at p. 5, § 6.5 at p. 19. Recent cases include Porter v. Porter, 472 So.2d 630 (Ala.1985); Mulsow v. Gerber Energy Corp., 237 Kan. 58, 697 P.2d 1269 (1985); LDDC, Inc. v. Pressley, 71 N.C.App. 431, 322 S.E.2d 416 (1984); Rouse v. Glascam Builders, Inc., 101 Wn.2d 127, 677 P.2d 125 (1984); Osborn v. Warner, 694 P.2d 730 (Wyo.1985).

6. E.g., where the conveyance was "to A and B."

ests of all co-tenants were equal or not,[7] or if the instrument gave some co-tenants estates in fee simple and other co-tenants estates for life,[8] or if the grantor expressed the intent to create a tenancy in common. *A fortiori,* a tenancy in common would be created where different co-tenants received their interests—whether or not identical—at different times by different instruments of transfer.[9]

In the early period of the common law, neither a tenancy in common nor a joint tenancy could be created except by *inter vivos* conveyance. After 1540, either type of concurrent estate could be created by will.[10] A tenancy in coparcenary, rather than a tenancy in common or a joint tenancy, would arise when two or more heirs took real property by descent—i.e., where female heirs inherited because no male heir survived the deceased owner of the fee simple estate, or where male heirs inherited by virtue of the Kentish custom of gavel-kind tenure.[11] An estate in coparcenary, like an estate in joint tenancy, was characterized by the unities of time, title, interest, and possession, but there was no right of survivorship among coparceners.[12] The undivided interest of a deceased coparcener passed to his or her heir (or heirs) by descent. Unlike joint tenants and tenants in common, coparceners could compel partition and thus obtain separate estates in specific parts of the property.[13] Even after the tenancy in common was judicially recognized in the fourteenth century, the power of a coparcener to compel partition was an important feature distinguishing tenancy in coparcenary from tenancy in common prior to 1539, when actions at law to compel partition of tenancies in common and joint tenancies were authorized by statute.[14] Since primogeniture has been completely abolished in the United States and heirs of equal degree, male or female, inherit equally, tenancy in coparcenary and tenancy in common would now seem to be identical for all practical purposes. Very few American cases (even the older ones) mention coparcenary as a separate form of concurrent ownership, and even when they do, it seems substantially the same as tenancy in common.[15] American intestate succession laws often provide expressly that heirs shall take as tenants in common, but even in the absence of such a provision it seems generally to be assumed that heirs take as tenants in common at the present time.

At the present time every American jurisdiction has, by statute, created a presumption in favor of tenancies in common as against joint tenancies, so

---

7. If the fractional interests were unequal, the unity of interest requirement was violated. Even if the fractional interests were equal, a tenancy in common was created "because the gift was to them as separate individuals and not to them as a unit." 2 Am. L.Prop. § 6.1 at p. 5.

8. In such a case, the unity of interest requirement was violated because the quantum of the estates of all the co-tenants was not identical.

9. E.g., where A and B were joint tenants and A conveyed his undivided interest to X, in which case B and X would become tenants in common.

10. By virtue of the Statute of Wills, 32 Hen. VIII, c. 1 (1540).

11. Co.Litt. * 163b, * 164a; 2 Bl.Comm. * 187; 4 Kent, Comm. * 366; 2 Am.L.Prop. § 6.1 at p. 3, § 6.7.

12. E.g., Gilpin v. Hollingsworth, 3 Md. 190 (1852).

13. Bracton, ff. 72 et seq., * 443b; 2 Am. L.Prop. § 6.1 at p. 3.

14. 31 Hen. VIII, c. 1 (1539); 32 Hen. VIII, c. 32 (1540). Prior to 1539, joint tenants and tenants in common could effect a voluntary partition by agreement. See post Section 5.11.

15. See Graham v. Graham, 22 Ky. (6 T.B.Mon.) 561, 17 Am.Dec. 166 (Ky.1828); Donnelly v. Turner, 60 Md. 81 (1882); Gilpin v. Hollingsworth, supra note 12; Phillips v. Wells, 147 Va. 1030, 133 S.E. 581 (1926).

that a transfer to two or more persons, other than husband and wife, in their own right, will create a tenancy in common unless the grantor clearly expresses the intent to create a joint tenancy.[16] If land is transferred to husband and wife in a jurisdiction where tenancies by the entirety have been abolished, the statutory presumption in favor of tenancies in common is applicable. But in a jurisdiction where tenancies by the entirety have not been abolished, a tenancy in common can be created between husband and wife only if the grantor clearly expresses the intent to create a tenancy in common, and a transfer to husband and wife, without more, will create a tenancy by the entirety, as at common law.[17] On the other hand, a conveyance to unmarried persons "as tenants by the entirety" will generally create a tenancy in common even if tenancies by the entirety have not been abolished.[18]

Since the interest of a tenant in common is alienable, as a general rule,[19] a tenant in common may, without the consent of his cotenants, transfer his interest by deed[20] or (pro tanto) by lease,[21] and he may mortgage his interest.[22] Moreover, since survivorship is not an incident of tenancy in common, the interest of a tenant in common may be devised by will and may pass by intestate succession to his heirs.[23]

Since the "unities" of time, title, and interest need not exist with respect to a tenancy in common,[24] tenants in common need not have acquired their interests at the same time, nor from the same source;[25] their estates need not be of the same quantity—e.g., some may be in fee simple and others only for life;[26] their estates need not be of the same quality—e.g., some may be legal and others equitable;[27] and all tenants in common need not have equal

16. See statutes listed in 2 Am.L.Prop. § 6.3 n. 1. Some of these statutes have been in effect since shortly after the American Revolution. The presumption applies whether or not the four unities are present.

17. E.g., Foster v. Schmiedeskamp, 260 Ark. 898, 545 S.W.2d 624 (1977); Campbell County Board of Education v. Boulevard Enterprises, Inc., 360 S.W.2d 744 (Ky.1962); Witzel v. Witzel, 386 P.2d 103 (Wyo.1963). Contra: Carver v. Gilbert, 387 P.2d 928, 32 A.L.R.3d 563 (Alaska 1963).

18. See post Section 5.5 note 11.

19. Restraints on alienation of the interest of a tenant in common are valid to the same extent as restraints upon like estates owned in severalty.

20. E.g., Moore v. Foshee, 251 Ala. 489, 38 So.2d 10 (1948); Wilk v. Vencill, 30 Cal.2d 104, 180 P.2d 351 (1947). A tenant in common cannot, of course, convey more than his own undivided interest, and a deed purporting to convey the entire premises by metes and bounds will only convey his undivided interest. E.g., Swindle v. Curry, 218 Ga. 552, 129 S.E.2d 144 (1962); Schank v. North American Royalties, Inc., 201 N.W.2d 419 (N.D.1972).

21. E.g., Sun Oil Co. v. Oswell, 258 Ala. 326, 62 So.2d 783 (1953); Schank v. North

American Royalties, Inc., supra note 20. Such a lease, of course, only makes the lessee a tenant in common for the lease term, and does not give the lessee an exclusive right to possession. E.g., Cook v. Hollyday, 186 Md. 42, 45 A.2d 768 (1946); Trowbridge v. Donner, 152 Neb. 206, 40 N.W.2d 655 (1950). See Annot., 49 A.L.R.2d 797 (1956).

22. E.g., Shreve v. Harvey, 74 N.J.Eq. 336, 70 A. 671 (Ch.1908); Z.V. Pate, Inc. v. Kollock, 202 S.C. 522, 25 S.E.2d 728 (1943).

23. 2 Am.L.Prop. § 6.10 at p. 46; 4 Thompson, Real Prop. § 1793 at p. 137, § 1795 at p. 145.

24. See authorities cited supra, note 5.

25. Thus, e.g., a tenancy in common will arise when one joint tenant "severs" the joint tenancy by conveying his interest to a "stranger." In such a case, obviously, the grantee obtains his interest at a different time and from a different source than the non-conveying joint tenant(s). For more on severance of joint tenancies, see post Section 5.3.

26. E.g., American Bank & Trust Co. v. Continental Investment Corp., 202 Okl. 341, 213 P.2d 861 (1949). See 2 Bl.Comm. * 191.

27. Comer v. Landrum, 277 S.W. 743 (Tex. Civ.App.1925).

fractional interests.[28] Only the "unity" of possession is required—i.e., all tenants in common must have equal rights of possession and use when the concurrent interests are "legal." [29]

When a tenancy in common arises by intestate succession, the shares of the cotenants are determined by the intestate succession law; in many, but not all cases, the shares will be equal. A deed or will may, of course, expressly provide that the interests of the cotenants shall be unequal. If the instrument does not specify the shares of each cotenant, it will be presumed that they take equal undivided interests,[30] but this presumption may be rebutted by proof, e.g., that the cotenants contributed unequal amounts toward the purchase price of the property and there is neither a family relationship among the cotenants nor any evidence of donative intent on the part of those who contributed more than their pro rata amounts toward the purchase price.[31] Although each tenant in common has an equal right to the possession and use of the entire property without regard to the quantum of his interest,[32] it will be necessary to determine the relative shares of the tenants upon transfer of some or all of their interests and when a voluntary or court-ordered partition takes place.

Persons owning undivided interests in subsurface minerals whether in fee simple or for a term of years, are usually tenants in common,[33] although they may be joint tenants if the intent to create a joint tenancy is expressed in the creating instrument and the requisite "unities" are present. But one who is not entitled to possession or to a present beneficial interest cannot be a tenant in common; [34] thus remaindermen or reversioners cannot be tenants in common either with a life tenant or among themselves,[35] although they may, like tenants in common, be subject to fiduciary duties among themselves.[36]

Although survivorship is not an incident of tenancies in common, many cases assert that the right of survivorship may be annexed to a tenancy in

28. E.g., Van Veen v. Van Veen, 213 Iowa 323, 238 N.W. 718 (1931); Roach v. Roach, 406 S.W.2d 731 (Ky.1966). See 2 Bl.Comm. * 191; 2 Am.L.Prop. § 6.5 at p. 19; 4 Thompson, Real Prop. § 173 at n. 30; Challis, Real Prop. 370 (3d ed. 1911). Equal shares will be presumed if shares are not specified in the deed or will. For a recent case, see Sanders v. Knapp, 674 P.2d 385 (Colo.App.1983).

29. See 2 Am.L.Prop. § 6.5; 2 Bl.Comm. * 191; Spencer v. Austin, 38 Vt. 258 (1865). See also Taylor v. Millard, 118 N.Y. 244, 23 N.E. 376, 6 L.R.A. 667 (1890). Each tenant in common holds an undivided fractional interest in each particle of the common property. State v. Hoskins, 357 Mo. 377, 208 S.W.2d 221 (1948); Succession of LeBlanc, 577 So.2d 105 (La.App.1991).

30. E.g., Caito v. United California Bank, 20 Cal.3d 694, 144 Cal.Rptr. 751, 576 P.2d 466 (1978); In re Estate of Anders, 238 Iowa 344, 26 N.W.2d 67 (1947); Hoover v. Haller, 146 Neb. 697, 21 N.W.2d 450 (1946).

31. People v. Varel, 351 Ill. 96, 184 N.E. 209 (1932); Williams v. Monzingo, 235 Iowa

434, 16 N.W.2d 619, 156 A.L.R. 508 (1944); Taylor v. Taylor, 310 Mich. 541, 17 N.W.2d 745 (1945); Succession of LeBlanc, supra note 29.

But see Miller v. Miller, 101 Or.App. 371, 790 P.2d 1184 (1990) (where cotenants expressly agreed that their shares should be equal, it was immaterial that one cotenant paid two-thirds of the purchase price when the property was acquired).

32. Supra note 29.

33. E.g., Skelly Oil Co. v. Wickham, 202 F.2d 442 (10th Cir.1953) (fee simple); Dampier v. Polk, 214 Miss. 65, 58 So.2d 44 (1952) (fee simple); Petroleum Exploration Corp. v. Hensley, 284 S.W.2d 828 (Ky.1955) (term of years).

34. Le Bus v. Le Bus, 269 S.W.2d 506 (Tex. Civ.App.1954) refused n.r.e.

35. E.g., Givens v. Givens, 387 S.W.2d 851 (Ky.1965); Cline v. Henry, 239 S.W.2d 205 (Tex.Civ.App.1951), refused n.r.e.

36. Givens v. Givens, supra note 35; Wilson v. Linder, 21 Idaho 576, 123 P. 487, 42 L.R.A.(N.S.) 242 (1912).

common if the instrument creating the tenancy in common so provides.[37] This means, apparently, that an instrument containing an express provision for survivorship will be held to create a tenancy in common for the lives of the cotenants, with a contingent remainder (usually in fee simple) in favor of the surviving cotenant. This result has been reached in a case where the conveyance was "to A and B and to the survivor of them"[38] although in jurisdictions where joint tenancies may still be created it would seem that the quoted language should simply create a joint tenancy.[39] The same result has also been reached in cases where an express attempt to create a joint tenancy is frustrated either because joint tenancies have been abolished by statute or because one of the requisite "unities" is lacking.[40]

As previously indicated,[41] the form of real estate ownership peculiar to "condominiums" is characterized by individual ownership of each unit (or apartment) and concurrent ownership of the condominium's common elements. Usually the unit owner's interest in the dwelling unit itself is said to be a fee simple, although it has been suggested that it would be advantageous to regard the unit owner's interest in the air space within his unit as some kind of easement.[42] The concurrent ownership of the common elements—the framework, walls, and roofs of buildings, basement areas in buildings, courtyards, grounds, and the like—seems invariably to be a tenancy in common.[43]

Condominium enabling legislation usually prohibits any action by individual unit owners to compel partition of the common elements and requires the unit owners to be organized into an association empowered to control and manage the entire condominium development, including common ele-

37. E.g., Mitchell v. Frederick, 166 Md. 42, 170 A. 733, 92 A.L.R. 1412 (1934) (dictum); Papke v. Pearson, 203 Minn. 130, 134, 280 N.W. 183, 184–185 (1938) (dictum); Anson v. Murphy, 149 Neb. 716, 32 N.W.2d 271 (1948); Burns v. Nolette, 83 N.H. 489, 144 A. 848, 67 A.L.R. 1051 (1929) (personalty); Pope v. Burgess, 230 N.C. 323, 325, 53 S.E.2d 159, 160 (1949). Accord: 4 Thompson, Real Prop. § 1793 at n. 36, § 1796 at p. 149. But see Hershy v. Clark, 35 Ark. 17, 37 Am.Rep. 1 (1879).

38. Bonner v. Pugh, 376 So.2d 1354 (Ala. 1979); Rowerdink v. Carothers, 334 Mich. 454, 54 N.W.2d 715 (1952), noted, 51 Mich.L.Rev. 756 (1953); Papke v. Pearson, supra note 37; Davis v. Davis, 223 S.C. 182, 75 S.E.2d 46 (1953). See also Hass v. Hass, 248 Wis. 212, 21 N.W.2d 398 (1946), rehearing denied 248 Wis. 212, 22 N.W.2d 151 (1946). But see Wright v. Smith, 257 Ala. 665, 60 So.2d 688 (1952); Hart v. Kanaye Nagasawa, 218 Cal. 685, 24 P.2d 815 (1933).

39. Cf. 2 H. Tiffany, Real Prop. § 424 (3d ed.): "[W]hen one makes a gift to two or more with the right of survivorship, it appears to be a reasonable conclusion that he has in mind an indestructible right of survivorship. The view that there is in such case a tenancy in common for life with a contingent remainder in favor of the survivor, or even that there is a tenancy in common in fee simple with an executory limitation in favor of the survivor, might seem more in accord with the intention of the grantor or testator."

40. E.g., Erickson v. Erickson, 167 Or. 1, 115 P.2d 172 (1941); Holbrook v. Holbrook, 240 Or. 567, 403 P.2d 12 (1965). See also Hass v. Hass, supra note 38. In this sort of case, where the grantor expressed the intent to create a joint tenancy, it is hard to see why the right of survivorship should be indestructible, since at common the right of survivorship could be destroyed by a transfer which "severed" the joint tenancy.

41. Ante Section 2.2.

42. 4B R. Powell, Real Property ¶ 633.8[4], arguing that the unit owner's "right to occupy the air space enclosed by his apartment * * * can be sufficient although it is classified as an easement appurtenant to the apartment wall, floors, and ceilings enclosing the space." The same authority also concedes, however, that "it should make little difference to the apartment owner whether his interest is described as ownership in fee simple of the space or an exclusive easement to occupy the space so long as the building stands."

43. 4B R. Powell, Real Property ¶ 633.20.

See Rouse v. Glascam Builders, Inc., 101 Wn.2d 127, 677 P.2d 125 (1984).

ments.[44] American condominium enabling acts usually list specific matters that shall be included in the condominium association's by-laws—e.g., building and common area maintenance, budgeting, assessment and collection of maintenance charges, approval and financing of capital improvements, and restrictions on use and on the transfer of individual units.[45] In addition, the statutes generally include provisions governing cases where a structure in a condominium development is totally or substantially destroyed.[46]

Provisions restricting the transfer of condominium units—usually by means of pre-emptive "rights of first refusal"—and provisions as to the effect of total or substantial destruction of buildings in which individual units are located may raise serious problems under the Rule Against Perpetuities. This was briefly considered ante in Section 3.18. Prohibitions against partition of the common elements are briefly considered post in Section 5.11. Provisions restricting the use of condominium units draw on the law of real covenants and equitable servitudes, which is dealt with at some length post in Chapter 8. Provisions with respect to the collection of maintenance charges assessed by the condominium association rely mainly on imposition of a lien upon the unit owner's entire property interest.[47] However, if personal liability is to be imposed on unit owners for failure to pay maintenance charges, the law of real covenants and equitable servitudes will again be implicated.

§ 5.3 Joint Tenancy—In General

As early as the thirteenth century the form of concurrent ownership known as joint tenancy was recognized.[1] For purposes of tenure and survivorship, each joint tenant was seized of the entire estate in which the joint tenancy existed, whether it was an estate in fee simple, in fee tail, or only for lives.[2] But for purposes of alienation, each joint tenant had only a fractional interest in the entire estate.[3] The joint tenancy was the preferred form of concurrent ownership because one of its inseparable incidents was the right of survivorship—i.e., the last surviving joint tenant became the sole owner of the entire estate in severalty.[4] The right of survivorship was not a

---

44. Id. ¶ 633.6[2].

45. Ibid.

46. Id. ¶ 633.12.

47. Id. ¶ 633.26[1].

§ 5.3

1. 2 Am.L.Prop. § 6.1 at p. 3.

For a good summary of the historical origins and characteristics of joint tenancies, see Spessard v. Spessard, 64 Md.App. 83, 494 A.2d 701 (1985).

2. Co.Litt. * 186a; Bl.Comm. * 182; 4 Kent, Comm. * 360, note (a); Challis, Real Prop. 367 (3d ed. 1911); 2 Am.L.Prop. § 6.1 at p. 4; 4 H. Tiffany, Real Prop. § 418 at p. 196 (3d ed. 1939).

3. Ibid.

4. Litt., Tenures § 280; 2 Bl.Comm. * 183; 4 Kent, Comm. * 360; 2 H. Tiffany, Real Prop. § 419 (3d ed. 1939). See, e.g., Henderson v.

Henderson, 59 Ariz. 53, 121 P.2d 437 (1942); McDonald v. Morley, 15 Cal.2d 409, 101 P.2d 690, 129 A.L.R. 810 (1940); In re Brose's Estate, 416 Pa. 386, 206 A.2d 301 (1965); Porter v. Porter, 472 So.2d 630 (Ala.1985); Wiggins v. Parson, 446 So.2d 169 (Fla.App.1984); Neaderhiser v. State Dept. of Social & Rehabilitation Services, 9 Kan.App.2d 115, 673 P.2d 462 (1983).

As previously noted (ante § 5.1 note 2), joint tenancies may be created in personalty as well as in realty. It is now very common for one person to deposit funds in either a savings account or a checking account in his own name and that of another, subject to withdrawal by either party. By the terms of the bank's signature card or its savings account book or certificate of deposit, the account is described as "joint" or the co-creditors are described as "joint tenants." There is also frequently a provision that upon the death of either co-creditor the balance in the account

future interest like a reversion or a remainder, however. The last surviving joint tenant became the sole owner because his original interest in the entire estate was left as the only interest after all the other joint tenants died.[5]

Although joint tenants had individual fractional interests, the essence of a joint tenancy was that there was a single, though concurrent, estate in the joint tenants as a unit.[6] From this basic concept there arose the doctrine that the four "unities of time, title, interest, and possession" were essential; i.e., that all the joint tenants must acquire their interests the same time [7] and by the same instrument (deed or will); and that the interests of the co-tenants must be identical as to individual fractional shares, quantum of estate,[8] and quality of estate (legal or equitable),[9] carrying with them equal rights of possession and enjoyment.

shall be payable to the "survivor." Such "joint and survivor" accounts have given rise to an enormous amount of litigation—usually focussing on the question whether the depositor really intended to make a gift of any present interest to the person named as co-creditor and the question whether a true joint tenancy with right of survivorship has been created. There has been a good deal of legislation designed primarily to protect the bank if it allows either of the co-creditors to withdraw or pays the balance to the survivor. But such legislation generally does little to resolve the questions that are most often litigated between the co-creditors or between the surviving co-creditor and the personal representative of the deceased co-creditor. As might be expected, the results reached by the courts in different jurisdictions are not in accord. As one commentator has pointed out,

"The difficulty the courts have had with joint accounts can be traced primarily to the insistence on forcing an essentially novel ownership arrangement into the mold of an existing set of legal principles. The joint account is fundamentally neither a common law joint tenancy, an ordinary inter vivos gift, a trust nor a will, yet it partakes of the features of all of these." Hines, Personal Property Joint Tenancies: More Law, Fact, and Fancy, 54 Minn.L.Rev. 509, 531 (1970).

Detailed treatment of joint bank accounts is beyond the scope of this book. Recent cases illustrative of the difficulties that courts have had in dealing with the legal rights arising when such accounts are created include the following: Citizens Bank of Batesville v. Estate of Pettyjohn, 282 Ark. 222, 667 S.W.2d 657 (1984); Morton v. McComb, 281 Ark. 125, 662 S.W.2d 471 (1983); In re Estate of Gainer, 466 So.2d 1055 (Fla.1985); In re Estate of Steppuhn, 221 Neb. 329, 377 N.W.2d 83 (1985).

5. E.g., Kleemann v. Sheridan, 75 Ariz. 311, 256 P.2d 553 (1953); Klajbor v. Klajbor, 406 Ill. 513, 94 N.E.2d 502 (1950); United Trust Co. v. Pyke, 199 Kan. 1, 427 P.2d 67 (1967); Harms v. Sprague, 105 Ill.2d 215, 85 Ill.Dec. 331, 473 N.E.2d 930 (1984).

6. "This is apparently the meaning of the statement in the books that each tenant holds 'per my et per tout' * * *." 2 H. Tiffany, Real Prop. § 418 at p. 196 (3d ed. 1939). Tiffany also says that the "doctrine of survivorship [in joint tenancy] appears to be the result of, or at least associated with, the theory that the joint tenants together own but one estate, a theory which, rigidly applied, would recognize no distinct interest in one to pass on to his heirs or devisees, his claim being, as against the others, merely extinguished in that case. The survivor takes no new title by survivorship, but holds under the deed by virtue of which he was originally seized of the whole." Id. § 419 at p. 198.

7. The requirement of unity of time was held not applicable, however, where the several co-tenants took by virtue of an executory limitation operating under the Statute of Uses or Statute of Wills. Sugden's Gilbert on Uses 135, note 10; 2 Jarman, Wills 118; Fearne, Contingent Remainders 313.

Modern cases generally state that the "four unities" are essential to creation of a joint tenancy. See, e.g., Harms v. Sprague, supra note 5. But modern cases also hold, in particular situations, that the "four unities" are not essential. See infra note 38; see also Nunn v. Keith, 289 Ala. 518, 524, 268 So.2d 792, 797 (1972), followed in Porter v. Porter, 472 So.2d 630 (Ala.1985).

8. Thus there can be no joint tenancy if one co-tenant has a fee simple and another has only a life estate. But an estate may be given to joint tenants for life, with a remainder to one of them in fee simple, in which case, if the one who has the remainder is not the survivor, the survivor will hold the entire property for the balance of his life, and will then be succeeded by the heirs or other successors of the remainderman as owners in fee simple. Co.Litt. * 188a; 2 Bl.Comm. * 181; 4 Kent, Comm. 357.

9. That an equitable joint tenancy can be created, see Edmonds v. Commissioner of Internal Revenue, 90 F.2d 14 (9th Cir.1937), certiorari denied 302 U.S. 713, 58 S.Ct. 32, 82

At common law any conveyance to two or more persons, not husband and wife, without further specification, would create a joint tenancy.[10] The same rule was applied to devises to two or more persons after the power to devise legal estates in land was conferred on owners of freehold estates in 1540.[11] But a joint tenancy could not arise by inheritance. As previously indicated,[12] when there was no male heir in closer or equal degree, female heirs would take concurrent estates as coparceners rather than as joint tenants.

An express conveyance or devise of an undivided interest to each of two or more persons would not create a joint tenancy at common law, even if the undivided interests were equal, because the transfer was to them as separate individuals rather than as a unit;[13] this violated the fundamental requirement that all joint tenants must hold "per tout" as well as "per my." And a joint tenancy would not result from either the conveyance of an entire estate to the grantor and another (or others) expressly as "joint tenants" or the conveyance of an undivided half interest to another.[14] In either case, the "unities of time and title" would be lacking because the intended joint tenants (including the grantor) would acquire their individual undivided interests at different times and would hold by different titles (i.e., the sources of their titles would not be the same).[15]

Although joint tenancies were favored by the English courts, the common law joint tenancy has been abolished by statute in some American jurisdictions and has been significantly modified in most of the other American jurisdictions.[16] But even where the joint tenancy has been abolished, courts have held that a transfer "to A and B, and to the survivor of them,"[17] or "to A and B as joint tenants, and to the survivor of them,"[18] or

L.Ed. 551 (1937); Lowry v. Lowry, 541 S.W.2d 128 (Tenn.1976), note, 7 Mem.St.L.Rev. 332 (1977).

10. Co.Litt. * 70b; 2 Bl.Comm. * 193; 2 H. Tiffany, Real Prop. § 421 at p. 201 (3d ed. 1939); 2 Am.L.Prop. § 6.21 at p. 3. It was unnecessary to say "as joint tenants" or to provide expressly for survivorship. Joint tenancy was apparently preferred for feudal reasons—i.e., because a feudal lord would prefer that each estate held of him by two or more tenants in a given tract should be a single estate continuing until the death of the survivor.

11. Statute of Wills, 32 Hen. VIII, c. 1 (1536).

12. See ante Section 5.2 between notes 10 and 11.

13. See 2 Am.L.Prop. § 6.1 at pp. 4–5.

14. E.g., Pegg v. Pegg, 165 Mich. 228, 130 N.W. 617, 33 L.R.A.(N.S.) 166 (1911); In re Walker's Estate, 340 Pa. 13, 16 A.2d 28, 132 A.L.R. 628 (1940), noted, 83 U.Pa.L.Rev. 681 (1935); Moe v. Krupke, 255 Wis. 33, 37 N.W.2d 865 (1949)—all holding that a tenancy in common was created.

15. Thus, in order to create a joint tenancy, the grantor had to convey the entire estate to a "straw man" who, by prior arrangement, would then convey it back to the grantor and another.

16. See, e.g., Oregon Rev.Stat. § 93.180 (abolishes joint tenancies, but see cases cited infra note 18); Ariz.Rev.Stat. § 33–431 (abolishes joint tenancies, except as to grants or devises in trust, or to executors, or to husbands and wives, but also provides that a deed or will may, "by express words, vest the estate in the survivor upon the death of a grantee or devisee"); Ill.—S.H.A. ch. 76, ¶¶ 1, 2 (abolishes joint tenancies, except as to executors and trustees, or where a will expresses intent to create a joint tenancy with survivorship in personal property); Kentucky Rev.Stat. §§ 381.120, 381.130 (abolishes joint tenancy, except as to executors and trustees, or "when it manifestly appears from the tenor of the instrument that the part of the one dying should belong to the others"); Ga.Code § 85–1002 (transfer shall create "interests in common without survivorship" unless intent to create joint tenancy is expressed); Mass.Gen. Laws Ann. c. 184, § 7 (same).

17. E.g., Houghton v. Brantingham, 86 Conn. 630, 86 A. 664 (1913); Withers v. Barnes, 95 Kan. 798, 149 P. 691, Ann.Cas. 1917B 55 (1915); Molloy v. Barkley, 219 Ky. 671, 294 S.W. 168 (1927).

the like, will create a concurrent estate for the life of the shorter-lived co-tenant, with an indestructible contingent remainder in fee simple to the survivor.

In many states there are statutes that do not purport to abolish joint tenancies, but which provide in substance that a transfer to two or more persons in their own right shall create a tenancy in common unless the transferor indicates that the transferees shall take as joint tenants. These statutes usually declare that such a transfer shall create a tenancy in common unless the transferees are "expressly declared to be joint tenants," [19] or are directed to take "as joint tenants and not as tenants in common," [20] or the instrument "expressly provides that the property is to be held in joint tenancy," [21] or "jointly with survivorship," [22] or some combination of these or similar expressions of intent.[23]

18. E.g., Erickson v. Erickson, 167 Or. 1, 115 P.2d 172 (1941); Holbrook v. Holbrook, 240 Or. 567, 403 P.2d 12 (1965); Gilbert v. Brown, 71 Or.App. 809, 693 P.2d 1330 (1985), review denied 300 Or. 367, 712 P.2d 109 (1985). But see In re Marriage of Leversee, 156 Cal.App.3d 891, 203 Cal.Rptr. 481 (1984) (statutory presumption in favor of community property arising when residence is acquired by spouses during marriage did not apply where spouses acquired property before marriage, and there was, instead, a presumption in favor of joint tenancy where parties took title "as joint tenants" and there was no express agreement to convert ownership into community property form; erroneous description of grantees as husband and wife had no legal effect).

19. Ark.Stat. § 50–411.

20. 25 Del.Code Ann. § 701.

21. Md.Code Real Property, § 2–117; Mont.Code Ann. § 70–1–307 (must "expressly" purport to create "joint tenancy"; no reference to "survivorship" expressly required); 60 Okl.Stat.Ann. § 74 (same). See Hill v. Hill, 672 P.2d 1149 (Okl.1983) ("since legislation neither defined the term ["joint tenancy"] nor used language indicating a contrary intent, it was to be presumed the term was used in its technical common law sense").

22. Official Code Ga.Ann. § 85–1002.

23. The Georgia and Massachusetts statutes are among the most comprehensive. The Georgia statute, supra notes 16, 22, provides that a transfer to two or more persons creates "interests in common without survivorship" unless the transfer is expressly made to the transferees as "joint tenants," "joint tenants and not as tenants in common," or "joint tenants with survivorship," or says they shall take "jointly with survivorship," or the instrument contains essentially the same language, in which case it "shall create a joint tenancy * * * that may be severed as to the interest of any owner by his lifetime transfer of all or part of his interest." Mass.Gen.Laws Ann. c.

184, § 7 (1977) provides that a transfer to two or more persons shall create a tenancy in common "unless it is expressed * * * that the grantees or devisees shall take jointly, or as joint tenants, or to them and the survivor of them, or unless it manifestly appears from the tenor of the instrument that it was intended to create an estate in joint tenancy." Kan. Stat.Ann. § 58–501 provides that "real or personal property granted or devised to two or more persons * * * shall create in them a tenancy in common * * * unless the language used in such grant or devise makes it clear that a joint tenancy was intended to be created," except where the grant or devise is to trustees. Ohio Rev.Code § 5302.17 provides a statutory deed form for creation of a "survivorship tenancy"; id. § 5202.20 provides that "any deed or will that shows a clear intent to create a survivorship tenancy shall be liberally construed to do so." These statutory provisions became effective April 4, 1985. Since the cotenancy is called a "survivorship tenancy" instead of a "joint tenancy," it is likely that there must be a clear reference to "survivorship" when the statutory form is not employed. Va.Code 1950, §§ 55–20, 55–21 provides that a conveyance to "joint tenants" without more creates a tenancy in common, but a conveyance to "joint tenants with right of survivorship" is effective according to its terms. See Jones v. Conwell, 227 Va. 176, 314 S.E.2d 61 (1984).

Many of the statutes reversing the common law presumption in favor of joint tenancies were originally enacted soon after the American Revolution. They are all based on a policy judgment that the reasons for the common law presumption in favor of joint tenancies disappeared with the demise of the feudal system, and a further policy judgment that the right of survivorship incident to joint tenancies is often productive of injustice and should not be recognized unless the transferor's intent to create such a right is clear. See 2 H. Tiffany, Real Prop. § 424 at n. 47 (3d ed. 1939).

Where the statute sets out several alternatives, and/or indicates that any language showing the intent to create a joint tenancy will be sufficient to overcome the new statutory presumption in favor of tenancies in common, the draftsman has substantial leeway as to the language he will employ to create a joint tenancy. Even where the statutory language is rather restrictive, it is generally unnecessary to use the exact words contained in the statute in order to indicate the intent to create a joint tenancy.[24] But the phrase "to A and B jointly," although it has sometimes been held sufficient for this purpose,[25] has often been held insufficient[26] and therefore should be avoided. And there is also a division of authority in those cases where the transfer is "to A and B and the survivor of them." In some cases, the survivorship language has been held to show the intent to create a joint tenancy, since survivorship is the most salient characteristic of the common law joint tenancy.[27] In other cases, however, it has been held that the express provision for survivorship results in creation of a concurrent estate for the life of the first transferee to die, with an indestructible contingent remainder in fee simple to the survivor.[28] In several states, the courts have reached the same conclusion even where the transfer is "to A and B as joint tenants and to the survivor of them."[29] But the prevailing rule is that such language creates a joint tenancy, in accordance with the clearly expressed intention of the transferor.[30]

24. E.g., Blumenthal v. Culver, 116 Iowa 326, 89 N.W. 1116 (1902); Petition of Buzenac, 50 R.I. 429, 148 A. 321 (1930); Palmer v. Flint, 156 Me. 103, 161 A.2d 837 (1960); Moxley v. Vaughn, 148 Mont. 30, 416 P.2d 536 (1966); Kilgore v. Parrott, 197 Okl. 77, 168 P.2d 886 (1946). See also Neb.Rev.Stat. § 76–205, applicable to all kinds of transfers, which simply provides that "the true intent of the parties" shall be controlling.

25. E.g., Case v. Owen, 139 Ind. 22, 38 N.E. 395 (1894); Murray v. Kator, 221 Mich. 101, 190 N.W. 667 (1922). But see Taylor v. Taylor, 310 Mich. 541, 17 N.W.2d 745, 157 A.L.R. 559 (1945) (doubting the *Murray* case).

26. E.g., Porter v. Porter, 472 So.2d 630 (Ala.1985); Switzer v. Pratt, 237 Iowa 788, 23 N.W.2d 837 (1946); Cohen v. Herbert, 205 Mo. 537, 104 S.W. 84 (1907); Overhelser v. Lackey, 207 N.Y. 229, 100 N.E. 738 (1913); Weber v. Nedin, 210 Wis. 39, 246 N.W. 307 (1933) (dictum). These decisions seem to rest on the idea that "jointly" is ambiguous and is as likely to be used to create a tenancy in common as a joint tenancy.

27. E.g., Wood v. Logue, 167 Iowa 436, 149 N.W. 613, Ann.Cas. 1917B 116 (1914); Blaine v. Dow, 111 Me. 480, 89 A. 1126 (1914); Weber v. Nadin, supra note 26. Presumably such a transfer would create a joint tenancy in states where a statute abolishes joint tenancies except when survivorship is expressly provided for. See, e.g., West's Fla.Stat.Ann. § 689.15.

28. See cases cited ante Section 5.2, note 37. Cf. Gagnon v. Pronovost, 96 N.H. 154, 71 A.2d 747 (1949) (deed to A and B "and to the

survivors of them" created tenancy in common).

29. E.g., Jones v. Snyder, 218 Mich. 446, 188 N.W. 505 (1922); Ames v. Cheyne, 290 Mich. 215, 287 N.W. 439 (1939), noted, 38 Mich.L.Rev. 875 (1940); Hunter v. Hunter, 320 S.W.2d 529 (Mo.1959); Williams v. Studstill, 251 Ga. 466, 306 S.E.2d 633 (1983).

The Alabama court has had a checkered history on this point. In Bernhard v. Bernhard, 278 Ala. 240, 177 So.2d 565 (1965), the court held that language which, at common law, would create a joint tenancy would, instead, create a tenancy in common with an "indestructible contingent remainder" to the survivor by virtue of a statute abolishing joint tenancy. *Bernhard* was overruled by Nunn v. Keith, 289 Ala. 518, 268 So.2d 792 (1972), where the court held that a "true joint tenancy" could still be created by using express survivorship language, in which case the right of survivorship could be destroyed by conveyance of either joint tenant's interest to a third party. Subsequently, in Durant v. Hamrick, 409 So.2d 731 (Ala.1981), the court held that *Bernhard* did not apply where a conveyance was made to two or more persons "as tenants in common, and to the survivor," in which case the word "survivor" created an "indestructible contingent remainder." Then, in Johnson v. Keener, 425 So.2d 1108 (Ala.1983), appeal after remand 447 So.2d 689 (1984), the court held that *Nunn* should not be applied retroactively, and that *Bernhard* would be controlling as to conveyances made before the decision in *Nunn*.

30. E.g., Palmer v. Flint, supra note 24.

Since the right of survivorship incident to a common law joint tenancy is destructible by "severance"—i.e., by transfer of one joint tenant's interest to a stranger—judicial recognition of an indestructible contingent remainder when there is express provision for a right of survivorship is quite inconsistent with the common law concept of joint tenancy. And it is also quite inconsistent with the policy underlying the legislation abolishing joint tenancy or creating a presumption in favor of tenancy in common, since it is clear that such legislation was based upon hostility toward the right of survivorship in a common law joint tenancy.[31]

Statutes abolishing joint tenancies or creating a presumption in favor of tenancy in common generally provide that any concurrent estate vested in executors or trustees shall be held in joint tenancy.[32] And even where the statutes do not expressly provide for trustees and executors to hold in joint tenancy, joint tenancy has generally been recognized when land is transferred to multiple executors or trustees.[33] In such cases, a right of survivorship is highly desirable so that the estate or trust may be administered without interruption when one fiduciary dies.

In jurisdictions where tenancies by the entirety have been abolished, a transfer to "H and W [husband and wife] as joint tenants, with right of survivorship" will create a joint tenancy between H and W if it would have done so had they not been husband and wife.[34] But in jurisdictions where tenancies by the entirety can still be created, the cases are divided as to whether such a transfer creates a joint tenancy[35] or a tenancy by the entirety.[36]

The old common law rule that a grantor could not create a joint tenancy by conveying to himself and another (or others), or by conveying an undivided interest to another, generally has been evaded by conveying the entire estate to a third party "straw man" who, by prearrangement, then conveys the estate back to the entire group of intended joint tenants (including the grantor). In some states, the need to use a "straw man" has been eliminated by statutes[37] or judicial decisions[38] allowing the creation of joint tenancies

31. "The effect of * * * [construing language of survivorship to create concurrent life estates with an indestructible contingent remainder to the survivor] is to swing back the pendulum even further than the common-law joint tenancy in upholding survivorship * * *." 4 G. Thompson, Real Prop. § 1775 at p. 14.

32. E.g., Ariz.Rev.Stat. § 33–431; Ill.—S.H.A. ch. 76, ¶ 2; Kentucky Rev.Stat. § 381.-130.

33. E.g., Saunders v. Schmaelzle, 49 Cal. 59 (1874); Stout v. Van Zante, 109 Or. 430, 220 P. 414 (1923); Franklin Inst. for Savings v. People's Savings Bank, 14 R.I. 632 (1885).

34. In such a case, the fact that H and W are husband and wife is not relevant in determining whether they take as true joint tenants or as concurrent owners for life with a contingent remainder in fee simple to the survivor.

35. E.g., Wilken v. Young, 144 Ind. 1, 41 N.E. 68 (1895); Kolker v. Gorn, 193 Md. 391, 67 A.2d 258 (1949); Witzel v. Witzel, 386 P.2d 103 (Wyo.1963).

36. E.g., Naler v. Ballew, 81 Ark. 328, 99 S.W. 72 (1907); Kollar v. Kollar, 155 Fla. 705, 21 So.2d 356 (1945); Hoag v. Hoag, 213 Mass. 50, 99 N.E. 521 (1912); Fulton v. Katsowney, 342 Mass. 503, 174 N.E.2d 366 (1961); Goethe v. Gmelin, 256 Mich. 112, 239 N.W. 347 (1931). But see Fekkes v. Hughes, 354 Mass. 303, 237 N.E.2d 19 (1968); Knight v. Knight, 62 Tenn. App. 70, 458 S.W.2d 803 (1970).

37. E.g., Mass.Gen.Laws Ann. c. 184, § 8; Mich.Comp.Laws Ann. § 565.49; Ohio Rev. Code § 5302.18; Wyo.Stat.1977, § 34–1–140.

38. E.g., Miller v. Riegler, 243 Ark. 251, 419 S.W.2d 599 (1967), noted, 23 Ark.L.Rev. 136 (1969) (personal property); Strout v. Burgess, 144 Me. 263, 68 A.2d 241 (1949); Crowell v. Milligan, 157 Neb. 127, 59 N.W.2d 346 (1953); Therrien v. Therrien, 94 N.H. 66, 46 A.2d 538 (1946).

by direct conveyance in such cases. Such statutes and decisions effectively eliminate, *pro tanto,* the requirement that there be unity of time and title in joint tenancies.[39]

The distinguishing feature of the joint tenancy is the right of survivorship incident to each joint tenant's present, undivided interest. If there are more than two joint tenants, the death of one increases the individual fractional shares of the survivors. In any case, the ultimate survivor becomes the sole owner in severalty.[40] If the ultimate survivor acquires a fee simple estate, he can convey it *inter vivos* or devise it by will,[41] and it will pass to his heirs if he dies intestate. If the ultimate survivor acquires only a life estate, it will, of course, terminate when he dies.

§ 5.4   Joint Tenancy—Conversion Into Tenancy in Common by Severance

As a general rule, the undivided fractional interest of each joint tenant is freely alienable without the consent of the other joint tenant(s).[1] But the transfer of one joint tenant's interest to a stranger will "sever" the interest transferred from the joint tenancy and defeat the survivorship right(s) of the other joint tenant(s) as to the interest transferred.[2] Thus a transfer of the

---

39. Although the "four unities" are still generally stated to be essential to creation of a joint tenancy, they have often been held unnecessary in particular situations. See supra note 7. Moreover, courts have frequently held that the "unity of possession" may exist even though by express agreement between the joint tenants one of them retains the exclusive right to the possession of, and/or income from, the jointly owned property. See, e.g., Miller v. Riegler, supra note 38; Tindall v. Yeats, 392 Ill. 502, 64 N.E.2d 903 (1946); Neaderhiser v. State Dept. of Social & Rehabilitation Services, 9 Kan.App.2d 115, 673 P.2d 462 (1983); Jones v. Cox, 629 S.W.2d 511 (Mo.App.1981).

40. E.g., Erwin v. Felter, 238 Ill. 36, 119 N.E. 926, L.R.A. 1918E 776 (1918); Switzer v. Pratt, 237 Iowa 788, 23 N.W.2d 837 (1946); Nussbacher v. Manderfeld, 64 Wyo. 55, 186 P.2d 548 (1947). The right of the survivor takes precedence over any devise or bequest made by the deceased joint tenant, since the latter has no interest that can outlive him. E.g., Cranston v. Winters, 238 N.W.2d 647 (N.D.1976); Bassler v. Rewodlinski, 130 Wis. 26, 109 N.W. 1032, 7 L.R.A.(N.S.) 701 (1906). In the event of simultaneous death of two or more joint tenants, Uniform Simultaneous Death Act § 3 provides that the property shall be divided into as many equal shares as there were joint tenants, and that each one's share shall be distributed as if he had survived the others. *Sed quaere* whether evidence is admissible to show that, in equity, the shares should be unequal. See In re Strong's Will, 171 Misc. 445, 12 N.Y.S.2d 544 (1939) (tenancy by the entirety; presumption of equal shares may be rebutted by proof of unequal contributions).

41. A will executed by the surviving joint tenant during his co-tenant's lifetime is effective to pass the estate in severalty resulting from survivorship, without the need to republish the will after the other co-tenant's death. Eckardt v. Osborne, 338 Ill. 611, 170 N.E. 774, 75 A.L.R. 509 (1930).

§ 5.4

1. Commercial Factors of Denver v. Clarke & Waggener, 684 P.2d 261 (Colo.App.1984) (unless parties are husband and wife and a written homestead declaration has been recorded); Hall v. Hamilton, 233 Kan. 880, 667 P.2d 350 (1983). Total or partial restraints on alienation are presumably valid only to the extent they would be valid if imposed on estates in severalty.

2. E.g., McLaughlin v. Cooper's Estate, 128 Conn. 557, 24 A.2d 502 (1942); Harms v. Sprague, 105 Ill.2d 215, 85 Ill.Dec. 331, 473 N.E.2d 930 (1984); Smith v. Smith, 290 Mich. 143, 287 N.W. 411, 124 A.L.R. 215 (1939); Mullikin v. Jones, 71 Nev. 14, 278 P.2d 876 (1955). "Severance" destroys the survivorship right(s) of the other joint tenant(s), and results from the destruction of the unities of time and title.

The result will, of course, be different in states where a conveyance to "A and B as joint tenants with right of survivorship" creates an estate for the joint lives of A and B with an indestructible remainder in fee simple to the survivor. Although one "joint tenant" may convey his entire interest to a third party without the other cotenant's consent, such a conveyance doesn't destroy the contingent remainder (right of survivorship). Albro v. Allen, 434 Mich. 271, 454 N.W.2d 85 (1990).

interest of one of two joint tenants to a stranger creates a tenancy in common between the transferee and the other (former) joint tenant.[3] If there were originally three or more joint tenants, transfer of the interest of one of them to a stranger makes the latter a tenant in common vis-a-vis the remaining joint tenants, who continue to be joint tenants as among themselves.[4]

If there were originally three or more joint tenants and one of them conveys his interest to another joint tenant, the grantee remains a joint tenant as to his original undivided interest but becomes, vis-a-vis the other joint tenants, a tenant in common as to the interest conveyed to him.[5] And if there were originally only two joint tenants, the effect of a conveyance of the undivided interest of one to the other will be to extinguish the joint tenancy by merger and give the grantee sole ownership of the estate in severalty.

Severance may result from the transfer of less than the entire interest of a joint tenant. Thus, if the estate subject to the joint tenancy is a fee simple, a conveyance by one joint tenant of his interest for the life of the transferee will result in a severance *pro tanto*.[6] In such case, if any of the joint tenants dies during the continuance of the life estate conveyed, there is no immediate right of survivorship;[7] but upon termination of the life estate the joint tenancy revives[8] or, if only one of the joint tenants is then living, he acquires sole ownership in severalty.

A joint tenant who purports to lease the entire fee simple estate in which the joint tenancy exists, without joinder in the lease by his co-tenants, cannot bind his co-tenants so as to give the lessee an exclusive right of possession,[9] but such a lease will be effective as to the lessor's undivided interest.[10] And one joint tenant may, of course, lease his own undivided interest. Whether such a lease will effect a severance has, however, been a subject of controversy since the time of Littleton and Coke.[11] In England, it now appears that such a lease completely severs the lessor's interest from

---

3. E.g., Handy v. Shiells, 190 Cal.App.3d 512, 235 Cal.Rptr. 543 (1987); Porter v. Porter, 381 Ill. 322, 45 N.E.2d 635 (1942); Wood v. Logue, 167 Iowa 436, 149 N.W. 613, Ann.Cas. 1917B 116 (1914); In re Estate of King, 261 Wis. 266, 52 N.W.2d 885 (1952).

In Minonk State Bank v. Grassman, 95 Ill.2d 392, 69 Ill.Dec. 387, 447 N.E.2d 822 (1983), the court held that one joint tenant, by virtue of a statute dispensing with the "straw man" requirement in the creation of joint tenancies, could convey to herself as a tenant in common and thus convert the joint tenancy into a tenancy in common.

4. E.g., Hammond v. McArthur, 30 Cal.2d 512, 183 P.2d 1 (1947); Jackson v. O'Connell, 23 Ill.2d 52, 177 N.E.2d 194 (1961) (dictum); Giles v. Sheridan, 179 Neb. 257, 137 N.W.2d 828 (1965).

5. E.g., Jackson v. O'Connell, supra note 4; Rendle v. Wiemeyer, 374 Mich. 30, 131 N.W.2d 45, 132 N.W.2d 606 (1965); Leonard v. Boswell, 197 Va. 713, 90 S.E.2d 872 (1956). Such a conveyance is technically a "release."

6. Hoover v. El Paso National Bank, 498 S.W.2d 276 (Tex.Civ.App.1973). See Litt. § 302; Co.Litt. * 191b.

7. Litt. §§ 302, 303. In such case the share of the deceased joint tenant passes to his heirs for the time being.

8. Hammond v. McArthur, supra note 4. See Co.Litt. * 193a; 2 Preston, Abstracts 59 (2nd ed. 1824). But see Comment, 25 Calif.L.Rev. 203, 206 (1937), arguing that total severance should result.

9. The other joint tenants will, of course, be bound if they authorize or ratify the lease.

10. E.g., Swartzbaugh v. Sampson, 11 Cal. App.2d 451, 54 P.2d 73 (1936).

11. Cf. Co.Litt. * 193a with 2 Bl.Comm. * 186. See Swenson & Degnan, Severance of Joint Tenancies, 38 Minn.L.Rev. 466, 472–474 (1954); 2 Am.L.Prop. § 6.2 at p. 10; Comment, 61 Calif.L.Rev. 231 (1973); Comment, 25 Calif.L.Rev. 203, 206–209 (1937); Comment, 8 Hastings L.J. 290, 293 (1957); Comment, 21 So.Cal.L.Rev. 295, 297 (1948).

the joint tenancy and destroys the right of survivorship as to the lessor's undivided interest,[12] although this seems inconsistent with the rule as to the effect of a transfer of a joint tenant's undivided interest for the transferee's life. In the United States there is little authority on the point, and two recent cases reached opposite results as to the effect of a lease given by one joint tenant.[13] In the case holding that such a lease does not sever the joint tenancy, the death of the lessor during the lease term necessarily terminated the lease and gave the surviving joint tenant the immediate right to possession.

An executory contract to convey one joint tenant's interest—assuming the contract is specifically enforceable—severs the vendor's undivided interest from the joint tenancy in equity, so that the vendor's successors in interest will be entitled to the purchase money if the vendor dies before the contract is performed.[14] But the courts are divided as to whether there is a severance, entitling each cotenant to a pro rata portion of the purchase money, when all the joint tenants join as vendors in the executory contract.[15]

It is well settled that a mortgage of the undivided interest of one joint tenant will effect a severance of that interest from the joint tenancy in jurisdictions which adhere to the "title" or "hybrid" theory of mortgages.[16] In these jurisdictions the mortgage has the same effect as an absolute conveyance, and a subsequent discharge of the mortgage will not revive the joint tenancy as to the mortgaged interest. But in jurisdictions adhering to the "lien" theory of mortgages, the cases are in conflict; some hold that no severance occurs when one joint tenant mortgages his undivided interest,[17] and other cases hold that there is a severance to the extent necessary to protect the mortgagee against loss of his security if the mortgagor predeceas-

---

12. Roe v. Lonsdale, 12 East. 39, 104 Eng. Rep. 16 (K.B.1810); Napier v. Williams, [1911] 1 Ch. 361. But see Sym's Case, Cro.Eliz. 33, 78 Eng.Rep. 299 (K.B.); Clerk v. Clerk, 2 Vern. 323, 23 Eng.Rep. 809 (Ch.1694).

13. Tenhet v. Boswell, 18 Cal.3d 150, 133 Cal.Rptr. 10, 554 P.2d 330 (1976) (neither temporary nor permanent severance; when lessor died, lease terminated and lessee's interest also terminated); Alexander v. Boyer, 253 Md. 511, 253 A.2d 359 (1969) (joint tenancy severed).

14. E.g., Kozacik v. Kozacik, 157 Fla. 597, 26 So.2d 659 (1946); Naiburg v. Hendriksen, 370 Ill. 502, 19 N.E.2d 348 (1939); Kurowski v. Retail Hardware Mutual Fire Insurance Co., 203 Wis. 644, 234 N.W. 900 (1931).

15. That a severance is effected, so that the vendors are entitled to the purchase money as tenants in common, see In re Baker's Estate, 247 Iowa 1380, 78 N.W.2d 863 (1956), noted, 42 Iowa L.Rev. 646 (1957), 55 Mich. L.Rev. 1194 (1957); Buford v. DahKle, 158 Neb. 39, 62 N.W.2d 252 (1954); Yannopoulos v. Sophos, 243 Pa.Super. 454, 365 A.2d 1312 (1976). That there is no severance, see Weise v. Kizer, 435 So.2d 381 (Fla.App.1983), petition for review denied 444 So.2d 417 (Fla.1984) ("the weight of authority, and the better view," is that there is no severance "unless there is an indication in the contract, or from

the circumstances, that the parties intended to sever and terminate the joint tenancy"); Watson v. Watson, 5 Ill.2d 526, 126 N.E.2d 220 (1955); but see, contra, Illinois Public Aid Commission v. Stille, 14 Ill.2d 344, 153 N.E.2d 59 (1958). See U.Ill.L.F. 658, 659–660, for discussion of the Illinois cases. See also Swenson & Degnan, supra note 11, at 476; Note, 41 Cornell L.Q. 154 (1955); Note, 34 Neb.L.Rev. 501 (1955); Comment, 24 Mo.L.Rev. 108 (1959). That an unexercised option to buy does not effect a severance, see Alexander v. Boyer, supra note 13.

16. E.g., Hammond v. McArthur, 30 Cal.2d 512, 183 P.2d 1 (1947) (dictum); Eder v. Rothamel, 202 Md. 189, 95 A.2d 860 (1953); Hardin v. Wolf, 318 Ill. 48, 148 N.E. 868 (1925) (under "hybrid" theory of mortgage, which gives mortgagor the right to possession till default).

But see, as to the rule in Illinois, Harms v. Sprague, 105 Ill.2d 215, 85 Ill.Dec. 331, 473 N.E.2d 930 (1984) (disavowing dicta in earlier cases and holding that a mortgage creates only a lien and therefore does not sever a joint tenancy).

17. Hammond v. McArthur, supra note 16; D.A.D., Inc. v. Moring, 218 So.2d 451 (Fla. 1969); Harms v. Sprague, supra note 16; American National Bank & Trust Co. v. McGinnis, 571 P.2d 1198 (Okl.1977).

es the other joint tenant(s), although the other joint tenant(s) will take the mortgagor's undivided interest by survivorship in such a case.[18] Under the latter view, if the other joint tenant(s) predecease the mortgagor while the mortgage is outstanding, the mortgagor should acquire the interests of the deceased joint tenant(s) by survivorship.

Severance of one joint tenant's undivided interest from the joint tenancy may result from an involuntary transfer of that interest—e.g., by virtue of a sale of the interest by the joint tenant's trustee in bankruptcy or by virtue of a sale on execution of a judgment against the joint tenant.[19] But there is a division of authority as to whether a mere levy of execution, or an attachment, without sale, effects a severance.[20] The mere docketing or recording of a judgment against a joint tenant, which creates a statutory judgment lien against the joint tenant's undivided interest and enables the judgment creditor to obtain a writ of execution, does not effect a severance.[21] A court-ordered mortgage foreclosure sale of one joint tenant's interest will, of course, sever a joint tenancy even in a "lien theory" state.

A joint tenancy may be severed by an express agreement between the joint tenants to hold as tenants in common,[22] or by such an agreement implied from conduct of the parties which is inconsistent with the continuance of a joint tenancy.[23]

§ 5.5 Tenancy by the Entirety

At common law any conveyance or (after 1540) any devise to a husband and wife created a tenancy by the entirety which was characterized by an

See also Coffman v. Adkins, 338 N.W.2d 540 (Iowa App.1983) (joint tenancy in certificate of deposit not severed when one joint tenant pledged certificate of deposit as security for note executed by him alone).

18. Wilkens v. Young, 144 Ind. 1, 41 N.E. 68 (1895).

19. Mangus v. Miller, 317 U.S. 178, 63 S.Ct. 182, 87 L.Ed. 169 (1942), rehearing denied 317 U.S. 712, 63 S.Ct. 432, 87 L.Ed. 567 (1943); New Haven Trolley & Bus Employees Credit Union v. Hill, 145 Conn. 332, 142 A.2d 730 (1958); Poulson v. Poulson, 145 Me. 15, 70 A.2d 868, 12 A.L.R.2d 939 (1950). Contra: Jackson v. Lacey, 408 Ill. 530, 97 N.E.2d 839 (1951). In any case, there is no severance till the redemption period expires without redemption having been effected.

20. Severance: Mangus v. Miller, supra note 19; Hammond v. McArthur, supra note 16; Frederick v. Shorman, 259 Iowa 1050, 147 N.W.2d 478 (1966); Ladd v. State ex rel. Oklahoma Tax Com'n, 688 P.2d 59 (Okl.1984). No severance: In re Rauer's Collection Co., 87 Cal.App.2d 248, 196 P.2d 803 (1948); Knibb v. Security Insurance Co., 121 R.I. 406, 399 A.2d 1214 (1979).

21. Frederick v. Shorman, supra note 20; Hughes v. Fairfield Lumber & Supply Co., 143 Conn. 427, 123 A.2d 195 (1956); Northern State Bank v. Toal, 69 Wis.2d 50, 230 N.W.2d 153 (1975).

22. E.g., California Trust Co. v. Anderson, 91 Cal.App.2d 832, 205 P.2d 1127 (1949).

23. E.g., Thomas v. Johnson, 12 Ill.App.3d 302, 297 N.E.2d 712 (1973); Mann v. Bradley, 188 Colo. 392, 535 P.2d 213 (1975); Carson v. Ellis, 186 Kan. 112, 348 P.2d 807 (1960); Neaderhiser v. State Dept. of Social & Rehabilitation Services, 9 Kan.App.2d 115, 673 P.2d 462 (1983) (dictum). But a joint tenancy is not necessarily "severed" by an agreement allocating income and/or possession to one of the joint tenants. Ibid. A final judgment for partition will, of course, terminate a joint tenancy; but commencement of a partition action, without more, is insufficient to terminate a joint tenancy because the action may be discontinued at any time before entry of a final judgment. Hence, if one joint tenant dies during pendency of a partition action, the property passes by right of survivorship to the other joint tenant(s). Allison v. Powell, 333 Pa.Super. 48, 481 A.2d 1215 (1984).

Whether a joint tenancy between spouses persists after a divorce decree is entered ordering the former spouses to join in sale of the property depends either upon the intent of the parties as evidenced in the divorce proceedings or upon the subjective or manifested intent of the trial judge. In re Marriage of Lutzke by Lutzke v. Lutzke, 122 Wis.2d 24, 361 N.W.2d 640 (1985).

indestructible right of survivorship, even if the instrument expressly provided that the grantees or devisees were to hold as joint tenants or as tenants in common.[1] A tenancy by the entirety was the only concurrent estate that could be created between husband and wife because they were deemed, at common law, to constitute a single person or entity.[2] In the nineteenth century, however, the single entity notion was almost wholly eliminated by adoption of the Married Women's Property Acts and the accompanying changes in social attitudes with respect to the relationship of husband and wife. In the United States, tenancies by the entirety have now been abolished in all but twenty jurisdictions.[3] Where tenancies by the entirety have been abolished, a conveyance to husband and wife will necessarily create either a tenancy in common or (where still permitted) a joint tenancy.

In jurisdictions where tenancies by the entirety have not been abolished, a conveyance or devise to husband and wife, without more, is presumed to create a tenancy by the entirety.[4] But some courts hold that, when real property passes to husband and wife by intestate succession they take as tenants in common rather than as tenants by the entirety because each spouse, as heir, takes a separate and distinct undivided interest not dependent upon their marital relationship.[5] And it is sometimes held, in reliance on a similar rationale, that a specific transfer of equal and identical undivided interests to husband and wife creates a tenancy in common rather than a tenancy by the entirety because the undivided interests in such case are transferred to them as individuals rather than as an entity.[6]

In jurisdictions where tenancies by the entirety have not been abolished, the courts will give effect to a clearly stated intent that transferees are to

---

§ 5.5

1. See 2 Bl.Comm. * 182; 2 Kent Comm. * 132; Pineo v. White, 320 Mass. 487, 70 N.E.2d 294 (1946); Stuckey v. Keefe's Executor, 26 Pa. 397 (1856); Heath v. Heath, 189 F.2d 697 (D.C.Cir.1951).

For a good summary of the historical origin and characteristics of the tenancy by the entirety, see Spessard v. Spessard, 64 Md.App. 83, 494 A.2d 701 (1985).

2. See 1 Bracton, lib. 5, f. 416; Litt., Tenures § 291; 2 Bl.Comm. * 182. There were said to be five unities in a tenancy by the entirety: time, title, interest, possession, and person.

3. Tenancies by the entirety can still be created in Arkansas, Delaware, District of Columbia, Florida, Indiana, Kentucky, Maryland, Massachusetts, Michigan, Missouri, New Jersey, New York, North Carolina, Oregon, Pennsylvania, Rhode Island, Tennessee, Vermont, Virginia, and Wyoming. See 4 Thompson, Real Prop. § 1784 at n. 13 and authorities cited. In most states where tenancies by the entirety can no longer be created, the courts held that the spousal unity necessary for such a tenancy was destroyed by enactment of the Married Women's Acts, which removed the common law disabilities of married women. In a few jurisdictions, abolition of tenancies by the entirety was held to result from enact-

ment of statutes which enumerated the permitted kinds of co-tenancies but omitted any mention of the tenancy by the entirety. And a few courts simply rejected the tenancy by the entirety as "repugnant to our institutions and to the American sense of justice to the heirs, and therefore not the common law." Prior to April 4, 1985, when the new Ohio Rev.Code §§ 5302.17–5302.21 became effective, former § 5302.17 authorized creation of tenancies by the entirety. See Donvito v. Criswell, 1 Ohio App.3d 53, 439 N.E.2d 467 (1982). Since April 4, 1985, it has been impossible to create such tenancies in Ohio, but Ohio Rev.Code § 5302.21 preserves tenancies by the entirety created and recorded prior to April 4, 1985.

4. Jenkins v. Simmons, 241 Ark. 242, 407 S.W.2d 105 (1966); Knapp v. Fredricksen, 148 Fla. 311, 4 So.2d 251 (1941); Young v. Cockman, 182 Md. 246, 34 A.2d 428, 149 A.L.R. 1006 (1943).

5. E.g., Knapp v. Windsor, 60 Mass. (6 Cush.) 156 (1850); Brown v. Baraboo, 90 Wis. 151, 62 N.W. 921, 30 L.R.A. 320 (1895). Contra: Gillan's Executors v. Dixon, 65 Pa. 395 (1870) (husband and wife, as sole heirs of their child, became tenants by the entirety).

6. E.g., Highsmith v. Page, 158 N.C. 226, 73 S.E. 998 (1912); Blease v. Anderson, 241 Pa. 198, 88 A. 365 (1913).

hold as tenants in common or (where still permitted) as joint tenants rather than as tenants by the entirety.[7] But there is a conflict of authority as to whether a transfer to husband and wife "as joint tenants [with right of survivorship] and not as tenants in common" will create a joint tenancy (where still permitted) or a tenancy by the entirety.[8]

In jurisdictions where tenancies by the entirety have not been abolished, a tenancy by the entirety may be created by a transfer to three or more persons, two of whom are husband and wife—e.g., by a transfer to H (husband), W (wife), and X, in which case H and W take an undivided one-half interest as tenants by the entirety, and X takes a one-half undivided interest as tenant in common vis-a-vis H and W.[9] But a tenancy by the entirety cannot be created even by a clear expression of intent if the transferees are not, in fact—though supposed to be—husband and wife, as, for example, where their purported marriage is void for some reason.[10] If the transferees are not husband and wife, they will take either as tenants in common or (where still permitted) as joint tenants. The modern constructional preference for tenancies in common has led some courts to find that a tenancy in common has been created;[11] but other courts have found that a joint tenancy (if still permitted) is created because it is more like the tenancy by the entirety which the transferor presumably intended to create.[12]

A good deal of litigation has resulted from attempts by one spouse to create a tenancy by the entirety by conveyance of an undivided interest to the other spouse or the entire estate to both spouses. At one time such transfers were uniformly held to create a tenancy in common because tenancies by the entirety could exist only if the four "unities" were present

7. E.g., Thornburg v. Wiggins, 135 Ind. 178, 34 N.E. 999, 22 L.R.A. 42 (1893); Baker v. Stewart, 40 Kan. 442, 19 P. 904, 2 L.R.A. 434 (1888); Hiles v. Fisher, 144 N.Y. 306, 39 N.E. 337, 30 L.R.A. 305 (1895). See also Carver v. Gilbert, 387 P.2d 928, 32 A.L.R.3d 563 (Alaska 1963).

8. Tenancy by the entirety: Naler v. Ballew, 81 Ark. 328, 99 S.W. 72 (1907); Hoag v. Hoag, 213 Mass. 50, 99 N.E. 521 (1912); Jurewicz v. Jurewicz, 317 Mass. 512, 58 N.E.2d 832 (1945); Goethe v. Gmelin, 256 Mich. 112, 239 N.W. 347 (1931). Joint tenancy: Wilken v. Young, 144 Ind. 1, 41 N.E. 68 (1895); Kolker v. Gorn, 193 Md. 391, 67 A.2d 258 (1949), noted 13 Md.L.Rev. 43 (1949). Cases holding that a tenancy by the entirety is created often rely on the theory that the quoted language is designed to rebut the presumption in favor of tenancies in common and that language otherwise effective to create a joint tenancy will create a tenancy by the entirety when the grantees are husband and wife.

9. E.g., Dennis v. Dennis, 152 Ark. 187, 238 S.W. 15 (1922); West Chicago Park Commissioners v. Coleman, 108 Ill. 591 (1884); Bartholomew v. Marshall, 257 App.Div. 1060, 13 N.Y.S.2d 568 (1939). See also Heatter v. Lucas, 367 Pa. 296, 80 A.2d 749 (1951); Margarite v. Ewald, 252 Pa.Super. 244, 381 A.2d 480 (1977). In both *Heatter and Margarite*, the

court said that a conveyance to three parties, two of whom are husband and wife, will produce a tenancy in common with the grantees holding equal shares unless the grantor clearly indicates that the husband and wife shall hold as tenants by the entirety. In both cases, the intent to create a tenancy by the entirety was held to be clearly shown by language identifying one grantee as the "wife" of another grantee. Three married couples, as grantees, may hold one-third shares in common, with each share held by husband and wife as tenants by the entirety. Burt v. Edmonds, 224 Tenn. 403, 456 S.W.2d 342 (1969).

10. Co.Litt. * 187b; Mitchell v. Frederick, 166 Md. 42, 170 A. 733, 92 A.L.R. 1412 (1934) (void marriage); Morris v. McCarty, 158 Mass. 11, 32 N.E. 938 (1893) (same); Emmons v. Sanders, 217 Or. 234, 342 P.2d 125 (1959) (same). See also Lopez v. Lopez, 250 Md. 491, 243 A.2d 588 (1968) (couple not married at time of conveyance).

11. E.g., Bove v. Bove, 394 Pa. 627, 149 A.2d 67 (1959); Hynes v. Hynes, 28 Wn.2d 660, 184 P.2d 68 (1947); Matter of Estate of Kappler, 418 Mich. 237, 341 N.W.2d 113 (1983); Reinhardt v. Diedricks, 439 So.2d 936 (Fla.App.1983), appeal after remand 466 So.2d 375 (1985).

12. E.g., Mitchell v. Frederick, supra note 10; Morris v. McCarty, supra note 10.

and, in such cases, the "unities of time and title" were lacking.[13] Hence it was necessary for the grantor to convey to a third party "straw man" who, by prearrangement, would then convey back to the spouses as tenants by the entirety. In some states, the need for a "straw man" has been eliminated by decisions holding that one spouse can create a tenancy by the entirety either by conveying an undivided interest to the other spouse or by conveying the entire estate to both spouses.[14] In other states, statutes now expressly authorize the creation of tenancies by the entirety by conveyances of the kinds under discussion.[15] Statutes authorizing conveyances by the owner to himself and another as joint tenants may, however, leave it doubtful as to whether such statutes apply to tenancies by the entirety.[16]

In the jurisdictions where a tenancy by the entirety can still be created, the Married Women's Property Acts were generally held to abolish the common law right of the husband to exclusive control of land held by the entirety and his right to convey or encumber the entire estate, subject to the wife's right of survivorship, without her consent.[17] Although tenancies by

13. Tenancy in common: Pegg v. Pegg, 165 Mich. 228, 130 N.W. 617, 33 L.R.A. 166 (1911); In re Walker's Estate, 340 Pa. 13, 16 A.2d 28, 132 A.L.R. 628 (1940), noted 7 U.Pitt.L.Rev. 164 (1941). Tenancy in common with right of survivorship added: Little River Bank & Trust Co. v. Eastman, 105 So.2d 912 (Fla.App. 1958). Common law joint tenancy: Tindall v. Yeats, 392 Ill. 502, 64 N.E.2d 903 (1946); Stuehm v. Mikulski, 139 Neb. 374, 297 N.W. 595, 137 A.L.R. 327 (1941); Lawton v. Lawton, 48 R.I. 134, 136 A. 241 (1927). In a few cases it has been held that a conveyance by one spouse to both spouses gives the entire estate to the other spouse in severalty. E.g., Hicks v. Sprankle, 149 Tenn. 310, 257 S.W. 1044 (1924); Wright v. Knapp, 183 Mich. 656, 150 N.W. 315 (1915).

14. E.g., Ebrite v. Brookhyser, 219 Ark. 676, 244 S.W.2d 625 (1951), noted, 51 Mich. L.Rev. 121 (1952); Johnson v. Landefeld, 138 .Fla. 511, 189 So. 666 (1939); Fay v. Smiley, 201 Iowa 1290, 207 N.W. 369 (1926); Therrien v. Therrien, 94 N.H. 66, 46 A.2d 538 (1946); Boehringer v. Schmid, 254 N.Y. 355, 173 N.E. 220 (1930); Jameson v. Jameson, 387 So.2d 351 (Fla.1980). See also Dutton v. Buckley, 116 Or. 661, 242 P. 626 (1926) (deed from husband to self and wife as tenants by the entirety gives wife a half interest in fee simple, with remainder in fee simple in the other half interest to become possessory at husband's death).

15. E.g., North Carolina Gen.Stat. § 39–13.3(b) (1976 repl.).

16. E.g., Lee's Estate v. Graber, 170 Colo. 419, 462 P.2d 492 (1969); Ames v. Chandler, 265 Mass. 428, 164 N.E. 616 (1929).

17. E.g., Cooper v. Maynard, 156 Fla. 534, 23 So.2d 734 (1945); Hiles v. Fisher, 144 N.Y. 306, 39 N.E. 337, 30 L.R.A. 305 (1895); Shapiro v. Shapiro, 424 Pa. 120, 224 A.2d 164 (1966). Contra: Licker v. Gluskin, 265 Mass. 403, 164

N.E. 613, 63 A.L.R. 231 (1929); Arrand v. Graham, 297 Mich. 559, 298 N.W. 281 (1941), rehearing denied 297 Mich. 559, 300 N.W. 16 (1941); In re Perry's Estate, 256 N.C. 65, 123 S.E.2d 99 (1961).

In 1976 the Massachusetts Declaration of Rights [Constitution] was amended to provide that "Equality under the law shall not be denied or abridged because of sex." (Art. 106 of Articles of Amendment, eff. Nov. 2, 1976). In 1979 Mass.Ann.Laws c. 209, § 1, was amended (eff. Feb. 11, 1980) to provide that "the interest of a debtor spouse in property held as tenants by the entirety shall not be subject to seizure or execution by a creditor of such debtor spouse so long as such property is the principal residence of the nondebtor spouse, provided, however, both spouses shall be liable jointly and severally for debts incurred on account of necessaries furnished to either spouse or to a member of their family." In D'Ercole v. D'Ercole, 407 F.Supp. 1377 (D.Mass.1976), it was held that the husband's control of property held in a common law tenancy by the entirety did not violate the 14th Amendment's equal protection clause. In West v. First Agricultural Bank, 382 Mass. 534, 419 N.E.2d 262 (1981), the court declined to decide the constitutionality of a common law tenancy by the entirety created prior adoption of Art. 106, expressing doubt as to whether Art. 106 was intended to have retroactive application. In Turner v. Greenaway, 391 Mass. 1002, 459 N.E.2d 821 (1984), the court refused to apply Mass.Gen.Laws Ann. c. 209, § 1, to a tenancy by the entirety created prior to the effective date of the 1979 amendment, although the creditor had seized the nondebtor spouse's principal residence after the effective date of the amendment. Mass. Gen.Laws Ann. c. 209, § 1A, added by Mass. Laws 1989, § 283, now provides that tenants by the entirety holding under a deed dated

the entirety are still not destructible by the unilateral act of either spouse, different courts have reached different conclusions as to the alienability of the spouse's interests in a tenancy by the entirety. In a few states it has been held that each spouse has an undivided one-half interest which he or she can convey or encumber at will, and which may be subjected to sale to satisfy his or her individual debts, although any conveyance, encumbrance, or involuntary sale of the interest of one spouse cannot deprive the other spouse of his or her right to possession or right of survivorship.[18] In a larger number of states, however, it has been held that neither spouse has any interest that can be separately conveyed or encumbered, or seized by the creditors of one spouse alone to satisfy their claims against that spouse; thus one spouse alone cannot convey, encumber, or subject to the satisfaction of creditors' claims either that spouse's possessory estate for the joint lives of the co-tenants or that spouse's contingent right of survivorship.[19]

Tenants by the entirety may, of course, join in making an effective conveyance or mortgage of their estate; and it appears that property held in a tenancy by the entirety may be subjected to the payment of the joint debts of the spouses and sold on execution.[20]

When one tenant by the entirety dies, the surviving spouse becomes the

prior to Feb. 11, 1980, may elect to have their tenancies treated as being subject to the 1974 amendment to Mass.Gen.Laws Ann. c. 209, § 1, if they execute and record a written and duly notarized statement of such election.

18. E.g., Schwind v. O'Halloran, 346 Mo. 486, 142 S.W.2d 55 (1940); Zanzonico v. Zanzonico, 24 N.J.Misc. 153, 46 A.2d 565, 166 A.L.R. 964 (1946); Hiles v. Fisher, supra note 17. *Zanzonico* was overruled in part by King v. Greene, 30 N.J. 395, 153 A.2d 49, 75 A.L.R.2d 1153 (1959), noted, 73 Harv.L.Rev. 792 (1960), 58 Mich.L.Rev. 601 (1960), 14 Rutgers L.Rev. 457 (1960), 5 Vill.L.Rev. 154 (1959), holding that a creditor's interest attaches to the debtor spouse's interest after the death of the other spouse. Cf. Stauffer v. Stauffer, 465 Pa. 558, 351 A.2d 236 (1976) (only survivorship right can be unilaterally transferred, or seized by creditors); Robinson v. Trousdale County, 516 S.W.2d 626 (Tenn.1974) (same).

19. E.g., Sawada v. Endo, 57 Hawaii 608, 561 P.2d 1291 (1977); Elko v. Elko, 187 Md. 161, 49 A.2d 441 (1946); Brownley v. Lincoln County, 218 Or. 7, 343 P.2d 529 (1959), noted, 39 Or.L.Rev. 194, 386 (1960); Arbesman v. Winer, 298 Md. 282, 468 A.2d 633 (1983) (neither spouse can make an effective lease without joinder of the other); Jones v. Conwell, 227 Va. 176, 314 S.E.2d 61 (1984). The rule stated in the text is still applicable in Ohio to tenancies by the entirety created before April 4, 1985, although such tenancies can no longer be created in Ohio. See supra note 3 for discussion of the current Ohio statute.

Cf. Branch Banking & Trust Co. v. Wright, 74 N.C.App. 550, 328 S.E.2d 840 (1985) (although marital home, held in a tenancy by the entirety, was conveyed to former wife pursuant to court order in divorce action, the lien of a trust deed mortgage given by husband alone during marriage attached to undivided one-half interest of property after conveyance to former wife because divorce decree converted tenancy from one by the entirety into one in common and made it subject to claims of husband's creditors pursuant to legislative intent to protect creditors of former spouses in "equitable distribution" of marital realty); Moehlenkamp v. Shatz, 396 N.E.2d 433 (Ind. App.1979) (mortgage executed by husband alone was binding on wife because husband for a long time had conducted a family business with wife's tacit approval and thus had implied authority to sign mortgage as her agent; wife failed to revoke husband's implied authority because she did not object to his signing her name on an earlier note and mortgage).

Until 1988 the New Jersey law was uncertain, but a 1988 statute (applicable to tenancies by the entirety created after its effective date) now provides that "Neither spouse may sever, alienate, or otherwise affect their interest in the tenancy by the entirety during the marriage or upon separation, without the written consent of both spouses." N.J.S.A. 46:3–17.4 (eff. May 6, 1988).

20. The power to convey includes, of course, the power to lease. But where land is leased by both spouses, the lease cannot be terminated by either spouse alone. Hence a notice of termination of a tenancy at will created by both spouses, given by one spouse alone, was not effective. Arbesman v. Winer, 298 Md. 282, 468 A.2d 633 (1983).

sole owner of the property in severalty [21] unless the survivorship right of the surviving spouse was previously conveyed or sold on execution in a jurisdiction where the survivorship right can be effectively conveyed by one spouse without the concurrence of the other and can be sold on execution to satisfy a judgment against one spouse.[22]

A tenancy by the entirety can, of course, be terminated by a conveyance (technically a "release") of the entire interest of one spouse to the other spouse.[23] And an absolute divorce or annulment will generally terminate a tenancy by the entirety and convert it into a tenancy in common.[24] In some jurisdictions, however, a divorce brings into operation a statutory provision for "equitable distribution of the property * * * which was legally and beneficially acquired by * * * [the spouses] or either of them during the marriage," [25] in which case the divorce will not necessarily convert a tenancy by the entirety into a tenancy in common. And a court may give effect to an express pre-divorce agreement preserving the right of survivorship as between the parties.[26] Where divorce converts a tenancy by the entirety into a

21. As previously indicated, the right of survivorship is indestructible and inalienable at common law. Illustrating the right of survivorship, see Baumgardner v. Kennedy, 343 So.2d 1323 (Fla.App.1977); Wenker v. Landon, 161 Or. 265, 88 P.2d 971 (1939) (husband murdered wife and killed himself; entire estate passed to his heir because statute forbidding *inheritance* by murderer from person murdered had no application). In the event of simultaneous death of the spouses, Uniform Simultaneous Death Act § 3 provides that the property shall be distributed one-half as if one spouse had survived, and the other half as if the other spouse had survived. But a court may hold that equality of interest is only presumed and that proof of unequal contributions will rebut the presumption. In re Strong's Will, 171 Misc. 445, 12 N.Y.S.2d 544 (1939).

22. See ante, text at note 18 and authorities cited.

23. E.g., Thornburg v. Wiggins, 135 Ind. 178, 34 N.E. 999, 22 L.R.A. 42 (1893); Backus v. Backus, 464 Pa. 380, 346 A.2d 790 (1975).

A judicial separation decree may also terminate a tenancy by the entirety. In re Estate of Violi, 65 N.Y.2d 392, 492 N.Y.S.2d 550, 482 N.E.2d 29 (1985). But execution of a contract to sell the land by husband and wife does not terminate a tenancy by the entirety unless the doctrine of equitable conversion is applicable upon execution of the contract. Matter of Houghton's Estate, 75 N.J. 462, 383 A.2d 713 (1978) (doctrine of equitable conversion held not applicable).

24. E.g., Donegan v. Donegan, 103 Ala. 488, 15 So. 823 (1894); Sebold v. Sebold, 444 F.2d 864 (D.C.Cir.1971); Wild v. Wild, 157 So.2d 532 (Fla.1963); Bernatavicius v. Bernatavicius, 259 Mass. 486, 156 N.E. 685, 52 A.L.R. 886 (1927); Matter of Estate of Violi, 65 N.Y.2d 392, 492 N.Y.S.2d 550, 482 N.E.2d 29 (1985) (but tenancy by the entirety is not converted into tenancy in common by provision in separation agreement for sale of marital home at a future date); Branch Banking & Trust Co. v. Wright, supra note 19; Rogers v. Kelly, 66 N.C.App. 264, 311 S.E.2d 43 (1984); Brown v. Prisel's Estate, 97 Mich.App. 188, 293 N.W.2d 729 (1980). The same general rule is now statutory in Arkansas and Pennsylvania. Ark.Stat. § 34–1215; 68 Penn.Stat. § 501. Prior to 1947, divorce had no effect on an Arkansas tenancy by the entirety, but Ark. Laws 1947, Act 340, empowered the court to abrogate a tenancy by the entirety upon dissolution of the marriage; and the 1975 amendment provided that divorce shall "automatically" dissolve a tenancy by the entirety "unless the court specifically provides otherwise." In Pennsylvania, prior to enactment of Penn. Laws 1949, Act 412, divorce did not affect a tenancy by the entirety. The Pennsylvania statute, supra, provides that each of the former spouses is entitled to one-half the property as a tenant in common with the other. The Arkansas and Pennsylvania statutes applied only prospectively. Hubbard v. Hubbard, 251 Ark. 465, 472 S.W.2d 937 (1971); Villanova v. Pollock, 264 Ark. 912, 576 S.W.2d 501 (1979); Backus v. Backus, 464 Pa. 380, 346 A.2d 790 (1975).

25. The statute quoted is New Jersey Stat. Ann. 2A:34–23, as amended by N.J.Laws 1971, c. 212. In all, some 38 states have similar statutes. Under these statutes it is immaterial whether legal title to the property is held by one spouse alone or by both spouses as concurrent owners. See, generally, Freed & Foster, Divorce in Fifty States: An Overview as of 1978, 13 Family L.Q. 105 (1979).

26. Heath v. Heath, 189 F.2d 697 (D.C.Cir. 1951) (also holding that a divorce leaves the status of a former tenancy by the entirety undefined till a court determines it; holding

tenancy in common, either co-tenant may, of course, compel a partition.[27]

Some jurisdictions still hold that a tenancy by the entirety cannot be created in personal property,[28] although the original basis for such holdings—the common law rule that a husband acquired absolute ownership of his wife's personal property [29]—has generally been eliminated by the Married Women's Property Acts. In most jurisdictions, however, a tenancy by the entirety can now be created in personal property if the parties indicate their intention to create a tenancy by the entirety.[30] But it may still be impossible in some jurisdictions to create a tenancy by the entirety in a bank account if the bank's rules allow either of the co-owners to withdraw funds because, in such case, the right of withdrawal amounts to a unilateral power to terminate the co-tenancy and is inconsistent with the basic nature of a tenancy by the entirety.[31]

In jurisdictions where tenancies by the entirety can still be created, they continue to be popular with laymen because they make it possible to transmit property to the surviving spouse without making a will and without the necessity for probate proceedings—and, in some jurisdictions, because tenancies by the entirety effectively shield property held by the entirety from seizure and sale to satisfy the claims of creditors of either spouse.

§ 5.6 Tenancy in Partnership

Prior to adoption of the Uniform Partnership Act [1] in a given jurisdiction, a tenancy in partnership was—in the United States—essentially a special type of tenancy in common. Since a partnership, apart from statute, is not a legal entity that can hold title to land,[2] title to partnership realty had to be held by the partners as concurrent owners.[3] Even where the four "unities" were all present, the partners could not hold as joint tenants because the right of survivorship characteristic of joint tenancies was clearly inconsistent with the rules of partnership law requiring that partnership property be applied to the extent necessary to satisfaction of partnership debts and adjustment of accounts between the partners upon dissolution of a partnership. Hence the legal title to partnership realty was generally held to be vested in the partners as tenants in common,[4] subject to a trust implied

---

disapproved and not followed in *Sebold,* supra note 24).

27. E.g., Bernatavicius v. Bernatavicius, supra note 24; Jones v. Conwell, supra note 19.

28. E.g., In re Blumenthal's Estate, 236 N.Y. 448, 141 N.E. 911, 30 A.L.R. 901 (1923); Hawthorne v. Hawthorne, 13 N.Y.2d 82, 242 N.Y.S.2d 50, 192 N.E.2d 20 (1963); Lovell v. Rowan Mut. Fire Ins. Co., 302 N.C. 150, 274 S.E.2d 170 (1981).

29. Co.Litt. *351.

30. E.g., Carlisle v. Parker, 38 Del. 83, 188 A. 67 (1936); Dodson v. National Title Insurance Co., 159 Fla. 371, 31 So.2d 402 (1947); Madden v. Gosztonyi Savings & Trust Co., 331 Pa. 476, 200 A. 624, 117 A.L.R. 904 (1938).

31. See Annot., 117 A.L.R. 915 (1938), 8 A.L.R. 1017 (1920).

§ 5.6

1. See 6 Uniform Laws Ann. (Master ed. 1969) for text of the Uniform Partnership Act.

2. E.g., Williams v. Dovell, 202 Md. 351, 96 A.2d 484 (1953). See Crane, Partnership 143 (1938).

3. E.g., Riddle v. Whitehill, 135 U.S. 621, 10 S.Ct. 924, 34 L.Ed. 282 (1889); Berg v. Johnson, 139 Ark. 243, 213 S.W. 393, 8 A.L.R. 489 (1919).

4. E.g., Darrow v. Calkins, 154 N.Y. 503, 49 N.E. 61, 48 L.R.A. 299 (1897); Adams v. Church, 42 Or. 270, 70 P. 1037, 59 L.R.A. 782 (1902). But if the partners make their intent to hold as joint tenants known, they may hold as joint tenants in trust for the partnership, in which case partnership creditors have a prior claim against the firm's property as against the surviving joint tenant. District of

in law requiring that the realty should be applied to firm purposes before it could be applied for the benefit of individual partners or their successors in interest.[5]

The Uniform Partnership Act, now in force in all American jurisdictions,[6] provides that "a partner is co-owner with his partners of specific partnership property holding as a tenant in partnership,"[7] that title to realty may be acquired in the partnership's firm name, and that when title is so acquired it can be conveyed only in the firm name.[8] When realty is acquired in the firm name, the partnership, as a legal entity, holds both the legal and equitable title thereto, and no trust exists as to such realty.[9] But the Uniform Partnership Act does not prevent the partners from taking title to realty in the name of one, several, or all of the partners.[10] In such a case, the legal title is held in trust for the benefit of the partnership;[11] and no interest in the realty can be transferred by inheritance, devise, or—except where the conveyance is to a purchaser for value and without notice of the trust in favor of the firm—by *inter vivos* conveyance.[12] Thus the legal title of all or some of the partners, individually, is "an empty technicality carrying with it no rights of substance."[13] Indeed, the interests of the individual partners are properly deemed to be personal rather than real property,[14] and it is quite immaterial whether the partners (if the legal title is held by two or more) are technically tenants in common or not.

§ 5.7　Transfer of a Cotenant's Undivided Interest

As we have seen, the individual undivided interests of tenants in common and joint tenants are transferable by *inter vivos* conveyance; the individual undivided interests of tenants in partnership are not transferable by *inter vivos* conveyance except to a purchaser for value and without notice that the land is partnership property; and the authorities are divided as to whether tenants by the entirety have any interest that may be transferred by *inter vivos* conveyance. In any case, a tenant by the entirety cannot convey his or her undivided interest in such a way as to destroy the other spouse's right of survivorship, whereas a joint tenant's conveyance of his interest (at least where it is absolute) "severs" it from the joint tenancy and destroys the right of survivorship as to that interest.[1]

Columbia v. Riggs National Bank of Washington, D.C., 335 A.2d 238 (D.C.App.1975).

5. E.g., Bank of Luverne v. Reddoch, 207 Ala. 297, 92 So. 848, 25 A.L.R. 381 (1921); Kruschke v. Stefan, 83 Wis. 373, 53 N.W. 679 (1892).

6. See table of jurisdictions where the Act has been adopted, 6 Uniform Laws Ann., 1982 Pocket Part p. 1. The Act was adopted by the Commissioners on Uniform State Laws in 1914.

7. Uniform Partnership Act § 25(1).

8. Id. § 8.

9. See Campbell, Partnership Real Estate: Effect of the Uniform Partnership Act on Conveyances to the Firm in the Firm Name, 14 Chi.-Kent L.Rev. 203 (1936); 2 Am.L.Prop. § 6.9 at p. 43.

10. E.g., Korziuk v. Korziuk, 13 Ill.2d 238, 148 N.E.2d 727 (1958).

11. 2 Am.L.Prop. § 6.9 at p. 43.

12. Id. at p. 44. The bona fide purchaser for value takes title free of the trust under Uniform Partnership Act § 10(1). See Ewing v. Caldwell, 243 N.C. 18, 89 S.E.2d 774 (1955).

13. 2 Am.L.Prop. § 6.9 at p. 44.

14. Uniform Partnership Act § 26. See Wharf v. Wharf, 306 Ill. 79, 137 N.E. 446 (1922); Vlamis v. De Weese, 216 Md. 384, 140 A.2d 665 (1958), noted 19 Md.L.Rev. 141 (1959).

§ 5.7

1. Ante, Sections 5.3, 5.4. See In re Marriage of Lutzke by Lutzke v. Lutzke, 122 Wis.2d 24, 361 N.W.2d 640 (1985) ("joint ten-

Transfer of a cotenant's undivided interest may be either by an absolute conveyance or by a lease for a term of years.[2] In either case, the transferee obtains only the transferor's concurrent rights of possession and use,[3] and any attempt to exclude the other cotenants from possession or to interfere with their use and enjoyment of the entire property will be tortious.[4]

Suppose a tenant in common or joint tenant, instead of conveying or leasing only an undivided interest, purports to convey or lease the entire property. This can only be effective to transfer the undivided interest of the transferor, of course.[5] But suppose a joint tenant or tenant in common purports to convey or lease a specific portion of the property by metes and bounds. Such a conveyance or lease amounts to a unilateral attempt to partition the property without the consent of the other cotenants. Although valid as between the parties, such a conveyance or lease is not binding on the other cotenants except as a transfer of the grantor's undivided interest in the portion of the property described in the instrument.[6] But if that portion is allotted to the grantor on partition or is otherwise acquired by him in severalty, the conveyance or lease may operate by way of estoppel to give the transferee sole ownership of the portion so allotted or acquired.[7] And in an action for partition by any cotenant, the court may allot to the transferor the specific portion previously sought to be transferred if this will not prejudice any of the other cotenants;[8] and the grantee or lessee may intervene in the partition action in order to have his interest in the property recognized and protected by the court.[9]

ant, absent some prohibition of specific nature, always has the power to sell his or her interest").

2. That a lease of one co-tenant's interest is valid, see Swartzbaugh v. Sampson, 11 Cal. App.2d 451, 54 P.2d 73 (1936) (dictum that he can convey or mortgage it). Kresha v. Kresha, 220 Neb. 598, 371 N.W.2d 280 (1985) (when one cotenant acquires sole ownership, she takes land subject to existing lease executed by other cotenant).

3. Washington Ins. Agency, Inc. v. Friedlander, 487 A.2d 599 (D.C.App.1985) (lessee became tenant in common of non-lessor cotenant where premises were capable of non-exclusive use, and was liable to lessor for full lease rent); Burack v. I. Burack, Inc., 128 Misc.2d 324, 490 N.Y.S.2d 82 (Yonkers City Ct.1985); Kassover v. Gordon Family Associates, Inc., 120 Misc.2d 196, 465 N.Y.S.2d 668 (N.Y.C.Civ. Ct.1983).

4. E.g., Swartzbaugh v. Sampson, Supra note 2 (dictum); Miller v. Gemricher, 191 Iowa 992, 183 N.W. 503 (1921); Cook v. Boehl, 188 Md. 581, 53 A.2d 555 (1947); Howard v. Manning, 79 Okl. 165, 192 P. 358, 12 A.L.R. 819 (1920); Rogers v. Kelly, 66 N.C.App. 264, 311 S.E.2d 43 (1984) (lessee liable to non-lessor cotenant for pro rata portion of reasonable rental value, as compensation for use and occupation where premises were not capable of non-exclusive use). The rule stated in the text is recognized in Dozier v. Wallace, 169

Ga.App. 126, 311 S.E.2d 839 (1983) (consent of one of three cotenants to sublease did not bind the other cotenants, and the latter could "refuse to recognize the right of possession in the sub-tenant and proceed to expel [it] from the rented premises as a mere intruder").

5. Ibid.

6. E.g., Russell v. Stylecraft, Inc., 286 Ala. 633, 244 So.2d 579 (1971); Elmore v. Elmore, 99 So.2d 265 (Fla.1957). Thompson v. Gaudette, 148 Me. 288, 92 A.2d 342 (1952); Landskroner v. McClure, 107 N.M. 773, 765 P.2d 189 (1988). If recognition of the transfer would prejudice the other co-tenants, the transfer may be set aside "in equity." Long v. Howard, 311 Ky. 66, 223 S.W.2d 376 (1949).

7. E.g., Barnes v. Lynch, 151 Mass. 510, 24 N.E. 783, 21 Am.St.Rep. 470 (1890); McElroy v. McLeay, 71 Vt. 396, 45 A. 898 (1899); Worthington v. Staunton, 16 W.Va. 208 (1880).

8. E.g., O'Neal v. Cooper, 191 Ala. 182, 67 So. 689 (1914); Pellow v. Artic Mining Co., 164 Mich. 87, 128 N.W. 918, 47 L.R.A.(N.S.) 573 (1910); Young v. Edwards, 33 S.C. 404, 11 S.E. 1066, 10 L.R.A. 55 (1890). Contra: Taylor v. Taylor, 243 N.C. 726, 92 S.E.2d 136 (1956), noted 35 N.C.L.Rev. 431 (1957).

9. E.g., Benedict v. Torrent, 83 Mich. 181, 47 N.W. 129, 11 L.R.A. 278 (1890); Seavey v. Green, 137 Or. 127, 1 P.2d 601, 75 A.L.R. 1451 (1931).

One tenant in common or joint tenant cannot, without the joinder of the other cotenants, grant an easement that will be valid against the other cotenants,[10] and because "[i]t involves an attempt by one cotenant, not to substitute another as cotenant in his place, as in the case of a conveyance or lease of his interest, but to enable a person, not a cotenant, to interfere, it may be perpetually, with the possession of the other cotenants."[11] But the grant is valid as against the grantor, and would be effective by way of estoppel if the grantor should later acquire in severalty any portion of the land required for the exercise of the easement.[12]

Direct restraints on the alienation of concurrent estates in fee simple are no more effective than direct restraints on the alienation of fee simple estates held in severalty, whether the restraints are of the "disabling," the "forfeiture," or the "promissory" type.[13] To avoid the common law rule against restraints on alienation, most condominium by-laws provide that the association shall have a pre-emptive right of first refusal when a condominium unit owner wishes to sell or lease his unit.[14] But this may raise serious problems under the Rule Against Perpetuities.[15] For discussion of these problems, see ante Section 3.18.

§ 5.8 Rights of Cotenants Inter Se—Possession and Use of the Realty—Accounting

Possession and use of realty subject to concurrent ownership by one cotenant is subject to the equal rights of possession and use of all the other cotenants.[1] But sole possession and use by one cotenant is not tortious or "adverse" as against the others so long as they are not excluded or "ousted" from possession by the cotenant in possession.[2] There is an exclusion or "ouster" only when the cotenant in possession refuses to allow another cotenant to share the possession after the latter has made a demand for possession;[3] where one cotenant purports to convey sole ownership of the

---

10. E.g., East Shore Co. v. Richmond Belt Railway, 172 Cal. 174, 155 P. 999 (1916); Burnham v. Baltimore Gas & Electric Co., 217 Md. 507, 144 A.2d 80 (1958); City Club of Auburn v. McGeer, 198 N.Y. 160, 91 N.E. 539 (1910), rehearing denied 198 N.Y. 609, 92 N.E. 105; LDDC, Inc. v. Pressley, 71 N.C.App. 431, 322 S.E.2d 416 (1984). Nor can one co-tenant authorize the police to search the common property without a warrant if another co-tenant is in possession and objects. Tompkins v. Superior Court, 59 Cal.2d 65, 27 Cal.Rptr. 889, 378 P.2d 113 (1963).

11. 2 Tiffany, Real Prop. § 456 at p. 274 (3d ed. 1939).

12. E.g., McElroy v. McLeay, supra note 7; White v. Manhattan Railway Co., 139 N.Y. 19, 34 N.E. 887 (1893).

The non-grantor cotenants may, of course, effectively ratify or consent to the grant of the easement and thus become bound by it. Keller v. Hartman, 175 W.Va. 418, 333 S.E.2d 89 (1985).

13. 4B R. Powell, Real Property ¶ 633.13[2] (Rohan rev. 1979).

14. Id. ¶ 633.14[2].

15. See ante Section 3.18 in text after note 16.

§ 5.8

1. E.g., Zaslow v. Kroenert, 29 Cal.2d 541, 176 P.2d 1 (1946); Watson v. Little, 224 S.C. 359, 79 S.E.2d 384 (1953); Coulbourn v. Armstrong, 243 N.C. 663, 91 S.E.2d 912 (1956).

2. E.g., Tarver v. Tarver, 258 Ala. 683, 65 So.2d 148 (1953); Johnson v. James, 237 Ark. 900, 377 S.W.2d 44 (1964); Hare v. Chisman, 230 Ind. 333, 101 N.E.2d 268 (1951); Bader v. Bader, 207 Okl. 683, 252 P.2d 427 (1953); McKnight v. Basilides, 19 Wn.2d 391, 143 P.2d 307 (1943); Diedricks v. Reinhardt, 466 So.2d 375 (Fla.App.1985); Evans v. Covington, 795 S.W.2d 806 (Tex.App.1990).

3. E.g., Zaslow v. Kroenert, supra note 1; Cameron v. Chicago, Milwaukee & St. Paul Railway Co., 60 Minn. 100, 61 N.W. 814 (1895).

land in severalty, the grantee enters into sole possession in reliance on the conveyance, and the other cotenants have notice of these facts;[4] or, generally, where one cotenant is in sole possession asserting a "hostile" claim of sole ownership in severalty and the other cotenants have notice of his claim.[5] Notice is required because, absent notice, each cotenant is entitled to assume that the possession of any other cotenant is consistent with the rights of all the cotenants to concurrent possession and use.[6]

An excluded or "ousted" cotenant has various remedies, the most important of which is ejectment, or its modern equivalent, coupled with a claim for mesne profits.[7] A judgment for the plaintiff will not result in dispossession of the defendant, but will restore the plaintiff's concurrent possession with the defendant[8] and will also award mesne profits—usually equal to the plaintiff's pro rata share of the reasonable value of the defendant's use and occupation of the land.[9]

If one cotenant was in sole possession of property subject to concurrent ownership but had not excluded the other cotenant(s), he was not accountable to the other cotenant(s) at common law for either the rental value of his use and occupation or for the actual net income he received from the property[10] unless (1) he was appointed bailiff or agent for the other coten-

4. E.g., West v. Evans, 29 Cal.2d 414, 175 P.2d 219 (1946); Whittington v. Cameron, 385 Ill. 99, 52 N.E.2d 134 (1943); Witherspoon v. Brummett, 50 N.M. 303, 176 P.2d 187 (1946). See Annot., 27 A.L.R. 8 (1923), id. 71 A.L.R. 444 (1931).

5. E.g., Johnson v. James, supra note 2; Blankenhorn v. Lenox, 123 Iowa 67, 98 N.W. 556 (1904); Saucier v. Kremer, 297 Mo. 461, 249 S.W. 640 (1923); Diedricks v. Reinhardt, supra note 3 (cotenant's sole possession deemed adverse to other cotenant after the latter began action to obtain joint possession; cotenant in possession was liable for one-half the reasonable rental value of the land from date complaint was filed); Evans v. Covington, supra note 2; Sweeney Land Co. v. Kimball, 786 P.2d 760 (Utah 1990); In re Estate of Neil, 152 Vt. 124, 565 A.2d 1309 (1989); Pendley v. Byrom, 703 S.W.2d 405 (Tex.App.1986), reversed 717 S.W.2d 602 (Tex.1986) (group of cotenants working interest in oil and gas leasehold were "bad faith trespassers" as matter of law where they asserted in pending litigation that other co-tenant's leasehold interest was invalid; the "bad faith trespassers" could not recover from other cotenant one-half of their cost incurred in drilling and operating oil and gas well). Cf. Coggan v. Coggan, 239 So.2d 17 (Fla.1970) (no ouster when one co-tenant sued for partition and the co-tenant in possession alleged in answer that plaintiff had no interest in the property).

6. E.g., Johnson v. James, supra note 2; Fallon v. Davidson, 137 Colo. 48, 320 P.2d 976 (1958), noted, 56 Mich.L.Rev. 1360 (1958); Diedricks v. Reinhardt, supra note 2; Evans v.

Covington, supra note 2; Sweeney Land Co. v. Kimball, supra note 5; In re Estate of Neil, supra note 5; Fairchild v. Fairchild, 106 Idaho 147, 676 P.2d 722 (1984). In the absence of notice of a "hostile" claim, a tenant who has acquired an outstanding "hostile" title is deemed to hold it for the benefit of his cotenants and not adversely to them. E.g., Leach v. Hall, 95 Iowa 611, 64 N.W. 790 (1895); Woods v. Richardson, 190 Tenn. 662, 231 S.W.2d 340 (1950).

7. It is no longer necessary to bring a separate trespass action for mesne profits after recovering possession in ejectment. E.g., Zapp v. Miller, 109 N.Y. 51, 15 N.E. 889 (1888).

8. E.g., Ewald v. Corbett, 32 Cal. 493 (1867); King v. Dickerman, 77 Mass. (11 Gray) 480 (1858).

9. E.g., Lane v. Harrold, 72 Pa. 267 (1872); Wait v. Richardson, 33 Vt. 190 (1860). But actual net income is sometimes awarded. See, e.g., Edwards v. Lee's Adm'r, 265 Ky. 418, 96 S.W.2d 1028 (1936). See also Stylianopoulos v. Stylianopoulos, 17 Mass.App. 64, 455 N.E.2d 477 (1983), review denied 390 Mass. 1107, 459 N.E.2d 824 (1984) (occupying cotenant liable for rental value only if he "ousted" other cotenant(s) or agreed to pay); Weaver v. American Nat. Bank, 452 So.2d 469 (Ala.1984).

10. E.g., Warner v. Warner, 248 Ala. 556, 28 So.2d 701 (1946); Desroches v. McCrary, 315 Mich. 611, 24 N.W.2d 511 (1946); Arnold v. De Booy, 161 Minn. 255, 201 N.W. 437, 39 A.L.R. 403 (1924); Beer v. Beer, 12 C.B. 60, 138 Eng.Rep. 823 (1852); Succession of Le-Blanc, 577 So.2d 105 (La.App.1991).

ant(s),[11] or (2) he had entered into a lease or rental agreement giving him the exclusive right to possession of the land for a term,[12] or (3) he was the guardian of or trustee for the other cotenant(s).[13] But the common law rule was changed in England by a statute enacted in 1704, commonly known as the Statute of Anne,[14] which provided that a cotenant must account, as bailiff, for any rents and profits he might receive from the property in excess of his just proportion. This statute has been narrowly construed in England so that it is applicable only to rents actually received by a cotenant from a third person [15]—not to income derived from a non-tortious use of the property by the cotenant himself, even though the income is obtained from exploitation of mineral or timber resources in a way that permanently reduces the value of the property.[16]

Most American jurisdictions have either substantially re-enacted the Statute of Anne [17] or have declared it to be part of their common law.[18] In most of these jurisdictions, the duty to account has been limited almost as narrowly as in England,[19] but the cotenant who derives income from a non-tortious use of the land that permanently reduces its value has generally been required to account to the other cotenants.[20] In a minority of the American jurisdictions, the duty to account applies more broadly whenever one cotenant derives any income from the sole possession of the property in

---

11. In the absence of an express agreement the co-tenant in possession was neither bailiff nor agent. Co.Litt. *200b.

12. In such case, the occupying co-tenant had to pay the agreed rent, or a reasonable rent if no definite rent was fixed. See, e.g., Burk v. Burk, 247 Ala. 91, 22 So.2d 609 (1945); Kites v. Church, 142 Mass. 586, 8 N.E. 743 (1886); Stylianopoulos v. Stylianopoulos, supra note 9.

13. The guardian or trustee was accountable for actual net income, or the reasonable rental value if there was no actual income. See, e.g., Minion v. Warner, 238 N.Y. 413, 144 N.E. 665, 41 A.L.R. 1412 (1924).

14. Stat. 4 Anne, c. 16, § 27 (1704). See, generally, 2 Am.L.Prop. § 6.14 at p. 59; Weible, Accountability of Cotenants, 29 Iowa L.Rev. 558, 559 (1944).

15. Job v. Patton, L.R. 20 Eq. 84 (1872).

16. E.g., Job v. Patton, supra note 15 (working of coal mine by one co-tenant).

17. The American statutes usually authorize an action both for an accounting and for recovery of "money had and received to the use of the plaintiff." 2 Am.L.Prop. § 6.14 n. 10.

18. E.g., Flack v. Gosnell, 76 Md. 88, 24 A. 414, 16 L.R.A. 547 (1892); Brown v. Wellington, 106 Mass. 318 (1871); Lancaster v. Flowers, 208 Pa. 199, 57 A. 526 (1904). See also Lohmann v. Lohmann, 50 N.J.Super. 37, 141 A.2d 84 (1958). But see Pico v. Columbet, 12 Cal. 414 (1859). Generally, see Comments, 42

Marquette L.Rev. 363 (1958), 12 Wyo.L.J. 156 (1958).

19. E.g., Dabney–Johnston Oil Corp. v. Walden, 4 Cal.2d 637, 52 P.2d 237 (1935); Coggan v. Coggan, 239 So.2d 17 (Fla.1970); Mastbaum v. Mastbaum, 126 N.J.Eq. 336, 9 A.2d 51 (1939); Le Barron v. House, 122 N.Y. 153, 25 N.E. 253, 9 L.R.A. 625 (1890); Diedricks v. Reinhardt, 466 So.2d 375 (Fla.App. 1985) (occupying cotenant not accountable for non-rent benefits, absent "ouster" or adverse possession); Smith v. Smith, 464 So.2d 1287 (Fla.App.1985) (occupying cotenant not accountable for his non-exclusive possession or the non-exclusive possession of his tenant). See also Baird v. Moore, 50 N.J.Super. 156, 141 A.2d 324 (1958) (equitable considerations led court not to charge tenant in possession with actual rents or rental value). Of course, an occupying cotenant is accountable for rents actually received by him. E.g., Albright v. Albright, 73 Or.App. 410, 699 P.2d 195 (1985).

20. McCord v. Oakland Quicksilver Mining Co., 64 Cal. 134, 27 P. 863 (1883); Abbey v. Wheeler, 170 N.Y. 122, 62 N.E. 1074 (1901), reargument denied 171 N.Y. 650, 63 N.E. 1115 (1902) (called "waste" but cotenant was accountable for net profits not liable for damages); Meeker v. Denver Producing & Refining Co., 199 Okl. 455, 188 P.2d 854 (1947); White v. Smyth, 147 Tex. 272, 214 S.W.2d 967 (1948), noted 27 Tex.L.Rev. 863 (1949) (co-tenant who mined and marketed rock asphalt was accountable for net profits from mining, processing and sale, not for value of asphalt in the ground).

the form of rents or otherwise.[21]   And in a few states, a cotenant in sole possession must account for the reasonable rental value of the land even if he derives no actual income from it.[22]   But there is no duty to account for income produced by improvements on the land made by the occupying cotenant alone.[23]

In some jurisdictions the interest of a cotenant subject to a duty to account for income received is also subject to an equitable lien,[24] but no such lien exists in most jurisdictions.[25]

Exclusive use of property subject to concurrent ownership by one cotenant may be tortious because he has "ousted" the other cotenants[26] or because he has committed waste.   Actions for waste against a fellow joint tenant or tenant in common were authorized in England in 1285,[27] and similar statutes have been enacted in most American jurisdictions.[28]   In England, however, the statute was given only limited application to cotenants in fee simple, on the ground that such cotenants were entitled to the same broad privileges of use and enjoyment as the sole owner of a defeasible fee simple estate[29]—i.e., a cotenant in fee simple would only be subject to an injunction for "waste" if he used the realty in a "malicious" or "unconscionable" manner.   Thus one cotenant in fee simple was not guilty of waste if he cut and sold mature timber that had no special ornamental value,[30] or opened and operated mines or quarries while in sole possession of the realty.[31]

The American case law as to "waste" is extremely confused.   Some cases hold or say that a cotenant is liable for waste if he cuts timber or opens new mines, oil and gas wells, or quarries;[32] other cases hold that such conduct

---

21. E.g., Armstrong v. Rodemacher, 199 Iowa 928, 203 N.W. 23 (1925); Lohmann v. Lohmann, supra note 18; Griffin v. Griffin, 82 S.C. 256, 64 S.E. 160 (1909). In Pennsylvania, cotenant in possession of mineral estate who develops the minerals is subject to duty to account to non-occupying cotenants for their pro rata share of income received by occupying cotenant. Lichtenfels v. Bridgeview Coal Co., 344 Pa.Super. 257, 496 A.2d 782 (1985).

22. McPherson v. McPherson, 33 N.C. 391 (1850); McKnight v. Basilides, 19 Wn.2d 391, 143 P.2d 307 (1943). See also Baird v. Moore, supra note 19.

In some states the occupying cotenant is liable for a proportionate share of the reasonable rental value of the land by virtue of a statute other than the Statute of Anne. See, e.g., West v. Weyer, 46 Ohio St. 66, 18 N.E. 537 (1888); Collins v. Jackson, 34 Ohio App.3d 101, 517 N.E.2d 269 (1986).

23. E.g., Hannah v. Carver, 121 Ind. 278, 23 N.E. 93 (1889); Van Ormer v. Harley, 102 Iowa 150, 71 N.W. 241 (1897); Larmon v. Larmon, 173 Ky. 477, 191 S.W. 110 (1917). Also see Haas v. Haas, 165 F.Supp. 701 (D.Del. 1958).

24. E.g., New Winder Lumber Co. v. Guest, 182 Ga. 859, 187 S.E. 63 (1936); Stevens v. Pels, 191 Iowa 176, 175 N.W. 303 (1919); Peets

v. Wright, 117 S.C. 409, 109 S.E. 649 (1921). See Note, 27 Harv.L.Rev. 397 (1914).

25. E.g., Griffin v. Ayers, 233 Ala. 389, 171 So. 719 (1936); Whitehurst v. Hinton, 209 N.C. 392, 184 S.E. 66 (1936); Tedder v. Tedder, 123 S.C. 346, 116 S.E. 436 (1923).

26. See text ante at notes 14–20.

27. Stat. of Westminster, 13 Edw. I, c. 22 (1285).

28. E.g., N.Y.—McKinney's R.P.L. § 525.

29. E.g., Martyn v. Knollys, 8 T.R. 145, 101 Eng.Rep. 1313 (1799); Job v. Patton, L.R. 20 Eq. 84 (1872).

30. Martyn v. Knollys, supra note 29.

31. Job v. Patton, supra note 29.

32. E.g., Clark v. Whitfield, 218 Ala. 593, 119 So. 631 (1929) (mining); Fitzhugh v. Norwood, 153 Ark. 412, 241 S.W. 8 (1922) (timber); Page v. Donnelly, 346 Mass. 768, 193 N.E.2d 682 (1963) (timber); Childs v. Kansas City, St. Joseph & Council Bluffs Railroad Co., 117 Mo. 414, 23 S.W. 373 (1893); Abbey v. Wheeler, 170 N.Y. 122, 62 N.E. 1074 (1901), reargument denied 171 N.Y. 650, 63 N.E. 1115 (1902); Cosgriff v. Dewey, 164 N.Y. 1, 58 N.E. 1 (1900); Cecil v. Clark, 49 W.Va. 459, 39 S.E. 202 (1901); Dotson v. Branham, 197 Va. 674, 90 S.E.2d 783 (1956) (mining).

does not constitute waste.[33] In most of the cases where American courts have said that a cotenant in fee simple was liable for waste because of such conduct, however, they have not imposed the usual penalties for waste, such as treble damages, but have simply required the defendant cotenant to account for the net profits derived from his use of the property.[34] Of course, if the cotenant in sole possession has "ousted" his cotenants and commits waste, the ousted cotenants may recover damages for "waste" as an alternative to recovering "mesne profits" in an ejectment action.[35]

§ 5.9   Rights of Cotenants Inter Se—Contribution Toward Carrying Charges of Common Property

When one cotenant pays more than his pro rata share of the cost of necessary repairs on the property, he may assert his equitable right to compel the other cotenants to contribute proportionately to the cost of the repairs in an accounting for rents and profits[1] or in the final settlement of accounts between the cotenants on partition.[2] Absent an agreement, express or implied, that the other cotenants will contribute, the cases are divided as to whether the cotenant who pays more than his pro rata share of the cost of repairs may maintain an independent action for contribution against the other cotenants.[3] If one looks only at what the courts say, the prevailing

See also Green v. Crawford, 662 S.W.2d 123 (Tex.App.1983), error refused n.r.e. (selling cotenants and vendees were liable for conversion of timber cut by vendees and removed from land, where timber cut was more than selling cotenants' pro rata share).

Choser Corp. v. Owens, 235 Va. 660, 370 S.E.2d 305 (1988) (when less than all cotenants authorized lessee to mine coal, mining constituted waste which the court would enjoin on petition of the other cotenants in order to prevent "irreparable harm").

33. E.g., McCord v. Oakland Quicksilver Mining Co., 64 Cal. 134, 27 P. 863 (1883); Meeker v. Denver Producing & Refining Co., 199 Okl. 455, 188 P.2d 854 (1947); White v. Smyth, 147 Tex. 272, 214 S.W.2d 967 (1948), noted 27 Tex.L.Rev. 863 (1949); Lichtenfels v. Bridgeview Coal Co., 344 Pa.Super. 257, 496 A.2d 782 (1985) (one cotenant cannot restrain another cotenant from realizing value of mineral estate by producing or consuming the minerals, but has a right to recover a pro rata share of the value of minerals extracted). In all these cases, the producing co-tenant was held accountable for net income, but was not liable for "waste".

34. See, e.g., Childs v. Kansas City, St. Joseph & Council Bluffs Railroad Co., Abbey v. Wheeler, Cosgriff v. Dewey, and Cecil v. Clark, supra note 32.

35. In some of the cases where the court purports to impose liability for "waste," the co-tenant charged with "waste" had ousted his co-tenants and could also have been liable for "mesne profits" in an ejectment action.

§ 5.9

1. E.g., Van Veen v. Van Veen, 213 Iowa 323, 236 N.W. 1, 238 N.W. 718 (1931); Pickering v. Pickering, 63 N.H. 468, 3 A. 744 (1885); Fassitt v. Seip, 249 Pa. 576, 95 A. 273, 6 A.L.R. 1671 (1915); Ward v. Ward's Heirs, 40 W.Va. 611, 21 S.E. 746, 29 L.R.A. 449 (1895).

2. E.g., In re Cochran's Real Estate, 31 Del.Ch. 545, 66 A.2d 497 (1949); Larmon v. Larmon, 173 Ky. 477, 191 S.W. 110 (1917); Williams v. Coombs, 88 Me. 183, 33 A. 1073 (1895); Hogan v. McMahon, 115 Md. 195, 80 A. 695 (1911); Stylianopoulos v. Stylianopoulos, 17 Mass.App.Ct. 64, 455 N.E.2d 477 (1983), review denied 390 Mass. 1107, 459 N.E.2d 824 (1984).

3. Co.Litt. * 300b; Shelangowski v. Schrack, 162 Iowa 176, 143 N.W. 1081 (1913); Calvert v. Aldrich, 99 Mass. 74 (1868); Barry v. Barry, 147 Neb. 1067, 26 N.W.2d 1 (1947); Baird v. Moore, 50 N.J.Super. 156, 141 A.2d 324 (1958); Johnson v. Hendrickson, 71 S.D. 392, 24 N.W.2d 914 (1946); Perez v. Hernandez, 658 S.W.2d 697 (Tex.App.1983) (cotenant who incurs expenses necessary for preservation of property, such as taxes, is entitled to reimbursement from other cotenants). "The question of how much should be expended on repairs, their character and extent, and whether as a matter of judgment such expenditures are justified is, fundamentally, only one of the many questions which may arise between the cotenants in their use and enjoyment of the common property. The law cannot possibly settle such details where the cotenants do not agree. * * * The law's remedy in all such cases is partition; * * * and in

view seems to allow the independent action for contribution provided the cotenant who makes the repairs has notified the other cotenants of the need for repairs. But in many of the cases announcing this view, the right to contribution was actually enforced in an action for an accounting for rents and profits or in a partition action, and the courts' statements as to the availability of an independent action for contribution are only dicta.[4] And the courts appear to be unanimous in holding that a cotenant who pays more than his pro rata share of the cost of improvements (as distinct from repairs) to the common property constructed without the consent of the other cotenants can obtain contribution only in the final accounting incident to a successful partition action.[5]

A cotenant, not in sole possession, who pays more than his pro rata share of property taxes or mortgage interest and/or principal has a right of contribution [6] which may be asserted either in an independent action,[7] an action for an accounting,[8] or a partition action.[9] If the cotenants are personally liable for the property taxes (not usually the case) or the mortgage payments (sometimes the case), a personal judgment may be rendered in an independent action for contribution.[10] If the cotenants are not personally liable, the right to contribution from those cotenants who have not paid their pro rata shares can be made effective only by obtaining judicial

that action he will be credited with * * * expenditures [for reasonable repairs] in the final accounting." 2 Am.L.Prop. § 6.18 at p. 78. But cf. Hahn v. Hahn, 297 S.W.2d 559 (Mo.1957).

4. E.g., Pickering v. Pickering, Fassitt v. Seip, supra note 1; Larmon v. Larmon, William v. Coombs, and Hogan v. McMahon, supra note 2.

5. E.g., Shelangowski v. Schrack, Barry v. Barry, and Baird v. Moore, supra note 3; Fassitt v. Seip and Ward v. Ward's Heirs, supra note 1; Perez v. Hernandez, supra note 3 (improving cotenant not entitled to reimbursement in independent action for cost of development of property as a citrus grove). "Improvements made by the voluntary action of one of the cotenants become part of the land and therefore all the cotenants can claim ownership, but in the absence of a contract to pay his share of the cost there is no reason, legal or equitable, why any other tenant should be required to contribute [either in an independent action or in an action for an account of rents and profits]." 2 Am.L.Prop. § 1.18 at p. 81. Also, see ante Section 5.12, text at note 20, and authorities cited.

Of course, credit may be awarded to an improving cotenant in the final accounting in a partition action. See post § 5.12.

6. Taxes: E.g., Cocks v. Simmons, 55 Ark. 104, 17 S.W. 594 (1891); Eads v. Retherford, 114 Ind. 273, 16 N.E. 587 (1888); Hogan v. McMahon, supra note 2; Van Veen v. Van Veen, supra note 1; Hogan v. McMahon, supra note 2; Kites v. Church, 142 Mass. 586, 8 N.E. 743 (1886); Woolston v. Pullen, 88 N.J.Eq. 35, 102 A. 461 (1917); Fassitt v. Seip,

supra note 1. Mortgage payments: E.g., Kelly v. Carmichael, 221 Ala. 371, 129 So. 81 (1930); Scanlon v. Parish, 85 Conn. 379, 82 A. 969 (1912); Laura v. Christian, 88 N.M. 127, 537 P.2d 1389 (1975); Connell v. Welch, 101 Wis. 8, 76 N.W. 596 (1898); Spessard v. Spessard, 64 Md.App. 83, 494 A.2d 701 (1985) (right to contribution recognized; rationale is that the non-paying cotenant's interest has been protected from extinction by tax sale or mortgage foreclosure). But the courts may reject particular contribution claims. See, e.g., Allen v. Allen, 687 S.W.2d 660 (Mo.App.1985) (occupying cotenant not entitled to contribution where rental value of land exceeded amount of taxes paid); Albright v. Albright, 73 Or. App. 410, 699 P.2d 195 (1985) (occupying cotenant not entitled to contribution where charges for some expenses were unjustified and occupying cotenant was liable for other cotenants' pro rata share of rents).

7. E.g., Eads v. Retherford, supra note 6; Kites v. Church, supra note 6.

8. E.g., Hogan v. McMahon, supra note 2; Fassitt v. Seip, supra note 1. See Annot., 27 A.L.R. 249 (1923).

9. E.g., Cocks v. Simmons, supra note 6; Van Veen v. Van Veen, supra 1; Hahn v. Hahn, supra note 3; Woolston v. Pullen, supra note 6; Spessard v. Spessard, supra note 6; Kamin–A–Kalaw v. Dulic, 322 Md. 49, 585 A.2d 216 (1991).

10. E.g., Troy v. Protestant Episcopal Church, 174 Ala. 380, 56 So. 982 (1911); Dickinson v. Williams, 65 Mass. (11 Cush.) 258 (1853) (mortgage was assumed).

recognition and enforcement of an equitable lien on the property [11] or by subrogation to and enforcement of the lien held by the taxing authority or mortgage holder, as the case may be.[12] In either case, the ultimate result will be a judicial sale of the property and an equitable distribution of the proceeds, as is frequently the case when the court enters an order for partition.[13]

If a cotenant who is in sole possession of the common property, though he has not excluded his cotenants, has paid taxes or made mortgage payments in excess of his pro rata share, he cannot obtain contribution in any form of action if the value of his use and occupation exceeds such payments.[14] A cotenant who has excluded his cotenants (and is therefore an adverse possessor) can never maintain an action for contribution against the cotenants,[15] but in an action by the cotenants to recover possession and mesne profits, he will be credited with the amounts in excess of his pro rata share expended for property taxes or mortgage payments.[16]

§ 5.10　Rights of Cotenants Inter Se—Acquisition of Outstanding Interests in Common Property

When cotenants acquire their concurrent interests at the same time, either by the same instrument or by inheritance from a common ancestor, they are held to be subject to fiduciary duties with respect to their dealings with the common property.[1] Since all joint tenants and most tenants in

11. E.g., Kelly v. Carmichael, supra note 6; Eads v. Retherford, supra note 6; Kirsch v. Scandia American Bank, 160 Minn. 269, 199 N.W. 881 (1924); Hahn v. Hahn, supra note 3; Connell v. Welch, supra note 6. But see Kites v. Church, supra note 6 (money judgment for contribution in suit on "account annexed").

12. E.g., Scanlon v. Parish, supra note 6; Hansen v. Cerro Gordo State Bank, 209 Iowa 1352, 230 N.W. 415 (1930). See also Baird v. Moore, supra note 3. Subrogation to the lien of the mortgage holder is possible only when the entire indebtedness is discharged. See L. Simpson, Suretyship § 47 (1950).

13. See post Section 5.13.

14. Ward v. Pipkin, 181 Ark. 736, 27 S.W.2d 523 (1930); Willmon v. Koyer, 168 Cal. 369, 143 P. 694, L.R.A. 1915B (1914); Ellis v. Snyder, 83 Kan. 638, 112 P. 594, 32 L.R.A. (N.S.) 233 (1911); Mastbaum v. Mastbaum, 126 N.J.Eq. 366, 9 A.2d 51 (1939); Roberts v. Roberts, 136 Tex. 255, 150 S.W.2d 236 (1941). In Ward v. Pipkin, supra, the court said it would be presumed that the benefits received by the occupying co-tenant were at least equal to the taxes paid, in the absence of evidence to the contrary.

15. E.g., Victoria Copper Mining Co. v. Rich, 193 Fed. 314 (6th Cir.1911) (conclusive presumption that benefits are at least equal to taxes paid); Appeal of Wistar, 125 Pa. 526, 17 A. 460, 11 Am.St.Rep. 917 (1889). But see Lovin v. Poss, 240 Ga. 848, 242 S.E.2d 609 (1978) (occupying co-tenant entitled to contribution in *his* action for equitable accounting).

16. E.g., Willmon v. Koyer, supra note 14; Engle v. Terrell, 281 Ky. 88, 134 S.W.2d 980 (1939); Smith v. Mount, 149 Mo.App. 668, 129 S.W. 722 (1910) (credit for taxes but not improvements; independent action after partition); Eaton v. Davis, 165 Va. 313, 182 S.E. 229 (1935) (improvements); Plebuch v. Barnes, 149 Wash. 221, 270 P. 823 (1928) (taxes and assessments).

See also Spessard v. Spessard, supra note 6 (husband's claim for contribution could be considered in determining monetary award to wife in divorce action).

§ 5.10

1. E.g., Minion v. Warner, 238 N.Y. 413, 144 N.E. 665, 41 A.L.R. 1412 (1924); Givens v. Givens, 387 S.W.2d 851 (Ky.1965) (dictum); Dampier v. Polk, 214 Miss. 65, 58 So.2d 44 (1952); Foster v. Hudson, 437 So.2d 528 (Ala. 1983). The requirements for a fiduciary relationship are, of course, always satisfied in a tenancy by the entirety or a joint tenancy. And some cases hold that there is a fiduciary relationship between tenants in common simply because of the "unity of possession," although the other unities are lacking. E.g., Smith v. Borradaile, 30 N.M. 62, 227 P. 602 (1922). Moreover, tenants in common may, by their own conduct, create a fiduciary relationship among themselves; e.g., the co-tenants may make one of their number an agent for the others, as in West v. Madansky, 80 Okl. 161, 194 P. 439 (1920).

common do, in fact, acquire their interests at the same time and from a common source, it seems clear that a fiduciary relationship exists among most groups of cotenants.

A major consequence of the existence of a fiduciary relationship among a group of cotenants is that an individual cotenant who acquires an outstanding superior title to the common property must hold it for the benefit of the other cotenants, provided they offer to contribute their pro rata shares of the cost of acquisition within a reasonable time.[2] This rule does not apply, however, if the outstanding superior title was acquired before the concurrent estate was created or after it ceased to exist.[3] Thus, e.g., if A takes a mortgage on Blackacre from the owner and subsequently A, B, and C become cotenants of Blackacre, A is not required to hold the mortgage for the benefit of B and C, and may enforce the mortgage as if he were a stranger rather than a cotenant. Similarly, there is no fiduciary duty to hold for the benefit of the other cotenants if A buys Blackacre, formerly concurrently owned by A, B, and C, after the expiration of any statutory redemption period, from a third person who purchased Blackacre at a tax sale, mortgage foreclosure sale, or execution sale.[4] But where A buys Blackacre, concurrently owned by A, B, and C, subject to a statutory right of redemption, at a tax, mortgage foreclosure, or execution sale, or redeems from such a sale, or buys from a third person who purchased at such a sale— thus acquiring title to the property while the concurrent estate still exists— the courts are divided as to whether A is subject to a fiduciary duty requiring him to hold the title for the benefit of B and C.[5]

Some of the cases permitting the purchasing cotenant (A, in the last example, above) to hold the title for his own sole benefit simply assert that the other cotenants, if adults, had an equal opportunity to bid at the sale— absent some fraudulent or other inequitable conduct on the part of the purchasing cotenant—and that there is thus no basis to hold that any one

---

2. E.g., Chatman v. Hall, 246 Ala. 403, 20 So.2d 713 (1945); Fuller v. McBurrows, 229 Ga. 422, 192 S.E.2d 144 (1972); Chapin v. Stewart, 71 Idaho 306, 230 P.2d 998 (1951); Givens v. Givens, 387 S.W.2d 851 (Ky.1965); Raker v. G.C. Murphy Co., 358 Pa. 339, 58 A.2d 18 (1948); Cecil v. Dollar, 147 Tex. 541, 218 S.W.2d 448 (1949); Finley v. Bailey, 440 So.2d 1019 (Ala.1983). See Annot., 54 A.L.R. 874 (1928).

3. E.g., Watson v. Edwards, 105 Cal. 70, 38 P. 527 (1894); Franklin v. Dragoo, 155 Ind. App. 682, 294 N.E.2d 165 (1973); Ford v. Jellico Grocery Co., 194 Ky. 552, 240 S.W. 65 (1922); Fuller v. Dennistoun, 164 Minn. 160, 204 N.W. 958 (1925).

4. E.g., Hurley v. Hurley, 148 Mass. 444, 19 N.E. 545, 2 L.R.A. 172 (1889); Franklin v. Dragoo, supra note 3; Hamilton v. Shaw, 286 S.C. 374, 334 S.E.2d 139 (App.1985) (provided there is no fraud or collusion).

5. That it must be so held, see, e.g., Batson v. Etheridge, 239 Ala. 535, 195 So. 873 (1940)

(tax sale); Hollaway v. Berenzen, 208 Ark. 849, 188 S.W.2d 298 (1945) (same); Pease v. Snyder, 169 Kan. 628, 220 P.2d 151 (1950) (execution sale); Carpenter v. Carpenter, 131 N.Y. 101, 29 N.E. 1013 (1892) (mortgage foreclosure sale); Rebelo v. Cardoso, 91 R.I. 153, 161 A.2d 806 (1960) (same); Stevahn v. Meidinger, 79 N.D. 323, 57 N.W.2d 1 (1952) (cotenant redeemed after mortgage foreclosure sale). See also Foster v. Hudson, supra note 1 (when property was reconveyed to cotenants after statutory redemption, the foreclosure sale was nullified and legal title restored to cotenants as if no sale ·had occurred; hence cotenants still owned undivided ¾ and ¼ interests, respectively, not equal interests as would be the case if they were acquiring title for the first time).

Contra, see, e.g., Plant v. Plant, 171 Cal. 765, 154 P. 1058 (1916); Wenzel v. O'Neal, 222 S.W. 392 (Mo.1920); Jackson v. Baird, 148 N.C. 29, 61 S.E. 632, 19 L.R.A. (N.S.) 591 (1908); Davis v. Solari, 132 Tenn. 225, 177 S.W. 939 (1915).

cotenant had a duty to purchase for the benefit of the others.[6] This rationale, however, ignores the basic assumption that the cotenants are subject to fiduciary duties, by virtue of their relationship, so long as that relationship continues.

Some cases requiring the cotenant who purchases at a tax sale to hold the title for the benefit of the other cotenants assert that all cotenants have a duty to pay property taxes on the common property and that no one cotenant, after failing to discharge that duty, can "take advantage of his own wrong" in order to acquire title to the property for his own sole benefit.[7] But this argument is not entirely persuasive, since property taxes normally do not impose any personal obligation on the property owner and can be collected only by enforcement of a lien on the property itself.[8] It is difficult to see why the failure to discharge that lien by payment is any more "wrongful" than the failure of a grantee who takes property "subject to" an outstanding mortgage, but without assuming any personal obligation to discharge that mortgage, to pay the mortgage debt.[9] It seems clear that the concept of fiduciary duty provides a better basis for requiring the purchasing cotenant to hold the title acquired at a tax sale for the benefit of all the cotenants; and in fact, that is generally the basis for similar holdings in cases involving purchase by one cotenant at a mortgage foreclosure or an execution sale.

Suppose one cotenant purchases the common property at a mortgage foreclosure or execution sale in a jurisdiction where there is no statutory right to redeem after the sale. Should the purchasing cotenant, in such a case, be held to acquire the title for the benefit of his cotenants, or to acquire the title for his own sole benefit? The cases give no clear answer to this question. As a matter of strict logic, it is arguable that the purchasing cotenant should acquire the title for his own sole benefit because he acquires it only upon termination of the concurrent estate which is the essential basis for recognition of a fiduciary relationship among the cotenants.

If the purchasing cotenant is guilty of fraud or other inequitable conduct in connection with the sale—e.g., if he has persuaded the other cotenants not to bid by representing that he will protect their interests—he obviously should not be allowed to "take advantage of his own wrong" and should be held to take title to the common property subject to a constructive trust in favor of the other cotenants.[10] And it is certainly arguable that, where the

---

6. E.g., Plant v. Plant, Wenzel v. O'Neal, Jackson v. Baird, Davis v. Solari—all supra note 5.

7. E.g., Batson v. Etheridge and Hollaway v. Berenzen, supra note 5.

8. Hamilton v. Shaw, supra note 4 (there is no duty on part of any cotenant to redeem common property from tax sale in the absence of a contractual duty to do so). The tax lien is enforced by a public sale of the property for non-payment of the taxes levied in particular years.

9. In most of the litigated cases the cotenants are not personally obligated to the mortgage holder, having acquired title by inheritance, devise, or purchase after the land

was mortgaged, and not having "assumed" the mortgage debt.

10. E.g., Caldwell v. Caldwell, 173 Ala. 216, 55 So. 515 (1911) (one co-tenant fraudulently arranged with others not to bid at sale, representing that he would give the others time to redeem); Cohen v. Friedman, 259 Ill. 416, 102 N.E. 815 (1913) (third person bought at sale under agreement with one co-tenant to convey to that co-tenant after statutory redemption period expired); Mosher v. Van Buskirk, 104 N.J.Eq. 89, 144 A. 446 (1929) (collusion by purchasing co-tenants as to infant co-tenants); Carpenter v. Carpenter, supra note 5 (foreclosure induced by co-tenants in order to buy in and destroy interests of infant co-tenants).

cotenants are personally liable for payment of a mortgage debt or a judgment, none of the cotenants should be allowed to improve his position by defaulting and then purchasing the common property at a mortgage foreclosure or execution sale because that would permit him to "take advantage of his own wrong." [11]

In order to assert their rights under the rule requiring the purchasing cotenant to hold the title he acquires for the benefit of all the cotenants, the other cotenants must, within a "reasonable time" after notice of the acquisition, either pay or offer to pay their pro rata shares of the amount expended by the purchasing cotenant to acquire title to the common property.[12] Failure to pay or offer to pay within a "reasonable time" will bar the rights of the other cotenants by virtue of the doctrines of repudiation, abandonment, laches, and/or estoppel.[13]

If the fiduciary duty rule is applied where one cotenant acquires the title subject to a statutory right of redemption, any of his cotenants may, of course, exercise that right within the period allowed by the statute. But the statutory period is usually quite short,[14] and statutory redemption requires tender of the entire amount paid for the property by the purchasing cotenant.[15] Under the fiduciary duty rule, on the other hand, any cotenant may preserve his rights by contributing only his pro rata share of the amount paid for the property by the purchasing cotenant,[16] and the "reasonable time" within which he must offer to contribute will generally be much longer than the statutory redemption period.[17]

See also Hamilton v. Shaw, supra note 4.

11. It has been so held, e.g., in Skolnick v. Skolnick, 131 Conn. 561, 41 A.2d 452 (1945); Hardin v. Council, 200 Ga. 822, 38 S.E.2d 549 (1946); Schilbach v. Schilbach, 171 Md. 405, 189 A. 432 (1936); Jolley v. Corry, 671 P.2d 139 (Utah 1983). A similar rule is applied where a grantee who assumes both the first and second mortgages on the property defaults on both and then buys in at the first mortgagee's foreclosure sale; in such case, the purchaser will "in equity" hold title subject to the second mortgage even though the second mortgagee's interest was foreclosed "at law." See, e.g., Hilton v. Bissell, 1 Sandf.Ch. 407 (N.Y.1844).

12. E.g., Draper v. Sewell, 263 Ala. 250, 82 So.2d 303 (1955); Smith v. Goethe, 159 Cal. 628, 115 P. 223 (1911); Wilson v. Linder, 21 Idaho 576, 123 P. 487, 42 L.R.A.(N.S.) 242 (1912); Mason v. Barrett, 295 Ky. 462, 174 S.W.2d 702 (1943); Duson v. Roos, 123 La. 835, 49 So. 590, 131 Am.St.Rep. 375 (1909). Toole v. Lawrence, 144 Neb. 779, 14 N.W.2d 607 (1944); Laura v. Christian, 88 N.M. 127, 537 P.2d 1389 (1975); Morris v. Roseberry, 46 W.Va. 24, 32 S.E. 1019 (1899). For additional cases, see Annot. 54 A.L.R. 875, at 910 (1928), id. 85 A.L.R. 1535, at 1538 (1933).

But see Jolley v. Corry, supra note 11 (where purchasing cotenant was the only one personally liable for mortgage debt, she was not entitled to contribution because she was merely paying her own debt rather than making an advance for the benefit of all the cotenants).

13. See cases cited supra note 12.

14. Periods range from six months to two years for redemption from mortgage foreclosure sales, but most such redemption statutes provide for a one-year period. In most of the twenty-six states with such statutes, the owners have the right to possession during the redemption period. See G. Osborne, G. Nelson, and D. Whitman, Real Estate Finance Law § 8.4 at p. 537 (1979).

15. See, e.g., Iowa Code Ann. § 628.11; Mich.Comp.Laws Ann. § 692.3140; Minn.Stat. Ann. § 580.23. For general discussion of statutory redemption from mortgage sales, see G. Osborne, G. Nelson, & D. Whitman, Real Estate Finance Laws §§ 8.4 through 8.7 (1979); G. Osborne, Mortgages §§ 8 and 307 through 310 (2d. ed. 1970).

16. See cases cited supra note 12.

17. The general principle is that delay becomes "unreasonable" only where there is a change of position or a change in the condition of the property that renders it inequitable to enforce the purchasing co-tenant's fiduciary duty—i.e., where the doctrine of laches or estoppel is applicable. See, e.g., Mason v. Barrett, supra note 12 (more than 20 years' delay not unreasonable where no change of position or change in condition of property); Duson v. Roos, supra note 29 (duty of purchas-

If one cotenant pays off and discharges an outstanding mortgage on the common property, he will have a lien to secure his right to pro rata contribution from the other cotenants.[18] If, instead, one cotenant buys the mortgage and takes an assignment of it, his position will be substantially the same (assuming there is a fiduciary relationship among the cotenants), since he must hold the mortgage for the benefit of the other cotenants.[19] In either case, each of the other cotenants may preserve his undivided interest by paying his pro rata share of the amount expended to pay off or acquire the mortgage within a "reasonable time."[20] If any cotenant fails to offer to contribute his pro rata share before the paying cotenant brings a suit to foreclose his lien or mortgage, or to quiet title, it is not clear whether the additional time allowed to the other cotenant for contribution would exceed, in any case, the usual "short period" allowed for equitable redemption prior to a judicial foreclosure sale.[21] Nor is it clear whether a court would delay an out-of-court foreclosure sale pursuant to an express power of sale in the mortgage in order to allow a cotenant to contribute his pro rata share of the amount expended by the paying cotenant.[22]

Cotenants for a term of years who acquire their interests at the same time may invoke the fiduciary duty rule so that a renewal of the lease or a new lease obtained by one cotenant will be held for the benefit of all, subject to the requirement that each must continue to contribute his pro rata share of the rent payable under the new or extended lease.[23] And the rule has been applied where one coremainderman acquires a term of years from the life tenant before the remainder becomes a present estate.[24] But the purchase of the life estate by one coremainderman,[25] or the purchase of the reversion by one colessee,[26] does not come within the rule because, in such cases, neither the life estate nor the reversion is a "hostile" interest vis-a-vis the non-purchasing coremaindermen or colessees. Nor does the fiduciary

ing co-tenant cannot be enforced where other co-tenants have waited to see whether the property will increase in value). But see Draper v. Sewell, supra note 12 (3 or 4 years' delay is unreasonable); Savage v. Bradley, 149 Ala. 169, 43 So. 20, 123 Am.St.Rep. 30 (1907) ("by analogy to the term fixed for the exercise of the statutory right of redemption, two years is the limit of time within which election by a co-tenant should be made in order to avail himself of the redemptioner's act").

18. See ante Section 5.9, text at note 11 and authorities cited. See also Laura v. Christian, supra note 12 (paying co-tenant sued to quiet title and another co-tenant claimed right to preserve his interest by making pro rata contribution; this right was recognized, subject to an expressly declared lien in favor of the paying co-tenant).

19. E.g., McArthur v. Dumaw, 328 Mich. 453, 43 N.W.2d 924 (1950); Jones v. Stanton, 11 Mo. 433 (1848). But see Patterson v. Wilson, 203 Okl. 527, 223 P.2d 770 (1950).

20. See cases cited supra notes 11, 17 and 18. Ordinarily, any person seeking to exercise an equitable right to redeem from a mortgage must pay the entire mortgage debt even

if he owns only a fractional interest in the property. E.g., Douglass v. Bishop, 27 Iowa 214 (1869); Lamson v. Drake, 105 Mass. 564 (1870); Hamilton v. Dobbs, 19 N.J.Eq. 227 (1868); Wunderle v. Ellis, 212 Pa. 618, 62 A. 106, 4 Ann.Cas. 806 (1905).

21. This period must be long enough to permit the foreclosure sale to be advertised as required by statute, but rarely exceeds three months.

22. In such cases, statutory advertisement requirements must also be satisfied, which will delay the sale for two or three months.

23. E.g., Thayer v. Leggett, 229 N.Y. 152, 128 N.E. 133 (1920); Weaver v. Akin, 48 W.Va. 456, 37 S.E. 600 (1900).

24. Givens v. Givens, 387 S.W.2d 851 (Ky. 1965).

25. E.g., Frank v. Frank, 305 Ill. 181, 137 N.E. 151 (1922); McLaughlin v. McLaughlin, 80 Md. 115, 30 A. 607 (1894).

26. E.g., Ramberg v. Wahlstrom, 140 Ill. 182, 29 N.E. 727, 33 Am.St.Rep. 227 (1892); Kershaw v. Simpson, 46 Wash. 313, 89 P. 889 (1907).

duty rule apply where one cotenant purchases the interest of another cotenant, either directly, or at a tax, mortgage foreclosure, or execution sale, or from a third party who purchased the interest at such a sale.[27]

§ 5.11 Partition—In General

Any kind of concurrent estate will, of course, be terminated and converted into an estate in severalty if all the undivided interests are united in one person by conveyance, devise, inheritance. In such case, the undivided interests merge to form a single estate in severalty.[1]

In fact, however, concurrent estates are most often terminated and converted into two or more estates in severalty by partition, either voluntary or involuntary.[2] A voluntary partition may be effected by an exchange of deeds among the cotenants, with all the cotenants joining in each deed in order to set off a particular parcel of the common property to one of the cotenants in severalty. Prior to the Statute of Frauds, a parol agreement for partition was valid if each cotenant then took exclusive possession of a separate portion of the common property pursuant to the agreement.[3] A parol agreement for partition was held void "at law" in England after enactment of the Statute of Frauds, and many American cases have followed the English precedents.[4] But parol agreements for partition have generally been enforced either on a part performance theory or on an estoppel theory where the cotenants take possession of separate portions of the property pursuant to the parol agreement and make improvements on the land or otherwise materially change position in reliance on the parol agreement.[5]

Where a voluntary partition of the common property into equally valuable portions is impossible, equality may be achieved by having the cotenants receiving more valuable portions make money payments, called

27. E.g., Brittin v. Handy, 20 Ark. 381, 73 Am.Dec. 497 (1859); Ziebarth v. Donaldson, 150 Minn. 308, 185 N.W. 377 (1921); Murray v. Murray, 159 Minn. 111, 198 N.W. 307 (1924); Snell v. Harrison, 104 Mo. 158, 16 S.W. 152 (1891); Colby v. Colby, 96 N.H. 452, 79 A.2d 343 (1951); Sharples Corp. v. Sinclair Wyoming Oil Co., 62 Wyo. 341, 167 P.2d 29 (1946), rehearing denied 62 Wyo. 341, 168 P.2d 565 (1946). *A fortiori*, the rule is inapplicable if one cotenant purchases at a sale for non-payment of taxes assessed only on another cotenant's undivided interest. E.g., Bennet v. North Colorado Springs Land & Improvement Co., 23 Colo. 470, 48 P. 812 (1897); Jesberg v. Klinger, 187 Kan. 582, 358 P.2d 770 (1961).

§ 5.11

1. See 2 Bl.Comm. *186, *195; 13 Rul.Cas. Law § 1162.

2. Generally, see 2 Am.L.Prop. §§ 6.19 through 6.26.

3. Co.Litt. *169a; Thomas v. Gyles, 2 Vern. 232, 23 Eng.Rep. 750 (1691). The transfer of possession was held to constitute a livery of seisin so as to transfer an interest in severalty.

4. E.g., Boyers v. Boyers, 310 Ky. 727, 221 S.W.2d 657 (1949); Duncan v. Sylvester, 16 Me. 388 (1839); Ballou v. Hale, 47 N.H. 347 (1867); Duckett v. Harrison, 235 N.C. 145, 69 S.E.2d 176 (1952); Virginia Coal & Iron Co. v. Richmond, 128 Va. 258, 104 S.E. 805 (1920). Contra, see, e.g., Shepard v. Rinks, 78 Ill. 188 (1875); Wood v. Fleet, 36 N.Y. 499 (1867); Hughes v. Kay, 194 Or. 519, 242 P.2d 788 (1952); Reynolds v. Mangrum, 250 S.W.2d 283 (Tex.Civ.App.1952).

5. E.g., Ellis v. Campbell, 84 Ark. 584, 106 S.W. 939 (1907) (part performance); Duffy v. Duffy, 243 Ill. 476, 90 N.E. 697 (1909) (same); Herrman v. Golden, 93 Ill.App.3d 937, 49 Ill. Dec. 543, 418 N.E.2d 187 (1981); Cooper v. Davis, 226 Md. 371, 174 A.2d 144 (1961) (same); Martin v. Taylor, 521 S.W.2d 581 (Tenn.1975) (same); Swift v. Swift, 121 Ark. 197, 180 S.W. 742 (1915) (estoppel); Brown v. Wheeler, 17 Conn. 345, 44 Am.Dec. 550 (1845) (same).

Some of the cases asserting that a patrol partition agreement is valid "at law" could have been decided on the basis of either part performance or estoppel. E.g., Wood v. Fleet, *supra* note 4.

"owelty" to the other cotenants.[6] And the cotenants may, of course, agree to sell the common property and divide the proceeds of sale where equal division is impossible or physical partition is not feasible at all.

If cotenants cannot agree on a voluntary partition, any cotenant except a tenant by the entirety can compel partition by an action for partition.[7] Although such an action was originally available only to coparceners,[8] it was made available to tenants in common and joint tenants by a statute of Henry VIII.[9] Thereafter, partition could be had either "at law" or "in equity," [10] but after 1833 partition "in equity" became exclusive in England.[11] In the United States the old distinction between partition "at law" and partition "in equity" appears to have little current significance, although in some states where there is statutory authorization for partition it is said that "equitable" partition is still available—in lieu of statutory partition—where special equities require protection.[12]

6. Gonzalez v. Gonzalez, 174 Cal. 588, 163 P. 993 (1917); Newsome v. Harrell, 168 N.C. 295, 84 S.E. 337 (1915); Schnell v. Schnell, 346 N.W.2d 713 (N.D.1984) (by statute); Wright v. Wright, 131 Ill.App.3d 46, 86 Ill.Dec. 342, 475 N.E.2d 556 (1985). The portion allotted to a co-tenant who is charged with owelty may be subjected to a lien to secure payment, if the parties so agree. E.g., Davis v. Williams, 148 Ky. 829, 147 S.W. 760 (1912).

7. E.g., Caruso v. Plunk, 574 So.2d 1230 (Fla.App.1991) (right to partition is absolute in absence of estoppel or waiver); Hall v. Hamilton, 233 Kan. 880, 667 P.2d 350 (1983) (property held in joint tenancy may be partitioned); Albro v. Allen, 434 Mich. 271, 454 N.W.2d 85 (1990) (although conveyance to A and B "with right of survivorship" creates concurrent life estates with a contingent remainder in fee simple to the survivor in Michigan, partition of life estates will be granted; but contingent remainder will not thereby be destroyed); Swartz v. Becker, 246 N.J.Super. 406, 587 A.2d 1295 (App.Div.1991) (partition granted despite defendant's claim that it would cause hardship); First Trust Co. v. Holt, 361 N.W.2d 476 (Minn.App.1985) (partition will be granted unless the right is waived or suspended by express contract); Prickett v. Moore, 684 P.2d 1191 (Okl.1984) (partition will be granted provided petitioning cotenant is *sui juris*).

Sometimes the statute authorizing partition actions provides that partition shall be ordered only if "the interest of the other person or persons * * * will not be prejudiced thereby." See, e.g., Harris v. Crowder, 174 W.Va. 83, 322 S.E.2d 854 (1984); Vincent v. Gustke, 175 W.Va. 521, 336 S.E.2d 33 (1985). In Hall v. Hamilton, supra, the court said that partition may be refused if "equity" so requires; and in Mulsow v. Gerber Energy Corp., 237 Kan. 58, 697 P.2d 1269 (1985) the court said partition may be refused if it would result in fraud or oppression. But the Arkansas court recently held that the Arkansas partition statute is not unconstitutional merely because it

might be employed to enable white speculators to buy black-owned land for less than its fair market value. McNeely v. Bone, 287 Ark. 339, 698 S.W.2d 512 (1985).

A tenancy by the entirety cannot be judicially partitioned—Jones v. Conwell, 227 Va. 176, 314 S.E.2d 61 (1984)—but judicial partition is available after divorce has converted a tenancy by the entirety into a tenancy in common—Butler v. Butler, 122 Mich.App. 361, 332 N.W.2d 488 (1983). On the other hand, partition of a cotenant's marital home will not be ordered so long as a cotenant's spouse has a right to possession thereof pursuant to a divorce decree. Salyers v. Good, 443 So.2d 152 (Fla.App.1983). And an outstanding dower interest in a cotenant's widow will preclude judicial partition, although other encumbrances will not do so. Daughtrey v. Daughtrey, 474 So.2d 598 (Miss.1985).

No statute of limitations is applicable to an action for partition because the cause of action is a continuing one so long as the cotenancy exists. Occhino v. Occhino, 164 Ariz. 482, 793 P.2d 1149 (App.1990). A pending partition action will not survive the death of a plaintiff joint tenant because filing the action does not sever the joint tenancy. Allison v. Powell, 333 Pa.Super. 48, 481 A.2d 1215 (1984).

8. See ante Section 5.2, text at notes 11–14.

9. 31 Hen. VIII, c. 1 (1939); 32 id. c. 32 (1540).

10. The English Chancery Court assumed jurisdiction over partitions at an early date, in cases where a physical division of the property without regard to the special equities of the parties would result in injustice. See Freeman, Cotenancy § 432 (2d ed. 1886); Story, Equity Jurisprudence § 872 (14th ed. 1918); Hill v. Reno, 112 Ill. 154, 159 (1883).

11. Stat. 3 & 4 Will. IV, c. 27, § 36 (1833).

12. Partition "in equity" is "made exclusive by statute in some of the states; and in

Cotenants in fee simple sometimes expressly or impliedly agree that none of them or their successors shall have the right to compel a partition by court action.[13] Such an agreement imposes a restraint on alienation which would ordinarily be void under the common law rule against restraints on alienation.[14] But an agreement prohibiting judicial partition of a concurrent estate in fee simple—enforceable in equity—will be sustained if its duration is limited to a "reasonable time," which may be as long as the period permitted by the Rule Against Perpetuities—"lives in being at the creation of the interests, plus a period in gross not exceeding twenty-one years."[15] Moreover, there are some cases sustaining "disabling" restraints on judicial partition imposed by the creator of a concurrent estate if they are limited to a "reasonable time."[16] Indeed, courts sometimes deny partition when this will defeat some purpose of the creator of a concurrent estate that is dependent upon the continued existence of that concurrent estate.[17] And some states have statutes expressly authorizing the creator of a concurrent estate to prohibit judicial partition of the estate.[18]

Condominium enabling legislation usually prohibits any action by individual unit owners to compel partition of the common elements of the condominium development.[19] Presumably statutory prohibitions against

---

all of them courts of equity or courts with equitable powers have jurisdiction over partition suits and exercise that jurisdiction to the practical exclusion of the ancient common law action. In several states statutory partition is provided for, but in those states, as in other states, courts of general equity jurisdiction have concurrent power to partition * * * in accordance with the principles of equity and these statutes provide for partition according to equitable principles." 2 Am.L.Prop. § 6.21 at p. 95.

See, e.g., Swartz v. Becker, supra note 7 (partition is primarily statutory in New Jersey, but is still within "the inherent power of the court's equity jurisdiction"); Lohmiller v. Weidenbaugh, 503 Pa. 329, 469 A.2d 578 (1983) (statutory action is not sole or exclusive remedy). Cf. Eller v. Eller, 168 A.D.2d 414, 562 N.Y.S.2d 540 (1990) (in statutory action the alleged "unclean hands" of plaintiff did not defeat the action where the facts relied on to show "unclean hands" were unrelated to the interests of the parties as tenants in common; *sed quaere* whether the court meant to imply that the result would be different in an "equitable" action).

13. Northern New Hampshire Mental Health and Developmental Services, Inc. v. Cannell, 134 N.H. 519, 593 A.2d 1161 (1991); Bessen v. Glatt, 170 A.D.2d 924, 566 N.Y.S.2d 750 (1991).

14. See ante Sections 2.2, 2.3, 2.11.

15. Ex parte Watts, 130 N.C. 237, 41 S.E. 289 (1902). Other cases holding the period of the restraint "reasonable" and therefore valid include Condrey v. Condrey, 92 So.2d 423 (Fla. 1957) (lives in being); Rosenberg v. Rosenberg,

413 Ill. 343, 108 N.E.2d 766 (1952) (same); Porter v. Tracey, 179 Iowa 1295, 162 N.W. 800 (1917) (not more than 21 years); Michalski v. Michalski, 50 N.J.Super. 454, 142 A.2d 645 (1958) (lives in being, but "changed circumstances" may make agreement unenforceable); Besson v. Glatt, supra note 13 (purchase option limited to lives of cotenants).

See also Schultheis v. Schultheis, 36 Wn. App. 588, 675 P.2d 634 (1984) (court may determine "reasonable time" when no time is specified), following suggestion in Robroy Land Co. v. Prather, 95 Wn.2d 66, 622 P.2d 367 (1980).

16. E.g., Trimble v. Fairbanks, 209 Ga. 741, 76 S.E.2d 16 (1953); Kepley v. Overton, 74 Ind. 448 (1881) (till a co-tenant reached a stated age); Freeland v. Andersen, 114 Neb. 822, 211 N.W. 167 (1926) (lives in being); In re Tombs' Estate, 155 Pa.Super. 605, 39 A.2d 367 (1944) (same). Presumably such restraints are enforcible by injunction.

17. E.g., Carter v. Weowna Beach Community Corp., 71 Wn.2d 498, 429 P.2d 201 (1967).

18. E.g., Ark.Stats. § 34–1814 (only when created by will); West's Ann.Ind.Code 32–4–5–5; Vernon's Ann.Missouri Stat. § 528.130.

19. "In the condominium structure, each participant has a separate property interest in his particular apartment plus an undivided interest in cotenancy as to the underlying fee and common elements. The right to partition is an established characteristic of tenancies in common. However, to permit a unit owner to bring an action to partition the common elements would shatter the whole condominium structure. Thus, to insure the continued oper-

partition are valid and are effective to prevent partition during the continuance of the condominium regime, although it has been suggested that [20]

> [p]erhaps it would be better if all the statutes contained a provision stating that neither the rule against perpetuities nor the common-law rule prohibiting restraints on alienation should be construed as invalidating any provision of the condominium act or any provisions in instruments executed in accordance with the act.

The right to bring an action for partition is generally restricted to owners of concurrent interests who have actual possession or an immediate right to possession,[21] except where the concurrent estate is subject to a leasehold estate, in which case the co-tenants—as reversioners—are "seised," though not "possessed" of the common property and may compel partition of the reversion.[22] In some states, there are statutes which expressly provide for partition among the owners of future interests when a life estate or defeasible fee estate is outstanding.[23] These statutes vary considerably, and some of them include important limitations on the right to compel partition. In some twenty states the statutes authorize partition only if the future interests are indefeasibly vested,[24] and even where the statutes do not so provide, there seems to be no decision ordering partition of future interests which are contingent or vested subject to defeasance. Because of the uncertainty as to whether a contingent or defeasible future interest will ever become possessory, it is unlikely that a court would authorize partition of such a future interest even if the statutory language were broad enough to permit it.

Where partition of future interests is authorized by statute, it is clear that a life tenant cannot be compelled to accept either a part of the property or a money payment in lieu of his life estate; the partition must be made subject to the life estate unless the life tenant consents to participate in the

---

ation of the regime, restraints on the right to partition must be effectively imposed." 4B R. Powell, Real Property ¶ 633.11[1] (Rohan rev. 1979).

"Condominium statutes generally recognize the threat posed by a possible partition proceeding and wisely provide that the common elements, both general and limited, shall remain undivided and that no apartment owner or any other person shall be permitted to bring any action for partition * * * of the ownership as long as the condominium regime is continued as to the particular building or buildings." Id. ¶ 633.11[4] at n. 16, citing many statutes.

20. Id. ¶ 633.11[4] between nn. 17 and 18. For such provisions see Utah Code Ann. 1953, 57–8–28; Vernon's Ann.Missouri Stat. § 448.-210.

21. E.g., Hausen v. Dahlquist, 232 Iowa 100, 5 N.W.2d 321 (1942); Baker v. Baker, 97 N.J.Eq. 306, 127 A. 657 (1925); Phillips v. Wells, 147 Va. 1030, 133 S.E. 581 (1926); Wagner v. Maskey, 353 N.W.2d 891 (Iowa App. 1984).

However, there is some authority allowing a judgment creditor or other lien creditor of a cotenant to bring action for partition in order to enforce the creditor's claim. E.g., Jones v. Conwell, 227 Va. 176, 314 S.E.2d 61 (1984); Harris v. Crowder, 174 W.Va. 83, 322 S.E.2d 854 (1984); Vincent v. Gustke, 175 W.Va. 521, 336 S.E.2d 33 (1985).

22. E.g., Watson v. Watson, 150 Mass. 84, 22 N.E. 438 (1889); Heintz v. Wilhelm, 151 Minn. 195, 186 N.W. 305 (1922); Peterman v. Kingsley, 140 Wis. 666, 123 N.W. 137 (1909). The tenant has no basis to object, since the partition will not affect his leasehold estate.

23. See 2 R. Powell, Real Property ¶ 290 for a detailed listing and discussion of these statutes.

24. For a listing of these statutes, see 2 R. Powell, Real Property ¶ 290 nn. 11, 12. Under these statutes only indefeasibly vested remainders and reversions in fee simple—and possibly executory interests that are certain to become possessory estates in fee simple absolute—can be partitioned. See discussion, op. cit. supra ¶ 290 at nn. 13–19.

partition.[25] But where the owner in severalty of a life estate is also co-owner of the reversion or remainder in fee simple, he has a right to compel partition.[26] If the partition is in kind, he will obtain his fractional share in possession in fee simple and his life estate will continue as to the share of the other co-remaindermen. If the partition is by sale, his consent as life tenant to the sale will permit a sale of the entire fee simple and an immediate division of all the proceeds.[27] And if the same person has an undivided interest for life and an undivided interest in the remainder or reversion in fee simple, he has a right to a complete partition in kind or a sale and immediate division of the proceeds under statutes authorizing partition between co-owners of future interests.[28]

§ 5.12 Partition—Parties and Final Accounting

In a partition action, all cotenants (or coowners of future interests if they can compel partition) must be joined either as plaintiffs or defendants.[1] The grantee of part of the common property by metes and bounds is a proper party[2] or, in some jurisdictions, a necessary party[3] who may intervene in the partition action to protect his or her interests.[4] If one cotenant's undivided interest is subject to an executory contract of sale, the vendor is a necessary party[5] and the purchaser is at least a proper party.[6] In some jurisdictions there are statutes that require joinder of the contract purchaser.[7]

A lessee of one cotenant's undivided interest is a necessary party in a partition action,[8] but a lessee of the entire property is not a necessary party because his leasehold estate will not be disturbed by partition.[9] For the

---

25. E.g., Powe v. Payne, 208 Ala. 527, 94 So. 587 (1922); Tolson v. Bryan, 130 Md. 338, 100 A. 366 (1917); Carson v. Hecke, 282 Mo. 580, 222 S.W. 850 (1920). That the life tenant is also owner of an undivided interest in the remainder does not give the other remaindermen the right to partition the life estate unless this right is expressly conferred by statute. Compare Soper v. Soper, 222 App.Div. 103, 225 N.Y.S. 3 (1927), with Tower v. Tower, 141 Ind. 223, 40 N.E. 747 (1894).

26. E.g., Chapman v. York, 212 Ala. 540, 103 So. 567 (1925); Shafer v. Covey, 90 Kan. 588, 135 P. 676 (1913).

27. Ibid.

28. E.g., Cottingham v. Love, 211 Ala. 152, 99 So. 907 (1924); Weedon v. Power, 202 Ky. 542, 260 S.W. 385 (1924); Bosley v. Burk, 154 Md. 27, 139 A. 543 (1927). If there is no such statute, only the concurrent life estate can be partitioned. E.g., Brown v. Brown, 67 W.Va. 251, 67 S.E. 596, 28 L.R.A.(N.S.) 125 (1910).

§ 5.12

1. E.g., Curtis v. Reilly, 188 Iowa 1217, 177 N.W. 535 (1920); Benedict v. Beurmann, 90 Mich. 396, 51 N.W. 461 (1892); Lohmiller v. Weidenbaugh, 503 Pa. 329, 469 A.2d 578 (1983).

2. E.g., Ferris v. Montgomery Land and Implement Co., 94 Ala. 557, 10 So. 607 (1892);

Phillips v. Wells, 147 Va. 1030, 133 S.E. 581 (1926).

3. E.g., Gates v. Salmon, 35 Cal. 576 (1868); Pellow v. Artic Mining Co., 164 Mich. 87, 128 N.W. 918, 47 L.R.A.(N.S.) 573 (1910).

4. E.g., Harrell v. Mason, 170 Ala. 282, 54 So. 105 (1911); Potter v. Wallace, 185 Ky. 528, 215 S.W. 538 (1919); Seavey v. Green, 137 Or. 127, 1 P.2d 601, 75 A.L.R. 1451 (1931).

5. E.g., Jones v. Napier, 93 Ga. 582, 20 S.E. 41 (1894); Crippen v. Spies, 255 App.Div. 411, 7 N.Y.S.2d 704 (1938).

6. E.g., Howard v. Morrissey, 71 Misc. 267, 130 N.Y.S. 322 (1911).

7. See, e.g., Rich v. Smith, 26 Cal.App. 775, 148 P. 545 (1915).

8. This results from the necessity of joining persons whose interests in the common property will be affected by partition, so that they will be bound by the court's judgment or decree.

But see Lichtenfels v. Bridgeview Coal Co., 344 Pa.Super. 257, 496 A.2d 782 (1985) (notice required only if lessee has "sufficient" interest in land).

9. The order for partition should, of course, be made subject to the lease. E.g., McLear v. Balmat, 194 App.Div. 827, 186 N.Y.S. 180

same reason, the holder of a mortgage or other lien on the entire property is not a necessary party.[10] Statutes often require joinder of the holder of a mortgage or other lien upon a single cotenant's interest in the common property.[11] In the absence of such a statute, the cases are divided as to whether the holder of a mortgage or other lien upon a single cotenant's interest is a necessary party in a partition action.[12] It would seem, on principle, that he should be considered a necessary party since his interest will be affected by the court's order for partition and the reasons given for not requiring joinder are unpersuasive.[13]

Since the partition of a concurrent life estate cannot, absent statutory authorization, affect the future interests limited after the life estate,[14] the owners of such future interests are not necessary parties in a partition action unless a statute expressly requires that they be joined. And the owners of contingent interests such as dower or curtesy generally need not be joined in a partition action unless joinder is required by statute.[15]

In the final accounting incident to every partition action, each cotenant may be charged with rents and profits actually received by him in excess of his pro rata share [16] or, where one cotenant has excluded the other cotenants, the mesne profits (usually the fair rental value).[17] Any cotenant may

(1921), affirmed 231 N.Y. 548, 132 N.E. 883, appeal granted 231 N.Y. 599, 132 N.E. 904; Hall v. Douglas, 104 W.Va. 286, 140 S.E. 4 (1927).

10. E.g., Graham v. Graham, 202 Ala. 56, 79 So. 450 (1918); Tompkins v. Kyle, 95 W.Va. 584, 122 S.E. 150 (1924). It has even been held that he is not a "proper" party. E.g., Neale v. Stamm, 100 N.J.Eq. 35, 135 A. 345 (1926).

11. See, e.g., Cheney v. Ricks, 168 Ill. 533, 48 N.E. 75 (1897) (mortgagee); Metcalf v. Hoopingardner, 45 Iowa 510 (1877) (judgment lienor). In some states, similar statutes are construed only as making holders of mortgages or other liens "proper" parties. See, e.g., Grogan v. Grogan, 177 S.W. 649 (Mo.1915).

12. That joinder is necessary, see, e.g., Bradley v. Fuller, 40 Mass. (23 Pick.) 1 (1839); Whitton v. Whitton, 38 N.H. 127, 75 Am.Dec. 163 (1859). That joinder is unnecessary, see, e.g., Graham v. Graham, supra note 10; Baltzell v. Daniel, 111 Fla. 303, 149 So. 639, 93 A.L.R. 1259 (1933); Baldwin v. Baldwin, 347 Ill. 351, 179 N.E. 859 (1932).

13. The cases holding joinder unnecessary cited supra note 12, are said, in 2 Am.L.Prop. § 6.24, p. 107, to be based on "the fundamental right of partition which is incident to all co-tenancies, so that the mortgagee or other lienor necessarily takes subject to it." But in other cases it is the very fact that one interest is subject to another interest that makes joinder of the subordinate interest necessary—as, e.g., in mortgage foreclosure actions. Another reason sometimes given for not requiring joinder is that the holder of a mortgage or other lien has no possessory estate in the land. But this is simply incorrect in "title" jurisdictions

and it is also incorrect with respect to the mortgagee's "title" after default in "hybrid" or "intermediate" jurisdictions. See G. Osborne, G. Nelson, and D. Whitman, Real Estate Financing § 1.5 (1979).

14. E.g., Jordan v. Walker, 201 Ala. 248, 77 So. 838 (1917); Whittaker v. Porter, 321 Ill. 368, 151 N.E. 905 (1926); Fox v. Greene, 289 Mich. 179, 286 N.W. 203 (1939).

15. E.g., Brady v. Paine, 391 Ill. 596, 63 N.E.2d 721 (1945) (dower); Turner v. Turner, 185 Va. 505, 39 S.E.2d 299 (1946) (dower); Hazelbaker v. Reber, 123 Kan. 131, 254 P. 407 (1927) (curtesy); Helmick v. Kraft, 84 W.Va. 159, 99 S.E. 325 (1919) (curtesy). Where curtesy initiate still exists as at common law, the cotenant's husband must, of course, be joined. E.g., Appeal of Welch, 126 Pa. 297, 17 A. 623 (1889); Helmick v. Kraft, supra.

16. See ante Section 5.8, text between notes 13 and 22, and authorities cited. Recent cases include Janik v. Janik, 474 N.E.2d 1054 (Ind.App.1985); Hawkins v. Hawkins, 11 Ohio Misc.2d 18, 464 N.E.2d 199 (Comm.Pl.1984).

Reimbursement will not be ordered if no demand for an accounting is made. Bessen v. Glatt, 170 A.D.2d 924, 566 N.Y.S.2d 750 (1991).

17. See ante Section 5.8, text between notes 7 and 8, and authorities cited. See Stylianopoulos v. Stylianopoulos, 17 Mass. App.Ct. 64, 455 N.E.2d 477 (1983), review denied 390 Mass. 1107, 459 N.E.2d 824 (1984). But see Sanborn v. Johns, 19 Mass.App.Ct. 721, 477 N.E.2d 196 (1985) ("choice of charges to be made * * * varies according to circumstances" and "rent may or may not be deducted from the share of the occupant").

also be charged for any waste he has committed.[18] And each cotenant will be credited with sums expended, beyond his pro rata share, for necessary repairs,[19] improvements (to the extent they have increased the value of the property),[20] taxes and payments of interest and/or principal on mortgages or other liens,[21] insurance for the common benefit,[22] or expended to protect the title.[23] But, absent an agreement therefor, a cotenant is not entitled to credit for the value of personal services in managing and caring for the property.[24]

When one cotenant is credited with the increase in value resulting from improvements which he has made at his own expense, the parcel allotted to the improving cotenant when there is a partition in kind will include the improvements if this is feasible.[25] Otherwise, the claim of any former cotenant for the balance due him pursuant to the final accounting will usually be enforced by imposition of a lien upon the parcels set off to the other former cotenants.[26] A personal judgment for such balance will be awarded only to the extent that some or all of the other cotenants were personally liable for the debts discharged by the claimant.[27] If there is a

18. See ante Section 5.7, text between notes 25 and 34, and authorities cited.

19. See ante Section 5.9, text between notes 1 and 4, and authorities cited. See also Janik v. Janik and Hawkins v. Hawkins, supra note 16.

20. E.g., Staples v. Pearson, 230 Ala. 62, 159 So. 488 (1935); Mastin v. Mastin's Administrators, 243 Ky. 830, 50 S.W.2d 77 (1932); Buschmeyer v. Eikermann, 378 S.W.2d 468 (Mo.1964) (cost or increase in value, whichever is less); Johnson v. Hendrickson, 71 S.D. 392, 24 N.W.2d 914 (1946); Cleveland v. Milner, 141 Tex. 120, 170 S.W.2d 472 (1943); White v. Pleasants, 227 Va. 508, 317 S.E.2d 489 (1984) (general rule recognized, but compensation denied where improver was lessee who had actual notice of an outstanding interest belonging to one other than lessor cotenant); Quillen v. Tull, 226 Va. 498, 312 S.E.2d 278 (1984) (enhancement rather than cost is basis for compensation); Janik v. Janik, supra note 16; Knowlton v. Knowlton, 673 S.W.2d 502 (Mo. App.1984) (general rule recognized, but "extent to which improvements are to be taken into account will reflect the equities"). See, also, ante Section 5.9 at note 5.

21. See ante Section 5.9, text between notes 6 and 9.

See also Janik v. Janik and Hawkins v. Hawkins, supra note 16.

22. Fenton v. Wendell, 116 Mich. 45, 74 N.W. 384 (1898); Clapp v. Hunter, 52 App.Div. 253, 65 N.Y.S. 411 (1900).

23. E.g., Schluter v. Sell, 194 S.W.2d 125 (Tex.Civ.App.1946); Blackwell v. McLean, 9 Wash. 301, 37 P. 317 (1894). See also In re Marriage of Leversee, 156 Cal.App.3d 891, 203 Cal.Rptr. 481 (1984) (former wife entitled to "equitable compensatory adjustment * * * for use of her separate funds for the down payment on the [marital] residence").

24. E.g., Goodenow v. Ewer, 16 Cal. 461 (1860); Shipman v. Shipman, 65 N.J.Eq. 556, 56 A. 694 (1904); Myers v. Bolton, 157 N.Y. 393, 52 N.E. 114 (1898), reargument denied 158 N.Y. 665, 52 N.E. 1125 (1899). Cf. Baird v. Moore, 50 N.J.Super. 156, 141 A.2d 324 (1958) (no credit for personal services, as such, but they may be taken into account as "part of the factual pattern relating to general improvement").

25. E.g., Hollis v. Watkins, 189 Ala. 292, 66 So. 29 (1914); Farley v. Stacey, 177 Ky. 109, 197 S.W. 636, 1 A.L.R. 1181 (1917); Fair v. Fair, 121 Mass. 559 (1877); Lawrence v. Donovan, 207 Mont. 130, 673 P.2d 130 (1983). Occasionally, where some of the improvements are allotted to co-tenants who contributed nothing to their cost, such co-tenants have been required to pay their pro rata shares of the increased value of the common property to the improving co-tenant. E.g., Ferris v. Montgomery Land & Implement Co., 94 Ala. 557, 10 So. 607 (1892) (but only when improving cotenant believed he was sole owner); Swift v. Swift, 121 Ark. 197, 180 S.W. 742 (1915). An allowance of additional land to the improving co-tenant has also been suggested when the improvements cannot be allotted entirely to him. E.g., Arnold v. De Booy, 161 Minn. 255, 201 N.W. 437 (1924).

26. E.g., Kelly v. Carmichael, 221 Ala. 371, 129 So. 81 (1930); Cocks v. Simmons, 55 Ark. 104, 17 S.W. 594 (1891); Hogan v. McMahon, 115 Md. 195, 80 A. 695 (1911); Giles v. Sheridan, 179 Neb. 257, 137 N.W.2d 828 (1965).

27. E.g., Scanlon v. Parish, 85 Conn. 379, 82 A. 969 (1912). See 2 Am.L.Prop. § 6.17 at p. 77, § 6.26 at p. 118. But see Goergen v. Maar, 2 A.D.2d 276, 153 N.Y.S.2d 826 (1956).

partition sale, the adjustment of all charges and credits will be made in determining what share of the sale proceeds shall be paid over to each former cotenant.[28]

§ 5.13 Partition—Physical Division or Sale and Division of Proceeds

In an action for partition, the court will generally first render an interlocutory judgment determining the share of each cotenant [1] and any other party properly joined in the action,[2] and further determining whether a physical division of the common property should be ordered or whether the property should be sold and the proceeds divided among those entitled to share as cotenants or otherwise.

When a concurrent estate is created by a deed or will that does not expressly provide to the contrary, it will be presumed that each concurrent owner obtains an equal undivided interest.[3] If the deed or will creating the concurrent estate expressly provides for unequal interests, it will necessarily create a tenancy in common and the cotenants will obtain the unequal interests specified in the instrument.[4] But even where unequal interests are not expressly provided for in the creating instrument, the presumption of equality may be rebutted for purposes of determining the share of each cotenant in a partition action, whether the concurrent estate is a joint tenancy [5] or a tenancy in common.[6] And where a tenancy in common arises

---

28. E.g., Killmer v. Wuchner, 79 Iowa 722, 45 N.W. 299, 8 L.R.A. 289 (1890) (improvements); Moore v. Thorp, 16 R.I. 655, 19 A. 321, 7 L.R.A. 731 (1889) (same); Ward v. Ward's Heirs, 40 W.Va. 611, 21 S.E. 746, 29 L.R.A. 449 (1895) (same). In the more frequent modern cases in which the property is sold, the adjustment of all these items becomes a simple matter of accounting in distributing the proceeds. 2 Am.L.Prop. § 6.26 at p. 118.

§ 5.13

1. E.g., Stoffer v. Verhellen, 195 Cal. 317, 231 P. 233 (1925); Provident Life & Trust Co. v. Wood, 96 W.Va. 516, 123 S.E. 276, 41 A.L.R. 570 (1924); Daughtrey v. Daughtrey, 474 So.2d 598 (Miss.1985) (determination of shares need not be made prior to order for sale, but better practice is to make such determination first). The court may appoint commissioners to determine the shares and their determination is entitled to judicial deference. Lawrence v. Donovan, 207 Mont. 130, 673 P.2d 130 (1983).

2. E.g., Arnold v. Arnold, 308 Ill. 365, 139 N.E. 592 (1923).

3. E.g., People v. Varel, 351 Ill. 96, 184 N.E. 209 (1932) (tenancy in common); Williams v. Monzingo, 235 Iowa 434, 16 N.W.2d 619, 156 A.L.R. 508 (1944) (same); Anderson v. Anderson, 137 Kan. 833, 22 P.2d 471 (1933) (same) rehearing denied 137 Kan. 77, 23 P.2d 474 (1933). In cases where the creating instrument clearly indicates that a joint tenancy is intended, the presumption of equality cannot be rebutted while the joint tenancy continues, but it is not controlling when a partition action is begun. See Jezo v. Jezo, 23 Wis.2d 399, 127 N.W.2d 246 (1964), rehearing denied 23 Wis.2d 399, 129 N.W.2d 195 (1964).

4. This is because the interests of joint tenants must be equal. If the instrument also expressly provides for a right of survivorship, it may be construed as creating a concurrent estate for lives with a contingent remainder in fee simple to the survivor, in which case only the concurrent life estate can be partitioned.

5. "The rule is * * * that the interests of joint tenants being equal during their lives, a presumption arises that upon dissolution of the joint tenancy during the lives of the cotenants, each is entitled to an equal share of the proceeds. This presumption is subject to rebuttal, however, and does not prevent proof from being introduced that the respective holdings and interests are unequal. This presumption may be rebutted by evidence showing the source of the actual cash outlay at the time of acquisition, the intent of the cotenant creating the joint tenancy to make a gift of the half-interest to the other cotenant, unequal contribution by way of money or services, unequal expenditures in improving the property or freeing it from encumbrances and clouds [on title], or other evidence raising inferences contrary to the idea of equal interest in the joint estate." Jezo v. Jezo, 23 Wis.2d 399, 406, 127 N.W.2d 246, 250 (1964), rehearing denied 23 Wis.2d 399, 129 N.W.2d 195.

by intestate succession, the shares of the cotenants may be either equal or unequal, depending on the intestate succession statute and the relationships among the cotenants.[7]

In earlier times, courts always ordered a partition in kind—i.e., a physical division of the common property—unless all the cotenants consented to a sale,[8] but all states now have statutory authorization for sale and division of the proceeds whenever a fair and equitable physical division of the property is impossible.[9] This is likely to be the case where the common property consists of a relatively small parcel of land improved with a single structure,[10] or an unimproved parcel of such size that a physical division

6. Williams v. Monzingo, supra note 3, at 442, 16 N.W.2d at 622; Brooks v. Kunz, 597 S.W.2d 183 (Mo.1980), appeal after remand 637 S.W.2d 135 (Mo.App.1982). See also Sebold v. Sebold, 444 F.2d 864 (D.C.Cir.1971), holding the interests of former tenants by the entirety were equal when the divorce converted the tenancy by the entirety into a tenancy in common, but recognizing that "the fact that the parties were [then] tenants in common * * * does not mean that each had to receive one-half of the property, for the rule is that, in a suit for partition, the court must first determine the respective shares which the parties hold in the property." Id. at 872. Generally, see Annot., 156 A.L.R. 508 (1945).

7. Thus, e.g., a surviving spouse and the children of a decedent may take unequal shares.

8. E.g., Chuck v. Gomes, 56 Hawaii 171, 532 P.2d 657 (1975); Bragg v. Lyon, 93 N.C. 151 (1885). See, generally, Freeman, Cotenancy § 537 et seq.; 3 Pomeroy, Equity Jurisprudence § 1390 (5th ed. Symon 1941); 2 H. Tiffany, Real Prop. § 479 at n. 44 (3d ed. 1939); 4 G. Thompson, Real Prop. § 1828 at p. 315 (1979 repl.); 2 Am.L.Prop. § 6.26 at n. 5.

9. E.g., Chuck v. Gomes, supra note 8; Nordhausen v. Christner, 215 Neb. 367, 338 N.W.2d 754 (1983) (sale proper where partition in kind would result in complex settlement granting parties rights they did not want or could not use); Cavanagh v. Cavanagh, 468 A.2d 286 (R.I.1983); White v. Pleasants, 227 Va. 508, 317 S.E.2d 489 (1984); Wilkins v. Wilkins, 175 W.Va. 787, 338 S.E.2d 388 (1985); McConnell v. McConnell, 449 So.2d 785 (Miss.1984) (where parties admitted physical partition was not feasible, court must order sale even though current economic conditions might preclude obtaining reasonable price). Murphy v. Daley, ___ Mass. ___, 582 A.2d 1212 (1990). However, the courts have generally held that partition in kind (physical division of the land) is favored and that the party seeking a sale has the burden of showing that partition in kind would be prejudicial to the parties. E.g., McNeely v. Bone, 287 Ark. 339, 698 S.W.2d 512 (1985) (expert testimony showed that no equitable physical division was possible); Filipetti v. Filipetti, 2

Conn.App. 456, 479 A.2d 1229 (1984), certification denied 194 Conn. 804, 482 A.2d 709 (1984); Delfino v. Vealencis, 181 Conn. 533, 436 A.2d 27 (1980) (trial court's conclusion that rights of parties would be promoted by sale not supported by findings of subordinate facts); Wright v. Wright, 131 Ill.App.3d 46, 86 Ill.Dec. 342, 475 N.E.2d 556 (1985); Swartz v. Becker, 246 N.J.Super. 406, 587 A.2d 1295 (1991); Chamberlain v. Beam, 63 N.C.App. 377, 304 S.E.2d 770 (1983); Miller v. Miller, 101 Or.App. 371, 790 P.2d 1184 (1990). Cf. Dickinson v. Killheffer, 497 A.2d 307 (R.I. 1985) (substantial evidence supported decision in favor of physical division, although this would create zoning problems and one parcel would have less frontage than the other).

Courts have generally held that they have no power to order one cotenant to sell the concurrently owned land to another cotenant. George v. Tanner, 108 Idaho 40, 696 P.2d 891 (1985); Janik v. Janik, 474 N.E.2d 1054 (Ind. App.1985). See also Jolly v. Knopf, 463 So.2d 150 (Ala.1985), invalidating Ala.Code 1975, § 35–6–100, which provides that on filing of petition for partition by sale the court may provide for purchase of the interests of petitioning cotenants by other cotenants without a public sale if the other cotenants wish to purchase. The court distinguished Madison v. Lambert, 399 So.2d 840 (Ala.1981), appeal after remand 428 So.2d 25 (1983), and held that the statute violates the equal protection guaranties in both the Alabama and United States constitutions because it permitted only defendant cotenants, and not petitioning cotenant, to purchase. The court remanded *Jolly* to "allow each of the seven co-owners * * * a right to purchase the interests of the others at such price as the others are willing to sell and the buyers are willing to pay," but the court failed to address the problem that will arise if there is no agreement between the parties on price. Presumably the court would then order a public sale and divide the proceeds. But see Andersen v. Andersen, 376 N.W.2d 711 (Minn.App.1985) (court ordered one cotenant to sell his interest to another in lieu of a public sale of common property).

10. E.g., Bell v. Smith, 24 Ky.Law Rep. 1328, 71 S.W. 433 (1903), rehearing denied 24

would substantially diminish the value of the property as a whole and/or produce very small parcels that would be practically unsalable.[11] In some cases, of course, inequality in the value of the parcels allocated to the former cotenants may be corrected by money payments called "owelty" as in cases of voluntary partition.[12] But most partition actions, in modern times, result in a court order for sale of the entire property and division of the proceeds.[13]

The judgment in a partition action binds all persons who were joined as parties.[14] Where the entire property is subject to a mortgage or similar lien, a physical division of the property will leave each separate portion of the property still subject to the security interest,[15] and if the property is sold subject to the mortgage or other lien, the purchaser will take it subject to the security interest. But if the holder of a mortgage or other lien on the entire property is joined in the partition action, the court may, in a proper case, order a sale free and clear and provide that the security interests shall attach to the proceeds of the sale.[16]

Where the undivided interest of one cotenant is subject to a mortgage or similar lien, the results of a physical division or a partition sale are similar to the results in cases where the security interest covers the entire property.[17]

Ky.Law Rep. 2095, 72 S.W. 1107 (1903); Blandin v. Blandin, 126 La. 819, 53 So. 15 (1910); McConnell v. McConnell, supra note 9. Indeed, the fact that the tract is very small, without more, may justify an order for sale. Swartz v. Becker, supra note 9. But see Delfino v. Vealancis, supra note 9. Cf. Marshall & Ilsley Bank v. De Wolf, 268 Wis. 244, 67 N.W.2d 380 (1954) (physical division of city lot improved with a 3–story building covering entire lot).

11. E.g., Phillips v. Phillips, 185 Ill. 629, 57 N.E. 796 (1900); Tichenor v. Rock, 140 Ky. 86, 130 S.W. 989 (1910) (each heir had a ¹/₁₄ interest in a 90–acre farm); Arnold v. Cesare, 137 Ariz. 48, 668 P.2d 891 (App.1983); Swartz v. Becker, supra note 9; Loupe v. Bybee, 570 So.2d 31 (La.App.1990); Halamka v. Halamka, 799 S.W.2d 351 (Tex.App.1990). Where the common property is a farm, physical division is likely both to cause diminution in the value of the whole and to produce parcels so small as to be unsalable. Physical division of substantial urban land parcels is also likely to reduce the value of the whole, whether or not the resulting lots are salable. See discussion of the judicial role in preventing uneconomic parcellization of inherited common property in Note, 23 U.Chi.L.Rev. 343 (1956).

12. E.g., Cooter v. Dearborn, 115 Ill. 509, 4 N.E. 388 (1886); Robinson's Administrator v. Alexander, 194 Ky. 494, 239 S.W. 786 (1922); Johnson v. Hendrickson, supra § 5.12 note 20; Von Herberg v. Von Herberg, 6 Wn.2d 100, 106 P.2d 737 (1940); Marshall & Ilsley Bank v. De Wolf, supra note 10; Filipetti v. Filipetti, supra note 9. Some statutes specifically authorize equalization by an order for payment of "owelty," but courts have the power to

order such payment even in the absence of express statutory authorization.

13. 2 Am.L.Prop. § 6.26 at p. 114. See, e.g., Cunningham v. Hastings, 556 N.E.2d 12 (Ind.App.1990) (proceeds should be equally divided; purchasing cotenant is not entitled to reimbursement for amount originally paid out of his own funds).

14. E.g., Henslee v. Williams, 253 Ala. 363, 44 So.2d 763 (1950); Southerland v. Potts, 234 N.C. 268, 67 S.E.2d 51 (1951).

15. E.g., Schuck v. Schuck, 413 Ill. 390, 108 N.E.2d 905 (1952), appeal transferred 347 Ill. App. 557, 107 N.E.2d 53 (1952); Washburn v. Washburn, 234 N.C. 370, 67 S.E.2d 264 (1951); Smith v. Smith, 206 Okl. 206, 242 P.2d 436 (1952).

16. This would seem appropriate if the debt secured by the mortgage or other lien is due and payable when the order for a partition sale is made or the secured creditor consents to acceleration of payment, in which case the court can order immediate payment out of the proceeds of the sale. Of course, if the holder of the mortgage or other lien is not a "proper" party and cannot be joined in the partition action, the court cannot order a sale free and clear of the security interest.

17. The mortgage or other lien will not be limited to the parcel set off to the former cotenant whose undivided interest was subject to the security interest if there is a physical division of the common property. If a sale is ordered, the entire property would remain subject to the security interest unless the sale is made free and clear of the security interest and that interest is transferred to the share of

Where there is an outstanding lease on the entire property, neither a physical division nor a sale will affect the lessee's estate and right to possession.[18] Where there is an outstanding lease on the undivided interest of one cotenant, a physical division of the property will result in the lessee's estate being limited to the parcel set off to his lessor.[19] But a sale of the entire property would, it seems, have to be made subject to the lease, which would make the lessee and the purchaser tenants in common for the balance of the lease term.[20]

In a jurisdiction where inchoate dower and/or curtesy are still recognized, a partition in kind will transfer the inchoate interest of a cotenant's spouse to the separate interest set off to that cotenant by the court's judgment.[21] And if the court orders a sale of the property, the inchoate dower or curtesy interest of a cotenant's spouse in the common property will be cut off—even when the spouse is not joined in the partition action [22]—and will attach to that cotenant's share of the proceeds of sale.[23]

§ 5.14 Community Property—In General

In the eight states of Arizona, California, Idaho, Louisiana, Nevada, New Mexico, Texas, and Washington a system of marital property exists, known as community property. It is in those places exclusive, a substitute for the common law marital property system of the other states. Community property is a European civil law institution. Its ancient well-springs are among the Visigoths; in modern times it is principally associated with the legal systems of France and Spain.[1] American community property law is primarily of Spanish origin, even in French Louisiana.[2] The system was

the proceeds allotted to the co-tenant whose undivided interest was previously subject to the security interest.

18. If the common property is sold, the court should expressly order the sale to be made subject to the lease. E.g., McLear v. Balmat, 194 App.Div. 827, 186 N.Y.S. 180 (1921), affirmed 231 N.Y. 548, 132 N.E. 883, appeal granted 231 N.Y. 599, 132 N.E. 904 (1921); Hall v. Douglas, 104 W.Va. 286, 140 S.E. 4 (1927).

19. E.g., Noble v. Beach, 21 Cal.2d 91, 130 P.2d 426 (1942). The lessee must, of course, be made a party in order to be bound by the partition judgment.

20. Since this would create an inconvenient situation for both the lessee and the purchaser, and might chill the bidding at the partition sale, a court would be justified in refusing to order a sale in such a case.

21. E.g., Potter v. Wheeler, 13 Mass. 504 (1816); Hinds v. Stevens, 45 Mo. 209 (1870); Lloyd v. Conover, 25 N.J.L. 47 (1855); Holley v. Glover, 36 S.C. 404, 15 S.E. 605, 16 L.R.A. 776 (1892). The spouse need not be joined in the partition action. Hinds v. Stevens, supra.

22. E.g., Davis v. Lang, 153 Ill. 175, 38 N.E. 635 (1894); Frahm v. Seaman, 179 Iowa 144, 159 N.W. 206 (1916); Hazelbaker v. Reber, 123

Kan. 131, 254 P. 407 (1927); Hinds v. Stevens, supra note 21; Holley v. Glover, supra note 21; Turner v. Turner, 185 Va. 505, 39 S.E.2d 299 (1946). Some courts, however, require joinder of each co-tenant's spouse. E.g., Warren v. Twilley, 10 Md. 39 (1873); Greiner v. Klein, 28 Mich. 12 (1873); Jordan v. Van Epps, 85 N.Y. 427 (1881).

23. See cases cited supra note 22. In Turner v. Turner, under a statute, the inchoate dower interest of a co-tenant's wife was "wiped out" by the partition sale and did not attach to the husband's share of the sale proceeds, even though the wife was not joined in the partition action.

§ 5.14

1. W. de Funiak & M. Vaughn, Principles of Community Property §§ 11.1, 19–36, 37–39 (2d ed. 1971) [hereinafter cited as "De Funiak & Vaughn"].

2. Id. at § 37; Cross, The Community Property Law in Washington, 49 Wash.L.Rev. 729, 733 (1974). Louisiana's code system of law is mostly adapted from French law, but its community property law seems to be of Spanish origin. When the United States acquired Louisiana from France in 1803–1804, Spain had just returned the territory to France after some three decades of Spanish rule.

established by the constitutions of California, Nevada, and Texas and by statute in the remaining five community property states.[3] In all the states community property has a statutory skeleton, fleshed out with numerous judicial precedents. Civil law sources today play hardly any role in American community property decisions, despite scholarly pleas that lawyers and judges should be more familiar with these sources.[4] Common law principles have had an effect on American community property law, as community property principles such as equality between spouses and marital partnership have much influenced the law of the whole country.[5] American community property law has become an indigenous system or, more precisely, eight common systems that differ in important details.

Underlying community property is the philosophical premise that husband and wife are equals. Together in marriage, they form a kind of marital partnership, not a business partnership, but analogous to it. Each may own property in his or her individual right, called "separate" property. Other property they own together equally as "community" property, whose closest analogue again is property of a business partnership.[6] Thus, characterization of property as separate or community is the crucial first step in determining the spouses' legal relationships with respect to it. Classification of their contract or tort obligations as community or separate is also important in determining liability. Dissolution of the marriage by death or divorce raises the problem: who shall receive the community property and be liable for community obligations? One is sometimes tempted to think of the community as a third entity in the marriage, but we must resist this temptation, for the respected sources say it is not, just as other respected sources say a business partnership is not.[7]

For a marital community to exist, a man and woman must have a relationship that the law recognizes as marriage. In most cases this is obvious because the spouses have gone through a valid ceremonial marriage. Only two of the community property states, Idaho and Texas, recognize common law marriages formed within their jurisdictions, and of course these two accept that as a valid marriage. The others will recognize common law marriages that were formed in other jurisdictions that recognize such marriages.[8] Under the doctrine of "putative marriage," the civil law extends the benefits of community property to one spouse or to both of them

---

3. West's Ann.Cal. Const.1879, Art. I, § 21; Nevada Const.1864, Art. IV, § 31; Vernon's Ann.Tex. Const.1876, Art. XVI, § 15; Ariz. Rev.Stats. § 25–211; Idaho Code § 32–903; La.—LSA–C.C. arts. 2325–2327; New Mexico Stats.Ann. § 40–3–8; West's Rev.Code Wash. Ann. § 26.16.030. Puerto Rico, whose law will not be further covered here, also has a community property system. 31 L.P.R.Ann. § 3621.

4. See De Funiak & Vaughn §§ 3–5.

5. For a discussion of the influence of principles associated with community property, see W. McClanahan, Community Property Law in the United States §§ 14.2, 14.3 (1982) [hereinafter cited as "McClanahan"].

6. The concept is that, while the marriage endures, the spouses have equal, undivided shares in the community property. While they may by agreement change the character from community to separate and vice versa, any property that is classified as community must be equal, which is not true of business partnership property. E.g., West's Ann.Cal. Civ.Code § 5105; La.—LSA–Civ.Code art. 2336; Nev.Rev.Stat.Ann. 123.225; Phillipson v. Board of Administration, 3 Cal.3d 32, 89 Cal.Rptr. 61, 473 P.2d 765 (1970).

7. See Household Finance Corp. v. Smith, 70 Wn.2d 401, 423 P.2d 621 (1967); Bortle v. Osborne, 155 Wash. 585, 285 P. 425 (1930); De Funiak & Vaughn § 95.

8. De Funiak & Vaughn § 55.1; Cross, The Community Property Law in Washington, 49 Wash.L.Rev. 729, 736 (1974).

who in good faith enter into a ceremonial marriage that proves to be legally invalid.[9] Louisiana has adopted the principle by statute.[10] In California, where the phrase "putative marriage" appears in a statute and in some court decisions, property may be divided as if it were community property upon "dissolution" of an innocent relationship, but the relationship is not called a marriage.[11] Texas decisions are in disarray, with some seeming to recognize the civil law putative marriage doctrine and some refusing to recognize it.[12] Elsewhere, to the extent the question of putative marriage has come up, the courts have generally not adopted the doctrine.[13] Nevertheless, when one or both parties are innocent of their unmarried condition, courts in community property states generally will divide property upon dissolution of the relationship on a basis that may approximate division of community property, on theories such as equitable division or partnership.[14] When the parties live together unmarried and both know it, then clearly no community property may exist either at civil law or under American community property law. Even then, however, courts, especially in recent years, may divide the property between them upon theories of deceit, implied contract, partnership, or restitution.[15]

§ 5.15 Community Property—Character of Ownership

When a marital community exists, all property rights held by either or both of the spouses are classified as either the "separate" property of one or as their "community" property. Subject to some qualifications that will be noted, each spouse owns his or her separate property in his or her own right, free from claims of the other spouse, just as if he or she were unmarried.[1]

---

9. Barkley v. Dumke, 99 Tex. 150, 87 S.W. 1147 (1905); De Funiak & Vaughn § 56. As Professor Harry M. Cross, in his typically incisive way, pointed out in a conversation with the writer of this section, it is not strictly accurate to speak of a putative "marriage" when only one spouse is innocent. It would be more precise in that circumstance to speak of a putative "spouse."—W.B.S.

10. La.—LSA–Civ.Code art. 96.

11. West's Ann.Cal.Civ.Code § 4452; In re Vargas' Estate, 36 Cal.App.3d 714, 111 Cal. Rptr. 779 (1974); De Funiak & Vaughn § 56.2; W. Reppy & C. Samuel, Community Property in the United States 335–36 (2d ed. 1982).

12. Lee v. Lee, 112 Tex. 392, 247 S.W. 828 (1923) (putative marriage); Barkley v. Dumke, 99 Tex. 150, 87 S.W. 1147 (1905) (putative marriage); Texas Employers Insurance Association v. Grimes, 153 Tex. 357, 269 S.W.2d 332 (1954) (no wrongful death benefits to "putative wife"); Fort Worth & Rio Grande Railway Co. v. Robertson, 103 Tex. 504, 131 S.W. 400 (1910), reversing 55 Tex.Civ.App. 309, 121 S.W. 202 (1909) (putative wife may not maintain survival action).

13. Poole v. Schrichte, 39 Wn.2d 558, 236 P.2d 1044 (1951); De Funiak & Vaughn §§ 56–56.8; Cross, The Community Property Law in Washington, 49 Wash.L.Rev. 729, 736 (1974).

14. In re Vargas' Estate, 36 Cal.App.3d 714, 111 Cal.Rptr. 779 (1974) ("equitable principles"); McGhee v. McGhee, 82 Idaho 367, 353 P.2d 760 (1960) ("constructive fraud" against innocent party); Poole v. Schrichte, 39 Wn.2d 558, 236 P.2d 1044 (1951) (partnership; alternative theory); Creasman v. Boyle, 31 Wn.2d 345, 196 P.2d 835 (1948) (resulting trust). In re Marriage of Lindsey, 101 Wn.2d 299, 678 P.2d 328 (1984), overruled *Creasman v. Boyle* on a different point than that for which it is cited here.

15. Carroll v. Lee, 148 Ariz. 10, 712 P.2d 923 (1986) (contract); Marvin v. Marvin, 18 Cal.3d 660, 134 Cal.Rptr. 815, 557 P.2d 106 (1976), appeal after remand 122 Cal.App.3d 871, 176 Cal.Rptr. 555 (1981); In re Cary's Marriage, 34 Cal.App.3d 345, 109 Cal.Rptr. 862 (1973); In re Marriage of Lindsey, 101 Wn.2d 299, 678 P.2d 328 (1984) ("just and equitable"); In re Estate of Thornton, 81 Wn.2d 72, 499 P.2d 864 (1972); Poole v. Schrichte, 39 Wn.2d 558, 236 P.2d 1044 (1951) (alternative approach).

§ 5.15

1. Ariz.Rev.Stat. §§ 25–214, 33–451; West's Ann.Cal.Civ.Code §§ 5102, 5107, 5108; Idaho Code §§ 32–903, 32–904, 15–1–201; La.—LSA–Civ.Code art. 2371; Nev.Rev.Stat. §§ 123.060, 123.170; New Mexico Stat.Ann.

All property acquired by either spouse before marriage—and this is the
feature that particularly distinguishes the Spanish "ganancial" system from
other European community property institutions—is that spouse's separate
property.[2] And property acquired by either one after marriage by gift,
devise, bequest, or inheritance is also separate.[3] In other words, acquisitions
after marriage that are donative or "lucrative," and so not acquired "oner-
ously" as the result of the effort, skill, or industry of either spouse, are
separate. The distinction between "lucrative" and "onerous" acquisitions
rests immediately upon the premise that community property is the product
of a husband-wife team, pulling together in harness. If a presently owned
asset has its source in a previously owned asset that was separate, such as
having been exchanged for it, the present asset is separate as long as it can
be traced to the previous one.[4] The natural produce of separate property,
rents, issues, and profits, is community property in Idaho, Louisiana, and
Texas (the "civil law" or "Spanish" rule) but separate property in the other
community property states (the "American" or "California" rule).[5] Where
rents, issues, and profits of separate property remain separate, to some
extent the income stream from the asset may be the result of one or both
spouse's "onerous" efforts; this is especially true when the assets are in a
going business. All agree that in principle the income is to that extent
community, but judicial formulas to measure the extent differ.[6] A similar
and partially overlapping problem arises upon dissolution of marriage when
it appears that the value of separate property has increased in part due to
market forces and in part due to spousal efforts; again, there is a complex
apportionment problem with various factors to be considered and differing
judicial formulas.[7] Gifts to both spouses are generally community, at least if

1978, § 40-3-3; Vernon's Tex.Codes Ann.,
Family Code § 5.21; West's Rev.Code Wash.
Ann. §§ 26.16.010, 26.16.020.

2. Ariz.Rev.Stat. § 25-213; West's Ann.
Cal.Civ.Code § 5107; Idaho Code §§ 32-903,
15-1-201; La.—LSA-Civ.Code art. 2341; Nev.
Rev.Stat.Ann. § 123.130; New Mexico Stat.
Ann. 1978, § 40-3-8; Vernon's Tex.Codes
Ann., Family Code § 5.01(a); West's Rev.Code
Wash.Ann. §§ 26.16.010, 26.16.020; De Fun-
iak & Vaughn §§ 58, 63, 64, 66; McClanahan
§§ 6.1-6.3.

3. See authorities cited in preceding footnote.

4. See In re Clark's Estate, 94 Cal.App.
453, 271 P. 542 (1928) (division of estate received in settlement of contested will was separate); De Funiak & Vaughn §§ 62, 69; W.
Brockelbank, The Community Property Law
of Idaho 134-38 (1962). The principle that a
previously owned separate asset may impart
its character to a present asset is variously
discussed as the "source" doctrine, as a "tracing," or as an exchange.

5. Ariz.Rev.Stat. § 25-213; West's Ann.
Cal.Civ.Code §§ 5107, 5108; Idaho Code § 32-
906(1); La.—LSA-Civ.Code art. 2339; Nev.
Rev.Stat.Ann. § 123.130; New Mexico Stat.
Ann.1978, § 40-3-8; West's Rev.Code Wash.

Ann. §§ 26.16.010, 26.16.020; Frame v.
Frame, 120 Tex. 61, 36 S.W.2d 152 (1931). In
Idaho, Louisiana, and, since a constitutional
amendment in 1980, Texas, it is possible for
the spouses to provide by agreement that
rents, issues, and profits of separate property
will be separate. McClanahan § 6.12. Cf.
Swope v. Swope, 112 Idaho 974, 739 P.2d 273
(1987), appeal after remand __ Idaho __, __
P.2d __ (1992) (earnings of separate-property
partnership are community).

6. The two best known formulas are contained in Pereira v. Pereira, 156 Cal. 1, 103 P.
488 (1909), and Van Camp v. Van Camp, 53
Cal.App. 17, 199 P. 885 (1921). See discussion
in McClanahan, § 6.18.

7. See Cockrill v. Cockrill, 124 Ariz. 50,
601 P.2d 1334 (1979), appeal after remand 139
Ariz. 72, 676 P.2d 1130 (1983); Beam v. Bank
of America, 6 Cal.3d 12, 98 Cal.Rptr. 137, 490
P.2d 257 (1971); Simplot v. Simplot, 96 Idaho
239, 526 P.2d 844 (1974); Speer v. Quinlan, 96
Idaho 119, 525 P.2d 314 (1973); Abraham v.
Abraham, 230 La. 78, 87 So.2d 735 (1956);
Cord v. Neuhoff, 94 Nev. 21, 573 P.2d 1170
(1978); Jensen v. Jensen, 665 S.W.2d 107 (Tex.
1984) ("reimbursement" theory); Vallone v.
Vallone, 644 S.W.2d 455 (Tex.1982); Norris v.
Vaughan, 152 Tex. 491, 260 S.W.2d 676 (1953);
McClanahan, § 6.18.

no arrangement is made otherwise, in part due to the presumption that assets received after marriage are community.[8] It is, however, possible for spouses to be tenants in common or, except in Louisiana, joint tenants with each other, owning their shares as separate property.[9]

Community property is nearly always described by exclusion. In the typical language of the Texas Family Code, "Community property consists of the property, other than separate property, acquired by either spouse during marriage."[10] Only the Louisiana Civil Code attempts an affirmative definition, "The community property comprises: property acquired during the existence of the legal regime through the effort, skill or industry of either spouse," etc.—and even it backstops the definition with, "and all other property not classified by law as separate property."[11] Thus is the American application of the civil law's distinction between "lucrative" and "onerous" acquisitions expressed. Statutes are also beginning to recognize a category called "quasi-community property." In general, this means property of spouses now residing in a community property state, acquired in another state, which would have been community property if it had been acquired in the community property state.[12]

The problem that most severely tests the basic distinction is characterization of personal injury damages. Originally the community property states classified them as community property, on the mechanical reasoning that the statutes said everything acquired after marriage was community property unless acquired by some form of donative transfer.[13] That united front has now broken down, as is usually the case when law changes, in a welter of confusion. Idaho still adheres to the traditional all-community view, though there is some question whether the rule is cracking.[14] Most of the other seven states now apportion personal injury awards, with those portions representing loss of earnings and community expenses being community and the portions representing pain, suffering, and loss of bodily parts as separate property of the injured spouse. Louisiana has reached that position by statute, and Arizona, Nevada, New Mexico, Texas and Washing-

---

8. Hamilton v. Hamilton, 381 So.2d 517 (La.App.1979) (apparent result); In re Salvini's Estate, 65 Wn.2d 442, 397 P.2d 811 (1964).

9. Ariz.Rev.Stat. § 33–431; West's Ann. Cal.Civ.Code § 5104; Idaho Code § 55–104; La.—LSA–Civ.Code art. 480 (ownership in "indivision"); Nev.Rev.Stat.Ann. § 123.030; New Mexico Stat.Ann. 1978, § 40–3–2; Vernon's Ann.Tex.Stats.Probate Code, § 46; West's Rev.Stat.Wash.Ann. §§ 64.28.010, 64.28.020; De Funiak & Vaughn § 134.

10. Vernon's Tex.Codes Ann., Family Code § 5.01(b). To similar effect, see Ariz.Rev.Code § 25–211; West's Ann.Cal.Civ.Code § 5110; Idaho Code § 32–906(1); Nev.Rev.Stat.Ann. § 123.220; New Mexico Stat.Ann.1978, § 40–3–8(B); West's Revised Code Wash.Ann. 26.-16.030.

11. La.—LSA–C.C. art. 2338.

12. The definition of "quasi-community property" usually also includes property re-

ceived in exchange for property that would have been community property if the spouse who acquired it had lived in the community property state when it was acquired. Some of the statutes attempt to make out-of-state realty quasi-community, and sôme do not. See West's Ann.Cal.Civ.Code § 4803 (out-of-state realty included); Idaho Code §§ 15–2–201, 15–2–209 (out-of-state realty not included); N.Mex.Stat.Ann. § 40–3–8 (out-of-state realty included); Vernon's Tex.Code Ann.Family Code § 3.63(b) (out-of-state realty included; words "quasi-community property" do not appear); West's Rev.Code Wash.Ann. § 26.16.-220 (quasi-community property of deceased persons; certain out-of-state realty included).

13. De Funiak & Vaughn § 82; McClanahan, § 6.27.

14. Rogers v. Yellowstone Park Co., 97 Idaho 14, 539 P.2d 566 (1974); Cross, The Community Property Law in Washington, 49 Wash.L.Rev. 729, 773–76 (1974).

ton have done so by court decision.[15] California, by statute and by force of decisions prior to the statute, has a jumbled scheme, whereby one spouse's personal injury damages in a suit against the other spouse are separate, but damages received by a spouse in a suit against a third person are always community when received, subject to possible reimbursement between spouses for certain expenses paid out of separate funds.[16]

Characterization problems that may be simpler theoretically than the problems with personal injury damages but that are practically more complex arise when assets are acquired partly with community and partly with separate funds or when property of one kind is improved with funds of the other kind. The proprietary nature of an asset, whether the title is separate or community, is fixed when it is "acquired" and does not change.[17] But in cases in which an asset is acquired over a period of time extending before and after marriage, mainly acquisitions by mortgage, real estate contract, other credit, or life insurance purchased with periodic premiums, the difficult problem is to determine when acquisition occurred. From state to state and even among the decisions of a given state, three doctrines are used to resolve the time-of-acquisition problems, namely the "inception-of-title" (when the credit transaction was initiated), "time-of-vesting" (when legal title vested), and "pro rata" (piecemeal division of ownership) theories.[18] Even when title or ownership of the asset is determined to be entirely separate or entirely community property, to the extent funds of the other kind have been spent in acquiring it, a claim against the ownership for reimbursement will arise. Similarly, when community funds have been spent to improve a separate asset or vice versa, a claim for reimbursement will arise.[19] Realistically, it is often easier to establish a community claim against separate assets than the other way around, because of a presumption some jurisdictions engage in that separate improvements on community assets are intended as a gift.[20] Indeed, the problems discussed in this paragraph are frequently associated with, if not resolved in the framework of, the presumption in favor of community property and the doctrine of tracing and commingling, to which we now move.

There is a presumption, by statute in four community property states and by decision in the other four, that property acquired during marriage is

15. La.—LSA–Civ.Code art. 2344; Jurek v. Jurek, 124 Ariz. 596, 606 P.2d 812 (1980); Graham v. Franco, 488 S.W.2d 390 (Tex.1972); Brown v. Brown, 100 Wn.2d 729, 675 P.2d 1207 (1984) (overruling prior decisions); McClanahan § 6.27; Akers, Blood and Money—Separate or Community Character of Personal Injury Recovery, 9 Texas Tech.L.Rev. 1, 2–14 (1977).

16. West's Ann.Cal.Civ.Code § 5126; McClanahan § 6.27.

17. De Funiak & Vaughn § 64; McClanahan § 6.3; Cross, The Community Property Law in Washington, 49 Wash.L.Rev. 729, 755 (1974).

18. E.g., Cosey v. Cosey, 364 So.2d 186 (La. App.1978), writ granted 366 So.2d 570, reversed on facts but legal theory left intact, 376 So.2d 486 (La.1979) (time-of-vesting rule);

McCurdy v. McCurdy, 372 S.W.2d 381 (Tex. Civ.App.1963), error refused (inception-of-title rule); Wilson v. Wilson, 35 Wn.2d 364, 212 P.2d 1022 (1949) (pro rata theory); In re Dougherty's Estate, 27 Wn.2d 11, 176 P.2d 335 (1947) (inception-of-title rule); W. Reppy & C. Samuel, Community Property in the United States 80–83 (2d ed. 1982).

19. See Hanrahan v. Sims, 20 Ariz.App. 313, 512 P.2d 617 (1973); Marriage of Moore, 28 Cal.3d 366, 168 Cal.Rptr. 662, 618 P.2d 208 (1980); Portillo v. Shappie, 97 N.M. 59, 636 P.2d 878 (1981) (value of community lien measured by value added by community labor).

20. See In re Warren's Marriage, 28 Cal. App.3d 777, 104 Cal.Rptr. 860 (1972); McClanahan § 6.16.

community.[21] In several jurisdictions there is an even broader presumption of community property if the only facts known are that parties are married and are possessed of assets.[22] Of course a presumption in favor of community property may be rebutted by proof that a particular asset was acquired before marriage or after marriage by gift, devise, bequest, or inheritance.[23] This may not be too difficult when a separate asset has been segregated and maintained as received, as a unitary parcel of real estate, a block of corporate stock, or a bank account scrupulously kept segregated. However, extremely complex problems arise in two common situations: (1) when the asset presently owned is not the original separate asset but is allegedly traceable back to it, usually through a series of exchanges, and (2) when separate and community funds or fungible goods have been commingled. We previously discussed the "tracing" doctrine in another context [24] and there saw that a presently owned asset is separate if it can be traced back to a "source" that was separate. However, as more time has elapsed between source and present asset and more tracing steps are required, or as community efforts or funds increasingly go into the asset, it becomes progressively more difficult to overcome the community property presumption. "Commingling" occurs when fungible separate and community property are intermixed; the usual example is a bank account into and from which separate and community funds are deposited and withdrawn. If that is all that is known, the presumption in favor of community property will prevail unless, according to some decisions, the amount of community property is "trifling" or "negligible." [25] To "uncommingle" the commingled mass essentially involves a process of tracing. If, as is rarely the case, the party maintaining, say, the bank account has kept records of each deposit and withdrawal in sufficient detail to identify its separate or community source or destination, the tracing can be accomplished. The less complete the records are, the more doubtful it becomes that the party seeking to establish that the mass is wholly or partly separate will succeed. Sometimes that party will benefit from the widely recognized "family expense" presumption that community funds, if available at a given time, are used for community living expenses.[26] Courts are divided over whether a party may offset total family expenses against total community income during the marriage ("total recapitulation" technique) or whether proof must relate to specific transactions.[27]

21. West's Ann.Cal.Civ.Code § 5110 (subject to exception of § 5111); La.—LSA–C.C. art. 2340; New Mexico Stat.Ann.1978 § 40–3–12(A); Vernon's Tex.Codes Ann., Family Code § 5.02; De Funiak & Vaughn §§ 60, 60.1.

22. State ex rel. Marshall v. Superior Court, 119 Wash. 631, 206 P. 362 (1922); McClanahan § 6.5; Cross, The Community Property Law in Washington, 49 Wash.L.Rev. 729, 747 (1974).

23. See, e.g., Duncan v. United States, 247 F.2d 845 (5th Cir.1957) (Texas law); See v. See, 64 Cal.2d 778, 51 Cal.Rptr. 888, 415 P.2d 776 (1966); De Funiak & Vaughn § 60; McClanahan § 6.5.

24. See note 20 and accompanying text, supra.

25. In re Mix's Marriage, 14 Cal.3d 604, 122 Cal.Rptr. 79, 536 P.2d 479 (1975); See v. See, 64 Cal.2d 778, 51 Cal.Rptr. 888, 415 P.2d 776 (1966); McClanahan § 6.8.

26. See See v. See, 64 Cal.2d 778, 51 Cal. Rptr. 888, 415 P.2d 776 (1966); W. Reppy & C. Samuel, Community Property in the United States 119 (2d ed. 1982); Comment, 19 Stan. L.Rev. 661 (1967) (critical of "family expense" doctrine).

27. See See v. See, 64 Cal.2d 778, 51 Cal. Rptr. 888, 415 P.2d 776 (1966) ("total recapitulation" not allowed); McClanahan § 6.8; W. Reppy & C. Samuel, Community Property Law in the United States 119–21 (2d ed. 1982).

California and Washington have statutes providing that when spouses are living "separate and apart" their "earnings and accumulations" are the separate property of the one acquiring them.[28] Idaho has a statute so providing for the wife only, but that statute was declared unconstitutional because of sex discrimination in Suter v. Suter.[29] Courts have had difficulty determining what "separate and apart" means, but it means more than a simple physical separation. At least it means that there is a permanent rupture of the marriage; some authorities even say the rupture must be so complete that both spouses have abandoned the marriage.[30] Even when no statutes govern the situation, courts have held in some cases that assets acquired after separation are not community property. This may be on the theory that the spouses had impliedly made a separate property agreement, that the non-acquiring spouse had abandoned the marriage, or that that spouse was estopped to assert a community claim.[31]

"Transmutation" is the spouses' conversion of separate into community property or vice versa, and all community property states allow it to some extent.[32] Transmutations are effected by two legal mechanisms, contractual agreement and gift.

As to contractual agreements, by statute those made before marriage must be in writing and generally must be acknowledged.[33] After marriage the members of a marital community are, with some limitations, permitted to contract with each other. One limitation is that they deal, not at arm's length, but from a position of trust and confidence, a principle the courts have most often applied to keep husbands from overreaching their wives.[34] Post-marital agreements may transmute all or some of one or both spouses' presently existing or after-acquired separate assets into community property or community assets into separate property. Consideration is present if there is an exchange of assets, if the agreement effects an exchange, or in any event, by virtue of the marriage.[35] Whether the agreement must be in writing or acknowledged depends generally upon statutes of frauds that

28. West's Ann.Cal.Civ.Code § 5118; West's Revised Code Wash.Ann. 26.16.140.

29. Idaho Code § 32–909; Suter v. Suter, 97 Idaho 461, 546 P.2d 1169 (1976).

30. Marriage of Baragry, 73 Cal.App.3d 444, 140 Cal.Rptr. 779 (1977); Makeig v. United Security Bank & Trust Co., 112 Cal.App. 138, 296 P. 673 (1931) (no "actual rupture" when living apart was supposedly to save money); Cross, The Community Property Law in Washington, 49 Wash.L.Rev. 729, 750–53 (1974). But cf. Loring v. Stuart, 79 Cal. 200, 21 P. 651 (1889), in which it seems the intent to break the marriage permanently was on the husband's side only.

31. Togliatti v. Robertson, 29 Wn.2d 844, 190 P.2d 575 (1948) (implied contract); McClanahan § 6.19.

32. As to pre-marital agreements, see Ariz. Rev.Stat. § 25–201; West's Ann.Cal.Civ.Code §§ 5200, 5201, 5202, 5311; Idaho Code §§ 32–905, 32–916, 32–917; La.—LSA–Civ.Code arts. 2328–2331, 2370; Nev.Rev.Stat.Ann. 123.010, 123.270; New Mexico Stat.Ann. 1978, §§ 40–

2–4, 40–2–7, 40–3–8; Vernon's Ann.Tex. Const. Art. XVI, § 15; Washington has no statute providing for pre-marital agreements. As to agreements during marriage, see Ariz. Rev.Stat. § 25–317 (upon separation or dissolution only); West's Ann.Cal.Civ.Code §§ 4802, 5103; Idaho Code § 32–906; La.— LSA–Civ.Code arts. 1743, 1746, 2329–2331, 2339, 2343; Nev.Rev.Stat.Ann. 123.070, 123.-080; New Mexico Stat.Ann. 1978, §§ 40–2–2, 40–3–8; Vernon's Ann.Tex. Const. Art. XVI, § 15 (including 1980 amendment); V.T.C.A., Family Code § 5.42; West's Rev.Code Wash. Ann. 26.16.050, 26.16.120, 26.16.210.

33. See statutes cited preceding note.

34. See, e.g., West's Ann.Cal.Civ.Code § 5103; Nev.Rev.Stat.Ann. 123.070; New Mexico Stat.Ann. 1978, § 40–2–2; West's Revised Code Wash.Ann. 26.16.210 (burden to prove good faith); De Funiak & Vaughn § 138.

35. Woods v. Security First National Bank, 46 Cal.2d 697, 299 P.2d 657 (1956); De Funiak & Vaughn § 136.

govern the transfer of the particular kind of assets involved. Transmutation of real property must be by a document that satisfies the local requirements for conveyances or contracts to convey, except in California, which has a remarkable doctrine allowing oral transmutation of real property.[36] Louisiana and Texas impose the strictest limitations upon post-marital transmutations, though, in keeping with a trend in all the community property states, they have relaxed the restrictions recently.[37] An oral transmutation may also be implied from such circumstances as the spouses treating certain assets as separate or community or from the form in which title is taken, but most jurisdictions probably require evidence sufficient to establish an agreement for transmutation.[38]

Transmutations may also occur by gift between the spouses, subject to the rules about forms of transfer just stated. In most community property states it tends to be easier to prove a gift of separate property to the community than the other way around, due to the presumption in favor of community property.[39] However, when the alleged gift is of an object, such as personal effects or jewelry, for the donee spouse's individual use, a gift should be easy to prove.[40] Conceptually, gifts of community property to one spouse as separate property are a transfer of only the other's community interest; therefore, as some statutes provide, only the donor spouse should have to make the transfer.[41]

§ 5.16 Community Property—Management, Disposition and Dissolution of Community Property

In community property states each spouse has the full power to manage and dispose of his or her separate property, as if he or she were single.[1] Of the community property, the husband historically was the manager, though even before the 1970's the tendency was toward the wife's increasing

---

36. Woods v. Security First National Bank, 46 Cal.2d 697, 299 P.2d 657 (1956), is a classic example of "bootstrapping." It holds an oral agreement purporting to transmute land from separate to community property was outside the statute of frauds because "executed"— "executed," apparently, because there was an agreement that "the property *had become* community property." All other states are believed to require a writing to transmute land. McClanahan § 8.16; W. Reppy & C. Samuel, Community Property in the United States 28 (2d ed. 1982).

37. La.—LSA—Civ.Code art. 2329; Vernon's Ann.Tex. Const. Art. 16, § 15; McClanahan § 8.13.

38. O'Connor v. Travelers Insurance Co., 169 Cal.App.2d 763, 337 P.2d 893 (1959) (individually maintained bank accounts; implied separate property agreement); Fletcher's Estate v. Jackson, 94 N.M. 572, 613 P.2d 714 (1980), cert. denied 94 N.M. 674, 615 P.2d 991 (1980) (taking title as joint tenants implied separate shares); In re Estate of Olson, 87 Wn.2d 855, 557 P.2d 302 (1976) (deed from third person to spouses as joint tenants created community property because they did not agree to separate shares by deed); W. Reppy

& C. Samuel, Community Property Law in the United States 31–32, 37–38 (2d ed. 1982).

39. In re Marriage of Lucas, 27 Cal.3d 808, 166 Cal.Rptr. 853, 614 P.2d 285 (1980); De Funiak & Vaughn § 147; Cross, The Community Property Law in Washington, 49 Wash. L.Rev. 729, 813–14 (1974). See also O'Neill v. O'Neill, 600 S.W.2d 493 (Ky.App.1980) (presumption in favor of Kentucky "marital property").

40. Johnson v. Dar Denne, 161 Wash. 496, 296 P. 1105 (1931); Cross, preceding note.

41. Idaho Code § 32–906; La.—LSA–Civ. Code art. 2343; Vernon's Tex.Code Ann., Family Code § 5.42; West's Revised Code Wash. Ann. 26.16.050; De Funiak & Vaughn § 147.

§ 5.16

1. Ariz.Rev.Stat. §§ 25–214, 33–451; West's Ann.Cal.Civ.Code §§ 5107, 5108; Idaho Code §§ 32–904, 32–906(1); La.—LSA–Civ. Code art. 2371; Nev.Rev.Stat.Ann. 123.170; New Mexico Stat.Ann. 1978, § 40–3–13(A); Vernon's Tex.Code Ann., Family Code § 5.21; West's Rev.Code Wash.Ann. 26.16.010, 26.16.- 020.

participation, as, for instance, in the requirement that both spouses join in conveyances of land.[2] Beginning with new Washington legislation in 1972, the historic scheme has been much changed. All community property states now vest general powers of management and disposition in each spouse, with exceptions to be noted. Everywhere but Texas, the statutes simply say either that spouses have equal management powers or, the equivalent, that each has full management powers.[3] Texas gives each spouse powers of management and disposition over "the community property that he or she would have owned if single," creating a presumption that property standing in the one's name or possession is subject to that one's management.[4] Exceptions to full individual powers frequently exist for acquisition or transfers of interests in land, for transfers of household necessities, for assets of a business in which both spouses participate, and occasionally for other specified assets. Where there are such exceptions, both spouses must join in the transaction.[5] To some extent one spouse alone may have enhanced powers of management in emergencies, such as when the other has disappeared or becomes incompetent to act.[6] In this connection, the statutory rule in several states, previously discussed, that a spouse's income is separate property when they are living separate and apart, may effectively enhance management powers. Death of a spouse dissolves the marital community, a subject that will be covered more generally below. In all community property jurisdictions, each spouse has statutory power to dispose by will of all his or her separate property[7] and one-half of the community property.[8]

The effect of American community property on liabilities of the spouses to third persons is pervasive—and all but incapable of meaningful general restatement.[9] With a force that varies from state to state, there is some

2. See De Funiak & Vaughn §§ 113, 115.1.

3. Ariz.Rev.Stat. § 25–214; West's Ann. Cal.Civ.Code § 5125; Idaho Code § 32–912; La.—LSA–Civ.Code art. 2346; Nev.Rev.Stat. Ann. 123.230; New Mexico Stat.Ann. 1978, § 40–3–14; West's Rev.Code Wash.Ann. 26.-16.030.

4. V.T.C.A., Family Code §§ 5.22, 5.24.

5. See statutes cited two notes above and also West's Ann.Cal.Civ.Code § 5127; La.—LSA–Civ.Code arts. 2347, 2349, 2350, 2351; New Mexico Stat.Ann. 1978, § 40–3–13.

6. West's Ann.Cal.Civ.Code § 5128; La.—LSA–Civ.Code art. 2355; New Mexico Stat. Ann. 1978, § 40–3–16; Vernon's Tex.Code Ann., Family Code §§ 5.25, 5.26. Beyond statutory provisions, there is some thought that a spouse who needs to act in an emergency should have enhanced powers of management and disposition. See McClanahan § 9.14; Cross, The Community Property Law in Washington, 49 Wash.L.Rev. 729, 787–88 (1974).

7. Ariz.Rev.Stat. § 14–3101(A); West's Ann.Cal.Prob.Code § [6101] Idaho Code § 15–3–101; La.—LSA–Civ.Code art. 1470; Nev. Rev.Stat.Ann. 133.030(1); New Mexico Stat. Ann. 1978, § 45–3–101(B); Vernon's Ann.Tex.

Stats.Prob.Code, § 58; West's Rev.Code Wash. Ann. 11.12.010; McClanahan § 4.24.

8. Ariz.Rev.Stat. § 14–3101(A); West's Ann.Cal.Prob.Code §§ [100, 6101] Idaho Code § 15–3–101; Nev.Rev.Stat.Ann. 123.250(1); New Mexico Stat.Ann. 1978, §§ 45–2–804(A), 45–8–9; Vernon's Ann.Tex.Stats.Prob.Code, § 58; West's Rev.Code Wash.Ann. 11.02.070; McClanahan § 4.26.

9. As evidence that it is difficult to agree even on a framework of analysis, see the three works from which the present discussion on liabilities is mainly drawn. De Funiak & Vaughn, Chap. 9, after stating some historical and preliminary matters, basically organizes the discussion around the various kinds of liabilities, taking up peculiarities of the states' doctrines within each of those categories. McClanahan, Chap. 10, which was contributed by Professor Frederick M. Hart, of the University of New Mexico School of Law, is organized similarly. But W. Reppy & C. Samuel, Community Property Law in the United States, Chap. 17, divides its discussion into two principal parts, one for those states that follow the "managerial system" and another for those that follow the "community debt system."

utility in thinking of separate and community liabilities, just as one thinks of separate and community assets.

There is general agreement that a liability either spouse had before marriage is separate. It is possible to incur separate liabilities after marriage, but this is less likely than if they were acquired before. In part this is due to a presumption that debts incurred during marriage are community debts; in part it is due to the broad general concepts that contractual obligations after marriage are on behalf of the community and that even tort liabilities arise during the conduct of activities that benefit the community.[10] Courts have made a total shambles of their attempts to define separate and community tort liability.[11] If it is found that an obligation is the separate obligation of one spouse, then that one's separate assets clearly may be reached to satisfy it, and if an obligation is community, community assets may be reached.[12] Separate assets of one spouse are not liable for the other spouse's separate obligations, except to a limited extent in several states that make the separate estates liable for family necessities.[13] The right of a separate creditor to reach community property exists to some extent now in all community property states, but it is utterly impossible to discern any general pattern. At the theoretical level, if one views the community as an entity, then its assets would tend to be insulated from separate claims; but if there is no entity and the spouses simply have some sort of co-tenancy interests in community assets, this would suggest that each one's share ought to be reachable.[14] Factors that may be important in different jurisdictions are whether the obligation arose in contract or tort, whether the obligation arose before or after marriage, whether the community assets to be reached are controlled by the debtor spouse, and whether the assets to be reached are earned income.[15] Some community property states have followed the so-called "managerial system," in which, as a general proposition, the community property that one spouse manages is liable for that one's separate obligations. Traditionally the husband was the manager. With the change to equal management since 1972, presumably the "managerial system" states have some doctrinal adjustments to make.[16]

Third persons who hold "community" claims may of course reach community property in satisfaction. Before the 1970's, when the husband, as community manager, was the spouse who had general power to obligate the community, creditors who had dealt with the wife might have to establish that she was the husband's agent or had the power to contract for family necessaries. Now, with generally equal management powers, those creditors should have an easier time. The right of the creditor who holds a claim against the community to reach separate assets is much clearer than the right of one who holds a separate claim to reach community assets.

---

10. See McClanahan §§ 10.2–10.4.

11. See, e.g., Babcock v. Tam, 156 F.2d 116 (9th Cir.1946); deElche v. Jacobsen, 95 Wn.2d 237, 622 P.2d 835 (1980).

12. McClanahan §§ 10.6, 10.8.

13. West's Ann.Cal.Civ.Code §§ [5120.130, 5120.140, 5132] La.—LSA–Civ.Code art. 2372; West's Rev.Code Wash.Ann. 26.16.205; McClanahan § 10.6.

14. For discussion of what are essentially the "entity" and "shares" theories, though perhaps couched in slightly different language, see the majority and dissenting opinions in deElche v. Jacobsen, 95 Wn.2d 237, 622 P.2d 835 (1980).

15. McClanahan § 10.7.

16. See W. Reppy & C. Samuel, Community Property Law in the United States 251–55 (2d ed. 1982).

Under Spanish law and generally in America, the one who holds a community obligation may reach the separate assets of the spouse who incurred the obligation, as well as the community assets.[17] There is in some states, however, a requirement that the creditor have exhausted community assets before seizing the separate property of the obligating spouse.[18] In addition, upon dissolution of the marital community, the spouse whose separate assets were used to pay community obligations may have a claim for reimbursement.[19]

Along with the marriage, the marital community is dissolved by death of a spouse or by divorce or annulment of the marriage. Of the spouses' testamentary powers of disposition, we have already spoken. As to a deceased spouse's separate property that has not been disposed of by will, except for Louisiana, which follows a civil law scheme of intestate distribution that is based upon different concepts than those of the common law, the property goes according to the state's statutory plan of descent or succession. These plans have their origins in the common law and are similar to the comparable statutory schemes of the common law states.[20] As to the decedent's half of the community property that is not given by will, the commonest plan is for that share to go to the surviving spouse.[21] In Arizona and Texas, the surviving spouse will or may have to share with children.[22]

When the marital community is dissolved by divorce or, as it is now usually called, dissolution, the judicial division of the spouses' assets is affected by whether they are separate or community. In Arizona, California, Idaho, and Louisiana, the judge must award separate property to the spouses who own it. However, statutes in California and Idaho allow alimony or support allowances to one spouse out of the other's separate property.[23] The other community property states do not strictly require separate property to be awarded to the owning spouse but instead allow it to be divided on an "equitable" basis; however, the fact that it is separate property is generally a factor in determining its destination.[24] As to community property, California, Louisiana, and New Mexico are known as "equal division" states, which require equal division of community property. This, however, means, not mathematically, but only "substantially," equal division, which allows the judge some leeway.[25] The remaining five jurisdic-

17. McClanahan § 10.9; Cross, The Community Property Law in Washington, 49 Wash.L.Rev. 729, 820 (1974).

18. Ariz.Rev.Stat. § 25–215; New Mexico Stat.Ann. 1978, § 40–3–11.

19. La.—LSA—Civ.Code art. 2365; W. Reppy & C. Samuel, Community Property Law in the United States 267 (2d ed. 1982).

20. Ariz.Rev.Stat. § 14–2101; West's Ann. Cal.Prob.Code § 6402, Idaho Code § 15–2–101; Nev.Rev.Stat.Ann. §§ 134.030–134.210, New Mexico Stat.Ann. 1978 §§ 45–2–102, 45–3–101; Vernon's Ann.Tex.Stats.Prob.Code §§ 37–39; West's Rev.Code Wash.Ann. 11.04.015; McClanahan § 4.25.

21. West's Ann.Cal.Prob.Code § [6401] Idaho Code § 15–2–102 (but see § 15–2–201 as to Idaho's "quasi-community property"); Nev.

Rev.Stat.Ann. § 123.250(1); New Mexico Stat. Ann. 1978, § 45–2–102; West's Rev.Code Wash.Ann. 11.04.015(1).

22. Ariz.Rev.Stat. § 14–2102 (children take only if there are children not issue of surviving spouse); Vernon's Ann.Tex.Stats.Prob. Code, § 45.

23. Ariz.Rev.Stat. § 25–318; West's Ann. Cal.Civ.Code § 4806; Idaho Code § 32–708 La.—LSA—Civ.Code art. 155; McClanahan § 12.3.

24. See Nev.Rev.Stat.Ann. § 125.150; New Mexico Stat.Ann. 1978, § 40–4–7; Vernon's Tex.Codes Ann., Family Code § 3.63; West's Rev.Code Wash.Ann. 26.09.050, 26.09.080.

25. West's Ann.Cal.Civ.Code §§ 4800, 4805, 4807; La.—LSA—Civ.Code art. 155; New Mexico Stat.Ann. §§ 1978 40–4–3, 40–4–20;

tions, which may be called "equitable division" states, allow the judge wide discretion in awarding the community property, with, again, the fact of its being community being one factor.[26] Perhaps it ought to be added in closing that the movement for equal rights of the sexes has brought many changes to both the law of community property and of marriage, changes that are likely not over yet.

§ 5.17 The Uniform Marital Property Act

The Commissioners on Uniform State Laws approved a new Uniform Marital Property Act in 1983.[1] The new Uniform Act is based on "community property" principles, and builds on provisions of the Uniform Probate Code[2] and the Uniform Marriage and Divorce Act[3] as well as the many statutes providing for "equitable apportionment" of spousal property upon dissolution of marriage.[4] UMPA fills a gap left by the Uniform Probate Code and the "equitable apportionment" statutes, which protect the "non-owning" spouse in common law jurisdictions only when the "owning" spouse dies first or the marriage is dissolved. UMPA, however, creates present shared property rights during the marriage with respect to property brought within the "marital property" regime during the marriage, and thus makes the division of property upon dissolution of the marriage and devolution of property upon the death of a spouse more predictable and less a product of the adversary process. Salient features of UMPA are as follows: (1) all property of the spouses is presumed to be marital property;[5] (2) each spouse has a present undivided one-half interest in marital property;[6] (3) property owned by a spouse at the "determination date" for classification is individual property if acquired (a) by gift or testamentary disposition from a third party, or (b) in exchange for or with the proceeds of other individual property, or from appreciation of the spouse's individual property, except to the extent that appreciation is classified by UMPA as marital property;[7] (4) ownership and management of marital property are carefully separated, and the right to manage and control marital property does not determine the classification of spousal property or rebut the presumption that all property

W. Reppy & C. Samuel, Community Property Law in the United States 297 (2d ed. 1982).

26. Ariz.Rev.Stat. § 25–318; Idaho Code § 32–712; Nev.Rev.Stat.Ann. § 125.150; Vernon's Tex.Codes Ann., Family Code § 3.63; West's Rev.Code Wash.Ann. 26.09.080; McClanahan §§ 12.6–12.14 (detailed, state-by-state analysis); W. Reppy & C. Samuel, Community Property Law in the United States 297 (2d ed. 1982).

§ 5.17

1. The text of UMPA, along with copious commentary, can be found in 9A Uniform Laws Annotated 21–58 (1986 Supp.).

2. The text of the Uniform Probate Code can be found in 9 Uniform Laws Annotated (1983).

3. The Uniform Marriage and Divorce Act can be found in 9A Uniform Laws Annotated 91–219 (1979).

4. See ante § 5.5, text at note 24 and authorities cited.

5. UMPA § 4(b). Unless classified otherwise, all spousal property is marital property. Id. § 4(a).

6. UMPA § 4(c).

7. UMPA § 5. Id. § 1(5) defines "determination date" as "the last to occur of the following: (i) marriage; (ii) 12:01 a.m. on the date of establishment of a marital domicile in this State; or (iii) 12:01 a.m. on the effective date of this [Act]." UMPA § 14(b) provides: "Application by one spouse of substantial labor, effort, inventiveness, physical or intellectual skill, creativity, or managerial activity on individual property of the other spouse creates marital property attributable to that application if: (i) reasonable compensation is not received for the application; and (ii) substantial appreciation of the individual property of the other spouse results from the application."

of the spouses is marital property;[8] (5) a spouse acting alone may manage and control marital property held in the name of that spouse alone or not held in the name of either spouse, or in the names of both spouses in the alternative,[9] but the spouses must act together to manage and control property held in the names of both spouses other than in the alternative;[10] (6) gifts of marital property by a spouse to a third party in a single year are significantly restricted in amount;[11] (7) the rights of bona fide purchasers for value who deal with one of the spouses are protected by a provision that such purchasers take marital property from a spouse having the right to manage and control that property free of claims of the other spouse;[12] (8) special provisions deal with the classification of life insurance policies and proceeds,[13] deferred employment benefits,[14] interspousal remedies,[15] and the effect of a judicial declaration that a purported marriage is invalid;[16] (9) upon dissolution of a valid marriage, each former spouse owns an undivided one-half interest in the former marital property as a tenant in common except as provided otherwise in a decree or written consent;[17] (10) at the death of a spouse domiciled in the state, all property owned by that spouse that was acquired during marriage and before the "determination date" which would have been marital property under UMPA if acquired after the effective date of the Act must be treated if it were marital property.[18] It is not clear, however, whether all, or only one-half, of the marital property is subject to probate administration on the death of one spouse.

An important feature of UMPA is that it permits spouses to change the classification of their property by gift or by marital property agreement[19] and, by marital property agreement, to (1) alter their rights and obligations in any of their property whenever and wherever acquired or located;[20] (2) alter the management and control of any of their property;[21] (3) provide for disposition of any of their property upon dissolution of the marriage, the death of a spouse, of the occurrence or nonoccurrence of any other event;[22] (4) modify or eliminate the obligation of spousal support;[23] (5) provide for making a will, trust, or other arrangement to carry out the agreement;[24] (6) provide that upon the death of either of them, any of their property, including after-acquired property, will pass without probate to a designated person, trust, or other entity by nontestamentary disposition;[25] and (7) provide for the choice of law to govern construction of the agreement.[26] The marital property agreement is enforceable without consideration;[27] and may

---

8. UMPA § 5(d).
9. UMPA § 5(d).
10. UMPA § 5(b).
11. UMPA § 6.
12. UMPA § 9.
13. UMPA § 12.
14. UMPA § 13.
15. UMPA § 15.
16. UMPA § 16.
17. UMPA § 17.
18. UMPA § 18.
19. UMPA § 7. Id. § 10(a) provides that "a marital property agreement must be a document signed by both spouses." Id. § 3 pro-

vides broadly that, with stated exceptions, "a marital property agreement may vary the effect of this [Act]."

20. UMPA § 10(c)(1).
21. UMPA § 10(c)(2).
22. UMPA § 10(c)(3).
23. UMPA § 10(c)(4).
24. UMPA § 10(c)(5).
25. UMPA § 10(c)(6).
26. UMPA § 10(c)(7).
27. UMPA § 10(a).

be amended or revoked by a later agreement.[28] Persons intending to marry may enter into a marital property agreement, but the agreement becomes effective only upon their marriage.[29] All marital property agreements are rendered unenforceable if the spouse against whom enforcement is sought proves unconscionability, lack of voluntary execution, or lack of fair and reasonable disclosure of the property or financial obligations of the other spouse or prospective spouse (absent written, voluntary waiver of the right to such disclosure by the spouse against whom enforcement is sought).[30] If a marital property agreement modifies or eliminates the right of spousal support and this later causes one spouse to be eligible for support under a program of public assistance at the time when the marriage is dissolved, the court may require the other spouse to provide support to the extent necessary to remove such eligibility, notwithstanding the terms of the agreement.[31]

To date, the only state to adopt UMPA is Wisconsin.[32] In addition to a number of minor changes in UMPA's language, the Wisconsin statute added a section entitled "Credit transactions with married persons,"[33] made substantial additions to the UMPA section entitled "Interspousal Remedies,"[34] and substituted for the UMPA section entitled "Estate by the Entireties" a section that preserves "Existing Joint Tenancies, Tenancies in Common, and Joint Accounts," "Buy–Sell Agreements," and "Transactions of Guaranty, Indemnity or Suretyship."[35] Since the adoption of the Marital Property Act makes important changes in Wisconsin law, it has, of course, produced a good deal of commentary.[36]

28. UMPA § 10(d).

29. UMPA § 10(e).

30. UMPA § 10(f), (g).

31. UMPA § 10(i).

32. Wis.Stat.Ann. ch. 766, enacted by 1983 Wis.Laws, Act 186, effective Jan. 1, 1986.

33. Wis.Stat.Ann. § 766.56.

34. Wis.Stat.Ann. § 766.70.

35. Wis.Stat.Ann. § 766.90.

36. For the texts of the Wisconsin Act and UMPA, printed together to facilitate comparison, see 57 Wis.Bar.Bull. No. 7, p. 40 (1984). Commentary includes Weisberger & Wilcox, A Brief Overview: The New Wisconsin Marital Property Act, id. 10; Furrh, A Look at Transition: Is the Marital Property Act Retroactive?, id. 15; Boykoff, The Marital Property Act and Wisconsin Taxation, id. 18; Bugge, Credit under Wisconsin's Marital Property Act, id. 21; Horton, Real Estate and Conveyancing under the Marital Property Act, id. 25; Robertson & Langer, Marital Agreements: An Important Financial Planning Tool, id. 29; Friedman, Accounting for WUMPA, id. 31; Brauer, The Impact of the Marital Property Act on Deferred Employment Benefits, id. 35; Schumaker, Life Insurance under the Marital Property Act, id. 37; Erlanger, Hughes & Weisberger, Better Worse Richer Poorer: Estate Planning under Wisconsin's Marital Property Act, 59 Wis.Bar Bull. No. 2, p. 14 (1986); Note, Uniform Marital Property Act: Suggested Revisions for Equality Between Spouses, 1987 U.Ill.L.Rev. 471; Parkinson, Who Needs the Uniform Marital Property Act?, 55 U.Cin. L.Rev. 677 (1987); Furrh, Divorce and the Marital Property Act?, 62 Wis.Law 23 (Jan. 1989).

Chapter 6

LANDLORD AND TENANT

Table of Sections

A. NATURE AND HISTORY OF LEASEHOLDS

§ 6.1 The Landlord–Tenant Relation

The early history of leaseholds was discussed in chapter 2. In medieval English law a "tenant" was anyone who held any estate in land in a tenurial relationship. This implied that another person, the "lord," had previously held the same or a larger estate in the land and had conveyed the tenant's estate to the tenant with the latter having to perform stated duties in return for as long as he held the tenancy. For instance, the king, ultimate owner of all land, might parcel out some land to one of his nobles in fee simple or for life, in return for which the noble would owe the king military or other service. The king was lord and the noble, tenant. If the noble similarly parceled out a portion of the same land, the process was called "subinfeudation" and created another lord-tenant relation, another rung on the feudal ladder.

One still occasionally sees definitions of "tenant" that are as broad as the description above.[1] However, the phrase "landlord and tenant" is today ordinarily understood and is used here in a narrower sense. A tenant is one who holds a possessory estate in land for a determinate period or at will by permission of another, the landlord, who holds an estate of larger duration in the same land.[2] Observe some matters implied by this definition. It

§ 6.1

1. See, e.g., Urban Investment & Development Co. v. Maurice L. Rothschild & Co., 25 Ill.App.3d 546, 323 N.E.2d 588 (1975); 1 American Law of Property § 3.2 (A.J. Casner ed. 1952). [Hereinafter cited as "A.L.P."]

2. See United States v. 15.3 Acres of Land, 154 F.Supp. 770 (M.D.Pa.1957); Chubb Group of Ins. Companies v. C.F. Murphy & Associ-ates, 656 S.W.2d 766 (Mo.App.1983) (court lists essentials of leasehold); Friend v. Gem International, Inc., 476 S.W.2d 134 (Mo.App.1971); Port of Coos Bay v. Department of Revenue, 298 Or. 229, 691 P.2d 100 (1984) (essence of leasehold is that tenant has sufficient control to have possession). Hughes v. Chehalis School District No. 302, 61 Wn.2d 222, 377 P.2d 642 (1963).

deliberately excludes leaseholds for life, though they are sometimes included as a form of leasehold.[3] This exclusion is because it is felt there should not be two estates, life estate and leasehold, of the same duration; the greater life estate should exclude the life leasehold. The word "possessory," though redundant in the sense that all estates are possessory, is to emphasize that a leasehold is truly an estate in land, albeit that it is not listed among the freehold estates. And the requirement that the landlord hold a longer estate than the tenant implies that the landlord has something left over after the end of the tenant's estate, a reversion in the landlord. Thus, during the existence of the leasehold there are at least two estates in the land, the tenant's present possessory estate and the landlord's future estate in reversion.

A leasehold may be carved out of any "larger" estate. For this purpose, all the freehold estates are larger. A leasehold tenant may also carve another leasehold of shorter duration, called a subleasehold, out of the head leasehold. The parties to this new arrangement are sublandlord and subtenant. In fact, the subtenant in turn should be able to create a sub-subtenancy and so on without theoretical end. All these propositions flow from the first principle, that a leasehold may be carved out of any larger estate. A corollary is that the holder of an estate who transfers all he has cannot create a leasehold, but effects what ought to be styled a conveyance when the transfer is of a freehold or an assignment when the estate transferred is a leasehold.

The transaction that creates a leasehold is called a leasing, lease, letting, demise, or renting. In popular parlance the word "lease" often refers to a documentary leasing instrument, although it seems proper to speak of an oral lease. Leases, particularly written ones, customarily contain a number of contractual covenants, virtually always including a tenant's covenant to pay rent. None of these covenants are necessary to the existence of the leasehold, which could for example be granted as a gift with no covenants by either party. However, because landlords generally expect rent, it is likely that a court would find an implied promise for rent unless the parties had overcome the implication. In addition, once the landlord-tenant relation was found to exist, the parties would have those rights and duties with which the relation is surrounded by judge-made and legislative law. That body of law is, of course, the bulk of the material in this chapter.

B. LEASEHOLDS DISTINGUISHED FROM OTHER RELATIONSHIPS

§ 6.2 Distinguished—License, Easement, or Profit

Courts have sometimes used false bases to distinguish leaseholds from licenses, easements, or profits. Decisions can be found in which a lease was said to be irrevocable and a license revocable.[1] This is a false distinction because, while a license is revocable, a tenancy at will, one form of leasehold, is, too. Moreover, many leases contain clauses allowing one or both parties to terminate. One may also find courts that purport to distinguish a license

---

3. See 1 A.L.P., supra note 1, at § 3.2.

§ **6.2**

1. A.L.P., supra note 1, at § 3.3.

on the ground that it is given without consideration, whereas a leasehold is given in consideration of rent.[2] This is no proper distinction because rent is not necessary for a leasehold, and the holder of a license may well have paid for it.

Other false examples might be added, but it is more profitable to determine what is the true point of distinction. It is simply this: a leasehold, being an estate, gives the right of possession or occupation, whereas licenses, easements, and profits involve only rights of use.[3] To be sure, there can be real problems distinguishing possession from use, but these problems are not peculiar to landlord-tenant law. They occur in other areas, such as in distinguishing adverse possession from adverse use or prescription. As long as the distinction is one the law of real property makes generally, the difficulty of making it is no argument against making it in landlord-tenant law.

One sometimes sees a court describe an easement or profit for so many years as being a leasehold in an easement or profit or some similar phrase.[4] A distinguished scholar has suggested that such an easement or profit should give rise to a landlord-tenant relationship, presumably with the usual incidents of that relationship.[5] However, on balance objections to this result, both technical and practical, probably make it unwise. On the technical side, an easement or profit does not fit the historical understanding that a leasehold is a possessory estate with a tenurial relationship. From a practical standpoint, it might be awkward to try to impose the incidents of this tenurial estate upon easements and profits.[6] It probably is better, then, to think of an easement or profit for so many years instead of a leasehold.

§ 6.3   Distinguished—Signs and Billboards

Someone wishing to give the traveling public a message may obtain the right to place a sign or billboard on another's land. Of course the installer may clearly become a tenant by leasing a specified parcel of land for the purpose. However, in most cases the relationship is not so clear, as when the right is only to erect a free standing sign in a field or on a roof or to paint the message on the landowner's wall. These cases really pose a specialized problem of distinguishing easements and licenses from lease-

---

2. Siver v. Atlantic Union College, 338 Mass. 212, 154 N.E.2d 360 (1958); Jewish Child Care Ass'n v. City of New York, 129 Misc.2d 871, 493 N.Y.S.2d 936 (1985) (occupancy without rent not leasehold but license).

3. Tanner Companies v. Arizona State Land Dept., 142 Ariz. 183, 688 P.2d 1075 (App. 1984) (right to remove clay only profit, not leasehold); Clayton County Bd. of Tax Assessors v. City of Atlanta, 164 Ga.App. 864, 298 S.E.2d 544 (1982) (right to operate commissary at airport mere "usufruct" or license, not leasehold); Hi-Rise Laundry Equip. Corp. v. Matrix Properties, Inc., 96 A.D.2d 930, 466 N.Y.S.2d 375 (1983) (right to occupy for 10 years upon rent was leasehold); Todd v. Krolick, 96 A.D.2d 695, 466 N.Y.S.2d 788 (1983), order affirmed 62 N.Y.2d 836, 477 N.Y.S.2d 609, 466 N.E.2d 149 (1984) (right to install

coin laundry equipment license, not leasehold); Mann Theatres Corp. v. Mid–Island Shopping Plaza Co., 94 A.D.2d 466, 464 N.Y.S.2d 793 (1983), affirmed 62 N.Y.2d 930, 479 N.Y.S.2d 213, 468 N.E.2d 51 (1984) (what parties called theater "operating agreement" was really assignment); Weathers v. M.C. Lininger & Sons, Inc., 68 Or.App. 30, 682 P.2d 770 (1984), review denied 297 Or. 492, 683 P.2d 1372 (1984) (agreement was for mineral lease, not license); Restatement (Second) of Property § 1.2 (1977); 1 A.L.P., supra note 1, at § 3.3.

4. E.g., Jordan v. Indianapolis Water Co., 159 Ind. 337, 64 N.E. 680 (1902); Knapp v. Crawford, 16 Wash. 524, 48 P. 261 (1897).

5. Walsh, Licenses and Tenancies for Years, 19 N.Y.U.L.Q.Rev. 333 (1942).

6. See 1 A.L.P., supra note 1, § 3.3.

holds. Similarly to what we saw in the preceding section, the question should be whether in all the circumstances the sign installer has possession of a defined area or only use. Crucial to the possession-use question is the underlying question whether the parties intend the installer to have exclusive control over a defined area.

When the sign is painted on a wall that is otherwise used by the landowner, we generally will conclude that the sign installer has only an easement for the sign and likely secondary easements to make temporary use of the owner's land for maintenance. Sign structures on roofs pose closer questions, since the sign installer intrudes more upon the landowner's exclusive occupation. However, in most cases, if the dominant function of the roof continues to be to shelter the landowner's building, the sign installer probably has an easement. Free standing signs on the ground would appear to pose the most difficult questions. If the parties' agreement is in substance that the sign installer is to have exclusive control over a defined plot of ground, a landlord-tenant relation should exist. If this is not clearly agreed, but if the billboard structure is large and so constructed that the landowner can make no substantial use of the area it encloses without interfering with the billboards, then this would seem to imply a leasehold. Most billboards, supported by a few posts separated by open spaces, probably do not, without more, imply a leasehold. Though we might engage in interesting (and probably endless) speculation about whether one may have an easement for a structure as substantial as, say, a house, the law conventionally allows easements for minor structures. Utility poles or the improvements upon a road easement are examples. By analogy, it is felt most courts would allow easements for fairly substantial billboards.[1]

§ 6.4 Distinguished—Concession on Business Premises

A merchandising entity that is in general possession of its business premises often contracts with others who carry on particular aspects of the business on parts of the premises. Examples of such "concessions" are departments in department stores and refreshment concessions in theaters. The parties' agreement may be called a "lease," the concessionaire may pay "rent," often based wholly or partly on the amount of its sales; the concession area will be more or less physically separated from the rest of the premises; employees of the larger business may be privileged to enter the concession area for stated purposes; and the larger business may be empowered to move the concessionaire around within the general premises. These are key factors in determining whether the concessionaire is a tenant. Other possible legal relationships are grantor and grantee of an easement, employer and employee, and licensor and licensee. The ultimate question should be whether the concessionaire has the right of possession; if so, he is a tenant. If the right is only of use, then the concessionaire will likely have an easement or a license. If the so-called concessionaire's relationship to the larger business is such that he is really an employee, then he has no relation

<hr>

§ 6.3

1. On the question of signs and billboards generally, see 1 A.L.P., supra note 1, at § 3.4.

to the land that can be called either possession or use, for his use of the premises is only for the employer.

The foregoing are the basic theoretical distinctions among several relationships that may exist. In practice, however, there seems to be much inconsistency among court decisions, with the landlord-tenant issue often being made to turn upon some detail of the parties' relationship.[1] With a number of factual variables likely to be present and a choice to be made from the several possible legal relationships, this is perhaps to be expected. In addition, the final question before the court in the concessionaire cases has usually been, not a landlord-tenant issue, but some other question, such as whether the larger business entity must pay employee benefits for the "concessionaire" or whether the larger entity is liable to the "concessionaire's" employee in a slip-and-fall case.[2] With the court's gaze being fixed upon some other kind of question, the landlord-tenant issue may not receive thorough attention or may even be colored by the other question. In a proper analysis, the ultimate determination is whether the concessionaire has possession on all the facts. Hardly ever will a single factor be determinative, but only a balancing of various often contradictory factors.

§ 6.5 Distinguished—Cropping Agreements

A "share-cropper" is a person who raises crops on land possessed by another, the two of them sharing the crops produced. Thus, the share-cropper does not have possession and is not a tenant, though he has a right in the nature of an easement to enter and produce crops. Obviously this relationship has much in common with an agricultural tenancy in which the tenant pays rent wholly or partly in crop shares. Some disagreement exists over whether a share-cropper should be classified as an employee or an independent contractor,[1] but it is not necessary to resolve that matter here, since neither relationship implies he is a tenant. The essential difference once again, easy to state but often difficult to determine, is in who has possession.

Whether the parties' relationship is landlord-tenant or some other depends upon their agreement and the surrounding circumstances. Important factors in the decisions have been whether the parties called their agreement a "lease," whether they used a lease form with customary leasing clauses, whether the alleged tenant has general rights to use the land for purposes beyond merely raising a crop, who furnishes supplies, and the

§ 6.4

1. Compare Friend v. Gem International, Inc., 476 S.W.2d 134 (Mo.App.1971), with Wandell v. Ross, 241 Mo.App. 1189, 245 S.W.2d 689 (1952). See 1 A.L.P., supra note 1, at § 3.5. Courts are not precise in distinguishing the words "concession" and "lease" from each other. See South Carolina Public Service Authority v. Summers, 282 S.C. 148, 318 S.E.2d 113 (1984) (property "leased" to "concessionaires"); McGary v. Westlake Investors, 99 Wn.2d 280, 661 P.2d 971 (1983) (parking "concession" was "leased").

2. E.g., Friend v. Gem International, Inc., 476 S.W.2d 134 (Mo.App.1971) (slip-and-fall case); George J. Wolff Co. v. Riley, 24 Wn.2d 62, 163 P.2d 179 (1945) (employee benefits).

§ 6.5

1. For statements that the cropper is an employee, see Davis v. Burton, 126 Mont. 137, 246 P.2d 236 (1952), and Hampton v. Struve, 160 Neb. 305, 70 N.W.2d 74 (1955). For the view that he is usually an independent contractor, see 1 A.L.P., supra note 1, at § 3.6. See generally Comment, 42 Iowa L.Rev. 650 (1957).

length of the agreement.[2] It has been suggested that if the alleged tenant both resides on the land and farms it under the agreement, this is usually conclusive that he has a leasehold, though the fact that he does not live there does not necessarily negative that estate.[3] However, residence on the premises hardly is an infallible test, since hired farm hands often are provided housing. The only safe statement is that we must examine the parties' total relationship to determine whether the alleged tenant has possession.

Policy considerations incline courts toward the landlord-tenant relationship in doubtful cases, perhaps with increasing force. Modern farming methods require assembly of large aggregations of land. The nation's recent history indicates that farmland leaseholds are being used increasingly to achieve this result.[4] Not only is it becoming statistically more likely that parties intended a lease, but a decision favoring a leasehold tends to promote a relationship the marketplace has found useful.

§ 6.6 Distinguished—Lodging Agreements

A "guest" is a transient occupant of quarters in a hotel, motel, or inn, while a "lodger," also called a "roomer" or "boarder," is a more permanent occupant. The distinction between "guest" and "lodger" may have legal significance, but it is beyond our present subject, which is to distinguish both of those relationships from that of a tenant. For our purposes, "lodger" may include "guest," for neither is a tenant. Neither has the right of possession, as contrasted with occupancy. On the categorizing of a person as a tenant or lodger may turn important legal consequences.[1]

As with the other non-tenant statuses we have been discussing, the basic theoretical distinction to be made here concerns possession: a tenant has possession, but a lodger does not. Again the difficulty is to identify those factual circumstances that will lead a court to choose one alternative or the other. Factors usually mentioned are whether the occupant's stay was short, whether the owner lived in the same building, whether the owner had free access to the room, whether the owner provided services such as maid service, whether the occupant shared bathroom facilities, whether the owner provided meals, whether the room was furnished, and whether the owner holds the premises out to the public as a place for travelers or lodgers. To the extent answers to these questions tend to be affirmative, to that extent the occupant is likely to be a lodger and not a possessory tenant.[2] No single

---

2. See Dopheide v. Schoeppner, 163 N.W.2d 360 (Iowa 1968); Davis v. Burton, 126 Mont. 137, 246 P.2d 236 (1952); Hampton v. Struve, 160 Neb. 305, 70 N.W.2d 74 (1955). See also Hofmann v. Hofmann, 94 Ill.2d 205, 68 Ill.Dec. 593, 446 N.E.2d 499 (1983), appeal after remand 125 Ill.App.3d 548, 81 Ill.Dec. 12, 466 N.E.2d 598 (1984), which suggests sharecropping is less formal and more temporary than leasehold.

3. 1 A.L.P., supra note 1, at § 3.6.

4. See Comment, 42 Iowa L.Rev. 650, 652 (1957).

§ 6.6

1. See Bourque v. Morris, 190 Conn. 364, 460 A.2d 1251 (1983) (distinguishes between "guest" and "lodger"). Introductions to the subject of lodger or guest versus tenant are in Restatement (Second) of Property § 1.2 (1977); 1 A.L.P., supra note 1, at § 3.7; and Comment, 64 Yale L.J. 391 (1955).

2. In addition to the secondary authorities cited in the preceding footnote, see Johnson v. Kolibas, 75 N.J.Super. 56, 182 A.2d 157 (1962), cert. denied 38 N.J. 310, 184 A.2d 422 (1962); Chawla v. Horch, 70 Misc.2d 290, 333 N.Y.S.2d 531 (1972); and Buck v. Del City Apartments, Inc., 431 P.2d 360 (Okl.1967).

factor is determinative. For instance, it is possible to be a tenant for only a few hours,[3] and to be a lodger (but hardly a "guest") for months or years.[4] The ultimate question is for the trier of fact.[5]

The most frequently litigated consequence of the lodger-tenant distinction seems to be the landowner's extent of liability to the occupant for the latter's personal injuries. An innkeeper, hotel or motel proprietor, or lodging house operator has greater duties of care for the occupant's personal safety than does a landlord.[6] A similar question is the standard for measuring the owner's liability for the occupant's loss of personalty from theft or casualty.[7] Another question that arises with some frequency is whether an occupant may be ousted from the premises without notice, which may be done if he is a lodger,[8] or whether he is a periodic tenant, who is generally entitled to advance notice.[9] Court decisions make these questions and some others turn on the lodger-tenant distinction, in spite of scholarly criticism that that distinction is not necessarily related to the differing questions presented.[10] Some modern legislation avoids the distinction altogether in certain cases by including lodgers within the definition of a "tenant."[11]

§ 6.7 Distinguished—Occupation Incidental to Employment

One may certainly be a tenant of a person who happens to be his employer. However, there are some employments in which the employee is required to occupy the employer's premises, not in a separate landlord-tenant relationship but in order to perform the duties of his job. A building caretaker is likely to be so employed. Such persons are not regarded as tenants, with the rights and duties that would imply, but as employees whose occupancy is in the employer's right and not the employee's possession.[1]

Crucial circumstances in determining whether an employee's occupancy is merely incidental to employment are whether the occupancy was granted as part of the hiring and whether occupancy was a necessary part of the job or at least for the employer's convenience. Recent decisions in the lower New York courts have indicated that if the occupant was originally a tenant

---

3. See Hughes v. Chehalis School District No. 302, 61 Wn.2d 222, 377 P.2d 642 (1963).

4. See Marden v. Radford, 229 Mo.App. 789, 84 S.W.2d 947 (1935).

5. Id.

6. See Marden v. Radford, 229 Mo.App. 789, 84 S.W.2d 947 (1935); Johnson v. Kolibas, 75 N.J.Super. 56, 182 A.2d 157 (1962), cert. denied 38 N.J. 310, 184 A.2d 422 (1962); Buck v. Del City Apartments, Inc., 431 P.2d 360 (Okl.1967).

7. See Chawla v. Horch, 70 Misc.2d 290, 333 N.Y.S.2d 531 (1972).

8. See Dewar v. Minneapolis Lodge, No. 44, B.P.O.E., 155 Minn. 98, 192 N.W. 358 (1923); Fischer v. Taub, 127 Misc.2d 518, 491 N.Y.S.2d 538 (1984) (residents of adult care home not "tenants," nor was it a "hotel").

9. Hundley v. Milner Hotel Management Co., 114 F.Supp. 206 (W.D.Ky.1953), affirmed 216 F.2d 613 (6th Cir.1954).

10. Comment, 64 Yale L.J. 391, 396, 410 (1955).

11. ABF Model Residential Landlord–Tenant Code §§ 1–204, 2–101 (1969); Uniform Residential Landlord and Tenant Act § 1.202. These statutes appear to include "lodgers" but not transient "guests" within the definition of "tenant."

§ 6.7

1. See Kwong v. Guido, 129 Misc.2d 211, 492 N.Y.S.2d 678 (1985) (does tenant who becomes building superintendent become employee in possession?). See generally Restatement (Second) of Property § 1.2, Illustration 4 (1977); 1 A.L.P., supra note 1, at § 3.8.

and then only later became an employee (building manager), this was conclusive that he was tenant separately from his employment.[2] Several other recent decisions around the country involve migrant agricultural workers who lived in cabins in their employers' company camps. The ultimate question at stake in these cases was whether the workers were tenants who enjoyed easements of access for visitors, who happened to be union organizers and volunteer attorneys. In all cases the workers were held to be tenants.[3] The suggestion is that employees who reside in a company town will usually be tenants, for even if the site is isolated so that other housing is not available, the housing is for the worker's convenience. In the Uniform Residential Landlord and Tenant Act, employees whose occupancy is "conditional upon employment in and about the premises" are excluded from the act's operation, but no such exclusion appears in the Model Residential Landlord–Tenant Code.[4]

What are the likely consequences of one's being an employee occupant instead of a tenant? The predominant consequence in the appellate decisions has been that if the occupant is not a tenant but is only a licensee, he is not entitled to the advance notice to quit generally allowed periodic tenants.[5] If occupancy is only as an incident to employment, then the only notice to vacate that the employer must give is that notice which, under the employment agreement, is required to terminate employment.[6] Of course the fact that the relationship is terminable at will does not necessarily mean it is only employee's occupation, since tenancies at will are terminable without advance notice unless a statute requires it.[7] Similarly, it is possible for an employee to be a true tenant and for the tenancy to end with the termination of employment if the parties so agree.[8]

§ 6.8 Distinguished—Contract Purchaser in Possession

Unlike the relationships distinguished from leaseholds in the preceding several sections, we now distinguish a relationship that carries the right to possess land, title to which is in another. The modern form of the real estate installment sale contract gives the purchaser possession while the contract is executory, yet legal title is retained by the vendor. To be sure, most jurisdictions recognize that the purchaser has equitable title during the executory period. It is in fact this equitable title that enables the courts generally to conclude that the purchaser's possession is not as tenant of the vendor but as equitable owner in his own right. Still, these matters understood, we can say at least that the purchaser, though not a tenant, does

---

2. Dobson Factors, Inc. v. Dattory, 80 Misc.2d 1054, 364 N.Y.S.2d 723 (1975); Mayer v. Norton, 62 Misc.2d 887, 310 N.Y.S.2d 576 (1970).

3. Franceschina v. Morgan, 346 F.Supp. 833 (S.D.Ind.1972); Folgueras v. Hassle, 331 F.Supp. 615 (W.D.Mich.1971); State v. Fox, 82 Wn.2d 289, 510 P.2d 230 (1973), certiorari denied 414 U.S. 1130, 94 S.Ct. 868, 38 L.Ed.2d 754 (1974).

4. ABF Model Residential Landlord–Tenant Code § 2–101 (1969); Uniform Residential Landlord and Tenant Act § 1.202.

5. See Dobson Factors, Inc. v. Dattory, 80 Misc.2d 1054, 364 N.Y.S.2d 723 (1975); Mayer v. Norton, 62 Misc.2d 887, 310 N.Y.S.2d 576 (1970); 1 A.L.P., supra note 1, at § 3.8.

6. See Johnson v. Simpson Oil Co., 394 S.W.2d 91 (Mo.App.1965).

7. Id.

8. See Coldiron v. Good Coal Co., 276 Ky.

possess land of which the legal or record title is in another.[1]

As just suggested the contract purchaser in possession is not viewed as a tenant; his relationship is *sui generis,* to be termed simply contract purchaser in possession.[2] There is even authority that if the contract gives the purchaser the right of possession, but he allows the vendor to remain in possession, the vendor becomes the purchaser's tenant.[3] Though many legal consequences may flow from the conclusion that the purchaser is not a tenant, several consequences have been in litigation frequently. A statutory scheme for summary possession may not be used by the vendor to evict a defaulting purchaser if the statute applies only to actions between landlords and tenants.[4] In case persons suffer injuries on the premises, the contract vendor's exposure to liability is different from, generally less than, that of a landlord.[5] A tenant who becomes a contract purchaser may thereby bear the risk of loss of the premises from a casualty such as fire.[6] And one who is in possession as contract purchaser does not owe rent, though of course he normally owes contract payments.[7]

§ 6.9   Distinguished—Mortgagee in Possession

The law governing mortgages contains a doctrine whereby a mortgagee who goes into possession of the mortgaged premises under certain circumstances is privileged to keep possession till the mortgage debt is paid or the mortgagor's interest is foreclosed. Courts disagree on what "certain circumstances" will allow this privilege. One formula is that the mortgagee has a kind of right, analogous to a pledge, to hold possession as security, in addition to his other rights under the mortgage.[1] Another theory is that the mortgagor expressly or impliedly "consents" to the mortgagee's holding possession for security.[2] Whatever the explanation, it is clear that the mortgagee in possession, though truly in possession in his own right, is not a tenant. It has been held, in fact, that if he is put into possession as a tenant, he is not "mortgagee in possession." [3]

While the status of mortgagee in possession is *sui generis* and is not that of a tenant, it is closer to a tenant's position than is the status of contract purchaser in possession. Perhaps the mortgagee in possession can roughly

833, 125 S.W.2d 757 (1939); Najewitz v. City of Seattle, 21 Wn.2d 656, 152 P.2d 722 (1944).

§ 6.8

1. See generally 1 A.L.P., supra note 1, at § 3.9; G. Osborne, G. Nelson & D. Whitman, Real Estate Finance Law § 3.25 (1979).

2. MacKenna v. Jordan, 123 Ga.App. 801, 182 S.E.2d 550 (1971); Misco Industries, Inc. v. Board of County Com'rs, 235 Kan. 958, 685 P.2d 866 (1984) (possessor held to be tenant, not contract purchaser); Shipley v. Bankers Life & Casualty Co., 377 P.2d 571 (Okl.1962); Strengowski v. Gomes, 128 Vt. 555, 268 A.2d 749 (1970); 1 A.L.P., supra note 1, at § 3.9.

3. Lasher v. Redevelopment Authority, 211 Pa.Super. 408, 236 A.2d 831 (1967).

4. Bemis v. Allen, 119 Iowa 160, 93 N.W. 50 (1903) (defendant held to be tenant); Kiernan v. Linnehan, 151 Mass. 543, 24 N.E. 907

(1890); Strengowski v. Gomes, 128 Vt. 555, 268 A.2d 749 (1970).

5. See MacKenna v. Jordan, 123 Ga.App. 801, 182 S.E.2d 550 (1971); Shipley v. Bankers Life & Casualty Co., 377 P.2d 571 (Okl.1962).

6. Ridenour v. France, 442 N.E.2d 716 (Ind. App.1982).

7. Ankeny v. Clark, 148 U.S. 345, 13 S.Ct. 617, 37 L.Ed. 475 (1893); Barrell v. Britton, 244 Mass. 273, 138 N.E. 579 (1923) (dictum).

§ 6.9

1. See Spect v. Spect, 88 Cal. 437, 26 P. 203 (1891).

2. See Barson v. Mulligan, 191 N.Y. 306, 84 N.E. 75 (1908), reversing 120 App.Div. 879, 105 N.Y.S. 1106 (1907).

3. Id.

be though of as a kind of caretaker. He does have duties of care and management, parallel to those of a responsible owner. He may lease out the land and collect rent from and deal with new or pre-existing tenants. If he does so, he may apply rental income to the mortgage debt after paying for necessary expenses, but he must strictly account for his dealings. Should he use the land for some profitable business of his own, such as farming, he is usually chargeable with the fair rental value. There seems little authority for whether he is liable for rental value if he neither rents out the land nor uses it himself, though this has been urged.[4]

§ 6.10 Conveyance or Contract?

When parties enter into a lease, have they executed a conveyance or a contract? A person who was otherwise learned in our law but for some reason of unsullied mind about landlord-tenant law would look at a lease and conclude it was both. It conveys a leasehold, a landed estate, and also contains more or less contractual undertakings, such as promises to pay rent, make repairs, pay taxes, procure insurance, and so forth. Logically and analytically it is correct to say a lease is both. Historically such a statement must be understood in a special way. Principles of real property law and of contract law are both applied, but not necessarily when reason would indicate. Rather than to try to discover general rules, it is more realistic to identify some situations in which the contract-conveyance choice matters and to discuss the law's response in those situations.

Once the law regarding landlord and tenant got beyond its earliest stages in England, when a tenant may have been regarded as having something like contractual rights, the subject was developed as a branch of real property law. A lease was usually spoken of as a conveyance and not a contract. An important consequence of this pigeonholing was that, when the law of contract developed the concept of dependency of covenants and, flowing from that concept, the equitable remedy of rescission for substantial failure of consideration, landlords and tenants did not share in that remedy. So, in theory the tenant's failure to pay rent or perform some other covenant did not justify the landlord's termination, nor did the landlord's breach excuse the tenant's performance. However, we find many sizable exceptions, some of them quite old, and the number is increasing. On the tenant's side, it has been true since the Middle Ages that an actual, physical eviction by the landlord excuses the tenant's performance. By an only slightly less ancient extension of the doctrine of actual eviction, a so-called constructive eviction, if due to the landlord's wrongful act or neglect, will likewise excuse the tenant if he vacates. On the landlord's side, statutes very generally give him the power to terminate on account of the tenant's failure to pay rent or, more or less, to perform other covenants. These matters will be covered in detail in subsequent sections, and to detail them here or to list supporting authorities would be repetitious. Even beyond these examples, we can find a few decisions, not necessarily brand new ones, either, that openly call a lease

---

4. For a detailed discussion of the matters summarized here, see G. Nelson and D. Whit- man, Real Estate Finance Law at §§ 4.24–4.32 (2d ed. 1985).

a "contract" and allow a remedy that operates like and is labeled "rescission." [1]

Another important consequence of categorizing a lease as solely a conveyance has been to deny tenants the benefits of implied warranties as to the condition of the premises. While that branch of contract law dealing with sales of goods long ago developed implied warranties of fitness for purpose and merchantability, real property law did not partake of this development historically. With conveyances, including leases as conveyances, the rule was rather *caveat emptor,* so that the tenant was generally out of luck if the premises, including buildings, proved defective or unsuitable for his purpose. Moreover, he generally could not maintain actions for injuries to himself or his belongings caused by defective conditions. Mitigating these rules, however, landlord-tenant law developed some exceptions, such as when a landlord knows of a hidden dangerous condition at the time of leasing, fails to tell the tenant, and the condition injures the tenant. Of far more sweeping importance than these exceptions, the entire edifice of *caveat emptor* has begun to collapse like a house of cards within the last few years. A number of courts have, with leasings of dwelling houses, simply abolished *caveat emptor* and have found implied warranties of fitness for human habitation.[2] More states have new residential landlord-tenant statutes accomplishing the same end. Traditional principles have, though, proved more resistant to change when commercial leaseholds are involved. Again, these matters will be detailed in their appropriate places.

Despite the oft-repeated traditional statements that leaseholds are only conveyances, there are some sizable areas in which pure contract principles have always governed. One such area is the interpretation of promissory language. If the question is whether a covenant to "insure" requires a policy with extended coverage or a policy for the full value of improvements, cases from the branch of contract law dealing with insurance will be controlling. Another pointed example is the familiar rule that leases will be construed against the landlord. This is an application of the contract rule of construing against the draftsman, who almost always is the landlord. We may also note that, while it is usually descriptive and not decisive, landlord-tenant decisions commonly, almost routinely, speak of a lease as a contract. No actual count has been made, but if all American decisions involving leases were lined up, it would not be surprising to find that the majority concern the interpretation of covenants and are resolved as contract cases.

To return to a point previously made, perhaps we can now better understand how leases are governed by a mixture of conveyancing and

§ 6.10

1. E.g., University Club v. Deakin, 265 Ill. 257, 106 N.E. 790 (1914); University Properties, Inc. v. Moss, 63 Wn.2d 619, 388 P.2d 543 (1964). The following decisions allowed "rescission" of leases, using that word. Uptegraft v. Scott, 169 Ga.App. 12, 311 S.E.2d 187 (1983); Select Properties, Ltd. v. Rando, 453 So.2d 980 (La.App.1984). In the following decisions "rescission" of leases was discussed but not allowed on the facts. Wooldridge v. Exxon Corp., 39 Conn.Sup. 190, 473 A.2d 1254

(1984); Braeside Realty Trust v. Cimino, 133 Ill.App.3d 1009, 89 Ill.Dec. 25, 479 N.E.2d 1031 (1985).

2. One state, Texas, has recently held that there is an implied warranty of suitability in the leasing of commercial premises. Davidow v. Inwood North Professional Group–Phase I, 747 S.W.2d 373 (Tex.1988); Coleman v. Rotana, Inc., 778 S.W.2d 867 (Tex.Civ.App.1989). Does this possibly signal a change in American law?

contract principles. Rightly understood, this has been true even traditionally. In addition, some of those areas that have been traditional preserves of conveyancing law are now being infiltrated by contract principles, sometimes quite precipitously.

§ 6.11 Nature of Tenant's Property Interest

A tenant has an estate in land in the strictest sense. He has the right to possession, the hallmark of every estate, for a determinant period of time. Yet, for purely historical reasons, this estate has not been listed as a freehold estate. Rather, it is classified as a non-freehold "chattel real," a species of personalty.[1] The freehold-chattel real distinction has lost most of its significance over the centuries, so that today it is generally accurate to think of a leasehold as simply an estate. In a moment, when we examine the several kinds of leasehold estates, we will be examining, as it were, subspecies of the species, "leasehold estate."

One area in which the peculiar concept of a chattel real still may be significant is the settlement of decedents' estates. In England before the Statute of Wills in 1540,[2] when personalty could be willed but realty could not, and even to some extent later,[3] this concept was important. Persons who took personalty by descent were also different in England from those who inherited land. To a much lesser extent, differences as to wills and between descent and inheritance existed in former times in the American colonies and states. Now, however, these differences have virtually disappeared, so that it can be said that a leasehold descends by intestacy or may be willed to the same persons as may take freehold estates.[4] There is, however, one probate situation in which the concept of chattel real has impact, and that concerns an estate the decedent has in land in a state other than that in which he is domiciled. As to personalty the decedent owns, though it may be physically located outside his domiciliary state, the law of the domicile usually controls disposition, and the personalty generally can be administered in the domiciliary probate court. A leasehold is considered personalty for these purposes. On the other hand, a freehold estate in land in another state is disposed of by the foreign state's laws, and an ancillary administration usually must be had over it in that state.[5]

§ 6.12 Nature of Landlord's Property Interest

The tenant's leasehold is an estate carved out of some estate of longer duration that the landlord holds. Thus, the landlord, though he has given the tenant a present possessory estate, has retained that future part of the

---

§ 6.11

1. See Callen v. Sherman's, Inc., 92 N.J. 114, 455 A.2d 1102 (1983) (leasehold is "property," entitled to constitutional protection). 2 F. Pollock & F. Maitland, History of English Law 106–17 (2d ed. 1898), traces the early history of the leasehold.

2. Stat. 32, Hen. 8, c. 1.

3. Some differences between testamentary gifts of realty and personalty remained until the Wills Act, 7 Wm. 4 and 1 Vict., c. 26 (1837). The most important was that a will operated on all personalty acquired before death, while it operated only on realty held at the date the will was executed. See T. Atkinson, Wills § 3 (2d ed. 1953).

4. T. Atkinson, Wills, preceding note, at § 4.

5. See In re Barclay's Estate, 1 Wn.2d 82, 95 P.2d 393 (1939); T. Atkinson, Wills, supra at §§ 106, 116, esp. p. 637; 6 W. Bowe & D. Parker, Page on Wills § 60.11 (1962).

longer estate that follows the end of the leasehold. In other words, the landlord has retained a reversion.[1] If the landlord held the fee simple, the reversion is in fee. It is possible, too, for the landlord's estate to be shorter in duration than a fee, so long as it is longer than the leasehold he gives. For example, the landlord may have a life estate. Even though he may be 100 years old and create a 99–year leasehold, we regard the leasehold conceptually as smaller than the life estate, so that in theory the life tenant has a reversion, however unlikely this is in practice. As another example, a tenant may create a sub-tenancy for a shorter time than the head leasehold. The head tenant becomes also a sub-landlord with a sub-tenant and a reversion in his own head leasehold; there is now a true second landlord-tenant relationship.

As a matter of interest, the landlord-tenant relationship is the surviving remnant of the tenurial relationship that dominated medieval English land law. This is not quite correct, for the leasehold is not descended from the medieval freehold; the present freehold estates are so descended, but they no longer carry tenure. The essence of tenure is that one person holds an estate of or under another person and owes the other continuing or recurring duties, such as the payment of rent, during the duration of the estate. With some inconsequentially rare exceptions, tenures do not exist in freehold estates in the United States.[2] With the leasehold, not only are the medieval words "lord" and "tenant" used, but the customary covenant to pay rent will make the relationship tenurial.

C.   CREATION OF THE LANDLORD– TENANT RELATIONSHIP

§ 6.13   Principles Applied to All Leaseholds

All leaseholds, it is often said, must be founded in an agreement between landlord and tenant.[1] Therefore, the parties must have the legal capacity to make such an agreement.[2] The statement about an agreement must be understood in a broad way. A rudimentary leasehold "agreement," which likely creates a tenancy at will, may arise by implication simply from the circumstance that the holder of an estate permits another to possess his

---

§ 6.12

1. In various ways the existence of a reversionary estate in the landlord is recognized. See, e.g., Mobil Oil Corp. v. Phoenix Central Christian Church, 138 Ariz. 397, 675 P.2d 284 (App.1983) (landlord and tenant have separate interests in condemnation award); Wing v. Martin, 107 Idaho 267, 688 P.2d 1172 (1984) (dictum that landlord has right to recover for permanent damage to reversion); Foertsch v. Schaus, 477 N.E.2d 566 (Ind.App.1985) (when landowner makes oil lease, he has right to only such oil as remains in ground after end of lease); Lentz Plumbing Co. v. Fee, 235 Kan. 266, 679 P.2d 736 (1984) (tenant has no general right to burden landlord's reversion with mechanic's lien).

2. The Statute Quia Emptores, 18 Edw. 1, cc. 1–3 (1290), forbade generally the subsequent creation of new tenures in freehold. However, an exception was allowed for freeholds created by the crown. Tenurial freeholds existed to some extent in some of the American colonies. Whether this has carried over into modern time is a debatable question. See 1 A.L.P., supra note 1, at § 1.41.

§ 6.13

1. See, e.g., McCarter v. Uban, 166 N.W.2d 910 (Iowa 1969); Faroldi v. Nungesser, 144 So.2d 568 (La.App.1962).

2. Tecklenburg v. Washington Gas & Electric Co., 40 Wn.2d 141, 241 P.2d 1172 (1952); Restatement (Second) of Property § 1.3 (1977).

land.[3] Absence of covenants, including a covenant for rent, would not defeat the existence of a landlord-tenant relationship. The possessor would not be a trespasser or adverse possessor.

When the alleged tenant has not taken possession, then the word "agreement" must refer more strictly to a verbalized exchange of undertakings. In the absence of a Statute of Frauds, an oral agreement is as good as a written one.[4] Whatever form the agreement is in, it must be sufficiently definite in its "essential" parts that a court can determine the parties' intent. The question of definiteness seems to be the same as in the law of contracts.[5] What are the "essential" parts of a lease is, however, a landlord-tenant question, as to which there is no categorical answer.

Courts often say that the essential items a lease agreement must cover to be enforced are identity of the parties, description of the premises, statement of the term, and amount of rent.[6] Even the amount of rent would not be material if the parties intended a rent-free leasehold, though perhaps agreement is essential if rent is intended. Description of the premises is a provision that has caused frequent problems. The usual judicial formula is that a description is adequate though it is not a formal legal description or even a complete informal one, if it gives a clue that, with extrinsic evidence, identifies the intended premises.[7] Street addresses and nicknames have been held adequate.[8] In some jurisdictions, stricter standards for descriptions may be the rule, possibly even requiring a legal description.[9] A saving principle, in its nature apt to save many questionable descriptions, is that an inadequate description is cured if the tenant takes possession.[10]

It is generally understood that the duration of a leasehold term must be stated, either explicitly or by reference to a formula by which it can be computed.[11] If this cannot be determined, the lease is not sufficiently definite to be enforced.[12] Perhaps the most crucial point in time to be fixed is the commencement of the term, for if this cannot be determined, no kind of tenancy can arise, whereas if only the extent of the term is in doubt, a tenancy at will might exist. The term may be fixed to commence in the future and upon an uncertain event, such as completion of structures on the

3. Compare Faroldi v. Nungesser, 144 So.2d 568 (La.App.1962), which holds that occupancy alone will not imply a leasehold.

4. Maccarini v. New Haven Trap Rock Co., 148 F.Supp. 271 (S.D.N.Y.1957), affirmed 249 F.2d 893 (2d Cir.1957); McCarter v. Uban, 166 N.W.2d 910 (Iowa 1969); Restatement (Second) of Property § 2.1 (1977).

5. See, e.g., In re Wonderfair Stores, Inc., 511 F.2d 1206 (9th Cir.1975); Walker v. Keith, 382 S.W.2d 198 (Ky.1964).

6. See Cook v. Hargis, 164 Colo. 368, 435 P.2d 385 (1967); McCarter v. Uban, 166 N.W.2d 910 (Iowa 1969); Rubin v. Josephson, 478 A.2d 665 (Me.1984) (covenant for rent was "material, essential and substantial"); King v. Oxford, 282 S.C. 307, 318 S.E.2d 125 (1984) (purchase option was not essential part of lease).

7. Consolidation Coal Co. v. Mineral Coal Co., 147 W.Va. 130, 126 S.E.2d 194 (1962);

Soppe v. Breed, 504 P.2d 1077 (Wyo.1973) (alternative ground).

8. Keck v. Brookfield, 2 Ariz.App. 424, 409 P.2d 583 (1965) (street address); Cook v. Hargis, 164 Colo. 368, 435 P.2d 385 (1967) ("Old Pine Theatre Building").

9. See Stoebuck, The Law Between Landlord and Tenant in Washington, 49 Wash. L.Rev. 291, 311–12 (1974).

10. McKennon v. Anderson, 49 Wn.2d 55, 298 P.2d 492 (1956); Soppe v. Breed, 504 P.2d 1077 (Wyo.1973) (alternative ground).

11. Restatement (Second) of Property § 1.4 (1977); 1 A.L.P., supra note 1, at § 3.14.

12. Cypert v. Holmes, 81 Ariz. 64, 299 P.2d 650 (1956); Adams v. Lay, 218 Ga. 451, 128 S.E.2d 502 (1962).

demised land.[13] Though the lease to commence *in futuro* is generally unexceptional, if it is to commence upon an uncertain event that may not occur within 21 years, it is arguable that this violates the rule against perpetuities.[14] This problem should be sidestepped by a simple proviso that the leasing will fail if the term does not commence within 21 years. As long as the term commences within the period of the rule, no perpetuity is created by a term of any length, even a hundred years or a thousand.[15] When the leasehold commences *in futuro,* the time before commencement is no part of the term, and the future tenant's right during this time is sometimes called *"interesse termini."*[16]

A special problem exists about leaseholds to commence upon completion of a commercial structure, such as a store in a shopping center. Presumably if substantial structures are to be erected before the term commences, this is a material enough condition that no lease or agreement for lease is enforceable unless the structures are described with some degree of particularity. Some decisions suggest that plans and specifications must be attached or incorporated in the agreement that are detailed enough to direct construction.[17] This seems an extreme position, and most courts would probably be satisfied in most cases with an agreement that enabled the court to determine the rough design of the buildings.[18] Obviously the parties' agreement and surrounding circumstances have much to do with the specificity that is required. Sometimes also the parties provide that building plans shall be satisfactory to one of them, giving rise to arguments that the agreement is too vague or is illusory. The expectable judicial response is that the party to be satisfied must act in good faith or not unreasonably disapprove, matters into which the court may inquire.[19]

A good many decisions deal with whether an agreement is a lease to commence *in futuro* or only a contract to make a lease. The major consequence of this distinction is the measure of damages to the landowner if the alleged tenant defaults. If the agreement is a lease, damages are the

---

13. Carolina Helicopter Corp. v. Cutter Realty Co., 263 N.C. 139, 139 S.E.2d 362 (1964) (term to commence when tenant got business permit); E.I. DuPont de Nemours & Co. v. Zale Corp., 462 S.W.2d 355 (Tex.Civ.App.1970), refused n.r.e., appeal after remand 494 S.W.2d 229 (1973) (term to commence when building erected). See also In re Wonderfair Stores, Inc., 511 F.2d 1206 (9th Cir.1975).

14. See Wong v. DiGrazia, 60 Cal.2d 525, 35 Cal.Rptr. 241, 386 P.2d 817 (1963). The court saved the future leasehold from the rule against perpetuities, but the ground of decision is somewhat unclear.

15. 1 A.L.P., supra note 1, at § 3.15.

16. See Arthur Treacher's Fish & Chips, of Fairfax, Inc. v. Chillum Terrace Limited Partnership, 272 Md. 720, 327 A.2d 282 (1974), appeal after remand 29 Md.App. 320, 347 A.2d 568 (1975); E.I. DuPont de Nemours & Co. v. Zale Corp., 462 S.W.2d 355 (Tex.Civ.App.1970), refused n.r.e., appeal after remand 494 S.W.2d 229 (1973). The phrase *"interesse termini"* has also been used to refer to a period of time after the stated term has begun, but in which the tenant has not taken possession. The

tenant has been said to have no estate during this period, which is curious, since generally one may have an estate by grant without possession. See 1 A.L.P., supra note 1, at § 3.22.

17. See Target Stores, Inc. v. Twin Plaza Co., 277 Minn. 481, 153 N.W.2d 832 (1967).

18. Brodsky v. Allen Hayosh Industries, Inc., 1 Mich.App. 591, 137 N.W.2d 771 (1965). See also In re Wonderfair Stores, Inc., 511 F.2d 1206 (9th Cir.1975); S. Jon Kreedman & Co. v. Meyers Brothers Parking–Western Corp., 58 Cal.App.3d 173, 130 Cal.Rptr. 41 (1976).

19. In re Wonderfair Stores, Inc., 511 F.2d 1206 (9th Cir.1975); S. Jon Kreedman & Co. v. Meyers Brothers Parking–Western Corp., 58 Cal.App.3d 173, 130 Cal.Rptr. 41 (1976). Cf. Saxon Theatre Corp. v. Sage, 347 Mass. 662, 200 N.E.2d 241 (1964), in which an agreement for a lease was held unenforceable when *both* parties were to agree to building plans and other matters.

unpaid rent, whereas damages are only the difference between the agreed rent and fair rental value if the agreement is a contract.[20] Other consequences may flow from the lease-contract-to-lease distinction, such as whether the landowner's trustee in bankruptcy must recognize a leasehold or whether the purported tenant has an interest that is subject to local real estate taxation.[21] Ultimately it is a question of fact whether the parties intended a contract or a lease. Factors may be whether they use the word "lease" or an equivalent, whether they intend to draw up a later agreement, and whether a document contains legally required elements for a lease.[22] The fact that the tenant is not to have possession immediately is of little consequence, for leases to commence *in futuro* are unexceptional, as we have seen. Even if the transaction is found to be a purported contract to lease, it may still be abortive for indefiniteness, on the contract law principle that a contract for a contract must contain the essential elements of the final agreement sufficiently for a court to enforce it. Thus, we still face questions similar to those faced with a lease itself, whether parties, premises, term, and so forth are spelled out with adequate specificity.[23]

Under one line of analysis, the differences between a lease and a contract for a lease may be obviated. It has been said that a contract to lease, at least if it is specifically enforceable, is a lease.[24] Theoretical support is not lacking, either on the basis that an enforceable agreement to make a contract amounts to the final contract [25] on the same basis that gives a contract purchaser of land equitable title.[26] Though the suggested analysis seems to have been little advanced, it should be considered in appropriate cases.

§ 6.14 Tenancy for Years—Nature

The distinguishing characteristic of a tenancy for years is that, by the parties' agreement, it is for a definite period, fixed in advance.[1] As we have

20. Lee Shops, Inc. v. Schatten–Cypress Co., 350 F.2d 12 (6th Cir.1965), certiorari denied 382 U.S. 980, 86 S.Ct. 552, 15 L.Ed.2d 470 (1960) (contract to lease); Handley v. Guasco, 165 Cal.App.2d 703, 332 P.2d 354 (1958) (contract to lease); Malani v. Clapp, 56 Hawaii 507, 542 P.2d 1265 (1975) (contract to lease); Gromelski v. Bruno, 336 Mass. 678, 147 N.E.2d 747 (1958) (lease); Maida v. Main Building, 473 S.W.2d 648 (Tex.Civ.App.1971) (lease). See also Wright v. Baumann, 239 Or. 410, 398 P.2d 119 (1965), appeal after remand 254 Or. 175, 458 P.2d 674 (1969).

21. In re Wonderfair Stores, Inc., 511 F.2d 1206 (9th Cir.1975) (bankruptcy); Motels of Maryland, Inc. v. Baltimore County, 244 Md. 306, 223 A.2d 609 (1966) (taxation).

22. See cases cited, preceding note, and 1 A.L.P., supra note 1, at § 3.17.

23. The question of the definiteness of a contract for a lease is on the margin of landlord-tenant law, since it is usually treated as part of contract law. For decisions on various aspects of the question, see M.N. Landau Stores, Inc. v. Daigle, 157 Me. 253, 170 A.2d

673 (1961); Saxon Theatre Corp. v. Sage, 347 Mass. 662, 200 N.E.2d 241 (1964); and Joseph v. Doraty, 77 O.L.A. 381, 144 N.E.2d 111 (Ohio App.1957).

24. Motels of Maryland, Inc. v. Baltimore County, 244 Md. 306, 223 A.2d 609 (1966) (apparent holding); Granva Corp. v. Heyder, 205 Va. 660, 139 S.E.2d 77 (1964) (dictum).

25. See 1 A. Corbin, Contracts § 29 (1963).

26. See 3 A.L.P., supra note 1, at § 11.22. Indeed, Williston urged that equitable conversion be applied to leases as well as contracts. 7 S. Williston, Contracts § 945 (3d ed. W. Jaeger ed. 1963).

§ 6.14

1. Waldrop v. Siebert, 286 Ala. 106, 237 So.2d 493 (1970) (dictum); F.H. Stoltze Land Co. v. Westberg, 63 Mont. 38, 206 P. 407 (1922). See also Union Bldg. Materials Corp. v. Kakaako Corp., 5 Hawaii App. 146, 682 P.2d 82 (1984) (leasehold stated to end at uncertain time was month-to-month tenancy, not tenancy for years).

seen, leaseholds may commence upon some uncertain future event, but once the tenancy for years begins, its term must be fixed. It is thus sometimes called a fixed-term tenancy. The term need not be literally for a year or multiple of a year; any fixed term, a month, a week, or even a few hours will suffice.[2] Bare essentials of the estate are the tenant's permissive possession of the landlord's land for such a fixed time.[3]

§ 6.15 Tenancy for Years—Statutes of Fraud

State statutes generally provide that leaseholds for over one year, or in some states a longer period, must be created by a written instrument. A few states require that all leaseholds be so created. Only Louisiana and New Mexico have no such statute.[1] To be a complete lease, the written document must contain the essential elements recently discussed.[2] Most disputes have been concerned with who must sign the instrument. Statutes sometimes require both parties to sign and sometimes the lessor alone, but the commonest requirement is that "the party to be charged" shall sign.[3] "The party to be charged" is the party against whom the lease is sought to be enforced.[4] This means, of course, that each party wants to insure that the other has signed.

An "informal" lease, one that fails to comply with the Statute of Frauds, does not by itself create either leasehold or duties. If, however, the tenant takes possession with the landowner's permission, some sort of leasehold, at least a tenancy at will, is created, not precisely by the informal instrument, but by the fact of permissive possession. Should the tenant, after entry, pay rent by an agreed period, such as $200 per month, this generally implies a periodic tenancy by that period. In some states when the informal lease provides for rent by periods, that much of the agreement will be enforced, so that upon permissive entry the tenant will have a periodic tenancy at that rent. It seems further that when a periodic tenancy does arise, the courts will charge the parties with the provisions of their informal lease, except for the agreement on the term.[5] This certainly should be the result, for parties may enter into a periodic tenancy orally and may in that form agree to such contractual matters as rent, repairs, and insurance.

Under the equitable doctrines of part performance and estoppel, which are not always carefully distinguished by the courts, an informal lease may

---

2. Hughes v. Chehalis School District No. 302, 61 Wn.2d 222, 377 P.2d 642 (1963).

3. Id.; Regan v. City of Seattle, 76 Wn.2d 501, 458 P.2d 12 (1969). But see Southern Airways Co. v. De Kalb County, 216 Ga. 358, 116 S.E.2d 602 (1960), which explains a peculiar doctrine, based on a Georgia statute, whereby a tenant for years is said not to have an estate in land.

§ 6.15

1. See Restatement (Second) of Property § 2.1, Statutory Note (1977).

2. An exchange of letters signed by the parties or letters aided by other documents may satisfy the requirement of a writing. Satterfield v. Pappas, 67 N.C.App. 28, 312

S.E.2d 511 (1984), review denied 311 N.C. 403, 319 S.E.2d 274 (1984) (correspondence between parties satisfied statute of frauds); Fuller v. Southland Corp., 57 N.C.App. 1, 290 S.E.2d 754 (1982), review denied 306 N.C. 556, 294 S.E.2d 223 (1982) (letter from tenant satisfied statute of frauds when ambiguities were clarified by other documents).

3. Id.

4. Restatement (Second) of Property § 2.2, Illustration 6 (1977). But it is possible for the phrase "party to be charged" to be interpreted "grantor," i.e., landlord alone. See Central Building Co. v. Keystone Shares Corp., 185 Wash. 645, 56 P.2d 697 (1936).

5. Restatement (Second) of Property § 2.3 (1977); 1 A.L.P., supra note 1, at § 3.20.

become specifically enforceable. Observe that we are speaking of excusing noncompliance with the statute and enforcing the lease document, not of enforcing a substitute agreement as we discussed in the preceding paragraph. A careful definition of the part performance doctrine is that it allows the enforcement of an informal agreement by a party who has acted under it and whose actions give independent evidence of the existence of the agreement. In other words, the actions are ones a party would not take unless he had an agreement of the sort claimed.[6] With a lease, this typically means a tenant goes into possession and makes substantial improvements of a permanent kind he would not make with a periodic or short-term tenancy.[7] When the estoppel theory is relied upon, the same sort of fact pattern is said to estop the landlord to deny that a tenant, who relied upon having a valid lease, had one.[8]

A, perhaps the most, frequently litigated question is what acts of the tenant will be sufficient to excuse the statute, on whichever theory is used. Courts seem generally agreed that possession and payment of rent alone will not do so; these acts are as consistent with a short-term as with a long-term leasehold. In addition there must be acts that bespeak a long-term leasehold, which almost always means valuable and permanent improvements by the tenant.[9] On principle it seems that payment of long-term rent, such as a lump-sum payment of several years' rent, might suffice, but whether this can be successfully argued is speculative.

There seem to be far more cases of tenants than of landlords seeking to enforce informal leases. When it is the landlord, one would look for his acts that were peculiarly referable to a long-term leasehold, particularly acts that he would not have done without such a leasehold. These are usually substantial landlord's improvements or alterations called for by the document, made at the tenant's request, or of a kind to suit the tenant's use.[10] Whether the tenant had taken possession or paid rent would seem immaterial, though this has usually been the fact and, however odd it seems, has been considered by some courts.[11]

§ 6.16 Periodic Tenancy—Nature

A periodic tenancy is of indefinite duration. It must have a definite commencement, but after that it continues on and on till one of the parties terminates it by notice to the other. So far, the periodic tenancy is like a tenancy at will; indeed, it developed out of the tenancy at will 400 or so

6. The classic exposition of the part performance theory is contained in Sleeth v. Sampson, 237 N.Y. 69, 142 N.E. 355 (1923), involving an informal mortgage.

7. See Walter C. Pressing Co. v. Hogan, 99 Ohio App. 319, 133 N.E.2d 419 (1954); Bennett v. Pratt, 228 Or. 474, 365 P.2d 622 (1961).

8. See Whitelock v. Leatherman, 460 F.2d 507 (10th Cir.1972); Delfino v. Paul Davies Chevrolet, Inc., 2 Ohio St.2d 282, 209 N.E.2d

194 (1965); Garbrick v. Franz, 13 Wn.2d 427, 125 P.2d 295 (1942).

9. Whitelock v. Leatherman, 460 F.2d 507 (10th Cir.1972); Walter C. Pressing Co. v. Hogan, 99 Ohio App. 319, 133 N.E.2d 419 (1954); Bennett v. Pratt, 228 Or. 474, 365 P.2d 622 (1961); 1 A.L.P., supra note 1, at § 3.21.

10. Annot., 101 A.L.R. 185 (1936).

11. See Omak Realty Investment Co. v. Dewey, 129 Wash. 385, 225 P. 236 (1924); Annot., 101 A.L.R. 185, 188–89 (1936).

years ago.[1] Its peculiar characteristic is that termination notice, to be effective, must be given a minimum time before the end of some recurring period. The recurring period, commonly a week, a month, or a year, is fixed by the parties by agreement, express or implied. So, for example, we may speak of a monthly periodic tenancy or of a "month-to-month" tenancy. This latter expression can be misleading, for it suggests a series of separate successive monthly terms, but that is incorrect; there is only one indefinite term.[2] In practice rent is almost inevitably paid by the same periods, though in theory there is no reason the parties might not, say, have a year-to-year leasehold with monthly rent if they so agree. However, unless their agreement were clear, a court would be likely to imply a periodic tenancy by the rental periods. The minimum time of notice to terminate will be prescribed by a rule of law. With the original periodic tenancies in England, yearly leaseholds of agricultural land, the period was six months, to make sure the tenant could harvest crops before being evicted.[3] In America statutes prescribe notice periods, running from seven days to one year. The shorter periods are for short-term leaseholds, and the longer periods tend to be for long-term or agricultural leaseholds.[4] Courts in some states use the terminology "tenancy at will" to refer to what has been described above as a periodic tenancy.[5] Historically there is reason for this, since, as mentioned, periodic tenancies developed out of estates at will. In cases where the terminology is used, the notice statutes are applied, so that the difference is only linguistic.

§ 6.17 Periodic Tenancy—Methods of Creation

Landlord and tenant may, of course, expressly agree for a periodic tenancy. Phrases such as "month-to-month," "monthly," or "periodic by the month" should suffice. Express agreement is usually found when the parties use a professionally drafted written lease.

No statistics have been sought, but experience indicates that the commonest form of periodic tenancy, indeed, the commonest form of any kind of tenancy, arises by a "general letting." The agreement is oral and probably largely implied at that. The premises are usually a dwelling and the parties relatively unsophisticated and casual in their dealings. They often discuss little more than the amount of rent, how often it will be paid, and who will pay which utility bills and possibly something about furnishings and damage to the premises and a damage deposit. For present purposes the crucial—and likely only relevant—fact is that they agreed on a stated period for rent. This is generally sufficient to imply a periodic tenancy by that period. The

§ 6.16

1. See State v. Fin & Feather Club, 316 A.2d 351, 357–58 (Me.1974); Rossow Oil Co., Inc. v. Heiman, 72 Wis.2d 696, 242 N.W.2d 176 (1976); 1 A.L.P., supra note 1, at § 3.23.

2. Janofsky v. Garland, 42 Cal.App.2d 655, 109 P.2d 750 (1941). But see Berlingo v. Sterling Ocean House, Inc., 497 A.2d 1031 (Conn. App.1985), where the court made the unfortunate statement that a month-to-month tenancy was a series of separate monthly tenancies. It was repeated upon rehearing in 5 Conn. App. 302, 504 A.2d 516 (1985).

3. See authorities cited in preceding note and also see Saracino v. Capital Properties Associates, Inc., 50 N.J.Super. 81, 141 A.2d 71 (1958) (dictum).

4. See Restatement (Second) of Property § 1.5, Statutory Note (1977).

5. See Donnelly Advertising Corp. v. Flaccomio, 216 Md. 113, 140 A.2d 165 (1958) ("a class of estates at will"); Maguire v. Haddad, 325 Mass. 590, 91 N.E.2d 769 (1950); 1 A.L.P., supra note 1, at § 3.23.

same implication arises even in the absence of an agreement for periodic rent if rent is actually paid and accepted by some period.[1]

A periodic tenancy may arise when a tenant holds over after his term has expired. Judging from the number of appellate decisions on the subject, this is a frequent source of controversy. When a term of years reaches its termination date or when a periodic tenancy or tenancy at will ends by notice, if the tenant wrongfully stays in possession, he initially enters that ephemeral and temporary status called tenancy at sufferance. That tenancy will be dealt with in a moment. At this point it is enough to know that one incident of the status is that the landlord has a power to transform the tenant at sufferance into a periodic tenant by electing to do so.[2] Certainly the landlord may make the election by express notice to the tenant.[3] More likely the election will be made by the tenant's tendering and the landlord's accepting rent for a time beyond the termination date. If the prior tenancy was periodic by periods less than a year, e.g., month to month, it seems the new tenancy will be by the same period.[4] But if the prior leasehold was for a term of a year or more, then, by the weight of authority, the new periodic tenancy is year to year.[5]

When the tenant becomes a periodic tenant by holding over, serious issues may arise about the provisions of the new leasing, particularly as to rent. If, in electing for the new tenancy, the landlord specifies a new amount of rent and the tenant does not contest it, then the tenant is liable

§ 6.17

1. Plank v. Bourdon, 173 Ga.App. 391, 326 S.E.2d 571 (1985) (tenant in possession while parties negotiated formal lease was periodic tenant); Ogden v. John Jay Esthetic Salons, Inc., 470 So.2d 521 (La.App.1985) (subtenant who remained in possession and paid rent after original tenant's term became new periodic tenant); Sacks v. Pleasant, 253 Md. 40, 251 A.2d 858 (1969) (apparent dictum); Longmier v. Kaufman, 663 S.W.2d 385 (Mo.App. 1983) (party who took possession and paid rent while he and owner orally negotiated five-year lease was periodic tenant); F.H. Stoltze Land Co. v. Westberg, 63 Mont. 38, 206 P. 407 (1922); Harry's Village, Inc. v. Egg Harbor Tp., 89 N.J. 576, 446 A.2d 862 (1982) (tenants who have no written leases but pay monthly rent are month-to-month tenants). Restatement (Second) of Property § 1.5 (1977); 1 A.L.P., supra note 1, at § 3.25. See also Evershed v. Berry, 20 Utah 2d 203, 436 P.2d 438 (1968); Uniform Residential Landlord–Tenant Act § 1.401(d).

2. Brown v. Music, Inc., 359 P.2d 295 (Alaska 1961) (dictum); Millhouse v. Drainage District No. 48, 304 S.W.2d 54 (Mo.App.1957) (dictum); Mack v. Fennell, 195 Pa.Super. 501, 171 A.2d 844 (1961). Cf. Bledsoe v. United States, 349 F.2d 605 (10th Cir.1965), and Leaders International Jewelry, Inc. v. Board of County Commissioners, 183 So.2d 242 (Fla. App.1966), cert. denied 188 So.2d 816 (Fla. 1966), cases in which statutes prevented holdover tenants from becoming periodic tenants.

3. David Properties, Inc. v. Selk, 151 So.2d 334 (Fla.App.1963).

4. Redevelopment Agency v. Superior Court, 13 Cal.App.3d 561, 91 Cal.Rptr. 886 (1970) (dictum); Governor Claiborne Apartments, Inc. v. Attaldo, 256 La. 218, 235 So.2d 574 (1970) (civil law doctrine of "reconduction"); Mid Continent Management Corp. v. Donnelly, 372 N.W.2d 814 (Minn.App.1985) (tenant who held over and paid rent became periodic tenant); Kiefer v. First Capitol Sports Center, Inc., 684 S.W.2d 483 (Mo.App.1984) (tenant who held over and paid rent was "tenant at will on a month to month basis"); Mississippi State Dep. of Public Welfare v. Howie, 449 So.2d 772 (Miss.1984) (tenant who held over and paid rent became periodic tenant); Mack v. Fennell, 195 Pa.Super. 501, 171 A.2d 844 (1961).

5. Butz v. Butz, 13 Ill.App.3d 341, 299 N.E.2d 782 (1973); Donnelly Advertising Corp. v. Flaccomio, 216 Md. 113, 140 A.2d 165 (1958); Mason v. Wierengo's Estate, 113 Mich. 151, 71 N.W. 489 (1897); Zola v. Havivi, 17 Misc.2d 366, 184 N.Y.S.2d 305 (1959); Williams v. King, 247 N.C. 581, 101 S.E.2d 308 (1958); Bergeron v. Forger, 125 Vt. 207, 214 A.2d 85 (1965); Rottman v. Bluebird Bakery, Inc., 3 Wis.2d 309, 88 N.W.2d 374 (1958) ("presumption" of year-to-year leasehold). Contra, Crechale & Polles, Inc. v. Smith, 295 So.2d 275 (Miss.1974), and Hofmann v. McCanlies, 76 N.M. 218, 413 P.2d 697 (1966), which are decisions that tenants for years who held over became monthly tenants by paying monthly rent.

for that amount.[6] While that result has been stated by the courts, one wonders if they would not limit the landlord's power to raise the rent to, say, a reasonable level. If the landlord notifies the tenant of a rent increase and the tenant protests it, perhaps verbally or perhaps by tendering only the old rent, then some decisions say there is no increase, though there seems to be a contrary view.[7] Whether the landlord has power to alter other leasing provisions is a question on which authority seems lacking, but it may be supposed he could do so to the extent he would be allowed to raise rent. If the landlord says nothing about new provisions, then it seems the provisions of the former lease will carry over unless they are found to be inconsistent with the new situation.[8]

Another situation in which a periodic tenancy arises is by the tenant's entry under an attempted lease for years that is not enforceable as such. Usually the lease is an "informal" one, an agreement that fails to conform to the Statute of Frauds when no circumstances are present to excuse the statute's operation. Nevertheless, the tenant enters permissively and very likely pays rent; obviously he is some kind of tenant. Even in the absence of a lease agreement, he would be a periodic tenant under a "general letting," as we have seen. Because we now suppose there was an agreement, the courts will enforce its provisions that do not run afoul of the Statute of Frauds, in other words, all provisions except as to the term. And even as to the term the informal agreement, though not enforceable as stated, will likely be the factual basis from which the court will fix a term. The general proposition seems to be that the rental periods stated in the informal agreement will be the tenancy periods, provided they do not exceed the maximum length allowed by the Statute of Frauds. Thus, if rent was stated in annual installments, the tenancy will be year to year[9] and month to month if stated monthly.[10] In a few states, however, it appears the periods are fixed by the way rent is actually paid and received.[11] If rent is neither stated nor paid, the tenancy is at will.[12] Presumably also, the periodic tenancy is called a tenancy at will in the jurisdictions that use the latter terminology.[13]

§ 6.18   Tenancy at Will—Nature

As its name suggests, a common-law tenancy at will is terminable at any time by either party. We speak now of tenancy at will as the phrase is

---

6. David Properties, Inc. v. Selk, 151 So.2d 334 (Fla.App.1963); Bhar Realty Corp. v. Becker, 49 N.J.Super. 585, 140 A.2d 756 (App. Div.1958).

7. See Moll v. Main Motor Co., 213 Ark. 28, 210 S.W.2d 321 (1948); Bhar Realty Corp. v. Becker, 49 N.J.Super. 585, 140 A.2d 756 (App.Div.1958) (dictum).

8. Barragan v. Munoz, 525 S.W.2d 559 (Tex.Civ.App.1975). See also Butz v. Butz, 13 Ill.App.3d 341, 299 N.E.2d 782 (1973), which holds that a purchase option did not carry over.

9. Darling Shops Delaware Corp. v. Baltimore Center Corp., 191 Md. 289, 60 A.2d 669 (1948); Arbenz v. Exley, Watkins & Co., 57 W.Va. 580, 50 S.E. 813 (1905).

10. Luster v. Cohon's Estate, 11 Ill.App.3d 608, 297 N.E.2d 335 (1973) (semble); Delfino v. Paul Davies Chevrolet, Inc., 2 Ohio St.2d 282, 209 N.E.2d 194 (1965); Logan v. Time Oil Co., 73 Wn.2d 161, 437 P.2d 192 (1968).

11. 1 A.L.P., supra note 1, at § 3.27.

12. Maccarini v. New Haven Trap Rock Co., 148 F.Supp. 271 (S.D.N.Y.1957), affirmed 249 F.2d 893 (2d Cir.1957); Parceluk v. Knudtson, 139 N.W.2d 864 (N.D.1966).

13. See, e.g., Gower v. Waters, 125 Me. 223, 132 A. 550 (1926), and Riedel v. Plymouth Redevelopment Authority, 354 Mass. 664, 241 N.E.2d 852 (1968).

generally and traditionally used, not as the phrase is used in a few states that thus label periodic tenancies. The status is considered a leasehold estate, since the tenant does have permissive possession of another's land.[1] Yet, because the permission may be revoked at any time, the possession is a most tenuous one; it is quite analogous to a license.

Owing to its insubstantial nature, a tenancy at will may not be assigned; an attempt terminates it.[2] So does the tenant's death.[3] The tenant at will should not be entitled to eminent domain compensation, since a conveyance is involved, but the decisions show some confusion on the point.[4]

§ 6.19   Tenancy at Will—Methods of Creation

Only in unusual circumstances is it possible to have a tenancy at will accompanied by rent. As we have seen, if rent is payable by a period, this generally implies a periodic tenancy. The parties might expressly agree that a tenancy with rent was at will, but this is unlikely. It seems therefore that a tenancy at will upon rent ordinarily exists only if the rent is not measured by a period, which practically means some form of rent in kind. This may occur if the tenant is put into possession with no agreed term but agrees only to make repairs or pay taxes.[1] An employee at will who is provided a home as part of his pay may be a tenant at will.[2] Obviously a permissive possession without any agreement for a term, money rent, or rent in kind is a tenancy at will.

The tenancy may arise in some situations that may generically be called holdovers. A grantor who remains in possession with the grantee's consent after conveyance may be a tenant at will.[3] Statutes may declare certain persons tenants at will who normally would occupy another relationship. Examples are holdover tenants and even trespassers.[4]

Disagreement exists about a tenant who holds for as long as he "desires" or "wishes." Such a tenant should be a tenant at will, on the reasoning that the holding at his will is by implication also at the landlord's will. This is the usual result, though the reasoning may be the doctrine of mutuality.[5]

§ 6.18

1. For a decision that distinguishes tenant at will from trespasser, see Nicholas v. Howard, 459 A.2d 1039 (D.C.App.1983).

2. Bellis v. Morgan Trucking, Inc., 375 F.Supp. 862 (D.Del.1974); 1 A.L.P., supra note 1, at § 3.28.

3. Dean v. Simpson, 235 Miss. 162, 108 So.2d 546 (1959); Paddock v. Clay, 138 Mont. 541, 357 P.2d 1 (1960).

4. See Lasher v. Redevelopment Authority, 211 Pa.Super. 408, 236 A.2d 831 (1967) (statute allowed $250 to any tenant); Lee v. Venable, 134 Ga.App. 92, 213 S.E.2d 188 (1975) (tenant at will allowed compensation); 1 A.L.P., supra note 1, at § 3.28 (no compensation allowed).

§ 6.19

1. See Maccarini v. New Haven Trap Rock Co., 148 F.Supp. 271 (S.D.N.Y.1957), affirmed 249 F.2d 893 (2d Cir.1957) (make repairs);

Parceluk v. Knudtson, 139 N.W.2d 864 (N.D. 1966) (repairs and taxes).

2. Najewitz v. City of Seattle, 21 Wn.2d 656, 152 P.2d 722 (1944).

3. Lasher v. Redevelopment Authority, 211 Pa.Super. 408, 236 A.2d 831 (1967).

4. See Townsend v. Singleton, 257 S.C. 1, 183 S.E.2d 893 (1971).

5. See Dwyer v. Graham, 99 Ill.2d 205, 75 Ill.Dec. 680, 457 N.E.2d 1239 (1983) (lease for as long as tenant desired was either no leasehold or at most tenancy at will); Foley v. Gamester, 271 Mass. 55, 170 N.E. 799 (1930); Nitschke v. Doggett, 489 S.W.2d 335 (Tex.Civ. App.1972), vacated 498 S.W.2d 339 (Tex.1973); 1 A.L.P., supra note 1, at § 3.30. See also Philpot v. Fields, 633 S.W.2d 546 (Tex.App. 1982) (lease for as long as tenant used premises for certain purpose was not merely tenancy at will); Day v. Kolar, 216 Neb. 47, 341 N.W.2d 598 (1983) (lease terminable by either

However, it is possible to find judicial decisions or statements that such an arrangement makes the possessor a life tenant.[6]

§ 6.20 Tenancy at Sufferance

Tenancy at sufferance is as illusory as the rings of Saturn viewed edge-on. It arises in one narrow situation only: when one who is tenant in one of the three other tenancies holds over (wrongfully) after the termination of that tenancy. The courts might have treated such a person as a trespasser, but that would produce certain inconveniences, such as making him a probable adverse possessor.[1] Hence, he is called tenant at sufferance, though it stretches the point to say his possession is permissive. It is so regarded, subject to the landlord's power to make it wrongful *ab initio,* but the tenancy is ephemeral and intended to be temporary.[2]

Ordinarily it is obvious when a tenant is holding over; however, some borderline situations produce litigation. The tenant's merely leaving items of personalty behind is not a holding over, since possession is required.[3] Courts are likely to excuse a holding over for a temporary period, such as for a few hours when the tenant is moving out.[4] A similar question, often discussed but upon which there is little authority, is whether the tenant's serious illness or similar misfortune will excuse a delayed quitting. The oft-cited New York decision in Herter v. Mullen [5] held no tenancy at sufferance arose when critical illness of a member of the tenant's family caused a lengthy delay, but it is not certain other courts would follow this precedent.[6] Another unclear situation arises when a tenant remains in occupation after title has been taken by condemnation. Since the condemnation not only transfers title but terminates existing leaseholds, it can be argued that, if the former tenant is not a trespasser, he begins a new leasehold that would

party "upon –0– days notice" was tenancy at will).

6. Collins v. Shanahan, 34 Colo.App. 82, 523 P.2d 999 (1974), affirmed in part, reversed in part 189 Colo. 169, 539 P.2d 1261 (1975). See also the strange case of Thompson v. Baxter, 107 Minn. 122, 119 N.W. 797 (1909), in which the court held that a possession upon monthly rent "while he shall wish to live there" was a life estate, but said in dictum that possession for as long as the tenant "wishes" would be a tenancy at will.

§ 6.20

1. See Rivera v. Santiago, 4 Conn.App. 608, 495 A.2d 1122 (1985) (tenant who remained in possession after landlord terminated leasehold became tenant at sufferance); St. Regis Pulp & Paper Corp. v. Floyd, 238 So.2d 740 (Miss. 1970); Hill v. Dobrowolski, 125 N.H. 572, 484 A.2d 1123 (1984) (tenancy at sufferance was true tenancy, so that landlord-tenant act applied). See also Small Business Inv. Co. v. Cavallo, 188 Conn. 286, 449 A.2d 988 (1982) (mortgagor who wrongfully continued in possession after foreclosure sale became tenant at sufferance).

2. There are many discussions of the nature and basic mechanism of tenancy at sufferance. For some of the more informative

discussions, see David Properties, Inc. v. Selk, 151 So.2d 334 (Fla.App.1963); Bradley v. Gallagher, 14 Ill.App.3d 652, 303 N.E.2d 251 (1973); Margosian v. Markarian, 288 Mass. 197, 192 N.E. 612 (1934) (tenant at sufferance a "bare licensee"); Warehouse Distributors, Inc. v. Prudential Storage & Van Corp., 208 Va. 784, 161 S.E.2d 86 (1968). But see Rise v. Steckel, 59 Or.App. 675, 652 P.2d 364 (1982), review denied 294 Or. 212, 656 P.2d 943 (1982) (life tenant who continued in possession when life estate ended upon his marriage was tenant at sufferance for 13 years, not adverse possessor). For an example of how statutes may affect tenancy at sufferance, see Townsend v. Singleton, 257 S.C. 1, 183 S.E.2d 893 (1971).

3. Brown v. Music, Inc., 359 P.2d 295 (Alaska 1961) (alternative ground).

4. Commonwealth Building Corp. v. Hirschfield, 307 Ill.App. 533, 30 N.E.2d 790 (1940).

5. 159 N.Y. 28, 53 N.E. 700 (1899).

6. For a contrary result see Mason v. Wierengo's Estate, 113 Mich. 151, 71 N.W. 489 (1897).

be either a tenancy at will or a periodic tenancy.[7] But he may be considered a tenant at sufferance if one reasons that he fits the definition of a tenant who holds over after termination.[8]

Assuming that a tenancy at sufferance has been found, the first important consequence or incident of the relation is that the landlord has a power to make the tenant either a trespasser or a periodic tenant retroactively to the beginning of the holdover period. Whether this power should be said to arise out of intention imputed to the parties or whether it has evolved into a rule of law is in debate, though American courts do not allow the tenant to defeat it. It generally is said that the landlord must exercise the power by making an election within a reasonable time. However, "reasonable" is not well defined, nor is there agreement whether his failure to act within a reasonable time will result in the tenant's being a trespasser, periodic tenant, or tenant at will.[9] Some decisions seem to imply that if no positive election is made to treat the tenant as having a new term, he is a trespasser.[10]

Although the clearest way for the landlord to elect to treat the tenant as a trespasser would be an express statement, the litigated cases seem to involve implied elections. The landlord's suit to evict the tenant may be such an election.[11] Actions that are inconsistent with treating the holdover tenant as having a new tenancy, such as leasing the premises to another, evince an election to make him a trespasser.[12] While, as we shall see, the landlord's accepting rent from the holdover tenant is likely to constitute an election to create a new tenancy, this may not be the case if the rent was accepted as a temporary expedient when the parties were negotiating for a possible new leasehold.[13] If the landlord's election is to treat the holdover tenant as a trespasser, then the landlord does not need to give a notice to terminate a tenancy in order to recover possession. An action to recover possession from a trespasser will suffice.[14]

The landlord's other choice is to treat the holdover tenant as a tenant under a new leasehold. In most jurisdictions the leasehold is regarded as a periodic tenancy, whose nature has been covered in the section entitled "Periodic Tenancy—Methods of Creation." Some jurisdictions consider the new tenancy to be one for years.[15] Express verbal or written statements to that effect are the clearest manner of election.[16] More frequently the

7. See Redevelopment Agency v. Superior Court, 13 Cal.App.3d 561, 91 Cal.Rptr. 886 (1970).

8. Lowell Housing Authority v. Save–Mor Furniture Stores, Inc., 346 Mass. 426, 193 N.E.2d 585 (1963).

9. See 1 A.L.P., supra note 1, at § 3.33.

10. See, e.g., Kilbourne v. Forester, 464 S.W.2d 770 (Mo.App.1970); Rottman v. Bluebird Bakery, Inc., 3 Wis.2d 309, 88 N.W.2d 374 (1958).

11. See Bledsoe v. United States, 349 F.2d 605 (10th Cir.1965); Kilbourne v. Forester, 464 S.W.2d 770 (Mo.App.1970). Cf. Gower v. Waters, 125 Me. 223, 132 A. 550 (1926); Baker v. Simonds, 79 Nev. 434, 386 P.2d 86 (1963).

12. Brown v. Music, Inc., 359 P.2d 295 (Alaska 1961).

13. Rottman v. Bluebird Bakery, Inc., 3 Wis.2d 309, 88 N.W.2d 374 (1958).

14. Bledsoe v. United States, 349 F.2d 605 (10th Cir.1965); Vandenbergh v. Davis, 190 Cal.App.2d 694, 12 Cal.Rptr. 222 (1961); Kilbourne v. Forester, 464 S.W.2d 770 (Mo.App. 1970). But see Fisher v. Parkwood, Inc., 213 A.2d 757 (D.C.App.1965), where a statute was held to require 30 days' notice.

15. 1 A.L.P., supra note 1, at § 3.35.

16. See David Properties, Inc. v. Selk, 151 So.2d 334 (Fla.App.1963); Fetting Manufacturing Jewelry Co. v. Waltz, 160 Md. 50, 152 A. 434 (1930) (apparently landlord notified tenant during negotiations).

election is implied by the tenant's paying and the landlord's accepting rent after the tenant becomes tenant at sufferance.[17]

D. TENANT'S RIGHT OF POSSESSION AND ENJOYMENT

§ 6.21 Landlord's Implied Covenant to Deliver Possession

Since the act of leasing is a conveyance of an estate, the landlord necessarily impliedly covenants that he has an estate out of which the leasehold can be carved and that he is not legally disabled from leasing. He also necessarily covenants that he will not personally prevent the tenant's taking possession and that no third person has a paramount legal right that will prevent such possession.[1] Our attention, however, is now focused on the further question whether the landlord impliedly warrants that there will be no third person wrongfully occupying the premises whose presence will physically block the tenant's initial entry. In other words, is there an implied warranty for actual possession? On this question American courts are divided.

One group of jurisdictions, which seems to be a clear majority, follow the so-called "English rule."[2] This rule is that the landlord impliedly warrants, and has a duty to see to it, that the premises will be free from the presence of a former tenant holding over or from some other person wrongfully in possession.[3] The same rule is embodied in the Uniform Residential Land-lord–Tenant Act and other legislation.[4] American decisions following this rule adopt the reasoning of earlier English opinions from which it was taken, that a tenant bargains for possession of premises, not for a chance at a lawsuit. It also is argued that the landlord ordinarily is in a better position than an incoming tenant to know if someone, particularly a holdover tenant, is in possession and to take action against that person.[5] For the breach of the warranty, the tenant may recover damages measured by the difference between rental value and agreed rent or may repudiate the lease.[6]

A minority of states follow the so-called "American rule," which of course is that the landlord does not impliedly warrant that the tenant shall

17. Chappell v. Reynolds, 206 Ark. 452, 176 S.W.2d 154 (1943); Bellows v. Ziv, 38 Ill.App.2d 342, 187 N.E.2d 265 (1962); Crechale & Polles, Inc. v. Smith, 295 So.2d 275 (Miss.1974); Williams v. King, 247 N.C. 581, 101 S.E.2d 308 (1958) (possibly dictum); Warehouse Distributors, Inc. v. Prudential Storage & Van Corp., 208 Va. 784, 161 S.E.2d 86 (1968) ("tenant at will"). But cf. Leaders International Jewelry, Inc. v. Board of County Commissioners, 183 So.2d 242 (Fla.App.1966), cert. denied 188 So.2d 816 (Fla.1966), where a statute required the landlord to give "written consent" to make a holdover tenant a "tenant at will."

§ 6.21

1. Hannan v. Dusch, 154 Va. 356, 153 S.E. 824 (1930) (dictum); Restatement (Second) of Property, § 4.2 (1977).

2. Annot., 96 A.L.R.3d 1155 (1979).

3. See King v. Reynolds, 67 Ala. 229 (1880); Hall v. Major, 312 So.2d 169 (La.App.1975), writ denied 313 So.2d 846 (La.1975); Adrian v. Rabinowitz, 116 N.J.L. 586, 186 A. 29 (1936); 1 A.L.P., supra note 1, at § 3.37. Annot., 96 A.L.R.3d 1155 (1979), collects many other decisions.

4. Uniform Residential Landlord–Tenant Act, § 2.103; New York Real Property Law, § 223–a.

5. See Sloan v. Hart, 150 N.C. 269, 63 S.E. 1037 (1909); Hannan v. Dusch, 154 Va. 356, 153 S.E. 824 (1930).

6. 1 A.L.P., supra note 1, at § 3.37; Annot., 104 A.L.R. 141 (1936), Supp.Annot., 88 A.L.R.2d 1024 (1963).

be able to have actual possession.[7]   Courts applying this rule regard it as unfair to charge the landlord with the wrongful act of a person he does not control.   They also note that the tenant, having the right to possession, can eject the trespasser as well as the landlord can.[8]

§ 6.22   Tenant's Possessory Interest

A tenant, having an estate in land, has the general and exclusive right of possession during the term.   He may exclude third persons and, with few exceptions, the landlord as well.   Of course, the leases frequently give landlords a privilege to enter for stated purposes, such as to inspect or to show the premises to prospective new tenants.   If the landlord has a duty to make certain repairs, he generally is privileged to enter for that purpose.   In the absence of some specific privilege to enter, it has been held that the landlord may enter to collect rent and to distrain where that is permitted.[1]

The tenant's estate may carry with it by implication rights in surrounding areas the landlord owns.   We speak of such diverse rights as easements over walkways and driveways; [2] the use of halls, stairs, and entrances,[3] the right to a view into windows or skylights,[4] and rights to use utilities and pipes serving the demised premises.[5]   In recent years much litigation has arisen over the rights of shopping center tenants to use and to prevent alteration of parking areas and other common areas.[6]   The theory upon which tenants have such implied rights is akin to the theory of easement by way of necessity but is not as strict.   A few older decisions contain language suggesting that the tenant has the implied right in the landlord's adjoining areas only if strict necessity exists.[7]   But the formula generally stated is that, while such rights will not arise out of mere convenience, they will be implied if they are "reasonably necessary" to the use of the demised premises.[8]   It is felt that the trend is to hold to a relaxed view of what

7.   Reynolds v. McEwen, 111 Cal.App.2d 540, 244 P.2d 961 (1952); Teitelbaum v. Direct Realty Co., 172 Misc. 48, 13 N.Y.S.2d 886 (1939); Hannan v. Dusch, 154 Va. 356, 153 S.E. 824 (1930).   The result in *Teitelbaum* has been reversed by N.Y.—McKinney's Real Property Law § 223–a.

8.   See principally Hannan v. Dusch, 154 Va. 356, 153 S.E. 824 (1930).   Also see Gazzolo v. Chambers, 73 Ill. 75 (1874); Snider v. Deban, 249 Mass. 59, 144 N.E. 69 (1924).   If the summary eviction statute allows only the new tenant to recover possession, this indicates the "American rule" should be followed.

§ 6.22

1.   1 A.L.P., supra note 1, at § 3.38.

2.   See, e.g., Owsley v. Hamner, 36 Cal.2d 710, 227 P.2d 263 (1951); Weigand v. American Stores Co., 346 Pa. 253, 29 A.2d 484 (1943); State v. Fox, 82 Wn.2d 289, 510 P.2d 230 (1973), certiorari denied 414 U.S. 1130, 94 S.Ct. 868, 38 L.Ed.2d 754 (1974).

3.   See, e.g., Martel v. Malone, 138 Conn. 385, 85 A.2d 246 (1951); Nyer v. Munoz–Mendoza, 385 Mass. 184, 430 N.E.2d 1214 (1982) (tenant had right to use exterior of door to her

apartment and to post signs on it).   Tremont Theater Amusement Co. v. Bruno, 225 Mass. 461, 114 N.E. 672 (1917); Konick v. Champneys, 108 Wash. 35, 183 P. 75 (1919).

4.   See, e.g., Owsley v. Hamner, 36 Cal.2d 710, 227 P.2d 263 (1951); O'Neill v. Breese, 3 Misc. 219, 23 N.Y.S. 526 (Sup.1893).

5.   See, e.g., Tong v. Feldman, 152 Md. 398, 136 A. 822 (1927) (gas pipe); Gans v. Hughes, 14 N.Y.S. 930 (City Ct.1891).

6.   LaPointe's, Inc. v. Beri, Inc., 73 Or.App. 773, 699 P.2d 1173 (1985) (shopping center lease interpreted to allow tenant's employees to park in parking lot).   See exhaustive annotation in 56 A.L.R.3d 596 (1974).

7.   E.g., Julius A. Bauer & Co. v. Chamberlain, 159 Iowa 12, 138 N.W. 903 (1912); Tong v. Feldman, 152 Md. 398, 136 A. 822 (1927).

8.   See Owsley v. Hamner, 36 Cal.2d 710, 227 P.2d 263 (1951); Devlin v. The Phoenix, Inc., 471 So.2d 93 (Fla.App.1985), review denied 480 So.2d 1295 (Fla.1985) (restaurant tenant in shopping center had implied easement for access and parking).   Weigand v. American Stores Co., 346 Pa. 253, 29 A.2d 484 (1943); Annot., 24 A.L.R.2d 123, 125–29 (1952).

"reasonably necessary" means.[9] Moreover, an easement or other right, if found to exist, may be used by the tenant's guests and those having business with him.[10]

Unless the leasing agreement limits his rights, the tenant has the right to use the premises for whatever purposes they are suited. He owns all crops that reach maturity during the term, even if they were growing when the term began.[11] Limitations on the tenant's rights of use are contained in the rules against waste, nuisance, and negligent damage, which will be covered next.

§ 6.23   Tenant's Mode of Use

A tenant, as holder of a present possessory estate followed by a reversion in the landlord, is subject to the rules against waste. The gist of it is that the holder of the present estate is to a considerable extent inhibited by the law of waste from permanently damaging the land or things on it, i.e., from doing damage that will still be present when the landlord's reversion becomes possessory. Cutting standing timber was the classic common-law example, but the prohibition is not absolute, for the holder of the present estate has always been allowed to cut timber for building repairs and fences, and to cut at least "small stuff" for firewood. In America, where clearing land for farming was a benefit, most courts have adopted the principle that it is not waste to cut timber to promote "good husbandry."[1] Other activities that may constitute waste are the razing of buildings; serious damage to their component parts; and improper farming, which may, for instance, cause soil erosion.[2]

Whether removal of minerals, such as coal and gravel, is waste involves a special aspect of the law on the subject. If a tenant leases land that already has ongoing mineral extractive operations, and if the lease does not prohibit it, it is not waste for him to continue to work the same mines or pits.[3] To an extent, the limits of which are not well defined, the tenant may even expand existing operations.[4] But he may not open new mines or pits

9. See especially Owsley v. Hamner, 36 Cal.2d 710, 227 P.2d 263 (1951), and the discussion of shopping center cases in Annot., 56 A.L.R.3d 596 (1974).

10. See Franceschina v. Morgan, 346 F.Supp. 833 (S.D.Ind.1972) (labor union organizer); State v. Fox, 82 Wn.2d 289, 510 P.2d 230 (1973), certiorari denied 414 U.S. 1130, 94 S.Ct. 868, 38 L.Ed.2d 754 (1974) (legal services lawyer); Konick v. Champneys, 108 Wash. 35, 183 P. 75 (1919) (grocer making delivery).

11. Munier v. Zachary, 138 Iowa 219, 114 N.W. 525 (1908); Long Island Oyster Co. v. Eagle Oyster Packing Co., 22 Wn.2d 322, 156 P.2d 222 (1945) (oysters treated as crop).

§ 6.23

1. See Kremer v. Rule, 209 Wis. 183, 244 N.W. 596 (1932); 1 A.L.P., supra note 1, at § 3.39; 5 Id., at §§ 20.1–20.4. Also see court's discussion in Melms v. Pabst Brewing Co., 104 Wis. 7, 79 N.W. 738 (1899).

2. See Sigsbee Holding Corp. v. Canavan, 39 Misc.2d 465, 240 N.Y.S.2d 900 (City Ct. 1963) (dictum); Graffell v. Honeysuckle, 30 Wn.2d 390, 191 P.2d 858 (1948) (damage to building components); Melms v. Pabst Brewing Co., 104 Wis. 7, 79 N.W. 738 (1899) (dictum, razing house); 5 A.L.P., supra note 1, at §§ 20.7, 20.9, 20.10; Niehuss, Alteration or Replacement of Buildings by the Long-term Lessee, 30 Mich.L.Rev. 386 (1932).

3. Cherokee Construction Co. v. Harris, 92 Ark. 260, 122 S.W. 485 (1909) (dictum); Schuylkill Trust Co. v. Schuylkill Mining Co., 358 Pa. 535, 57 A.2d 833 (1948) (dictum); 5 A.L.P., supra note 1, at § 20.6.

4. See Westmoreland Coal Co.'s Appeal, 85 Pa. 344 (1877); 5 A.L.P., supra note 1, at p. 90, n. 3.

on the leased land.[5]

Our law of waste also includes the doctrine known as "meliorating waste." This doctrine is that a permanent harm to the freehold that increases the land's value is not actionable, though it technically is called waste.[6] In America the decisions allowing tenants to clear farmland of timber may be analyzed as meliorating waste cases and would be the commonest application of the doctrine. Melms v. Pabst Brewing Co.,[7] a leading but unusual case, discussed the doctrine in connection with the razing of a house when that increased the land's value. How broadly one applies the doctrine depends largely upon whether one views waste as causing economic rather than physical harm.[8]

In addition to a duty not affirmatively to waste the premises, so-called "commissive" waste, a tenant is under a duty to take reasonable steps to prevent waste, i.e., not to permit it.[9] This means the tenant has a common-law duty to make such repairs as will prevent waste to the land or to its improvements. In practice this most frequently means the tenant must keep buildings enough sealed that the elements will not enter and cause waste, though one can imagine he might also have to prevent wasting of the soil itself from various causes. It is difficult to give a definition of the duty that has universal application; circumstances shape the duty, in other words.[10] This is the only common-law duty that the tenant, or the landlord either, has to make repairs.

Beyond the duties not to permit or commit waste, the courts have often recognized that a tenant has a duty not to cause specific damage to the premises intentionally or negligently.[11] The duty here is affirmative, not to do damage; in this respect it is like the duty not to commit waste. But, for the landlord to have a cause of action, the harm done need not be (though it may be) as serious as the harm necessary to constitute waste.

Finally, the law of nuisance imposes limitations upon the tenant's mode of use. Of course the tenant, along with other possessors of land, owes a duty to nearby landowners not to commit nuisances. The general subject of nuisance will be covered elsewhere in this treatise. A tenant, however, also owes a duty to his landlord not to engage in nuisances.[12] This duty

---

5. Schuylkill Trust Co. v. Schuylkill Mining Co., 358 Pa. 535, 57 A.2d 833 (1948) (dictum); Westmoreland Coal Co.'s Appeal, 85 Pa. 344 (1877); Kremer v. Rule, 209 Wis. 183, 244 N.W. 596 (1932) (mortgagor).

6. See Melms v. Pabst Brewing Co., 104 Wis. 7, 79 N.W. 738 (1899); 5 A.L.P., supra note 1, at § 20.11. The *Melms* case, which involved a life tenant and the holders of a reversion, suggested there would be less reason to apply the meliorating waste doctrine to a leasehold tenant than to a life tenant. It seems unlikely that the doctrine would be applied to relatively short leaseholds.

7. 104 Wis. 7, 79 N.W. 738 (1899).

8. See Niehuss, supra note 2, this section.

9. Glenn R. Sewell Sheet Metal, Inc. v. Loverde, 70 Cal.2d 666, 75 Cal.Rptr. 889, 451 P.2d 721 (1969) (dictum); Hooker v. Goodwin,

91 Conn. 463, 99 A. 1059 (1917) (life tenant); Grimm v. Grimm, 153 Ga. 655, 113 S.E. 91 (1922) (life tenant); Gade v. National Creamery Co., 324 Mass. 515, 87 N.E.2d 180 (1949) (dictum); 1 A.L.P., supra note 1, at § 3.78; 5 Id., at § 20.12.

10. See 5 A.L.P., supra note 1, at § 20.12.

11. United States v. Bostwick, 94 U.S. (4 Otto) 53, 24 L.Ed. 65 (1877); Precisionware, Inc. v. Madison County Tobacco Warehouse, Inc., 411 F.2d 42 (5th Cir.1969); Gade v. National Creamery Co., 324 Mass. 515, 87 N.E.2d 180 (1949); Annot., 10 A.L.R.2d 1012 (1950). See also King v. Cooney–Eckstein Co., 66 Fla. 246, 63 So. 659 (1913).

12. Mosby v. Manhattan Oil Co., 52 F.2d 364 (8th Cir.1931), certiorari denied 284 U.S. 677, 52 S.Ct. 131, 76 L.Ed. 572 (1931); Hall v. Smith–McKenney Co., 162 Ky. 159, 172 S.W.

apparently is implied in the landlord-tenant relation. Also, especially if the tenant's activity is illegal, the landlord might have an interest in avoiding penalties against himself.

§ 6.24 Covenants Limiting Tenant's Use

In addition to the limitations on use imposed on the tenant by the rules against waste, negligent use, and nuisance discussed above, the lease may contain covenants limiting use. As a general proposition, such covenants are permitted.[1] They are restrictive covenants, burdening the tenant's leasehold estate, which, if they meet the requirements for running covenants, will burden the tenant's assignees. However, both because the law does not favor burdens on land and because the language of a lease is usually construed against the landlord, courts are wont to limit the scope of the restrictions by a strict or literal reading.[2] A frequent application of this principle is in the rule that a lease clause that authorizes or even requires the premises to be used for a stated purpose does not prohibit other uses.[3] Thus, a landlord who would limit uses to, say, a grocery and delicatessen should insure that the tenant covenants to use the premises "only" for those purposes or for those purposes "and no other purposes."

Traditionally covenants restricting use may arise or be amended only by contractual agreement of both parties. Under the Uniform Residential Landlord and Tenant Act and statutes based upon it, the landlord has a limited power unilaterally to impose and amend "a rule or regulation * * * concerning the tenant's use and occupancy of the premises."[4] Such rules may be, generally, only for the welfare of other tenants or to prevent abusive use of the premises, must apply to all tenants in the case of multiple dwellings, and may not work "substantial modification of his [tenant's] bargain."

§ 6.25 Tenant's Duty to Occupy and Use

As the holder of an estate in land, the tenant has a right of possession. Keeping in mind the distinction between right and duty, American courts have adopted the general rule that, in the absence of a covenant to do so, the

125 (1915). See also Louisiana Leasing Co. v. Sokolow, 48 Misc.2d 1014, 266 N.Y.S.2d 447 (1966) (breach of covenant not to disturb); Stroup v. Conant, 268 Or. 292, 520 P.2d 337 (1974).

§ 6.24

1. Denecke v. Henry F. Miller & Son, 142 Iowa 486, 119 N.W. 380 (1909); Dennis & Jimmy's Food Corp. v. Milton Co., 99 A.D.2d 477, 470 N.Y.S.2d 412 (1984), affirmed 62 N.Y.2d 613, 476 N.Y.S.2d 116, 464 N.E.2d 484 (1984) (lease clause limiting use solely to delicatessen and grocery did not allow tenant to install video games). Davis v. Driver, 271 S.W. 435 (Tex.Civ.App.1925); 1 A.L.P., supra note 1, at § 3.40.

2. Otting v. Gradsky, 294 Ky. 779, 172 S.W.2d 554 (1943); Mutual Paper Co. v. Hoague–Sprague Corp., 297 Mass. 294, 8 N.E.2d

802 (1937). See also Ray–Ron Corp. v. DMY Realty Co., 500 N.E.2d 1163 (Ind.1986); Louisiana Leasing Co. v. Sokolow, 48 Misc.2d 1014, 266 N.Y.S.2d 447 (1966).

3. Cox v. Ford Leasing Dev. Co., 170 Ga. App. 81, 316 S.E.2d 182 (1984) (lease recital that tenant intended to use premises for certain business did not prevent other use); Otting v. Gradsky, 294 Ky. 779, 172 S.W.2d 554 (1943); Noon v. Mironski, 58 Wash. 453, 108 P. 1069 (1910) (alternative ground); Annot., 148 A.L.R. 583 (1944). Contra, Chandler v. Hart, 161 Cal. 405, 119 P. 516 (1911) (dictum); Asa G. Candler v. Georgia Theater Co., 148 Ga. 188, 96 S.E. 226 (1918), which say or hold that a tenant's covenant to use premises for a stated purpose implies a promise not to use them for other purposes.

4. Uniform Residential Landlord and Tenant Act § 3.102.

tenant has no duty to take possession, or to make any particular use, of the premises.[1] This is usually true even if the lease specifies an exclusive manner in which the premises may be used, as long as the court does not interpret the lease to require that use.[2] Scholarly argument has been made that the duty not to permit waste should imply a duty to occupy, but such is not the decisional law.[3] There is, however, some basis to believe a court might require a tenant to occupy if the premises are actually deteriorating from vacancy.[4]

Courts may make an exception to the general rule stated above in the case of certain commercial leases in which rent is a percentage of sales on the premises. Indeed, if a court will infer a duty, it will be a duty not only to occupy but to conduct the business. The theory is that if rent is to be based upon sales, the parties must have intended that sales would be made. Traditionally and in most decisions in the area, courts have refused to make the inference if there is more than a nominal fixed minimum rent in addition to the percentage rent.[5] When the inference has been made, there has nearly always been no fixed minimum or only a nominal minimum, such as ten dollars a month.[6] Recently a few courts have been willing to consider making the inference when the fixed rent was more than nominal, but it is not clear if this is the trend.[7]

§ 6.26 Covenants to Protect Tenant's Business

In commercial leases one often finds covenants by the landlord not to conduct, or permit to be conducted, stated activities on his land outside the demised premises. Typical is a covenant by the landlord of a shopping center, providing that this tenant shall have the exclusive right to conduct a described business within the shopping center. Such a clause is popularly called an "exclusive clause." If the landlord further covenants that he will not use land beyond the shopping center perimeter for the described business, the covenant is labeled a "radius clause." Either clause is a restrictive covenant, in which the tenant's premises are the benefitted estate and the

§ 6.25

1. Security Builders, Inc. v. Southwest Drug Co., 244 Miss. 877, 147 So.2d 635 (1962), motion overruled 149 So.2d 319 (Miss.1963) (alternative ground); Davis v. Wickline, 205 Va. 166, 135 S.E.2d 812 (1964); Annot., 40 A.L.R.3d 971, 973–74 (1971); Annot., 46 A.L.R. 1134 (1927).

2. See Weil v. Ann Lewis Shops, Inc., 281 S.W.2d 651 (Tex.Civ.App.1955), error refused; Davis v. Wickline, 205 Va. 166, 135 S.E.2d 812 (1964); Annot., 40 A.L.R.3d 971, 975–77 (1971).

3. See 1 A.L.P., supra note 1, at § 3.41.

4. See Asling v. McAllister–Fitzgerald Lumber Co., 120 Kan. 455, 244 P. 16 (1926).

5. See Percoff v. Solomon, 259 Ala. 482, 67 So.2d 31 (1953); Hicks v. Whelan Drug Co., 131 Cal.App.2d 110, 280 P.2d 104 (1955); Chicago Title & Trust Co. v. Southland Corp., 111 Ill.App.3d 67, 66 Ill.Dec. 611, 443 N.E.2d 294 (1982) (no implied covenant to continue in business); Stop & Shop, Inc. v. Ganem, 347 Mass. 697, 200 N.E.2d 248 (1964); Tuttle v. W.T. Grant Co., 5 A.D.2d 370, 171 N.Y.S.2d 954 (1958), affirmed 6 N.Y.2d 754, 186 N.Y.S.2d 655, 159 N.E.2d 202 (1959); Jenkins v. Rose's 5, 10 & 25¢ Stores, Inc., 213 N.C. 606, 197 S.E. 174 (1938); Palm v. Mortgage Investment Co., 229 S.W.2d 869 (Tex.Civ.App.1950); Annot., 38 A.L.R.2d 1113 (1954).

6. See Sinclair Refining Co. v. Giddens, 54 Ga.App. 69, 187 S.E. 201 (1936); Seggebruch v. Stosor, 309 Ill.App. 385, 33 N.E.2d 159 (1941); Marvin Drug Co. v. Couch, 134 S.W.2d 356 (Tex.Civ.App.1939), error dismissed. Typical cases are "filling station cases," such as *Giddens* and *Seggebruch,* in which rent was so much per gallon of gasoline the tenant sold, with a nominal fixed rent.

7. See Professional Building of Eureka, Inc. v. Anita Frocks, Inc., 178 Cal.App.2d 276, 2 Cal.Rptr. 914 (1960); Simhawk Corp. v. Egler, 52 Ill.App.2d 449, 202 N.E.2d 49 (1964); Note, 61 Harv.L.Rev. 317 (1948); Note, 51 Minn.L.Rev. 1139 (1967).

landlord's other premises the burdened estate. Such clauses are in general legally permissible, but with some qualifications.[1]

Courts frequently say that the restrictive covenants here being discussed, though permissible, are to be strictly construed.[2] Such clauses are rarely implied,[3] though in a few cases courts may have found such an implication from the presence of a percentage rent clause.[4] Reasons for a narrow reading are that restrictive covenants are often said to be so read and also that the covenant restrains competition.

The latter point, restraining competition, gives rise to an argument of increasing concern to commercial landlords and tenants.[5] Under the common-law policy against restraints on free trade, the argument has long been made that covenants restricting business activities are void. This argument generally fails, because of the exception that allows such private agreements if they are limited in time or place and if the parties find them utile.[6] In recent years attacks upon exclusive clauses have in a number of cases been based upon state and federal antitrust acts. As best one can judge a new and developing area of law, it seems that such attacks will fail in the ordinary case in which a simple exclusive clause, or even the interlocking network of simple exclusive clauses found in a shopping center, are in issue.[7] However, the parties should have a concern about violating antitrust laws if their clause would allow what might be called an "aggravated" form of tenant's exclusive. An example is a clause that allows the major shopping center tenant to have veto powers over the admission of new tenants or over their manner of doing business.[8]

What are the tenant's remedies if the landlord breaches or threatens to breach an exclusive or radius clause? Damages are available, though tenants seldom would find this remedy adequate. The usual measure of damages is the difference in rental value between the value of the tenant's

§ 6.26

1. Covenants of the kind discussed are the subject of an exhaustive annotation in 97 A.L.R.2d 4–135 (1964).

2. See, e.g., Norwood Shopping Center, Inc. v. MKR Corp., 135 So.2d 448 (Fla.App.1961); Crest Commercial, Inc. v. Union–Hall, Inc., 104 Ill.App.2d 110, 243 N.E.2d 652 (1968).

3. See Crest Commercial, Inc. v. Union–Hall, Inc., 104 Ill.App.2d 110, 243 N.E.2d 652 (1968); Great Atlantic & Pacific Tea Co. v. Bailey, 421 Pa. 540, 220 A.2d 1 (1966).

4. See Carter v. Adler, 138 Cal.App.2d 63, 291 P.2d 111 (1955) (apparent alternative ground); Tabet v. Sprouse–Reitz Co., 75 N.M. 645, 409 P.2d 497 (1966). The reasoning in such decisions is that, since the parties agreed on percentage rent, they must have intended that the landlord would not derogate from the tenant's ability to make the sales upon which rent was to be based.

5. As evidence of this concern, and also for a summary of many decisions, see International Council of Shopping Centers, Legal Bulle-

tin, Commercial Restrictions in Shopping Center Agreements (1973).

6. See Goldberg v. Tri–States Theatre Corp., 126 F.2d 26 (8th Cir.1942); Colby v. McLaughlin, 50 Wn.2d 152, 310 P.2d 527 (1957).

7. See Dalmo Sales Co. v. Tysons Corner Regional Shopping Center, 308 F.Supp. 988 (D.D.C.1970), affirmed 429 F.2d 206 (D.C.Cir. 1970) (preliminary injunction denied); Savon Gas Stations No. Six, Inc. v. Shell Oil Co., 309 F.2d 306 (4th Cir.1962), certiorari denied 372 U.S. 911, 83 S.Ct. 725, 9 L.Ed.2d 719 (1963); Optivision, Inc. v. Syracuse Shopping Center Associates, 472 F.Supp. 665 (N.D.N.Y.1979); Elida, Inc. v. Harmor Realty Corp., 177 Conn. 218, 413 A.2d 1226 (1979).

8. See In re Tysons Corner Regional Shopping Center, 85 F.T.C. 970 (1975). A consent order forbade a major tenant from engaging in the acts described in text. But see Dalmo Sales Co. v. Tysons Corner Regional Shopping Center, 308 F.Supp. 988 (D.D.C.1970), affirmed 429 F.2d 206 (D.C.Cir.1970). For a discussion of the antitrust dangers of exclusive clauses,

leasehold with the breach and if there had been no breach, but evidence of the tenant's lost profits may be relevant to this measure.[9] Injunction against the landlord is also a possible, and effective, remedy if it can be obtained before the landlord has consummated the competing lease. But if that lease has already been executed to a tenant who has no notice of the exclusive clause, then this other tenant cannot be enjoined, which blocks enjoining the landlord.[10] An injunction is allowed against the landlord and a competing tenant who had notice.[11] And, as yet another possible remedy, a few decisions have held the landlord's breach of an exclusive clause justifies the tenant's terminating the leasehold. One theory is that the breach constitutes a constructive eviction.[12] The second theory, which is quite novel in that it implies the dependency of lease covenants, is that the landlord's breach is a substantial one, giving the tenant a power to rescind.[13]

§ 6.27 Illegal Use—Existing at Time of Leasing

To begin at a known point, it can be said that if a lease limits the use of premises to a purpose that is then forbidden by law, the attempted leasing is void.[1] All permitted uses must be illegal; if some uses are illegal and some legal, the leasing is valid.[2] At work here is the contract doctrine of illegality, providing an instance in which contract law principles have replaced conveyancing principles in landlord-tenant law. If strict conveyancing theory were applied, illegality would not affect the existence of the leasehold estate; the tenant, indeed, could have his estate without physical possession.

There are not many cases in which the parties' agreement expressly limits use to an illegal activity. More cases involve a pattern in which the agreement, on its face, imposes no such limitation, but the tenant in fact intends to make a use that is then illegal. Unless the landlord knows of this intent, the validity of the leasing is not affected. If, however, he knows of the intended illegal use, this is enough, under some decisions, to invalidate the leasing.[3] Under other decisions, however, the landlord's mere knowledge is not enough. He must in some way participate in the illegality, though it is not clear just what actions amount to participation.[4]

see Baum, Lessors' Covenants Restricting Competition, 1965 U.Ill.L.F. 228.

9. Fontainbleau Hotel Corp. v. Crossman, 323 F.2d 937 (5th Cir.1963); Parker v. Levin, 285 Mass. 125, 188 N.E. 502 (1934); Annot., 97 A.L.R.2d 4, 111–19 (1964).

10. See Skaggs v. Jensen, 94 Idaho 179, 484 P.2d 728 (1971); Meredith Hardware, Inc. v. Belknap Realty Trust, 117 N.H. 22, 369 A.2d 204 (1977); Annot., 97 A.L.R.2d 4, 88–96, 120–22 (1964).

11. See Fontainbleau Hotel Corp. v. Crossman, 323 F.2d 937 (5th Cir.1963); Hildebrand v. Stonecrest Corp., 174 Cal.App.2d 158, 344 P.2d 378 (1959).

12. See Kulawitz v. Pacific Woodenware & Paper Co., 25 Cal.2d 664, 155 P.2d 24 (1944).

13. See University Club v. Deakin, 265 Ill. 257, 106 N.E. 790 (1914).

§ 6.27

1. Musco v. Torello, 102 Conn. 346, 128 A. 645 (1925) (dictum); Warshawsky v. American Automotive Products Co., 12 Ill.App.2d 178, 138 N.E.2d 816 (1956) (dictum); Restatement (Second) of Property § 12.4 (1977); 1 A.L.P., supra note 1, § 3.43.

2. Warshawsky v. American Automotive Products Co., 12 Ill.App.2d 178, 138 N.E.2d 816 (1956) (alternative ground); Stern Holding Co. v. O'Connor, 119 N.J.L. 291, 196 A. 432 (1938); Restatement (Second) of Property § 12.4 (1977).

3. See, e.g., Dougherty v. Seymour, 16 Colo. 289, 26 P. 823 (1891); Musco v. Torello, 102 Conn. 346, 128 A. 645 (1925); Annot., 166 A.L.R. 1353, 1374–79 (1947).

4. See Hoefeld v. Ozello, 290 Ill. 147, 125 N.E. 5 (1919); Fuchs v. Goe, 62 Wyo. 134, 163

Violations of zoning ordinances present a special situation. In some cases in which the lease is for a purpose that violates zoning, the courts have held the leasing valid or invalid on the principles stated above, the same as for other kinds of illegality.[5] Other courts, however, refuse to apply the illegality invalidity doctrine, at least where, as is usually the case, zoning ordinances allow for nonconforming uses, variances, special permits, and the like.[6] These courts reason that the parties may have written their lease intending that zoning relief would be obtained, though it would seem to be a question of fact whether they did so. Some courts may simply feel zoning restrictions are different from, say, an ordinance or statute prohibiting prostitution. In any event, a tenant who is concerned about zoning should always expressly reserve a power to terminate if the intended use cannot be made.

Finally on the problem of illegality, we consider whether a leasing is void if the physical condition of the premises violates a local housing code or statute. Brown v. Southall Realty Co.,[7] in the District of Columbia, created quite a stir a few years ago by holding a lease of such premises void. Merely to raise the illegality issue on these facts fills the air with profound questions about how serious and direct illegality must be to prevent an enforceable agreement. These are questions of contract law, beyond the scope of this treatise.[8] Brown's doctrine seemingly will not catch on; the decision has become pretty much isolated. It produced "inconveniences" in the jurisdiction where decided [9] and seems to have been generally ignored or rejected elsewhere.[10] As a remedy for the problem of rundown housing, Brown's illegality theory has been bypassed in favor of the theory of implied warranty of fitness.[11]

P.2d 783 (1945). 1 A.L.P., supra note 1, at § 3.43, takes the position that the majority rule is that the landlord's mere knowledge makes the lease unenforceable. But Annot., 166 A.L.R. 1353, 1374–79 (1947), marshals decisions to show that, while mere knowledge is enough in nearly all cases in which prostitution is the illegal activity, where gambling or illegal liquor sales is the activity, the landlord must participate.

5. See Walker v. Southern Trucking Corp., 283 Ala. 551, 219 So.2d 379 (1969); Becerra v. Hochberg, 193 Cal.App.2d 431, 14 Cal.Rptr. 101 (1961) (rule stated, not applied on facts); Sippin v. Ellam, 24 Conn.App. 385, 588 A.2d 660 (1991) (both zoning and restrictive covenant prohibited intended use); Ober v. Metropolitan Life Insurance Co., 157 Misc. 869, 284 N.Y.S. 966 (1935); Annot., 37 A.L.R.3d 1018, 1031–35 (1971).

6. See Entrepreneur, Ltd. v. Yasuna, 498 A.2d 1151 (D.C.App.1985) (lease for purpose not allowed by zoning was valid; parties may have contemplated zoning permit); Warshawsky v. American Automotive Products Co., 12 Ill.App.2d 178, 138 N.E.2d 816 (1956); Schlesinger v. Levine, 28 Misc.2d 654, 212 N.Y.S.2d 904 (1961); Young v. Texas Co., 8 Utah 2d 206,

331 P.2d 1099 (1958); Pennsylvania State Shopping Plazas, Inc. v. Olive, 202 Va. 862, 120 S.E.2d 372 (1961).

7. 237 A.2d 834 (D.C.App.1968).

8. See 6A A. Corbin, Contracts §§ 1373–78 (1962).

9. See Robinson v. Diamond Housing Corp., 463 F.2d 853 (D.C.Cir.1972).

10. See especially Saunders v. First National Realty Corp., 245 A.2d 836 (D.C.App. 1968) (Brown limited); Posnanski v. Hood, 46 Wis.2d 172, 174 N.W.2d 528 (1970) (Brown rejected). But see King v. Moorehead, 495 S.W.2d 65 (Mo.App.1973), where the court apparently held Brown's illegality defense was available to a tenant as an alternative to the theory of implied warranty of habitability.

11. See especially Javins v. First National Realty Corp., 138 U.S.App.D.C. 369, 428 F.2d 1071 (1970), certiorari denied 400 U.S. 925, 91 S.Ct. 186, 27 L.Ed.2d 185 (1970), and Pines v. Perssion, 14 Wis.2d 590, 111 N.W.2d 409 (1961). See also, e.g., Lemle v. Breeden, 51 Hawaii 426, 462 P.2d 470 (1969); Jack Spring, Inc. v. Little, 50 Ill.2d 351, 280 N.E.2d 208 (1972); Kline v. Burns, 111 N.H. 87, 276 A.2d 248 (1971); Marini v. Ireland, 56 N.J. 130, 265

§ 6.28 Illegal Use—Supervening Illegality

We assume now that the use of the premises contemplated by the parties' agreement, and indeed the tenant's actual use, are initially permitted by law but become illegal by subsequent changes in the law. The consequences of this will be discussed more fully near the end of this chapter under the heading "Frustration of Purpose," but will be briefly summarized here.

If the lease limits the tenant's use of the premises solely to the use that becomes illegal, the leasehold terminates in most jurisdictions.[1] The same is true if the tenant's main or principal activity becomes illegal, though a minor part remains legal.[2] The corollary seems true, that if the part that remains legal is found to be a major part of the activity, the lease is not voided.[3] Some courts, contrary to the result in most jurisdictions, do not allow the lease to terminate on account of supervening illegality.[4] These courts reason that the tenant should have anticipated the possibility of illegality and have inserted a termination clause in the lease. In cases where the evidence shows the tenant should in fact have contemplated that his use might become illegal, it appears the courts generally will enforce the lease against him despite supervening illegality.[5] Similar are cases in which a tenant cannot carry on intended activity, not because the activity is illegal per se, but because he cannot obtain a necessary permit or license for the activity. Most courts will not set the lease aside for that reason, but some have done so.[6]

E. INTERFERENCE WITH TENANT'S POSSESSION

§ 6.29 Implied Covenant of Power to Lease

It is well to be reminded that a lease is most fundamentally a conveyance. Though contractual undertakings usually take up most of the space, the only essential part is the landlord's conveyance of a leasehold estate. Necessarily implied in this act of conveyance, as with other conveyances, is a representation by the grantor that he has legal power to make the conveyance described.[1] This representation is called a "covenant," but, since it is a

---

A.2d 526 (1970); Foisy v. Wyman, 83 Wn.2d 22, 515 P.2d 160 (1973).

§ 6.28

1. E.g., Greil Brothers Co. v. Mabson, 179 Ala. 444, 60 So. 876 (1912); Brunswick–Balke–Collender Co. v. Seattle Brewing & Malting Co., 98 Wash. 12, 167 P. 58 (1917); 1 A.L.P., supra note 1, at § 3.44.

2. Doherty v. Monroe Eckstein Brewing Co., 115 Misc. 175, 187 N.Y.S. 633 (1921), affirmed 198 App.Div. 708, 191 N.Y.S. 59 (1921); Stratford, Inc. v. Seattle Brewing & Malting Co., 94 Wash. 125, 162 P. 31 (1916). But see O'Byrne v. Henley, 161 Ala. 620, 50 So. 83 (1909).

3. Standard Brewing Co. v. Weil, 129 Md. 487, 99 A. 661 (1916) (alternative ground); Warm Springs Co. v. Salt Lake City, 50 Utah 58, 165 P. 788 (1917).

4. See, e.g., Standard Brewing Co. v. Weil, 129 Md. 487, 99 A. 661 (1916) (alternative ground); Imbeschied v. Lerner, 241 Mass. 199, 135 N.E. 219 (1922); Annot., 22 A.L.R. 821, 830–34 (1923).

5. See Nebaco, Inc. v. Riverview Realty Co., 87 Nev. 55, 482 P.2d 305 (1971); North American Capital Corp. v. McCants, 510 S.W.2d 901 (Tenn.1974).

6. Rowe v. Wells Fargo Realty, Inc., 166 Cal.App.3d 310, 212 Cal.Rptr. 374 (1985) (tenant's setting furnace thermostat below temperature permitted by federal regulation did not make use of premises for "unlawful purpose"). See Annot., 89 A.L.R.3d 329 (1979).

§ 6.29

1. Restatement (Second) of Property § 4.2, Comment b (1977); 1 A.L.P., supra note 1, at § 3.46. See Hannan v. Dusch, 154 Va. 356, 153 S.E. 824 (1930).

statement of a supposed state of affairs then existing and not an undertaking to do something, it is more precisely a "warranty."

Observe that the representation is not that the landlord has title, but that he simply has a power to convey a leasehold. In most cases, of course, he has that power as an incident of ownership; however, it would be possible for him to have a power of conveyance beyond any interest he has in the land.[2] Since the warranty is as to the state of affairs at one instant in time, the point of leasing, breach will occur only if the landlord lacks a power to convey at that time.

§ 6.30   Implied Covenant of Quiet Enjoyment

There is implied in every leasing a covenant of quiet enjoyment.[1] It is both a covenant and a warranty. The landlord warrants that the tenant will not be disturbed in possession by any other person with a superior legal right to possession. In case of disturbance, the landlord covenants to defend the tenant. Moreover, the landlord covenants not to evict the tenant himself, actually or constructively. Thus, the covenant is breached only if, during his term, the tenant is disturbed by a third person or by the landlord.

§ 6.31   Quiet Enjoyment—Interference by Third Persons

Interference with the tenant's possession by trespassers or wrongdoers does not work a breach of the warranty of quiet enjoyment, but only interference by persons having "paramount title." It further appears that in a majority of decisions on the issue, the warranty is breached only when the third-person interference comes to an actual dispossession of the tenant.[1] Probably the most common manner in which this occurs is foreclosure of a mortgage by a mortgagee who has priority over the tenant, followed by sale and possession by the purchaser.[2] Dispossession or exclusion by a prior tenant whose term has not ended is another example.[3] It would seem also

---

2. See Givens v. Givens, 387 S.W.2d 851 (Ky.1965).

§ 6.30

1. Standard Livestock Co. v. Pentz, 204 Cal. 618, 269 P. 645 (1928); Hankins v. Smith, 103 Fla. 892, 138 So. 494 (1931); Kuiken v. Garrett, 243 Iowa 785, 51 N.W.2d 149 (1952); Dobbins v. Paul, 71 N.C.App. 113, 321 S.E.2d 537 (1984) (covenant of quiet enjoyment implied in every lease); 2401 Pennsylvania Ave. Corp. v. Federation of Jewish Agencies, 507 Pa. 166, 489 A.2d 733 (1985) (landlord breached new tenant's implied covenant of quiet enjoyment by extending leasehold of holdover tenant); Hannan v. Dusch, 154 Va. 356, 153 S.E. 824 (1930) (dictum); Annot., 62 A.L.R. 1257, 1258–63 (1929), Supp., 41 A.L.R.2d 1414, 1420–22 (1955). The A.L.R. annotations cite an enormous number of decisions in support of the statement in text. The only major exception seems to be in New Jersey, where the warranty is not implied merely from the landlord-tenant relationship. Ellis v. McDermott, 7 N.J.Misc. 757, 147 A. 236 (1929); Mershon v. Williams, 63 N.J.L. 398, 44 A. 211 (1899).

§ 6.31

1. E.g., Standard Livestock Co. v. Pentz, 204 Cal. 618, 269 P. 645 (1928); Hyman v. Fischer, 184 Misc. 90, 52 N.Y.S.2d 553 (1944); 1 A.L.P., supra note 1, at § 3.48. But see the annotations in 62 A.L.R. 1257 (1929), and 41 A.L.R.2d 1414 (1955). Their textual statements suggest actual dispossession is not necessary. However, it appears A.L.R. has not distinguished between cases in which interference against the tenant is by a third person and when it is by the landlord. As we shall see, acts short of actual, or even constructive, eviction, e.g., trespasses or nuisances, have sometimes been held to breach the covenant of quiet enjoyment when the acts are laid to the landlord.

2. Standard Livestock Co. v. Pentz, 204 Cal. 618, 269 P. 645 (1928), is a foreclosure case, but there was no dispossession.

3. See, e.g., Sandall v. Hoskins, 104 Utah 50, 137 P.2d 819 (1943).

that if the holder of a life estate leases for a term that has not ended at his death, entry by the reversioner or remainderman breaches the warranty.

§ 6.32 Quiet Enjoyment—Actual Eviction

The preceding section considered dispossession by a third person who had a right of possession superior to the tenant's. Here we consider dispossession, i.e., eviction, by the landlord himself. Whereas the third person's dispossession had to be by legal right to cause a breach of the covenant of quiet enjoyment, here the covenant is breached when the landlord's act is decidedly wrongful. Indeed, it is hard to imagine that the tenant could be a tenant if the landowner had the right of possession.

In an actual eviction the landlord physically forces the tenant off the premises or enters and wrongfully excludes the tenant.[1] Of course the tenant has an action for damages for trespass, as well as actions to regain possession by ejectment and, likely, statutory forcible entry. More remarkably, and of more interest to most tenants, the eviction empowers the tenant to terminate the leasehold or at least to suspend paying rent. The reasons for this remarkable remedy and the mechanism by which it operates want some explaining, for they have not sufficiently excited scholarly curiosity.

The remedy is of some antiquity; it is mentioned by Lord Coke in a manner suggesting it was old in his time.[2] Traditionally all that was said was that if the landlord wrongfully evicted the tenant, the latter might suspend paying rent during the period of eviction.[3] That is to say, neither the leasehold nor the other lease covenants are terminable, only the covenant to pay rent is suspended and only while the eviction lasts. Some American decisions of fairly recent date seem to support this proposition.[4] It is believed, however, that most American courts today, if squarely faced with the issue, would allow the tenant to terminate all obligations and the leasehold itself.[5] The next paragraph will aid in explaining why this is believed to be so.

§ 6.32

1. See Barash v. Pennsylvania Terminal Real Estate Corp., 26 N.Y.2d 77, 308 N.Y.S.2d 649, 256 N.E.2d 707 (1970) (distinguishing actual and constructive evictions); Olin v. Goehler, 39 Wn.App. 688, 694 P.2d 1129 (1985) (landlord breaches implied covenant of quiet enjoyment by wrongfully locking out tenant); 1 A.L.P., supra note 1, at § 3.49.

2. E. Coke, Littleton *148b, *292b. The scope of the present work does not justify pushing research on the eviction doctrine back to about the year 1600. Someone should do this.

3. See, e.g., Id.; Clun's Case, 10 Co.Rep. 127a, 77 Eng.Rep. 1117 (1614); Collins v. Harding, Cro.Eliz. 606, 78 Eng.Rep. 848 (1598); 7 W. Holdsworth, History of English Law 267–70 (1925).

4. See, e.g., Automobile Supply Co. v. Scene–In–Action Corp., 340 Ill. 196, 172 N.E. 35 (1930) (dictum); Smith v. McEnany, 170 Mass. 26, 48 N.E. 781 (1897). Most actual or constructive eviction cases are ones in which the landlord sues for rent, not to enforce some other covenant. Thus, statements that rent is suspended are not directed toward a contested issue in most cases.

5. See, e.g., Kulawitz v. Pacific Woodenware & Paper Co., 25 Cal.2d 664, 155 P.2d 24 (1944); J.C. Penney Co. v. Birrell, 95 Colo. 59, 32 P.2d 805 (1934); Charles E. Burt, Inc. v. Seven Grand Corp., 340 Mass. 124, 163 N.E.2d 4 (1959); 1 A.L.P., supra note 1, at § 3.51. In part the statement in text is based upon decisions that allow the tenant to terminate on the contract theory of rescission. On this see, e.g., University Club v. Deakin, 265 Ill. 257, 106 N.E. 790 (1914); Stifter v. Hartman, 225 Mich. 101, 195 N.W. 673 (1923); Higgins v. Whiting, 102 N.J.L. 279, 131 A. 879 (1926); Ringwood Associates, Limited v. Jack's of Route 23, Inc., 166 N.J.Super. 36, 398 A.2d 1315 (1979); University Properties, Inc. v. Moss, 63 Wn.2d 619, 388 P.2d 543 (1964); Restatement (Second) of Property § 7.1 (1977).

What is the legal theory or mechanism by which eviction excuses the tenant's performance? Historically the reason given was that rent reserved by a landlord was to be paid out of the produce of the land. Therefore, if the tenant was wrongfully ousted, he was denied the source of rent, which was suspended.[6] This was the same concept that underlay the common-law rule that rent is not due till the end of the term, i.e., until crops could be harvested. Whether the concept should be applied to leaseholds, especially residential ones, that do not provide the tenant with produce is a problem that seems not to have been considered. In any event, the historical concept avoids the question whether the rule suspending the tenant's duty to pay rent was really an ancient application of the contract doctrine of dependency of covenants to leases. In American jurisprudence, though, the standard mechanism described by the court is dependency of covenants.[7] Indeed, Dyett v. Pendleton,[8] the earliest constructive eviction decision in America (the difference between actual and constructive evictions does not matter here), reads much like a contract case. It can be said, therefore, that the rule allowing the tenant either to suspend rent or to terminate for an eviction exists as a large exception to the leasing-conveyancing doctrine of independence of covenants. This in turn tends to support the conclusion of the last paragraph, that courts will allow the tenant to terminate all obligations, a result that is essentially rescission in the contract sense.

Rescission is supposedly not available to landlord and tenant, since that remedy implies the dependency of contractual covenants. Perhaps it is heresy to suggest it, but there is evidence that courts have in fact allowed a remedy called rescission much more frequently than we are supposed to think.[9] Independence of covenants and unavailability of rescission are the traditional principles. However, the suggestion is that the law of contract is rapidly overtaking traditional conveyancing doctrine in these areas. Whether what has been called rescission is truly the contract remedy of that name or is a *sui generis* remedy is a question that has not been aired. The problem is, if it is truly rescission, should not the court put the parties back into their status before the lease? This is by no means an easy question to answer even in contract law,[10] but the leasing rescission opinions seem to assume the tenant may terminate without even discussing that question.[11] It may be then that we should speak of power of termination, not of rescission.

6. See authorities cited in note 3, this section.

7. See, e.g., Kulawitz v. Pacific Woodenware & Paper Co., 25 Cal.2d 664, 155 P.2d 24 (1944); Charles E. Burt, Inc. v. Seven Grand Corp., 340 Mass. 124, 163 N.E.2d 4 (1959); Dolph v. Barry, 165 Mo.App. 659, 148 S.W. 196 (1912); Higgins v. Whiting, 102 N.J.L. 279, 131 A. 879 (1926); Fifth Avenue Building Co. v. Kernochan, 221 N.Y. 370, 117 N.E. 579 (1917), reargument denied 222 N.Y. 525, 118 N.E. 1057 (1917).

8. 8 Cow. 727 (N.Y.1826).

9. Research on the doctrines of actual and constructive eviction turned up incidentally a surprising number of opinions in which the courts purport to allow "rescission" or at least allow escape from obligation on the ground of dependency. See authorities cited in note 5, this section. Also see some of the recent decisions on implied warranties of habitability, such as King v. Moorehead, 495 S.W.2d 65 (Mo.App.1973).

10. See Restatement of Restitution § 65 (1937); 12 S. Williston, Contracts §§ 1455, 1460, 1460A (3d ed. W. Jaeger ed. 1970).

11. But see Kulawitz v. Pacific Woodenware & Paper Co., 25 Cal.2d 664, 155 P.2d 24 (1944), where the court in passing said a tenant could not have rescission because he did not offer to pay back rent.

One final point needs to be noted about the actual eviction doctrine as it has existed historically. A partial actual eviction, that is, eviction from only part of the demised premises, suspends the tenant's duty to pay every penny of the rent.[12] The reason assigned, more talismanic than rational, is that the landlord, as wrongdoer, will not be permitted to apportion his wrong.

§ 6.33 Quiet Enjoyment—Constructive Eviction

Both historically and functionally, the doctrine of constructive eviction is an extension of the doctrine of actual eviction. Here the concept is that, because of some wrongful act or omission by the landlord, the premises become uninhabitable ("untenantable") for the intended purposes. The tenant is not physically evicted or excluded—but he might as well be. In fact, to be able to invoke the eviction remedy of rent suspension or termination, the tenant must complete the eviction cycle by moving out. Thus, there is an eviction, though constructive instead of actual.[1]

As an actual eviction by the landlord is wrongful, so must a constructive eviction be caused by a wrong laid to the landlord. A classic hypothetical instance would be the landlord's removal of all windows and doors in the middle of a hard winter. Sometimes the landlord's acts or wrongful omissions outside the leased premises may release disturbances or substances that invade the premises. Examples are flooding or rodents originating from common areas under the landlord's control [2] or a nuisance emanating from the landlord's nearby brothel.[3] Many decisions, especially recent ones, go so far as to impute to the landlord nuisances caused by his other tenants,[4] but other opinions refuse to charge him with another's wrong.[5] Frequently the landlord's wrong consists of failing to make repairs the lease requires of him.[6] Most frequently the landlord's wrong seems to be the failure to

12. Dolph v. Barry, 165 Mo.App. 659, 148 S.W. 196 (1912) (dictum); Barash v. Pennsylvania Terminal Real Estate Corp., 26 N.Y.2d 77, 308 N.Y.S.2d 649, 256 N.E.2d 707 (1970) (dictum); E. Coke, Littleton *148b; 7 W. Holdsworth, History of English Law 270 (1925). But cf. the rule that if the tenant is evicted from part of the premises by a third person who has paramount title, rent is apportioned. Fifth Avenue Building Co. v. Kernochan, 221 N.Y. 370, 117 N.E. 579 (1917), reargument denied 222 N.Y. 525, 118 N.E. 1057 (1917). E. Coke, supra at *148a, 148b; 7 W. Holdsworth, supra at 267–70.

§ 6.33

1. For general discussions of constructive eviction, see 1 A.L.P., supra note 1, at §§ 3.51, 3.52; Annot., 62 A.L.R. 1257 (1929), Supp., 41 A.L.R.2d 1414 (1955); Note, 19 Harv.L.Rev. 50 (1905).

2. See Simon v. Solomon, 385 Mass. 91, 431 N.E.2d 556 (1982) (repeated flooding from adjoining areas constituted constructive eviction); Reste Realty Corp. v. Cooper, 53 N.J. 444, 251 A.2d 268 (1969). Also see Jacobs v.

Morand, 59 Misc. 200, 110 N.Y.S. 208 (1908) (bugs).

3. See Dyett v. Pendleton, 8 Cow. 727 (N.Y. 1826).

4. Milheim v. Baxter, 46 Colo. 155, 103 P. 376 (1909) (brothel); Barton v. Mitchell Co., 507 So.2d 148 (Fla.App.1987) (adjacent tenant, exercise studio); Bocchini v. Gorn Management Co., 69 Md.App. 1, 515 A.2d 1179 (1986) (noisy tenants in apartment above); Q C Corp. v. Maryland Port Administration, 68 Md.App. 181, 510 A.2d 1101 (1986) (adjacent tenant had chrome waste landfill); Phyfe v. Dale, 72 Misc. 383, 130 N.Y.S. 231 (1911) (brothel).

5. E.g., Stewart v. Lawson, 199 Mich. 497, 165 N.W. 716 (1917).

6. See Wood v. Gabler, 229 Mo.App. 1188, 70 S.W.2d 110 (1934) (alternative ground); Dolph v. Barry, 165 Mo.App. 659, 148 S.W. 196 (1912). See also J.C. Penney Co. v. Birrell, 95 Colo. 59, 32 P.2d 805 (1934). But cf. the strange opinion in Stewart v. Childs Co., 86 N.J.L. 648, 92 A. 392 (1914), where the court seems to say there is no constructive eviction unless the landlord intends to force the tenant out.

provide promised utilities, such as heat.[7] It seems that the landlord's failure to make repairs or to provide utilities required by statute or ordinance should be the basis for constructive eviction, but court decisions to date are split on whether, in effect, these public duties will be read into the landlord-tenant agreement.[8] There is even a little authority stretching constructive eviction to include the landlord's breach of a covenant giving the tenant exclusive right to conduct a described business.[9]

Not only must the interference be laid to the landlord's wrong, but it must be of such severity that the premises become "untenantable"—uninhabitable as a residence or unusable for the tenant's business. The cases described in the preceding paragraph give the flavor of what sorts of interferences may cause that condition. In pure form the concept is that the effect on the tenant is as bad as if the landlord had actually evicted him. However, in actual decisions a lesser test satisfies, something like, "Should a tenant be expected to continue to occupy the premises under these conditions?" Because of lack of repairs,[10] of essential utilities,[11] or invasions by pests, rodents, water, or nuisances,[12] things come to that pass. While the interference cannot be a one-time or isolated occurrence, it need not be literally continuous, but may be intermittent.[13] In nearly all the examples given there is some interference with the tenant's physical use of the premises. However, those decisions that find constructive eviction in the landlord's breach of an exclusive business clause protect the tenant's economic enjoyment.[14]

If the tenant wishes to have the peculiar eviction remedy, rent suspension (or termination, it may be), he must have vacated the premises.[15] To be sure, whether or not the tenant vacates, he may have damages, generally in the amount of the diminution in rental value. But it is usually the peculiar remedy that is desired, and the vacation requirement is a serious stumbling block. First, in residential tenancies of low-quality housing, the tenant likely has little choice of an alternative home, and the alternative may be as rundown as the present one. Moreover, since such tenancies are generally short-term periodic ones, it is largely academic whether the tenant vacates under constructive eviction or simply by giving notice. Second, with any tenancy, residential or commercial, a tenant who vacates upon what appears

7. Automobile Supply Co. v. Scene–In–Action Corp., 340 Ill. 196, 172 N.E. 35 (1930) (heat; dictum); Charles E. Burt, Inc. v. Seven Grand Corp., 340 Mass. 124, 163 N.E.2d 4 (1959) (electricity, heat, elevator); Shindler v. Grove Hall Kosher Delicatessen & Lunch, Inc., 282 Mass. 32, 184 N.E. 673 (1933) (heating system); Barash v. Pennsylvania Terminal Real Estate Corp., 26 N.Y.2d 77, 308 N.Y.S.2d 649, 256 N.E.2d 707 (1970) (air conditioning; dictum).

8. See Thompson v. Shoemaker, 7 N.C.App. 687, 173 S.E.2d 627 (1970); Annot., 86 A.L.R.3d 352 (1978).

9. In re Consumers World, Inc., 160 F.Supp. 238 (D.C.Mass.1958) (language of both constructive eviction and rescission); Kulawitz v. Pacific Woodenware & Paper Co., 25 Cal.2d 664, 155 P.2d 24 (1944).

10. See note 6, this section. See also Middagh v. Stanal Sound Ltd., 222 Neb. 54, 382 N.W.2d 303 (1986) (landlord's failure to build promised fence did not make premises untenantable).

11. See note 7, this section.

12. See notes 2, 3, 4, this section.

13. Reste Realty Corp. v. Cooper, 53 N.J. 444, 251 A.2d 268 (1969).

14. See Kulawitz v. Pacific Woodenware & Paper Co., 25 Cal.2d 664, 155 P.2d 24 (1944).

15. Automobile Supply Co. v. Scene–In–Action Corp., 340 Ill. 196, 172 N.E. 35 (1930); Barash v. Pennsylvania Terminal Real Estate Corp., 26 N.Y.2d 77, 308 N.Y.S.2d 649, 256 N.E.2d 707 (1970); Thompson v. Shoemaker, 7 N.C.App. 687, 173 S.E.2d 627 (1970).

to be a constructive eviction gambles that a court will agree. Massachusetts has allowed the tenant to hedge against that gamble by maintaining a declaratory judgment action.[16] Other states should follow this sensible procedure.

Not only must the tenant vacate to complete a constructive eviction, but he must do so within a reasonable time after the interference justifies it.[17] Certainly it is too late for the tenant to quit when his leasehold has otherwise come to an end. If he uses the constructive eviction as a defense to paying rent, the defense is not good against rent that came due before he vacated. Nor is the tenant privileged to vacate after the interference has abated.[18] What is a reasonable time to quit is a question of fact in the circumstances of the case. Vacation within a month of the onset of untenantability seems generally to be safe.[19] The period of reasonable time may be extended by various factors, such as the tenant's difficulty in finding new premises, difficulty in removing personal items or fixtures, and the tenant's serious illness.[20] If the landlord promises to correct the defective conditions and then delays doing so, this particularly justifies the tenant's delay in vacating.[21]

§ 6.34 Interference by Strangers to Title

Interference with the tenant's possession by persons other than, and not acting for, the landlord who have no legal right so to interfere is no breach of the warranty, or covenant, of quiet enjoyment.[1] Such persons, who are neither the landlord nor one acting under his authority nor holders of title paramount, are called "strangers to title." Of course they may be, and probably are, liable to the tenant for trespass or disseisin, but the landlord is not liable. A limitation of sorts upon this statement exists in those cases, discussed in the preceding section, in which courts find a constructive eviction from activities carried on by the landlord's other tenants. In general, though, in the absence of his covenant to do so, the landlord does not warrant against interference by strangers to title.

§ 6.35 Condemnation

The taking of all or part of leased land, or of some interest in it, such as an easement, by a public entity under the power of eminent domain is not a

---

16. Charles E. Burt, Inc. v. Seven Grand Corp., 340 Mass. 124, 163 N.E.2d 4 (1959).

17. See the exhaustive annotation in 91 A.L.R.2d 638 (1963); and also 1 A.L.P., supra note 1, at § 3.51.

18. Gateway Co. v. Charlotte Theatres, Inc., 297 F.2d 483 (1st Cir.1961); Merritt v. Tague, 94 Mont. 595, 23 P.2d 340 (1933).

19. See Annot., 91 A.L.R.2d 638, 646–51 (1963). But see Automobile Supply Co. v. Scene–In–Action Corp., 340 Ill. 196, 172 N.E. 35 (1930), which suggests three weeks was too long.

20. See Greenstein v. Conradi, 161 Minn. 234, 201 N.W. 602 (1924) (delay in finding new premises); Rome v. Johnson, 274 Mass. 444,

174 N.E. 716 (1931) (court lists several factors); Leider v. 80 William St. Co., 22 A.D.2d 952, 255 N.Y.S.2d 999 (1964) (delay in commencement of another leasehold).

21. See Reste Realty Corp. v. Cooper, 53 N.J. 444, 251 A.2d 268 (1969); Rockrose Associates v. Peters, 81 Misc.2d 971, 366 N.Y.S.2d 567 (1975); Annot., 91 A.L.R.2d 638, 655–58 (1963).

§ 6.34

1. Blomberg v. Evans, 194 N.C. 113, 138 S.E. 593 (1927); Johnson–Lieber Co. v. Berlin Machine Works, 87 Wash. 426, 151 P. 778 (1915); Paradine v. Jane, Aleyn 27, 82 Eng. Rep. 897 (K.B.1647); 1 A.L.P., supra note 1, at § 3.53.

breach of the landlord's warranty of quiet enjoyment.[1] Sometimes this is said to be so because the parties contemplated the possibility of condemnation, but it seems sufficient to say the condemnation occurs through no fault of the landlord. Even though there is no breach of the warranty, condemnation impacts upon the landlord-tenant relationship. The most orderly way to approach the subject is to consider two basic fact patterns, one in which all the leased land is taken, and the other in which only a physical part is taken.[2]

It is agreed all around that if the demised land is wholly taken by eminent domain, the leasehold and all duties under the lease, including the tenant's duty to pay rent, are terminated.[3] However, the tenant will be entitled to share in the compensation award in some cases. The nearly universal rule is that the condemnor pays only one award, as if the fee simple title were not subject to the leasehold; i.e., the leasehold and the reversion are not valued separately.[4] To the extent the tenant has a "bonus value" in the leasehold, i.e., the sum by which the fair market value of the leasehold for the remainder of the term exceeds the cost of the tenant's obligations under the lease, the tenant is entitled to share.[5] The landlord is entitled to the balance of the award.[6] Of course if the tenant has a zero or negative bonus value, he does not share.

When only a physical part of the leased premises is taken, the legal situation is more complicated. Logically the tenant's duty to pay rent should be abated pro rata, as most commentators have advocated.[7] Howev-

---

§ 6.35

1. Cornell–Andrews Smelting Co. v. Boston & Providence Railroad Corp., 202 Mass. 585, 89 N.E. 118 (1909); Hockersmith v. Sullivan, 71 Wash. 244, 128 P. 222 (1912); 1 A.L.P., supra note 1, at § 3.54; Annot., 62 A.L.R. 1257, 1297–98 (1929), Supp., 41 A.L.R.2d 1414, 1442–45 (1955).

2. This treatise considers only the two common situations described in the text. Other problems, such as governmental takings of the leasehold estate, are left to eminent domain treatises.

3. Corrigan v. City of Chicago, 144 Ill. 537, 33 N.E. 746 (1893); Goodyear Shoe Machinery Co. v. Boston Terminal Co., 176 Mass. 115, 57 N.E. 214 (1900) (dictum); Annot., 43 A.L.R. 1176, 1176–77 (1926), Supp., 163 A.L.R. 679, 680–81 (1946); 1 A.L.P., supra note 1, at § 3.54; 2 P. Nichols, Eminent Domain § 5.06[3] (3d ed. J. Sackman ed. 1980); Polasky, The Condemnation of Leasehold Interests, 48 Va.L.Rev. 477 (1962).

4. J.J. Newberry Co. v. City of East Chicago, 441 N.E.2d 39 (Ind.App.1982) (total of landlord's and tenant's awards may not exceed market value of fee); Kentucky Department of Highways v. Sherrod, 367 S.W.2d 844 (Ky. 1963); 4 P. Nichols, Eminent Domain §§ 12.-36[1], 12.36[2] (3d ed. J. Sackman ed. 1980). However, the existence of a leasehold and the amount of rent may affect the valuation of the fee simple estate. See 4 Id. § 12.3122.

5. Alamo Land & Cattle Co. v. Arizona, 424 U.S. 295, 96 S.Ct. 910, 47 L.Ed.2d 1 (1976); United States v. Petty Motor Co., 327 U.S. 372, 66 S.Ct. 596, 90 L.Ed. 729 (1946), rehearing denied 327 U.S. 818, 66 S.Ct. 813, 90 L.Ed. 1040 (1946); Corrigan v. City of Chicago, 144 Ill. 537, 33 N.E. 746 (1893); J.J. Newberry Co. v. City of East Chicago, supra note 4 (tenant is entitled only to bonus value of leasehold; court rejects "capitalization of income" formula); Annot., 3 A.L.R.2d 286, 290–94 (1949); 1 A.L.P., supra note 1, at § 3.54; 4 Id. at § 12.-42[3]; Restatement (Second) of Property § 8.2(2)(a) (1977). See also State ex rel. State Highway Comm'n v. St. Charles County Assocs., 698 S.W.2d 34 (Mo.App.1985) (month-to-month tenant not entitled to share in condemnation award). The amount of the tenant's award is the discounted present value of his "bonus value."

6. But see Restatement (Second) of Property § 8.2(2)(a) (1977), which adopts a formula for proportioning an award between landlord and tenant when the separate values of leasehold and reversion total more or less than the award the condemnee has paid into court.

7. E.g., 1 A.L.P., supra note 1, at § 3.54; 2 P. Nichols, Eminent Domain § 5.06[3] (3d ed. J. Sackman ed. 1980); Restatement (Second) of Property §§ 8.1(2)(b), 8.2(2)(b), 11.1. Nichols and the Restatement also advocate that the taking of so much of the land as significantly to interfere with the tenant's use should terminate the lease.

er, the predominant rule in the courts is that the tenant must continue to pay the entire rent, so that he pays for the portion of the premises of which he has lost possession.[8] Therefore, the tenant may be entitled to a share of the condemnation award that is comprised of two components. He will always receive that sum which, when capitalized over the time remaining in the term, will produce a fund equal to the rent allocated to the part of the premises taken. In addition, in cases where the tenant has a bonus value as described in the preceding paragraph, he will be entitled to a discounted amount equal to the portion of the bonus value allocated to the part of the premises taken.[9] These are the usual formulas, though different approaches have on occasion been invoked in unusual cases.[10] Of course landlord and tenant may specifically agree in their lease for the consequences of condemnation, and their agreement will be enforced.[11] In any longterm lease or one in which condemnation may be anticipated, such a clause should be included.

We should emphasize that the apportionment formulations stated in the two preceding paragraphs apply only when the estate condemned is the fee simple or at least of a greater length than the remaining time of the leasehold. An entity that has eminent domain power may condemn lesser interests in the land, such as the leasehold alone or even an estate of shorter duration. In such a case, since the reversion is not affected, the landlord has no interest in the condemnation award, which goes entirely to the tenant.[12]

F. CONDITION OF THE PREMISES

§ 6.36   Fitness of Premises for Intended Use—Traditional Rules

The common law concept of a lease as primarily a conveyance of the leasehold estate resulted in the general application, until quite recently, of the doctrine of *caveat emptor* with respect to the condition of the leased premises at the inception of a tenancy; the landlord ordinarily did not impliedly warrant that the leased premises were suitable for the intended

---

8. See Stubbings v. Village of Evanston, 136 Ill. 37, 26 N.E. 577 (1891); Elliott v. Joseph, 163 Tex. 71, 351 S.W.2d 879 (1961); Olson Land Co. v. Alki Park Co., 63 Wash. 521, 115 P. 1083 (1911); Annot., 43 A.L.R. 1176, 1177–83 (1926), Supp., 163 A.L.R. 679, 682–85 (1946). Examination of the A.L.R. annotations suggests the law has regressed, i.e., that the few decisions requiring pro rata rent abatement tend to be old ones, with the trend being toward the rule stated in text.

9. See authorities in preceding note and also Mobil Oil Corp. v. Phoenix Central Christian Church, 138 Ariz. 397, 675 P.2d 284 (App. 1983) (tenant entitled to difference between fair market value of leasehold before and after taking; "capitalization" formula rejected); Kentucky Department of Highways v. Sherrod, 367 S.W.2d 844 (Ky.1963); and 1 A.L.P., supra note 1, at § 3.54.

10. See, e.g., Department of Public Works & Buildings v. Metropolitan Life Insurance Co., 42 Ill.App.2d 378, 192 N.E.2d 607 (1963)

(long-term leasehold valued as if it were fee); Korf v. Fleming, 239 Iowa 501, 32 N.W.2d 85 (1948) (farm leasehold, difficult to value).

11. See State v. Garley, 111 N.M. 383, 806 P.2d 32 (1991), for a clause, which the court enforced, that provided that upon condemnation the leasehold terminated and the landlord got the entire award.

12. See Almota Farmers Elevator & Warehouse Co. v. United States, 409 U.S. 470, 93 S.Ct. 791, 35 L.Ed.2d 1 (1973); United States v. General Motors Corp., 323 U.S. 373, 65 S.Ct. 357, 89 L.Ed. 311 (1945); 2 P. Nichols, Eminent Domain § 5.06 (3d ed. J. Sackman ed. 1980). Cf. Leonard v. Autocar Sales & Service Co., 392 Ill. 182, 64 N.E.2d 477 (1945), certiorari denied 327 U.S. 804, 66 S.Ct. 968, 90 L.Ed. 1029 (1946), rehearing denied 328 U.S. 878, 66 S.Ct. 1118, 90 L.Ed. 1646 (1946), rehearing denied 328 U.S. 879, 66 S.Ct. 1339, 90 L.Ed. 1647 (1946) (condemnation for time shorter than leasehold does not end it).

use, whether that use was agricultural, residential, commercial, or industrial.[1] Hence the tenant generally could not assert, either as a basis for recovery of damages in tort or as a defense to an action by the landlord for unpaid rent, that the premises were not suitable for the tenant's use in the absence of an express warranty of fitness. *A fortiori,* the tenant could not terminate or "rescind" the lease on the ground that the premises were not suitable for his use.[2]

Whether or not the leased premises were suitable for the tenant's use at the beginning of the lease term, the common law did not impose on the landlord any duty to make repairs required to make or keep the premises suitable for the tenant's use.[3] Instead, as we have already seen, the common law imposed on the tenant a minimal duty to keep the buildings on the leased premises well enough sealed against the "wind and weather" as to prevent "permissive waste."[4] This was the only duty with respect to repairs imposed by the common law on either the landlord or the tenant.

When the lease contained an express covenant by the landlord to keep the premises in repair, or to make certain specified kinds of repairs, the lessee's remedy for breach of the lessor's covenant was to make the required repairs, if minor in character, and then to seek reimbursement by bringing

§ 6.36

1. Little Rock Ice Co. v. Consumers' Ice Co., 114 Ark. 532, 170 S.W. 241 (1914); Davidson v. Fischer, 11 Colo. 583, 19 P. 652 (1888); Valin v. Jewell, 88 Conn. 151, 90 A. 36 (1914); Lawler v. Capital City Life Insurance Co., 62 App.D.C. 391, 68 F.2d 438 (1933); Boyer v. Commercial Building Investment Co., 110 Iowa 491, 81 N.W. 720 (1900); Smith v. State, 92 Md. 518, 48 A. 92 (1901); Anderson Drive–In Theatre v. Kirkpatrick, 123 Ind.App. 388, 110 N.E.2d 506 (1953); Causey v. Norwood, 170 Miss. 874, 156 So. 592 (1934); Arbuckle Realty Trust v. Rosson, 180 Okl. 20, 67 P.2d 444 (1937). Cases are collected in 48 Am.Jur. Landlord and Tenant § 768 (no implied warranty of fitness) and § 769 (no implied warranty of habitability). It should be noted, however, that the landlord did have a common law duty to disclose the existence of substantial "latent" defects in the leased premises that were known to him, if the tenant did not know of them; and if the tenant or members of his family suffered personal injury as a result of such defects not disclosed by the landlord, the landlord was liable for damages in tort. E.g., Sunasack v. Morey, 196 Ill. 569, 63 N.E. 1039 (1902); Moore v. Parker, 63 Kan. 52, 64 P. 975 (1901); Steefel v. Rothschild, 179 N.Y. 273, 72 N.E. 112, 1 Ann.Cas. 676 (1904); Perkins v. Marsh, 179 Wash. 362, 37 P.2d 689 (1934); Marsh v. Bliss Realty, Inc., 97 R.I. 27, 195 A.2d 331 (1963). In some states a landlord may be charged with knowledge of "latent" defects which he could have discovered by the exercise of reasonable care, and may be held liable for injuries to the tenant or the tenant's family resulting from such defects unless the tenant is also chargeable with

knowledge of those defects. E.g., Anderson v. Hamilton Gardens, Inc., 154 Conn. 719, 222 A.2d 809 (1966); Reckert v. Roco Petroleum Corp., 411 S.W.2d 199 (Mo.1966). In a few states the landlord is not liable unless he has actual knowledge of the "latent" defects and the tenant is not chargeable with the knowledge that a reasonable inspection would have revealed. E.g., Hendricks v. Socony Mobil Oil Co., 45 Ill.App.2d 44, 195 N.E.2d 1 (1963). Generally, see W. Prosser, Torts § 63 (4th ed. 1971).

2. Even if there were an express warranty of suitability for use the traditional doctrine that lease covenants are "independent" would preclude termination or "rescission." See ante Section 6.11. However, it is possible that the landlord's failure to disclose a known but "latent" defect that creates an unreasonable risk of harm to the tenant might be deemed a species of "fraud" that would justify the tenant in "rescinding" or setting aside the lease when he discovers the defect.

3. E.g., Friedman v. Le Noir, 73 Ariz. 333, 241 P.2d 779 (1952); Chambers v. Lowe, 117 Conn. 624, 169 A. 912 (1933); Duthie v. Haas, 71 Idaho 368, 232 P.2d 971 (1951); Divines v. Dickinson, 189 Iowa 194, 174 N.W. 8, 12 A.L.R. 155 (1919); Sipprell v. Merner Motors, 164 Neb. 447, 82 N.W.2d 648 (1957); Harrill v. Sinclair Refining Co., 225 N.C. 421, 35 S.E.2d 240 (1945); Lyman v. Cowen, 167 Okl. 574, 31 P.2d 108 (1934); Irish v. Rosenbaum Co., 348 Pa. 194, 34 A.2d 486 (1943); K.W. Corby Co. v. Zimmer, 99 A.2d 485 (D.C.Mun.App.1953). Cases are collected in 49 Am.Jur.2d Landlord and Tenant § 774.

4. Ante Sections 4.4, 6.24.

an action against the lessor for breach of the covenant.[5] If the lessor failed to make major repairs required by his express covenant, the lessee could either make the repairs and sue for reimbursement or, at his option, simply bring an action for breach of the lessor's covenant.[6] But the lessee could not withhold the rent because of the lessor's breach of covenant; nor, until early in the nineteenth century, could the lessee terminate the lease, absent an express provision in the lease authorizing termination for breach of the lessor's covenants.[7] As we have seen, only a breach of the lessor's express or implied covenant of quiet enjoyment—in the form of an actual eviction of the lessee by the lessor or by one asserting a paramount title—would justify the lessee in withholding rent and allow him to terminate the lease.[8]

Moreover, the common law imposed no duty on the lessor to furnish any services in connection with the leasing of realty, regardless of the purpose for which the lease was made.[9] And if the lease contained an express covenant by the lessor to supply services such as water and heat—as might be the case when he leased a unit in a multi-family dwelling house—the lessee's remedies for breach of the covenant were limited to those available when there was a breach by the lessor of an express covenant to repair.[10]

The common law rules set out above were probably fair and workable in an agrarian society where multi-family dwelling houses were uncommon, materials required for repairs were simple and easy to obtain, and lessees were generally as capable of carrying out needed repairs as lessors were.[11] Presumably rents were ordinarily fixed on the basis of these common law rules.[12]

In the course of the nineteenth century, as the United States became more and more a nation of cities, the courts came to recognize various

---

5. E.g., Young v. Berman, 96 Ark. 78, 131 S.W. 62 (1910); Olinger v. Reahard, 117 Ind. App. 172, 70 N.E.2d 436 (1947); Warner Brothers Pictures, Inc. v. Southern Tier Theatre Co., 279 App.Div. 309, 109 N.Y.S.2d 781 (1952); Pappas v. Zerwoodis, 21 Wn.2d 725, 153 P.2d 170 (1944).

6. Young v. Berman, supra note 5; Borochoff Properties, Inc. v. Creative Printing Enterprises, Inc., 233 Ga. 279, 210 S.E.2d 809 (1974); Charles E. Burt, Inc. v. Seven Grand Corp., 340 Mass. 124, 163 N.E.2d 4 (1959); Parker v. Meadows, 86 Tenn. 181, 6 S.W. 49 (1887). The measure of damages is usually the difference in rental value of the leased premises with and without the repairs. E.g., Koneman v. Seymour, 176 Ill.App. 629 (1913); Williams v. Fenster, 103 N.J.L. 566, 137 A. 406 (1926). But cf. Cato Ladies Modes of North Carolina, Inc. v. Pope, 21 N.C.App. 133, 203 S.E.2d 405 (1974) (damages are the reasonable cost of repairs plus compensation for loss resulting from breach). Older cases are collected in 28 A.L.R. 1448, 1494 (1924), 116 id. 1228 (1938).

7. The reason, of course, was the doctrine that covenants in leases were "independent," so that performance by the landlord of his covenants was not a condition precedent to

the tenant's duty to perform his covenants. See ante, Section 6.11.

8. See ante Sections 6.31, 6.32.

9. Prior to the middle of the nineteenth century, of course, few, if any, services were available even where a lease covered a rental unit in a multi-family dwelling house.

10. See supra note 7.

11. As one commentator has observed:

It all made sense back in those days with the landlord off on the hunt or drinking port in the quiet of the evening, and the tenant asking to be left alone to tend his fences and to shear his sheep. The heart of the system was land and its possession. The model landlord was the one who did the least. The tenant, in turn, was expected to run the farm, to be the omnicompetent man fully prepared to see to his own shelter, heat and light. T. Quinn and E. Phillips, The Law of Landlord–Tenant: A Critical Evaluation of the Past With Guidelines for the Future, 38 Fordham L.Rev. 225, 231 (1969).

12. This would certainly have been true whenever the supply and the demand for rental properties was in reasonable balance.

exceptions to the doctrine of *caveat emptor* and the rule that landlords were subject to no implied duties to repair or supply services. Thus, e.g., it was held that a landlord who leased premises on a "furnished" basis for a short term had a duty to put them in a "habitable" condition before the tenant took possession,[13] and that a landlord must put the premises into a condition suitable for the intended use when the lease restricted the tenant to a specified use and the lease was made before completion of the construction or alteration of the premises.[14] Moreover, the courts also came to hold that a landlord had a common law duty to maintain all the "common areas" over which he retained control when he leased two or more rental units on the same parcel of land—e.g., the stairways, corridors, elevators, lobbies, and grounds of an apartment building—in a reasonably safe condition for the use of his tenants.[15] And the courts later expanded the "common areas" rule to include facilities located within individual rental units which were connected to a central system—e.g., a central heating, hot water, or electric supply system.[16]

Tenants' rights were further expanded by judicial recognition and development of the doctrine of "constructive eviction" in the nineteenth century. As we have seen,[17] the courts' initial insistence that a tenant would be justified in vacating the leased premises and asserting that he had been constructively evicted only on the basis of affirmative acts of the landlord which rendered the premises untenantable [18] was later relaxed, and the courts came to hold that a constructive eviction could be predicated on the lessor's breach of any express or implied covenant, or any judicially recognized duty as to maintenance of common areas or service systems.[19] Thus e.g., a tenant who vacated the leased premises within a reasonable time could assert that he had been constructively evicted on the ground that the

---

13. Smith v. Marrable, 11 M. & W. 5, 152 Eng.Rep. 693 (Ex.1843), is the leading case. Accord: Young v. Povich, 121 Me. 141, 116 A. 26, 29 A.L.R. 48 (1922); Hacker v. Nitschke, 310 Mass. 754, 39 N.E.2d 644 (1942).

14. E.g., Woolford v. Electric Appliances, 24 Cal.App.2d 385, 75 P.2d 112 (1938); J.D. Young Corp. v. McClintic, 26 S.W.2d 460 (Tex. Civ.App.1930); The Hardman Estate v. McNair, 61 Wash. 74, 111 P. 1059 (1910).

15. E.g., Schedler v. Wagner, 37 Wn.2d 612, 225 P.2d 213 (1950), adhered to 37 Wn.2d 612, 230 P.2d 600 (1951); Inglehardt v. Mueller, 156 Wis. 609, 146 N.W. 808 (1914). Most of the cases recognizing such a duty are cases where the tenant sought to impose tort liability on the landlord because of physical injuries suffered by him or members of his family as a result of unsafe conditions in "common areas." See W. Prosser, Torts § 63 at pp. 405–408 (4th ed. 1971).

16. Allen v. William H. Hall Free Library, 68 R.I. 80, 26 A.2d 751 (1942); Conroy v. 10 Brewster Avenue Corp., 97 N.J.Super. 75, 234 A.2d 415 (1967), cert. denied 51 N.J. 276, 239 A.2d 664 (1968); Marsh v. Riley, 118 W.Va. 52, 188 S.E. 748 (1936); Gladden v. Walker & Dunlop, 83 U.S.App.D.C. 224, 168 F.2d 321

(1948). Here again, however, the duty was generally recognized only as a basis for imposing tort liability on the landlord. See W. Prosser, Torts § 63 at p. 406 (4th ed. 1971).

17. Ante, Section 6.33.

18. Such acts of the landlord would necessarily consist either of repeated trespasses or nuisances.

19. Ante, Section 6.33 at notes 6 through 9 and authorities cited. Other authorities include Gibbons v. Hoefeld, 299 Ill. 455, 132 N.E. 425 (1921), noted 16 Ill.L.Rev. 535 (1922) (covenant to waterproof basement); Kinsey v. Zimmerman, 329 Ill. 75, 160 N.E. 155 (1928) (covenant to mend leaking pipes); Shindler v. Grove Hall Kosher Delicatessen & Lunch, 282 Mass. 32, 184 N.E. 673 (1933) (covenant to supply heat); McCall v. New York Life Insurance Co., 201 Mass. 223, 87 N.E. 582, 21 L.R.A.(N.S.) 38 (1909) (elevator service); Reste Realty Corp. v. Cooper, 53 N.J. 444, 251 A.2d 268 (1969) (oral promise to seal outside driveway and basement wall, semble); Jackson v. Paterno, 58 Misc. 201, 108 N.Y.S. 1073 (Sup. Ct.App.Term 1908), affirmed 128 App.Div. 474, 112 N.Y.S. 924 (1908) (covenant to supply heat was implied from express covenant of quiet enjoyment; dictum).

landlord's failure to perform an express covenant to make repairs or to provide essential services to the tenant made the leased premises untenantable.[20] As the New Jersey court recently observed,[21]

> The inference to be drawn from the cases is that the remedy of constructive eviction probably evolved from a desire by the courts to relieve the tenant from the harsh burden imposed by common law rules which applied principles of *caveat emptor* to the letting, rejected an implied warranty of habitability, and ordinarily treated undertakings of the landlord in a lease as independent covenants. To alleviate the tenant's burden, the courts broadened the scope of the long-recognized covenant of quiet enjoyment * * * to include the right of the tenant to have the beneficial enjoyment and use of the premises for the agreed term.

When fully developed, the constructive eviction doctrine, in substance, gave a tenant the power to terminate the lease if the landlord's breach of duty made the leased premises untenantable.[22]

The changes in the common law summarized above, including development of the constructive eviction doctrine, constituted a nineteenth (and early twentieth) century response to the problems of an increasingly urban society and, in cases where the constructive eviction doctrine was applied to rental housing, a partial recognition of the residential tenant's right to a habitable dwelling rather than just the right to possession of the premises. But this right was only partially protected, because—

1. Neither contractual remedies nor the power to terminate the lease because of constructive eviction were ordinarily available to the tenant unless the lessor had expressly covenanted to keep the premises in repair or to provide essential services. But low-income tenants rarely had sufficient bargaining power to compel landlords to enter into any express covenants in favor of their tenants. In the absence of such express covenants, the constructive eviction doctrine was available to a tenant only in cases where failure to maintain common areas in a reasonably safe condition made the leased premises untenantable, or where the courts would "imply" a duty on the part of the landlord to supply essential services.

2. A tenant who vacated leased premises in reliance on the constructive eviction doctrine was always subject to the risk that, in a later action by the landlord for unpaid rent, the court would find either that the landlord's breach of duty did not interfere so substantially with the tenant's use and enjoyment as to justify the tenant in vacating, or that the tenant had failed to vacate within a "reasonable time."[23] Either finding would result in the

---

20. Ante Section 6.33.

21. Reste Realty Corp. v. Cooper, supra note 19, 53 N.J. at 460, 251 A.2d at 276.

22. Ante Section 6.33. Originally, it appears that the constructive eviction doctrine only gave tenants a defense against actions for rent, but the tenant's power to terminate was later recognized.

23. As to the requirement of vacating within a "reasonable time," see ante, Section 6.33 at notes 17 through 21 and authorities

cited. Illustrative cases where the tenant was held to have waited an "unreasonable time" include the following: Stone v. Sullivan, 300 Mass. 450, 15 N.E.2d 476, 116 A.L.R. 1223 (1938) (10 months); Palumbo v. Olympia Theatres, 276 Mass. 84, 176 N.E. 815, 75 A.L.R. 1111 (1931) (11 months); Merritt v. Tague, 94 Mont. 595, 23 P.2d 340 (1933) (2 months). Compare Reste Realty Corp. v. Cooper, supra note 19 ("reasonable" for the lessee to remain in possession for about three and one-half years after flooding of leased premises by rain

tenant's remaining liable for rent for the entire balance of the lease term despite the fact that the tenant had vacated long before the action for unpaid rent was brought.[24]

3.   Reliance on the constructive eviction doctrine was not feasible in areas where there was a substantial shortage of rental housing, since a tenant who vacated leased premises would find it hard to obtain substitute housing.

4.   If the tenant remained in possession and attempted to defeat a summary action to evict him for nonpayment of rent by alleging the landlord's breach of covenant, it was uniformly held that such a defense was inadmissible because it was not germane.[25]

5.   Many—perhaps most—low-income tenants were tenants from month-to-month or from week-to-week, which placed them in a very vulnerable position if they sued their landlords for breach of an express covenant to repair or to provide essential services, because their tenancies could be terminated, without cause, by the landlords' giving the notice required at common law or by statute.[26]

§ 6.37   Statutory Modifications of the Traditional Rules: The Housing Code Approach

Another legislative approach to modification of the traditional rules as to the condition of leased premises was the adoption, in the second half of the nineteenth century, of "tenement house laws" and, in the twentieth century, "housing codes."[1]   The direct ancestor of all modern "housing codes" is the New York Tenement House Law of 1867, which applied only to lodging houses and multiple dwellings located in New York City.[2]   This statute contained nineteen sections mandating (*inter alia*) that "tenement" houses should have water-tight roofs, adequate chimneys, fire escapes, ventilators, and refuse containers, and "good and sufficient water closets or privies."[3]   That the principal purpose of the statute was to safeguard public health is evidenced by the designation of the Metropolitan Board of Health

water began; until about nine months before the lessee vacated, the lessor's resident manager made repeated, good faith attempts to deal with the flooding problem).

24.   Charles E. Burt, Inc. v. Seven Grand Corp., 340 Mass. 124, 163 N.E.2d 4 (1959) indicates that the difficulty may be obviated by a suit for a declaratory judgment and/or for rescission. The *Seven Grand* case held that the tenant was entitled to a declaration that it was "entitled to abandon the premises within a reasonable time [after the court's judgment] and to treat Seven Grand's conduct as a constructive eviction," and also to recover damages "for Seven Grand's past actions."

25.   As to the scope of the summary action to evict, generally, see post Section 6.77 and authorities cited. For a good discussion of the classical rule sharply limiting the available defenses, see Jack Spring, Inc. v. Little, 50 Ill.2d 351, 280 N.E.2d 208 (1972); Lindsey v.

Normet, 405 U.S. 56, 92 S.Ct. 862, 31 L.Ed.2d 36 (1972). For additional authorities, see 52A C.J.S. Landlord & Tenant § 755.

26.   See § 6.72.

§ 6.37

1.   Generally, see F. Grad, Legal Remedies for Housing Code Violations 1–6 (Research Report 14, prepared for the National Commission on Urban Problems, 1968); L. Friedman, Government and Slum Housing 25–55 (1968); Abbott, Housing Policy, Housing Codes and Tenant Remedies: An Integration, 56 B.U.L.Rev. 1, 40–48 (1976); Cunningham, The New Implied and Statutory Warranties of Habitability in Residential Leases: From Contract to Status, 16 Urban L.Annual 3, 10–51 (1979).

2.   L. Friedman, supra note 1, at 26–27.

3.   New York Laws 1867, c. 908, §§ 1–19.

(created the previous year) as the enforcement agency.[4] Massachusetts enacted a statute applicable only to Boston and patterned on the 1867 New York statute in 1868.[5] In New York, the need for a more comprehensive housing law was forcefully demonstrated by Riis, DeForest, and Veiller,[6] whose efforts led to enactment of a new Tenement House Law (applicable to New York City and Buffalo) in 1901.[7] The 1901 statute increased the number of sections setting out minimum standards from nineteen to one hundred and provided for a system of tenement house registration and occupancy permits.[8]

The pioneering New York and Massachusetts tenement house laws provided the basis for the modern "housing code," defined as follows: [9]

> A housing code deals with the owner's and occupant's duty to keep existing housing in decent condition—to see to it that it is not occupied by more persons than are legally permitted for housing accommodations of that size; to keep it in proper repair; to maintain it in a sanitary condition; to see that it remains properly ventilated and lighted; to make sure that it has the required facilities for fire safety; that required machinery—elevators, boilers and heating plants, etc.—are kept in working order; and that required services—heat, hot and cold water— are provided in accordance with minimal requirements of law.

There are broad similarities in the current housing codes of different municipalities, most of which are based to a considerable extent on one of four or five model codes, which are themselves quite similar. In addition to municipal housing codes, there are several state housing codes. The substantive content of state housing codes is substantially like that of the model codes and their municipal derivatives. Some of the state housing codes apply statewide; others are applicable only to certain cities or to municipalities falling in certain classifications. Some are "mandatory" but allow

---

4. Ibid. See also New York Laws 1866, c. 74, §§ 1–33.

5. Mass.Gen.Laws Ann. c. 281, §§ 1–18.

6. See The Tenement House Problem (R. DeForest & L. Veiller eds. 1903); Riis, The Clearing of Mulberry Bend, 12 Rev. of Reviews 172 (1895); Veiller, The Tenement House Exhibition of 1899, 10 Charities Rev. 19 (1900).

7. New York Laws 1901, c. 334, §§ 1–149.

8. Ibid.

9. F. Grad, supra note 1, at 2. As Grad points out, the term "housing code" really means more than a particular municipal ordinance: "Realistically, it includes the entire body of state and local law that prescribes housing standards and that may be relied upon to provide the source of power or authority for enforcement sanctions and remedies." Id. at 8. In some municipalities, "housing code" elements are lumped together with elements of building codes, plumbing codes, electrical codes, and the like. On the other hand, a provision for a minimum number of windows in a dwelling unit might be contained either in a "housing code" or a "building code"; and minimum plumbing standards might be included in either a "housing," "building," or "plumbing code." But, for present purposes, the "housing code" should be clearly distinguished from the other types of regulatory ordinances.

"Building codes," "plumbing codes," and "electrical codes" all specify structural standards, materials, and requirements for new or substantially remodeled buildings of all types, but they impose no continuing requirements as to maintenance or provision of services to tenants. "Housing codes," as that term is used herein, apply only to dwelling units— primarily rental units—and they impose only ongoing requirements as to maintenance and provision of services. When a "housing code" is enacted or amended, the new regulations generally apply to existing housing; but when a "building code," "plumbing code," or "electrical code" is adopted or amended, the new or amended regulations ordinarily apply only to buildings constructed or substantially remodeled after adoption or amendment of the regulations.

municipalities to adopt more stringent requirements; others are "option-al"—i.e., municipalities may, but need not, adopt them as local ordinances.[10]

A housing code generally provides minimum standards in regard to four different features of the housing it regulates: (1) structural elements such as walls, roofs, ceilings, floors, windows, and staircases; (2) facilities such as toilets, sinks, bathtubs, radiators or other heating fixtures, stoves, electrical outlets, window screens, and door and window locks; (3) services such as heat, hot and cold water, sanitary sewage disposal, electricity, elevator service, central air conditioning, and repair and maintenance services for each dwelling unit; and (4) occupancy standards setting limits on the number of occupants per dwelling or per bedroom.[11]

Housing codes were still not very common in 1954; there were then only some fifty-six codes in force in the United States.[12] But the "workable program" requirement of the 1954 Federal Housing Act[13] gave impetus to the spread of housing codes; and further impetus was provided by the 1964 Federal Housing Act amendments which require the Federal Housing Administration to refuse certification or recertification of local "workable programs" unless the localities in question have had housing codes in effect for at least six months and are able to satisfy the Administrator that effective code enforcement programs are being carried out.[14] Under the stimulus of this Federal legislation, at least 4,904 communities had local housing codes in force by 1968, and at least six states then had state-wide housing codes in force.[15]

Until very recently, violation of a housing code provision was not considered a breach of any duty owed by the landlord directly to his tenants, and tenants had no direct remedies when code violations occurred. Enforcement of the early tenement house laws was delegated to local administrative agencies charged with a duty to inspect buildings covered by such laws both on a regular periodic basis and in response to tenant complaints, and this has continued to be the normal mode of enforcement of modern housing codes.[16] If the issuance of a violation notice and one or more informal or

10. See E. Mood, The Development, Objectives, and Adequacy of Current Housing Code Standards, In Housing Code Standards: Three Critical Studies (prepared for National Comm'n on Urban Problems, Research Rep. No. 19, 1969), surveying the requirements of four model housing codes; nine state housing codes, and sixteen city or county housing codes.

11. Abbott, supra note 1, at 40. For a more extended discussion of the contents of housing codes, see Grad, Hack and McAvoy, Housing Codes and Their Enforcement 195–216 (study prepared for HUD, 1966). Mood, supra note 10, at 13, 18, makes the following critique:

Housing legislation usually implies the existence of criteria of acceptability. It suggests that data are available which separate with precision unfit, unsanitary, unsafe, and inadequate housing from that which is decent, clean, safe and sanitary. Unfortunately, such a bank of data does not exist

* * * The state of the art today is such that currently there is no single comprehensive evaluation procedure available that will clearly and concisely delineate the presence or absence of a relationship even between the quality of housing and health.

12. Urban Renewal Admin., Housing & Home Finance Agency, Urban Renewal Bull. No. 3, Provisions of Housing Codes in Various American Cities.

13. Housing Act of 1954, ch. 649, § 303, 68 Stat. 623, as amended, 42 U.S.C.A. § 1451(c).

14. Housing Act of 1964, § 301(a), 78 Stat. 784, as amended, 42 U.S.C.A. § 1451(c).

15. National Comm'n on Urban Problems, Building the American City, H.R.Doc. No. 91–34, 91st Cong., 1st Sess. 276–77 (1968).

16. F. Grad, supra note 1, at 5. When a housing code enforcement officer discovers and reports code violations, the code enforcement agency usually sends a violation notice

formal administrative hearings do not lead to correction of the violation, the enforcement agency has traditionally been authorized to obtain an order for vacation of the building, followed by an order for demolition if the owner does not correct the violation within a designated time; [17] and to bring a criminal action against the building owner.[18] In some states additional modes of agency enforcement are authorized; these may include obtaining a mandatory injunction requiring the building owner to bring his building into compliance with the housing code,[19] suits to impose a "civil" penalty on the building owner,[20] direct agency action to correct code violations by making repairs and improvements,[21] and suits for appointment of a receiver to take over the building and apply its rents to correction of code violations.[22]

If some or all of the traditional modes of housing code enforcement listed above had proven effective, it is possible that the "revolution" of the 1960's and 1970's in landlord-tenant law would not have occurred. But all observers agree that local governments have been notably unsuccessful in code enforcement.[23] In part the lack of success stems from the institutions charged with enforcement. Most code enforcement agencies are understaffed and underfunded because of the low level of public awareness of code enforcement problems and lukewarm support by local elected officials.[24] Periodic inspections are not carried out on any regular schedule and, since housing inspectors are not very well paid, code enforcement has been hindered by corruption.[25] Even honest housing inspectors may grow discouraged and apathetic because of the ease with which landlords can obtain "variances," [26] and public prosecutors rarely demonstrate much zeal in code enforcement.[27]

to the owner of the building with a request that the violations be corrected. If the violation notice does not produce corrective action, the owner may be invited to discuss the reported code violations informally at the agency's office; or the agency may issue a formal "show cause order" demanding that the owner show cause why the agency should not initiate an enforcement action against him because of the reported code violations. Formal administrative hearings before a hearing officer may be used to determine initially whether the reported conditions actually constitute code violations. More often, however, the reporting of a violation by the inspector is itself an administrative determination that a violation exists, and the administrative hearing is in substance an appeal from the inspector's determination. Id. at 14–19.

17. For full discussion, see id. at 56–61.

18. For full discussion, see id. at 22–33.

19. For full discussion, see id. at 40–42.

20. For full discussion, see id. at 34–39.

21. For full discussion, see id. at 62–69.

22. For full discussion, see id. at 42–55.

23. The literature is voluminous. See, e.g., M. Teitz and S. Rosenthal, Housing Code Enforcement in New York City (1971); B. Lieberman, Local Administration and Enforcement of Housing Codes: A Survey of 39 Cities

(1969); J. Slavet and M. Levin, New Approaches to Housing Code Administration (Research Report 17, for National Commission on Urban Problems, 1969); F. Grad, supra note 1; Abbott, supra note 1, at 49–56.

24. Abbott, supra note 1, at 54–55.

25. See J. Slavet and M. Levin, New Approaches to Housing Code Administration 179 (Research Report 17, prepared for The National Commission on Urban Problems, 1969).

26. Lieberman reported that most code enforcement personnel believed that variance boards act on the basis of political considerations or emotion. "The results are disrespect for the inspector and his superiors; ineffective systematic code compliance programs; and disrespect for local regulatory measures." B. Lieberman, Local Administration and Enforcement of Housing Codes: A Survey of 39 Cities 23 (1969).

27. " * * * Few housing code enforcement agencies have legal staffs of their own, and even the ones that do must usually bring prosecutions through the municipality's regular legal department; i.e., through the city attorney or corporation counsel, or through the city or county prosecutor. In the usual course, the municipal law officer or his deputies have little experience or knowledge of housing matters and tend to regard housing

Each of the modes of housing code enforcement listed above is subject to its own peculiar problems.[28] In addition, most of them share at least one common problem: the difficulty of obtaining personal jurisdiction over the owner of a non-complying building—a result of the common practice of placing the title to low-income multi-family dwelling houses in corporations whose officers and offices cannot be located and whose agents cannot identify their principals.[29] Consequently, some states began to adopt new legislation authorizing tenants to withhold rent when their landlords failed to correct serious housing code violations which rendered their rental units "uninhabitable." Although two states adopted legislation of this type before New York,[30] the New York legislation of 1929 [31] was the first significant rent withholding statute. Additional significant New York rent withholding legislation was enacted in 1939 and in the 1960's,[32] and a number of other states enacted rent withholding legislation in the 1960's.[33] This legislation generally authorizes withholding of rent while serious code violations persist, and leaves for judicial determination the question whether a particular code violation or combination of violations is, in fact, serious enough to justify the withholding of rent. Most of the statutes also require a tenant to show, in order to justify rent withholding, that an official inspection of his dwelling unit was made and that the inspecting officer reported one or more code violations to the code enforcement agency.

The statutes authorizing tenants to withhold rent because of serious housing code violations do not, in terms, alter the contractual rights and duties of landlords and tenants. In substance, however, they make the tenant's duty to pay rent conditional upon the landlord's compliance with applicable housing code provisions designed to assure that premises leased for residential use shall be in a habitable condition throughout the duration of the tenancy. Some of these statutes apply to all kinds of rental housing; some apply only to multi-family dwellings—usually defined as buildings with three or more dwelling units; and some have an even more limited application. Many of the statutes include or are coupled with provisions designed

prosecutions as a very minor, troublesome, and unexciting area for the application of their legal expertise. Even in large cities, where hundreds and thousands of housing cases may be brought each year, they represent a low-prestige area of activity, for a young lawyer in the city's legal department gains neither friends nor glory by successfully prosecuting housing cases." F. Grad, supra note 1, at 25. See also Philadelphia Housing Ass'n, Impediments to Housing Code Compliance iv (1963), cited by Grad. And see Abbott, supra note 1, at 53–54.

28. For a more detailed discussion, see Cunningham, supra note 1, at 16–23.

29. Abbott, supra note 1, at 50. For a more detailed discussion of the problem, see F. Grad, supra note 1, Ch. X ("The Phantom Landlord: Finding the Absentee Landlord").

30. See Conn.Gen.Stat.Ann. §§ 19–371, 19–400 (originally enacted in 1905, this statute provided that failure to obtain a certificate of compliance with the state housing law should

(C., S.&W.) Prop. 2d HB —8

bar any action by the landlord to recover rent or to evict for nonpayment of rent; the statute, in its present form, is applicable to all multi-family housing except public housing); Iowa Code Ann. § 413.106 (originally enacted in 1919, the statute was similar to the Connecticut statute). See Cunningham, supra note 1, at 23.

31. N.Y.—McKinney's Multiple Dwelling Law § 302. The Multiple Dwelling Law was enacted in 1929 to replace the 1901 Tenement House Law; Buffalo, however, remained subject to the latter until 1950, when it was brought under the Multiple Dwelling Law. Section 302 of the latter was similar to the Connecticut and Iowa rent withholding statutes, supra note 30.

32. See discussion of these statutes in Cunningham, supra note 1, at 24, 26–35.

33. See discussion of these statutes in Cunningham, supra note 1, at 35–51, and other discussions of these statutes cited id., at 25 n. 97.

to protect the tenant from retaliatory action by the landlord, and most of the statutes expressly prohibit any waiver of the tenant's right to withhold rent because of serious housing code violations. But the statutes differ substantially with respect to the way in which rent withholding may be initiated and other matters. These differences are considered in the section on rent withholding as a tenant remedy for the landlord's breach of his duty to keep the leased premises in a habitable condition.

In Brown v. Southall Realty Co.,[34] the District of Columbia Court of Appeals held that a tenant could successfully avoid liability for unpaid rent by proving that serious violations of the D.C. Housing Regulations existed on the premises when the tenancy began, although the Regulations did not expressly authorize tenants to set up such violations as a defense to a landlord's action for unpaid rent. In so holding, the D.C. Appeals Court relied on a section of the Regulations which prohibited the renting of "any habitation * * * unless such habitation and its furnishings are in a clean, safe, and sanitary condition, in repair, and free from rodents and vermin," [35] and upon another provision of the Housing Regulations which required all "premises accommodating one or more habitations" to "be maintained and kept in repair so as to provide decent living accommodations for the occupants." [36] The latter provision also included a statement that its purpose was to "make a premises or a neighborhood healthy and safe" rather than merely to require "basic repairs and maintenance to keep out the elements." [37] Brushing aside the landlord's contention that the Housing Regulations were not intended to make a lease voidable because there were violations on the leased premises, the *Brown* court held the lease "void as an illegal contract" after pointing out that "the violations known by" the landlord "to be existing * * * at the time of the signing of the lease agreement were of a nature to make the 'habitation' unsafe and unsanitary," and to establish that the premises had not been "maintained or repaired to the degree contemplated by the regulations." [38]

In Saunders v. First National Realty Corp.,[39] the D.C. Court of Appeals refused to extend the *Brown* "illegal contract" doctrine to cases where the alleged housing code violations were not proved to have been present at the beginning of the defendants' tenancies. The *Brown* doctrine was later extended to such cases when the "illegal contract" doctrine was incorporated in the District of Columbia Landlord–Tenant Code,[40] but at least one subse-

---

34. 237 A.2d 834 (D.C.App.1968).

35. D.C. Housing Regs. § 2304.

36. Id. § 2501.

37. Ibid.

38. 237 A.2d at 836. The "illegal contract" doctrine has also been adopted in Missouri, but there a tenant must elect between the "illegal contract" doctrine and the "implied" warranty of habitability in litigation with his landlord—King v. Moorehead, 495 S.W.2d 65 (Mo.App.1973)—and failure to plead the "illegal contract" defense affirmatively will result in a waiver of that defense—Detling v. Edelbrock, 671 S.W.2d 265 (Mo.1984).

But in Kentucky the "illegal contract" doctrine, as well as the "implied" warranty of habitability, has been rejected. Miles v. Shauntee, 664 S.W.2d 512 (Ky.1983).

39. 245 A.2d 836 (D.C.App.1968), reversed on another point, sub nom. Javins v. First National Realty Corp., 428 F.2d 1071 (D.C.Cir. 1970), certiorari denied 400 U.S. 925, 91 S.Ct. 186, 27 L.Ed.2d 185 (1970). For more on the *Javins* case, see post Section 6.38.

40. D.C. Landlord–Tenant Regulations § 2902.1 (1970), allowing the "illegal contract" defense whether the housing code violations arise before or after the beginning of the tenancy.

quent District of Columbia case [41] ignored the Code provision and refused to apply the "illegal contract" doctrine in a case where housing code violations only arose "after commencement of the lease."

In *Brown,* the tenant had already abandoned the premises, and the court had no occasion to decide whether a tenant who invoked the "illegal contract" defense could remain in possession without paying the agreed rent. In subsequent cases, the District of Columbia courts decided that a tenant who remained in possession and later invoked the "illegal contract" defense was a statutory "tenant at sufferance," not liable for the agreed rent but liable on a quasi-contractual basis for the reasonable rental value of the premises; [42] and that the landlord could not terminate the "tenancy at sufferance" by giving the statutory notice unless (a) the landlord should elect to go out of the rental housing business or (b) the trier of fact should find that the landlord was financially incapable of correcting the housing code violations and that the landlord had no "retaliatory" motive in seeking to evict the tenant.[43] The latter holding led Judge Robb, dissenting, to say that "[t]he theory of the majority seems to be that if not an outlaw a landlord is at least a public utility, subject to regulation by the court in conformity with its concept of public convenience and necessity * * * which in practical application will commit to the discretion of a jury the management of the landlord's business and property." [44]

The "illegal contract" doctrine has gained few adherents outside the District of Columbia.[45]

§ 6.38　The Judge–Made "Implied" Warranty of Habitability

Although legislation furnished the major component in the rapid shift from *caveat emptor* to imposition of a duty on landlords to put and keep premises leased for residential use in a habitable condition, the new legislation enacted for this purpose in the 1960s and 1970s, by and large, has attracted less attention than the dramatic expansion of tenants' rights by judicial decisions holding that a "warranty of habitability" must be "implied" in all or most residential leases.

As early as 1931 the Minnesota Supreme Court held that there was an "implied" warranty of habitability in the leasing of an apartment in a modern apartment building, whether furnished or not, and whether the lease was for a long or a short term.[1] But this decision had no discernible influence on the development of landlord-tenant law, and the "revolution" in

---

41. Winchester Management Corp. v. Staten, 361 A.2d 187 (D.C.App.1976).

42. Davis, Inc. v. Slade, 271 A.2d 412 (D.C.App.1970).

43. Robinson v. Diamond Housing Corp., 463 F.2d 853 (D.C.Cir.1972).

44. 463 A.2d at 871.

45. The "illegal contract" doctrine was recognized in King v. Moorehead, 495 S.W.2d 65 (Mo.App.1973), where the court also adopted the "implied warranty of habitability" doctrine and held that a tenant must elect between them in defending an action by the landlord to recover rent. In Glyco v. Schultz, 35 Ohio Misc. 25, 289 N.E.2d 919 (1972), the Municipal Court of Sylvania, Ohio, also recognized both the "illegal contract" doctrine and the "implied warranty of habitability" doctrine, but did not indicate that the tenant must elect between them.

§ 6.38

1. Delamater v. Foreman, 184 Minn. 428, 239 N.W. 148 (1931).

landlord-tenant law centering on the "implied" warranty of habitability did not occur until the 1960s. The modern era of judicial activism in expanding tenants' rights began only in 1961 with the decision of the Wisconsin Supreme Court in Pines v. Perssion,[2] where the court held that the traditional rule of *caveat emptor* should be rejected and that a warranty of habitability should be implied in every residential lease.

In Pines v. Perssion, the Wisconsin court seems to have believed that recognition of an "implied" warranty of habitability would provide an effective, though indirect, way to enforce state and municipal housing codes, noting that the traditional *caveat emptor* rule was "inconsistent with the current legislative policy concerning housing standards" as exemplified in "legislative and administrative rules, such as the safeplace statute, building codes and health regulations," all of which "impose certain duties on a property owner with respect to the condition of his premises."[3] Although Pines v. Perssion was arguably later overruled *sub silentio,*[4] and has in any case been at least partly superseded by subsequent Wisconsin legislation,[5] the highest courts of at least fifteen other jurisdictions followed the Wisconsin court's lead in adopting an "implied" warranty of habitability. These jurisdictions are California,[6] the District of Columbia,[7] Hawaii,[8] Illinois,[9] Iowa,[10] Kansas,[11] Massachusetts,[12] Missouri,[13] New Hampshire,[14] New Jer-

2. 14 Wis.2d 590, 111 N.W.2d 409 (1961).

3. Id. at 595–596, 111 N.W.2d at 412–413.

4. See Posnanski v. Hood, 46 Wis.2d 172, 174 N.W.2d 528 (1970), where the court not only rejected the "illegal contract" theory as a basis for invalidating a lease of premises on which there were alleged to be a number of housing code violations, but also "rejected the claim that the housing regulations abrogated the common law relation between landlord and tenant so as to create a contractual duty on the landlord to comply with the regulations." Although it is not clear whether the alleged code violations were in existence when the lease was made—and hence not clear that the rule of Pines v. Perssion would be applicable—the court used broad language in *Posnanski* indicating that it believed that housing code standards could not be used as a basis for imposing on the landlord a duty to comply with code standards because the legislature intended "a method of enforcement based entirely upon orders issued by the commissioner of health." This broad language is at least arguably inconsistent with the holding and rationale in *Pines.* However, *Pines* is not even cited in *Posnanski*—nor has it been cited in any subsequent Wisconsin Supreme Court opinion in support of a holding that a warranty of habitability should be implied in residential leases. See Earl Milliken, Inc. v. Allen, 21 Wis.2d 497, 124 N.W.2d 651, 654 n. 1 (1963); Dickhut v. Norton, 45 Wis.2d 389, 173

N.W.2d 297, 300, 304 (1970)—both of which were decided before *Posnanski.* See also State ex rel. Michalek v. LeGrand, 77 Wis.2d 520, 253 N.W.2d 505, 509 (1977).

5. Wis.Stat.Ann. § 704.07.

6. Green v. Superior Court, 10 Cal.3d 616, 111 Cal.Rptr. 704, 517 P.2d 1168 (1974).

7. Javins v. First National Realty Corp., 428 F.2d 1071 (D.C.Cir.1970), certiorari denied 400 U.S. 925, 91 S.Ct. 186, 27 L.Ed.2d 185 (1970).

8. Lemle v. Breeden, 51 Hawaii 426, 462 P.2d 470 (1969); Lund v. MacArthur, 51 Hawaii 473, 462 P.2d 482 (1969).

9. Jack Spring v. Little, 50 Ill.2d 351, 280 N.E.2d 208 (1972); Pole Realty Co. v. Sorrells, 84 Ill.2d 178, 49 Ill.Dec. 283, 417 N.E.2d 1297 (1981).

10. Mease v. Fox, 200 N.W.2d 791 (Iowa 1972).

11. Steele v. Latimer, 214 Kan. 329, 521 P.2d 304 (1974).

12. Boston Housing Authority v. Hemingway, 363 Mass. 184, 293 N.E.2d 831 (1973).

13. Detling v. Edelbrock, 671 S.W.2d 265 (Mo.1984), adopting the views set forth in King v. Moorehead, 495 S.W.2d 65 (Mo.App. 1973).

14. Kline v. Burns, 111 N.H. 87, 276 A.2d 248 (1971).

sey,[15] Pennsylvania,[16] Texas,[17] Vermont,[18] Washington,[19] and West Virginia.[20] In addition, lower courts have recognized the "implied" warranty in Indiana,[21] New York,[22] and Ohio.[23] In Hawaii, Iowa, Ohio, Texas, Vermont, and Washington, however, the judge-made "implied" warranty of habitability has been entirely or largely superseded by comprehensive residential landlord-tenant statutes imposing on landlords a duty—set out in detail—to put and keep the leased premises in a habitable condition.[24] And the "implied" warranty has also been put into statutory form in the District of Columbia, New York, North Carolina, and Utah, although these jurisdictions have not enacted comprehensive new landlord-tenant legislation.[25]

In jurisdictions where the new tenant's right to a habitable dwelling is based only on judicial decisions recognizing an "implied warranty of habitability," it is not always clear just what rental housing is subject to the "implied" warranty. In Javins v. First Nat. Realty Corp.,[26] the court held that the District of Columbia housing code required "implication" of a warranty of habitability in the leasing of all housing covered by the code, and also suggested that, even without reference to the code, a warranty of habitability should "be implied into all contracts for urban dwellings" as a matter of common law.[27] The latter suggestion really had no significance with respect to the District of Columbia, however, since the D.C. housing code applied to "any habitation" in the District [28] and all rental housing in the District is clearly "urban." A later decision by a lower court has interpreted *Javins* as applying only to dwelling units covered by the D.C. housing code.[29]

After *Javins,* the highest courts of California, Illinois, Iowa, Massachusetts, New Jersey, Pennsylvania, Washington, and West Virginia held that the new warranty of habitability should be "implied" in all residential leases; [30] and in Iowa, Washington, and West Virginia, this broad coverage

15. Marini v. Ireland, 56 N.J. 130, 265 A.2d 526 (1970); Berzito v. Gambino, 63 N.J. 460, 308 A.2d 17 (1973).

16. Pugh v. Holmes, 486 Pa. 272, 405 A.2d 897 (1979).

17. Kamarath v. Bennett, 568 S.W.2d 658 (Tex.1978).

18. Hilder v. St. Peter, 144 Vt. 150, 478 A.2d 202 (1984).

19. Foisy v. Wyman, 83 Wn.2d 22, 515 P.2d 160 (1973).

20. Teller v. McCoy, 162 W.Va. 367, 253 S.E.2d 114 (1978) (court held that a common law warranty should be "implied" where case arose after adoption of a statute establishing a warranty of habitability but before the statute became effective).

21. Old Town Development Co. v. Langford, 349 N.E.2d 744 (Ind.App.1976), superseded 267 Ind. 176, 369 N.E.2d 404 (1977); Breezewood Management Co. v. Maltbie, 411 N.E.2d 670 (Ind.App.1980).

22. Tonetti v. Penati, 48 A.D.2d 25, 367 N.Y.S.2d 804 (2d Dept.1975).

23. Glyco v. Schultz, 35 Ohio Misc. 25, 289 N.E.2d 919 (Mun.Ct.1972).

24. Post Section 6.39, note 15. In Washington, the "implied" warranty doctrine of Foisy v. Wyman, supra note 19, remains applicable to residential leases not covered by the Washington statute, the most important of which are leases of houses on farms.

In Texas, on the other hand, the comprehensive new landlord-tenant legislation expressly preempts and supersedes any judge-made "implied" warranty of habitability.

25. D.C. Landlord–Tenant Regulations § 2902.2 (1970); N.Y.—McKinney's Real Prop. Law § 235–b; West Virginia Code, § 37–6–30; N.C.Gen.Stat. § 42–42 (1984); Utah Code Ann. §§ 57–22–1 to 57–22–6 (1990).

26. Supra note 7.

27. 428 F.2d at 1080.

28. District of Columbia, Landlord–Tenant Regulations §§ 2304, 2501 (1970).

29. Winchester Management Corp. v. Staten, 361 A.2d 187 (D.C.App.1976).

30. Green v. Superior Court, supra note 6; Pole Realty Co. v. Sorrells, supra note 9; Mease v. Fox, supra note 10; Marini v. Ireland, supra note 15; Pugh v. Holmes, supra

was confirmed by legislation establishing a statutory warranty of habitability.[31] In New Hampshire, on the other hand, the "implied" warranty is limited to multi-family dwelling units;[32] in Kansas, the "implied" warranty was originally limited to "urban residential property,"[33] but was later broadened by statute to cover all property leased for residential use.[34]

Where the courts have "implied" a warranty of habitability in residential leases without the aid of legislation, the relationship between the new "implied" warranty and the standards set out in applicable housing codes is not always clear. In general, the cases indicate that proof of housing code violations having a substantial adverse impact on health and/or safety will be sufficient to establish a breach of the "implied" warranty.[35] On the other hand, most of the cases recognize that some housing code violations, standing alone, do not pose any substantial threat to the health or safety of tenants, and hence that a breach of the "implied" warranty is not proved merely by proof of the existence of a code violation (or violations).[36] As the court observed in *Javins,* "one or two minor violations standing alone, which do not affect habitability, are *de minimis.*"[37]

Assuming that most courts will not find a breach of the implied warranty of habitability on the basis of housing code violations unless the code violations are serious enough to pose a threat to the health or safety of the tenant, the question remains whether a breach may be found where there is no code violation at all. It is not clear what position the *Javins* court would have taken on this question, but the District of Columbia Court of Appeals subsequently interpreted *Javins* as holding that the implied warranty is measured solely "by the standards set out in the [D.C.] Housing Regulations" and has refused to "stray from or expand upon that holding."[38] In several other jurisdictions, however, the courts have defined the implied warranty of habitability broadly enough to include all cases where the leased premises are unfit for human habitation because of health or safety hazards, whether or not there is a violation of any housing code provision.[39] Thus

note 16; Kamarath v. Bennett, supra note 17; Foisy v. Wyman, supra note 19; Teller v. McCoy, supra note 20.

31. See post Section 6.39, notes 15, 28.

32. Kline v. Burns, supra note 14.

33. Steele v. Latimer, supra note 11.

34. See post Section 6.40, note 1.

35. Javins v. First National Realty Corp., supra note 7; Green v. Superior Court, supra note 6; Jack Spring v. Little, supra note 9; Boston Housing Authority v. Hemingway, supra note 12; King v. Moorehead, supra note 13; Kline v. Burns, supra note 14; Berzito v. Gambino, supra note 15; Pugh v. Holmes, supra note 16; Foisy v. Wyman, supra note 19; Teller v. McCoy, supra note 20.

36. Javins v. First National Realty Corp., supra note 7; Green v. Superior Court, supra note 6; Lund v. MacArthur, supra note 8; Boston Housing Authority v. Hemingway, supra note 12; King v. Moorehead, supra note 13; Berzito v. Gambino, supra note 15; Foisy v. Wyman, supra note 19; Knight v. Hallsthammar, 29 Cal.3d 46, 171 Cal.Rptr. 707, 623

P.2d 268 (1981); Detling v. Edelbrock, 671 S.W.2d 265 (Mo.1984). But see Breezewood Management Co. v. Maltbie, 411 N.E.2d 670 (Ind.App.1980) (evidence that there were "numerous housing code violations" was sufficient to sustain a finding that the "implied" warranty was breached).

37. 428 F.2d at 1082 n. 63.

38. Winchester Management Corp. v. Staten, 361 A.2d 187, 190 (D.C.App.1976).

39. Green v. Superior Court, 10 Cal.3d 616, 111 Cal.Rptr. 704, 517 P.2d 1168 (1974); Lemle v. Breeden, 51 Hawaii 426, 462 P.2d 470 (1969); Glasoe v. Trinkle, 107 Ill.2d 1, 88 Ill.Dec. 895, 479 N.E.2d 915 (1985); Mease v. Fox, 200 N.W.2d 791 (Iowa 1972); Old Town Development Co. v. Langford, 349 N.E.2d 744 (Ind.App.1976) superseded 267 Ind. 176, 369 N.E.2d 404 (1977); Boston Housing Authority v. Hemingway, 363 Mass. 184, 293 N.E.2d 831 (1973); King v. Moorehead, 495 S.W.2d 65 (Mo.App.1973); Kline v. Burns, 111 N.H. 87, 276 A.2d 248 (1971); Marini v. Ireland, 56 N.J. 130, 265 A.2d 526 (1970); Berzito v. Gambino,

several courts [40] have stated that whether defects are so substantial as to render the leased premises unsafe or unsanitary, and thus unfit for habitation, is a factual issue to be determined in light of the circumstances of each case; that ordinarily one such circumstance would be whether the alleged defect violates an applicable housing code; and that other factors to be considered are the nature of the defect, its effect on safety and sanitation, the length of time it has persisted, the age of the structure, and the amount of the rent.

Although most of the court opinions focus on "defects" in the premises serious enough to pose a threat to the health and safety of the tenant, it seems clear that the implied warranty generally requires the provision of "essential" or "vital" services such as hot water, heat, and elevators (in high rise buildings), even if these services are not strictly necessary to protect the tenant's health or safety.[41] Of course, where a housing code is applicable, it will usually require that such services be provided by the landlord.[42]

To the extent that the landlord's obligation is to assure that the leased premises are habitable at the beginning of the tenancy, the further question may arise as to whether the obligation covers "patent" as well as "latent" defects. In Pines v. Perssion,[43] many of the defects that made the premises "uninhabitable" were "patent," but some were "latent." The court, however, said nothing to suggest any distinction between "patent" and "latent" with respect to the newly discovered implied warranty. In Lemle v. Breeden [44] and Lund v. MacArthur,[45] all the defects appear to have been "latent," but the court did not indicate that this was significant. In Javins v. First

63 N.J. 460, 308 A.2d 17 (1973); Tonetti v. Penati, 48 A.D.2d 25, 367 N.Y.S.2d 804 (2d Dept.1975); Pugh v. Holmes, 486 Pa. 272, 405 A.2d 897 (1979).

40. E.g., Mease v. Fox, Boston Housing Authority v. Hemingway, King v. Moorehead, Kline v. Burns, Marini v. Ireland, and Berzito v. Gambino, supra note 39; Knight v. Hallsthammar, supra note 36 (landlord's noncompliance with applicable housing and building codes may or may not constitute a breach of the "implied" warranty of habitability, but the court would not try to lay down precise rules defining "habitability"); Detling v. Edelbrock, supra note 36 ("habitability is to be measured by community standards, reflected in most cases in local housing and property maintenance codes"; to establish a breach of the implied warranty, the tenant must allege and prove conditions making the premises "unsafe and unsanitary"). Many cases emphasize that defects in the premises or failures in provision of services must have "a serious and substantial relationship to the rental value"—Doric Realty Co. v. Union City Rent Leveling Bd., 182 N.J.Super. 486, 442 A.2d 652 (Law Div.1981)—or "be such as to render the premises uninhabitable in the eyes of a reasonable person"—Berzito v. Gambino, supra note 39. See also Allen v. Housing Authority of Chester County, 683 F.2d 75 (3d Cir.1982) (under Pennsylvania law, an apartment was

clearly "uninhabitable" where there was an "almost daily * * * problem of overflowing water coming from [tenant's] bathroom toilet and sink" which at times "contained human waste which flooded throughout her apartment reaching levels of several inches, forcing her and her three children on several occasions to evacuate the apartment").

41. Winchester Development Corp. v. Staten, supra note 38 (hot water, but not air conditioning, is required by housing code and, thus, by the implied warranty); Marini v. Ireland, supra note 39 ("facilities vital to the use of the premises for residential purposes"); Berzito v. Gambino, supra note 39 (same); Academy Spires, Inc. v. Brown, 111 N.J.Super. 477, 268 A.2d 556 (County Dist.Ct.1970) (garbage disposal, hot water, elevator service); Park Hill Terrace Associates v. Glennon, 146 N.J.Super. 271, 369 A.2d 938 (App.Div.1977), cert. denied 74 N.J. 250, 377 A.2d 657 (1977) (air conditioning); Pugh v. Holmes, supra note 39 (hot water); Foisy v. Wyman, 83 Wn.2d 22, 515 P.2d 160 (1973) (same).

42. E.g., Winchester Development Corp. v. Staten, supra note 38.

43. 14 Wis.2d 590, 111 N.W.2d 409 (1961).

44. Supra note 39.

45. Ibid.

Nat. Realty Corp.,[46] the tenants offered to prove that there were some 1500 violations of the District of Columbia housing code, but they conceded that "this offer of proof reached only violations which have arisen since the term of the lease had commenced." [47] Thus the court had no reason to discuss the question whether the newly discovered implied warranty would cover patent defects existing at the beginning of the lease term. But the *Javins* opinion does include a dictum that the shortage of housing in the District of Columbia compels tenants to accept rental units notwithstanding observable defects; [48] and the court's emphasis on the need to give tenants new remedies to enforce their right to a habitable dwelling that substantially complies with the housing code suggests that the *Javins* court would draw no distinction between "latent" and "patent" defects.

In New Jersey, on the other hand, it has been held that the warranty of habitability implied in a residential letting is "that at the inception of the lease, there are no *latent* defects in facilities vital to the use of the premises for residential purposes because of original faulty construction or deterioration from age or normal usage." [49] This language was later adopted by the New Hampshire [50] and Iowa courts.[51] But the significance of the "latent" defect limitation is hard to determine, since the Iowa, New Hampshire, and New Jersey courts have all held that the implied warranty also includes a continuing duty to keep the premises in a habitable condition.[52] It is probable that this continuing duty extends to the repair of "patent" as well as "latent" defects.[53] And in Massachusetts it is clear that the implied warranty of habitability covers both "latent" and "patent" defects existing at the beginning of the tenancy.[54]

The opinion in Pines v. Perssion,[55] proclaiming the existence of an

---

46. 428 F.2d 1071 (D.C.Cir.1970), certiorari denied 400 U.S. 925, 91 S.Ct. 186, 27 L.Ed.2d 185 (1970).

47. 428 F.2d at 1073.

48. 428 F.2d at 1079 n. 42.

49. Marini v. Ireland, 56 N.J. at 144, 265 A.2d at 534 (emphasis added). The quoted language was repeated with approval in Berzito v. Gambino, 63 N.J. at 466, 308 A.2d at 20. The *Berzito* case involved an express rather than an implied warranty of habitability, and the only real issue was the scope of the remedies for breach of such a warranty, whether express or implied.

50. Kline v. Burns, 111 N.H. 87, 276 A.2d 248 (1971).

51. Mease v. Fox, 200 N.W.2d 791 (Iowa 1972).

52. Mease v. Fox, supra note 51; Kline v. Burns, supra note 50; Marini v. Ireland, 56 N.J. 130, 144, 265 A.2d 526, 534 (1970). In Iowa, the implied warranty of habitability recognized in Mease v. Fox has been superseded by the statutory warranty of habitability established by Iowa Code Ann. § 562A.15, which clearly covers both "latent" and "patent" defects (based on Uniform Residential Landlord and Tenant Act § 2.104(a) (1972)).

53. It should be noted that both Mease v. Fox, supra note 51, and Berzito v. Gambino, supra note 49 (quoting *Mease*) contain statements that the court should consider, in a particular case, "whether the tenant voluntarily, knowingly and intelligently waived the defects." This clearly suggests that merely accepting possession when "patent" defects exist would not satisfy the stated requirement that any waiver should be made "knowingly and intelligently." The requirement that there be existing latent defects before there can be a breach of the implied warranty seems to have been abandoned in later New Jersey cases. See, e.g., Trentacost v. Brussel, 82 N.J. 214, 412 A.2d 436 (1980); Chess v. Muhammad, 179 N.J.Super. 75, 430 A.2d 928 (App. Div.1981); Housing Authority of City of Newark v. Scott, 137 N.J.Super. 110, 348 A.2d 195 (App.Div.1975); Drew v. Pullen, 172 N.J.Super. 570, 412 A.2d 1331 (App.Div.1980).

54. Boston Housing Authority v. Hemingway, 363 Mass. 184, 199, 293 N.E.2d 831, 843 (1973) (implied warranty that "at the inception of the rental there are *no latent or patent defects* in facilities vital to the use of the premises for residential purposes"). (Emphasis added.)

55. 14 Wis.2d 590, 111 N.W.2d 409 (1961).

"implied" warranty that residential premises are habitable at the inception of a tenancy, contains no language indicating that there is also a continuing duty of the landlord to maintain the premises in a habitable condition, although the legislative policy embodied in housing codes arguably supports the view that there should be such a continuing duty running directly from landlord to tenant and enforceable by "private" tenant remedies. And neither of the "implied" warranty cases from Hawaii [56] contains any language suggesting that the implied warranty includes any continuing duty of the landlord to maintain the premises in habitable condition. But in Javins v. First Nat. Realty Corp.[57] the sole issue was whether the landlord was subject to such a continuing duty—more precisely, whether he had a duty to correct numerous housing code violations which were assumed to have "arisen since the term of the lease commenced." The *Javins* court's affirmative answer is clearly not based on the supposed analogy to the "consumer protection" cases relied on by Judge Wright,[58] but it does seem to be justified by the policy underlying the District of Columbia housing code. Since *Javins*, although most of the cases have involved defective conditions in existence at the beginning of the tenancy, the courts have consistently said that the new "implied" warranty includes a continuing duty to maintain the dwelling unit in a habitable condition—i.e., to make all repairs necessary to keep the premises habitable, whether the conditions requiring the repairs existed when the tenancy began or only arose later.[59] None of the opinions limits the landlord's duty of repair to those "latent" conditions existing at the inception of the tenancy which first become apparent during the course of the tenancy.[60]

In jurisdictions where the courts have rejected any distinction between "latent" and "patent" defects existing when the tenancy commences and have held that the "implied" warranty of habitability includes a continuing duty to keep the leased premises in a habitable condition, it is clear that the "implied" warranty of habitability is not a true common law implied warranty at all, and that the supposed analogy to the "consumer protection" rules developed in the commercial law field, relied upon by the *Javins* court, is mistaken. Neither the common law warranties of fitness and quality implied in sales of goods nor their modern statutory counterparts under the Uniform Commercial Code include any continuing duty to repair defects arising from the normal use of the goods after acquisition by the buyer; and such implied or statutory warranties do not cover patent defects discoverable

---

56. Lemle v. Breeden, 51 Hawaii 426, 462 P.2d 470 (1969); Lund v. MacArthur, 51 Hawaii 473, 462 P.2d 482 (1969).

57. 428 F.2d 1071 (D.C.Cir.1970), certiorari denied 400 U.S. 925, 91 S.Ct. 186, 27 L.Ed.2d 185 (1970).

58. Id. at 1079.

59. E.g., Green v. Superior Court, 10 Cal.3d 616, 111 Cal.Rptr. 704, 517 P.2d 1168 (1974); Jack Spring, Inc. v. Little, 50 Ill.2d 351, 280 N.E.2d 208 (1972); Boston Housing Authority v. Hemingway, supra note 54; Marini v. Ireland, 56 N.J. 130, 144, 265 A.2d 526, 534 (1970); Berzito v. Gambino, 63 N.J. 460, 308 A.2d 17 (1973); Pugh v. Holmes, 486 Pa. 272,

405 A.2d 897 (1979); Foisy v. Wyman, 83 Wn.2d 22, 515 P.2d 160 (1973).

60. Ibid. In Knight v. Hallsthammar, 29 Cal.3d 46, 171 Cal.Rptr. 707, 623 P.2d 268 (1981), the court expressly rejected any limitation of the "implied" warranty of habitability to cases where the defect is "latent," stating that the policy considerations underlying the imposition of the warranty compelled the conclusion that "a tenant's lack of knowledge of the defects is not a prerequisite to the landlord's breach of the warranty." See also cases cited supra note 53.

by a reasonable inspection.[61] In fact, the new judicially-created "implied" warranty of habitability represents "a judicial recognition of the largely accomplished fact of the transition of residential lease law from the private law fields of property and contract to an area in which public regulatory law predominates"[62]—a point that is emphasized by the general refusal of the courts to give effect to even the most explicit waiver by the tenant of the protection afforded him by the "implied" warranty of habitability.[63]

Where the landlord's duty to keep the leased premises in repair is based on a judicially-created "implied" warranty of habitability, it would seem that the landlord should not be deemed to be in breach of his duty unless he fails to make the necessary repairs within a reasonable time after receiving notice of the defective condition(s) requiring repair—at least where the defective condition(s) only arise, or become "patent," after the tenancy begins.[64] The Massachusetts intermediate court recently said that the tenant was entitled to damages from "the time the landlord first knew or

---

61. As to common law implied warranties in the sale of goods, see, e.g., Remy, Schmidt & Pleissner v. Healy, 161 Mich. 266, 268, 126 N.W. 202, 203, 29 L.R.A.(N.S.) 139 (1910): "It is a settled rule that one who buys an article which is present and subject to his inspection cannot afterwards assert an implied warranty of fitness, quality, or condition in the absence of fraud, except possibly where the seller is the manufacturer or grower, or the vendor of articles intended for consumption as food; *caveat emptor* is the invariable rule." As to the statutory warranties on the sale of goods under the Uniform Commercial Code, see U.C.C. §§ 2–314 through 2–317. "If the warranty were limited to latent defects existing at the commencement of the tenancy, the analogy to consumer protection principles in the law of sales would be sound. But the warranty extends to patent defects and imposes an ongoing duty to repair on the landlord. Hence, the analogy breaks down. * * * Because residential premises are seldom leased without an inspection by the prospective tenant, the UCC would suggest that he takes subject to obvious defects, and the defects would presumably be reflected in the rent he agreed to pay. Additionally, the UCC provides no implied warranty that the seller will repair defects arising from ordinary deterioration of durable goods over time. Only when a defect latent at the time of sale becomes patent does the implied warranty of merchantability afford the buyer a remedy." Abbott, Housing Policy, Housing Codes and Tenant Remedies: An Integration, 56 B.U.L.Rev. 1, 31–32 (1976). The overall critique of the *Javins* rationale in Abbott's article is excellent. See id. at 25–40.

62. Glendon, The Transformation of American Landlord–Tenant Law, 23 B.C.L.Rev. 503, 552 (1982).

63. Although the courts indicated a willingness to consider "whether the tenant [in a particular case] voluntarily, knowingly and intelligently waived the [existing, patent] de-

fects, or is estopped to raise the question of the breach" in Mease v. Fox, 200 N.W.2d 791, 797 (Iowa 1972), and in Berzito v. Gambino, 63 N.J. 460, 470, 308 A.2d 17, 22 (1973) (quoting from *Mease*), the Berzito court, on the facts, sustained the trial court's conclusion that "the scarcity in the Elizabeth [New Jersey] area of available housing for low-income families with children" precluded an effective waiver where a tenant moved into substandard housing and paid the agreed rent for almost a year and a half. In Javins v. First National Realty Corp., 428 F.2d 1071, 1080 n. 49, 1082 n. 58 (D.C.Cir. 1970), certiorari denied 400 U.S. 925, 91 S.Ct. 186, 27 L.Ed.2d 185 (1970), the court refused to consider whether the tenant's express covenant to repair constituted a waiver of the "implied" warranty of habitability because "the implied warranty of the landlord could not be excluded" and any private agreement to shift the burden of compliance with the housing code to the tenant would be "illegal and unenforceable." Most of the other cases have followed *Javins* in holding or stating that the "implied" warranty of habitability cannot be waived. See, e.g., Green v. Superior Court, Boston Housing Authority v. Hemingway, and Foisy v. Wyman, supra note 59. None of the cases dealt with a fact situation like that envisaged by URLTA § 2.104(c), (d), where the parties make a separate written agreement, for an adequate consideration, to shift some of the repair obligations of the landlord to the tenant.

See also Knight v. Hallsthammar, supra note 60.

64. This is the rule in cases where the lease contains an express covenant by the landlord to make repairs on the leased premises. E.g., Chambers v. Lindsey, 171 Ala. 158, 55 So. 150 (1911); Bowling v. Carroll, 122 Ark. 23, 182 S.W. 514 (1916); Woodbury Co. v. Williams Tackaberry Co., 166 Iowa 642, 148 N.W. 639 (1914).

was notified of" any defective condition(s) "shown to have arisen during the tenancy." [65]   But this statement, insofar as it purports to deny the landlord any time to repair the defects after learning of them, is only a dictum, since the evidence revealed "that the landlord knew of the [defective] conditions in the apartment at the inception of the tenancy." [66]

All the cases recognize that the "implied" warranty of habitability does not cover conditions resulting from the deliberate or negligent conduct of the tenant or anyone for whose conduct the tenant is responsible.

The original Restatement of the Law of Property [67] did not undertake to restate the law of landlord and tenant. The Second Restatement of the Law of Property,[68] however, includes a comprehensive restatement of the law of landlord and tenant; the provisions dealing with the allocation of duties with respect to the condition of leased premises form the subject matter of Chapter 5 of the Second Restatement.[69] Sections 5.1 and 5.2 state that there is an implied warranty (without using that term) that property leased for residential use will be suitable for such use both when the lease is made and at the date when the tenant is entitled to possession. The draftsman's comment states that the leased property "is unsuitable for residential purposes if it would be unsafe or unhealthy for the tenant to enter on the leased property and use it as a residence"; that "[a] significant violation of any controlling building or sanitary code, or similar public regulation, which has a substantial impact upon safety or health, is *conclusive* that the premises are unsafe or unhealthy, but other modes of proof are acceptable"; and that "[t]he premises may not be unsafe or unhealthy to occupy but may [nevertheless] be unsuitable for residential purposes." [70] Section 5.5 creates a separate "obligation of the landlord to keep leased property in repair," which includes, but is not limited to, a duty to keep the leased premises in compliance with applicable housing code provisions. Chapter 5, as a whole, appears to be based largely on those sections of the Uniform Residential Landlord and Tenant Act which impose on landlords a duty to put and keep the premises in a habitable condition and detail the remedies available to tenants when there is a breach of this duty.[71] It thus more nearly approximates a restatement of the current statutory law with respect to these duties than a restatement of the current case law.

Special Note: The Implied Warranty of Fitness
for Intended Use in Commercial Leases

The "implied warranty" concept has not generally been extended to commercial leases. In Davidow v. Inwood North Professional Group–Phase

---

65. McKenna v. Begin, 3 Mass.App.Ct. 168, 325 N.E.2d 587, 592 (1975), appeal after remand 5 Mass.App.Ct. 304, 362 N.E.2d 548 (1977).

66. Id. at 589. But the *McKenna* dictum was confirmed by a square holding in Berman & Sons, Inc. v. Jefferson, 379 Mass. 196, 396 N.E.2d 981 (1979). To the same effect, see Knight v. Hallsthammar, supra note 60 (immediate breach of warranty when landlord had notice of conditions making premises un-

inhabitable, not caused by tenants, and landlord was not entitled to "reasonable time to repair").

67. Am.L.Inst., Rest.Prop. (1936–44).

68. Am.L.Inst., Rest.Prop.2d (1977).

69. Id., Landlord and Tenant, Ch. 5 (1977).

70. Id., Landlord and Tenant, § 5.1, Comment e (1977) (emphasis supplied).

71. See post Section 6.39.

I,[72] however, the Texas Supreme Court held that there is an implied warranty of suitability in a commercial lease that the premises are suitable for their intended purpose. * * * This warranty means that at the inception of the lease there are no latent defects in the facilities that are vital to the premises for their intended commercial purposes and that these essential facilities will remain in a suitable condition.[73]

§ 6.39 Statutory Warranties of Habitability in Residential Leases

Unlike the English common law, the French civil law in force in Louisiana at the beginning of the nineteenth century imposed on the lessor, in the absence of a contrary agreement, a duty to deliver the premises to the lessee in a condition suitable for the lessee's intended use, and to make all major repairs on the premises not made necessary by the lessee's wrongful conduct. This duty has been carried forward in successive revisions of the Louisiana Civil Code, and is still applicable in Louisiana.[1]

Early in their history, California, Georgia, Montana, and the Dakota Territory enacted the proposed Civil Code drafted by David Dudley Field.[2] As enacted in all these jurisdictions except Georgia, the Field Civil Code contained provisions—probably derived from the French Civil Code—that imposed on the lessor of a building intended for human habitation a duty to "put it into a condition fit for such occupation, and to repair all subsequent dilapidations thereof, which render it untenantable." These Field Civil Code provisions were carried over to the subsequently enacted Civil Codes of North and South Dakota and, still later, were enacted in Oklahoma.[3]

---

72. 747 S.W.2d 373 (Tex.1988). The premises in question had been leased for use as a doctor's office.

73. Id. at 377. The court also said: "The existence of a breach of the implied warranty of suitability in commercial leases is usually a fact question to be determined from the particular circumstances of each case. Among the factors to be considered * * * are: its effect on the tenant's use of the premises; the length of time the defect persisted; the age of the structure; the amount of the rent; the area in which the premises are located; whether the tenant waived the defects; and whether the defect resulted from any unusual or abnormal use by the tenant." Ibid. The court described the "defects" in *Davidow* as follows:

"The air conditioning did not work properly, often causing temperatures inside the office to rise above eighty-five degrees. The roof leaked whenever it rained, resulting in stained tiles and rotting, mildewed carpet. Patients were directed away from certain areas during rain so that they could not be dripped upon in the waiting room. Pests and rodents often infested the office. The hallways remained dark because hallway lights were unreplaced for months. Cleaning and maintenance were not provided. The parking lot was constantly filled with trash. Hot water was not provided, and on one occasion Dr.

Davidow went without electricity for several days because Inwood failed to pay the electric bill. Several burglaries and various acts of vandalism occurred." 747 S.W.2d at 375.

§ 6.39

1. La.—LSA–C.C. arts. 2692, 2693, 2695. See also id. art. 2717, imposing on the landlord a duty to make even minor repairs required by "unforeseen events or decay." The lessee, on the other hand, is responsible for other minor repairs customarily undertaken by tenants unless there is a contrary agreement between the parties. Id. art. 2716.

2. See A. Reppy, The Field Codification Concept, in David Dudley Field Centenary Essays 17, 48 (A. Reppy ed. 1949). The Field Civil Code was designed for adoption in New York, but was rejected by the New York legislature.

3. These provisions constituted sections 990 and 991 of the Field Civil Code. Their derivatives constitute West's Ann.Cal.Civ. Code §§ 1941, 1942; North Dakota Cent.Code 47–16–13, 47–16–13.1; and South Dakota Codified Laws 43–32–8, 43–32–9. Until recently, provisions derived from the Field Civil Code also constituted Mont.Rev.Codes 1947, §§ 42–201, 42–202, repealed in 1977; and 41 Okla. Stat.Ann., §§ 31, 32, repealed in 1978. Reppy,

Although Georgia substantially enacted the Field Civil Code even before California did,[4] the provision requiring landlords to put and keep leased premises in a tenantable condition was significantly altered. As the Georgia Supreme Court has said,[5] "[w]here an estate for years is created, our Civil Code, * * * following the common law, makes the tenant bound for all repairs or other expense necessary for the preservation and protection of the property * * *."[6] But the Georgia Civil Code also recognizes a form of landlord-tenant relationship where the tenant has a "usufruct" instead of an estate for years,[7] and a lease for a period of less than five years is presumed to create a "usufruct" rather than an estate for years.[8] Where only a "usufruct" is created, "the civil law is adopted [in Georgia], and the landlord must keep the premises in repair."[9] Moreover, the landlord must have the premises in a condition fit for the tenant's intended use at the beginning of the tenancy "if full rent is reserved."[10] The Georgia Civil Code provisions as to the landlord's duty when a "usufruct" is created are not limited to residential leases; but the parties are free to draft the lease so as to create an estate for years rather than a "usufruct" even if the term is less than five years,[11] in which case the landlord is not subject to any statutory duty as to the condition of the leased premises.

No other American jurisdiction followed the lead of California, Georgia, Montana, the Dakotas, and Oklahoma in adopting the Field Civil Code provision imposing a duty on landlords to keep the leased premises in tenantable condition. In California, a 1970 amendment detailed the conditions deemed to make a dwelling untenantable and provided additional protection for residential tenants.[12] In both North and South Dakota, the statutory rights of residential tenants were enlarged by recent amendments

supra note 2, says the Field Civil Code was enacted in California in 1866, but I cannot trace West's Ann.Cal.Civ.Code §§ 1941 and 1942 back beyond 1872. See Legislative History of these sections in West's Ann.Cal.Civ. Code. Reppy, supra note 2, also says that the Field Civil Code was adopted in Montana and in the Dakota Territory in 1872. But the legislative history of the Montana, North Dakota, and South Dakota provisions, supra, indicates that they were derived from the California Civil Code provisions rather than directly from the Field Civil Code. Former 41 Okla.Stat.Ann. §§ 31, 32, were derived from Okla.Stat.1900 §§ 930, 931, which in turn were derived from Dak.Terr.Comp.Laws 1887, §§ 3737, 3738.

4. See Reppy, supra note 2, n. 159, stating that Georgia adopted the Field Civil Code in 1863.

5. Mayer v. Morehead, 106 Ga. 434, 435, 32 S.E. 349 (1899).

6. The "common law rule" is codified in Official Code Ga.Ann. § 44–6–105 (1981 recodification; formerly § 85–805).

7. Official Code Ga.Ann. § 44–7–1(a) (1981 recodification; formerly § 61–101(a)). "In such a case, no estate passes out of the land-

lord and the tenant has only a usufruct which may not be conveyed except by the landlord's consent and which is not subject to levy and sale." Ibid.

8. Official Code Ga.Ann. §§ 44–6–100(a), 44–7–1(b) (1981 recodification; formerly §§ 85–801(a), 61–101(b)); Warehouses, Inc. v. Wetherbee, 203 Ga. 483, 46 S.E.2d 894 (1948).

9. Mayer v. Morehead, supra note 5. The "civil law rule," applicable to a "usufruct," is codified in Official Code Ga.Ann. § 44–7–13 (1981 recodification; formerly § 61–111).

10. E.g., Whittle v. Webster, 55 Ga. 180 (1875); Driver v. Maxwell, 56 Ga. 11 (1876).

11. Official Code Ga.Ann. § 44–7–1(b) (1981 recodification; formerly § 61–101(b); lease must expressly provide for creation of an estate for years rather than a "usufruct").

12. West's Ann.Cal.Civ.Code § 1941.1.

In Knight v. Hallsthammar, 29 Cal.3d 46, 171 Cal.Rptr. 707, 623 P.2d 268 (1981), the court held that the standards set out in § 1941.1 may, depending on the circumstances, be relevant to a determination of "uninhabitability," although § 1941.1 is not controlling as to breach of the "implied" warranty of habitability.

substantially like those enacted in 1970 in California.[13] In Montana and Oklahoma, however, the old provisions derived from the Field Civil Code have recently been superseded by comprehensive new legislation based upon the Uniform Residential Landlord and Tenant Act (hereafter called the URLTA).[14]

At least twenty states (including Montana and Oklahoma) have in recent years enacted legislation, based on the URLTA,[15] which includes detailed provisions imposing on landlords a duty to put and keep premises

13. See North Dakota Cent.Code §§ 47–16–13.1, 47–16–13.2, 47–16–14; South Dakota Codified Laws §§ 43–32–8, 43–32–9, 43–32–10.

14. The URLTA was published in final form and recommended for adoption by the several states in 1972. A few minor amendments were adopted by the Commissioners in 1974. All the recent amendments to the California, North Dakota, and South Dakota Civil Code provisions dealing with the condition of the leased premises seem to be based on the URLTA.

For the text of the URLTA and the Commissioners' Comments, see 7B Uniform Laws Annotated (1985). The 1974 amendments may be found in id., 1991 Pocket Part.

15. Alaska Stat. §§ 34.03.010 to 34.03.380; Ariz.Rev.Stat. §§ 33–1301 to 33–1381; Conn. Gen.Stat. §§ 47a–1 to 42a–20; West's Fla.Stat. Ann. §§ 83–40 to 83.63; Iowa Code Ann. §§ 562A.1 to 562A.37; Kan.Stat.Ann. §§ 58–2540 to 58–2573; Ky.Rev.Stat. §§ 383.505 to 383.715; Mont.Code Ann. §§ 70–24–101 to 70–24–442; Neb.Rev.Stat. §§ 76–1401 to 76–1449; Nev.Rev.Stat.Ann. §§ 118A.010 to 118A.530; N.M.Stat.Ann. §§ 47–8–1 to 47–8–51; Ohio Rev.Code §§ 5321.01 to 5321.19; 41 Okl.Stat. Ann. §§ 101 to 135; Or.Rev.Stat. §§ 90.100 to 90.435; R.I.Gen.Laws 1956, §§ 34–18–1 to 34–18–56; S.C.Code §§ 27–40–10 to 27–40–940; Tenn.Code Ann. §§ 66–28–101 to 66–28–516; Va.Code 1950, §§ 55–248.2 to 55–248.40; 9 Vt.Stat.Ann. §§ 4451 to 4468; West's Rev. Code Wash.Ann. §§ 59.18.010 to 59.18.900. (See also West's Rev.Code Wash.Ann. §§ 59.-20.010 to 59.20.900 [Mobile Home Landlord–Tenant Act.])

The list of states where the URLTA has been substantially enacted to be found in 7B Uniform Laws Annotated is inaccurate. It omits Connecticut, Nevada, Ohio, Oklahoma, Rhode Island, and Washington. In addition, Hawaii, listed in 7B ULA, appears to be based on the Model Residential Landlord–Tenant Code rather than the URLTA. See note 16, infra.

As originally enacted the Kentucky statute, supra, applied only to two counties; it was held to be unconstitutional in Miles v. Shauntee, 664 S.W.2d 512 (Ky.1983) on the ground that there was no reasonable relation between the statute's purpose and the limitation of its applicability to only two counties. In 1984 the statute was re-enacted as an enabling act applicable to all units of local government in Kentucky. As re-enacted, the statute provides that its provisions "shall be adopted in their entirety and without amendments," thus presenting Kentucky local governing bodies with an "all or nothing" approach. Failure to adopt the Kentucky statute, as re-enacted, will leave the common law in force, with the result—as held in *Miles,* supra—that no "implied" warranty of habitability will be applicable.

The Connecticut legislation, supra, was held to be inapplicable on the facts in Johnson v. Fuller, 190 Conn. 552, 461 A.2d 988 (1983), because the trial court found that for the purpose for which defendants (tenants) were using them were habitable. Although the court quoted a statement from a case antedating enactment of the URLTA in Connecticut asserting that "[i]n general, there is no implied warranty of habitability," the court clearly did not refuse to recognize the warranty of habitability contained in Conn.Gen.Stat. § 47a–7(a)(2). The contrary conclusion in Note, The Uncertain Status of the Implied Warranty of Habitability in Connecticut, 10 Univ. of Bridgeport L.Rev. 465, 479 (1990), is clearly erroneous. The *Johnson* court's quotation was apparently intended simply to indicate that at common law there was no "implied" warranty of habitability, although the relevance of this observation is unclear, given the finding that there was no breach of the statutory warranty of habitability. The *Johnson* court's additional statement that "the defect in the septic system, to wit, a broken sewer pipe * * * did not arise until * * * more than six months after the defendants (tenants) entered into possession" also seems irrelevant unless the court assumed that a warranty of habitability would not obligate the landlord to repair defects arising after the tenancy began, even if such a warranty existed in Connecticut.

The Washington version of the URLTA—which probably varies more from the text of the URLTA as approved by the Commissioners than the versions adopted in other state—has been held to preempt the field of residential landlord-tenant relations, and hence to exclude any application of the state's Consumer Protection Act. State v. Schwab, 103 Wn.2d 542, 693 P.2d 108 (1985).

leased for residential use in a habitable condition and prescribing in detail the remedies available to tenants when there is a breach of the landlord's duty. At least two other states have recently enacted similar comprehensive legislation based on the American Bar Foundation's Model Residential Landlord–Tenant Code (hereafter called the Model Code), which was itself the starting point for development of the URLTA.[16] Both the URLTA and the Model Code provide, in substance (although the term is not used), that every residential lease includes a "warranty of habitability" coupled with a continuing duty to keep the leased premises in a habitable condition.

Both the URLTA and the Model Code are applicable to substantially all residential rental units within a state, not just to rental units in multi-family dwellings or to housing covered by state or local housing codes.[17] The URLTA imposes on landlords a duty to "comply with the requirements of applicable building and housing codes materially affecting health and safety,"[18] and in addition requires landlords to "make all repairs * * * necessary to put and keep the premises in a fit and habitable condition," to "keep all common areas of the premises in a clean and safe condition," to "maintain in good and safe working order and condition all * * * facilities and appliances * * * supplied or required to be supplied by" the landlord, and to provide adequate waste disposal, water, and heat.[19] If the duty of compliance with the applicable building and housing codes "is greater than any duty imposed by" the specific provisions set out in the URLTA, "the landlord's duty shall be determined by reference to" the building and housing code provisions.[20] The duties imposed on landlords by the Model Code are substantially the same as those imposed by the URLTA,[21] although there are important differences in the sections dealing with remedies.[22]

Although the landlord-tenant codes based on the URLTA are generally quite similar, several states, in enacting their versions of the URLTA, have

16. The Model Code (Tentative Draft) was completed and published in 1969. 25 Del.C. §§ 5501 to 5517 and Hawaii Rev.Stat.Ann. §§ 521–1 to 521–77 appear to be based on the Model Code, or possibly on an early draft of the URLTA which resembled the Model Code more closely than the final version of the URLTA.

17. See URLTA § 1.201; ABF Model Code § 1–104. URLTA § 1.201 lists the following exceptions to the URLTA's coverage:

"(1) residence at an institution, public or private, if incidental to detention or of the provision of medical, geriatric, educational, counseling, religious, or similar service;

"(2) occupancy under a contract of sale of a dwelling unit or the property of which it is a part, if the occupant is the purchaser or a person who succeeds to his interest;

"(3) occupancy by a member of a fraternal or social organization in the portion of a structure operated for the benefit of the organization;

"(4) transient occupancy in a hotel, or motel [or lodgings [subject to a state tran-

sient lodgings or room occupancy excise tax act]];

"(5) occupancy by an employee of a landlord whose right to occupancy is conditional upon employment in and about the premises;

"(6) occupancy by an owner of a condominium unit or a holder of a proprietary lease in a cooperative;

"(7) occupancy under a rental agreement covering premises used by the occupant primarily for agricultural purposes."

18. URLTA § 2.104(a)(1).

19. Id. § 2.104(a)(2) through (6).

20. Id. § 2.104(b). The Commissioners' Comment to § 2.104 states that it "follows the warranty of habitability doctrine" judicially developed in a number of jurisdictions such as California, Washington, D.C., Hawaii, Illinois, Michigan, New Hampshire, New Jersey, and Washington.

21. Model ABF Code § 2–201.

22. See post Sections 6.41 through 6.45.

made substantial changes in the coverage of the statute [23] and/or in the scope of the duty imposed on the landlord to put and keep the leased premises in a habitable condition.[24] It is clear, however, that the statutes based on the URLTA impose a greater duty on landlords than do the statutes previously considered in the section dealing with "The Housing Code Approach," for the URLTA-derived statutes require a landlord to keep a rented dwelling unit habitable even if it is not covered by a housing code at all, and to keep it in compliance with standards that may be higher than those imposed by the applicable housing code where the premises are subject to housing code requirements. Statutes based on the URLTA generally do not expressly provide that the landlord must have a rented dwelling unit "habitable" at the beginning of the tenancy, but a careful reading of the provisions as to the landlord's duty together with the provisions as to remedies for breach of the duty makes it clear that there is an immediate breach of the landlord's duty if the dwelling unit is not habitable at the beginning of the tenancy, although some remedies may not be utilized by the tenant until a stated time after the landlord has been notified of the breach, during which time the landlord has an opportunity to cure the breach.[25]

---

23. E.g., Ariz.Rev.Stat. § 33–1308(7) and West's Rev.Code Wash.Ann. 59.18.040(7) exclude public housing; Hawaii Rev.Stat.Ann. § 521–7(7) excludes leases for 15 years or more, and Neb.Rev.Stat. § 76–1408(8) excludes leases for 5 years or more; and Va.Code 1950, § 55–248.5(10) excludes any single-family residence whose landlord owns ten or more residences.

A summary of some of the changes may be found in 7B Uniform Laws Annotated (1991 Pocket Part), but it is there indicated that in many states there are numerous variations from the text of the URLTA which cannot be clearly identified in the annotations.

24. West's Rev.Code Wash.Ann. 59.18.060, e.g., states the landlord's duty in more detail:

"The landlord will at all times during the tenancy keep the premises fit for human habitation, and shall in particular:

(1) Maintain the premises to substantially comply with any applicable code, statute, ordinance, or regulation governing their maintenance or operation, which the legislative body enacting the applicable code, statute, ordinance or regulation could enforce as to the premises rented;

(2) Maintain the roofs, floors, walls, chimneys, fireplaces, foundations, and all other structural components in reasonably good repair so as to be usable and capable of resisting any and all normal forces and loads to which they may be subjected;

(3) Keep any shared or common areas reasonably clean, sanitary, and safe from defects increasing the hazards of fire or accident;

(4) Provide a reasonable program for the control of infestation by insects, rodents, and other pests at the initiation of the tenancy and control infestation during tenancy except where such infestation is caused by the tenant;

(5) Except where the condition is attributable to normal wear and tear, make repairs and arrangements necessary to put and keep the premises in as good condition as it by law or rental agreement should have been, at the commencement of the tenancy;

(6) Provide reasonably adequate locks and furnish keys to the tenant;

(7) Maintain all electrical, plumbing, heating, and other facilities and appliances supplied by him in reasonably good working order;

(8) Maintain the dwelling unit in reasonably weather-tight condition;

(9) Except in the case of a single family residence, provide and maintain appropriate receptacles in common areas for the removal of ashes, rubbish, and garbage, incidental to the occupancy and arrange for the reasonable and regular removal of such waste.

(10) Except where the building is not equipped for the purpose, provide facilities adequate to supply heat and water and hot water as reasonably required by the tenant."

Compare 41 Okla.Stat.Ann. § 118, which omits any reference to building or housing codes and expressly limits the duties of the landlord with respect to "common areas," waste disposal, and supplying heat and water to rental units within a multi-family dwelling.

25. URLTA §§ 2.104, 4.101, 4.103, 4.104; Model ABF Code §§ 2–203 through 2–207.

It is also clear that the URLTA, the Model Code, and all the statutes based on one or the other, make no distinction between "latent" and "patent" defects in existence at the inception of the tenancy.[26] There is nothing in the URLTA, Model Code, or the statutes based on one or the other, to suggest that the tenant may not treat serious "patent" defects as causing an immediate breach of the statutory warranty of habitability, or that such defects are not subject to the landlord's duty to "make all repairs * * * necessary to put and keep the premises in a fit and habitable condition."

In recent years a number of jurisdictions have enacted new landlord-tenant legislation, not based on the URLTA or the Model Code, which imposes on the landlord a duty similar to that imposed by the URLTA—a duty to provide the tenant with a habitable dwelling.[27] Some of this legislation provides a comprehensive new landlord-tenant code somewhat like the URLTA, although not based upon it, and some of the legislation merely superimposes the new statutory duty with respect to habitability upon pre-existing judge-made and statutory landlord-tenant law. Legislation of the first type is exemplified by the Texas statute.[28] Legislation of the second type is more common, but varies considerably in content.[29] For example, the Maine and New York statutes[30] create a warranty that premises leased for residential use *are* habitable, without creating an express duty to *keep* them in a habitable condition, but the Idaho, Michigan, Minnesota, and West Virginia statutes,[31] in addition, expressly require the landlord to *keep* the premises in a habitable condition. The Michigan, Minnesota, and West Virginia statutes[32] also require the landlord to keep the premises in compliance with applicable housing codes. The Wisconsin statute[33] imposes a duty on the landlord to maintain the premises in a habitable condition but does not expressly state that there is any "warranty" or "covenant" that the premises are habitable at the beginning of the tenancy. Some of the new statutes not based upon the URLTA or the Model Code expressly provide for tenant remedies when there is a breach of the landlord's duties,[34] and where the statutes do not so provide, the courts have nevertheless provided "contractual" remedies on the theory that performance of the landlord's duty is a condition precedent to performance of the

---

26. Cf. Kline v. Burns, 111 N.H. 87, 276 A.2d 248 (1971) ("implied warranty of habitability * * * [which means] that at the inception of the rental there are no latent defects in facilities vital to the use of the premises for residential purposes and that these essential facilities will remain during the entire term in a condition which makes the property livable").

27. This legislation includes D.C. Landlord–Tenant Regulations § 2902.2 (1970); Idaho Code §§ 6–320 to 6–323; 14 Me.Rev.Stat. Ann. § 6021; Md.Code, Real Prop., § 8–211 et seq.; Mich.Comp.Laws Ann. § 554.139; Minn. Stat.Ann. § 504.18; N.Y.—McKinney's Real Prop.Law § 235–b; N.C.Gen.Stat. §§ 42–42 to 42–44 (1974); Vernon's Tex.C.A.Prop.Code

§§ 92.051 to 92.262 (1991); Utah Code Ann. §§ 57–22–1 to 57–22–5; W.Va.Code, § 37–6–30; Wis.Stat.Ann. § 704.07.

28. Supra note 27.

29. See D.C., Idaho, Maryland, Michigan, Minnesota, New York, North Carolina, Utah, West Virginia, and Wisconsin legislation, supra note 27.

30. Supra note 27.

31. Ibid.

32. Ibid.

33. Ibid.

34. E.g., the Idaho, Maine, and Wisconsin statutes, supra note 27.

tenant's duties.[35] The Maine statute [36] provides: "Municipalities of this State are empowered to adopt or retain more stringent standards by ordinance, laws or regulations [than are] provided by this section. Any less stringent ordinance, law or regulation establishing standards are [sic] invalid and of no force and suspended by this section."

Presumably in jurisdictions where the courts first recognized an implied warranty of habitability and the legislatures later enacted comprehensive statutes imposing a duty on residential landlords to put and keep leased dwelling units in habitable condition and detailing the remedies available to tenants for breach of this duty, these statutes have largely, if not entirely, pre-empted the field.[37] By contrast, where the legislature has merely provided new tenant remedies for violation of applicable housing codes, the courts have sometimes also recognized an implied warranty of habitability and allowed additional remedies for breach of the implied warranty.[38] And in California, where there has for over a century been a statutory warranty of fitness for use and a landlord duty to keep leased premises in repair, the courts have recognized an implied warranty of habitability as well, and have allowed remedies for breach of the implied warranty in addition to the specifically prescribed remedies for breach of the statutory warranty of habitability.[39]

§ 6.40 Can the Benefit of the Warranty of Habitability Be Waived?

The original California, Montana, North Dakota, South Dakota, and Oklahoma Civil Code provisions imposing a duty on landlords to put and keep leased premises in a tenantable condition were, from an early date, capable of being waived by "an agreement to the contrary." [1] But a 1970 amendment to the California provision invalidates any waiver of the tenant's rights "with respect to any condition which renders the premises untenantable" unless the tenant agrees "to improve, repair or maintain all or stipulated portions of the dwelling as part of the consideration for the rental"; [2] and a 1976 amendment to the South Dakota provision provides

35. See discussion of tenant's remedies infra Sections 6.41 through 6.45.

36. 14 Me.Rev.Stat.Ann. § 6021 (concluding paragraph).

37. For an instance where the implied warranty has broader coverage than the statutory warranty, see ante Section 6.38, note 23.

Vernon's Tex.C.A., Prop.Code §§ 92.061 expressly provides that the duties of the landlord and the remedies of the tenant under §§ 92.051 to 92.061 "are in lieu of existing common law and other statutory law warranties and duties of landlords for maintenance, repair, security, habitability, and nonretaliation, and remedies of tenants for a violation of those warranties and duties."

38. This is the case in Massachusetts. Compare Mass.Gen.Laws Ann. c. 239, § 8A and c. 111, §§ 127A–127N with Boston Housing Authority v. Hemingway, 363 Mass. 184,

293 N.E.2d 831 (1973). Both of the cited statutes were originally enacted in 1965.

39. Compare   West's   Ann.Cal.Civ.Code §§ 1941, 1942 with Green v. Superior Court, 10 Cal.2d 616, 111 Cal.Rptr. 704, 517 P.2d 1168 (1974).

§ 6.40

1. The quoted language was added to West's Ann.Cal.Civ.Code § 1941 in 1873–74 (see Legislative History, West's Session Laws 1972), and was apparently added later to the cognate provisions in Montana, the Dakota Territory, and Oklahoma. If the lessor's duty is negated by "an agreement to the contrary," the lessee cannot, of course, utilize either of the remedies provided in West's Ann.Cal.Civ. Code § 1942. See, e.g., Curtis v. Arnold, 43 Cal.App. 97, 184 P. 510 (1919); Arnold v. Krigbaum, 169 Cal. 143, 146 P. 423 (1915).

2. West's Ann.Cal.Civ.Code § 1942.1.

that the parties to a lease "may not waive or modify the requirements imposed by" the statute, with the single exception that "the lessor may agree with the lessee that the lessee shall perform specified repairs or maintenance in lieu of rent."[3]

Most of the statutes based on the URLTA contain, in substance, the URLTA provision that no rental agreement may include any agreement waiving the tenant's rights or remedies under the statute,[4] subject to the following exceptions:[5]

(c) The landlord and tenant of a single family residence may agree in writing that the tenant perform the landlord duties * * * [with respect to providing facilities for waste removal and supplying running water, hot water, and heat] and also specified repairs, maintenance tasks, alterations, and remodeling, but only if the transaction is entered into in good faith and not for the purpose of evading the obligations of the landlord.

(d) The landlord and tenant of any dwelling unit other than a single family residence may agree that the tenant is to perform specified repairs, maintenance tasks, alterations, or remodeling only if (1) the agreement of the parties is entered into in good faith and not for the purpose of evading the obligations of the landlord and is set forth in a separate writing, (2) the work is not necessary to cure noncompliance with * * * [the requirements of applicable building or housing codes materially affecting health and safety]; and (3) the agreement does not diminish or affect the obligation of the landlord to other tenants in the premises.

(e) The landlord may not treat performance of the separate written agreement described in subsection (c) as a condition to any obligation or performance of any rental agreement.

Although paragraph (c), above, does not expressly say that the written agreement between the landlord and tenant of a single family dwelling may not be included in the lease itself, a separate written agreement may arguably be required by the more general URLTA provision that any waiver clause prohibited by statute which is "included in a rental agreement is unenforceable."[6] The general anti-waiver section of the URLTA also contains a curious additional provision that, "[i]f a landlord deliberately uses a

See Knight v. Hallsthammar, 29 Cal.3d 46, 171 Cal.Rptr. 707, 623 P.2d 268 (1981) (tenants did not waive benefit of "implied" warranty, despite their possible failure to inspect the premises and their continued occupancy of the premises after discovery of defects; the court relied both on the statutory scheme of which § 1942.1 is a part and on the policy considerations underlying the "implied" warranty of habitability).

3. South Dakota Codified Law 43–32–8.

4. URLTA § 1.403. The Commissioners' Comment indicates that the purpose of this provision is to invalidate "adhesive clauses" in form leases "provided by landlords."

5. URLTA § 2.104(c), (d), (e).

The amendments approved by the Commissioners in 1974 deleted the phrase "and not for the purpose of evading the obligations of the landlord" in § 2.104(c), (d)(1). The original wording, as set out in the text herein, remains in force in Alaska, Arizona, Kansas, Kentucky, Montana, Nebraska, and New Mexico. The amended version is in force in Iowa. In Connecticut, Nevada, Rhode Island, Oregon, Tennessee, and Virginia subsection (d)(1) is omitted and these state's version of subsection (c) omits "and not for the purpose of evading the obligations of the landlord." In Florida, Ohio, Vermont, and Washington both subsection (c) and (d)(1) are omitted.

6. Id. § 1.403(b).

rental agreement containing provisions known by him to be prohibited, the tenant may recover in addition to his actual damages an amount up to [3] month's periodic rent and reasonable attorney's fees." [7] This seems a rather drastic penalty for use of a standard form lease that may purport to impose on the tenant the duty to make repairs within his own dwelling unit, but was apparently included for its *in terrorem* effect. Presumably the penalty is recoverable only if "actual damages" resulting from inclusion of a prohibited provision can be proved, although this is not entirely clear. If the agreement shifting repair duties to the tenant is placed in a separate written agreement that satisfies paragraphs (c) through (e), above,[8] it would seem that no penalty should be imposed on the landlord simply because the same agreement was also included in the lease.

There are significant variations from the URLTA waiver provisions set out above, in some of the states with statutes based on the URLTA—e.g., Kentucky,[9] Oregon,[10] and Washington.[11] The statutes based on the Model Code are substantially like those based on the URLTA insofar as they generally prohibit any effective waiver of the tenant's rights under the statutes and then expressly provide for agreements that shift the burden of maintenance, to a limited extent, from the landlord to the tenant. The Delaware statute [12] follows the Model Code [13] in requiring the agreement to be placed in a "conspicuous writing independent of the rental agreement" and to be "supported by adequate consideration apart from the rental

---

7. Ibid.

8. Supra note 5 and text therewith.

9. Kentucky Rev.Stat. 383.595, cognate with URLTA § 2.104, does not include in its para. (c) any authorization to shift to the tenant the duty of supplying facilities for waste removal, and omits para. (e) altogether.

See supra Section 6.39 note 15 for discussion of the Kentucky statute's current status as a municipal government enabling act rather than a statutory mandate applicable on a state-wide basis.

10. Oregon Rev.Stat. 91.770(2) cognate with URLTA § 2.104, includes the following provisions in lieu of id. paras. (c) through (e):

"The landlord and tenant may agree in writing that the tenant is to perform specified repairs, maintenance tasks and minor remodeling only if:

(a) The agreement of the parties is entered into in good faith and not for the purpose of evading the obligations of the landlord;

(b) The agreement does not diminish the obligations of the landlord to other tenants in the premises; and

(c) The terms and conditions of the agreement are clearly and fairly disclosed and adequate consideration for the agreement is specifically stated."

11. West's Rev.Code Wash.Ann. 59.18.360 allows agreements exempting the parties from the statute's protective provisions, subject to the following limitations:

"(1) The agreement may not appear in a standard form lease or rental agreement;

(2) There is no substantial inequality in the bargaining position of the two parties;

(3) The exemption does not violate the public policy of this state in favor of the ensuring safe, and sanitary housing; and

(4) Either the local county prosecutor's office or the consumer protection division of the attorney general's office or the attorney for the tenant has approved in writing the application for exemption as complying with subsections (1) through (3) of this section."

This provision leaves a number of questions for future judicial decision. For example, whether the public policy mentioned in subsection (3) is violated (a) by any violation of an applicable housing or building code, no matter how trivial, and (b) by the existence of conditions that render the leased premises unsafe or unsanitary but are not violations of any applicable housing or building code; and whether the approval of a proposed waiver by the local prosecutor's office, consumer protection division of the attorney general's office, or the tenant's attorney is binding on the tenant. It would seem that the tenant should be estopped when the approval is given by his own attorney; but it is not so clear that he should be estopped when the approval is given by either of the other agencies mentioned in subsection (4).

12. 25 Del.C. § 5115.

13. Model ABF Code § 2–203(2), (3).

agreement"; but the Hawaii statute,[14] also based on the Model Code, omits these requirements for an effective waiver.

Of those statutes which create a warranty of habitability but are not part of a comprehensive new landlord-tenant code based on the URLTA or the Model Act, the Michigan and Rhode Island statutes authorize a "modification" of the statutory warranty or covenant of habitability where the lease or letting has a term of "at least 1 year" (Michigan)[15] or of "nine months or more" (Rhode Island).[16] Neither the Michigan nor the Rhode Island statute expressly requires the modification to be embodied in a separate written agreement or even to be in writing. The Minnesota statute,[17] which is otherwise very similar to Michigan's, declares that the parties to a lease "may not waive or modify the covenants imposed by" the statute. The Maine statute [18] provides that "[a] written agreement whereby the tenant accepts certain specified conditions which may violate the warranty of fitness for human habitation in return for a stated reduction in rent or other specified fair consideration shall be binding on the tenant and the landlord. Any [other] agreement * * * by a tenant to waive any of the rights or benefits provided by this section shall be void." The New York statute simply states that any waiver or modification agreement "shall be void as contrary to public policy." [19] The West Virginia statute [20] says nothing about waiver, but the West Virginia court has recently said that a waiver of "the protection accorded by the implied warranty and the statutes" giving the same protection to residential tenants is "against public policy." [21]

Where "implied" warranties of habitability have been judicially created, without express statutory provision therefor, most of the cases have followed Javins v. First National Realty Corp.[22] in rejecting the possibility of an effective waiver of the protection afforded to tenants by the "implied" warranty. None of the cases,[23] however, has dealt with the fact situation envisaged by the URLTA, where the parties enter into a separate written

---

14. Hawaii Rev.Stat.Ann. § 521–42.

15. Mich.Comp.Laws Ann. § 554.139.

16. Rhode Island Gen.Laws 1956, § 34–18–16.

17. Minn.Stat.Ann. § 504.18.

18. 14 Me.Rev.Stat.Ann. § 6021(5).

19. N.Y.—McKinney's Real Prop.Law § 235b.

20. West Va.Code, § 37–6–30, which is based on URLTA § 2.104.

21. Teller v. McCoy, 162 W.Va. 367, 253 S.E.2d 114 (1978) (holding that an "implied" warranty of habitability identical with the new statutory warranty—supra note 20—was already in force prior to enactment of statute).

22. 428 F.2d 1071, 1080 n. 49, 1082 n. 58 (D.C.Cir.1970) certiorari denied 400 U.S. 925, 91 S.Ct. 186, 27 L.Ed.2d 185 (1970) (court refused to consider whether tenant's express covenant to repair constituted a waiver of the "implied" warranty of habitability because it could not be waived; any agreement to shift the burden of compliance with the housing code to the tenant would be illegal and unenforceable).

23. See, holding or saying that any attempted waiver is invalid, Green v. Superior Court, 10 Cal.3d 616, 625 n. 9, 111 Cal.Rptr. 704, 709 n. 9, 517 P.2d 1168, 1173 n. 9 (1974) ("landlords generally [should] not be permitted to use their superior bargaining power to negate the warranty of habitability rule"); Knight v. Hallsthammer, 29 Cal.3d 46, 171 Cal.Rptr. 707, 623 P.2d 268 (1981) (tenant's knowledge of defects in apartment at beginning of tenancy does not waive right to assert "implied" warranty of habitability in landlord's unlawful detainer action); Boston Housing Authority v. Hemingway, 363 Mass. 184, 199, 293 N.E.2d 831, 843 (1973) ("This warranty (in so far as it is based on the State Sanitary Code and local health regulations) cannot be waived by any provision in the lease"); Foisy v. Wyman, 83 Wn.2d 22, 28, 515 P.2d 160, 164 (1973) ("this type of bargaining by the landlord with the tenant is contrary to public policy and the purpose of the doctrine of implied warranty"); Teller v. McCoy, supra note 21.

agreement, for an adequate consideration, to shift at least some maintenance duties from the landlord to the tenant.

In those states where the courts have not yet decided whether the benefit of the "implied" warranty of habitability can be waived, Section 5.6 of the Landlord and Tenant part of the Second Property Restatement [24] seems likely to influence future judicial decisions on that point. Section 5.6 allows the parties by agreement "to increase or decrease what would otherwise be the obligations of the landlord with respect to the condition of the leased property and * * * to expand or contract what would otherwise be the remedies available to the tenant for the breach of those obligations," provided the agreement is not "unconscionable or significantly against public policy." A wide variety of factors "which may be considered in determining whether an agreement in a lease is in whole or in part unenforceable because unconscionable or against public policy" is listed in a Comment.[25]

The Second Property Restatement unequivocally states in another Comment that "[t]he tenant as a matter of law is unable to waive any remedies [for breach of the landlord's duty] available to him at the time of entry, if at the time of entry it would be unsafe or unhealthy to use the leased premises in the manner contemplated by the parties," [26] and further states in a Reporter's Note that "[t]he rule of this section does not allow waiver of housing code violations" because of "public policy considerations." [27] The latter statement clearly goes beyond a mere refusal to allow waiver when there are conditions on the leased premises hazardous to health or safety, since it is obvious that not all housing code violations endanger health or safety and that many violations are quite trivial in character.[28]

---

24. Am.L.Inst., Rest.Prop.2d, Landlord and Tenant § 5.6 (1977).

25. Id., § 5.6, Comment e (emphasis added).

26. Id., § 5.3, Comment c. The following factors would seem to be the most relevant to residential leases:

(1) Whether and to what extent the agreement will be counter to the policy underlying statutory or regulatory provisions, especially those relating to the public health and safety and those relating to the tenants of moderate income in multi-unit residential * * * properties;

(2) Whether the agreement * * * appears in a lease of * * * a substantial residence or estate designed for single family occupancy, * * * concerning which freedom of negotiation is usually permissible;

(3) Whether and to what extent the agreement * * * appears to have been the result of conscious negotiations for the distribution of risks as part of the total bargain contained in the lease;

(4) Whether the provision appears to be part of an unduly harsh and unreasonable standard, "boilerplate" lease document;

(5) Whether and to what extent the parties or either of them, habitually (or on a discriminatory basis) disregard and do not enforce the agreement * * * in actual operations under the lease or, in the case of a landlord, under similar leases;

(6) Whether and to what extent the agreement * * * (especially if it relates to low or moderate income residential property) imposes unconscionable * * * burdens on persons who are financially ill-equipped to assume those burdens and who may have had significant inequality of bargaining power;

(7) Whether and to what extent the parties were each represented by counsel in the course of negotiating the lease.

Note, however, that Comment d, § 5.3 (Landlord–Tenant part) provides: "The parties may expressly or impliedly agree that the landlord is to have a reasonable time after the tenant's entry to make the condition of the leased property suitable for the use contemplated by the parties. * * * In this situation the reasonable time is measured from the date of the tenant's entry."

27. Id. § 5.3, Reporter's Note 3.

28. Although id. § 5.1 creates a "implied" warranty of suitability for residential use that would not be broken by unsubstantial housing

The general tendency of the legislatures and the courts to prohibit waivers of the tenant's rights under statutory or judicially created warranties of habitability illustrates the point—extensively documented in a recent article—that the period from 1960 to the present has witnessed "the transition of residential leases from the private law fields of property and contract to an area in which public regulatory law predominates." [29]

§ 6.41   Remedies for Landlord's Breach of Duty—Termination

Breach of the statutory warranty of habitability adopted at an early date in California and several other states gives the tenant the right to terminate the tenancy and avoid any further liability for rent.[1]   The same remedy for breach is provided in those jurisdictions which have adopted comprehensive landlord-tenant codes based on the Uniform Residential Landlord and Tenant Act, provided the landlord's breach of duty "materially" affects the tenant's health and safety and the tenant complies with stated "notice" requirements.[2]

Where the duty to put and keep the premises in habitable condition is imposed on the landlord by judicial decision rather than by statute, the courts have generally held (or said) that performance of the landlord's warranty obligation and performance of the tenant's obligations are mutual-

---

code violations—see Comment e following the § 5.1 blackletter—§ 5.5 creates (*inter alia*) a continuing duty of the landlord "to keep the leased property in a condition that meets the requirements of governing health, safety, and housing codes" not qualified by any language indicating that the duty is only to keep the property free from substantial code violations that affect health or safety. It thus appears that the draftsman's intent was not to allow effective waiver of the tenant's right to have full compliance with all housing code requirements, however unsubstantial, or even trivial, in nature.

29.   Glendon, The Transformation of American Landlord–Tenant Law, 23 B.C.L.Rev. 503, 552 (1982).

§ 6.41

1.   West's Ann.Cal.Civ.Code § 1942; La.— LSA–C.C. art. 2729 (breach may "give cause for a dissolution of the lease"); North Dakota Cent.Code 47–16–13; South Dakota Codified Law 43–32–9.

2.   URLTA § 4.101(a) provides as follows:

Except as provided in this Act, if there is a material noncompliance by the landlord with the rental agreement or a noncompliance with Section 2.104 materially affecting health and safety, the tenant may deliver a written notice to the landlord specifying the acts and omissions constituting the breach and that the rental agreement will terminate upon a date not less than [30] days after receipt of the notice if the breach is not remedied in [14] days, and the rental agreement shall terminate as provided in the notice subject to the following:

(1) If the breach is remedial by repairs, the payment of damages or otherwise and the landlord adequately remedies the breach before the date specified in the notice, the rental agreement shall not terminate by reason of the breach.

(2) If substantially the same act or omission which constituted a prior noncompliance of which notice was given recurs within [6] months, the tenant may terminate the rental agreement upon at least [14 days'] written notice specifying the breach and the date of termination of the rental agreement.

(3) The tenant may not terminate for a condition caused by the deliberate or negligent act or omission of the tenant, a member of his family, or other person on the premises with his consent.

The state statutes modelled on this URLTA vary in the time periods specified for remedy of the landlord's breach of the statutory warranty of habitability and for termination of the rental agreement.   E.g., Conn.Gen.Stat. Ann. § 47a–12(a) provides in part that "[i]f the breach is not remedied in twenty-one days, the rental agreement shall terminate nine days thereafter. If substantially the same act or omission which constituted a prior noncompliance of which notice was given, recurs within six months of the first act of noncompliance, the tenant may terminate the rental agreement upon at least fourteen days written notice specifying (1) the date the breach complained of occurred and (2) the date the tenant intends to terminate the rental agreement by vacating the premises, which date shall be within thirty days of such breach."

ly dependent and, consequently, that the landlord's breach of the implied warranty of habitability entitles the tenant to terminate the lease and avoid further rent liability.[3] In jurisdictions where there is a statutory warranty of habitability not accompanied by any express provision as to the remedies for breach, the tenant presumably has the same option to terminate as in jurisdictions where recognition of the implied warranty of habitability is entirely a result of judicial action.[4] Whatever the source of the new rule imposing on the landlord a duty to put and keep the premises leased for residential use in "habitable" condition, the tenant must vacate the premises if he wishes to terminate the tenancy. If the tenant is willing to vacate the premises, he may, in substance, treat the landlord's breach of duty as a "constructive eviction."[5]

The traditional rule is that a tenant cannot assert that he has been constructively evicted and avoid liability for further rent unless he has vacated the premises within a reasonable time after the landlord's breach of duty occurs.[6] When termination for breach of the implied warranty of habitability is the basis of the tenant's defense, however, it may well be that the "reasonable time" limitation will be relaxed or even eliminated since most courts have held that a tenant may withhold rent because of a breach of the implied warranty without having to vacate the premises. Courts may well decide that a tenant, after a breach of the implied warranty, may stay in possession and withhold rent for a very substantial time without forfeiting the right ultimately to terminate the lease and vacate the premises. In any case, where there is a serious shortage of rental housing the courts are likely to hold that even a long delay before terminating the lease and vacating the premises is "reasonable." But the tenant's right to terminate is still likely to depend in part upon his having taken reasonable steps to notify the

---

3. Termination—often called "rescission" in the cases—requires the tenant to vacate the premises and is, obviously, very similar to a traditional "constructive eviction" based on the landlord's failure to perform an express covenant to maintain the premises in a habitable condition, to keep it in repair, or to provide essential services. The termination remedy is recognized in Javins v. First National Realty Corp., 428 F.2d 1071 (D.C.Cir.1970), certiorari denied 400 U.S. 925, 91 S.Ct. 186, 27 L.Ed.2d 185 (1970) (dictum: all contract remedies are extended—428 F.2d at 1082 n. 61); Lemle v. Breeden, 51 Hawaii 426, 462 P.2d 470 (1969); Lund v. MacArthur, 51 Hawaii 473, 462 P.2d 482 (1969); Old Town Development Co. v. Langford, 349 N.E.2d 744 (Ind. App.1976), superseded 267 Ind. 176, 369 N.E.2d 404 (1977) (dictum); Steele v. Latimer, 214 Kan. 329, 521 P.2d 304 (1974) (dictum: "traditional remedies for breach of contract are available to the tenant"); Boston Housing Authority v. Hemingway, 363 Mass. 184, 293 N.E.2d 831 (1973) (dictum); King v. Moorehead, 495 S.W.2d 65 (Mo.App.1973) (dictum: "the basic remedies for contract law, including * * * rescission, * * * are available to the tenant"); Kline v. Burns, 111 N.H. 87, 276 A.2d 248 (1971) (dictum—same); Marini v. Ireland, 56 N.J. 130, 265 A.2d 526 (1970) (dic-

tum); Tonetti v. Penati, 48 A.D.2d 25, 367 N.Y.S.2d 804 (2d Dept.1975) (holding); Pugh v. Holmes, 486 Pa. 272, 405 A.2d 897 (1979) (dictum: "tenant may vacate the premises where the landlord materially breaches the implied warranty of habitability. * * * Surrender of possession by the tenant would terminate his obligation to pay rent under the lease"); Teller v. McCoy, 162 W.Va. 367, 253 S.E.2d 114 (1978) ("material breach * * * [gives the tenant the remedy of] rescission"). Termination is also authorized by Rest.Prop. 2d, Landlord & Tenant §§ 5.1(1), 5.4(1) and 5.5(4). Id. § 10.1 prescribes the procedure for termination.

4. Wis.Stat.Ann. 704.107, e.g., expressly provides for termination upon breach of the landlord's statutory duty. Some of the statutes creating warranties or covenants of habitability, however, do not expressly provide for any remedies in the event of breach of the landlord's duty. See, e.g., Mich.Comp.Laws Ann. § 554.139; Minn.Stat.Ann. § 504–18; N.Y.—McKinney's Real Prop.Law § 235–b.

5. See ante Section 6.33.

6. E.g., Reste Realty Corp. v. Cooper, 53 N.J. 444, 251 A.2d 268 (1969) (holding; case involved commercial lease, however).

landlord of his decision to terminate and the reason for termination, and the continuance of the landlord's breach until the time specified for termination.[7]

As previously indicated, the tenant cannot terminate or "rescind" the lease because of the landlord's breach of duty without vacating the premises. But the question whether the tenant was entitled to terminate is likely to be tested in an action by the landlord for recovery of unpaid rent. If the court finds that the tenant was not in fact entitled to terminate the lease—either because there was no breach of the landlord's duty, or because the tenant failed to vacate within a reasonable time, or because the tenant failed to give notices required by statute, or because the landlord cured the breach before the tenant vacated—the defense will be rejected and the tenant will remain liable for the agreed rent for the balance of the lease term.[8] Hence, if there is any doubt as to the tenant's right to terminate, it will be advisable for him to obtain a declaratory judgment as to his rights before vacating, as the tenant did in Charles E. Burt, Inc. v. Seven Grand Corp.[9] Although none of the statutes authorizing termination expressly provides for such a declaratory judgment, it seems clear that none of them would preclude it if declaratory judgments are otherwise available in the jurisdiction.

Assuming that the tenant has effectively terminated the lease because of the landlord's breach of an implied warranty of habitability, or the statutory equivalent, thus relieving himself of further liability for rent under the lease, the tenant is also entitled to a judgment either for restitution or for damages. If the tenant has paid rent in advance or made a security deposit and later terminates the lease before his right to possession accrues, he is clearly entitled to recover all the advance rent paid plus any security deposit either on a restitutionary theory or as damages.[10] In the more common situation where the tenant terminates and vacates the premises after having been in possession, most of the cases hold that the tenant is liable for the agreed rent for the period of his possession, subject to an offsetting claim for damages for the landlord's breach of the warranty of habitability.[11] The URLTA adopts the same rule.[12]

7. Compare "notice" requirements in URLTA § 4.101(a), supra note 2. Model ABF Code § 2–205 does not require notice to the landlord if "the condition renders the dwelling unit uninhabitable or poses an imminent threat to the health or safety of any occupant." Rest.Prop.2d, Landlord & Tenant § 10.1 requires the tenant to vacate and to take "reasonable steps to assure that the landlord has knowledge of his decision to terminate the lease and the reason therefor."

8. See, e.g., Reste Realty Corp. v. Cooper, supra note 6; Lemle v. Breeden, 51 Hawaii 426, 462 P.2d 470 (1969).

9. 340 Mass. 124, 163 N.E.2d 4 (1959) ("The trial judge could properly (1) declare that Seven Grand's material breach of the lease constituted, or would constitute, a constructive eviction upon Burt's abandonment of the premises, and that Burt, upon such abandonment, was or would be excused from further perfor-

mance of the lease, and (2) assess damages." Id. at 130, 163 N.E.2d at 7.)

10. In such a case, where the lease never becomes operative as a "conveyance," the tenant's right to recover back anything paid on the "lease contract" is clear; and if the tenant seeks nothing more, it is immaterial whether the tenant relies on a restitutionary or a damage theory. The tenant may, of course, assert his claim either in an independent action or as a counterclaim in an action by the landlord for rent.

11. E.g., Lund v. MacArthur, 51 Hawaii 473, 462 P.2d 482 (1969); Mease v. Fox, 200 N.W.2d 791 (Iowa 1972); Berzito v. Gambino, 63 N.J. 460, 308 A.2d 17 (1973). Cf. Pines v. Perssion, 14 Wis.2d 590, 597, 111 N.W.2d 409, 413 (1961), where the court said that the landlord's breach of duty relieved the tenants of any "liability for rent under the lease and their only liability is for the reasonable rental

12. See note 12 on page 324.

§ 6.42 Remedies for Breach of the Landlord's Duty—Damages

There seems to be unanimous agreement that a breach of the landlord's "implied" or statutory duty to put and keep the leased premises in a habitable condition entitles the tenant to a damage recovery, whether the tenant does or does not terminate the lease.[1] As several courts have pointed out, the tenant may often prefer not to terminate the lease because it would be difficult for him to find another place to live in most urban areas, which are generally characterized by a "scarcity of adequate low cost housing."[2]

The Uniform Residential Landlord and Tenant Act[3] and all the statutes based on the URLTA expressly authorize the recovery of damages by the tenant for breach of the landlord's basic duty to put and keep the premises in a habitable condition. Neither the Model Residential Landlord–Tenant Code nor the two statutes based on the Model Code contains such authorization. Nor does the URLTA contain any general formula for measuring the tenant's damages when there is a breach of the landlord's statutory duty. But both the URLTA and the Model Act in effect supply a special damage formula in sections authorizing self-help remedies in cases where the landlord (1) fails to keep leased premises in a safe and sanitary condition and/or (2) to provide essential services, as required by the lease ("rental agreement") and/or any applicable housing code.[4] The statutes based on the

---

12.¤H See note 12 on page 324.value of the premises during the time of actual occupancy," but did not indicate whether the breach simply suspended the tenants' duty to pay rent, leaving the lease otherwise in force, or made the lease void *ab initio* so that the tenant was only a tenant at will or from period to period.

12. URLTA § 4.101(b), (c).

§ 6.42

1. Steele v. Latimer, 214 Kan. 329, 521 P.2d 304 (1974), seems to be the only appellate case where the tenant stayed in possession and sued for damages. But most of the cases allowing the tenant to sue or counterclaim for damages after vacating the leased premises indicate that the damage remedy would have been available whether or not the tenant chose to vacate (and thus terminate the lease) or stay in possession (and thus "affirm" the lease). Accord: Rest.Prop.2d Landlord and Tenant §§ 5.1, 5.2, 5.4, 5.5, 10.2 (1977). The right to recover damages was recognized in Detling v. Edelbrock, 671 S.W.2d 265 (Mo. 1984), although the tenants apparently did not originally seek damages.

It should be emphasized that the tenant, after terminating or "rescinding" the lease because of the landlord's breach of duty, may generally recover all the damages to which he is entitled either in an independent action or by counterclaim in an action by the landlord for unpaid rent. As a practical matter, the issue is likely to be raised only if the landlord elects to sue for unpaid rent, so the tenant's right to recover damages is most often asserted by way of counterclaim. See, e.g., Lemle v. Breeden, 51 Hawaii 426, 462 P.2d 470 (1969);

Lund v. MacArthur, 51 Hawaii 473, 462 P.2d 482 (1969); Mease v. Fox, 200 N.W.2d 791 (Iowa 1972); Boston Housing Authority v. Hemingway, 363 Mass. 184, 293 N.E.2d 831 (1973); King v. Moorehead, 495 S.W.2d 65 (Mo.App.1973). Compare Berzito v. Gambino, 63 N.J. 460, 308 A.2d 17 (1973), where the tenant sued to recover part of the rent already paid and the landlord counterclaimed for the amount of rent remitted to the plaintiff in an earlier eviction action.

2. Green v. Superior Court, 10 Cal.2d 616, 627, 111 Cal.Rptr. 704, 711, 517 P.2d 1168, 1173 (1974).

3. URLTA § 4.101(b).

4. URLTA §§ 4.103, 4.104; Model ABF Code §§ 2–206, 2–207. These sections basically authorize self-help remedies for tenants when the landlord fails to comply with the statutory warranty of habitability contained in the URLTA and the Model ABF Code, respectively. URLTA § 4.103 authorizes "self-help for minor defects," but as an alternative authorizes a recovery of damages under § 4.101(b) "if the landlord fails to comply with the rental agreement or Section 2.04, and the reasonable cost of compliance is less than [$100] or an amount equal to [one-half] the periodic rent, whichever is greater." URLTA § 4.104 authorizes self help when there is a "wrongful failure [by the landlord] to supply heat, water, hot water, or other essential service," but as an alternative authorizes the tenant to "recover damages based upon the diminution in the fair rental value of the dwelling unit." In Austin v. Danford, 62 Or. App. 242, 660 P.2d 698 (1983), the court stated

URLTA all contain the URLTA provisions on these points. The Delaware statute, based on the Model Code, contains the very similar Model Code provisions on these points.[5] The Hawaii statute, also based on the Model Code, contains the Model Code's provisions as to self-help when the landlord fails to keep the premises in a safe and sanitary condition [6] but omits the Code's provisions for self-help when the landlord fails to supply essential services.

Most of the cases treat a breach of the warranty of habitability as a breach of contract, whether the warranty is judicially "implied" or imposed by statute. But the courts have developed three different formulas for measuring the damages for breach of the "implied" warranty of habitability: *first,* that the damages should be measured by "the difference between the agreed rent [provided for in the lease] and the fair rental value of the premises as they were during their occupancy by the tenant in the unsafe, unsanitary or unfit condition" which makes them uninhabitable,[7] *second,* that damages should be measured by "the difference between the fair rental value of the premises if they had been as warranted and the fair rental value of the premises as they were during the occupancy in the unsafe or unsanitary condition"; [8] and *third,* drawing upon the Model Code's percentage rent abatement formula,[9] that the agreed rent should be reduced by a percentage equal to the percentage of the tenant's rightful use and enjoyment which has been lost to him because of the breach.[10] Presumably, in states where there is a statute establishing a warranty of habitability which does not expressly state what the measure of damages shall be—or does not

---

that whether a particular habitability requirement is an "essential service" within the meaning of Oregon's version of URLTA § 4.104 (which contains no definition of "essential service") must be determined on the facts of each case, but made no such determination because it concluded that the landlords clearly did not "willfully" or "negligently" refuse to supply any "essential service."

5. See 25 Del.C. §§ 5306, 5307.

6. See Hawaii Rev.Stat.Ann. § 521–64(b).

7. E.g., Kline v. Burns, 111 N.H. 87, 93–94, 276 A.2d 248, 252 (1971) (tenant did not terminate, but was evicted by summary process; the only issue on appeal was the balance due the landlord for unpaid rent); Glyco v. Schultz, 35 Ohio Misc. 25, 34, 289 N.E.2d 919, 925 (Mun.Ct.1972). This formula seems to assume that the "agreed rent" is "the fair rental value of the premises if they had been as warranted." This was expressly stated by the court in Lane v. Kelley, 57 Or.App. 197, 643 P.2d 1375 (1982), review denied 293 Or. 394, 650 P.2d 927 (1982). Compare Berzito v. Gambino, 63 N.J. 460, 469, 308 A.2d 17, 22 (1973) ("tenant will be charged only with the rental value of the property in its imperfect condition during his period of occupancy").

8. E.g., Green v. Superior Court, 10 Cal.3d 616, 638, 111 Cal.Rptr. 704, 517 P.2d 1168, 1183 (1974); Breezewood Management Co. v. Maltbie, 411 N.E.2d 670, 675 (Ind.App.1980); Steele v. Latimer, 214 Kan. 329, 337, 521 P.2d 304, 311 (1974); Love v. Monarch Apartments, 13 Kan.App.2d 341, 345, 771 P.2d 79, 83 (1989) (court also said action for breach of statutory warranty is "essentially" breach of contract action); Boston Housing Authority v. Hemingway, 363 Mass. 184, 203, 293 N.E.2d 831, 845 (1973). This formula seems to assume that the "agreed rent" is less than the "fair rental value of the premises if they had been as warranted."

9. Model ABF Code § 2–207 (tenant may "keep 25 percent of the rent accruing during any period when hot water, heat or water is not supplied").

10. All of the following cases actually involve an application of the "percentage diminution" approach in determining the rent abatement to be allowed when a tenant sets up the breach of warranty as a defense in a summary action to evict for nonpayment of rent: Academy Spires, Inc. v. Brown, 111 N.J.Super. 477, 268 A.2d 556 (County Dist.Ct. 1970); Morbeth Realty Corp. v. Rosenshine, 67 Misc.2d 325, 323 N.Y.S.2d 363 (N.Y.City Civ. Ct.1971) (20% reduction); Morbeth Realty Corp. v. Velez, 73 Misc.2d 996, 343 N.Y.S.2d 406 (N.Y.City Civ.Ct.1973) (50% reduction); Glyco v. Schultz, supra note 7 (2/3 reduction). See also Cooks v. Fowler, 455 F.2d 1281 (D.C.Cir.1971) (1/3 reduction in determining amount tenant must deposit in court pending appeal from landlord's judgment for possession for nonpayment of rent).

even provide expressly for recovery of damages for breach of the warranty—the courts are free to adopt any of the three damage formulas set out above.

Either the first or the second damage formula set out above is workable if the dwelling unit is in compliance with the warranty of habitability at the beginning of the tenancy and later becomes "uninhabitable," in which case the "agreed rent" and the "fair rental value as warranted" are *prima facie* the same. But suppose "patent" conditions rendering the dwelling unit "uninhabitable" exist at the beginning of the tenancy—a situation which "is common in the low income housing market, particularly with respect to the worst units and the neediest tenants." [11] In such a case the "fair rental value of the premises as they were during occupancy" may be exactly equal to the "agreed rent." Under the first damage formula, the tenant will then be unable to prove any damages, at least where the condition of the dwelling unit has not worsened since the beginning of the tenancy. And under the second formula the tenant would theoretically be able to recover the excess value of the dwelling unit "as warranted" over the "agreed rent," which would produce the patently absurd result that the landlord would have to pay the tenant for occupying the unit.[12]

Some of the difficulties inherent in the second damage formula set out above are illustrated in McKenna v. Begin,[13] where, on the second appeal,[14] the trial judge was directed to abandon that damage formula and to "assess the major code violations and determine the percentage by which the use and enjoyment of the apartment has been diminished by the existence of those violations * * * and then assess as damages that percentage of McKenna's weekly rent for each of the weeks during which the defect remained unrepaired"—thus adopting the third damage formula derived from the Model Code. As in both McKenna v. Begin and Academy Spires, Inc. v. Brown [15] (relied on by the *Begin* court), this third formula is essentially a practical expedient to avoid the difficulty of determining the damages under either of the other formulas and make it unnecessary for the tenant to bear the cost of producing an expert witness to supply testimony required by either of the other formulas.[16]

11. Abbott, Housing Policy, Housing Codes and Tenant Remedies: An Integration, 56 B.U.L.Rev. 1, 21 (1976).

12. Id. at 22.

13. 3 Mass.App.Ct. 168, 325 N.E.2d 587 (1975) (1st appeal); 5 Mass.App.Ct. 304, 362 N.E.2d 548 (1977) (2nd appeal). On the 1st appeal, the court rejected the possibility that the landlord might be required to pay the tenant for living in a "patently" defective dwelling unit—which would be the logical result of the adoption of the second damage formula in Boston Housing Authority v. Hemingway, 363 Mass. 184, 203, 293 N.E.2d 831, 845 (1973); but the court further held that the trial judge erred in taking the "agreed rent" as "evidence of the value of the premises in a defective condition" because this would make any "rental of defective premises * * * tantamount to a waiver of the statutory provisions for enforcement of the State Sanitary Code and the landlord's implied obligation to let and maintain the premises in a habitable condition." This made it hard for the trial judge, on remand, to determine the fair rental value of the tenant's patently defective dwelling unit and led him finally to hold that the fair rental value was the agreed rent less the amortized cost of repairing the major code violations.

14. 5 Mass.App.Ct. 304, 362 N.E.2d 548, 553 (1977).

15. 111 N.J.Super. 477, 268 A.2d 556 (County Dist.Ct.1970).

16. Cf. Moskovitz, The Implied Warranty of Habitability: A New Doctrine Raising New Issues, 62 Calif.L.Rev. 1444, 1470 (1974) (tenant should be compensated for discomfort and annoyance); Sax & Hiestand, Slumlordism as a Tort, 65 Mich.L.Rev. 869, 875, 913 (1967) (deterrence and punishment should be the prime objectives); Abbott, Housing Policy, Housing Codes, and Tenant Remedies: An In-

In Iowa and Missouri (intermediate court decision only) the determination of damages for breach of the implied warranty of habitability has been complicated by decisions adopting a two-tiered formula. In Mease v. Fox,[17] the Iowa Supreme Court held that, with respect to the tenant's period of occupancy, the first damage formula set out above should be applied;[18] but, with respect to the period after the tenant vacated the premises, the second damage formula should be applied because the tenant, after he vacates, "is then unaffected by the condition of the premises," and for the balance of the lease term has simply "lost the benefit of his bargain, assuming that he had an advantageous lease."[19] And in King v. Moorehead,[20] the Missouri intermediate appellate court adopted the same two-tiered formula.[21]

In addition to damages computed according to one or the other of the damage formulas discussed above, it seems clear that, in cases where the tenant elects to remain in possession after breach of the landlord's duty to put and keep the leased premises in a habitable condition, the tenant should be awarded "consequential" damages resulting from losses that were "foreseeable" unless a statute expressly bars such an award.[22] Statutes based on the URLTA and the Model Code which authorize self-help remedies such as "repair-and-deduct" in substance authorize recovery of "consequential damages."[23] The Maine statute, on the other hand, expressly prohibits recovery of "consequential damages * * * for breach of the warranty [of habitability]."[24] A number of New York lower courts have held that where breach of the warranty of habitability consists of a failure to provide essential services such as heat and hot water, the measure of damages is either (1) the difference in value of the leased premises with and without such services,[25] or (2) the actual monetary loss suffered by the tenant,[26] or (3) some other practical measure of damages fair to both parties.[27]

The Second Property Restatement's Landlord and Tenant part rejects the traditional division between "general" and "special" damages and simply

---

tegration, 56 B.U.L.Rev. 1, at 24 (1976) (under the "percentage diminution" formula, "the tenant's recovery really amounts to a civil fine levied on the landlord which recaptures some or all of the contract rent depending upon the court's judgment as to the condition of the [dwelling] unit.")

17. 200 N.W.2d 791 (Iowa 1972).

18. Id. at 797.

19. Ibid. Meese v. Fox was followed in Roeder v. Nolan, 321 N.W.2d 1, 5 (Iowa 1982).

20. 495 S.W.2d 65 (Mo.App.1973).

21. Id. at 76. Detling v. Edelbrock, 671 S.W.2d 265 (Mo.1984), although it accepts the "implied" warranty of habitability theory enunciated in King v. Moorehead, did not adopt the two-tiered damage formula. But the *Detling* court did state that "tenants may seek to recover damages for the impaired enjoyment of the premises and consequential damages."

22. Such damages are within the limits set by Hadley v. Baxendale, 9 Exch. 341 (1854).

Accord: Rest.Prop.2d Landlord and Tenant § 10.2(2), (3); see Comments c and d thereto.

Recent cases include Detling v. Edelbrock, supra note 21; Love v. Monarch Apartments, 13 Kan.App.2d 341, 345, 771 P.2d 79, 83 (1989) (tenant may recover "any consequential damages flowing from" landlord's breach if such damages "may fairly be considered as arising, in the usual course of things, from the breach itself" or "may reasonably be assumed to have been within the contemplation of both parties as the probable result of the breach.").

23. Supra note 4.

24. 14 Maine Rev.Stat.Ann. § 6021.

25. Leris Realty Corp. v. Robbins, 95 Misc.2d 712, 408 N.Y.S.2d 166 (N.Y.Civ.Ct. 1978); Goldner v. Doknovitch, 88 Misc.2d 88, 388 N.Y.S.2d 504 (Sup.Ct.1976); Whitehouse Estates, Inc. v. Thomson, 87 Misc.2d 813, 386 N.Y.S.2d 733 (N.Y.City Civ.Ct.1976).

26. Goldner v. Doknovitch, supra note 25.

27. Goldner v. Doknovitch, supra note 25.

lists all items of damage individually "so that the court may apply them individually or in combination to achieve the goal of proper compensation to the tenant without double recovery." [28]   Perhaps the most interesting feature of the section on damages is the provision for recovery of "the fair market value of the lease on the date he terminates the lease." [29]   Although the Second Property Restatement provides no formula for determining "the fair market value of the lease," a Reporter's Note to Section 10.2 asserts that "fair market value" is "believed to be the equivalent" of "the difference between the fair rental value of the property and the agreed rental value." [30] Unfortunately, "fair rental value" is not defined, but presumably the term means the fair rental value of the premises if they had been as warranted. If so, the "fair market value" damage formula of the Second Property Restatement is identical with the second formula set out above—and with the "benefit of the bargain" formula held in *Mease* and in *King* to be applicable for the period after the tenant vacates.[31]

The Second Property Restatement also expressly includes, as items of damages recoverable by the tenant for breach of the landlord's duty, expenditures by the tenant for "substituted premises" [32] or "eliminating the default";[33] "reasonable relocation costs" when "the tenant is entitled to terminate the lease and does so";[34] and, to the extent that "the landlord at the time the lease was made could reasonably have foreseen" them, "the loss sustained by the tenant due to reasonable expenditures * * * before the landlord's default." [35]   Whether the Second Property Restatement's listing of items of damages will influence the courts in determining the appropriate measure of damages for breach of an "implied" warranty of habitability remains to be seen.

Any claim by the tenant for damages for breach of the landlord's statutory or "implied" warranty of habitability may, of course, be asserted either by a direct action or by way of counterclaim in an action by the landlord to recover unpaid rent.   Such a claim may also be asserted by the tenant as a defense to an action by the landlord to evict the tenant for nonpayment of rent.   In the latter case, however, the courts often speak of an "abatement of the rent" instead of a "counterclaim for damages."   The tenant's ability to assert a claim for "abatement of the rent" or a "counterclaim for damages" is discussed in the next Section.

Up to this point the discussion has been concerned with damages for one common type of economic injury resulting from breach of the warranty of habitability—reduction in rental value caused by breach of the warranty, determined in accordance with one of the damage formulas hitherto discussed.   But breach of the warranty of habitability may be the actual cause of other kinds of injury to the tenant or members of the tenant's family, such as injury to personal property of the tenant on the premises, physical injury to the tenant or his family, and injury in the form of emotional distress.

---

28. Am.L.Inst., Rest., Prop.2d Landlord and Tenant, § 10.2, Comment a.

29. Id. § 10.2(1).

30. Id., Reporter's Note, para. 1.

31. See discussion in text ante between notes 11 and 15.

32. Supra note 28, § 10.2(4).

33. Id. § 10.2(6).

34. Id. § 10.2(3).

35. Id. § 10.2(2).

Damages for physical injury to the tenant or members of his family are discussed hereafter in Section 6.46, and will not be further discussed here. At least one case has denied any recovery for destruction of a tenant's personal property,[36] although injury to the tenant's personal property is a reasonably foreseeable consequence of noncompliance with several of the duties generally imposed on the landlord by both judge-made and statutory warranties of habitability.[37] On the other hand, at least one court has allowed damages for "tangible consequences" of a breach of warranty such as physical illness, medical bills, inability to sleep, and inability to eat or work in one's dwelling.[38] That court, however, denied recovery for "the strain or preoccupation and vexation" resulting from a continuing dispute with the landlord.[39] And a few cases have allowed recovery of damages for "intentional," "wanton or willful," or "reckless" infliction of "emotional distress" resulting from breach of the warranty of habitability.[40] In most, if not all of these cases, recovery was based on the theory that the landlord's breach of warranty amounted to a tort when it caused "emotional distress" to the tenant.[41]

Although "no matter how reprehensible the breach, damages that are punitive, in the sense of being in excess of those required to compensate the injured party for his lost expectation, are not ordinarily awarded for breach of contract," punitive damages have been awarded when the breach of contract is in some respect tortious.[42] Hence it is not surprising that at least two courts have approved the award of punitive damages when a breach of the warranty of habitability was accompanied by conduct of the landlord characterized by the court as "culpable and demeaning * * * and clearly expressive of a wanton disregard of plaintiff's rights"[43] or as "outrageous."[44]

§ 6.43 Remedies for Landlord's Breach of Duty—Rent Withholding and Abatement

Except when there was a breach of the landlord's express or implied covenant of quiet enjoyment, the traditional common law doctrine that lease covenants are "independent" deprived the tenant of any remedy for the landlord's breach of covenant except an action or counterclaim for damages.[1]

36. Abram v. Litman, 150 Ill.App.3d 174, 103 Ill.Dec. 349, 501 N.E.2d 370 (1986), appeal denied 114 Ill.2d 543, 108 Ill.Dec. 414, 508 N.E.2d 725 (1987) (personal property was destroyed by fire caused by faulty wiring, alleged to have made premises uninhabitable and unreasonably dangerous; the court also denied recovery in tort because the defect was "latent" and landlord did know of its existence).

37. For a good general discussion of contract liability for "consequential damages," see E. Farnsworth, Contracts § 12.14 (1982).

38. Brewer v. Erwin, 287 Or. 435, 600 P.2d 398 (1979), appeal after remand 61 Or.App. 642, 658 P.2d 1180 (1983).

39. Ibid.

40. Simon v. Solomon, 385 Mass. 91, 431 N.E.2d 556 (1982); Hilder v. St. Peter, 144 Vt. 150, 478 A.2d 202 (1984); Fair v. Negley, 257 Pa.Super. 50, 390 A.2d 240 (1978); Beasley v. Freedman, 256 Pa.Super. 208, 389 A.2d 1087 (1978).

41. This is consistent with the generally accepted view that damages for "physical injury" resulting from breach of the warranty of habitability can only give rise to "tort," not "contract" damages.

42. E. Farnsworth, supra note 37, § 12.8 at pp. 842–843 (1982).

43. Hilder v. St. Peter, supra note 40.

44. 49 Prospect Street Tenants Ass'n v. Sheva Gardens, Inc., 227 N.J.Super. 449, 547 A.2d 1134 (App.Div.1988).

§ 6.43

1. See, e.g., Green v. Superior Court, 10 Cal.3d 616, 622, 111 Cal.Rptr. 704, 707, 517 P.2d 1168, 1172 (1974) ("a lessee's covenant to

Although the doctrine of "constructive eviction" authorized the tenant to vacate the premises and treat the landlord's failure to perform an obligation to keep the leased premises habitable as a breach of the covenant of quiet enjoyment, the tenant had no right to remain in possession and withhold rent because of the landlord's breach.[2] Because the landlord could always summarily evict the tenant for nonpayment of rent despite his own breach, even where the landlord failed to perform an express covenant to put and keep the premises in habitable condition, the tenant was often faced with a dilemma: he must either "continue to pay rent and endure the conditions of untenantability or abandon the premises and hope to find another dwelling which, in these times of severe housing shortage, is likely to be as uninhabitable as the last."[3]

As we have already seen,[4] legislation authorizing a residential tenant to withhold rent because of serious housing code violations was enacted in a few states long before the "revolution" in landlord-tenant law which took place in the 1960's and 1970's, and many new (and more effective) rent withholding statutes were enacted during the 1960's.[5] Most of these new statutes require payment of withheld rents either into court or to some other agency, to be held in escrow pending correction of the code violations which are the basis of the tenant's right to withhold the rent.[6] Some of the statutes require the tenant to bring suit and obtain a court order for rent withholding.[7] Others do not require the tenant to bring suit but simply allow the tenant to set up the landlord's violations of the housing code as a defense to any action by the landlord to recover unpaid rent or to evict the tenant for nonpayment of rent.[8] Some of the statutes provide for application of the withheld rents—under the direction of the court or some other

pay rent was considered at common law as independent of the lessor's covenants"); Boston Housing Authority v. Hemingway, 363 Mass. 184, 188, 293 N.E.2d 831, 837 (1973) (under the "doctrine of * * * independent covenants between the landlord and the tenant * * * even where the landlord is bound by custom or express covenant to repair, and by his failure to do so the premises become uninhabitable, * * * the tenant has no right * * * to refuse to pay the rent according to his covenant, but his only remedy is by action for damages").

2. Boston Housing Authority v. Hemingway, supra note 1; King v. Moorehead, 495 S.W.2d 65, 76 (Mo.App.1973) ("Abandonment was required to maintain the fiction of an eviction and thus the breach of the dependent covenant of quiet enjoyment. The effect of the abandonment requirement was to prevent a tenant from remaining in possession without paying rent."); Two Rector Street Corp. v. Bein, 226 App.Div. 73, 76, 234 N.Y.S. 409, 412 (1929) ("tenant cannot claim uninhabitability and at the same time continue to inhabit").

3. King v. Moorehead, supra note 1, at 76–77.

4. Ante Section 6.37.

5. Conn.Gen.Stat.Ann. §§ 19–347k through 19–347r; Mass.Gen.Laws Ann. c. 111, §§ 127A through 127H, and c. 239, § 8A; Mich.Comp.

Laws Ann. § 125.520; Vernon's Ann.Missouri Stat. §§ 441.500 through 441.620; New Jersey Stat.Ann. 24:42–85 through 24:42–96; N.Y.—McKinney's Multiple Dwelling Law § 302–a; N.Y.—McKinney's Real Prop.Actions & Proc. Law Art. 7–A; 35 Pa.Stat. § 1700–1; Rhode Island Gen.Laws 1956, § 45–24.2–11; Tenn. Code Ann. §§ 55–5501 through 55–5507.

The New Jersey statute allows, but does not require, an action by the tenant to establish a right to deposit withheld rents when his dwelling unit fails to meet "minimum standards of safety and sanitation." See Drew v. Pullen, 172 N.J.Super. 570, 412 A.2d 1331 (App.Div.1980).

6. E.g., Mass.Gen.Laws Ann. c. 111, §§ 127F, 127H, and c. 239, § 8A (into court); N.Y.—McKinney's Multiple Dwelling Law § 302–a (to court appointed administrator); 35 Pa.Stat. § 1700–1 ("escrow account in a bank or trust company approved by the city or county").

7. E.g., Mass.Gen.Laws Ann. c. 111, §§ 127C–127H;   N.Y.—McKinney's   Real Prop.Actions & Proc Law Art. 7–A.

8. E.g., N.Y.—McKinney's Multiple Dwelling Law § 302–a; 35 Pa.Stat. § 1700–1.

agency—to correction of the housing code violations;[9] others do not. Some of the statutes provide for rent abatement (reduction),[10] or even—if the landlord fails to correct the code violations within a stated time—forfeiture of the rent withheld.[11]

In those states where the courts have imposed an implied warranty of habitability on residential lessors without statutory authority, and in those states where the statutory warranty says nothing as to remedies, it has generally been held that the tenant may set up any breach of the warranty either as the basis for a counterclaim in an action by the landlord to recover rent or as a defense in a summary action by the landlord to evict for nonpayment of rent.[12] This, in effect, gives the tenant the right to withhold the rent, retain possession of the premises, and ultimately to obtain a judicially determined abatement of the agreed rent because of the landlord's breach. The cases which recognize the tenant's right to withhold rent in the absence of express statutory authorization generally base the right on one or the other, or both, of two propositions: (1) that the landlord's implied warranty of habitability and the tenant's covenant to pay rent are "mutually dependent" rather than "independent";[13] and (2) that a breach of the landlord's implied warranty is "germane" to the purpose of the summary eviction action.[14]

The first case to recognize a tenant's right to withhold rent because of the landlord's breach of the implied warranty of habitability was Javins v. First National Realty Corp.,[15] where the court, addressing the question whether the tenant could be evicted for nonpayment of rent, held as follows:[16]

9. E.g., Mass.Gen.Laws Ann. c. 111, §§ 127F, 127H, and c. 239, § 8A; N.Y.—McKinney's Real Prop.Actions & Proc.Law § 778.

10. E.g., Mass.Gen.Laws Ann. c. 111, § 127F, and c. 239, § 8A.

11. E.g., N.Y.—McKinney's Multiple Dwelling Law § 302–a; 35 Pa.Stat. § 1700–1.

12. E.g., Green v. Superior Court, 10 Cal.3d 616, 111 Cal.Rptr. 704, 517 P.2d 1168 (1974); Javins v. First National Realty Corp., 428 F.2d 1071 (D.C.Cir.1970), certiorari denied 400 U.S. 925, 91 S.Ct. 186, 27 L.Ed.2d 185 (1970); Bell v. Tsintolas Realty Co., 430 F.2d 474 (D.C.Cir. 1970); Cooks v. Fowler, 455 F.2d 1281 (D.C.Cir.1971); Jack Spring, Inc. v. Little, 50 Ill.2d 351, 280 N.E.2d 208 (1972); King v. Moorehead, 495 S.W.2d 65 (Mo.App.1973); Boston Housing Authority v. Hemingway, 363 Mass. 184, 293 N.E.2d 831 (1973) (but only if statutory withholding procedure is used—see ante in text at notes 5–10); Detling v. Edelbrock, 671 S.W.2d 265 (Mo.1984); Marini v. Ireland, 56 N.J. 130, 265 A.2d 526 (1970); Pugh v. Holmes, 486 Pa. 272, 405 A.2d 897 (1979); Teller v. McCoy, 162 W.Va. 367, 253 S.E.2d 114 (1978). Accord: Foisy v. Wyman, 83 Wn.2d 22, 515 P.2d 160 (1973) (case decided on basis of "implied" warranty of habitability, though URLTA was adopted before the appeal

was decided); Fritz v. Warthen, 298 Minn. 54, 213 N.W.2d 339 (1973) (statutory warranty of habitability with no express provision as to counterclaim in eviction action); Rome v. Walker, 38 Mich.App. 458, 196 N.W.2d 850 (1972) (same).

13. E.g., Green v. Superior Court, Javins v. First National Realty Corp., Boston Housing Authority v. Hemingway, King v. Moorehead, Marini v. Ireland, Pugh v. Holmes, Teller v. McCoy, Fritz v. Warthen, Rome v. Walker, supra note 12.

14. E.g., Green v. Superior Court, Jack Spring, Inc. v. Little, Marini v. Ireland, Teller v. McCoy, Foisy v. Wyman, supra note 12. Most of the cases allowing the defense simply assume that the breach of warranty is germane.

15. Supra note 12.

16. Supra note 12, at 1082. The *Javins* language was substantially approved in Pugh v. Holmes, 486 Pa. 272, 405 A.2d 897 (1979); but in Allen v. Housing Authority of County of Chester, 683 F.2d 75 (3d Cir.1982), the court, applying Pennsylvania law, was unable to determine from the record whether the tenant's "total withholding of rent" was justified.

* * * Under contract principles, * * * the tenant's obligation to pay rent is dependent upon the landlord's performance of his obligations, including his warranty to maintain the premises in habitable condition. In order to determine whether any rent is owed to the landlord, the tenants must be given an opportunity to prove the housing code violations alleged as a breach of the landlord's warranty.

At trial, the finder of fact must make two findings: (1) whether the alleged violations existed during the period for which past due rent is claimed, and (2) what portion, if any or all, of the tenant's obligation to pay rent was suspended by the landlord's breach. If no part of the tenant's rental obligation is found to have been suspended, then a judgment for possession may issue forthwith. On the other hand, if the jury determines that the entire rental obligation has been extinguished by the landlord's total breach, then the action for possession on the ground of nonpayment must fail.

The jury may find that part of the tenant's rental obligation has been suspended but that part of the unpaid back rent is indeed owed to the landlord. In these circumstances, no judgment for possession should issue if the tenant agrees to pay the partial rent found to be due. If the tenant refuses to pay the partial amount, a judgment for possession may then be entered.

The court's use of the terms "suspension" and "extinguishment" is rather puzzling. It may be that the court simply meant that the damages for breach of the "implied" warranty of habitability must be set off against the rent claimed by the landlord, and that the tenant must be given a chance to pay any balance found due to landlord before he could be evicted for nonpayment of rent. But it sounds as though the court thought the breach of warranty (if proved) would operate directly to reduce—or even extinguish—the tenant's obligation to pay rent during any period when the leased premises were "uninhabitable." [17] However, at least where the tenant does not try to prove consequential damages, the result should be the same on a set-off theory as it would be on direct reduction theory. The latter theory, however, would presumably not allow recovery of consequential damages.

Like the URLTA, which contains no formula for measuring damages, the *Javins* decision is devoid of any formula for determining "what portion, if any or all, of the tenant's obligation to pay rent was suspended by the landlord's breach." [18] In a later decision, the U.S. Court of Appeals for the D.C. Circuit adopted a kind of "percentage diminution" approach in deter-

17. The *Javins* language as to the dependency of landlord's and tenant's covenants is drawn from Pines v. Perssion, 14 Wis.2d 590, 597, 111 N.W.2d 409, 413 (1961), where the court held that the lease was void when the tenants elected to vacate the premises, leaving the tenants liable only for the value of their use and occupation rather than the agreed rent; but the *Javins* court clearly does not hold that the landlord's breach of the "implied" warranty of habitability gives the tenants the right to avoid the lease while they remained in possession. Perhaps the *Javins* court simply meant that the landlord's breach of the "implied" warranty suspended the tenant's contractual obligation to pay the agreed rent, pending a final determination of the amount of rent actually due to the landlord after deduction of the tenant's damages. Presumably, the tenant's entire obligation to pay rent would be extinguished if the tenant continued to pay the agreed rent after the breach and thus built up a credit which, when added to the tenant's damages for the period when the tenant withheld the rent, was in excess of the agreed rent for that period.

18. Supra note 12, at 1082.

mining the amount to be deposited in court by the tenant under a "protective order," pending an appeal from the trial court's judgment evicting the tenant for nonpayment of rent; but the court made it clear that it was not making "a final decision as to abatement of rent" to which the tenant was entitled because of the breach of warranty, and that its formula for determining the amount to be paid into court under a "protective order" would not necessarily be applied in making such a final decision.[19] The "percentage diminution" approach has also been used by several trial courts in determining the amount of "rent abatement" when the tenant asserts and proves a breach of the "implied" warranty of habitability in a summary action to evict for nonpayment of rent.[20]

Among the post-*Javins* cases recognizing an "implied" warranty of habitability and allowing the tenant to set up a breach of the warranty as a defense in a summary action to evict for nonpayment of rent, Jack Spring, Inc. v. Little [21] is especially interesting. The landlord's breach of warranty was held to be "germane" to the distinctive purpose of the summary action because a 1937 amendment of the Illinois Forcible Entry and Detainer Act authorized a judgment for the landlord for unpaid rent in such an action.[22] And the court clearly regarded the landlord's breach of the "implied" warranty as giving the tenant a claim for "damages" which could be set off against the landlord's rent claim in the summary action, not as directly reducing the "rent" due under the lease.[23]

---

19. Cooks v. Fowler, 455 F.2d 1281, 1282–83 (D.C.Cir.1971). The court adopted the "percentage diminution" approach because no evidence was introduced at the trial as to the rental value of the premises "as is"—i.e., with substantial housing code violations. The court's initial assumption that the agreed rent was "evidence of the occupancy value of the apartment if it fully complied with applicable housing regulations" is questionable. It is more likely that it was evidence of the value of the apartment "as is," since the housing code violations were apparently "patent" and were in existence when the tenancy began.

See also the second appeal in Cooks v. Fowler, 459 F.2d 1269 (D.C.Cir.1971).

20. E.g., Academy Spires, Inc. v. Brown, 111 N.J.Super. 477, 268 A.2d 556 (Essex Co. Ct.1970) (25% reduction); Morbeth Realty Corp. v. Velez, 73 Misc.2d 996, 343 N.Y.S.2d 406 (Civ.Ct.N.Y.1973) (50% reduction); Morbeth Realty Corp. v. Rosenshine, 67 Misc.2d 325, 323 N.Y.S.2d 363 (Civ.Ct.N.Y.1971) (20% reduction); Glyco v. Schultz, 35 Ohio Misc.25, 289 N.E.2d 919 (Sylvania Mun.Ct.1972) (⅓ reduction).

21. 50 Ill.2d 351, 280 N.E.2d 208 (1972).

22. The statute is Ill.Rev.Stat.1977, ch. 57, § 5. The court's rationale was as follows:

* * * To hold that a landlord, at his option, may expand the issues in a proceeding brought under the statute and the tenant may not is violative of common sense and accepted rules of statutory interpretation. * * * In these cases there is no question that * * * unless, as claimed by plaintiffs, rent is due and remains unpaid, possession is not "unlawfully withheld." It is apparent, therefore, that even though the plaintiffs do not seek to recover rent in these actions, the question of whether rent is due and owing is not only germane, but in these cases where the right to possession is asserted solely by reason of nonpayment, is the crucial and decisive issue for determination. * * * It would be paradoxical, indeed, to hold that if these were actions to recover sums owed for rent the defendants would be permitted to prove that damages suffered as the result of the plaintiffs' breach of warranty equalled or exceeded the rent claimed to be due, and therefore, no rent was owed, and at the same time hold that because the plaintiffs seek possession of the premises, to which admittedly they are not entitled unless rent is due and unpaid after demand, the defendants are precluded from proving that because of the breach of warranty no rent is in fact owed. The argument that the landlord's claim is for rent and the tenant's for damages should not be permitted to obfuscate the sole and decisive issue, which simply stated is whether the tenants owe the landlords rent which is due and remains unpaid.

50 Ill.2d at 358–359, 280 N.E.2d at 213.

23. Ibid.

It seems generally to have been assumed that the *Jack Spring* case adopts the *Javins* rule [24] that if the tenant is found to owe some, but not all, of the rent claimed by the landlord, the court should give the tenant a short grace period to pay the amount found due and that eviction should be ordered only if the tenant fails to pay within the time allowed. But a careful reading of the *Jack Spring* opinion does not bear out this assumption. The Illinois court, in substance, said only that the tenant should be "permitted to prove that damages suffered as a result of the plaintiff's breach of warranty equalled or exceeded the rent claimed to be due, and therefore, no rent was owed"; and that "the sole and decisive issue * * * is whether the tenants owe the landlord rent which is due and remains unpaid." [25] This language has been literally construed by the Illinois intermediate appellate court to mean, that, even if the breach of warranty is proved by the tenant, he cannot escape eviction for nonpayment of rent unless he satisfies the trier of fact that "the damages for breach of the warranty equal or exceed the rent claimed to be due," so that no rent "is due and remains unpaid." [26] Such a rule seems inconsistent with settled doctrines as to equitable relief against forfeiture and, as a practical matter, makes rent withholding a risky venture for a tenant.

The New Jersey court has clearly adopted the view that the landlord's breach of the implied warranty of habitability gives the tenant a damage claim that may be asserted "by way of defense and set off" in a summary eviction action and that since "equitable as well as legal defenses" are available in such actions the tenant may avoid eviction by showing "absolution from payment *in whole or in part* * * * in a dispossess action." [27] This presumably means that, if the tenant shows that the landlord is entitled to less rent than he claims because of the set-off of damages for breach of warranty, the tenant may retain possession by paying the amount found to be "due, unpaid, and owing" within whatever time the court specifies. This is essentially the *Javins* rule.

Massachusetts, like Washington, has both case law recognizing an implied warranty of habitability in residential leases and legislation imposing on landlords a duty to put and keep the lease premises in habitable condition. The Massachusetts legislation, however, takes the form of a specific statutory authorization for rent withholding when the landlord fails to perform his duty. In Boston Housing Authority v. Hemingway,[28] although the Massachusetts court held that the landlord's implied warranty and the tenant's obligation to pay rent should be deemed to "constitute interdependent and mutual considerations," [29] the court nevertheless held that the tenant could not use the landlord's breach of the implied warranty as a defense against summary eviction because he had failed to follow the statutory rent withholding procedure,[30] which required a written notice to

24. 428 F.2d at 1083.

25. 50 Ill.2d at 359, 280 N.E.2d at 213.

26. E.g., Lensey Corp. v. Wong, 83 Ill. App.3d 207, 38 Ill.Dec. 612, 403 N.E.2d 1066 (1980); South Austin Realty Ass'n v. Sombright, 47 Ill.App.3d 89, 5 Ill.Dec. 472, 361 N.E.2d 795 (1977).

27. Marini v. Ireland, 56 N.J. 130, 140, 265 A.2d 526, 531 (1970) (emphasis added).

28. 363 Mass. 184, 293 N.E.2d 831 (1973).

29. Id. at 198, 293 N.E.2d at 842.

30. Id. at 203, 293 N.E.2d at 845.

See also Berman & Sons, Inc. v. Jefferson, 379 Mass. 196, 396 N.E.2d 981 (1979) ("rent

the landlord of the tenant's intention to withhold the rent.[31]

It is possible that the tenant's claim for damages for breach of the implied or statutory warranty of habitability might exceed the landlord's claim for unpaid rent in some cases. In such case, the landlord's rent claim (to use the *Javins* terminology) would be "extinguished." The URLTA clearly authorizes a judgment in favor of the tenant for the amount by which his damages for breach of the warranty exceed the rent, when the tenant files a counterclaim for breach of the statutory warranty of habitability.[32] Where legislation based on the URLTA has not been adopted but the summary eviction statute authorizes a judgment in favor of the landlord for unpaid rent, it is possible that a judgment for the tenant for the excess of damages over the rent due might be entered in the tenant's favor when he counterclaims for breach of warranty. If the tenant is not allowed to recover such excess in the summary eviction action, he can presumably set up the breach of warranty as a defense and then bring a separate action for the amount by which his damages exceed the rent due.

Although there is clearly a strong trend toward admitting proof of the landlord's breach of his warranty of habitability as a defense in summary actions to evict for nonpayment of rent, it is also clear that the United States Constitution does not require state courts to recognize the breach of warranty as a defense in such actions. In Lindsey v. Normet[33] the United States Supreme Court rejected a contention that the Oregon summary eviction statute violates the Fourteenth Amendment because (as judicially construed in Oregon) it precludes "consideration of defenses based on the landlord's duty to maintain the premises"—a duty not yet established in Oregon at the time of the *Normet* decision. The court said, *inter alia,* that "[t]he Constitution has not federalized the substantive law of landlord-tenant relations, * * * and we see nothing to forbid Oregon from treating the undertakings of the tenant and those of the landlord as independent rather than dependent covenants."[34] It seems clear that the court also thought the Fourteenth Amendment does not require Oregon (or any state) to impose a warranty of habitability upon residential lessors.

Under the Uniform Residential Landlord and Tenant Act and most of the statutes modelled on it, the tenant may set up the landlord's breach of his duty to put and keep the premises in a habitable condition by way of counterclaim and defense in any action by the landlord to evict the tenant

abatement" was authorized by *Hemingway,* "as a matter of common law," while Mass. Gen.Laws Ann. c. 239, § 8A, "provides for rent withholding, not rent abatement"—indicating that the right to "abatement" may be enforced by a court whether or not the tenant "withheld" rent as it accrued).

31. Mass.Gen.Laws Ann. c. 239, § 8A, as it stood in 1973. The written notice requirement was eliminated by Mass.Gen.Laws Ann. c. 963, § 1.

32. URLTA § 4.105(a) (1972).

In Pennsylvania, although the right to set up a breach of the "implied" warranty of habitability as a defense to a landlord's action

to recover rent was recognized as a matter of common law in Pugh v. Holmes, 486 Pa. 272, 405 A.2d 897 (1979), it was held in Glickman Real Estate Development v. Korf, 300 Pa.Super. 202, 446 A.2d 300 (1982), that a tenant may not withhold rent and defend an action for rent on breach of warranty grounds unless the rent was paid into escrow as required by the Pennsylvania Rent Withholding Act.

33. 405 U.S. 56, 92 S.Ct. 862, 31 L.Ed.2d 36 (1972).

34. Id. at 68, 92 S.Ct. at 871, 31 L.Ed.2d at 47. The court rejected arguments of the tenant based on both the due process and equal protection clauses of the Fourteenth Amendment.

for nonpayment of rent.[35]   In addition, the court is authorized to "order the tenant to pay into court all or part of the rent accrued and thereafter accruing, and * * * determine the amount due to each party," and, in an eviction action, to enter judgment for the tenant if no rent remains due to the landlord after the net amount determined to be owing from one party to the other is paid.[36]   This provision is rather cryptic, but seems generally to have been construed to empower the tenant to "withhold" rent when the landlord violates his obligation to put and keep the premises in a habitable condition, and to preclude eviction of the tenant for nonpayment of rent if (a) it is finally determined that he owes nothing or (b) he pays, within a time fixed by the court, the net amount found to be owing to the landlord.   In Oregon, for example, where the cognate provision is almost, although not quite, identical with the URLTA provision under discussion, the court said: [37]

> The language at issue appears to us unambiguous: if a tenant counterclaims and tenders into court any outstanding rent, the tenant is entitled to retain possession provided the counterclaim award *plus* the tendered rent equal or exceed the amount of rent adjudicated due. * * * [F]or purposes of the [Oregon] statutory scheme, a tenant is not in default of rent and a landlord is not entitled to terminate the lease for nonpayment of rent if the tenant has refused to pay the rent because of some default of the landlord's which entitles her to damages and she tenders sufficient funds into court to cover any rent that may ultimately be determined to be due.

> The net effect of all this is an implicit withholding remedy * * *. Withholding effectively shifts to the landlord the burden to commence any litigation necessary to determine the parties' rights in the dispute and, further, confronts the landlord with the risk of becoming liable for costs and attorney fees if the tenant "prevails."   Withholding at first blush appears to be a rather formidable weapon in the tenant's arsenal. On closer inspection, however, this withholding remedy is narrowly circumscribed and comports well with the [Oregon statutory] policy of achieving a fair balance between the rights of tenants and landlords.

Unlike the URLTA, the Oregon Residential Landlord and Tenant Act expressly authorizes the court, at any time, to release money paid into court to either party "if the parties agree or if the court finds such party to be entitled to the sum so released." [38]   Although the statute doesn't expressly say so, it would seem that any money so released could be used for making repairs necessary to bring the leased premises into compliance with the statutory warranty of habitability.

In Washington, the URLTA provision here under discussion has been omitted from the legislation establishing a warranty of habitability in

35.   URLTA § 4.105(a) (1972).

See McCall v. Fickes, 556 P.2d 535 (Alaska 1976).

36.   Ibid.   The Commissioners' Comment adds the following: "It is anticipated that upon the filing of the counterclaim the court will enter the order deemed appropriate by him concerning the payment of rent in order to protect the interests of the parties."   URL-

TA § 4.105(b) (1972) provides that, "In an action for rent when the tenant is not in possession, he may [counterclaim] as provided in subsection (a) but is not required to pay any rent into court."

37.   Napolski v. Champney, 295 Or. 408, 416–420, 667 P.2d 1013, 1019–1020 (1983).

38.   Or.Rev.Stat. § 91.810(1).

residential leases. In place of this provision, the Washington statute sets out a general rule that the tenant "shall be current in the payment of rent before exercising any of the remedies accorded him" and then qualifies this rule by a provision that the rule "shall not be construed as limiting the tenant's right in an unlawful detainer [summary eviction] proceeding to raise the defense that there is no rent due and owing." [39] Since the tenant is always entitled to show that all rent required under the lease has been paid as a defense in a summary eviction action, it would seem that the Washington statutory provision was intended to allow the tenant who wishes to set up the landlord's breach of the statutory warranty of habitability to allege that the damages caused by the breach are at least equal to the rent claimed, and hence that "there is no rent due and owing." Otherwise, the provision adds nothing to the general rule that would apply had Washington not (in substance) adopted the URLTA. If this construction of the Washington statute is correct it would, like the other statutes based on the URLTA, implicitly authorize the "withholding" of rent by the tenant in order to shift to the landlord the burden of initiating any litigation necessary to determine the parties' rights with respect to the landlord's compliance with the statutory warranty of habitability.

Unlike most of the legislation based on the URLTA, the Washington statute expressly provides that, if the landlord fails to comply with the statutory warranty of habitability and the local government, after inspecting the premises, certifies that conditions exist that make the premises substantially unfit for human habitation or can be a substantial risk to the health and safety of the tenant, and if the tenant makes a good faith determination that he or she is unable to repair the condition described in such certification, "the tenant shall then either pay the periodic rent due to the landlord or deposit all periodic then called for in the rental agreement and all rent thereafter called for in the rental agreement into an escrow account maintained by a person authorized by law to set up and maintain escrow accounts." [40] If the tenant elects this remedy, it will be the exclusive remedy with respect to defects described in the certification by the local government, except for "an action in an appropriate court, or an arbitration if so agreed, to determine past, present, or future diminution in rental value of the premises due to any defective condition." [41] Presumably payment of rent into escrow will satisfy the statutory requirement, discussed above, that the tenant "shall be current in the payment of rent before exercising any of the remedies accorded him" by the Washington statute.

The Model Residential Landlord–Tenant Code contains no provision authorizing the tenant set up the landlord's breach of his duty to put and keep the premises in a habitable condition as a defense in a summary action to evict the tenant for nonpayment of rent. Neither the Delaware nor the Hawaii statutes modelled on the Model Act originally contained any such provision. However, in Lau v. Bautista [42] the Hawaii Supreme Court held that "where a landlord brings an action for summary possession based on the tenant's failure to pay rent, the tenant may assert the landlord's breach

39. West's Rev.Code Wash.Ann. § 59.18.-410.

40. Id. § 58.18.115.

41. Ibid.

42. 61 Hawaii 144, 598 P.2d 161 (1979).

of an *implied* warranty of habitability as an affirmative defense" [43]—without explaining why a warranty of habitability should be "implied" in a state which had enacted the Model Code seven years earlier.[44]   Moreover, the court did not refer—perhaps because it was enacted after the relevant events in *Lau*—to a 1978 amendment of Hawaii's version of the Model Code [45] which (although badly drafted) seems to authorize rent withholding and assertion of any breach of the landlord's statutory warranty of habitability as an affirmative defense in a summary action to evict the tenant for nonpayment of rent.

The "rent withholding" remedy available under the Uniform Residential Landlord and Tenant Act and in connection with judicially created implied warranties of habitability should be compared with the remedy provided by the free-standing "rent withholding" statutes previously discussed, some of which provide for release of rents paid into court or into escrow in order to enable the landlord to carry out necessary repairs on the leased premises. In jurisdictions where there are no applicable statutory provisions with respect to rent withholding, the courts may well be influenced, as time goes on, by the provisions with respect to "rent abatement" and "rent withholding" contained in the Second Property Restatement.[46]

Section 11.1 of the Second Property Restatement provides (*inter alia*) that "[a]batement is allowed until the default [of the landlord] is eliminated or the lease terminates, whichever first occurs," and the manner of accomplishing rent abatement is set out in a comment to Section 11.1,[47] as follows:

> Frequently the rent abatement will be accomplished in a judicial proceeding brought by the landlord to evict the tenant for the failure to pay the rent [i.e., when the tenant has been withholding the rent].   In this proceeding, if the tenant is entitled to abate the rent, he is entitled to defend against eviction by establishing his right to abate the rent and paying to the landlord the amount of the abated rent as judicially determined in the proceeding.   If the tenant has paid the rent stipulated in the lease during the period of time when he was entitled to an

---

43. Id. at 149, 598 P.2d at 165 (emphasis added).

44. It might be supposed that Hawaii Rev. Stat.Ann. §§ 521–1 through 521–76, originally enacted in 1972 as a comprehensive new landlord-tenant code, would be deemed to supersede the "implied" warranty of habitability which was first judicially recognized in Hawaii in Lemle v. Breeden, 51 Hawaii 426, 462 P.2d 470 (1969). Lau v. Bautista contains no mention of the statutory warranty of habitability created by Hawaii Rev.Stat.Ann. § 521–42.

45. Hawaii Rev.Stat.Ann. § 521–78, added by Hawaii Laws 1978, Act 75, § 2, which authorizes the court in any "proceeding in which the payment or nonpayment of rent is in dispute" to "order the tenant to deposit any disputed rent as it becomes due into the court" and to "hold in trust any rent [so] deposited," and to "order payment of such money * * * or part thereof to the landlord if the court finds that the rent is due and has not been paid * * * and that the tenant did not have any basis to withhold, deduct, or otherwise set off the rent not paid." But "[t]he court shall order payment of such money * * * or portion thereof to the tenant if the court finds that the rent is not due or has been paid, or that the tenant had a basis to withhold, deduct, or otherwise set off the rent not paid." Although the reference to the tenant's right to "deduct * * * rent not paid" seems to be based on an express authorization to "repair and deduct," the provision quoted above also seems—although not very well drafted—to authorize the tenant to "withhold" rent because of a breach of the statutory warranty of habitability and to "set off" his damages against the rent claimed in a summary action to evict for nonpayment of rent.

46. Am.L.Inst., Rest.Prop.2d §§ 11.1, 11.3 (1977).

47. Id. § 11.1, Comment b.

abatement * * *, he is entitled to sue for the excess he has paid * * * and the judicial proceeding will establish the proper amount of the abated rent for the period of the landlord's default.

This Comment demonstrates both the close relationship between the concepts of "rent abatement" and "rent withholding" [48] and the fact the "rent abatement" is actually the result of setting off the tenant's damages for the period of the landlord's default against the agreed rent for that period.[49] As was previously indicated, the Second Property Restatement adopts a modified "percentage diminution" formula for determining the amount of rent abatement to which the tenant is entitled.[50]

Section 11.3 of the Second Property Restatement provides as follows:

> If the tenant is entitled to withhold the rent, the tenant, after proper notice to the landlord, may place in escrow the rent thereafter becoming due until the default is eliminated or the lease terminates, whichever first occurs. Whenever there has been a proper abatement of the rent, only the abated rent is placed in escrow.

However, there is no apparent advantage to the tenant in adopting the "rent withholding" remedy, since he can always simply withhold all the rent when the landlord is in default and thus force the landlord to bring an action to recover the unpaid rent and/or to evict the tenant for nonpayment of rent. In such an action, the tenant may always assert his right to "damages" or "rent abatement" by an appropriate counterclaim or defense. The provision as to placing "only the abated rent" in escrow when there has been "a proper abatement of the rent" apparently assumes that the amount of the "proper abatement of the rent" abatement has been judicially determined, but it is not clear whether it is also assumed the court will retain jurisdiction of the case until the landlord's default is eliminated or the lease terminates.

A series of comments to Section 11.3 [51] makes clear that the rent can be placed in a private escrow account with a person or organization selected by the tenant "whom he in good faith believes to be responsible"; that the cost of the escrow is payable out of the funds held in escrow; that placing the rent in escrow "immunizes the tenant from dispossession for nonpayment of rent if he is entitled to withhold"; that the landlord, if he believes the amount deposited in escrow is incorrect, "may contest the amount in court"; that the landlord may, "upon giving proper assurances," use the money in escrow to eliminate the default and may, in any case, collect the escrowed rent when he has remedied the default; that if the landlord claims he is not in default, "he should be able to litigate that issue immediately upon the first nonpayment of rent in a summary proceeding"; and that the landlord

---

48. As indicated by the bracketed interpolation in the text quoted at note 47, supra, "rent withholding" is likely to precipitate the summary action to evict for nonpayment of rent in which the tenant will exercise his right to have a "rent abatement."

49. Apparently the Second Property Restatement uses the term "damages" to describe the tenant's right to recover monetary compensation for the landlord's default either by a direct action or on a counterclaim in an action by the landlord to recover rent, and

term "rent abatement" describe the tenant's right to interpose his claim for monetary compensation in an action by the landlord to evict the tenant for nonpayment of rent.

50. Id. § 11.1 provides: "If the tenant is entitled to an abatement of the rent, the rent is abated to the amount of that proportion of the rent which the fair rental value after the event giving the right to abate bears to the fair rental value before the event."

51. Id. § 11.3, Comments e and g.

is entitled to the escrowed rent at the end of the lease term if he does not elect to eliminate the default. If the tenant has paid the entire rent stipulated in the lease into escrow and the landlord does not elect to eliminate his default, the tenant may sue for damages and, upon obtaining judgment, seize and apply the escrowed rent to the satisfaction of his judgment if the landlord has not yet withdrawn the rent from escrow.[52]

Comments to Sections 11.1 and 11.3 [53] assert that the "rent abatement" and "rent withholding" remedies may be made unavailable by an agreement between the parties unless the agreement is "unconscionable." In view of the strong judicial and legislative hostility to allowing waivers of the tenant's rights in connection with the "implied" or statutory warranty of habitability in residential leases, it seems unlikely that many courts will follow the Second Property Restatement in allowing the parties to abrogate the "rent abatement" and "rent withholding" remedies by contract.

In those jurisdictions where tenants are permitted to set up the landlord's breach of the implied or statutory warranty of habitability as a defense in summary actions to evict for nonpayment of rent, and are also permitted to pay whatever rent is ultimately found to be due within a fixed period, tenants are in substance now authorized to withhold all the rent otherwise payable whenever a breach of the warranty occurs. However, as we have seen, determination of the fair rental value of the leased premises either "as warranted" or "as is," will often be difficult. And if the tenant is withholding all the rent, the landlord runs the risk that the tenant may ultimately be unwilling or unable to pay the amount found by the court to be due and owing. Hence the court may, in appropriate cases, enter a "protective order" requiring the tenant to pay all or part of the rent claimed into court until it is finally determined whether there is a breach of the implied or statutory warranty and, if so, how large an abatement of rent the court should grant. The Uniform Residential Landlord and Tenant Act expressly provides for an order requiring payment of some or all of the "rent accrued and thereafter accruing" into court pending final resolution of the case.[54] In *Javins,* the United States Court of Appeals for the District of Columbia Circuit recognized the propriety of such an order,[55] and similar orders for

---

52. Id. § 11.3, Comment d. Compare id. § 11.1, Comment b, second para.

53. Id. § 11.1, Comment a, § 11.3, Comment a. As to unconscionability, see id. § 5.6.

54. URLTA § 4.105.

55. Javins v. First National Realty Corp., 428 F.2d 1071 (D.C.Cir.1970), certiorari denied 400 U.S. 925, 91 S.Ct. 186, 27 L.Ed.2d 185 (1970), where the court said:

Appellants in the present cases offered to pay rent into the registry of the court during the present action. We think this is an excellent protective measure. If the tenant defends against an action for possession on the basis of breach of the landlord's warranty of habitability, the trial court may require the tenant to make future rent payments into the registry of the court as they become due; such a procedure would be

appropriate only while the tenant remains in possession. The escrowed money will, however, represent rent for the period between the time the landlord files suit and the time the case comes to trial. In the normal course of litigation, the only factual question at trial would be the condition of the apartment during the time the landlord alleged rent was due and not paid.

Id. at 1083 n. 67.

See also Bell v. Tsintolas Realty Co., 430 F.2d 474 (D.C.Cir.1970) ("we suggest that in such a case the court investigate the possibility of providing the landlord the protection of reasonable interim rent short of the agreed upon rent"); Cooks v. Fowler, 455 F.2d 1281 (D.C.Cir.1971) (tenant ordered to pay ⅔ of the agreed rent during pendency of an appeal from a judgment for the landlord in a summary eviction action).

payment of rent into court have also been held necessary or proper in California,[56] Minnesota,[57] Missouri,[58] and West Virginia.[59]

§ 6.44   Remedies for Landlord's Breach of Duty—Self–Help

The early statutes derived from the civil law—including those based on the Field Civil Code—all provided the tenant with a self-help remedy for breach of the landlord's obligation to provide the tenant with "habitable" premises—i.e., these statutes all authorize the tenant to make the repairs necessary to put the premises in a habitable condition and to deduct the cost of the repairs from the agreed rent. Thus, e.g., the Louisiana Civil Code gives the lessee a right, when repairs are required, to call upon the lessor to make the repairs and, if the lessor fails to do so, "the lessee may himself cause them to be made, and deduct the price from the rent due [and to become due], on proving that the repairs were indispensable, and that the price which he has paid was just and reasonable."[1] The lessor's breach of his duty to make repairs does not justify rent withholding by the lessee in Louisiana except when the tenant elects to use the "repair-and-deduct" remedy or to "dissolve" (terminate) the lease.[2]

56. Green v. Superior Court, 10 Cal.3d 616, 111 Cal.Rptr. 704, 517 P.2d 1168 (1974) (protective order proper); Hinson v. Delis, 26 Cal. App.3d 62, 71, 102 Cal.Rptr. 661, 666 (1972) (same).

See also Medford v. Superior Ct. for County of Los Angeles, 140 Cal.App.3d 236, 189 Cal. Rptr. 227 (1983), where the court said: "Even in the context of unlawful detainer actions, depositing disputed back rent and accrued damages bears no rational relation to protecting the landlord from delays incident to the filing of the cross-complaint. * * * It is clear from Green that a tenant in possession can only be required to pay into court rent which accrues after she files her answer alleging breach of the warranty of habitability. * * * The landlord gains sufficient protection from the deposit of the contract rent as it becomes due. A fortiori, when the tenant has vacated the premises, there is no basis for ordering past rent and damages to be deposited for the protection of the landlord. 'Judicial protection of the landlord, whether pretrial or post-trial can be justified only within the area of fair compensation for the possession he loses during the period of litigation.' " (189 Cal. Rptr. at 230, citing Cooks v. Fowler, supra note 55.)

57. Fritz v. Warthen, 298 Minn. 54, 61, 213 N.W.2d 339, 343 (1973): "once the trial court has determined that a fact question exists as to the breach of the covenant of habitability, that court will order the tenant to pay the rent to be withheld from the landlord into court * * *. The court under its inherent powers may order payment of amounts out of this fund to enable the landlord to make repairs or meet his obligations on the property or for other appropriate purposes. * * * the trial court, in lieu of ordering the rent paid

into court * * * may order that it be deposited in escrow * * * or, in lieu of the payment of rents, may require adequate security therefor if such a procedure is more suitable under the circumstances."

58. King v. Moorehead, 495 S.W.2d 65, 77 (Mo.App.1973): "A tenant who retains possession, however, shall be required to deposit the rent as it becomes due, in *custodia legis* pending the litigation. * * * This procedure assures that those rents adjudicated for distribution to him will be available to correct the defects in habitability, and will also encourage the landlord to minimize the tenant's damages by making tenantable repairs at the earliest time. Also, for good cause and in a manner consistent with the ultimate right between the parties, a trial court will have discretion to make partial distribution to the landlord before final adjudication when to deny it would result in irreparable loss to him."

59. Teller v. McCoy, 162 W.Va. 367, 253 S.E.2d 114 (1978).

§ 6.44

1. La.—LSA—Civ.Code art. 2694. The bracketed words, "and to become due," are in the original French text, but were inadvertently omitted in the English translation of the French text made in 1825.

2. Bruno v. Louisiana School Supply Co., 274 So.2d 710 (La.App.1973); Leggio v. Manion, 172 So.2d 748 (La.App.1965); Mullen v. Kerlec, 115 La. 783, 40 So. 46 (1905). All three cases allow eviction of the tenant for nonpayment of rent where he had not made the repairs; but note the discussion in *Leggio*, 172 So.2d at 750, implying that the tenant has a reasonable time in which to begin the re-

The Georgia Civil Code also provides the tenant with a "repair-and-deduct" remedy when the lease creates only a "usufruct" and the landlord fails to keep the premises reasonably fit for the purposes for which it is intended to be used.[3] As in Louisiana, the landlord must have received notice of the condition requiring repair before this remedy becomes available to the tenant.[4]

In the other states which enacted the Field Civil Code or parts thereof dealing with the landlord-tenant relationship—California, Montana, Oklahoma, and North and South Dakota—the "repair-and-deduct" remedy was also provided to tenants in cases where the landlord failed to perform his statutory duty to keep the premises in a "habitable" condition within a reasonable time after notice of the need for repairs.[5] In California and Montana, however, early amendments limited the amount that could be deducted to one month's rent,[6] which precluded use of the "repair-and-deduct" remedy when major repairs were required to make the premises "habitable." In California this remedy was further limited by a 1970 amendment which provided that it "shall not be available to the lessee more than once in any twelve-month period."[7] In Montana and Oklahoma, the old provisions derived from the Field Civil Code have recently been superseded by comprehensive landlord-tenant legislation based upon the Uniform Residential Landlord and Tenant Act.[8]

The URLTA not only authorizes the tenant to "repair-and-deduct"—subject to a limitation on the maximum amount that may be deducted[9]—but also authorizes additional self-help remedies when the landlord "willfully or negligently fails to supply heat, running water, hot water, electric, gas, or other essential services."[10] These additional remedies include procuring "reasonable amounts" of such services during the period of the landlord's default and deducting "their actual and reasonable cost," or procuring "reasonable substitute housing" during the period of the landlord's default, in which case the tenant is excused from paying rent for the period of the landlord's default.[11] None of these self-help remedies is available, however,

---

pairs after exercising the privilege of retaining the rent.

3. E.g., Lewis & Co. v. Chisholm, 68 Ga. 40 (1881); Valdes Hotel Co. v. Ferrell, 17 Ga.App. 93, 86 S.E. 333 (1915).

4. E.g., Ocean Steamship Co. v. Hamilton, 112 Ga. 901, 38 S.E. 204 (1901); J.P. White & Co. v. Montgomery, 58 Ga. 204 (1877).

5. West's Ann.Cal.Civ.Code § 1942; Rev. Code Mont.1947, § 42–202 (now repealed); 41 Okla.Stat.Ann. § 31 (now repealed); North Dakota Cent.Code 47–16–13 (also authorizing recovery of the lessee's repair expenditures "in any other lawful manner from the lessor"); South Dakota Codified Laws 43–32–9.

6. See West's Ann.Cal.Civ.Code § 1942.

7. West's Ann.Cal.Civ.Code § 1942(a). Id. § 1942(b), also added in 1970, provides: "For the purpose of this section, if a lessee acts to repair and deduct after the 30th day following notice, he is presumed to have acted after a reasonable time. The presumption estab-

lished by this subdivision is a presumption affecting the burden of producing evidence."

8. See ante Section 6.39.

9. URLTA § 4.103 (1972). The limitation on the amount deductible applies when "the reasonable cost of compliance" is less than a stated dollar amount or a stated percentage of the periodic rent, which ever amount is greater. In the alternative, the tenant may elect to "recover damages for the breach under Section 4.101(b)" as previously discussed in Section 6.42 of this book.

10. Id. § 4.104.

11. Id. § 4.104(a)(1), (3). Alternatively, the tenant may "recover damages based upon the diminution in the fair rental value of the dwelling unit" under URLTA § 4.104(a)(2); and if the tenant elects to "procure reasonable substitute housing during the period of the landlord's noncompliance," id. § 104(b) also authorizes him to "recover the actual and reasonable cost or fair and reasonable value of

until the tenant has given "written notice to the landlord specifying the breach." [12] Some of the states which have enacted legislation based on the URLTA have either omitted these self-help provisions or have substantially changed them.[13] The Model Code contains provisions similar to those in the URLTA;[14] these have been adopted in Delaware [15] and—in part—in Hawaii.[16]

Although the "repair-and-deduct" remedy has generally been a creature of statute, it was authorized by judicial decision in Pines v. Perssion,[17] and was subsequently authorized by judicial decisions in New Jersey and New York. In both Marini v. Ireland,[18] the leading New Jersey case, and Jackson v. Rivera,[19] the leading New York case, the repairs had in fact been completed and the courts did not discuss the question whether the actual completion of the necessary repairs is a prerequisite to the tenant's right to deduct the repair costs. It would seem that completion of the repairs should generally be required, and that the landlord is entitled to have satisfactory evidence of the completion of the repairs and their cost, as is required by many of the statutes authorizing the "repair-and-deduct" remedy.[20] In Marini v. Ireland the court did not consider whether the tenant should be required to submit such evidence to the landlord, but in fact the tenant had done so. In Jackson v. Rivera the court permitted the tenant to deduct part of the amount claimed, but refused to allow deduction of the remainder of that amount because she failed to prove she had made the expenditures claimed.[21]

As courts come to recognize the "repair-and-deduct" remedy in states where there is no statutory basis for the remedy, the courts are likely to be influenced by Section 11.2 of the Second Property Restatement, which

---

the substitute housing not in excess of an amount equal to the periodic rent." Moreover, id. § 4.104(b) authorizes recovery of "reasonable attorney's fees" if the tenant exercises his rights under id. § 4.104(a). However, if the tenant proceeds under id. § 4.104, id. § 4.104(c) provides that "he may not proceed under Section 4.101 or Section 4.103 for that breach."

12. Id. § 4.104(a) (first para.).

13. E.g., both the Florida and the Kansas versions of the URLTA completely omit URLTA §§ 4.103, 4.104 (1972); Iowa Code Ann. § 526A.23 contains the substance of URLTA § 4.104, but URLTA § 4.103 is completely omitted; Washington completely omitted URLTA § 4.104 and substantially changed URLTA § 4.103—see West's Rev.Code Wash. Ann. 59.18.100. On the other hand, both of the self-help sections of the URLTA are included, without substantial change, in Nev. Rev.Stat.Ann. 118A.360, 118A.380, and in 41 Okla.Stat.1981, § 121.

14. Model ABF Code §§ 2–206, 2–607 (1969).

15. 25 Del.Code §§ 5306, 5307.

16. Hawaii Rev.Stat.Ann. § 521–64 contains a substantially modified version of Mod-

el Code § 2–206; Model Code § 2–207 is completely omitted.

17. 14 Wis.2d 590, 111 N.W.2d 409 (1961).

18. 56 N.J. 130, 146, 265 A.2d 526, 535 (1970): "If * * * a landlord fails to make repairs and replacements of vital facilities necessary to maintain the premises in a livable condition for a period of time adequate to accomplish such repair and replacements, the tenant may cause the same to be done and deduct the cost thereof from future rents. The tenant's recourse to such self-help must be preceded by timely and adequate notice to the landlord of the faulty condition in order to accord him the opportunity to make the necessary replacement or repair. If the tenant is unable to give such notice after a reasonable attempt, he may nonetheless proceed."

19. 65 Misc.2d 468, 318 N.Y.S.2d 7 (City Civ.Ct.1971).

20. See statutes cited supra, notes 1–16.

21. The court in Jackson v. Rivera permitted the tenant to deduct the cost of repairing a defective toilet; but refused to allow her to deduct expenditures to replace a front door and repair a window because she failed to sustain the burden of proving she had made the expenditures.

broadly authorizes the tenant, after proper notice to the landlord, to "deduct from his rent reasonable costs incurred in eliminating" any default of the landlord which entitles the tenant to "apply his rent to eliminate the * * * default." Section 11.2 does not impose maximum limits on the amount of rent that may be deducted as do most of the statutes which authorize the "repair-and-deduct" remedy; but it does include comments which set out guidelines for the tenant's use of this remedy, including the following:

> Since the tenant must present evidence that the sum deducted from the rent has been applied to the elimination of the landlord's default, generally he may not begin making deductions until the default has been eliminated and may not deduct from rents which are already in arrears when he eliminates the default. In special situations, after giving adequate assurance that the work will be completed, the tenant may make appropriate deductions from the rent during the progress of the work. A special situation would be present if the work involved emergency repairs and the tenant did not have readily available funds other than the rent money.

> The default must be one which the tenant can and does eliminate and one that can be eliminated at a cost that does not exceed the amount of the rent that will be available to apply against the cost. * * *

> If the default for which rent application is available involves the condition of the leased premises, the repairs made by the tenant at the landlord's expense should be commensurate with the age and overall condition of the premises, the condition of the surrounding neighborhood, and the alternative uses to which the premises might be put, in order for them to meet the test of being accomplished at a reasonable cost.

The Second Property Restatement also expressly includes, as items of damages recoverable by the tenant for breach of the landlord's duty, expenditures by the tenant for "substituted premises" [22] or "eliminating the default"; [23] "reasonable relocation costs" when "the tenant is entitled to terminate the lease and does so"; [24] and, to the extent that "the landlord at the time the lease was made could reasonably have foreseen" them, "the loss sustained by the tenant due to reasonable expenditures * * * before the landlord's default." [25] Whether the Second Property Restatement's listing of items of damages will influence the courts in determining the appropriate measure of damages for breach of an "implied" warranty of habitability remains to be seen.

In jurisdictions where the tenant's right to "repair-and-deduct" is recognized by statute or by judicial decision, it would seem that tenants should be required to utilize this self-help remedy if the landlord's breach of duty can be cured through an exercise of the right to "repair-and-deduct" without substantial inconvenience to the tenant and at a cost less than the damages that would accrue if the breach went unsecured for a substantial time. This would involve only an application of the general rule (applied in both

22. Rest.Prop.2d § 10.2(4).

23. Id. § 10.2(6).

24. Id. § 10.2(3).

25. Id. § 10.2(2).

contract and tort law) which requires the injured party to take reasonable action to mitigate the damages arising from the other party's breach of duty, and would result in limitation of the tenant's damages for breach of the landlord's duty to the reasonable cost of repairs in cases where the tenant's exercise of his right to "repair-and-deduct" would not involve substantial inconvenience.

Except in situations where the obligation to mitigate damages arises, a tenant may, when there is a breach of the warranty of habitability, elect among the various remedies available to him if he decides not to terminate the lease.

§ 6.45 Remedies for Breach of Landlord's Duty—Specific Performance and Receivership

In Lemle v. Breeden[1] the court said that breach of the landlord's implied warranty of habitability makes available to the tenant "the basic contract remedies of damages, reformation and rescission." This language has been repeated in most of the subsequent cases in which an implied warranty of habitability is recognized by the court.[2] "Rescission," accompanied by vacation of the leased premises, really amounts to "termination" of the lease or to "constructive eviction," and has already been discussed. It is not immediately apparent how the remedy of "reformation" can aid a tenant when there is a breach of the implied warranty of habitability.

Perhaps the statement in Lemle v. Breeden and the other cases should simply be dismissed as judicial hyperbole. But some attention should be given to the statement in Javins v. First National Realty Corp. that, "[i]n extending all contract remedies for breach to the parties to a lease, we include an action for specific performance of the landlord's implied warranty of habitability."[3] This statement is, of course, *obiter dictum;* specific performance was neither sought nor granted in *Javins.* In Steele v. Latimer[4] the tenant sought both damages and specific performance—i.e., an injunction against further violation of the housing code—but the court devoted most of its opinion to the question whether a warranty of habitability should be implied. The opinion contains no mention of the possibility of specific performance, although the court did paraphrase the *Lemle* dictum that "traditional remedies for breach of contract are available to the tenant."[5] No other appellate opinion has been found in which the tenant actually sought specific performance of the landlord's duty to put and keep

§ 6.45

1. 51 Hawaii 426, 436, 462 P.2d 470, 475 (1969).

2. Old Town Development Co. v. Langford, 349 N.E.2d 744, 761 (Ind.App.1976), superseded 267 Ind. 176, 369 N.E.2d 404 (1977); Steele v. Latimer, 214 Kan. 329, 336, 521 P.2d 304, 310 (1974); King v. Moorehead, 495 S.W.2d 65, 76 (Mo.App.1973); Kline v. Burns, 111 N.H. 87, 93, 276 A.2d 248, 252 (1971).

In Detling v. Edelbrock, 671 S.W.2d 265 (Mo.1984), the court said the tenant is entitled to pursue "traditional contract remedies" upon proof of a breach of the warranty of habitability in a case where the tenants initially sought specific performance of express and implied lease covenants and the trial court actually entered an order for specific performance after a receiver appointed by the court failed to obtain a loan in order to finance necessary repairs.

3. Javins v. First National Realty Corp., 428 F.2d 1071, 1082 n. 61 (D.C.Cir.1970), certiorari denied 400 U.S. 925, 91 S.Ct. 186, 27 L.Ed.2d 185 (1970).

4. Supra note 2.

5. Id. at 336, 521 P.2d at 310.

the premises habitable, although there is some authority in support of a tenant's right to have specific performance of an express covenant by the landlord to keep the premises in repair.[6]

Certainly specific performance (mandatory injunction) could be an extremely valuable remedy in cases where the tenant does not wish to terminate the lease because of the landlord's breach of the "implied" or statutory warranty of habitability, and also does not wish to wait for the landlord to sue him for rent and/or for possession. In view of the disadvantages involved in the use of any of the "legal" remedies of the tenant—e.g., the difficulty of finding alternative housing if he vacates the leased premises, and the likelihood that the tenant will be involved in protracted litigation without necessarily getting the landlord to put the premises in habitable condition if the tenant remains in possession and relies on his rent abatement and/or damage remedies—it is arguable that all the tenant's "legal" remedies are inadequate and that he is entitled to the "equitable" remedy of specific performance. A court order requiring the landlord to perform his warranty obligation or face punishment for contempt is certainly likely to be more effective than the traditional techniques used by local administrative agencies to enforce housing codes.

Specific performance is no panacea, however. Some of the factors that make traditional administrative agency enforcement of housing codes ineffective in practice may also make specific performance ineffective—e.g., the financial inability of the owners of slum housing to make the expensive repairs and improvements necessary to comply with the warranty of habitability, and the difficulty of locating the owner of such housing if he decides simply to abandon his property rather than put it into habitable condition. Moreover, tenants of slum housing are usually only periodic tenants who are unlikely to be interested in compelling the landlord to make expensive repairs and improvements that will primarily benefit subsequent tenants. And judicial reluctance to supervise the correction of multiple defects in rental housing might well result in restricting the specific performance remedy to cases involving a single serious defect.[7]

Some of the free-standing "rent withholding" statutes authorize, as an additional tenant remedy, the appointment of a receiver to take possession and control of the leased premises, collect rents from the tenants, and make all repairs necessary to bring the premises into conformity with the applicable housing code. Although authorized by statute, receivership is, of course,

---

6. Jones v. Parker, 163 Mass. 564, 40 N.E. 1044 (1895). See Darnall v. Day, 240 Iowa 665, 37 N.W.2d 277 (1949) (relief refused because inequitable under the circumstances). Contra: Beck v. Allison, 56 N.Y. 366 (1874). But see Detling v. Edelbrock, supra note 2. In 1983 the Connecticut version of the URLTA was amended to add Conn.Gen.Stat.Ann. § 47a–14h, which has been described as giving tenants a private cause of action to enforce housing codes. See Dugan v. Milledge, 196 Conn. 591, 494 A.2d 1203 (1985). *Inter alia,* the new statutory provision authorizes courts to enter orders "compelling the landlord to comply with his duties under local, state or federal law"—i.e., to order specific perfor-

mance—upon the complaint of any tenant. Conn.Gen.Stat.Ann. § 47a–14h(e)(1).

7. See Abbott, Housing Policy, Housing Codes and Tenant Remedies: An Integration, 56 B.U.L.Rev. 1, 64 (1976). Abbott concludes, despite the potential difficulties in reliance on mandatory injunctions for specific enforcement of housing codes, that it should be the *only* private tenant remedy in cases where the leased premises are not subject to latent defects at the beginning of the tenancy and the landlord fails to make the repairs necessary to comply with the minimum housing code standards (as defined by the author). Id. at 135–136.

a traditional "equitable" remedy, and may be viewed as an alternative method of specifically enforcing the landlord's duty to put and keep the premises in compliance with the housing code. The New York and Connecticut statutes allow the court to appoint a receiver (called an "administrator" in New York) in a proceeding initiated by a stated percentage of the tenants in any building containing more than a stated number of rental units.[8] The Massachusetts statute allows tenants to combine the rent withholding remedy with receivership, but it does not make the right of tenants to withhold rent dependent on appointment of a receiver as is the case under the New York statute.[9]

§ 6.46   Landlord's Liability for Personal Injuries

This section considers a subject that lies along the boundary between tort law and property law, the liability of a landlord to the tenant and to others for personal injuries they suffer on the leased premises or on common areas associated with the leased premises. Because of the "boundary" phenomenon, it will be useful to compare the very general discussion here, written from a property-law perspective, with discussions approached from a tort-law point of view.[1] Landlords' tort liability is currently in a state of flux, caused by changes in landlords' repair duties to residential tenants and to the shifts in public policy that underlie those changes. Therefore, this section is divided into several subdivisions that are suggested by the developments going on. We will first discuss the traditional rules governing landlords' limited tort liability, then we will move to recent doctrines that more or less expand that liability. The next section will deal with another developing subject, landlords' liability for injuries caused by criminal acts of third persons.

The Traditional View

Controlling decisions in most American jurisdictions still subscribe to what is called here the "traditional view" of landlords' liability to the tenant

---

8. N.Y.—McKinney's Real Prop. Actions & Proc. Law Art. 7A (the special proceeding can be initiated by one-third of the tenants in any building containing six or more rental units); Conn.Gen.Stat.Ann. §§ 47a–14a through 47A–14g, enacted in 1979 and replacing id. §§ 19–347k through 19–347q. The original Connecticut legislation was obviously modelled on the cited New York statute. Conn.Gen.Stat.Ann. § 47a–14h(3)(2) authorizes courts to enter an order "appointing a receiver to collect rent or to correct conditions in the property which violate local, state or federal law" upon the complaint of any tenant. This provision authorizes the appointment of a receiver upon institution of an enforcement action by a single tenant.

9. Mass.Gen.Laws Ann. c. 111, § 127H.

§ 6.46

1. Two introductory tort-law discussions, often cited, are Restatement (Second) of Torts §§ 355–62 (1965), and D. Dobbs, R. Keeton & D. Owen, Prosser and Keeton on Torts § 63

(5th ed. 1984) [hereinafter cited as "Prosser and Keeton on Torts"]. From a property-law perspective, Restatement (Second) of Property §§ 17.1–17.7 (1977), generally tracks Restatement (Second) of Torts, with some significant additions; and Browder, The Taming of a Duty—The Tort Liability of Landlords, 81 Mich.L.Rev. 99 (1982) [hereinafter cited as "Browder, Taming of a Duty"], is highly recommended. Several American Law Reports annotations are useful for research purposes. See especially Annot., Strict Liability of Landlord for Injury or Death of Tenant or Third Person Caused by Defect in Premises Leased for Residential Use, 48 A.L.R.4th 638 (1986); Annot., Modern Status of Landlord's Tort Liability for Injury or Death of Tenant or Third Person Caused by Dangerous Condition of Premises, 64 A.L.R.3d 339 (1975); Annot., Landlord's Obligation to Protect Tenant Against Criminal Activities of Third Persons, 43 A.L.R.3d 331 (1972).

and others for personal injuries on or about the leased premises.[2] This view starts out with the general proposition that a landlord is not so liable, then proceeds to a series of exceptions, under which he may be liable. The general rule of nonliability flows from two fundamental traditional principles of landlord-tenant law, which we see in other sections of this chapter, namely the doctrine of caveat emptor and the concept that the tenant, having an estate in land with the sole right of possession, is responsible for what goes on on the land. However, even within courts that subscribe to the traditional view, two developments are going on that have effectively increased the landlord's exposure to liability. First, as we know, the doctrine of caveat emptor is weakening. Second, the exceptions have been enlarged over the years, so that the exceptions have eaten heavily into the general rule.[3] Underlying these developments is the shift in public policy that has for some years now tended to make landlord-tenant law more favorable to residential tenants and less favorable to landlords. Nevertheless, under the traditional view, orderly analysis of tort liability should begin with the general proposition that the landlord is not liable, and then one should move to the exceptions, to see if any of them fit the facts of the particular case.

Before we begin to describe the exceptions referred to, it will clarify our discussion to understand a principle that, save for one of the exceptions, runs through the law of landlord tort liability. A landlord's liability, if any, is the same to third persons who are on or about the leased premises with the tenant's permission as it is to the tenant personally. Third persons include not only members of the tenant's family, but also guests and invitees. One consequence of this principle is that a defense the landlord would have against the tenant is also available when a third person is the one injured. For instance, if the tenant's knowledge of a dangerous condition would give the landlord a defense against the tenant for an injury from that condition, the tenant's knowledge also gives a defense in a suit by an injured third person.[4] The one exception to which this principle does not apply is the exception whereby the landlord may be liable to third persons on premises that are leased for admission of members of the public. This is simply because the landlord has no liability to tenants under this exception.

The first so-called exception is that a landlord is liable to the tenant and others for personal injuries that are caused to them on "common areas" by the landlord's failure to use reasonable care in maintaining those areas.[5] Common areas are areas not within the leased premises but within the landlord's control and that are used in connection with the leased premises, such as hallways, stairways, walkways, driveways, entrances, and laundry

---

2. See the leading decision in Borders v. Roseberry, 216 Kan. 486, 532 P.2d 1366 (1975), and also Restatement (Second) of Property §§ 17.1–17.7 (1977); Restatement (Second) of Torts §§ 355–62 (1965). The Restatement of Property generally tracks the Restatement of Torts, with some greater precision in language, but with a significant change in § 17.6, which will be discussed later in this section.

3. See Restatement (Second) of Property, Ch. 17, Introductory Note (1977); Browder, Taming of a Duty, supra n. 1, at 99–102.

4. See Borders v. Roseberry, 216 Kan. 486, 532 P.2d 1366 (1975).

5. Paul v. Sharpe, 181 Ga.App. 443, 352 S.E.2d 626 (1987); Borders v. Roseberry, 216 Kan. 486, 532 P.2d 1366 (1975) (held not applicable on facts); Cappaert v. Junker, 413 So.2d 378 (Miss.1982); Kennett v. Yates, 41 Wn.2d 558, 250 P.2d 962 (1952); Restatement (Second) of Property § 17.3 (1977); Restatement (Second) of Torts § 361 (1965); Prosser and Keeton on Torts, supra n. 1; Browder, Taming of a Duty, supra n. 1, at 102–03.

rooms. While this "exception" probably accounts for the largest number of personal injury suits by tenants against landlords, it is not really an exception at all. The reason is that common areas are by definition outside the premises leased to any tenant; they are the landlord's land, just as the front porch of a private home is under the general possession and control of the owner, though persons having legitimate purposes are permitted to enter. It is quite incidental to the landlord-tenant relationship that a tenant or perhaps a tenant's invitee happens to be injured on a common area; the landlord is equally liable to anyone who has a legitimate reason to be there. Nonetheless, the landlord's liability is well settled and is commonly listed as an exception in landlord-tenant law.

Under the second exception, the "latent-defects" exception, a landlord may be liable to the tenant and others for injuries caused by "latent" defects that exist on the premises when the leasehold begins. A "latent" defect is one that is, or reasonably should be known, to the landlord, of which the tenant does not know or have reason to know. Generally this means a concealed defect. At an earlier time, some courts required the landlord to have actual knowledge of the defect,[6] but, as a part of the historical expansion of the exceptions, courts today are satisfied if the landlord either knows or reasonably should know of the defect.[7] "Latent" also implies that the landlord may avoid liability to the tenant or others under this exception by disclosing the defect to the tenant. The two Restatements make a distinction between a landlord who simply fails to disclose and one who actively conceals a known or knowable latent defect. In the former case, they say the landlord's liability ends after the tenant has had a reasonable opportunity to discover the condition, but in the case of active concealment, they say the landlord's liability continues until the tenant actually discovers the condition.[8]

Courts are still divided on the third exception, whether a landlord may be liable for personal injuries on the premises that are caused by conditions he has covenanted to repair but, in breach of the covenant, has failed to repair.[9] But the exception creating liability has increasingly gained ground and is now the majority view; this is a major area in which landlords' tort liability is expanding.[10] The older view is that breach of the covenant to repair gives rise to only an action for breach of contract.[11] Both of the Restatements, as well as other leading secondary authorities, endorse the rule that a landlord is liable in tort if he has notice of the need for agreed repairs, fails to exercise reasonable care to make the repairs, the disrepair

6. See W. Prosser, Torts § 81 (1941).

7. See City of Yuma v. Evans, 85 Ariz. 229, 336 P.2d 135 (1959) (long-standing defect); Borders v. Roseberry, 216 Kan. 486, 532 P.2d 1366 (1975) (tenant had actual knowledge); Freitag v. Evenson, 232 Or. 225, 375 P.2d 69 (1962) (landlord had done work that should have disclosed); Restatement (Second) or Property § 17.1 (1977); Restatement (Second) of Torts § 358 (1965); Prosser and Keeton on Torts, supra n. 1.

8. Restatement (Second) of Property § 17.1 (1977); Restatement (Second) of Torts § 358 (1965).

9. See Restatement (Second) of Property § 17.5, Reporter's Note 4 (1977), for exhaustive citation of decisions from American courts.

10. See, e.g., Williams v. Davis, 188 Kan. 385, 362 P.2d 641 (1961), overruling Murrell v. Crawford, 102 Kan. 118, 169 P. 561 (1918); Teglo v. Porter, 65 Wn.2d 772, 399 P.2d 519 (1965); Browder, Taming of a Duty, supra n. 1, at 104.

11. See, e.g., Murrell v. Crawford, 102 Kan. 118, 169 P. 561 (1918) (citing many authorities); W. Prosser, Torts § 81 (1941) (stating older view as majority rule).

creates an unreasonable risk of harm, and the disrepair causes injury to the tenant or others who are on the premises with the tenant's permission.[12] Unless the leasing agreement gives the landlord a duty to inspect for needed repairs, his duty to repair does not arise until he has notice that repairs are needed. Ordinarily, then, when the need arises after the tenant is in possession, it will be notice from the tenant that fixes the landlord's duty. Even after that, the Restatements say that the landlord is liable only if he fails to exercise reasonable diligence and care in making the repairs.[13] A potentially important question, upon which there is little authority, is whether a landlord who has not covenanted in the leasing agreement to make repairs may impliedly acquire that duty by gratuitously making them during the term. If so, many landlords would acquire the duty, especially in informal leasing arrangements. The authors believe no such duty should be implied.[14] A technical reason is that there is no contractual consideration for the gratuitous undertaking.[15] At the policy level, it would be unwise to discourage gratuitous repairs by penalizing the landlord for making them.

As another exception to the rule of no liability, a landlord may be liable for personal injuries caused by his negligence in making repairs that he undertakes to make, whether or not he was contractually obligated to make them. The Restatements say the landlord is liable only if the attempted repairs make the defective condition more dangerous or give a deceptive appearance of safety and if the tenant does not know or have reason to know of those facts.[16] So, for instance, if the landlord has only partially completed a repair job and has left the premises in a dangerous condition, but this condition is obvious to the tenant, there is no liability to the tenant or others under this exception.[17] A number of courts have gone beyond the Restatements' position, by holding that the landlord may be liable by negligently failing to make attempted repairs or by making them shoddily, even though the work did not worsen the condition or make it deceptively appear safe.[18]

A landlord who leases premises that are to be used for admission of the public (public areas) may be liable to members of the public who are injured by defective conditions that existed on the public areas at the time of leasing. Here the landlord's duty is not to the tenant but to third persons who enter the premises for the purposes for which they are open to the public.[19] Public

12. Restatement (Second) of Property § 17.5 (1977); Restatement (Second) of Torts § 357 (1965); Prosser and Keeton on Torts, supra n. 1; Browder, Taming of a Duty, supra n. 1, at 104.

13. Restatement (Second) of Property § 17.5, Comments c and d (1977).

14. Accord, Flynn v. Pan American Hotel Co., 143 Tex. 219, 183 S.W.2d 446 (1944).

15. See Restatement (Second) of Property § 17.5, Reporter's Note 6 (1977).

16. Restatement (Second) of Property § 17.7 (1977); Restatement (Second) of Torts § 362 (1965).

17. Borders v. Roseberry, 216 Kan. 486, 532 P.2d 1366 (1975).

18. Janofsky v. Garland, 42 Cal.App.2d 655, 109 P.2d 750 (1941); Marks v. Nambil

Realty Co., 245 N.Y. 256, 157 N.E. 129 (1927); Restatement (Second) of Property § 17.7, Reporter's Note 4 (1977); Prosser and Keeton on Torts, supra n. 1.

19. In general, the landlord owes the duty only to persons who enter public areas for purposes for which they are open to the public, not to persons who enter for other purposes. Compare Sherwood Brothers v. Eckard, 204 Md. 485, 105 A.2d 207 (1954), and Van Avery v. Platte Valley Land & Inv. Co., 133 Neb. 314, 275 N.W. 288 (1937), cases in which recovery was denied; with Hayes v. Richfield Oil Corp., 38 Cal.2d 375, 240 P.2d 580 (1952), and Hamilton v. Union Oil Co., 216 Or. 354, 339 P.2d 440 (1959), cases in which landlords were held liable. See also Annot., 17 A.L.R.3d 873 (1968).

areas certainly include such places as stadiums, amusement parks, lecture halls, and hotels. Some early authority limited this exception to such places where masses of persons would congregate.[20] However, by the overwhelming weight of authority, while the exception does not extend to private places such as dwellings or the private parts of commercial premises, it does extend to places where small numbers of the public are to be admitted, such as stores, shops, restaurants, motels, and professional offices.[21] The landlord is liable if he knows or reasonably should know of a defective condition that poses an unreasonable risk of harm to the public and fails to repair it or reasonably to provide for its repair. The tenant's mere knowledge of the defect does not relieve the landlord of liability, since the duty is not to the tenant. However, if the tenant promises to repair the condition and not to admit members of the public until he has repaired it, this relieves the landlord of liability, provided the tenant's promise is a credible one in the circumstances.[22]

Several preceding sections of this chapter, especially sections 6.38 to 6.40, discussed the creation in the last 25 or 30 years of judicially implied and statutory landlords' warranties of habitability in residential leases. In fact these warranties impose on residential landlords a continuing duty to keep the premises fit for human habitation and often to keep certain specified items in repair. Now that such warranties exist in most states, the question is being presented, to what extent is a landlord liable for a tort injury when the proximate cause of the injury is a defective condition that the landlord failed to repair, in violation of such a warranty?[23] In jurisdictions in which a landlord may be liable for tort injuries caused by the landlord's failure to make covenanted repairs, which, as we just saw, is a growing number of jurisdictions, it seems logically that the landlord might be liable on some basis for injuries flowing from breach of warranty. If tort liability may flow from breach of a repair duty created by contract with the tenant, it is logical to say that such liability may flow from breach of a repair duty created by a judicially implied or statutory warranty. Actual court decisions on the question thus far identify three possible answers to the liability question, which will now be discussed in the next four paragraphs.

First, it is possible that no tort liability will attach on account of the landlord's breach of warranty. A leading decision for this position is

20. The first Restatement of Torts took this position. Restatement of Torts § 359 (1939).

21. Restatement (Second) of Property § 17.2, Comment d. (1977); Restatement (Second) of Torts § 359, Comment c. (1965); Prosser and Keeton on Torts, supra n. 1. However, when part of the premises are public areas and part are private, the landlord is not liable under this exception for injuries that occur on the private areas. See Brenner v. Central Realty Co., 130 Conn. 666, 37 A.2d 230 (1944) (storage room); Wilson v. Dowtin, 215 N.C. 547, 2 S.E.2d 576 (1939) (storage room).

22. Maglin v. Peoples City Bank, 141 Pa.Super. 329, 14 A.2d 827 (1940); Restatement (Second) of Property § 17.2, Illustration

10 (1977); Prosser and Keeton on Torts, supra n. 1. The landlord is not relieved of liability by the tenant's promise to repair if it is apparent that members of the public will be invited before the tenant has time to make the repairs. See Warner v. Lucey, 207 App.Div. 241, 201 N.Y.S. 658 (1923), affirmed 238 N.Y. 638, 144 N.E. 924 (1924); Folkman v. Lauer, 244 Pa. 605, 91 A. 218 (1914).

23. The discussion here of a developing area of law that has not yet "jelled" must be cursory. For a thorough and thoughtful exploration of developments in this area, see Browder, Taming of a Duty, supra n. 1, at 109–41, which is relied upon here.

Dapkunas v. Cagle, from the Illinois Court of Appeals, which refused to create a new exception to the general common-law rule that landlords are not liable for tort injuries.[24] Though Illinois had previously adopted a judicial implied warranty of habitability,[25] *Dapkunas* reasoned simply that the warranty was not intended to create tort liability. The decision has influenced several Illinois appellate court decisions, but does not seem to be attracting adherents elsewhere.[26]

A second possible answer, which, with some variations, seems to be gathering the most support, is that the landlord's breach of an implied or statutory warranty gives rise to tort liability if he negligently or unreasonably failed to make the required repairs.[27] It needs to be emphasized that liability on this basis applies only to residential premises, since implied or statutory warranties have not generally been extended to commercial tenants.[28] The Restatement (Second) of Property states the rule to be that a landlord is liable if he breaches an implied warranty or statutory duty to repair, if this is the cause of tort injury, and "if he has failed to exercise reasonable care to repair the condition." [29] *Dwyer v. Skyline Apartments, Inc.,*[30] a 1973 decision from New Jersey, was the first decision for this position and remains the leading case. Since then, of the states that have had decisions on the question of landlords' tort liability for violation of implied warranties or statutory duties, a plurality, if not a majority, are in general agreement with *Dwyer*'s and the Restatement's position.[31] If the landlord is liable only for negligence or lack of reasonable care, this implies, for one thing, that he shall have had notice of the defect that caused the injury and a reasonable opportunity to repair it.[32] Also, though there seems to be no specific authority for this, it seems the landlord should not be liable if the condition he failed to correct in breach of the implied or statutory duty did not create an unreasonable risk of harm.

A variation on the negligence doctrine described in the preceding paragraph has appeared in a few decisions. It has been said or suggested that the landlord is liable in tort for negligently failing to make the repairs

24. 42 Ill.App.3d 644, 1 Ill.Dec. 387, 356 N.E.2d 575 (1976).

25. See Jack Spring, Inc. v. Little, 50 Ill.2d 351, 280 N.E.2d 208 (1972).

26. See Browder, Taming of a Duty, supra n. 1, at 116–18.

27. For full discussion, see Browder, Taming of a Duty, supra n. 1, at 122–35.

28. However, Texas has extended a judicially implied warranty to commercial tenants. Davidow v. Inwood North Professional Group–Phase I, 747 S.W.2d 373 (Tex.1988). Whether this implies a commercial landlord's tort liability is not yet known.

29. Restatement (Second) of Property § 17.6 (1977).

30. 123 N.J.Super. 48, 301 A.2d 463 (1973) affirmed 63 N.J. 577, 311 A.2d 1 (1973).

31. The following decisions give general support to the statement in text, though not all do so explicitly: Thompson v. Crownover, 259 Ga. 126, 377 S.E.2d 660 (1989); Jackson v. Wood, 11 Kan.App.2d 478, 726 P.2d 796 (1986); Crowell v. McCaffrey, 377 Mass. 443, 386 N.E.2d 1256 (1979) (alternative ground); Henderson v. W.C. Hass Realty Management, Inc., 561 S.W.2d 382 (Mo.App.1977); Humbert v. Sellars, 300 Or. 113, 708 P.2d 344 (1985); Rivera v. Selfon Home Repairs & Imp. Co., 294 Pa.Super 41, 439 A.2d 739 (1982); Porter v. Lumbermen's Inv. Corp., 606 S.W.2d 715 (Tex.Civ.App.1980); Lincoln v. Farnkoff, 26 Wn.App. 717, 613 P.2d 1212 (1980). See Browder, Taming of a Duty, supra n. 1, at 122–35.

32. See Henderson v. W.C. Hass Realty Management, Inc., 561 S.W.2d 382 (Mo.App. 1977); Rivera v. Selfon Home Repairs & Imp. Co., 294 Pa.Super. 41, 439 A.2d 739 (1982); Lincoln v. Farnkoff, 26 Wn.App. 717, 613 P.2d 1212 (1980); Restatement (Second) of Property § 17.6, Comment c (1977).

required by a residential landlord-tenant statute, and violation of the statute is said to be negligence per se.[33] These decisions appear in essence to be following the rule stated in Restatement (Second) of Torts,[34] that violation of a safety statute is negligence per se. However, on that point the Restatement of Torts imposes so many qualifications that the actual working of its rule is not much different from ordinary negligence.[35]

The third possible answer is that landlords are strictly liable for personal injuries caused by defects they have failed to correct in violation of an implied or statutory duty to repair. Kaplan v. Coulston,[36] a decision of the Civil Court of New York, held there was strict liability under the warranty provisions of the New York Real Property Law, but there is little other authority for that position.[37] A number of the decisions cited in the preceding paragraph rejected strict liability. Kaplan's rationale was an extension of the tort doctrine of products liability.

Liability Based Upon Ordinary Negligence Doctrine

Thus far in this section, in discussing the "traditional doctrine" of landlords' liability for tort injuries, the question of landlords' liability has been set off from the main body of ordinary negligence law. The traditional doctrine first assumes a general rule that the landlord is not liable, then creates a series of extensive exceptions under which landlords may be liable. In 1973, Sargent v. Ross,[38] took a fresh approach, declaring that a landlord is liable to the tenant or others for injuries on or about the premises if the landlord failed to exercise reasonable care in all the circumstances. This is the ordinary doctrine of liability for negligence. A guest of the tenant, a small child whom the tenant was baby-sitting, was killed when she fell off an outside stairway leading up to the tenant's second-floor apartment. Allegedly, the landlord was negligent in having a stairway that was too steep, with an inadequate railing. Plaintiff, the child's mother, argued that the stairway was a common area, so as to invoke the exception (see above) that landlords are liable for lack of reasonable care in maintaining common areas, whereas the landlord defended on the ground that the stairway was part of the leased premises, under the tenant's control. These factual distinctions the court sidestepped by announcing that the traditional rule with the traditional exceptions were no longer relevant, but that legal liability was henceforth to be based upon ordinary negligence. "A landlord must act as a reasonable person under all of the circumstances, including

---

33. See especially Shroades v. Rental Homes, Inc., 68 Ohio St.2d 20, 427 N.E.2d 774 (1981), overruling Thrash v. Hill, 63 Ohio St.2d 178, 407 N.E.2d 495 (1980); Browder, Taming of a Duty, supra n. 1, at 127–35. See also Clarke v. O'Connor, 435 F.2d 104 (D.C.Cir. 1970).

34. Restatement (Second) of Torts § 288A(b) 1965.

35. See Browder, Taming of a Duty, supra n. 1, at 132–33.

36. 85 Misc.2d 745, 381 N.Y.S.2d 634 (City Civ.Ct.1976).

37. An argument for strict liability is made in Love, Landlord's Liability for Defective Premises: Caveat Lessee, Negligence, or Strict Liability?, 1975 Wis.L.Rev. 19. The argument there is for broader strict liability, not limited to statutory breaches. Similarly, see Becker v. IRM Corp., 38 Cal.3d 454, 213 Cal. Rptr. 213, 698 P.2d 116 (1985), in which the California Supreme Court imposed strict liability on residential landlords on common law grounds. The Becker case will be discussed later in this section.

38. 113 N.H. 388, 308 A.2d 528 (1973).

the likelihood of injury to others, the probable seriousness of such injuries, and the burden of reducing or avoiding the risk." [39] The court said questions of control, hidden defects, and common areas were only factors to be considered. On the doctrine announced, the court affirmed a jury verdict for the plaintiff, even though the trial judge had given instructions under the traditional doctrine with its exceptions.

Sargent has attracted a following in several jurisdictions, including the Wisconsin decision in Pagelsdorf v. Safeco Insurance Co. of America,[40] which has itself become a leading decision. Besides Wisconsin, a half dozen or more states—the number is growing and therefore outdated when written— have adopted the Sargent position across the board or at least as to certain facts.[41] Some of the decisions basing liability upon violation of implied or statutory warranties, previously cited in this section, also contain language more or less suggesting approval of the Sargent doctrine. The doctrine has been rejected in at least two decisions, though the grounds for rejection would not necessarily apply in other courts.[42]

On balance, Sargent has met with approval, though, considering that it came down in 1973, it is not a wildfire. However, when one considers the expansion of the exceptions to the traditional doctrine, especially the exception for residential landlords' breaches of implied and statutory warranties, together with the Sargent doctrine, the landlord's general immunity from tort liability has been very much eroded in recent years. It may be said that the traditional general rule of no liability has become the exception as to residential landlords. It must be emphasized that the changes we have discussed affect only residential landlords, as there is so far no discernible movement to extend those changes to landlords of commercial or other non-residential real estate.

Strict Liability

The California Supreme Court's 1985 decision in Becker v. IRM Corporation [43] has generated much attention, more for the novelty of its position than for its persuasiveness. Becker holds that a landlord of residential premises is strictly liable to a tenant for injuries caused by a defect that existed at the time of leasing. The court's rationale was based upon products liability cases from the field of torts. Underlying the decision is a policy of risk shifting, to shift the risk of liability for the tenant's injuries, and so the practical necessity to insure against those risks, to the landlord.

So far, Becker has brought little reaction from other courts, and that

---

39. Sargent v. Ross, 113 N.H. 388, 308 A.2d 528, 534 (1973).

40. 91 Wis.2d 734, 284 N.W.2d 55 (1979).

41. See Stephens v. Stearns, 678 P.2d 41 (Idaho 1984); Young v. Garwacki, 380 Mass. 162, 402 N.E.2d 1045 (1980); Turpel v. Sayles, 101 Nev. 35, 692 P.2d 1290 (1985); Williams v. Melby, 699 P.2d 723 (Utah 1985). See also Presson v. Mountain States Properties, Inc., 18 Ariz.App. 176, 501 P.2d 17 (1972), and Mansur v. Eubanks, 401 So.2d 1328 (Fla.1981),

which appear to follow Sargent's doctrine in limited factual patterns.

42. See Murphy v. Hendrix, 500 So.2d 8 (Ala.1986) (court rejects implied warranty of habitability or any broadened rule of liability); Broughton v. Maes, 378 N.W.2d 134 (Minn. App.1985) (court rejects broadened rule of liability because no state supreme court decision doing so).

43. 38 Cal.3d 454, 213 Cal.Rptr. 213, 698 P.2d 116 (1985). Becker is the subject of Annot., 48 A.L.R.4th 638 (1986).

negative.[44]   A California court of appeals has refused to extend it to commercial leases, on the ground that *Becker*'s underlying policies should apply only to residential landlords and tenants.[45]   The evidence is that courts are not willing to make landlords insurers that defects in the premises will not injure their tenants.

It should be noted that Louisiana has long had a statutory rule that imposes strict liability upon landlords for injuries caused by defects in the premises that exist at the beginning of the lease.[46]   Of course, this creates no precedent for other states.   Studies disagree upon whether, or how much, strict liability may drive up landlords' insurance rates in Louisiana.[47]   Apparently, however, the rule is not viewed in Louisiana as causing insuperable hardship to landlords.

Exculpatory Clauses

Since landlords generally draft the written leases used in routine lettings of land, it would not be surprising to see them insert a clause that purports to relieve themselves from their otherwise legal liability for tort injury.   Such clauses, generically called "exculpatory clauses," take various forms, but their general import is that the tenant relieves the landlord from liability or "waives" any claim for injuries upon the demised premises and upon associated common areas.   Under the concept of freedom to contract, such clauses were traditionally enforced.[48]   However, because such clauses were generally not bargained for by tenants with equal bargaining power, they were not judicial favorites;   courts often found ways not to enforce them.[49]

In recent years the tide has been running strongly against the enforceability of exculpatory clauses in residential leases.   As part of the revolution in residential landlord-tenant law that began in the mid–1960's, both court decisions and statutes have either invalidated such clauses or sharply restricted their operation.   Some judicial decisions have invalidated them wholesale in residential leasings on public policy grounds.[50]   Others have done so insofar as the clauses would exculpate a landlord for "active" negligence or upon a showing of an actual inequality in bargaining power.[51]   Perhaps more importantly in the long run, the residential landlord-tenant statutes that have been adopted in a number of states outlaw such clauses or severely restrict their operation.   The Uniform Residential Landlord–Tenant Act, for instance, contains a general prohibition of exculpatory clauses, subject to some exceptions where they may be permitted under certain

44. See Fitzgerald v. Cestari, 569 So.2d 1258 (Fla.1990) (briefly cited; rejected); Armstrong v. Cione, 69 Hawaii 176, 738 P.2d 79 (1987) (rejected).

45. Muro v. Superior Court, 184 Cal. App.3d 1089, 229 Cal.Rptr. 383 (1986).

46. LSA–Civ.Code § 2695.

47. See Browder, Taming of a Duty, supra n. 1, at 138–41.

48. See, e.g., O'Callaghan v. Waller & Beckwith Realty Co., 15 Ill.2d 436, 155 N.E.2d 545 (1958); Manaster v. Gopin, 330 Mass. 569, 116 N.E.2d 134 (1953); Broderson v. Rainier

Nat. Park Co., 187 Wash. 399, 60 P.2d 234 (1936), overruled, Baker v. City of Seattle, 79 Wn.2d 198, 484 P.2d 405 (1971); 6 S. Williston, Contracts § 1751C (Rev.Ed.1938).

49. See McCutcheon v. United Homes Corp., 79 Wn.2d 443, 486 P.2d 1093 (1971); 6 S. Williston, Contracts § 1751C (Rev.Ed.1938).

50. See Cappaert v. Junker, 413 So.2d 378 (Miss.1982); McCutcheon v. United Homes Corp., 79 Wn.2d 443, 486 P.2d 1093 (1971).

51. Browder, Taming of a Duty, supra n. 1, at 141–42.

conditions.[52] All in all, then, exculpatory clauses in residential leases are now of doubtful effect in most jurisdictions. However, there is no indication that they are any less enforceable in commercial leases than they traditionally were.

§ 6.47 Landlord's Liability for Criminal Acts

Under traditional landlord-tenant law, landlords were not liable to tenants and others on the premises for injuries to their persons or property caused by the criminal acts of third persons. One reason was the landlord's limited liability for torts, and another was the reluctance of traditional tort law to allow a defendant to be liable for injuries caused by the intervention of third-party criminals. With the weakening of both of these reasons within the past 20 to 30 years, a large majority of American courts that have considered the subject have become willing to hold landlords liable if the right facts are present.[1] The leading decision in Kline v. 1500 Massachusetts Avenue Apartment Corporation,[2] from the D.C. Circuit in 1970, has been cited as marking this change. A landlord was held liable to a tenant who was criminally assaulted in her apartment house hallway. In most decisions, liability is founded in tort negligence, though some decisions have based liability upon contract. *Kline,* for instance, seems to be mostly a tort case, but contractual obligation plays a role. By far most of the decisions have involved residential landlords, but commercial landlords have also been held liable in a few cases.

All the courts say the landlord is not the tenant's insurer against crimes: the landlord is not strictly liable for crimes against tenants or others on or about the leased premises.[3] Some decisions have denied that landlords have a special relationship to tenants that would create a duty to protect against criminal acts, similar to the relationship of carrier to passenger or of innkeeper to guest, but other decisions seem to flirt with, perhaps to find, such a relationship.[4] This question appears important in the abstract, because if the special relationship exists, one does not have to look further to

---

52. Unif. Residential Landlord–Tenant Act §§ 1.403, 2.104. Other statutes are reviewed in Browder, Taming of a Duty, supra n. 1, at 142–43.

§ 6.47

1. For discussions of the shift in American law, see Jackson v. Warner Holdings, Ltd., 617 F.Supp. 646 (W.D.Ark.1985); and Browder, The Taming of a Duty—The Tort Liability of Landlords, 81 Mich.L.Rev. 99 (1982) [hereinafter cited as "Browder, Taming of a Duty"]. Though a number of significant decisions have come down since Professor Browder's article, it is surprising how useful and up-to-date the article is. D. Dobbs, R. Keeton & D. Owen, Prosser and Keeton on Torts § 63 (5th ed. 1984), devotes only one paragraph to landlords' liability for criminal acts. Restatement (Second) of Property § 17.3, Comment 1 (1977), states that a landlord may be liable to a tenant for criminal intrusion caused by the landlord's failure to exercise reasonable care to provide an adequate door lock on the ten-

ant's apartment. See also Restatement (Second) of Torts §§ 302B, 448, 449 (1965), which, though not mentioning landlords specifically, allow tort liability for creating an unreasonable risk of criminal acts.

2. 439 F.2d 477 (D.C.Cir.1970).

3. See, e.g., Kline v. 1500 Massachusetts Avenue Apartment Corp., 439 F.2d 477 (D.C.Cir.1970); Trentacost v. Brussel, 82 N.J. 214, 412 A.2d 436 (1980); Lay v. Dworman, 732 P.2d 455 (Okl.1986) (landlord not "quasi-guarantor" of tenant's safety).

4. Compare Kline v. 1500 Massachusetts Avenue Apartment Corp., 439 F.2d 477 (D.C.Cir.1970), and Jackson v. Warner Holdings, Ltd., 617 F.Supp. 646 (W.D.Ark.1985), which seem to discover some kind of special relationship, with Scott v. Watson, 278 Md. 160, 359 A.2d 548 (1976), and Lay v. Dworman, 732 P.2d 455 (Okl.1986), which, though allowing landlords to be liable in negligence, denied that a special relationship existed.

find a duty to protect the tenant.   In several decisions, notably Pippin v. Chicago Housing Authority,[5] from Illinois, Feld v. Merriam,[6] from Pennsylvania, and Virginia's decision in Gulf Reston, Inc. v. Rogers,[7] sweeping statements have been made that landlords are not liable for criminal injuries because there is no special relationship.   But the effect of those statements has been largely undercut by alternative theories of liability that were announced either in the decisions themselves or in later decisions in those jurisdictions.[8]   Moreover, the force of *Pippin, Feld,* and *Gulf Reston* is blunted because in all three cases it is very doubtful that the intervention of criminal acts was foreseeable, which is generally a prerequisite to liability. In practice, the existence of a special relationship has not proved crucial.   As we will see in a moment, in most decisions, from most jurisdictions that have faced the liability question since 1970, landlords have been held on one basis or another to have a duty to exercise reasonable care in providing and maintaining security devices to prevent crime.   If one simply counts up results, far more appellate decisions have held landlords liable for injuries from criminal acts since 1970 than have denied liability.   And even in those several jurisdictions that formerly appeared sweepingly to deny liability, there has been a shift away from that position.

Assuming a court determines that a landlord has a duty to provide devices and systems that will guard against crime, such as locks, secure doors and windows, alarms, and guards, at what point will a failure of such devices and systems make the landlord liable for criminal injuries?   Of course it must be shown that the failure to provide or to maintain security facilitated the commission of a crime that caused an injury.[9]   The predominant theory is that the landlord's liability, if any, lies in the tort law of negligence.   Most decisions go on the theory that the landlord is liable if, having a duty to provide security, he fails unreasonably to perform that

---

5.   78 Ill.2d 204, 35 Ill.Dec. 530, 399 N.E.2d 596 (1979).

6.   506 Pa. 383, 485 A.2d 742 (1984).

7.   215 Va. 155, 207 S.E.2d 841 (1974).

8.   See Rowe v. State Bank of Lombard, 125 Ill.2d 203, 126 Ill.Dec. 519, 531 N.E.2d 1358 (1988) (liability for inadequate voluntary security measures; held adequate here); Phillips v. Chicago Housing Auth., 89 Ill.2d 122, 59 Ill.Dec. 281, 431 N.E.2d 1038 (1982) (liability for voluntary security measures that failed); Feld v. Merriam, 506 Pa. 383, 485 A.2d 742 (1984) (liability for inadequate voluntary security measures; alternative theory); Klingbeil Management Group Co. v. Vito, 233 Va. 445, 357 S.E.2d 200 (1987) (implied that landlord would be liable for failing to provide lock if statute had required it); Richmond Medical Supply Co. v. Clifton, 235 Va. 584, 369 S.E.2d 407 (1988) (liability based upon breach of contract to repair).   Browder, Taming of a Duty, supra n. 1, at 148–49, traces the change in Illinois law, but somewhat understates the extent of that change.

9.   This obvious element must be present for liability, though no serious discussion has been found on just how much the landlord's failure must facilitate commission of the crime.   About as definite a statement as will be found is that the landlord's "negligent act or omission was a substantial factor in bringing about the injury."   Nixon v. Mr. Property Management Co., 690 S.W.2d 546 (Tex.1985). In discussions of proximate cause, foreseeability has been a far more important issue than cause in fact.   Apparently it is enough to show that in fact the criminal gained entry through the failed system or that the landlord's breach otherwise enabled the criminal to commit the crime, even if the crime might have been committed otherwise.   See Duncavage v. Allen, 147 Ill.App.3d 88, 100 Ill.Dec. 455, 497 N.E.2d 433 (1986), appeal denied 113 Ill.2d 573, 106 Ill.Dec. 46, 505 N.E.2d 352 (1987) (intruder used ladder landlord left out); Scott v. Watson, 278 Md. 160, 359 A.2d 548 (1976) (landlord's neglect in "stream of events" that led to crime).   And see Aaron v. Havens, 758 S.W.2d 446 (Mo.App.1988) (landlord not liable when criminal gained entry because tenant left her keys in lock).

particular duty, thereby facilitating the commission of the crime that injures the tenant or others on the leased premises or on common areas.[10] The extent of duty may differ from jurisdiction to jurisdiction, but once that duty is defined, no post–1970 decision has been found in which the landlord has not been held to be liable for foreseeable criminal injuries caused by an unreasonable failure to perform that duty. For instance, the supreme courts of Illinois, Pennsylvania, and Virginia have held that landlords have no general duty to provide security against criminal activity on common areas. However, Illinois and Pennsylvania have held that landlords have a duty to carry out security programs voluntarily undertaken, and Virginia has held a landlord may contractually undertake a duty to safeguard and has implied that a landlord-tenant statute may establish a duty to safeguard. To the extent of the duties thus defined, those states subscribe to the rule that a landlord may be liable to a tenant for criminal acts facilitated by an unreasonable failure to perform those duties.[11] Another possible basis for liability is the landlord's negligent choice of employees who commit criminal acts or of independent guard services who fail to prevent crimes they are hired to prevent.[12]

10. Decisions that clearly employ this theory are: Kline v. 1500 Massachusetts Avenue Apartment Corp., 439 F.2d 477 (D.C.Cir.1970) (duty to secure common areas); Jackson v. Warner Holdings, Ltd., 617 F.Supp. 646 (W.D.Ark.1985) (duty to provide locks on apartment door); Czerwinski v. Sunrise Point Condominium, 540 So.2d 199 (Fla.App.1989) (duty to safeguard common areas and ladder); Paterson v. Deeb, 472 So.2d 1210 (Fla.App. 1985), review denied 484 So.2d 8 (Fla.1986) (duty to secure common areas as required by statute); Holley v. Mt. Zion Terrace Apartments, Inc., 382 So.2d 98 (Fla.App.1980) (duty to secure common areas); Rowe v. State Bank of Lombard, 125 Ill.2d 203, 126 Ill.Dec. 519, 531 N.E.2d 1358 (1988) (duty to account for missing pass keys; dictum on duty to carry out voluntary security measures); Phillips v. Chicago Housing Auth., 89 Ill.2d 122, 59 Ill. Dec. 281, 431 N.E.2d 1038 (1982) (duty to carry out security measures voluntarily undertaken); Rabel v. Illinois Wesleyan University, 161 Ill.App.3d 348, 112 Ill.Dec. 889, 514 N.E.2d 552 (1987) (landlord held to have reasonably carried out voluntary security measures); Duncavage v. Allen, 147 Ill.App.3d 88, 100 Ill.Dec. 455, 497 N.E.2d 433 (1986), appeal denied 113 Ill.2d 573, 106 Ill.Dec. 46, 505 N.E.2d 352 (1987) (duty to secure common areas and safeguard ladder); Brichacek v. Hiskey, 401 N.W.2d 44 (Iowa 1987) (landlord provided reasonably secure locks, as required by implied warranty of habitability); Scott v. Watson, 278 Md. 160, 359 A.2d 548 (1976) (landlord owes duty to use reasonable care in securing common areas); Samson v. Saginaw Professional Bldg., Inc., 393 Mich. 393, 224 N.W.2d 843 (1975) (landlord liable for safeguarding common areas against dangerous persons); Johnston v. Harris, 387 Mich. 569, 198 N.W.2d 409 (1972) (landlord liable for failing to use reasonable care to safeguard common area); Aaron v. Havens, 758 S.W.2d 446 (Mo.1988) (duty to safeguard common area); Trentacost v. Brussel, 82 N.J. 214, 412 A.2d 436 (1980) (duty under both common law and implied warranty of habitability to provide locks to common area); Lay v. Dworman, 732 P.2d 455 (Okl.1986) (landlord's duty to secure common areas and to fix lock on tenant's apartment as agreed); Feld v. Merriam, 506 Pa. 383, 485 A.2d 742 (1984) (no general duty to maintain common areas, but duty to carry out voluntary security program).

11. See Phillips v. Chicago Housing Auth., 89 Ill.2d 122, 59 Ill.Dec. 281, 431 N.E.2d 1038 (1982) (duty to carry out security measures voluntarily undertaken); Pippin v. Chicago Housing Auth., 78 Ill.2d 204, 35 Ill.Dec. 530, 399 N.E.2d 596 (1979) (no general duty); Feld v. Merriam, 506 Pa. 383, 485 A.2d 742 (1984) (no general duty, but duty to carry out voluntary program); Richmond Medical Supply Co. v. Clifton, 235 Va. 584, 369 S.E.2d 407 (1988) (contractual duty); Klingbeil Management Group Co. v. Vito, 233 Va. 445, 357 S.E.2d 200 (1987) (implied that statute may impose duty); Gulf Reston, Inc. v. Rogers, 215 Va. 155, 207 S.E.2d 841 (1974) (no general duty on common areas). Duncavage v. Allen, 147 Ill.App.3d 88, 100 Ill.Dec. 455, 497 N.E.2d 433 (1986), appeal denied 113 Ill.2d 573, 106 Ill.Dec. 46, 505 N.E.2d 352 (1987), holds that a landlord has a general duty to safeguard common areas against criminal intrusion, which seems to go beyond the duties established by the Supreme Court of Illinois.

12. See Pippin v. Chicago Housing Auth., 78 Ill.2d 204, 35 Ill.Dec. 530, 399 N.E.2d 596 (1979) (guard service); Annot., 38 A.L.R.4th 240 (1985) (employees).

In decisions that turn upon the landlord's negligent failure to perform a duty, the critical issue has most frequently been foreseeability, whether the landlord should have foreseen the intervention of third-party criminal acts. That is natural, given the reluctance of tort law to require defendants to anticipate that kind of intervening cause. Of course crime may occur anywhere, but landlords are not held to anticipate it everywhere; there must be some special reason to expect it at the particular location. Usually this reason is provided by a history of crimes perpetrated or attempted on the tenant's premises or in a building in which the premises are located.[13] In some cases the tenant has personally complained of criminal activities to the landlord and has expressed fear for his or her safety.[14] Perhaps it is true, as some decisions say, that the landlord must be able to foresee criminal acts on his property and not merely in the neighborhood, but courts routinely accept evidence of criminal activity in the neighborhood.[15] Prior crimes need not be of the same kind as that suffered by the plaintiff.[16] It may be possible for an isolated crime to be foreseeable, but this is the unusual case.[17]

A contract theory of liability has been relied upon in a few decisions. Presumably this theory is available only to a tenant plaintiff, with whom the landlord has a contractual relationship. Virginia, which has refused to hold landlords to a general duty to protect tenants against crimes on common areas, has held that a landlord might be liable for a crime that was facilitated by its breach of a contractual promise to repair a door.[18] Also, in

13. See, e.g., Kline v. 1500 Massachusetts Avenue Apartment Corp., 439 F.2d 477 (D.C.Cir.1970) (prior crimes on common areas); Holley v. Mt. Zion Terrace Apartments, Inc., 382 So.2d 98 (Fla.App.1980) (many crimes on common areas); Scott v. Watson, 278 Md. 160, 359 A.2d 548 (1976) (prior crimes on common areas); Aaron v. Havens, 758 S.W.2d 446 (Mo. 1988) (prior attempt to break into plaintiff's apartment). But see Paterson v. Deeb, 472 So.2d 1210 (Fla.App.1985), review denied 484 So.2d 8 (Fla.1986), where the court said that foreseeability need not be proven when the tenant's action is based upon the landlord's failure to provide security devices required by statute.

14. See, e.g., Kline v. 1500 Massachusetts Avenue Apartment Corp., 439 F.2d 477 (D.C.Cir.1970); Aaron v. Havens, 758 S.W.2d 446 (Mo.1988); Frances T. v. Village Green Owners Ass'n, 42 Cal.3d 490, 229 Cal.Rptr. 456, 723 P.2d 573 (1986) (condominium case).

15. Czerwinski v. Sunrise Point Condominium, 540 So.2d 199 (Fla.App.1989) (court looks for evidence of crimes on premises); Scott v. Watson, 278 Md. 160, 359 A.2d 548 (1976) (court says neighborhood crimes not enough). But see Kline v. 1500 Massachusetts Avenue Apartment Corp., 439 F.2d 477 (D.C.Cir.1970); Trentacost v. Brussel, 82 N.J. 214, 412 A.2d 436 (1980) (police officers testified to many crimes in neighborhood). Browder, Taming of a Duty, supra n. 1, at 150, views Trentacost v. Brussel as dispensing with foreseeability—

with holding landlords "strictly accountable for every crime committed on their property." The decision is liberal, but one need not take that extreme a view.

16. See, e.g., Czerwinski v. Sunrise Point Condominium, 540 So.2d 199 (Fla.App.1989); Nixon v. Mr. Property Management Co., Inc., 690 S.W.2d 546 (Tex.1985). It may well be, however, that prior crimes must involve some violence or threat of violence when the crime against the plaintiff involves violence.

17. As previously suggested in this section, unforeseeability of isolated incidents was apparently the underlying problem that bothered the courts in Pippin v. Chicago Housing Auth., 78 Ill.2d 204, 35 Ill.Dec. 530, 399 N.E.2d 596 (1979), and Gulf Reston, Inc. v. Rogers, 215 Va. 155, 207 S.E.2d 841 (1974). See also Rabel v. Illinois Wesleyan University, 161 Ill. App.3d 348, 112 Ill.Dec. 889, 514 N.E.2d 552 (1987), appeal denied 118 Ill.2d 551, 117 Ill. Dec. 231, 520 N.E.2d 392 (1988). Samson v. Saginaw Professional Bldg., Inc., 393 Mich. 393, 224 N.W.2d 843 (1975), is the "unusual case." There, owners of an office building were held liable for an assault committed in an elevator by a patient of a mental-health clinic in the building, though there had been no prior assault, because persons working in the building had repeatedly expressed fears of such assaults to the building management.

18. Richmond Medical Supply Co. v. Clifton, 235 Va. 584, 369 S.E.2d 407 (1988). Cf.

those several decisions that have said or held that a landlord may be liable for negligently failing to perform security measures he has undertaken, the courts have said the measures may be ones the landlord undertakes by *agreement* or voluntarily.[19] Kline v. 1500 Massachusetts Avenue Apartment Corporation [20] is interesting, in that the court determined that, by providing a certain level of guard and security services at the commencement of the tenant's leasehold, the landlord had impliedly contracted to continue services at that level. It is unclear whether the court finally holds, as an alternative to recovery for tort negligence, that the landlord was separately liable in contract or whether the implied contractual obligation somehow enhanced the tort duty of care. Except in *Kline,* there is little evidence in the decisions reviewed here that courts are willing to imply contractual promises by landlords to provide security.[21]

A small body of recent authority suggests that a landlord's liability for criminal injury may be based upon his failure to provide locks or similar security devices required by statute or ordinance or by an implied warranty of habitability. Courts have been reluctant to hold that statutes or ordinances that, in general terms, require "safe and decent" premises impose upon landlords a duty to provide security devices to prevent crime.[22] However, when a statute or ordinance specifically requires security devices, usually locks, several decisions indicate that a landlord's liability for criminal injury may be predicated upon a failure to provide an adequate device when that facilitates criminal entry. There is not enough authority to say just what is the precise legal effect of the breach, except that the statute or ordinance creates a duty and breach is at least some evidence of negligence.[23] Two decisions say that foreseeability need not be specifically shown when the landlord has breached a statute or ordinance that requires a security device, since the obvious purpose of the legislative act is to prevent unauthorized entry.[24] It is too early to say whether a landlord's breach of a judicially implied warranty of habitability of residential premises can give rise to liability for criminal acts. A serious problem with the theory is that a court first must determine that "habitability" includes the provision and maintenance of a specific security device whose absence facilitated criminal entry. Trentacost v. Brussel,[25] from New Jersey, was willing to conclude that

Gulf Reston, Inc. v. Rogers, 215 Va. 155, 207 S.E.2d 841 (1974), where the same court held there was no general duty to prevent crimes.

19. See Pippin v. Chicago Housing Auth., 78 Ill.2d 204, 35 Ill.Dec. 530, 399 N.E.2d 596 (1979); Feld v. Merriam, 506 Pa. 383, 485 A.2d 742 (1984).

20. 439 F.2d 477 (D.C.Cir.1970).

21. In this connection, see Lay v. Dworman, 732 P.2d 455 (Okl.1986), where the court refused to hold that a landlord's verbal statements that an apartment complex was secure implied a contractual promise.

22. See Pippin v. Chicago Housing Auth., 78 Ill.2d 204, 35 Ill.Dec. 530, 399 N.E.2d 596 (1979); Mengel v. Rosen, 735 P.2d 560 (Okl. 1987); Annot., 43 A.L.R.3d 331, 344 (1972).

23. See Paterson v. Deeb, 472 So.2d 1210 (Fla.App.1985), review denied 484 So.2d 8 (Fla.

1986) ("at least evidence of negligence"); Brichacek v. Hiskey, 401 N.W.2d 44 (Iowa 1987) ("a standard of conduct in determining negligence"; dictum); Trentacost v. Brussel, 82 N.J. 214, 412 A.2d 436 (1980) ("evidence of defendant's negligence"); Nixon v. Mr. Property Management Co., Inc., 690 S.W.2d 546 (Tex.1985) ("negligent per se"). See also Klingbeil Management Group Co. v. Vito, 233 Va. 445, 357 S.E.2d 200 (1987), which holds a landlord was not liable for a door lock that did not conform to a city ordinance, but implies that it might have been liable if the lock had failed to conform to the state statute that superseded the ordinance.

24. Paterson v. Deeb, 472 So.2d 1210 (Fla. App.1985), review denied 484 So.2d 8 (Fla. 1986); Trentacost v. Brussel, 82 N.J. 214, 412 A.2d 436 (1980).

25. 82 N.J. 214, 412 A.2d 436 (1980).

habitable premises were those protected by adequate locks on common-area entrances. The Iowa Supreme Court said that habitability meant a tenant's apartment had a secure lock, but the court did so because it found the judicially implied warranty incorporated a statutory locking requirement, which, in the end, the landlord was held to have met adequately.[26]

In the preceding section, when examining landlords' liability for tort injuries not caused by criminal acts, we saw that they have much greater exposure for liability for injuries that occur on common areas than for injuries that occur upon premises leased to a tenant. This phenomenon is due to the simple fact that the landlord always owes both the tenant and third persons a duty to maintain common areas with reasonable care, whereas most courts impose tort liability upon the landlord for injuries on leased premises only under several exceptions. One might suppose the same thing would be true with injuries caused by third-party criminal acts—that landlords would be liable far more often for injuries that occur on common areas than on the leased premises. In fact, however, the place of injury has proven insignificant in the criminal-act cases. To be sure, in some leading cases, such as Kline v. 1500 Massachusetts Avenue Apartment Corporation[27] and Trentacost v. Brussel,[28] landlords have been liable for injuries that occurred on common areas. But they have also been held liable for criminal injuries suffered within leased apartments and offices, with courts making no issue about where the crimes occurred.[29] The difference between the ordinary personal injury case and the criminal-act case is due to the fact that in the former group, injury occurs at the location of the defect that causes it, while in the latter group of cases, the defect is generally a lack of security that admits a criminal who may commit the crime on a common area, but may just as well commit it within an apartment or office leased to a tenant.

What is significant, therefore, is not the location where the crime is committed, but the location of the defect that facilitates the criminal act. Since the landlord has a common-law duty to maintain common areas with reasonable care, his duty is clear. Even Pippin v. Chicago Housing Authority,[30] Feld v. Merriam,[31] and Gulf Reston, Inc. v. Rogers,[32] the best known decisions to hold that landlords have no general liability for criminal injuries on common areas, so held, not because they doubted that landlords had a duty to maintain common areas, but because they felt third-party crimes were not foreseeable. Most of the decisions cited in this section involved proven or alleged inadequacies in common-area security. When the defect that facilitates the crime exists on the leased premises, such as a missing or defective lock on a door or window, then a court should have to find the landlord has a special duty to provide or to fix it. One would expect rather particular discussion of the basis for this duty, to overcome the general

---

26. Brichacek v. Hiskey, 401 N.W.2d 44 (Iowa 1987).

27. 439 F.2d 477 (D.C.Cir.1970).

28. 82 N.J. 214, 412 A.2d 436 (1980).

29. See, e.g., Holley v. Mt. Zion Terrace Apartments, Inc., 382 So.2d 98 (Fla.App.1980); Aaron v. Havens, 758 S.W.2d 446 (Mo.1988); Lay v. Dworman, 732 P.2d 455 (Okl.1986);

Richmond Medical Supply Co. v. Clifton, 235 Va. 584, 369 S.E.2d 407 (1988).

30. 78 Ill.2d 204, 35 Ill.Dec. 530, 399 N.E.2d 596 (1979).

31. 506 Pa. 383, 485 A.2d 742 (1984).

32. 215 Va. 155, 207 S.E.2d 841 (1974).

common-law rule that the landlord has no duty to repair leased premises. Some decisions do have such particular discussion, such as the Virginia case in which the written lease expressly required the landlord to make certain (unmade) repairs to the door by which the criminal entered [33] or the cases in which courts cite statutes or ordinances that specifically require landlords to provide secure door locks.[34] In some other decisions, however, courts have, with little consideration of the source of the duty, imposed upon landlords a duty to provide and maintain locks upon doors and windows of the leased premises themselves.[35] Perhaps these latter decisions are explained by a remark in the Restatement (Second) of Property: "In addition, other parts of the property [besides common areas], such as door locks on the entrance to the tenant's apartment or office, may be effectively retained in the landlord's control in the sense that the landlord is the only one with the authority to make necessary changes in order to avoid unreasonable risk of harm." [36]

By far most of the criminal-injury cases have involved personal injuries or death to tenants and others by assault, rape, and murder. In such cases, landlords' liability, if any, is determined under the principles of law already discussed in this section. Is there a difference in the landlord's liability for a tenant's loss of property by some form of larceny? No reason appears in principle why there should be such a difference. A number of the personal injury cases involve robbery as well as assault, and the courts have not paid special attention to that fact in determining liability.[37] It may be that, through the years, tenants have lost slightly more property-loss cases than personal injury cases,[38] but only one recent decision, from a California Court of Appeal, has been found that says landlords cannot be liable for tenants' loss of property.[39] However, any difference in results is probably explained by the fact that property-loss cases tend to pose somewhat different issues of law or fact than do personal injury cases. Foreseeability of crimes against property is based upon somewhat different facts than foreseeability of crimes against the person, but in principle the issue seems to be treated the same in both classes of cases. In a leading property-loss case (burglary), Braitman v. Overlook Terrace Corporation, foreseeability was as easily established as in

---

33. Richmond Medical Supply Co. v. Clifton, 235 Va. 584, 369 S.E.2d 407 (1988).

34. See Paterson v. Deeb, 472 So.2d 1210 (Fla.App.1985), review denied 484 So.2d 8 (Fla. 1986); Brichacek v. Hiskey, 401 N.W.2d 44 (Iowa 1987) (but landlord held to have complied with housing code); Klingbeil Management Group Co. v. Vito, 233 Va. 445, 357 S.E.2d 200 (1987) (but landlord held to have complied with only applicable statute).

35. See Duncavage v. Allen, 147 Ill.App.3d 88, 100 Ill.Dec. 455, 497 N.E.2d 433 (1986) (unlockable window, but also problems in common areas); Lay v. Dworman, 732 P.2d 455 (Okl.1986) (defective lock on sliding glass door to apartment).

36. Restatement (Second) of Property § 17.3, Comment *l* (1977). See also Braitman v. Overlook Terrace Corp., 68 N.J. 368, 346 A.2d 76 (1975).

37. See, e.g., Kline v. 1500 Massachusetts Avenue Apartment Corp., 439 F.2d 477 (D.C.Cir.1970); Samson v. Saginaw Professional Bldg., Inc., 393 Mich. 393, 224 N.W.2d 843 (1975); Trentacost v. Brussel, 82 N.J. 214, 412 A.2d 436 (1980).

38. See Annot., 43 A.L.R.3d 331, 356–59 (1972), and 1990 Supplement 31–32. However, most of the decisions noted in the original annotation are old ones, decided in an era when landlords were generally held not liable for criminal acts.

39. Royal Neckwear Co., Inc. v. Century City, Inc., 205 Cal.App.3d 1146, 252 Cal.Rptr. 810 (1988), holds that a "commercial landlord" does not owe a duty to its tenant "to safeguard that tenant's *property* from reasonably foreseeable criminal activity by third parties." (Emphasis by court.)

most personal injury cases.[40] Since thefts in tenants' apartments are often committed by employees of the landlord, liability for property loss may also be predicated upon the landlord's position as employer. Courts have tended not to impose liability on the doctrine of respondeat superior, on the ground that acts of thievery are not within the scope of the employment. However, a landlord may be liable if it can be shown that he was negligent in hiring, supervising, or retaining an untrustworthy employee.[41]

Only a few criminal-injury cases have been brought by commercial tenants, but the indication is that landlords may be liable to commercial tenants as well as to residential ones. At least, courts have not stated a preference for one class of plaintiffs over the other.[42] However, as a practical matter, there are several reasons commercial landlords are less likely to be liable than residential ones. Courts' special concern for the welfare of residential tenants in recent years is well known and must have an effect, though this cannot be quantified. Also, the judicially implied and statutory warranties of habitability, which have in some cases been the basis for a landlord's duty to secure residential premises against criminal intrusion, are not available to commercial tenants. On the other hand, commercial tenants may more frequently than residential ones obtain express landlords' repair covenants, which can be the basis for a duty to secure the premises.[43] But statistically, for what that is worth, we have to say that there have been far more residential than commercial plaintiffs in criminal-injury cases.

G. ANNEXATION OF BUILDINGS AND IMPROVEMENTS

§ 6.48 Ownership and Removal of Things Annexed

During the term of his leasehold the tenant may erect new buildings or other permanent improvements upon the premises or may install new components or chattels upon existing buildings or improvements. Such additions may be a form of waste if made wrongfully,[1] but we will assume for present purposes that they are permitted. The question to be pursued here is, does the tenant own the additions, so that he may remove them? We are working in the subject of fixtures law, which is treated generally elsewhere in this treatise, so that we now will briefly explore only those aspects that pertain especially to landlord and tenant. Moreover, we will not consider

40. 68 N.J. 368, 346 A.2d 76 (1975). The only evidence of foreseeability seems to have been that the landlord knew the deadbolt lock on the plaintiff's door was broken and that other burglaries had occurred "in the vicinity of defendant's building."

41. Annot., 38 A.L.R.4th 240 (1985).

42. Samson v. Saginaw Professional Bldg., Inc., 393 Mich. 393, 224 N.W.2d 843 (1975) (landlord liable to employee of tenant of office building); Richmond Medical Supply Co. v. Clifton, 235 Va. 584, 369 S.E.2d 407 (1988) (landlord may be liable to commercial tenant for theft; remanded for trial); Annot., 43 A.L.R.3d 331, 363 (1972). But see Royal Neck-

wear Co., Inc. v. Century City, Inc., 205 Cal. App.3d 1146, 252 Cal.Rptr. 810 (1988), which holds that a "commercial landlord" does not owe a duty to its tenant "to safeguard that tenant's *property* from reasonably foreseeable criminal activity by third parties." (Emphasis by court on word "property.")

43. See Richmond Medical Supply Co. v. Clifton, 235 Va. 584, 369 S.E.2d 407 (1988), where an express covenant to repair a defective door created the duty.

§ 6.48

1. 1 A.L.P., supra note 1, at § 3.39.

the effect of lease clauses covering ownership and removal, beyond observing that such clauses are common and generally controlling when they exist.

By the doctrine of "accessions," if one person annexes chattels to land owned by another under such circumstances that the law will not permit their removal, ownership of the chattels passes to the landowner.[2] Therefore, the important matter is to describe the circumstances that will block removal, i.e., that make the annexed chattels "fixtures" (not to be confused with a tenant's "trade fixtures"). Of this some useful general principles can be stated. The following factors militate against removal and their opposites, in favor of removal: (1) the chattels are firmly imbedded in or connected to the soil or to some pre-existing fixture; (2) the chattels are peculiarly adapted or fitted to the particular premises; (3) removal of the chattels would largely destroy them or damage the premises; and (4) the annexor had a substantial and permanent interest in the land, a fee simple estate being the greatest such interest. English courts, at an early time at least, strongly emphasized the first factor. American courts now are fond of saying the removal-fixture question turns upon the intention of the parties as shown by the circumstances.[3] Since the parties' actual intent is seldom known or sought, it is questionable how useful it is to "filter" the several factors, which are the real determinants, through some synthesized intent.

When a tenant installs chattels that may be fixtures upon the demised premises, factors 2 and 4 above are likely to be crucial. Even traditional English law, and certainly American law, have long been most liberal in allowing a tenant to remove so-called "trade fixtures."[4] Since items thus labeled are removable, it is questionable whether the word "fixtures" ought to be used at all; surely it is used differently than "fixtures" is used generally.[5] In any event, a trade fixture, strictly speaking an item used by a tenant in a trade or business on the premises, may almost always be removed, up to the point that factor 3 is definitely involved, that is, until serious damage would be done by removal.[6] Very substantial items, even buildings and large objects installed in a building, have been allowed to be removed.[7] Moreover, the courts commonly include under the trade fixture

2. See 5 A.L.P., supra note 1, at §§ 19.1–19.3.

3. For general support for the last three sentences, see 5 A.L.P., supra note 1, at §§ 19.1–19.3; 5 R. Powell, Real Property ¶¶ 651, 652 (P. Rohan rev. ed. 1990); 2 H. Tiffany, Real Property §§ 606–611 (3d ed. 1939).

4. See especially Van Ness v. Pacard, 27 U.S. (2 Pet.) 137, 7 L.Ed. 374 (1829); Handler v. Horns, 2 N.J. 18, 65 A.2d 523 (1949); Ballard v. Alaska Theater Co., 93 Wash. 655, 161 P. 478 (1916); Old Line Life Insurance Co. v. Hawn, 225 Wis. 627, 275 N.W. 542 (1937).

5. See Black's Law Dictionary 638 (6th ed. 1990).

6. If substantial and unrepairable damage would be done to the premises, not even trade fixtures may be removed. Neely v. Jacobs, 673 S.W.2d 705 (Tex.App.1984) (hydraulic lifts, attached to building, might be removed); Jim

Walter Window Components v. Turnpike Dist. Center, 642 S.W.2d 3 (Tex.App.1982), error refused n.r.e. (electrical equipment were trade fixtures that might be removed when slight damage from removal could be repaired); Connelly v. Art & Gary, Inc., 630 S.W.2d 514 (Tex.App.1982), error refused n.r.e. (sign was not trade fixture and could not be removed when it would leave concrete footing and iron pipe in ground); Delano v. Tennent, 138 Wash. 39, 244 P. 273 (1926) (alternative ground).

7. See, e.g., Van Ness v. Pacard, 27 U.S. (2 Pet.) 137, 7 L.Ed. 374 (1829) (house); Cameron v. Oakland County Gas & Oil Co., 277 Mich. 442, 269 N.W. 227 (1936) (service station buildings); Ballard v. Alaska Theater Co., 93 Wash. 655, 161 P. 478 (1916) (built-in theater pipe organ, etc.); Old Line Life Ins. Co. v. Hawn, 225 Wis. 627, 275 N.W. 542 (1937) (small farm buildings, furnace, etc.).

umbrella items that may not strictly be used in a business but that may be for domestic use or only ornamental.[8] The trade-fixture doctrine will, upon analysis, be seen to be an application of the opposite of factor 2 above; the items are ones the tenant might find useful at another location.

Indeed, it is questionable whether the trade-fixture doctrine should be set apart as it has been. In most leasings the opposite of factor 4 will militate more or less in favor of removability, for the annexing tenant always has a temporary estate in the land. The shorter time the leasehold has to run, the more likely the tenant should be allowed to remove chattels he has annexed. Of course it does not matter whether the item is a trade fixture or how it is used, as far as this factor goes.

The upshot of the foregoing analysis is that tenants are likely to be able to remove chattels they annex. Principal limiting circumstances are factors 1 and 3 above. One would not expect a tenant to be able to remove construction materials incorporated into an existing structure, such as bricks, nails, and lumber used in repairs (factor 1). Nor may items be removed if to do so would cause major irreparable damage to the land (item 3). And of course when a tenant is allowed to remove chattels, he must repair damage thereby done.

§ 6.49   Payment for Annexations

Upon quitting demised premises a tenant will presumably leave behind those annexed items that, under the principles just discussed, may not legally be removed. As indicated, these items are by accession realty and are owned by the landlord. In the absence of a promise to do so, the landlord is under no duty to pay for these annexations.[1] The practical implication from all this is that in any leasing in which substantial tenant's improvements are foreseeable, the lease should expressly provide for removal, payment, and other details.

H. RENT AND SECURITY

§ 6.50   Duty to Pay Rent

The payment of rent is not essential to the existence of a leasehold, which may, like other estates, be transferred gratuitously. At least if the parties agree that no rent shall be paid, none is due.[1] Normally, of course, rent is due upon an express agreement for it, the strongest form of agreement being a covenant to pay and not merely a clause reserving rent.[2]

---

8. See Old Line Life Insurance Co. v. Hawn, 225 Wis. 627, 275 N.W. 542 (1937) (furnace used in farm home).

§ 6.49

1. Hughes v. Kershow, 42 Colo. 210, 93 P. 1116 (1908) (by implication); Najewitz v. City of Seattle, 21 Wn.2d 656, 152 P.2d 722 (1944).

§ 6.50

1. See Altman v. Alaska Truss & Mfg. Co., 677 P.2d 1215 (Alaska 1983) (tenant does not owe rent if parties tacitly agree none is due, but rent becomes due if landlord later de-

mands it); Pinnell v. Woods, 275 Ky. 290, 121 S.W.2d 679 (1938); Enslein v. Enslein, 84 Ohio App. 259, 82 N.E.2d 555 (1948); Najewitz v. City of Seattle, 21 Wn.2d 656, 152 P.2d 722 (1944).

2. The reason for preferring an express covenant is that, when there is only a reservation, a few decisions hold that assignment of the leasehold releases the tenant from paying rent. See discussion in Consumers' Ice Co. v. Bixler, 84 Md. 437, 35 A. 1086 (1896). But cf. Samuels v. Ottinger, 169 Cal. 209, 146 P. 638 (1915) (rent "payable").

Commercial leases especially often contain elaborate, lengthy provisions for rent and attendant matters, the interpretation of which is contained in a huge volume of litigation that is beyond the scope of this treatise. In the absence of any agreement for or against rent, one who permissively occupies another's land generally owes the reasonable value of the occupancy unless there are circumstances negativing such liability. There is some question about the mechanism by which this occurs. A 1738 English statute allowed the owner of land to recover reasonable use value from one who occupied it without an express agreement for rent.[3] Many of the United States have similar statutes.[4] Both the Uniform Residential Landlord and Tenant Act and the Model Residential Landlord–Tenant Code provide for reasonable rental value in the absence of rent agreement.[5] In other jurisdictions there is, by judicial rule, an implied contractual duty to pay reasonable use value, though there appears to be some disagreement whether this should be labeled a duty implied in law or in fact.[6] It is clear, however, that nothing is owing if the circumstances negative such intent, as where an employee occupies as part of his duties or where a contract purchaser goes into possession and the sale goes through.[7] There also is a question whether the owner's recovery should be called "rent" or only "reasonable use value." The Restatement takes the position it is not rent, but some decisions label the recovery "rent," apparently on the theory that the implied agreement is one for rent.[8]

A problem on which there is hardly any appellate litigation but which may become increasingly important is who is liable for rent when there are two or more tenants of the same premises.[9] Unless the tenants and the landlord agree otherwise, where more than one tenant makes the leasing agreement, it seems they are all jointly liable for rent.[10] This result is explained by the principles governing the obligations of joint contractual promisors.[11]

§ 6.51 Percentage Rent Clauses

In commercial leases to retail stores, it has become commonplace for part of the rent, sometimes all or nearly all, to be expressed as a percentage

---

3. 11 Geo. 2, c. 19, § 14 (1738).

4. 1 A.L.P., supra note 1, at § 3.64, n. 2.

5. Uniform Residential Landlord and Tenant Act § 1.401(b) ("fair rental value"); Model Residential Landlord–Tenant Code § 2–301(1).

6. See, e.g., Lazarus v. Phelps, 152 U.S. 81, 14 S.Ct. 477, 38 L.Ed. 363 (1894) (implied in law); Carpenter v. United States, 84 U.S. (17 Wall.) 489, 21 L.Ed. 680 (1873) (implied in law; dictum); Gunn v. Scovil, 4 Day 228 (Conn. 1810) (action in *indebitatus assumpsit*); Webb v. Young, 338 So.2d 767 (La.App.1976), application denied 341 So.2d 419 (La.1977) ("*quantum meruit*" recovery); Dwight v. Cutler, 3 Mich. 566 (1855) (implied in fact?); Enslein v. Enslein, 84 Ohio App. 259, 82 N.E.2d 555 (1948).

7. See Carpenter v. United States, 84 U.S. (17 Wall.) 489, 21 L.Ed. 680 (1873) (contract purchaser); Najewitz v. City of Seattle, 21 Wn.2d 656, 152 P.2d 722 (1944) (employee).

But if a sale fails to close, then the contract purchaser usually owes for a period of occupancy. Carpenter v. United States, supra (dictum); Webb v. Young, 338 So.2d 767 (La.App. 1976), application denied 341 So.2d 419 (La. 1977).

8. Compare Restatement (Second) of Property § 12.1, Comment b and Reporter's Note 4 (1977), with, e.g., Carpenter v. United States, 84 U.S. (17 Wall.) 489, 494, 21 L.Ed. 680 (1873) ("reasonable rent"); Enslein v. Enslein, 84 Ohio App. 259, 82 N.E.2d 555 (1948) ("reasonable rental").

9. The occupation of communal houses, occurring especially around college campuses, increases the importance of the problem.

10. Sentliffer v. Jacobs, 84 N.J.L. 128, 86 A. 929 (1913). Cf. Libby v. Perry, 311 A.2d 527 (Me.1973).

11. See 4 A. Corbin, Contracts §§ 925, 926, 928 (1951).

of the tenant's sales on the premises. In this way the landlord shares in the tenant's good (or bad) fortune. Of more importance in recent decades, percentage rent gives the landlord a kind of built-in rent adjustment, a hedge against inflation, since the tenant's prices will usually approximate a general rise in prices. Percentage rental is now almost always based upon "gross sales," though "net sales" used to be used sometimes; gross sales is far preferable because it can be computed with less elements, and less chance for controversy, than net sales. The commonest formula gives the landlord a fixed minimum rent, plus a percentage "override" on sales over a stated amount per some period, often declining percentages at ascending stages of sales. Not only is a well drafted percentage clause a finely tuned, sophisticated piece of drafting, but the landlord, once he has tied his fortunes to the tenant's, will want further clauses in aid of percentage rental. The tenant will generally covenant concerning conduct of the business, noncompetition, accounting for sales, and so forth.[1]

Percentage rent clauses are unquestionably legally enforceable. Courts have, if anything, tended to enforce their language broadly, not unfavorably to landlords.[2] Litigation about such clauses is usually over their specific interpretation or over the question whether a percentage rent clause implies further covenants in aid of percentage rental. For instance, does the existence of a percentage rent clause imply that the tenant will keep long business hours, not open a nearby competing business, or otherwise conduct the business so as to maximize sales when the lease contains no express undertakings of these kinds? Case law has generally implied reasonable obligations of these sorts when percentage rent was the only rent or when fixed minimum rent was nominal, reasoning that the implication was natural when payment of rent totally depended on business practices.[3] But when there has been any fixed minimum rent above a nominal sum, courts have generally refused to imply further covenants, without inquiring into how substantial the fixed minimum is.[4] A few decisions, perhaps representing a trend, have been willing to turn the question of implied covenants on an examination of the surrounding circumstances, an approach favored by some law review notes.[5]

§ 6.51

1. For background on percentage rent, practical tips, and forms, see Colbourn, A Guide to Problems in Shopping Center Leases, 29 Brooklyn L.Rev. 56 (1962); Kranzdorf, Problems of the Developer, 1965 U.Ill.L.F. 173, 187–88, 197–99; Note, 61 Harv.L.Rev. 317 (1948).

2. See, e.g., Gamble–Skogmo, Inc. v. McNair Realty Co., 98 F.Supp. 440 (D.Mont. 1951), affirmed 193 F.2d 876 (9th Cir.1952); Professional Building of Eureka, Inc. v. Anita Frocks, Inc., 178 Cal.App.2d 276, 2 Cal.Rptr. 914 (1960); and Cissna Loan Co. v. Baron, 149 Wash. 386, 270 P. 1022 (1928), examples of decisions giving broad meanings to percentage rent clauses.

3. E.g., Sinclair Refining Co. v. Giddens, 54 Ga.App. 69, 187 S.E. 201 (1936); Marvin Drug Co. v. Couch, 134 S.W.2d 356 (Tex.Civ.App.

1939); Reeker v. Remour, 40 Wn.2d 519, 244 P.2d 270 (1952).

4. E.g., Hicks v. Whelan Drug Co., 131 Cal.App.2d 110, 280 P.2d 104 (1955); Percoff v. Solomon, 259 Ala. 482, 67 So.2d 31 (1953); Stop & Shop, Inc. v. Ganem, 347 Mass. 697, 200 N.E.2d 248 (1964); Tuttle v. W.T. Grant Co., 5 A.D.2d 370, 171 N.Y.S.2d 954 (1958), reversed 6 N.Y.2d 754, 186 N.Y.S.2d 655, 159 N.E.2d 202 (1959); Mercury Inv. Co. v. F.W. Woolworth Co., 706 P.2d 523 (Okl.1985) (no implied covenant to conduct business so as to maximize sales when lease provided for substantial minimum rent). Palm v. Mortgage Investment Co., 229 S.W.2d 869 (Tex.Civ.App. 1950).

5. See College Block v. Atlantic Richfield Co., 200 Cal.App.3d 524, 246 Cal.Rptr. 340 (1988) (court willing to consider whether $1,000 per month was more than nominal rent); Professional Building of Eureka, Inc. v.

§ 6.52   Rent Adjusting Formulas

Anytime a leasehold may run longer than the parties are willing to predict economic conditions, they should consider incorporating a rent adjusting formula, even if there is also percentage rent. Enforceability of such formulas is not in doubt;[1] the problem is in the clear drafting of a formula that is workable and will not produce controversy. Obviously any formula should not depend upon the discretion of either or both parties. A favorite technique is to base rent adjustments on independent appraisals at stated intervals, such as every five years. This plan will work, but it is expensive because there should be three appraisers who should be professionals and it is cumbersome. Also, draftsmen should be aware that a court may treat the appraisers' or rent arbiters' decision as binding and conclusive in the absence of fraud or bad faith.[2]

There is no reason rent cannot be tied to some generally available index, such as the Department of Commerce Consumer Price Index or perhaps some sort of local index. An error in using such an index, at least in theory, is that it is not an index of real estate values and particularly not of the value of the demised premises. However, considering the cost and difficulty of the appraisal method, indexation may be better than nothing in many cases. As a last resort, a lease could provide for fixed increases at stated intervals, a crude method, literally only better than nothing.

§ 6.53   Rent Modification Agreements

The parties to a lease, no less than the parties to a contract, may expressly modify their covenants, including the rental covenant. Questions concern not whether they may do this but how. Issues most litigated have been whether the modification agreement is supported by consideration and whether it is in a form to comply with the Statute of Frauds.

In principle an agreement to increase or decrease rent, being either a promise by the tenant to do more than his legal due or by the landlord to accept less, must be supported by fresh consideration.[1] However, we must hasten to say, in practice courts have often been assiduous to find consideration. When the agreement is to reduce rent, consideration may be present in the tenant's new promise to occupy the premises, to make repairs or

Anita Frocks, Inc., 178 Cal.App.2d 276, 2 Cal. Rptr. 914 (1960); Bastian v. Albertson's, Inc., 102 Idaho 909, 643 P.2d 1079 (App.1982) (when lease provided minimum rent of $1,000 per month, court would not infer covenant to remain in possession but did infer covenant to pay reasonable rent beyond minimum); Simhawk Corp. v. Egler, 52 Ill.App.2d 449, 202 N.E.2d 49 (1964); Note, 61 Harv.L.Rev. 317 (1948); Note, 51 Minn.L.Rev. 1139 (1967).

§ 6.52

1. McMillan v. Great Northern Railway Co., 45 Wn.2d 802, 278 P.2d 316 (1954); 1 A.L.P. supra note 1, at § 3.68. The percent-

age rental decisions, cited in the preceding section, also tend to support the validity of other variable rent devices.

2. Rice v. Ritz Associates, Inc., 58 N.Y.2d 923, 460 N.Y.S.2d 510, 447 N.E.2d 58 (1983), reargument denied 59 N.Y.2d 762, 463 N.Y.S.2d 1030, 450 N.E.2d 254 (1983).

§ 6.53

1. United States v. Bostwick, 94 U.S. (4 Otto) 53, 24 L.Ed. 65 (1876); Green v. Millman Brothers, Inc., 7 Mich.App. 450, 151 N.W.2d 860 (1967); Annot., 43 A.L.R. 1451, 1478–83 (1926), Supp., 93 A.L.R. 1404, 1406–07 (1934); Annot., 30 A.L.R.3d 1259, 1262–67 (1970).

improvements, or to surrender up a portion of the premises.[2] Some decisions even go so far as to find consideration when the rent reduction is designed to alleviate a tenant's financial difficulties, reasoning it is worth something to the landlord to keep the tenant afloat and not abandoning the premises.[3] But other decisions, reasoning that such a tenant incurs no new legal liability, refuse to find consideration in these circumstances.[4] Cases involving rent increases are fewer in number than those involving reductions, but fresh consideration seems to have been required here, too. Such consideration might be in the landlord's extending the term, committing himself not to give notice to terminate, or allowing the tenant to use the land in some manner previously forbidden.[5]

A Statute of Frauds issue is presented when the lease either was, or was required to be, in written or other formal form and a rent modification agreement is in less formal form. Questions are ones of contract law, not peculiarly of landlord-tenant law. As Corbin reminds us, modification agreements really have a double aspect: they are rescissions of part of the original agreement, and they are new agreements for substituted provisions.[6] As to their rescission aspect, the Statute does not apply, for a formal contract may be rescinded informally.[7] As to the substituted provisions, however, there may be a Statute of Frauds problem. Obviously if the original lease was permitted to be and was made informally, an equally informal rent modification is permitted. Or if the original lease was made formally but the Statute would permit such a lease to be made informally, then the rent adjustment agreement may be informal; except for the Statute, an oral and written agreement are of equal dignity.[8] When the Statute of Frauds required the original lease to be in a certain form, then we need to know how long the lease has to run at the date of the modification agreement. If this time is short enough that an oral lease for that time would be permitted by the Statute, then an informal modification for the balance of the term should be valid but otherwise not.[9] This is correct under Corbin's analysis since the substituted provision rests "on its own bottom" as a new agreement. Perhaps, however, the cautious draftsman will put the modification agreement in formal form any time the original lease was so required to be, because some decisions make the sweeping statement that

2. E.g., Cohen v. Homonoff, 311 Mass. 374, 41 N.E.2d 193 (1942) (occupancy); Segal v. M.H. Harris, Inc., 124 N.J.L. 31, 10 A.2d 748 (1940) (partial surrender); Natelsohn v. Reich, 50 Misc. 585, 99 N.Y.S. 327 (1906) (repairs); Annot., 30 A.L.R.3d 1259, 1278–86 (1970).

3. E.g., Ma–Beha Co. v. ACME Realty Co., 286 Ky. 382, 150 S.W.2d 1 (1941) (alternative ground); William Lindeke Land Co. v. Kalman, 190 Minn. 601, 252 N.W. 650 (1934); Annot., 30 A.L.R.3d 1259, 1288–93 (1970).

4. E.g., Green v. Millman Brothers, Inc., 7 Mich.App. 450, 151 N.W.2d 860 (1967); Levine v. Blumenthal, 117 N.J.L. 23, 186 A. 457 (1936), affirmed per curiam, 117 N.J.L. 426, 189 A. 54 (1937). See Annot., 30 A.L.R.3d 1259, 1293–94 (1970).

5. E.g., Anderson v. Miller, 76 Ind.App. 681, 133 N.E. 29 (1921) (dictum) (agreement not to terminate); Jensen v. Anderson, 50 Utah 515, 167 P. 811 (1917) (increased use permitted). See Annot., 43 A.L.R. 1451, 1477–78 (1926).

6. 2 A. Corbin, Contracts § 303 (1950).

7. Id.; 4 S. Williston, Contracts § 592 (3d ed. W. Jaeger ed. 1961).

8. See Teal v. Bilby, 123 U.S. 572, 8 S.Ct. 239, 31 L.Ed. 263 (1887) (contract to agist cattle); Anderson v. Miller, 76 Ind.App. 681, 133 N.E. 29 (1921); 2 A. Corbin, Contracts, supra note 6, this section, at § 301.

9. Tashjian v. Karp, 277 Mass. 42, 177 N.E. 816 (1931); Sherman Clay & Co. v. Buffum & Pendleton, Inc., 91 Or. 352, 179 P. 241 (1919); Restatement (Second) of Property, § 2.4, Comment b (1977); 1 A.L.P., supra note 1, at § 3.70. See Parrish v. Haynes, 62 F.2d 105 (5th Cir.1932); Jewell v. Irvmac Shoe Shops, Inc., 19 Misc.2d 815, 187 N.Y.S.2d 412 (1959).

that is necessary.[10]   In these decisions the theory, contrary to Corbin's, is that the modified provision is part of an agreement the whole of which is within the Statute.[11]

Even when a rent modification agreement falls under the Statute's interdiction, it may be saved in a couple of cases.   First, under the doctrine that the Statute does not apply to fully executed informal agreements, when the tenant has paid and the landlord accepted modified rent under such an agreement, then generally neither party is allowed to recover the difference between the amounts paid and the original rent.[12]   Second, as to future rental payments, there is the possibility that the informal modification agreement may be taken out of the Statute's operation by the familiar doctrines of estoppel or part performance.[13]

§ 6.54   Rent Acceleration Clauses

A rent acceleration clause empowers the landlord to advance the due date of future rent installments in the event the tenant defaults in any installment or, as such clauses are generally drafted, breaches any covenant. One reason a landlord would wish such a clause is that the application of the contract doctrine of breach by anticipatory repudiation to landlord and tenant is somewhat problematical.[1]   The main advantage of an acceleration clause, however, is an important practical one.   If the tenant is on the verge of default or possibly has had some minor defaults and is on the verge of serious ones, the landlord's threat to accelerate all future rent can be a powerful lever to induce strict rectitude.

Indeed, it is the power of the lever that gives rise to a legal argument against acceleration clauses.   Most decisions on the question, a number of them from one jurisdiction, Pennsylvania, have upheld the validity of such clauses.[2]   Reasoning is that parties have freedom to contract and also that

---

10. E.g., Bonicamp v. Starbuck, 25 Okl. 483, 106 P. 839 (1910); Vance Lumber Co. v. Tall's Travel Shops, Inc., 19 Wn.2d 414, 142 P.2d 904 (1943).   See generally Annot., 17 A.L.R. 10 (1922).   Supp., 28 A.L.R. 1095 (1924), 80 A.L.R. 539 (1932), 118 A.L.R. 1511 (1939).

11. In addition to the *Bonicamp* case and the A.L.R. annotations cited in the preceding note, see Arkmo Lumber Co. v. Cantrell, 159 Ark. 445, 252 S.W. 901 (1923).

12. E.g., Central Sav. Bank v. Fashoda, Inc., 94 A.D.2d 927, 463 N.Y.S.2d 335 (1983), affirmed 62 N.Y.2d 721, 476 N.Y.S.2d 828, 465 N.E.2d 367 (1984); Bamberger Co. v. Certified Productions, 88 Utah 194, 48 P.2d 489 (1935), adhered to 88 Utah 213, 53 P.2d 1153 (1936); Oregon & Washington Railroad Co. v. Elliott Bay Mill & Lumber Co., 70 Wash. 148, 126 P. 406 (1912); Annot., 17 A.L.R. 10 (1922), Supp., 28 A.L.R. 1095 (1924), 80 A.L.R. 539 (1932), 118 A.L.R. 1511 (1939).

13. See generally Restatement (Second) of Property, § 2.3 (1977); 1 A.L.P., supra note 1, at § 3.21; 2 A. Corbin, Contracts, supra note 6, this section, at § 308.

§ 6.54

1. Most American courts now probably apply the anticipatory breach doctrine to leases.

See Farmers & Bankers Life Insurance Co. v. St. Regis Paper Co., 456 F.2d 347 (5th Cir. 1972); Hawkinson v. Johnston, 122 F.2d 724 (8th Cir.1941), certiorari denied 314 U.S. 694, 62 S.Ct. 365, 86 L.Ed. 555 (1941); Szabo Associates, Inc. v. Peachtree Piedmont Associates, 141 Ga.App. 654, 234 S.E.2d 119 (1977).   However, the doctrine was not a traditional part of landlord-tenant law, and some courts have refused to apply it.   E.g., Wells v. Twenty-First St. Realty Co., 12 F.2d 237 (6th Cir.1926); People ex rel. Nelson v. West Town State Bank, 373 Ill. 106, 25 N.E.2d 509 (1940).   For general discussions see Annot., 137 A.L.R. 432 (1942); 1 A.L.P., supra note 1, at §§ 3.11, 3.74.

2. Maddox v. Hobbie, 228 Ala. 80, 152 So. 222 (1934); Shepard Realty Co. v. United Shoe Stores Co., 193 La. 211, 190 So. 383 (1939); Belnord Realty Co. v. Levison, 204 App.Div. 415, 198 N.Y.S. 184 (1923); Platt v. Johnson, 168 Pa. 47, 31 A. 935 (1895); American Seating Co. v. Murdock, 111 Pa.Super. 242, 169 A. 250 (1933); Annot., 58 A.L.R. 300 (1929), Supp., 128 A.L.R. 750 (1940).   See Snyder v. Exum, 227 Va. 373, 315 S.E.2d 216 (1984) (decision suggests it is safer for landlord to have power to accelerate than to have automatic acceleration clause).

they might have agreed that the entire rent was due at the beginning of the term. A smaller group of decisions have refused to enforce rent acceleration clauses, on the ground that they provide for a penalty.[3] The same question arises in testing the validity of a liquidated damages clause; indeed, acceleration clauses are viewed as a form of liquidated damages clause. Therefore, a court that is inclined to question an acceleration clause will be most upset by one that allows acceleration of a large amount of rent for minor breaches.[4] Even courts that generally enforce acceleration clauses will not allow the landlord both to terminate the leasehold and to recover the sum of accelerated rent for the balance of the term.[5]

§ 6.55 Government Regulation of Rent

During periods that are designated as emergencies, federal, state, or local governments sometimes legislatively control maximum rents to which residential landlords and tenants may agree. America's first rent controls were imposed by the District of Columbia during a housing shortage that followed World War I. During World War II, federal rent controls were imposed in certain areas as part of a general system of price control established by the Emergency Price Control Act of 1942. Again, federal controls existed in a few areas under the Economic Stabilization Act of 1970, which expired in 1974. State and local residential rent controls have continued in several states since World War II, even increasing in number since the early 1970's.[1] It seems that a dozen or so states have statutes that enable their cities or counties to enact systems of peacetime residential rent control.[2] Not all localities within those states have adopted rent controls, but over 200 have done so.[3]

Under the United States Constitution, the validity of federal rent control during wartime was established by the Supreme Court in *Bowles v.*

3. In re Barnett, 12 F.2d 73 (2d Cir.1926), cert. denied 273 U.S. 699, 47 S.Ct. 94, 71 L.Ed. 846 (1926) (New York law, alternative ground); Ricker v. Rombough, 120 Cal.App.2d Supp. 912, 261 P.2d 328 (1953); 884 West End Ave. Corp. v. Pearlman, 201 App.Div. 12, 193 N.Y.S. 670 (1922), affirmed per curiam, 234 N.Y. 589, 138 N.E. 458 (1922); Fifty States Management Corp. v. Pioneer Auto Parks, Inc., 64 A.D.2d 836, 407 N.Y.S.2d 318 (1978), reversed 46 N.Y.2d 573, 475 N.Y.S.2d 800, 389 N.E.2d 113 (1979) (clause void "under the particular circumstances of this case"). See generally the A.L.R. annotations cited in the preceding note. Note that there is some conflict in the New York decisions. See also Frey v. Abdo, 441 So.2d 1383 (Miss.1983) (acceleration's being harsh remedy, court will not find acceleration clause if language is not clear); Saladino v. Rault Petroleum Corp., 436 So.2d 714 (La.App.1983) (to accelerate, landlord had to comply strictly with notice provisions of lease).

4. See especially 884 West End Ave. Corp. v. Pearlman, preceding note.

5. See In re Barnett, 12 F.2d 73 (2d Cir. 1926) (alternative ground); Maddox v. Hobbie, 228 Ala. 80, 152 So. 222 (1934) (dictum); Gen-

try v. Recreation, Inc., 192 S.C. 429, 7 S.E.2d 63 (1940); Annot., 58 A.L.R. 300, 306 (1929), Supp., 128 A.L.R. 750, 755 (1940). But see Caplan v. Latter & Blum, Inc., 462 So.2d 229 (La.App.1984), reversed on other grounds 468 So.2d 1188 (La.1985) (tenant who abandoned premises owed accelerated rent for balance of term, but landlord had to credit rent received from new tenant).

§ 6.55

1. See Note, Rent Control and Landlords' Property Right: The Reasonable Return Doctrine Revived, 33 Rutgers L.Rev. 165, 165–68 (1980).

2. A count made in 1977 showed 10 states with rent-control enabling acts. They were Alaska, Connecticut, District of Columbia, Hawaii, Maine, Massachusetts, New York, Puerto Rico, Texas, and the Virgin Islands. Restatement (Second) of Property § 12.1, Statutory Note 4 (1977). In addition, other states, including California, Florida, and New Jersey, are known to have rent controls in some localities.

3. Report of the President's Commission on Housing, p. 91 (1982).

Willingham in 1944.[4] *Block v. Hirsh* upheld the constitutionality of the peacetime controls that existed in the District of Columbia following World War I.[5] There was once a question whether rent controls had to be justified by an emergency and thus had to be temporary.[6] However, the Supreme Court's decision in *Pennell v. City of San Jose* in 1988 leaves no question that peacetime controls are constitutionally permissible in areas that have housing shortages.[7] The Court has also rejected an argument that the Berkeley, California, rent control ordinance violated the Federal Sherman Antitrust Act.[8]

Much recent litigation, especially in California, New Jersey, and New York, makes it clear that, at least in those jurisdictions, there is no question that peacetime rent control is in general valid. However, it seems to be accepted that a given rent control system may be invalid as a taking or perhaps as a denial of due process if it denies a particular landlord profitable use of his land.[9] The Supreme Court in *Pennell v. City of San Jose* also seems to accept the proposition that an ordinance may amount to a taking if it denies the landlord profitable use of the land.

Where state rent control exists, it generally is administered by local governments under state enabling acts that specifically authorize the local entities to engage in the function. In the absence of specific enabling legislation, there is a split of authority over whether local governments may adopt rent controls under their general police powers.[10]

Rent regulation of a limited kind exists in those states that have adopted residential landlord-tenant statutes with provisions against what is generically called "retaliatory eviction." Going back to Edwards v. Habib [11] in 1968, decisions in several jurisdictions concluded it was against public policy for a landlord to attempt to evict a residential tenant to retaliate for the tenant's taking some action, such as complaining to public officers or bringing a court suit, on account of the landlord's breach of a duty to keep

4. Bowles v. Willingham, 321 U.S. 503, 64 S.Ct. 641, 88 L.Ed. 892 (1944).

5. Block v. Hirsh, 256 U.S. 135, 41 S.Ct. 458, 65 L.Ed. 865 (1921) (District of Columbia); Teeval Co. v. Stern, 301 N.Y. 346, 93 N.E.2d 884 (1950).

6. Teeval Co. v. Stern, 301 N.Y. 346, 93 N.E.2d 884 (1950) (dictum); Meyers v. New York States Division of Housing, etc., 36 A.D.2d 166, 319 N.Y.S.2d 522 (1971) (dictum).

7. Pennell v. City of San Jose, 485 U.S. 1, 108 S.Ct. 849, 99 L.Ed.2d 1 (1988).

8. Fisher v. City of Berkeley, 475 U.S. 260, 106 S.Ct. 1045, 89 L.Ed.2d 206 (1986), rehearing denied 475 U.S. 1150, 106 S.Ct. 1806, 90 L.Ed.2d 350 (1986).

9. See Nash v. City of Santa Monica, 37 Cal.3d 97, 207 Cal.Rptr. 285, 688 P.2d 894 (1984), appeal dismissed 470 U.S. 1046, 105 S.Ct. 1740, 84 L.Ed.2d 807 (1985) (ordinance constitutional that restricted landlord's ability to evict tenants or to demolish rental units; far-reaching decision); Birkenfeld v. City of Berkeley, 17 Cal.3d 129, 130 Cal.Rptr. 465, 550 P.2d 1001 (1976) (leading case, cited in all

subsequent California decisions); Cotati Alliance for Better Housing v. City of Cotati, 148 Cal.App.3d 280, 195 Cal.Rptr. 825 (1983) (rent control ordinance constitutional); Orange Taxpayers Council, Inc. v. City of Orange, 83 N.J. 246, 416 A.2d 353 (1980) (ordinance valid, even though it allowed rent increase only when premises were in substantial compliance with housing codes); Helmsley v. Borough of Fort Lee, 78 N.J. 200, 394 A.2d 65 (1978), appeal dismissed 440 U.S. 978, 99 S.Ct. 1782, 60 L.Ed.2d 237 (1979) (to extent ordinance did not allow "reasonable return," it was void); Windman v. City of Englewood, 200 N.J.Super. 218, 491 A.2d 32 (1985) (rent rollback upheld).

10. E.g., Heubeck v. City of Baltimore, 205 Md. 203, 107 A.2d 99 (1954) (may adopt); Tietjens v. City of St. Louis, 359 Mo. 439, 222 S.W.2d 70 (1949) (may not adopt); Inganamort v. Borough of Fort Lee, 62 N.J. 521, 303 A.2d 298 (1973), appeal after remand 72 N.J. 412, 371 A.2d 34 (1977) (may adopt).

11. 397 F.2d 687 (D.C.Cir.1968), certiorari denied 393 U.S. 1016, 89 S.Ct. 618, 21 L.Ed.2d 560 (1969). *Edwards* has been followed by a number of other decisions around the country,

the premises in repair. Since that date a number of jurisdictions have enacted residential landlord-tenant acts with similar but broader anti-retaliatory sections.[12] Both the Uniform Residential Landlord and Tenant Act and the Model Residential Landlord–Tenant Code contain such sections.[13] These broader statutory provisions prohibit not only retaliatory evictions but also other kinds of retaliatory actions, including rent increases. Usually the statutes either create a presumption that a rent increase attempted after the tenant's action is retaliatory or prohibit a rent increase for a stated time after such action, with exceptions for certain bona fide increases. Therefore, where such a statutory provision is in effect, when a tenant has taken action of the kind described, the landlord is under a disability, at least for a prescribed period, to increase rent.

§ 6.56 Actions for Rent–Estoppel to Deny Title

We saw in a prior section that, unless the parties have agreed there shall be none, a tenant has a duty to pay rent. This duty almost always arises upon an express covenant for or reservation of rent, and if there is no such provision, upon an implied obligation to pay reasonable rental value. These duties measure the extent of the landlord's recovery in an action for rent.

The general statement is sometimes made that in an action for rent a tenant is estopped to defend by setting up a title adverse to his landlord's. This statement must be understood with some qualifications. First, implicit in the statement itself, it must have been established that the parties were landlord and tenant.[1] Second, the estoppel is only as to the landlord's title at the inception of the leasehold; thus, a tenant may assert that the landlord's title passed to a third person or even to the tenant after the term began.[2] Third, the tenant is not estopped if he has been kept out of or ousted from possession by someone with paramount title, since the reason for the estoppel is that the tenant has gotten what he bargained for in the lease. There is a split of authority on the question whether a tenant is estopped to set up his own title when he was already in possession at the time he made a lease with the adverse party.[3] Fourth, there is no estoppel if the putative tenant was induced to make the lease by the landlord's fraud or misrepresentation or, some decisions say, by the tenant's mistake as to the landlord's title.[4] Perhaps it is appropriate to remark that, considering all the qualifications, the tenant's estoppel serves a quite limited purpose in actions for rent.

of which Dickhut v. Norton, 45 Wis.2d 389, 173 N.W.2d 297 (1970), is perhaps best known.

12. See Cunningham, The New Implied and Statutory Warranties of Habitability in Residential Leases: From Contract to Status, 16 Urban Law Annual 3, 126–35 (1979).

13. Uniform Residential Landlord and Tenant Act § 5.101; Model Residential Landlord–Tenant Code § 2–407.

§ 6.56

1. See Lund v. Gray Line Water Tours, Inc., 277 S.C. 447, 289 S.E.2d 404 (1982) (tenant estopped to deny landlord's title; alternative holding). Lockwood v. Carter Oil Co., 73 W.Va. 175, 80 S.E. 814 (1913) (oil lease);

Smith v. Smith, 81 Tex. 45, 16 S.W. 637 (1891); 1 A.L.P., supra note 1, at § 3.65.

2. E.g., Seivert v. Powell, 191 Or. 637, 232 P.2d 806 (1951) (conveyance to third person); Holzer v. Rhodes, 24 Wn.2d 184, 163 P.2d 811 (1945) (tenant purchased tax title).

3. Annot., 98 A.L.R. 545 (1935); Annot., 87 A.L.R.2d 602 (1963) (oil and gas leases); 1 A.L.P., supra note 1, at § 3.65. Some decisions even conclude a tenant is not estopped if he voluntarily refrains from entering into possession.

4. Williams v. Higgason, 205 Ga. 349, 53 S.E.2d 473 (1949); Gray v. Whitla, 70 Okl. 288, 174 P. 239 (1918); Annot., 2 A.L.R. 359 (1919).

§ 6.57 Distraint

Under the ancient common-law right of distraint, or "distress" as it is often called, the landlord is allowed to enter the demised premises and to seize goods found there for the collection of unpaid rent. He could seize and hold any goods found on the premises, even those being sold to the tenant on conditional sale or the goods of a third person.[1] Once the landlord had the goods in his possession, he had what amounted to a common-law holding lien; he could not sell the goods, but he could hold them "hostage" until the tenant made up the rent default.[2]

In America distraint as known at common law has fallen on evil times, so that, one way or another, it no longer generally exists. A few jurisdictions never did adopt it.[3] Others have refused to apply the doctrine because it has been expressly or impliedly abolished by some statute.[4] Both the Uniform Residential Landlord and Tenant Act and the Model Residential Landlord–Tenant Code expressly abolish distraint.[5] In states where distress still exists, it is generally governed by statutes that more or less modify its common-law form.[6] At least where such statutes require some state official to participate in the seizure proceedings, they may deny due process on the ground that they authorize seizure without a prior hearing.[7] If no state officer is involved, as he was not with common-law distraint, then the due process attack is harder to make, but it has been made successfully.[8]

§ 6.58 Landlords' Statutory Liens

As just mentioned, in most jurisdictions common-law distraint has either been codified or has been replaced with statutory landlords' liens. Statutory liens are more common than codified distraint. Because the lien statutes are highly individual from state to state, one must examine the statutes of a

§ 6.57

1. See Annot., 45 A.L.R. 949, 952–53 (1926) (conditional sale); Annot., 62 A.L.R. 1106, 1107–11 (1929).

2. In addition to the A.L.R. annotations cited in the preceding note, see discussions in Henderson v. Mayer, 225 U.S. 631, 32 S.Ct. 699, 56 L.Ed. 1233 (1912); Jones v. Ford, 254 Fed. 645 (8th Cir.1918); 2 H. Tiffany, Landlord and Tenant §§ 325–46 (1912).

3. E.g., Jones v. Ford, 254 Fed. 645 (8th Cir.1918) (Missouri law); 2 H. Tiffany, preceding note, at § 325.

4. See, e.g., Webb v. Sharp, 80 U.S. (13 Wall.) 14, 20 L.Ed. 478 (1871) (District of Columbia); P.F. Scheidelman & Sons, Inc. v. Webster Basket Co., 143 Misc. 836, 257 N.Y.S. 552 (1932), affirmed 236 A.D. 774, 259 N.Y.S. 963 (1932); Annot., 9 A.L.R. 300, 300–01 (1920).

5. Uniform Residential Landlord and Tenant Act § 4.205(b); Model Residential Landlord–Tenant Code § 3–403(2).

6. See Janes v. Country Escrow Service, 135 Ariz. 231, 660 P.2d 482 (App.1982) (landlord entitled to distrain tenant's goods for

unpaid rent under statute, even though he had wrongfully evicted tenant). For a list of statutes, see Restatement (Second) of Property, § 12.1, Statutory Note 5 (1977).

7. See Fuentes v. Shevin, 407 U.S. 67, 92 S.Ct. 1983, 32 L.Ed.2d 556 (1972), rehearing denied 409 U.S. 902, 93 S.Ct. 177, 34 L.Ed.2d 165 (1972); Sniadach v. Family Finance Corp., 395 U.S. 337, 89 S.Ct. 1820, 23 L.Ed.2d 349 (1969); Callen v. Sherman's, Inc., 92 N.J. 114, 455 A.2d 1102 (1983) (statutory distraint by sheriff violated due process because no prior hearing, but tenant suffered no damage in this case); Van Ness Industries, Inc. v. Claremont Painting & Decorating Co., 129 N.J.Super. 507, 324 A.2d 102 (Ch.Div.1974); Restatement (Second) of Property, § 12.1, Reporter's Note 12 (1977), cites a number of decisions that have invalidated distraint and lien statutes for lack of prior hearing.

8. Gross v. Fox, 349 F.Supp. 1164 (E.D.Pa. 1972), vacated 496 F.2d 1153 (3d Cir.1974). See also Hall v. Garson, 468 F.2d 845 (5th Cir.1972), and Barber v. Rader, 350 F.Supp. 183 (S.D.Fla.1972), which strike down state "lien" statutes that provided landlords could seize tenants' goods by self-help.

given state. Commonly found features are: there may be separate provisions for liens on crops or other tenant's goods or both. Liens attach only to items the tenant owns, not, for instance, to third persons' goods, to goods the tenant is purchasing by conditional sale, or to items sold to bona fide purchasers. A lien may be to secure rent or both rent and the tenant's other covenants. The device being a true lien, analogous to a mechanic's lien, there will be procedures for foreclosure and sale. Some statutes provide for seizure of the tenant's goods by a public officer, by a procedure similar to pre-judgment attachment.[1]

Especially when this last feature is present, there are serious questions about the constitutionality of landlords' lien statutes. The most likely objection is that of Fuentes v. Shevin and Sniadach v. Family Finance Corporation, that seizure by state officers without a hearing deprives the tenant of property without due process of law.[2] On that ground a number of landlords' lien statutes have been struck down around the country.[3] Even when the statute provides for seizure by the landlord rather than by state officers, so that state action is harder to find, several lien statutes have been held to deny due process.[4] Another possible constitutional objection is that invasion of the tenant's premises by a public officer, conceivably even by the landlord, amounts to an unreasonable search and seizure, in violation of the fourth amendment. Some courts have adopted this argument in pre-judgment replevin cases; some have rejected it.[5] Finally, it seems an argument could be mounted that seizure without a prior hearing was against public policy.[6] Perhaps it may be remarked that statutory rent liens, though less outmoded than common-law distraint, are also in decline. They, like distraint, are abolished in both the Uniform Residential Landlord and Tenant Act and the Model Residential Landlord–Tenant Code.[7]

§ 6.59 Security and Damage Deposits

Presumably on the theory of "a bird in the hand," landlords frequently require their tenants to deposit a sum of money with them at the beginning of the term, to serve as security for the tenant's paying rent and performing

---

§ 6.58

1. See especially Restatement (Second) of Property § 12.1, Statutory Note 5 (1977), which summarizes lien statutes for 28 states. It separately lists statutes codifying distraint for 16 states. For other discussions of lien statutes, see Annot., 9 A.L.R. 300 (1920), and 1 A.L.P., supra note 1, at § 3.72. See also Sachs v. Curry–Thomas Hardware, Inc., 464 So.2d 597 (Fla.App.1985) (landlord's statutory lien, which had attached to tenant's business fixtures, continued when tenant assigned lease and sold fixtures to assignee); Dwyer v. Cooksville Grain Co., 117 Ill.App.3d 1001, 73 Ill.Dec. 497, 454 N.E.2d 357 (1983) (landlord's statutory lien had priority over tenant's lender's U.C.C. security interest in proceeds from sale of crops).

2. Fuentes v. Shevin, 407 U.S. 67, 92 S.Ct. 1983, 32 L.Ed.2d 556 (1972), rehearing denied 409 U.S. 902, 93 S.Ct. 177, 34 L.Ed.2d 165 (1972) (pre-judgment replevin); Sniadach v. Family Finance Corp., 395 U.S. 337, 89 S.Ct. 1820, 23 L.Ed.2d 349 (1969) (pre-judgment garnishment).

3. See Annot., 18 A.L.R. Fed. 223, 276–80 (1974); Restatement (Second) of Property § 12.1, Reporter's Note 12 (1977).

4. Hall v. Garson, 468 F.2d 845 (5th Cir. 1972); Barber v. Rader, 350 F.Supp. 183 (S.D.Fla.1972). See also Gross v. Fox, 349 F.Supp. 1164 (E.D.Pa.1972), vacated 496 F.2d 1153 (3d Cir.1974) (distraint statute).

5. See Annot., 18 A.L.R. Fed. 223, 248–50 (1974).

6. Cf. Bass v. Boetel & Co., 191 Neb. 733, 217 N.W.2d 804 (1974) (lease clause authorizing self-help seizure).

7. Uniform Residential Landlord and Tenant Act § 4.205(a); Model Landlord–Tenant Code § 3.403(1).

other lease covenants. A specialized form of security deposit is the so-called "damage deposit," which the landlord holds to cover the cost of repairing physical damage or perhaps extraordinary cleaning costs caused by the tenant's acts. It is common for leases to require both deposits to secure rent and performance and to pay for damage. Both kinds will, unless the context indicates otherwise, be treated here as forms of security deposits.

Lease clauses for cash deposits are too varied to cover in detail, but they commonly establish one of three basic mechanisms: (1) The tenant deposits a sum of money or of securities, against which the landlord may draw to make up any default or to pay for damage. (2) The deposit will be forfeited if the tenant defaults. (3) The deposit is denominated advance rent, usually for one or more rent periods at the end of the leasehold. We will discuss each of these, then will take up some problems pertaining to security deposits generally.

The first and most straightforward mechanism is for the tenant to deposit money or securities upon the understanding that the landlord may draw upon the fund to make up for the tenant's defaults or to pay for physical damage but that all sums not thus withdrawn will be returned to the tenant at the end of the term. Courts agree that the fund remains the tenant's property; for instance, with this kind of deposit, the landlord does not receive income for federal income tax purposes when the deposit is made but only if and when a breach occurs.[1] There is disagreement, however, over the relationship between landlord and tenant with respect to the fund. Most courts consider the landlord to be the tenant's debtor.[2] A few states, New Jersey notably, regard the parties as pledgor and pledgee.[3] Under the creditor-debtor view or the pledgor-pledgee view, the landlord generally is not required to keep the deposit separate from his own funds or to pay interest on it unless, as in a number of jurisdictions, a statute imposes one or both duties.[4] In New York, by virtue of a statute, the landlord has long been considered a trustee of the deposit, which he may not commingle.[5] Under any view of the landlord-tenant relationship, with the type of deposit now being discussed, the landlord has a duty to account to the tenant for anything he withdraws from the fund.[6] All that has been said in this paragraph must be read together with a later paragraph that will summarize important statutory impacts upon security deposits in general.

A second form of security clause is one that, on its face anyway, allows that landlord to retain the entire deposit if the tenant breaches in any way. This is in essence a liquidated damages mechanism. Questions about commingling, interest payment, federal income tax, and accounting should be

---

§ 6.59

1. Astor Holding Co. v. Commissioner, 135 F.2d 47 (5th Cir.1943) (dictum); Warren Service Corp. v. Commissioner, 110 F.2d 723 (2d Cir.1940).

2. Mallory Associates v. Barving Realty Co., 300 N.Y. 297, 90 N.E.2d 468 (1949) (dictum); Commercial National Bank v. Cutter Realty Co., 205 N.C. 99, 170 S.E. 139 (1933); 1 A.L.P., supra note 1, at § 3.73; Restatement (Second) of Property § 12.1, Comment 1 (1977).

3. E.g., Rasmussen v. Helen Realty Co., 92 Ind.App. 278, 168 N.E. 717 (1929) (parties agreed deposit was "collateral"); Partington v. Miller, 122 N.J.L. 388, 5 A.2d 468 (1939).

4. See Restatement (Second) of Property § 12.1, Comment 1, Statutory Note 6, and Reporter's Note 11 (1977).

5. See Mallory Associates v. Barving Realty Co., 300 N.Y. 297, 90 N.E.2d 468 (1949).

6. Restatement (Second) of Property § 12.1, Comment 1 and Reporter's Note 11 (1977).

resolved the same as for the deposit described in the preceding paragraph. A new issue is whether the provision for liquidated damages may be declared void on the ground that it calls for a penalty. Decided cases go both ways on this question.[7] The correct approach, which seems to reconcile most of the decisions, is to begin with the principle that parties may agree for liquidated damages as long as the amount is "reasonable." To test reasonableness, we place ourselves in the position of the parties when they made their agreement and then ask whether, looking ahead, the amount provided for liquidated damages bore a reasonable relationship to actual damages that might have been anticipated. If so, the provision is valid; if not, it is void.[8] Other factors sometimes mentioned, such as uncertainty of actual damages, length of leasehold, and variation in importance of various lease covenants, should be considered as elements of the general reasonableness test.

The third form of security device, the prepayment of rent for the last period or periods of the term, is not truly a "deposit." When paid at the commencement of the term, the money is the landlord's absolute property. He is required to include it in that year's income for federal income tax purposes.[9] Though it is probably not often done, because advance rent and a security deposit serve overlapping functions, there seems no reason the parties might not use both devices, which do not completely overlap. Apparently the main legal reason a landlord would want rent in advance for the latter part of the term is to avoid the common-law rule that if the landlord entered during the term because the lease authorized it for the tenant's breach, the landlord could not recover rent for the balance of the term. When courts have been willing to categorize the sum paid as being advance rent, they have generally allowed the landlord to retain the advance rent upon his reentry.[10] Some courts, however, have had a tendency to interpret loosely drawn clauses to call for security deposits instead of advance rent, with the result that the landlord receives only actual damages.[11]

With either kind of true security deposit, a problem arises if the landlord conveys the reversion. Is the grantee liable to pay over to the tenant the deposit or that portion to which the tenant is entitled at the end of the term? The question is usually viewed as being whether the landlord's express or implied promise to return is a covenant the burden of which runs with the reversion. At the heart of this question, the narrow issue is whether such a burden touches and concerns the reversion. On this, the few courts that have faced the issue have reached opposite conclusions.[12] It

---

7. See Annot., 106 A.L.R. 292 (1937), which collects many decisions, and 1 A.L.P., supra note 1, at § 3.73.

8. See, among many decisions, Burns Trading Co. v. Welborn, 81 F.2d 691 (10th Cir. 1936), certiorari denied 298 U.S. 672, 56 S.Ct. 936, 80 L.Ed. 1394 (1936); Barrett v. Monro, 69 Wash. 229, 124 P. 369 (1912). See generally Annot., 106 A.L.R. 292 (1937).

9. Hyde Park Realty v. Commissioner, 211 F.2d 462 (2d Cir.1954); Astor Holding Co. v. Commissioner, 135 F.2d 47 (5th Cir.1943).

10. E.g., Lochner v. Martin, 218 Md. 519, 147 A.2d 749 (1959); Dutton v. Christie, 63 Wash. 372, 115 P. 856 (1911). See discussion

and decisions cited, Annot., 27 A.L.R.2d 656 (1953); Restatement (Second) of Property § 12.1, Reporter's Note 11 (1977).

11. In addition to the A.L.R. annotation and Restatement citations in the preceding note, see 1 A.L.P., supra note 1, at § 3.73.

12. Moskin v. Goldstein, 225 Mich. 389, 196 N.W. 415 (1923) (grantee is bound to refund tenant); Mallory Associates, Inc. v. Barving Realty Co., 300 N.Y. 297, 90 N.E.2d 468 (1949) ("personal covenant"; dictum); Kaufman v. Williams, 92 N.J.L. 182, 104 A. 202 (1918) (N.J. theory that landlord is pledgee). See also Richards v. Browning, 214 App.Div. 665, 212 N.Y.S. 738 (1925), appeal dismissed

seems clear that if the sum paid by the tenant is advance rent, he is entitled to have it applied to the agreed rental period, whether or not the landlord has conveyed the reversion.

In the event of the tenant's becoming a bankrupt, the landlord's holding of a security deposit will affect his claim against the bankrupt. The amount of the deposit must be credited against this claim. Indeed, in the unlikely event the deposit is more than the claim, it seems the overplus must be paid to the bankruptcy trustee.[13] For advance rent, the same rules would presumably hold.

Statutes in most states affect, to a greater or lesser extent, what has been said thus far about security and damage deposits.[14] Likewise, the Uniform Residential Landlord and Tenant Act and the Model Residential Landlord–Tenant Code regulate such deposits.[15] Reference must be had to the quite varied statutes for details. Matters often regulated are maximum amounts of deposits, separation of the deposit from the landlord's personal funds, payment of interest, items deposits may secure, the landlord's duty to render an accounting, the landlord's duty to give notice of items of physical damage, attorneys' fees and perhaps penalties to a tenant who has to sue for reimbursement, and provisions that the landlord's grantee is bound. Most statutes apply only to residential leases. A question that will have to be resolved is whether advance rent is a "security deposit" under such statutes. It would seem that if the sum paid is clearly advance rent, after allowing for the fact that in doubtful cases some courts prefer to describe sums as deposits, most statutes should not apply.

Statutes regulating landlords' retention of residential tenants' security deposits are spawning a tremendous amount of litigation. In general, such statutes are designed to give tenants protection the common law never afforded, and courts tend to interpret the statutes against landlords.[16] Judging from the large volume of litigation, it seems landlords have not yet become familiar with the provisions of the comparatively recent statutes. In order to be entitled to retain security deposits, landlords may be required to give tenants itemized lists of claimed damages and perhaps even receipts for items the landlord has had repaired or replaced.[17] Wrongful withholding of a security deposit, whether because there was no ground to hold it or because he failed to comply with technical conditions of the statute, may

242 N.Y. 539, 152 N.E. 418 (1926) (original owner must return; deposit does not "go with the land"); Mullendore Theatres, Inc. v. Growth Realty Investors Co., 39 Wn.App. 64, 691 P.2d 970 (1984) (landlord's covenant to return security deposit only personal covenant that did not bind landlord's grantee). See also Vinton v. Demetrion, 19 Mass.App.Ct. 948, 473 N.E.2d 207 (1985) (landlord's grantee has statutory duty to return residential tenant's security deposit).

13. Oldden v. Tonto Realty Corp., 143 F.2d 916 (2d Cir.1944); 3 W. Collier, Bankruptcy § 502.02[7][d] (15th ed. 1980).

14. Statutes from 30 states are cited and summarized in Restatement (Second) of Property § 12.1, Statutory Note 6 (1977).

15. Uniform Residential Landlord and Tenant Act § 2.101; Model Residential Landlord–Tenant Code § 2–401.

16. See, e.g., Mellor v. Berman, 390 Mass. 275, 454 N.E.2d 907 (1983); Mitchell v. Preusse, 358 N.W.2d 511 (N.D.1984); and Shands v. Castrovinci, 115 Wis.2d 352, 340 N.W.2d 506 (1983), as examples of interpretation against landlords.

17. See Mallah v. Barkauskas, 130 Ill. App.3d 815, 85 Ill.Dec. 926, 474 N.E.2d 886 (1985) (receipts); Ackerman v. Little, 679 S.W.2d 70 (Tex.App.1984) (itemized list).

subject the landlord to double or treble damages or the tenant's attorney fees.[18]

Tenants also may be caught unawares by provisions of some of the residential security deposit statutes. Again judging from recent decisions, it seems tenants may overlook a requirement of some statutes that, in order to be entitled to return of their deposits, they must give the landlord their forwarding address.[19] So, it seems that lawyers who represent either landlords or tenants should, if they are consulted in time, instruct their clients about strict observance of the requirements of security deposit statutes.

I. TAXES AND INSURANCE

§ 6.60 Taxes and Assessments

Nothing in the ordinary leasing situation implies a tenant's duty to pay real estate taxes or special assessments on the demised premises.[1] If the tenant has the duty, it is usually under a covenant in the lease. There are, however, a few circumstances out of which courts may imply a tenant's duty. He generally has the duty to pay an increase in the taxes caused by his construction of improvements that he will use up or get to keep.[2] The tenant of a leasehold that is perpetual or of a term of 99 years or more is, by a number of decisions, taxable, on the theory that he either owns the fee or something equivalent.[3] Landlords have sometimes argued that a tenant's duty should be implied when the tenant has been voluntarily paying taxes or when he has a purchase option. Courts have been unreceptive to these arguments, there being a general indisposition to fasten liability on the tenant except in clear cases.[4]

On the landlord's side, still assuming no lease clause governs, the opinions often say the landlord has a "duty" to pay real estate taxes.[5] While the landlord, as owner, is generally liable to lose his land if taxes are not paid, it seems inaccurate to say he owes the tenant a duty, for breach of

---

18. See Rohrbaugh v. Estate of Stern, 305 Md. 443, 505 A.2d 113 (1986) (treble amount wrongfully withheld, plus attorney fees); Mellor v. Berman, 390 Mass. 275, 454 N.E.2d 907 (1983) (treble damages); Mitchell v. Preusse, 358 N.W.2d 511 (N.D.1984) (treble damages); Vardeman v. Llewellyn, 17 Ohio St.3d 24, 476 N.E.2d 1038 (1985) (double damages but only as to amount wrongfully withheld); Ackerman v. Little, 679 S.W.2d 70 (Tex.App.1984) (treble damages); Shands v. Castrovinci, 115 Wis.2d 352, 340 N.W.2d 506 (1983) (tenant awarded attorney fees though represented by legal services office free); Paulik v. Coombs, 120 Wis.2d 431, 355 N.W.2d 357 (App.1984) (double damages, attorney fees).

19. See Oak Park Village v. Gorton, 128 Mich.App. 671, 341 N.W.2d 788 (1983); Dow v. Carter, 122 N.H. 395, 445 A.2d 1100 (1982).

§ 6.60

1. E.g., Beck v. F.W. Woolworth Co., 111 F.Supp. 824 (N.D.Iowa 1953) (dictum); Wycoff v. Gavriloff Motors, Inc., 362 Mich. 582, 107 N.W.2d 820 (1961) (dictum); Annot., 86

A.L.R.2d 670, 673–78 (1962); 1 A.L.P., supra note 1, at § 3.76.

2. E.g., Beck v. F.W. Woolworth Co., 111 F.Supp. 824 (N.D.Iowa 1953) (dictum); Wycoff v. Gavriloff Motors, Inc., 362 Mich. 582, 107 N.W.2d 820 (1961), Annot., 86 A.L.R.2d 670, 682–85 (1962), but n.b. that the tenant is not liable to the landlord to pay a tax increase if the improvements become the landlord's. See Beck v. F.W. Woolworth Co., supra, and the A.L.R. Annot., supra, at 685–88.

3. E.g., Piper v. Town of Meredith, 83 N.Y. 107, 139 A. 294 (1927); City of Norfolk v. J.W. Perry Co., 108 Va. 28, 61 S.E. 867 (1908), affirmed 220 U.S. 472, 31 S.Ct. 465, 55 L.Ed. 548 (1911) (alternative ground); Annot., 55 A.L.R. 154 (1928).

4. Annot., 86 A.L.R.2d 670, 681–82 (1962).

5. E.g., Sherman v. Spalding, 126 Mich. 561, 85 N.W. 1129 (1901); City of Norfolk v. J.W. Perry Co., 108 Va. 28, 61 S.E. 867 (1908), affirmed 220 U.S. 472, 31 S.Ct. 465, 55 L.Ed. 548 (1911).

which the tenant has an action at law. If the landlord fails to pay the taxes for so long that the land is sold at tax sale, there may be a breach of the covenant of quiet enjoyment. Even then, that point will be reached only when the purchaser at the tax sale actually disturbs the tenant in possession.[6] Only in that sense should it be said the landlord owes the tenant a duty, though as a practical matter he had better pay the taxes if the tenant is not obligated to do so.

Commercial and long-term residential leases frequently contain clauses requiring the tenant to pay all or some part of the real estate taxes. Especially in a "net" lease, he may be required to pay all taxes and assessments. A more limited form of clause requires the tenant to pay tax increases that flow from improvements the tenant makes.[7] In many modern commercial leases, the so-called "tax stop" clause is found, requiring the tenant to pay, generally as additional rent, increases in real estate taxes that come along after the term begins.[8] This listing is suggestive rather than exhaustive, nor is it possible here to open up the many questions of construction of tax clauses. One point that needs to be made, however, is that, especially from the landlord's perspective, tenants' covenants to pay taxes must be clearly and expressly drafted. Reference was previously made to the indisposition courts usually have to impose tax liability on a tenant. It has generally been held that a covenant to pay "taxes" does not impose a duty to pay special assessments.[9] In other ways, it may be said that the courts display a distinct tendency to interpret tax clauses narrowly, in the tenant's favor.[10]

§ 6.61 Insurance

Both landlord and tenant have insurable interests in the demised premises, the landlord's being that part of the entire insurable interest that is apportionable to the reversion and the tenant's being the part apportionable to the leasehold. However, absent a covenant to do so, neither one has any duty to procure fire or casualty insurance.[1] If either party voluntarily insures his interest in his own name, the other has nothing to say about what he does with the proceeds.[2] Even if the voluntary insured takes out insurance in an amount larger than his insurable interest, i.e., over-insures, most courts reach the same result, though a few decisions require him to

6. See Barry v. Frankini, 287 Mass. 196, 191 N.E. 651 (1934); Rustin Co. v. Bowen, 129 N.J.L. 505, 30 A.2d 70 (1943); Restatement (Second) of Property § 4.3, Reporter's Note 3 (1977).

7. Tiara Corp. v. Delta Elec. Co., 424 So.2d 459 (La.App.1982) (lease clause interpreted to require tenant to reimburse landlord for tax increase caused by tenant's improvements). For discussion of cases involving a related question, see Annot., 68 A.L.R.2d 1289 (1959).

8. For decisions construing such tax-stop clauses, see Annot., 48 A.L.R.3d 287 (1973).

9. Annot., 63 A.L.R. 1391 (1929).

10. See, e.g., First Nat. Bank of Highland Park v. Mid–Central Food Sales, Inc., 129 Ill. App.3d 1002, 85 Ill.Dec. 4, 473 N.E.2d 372

(1984) (lease clause requiring tenant to pay taxes when due during lease term obligated tenant to pay prorata taxes for last partial year of lease); Beck v. F.W. Woolworth Co., 111 F.Supp. 824 (N.D.Iowa 1953); Gold Medal Stamp Co. v. Carver, 359 Mass. 681, 270 N.E.2d 834 (1971); Annot., 48 A.L.R.3d 287 (1973).

§ 6.61

1. Carolina Helicopter Corp. v. Cutter Realty Co., 263 N.C. 139, 139 S.E.2d 362 (1964) (dictum); Gebhart v. Huffman, 326 N.W.2d 891 (S.D.1982) (tenant had no common law or implied duty to procure casualty insurance); Hart v. Hart, 117 Wis. 639, 94 N.W. 890 (1903) (dictum); 1 A.L.P., supra note 1, at § 3.75.

2. Annot., 66 A.L.R. 864 (1930).

account to the other for a share.[3] However, should the voluntary insured take out a policy payable jointly to himself and the other party, then a handful of decisions hold they share the proceeds according to their interests.[4]

Leases, particularly commercial or long-term ones, often contain covenants by one party, usually the tenant, to procure insurance. A well drafted insurance clause should specify the kind of insurance (fire and other casualty?), the amount (full insurable value?), to whom payable (to landlord and tenant as their interests shall appear?), and how and by whom proceeds are to be applied. This clause must be coordinated with any repair clauses and with clauses providing for termination or alteration of the leasing relationship in the event of whole or partial destruction. When one party covenants to insure, he is liable to the other for the other's share of proceeds from any policy he takes out, whether or not the policy on its face runs to both parties.[5] If the lease requires insurance proceeds to be applied to repairs ("coupled with" a repair clause), American courts agree that the burden of the covenant runs with the estate of the covenanting party, so as to bind a grantee or assignee.[6] Owing, however, to dictum in the old case of Masury v. Southworth, when the proceeds are not required to be applied to repairs ("bare" insurance clause), the courts are split on whether the burden of the covenant runs.[7]

J. RENEWALS AND EXTENSIONS

§ 6.62 Distinction Between Renewals and Extensions

Leases for years may contain clauses giving tenants power to be tenants for one or more terms beyond the end of the original term. Two mechanisms serve that purpose, a power to compel a new lease and a power to extend the original term. For many purposes the parties may not much care which mechanism they employ, but in a couple of ways there are significant differences. If there is to be a new lease, one will have to be executed, which of course is not the case with an extension of the original lease. And, whereas the tenant's act of simply holding over will generally be a sufficient election to extend, something more is required to elect a new lease, probably the tendering of a lease or at a minimum notice before the end of the original term.[1]

3. Miller v. Gold Beach Packing Co., 131 Or. 302, 282 P. 764 (1929); Id.

4. Ingold v. Phoenix Assurance Co., 230 N.C. 142, 52 S.E.2d 366 (1949); Annot., 8 A.L.R.2d 1445 (1949).

5. See Meyer v. Caribbean Interiors Inc., 435 So.2d 936 (Fla.App.1983) (clauses in commercial lease exculpating landlord for liability and requiring tenant to purchase casualty insurance on roof were enforceable, even though repair clause required landlord to repair roof); Annot., 66 A.L.R. 864, 866–67 (1930).

6. E.g., Masury v. Southworth, 9 Ohio St. 340 (1859); Burton v. Chesapeake Box & Lumber Corp., 190 Va. 755, 57 S.E.2d 904 (1950) (dictum); Annot., 18 A.L.R.2d 1051 (1951).

7. See Masury v. Southworth, 9 Ohio St. 340 (1859) (dictum); Burton v. Chesapeake Box & Lumber Corp., 190 Va. 755, 57 S.E.2d 904 (1950); Annot., 18 A.L.R.2d 1051 (1951).

§ 6.62

1. See Riggs v. United States, 12 F.2d 85 (E.D.S.C.1926) (renewal); Shannon v. Jacobson, 262 Mass. 463, 160 N.E. 245 (1928) (extension); Annot., 172 A.L.R. 1205, 1219–22 (1948). But some courts may make no distinction between the kinds of notice required for renewals and extensions. See, e.g., Riverside Land Co. v. Big Rock Stone & Material Co., 183 Ark. 1061, 40 S.W.2d 423 (1931).

Parties who wish one of the above arrangements should "watch their language." Use of the word "extend" or "extension" is reasonably safe; the courts are generally agreed that this denotes continuation of the original term, not a new lease.[2] Unadorned use of the word "renew" or "renewal," however, is inadvisable as a general matter. This word may well, in some courts, be interpreted to refer to a new lease.[3] But in many courts that word is not considered conclusive, so that the courts will look to other circumstances to determine if the parties intended an extension or a new lease.[4] It is fair to say there is a judicial preference for an extension.

§ 6.63   Operation of Renewal/Extension Provisions

A well drafted renewal or extension clause specifies how many renewals or extensions the tenant may have and which provisions, if any, such as amount of rent or length of term are to be adjusted. When the language is general or vague as to the number of renewals or extensions, even when they are referred to in the plural, courts usually allow the tenant to have only one.[1] If the clause provides for renewal or extension but does not specify for what term or upon what provisions, the courts imply that it shall be for the same term as the original one [2] and with the same provisions, including the rental agreement.[3] In line with what was just said, the renewal or extension clause is not included, for this would work perpetually.[4] If, however, the renewal or extension clause states that some or all the key provisions, especially rent shall be determined by the parties' future agreement or words to that effect, then the courts generally refuse to enforce the clause on the ground it is indefinite.[5] A few decisions, perhaps forming some trend,

2. See, e.g., Riverside Land Co. v. Big Rock Stone & Material Co., 183 Ark. 1061, 40 S.W.2d 423 (1931); Shannon v. Jacobson, 262 Mass. 463, 160 N.E. 245 (1928); Annot., 172 A.L.R. 1205, 1219–22 (1948).

3. E.g., Riggs v. United States, 12 F.2d 85 (E.D.S.C.1926); Shannon v. Jacobson, 262 Mass. 463, 160 N.E. 245 (1928) (dictum); Annot., 172 A.L.R. 1205, 1210–1212 (1948).

4. HLM Realty Corp. v. Morreale, 394 Mass. 714, 477 N.E.2d 394 (1985) (critical distinction is whether some additional act is necessary, not whether option is called "renewal" or "extension"); Anderson v. Lissandri, 19 Mass.App.Ct. 191, 472 N.E.2d 1365 (1985) (use of word "renewal" not conclusive where circumstances show parties intended extension). See Blanck v. Kimland Realty Co., 122 Conn. 317, 189 A. 176 (1937). See Med–Care Associates, Inc. v. Noot, 329 N.W.2d 549 (Minn.1983) (legislature's use of word "renewal" held to include extensions); Dubinsky Realty, Inc. v. Vactec, Inc., 637 S.W.2d 190 (Mo.App.1982) (dictum that Missouri courts usually ignore technical distinction between renewals and extensions); Jador Service Co. v. Werbel, 140 N.J.Eq. 188, 53 A.2d 182 (1947); Annot., 172 A.L.R. 1205, 1222–25 (1948).

§ 6.63

1. E.g., Geyer v. Lietzan, 230 Ind. 404, 103 N.E.2d 199 (1952); Potter v. Henry Field Seed Co., 239 Iowa 920, 32 N.W.2d 385 (1948); Thomas v. Knight, 457 So.2d 1207 (La.App. 1984) (when lease unclear on number of renewals, tenant has only one). Annot., 31 A.L.R.2d 607, 611–13 (1953).

2. E.g., Mutual Paper Co. v. Hoague–Sprague Corp., 297 Mass. 294, 8 N.E.2d 802 (1937); Starr v. Holck, 318 Mich. 452, 28 N.W.2d 289 (1947); Annot., 172 A.L.R. 421, 422–24 (1948).

3. Johnson v. Hudson, 420 So.2d 85 (Ala. 1982) (extension agreement with no rent stated for extension contemplated continuation of original rent); Penilla v. Gerstenkorn, 86 Cal. App. 668, 261 P. 488 (1927); 58–59 Realty Corp. v. Park Central Valet, Inc., 252 App.Div. 72, 297 N.Y.S. 40 (1937) (dictum); Annot., 30 A.L.R. 572, 577–79 (1924), Supp., 68 A.L.R. 157, 158–59 (1930), Supp., 166 A.L.R. 1237, 1243 (1947).

4. See the *Johnson* and *Penilla* cases, cited in the preceding note.

5. E.g., Lonoke Nursing Home, Inc. v. Wayne & Neil Bennett Family Partnership, 12 Ark.App. 282, 676 S.W.2d 461 (1984), opinion supplemented 12 Ark.App. 282, 679 S.W.2d 823 (1984) (renewal of nursing home lease, to be on terms "compatible to similar facilities," too vague to be enforced); Etco Corp. v. Hauer, 161 Cal.App.3d 1154, 208 Cal.

have enforced clauses calling for rent to be set by future agreement, the courts being willing to determine a "reasonable" rent.[6] Of course there is nothing wrong with a formula that leaves the fixing of rent or other provisions to some external standard, such as appraisal, arbitration, or an economic index.[7]

Since renewal or extension is at the tenant's election, he must sufficiently act to make the election. A well drafted clause states expressly what notice or other acts the tenant must do, when these must be done, and that the election is lost if they are not done in the manner and within the time specified. The landlord normally should insist that the tenant must make an irrevocable election by an appropriate fixed time before the end of the term. If the clause is clear on these matters, the courts will usually make the tenant's strict compliance a condition precedent to renewal or extension.[8] There are, however, some circumstances, such as mistake, unexpected and excusable delay, and landlord's waiver, in which equity courts may excuse late election, especially if the lease does not make time of the essence.[9] Should the renewal or extension clause require notice but not specify when it must be given, notice by the end of the term is adequate.[10] If written notice is not required, oral notice is as good as written.[11] Differences of opinion surround the question whether a tenant's act of holding over and paying rent amounts to an election to renew or extend in cases where the

Rptr. 118 (1984) (renewal agreement with rent to be fixed "by mutual agreement" too vague to be enforced); Camichos v. Diana Stores Corp., 157 Fla. 349, 25 So.2d 864 (1946); State ex. rel. Johnson v. Blair, 351 Mo. 1072, 174 S.W.2d 851 (1943); R.A.S., Inc. v. Crowley, 217 Neb. 811, 351 N.W.2d 414 (1984) (renewal agreement to be on terms "satisfactory and acceptable" to parties was too vague to be enforced); R.J. Reynolds Realty Co. v. Logan, 216 N.C. 26, 3 S.E.2d 280 (1939); Annot., 30 A.L.R. 572, 573–75 (1924), Supp., 68 A.L.R. 157, 157–58 (1930), Supp., 166 A.L.R. 1237, 1238–42 (1947).

6. E.g., Edwards v. Tobin, 132 Or. 38, 284 P. 562 (1930); Rainwater v. Hobeika, 208 S.C. 433, 38 S.E.2d 495 (1946); Young v. Nelson, 121 Wash. 285, 209 P. 515 (1922). See the A.L.R. annotation and supplements cited in the preceding note.

7. See the A.L.R. annotation and supplements cited above.

8. E.g., La Salle Nat. Bank v. Graham, 119 Ill.App.3d 85, 74 Ill.Dec. 821, 456 N.E.2d 323 (1983) (no renewal when tenant negligently failed to give required written notice of renewal); Gurunian v. Grossman, 331 Mich. 412, 49 N.W.2d 354 (1951); Wayside Homes, Inc. v. Purcelli, 104 A.D.2d 650, 480 N.Y.S.2d 29 (1984), appeal denied 64 N.Y.2d 602, 485 N.Y.S.2d 1027, 475 N.E.2d 126 (1984) (when lease required six months' notice for renewal, notice less than two months in advance was not sufficient); Royer v. Honrine, 68 N.C.App. 664, 316 S.E.2d 93 (1984) (when tenant of renewable lease held over but paid only origi-

nal rent and not stated increased rent for renewal term, there was no renewal); Jones v. Dexter, 48 Wn.2d 224, 292 P.2d 369 (1956); Annot., 51 A.L.R.2d 1404, 1406–12 (1957); Annot., 44 A.L.R.2d 1359, 1362 (1955). See Anthony v. Ausburn, 254 Ga. 472, 330 S.E.2d 724 (1985), on remand 175 Ga.App. 857, 335 S.E.2d 746 (1985) (renewal notice not effective until landlord received it).

9. R & R of Conn., Inc. v. Stiegler, 4 Conn. App. 240, 493 A.2d 293 (1985) (in determining whether equity will excuse late notice, tenant's degree of negligence in being late should be considered). But see Ceres Terminals, Inc. v. Chicago City Bank & Trust Co., 117 Ill. App.3d 399, 72 Ill.Dec. 860, 453 N.E.2d 735 (1983) (facts not sufficient to give tenant equitable relief from late renewal notice); Lemay v. Rouse, 122 N.H. 349, 444 A.2d 553 (1982) (fact that tenant would lose rent from subtenant was no such hardship as to excuse late renewal notice). For an extensive catalog of such circumstances, see Annot., 27 A.L.R. 981 (1923), Supp., 44 A.L.R.2d 1359 (1955).

10. See Penilla v. Gerstenkorn, 86 Cal. App. 668, 261 P. 488 (1927); Caito v. Ferri, 44 R.I. 261, 116 A. 897 (1922) (two days after term ended). Some courts have even allowed tenants to give notice a short time after the term ends. See Caito, supra, and Annot., 27 A.L.R. 981 (1923), Supp., 44 A.L.R.2d 1359 (1955).

11. E.g., Economy Stores, Inc. v. Moran, 178 Miss. 62, 172 So. 865 (1937); Caito v. Ferri, 44 R.I. 261, 116 A. 897 (1922); Annot., 51 A.L.R.2d 1404, 1412–13 (1957).

clause does not specify the manner in which he shall elect. The general principle is that he must reasonably manifest his election; the difference concerns whether holding over meets that test. When the clause clearly is for an extension or, though couched in ambiguous language or renewal language, is interpreted as being for an extension, then holding over and paying rent generally is held sufficient for the election.[12] But if a renewal clause is strictly interpreted to require a new lease, then a holding over is generally not regarded sufficient to constitute an election; some communicated manifestation is required.[13]

§ 6.64 Perpetual Renewals

Perpetual renewals are allowed and are considered to amount to a conveyance in fee simple.[1] They do not violate the Rule Against Perpetuities because the grantee has a vested, indeed a presently possessory, estate.[2] However, courts strongly disfavor perpetual renewals and will if possible interpret language so as to avoid their existence.[3] We have previously seen one technique by which this may be accomplished, the rule that the courts usually take indefinite references to the number of renewals to mean only one.

K. PURCHASE OPTIONS

§ 6.65 Nature and Creation of Purchase Options

A lease may contain a grant to the tenant of an option to purchase the demised premises. Two forms of option are in common usage, the "straight option" and the "right of first refusal." With the first form, the tenant has a power to compel the landlord to convey the reversion to him at a fixed or determinable price at any time during all or a stated portion of the leasehold term. The second form of option disables the landlord from conveying the reversion to any third person without first offering it to the tenant, usually at the same price the third person has offered. From the tenant's perspec-

---

12. E.g., Riverside Land Co. v. Big Rock Stone & Material Co., 183 Ark. 1061, 40 S.W.2d 423 (1931); Blanck v. Kimland Realty Co., 122 Conn. 317, 189 A. 176 (1937); Jador Service Co. v. Werbel, 140 N.J.Eq. 188, 53 A.2d 182 (1947) (dictum); Annot., 172 A.L.R. 1205, 1219–22, 1237–40 (1948).

13. E.g., Riggs v. United States, 12 F.2d 85 (E.D.S.C.1926) (alternative ground); Potter v. Henry Field Seed Co., 239 Iowa 920, 32 N.W.2d 385 (1948); Annot., 172 A.L.R. 1205, 1206–10, 1217–19 (1948).

§ 6.64

1. Williams v. J.M. High Co., 200 Ga. 230, 36 S.E.2d 667 (1946) (dictum); Department of Natural Resources v. Board of Trustees of Westminster Church of Detroit, 114 Mich. App. 99, 318 N.W.2d 830 (1982) (renewal from year to year so long as tenant used premises for stated purpose was valid perpetual renewal clause); Burns v. City of New York, 213 N.Y. 516, 108 N.E. 77 (1915), motion to amend

remittitur granted 214 N.Y. 658, 108 N.E. 1090 (1915); Tipton v. North, 185 Okl. 365, 92 P.2d 364 (1939); Annot., 31 A.L.R.2d 607, 622–24 (1953); 1 A.L.P., supra note 1, at § 3.87.

2. In addition to the cases cited in the preceding note, see Annot., 3 A.L.R. 498 (1919), Supp., 162 A.L.R. 1147 (1946).

3. McLean v. United States, 316 F.Supp. 827 (E.D.Va.1970); Nakdimen v. Atkinson Improvement Co., 149 Ark. 448, 233 S.W. 694 (1921); Lonergan v. Connecticut Food Store, Inc., 168 Conn. 122, 357 A.2d 910 (1975); Sheradsky v. Basadre, 452 So.2d 599 (Fla.App. 1984), review denied 461 So.2d 113 (Fla.1985) (no perpetual renewal when language was unclear). See Thomas v. Knight, 457 So.2d 1207 (La.App.1984) (when lease did not state number of renewals, not perpetual but only one); Lattimore v. Fisher's Food Shoppe, Inc., 313 N.C. 467, 329 S.E.2d 346 (1985) (automatic-renewal clause did not create perpetual renewals); Annot., 31 A.L.R.2d 607, 623–30 (1953).

tive, this second form is an option to purchase upon the conditions that the landlord has received an offer and desires to sell on the offered terms.[1]

Since either form of option exists only by virtue of specific language in the lease, problems of creation are basically drafting problems. An option, being a contract of irrevocable offer, must be supported by consideration, but this is no problem in a lease because of the various valuable exchanges.[2]

Serious problems do arise over definiteness of terms, particularly price and mode of payment, as an option has the aspect of a contract to consummate further contractual undertakings. In general, the terms of a straight option must be stated with the same particularity as would the terms of any offer.[3] With a right of first refusal, of course, the terms are determined by the third person's offer and are definite enough because they are controlled by an external standard. Much litigation has arisen over whether certain language created a straight option or right of first refusal. Generalizations are difficult. Language of specific leases is too varied for decisions to produce rules, and it cannot even be said that courts generally prefer one device over the other. Draftsmen should be careful not to mix language usually associated with a straight option with customary first refusal language. The word "first," even when connected with "refusal" or "privilege," may be regarded as ambiguous, and provisions for a stated price or for exercise of the optionee's right at anytime within a stated timespan suggest a straight option.[4] Especially when a right of first refusal is intended, the mechanism should be spelled out.

§ 6.66   Operation and Exercise of Purchase Options

Leases frequently grant options for only a stated portion of the leasehold term; longterm commercial leases may contain an elaborate series of options, exercisable during successive stages upon differing terms. If the lease does not limit the time when the option may be exercised, it endures during the term plus any extensions or renewals.[1] That the lease has a very long

§ 6.65

1. Corbin disagrees that a first refusal is an option. See 1A A. Corbin, Contracts § 261 (1963).
2. Id. at §§ 259, 266.
3. Id. at § 266.
4. See Annot., 34 A.L.R.2d 1158 (1954).

§ 6.66

1. Moiger v. Johnson, 180 F.2d 777 (D.C.Cir.1950) (extension); Hindu Incense Manufacturing Co. v. MacKenzie, 403 Ill. 390, 86 N.E.2d 214 (1949) (renewal); Taylor v. Wells, 188 Or. 648, 217 P.2d 236 (1950) (during term); Durepo v. May, 73 R.I. 71, 54 A.2d 15 (1947) (during term); Exxon Corp. v. Pollman, 729 S.W.2d 302 (Tex.App.1986) (during extension); Annot., 15 A.L.R.3d 470, 472–82 (1976) (extensions and renewals). A few courts have made a distinction between extensions and renewals, saying or holding that purchase options do not carry over to renewals. See Seefeldt v. Keske, 14 Wis.2d 438, 111 N.W.2d 574 (1961); A.L.R. Annot., supra at 482–83. Also,

of course, a court, in interpreting disputed language in a lease, may find the parties did not intend a purchase option to continue during extension or renewal. See, e.g., Denver Plastics, Inc. v. Snyder, 160 Colo. 232, 416 P.2d 370 (1966). Several cases have posed the interesting question whether, when a lease contains both a purchase option at a fixed price and a right of first refusal, the tenant may exercise the fixed-price option after being notified that the landlord has received an offer of purchase at a higher price. Texaco, Inc. v. Creel, 310 N.C. 695, 314 S.E.2d 506 (1984), and Amoco Oil Co. v. Snyder, 505 Pa. 214, 478 A.2d 795 (1984), hold that the tenant may exercise the fixed-price option, though the Creel decision turns somewhat upon the language of the lease. The contrary result was reached in Tantleff v. Truscelli, 110 A.D.2d 240, 493 N.Y.S.2d 979 (1985), affirmed 69 N.Y.2d 769, 513 N.Y.S.2d 113, 505 N.E.2d 623 (1987), where the court reasoned that, to harmonize the two inconsistent provisions, the lease should be read to allow exercise of the

term or even that it is perpetually renewable does not void a purchase option, for American courts do not apply the Rule Against Perpetuities to options in leases.[2] Whether termination of a leasehold before its expiry terminates a purchase option turns in general upon whether one views the option as existing independently of the other lease provisions.[3] If the tenant assigns the leasehold, the assignee generally may exercise a purchase option, which is considered a running covenant.[4]

Upon due exercise of a purchase option, the landlord-tenant relation ends; the parties become vendor and vendee.[5] In a handful of decisions, courts have even, for some purposes, invoked a fiction of relation back, to make the equitable passage of title effective as of the date the option was given. This has been done to give the optionee tenant condemnation awards [6] and casualty insurance proceeds [7] that have been received prior to the option's exercise. When, however, an optionor or optionee has died during the option period and there is a dispute between rival claimants to his estate, most American courts refuse to relate the passage of title back to the date the option was given.[8] And finally, landlords should be aware that, because of the relation-back doctrine, the existence of a lease purchase option may hinder their mortgage financing.[9]

L. TRANSFERS BY LANDLORD OR TENANT

§ 6.67 Tenant's Transfers in General

A tenant, having an estate in land, may as a general proposition transfer it or lesser interests carved out of it.[1] Transfers of possession are subdivided into two species, assignments and subleasings, which will be distinguished and explored presently. A tenant may also create non-possessory interests, such as easements or licenses, within his leasehold, but little attention has been paid to these.

We must somewhat qualify what was just said. It is doubtful that a tenant at will, one whose so-called leasehold is terminable at the landlord's

---

fixed-price option only until the right of first refusal became operative.

2. Keogh v. Peck, 316 Ill. 318, 147 N.E. 266 (1925); Hollander v. Central Metal & Supply Co., 109 Md. 131, 71 A. 442 (1908).

3. E.g., Spindler v. Valparaiso Lodge, 223 Ind. 276, 59 N.E.2d 895 (1945) (new lease when old ended); Estfan v. Hawks, 166 Kan. 712, 204 P.2d 780 (1949); Annot., 10 A.L.R.2d 884 (1950).

4. E.g., Bewick v. Mecham, 26 Cal.2d 92, 156 P.2d 757 (1945); Gilbert v. Van Kleeck, 284 App.Div. 611, 132 N.Y.S.2d 580 (1954), motion denied 284 App.Div. 857, 134 N.Y.S.2d 193 (1954), appeal dismissed 308 N.Y. 882, 126 N.E.2d 383 (1955), motion denied 308 N.Y. 1045, 127 N.E.2d 873 (1955); Randolph v. Koury Corp., 173 W.Va. 96, 312 S.E.2d 759 (1984) (option passes with assignment of lease in absence of clear language prohibiting it); Annot., 45 A.L.R.2d 1034 (1956).

5. Willard v. Tayloe, 75 U.S. (8 Wall.) 557, 19 L.Ed. 501 (1870); Gassert v. Anderson, 201 Minn. 515, 276 N.W. 808 (1937).

6. Cullen & Vaughn Co. v. Bender Co., 122 Ohio St. 82, 170 N.E. 633 (1930); Annot., 68 A.L.R. 1338 (1930).

7. Schnee v. Elston, 299 Pa. 100, 149 A. 108 (1930).

8. 1 A.L.P., supra note 1, at § 3.84; Annot., 172 A.L.R. 438 (1948).

9. If the lease with purchase option is prior to the mortgage and if the exercise relates back to the making of the lease, then the tenant would acquire title prior to the mortgage. The danger that this might occur causes sophisticated mortgage lenders to object to the option. See, International Council of Shopping Centers, Shopping Center Report No. 13, A Lender's Examination of Shopping Center Leases 8 (1964). See also Crowley v. Byrne, 71 Wash. 444, 129 P. 113 (1912).

§ 6.67

1. See generally, Annot., 23 A.L.R. 135 (1923), Supp., 70 A.L.R. 486 (1931).

will, has a sufficient interest to be transferred. Several decisions have held that the purported transferee becomes only a trespasser against the landowner.[2] A more important limitation on transfer arises from the common practice of inserting lease clauses that prohibit or inhibit assignment or subletting. Such clauses are generally valid, as we shall see in a later section on the subject.

§ 6.68 Assignment and Sublease Distinguished

The distinction between assignment and subletting is important and technical: important, because quite different legal relations go with each transaction; technical, because the courts generally turn the distinction upon a fixed legal test rather than upon the parties' intent.[1] With an assignment the tenant transfers the right of possession to all or part of the premises for the full time remaining on the term. With a sublease the tenant transfers the right of possession to all or part of the premises for a time, be it 10 years or a day, less than the full time remaining. Expressed conceptually, with a sublease the tenant retains a reversion in his own leasehold following the subtenancy; with an assignment he does not.[2]

Within this test, some questions still arise. A minority of courts, following Massachusetts, have held that if the tenant otherwise transfers the balance of the term but reserves a power of termination (e.g., for the transferee's breach), the transfer is a subletting.[3] The subtenant has an estate analogous to a fee upon condition subsequent and the head tenant an interest analogous to a right of entry (power of termination). Since the right of entry is classified only as an "interest" and not an "estate"[4] and since a right of entry upon a leasehold is not of as much substance as one upon a fee simple, the underlying question is whether it is a sufficient interest to convert an otherwise assignment into a subleasing.

The question also has arisen whether a transfer for the full balance of the term but of only a portion of the premises is an assignment or a

2. Hunnicutt v. Head, 179 Ala. 567, 60 So. 831 (1912); Ferrigno v. O'Connell, 315 Mass. 536, 53 N.E.2d 384 (1944) (dictum); Annot., 167 A.L.R. 1040 (1947). But cf., Anderson v. Ries, 222 Minn. 408, 24 N.W.2d 717 (1946) (landlord may not evict tenant at will's subtenant without evicting tenant); Public Service Co. v. Voudoumas, 84 N.H. 387, 151 A. 81 (1930) (tenant at will's subletting is good as between himself and subtenant).

§ 6.68

1. Tidewater Investors, Ltd. v. United Dominion Realty Trust, Inc., 804 F.2d 293 (4th Cir.1986) (transfer of full term assignment, though parties called it "sublease"). But see Jaber v. Miller, 219 Ark. 59, 239 S.W.2d 760 (1951), urging intent as the test. However, the result, that there was an assignment, would have been reached under the traditional test.

2. E.g., Haynes v. Eagle–Picher Co., 295 F.2d 761 (10th Cir.1961), certiorari denied 369 U.S. 828, 82 S.Ct. 846, 7 L.Ed.2d 794 (1962);

Jaber v. Miller, 219 Ark. 59, 239 S.W.2d 760 (1951) (dictum); V.O.B. Co. v. Hang It Up, Inc., 691 P.2d 1157 (Colo.App.1984) (when tenant transferred less than entire interest, it was sublease, though parties did not use that word); 24 Broad Street Corp. v. Quinn, 19 N.J.Super. 21, 87 A.2d 759 (1952) (dictum); Conklin Dev. Corp. v. Acme Markets, Inc., 89 A.D.2d 769, 453 N.Y.S.2d 930 (1982), appeal dismissed 58 N.Y.2d 929, 460 N.Y.S.2d 532, 447 N.E.2d 80 (1983) (transfer was sublease when tenant did not transfer full term and retained some rights under lease); Amco Trust, Inc. v. Naylor, 159 Tex. 146, 317 S.W.2d 47 (1958); L & M Corp. v. Loader, 688 P.2d 448 (Utah 1984) (transfer of entire term is assignment); 1 A.L.P., supra note 1, at § 3.57.

3. Hartman Ranch Co. v. Associated Oil Co., 10 Cal.2d 232, 73 P.2d 1163 (1937); Dunlap v. Bullard, 131 Mass. 161 (1881); Davis v. Vidal, 105 Tex. 444, 151 S.W. 290 (1912).

4. See 1 L. Simes & A. Smith, Future Interests § 35 (2d ed. 1956).

subletting. It is properly an assignment that has been called an assignment pro tanto.[5]

§ 6.69 Assignments

Assignment creates an interesting network of legal relations. The assignee, who acquires the tenant's entire estate, comes into privity of estate with the landlord, i.e., the leasehold and the reversion adjoin. Under both real covenant and equitable servitude theories, the assignee is liable to the landlord to perform all tenant's covenants in the lease whose burden runs with the leasehold, including a rent covenant.[1] Obversely, if an assignee reassigns and so divests himself of the leasehold, then he owes no further duties to the landlord unless the purported assignment was a sham.[2] It is possible, though, that in taking the assignment, the assignee has expressly made a fresh covenant to perform the tenant's duties—"assumed," as the expression goes in mortgage law. In that event reassignment will not relieve the assignee; he has lost his liability to the landlord on privity of estate but not on privity of contract unless the landlord releases him.[3] Along with acquisition of duties to the landlord, the assignee naturally acquires the right to the landlord's performance of all his covenants whose benefit runs with the leasehold; privity of estate cuts both ways.

Assignment does not relieve the assignor tenant of the duty to perform his covenants in the lease.[4] This is because the tenant made contractual promises in the lease and still remains liable, as it is said, on privity of contract. It is quite true then that, as to those tenant's covenants whose burden runs, the landlord now may come against both tenant and assignee.

5. Only a few decisions, generally old ones, call this a sublease. See, e.g., Fulton v. Stuart, 2 Ohio 215 (1825); Shannon v. Grindstaff, 11 Wash. 536, 40 P. 123 (1895) (alternative ground?). A large majority of decisions correctly recognize the transfer as a partial or pro tanto assignment. E.g., Waller v. Commissioner, 40 F.2d 892 (5th Cir.1930), certiorari denied 282 U.S. 889, 51 S.Ct. 101, 75 L.Ed. 784 (1930); Sheridan v. O.E. Doherty, Inc., 106 Wash. 561, 181 P. 16 (1919) (contrary to *Shannon,* supra); Annot., 99 A.L.R. 220 (1935).

§ 6.69

1. Samuels v. Ottinger, 169 Cal. 209, 146 P. 638 (1915) (dictum); Reid v. Wiessner & Sons Brewing Co., 88 Md. 234, 40 A. 877 (1898) (dictum); Gerber v. Pecht, 15 N.J. 29, 104 A.2d 41 (1954) (dictum); Masury v. Southworth, 9 Ohio St. 340 (1859); Cauble v. Hanson, 249 S.W. 175 (Tex.Com.App.1923) (dictum). See Childs v. Warner Brothers Southern Theatres, Inc., 200 N.C. 333, 156 S.E. 923 (1931) (implied holding). See also Price v. S.S. Fuller, Inc., 639 P.2d 1003 (Alaska 1982) (assignee was liable to pay rent to landlord, even though landlord had released assignor tenant from liability).

2. Reid v. Wiessner & Sons Brewing Co., 88 Md. 234, 40 A. 877 (1898); Packard–Bamberger & Co. v. Maloof, 83 N.J.Super. 273, 199 A.2d 400 (1964), reversed 89 N.J.Super. 128,

214 A.2d 45 (1965) (dictum); A.D. Juilliard & Co. v. American Woolen Co., 69 R.I. 215, 32 A.2d 800 (1943) (involves alleged sham assignment). See also Childs v. Warner Brothers Southern Theatres, Inc., 200 N.C. 333, 156 S.E. 923 (1931) (reassignment in breach of covenant not to assign).

3. Reid v. Wiessner & Sons Brewing Co., 88 Md. 234, 40 A. 877 (1898) (dictum); Packard–Bamberger & Co. v. Maloof, 83 N.J.Super. 273, 199 A.2d 400 (1964), reversed 89 N.J.Super. 128, 214 A.2d 45 (1965) (alternative ground); A.D. Juilliard & Co. v. American Woolen Co., 69 R.I. 215, 32 A.2d 800 (1943) (dictum).

4. Samuels v. Ottinger, 169 Cal. 209, 146 P. 638 (1915); Net Realty Holding Trust v. Giannini, 13 Mass.App.Ct. 273, 432 N.E.2d 120 (1982), review denied 386 Mass. 1102, 440 N.E.2d 1175 (1982) (assignment does not relieve original tenant from duty to pay rent); Gerber v. Pecht, 15 N.J. 29, 104 A.2d 41 (1954); Goldome v. Bonuch, 112 A.D.2d 1025, 493 N.Y.S.2d 22 (1985), appeal granted 66 N.Y.2d 604, 498 N.Y.S.2d 1024, 489 N.E.2d 769 (1985) (assignment does not relieve original tenant from duty to pay rent); Hoffman v. Junior Vogue, Inc., 91 A.D.2d 703, 457 N.Y.S.2d 601 (1982) (assignment does not relieve original tenant from duty to pay rent); Cauble v. Hanson, 249 S.W. 175 (Tex.Com. App.1923).

Of course the landlord, if he is willing, may release the tenant from personal liability, but this generally is not implied from the landlord's consenting to the assignment and certainly not from his simply accepting the assignee's performance.[5] The tenant, who has assigned the leasehold and has no further interest in the land, probably cannot enforce the landlord's covenants.[6]

Legal relations between tenant and assignee are the most interesting of all. Because the assignee has, impliedly if not expressly, undertaken with the tenant to perform the latter's running covenants, as to these covenants, as far as the tenant is concerned, the assignee has a primary duty to perform them. And, as far as the assignee is concerned, it follows that the tenant's concurrent duty to the landlord to perform these same covenants becomes a secondary duty. Out of this primary-secondary order of duties arises a suretyship relation, with the assignee the principal and the tenant the surety. So, if the landlord compels the tenant to perform one of these duties, the tenant may come back on the assignee. It should also follow, as a principle of suretyship law, that the landlord's release of the principal-assignee from some major duty or the material alteration of the duties, such as by significantly raising or lowering rent or postponing due dates, will release the tenant from all duties of which he is surety.[7]

§ 6.70 Subleases

The word "subtenancy" is particularly expressive. We have already seen that with a subtenancy the tenant transfers his right of possession for a time shorter than the balance of his leasehold, so that he retains a reversion within that leasehold. Therefore, the subtenant is not in privity of estate with the head landlord nor, of course, in contractual privity. But, being in rightful possession for a time, he is a tenant with a leasehold estate that is carved out of the head leasehold. Between the head tenant, who may also be called the sublandlord, and the subtenant there is a true landlord-tenant relationship. In general the legal rules attending that relationship are those discussed here for the head landlord and head tenant.[1] The subtenant has a direct landlord-tenant relationship with the head tenant but no direct relationship with the head landlord. That is why if two tenants agree between themselves to divide up the premises and the rent, but both have gained possession through the landlord, they are not tenant and subtenant but co-tenants who each owe the full rent to the landlord.[2]

5. Gerber v. Pecht, 15 N.J. 29, 104 A.2d 41 (1954); Cauble v. Hanson, 249 S.W. 175 (Tex. Com.App.1923).

6. Murray Hill Mello Corp. v. Bonne Bouchee Restaurant, Inc., 113 Misc.2d 683, 449 N.Y.S.2d 870 (1982) (assignee has privity of estate with landlord). See Restatement (Second) of Property § 16.2 (1977); Stoebuck, Running Covenants: An Analytical Primer, 53 Wash.L.Rev. 861, 887 (1977).

7. See 1 A.L.P., supra note 1, at § 3.61; Annot., 99 A.L.R. 1238 (1935).

§ 6.70

1. General discussions of these well known concepts will be found in, e.g., Haynes v. Eagle–Picher Co., 295 F.2d 761 (10th Cir.1961), certiorari denied 369 U.S. 828, 82 S.Ct. 846, 7 L.Ed.2d 794 (1962); Hartman Ranch Co. v. Associated Oil Co., 10 Cal.2d 232, 73 P.2d 1163 (1937); Amco Trust, Inc. v. Naylor, 159 Tex. 146, 317 S.W.2d 47 (1958); and 1 A.L.P., supra note 1, at § 3.62.

2. Sentliffer v. Jacobs, 84 N.J.L. 128, 86 A. 929 (1913).

Lacking privity, a subtenant is not liable to the landlord to pay rent or perform any covenant of the head lease as a real covenant.[3] However, under equitable servitude theory no privity is required. Probably any possessor, certainly a subtenant, who has notice will be bound by covenants that touch and concern the land.[4] A subtenant will normally have actual knowledge of the head lease's contents and in any event will almost certainly have constructive notice. The maddeningly elusive issue is whether equity will compel the subtenant to perform head lease covenants for the payment of money, chiefly the rent covenant. It has been said equity will not, because equity will not award damages.[5] The issue is not that simple. For one thing, the argument can be made that equity is ordering, not damages, but performance of the very thing promised, which happens to be paying money. There are in fact decisions in which courts do enforce as equitable servitudes promises contained in deeds to pay money.[6] Moreover, it is not uncommon for equity courts to order a contract purchaser of land specifically to pay the purchase price and to accept a deed.[7] It is quite possible, then, that the head tenant's covenants to pay money will be enforced as equitable servitudes against a subtenant, subject to equity's discretion to limit or withhold the remedy.[8]

Aside from either of the running covenant doctrines, a subtenant may have some liability to the head landlord. It is possible that the subtenant may make promises to the head tenant or to the landlord to pay rent or to perform some acts directly to the latter.[9] A subtenant may become liable to the landlord for tortious damage to the premises, and the head tenant may also be vicariously liable.[10]

Since the subtenancy is carved out of the head leasehold, an early termination of the head tenancy should cause the subtenancy to fall in. Anyone taking a subtenancy should be aware of his vulnerability in this respect and should have some arrangements with the tenant or head landlord to protect himself. If the landlord exercises a power to terminate on account of the head tenant's breach, this will bring down the subtenancy,

---

3. Bordelon v. Bordelon, 434 So.2d 633 (La. App.1983) (landlord may not enforce clause in his tenant's lease with subtenant); Davis v. Vidal, 105 Tex. 444, 151 S.W. 290 (1912); Stoebuck, supra note 6, § 6.69, at 876–77. Also, the subtenancy relationship does not empower the subtenant to enforce against the head tenant the latter's covenants in the head lease. Summit Foods, Inc. v. Greyhound Food Management, Inc., 752 F.Supp. 363 (D.Colo. 1990).

4. Oliver v. Hewitt, 191 Va. 163, 60 S.E.2d 1 (1950); Stoebuck, supra note 6, § 6.69, at 897–98.

5. 1 A.L.P., supra note 1, at § 3.62.

6. E.g., Everett Factories & Terminal Corp. v. Oldetyme Distillers Corp., 300 Mass. 499, 15 N.E.2d 829 (1938) (covenant to pay expenses of easement); Rodruck v. Sand Point Maintenance Commission, 48 Wn.2d 565, 295 P.2d 714 (1956) (covenant to pay assessments to homeowners' association).

7. D. Dobbs, Remedies § 12.13 (1973).

8. Suppose the head lease calls for rent of $500 per month and the sublease, only $400. Or suppose the subtenant takes only a portion of the premises for a lower rent than the head tenant's rent for the entire premises. In such cases equity might require the subtenant to pay the head landlord only part of the head lease rent.

9. See Goldberg v. L.H. Realty Corp., 227 Miss. 345, 86 So.2d 326 (1956), which holds that the subtenant expressly and impliedly promised to pay the landlord rent.

10. On this latter point, see Dozier v. Wallace, 169 Ga.App. 126, 311 S.E.2d 839 (1983) (head tenant remains liable to landlord after sublease); Marcellus v. K.O.V., Inc., 5 Kan. App.2d 339, 615 P.2d 170 (1980); Lustig v. U.M.C. Industries, Inc., 637 S.W.2d 55 (Mo. App.1982) (head tenant liable to landlord for waste on premises done by tenant's subtenant); Dixie Fire & Casualty Co. v. Esso Standard Oil Co., 265 N.C. 121, 143 S.E.2d 279 (1965).

too.[11] However, the courts draw the line, on equitable principles, and will not allow the head tenant to terminate a sublease by a voluntary surrender of the head lease.[12] The traditional common-law rule was even that this act released the subtenant from liability for rent to anyone, but more recent decisions hold him liable to perform the running covenants of the head lease.[13]

§ 6.71 Tenant's Covenants Against Transfer

Clauses restricting the tenant's power to assign or sublease are "boiler-plate." The simplest drafting says that the tenant may not assign or may not sublease or may not do either. More common is a clause requiring the landlord's consent for such acts, which is functionally the same as the first clause, because the parties may always modify their lease by agreeing to a transfer. An attempt to balance the parties' interests is a clause requiring the landlord's consent but limiting his privilege to refuse, usually by saying he shall not unreasonably withhold consent.

Clauses restricting transfer are enforced, but they are not judicial favorites. They run contrary to the policy against restraints on alienation. However, the policy is not absolute but permits restraints when they serve good purposes. A landlord has such purposes, to be assured that those in possession of the land he owns will not waste it and, as it usually works out in practice, will be able to perform his tenant's covenants. Therefore, any of the clauses described in the preceding paragraph are honored in court.[1] In various ways, though, courts strictly interpret the clauses.

A clause restraining "assignment" will not be interpreted to prevent subleasing,[2] nor will a clause prohibiting "subleasing" usually prevent assignment.[3] Hence, landlords ordinarily want the clause expressly to restrain

11. Brock v. Desmond & Co., 154 Ala. 634, 45 So. 665 (1908); V.O.B. Co. v. Hang It Up, Inc., 691 P.2d 1157 (Colo.App.1984) (sublease falls in if head landlord terminates head lease because of head tenant's defaults); Wehrle v. Landsman, 23 N.J.Super. 40, 92 A.2d 525 (1952); Shepard v. Dye, 137 Wash. 180, 242 P. 381 (1926). See also Minister, Elders & Deacons of Reformed Protestant Dutch Church of City of New York v. 198 Broadway, Inc., 59 N.Y.2d 170, 464 N.Y.S.2d 406, 451 N.E.2d 164 (1983) (subtenant, whose sublease contained renewal option, had no power to compel head tenant to exercise renewal option in head lease); Asherson v. Schuman, 106 A.D.2d 340, 483 N.Y.S.2d 253 (1984) (landlord could evict subtenant who held over after expiration of term of head lease).

12. E.g., Goldberg v. Tri–States Theatre Corp., 126 F.2d 26 (8th Cir.1942); Byrd v. Peterson, 66 Ariz. 253, 186 P.2d 955 (1947).

13. Warnert v. MGM Properties, 362 N.W.2d 364 (Minn.App.1985) (subtenant entitled to continue in possession after head tenant surrendered possession in mid-term); 1 A.L.P., supra note 1, at § 3.62; Annot., 18 A.L.R. 957, 963–65 (1922), Supp., 58 A.L.R. 906 (1929). But see Gordon v. Schneiker, 699 P.2d 3 (Colo.App.1984) (termination of head lease

by agreement of landlord and head tenant caused sublease to fall in).

§ 6.71

1. See, e.g., Gruman v. Investors Diversified Services, Inc., 247 Minn. 502, 78 N.W.2d 377 (1956); Dress Shirt Sales, Inc. v. Hotel Martinique Associates, 12 N.Y.2d 339, 239 N.Y.S.2d 660, 190 N.E.2d 10 (1963); Coulos v. Desimone, 34 Wn.2d 87, 208 P.2d 105 (1949). See also Tage II Corp. v. Ducas (U.S.) Realty Corp., 17 Mass.App.Ct. 664, 461 N.E.2d 1222 (1984) (to accept assignment by accepting rent from assignee, landlord must have reasonable notice rent is coming from assignee).

2. 24 Broad Street Corp. v. Quinn, 19 N.J.Super. 21, 87 A.2d 759 (1952); Burns v. Dufresne, 67 Wash. 158, 121 P. 46 (1912); Annot., 74 A.L.R. 1018 (1931); Restatement (Second) of Property § 15.2, Reporter's Note 5 (1977).

3. Cities Service Oil Co. v. Taylor, 242 Ky. 157, 45 S.W.2d 1039 (1932); Presby v. Benjamin, 169 N.Y. 377, 62 N.E. 430 (1902) (dictum); Willenbrock v. Latulippe, 125 Wash. 168, 215 P. 330 (1923); Annot., 7 A.L.R. 249 (1920), Supp., 79 A.L.R. 1379 (1932).

both. Some decisions hold that a tenant does not violate a no-subleasing clause who sublets a physical portion of the premises.[4] Nonconsensual transfers and transfers by operation of law, including inheritance and even devises, generally do not fall within the interdiction of a non-transfer clause unless the clause specifically mentions them.[5] In a lien theory state a tenant's mortgaging the leasehold does not violate a clause against transfer, but it may in a title theory state.[6] If the mortgage is foreclosed by sale, this also has in a majority of cases been held not to violate the clause, which seems correct, since the sale is involuntary.[7] Licensing the premises, such as by an agricultural tenant's granting grazing rights, usually does not breach a clause prohibiting transfer.[8] In the ways described and in other ways, the courts manifest a disposition to interpret the restraining clauses tightly.

The English Rule in *Dumpor's Case* [9] may be regarded as a manifestation of the same attitude. In substance the rule provides that, if a landlord whose consent is necessary to an assignment gives consent to one particular assignment without restricting future assignments, they may be made without his consent. Though the rule has been abolished in its homeland [10] and often criticized in America even by courts applying it, it has been said, usually in dictum, to be the American majority rule.[11] Because it is difficult to support the rule in logic, courts that have purported to follow it have reined in its application. It is not applied to a provision requiring consent for subleasing.[12] As previously suggested, the landlord may avert the rule's application by reserving the privilege to restrict future assignments in giving

4. Drake v. Eggleston, 123 Ind.App. 306, 108 N.E.2d 67 (1952), rehearing denied 123 Ind.App. 306, 108 N.E.2d 901 (1952); Denecke v. Henry F. Miller & Son, 142 Iowa 486, 119 N.W. 380 (1909) (dictum); Presby v. Benjamin, 169 N.Y. 377, 62 N.E. 430 (1902) (dictum); Annot., 56 A.L.R.2d 1002 (1957).

5. Gazlay v. Williams, 210 U.S. 41, 28 S.Ct. 687, 52 L.Ed. 950 (1908) (transfer to bankruptcy trustee); Francis v. Ferguson, 246 N.Y. 516, 159 N.E. 416 (1927) (transfer to and by executors); Powell v. Nichols, 26 Okl. 734, 110 P. 762 (1910) (execution by tenant's creditors); Annot., 46 A.L.R. 847 (1927); Restatement (Second) of Property § 15.2, Reporter's Note 5 (1977).

6. Chapman v. Great Western Gypsum Co., 216 Cal. 420, 14 P.2d 758 (1932) (lien theory); Becker v. Werner, 98 Pa. 555 (1881) (title theory).

7. Crouse v. Michell, 130 Mich. 347, 90 N.W. 32 (1902); Riggs v. Pursell, 66 N.Y. 193 (1876); Annot., 46 A.L.R. 847, 850–51 (1927). Contra, West Shore Railroad Co. v. Wenner, 70 N.J.L. 233, 57 A. 408 (1904), affirmed 71 N.J.L. 682, 60 A. 1134 (1905). See also Lipsker v. Billings Boot Shop, 129 Mont. 420, 288 P.2d 660 (1955).

8. Annot., 71 A.L.R.3d 780 (1976); Annot. 89 A.L.R. 1325 (1934); Restatement (Second) of Property § 15.2, Reporter's Note 5 (1977). Cf. Presby v. Benjamin, 169 N.Y. 377, 62 N.E. 430 (1902) (caretaker in premises). But see Enders v. Wesley W. Hubbard & Sons, Inc., 95

Idaho 590, 513 P.2d 992 (1973), appeal after remand 95 Idaho 908, 523 P.2d 40 (1974) (allowing another to graze, a breach when land used only for grazing).

9. 4 Coke 119b, 76 Eng.Rep. 1110 (K.B. 1603).

10. Law of Property Act, 22 & 23 Vict., c. 35, § 1 (1859).

11. German–American Savings Bank v. Gollmer, 155 Cal. 683, 102 P. 932 (1909) (dictum); Reid v. John F. Wiessner & Sons Brewing Co., 88 Md. 234, 40 A. 877 (1898); Aste v. Putnam's Hotel Co., 247 Mass. 147, 141 N.E. 666 (1923); Easley Coal Co. v. Brush Creek Coal Co., 91 W.Va. 291, 112 S.E. 512 (1922); Annot., 31 A.L.R. 153 (1924), Supp., 32 A.L.R. 1080 (1924). Contra, Packard–Bamberger & Co. v. Maloof, 83 N.J.Super. 273, 199 A.2d 400 (1964), reversed 89 N.J.Super. 128, 214 A.2d 45 (1965) (by implication); Childs v. Warner Brothers Southern Theatres, 200 N.C. 333, 156 S.E. 923 (1931); Reynolds v. McCullough, 739 S.W.2d 424 (Tex.App.1987) (rule rejected by implication); Investors' Guaranty Corp. v. Thomson, 31 Wyo. 264, 225 P. 590 (1924); Restatement (Second) of Property § 16.1, Comment g (1977).

12. German–American Savings Bank v. Gollmer, 155 Cal. 683, 102 P. 932 (1909) (dictum); Miller v. Newton–Humphreville Co., 116 A. 325 (N.J.Eq.1920); Annot., 31 A.L.R. 153, 157–59 (1924).

consent to a prior assignment. Clauses restricting transfer commonly contain a proviso that the giving of consent shall not end the need for future consent, and this also is believed to be effective.[13]

When the restraining clause says, without qualification, that the landlord's consent is required for the tenant's transfer, then it is quite generally held that he may withhold consent without having to give a reason.[14] However, several recent decisions, of which the best known is *Kendall v. Ernest Pestana, Inc.,* from California, have held that, at least when the landlord withholds consent to force a higher rent upon assignment, he must have a reasonable basis for withholding.[15] It may strengthen the landlord's position to insert specific language that consent may be withheld for any or for no reason.[16] A tenant, on the other hand, may wish to have the clause say the landlord shall not "unreasonably" withhold consent or words to that effect. Such limits on the landlord are enforced, though, reasonableness being a factual question, results may vary.[17]

Landlords normally want to have a consent clause coupled with a power to terminate the leasehold if the tenant or his transferee attempts a transfer without consent. It seems that when a transfer is in fact made without the required consent, the transfer is nevertheless valid.[18] Without a power to terminate, the landlord has a damages action. He might enjoin a threatened nonconsensual transfer before it occurred but apparently could not "unring the bell" by a decree dissolving an accomplished transfer.[19] Termination under a power seems useful, therefore, and the threat of termination must be a strong deterrent against breach.

§ 6.72 Transfers by Landlord

A landlord may convey his reversion, usually by a deed to the fee. Almost always the grantee will take subject to the ongoing leasehold. It is

13. See Merritt v. Kay, 54 App.D.C. 152, 295 Fed. 973 (1924); 1 A.L.P., supra note 1, at § 3.58.

14. Friedman v. Thomas J. Fisher & Co., 88 A.2d 321 (D.C.Mun.App.1952); Gruman v. Investors Diversified Services, Inc., 247 Minn. 502, 78 N.W.2d 377 (1956); Dress Shirt Sales, Inc. v. Hotel Martinique Associates, 12 N.Y.2d 339, 239 N.Y.S.2d 660, 190 N.E.2d 10 (1963); Coulos v. Desimone, 34 Wn.2d 87, 208 P.2d 105 (1949); Annot., 31 A.L.R.2d 831, 831–34 (1953). Accord, Herlou Card Shop, Inc. v. Prudential Insurance Co., 73 A.D.2d 562, 422 N.Y.S.2d 708 (1979).

15. Kendall v. Ernest Pestana, Inc., 40 Cal.3d 488, 220 Cal.Rptr. 818, 709 P.2d 837 (1985). Accord, Campbell v. Westdahl, 148 Ariz. 432, 715 P.2d 288 (App.1985); Jack Frost Sales, Inc. v. Harris Trust & Sav. Bank, 104 Ill.App.3d 933, 60 Ill.Dec. 703, 433 N.E.2d 941 (1982). Contra, Reynolds v. McCullough, 739 S.W.2d 424 (Tex.App.1987), which expressly rejects the California position. In some states that reject the *Kendall* position, the tenant may produce a similar result by (wrongfully) quitting the premises when the landlord un-

reasonably refuses to consent to a proffered assignee. If the state is one that requires the landlord to mitigate by making reasonable attempts to relet, to avoid termination by surrender, and if the landlord persists in refusing to let the proffered assignee (now proffered as a substitute tenant), then this will work a termination. See Bert Bidwell Inv. Corp. v. LaSalle & Schiffer, P.C., 797 P.2d 811 (Colo. App.1990).

16. See Annot., 31 A.L.R.2d 831, 834–35 (1953); Restatement (Second) of Property § 15.2 (1977).

17. See Fahrenwald v. LaBonte, 103 Idaho 751, 653 P.2d 806 (1982) (landlord's refusal to consent was reasonable when landlord had reason to doubt proposed assignee's financial stability); Annot., 54 A.L.R.3d 679 (1973).

18. People v. Klopstock, 24 Cal.2d 897, 151 P.2d 641 (1944). But see Reynolds v. McCullough, 739 S.W.2d 424 (Tex.App.1987), which holds that a landlord has an implied power to terminate if a tenant breaches a clause forbidding assignment.

19. See 1 A.L.P., supra note 1, at § 3.58.

possible but very unlikely for the grantee to take free of the leasehold by force of a recording act. For this to occur, the following conditions would have to coincide: (1) the leasehold would be of such a length as to require the lease to be recorded to protect the tenant's priority; (2) the lease would be unrecorded; (3) the grantee would have given value; (4) the grantee would have no notice of the tenancy; and (5) the tenant could not be in possession, for possession would give the grantee inquiry notice.[1] In states with race-notice recording acts, the conveyance would also have to be recorded before the lease was recorded. The landlord may mortgage the reversion instead of conveying it, in which event the statements just made would govern priority between mortgagee and tenant.

The grantee, as owner of the reversion, comes into privity and has a direct relationship with the tenant. A few decisions have even gone so far as to consider the grantee a substitute landlord, meaning that in every respect the grantee has the right to performance of the tenant's lease covenants and the duty to perform all landlord's covenants.[2] This goes too far. We previously saw that when it is the leasehold that is assigned, the assignee has the benefit of, and must perform, only those covenants, the benefit and burden of which runs. By the correct theory, the same is true when a grantee of the reversion comes into privity with the tenant: each has the burden to perform, and the right to enforce, only those covenants that run.[3] As a practical matter, these include most of the tenant's valuable covenants, such as rent covenants, and most of the landlord's covenants. However, if the grantee and the tenant want to be sure all covenants are binding between them, they must make a new lease or adopt the existing lease contractually.

Under the original common-law rule, the tenant had to "attorn" to the grantee before rights or duties existed between them. This meant the tenant had to recognize the grantee, usually by paying him rent. In England the Statute of Anne of 1705[4] ended the requirement for attornment. American states, by statutes similar to the Statute of Anne, by including it within the received common law, or by judicial decision, have abandoned the requirement as well.[5]

M. TERMINATION

§ 6.73 Normal End of Term—Tenancy for Years

A tenancy for years, or fixed-term tenancy, terminates automatically at the agreed end of the term. Neither party need give notice or do any act to

---

§ 6.72

1. See 1 A.L.P., supra note, at § 3.59.

2. See, e.g., F. Groos & Co. v. Chittim, 100 S.W. 1006 (Tex.Civ.App.1907); Annot., 14 A.L.R. 664, 678 (1921).

3. Mrotek Enterprises, Inc. v. Dryer, 256 A.2d 557 (D.C.App.1969) (landlord's covenant to appoint agent for service of process did not bind grantee of reversion because not running covenant). See Savings, Inc. v. City of Blytheville, 240 Ark. 558, 401 S.W.2d 26 (1966); P.M.K., Inc. v. Folsom Heights Dev. Co., 692 S.W.2d 395 (Mo.App.1985) (landlord's covenant to return security deposit did not bind grantee of reversion because not running covenant); Masury v. Southworth, 9 Ohio St. 340

(1859) (court's discussion). Mullendore Theatres, Inc. v. Growth Realty Investors Co., 39 Wn.App. 64, 691 P.2d 970 (1984) (landlord's covenant to return security deposit did not bind grantee of reversion because not running covenant). See also Stroshein v. Harbour Hall Inlet Club II Condo. Ass'n, Inc., 418 So.2d 473 (Fla.App.1982) (after landlord conveyed reversion, he had no duty to perform covenants that ran with transfer of reversion).

4. 4 Anne, c. 16, §§ 9, 10.

5. See Glidden v. Second Avenue Investment Co., 125 Minn. 471, 147 N.W. 658 (1914) (dictum); Northern Pacific Railway Co. v. McClure, 9 N.D. 73, 81 N.W. 52 (1899) (dictum); 1 A.L.P. supra note 1, at § 3.60.

make it end, for the simple reason that the parties' agreement has already limited the leasehold's life.[1] When the agreed period is for some definite calendar period, such as a month or day, the term ends at the end of the last day of that period.[2] If the tenant holds over without the landlord's consent, he becomes tenant at sufferance, a subject discussed previously in this chapter.

§ 6.74 Normal End of Term—Periodic Tenancy

As explained earlier in the chapter, a periodic tenancy, which developed out of the tenancy at will, has a term of indefinite duration that is normally ended at the end of some rental period by notice of one of the parties to the other. Statutes prescribe the length of notice that must be given, the time usually being counted backward from the end of one of the periods of the leasehold. The various statutes prescribe times varying from seven days to one year. A given state may prescribe different times for different kinds of land. Shorter periods of notice are likely to be for short-term leaseholds and longer periods for agricultural and long-term leaseholds.[1]

To know the proper form of notice and manner of delivery, one must consult the controlling statute, which presumably is mandatory. Notices may be oral unless, as is apt to be the case, the lease or the applicable statute requires written notice. Generally speaking, a well prepared notice will identify the sender as landlord or tenant and the recipient as the other; will identify the premises; will state that it is a notice to terminate; and will expressly designate the day of termination. In keeping with the usual rule, the notice is effective when delivered. Length of notice is computed by excluding the day of service and including the designated termination day.[2]

§ 6.73

1. Minor v. Hicks, 235 Ala. 686, 180 So. 689 (1938); Chappell v. Reynolds, 206 Ark. 452, 176 S.W.2d 154 (1943) (semble); Tredick v. Birrer, 109 Kan. 488, 200 P. 272 (1921); Frenchtown Villa v. Meadors, 117 Mich.App. 683, 324 N.W.2d 133 (1982) (because term for years ended automatically at end of term, landlord's demand of possession could not be retaliatory eviction). See also Gothard v. Murphy Oil Corp., 659 S.W.2d 26 (Tenn.App. 1983) (fifteen-year leasehold commencing 1 January 1967 ended automatically 31 December 1981, not 31 December 1982 as lease said).

2. Minor v. Hicks, 235 Ala. 686, 180 So. 689 (1938).

§ 6.74

1. See Restatement (Second) of Property § 1.5, Statutory Note (1977), for a listing and analysis of the many state statutes. For sample discussions of the operation of various notice statutes, see Darling Shops Delaware Corp. v. Baltimore Center Corp., 191 Md. 289, 60 A.2d 669 (1948); 28 Mott Street Co. v. Summit Import Corp., 34 A.D.2d 144, 310 N.Y.S.2d 93 (1970), affirmed 28 N.Y.2d 508,

319 N.Y.S.2d 65, 267 N.E.2d 880 (1971); Arbenz v. Exley, Watkins & Co., 57 W.Va. 580, 50 S.E. 813 (1905); Annot., 86 A.L.R. 1346 (1933); C. Donahue, T. Kauper & P. Martin, Cases and Materials on Property [864–65 (2d ed. 1983).]

2. See Ogden v. John Jay Esthetic Salons, Inc., 470 So.2d 521 (La.App.1985) (letter notifying tenant to quit complied with statutory requirement of "written" notice); Pertillo v. Forest Ridge Ltd., 166 Ga.App. 552, 304 S.E.2d 925 (1983) (notice to quit may be effective only at end of a tenancy period, which may be further away than the days of advance notice required by statute); Worthington v. Moreland Motor Truck Co., 140 Wash. 528, 250 P. 30 (1926); Arbenz v. Exley, Watkins & Co., 57 W.Va. 580, 50 S.E. 813 (1905); Annot., 86 A.L.R. 1346 (1933); 1 A.L.P. supra note 1, at § 3.90; C. Donahue, T. Kauper & P. Martin, Cases and Materials on Property 864–65 (2d ed. 1983); Restatement (Second) of Property § 1.5 (1977). See also Buss v. Gruis, 320 N.W.2d 549 (Iowa 1982) (notice sent by ordinary mail was not effective, though actually received, when statute required certified mail); Harry's Village, Inc. v. Egg Harbor Tp.,

A nettlesome question arises over what may be called the landlord's "notice in the alternative." In its typical form this notice tells the tenant either to quit the premises on a designated day (which we assume to be a permitted termination date) or, if the tenant does not quit, to render an amended performance, usually to pay more rent. Courts are split over the effect of such a notice. Most courts hold the tenant liable for the amended performance if he remains in possession and fails to dispute the proposed amendment.[3] Since the tenant's new liability is founded in his implied assent to the proposed amendment, his expressed dissent would presumably prevent the change, though authority on the point seems mostly dictum.[4] By a minority view, the alternative form of notice, being neither fish nor fowl, has no effect, either to amend or to terminate.[5]

§ 6.75 Normal End of Term—Tenancy at Will

As its name suggests, a tenancy at will extends only so long as both parties desire it. At common law it is instantly terminable by either party's indicating that he wishes it to end. In practice this wish is normally expressed in the form of one's notice to the other, though other inconsistent acts, such as a demand for possession, landlord's conveyance, or tenant's attempt to assign, also suffice. The courts do, however, allow the tenant a reasonable time to remove possessions.[1]

About half the American states have statutes requiring advance notice to terminate a tenancy at will. Required notice periods run from three days (Colorado) to three months (Minnesota), with 30 days or one month being the commonest period.[2] Such a requirement converts the tenancy at will into a periodic tenancy in effect, if perhaps not in strict theory. Indeed, Massachusetts uses the phrase "tenancy at will" to refer to what has traditionally been known as a periodic tenancy.[3]

§ 6.76 Normal End of Term—Tenancy at Sufferance

As noted earlier in the chapter, it stretches the imagination to say that a tenant at sufferance, who becomes such by a non-permissive holding over, is truly a tenant. But if he is, his tenancy does not come to an end in any

89 N.J. 576, 446 A.2d 862 (1982) (notice that demanded possession on date that was not end of a tenancy period substantially complied with statutory requirements and was effective at end of next full tenancy period). But see Steele v. Murphy, 279 Ark. 235, 650 S.W.2d 573 (1983) (under statute that required landlord to "give" notice of termination, notice was effective when mailed, despite usual rule that notice is effective when received).

3. Garrity v. United States, 107 Ct.Cl. 92, 67 F.Supp. 821 (1946); Welk v. Bidwell, 136 Conn. 603, 73 A.2d 295 (1950); Heckman v. Walker, 167 Neb. 216, 92 N.W.2d 548 (1958); Bhar Realty Corp. v. Becker, 49 N.J.Super. 585, 140 A.2d 756 (1958). Cf. Annot., 109 A.L.R. 197 (1937), which deals with landlords' notices purporting to amend lease provisions when such notices are not conjoined with a notice to quit.

4. Moll v. Main Motor Co., 213 Ark. 28, 210 S.W.2d 321 (1948). See authorities in preceding note.

5. Maguire v. Haddad, 325 Mass. 590, 91 N.E.2d 769 (1950).

§ 6.75

1. 1 A.L.P. supra note 1, at § 3.91; Restatement (Second) of Property § 1.6 (1977). See also Day v. Kolar, 216 Neb. 47, 341 N.W.2d 598 (1983) (lease that allowed either party to terminate "upon –0– days notice" was tenancy at will that was terminable at any time).

2. See Restatement (Second) of Property § 1.6, Statutory Note 3 (1977).

3. See Mass.Gen.Laws Ann. c. 186, § 12; Maguire v. Haddad, 325 Mass. 590, 91 N.E.2d 769 (1950).

regular way. The relationship, temporary by nature, usually is brought to an end by the tenant's being thrust into one of two other relationships, trespasser or periodic tenant. It will be recalled that the landlord has a power, exercisable for a "reasonable time" after the tenancy at sufferance begins, to transform the holdover tenant into one of these two statuses. Even if the landlord fails to make the election within that time, the tenancy at sufferance ends, though the little authority on the subject disagrees on whether the tenant then is trespasser, periodic tenant, or tenant at will. At all odds, we can say the tenancy at sufferance will terminate after a temporary lifespan.[1]

§ 6.77 Tenancy Upon Special Limitation

Students of real property law are familiar with the fee simple determinable and with other freehold estates upon special limitation. A fee or other freehold estate may be created to endure only "so long as" a given state of affairs obtains, e.g., so long as a school is maintained or so long as liquor is not sold. The continuation of the described condition, e.g., "dryness" or "school-ness," is necessary to support the estate. If and when that state of affairs ceases to continue, the estate falls in, automatically, without entry or other act by the holder of the succeeding estate.

Leaseholds may be similarly limited. It would be quite proper to speak of them as "leaseholds upon special limitation," but in popular parlance they are called "leases with automatic termination clauses." Terminating events one frequently finds include the tenant's illegal activities on the premises, insolvency or bankruptcy, death, and vacating the premises and the landlord's sale of the reversion. Upon the event's happening, the leasehold automatically ends.[1]

Automatic termination clauses are to be disfavored, in two senses. At the practical level, the party for whose benefit a termination clause exists would nearly always be better served to have the form of clause that will be described in the next section, a clause giving that party a power to terminate if the stated event occurs. Thus, the party may postpone the decision whether to terminate until the event occurs, when, in the light of a known situation, it may well seem better not to bring the leasehold down. At the level of legal principle, the courts are, because of the sudden-death operation of the clause and because parties are unlikely to intend it, reluctant to read language to mean automatic termination. The courts will do so only if the language leaves no doubt that was the parties' intent.[2] There is one situation in particular in which courts may and should refuse to find automatic termination, where the leasehold is said to terminate upon the

§ 6.76

1. See Dvoracek v. Gillies, 363 N.W.2d 99 (Minn.App.1985) (when tenant held over after leasehold ended, he was tenant at sufferance who could be ousted without further notice); § 6.20, supra.

§ 6.77

1. See Remedco Corp. v. Bryn Mawr Hotel Corp., 45 Misc.2d 586, 257 N.Y.S.2d 525 (Civ. Ct.1965); Jamaica Builders Supply Corp. v. Buttelman, 25 Misc.2d 326, 205 N.Y.S.2d 303

(Mun.Ct.1960) (court's discussion); Restatement (Second) of Property § 1.7 (1977).

2. Jamaica Builders Supply Corp. v. Buttelman, 25 Misc.2d 326, 205 N.Y.S.2d 303 (Mun.Ct.1960); Restatement (Second) of Property § 1.7 (1977). Compare Remedco Corp. v. Bryn Mawr Hotel Corp., 45 Misc.2d 586, 257 N.Y.S.2d 525 (Civ.Ct.1965), where the court held that "shall immediately cease and determine" meant automatic termination.

tenant's failure to pay rent or breach of some other lease covenant.[3] It is hardly conceivable that a landlord would intend to give the tenant, in effect, an election to terminate by his own breach; indeed, to allow this may violate public policy.

§ 6.78 Powers of Termination

In the absence of a statute or lease clause authorizing it, neither landlord nor tenant is traditionally empowered to terminate a leasehold on account of the other's breach. Decisions, previously discussed in section 6.40, that allow the tenant to terminate because of the landlord's breach of a warranty of habitability may be an exception. Though there are probably a few decisions allowing it,[1] the contract doctrine of rescission is not a traditionally accepted part of landlord-tenant law. However, leases frequently contain clauses giving one party or the other a power to terminate the leasehold and the parties' contractual obligations if certain conditions exist. Such clauses are commonly called "forfeiture" clauses, but "power of termination" is more precise. Conditions that trigger the power are usually a breach by the burdened party or the events, described in the preceding section, that might cause automatic termination. Leases more frequently confer termination powers on the landlord than on the tenant, but it may work either way. Unlike automatic termination, a power of termination clause allows the benefitted party to elect whether there shall be a termination. A threat of exercise powerfully restrains the burdened party from breaching or otherwise triggering the power.

No termination occurs until the party who has the power exercises it in some unequivocal way.[2] When the landlord holds the power, he may exercise it by entry or by a court action for possession.[3] If the lease permits it, the power may be exercised by a notice. However, any special requirements, such as giving a period of advance notice, must be satisfied.[4]

Because the courts regard termination as a forfeiture, they tend to be chary in finding it has occurred. This explains the need for unequivocal exercise, just noted. It also explains why, in general, courts incline to restrictive interpretation of termination language. Two particular doctrines impose limitations on the exercise of powers of termination, the doctrines of waiver, so called, and estoppel.

Waiver may occur when the burdened party breaches and a termination might be declared, but, before termination, the benefitted party expressly or impliedly recognizes the tenancy as continuing. The commonest example is a breach by the tenant and known to the landlord, followed by the landlord's

---

3. See Entrepreneur, Ltd. v. Yasuna, 498 A.2d 1151 (D.C.App.1985) (though lease clause said lease would terminate if tenant used premises for any unlawful purpose, court read clause to allow landlord power to terminate); Cochran v. Lakota Land & Water Co., 171 Wash. 155, 17 P.2d 861 (1933), rehearing denied 171 Wash. 155, 19 P.2d 927 (1933).

§ 6.78

1. E.g., University Properties, Inc. v. Moss, 63 Wn.2d 619, 388 P.2d 543 (1964).

2. Padilla v. Sais, 76 N.M. 247, 414 P.2d 223 (1966); Larsen v. Sjogren, 67 Wyo. 447, 226 P.2d 177 (1951).

3. Id. (dictum).

4. Joseph J. Freed & Assocs., Inc. v. Cassinelli Apparel Corp., 23 Ohio St.3d 94, 491 N.E.2d 1109 (1986) (termination by 10–day notice); Gray v. Gregory, 36 Wn.2d 416, 218 P.2d 307 (1950).

acceptance of rent due for a period after the breach; no termination may then be predicated on that breach.[5] Similar is the situation in which the tenant assigned in violation of a no-assignment clause, but the landlord accepts rent from the assignee; he is said to have waived any power to terminate.[6] The waiver is only as to breaches that have previously occurred, not for later repetitions of the same breach or for a later period of a continuing breach.[7] "Waiver" is a chameleon word, incapable of precise definition, a collection of equitable doctrines invoked in differing situations for differing reasons. In the situation we are considering, the courts may find a waiver because they dislike forfeitures.[8] Another plausible basis is that the benefitted party has made a binding election not to pursue the termination remedy.[9]

Waiver is often confused with another equitable doctrine, estoppel. It is possible for a party to a lease who has the benefit of a power of termination to be estopped from exercising the power, at least to a certain extent. Two such situations will be identified. First, suppose a landlord has a power to terminate for the tenant's breach of, say, a covenant not to alter the premises. Not only does the tenant make forbidden alterations, but the landlord either stands by or assists the tenant in doing so. As to that breach, the landlord, having sanctioned the breach is estopped from terminating.[10] In the second situation the benefitted party, usually the landlord, has repeatedly tolerated the other's late performance, e.g., late rent payment. The next time that performance is late, the benefitted party will be allowed to terminate only after a grace period comparable to the periods customarily tolerated unless he has given notice that late performance will no longer be accepted.[11]

When the burdened party's breach is only the failure to pay a sum of money, equity will usually bar the other party from exercising a power of termination, on the condition the money is paid. The remedy is within the equity court's discretion, which means the court will balance the equities and hardships of both parties. Factors favoring the burdened party include a showing that his monetary loss from forfeiture will be large, that his breach is slight, that he has previously had a good performance record, that

---

5. E.g., Goldberg v. Pearl, 306 Ill. 436, 138 N.E. 141 (1923) (alternative ground); Woollard v. Schaffer Stores Co., 272 N.Y. 304, 5 N.E.2d 829 (1936), amend. of remittitur denied 273 N.Y. 527, 7 N.E.2d 676 (1937); Annot., 109 A.L.R. 1267, 1267–77 (1937). See also Annot., 49 A.L.R. 830, 833 (1927).

6. E.g., Buchanan v. Banta, 204 Cal. 73, 266 P. 547 (1928); Johnson v. Hotel Lawrence Corp., 337 Ill. 345, 169 N.E. 240 (1929); Towle v. Commissioner of Banks, 246 Mass. 161, 140 N.E. 747 (1923) (banking commissioner took over tenant's premises); Annot., 109 A.L.R. 1267, 1267–77 (1937); Annot., 118 A.L.R. 124, 124–31 (1939).

7. Sherrill v. Harlan Theater Co., 256 Ky. 150, 75 S.W.2d 775 (1934); Shepard v. Dye, 137 Wash. 180, 242 P. 381 (1926); Annot., 109 A.L.R. 1267, 1277–79 (1937).

8. See C & A Land Co. v. Rudolf Inv. Corp., 163 Ga.App. 832, 296 S.E.2d 149 (1982) (landlord waived power to terminate by retaining, without cashing rent checks for months prior to notice of termination); Quinn v. Cardinal Foods, Inc., 20 Ohio App.3d 194, 485 N.E.2d 741 (1984) (landlord waived power to terminate by accepting rent after notice to terminate). But see Riverside Dev. Co. v. Ritchie, 103 Idaho 515, 650 P.2d 657 (1982) (landlord did not waive power to terminate by accepting rent after notice was given). 3A A. Corbin, Contracts § 754 (1960), suggests this rationale.

9. This is suggested in 5 S. Williston, Contracts § 687 (3d ed. 1961).

10. See Annot., 76 A.L.R. 304, 317–19 (1932).

11. 1 A.L.P., supra note 1, at § 3.95.

he has acted in good faith, or that the other party is trying to take advantage of the situation. The party holding the power is favored by the opposites of those factors or by a showing that to deny termination will cause him a hardship.[12] Termination is likely to be allowed if the tenant has repeatedly defaulted in paying rent. At work here is the maxim that equity abhors a forfeiture. The process by which equity intervenes is essentially the same as that by which equity developed the modern mortgage.

Leases frequently contain clauses empowering the landlord or tenant to terminate if the other becomes insolvent or is declared a bankrupt. Under the current Bankruptcy Code, such a clause is unenforceable.[13]

§ 6.79 Summary Eviction Statutes

Every state, as well as the District of Columbia, Guam, Puerto Rico, and the Virgin Islands, has some form of statute allowing the landlord to evict a tenant who breaches his lease covenants, by a special, summary proceeding. All but a few jurisdictions allow the landlord to use the action even though the lease does not contain a termination clause.[1] In a broad sense, these statutes constitute an exception to the traditional common-law rule that one may not rescind a lease.

The types of breaches that will trigger the statutory remedy known as summary eviction or unlawful detainer may be limited. Some statutes allow the remedy only for nonpayment of rent; others may allow it for other kinds of breaches, some for any tenant's breach. The usual scheme is that the landlord must give the tenant a notice in a prescribed manner, requiring the tenant either to cure the breach, if it is curable, within a certain period of time or to vacate. Times of notice, generally short, vary from state to state and according to the nature of the breach; from three to 10 days' notice is typical for a rent default. If the tenant vacates, lease and leasehold terminate. If not, the tenant falls into a status usually called "unlawful detainer."[2] At that point the landlord has the summary court action for possession and, in most states, for back rent with perhaps a penalty.[3] In Lindsey v. Normet the United States Supreme Court upheld the constitution-

---

12. E.g., Gamble–Skogmo, Inc. v. McNair Realty Co., 98 F.Supp. 440 (D.Mont.1951), affirmed per curiam, 193 F.2d 876 (9th Cir. 1952); Humphrey v. Humphrey, 254 Ala. 395, 48 So.2d 424 (1950). See the extensive coverage in Annot., 16 A.L.R. 437 (1922), Supp., 31 A.L.R.2d 321 (1953). See also Entrepreneur, Ltd. v. Yasuna, 498 A.2d 1151 (D.C.App.1985) (landlord could not terminate for tenant's technical breach of failure to apply for business permit); Dillingham Commercial Co. v. Spears, 641 P.2d 1 (Alaska 1982) (landlord could not terminate for tenant's slight breach of failing to pay real estate taxes); Housing Auth. of City of Mansfield v. Rovig, 676 S.W.2d 314 (Mo.App.1984) (landlord could not terminate for tenant's minor breach of keeping a dog).

13. 11 U.S.C.A. § 365(e); 2 W. Collier, Bankruptcy ¶ 365.06 (15th ed. 1980).

§ 6.79

1. Restatement (Second) of Property § 12.1, Statutory Note 1 (1977), contains a complete list of the statutes, with brief descriptions.

2. But the tenant is called "tenant at sufferance" in some states. See Gower v. Waters, 125 Me. 223, 132 A. 550 (1926); Margosian v. Markarian, 288 Mass. 197, 192 N.E. 612 (1934).

3. For general descriptions of summary eviction statutes, see C. Donahue, T. Kauper & P. Martin, Cases and Materials on Property [852–53 (2d ed. 1983);] Restatement (Second) of Property § 12.1, Statutory Note 1 (1977); Gibbons, Residential Landlord–Tenant Law: A Survey of Modern Problems With Reference to the Proposed Model Code, 21 Hastings L.J. 369, 372–78 (1970).

ality of the summary form of action with accelerated trial date.[4]

Because the statutory actions are summary, courts have traditionally limited the issues to whether the tenant has committed the breach alleged. Most frequently this principle has been applied to prevent a tenant's presenting evidence of an offset or counterclaim against his unpaid rent. If rent is unpaid, he is liable to be placed in unlawful detainer, and his affirmative claim will have to await a separate action.[5] Lindsey v. Normet held this limitation of issues valid.[6] In recent years, however, the traditional rule has been changed in a number of jurisdictions, to allow tenants to prove offsets or counterclaims against unpaid rent. The decisions in which this has occurred have generally involved a residential tenant who claimed an offset for breach of the landlord's newly found implied warranty of habitability.[7] In popular parlance, this allows a form of "rent withholding" by a tenant whose premises do not come up to the habitability standard. A number of states that have recently adopted residential landlord-tenant codes, exemplified by the Uniform Residential Landlord and Tenant Act and the Model Residential Landlord–Tenant Code, have accomplished the same result legislatively.[8]

Under some summary eviction statutes, the landlord's sole remedy is possession. Most statutes also permit recovery of rent due, and some permit even a penalty in a multiple of the rent, such as double. When there is a statutory penalty, courts certainly may award it, but they have frequently refused to do so when tenants have had a reasonable excuse for holding over after the statutory notice to quit.[9]

§ 6.80　Eviction by Self–Help

In approaching the tortured subject of eviction by self-help, we must carefully describe the setting of the problem. We assume that the tenant's

4. Lindsey v. Normet, 405 U.S. 56, 92 S.Ct. 862, 31 L.Ed.2d 36 (1972). However, the Court struck down a requirement that the tenant, to appeal in a summary eviction action, post a bond in double the amount of rent expected to be owing.

5. E.g., People ex rel. Tuttle v. Walton, 2 Thompson & Cook 533 (N.Y.Sup.Ct.1874); Class v. Carter, 293 Or. 147, 645 P.2d 536 (1982) (in unlawful detainer action, tenant may not claim offsetting damages for landlord's breach); Sundholm v. Patch, 62 Wn.2d 244, 382 P.2d 262 (1963); Gibbons, supra note 3, this section.

6. 405 U.S. 56, 92 S.Ct. 862, 31 L.Ed.2d 36 (1972).

7. Jack Spring, Inc. v. Little, 50 Ill.2d 351, 280 N.E.2d 208 (1972); Marini v. Ireland, 56 N.J. 130, 265 A.2d 526 (1970); Academy Spires, Inc. v. Brown, 111 N.J.Super. 477, 268 A.2d 556 (1970); Foisy v. Wyman, 83 Wn.2d 22, 515 P.2d 160 (1973). See also Javins v. First National Realty Corp., 428 F.2d 1071 (D.C.Cir.1970), certiorari denied 400 U.S. 925, 91 S.Ct. 186, 27 L.Ed.2d 185 (1970) (offset

allowed by court rule). Some decisions seem to take the position, difficult to understand in principle, that, while the tenant may offset damages caused by the landlord's breach of an implied warranty of habitability, he may not offset damages for the landlord's breach of an express lease covenant. See Winchester Management Corp. v. Staten, 361 A.2d 187 (D.C.App.1976); Timber Ridge Town House v. Dietz, 133 N.J.Super. 577, 338 A.2d 21 (1975). Since the offset has been associated with implied warranties of residential habitability, is it possible the courts will still not allow commercial tenants to offset in summary eviction actions? If so, on what principled ground?

8. Uniform Residential Landlord and Tenant Act § 4.105; Model Residential Landlord–Tenant Code § 3–210. See Cunningham, The New Implied and Statutory Warranties of Habitability in Residential Leases: From Contract to Status, 16 Urban L.Ann. 3, 113–26 (1979).

9. See Jones v. Taylor, 136 Ky. 39, 123 S.W. 326 (1909) (tenant "in good faith"); Feiges v. Racine Dry Goods Co., 231 Wis. 270, 285 N.W. 799 (1939) (tenant's employees on strike).

leasehold has terminated in some manner. However, he fails to quit the premises. If the tenant has abandoned the premises, i.e., vacated without an intent to return, then of course the landlord may re-enter; he is not evicting the tenant if the tenant has already given up possession. We assume that the tenant is a wrongful holdover, that the landlord is legally entitled to possession, and indeed that the landlord might prevail in a summary eviction or other possessory action. The landlord, though, eschews expensive, cumbersome legal processes and attempts to regain possession by some form of self-help, such as by entering while the tenant is away and changing the locks or even by entering and forcing out a tenant who is present. To what extent may the landlord lawfully use such self-help?

English history is still relevant to this question. Before 1381 the landlord was privileged to oust a holdover tenant by any force short of serious injury or death. In 1381 the Statute of Forcible Entry [1] made it a crime for the landlord (or anyone) to enter by self-help except in a "peaceable and easy manner." The judicial doctrine came to be that, since the statute was a criminal one, a landlord's entry was not a trespass *quare clausum fregit*. However, any touching of the person or goods of the tenant or his family would be a tort. Newton v. Harland, in 1840, was the leading decision recognizing this doctrine.[2] In effect, then, the landlord was privileged to enter in the tenant's absence or peaceably in his presence but not to use any force whatever to remove the tenant or his goods. *Newton* was overruled in 1920 in Hemmings v. Stoke Poges Golf Club, Ltd.,[3] and the current English rule became that the landlord is privileged to use such reasonable force as is necessary to expel the holdover tenant.[4]

It will be perceived that, as the law was developed, we have two basic questions: (1) is it trespass, *q.c.f.* for the landlord to enter; and (2) what degree of force, if any, is the landlord privileged to use to remove persons or goods? American courts take different positions on these questions. Failure to separate the questions contributes to the general confusion. In addition to a court's philosophy about the use of self-help to regain possession, a couple of special factors may influence a decision. As previously noted, every jurisdiction has some form of statutory summary eviction procedure. Some courts have been moved by the argument that the special summary procedure is a trade-off for self-help, so that legal proceedings for eviction should be exclusive.[5] Second, many jurisdictions have forcible entry statutes similar to the 1381 English statute or have incorporated the principles of the English statute as a received part of the common law. It is possible for a court to disagree with the position the English always took, that the statute did not define a civil trespass. In other words, some American courts are

---

§ 6.80

1. 5 Rich. 2, c. 7.

2. 1 Man. & G. 644, 133 Eng.Rep. 490. The court's lengthy discussions of the doctrine are technically dicta, since the case was sent back for determination of additional facts twice, and there was no appeal on this point from the last remand.

3. [1920] 1 K.B. 720.

4. For reviews of the English legal history on the subject, see City of Chicago v. Chicago Steamship Lines, 328 Ill. 309, 159 N.E. 301 (1927); Annot., 6 A.L.R.3d 177 (1966); 1 F. Harper, F. James and O. Gray, Torts § 3.15 (2d ed. 1986); [W. Prosser and W. Keeton, Torts § 23 (5th ed. 1984).]

5. See, e.g., Spencer v. Commercial Co., 30 Wash. 520, 71 P. 53 (1902).

persuaded that a landlord's forcible entry is a civil wrong.[6] Varying statutory and judicial definitions of "forcible" complicate matters further.

The rule in some jurisdictions, simple to state and to apply, is that the landlord is not privileged to enter premises held by a holdover tenant. Any entry is a trespass; the landlord may use only legal process.[7] As just suggested, arguments for this position are sometimes based upon summary eviction and forcible entry statutes, as well as upon a policy to avoid breaches of the peace. This rule has traditionally been regarded as a distinct minority one,[8] and it still probably is as far as case law goes. However, there appears to be a trend toward the rule in judicial decisions.[9] It is the rule advocated by the Restatement (Second) of Property and is embodied in the Uniform Residential Landlord and Tenant Act and the Model Residential Landlord–Tenant Code.[10] Considering the number of states that have adopted versions of the Uniform Act or Model Act or some similar legislation, plus those that have adopted the rule by court decision, it seems that it is the governing rule of law between *residential* landlords and tenants in half or slightly more states.[11] Between landlords and tenants to whom these statutes do not apply, the rule forbidding the landlord to enter remains a minority rule.

As just stated, on the question of trespass to land, the traditional majority rule is that the landlord is privileged to enter upon a holdover tenant. (We are still not discussing touchings of the tenant or his goods.) But even in states that allow the landlord this privilege, most say the landlord's entry must be by "peaceable" means; otherwise, it will be an unlawful forcible entry. What is "peaceable" varies so widely from state to state and from case to case that generalizations are not useful. Entry upon open land or, without physical entry, by inducing subtenants to pay their rent to the landowner, is likely to be "peaceable." Entry by trick, by pass key, or simply by walking through an unlocked door may or may not be allowed. Breaking in by forcing a lock, door, or window is sometimes called "peaceable" but is likely not to be.[12] "Peaceable" entries are usually made

---

6. See, e.g., Jordan v. Talbot, 55 Cal.2d 597, 12 Cal.Rptr. 488, 361 P.2d 20 (1961).

7. E.g., Gorman v. Ratliff, 289 Ark. 332, 712 S.W.2d 888 (1986) (no self-help); Jordan v. Talbot, 55 Cal.2d 597, 12 Cal.Rptr. 488, 361 P.2d 20 (1961); See Bedi v. McMullan, 160 Cal.App.3d 272, 206 Cal.Rptr. 578 (1984) (illegal forcible entry by landlord when sheriff entered on tenant under writ of restitution that was void); Spencer v. Commercial Co., 30 Wash. 520, 71 P. 53 (1902). See Annot., 6 A.L.R.3d 177, 186–89 (1966), for citations to decisions from 13 states for this position.

8. See Moriarity v. Dziak, 435 So.2d 35 (Ala.1983) (landlord's reentry proper when lease allowed reentry upon default, tenant was in default, and landlord had demanded rent); Annot., 6 A.L.R.3d 177, 186 (1966); 1 F. Harper, F. James and O. Gray, Torts § 1.12 (2d ed. 1986); Restatement (Second) of Property § 14.1, Statutory Note 7, and § 14.2, Reporter's Note 1 (1977).

9. Annot., 6 A.L.R.3d 177, 186 (1977).

See also Gorman v. Ratliff, 289 Ark. 332, 712 S.W.2d 888 (1986).

10. Restatement (Second) of Property § 14.2 (1977); Uniform Residential Landlord and Tenant Act § 4.207; Model Residential Landlord–Tenant Code § 2–408.

11. This statement may be supported by comparing and making inferences from the following sources: 7A Uniform Laws Annotated 499, 553 (1978 & 1981 Pocket Part); Annot., 6 A.L.R.3d 177, 186–89 (1966); Restatement (Second) of Property § 14.1, Statutory Note 7 (1977); Cunningham, The New Implied and Statutory Warranties of Habitability in Residential Leases: From Contract to Status, 16 Urban L.Ann. 3, 7, nn. 10 & 11 (1979).

12. See Annot., 6 A.L.R.3d 177, 189–94, 199–222 (1966); 1 F. Harper, F. James and O. Gray, Torts § 1.12 (2d ed. 1986)

in the tenant's absence; any confrontation between landlord and tenant seems to make it more likely that a court will find the means of entry were forcible.

Even if the landlord is permitted to, and does, make a "peaceable" entry, his ensuing exclusion of the tenant may, in some jurisdictions, yet be wrongful. Forcible entry statutes often also prohibit forcible "detainer." The word "detainer" usually refers to a tenant's wrongful possession, but a few states have also held landlords liable for unlawful detainer for wrongfully excluding tenants. Again, there is a variety of judicial opinion about what actions are forcible and what "peaceable." Decisions have held it wrongful for the landlord to exclude the tenant by removing doors or windows, terminating utilities, by threatening the tenant, or even by changing locks.[13] Indeed, residential landlord-tenant statutes may subject the landlord to severe penalties for cutting off utilities.[14] Examination of decisions often leaves one in doubt whether a court regarded such actions as a forcible entry or a forcible detainer or possibly an assault upon the tenant's person. Also, when a state refuses to allow mild forms of exclusion, such as changing locks, one may question whether a landlord in that state has any practical way to exclude a tenant who wishes to re-enter.

We now turn to the question whether the landlord may use force against the holdover tenant's, or his family's, person or goods. For this purpose we assume that, under the law of the jurisdiction, the landlord's entry upon and detention of the premises are by privileged means. It is here that the different formulas of the English decisions in Newton v. Harland and Hemmings v. Stoke Poges Golf Club are particularly relevant. No American jurisdiction will allow the landlord to use more force against the tenant, his family or goods, than is reasonably necessary to evict.[15] That is, the current English rule of *Hemmings* is the "bottom line" in America. There also is a following, by probably more states, for *Newton's* former English rule, that the landlord is not privileged to touch the tenant, his family, or goods at all.[16] Once more, it should be observed that judicial opinions often do not neatly separate questions of trespass to land from torts against persons and goods; those distinctions are urged here, to promote clearer analysis of a confused area.

Leases sometimes contain a clause purporting to allow the landlord to use self-help to evict the tenant if he holds over. A majority of decisions have enforced such clauses, so as to confer on the landlord privileges of self-

---

13. See, e.g., Jordan v. Talbot, 55 Cal.2d 597, 12 Cal.Rptr. 488, 361 P.2d 20 (1961) (threats); Pelavin v. Misner, 241 Mich. 209, 217 N.W. 36 (1928), affirmed 343 Mich. 516, 220 N.W. 665 (1928) (locking tenant out); Paxton v. Fisher, 86 Utah 408, 45 P.2d 903 (1935) (contract purchaser vs. tenant); Annot., 6 A.L.R.3d 177, 199–210 (1966).

14. E.g., Uniform Residential Landlord and Tenant Act § 4.104; Kinney v. Vaccari, 27 Cal.3d 348, 165 Cal.Rptr. 787, 612 P.2d 877 (1980) ($36,000 penalty, plus $7,901 actual damages, plus $5,600 attorney fees).

15. See Gower v. Waters, 125 Me. 223, 132 A. 550 (1926); Shorter v. Shelton, 183 Va. 819, 33 S.E.2d 643 (1945); Annot., 6 A.L.R.3d 177, 182–86 (1966); 1 F. Harper, F. James and O. Gray, Torts § 3.15 (2d ed. 1986). Restatement (Second) of Property § 14.1, Statutory Note 7, and § 14.2, Reporter's Note (1977).

16. Maddix v. Gammon, 293 Ky. 540, 169 S.W.2d 594 (1943) (tenant's family); Rivers v. Tessitore, 165 So.2d 888 (La.App.1964) (tenant's goods); Annot., 6 A.L.R.3d 177, 181, 222–37 (1966); [W. Prosser and W. Keeton, Torts § 23 (5th ed. 1984).] Restatement (Second) of Property § 14.2, Reporter's Note 4 (1977).

help that applicable rules of law would otherwise deny him.[17] By the minority position, such clauses contravene public policy and are void.[18] There is some reason to doubt the majority position's vitality, as most of its decisions are old. The Restatement advocates the minority view.[19] Also, recent residential landlord-tenant codes, such as the Uniform Act, may forbid self-help clauses.[20]

Perhaps the preceding discussion of self-help eviction has done no more than to convince of the assertion, made at the beginning of the section, that the subject is a "tortured" one. It is withal an important one, too much ignored, that deserves far more exhaustive treatment than can be given in this place. How many lawyers have received telephone calls from landlord clients, who say they are standing on the sidewalk and want to know just how far they may go to effect entry? Unless the lawyer has previously determined that his jurisdiction permits certain steps in self-help, his only safe advice for the moment is that the client should attempt no form of entry.

§ 6.81 Legal Inhibitions on Evictions

Under this heading we will discuss several subjects that have no connection, except that they all involve situations in which there are legal restrictions on a landlord's capacity to maintain an action to evict a tenant. Major attention will be given to the doctrine against "retaliatory evictions" that has arisen by judicial decision or legislation in a number of jurisdictions in recent years. Brief mentions also will be made to alert readers that evictions may be regulated in certain circumstances, such as when there is public housing or rent control or when the tenant is in military service.

The subject of "retaliatory eviction" began in 1968 in the District of Columbia Circuit Court opinion in Edwards v. Habib.[1] After the tenant reported the landlord's housing code violation to public authorities, the landlord gave a notice to terminate the tenancy and began a summary eviction action. In that action the tenant was held to have a defense if she could prove the landlord acted in retaliation for her report. The decision was based upon the policy ground that to allow retaliatory eviction would tend to thwart the purpose of a housing code. *Edwards* has been followed in decisions in some six or seven states.[2] Presumably the retaliatory eviction

---

17. E.g., Goshen v. People, 22 Colo. 270, 44 P. 503 (1896); Annot., 6 A.L.R.3d 177, 194–99 (1966); Restatement (Second) of Property § 14.2, Reporter's Note 5 (1977).

18. Jordan v. Talbot, 55 Cal.2d 597, 12 Cal.Rptr. 488, 361 P.2d 20 (1961); Bass v. Boetel & Co., 191 Neb. 733, 217 N.W.2d 804 (1974). Also see the A.L.R. and Restatement citations in the preceding note.

19. Restatement (Second) of Property § 14.2(2) (1977).

20. Uniform Residential Landlord and Tenant Act §§ 1.403(a)(1), 4.207, and 4.302(b) appears to forbid such agreements.

§ 6.81

1. 397 F.2d 687 (D.C.Cir.1968), certiorari denied 393 U.S. 1016, 89 S.Ct. 618, 21 L.Ed.2d 560 (1969).

2. Schweiger v. Superior Court, 3 Cal.3d 507, 90 Cal.Rptr. 729, 476 P.2d 97 (1970); Dickhut v. Norton, 45 Wis.2d 389, 173 N.W.2d 297 (1970); Annot., 40 A.L.R.3d 753 (1971 and 1991 supp.); Cunningham, supra note 11, § 6.80 at 135–37. Contra, Mobilia, Inc. v. Santos, 4 Conn.App. 128, 492 A.2d 544 (1985) (court refused to allow retaliatory eviction defense in summary eviction action against residential tenant). See also Custom Parking, Inc. v. Superior Court of State for County of Marin, 138 Cal.App.3d 90, 187 Cal.Rptr. 674 (1982), which held that a defense of retaliatory

defense would, where available, be extended to tenants who exercise other legal remedies than reporting housing code violations, such as attempting to enforce landlords' statutory or implied warranties of habitability.[3] Indications so far are that the defense is available only to residential tenants.

Some 30 states have adopted residential landlord-tenant statutes that embody versions of the retaliatory eviction principle. The Uniform Residential Landlord and Tenant Act, which is the source for over half of these statutes, and also the Model Residential Landlord–Tenant Code contain anti-retaliatory eviction provisions.[4] State statutes vary widely, with some statutes more or less complete than others. Features that may be found are as follows: The landlord is forbidden not only to evict in retaliation, but also to engage in certain other forms of retaliatory conduct, such as increasing rent or decreasing services. The tenant is protected in joining a tenants' union, as well as in reporting housing code violations and in pursuing remedies under the residential landlord-tenant act. A presumption is created that, if the landlord attempts a listed form of conduct within a certain time (perhaps 90 days to one year) after the tenant has taken his protected action, the landlord's conduct is retaliatory. Exceptions in the landlord's favor exist if the tenant is himself at fault in certain ways, including being in default in paying rent, which raises doubt as to the efficacy of the tenant's remedy of rent withholding. It appears that most of the states with statutes are ones that also have retaliatory eviction decisions but that two or three states plus the District of Columbia have decisions and no statutes. Thus, the total number of jurisdictions that, in some way and to some degree, prohibit retaliatory evictions of residential tenants is in the vicinity of 30.[5]

Several specialized situations exist in which landlords are regulated by law in evicting tenants. This is true under regulations of the Department of Housing and Urban Development that pertain to federally assisted publicly owned housing.[6] State statutes or local ordinances and regulations may similarly regulate public housing.[7] On a related subject, whenever there is legislative rent control, national or local, one may expect to find restrictions on evictions as a part of the scheme.[8]

eviction could be asserted in a summary eviction action by a *commercial* tenant. The decision may be the only one allowing the defense to a commercial tenant.

3. Pohlman v. Metropolitan Trailer Park, Inc., 126 N.J.Super. 114, 312 A.2d 888 (Ch.Div. 1973), even allowed the defense against a landlord who sought to evict a tenant who had opposed the landlord's application for rezoning the premises. See also Hernandez v. Stabach, 145 Cal.App.3d 309, 193 Cal.Rptr. 350 (1983) (court may enjoin landlord from threatened retaliatory eviction or action).

4. Uniform Residential Landlord and Tenant Act § 5.101; Model Residential Landlord Tenant Code § 2–407.

5. See Cunningham, supra note 11, § 6.80, at 7, 126–37. May a landlord's refusal to renew a fixed-term tenancy be a retaliatory eviction? Van Buren Apts. v. Adams, 145 Ariz. 325, 701 P.2d 583 (App.1984), decided

this question in the affirmative, and Frenchtown Villa v. Meadors, 117 Mich.App. 683, 324 N.W.2d 133 (1982), decided in the negative.

6. See 24 C.F.R. §§ 450.1–450.10; Thorpe v. Housing Authority, 393 U.S. 268, 89 S.Ct. 518, 21 L.Ed.2d 474 (1969); Caulder v. Durham Housing Authority, 433 F.2d 998 (4th Cir.1970), certiorari denied 401 U.S. 1003, 91 S.Ct. 1228, 28 L.Ed.2d 539 (1971); Housing Authority v. Mosby, 53 Wis.2d 275, 192 N.W.2d 913 (1972). See also Joy v. Daniels, 479 F.2d 1236 (4th Cir.1973); Kutcher v. Housing Authority, 20 N.J. 181, 119 A.2d 1 (1955).

7. See Escalera v. New York City Housing Authority, 425 F.2d 853 (2d Cir.1970), certiorari denied 400 U.S. 853, 91 S.Ct. 54, 27 L.Ed.2d 91 (1970); Sanders v. Cruise, 10 Misc.2d 533, 173 N.Y.S.2d 871 (1958).

8. See Block v. Hirsh, 256 U.S. 135, 41 S.Ct. 458, 65 L.Ed. 865 (1921); 1 A.L.P., supra note 1, at § 3.93.

The Soldiers' and Sailors' Civil Relief Act of 1940 [9] restricts evictions in some cases. Whenever a dwelling is occupied by the spouse, children, or other dependents of a person in military service and the rent is $150 or less per month, eviction may be delayed as long as three months. In commencing an eviction action, a landlord who knows of it must disclose the serviceperson's military status. The Act also allows the military member to terminate tenancies commenced before his entry into the armed services where he or his family have occupied the premises.

§ 6.82 Surrender

"Surrender" is the early termination of a leasehold by either the parties' agreement or by the doctrine, to be discussed in a moment, known as "operation of law." Surrender by agreement is like modification or cancellation of a contract. There may be essentially contract law problems, such as whether the parties' words amount to a termination agreement. The largest problem, however, is whether the agreement, to be enforceable, must be made in some special form required by a Statute of Frauds. Some American statutes, patterned after the English Statute of Frauds of 1677, expressly require "surrenders" to be in writing. Under such statutes, some courts hold that all surrender agreements, to be enforced, must be in writing, regardless of whether the original lease had to be written and of how long it has to run. Other courts gloss such statutes, however, holding an oral agreement enforceable if the time yet to run is short enough that a leasehold for that duration might be created by parol. Some statutes that require surrenders in general to be in writing, expressly except leaseholds having only certain short terms to run. Unlike the pattern of the English statute, some American Statutes of Frauds do not specifically mention surrenders. Under statutes of this type, it seems safe to say that if the original lease did not have to be in writing, a surrender agreement need not be. But if the original lease was within the statute, there is a split of authority, some courts concluding the surrender agreement must be in writing and others holding it must be only if the time to run is so long that a term of that length must be by a written instrument.[1]

The English Statute of Frauds excepted from its requirements surrenders that occurred "by operation of law." This is in keeping with a general principle that courts will not raise the statute against mechanisms of their own creation. A surrender by operation of law occurs when the tenant abandons the premises and the landlord accepts them back for his own account.[2] Another rationale to avoid the Statute of Frauds is that it should not apply when the parties' intent is evidenced by non-verbal acts. Similarly, some "operation-of-law" cases are ones in which the parties made an oral surrender agreement, arguably unenforceable as such, but the tenant then abandoned. Courts may speak of the agreement as "executed."[3]

---

9. 50 U.S.C.A. §§ 501–90.

§ 6.82

1. See 1 A.L.P., supra note 1, at § 3.99; Annot., 78 A.L.R.2d 933, 941–49 (1961).

2. See discussion in, e.g., Riggs v. Murdock, 10 Ariz.App. 248, 458 P.2d 115 (1969);

McGrath v. Shalett, 114 Conn. 622, 159 A. 633 (1932); Liberty Plan Co. v. Adwan, 370 P.2d 928 (Okl.1962).

3. See Annot., 78 A.L.R.2d 933, 939, n. 9 (1961).

Abandonment does not alone work a surrender by operation of law; the landlord must accept the premises back "for his own account" to complete the termination. More precisely, the tenant's abandonment confers upon the landlord three choices: (1) to complete surrender and termination by re-entering for his own account; (2) to do nothing and so to keep the leasehold, and the tenant's duty to pay rent, going; or (3) to re-enter and re-let "for the tenant's account," charging to the tenant any difference between his agreed rent and the rent received from the replacement tenant. Such at least is the traditional view.[4] No question exists that the landlord may effect the first option.

Today the question is whether the second option still exists or whether the landlord has only the first and third. If he does not wish to terminate, must he, as it is said, at least make a reasonable attempt to re-let the premises for the tenant's account, to mitigate his own damages? The courts speak of this as a "duty" to mitigate. It is not a duty but, in Hohfeldian terms, a "disability"; failure to do it gives the tenant a defense to an action for rent but not an affirmative claim for relief. Traditionally, and still by the majority of decided cases, the contracts law doctrine of mitigation of damages does not apply; the landlord suffers no legal detriment by choosing the second option.[5] The Restatement (Second) of Property, which usually does not hesitate to keep up with, or ahead of, trends in landlord-tenant law, adopts this view.[6] In this area a strong minority position and the trend is that the landlord is under a disability to re-let for the tenant's account, to mitigate damages.[7] Both the Uniform Residential Landlord and Tenant Act and the Model Residential Landlord–Tenant Code incorporate forms of the mitigation requirement.[8] Taking into account the states that have adopted these acts, as well as other statutes requiring mitigation, it is likely that, by legislation or court decision, a majority of states place residential landlords under a disability for failing to mitigate.[9]

A landlord who, voluntarily or by compulsion of law, undertakes to mitigate is in a ticklish position. If he re-enters and re-lets "for the tenant's account," the leasehold is not terminated, and the tenant is liable for any loss of rent. Particularly where mitigation is a legal requirement, the tenant should also be liable for the landlord's reasonable expenses of re-

---

4. In addition to the decisions cited in the next footnote, see Sagamore Corp. v. Willcutt, 120 Conn. 315, 180 A. 464 (1935); Novak v. Fontaine Furniture Co., 84 N.H. 93, 146 A. 525 (1929).

5. E.g., Riggs v. Murdock, 10 Ariz.App. 248, 458 P.2d 115 (1969); McGrath v. Shalett, 114 Conn. 622, 159 A. 633 (1932) (dictum); Heckel v. Griese, 12 N.J.Misc. 211, 171 A. 148 (1934); Tanella v. Rettagliata, 120 N.J.Super. 400, 294 A.2d 431 (1972) (dictum); Liberty Plan Co. v. Adwan, 370 P.2d 928 (Okl.1962) (dictum); Restatement (Second) of Property § 12.1(3), Comment i, and Reporter's Note 8 (1977). Contra, Sommer v. Kridel, 74 N.J. 446, 378 A.2d 767 (1977), which overruled *Heckel*, supra, and other prior New Jersey decisions.

6. See preceding note.

7. Vawter v. McKissick, 159 N.W.2d 538 (Iowa 1968); Sommer v. Kridel, 74 N.J. 446, 378 A.2d 767 (1977) (overruling older decisions); Wright v. Baumann, 239 Or. 410, 398 P.2d 119 (1965), appeal after remand 254 Or. 175, 458 P.2d 674 (1969) (alternative ground; contrary to older decisions); Myers v. Western Farmers Association, 75 Wn.2d 133, 449 P.2d 104 (1969) (strong dictum); Restatement (Second) of Property § 12.1, Reporter's Note 8 (1977).

8. Uniform Residential Landlord and Tenant Act § 4.203(c); Model Residential Landlord–Tenant Code § 2–308(4).

9. See Restatement (Second) of Property § 12.1, Statutory Note 7 (1977).

letting.[10] But if the landlord goes too far and acts "for his own account," then the leasehold will terminate by operation of law and the tenant's liability under the lease end. When the landlord's actions cross the line is a question of fact, sometimes of degree. Such acts as accepting back keys, entering the premises, advertising them for rent, cleaning and even to a certain extent altering them, and re-letting them do not ordinarily cause termination by surrender, since these acts are necessary for the tenant's account.[11] After all, there will be no mitigation unless the landlord either acquires a new tenant or makes reasonable attempts to do so. However, he may go too far and act for his own account. If he makes alterations greater than those required to re-let, this will give the tenant an argument that the landlord has accepted surrender, though the argument has not often been successful.[12] Re-letting for a term longer than the tenant's term is generally considered so inconsistent with continuation of the leasehold as to work a surrender, though there are contrary decisions.[13] Some states have adopted the rule that, to avoid surrender, the landlord who wishes to enter to mitigate must expressly notify the tenant of that purpose.[14] Even where it is not required, the landlord's position is much strengthened by such a clear, written notice.[15] Moreover, if the lease so provides, the landlord may recover the difference between agreed rent and fair market value for the remainder of the agreed leasehold term after a surrender.

§ 6.83   Merger

As a general proposition, when a leasehold and the estate immediately following it come together in the same person, the leasehold is extinguished by being merged into the following estate. The following estate may be a reversion or remainder in fee or for life or another leasehold of longer duration; any such estate will be "larger" in legal concept than the leasehold in question. No merger will occur unless the leasehold and the

---

10. See Ross v. Smigelski, 42 Wis.2d 185, 166 N.W.2d 243 (1969).

11. See, e.g., American Nat. Bank & Trust Co. v. Hoyne Industries, Inc., 738 F.Supp. 297 (N.D.Ill.1990) (landlord may attempt to re-let at higher rent when lease allows this); Riggs v. Murdock, 10 Ariz.App. 248, 458 P.2d 115 (1969); McGrath v. Shalett, 114 Conn. 622, 159 A. 633 (1932); Owens v. Ramsey, 213 Ky. 279, 280 S.W. 1112 (1926); Dahl v. Comber, 444 A.2d 392 (Me.1982) (landlord did not accept surrender of premises by reletting parts of them for terms not longer than original tenant's term); Windsor Real Estate & Mortg. Co. v. Ruma, 674 S.W.2d 252 (Mo.App.1984), appeal after remand 710 S.W.2d 316 (1986) (landlord did not accept surrender of premises by attempting to relet); Novak v. Fontaine Furniture Co., 84 N.H. 93, 146 A. 525 (1929); Armijo v. Pettit, 32 N.M. 469, 259 P. 620 (1927); Liberty Plan Co. v. Adwan, 370 P.2d 928 (Okl.1962); Washington Securities Co. v. Oppenheimer & Co., 163 Wash. 338, 1 P.2d 236 (1931); Annot., 3 A.L.R. 1080 (1919), Supp. by Annots., 52 A.L.R. 154 (1928), 61 A.L.R. 773 (1929), 110 A.L.R. 368 (1937).

12. See H.S. Chase & Co. v. Evans, 178 Iowa 885, 160 N.W. 346 (1916) (evidence of extent of repairs relevant); Washington Securities Co. v. Oppenheimer & Co., 163 Wash. 338, 1 P.2d 236 (1931) (argument made but unsuccessful).

13. Welcome v. Hess, 90 Cal. 507, 27 P. 369 (1891); Michigan Lafayette Building Co. v. Continental Bank, 261 Mich. 256, 246 N.W. 53 (1933) (dictum); In re Adams' Estate, 149 Misc. 289, 267 N.Y.S. 910 (1933); Casper National Bank v. Curry, 51 Wyo. 284, 65 P.2d 1116 (1937) (one of several factors). Contra, McGrath v. Shalett, 114 Conn. 622, 159 A. 633 (1932); Armijo v. Pettit, 32 N.M. 469, 259 P. 620 (1927). For discussion of other decisions, see A.L.R. annotations, note 11, this section. See also Mesilla Valley Mall Co. v. Crown Industries, 111 N.M. 663, 808 P.2d 633 (1991) (landlord's re-letting rent-free to charitable organization accepted surrender).

14. Bernard v. Renard, 175 Cal. 230, 165 P. 694 (1917); Casper National Bank v. Curry, 51 Wyo. 284, 65 P.2d 1116 (1937).

15. See especially Liberty Plan Co. v. Adwan, 370 P.2d 928 (Okl.1962).

following estate are adjoining, as the word "immediately" connotes. Extinction of the leasehold estate also terminates the rights and duties of the parties as landlord and tenant.[1]

Merger does not operate with mechanical absoluteness; courts may refuse to find a merger where it normally occurs. Whether this is due to the intervention of equity need not be resolved here. It sometimes is said that no merger will occur when this would be contrary to the parties' apparent intent or would defeat their expectations.[2] A frequent application of this principle is that a merger will not happen when the two interests in land were created at the same time; their creator surely would not have intended to establish two separate interests only to have them merge. An application particularly to leaseholds is that, where there is a sublease and the head tenant surrenders to the head landlord, there will be no merger in the latter that will extinguish the sublease. Rather, the head landlord is viewed as acquiring the subtenant as his direct tenant.[3]

§ 6.84 Expiration of Landlord's Estate

Since a leasehold is carved out of an estate of longer duration, anything that brings that estate to an end before the agreed termination date of the leasehold should cause the leasehold to fall in. Such is the result in the decided cases except where, rarely, a statute provides for the leasehold's continuation. The cases so deciding generally are ones in which a life tenant creates a leasehold then dies before the end of the tenancy.[1] Though the leasehold ends, the tenant may be allowed to enter later for certain limited purposes. If he has growing crops, he is permitted to enter to cultivate and harvest them. Decisions are in conflict, however, over whether the tenant is privileged to enter to remove tenant's fixtures that a tenant would be allowed to remove before the end of his term.[2]

§ 6.85 Death of a Party

With a common-law tenancy at will, which either party may terminate any time at pleasure, death of either landlord or tenant terminates the

§ 6.83

1. For specific support for the statements in this paragraph and for generally helpful discussions of merger, see Ferguson v. Etter, 21 Ark. 160, 76 Am.Dec. 361 (1860); Erving v. Jas. H. Goodman & Co. Bank, 171 Cal. 559, 153 P. 945 (1915); Liebschutz v. Moore, 70 Ind. 142 (1880); Hudson Brothers Commission Co. v. Glencoe Sand & Gravel Co., 140 Mo. 103, 41 S.W. 450 (1897); Tolsma v. Adair, 32 Wash. 383, 73 P. 347 (1903); Annot., 143 A.L.R. 93 (1943); 1 A.L.P., supra note 1, at § 3.100; Restatement of Property § 238, Comment d (1936).

2. See, e.g., Mobley v. Harkins, 14 Wn.2d 276, 128 P.2d 289 (1942); Annot., 143 A.L.R. 93, 107–11 (1943).

3. Metropolitan Life Insurance Co. v. Hellinger, 246 App.Div. 7, 284 N.Y.S. 432 (1935), affirmed 272 N.Y. 24, 3 N.E.2d 621 (1936);

Hessel v. Johnson, 129 Pa. 173, 18 A. 754 (1889); 1 A.L.P. supra note 1, at § 3.100.

§ 6.84

1. E.g., Sanders v. Sutlive Brothers & Co., 187 Iowa 300, 174 N.W. 267 (1919); Haywood v. Briggs, 227 N.C. 108, 41 S.E.2d 289 (1947); Kerns v. Pickett, 47 Wn.2d 184, 287 P.2d 88 (1955) (apparent dictum); Annot., 6 A.L.R. 1506 (1920), Supp., 171 A.L.R. 489 (1947); 1 A.L.P., supra note 1, at § 3.101. But see Ganzer v. Pfab, 360 N.W.2d 754 (Iowa 1985) (when landlord, who was contract purchaser of farm land, had his contract forfeited, his tenant's leasehold continued for following crop year, to prevent loss of crops).

2. See, e.g., Ray v. Young, 160 Iowa 613, 142 N.W. 393 (1913) (reasonable time to remove); Haywood v. Briggs, 227 N.C. 108, 41 S.E.2d 289 (1947) (may not remove).

tenancy.[1] With more substantial leaseholds, tenancies for years and periodic tenancies, death of the landlord or of the tenant does not generally work a termination.[2] So, the landlord's underlying estate passes to his heirs or devisees subject to the leasehold, and the leasehold, viewed as a chattel real, passes as personalty to the tenant's estate. Slightly qualifying what was said, there may be some tendency in the courts, when the tenant has died and his estate wants to escape from the leasehold, to find a way to terminate the lease. For instance, some courts have stated an exception from contract law, whereby death will terminate a leasehold if it is found to be of a "personal nature."[3]

§ 6.86 Destruction of Building

The basic common-law rule is that destruction of a building, even the sole building, on the demised premises by a casualty not the fault of either party does not affect the length of the term.[1] A leasehold estate in Blackacre is what the tenant rented, and estate and land are still there. Naturally, the harshness of the rule causes the tenant to insert in any well drafted lease clauses providing perhaps a range of remedies for different degrees of destruction and ultimately a power of termination in case of destruction beyond a certain extent.

We must add that the general rule is subject to a sizable exception and has also fallen victim to some statutory and other limitations. An exception has long existed in American courts when the leasehold is in rooms only, within the building that is destroyed.[2] The tenant leased only building space and has lost everything. Large and growing limitations are placed on the rule by two kinds of statutes. First, before the residential landlord-tenant statutes of the 1970's began, a number of states, apparently just

§ 6.85

1. Perry v. Veal, 142 Ky. 441, 134 S.W. 458 (1911); Hancock v. Maurer, 103 Okl. 196, 229 P. 611 (1924); Annot., 68 A.L.R. 590, 595–96 (1930).

2. Kensington Associates v. Moss, 426 So.2d 1076 (Fla.App.1983), petition for review denied 434 So.2d 888 (Fla.1983) (when lease bound tenant's heirs, successors, and assigns, tenant's death did not terminate leasehold); In re Estate of Conklin, 116 Ill.App.3d 426, 72 Ill.Dec. 59, 451 N.E.2d 1382 (1983) (death of tenant did not terminate leasehold); Israel v. Beale, 270 Mass. 61, 169 N.E. 777 (1930); In re Lewis' Estate, 492 S.W.2d 385 (Mo.App.1973); Gross v. Peskin, 101 N.J.Super. 468, 244 A.2d 692 (1968); Joint Properties Owners, Inc. v. Deri, 127 Misc.2d 26, 488 N.Y.S.2d 948 (1985), judgment reversed 113 A.D.2d 691, 497 N.Y.S.2d 658 (1986) (dictum that tenant's death normally does not terminate leasehold, but N.Y. Statute allowed landlord to terminate). Frazier v. Wynn, 459 S.W.2d 895 (Tex. Civ.App.1970), reversed on another ground 472 S.W.2d 750 (Tex.1971), appeal after remand 492 S.W.2d 54 (1973), refused n.r.e.; Annot., 68 A.L.R. 590, 590–95 (1930); 1 A.L.P., supra note 1, at § 3.102.

3. Goodman v. Jardine, 353 So.2d 896 (Fla. App.1977); In re Lewis' Estate, 492 S.W.2d 385 (Mo.App.1973) (dictum). See also Schnee v. Jonas Equities, Inc., 103 Misc.2d 625, 426 N.Y.S.2d 431 (1980) (vacancy from tenant's death caused termination "by operation of law").

§ 6.86

1. Chambers v. North River Line, 179 N.C. 199, 102 S.E. 198 (1920); Evco Corp. v. Ross, 528 S.W.2d 20 (Tenn.1975) (dictum); Gonzalez v. Cavazos, 601 S.W.2d 202 (Tex.Civ.App.1980); 1 A.L.P. supra note 1, at § 3.103; Restatement (Second) of Property § 5.4, Reporter's Note 4 (1977).

2. Solomon v. Neisner Brothers, 93 F.Supp. 310 (M.D.Pa.1950), affirmed 187 F.2d 735 (3d Cir.1951) (dictum); Martin Emerich Outfitting Co. v. Siegel, Cooper & Co., 237 Ill. 610, 86 N.E. 1104 (1908); Crow Lumber & Building Materials Co. v. Washington County Library Board, 428 S.W.2d 758 (Mo.App.1968); 1 A.L.P. supra preceding note; Restatement (Second) of Property, supra preceding note.

under 20, had adopted statutes reversing or modifying the rule. Most of these allow the tenant to terminate at once in case of destruction; some allow termination only after a rent-free period during which the landlord might rebuild. Most of these statutes apply to both commercial and residential leaseholds, a few to residential only.[3] In addition to these "traditional" statutes, it seems that about 10 more states have adopted residential landlord-tenant acts that empower the tenant to terminate in case of casualty destruction.[4]

A further limitation on the common-law rule must exist where, by residential landlord-tenant acts or by decisions following Javins v. First National Realty Corp.,[5] courts have created an implied warranty of fitness in residential leases. If premises are destroyed and the landlord fails to rebuild, this certainly breaches the warranty. The Restatement takes the position that the tenant then has, among other remedies, a power to terminate.[6] In any event, the tenant may achieve the same result by invoking the traditional doctrine of constructive eviction.

§ 6.87 Frustration of Purpose

This section is a companion to section 6.28, which should be read before going on. We there saw that if a lease limits the tenant to a certain use of the premises and that use subsequently becomes prohibited by law, in most jurisdictions the tenant is wholly excused from performing. Even if the uses limited do not all become illegal, if the main or principal use is made illegal, most courts excuse the tenant. A minority of decisions on point disagree with these propositions. It now remains to state the theory upon which the majority excuses performance.

It is clear that we have at work here a theory adopted from the law of contracts; this is one of many modern examples of contract law's growing influence in landlord-tenant relations. What is not so clear is whether the theory ought to be called "impossibility of performance" or "frustration of purpose." The subject is often discussed under the heading, "impossibility of performance." [1] "Frustration of purpose" or "commercial frustration" seems the accurate description, however, as most respected commentators contend.[2] The doctrine of impossibility excuses the promisor's performance of the duty that has become impossible (illegal). That ordinarily does not fit our case because the clause limiting use is not a promised performance by either party. In a few cases, where the tenant has both covenanted to occupy and to use for a stated purpose and no other, he probably has

---

3. See 1 A.L.P. supra note 1, at p. 398, n. 8; Restatement (Second) of Property Ch. 5, Statutory Note 2 (1977).

4. See Restatement (Second) of Property, supra preceding note; 7B Uniform Laws Annotated 427, 487–88 (1985 and 1991 pocket part).

5. 428 F.2d 1071 (D.C.Cir.1970), certiorari denied 400 U.S. 925, 91 S.Ct. 186, 27 L.Ed.2d 185 (1970).

6. Restatement (Second) of Property § 5.4(1) and Reporter's Note 9 (1977).

§ 6.87

1. See Annot., 84 A.L.R.2d 12, 43–48 (1962).

2. See Lloyd v. Murphy, 25 Cal.2d 48, 153 P.2d 47 (1944); 1 A.L.P. supra note 1, at § 3.104; 6 A. Corbin, Contracts § 1320 (1962); 18 S. Williston, Contracts § 1955 (3d ed. 1978). Cf. Restatement of Contracts §§ 288, 290, 458 (1932), which, while not giving landlord-tenant examples, apparently would include supervening illegal use under "frustration"—except that § 290 says the contracts rule does not apply to leases.

promised to do so, but the impossibility doctrine excuses only *that* performance, not the performance of other covenants such as the covenant to pay rent.[3] Rescission is not the theory, for the landlord has breached no duty. Rather, because there has been frustration of an object of the agreement that certainly was fundamental to the tenant, and even to both parties, the law excuses the tenant's whole performance. Perhaps the underlying mechanism is that of implied condition. And, the final step, the tenant's performance being excused, so is the landlord's because he suffers a total failure of consideration.[4]

3. See especially Restatement of Contracts, Second §§ 261, 264, 265, 267 (1981).

4. See Restatement of Contracts, Second § 237 (1981).

Chapter 7

RIGHTS INCIDENT TO POSSESSION OF LAND

Table of Sections

This chapter deals with certain rights enjoyed by one who is entitled to possession of land that are a consequence of possession. Sometimes these rights are said to be ones "naturally" incident to the possession of land, to distinguish them from other rights, such as the benefit of easements or restrictive covenants, that arise only by special arrangements. The rights of which we speak thus normally come with possession, and if they do not, it is because the possessor has given them up. We shall discuss the rights to be free from physical intrusions and nuisances and rights in lateral and subjacent support, flowing streams, underground water, and surface water.

The matters discussed in this chapter lie along the boundary between property law and tort law. Since this is a treatise on property law, we view these matters from the side of the possessor, in other words, the "rights" side. Tort law views them from the side of other persons who have correlative "duties" not to invade these rights. In treatises on tort law, the subjects we discuss here will be found under the headings of trespass, nuisance, and, to some extent, negligence.

§ 7.1 Freedom From Physical Intrusion

In many and various ways expositors of our law have spoken of the landowner's absolute right to exclude physical intrusions. There is Pitt's ringing declaration that "the poorest man may in his cottage bid defiance to all the force of the Crown. * * * the King of England cannot enter. * * *"[1] Blackstone wrote of the right of property's being "that sole and despotic dominion which one man claims and exercises over the external things of the world, in total exclusion of the right of any other individual in the universe."[2] To some jurisprudents "the essence of private property is

---

§ 7.1
1. W. Pitt, Speech on the Excise Bill.

2. 2 W. Blackstone, Commentaries *2.

always the right to exclude others."[3] We will see presently that the right to exclude others is not absolute; not only may others enter with the rightful possessor's permission but in a few cases, against his will. In the main, however, it is true that the right physically to exclude others is the most nearly absolute of the many property rights that flow from the ownership or other rightful possession of land. A recent decision of the United States Supreme Court reminds us anew that the owner may generally insist strictly upon excluding others, without their competing claims being balanced in, as is often done with other property rights.[4]

Unless it is with the possessor's permission or is excused as privileged, any knowing entry upon the possessor's land is wrongful: it is a trespass. Permissive entries are the subjects of other large parts of this treatise, such as tenancies, easements, profits, and licenses. Principal categories of other privileged entries will be described in this section below. Not only is the trespasser liable for actual damages done, he is liable for nominal damages if there is no actual damage. Subject to equity's discretion to withhold its remedies, continuing or threatened trespasses may also be enjoined. Even an unknowing non-permissive and unprivileged entry is wrongful if it is negligent or the result of extrahazardous activity, though apparently not if it is by excusable mistake.[5]

Trespassory invasions may be committed not only by the trespasser in person but also by instrumentalities under his control. Examples are objects placed or left on the plaintiff's land; projectiles or aircraft propelled through owned airspace; and, where open-range rules do not apply, animals allowed to wander.[6] At some point the law of trespass shades into the law of nuisance. Instrumentalities that can cause trespass are generally objects such as those just suggested that have size and weight, whereas nuisances are generally caused by "nonphysical" forces such as noise, odors, and vibration. As we will see later in this chapter, substances such as dust and smoke are often nuisance-causing agents, though they do have minute physical size and weight. An argument can be made, for which there is some authority, that invasions by such substances should be trespasses.[7]

Most trespasses occur on the surface of the plaintiff's land. However, they may also occur below the surface, since ownership is viewed as extend-

---

3. Cohen, Property and Sovereignty, 13 Corn.L.Q. 8, 12 (1927).

4. Loretto v. Teleprompter Manhattan CATV Corp., 458 U.S. 419, 102 S.Ct. 3164, 73 L.Ed.2d 868 (1982), on remand 58 N.Y.2d 143, 58 N.Y.S.2d 743, 446 N.E.2d 428 (1983). This eminent domain decision turns upon the principle that even a slight permanent, physical invasion done under authority of government is a "taking." See also Kaiser Aetna v. United States, 444 U.S. 164, 100 S.Ct. 383, 62 L.Ed.2d 332 (1979).

5. 6A American Law of Property §§ 28.1, 28.12, 28.17 (A.J. Casner ed. 1954); Restatement of Torts Second §§ 158, 162, 163–166 (1965).

6. United States v. Causby, 328 U.S. 256, 66 S.Ct. 1062, 90 L.Ed. 1206 (1946) (aircraft);

Portsmouth Harbor Land & Hotel Co. v. United States, 260 U.S. 327, 43 S.Ct. 135, 67 L.Ed. 287 (1922) (artillery projectiles); Herrin v. Sutherland, 74 Mont. 587, 241 P. 328 (1925) (shotgun pellets); Annot., 42 A.L.R. 945 (1926); 6A American Law of Property §§ 28.2, 28.4 (A.J. Casner ed. 1954); Restatement of Torts Second §§ 159–61 (1965).

7. Martin v. Reynolds Metals Co., 221 Or. 86, 342 P.2d 790 (1959), certiorari denied 362 U.S. 918, 80 S.Ct. 672, 4 L.Ed.2d 739 (1960), holds that "gases and particulates" containing fluoride compounds caused a trespass. The court even speculates that bright lights might cause a trespass. But see Amphitheaters, Inc. v. Portland Meadows, 184 Or. 336, 198 P.2d 847 (1948), which holds bright lights were not a trespass.

ing downward indefinitely. Invasions by encroaching building foundations and mining tunnels and by passing through caves under the owner's land may be trespasses.[8] As suggested above, to the extent the surface owner owns the airspace above his land, the unauthorized and unprivileged passage through it is a trespass.[9] With aircraft overflights, it has become clear that landowners do not, as once stated, own "to the heavens," though the extent of ownership is in some doubt. However high it goes, passage through it may be a trespass.

Nonpermissive entries are not wrongful, and thus not a trespass, if they are privileged. There are a surprising number of privileges, so many that the Restatement of Torts, Second, devotes an entire chapter to them.[10] A large group of privileges are founded in transactions between the possessor of the land and the entrant. Examples are entries by departing tenants, licensees, vendors, landlords, and mortgagors to return within a reasonable time to remove things they are entitled to possess. Another large group of privileges do not depend upon any present or former special relationship between possessor and entrant but are based upon some claim of the entrant's that, in the balance, is stronger than the possessor's right to exclude others. Entries by public officers, such as police (with or sometimes even without a warrant), health and fire inspectors, and process servers are examples.[11] Private individuals may also enter in certain situations, such as to retrieve their goods that have accidentally gone onto the land, to detour around a blocked public highway, or to abate a private nuisance. In recent years the United States Supreme Court has allowed private persons to enter shopping centers to disseminate information, in pursuit of their privilege of free speech; however, the parameters of this form of privileged entry are still ill defined.[12]

Examination of the privilege cases will show some general principles that run through all of them. Entry may be only for the limited purposes for which a particular privilege exists. Similarly, the right to remain is temporary, for only as long as needed to accomplish the privileged purpose. Privileged entrants are immune from liability for minor damage to the premises if necessary to accomplish the permitted purpose, but they may be liable for substantial harm though done necessarily and unavoidably. How-

8. Edwards v. Sims, 232 Ky. 791, 24 S.W.2d 619 (1929) (Great Onyx Cave); Marengo Cave Co. v. Ross, 212 Ind. 624, 10 N.E.2d 917 (1937) (cave; dictum); 6A American Law of Property § 28.3 (A.J. Casner ed. 1954); Restatement of Torts Second § 159(1) (1965).

9. See authorities cited in note 6, supra.

10. Restatement of Torts Second Ch. 8, §§ 167–215 (1965). Also see the discussion in 6A American Law of Property §§ 28.9–28.11 (A.J. Casner ed. 1954). Reference is made to these sections for what appears to be the most extended current discussion of privileged entry.

11. The subject of entry by governmental officers rapidly becomes a constitutional question of search and seizure. For something of this tangled web, see, e.g., Zurcher v. Stanford Daily, 436 U.S. 547, 98 S.Ct. 1970, 56 L.Ed.2d 525 (1978), rehearing denied 439 U.S. 885, 99

S.Ct. 231, 58 L.Ed.2d 200 (1978); Marshall v. Barlow's, Inc., 436 U.S. 307, 98 S.Ct. 1816, 56 L.Ed.2d 305 (1978); Colonnade Catering Corp. v. United States, 397 U.S. 72, 90 S.Ct. 774, 25 L.Ed.2d 60 (1970); See v. City of Seattle, 387 U.S. 541, 87 S.Ct. 1737, 18 L.Ed.2d 943 (1967); Camara v. Municipal Court, 387 U.S. 523, 87 S.Ct. 1727, 18 L.Ed.2d 930 (1967).

12. See Prune Yard Shopping Center v. Robins, 447 U.S. 74, 100 S.Ct. 2035, 64 L.Ed.2d 741 (1980); Hudgens v. NLRB, 424 U.S. 507, 96 S.Ct. 1029, 47 L.Ed.2d 196 (1976); Lloyd Corp., Limited v. Tanner, 407 U.S. 551, 92 S.Ct. 2219, 33 L.Ed.2d 131 (1972), conformed to 463 F.2d 1095 (9th Cir.); Amalgamated Food Employees Union Local 590 v. Logan Valley Plaza, Inc., 391 U.S. 308, 88 S.Ct. 1601, 20 L.Ed.2d 603 (1968).

ever, they are liable for harm to the premises caused by negligence or by exceeding the limits of the privilege. Although the examples of privileged entry demonstrate that the possessor's right to exclude others is not absolute, the restrictions on the privileges also show that exclusion is the norm.

§ 7.2   Freedom From Nuisance

A "nuisance" is a state of affairs. To conduct a nuisance is a tort. In tort law the word "nuisance" has had an extremely elastic meaning; sometimes it is little more than a pejorative term, a weasel word used as a substitute for reasoning.[1] As used here, "nuisance" refers only to what seems to be by far the largest branch of the subject, cases in which the defendant maintains on his land a condition that interferes with the plaintiff's use and enjoyment of land the plaintiff possesses. Our plaintiff's right as possessor is the right to be free from nuisance.

The general distinction between a nuisance and a trespass is that the trespass flows from a physical invasion and the nuisance does not. As mentioned in the preceding section, the physical and non-physical shade together in certain classes of cases.[2] Typical nuisance-causing agents are noise, dust, smoke, odors, other airborne or water-borne contaminants, vermin, insects, and vibration; the list is not exhaustive.[3]

With some minor variation in language, the courts pretty uniformly define a nuisance as an "unreasonable" activity or condition on the defendant's land that "substantially" or "unreasonably" interferes with the plaintiff's use and enjoyment of his land.[4] The Restatement of Torts calls nuisances thus defined "intentional" nuisances. It also has another category of "unintentional" nuisances, which it defines as conduct that would be actionable under rules for negligence and extrahazardous activity.[5] The category of "unintentional" nuisances is confusing, though no doubt courts have sometimes spoken of negligent, etc., harm to land as a "nuisance." First, it seems redundant to say a plaintiff has a "nuisance" cause of action

§ 7.2

1. See W. Prosser and W. Keeton, Torts §§ 86, 87 (5th ed. 1984).

2. See Martin v. Reynolds Metals Co., 221 Or. 86, 342 P.2d 790 (1959), certiorari denied 362 U.S. 918, 80 S.Ct. 672, 4 L.Ed.2d 739 (1960) (gases and particulate matter). Cf. Boomer v. Atlantic Cement Co., 26 N.Y.2d 219, 309 N.Y.S.2d 312, 257 N.E.2d 870 (1970), on remand 72 Misc.2d 834, 340 N.Y.S.2d 97 (1972), affirmed 42 A.D.2d 496, 349 N.Y.S.2d 199 (1973) (cement dust); Amphitheaters, Inc. v. Portland Meadows, 184 Or. 336, 198 P.2d 847 (1948) (bright lights); Riblet v. Spokane–Portland Cement Co., 41 Wn.2d 249, 248 P.2d 380 (1952) (cement dust).

3. See, e.g., Spur Industries, Inc. v. Del E. Webb Development Co., 108 Ariz. 178, 494 P.2d 700 (1972) (flies, odors); Schlotfelt v. Vinton Farmers' Supply Co., 252 Iowa 1102, 109 N.W.2d 695 (1961) (noise, dust); Pendoley v. Ferreira, 345 Mass. 309, 187 N.E.2d 142 (1963) (smelly piggery); Boomer v. Atlantic Cement

Co., 26 N.Y.2d 219, 309 N.Y.S.2d 312, 257 N.E.2d 870 (1970), on remand 72 Misc.2d 834, 340 N.Y.S.2d 97 (1972), affirmed 42 A.D.2d 496, 349 N.Y.S.2d 199 (1973) (cement dust); Campbell v. Seamen, 63 N.Y. 568 (1876) (acid fumes); Morgan v. High Penn Oil Co., 238 N.C. 185, 77 S.E.2d 682 (1953) (gases and odors); Estancias Dallas Corp. v. Schultz, 500 S.W.2d 217 (Tex.Civ.App.1973), refused n.r.e. (noise, vibration).

4. In addition to the cases cited in the preceding note, see Bove v. Donner–Hanna Coke Corp., 236 App.Div. 37, 258 N.Y.S. 229 (1932), motion denied 236 App.Div. 775, 258 N.Y.S. 1075 (1932); W. Prosser, Torts § 87 (4th ed. 1971); Restatement (Second) of Torts § 822 (1979). See also the definition in Restatement (First) of Torts § 822 (1939), which has probably been cited by the courts more than any other definition of nuisance.

5. Restatement (Second) of Torts § 822(b) (1979); Restatement (First) of Torts § 822(d)(ii) (1939).

when the cause of action really arises under some other theory. The Restatement itself asserts the generally accepted axiom that the existence of a nuisance does not depend upon the quality of the defendant's conduct.[6] Second, it is hard to imagine a defendant, particularly by the time the matter reaches a court, who unintentionally or unknowingly carries on an activity that appreciably invades his neighbor's land unless it is one of the rare cases in which courts label a single act a nuisance. In any event, none of the decisions discussed here were of that sort. It will then be orderly for us to arrange the following discussion under the two main heads for "intentional" nuisance, the question of the defendant's "unreasonable" conduct and the question of "substantial" harm to the plaintiff.

Whether the defendant's use of his own land is "unreasonable" is of course a mixed question of fact and law. Certain kinds of activities constitute a nuisance anywhere, such as maliciously designing to harm a neighbor, acts forbidden by statute, and activities openly carried on that a court considers flagrantly against accepted moral standards.[7] When one gets beyond these activities, it may be said that no activity is necessarily a nuisance at all times and places. In Justice Sutherland's famous sentence, "A nuisance may be merely a right thing in the wrong place,—like a pig in the parlor instead of the barnyard."[8] The trier of fact may consider all relevant circumstances, so that an enumeration of them is suggestive only. Factors that often predispose to a finding of nuisance include these: the activity is not customary for or suited to the area; the activity causes observable effects that most of us would find disagreeable, independently of whether they in fact harm the plaintiff; the activity is carried on by methods that produce more disturbance than other available methods; the activity is of little value to the defendant; the activity is unimportant to society; and the defendant's activity was begun after the plaintiff began the present use of his land. Opposites of these factors tend to show that the defendant's activity is reasonable.[9] No single factor is conclusive for all cases. Despite statements in some decisions that an activity permitted by zoning cannot be a nuisance, this too is correctly considered only a factor.[10] There also has sometimes been confusion about whether an activity not originally a nuisance may become one because the area in which it is located

---

6. Morgan v. High Penn Oil Co., 238 N.C. 185, 77 S.E.2d 682 (1953); W. Prosser and W. Keeton, Torts, § 87 (5th ed. 1984); Restatement (Second) of Torts § 822, Comment b (1979).

7. Restatement (Second) of Torts § 829 (1979).

8. Village of Euclid v. Ambler Realty Co., 272 U.S. 365, 388, 47 S.Ct. 114, 118, 71 L.Ed. 303 (1926).

9. Schlotfelt v. Vinton Farmers' Supply Co., 252 Iowa 1102, 109 N.W.2d 695 (1961) (unsuited; plaintiff there first); Pendoley v. Ferreira, 345 Mass. 309, 187 N.E.2d 142 (1963) (unsuited; defendant there first, but area changed); Bove v. Donner–Hanna Coke Corp., 236 App.Div. 37, 258 N.Y.S. 229 (1932), motion denied 236 App.Div. 775, 258 N.Y.S. 1075

(1932) (defendant's use suited to area); Morgan v. High Penn Oil Co., 238 N.C. 185, 77 S.E.2d 682 (1953) (defendant's refinery operated efficiently, but severe gases and odors); Amphitheaters, Inc. v. Portland Meadows, 184 Or. 336, 198 P.2d 847 (1948) (defendant's racetrack suited to area); Estancias Dallas Corp. v. Schultz, 500 S.W.2d 217 (Tex.Civ.App.1973), refused n.r.e. (noise, near homes, severe); W. Prosser and W. Keeton, Torts § 87 (5th ed. 1984); Restatement (Second) of Torts §§ 826–831 (1979).

10. Compare Weltshe v. Graf, 323 Mass. 498, 82 N.E.2d 795 (1948) (only a factor); with Bove v. Donner–Hanna Coke Corp., 236 App. Div. 37, 258 N.Y.S. 229 (1932), motion denied 236 App.Div. 775, 258 N.Y.S. 1075 (1932) ("not for the court" to "override" zoning).

changes. It clearly may so become, as the courts generally hold.[11] The related question whether "coming to a nuisance" is a defense will be discussed presently. Another question that occasionally arises is whether one may commit a nuisance by refusing to alter his land's natural condition, as by failing to cut weeds or to spray for insects. Despite arguments to the contrary, courts overwhelmingly hold that it is not wrongful to fail to correct a natural condition, though it may be wrongful to fail to abate an artificial one.[12]

An interesting question, upon which there has been some litigation but not enough searching analysis, is whether blockage of light, air, and view can cause a nuisance. Most courts that have faced the question have said or held that the plaintiff landowner has no protected right to a view and thus no cause of action. These courts have generally refused to consider the economic impact loss of light, air, or view has upon the plaintiff, saying merely that a blocking structure cannot be a nuisance.[13] Sometimes it has been said that plaintiff landowners have no protectable interest in sunlight.[14] However, at least two courts have recognized that a landowner may have a cause of action against another landowner who blocks his sunlight and air flow.[15] Courts have failed to probe a fundamental concept of nuisance law that underlies the light-air-view cases. How should we define the property interest that the law of nuisance protects? Is it necessary to say that the plaintiff has a specifically defined property interest in light, air, and view, as discrete kinds of "property," or should we define the protected property interest more broadly as use and enjoyment of the land? If we must define the protected interests narrowly and discretely, then it is probably true that the plaintiff has no protectable interest. But if the interest is defined broadly as "use and enjoyment," then in many cases a plaintiff can show that blockage has caused a severe loss of use and enjoyment and can, indeed, measure the loss by proof of substantial loss of market value. The plaintiff would not automatically lose, but at that point the analysis would shift to considering the reasonableness of the defendant's activity and balancing the two parties' interests. Thus, the light-air-view cases deserve a more searching analysis than they have had.

Even though a defendant's activities may be outrageously unreasonable, they will not be actionable as a nuisance, at least not as a "private" nuisance, unless they cause "substantial" harm to the plaintiff's use and enjoyment of land. Once again, the question of what is "substantial" is a mixed question of fact and law, the resolution of which depends upon

---

11. Pendoley v. Ferreira, 345 Mass. 309, 187 N.E.2d 142 (1963); Bove v. Donner–Hanna Coke Corp., 236 App.Div. 37, 258 N.Y.S. 229 (1932), motion denied 236 App.Div. 775, 258 N.Y.S. 1075 (1932); Annot., 42 A.L.R.3d 344, 364–68 (1972).

12. See Bandy v. Bosie, 132 Ill.App.3d 832, 87 Ill.Dec. 714, 477 N.E.2d 840 (1985) (natural trees); Merriam v. McConnell, 31 Ill.App.2d 241, 175 N.E.2d 293 (1961) (natural condition); Andrews v. Andrews, 242 N.C. 382, 88 S.E.2d 88 (1955) (artificial condition); Annot., 83 A.L.R.2d 936 (1962); Restatement (Second) of Torts § 839 (1979); Noel, Nuisances from Land in its Natural Condition, 56 Harv.L.Rev. 772 (1943) (critical of general rule).

13. See Venuto v. Owens–Corning Fiberglas Corp., 22 Cal.App.3d 116, 99 Cal.Rptr. 350 (1971); Mohr v. Midas Realty Corp., 431 N.W.2d 380 (Iowa 1988); Scharlack v. Gulf Oil Corp., 368 S.W.2d 705 (Tex.Civ.App.1963); Collinson v. John L. Scott, Inc., 55 Wn.App. 481, 778 P.2d 534 (1989).

14. E.g., Sher v. Leiderman, 181 Cal. App.3d 867, 226 Cal.Rptr. 698 (1986).

15. Tenn v. 889 Associates, Ltd., 127 N.H. 321, 500 A.2d 366 (1985); Prah v. Maretti, 108 Wis.2d 223, 321 N.W.2d 182 (1982).

consideration of all the circumstances. Factors frequently considered as tending to show substantial harm include: the plaintiff's loss is financially large; there is observable physical damage to his premises; persons on his land suffer observable physical harm or mental anguish; it would be costly or difficult for the plaintiff to avoid the harm; and the harm is of long duration or unremitting. Opposites of these factors tend to show that the harm is not substantial.[16] No single factor is necessarily controlling. Nuisance defendants sometimes try to defend by showing that the plaintiff acquired possession of his land after the defendant's activity was already established—the so-called "coming to the nuisance" defense. It is generally recognized as one relevant factor, particularly if the plaintiff had full knowledge of the defendant's activities, and it may tend to diminish the plaintiff's chance to get an injunction. But there is hardly any authority for its being an absolute defense.[17] Whether the interference with the plaintiff is substantial is measured from the viewpoint of a person of ordinary sensitivity, making an ordinarily sensitive use of land, not from the viewpoint of this particular plaintiff or use.[18] For this reason, defendants have argued that something that causes only mental disturbance, such as a nearby cemetery or funeral home, cannot be a nuisance. However, the courts generally decide that such activities may be nuisances if the distress or fear they engender would cause substantial harm to an ordinary person.[19]

So far we have discussed what are known as "private" nuisances, as contrasted with "public" nuisances. The term "public nuisance" plays a special role in the history of nuisance law.[20] Today, however, the difference between a public and private nuisance is chiefly a matter of degree. The basic distinction is that, whereas a private nuisance affects one or a limited number of plaintiffs, a public nuisance is viewed as being so serious that it affects the public generally or at least a large number of the public.[21] Illegal

16. Spur Industries, Inc. v. Del E. Webb Development Co., 108 Ariz. 178, 494 P.2d 700 (1972) (dwellings out of place in rural area; dictum); Nicholson v. Connecticut Half–Way House, Inc., 153 Conn. 507, 218 A.2d 383 (1966) (vague future harm; loss of value); Schlotfelt v. Vinton Farmers' Supply Co., 252 Iowa 1102, 109 N.W.2d 695 (1961) (plaintiff's home, in suitable area, there first); Pendoley v. Ferreira, 345 Mass. 309, 187 N.E.2d 142 (1963) (plaintiff's home in residential area); Robie v. Lillis, 112 N.H. 492, 299 A.2d 155 (1972) (harm to plaintiffs fairly ordinary for area); Campbell v. Seamen, 63 N.Y. 568 (1876) (irreplaceable trees destroyed); Bove v. Donner–Hanna Coke Corp., 236 App.Div. 37, 258 N.Y.S. 229 (1932), motion denied 236 App.Div. 775, 258 N.Y.S. 1075 (1932) (plaintiff's home in industrial area); Amphitheaters, Inc. v. Portland Meadows, 184 Or. 336, 198 P.2d 847 (1948) (plaintiff's use abnormally sensitive); W. Prosser and W. Keeton, Torts, § 87 (5th ed. 1984); Restatement (Second) of Torts §§ 827, 829, 829A, 831 (1979).

17. Spur Industries, Inc. v. Del E. Webb Development Co., 108 Ariz. 178, 494 P.2d 700 (1972) (defense recognized, but exception found); Schlotfelt v. Vinton Farmers' Supply

Co., 252 Iowa 1102, 109 N.W.2d 695 (1961) (priority of occupation a "circumstance"); Patton v. Westwood Country Club Co., 18 Ohio App.2d 137, 247 N.E.2d 761 (1969) (factor against plaintiff; no injunction); Annot., 42 A.L.R.3d 344 (1972).

18. Schlotfelt v. Vinton Farmers' Supply Co., 252 Iowa 1102, 109 N.W.2d 695 (1961); Campbell v. Seamen, 63 N.Y. 568 (1876); Amphitheaters, Inc. v. Portland Meadows, 184 Or. 336, 198 P.2d 847 (1948); Restatement (Second) of Torts § 827, Comment e (1979).

19. Powell v. Taylor, 222 Ark. 896, 263 S.W.2d 906 (1954) (funeral home); Jones v. Trawick, 75 So.2d 785 (Fla.1954) (cemetery); W. Prosser and W. Keeton, Torts, § 87 (5th ed. 1984). But cf. McCaw v. Harrison, 259 S.W.2d 457 (Ky.1953) (cemetery); Nicholson v. Connecticut Half–Way House, Inc., 153 Conn. 507, 218 A.2d 383 (1966) (halfway house for ex-prisoners).

20. See W. Prosser and W. Keeton, Torts §§ 86, 90 (5th ed. 1984); Restatement (Second) of Torts § 821B, Comment a (1979).

21. Spur Industries, Inc. v. Del E. Webb Development Co., 108 Ariz. 178, 494 P.2d 700

uses of land, such as houses of prostitution or illegal gambling places are one group; ordinances sometimes declare them public nuisances. But not all public nuisances are illegal activities; many are the same kinds of activities that are private nuisances (indeed, they are both), except that they have such a pervasive, widespread effect as to harm a large number of the public.[22] Even though a public nuisance affects the public generally, the traditional rule is that the only person who may maintain an action for damages or for an abating injunction is a land possessor who is specially affected, which means one against whom it is a private nuisance, or a public prosecutor. The Restatement of Torts, however, advocates that any affected member of the public should be able to maintain an abatement action.[23]

The successful plaintiff in a nuisance action may always recover such damages as he can prove, measured by loss of rental value for a temporary nuisance or by loss of market value for a permanent nuisance.[24] Plaintiffs usually prefer injunctions to damages, for obvious reasons. Except possibly in a few jurisdictions where injunctions against nuisances are said to be a matter of right, injunctions, being an equitable remedy, are regarded as being within the court's discretion. Thus, in most states various equitable defenses may bar an injunction even though the common law remedy of damages will be given. The particular equitable defense most important to us at this point is called either "balancing the equities" or "balancing the hardships"; the latter phrase fits our situation better. Roughly stated, the court may refuse to issue an injunction if it would do more harm than good. The court will balance the hardship from the plaintiff's side if the injunction is not issued, against the hardship from the defendant's side if it is. In assessing the respective hardships, the court will consider generally the same factors that were described above when the questions of "unreasonable" use and "substantial" interference were discussed.[25] At this stage economic and social effects of an injunction vel non on the community may be crucial. For instance, the court may refuse to enjoin a commercial enterprise when this would cause much unemployment or otherwise disadvantage the community.[26] In any event, if an injunction is issued, equity always tailors it to the case. Rather than to enjoin the defendant complete-

---

(1972); Robie v. Lillis, 112 N.H. 492, 299 A.2d 155 (1972) (dictum).

22. Spur Industries, Inc. v. Del E. Webb Development Co., 108 Ariz. 178, 494 P.2d 700 (1972) (cattle feedlot); Town of Preble v. Song Mountain, Inc., 62 Misc.2d 353, 308 N.Y.S.2d 1001 (1970) (rock concert); W. Prosser and W. Keeton, Torts §§ 86, 90 (5th ed. 1984). Restatement (Second) of Torts § 821B (1979).

23. Restatement (Second) of Torts § 821C (1979).

24. W. Prosser and W. Keeton, Torts § 89 (5th ed. 1984). See Boomer v. Atlantic Cement Co., 26 N.Y.2d 219, 309 N.Y.S.2d 312, 257 N.E.2d 870 (1970), on remand 72 Misc.2d 834, 340 N.Y.S.2d 97 (1972), affirmed 42 A.D.2d 496, 349 N.Y.S.2d 199 (1973); Restatement (Second) of Torts § 822, Comment d (1979).

25. Nicholson v. Connecticut Half–Way House, Inc., 153 Conn. 507, 218 A.2d 383 (1966); Schlotfelt v. Vinton Farmers' Supply Co., 252 Iowa 1102, 109 N.W.2d 695 (1961); Robie v. Lillis, 112 N.H. 492, 299 A.2d 155 (1972) (dictum); Campbell v. Seamen, 63 N.Y. 568 (1876); Estancias Dallas Corp. v. Schultz, 500 S.W.2d 217 (Tex.Civ.App.1973), refused n.r.e.; Mathewson v. Primeau, 64 Wn.2d 929, 395 P.2d 183 (1964).

26. Harrisonville v. W.S. Dickey Clay Manufacturing Co., 289 U.S. 334, 53 S.Ct. 602, 77 L.Ed. 1208 (1933); Boomer v. Atlantic Cement Co., 26 N.Y.2d 219, 309 N.Y.S.2d 312, 257 N.E.2d 870 (1970), on remand 72 Misc.2d 834, 340 N.Y.S.2d 97 (1972) affirmed 42 A.D.2d 496, 349 N.Y.S.2d 199 (1973) (injunction "granted" but to be "vacated"); W. Prosser and W. Keeton, Torts § 89 (5th ed. 1984).

ly, the court will if possible issue a partial injunction, zeroing in on certain features of the defendant's activities, such as time, manner, and place.[27]

§ 7.3 Right to Support

Possessors of land have a common-law or "natural" right against other persons for two kinds of support for their land, the rights to "lateral support" and "subjacent support." Lateral support is support in a vertical plane from the adjoining lands of other persons. Subjacent support is support in a horizontal plane from underlying strata of earth owned or occupied by other persons. We will discuss these two subjects in the order mentioned.

The right of lateral support is the right to have one's land, in its natural condition, i.e., as if it were not burdened by structures or other weighty objects, supported by the adjacent neighbors' land. This right is an absolute one, traditionally thought of as a servitude burdening the adjoining land. Therefore, the neighbor is strictly liable for removing support, which usually occurs by his excavating on his land.[1] Implicit in this statement is the rule that the neighbor is not strictly liable if the plaintiff's land would have been adequately supported if it had been in its natural condition, unburdened by buildings or other artificial weight.[2] Note that we here are speaking only of the property right to support, i.e., strict liability. One's neighbor may well be liable for harm to weight-burdened land on some other theory, such as negligence or malicious harm, tort theories beyond the scope of this treatise. Since the right-duty is to have and maintain support, the plaintiff has a cause of action as soon as the neighbor removes support, even if no subsidence has yet occurred. However, no action for damages may be maintained until subsidence causes provable damage, though it seems an action for an injunction should be possible.[3]

A defendant whose activities, such as excavating, would cause a loss of lateral support to his neighbor's land, may avoid liability by providing artificial support by a retaining wall or some similar installation. He will escape liability so long as the artificial support does in fact do its job. But if he fails to maintain it or it otherwise fails to keep lateral support up to the legally required standard, the defendant will then become liable.[4]

27. E.g., Weltshe v. Graf, 323 Mass. 498, 82 N.E.2d 795 (1948) (hours of operation); Pendoley v. Ferreira, 345 Mass. 309, 187 N.E.2d 142 (1963) (injunction granted but delayed); Payne v. Johnson, 20 Wn.2d 24, 145 P.2d 552 (1944) (manner of operation).

§ 7.3

1. Holtz v. Superior Court, 3 Cal.3d 296, 90 Cal.Rptr. 345, 475 P.2d 441 (1970) (implied); Moellering v. Evans, 121 Ind. 195, 22 N.E. 989 (1889); Levi v. Schwartz, 201 Md. 575, 95 A.2d 322 (1953) (dictum); Prete v. Cray, 49 R.I. 209, 141 A. 609 (1928). See discussion of this and related points in 6A American Law of Property §§ 28.36, 28.39–28.42 (A.J. Casner ed. 1954), and Restatement (Second) of Torts §§ 817–819

(1979). These two treatises may sometimes be drawn upon in this section without further attribution, to save repeated citations. See also Annot., 33 A.L.R.2d 111, 112–20 (1954); Annot., 50 A.L.R. 486, 486–98 (1927), Supp., 59 A.L.R. 1252 (1929).

2. Moellering v. Evans, 121 Ind. 195, 22 N.E. 989 (1889); Spall v. Janota, 406 N.E.2d 378 (Ind.App.1980). See generally the authorities cited in the preceding note.

3. See Restatement (Second) of Torts, Ch. 9, Scope and Introductory Note; §§ 817, Comment i, and 936, Comment e (1979).

4. Gorton v. Schofield, 311 Mass. 352, 41 N.E.2d 12 (1942); Restatement (Second) of Torts § 817, Comment k (1979).

It will be noted that, in defining the property right of lateral support, the text above carefully states that it is a right to support from "adjacent" land.   There is controversy whether the right extends to support from neighboring but non-adjacent land.   The Restatement of Torts, Second, states that it does so extend, and American Law of Property apparently advocates it.[5]   As to the decided cases, it seems that, while non-adjacent neighbors have sometimes been held liable for causing subsidence, this has nearly always been on a theory of negligence, not of absolute liability.[6]   For that reason, lateral support, as a real property right, probably does not extend to a right of support from non-adjacent lands.

A question that sometimes arises is whether a plaintiff may recover for damage to his buildings that happen to be on the land when the defendant is liable for damage to the bare land for destroying lateral support.   The question assumes the defendant removed lateral support, that the plaintiff's land subsided and would have subsided without the weight of buildings on it.   We may assume the defendant is liable for damages for the diminution in value of the bare land.   At issue is whether he is also liable for damages for the harm to the building.   By the English rule and the very decided weight of American authority, he is.[7]   A few decisions that deny damages to the building reason that, since the defendant's duty is only to support the unburdened land, his liability for damages should exist only to the same extent.[8]

Turning to the subject of subjacent support, it was defined in the beginning of this section as a right to have one's land supported "in a horizontal plane from underlying strata of earth owned and occupied by other persons."   This generally implies a severance of one or more estates in layers of underlying earth from the estate in the surface, with the underlying layers being owned, occupied, or used by others than the holder of the surface estate.   Potential defendants thus are, by definition, limited to such underlying owners or users, and potential plaintiffs are limited to the possessor of the surface or of some layer above the defendant.   An exception, in some jurisdictions, exists in cases in which a neighbor removes underground water in such quantities as to drain the water from under the plaintiff's land and to cause the plaintiff's land to subside.   The Restatement of Torts, Second, some text writers, and some decisions take the position that the neighbor should be liable for the loss of subjacent support.[9]   It appears, however, that the majority of courts deciding the question have refused to extend liability, on the theory that subjacent support means support from solid substances in the earth, not from underground water.[10]

5.   Restatement (Second) of Torts § 817, Comment g (1979); 6A American Law of Property § 28.39 (A.J. Casner ed. 1954).

6.   See United States v. Peachy, 36 F. 160 (S.D.Ohio 1888); Puckett v. Sullivan, 190 Cal. App.2d 489, 12 Cal.Rptr. 55 (1961); Annot., 87 A.L.R.2d 710 (1963).

7.   Smith v. Howard, 201 Ky. 249, 256 S.W. 402 (1923); Prete v. Cray, 49 R.I. 209, 141 A. 609 (1928); Annot., 50 A.L.R. 486 (1927), Supp., 59 A.L.R. 1252 (1929).

8.   See Moellering v. Evans, 121 Ind. 195, 22 N.E. 989 (1889); A.L.R.Annots., preceding note.

9.   6A American Law of Property § 28.46 (A.J. Casner ed. 1954); Restatement (Second) of Torts § 818 (1979).

10.   See Finley v. Teeter Stone, Inc., 251 Md. 428, 248 A.2d 106 (1968); Annot., 4 A.L.R. 1104 (1919).

The right of subjacent support is quite similar to the right to lateral support, except in a horizontal plane. One difference is in the defendant's exposure to liability for failing to support land burdened by weighty structures. With lateral support, it will be recalled, the duty is only to preserve support for the land as if it were unburdened by structures. Technically, this is also usually stated to be the extent of the defendant's duty to maintain subjacent support.[11] What appears to be a minority of courts have adopted the rule that the subjacent defendant owes a duty to support the surface with the structures that were on it at the date of severance.[12] There seems to be agreement that the defendant owes no duty to support structures added later. As a practical matter, however, a rule of evidence is likely to cause the defendant to be liable for land burdened by buildings that fall in, whether the buildings were emplaced before or after severance. The courts generally are agreed that the burden of proof is on the defendant to show that the land would not have subsided in its unburdened condition, i.e., that the buildings caused it. Because proof of actual cause is difficult in these cases, the plaintiff is likely to win on this otherwise troublesome point.[13] If the defendant is liable at all, he will be liable for damage to improvements on the overlying land as well as for damage to the land itself.

§ 7.4 Rights to Streams and Lakes (Riparian Rights)

An owner or possessor of land that has a boundary on a natural stream, pond, or lake is commonly called a "riparian" proprietor. Perhaps the word "littoral" is technically more correct for an owner on a pond or lake, but the word "riparian" will be used here for convenience. Riparian possessors have certain rights to the water, incident to their rights of possession. These include rights to have the body of water remain in more or less its natural quantity and quality, limited use and consumption, access, and accretion and reliction.[1] In the nature of things, however, these rights cannot be absolute. Unless a given person owns all the riparian land around a pond or lake, there are others bounding on the same stream or body of water who have the same claims to riparian rights, competing claims. Then the public may also have claims to a certain extent to use the water, especially if it is navigable. So, the study of riparian rights is not only an investigation of the rights of an individual owner; it is a study of competing claims, of shared rights in a limited resource.

---

11. Colorado Fuel & Iron Corp. v. Salardino, 125 Colo. 516, 245 P.2d 461 (1952); Annot., 32 A.L.R.2d 1309, 1310–13 (1953); Restatement (Second) of Torts § 820, Comment c (1979). See Platts v. Sacramento Northern Ry., 205 Cal.App.3d 1025, 253 Cal.Rptr. 269 (1988) (absolute duty to maintain land in natural condition; dictum).

12. Annot., 32 A.L.R.2d 1309, 1310–18, 1325–29 (1953). 6A American Law of Property § 28.44 (A.J. Casner ed. 1954), states the rule to be that the duty is to support buildings that were there at the date of severance.

13. See authorities cited in preceding note plus Restatement (Second) of Torts § 820, Comment d (1979).

§ 7.4

1. 1 H. Farnham, Waters and Water Rights 278–347 (1904); Wiel, Running Water, 22 Harv.L.Rev. 190 (1909). On the right of access, see Comment Note, 89 A.L.R. 1156 (1934). See also Horry County v. Woodward, 282 S.C. 366, 318 S.E.2d 584 (1984) (when stream shifts so far that it cuts into land that never had waterfront, but had fixed upland boundary, then shifts back toward its original location, fixed boundary is restored along its original line and is fixed there once again).

The English common-law doctrine of riparian rights, received in the early American cases, is known as the "natural flow" doctrine. Developed mostly with reference to flowing streams, its basic thesis is that the various owners on a body of water have use rights, but, with minor exceptions, none is permitted to reduce the water to ownership. There is concern for the lower owners on a stream; ideally, they should, under the natural flow doctrine, receive as much and as good water as the upper owners. Of course if this were taken literally, no owner, except possibly the lowest, could even touch the water, for this would in some degree alter it. The doctrine permits every owner to consume as much water as needed for "domestic" purposes, which generally means for personal human consumption, drinking, bathing, etc., and for watering domestic animals. Beyond this, the owner may use the water for "reasonable" artificial or commercial purposes, subject to the very large proviso that he may not substantially or materially diminish the quantity or quality of water.[2] Certainly no water may be transported to land beyond the riparian land.

As must be apparent, the natural flow doctrine bears the stamp of an agrarian society; it is not designed to promote irrigation or commercial use of water. If any use may be made for these purposes, it is slight indeed. Many cases involved some variant of the question whether a mill owner, usually one with a dam to impound a pond to feed the mill, might temporarily detain water and to some extent use it up in manufacturing processes and by evaporation.[3] As the industrial revolution progressed in America and it became increasingly apparent that the natural flow theory inhibited important developments, the courts began to modify the doctrine. Though they did not always say so, the tendency was to move toward—at least to introduce elements of—the "reasonable use" doctrine that will be discussed in a moment. Possibly a court would expand the notion of what were "domestic" uses [4] or possibly there would be an expansion of how much water could be detained or consumed in commercial uses.[5]

Modernly the large majority of states, except those that have an appropriation system, to be described presently, follow some version of the "reasonable use" doctrine. Even some with appropriation systems may have a dual system, with the other part being the reasonable use doctrine. In broad concept the reasonable use doctrine says that a riparian owner may make any and all reasonable uses of the water, as long they do not unreasonably interfere with the other riparian owners' opportunity for reasonable use. An underlying policy is that, instead of water being preserved in its natural quantity and quality, it should be used, even totally, to serve human

---

2. Scranton Gas & Water Co. v. Delaware, Lackawanna & Western Railroad Co., 240 Pa. 604, 88 A. 24 (1913); Filbert v. Dechert, 22 Pa.Super. 362 (1903); 6A American Law of Property §§ 28.56, 28.57 (A.J. Casner ed. 1954); Restatement (Second) of Torts, Ch. 41, Introductory Note on the Nature of Riparian Rights and Legal Theories for Determination of the Rights (1979).

3. See, e.g., Evans v. Merriweather, 4 Ill. 492 (1842); Gehlen v. Knorr, 101 Iowa 700, 70 N.W. 757 (1897). Annot., 70 A.L.R. 220 (1931),

lists many cases involving mills. See also Annot., 9 A.L.R. 1211 (1920), reporting cases on increased velocity and volume.

4. E.g., Filbert v. Dechert, 22 Pa.Super. 362 (1903) (water for 800 hospital inmates "domestic" use).

5. E.g., Evans v. Merriweather, 4 Ill. 492 (1842) ("reasonable" use for "artificial" purposes; dictum); Gehlen v. Knorr, 101 Iowa 700, 70 N.W. 757 (1897) (detaining water in pond).

endeavors. There is also a concern that the natural flow theory favored the lower owners on a stream at the expense of upper owners.[6]

Whether and to what extent a given use shall be allowed under the reasonable use doctrine depends upon the weighing of factors on the would-be user's side and balancing them against similar factors on the side of other riparian owners. No list of factors is exhaustive, because the court will consider all the circumstances that are relevant in a given case.[7] However, factors that frequently are important are the purposes of the various uses, their economic value and importance to the owners and to the community, their social value, how much a given use impinges upon the other riparian owners, how appropriate a use is to the particular body of water, and the cost and practicality of adjusting a given use or the other uses.[8] In theory no single factor is conclusive. In practice, however, there is a kind of ranking of uses, either favored or unfavored ones, that may prove conclusive or nigh to it. Domestic uses are so favored that they will generally prevail over other uses. Indeed, some courts state a two-tiered doctrine, essentially a carryover from the natural flow theory, in which they recognize domestic uses as a preferred category and then other reasonable uses as a second category.[9] In arid regions of the West, irrigation may be a use favored over all other uses except domestic uses.[10] While the reasonable use doctrine generally permits water to be transported to and used on non-riparian lands, uses there may be in some way disfavored over uses on riparian lands.[11] The result of all this is that the reasonable use doctrine is flexible, applied with local variations in the states that follow it.

In the seventeen states west of the ninety-eighth meridian, another system of water law, some form of a statutory "appropriation" system, is exclusively or partly in effect. Really, there is not one system but seventeen. In the states of Arizona, Colorado, Idaho, Montana, Nevada, New Mexico, Utah, and Wyoming, forming an arid inner core, an appropriation system is the exclusive system. This is called the "Colorado doctrine." The less arid states on the eastern and western fringes, California, Kansas, Nebraska, North Dakota, Oklahoma, Oregon, South Dakota, Texas, and Washington, follow combinations of both appropriation and reasonable use doctrines. This is known as the "California doctrine." [12]

---

6. See Gehlen v. Knorr, 101 Iowa 700, 70 N.W. 757 (1897); Dumont v. Kellogg, 29 Mich. 420 (1874).

7. See Stratton v. Mt. Hermon Boys' School, 216 Mass. 83, 103 N.E. 87 (1913); Dumont v. Kellogg, 29 Mich. 420 (1874).

8. A listing of factors is contained in Restatement (Second) of Torts § 850A (1979).

9. See Evans v. Merriweather, 4 Ill. 492 (1842) (dictum); Stratton v. Mt. Hermon Boys' School, 216 Mass. 83, 103 N.E. 87 (1913) (dictum); 6A American Law of Property § 28.57 (A.J. Casner ed. 1954).

10. E.g., Herminghaus v. Southern California Edison Co., 200 Cal. 81, 252 P. 607 (1926), certiorari dismissed 275 U.S. 486, 48 S.Ct. 27, 72 L.Ed. 387 (1927); 6A American Law of Property § 28.57 (A.J. Casner ed. 1954).

11. See, e.g., West's Ann.Cal. Water Code § 1254; Osterman v. Central Nebraska Public Power & Irrigation District, 131 Neb. 356, 268 N.W. 334 (1936). See generally Trelease, Coordination of Riparian and Appropriative Rights to the Use of Water, 33 Tex.L.Rev. 24, 41 (1954).

12. Standard backgrounds on appropriation systems, of both the California and Colorado types, are in W. Hutchins, Selected Problems in the Law of Water Rights in the West 27–109 (1942), and Trelease, Coordination of Riparian and Appropriative Rights to the Use of Water, 33 Tex.L.Rev. 24 (1954). These works are the source for much of what will be said here on appropriation systems. For a historical discussion of the appropriation system, tracing it back to the miners' law of the California gold rush, see Justice Field's opin-

To anyone who reads the list of states above and who has any familiarity with American geography, it will come as no surprise to learn that the underlying purpose of an appropriation system is to assure that scarce water resources are put to use, rather than being conserved or apportioned among all riparian owners. The basic appropriation principle is that one, not necessarily a riparian owner, who makes a prior use of water for some "beneficial" purpose may gain the right to continue doing so.[13] Under most systems the prior appropriator's right is subject to being diminished by a later claimant who can establish a need for water for a preferred beneficial purpose. However, since water rights are viewed as property rights, the diminished prior appropriator must be compensated. Water statutes may list preferred uses, but nevertheless litigation arises over what is a beneficial or preferred use.[14] The entire appropriation system will be under the control of a state agency, which will issue water permits, iron out disputes, and enforce the water code through local officers who have such titles as "stream wardens" or "water masters."[15]

The "California" systems, in which appropriation rights and common-law rights under the reasonable use doctrine are mixed in various ways, are bound to breed conflicts. Of course the conflicts would be much worse if the Western states still applied the natural flow doctrine, with its insistence that a stream be kept at full flow and that water be used only on riparian land, as California once did.[16] Even with the reasonable use doctrine, there are serious conflicts between a permit holder who claims by prior appropriation and a riparian owner who comes along later and claims under riparian rights. Or a later appropriator may take rights from a prior riparian owner, who will generally be entitled to compensation.[17] Another frequent conflict concerns water transported for use beyond riparian land, particularly on land beyond the watershed of the stream from which taken.[18]

On navigable water a major limitation on the riparian owner's rights is imposed by what is commonly called the "navigation servitudes" held by the Federal Government and to a much lesser extent by state governments. Under an extension of the commerce clause of the United States Constitution, the Federal Government has the power to regulate and improve navigation.[19] It is well settled that this gives the Government not only the power to regulate water traffic but also to build and to license the building of structures in navigable water, which in recent history has significantly included power dams. In those few instances in which Congress has not

ion in Jennison v. Kirk, 98 U.S. (8 Otto) 453, 25 L.Ed. 240 (1878).

13. See the classic discussion in Coffin v. Left Hand Ditch Co., 6 Colo. 443 (1882).

14. See, e.g., State v. Idaho Department of Water Administration, 96 Idaho 440, 530 P.2d 924 (1974) (Is scenic preservation a beneficial use?).

15. See, e.g., West's Ann.Cal. Water Code §§ 1201–1675; West's Rev.Code Wash.Ann. chs. 90.03–90.16.

16. See Lux v. Haggin, 69 Cal. 255, 4 P. 919 (1884), and Lux v. Haggin, 69 Cal. 255, 10 P. 674 (1886).

17. See Trelease, Coordination of Riparian and Appropriative Rights to the Use of Water, 33 Tex.L.Rev. 24 (1954); Stoebuck, Condemnation of Riparian Rights, a Species of Taking Without Touching, 30 La.L.Rev. 394, 413–16 (1970).

18. Osterman v. Central Nebraska Public Power & Irrigation District, 131 Neb. 356, 268 N.W. 334 (1936) (not beyond the watershed); Trelease, preceding note.

19. U.S. Const. Art. I, § 8, cl. 3; Gibbons v. Ogden, 22 U.S. (9 Wheat.) 1, 6 L.Ed. 23 (1824).

exercised it, states also have the power.[20] The navigation servitude doctrine says that private riparian rights are held subject to a "servitude" held by the Government to do and to license the doing of things under the navigation power. So the reasoning goes, it is no wrong to the riparian owner to interfere with his riparian rights, either those arising at common law or under an appropriation system, if the interference was by activity pursuant to the navigation power, because his rights were always subject to the power. Why government should be able to interfere with property rights under the navigation power when it cannot so interfere under other powers has never been satisfactorily explained, and the navigation servitude doctrine has been roundly criticized by legal writers. Nevertheless, there it is.[21]

It is clear that the riparian owner has no redress for loss of riparian rights when the impact falls out beyond the line that divides his upland or fast land from the adjacent water. Such noncompensable impacts may interfere with access to the water, water level (including loss of power-site value), and the right to use the water (port-site value).[22] Even if the upland owner also owns the bed under the water, the bed is subject to the servitude.[23] However, it is clear that the servitude stops at the point where water or bed ends and upland begins.[24] Where that line is seems now to be a matter of state law, though perhaps the Supreme Court still has some work to do to make that entirely clear.[25] It is also believed that the servitude does not burden riparian rights in non-navigable streams,[26] but Supreme Court decisions leave that point in some doubt, too.[27]

In addition to navigation servitudes, private riparian rights may be subject to the public's right to boat and perhaps to use the water for recreational purposes. This is true on navigable waters, and some courts have extended the public rights to some extent onto waters that would not

---

20. United States v. Bellingham Bay Boom Co., 176 U.S. 211, 20 S.Ct. 343, 44 L.Ed. 437 (1900); Colberg, Inc. v. State ex rel. Department of Public Works, 67 Cal.2d 408, 62 Cal. Rptr. 401, 432 P.2d 3 (1967), certiorari denied 390 U.S. 949, 88 S.Ct. 1037, 19 L.Ed.2d 1139 (1968).

21. This entire discussion of the navigation servitude is based largely upon Stoebuck, Condemnation of Riparian Rights, a Species of Taking Without Touching, 30 La.L.Rev. 394, 421–39 (1970).

22. United States v. Rands, 389 U.S. 121, 88 S.Ct. 265, 19 L.Ed.2d 329 (1967) (port site); United States v. Twin City Power Co., 350 U.S. 222, 76 S.Ct. 259, 100 L.Ed. 240 (1956), rehearing denied 350 U.S. 1009, 76 S.Ct. 648, 100 L.Ed. 871 (1956) (water site; power site); United States v. Willow River Power Co., 324 U.S. 499, 65 S.Ct. 761, 89 L.Ed. 1101 (1945) (water level; power site); United States v. Chandler–Dunbar Water Power Co., 229 U.S. 53, 33 S.Ct. 667, 57 L.Ed. 1063 (1913) (mostly water level, power site).

23. United States v. Cherokee Nation, 480 U.S. 700, 107 S.Ct. 1487, 94 L.Ed.2d 704 (1987), appeal after remand 937 F.2d 1539 (10th Cir. 1991); Lewis Blue Point Oyster Cultivation Co. v. Briggs, 229 U.S. 82, 33 S.Ct. 679, 57 L.Ed. 1083 (1913).

24. United States v. Kansas City Life Insurance Co., 339 U.S. 799, 70 S.Ct. 885, 94 L.Ed. 1277 (1950).

25. See Oregon ex rel. State Land Board v. Corvallis Sand & Gravel Co., 429 U.S. 363, 97 S.Ct. 582, 50 L.Ed.2d 550 (1977), on remand 283 Or. 147, 582 P.2d 1352 (1978). See also Phillips Petroleum Co. v. Mississippi, 484 U.S. 469, 108 S.Ct. 791, 98 L.Ed.2d 877 (1988), rehearing denied 486 U.S. 1018, 108 S.Ct. 1760, 100 L.Ed.2d 221 (1988) (state owned to tide line, upward of navigation line, when it claimed to that line); Utah Div. of State Lands v. United States, 482 U.S. 193, 107 S.Ct. 2318, 96 L.Ed.2d 162 (1987), on remand 846 F.2d 613 (10th Cir.1988) (state owned lake bed).

26. United States v. Cress and United States v. Kelly, 243 U.S. 316, 37 S.Ct. 380, 61 L.Ed. 746 (1917).

27. See United States v. Grand River Dam Authority, 363 U.S. 229, 80 S.Ct. 1134, 4 L.Ed.2d 1186 (1960), rehearing denied 364 U.S. 855, 81 S.Ct. 33, 5 L.Ed.2d 79 (1960); United States v. Willow River Power Co., 324 U.S. 499, 65 S.Ct. 761, 89 L.Ed. 1101 (1945).

for other purposes be considered navigable.[28] And so we return to a point made in the beginning of this section, that the study of riparian rights is in large part a study of competing claims to a limited resource. Riparian rights are not absolute. They are shared with the rights of other riparian owners and even, to some extent, with rights of the public.

§ 7.5 Rights to Underground Water

Water collects in useful concentrations under the surface of the earth in permeable rock, sand, or gravel, in basins or reservoirs known as "aquifers." From thence surface possessors may obtain it from natural springs and pools and from artificial wells. Since an aquifer generally underlies the lands of many persons, withdrawals of water from it by one person will more or less lower its upper level, known as the "water table." Withdrawals by many commercial or municipal users, employing large mechanical pumps, may lower the table appreciably, causing other possessors within the aquifer to suffer a loss of supply and perhaps to have to extend their own wells deeper. Competing claims to a limited common resource cause disputes that find their way into the courts. This section deals with the principles of law that attempt to resolve those disputes.

Under the traditional principles in general use, the first step in analysis of an underground water dispute is to ask whether the water in question flows in a defined underground stream. Most underground water does not do so; most is diffused or "percolating" water that seeps and trickles through the permeable strata. The judicial presumption is that a supply of water is percolating water, so that the burden is on the one who claims it, to prove the water flows in a stream. Evidence of an underground stream with defined banks and bed is from test borings, observations of the stream appearing from or disappearing into the earth, surface sounds of flowing water, vegetation on the surface, and other signs. When a court determines that underground water is flowing in a stream, it applies in general the same principles of riparian or appropriation law it applies to a flowing surface stream. The rules governing riparian and appropriation rights we studied in the last section generally apply.[1]

If the underground water supply is determined to be percolating rather than a stream, then, as far as judge-made law goes, disputes will be settled under one of three doctrines. The oldest, most traditional of the three is the

---

28. See Annot., 6 A.L.R.4th 1030 (1981). See also Anderson v. Bell, 433 So.2d 1202 (Fla.1983), reversing 411 So.2d 948 (Fla.App. 1982) (riparian landowner who owned portion of bed of non-navigable artificial lake not allowed to use waters over portion of bed owned by another); Black v. Williams, 417 So.2d 911 (Miss.1982) (riparian landowner who owned portion of bed of non-navigable lake had right to exclude other riparian owners from water above his portion).

§ 7.5

1. Bristor v. Cheatham, 75 Ariz. 227, 255 P.2d 173 (1953); Finley v. Teeter Stone, Inc., 251 Md. 428, 248 A.2d 106 (1968) (dictum); Higday v. Nickolaus, 469 S.W.2d 859 (Mo.App. 1971) (dictum); 6A American Law of Property

§ 28.65 (A.J. Casner ed. 1954); J. Sax, Water Law, Planning & Policy 459 (1968). A major annotation, covering all the law of underground water, is contained in 55 A.L.R. 1385–1566 (1928), supplemented by Annot., 109 A.L.R. 395–422 (1937). Pages 1487–1501 and 415–16, respectively, deal with underground streams. See also Annot., 29 A.L.R.2d 1354 (1953), on the subject of obstruction and diversion of underground waters. The American Law Institute, in a missionary effort to reform the law of underground water, has adopted rules that, inter alia, abolish the distinction between underground streams and percolating water. Restatement (Second) of Torts § 858 and Introductory Note thereto (1979).

English doctrine of Acton v. Blundell, sometimes called the "absolute ownership" doctrine.[2] This doctrine may be stated very simply: a possessor of land may withdraw as much underground water as he wishes, for whatever purposes he wishes, and let his neighbors look elsewhere than the law for relief. About the only limit is that one may not withdraw water for the malicious purpose of injuring others. The English rule became the traditional, and once prevailing, rule in American courts, still followed in some places.[3] For many years the trend of American decisions has been against the English doctrine, so that today it takes second place to the rule of "reasonable use," to be discussed next.

The "reasonable use" doctrine, sometimes called the "American doctrine" or doctrine of "correlative rights," traces back to dictum in Bassett v. Salisbury Manufacturing Company, an 1862 decision involving surface waters.[4] The court there suggested that the use of underground water should be regulated by a rule of "reasonable use," a suggestion that Lord Wensleydale had previously made in one of the English decisions that followed Acton v. Blundell, Chasemore v. Richards.[5] *Bassett's* dictum bore fruit about forty years later, after American courts became disillusioned by the way the absolute ownership rule allowed municipalities to dry up aquifers by transporting huge amounts of water off the overlying lands. Decisions began coming down in which cities were enjoined from this practice on the ground that the right to underground water was only for "reasonable uses."[6] As the doctrine has developed, it generally has been held that all uses of water upon the land from which it is extracted are "reasonable," even if they more or less deplete the supply to the harm of neighbors, unless the purpose is malicious or the water simply wasted.[7] But, as the origins of the doctrine suggest, when the question is whether water may be transported off that land for use elsewhere, this is usually found "unreasonable," though it has sometimes been permitted. Authorities are not all agreed, but a principle that seems to harmonize the decisions is that water may be extracted for use elsewhere only up to the point that it begins to injure owners within the aquifer.[8] As already mentioned, the reasonable use doctrine has become the

2. 12 Mees. & W. 324, 152 Eng.Rep. 1223 (Exch.1843). Dickinson v. Grand Junction Canal Co., 7 Exch. 282, 155 Eng.Rep. 953 (1852), seemed to limit and question Acton. But the House of Lords fully reaffirmed Acton v. Blundell in Chasemore v. Richards, 7 H.L.C. 349, 11 Eng.Rep. 140 (1859).

3. Bristor v. Cheatham, 75 Ariz. 227, 255 P.2d 173 (1953) (dictum); Finley v. Teeter Stone, Inc., 251 Md. 428, 248 A.2d 106 (1968) (dictum?); Meeker v. City of East Orange, 77 N.J.L. 623, 74 A. 379 (1909) (dictum); Higday v. Nickolaus, 469 S.W.2d 859 (Mo.App.1971) (dictum); City of Corpus Christi v. City of Pleasanton, 154 Tex. 289, 276 S.W.2d 798 (1955) (rule of decision); Annot., 55 A.L.R. 1385, 1390–98 (1928), Supp., 109 A.L.R. 395, 397–99 (1937); J. Sax, Water Law, Planning & Policy 460–61 (1968).

4. 43 N.H. 569 (1862). Accord, Swett v. Cutts, 50 N.H. 439 (1870).

5. 7 H.L.C. 349, 11 Eng.Rep. 140 (1859).

6. See especially Katz v. Walkinshaw, 141 Cal. 116, 70 P. 663 (1902) reversed 141 Cal. 116, 74 P. 766 (1903) ("reasonable use" and "correlative rights" used interchangeably); Forbell v. City of New York, 164 N.Y. 522, 58 N.E. 644 (1900). See generally Annot., 55 A.L.R. 1385, 1398–1404 (1928), Supp., 109 A.L.R. 395, 399–402 (1937).

7. See Farmers Investment Co. v. Bettwy, 113 Ariz. 520, 558 P.2d 14 (1976) (dictum); 6A American Law of Property § 28.66 (A.J. Casner ed. 1954) Restatement (Second) of Torts, Introductory Note to § 858 (1979); J. Sax, Water Law, Policy & Planning 462 (1968); Annot., 55 A.L.R. 1385, 1398–1421 (1928), Supp., 109 A.L.R. 395, 399–405 (1937).

8. Farmers Investment Co. v. Bettwy, 113 Ariz. 520, 558 P.2d 14 (1976); Finley v. Teeter Stone, Inc., 251 Md. 428, 248 A.2d 106 (1968) (dictum); Higday v. Nickolaus, 469 S.W.2d 859 (Mo.App.1971); Meeker v. City of East Orange, 77 N.J.L. 623, 74 A. 379 (1909). Also see

rule of decision in the large majority of American jurisdictions. Its main thrust has been substantially to undo the old English doctrine as to water used off the premises from which extracted, but it has only slightly altered the rights to the use of water upon that land.

California has developed a variant of the reasonable use doctrine, known as the "correlative rights" doctrine, and it does somewhat more alter the rights to use of water upon the land from which extracted. Owners of land within an aquifer are viewed as having equal rights to put the water to beneficial uses upon those lands. However, an owner's rights do not extend to depleting his neighbor's supply, at least not seriously so, for in the event of a water shortage, a court may apportion the supply that is available among all the owners. It is sometimes said that this is the application of the reasonable use doctrine of flowing streams to underground water. In an arid state, where shortages are frequent or chronic, this may produce a practical result significantly different than would the normal reasonable use doctrine. As to uses outside the land from which the water is drawn, for municipal and other uses, the rule is similar to that under the ordinary reasonable use doctrine: water may be transported only if the overlying owners have been fully supplied.[9]

To a greater or lesser extent in various states, statutes have altered the law of underground water. A waterwell permit may be required, and while this may in some states be only a formality that does not change the applicant's substantive rights to take water, it may in other states somewhat alter those rights. Much larger alterations of rights have been wrought in a number of the arid Western states. Historically, underground waters were not placed under the statutory appropriation systems that have long applied to streams and lakes in those states.[10] Today, however, most of the Western states that have statutory appropriation systems for streams and lakes (described in the preceding section) have also adapted the same systems to underground waters. This generally implies a preference for beneficial uses that existed prior to the adoption of the statute, a registration and permit system, and administration by a state agency. It also implies a mixed appropriation-common-law system in states where the so-called "California" doctrine obtains.[11]

---

all the secondary authorities cited in the preceding footnote, some of which state the rules governing off-premises use of water somewhat differently.

9. City of Pasadena v. City of Alhambra, 33 Cal.2d 908, 207 P.2d 17 (1949), certiorari denied 339 U.S. 937, 70 S.Ct. 671, 94 L.Ed. 1354 (1950); Katz v. Walkinshaw, 141 Cal. 116, 70 P. 663 (1902), reversed 141 Cal. 116, 74 P. 766 (1903); 6A American Law of Property § 28.66 (A.J. Casner ed. 1954); Annot., 109 A.L.R. 395, 399–401 (1937); Restatement (Second) of Torts, Introductory Note to § 858 (1979); J. Sax, Water Law, Planning & Policy 462–63 (1968); Hutchins, Trends in the Statutory Law of Ground Water in the Western States, 34 Tex.L.Rev. 157 (1955).

10. See Annot., 55 A.L.R. 1385, 1450–51 (1928), Supp., 109 A.L.R. 395, 408–12 (1937). Interestingly, an examination of the two A.L.R. annotations suggests that, by the time the supplemental one came along, there was some movement toward subjecting underground water to appropriation systems.

11. Detailed examination of statutory appropriation systems is beyond the scope of this Hornbook. For support for the statements in this paragraph and for a start on further study, see Supplement to American Law of Property § 28.67 (1977); J. Sax, Water Law, Policy & Planning 463–68 (1968); Hutchins, Trends in the Statutory Law of Ground Water in the Western States, 34 Tex.L.Rev. 157 (1955).

§ 7.6 Diffuse Surface Water

Diffuse surface water is drainage water from rain, melting snow, and springs that runs over the surface of the earth or perhaps stands in a marsh but does not amount to a stream. The factual situations that give rise to legal problems are usually different, the opposite, in a sense, from those we saw with stream, lake, or underground water in the preceding two sections. There the problems generally arose because neighbors contended to get ahold of a quantity of water. Here the problems usually arise because owners want to get rid of surface water and, in so doing, cast it upon their neighbors, who do not want it either. Occasionally a case comes along in which one neighbor wants to use the diffuse surface water and complains that his neighbor wrongfully impounded it first. The rule in such cases is that whoever impounds the water may have all he can get, unless possibly his motive was malicious.[1] Usually, however, an upper owner precipitates the dispute by doing something on his land that allegedly increases the quantity or force of the surface water as it flows onto a lower neighbor's land. It is also possible for a lower owner to back up the water onto a higher neighbor by damming or filling, but this variation from the usual fact pattern seems to make no difference in the legal principles a court will apply.[2] In the resolution of such disputes, the courts are split among three doctrines, the "common enemy," "civil law," and "reasonable use" doctrines.

The common enemy doctrine is simple in its pristine form: a landowner is privileged to use any and all methods to get rid of surface water and is not liable to his neighbors for flooding them. They in turn may do the same. Surface water is considered an outlaw or common enemy; a high value is placed upon getting rid of it to develop land.[3] States that follow the doctrine generally do so with varying modifications that may considerably soften its seeming harshness. A frequent modification is that an owner is not privileged artificially to collect water and to expel it in a larger quantity than, or in a place or manner different from, the natural flow.[4] Courts often make a distinction between increased runoff that is incidental to grading or improving land, which is said to be privileged, and increased runoff caused by alterations undertaken merely to deflect water, which may create liability.[5]

§ 7.6

1. Terry v. Heppner, 59 S.D. 317, 239 N.W. 759 (1931); Restatement (Second) of Torts § 864 (1979); J. Sax, Water Law, Policy & Planning 489 (1968).

2. See Pendergrast v. Aiken, 293 N.C. 201, 236 S.E.2d 787 (1977); Carland v. Aurin, 103 Tenn. 555, 53 S.W. 940 (1899).

3. For particularly apt descriptions of the common enemy rule, see Keys v. Romley, 64 Cal.2d 396, 50 Cal.Rptr. 273, 412 P.2d 529 (1966); Yonadi v. Homestead Country Homes, Inc., 35 N.J.Super. 514, 114 A.2d 564 (App.Div. 1955), petition denied 42 N.J.Super. 521, 127 A.2d 198 (1956); Butler v. Bruno, 115 R.I. 264, 341 A.2d 735 (1975); Carland v. Aurin, 103 Tenn. 555, 53 S.W. 940 (1899).

4. Butler v. Bruno, 115 R.I. 264, 341 A.2d 735 (1975) (dictum); Wilber Development Corp. v. Les Rowland Construction, Inc., 83

Wn.2d 871, 523 P.2d 186 (1974); King County v. Boeing Co., 62 Wn.2d 545, 384 P.2d 122 (1963); Island County v. Mackie, 36 Wn.App. 385, 675 P.2d 607 (1984) (exception to common enemy rule is that landowner is liable for damage caused by his diverting natural drain onto another's land); Annot., 93 A.L.R.3d 1193, 1203–07 (1979); Annot., 12 A.L.R.2d 1338, 1344–46 (1950). But cf. Yonadi v. Homestead Country Homes, Inc., 35 N.J.Super. 514, 114 A.2d 564 (App.Div.1955) petition denied 42 N.J.Super. 521, 127 A.2d 198 (1956) (increased force permitted). The annotation in 93 A.L.R.3d is comprehensive, a good place to start research.

5. See Jordan v. St. Paul, Minneapolis & Manitoba Railway Co., 42 Minn. 172, 43 N.W. 849 (1889); Mason v. Lamb, 189 Va. 348, 53 S.E.2d 7 (1949); A.L.R. annotations, preceding note.

Sometimes courts following the common enemy rule look into the landowner's purpose for altering drainage and even suggest he might be liable for increased runoff if that purpose or the manner of alteration is not reasonable.[6]

Subject to the modifications suggested above, it appears some form of the common enemy rule is employed in perhaps seventeen states. The number was larger twenty or so years ago, with several states having slipped away to the reasonable use rule.[7] Several of the states appearing to employ the common enemy doctrine also have decisions containing language appropriate to the civil law rule and perhaps turning on that rule. Moreover, modifications to both the common enemy and civil law doctrines have tended to blur the distinctions between them.[8] While courts still resolve some surface water controversies by asserting the common enemy rule in absolute terms, it would be unsafe to assume that any given court would so apply the rule to all cases.

The civil law rule, as its name suggests, comes from a Louisiana decision, which was Orleans Navigation Company v. New Orleans in 1812.[9] This rule in its pure form is the opposite of the common enemy rule, for it says that a landowner who interferes with the natural flow of surface water is strictly liable for any harm this causes his neighbors. When the doctrine is cast in property law terms, land is said to be burdened with a servitude in favor of neighboring land, that natural drainage will not be altered.[10] Again, the civil law doctrine, like the common enemy doctrine, has been encumbered with significant modifications. Most of these have been appended because, if applied literally, the civil law rule inhibits land development. A modification in some jurisdictions is that the common enemy rule, or at least a civil law rule with "balancing," instead of the strict civil law rule will be applied to urban land.[11] Even in rural areas, some courts modify the civil law rule to allow farmers to accelerate the flow of drainage if needed for "good husbandry," so long as they confine the flow to natural channels.[12] These are not the only modifications; there are others and sometimes decisions that contain language suggestive of the reasonable use doctrine.[13]

6. See Morris v. McNicol, 83 Wn.2d 491, 519 P.2d 7 (1974); A.L.R. annotations, preceding note.

7. Compare the counts that have appeared through the years in Carland v. Aurin, 103 Tenn. 555, 53 S.W. 940 (1899); Yonadi v. Homestead Country Homes, Inc., 35 N.J.Super. 514, 114 A.2d 564 (App.Div.1955), petition denied 42 N.J.Super. 521, 127 A.2d 198 (1956); Keys v. Romley, 64 Cal.2d 396, 50 Cal.Rptr. 273, 412 P.2d 529 (1966); Pendergrast v. Aiken, 293 N.C. 201, 236 S.E.2d 787 (1977); and Annot., 93 A.L.R.3d 1193, 1199–1201 (1979).

8. See Butler v. Bruno, 115 R.I. 264, 341 A.2d 735 (1975); Annot., 93 A.L.R.3d 1193 (1979); Annot., 12 A.L.R.2d 1338 (1950).

9. 1 La. (2 Mart. [O.S.]) 214 (1812).

10. See discussions in Keys v. Romley, 64 Cal.2d 396, 50 Cal.Rptr. 273, 412 P.2d 529

(1966); Armstrong v. Francis Corp., 20 N.J. 320, 120 A.2d 4 (1956) (dictum); Pendergrast v. Aiken, 293 N.C. 201, 236 S.E.2d 787 (1977) (dictum); Carland v. Aurin, 103 Tenn. 555, 53 S.W. 940 (1899); Annot., 93 A.L.R.3d 1193, 1207–11 (1979).

11. See Keys v. Romley, 64 Cal.2d 396, 50 Cal.Rptr. 273, 412 P.2d 529 (1966) ("balancing"); Annot., 93 A.L.R.3d 1193, 1212–14 (1979). Some states have rejected the urban-land exception. Carland v. Aurin, 103 Tenn. 555, 53 S.W. 940 (1899); Annot., supra, at 1214–15.

12. See Butler v. Bruno, 115 R.I. 264, 341 A.2d 735 (1975) (dictum); Annot., 93 A.L.R.3d 1193, 1215–16 (1979).

13. See Keys v. Romley, 64 Cal.2d 396, 50 Cal.Rptr. 273, 412 P.2d 529 (1966).

The civil law doctrine, often modified as indicated, appears to be adopted in more states than the common enemy doctrine, apparently twenty-five or so.[14] In a few of these there are also decisions that suggest or follow the common enemy or reasonable use doctrines. Through the years, up until the last few years, both the civil law and common enemy doctrines gained adherents, but the ratio between them seemed not to have varied much.[15] In recent years the reasonable use rule, to which we next turn, has been the growth area, partly by picking up uncommitted states and partly by wooing states away from one of the more traditional doctrines.

The reasonable use doctrine is traced back to New Hampshire, to the 1870 decision in Swett v. Cutts, a decision linked with New Hampshire's slightly earlier decision founding the same doctrine for underground water.[16] To state it succinctly, the doctrine is that an owner is privileged to make reasonable use of his land and in so doing, to alter the drainage of surface water up to the point that the alteration causes unreasonable interference with his neighbors' use of their land.[17] Thus, the question of liability is one of mixed fact and law. Factors that often are considered are how necessary it is for the actor to alter the drainage that reaches his neighbor, whether the actor acted with care, whether better methods of drainage are feasible, and the degree of harm to the neighbor. The decision making process is one of balancing the factors.[18] Simply to state the doctrine makes it apparent that its foundations are more in the law of torts than of property. It has been described as the application of nuisance law principles to surface water.[19] Indeed, the Restatement of Torts, Second treats the law governing surface drainage as a branch of the law of nuisance.[20]

No doubt we have been experiencing a movement toward the reasonable use rule for the past twenty-five years or so. Several jurisdictions have expressly departed the common enemy or civil law rules for it.[21] Other jurisdictions have gone to the reasonable use doctrine partially, as for urban land or other limited situations. Previously uncommitted courts seem more attracted to it than to the two traditional doctrines. It is the principal rule of decision in perhaps ten states.[22] We have already noted that decisions in states generally following one or the other of these two doctrines often more or less contain language imparting the flavor of the reasonable use doctrine.

It is a truism to say we are in a period of historical movement; we always are. But with the law of diffuse surface waters, it is more than

---

14. See the "nose counts" in Keys v. Romley, id., and Annot., 93 A.L.R.3d 1193, 1207–11 (1979).

15. Compare the counts in Carland v. Aurin, 103 Tenn. 555, 53 S.W. 940 (1899), and Annot., 93 A.L.R.3d 1193 (1979).

16. Swett v. Cutts, 50 N.H. 439 (1870). The earlier decision was Bassett v. Salisbury Manufacturing Co., 43 N.H. 569 (1862).

17. See Enderson v. Kelehan, 226 Minn. 163, 32 N.W.2d 286 (1948); Armstrong v. Francis Corp., 20 N.J. 320, 120 A.2d 4 (1956); Pendergrast v. Aiken, 293 N.C. 201, 236 S.E.2d 787 (1977); Butler v. Bruno, 115 R.I. 264, 341 A.2d 735 (1975); Annot., 93 A.L.R.3d 1193, 1216–21 (1979).

18. See especially Enderson v. Kelehan, 226 Minn. 163, 32 N.W.2d 286 (1948); Butler v. Bruno, 115 R.I. 264, 341 A.2d 735 (1975).

19. Pendergrast v. Aiken, 293 N.C. 201, 236 S.E.2d 787 (1977).

20. Restatement (Second) of Torts § 833 (1979).

21. E.g., Armstrong v. Francis Corp., 20 N.J. 320, 120 A.2d 4 (1956); Pendergrast v. Aiken, 293 N.C. 201, 236 S.E.2d 787 (1977); Butler v. Bruno, 115 R.I. 264, 341 A.2d 735 (1975). See Annot., 93 A.L.R.3d 1193, 1216–21 (1979).

22. See Annot., 93 A.L.R.3d, preceding note.

truism. Two opposite streams, common enemy and civil law doctrines, tend to merge. One may not confidently predict the outcome of a given dispute simply by knowing to which of the two doctrines the jurisdiction nominally adheres. In between the two rules flows the reasonable use doctrine, which swells as courts edge over toward or actually join it. One who is caught up in a historic development or, to continue the metaphor, a flood has not the best perspective to predict its course. In this case, however, it seems pretty sure that the principle of reasonable use, though now a minority position in a number of states, will increasingly govern the law of surface waters in the near future. Its counterparts already predominate in the law of riparian and underground waters.

Chapter 8

SERVITUDES

Table of Sections

A. EASEMENTS AND PROFITS

B. RUNNING COVENANTS

A. EASEMENTS AND PROFITS

§ 8.1 Nature of Easements and Profits

Easements and profits a prendre (just "profits" to their friends), like diamonds, present different facets from different angles. To those who hold them, they are rights or interests in land. To distinguish them from estates in land, they do not give the holder a right of possession but a right to use or to take something from land, the possessory estates in which are owned by others. Viewed from this other person's angle, an easement or profit is a burden—an encumbrance—upon that person's estate. Some of the sticks have been taken from the bundle that comprise the estate and have been transferred to the holder of the easement or profit.[1]

The ancient phrase "incorporeal hereditaments" is still sometimes used to refer to easements and profits.[2] "Hereditament" signified in medieval law that the interest was inheritable, thus, a species of real property. The word "incorporeal" in old law denoted that such interests, being non-possessory, were not created or transferred by livery of seisin, as estates were, but lay in grant by a written, originally sealed, instrument.[3] Thus, "incorporeal" means simply "non-possessory." Today, however, the word carries inaccurate connotations that easements and profits are non-physical interests, contrasted with physical estates. In the first place, all interests in land are non-physical concepts, legally protected rights. Second, the uses that may be exercised by the holder of a servitude are as physical as the possession that goes with an estate; they are simply different kinds of physical acts. It would be better if "incorporeal hereditaments" were dropped from the legal language. Anyway, most persons find the phrase impossible to pronounce.

Modernly, when both servitudes and estates are generally created and transferred by the same kinds of instruments and usually pass under the same statutes of inheritance, their chief distinction is that the former give rights of "use" and the latter, rights of "possession." In most cases the distinction can be observed clearly enough. Typical easements are for driveways, roads, rail lines, walkways, and pipe and other utility lines. Profits are usually to remove from the soil substances like minerals, gravel, and timber. Of course possession also includes these uses, but they are limited rights, whereas possession includes all kinds of use and enjoyment that the law allows. The conveyance of an estate, by words sufficient to make the transfer, carries the full rights. But it would hardly do to grant simply an "easement"; its purpose must also be stated, which at once defines and limits the permitted uses. Possession means exclusive occupation, which means that the possessor may wholly exclude all others from all parts of the land, without having to show they will actually interfere with any aspect of use and enjoyment. With an easement or profit, the right to exclude others extends only so far as to prevent their interference with the servitude's particular purpose.[4]

§ 8.1

1. For useful discussions of the law of easements and profits, see 2 American Law of Property §§ 8.1–8.108 (A.J. Casner ed. 1952); Restatement of Property §§ 450–521 (1944); 3 H. Tiffany, Real Property §§ 756–847 (3d ed. 1939). The Restatement tried—and failed—to eliminate the verbal distinction between easements and profits.

2. E.g., Stanton v. T.L. Herbert & Sons, 141 Tenn. 440, 211 S.W. 353 (1919); Cottrell v.

Nurnberger, 131 W.Va. 391, 47 S.E.2d 454 (1948).

3. Cottrell v. Nurnberger, 131 W.Va. 391, 47 S.E.2d 454 (1948); 2 American Law of Property, supra note 1, at §§ 8.15–8.17.

4. Restatement of Property § 450, Comment b (1944). See also Howard v. County of Amador, 220 Cal.App.3d 962, 269 Cal.Rptr. 807 (1990) (what parties called "mineral lease" was not possessory estate but only profit); Avery Dev. Corp. v. Village by the Sea

Use is difficult to distinguish from possession in some cases. Grantors occasionally create "exclusive" easements or profits. Courts may treat such interests as being or "almost" being possessory estates in the area or substance covered by the easement or profit.[5] At the opposite extreme, there might be only an easement or profit if the grantor gave a deed that granted what appeared to be an estate but excepted for himself such extensive rights that the grantee could exercise only limited uses.[6] Easement and profit rights generally include the right more or less to improve the burdened land, perhaps only to gravel a road, but perhaps to erect and maintain more substantial structures, such as bridges, pipelines, and even buildings that facilitate use of the easement or profit. The question arises whether a point is reached at which structures become so substantial that we should say the rights are those of occupation or possession and not only use. Can one have an easement for a large office building or even a dwelling house, for instance? To determine if the interest is an estate or servitude, courts look at the total circumstances, not only the labels the parties used but also the kinds of activities in which the grantee may engage. At least the existence of permanent, substantial structures militates strongly in favor of an estate.[7]

One basic distinction is between easements and profits. As already suggested, the general distinction is that easements allow some use to be made of the burdened land, while profits allow some substance to be severed and removed. Examples were given in the preceding paragraph. Though the distinction is easily observed in most cases, there are some situations in which complications occur. One of these is that a profit nearly always is accompanied by easement rights, implied, if not, as should be done, expressly spelled out in the grant. A profit to remove any substance must necessarily carry with it access over the burdened land sufficient to reach, work, and remove the substance. These secondary easements may, of course, become quite extensive if heavy equipment is needed to extract and remove the substance.[8]

Borderline situations exist, in which we find disagreement over whether a right should be classified as an easement or profit. These generally involve rights to enter an owner's land to remove things that he may not own. Rights to fish in a stream or to hunt for wild animals are examples. Similar is a right to take water from a stream or spring. Of course, these

Condominium Apartments, Inc., 567 So.2d 447 (Fla.App.1990) (easement holder may not make use of servient land beyond what easement allows); Messer v. Leveson, 23 A.D.2d 834, 259 N.Y.S.2d 662 (1965).

5. See discussions in City of Pasadena v. California—Michigan Land & Water Co., 17 Cal.2d 576, 110 P.2d 983 (1941); Stanton v. T.L. Herbert & Sons, 141 Tenn. 440, 211 S.W. 353 (1919).

6. See the intriguing case of Deterding v. United States, 107 Ct.Cl. 656, 69 F.Supp. 214 (1947).

7. See Lynch v. Cypert, 227 Ark. 907, 302 S.W.2d 284 (1957) (railroad depot); Standard Oil Co. v. Buchi, 72 N.J.Eq. 492, 66 A. 427 (1907) (underground oil pipeline); Miller v. City of New York, 15 N.Y.2d 34, 255 N.Y.S.2d 78, 203 N.E.2d 478 (1964) (driving range and buildings in city park); Texas & Pacific Railway Co. v. Martin, 123 Tex. 383, 71 S.W.2d 867 (1934), certiorari denied 293 U.S. 598, 55 S.Ct. 121, 79 L.Ed. 691 (1934). See also Farnes v. Lane, 281 Minn. 222, 161 N.W.2d 297 (1968) (boat dock may be part of easement).

8. See, e.g., Callahan v. Martin, 3 Cal.2d 110, 43 P.2d 788 (1935); Wardell v. Watson, 93 Mo. 107, 5 S.W. 605 (1887).

involve easements to enter and to move around,[9] but can there be a profit when the landowner does not own the fish, game, or water? The large majority of courts agree there can be a profit in fish and game, even though the landowner does not own the wild creatures.[10] In part the American courts' position is based upon the precedent of English decisions that were rendered at a time when landowners did own wild animals on their land.[11] With the grant of the right to take water from a stream, spring, or lake, where the landowner does not own the water, the right is generally labeled an easement.[12] Of course if the landowner has reduced fish, animals or water to ownership by capture or impoundment, then he may grant a profit in them.[13]

Easements and profits are to be distinguished from licenses. They all involve similar kinds of land use. The fundamental difference is that a license is terminable at the will of the creator landowner, whereas easements and profits exist for a determinate time or "perpetually."[14] In Hohfeldian terminology (this is one of Hohfeld's classic examples), while easements and profits are "rights," a license is only a "privilege."[15] Easements and profits are interests in land; licenses are not. Licenses may be granted orally; easements and profits are subject to the Statute of Frauds. In difficult cases, when the parties' words and actions are unclear, courts often say that it is a matter of their intent which relationship was meant.[16] There may be some cases in which the ultimate reasoning should be that the parties simply could not have intended to create a right in land, such as cases involving admission to public places of entertainment.[17] But, as is often true in legal reasoning, talk about "intent" usually only interposes an unnecessary, and in that sense false, step in the process of synthesis that begins with factors and ends with a conclusion. It is the factors that count. Factors that indicate a relationship is an easement or profit and not a license are that it is for a specified time, that it is for a designated area, that substantial consideration was paid for it, and that the holder is allowed to

---

9. At times questions have been raised whether there could be an easement to wander at large about another's land. See notes 19–22 and accompanying text, infra this section.

10. E.g., St. Helen Shooting Club v. Mogle, 234 Mich. 60, 207 N.W. 915 (1926); Anderson v. Gipson, 144 S.W.2d 948 (Tex.Civ.App.1940); Annot., 49 A.L.R.2d 1395, 1397–99 (1956); Restatement of Property § 450, Comment g (1944).

11. See Hanson v. Fergus Falls National Bank & Trust Co., 242 Minn. 498, 65 N.W.2d 857 (1954); Annot., 49 A.L.R.2d 1395, 1396 (1956).

12. Saratoga State Waters Corp. v. Pratt, 227 N.Y. 429, 125 N.E. 834 (1920); Diffendal v. Virginia Midland Railway Co., 86 Va. 459, 10 S.E. 536 (1890); 3 H. Tiffany, Real Property § 841 (3d ed. 1939). For an argument that rights to water should be called profits and citation of authorities, some of which support the argument, see C. Clark, Real Covenants and Other Interests Which "Run with Land" 86–87 (2d ed. 1947).

13. See Loch Sheldrake Associates v. Evans, 306 N.Y. 297, 118 N.E.2d 444 (1954).

14. Easements and profits that have no express or implied termination date are often called "perpetual." This is not strictly accurate, since they are carved out of estates. Even the fee simple may come to an end by escheat.

15. Hohfeld, Some Fundamental Legal Conceptions as Applied in Judicial Reasoning, 23 Yale L.J. 16, 43–44 (1913).

16. See, e.g., Hubbard v. Brown, 50 Cal.3d 189, 266 Cal.Rptr. 491, 785 P.2d 1183 (1990) (Forest Service grazing permit was "interest" in land); McCastle v. Scanlon, 337 Mich. 122, 59 N.W.2d 114 (1953); Kansas City Area Transportation Authority v. Ashley, 485 S.W.2d 641 (Mo.App.1972).

17. See Marrone v. Washington Jockey Club, 227 U.S. 633, 33 S.Ct. 401, 57 L.Ed. 679 (1913).

make improvements and repairs or somehow exercise control.[18] Opposites of these factors suggest a license. A finding that the relationship could not be terminated at the landowner's will should be conclusive of an easement or profit.

Some question has existed whether one may have an easement to roam at large over another's land. The question is associated with easements for hunting, fishing, and other recreational pursuits. In part the question arises because of statements in English cases that "incidents of a novel kind" should not be allowed.[19] That reason no longer has force. Perhaps also there is some vague notion that a right to wander about, having no fixed locus, is too indefinite to be enforced. In any event, many American decisions recognize and enforce hunting and fishing easements.[20] Some states have statutes specifically allowing such easements.[21] It is doubtful that an easement to roam can be created as an implied easement because of its not being "apparent." [22] As a general proposition, however, there is no serious question that such easements are perfectly proper today.

The phrase "negative easement" is widely used by the courts and by legal writers. By ancient and honorable phraseology, we have a specialized form of "negative easement" called an "easement of light, air, and view." [23] As the term is used, a "negative easement" is like the "affirmative" easements we have been examining in that they both impose a burden or servitude upon the grantor's land. The difference is that, whereas an "affirmative" easement allows its holder to go upon and to make specified uses of the burdened land, a "negative easement" gives its holder a right to require the owner of the burdened land to do or not to do specified things with respect to that land but not to go upon or to use it. This meaning makes "negative easement" synonymous with covenantal land restrictions. When the term is used, it generally denotes a restriction that burdens one parcel of land and benefits a separate parcel; it would not ordinarily be used to describe burdens and benefits to two estates in the same parcel, such as covenants between landlord and tenant usually are. "Negative easement" will not be used in this treatise to refer to restrictive covenants. If a "negative easement" were truly a form of easement, then the special rules

---

18. Examination of the following decisions will show one or more of the factors at work in each case: South Center Department Store, Inc. v. South Parkway Building Corp., 19 Ill. App.2d 61, 153 N.E.2d 241 (1958) (no license; owner had general control); Baseball Publishing Co. v. Bruton, 302 Mass. 54, 18 N.E.2d 362 (1938); Kansas City Area Transportation Authority v. Ashley, 485 S.W.2d 641 (Mo.App. 1972); Standard Oil Co. v. Buchi, 72 N.J.Eq. 492, 66 A. 427 (1907); Miller v. City of New York, 15 N.Y.2d 34, 255 N.Y.S.2d 78, 203 N.E.2d 478 (1964); Reliable Washer Service v. Delmar Associates, 49 Misc.2d 348, 267 N.Y.S.2d 419 (1966). But see the unsound decisions in McCastle v. Scanlon, 337 Mich. 122, 59 N.W.2d 114 (1953), in which the written grant to take timber for one year was held only a license.

19. See Keppell v. Bailey, 2 My. & K. 517, 39 Eng.Rep. 1042 (Ch. 1834); Drye v. Eagle

Rock Ranch, Inc., 364 S.W.2d 196 (Tex.1962); Conrad, Easement Novelties, 30 Cal.L.Rev. 125 (1942).

20. See, e.g., St. Helen Shooting Club v. Mogle, 234 Mich. 60, 207 N.W. 915 (1926) (hunting); Anderson v. Gipson, 144 S.W.2d 948 (Tex.Civ.App.1940) (hunting); Cottrell v. Nurnberger, 131 W.Va. 391, 47 S.E.2d 454 (1948) (recreational area); Annot., 49 A.L.R.2d 1395 (1956).

21. Drye v. Eagle Rock Ranch, Inc., 364 S.W.2d 196 (Tex.1962).

22. Id.

23. See, e.g., Thruston v. Minke, 32 Md. 487 (1870); Sanborn v. McLean, 233 Mich. 227, 206 N.W. 496 (1925); Hopkins The Florist, Inc. v. Fleming, 112 Vt. 389, 26 A.2d 96 (1942); 2 American Law of Property, supra note 1, at § 8.12; Restatement of Property § 452 (1944).

that attend the creation and running of covenants would not apply.[24] Indeed, the present chapter will conclude with the thought that such a development would be logical and desirable. That, however, has not been the consequence when the term is used, except perhaps rarely.[25] Unless a court truly intends that consequence, it should be wary in using the phrase "negative easement."

Easements and covenantal restrictions are similar to certain "natural rights" that are incidents of land ownership. They are of the same "stuff," but they differ in that natural rights inhere by law and easements and profits exist only when specifically created. Examples of natural rights are riparian rights, lateral and subjacent support, and freedom from nuisances. From the viewpoint of a landowner who enjoys these rights, they are incidents of property and give rights against others, usually neighbors, who have duties not to interfere. From the neighbor's perspective, the duties impose burdens on them in the use of their land, quite similar to convenantal restrictions. Of course natural rights and duties are more or less reciprocal among owners.

§ 8.2 Easements and Profits Appurtenant and in Gross

An easement or profit "appurtenant" is one whose benefits serve a parcel of land. More exactly, it serves the owner of that land in a way that cannot be separated from his rights in the land. It in fact becomes a right in that land and, as we shall see, passes with the title. Typical examples of easements appurtenant are walkways, driveways, and utility lines across Whiteacre, leading to adjoining or nearby Blackacre. Profits appurtenant, though less numerous than easements appurtenant, include rights to take timber or some substance from the soil of Whiteacre, to be used for some purpose on Blackacre. We speak of the benefitted parcel, Blackacre, as the "dominant tenement" and of the burdened parcel, Whiteacre, as the "servient tenement."[1]

Easements or profits "in gross" are those whose benefits serve their holder only personally, not in connection with his ownership or use of any specific parcel of land. Whatever doubt there may be in England about the existence of easements in gross,[2] they exist in the United States and in large numbers. Examples are easements for utilities held by utility companies, street easements, and railroad easements. Profits in gross include rights to remove timber or substances from the soil when the holder of the right is not limited to using the several items on specific land. Thus, there is no parcel we can call dominant, which of course means the easement right cannot pass

24. See Trustees of Columbia College v. Lynch, 70 N.Y. 440 (1877); Fitzstephens v. Watson, 218 Or. 185, 344 P.2d 221 (1959).

25. One clear example of a court's applying easement rules to a restrictive covenant is in Trustees of Columbia College v. Lynch, 70 N.Y. 440 (1877). See also Waldrop v. Town of Brevard, 233 N.C. 26, 62 S.E.2d 512 (1950).

§ 8.2

1. For discussions of the basic principles in this paragraph, see Martin v. Music, 254

S.W.2d 701 (Ky.1953); Shingleton v. State, 260 N.C. 451, 133 S.E.2d 183 (1963); 2 American Law of Property, supra note 1, at §§ 8.6, 8.7; Restatement of Property §§ 453, 455, 456 (1944).

2. See 2 American Law of Property, supra note 1, at § 8.9, n. 1.

with the title to any land. We will see, in fact, that there is some question about the extent to which easements (not so much profits) in gross may be assigned. It is proper to speak of land burdened by an easement or profit in gross as a "servient tenement."[3]

Whether an easement or profit is appurtenant or in gross depends upon surrounding circumstances equally with the language of its creation. With easements, though probably not with profits, the courts quite generally have a strong preference for the appurtenant kind.[4] A typical example occurs when the owner of Whiteacre grants the owner of neighboring Blackacre an easement, using such language as "an easement for driveway purposes across the south 18 feet of Whiteacre." Were the instrument more fully drafted, it would indicate that the easement was to serve Blackacre, but assume this was (typically) not done. If Whiteacre and Blackacre are so situated that an easement in the location serves Blackacre, a court will almost surely observe that fact and that the parties owned the two parcels and will find the easement appurtenant.[5] Another fact that courts often say indicates appurtenance is that the instrument creating an easement contains words of inheritance.[6] When an easement is held to be in gross, it is usually because its holder owned no land that was so situated as to be served or benefited by it.[7] With profits a prendre, though the question seems hardly to have been considered, it would seem that by their nature they are more likely to be in gross than are easements. The mere fact that the holder owned adjoining land should not suggest appurtenance; it should take

3. For discussions of the general nature of easements and profits in gross, see Stockdale v. Yerden, 220 Mich. 444, 190 N.W. 225 (1922); Standard Oil Co. v. Buchi, 72 N.J.Eq. 492, 66 A. 427 (1907); Loch Sheldrake Associates v. Evans, 306 N.Y. 297, 118 N.E.2d 444 (1954); 2 American Law of Property, supra note 1, at § 8.9; Restatement of Property §§ 454, 455 (1944).

4. See especially Cushman v. Davis, 80 Cal. App.3d 731, 145 Cal.Rptr. 791 (1978); Martin v. Music, 254 S.W.2d 701 (Ky.1953); Shingleton v. State, 260 N.C. 451, 133 S.E.2d 183 (1963). But see Gilbert v. Workman's Circle Camp, 28 A.D.2d 734, 282 N.Y.S.2d 293 (1967) (semble; facts incomplete); Douglas v. Medical Investors, Inc., 256 S.C. 440, 182 S.E.2d 720 (1971). For a suggestion that the preference for appurtenance does not apply to profits, see Loch Sheldrake Associates v. Evans, 306 N.Y. 297, 118 N.E.2d 444 (1954).

5. See Moylan v. Dykes, 181 Cal.App.3d 561, 226 Cal.Rptr. 673 (1986); Martin v. Music, 254 S.W.2d 701 (Ky.1953); Shingleton v. State, 260 N.C. 451, 133 S.E.2d 183 (1963); Siferd v. Stambor, 5 Ohio App.2d 79, 214 N.E.2d 106 (1966); Garza v. Grayson, 255 Or. 413, 467 P.2d 960 (1970); Maranatha Settlement Association, Inc. v. Evans, 385 Pa. 208, 122 A.2d 679 (1956); Green v. Lupo, 32 Wn. App. 318, 647 P.2d 51 (1982) (under presumption that easements are appurtenant, easement "for ingress and egress" was appurtenant). But see Douglas v. Medical Investors,

Inc., 256 S.C. 440, 182 S.E.2d 720 (1971). See also, Kanefsky v. Dratch Construction Co., 376 Pa. 188, 101 A.2d 923 (1954).

6. See Siferd v. Stambor, 5 Ohio App.2d 79, 214 N.E.2d 106 (1966); Maranatha Settlement Association, Inc. v. Evans, 385 Pa. 208, 122 A.2d 679 (1956).

7. See Baseball Publishing Co. v. Bruton, 302 Mass. 54, 18 N.E.2d 362 (1938) (advertising sign on wall); Johnston v. Michigan Consolidated Gas Co., 337 Mich. 572, 60 N.W.2d 464 (1953) (pipeline easement); Boatman v. Lasley, 23 Ohio St. 614 (1873) (holder owned no land when easement granted); Miller v. Lutheran Conference & Camp Association, 331 Pa. 241, 200 A. 646 (1938) (recreational easement on lake). See also State ex rel. Haman v. Fox, 100 Idaho 140, 594 P.2d 1093 (1979) (easement to public must be in gross; dictum); Stockdale v. Yerden, 220 Mich. 444, 190 N.W. 225 (1922) (easement is in gross if part of profit in gross); Standard Oil Co. v. Buchi, 72 N.J.Eq. 492, 66 A. 427 (1907) (pipeline rights were "estate" but not appurtenant). Railroad easements have presented a problem. They should be classified as easements in gross, since it stretches the facts to say they serve any land owned by the railroad. But, to avoid the question whether easements in gross are alienable, courts sometimes classify railroad easements as sui generis or even as appurtenant to the whole rail system. See Geffine v. Thompson, 76 Ohio App. 64, 62 N.E.2d 590 (1945) (dictum).

specific language or some peculiarity in the nature of the profit that indicates it is usable only in connection with the other land.[8]

Whether an easement or profit is appurtenant or in gross usually is consequential when the ultimate question is whether it is assignable or whether it passes with the title of land to which it may be appurtenant. As we will discuss in a later section of this chapter, there has been some doubt about the assignability of easements in gross.

§ 8.3   Creation of Easements and Profits by Express Act

Questions of whether "incorporeal hereditaments" could be created by livery of seisin or only by a grant under seal, important in old English law,[1] are no longer so. Since we regard easements and profits as interests in land, the draftsman should create them in instruments that comply with the Statute of Frauds for deeds or with the Statute of Wills.[2] Whether the grant of a "perpetual" easement, one having the duration of a fee simple estate, should contain words of inheritance is a debated point.[3] A safe practice is to use words of inheritance in a deed whenever state law requires them for a conveyance in fee. Since words of inheritance are not required to devise fee simple estates, such words are not necessary to create easements in wills.[4] The basic rules of form stated in this paragraph should be followed by draftsmen. We will see later that there are doctrines, essentially exceptions to the Statute of Frauds, by which informal agreements are sometimes saved, but these are for the litigating lawyer who must salvage someone else's mistakes, not for the draftsman.

For some reason, easements seem to evoke careless drafting. The instrument should say that the grantor or testator "grants" "an easement [or profit] for the purpose of" such and such to the grantee. One should avoid words of grant like "convey and warrant" or "quitclaim and convey," which suggest estates in land.[5] The thing conveyed should be described as an "easement" or "profit" or, if in doubt, a "right to use" but never as a "strip of land," "right of way," or the like. These latter phrases are very suggestive of an estate and have caused terrible problems, especially in any number of railroad cases.[6] Chronic problems in drafting are inadequate

---

8. See Loch Sheldrake Associates v. Evans, 306 N.Y. 297, 118 N.E.2d 444 (1954); Restatement of Property § 453, Illustration 2 (1944); 3 H. Tiffany, Real Property § 843 (3d ed. 1939).

§ 8.3

1. See note 3 and accompanying text, supra § 8.1.

2. Camp v. Milam, 291 Ala. 12, 277 So.2d 95 (1973) (dictum); City of New York v. New York & South Brooklyn Ferry & Steam Transportation Co., 231 N.Y. 18, 131 N.E. 554 (1921), reargument denied 231 N.Y. 598, 132 N.E. 903 (1921); 2 American Law of Property, supra note 1, at § 8.20; Restatement of Property §§ 466, 467, 469 (1944).

3. See 2 American Law of Property, supra note 1, at § 8.23; Restatement of Property § 468 (1944).

4. Restatement of Property § 470 (1944).

5. See Deterding v. United States, 107 Ct. Cl. 656, 69 F.Supp. 214 (1947); Johnson v. Ocean Shore Railroad Co., 16 Cal.App.3d 429, 94 Cal.Rptr. 68 (1971); Annot., 136 A.L.R. 379 (1942). Indeed, statutes may provide that "convey" transfers an estate; Midland Valley Railroad Co. v. Arrow Industrial Manufacturing Co., 297 P.2d 410 (Okl.1956).

6. See Johnson v. Ocean Shore Railroad Co., 16 Cal.App.3d 429, 94 Cal.Rptr. 68 (1971) ("strip of ground"); Minneapolis Athletic Club v. Cohler, 287 Minn. 254, 177 N.W.2d 786 (1970) ("right of way"); Midland Valley Railroad Co. v. Arrow Industrial Manufacturing Co., 297 P.2d 410 (Okl.1956) ("strip of land for a right of way"); Rod v. Campion, 464 S.W.2d 922 (Tex.Civ.App.1971) ("lane"); Annot., 6 A.L.R.3d 973 (1966); Annot., 136 A.L.R. 379 (1942).

descriptions of the area covered by an easement or profit; its purposes; and what might be called "secondary easements," such as rights to improve and maintain. Courts go a long way in establishing the location and width of easements when the parties do not describe these matters adequately; even when no location is stated, a reasonable and convenient location will be fixed.[7] Nevertheless, the draftsman's standard is to describe location by metes and bounds so clearly that a surveyor can run out the area from the instrument; in exceptional cases description by reference to an existing location may have to suffice.

Instruments creating easements are sometimes called "agreements." The word is not appropriate to refer to a deed that creates a single easement. Perhaps it better suits an instrument creating mutual easements, such as for a driveway along a property line, though "deed for mutual easements" or "cross-easements" still seems more accurate. Whatever it is called, the instrument should comply with the Statute of Frauds for deeds.

Frequently the grantor of a parcel of land wishes to have an easement or profit upon it after the conveyance, usually when he retains title to an adjoining parcel. In early English law, and to a lesser extent in early American law, there were serious questions about how, and upon what theory, this might be accomplished.[8] Today it is settled that it may be done by what is properly called "reservation." The grantor's instrument of conveyance may simply provide that "grantor reserves" an easement or profit, describing its purposes, location, and duration according to the principles for granting such interests discussed above.[9] "Reservations" are confused with "exceptions," deeds often saying that the grantor "excepts" an easement or profit. Properly, an exception is the withholding of title to a piece of a larger parcel of land, e.g., "all of Blackacre except the east 10 feet thereof." It is true that modern courts will attempt to discern the parties' true intent, even if they use "except" instead of "reserve."[10] But draftsmen should use "reservation," first, because it is technically correct and, second, because "exception" may create genuine ambiguity when combined with certain other words.[11]

Many jurisdictions follow the rule that a grantor may not reserve an

7. Cox v. Glenbrook Co., 78 Nev. 254, 371 P.2d 647 (1962) (width); Alban v. R.K. Co., 15 Ohio St.2d 229, 239 N.E.2d 22 (1968) (no location stated); Clearwater Realty Co. v. Bouchard, 146 Vt. 359, 505 A.2d 1189 (1985); Cushman Virginia Corp. v. Barnes, 204 Va. 245, 129 S.E.2d 633 (1963) (width); Annot., 110 A.L.R. 174 (1937). If no location is stated in the grant, the owner of the servient tenement is given first choice of location, provided he chooses a reasonable one. *Alban* and A.L.R.Annot., supra.

8. For the tortured history of these matters, see 2 American Law of Property, supra note 1 at §§ 8.24–8.28; Restatement of Property § 473, Comment a (1944); Madden, Cre-

ation of Easements by Exception, 32 W.Va. L.Q. 33 (1925).

9. Id.; Petersen v. Friedman, 162 Cal. App.2d 245, 328 P.2d 264 (1958); McDermott v. Dodd, 326 Mass. 54, 92 N.E.2d 875 (1950); Mitchell v. Castellaw, 151 Tex. 56, 246 S.W.2d 163 (1952).

10. Coon v. Sonoma Magnesite Co., 182 Cal. 597, 189 P. 271 (1920); McDermott v. Dodd, 326 Mass. 54, 92 N.E.2d 875 (1950); Restatement of Property § 473, Comment a (1944).

11. See, e.g., Coon v. Sonoma Magnesite Co., 182 Cal. 597, 189 P. 271 (1920), where the court wrestles with the phrase "saving and

easement or profit in favor of a third person.[12] The theory of course is that the stranger has no interest in the land conveyed, out of which he might reserve an easement or profit. Legal writers are critical of the rule, and the Restatement of Property refuses to adopt it.[13] A minority of jurisdictions, probably representing a trend, do allow easements and profits to be created in favor of third persons by language of reservation.[14] They reason either that the intent of the parties to the deed should be followed, disregarding language technicalities, or that the reservation operates as a grant from the grantee of the deed. In jurisdictions where there is doubt, the draftsman may finesse the problem simply by having the grantor make separate grants of the estate and of the easement in the same deed.

§ 8.4 Easements Implied From Prior Use

This and the next two sections will discuss three fact patterns in which easements may be created by implication. In all the patterns the implication arises in connection with conveyances of estates in land. However, in none of the three cases is the language of the conveyance a significant factor or element. Rather, the implication of an easement arises out of a pattern of circumstances surrounding the conveyance. Since a court that finds such an easement does not purport to find it in the language of the conveyance, there is no Statute of Frauds problem as to the easement itself, though presumably the Statute applies to the conveyance of the estate.[1]

The first kind of implied easement is often called simply an "implied easement," though the phrase "easement implied from prior use" better distinguishes it from the other two varieties. Its essential elements may be quickly sketched: (1) a conveyance (2) of a physical part only of the grantor's land (hence, he retains part, usually adjoining the part conveyed); (3) before the conveyance there was a usage on the land that, had the two parts then been severed, could have been the subject of an easement appurtenant to one and servient upon the other; (4) this usage is, more or less, "necessary" to the use of the part to which it would be appurtenant; and (5) the usage is "apparent."[2] The grantor is sometimes called a "common grantor," which

excepting therefrom a strip of land. * * * "
See also Annot., 139 A.L.R. 1339 (1942).

12. E.g., Davis v. Gowen, 83 Idaho 204, 360 P.2d 403 (1961); Haverhill Savings Bank v. Griffin, 184 Mass. 419, 68 N.E. 839 (1903); First National Bank v. Laperle, 117 Vt. 144, 86 A.2d 635 (1952); Pitman v. Sweeney, 34 Wn.App. 321, 661 P.2d 153 (1983) (grantor may not reserve easement in favor of third person; said to be majority rule). The decisions are exhaustively reviewed in Annot., 88 A.L.R.2d 1199 (1963).

13. E.g., 2 American Law of Property, supra note 1, at § 8.29; Restatement of Property § 472, Comment b (1944).

14. Willard v. First Church of Christ, Scientist, Pacifica, 7 Cal.3d 473, 102 Cal.Rptr. 739, 498 P.2d 987 (1972); Townsend v. Cable, 378 S.W.2d 806 (Ky.1964); Garza v. Grayson, 255 Or. 413, 467 P.2d 960 (1970).

§ 8.4

1. See Restatement of Property § 475, Comment b (1944). See also Kincaid v. Yount, 9 Ohio App.3d 145, 459 N.E.2d 235 (1983) (implied easement may not be acquired across registered-title land unless it is on register of title).

2. See generally Romanchuk v. Plotkin, 215 Minn. 156, 9 N.W.2d 421 (1943); Westbrook v. Wright, 477 S.W.2d 663 (Tex.Civ.App. 1972); Adams v. Cullen, 44 Wn.2d 502, 268 P.2d 451 (1954); 2 American Law of Property, supra note 1, at §§ 8.32, 8.37–8.42; 3 H. Tiffany, supra note 1, at § 7.91. Cf. Restatement of Property § 476 (1944), which discusses several factors that include those mentioned here in text. But cf. Boudreau v. Coleman, 29 Mass.App.Ct. 621, 564 N.E.2d 1 (1990), which, instead of ticking off the several factors listed in text, looks at large at the circumstances, to determine whether a grantor intended to reserve a roadway easement.

is accurate only if he conveys the retained parcel after conveying the first one. To provide a mechanism by which implied easements arise, some courts say the grantor conveys the granted parcel together with a pre-existing easement upon the retained parcel or subject to a pre-existing easement upon it appurtenant to his retained parcel. (Implied easements in favor of the grantor raise a special issue we will discuss in a moment.) The question then arises, seeing that both parcels were in the grantor's sole, unitary ownership prior to the conveyance, how could he have an easement over his own land? To answer this, the courts indulge in the fiction that a "quasi easement" pre-existed.[3] This theory, apparently connected with an outmoded piece of medieval learning that explained easements reserved by grantors,[4] seems quite superfluous. It is sufficient and simpler, and therefore more satisfactory, to say, as some authorities do, that the easement arises initially by implication in the grantor's conveyance.[5]

Elements 4 and 5 above have produced most of the litigation. On 4, the word "necessary" covers a broad spectrum. Some courts, at least verbally, cling to the notion that the usage must be strictly necessary to the use and enjoyment of the dominant parcel.[6] A more relaxed standard of "reasonable necessity" describes the stance most courts take.[7] So relaxed does "reasonable necessity" become in some decisions that it seems to mean only that the continued usage will be convenient to enjoyment of the dominant tenement.[8] What "necessity" means in a given case depends much on the circumstances. Most courts, except those that hold to strict necessity, will find the requirement satisfied if the owner of the dominant tenement would be put to appreciable expense to provide a substitute for the claimed easement.

Element 5 requires that the pre-existing use be "apparent," so that continuance can be within the grantor's and grantee's contemplation. No difficulty is met in satisfying this element when the use is visible by casual observation, as with a well established roadway or other surface use. Difficult cases are those that involve underground uses, such as sewer or other utility lines. A number of interesting decisions, which are favorites of law school casebooks, hold that such underground lines are sufficiently "apparent."[9] These decisions reason that, while the underground line is not visible to the casual observer, it is discoverable by inspection of utility connections

3. E.g., Harrison v. Heald, 360 Mich. 203, 103 N.W.2d 348 (1960); Romanchuk v. Plotkin, 215 Minn. 156, 9 N.W.2d 421 (1943); Wiesel v. Smira, 49 R.I. 246, 142 A. 148 (1928).

4. See 2 American Law of Property §§ 8.24–8.26, 8.27 n. 1 (A.J. Casner ed. 1952); Madden, Creation of Easements by Exception, 32 W.Va.L.Q. 33 (1925), esp. pp. 48–49.

5. See, e.g., Wymer v. Dagnillo, 162 N.W.2d 514 (Iowa 1968); Restatement of Property §§ 474, 476, Comment i (1944).

6. Wymer v. Dagnillo, 162 N.W.2d 514 (Iowa 1968) ("essential"); Haase v. Zobkiw, 36 A.D.2d 821, 321 N.Y.S.2d 152 (1971); Mitchell v. Castellaw, 151 Tex. 56, 246 S.W.2d 163 (1952); Ward v. Slavecek, 466 S.W.2d 91 (Tex. Civ.App.1971).

7. See Romanchuk v. Plotkin, 215 Minn. 156, 9 N.W.2d 421 (1943); Van Sandt v. Royster, 148 Kan. 495, 83 P.2d 698 (1938); Westbrook v. Wright, 477 S.W.2d 663 (Tex.Civ.App. 1972); Hellberg v. Coffin Sheep Co., 66 Wn.2d 664, 404 P.2d 770 (1965) (dictum?); Adams v. Cullen, 44 Wn.2d 502, 268 P.2d 451 (1954) (dictum); 2 American Law of Property, supra note 1, at § 8.39.

8. Romanchuk v. Plotkin, 215 Minn. 156, 9 N.W.2d 421 (1943); Westbrook v. Wright, 477 S.W.2d 663 (Tex.Civ.App.1972) ("necessary for the convenient and quiet enjoyment").

9. Van Sandt v. Royster, 148 Kan. 495, 83 P.2d 698 (1938); Romanchuk v. Plotkin, 215 Minn. 156, 9 N.W.2d 421 (1943); Wiesel v. Smira, 49 R.I. 246, 142 A. 148 (1928); Westbrook v. Wright, 477 S.W.2d 663 (Tex.Civ.App. 1972).

that are visible. Thus, it can be said that "apparent" includes "reasonably discoverable." [10]

In the older decisions another element was added, that an easement implied from prior use had to be "continuous." This was critical in roadway and driveway easement cases, for if the use had to be literally continuous, the intermittent use of an access way would not qualify.[11] Such an element has pretty much disappeared now, though it may occasionally surface in comparatively recent decisions.[12] Generally now the courts either do not mention the element at all or find that intermittent use is continuous enough or treat the element of visible use as the important question, with continuity being only an aspect of visibility.[13]

Serious question has been raised whether an implied easement in favor of the grantor's retained land, i.e., an implied reserved easement, should be allowed. Concern arises from the principle that a grantor may not derogate from his own grant and the companion rule of construction that a deed is construed against the grantor. When an easement is implied in favor of the grantor, this detracts from the estate the deed's words appear to convey. On this account a number of decisions hold or say that a reserved easement will be implied only when it is strictly necessary to the use of the grantor's retained parcel.[14] However, the distinction between granted and reserved implied easements is not always observed, and it appears less pronounced now than it was, say, early in the century.[15] It probably puts the matter in perspective simply to say a court may be less disposed to find, and to require stronger proof of, a reserved than a granted implied easement.[16]

§ 8.5 Easements Implied From Necessity

The second kind of implied easement is usually called a "way of necessity." Its essential elements are: (1) a conveyance (2) of a physical part only of the grantor's land (hence, he retains part, usually adjoining the part conveyed); and (3) after severance of the two parcels, it is "necessary" to pass over one of them to reach any public street or road from the other.

---

10. See Restatement of Property § 476, Comment j (1944) ("within the possibility of their knowledge"). See also the interesting decision in George v. Goshgarian, 139 Cal. App.3d 856, 189 Cal.Rptr. 94 (1983), which held that an easement for a power line to lot 62 from a main power line running across adjoining lot 115 could be implied, even though there was no line leading onto lot 62 at the moment of severance of the two lots, because, from the position of the power line running across lot 115 and the juxtaposition of the lots, a jury could conclude that a buyer of lot 62 would believe that the power line was intended to serve lot 62. The decision dispenses with the usual requirement that a "quasi easement" be in existence at the moment of severance.

11. Annot., 34 A.L.R. 233 (1925); Note, 1 Calif.L.Rev. 275 (1913).

12. See Milewski v. Wolski, 314 Mich. 445, 22 N.W.2d 831 (1946); Burling v. Leiter, 272

Mich. 448, 262 N.W. 388 (1935) (alternative ground).

13. 2 American Law of Property § 8.41 (A.J. Casner ed. 1952); Annot., 34 A.L.R. 233 (1925), Supp., 100 A.L.R. 1321 (1936), Supp., 164 A.L.R. 1001 (1946).

14. Van Sandt v. Royster, 148 Kan. 495, 83 P.2d 698 (1938); Brown v. Fuller, 165 Mich. 162, 130 N.W. 621 (1911); Toothe v. Bryce, 59 N.J.Eq. 589, 25 A. 182 (1892) (dictum, but classic discussion); Wiesel v. Smira, 49 R.I. 246, 142 A. 148 (1928); Annot., 58 A.L.R. 824, 837–42 (1929).

15. Compare Harrison v. Heald, 360 Mich. 203, 103 N.W.2d 348 (1960), with Brown v. Fuller, 165 Mich. 162, 130 N.W. 621 (1938). See Annot., 58 A.L.R. 824, 840–42 (1929).

16. See Restatement of Property § 476, Comment c (1944).

Elements 1 and 2 are the same as for the implied easements discussed in the preceding section. The essential difference between the two kinds of easements is that, while with the former kind, a pre-existing use had to be present, there is now no such requirement. Rather, the severance will more or less landlock one of the parcels unless its owner is given implied access over the other parcel. Whether it must be totally landlocked goes to the question of what "necessary" means, which we will discuss. Obviously there may be cases in which both theories fit, as when a conveyance will landlock one parcel unless a pre-existing road over the other may be used.[1]

May an easement arise out of necessity, without a pre-existing usage, for some purpose other than for ingress and egress? Might a grantee, for instance, make out a claim of necessity to run utility lines over his grantor's remaining land? Authority seems lacking on the precise question. Courts generally deny easements of necessity for light and air, usually stating that an easement for these purposes may be created in America only by grant.[2] If a deed states that the land conveyed is to be used for a certain purpose, such as to operate a particular business, this may imply such easements as are reasonably necessary to conduct that activity.[3] That, however, adds an additional element to the ones we are supposing. In the present state of the law, it seems easements implied from necessity are synonymous with ways of necessity. It would normally be harder to make out a case of necessity for some use, such as utility lines, other than access. Notwithstanding its novelty, the argument would seem plausible in a strong case.

Nearly all the litigation on ways of necessity is over the third element, about what "necessary," means. Certainly, if the conveyance will result in either the granted or retained parcel's being literally without access to the outside world—landlocked—this meets the strictest definitions.[4] One would suppose the necessity here must be, if not absolute, much more nearly so than with easements implied from pre-existing use. If the claimant has free access to some part of his land, he cannot make out a way of necessity to another part just because it would be more convenient.[5] However, while some courts may insist on the land's being landlocked, most recognize a degree of flexibility. Sometimes it is said the claimant is entitled to sufficient access to make "effective use" of his land. This might be lacking if the only established roadway were, for instance, narrow or flooded much of the time.[6] A recent study of all the decisions of a single state showed they had made no distinction between the degree of necessity required for a way

---

§ 8.5

1. Hellberg v. Coffin Sheep Co., 66 Wn.2d 664, 404 P.2d 770 (1965), is such a case. See also Koonce v. J.E. Brite Estate, 663 S.W.2d 451 (Tex.1984) (no way of necessity unless the alleged dominant and servient tenements were owned as a unit prior to separation).

2. E.g., Fontainebleau Hotel Corp. v. Forty-Five Twenty-Five, Inc., 114 So.2d 357 (Fla. App.1959), cert. denied 117 So.2d 842 (Fla. 1960); Maioriello v. Arlotta, 364 Pa. 557, 73 A.2d 374 (1950).

3. 3 H. Tiffany, Real Property § 792 (3d ed. 1939).

4. See, e.g., Finn v. Williams, 376 Ill. 95, 33 N.E.2d 226 (1941); Horner v. Heersche, 202 Kan. 250, 447 P.2d 811 (1968); Soltis v. Miller, 444 Pa. 357, 282 A.2d 369 (1971); Hellberg v. Coffin Sheep Co., 66 Wn.2d 664, 404 P.2d 770 (1965) (alternative ground).

5. Hunt v. Zimmerman, 139 Ind.App. 242, 216 N.E.2d 854 (1966), rehearing denied 139 Ind.App. 242, 218 N.E.2d 709 (1966).

6. See State v. Deal, 191 Or. 661, 233 P.2d 242 (1951); Restatement of Property § 476,

of necessity and that for an easement implied from pre-existing use.[7] That is going too far; it makes the elements of pre-existing and apparent use count for nothing in the process of implication.

The claimant cannot make out necessity if he has access over other land of his that adjoins the would-be dominant tenement.[8] But he can if a stranger owns the adjoining land; he has no claim of access over the stranger's land that reduces the necessity.[9] Whether access to a navigable body of water will defeat a claim of necessity is a question on which the several decisions are in conflict. A strong majority of older decisions held the claim was defeated, but the recent trend has been to allow the claim of necessity if the water access does not permit effective use of the dominant tenement.[10] The trend is symptomatic of a general tendency toward a flexible understanding of "necessity."

Necessity for the easement must exist at the moment of severance; a necessity arising later will have no effect.[11] The easement's purposes will be initially defined by the necessity then existing, but, similarly to a granted easement of general access, its permitted scope is capable of gradual change to keep pace with reasonable changes in uses of the dominant tenement.[12] Location of the route of a way of necessity is more difficult than with an easement implied from pre-existing use because, by definition, no location is established on the ground. It seems that the owner of the servient estate is given the first opportunity to select the route, and then, if he fails to do so, the other party may choose. If they cannot agree, a court of equity will fix the location, having regard for not only the shortest route but for all other factors that bear upon the most convenient and suitable route.[13]

§ 8.6 Easements Implied From Plat

A purchaser who acquires a lot in a platted subdivision will, to an extent that varies from state to state, acquire implied private easements to use streets and alleys and perhaps parks and playgrounds shown on the plat.

Comment g (1944).

7. Glenn, Implied Easements in the North Carolina Courts: An Essay on the Meaning of "Necessary," 58 N.C.L.Rev. 223 (1980).

8. Bully Hill Copper Mining & Smelting Co. v. Bruson, 4 Cal.App. 180, 87 P. 237 (1906); Gaines v. Lunsford, 120 Ga. 370, 47 S.E. 967 (1904) (private condemnation statute). See also Witten v. Murphy, 71 Or.App. 511, 692 P.2d 715 (1984), review denied 298 Or. 773, 697 P.2d 556 (1985) (under statute allowing condemnation of way of necessity, claimant cannot establish necessity when he had access to road over other neighbors' lands). Of course if the claimant cannot get access over his adjoining land because of a physical barrier such as a stream or cliff, this will not defeat his claim of necessity. Wiese v. Thien, 279 Mo. 524, 214 S.W. 853 (1919); Annot., 5 A.L.R. 1557 (1920).

9. Finn v. Williams, 376 Ill. 95, 33 N.E.2d 226 (1941). Cf. Robertson v. Robertson, 214 Va. 76, 197 S.E.2d 183 (1973).

10. E.g., the claim of necessity was denied in Kingsley v. Gouldsborough Land Improvement Co., 86 Me. 279, 29 A. 1074 (1894), and Bauman v. Wagner, 146 App.Div. 191, 130 N.Y.S. 1016 (1911), but allowed in Redman v. Kidwell, 180 So.2d 682 (Fla.App.1965), cert. denied 188 So.2d 806 (Fla.1966), and Hancock v. Henderson, 236 Md. 98, 202 A.2d 599 (1964). See also Hellberg v. Coffin Sheep Co., 66 Wn.2d 664, 404 P.2d 770 (1965), where the land adjoined a navigable river, but no issue was made of the fact. Compare Annot. 9 A.L.R.3d 600 (1966), with the Annot. it supersedes in 38 A.L.R. 1310 (1925).

11. Leonard v. Bailwitz, 148 Conn. 8, 166 A.2d 451 (1960); Othen v. Rosier, 148 Tex. 485, 226 S.W.2d 622 (1950).

12. Soltis v. Miller, 444 Pa. 357, 282 A.2d 369 (1971).

13. Hancock v. Henderson, 236 Md. 98, 202 A.2d 599 (1964); Higbee Fishing Club v. Atlantic City Electric Co., 78 N.J.Eq. 434, 79 A. 326 (1911); Annot., 68 A.L.R. 528 (1930).

Litigation over such easements seldom arises in states in which the act of subdividing automatically dedicates to public use those easements displayed on the plat. This is not because the individual lot owners might not claim private easements in addition to the public's easements but for the practical reason that they are usually content to exercise the right as members of the public.[1] In other states, where the act of platting does not necessarily dedicate to the public, an individual lot purchaser's claim to a private easement is more likely to be crucial. The purchaser's claim may sound in estoppel, based upon his having bought in reliance upon the availability of the easements shown on the plat.[2] Or—and this is the focus of our attention—his theory may be that easements were implied by his purchase by incorporating by reference the plat that showed the easement areas.

Private easements in platted streets and other access ways have been held to exist to some extent in all jurisdictions that have decided the question.[3] The question upon which there is a difference of opinion is the extent to which the lot owner has easements over the access ways. On this there are three general positions or rules. First is the so-called "broad" or "unity" rule, that the owner has a private easement over all parts of all ways shown on the plat.[4] Next is the "intermediate," "beneficial," or "full enjoyment" rule, which essentially is that the owner has private access easements over such platted ways as are reasonably beneficial to the use of his lot. This generally means he may not be denied use of any way if the deprivation would diminish his lot's market value.[5] Finally, the "narrow" or "necessary" rule is that the owner has private easements over only his abutting street and such connecting streets as are necessary to give access to the system of public streets and roads.[6] Examination of the decisions indicates that the three positions are not as neatly compartmentalized as their statements might seem. In several jurisdictions there are conflicting decisions, in which both the "narrow" rule and one of the broader rules are applied.[7] Some decisions that seem to fall into the "narrow" category are ones in which the courts have no occasion to consider a broader rule, because the facts show lot owners truly need to use platted streets to reach public ways. It is common to find courts in their reasoning using language of both estoppel and implied grant. Also, there is a tendency in some opinions to intermix a theory of implied private easement with the doctrine of dedica-

§ 8.6

1. See Scott v. Snyder, 73 Ohio App. 424, 54 N.E.2d 157 (1943); Shertzer v. Hillman Investment Co., 52 Wash. 492, 100 P. 982 (1909); Annot., 7 A.L.R.2d 607, 608–09 (1949).

2. See, e.g., Lindsay v. James, 188 Va. 646, 51 S.E.2d 326 (1949).

3. Annot., 7 A.L.R.2d 607, 612 (1949).

4. E.g., Trustees of Schools v. Dassow, 321 Ill. 346, 151 N.E. 896 (1926); Krzewinski v. Eaton Homes, Inc., 108 Ohio App. 175, 161 N.E.2d 88 (1958), appeal dismissed 169 Ohio St. 86, 157 N.E.2d 339 (1959) (dictum?); Annot., 7 A.L.R.2d 607, 613–33 (1949).

5. E.g., Lake Garda Co. v. D'Arche, 135 Conn. 449, 66 A.2d 120 (1949); Lindsay v. James, 188 Va. 646, 51 S.E.2d 326 (1949) (some

dependence on estoppel theory); Annot., 7 A.L.R.2d 607, 633–39 (1949).

6. E.g., Wellwood v. Havrah Mishna Anshi Sphard Cemetery Corp., 254 Mass. 350, 150 N.E. 203 (1926); In re Wooley Avenue, 270 N.Y. 368, 1 N.E.2d 467 (1936); In re East 177th St., 239 N.Y. 119, 145 N.E. 903 (1924); Annot., 7 A.L.R.2d 607, 639–43 (1949). N.b., however, that there are some New York decisions that appear to follow one of the broader rules. Annot., 7 A.L.R.2d, supra, at 643–47.

7. See the New York citations, id., and in general see Annot., 7 A.L.R.2d 607, 643–50 (1949).

tion to public use.[8] The suggestion is strong that, in a number of jurisdictions at least, litigants should not feel strictly bound by the language of all the decisions.

Besides the cases involving platted streets, there are a smaller number that deal with implied private easements for platted parks and playgrounds. As must be apparent, it will be difficult for a lot owner to succeed unless the court adopts the "broad" or "unity" rule of implication. By far most of the decisions implying private easements for these purposes do employ the "broad" rule.[9] A few courts, however, have stretched one of the narrower rules to fit the case of parks.[10] Again, as with street easements, one finds implied private easement theory intermixed with doctrines of estoppel and of public dedication.

§ 8.7   Easements by Prescription

This section may profitably be read together with section 11.7, covering adverse possession. Though the history of the two institutions is much different, in America today prescription and adverse possession have been blended.[1] With some differences that will be noted, it is accurate enough as a working doctrine to substitute "adverse use" (or "user") for "prescription," as courts commonly do.[2] The chief distinction is that in adverse possession the claimant occupies or possesses the disseisee's land, whereas in prescription he makes some easement-like use of it. As with adverse possession, if the prescriptive acts continue for the period of the statute of limitations, the prescriber acquires rights that correspond to the nature of use. Possession being the right carried by an estate, adverse possession creates an estate. Use being the right carried by an easement, adverse use creates an easement. To consummate the parallel with adverse possession, we may define prescription as the actual, open, notorious, hostile, "continuous," and "exclusive" *use* of another's land. "Continuous" and "exclusive" were put in quotations because these elements have a somewhat different meaning in the law of prescription than in adverse possession.

American prescription decisions discuss the doctrine or fiction of "lost grant" or "presumed grant," usually erroneously. Particularly objectionable are those opinions that say the doctrine is the foundation or origin of prescription.[3] In fact the doctrine developed in English law hundreds of years after prescription was established as a means of acquiring easements and related "incorporeal" interests. At that time, and indeed until 1832,

---

8. Examination of the decisions cited in the preceding four footnotes will show these conflicts and problems. For a general discussion, see Annot., 7 A.L.R.2d 607 (1949).

9. E.g., Caffey v. Parris, 186 Ga. 303, 197 S.E. 898 (1938); Schurtz v. Wescott, 286 Mich. 691, 282 N.W. 870 (1938); Putnam v. Dickinson, 142 N.W.2d 111 (N.D.1966) (some estoppel reasoning); Eidelbach v. Davis, 99 S.W.2d 1067 (Tex.Civ.App.1936), error dismissed (relief denied); Annot., 7 A.L.R.2d 607, 650–51 (1949).

10. See Annot., 7 A.L.R.2d 607, 660–67 (1949).

§ 8.7

1. See Stoebuck, The Fiction of Presumed Grant, 15 Kan.L.Rev. 17 (1966).

2. E.g., Truc v. Field, 269 Mass. 524, 169 N.E. 428 (1930); Romans v. Nadler, 217 Minn. 174, 14 N.W.2d 482 (1944); Winterringer v. Price, 370 P.2d 918 (Okl.1961); State ex rel. Shorett v. Blue Ridge Club, Inc., 22 Wn.2d 487, 156 P.2d 667 (1945).

3. E.g., Romans v. Nadler, 217 Minn. 174, 14 N.W.2d 482 (1944); Hester v. Sawyers, 41 N.M. 497, 71 P.2d 646 (1937); Big Cottonwood Tanner Ditch Co. v. Moyle, 109 Utah 213, 174 P.2d 148 (1946); Shellow v. Hagen, 9 Wis.2d 506, 101 N.W.2d 694 (1960).

English prescription theory depended upon a presumption that the prescriptive use dated back to "time immemorial," 3 September 1189, the day on which Richard I ascended the throne. To assist in establishing that presumption, a second presumption was created, that proof of use of an easement for the period of the statute of limitations raised an inference of a grant, now lost.[4] Lost grant is part of the historical development of American prescription law, but that is all. The blending of prescription and adverse possession, whether right or wrong in history and theory, has in fact made title arise simply by the running of the applicable statute of limitations. There is no need to presume usage back to 1189 (in America?) and so no need to presume a lost grant. Except for historical purposes, discussions of the subject should drop out of the legal literature.

It was just suggested that the elements for adverse use are enough the same as for adverse possession that the section on that subject is generally applicable here. Some differences need to be pointed out, however. The most basic difference is between "use" and "possession," for that determines whether activities that are adverse will gain an easement or estate for the claimant. Usually it is obvious whether the activity is only use, such as passing over land, or possession, marked by occupation, fencing, or permanent improvements. But there are some situations in which the distinction is difficult. The maintaining of a paved driveway is usually treated as a prescriptive use,[5] but its permanent, continuous, and substantial nature might lead a court to consider it possessory.[6] In the handful of cases involving overhanging house eaves, the courts have treated them as use and not possession.[7] There has been little attempt to formulate a test to distinguish use from possession. It seems the test should flow from the principle that possession implies not only the possessor's use but his exclusion of others, while use involves only limited activities that do not imply or require that others be excluded. Thus, in distinguishing adverse use from adverse possession, we are not ultimately concerned with the substantiality of physical objects but with whether the claimant's uses and purposes are inconsistent with other persons' shared uses.

We will see that adverse possession must be "hostile," which means it must be without the record owner's permission. This is true also of prescription, but some peculiar recurring fact patterns introduce special problems. Cases in which neighbors maintain a common driveway by oral agreement are one example. If they had made a written cross-easement agreement that complied with the Statute of Frauds, then each one would have an easement over his neighbor's land by formal grant. When the agreement is oral, however, whether each one acquires a prescriptive easement over his neighbor depends upon how a given court characterizes their transaction. Some courts reason that, while the oral agreement fails as a conveyance, it still has effect as mutual oral licenses, so that each one's use of his

---

4. For further details, see 2 American Law of Property, supra note 51, at §§ 8.48–8.51; Stoebuck, supra note 1, this section.

5. E.g., Shanks v. Floom, 162 Ohio St. 479, 124 N.E.2d 416 (1955); Johnson v. Whelan, 171 Okl. 243, 42 P.2d 882 (1935). See Annot., 27 A.L.R.2d 332 (1953).

6. See Predham v. Holfester, 32 N.J.Super. 419, 108 A.2d 458 (App.Div.1954), where the court, though finally holding the claim was not hostile, spoke of a driveway as "possession."

7. Romans v. Nadler, 217 Minn. 174, 14 N.W.2d 482 (1944); Annot., 58 A.L.R. 1037, 1038–39 (1929).

neighbor's strip is permissive and cannot be prescriptive.[8] Other courts regard the oral agreement as a complete nullity, neither conveyance nor license, so that each neighbor is using the other's land hostilely, without permission.[9]

Some of the common driveway cases turn in part upon a judicial presumption that one's use of another's land is, according to some decisions, hostile or, according to other decisions, permissive. This gets us into the question of whether there is or should be a general presumption that unexplained use is hostile or permissive. If a court indulges in the general presumption that unexplained use is permissive, then the adverse claimant has the burden to go forward with evidence showing hostility.[10] A presumption of permissiveness seems to flow from the concept that prescriptive rights are founded in the owner's "acquiescence," which in turn seems to be connected with mistaken notions about the doctrine of lost (or presumed) grant. As we saw, it is simply wrong, especially in America, to say prescriptive easements are founded in a lost grant. Prescriptive rights, like adverse possession title, are today founded in wrongful, hostile, trespassory acts that ripen into title when the statute of limitations bars the owner's action of trespass or ejectment. To talk about acquiescence or any kind of permission is to come back full circle on the true theory. Moreover, to indulge in a generalized presumption that an intruder is anything but a trespasser is contrary to the basic principle that the whole world must stay off the owner's land unless he affirmatively admits them. Better are the decisions that indulge in the presumption that the unexplained use or occupation of another's land is hostile.[11] Then if the owner wishes to rebut by showing permission, he may do so by proof of specific facts that should be known to him or his predecessors.

The foregoing is not to say that permission may not in a proper case be implied in fact. Some courts recognize a presumption that use of unenclosed and unoccupied land is permissive.[12] It is said that, since owners of such land ordinarily allow others to make light, occasional uses, permission is presumed. Another time courts speak of "presumption" is when the owner originally gave knowing permission by agreement or license and then the use allegedly became hostile later. The adverse claimant has a burden to show notorious acts beyond the scope of the permission, such as fencing, or words that clearly show the transformation from permissive to hostile.[13] At work here seems to be a doctrine analogous to ouster in adverse possession.

---

8. Mueller v. Keller, 18 Ill.2d 334, 164 N.E.2d 28 (1960); Sexton v. Holt, 91 Kan. 26, 136 P. 934 (1913); Annot., 27 A.L.R.2d 332, 359–62 (1953).

9. Alstad v. Boyer, 228 Minn. 307, 37 N.W.2d 372 (1949); Shanks v. Floom, 162 Ohio St. 479, 124 N.E.2d 416 (1955); Annot., 27 A.L.R.2d 332 (1953).

10. E.g., Mueller v. Keller, 18 Ill.2d 334, 164 N.E.2d 28 (1960); Dartnell v. Bidwell, 115 Me. 227, 98 A. 743 (1916).

11. See Alstad v. Boyer, 228 Minn. 307, 37 N.W.2d 372 (1949); Shanks v. Floom, 162 Ohio St. 479, 124 N.E.2d 416 (1955).

12. E.g., Hester v. Sawyers, 41 N.M. 497, 71 P.2d 646 (1937) (dictum); State ex rel. Shorett v. Blue Ridge Club, 22 Wn.2d 487, 156 P.2d 667 (1945); Shellow v. Hagen, 9 Wis.2d 506, 101 N.W.2d 694 (1960) (dictum).

13. Hester v. Sawyers, 41 N.M. 497, 71 P.2d 646 (1937); Lunt v. Kitchens, 123 Utah 488, 260 P.2d 535 (1953). Cf. Mueller v. Keller, 18 Ill.2d 334, 164 N.E.2d 28 (1960); Holbrook v. Taylor, 532 S.W.2d 763 (Ky.1976).

Consider a question that is the opposite of the last one. If an adverse claimant begins using the owner's land in a way that is hostile and otherwise prescriptive, how may the use become permissive? Clearly it may if the parties execute a formal easement agreement or agree to an informal license. However, the slight authority on the question holds that unilateral, unsolicited consent by the owner to the user does not interrupt a period of adverse use already begun.[14] The decisions purport to distinguish "permission" from "consent," which they equate with the "acquiescence" that is supposedly the "foundation" of prescription. Fallacies of the "acquiescence" doctrine were previously pointed out. Thus, the notion that unsolicited consent is not permission seems to rest on a weak theoretical basis. Moreover it is harsh on the landowner who discovers a prescriptive use on his land, for it apparently leaves him no sure way to stop it short of a lawsuit or a physical confrontation.[15] For both theoretical and practical reasons, an owner who discovers adverse use (or possession) should be able to "thrust" permission on the wrongdoer, perhaps by giving and recording a notice.

Exclusivity of possession is one of the essential elements of adverse possession, meaning that it may not be shared with the owner. If this element exists at all in prescription, it is only in a special and narrow way. In the nature of things, when there is an easement, a limited use of an owner's land, the owner may legally make any use of the easement area that does not actually interfere with the easement. And so with prescriptive easements. The owner, or presumably anyone else, may use the easement area in any way that does not prevent the claimed adverse use.[16] Only in that limited sense can it be said the adverse use must be exclusive, almost a play on words. In a different meaning of exclusivity, however, some decisions have adopted the rule that the public at large cannot prescribe.[17] Often these decisions involve public use of unenclosed, unoccupied land, so that courts may also reason the use is impliedly permissive. Prescription by a large but definable group, such as the members of a large organization, is generally allowed.[18] Some courts do allow the public to prescribe, though they seem to require strong proof of hostility, again perhaps because cases

14. Naporra v. Weckwerth, 178 Minn. 203, 226 N.W. 569 (1929); Huff v. Northern Pacific Railway Co., 38 Wn.2d 103, 228 P.2d 121 (1951); Annot., 65 A.L.R. 128 (1930) (citing only *Naporra* case). Cf. Cremer v. Cremer Rodeo Land & Livestock Co., 192 Mont. 208, 627 P.2d 1199 (1981); Macias v. Guymon Industrial Foundation, 595 P.2d 430 (Okl.1979).

15. If unsolicited consent will not stop adverse use, consider these examples: (1) The landowner is a shopping center, and certain individuals regularly cut through the parking area on their way to and from work. Consent in the form of signboards will have no legal effect. Barring access with gates or chains is wholly impractical. So is (are?) a lawsuit (lawsuits?). (2) The owner brings an action of trespass and prevails. The court awards damages, probably nominal, but refuses an injunction on some equitable ground such as balancing hardships. See Crescent Mining Co. v.

Silver King Mining Co., 17 Utah 444, 54 P. 244 (1898). Will the use continue to run the statute of limitations?

16. Fowler v. Matthews, 204 S.W.2d 80 (Tex.Civ.App.1947); Shellow v. Hagen, 9 Wis.2d 506, 101 N.W.2d 694 (1960). But see Othen v. Rosier, 148 Tex. 485, 226 S.W.2d 622 (1950).

17. E.g., State ex rel. Haman v. Fox, 100 Idaho 140, 594 P.2d 1093 (1979); Scoville v. Fisher, 181 Neb. 496, 149 N.W.2d 339 (1967).

18. See, e.g., Confederated Salish & Kootenai Tribes v. Vulles, 437 F.2d 177 (9th Cir. 1971) (Indian tribe); Williams v. Harrsch, 58 Or.App. 301, 648 P.2d 386 (1982), review denied 293 Or. 634, 652 P.2d 810 (1982) (public, as well as individual claimant, acquired prescriptive easement for recreational purposes); Mountaineers v. Wymer, 56 Wn.2d 721, 355 P.2d 341 (1960) (hiking and climbing club).

often involve unenclosed, unoccupied land.[19] Where the public is so allowed, it generally is held that an individual may not obtain a private prescriptive easement by making only the same use the public makes.[20]

The element of continuity, necessary to adverse possession, is part of prescription but with a meaning adapted to the nature of easements. In the typical adverse possession case, even though the disseisor is not bodily on the land every minute, he has some sort of improvements that stay there. Cases of intermittent use of wild and unenclosed land create division in the courts, though adverse possession is in theory possible.[21] An easement is like that; its holder uses it intermittently, as he has need. In prescription cases the courts accept as continuous enough a frequency of use that is normal for the kind of easement claimed.[22]

Adverse possession elements of "actual," "open," and "notorious," closely related factually, are also prescription elements. Obviously the adverse claimant must make some physical use, and it must have some degree of definiteness.[23] Most prescriptive easements are for walkways, driveways, or roads on the surface, so that if there is use at all, it is open, visible, and confined to a fairly well defined area. While slight variations in the line of travel are acceptable, it often is said that the prescriptive use of an access way must follow a definite or ascertainable route.[24] However, if a jurisdiction permits easements to wander over land for recreational purposes, it should be possible to establish such an easement by prescription, though proof may be difficult.[25] Prescriptive easements for drains, pipes, or sewers pose a special problem. If they are on the surface, the use is usually open and notorious. But if they are concealed beneath the ground, they generally have been held not to be so.[26]

Some states have special statutes of limitation that not only establish a limitation period but list elements of adverse possession. When such statutes list elements not part of the common law, usually color of title or payment of taxes, the question has sometimes arisen whether these elements shall be required for prescriptive easements. Because of the blending of adverse possession and prescription in America, previously noted, some

19. E.g., State ex rel. Thornton v. Hay, 254 Or. 584, 462 P.2d 671 (1969) (dictum); Fowler v. Matthews, 204 S.W.2d 80 (Tex.Civ.App. 1947); Gray v. McDonald, 46 Wn.2d 574, 283 P.2d 135 (1955).

20. Pirman v. Confer, 273 N.Y. 357, 7 N.E.2d 262 (1937), reargument denied 274 N.Y. 570, 10 N.E.2d 556 (1937), motion granted 275 N.Y. 624, 11 N.E.2d 788 (1937); Annot., 111 A.L.R. 221 (1937).

21. Compare Monroe v. Rawlings, 331 Mich. 49, 49 N.W.2d 55 (1951), with Murray v. Bousquet, 154 Wash. 42, 280 P. 935 (1929).

22. Confederated Salish & Kootenai Tribes v. Vulles, 437 F.2d 177 (9th Cir.1971) (use "continuous"); Holbrook v. Taylor, 532 S.W.2d 763 (Ky.1976) (not "continuous"); Romans v. Nadler, 217 Minn. 174, 14 N.W.2d 482 (1944) (use twice a year not "continuous"); Shellow v. Hagen, 9 Wis.2d 506, 101 N.W.2d 694 (1960) (use during summers "continuous").

23. Shellow v. Hagen, 9 Wis.2d 506, 101 N.W.2d 694 (1960). Cf. Parker & Edgarton v. Foote, 19 Wend. 309 (N.Y.1838) (no prescriptive easement for light and air; no physical use).

24. Nelms v. Steelhammer, 225 Ark. 429, 283 S.W.2d 118 (1955); Descheemaeker v. Anderson, 131 Mont. 322, 310 P.2d 587 (1957); Othen v. Rosier, 148 Tex. 485, 226 S.W.2d 622 (1950).

25. Vigil v. Baltzley, 79 N.M. 659, 448 P.2d 171 (1968); State ex rel. Thornton v. Hay, 254 Or. 584, 462 P.2d 671 (1969) (dictum); Anderson v. Osguthorpe, 29 Utah 2d 32, 504 P.2d 1000 (1972); 4 H. Tiffany, Real Property § 1194 (3d ed. 1975). But see State ex rel. Haman v. Fox, 100 Idaho 140, 594 P.2d 1093 (1979).

26. See Annot., 55 A.L.R.2d 1144 (1957).

courts have required the additional elements.[27] Other courts take the contrary view, that the only part of the statute that applies to prescription is the limitation period.[28] This latter view seems the better, on the theory that the elements of prescription arose and exist by judge-made law, independent of any statute of limitations. Indeed, the elements developed in the law of prescription first and were in America incorporated into adverse possession. Also, it is unrealistic to require a prescriptive user to pay taxes, because they will not be separately assessed to him.

§ 8.8 Creation by Estoppel or Part Performance

"In every American jurisdiction except North Carolina, a person may become unconditionally entitled to the use of land through an oral agreement followed by certain types of conduct. * * * Pursuant to the agreement, the licensee must have expended money, property or labor which he would not have spent but for the license, and the licensor must have had reason to anticipate the expenditure."[1] The result on the facts seems clear enough. It is when they attempt to state its theoretical or doctrinal basis that courts run into trouble.

Courts have used a number of descriptive phrases for the underlying theory. "Irrevocable license" is one, which describes the result but gives little clue to the mechanism at work. All it suggests is that a license, ordinarily not an interest in land and revocable, has been transformed into a corresponding interest in land, an easement or profit. Alternative phrases, "licenses irrevocable in equity," "easements in equity," and "oral contracts enforceable in equity," suffer from the same shortcoming.[2] Equity has no general rule that all oral conveyances are taken out of the Statute of Frauds but only specific doctrines, limited to certain fact patterns.

A lot of the verbiage on "irrevocable licenses" or "oral easements" has made the subject far more mysterious than it needs to be. All we are doing is to take an oral agreement for an interest in land out of the Statute of Frauds or, as Corbin said, finding facts that block the Statute's application.[3] There are two recognized equitable doctrines to accomplish this, estoppel and part performance. Under one or the other doctrine oral conveyances or agreements to convey interests in land, even the fee simple estate, can be enforced. Surely a doctrine powerful enough to uphold the oral conveyance

---

27. Annot., 112 A.L.R. 545 (1938).

28. Hester v. Sawyers, 41 N.M. 497, 71 P.2d 646 (1937); Id.

§ 8.8

1. Conard, Unwritten Agreements for the Use of Land, 14 Rocky Mtn.L.Rev. 153–65, 294–314, 313 (1942). Research, in the West Digest system and by electronic search, fails to disclose a North Carolina decision since the date of Professor Conard's article that allows an oral easement to be enforced. It seems that North Carolina rejects the theories of equitable estoppel and part performance for the creation of any interest in land. However, the state allows the oral grantee restriction for expenditures. Pickelsimer v. Pickel-

simer, 257 N.C. 696, 127 S.E.2d 557 (1962). See generally N.C.Gen.Stats. § 22–2; Sanders v. Wilkerson, 285 N.C. 215, 204 S.E.2d 17 (1974); Hill v. Smith, 51 N.C.App. 670, 277 S.E.2d 542 (1981), review denied 303 N.C. 543, 281 S.E.2d 392 (1981); Simmons v. Morton, 1 N.C.App. 308, 161 S.E.2d 222 (1968). Since it is unlikely that any jurisdiction has adopted the North Carolina position since 1942, Professor Conard's quoted statement must be as accurate now as when he wrote it.

2. E.g., Croasdale v. Lanigan, 129 N.Y. 604, 29 N.E. 824 (1892) ("license * * * irrevocable"). See Conard, preceding note.

3. 2 A. Corbin, Contracts § 276 (1950).

of a fee estate ought to suffice for the oral conveyance of an easement or profit, a much lesser interest.

Judge Clark argued that estoppel is the true basis for enforcing oral easements.[4] If this theory is employed, one reasons as follows: the oral grantor represented to the grantee that he had an easement or profit upon the grantor's land; in reliance upon the representation, the grantee expended money or labor or made improvements upon or with reference to the easement or profit—detrimental reliance; and therefore, the grantor became estopped to deny the easement or profit. The theory fits the fact pattern we have supposed, and it seems now to be the theory predominantly used in the decisions.[5] Some decisions contain even stronger language, that to allow the oral grantor to renege would work a "fraud" on the grantee.[6] Not only is there seldom true fraud present, as Clark pointed out,[7] but, even if the grantor did have fraudulent intent, the estoppel theory is as far as one needs to go to resolve the case. One should not waste a cannon to kill a rabbit.

The same facts that invoke the estoppel theory will usually support the equitable part performance theory. Here the reasoning is that the oral grantee's acts, making improvements of a kind one would make if one had an easement or profit, give tangible evidence, independent of the spoken words, that such an interest exists. The acts themselves "speak of" an easement or profit; the trier of fact need not rely on the oral statements alone.[8] Though Judge Clark preferred estoppel, some courts have adopted the part performance theory.[9] We do not need to make a choice between the two theories here. Both are recognized equitable theories to excuse the operation of the Statute of Frauds upon oral conveyances.

§ 8.9   Scope of Easements and Profits

The "scope" of an easement or profit is what its holder may do with it, the purposes for which it may be used. This section will also include something about locating easements. As a general point of beginning, it may be said that scope and location are determined by the creating words of a deed or enforceable oral representation when an easement or profit is expressly created, or by the events that create an easement by prescription or implication. If the words or events make the scope or location perfectly clear, there is no problem that presently concerns us.[1] Only when the operative words or events leave one of these matters unclear, do we have a problem. Prescriptive and implied servitudes are always likely to present

---

4. C. Clark, Real Covenants and Other Interests Which "Run with Land" 59–64 (2d ed. 1947).

5. E.g., Camp v. Milam, 291 Ala. 12, 277 So.2d 95 (1973); Holbrook v. Taylor, 532 S.W.2d 763 (Ky.1976); Cooke v. Ramponi, 38 Cal.2d 282, 239 P.2d 638 (1952) (also discussion of part performance theory); Stoner v. Zucker, 148 Cal. 516, 83 P. 808 (1906); Ricenbaw v. Kraus, 157 Neb. 723, 61 N.W.2d 350 (1953). Cf. Vrazel v. Skrabanek, 725 S.W.2d 709 (Tex. 1987) (landowner estopped to deny use of road, though he had made no oral agreement it could be used).

6. E.g., Stoner v. Zucker, 148 Cal. 516, 83 P. 808 (1906); Mueller v. Keller, 18 Ill.2d 334, 164 N.E.2d 28 (1960).

7. Clark, supra note 4, this section.

8. The classic exposition of this theory is by Justice Cardozo in Sleeth v. Sampson, 237 N.Y. 69, 142 N.E. 355 (1923).

9. E.g., Camp v. Milam, 291 Ala. 12, 277 So.2d 95 (1973) ("executed license" and also "estoppel"); Buckles–Irvine Coal Co. v. Kennedy Coal Corp., 134 Va. 1, 114 S.E. 233 (1922).

§ 8.9

1. See Wilson v. Abrams, 1 Cal.App.3d 1030, 82 Cal.Rptr. 272 (1969).

questions of scope or location, since the events giving rise to them are not communicative acts. Even with easements and profits created by direct verbal act, draftsmen have a deplorable tendency to be vague about scope and location.

The draftsman should describe the location of an easement or profit so that a surveyor can run out the location by reference to the document alone. Expressions like "over the south 20 feet of Lot 2" or a metes and bounds description are best. In a pinch, such as when the parties will not pay for a survey of a sinuous roadway, it may be necessary to refer to an existing road or other feature, describing its general location as accurately as possible. Incorporation by reference of a plot plan may help. When the grant is entirely vague, as "a roadway [how wide?] across Blackacre from the county road to Whiteacre [what route?]," many decisions hold that, rather than for the grant to fail, a way that is reasonable and convenient for both parties is implied. The grantor has the power in the first instance to fix a reasonable and convenient location. If he fails to act, the grantee may fix the location. If the parties establish an easement on the ground by use and acquiesce in it, this will fix the location. What is a reasonable and convenient location is a judicial question, so that a court will have to fix it if the parties disagree.[2] Once the location is definitely determined, the holder cannot be compelled to accept a substitute route.[3]

Just as draftsmen are often lax in describing location, so too they frequently fail to describe the scope or purposes of an easement or profit with sufficient particularity. Precise drafting, instead of simply saying, "a driveway" or "a pipeline easement," might spell out the kind, maximum weight, and number per day of vehicles or the maximum number and size of pipes. In some cases it may be appropriate to limit the uses by reference to the activities on the dominant tenement that the easement may serve, e.g., "for vehicles to serve one single-family residence only." Attention should be given to "secondary easements," such as the easement holder's rights to improve and maintain an easement or profit. In the absence of an agreement on the subject, the owner of the servient tenement has no duty to maintain the easement; that is up to the easement holder. It should also follow that the easement holder is liable to third persons for injuries caused them by lack of maintenance.[4] When details about "secondary easements" are not spelled out, the general principle is that "reasonable" uses are implied. What is reasonable depends upon the surrounding circumstances, most importantly, in the case of an easement appurtenant, the activities that one might be expected to conduct on the dominant tenement.[5]

As just suggested, when the creating language is general, an appurtenant easement may be used to support, not only the activities carried on on

---

2. See Ingelson v. Olson, 199 Minn. 422, 272 N.W. 270 (1937); Alban v. R.K. Co., 15 Ohio St.2d 229, 239 N.E.2d 22 (1968); Clearwater Realty Co. v. Bouchard, 146 Vt. 359, 505 A.2d 1189 (1985); 2 American Law of Property § 8.66 (A.J. Casner ed. 1952); Annot., 110 A.L.R. 174 (1937).

3. Sakansky v. Wein, 86 N.H. 337, 169 A. 1 (1933).

4. See Reyna v. Ayco Dev. Corp., 788 S.W.2d 722 (Tex.App.1990).

5. See, e.g., Farnes v. Lane, 281 Minn. 222, 161 N.W.2d 297 (1968) (Does road to a lake include a boat pier?); Sakansky v. Wein, 86 N.H. 337, 169 A. 1 (1933) (How much headroom for a driveway?); Shingleton v. State, 260 N.C. 451, 133 S.E.2d 183 (1963) (Use related to dominant tenement).

the dominant tenement at the time of creation, but to a certain extent changing future activities. The permitted purposes are subject to a degree of change or growth; the question is, how much? Perhaps the best formula is that the purposes may keep up with those changes that might be reasonably anticipated for the dominant tenement—evolutionary but not revolutionary changes.[6] So, for instance, a general passway easement permits gradually changing uses, to correspond with normal changes in modes of transportation and normal development of the dominant tenement.[7] Similar principles govern growth and changes in easements created by prescription or by implication from prior use or from necessity, but the manner of creation poses special problems in applying the principles. These problems lie more in defining the purposes originally permitted than they do in determining the permissible degree of change or growth after that point. With an easement created by implication from prior use, we should be able to determine the originally permitted uses by what they were when the two parcels were severed.[8] When the implied easement is a way of necessity, we must determine the original location and scope from what is then necessary, which may be a difficult task factually.[9] The original scope and location of a prescriptive easement are determined by the kind of adverse use made during the prescriptive period, allowing for some flexibility of use. Once we describe the original scope and location of an easement created by implication or prescription, it should be subject to change and growth in the same way as would a granted easement of the same original description.[10]

An easement appurtenant may be used to serve only the land to which it is appurtenant. It cannot, for instance, be used to pass over the dominant tenement to reach another parcel.[11] Nor may it be used to serve integrated, inseparable activities conducted in a building that sits astride the dominant tenement and an adjoining parcel. As long as the usage cannot be separated, a court will enjoin any use of the easement.[12] There is even authority

6. See Petersen v. Friedman, 162 Cal. App.2d 245, 328 P.2d 264 (1958); Birdsey v. Kosienski, 140 Conn. 403, 101 A.2d 274 (1953); Cameron v. Barton, 272 S.W.2d 40 (Ky.1954). Much interest has focused recently on the "rails to trails" question: when a railroad abandons a rail line, may its "railroad" easement be used as a public recreational trail? Is a recreational trail within the scope of a railroad easement? Courts are divided on this issue. See, e.g., State by Washington Wildlife Preservation, Inc. v. State, Dept. of Natural Resources, 329 N.W.2d 543 (Minn.1983), cert. denied 463 U.S. 1209, 103 S.Ct. 3540, 77 L.Ed.2d 1390 (1983) (yes); Lawson v. State, 107 Wn.2d 444, 730 P.2d 1308 (1986) (no). In Preseault v. Interstate Commerce Com'n, 494 U.S. 1, 110 S.Ct. 914, 108 L.Ed.2d 1 (1990), the Supreme Court avoided answering the issue, though they held that if the trail was not within the scope, compulsory conversion would be a taking.

7. See Birdsey and Cameron cases, preceding note; Miller v. Street, 663 S.W.2d 797 (Tenn.App.1983) (right to take water from spring, originally by bucket, could change to allow piping of water).

8. See Fristoe v. Drapeau, 35 Cal.2d 5, 215 P.2d 729 (1950).

9. See Soltis v. Miller, 444 Pa. 357, 282 A.2d 369 (1971).

10. See Baldwin v. Boston & Maine Railroad, 181 Mass. 166, 63 N.E. 428 (1902) (prescriptive easement). General discussions of scope and change in implied and prescriptive easements will be found in 2 American Law of Property, supra note 1, at §§ 8.68, 8.69, and Restatement of Property §§ 477–81 (1944). While these two sources formulate the principles somewhat differently than they are stated here, the meanings are generally consistent.

11. Crimmins v. Gould, 149 Cal.App.2d 383, 308 P.2d 786 (1957); Kanefsky v. Dratch Construction Co., 376 Pa. 188, 101 A.2d 923 (1954); S.S. Kresge Co. v. Winkelman Realty Co., 260 Wis. 372, 50 N.W.2d 920 (1952).

12. Penn Bowling Recreation Center, Inc. v. Hot Shoppes, 179 F.2d 64 (D.C.Cir.1949); McCullough v. Broad Exchange Co., 101 App. Div. 566, 92 N.Y.S. 533 (1905), affirmed 184 N.Y. 592, 77 N.E. 1191 (1906). Accord Brown

that if the inseparable use is permanent, rather than simply to issue a permanent injunction, the court will declare the easement extinguished.[13] While the appurtenant easement may serve only the dominant tenement, unless it is limited by its creating language, it may be used to serve all parts of that tenement. The question usually arises when land is subdivided into lots or parcels after the easement is granted. In such cases the usual result is that subdivision does not per se prevent the easement's serving the individual parts.[14] Of course if development of the subdivided land will cause the easement to be surcharged—used beyond ways that might have been reasonably anticipated—then the excess use will not be permitted.[15]

Deeds for railroad right of ways present special problems that might be called scope problems. Here the issue is whether the railroad gets an estate, a fee simple absolute or perhaps a defeasible fee, or only an easement of passage. To a considerable extent the question arises out of the use of words of grant such as "land," "strip," and "right of way," certain words in habendum clauses, and words of purpose such as "for railway purposes." It also seems to some extent that the nature of railroad operations, which, if the railroad company has an easement, largely exclude the owner of the servient tenement from any shared use, add to the confusion. In any event, the decisions are in considerable disarray.[16] To attempt statements beyond that would unduly lengthen the discussion.

Since an easement or profit gives only limited uses of the servient land, the person entitled to general possession may make all other uses that do not unreasonably interfere with the easement or profit.[17] If the easement holder is not at the time using a certain part of the easement area, the owner of the servient tenement may use that area, subject to the easement holder's right to use it later.[18] The concurrent rights the owner has, he may transfer to

v. Voss, 38 Wn.App. 777, 689 P.2d 1111 (1984), judgment reversed 105 Wn.2d 366, 715 P.2d 514 (1986) (easement appurtenant could not be used to serve house that sat astride property line between dominant tenement and another parcel, but injunction denied on equitable grounds).

13. *Penn Bowling* case, preceding note.

14. Moylan v. Dykes, 181 Cal.App.3d 561, 226 Cal.Rptr. 673 (1986) (appurtenant roadway easement serves both halves of land after dominant tenement is divided); Martin v. Music, 254 S.W.2d 701 (Ky.1953); Bang v. Forman, 244 Mich. 571, 222 N.W. 96 (1928) (dictum); Cox v. Glenbrook Co., 78 Nev. 254, 371 P.2d 647 (1962); Cushman Virginia Corp. v. Barnes, 204 Va. 245, 129 S.E.2d 633 (1963).

15. This point was previously covered. Also see Martin v. Music (dictum), and Bang v. Forman, preceding note.

16. E.g., Johnson v. Ocean Shore Railroad Co., 16 Cal.App.3d 429, 94 Cal.Rptr. 68 (1971); Sowers v. Illinois Central Gulf R. Co., 152 Ill.App.3d 163, 105 Ill.Dec. 76, 503 N.E.2d 1082 (1987) (deeds that said "convey * * * strip of land" or "convey and warrant ... right of way" all conveyed fee simple estate); Harvest Queen Mill & Elevator Co. v. Sanders,

189 Kan. 536, 370 P.2d 419 (1962); City of Port Isabel v. Missouri Pacific R. Co., 729 S.W.2d 939 (Tex.App.1987) (deed that said "conveys in fee simple * * * a right-of-way" conveyed only easement). See Annot., 6 A.L.R.3d 973–1039 (1966).

17. Harding v. Pinello, 518 P.2d 846 (Colo. App.1973) (locked gate not reasonable); Minneapolis Athletic Club v. Cohler, 287 Minn. 254, 177 N.W.2d 786 (1970); Messer v. Leveson, 23 A.D.2d 834, 259 N.Y.S.2d 662 (1965) (locked gate reasonable); Shingleton v. State, 260 N.C. 451, 133 S.E.2d 183 (1963) (locked gate reasonable); Energy Transportation Systems, Inc. v. Kansas City Southern Railway Co., 638 P.2d 459 (Okl.1981). See Borrowman v. Howland, 119 Ill.App.3d 493, 75 Ill.Dec. 313, 457 N.E.2d 103 (1983) (owner of servient tenement could not maintain shed over area of drainage ditch easement because it would interfere with the right to maintain the easement). See also Deterding v. United States, 107 Ct.Cl. 656, 69 F.Supp. 214 (1947).

18. City of Pasadena v. California–Michigan Land & Water Co., 17 Cal.2d 576, 110 P.2d 983 (1941); Alban v. R.K. Co., 15 Ohio St.2d 229, 239 N.E.2d 22 (1968); Thompson v. Smith, 59 Wn.2d 397, 367 P.2d 798 (1962).

third persons.[19]

§ 8.10   Transfer of Easements and Profits

The word "appurtenant" signifies that an easement appurtenant is attached to and a part of the right of possession of its dominant tenement. Use of the easement is one of the incidents of ownership of the dominant tenement, though of course this incident is enjoyed upon other land. Therefore, any act that is sufficient to transfer title or even rightful possession of the dominant tenement will carry the easement rights with it. No mention need be made of the easement; it goes along like a dog's tail goes along with a sale of the dog. Nor may the easement be transferred separately from the dominant tenement, for "appurtenant" also signifies that the easement may serve only the dominant tenement, as we have seen.[1]

Easements in gross present a different problem. Since there is no dominant tenement to which they are appurtenant, if they can pass at all, it must be by an independent act of transfer of the easement itself. Though easements in gross exist freely and in large numbers in America, probably because English law traditionally questioned their existence,[2] there has been some question about their transferability even in America. It is clear that easements in gross for commercial purposes are alienable.[3] Any other rule would be disastrous for, say, a public utility company that sought to transfer its utility easements to another company. The word "commercial" here does not refer only to easements held for use in a business but also to easements held by private persons that have economic value, as contrasted with a purpose of the holder's personal pleasure. Such "personal" easements in gross, of which examples are easements for the holder's recreation, are probably not alienable, though authority for the proposition seems to be speculative discussion more than caselaw.[4] Behind the commercial-personal dichotomy is the principle of intent, that the grantor would not intend the holder to transfer an easement that was for the limited purpose of serving the holder's person. Indeed, the Restatement, which has done much to shape the law in this area, would make the question of alienability of

19. City of Pasadena v. California–Michigan Land & Water Co., 17 Cal.2d 576, 110 P.2d 983 (1941).

§ 8.10

1. 2 American Law of Property, supra note 1, at § 8.71; Restatement of Property § 487 (1944).

2. See note 7, supra § 8.9, and related text.

3. Johnston v. Michigan Consolidated Gas Co., 337 Mich. 572, 60 N.W.2d 464 (1953); Kansas City Area Transportation Authority v. Ashley, 485 S.W.2d 641 (Mo.App.1972) (dictum); Geffine v. Thompson, 76 Ohio App. 64, 62 N.E.2d 590 (1945); Miller v. Lutheran Conference & Camp Association, 331 Pa. 241, 200 A. 646 (1938); Douglas v. Medical Investors, Inc., 256 S.C. 440, 182 S.E.2d 720 (1971). But see Stockdale v. Yerden, 220 Mich. 444, 190

N.W. 225 (1922) (easement to remove timber not alienable); Restatement of Property § 489 (1944). But cf. McCastle v. Scanlon, 337 Mich. 122, 59 N.W.2d 114 (1953) ("license" to remove timber for one year not alienable). For evidence that the transferability of easements in gross is still unsettled, see Note, *The Easement in Gross Revisited: Transferability and Divisibility Since 1945*, 39 Vand.L.Rev. 109 (1986).

4. See 2 American Law of Property, supra note 1, at §§ 8.75–8.83; Restatement of Property § 491 (1944). See also Simes, Assignability of Easements in Gross in American Law, 22 Mich.L.Rev. 521 (1924); Note, 40 Dick.L.Rev. 46 (1935); and Comment (signed "W.R.V.": William R. Vance), 32 Yale L.J. 813 (1923), all of which advocate assignability of easements in gross without making the commercial-personal distinction.

easements in gross turn upon "the manner or the terms of their creation." [5]

In contrast with easements in gross, profits a prendre in gross are freely alienable. This has been clearly understood since at least *Mountjoy's Case* in 1583.[6] Since nearly all profits are in gross, nearly all are separately alienable. We will see in the next section that there are serious questions about their divisibility or apportionability, but not about alienability per se.

§ 8.11 Divisibility or Apportionability of Easements and Profits

We previously discussed whether an easement appurtenant continues to serve a dominant tenement that is divided into parcels.[1] For easements or profits in gross, which have no dominant tenement, the corresponding question is whether they may be divided or apportioned by being transferred to more than one person. An easement or profit that may be so transferred was traditionally called "admeasurable." The underlying problem is that, to allow more than one person to use an easement or to exploit a profit when it was created for only one, may work a surcharge or additional burden upon that granted.[2] The key to solving the problem is to determine what is the "measure" of the easement or profit.

When the grantee received an "exclusive" easement or profit, the right to make sole use of the easement or to take all of a substance from the land, then he may transfer to as many other persons as he wishes.[3] No surcharge is worked by the division because any number of grantees cannot use any more than was granted; the measure was "all." Similarly, it should follow that if the creating instrument established an absolute measure less than all, such as so many passages per day or so many tons of rock per day, the right may be divided. Usage by the several grantees could not exceed that granted.

Divisibility problems are acute when the easement or profit is not exclusive and does not contain an absolute measure. Examples are "an easement of passage" or "a right to remove rock." Courts sometimes say flatly that a non-exclusive easement of profit is not divisible.[4] It seems more accurate, however, to say that whether a non-exclusive easement or profit may be divided depends ultimately upon the grantor's intent. If the creat-

---

5. Restatement of Property, supra, preceding note.

6. Earl of Huntington v. Lord Mountjoy, 1 And. 307, 123 Eng.Rep. 488, Godb. 17, 78 Eng. Rep. 11 (C.P. 1583). Accord, Loch Sheldrake Associates v. Evans, 306 N.Y. 297, 118 N.E.2d 444 (1954); Stanton v. T.L. Herbert & Sons, 141 Tenn. 440, 211 S.W. 353 (1919); Co.Litt. * 164 b. (analyzing *Mountjoy's Case*).

§ 8.11

1. See § 8.9, supra.

2. See Jolliff v. Hardin Cable Television Co., 26 Ohio St.2d 103, 269 N.E.2d 588 (1971), reversing 22 Ohio App.2d 49, 258 N.E.2d 244 (1970); Hinds v. Phillips Petroleum Co., 591 P.2d 697 (Okl.1979); Stanton v. T.L. Herbert & Sons, 141 Tenn. 440, 211 S.W. 353 (1919).

3. Hoffman v. Capitol Cablevision System, Inc., 52 A.D.2d 313, 383 N.Y.S.2d 674 (1976), appeal denied 40 N.Y.2d 806, 390 N.Y.S.2d 1025, 359 N.E.2d 438 (1976); Hinds v. Phillips Petroleum Co., 591 P.2d 697 (Okl.1979); Stanton v. T.L. Herbert & Sons, 141 Tenn. 440, 211 S.W. 353 (1919) (dictum); Restatement of Property § 493, Comment b (1944). See also Jolliff v. Hardin Cable Television Co., 22 Ohio App.2d 49, 258 N.E.2d 244 (1970) (dictum), reversed 26 Ohio St.2d 103, 269 N.E.2d 588 (1971).

4. E.g., Jolliff v. Hardin Cable Television Co., 22 Ohio App.2d 49, 258 N.E.2d 244 (1970), reversed 26 Ohio St.2d 103, 269 N.E.2d 588 (1971); Stanton v. T.L. Herbert & Sons, 141 Tenn. 440, 211 S.W. 353 (1919).

ing instrument contains language that shows he anticipated or was willing that it might be divided, then it may be.[5] Some recent decisions have even found such a willingness when the right was granted to the grantee, "its successors and assigns." [6] The fact that an easement or profit is non-exclusive is a powerful factor tending to show, or even raising a presumption, that divisibility was not intended, but it is not always conclusive.[7] An exception of sorts to what has been said, recognized since *Mountjoy's Case,* is that it is no division to transfer an easement or profit to two or more persons who will use it "as one stock." [8] Persons who act "as one stock" are usually partners, joint venturers, or a corporation.

§ 8.12   Termination of Easements and Profits

The most obvious way in which an easement or profit may be terminated is by the holder's express release to the owner of the servient tenement. This should be accomplished in an instrument executed with the same formalities required to grant an easement or profit, generally a deed in the form required to convey an estate in land.[1]

Like other interests in land, easements may be limited to a definite time by their creating language. Presumably, a servitude not so limited, sometimes misnamed a perpetual easement or profit, will have the duration of the estate of him who created it, usually a fee simple estate. But there is no reason a servitude cannot be granted expressly for the duration of a lesser estate, such as a defeasible fee, a life estate, or an estate for years.[2] Such an interest should not, for instance, be called a leasehold but an easement or profit of the duration of a leasehold or simply an easement or profit for so many years. Express time limits do not seem very common, but they can be useful and should be considered.

A servitude's duration may be limited by implication as well as by express language. This is most likely to occur when an easement or profit was created for a certain purpose but can no longer serve that purpose. For example, a pipeline easement for transporting only coal slurry comes to an end when the easement holder no longer has slurry to transport.[3] The

---

5. Hoffman v. Capitol Cablevision System, Inc., 52 A.D.2d 313, 383 N.Y.S.2d 674 (1976), appeal denied 40 N.Y.2d 806, 390 N.Y.S.2d 1025, 359 N.E.2d 438 (1976); Jolliff v. Hardin Cable Television Co., 26 Ohio St. 103, 269 N.E.2d 588 (1971), reversing 22 Ohio App.2d 49, 258 N.E.2d 244 (1970); Restatement of Property § 493, Ill. 4 (1944). Increasingly, American courts are making the question of divisibility turn upon the parties' intent instead upon a formulaic doctrine. See Note, *The Easement in Gross Revisited: Transferability and Divisibility Since 1945,* 39 Vand. L.Rev. 109 (1986).

6. *Hoffman* and *Jolliff* cases, preceding note.

7. 2 American Law of Property, supra note 1, at § 8.84; Restatement of Property § 493, Comment d (1944).

8. Earl of Huntington v. Lord Mountjoy, 1 And. 307, 123 Eng.Rep. 488, Godb. 17, 78 Eng.

Rep. 11 (C.P.1583). Accord, Miller v. Lutheran Conference & Camp Association, 331 Pa. 241, 200 A. 646 (1938); Annot., 130 A.L.R. 1253, 1268–69 (1941); Co.Litt. * 164b.

§ 8.12

1. 2 American Law of Property, supra note 1, at § 8.95; 3 H. Tiffany, Real Property § 824 (3d ed. 1939).

2. See Miller v. City of New York, 15 N.Y.2d 34, 255 N.Y.S.2d 78, 203 N.E.2d 478 (1964); 2 American Law of Property, supra note 1, at § 8.87.

3. See Pavlik v. Consolidation Coal Co., 456 F.2d 378 (6th Cir.1972) (under language of easement deed, cessation of coal slurry triggered termination clause); Fox Investments v. Thomas, 431 So.2d 1021 (Fla.App.1983) (easement of necessity terminated when its holder obtained another satisfactory outlet to highway); Lawson v. State, 107 Wn.2d 444, 730

broader the purposes, the less likely the servitude will end, for all its purposes must have permanently ended.[4] Of course there may be hot debate over the facts, as to both the scope of the servitude and whether it can no longer serve any intended purpose.[5]

Another way in which some easements may end by implication is by the destruction of a structure on the servient tenement in which they exist. The decided cases involve either an easement of passage through a building that is destroyed or an easement in a party wall that is altered or destroyed. With easements through buildings, the general rule is that they are limited to the life of the specific building, whose destruction terminates the easement.[6] The easement is not revived through a replacement building unless the court finds the parties intended it should be.[7] There is a split of authority over whether the owner of the servient tenement may voluntarily raze the building or whether he must suffer the easement to continue until the building's destruction from natural causes.[8] In the case of party walls, most decisions hold that destruction of both buildings and of the wall terminates each adjoining owner's easement. Apparently a few decisions have allowed the easements to continue in a new wall. Destruction of one building has been held to terminate the party wall easement for that building but not for the remaining building.[9] Party walls may also terminate by implication when they become inadequate or dangerous to support the original buildings or to support larger buildings that changed conditions make it appropriate to build.[10]

To the extent the acquired estate allows the same use as the easement or profit did, an easement or profit is extinguished when its holder acquires an estate in the servient tenement.[11] The servitude is said to merge into the estate, which simply means an owner may not twice have the same rights of use in the same land. By the strong majority position, the easement is not revived if its former holder divests himself of the estate.[12] A few jurisdic-

---

P.2d 1308 (1986) (abandonment of rail line terminated railroad easement). Cf. Preseault v. Interstate Commerce Com'n, 494 U.S. 1, 110 S.Ct. 914, 108 L.Ed.2d 1 (1990) (Court avoids deciding question of termination of railroad easement).

4. See First National Bank v. Konner, 373 Mass. 463, 367 N.E.2d 1174 (1977); First National Trust & Savings Bank v. Raphael, 201 Va. 718, 113 S.E.2d 683 (1960).

5. In addition to the *Pavlik* case (purpose ended), the *Konner* case (purposes not totally ended), and the *Raphael* case (broad purpose intended), cited in the two preceding notes, see Hopkins The Florist v. Fleming, 112 Vt. 389, 26 A.2d 96 (1942) (narrow purpose; easement terminated).

6. Union National Bank v. Nesmith, 238 Mass. 247, 130 N.E. 251 (1921); Rudderham v. Emery Brothers, 46 R.I. 171, 125 A. 291 (1924); Annot., 34 A.L.R. 606 (1925), Supp., 154 A.L.R. 82 (1945).

7. See Rudderham v. Emery Brothers, 46 R.I. 171, 125 A. 291 (1924) (not revived); Annot., 34 A.L.R. 606 (1925) Supp., 154 A.L.R. 82 (1945).

8. Compare Rothschild v. Wolf, 20 Cal.2d 17, 123 P.2d 483 (1942) (owner may not raze), with Union National Bank v. Nesmith, 238 Mass. 247, 130 N.E. 251 (1921) (owner may raze). Even in states that say the owner may not voluntarily raze the building, should there not be an implied outer limit to how long he must maintain an old building for the sake of the easement? Should not the draftsman avoid the question by some limit on the easement's life?

9. Annot., 85 A.L.R. 288 (1933); 3 H. Tiffany Real Property, supra note 1, this section, at § 818.

10. S.S. Kresge Co. v. Garrick Realty Co., 209 Wis. 305, 245 N.W. 118 (1932); Annot., 85 A.L.R. 288, 293 (1933).

11. Witt v. Reavis, 284 Or. 503, 587 P.2d 1005 (1978); 2 American Law of Property, supra note 1, at §§ 8.90, 8.93; Restatement of Property §§ 497, 499 (1944).

12. Witt v. Reavis, 284 Or. 503, 587 P.2d 1005 (1978); 2 American Law of Property, supra note 1, at § 8.91; Restatement of Property § 497, Comment h (1944).

tions, notably Pennsylvania, allow revival in certain circumstances.[13]

It is generally said that easements, and perhaps profits, may be terminated by abandonment, which requires two elements, a cessation of use and an intent to relinquish.[14] This is a strange doctrine. Our law knows no doctrine of abandonment of estates in land; we do not conceive of unowned land. Abandonment of chattels is well recognized; they may become unowned, available for new ownership by whoever will take them into possession with intent to own. Abandonment of servitudes, however, cannot result in their being unowned in this way but must operate as a release to the owner of the servient estate. In this sense, there are some decisions in which it has been held that an abandonment occurred.[15] Far more decisions contain dictum about abandonment or contain facts that permit termination on some other theory.[16] Many of these decisions find that, while the easement holder ceased to use the easement, he had no intent to abandon.[17] It seems fair to conclude that, while our law recognizes a doctrine of abandonment of easements, it is not a judicial favorite, and intent is likely to be difficult to establish.

Servitudes may be extinguished by adverse possession or prescription by the owner of the servient tenement or by a third person. To be adverse, the possession or use must be under the usual conditions of adversity, actual, open, notorious, hostile or nonpermissive, and continuous, for the period of the statute of limitations.[18] Mere non-use by the easement holder will not suffice for adverse possession or use, just as it will not alone suffice for abandonment. Rather, the adverse claimant must do something that wrongfully and physically prevents the easement or profit to be used—that is in that sense inconsistent with it. Particularly when the adverse claimant is the owner of the servient tenement, this may imply severe interference, because of the principle that he may make any use not inconsistent with the servitude. For instance, it is usually rightful and consistent for the owner to maintain a reasonable gate across a roadway easement.[19] With an easement

---

13. Schwoyer v. Smith, 388 Pa. 637, 131 A.2d 385 (1957); Witt v. Reavis, 284 Or. 503, 587 P.2d 1005 (1978) (dictum); 3 H. Tiffany, Real Property, supra note 1, this section at § 822.

14. 2 American Law of Property, supra note 1, at §§ 8.96–8.98; Restatement of Property § 504 (1944); 3 H. Tiffany, Real Property, supra note 1, this section, at § 825. See the exhaustive annotation on the subject in 25 A.L.R.2d 1265, 1272–1322 (1952).

15. E.g., D.C. Transit System, Inc. v. State Roads Commission, 265 Md. 622, 290 A.2d 807 (1972); Carr v. Bartell, 305 Mich. 317, 9 N.W.2d 556 (1943); Hatcher v. Chesner, 422 Pa. 138, 221 A.2d 305 (1966).

16. See Simonton, Abandonment of Interests in Land, 25 Ill.L.Rev. 261 (1930). Also see discussions cited in next note.

17. E.g., Pencader Associates, Inc. v. Glasgow Trust, 446 A.2d 1097 (Del.1982) (mere non-use of easement for 170 [!] years did not constitute abandonment); Kurz v. Blume, 407

Ill. 383, 95 N.E.2d 338 (1950); First National Bank v. Konner, 373 Mass. 463, 367 N.E.2d 1174 (1977); Sabados v. Kiraly, 258 Pa.Super. 532, 393 A.2d 486 (1978); Spangler v. Schaus, 106 R.I. 795, 264 A.2d 161 (1970); Miller v. Street, 663 S.W.2d 797 (Tenn.App.1983) (though use of profit in spring was irregular, when it continued over a number of years, there was no abandonment). Cushman Virginia Corp. v. Barnes, 204 Va. 245, 129 S.E.2d 633 (1963); Lindsey v. Clark, 193 Va. 522, 69 S.E.2d 342 (1952).

18. See Kurz v. Blume, 407 Ill. 383, 95 N.E.2d 338 (1950); Hatcher v. Chesner, 422 Pa. 138, 221 A.2d 305 (1966) (dictum); 2 American Law of Property, supra note 1, at § 8.102; Restatement of Property § 506 (1944). The subject of adverse possession or use against easements is treated exhaustively in Annot., 25 A.L.R.2d 1265, 1322–37 (1952).

19. See note 16, § 8.9 supra, and related text. But see Strahan v. Bush, 237 Mont. 265, 773 P.2d 718 (1989) (locked gate may be unreasonable interference in some circumstances);

of passage, while there is no rule that the interference must be by a solid structure such as a building or wall, that seems to have been the situation in most cases of extinguishment.[20]

Though the owner of the servient tenement likely can enjoin the holder's misuse, overuse, or surcharge of an easement, misuse does not normally terminate it.[21] In a few decisions, however, it has been held or said that an easement may be declared terminated if the misuse was under such circumstances that an injunction would have issued to forbid use of the easement permanently. These cases are usually ones in which the owner of an appurtenant easement of passage has built a permanent structure that sits astride both the dominant tenement and another adjoining parcel. As we know, it will be a surcharge to use the easement to serve the adjoining parcel. If the structure is so arranged that the activities inside are conducted as an integrated, inseparable whole, then an injunction would have to forbid all use and permanently, in the sense that a building is permanent. On the reasoning that a permanent injunction is tantamount to extinction, some courts declare that the easement may be terminated.[22] It seems clear that, for termination, the misuse must be more than only minor or technical.[23] Some courts are unwilling to declare termination, even when they will issue a permanent injunction.[24] Those courts that are willing to terminate, seem to do so reluctantly, only if permitted and forbidden uses cannot be separated.[25]

B. RUNNING COVENANTS

§ 8.13 Introduction to Running Covenants

The word "covenant" sometimes signifies an agreement between two persons and sometimes a promise contained in such an agreement. As used here, "covenant" is taken to mean a promise by one person to another to do or to refrain from doing something, which promise the covenantee may enforce at law against the covenantor. The covenants we here consider have the peculiar quality of "running" to persons who subsequently have certain connections with the same land or lands with which the covenantor or covenantee, or both, were connected. One should dwell for a moment on the fact that a covenant has two sides to it. The covenantor's side is a duty to do or to refrain as promised. In the law of running covenants this is usually spoken of as the "burden" side. On the covenantee's side is the right to have

Flynn v. Siren, 219 Mont. 359, 711 P.2d 1371 (1986) (ditto *Strahan,* supra). Cf. National Properties Corp. v. Polk County, 386 N.W.2d 98 (Iowa 1986) (easement, though created by prescription, not lost by mere non-use, but may be lost by adverse possession).

20. See Annot., 25 A.L.R.2d 1265, 1325–32 (1952).

21. Gagnon v. Carrier, 96 N.H. 409, 77 A.2d 868 (1951); Hoak v. Ferguson, 255 S.W.2d 258 (Tex.Civ.App.1953), refused n.r.e.; Annot., 16 A.L.R.2d 609 (1951).

22. Penn Bowling Recreation Center v. Hot Shoppes, Inc., 179 F.2d 64 (D.C.App.1949); Crimmins v. Gould, 149 Cal.App.2d 383, 308

P.2d 786 (1957); Leasehold Estates, Inc. v. Fulbro Holding Co., 47 N.J.Super. 534, 136 A.2d 423 (1957) (court speaks of "abandonment").

23. Paul v. Blakely, 243 Iowa 355, 51 N.W.2d 405 (1952); Vieth v. Dorsch, 272 Wis. 17, 79 N.W.2d 96 (1956).

24. McCullough v. Broad Exchange Co., 101 App.Div. 566, 92 N.Y.S. 533 (1905), affirmed 184 N.Y. 592, 77 N.E. 1191 (1906); Deavitt v. Washington County, 75 Vt. 156, 53 A. 563 (1903) ("forfeiture is not the remedy" for misuse).

25. See Penn Bowling Recreation Center v. Hot Shoppes, Inc., 179 F.2d 64 (D.C.App.1949).

this duty performed, usually spoken of in the law of running covenants as the "benefit" side.

In their nature, covenants are first cousins to easements appurtenant. The burdened land corresponds to a servient tenement, the benefitted land, to a dominant tenement. In concept, the main difference between easements and covenants is that, whereas an easement allows its holder to go upon and to do something upon the servient tenement, the beneficiary of a covenant may not enter the burdened land, but may require the owner of that land to do, or more likely not to do, something on that land. This "something" is regarded by the parties as benefitting the beneficiary's land. Because of the relationship between easements and covenants, covenants are sometimes called "negative easements," [1] but that phrase is not used here because it can, if taken too literally, produce unusual consequences.

Since covenants impose restrictions upon use and enjoyment of the burdened land, they are burdens or clouds upon title. In theory they make title less marketable, against the law's long bias in favor of unencumbered, marketable title. Hence, the traditional view is that covenants that burden title will be interpreted narrowly. Courts still sometimes assert, even apply, the traditional rule, to give a narrow application to the language creating a covenant.[2] But they do so selectively. The reality is that many covenants are given expanded scope because their practical effect is to benefit the burdened land. Reciprocal subdivision covenants, in which all or nearly all the lots in a subdivision are both burdened and benefitted by uniform covenants, which represent the large bulk of covenants today, are usually interpreted very liberally.[3] As we all know, home buyers regard a tight system of restrictive covenants as desirable; they are willing to pay more for homes protected (and restricted) by such covenants than for homes not so protected. While subdivision covenants are still as much burdens on legal title as ever, modern legal thinking focuses upon their effect upon use, enjoyment, and value in the marketplace.

Within the past few years, there has been a rash of litigation concerning group homes for physically or mentally disabled persons, and a number of

§ 8.13

1. See, e.g., City of Olympia v. Palzer, 107 Wn.2d 225, 728 P.2d 135 (1986).

2. See, e.g., Belleview Const. Co., Inc. v. Rugby Hall Community Ass'n, Inc., 321 Md. 152, 582 A.2d 493 (1990) (in case of doubt, construe against restriction); Holtmeyer v. Roseman, 731 S.W.2d 484 (Mo.App.1987) (mobile home with wheels and axles removed was not "trailer" or "structure of a temporary character"); Charping v. J.P. Scurry & Co., Inc., 296 S.C. 312, 372 S.E.2d 120 (App.1988) ("historical disfavor for restrictive covenants"); Permian Basin Centers For Mental Health and Mental Retardation v. Alsobrook, 723 S.W.2d 774 (Tex.App.1986) (group home for mentally retarded not "single-family dwelling"); J.P. Building Enterprises, Inc. v. Timberwood Dev. Co., 718 S.W.2d 841 (Tex. App.1986) (restrictions to be construed in favor of free and unrestricted use of land; meaning not to be extended).

3. Examination of cases involving subdivision covenants, to be cited later in this chapter, especially those that operate as equitable restrictions, will show that courts generally apply them quite liberally. For instance, decisions such as Kell v. Bella Vista Village Property Owners Ass'n, 258 Ark. 757, 528 S.W.2d 651 (1975), and Rodruck v. Sand Point Maintenance Com'n, 48 Wn.2d 565, 295 P.2d 714 (1956), which allow homeowners' associations to enforce covenants that, strictly speaking, are made only among the individual landowners, work a considerable extension of subdivision reciprocal covenants. See also Sherwood Estates Homes Ass'n, Inc. v. McConnell, 714 S.W.2d 848 (Mo.App.1986) (restriction against "structure" prevented dog pen); Albert v. Orwige, 731 S.W.2d 63 (Tenn.App.1987) (factory-built home violated covenant against "mobile home").

cases have asked whether such homes violate restrictive covenants. These cases tend to present the question of broad or narrow interpretation in a setting that produces cross currents at the policy level. Suppose the group home seeks to locate in a neighborhood in which subdivision covenants limit usage to "residential" or "single-family dwellings." A broad, liberal application of the restriction will tend to expand it to restrict the non-traditional use of a group home. Some courts have given a broad application and have kept out group homes, though of course individual cases turn to some extent upon the precise language of the covenant and the precise nature of the group home.[4] Other courts have narrowed the ambit of restrictive covenants and have allowed group homes by holding that words such as "residence" or "single-family residence" did not apply to the kinds of persons who resided within a building, but to the physical configuration of the building.[5] Another possibility, especially if a plaintiff seeks to enjoin violation of the covenant, is to conclude that the group home violates the covenant (i.e., tending to be a broad application of the covenant) and then to refuse the injunction on one basis or another.[6]

Our focus will be not on the covenant per se, but on the question whether one or the other side of it has the quality of running. That question has from ancient times been treated as part of the law of real property.[7] The reason is that "runningness" is connected with the acquisition of some sort of interest in land; the benefit or burden is said to "run with" land or with an estate in land. In the law of contracts, rights or benefits may be assigned and duties or burdens delegated by the original parties. In the branch of property law dealing with running covenants, express assignment or delegation does not occur. Rather, remote persons are benefited or burdened because they acquire an interest in land that carries the benefit or burden along with it, provided certain other conditions required by law are met. It is our purpose to define and to understand all those elements that must be present for running to occur.

4. See, e.g., Shaver v. Hunter, 626 S.W.2d 574 (Tex.Civ.App.1981), certiorari denied 459 U.S. 1016, 103 S.Ct. 377, 74 L.Ed.2d 510 (1982) ("family" includes only related persons); Omega Corp. of Chesterfield v. Malloy, 228 Va. 12, 319 S.E.2d 728 (1984), certiorari denied 469 U.S. 1192, 105 S.Ct. 967, 83 L.Ed.2d 971 (1985) (supervision over residents by governmental employees made building "facility," not single-family home). See also Westwood Homeowners Ass'n v. Tenhoff, 155 Ariz. 229, 745 P.2d 976 (App.1987), in which the court held a group home for developmentally disabled persons violated a covenant against hospitals or sanitariums, but that the covenant was unenforceable on public policy grounds.

5. See Blevins v. Barry–Lawrence County Ass'n for Retarded Citizens, 707 S.W.2d 407 (Mo.1986); Knudtson v. Trainor, 216 Neb. 653, 345 N.W.2d 4 (1984); Beres v. Hope Homes, Inc., 6 Ohio App.3d 71, 453 N.E.2d 1119 (1982), certiorari denied 464 U.S. 937, 104 S.Ct. 347, 78 L.Ed.2d 313 (1983); Permian Basin Centers For Mental Health and Mental Retardation v. Alsobrook, 723 S.W.2d 774 (Tex.App.1986).

See also Beverly Island Ass'n v. Zinger, 113 Mich.App. 322, 317 N.W.2d 611 (1982) (group home was used for "residential purposes" as restriction required).

6. See Westwood Homeowners Ass'n v. Tenhoff, 155 Ariz. 229, 745 P.2d 976 (App. 1987) (group home violated covenant, but covenant unenforceable on public policy grounds); Crane Neck Ass'n, Inc. v. New York City/ Long Island County Services Group, 61 N.Y.2d 154, 472 N.Y.S.2d 901, 460 N.E.2d 1336 (1984), appeal dismissed, certiorari denied 469 U.S. 804, 105 S.Ct. 60, 83 L.Ed.2d 11 (1984) (group home violated covenant, but court exercised equitable discretion to deny injunction).

7. Bordwell, The Running of Covenants— No Anomaly, 36 Iowa L.Rev. 1, 1–8 (1950). With permission of the Washington Law Review and of Fred B. Rothman Company, sections 8.13–8.33 of this treatise are largely a reprint of Stoebuck, Running Covenants: An Analytical Primer, 53 Wash.L.Rev. 861 (1977).

By convention and as a historical fact, running covenants are of two kinds. Covenants that run under doctrine developed in the English common law courts of Common Pleas and King's Bench are known as covenants running at law or, more generally, "real covenants." They will be assumed here to trace back to *Spencer's Case* [8] in 1583; we will not enter into the debate about more ancient antecedents. The second kind of covenant runs under doctrine originating in the English Chancery Court in the 1848 decision in Tulk v. Moxhay.[9] They will be called by the neutral term "equitable restrictions" here, though the contemporary name is usually "equitable servitudes." We will discuss real covenants first, because for historical and analytical reasons it is best to unfold equitable restrictions by reference back to real covenants. At the end of the discussion of equitable restrictions we will explore modern judicial developments by which covenants, usually associated with residential subdivisions, are made to run under theories that sometimes appear to be extensions of the equity doctrine and sometimes appear inexplicable under any traditional doctrine.

It will be convenient now, and more importantly will promote analysis, to organize the discussion of real covenants according to their elements. The outline that will be followed is a variant of that adopted by the leading writer on the subject, Judge Charles E. Clark, and often used by the courts: [10] (1) form of the covenant; (2) whether the covenanting parties intended the covenant to run; (3) whether the covenant touches and concerns; (4) whether there is privity between one or both of the covenanting parties and the remote party or parties sought to be benefited or burdened (called "vertical privity"); and (5) whether there is privity between the original covenanting parties (called "horizontal privity"). After these elements have been explored, certain questions relating generally to real covenants will be taken up.

§ 8.14 Form of Real Covenants

For a covenant to be enforceable by or against a remote party, it must have been enforceable between the covenanting parties. This is a question of contract law into which we will not venture, except to say the question seldom arises. A more important issue is whether a real covenant must be in such a form as will satisfy the Statute of Frauds regulating transfer of interests in land.[1] Underneath this issue is the more fundamental question whether real covenants are interests in land or whether they are contract

---

8. 5 Co. 16a, 77 Eng.Rep. 72 (Q.B.1583).

9. 2 Phil. 774, 41 Eng.Rep. 1143 (Ch.1848). For the view that, before Tulk v. Moxhay, American courts developed indigenous theories that subsumed both *Spencer's Case* and *Tulk,* see Reichman, Toward a Unified Concept of Servitudes, 55 S.Cal.L.Rev. 1179, 1188–1211 (1982).

10. C. Clark, Real Covenants and Other Interests Which "Run With Land" 94 (2d ed. 1947).

§ 8.14

1. The question first becomes important in a context indirectly related to our subject, in determining whether running covenants are a form of "property" for which eminent domain compensation must be paid in certain situations. A majority of the courts that have considered that question have resolved it affirmatively. See Washington Suburban Sanitary Com'n v. Frankel, 57 Md.App. 419, 470 A.2d 813 (1984), vacated on other grounds 302 Md. 301, 487 A.2d 651 (1984) (equitable land restriction was "property," for which compensation had to be paid when burdened land was condemned); Stoebuck, Condemnation of Rights the Condemnee Holds in Lands of Another, 56 Iowa L.Rev. 293, 301–10 (1970).

rights that are made to run by their connection with estates in land. If they are interests in land, then it should follow in theory that either they must be entered into in a document that meets the requirements of the Statute of Frauds or the operation of the statute must be excused in some recognized way.[2] Exactly the same issue and question arise in connection with equitable restrictions. The courts have usually made no distinction between legal and equitable restrictions in discussing the Statute of Frauds, though perhaps they have tended to excuse the statute more readily with equitable restrictions. In any event, it seems valid for purposes of the Statute of Frauds to discuss both legal and equitable restrictions collectively as "running covenants."

In deciding whether the real property Statute of Frauds applies to the creation of running covenants, the Restatement of Property and most writers on the subject agree that running covenants, as proprietary interests in land, must be created in conformity with the Statute of Frauds.[3] The decisions are split, but apparently most courts also adopt the preceding position.[4]

A substantial minority, however, have held that the Statute of Frauds does not apply to running covenants because they are not interests in land. The majority stance coincides better with the concept that proprietary interests in land are the total bundle of rights that the holder enjoys. One who restricts his previously enjoyed rights by covenanting not to exercise some of them (for instance, by covenanting not to erect certain kinds of structures) has certainly diminished his quantum of ownership in his land.[5]

As a practical matter, the Statute of Frauds seldom proves an insurmountable obstacle to establishing a running covenant. In the first place, as Sims estimated, probably over ninety percent of the real property covenants that are attempted are included in a writing that satisfies the Statute, such as a deed, easement agreement, or lease.[6] Even if the formalities have not been observed, the covenant may be saved in several other ways.[7] Thus in

---

2. See Miller v. Lawlor, 245 Iowa 1144, 66 N.W.2d 267 (1954).

3. C. Clark, note 4, § 8.13 supra, at 94; R. Powell & P. Rohan, Real Property ¶ 672 (abr. ed. 1968); Restatement of Property § 522 (1944); Cross, Interplay Between Property Law Change and Constitutional Barriers to Property Law Reform, 35 N.Y.U.L.Rev. 1317, 1322 (1960).

4. R. Powell & P. Rohan, preceding note; Restatement of Property § 522 (1944). However, writing in 1944, Sims counted nine states that had agreed that running covenants were property interests within the Statute of Frauds and 14 states that had determined they were not. Sims, The Law of Real Covenants: Exceptions to the Restatement of the Subject by the American Law Institute, 30 Cornell L.Q. 1, 27–30 (1944).

For the minority position see Johnson v. Mt. Baker Park Presbyterian Church, 113 Wash. 458, 194 P. 536 (1920) and Sims, supra at 27–30. See Stoebuck, note 1, this section, at 302–

06, for the proposition that the decisions denying the proprietary nature of running covenants are probably a minority.

5. It may be observed that running covenants are similar in their nature and in their benefiting and burdening effects to easements, which clearly must be created in compliance with the Statute of Frauds.

6. Sims, note 4, this section, at 28.

7. The well known doctrines of estoppel and part performance, by which informal conveyances may be taken out of the Statute of Frauds apply. See 4 H. Tiffany, Real Property §§ 1235, 1236 (3rd ed. 1975), for a discussion of the estoppel and part performance doctrines that analyzes both of them as forms of estoppel. Justice Cardozo's opinion in Sleeth v. Sampson, 237 N.Y. 69, 142 N.E. 355 (1923), gives a classic description of part performance as a doctrine independent of estoppel. There has been special relaxation of the Statute in connection with running covenants. A major example is the rule, generally fol-

theory the Statute applies, but in practice it does not frequently bar the covenant.

§ 8.15   Real Covenants Must Touch and Concern

Whatever other attributes a real covenant may have, unless its benefit "touches and concerns" some estate in land, the benefit cannot run to the covenantee's grantee. Similarly, unless the burden "touches and concerns" some estate in land, the burden cannot run. To emphasize the point, suppose that in a lease that both parties executed in compliance with the Statute of Frauds the tenant covenanted to paint the landlord's portrait. Suppose further the parties expressly agreed that "this covenant shall be a covenant running with the land, binding and benefiting the parties' grantees and assigns forever and ever." That covenant should be held not to bind the tenant's assignee, because painting a portrait has nothing to do with land or leasehold or with being a tenant. Nor would the benefit be enforceable by the landlord's grantee, who would have no interest unique to his owning the reversion in having the landlord's (or his own) portrait done.

Touch and concern is a concept, and like all concepts has space and content that can be explored and felt better than it can be defined. The clearest example of a covenant that meets the requirement is one calling for the doing of a physical thing to land. The tenant's covenant to build a wall in *Spencer's Case* was of this sort; so is a covenant to repair. Perhaps we may also say that covenants to refrain from doing a physical thing to land, such as covenants not to plow the soil, not to build a structure, or not to build multifamily dwellings, fit into this category too. At any rate the courts have no difficulty finding that these covenants touch and concern the land.[1]

If there ever was a rule that a running covenant had to touch and concern land in a physical sense, it has long since been abandoned in America.[2] The most that can be said concerning American doctrine is that the meaning of touch and concern tends to become less clear as physical

---

lowed, that when a deed contains a grantee's covenant, the grantee makes the covenant in due form by accepting the deed, though he does not sign it. C. Clark supra note 81, at 94. Courts commonly enforce grantees' covenants without discussing the nonsigning, where the grantee has not signed the deed. E.g., Sanborn v. McLean, 233 Mich. 227, 206 N.W. 496 (1925); Vogeler v. Alwyn Improvement Corp., 247 N.Y. 131, 159 N.E. 886 (1928); Rodruck v. Sand Point Maintenance Commission, 48 Wn.2d 565, 295 P.2d 714 (1956). In general, the courts seem to take a relaxed view of the Statute of Frauds in running covenant cases. Still, of course, the careful draftsman will always place the covenant in a document that complies with the statute. It would be well also to have grantees formally execute conveyances containing grantees' covenants.

§ 8.15

1. Thurston v. Minke, 32 Md. 487 (1870); C. Clark, note 10, § 8.13 supra, at 98–100.

Restrictions against building have usually arisen in cases in which the theory appears to be equitable restrictions rather than real covenants, but those decisions seem pertinent here. See, e.g., Sanborn v. McLean, 233 Mich. 227, 206 N.W. 496 (1925); Booth v. Knipe, 225 N.Y. 390, 122 N.E. 202 (1919); Johnson v. Mt. Baker Park Presbyterian Church, 113 Wash. 458, 194 P. 536 (1920); Tulk v. Moxhay, 2 Phil. 774, 41 Eng.Rep. 1143 (Ch.1848). Cf. Bremmeyer Excavating, Inc. v. McKenna, 44 Wn.App. 267, 721 P.2d 567 (1986) (excavation contractor's contract to excavate land did not touch and concern).

2. See Masury v. Southworth, 9 Ohio St. 340 (1859), an old case, an influential one, and not a liberal one, but a case in which the court certainly did not insist upon a physical touching; and see Flying Diamond Oil Corp. v. Newton Sheep Co., 776 P.2d 618 (Utah 1989) (covenant to pay oil and gas royalty touches and concerns; court repudiated earlier decision requiring physical acts on land).

contact becomes less direct. One problem area has been whether covenants to pay a sum of money touch and concern. For example, covenants to purchase insurance are, under the influence of the old case of Masury v. Southworth,[3] in some doubt. *Masury* and decisions following it hold that a "bare" covenant to insure will not run;[4] the insurance covenant will run only if it is coupled with a covenant to invest the insurance proceeds in restoring the damaged premises. Under this traditional view the investment of proceeds provides a kind of indirect physical connection between insurance and land. Clark, on the other hand, advocates that a "bare" covenant should run. While there may be a trend toward his position, case authority seems skimpy.[5] As to other forms of covenants to pay money, there is little doubt of their touching and concerning when the payment is for the use of land or to pay for improvements. A number of decisions so hold with respect to a landowner's promise to repay a neighbor for a portion of the cost of a party wall if, in the future, the landowner erects a building that uses the wall.[6] However, when the promise is to pay a portion for a wall being built regardless of future use, the covenant has usually been held not to run, though the reason appears more to be that the parties did not intend it to run than that it does not touch and concern.[7] Controversy has existed over whether covenants to pay real estate taxes and assessments touch and concern, but the better view and probably the trend is that they do.[8] Leading cases on the subject are split over whether a landlord's covenant to repay the tenant's security deposit touches and concerns.[9]

As a final example of money covenants, we should note that the covenant to pay rent touches and concerns; about this there is no argument.[10] Because the payment of rent is not even indirectly connected to the land, this judicial solidarity is somewhat remarkable.[11] To say that rent

---

3. Id.

4. E.g., Spillane v. Yarmalowicz, 252 Mass. 168, 147 N.E. 571 (1925); Burton v. Chesapeake Box & Lumber Corp., 190 Va. 755, 57 S.E.2d 904 (1950).

5. See St. Regis Restaurant Inc. v. Powers, 219 App.Div. 321, 219 N.Y.S. 684 (1927) (dictum); C. Clark, note 10, § 8.13 supra, at 98–100; Bigelow, The Content of Covenants in Leases, 12 Mich.L.Rev. 639, 644 (1914). Note also the court's discussion in Burton v. Chesapeake Box & Lumber Corp., 190 Va. 755, 57 S.E.2d 904 (1950).

6. Mackin v. Haven, 187 Ill. 480, 58 N.E. 448 (1900); Conduitt v. Ross, 102 Ind. 166, 26 N.E. 198 (1885); Bennett v. Sheinwald, 252 Mass. 23, 147 N.E. 28 (1925).

7. Gibson v. Holden, 115 Ill. 199, 3 N.E. 282 (1885); Sebald v. Mulholland, 155 N.Y. 455, 50 N.E. 260 (1898); Meado–Lawn Homes, Inc. v. Westchester Lighting Co., 171 Misc. 669, 13 N.Y.S.2d 709 (Sup.Ct.1939), affirmed 259 App.Div. 810, 20 N.Y.S.2d 396 (1940), affirmed 284 N.Y. 667, 30 N.E.2d 608 (1940). But see King v. Wight, 155 Mass. 444, 29 N.E. 644 (1891).

8. Security System Co. v. S.S. Pierce Co., 258 Mass. 4, 154 N.E. 190 (1926) (dictum);

Maher v. Cleveland Union Stockyards Co., 55 Ohio App. 412, 9 N.E.2d 995 (1936); C. Clark, note 10, § 8.13 supra, at 98–100.

9. Compare Moskin v. Goldstein, 225 Mich. 389, 196 N.W. 415 (1923) (covenant touches and concerns), with Richards v. Browning, 214 App.Div. 665, 212 N.Y.S. 738 (1925), dismissed 242 N.Y. 539, 152 N.E. 418 (1926) (covenant does not touch and concern). See C. Clark, note 10, § 8.13 supra, at 98–100.

10. See, e.g., Abbott v. Bob's U–Drive, 222 Or. 147, 352 P.2d 598 (1960); 2 American Law of Property § 9.4, at 351 n. 55 (A.J. Casner ed. 1952); 1 H. Tiffany, Real Property § 126, at 207 (3d ed. 1939); Annot., 41 A.L.R. 1363, 1370 (1926); Annot., 102 A.L.R. 781, 784 (1936).

11. It might be argued that covenants to pay rent run under the English Statute, 32 Hen. 8, c. 34 (1540), assuming it has become part of American common law. On its face, the statute does seem to say that all the tenant's lease covenants bind his assignees. However, Spencer's Case, 5 Co. 16a, 77 Eng. Rep. 72 (Q.B.1583), in effect glosses the statute by allowing lease covenants to run only if they touch and concern. In historical perspective, that is the role of Spencer's Case. We are thus thrown back upon the question whether payment of rent touches and concerns.

touches the leasehold estate because it is necessary to preserve that estate to the tenant is bootstrapping. It is odd that United States courts, which have no trouble with the running of rent, should disagree over the running of a covenant to insure. Occasionally one sees the argument that a certain questionable tenant's covenant touches and concerns because, being bargained for and having value, the covenant is "additional rent."[12] This argument says too much. It means that every one of the tenant's covenants will run, even the symbolic covenant to paint the landlord's portrait. Furthermore, the "additional rent" theory does not hold for the landlord's covenants; thus, it produces an undesirably asymmetrical result.

Covenants restricting business activity on a described parcel of land have been a fruitful source of controversy. For many years Massachusetts followed Holmes' decision, in Norcross v. James[13] that such covenants do not touch and concern because they regulate the personal conduct of business only.[14] But Massachusetts first weakened,[15] then, in Whitinsville Plaza, Inc. v. Kotseas,[16] finally overruled *Norcross.* Other jurisdictions have generally not had Massachusetts's problems; covenants restricting the conduct of business on specified land touch and concern.[17] Typically, such a covenant, if properly drafted, will read that a parcel will not be used for a particular business. This type of covenant should be distinguished from promises that the covenantor, as an individual, will not engage in such and such a business; the latter covenants do not touch and concern because they do not relate to specific land.[18] When the covenant refers to identifiable land it is hard to escape the conclusion that it touches and concerns, because it certainly restricts the use of that land.

Examples of other, miscellaneous covenants which have been held to touch and concern as real covenants will help impart the flavor of the concept. Purchase options in a lease, while there may have been some doubt about them formerly, may be expected to touch and concern.[19] A tenant's covenant to indemnify his landlord has been controversial in this respect.[20] One comparatively recent and liberal decision holds that a lease covenant to arbitrate differences arising under the lease touches and concerns.[21] Surely a covenant restricting the use of land to certain purposes or to certain kinds

---

12. E.g., St. Regis Restaurant Inc. v. Powers, 219 App.Div. 321, 219 N.Y.S. 684 (1927).

13. 140 Mass. 188, 2 N.E. 946 (1885). *Norcross,* read literally, said it was the benefit of the covenant that did not add to the "quiet enjoyment" of the benefitted land.

14. Shell Oil Co. v. Henry Ouellette & Sons, 352 Mass. 725, 227 N.E.2d 509 (1967); Shade v. M. O'Keeffe, Inc., 260 Mass. 180, 156 N.E. 867 (1927).

15. Shell Oil Co. v. Henry Ouellette & Sons, 352 Mass. 725, 227 N.E.2d 509 (1967).

16. 378 Mass. 85, 390 N.E.2d 243 (1979). The *Shade* and *Ouellette* cases, supra note 14, this section, were also overruled to the extent they conflicted.

17. E.g., Dick v. Sears–Roebuck & Co., 115 Conn. 122, 160 A. 432 (1932); Natural Products Co. v. Dolese & Shepard Co., 309 Ill. 230, 140 N.E. 840 (1923).

18. Savings, Inc. v. City of Blytheville, 240 Ark. 558, 401 S.W.2d 26 (1966); Hebert v. Dupaty, 42 La.Ann. 343, 7 So. 580 (1890).

19. H.J. Lewis Oyster Co. v. West, 93 Conn. 518, 107 A. 138 (1919); Keogh v. Peck, 316 Ill. 318, 147 N.E. 266 (1925); C. Clark, note 10, § 8.13 supra, at 98–100.

20. Compare Atwood v. Chicago, Milwaukee & St. Paul Railway Co., 313 Ill. 59, 144 N.E. 351 (1924) (does not touch and concern), with Northern Pacific Railway v. McClure, 9 N.D. 73, 81 N.W. 52 (1899) (does touch and concern).

21. Abbott v. Bob's U–Drive, 222 Or. 147, 352 P.2d 598 (1960). Cf. Waldrop v. Town of Brevard, 233 N.C. 26, 62 S.E.2d 512 (1950) (covenant not to sue neighbor for nuisance); Muldawer v. Stribling, 243 Ga. 673, 256 S.E.2d 357 (1979) (covenant not to apply for rezoning).

of buildings touches and concerns as a real covenant, though historically it has been dealt with as an equitable restriction.[22]

Because New York has had trouble with covenants to do an affirmative act, writers have felt obliged to discuss them.[23] In 1913, the New York Court of Appeals held, in Miller v. Clary,[24] that a covenant to provide power to neighboring land via a turning shaft did not run because affirmative covenants, with specified exceptions, could not touch and concern. For some years, the New York courts weakened the case by chipping away at it.[25] Finally, in 1959, Miller v. Clary was destroyed for all practical purposes by being limited so disingenuously as to leave no room for its rule to operate.[26] Other American courts hold that both affirmative and negative covenants run,[27] so that there is no longer disagreement on the point. Indeed, many of the covenants described previously as touching and concerning, including all those for the payment of money, are affirmative.

To sum up on the touch and concern element, the trend in American courts has been and is to move away from any requirement of physical touching. Two very influential tests which probably express the current attitude of the courts were advanced by Dean Harry Bigelow and by Judge Charles E. Clark. Bigelow, in an article on lease covenants, advocated that the burden side should run if the covenant limited the covenantor's rights, privileges, or powers as a tenant or landowner, and that the benefit should run if the covenant made the rights, privileges, or powers of the covenantee's leasehold or reversion more valuable or if he were relieved of all or part of his duties.[28] Clark, endorsing the Bigelow test, restated it thus:

> If the promisor's legal relations in respect to the land in question are lessened—his legal interest as owner rendered less valuable by the promise—the burden of the covenant touches or concerns that land; if the promisee's legal relations in respect to that land are increased—his legal interest as owner rendered more valuable by the promise—the benefit of the covenant touches or concerns that land.[29]

22. See Tulk v. Moxhay, 2 Phil. 774, 41 Eng.Rep. 1143 (Ch.1848). Note also the leading American decisions of Van Sant v. Rose, 260 Ill. 401, 103 N.E. 194 (1913); Snow v. Van Dam, 291 Mass. 477, 197 N.E. 224 (1935); Sanborn v. McLean, 233 Mich. 227, 206 N.W. 496 (1925); Booth v. Knipe, 225 N.Y. 390, 122 N.E. 202 (1919); and Finley v. Glenn, 303 Pa. 131, 154 A. 299 (1931).

23. 2 American Law of Property § 916 (A.J. Casner ed. 1952); C. Clark, note 10, § 8.13 supra, at 100 n. 22; R. Powell & P. Rohan, note 3, § 8.14 supra, at ¶ 677; 3 H. Tiffany, Real Property § 854 (3d ed. 1939).

24. 210 N.Y. 127, 103 N.E. 1114 (1913).

25. E.g., Neponsit Property Owners' Association v. Emigrant Industrial Savings Bank, 278 N.Y. 248, 15 N.E.2d 793 (1938), reargument denied 278 N.Y. 704, 16 N.E.2d 852 (1938); Greenfarb v. R.S.K. Realty Corp., 256 N.Y. 130, 175 N.E. 649 (1931), reargument denied 256 N.Y. 678, 177 N.E. 190 (1931).

26. Nicholson v. 300 Broadway Realty Corp., 7 N.Y.2d 240, 196 N.Y.S.2d 945, 164 N.E.2d 832 (1959). The *Nicholson* court, which allowed the running of a covenant to supply steam heat to neighboring land, said affirmative covenants would run provided (1) the covenanting parties intended it, (2) there was privity of estate between the covenantor and the third person sought to be bound, and (3) the covenant touched and concerned (which was the very question the court set out to answer). These are simply the accepted elements for the running of any real covenant. Accord, Martin v. City of Glens Falls, 27 Misc.2d 925, 210 N.Y.S.2d 372 (1961). But see Eagle Enterprises, Inc. v. Gross, 39 N.Y.2d 505, 384 N.Y.S.2d 717, 349 N.E.2d 816 (1976).

27. Annot., 41 A.L.R. 1363 (1926); Annot., 102 A.L.R. 781 (1936). Accord, 2 American Law of Property § 9.16 (A.J. Casner ed. 1952).

28. Bigelow, note 5, § 8.15 supra, at 645.

29. C. Clark, note 10, § 8.13 supra, at 97.

Observe two things in particular about the Bigelow–Clark formulation: (1) it relates benefit and burden to the estates instead of to physical land, and (2) it measures benefit and burden by economic impact. The Bigelow and Clark tests, or their combination, have been accepted by a number of courts and writers.[30] If the Bigelow–Clark test is vague, it is still more successful than other formulas in defining a concept as intangible as touch and concern.

§ 8.16　Intent to Bind Successors to Real Covenants

The main issue in *Spencer's Case*[1] was whether a covenantor's successors could be bound by the covenant unless the covenanting parties agreed that the covenant should bind "assigns," using that precise word. Holding that the word "assigns" had to be used if the covenant related to a thing not *in esse,* the court said in dictum that the word did not have to be used if the covenant concerned a thing already existing. All this learning has largely been lost in the American cases. No American decision has been found that makes anything of the distinction between things that are or are not *in esse.* Also, there seems to be no extant requirement that the express word "assigns" ever be used. Instead, American courts look for the covenanting parties' "intent" that the covenant shall run.[2]

Intent is to be found from all the circumstances surrounding the covenant. Obviously the use of the word "assigns" is highly persuasive of an intent to bind successors. The thorough draftsman will use language to the effect that "this covenant is intended to be a running covenant, burdening and benefiting the parties' successors and assigns." Few recent decisions contain much discussion of the intent element; rather, the courts seem to conclude that it is or is not present from the nature of the covenant. A covenant that is found to be of a "personal" kind, such as one owner's promise to pay his neighbor for something the neighbor has already done, will be said not to be intended to run.[3] Conversely, when the covenanted performance is not merely personal but is connected with land, then the courts seem to assume that the parties intended it to run.[4] This comes very close to saying that a covenant that touches and concerns will impliedly be intended to run. Perhaps no authority has put it quite so bluntly, but that is very nearly what has happened. The logical conclusion of that process is

30. E.g., Abbott v. Bob's U–Drive, 222 Or. 147, 352 P.2d 598 (1960); City of Reno v. Matley, 79 Nev. 49, 378 P.2d 256 (1963); Neponsit Property Owners' Association v. Emigrant Industrial Savings Bank, 278 N.Y. 248, 15 N.E.2d 793 (1938); R. Powell & P. Rohan, note 3, § 8.14 supra, at ¶ 675; Williams, Restrictions on the Use of Land: Covenants Running with the Land at Law, 27 Tex.L.Rev. 419, 429–30 (1949).

§ 8.16

1. 5 Co. 16a, 77 Eng.Rep. 72 (Q.B.1583).

2. Masury v. Southworth, 9 Ohio St. 340 (1859); C. Clark, note 10, § 8.13 supra, at 95–96; Williams, note 30, § 8.15 supra, at 419, 423–24; 28 Ore.L.Rev. 180, 180–84 (1949). England has expressly abolished the rule in

Spencer's Case about the word "assigns," first by decision and then by statute. See Law of Property Act, 1925, 15 & 16 Geo. 5, c. 20, § 79 (1925); 28 Ore.L.Rev., supra.

3. Gibson v. Holden, 115 Ill. 199, 3 N.E. 282 (1885); Suttle v. Bailey, 68 N.M. 283, 361 P.2d 325 (1961); Sebald v. Mulholland, 155 N.Y. 455, 50 N.E. 260 (1898); Meado–Lawn Homes v. Westchester Lighting Co., 171 Misc. 669, 13 N.Y.S.2d 709 (1939), affirmed 259 App. Div. 810, 20 N.Y.S.2d 396 (1940), affirmed 284 N.Y. 667, 30 N.E.2d 608 (1940).

4. See Keogh v. Peck, 316 Ill. 318, 147 N.E. 266 (1925); King v. Wight, 155 Mass. 444, 29 N.E. 644 (1892). But see Charping v. J.P. Scurry & Co., Inc., 296 S.C. 312, 372 S.E.2d 120 (App.1988) (court apparently required express statement of intent to run).

to make intent disappear as a discrete element, though it is probably premature to suppose that this has in fact occurred.

We should also observe that the burden side of a covenant may be intended to run and the benefit side not so intended or vice versa. A common example occurs when the covenantor makes a promise that clearly burdens his land, e.g., a building restriction, but the covenantee owns only land situated so far away as not to be benefited by the restriction. One analysis is that the covenant's benefit does not touch and concern, and therefore does not run with, the covenantee's distant parcel. Another analysis leading to the same end is that the parties would not, in the absence of express words, be presumed to intend the benefit to run. Of course, even if they did use express words, the benefit could not run if it did not also touch and concern; so, perhaps this element should be said to be the ultimate factor in the example given.

§ 8.17 Vertical Privity With Real Covenants (A Bird on a Wagon)

When discussing real covenants, to be distinguished from equitable restrictions particularly in this respect, one should emphasize that they run with *estates* in land. That is, the burden passes with a transfer of the estate the covenantor held in the burdened land; and the benefit passes with a transfer of the estate, or at least some lesser estate carved out of the estate, that the covenantee held in the benefited land. It is, therefore, more precise to say that the respective *estates,* and not "lands," are benefited and burdened.[1] As the quaint phrase puts it, real covenants run along with estates as a bird rides on a wagon.[2]

The most obvious implication of this principle is that the burden of a real covenant may be enforced against remote parties only when they have succeeded to the covenantor's estate in land. Such parties stand in privity of estate with the covenantor. For the running of benefits, however, the rule is relaxed somewhat. Benefits generally may be enforced by a grantee who succeeds to either the promisee's estate or to a lesser estate carved out of that estate.[3] In either case, of course, the estate succeeded to must be one touched and concerned by the burden or benefit. An exception of sorts to the basic rule has been worked out in some cases in which homeowners' associations have been allowed to enforce subdivision restrictive covenants on behalf of landowners who were successors to the benefited estate.[4] The

§ 8.17

1. Amco Trust, Inc. v. Naylor, 159 Tex. 146, 317 S.W.2d 47 (1958); C. Clark, note 10, § 8.13 supra, at 93–94; Bordwell, note 7, § 8.13 supra, at 3. The Restatement of Property takes the position that the burden side of a covenant may run only with the covenantor's estate, but that the requirement is relaxed for the benefit side, so that it may run with any interest in the benefited land. Restatement of Property §§ 535, 547 (1944). Under Holmes' peculiar history of real covenants, benefit and burden would be attached to land rather than to estates. O. Holmes, The Common Law 395–407 (1881).

2. Powell uses the phrase "bird on a wagon," but does not attribute the source. 5 R. Powell, Real Property ¶ 670 (P. Rohan rev. ed. 1990). It must, from the sound of it, have been coined by some old English judge.

3. Alexander's Department Stores of New Jersey, Inc. v. Arnold Constable Corp., 105 N.J.Super. 14, 250 A.2d 792 (1969); 2 American Law of Property § 9.20 (A.J. Casner ed. 1952); Restatement of Property § 547 (1944).

4. Merrionette Manor Homes Improvement Association v. Heda, 11 Ill.App.2d 186, 136 N.E.2d 556 (1956); Neponsit Property Owners' Association v. Emigrant Industrial

theory of these cases seems to be that an association that is expressly designated as having power to enforce the covenant acts as agent for the benefited landowners.

Because estates and not land are benefited and burdened, it is possible to have both the benefited and burdened estates in the same land, as well as to have them in separate parcels. A most common example of the former arrangement occurs when the covenant is made between landlord and tenant. Running covenants in a lease usually run with the leasehold and the reversion in the demised parcel, though it is possible to have either side of the covenant relate to an estate in other land.[5] When covenants are made between persons whose estates are in different parcels, then of course benefited and burdened estates will not be in the same land.

§ 8.18　Horizontal Privity With Real Covenants

Let us be very careful to distinguish the two types of privity. The preceding section has discussed privity of estate as a succession of ownership between covenantor or covenantee and a remote person to be bound or benefited by the covenant. This is commonly (though not universally) termed "vertical privity," because the remote party usually appears beneath the covenantor or covenantee in a diagram of the transaction such as a law teacher might draw on the blackboard. "Horizontal privity"[1] refers to a relationship between the original parties, covenantor and covenantee, which the law teacher might diagram by a horizontal line.[2] One of the chronically maddening features of writings on real covenants is that authors use the term "privity" without signalling which of these two entirely different kinds

Savings Bank, 278 N.Y. 248, 15 N.E.2d 793 (1938).

5. See Thruston v. Minke, 32 Md. 487 (1870).

§ 8.18

1. The subject of horizontal privity spawned a most remarkable and acrimonious flurry of literature a few years ago. It is not our purpose to resurrect this unfortunate exchange any further than to show that it has affected leading writings on real covenants. Occasion for this literary activity was the impending publication of the Restatement of Property in 1944. Section 534 of the Restatement imposes a requirement that the covenants have been created in connection with the transfer or creation of certain interests in land. Section 537 adds the further requirements that benefit or burden touch and concern land in a physical way and that there be a "reasonable relation" between benefit and burden. It is apparent that the reporter for this part of the Restatement, Professor Oliver Rundell, wished for policy reasons to limit the incidence of real covenants by imposing restrictions upon them. Judge Clark sprang to the attack, producing the second edition of his book on covenants, in which he added material not only denying the validity of §§ 534 and 537, but also bitterly criticizing Professor Run-

dell's handling of his duties as reporter. C. Clark, note 4, § 8.13 supra, at 217–26, 241–49. Clark appears to have overstated his case with respect to § 534, as will be seen momentarily. We have already seen that the first part of § 537, defining the touch and concern element in a physical way, is too restrictive. The latter clause of § 537, using the phrase "reasonable relation," seems quite unsupportable. Most subsequent scholars on real covenants have, like Judge Clark, been critical of the Restatement, especially of § 537, which has little credit, 3 H. Tiffany Real Property § 851 (3d ed. 1939); Newman & Losey, Covenants Running with the Land, and Equitable Servitudes: Two Concepts, or One?, 21 Hastings L.J. 1319, 1330 (1970); Sims, note 4, § 8.14 supra, at 30–33; Walsh, Covenants Running with the Land, 21 N.Y.U.L.Q.Rev. 28, 55–59 (1946).

2. We will not discuss whether there must be some relationship in addition to covenantor-covenantee between the original parties if their covenant is to be capable of running. Must they, for instance, be landlord and tenant or grantor and grantee, and must the covenant be made as part of the creation of that relationship?

of privity they are discussing.[3]

There is some authority for saying that horizontal privity will not be required for the *benefit* side of a covenant to run, though some form of horizontal privity might be necessary to the running of the *burden* side.[4] Some writers deny that such a distinction does, or should exist.[5] The usual justification for the distinction lies in the broad policy against encumbering land titles; a burden is an encumbrance, while a benefit is not. So, the argument runs, tighter restrictions should be imposed upon the running of burdens than of benefits. This argument is inconclusive as far as the present subject is concerned, for it does not indicate why horizontal privity should be the point at which to do the tightening—only that tightening should be done on the burden side. It has also been suggested that the horizontal privity requirement insures that the covenant will be contained in a document that is clearly recordable and that will thereby give notice.[6] Despite somewhat shaky underpinnings in either theory or authority for treating horizontal privity differently on the burden and benefit sides, we will consider them separately.

In American law, the most restrictive form of horizontal privity is commonly called "Massachusetts privity." This term refers to Hurd v. Curtis,[7] the famous 1837 decision which established the rule that a covenant would not run[8] unless it had been made in a transaction that left the original covenanting parties in privity of estate. By this the court meant that the parties must, as a result of the transaction, end up holding simultaneous interests in the same parcel of land. Taken strictly, this would mean the covenanting parties would create a relationship in which one held a lesser estate carved out of the other's larger estate in the same land, that is, a tenurial relationship. In practical, modern terms this generally means a landlord-tenant relationship. However, in Morse v. Aldrich,[9] decided the same year, the Massachusetts court held that the burden of a covenant made to settle a dispute over use of an easement also ran. The Massachusetts doctrine as set forth in these cases still controls there and was adopted in Nevada in Wheeler v. Schad.[10] It seems not to have force elsewhere.

The recent Massachusetts decision in Whitinsville Plaza, Inc. v. Kotseas [11] appears to have undercut *Hurd* and *Morse,* if not overruled them by implication. A grantor conveyed part of a parcel by deed, inserting in the deed covenants restricting business activities on both the land conveyed and

---

3. See, e.g., C. Clark, note 4, § 8.13 supra, at 93–94. The author discusses vertical privity, then switches to what, from the context, has to be horizontal privity, all the time using the bare word "privity."

4. City of Reno v. Matley, 79 Nev. 49, 378 P.2d 256 (1963); Restatement of Property § 548 (1944); 3 H. Tiffany, Real Property § 849 (3d ed. 1939) ("The authorities are about equally divided upon the question"); Walsh, supra note 1 this section, at 31; Williams, note 30, § 8.15 supra.

5. C. Clark, Real Covenants and Other Interests Which "Run With Land" 131 (2d ed. 1947); 5 R. Powell, note 2, § 8.17 supra, § 673.

6. See Browder, Running Covenants and Public Policy, 77 Mich.L.Rev. 12, 25–26 (1978); Reichman, Toward a Unified Concept of Servitudes, 55 S.Cal.L.Rev. 1177, 1219–21 (1982).

7. 36 Mass. (19 Pick.) 459 (1837).

8. It was the burden side, but the court did not emphasize this fact.

9. 36 Mass. (19 Pick.) 449 (1837).

10. 7 Nev. 204 (1871). In Nevada, Wheeler v. Schad has been limited to the running of burdens and held not to govern the running of benefits. City of Reno v. Matley, 79 Nev. 49, 378 P.2d 256 (1963).

11. 378 Mass. 85, 390 N.E.2d 243 (1979).

the adjoining land retained. Under the heading "real covenant analysis," the Supreme Judicial Court made the following statement, apparently a holding: "The deed also grants mutual easements sufficient to satisfy the requirement that Plaza and CVS be in privity of estate. See, e.g., Morse v. Aldrich, * * * (action at law)." As far as the court's decision shows, the only "easements" in the deed were the mutual restrictive covenants. Perhaps the decision can be limited to cases involving two-way restrictions; perhaps there is no holding that a one-way covenant may be "bootstrapped" into an "easement." Also, the court apparently did not realize the implications of its own statement. Still and all, the status of traditional "Massachusetts privity" seems very clouded.

After the traditional Massachusetts doctrine, the most restrictive rule is that the burden will run only if the covenant was made in connection with the transfer of some interest in land between covenantor and covenantee in addition to the covenant itself. Of course this includes leaseholds and easements.[12] More importantly, it includes conveyances in fee, which do not satisfy the traditional Massachusetts rule. This difference, in practical application chiefly distinguishes the two rules.[13] A thin plurality of appellate decision seems to support the Restatement's assertion that this was the American position.[14]

The third view, Judge Clark's, is that there should be no requirement of horizontal privity for the running of the burden of a real covenant. We have just seen that several states have espoused this position, which writers on the subject tend to favor.[15] Very likely the trend of decisional law, to the extent there is a trend, favors the Clark position. An article published in 1970 noted that only one state, Oregon, had adopted a horizontal privity requirement in the preceding twenty-seven years.[16] Modern thinking on covenants certainly militates against the requirement, because, instead of

12. 165 Broadway Building, Inc. v. City Investing Co., 120 F.2d 813 (2d Cir.1941), certiorari denied 314 U.S. 682, 62 S.Ct. 186, 86 L.Ed. 546 (1941) (easement); Carlson v. Libby, 137 Conn. 362, 77 A.2d 332 (1950) (easement); Conduitt v. Ross, 102 Ind. 166, 26 N.E. 198 (1885) (easement); Nye v. Hoyle, 120 N.Y. 195, 24 N.E. 1 (1890) (cross-easement); Northern Pacific Railway v. McClure, 9 N.D. 73, 81 N.W. 52 (1899) (leasehold); Flying Diamond Oil Corp. v. Newton Sheep Co., 776 P.2d 618 (Utah 1989) (easements).

13. E.g., H.J. Lewis Oyster Co. v. West, 93 Conn. 518, 107 A. 138 (1919); Muldawer v. Stribling, 243 Ga. 673, 256 S.E.2d 357 (1979); Natural Products Co. v. Dolese & Shepard Co., 309 Ill. 230, 140 N.E. 840 (1923); Newman & Losey, note 1, this section, at 1328–29; Sims, note 4, § 8.14 supra, at 30–33; Williams, note 30, § 8.15 supra, at 440–43.

14. Clear Lake Apartments, Inc. v. Clear Lake Utilities Co., 537 S.W.2d 48 (Tex.Civ. App.1976), modified 549 S.W.2d 385 (Tex.1977) (alternative ground); Bremmeyer Excavating, Inc. v. McKenna, 44 Wn.App. 267, 721 P.2d 567 (1986) (no transfer; does not run); Restatement of Property § 534 (1944). In his eagerness to refute the Restatement position, Judge Clark, with an elaborate argument on

the cases, denied that any appreciable number of jurisdictions required horizontal privity. See C. Clark, supra note 5, this section, at 127–28, 218, 226–41, 249–59. It appears, however, that a slight majority of the jurisdictions that have decided the issue have required horizontal privity either in the Massachusetts sense or in the sense of some kind of transfer between covenantor and covenantee. Newman & Losey, note 1, this section, at 1328–29; Sims, note 4, § 8.14 supra, at 30–33; Walsh, note 1, this section, at 30–31; Williams, note 30, § 8.15 supra, at 440–43. "Nose counts" vary, but the most recent and convincing article on the point lists seven states plus Massachusetts for that position, against six states that seem to have dispensed with any requirement of horizontal privity. Newman & Losey, supra, at 1328–29.

15. Besides Clark, see 3 H. Tiffany, Real Property § 851, at 452 (3d ed. 1939); Newman & Losey, note 1, this section, at 1331; Sims, note 4, § 8.14 supra, at 30–33; Walsh, note 1, this section, at 41–44.

16. Newman & Losey, note 1, this section, at 1330.

being disfavored as title burdens, covenant restrictions are now favored as a mode of preserving neighborhood plans. The issue will probably die before it is resolved, because the courts now rely heavily upon theories of equitable restrictions and little upon real covenant doctrine.

As noted previously, there is some authority for saying that, even if horizontal privity is required for the running of burdens, it is not required for the running of the benefit side—though the distinction also has been denied.[17] The Restatement takes the position that horizontal privity is not an element for the running of benefits,[18] and here Clark agrees in the limited sense that he does not accept the requirement for either benefit or burden side.[19] Case authority on the precise issue is slight. Nevada, which had required Massachusetts privity for the running of a burden,[20] has expressly held that no horizontal privity is needed on the benefit side.[21] The policy against encumbrances, which has traditionally made courts disfavor and impose restrictions upon the running of burdens, does not extend to the running of benefits; as we have seen, a number of courts do not require horizontal privity even on the burden side. Considering all the enumerated factors, it seems justifiable to conclude that horizontal privity is not required by most American courts for the running of the benefit side of a real covenant.

§ 8.19 Separate Running of Benefit and Burden

We have here assumed that one should consider separately the running of benefit and burden. Hence, the frequent use of the phrase "burden side" and "benefit side." However, almost any case on real (or equitable) covenants will find the court speaking of the running of "the covenant." Usually nothing turns on this and no harm is done, for the question before the court will be whether a remote party is liable for the burden or is entitled to the right of the benefit; occasionally both parties are remote, so that there are really questions of the running of both sides. Reading the decision, we can say that the court did or did not allow the burden side, benefit side, or both sides to run.

Occasionally it matters whether we are precise in thinking separately of benefit and burden. The Nevada Supreme Court did so when, as just recounted, it distinguished the benefit from the burden side as to the issue of horizontal privity.[1] Another example of when the distinction matters occurs when one side of a covenant touches and concerns land, but the other side does not—that is, when it is "in gross." Suppose, in a transaction conveying his land and selling the business upon it, a businessman covenants that he personally will not compete with that business. A few decisions have held that one side of a covenant will not run unless the other side also touches and concerns and otherwise meets the requirements to run.[2] In the strictest

17. See notes 4 & 5, this section.

18. Restatement of Property § 548 (1944).

19. C. Clark, note 5, this section.

20. Wheeler v. Schad, 7 Nev. 204 (1871).

21. City of Reno v. Matley, 79 Nev. 49, 378 P.2d 256 (1963).

§ 8.19

1. See text accompanying notes 20 & 21, § 8.18 supra.

2. E.g., Lincoln v. Burrage, 177 Mass. 378, 59 N.E. 67 (1901); Caullett v. Stanley Stilwell & Sons, Inc., 67 N.J.Super. 111, 170 A.2d 52 (1961). Contra Streams Sports Club, Ltd. v. Richmond, 109 Ill.App.3d 689, 65 Ill.Dec. 248,

sense this view does not deny the existence of separate sides—it explicitly recognizes them—but it does tie them together. By far the preferable and, it is believed, usual view is that the running of burden and benefit should be tested separately.[3]

Separation of benefit and burden has been discussed in one further context, of which the leading case of Thruston v. Minke [4] affords an example. Leased property was adjacent to a hotel on property also owned by the landlord. The tenant covenanted not to build a structure over three stories high. The trial judge appeared to conclude that the benefit of the covenant had to run with the landlord's reversion in the demised premises (which he had conveyed), but the appellate court correctly determined that the benefit was for the landlord's fee estate in the adjoining hotel land (which he had retained). Strictly speaking, the issue was whether burden and benefit must be in the same land, and the case stands for the proposition we have previously established: real covenants run with estates and not with land. This means, and Thruston v. Minke holds, that the benefit runs with one estate, the burden with another, and the estates may exist in separate parcels of land as well as in the same parcel.

§ 8.20 Termination of Real Covenants

As with other interests in land, a real covenant may end at a fixed time if the parties creating it so intend. Of course the clearest manifestation of their intent is express language in the instrument creating the covenant, e.g., "A covenants that, for a period of 25 years from the date hereof, * * *" Covenants, particularly those involving a number of owners, may provide some method for the owners to work a termination at any time. Some states have statutes like the Massachusetts law limiting the duration of covenants to thirty years. In any event, the person having the benefit of a real covenant may extinguish it by a formal release, which should be in deed form.[1] These modes of termination are pretty much self-explanatory.

More attention must be given to the so-called "change of neighborhood" doctrine. So great is the confusion about the basic nature and operation of this doctrine that, so far as one can cite authority, it is not clear whether the doctrine should apply to real covenants as well as to equitable restrictions and, if it should apply, how it should apply. An attempt will be made here to unwind the complications and to arrive at an analysis that will place the doctrine on a sound foundation with respect to real covenants.

Briefly, the change of neighborhood doctrine becomes an issue when the neighborhood in which the burdened land is located has so changed that a court ought (under one theory) to declare the covenant terminated or at least

440 N.E.2d 1264 (1982), affirmed 99 Ill.2d 182, 75 Ill.Dec. 667, 457 N.E.2d 1226 (1983) (burden side of covenant may run though benefit side is in gross and cannot run; dictum).

3. For a cogent argument that courts should not mechanically refuse to let the burden side run when the benefit is in gross, see Roberts, *Promises Respecting Land Use—Can Benefits Be Held in Gross?* 51 Mo.L.Rev. 933 (1986).

4. 32 Md. 487 (1870).

§ 8.20

1. The most extended discussion of the modes of termination listed in this paragraph is in 5 R. Powell, note 2, § 8.17 supra, at ¶ 679.

(under a second theory) ought to refuse to enforce it.[2] It is usually said that the change must be physical and substantial and, of course, must have produced a use of land contrary to the restrictions of the covenant.[3] Courts look for a change that affects the general vicinity and not merely a few parcels.[4] When the restrictions in question blanket a whole subdivision or area covered by a common plan of development, it is frequently said that the changes must have occurred within the bounds of that area.[5] The ultimate test of a change sufficient to invoke the doctrine is most often stated to be such a change as has caused the restriction to become outmoded and to have lost its usefulness, so that its benefits have already been substantially lost.[6] Sometimes it is also said that the change must be such as would make it "inequitable" to enforce the restriction.[7] Addition of this last bit of language implies a theory (which will be explored later) that limits the extent to which the change of neighborhood doctrine applies to real covenants. Finally, judicial opinions sometimes state that changes in zoning and loss of value to the benefited land do not establish a sufficient change of neighborhood,[8] though they may be evidence of it.

The extent to which the change of neighborhood doctrine should apply to real covenants depends on the theory upon which it operates. The theory most often advanced is that it is an equitable defense to an action to enforce the burden of the covenant, probably a form of balancing the equities.[9] When the suit is to enforce a real covenant, the question is, to what extent may an equitable defense be raised to a common-law cause of action? If the

2. See Osborne v. Hewitt, 335 S.W.2d 922 (Ky.1960); Chevy Chase Village v. Jaggers, 261 Md. 309, 275 A.2d 167 (1971); Jackson v. Stevenson, 156 Mass. 496, 31 N.E. 691 (1892); 2 American Law of Property § 9.22 (A.J. Casner ed. 1952); 5 R. Powell, note 2, § 8.17 supra, at ¶ 679; Restatement of Property § 564 (1944); 3 H. Tiffany, Real Property § 875 (3d ed. 1939). Some of these sources discuss the change of neighborhood doctrine as a branch of the law of equitable restrictions, but we are assuming for our discussion that the doctrine applies as well to real covenants.

3. See 5 R. Powell, note 2, § 8.17 supra, at ¶ 679; Restatement of Property § 564 (1944).

4. E.g., Chevy Chase Village v. Jaggers, 261 Md. 309, 275 A.2d 167 (1971); Cilberti v. Angilletta, 61 Misc.2d 13, 304 N.Y.S.2d 673 (1969). See Tanglewood Homes Ass'n, Inc. v. Henke, 728 S.W.2d 39 (Tex.App.1987) (violation of covenant on 5 out of 56 lots not "abandonment").

5. Osborne v. Hewitt, 335 S.W.2d 922 (Ky. 1960); Western Land Co. v. Truskolaski, 88 Nev. 200, 495 P.2d 624 (1972); Cilberti v. Angilletta, 61 Misc.2d 13, 304 N.Y.S.2d 673 (1969); 5 R. Powell, note 2, § 8.17 supra, at ¶ 679; 3 H. Tiffany, Real Property § 875 (3d ed. 1939).

6. Osborne v. Hewitt, 335 S.W.2d 922 (Ky. 1960); Chevy Chase Village v. Jaggers, 261 Md. 309, 275 A.2d 167 (1971); Jackson v. Stevenson, 156 Mass. 496, 31 N.E. 691 (1892);

Ginsberg v. Yeshiva of Far Rockaway, 45 A.D.2d 334, 358 N.Y.S.2d 477 (1974), affirmed 36 N.Y.2d 706, 366 N.Y.S.2d 418, 325 N.E.2d 876 (1975); Cowling v. Colligan, 158 Tex. 458, 312 S.W.2d 943 (1958); 5 R. Powell, note 2, § 8.17 supra, at ¶ 679; Restatement of Property § 564 (1944); 3 H. Tiffany, Real Property § 875 (3d ed. 1939). See El Di, Inc. v. Town of Bethany Beach, 477 A.2d 1066 (Del.1984) (change of restricted area from residential to commercial and violation of no-liquor restriction, to some extent within restricted area and more so outside it, justified termination of no-liquor restriction).

7. Jackson v. Stevenson, 156 Mass. 496, 31 N.E. 691 (1892); McClure v. Leaycraft, 183 N.Y. 36, 75 N.E. 961 (1905); 2 American Law of Property § 9.22 (A.J. Casner ed. 1952); Restatement of Property § 564 (1944).

8. Goodman v. Superior Court of State of Arizona In and For Pima County, 137 Ariz. 348, 670 P.2d 746 (App.1983) (mere change in value does not terminate restrictive covenant); Shalimar Ass'n v. D.O.C. Enterprises, Ltd., 142 Ariz. 36, 688 P.2d 682 (App.1984) (fact that enforcement of restrictive covenant would make use of restricted premises unprofitable does not terminate covenant); Osborne v. Hewitt, 335 S.W.2d 922 (Ky.1960); Western Land Co. v. Truskolaski, 88 Nev. 200, 495 P.2d 624 (1972); Cilberti v. Angilletta, 61 Misc.2d 13, 304 N.Y.S.2d 673 (1969).

9. See authorities cited at note 7, this section.

plaintiff seeks an equitable remedy on his common-law covenant—an injunction—he may be denied that specific relief. However, the plaintiff still would seem to have the ordinary common-law remedy of damages; moreover, the covenant itself would be as alive as ever. This is in fact the result the Restatement adopts, and some cases support it.[10]

The result seems awkward and unsatisfactory. Most recent legal writers, and some courts, have sought to find a theory under which the change of neighborhood doctrine can not only deny equitable relief, but can be said to terminate the covenant.[11] Indeed, Professor Harry M. Cross found in 1960 that "there is essentially no indication in cases in the last twenty-five years that the character of the restriction is of the least importance" in application of the doctrine.[12] One possibility would be to allow the change of neighborhood doctrine, admitting that it is an equitable defense in origin, to be transformed into a defense to the common-law cause of action. Two problems arise, though perhaps neither is intolerable. First, not all equitable remedies have been transformed;[13] it might be a bit awkward to transform what seems to be a form of balancing the equities. Second, even if the equitable defense is transformed, it still is only a defense in bar of remedies, leaving the nagging question whether barring remedies terminates underlying rights. In this case the question is more than an abstract, jurisprudential exercise, for the burden of the covenant might still be regarded as a cloud on title.

A satisfactory solution is found in a theory suggested by Dean Roscoe Pound: "It is submitted that the sound course is to hold that when the purpose of the restrictions can no longer be carried out the servitude comes to an end; that the duration of the servitude is determined by its purpose."[14] He was writing specifically of equitable restrictions, but the theory can be applied equally well to real covenants. The basic mechanism is a judicial inference that the covenanting parties intended the covenant to last only so long as it served their purpose. An analogue is found in the doctrine that an easement terminates when the purpose for which it was created comes to an end.[15] That is precisely the state of affairs tested by the change of neighborhood doctrine. Because the covenant itself is at an end, both right and remedy are barred.

§ 8.21   Remedies for Breach of Real Covenants

Assuming that a person liable to perform the burden of a real covenant has breached it, the person entitled to enforce it may recover money

10. Jackson v. Stevenson, 156 Mass. 496, 31 N.E. 691 (1892); McClure v. Leaycraft, 183 N.Y. 36, 75 N.E. 961 (1905) (dictum); 2 American Law of Property § 9.22 (A.J. Casner ed. 1952); 5 R. Powell, note 2, § 8.17 supra, at ¶ 679; Restatement of Property § 564 (1944).

11. 2 American Law of Property § 9.22 (A.J. Casner ed. 1952); C. Clark, note 5, § 8.18 supra, at 184–86; 5 R. Powell, note 2, § 8.17 supra, at ¶ 679; 3 H. Tiffany, Real Property § 875 (3d ed. 1939); Cross, Interplay Between Property Law Change and Constitutional Barriers to Property Law Reform, 35 N.Y.U.L.Rev. 1317, 1325–26 (1960); Pound, The Progress of the Law, 1918–1919, Equity, 33 Harv.L.Rev. 813, 821 (1920).

12. Cross, preceding note, at 1326.

13. See D. Dobbs, Remedies § 2.4 (1973).

14. Pound, note 11, this section.

15. See Union National Bank v. Nesmith, 238 Mass. 247, 130 N.E. 251 (1921); 3 H. Tiffany, Real Property § 817 (3d ed. 1939); § 8.12, supra.

damages for the breach. The covenant is a common law creation and
damages are the common law remedy. As a practical matter, the beneficiary usually prefers an injunction against future breach of the covenant,
together with any damages that may be due for past breaches. Although
injunction is an equitable remedy and may once have been thought of as
extraordinary, it is today routinely available on the theory that the legal
remedy is inadequate to prevent future injury to unique property interests.[1]
As an equitable remedy, an injunction may of course be denied in a
particular case because of an equity defense such as laches, unclean hands,
or balancing hardships.[2]

Even though he has conveyed his land to a grantee who is liable for
performing the burden of a real covenant, in some cases the original
covenantor may still be liable. His promise had a dual nature: as a
contract, it bound him personally; as a covenant it bound his privies. It
would seem in theory, therefore, that if the burdened estate has been
conveyed but the benefited estate is still held by the original covenantee, he
should be able to both pursue the grantee on the running covenant and his
covenantee under "privity of contract," as it is called. That does indeed
seem to be the result in the courts upon covenants contained in leases.
Between themselves the covenantor and his grantee stand in a suretyship
relation, the grantee being primarily liable and the covenantor only second-
arily so.[3] However, when the covenant is contained in a conveyance in fee, a
number of decisions refuse to hold the original covenantor liable after he has
conveyed to a grantee. Particularly when the covenant is to be performed
upon the burdened land, such as a covenant to repair or to refrain from
building in a certain way, one can reason that the original parties intended
the covenant to be performed only by the person who possessed the land
from time to time.[4] The Restatement of Property suggests that covenants to
pay money, since they are not to be performed on the land, may continue to
bind the covenantor after his conveyance.[5] In a situation that is the
opposite of the one we have been discussing, when it is the covenantee and
not the covenantor who has conveyed, there is general agreement that the
original covenantee loses the right to enforce the covenant.[6]

§ 8.22 Equitable Restrictions—Introduction

Background

We now begin a whole new ballgame. Covenants that run in equity,
which will here be called by the neutral name "equitable restrictions," are
today usually known as "equitable servitudes." They were created in 1848

§ 8.21

1. See Cross, note 11, § 8.20 supra, at
1325–26. See also W.F. White Land Co. v.
Christenson, 14 S.W.2d 369 (Tex.Civ.App.
1928), where the court enforces a "covenant"
by injunction.

2. See Gaskin v. Harris, 82 N.M. 336, 481
P.2d 698 (1971) (injunction granted).

3. Gerber v. Pecht, 15 N.J. 29, 104 A.2d 41
(1954).

4. 2 American Law of Property § 9.18 (A.J.
Casner ed. 1952); Restatement of Property
§ 538, Comments a & c, Ill. 2 (1944).

5. Restatement of Property § 538, Comment c & Ill. 1 (1944).

6. Restatement of Property §§ 549, 550
(1944).

as a result of Lord Chancellor Cottenham's decision in Tulk v. Moxhay.[1] One must realize that the equity chancellors were completely independent of the common law courts, literally a law unto themselves.[2]

The decision in Tulk v. Moxhay was, in fact, precisely contrary to English common law of real covenants, which, as we have seen, did not and still does not in England allow the running of burdens that originate in a conveyance in fee. This indicates that equitable restrictions are a separate subject from real covenants and should be approached that way.

Tulk v. Moxhay concerned a covenant in a deed whereby the grantee of Leicester Square promised for himself, his heirs, and assigns, to maintain the square as a pleasure garden for the benefit of dwelling lots around the square. Owners of surrounding lots, upon payment of a fee, were to have access to the garden. The grantee conveyed the square which by further conveyances came to the defendant, who, though he well knew of the covenant, intended to build houses upon the square. Plaintiff was the original grantor-covenantee so that there was no question of the running of the benefit but only of the burden, which, as mentioned, did not run at common law. In Chancery, though, said Lord Cottenham, there was "an equity attached to the property" which bound anyone who took with notice of it.[3] It would be "inequitable," he said, for the original covenantor to shed the burden simply by selling the land. What was the mechanism underlying the decision? The question has caused much debate among scholars, for Tulk v. Moxhay did not resolve it.

Some distinguished scholars have argued that equitable restrictions run under a contract theory, in which the promise is enforced against third persons. For example, Professor James Barr Ames thought prevention of unjust enrichment was the basis.[4] Dean Harlan F. Stone favored a variant of specific performance,[5] as does Tiffany's treatise.[6] Language in Tulk v. Moxhay about a "contract" tends to support a contract theory, and in certain situations such a theory works well. These matters will be discussed in detail later.

On the other side are scholars who consider equitable restrictions as creating servitudes on the burdened land, similar to easements; hence the name "equitable servitudes." Under this theory, the land itself, not estates in it, becomes burdened with the covenant; as the expression goes, the servitude "sinks its tentacles into the soil." As one might suppose, real

---

§ 8.22

1. 2 Phil. 774, 41 Eng.Rep. 1143 (Ch. 1848). But cf. Reichman, Toward a Unified Concept of Servitudes, 55 S.Cal.L.Rev. 1177, 1188–1211 (1982), which presents evidence that American courts enforced the equivalent of equitable restrictions before Tulk v. Moxhay was decided.

2. If there had ever been any doubt of this, it had long ago been settled in one of the famous constitutional struggles of English history. At the beginning of the 17th century, Lord Coke, Chief Justice of King's Bench, had taken on both Chancery and King James, claiming in essence that the law courts could

control decisions of equity. Coke lost the battle, lost his job, and was lucky not to lose his neck; after that, until Parliament established a unified court system in 1875, the chancellor's independence was assured.

3. 2 Phil. at 778, 41 Eng.Rep. at 1144.

4. Ames, Specific Performance For and Against Strangers to the Contract, 17 Harv. L.Rev. 174, 177–79 (1904).

5. Stone, The Equitable Rights and Liabilities of Strangers to a Contract, 18 Colum.L.Rev. 291, 294–96 (1918).

6. 3 H. Tiffany, Real Property § 861, at 489 (3d ed. 1939).

property teachers tend to favor this theory. Adherents include Judge Clark,[7] Dean Roscoe Pound,[8] Professor Richard R. Powell,[9] Professor William F. Walsh,[10] and the Restatement of Property.[11] Not only the recent writers but also the recent case law tends strongly to employ the equitable servitude theory.[12] It has become the accepted doctrine in England.[13] As with the contract theory, the servitude theory creates problems in certain situations, as we will see as we go along. While neither theory can completely explain the operation of equitable restrictions as they have developed in the courts, the servitude theory has by far the better of it.

One other general observation ought to be made about equitable restrictions: They have nearly replaced real covenants in the courts today.[14] Recent court decisions rarely turn upon real covenant doctrine. Plaintiffs can usually employ equitable-restriction theory except possibly in two situations: when they seek money damages, which equity ordinarily will not grant; and, in perhaps a few jurisdictions, where courts will not enforce affirmative covenants in equity. Most recent litigation concerning running covenants involves subdivision covenants whose operation can be explained best, or only, by equitable theory. Landlord and tenant covenants comprise most of the modern examples of real covenants. Increasingly, one finds decisions that do not articulate any clear theory but which must go upon equitable theory or, more and more, upon extensions of it that might be termed "second-generation" theories.

As was done with real covenants, the detailed discussion of equitable restrictions will be subdivided according to their elements. These are: (1) form of the covenant; (2) intent of the covenanting parties that the covenant shall run; (3) the requirement of touch and concern; (4) (horizontal) privity between the covenanting parties; (5) benefit or burden to successors of the covenanting parties; and (6) notice. Following these subdivisions there will be analysis of several specific problems; and finally we will explore modern extensions of equitable restriction theory, especially as it has developed in the residential subdivision cases.

§ 8.23 Form of the Covenant in Equity

Most of what was said under the same heading in the prior discussion of real covenants should apply here, too. We presuppose that there is a covenant that, under the rules of contract interpretation, is binding between covenantor and covenantee. Obviously the language of the covenant must be such that a court can conclude that the parties intended to burden land

---

7. C. Clark, note 5 § 8.18 supra, at 174–75.

8. Pound, note 11, § 8.20 supra, at 813–15.

9. 5 R. Powell, Real Property ¶ 670 (P. Rohan rev. ed. 1990) (the contract theory is "historically correct, but presently inadequate").

10. Walsh, Equitable Easements and Restrictions, 2 Rocky Mtn.L.Rev. 234, 236 (1930).

11. Restatement of Property § 539, Comment a (1944).

12. 2 American Law of Property § 9.24 (A.J. Casner ed. 1952); 5 R. Powell, note 9, this section, ¶ 670 ("the great weight of authority"); L. Simes & C. Taylor, The Improvement of Conveyancing by Legislation 219 (1960).

13. London County Council v. Allen, [1914] 3 K.B. 642 (C.A.); Hayton, Restrictive Covenants as Property Interests, 87 L.Q.Rev. 539, 540–41 (1971).

14. Cross, note 11, § 8.20 supra, at 1327.

and not to bind the covenantor to perform some personal act.[1] Detailed exploration of this matter will be made later in the discussions of intent and of touch and concern.

A great divergence of result and of theory attends the question whether equitable restrictions must be created in an instrument that complies with the Statute of Frauds. At one end of the spectrum are those decisions that argue that the statute does not apply at all, because equitable restrictions are contract rights and not interests in land.[2] Henry Upson Sims, writing in 1944, counted fourteen states that had adopted this position, against nine that had done otherwise.[3] Tiffany on Real Property seems to be the only major treatise in current use that agrees with this conclusion and reasoning.[4] In view of the fact that both decisions and writers have come to regard equitable restrictions as interests in land,[5] it is doubtful that this conclusion on the Statute of Frauds could now be said to be the majority position.

The opposing view, that equitable restrictions as interests in land must comply with the Statute of Frauds, was adopted in the Restatement of Property,[6] by Clark,[7] by Powell,[8] and apparently by the American Law of Property.[9] As a practical matter, it may well be that the supposed application of the Statute of Frauds does not serve to invalidate many more covenants than if the Statute were not applied. Obviously, the large majority of covenants will be contained in instruments that comply with every required formality. Exceptions to the applicability of the Statute save most of the rest. As the cases occur today, equitable restrictions are generally associated with subdivision development; they will either be made by the land developer-grantor or by a lot purchaser-grantee. Possibly the developer will expressly burden his other lots in the deed; because he executes the deed, this ordinarily poses no Statute of Frauds problem. Such a problem will arise when the grantee or a successor of the developer-grantor attempts to establish in court that the developer made the covenant only orally and impliedly, e.g., via sales literature, salesman's representations, and by the fact that he developed the subdivision in line with the alleged restriction under a common plan of development; we will discuss the so-called "common plan" or "common scheme" later. If the court is convinced that the developer-grantor did orally and impliedly covenant to restrict his other lots, that covenant must be taken out of the Statute of Frauds if it is to have legal life even between the original parties. That means application of either the doctrine of part performance or the doctrine of equitable estoppel. Fortunately, the fact pattern that produces the problem tends to solve it as

§ 8.23

1. Compare Buckley v. Mooney, 339 Mich. 398, 63 N.W.2d 655 (1954), with Finley v. Glenn, 303 Pa. 131, 154 A. 299 (1931).

2. Johnson v. Mt. Baker Park Presbyterian Church, 113 Wash. 458, 194 P. 536 (1920); C. Clark, Real Covenants and Other Interests Which "Run With Land" 178 (2d ed. 1947); Sims, The Law of Real Covenants: Exceptions to the Restatement of the Subject by the American Law Institute, 30 Cornell L.Q. 1, 27–28 (1944).

3. Sims, preceding note, at 27–30.

4. 3 H. Tiffany, Real Property § 860 (3d ed. 1939).

5. See text accompanying notes 7–13, § 8.22 supra.

6. Restatement of property § 539, Comment j (1944).

7. C. Clark, note 2, this section, at 178.

8. 5 R. Powell, note 9, § 8.22 supra, at ¶ 671.

9. 2 American Law of Property § 9.25 (A.J. Casner ed. 1952).

well.[10] The lot purchaser has relied upon the developer's representations in buying his lot, so that it should ordinarily be workable to estop the developer and his successors from asserting the Statute. On the other side of the purchase-sale arrangement, a problem arises when the deed contains a covenant purporting to burden the purchaser-grantee's lot. The problem is, that grantee does not customarily sign the deed. Here the courts have almost universally held that the grantee is bound by covenants in the deed by his accepting it. Sometimes it is reasoned that the grantor's signature is all that the Statute of Frauds requires; sometimes other reasons, or none, are given.[11]

One must also concede that American courts have taken a considerably more relaxed view of the Statute of Frauds in recent equitable restrictions.[12] That is apparent from the preceding discussion. Under the correct principle that equitable restrictions are interests in land, however, the Statute of Frauds should apply to their creation, subject to its exceptions. To avoid uncertainty and litigation in deeds setting up subdivision covenants, the draftsman should have the developer expressly burden his retained land and have the grantee execute the deeds with due formality.

§ 8.24 Equitable Restrictions Must Touch and Concern

To run, equitable restrictions must touch and concern benefited and burdened land, and the requirement should be exactly the same as for real covenants.[1] The prior discussion of the touch and concern requirement for real covenants in section 8.15 is generally applicable here and will not be repeated. Statements have occasionally been made that the touch and concern requirement is not as restrictive or rigorous for equitable restrictions as for real covenants.[2] This is true in a sense as a matter of history, because equitable theory has come to be used more and more and real covenant theory less and less during a period when the courts have generally relaxed the restrictions on covenants for policy reasons. In principle, though, there is as much reason to require an equitable restriction to touch and concern as there is when a real covenant is involved. It is this quality that justifies our attaching them to land or to estates in land—that most fundamentally distinguishes them from a covenant to paint someone's portrait.

On the other side of the balance sheet, there is one kind of equitable restriction which, it can be argued, should not touch and concern: the covenant to do an affirmative act. In fact, most courts have held that

10. The mechanism for this is spelled out in 5 R. Powell, note 9, § 8.22 supra, at ¶ 671.

11. See 2 American Law of Property § 9.25 (A.J. Casner ed. 1952); 5 R. Powell, note 9, § 8.22 supra, ¶ 671.

12. California takes the strictest view of any state on oral covenants. There is a question whether California regards the issue as one of the Statute of Frauds or of the parol evidence rule. See Riley v. Bear Creek Planning Committee, 17 Cal.3d 500, 131 Cal.Rptr. 381, 551 P.2d 1213 (1976); Werner v. Graham,

181 Cal. 174, 183 P. 945 (1919); Murry v. Lovell, 132 Cal.App.2d 30, 281 P.2d 316 (1955).

§ 8.24

1. See 2 American Law of Property § 9.28 (A.J. Casner ed. 1952); 5 R. Powell, note 9, § 8.22 supra, at ¶ 673. The treatises treat the touch and concern element the same for both real covenants and equitable restrictions.

2. E.g., Hodge v. Sloan, 107 N.Y. 244, 17 N.E. 335 (1887). Pittsburg, Cincinnati & St. Louis Railway Co. v. Bosworth, 46 Ohio St. 81, 18 N.E. 533 (1888) (dictum).

affirmative equitable restrictions do touch and concern,[3] but theoretical justification is complicated. If, as we should, we follow the theory that equitable restrictions are interests in land similar to easements, how is it possible to have an easement requiring the owner of the servient estate to do affirmative acts? Upon posing this question, Judge Clark concluded that present thinking should allow only negative equitable restrictions—that affirmative ones should "wait upon the development of a more enlightened policy."[4] The answer, enlightened or not, that supports what the courts have in fact done is that equitable restrictions are not easements; perhaps the word "similar" is too strong. Perhaps we should say only that they are something like easements or interests in land of that general family. Statistically it happens that most equitable covenants today are negative; the covenants limiting structures to single-family dwellings are typical. But there is not much question that covenants to join homeowners' associations and to support them and pay their dues, all affirmative undertakings, will run as well.[5] Whether covenants to buy services exclusively from a certain promisee touch and concern the promisor's land is a puzzling and controversial question.[6]

Perhaps this is the place to raise a question that has not received enough attention: whether an equitable covenant may burden land the covenantor does not now own but later acquires. For example, if *A* conveys or leases land to *B* that *B* intends to use for a certain business, *A* may covenant in the deed or lease that no similar business will be operated on any land which *A* now or hereafter occupies or owns within a radius of two miles. Such clauses, called "radius" clauses, are sometimes given by shopping center owners to their tenants. Will the covenant burden land within the radius that *A* later acquires? Presumably the land would not be bound until *A* acquired it,[7] but in basic equitable restriction theory no reason appears why the land should not be burdened at that time. The slight authority on the subject supports this conclusion.[8] Two theoretical problems arise. One is whether the covenant can sufficiently describe after-acquired land, and the other is whether a previously recorded instrument containing the covenant will give notice to a purchaser of the after-acquired land.

3. Everett Factories & Terminal Corp. v. Oldetyme Distillers Corp., 300 Mass. 499, 15 N.E.2d 829 (1938); Bald Eagle Valley Railroad Co. v. Nittany Valley Railroad Co., 171 Pa. 284, 33 A. 239 (1895); Annot., 41 A.L.R. 1363, 1364 (1926); Annot., 102 A.L.R. 781, 784 (1936); Newman & Losey, note 1, § 8.18 supra, at 1339.

4. C. Clark, note 2, § 8.23 supra, at 180–81.

5. Kell v. Bella Vista Village Property Owners Association, 258 Ark. 757, 528 S.W.2d 651 (1975); Rodruck v. Sand Point Maintenance Commission, 48 Wn.2d 565, 295 P.2d 714 (1956). Cf. Rhue v. Cheyenne Homes, Inc., 168 Colo. 6, 449 P.2d 361 (1969) (architectural committee).

6. See Pratte v. Balatsos, 99 N.H. 430, 113 A.2d 492 (1955) (yes); Clear Lake Apartments, Inc. v. Clear Lake Utilities Co., 537 S.W.2d 48 (Tex.Civ.App.1976), modified 549 S.W.2d 385 (Tex.1977) (no). See Eagle Enterprises, Inc. v. Gross, 39 N.Y.2d 505, 384 N.Y.S.2d 717, 349 N.E.2d 816 (1976).

7. See Hazen v. Mathews, 184 Mass. 388, 68 N.E. 838 (1903).

8. Guaranty Trust Co. v. New York & Queens County Railway Co., 253 N.Y. 190, 170 N.E. 887 (1930) (dictum), appeal dismissed 282 U.S. 803, 51 S.Ct. 86, 75 L.Ed. 722 (1930); Lewis v. Gollner, 129 N.Y. 227, 29 N.E. 81 (1891); 2 American Law of Property § 9.35 (A.J. Casner ed. 1952). American Law of Property suggests the covenant could attach to the after-acquired land under the contract theory of equitable restrictions but not under the servitude theory. However, by analogy to the real property doctrine of after-acquired title, it seems that after-acquired land might be impressed with the burden.

§ 8.25 Intent to Bind Successors by Equitable Restrictions

Again, one must discuss the running of benefits and burdens separately. On the burden side, there seems to be no requirement that the parties to an equitable restriction have a specific intent that it shall run. With real covenants, *Spencer's Case*[1] held that a covenant relating to a thing not then in existence would run only if the parties used the word "assigns." Because equitable restrictions have never been controlled by *Spencer's Case,* the courts have not had to deal with the word "assigns" and apparently have not developed an intent doctrine paralleling that for real covenants. Little discussion of such a doctrine has been found in the case law.[2]

When we consider the benefit side, we find statements that the benefit of an equitable restriction will run only if the covenanting parties intend it.[3] Sometimes this means only that the benefit side may not run to anyone if the thing to be done or refrained from by the covenantor is for the covenantee's personal benefit only, if it does not benefit some land of his.[4] This is obvious; a benefit cannot run with any land if it is in gross. In some decisions statements about intent deal with the issue of whose land is intended to be benefited by a covenant, assuming it is of a kind that touches and concerns land. If a court is willing to employ third-party-beneficiary theory, it is possible for the parties to attach the benefit to a third person's land by an express statement.[5] In addition, third parties are sometimes allowed to enforce a covenant when the covenant is part of a common plan of development and they have land within the area covered by this plan. In substance, the court infers that, because the covenant was part of the common plan for the area, the covenant was intended to benefit (and also burden) all parcels within the area.[6] Some courts employ a different theory, known as "implied reciprocal servitudes," for making common-plan covenants attach; a detailed comparison of that theory and a third-party-beneficiary, or contract, doctrine will be made later.[7]

Intent to benefit may be inferred in one other situation which, although it is common, has not been much analyzed. Suppose *A* covenants with *B* not to build certain kinds of structures on his (*A* 's) land. *B* owns adjacent land that will be greatly benefited, but the covenant does not expressly refer to *B* 's land. Courts routinely infer that the benefit attaches to and runs with *B* 's adjacent land.[8] If the covenantee does not own land which is both

---

§ 8.25

1. 5 Co. 16a, 77 Eng.Rep. 72 (Q.B.1583).

2. For as extended a discussion as one is likely to find, see Coomes v. Aero Theatre & Shopping Center, 207 Md. 432, 114 A.2d 631 (1955).

3. See 2 American Law of Property § 9.29 (A.J. Casner ed. 1952).

4. Stegall v. Housing Authority, 278 N.C. 95, 178 S.E.2d 824 (1971) (apparent basis for decision); Clark v. Guy Drews Post of American Legion, 247 Wis. 48, 18 N.W.2d 322 (1945).

5. Vogeler v. Alwyn Improvement Corp., 247 N.Y. 131, 159 N.E. 886 (1928). Cf. Hazen v. Mathews, 184 Mass. 388, 68 N.E. 838 (1903)

(where the court refused to apply third-party beneficiary theory).

6. Rodgers v. Reimann, 227 Or. 62, 361 P.2d 101, 103–04 (1961) (dictum); 2 American Law of Property § 9.29, at 417–18 (A.J. Casner ed. 1952); 5 R. Powell, note 9, § 8.22 supra, at ¶ 673.

7. See § 8.32, infra.

8. Bauby v. Krasow, 107 Conn. 109, 139 A. 508 (1927); Clem v. Valentine, 155 Md. 19, 141 A. 710 (1928); Peck v. Conway, 119 Mass. 546 (1876); 2 American Law of Property § 9.29, at 417 (A.J. Casner ed. 1952).

nearby and capable of being benefited, the benefit will not attach to land he owns some distance away.[9]

§ 8.26 Horizontal Privity Not Required With Equitable Restrictions

A major difference between real covenants and equitable restrictions is that the latter may run even if they are not created in connection with the transfer of an interest in land. In other words, horizontal privity, as the phrase was used in discussing real covenants,[1] is not an element of equitable restrictions.[2] In practice, equitable restrictions are usually made in an instrument of conveyance, today typically a deed to a lot in a subdivision, which satisfies the horizontal privity requirement in most states. But they need not be so made, and the reason is obvious enough: they are self-contained equitable interests in land that do not ride along on any other interest or estate.[3] This point should not be confused with the requirement that equitable restrictions should either conform to the Statute of Frauds or fall within one of its exceptions.[4]

§ 8.27 Equitable Restrictions Run With Burdened Land (Sink Their Roots Into the Soil)

This section corresponds to the discussion of "vertical privity" for real covenants.[1] We saw, in that discussion, that real covenants run with estates in land; hence, the simile that they ride with estates "like a bird on a wagon." The corresponding simile for equitable restrictions is that they "sink their roots into the soil." By this we mean the land itself—more precisely, every possessory interest in it—is bound by the equitable covenant.[2] Anyone who succeeds the covenantor as possessor of the burdened land may be bound, whether or not he happens to hold the covenantor's precise estate. Thus, a tenant[3] or a contract purchaser who does not have title[4] may be bound; there is some suggestion that even an adverse possessor may be bound.[5]

---

9. See Stegall v. Housing Authority, 278 N.C. 95, 178 S.E.2d 824 (1971).

§ 8.26

1. See § 8.18, supra.

2. E.g., St. Clair v. Krueger, 115 Idaho 702, 769 P.2d 579 (1989) ("horizontal privity is not required"); Pratte v. Balatsos, 99 N.H. 430, 113 A.2d 492 (1955); Lewis v. Gollner, 129 N.Y. 227, 29 N.E. 81 (1891); Bald Eagle Valley Railroad Co. v. Nittany Valley Railroad Co., 171 Pa. 284, 33 A. 239 (1895) (by implication). See 2 American Law of Property § 9.26 (A.J. Casner ed. 1952); 5 R. Powell, note 9, § 8.22 supra, at ¶ 673; Restatement of Property § 539, Comment a (1944); Newman & Losey, Covenants Running With the Land and Equitable Servitudes: Two Concepts, or One?, 21 Hastings L.J. 1319, 1327–28 (1970). Newman & Losey have the most definitive discussion; they count several states that have rejected horizontal privity for equitable restrictions and report that no state has required it.

3. Restatement of Property § 539 (1944), especially Comments a and i, is wonderfully incisive on the basic nature of "equitable obligations," as the Restatement calls them.

4. See § 8.23 supra.

§ 8.27

1. See § 8.17 supra.

2. 2 American Law of Property § 9.27 (A.J. Casner ed. 1952); C. Clark, note 2, § 8.23 supra, at 93–94; Restatement of Property § 539, Comment i (1944); Bordwell, The Running of Covenants—No Anomaly, 36 Iowa L.Rev. 1, 3 (1950).

3. Oliver v. Hewitt, 191 Va. 163, 60 S.E.2d 1 (1950).

4. Huber v. Guglielmi, 29 Ohio App. 290, 163 N.E. 571 (1928).

5. See Restatement of Property § 539, Illustration 3 (1944).

The underlying theory should be obvious enough by now. As we have previously seen, both American and English courts and writers have pretty much come to agree that equitable servitudes are equitable interests in land in the same family as easements.[6] Application of this basic concept to the subject at hand is well stated in the Restatement of Property's brief but trenchant discussion of equitable restrictions:

> The burden of this equitable interest binds all those having interests in the land subordinate to or arising posterior to that of the promisor who possesses the land without defense to it regardless of whether they have the same estate the promisor had or whether they succeeded him in anything other than possession.[7]

§ 8.28 Notice/Value and the Running of Equitable Restrictions

We come now to the aspect which most decisively distinguishes the theory of equitable restrictions from the theory of real covenants. "[F]or if an equity is attached to the property by the owner," said the court in Tulk v. Moxhay,[1] "no one purchasing with notice of that equity can stand in a different situation from the party from whom he purchases." In Tulk v. Moxhay the purchaser who was bound by the covenant had "actual notice," subjective awareness induced by communicated information, of the covenant. It has never been doubted that such actual notice is sufficient to fasten an equitable restriction upon a successor to the burdened land, provided of course the other elements for running are present.[2]

By far the commonest form of notice in American cases today is "constructive notice" through the operation of recording acts. In fact, the recognition of this form of notice has largely made possible the widespread application of equitable restriction theory and has enabled it to eclipse real covenant theory. It is settled, to the point of being commonplace, that one who acquires an interest in land is charged with notice of an equitable restriction that is contained in a duly recorded prior instrument in his chain of title.[3] Some doubt exists about constructive notice, however, when the prior instrument is outside the direct chain of title. Suppose *A,* who owns both Blackacre and Whiteacre, conveys Whiteacre to *B* and covenants in the deed that nothing but a single-family dwelling will be built on Blackacre; i.e., the deed is to Whiteacre, but Blackacre is the burdened land. Assume

---

6. See § 8.22 supra.

7. Restatement of Property § 539, Comment i (1944).

§ 8.28

1. 2 Phil. 774, 778, 41 Eng.Rep. 1143, 1144 (Ch. 1848).

2. The proposition about actual notice being part of Tulk v. Moxhay, hardly needs documentation. But because it is customary to support important statements, see, e.g., Bauby v. Krasow, 107 Conn. 109, 139 A. 508 (1927); Sanborn v. McLean, 233 Mich. 227, 206 N.W. 496 (1925) (dictum); Pratte v. Balatsos, 99 N.H. 430, 113 A.2d 492 (1955); Hodge v. Sloan, 107 N.Y. 244, 17 N.E. 335 (1887); Selected Lands Corp. v. Speich, 702 S.W.2d 197 (Tex.App.1985), opinion supplemented 709 S.W.2d 1 (1985) (actual notice of restrictive covenant is sufficient notice); 3 H. Tiffany, Real Property § 863 (3d ed. 1939).

3. Wiegman v. Kusel, 270 Ill. 520, 110 N.E. 884 (1915); Everett Factories & Terminal Corp. v. Oldetyme Distillers Corp., 300 Mass. 499, 15 N.E.2d 829 (1938); Oliver v. Hewitt, 191 Va. 163, 60 S.E.2d 1 (1950); 2 American Law of Property § 9.24 (A.J. Casner ed. 1952); C. Clark, note 2, § 8.23 supra, at 183–84; 5 R. Powell, note 9, § 8.22 supra, at ¶ 670; Restatement of Property § 539, Comments *l* and m (1944); 3 H. Tiffany, Real Property § 863 (3d ed. 1939).

the deed is properly recorded at once. Will *C,* a subsequent purchaser of Blackacre, who has no other notice of the covenant, have constructive notice of it via the recording of the *A–B* deed? One line of cases, represented by Finley v. Glenn,[4] says yes; another line, represented by Glorieux v. Lighthipe,[5] says no. The *Finley* line of cases hold that, because recorded deeds are indexed under the name of the grantor in the typical grantor-grantee index, and because *C* is liable to search the index under the name of his prior grantor, *A,* he is charged with discovering the *A–B* deed. *Glorieux* finds it an intolerable burden to require *C* to examine deeds *A* has given to land other than Blackacre itself.

Some decisions suggest that there is a kind of constructive notice besides recording notice. Sanborn v. McLean,[6] a leading and very instructive, though perhaps extreme, equitable restriction case, apparently held that, because of the uniform appearance of the area, a purchaser of a lot in a subdivision was charged with knowledge that all lots were restricted to private dwellings. The court said that anyone purchasing would thereby have either constructive notice of the uniform restriction or at least inquiry notice to make a further investigation to determine if the restriction had been recorded. Other decisions may be suggesting something similar.[7]

So far we have spoken only of the effect of notice upon acquirers of the land burdened by an equitable restriction. It also appears that the acquirer, even though he has neither actual nor constructive notice, will be free of the covenant only if he has given value for the land.[8] To state the proposition conversely, the equitable restriction binds any successor to the burdened land who is not a bona fide purchaser. The implications of this statement seem never to have been fully spelled out—certainly they have never been appreciated to any extent. Yet, the proposition describes the single most important characteristic of equitable restrictions.

Section 539 of the Restatement of Property, especially Comments *a, i,* and *l,* describe "equitable obligations" and "equitable interests" that are "subject to the rule that equitable interests in a given tract of land are *cut off* by a transfer of the legal title to the land to an *innocent purchaser for value.* As against such a purchaser, the equitable interests *cease to be effective.*"[9] There are indeed other kinds of equitable interests in land, of which the most frequent examples are equitable liens and beneficial interests in trust. And there is an established doctrine that such equitable interests are ineffective against a subsequent grantee, provided he is inno-

---

4. 303 Pa. 131, 154 A. 299 (1931). See also Sanborn v. McLean, 233 Mich. 227, 206 N.W. 496 (1925).

5. 88 N.J.L. 199, 96 A. 94 (1915).

6. 233 Mich. 227, 206 N.W. 496 (1925).

7. See, e.g., Shalimar Ass'n v. D.O.C. Enterprises, Ltd., 142 Ariz. 36, 688 P.2d 682 (App.1984) (notice of restrictive covenant exists if reasonably careful inspection of premises would disclose need for inquiry); Hagan v. Sabal Palms, Inc., 186 So.2d 302 (Fla.App. 1966), cert. denied 192 So.2d 489 (Fla.1966);

Turner v. Brocato, 206 Md. 336, 111 A.2d 855 (1955).

8. C. Clark, supra note 87 at 183; Restatement of Property § 539, Comment *l* (1944); 3 H. Tiffany, Real Property § 861 (3d ed. 1939).

9. Restatement of Property § 539, Comment *l* (1944) (emphasis added). See also Murphy v. City of Seattle, 32 Wn.App. 386, 647 P.2d 540 (1982) (no notice of restrictive covenant that was contained in court records but not recorded in land records).

cent of their existence and purchases for value, i.e., is a bona fide purchaser.[10] This family of equitable interests was ancient in Chancery when Lord Cottenham gave the opinion in Tulk v. Moxhay, which explains why he spoke of "an equity attached to land."[11] It is both sound and utilitarian theory today to phrase the so-called "notice" requirement thusly: Equitable restrictions are equitable interests in land that are good against subsequent possessors who are not bona fide purchasers.

§ 8.29   Separate Running of Benefit and Burden

This section parallels part of what is contained under the same heading in the previous examination of real covenants.[1] The general issue that has concerned courts is whether the benefit side and the burden side of an equitable restriction should be considered to exist separately. We have consistently spoken of them separately, and the decisions generally agree that they are best considered separately.

The more precise issue has been whether both sides of the restriction must touch and concern and otherwise meet the requirements for running for either side to run. More specifically, some decisions have raised the question whether the burden side shall be allowed to run if the benefit side is "in gross," i.e., if the benefit side does not touch and concern any land. In England it has been held that the burden side cannot run in this situation, supposedly pursuant to the English rule against easements in gross. American decisions have split on the point, some allowing the burden side to run and some not. In America, where easements in gross are recognized, it seems the burden side should run, even if the benefit side is in gross.

§ 8.30   Termination of Equitable Restrictions

In section 8.20, we discussed the termination of running covenants. That discussion applies equally to real covenants and equitable restrictions and should be re-read at this point.

We will repeat one matter, simply for emphasis. In discussing the change of neighborhood doctrine, we saw that, under the preferred theory, it operates to terminate the covenantal right and not merely to bar a remedy. However, there is another doctrine, essentially that of balancing the equities, by which only equitable remedies, usually an injunction, are barred. When this latter doctrine is applied to a real covenant, though the benefitted party cannot have an injunction, he should still be able to recover damages. But if we apply this latter doctrine to an equitable restriction, the result for the benefitted party may be more serious. As we will see in the next section, equity courts have traditionally been reluctant to award money damages, though it is not unknown. Also, with the merger of law and equity in American courts, this traditional reluctance has diminished. Nevertheless, in theory it may be more difficult to persuade the equity court to award

---

10. Martin v. Bowen, 51 N.J.Eq. 452, 26 A. 823 (1893); Cave v. Cave, 15 Ch.D. 639 (1880); 4 A. Scott, Trusts §§ 284, 287–289 (4th ed., Fratcher 1989).

11. 2 Phil. 774, 41 Eng.Rep. 1143 (Ch. 1848).

§ 8.29

1. See § 8.19 supra.

damages in this situation than to get damages at law upon a real covenant.[1]

§ 8.31   Remedies for Breach of Equitable Restrictions

General principles distinguishing the equity-common law systems of relief[1] support some propositions for us at this juncture. First, an equitable remedy, an injunction, is available to prevent future breach of an equitable restriction. Moreover, because damages would ordinarily be inadequate to remedy future breach of a common law real covenant, equity should in most cases be willing to enjoin that breach also.[2] One cannot agree with the writer who claimed that all cases in which an injunction is given therefore involve equitable restrictions.[3] Conversely, however, the fact that damages are granted does tell us, under traditional equity and common law principles, that the covenant is probably a real covenant. Note the word "probably" must be inserted because equity occasionally would give money damages if for some reason its preferred specific remedy, injunction, could not be given. This has been called equity's "cleanup" jurisdiction.[4] An example might arise when the plaintiff sued to enjoin breach of an equitable restriction but during the pendency of the action the defendant sold the land to a bona fide purchaser to whom the restriction did not run and against whom the court could not issue an injunction. In such a case, an equity court might decree that the plaintiff was entitled to equitable damages for the defendant's past breaches. Such cases are rare.

The situation is more complex in America today, because most states have merged the functions of law and equity into unified court systems. Many of the historical distinctions between law and equity have broken down. Still, judges and lawyers have a notion of the differences between equitable and legal courses of action; there must be a general awareness of the origins of real covenants and equitable restrictions. It would be fairly novel for a merged court to grant damages for breach of an equitable

§ 8.30

1. See Jackson v. Stevenson, 156 Mass. 496, 31 N.E. 691 (1892); McClure v. Leaycraft, 183 N.Y. 36, 75 N.E. 961 (1905) (dictum); 2 American Law of Property § 9.39 (A.J. Casner ed. 1952); 5 R. Powell, Real Property ¶ 676 (P. Rohan rev. ed. 1990); Restatement of Property § 564, Comment d (1944).

§ 8.31

1. Equity, as a separate, coordinate system, had (and still has) two functions; the remedial, that of fashioning remedies, and the substantive, that of originating theories of recovery. Its remedial side has been the more important and receives the most attention in law schools; we are especially familiar with injunctions and specific performance. On its less well known substantive side, equity's great contributions were the trust, the equity of redemption in mortgages, and, of course, the equitable restrictions we are discussing. Equitable remedies were, naturally, available in chancery to vindicate equitable substantive claims, but equity never gave common law remedies as such, though certain equitable remedies paralleled the legal ones. For their part, the common law courts neither recognized equitable causes of action nor gave equitable relief, though law, too, developed a few theories of recovery and a few remedies similar to those in equity. In equity, however, it was not only possible but the ordinary course to give equitable forms of relief on a common law cause of action, provided the chancellor was convinced the remedy available in law, usually damages, was "inadequate." D. Dobbs, Remedies §§ 2.1–2.5 (1973).

2. See Cross, Interplay Between Property Law Change and Constitutional Barriers to Property Law Reform, 35 N.Y.U.L.Rev. 1317, 1317–20 (1960). But see Amana Society v. Colony Inn, Inc., 315 N.W.2d 101 (Iowa 1982) (restrictive covenant was too broadly worded to be enforced by injunction).

3. See Newman & Losey, note 2, § 8.26 supra, at 1319.

4. See D. Dobbs, Remedies § 2.7 (1973).

restriction, though there is perhaps some indication of movement in that direction.[5] Of course an injunction is usually the preferred remedy.

§ 8.32 Equitable Restrictions in Subdivisions

Today running covenants are generally found in connection with residential subdivisions; indeed, the subject of running covenants has become virtually synonymous with subdivision restrictions. Although they are very common and as well known to the public as to the legal profession, the theoretical mechanism by which such restrictions operate is exceedingly complicated and not at all well understood. In truth this is partly because courts, in their desire to enforce subdivision restrictions for policy reasons, have outrun their understanding of theory. However, most subdivision decisions can be explained under an extension of equitable theory, which is what the courts usually seem to have in mind, though many decisions might be as well explained with no greater extension of real covenant doctrine. Most of what follows would seem to apply also to covenants regulating use of common areas in a condominium.

This section can be understood only by those who have a firm working grasp on all the preceding sections, especially those on equitable restrictions. Propositions previously established will be drawn upon and used without citation of further authority or specific reference to prior sections. In a sense the present section is the culmination of what has gone before, bringing together and applying the principles worked out. In another sense, the section is an attempt to state a sound, usable theoretical basis for the dominant form of running covenant.

Implied Reciprocal Servitudes

The theory to be traced in the examples to follow is known as the "implied reciprocal servitude" or "implied reciprocal negative easement" theory. Suppose first a comparatively simple and ideal plan of subdivision restrictions. The developer of fifty lots, as he sells each one, inserts in each deed in uniform language a covenant by the grantee that the lot will contain no structure other than a single-family dwelling and also an express grantor's covenant similarly burdening all other lots in the subdivision that the developer still owns. The execution, delivery, and acceptance of that deed, whether it is signed by both grantor and grantee or by the grantor alone, will impose reciprocal benefits and burdens enforceable between the original parties against their respective lands. E.g., when the first lot is sold (let us call it Lot 1 and assume Lots 2, 3, 4, etc. will be sold in numerical order), it will be burdened by the restriction, of which the beneficiary will be the developer. And the developer's remaining lots will be burdened by the same restriction, of which the grantee of Lot 1 is beneficiary. Now suppose the developer sells Lot 2, with the same deed restrictions. What if the buyer of Lot 2 begins to build a service station on it? It seems the developer may enforce the covenant, as a contractual covenant, against Lot 2's owner; but may the owner of Lot 1 enforce it? He may if the burden runs with Lot 2.

Does the covenant run as a real covenant? The elements are: (1) a promise which is enforceable between the original parties; (2) which touches

5. Miller v. McCamish, 78 Wn.2d 821, 479 P.2d 919 (1971).

and concerns; (3) which the parties intended to bind privies; (4) which is, by the bare majority rule, created in an instrument leasing or conveying some interest in land (horizontal privity); and (5) which is sought to be enforced by or against an original party or one in vertical privity. It seems that all the elements are accounted for—but the covenant may not be enforced against Lot 2. We did not say the deed to Lot 1 was recorded, and it is the covenant the developer made in the deed (not the covenant which the owner of Lot 2 made in his deed) that the owner of Lot 1 is trying to enforce as a running covenant against the grantee of Lot 2. Typical American recording acts intervene to make the restriction on Lot 2 void against the subsequent purchaser of that lot, provided the instrument containing the restriction has not been recorded and the purchaser has given value and has no actual or constructive notice of the restriction.[1] This has the practical effect of making notice, through recording or otherwise, a requirement of real covenants in virtually all cases. We will dwell later upon the similarity to equitable restrictions they thus acquire. If the deed to Lot 1 was recorded or (infrequent in practice) if the purchaser of Lot 2 knew of the restriction, then the recording act impediment would disappear, and he should be bound under real covenant theory. It may be possible to argue, following Glorieux v. Lighthipe's [2] analysis, that a purchaser of Lot 2 should not be bound by a deed out of his chain of title, but somehow this seems to be overlooked in today's decisions.

Suppose now it is Lot 1 upon which the service station is being erected, Lot 2 having been sold. If Lot 1 is still in the original grantee's ownership, it takes no explanation to see that the benefit already attached to Lot 2 will have run to its purchaser. Recording or other notice is immaterial, because the burden side does not have to run, and because the grantee of benefited land, who is the subsequent grantee under the recording acts, is not the one whose instrument is voided by non-recording. If Lot 1 had been conveyed by its original purchaser to a second grantee, Lot 1 in this grantee's hands would be bound only if the original deed to it was recorded or the second grantee had notice or failed to give value. We would then have essentially the same analysis as in the preceding paragraph, except there would be no issue about whether the original deed to Lot 1 was out of the second grantee's chain of title.

It remains to be said—perhaps it is already obvious—that the foregoing analyses may also be worked between the original owner or subsequent grantees of Lot 1 and the purchaser and successors of lots 3 through 50. The same is true between the owners and successors of any two of the lots. We are still supposing, bear in mind, that express grantor and grantee covenants were inserted in all fifty deeds. As a result, we have a complete network of reciprocal and mutually enforceable covenants, which run under the common law real covenant doctrine (provided the recording act requirements are met).

§ 8.32

1. Cross, note 2, § 8.31 supra, at 1324; Newman & Losey, note 2, § 8.26 supra, at 1340–42.

2. 88 N.J.L. 199, 96 A. 94 (1915).

Now let us see how the same network of covenants work under equitable restriction theory. The elements, we know, are: (1) a promise which is enforceable between the original parties; (2) which touches and concerns; (3) which the parties intended to bind successors; and (4) which is sought to be enforced by an original party or a successor, against an original party or a successor in possession; (5) who has notice of the covenant or has not given value. Comparing this list with the five elements given for real covenants, we see that we have dropped the requirements for horizontal and vertical privity and have added the notice/value and succession elements. Theoretically, these may seem like substantial changes; in practice, they will seldom produce different results. First, the intervention of typical recording acts has, as noted, essentially added a notice/value requirement to real covenants. Second, horizontal privity is normally present because covenants are almost always made in deeds, leases, or other conveyances. Finally, the remote party seeking to enforce a covenant or against whom it is sought to be enforced is usually in vertical privity of estate with an original party; occasionally he may be the party's tenant, rarely a mere possessor. This gives some suggestion of the range of situations in which either real covenant and equitable restriction theory might apply and the other not be workable. A bit of reflection will demonstrate, however, that equitable theory can virtually always be applied if real covenant theory can be. It is, in fact, an interesting exercise and wonderful mental gymnastics to try to devise hypothetical situations in which this is not so.[3] This is why it has been observed that the much broader equitable theory has nearly swallowed up real covenants.[4]

We were supposing a system of subdivision covenants in which there were uniform and express grantor and grantee covenants in all fifty deeds. It should be apparent by now that, in the examples we put, the results will in all cases be the same whether an equitable restriction theory or a real covenant theory is used. Notice, via recording or otherwise, remains a critical element, though now it is not only because of the recording act, but also because of the specific notice requirement of the equitable theory.

We shall now introduce some variables into our hypothetical fact pattern. Assume that the developer-grantor does not insert an express grantor's covenant into any deed, though he continues to insert the uniform grantee's covenant in all fifty deeds. This is actually a frequent pattern. No new problem exists as long as the developer or one of his purchasers is trying to enforce the restriction against another purchaser who has, as grantee of a lot, expressly made a covenant or against a successor to such an express covenantor. We may run out the analyses previously traced. The result of doing so is that the owner of a given lot may enforce the covenant

3. Here is one such situation to stimulate thinking: A covenant is contained in an instrument that is not of a kind the recording act "requires" to be recorded (i.e. make void against a subsequent bona fide purchaser if not recorded). For example, let us assume the covenant is made by the tenant in a short-term lease that, because it is only for a short term, is not mentioned in the recording act. The lease is not in fact recorded. Later the tenant assigned his leasehold for value in another instrument. Because the assignee does not see the lease and has no other form of notice of the covenant, it cannot run in equity, though it appears to run under the real covenant theory.

4. Cross, note 2, § 8.31, supra, at 1324; Newman & Losey, note 2, § 8.26 supra, at 1344.

against the owner of a lot previously purchased, but the owner of a previously purchased lot may not enforce a covenant against the owner of a subsequently purchased lot. E.g., the purchaser of Lot 2 may go against the grantee of Lot 1, or the grantee of Lot 50 against the purchasers of lots 1–49, but the purchaser of Lot 1 may not go against the grantee of Lot 2 nor the grantee of Lot 2 against the purchasers of lots 3–50. This is because subsequent lots, to be burdened in favor of prior lots, must be burdened while in the hands of the developer-common grantor. In our example, this means he must make a covenant in the deed to a prior grantee burdening the lots that then remain unsold, but here, the grantor has made no covenants in his deeds.

Is there any way we can find a covenant by the common grantor? If we can, it must be an informal covenant, and this is where the so-called "common plan" of development enters. Suppose that when Developer sold Lot 1, he represented to the purchaser of Lot 1 through agents, sales literature, and the like that "all fifty lots of this subdivision are going to be developed as a high class residential area—single-family homes exclusively." Furthermore, the layout of the lots and, to the extent homes may have been built in advance of sales, the overall appearance is consistent with the representations. The court, favoring the existence of such covenants, is willing to infer that Developer has orally-impliedly covenanted to the purchaser of Lot 1 that lots 2–50, still owned by Developer, were then burdened by the restriction. Because the promise is parol, there is a problem with the Statute of Frauds, but as we have seen, this may be sidestepped by a theory of estoppel or part performance or by the court's simply looking the other way.[5] So, as between Developer and purchaser of Lot 1, Developer is bound as to his remaining lots 2–50. As these lots are sold, their purchasers are also bound to the purchaser of Lot 1, provided the recording act and notice requirements are met. That is a difficult problem that requires us to pause.

Because the covenant burdening a subsequently sold lot—let us use Lot 25 as an example—was made only orally and impliedly by Developer, a purchaser of Lot 25 cannot find it as a grantor's covenant written in the deeds to lots 1–24, even if he is charged with notice of the contents of those deeds. The leading case to go into this question is Sanborn v. McLean, a 1925 Michigan decision.[6] The defendant, a subsequent lot purchaser, was held to have notice from what the court seems to regard as a combination of factors. The defendant could see that twenty prior recorded deeds all bound grantees to a more or less uniform single-family-dwelling restriction. He could then see that the subdivision was developing in that uniform way. From these facts, the defendant was charged, as a matter of law, with sufficient information to conclude that the developer had impliedly burdened land remaining in the developer's hands, including the lot subsequently sold to the defendant, when he sold lots prior to the defendant's lot. Sanborn v. McLean is a very liberal decision, and there are some factual difficulties the court overlooks. For instance, the restriction had to have attached at the

---

5. See Warren v. Detlefsen, 281 Ark. 196, 663 S.W.2d 710 (1984) (though deeds limited use to "residential purposes," restriction was to single-family residences because of developer's oral representations); Johnson v. Mt. Baker Park Presbyterian Church, 113 Wash. 458, 194 P. 536 (1920).

6. 233 Mich. 227, 206 N.W. 496 (1925). See also § 8.28 supra. Accord, Turner v. Brocato, 206 Md. 336, 111 A.2d 855 (1955).

time the defendant's lot was originally sold, some years before it was resold to the defendant. But it is not clear what representations the developer then made, nor is it clear that a common plan of development was visible. Nevertheless, *Sanborn* does set out the mechanism that has to be used to give notice.

Let us introduce yet another variable into the basic hypothetical example. Suppose Developer, in selling his fifty lots, (1) makes no express grantor's covenant and (2) inserts grantees' covenants in only some rather than all of the deeds; say, in deeds to Lots numbers 6–20 and 26–50. Sanborn v. McLean is an example of a case in which only part of the lots were expressly restricted. Factor (1) we have just discussed and we may simply carry that discussion in our minds. Factor (2), however, is new and critical. First, is there any way Lot 1 can be burdened? It seems not. The purchaser of that lot made no covenant burdening it, and unless the burden attached at that point, it could not be attached later in transactions between persons who had no interest in Lot 1.[7] Is it possible that Lot 1 may have the benefit of restrictions burdening later lots? Under the theory we are discussing, that is possible but very unlikely. (It is more likely under the third-party-beneficiary theory we will soon discuss). If Developer made strong representations to the purchaser of Lot 1 that lots 2–50 were restricted, arguably, the purchaser of Lot 1 could enforce the representations, if we assume they could be taken out of the Statute of Frauds. But courts put so much weight on the existence of a common plan, manifest in a pattern of deed covenants or on the ground that the inference would probably not be made when, as here, the plan is not yet manifest.[8] Purchasers of lots 2–5 probably will be treated the same way as Lot 1. The only difference with them is that one, two, three, or four prior lots may have in fact been improved in a uniform manner; however, courts generally do not regard coincidental development (development not pursuant to a pattern of deed restrictions) as establishing a common plan.[9] The original grantees of lots 6–20, however, have expressly burdened their lots. Under principles we have already developed, it is clear that *within* this group, which consists of the purchasers of lots 6–20, the subsequent purchasers and their successors may enforce the restriction against prior purchasers and their successors. The subsequent purchasers have acquired from Developer lots with the benefit of express covenants that prior purchasers made to Developer for the benefit of the subsequent lots he then still owned. However, it is more difficult to make the benefit of the covenants run backward, e.g., to give the prior purchaser and his successors of Lot 6 an action against the subsequent purchasers and their successors of lots 7–20. This can be accomplished, under the theory we are now exploring, only if a court is willing to infer the oral, implied promise back from Developer to the original purchaser of Lot 6.

---

7. See, Id.; Riley v. Bear Creek Planning Committee, 17 Cal.3d 500, 131 Cal.Rptr. 381, 551 P.2d 1213 (1976); Jones v. Gaddy, 259 Ga. 356, 380 S.E.2d 706 (1989) (grantee who took title before covenant imposed could not enforce it, but grantees who took title afterward could).

8. See Buckley v. Mooney, 339 Mich. 398, 63 N.W.2d 655 (1954); Rodgers v. Reimann, 227 Or. 62, 361 P.2d 101 (1961).

9. Hamlen v. Keith, 171 Mass. 77, 50 N.E. 462 (1898). But see Ward v. Prudential Insurance Co. of America, 299 Mass. 559, 13 N.E.2d 411 (1938); Buckley v. Mooney, 339 Mich. 398, 63 N.W.2d 655 (1954); Johnson v. Mt. Baker Park Presbyterian Church, 113 Wash. 458, 194 P. 536 (1920).

We have seen that this depends upon Developer's representations, together with the existence of the common plan. (We will soon discuss the third-party-beneficiary theory, which some courts use to reach this result.) The problem, of course, is that the common plan, an important factor in the implication process, is a snowballing condition; it is much more apparent when Lot 20 is sold than when Lot 6 is. Decisions on the question apparently allow the purchaser of Lot 6 to enforce the covenant against the later lot-owners to the extent the Developer contemplated the restrictions when Lot 6 was sold and represented them to the purchaser.[10] In this the courts, despite the obvious logical lacuna, seem often to look to the later uniform development as evidence of what the plan was originally.[11]

The "implied reciprocal servitude" or "implied reciprocal negative easement" theory builds upon the concept that running covenants are interests in land of the family of servitudes or easements. Real covenant doctrine as well as equitable restriction doctrine may usually be stretched to fit the theory, though, as the phrase "reciprocal servitude" implies, the courts seem to be contemplating predominantly the equitable doctrine. The important point is that one or the other, or both, of the established doctrines fits and is being employed, though it may be that the courts themselves do not always see just how this is so. There is certainly a stretching of the elements or of the facts to fit the elements, but the elements may be accounted for. And actually the stretching is not as great as it may seem. Courts are working principally with the requirement that a covenant be made, and are allowing it to be implied; then, to a certain extent, they are allowing the notice/recording requirement to be relaxed somewhat. Other elements are present in traditional forms.

Third–Party–Beneficiary Theory

Instead of the implied reciprocal servitude theory, some courts employ what is known as the "third-party-beneficiary" theory. This approach, which is espoused and clearly explained in the Restatement of Property,[12] is employed by some courts to make the benefit of subdivision covenants run "backward." Earlier, we saw that using the implied reciprocal servitude theory to make the benefit run backward can prove awkward. The third-party-beneficiary doctrine is easier to apply in the particular situation; however, it is subject to the fundamental objection that it supposes equitable restrictions, at least on the benefit side, to be contract rights rather than interests in land.

An example we previously used will illustrate operation of the third-party-beneficiary theory. Suppose again that Developer, in selling his fifty lots, (1) makes no express grantor's covenants and (2) inserts grantee's covenants in the deeds to only lots 6–20 and 25–50. Now is there a way that the purchaser of Lot 1 may have the benefit of the promises burdening lots 6–20 and 25–50? There is if a court is willing to make the purchaser of Lot 1 and his successors third-party-beneficiaries of the covenants made by the

---

10. 2 American Law of Property § 9.30 (A.J. Casner ed. 1952). However, it seems clear that to be burdened by the restrictive covenant, a parcel of land must be within the area covered by the common plan. Olson v. Albert, 523 A.2d 585 (Me.1987); Chase v. Burrell, 474 A.2d 180 (Me.1984).

11. Sanborn v. McLean, 233 Mich. 227, 206 N.W. 496 (1925).

12. Restatement of Property § 541 (1944).

grantees of these latter groups of lots. Of course if the latter grantees had expressly recited that "this covenant is intended to be for the benefit of Lot 1," that should suffice. The real question is whether a court will infer such a recital. Again, the existence of a common plan of development becomes the key factor. From it courts which adopt the third-party-beneficiary theory are willing to infer that the covenants made by subsequent grantees, burdening in our example lots 6–20 and 25–50, were intended for the benefit of previously conveyed lots, numbers 1–5 and 21–24 in the example.[13] In fact, it can as plausibly be said that a grantee who makes the covenant intends it for the benefit of all owners, previous or subsequent, who acquire lots within the area covered by the common plan. Many judicial opinions seem to make that broad statement.[14] Subsequent purchasers, however, who are generally protected by the implied reciprocal servitude theory, have little need to rely upon the third-party-beneficiary theory and may create unnecessary problems by so relying.[15]

With either the implied reciprocal servitude or third-party-beneficiary theories, we have seen that it is crucial to determine if a common plan of development exists. Whether it exists is a question of fact, depending upon the concurrence of several factors. The basic pattern requires that the restriction in question be included in deeds to lots in a certain area, usually a subdivision, and actually followed on the ground.[16] Restrictions do not have to be in every deed, but they must be "general." No precise percentage can be given, since generality is a factual conclusion. In most cases the restriction has appeared in a large majority of the deeds although in Sanborn v. McLean,[17] the court, liberal here as on other points, found fifty-three out of ninety-one deeds sufficient. Nor does the restrictive language have to be identical from deed to deed; a common pattern is sufficient. As to the development on the ground, it too need only "generally" conform to the deed restrictions. It need not be observed in every lot nor uniformly in those lots in which it is observed. It should also be noted that a uniform or common plan is not always one that calls for every lot to be developed with the same restrictions. For instance, if the original plan called for several hundred lots to be restricted to single family dwellings, but for a few appropriately located lots to be set aside for, say, a school, a fire station, and a reasonable number of businesses to serve the residential area, all the lots might be said to be included in the common plan. While the most promi-

---

13. This mechanism is brought out clearly in Rodgers v. Reimann, 227 Or. 62, 361 P.2d 101 (1961), and in Restatement of Property § 541 (1944).

14. E.g., Wiegman v. Kusel, 270 Ill. 520, 110 N.E. 884 (1915); Snow v. Van Dam, 291 Mass. 477, 197 N.E. 224 (1935); Evans v. Foss, 194 Mass. 513, 80 N.E. 587 (1907); Booth v. Knipe, 225 N.Y. 390, 122 N.E. 202 (1919).

15. See Restatement of Property § 541, Comment f (1944).

16. See Wiegman v. Kusel, 270 Ill. 520, 110 N.E. 884 (1915); Clark v. McGee, 159 Ill. 518, 42 N.E. 965 (1896) (no common plan existed); Ward v. Prudential Insurance Co. of America, 299 Mass. 559, 13 N.E.2d 411 (1938); Snow v. Van Dam, 291 Mass. 477, 197 N.E. 224 (1935); Hamlen v. Keith, 171 Mass. 77, 50 N.E. 462

(1898) (no common plan existed); Olson v. Albert, 523 A.2d 585 (Me.1987) (four out of 16 lots not common plan); Buckley v. Mooney, 339 Mich. 398, 63 N.W.2d 655 (1954) (no common plan existed); Sanborn v. McLean, 233 Mich. 227, 206 N.W. 496 (1925); Booth v. Knipe, 225 N.Y. 390, 122 N.E. 202 (1919); Scaling v. Sutton, 167 S.W.2d 275 (Tex.Civ. App.1942), error refused; Johnson v. Mt. Baker Park Presbyterian Church, 113 Wash. 458, 194 P. 536 (1920). See also Nelle v. Loch Haven Homeowners' Ass'n, Inc., 413 So.2d 28 (Fla.1982) (developer's reserved power to modify subdivision restrictions does not negate existence of common plan).

17. 233 Mich. 227, 206 N.W. 496 (1925).

nent factors in a common plan are the deed restrictions and the pattern of physical development, representations made by the developer and his agents, orally or in literature, that the area is being developed according to a common plan are also of some importance. To sum up, existence of a common plan is a question of fact dependent upon a combination of the factors mentioned.

§ 8.33 "Second–Generation" Cases

There are some decisions, tending to be recent ones, in which running covenants appear to be worked out on other than real covenant or equitable restriction theories. Quite a few of the subdivision opinions cited in the last section make only elliptical reference to either theory, and there are some decisions in which the courts enforce running covenants without relying rhetorically upon either of the traditional theories at all.

First are a group of subdivision cases in which courts make some variation of this statement: When a common plan of development has been found to exist, with covenants by grantees of the lots and reciprocal covenants by the common grantor, the covenants may be enforced by or against the owner of any lot.[1] Such a statement, being but a conclusion, invites speculation as to its theoretical base. One explanation, of course, is simply to say that the result in the case is based upon some recognized extension or variation of equitable restriction doctrine, such as we traced in the preceding section. As we saw, to make the benefit of the covenant run backward as well as forward in some contexts, it might be necessary to resort to third-party-beneficiary theory in addition to, or in lieu of, implied reciprocal covenant theory. Possibly other courts may be willing to follow the Supreme Court of Oregon, which said in Rodgers v. Reimann[2] that it was willing to employ these theories alternatively if necessary. There is a question of judgment and of scholarly accuracy, however, about how far one ought to go in rationalizing a decision on some theory, however plausible, that the court itself did not suggest. It seems more accurate, then, to accept the thesis that at least a few of the subdivision decisions are *sui generis,* as the Massachusetts Supreme Judicial Court implied in Snow v. Van Dam.[3] One suspects that such decisions are not so much aberrant as they are precursory.

Some comparatively recent subdivision decisions have allowed homeowners' associations to enforce common plan covenants. The cases involve lot owners' restrictive covenants that require the owners to pay dues or maintenance assessments to the association[4] or to have its permission to erect buildings.[5] Under a true running covenant theory, the benefit of a

---

§ 8.33

1. Clark v. McGee, 159 Ill. 518, 42 N.E. 965 (1896); Snow v. Van Dam, 291 Mass. 477, 197 N.E. 224 (1935); Scaling v. Sutton, 167 S.W.2d 275 (Tex.Civ.App.1942), error refused; L. Simes & C. Taylor, The Improvement of Conveyancing by Legislation 220 (1960). See also Chief Justice Cardozo's suggestion in the penultimate paragraph of Bristol v. Woodward, 251 N.Y. 275, 167 N.E. 441 (1929).

2. 227 Or. 62, 361 P.2d 101 (1961) (dictum).

3. 291 Mass. 477, 197 N.E. 224 (1935).

4. Rodruck v. Sand Point Maintenance Commission, 48 Wn.2d 565, 295 P.2d 714 (1956).

5. See Hannula v. Hacienda Homes, 34 Cal.2d 442, 211 P.2d 302 (1949); Jones v. Northwest Real Estate Co., 149 Md. 271, 131 A. 446 (1925); Normandy Square Ass'n, Inc. v. Ells, 213 Neb. 60, 327 N.W.2d 101 (1982) (court upheld broad powers of architectural committee to disapprove of proposed structures);

covenant should be enforceable only by one who owns land benefited by the covenant.[6] In many situations the homeowners' association may own land within the subdivision that might be said to be benefited, such as a clubhouse or recreational facilities. It seems, however, that the decisions referred to do not contemplate the association's vindicating its own rights as landowner as much as they regard it as third-party beneficiary of the promise and as trustee to seek enforcement for the lot owners.[7] Whether one wants to label this reasoning a departure from traditional running covenant theory or simply the appending of other doctrines to such theory, it opens up a new dimension for subdivision restrictions. Clearly, here is another case in which American courts are persuaded of the socioeconomic utility of private land use controls.

We come finally to a "second-generation" theory that might be described as the natural evolution of equitable restrictions. It will be recalled that courts commonly term these "negative easements." What if we were to say literally that an equitable restriction, whether it is negative or affirmative, is a kind of easement, or at least enough like an easement, that it may be created and may pass as does an easement? The chief result of such reasoning would be to remove the requirement that a successor to the burdened land is bound only if he has notice of the restriction. While this is a sharp departure from the original theory of Tulk v. Moxhay,[8] with its emphasis on the element of notice, in practice it would cause only a ripple—notice nearly always comes through the operation of American recording acts anyway. A purchaser is not bound by a granted easement unless he has notice of it or is charged with notice by the recording of an instrument creating or identifying it.[9] The theory here described is suggested strongly by the 1877 New York opinion in Trustees of Columbia College v. Lynch.[10] It is true that the court speaks of "negative easements" and "equities" as well as of "easements," but it seems to have in mind a more literal affinity between easements and "negative easements" than have other courts using the latter term. Possibly the courts have not more pressed the "true easement" theory precisely because traditional equitable easement theory, combined with the recording acts, produces such similar results. The idea commends itself. To treat running covenants as easements would be a natural step that would cause little practical dislocation. And it would vastly simplify a complex subject.

Whiteco Metrocom, Inc. v. Industrial Properties Corp., 711 S.W.2d 81 (Tex.App.1986) (covenant requiring developer's approval of building plans was enforceable). See also Ardmore Park Subdivision Ass'n, Inc. v. Simon, 117 Mich.App. 57, 323 N.W.2d 591 (1982) (when restrictive covenant allowed majority of owners to modify restrictions, decision of majority was binding on all owners). Covenants that create powers for future exercise, such as covenants requiring architectural approval, covenants allowing homeowners to amend other covenants, and covenants requiring homeowners to be bound by decisions of a homeowners' association, seem to be growing in number and to be generally enforceable. Such covenants are very powerful, for they have a kind of multiplier effect.

6. See A. Casner & W. Leach, Cases and Text on Property 1073 (2d ed. 1969); Annot., 19 A.L.R.2d 1274, 1276 (1951).

7. This is explicitly stated in Merrionette Manor Homes Improvement Association v. Heda, 11 Ill.App.2d 186, 136 N.E.2d 556 (1956), and seems implicit in the decisions cited in notes 4 & 5, this section.

8. 2 Phil. 774, 41 Eng.Rep. 1143 (Ch. 1848).

9. 6A R. Powell, Real Property ¶¶ 904, 905 (P. Rohan rev. ed. 1990). See also 5 H. Tiffany, Real Property § 1263 (3d ed. 1939) (party walls). Most recording acts provide for the recording of easements. See, e.g., West's Rev. Code Wash.Ann. 65.08.060–65.08.070.

10. 70 N.Y. 440 (1877).

Chapter 9

GOVERNMENT CONTROL OF LAND USE

Table of Sections

A. THE CONSTITUTIONAL BASIS FOR GOVERNMENT CONTROL OF LAND USE

§ 9.1 Eminent Domain

Governments at the federal, state, or local levels may control the use of land in a variety of ways. Direct control is usually effected either by acquiring a recognized estate or interest in a particular parcel (or parcels) of land or by restricting the use of land by regulations based on the "police

505

power." Governments may acquire estates or interests in land by gift, by purchase, or by exercising their power of eminent domain. In this section we shall briefly consider the eminent domain power.

It is universally accepted that the power of eminent domain—the power to "take" private property for public use (or for a public purpose) without the owner's consent—is an inherent power of the federal and state governments, a necessary attribute of sovereignty.[1] The states may delegate the power to local units of government such as counties and municipal corporations. Moreover, despite the basic concept that eminent domain is a governmental power, the power of eminent domain may be—and has frequently been—delegated to private corporations, such as railroad and utility companies, which provide public service.[2]

Constitutional provisions do not create or grant the power of eminent domain to the state and federal governments. Rather both state and federal constitutions limit the power by requiring state and federal governments (and other entities to which the power is properly delegated) to pay for what they "take." The Fifth Amendment to the United States Constitution provides that "private property" shall not be "taken for public use [by the federal government] without just compensation." Although this clause does not, of its own force, apply to the states, it has been settled since 1897 that the "due process" clause of the Fourteenth Amendment makes this federal guarantee of just compensation applicable to the states,[3] thus providing a minimum level of protection for private property rights throughout the United States. In addition, all but three state constitutions expressly prohibit the taking of private property for public use without just compensation, and the other three have been construed to impose the same prohibition, although they do not do so expressly.[4]

§ 9.1

1. Kohl v. United States, 91 U.S. (1 Otto) 367, 23 L.Ed. 449 (1875), is the classic decision. Others are, e.g., United States v. Jones, 109 U.S. 513, 3 S.Ct. 346, 27 L.Ed. 1015 (1883); Bonaparte v. Camden & A.R. Co., 3 Fed.Cas. 821 (D.N.J.1830); Cairo & Fulton Railroad Co. v. Turner, 31 Ark. 494 (1876); and Sinnickson v. Johnson, 17 N.J.Law 129 (1839).

2. The seriatim opinions, especially Senator Tracy's, in Bloodgood v. Mohawk & Hudson River Railroad, 18 Wend. 9 (N.Y.1837), present the issue starkly. See also Stoebuck, A General Theory of Eminent Domain, 47 Wash.L.Rev. 553, 588–99 (1972); Comment, The Public Use Limitation on Eminent Domain: An Advance Requiem, 58 Yale L.J. 599 (1949).

3. Chicago, Burlington & Quincy Railroad Co. v. City of Chicago, 166 U.S. 226, 17 S.Ct. 581, 41 L.Ed. 979 (1897). Although in subsequent cases the courts have spoken of the "incorporation" of the Fifth Amendment's "taking" clause into the Fourteenth Amendment's "due process" clause, the Chicago, Burlington & Quincy Railroad Co. case does not use an "incorporation" rationale; instead, it holds that substantive "due process" requires payment of "just compensation" whenever pri-

vate property is "taken for public use." See J. Nowak, R. Rotunda & J. Young, Constitutional Law 412–15 (1978). Some confusion results from loose judicial statements that challenges to local land use regulations alleging a *de facto* "taking" are based on the Fifth Amendment. See, e.g., Penn Central Transportation Co. v. City of New York, 438 U.S. 104, 122, 98 S.Ct. 2646, 2658, 57 L.Ed.2d 631 (1978), rehearing denied 439 U.S. 883, 99 S.Ct. 226, 58 L.Ed.2d 198 (1978).

4. 1 P. Nichols, The Law of Eminent Domain § 1.3 at 78–79 (3d ed. J. Sackman rev. 1979). The three states are Kansas, North Carolina, and Virginia. The Kansas constitution expressly requires payment of compensation when private corporations acquire land for right of way use. Kan.—K.S.A. Const. Art. 12, § 4. The constitutions of the other 47 states contain "taking" clauses essentially like the "taking" clause of the Fifth Amendment, except that 26 of these states also require payment of compensation for property that is "damaged" as well as for property that is "taken." The "damaged" language tends to facilitate the award of compensation for certain nontrespassory interferences with private property and for trespassory but unintended interferences, where the courts might other-

We shall now look briefly at the meaning of the four elements of the typical constitutional "taking" clause.

Private Property

Eminent domain always concerns "property." In the bulk of eminent domain cases, it is obvious that governmental activity has affected an owner's property. The governmental entity seeks to acquire a well recognized legal species of property, the fee, an easement, or perhaps a leasehold, and it plans to occupy or use the area with something like a road, building, or park. There are, however, kinds of cases that do test the question, what is "property"? They are cases in which an alleged taking of property occurs without the governmental entity's necessarily touching the condemnee's land; we may categorize these as "nontrespassory taking" cases.

A typical nontrespassory taking case, and the most frequent kind, is one in which a state or local government has altered, or is about to alter, a landowner's access onto an abutting street or road.[5] The alteration might be caused by a physical barrier, such as a fence, or by a regulation restricting access. Assuming the public way is a "landservice" way, then the abutting owner has, by judge-made law, a right of reasonable ingress and egress to and from the road. Will the proposed alteration of this right amount to a taking of the owner's property, for which compensation is due? The underlying question is, what is "property" as used in a constitutional eminent domain clause? If one analyzes the owner's access right under accepted principles of the law of real property as it is taught today, it is clear the owner has an easement, appurtenant to his land and burdening the state's roadway. Easements are certainly forms of "property." It seems to follow that if the diminution of access is severe enough to invade the "reasonable" access, the owner has been deprived of property and ought to be compensated. That would in fact generally be the result in American courts today.[6] But through much of the 19th century it was not the result, on the rationale that "property" in a constitution had its "plain and popular" meaning of "physical" land instead of the legal abstraction of "property rights.[7]" The older concept was summed up in the phrase, "no taking without a touching."

Today it can pretty generally be said that eminent domain law accepts "property" as an abstract legal construct. Thus, compensation may be had on account of nontrespassory interferences by governmental entities that cause owners to lose air space rights;[8] that cause loss of riparian rights;[9] and that seriously interfere with many other interests normally regarded as property rights, such as easements, profits, restrictive covenants, and rights of lateral support that are extinguished when the land they burden is

wise find only noncompensable "consequential damaging" rather than a compensable "taking." Stoebuck, supra note 2 at 555.

5. For a fuller exploration of what is being said here, see Stoebuck, The Property Right of Access Versus the Power of Eminent Domain, 47 Texas L.Rev. 733 (1969).

6. See, e.g., McCandless v. City of Los Angeles, 214 Cal. 67, 4 P.2d 139 (1931); Iowa State Highway Commission v. Smith, 248

Iowa 869, 82 N.W.2d 755 (1957); Stoebuck, preceding note, at 741–57.

7. See, e.g., Callender v. Marsh, 18 Mass. (1 Pick.) 418 (1823).

8. See Stoebuck, Condemnation by Nuisance: The Airport Cases in Retrospect and Prospect, 71 Dick.L.Rev. 207 (1967).

9. See Stoebuck, Condemnation of Riparian Rights, A Species of Taking Without Touching, 30 La.L.Rev. 394 (1970).

condemned.[10]   Older notions that some physical trespass is required for a taking of property occasionally influence decisions.[11]   In the main, however, it can be said that if government, in furthering some activity it carries on, destroys or substantially diminishes a landowner's interests that would be considered property rights under the normal principles of property law, a taking of property has occurred.

In many of the nontrespassory "taking" cases mentioned in the preceding paragraph, the government did not really intend to acquire any property right by virtue of the activities alleged by the landowner to amount to a "taking of private property," and did not institute a formal eminent domain (or condemnation) proceeding to acquire that property right.[12]   In such cases, the landowner usually brings an "inverse condemnation" action alleging that his property was, in fact, "taken for public use" and asking the court to determine the compensation to which he is constitutionally entitled.[13]   And "inverse condemnation" actions are often brought in cases where there was a trespassory, though unintended, interference with the landowner's property rights—e.g., where there are frequent, low-level, direct overflights of his land by aircraft taking off from and landing at a nearby major public airport,[14] or where road construction or repair activity causes the flooding of nearby land,[15] the deposit of unwanted soil on nearby land,[16] or the sliding or erosion of nearby land.[17]

Taken

Not only must property be affected, but it must be "taken" for an act of eminent domain to have occurred and for compensation to be due.[18]   In the vast bulk of eminent domain cases, there is no issue whether a taking has occurred.   In the common examples given previously, governmental expropriation of land for roads, buildings, parks, and so forth, land is taken in the most literal sense; it will be entered and used physically.   The governmental entity, by force of the condemnation decree, receives a transfer of the condemnee's title, easement, or other interest.   An instrument of conveyance serves precisely the same purposes and is routinely used when condemnor and condemnee can agree on the price without trial.   We might call such takings "physical appropriations."   Yet if "property" is recognized as a non-physical legal construct, it should be possible to have non-physical takings, and it is.

---

10. See Stoebuck, Condemnation of Rights the Condemnee Holds in Lands of Others, 56 Iowa L.Rev. 293 (1970).

11. See, e.g., Batten v. United States, 306 F.2d 580 (10th Cir.1962), certiorari denied 371 U.S. 955, 83 S.Ct. 506, 9 L.Ed.2d 502 (1963), rehearing denied 372 U.S. 925, 83 S.Ct. 718, 9 L.Ed.2d 731 (1963).

12. E.g., the airport "nuisance" cases discussed in Stoebuck, supra note 8.

13. Ibid.

14. E.g., United States v. Causby, 328 U.S. 256, 66 S.Ct. 1062, 90 L.Ed. 1206 (1946) (not clear whether "taking" resulted from "trespass" or from "nuisance" effects of direct overflights); Griggs v. Allegheny County, 369 U.S. 84, 82 S.Ct. 531, 7 L.Ed.2d 585 (1962),

rehearing denied 369 U.S. 857, 82 S.Ct. 931, 8 L.Ed.2d 16 (1962).

15. E.g., Pumpelly v. Green Bay & Mississippi Canal Co., 80 U.S. (13 Wall.) 166, 20 L.Ed. 557 (1871); Bauer v. County of Ventura, 45 Cal.2d 276, 289 P.2d 1 (1955).

16. E.g., Wong Kee Jun v. City of Seattle, 143 Wash. 479, 255 P. 645 (1927).

17. E.g., Wong Kee Jun v. City of Seattle, supra note 16; Albers v. County of Los Angeles, 62 Cal.2d 250, 42 Cal.Rptr. 89, 398 P.2d 129 (1965).

18. Except where the state constitution requires payment of compensation for "damaging" as well as for "taking" private property. See supra note 4.

The most interesting "taking" issues are those raised by nontrespassory acts and by trespassory but unintended acts of the kinds discussed above in connection with "private property." To return to the previous example involving an abutting landowner's loss of street access, how does the taking occur? What is the mechanism? Before the governmental entity diminished the access, the owner had "reasonable" access. It was an easement, appurtenant to his land and burdening the government's real property interest in its street. If we assume it has been wholly shut up or unreasonably diminished, the owner has in effect been compelled to give a whole or partial release of the easement, as if it had been done by a deed of release. The owner has lost some of his property rights, and government's property rights have been increased by the removal of a burden on its street. Similar increases-decreases, i.e., transfers from owner to government, go on whenever nontrespassory governmental activity takes other property rights of the kinds suggested above, easements, profits, restrictive covenants, lateral support, and so forth. And in those cases where there is a substantial and continuing trespassory, though unintentional, interference with private property rights, the interest "taken" will usually be an easement of some kind—e.g., a "flowage (flooding) easement."

It is important to understand the foregoing discussion of the principles of "property" and "taking" and to see their application in the nontrespassory cases. In the next section we will explore the question whether, and if so when, governmental regulations that diminish a landowner's use and enjoyment of and can amount to a *de facto* taking of property. This is perhaps the most burning legal question that today surrounds the growing number of land-use regulations. A satisfactory answer has eluded our courts, especially the United States Supreme Court, for a hundred years.[19]

Public purpose

Constitutional eminent domain clauses generally contain the words "public use"—"private property shall not be taken for *public use* without just compensation." From the position of the words in the phrase, the reader might assume they were merely descriptive and did not impose a limitation on governmental use of the eminent domain power. After all, it does not say private property shall not be taken "except for" public use. However, since Hugo Grotius and other Continental jurisprudential writers first discussed eminent domain in the 17th century, the belief has been afoot that the purposes for which government might exercise its power of eminent domain should be somewhat more limited than those purposes that justify use of other powers.[20] For whatever reasons, the words "public use" are regarded as imposing some limitation on the exercise of the power, though, as we will see, it is not usually a very great restraint.

19. See especially Penn Central Transportation Co. v. City of New York, 438 U.S. 104, 98 S.Ct. 2646, 57 L.Ed.2d 631 (1978), rehearing denied 439 U.S. 883, 99 S.Ct. 226, 58 L.Ed.2d 198 (1978), where the Court admitted that it had been unable to find a satisfactory test for "regulatory takings."

20. See Bloodgood v. Mohawk & Hudson River Railroad, 18 Wend. 9 (N.Y.1837); H.

Grotius, De Jure Belli ac Pacis 385 (F. Kelsey transl.1925); C. Van Bynkershoek, Quaestionum Juris Publici 218 (T. Frank transl.1930); Stoebuck, supra note 2, at 588–99; Comment, The Public Use Limitation on Eminent Domain: An Advance Requiem, 58 Yale L.J. 599 (1949).

An extreme view, hardly ever applied in the cases, is that eminent domain may be used only to acquire interests in land that will physically be occupied or used by the public.[21]   In a few states, under the influence of state constitutional provisions, governmental entities may not condemn land to convey or lease it to private persons for their use.[22]   Perhaps the most persistent "public use" question arises in connection with so-called "excess condemnations" when a public entity proposes to condemn more land than it needs for a project or when it proposes to condemn land but has a project only vaguely in mind.   Courts have widely varying conceptions of how definitely fixed a project must be for public use to be present.[23]

Though the public use concept does impose some limitations on the occasions when governmental entities may employ eminent domain, as previously suggested, the restraint is not great.   The prevailing American view is similar to that spelled out by the Supreme Court in its leading decision in Berman v. Parker.[24]   There the question was whether the District of Columbia government might condemn land for urban renewal, land that was to be reconveyed to private developers who would redevelop it according to the renewal plan.   How could land be taken for "public use" if it was going to end up in private hands?   The Court's answer was that "use" meant, not who would physically use the land, but the purposes the government had for the project: to clear slums and to make the city more attractive.   Governmental power to do these things existed in the police power; eminent domain was a sort of ancillary power to accomplish these purposes that were justified by the police power.   Thus, the phrase "public use" was in *Berman,* and may today generally be, restated to mean "public purpose."   If the object be one government may pursue under one of its powers, then eminent domain may be used to pursue it.   Viewed thus, eminent domain may be employed in nearly all situations in which other governmental powers may be exercised.   Under this broad definition of "public use," the courts have upheld the use of eminent domain to acquire land simply for the purpose of commercial or industrial redevelopment.[25]

Recent decisions of the Michigan Supreme Court and of the United States Supreme Court raise the question whether the "public use" requirement imposes any real limitation upon governmental power to "take" private property for purposes that the government believes to be desirable.

---

21. See *Bloodgood* case, Stoebuck, and Comment, preceding note.

22. See, e.g., In re City of Seattle, 96 Wn.2d 616, 638 P.2d 549 (1981).   See also Coquina Oil Corp. v. Harry Kourlis Ranch, 643 P.2d 519 (Colo.1982).

23. Compare City of St. Petersburg v. Vinoy Park Hotel Co., 352 So.2d 149 (Fla.App. 1977) (sufficient public use; future park); with Salt Lake County v. Ramoselli, 567 P.2d 182 (Utah 1977) (not sufficient public use; future park).

24. 348 U.S. 26, 75 S.Ct. 98, 99 L.Ed. 27 (1954).

25. E.g., Courtesy Sandwich Shop, Inc. v. Port of New York Authority, 12 N.Y.2d 379, 240 N.Y.S.2d 1, 190 N.E.2d 402 (1963), appeal

dismissed 375 U.S. 78, 84 S.Ct. 194, 11 L.Ed.2d 141 (1963), rehearing denied 375 U.S. 960, 84 S.Ct. 440, 11 L.Ed.2d 318 (1963).   "Public purpose" sufficient to justify use of the eminent domain power has even been found where the property condemned was not "blighted" and was to be immediately resold to a private business organization (General Motors) which planned to build a large manufacturing facility on it.   Poletown Neighborhood Council v. City of Detroit, 410 Mich. 616, 304 N.W.2d 455 (1981) (purpose of condemnation and private redevelopment was to improve the economic condition of Detroit by providing new jobs and tax base; the court said the test of "public purpose" is whether there is "substantial proof that the public is primarily to be benefitted").

In Poletown Neighborhood Council v. City of Detroit,[26] the Michigan court approved the use of eminent domain by Detroit to acquire a large tract of land to be conveyed to General Motors Corporation as a site for construction of an automobile assembly plant. The court said that the test of constitutionality was whether the proposed condemnation was for "the primary benefit of the public or the private user," and sustained Detroit's action because eminent domain was "to be used in this instance primarily to accomplish the essential public purposes of alleviating unemployment and revitalizing the economic base of the community." The benefit to the private interest of General Motors was held to be "merely incidental." In Hawaii Housing Authority v. Midkiff,[27] the United States Supreme Court sustained a Hawaiian statute authorizing the state to take the fee simple title to realty from owner-lessors and transfer it to lessees in order to reduce the concentration of fee simple ownership.[28] In so holding, the Court relied largely upon Berman v. Parker, and summarized its reasoning in the following passage: [29]

> The mere fact that property taken outright by eminent domain is transferred * * * to private beneficiaries does not condemn that taking as having only a private purpose. The Court long ago rejected any literal requirement that condemned property be put into use for the general public. * * * As the unique way titles were held in Hawaii skewed the land market, exercise of the power of eminent domain was justified. * * * The Hawaii legislature enacted its Land Reform Act not to benefit a particular class of identifiable individuals but to attack certain perceived evils of concentrated property ownership in Hawaii—a legitimate public purpose. Use of the condemnation power for this purpose is not irrational.

Just compensation

In the overwhelming majority of eminent domain cases, there is no question whether a taking of property has occurred or whether it is for a public purpose, but only a question of "just compensation": how much does the condemnee get? We can attempt only the barest review of the most basic legal principles here, for just compensation is a question for the trier of fact. Volumes have been written on how to persuade juries to enlarge (or

---

26. 410 Mich. 616, 304 N.W.2d 455 (1981).

27. 467 U.S. 229, 104 S.Ct. 2321, 81 L.Ed.2d 186 (1984), on remand 740 F.2d 15 (9th Cir. 1984).

28. The Hawaii Legislature had determined that almost one-half the state's land was owned by the State and Federal Governments; that another 47% was in the hands of only 72 private owners; and that 18 landholders with tracts of 21,000 acres or more owned more than 40% of the 47% held by private owners.

29. 467 U.S. at 243–245, 104 S.Ct. at 2331, 81 L.Ed. at 199–200. Also see City of Oakland v. Oakland Raiders, 32 Cal.3d 60, 183 Cal. Rptr. 673, 646 P.2d 835 (1982), appeal after remand 136 Cal.App.3d 565, 186 Cal.Rptr. 326 (1982), holding that Oakland had stated a cause of action for condemnation of the Oakland Raiders' franchise and other assets, and rejecting the contention of the defendant that the taking contemplated by the City could not, as a matter of law, be for any "public use" within the City's authority. The court said, *inter alia,* that a "public use" is "a use which concerns the whole community or promotes the general interest in its relation to any legitimate object of government," but that it is "not essential that the entire community, or even any considerable portion thereof, shall directly enjoy or participate * * * in order to constitute a public use."

limit) verdicts and how to select and manage the real estate appraisers who inevitably testify as valuation experts.[30]

The most basic legal principle is that "just compensation" equals fair market value, generally in cash.[31] In cases in which part of an owner's land is taken and part remains, he may be entitled to "severance damages" suffered by the remaining part, in addition to compensation for the part taken.[32] This may occur, for instance, when the project for which the taking is made will interfere with use of the remaining land or when the simple fact that the two parts can no longer be used together reduces the value of the remaining part. Sometimes in cases of partial takings the remaining part is benefitted by the to-be presence of the project; a new highway may help land values a lot. Some jurisdictions do not allow the value of these benefits to be offset against the owner's award, but most jurisdictions to some extent allow benefits to be offset against either the entire award or against any part of it that is for severance damages.[33] When leased land is condemned special problems arise in apportioning the award between landlord and tenant. Though the total award should not be greater than if there were no leasehold, the tenant may be entitled to receive part of it.[34]

Many other details and specialized rules of "just compensation" might be discussed. It is time, however, to return to the main subject of this chapter, governmental control of land use by regulations based upon the police power, and to see in more detail how eminent domain bears upon that subject.

§ 9.2 The Police Power, Due Process, and the "Taking" Issue

(a) Introduction

As previously indicated, governments may control land use by regulation rather than by acquisition. The power of the federal government to regulate is derived from the various express power delegations in the United States Constitution. State governments, on the other hand, may regulate land use by virtue of their inherent powers, confirmed in the Tenth Amendment to the United States Constitution, and may delegate their powers to units of local government. When state and local governments regulate land

---

30. E.g., 4 & 5 P. Nichols, Eminent Domain (J. Sackman 3d ed. 1981); 1 & 2 L. Orgel, Valuation (1953).

31. Some representative leading decisions are Shoemaker v. United States, 147 U.S. 282, 13 S.Ct. 361, 37 L.Ed. 170 (1893); Riley v. District of Columbia Redevelopment Land Agency, 246 F.2d 641 (D.C.Cir.1957); Vanhorne's Lessee v. Dorrance, (Fed.Case No. 16,-857), 2 U.S. (2 Dall.) 304, 1 L.Ed. 391 (1795). In all the law of eminent domain, there is no more trenchant decision than Vanhorne v. Dorrance. There are perhaps some situations in which the fair market value test breaks down, as when the condemnee owns something for which there is no market. For an application of the "substitute facilities" doctrine to such a case, see City of Tulsa v. Mingo School District, 559 P.2d 487 (Okl.App.1976).

32. See generally Sharp v. United States, 191 U.S. 341, 24 S.Ct. 114, 48 L.Ed. 211 (1903); 4A P. Nichols, supra note 18, at secs. 14.2–14.4.

33. See generally Chiesa v. State, 36 N.Y.2d 21, 364 N.Y.S.2d 848, 324 N.E.2d 329 (1974); 3 P. Nichols, supra note 18, at sec. 8.62. A refinement, not noted in text, is that in many jurisdictions offsetting benefits are considered only to the extent they are "special" benefits, those that accrue peculiarly to this owner or only to a few similarly situated owners and not generally to large numbers of persons.

34. See generally Department of Public Works v. Metropolitan Life Insurance Co., 42 Ill.App.2d 378, 192 N.E.2d 607 (1963); 7A P. Nichols, supra note 18, at secs. 11.01–12.05.

use, it is almost invariably said that they are exercising the "police power." Although definitions of the "police power" may vary a bit from one judicial opinion to the next, all courts would undoubtedly accept the following definition: the police power is the power of government to regulate human conduct to protect or promote "public health, safety, or the general welfare."[1]

The power of the federal government to regulate land use is expressly limited by the "due process" and "taking" clauses of the Fifth Amendment to the United States Constitution.[2] Although the Fourteenth Amendment contains no "taking" clause, it has long been settled that the "due process" clause makes the "taking" clause of the Fifth amendment applicable to the states.[3] Thus the states (and their political subdivisions) are subject to limitations under the Fourteenth Amendment that are identical with the limitations imposed on the federal government by the Fifth Amendment, as well as the "equal protection" guarantee expressly included in the Fourteenth Amendment.[4] In addition, the power of state and local governments is expressly limited by "due process" and/or "taking" clauses in the various state constitutions.

State statutes and local ordinances regulating land use are frequently challenged on the ground that they deprive the landowner of property without "substantive due process"—as distinct from "procedural due process"—and/or amount to a *de facto* "taking of private property for public use without just compensation." Unfortunately, it is often unclear whether the challenge is based on the state constitution or on the Fourteenth Amendment, and the courts generally do not distinguish clearly between "substantive due process" and "taking" arguments. Where the challenge is based (at

§ 9.2

1. E.g., Village of Euclid v. Ambler Realty Co., 272 U.S. 365, 395, 47 S.Ct. 114, 121, 71 L.Ed. 303 (1926) (local zoning ordinance was valid exercise of police power unless "clearly arbitrary and unreasonable, having no substantial relation to the public health, safety, morals, or general welfare."). It is obvious that "health," "safety," and "morals" are simply specific aspects of the "general welfare." Some of the earlier cases often expressly mentioned other aspects of the general welfare such as "public convenience and prosperity."

2. "No person shall * * * be deprived of life, liberty, or property, without due process of law; nor shall private property be taken for public use, without just compensation."

3. The first case clearly so holding is Chicago, Burlington & Quincy Railroad Co. v. City of Chicago, 166 U.S. 226, 17 S.Ct. 581, 41 L.Ed. 979 (1897). For further discussion, see ante Section 9.1 note 3.

4. State and local land use regulations are also, of course, subject to the Fourteenth Amendment's "equal protection" clause. Consequently, denial of equal protection is sometimes the basis of a successful challenge to land use regulations which are alleged to single out the challenger for more onerous treatment than other landowners who are similarly situated. See, Ronda Realty Corp. v. Lawton, 414 Ill. 313, 111 N.E.2d 310 (1953). Churches and religious organizations may sometimes successfully challenge land use regulations on the ground that they infringe the "free exercise" clause of the First Amendment, as made applicable to the states by the Fourteenth Amendment. See e.g., Westchester Reform Temple v. Brown, 22 N.Y.2d 488, 293 N.Y.S.2d 297, 239 N.E.2d 891 (1968); State ex rel. Wenatchee Congregation of Jehovah's Witnesses v. City of Wenatchee, 50 Wn.2d 378, 312 P.2d 195 (1957). But see Corporation of Presiding Bishop v. City of Porterville, 90 Cal.App.2d 656, 203 P.2d 823 (1949). Organizations in the business of disseminating information, such as bookstores and movie theaters, have also successfully challenged land use regulations on the ground that they violate the First Amendment's guarantee of free speech as made applicable to the states by the Fourteenth Amendment. See, e.g., Schad v. Borough of Mount Ephraim, 452 U.S. 61, 101 S.Ct. 2176, 68 L.Ed.2d 671 (1981). Cf. Young v. American Mini Theatres, 427 U.S. 50, 96 S.Ct. 2440, 49 L.Ed.2d 310 (1976), rehearing denied 429 U.S. 873, 97 S.Ct. 191, 50 L.Ed.2d 155 (1976).

least partly) on the Fourteenth Amendment, this is understandable, since the Fourteenth Amendment (as noted above) contains no "taking" clause and the "taking" challenge is thus always, in a sense, a "substantive due process" challenge; a land use regulation that amounts to a *de facto* "taking" violates the Fourteenth Amendment *only* because it is deemed, *ipso facto,* to deprive the landowner of his property "without due process of law."

(b) The Supreme Court Cases from Mugler v. Kansas to Nectow v. Cambridge

Further confusion has arisen in land use regulation cases because the United States Supreme Court—which establishes the minimum constitutional limitations on the exercise of state and local police power—has not developed any consistent standard to determine the validity of police power regulations challenged under the Fourteenth Amendment. In Mugler v. Kansas,[5] where the Court upheld a Kansas statute that prohibited the manufacture of intoxicating liquors, the Court applied a substantive due process test but declared that the Fourteenth Amendment's due process clause was not "designed to interfere with the power of the States, sometimes termed police power, to prescribe regulations to promote the health, peace, morals, education and good order of the people, and to legislate so as to increase the industries of the State, develop its resources, and add to its wealth and prosperity."[6] Hence, said the Court, the police power of the States "cannot be burdened with the condition that the State must compensate * * * individual owners of property for pecuniary losses they may sustain, by their not being permitted, by a *noxious* use of their property, to inflict injury on the community."[7] The Court also said that a valid legislative act prohibiting the use of property in a manner declared by a state to be "injurious to the health, safety, morals, or safety of the community is not an appropriation of property for the public benefit in the sense in which a taking of the property by the exercise of the State's power of eminent domain is such a taking or appropriation."[8] And the Court adopted a deferential attitude with respect to the legislative determination that the manufacture of liquor was "injurious" to the public.[9]

A few years later, in Lawton v. Steele,[10] the Court, in upholding a New York statute that authorized seizure and destruction of illegal fishing nets without compensating the owners, said that a purported exercise of the police power is valid under the Fourteenth Amendment if it appears, "first, that the interests of the public * * * require such interference; second, that the means are reasonably necessary for the accomplishment of the purpose, and not unduly oppressive on individuals."[11] This has long been considered the classic statement of the concept of "substantive due process." Unfortunately, however, *Lawton* did not indicate the relative weight to be attached to each of the designated factors, proper governmental purpose, reasonable means to achieve the purpose, and the adverse impact of the regulation on the landowner affected by it. In many state cases involving challenges to

---

5. 123 U.S. 623, 8 S.Ct. 273, 31 L.Ed. 205 (1887).

6. 123 U.S. at 663, 8 S.Ct. at 298.

7. 123 U.S. at 669, 8 S.Ct. at 301.

8. 123 U.S. at 668, 8 S.Ct. at 301.

9. 123 U.S. at 660, 8 S.Ct. at 296.

10. 152 U.S. 133, 14 S.Ct. 499, 38 L.Ed. 385 (1894).

11. 152 U.S. at 137, 14 S.Ct. at 501.

the validity of land use regulations, the courts seem to accept the *Lawton* substantive due process formula as a basis for "balancing" the importance of the public purpose and the reasonableness of the means against the adverse (usually economic) impact on the landowner.[12]

In two important cases decided after *Lawton*, the Supreme Court seemed to revert to the *Mugler* test of validity and to ignore arguments that the regulations under attack were "unduly oppressive." In Reinman v. City of Little Rock,[13] the Court upheld an ordinance prohibiting the operation of livery stables in downtown Little Rock, asserting that the only constitutional limitation on the police power of the states is that it cannot be exercised arbitrarily or with unjust discrimination. In Hadacheck v. Sebastian,[14] the Court sustained a Los Angeles ordinance prohibiting the manufacture of bricks in a designated part of the city where Hadacheck owned a brick factory and a valuable deposit of "brick clay" which he was making into bricks "on site." The Court did not directly address Hadacheck's allegation (supported by affidavit) that the ordinance reduced the value of his land from $800,000 to $60,000. Instead, the Court declared,

> We are dealing with one of the most essential powers of government, one that is the least limitable [the police power]. It may, indeed, seem harsh in its exercise, usually is on some individual, but the imperative necessity for its exercise precludes any limitation upon it when not exerted arbitrarily. A vested interest cannot be asserted against it because of conditions once obtaining. * * * To so hold would preclude development and fix a city forever in its primitive conditions. There must be progress, and if in its march private interests are in the way, they must yield to the good of the community.[15]

Despite the Supreme court's ringing indorsement of the police power and its failure to consider how "oppressive" the regulations upheld in *Reinman* and *Hadacheck* might be from the viewpoint of the owners of livery stables and brick factories, respectively, the Court proceeded only a few years later, in Pennsylvania Coal Co. v. Mahon,[16] to strike down a state statute forbidding the mining of coal in certain areas so as to cause subsidence of the surface.[17] The action was brought by Mahon to prevent the Pennsylvania Coal company from mining under their property in viola-

---

12. E.g., Hartung v. Village of Skokie, 22 Ill.2d 485, 177 N.E.2d 328 (1961). In many of the cases the "balancing" test is implicit rather than explicit. Since the "balancing" test presumably attempts to measure net social gains against the economic loss to individual landowners, it is basically a utilitarian test. Some critics have questioned the fairness of using the "balancing" test. See, e.g., Michelman, Property, Utility, and Fairness: Comments on the Ethical Foundations of "Just Compensation" Law, 80 Harv.L.Rev. 1165 (1967). In any case, it is far from clear that courts are really capable of applying the "balancing" test, since it requires courts to make subjective evaluations of the public interests that may rightfully serve to balance economic losses to landowners. In a sense, this is like "balancing" apples against oranges.

13. 237 U.S. 171, 35 S.Ct. 511, 59 L.Ed. 900 (1914).

14. 239 U.S. 394, 36 S.Ct. 143, 60 L.Ed. 348 (1915).

15. 239 U.S. at 410, 36 S.Ct. at 145.

16. 260 U.S. 393, 43 S.Ct. 158, 67 L.Ed. 322 (1922).

17. The statute, Pennsylvania's Kohler Act, prohibited the mining of anthracite coal within the limits of a city in such a manner or to such an extent "as to cause the * * * subsidence of any dwelling or other structure used as human habitation, or any factory, store, or other industrial or mercantile establishment in which human labor is employed" as well as mining so as to cause the subsidence of public streets or public buildings.

tion of the statutory prohibition. Justice Holmes began his opinion for the majority by stating that, "if we were called upon to deal with the plaintiff's position alone, we should think it clear that the statute does not disclose a public interest sufficient to justify so extensive a destruction of the defendant's constitutionally protected right." [18] Justice Holmes then proceeded to consider the "general validity" of the statute [19] and held that, although the Court would assume that "an exigency existed that would warrant the exercise of eminent domain," [20] the statute nevertheless was invalid "so far as it affects the mining of coal under streets or cities where the right to mine such coal has been reserved" by the coal company, because the statute made it "commercially impractical to mine certain coal," which had "very nearly the same effect for constitutional purposes as appropriating or destroying it." [21] In the course of his opinion, Justice Holmes made the oft-repeated statement that "[t]he general rule * * * is that while property may be regulated to a certain extent, if regulation goes too far it will be recognized as a taking. * * * [T]his is a question of degree—and therefore cannot be disposed of by general propositions. But we regard this [case] as going beyond any of the cases decided by this Court." [22]

18. 260 U.S. at 414, 43 S.Ct. at 159. Justice Holmes also said: "The extent of the public interest is shown by the statute to be limited, since the statute ordinarily does not apply to land when the surface is owned by the owner of the coal. Furthermore, it is not justified as a protection of personal safety. That could be provided for by notice. Indeed the very foundation of this bill is that the defendant gave timely notice of its intent to mine under the house. On the other hand the extent of the taking is great. It purports to abolish what is recognized in Pennsylvania as an estate in land—a very valuable estate—and what is declared by the Court below to be a contract hitherto binding the defendants." Ibid.

19. 260 U.S. at 414, 43 S.Ct. at 159–160. Justice Holmes said that "the case has been treated as one in which the general validity of the act should be discussed. The Attorney General of the State, the City of Scranton, and the representatives of other extensive interests were allowed to take part in the argument below and have submitted their contentions here. It seems, therefore, to be our duty to go farther in the statement of our opinion, in order that it may be known at once, and that further suits should not be brought in vain." Ibid.

20. 260 U.S. at 416, 43 S.Ct. at 160.

21. 260 U.S. at 414, 43 S.Ct. at 160.

22. 260 U.S. at 415–416, 43 S.Ct. at 160. Justice Holmes also said: "Government could hardly go on if to some extent values incident to property could not be diminished without paying for every such change in the general law. As long recognized, some values are enjoyed under the implied limitation and must yield to the police power. But obviously the implied limitation must have its limits or the contract and due process clauses are gone. One fact for consideration in determining such limits is the extent of the diminution. When it reaches a certain magnitude, in most if not in all cases there must be an exercise of eminent domain and compensation to sustain the act. The greatest weight is given to the judgment of the legislature, but it is always open to the interested parties to contend that the legislature has gone beyond its constitutional power." 260 U.S. at 413, 43 S.Ct. at 159.

There is nothing in either the majority opinion by Justice Holmes or the dissent by Justice Brandeis to indicate what percentage of the remaining underground coal owned by defendant coal company would have to be left in place to satisfy the Kohler Act, nor is there anything in either opinion to indicate the dollar value of such coal. The Brandeis dissent argued that, "If we are to consider the value of the coal kept in place by the [statutory] restriction, we should compare it with the value of all other parts of the land. That is, with the value not of the coal alone, but with the value of the whole property. The rights of an owner as against the public are not increased by dividing the interests in his property into surface and subsoil." 260 U.S. at 419, 43 S.Ct. at 161. Brandeis also rejected the basic Holmesian analysis, arguing that, in accord with Mugler v. Kansas, supra note 5, a governmental restriction "imposed to protect the public health, safety or morals from dangers threatened is not a taking" because the government "merely prevents the owner from making a use which interferes with paramount rights of the public." 260 U.S. at 417, 43 S.Ct. at 161.

In *Pennsylvania Coal* Justice Holmes did not cite *Mugler, Lawton, Reinman,* or *Hadacheck*. It can be argued that his opinion simply applied the *Lawton* test and that "too far" was merely a synonym for "unduly oppressive." It is clear, however, that Holmes did not purport to "balance" the statutory purpose and the means against the adverse impact on coal mine owners. Instead, he appeared to hold that when the regulation goes "too far"—i.e., is so restrictive as to deprive the landowner of most of the value of his property—it must be struck down as an unconstitutional "taking" even though the purpose of the statute is clearly to protect the public from great harm and the means adopted to achieve the purpose is clearly reasonable.

In Village of Euclid v. Ambler Realty Co.,[23] the Court sustained the then new "zoning" technique for regulating urban land uses in principle as against a substantive due process challenge based on the argument that land use regulation by "zoning" was inherently "arbitrary and unreasonable, having no substantial relation to the public health, safety, morals, or general welfare." [24] The Realty Company also seems to have argued that the Euclid ordinance, in fact, reduced the value of its property so greatly as to amount to a *de facto* "taking," [25] but the Court simply ignored this argument.[26] And in Nectow v. Cambridge [27] the Court invalidated the residential zoning classification placed on a particular tract of land *not* because it amounted to a *de facto* "taking" but because it did not promote "the health, safety, convenience and general welfare of the inhabitants of the part of the city affect" by that classification [28]—i.e., because it denied the landowner substantive due process.

---

23. 272 U.S. 365, 47 S.Ct. 114, 71 L.Ed. 303 (1926).

24. The Court adopted a deferential attitude to the local legislative body. After discussing the possible rational bases for a comprehensive zoning ordinance like that of the Village of Euclid, the Court said:

> If these reasons * * * do not demonstrate the wisdom or sound policy in all respects of these restrictions which we have indicated as pertinent to the inquiry, at least, the reasons are sufficiently cogent to preclude us from saying as it must be said before the ordinance can be declared unconstitutional, that such provisions are clearly arbitrary and unreasonable, having no substantial relation to the public health, safety, morals, or general welfare.

25. Although the proof was apparently not too convincing, the Ambler Realty Co. alleged that some of its land was well suited to industrial development and would be worth $10,000 per acre for industrial use, but was worth only $2,500 per acre under the residential use classification imposed it by the zoning ordinance. Similarly, it was alleged "that the first 200 feet of the parcel back from Euclid Avenue [the main street of Euclid], if unrestricted in respect of use, has a value of $150 per front foot, but if limited to residential uses [as it

was by the zoning ordinance], and ordinary mercantile businesses be excluded therefrom, its value is not in excess of $50 per front foot."

26. The Court said, "it is enough for us to determine, as we do, that the ordinance in its general scope and dominant features, so far as its provisions are here involved, is a valid exercise of authority." 272 U.S. at 397, 47 S.Ct. at 121. In thus limiting its review of the Euclid zoning ordinance, the Court seems largely to have adopted the position taken in Alfred Bettman's *amicus curiae* brief, which was "designed to discuss solely the question of the constitutionality of comprehensive zoning" and not to deal with "the reasonableness or arbitrariness of the Euclid Village ordinance itself in its districting of the particular property of the appellee." See A. Bettman, City and Regional Planning Papers 157 (1946).

27. 277 U.S. 183, 48 S.Ct. 447, 72 L.Ed. 842 (1928).

28. The Court accepted the finding of the master appointed by the Massachusetts trial court, which used the language quoted in the text. The Court also said that the evidence clearly showed that the invasion of the plaintiff's property rights by the residential use classification was "serious and highly injurious," and "since a necessary basis for the support of that invasion is wanting, the action

(c) The Supreme Court Cases from Nectow v. Cambridge to Lucas to
South Carolina Coastal Council

During the late 1930s, after the defeat of President Roosevelt's "court
packing" proposal, the Supreme Court practically abandoned the substantive
due process concept with respect to the regulation of business activity. For
several decades it seemed clear that the Court would almost never strike
down legislation regulating such activity on substantive due process
grounds.[29] But the Supreme Court in a series of land use cases beginning in
the 1950s cited both *Mahon* and *Nectow* with approval and made it clear
that both the "taking" doctrine and the substantive due process doctrine
were still alive.[30]

Penn Central Transportation Co. v. City of New York [31] contains a full-
scale review of the "regulatory taking" issue by the Supreme court. The
Court summarized all its prior "taking" cases, citing with apparent approval—and without any express recognition of the extent to which these prior
"taking" cases are inconsistent—*Mugler, Reinman, Hadacheck, Mahon, Euclid,* and *Nectow*. The Court then decided, without explaining why, that the
Mahon "too far" test should be applied and held that the New York city
landmark preservation ordinance before the Court did not go "too far," and
thus constituted a valid exercise of the police power, because it permitted "a
reasonable beneficial use of the landmark site." [32] Further language in the
opinion indicates that the Court equated "reasonable beneficial use" with a
"reasonable return" on the landmark owner's investment in the Grand
Central Terminal building.[33]

The majority opinion in *Penn Central* certainly does little to clear up the
existing confusion arising from the unresolved tension between the inconsistent *Mugler* and *Mahon* approaches to "regulatory taking" issues. Once it is
determined, on some basis, that the *Mahon* approach should be applied, the
Penn Central "reasonable beneficial use" or "reasonable return on investment" test may be some improvement on the original *Mahon* "too far" test;
but it does not really make prediction of the results much easier in "regula-

of the zoning authorities comes within the ban
of the Fourteenth Amendment and cannot be
sustained." 277 U.S. at 188, 48 S.Ct. at 448.

29. See especially United States v. Caro-
lene Products Co., 304 U.S. 144, 152 n. 4, 58
S.Ct. 778, 783 n. 4, 82 L.Ed. 1234 (1938); Olsen
v. Nebraska, 313 U.S. 236, 61 S.Ct. 862, 85
L.Ed. 1305 (1941); Williamson v. Lee Optical
Co., 348 U.S. 483, 75 S.Ct. 461, 99 L.Ed. 563
(1955), rehearing denied 349 U.S. 925, 75 S.Ct.
657, 99 L.Ed. 1256 (1955); and North Dakota
Board of Pharmacy v. Snyder's Drug Stores,
414 U.S. 156, 94 S.Ct. 407, 38 L.Ed.2d 379
(1973), on remand 219 N.W.2d 140 (N.D.1974).
See generally, McCloskey, Economic Due Process and the Supreme Court: Exhumation and
Reburial, 1962 Sup.Ct.Rev. 34.10.

30. See, e.g., Goldblatt v. Town of Hempstead, 369 U.S. 590, 82 S.Ct. 987, 8 L.Ed.2d 130
(1962); Moore v. East Cleveland, 431 U.S. 494,
97 S.Ct. 1932, 52 L.Ed.2d 531 (1977) (opinions
of Stevens and White, JJ.); Penn Central

Transportation Co. v. City of New York, 438
U.S. 104, 98 S.Ct. 2646, 57 L.Ed.2d 631 (1978),
rehearing denied 439 U.S. 883, 99 S.Ct. 226, 58
L.Ed.2d 198 (1978). See also the recent cases
sustaining procedural due process requirements in order to protect economic interests—
e.g., Lynch v. Household Finance Corp., 405
U.S. 538, 92 S.Ct. 1113, 31 L.Ed.2d 424 (1972),
rehearing denied 406 U.S. 911, 92 S.Ct. 1611,
31 L.Ed.2d 822 (1972); Fuentes v. Shevin, 407
U.S. 67, 92 S.Ct. 1983, 32 L.Ed.2d 556 (1972),
rehearing denied 409 U.S. 902, 93 S.Ct. 177, 34
L.Ed.2d 165 (1972); Sniadach v. Family Finance Corp., 395 U.S. 337, 89 S.Ct. 1820, 23
L.Ed.2d 349 (1969). Lynch v. Household Finance Co., 405 U.S. at 552, 92 S.Ct. at 1122,
contains a strong affirmation of the importance of constitutional protection of "property" as well as "personal" rights.

31. Supra note 27.

32. 438 U.S. at 138, 98 S.Ct. at 2666.

33. 438 U.S. at 136, 98 S.Ct. at 2665.

tory taking" cases than was previously the case.[34] More important, perhaps, is the explicit statement in the *Penn Central* majority opinion that " 'Taking' jurisprudence does not divide a single parcel into discrete segments and attempt to determine whether rights in a particular segment have been entirely abrogated," but rather focuses "on the nature and extent of the interference with [the owner's] rights in the parcel as a whole." [35] This statement apparently repudiates the Court's approach in *Mahon,* where it seems to have focused entirely on the coal that was required by statute to be left in the ground, and to adopt the contrary view expressed by Justice Brandeis in his *Mahon* dissent.[36]

Unfortunately, Justice Brennan's opinion for the majority in *Penn Central* contains a confusing mixture of substantive due process, equal protection, and "taking" analysis, and does little to clarify the standards to be applied in "taking" cases.[37] Justice Brennan's statement that "a use restriction on real property may constitute a 'taking' if not reasonably necessary to the effectuation of a substantial public purpose," [38] would appear to be the principal source of the notion, adopted in several more recent Supreme Court cases, that a "taking" occurs whenever a land use regulation violates substantive due process either because it lacks a proper public purpose or is not reasonably calculated to achieve such a purpose.[39] This is both confusing and incorrect. Although it is clear that every "taking" violates the Fourteenth Amendment's due process clause, it does not follow that every violation of that clause is a "taking." A regulation may clearly violate the due process clause because "it is not necessary to effectuate a substantial public purpose" without causing sufficient economic injury to amount to a "taking." [40]

34. It is not absolutely clear that the Court really intended to equate "reasonable beneficial use" with "reasonable return on investment." See supra in text at notecall 33. Moreover, the Court, in listing relevant considerations in "taking" cases, stated that one relevant consideration is whether the regulatory measure alleged to amount to a *de facto* "taking" frustrates the landowner's "distinct investment-backed expectations," citing Pennsylvania Coal Co. v. Mahon, supra note 16, but did not attempt to define "distinct investment-backed expectations." This term is not used in the *Pennsylvania Coal* majority opinion, nor is it used in Goldblatt v. Town of Hempstead, supra note 27, which Justice Brennan also cited in his majority opinion in *Penn Central* as adopting the "distinct investment-backed investment expectations" test. All these "taking" tests have been mentioned in decisions subsequent to *Penn Central,* along with an "economically viable use" test attributed to the *Penn Central* majority opinion in Agins v. City of Tiburon, 447 U.S. 255, 260, 100 S.Ct. 2138, 2141, 65 L.Ed.2d 106 (1980), although not actually mentioned in *Penn Central.*

35. 438 U.S. at 130, 98 S.Ct. at 2662.

36. See supra note 22 (second para.).

37. See 438 U.S. at 123–131, 135–138 ("taking" analysis), and 131–135 ("due process" and "equal protection" analysis), 98 S.Ct. at 2658–2662, 2665–2666 ("taking" analysis), and 2663–2665 ("due process" and "equal protection" analysis).

38. 438 U.S. at 127, 98 S.Ct. at 2660 (citing *Goldblatt,* supra note 30, and Nectow, supra note 27).

39. See Keystone Bituminous Coal Association v. De Benedictis, infra note 41; Nollan v. California Coastal Commission, infra note 51; and First Evangelical Lutheran Church, infra note 66.

40. See Wiseman, When the End Justifies the Means: Understanding Takings Jurisprudence in a Legal System with Integrity, 63 St. John's L.Rev. 433, 447–451 (1989).

An excellent discussion of the "separation" and the "unification" models of the proper relation between "due process" and "taking" can be found in Davis & Glickman, To The Promised Land: A Century of Wandering and a Final Homeland For The Due Process and Taking Clauses, 68 Oregon L.Rev. 393 (1989), reprinted in 1991 Land Use & Environmental Law Review 211.

The next important United States Supreme Court case after *Penn Central* was Keystone Bituminous Coal Association v. De Benedictis,[41] where the Court sustained a Pennsylvania statute (hereafter referred to as the Subsidence Act)[42] that is very similar to the Kohler Act struck down in Pennsylvania Coal Co. v. Mahon. Despite the similarity of the two statutes, Justice Stevens in his majority opinion in *Keystone* distinguished *Pennsylvania Coal* on various grounds and thus was able to conclude that the Subsidence Act was not invalid as an uncompensated "taking" of the bituminous coal mining companies' property. Many of the grounds used by Justice Stevens to distinguish the two cases are unpersuasive to the writer, particularly Justice Stevens' conclusions (1) that the principal part of Justice Homes' *Pennsylvania Coal* opinion, which addressed the "general validity" of the Kohler Act, was merely "advisory" and therefore not a precedent to be followed in deciding *Keystone Bituminous;*[43] (2) that in *Pennsylvania Coal* Justice Holmes concluded that the Kohler Act was "enacted solely for the benefit of private parties" and "served only private interests";[44] and (3) that in *Pennsylvania Coal* Justice Holmes concluded that the Kohler Act made it impossible to mine anthracite coal profitably in the area covered by the Act.[45]

In *Keystone* The Supreme Court seems, in substance, to have adopted two of the principal arguments upon which Justice Brandeis rested his dissent in *Pennsylvania Coal*: (1) that if the court is "to consider the value of the coal kept in place by the [statutory] restriction," the court should compare that value with "the value of all other parts of the land," and (2) that an owner's rights against the public are not increased by dividing the interests in his property into surface subsoil.[46] The *Keystone Court* clearly accepted these arguments insofar as it rested its decision on a holding that the 27 million tons of coal that the Subsidence Act would require to be left in place "do not constitute a separate segment of property for takings law purposes,"[47] and insofar as the Court refused to recognize the "support estate" as a separate property interest that could be deemed to have been "taken" as a result of enactment of the Subsidence Act, despite the fact that the "support estate" was clearly so recognized by Pennsylvania law.[48]

---

41. 480 U.S. 470, 107 S.Ct. 1232, 94 L.Ed.2d 472 (1987).

42. Bituminous Mine Subsidence and Land Conservation Act, 52 Pa.Stat.Ann., § 4 of the Act prohibits mining that causes subsidence damage to any public buildings and noncommercial buildings generally used by the public, any dwellings used for human habitation, and any cemeteries. Since 1966 the Pennsylvania Department of Environmental Resources has applied a formula that generally requires 50% of the coal beneath structures protected by § 4 to be kept in place in order to provide surface support. Sec. 6 of the act authorizes the DER to revoke a mining permit if the removal of coal causes damage to a structure or area protected by § 4 and the coal operator has not within six months either repaired the damage, satisfied any claim arising therefrom, or deposited a sum equal to the

reasonable cost of repair with the DER as security.

43. 480 U.S. at 483–484, 107 S.Ct. at 1241.

44. 480 U.S. at 484–486, 107 S.Ct. at 1241–1243.

45. 480 U.S. at 493, 499, 107 S.Ct. at 1246, 1249.

46. See supra note 22, for Brandeis' language. In *Keystone Bituminous,* Justice Stevens did not cite or quote Brandeis' dissent; instead Stevens quoted Justice Brennan's reformulation of Brandeis' views in *Penn Central,* which is set out ante in text between notecalls 35 and 36.

47. 480 U.S. at 498–499, 107 S.Ct. at 1248–1249.

48. 480 U.S. at 500–502, 107 S.Ct. at 1249–1250.

In view of the significant change in the personnel of the United States Supreme Court since *Keystone* was decided,[49] its continuing viability as a precedent is unclear. Three subsequent "taking" decisions suggest that the new conservative majority of the Court is now in the process of adopting a more property-protective attitude than the attitude displayed in *Penn Central* and *Keystone*.[50]

In Nollan v. California Coastal Commission,[51] the Court held that a "condition" requiring donation of an easement in order to obtain a building permit was invalid as a "taking" because the condition did not "substantially advance" the "legitimate state interest" which allegedly justified imposition of the condition. Justice Scalia, writing for the *Nollan* majority, stated that exacting the grant of an easement without providing compensation would effect a *de facto* "taking" unless the exaction would substantially mitigate some "harm" that would otherwise be visited upon the public by construction of a house on a beachfront lot.[52] The California Coastal Commission argued that the "harm" from which the easement would protect the public was "blockage of the view of the ocean" from the street upon which the Nollan's lot fronted, creating a "psychological barrier" to using the beach resulting from a developed beachfront, and "congestion on the public beaches" which were located a quarter of a mile north and 1800 feet south of the Nollans' lot.[53] The Commission also argued that this "harm" could be prevented by requiring donation of a lateral easement along the Nollans' beachfront between their seawall and the mean high water mark of the ocean.[54] The Court rejected this argument because "[i]t is quite impossible to understand how a requirement that people already on the beaches be able to walk across the Nollans' property reduces any obstacles to viewing the beach created by the new house * * * or how it lowers any 'psychological barrier' to using the public beaches * * * or how it helps to remedy any additional congestion on them." [55] Hence, the Court held, the "essential nexus" between the purpose of the condition attached to the grant of a building permit and the means selected to achieve that purpose was completely lacking.[56] The Court said that in a "taking" case, the "essential nexus" requirement is met only if the challenged regulation "substantially advances" a "legitimate state interest," [57] a requirement clearly not satisfied in *Nollan*. Indeed, the Court clearly indicated that the condition attached to issuance of a building permit did not even satisfy the less demanding requirement that the state "could rationally have decided" that the condition "might achieve the state's objective," which the court said was appropri-

---

49. Of the Justices who voted with Justice Stevens to make up a majority in *Keystone Bituminous,* only Justices Blackmun and White are still members of the Court.

50. This wing of the Court now generally includes Chief Justice Rehnquist and Justices Kennedy, O'Connor, Souter, Thomas, and White.

51. 483 U.S. 825, 107 S.Ct. 3141, 97 L.Ed.2d 677 (1987).

52. 483 U.S. at 838, 107 S.Ct. at 3148. In support of this conclusion Justice Scalia cited a large number of state court cases in which— although he did not advert to the fact—the

validity of subdivision exactions such as mandatory dedications of land for new streets, parks, and school sites were challenged by land developers. For more on subdivision exactions, see post Section 9.17.

53. 483 U.S. at 828, 835, 838, 107 S.Ct. at 3143, 3147, 3149.

54. 483 U.S. at 829, 838, 107 S.Ct. at 3144, 3149.

55. 483 U.S. at 838–839, 107 S.Ct. at 3149.

56. 483 U.S. at 837, 838, 107 S.Ct. at 3148.

57. 483 U.S. at 834, 107 S.Ct. at 3147.

ate in "due process" and "equal protection" cases but not in "taking" cases.[58] But it is not clear why this distinction is significant in a case like *Nollan,* where the requirement that an easement be donated to the Coastal Commission was invalid both as a violation of substantive due process and as an uncompensated "taking." [59]

Until the late 1970s it was generally assumed that, even if land use regulations were found to effect an uncompensated "taking," only specific relief such as a declaratory judgment, an injunction, or mandamus was available to the victorious plaintiff.[60] Beginning with San Diego Gas & Electric Co. v. City of San Diego,[61] however, the Supreme Court indicated that, in an appropriate case, it would be willing to address the question whether compensation should be awarded for a "regulatory taking" instead of, or in addition to, specific relief. In *San Diego Gas,* the Court ultimately dismissed the appeal on the ground that it lacked jurisdiction because there was no final California court judgment; [62] but Justice Brennan, in a dissent supported by three other members of the Court, argued that the Court should decide the case on the merits and hold that compensation for a "regulatory taking" was mandated by the Fifth Amendment as made applicable to the states by the Fourteenth Amendment.[63] Justice Brennan's opinion was thought by many to foreshadow a future majority decision establishing an "inverse condemnation" remedy for "regulatory takings" because, although Justice Rehnquist voted to dismiss the *San Diego Gas* appeal, he said in a concurring opinion that on the merits he would have "little difficulty in agreeing with" much of what Justice Brennan said in his dissent.[64]

58.   483 U.S. at 838, 834 n. 3, 107 S.Ct. at 3148, 3147 n. 3.

59.   See Wiseman, supra note 40.

60.   The posture of the parties in Pennsylvania Coal Co. v. Mahon, 260 U.S. 393, 43 S.Ct. 158, 67 L.Ed. 322 (1922), was such that compensation could neither have been sought nor awarded.   Compensation was not sought in Euclid v. Ambler Realty Co., 272 U.S. 365, 47 S.Ct. 114, 71 L.Ed. 303 (1926) or in Goldblatt v. Town of Hempstead, 369 U.S. 590, 82 S.Ct. 987, 8 L.Ed.2d 130 (1962).   In Penn Central Transportation Co. v. City of New York, 438 U.S. 104, 98 S.Ct. 2646, 57 L.Ed.2d 631 (1978), Justice Brennan said in a footnote that "[a]s is implicit in our opinion we do not embrace the proposition that a 'taking' can never occur unless government has transferred [sic] physical control over a portion of a parcel," but it is not clear whether the majority thought compensation might be payable for a "regulatory taking."   No compensation was sought in either Keystone Bituminous Coal Association v. De Benedictis, 480 U.S. 470, 107 S.Ct. 1232, 94 L.Ed.2d 472 (1987), or Nollan v. California Coastal Commission, 483 U.S. 825, 107 S.Ct. 3141, 97 L.Ed.2d 677 (1987).   In both Fred French Investing Co. v. City of New York, 39 N.Y.2d 587, 385 N.Y.S.2d 5, 350 N.E.2d 381 (1976), and Agins v. City of Tiburon, 24 Cal.2d 266, 157 Cal.Rptr. 372, 598 P.2d 25 (1979), it was held that land use regulations

that "went too far" could not amount to "takings" and, consequently, that no compensation could be granted when regulations "went too far."   On the other hand, compensation was awarded for a "regulatory taking" in Gordon v. City of Warren, 579 F.2d 386 (6th Cir.1978), Arastra Limited Partnership v. City of Palo Alto, 401 F.Supp. 962 (N.D.Cal.1975), and City of Austin v. Teague, 570 S.W.2d 389 (Tex. 1978).   In *Gordon* and *Teague,* the land use regulations in question were invalidated and compensation for the "temporary taking" while the regulations were in force was awarded to the landowner.   In *Arastra,* compensation for a "permanent taking" was awarded and the city acquired a fee simple in the land "taken."   For an exhaustive argument against allowing compensation when land use regulations go too far, see Williams, Smith, Siemon, Mandelker & Babcock, The White River Junction Manifesto, 9 Vt.L.Rev. 193 (1984).

61.   450 U.S. 621, 101 S.Ct. 1287, 67 L.Ed.2d 551 (1981).

62.   The majority opinion was written by Justice Blackmun, who was joined by four other Justices.

63.   Justices Stewart, Marshall, and Powell joined Justice Brennan in dissent.

64.   450 U.S. at 633, 101 S.Ct. at 1294–1295.

In two cases subsequent to *San Diego Gas* the Court was also presented with occasions for addressing the compensation issue, but in both cases the Court refused to do so on the ground that the issue was not yet "ripe" for decision.[65] The "taking mavens" were finally rewarded in 1987 when the Supreme Court reviewed a case where the compensation issue was neatly isolated by a final California appellate court decision holding that an "inverse condemnation" complaint failed to state a cause of action because it was settled by a California Supreme Court decision [66] that compensation was never available as a remedy for a "regulatory taking." In that case, First English Evangelical Lutheran Church v. County of Los Angeles, Cal., Glendale,[67] the United States Supreme Court adopted the rationale of Justice Brennan's *San Diego Gas* dissent, holding that the Fifth Amendment, as made applicable to the states by the Fourteenth Amendment, mandates payment of "just compensation" for a "regulatory taking." [68] The Court stated that, assuming the challenged regulations effected a *de facto* "taking," the local governing body could elect either to keep them in force by exercising its power of eminent domain or to "acquiesce" in a judgment invalidating the regulations; if it elected to "acquiesce," the municipality would have to pay "just compensation" for the "temporary taking" during the period when the invalid regulations were in force.[69] Unfortunately, however, Justice Rehnquist's opinion did not deal with a variety of important questions: how courts should determine when a "temporary taking" commences[70] how "just compensation" for a "temporary taking" is to be calculat-

65. The cases are Williamson County Regional Planning Commission v. Hamilton Bank, 473 U.S. 172, 105 S.Ct. 3108, 87 L.Ed.2d 126 (1985), and MacDonald, Sommer & Frates v. Yolo County, 477 U.S. 340, 106 S.Ct. 2561, 91 L.Ed.2d 285 (1986) rehearing 478 U.S. 1035, 107 S.Ct. 22, 92 L.Ed.2d 773 (1986). Both cases are treated in more detail post in Section 9.23.

66. Agins v. City of Tiburon, 24 Cal.2d 266, 157 Cal.Rptr. 372, 598 P.2d 25 (1979), aff'd without reaching the compensation issue, 447 U.S. 255, 100 S.Ct. 2138, 65 L.Ed.2d 106 (1980).

67. 482 U.S. 304, 107 S.Ct. 2378, 96 L.Ed.2d 250 (1987).

68. 482 U.S. at 314–317, 107 S.Ct. at 2385–2387. Chief Justice Rehnquist relied on the language of the Fifth Amendment's "just compensation" clause, as made applicable to the states by the Fourteenth Amendment's "due process" clause, which he said was "self-executing." See 482 U.S. at 315, 107 S.Ct. at 2386. The Chief Justice did not adduce any policy considerations in support of the Court's decision, apparently regarding such considerations as irrelevant. Justice Brennan had taken the same view in *San Diego Gas.* See 450 U.S. at 660–661, 101 S.Ct. at 1309.

69. 482 at 317–312, 107 S.Ct. at 2387–2389. Chief Justice Rehnquist stated that " 'temporary' takings which, as here, deny a landowner all use of his property are not different in kind from permanent takings, for which the Constitution clearly requires compensation," noting that the Court found "substantial guidance in cases where the government has only temporarily exercised its right to use private property." See 482 U.S. at 318, 107 S.Ct. at 2387, 2388.

70. In Hernandez v. City of Lafayette, 643 F.2d 1188 (5th Cir.1981), decided after *San Diego Gas* and before *First Church,* the court indicated that where "the application of a general zoning ordinance to a particular person's property does not initially deny the owner an economically viable use * * * but thereafter does come to result in such a denial due to changing circumstances, or where a zoning classification initially denies a property owner an economically viable use," the landowner must bring his objections to the zoning regulations to the attention of the local governing bodies, and that no "taking" could occur until the governing body has failed to "correct the inequity" by repealing or amending the regulations within a reasonable time. Some commentators have suggested that no "taking" should be deemed to occur until the complaining landowner has either sought and failed to obtain a variance or has brought an action to invalidate the land use regulations to which he objects. Where the alleged "taking" results from the landowner's inability to obtain some necessary development permit (e.g., subdivision approval), both *Williamson County* and *Yolo County* (supra note 65) establish that the landowner must have exhausted both his administrative and his judicial remedies under state law before he can bring a constitutional "inverse condemnation" action in a federal court. For citations, see supra note 65. *Williamson County* and *Yolo County* are treated in more detail post in Section 9.23.

ed,[71] whether "just compensation" must be paid only where, as the Court assumed was the case in *First Church,* the challenged land use regulations deny the landowner "all use" of the land,[72] and whether the same rules with respect to compensation should apply in both "inverse condemnation" actions based directly on the Fifth and Fourteenth Amendments and actions based on 42 U.S.C.A. § 1983.[73] The Court's assumption that the challenged regulations in First Church denied "all use" to the landowner may reflect the Court's unwillingness to lay down a definitive standard for determining whether a "regulatory taking" has occurred.

Lucas v. South Carolina Coastal Council,[74] decided June 29, 1992, marks the partial triumph of the "conservative" wing of the United States Supreme Court with respect to the "regulatory taking" question, although it is unclear what the ultimate significance of the decision will be. *Lucas* clearly raises a number of issues that cannot be resolved without further litigation.

Lucas bought two residentially zoned lots on a South Carolina barrier island in 1986 with the intention of building houses on both lots at some indeterminate future time. Houses had previously been erected on the immediately adjacent lots. When Lucas bought his lots he could have built

---

71. Presumably the interest "temporarily taken" would be a negative easement that precludes certain land uses, but there is no established market for such negative easements. Hence the conventional "market value" formula for determining the value of land "taken" in fee simple in formal eminent domain proceedings is hard to apply. When affirmative easements in fee simple are "taken" in formal eminent domain proceedings, the value of the easement is generally held to be the difference in the value of the land free of and the value subject to the easement. When negative easements (e.g., "scenic" and "open-space" easements) are "taken" in formal eminent domain proceedings, the same method for determining the value of the easement "taken" seems appropriate. In cases where a negative easement is "temporarily taken" by a formal exercise of the eminent domain power, it would seem that the value of the easement "taken" might be deemed to be the difference between the rental value of the land during the "temporary taking" free from and subject to the easement, and that the same formula might be applied to "temporary regulatory takings." But "rental value" may not be an appropriate standard when land is held not for production of rental income but for development and sale. It would seem that courts might in some cases find that the value of the negative easement "temporarily taken" is equal to the value of an option to purchase the land for the period of the "taking." In *San Diego Gas,* Justice Brennan noted that "the Constitution does not embody any specific procedure or form of remedy that the States must adopt," and said that "[t]he States should be free to experiment in the implementation of" the Constitutional mandate that

"just compensation" shall be paid for private property "taken for public use." See 450 U.S. at 660, 101 S.Ct. at 1308.

72. 482 U.S. at 321, 107 S.Ct. at 2389, where the Court said: " * * * the allegation of the complaint which we treat as true for purposes of our decision was that the ordinance in question denied appellant all use of its property. We limit our holding to the facts presented, and of course do not deal with the quite different questions that would arise in the case of normal delays in obtaining building permits, changes in zoning ordinances, variances, and the like which are not before us." It is possible when Chief Justice Rehnquist used the term "all use" he meant "all economically viable use," which in recent cases has appeared to be a crucial factor in the Court's decisions as to whether a "regulatory taking" has occurred. On remand of *First Church,* the California Court of Appeals, without returning the case to the trial court for rehearing, made its own determination that the complaint failed to state a cause of action for compensation because the challenged ordinance substantially advanced a legitimate government purpose and did not deny the plaintiff all use of his property. 258 Cal.Rptr. 893 (1989).

73. For a discussion of actions under 42 U.S.C.A. § 1983, see post part (c) of this Section.

74. 112 S.Ct. 2886, 120 L.Ed.2d 798 (1992). The Court granted certiorari in another case that raised the same issue, Esposito v. South Carolina Coastal Council, 939 F.2d 165 (4th Cir.1991), but dismissed the writ of certiorari on the day Lucas v. South Carolina Coastal Council was decided.

houses on them as a matter of right; but in 1988 the South Carolina legislature adopted the state's Beachfront Management Act, which allegedly prohibited Lucas from building any permanent structures (including houses) on his lots.[75] Without applying for possible administrative relief,[76] Lucas brought suit against the South Carolina Coastal Council, which administered the Beachfront Management Act, to obtain compensation for an alleged "regulatory taking" of his property rights in his beachfront lots. Lucas conceded that the Act was a "lawful exercise of the State's police power" but contended that the ban on construction deprived him of all "economically viable use" of his lots. At the trial Lucas testified that plans for construction of houses on his lots had been prepared, but that he was "in no hurry" to build because the lots were appreciating in value. The trial court held that the Beachfront Management Act effected a "regulatory taking" of Lucas's property and award him $1,200,000 as compensation—obviously on the theory that the "regulatory taking" was "permanent."

The South Carolina Supreme Court reversed the trial court's judgment,[77] relying on a line of United States Supreme Court cases [78] holding that no compensable "taking" can result from regulation of property to prevent "harmful or noxious" uses akin to public nuisances, regardless of the impact of the regulation on the value of the property. The South Carolina Supreme Court also held that it was bound to accept the uncontested finding of the South Carolina legislature that new construction seaward of the "setback line" established by the Beachfront Management Act—where Lucas's lots were located—would cause "great public harm." [79] The South Carolina Supreme Court refused to consider the effect of a 1990 amendment to the Beachfront Management Act that would have enabled Lucas to apply for a "special permit" for construction of houses on his lots—an amendment adopted after *Lucas* was briefed and argued in the state Supreme Court.[80]

---

75. 16A S.C. Code §§ 48–39–250 through 48–43–580 (Supp.1991). This enactment supplemented South Carolina's Coastal Zone Management Act, 16A S.C. Code §§ 48–39–10 et seq. (1987), enacted in 1977 in response to Congress's passage of the federal Coastal Zone Management Act of 1972, as amended, 16 U.S.C.A. § 1451 et seq.

The 1988 Act required establishment of a "baseline" for each "standard erosion zone * * * at the location of the crest of the primary oceanfront sand dune in that zone," and further required establishment of a "setback line * * * landward of the baseline a distance which is forty times the average erosion rate or not less than twenty feet from the baseline for each erosion zone." Lucas's two lots were located entirely seaward of the applicable "setback line," where permanent buildings were prohibited.

76. 16A S.C. Code § 48–39–280(E) provides: "A landowner claiming ownership of property * * * who feels that the final or revised setback line, baseline, or erosion rate as adopted is in error, upon submittal of substantiating evidence, must be granted a review of the setback line, baseline, or erosion rate, or a review of all three * * *."

77. Lucas v. South Carolina Coastal Council, 304 S.C. 376, 404 S.E.2d 895 (1991), judgment reversed ___ U.S. ___, 112 S.Ct. 2886, 120 L.Ed.2d 798 (1992).

78. These cases included Mugler v. Kansas, Hadacheck v. Sebastion, and Keyston Bituminous Coal Ass'n v. DeBenedictis, all discussed ante in this section.

79. "By failing to contest these legislative findings, Lucas concedes that the beach/dune area of South Carolina's shores is an extremely valuable public resource; that the erection of new construction, *inter alia*, contributes to the erosion and destruction of this public resource; and that discouraging new construction in close proximity to the beach/dune area is necessary to prevent great public harm." 404 S.E.2d at 898.

80. "We do not address the issue, not raised in this case, of whether Lucas may build a habitable structure under the provisions and procedures of the 1990 amendments to the Beachfront Management Act." 404 S.E.2d at 902 n. 8. The 1990 amendments in question are codified as 16A S.C. Code § 48–39–290(D), which provides, *inter alia*: "If an applicant requests a permit to build or rebuild

The United States Supreme Court granted certiorari in *Lucas* and subsequently reversed the judgment of the South Carolina Supreme Court and remanded the case to the state courts for further proceedings.[81]   The Court's opinion was written by Justice Scalia,[82] who was joined by Chief Justice Rehnquist and Justices White, O'Connor, and Thomas.   Justice Kennedy filed an opinion concurring in the Court's judgment but rejecting its rationale.[83]   Justices Blackmun and Stevens wrote separate dissenting opinions rejecting both the Court's judgment and its rationale.[84]   Justice Souter filed a separate "statement" indicating why he thought the writ of certiorari had been "improvidently granted." [85]   Thus, in contrast to the Pennsylvania "abortion case" decided the same day,[86] *Lucas* failed to produce a result controlled by the supposedly "moderate conservative" bloc made up of Justices O'Connor, Kennedy, and Souter.

The principal issues addressed by the United States Supreme Court in *Lucas* were (1) whether the "regulatory taking" issue was "ripe" for decision; (2) what legal standard should be applied in determining whether the Beachfront Management Act effected a "regulatory taking" requiring a payment of compensation to Lucas; (3) whether the uncontested findings of the South Carolina legislature as to the public harm that would be caused by building development on the beachfront should be presumed to be sufficient to sustain the Beachfront Management Act's restrictions on such development; and (4) whether the trial court's uncontested finding that the Act's restrictions on such development rendered Lucas's two beachfront lots "valueless" was conclusive.

With respect to the "ripeness" issue, Justice Scalia apparently conceded (without discussing the point) that *Lucas* was not "ripe" for review insofar as the petitioner sought compensation for a *permanent* "regulatory taking," in

a structure * * * seaward of the baseline that is not otherwise allowed * * *, the council may issue a special permit * * * authorizing construction or reconstruction on a primary beachfront sand dune or on the active beach and, if the beach erodes to the extent the permitted structure becomes situated on the active beach, the permittee agrees to remove the structure from the active beach if the council orders the removal. However, the use of the property authorized under this provision, in the determination of the council, must not be detrimental to the public health, safety, or welfare."

81. Lucas v. South Carolina Coastal Council, 112 S.Ct. 2886, 120 L.Ed.2d 798 (1992).

82. 112 S.Ct. at 2889, 120 L.Ed.2d at 807. The *Lucas* majority consists of justices who, previously, were generally classified as "conservative" on "property" issues, plus the most recently appointed member of the Court, Justice Thomas. Chief Justice Rehnquist and Justices Scalia and O'Connor dissented in *Keystone Bituminous,* supra note 41. Chief Justice Rehnquist and Justices Scalia, O'Connor, and White were in the majority in *Nollan,* supra note 51. Chief Justice Rehnquist and Justices Scalia and White were in the majori-

ty in *First Church,* while Justice O'Connor joined the dissent.

83. 112 S.Ct. at 2889, 120 L.Ed.2d at 807. Since Justice Kennedy voted with the majority to remand *Lucas* for further deliberations, he could not form part of a "moderate conservative" bloc that might have controlled the result in *Lucas.*

84. 112 S.Ct. at 2904, 120 L.Ed.2d at 825 (Blackmun) and 112 S.Ct. at 2917, 120 L.Ed.2d at 842 (Stevens). Justices Blackmun and Stevens have in the past consistently formed part of the "liberal" bloc that controlled results in "regulatory taking" cases decided by the Court prior to *Nollan* and *First Church.*

85. 112 S.Ct. at 2925, 120 L.Ed.2d at 851. Justice Souter's "statement" indicates that he "would dismiss the writ of certiorari * * * as having been granted improvidently" because "the questionable conclusion of total deprivation" of the owner's "entire economic interest in the subject property" could not be properly reviewed and the Court was therefore precluded from attempting to clarify the concept of total (and in the Court' view, categorically compensable) taking.

86. Planned Parenthood of Southeastern Pennsylvania v. Casey, 112 S.Ct. 2791, 120 L.Ed.2d 674 (1992).

light of the 1990 amendment to the Beachfront Management Act authorizing "special permits" for construction seaward of the "baseline" established by the Act,[87] but Justice Scalia expressly held that the question whether there had been a *temporary* "regulatory taking" during the period between initial enactment and amendment of the Act was "ripe" for review because the South Carolina Coastal Council stipulated in the trial court that no building permit would have been issued under the Act as originally enacted even if Lucas had applied for a building permit.[88] Justice Blackmun, in his dissent, appears to have ignored this stipulation.[89] Justice Stevens, on the other hand, argued that it was impossible to be sure that even a *temporary* "regulatory taking" occurred "because the record does not tell us whether his building plans were even temporarily frustrated by the enactment of" the Act.[90] Justice Stevens also noted that "until he exhausts his right to apply for a special permit" under the 1990 amendment, "petitioner is not entitled to an adjudication by this Court of his permanent takings claim." [91]

With respect to the legal standard to be applied to Lucas's claim that the Beachfront Management Act effected a "regulatory taking" of his property that entitled him to receive just compensation, Justice Scalia, in his opinion for the Court, broke new ground and largely repudiated the earlier United States Supreme Court "regulatory taking" cases.[92] Justice Scalia held that the "prevention of harm" standard employed by the South Carolina Supreme Court should not be applied, where (as in *Lucas*) regulations deprive a property owner of "all economically beneficial or productive use" of his land.[93] Such regulations, said Justice Scalia, constitute one of the two "discrete categories of regulatory action" which, "without the usual case-specific inquiry into the public interest advanced by the restraint," generally require payment of just compensation.[94] When such regulations are challenged, the constitutional obligation to pay just compensation cannot be avoided simply by arguing that the regulations were adopted in order to prevent "harmful or noxious" uses of the land, because the distinction between "harm-preventing" and "benefit-conferring" regulations is "difficult if not impossible to discern on an objective, value-free basis." [95] Such regulations will be sustained without payment of just compensation *only if* the State can identify preexisting "background principles of nuisance and

87. Supra note 80.

88. 112 S.Ct. at 2891, 120 L.Ed.2d at 810 n. 3, citing Record 14 (stipulations).

89. Justice Blackmun said, 112 S.Ct. at 2907, 120 L.Ed.2d at 830: "Under the Beachfront Management Act, petitioner was entitled to challenge the setback line or the baseline or the erosion rate applied to his property in formal administrative, followed by judicial proceedings. S.C.Code § 48–39–280(E) (Supp. 1991)." See supra note 76. But the Beachfront Management Council's stipulation—see supra note 88—would seem to make Justice Blackmun's statement irrelevant.

90. 112 S.Ct. at 2907, 120 L.Ed.2d at 892.

91. Ibid. Justice Stevens also said: "if we assume that petitioner is now able to build on the lot, the only injury that he may have suffered is the delay caused by the temporary existence of the absolute ban on construction." Ibid.

92. 112 S.Ct. at 2812–2900, 120 L.Ed.2d at 812–820.

93. 112 S.Ct. at 2897–2899, 120 L.Ed.2d at 817–819.

94. 112 S.Ct. at 2893, 120 L.Ed.2d at 812. The other such "discrete category" consists of "regulations that compel the property owner to suffer a physical 'invasion' of his property. In general (at least with regard to permanent invasions), no matter how minute the intrusion, and no matter how weighty the public purpose behind it, we have required compensation." 112 S.Ct. Ibid. citing Loretto v. Teleprompter Manhattan CATV Corp., 458 U.S. at 419 (1982).

95. 112 S.Ct. at 2897–2899, 120 L.Ed.2d at 818–819.

property law" prohibiting the uses proscribed by the regulations.[96]   The reasons for this exception from the general rule is that the right to make uses of land that would constitute nuisances at common law is not "part of" the owner's title, so that he had no legitimate expectation, when he bought the land, of putting it to such uses.[97]

The Court's answer to the question whether the uncontested legislative findings upon which the Beachfront Management Act was based were sufficient to bring the Act within the exception to the general rule requiring payment of just compensation announced by the Court was "no."   The Court said:[98]

> [T]he legislature's recitation of a noxious use classification cannot be the basis for departing from our categorical rule that total regulatory takings must be compensated.   If it were, departure would virtually always be allowed.   * * * [T]o win its case South Carolina must do more than proffer the legislature's declaration that the uses Lucas desires are inconsistent with the public interest, or the conclusory assertion that they violate a common-law maxim such as *sic utere tuo ut alienum non laedas*.   As we have said, a "State, by *ipse dixit*, may not transform private property into public property without compensation."

Although it is not entirely clear, the passage quoted seems to mean that the Court rejects the usual presumption of the validity of legislative action unless it is shown to be invalid when compensation is sought for a "regulatory taking" alleged to have deprived private property of all "economic value."

The Court found the predicate for application of its new "categorical" rule as to imposition of an obligation to pay just compensation in the trial court's finding that Lucas's two beachfront lots were "rendered valueless" by the Beachfront Management Act.   Since South Carolina did not challenge this trial court finding when Lucas applied for certiorari, the Court refused to consider South Carolina's argument, contained in its brief on the merits, that the trial court's finding was erroneous.[99]

Although Justice Kennedy concurred in the Court's judgment remanding *Lucas* to the State courts for further deliberation, his opinion set out a much broader definition of the police power than did the Court's opinion. He said:

> The common law of nuisance is too narrow a confine for the exercise of regulatory power in a complex and interdependent society.   * * * The State should not be prevented from enacting new regulatory initiatives

96. 112 S.Ct. at 2899–2900, 120 L.Ed.2d at 820–821. "A law or decree with such effect must * * * do no more than duplicate the result that could have been achieved by the courts—by adjacent landowners (other uniquely affected persons) under the State's law of private nuisance, or by the State's law of private nuisance, or by the State under its complementary power to abate nuisances that affect the public generally, or otherwise. 112 S.Ct. at 2900, 120 L.Ed.2d at 821. *Sed quaere* what Justice Scalia had in mind when he used the term "decree" in connection with legisla-

tive action pursuant to the state's police power.

97. 112 S.Ct. at 2899, 120 L.Ed.2d at 820. "This accords * * * with our 'takings' jurisprudence, which has traditionally been guided by the understandings of our citizens regarding the content of, and the State's power over, the 'bundle of rights' that they acquire when they obtain title to property." Ibid.

98. 112 S.Ct. at 2899, 2901, 120 L.Ed.2d at 820, 822–823.

99. 112 S.Ct. at 2896, 120 L.Ed.2d at 816, text at note call 9 and n. 9.

in response to changing conditions, and courts must consider all reasonable expectations whatever their source. The Takings Clause does not require a static body of State property law; it protects private expectations to ensure private investment. I agree with the Court that nuisance prevention accords with the most common expectations of property owners who face regulation, but I do not believe that this can be the sole source of State authority.[100]

This comes very close to the views asserted in the dissenting opinions of Justice Blackmun and Justice Stevens.

Both Justice Blackmun and Justice Stevens rejected the Court's new formulation of the legal standard for determining whether a regulation that deprives land of "all economic or productive value" requires payment of compensation to sustain it. Justice Blackmun began by asserting that, in a long line of cases beginning with Mugler v. Kansas, the Court "repeatedly has recognized the ability of government, in certain circumstances, to regulate property without compensation no matter how adverse the financial effect on the owner may be," and that "[i]n none of these cases did the court suggest that the right of a State to prohibit certain activities without paying compensation turned on the availability of some residual value use."[101] Justice Blackmun then concluded that

These cases rest on the principle that the State has full power to prohibit an owner's use of property if it is harmful to the public. * * * It would make no sense under this theory to suggest that an owner has a constitutional right to harm others, if only he makes the proper showing of loss.[102]

Justice Blackmun continued his critique of the Court's opinion by asserting that "the threshold inquiry for imposition of the Court's new rule, 'deprivation of all economically valuable use,' itself cannot be determined objectively" because, "[a]s the Court admits, whether the owner has been deprived of all economic value of his property will depend on how 'property' is defined."[103] And Justice Blackmun further criticized the Court's "new rule" on two additional grounds: (1) "Nothing in the discussions of Congress concerning the taking clause indicates that the clause was limited by the common law nuisance doctrine";[104] and (2) "In determining what is a nuisance at common law, state courts make exactly the same decision that the Court finds so troubling when made by the South Carolina General Assembly today: they determine whether the use is harmful."[105]

Justice Blackmun also argued that there was no evidence in the record supporting the trial court's conclusion that the damage to the lots owned by

100. 112 S.Ct. at 2903, 120 L.Ed.2d at 825.

101. 112 S.Ct. at 2910, 2911, 120 L.Ed.2d at 833, 835.

102. 112 S.Ct. at 2912, 120 L.Ed.2d at 835, 836.

103. 112 S.Ct. at 2913, 120 L.Ed.2d at 837. Justice Blackmun went on to point out that "The composition of the denominator in our 'deprivation fraction' is the dispositive inquiry. Yet there is no 'objective' way to define what that denominator should be." Ibid.

104. 112 S.Ct. at 2916, 120 L.Ed.2d at 841. Justice Blackmun went on to point out that "Common law courts themselves rejected such an understanding. They regularly recognized that it is 'for the legislature to interpose, and by positive enactment to prohibit a use of property which would be injurious to the public." Ibid.

105. 112 S.Ct. at 2914, 120 L.Ed.2d at 838.

Lucas was "total"; [106] and he further argued that, in the absence of "some factual foundation of record" controverting the legislative finding as to the harm that beachfront development would cause, that finding should have been accepted by the Court.[107]

Justice Stevens, in his dissenting opinion, advanced most of the arguments advanced by Justice Blackmun, but on some points his emphasis was somewhat different.[108]

The authors of this book are inclined to agree with Justice Blackmun's concluding statement about the *Lucas* case: [109]

> The Court makes sweeping and * * * misguided and unsupported changes in our taking doctrine. While it limits these changes to the most narrow subset of government regulation[s]—those that eliminate all economic value from land—these changes go far beyond what is necessary to secure petitioner Lucas's private benefit. One hopes they do not go beyond the narrow confines the Court assigns to them today.

(d) Section 1983 of the Federal Civil Rights Act: A Statutory Remedy for Violation of Constitutional Rights

Section 1983 of the Federal Civil Rights Act [110] provides as follows:

Every person who, under color of any statute, ordinance, custom or usage, of any State or Territory, subjects or causes to be subjected, any citizen of the United States or other person within the jurisdiction thereof to the deprivation of any rights, privileges, or immunities secured by the Constitution and the laws, shall be liable to the party injured in an action at law or suit in equity, or other proper proceeding for redress.

Until 1978 neither states nor local governing bodies were deemed to be "persons" and hence were not subject to Section 1983 liability,[111] but in Monell v. Dept. of Social Services [112] the Supreme Court held that "local governing bodies * * * can be sued directly under § 1983 for monetary,

---

106. 112 S.Ct. at 2908, 120 L.Ed.2d at 831. Justice Blackmun went on to point out that Lucas still retained the right to exclude others, "one of the essential sticks in the bundle of rights that are commonly characterized as property," and "the right to alienate the land, which would have value for neighbors and for those prepared to enjoy proximity to the ocean without a house." In addition, Lucas retained the exclusive right to "picnic, swim, camp in a tent, or live on the property in a movable trailer"—all of which have been recognized by state courts as giving the land "economic value." Ibid.

107. 112 S.Ct. at 2909, 120 L.Ed.2d at 832, pointing out that "this Court has always required plaintiffs challenging the constitutionality of an ordinance to provide 'some factual foundation of record' that contravenes the legislative findings."

108. See, e.g., 112 S.Ct. at 2919, 2920, 120 L.Ed.2d at 844, 845, where Justice Stevens said: "in addition to lacking support in past decisions, the Court's new rule is wholly arbitrary. A landowner whose property is dimin-

ished in value [by] 95% recovers nothing, while an owner whose property is diminished in value [by] 100% recovers the land's full value," and that the rule may lead land developers to market "specialized estates to take advantage of the Court's new rule." Thus, said Justice Stevens, "the categorical rule will likely have one of two effects: Either courts will alter the 'denominator' in the takings 'fraction' rendering the Court's categorical rule meaningless, or investors will manipulate the relevant property interests, giving the Court's rule sweeping effect"—neither of which would be "desirable or appropriate" and both of which "are distortions of our takings jurisprudence."

109. 112 S.Ct. at 2917, 120 L.Ed.2d at 841, 842.

110. Section 1983 of the Federal Civil Rights Act, originally enacted in 1871, is now codified as 42 U.S.C.A. § 1983.

111. Monroe v. Pape, 365 U.S. 167, 81 S.Ct. 473, 5 L.Ed.2d 492 (1961).

112. 436 U.S. 658, 98 S.Ct. 2018, 56 L.Ed.2d 611 (1978).

declaratory, or injunctive relief where * * * the action that is alleged to be unconstitutional implements or executes a policy statement, ordinance, regulation, or decision officially adopted and promulgated by that body's officers. Moreover, * * * local governments * * * may be sued for constitutional deprivations visited pursuant to governmental 'custom' even though such a custom has not received formal approval through the body's official decisionmaking channels." [113] Two years later, in Owen v. City of Independence,[114] the Court held that a municipality has no immunity from liability under § 1983 when it deprives any person of his constitutional rights, and may not assert the good faith of its officers as a defense, whether the municipality was performing "governmental" or "proprietary" functions and without regard to whether its actions were "discretionary" or "ministerial" in nature. In Pembaur v. City of Cincinnati,[115] however, a Supreme Court plurality held that municipal liability under § 1983 attaches when—and only when—"a deliberate choice is made to follow a course of action from among various alternatives by the official or officials responsible for establishing a final policy with respect to the subject matter in question."

In *Monell* [116] the Supreme Court reaffirmed prior decisions holding that the states are not "persons" and therefore cannot be held liable under § 1983. Prior to *Monell*, in Tenney v. Brandhove,[117] the Court held that state legislators, individually, were absolutely immune from § 1983 liability. In Lake Country Estates, Inc. v. Tahoe Regional Planning Agency,[118] the Court extended absolute immunity to state legislators serving on a bi-state regional planning agency, but the Court reserved its decision as to whether members of local governing bodies are also absolutely immune to § 1983 liability. Subsequent lower federal court decisions [119] have extended absolute liability to members of local governing bodies when they perform "legislative" functions. When local governing bodies perform "adjudicative" functions—e.g., granting or denying applications for zoning variances—they would appear to be absolutely immune to § 1983 liability, since both federal agencies and officials and local agencies and officials are immune when they perform "adjudicative" functions.[120] But when local government agencies

---

113. 436 U.S. at 690, 98 S.Ct. at 2035.

114. 445 U.S. 622, 100 S.Ct. 1398, 63 L.Ed.2d 673 (1980).

115. 475 U.S. 469, 106 S.Ct. 1292, 89 L.Ed.2d 452 (1986).

116. Supra note 79.

117. 341 U.S. 367, 71 S.Ct. 783, 95 L.Ed. 1019 (1951).

118. 440 U.S. 391, 99 S.Ct. 1171, 59 L.Ed.2d 401 (1979), on remand 474 F.Supp. 901 (D.Nev. 1979).

119. Baytree of Inverrary Realty Partners v. City of Lauderhill, 873 F.2d 1407 (11th Cir.1989); Culebras Enterprises Corp. v. Rivera Rios, 813 F.2d 506 (1st Cir.1987); Kuzinich v. County of Santa Clara, 689 F.2d 1345 (9th Cir.1982); Bruce v. Riddle, 631 F.2d 272 (4th Cir.1980); Gorman Towers, Inc. v. Bogoslavsky, 626 F.2d 607 (8th Cir.1980).

120. In Butz v. Economou, 438 U.S. 478, 98 S.Ct. 2894, 57 L.Ed.2d 895 (1978), on remand 466 F.Supp. 1351 (S.D.N.Y.1979), the Supreme Court conferred absolute immunity on federal officials who commenced an adjudicatory proceeding against the plaintiff, noting that adjudication by federal agencies is "functionally comparable" to adjudication by judges and should enjoy the same absolute immunity from § 1983 liability. Local agency determinations were held sufficiently adjudicative to qualify for absolute immunity in a number of cases, e.g., Anastasio v. Planning Board, 209 N.J.Super. 499, 507 A.2d 1194 (App.Div.1986), cert. denied 107 N.J. 46, 526 A.2d 136 (1986); Centennial Land & Development Co. v. Township of Medford, 165 N.J.Super. 220, 397 A.2d 1136 (L.Div.1979).

and officials perform strictly "administrative" functions they are entitled only to limited "good faith" immunity to § 1983 liability.[121] Unfortunately, it is sometimes difficult to determine what functions are "adjudicatory" and what functions are "administrative" in nature.[122]

After first adopting a rigorous test of "good faith," [123] the Supreme Court later adopted a more relaxed test under which "government officials performing discretionary functions generally are shielded from liability insofar as their conduct does not violate clearly established statutory or constitutional rights of which a reasonable person would have known." [124] Application of this objective "good faith" test was subsequently held to require a fact-specific inquiry to determine whether the official (or agency) could reasonably have believed that its action was constitutional in light of the clearly established constitutional right and the available facts.[125]

In theory, § 1983 actions may be commenced in either a state or a federal court unless access to the federal courts is barred by the "abstention" doctrine or the "ripeness" doctrines to be discussed hereafter.[126] But it is clear that "inverse condemnation" suits seeking compensation for *de facto* "regulatory takings," unlike actions to obtain injunctive or declaratory relief for violations of substantive due process, must be commenced in the state courts because, since First English Evangelical Lutheran Church v. County of Los Angeles, Cal., Glendale,[127] all state courts are constitutionally obligated to award compensation for "regulatory takings." And even § 1983 actions seeking only injunctive or declaratory relief that satisfy the "ripeness" requirement may be dismissed by federal courts pursuant to a doctrine, recently developed in a few United States Court of Appeals cases, under which "run of the mill" disputes between land developers or landown-

---

121. Bateson v. Geisse, 857 F.2d 1300 (9th Cir.1988) (permit denied); Sullivan v. Town of Salem, 805 F.2d 81 (2d Cir.1986) (permit denied); Cutting v. Muzzey, 724 F.2d 259 (1st Cir.1984).

122. Granting or denying an application for a zoning variance, for example, is sometimes termed "adjudicative" and sometimes termed "administrative." The former would appear to be more accurate. Actions of a local governing body may be "adjudicative" or "administrative" rather than "legislative." See, e.g., Haskell v. Washington Tp., 864 F.2d 1266 (6th Cir.1988), appeal after remand 891 F.2d 132 (1989), holding that local governing body's action is "legislative" if its purpose is to establish a general rule, but administrative if it singles out individuals for disparate treatment. Its action is "adjudicative" when it grants a variance.

123. Scheuer v. Rhodes, 416 U.S. 232, 94 S.Ct. 1683, 40 L.Ed.2d 90 (1974).

124. Harlow v. Fitzgerald, 457 U.S. 800, 102 S.Ct. 2727, 73 L.Ed.2d 396 (1982). See further Davis v. Scherer, 468 U.S. 183, 104 S.Ct. 3012, 92 L.Ed.2d 139 (1984) (immunity available only if defendant violated clearly established constitutional right). In Negin v.

City of Mentor, 601 F.Supp. 1502 (N.D.Ohio 1985), where a zoning board of appeals denied a variance and the state supreme court later declared the zoning ordinance unconstitutional, the federal court held that the board members had acted in good faith because "they could not reasonably have been expected to recognize," before the state court decision, that the ordinance was unconstitutional. Other federal cases applying *Harlow* to land use cases include Culebras Enterprises, supra note 123 (development moratorium); Kaplan v. Clear Lake City Water Authority, 794 F.2d 1059 (5th Cir.1986) (refusal to extend water and sewer service).

125. Anderson v. Creighton, 483 U.S. 635, 107 S.Ct. 3034, 97 L.Ed.2d 523 (1987), on remand 724 F.Supp. 654 (D.Minn.1989), judgment affirmed 922 F.2d 443 (8th Cir.1990). Because so many land use cases brought under § 1983 are fact-specific, one authority suggests that *Creighton* "should lead to an expansion of official immunity in such cases." D. Mandelker, Land Use Law (2d ed. 1988), 1991 Cum.Supp. at 50.

126. See discussion post Section 9.23.

127. See discussion of *First Church,* ante in part (b) of this Section at notes 69–75.

ers and local government agencies or officials have been held not to raise a substantial federal question.[128]

It is clear that a landowner may obtain any appropriate form of relief—injunctive, declaratory, or monetary—for violations of substantive or procedural due process.[129] Actionable violations of substantive due process may be found either because land use regulations are not intended to protect any legitimate government interest or because they are not well-designed to do so.[130] Although the Supreme Court has not yet expressly indicated whether a plaintiff may recover damages under § 1983 for a "temporary regulatory taking," lower federal courts have allowed recovery of such damages.[131] A § 1983 action for damages may, in some cases, be more advantageous to the plaintiff than an "inverse condemnation" action directly under the Fifth and Fourteenth Amendments. Since a § 1983 action is viewed by the courts as a constitutional "tort" action,[132] consequential as well as direct damages may be awarded, and determination of "damages" in a § 1983 action may be easier than determination of "just compensation" in an "inverse condemnation" action because of the difficulty of defining and valuing the interest "taken."[133] Moreover, a victorious § 1983 plaintiff has a statutory right to recover attorney's fees,[134] if he is successful on any "significant issue in litigation which achieves some benefits"[135] or obtains a favorable settlement of his claim.[136] In addition, punitive damages may be awarded against municipal officials[137]—though not against municipalities[138]—whether or not

128. See, e.g., Creative Environments, Inc. v. Estabrook, 680 F.2d 822 (1st Cir.1982), cert. denied, 459 U.S. 989, 103 S.Ct. 345, 74 L.Ed.2d 385 (1982) (rejection of subdivision application); Cloutier v. Town of Epping, 714 F.2d 1184 (1st Cir.1983) (revocation of sewer connection permits and other permits); Hynes v. Pasco County, 801 F.2d 1269 (11th Cir.1986) (revocation of building permits); Smith v. City of Picayune, 795 F.2d 482 (5th Cir.1986) (rezoning refused); Burrell v. City of Kankakee, 815 F.2d 1127 (7th Cir.1987) (rezoning refused).

129. Although an intent to violate the Constitution is not generally required for § 1983 liability—see Monroe v. Pape, 365 U.S. 167, 81 S.Ct. 473, 5 L.Ed.2d 492 (1961)—§ 1983 liability for procedural due process violations will only be imposed for intentional violations. Daniels v. Williams, 474 U.S. 327, 106 S.Ct. 662, 88 L.Ed.2d 662 (1986).

130. Regulations not intended to protect or promote legitimate government interests— e.g., health, safety, or general welfare—are not within the police power of the states. In Wheeler v. City of Pleasant Grove (II), 833 F.2d 267 (11th Cir.1987), rehearing denied 844 F.2d 794 (1988), the court said that, although "[t]echnically the fifth amendment is not applicable where there has been no 'public use' because the land use regulation that effected the taking was not enacted in furtherance of the public health, safety, morals, or general welfare," the affected landowner "may nevertheless have a damage cause of action under section 1983 since the taking may violate his

fourteenth amendment rights to due process." (Id. at 270, n. 3.)

131. Heritage Homes of Attleboro, Inc. v. Seekonk Water District, 648 F.2d 761 (1st Cir. 1981), cert. denied 454 U.S. 898, 102 S.Ct. 398, 70 L.Ed.2d 213 (1981). See also Wheeler v. City of Pleasant Grove (II), supra note 130; Cordeco Development Corp. v. Santiago Vasquez, 539 F.2d 256 (1st Cir.1976), cert. denied 429 U.S. 978, 97 S.Ct. 488, 50 L.Ed.2d 586 (1976).

132. See D. Mandelker, Land Use Law § 8.35 at n. 169 (2d ed. 1988), citing Memphis Community School District v. Stachura, 477 U.S. 299, 106 S.Ct. 2537, 91 L.Ed.2d 249 (1986), on remand 803 F.2d 721 (6th Cir.1986); Carey v. Piphus, 435 U.S. 247, 98 S.Ct. 1042, 55 L.Ed.2d 252 (1978).

133. See discussion supra note 73.

134. The right to an award of attorney's fees is contained in 42 U.S.C.A. § 1988, and is applicable in both state and federal courts. Maine v. Thiboutot, 448 U.S. 1, 100 S.Ct. 2502, 65 L.Ed.2d 555 (1980).

135. Hensley v. Eckerhart, 461 U.S. 424, 103 S.Ct. 1933, 76 L.Ed.2d 40 (1983).

136. Maher v. Gagne, 448 U.S. 122, 100 S.Ct. 2570, 65 L.Ed.2d 653 (1980).

137. Smith v. Wade, 461 U.S. 30, 103 S.Ct. 1625, 75 L.Ed.2d 632 (1983).

138. City of Newport v. Fact Concerts, Inc., 453 U.S. 247, 101 S.Ct. 2748, 69 L.Ed.2d 616 (1981).

the plaintiff can prove any actual damages.[139]   Finally, the "exhaustion of remedies" component of the "ripeness" doctrine is applicable in "inverse condemnation" actions but not in § 1983 actions.[140]

§ 9.2A   Land Use Litigation: State or Federal Forum?

(a) Land Use Litigation in the State Courts

Until about twenty years ago most cases challenging local land use controls were commenced in a state court.[1]   In state court litigation, the plaintiff may challenge the validity of local land use regulations on either statutory or constitutional grounds—that is, on the ground that particular regulations are *ultra vires* or that they violate applicable provisions of the state or federal constitution—or on both grounds.   Federal constitutional challenges are generally based on the "due process" or the "equal protection" clause of the Fourteenth Amendment.   As we have seen, land use controls may be challenged as effecting *de facto* "regulatory takings" because the Fourteenth Amendment's "due process" clause is held to make the Fifth Amendment's "taking" clause applicable to the states.[2]   State court constitutional challenges may be based on state constitutional analogues of the federal "due process" or "equal protection" clauses.[3]   However, state court land use decisions—particularly in the earlier cases—do not always make it clear whether the court is relying on state or federal constitutional provisions when they strike down land use regulations as "unreasonable," "arbitrary," or "capricious."   In many cases state court decisions have been based on an explicit or implicit balancing of the public interest sought to be protected by the regulations as against the adverse economic impact of the regulations upon the plaintiff,[4] but some decisions have followed Mugler v. Kansas[5] in holding that a strong public purpose will sustain almost any land use regulations without regard to the severity of its impact on the plaintiff.[6]

139.   Carey v. Piphus, supra note 132.

140.   Williamson County Regional Planning Commission v. Hamilton Bank, 473 U.S. 172, 105 S.Ct. 3108, 87 L.Ed.2d 126 (1985). However, the prerequisite of a final definitive decision by the initial state decision-maker does apply in § 1983 actions.

§ 9.2A

1.   Compare the number of state court cases with the number of federal court cases listed in the table of cases in D. Mandelker, Land Use Law (2d ed. 1988).

2.   See ante Section 9.2.

3.   Some states do not have "due process" and "equal protection" clauses in their state constitutions.   In some states a "declaration of rights" originally adopted in the 18th century has been treated as a "due process" clause.   See, e.g., N.J.S.A. Const. art. I, par. 1, which was so construed in Southern Burlington County NAACP v. Mount Laurel Tp., 67 N.J. 151, 336 A.2d 713 (1975), cert. denied 423 U.S. 808, 96 S.Ct. 18, 46 L.Ed.2d 28 (1975).

4.   These cases appear to be applying the rule laid down in Lawton v. Steele, 152 U.S.

133, 14 S.Ct. 499, 38 L.Ed. 385 (1894).   Examples include Hartung v. Village of Skokie, 22 Ill.2d 485, 177 N.E.2d 328 (1961).

5.   123 U.S. 623, 8 S.Ct. 273, 31 L.Ed. 205 (1887).

6.   See, e.g., Consolidated Rock Products Co. v. City of Los Angeles, 57 Cal.2d 515, 20 Cal.Rptr. 638, 370 P.2d 342 (1962), appeal dismissed 371 U.S. 36, 83 S.Ct. 145, 9 L.Ed.2d 112 (1962).   Cf. Agins v. City of Tiburon, 24 Cal.3d 266, 157 Cal.Rptr. 372, 598 P.2d 25 (1979), affirmed 447 U.S. 255, 100 S.Ct. 2138, 65 L.Ed.2d 106 (1980).   In cases involving subdivision exactions and other development charges, the state courts have required some "nexus" between the exactions imposed and the public harms the exactions are supposed to mitigate.   See post Section 9.17.   This "nexus" requirement was applied by the United States Supreme Court in Nollan v. California Coastal Commission, 483 U.S. 825, 107 S.Ct. 3141, 97 L.Ed.2d 677 (1987), discussed ante Section 9.2 in text between notes 52 and 59. Since *Nollan*, some state courts may require a stronger "nexus" than they did prior to *Nollan*.   See, e.g., Surfside Colony, Ltd. v. Califor-

On the other hand, some recent cases have adopted tests laid down in recent U.S. Supreme Court cases, such as the "investment-backed expectation" test;[7] and "downzoning" to reduce condemnation costs has often been held to effect an unconstitutional taking.[8]

When challenges to land use regulations are initiated in state courts, a successful plaintiff may obtain an injunction against enforcement of the invalid regulation[9] or a declaration that it is invalid,[10] or sometimes both. When a local governing body adopts land use regulations—e.g., zoning regulations—which a landowner believes to be unduly restrictive, he can bring an action to enjoin enforcement of the regulations on the ground that "as applied" they deprive him of property without due process of law and/or that they effect a *de facto* "taking," or on the ground that they are *ultra vires* and therefore illegal. A declaratory judgment action can be brought to challenge land use regulations even though the plaintiff has suffered no actual harm, but a justiciable controversy must exist and the plaintiff must satisfy "standing" requirements. Thus a court may not entertain a declaratory judgment action to challenge a zoning ordinance as "facially" unconstitutional unless he has been adversely affected by a permit denial or other detrimental local government action. And a declaratory judgment is not available when there is specific provision in the enabling statute for a different and exclusive means of judicial review—for example, when the enabling act provides for review of decisions of the zoning board of adjustment or the planning commission by way of mandamus or certiorari. Mandamus[11] is an "extraordinary" remedy that may enable a landowner to obtain affirmative relief, such as the issuance of a building permit, where a local land use agency or official has a legal duty to issue the permit and the landowner has no other adequate remedy. Certiorari[12] is also an "extraordinary" remedy available to review administrative or quasi-judicial actions which are "discretionary" in nature, such as the refusal of a zoning board of adjustment to grant a variance or a special exception. State zoning enabling acts based on the Standard State Zoning Enabling Act specifically authorize review by way of certiorari of actions of the board of adjustment alleged to be "illegal."[13]

As a general rule, a landowner cannot challenge the validity of zoning or other land use regulations in a state court unless he has exhausted his administrative remedies by seeking an administrative interpretation of the

---

nia Coastal Commission, 226 Cal.App.3d 1260, 277 Cal.Rptr. 371 (1991) (involving the same land use regulations that gave rise to the litigation in *Nollan*).

7. Kempf v. City of Iowa City, 402 N.W.2d 393 (Iowa 1987) ("balancing" test favored property owner, but even without applying that test, the challenged rezoning was invalid because it made any development economically unfeasible and frustrated the developer's "reasonable investment-backed expectation").

8. E.g., Riggs v. Long Beach Tp., 109 N.J. 601, 538 A.2d 808 (1988); Gordon v. City of Warren, 388 Mich. 82, 199 N.W.2d 465 (1972).

9. For a good brief discussion of injunctive relief, see D. Mandelker, Land Use Law § 8.14 (2d ed. 1988).

10. For a good brief discussion of declaratory relief, see D. Mandelker, Land Use Law § 8.15 (2d ed. 1988).

11. For a good brief discussion of mandamus relief, see D. Mandelker, Land Use Law § 8.13 (2d ed. 1988).

12. For a good brief discussion of relief by way of certiorari, see D. Mandelker, Land Use Law § 8.12 (2d ed. 1988).

13. The authorization is in Standard Act § 7. "This provision, although it authorizes judicial review by way of 'certiorari,' is more properly characterized as a statutory appeal." D. Mandelker, Land Use Law § 8.12 (2d ed. 1988).

regulations, a special exception, or a variance.[14] In most states, a landowner is not required to seek relief from the local legislative body by way of an amendment of the regulations.[15] Exhaustion of administrative remedies is not, of course, required if there is no adequate administrative remedy,[16] nor is it required when a landowner claims the land use regulations are facially invalid rather than invalid "as applied"[17] or when any attempt to obtain administrative relief would be futile.[18]

Prior to San Diego Gas & Electric Co. v. City of San Diego,[19] most state courts held that compensation could not be awarded when land use regulations were invalidated on "due process" or "taking" grounds. After *San Diego Gas,* but before the Supreme Court's landmark decision in First English Evangelical Lutheran Church of Glendale v. County of Los Angeles, Cal.,[20] several state courts held for the first time that compensation should be awarded when it was found that a "regulatory taking" had occurred.[21] These courts all relied upon their own state constitutions, but several of them indicated that they found the reasoning in Justice Brennan's *San Diego Gas* dissent persuasive.[22] After *First Church* it is clear that state courts, as well as the lower federal courts, are constitutionally bound to award compensation for a "regulatory taking" by virtue of the "supremacy" clause of the United States Constitution,[23] whether the "taking" is perma-

14. The "exhaustion" requirement is designed to give an administrative agency an opportunity to grant administrative relief that will make a court challenge unnecessary. In some states, "exhaustion" is a jurisdictional requirement. Poe v. City of Baltimore, 241 Md. 303, 216 A.2d 707 (1966); Nodell Inv. Corp. v. City of Glendale, 78 Wis.2d 416, 254 N.W.2d 310 (1977). Contra: Boomhower v. Cerro Gordo County Bd. of Supervisors, 173 N.W.2d 95 (Iowa 1969). Some state courts have now equated the "exhaustion" rule with the "ripeness" doctrine adopted by the United States Supreme Court in "taking" cases. April v. City of Broken Arrow, 775 P.2d 1347 (Okl.1989); Estate of Friedman v. Pierce City, 112 Wn.2d 68, 768 P.2d 462 (1989). See also Ben Lomond, Inc. v. Municipality of Anchorage, 761 P.2d 119 (Alaska 1988).

15. G.S.T. v. City of Avon Lake, 48 Ohio St.2d 63, 357 N.E.2d 38 (1976).

16. This may be the case, e.g., where the zoning enabling act forbids the granting of "use variances." See Sinclair Pipe Line Co. v. Village of Richton Park, 19 Ill.2d 370, 167 N.E.2d 406 (1960).

17. Golden Gate Corp. v. Town of Narragansett, 116 R.I. 552, 359 A.2d 321 (1976); Deal Gardens, Inc. v. Board of Trustees, 48 N.J. 492, 226 A.2d 607 (1967); Poe v. City of Baltimore, supra note 14.

18. Application would be futile, in most cases, because the municipality's opposition to a proposed land development is clear and a denial of administrative relief is inevitable. See, e.g., League of Women Voters v. Outagamie County, 113 Wis.2d 313, 334 N.W.2d 887 (1983); Ogo Associates v. City of Torrance, 37

Cal.App.3d 830, 112 Cal.Rptr. 761 (1974); see Karches v. City of Cincinnati, 38 Ohio St.3d 12, 526 N.E.2d 1350 (1988). But see Presbytery of Seattle v. King County, 114 Wn.2d 320, 787 P.2d 907 (1990), cert. denied __ U.S. __, 111 S.Ct. 284, 112 L.Ed.2d 238 (1990) (futility exception disfavored, and not found when ordinance could be interpreted to allow reasonable use of land); Estate of Friedman, supra note 12 (general belief of county officials as to use of land was not sufficient to invoke futility exception).

19. 450 U.S. 621, 101 S.Ct. 1287, 67 L.Ed.2d 551 (1981). See discussion of this case ante Section 9.2, in text at notes 61 to 65.

20. 482 U.S. 304, 107 S.Ct. 2378, 96 L.Ed.2d 250 (1987), on remand 210 Cal.App.3d 1353, 258 Cal.Rptr. 893 (1989), discussed ante in Section 9.2 at notes 67 to 76.

21. See, e.g., Burrows v. City of Keene, 121 N.H. 590, 432 A.2d 15 (1981); Sheerr v. Evesham Tp., 184 N.J.Super. 11, 445 A.2d 46 (Law Div.1982); Rippley v. City of Lincoln, 330 N.W.2d 505 (N.D.1983); Annicelli v. Town of South Kingston, 463 A.2d 133 (R.I.1983); Zinn v. State, 112 Wis.2d 417, 334 N.W.2d 67 (1983); Corrigan v. City of Scottsdale, 149 Ariz. 538, 720 P.2d 513 (1986).

22. See, e.g., *Rippley* and *Zinn,* supra note 21. But see *Scheerr,* supra note 21, where the court observed that the Brennan *San Diego Gas* dissent was "not yet law" and that it "provided little precedential help in the present case."

23. U.S. Const. Art. VI, § 2. See Mills v. Rogers, 457 U.S. 291, 300, 102 S.Ct. 2442,

nent or temporary. But the state courts still have considerable leeway in deciding whether a "regulatory taking" has occurred because the Supreme Court has not yet laid down any clear standard for determining when land use regulations effect a "regulatory taking." [24] Moreover, even if the Supreme Court does succeed in laying down such a standard, that standard will establish only the minimum level of protection for property rights under the United States Constitution. The state courts will retain the power to interpret their own constitutions in such a way as to provide greater protection for property rights as against the governmental power to regulate land use.[25]

If a landowner wishes to lay a foundation for United States Supreme Court review of an action seeking compensation for a *de facto* "regulatory taking," he must bring the action in a state court because of the holding in Williamson County Regional Planning Commission v. Hamilton Bank [26] that state court "inverse condemnation" remedies must be exhausted before the Supreme Court will review a "regulatory taking" claim. This is true whether the "inverse condemnation" claim invokes only the Fourteenth Amendment or only § 1983 of the Federal Civil Rights Act, or both.[27]

(b) Barriers to Litigation of Due Process and Taking Claims in the Federal Courts

(1) The "Ripeness" Doctrine

The "ripeness" doctrine now applied in the federal courts, including the United States Supreme Court, seems to have originated in Penn Central Transportation Co. v. City of New York,[28] where, after determining that the New York City Landmark Preservation ordinance was not invalid either because it violated substantive due process or because it effected a "regulatory taking" without compensation, the Court added as a sort of after thought that, "While the [Landmark] Commission's actions in denying applications to construct an office building in excess of 50 stories above the Terminal may indicate that it will refuse to issue a certificate of appropriateness for any comparably sized structure, nothing the commission has said or done suggests an intent to prohibit *any* construction above the Terminal. * * * Since

2448, 73 L.Ed.2d 16 (1982), which makes it clear that the requirements of the United States Constitution as construed by the Supreme Court establish the minimum level of protection to which litigants are entitled, whether they sue in state or federal courts.

Recent state court decisions holding that compensation must be paid when there is a "regulatory taking" include Orlando/Orange County Expressway Authority v. W & F Agrigrowth–Fernfield, Ltd., 582 So.2d 790 (Fla. App.1991), review denied 591 So.2d 183 (Fla. 1991); Joint Ventures, Inc. v. Department of Transportation, 563 So.2d 622 (Fla.1990) (but the court said the "inverse condemnation" remedy is not the equivalent of the property owner's remedy when formal eminent domain proceedings are brought). Cf. California Coastal Commission v. Superior Court, 210 Cal.App.3d 1488, 258 Cal.Rptr. 567 (1989) (landowner who has complied with dedication requirement imposed as condition of develop-

ment approval and has not pursued available administrative review procedures is barred by res judicata from later bringing an inverse condemnation action).

24. See discussion ante Section 9.2.

25. See, e.g., Southern Burlington County NAACP v. Mount Laurel Tp., supra note 3, where the court insulated its decision from challenge in the United States Supreme Court by basing it solely on the New Jersey constitution.

26. 473 U.S. 172, 105 S.Ct. 3108, 87 L.Ed.2d 126 (1985). For fuller discussion of Williamson County, see post, this Section, in text at notes 31–36.

27. See infra note 36.

28. 438 U.S. 104, 98 S.Ct. 2646, 57 L.Ed.2d 631 (1978), rehearing denied 439 U.S. 883, 99 S.Ct. 226, 58 L.Ed.2d 198 (1978).

appellants have not sought approval for the construction of a smaller structure, we do not know that appellants will be denied any use of any portion of the airspace above the Terminal." [29]   Later, in Agins v. City of Tiburon,[30] where a landowner challenged a zoning ordinance amendment that placed his land in a district that allowed single-family dwellings at a density ranging from one dwelling per acre to one dwelling per five acres, and which required developers to submit a development plan to allow the city to decide how many dwellings would be allowed within this density range, the Court dismissed the appeal, in part, because "the appellants have not submitted a plan for development of their property * * * there is as yet no concrete controversy regarding the application of the specific zoning provisions." [31]   The Court also noted that the landowners were "free to pursue their reasonable investment-backed expectations by submitting a development plan to the local officials." [32]   These statements were repeated in Williamson County Regional Planning Com'n v. Hamilton Bank,[33] where the Planning Commission's rejection of a final subdivision development plan ultimately led to an action by the developer's successor in interest under 42 U.S.C.A. § 1983 [34] seeking to recover "damages" on the ground (*inter alia*) that this refusal effected a "regulatory taking."   The Supreme Court was unwilling to resolve the "taking" issue because the developer's failure to apply to the Planning Commission for a variance made it impossible for the Court to determine whether the Commission's action had denied the developer any "economic benefit" from the land.[35]   The Court held that "exhaustion of remedies" was not a jurisdictional requirement because the action was brought under Section 1983 rather than directly under the Fourteenth Amendment, but held that a Section 1983 action may not be brought until "the initial [government] decision-maker has arrived at a definitive position" on the issue in dispute "that inflicts an actual concrete injury" upon the plaintiff.[36]   In addition, the Court held that the "compensation" issue was not "ripe" for decision because no effort had been made to obtain compensation "through the procedures the State had provided for doing so." [37]   This additional requirement is apparently applicable to "inverse condemnation" actions brought directly under the fifth Amendment as made applicable to the states by the Fourteenth Amendment as well as to Section 1983 actions.[38]

29. 438 U.S. at 136, 98 S.Ct. at 2645.

30. 447 U.S. 255, 100 S.Ct. 2138, 65 L.Ed.2d 106 (1980).

31. 447 U.S. at 260, 100 S.Ct. at 2141.

32. 447 U.S. at 262, 100 S.Ct. at 2142.

33. 473 U.S. 172, 105 S.Ct. 3108, 87 L.Ed.2d 126 (1985), on remand 779 F.2d 50 (6th Cir. 1985).

34. See discussion of relief under Section 1983.

35. 473 U.S. at 191, 105 S.Ct. at 3119.

36. 473 U.S. at 190–194, 105 S.Ct. at 3118– 3120. In addition to *Agins* and *Penn Central* the Court cited Hodel v. Virginia Surface Mining & Reclamation Ass'n, 452 U.S. 264, 101 S.Ct. 2352, 69 L.Ed.2d 1 (1981), in support of its holding. In *Hodel*, the Court said:

"There is no indication in the record that appellees have availed themselves of the op-

portunities provided by the Act to obtain administrative relief by requesting either a variance * * * or a waiver. * * * If [the property owners] were to seek administrative relief under these procedures, a mutually acceptable solution might well be reached with regard to individual properties, thereby obviating any need to address the constitutional questions." 452 U.S. at 297, 101 S.Ct. at 2371.

37. 473 U.S. at 194–197, 105 S.Ct. at 3120– 3121, citing *Hodel,* supra note 34, 452 U.S. at 297 n. 40, 101 S.Ct. at 2374 n. 40.

38. This is implicit rather than explicit in *Williamson County.* But it would clearly be nonsensical not to apply the requirement in actions brought directly under the Fifth and Fourteenth Amendments while applying the requirement to § 1983 actions based on an alleged violation of the Fifth and Fourteenth amendments.

In MacDonald, Sommer & Frates v. Yolo County,[39] the plaintiff, after the County had rejected an application for approval of a proposed residential development, brought an action based on both the Fourteenth Amendment and Section 1983 to obtain compensation on the theory that this rejection effected a *de facto* "regulatory taking." Although the plaintiff alleged that the position taken by the County made it clear that any application either for a variance or for approval for a less intensive land development would have been futile, the Court again refused to resolve the "compensation," issue stating that the plaintiff had failed to obtain "the [County] Board's final, definitive position regarding how it will apply the [land use] regulations at issue to the particular land in question" because the plaintiff had submitted only one subdivision plan and the state court decision left open "the possibility that some development will be permitted." [40]

Taken together, the United States Supreme Court cases discussed above establish the basic contours of the "ripeness" doctrine. The only substantial difference between the doctrine's application in "inverse condemnation" actions based directly on the Fourteenth Amendment and "damage" actions based on Section 1983 would appear to be that, in the former, all administrative remedies must be exhausted, while in the latter only the remedies available from the "initial decision-maker" need be exhausted. *Yolo County* appears to require submission of alternative development plans to the "initial decision-maker" unless this would clearly be futile, whether the action is based directly on the Fourteenth Amendment or is based on Section 1983.[41] When a landowner seeks approval of a proposed development requiring subdivision of the land, the "initial decision-maker" will be either the local planning board (or commission) or the local governing body.[42] When a proposed development does not require subdivision of the land, the "initial decision-maker" will usually be the local zoning administrator or building department.[43]

Although the Supreme Court has not made it clear, the "ripeness" doctrine applies only to "as applied" as distinguished from "facial" constitutional or Section 1983 claims.[44] Although the doctrine was originally applied only to "taking" claims seeking compensation, some lower federal

39. 477 U.S. 340, 106 S.Ct. 2561, 91 L.Ed.2d 285 (1986), rehearing denied 478 U.S. 1035, 107 S.Ct. 22, 92 L.Ed.2d 773 (1986).

40. 477 U.S. at 351–353, 106 S.Ct. at 2567–2568. The Court also repeated the *Williamson County* requirement that the plaintiff must seek compensation through available state court procedures before seeking review in the United States Supreme Court. 477 U.S. at 350, 106 S.Ct. at 2566–2567. This appears to be *obiter dictum,* however, since the plaintiff had, in fact, unsuccessfully sought to obtain compensation in the California court. The plaintiff's lack of success was predictable in light of the California Supreme Court's holding that compensation may never be awarded in a "regulatory taking" case. See Agins v. City of Tiburon, 24 Cal.3d 266, 157 Cal.Rptr. 372, 598 P.2d 25 (1979).

41. 477 U.S. at 351–353, 106 S.Ct. at 2567–2568.

(C., S.&W.) Prop. 2d HB —13

42. As to administration of subdivision controls, see ante Section 9.16.

43. This is usually the case when the tract to be developed is small—e.g., a single residential lot. But when approval is sought for a large-scale development the developer may have to submit a site plan. See ante Section 9.16. In that case, the "initial decision-maker" is likely to be either the local planning board (or commission) or the local governing body.

44. See Keystone Bituminous Coal Association v. DeBenedictis, ante Section 9.2, note 41, where the Supreme Court said, however, that plaintiffs faced "an uphill battle in making a facial attack on [a regulation] as a 'taking.' " (480 U.S. at 495, 107 S.Ct. at 1247.) The only appropriate remedy when a "facial" challenge is successful is invalidation of the regulation.

courts now apply the doctrine to substantive due process and equal protection claims,[45] but they appear to apply the doctrine less stringently to substantive due process and equal protection claims.[46] The lower federal courts have sought to refine the "ripeness" doctrine in subsequent cases, but the effort has not been notably successful.[47]

The final "ripeness" requirement—that the plaintiff must have exhausted his state court remedy when he seeks compensation for a *de facto* "regulatory taking"—appears on its face to be quite straightforward. Before the United States Supreme Court's decision in *First Church*, this requirement was applicable only if a state court had already recognized a right to obtain compensation for a "regulatory taking." [48] But since *First Church* was decided, every state court is subject to the United States Supreme Court's ruling that payment of "just compensation" for a "regulatory taking" is mandated by the Fifth Amendment as made applicable to the states by the Fourteenth Amendment's "due process" clause. Thus "just compensation" is now available in every state court, and no action can be initiated

---

45. See, e.g., Kinzli v. City of Santa Cruz, 818 F.2d 1449 (9th Cir.1987), modified 830 F.2d 968 (1987), cert. denied 484 U.S. 1043, 108 S.Ct. 775, 98 L.Ed.2d 861 (1988); Unity Ventures v. County of Lake, 841 F.2d 770 (7th Cir.1988), cert. denied 488 U.S. 891, 109 S.Ct. 226, 102 L.Ed.2d 216 (1988); Ochoa Realty Corp. v. Faria, 815 F.2d 812 (1st Cir.1987); Golemis v. Kirby, 632 F.Supp. 159 (D.R.I.1985).

46. Harris v. County of Riverside, 904 F.2d 497 (9th Cir.1990); Greenbriar, Ltd. v. City of Alabaster, 881 F.2d 1570 (11th Cir.1989), rehearing denied 893 F.2d 346 (1989); Herrington v. Sonoma County, 834 F.2d 1488 (9th Cir.1987), cert. denied 489 U.S. 1090, 109 S.Ct. 1557, 103 L.Ed.2d 860 (1989).

47. Compare Herrington v. County of Sonoma, 834 F.2d 1488 (9th Cir.1987), cert. denied 489 U.S. 1090, 109 S.Ct. 1557, 103 L.Ed.2d 860 (1989) with Lake Nacimiento Ranch Co. v. County of San Luis Obispo, 830 F.2d 977 (9th Cir.1987), and Shelter Creek Development Corp. v. City of Oxnard, 838 F.2d 375 (9th Cir.1988), cert. denied 488 U.S. 851, 109 S.Ct. 134, 102 L.Ed.2d 106 (1988). In *Herrington,* the court held that the "finality" requirement was satisfied, although plaintiff had applied neither for a development permit nor, of course, for a variance, because of the County's determination that the proposed development was inconsistent with the County's General Plan. This holding is clearly correct, since the ordinance establishing the General Plan did not allow any development that was inconsistent with the General Plan either upon an original application or upon application for a variance. But in *Lake Nacimiento* it was held that the "finality" requirement was not satisfied because plaintiff had not sought approval of a development plan that would permit economically viable use of the land instead of seeking to have the General Plan amended, where the only uses permitted by the General Plan were not economically

viable. This holding would seem to be incorrect, since any application for approval of a plan that would permit an economically viable use would have been inconsistent with the General Plan and would certainly have been rejected, and would therefore have been futile. In *Shelter Creek,* on the other hand, plaintiff had obtained a ruling from the California Supreme Court that plaintiff need not obtain a special use permit before converting a rental apartment complex into a stock cooperative, and had then sought relief in federal court when the City blocked the proposed conversion. The United States District Court decided for the City on the merits. On appeal, the Court of Appeals dismissed the case for lack of federal jurisdiction on the ground that the case was not "ripe" because plaintiff had not applied for a special use permit. In response to plaintiff's argument that a special use permit was unnecessary by virtue of the California Supreme Court holding, the Court of Appeals, in language reminiscent of Alice in Wonderland, said:

> That holding was based on state law. As a matter of federal law, however, a federal court cannot entertain a challenge to application of a land use ordinance absent a final and authoritative decision by the appropriate administrative body. The federal requirement cannot be altered or abrogated by a decision of a state court construing its own law. (838 F.2d 380).

48. The right to compensation for a "regulatory taking" was recognized, prior to First Church, in several state court cases—e.g., Corrigan v. City of Scottsdale, 149 Ariz. 538, 720 P.2d 513 (1986); Burrows v. City of Keene, 121 N.H. 590, 432 A.2d 15 (1981); Minch v. City of Fargo, 297 N.W.2d 785 (N.D.1980), appeal after remand 332 N.W.2d 71 (1983); Rippley v. City of Lincoln, 330 N.W.2d 505 (N.D.1983);

in any federal court until the plaintiff has exhausted his federal constitutional remedy in the appropriate state courts.[49]

In view of the requirement that state court "inverse condemnation" remedies be exhausted in "regulatory taking" cases, the other "ripeness" requirements—exhaustion of state administrative remedies and filing a "meaningful" development application—no longer have independent significance in "inverse condemnation" cases, although under state law this requirement will usually be a prerequisite to seeking compensation in the state court.[50] But the exhaustion of state administrative remedies remains crucially important in cases where the plaintiff seeks only to invalidate land use regulations by suing in a federal court; in such cases, it would make no sense to require an effort to obtain compensation in the state court as a prerequisite to seeking review in the United States Supreme Court.

(2) The "Abstention" Doctrine

Another judicially created restriction on federal jurisdiction in land use cases is the so-called "abstention" doctrine, which originated in three United States Supreme Court cases: Railroad Com'n v. Pullman Co.,[51] Burford v. Sun Oil Co.,[52] and Younger v. Harris.[53] In *Pullman,* the Court held that federal courts should abstain from exercising their jurisdiction if resolution of a difficult and unsettled state law question would make it unnecessary to decide a federal constitutional issue, especially if the state law question "touches a sensitive area of social policy upon which the federal courts ought not to enter unless no alternative to its adjudication is open." Recently, in Hawaii Housing Auth. v. Midkiff,[54] the Court said that a state law must be "fairly subject" to an interpretation that would make it unnecessary to decide any federal constitutional question before the *Pullman* abstention doctrine should be applied. The federal courts have, in fact, applied the *Pullman* abstention doctrine in land use cases where state law was unsettled.[55] "Mirror image" constitutional problems may arise when a litigant

---

City of Austin v. Teague, 570 S.W.2d 389 (Tex. 1978).

49. Four Seasons Apartment v. City of Mayfield Heights, 775 F.2d 150 (6th Cir.1985); Culebras Enterprises Corp. v. Rivera Rios, 813 F.2d 506 (1st Cir.1987); Boothe v. Manatee County, 812 F.2d 1372 (11th Cir.1987), rehearing denied 818 F.2d 871 (1987); Austin v. City & County of Honolulu, 840 F.2d 678 (9th Cir. 1988), cert. denied 488 U.S. 852, 109 S.Ct. 136, 102 L.Ed.2d 109 (1988). The requirement has been applied retroactively to cases begun in the federal court before *Williamson County* was decided. See, e.g., *Austin,* supra, where the court explained that lack of "ripeness" deprives the court of jurisdiction and, therefore, that such a jurisdictional ruling must necessarily be retroactive.

50. See discussion of land use cases involving "due process" and "taking" claims in the state court, post part (e) of this Section.

51. 312 U.S. 496, 61 S.Ct. 643, 85 L.Ed. 971 (1941).

52. 319 U.S. 315, 63 S.Ct. 1098, 87 L.Ed. 1424 (1943).

53. 401 U.S. 37, 91 S.Ct. 746, 27 L.Ed.2d 669 (1971).

54. 467 U.S. 229, 104 S.Ct. 2321, 81 L.Ed.2d 186 (1984), on remand 740 F.2d 15 (9th Cir. 1984).

55. Kollsman v. City of Los Angeles, 737 F.2d 830 (9th Cir.1984), cert. denied 469 U.S. 1211, 105 S.Ct. 1179, 84 L.Ed.2d 327 (1985) (whether plaintiff's subdivision should be deemed "approved" depended on interlocking state statutes whose construction was unsettled); C–Y Development Co. v. City of Redlands, 703 F.2d 375 (9th Cir.1983) (denial of development permit under growth-management ordinance raised unsettled questions concerning the application of certain ordinance provisions); Caleb Stowe Associates, Ltd. v. Albemarle County, 724 F.2d 1079 (4th Cir.1984). The federal courts have refused to apply the *Pullman* abstention doctrine where relevant state law questions are settled. See, e.g., Urbanizadora Versalles, Inc. v. Rivera Rios, 701 F.2d 993 (1st Cir.1983). Federal courts often refuse to abstain in land use cases involving civil rights or First Amendment rights. See Cinema Arts, Inc. v. Clark Coun-

asks a federal court to abstain in order to allow a state court to interpret a state constitutional provision substantially similar to a federal constitutional provision—e.g., a state constitutional "taking" clause very similar to the Fifth Amendment's "taking" clause as made applicable to the states by the Fourteenth Amendment's "due process" clause. Several lower federal courts have invoked the *Pullman* abstention doctrine in such a case, but the Supreme Court held in *Midkiff* that abstention is inappropriate in such a case.[56]

In Burford v. Sun Oil Co.,[57] the Supreme Court extended the *Pullman* abstention doctrine to a case where, the Court said, federal intervention would lead to conflicts in the interpretation of state law that might endanger state policies. But in New Orleans Public Service, Inc. v. Council of City of New Orleans,[58] the Court limited the *Burford* abstention doctrine, holding that the doctrine was not applicable to a claim that a city council utility rate order was preempted by a federal statute. The Court said that the *Burford* doctrine does not always require abstention when there is a complex state regulatory system or a potential for conflict between state and federal law or policy. Consequently, said the Court, *Burford* abstention wasn't required in the *New Orleans* case because it turned on the federal preemption issue and only a facial review of the city council's rate order was necessary. Presumably the Court would reach the same result where a case involving a substantial federal question also involves a facial challenge to a local zoning ordinance.

Many *Burford* abstention cases may involve unsettled state law issues. Thus *Burford* and *Pullman* abstention may both be appropriate in a given case. The courts have applied a combined *Burford–Pullman* analysis in land use cases where the court held that abstention was proper.[59]

In Younger v. Harris,[60] the Supreme Court held that federal courts should abstain from enjoining pending state court criminal proceedings if the defendant in such a case can make an adequate federal defense in the state court proceeding and abstention would not cause irreparable injury to the defendant.[61] But the *Younger* doctrine as originally formulated rarely requires federal abstention in land use cases because criminal prosecution in land use cases is rare. The extension of the *Younger* doctrine to pending

ty, 722 F.2d 579 (9th Cir.1983) (First Amendment rights.).

56. 467 U.S. at 237 n. 4, 104 S.Ct. at 2327 n. 4.

57. Supra note 50. The *Burford* abstention doctrine was further explained in Colorado River Water Conservation District v. United States, 424 U.S. 800, 96 S.Ct. 1236, 47 L.Ed.2d 483 (1976), rehearing denied 426 U.S. 912, 96 S.Ct. 2239, 48 L.Ed.2d 839 (1976), where the Court said: "Abstention is also appropriate where there have been presented difficult questions of state law bearing on policy problems of substantial public import whose importance transcends the result in the case then at bar. * * * It is enough that exercise of federal review of the question * * * would be disruptive of state efforts to establish a coherent policy with respect to a

matter of substantial public concern * * *." 424 U.S. at 814, 96 S.Ct. at 1244.

58. 491 U.S. 350, 109 S.Ct. 2506, 105 L.Ed.2d 298 (1989), appeal after remand 911 F.2d 993 (5th Cir.1990).

59. Corder v. City of Sherwood, 579 F.Supp. 1042 (E.D.Ark.1984); Kent Island Joint Venture v. Smith, 452 F.Supp. 455 (D.Md.1978).

60. 401 U.S. 37, 91 S.Ct. 746, 27 L.Ed.2d 669 (1971).

61. *Younger* abstention is required even though the federal case is filed before the state case if "proceedings of substance" on the merits have not taken place in the federal court when the state court action is filed. Hicks v. Miranda, 422 U.S. 332, 95 S.Ct. 2281, 45 L.Ed.2d 223 (1975).

state civil proceedings implicating important state interests in Middlesex County Ethics Comm. v. Garden State Bar Ass'n [62] and to state administrative proceedings in Ohio Civil Rights Comm. v. Dayton Christian schools [63] might theoretically have led to application of the *Younger* doctrine to civil cases involving land use disputes. But in *New Orleans* [64] the Court held that *Younger* abstention is inapplicable when proceedings to challenge state legislative and executive actions are pending in state court.

The various "abstention" doctrines discussed above are potentially applicable whenever a landowner seeks to invalidate land use regulations on substantive due process or equal protection ground, provided he does not also seek to obtain compensation on the theory that the regulations are so restrictive as to effect a "regulatory taking." But when a landowner does seek to obtain compensation on that theory, the "abstention" doctrines no longer have any significance because, in such a case, *Williamson County* [65] clearly requires the landowner first to seek compensation in the state courts.

B.   CONTROL OF LAND USE BY ZONING

§ 9.3   The Early History of Zoning

In urban areas the most important form of governmental land use control based upon the police power is "zoning." [1] It has been said that "[t]he essence of zoning is territorial division in keeping with the character of the lands and structures and their peculiar suitability for particular uses, and uniformity of use within the division." [2] Historically, zoning is an extension of the concept of public nuisance by legislation. During the colonial period preceding the formation of the United States, municipalities in the British colonies frequently enacted regulatory ordinances banning slaughter houses, gunpowder mills, and the like to the outskirts of the municipality. [3] Later many municipalities established "fire districts" in which wooden buildings were prohibited. In 1889 a Wisconsin statute authorized cities to create districts with building regulations which differed from district to district according to the fire risks involved. [4] In the same year building height restrictions were enacted in Washington, D.C. Similar restrictions adopted in Boston were held constitutional in 1909. [5] But New York City was the first American municipality to adopt a comprehensive scheme of building and land use regulations based upon the creation of a number of districts or zones. The Building Zone Resolution adopted by New York City in 1916, after three years of careful study, established three

62. 457 U.S. 423, 102 S.Ct. 2515, 73 L.Ed.2d 116 (1982), on remand 687 F.2d 801 (3d Cir. 1982).

63. 477 U.S. 619, 106 S.Ct. 2718, 91 L.Ed.2d 512 (1986).

64. Supra note 58.

65. See discussion of *Williamson County* ante in text at notes 35–37.

§ 9.3

1. The most useful multi-volume treatises on zoning are N. Williams, American Land Planning Law (5 vols., 1975 and annual sup-

plements); R. Anderson, American Law of Zoning (5 vols., 2d ed. 1976 and annual supplements). The best single-volume text is D. Mandelker, Land Use Law (1982).

2. Katobimar Realty Co. v. Webster, 20 N.J. 114, 118 A.2d 824 (1955).

3. E.g., Acts & Resolves of the Province of Massachusetts Bay 1692–93, ch. 23.

4. See Solberg, Rural Zoning in the United States (Ag.Info.Bull. 59, U.S.D.A.1952).

5. Welch v. Swasey, 214 U.S. 91, 29 S.Ct. 567, 53 L.Ed. 923 (1909).

separate classes of districts, dealing respectively with the use of land and buildings, height of buildings, and land coverage, with each class of districts represented on a different set of maps.[6] "Use" districts were classified either as residence, business, or unrestricted. In residence districts, trade and industry of every kind were prohibited. In business districts, specified trades and industries—mainly nuisance-creating industries such as boiler-making, ammonia manufacturing, and the like—were prohibited; residences and all other kinds of trade and industry were permitted. In unrestricted districts any kind of land use was permitted. The regulations were prospective in their operation, and were intended to supply a rational basis for future building development in New York City.

Although the 1916 New York City Building Zone Resolution was adopted under the authority of a special enabling act, the New York Legislature shortly thereafter adopted a general zoning enabling act for cities. As zoning spread to other parts of the United States, the enactment of local zoning ordinances was generally preceded by adoption of general zoning enabling legislation. By 1926, all but five of the then forty-eight states had adopted zoning enabling legislation, and some 420 municipalities had enacted zoning ordinances. Until 1923 most of the new state zoning enabling acts were modelled on the New York zoning enabling legislation. In January of 1923 the United States Department of Commerce published the first draft of a Standard State Zoning Enabling Act, which departed in some respects from the New York zoning enabling legislation. The Standard Act, revised and republished in 1924 and again in 1926, was the model for most of the zoning enabling legislation adopted after 1923.[7] At the present time all fifty states have enacted zoning enabling legislation for municipalities, and upwards of three-quarters of the states also have enacted zoning enabling legislation for counties.[8] Although zoning enabling legislation currently in force often embodies very substantial changes from the enabling acts originally adopted, probably a majority of the current statutes still retains the substance of the New York or Standard Act models. *Inter alia,* most of the current zoning enabling acts still contain, either in identical or substantially similar language, the basic grant of power included in Sections 1 through 3 of the Standard Act, as follows:

> Sec. 1. For the purpose of promoting health, safety, morals, or the general welfare of the community, the legislative body of cities and incorporated villages is hereby empowered to regulate and restrict the height, number of stories, and size of buildings and other structures, the percentage of lot that may be occupied, the size of yards, courts, and other open spaces, the density of population, and the location and use of

---

6. For a discussion of the 1916 New York City Building Zone Resolution and its drafting, see E. Bassett, Zoning 7–8, 20–29 (1940); McGoldrick, et al., Building Regulations in New York City 91–95 (1944); S. Toll, Zoned American 78–187 (1969).

7. The Standard State Zoning Enabling Act (hereafter "Standard Act" in text and "SSZEA" in footnotes) is no longer in print in its original form as a publication of the U.S. Dept. of Commerce, but is reprinted in full, with the draftsmen's footnotes, as Appendix A, Am.L.Inst., A Model Land Development Code, Tent. Draft 1, p. 210 (1968). It is also reprinted, without the footnotes, in O. Browder, R. Cunningham, J. Julin & A. Smith, Basic Property Law 1116 (3d ed. 1979); and D. Mandelker & R. Cunningham, Planning and Control of Land Development 217 (1979).

8. Cunningham, Land–Use Control—The State and Local Programs, 50 Iowa L.Rev. 367, 368 (1965).

buildings, structures, and land for trade, industry, residence, or other purposes.

Sec. 2. For any or all of said purposes the local legislative body may divide the municipality into districts of such number, shape, and area as may be deemed best suited to carry out the purposes of this act; and within such districts it may regulate and restrict the erection, construction, reconstruction, alteration, repair, or use of buildings, structures, or land. All such regulations shall be uniform for each class or kind of buildings throughout each district, but the regulations in one district may differ from those in other districts.

Sec. 3. Such regulations shall be made in accordance with a comprehensive plan and designed to lessen congestion in the streets; to secure safety from fire, panic, and other dangers; to promote health and the general welfare; to provide adequate light and air; to prevent the overcrowding of land; to avoid undue concentration of population; to facilitate the adequate provision of transportation, water, sewerage, schools, parks, and other public requirements. Such regulations shall be made with reasonable consideration, among other things, to the character of the district and its peculiar suitability for particular uses, and with a view to conserving the value of buildings and encouraging the most appropriate use of land throughout such municipality.

Prior to 1926 the new zoning technique for controlling land use in urban areas had survived constitutional attack in a majority of the jurisdictions in which its constitutionality had been challenged,[9] but the zoning technique had been held unconstitutional in several states.[10] If the United States Supreme Court had held the new zoning technique to be unconstitutional, it would, of course, have had to be abandoned. But, in Euclid v. Ambler Realty Co.,[11] the Court held that the new zoning technique did not, in principle, violate the due process clause of the Fourteenth Amendment. Although the plaintiff alleged that the Euclid zoning ordinance, as applied to land which it held for future industrial and commercial development, reduced the value of that land by about seventy-five percent, the court did not really deal with this allegation—which was the basis for a substantive due process argument apparently premised on the "not too oppressive" branch of the Lawton v. Steele [12] substantive due process test. Instead, the Court considered only the "facial" validity of the zoning ordinance—in its "general scope and dominant features" [13]—and concluded that the reasons urged in support of the ordi-

---

9. These jurisdictions were California, Illinois, Kansas, Louisiana, Massachusetts, Minnesota, New York, Ohio, Oregon, and Wisconsin. See Brief *amicus curiae* filed by A. Bettman, as counsel for the Nat. Conf. on City Planning, the Nat. Housing Ass'n, and the Mass. Fed. of Town Planning Boards, in Euclid v. Ambler Realty Co., 272 U.S. 365, 47 S.Ct. 114, 71 L.Ed. 303 (1926). This brief is reprinted in A. Bettman, City and Regional Planning Papers 157 (1946).

10. These jurisdictions were Delaware, Georgia, Maryland, Missouri, and New Jersey. See A. Bettman, Brief, supra note 9.

11. Supra note 9.

12. 152 U.S. 133, 14 S.Ct. 499, 38 L.Ed. 385 (1894). See discussion ante Section 9.2 at note 10 and ff.

13. The Bettman Brief *amicus curiae*, supra note 9, asked the Court to limit its review of "comprehensive zoning" in this way, instead of considering "the contentions of the parties" as to "the reasonableness or arbitrariness of the Euclid Village ordinance itself in its districting of the particular property of the appellee."

nance were "sufficiently cogent to preclude" the Court from saying that the ordinance was "clearly arbitrary and unreasonable, having no substantial relationship to the public health, safety, morals, or general welfare." [14]

In reaching this conclusion, the *Euclid* Court found that the general exclusion of "all industrial establishments" from all but two of the six "use" districts created by the Euclid zoning ordinance was clearly a reasonable exercise of the police power, relying heavily on the analogy to the law of nuisance, "although some industries of an innocent character might fall within the proscribed class." [15] The Court had somewhat greater difficulty in determining the validity of "the provisions of the ordinance excluding from residential districts apartment houses, business houses, retail stores and shops, and other like establishments," which it characterized as "really the crux of the more recent zoning legislation." [16] The Court decided, however, that such provisions could be sustained on the basis of studies indicating that the segregation of one- and two-family dwellings from both businesses and apartments had a rational basis because this

> will make it easier to provide fire apparatus suitable for the character and intensity of the development of each section; * * * will increase the safety and security of home life, greatly tend to prevent accidents, especially to children, by reducing the traffic and resulting confusion in residential sections, decrease noise and other conditions which produce or intensify nervous disorders, preserve a more favorable environment in which to rear children, etc.[17]

The exclusion of apartment houses from one- and two-family districts—the most controversial form of segregation—was held to be justified on the basis of studies providing a rational basis to believe that the development of detached house sections is greatly retarded by the coming of apartment houses, which has sometimes resulted in destroying the entire section for private house purposes; that in such sections very often the apartment house is a mere parasite, constructed in order to take advantage of the open space and attractive surrounding created by the residential character of the district.[18]

The *Euclid* opinion closed with a warning that "when, if ever, the provisions set forth in the ordinance in tedious and minute detail, come to be concretely applied to particular premises, * * * or to particular conditions, or to be considered in connection with specific complaints, some of them, or even many of them, may be found to be clearly arbitrary and unreasonable." [19] This dictum—which uses substantive due process rather than "taking" language—seemed to foreshadow a continuing "watchdog" role for the Supreme Court in zoning cases. During the next few years, the Supreme Court did, in fact, review several zoning cases, and in Nectow v. City of Cambridge [20] it invalidated, as a violation of substantive due process, a residential use classification as applied to a small part of the plaintiff's

---

14. 272 U.S. at 395, 47 S.Ct. at 121. The Court employed the "deferential" standard of review and, in substance, recognized a presumption that the zoning ordinance was valid.

15. See 272 U.S. at 388, 47 S.Ct. at 119.

16. See 272 U.S. at 390, 47 S.Ct. at 119.

17. See 272 U.S. at 394, 47 S.Ct. at 120.

18. Ibid.

19. See 272 U.S. at 395, 47 S.Ct. at 121.

20. 277 U.S. 183, 48 S.Ct. 447, 72 L.Ed. 842 (1928).

land.[21] But the Supreme Court consistently refused to review zoning cases during the period from 1928 to 1962, and did not again become active in reviewing zoning cases until the mid–1970's. Consequently, for almost half a century the state courts were primarily responsible for developing the law of zoning. During this period, with the validity of zoning in principle established by *Euclid*,[22] the state courts reached varying conclusions as to the applicability of the substantive due process and "taking" tests to zoning cases.[23]

§ 9.4   Zoning to Segregate Land Uses and Building Types

In accordance with the basic grant of power contained in Sections 1 through 3 of the Standard Act and its current equivalents, most local zoning ordinances divide the relevant area—either a municipality or a county—into two or more districts and prescribe "use," "bulk," and "area" or "density" regulations for each district. The ordinance includes a zoning map which delineates the various districts, and the text of the ordinance sets out the regulations applicable in each district.

The 1916 New York City Building Zone Resolution created three "use" districts: residential, business, and unrestricted. Modern zoning ordinances usually create a much larger number of districts—often there are several residence districts, several business districts, and one or more industrial districts.[1] The 1916 New York City Building Zone Resolution drew no distinctions between different residential building types, but other municipalities soon began to create residence districts in which single-family dwellings were the only principal structures permitted. Even before *Euclid* was decided, exclusive single-family residence districts were sustained by state courts,[2] and the United States Supreme Court ultimately—at least by implication—established the validity of exclusive single-family zoning in Belle Terre v. Boraas.[3]

21. The Court relied on the finding of a master appointed by the state trial court to the effect that "the districting of the plaintiff's land in a residence district would not promote the health, safety convenience and general welfare of the inhabitants of that part of the defendant city." Although the Court concluded that "because of the industrial and railroad purposes to which the immediately adjoining lands * * * have been devoted and for which they are zoned, the locus is of comparatively little value for the limited uses permitted by the zoning ordinance," the Court did *not* hold that the ordinance amounted to a *de facto* "taking" nor did it cite Pennsylvania Coal Co. v. Mahon, 260 U.S. 393, 43 S.Ct. 158, 67 L.Ed. 322 (1922), discussed ante Section 9.2 at note 16 and ff.

22. In some states where comprehensive zoning was held to violate the state constitutions—e.g., Georgia and New Jersey—constitutional amendments were required to legalize the comprehensive zoning technique.

23. In many cases it is not clear whether the courts are applying a constitutional or a statutory test (i.e., are the zoning regulations *ultra vires*). Even where a court bases its decision on constitutional grounds it is often unclear whether the court is relying on the state or the federal constitution, or both, perhaps because the courts assume that it makes no difference.

§ 9.4

1. See, e.g., the Euclid Village zoning ordinance upheld in Village of Euclid v. Ambler Realty Co., 272 U.S. 365, 47 S.Ct. 114, 71 L.Ed. 303 (1926). Cf. the Model Zoning Ordinance prepared by the American Society of Planning Officials (3d ed. 1966) for use in small towns, which provides only for "Residential Districts" (permitting only one single-family dwelling as a principal "use" on each lot), "Multifamily Districts," and "Neighborhood Business Districts" (excluding industrial uses).

2. E.g., Brett v. Building Commissioner of Brookline, 250 Mass. 73, 145 N.E. 269 (1924).

3. 416 U.S. 1, 94 S.Ct. 1536, 39 L.Ed.2d 797 (1974).

Occasionally local governments in small, substantially built-up "bedroom" communities have zoned the entire municipal area exclusively for single-family dwellings. When this practice has been challenged, it has sometimes been held invalid on the ground that the zoning enabling act requires creation of more than one district, but it seems unlikely that many courts would adopt such a mechanical approach to the problem at the present time.[4] In Belle Terre v. Boraas,[5] the United States Supreme Court upheld a zoning ordinance which, in a village of 700 people almost entirely built up with single-family dwellings, permitted only "one-family dwellings, excluding lodging houses, boarding houses, fraternity houses, or multiple-dwelling houses."

In *Belle Terre* the Court also sustained the zoning ordinance's definition of a "family" as "[o]ne or more persons related by blood, adoption, or marriage, living and cooking together as a single housekeeping unit * * * [or a] number of persons but not exceeding two (2) living and cooking together as a single housekeeping unit though not related by blood, adoption or marriage." The limitation of unrelated occupants to two persons was challenged on the basis of allegations that it interfered with a constitutionally-protected "right to travel" and that it was not designed to achieve any legitimate governmental purpose but was, instead, designed to achieve social homogeneity and to exclude persons whose life style was different from that of the existing population of the village of Belle Terre.[6] In explaining the court's decision, Justice Douglas said that the police power may properly be used "to lay out zones where family values, youth values, and the blessings of quiet seclusion and clean air make the area a sanctuary for people."[7]

4. See City of Moline Acres v. Heidbreder, 367 S.W.2d 568 (Mo.1963) (single district zoning invalid), followed in Gunderson v. Village of Bingham Farms, 372 Mich. 352, 126 N.W.2d 715 (1964), but overruled in McDermott v. Village of Calverton Park, 454 S.W.2d 577 (Mo.1970) (single district zoning valid). See also Bartolomeo v. Town of Paradise Valley, 129 Ariz. 409, 631 P.2d 564 (1981) (single residential district, with special permit required for non-residential use, held valid).

5. Supra note 3. Accord: In re McGinnis, 68 Pa.Cmwlth. 57, 448 A.2d 108 (1982).

6. The Belle Terre ordinance was challenged by the owners of a "single-family" house who had originally leased it to one university student. Later, a second student became a co-lessee and, still later, four other students "moved into the house." When the village served the owners with an "Order to Remedy Violations" of the ordinance, the owners and three of the student occupants sued for an injunction under 42 U.S.C.A. § 1983 and for a declaration that the restrictive definition of "family" in the ordinance was unconstitutional.

7. 416 U.S. at 9, 94 S.Ct. at 1541. Justice Douglas said that the record did not support the allegations that the restrictive definition of "family" in the ordinance interfered with the "right to travel" and was intended to further impermissible purposes. He therefore decided the case on traditional substantive due process grounds, paying the usual deference to the local legislative judgment that the maximum number of unrelated persons who might occupy a "single-family" house should be two rather than "three or four."

Cf. the dissenting opinion of Justice Marshall, who concluded that the Belle Terre ordinance "creates a classification which impinges upon fundamental personal rights" and thus "can withstand constitutional scrutiny only upon a clear showing that the burden imposed is necessary to protect a compelling and substantial governmental interest." He held that no such interest had been demonstrated. See 416 U.S. at 15, 94 S.Ct. at 1544.

For critical comment on *Belle Terre,* see, e.g., 3 N. Williams, Am. Land Planning Law 91–103 (1975); Hartman, Village of Belle Terre v. Boraas: Belle Terre is a Nice Place to Visit—But Only "Families" May Live There, 8 Urb.L.Ann. 193 (1974); Note, Village of Belle Terre v. Boraas: "A Sanctuary for People," 9 U.S.F.L.Rev. 391 (1974).

Compare *Belle Terre* with Moore v. City of East Cleveland, 431 U.S. 494, 97 S.Ct. 1932, 52 L.Ed.2d 531 (1977), striking down a local housing code provision restricting the number of *related* individuals who could live in a "single-family" house. No single rationale command-

Despite the decision of the United States Supreme Court in the *Belle Terre* case, the recent trend in the state courts has been to invalidate, on state statutory or constitutional grounds, restrictive definitions of "family" like those sustained in *Belle Terre*. In State v. Baker,[8] the New Jersey Supreme Court held that the New Jersey constitution invalidates zoning ordinance provisions that "condition residence upon the number of unrelated persons present within the household" because, "[g]iven the availability of less restrictive alternative, such regulations are unsufficiently related to the perceived social ills which they were intended to ameliorate."[9] The Pennsylvania Commonwealth Court, the New York Court of Appeals, and the Supreme Court of Michigan have all reached the same result on substantially the same ground.[10] And the California Supreme Court recently held a similarly restrictive zoning ordinance definition of "family" unconstitutional,[11] not because—as was held in New Jersey and Pennsylvania—it violated substantive due process but because it violated an express provision of the

ed majority support, but all the justices who voted to strike down the provision in question relied on substantive due process, with emphasis on the sanctity of the family.

8. 81 N.J. 99, 405 A.2d 368 (1979).

9. 81 N.J. at 114, 405 A.2d at 375. The Court found the reasoning of *Belle Terre* to be both unpersuasive and inconsistent with prior New Jersey cases, pointing out that the Court remained "free to interpret [New Jersey's] constitution and statutes more stringently" than the United States Supreme Court's interpretations of the Fourteenth Amendment. It is not clear whether the *Baker* opinion uses the traditional substantive due process test of "minimum rationality" or the "strict scrutiny—compelling government interest" test applied where "fundamental personal rights" are restricted, or perhaps some intermediate test.

See also Borough of Glassboro v. Vallorosi, 117 N.J. 421, 568 A.2d 888 (1990) (ten college students constituted a "family" within the meaning of an ordinance defining a "family" as "one or more persons occupying a dwelling unit as a single nonprofit housekeeping unit, who are living together as a stable and permanent living unit, being a traditional family unit or the functional equivalency [sic] thereof").

10. *Pennsylvania:* Children's Home of Easton v. City of Easton, 53 Pa.Cmwlth. 216, 417 A.2d 830 (1980); Hopkins v. Zoning Hearing Board of Abington Township, 55 Pa.Cmwlth. 365, 423 A.2d 1082 (1980). But see In re McGinnis, 68 Pa.Cmwlth. 57, 448 A.2d 108, 112 n. 2 (1982), following *Belle Terre* and distinguishing the *Easton* and *Abington Tp.* cases.

New York: Baer v. Brookhaven, 73 N.Y.2d 942, 540 N.Y.S.2d 234, 537 N.E.2d 619 (1989) (The court struck down an ordinance provision similar to that sustained by the United States Supreme Court in *Belle Terre*, supra note 5; the ordinance did not restrict the size

of a "traditional" family but limited the size of a "functionally equivalent" family to four unrelated adults. The court acknowledged that the validity of such a provision under the United States Constitution was established by *Belle Terre*, but the court held that it violated New York's state constitution.).

Michigan: Charter Tp. of Delta v. Dinolfo, 419 Mich. 253, 351 N.W.2d 831 (1984) (ordinance which prohibited defendant couples from including six unrelated adults in their households was not reasonably related to achievement of the stated objectives of the ordinance—maintenance of property values, preservation of traditional family values, and population and density control—and thus deprived defendants of their property without due process in violation of Michigan state constitution; rationale of *Belle Terre* not applicable).

Belle Terre was cited approvingly in two cases sustaining restrictive definitions of "family" for zoning purposes: Town of Durham v. White Enterprises, Inc., 115 N.H. 645, 348 A.2d 706 (1975), and Rademan v. City & County of Denver, 186 Colo. 250, 526 P.2d 1325 (1974). But Rademan was qualified in Zavala v. City & County of Denver, 759 P.2d 664 (Colo.1988). Carroll v. Washington Tp. Zoning Com'n, 63 Ohio St. 249, 408 N.E.2d 191 (1980), sustained the exclusion of foster homes from single-family districts without mention of *Belle Terre;* but *Carroll* was qualified and perhaps overruled in Saunders v. Clark County Zoning Dept., 66 Ohio St.2d 259, 421 N.E.2d 152 (1981). See also Life Concepts v. Harden, 562 So.2d 726 (Fla.App.1990) (ordinance was not unconstitutionally vague in requiring group home's maximum number of occupants to be "compatible with the surrounding [land] uses").

11. City of Santa Barbara v. Adamson, 27 Cal.3d 123, 164 Cal.Rptr. 539, 610 P.2d 436 (1980).

California constitution protecting "privacy." [12] Elsewhere, state courts have sometimes construed local zoning ordinances to permit "group homes" in single-family residence districts despite restrictive definitions of "family" in the ordinance.[13] And in those states where there is state legislation authorizing establishment of "group" homes, some state courts have decided—in the face of restrictive definitions of "family" in local zoning ordinances—that "group homes" must be permitted in single-family residence districts on the basis of "state governmental immunity" or "overriding state policy." [14]

In City of Cleburne, Texas v. Cleburne Living Center,[15] the United States Supreme Court struck down the city's zoning provision—construed by the city to be applicable to group homes for retarded persons—requiring a special use permit for "hospitals, for the insane or feebleminded, or alcoholic or drug addicts, or penal or correctional institutions"—as applied to a group home for retarded persons that the Living Center sought to establish in a single-family residence zone. Although the Court held that mental retardation is not a "suspect" or "quasi-suspect" classification, and that middle-level "strict scrutiny" was not called for, the Court nevertheless held that the special use permit requirement failed to meet the "rational relationship" test applied in the general run of cases where government regulations are challenged under the equal protection clause. Since apartment houses,

12. 27 Cal.3d at 129, 610 P.2d at 439. The California and New Jersey constitutional provisions relied on in *Adamson* and *Baker,* respectively, are almost identical. Both, in fact, include "the right to privacy" among "the natural and unalienable rights" protected against government interference. These provisions have been construed as embodying a guaranty of substantive due process analogous to the Fourteenth Amendment's guaranty of due process.

See also City of Chula Vista v. Pagard, 171 Cal.Rptr. 738 (Cal.App.1981), accord with *Adamson. Belle Terre* has some support among the state courts—e.g., Carroll v. Washington Township Zoning Commission, 63 Ohio 2d 249, 408 N.E.2d 191 (1980). But see Saunders v. Clark County Zoning Department, 66 Ohio 2d 259, 421 N.E.2d 152 (1981).

13. E.g., City of White Plains v. Ferraioli, 34 N.Y.2d 300, 357 N.Y.S.2d 449, 313 N.E.2d 756 (1974); Hessling v. City of Broomfield, 193 Colo. 124, 563 P.2d 12 (1977).

14. E.g., People v. St. Agatha Home for Children, 47 N.Y.2d 46, 416 N.Y.S.2d 577, 389 N.E.2d 1098 (1979), certiorari denied 444 U.S. 869, 100 S.Ct. 145, 62 L.Ed.2d 94 (1979) (state governmental immunity); Abbott House v. Village of Tarrytown, 34 A.D.2d 821, 312 N.Y.S.2d 841 (1970). Incorporated Village of Nyack v. Daytop Village, Inc., 173 A.D.2d 778, 570 N.Y.S.2d 836 (1991) (state immunity for licensed drug treatment facility); Herrmann v. County Com'rs, 246 Kan. 152, 785 P.2d 1003 (1990). However, a state policy in favor of group homes will not necessarily override reasonable local zoning restrictions. See, e.g., People v. Renaissance Project, Inc., 36 N.Y.2d

65, 364 N.Y.S.2d 885, 324 N.E.2d 355 (1975). Where the legislative intent is not clear, the courts have usually used a balancing test, weighing the broader state interest promoted by locating a group home in a single-family district against the impact of such a location on the legitimate local interest served by the zoning regulations. See, e.g., Berger v. State, 71 N.J. 206, 364 A.2d 993 (1976).

For a list of statutes authorizing group homes in single-family districts, see Hopperton, A State Legislative Strategy for Ending Exclusionary Zoning of Community Homes, 19 Urb.L.Ann. 47 (1980). See also 19 Urb.L.Ann. 77 (1980) for the text of a Model Zoning Act provision authorizing group homes with six or fewer residents in all residential districts as a matter of right. The Model Act also invalidates any restrictive covenant precluding use of residential structures as group homes.

See also Northern Maine General Hospital v. Ricker, 572 A.2d 479 (Me.1990) (group home for male adolescents was previously allowed as special exception in residential zone; but refusal to grant special exception for pre-release half-way house for adult male felons was justified because such a half-way house was significantly more objectionable). Cf. Pinellas County Bd. of Adjustment v. Carlson, 536 So.2d 1062 (Fla.App.1988) (denial of special exception for group home for ten elderly persons was abuse of discretion where the statutory criteria were satisfied and there was no substantial evidence that group home use would be adverse to the public interest).

15. 473 U.S. 432, 105A S.Ct. 3249, 87 L.Ed.2d 313 (1985).

boarding houses, fraternity houses, hospitals, and nursing homes are not required to obtain special use permits, and since the Court could not find any rational basis for treating group homes for the mentally retarded differently, the Court found that the special use permit requirement as applied to group homes for the mentally retarded did not serve any legitimate government interest, but seemed to be based only on irrational prejudice against the mentally retarded. Justices Marshall, Brennan, and Blackmun, concurring,[16] said that the decision was in fact based on a "heightened scrutiny" analysis—noting that under the traditional "rational relationship" test the Court does not sift through the record for firm factual bases for each government policy decision—and declared that "heightened scrutiny" was appropriate in *Cleburne* because the interest of the mentally retarded in establishing group homes is substantial, and because the mentally retarded have historically suffered from discrimination. Hence, the three justices stated, the ordinance should have been found unconstitutional on its face.

Although the separation of residential from non-residential land uses, and even the exclusion of apartments from a one- and two-family residence district, was approved in principle in *Euclid*,[17] the validity of particular residential zoning classifications as applied to particular tracts of land is frequently litigated in the state courts. Occasionally a residential use classification is held invalid as a *de facto* "taking" under the *Mahon*[18] "taking" test. Thus, for example, a residential use classification was held invalid as a *de facto* "taking" in Arverne Bay Const. Co. v. Thatcher,[19] despite the court's recognition of the great public benefit that would result from reserving the area in question for future residential development. More often, however, the courts seem to use a Lawton v. Steele[20] "balancing" test in determining the validity of a residential use classification.

Landowners and land developers, in a typical case, challenge the validity of a residential use classification that excludes non-residential uses or, more frequently, excludes all land uses except use for single-family dwellings. In deciding such cases, the state courts usually examine the existing zoning and actual development of the area surrounding the plaintiff's land. If the surrounding area is zoned and/or developed for uses consistent with the uses permitted on the plaintiff's land, the courts are likely to conclude that the zoning of the plaintiff's land violates neither substantive due process nor equal protection guarantees and sustain the zoning classification.[21] But a more difficult problem arises when the area surrounding the plaintiff's land is zoned for or actually developed with a mixture of single-family, apartment, and/or non-residential uses. In such cases, state courts often strike down the classification of the plaintiff's land as "arbitrary," "unreasonable," and/or "capricious."[22]

16. 473 U.S. at 455, 105A S.Ct. at 3262, 87 L.Ed.2d at 330.

17. Village of Euclid v. Ambler Realty Co., 272 U.S. 365, 47 S.Ct. 114, 71 L.Ed. 303 (1926).

18. Pennsylvania Coal Co. v. Mahon, 260 U.S. 393, 43 S.Ct. 158, 67 L.Ed. 322 (1922).

19. 278 N.Y. 222, 15 N.E.2d 587 (1938) (surrounding area was largely undeveloped and existing "noxious" uses made the area unsuitable for residential development).

20. 152 U.S. 133, 14 S.Ct. 499, 38 L.Ed. 385 (1894).

21. E.g., Township of West Bloomfield v. Chapman, 351 Mich. 606, 88 N.W.2d 377 (1958). See also Krause v. City of Royal Oak, 11 Mich.App. 183, 160 N.W.2d 769 (1968).

22. E.g., Stevens v. Town of Huntington, 20 N.Y. 352, 283 N.Y.S.2d 16, 229 N.E.2d 591 (1967); Dequindre Development Co. v. Charter Township of Warren, 359 Mich. 634, 103

Although a few state courts have held that every "legitimate" type of land use must be allowed somewhere in each community,[23] the prevailing view is to the contrary.[24] However, if the zoning ordinance excludes a type of housing designed to meet the needs of "low" and/or "moderate" income households—e.g., mobile homes or high-density apartments—such exclusion is likely to be held invalid on either state statutory or constitutional grounds, or both.[25] This matter will be considered in greater detail in later sections devoted to "exclusionary" land use controls.[26]

During the early years of zoning, it was customary to create "cumulative" non-residential use districts in which residential uses and all the so-called "higher" uses were permitted.[27] Thus, for example, there might be no restrictions on the uses permitted in the least restrictive use district, such as a heavy industrial district. But after the second world war local officials began to recognize that it is often undesirable to allow the intrusion of residential uses into business and industrial districts or the intrusion of

---

N.W.2d 600 (1960); Rhein v. City of Frontenac, 809 S.W.2d 107 (Mo.App.1991) (residential zoning was unreasonable when it renders property's value markedly less than it would be if zoned for commercial use and the property's location in the center of existing commercial development makes it undesirable for residential use; property should be rezoned for commercial use).

In recent years, state courts have tended to adopt terminology utilized in recent United States Supreme Court cases where land use regulations are challenged on substantive due process and/or "taking" grounds. See, e.g., Columbia Oldsmobile, Inc. v. City of Montgomery, 56 Ohio St.3d 60, 564 N.E.2d 455 (1990), rehearing denied 57 Ohio St.3d 706, 566 N.E.2d 171 (1991) (residential zoning of 11.5 acre parcel was valid because "it substantially advances a legitimate government interest" and permits an "economically viable" use of the parcel).

23. E.g., Exton Quarries, Inc. v. Zoning Board of Adjustment, 425 Pa. 43, 228 A.2d 169 (1967); Appeal of Girsh, 437 Pa. 237, 263 A.2d 395 (1970); Beaver Gasoline Co. v. Zoning Hearing Board, 445 Pa. 571, 285 A.2d 501 (1971).

24. E.g., Duffcon Concrete Products v. Borough of Cresskill, 1 N.J. 509, 64 A.2d 347 (1949); Town of Los Altos Hills v. Adobe Creek Properties, Inc., 32 Cal.App.3d 488, 108 Cal.Rptr. 271 (1973).

25. E.g., Appeal of Girsh, supra note 23 (apartment exclusion invalid); Camp Hill Development Co. v. Zoning Board of Adjustment, 13 Pa.Cmwlth. 519, 319 A.2d 197 (1974) (same—"townhouses"); Dublin Properties v. Board of Commissioners, 21 Pa.Cmwlth. 54, 342 A.2d 821 (1975) (same); Oak Forest Mobile Home Park, Inc. v. City of Oak Forest, 27 Ill.App.3d 303, 326 N.E.2d 473 (1975) (mobile homes); Robinson Township v. Knoll, 410 Mich. 293, 302 N.W.2d 146 (1981) (same). See

also Town of Glocester v. Olivo's Mobile Home Court, Inc., 111 R.I. 120, 300 A.2d 465 (1973) (limitation to 30 units, in mobile parks only, held invalid).

Most states now prohibit, by statute or judicial decision, the blanket exclusion of mobile homes from single-family residence districts. See, e.g., Geiger v. Zoning Hearing Board of Tp. of North Whitehall, 85 Pa.Cmwlth. 362, 481 A.2d 1249 (1984), order affirmed 510 Pa. 231, 507 A.2d 361 (1986) (mobile homes cannot be relegated to designated mobile home parks); Cannon v. Coweta County, 260 Ga. 56, 389 S.E.2d 329 (1990) (prohibition of "manufactured homes" from all residential districts is not justifiable as an exercise of the police power for the purpose of protecting property values, "given the availability of mitigation measures, modern improvements in manufactured homes, and the oppressive impact of the ordinance on persons needing manufactured homes"). Local governments have responded by imposing dimensional limitations on mobile homes that purport to insure the compatibility of such homes with site-built homes in single-family residence districts. These dimensional limitations have had a mixed reception in the courts. See, e.g., Bunker Hill Tp. v. Goodnoe, 125 Mich.App. 794, 337 N.E.2d 27 (1983) (valid); Tyrone Tp. v. Crouch, 129 Mich.App. 388, 341 N.W.2d 218 (1983), affirmed 426 Mich. 642, 397 N.W.2d 166 (1986) (invalid); See also Duggins v. Town of Walnut Cove, 63 N.C.App. 684, 306 S.E.2d 186 (1983), review denied 309 N.C. 819, 310 S.E.2d 348 (1983), sustaining an ordinance excluding "mobile"—as distinct from "modular"—homes from single-family residence districts.

26. In the full-blown "exclusionary zoning" cases, total exclusion of and unreasonable restrictions on mobile homes have generally been invalidated.

27. See, e.g., Euclid zoning ordinance sustained in Euclid v. Ambler Realty Co., supra note 1.

general business uses into industrial districts.[28] Consequently, many local governments began to create exclusive business districts and exclusive industrial districts. When these exclusive business or industrial districts were challenged as not being substantially related to proper police power and zoning purposes, they were held invalid in a few early cases.[29] But since the mid–1950s all the cases have sustained "exclusive" industrial and commercial zoning in principle.[30]

For many years planners and zoning experts have advocated "industrial performance zoning" as a more sophisticated way to deal with land use compatibility (externality) problems caused by industrial land uses. The traditional "Euclidean" zoning technique is inadequate to deal with these problems because uses permitted within a given industrial district may produce quite different effects on the surrounding areas.[31] "Industrial performance zoning" seeks to deal with these problems by imposing standards for industrial uses with respect to noise, vibrations, smoke, odors, and other air pollutants. "Industrial performance zoning" of this type was upheld in DeCoals, Inc. v. Board of Zoning Appeals,[32] where a building permit for a proposed industrial use was denied because the proposed use would not comply with dust, noise, and sound performance standards.[33]

Although theoretically a good technique for regulating the negative externalities of industrial uses, administration of performance standards is expensive and difficult. Moreover, few communities are likely to impose drastic remedies on non-complying industrial uses. And the obvious overlap with the national air pollution control program may present additional problems.

Zoning ordinances that regulate "sex businesses"—"adult" bookstores and movie theaters and live entertainment in commercial establishments—present difficult constitutional issues in view of the United States Supreme Court's extension of free-speech protection to commercial speech.[34] Local zoning ordinances regulating sex businesses usually adopt one of two possible strategies: either such businesses are required to be spaced at reasonable distances from one another, or they are required to be concentrated in so-called "combat zones." In either case, sex businesses are forbidden to locate within a specified distance of residential areas. The obvious purpose of such

28. See, e.g., Urb.Land Inst.Tech.Bull. 10, Prohibition of Residential Developments in Industrial Districts (Mott & Wehrly, Nov. 1948); Brennan, J., dissenting in Katobimar Realty Co. v. Webster, 20 N.J. 114, 129, 118 A.2d 824, 832 (1955).

29. E.g., Katobimar Realty Co. v. Webster, supra note 28; Corthouts v. Town of Newington, 140 Conn. 284, 99 A.2d 112, 38 A.L.R.2d 1136 (1953).

30. E.g., Kozesnik v. Township of Montgomery, 24 N.J. 154, 131 A.2d 1 (1957); Roney v. Board of Supervisors, 138 Cal.App.2d 740, 292 P.2d 529 (1956); People ex rel. Skokie Town House Builders, Inc. v. Morton Grove, 16 Ill.2d 183, 157 N.E.2d 33 (1959); Gruble v. McLaughlin, 286 F.Supp. 24 (D.V.I.1968). Even very specialized commercial districts are now generally sustained. E.g., Forte v. Bor-

ough of Tenafly, 106 N.J.Super. 346, 255 A.2d 804 (1969), petition for certiorari denied 54 N.J. 560, 258 A.2d 13 (1969).

31. To some extent, this problem has been met by creating several different, narrowly restricted, industrial districts.

32. 168 W.Va. 339, 284 S.E.2d 856 (1981).

33. The court held that industrial performance standards are clearly within the zoning power. The court also refused to set aside the local legislative judgment that emission of dust "of any kind" should be prohibited, despite allegations of "technical infeasibility" and "economic hardship," noting that "technology forcing" air pollution regulations have often been upheld by the courts.

34. Generally, see D. Mandelker, Land Use Law §§ 5.38–5.40 (1982).

requirements is to minimize the detrimental influence of sex businesses on both commercial and residential areas.

In Young v. American Mini Theatres, Inc.,[35] the United States Supreme Court sustained a Detroit zoning ordinance provision that required sex businesses (as defined in the ordinance) to be spaced at least 1,000 feet apart and prohibited them within 500 feet of a residential area. Justice Stevens wrote a plurality opinion in which Justice Powell concurred. Both the plurality and Justice Powell agreed that the Detroit ordinance was not intended to regulate "speech" and only incidentally affected "speech" in the process of regulating land use. However, the plurality thought that "adult" sexual expression was entitled to less protection under the First Amendment than political speech, while Justice Powell thought there was no difference in the protection afforded these two types of "speech" under the First Amendment.

Subsequently, the United States Supreme Court, in Schad v. Borough of Mount Ephraim,[36] struck down a zoning ordinance that the court interpreted as excluding all live entertainment—including nude dancing—in commercial establishments. The court distinguished *Mini Theatres* because (1) it did not exclude sex business but only required their dispersion, and (2) because there was considerable evidence in *Mini Theatres* that sex businesses were detrimental to nearby residential and commercial areas but there was no evidence in *Schad* that "live entertainment is incompatible with the [commercial] uses presently permitted in the Borough." [37] In a concurring opinion, Justice Blackmun stated that the usual presumption of constitutionality generally applicable to zoning ordinances carries "little weight" when a zoning regulation burdens free speech.

Until its recent decision in Renton v. Playtime Theatres,[38] the United States Supreme Court had not reviewed a case challenging the concentration strategy for dealing with sex businesses. The state court cases are in conflict. In Northend Cinema, Inc. v. City of Seattle,[39] the court sustained a zoning ordinance amendment confining sex businesses to certain downtown business areas even though the amendment also provided for the gradual elimination of all sex businesses. In other cases the courts have struck down zoning regulations requiring concentration of sex businesses,[40] either on the ground that they result in effective total exclusion or limit sex businesses to unsuitable locations, or because the courts hold that zoning may not be used to bring about the gradual elimination of sex businesses. And the courts

35. 427 U.S. 50, 96 S.Ct. 2440, 49 L.Ed.2d 310 (1976), rehearing denied 429 U.S. 873, 97 S.Ct. 191, 50 L.Ed.2d 155 (1970).

36. 452 U.S. 61, 101 S.Ct. 2176, 68 L.Ed.2d 671 (1981).

37. 452 U.S. at 75, 101 S.Ct. at 2186. The Court also rejected the argument that the exclusion in *Schad* was valid because "live entertainment" and nude dancing were available outside the borough limits.

38. 475 U.S. 41, 106 S.Ct. 925, 89 L.Ed.2d 29 (1986), rehearing denied 475 U.S. 1132, 106 S.Ct. 1663, 90 L.Ed.2d 205 (1986).

39. 90 Wn.2d 709, 585 P.2d 1153 (1978), certiorari denied 441 U.S. 946, 99 S.Ct. 2166, 60 L.Ed.2d 1048 (1979).

40. E.g., Keego Harbor Co. v. City of Keego Harbor, 657 F.2d 94 (6th Cir.1981); CLR Corp. v. Henline, 520 F.Supp. 760 (W.D.Mich.1981), judgment affirmed 702 F.2d 637 (6th Cir.1983); Purple Onion, Inc. v. Jackson, 511 F.Supp. 1207 (N.D.Ga.1981); Ellwest Stereo Theaters Inc. v. Byrd, 472 F.Supp. 702 (N.D.Tex.1979); Bayside Enterprises, Inc. v. Carson, 450 F.Supp. 696 (M.D.Fla.1978).

have also sometimes invalidated classification of sex businesses as special exception or conditional uses.[41]

In City of Renton v. Playtime Theatres, Inc.,[42] the Court sustained an ordinance that prohibits adult motion picture theatres from locating within 1,000 feet of any residential zone, single- or multiple-family dwelling, church, park, or school. Relying heavily on *Mini Theatres,* the Court held:

(1) Since the ordinance does not ban adult theatres altogether, it constitutes a form of time, place and manner regulation and is valid if designed to serve a substantial government interest and does not unreasonably restrict alternative avenues of communication;

(2) The District Court's finding that the Renton City Council's "predominant" concerns were with the secondary effects of adult theatres on the surrounding area, not with the content of the adult films, was sufficient to establish that the purpose of the ordinance was unrelated to suppression of free expression and thus was a "content-neutral" speech regulation.

(3) The ordinance is designed to serve a substantial government interest while allowing reasonable avenues for communication, and the city could elect to regulate adult theatres either by dispersing them or concentrating them.

The extent to which zoning may constitutionally regulate the location of religious uses is not entirely clear. State courts have traditionally applied a substantive due process test. A majority of the cases have given special protection to religious uses by reversing the usual presumption of constitutionality.[43] However, courts following the majority view may sustain reasonable site development regulations.[44] A minority of the cases adopt the usual presumption of constitutionality and apply a "balancing test" with respect to zoning that regulates the location of religious uses.[45] In recent federal court cases, zoning restrictions on religious uses have been reviewed under both the "free exercise" and the "establishment" clauses of the First Amendment, with mixed results. Some of these cases have simply involved zoning

---

41. E.g., Entertainment Concepts, Inc., III v. Maciejewski, 631 F.2d 497 (7th Cir.1980), certiorari denied 450 U.S. 919, 101 S.Ct. 1366, 67 L.Ed.2d 346 (1981), on remand 514 F.Supp. 1378 (N.D.Ill.1981).

42. Supra note 38. Cases in which regulation of "adult" land uses is challenged continue to arise. Compare, e.g., International Eateries of America, Inc. v. Broward County, 941 F.2d 1157 (11th Cir.1991), cert. denied ___ U.S. ___, 112 S.Ct. 1294, 117 L.Ed.2d 517 (1992) (ordinance prohibited "adult" nightclubs within 500 feet of residential districts held constitutional), and City of Portland v. Tidyman, 306 Or. 174, 759 P.2d 242 (1988) (ordinance requiring "adult" businesses to locate only in certain districts and imposing space limitations on such businesses violates Oregon state constitution when such businesses produce no harmful effects).

43. See, e.g., Jehovah's Witnesses Assembly Hall v. Woolwich Tp., 220 N.J.Super. 381, 532 A.2d 276 (L.Div.1987); City of Englewood v. Apostolic Christian Church, 146 Colo. 374, 362 P.2d 172 (1961); State ex rel. Lake Drive Baptist Church v. Bayside Board of Trustees, 12 Wis.2d 585, 108 N.E.2d 288 (1961).

44. See, e.g., Bd. of Zoning Appeals v. Decatur, Indiana Congregation of Jehovah's Witnesses, 233 Ind. 83, 117 N.E.2d 115 (1954) (setback sustained).

45. See, e.g., Cornell University v. Bagnardi, 68 N.Y.2d 583, 510 N.Y.S.2d 861, 503 N.E.2d 509 (1986); Seward Chapel, Inc. v. City of Seward, 655 P.2d 1293 (Alaska 1982); Corporation of Presiding Bishop of Church of Jesus Christ of Latter–Day Saints v. City of Porterville, 90 Cal.2d 656, 203 P.2d 823 (1949), appeal dismissed 338 U.S. 805, 70 S.Ct. 78, 94 L.Ed. 487 (1949). The challenged zoning regulations were sustained in these cases.

restrictions on the location of religious uses.[46]   Other cases have involved government refusals to permit demolition or substantial alteration of religious buildings pursuant to "landmark" designation.   These cases will be discussed post in Section 9.20.   One case involved a statute imposing restrictions on issuance of liquor licenses on the basis of proximity of the business seeking a liquor license to churches or schools.[47]

§ 9.5   Zoning to Control Bulk of Structures and Density of Development

The Standard State Zoning Enabling Act expressly empowered local governments "to regulate and restrict the height, number of stories, and size of buildings and other structures, the percentage of lot that may be occupied, the size of yards, courts, and other open spaces, [and] the density of population."[1]   All the current zoning enabling acts contain substantially the same grant of power to regulate the bulk of structures, the relation between structures and the open space surrounding them, lot sizes, and the density of population.

Restrictions on the height of buildings are one of the oldest forms of land use control in the United States.   In New York, Boston, and Baltimore, such restrictions were adopted long before there were any comprehensive zoning ordinances, in an attempt to deal with the problem of growing congestion in urban areas in the late nineteenth century.   The constitutionality of municipal regulations fixing maximum building heights and creating different districts with different maximum height limits was established, when challenged as a violation of the Fourteenth Amendment, in Welch v. Swasey.[2]   But the reasonableness of particular height limits is always subject to judicial review.   Although maximum height limits in both business and residence districts have generally been sustained,[3] minimum height limits have usually been held invalid.[4]

The 1916 New York City Building Zone Resolution included height and land coverage regulations primarily designed to assure adequate light and air and based on "light angles."   The theory of the "light angle" was that building walls must stay behind an inclined plane which rose from the center of the street and, by "leaning" against buildings fronting on the

46. See, e.g., Lakewood, Ohio Congregation of Jehovah's Witnesses v. City of Lakewood, 699 F.2d 303 (6th Cir.1983) cert. denied 464 U.S. 815, 104 S.Ct. 72, 78 L.Ed.2d 85 (1983); Grosz v. City of Miami Beach, 721 F.2d 729 (11th Cir.1983), rehearing denied 727 F.2d 1116 (1984); both cases upheld the challenged zoning regulations. Compare Islamic Center of Mississippi, Inc. v. City of Starkville, 840 F.2d 292 (5th Cir.1988) (imposition of undue burden on Muslims denied "free exercise").

47. Larkin v. Grendel's Den, Inc., 459 U.S. 116, 103 S.Ct. 505, 74 L.Ed.2d 297 (1982) (held to violate the "establishment" clause).

§ 9.5

1. SSZEA § 1 (1926).

2. 214 U.S. 91, 29 S.Ct. 567, 53 L.Ed. 923 (1909).

3. E.g., LaSalle National Bank of Chicago v. City of Evanston, 57 Ill.2d 415, 312 N.E.2d 625 (1974); Loyola Federal Savings & Loan Association v. Buschman, 227 Md. 243, 176 A.2d 355 (1961); William C. Haas & Co. v. City and County of San Francisco, 605 F.2d 1117 (9th Cir.1979), cert. denied 445 U.S. 928, 100 S.Ct. 1315, 63 L.Ed.2d 761 (1980); see also Penn Central Transportation Co. v. City of New York, 438 U.S. 104, 98 S.Ct. 2646, 57 L.Ed.2d 631 (1978), rehearing denied 439 U.S. 883, 99 S.Ct. 226, 58 L.Ed.2d 198 (1978). Contra: LaSalle National Bank of Chicago v. City of Chicago, 5 Ill.2d 344, 125 N.E.2d 609 (1955).

4. See, e.g., 122 Main Street Corp. v. City of Brockton, 323 Mass. 646, 84 N.E.2d 13 (1949).

street, defined an angle of light coming down into the street.[5] The 1916 New York Resolution also included requirements for yards and courts in its land coverage regulations. The general validity of land coverage regulations as against challenges based on the Fourteenth Amendment was established by Gorieb v. Fox,[6] which sustained regulations requiring that all new buildings should be set back from the street a distance as great as the setbacks of 60 percent of the existing houses in a block.

Many present-day zoning ordinances seek to control the bulk of structures and the relationship between structures and open spaces around them in urban central business districts through the use of "floor area ratios" and "open space ratios."[7] A "floor area ratio" (FAR) regulates the amount of permitted floor space on a given lot by specifying a mathematical relationship between the area of the lot and the floor space area allowed on the lot; the FAR is equal to the height of the building in stories times the percentage of the lot covered. Thus, for example, a FAR of 1.0 would permit either a one-story building covering the entire lot, or a ten-story building covering ten percent of the lot. An "open space ratio" is the mathematical ratio between the amount of floor space on a lot and the area left open, including parking areas—and is often coupled with "bonuses" for additional open space at ground level provided by relaxation of the applicable FAR.[8]

Outside urban central business districts, most zoning ordinances try to control lot coverage and density of population by the use of front, side, and rear setbacks, minimum lot frontage requirements, restrictions on the percentage of a lot that may be covered by structures, and minimum lot size requirements.[9] Most local governments now control the density of population in apartment developments by limiting the number of dwelling units that may be built upon an acre of land. And suburban communities in some parts of the United States have imposed minimum single-family dwelling floor area requirements.

Except for minimum single-family dwelling floor area requirements—which now seem to be invalid per se in most states [10]—zoning regulations of the types listed in the preceding paragraph have generally been sustained in principle against challenges based on the Fourteenth Amendment, although particular regulations have sometimes been held to be "unreasonable" and therefore invalid. Minimum lot size requirements have been challenged more frequently than any other type of area or density restrictions, and they

---

5. See 1 N. Williams, Am.Land Planning Law § 35.09 (1974); 3 id. §§ 70.02, 70.06 (1975). See also Toll, Zoned American 163–164 (1969).

6. 274 U.S. 603, 47 S.Ct. 675, 71 L.Ed. 1228 (1927).

7. See 1 N. Williams, Am.Land Planning Law ch. 37 (1974 and Supp.1982); 3 id. ch. 70 (1975 and Supp.1982).

8. 3 id. §§ 70.10, 70.11 (1975 and Supp. 1982).

9. See 1 id. ch. 37 (1974 and Supp.1982); 2 id. ch. 38 (1974 and Supp.1982).

10. E.g., Home Builders League of South Jersey, Inc. v. Township of Berlin, 81 N.J. 127, 405 A.2d 381 (1979), overruling Lionshead Lake, Inc. v. Wayne Township, 10 N.J. 165, 89 A.2d 693 (1952), appeal dismissed 344 U.S. 919, 73 S.Ct. 386, 97 L.Ed. 708 (1953) (the leading case sustaining minimum floor area requirements); Appeal of Medinger, 377 Pa. 217, 104 A.2d 118 (1954); Northwood Properties Co. v. Perkins, 325 Mich. 419, 39 N.W.2d 25 (1949); Builders Service Corp. v. Planning and Zoning Com'n, 208 Conn. 267, 545 A.2d 530 (1988) (zoning regulations establishing different minimum floor areas for single-family houses in different districts, not tied to occupancy, are invalid because they serve no legitimate zoning purpose other than "conserving the value of buildings").

have generally been sustained by state courts on the ground that they protect or promote public health, safety, or general welfare in one or more of the following ways:

(a) Preservation of the semi-rural character and appearance of suburban communities by assuring sufficient open space around buildings; [11]

(b) Preservation of specific historic sites and buildings in their historic settings; [12]

(c) Preservation for low density development of sites not easily buildable at higher densities because of their topography; [13]

(d) Provision of large enough building sites to assure a safe water supply and safe on-site sewage disposal in areas without a public water supply and without public sanitary sewers; [14]

(e) Preservation of the natural capacity of the soil to absorb rainfall by limiting the area built upon, thus protecting land and buildings against flooding and soil erosion; [15]

(f) Regulation of the rate and pattern of suburban growth to assure orderly, efficient, and economical expansion of necessary public facilities such as sewers, water mains, and schools; [16]

(g) Implementation of specific planning principles as to the proper organization of residential areas and location of public schools; [17]

(h) Preservation of community identity by providing predominantly open areas ("green belts") between suburban communities; [18]

(i) Provision of some "high class" low-density residential areas in order to prevent the "blanketing" of undeveloped areas in the community with small, low-cost houses, thus maintaining community balance and the community tax base; [19]

(j) Protection of the value of existing houses on large lots against the depreciation that would result "if sections here and there are developed with

11. E.g., Senior v. Zoning Commission of New Canaan, 146 Conn. 531, 153 A.2d 415 (1959), appeal dismissed 363 U.S. 143, 80 S.Ct. 1083, 4 L.Ed.2d 1145 (1960) (4 acres); Fischer v. Bedminister Township, 11 N.J. 194, 93 A.2d 378 (1952) (5 acres); Flora Realty & Investment Co. v. City of Ladue, 362 Mo. 1025, 246 S.W.2d 771 (1952), appeal dismissed 344 U.S. 802, 73 S.Ct. 41, 97 L.Ed. 626 (1952) (3 acres); Levitt v. Incorporated Village of Sands Point, 6 N.Y.2d 269, 189 N.Y.S.2d 212, 160 N.E.2d 501 (1959) (2 acres).

12. E.g., County Commissioners v. Miles, 246 Md. 355, 228 A.2d 450 (1967) (5 acres).

13. E.g., Metropolitan Homes, Inc. v. Town Plan & Zoning Commission, 152 Conn. 7, 202 A.2d 241 (1964) (30,000 sq. ft.). See also Senior v. Zoning Commission of New Canaan, supra note 11; Honeck v. County of Cook, 12 Ill.2d 257, 146 N.E.2d 35 (1957) (5 acres); Flora Realty & Investment Co. v. City of Ladue, supra note 11.

14. De Mars v. Zoning Commission, 142 Conn. 580, 115 A.2d 653 (1955) (1 acre); Zygmont v. Planning & Zoning Commission, 152 Conn. 550, 210 A.2d 172 (1965) (4 acres); Salamar Builders Corp. v. Tuttle, 29 N.Y.2d 221, 325 N.Y.S.2d 933, 275 N.E.2d 585 (1971) (2 acres).

15. Bogert v. Washington Township, 25 N.J. 57, 135 A.2d 1 (1957) (1 acre).

16. Flora Realty & Investment Co. v. City of Ladue, supra note 11; Rockaway Estates v. Rockaway Township, 38 N.J.Super. 468, 119 A.2d 461 (App.Div.1955).

17. Padover v. Farmington Township, 374 Mich. 622, 132 N.W.2d 687 (1965) (20,000 sq. ft.).

18. Norbeck Village Joint Venture v. Montgomery County Council, 254 Md. 59, 254 A.2d 700 (1969) (2 acres).

19. Clary v. Borough of Eatontown, 41 N.J.Super. 47, 124 A.2d 54 (1956) (½ acre).

smaller lots." [20]

In Pennsylvania and, probably, in Massachusetts, the validity of lot sizes larger than one acre is highly questionable. The Pennsylvania court has invalidated two, three, and four acre lot minimums on the ground that, when the asserted justifications are balanced against the loss in value suffered by the landowner and the exclusionary effect of large lot minimums on less-than-affluent homebuyers, large minimum lot size requirements violate the constitutional guarantee of substantive due process.[21] In Massachusetts, the action of a suburban community in zoning one-third of its area for lots with a minimum size of two and one-half acres was held to be confiscatory and to be an improper attempt to use zoning as a substitute for condemnation in order to preserve open space.[22] And drastic "downzoning" amendments which increased the minimum lot size to five or ten acres in order to prevent development of open space have been held to constitute a *de facto* "taking" in California.[23]

Even in states where large-lot zoning has withstood constitutional challenge, the courts in recent years have viewed it as one factor which, along with other factors such as total or near-total exclusion of mobile homes and apartments, may lead to the conclusion that an entire municipal zoning ordinance is so "exclusionary" as to violate constitutional guarantees of substantive due process and equal protection. "Exclusionary" zoning and other "exclusionary" land use controls are considered in a later part of this Chapter.[24]

§ 9.6   Zoning and Nonconforming Uses

As one of our leading authorities on American zoning law has observed,[1]

---

20. Flora Realty & Investment Co., supra note 11.

21. See National Land & Investment Co. v. Kohn, 419 Pa. 504, 215 A.2d 597 (1965) (4 acres, invalid); Concord Township Appeal, 439 Pa. 466, 268 A.2d 765 (1970) (2 acres, invalid; reported in A.2d sub nom. Appeal of Kit–Mar Builders, Inc.). One-acre minimums were sustained in Bilbar Construction Co. v. Easttown Township, 393 Pa. 62, 141 A.2d 851 (1958). Concord Township Appeal may have been qualified by subsequent Pennsylvania Commonwealth Court cases such as DeCaro v. Washington Township, 21 Pa.Cmwlth. 252, 344 A.2d 725 (1975), and Delaware County Investment Corp. v. Zoning Hearing Board, 22 Pa.Cmwlth. 12, 347 A.2d 513 (1975), which have sustained lot minimums of more than one acre where the zoning ordinance, as a whole, was not found to be "exclusionary."

22. Aronson v. Town of Sharon, 346 Mass. 598, 195 N.E.2d 341 (1964). One-acre lot minimums were sustained in Simon v. Town of Needham, 311 Mass. 560, 42 N.E.2d 516 (1942), probably the first "acreage zoning" case.

23. See, e.g., Eldridge v. City of Palo Alto, 57 Cal.App.3d 613, 129 Cal.Rptr. 575 (1976)

(complaint held to state cause of action for "taking" where land was "downzoned" from 1–acre to 10–acre lot minimums); Arastra Limited Partnership v. City of Palo Alto, 401 F.Supp. 962 (N.D.Cal.1975), vacated after an out-of-court monetary settlement, 417 F.Supp. 1125 (1976) ("downzoning from 1–acre to 5–acre lot minimums found to be a "taking"). See also San Diego Gas & Electric Co. v. City of San Diego, 81 Cal.App.3d 844, 146 Cal.Rptr. 103 (1978), reversed on remand from Calif.Sup.Ct., in an unpublished opinion, and appeal dismissed 450 U.S. 621, 101 S.Ct. 1287, 67 L.Ed.2d 551 (1981) (state appellate court sustained trial court's finding that rezoning land from industrial to agricultural classification and "downzoning" some agriculturally zoned land from 1–acre to 10–acre lot minimums amounted to a *de facto* "taking").

24. See post Sections 9.12, 9.14.

§ 9.6

1. R. Babcock, The Illinois Supreme Court and Zoning: A Study in Uncertainty, 15 U.Chi.L.Rev. 87, 94 (1947). Generally, as to nonconforming uses, see 4 N. Williams, Am. Land Planning Law chaps. 109–117 (1975 and Supp.1982).

The haphazard growth of our cities and villages has resulted in an interlarding of strips of residential areas with stores, gas stations, and even heavy industrial properties. To superimpose a [zoning] use map upon an established urban area must inevitably result in creating large numbers of nonconforming uses * * *.

The draftsmen of the Standard State Zoning Enabling Act omitted any reference to nonconforming uses—uses lawfully established at particular sites before enactment of an original zoning ordinance or an amendment thereto prohibiting such uses at those sites—and the early zoning enabling legislation (including the pioneering New York legislation) was also silent with respect to nonconforming uses. The omission of any reference to nonconforming uses seems to have been prudential; the draftsmen of the Standard Act apparently feared that if they authorized elimination of nonconforming uses without compensation legislatures would hesitate to enact enabling legislation and courts might declare enacted legislation unconstitutional.[2] A few states enacted enabling acts which expressly provided that nonconforming uses could not be eliminated without payment of compensation.[3] And in cases where the zoning enabling act was silent as to nonconforming uses, early zoning ordinances almost invariably contained express provisions authorizing the continuance of nonconforming uses, although many ordinances also included a wide variety of restrictive regulations designed to hasten the ultimate disappearance of nonconforming uses. Such provisions, still a feature of many local zoning ordinances, typically prohibit or severely limit the physical extension of nonconforming uses,[4] impose restrictions on the repair, alteration, or reconstruction of nonconforming structures,[5] and prohibit the resumption of nonconforming uses after "abandonment" or "discontinuance."[6]

In practice, nonconforming uses have not tended to disappear as the zoning pioneers expected they would. In some cases—for example, where there is a neighborhood grocery store in a residence district—the nonconforming use enjoys a monopoly position which has tended to insure its continuance. Beginning in the 1950's there was a trend toward adoption of zoning ordinance amendments that required termination of nonconforming uses within a time or times specified in the ordinance. Such provisions came to be known as "amortization" provisions, apparently because it was thought that the owner of a nonconforming use could recover, or "amortize," all or a major part of his investment in the use during the period during which it was authorized to continue. The kinds of nonconforming uses required to be terminated upon "amortization" vary widely. Some ordinances only require termination of particular uses, such as billboards, garages, gasoline stations, and junk yards. Others require termination of substantially all nonconforming uses. And the ordinances usually provide

2. See Comment, 39 Yale L.J. 735, 737 (1930); E. Bassett, Zoning 108, 112 (1940); Note, 35 Va.L.Rev. 348, 352 (1949).

3. E.g., Mich.Comp.Laws Ann. § 125.583a.

4. See, e.g., Martin v. Cestone, 33 N.J.Super. 267, 110 A.2d 54 (1954). Generally, see 4 N.Williams, Am.Land Planning Law ch. 113 (1975 and Supp.1982).

5. See, e.g., Application of O'Neal, 243 N.C. 714, 92 S.E.2d 189 (1956); Granger v. Board of Adjustment, 241 Iowa 1356, 44 N.W.2d 399 (1950). Generally, see 4 N.Williams, Am.Land Planning Law ch. 114 (1975 and Supp.1982).

6. See Annot., 56 A.L.R.3d 14, 43–46 (1974); 4 N. Williams, Am.Land Planning Law ch. 115 (1975 and Supp.1982).

different period of "amortization" for different types of non-conforming uses. In general, short periods such as one or two years are provided for "open land" uses or nonconforming uses in conforming structures. Much longer periods—often as much as ten or twenty years—are provided for nonconforming structures which cannot be brought into conformance with the zoning ordinance at reasonable expense.[7]

A few early cases sustained, without much discussion, zoning ordinance provisions requiring termination of nonconforming uses either immediately or after a relatively short time.[8] Since 1950, the cases have been in conflict, but a majority of the cases sustains mandatory termination requirements where, on the facts, the "amortization" period is found to be "reasonable."[9] In most of the cases where the "amortization" technique was sustained, the nonconforming use required to be terminated was nuisance-like and did not involve a large capital investment by the landowner—e.g., billboards, junk yards, and the like.[10]

In the last decade or so, local zoning administrators have expressed their disenchantment with the "amortization" technique.[11] The American Law

7. Generally, see R. Scott, the Effect of Nonconforming Land–Use Amortization (Am. Soc. of Planning Officials, Planning Advis.Serv.Report 280, May 1972); 4 N.Williams, Am.Land Planning Law ch. 116 (1975 and Supp.1982).

8. E.g., Reinman v. City of Little Rock, 237 U.S. 171, 35 S.Ct. 511, 59 L.Ed. 900 (1914); Hadacheck v. Sebastian, 239 U.S. 394, 36 S.Ct. 143, 60 L.Ed. 348 (1915); State ex rel. Dema Realty Co. v. McDonald, 168 La. 172, 121 So. 613 (1929), appeal dismissed 280 U.S. 556, 50 S.Ct. 6, 74 L.Ed. 612 (1929); State ex rel. Dema Realty Co. v. Jacoby, 168 La. 752, 123 So. 314 (1929); Standard Oil Co. v. City of Tallahassee, 87 F.Supp. 145 (N.D.Fla.1949), affirmed 183 F.2d 410 (5th Cir.1950), cert. denied 340 U.S. 892, 71 S.Ct. 208, 95 L.Ed. 647 (1950).

9. E.g., Livingston Rock & Gravel Co. v. County of Los Angeles, 43 Cal.2d 121, 272 P.2d 4 (1954); City of Los Angeles v. Gage, 127 Cal.App.2d 442, 274 P.2d 34 (1954); Spurgeon v. Board of Commissioners of Shawnee County, 181 Kan. 1008, 317 P.2d 798 (1957); Grant v. Mayor & City Council of Baltimore, 212 Md. 301, 129 A.2d 363 (1957); Stoner McCray System v. City of Des Moines, 247 Iowa 1313, 78 N.W.2d 843 (1956); Harbison v. City of Buffalo, 4 N.Y.2d 553, 176 N.Y.S.2d 598, 152 N.E.2d 42 (1958); Hatfield v. City of Fayetteville, 278 Ark. 544, 647 S.W.2d 450 (1983); New Castle v. Rollins Outdoor Advertising, Inc., 475 A.2d 355 (Del.1984).

Recent cases upholding required amortization of nonconforming uses include the following: Tahoe Regional Planning Agency v. King, 233 Cal.App.3d 1365, 285 Cal.Reptr. 335 (1991) (5 year amortization period was reasonable on basis of the following criteria: the owner's investment in nonconforming signs,

their actual or depreciated value, dates of construction, depreciation for tax purposes, salvage value, remaining useful life, remaining term of the lease under which signs were maintained, and harm to the public if signs remained in place beyond the end of the amortization period); Metromedia, Inc. v. City of San Diego, 26 Cal.3d 848, 164 Cal.Rptr. 510, 610 P.2d 407 (1980), reversed on other grounds 453 U.S. 490, 101 S.Ct. 2882, 69 L.Ed.2d 800 (1981) (upholding amortization schedule requiring nonconforming signs to be removed within one to five years, depending on the "adjusted market value" of each sign, defined as the sign's original cost less ten percent of the original cost for each year the sign was in place before effective date of ordinance); Lone v. Montgomery County, 85 Md.App. 477, 584 A.2d 142 (1991) (ten year amortization period was reasonable on the facts because it allowed lost investment to be recouped).

Contra: O'Connor v. City of Moscow, 69 Idaho 37, 202 P.2d 401, 9 A.L.R.2d 1031 (1949); Ailes v. Decatur County Area Planning Commission, 448 N.E.2d 1057 (Ind.1983); City of Akron v. Chapman, 160 Ohio 382, 116 N.E.2d 697, 42 A.L.R.2d 1140 (1953); Art Neon Co. v. City & County of Denver, 488 F.2d 118 (10th Cir.1973), cert. denied 417 U.S. 932, 94 S.Ct. 2644, 41 L.Ed.2d 236 (1974) (requiring removal of signs over a five year period pursuant to amortization schedule based on replacement costs of individual signs was invalid, because replacement costs were "not related to any of the relevant factors")

10. See R. Scott, supra note 7; Am.L.Inst., Model Land Development Code, Commentary to Art. 4 (1976).

11. See R. Scott, supra note 7.

Institute's position is expressed in the following excerpt from its Commentary to Article 4 of the Model Land Development Code: [12]

> [T]he existing law of nonconforming uses consists of ineffective or unenforced regulations that seek to promote a poorly-defined concept—conformity—the value of which seems increasingly questionable. Considerable confusion has resulted. * * * The difference between a nonconforming building and a building constructed in violation of law becomes increasingly fuzzy, and boards of adjustment regularly grant variances from any attempt by the zoning officials to limit the expansion of nonconforming uses. Nuisance-type ordinances are likely to be more effective means of eliminating noxious uses than any regulations artificially based on the desire to promote homogeneous land uses.

The role of the zoning board of adjustment (or appeals) in granting "variances"—alluded to in the foregoing passage—will be considered in the next section.[13] In a succeeding section[14] we will consider the "wait and see" zoning technique which the Model Code draftsmen believed to be one of the factors militating against effective use of the "amortization" technique to compel termination of nonconforming uses.

§ 9.7 Zoning Administration—Variances

The zoning pioneers seem to have thought that, once a community had enacted its first zoning ordinance, the need for change would be minimal. Nevertheless, the early New York zoning legislation and the Standard State Zoning Act provided three mechanisms for change: (1) the "variance," (2) the "special exception," and (3) the "amendment." The first two were to be administered by a board of appeals (New York) or board of adjustment (Standard Act) upon applications from individual landowners. Amendments, on the other hand, were to be adopted by the local legislative body in the same manner as any other ordinance.

The New York general zoning enabling acts, as amended in 1920, authorized the board of appeals, where "there are practical difficulties or unnecessary hardship in the way of carrying out the strict letter of" the zoning ordinance,

> to vary or modify any of its rules, regulations or provisions relating to the construction, structural changes in, equipment, or alteration of buildings or structures, or the use of land, buildings or structures, so that the spirit of the ordinance shall be observed, public safety secured and substantial justice done.[1]

Section 7 of the Standard Act included similar language empowering the board of adjustment to grant,[2]

---

12. Am.L.Inst., Model Land Development Code at 150–158 (1976).

13. Post Section 9.7.

14. Post Section 9.9.

§ 9.7

1. Substantially identical language is still contained in New York—McKinney's Town Law § 267(5) and in New York—McKinney's Village Law § 7–712(2)(c). The 1917 General City Zoning Enabling Act merely provided that a zoning board of appeals should be created with the power to "vary the application of zoning regulations in harmony with their general purpose and intent and in accordance with the general or specific rules contained therein."

2. SSZEA § 7 (1926).

in specific cases such variance from the terms of the ordinance as will not be contrary to the public interest where, owing to special conditions, a literal enforcement of the provisions of the ordinance will result in unnecessary hardship, and so that the spirit of the ordinance shall be observed and substantial justice done.

In a few early cases this provision was held unconstitutional because it did not provide an adequate standard to guide the board of appeals in the exercise of its discretionary power to grant variances.[3] The "unnecessary hardship" standard is now generally held to be constitutionally adequate, but there is no uniformity in the interpretation of this standard in the various states. The strictest interpretation, adopted in several of the states where zoning litigation is very common, is that laid down by the New York Court of Appeals in Otto v. Steinhilber: [4]

> Before the Board may exercise its discretion and grant a variance upon the ground of unnecessary hardship, the record must show that (1) the land in question cannot yield a reasonable return if used only for a purpose allowed in that zone; (2) that the plight of the owner is due to unique circumstances and not to the general conditions in the neighborhood which may reflect the unreasonableness of the zoning ordinance itself; and (3) that the use to be authorized by the variance will not alter the essential character of the locality.

This interpretation of the "unnecessary hardship" standard is consistent with the view that the authority to grant variances was given to the zoning board of appeals (or adjustment) in order to provide a safety valve in cases where the zoning regulations, as applied to a particular parcel of land, impose so great a hardship on the landowner as to invite a constitutional attack on the regulations as applied.

In some states the strict *Steinhilber* rule has not been adopted and the courts have held that a variance may be granted almost as a matter of course where the zoning regulations seem to be rather restrictive.[5] And in many states the cases dealing with the question of standards for granting a

---

3. Welton v. Hamilton, 344 Ill. 82, 176 N.E. 333 (1931), overruled in Heft v. Zoning Board of Appeals, 31 Ill.2d 266, 201 N.E.2d 364 (1964); Jack Lewis, Inc. v. Mayor & City Council of Baltimore, 164 Md. 146, 164 A. 220 (1933), appeal dismissed 290 U.S. 585, 54 S.Ct. 56, 78 L.Ed. 517 (1933).

4. 282 N.Y. 71, 76, 24 N.E.2d 851, 853 (1939). This standard, which was applied by the New York courts until 1966, was also, in substance, adopted in Massachusetts, Pennsylvania, Michigan, and, with respect to one type of variance, New Jersey. See 5 N. Williams, Am. Land Planning Law chaps. 134 (Massachusetts) and 136 (Pennsylvania), and, as to Michigan law, Puritan–Greenfield Improvement Association v. Leo, 7 Mich.App. 659, 153 N.W.2d 162 (1967). The New Jersey law as to variances is summarized in 5 N. Williams, Am. Land Planning Law § 138.03, as follows:

"[The] two types of so-called variances in New Jersey are strikingly different: in fact,

the second one * * * is not a variance at all but a type of special permit without standards [allowing relaxation of use restrictions] * * *. The first type, dealing with bulk variances, has strict standards, and the local board of adjustment has the power to grant these. The other type * * * has very loose standards; the board of adjustment may recommend these, but they must actually be granted by the governing body."

See further discussion of the "second type" of "variance," allowed upon a showing of "special reasons," post Section 9.8 in text between notes 21 and 24.

5. E.g., Nelson v. Board of Zoning Appeals of Indianapolis, 240 Ind. 212, 162 N.E.2d 449 (1959); Kessler–Allisonville Civic League, Inc. v. Marion County Board of Zoning Appeals, 137 Ind.App. 610, 209 N.E.2d 43 (1965). But see The Light Co. v. Houghton, 141 Ind.App. 93, 226 N.E.2d 341 (1967).

variance leave the law in such confusion as to make useful generalization impossible.[6]

Although most of the zoning enabling statutes do not make any distinction between "use" variances and "area, bulk, or density" variances,[7] the courts in a few states have held that the zoning board of appeals (or adjustment) has no power to grant "use" variances because this is tantamount to "rezoning," which requires amendment of the zoning ordinance by the local governing body.[8] In New York, on the other hand, the courts—without any statutory warrant—have established different standards for granting "use" variances and what they call "area" variances, holding that "[a]n applicant for an area variance need not establish special hardship" and should be granted an area variance "on the ground of practical difficulties alone." [9] The reason given is that "[w]hen the variance is one of area only, there is no change in the character of the zoned district and the neighborhood considerations are not as strong as in [the case of] a use variance." [10]

The New York courts have not, unfortunately, clearly defined what they mean by "area" variances or "practical difficulties," although it is clear that the latter standard is much less strict than the "unnecessary hardship" standard for "use" variances. It seems probable that "area" variances will be held to include "bulk" and "density" variances. In Wilcox v. Zoning Board of Appeals,[11] the New York Court of Appeals sustained a variance allowing an increase in density in an apartment development as an "area" variance, despite the fact that this variance would arguably change "the character of the zoned district" substantially. In other states where the zoning enabling act provides for granting variances in cases of "practical difficulties" as well as "unnecessary hardship," it is not yet clear how many courts will follow the New York "area" variance rule.[12]

Most courts have held that the zoning board of appeals (or adjustment) has the power to attach appropriate conditions to the grant of any variance in order to satisfy the "negative standard"—i.e., to protect the "essential character of the locality"—although the enabling acts generally do not

---

6. New York now falls in this category. See 5 N. Williams, Am. Land Planning Law §§ 135.04, 135.05. Connecticut also seems to fall into this category, but for different reasons than New York. See 5 N. Williams, Am. Planning Law § 136.02, pointing out that, "so far as both the language and most of the holdings go, there is no appreciable difference between the Connecticut law on variances and that of Massachusetts, or New York before 1967. The problem is that there is a separate line of Connecticut cases, which say more or less the opposite." (Id. § 136.02.) A "clear break in the direction of tightening up on variances (and particularly on use variances) in Connecticut" in a 1965 case, along with more recent Connecticut cases, has left the Connecticut standard for variances uncertain. (Id. § 136.04.)

7. A "use" variance allows a land use or building type other than that permitted by the generally applicable district regulations. An "area," "bulk" or "density" variance al-

lows land development with less open space, larger structures, or more units per acre than is permitted by the generally applicable district regulations.

8. E.g., Josephson v. Autrey, 96 So.2d 784 (Fla.1957); Bray v. Beyer, 292 Ky. 162, 166 S.W.2d 290 (1942); Lee v. Board of Adjustment, 226 N.C. 107, 37 S.E.2d 128 (1946). In a few states the zoning enabling act expressly forbids the granting of "use" variances. E.g., West's Ann.Cal.Gov.Code § 65906.

9. Matter of Hoffman v. Harris, 17 N.Y.2d 138, 144, 269 N.Y.S.2d 119, 123, 216 N.E.2d 326, 330 (1966).

10. Id., 17 N.Y.2d at 144, 269 N.Y.S.2d at 123, 216 N.E.2d at 330.

11. 17 N.Y.2d 249, 270 N.Y.S.2d 569, 217 N.E.2d 633 (1966).

12. See Puritan–Greenfield Improvement Association v. Leo, supra note 4.

expressly confer such power on the board.[13] Municipal zoning ordinances often expressly authorize the board to impose conditions when a variance is granted, although this seems to be unnecessary. The courts have generally held that conditions attached to variances must relate to the use of the land itself, rather than to the person who owns or occupies the land.[14] Conditions imposing requirements as to access, paving of access roads, and landscaping are generally held valid.[15] Conditions limiting the hours of operation or imposing a time limit on the variance are sometimes invalidated on the ground that they do not relate to land use.[16] In a few cases conditions requiring dedication of land for street widening have been sustained where a proposed development will generate sufficient traffic to justify the requirement.[17]

If the zoning boards of appeals (or adjustment) had generally adhered to the statutory "unnecessary hardship" standard for granting variances (as expanded by judicial formulas like that in Otto v. Steinhilber),[18] the variance might have performed, in practice, its theoretical function of relieving individual hardships resulting from special conditions and protecting the zoning regulations from piecemeal challenge on constitutional grounds. But, in practice, many local zoning boards freely grant variances simply to enable individual landowners to convert their land to a more profitable use.[19] This seems to be a result of various factors: heavy case loads, lack of expertise, political influence, and outright bribery. If the grant of a variance is appealed by "aggrieved parties," the courts can reverse the board of appeals (or adjustment) on the ground that the variance was improperly granted. But there is no appeal in most cases, and thus no opportunity for judicial review. The frequent and indiscriminate granting of variances without proof of "unnecessary hardship" has resulted, in many urban areas, in substantial erosion of the uniformity of the zoning regulations applicable in particular districts.[20]

When courts review decisions of the zoning board of appeals (or adjustment) on variance applications, the board's actions have consistently been characterized by the courts as "administrative" or "quasi-judicial" or "adjudicative."[21] Hence the courts have often invoked procedural due process

---

13. See, generally, 3 A. Rathkopf, Law of Zoning and Planning ch. 40 (4th ed. 1983). Some current zoning enabling acts do specifically authorize imposition of conditions when variances are granted. E.g., West's Ann.Cal. Gov.Code § 65906; Mass.Gen.Laws Ann. c. 40A, § 10.

14. 3 A. Rathkopf, supra note 13, § 40.02.

15. E.g., Wright v. Zoning Board of Appeals, 174 Conn. 488, 391 A.2d 146 (1978); Nicholson v. Zoning Board of Adjustment, 392 Pa. 278, 140 A.2d 604 (1958).

16. E.g., Bora v. Zoning Board of Appeals, 161 Conn. 297, 288 A.2d 89 (1971) (hours of operation) Huntington v. Zoning Board of Appeals, 12 Mass.App.Ct. 710, 428 N.E.2d 826 (1981) (time limit).

17. E.g., Bringle v. Board of Supervisors, 54 Cal.2d 86, 4 Cal.Rptr. 493, 351 P.2d 765 (1960); Alperin v. Mayor & Township Commit-

tee, 91 N.J.Super. 190, 219 A.2d 628 (Ch.Div. 1966). Cf. Scrutton v. County of Sacramento, 275 Cal.App.2d 412, 79 Cal.Rptr. 872 (1969).

18. Supra note 5.

19. See Dukeminier & Stapleton, The Zoning Board of Adjustment: A Case Study in Misrule, 50 Ky.L.J. 273 (1962); Comment, 50 Calif.L.Rev. 101 (1962).

20. See Am.L.Inst., Model Land Development Code, Art. 4 Commentary, ante Section 9.6 at note 12, for discussion of the relation between nonconforming uses and the practice of granting variances without regard to the statutory criteria.

21. For a good general discussion of the distinction between policy-making and policy-application, with particular reference to the functions of zoning agencies, see Mandelker, Delegation of Power and Function in Zoning Administration, 1963 Wash.U.L.Q. 60.

requirements such as a requirement that the board shall create a written record and make findings of fact as a basis for its decision.[22]   And the courts have consistently overturned board decisions not based upon substantial evidence contained in the record and (where required) the board's findings.[23] But in Shelton v. City of College Station,[24] the United States Court of Appeals for the Fifth Circuit recently held that decisions of the zoning board of appeals should be considered to be "quasi-legislative" and that the board's decision must be sustained if there is any rational basis for its decision, even though the decision may not be supported by any evidence in the record.[25] Since the characterization of board action as "quasi-legislative" and the application of a substantive due process test appropriate in judicial review of legislative action is contrary to the uniform state court approach, the Fifth Circuit's decision seems to be designed to discourage resort to the federal courts (in the 5th Circuit, at least) when the action of a zoning board of appeals in granting or denying a variance is challenged.

§ 9.8   Zoning Administration—Special Exceptions, Special Uses and Conditional Uses

The Standard State Zoning Enabling Act conferred on the zoning board of adjustment an additional power not given to the zoning board of appeals by the original New York zoning enabling legislation.   Section 7 of the Standard Act empowered the board of adjustment "[t]o hear and decide special exceptions to the terms of the ordinance upon which such board is required to pass under such ordinance." [1]   Since this language is similar to the 1917 legislative authorization for the New York City governing body to empower its board of appeals "to determine and vary" the zoning regulations "in accordance with general or specific rules therein contained," [2] it is hardly surprising to find that, in early cases, courts often had difficulty in distinguishing "variances" from "special exceptions" under enabling statutes based on the Standard Act.[3]   The distinction was not yet recognized when Metzenbaum [4] and Bassett [5] wrote their pioneering treatises on zoning.   It is now generally understood, however, that a "special exception" is a use

22.   See Topanga Ass'n for a Scenic Community v. Los Angeles County, 11 Cal.3d 506, 113 Cal.Rptr. 836, 522 P.2d 12 (1974).   Some state zoning enabling acts expressly require findings.   E.g., Ill.—Smith–Hurd Ann. ch. 24, ¶ 11–13–11.

23.   See D. Mandelker, Land Use Law 173 (1982) (also noting that the SSZEA § 7 authorizes the court to take additional evidence, and that some courts interpret this as authorizing a *de novo* trial, with appellate review based on the trial court record rather than the board proceedings).

24.   780 F.2d 475 (5th Cir.1986) (en banc), certiorari denied 477 U.S. 905, 106 S.Ct. 3276, 91 L.Ed.2d 566 (1986).

25.   The majority relied, in support of its decision, entirely on cases characterizing zoning amendments enacted by the local legislative body as "legislative"—where the amendment changed the zoning classification of a substantial   area—or   "quasi-legislative"—

where the amendment rezoned a single property.   The majority opinion was concurred in by nine judges; one judge concurred only in the result; and five judges dissented on the ground that the majority's characterization of the action of a zoning board of appeals in variance cases as "quasi-legislative" was erroneous and, consequently, that the majority had applied the wrong standard of judicial review in the case at hand.

§ 9.8

1.   SSZEA § 1(1926).

2.   See ante Section 9.7 note 1.

3.   The Rhode Island courts seem to have had unusual difficulty in making the distinction.   See 5 N. Williams, Am.Land Planning Law § 139.02 (1975).

4.   See J. Metzenbaum, Law of Zoning ch. 9 (1st ed. 1930).

5.   See E. Bassett, Zoning ch. 6 (1940).

specifically authorized in one or more districts, but only upon specific approval by the zoning board of appeals (or adjustment) in individual cases rather than as a matter of right.[6] Unlike a variance, a special exception may be approved without any showing of "unnecessary hardship" or "practical difficulties." The following passage from Tullo v. Millburn Township[7] is the classic statement of the nature and purpose of the special exception:

> The theory is that certain uses, considered by the local legislative body to be essential or desirable for the welfare of the community and its citizenry or substantial segments of it, are entirely appropriate and not essentially incompatible within the basic uses in any zone (or in particular zones), but not at every or any location therein or without restrictions or conditions being imposed by reason of special problems the use or its particular location in relation to neighboring properties presents from a zoning standpoint, such as traffic congestion, safety, health, noise, and the like. The enabling act therefore permits the local ordinance to require approval of the local administrative agency as to the location of such use within the zone. If the board finds compliance with the standards or requisites set forth in the ordinance, the right to the exception exists, subject to such specific safeguarding conditions as the agency may impose by reason of the nature, location and incidents of the particular use. Without intending here to be inclusive or to prescribe limits, the uses so treated are generally those serving considerable numbers of people, such as private schools, clubs, hospitals and even churches, as distinguished from governmental structures or activities on the one hand and strictly individual residences or businesses on the other. This method of zoning treatment is also frequently extended to certain unusual kinds of strictly private business or activity which, though desirable and compatible may by their nature present peculiar zoning problems or have unduly unfavorable effect on their neighbors if not specifically regulated. Gasoline stations * * * are an example of this second category. The point is that such special uses are permissive in the particular zone under the ordinance and neither non-conforming nor akin to a variance.

In some states the term "special use" or "conditional use" is employed instead of "special exception."[8] In states where the enabling act still retains the Standard Act language, attempted delegation of the "special exception" approval power to the local planning commission or governing body have generally been held invalid;[9] but the New Jersey courts have upheld zoning ordinances providing that the board of adjustment shall

---

6. Generally, see D. Mandelker, Land Use Law §§ 6.48–6.56 (1982); 5 N. Williams, Am. Land Planning Law chaps. 148–151 (1975 and 1982 Supp.) (using term "special permit").

7. 54 N.J.Super. 483, 490–91, 149 A.2d 620, 624–25 (1959).

8. See D. Mandelker, Land Use Law § 6.48 (1982); 5 N. Williams, Am.Land Planning Law § 148.07 (1975). The term "conditional use" is employed, e.g., in West's Ann.Cal.Gov.Code § 65901. That "special exception" and "special use" are identical, see Depue v. City of Clinton, 160 N.W.2d 860 (Iowa 1968).

9. E.g., Langer v. Planning & Zoning Commission, 163 Conn. 453, 313 A.2d 44 (1972); Franklin County v. Webster, 400 S.W.2d 693 (Ky.1966) (planning commission); Swimming River Golf & Country Club, Inc. v. Borough of New Shrewsbury, 30 N.J. 132, 152 A.2d 135 (1959) (same); Depue v. City of Clinton, 160 N.W.2d 860 (Iowa 1968) (governing body); State ex rel. Skelly Oil Co. v. Common Council, 58 Wis.2d 695, 207 N.W.2d 585 (1973) (same).

merely recommend approval or disapproval of a "special exception" request, with the final decision reserved to the local governing body.[10] In states where the enabling act does not specifically delegate the power to approve "special exceptions," "special uses," or "conditional uses" to the board of appeals (or adjustment), a reservation of that power to the local governing body has been upheld.[11] And in some states the enabling authorizes delegation of that power to either of two or more local bodies.[12]

Although the courts are divided on the issue whether a local governing body acts "administratively" or "legislatively" when it approves or disapproves an application for a special exception, special use, or conditional use [13] it is clear that the zoning board of appeals (or adjustment) acts "administratively" when it passes upon such an application. It is a truism that local "administrative" action must be restrained by standards designed to prevent an arbitrary exercise of discretion by the administrative agency.[14] Hence the courts have generally struck down delegations to zoning boards of appeal (or adjustment) of the power to pass upon applications for special exceptions, special uses, or conditional uses when the zoning ordinance provides no standards whatever.[15] On the other hand, the courts have almost uniformly sustained simple "nuisance" standards—i.e., negatively phrased provisions prohibiting approval of such uses if they will create substantial negative externalities such as increased traffic congestion, increased noise, or increased air pollution.[16] And the courts are divided as to the adequacy of simple "general welfare" standards—i.e., provisions authorizing approval of requests for special exceptions, special uses, or conditional uses when this will protect or promote "public health, safety, or general welfare."[17] When

10. See Schmidt v. Board of Adjustment, 9 N.J. 405, 88 A.2d 607 (1952).

11. E.g., Kotrich v. County of DuPage, 19 Ill.2d 181, 166 N.E.2d 601 (1960), appeal dismissed 364 U.S. 475, 81 S.Ct. 243, 5 L.Ed.2d 221 (1960); Corporation Way Realty Trust v. Building Commissioner of Medford, 348 Mass. 732, 205 N.E.2d 718 (1965); Detroit Osteopathic Hospital Corp. v. City of Southfield, 377 Mich. 128, 139 N.W.2d 728 (1966) (but note that governing body is authorized to serve as "zoning board of appeals" in Michigan).

12. E.g., West's Ann.Cal.Gov.Code §§ 65901–65904 allows delegation to either a zoning administrator, a planning commissioner, or a board of appeals, or retention of the power by the local governing body.

13. That it acts "administratively," see, e.g., Wheeler v. Gregg, 90 Cal.App.2d 348, 203 P.2d 37 (1949); Osius v. City of St. Clair Shores, 344 Mich. 693, 75 N.W.2d 25 (1956); State ex rel. Ludlow v. Guffey, 306 S.W.2d 552 (Mo.1957). But see, holding that it acts "legislatively," see Kotrich v. County of DuPage, supra note 11; Green Point Savings Bank v. Board of Zoning Appeals, 281 N.Y. 534, 24 N.E.2d 319 (1939), appeal dismissed 309 U.S. 633, 60 S.Ct. 719, 84 L.Ed. 990 (1940).

14. Generally, see D. Mandelker, Land Use Law § 6.2 (1982).

15. E.g., City of St. Petersburg v. Schweitzer, 297 So.2d 74 (Fla.App.1974), certiorari denied 308 So.2d 114 (Fla.1975); Smith v. Board of Appeals of Fall River, 319 Mass. 341, 65 N.E.2d 547 (1946); Ostrand v. Village of North St. Paul, 275 Minn. 440, 147 N.W.2d 571 (1966); State ex rel. Humble Oil & Refining Co. v. Wahner, 25 Wis.2d 1, 130 N.W.2d 304 (1964).

16. E.g., Certain–Teed Products Corp. v. Paris Township, 351 Mich. 434, 88 N.W.2d 705 (1958); Ours Properties, Inc. v. Ley, 198 Va. 848, 96 S.E.2d 754 (1957). Contra: Kenville Realty Corp. v. Board of Zoning Appeals, 48 Misc.2d 666, 265 N.Y.S.2d 522 (1965). Cases holding the "nuisance" standard adequate are based on the presumption that special exceptions, special uses, or conditional uses are compatible with other uses allowed in the district in which they may be authorized by the administrative decision.

17. *Adequate:* E.g., Schultz v. Board of Adjustment, 258 Iowa 804, 139 N.W.2d 448 (1966); Mobil Oil Corp. v. City of Clawson, 36 Mich.App. 46, 193 N.W.2d 346 (1971); Peachtree Development Co. v. Paul, 67 Ohio St.2d 345, 423 N.E.2d 1087 (1981). *Inadequate:* E.g., Redwood City Co. of Jehovah's Witnesses v. City of Menlo Park, 167 Cal.App.2d 686, 335 P.2d 195 (1959); Clark v. Board of Appeals, 348 Mass. 407, 204 N.E.2d 434 (1975); Osius v. City of St. Clair Shores, supra note 13.

courts hold such standards to be inadequate, they sometimes state that it is inappropriate to allow an unelected "administrative" agency to make zoning policy on the basis of the general standard applicable to "legislative" bodies.

Some zoning ordinances contain quite specific and detailed standards as a basis for approving or disapproving requests for special exceptions, special uses, or conditional uses, with or without a reservation of discretion to disapprove an application on ground that it will cause substantial negative externalities or will not promote the general welfare.[18] Such standards are almost always sustained when challenged as insufficient.[19] Indeed, at least where there is no residual discretion to disapprove on nuisance or general welfare grounds, courts have sometimes held that compliance with all the specific standards in the zoning ordinance entitles the applicant as a matter of right to approval of his request for a special exception, special use, or conditional use.[20]

In two states, zoning enabling act provisions with respect to "special exceptions" and "variances," respectively, would appear practically to allow municipalities to establish land use licensing systems. In Rhode Island the statute authorizes the "board of review" to "make special exceptions to the terms of the ordinance * * * where such exception is reasonably necessary for the convenience or welfare of the public."[21] In New Jersey the statute authorizes the governing body to grant what is misleadingly called a "variance," on recommendation of the board of adjustment, "in particular cases and for special reasons" if "such relief can be granted without substantial detriment to the public good and will not substantially impair the intent and purpose of the * * * zoning ordinance."[22] These statutory provisions appear to authorize the local zoning board to permit any use whatever in any district, without proof of hardship to the landowner, on the basis of extremely vague and general standards.[23] The New Jersey courts have not been notably successful in articulating more specific standards for "special reasons" variances,[24] although the New Jersey Supreme Court has made it clear

18. See ante, the quotation in the text following note 7, where Justice Hall seems to assume that the zoning ordinance will contain pretty definite standards.

19. E.g., St. John's Roman Catholic Church Corp. v. Town of Darien, 149 Conn. 712, 184 A.2d 42 (1962); Mirschel v. Weissenberger, 277 App.Div. 1039, 100 N.Y.S.2d 452 (1950); Kline v. Louisville & Jefferson County Board of Zoning Adjustment & Appeals, 325 S.W.2d 324 (Ky.1959).

20. E.g., Lazarus v. Village of Northbrook, 31 Ill.2d 146, 199 N.E.2d 797 (1964); C.R. Investments, Inc. v. Village of Shoreview, 304 N.W.2d 320 (Minn.1981); Verona, Inc. v. West Caldwell, 49 N.J. 274, 229 A.2d 651 (1967).

21. Rhode Island Gen.Laws 1956, § 45–24–13, which is derived from the original Rhode Island zoning enabling act (Rhode Island Laws 1923, c. 430, § 2).

22. New Jersey Stat.Ann. 40:55–39(d). This provision authorizes "use" variances, and empowers the local governing body to make the final decision after receiving a recommen-

dation from the board of adjustment. As indicated ante Section 9.7 note 5, the New Jersey "special reasons" variance is really a "special use permit," not limited as to the kinds of nonconforming uses that may be authorized, rather than a true "variance." The broad authorization to grant "special reasons" variances would seem largely to emasculate the rather strict standards for granting "conditional uses * * * according to definite specifications and standards" imposed on the planning board by New Jersey Stat.Ann. 40:55D–67.

23. See 5 N. Williams, Am.Land Planning Law §§ 149.16–149.20 (1975 and Supp.1982).

24. See, e.g., Ward v. Scott, 11 N.J. 117, 93 A.2d 385 (1952); Andrews v. Board of Adjustment, 30 N.J. 245, 152 A.2d 580 (1959); Black v. Town of Montclair, 34 N.J. 105, 167 A.2d 388 (1961); Yahnel v. Board of Adjustment, 79 N.J.Super. 509, 192 A.2d 177 (App.Div.1963), certification denied 41 N.J. 116, 195 A.2d 15 (1963); Kramer v. Board of Adjustment, 45 N.J. 268, 212 A.2d 153 (1965); Brown Boveri,

that municipalities may not substitute licensing for zoning as their primary growth control technique.[25]

The Standard Act[26] and most current zoning enabling acts expressly authorize the imposition of conditions when special exceptions, special uses, or conditional uses are approved. The courts generally insist that such conditions relate to the use of the land as to which approval is granted.[27]

It is clear that the draftsmen of the Standard Act intended that large-scale changes in the municipal zoning pattern should be effected by amendment of the zoning ordinance rather than by means of "special exceptions."[28] Although the "special exception" has sometimes been misused to effect large-scale rezonings without a formal amendment, most large-scale (as well as many small-scale) zoning changes are, in fact, brought about by the amendment process.

The United States Supreme Court recently struck down a zoning ordinance provision requiring a special use permit for location of a group home for mentally retarded persons in any district on the ground that this requirement violated the equal protection clause of the Fourteenth Amendment.[29]

§ 9.9 Zoning Administration—Rezoning Amendments

All the zoning enabling acts authorize the local governing body to change the zoning regulations and the district boundaries by amending the zoning ordinance.[1] Although it is not expressly stated in the early New

Inc. v. Township Committee of North Brunswick, 160 N.J.Super. 179, 389 A.2d 483 (App. Div.1978); Castroll v. Township of Franklin, 161 N.J.Super. 190, 391 A.2d 544 (App.Div. 1978).

Medici v. BPR Co., 107 N.J. 1, 526 A.2d 109 (1987) (statutory policy favors "zoning by ordinance rather than by variance" in absence of "hardship"; this policy requires applicant to show "special reasons," including proof that the site in question is specially suited for the proposed use, when no "hardship" is shown).

25. Rockhill v. Chesterfield Township, 23 N.J. 117, 128 A.2d 473 (1957) (township entirely zoned for agriculture and single-family dwellings "as of right," with almost all other uses to be allowed by special permit pursuant to broad, general standards; held invalid).

26. SSZEA & 7 (1926).

27. E.g., Middlesex & Boston Street Railway Co. v. Board of Aldermen, 371 Mass. 849, 359 N.E.2d 1279 (1977); Exxon, Inc. v. City of Frederick, 36 Md.App. 703, 375 A.2d 34 (1977); Mechem v. City of Santa Fe, 96 N.M. 668, 634 P.2d 690 (1981).

But see Cupp v. Board of Supervisors of Fairfax County, 227 Va. 580, 318 S.E.2d 407 (1984), holding that conditions such as required land donations and off-site improvements cannot be imposed when a special use permit is sought because such conditions are *ultra vires* and were unrelated (in this case) to

any problem generated by the proposed use of the property in question. The court clearly adopted, as the second ground for its decision, what is generally termed the "rational nexus" doctrine in subdivision exaction cases. See post § 9.17 at note 14.

28. See SCIT, Inc. v. Planning Bd. of Braintree, 19 Mass.App.Ct. 101, 472 N.E.2d 269 (1984), holding that a zoning bylaw making all uses in a business district subject to issuance of a special permit violated two provisions of the zoning enabling act: (1) that zoning regulations should be uniform for each class of building or use within a district; and (2) that special permits shall be issued only for "specific types of uses." The court said that the enabling act does not contemplate the "conferral on local zoning boards of a roving and virtually unlimited power to discriminate as to uses between landowners similarly situated."

29. City of Cleburne, Texas v. Cleburne Living Center, 473 U.S. 432, 105 S.Ct. 3249, 87 L.Ed.2d 313 (1985), discussed in more detail ante § 9.4 at note call 14.5.

§ 9.9

1. SSZEA § 5 (1967) provided for amendments of the zoning "regulations, restrictions, and boundaries," subject to the same provisions "relative to public hearings and official notice" as were applicable to enactment of an original zoning ordinance.

York zoning enabling legislation or in the Standard State Zoning Enabling Act, it is reasonably clear that the basis for amending the zoning ordinance was intended to be the same as that for enacting an original zoning ordinance—promoting health, safety, morals, or the general welfare. Seemingly the draftsmen of the early zoning legislation expected that most communities would find it unnecessary to amend their zoning ordinances (once enacted) very frequently, and thought the amendment process would ordinarily be used only to change the regulations applicable to sizeable areas in response either to changed conditions or a change in the local legislative policy with respect to land use and urban development. But established neighborhoods were protected against unwelcome change by a provision requiring a three-fourths vote of the entire membership of the local legislative body to enact a rezoning amendment over the written protest of the owners of twenty percent of the land most directly affected by the amendment.[2]

The expectations of the zoning pioneers with respect to the stability of the original zoning regulations and the infrequency of rezoning amendments were not borne out by actual experience. Even before World War II, some local legislative bodies adopted the practice of enacting frequent rezoning amendments, generally in response to specific requests from landowners or developers to rezone land on which immediate development was planned.[3] And after World War II this practice was combined with what has come to be called "wait and see" zoning, which requires that most of the undeveloped land in a suburban community be zoned for uses and/or at densities that will not permit any profitable development at all. Thus no new development can occur without a rezoning amendment changing the land to a classification that will permit the proposed development.[4] In making the decision to rezone or not, the local authorities will usually take into account—contrary to formal zoning theory—the "personal" characteristics of each developer with respect to "financial capacity, reputation for quality, and record of good management."[5]

Any amendment of the sort required by the "wait and see" technique— an amendment rezoning a single tract of land in response to a request from

---

2. SSZEA § 5 (1926). The validity of the "protest" provision was settled in early cases in New York and elsewhere. E.g., Morrill Realty Corp. v. Rayon Holding Corp., 254 N.Y. 268, 172 N.E. 494 (1930); Russell v. Murphy, 177 Okl. 255, 58 P.2d 560 (1936); Rhode Island Episcopal Convention v. Providence City Council, 52 R.I. 182, 159 A. 647 (1932); Holzbauer v. Ritter, 184 Wis. 35, 198 N.W. 852 (1924). See also Northwood Properties Co. v. Perkins, 325 Mich. 419, 39 N.W.2d 25 (1949); Leighton v. City of Minneapolis, 16 F.Supp. 101 (D.Minn.1936). Cf. Washington ex rel. Seattle Title & Trust Co. v. Roberge, 278 U.S. 116, 49 S.Ct. 50, 73 L.Ed. 210 (1928), striking down an ordinance provision prohibiting a "home" for children or for old people in a residential district unless approved by the owners of ⅔ of the property within 400 feet of the proposed "home." If the statute does not distinguish between amendments initiated by

the local governing body and those initiated by petition of a landowner, the "protest" provision applies to both. Morrill Realty Corp. v. Rayon Holding Corp., supra.

3. See, e.g., Mueller v. Hoffmeister Undertaking & Livery Co., 343 Mo. 430, 121 S.W.2d 775 (1938); Linden Methodist Episcopal Church v. Linden, 113 N.J.L. 188, 173 A. 593 (1934).

4. See, e.g., Krasnowiecki, Abolish Zoning, 31 Syracuse L.Rev. 719, 734–741 (1980) (using the term "short zoning" rather than "wait and see zoning"). Cf. D. Mandelker, Land Use Law 285 (1982). To some extent, of course, development may be "licensed" by approval of a "variance" or "special exception." See ante Sections 9.7, 9.8.

5. See Krasnowiecki, supra note 4, at 729–731.

the owner or from a developer who holds an option to purchase the tract—is very likely to be challenged by unhappy neighbors on the ground that the rezoning constitutes illegal "spot zoning." [6] The courts have frequently held that such single-tract rezoning, "which gives to a single lot or a small area privileges which are not extended to other land in the vicinity is in general against sound public policy and obnoxious to the law." [7] The basis for such holdings seems to be that such "spot zoning" (1) is discriminatory—i.e., denies equal treatment to persons similarly situated; (2) is not "in accordance with a comprehensive plan" as required by the zoning enabling act; [8] and/or (3) is intended to benefit "a particular individual or group of individuals" rather than to promote "the good of the community as a whole." [9]

When a rezoning amendment is challenged as not "in accordance with a comprehensive plan," it might be supposed that the challenger would only need to point to an existing "comprehensive plan" adopted by the local authorities and then show that the amendment is inconsistent with that plan. But, unfortunately, "zoning" preceded "planning" in most communities.[10] Hence all courts, until quite recently, held that the zoning enabling act should not be construed to require "that the comprehensive plan shall exist in some physical form outside the ordinance itself," and that the "comprehensive plan" need only be discernable from an examination of the zoning ordinance itself.[11] Consequently, the courts have found it difficult to assign any independent meaning to the requirement that zoning regulations be "in accordance with a comprehensive plan," [12] and, as Norman Williams, Jr., has pointed out, the "spot zoning" and "comprehensive plan" challenges have become "merely two sides of the same coin." [13] Thus, if a zoning change is "in accordance with a comprehensive plan" it cannot be invalid as illegal "spot zoning," and if it constitutes illegal "spot zoning" it cannot be "in accordance with a comprehensive plan."

In cases where a rezoning amendment is challenged by neighboring landowners either as illegal "spot zoning" or as not "in accordance with a comprehensive plan," or both, the courts tend to give weight to the same basic elements: (1) whether the uses permitted on the rezoned tract—usually more intensive and more profitable—are compatible with the actual and

6. Generally, as to "spot zoning," see D. Mandelker, Land Use Law § 6.23 (1982); 1 N. Williams, Am.Land Planning Law ch. 27 (1974 and Supp.1982); 2A Rathkopf, Law of Zoning and Planning ch. 26 (1983).

7. Kuehne v. Town of East Hartford, 136 Conn. 452, 460, 72 A.2d 474, 478 (1950).

8. All zoning enabling acts contain either verbatim or in substance the SSZEA § 3 (1926) requirement that the zoning regulations "shall be made in accordance with a comprehensive plan."

For a discussion of the relationship between the "comprehensive plan" and the zoning ordinance, see post Section 9.10.

9. Kuehne v. Town of East Hartford, 136 Conn. 452, 461, 72 A.2d 474, 478 (1950).

The quoted language from *Kuehne* is echoed in a legion of other cases—e.g., Appeal of Mulac, 418 Pa. 207, 210, 210 A.2d 275, 277

(1965) (spot zoning is a "singling out of one lot or a small area for different treatment from that accorded to similar surrounding land indistinguishable from it in character, for the economic benefit of the owner or to his economic detriment"). Most spot zoning cases involve disparate treatment "for the economic benefit of the owner" of the rezoned land.

10. See, e.g., Kozesnik v. Township of Montgomery, 24 N.J. 154, 165, 131 A.2d 1, 7 (1957); Haar, In Accordance with a Comprehensive Plan, 68 Harv.L.Rev. 1154, 1157 (1955).

11. See, e.g., Kozesnik v. Township of Montgomery, 24 N.J. 154, 166, 131 A.2d 1, 7–8 (1957).

12. See Haar, supra note 10, at 1156–57, 1173.

13. 1 N. Williams, Am.Land Planning Law § 27.01 (1974).

permitted uses in the area surrounding the rezoned tract; (2) whether the rezoned tract is small or large; (3) whether the rezoned tract is entirely (or almost entirely) owned by one or a few persons; and (4) whether the legislative motive appears to be to promote "the good of the community as a whole" or only to benefit one or a few persons.[14]

A number of the state courts, in an effort to deal with cases where a rezoning amendment is attacked as illegal "spot zoning"[15] and/or as not "in accordance with a comprehensive plan" have adopted the rule that a rezoning amendment affecting only a relatively small parcel—especially if it is owned by one or a few individuals—can only be sustained if the local government shows that the rezoning was justified by either "changed conditions"[16] or "original mistake" in zoning the tract in question.[17] And even in states where the "change of condition or original mistake" rule is not rigidly applied, proof of either "change of condition" or "original mistake" may be given substantial weight when a rezoning amendment is attached as illegal "spot zoning." [18]

Until recently, the Oregon courts tended to give a good deal of weight to "change of condition" and "original mistake" in cases where rezoning amendments were challenged as illegal "spot zoning" and/or as not "in accordance with a comprehensive plan," but rezoning amendments were treated, in the traditional manner, as "legislative acts" entitled to a presumption of validity.[19] In Fasano v. Board of County Commissioners of Washington County,[20] however, the Oregon Supreme Court held that a single-tract rezoning should henceforth be treated as a "quasi-judicial" rather than a "legislative" act. This meant that rezoning amendments would be subject to a much stricter standard of judicial review than under the traditional view that such amendments are "legislative acts." In addition, the *Fasano* Court held that, to withstand judicial review when challenged as illegal "spot zoning," the proponents of a rezoning amendment would henceforth be required to prove that "the change is in conformance with the comprehensive plan," that "there is a public need for a change of

---

14. Id. §§ 27.01–27.05.

15. Jacobs, Visconsi & Jacobs, Co. v. City of Lawrence, Kansas, 927 F.2d 1111 (10th Cir. 1991) (refusal to rezone area outside central business district for a shopping mall does not violate due process or equal protection when comprehensive plan provides that central business district shall be the region's only retail business center).

16. William S. Hart Union High School District v. Regional Planning Com'n, 226 Cal. App.3d 1612, 277 Cal.Rptr. 645 (1991).

17. Generally, see D. Mandelker, Land Use Law § 6.25 (1982); 1 N. Williams, Am.Land Planning Law § 32.01 (1974 and Supp.1982). Although the "change or mistake" rule seems to have originated in Maryland, it was also adopted in Connecticut, Mississippi, New Mexico, and Washington, at least in modified form. See, e.g., MacDonald v. Board of County Commissioners, 238 Md. 549, 210 A.2d 325 (1965); Zoning Commission v. New Canaan Building Co., 146 Conn. 170, 148 A.2d 330 (1959); Lewis v. City of Jackson, 184 So.2d 384

(Miss.1966); Miller v. City of Albuquerque, 89 N.M. 503, 554 P.2d 665 (1976); Hayden v. City of Port Townsend, 93 Wn.2d 870, 613 P.2d 1164 (1980). The rule is now codified in Maryland Code art 66B, § 4.05(a).

18. E.g., King's Mill Homeowners Association v. City of Westminster, 192 Colo. 305, 557 P.2d 1186 (1976); Lanner v. Board of Appeals, 348 Mass. 220, 202 N.E.2d 777 (1964). The "change or mistake" rule has been expressly rejected in some states. E.g., Dye v. City of Phoenix, 25 Ariz. 193, 542 P.2d 31 (App.1975); Conner v. Shellburne, Inc., 281 A.2d 608 (Del. 1971), on remand 315 A.2d 620 (Del. Ch.1974) affirmed 336 A.2d 568 (1975); Oka v. Cole, 145 So.2d 233 (Fla.1962), conformed to 145 So.2d 900 (Fla.App.1962).

19. E.g., Roseta v. County of Washington, 254 Or. 161, 458 P.2d 405, 40 A.L.R.3d 364 (1969).

20. 264 Or. 574, 507 P.2d 23 (1973).

the kind in question," and that the public need "will be best served by changing the classification of the particular piece of property [rezoned] * * * as compared with other available property." [21] The *Fasano* doctrine was subsequently modified in Oregon as a result of the enactment of comprehensive statewide planning and land use control legislation [22] which, it was held in Neuberger v. City of Portland,[23] makes it unnecessary to prove either "public need" or that the land rezoned is the only suitable land available for the proposed development.[24]

The *Fasano* holding that single-tract rezonings should be treated as "quasi-judicial" rather that "legislative"—an idea which is ultimately traceable to Professor Jan Krasnowiecki [25]—has been adopted in several states [26] and expressly rejected in others.[27] In Oregon, it has been the basis for widespread adoption of a procedure in which hearings on rezoning applications from land developers are conducted by a hearing examiner, who then reports his findings and recommendations to the local governing body for final action on the application.

Shortly after World War II, some municipalities sought to make advance provision for new land uses or building types and, perhaps, to avoid charges that rezoning amendments constituted illegal "spot zoning" by creating so-

21. 264 Or. at 583–584, 507 P.2d at 28.

22. See Or.Rev.Stat. 197.010 et seq., 227.-175(3). See D. Mandelker & R. Cunningham, Planning and Control of Land Development 1228–1244 (1979) for a brief summary of the Oregon legislation.

23. 288 Or. 155, 603 P.2d 771 (1979), rehearing denied 288 Or. 585, 607 P.2d 722 (1980).

24. The court concluded that these requirements were not imposed on local governments by either the "goals" or the "guidelines" developed and promulgated by the Oregon Land Conservation and Development Commission.

25. See J. Krasnowiecki, The Basic System of Land Use Control: Legislative Preregulation v. Administrative Discretion, in The New Zoning 3 (N. Marcus & M. Groves eds. 1970); J. Krasnowiecki, Model Land Use and Development Planning Code § 208(2), in Maryland Planning Law Study Comm'n Final Report at 103 (1969). The idea was picked up in a student comment, see Zoning Amendments—The Product of Judicial or Quasi–Judicial Action, 33 Ohio St.L.J. 130, 136–39 (1972), and then adopted in *Fasano,* supra note 20.

26. E.g., Snyder v. City of Lakewood, 189 Colo. 421, 542 P.2d 371 (1975); Golden v. City of Overland Park, 224 Kan. 591, 584 P.2d 130 (1978); Lowe v. City of Missoula, 165 Mont. 38, 525 P.2d 551 (1974); Parkridge v. City of Seattle, 89 Wn.2d 454, 573 P.2d 359 (1978); Tate v. Miles, 503 A.2d 187 (Del.1986). Some of these cases applied the *Fasano* rule to denials of rezoning applications as well as approvals. But the Colorado court has qualified if not overruled *Snyder,* supra, in three cases where it held rezoning amendments to be "legislative" to the extent that they may be over-

turned by referendum. See 638 P.2d 297 (Colo.1981).

27. Wait v. City of Scottsdale, 127 Ariz. 107, 618 P.2d 601 (1980); Arnel Development Co. v. City of Costa Mesa, 28 Cal.3d 511, 169 Cal.Rptr. 904, 620 P.2d 565 (1980); Florida Land Co. v. City of Winter Springs, 427 So.2d 170 (Fla.1983); Hall Paving Co. v. Hall County, 237 Ga. 14, 226 S.E.2d 728 (1976); Pemberton v. Montgomery County, 275 Md. 363, 340 A.2d 240 (1975); Kirk v. Tyrone Township, 398 Mich. 429, 247 N.W.2d 848 (1976); State v. City of Rochester, 268 N.W.2d 885 (Minn. 1978); Quinn v. Town of Dodgeville, 122 Wis.2d 570, 364 N.W.2d 149 (1985) (exercise of town's veto power over county zoning decision changing district boundaries within town was a "legislative" act and was entitled to a presumption of validity). For the background of Kirk v. Tyrone Township, see Cunningham, Reflections on Stare Decisis in Michigan: The Rise and Fall of the "Rezoning as Administrative Act" Doctrine, 75 Mich.L.Rev. 983 (1977). West's Ann.Cal.Gov.Code § 65301.5 now provides expressly that adoption of a rezoning amendment is a "legislative" act.

The *Fasano* rule was also rejected in City of Eastlake v. Forest City Enterprises, Inc., 426 U.S. 668, 96 S.Ct. 2358, 49 L.Ed.2d 132 (1976), on remand 48 Ohio St.2d 47, 356 N.E.2d 499 (1976), sustaining an ordinance requiring a referendum, with a favorable vote of 55%, to give effect to any zoning change adopted by the city council.

Accord: R.G. Moore Bldg. Corp. v. Committee for Repeal of Ordinance, 239 Va. 484, 391 S.E.2d 587 (1990) (rezoning is "legislative," and hence subject to referendum).

called "floating zone" classifications which were not initially made applicable to any particular tract of land—i.e., were not put on the zoning map. Thus, e.g., Tarrytown, New York, adopted an ordinance establishing a new "Residence B–B" classification which allowed garden apartments in one- and two-family districts, but did not immediately rezone any particular tract or tracts of land to the new classification. Instead, the ordinance provided that the boundaries of any new "Residence B–B" district were to be "fixed by amendment of the official village building zone map" after approval of an application for rezoning of a particular tract by the village planning board or, if the planning board should withhold approval, by the village governing body. No tract of land was eligible for rezoning to the new classification unless it had a minimum area of ten acres, and the "Residence B–B" classification included strict height limits and open space requirements.

In Rodgers v. Village of Tarrytown,[28] the New York Court of Appeals sustained the new "floating zone" technique as against challenge on the grounds that it (1) authorized "spot zoning" not "in accordance with a comprehensive plan"; (2) constituted a device for "the granting of a 'variance'" by the local governing body; and (3) "set no boundaries for the new district and made no changes on the building zone map."[29] Although the "floating zone" technique has generally been upheld when challenged,[30] its objectives can generally be achieved by the use of special exceptions and only the specialized "planned unit development" form of "floating zone" has come into general use.[31] Once a "floating zone" classification is applied to a particular tract by a rezoning amendment, the fact that it originally "floated" has no significance.

Local authorities who adopt the "wait and see" approach often wish to "tailor" the regulations applicable to a tract that is to be rezoned in such a way as to (1) protect neighboring land from negative externalities generated by the development proposed for the rezoned tract, and (2) assure that the developer does not, after obtaining the desired rezoning, submit plans for a development that is permissible under the new zoning classification but quite different from the development originally proposed. The requisite "tailoring" might conceivably be achieved by creating in advance, "a whole range of much more sophisticated districts [than are generally found in zoning ordinances], many of these districts originally 'floaters,'" thus enabling the local authorities to "pick the district that is closest to the

---

28. 302 N.Y. 115, 96 N.E.2d 731 (1951).

29. See D. Mandelker, Land Use Law § 6.58 (1982).

30. E.g., Sheridan v. Planning Board, 159 Conn. 1, 266 A.2d 396 (1969); Bellemeade Co. v. Priddle, 503 S.W.2d 734 (Ky.1973); Baylis v. City of Baltimore, 219 Md. 164, 148 A.2d 429 (1959); Beyer v. Burns, 150 Misc.2d 10, 567 N.Y.S.2d 599 (1991) (2–year floating zone for senior citizen housing is valid). Pennsylvania initially struck down the "floating zone" technique in Eves v. Zoning Board of Adjustment, 401 Pa. 211, 164 A.2d 7 (1960), but *Eves* has in substance been overruled. See Donahue v. Zoning Board of Adjustment, 412 Pa. 332, 194 A.2d 610 (1963); Raum v. Board of Supervisors, 20 Pa.Cmwlth. 426, 342 A.2d 450 (1975), appeal after remand 29 Pa.Cmwlth. 9, 370 A.2d 777 (1977); Klem v. Zoning Hearing Board, 35 Pa.Cmwlth. 560, 387 A.2d 667 (1978).

"Floating zones" have been sustained even when inconsistent with a local comprehensive plan. Loh v. Town Planning & Zoning Commission, 161 Conn. 32, 282 A.2d 894 (1971).

31. "Planned unit development" (PUD) is considered post in Section 9.11. The "floating zone" technique, in general, allows the governing body to keep the zoning board of appeals (or adjustment) out of the approval process and to utilize the planning commission as an advisory agency.

particular proposal made by the developer." [32] But many local governing bodies want greater flexibility than would be possible with "pre-set" classifications, and therefore resort to what is termed either "conditional" or "contract" zoning.[33]

There are many variations, but "conditional" or "contract" zoning generally involves rezoning a tract subject to conditions or covenants that will restrict the developer (and its successors in interest) to the specific uses and building types proposed when rezoning is sought, and will also require the developer (and its successors in interest) to observe specified restrictions and design requirements that may go far beyond those embodied in the new zoning classification. Typically, the developer is required to leave more open space on the tract than would be required by the new zoning classification, to provide landscaped buffer areas along the boundaries of the tract, and to comply with appropriate "performance standards" designed to minimize negative externalities such as light, noise, and emissions of smoke.

"Conditional" or "contract" zoning has generally been sustained as against attacks by both neighboring landowners and by developers who do not wish to comply with the conditions to which they have agreed, after their land is rezoned.[34] But the judicial opinions are not notable for clarity of analysis and often make the decision turn upon issues that seem relatively unimportant.[35] Although some scholarly commentators disapprove of "conditional" or "contract" zoning,[36] it is hard to see why this zoning technique is any more objectionable than the well-accepted practice of imposing *ad hoc* conditions when a variance or a special exception (or special use or conditional use) is approved,[37] and the equally well-accepted practice of imposing conditions not expressly set out in the subdivision regulations when new subdivision developments are approved.[38] In all these cases the additional protective conditions imposed by the municipality obviously benefit neighboring landowners. If the municipality imposes unreasonably onerous con-

32. Krasnowiecki, Abolish Zoning, 31 Syracuse L.Rev. 719, 741 (1980).

33. Generally, see Comment, Contract and Conditional Zoning: A Tool for Zoning Flexibility, 23 Hastings L.J. 825 (1972); D. Mandelker, Land Use Law § 6.59 (1982).

34. E.g., Scrutton v. County of Sacramento, 275 Cal.App.2d 412, 79 Cal.Rptr. 872 (1969); Cross v. Hall County, 238 Ga. 709, 235 S.E.2d 379 (1977); Sylvania Electric Products, Inc. v. City of Newton, 344 Mass. 428, 183 N.E.2d 118 (1962); Bucholz v. City of Omaha, 174 Neb. 862, 120 N.W.2d 270 (1963); Church v. Town of Islip, 8 N.Y.2d 254, 203 N.Y.S.2d 866, 168 N.E.2d 680 (1960); Collard v. Incorporated Village of Flower Hill, 52 N.Y.2d 594, 439 N.Y.S.2d 326, 421 N.E.2d 818 (1981); Gladwyne Colony, Inc. v. Township of Lower Merion, 409 Pa. 441, 187 A.2d 549 (1963); State, Myhre v. City of Spokane, 70 Wn.2d 207, 422 P.2d 790 (1967); Housing and Redevelopment Authority v. Jorgensen, 328 N.W.2d 740 (Minn.1983). Contra: Hartnett v. Austin, 93 So.2d 86 (Fla.1956); Cederberg v. City of Rockford, 8 Ill.App.3d 984, 291 N.E.2d 249 (1972); Carlino v. Whitpain Investors, 499

Pa. 498, 453 A.2d 1385 (1982). But see Broward County v. Griffey, 366 So.2d 869 (Fla. App.1979), cert. denied 385 So.2d 757 (Fla. 1980), as to current Florida law.

35. Although rezoning based on a prior executory bilateral contract by which a municipality promises to rezone in consideration of a developer's promise observe additional restrictions may be objectionable, it is hard to see why courts should not approve (1) rezonings subject to an express condition that the developer agree to additional restrictions, and (2) rezonings subject to no express conditions but accompanied by collateral restrictive covenants contemporaneously executed by the developer.

See Comment, supra note 33, which contains a very elaborate classification of "contract" and "conditional" rezoning techniques.

36. E.g., Krasnowiecki, supra note 30, at 738; D. Mandelker, Land Use Law 180 (1982). Cf. Comment, supra note 33.

37. See ante Section 917 in text at notes 13–17, and Section 9.8 in text at notes 26, 27.

38. See post Section 9.16.

ditions on land developers, they presumably can obtain appropriate judicial relief in all these analogous cases.

Under the "wait and see" approach used in most communities with a substantial amount of undeveloped land, any new development that requires subdivision of raw land will also require rezoning. Thus the local planning commission and local governing body will have a chance to look at the proposed subdivision development for the first time when the developer submits an application for rezoning. Later, during the subdivision plat review, the local authorities may impose protective conditions of the sort that might otherwise be imposed as a result of negotiations between the developer and the local authorities when the rezoning application is under consideration. When a proposed development does not require subdivision of the land, many communities now require submission of a "site plan" for review in connection with the rezoning application.[39] The site plan review process may, to a considerable extent, provide an opportunity to impose protective conditions when the land in question is rezoned so as to allow the proposed development.

Because residential and other land development projects have become larger in scope, requiring more time for completion, changes in applicable zoning regulations often affect developments in progress when the zoning changes are made. In such cases, the developer often argues that he is entitled to proceed with the development as planned either because he has acquired a "vested right" in the prior zoning or on the ground that the municipality is "estopped" from applying the zoning change to the development in progress.[40] The "vested rights" argument is based on the theory that the developer has acquired constitutionally protected property rights in the development in progress. The "estoppel" theory is based on the equitable doctrine which protects good faith change of position in reliance upon some act or omission of the municipality.

Analytically, these theories are quite distinct, although many courts have failed to distinguish clearly between the "vested rights" and "estoppel" theories when they consider whether a developer has a right to proceed under the prior zoning regulations. Under the "vested rights" theory, the developer's right to proceed may date either from the time he applies for the first "permit" required by the applicable regulations—usually a building permit, a site plan approval, or a subdivision approval—or the actual issuance of the required "permit," provided the issuance of the "permit" is not illegal.[41] Under the "estoppel" theory, the developer's right to proceed is protected only when, after obtaining the required "permit," he takes action pursuant to the "permit" amounting to "substantial" detrimental reliance.[42]

39. See post Section 9.15.

40. The discussion of these topics is based largely on the discussion in D. Mandelker, Land Use Law §§ 6.11 through 6.22 (2d ed. 1988).

41. D. Mandelker, supra note 40, §§ 6.14, 6.15. If development occurs on a single lot, the first "permit" required will ordinarily be a building permit, although in some cases it will be "site plan approval." When development requires approval of a subdivision plat, "subdivision approval" is the "first permit." See, e.g., Western Land Equities, Inc. v. City of Logan, 617 P.2d 388 (Utah 1980); Littlefield v. Inhabitants of Town of Lyman, 447 A.2d 1231 (Me.1982). Subdivision and review procedure is considered post, Section 9.16.

42. D. Mandelker, supra note 40, §§ 6.18, 6.19. But Professor Mandelker's statement, id. § 6.12, that "[t]he factual basis for showing a vested right is the same as the factual basis

In applying the "estoppel" theory, the courts have developed three different formulations of the "substantial" detrimental reliance test: (1) A majority hold that the developer must have devoted a "set quantum" of expenditures to the project—which, of course, raises difficult questions as to precisely how much expenditure is required to meet this test.[43] (2) Other courts have adopted a "ratio" test, which requires that the expenditures must represent a substantial percentage of the total estimated cost of the project.[44] (3) A few courts have rejected both "set quantum" and "ratio" tests for "substantial" detrimental reliance and have adopted a "balancing" test under which the developer's expenditures are only one factor to be considered.[45] The "balancing" test allows the court to assess the "before-and-after" impact of a zoning change, which may not be fairly determined by applying either the "set quantum" or the "ratio" test—for example, in cases where a developer whose expenditures have been relatively small may face much greater costs if the zoning change is substantial.[46] The developer's incurring preliminary contractual and financial obligations may be sufficient to create an "estoppel," but the cost of purchasing land for the proposed development is generally held to be insufficient.[47]

In addition to applying one of the tests discussed in the preceding paragraph, most courts also require an actual beginning of construction before the zoning change becomes effective.[48] Completion of a structure is generally sufficient.[49] In some jurisdictions, completion of necessary land excavation is also sufficient,[50] but site preparation falling short of completion of the necessary excavation is generally insufficient.[51]

"Good faith" is an additional requirement for a successful claim of "vested rights" or "estoppel."[52] "Good faith" usually means that the developer must have "proceeded at a normal pace in the absence of any indication that a zoning change might occur."[53] On the other hand, if the developer "rushed to begin or complete his project with knowledge of a possible zoning

---

for proving and estoppel" is inaccurate; "estoppel" requires proof of "substantial" detrimental reliance, while creation of a "vested right" does not, as indicated herein, require any reliance. However, where there is "substantial" detrimental reliance upon issuance of the first required "permit," the developer may be entitled to proceed under either the "vested right" theory of the "estoppel" theory.

43. D. Mandelker, supra note 40, § 6.19 at n. 64 and cases cited.

44. D. Mandelker, supra note 40, § 6.19 at n. 65 and cases cited.

45. D. Mandelker, supra note 40, § 6.19, quoting from Tremarco Corp. v. Garzio, 32 N.J. 448, 161 A.2d 241, 245 (1960), as follows:

"The ultimate objective is fairness to both the public and the individual property owner. We think there is no profit in attempting to fix some precise concept of the nature and *quantum* of the reliance which will suffice. Rather a balance must be struck between the interests of the permittee and the right and duty of the municipality * * *

[to implement planning and zoning for the general welfare]."

See also Mays–Ott Co. v. Town of Nags Head, 751 F.Supp. 82 (E.D.N.C.1990) (right to complete development is "vested" when refusal to extend expired site plan would cause developer to lose $256,000 and public interest is small).

46. D. Mandelker, supra note 40, § 6.19.

47. D. Mandelker, supra note 40, § 6.20 at nn. 71, 72 and cases cited.

48. D. Mandelker, supra note 40, § 6.20 at n. 67 and cases cited.

49. D. Mandelker, supra note 40, § 6.20 at n. 68 and cases cited.

50. D. Mandelker, supra note 40, § 6.20 at n. 69 and cases cited.

51. D. Mandelker, supra note 40, § 6.20 at n. 70 and cases cited.

52. D. Mandelker, supra note 40, § 6.17.

53. D. Mandelker, supra note 40, § 6.17 at n. 57 and cases cited.

change" he is generally held to have acted in "bad faith." [54]   Although "good faith" would seem to be a subjective test, some courts have adopted a more objective test—whether the developer's conduct was that of a reasonable developer acting in the same circumstances.[55]   Under the objective test, a court may find that the developer acted in "good faith" even though he knew that a revision of the zoning regulations applicable to his land was pending.[56] Under the subjective test, the courts generally infer "bad faith" from such knowledge.   Under either test, the courts require "some positive indication that a revision of the zoning ordinance was actually contemplated by the local governing body before they will hold that knowledge of a pending revision is bad faith" and "mere knowledge of pending studies, or a landowner's expectation that political change may bring a revision of the ordinance, may not be enough." [57]

Because of substantial confusion in many jurisdictions as to the standards to be applied under either the "vested rights" or the "estoppel" theory, some states have added provisions to their enabling acts and some municipalities have added provisions to their land use ordinances designed to clarify the rules as to when a developer will be protected against any subsequent change in the applicable land use regulations.[58]   In addition, some states protect developers by authorizing the execution of development agreements between a developer and municipalities with respect to permitted uses and densities, maximum height and size of buildings, reservation or dedication of land for public use or payment of fees in lieu thereof, the allocation of responsibility for the timing and construction of public facilities, and similar questions.[59]   Such agreements obviously raise constitutional issues—e.g., whether a freeze on land use regulations is an unconstitutional "bargaining away of the police power." [60]   However, the courts have sustained agreements under which a landowner agrees to allow his land to be annexed by a municipality in return for the municipality's promise to provide public services, especially when the agreement is authorized by statute.[61]

§ 9.10 Zoning and Planning

As we saw in the preceding section, the prevailing rule is that the "in accordance with a comprehensive plan" provision in zoning enabling legislation does not require, as a prerequisite to exercise of the zoning power, that the planning commission or local governing body shall prepare and adopt a land use plan of the type authorized by the local planning enabling acts. Moreover, even when such a comprehensive land use plan has been adopted,

---

54. D. Mandelker, supra note 40, § 6.17 at n. 58 and cases cited.

55. D. Mandelker, supra note 40, § 6.17 at n. 59 and cases cited.

56. D. Mandelker, supra note 40, § 6.17 at n. 60 and cases cited.

57. D. Mandelker, supra note 40, § 6.17 at n. 61 and cases cited.

58. D. Mandelker, supra note 40, § 6.21.

59. D. Mandelker, supra note 40, § 6.23, citing West's Ann.Cal.Gov't Code §§ 65864–65869.5, West's Fla.Stat.Ann. §§ 163.3220–

163.3243, Hawaii Rev.Stat.Ann. §§ 46–121 through 46–132, and Nev.Rev.Stat.Ann. §§ 278.0201–278.0207.

60. D. Mandelker, supra note 40, § 6.23 at n. 83 and cases cited.

61. D. Mandelker, supra note 40, § 6.23 at n. 82 and cases cited. Cf. the "contract" and "conditional" zoning cases discussed ante in this Section.

the courts have not always invalidated zoning regulations that are inconsistent with the plan,[1] although consistency with the plan weighs heavily in favor of validity.[2]

In a number of states the relationship between planning and zoning has undergone substantial change in recent years. As we have already seen, the Oregon Supreme Court held (*inter alia*) in Fasano v. Board of County Commissioners of Washington County[3] that rezoning decisions must be based on the comprehensive land use plan previously adopted by the county planning commission. But *Fasano* was applicable only to *rezoning* decisions. Two years after *Fasano,* the Oregon Supreme Court held, in *Baker v. City of Milwaukie,*[4] that existing zoning regulations must be changed to conform to a subsequently adopted comprehensive land use plan. Although it was not clear that the Oregon planning statute then required that municipalities should adopt a comprehensive plan, the court held that, at least where a municipality has adopted a comprehensive plan, the plan is controlling as against inconsistent zoning regulations that would permit more intensive development on a given tract than would the comprehensive plan. Subsequently, an intermediate appellate court held that a municipality need not revise zoning regulations to conform to a subsequent comprehensive plan permitting more intensive development.[5]

Shortly after the *Baker* decision, the Oregon legislature enacted legislation requiring all local governments (municipalities as well as counties) to adopt comprehensive land use plans, based upon comprehensive statewide planning goals formulated by a state Land Conservation and Development Commission, and to make all zoning and other land use regulations conform to the local comprehensive plan.[6] Subsequently, the Oregon Supreme Court held, in Neuberger v. City of Portland,[7] that the proponent of a rezoning amendment need not prove either "public need" or that the land sought to be rezoned is the only suitable land available for the development for which rezoning is sought, because there is "no statutory or LCDC requirement"[8] to that effect. The Oregon planning legislation, which provides for state-level review of all local plans and regulatory ordinances to determine whether

§ 9.10

1. E.g., Rosenberg v. Planning Board, 155 Conn. 636, 236 A.2d 895 (1967); Cascio v. Town Council, 158 Conn. 111, 256 A.2d 685 (1969); Nottingham Village, Inc. v. Baltimore County, 266 Md. 339, 292 A.2d 680 (1972); Miller v. Abrahams, 239 Md. 263, 211 A.2d 309 (1965); Ward v. Knippenberg, 416 S.W.2d 746 (Ky.1967); Biske v. City of Troy, 381 Mich. 611, 166 N.W.2d 453 (1969) (plan adopted by planning comm'n but not by governing body); Cheney v. Village 2 at New Hope, Inc., 429 Pa. 626, 241 A.2d 81 (1968); Sharninghouse v. City of Bellingham, 4 Wn.App. 198, 480 P.2d 233 (1971).

2. E.g., Scull v. Coleman, 251 Md. 6, 246 A.2d 223 (1968); Norbeck Village Joint Venture v. Montgomery County Council, 254 Md. 59, 254 A.2d 700 (1969).

3. 264 Or. 574, 507 P.2d 23 (1973).

4. 271 Or. 500, 533 P.2d 772 (1975).

5. Pohrman v. Klamath County Commissioners, 25 Or.App. 613, 550 P.2d 1236 (1976).

6. See Or.Rev.Stat. ch. 197.

7. 288 Or. 155, 603 P.2d 771 (1979), rehearing denied 288 Or. 585, 607 P.2d 722 (1980).

8. "LCDC" is the common acronym for Land Conservation and Development Commission, the Oregon state land use planning and control agency. The LCDC establishes both "goals," which are mandatory, and "guidelines," which are only advisory, for local land use planning and control agencies. For a recent judicial discussion of LCDC "goals," see Willamette University v. Land Conservation Development Commission, 45 Or.App. 355, 608 P.2d 1178 (1980).

they comply with the statewide planning goals, recently survived a third attempt at repeal through a statewide public referendum.[9]

California was one of the first states to make local comprehensive planning mandatory.[10] The comprehensive planning legislation is quite detailed, setting out both mandatory and optional plan elements for inclusion in local comprehensive plans. However, the only substantive policies are those laid down for the "housing element" of the local plan, which must "make adequate provision for the housing needs of all economic segments of the community."[11] The California zoning enabling statute requires all local zoning ordinances (both municipal and county) to be consistent with the local comprehensive land use plan, and defines "consistent" to mean that "[t]he various land uses authorized by the ordinance are [to be] compatible with the objectives, policies, general land uses and programs specified in [the] plan."[12] This statutory definition of "consistent" was later amplified by a Guideline issued by the California Office of Planning and Research, which provides that the consistency requirement is satisfied if local regulatory ordinances "will not inhibit or obstruct the attainment of" the policies articulated in the local comprehensive plan. Compliance with the consistency requirement can be enforced by court action.[13]

The Florida Local Government Comprehensive Planning Act of 1975,[14] like the California comprehensive planning legislation, mandates planning by all Florida counties, municipalities, and special districts. County plans are controlling in municipalities and special districts that fail to prepare comprehensive plans, and the state may impose its own plan on any county that fails to prepare a comprehensive plan. Both mandatory and optional elements of the local comprehensive plan are set out in great detail in the statute.[15] Among the mandatory elements is a "housing element" requiring provision for low- and moderate-income housing needs.[16] The statute includes the following "consistency" provision: "After a comprehensive plan * * * has been adopted * * * all development undertaken by, and all actions taken in regard to development orders by, government agencies in regard to such plan * * * shall be consistent with such plan. * * * All land development regulations enacted or amended shall be consistent with the adopted comprehensive plan."[17] This requirement is reinforced by a statement that the intent of the planning act is that local land development regulations shall implement the comprehensive plan, and a provision for judicial review of the consistency of governmental actions or land development regulations with the plan.[18]

9. See 49 Planning, No. 1, January 1983, p. 7.

10. See West's Ann.Cal.Gov.Code § 65300 et seq. for the current planning legislation.

11. West's Ann.Cal.Gov.Code § 65302(c). See also id. §§ 65583, 65584.

12. West's Ann.Cal.Gov.Code § 65860(a) (iii). There is a comparable requirement for local and subdivision regulations; see id. § 66473.5.

13. J. DiMento, the Consistency Doctrine and the Limits of Planning (1980); Catalano &

DiMento, Mandating Consistency Between General Plans and Zoning Ordinances: The California Experience, 8 Nat.Res.Law 455 (1975).

14. Local Government Comprehensive Planning Act of 1975, West's Fla.Stat.Ann. §§ 163.3161–163.3211.

15. Id. § 163.3177.

16. Id. § 163.3177(6)(f).

17. Id. § 163.3194(1).

18. Id. § 163.3201.

A few other states also have legislation requiring preparation and adoption of local comprehensive plans and consistency of zoning regulations with the adopted land use plan.[19]

Those who advocate mandatory comprehensive planning and consistency of land use regulations with comprehensive plans are,[20] of course, heartened by the adoption of legislation like that recently enacted in Oregon, California, and Florida. But there are those who take a rather dim view of the traditional planning process, even as modified by recent legislation in states like Oregon, California, and Florida. The American Law Institute's Model Land Development Code does not require local comprehensive planning, and drops the list of planning elements that has been traditional in state planning legislation.[21] Both Professor Tarlock[22] and Professor Krasnowiecki[23] have recently published vigorous dissents to the view that land use regulations should be required to be consistent with the local comprehensive plan, if there is one. Professor Krasnowiecki proposes, instead,

> that the prevailing emphasis on a plan should be abandoned, and, instead, that decisions in the field should be supported by an ongoing planning system—a series of annual reports. These reports should contain, among other elements, a stock-taking element, short and long range projection elements, and a reasoning element that would explain or criticize failure to follow the projections of the last annual report, reconcile various actions taken during the report period, and so forth. This approach [would treat] planning as a system that enters into actual decisions in the field in a manner that allows the system to be shaped by, as well as to shape, the decisions.[24]

In recent years, largely as a result of federal subsidy programs that require "planning," several states have adopted legislation providing for development of land use and development plans for an entire state, and also providing for a significant amount of direct regulation of land use and development by state agencies. The Oregon legislation discussed previously in this section[25] is a good example. The Oregon legislation lodges the

19. E.g., Ariz.Rev.Stat. § 9–462.01E (municipalities); Nev.Rev.Stat.Ann. 278.150, 278.-160(1)(e), 278.250(2).

20. For early advocacy of these requirements, see Haar, In Accordance with a Comprehensive Plan, 68 Harv.L.Rev. 1154 (1955); Haar, The Master Plan: An Impermanent Constitution, 20 L. & Contemp.Prob. 353 91955). For more recent support of these requirements, see Report of ABA's Advisory Comm'n on Housing and Urban Growth, Housing for All under Law 408–410 (R. Fishman ed. 1978); D. Mandelker, The Role of the Local Comprehensive Plan in Land Use Regulation, 74 Mich.L.Rev. 900, 944–973 (1976).

21. See Am.L.Inst., Model Land Development Code § 3.102 (1975); id., Commentary at p. 119. The Model Code incorporates proposals set out in Bolan, Emerging Views of Planning, 31 J.Inst. of Planners 233 (1967).

22. Tarlock, Consistency with Adopted Land Use Plans as a Standard of Judicial

Review: The Case Against, 9 Urb.L.Ann. 69 (1975).

23. Krasnowiecki, Abolish Zoning, 31 Syracuse L.Rev. 719, 747–48 (1980).

24. Id. at 747–48. Krasnowiecki further proposes that "the states should enact new land-use control enabling legislation for substantially undeveloped communities" that will prohibit "self-administering standards" so that matters such as "lot size, use, height, density, or bulk * * * may only be regulated by a decision made in each particular case, based on reasons that must be articulated," arguing that "the case by case approach to land use control cannot be wished or legislated away because it is dictated by some urgent social and political realities, many of which are not intrinsically bad." Id. at 750, 753. Compare Kmiec, Deregulating Land Use: An Alternative Free Enterprise Development System, 130 U.Pa.L.Rev. 28 (1982).

25. Ante in text at notes 6–8.

responsibility for statewide planning in a Land Conservation and Development Commission (LCDC) served by staff located in the state Land Conservation and Development Department. Both the LCDC and the Department are subject to advice from a Joint Legislative Committee on Land Use. The Oregon legislation not only provides for adoption of "goals" and "guidelines" by the LCDC and review by the LCDC of locally adopted comprehensive plans,[26] but also provides for direct state level regulation of activities of statewide significance such as the planning and siting of public transportation facilities, public sewerage systems, public water supply systems, solid waste disposal sites, and public schools.[27] In general, these provisions for control of public developments of statewide significance parallel similar provisions in the American Law Institute's Model Land Development Code,[28] except that the Code provides for state review of local decisions on such developments and does not provide for issuance of state permits for such developments. Like the Model Code, the Oregon legislation also provides for the designation by the legislature of geographic areas of critical state concern.[29] The Oregon legislation further empowers the LCDC to regulate land use and development in such areas.[30]

Florida has adopted legislation [31] generally similar to the Oregon legislation and also based on the American Law Institute's Model Land Development Code.[32] But there are significant differences. The Oregon legislation links state-level planning with a mandatory local planning and regulatory consistency requirement. The Florida legislation does not really link the state-level land use planning and regulatory powers with the mandatory local-level planning and land use control system.[33] And the Florida legislation, unlike the Oregon legislation (and unlike the Model Code) authorizes the State Land Planning Agency to designate Regional Planning Agencies to perform an advisory role in the new statutory process required to obtain a permit for a "development of regional impact" (DRI).[34]

Other states have also recently enacted legislation, not based on the American Law Institute's Model Land Development Code, which provides for significant state level land use planning and regulatory activity.[35]

§ 9.11　Planned Unit Development

As Professor Daniel Mandelker has pointed out,[1]

Modern developers often plan and build residential developments as a single project, sometimes mixing both single-family and multifamily

26. See Oregon Rev.Stat. 197.015(7), 197.-015(8), 197.175, 197.185, 197.190, 197.230(1), 197.275, 197.300.

27. Id. 197.400. These activities may not be initiated without an LCDC permit. Id. 197.415.

28. Am.L.Inst., Model Land Development Code art. 7 (1976).

29. See Oregon Rev.Stat. 197.405(2).

30. Ibid.

31. Environmental Land and Water Management Act of 1972, West's Fla.Stat.Ann. ch. 380.

32. Supra note 28.

33. Compare West's Fla.Stat.Ann. ch. 380; West's Fla.Stat.Ann. §§ 163.3161–163.3211.

34. West's Fla.Stat.Ann. § 380.06.

35. See, e.g., Hawaii Rev.Stat.Ann. chs. 205, 205A, 206, 206E, 223, 224, 225 (see also id. chaps. 171–196); 10 Vermont Stat.Ann. ch. 151.

§ 9.11

1. D. Mandelker, Land Use Law 273 (1982).

dwellings. The application of conventional zoning to these large-scale developments presents a number of problems. Site development regulations governing lot sizes and setbacks often produce a monotonous uniformity. Because the conventional zoning ordinance does not allow the developer to trade off higher densities for the preservation of natural and unbuildable areas, the developer usually builds on all of her site and may destroy natural and environmentally important areas in the process. Developments containing both single-family and multifamily dwellings are also difficult to handle under conventional zoning. A development containing both types of dwellings will require two or more zoning districts, making it difficult to integrate and control the development under a single set of land use controls.

In an attempt to overcome these difficulties, the concept of "planned unit development" (PUD) was introduced about twenty years ago.[2] In the simplest form of PUD, usually limited to single-family dwellings, densities and uses in the project area are not changed, but densities are increased in one part of the project area in return for restrictions which preclude any building in other parts of the project area. In this form of PUD, often called a "cluster development," increased density in the area where building is permitted is traded for substantial open space in other areas. More complex PUDs may allow a mixture of residential building types, with or without an increase in overall density, or even an ancillary commercial area to serve the residents of the PUD. In either its simplest or in more complex forms, a PUD is always based on a project development plan which must be approved by the local authorities after review. Since the zoning map does not, prior to approval, show any PUD classification for the project area, and since the review process usually involves a good deal of negotiation with regard to project design and densities, the PUD clearly combines elements of the "floating zone" technique and the "conditional" rezoning technique.[3]

The earliest PUDs were authorized by local ordinances which in turn, were based on zoning enabling legislation based on the Standard State Zoning Enabling Act or the early New York zoning planning and zoning enabling statutes.[4] In the early cases, these ordinances were challenged on the ground that they were *ultra vires* because the zoning enabling act did not confer on local regulatory agencies such as the planning commission or the zoning board of appeals (or adjustment) the review powers commonly delegated to them by such ordinances, and/or because the mixture of densities and building types permitted in different parts of the project area violated the enabling act requirement that all zoning regulations "shall be uniform for each class or kind of building throughout each district."[5] But the courts have generally rejected such challenges.[6]

---

2. See Symposium, Planned Unit Development, 114 U.Pa.L.Rev. (1965).

3. See ante Section 9.9.

4. For an argument that PUD was authorized by Bassett's 1925 Model Planning Act, § 12, enacted in New York in 1927, see Krasnowiecki, Planned Unit Development: A Challenge to Established Theory and Practice of Land Use Control, in Symposium, supra note 2, at 48.

5. See, e.g., Cheney v. Village 2 at New Hope, Inc., 429 Pa. 626, 241 A.2d 81 (1968).

6. Ibid. See also Chrinko v. South Brunswick Township Planning Board, 77 N.J.Super, 594, 187 A.2d 221 (L.Div.1963); Orinda Homeowners Committee v. Board of Supervisors, 11 Cal.App.3d 768, 90 Cal.Rptr. 88 (1970).

The courts have also rejected challenges to PUD ordinances based on the argument that the bargaining and negotiation typical of the PUD review process constitutes invalid "contract zoning" [7] and the argument that approval of a PUD project is invalid as "spot zoning" that is not "in accordance with a comprehensive plan." [8]

A model PUD enabling statute was proposed in 1965 [9] to eliminate problems arising when local PUD ordinances have to be based on zoning enabling legislation derived from the Standard Act or the early New York zoning legislation. The model statute authorizes designation of a single local review agency with authority to issue a permit covering all aspects of the proposed PUD project, subject to a set of detailed standards set out in the local PUD ordinance, and characterizes the action of the review agency as adjudicative. An outline plan is not expressly required by the model statute, but both a tentative and a final approval of the PUD project plan are required, and the PUD developer is protected against changes in the PUD regulations after final approval has been granted.

Several states [10] have enacted the model PUD enabling statute. A few states have enacted less detailed PUD enabling statutes.[11] New York has enacted legislation authorizing approval of density transfer PUDs in the subdivision control process.[12] Where the model PUD enabling statute has been adopted, the cases have divided on the question whether local governments may enact PUD ordinances that do not comply with the enabling statute.[13]

In 1980 the Commissioners on Uniform State Laws promulgated a Uniform Planned Community Act [14] which, they asserted, is intended "to track the Uniform Condominium Act" as far as possible. To date, it does not appear that this Uniform Act has been adopted in any jurisdiction. In 1982 the Commissioners on Uniform State Laws promulgated a Uniform Common Interest Ownership Act [15] which is intended to combine under a single umbrella the Uniform Condominium Act, the Uniform Planned Community Act, and the Model Real Estate Cooperative Act (1981). To date, it does not appear that the Uniform Common Interest Ownership Act has been enacted in any jurisdiction.

Whether the authority for PUDs is derived from specific enabling legislation or from a traditional zoning enabling legislation modelled on the

7. E.g., Rutland Environmental Protection Association v. Kane County, 31 Ill.App.3d 82, 334 N.E.2d 215 (1975), certiorari denied 425 U.S. 913, 96 S.Ct. 1510, 47 L.Ed.2d 764 (1976).

8. Cheney v. Village 2 at New Hope, Inc., supra note 5.

9. Krasnowiecki, Babcock & McBride, Model State Statute, in Symposium, supra note 2, at 136–170.

10. E.g., Conn.Gen.Stat.Ann. ch. 124a (§§ 8–13b through 8–13k) 53 Penn.Stat. §§ 10701–10711.

11. E.g., Mich.Comp.Laws Ann. §§ 125.-584b, 125.584c; Ohio Rev.Code §§ 303.022 (county rural zoning), 519.021 (township zoning).

12. E.g., New York—McKinney's Town Law § 281.

13. Compare Niccollai v. Planning Board, 148 N.J.Super. 150, 372 A.2d 352 (App.Div. 1977), cert. denied 75 N.J. 11, 379 A.2d 242 (1977) with Raum v. Board of Supervisors, 20 Pa.Cmwlth. 426, 342 A.2d 450 (1975), appeal after remand 29 Pa.Cmwlth. 9, 370 A.2d 777 (1977).

14. See 7A Uniform Laws Ann.Supp.1983, p. 55.

15. See 7 Uniform Laws Ann.Supp.1983, p. 61.

Standard Act or the early New York enabling statutes, regulation of PUDs at the local level depends upon enactment of an appropriate local ordinance, which must include a set of standards for PUD approval.[16] The standards usually cover all aspects of the PUD, such as land uses, building types, densities, site development requirements, the provision of common open space, and overall project design. Some local PUD ordinances treat the PUD zoning classification as a "floating zone" and require rezoning of a proposed project area to the PUD classification by the local governing body.[17] Other ordinances simply authorize approval of PUD projects by the planning commission or the zoning board of appeals (or adjustment) as a kind of special exception or conditional use within designated districts.[18]

The typical PUD ordinance requires the developer to submit and obtain approval of both a preliminary plan and a final plan of his proposed PUD project. Sometimes the ordinance also requires the developer to submit an outline or sketch plan showing proposed densities, building types, and land uses, before submitting a detailed preliminary plan. The similarity of the PUD review process to the subdivision review process considered post in Section 16 is obvious. Indeed, PUD ordinances often provide for integration of the PUD and subdivision review processes, so that the developer can submit his entire plan to a single agency and receive a single approval of both the preliminary and final PUD plans. Such a unified review process is possible wherever the reviewing agency—usually the planning commission— has authority to approve both PUDs and subdivisions.[19]

Where the local PUD ordinance sets out detailed standards and does not expressly reserve to the local authorities the power to reject an application for PUD approval even when all the detailed standards are met, the cases are divided. Some cases hold that rejection is permitted,[20] other cases have reversed PUD denials not based on the standards included in the ordinance.[21]

Problems arising after the final approval of a PUD plan may require changes in the plan. If the PUD was approved by an administrative agency such as the planning commission as a kind of special exception, changes in the plan may also be approved by the same agency provided there is no change in permitted land uses that would require rezoning.[22] But if the local governing body approved the final plan and rezoned the PUD project area to a PUD classification on the basis of the final plan, substantial

16. See Tri–State Generation & Transmission Co. v. City of Thornton, 647 P.2d 670 (Colo.1982).

17. See, e.g., Cheney v. Village 2 at New Hope, Inc., supra note 5; Todd Mart, Inc. v. Town Board of Webster, 49 A.D.2d 12, 370 N.Y.S.2d 683 (1975); Town of North Hempstead v. Village of North Hills, 38 N.Y.2d 334, 379 N.Y.S.2d 792, 342 N.E.2d 566 (1975).

18. See, e.g., Appeal of Moreland, 497 P.2d 1287 (Okl.1972) (valid); Chandler v. Kroiss, 291 Minn. 196, 190 N.W.2d 472 (1971) (same). But see Lutz v. City of Longview, 83 Wn.2d 566, 520 P.2d 1374 (1974) (invalid).

19. See Prince George's County v. M & B Construction Corp., 267 Md. 338, 297 A.2d 683

(1972), holding that the power to approve density transfer PUDs was properly delegated to the planning commission in the exercise of its subdivision control powers.

20. E.g., Ford Leasing Development Co. v. Board of County Commissioners, 186 Colo. 418, 528 P.2d 237 (1974); Coronet Homes, Inc. v. McKenzie, 84 Nev. 250, 439 P.2d 219 (1968).

21. E.g., RK Development Corp. v. City of Norwalk, 156 Conn. 369, 242 A.2d 781 (1968); Hall v. Korth, 244 So.2d 766 (Fla.App.1971); LaSalle National Bank v. County of Lake, 27 Ill.App.3d 10, 325 N.E.2d 105 (1975).

22. E.g., Chandler v. Kroiss, supra note 18.

changes in the plan will require adoption of a rezoning amendment by the local governing body.[23] At least where authorized by the PUD ordinance, it would seem that minor changes could be made administratively, however.

Since PUD ordinances always require that a substantial part of any project site be left unbuilt as common open space, and since many PUD plans call for development of the common open space (or part of it, at least) for recreational use, some provision must obviously be made for continuing maintenance and management of the common open space.[24] PUD ordinances ordinarily do not require the common open space to be dedicated to public use and usually provide that ownership shall be vested in a property owner's association whose membership includes all owners of property within the project. Thus the maintenance and management of the common open space becomes the responsibility of the association's board of directors. In order to defray the costs of maintenance and management, the board of directors is usually empowered to fix and collect an annual fee from each property owner. The obligation to pay the annual fee is specifically made a lien upon each owner's interest so that successors of the original purchasers will be bound.[25] In this respect the provisions for maintenance and management are similar to the provisions adopted for the same purpose in condominium projects.[26]

§ 9.12   "Exclusionary Zoning" in the State Courts

The courts of New Jersey, Pennsylvania, and New York have been willing to adjudicate cases in which local zoning ordinances were attacked on the ground that, taken in their entirety, they are "exclusionary"—i.e., that they effectively preclude construction of any substantial amount of housing within the financial reach of low- and moderate-income families, and thus do not promote the general welfare. Exclusionary zoning litigation in these states has been facilitated by much more relaxed "standing" rules than those applied in the federal courts. Thus these courts have permitted nonresidents to initiate exclusionary zoning cases,[1] and they generally have not required that the plaintiffs have an interest in a site-specific low- or moderate-income housing project as a condition of bringing suit.[2] And these

---

23. E.g., Millbrae Association for Residential Survival v. City of Millbrae, 262 Cal. App.2d 222, 69 Cal.Rptr. 251 (1968).

24. See, generally, FHA Land Planning Bulletin 6, Planned Unit Development with a Homes Association (1963); Krasowiecki–Babcock & McBride, Model State Statutes, in Symposium, supra note 2, at 146–150; Uniform Planned Communities Act art. 3 (1980), 7A Uniform Laws Ann., Supp.1983, pp. 112–133; Uniform Common Interest Ownership Act art. 3 (1982), 7 Uniform Laws Ann., Supp. 1983, pp. 83–96.

25. See Uniform Planned Communities Act § 3–116 (1980), 7A Uniform Laws Ann., Supp.1983, p. 129; Uniform Common Interest Ownership Act § 3–116 (1982), 7 Uniform Laws Ann., Supp.1983, p. 93.

26. See Uniform Condominium Act art. 3 (1980), 7 Uniform Laws Ann., Supp.1983, pp. 178–200.

§ 9.12

1. E.g., Southern Burlington County NAACP v. Township of Mount Laurel, 67 N.J. 151, 336 A.2d 713 (1975), appeal dismissed and certiorari denied 423 U.S. 808, 96 S.Ct. 18, 46 L.Ed.2d 28 (1975), hereafter referred to as *Mount Laurel* I; Home Builders League v. Township of Berlin, 81 N.J. 127, 405 A.2d 381 (1979).

2. E.g., *Mount Laurel* I, supra note 1. But many exclusionary zoning cases arise from municipal refusal to rezone a specific site to permit construction of low- or moderate-income housing. E.g., Oakwood at Madison, Inc. v. Township of Madison, 72 N.J. 481, 371 A.2d 1192 (1977).

courts have not required any showing of racially discriminatory zoning as a condition of granting relief in exclusionary zoning cases.[3]

Professor Norman Williams, Jr., has listed six major exclusionary zoning techniques: (1) exclusion of multiple family dwellings; (2) restrictions on the number of bedrooms in multiple family dwellings; (3) exclusion of mobile homes; (4) minimum size building requirements; (5) minimum lot size requirements; and (6) minimum lot width requirements.[4] It seems clear that the first three have the most significant exclusionary effect since they prohibit the least expensive forms of housing—multi-family dwellings and mobile homes—and exclude renter-families with children. The last three zoning techniques apply only to single-family dwellings and probably have less significant exclusionary effects than the first three, although much of the discussion of exclusionary zoning in the law journals has focused on large minimum lot size requirements. It is likely that large minimum lot size requirements do increase housing costs in suburban communities to some extent, but the effect of such requirements is far from clear.[5]

The leading state exclusionary zoning case is Southern Burlington County NAACP v. Township of Mt. Laurel, which has now been twice reviewed by the New Jersey Supreme Court.[6] On the first appeal, the New Jersey court concluded that the township had over-zoned for industry—preventing any development of a large amount of vacant land—and that the residential zoning classifications placed upon the rest of the township's undeveloped land would "realistically allow only homes within the financial reach of persons of at least middle income" and would exclude "low and moderate income families."[7]

On the basis of New Jersey's state constitutional provision guaranteeing to all persons the "natural and unalienable" right "of acquiring, possessing, and protecting property"[8]—which the court viewed as incorporating "requirements of substantive due process and equal protection of the laws"—the court held the Mt. Laurel zoning ordinance invalid to the extent that it failed, "by its land use regulations, to make realistically possible the opportunity for an appropriate variety and choice of housing for all categories of people who may desire to live there, * * * including all those of low and moderate income,"[9]—and thus failed to promote the general welfare.[10]

3. See, e.g., cases supra notes 1 and 2.

4. See 2 N. Williams, Am. Land Planning Law chs. 62–65 (1974); 3 id. ch. 66.

5. See Urban Land Inst. Tech. Bull. 32, The Effects of Large Lot Sizes on Residential Development (1958); Coke & Liebman, Political Values and Population Density Control, 37 Land Econ. 347 (1961); Am.Soc. of Planning Officials, New Directions in Connecticut Planning Legislation (1967); Report of the Nat. Comm'n on Urban Problems to the Congress and President, Building the American City, HR Doc. 9134, 91st Cong., 1st Sess. (1968) (the Douglas Comm'n Report); Sternlieb and Sagalyn, Zoning and Housing Costs (1971); E. Bergman et al., External Validity of Policy Related Research on Development Controls and Housing Costs (Dept. of City and Regional Planning, Univ. of North Carolina, 1974).

6. The first appeal was decided in 1975; see supra note 1. The second *Mount Laurel* appeal, along with 7 companion cases, was decided in 1983: Southern Burlington County NAACP v. Township of Mount Laurel, 92 N.J. 158, 456 A.2d 390 (1983), hereafter referred to as *Mount Laurel* II.

7. See 67 N.J. at 161–173, 336 A.2d at 718–724.

8. N.J.S.A. Const. Art. 1, par. 1, quoted in 67 N.J. at 175 n. 11, 336 A.2d at 725 n. 11.

9. See 67 N.J. at 179–188, 336 A.2d at 727–731. The decision was expressly based on the New Jersey Constitution in order to preclude reversal by the United States Supreme Court.

10. See 67 N.J. at 187, 336 A.2d at 732.

More specifically, the Court held that Mount Laurel "must permit multi-family housing, without bedroom or similar restrictions, as well as small dwellings on very small lots, low cost housing of other types and, in general, high density zoning," [11] and, further, that "[t]he amount of land removed from residential use by allocation to industrial and commercial purposes must be reasonably related to the present and future potential for such purposes."

Since it was obvious that not every New Jersey "developing" municipality could be required to accommodate all the low- and moderate-income persons who might wish to reside in it, the *Mount Laurel* opinion purported to provide a general formula to measure compliance with the Court's mandate, as follows: each "developing" municipality must zone in such a way as to accommodate "the municipality's fair share of the present and prospective regional need" for low- and moderate-income housing. [12] In addition, the Court strongly implied that it would set out a more detailed definition of "fair share" and "regional need" in a then-pending case, Oakwood at Madison, Inc. v. Township of Madison. [13]

Oakwood at Madison disappointed those who hoped that it would clarify the issues left unsettled in *Mt. Laurel*. The *Oakwood at Madison* opinion did not formulate a helpful definition of either "fair share" or "region," and it substituted the concept of "least cost housing" for "low- and moderate-income housing." [14] But in its second *Mt. Laurel* opinion the New Jersey Court reaffirmed and extended its *Mt. Laurel* I holdings.

In *Mt. Laurel* II, [15] the New Jersey Court held that (1) the duty to provide a realistic opportunity to accommodate a fair share of the regional need for low- and moderate-income housing extends to all municipalities, any part of which is designated by the State Development Guide Plan as a "growth" area, whether the municipality as a whole is or is not a "developing" municipality; [16] (2) in exclusionary zoning litigation, challengers may still make a *prima facie* case for invalidity by proving that the zoning ordinance in fact substantially limits construction of low- and moderate-income housing; [17] (3) a municipality, in order to rebut the *prima facie* case, must introduce "numerical" evidence of the number of units needed immediately and within a reasonable time in the future, and cannot satisfy its burden

11. Ibid.

12. See 67 N.J. at 188, 336 A.2d at 732.

13. Supra note 2.

14. See 72 N.J. at 510–514, 371 A.2d at 1206–1208. This retreat from *Mount Laurel* I was based on the Court's conclusion that (1) "private enterprise will not in the current and prospective economy without subsidization or external incentive of some kind construct new housing affordable by the low income population and by a large proportion of those of moderate income," and (2) "sources extraneous to the unaided private building industry cannot be depended upon to produce any substantial proportion of the housing needed and affordable by most of the lower income population." The Court also adopted the theory that low- and moderate-income households would benefit through "filtering down" from an increase in "the total supply of available housing." Pascack Association, Limited v. Township of Washington, 74 N.J. 470, 379 A.2d 6 (1977) seemed to mark a further retreat from *Mount Laurel* I in holding that the *Mount Laurel* doctrine was not applicable at all in fully developed communities. Accord: Fobe Associates v. Mayor and Council and Board of Adjustment, 74 N.J. 519, 379 A.2d 31 (1977).

15. Southern Burlington County N.A.A.C.P. v. Mount Laurel, 92 N.J. 158, 456 A.2d 390 (1983).

16. 456 A.2d at 422–435.

17. 456 A.2d at 422.

simply by showing that it has made a "bona fide effort" to eliminate exclusionary land use regulations as indicated in *Oakwood at Madison;* [18] and (4) if removal of exclusionary land use regulations will not, without more, provide a "reasonable opportunity" for construction of low- and moderate-income housing, a municipality must co-operate with the attempts of land developers to obtain federal housing subsidies, and must also undertake various forms of "inclusionary zoning" such as density bonuses to developers who voluntarily provide units for low- and moderate-income households and mandatory provisions requiring developers to set aside some of their dwelling units for low- and moderate-income households. [19]

Mt. Laurel II also provides for the appointment, on a regional assignment basis, of three trial judges to hear all exclusionary zoning cases. [20] By this device the New Jersey Supreme Court apparently hopes to enable the assigned judges to develop special expertise in dealing with exclusionary zoning cases and to afford expeditious relief to aggrieved parties. In addition, *Mount Laurel* II provides that, [21]

> If a trial court determines that a municipality has not met its *Mount Laurel* obligation, it *shall* order the municipality to revise its zoning ordinance within a set time period to comply with the constitutional mandate; if the municipality fails adequately to revise its ordinance within that time, the court shall implement the remedies for noncompliance outlined below; and if plaintiff is a developer, the court shall determine whether a builder's remedy should be granted.

The "builder's remedy" mentioned in the excerpt above is simply a judicial grant of permission for a plaintiff developer to proceed with his proposed development. [22] Other remedies made available under *Mt. Laurel* II include (1) appointment of a master to "facilitate" revision of local zoning ordinances—a remedy that is discretionary but said to be "desirable in many cases" [23]—and (2) orders of the following types: [24]

> (1) that the municipality adopt such resolutions and ordinances, including particular amendments to its zoning ordinance, and other land use regulations, as will enable it to meet its *Mount Laurel* obligations;

> (2) that certain types of projects or construction as may be specified by the trial court be delayed within the municipality until its ordinance is satisfactorily revised, or until all or part of its fair share of lower income housing is constructed and/or firm commitments for its construction have been made by responsible developers;

> (3) that the zoning ordinance and other land use regulations of the municipality be deemed void in whole or in part so as to relax or eliminate building and use restrictions in all or selected portions of the municipality (the court may condition this remedy upon failure of the

18. 456 A.2d at 421–422.

19. 456 A.2d at 441–452.

20. 456 A.2d at 459.

21. 456 A.2d at 452.

22. 456 A.2d at 452–453. This remedy was granted in Oakwood at Madison v. Township of Madison, supra note 2.

23. 456 A.2d at 453–454.

24. 456 A.2d at 455.

municipality to adopt resolutions or ordinances mentioned in (1) above); and

(4) that particular applications to construct housing that includes lower income units be approved by the municipality, or any officer, board, agency, authority (independent or otherwise) or division thereof.

Most of the commentary since *Mt. Laurel* II has been favorable, although some has been critical.[25] In particular, some critics have asserted that the State Development Guide Plan is already out-of-date;[26] that, by and large, it designates as "growth areas" those communities where substantial growth has occurred during the past decade, thus exempting from Mt. Laurel "inclusionary zoning" requirements those communities that have most successfully limited growth in the past by "exclusionary zoning";[27] and that there is no assurance that "growth areas" shown on the SDGP are designated as "growth areas" on other statewide plans, such as those of the New Jersey Department of Environmental Protection.[28]

The New York courts have also developed a rule invalidating exclusionary zoning ordinances. In Berenson v. Town of New Castle,[29] New York's highest court adopted a two-tiered test of validity: (1) does the challenged zoning ordinance "provide for the development of a balanced, cohesive community which will make efficient use of the town's available land"; and (2) does the ordinance enable the municipality to accommodate otherwise unmet regional housing needs, in light of the needs of county and metropolitan area residents to live near their places of employment? But the New York court made it clear that it was not mandating "a certain relative proportion between various types of development."[30]

After remand in *Berenson,* the intermediate appellate court affirmed the trial court's order that the municipality should rezone plaintiff's land for multifamily use, but it reversed the trial court's order mandating a specific allowable density of development and directing issuance of a building permit to the developer upon compliance with the revised zoning regulations, asserting that issuance of a building permit would also depend on compliance with the New York Freshwater Wetlands Act.[31]

---

25. See, e.g., 35 Land Use L. & Zoning Dig. No. 3, pp. 3–12 (March 1983); Potomac Inst., Metro. Housing Memorandum, Feb. 1983; National Law Journal, March 14, 1983, p. 11.

26. See De Palma, N.J. Housing Woes Are All Over the Map, N.Y. Times, April 17, 1983, p. 6E.

27. Ibid.

28. Washburn, Some Unresolved Issues in Mount Laurel II, 35 Land Use L. & Zoning Dig. No. 3, p. 6 (March 1983). "For example, the New Jersey Department of Environmental Protection has prohibited sewer connections in numerous towns throughout the state because of inadequate capacity or failure to meet proper treatment standards. Many of these sewer bans prevent development, whether for low-income housing or otherwise, in areas designated as growth zones in the SDGP. Other plans indicate that various

SDGP growth areas cannot support construction due to their need to maintain water quality standards and preserve open space or agricultural lands. An ironic example of that issue concerns the Davis Enterprises mobile home park. The supreme court affirmed the builder's remedy in order to permit the park to be built in Mount Laurel Township. However, the Mount Laurel sewer authority does not have sufficient capacity to service the mobile home park (an issue that is currently in litigation), and the development site is classified as farmland by the U.S. Department of Agriculture." Id. at p. 7.

29. 38 N.Y.2d 102, 378 N.Y.S.2d 672, 341 N.E.2d 236 (1975).

30. 38 N.Y.2d at 109, 378 N.Y.S.2d at 679–680, 341 N.E.2d at 241.

31. Berenson v. Town of New Castle, 67 A.2d 506, 415 N.Y.S.2d 669 (1979).

In a later case,[32] the New York Court of Appeals seemingly modified its *Berenson* ruling somewhat, holding that a zoning ordinance alleged to be "exclusionary" is still entitled to the traditional presumption of validity unless it shows on its face that it was enacted for an impermissible purpose; and that this presumption can only be rebutted by showing that the ordinance was, in fact, enacted for an impermissible purpose or "without proper regard to local and regional housing needs and has an exclusionary effect." [33] On the facts, the Court held that a five-acre minimum lot size requirement "within a coherent area characterized by estate-type development * * * and generally bounded by properties developed on a large lot basis" was valid. The Court said the large lot zoning was not facially invalid because such zoning may have legitimate purposes—e.g., preservation of open space. And the Court found insufficient proof of either an improper purpose or of exclusionary effect—e.g., "no proof that persons of low or moderate incomes were foreclosed from housing in the general region because of the unavailability of properly zoned land." [34]

Pennsylvania, like New Jersey and New York, has in recent years developed rules invalidating exclusionary zoning. In Township of Williston v. Chesterdale Farms,[35] the Pennsylvania Supreme Court seemed to adopt the New Jersey "fair share" rule. But in Surrick v. Zoning Hearing Bd.,[36] the Court said that the "fair share" doctrine stated only a "general precept" and proceeded to apply a substantive due process test—"whether the zoning formulas fashioned by [local government] entities reflect a balanced and weighted consideration of the many factors that bear upon local and regional housing needs and development" [37]—as a basis for invalidating the almost total exclusion of apartments from a Philadelphia suburb. (Total exclusion of apartments had been held invalid much earlier.) For the benefit of Pennsylvania trial courts, the Supreme Court further stated that, if a trial court determines that a particular municipality is a logical place for high density housing development because it is part of a growing metropolitan area and has land available for such development, the court should apply an "exclusionary impact" test to determine whether the zoning ordinance denies substantive due process. Thus a zoning ordinance that zones a disproportionately small portion of the municipal area for multifamily development may be invalid although it does not totally exclude such development.[38]

The Pennsylvania intermediate appellate court has generally adhered to the *Surrick* doctrine,[39] although it has sometimes seemed more cautious than the Pennsylvania Supreme Court in exclusionary zoning cases. The post-*Surrick* cases in the intermediate appellate court have refused to interpret

---

32. Kurzius, Inc. v. Incorporated Village of Upper Brookville, 51 N.Y.2d 338, 434 N.Y.S.2d 180, 414 N.E.2d 680 (1980), cert. denied 450 U.S. 1042, 101 S.Ct. 1761, 68 L.Ed.2d 240 (1981).

33. 51 N.Y.2d at 344–345, 434 N.Y.S.2d at 182–183, 414 N.E.2d at 683–684.

34. 51 N.Y.2d at 345–347, 434 N.Y.S.2d at 183–185, 414 N.E.2d at 684–685.

35. 462 Pa. 445, 341 A.2d 466 (1975).

36. 476 Pa. 182, 382 A.2d 105 (1977).

37. 476 Pa. at 191, 382 A.2d at 109–110.

38. 476 Pa. at 194–195, 382 A.2d at 111.

39. E.g., In re Appeal of Elocin, Inc., 66

the most recent (but pre-*Surrick*) Supreme Court case [40] as holding minimum lot sizes greater than one acre to be invalid *per se,* and have either sustained or struck down large lot size requirements depending on whether the land available for higher density development was sufficient to accommodate metropolitan growth or not.[41] When existing zoning regulations are invalidated in Pennsylvania, the "builder's remedy"—granting permission for his proposed development—is practically assured by statutes (codifying prior case law) providing for that remedy if the developer's site is suitable for the proposed development and public facilities available at that site are adequate.[42]

The New Hampshire Supreme Court recently struck down a town zoning ordinance effectively limiting "affordable" housing to only 1.7 percent of the town's areas and requiring developers to pay for experts to assist the town in assessing the impact of any proposed planning unit developments.[43] In addition, the court awarded a "builder's remedy" to the plaintiff developer.[44] The New Hampshire court did not impose a *Mount Laurel* II duty with respect to accommodation of a "fair share of the regional need for low and moderate income housing" as a basis for calculating how many new housing units a municipality should seek to accommodate. But the recently established New Hampshire regional planning process [45] has already produced "fair share" numbers for each municipality in each planning region.[46] In

Pa.Cmwlth. 28, 443 A.2d 1333 (1982).

40. Appeal of Concord Township, 439 Pa. 466, 268 A.2d 765 (1970).

41. See, e.g., Martin v. Township of Millcreek, 50 Pa.Cmwlth. 249, 413 A.2d 764 (1980); Application of Wetherill, 45 Pa.Cmwlth. 303, 406 A.2d 827 (1979). These decisions were foreshadowed in DeCaro v. Washington Township, 21 Pa.Cmwlth. 252, 344 A.2d 725 (1975).

42. 53 Penn.Stat. §§ 10609.1, 11004(1)(c), 11011(2).

43. Britton v. Town of Chester, 134 N.H. 434, 595 A.2d 492 (1991). The term "affordable" is now in common use to describe what was called "low- and moderate-income" housing in *Mount Laurel* II. The *Britton* decision, unlike the two *Mount Laurel* decisions, was not constitutionally based; instead it was based entirely on the New Hampshire court's holding that the town's existing zoning ordinance did not promote "the health, safety, or the general welfare of the community" and hence was *ultra vires* because it did not advance the purposes set forth in New Hampshire's zoning enabling act.

44. In awarding a "builder's remedy," the New Hampshire court explicitly rejected the *Mount Laurel* II holding that the victorious builder-plaintiff in an "exclusionary zoning" case is virtually entitled to a "builder's remedy". Under *Britton,* it is clearly discretionary with the court whether to grant a "builder's remedy" or not.

45. Statutory provisions authorizing creation of regional planning commissions and defining their powers are contained in

N.H.Rev.Stat.Ann. §§ 36.45 through 36.58 (1986 and 1991 Cum.Supp.). Id. § 36.47, Para. 1, provides (*inter alia*) that "[a] regional planning commission's powers shall be advisory, and shall generally pertain to the development of the region within its jurisdiction as a whole. * * * The area of jurisdiction of a regional planning commission shall include the areas of the respective municipalities within the delineated planning region." In *Britton,* the court made no attempt to delineate the "region" of which Chester was a part. It was, in fact, located within the Southern New Hampshire Planning Commission Region, for which the Southern New Hampshire Planning Commission had (in June, 1988) completed the "housing element of the Land Use Plan 2010" which identified a total "affordable housing" need for the region of 8,322 units based on the 1980 census. Chester's adjusted "fair share" allocation was 90 units. Chester's own master plan, which assumed the relevant region to be Rockingham County, called for 67 units of "affordable housing." Amicus Curiae Brief in Britton v. Town of Chester, supra note 43, reprinted in 40 Wash. U.J. of Urban & Contemp.Law 3, at 20 n. 50.

46. Payne, Exclusionary Zoning and the "Chester Doctrine," 20 Real Est.L.J. 366, at 327 (1992) ("the most sensible conclusion is that in revising its ordinance Chester must acknowledge the state's fair share calculation unless it can explain why that calculation is incorrect, and it must rezone sufficient land with affordability controls (inclusionary zoning) to meet that obligation unless it can demonstrate that the need will be met in other ways").

the future it seems probable that the New Hampshire courts will require municipalities to use these "fair share" numbers as a basis for rezoning land for the construction of "affordable housing".

There is language in some Michigan court opinions [47] and in the state's township zoning enabling act [48] indicating that exclusionary zoning may be invalid there. And the California Supreme Court recently adverted to "the conflict between * * * [s]uburban residents who seek to overcome problems of inadequate schools and public facilities" and who "may assert a vital interest in limiting immigration to their community," and "[o]utsiders searching for a place to live in the face of a growing shortage of adequate housing, and hoping to share in the perceived benefits of suburban life, [who] may present a countervailing interest opposing barriers to immigration." [49] But in most states the courts have not yet been forced to consider seriously the exclusionary zoning problem. And even if exclusionary zoning cases do come before the courts in states other than New Hampshire, New Jersey, New York and Pennsylvania in the next few years, it seems unlikely that courts in states where the judges must face the electorate will undertake the deep involvement in politically sensitive local decision-making demanded by the New Jersey Court's decision in *Mount Laurel* II.[50]

Although elaborate "growth management" programs of the sort considered in a later section of this book [51] are likely to have a substantial "exclusionary" effect, the leading decisions upholding such programs, while recognizing their "exclusionary" potential, conclude that the particular "growth management" programs before the court were not, in fact, "exclusionary." [52]

§ 9.13 State "Inclusionary Zoning" Legislation

(a) The New Jersey Legislation

In 1985 the New Jersey legislature enacted a Fair Housing Law [1] which restates the *Mount Laurel* I requirements that every municipality in a "growth area" has a constitutional duty to provide through its land use regulations a realistic opportunity for a fair share of its region's present and prospective need for housing for low- and moderate-income families, and

---

47. See Kropf v. City of Sterling Heights, 391 Mich. 139, 155–156, 215 N.W.2d 179, 185 (1974).

48. Mich.Comp.Laws Ann. §§ 125, 297a (township zoning act), 125.592 (city and village zoning act).

49. Associated Home Builders v. City of Livermore, 18 Cal.3d 582, 608–609, 135 Cal. Rptr. 41, 56–57, 557 P.2d 473, 488, 92 A.L.R.3d 1038 (1976).

50. For a warning that such involvement may require the New Jersey courts to undertake legislative and administrative tasks for which they are not well-equipped, see the opinions of Schreiber, Mountain, and Clifford, JJ., concurring in part and dissenting in part, in Oakwood at Madison v. Township of Madison, 72 N.J. at 619–638, 371 A.2d at 1261–1271

(1977). See also Judge Conford's opinion for the majority in Pascack Association, Limited v. Township of Washington, 74 N.J. 470, 379 A.2d 6 (1977).

51. Post Section 9.18.

52. See Associated Home Builders Ass'n case, supra note 49, which challenged the validity of a moratorium on issuance of residential building permits. As the court noted, "it impartially bans all residential construction, expensive or inexpensive * * * [and] plaintiff * * * has eschewed reliance upon any claim that the ordinance discriminates on a basis of race or wealth." 18 Cal.3d at 602, 135 Cal. Rptr. at 52, 557 P.2d at 484.

§ 9.13

1. N.J.Stat.Ann. §§ 52:27D–301 through –304.

which then prescribes a variety of methods to fulfill the *Mount Laurel* requirements. More specifically, the Fair Housing Law provides for:

(1) the creation of a Council of Affordable Housing to determine regions in the state and calculate regional housing needs and municipal fair shares of those needs; (2) a procedure by which municipalities may obtain "substantive certification" of their zoning ordinances; (3) a mediation and review process to hear objections to a municipality's petition for substantive review; (4) a procedure by which a municipality may propose that a portion of its fair share be met through a "regional contribution agreement"; (5) a procedure by which a defendant municipality may be allowed to "phase in" its fair share obligation; (6) a program of financial assistance to help municipalities provide affordable low- and moderate-income housing; (7) authorization for the State Housing and Mortgage Finance Agency to administer resale controls, rent controls, and other aspects of administration of the low- and moderate-income housing; (8) a temporary moratorium on the builder's remedy; (9) amendment of the zoning enabling legislation requiring a housing element to be part of the municipal master plan; and (10) a six-year period of repose for municipalities that settle zoning legislation.[2]

The New Jersey Fair Housing Act establishes a new state agency, a Council on Affordable Housing, with "primary jurisdiction for the administration of housing obligations in accordance with sound regional planning considerations."[3] This means that the Council, in cooperation with New Jersey municipalities, has the responsibility for dividing New Jersey into "housing regions" and establishing the local "fair shares" of low- and moderate-income housing to be assigned to each municipality. The Council, since its establishment, has divided the state into six regions, each consisting of two to four counties; has established guidelines for determining the fair shares for each municipality; and has made an estimate of the total need for low- and moderate-income housing for the state and for each region. The Council is authorized to certify municipal housing plans, including its fair share estimates, and has the power to modify the fair share estimates submitted by municipalities.

The heart of the New Jersey Fair Housing Act is a section[4] which provides as follows:

"A municipality's housing element shall be designed to achieve the goal of access to affordable housing to meet present and prospective housing needs, with particular attention to low- and moderate-income housing, and shall contain at least:

"a. An inventory of the municipality's housing stock by age, condition, purchase or rental value, occupancy characteristics, and type, including the number of units affordable to low- and moderate-income households and substandard housing capable of being rehabilitated, and in conducting this inventory the municipality shall have access, on a confidential basis for the sole purpose of conducting the inventory, to all

2. This summary is drawn from Rose, New Jersey Enacts a Fair Housing Law, 14 Real Est.L.J. 195, at 196 (1986).

3. N.J.Stat.Ann. § 52:27D–304.

4. Id. § 52:27D–310.

necessary property tax assessment records and information in the assessor's office, including but not limited to the property record cards;

"b. A projection of the municipality's housing stock, including the probable future construction of low and moderate income housing, for the next six years, taking into account, but not necessarily limited to, construction permits issued, approvals of applications for development and probable residential development of lands;

"c. An analysis of the municipality's demographic characteristics, including but not necessarily limited to, household size, income level and age;

"d. An analysis of the existing and probable future employment characteristics of the municipality;

"e. A determination of the municipality's present and prospective fair share for low and moderate income housing and its capacity to accommodate its present and prospective housing needs, including its fair share for low and moderate income housing; and

"f. A consideration of the lands that are most appropriate for construction of low and moderate income housing and of the existing structures most appropriate for conversion to, or rehabilitation for, low and moderate income housing, including a consideration of lands of developers who have expressed a commitment to provide low and moderate income housing."

The Fair Housing Act[5] requires a municipality to "establish that its land use and other relevant ordinances have been revised to incorporate the provisions for low and moderate income housing" contained in its housing plan element; and further requires a municipality, in preparing the housing plan, to "consider the following techniques for providing low and moderate income housing within the municipality, as well as such other techniques as may be published by the council [Council on Affordable Housing] or proposed by the municipality:

"(1) Rezoning for densities necessary to assure the economic viability of any inclusionary developments, either through mandatory set-asides or density bonuses, as may be necessary to meet all or part of the municipality's fair share;

"(2) Determination of the total residential zoning necessary to assure that the municipality's fair share is achieved;

"(3) Determination of measures that the municipality will take to assure that low and moderate income units remain affordable to low and moderate income households for an appropriate period of not less than six years;

"(4) A plan for infrastructure expansion and rehabilitation if necessary to assure the achievement of the municipality's fair share of low and moderate income housing;

---

5.   Id. § 52:27D–311.

"(5) Donation or use of municipally owned land or land condemned by the municipality for purposes of providing low and moderate income housing;

"(6) Tax abatements for purposes of providing low and moderate income housing;

"(7) Utilization of funds obtained from any State or federal subsidy toward the construction of low and moderate income housing; and

"(8) Utilization of municipally generated funds towards the construction of low and moderate income housing."

Compliance with the foregoing provisions is a prerequisite to exercise of the zoning power because the zoning enabling act requires adoption of the "land use plan element and the housing plan element" of the municipal "master plan" before a municipality can either adopt or amend a zoning ordinance.[6]

Flexibility in pursuit of the objectives of the Fair Housing Act is sought to be provided by a section [7] that authorizes any municipality, after substantive certification of its housing plan element by the Council on Affordable Housing, to transfer up to fifty percent of its "fair share" housing units (not including any part of its "indigenous need") to another municipality in the same region by a "regional cooperation agreement," subject to the approval of the Council and County Planning Board. At least one-half of the units transferred must be in the low-income category. Regional cooperation agreements provide for monetary contributions by the "sending" to the "receiving" municipality (usually $15,000 to $25,000 per unit at the present time), and state funds are available to the "receiving" municipality to assist in the rehabilitation of older housing for low- and moderate-income persons.

The constitutionality of the Fair Housing Law was established by Hills Dev. Co. v. Township of Bernards.[8] The New Jersey Supreme Court, recognizing that the Law "represents an unprecedented willingness by the Governor and the Legislature to face the *Mount Laurel* issue after unprecedented decisions by this Court," held that (1) the constitutional obligation of municipalities to provide fair shares of lower income housing does not contain any implicit time table; (2) delay in the satisfaction of this constitutional obligation, when required in order to allow the Council on Affordable Housing to do its job well, does not render the Law unconstitutional; (3) since the builder's remedy is not constitutionally mandated, the moratorium on that remedy imposed by the Law is not unconstitutional; (4) since the Law does not preclude judicial review of a municipal ordinance once the Council of Affordable Housing has acted on that ordinance or a municipality is sued before the Council has acted, the Law does not interfere impermissibly with the right of judicial review under the New Jersey constitutional provision prohibiting interference with the Supreme Court's exclusive control over actions in lieu of prerogative writs; (5) the presumption of correctness attached to the Council on Affordable Housing's determinations as to whether a municipality's constitutional obligation to provide its fair share of lower income housing is satisfied does not strip the judiciary of its power to invalidate illegal or unconstitutional actions and thus does not violate the

6. Id. § 40:44D–62.
7. Id. § 52:27D–312.

8. 103 N.J. 1, 510 A.2d 621 (1986).

right of judicial review under the New Jersey Constitution; (6) the moratorium on the judicial grant of the builder's remedy does not constitute a usurpation of the judiciary's exclusive constitutional power to prescribe the relief to be granted in any action in lieu of prerogative writs. Moreover, the Court held, even if it were to find a constitutional requirement that the courts must grant a builder's remedy in certain or all cases where a builder's action results in enforcement of a municipality's fair share obligation, the Court would recognize the legislative moratorium as a matter of comity.

Although the court recognized that it was possible that "the Act simply will not achieve the construction of lower income housing," it said that it could not declare the Act unconstitutional on the basis of mere "speculation," and that the presumption of constitutionality must prevail.[9] But the court indicated that it was not relinquishing its right to reassert judicial control in ringing language: [10]

> "No one should assume that our exercise of comity today signals a weakening of our resolve to enforce the constitutional rights of New Jersey's lower income citizens. The constitutional obligation has not changed; the judiciary's ultimate duty to enforce it has not changed; our determination to perform that duty has not changed."

The New Jersey Fair Housing Act has been subjected to a good deal of criticism. Much of the criticism has been aimed at the Act's provision for transfer of up to fifty percent of one municipality's "fair share" obligation to another municipality in the same region pursuant to a "regional contribution agreement" approved by the Council on Affordable Housing and the county planning board. A "regional contribution agreement" allows the "fair share" transfer upon payment of agreed compensation by the "sending" district to the "receiving" district. One critic[11] has argued that such agreements, intended to "provide a way for suburban municipalities to compensate cities for the burden they bear as a result of the suburbs' exclusionary zoning laws"—the burden of absorbing "poor and underemployed people who are drawn to the region by its economic development but who cannot earn wages sufficient to enable them to afford decent housing

---

9. Id. at 43, 510 A.2d at 643.

10. Id. at 65, 510 A.2d at 653. The New Jersey courts have approved most of the regulations adopted by the Council on Affordable Housing establishing rules for determination of municipal "fair shares." See Township of Bernards v. State Dept. of Community Affairs, 233 N.J.Super. 1, 558 A.2d 1 (App.Div.1989), certification denied 118 N.J. 194, 570 A.2d 959 (1989); In re Tp. of Warren, 247 N.J.Super. 146, 588 A.2d 1227 (App.Div.1991), cert. denied 127 N.J. 557, 606 A.2d 369 (1992); In re Petition by Tp. of Denville, 247 N.J.Super. 186, 588 A.2d 1248 (App.Div.1991), certification denied 127 N.J. 557, 606 A.2d 369 (1992); In re Petition by Tp. of Roseland, 247 N.J.Super. 203, 588 A.2d 1256 (App.Div.1991), cert. denied 127 N.J. 557, 606 A.2d 369 (1992). See also Van Dalen v. Washington Tp., 120 N.J. 234, 576 A.2d 819 (1990) (Council on Affordable Housing has discretion to use State Devel-

opment Guide Plan in allocating a municipality's "fair share" of low- and moderate-income housing, although that plan was never officially adopted). Partly in response to Mount Laurel II, the legislature adopted a new State Planning Act authorizing a new State Planning Commission to prepare a State Development and Redevelopment Plan. See N.J.Stat.Ann. §§ 52:18A–196 through 52:18A–207. The Plan, which is expected to be completed in 1993, is to "provide a coordinated, integrated and comprehensive plan for the growth, development, renewal and conservation of the State and its regions and * * * shall identify areas for growth, agriculture, open space conservation and other appropriate designations." Id. § 52:18A–199(a).

11. McDougall, Regional Contribution Agreements: Compensation for Exclusionary Zoning, 60 Temple L.Q. 665, at 666–667, 691 (1987).

there"—are likely to prove effective in correcting inequities between suburbs and central cities in view of the "real bargain imbalance between suburbs and cities." Another critic [12] has taken the same view, noting that "to the extent the new inexpensive housing is * * * placed in older urban centers, the program does not deal with some of the broader issues involved in exclusionary zoning—access to new suburban jobs and to better suburban schools. And still another critic [13] has asserted that the Council on Affordable Housing has "drawn regional housing lines so that the greatest sources of need (in the older, urban counties) are walled-off from the greatest source of supply (in the rapidly developing central part of the state)." [14]

The only empirical study of the results of enactment of the New Jersey Fair Housing Act, published in 1989,[15] reveals the following facts: [16]

> The survey of 54 municipalities which have affordable housing plans discloses a total of 2,830 units completed, either in set-aside developments or through other methods. An additional 11,133 units are under development and are either being built or are very likely to be built over the next few years, bringing a total of actual or likely units to slightly over 14,000. A further 8,740 units have been proposed by the affordable housing plans but have not yet reached the stage of specific development.

> Two distinct patterns of construction of affordable units have emerged. Among units in set-aside developments built by the private sector, sale units predominate. Age-restricted units are not a major component of set-aside developments. The dominance of inclusionary developments in meeting municipal housing obligations, moreover, emphasizes the extent to which New Jersey's affordable housing policy is tied to prevailing economic forces, which have produced a robust housing market in recent years but which could see diminished opportunity in times of economic retrenchment.

> Housing built through other methods, usually by non-profit agencies or the public sector, compensates for the imbalances in set-aside developments to some extent by providing more low-income units and more rentals. However, because of the availability of federal subsidies for senior citizen housing, use of other methods tends to be dominated by age-restricted units, leaving younger low-income households seeking rental units with very few choices. In addition, the total number of units produced by other methods is much less than the number produced in set-aside developments, so that the set-aside pattern tends to dominate the overall numbers.

(b) Other State Legislation

Even without pressure from the courts, the legislatures in several states have recently adopted "inclusionary" housing legislation, and some local

---

12. N. Williams, Am. Land Planning Law § 66.61.50 (1991 Cum.Supp. at 27, n. 14).

13. Payne, Rethinking Fair Share: Enforcement of Affordable Housing Policies, 16 Real Est.L.J. 20, at 30 (1987).

14. See also Rose, supra note 2; The Fair Housing Act: Meeting the Mount Laurel Obligation With a Statewide Plan, 9 Seton Hall Legis.J. 585 (1986); Franzese, The New Jersey Supreme Court's Judicious Retreat, 18 Seton Hall L.Rev. 30 (1988).

15. Lamar, Mallach & Payne, Mount Laurel at Work: Affordable Housing in New Jersey, 1983–1988, 41 Rutgers L.Rev. 1197 (1989).

16. Id. at 1215.

governments have adopted "inclusionary" housing ordinances without the support of any state legislation on the subject. Among the states with "inclusionary" housing legislation, California and Oregon, in effect, impose a low- and moderate-income "fair share" requirement on local governments, while Massachusetts has a state agency—the Housing Appeals Committee—empowered to override local decisions that deny approval to federal- or state-subsidized low- or moderate-income housing projects.

As we have seen,[17] Oregon has adopted statewide land use planning and control legislation requiring all local governments to adopt both comprehensive plans and implement land use regulations that comply with state goals with respect to "matters of statewide concern" and with planning goals promulgated by the Oregon Land Conservation and Development Commission. The statute expressly declares that "availability of housing for persons of lower, middle and fixed income is a matter of statewide concern,"[18] and further provides that "[w]hen a need has been shown for housing within an urban growth boundary at particular price ranges and rent levels, needed housing shall be permitted in a zone of sufficient buildable land to satisfy that need."[19] And the statute defines "needed housing" as "housing that includes, but is not limited to, attached and detached single family housing for both owner and renter occupancy and manufactured homes * * * located in either mobile home parks or subdivisions."[20]

In order to carry out their statutory duties, Oregon local governments must determine and seek to meet housing needs at all income levels, but in doing so, they may determine how to designate "buildable lands"[21] and may provide for needed housing either by "as of right" zoning or by means of flexible zoning procedures such as floating zones and conditional use permits. Standards for such flexible procedures must be "clear and objective" and may not have the effect, either singly or in combination, "of discouraging the needed housing types through unreasonable cost or delay."[22]

California's statutory scheme is more complicated than Oregon's. The California comprehensive planning legislation requires inclusion of a "housing element" and a "housing program" in municipal and county comprehensive plans, which are themselves required.[23] The "housing element" of the local comprehensive plan must include an "assessment of housing needs and an inventory of resources and constraints relevant to the meeting of these needs."[24] The analysis of housing needs "shall include the locality's share of the regional housing need,"[25] and the statute specifies the criteria for distribution of the regional housing need, which is to be determined by regional councils of government or, where such councils do not exist, by the state housing and community development department:

17. See ante Section 9.10.

18. Or.Rev.Stat. 197.307(1)

19. Id. 197.307(2).

20. Id. 197.303.

21. " 'Buildable lands' means lands in urban or urbanizable areas that are suitable, available and necessary for residential uses." Or.Rev.Stat. 197.295(1).

22. Or.Rev.Stat. 197.307(4).

23. West's Ann.Cal.Gov.Code §§ 65583–65589.

24. Id. § 65583(a).

25. Id. § 65583(a)(1).

[T]he distribution of regional housing needs shall, based upon available data, take into consideration market demand for housing employment opportunities, the availability of suitable sites and public facilities, commuting patterns, type and tenure of housing need, and the housing needs of farmworkers. The distribution shall seek to avoid further impaction of localities with relatively high proportions of lower income households.[26]

The California planning and zoning legislation also prohibits discrimination against low- and moderate-income and governmentally assisted or subsidized housing,[27] requires local governments to "zone sufficient vacant land for residential use with appropriate standards * * * to meet housing needs as identified in the general plan," [28] provides that manufactured housing (including mobile homes) is a permitted use in single-family residence districts (subject to nondiscriminatory building and land use regulations),[29] and further provides that a local ordinance "directly" restricting building permits or buildable lots is "presumed to have an impact on the supply of residential lots available in the municipality and the surrounding area" so as to impose on the local government the burden of justifying such restrictions.[30] And, finally, the California legislation provides for a twenty-five percent "density bonus" or alternative incentives for residential developers who set aside at least twenty-five percent of their dwelling units for low- and/or moderate-income households.[31]

The Massachusetts "anti-snob zoning" law [32] proceeds on a different principle than the Oregon and California legislation. The Massachusetts statute authorizes a qualified developer to apply to a local board of appeals for approval of a subsidized low- or moderate-income housing project. The board may issue a comprehensive permit for the project, deny approval, or issue a permit subject to conditions.[33] The statutory standard for local board decisions is that proposed projects are to be approved if they are "consistent with local needs." [34] But the statute further provides that the local board need not approve a project if (1) "low- or moderate-income housing exists which is in excess of ten per cent of the [municipality's] housing units reported in the latest decennial census" or (2) such housing exists "on sites comprising one and one half per cent or more of the total land area zoned for residential, commercial or industrial use" or (3) "the application before the [local] board would result in the commencement of construction of such housing on sites comprising more than three-tenths of one per cent of such land area or ten acres, whichever is larger, in any one calendar year." [35] These qualifications substantially limit the impact of the Massachusetts law.

When a local housing board of appeals denies approval to a proposed low- and/or moderate-income housing project or imposes unacceptable conditions on approval, the developer may appeal to the state Housing Appeals

---

26. Id. § 65584.

27. Id. § 65008.

28. Id. § 65913.1.

29. Id. § 65852.2. Id. § 65852.7 makes a "mobilehome park" a "permitted use" on all land planned and zoned for residential land use as designated by the applicable general plan, subject to the local government's right to "require a use permit."

30. West's Ann.Cal.Evidence Code § 669.5.

31. West's Ann.Cal.Gov.Code §§ 65915–65918.

32. Mass.Gen.Laws Ann. c. 40B, §§ 20–23.

33. Id. c. 40B, § 21.

34. Id. c. 40B, § 23.

35. Id. c. 40B, § 20.

Committee.[36] If the Committee finds, in case of a denial, that the local board's decision was "unreasonable and not consistent with local needs," it must vacate the local board's decision and order issuance of a comprehensive permit for the proposed project.[37] And if, in the case of a conditional approval, the Committee finds that the local board's decision was "not consistent with local needs" and that the conditions imposed by the local board were "uneconomic," the Committee "shall order such board to modify or remove any such condition * * * so as to make the proposal no longer uneconomic." [38]

The Massachusetts Housing Appeals Committee cannot find the local board's action in denying or imposing conditions on approval of a proposed project inconsistent with local needs if the statutory conditions for board denial of project approval are satisfied.[39] If they are not satisfied, the Committee must balance the regional need for low- and moderate-income housing against the municipality's interest in enforcing its zoning and building regulations.[40] The Committee may find the conditions imposed on project approval to be "uneconomic" if, where the developer is a public agency or nonprofit corporation, it cannot build or operate the project without "financial loss" or, where the developer is a limited dividend corporation, it cannot "realize a reasonable return on the construction or operation of the project within the [rental] limits set by the subsidizing agency." [41]

The Massachusetts "anti-snob zoning" law was sustained in Board of Appeals of Hanover v. Housing Appeals Committee,[42] as against attack on the grounds that it violated the state Home Rule statute if construed to authorize the Committee to override local zoning regulations, that it constituted an improper delegation of power without adequate standards, and that it authorized illegal "spot zoning." Subsequent decisions have placed some restrictions on the Committee's power, however. For example, a municipality's decision to acquire for conservation purposes a tract of land to which an appeal was pending has been held not subject to Committee review,[43] and it has been held that the Committee may not authorize noncompliance with the state building code.[44]

Although prediction is hazardous, it seems likely that if and when new "inclusionary" housing programs are instituted in the future they will tend to follow the Oregon or California models rather than the Massachusetts model, and that they will result almost entirely from legislative rather than judicial initiative.

As previously indicated ante in Section 9.12, New Hampshire has enacted statutory provisions authorizing creation of regional planning commissions which have already identified a total "affordable housing" need for New Hampshire's "regions." [45] However, the powers of regional planning

---

36. Id. c. 40B, § 22.

37. Id. c. 40B, § 23.

38. Ibid.

39. Ibid.

40. Ibid.

41. Ibid.

42. 363 Mass. 339, 294 N.E.2d 393 (1973).

43. Town of Chelmsford v. DiBiase, 370 Mass. 90, 345 N.E.2d 373 (1976).

44. Board of Appeals v. Housing Appeals Committee, 4 Mass.App.Ct. 676, 357 N.E.2d 936 (1976).

45. See ante Section 9.12 n. 45.

commissions are only "advisory." [46]   Hence the allocation of "affordable housing" units and determinations of "fair shares" by regional planning commissions may have little practical effect unless the New Hampshire Supreme Court is willing to declare that municipalities are legally or constitutionally obligated to accept the determinations of the regional planning commissions.   In Britton v. Town of Chester, 134 N.H. 434, 595 A.2d 492 (1991), discussed ante in Section 9.12, the Court did not refer to the regional planning process in holding that a municipal zoning ordinance was invalid because it was "exclusionary" and did not promote "the general welfare.   Nor did the Court refer to a statutory provision enacted in 1990 [47] which provides as follows:

> All citizens of the state benefit from a balanced supply of housing which is affordable to persons and families of low and moderate income. Establishment of housing which is decent, safe, sanitary and affordable to low and moderate income persons and families is in the best interests of each community and the state of New Hampshire, and serves a vital public need.   Opportunity for development of such housing, including so-called cluster development and the development of multi-family structures, should not be prohibited or discouraged by use of municipal planning and zoning powers or by unreasonable interpretation of such powers.

As has previously been suggested,[48] it is possible and even likely that the New Hampshire Supreme Court in later cases will rely upon this statutory provision and utilize the "fair share of affordable housing" units determined by regional planning commissions as a basis for enforcing its declared hostility to "exclusionary" zoning.

§ 9.14   "Exclusionary Zoning" in the Federal Courts

Local zoning ordinances have occasionally been challenged in the federal courts either on constitutional "equal protection" grounds or on the ground that they violate the federal Fair Housing Act.   In either case, the plaintiff must allege and prove racial—not merely economic—discrimination.[1]   And since land developers are not generally interested in bringing "equal protection" suits which require a showing that the proposed development which is

---

46.   N.H.Rev.Stat.Ann. § 36.47 ("A regional planning commission's powers shall be advisory, and shall generally pertain to the development of the region within its jurisdiction").

47.   N.H.Rev.Stat.Ann. § 672:1, para. III–e, added by N.H.New Laws 1990, c. 174–1, para. III–d.   See also id. § 674:21, added in 1984 and amended in 1991, which authorizes the adoption of "innovative land use control ordinances" by New Hampshire municipalities. The list of "innovative land use controls" includes "inclusionary zoning," which is defined as follows:

" * * * land use control regulations which provide a voluntary incentive or benefit to a property owner in order to induce the property owner to produce housing units which are affordable to persons or families of low and moderate income * * * [including] but

not limited to, density bonuses, growth control exceptions, and a streamlined application procedure."

48.   Ante Section 9.12 at notecall 47.

§ 9.14

1.   It is clear that there is no "fundamental right" to housing as a matter of substantive due process under the Fourteenth Amendment—see Lindsey v. Normet, 405 U.S. 56, 92 S.Ct. 862, 31 L.Ed.2d 36 (1972) —and that discrimination against "the poor" does not violate the Fourteenth Amendment's equal protection clause if there is any rational basis for the legislative classification that results in such discrimination—see James v. Valtierra, 402 U.S. 137, 91 S.Ct. 1331, 28 L.Ed.2d 678 (1971).

blocked by the existing zoning regulations would be racially integrated, most "equal protection" suits have been brought by non-profit organizations interested in "opening up the suburbs" for blacks and hispanics. But cases brought by such non-profit organizations have rarely succeeded in producing a decision on the merits because of the restrictive "standing" rules developed by the Supreme Court.

The Supreme Court's "standing" rules now generally require a plaintiff to show that the local zoning regulations which are challenged on "equal protection" grounds have caused him or her to suffer "injury in fact" and to show that he or she would be personally benefited if the court should grant the relief sought.[2] In Warth v. Seldin,[3] where a number of non-resident plaintiffs (mainly non-profit organizations) challenged an ordinance zoning practically all of Penfield (New York, a suburb of Rochester) for single-family dwellings only, the court held that neither requirement was met, stating that there must be proof of "specific, concrete facts demonstrating" harm to the plaintiffs caused by the existing zoning of Penfield, as well as proof that they "personally would benefit from the court's intervention." In a footnote,[4] the Court added that "usually the initial focus should be on a particular project." Although the federal courts have subsequently relaxed the "personal benefit" requirement a bit, so that a showing that the relief sought would probably benefit the plaintiff is sufficient to satisfy the "personal benefit" standing requirement,[5] the courts continue to find standing only where the allegedly exclusionary zoning has blocked a site-specific project which has at least gone beyond the planning stage.

Another barrier to granting relief on "equal protection" grounds in exclusionary zoning cases was erected in Village of Arlington Heights v. Metropolitan Housing Development Corp.,[6] where the Supreme Court held that an allegedly exclusionary zoning ordinance cannot be struck down on "equal protection" grounds unless there is proof of an actual racially discriminatory intent on the part of the local officials.[7] In an extended dictum,[8] the Court discussed the kinds of evidence that might tend to show discriminatory intent—evidence of "a clear pattern unexplainable on grounds other than race" even where "the governing legislation appears neutral on its face," and of substantive departures from an established zoning policy in reaching the zoning decision that barred the proposed site-specific project. Having concluded that the evidence was insufficient to "warrant overturning the concurrent findings of both courts below" that discriminatory intent was not proved in *Arlington Heights,* the Court remanded the case for further consideration of plaintiffs' claims that the refusal of the village to rezone for the proposed housing project constituted a

2. Warth v. Seldin, 422 U.S. 490, 95 S.Ct. 2197, 45 L.Ed.2d 343 (1975).

3. Supra note 2.

4. 422 U.S. at 508 n. 18, 95 S.Ct. at 2210 n. 18.

5. See Village of Arlington Heights v. Metropolitan Housing Development Corp., 429 U.S. 252, 97 S.Ct. 555, 50 L.Ed.2d 450 (1977), on remand 558 F.2d 1283 (7th Cir.1977), certiorari denied 434 U.S. 1025, 98 S.Ct. 752, 54 L.Ed.2d 772 (1978), on remand 469 F.Supp. 836

(N.D.Ill.1979), affirmed 616 F.2d 1006 (7th Cir. 1980).

6. Supra note 5.

7. 429 U.S. at 264, 97 S.Ct. at 563. In so holding, the Court relied on Washington v. Davis, 426 U.S. 229, 96 S.Ct. 2040, 48 L.Ed.2d 597 (1976), decided after the *Arlington Heights* case was decided by the 7th Circuit Court of Appeals.

8. 429 U.S. at 266, 97 S.Ct. 564.

violation of the federal Fair Housing Act (Title VIII of the Civil Rights Act of 1968).[9]

On remand in *Arlington Heights*,[10] the Seventh Circuit set out the following four-part test as a basis for determining whether a local decision not to rezone to permit construction of a site-specific housing project constitutes a violation of the Fair Housing Act: (1) is there "some evidence" of discriminatory intent (though not sufficient to amount to a denial of equal protection); (2) how substantial is the racially discriminatory effect; (3) did the municipality act within the scope of its statutory authority; and (4) does the plaintiff seek to compel the defendant to construct integrated housing or take affirmative steps to insure that integrated housing is built—in which case the courts ought to be more reluctant to grant relief—or does "the plaintiff only wish to build integrated housing on his own land and to enjoin the defendant from interfering with that construction—in which case the courts should be more willing to grant relief.

The Court of Appeals ultimately concluded, in *Arlington Heights*, that items (1) and (3) weighed in favor of the defendant, while item (4) weighed in favor of the plaintiff, and that item (2) should be decisive. After reviewing the evidence the Court decided [11] that the plaintiff was entitled to the relief sought—rezoning the proposed project site to permit the proposed development—unless the defendant could carry the burden of identifying a parcel of land within Arlington Heights both properly zoned and suitable for low-cost housing under federal standards; and that if the defendant failed to satisfy this burden, "the district court should conclude that the Village's refusal to rezone effectively precluded plaintiffs from constructing low-cost housing within Arlington Heights, and should grant plaintiffs the relief they seek."

It is hard to see how parts (1), (3), or (4) of the fourfold test proposed by the Seventh Circuit are relevant to the question whether the failure of a local governing body to rezone has a substantial enough racially discriminatory effect to constitute a violation of the Fair Housing Act. And it is questionable whether the court was justified in placing the burden of proof with respect to the availability of a suitable alternative project site on the defendant. But in a pre-*Arlington Heights* case, United States v. City of Black Jack,[12] the Eighth Circuit took an even more liberal view of the application of the Fair Housing Act to racially discriminatory exclusionary zoning. In *Black Jack,* the court held that proof of a total exclusion of multifamily housing created a *prima facie* case of racial discrimination which shifted to the defendant the burden of showing a "compelling governmental interest" that would justify such exclusionary zoning. This approach to litigation under the Fair Housing Act is, of course, substantially like the "strict scrutiny" approach generally adopted by the United States Supreme Court in racial discrimination cases under the equal protection clause of the Fourteenth Amendment.

9. 429 U.S. at 271, 97 S.Ct. 566.

10. Metropolitan Housing Development Corp. v. Village of Arlington Heights, 558 F.2d 1283 (7th Cir.1977), certiorari denied 434 U.S. 1025, 98 S.Ct. 752, 54 L.Ed.2d 772 (1978), on remand 469 F.Supp. 836 (N.D.Ill.1979), affirmed 616 F.2d 1006 (7th Cir.1980).

11. 558 F.2d at 1295.

12. 508 F.2d 1179 (8th Cir.1974), certiorari denied 422 U.S. 1042, 95 S.Ct. 2656, 45 L.Ed.2d 694 (1975), rehearing denied 423 U.S. 884, 96 S.Ct. 158, 46 L.Ed.2d 115 (1975).

In *Black Jack*[13] the Eighth Circuit concluded that the defendant's evidence as to the adverse effect of multifamily housing development on property values, road and traffic problems, and school overcrowding did not establish a "compelling government interest" and held the Black Jack zoning ordinance invalid insofar as it excluded all multifamily housing development. On the facts, it seems probable that the Supreme Court would, in any case, have found racially discriminatory intent on the basis of the "substantive departure" from prior zoning policy when the newly incorporated City of Black Jack zoned out all multifamily housing.

In United States v. City of Black Jack[14] there was, of course, no standing problem because the suit was brought by the United States on the basis of an express provision authorizing suits by the United States to enforce the Fair Housing Act of 1968. Such suits may be the best method of challenging racially discriminatory zoning, since the United States clearly has standing and no proof of discriminatory intent is required. The most recent large-scale suit of this type is United States v. City of Parma,[15] where the Sixth Circuit Court of Appeals sustained a sweeping District Court finding that Parma, Ohio was guilty of racial discrimination in violation of the 1968 Fair Housing Act.

The *City of Parma* finding of racial discrimination was based on an entire "pattern and practice" of racially discriminatory conduct, rather than the local zoning ordinance alone. Although the holding of the Supreme Court in *Arlington Heights* would seem to have made it unnecessary, both the trial and appellate courts found that Parma's land use regulations and municipal conduct in general were both motivated by a racially discriminatory intent and produced a racially discriminatory effect. The Court of Appeals also devoted part of its opinion to determining that the 1968 Fair Housing Act invalidates municipal as well as private discrimination, although this would hardly seem necessary after the *Black Jack* and *Arlington Heights* decisions. More important, however, the Court of Appeals not only affirmed the District Court's invalidation of Parma's ordinance requiring a public referendum on all proposals for construction of low-income housing, but also approved most of the extensive District Court remedial order requiring affirmative action by Parma. This order included requirements that Parma should adopt an educational program for the city officials and employees responsible for carrying out the order, adopt a resolution welcoming all persons of good will to the city, set up a fair housing committee to develop plans and to monitor compliance with the order, and participate in a variety of public housing and housing subsidy programs. On the other hand, the Court of Appeals set aside those portions of the District Court's order requiring the city to make all efforts to ensure that at least 133 units of low- and moderate-income housing should be constructed each year and appointing a special master to oversee the city's compliance with the order.

The most recent federal Fair Housing Act case is Huntington Branch, N.A.A.C.P. v. Town of Huntington,[16] where the Second Circuit adopted a somewhat different approach to the problem of racial discrimination in

---

13. Supra note 12.

14. Ibid.

15. 661 F.2d 562 (6th Cir.1981).

16. 844 F.2d 926 (2d Cir.1988).

housing. The Court of Appeals held that a plaintiff need not prove discriminatory intent in a case brought under the Fair Housing Act but may rely upon proof of discriminatory impact—as in cases brought under the federal Equal Employment Opportunity Act—in order to establish that a facially neutral government policy, such as a refusal to rezone, violates the Fair Housing Act. The Court held that the plaintiff had established a prima facie case by showing that the town's refusal to rezone land in a white neighborhood for federally subsidized multifamily housing had a discriminatory effect on black persons by showing that a larger proportion of blacks than whites needed affordable housing.[17] The Court further held that the Town had failed to justify this discriminatory impact by showing (1) that there was no feasible alternative, such as housing project design modifications, that would be less discriminatory; and (2) that there were bona fide and legitimate reasons for the town's refusal to rezone. The second prong of the Court's holding was based on its conclusion that the Town had failed to show a "substantial" government concern that would justify a decision not to rezone by a "reasonable" Town official. The Court granted site-specific relief to the plaintiff to remedy the Fair Housing Act violation.

The judgment of the Court of Appeals in *Huntington Branch* was affirmed by the United States Supreme Court in a per curiam opinion[18] stating that, "[w]ithout endorsing the precise analysis of the Court of Appeals, we are satisfied on this record that disparate impact was shown, and the justification proffered to rebut the *prima facie* case was inadequate." Although the Town argued that proof of "disparate impact," without proof of actual "discriminatory intent," should not justify a finding that the Fair Housing Act was violated, the Supreme Court refused, on technical grounds, to address this argument.[19]

One's confidence in the will and the ability of federal courts to bring about the practical results envisioned in their opinions is not strengthened by observing the ultimate outcome in the *Arlington Heights* case.[20] Instead of rezoning the original project site for the low-income housing which Metropolitan Housing Development Corporation sought to build, the village ultimately agreed to annex land located in an unincorporated area between Arlington Heights and Mount Prospect (a nearby municipality) and rezone it to conform with the Corporation's planned use, and this agreement was incorporated in a District Court consent decree.[21]

---

17. Rezoning of the land in question was sought by plaintiff because privately constructed multi-family housing was limited by the Huntington zoning ordinance to an urban renewal area largely occupied by racial minorities.

18. Town of Huntington v. Huntington Branch, N.A.A.C.P., 488 U.S. 15, 109 S.Ct. 276, 102 L.Ed.2d 180 (1988).

19. The grounds for refusal to address the issue were (1) the Court of Appeals' holding that the Town's refusal to rezone violated the Fair Housing Act should have been challenged by petition for certiorari rather than by appeal, and (2) that the Town had "conceded the applicability of the disparate impact test under Title VIII"—the Fair Housing Act—in a facial challenge to the zoning ordinance itself.

20. Supra note 6.

21. Metropolitan Housing Development Corp. v. Village of Arlington Heights, 469 F.Supp. 836 (N.D.Ill.1979), affirmed 616 F.2d 1006 (7th Cir.1980).

C.   NON–ZONING LAND USE CONTROLS

§ 9.15   Subdivision Control and Site Plan Review—In General

Another important technique of governmental land use control—separate from but closely related to "zoning"—is "land subdivision control." Raw land which is used for agriculture or other non-urban purposes is usually held in relatively large tracts. If it is to be made available for single-family residential development, it must first be subdivided into blocks and lots which are suitable as sites for residential structures.[1] Thus the subdivision of raw land provides a strategic point at which local governments may intervene to control the pattern of future urban land development.

The regulation of the land subdivision process in the United States began long before 1900. Indeed, the rectangular survey of the public domain of the United States carried out pursuant to the Northwest Ordinance of 1785 constituted a rudimentary framework for control of land subdivision, since subsequent transfers of surveyed farm land usually involved survey "sections" or some fraction thereof, such as a "quarter-section." After 1844 so-called "town site laws" were passed to regulate the division of public domain lands for town development. But both the federal statutes dealing with the public domain and the early state statutes regulating land subdivision were primarily designed to assure that adequate engineering data would be supplied and that recorded subdivision plats would be as accurate as possible. As late as 1928, only a few states had legislation imposing any substantial design or infrastructure requirements upon subdividers.[2]

Drawing on existing New York land planning and subdivision control legislation, a committee appointed by the United States Department of Commerce prepared and, in 1928, published the Standard City Planning Enabling Act.[3] Title I of the Standard Act was concerned with "planning" in the literal sense and authorized municipalities to create planning commissions which were authorized and directed "to make and adopt a master plan for the physical development of the municipality, including any areas outside of its boundaries which, in the commission's judgment, bear relation to the planning of such municipality." Title II of the Standard Act authorized any municipal planning commission, after "adopting a major street plan of the territory within its subdivision jurisdiction or part thereof," to "adopt regulations governing the subdivision of land within its jurisdiction" and providing for

> the proper arrangement of streets in relation to other existing streets and to the master plan, for adequate and convenient open spaces for traffic, utilities, access of fire-fighting apparatus, recreation, light and air, and for the avoidance of congestion of population, including minimum width and area of lots.[4]

---

§ 9.15

1. Subdivision of a tract may also be required in some cases when a large-scale industrial or commercial development is contemplated—e.g., when a developer initiates an "industrial village" development.

2. Generally, see Melli, Subdivision Control in Wisconsin, 1953 Wis.L.Rev. 389.

3. The Standard Act (hereafter termed SCPEA) is no longer in print in its original form as a publication of the U.S. Dept. of Commerce, but it is reprinted in full, with the draftsmen's footnotes, as Appendix B in Am. L.Inst., Model Land Development Code, Tentative Draft 1 (1968).

4. SCPEA §§ 13, 14 (1928).

Although minimum lot width and area requirements are usually contained in the local zoning ordinance, they are sometimes included in the subdivision regulations. See also Town of Sun Prairie v. Storms, 110 Wis.2d 58, 327 N.W.2d 642 (1983), holding that municipalities may enforce minimum lot size requirements, pursuant to a statute fixing mini-

The Standard Act defined the "subdivision jurisdiction" of a municipal planning commission as including all land within the corporate limits of a municipality and "all land lying within 5 miles of the corporate limits of the municipality and not located in any other municipality."[5] Within this jurisdiction, a municipal planning commission was, in effect, both a legislative body in enacting subdivision regulations and an administrative body in applying the regulations to individual applications for subdivision plat approval. Some of the current enabling statutes also provide for extraterritorial exercise of the subdivision control power.[6] Although rarely challenged, the grant of extra-territorial jurisdiction has generally been sustained.[7]

The Standard Act substantially restricted the power of a municipality to accept or improve new streets, to install or authorize installation of utility lines in new streets, or to issue permits for building construction on new streets after the municipal planning commission adopted a major street plan, unless the new streets were within a subdivision approved by the planning commission.[8] In addition, the Standard Act provided that, where a major street plan had been adopted, "no plat of a subdivision * * * shall be filed or recorded until it shall have been approved by such planning commission,"[9] and further provided for the imposition of a civil penalty or the issuance of an injunction whenever a subdivider "transfers or sells or agrees to sell or negotiates to sell any land by reference to or exhibition of or by other use of a plat of a subdivision, before such plat has been approved by the planning commission and recorded," even if the land is sold or conveyed by "metes and bounds."[10]

Most current subdivision control enabling legislation can be traced back either to Title II of the Standard City Planning Act or to one of the Model Municipal Subdivision Regulation Acts published in the Harvard City Planning Series in the mid–1930's.[11] The latter were principally drafted by persons who had participated in drafting the Standard Act,[12] and did not differ substantially from the Standard Act. Many current subdivision control enabling statutes authorize local agencies to require subdividers to install an even wider range of infrastructure "improvements" than did the Standard Act;[13] authorize local agencies to require subdividers to convey or dedicate land to the local government or to a school district for use as parks, playgrounds, or school sites;[14] require approval of subdivisions by specified local and state agencies such as health departments, water departments, and highway commissions;[15] and authorize local or state agencies to refuse

---

mum lots sizes on a statewide basis, although the requirements have not been adopted at the local level by procedures mandated for adoption of zoning regulations.

5. Id. § 12.

6. At least nineteen states have such provisions.

7. See, e.g., Petterson v. City of Naperville, 9 Ill.2d 233, 137 N.E.2d 371 (1956).

8. SCPEA § 15.

9. Id. § 13.

10. Id. § 16.

11. E.g., A. Bettman, Municipal Subdivision Regulation Act, in E. Bassett, A. Bettman, F. Williams & Whitten, Model Laws for Planning Cities, Counties and States (Harvard City Planning Series 1935).

12. The draftsmen were Edward Bassett and Alfred Bettman.

13. E.g., West's Ann.Cal.Gov.Code § 66419.

14. Id. §§ 66477, 66478.

15. E.g., Mich.Comp.Laws Ann. §§ 560.- 114–560.119.

subdivision approval entirely in certain instances.[16]   In some jurisdictions, the enabling statutes require local subdivision regulations to be adopted by the local governing body (after they have been prepared and recommended by the planning commission) [17] and/or require individual subdivision plats to be approved by the local governing body as well as by the planning commission.[18]

Some current subdivision control enabling statutes expressly provide that land subdivisions must comply with local zoning regulations,[19] and in the few cases where the issue has been litigated it has generally been held that local subdivision agencies have the power to deny approval of subdivision plats when the subdivision does not comply with the local zoning ordinance.[20]   In a few states, land subdivisions are expressly required to be consistent with the local comprehensive plan.[21]   In these states subdivision approval must be withheld if the subdivision is inconsistent with the plan, even if it fully complies with the local zoning and subdivision regulations.[22]

The Standard City Planning Enabling Act defined "subdivision" as "the division of a lot, tract, or parcel of land into two or more lots, plats, sites, or other divisions of land for the purpose, whether immediate or future, of sale or of building development." [23]   Most current subdivision statutes, however, either exempt or authorize the local authorities to exempt land subdivisions that create less than a specified number of new lots (e.g., four lots) or create only lots larger than a specified size (e.g., five acres), or that do not require creation of a new street.[24]

The subdivision control enabling acts generally authorize the local subdivision control agency—whether it is the planning board or the local governing body—to disapprove proposed subdivisions for failure to comply with the locally adopted subdivision regulations with respect to street, block, and lot layout, improvement of internal subdivision streets, and installation of utility lines.[25]   In addition, modern enabling acts often authorize rejection of proposed subdivisions on the ground that they would cause serious traffic problems because of the inadequacy of existing access by public roads, or on the ground that the peculiar topography or soil conditions of the site make it unsuitable for development until public water, sewer, or drainage facilities have been extended to the site.[26]   Rejection of proposed subdivisions on such grounds, when authorized by statute has generally been sustained.[27]   And in some cases it would seem that subdivision approval may be permanently

---

16. E.g., Ariz.Rev.Stat. § 9–463.01(C)(4); New Hamp.Rev.Stat.Ann. 36:21.

17. E.g., West's Ann.Cal.Gov.Code § 66411.

18. E.g., Mich.Comp.Laws Ann. §§ 560.120, 560.167.

19. E.g., New Jersey Stat.Ann. 40:55D–38(d). West's Ann.Cal.Gov.Code § 66473.5 requires compliance with local general plans.

20. See, e.g., People v. City of Park Ridge, 25 Ill.App. 424, 166 N.E.2d 635 (1960).

21. E.g., West's Ann.Cal.Gov.Code § 66473.5.

22. Ibid.

23. SCPEA § 1 (1928).

24. E.g., West's Ann.Cal.Gov.Code § 66426; Mich.Comp.Laws Ann. § 560.102(d); New Jersey Stat.Ann. 40:55D–7.

25. E.g., West's Ann.Cal.Gov.Code §§ 66474–66474.2; Mich.Comp.Laws Ann. §§ 560.105–560.106.

26. See, e.g., West's Ann.Cal.Gov.Code § 66474(c), (d), (f); Mich.Comp.Laws Ann. §§ 560.105(g), 560.114, 560.117, 560.118.

27. See, e.g., Garipay v. Town of Hanover, 116 N.H. 34, 351 A.2d 64 (1976) (inadequate public access road); Hamilton v. Planning Board, 4 Mass.App.Ct. 802, 345 N.E.2d 906 (1976); Christianson v. Gasvoda, 242 Mont. 212, 789 P.2d 1234 (1990) (flooding problems).

withheld—e.g., where the site of the proposed subdivision is located in the main floodway of a flood plain or in a wetlands area where dredging and filling are prohibited.[28]

Because subdivision controls are only applicable to land development involving subdivision of a substantial tract into smaller parcels ("lots"), local governments could not rely on their delegated subdivision control powers to regulate large-scale land development that did not require subdivision of the tract to be developed—e.g., many large-scale apartment and industrial projects. To deal with this problem, "site plan" review procedures were established by many communities during the 1960s without any express statutory authorization.[29] In a few early cases it was held that site plan review procedures were impliedly authorized by the zoning enabling acts, although not expressly mentioned therein, in connection with applications for variances, special exceptions (or special uses or conditional uses) or rezoning amendments.[30] More recently, a number of states have adopted enabling legislation expressly authorizing site plan review procedures.[31] In many states, however, the scope of the local power to impose site plan review requirements is still unclear.

Although site plan review procedures were originally designed to give local governments some control over the physical layout and facilities of land development that did not require subdivision of the land, some enabling legislation now permits local governments to require submission of site plans even where the land is to be subdivided.[32] Although such enabling legislation does not make this clear, the purpose is apparently to enable local governments to get an advance look at a proposed subdivision development— as well as a development not involving subdivision—when a request for rezoning to a classification that will permit the proposed development is submitted pursuant to the usual "wait and see" zoning practice. In addition, local governments have used the site plan review procedure as a basis for imposing requirements as to "[p]reservation of existing natural resources on the site; * * * [s]afe and efficient vehicular and pedestrian circulation, parking and loading; * * * [s]creening, landscaping and location of structures; * * * [e]xterior lighting needed for safety reasons in addition to any requirements for street lighting; and * * * [c]onservation of energy and use

---

28. See post Section 9.21.

29. Generally, see D. Mandelker, Land Use Law § 6.63 (1982); 5 N. Williams, Am.Land Planning Law § 152.01 (1975 and Supp.1982).

30. See, e.g., McCrann v. Town Plan and Zoning Commission, 161 Conn. 65, 282 A.2d 900 (1971); Sun Oil Co. v. Zoning Board of Adjustment, 403 Pa. 409, 169 A.2d 294 (1961); Wilson v. Borough of Mountainside, 42 N.J. 426, 201 A.2d 540 (1964). Contra: Coolidge v. Planning Board of North Andover, 337 Mass. 648, 151 N.E.2d 51 (1958).

31. E.g., Mich.Comp.Laws Ann. § 125.-584d; New Jersey Stat.Ann. 40:55D-44, 40:55D-46, 40:55D-46.1. New Jersey Stat.Ann. 40:55D-7 defines "site plan" as follows:

a development plan of one or more lots on which is shown (1) the existing and proposed conditions of the lot, including but not necessarily limited to topography, vegetation, drainage, flood plains, marshes and waterways, (2) the location of all existing and proposed buildings, drives, parking spaces, walkways, means of ingress and egress, drainage facilities, utility services, landscaping, structures and signs, lighting, and screening devices, and (3) any other information in order to make an informed determination pursuant to an ordinance requiring review and approval of site plans by the planning board * * *.

32. See definition of "site plan," supra note 31.

of renewable energy sources," [33] as well as monetary contributions for off-tract water, sewer, drainage, and street improvements,[34] and reservations of land for public use.[35]

§ 9.16 Subdivision and Site Plan Review Procedure

Local subdivision regulations usually specify the review procedure to be followed in obtaining approval of a "non-exempt" or "major" subdivision. Although it is usually not specifically authorized by statute, the initial stage is usually an informal "pre-application" review of the proposed subdivision based on a sketch map of the tract and a location map showing the relationship of the proposed subdivision to existing development and the community facilities required to service the subdivision.[1] The sketch map and location map are generally reviewed by the professional planning staff and other local officials such as the municipal engineer to determine whether the proposed subdivision is consistent with the local comprehensive land use plan (if any), whether it satisfies municipal subdivision design standards and improvement requirements, and whether the site is suitable with respect to topography, drainage, etc. The results of this informal review are then discussed with the subdivider, who is informed of any changes necessary to comply with the subdivision regulations and the comprehensive plan. Suggestions for improvement of the subdivision design are often made at this stage.

After the "pre-application" review, if any, the subdivider must usually submit a "tentative" or "preliminary" plat of the proposed subdivision to the planning commission.[2] While the name suggests that approval of this plat is only "tentative" or "preliminary," nothing could be further from the truth, for approval of the "tentative" or "preliminary" plat authorizes the laying out and improvement of streets, installation of sewer and utility lines and, in some cases, construction of houses.[3] Because the decision to approve or deny approval is so important, the subdivision regulations generally set out in considerable detail the information to be shown on or to accompany the "tentative" or "preliminary" plat.[4] The plat must be submitted in sufficient time and with enough copies to allow for consideration and recommendations by a variety of local agencies such as the municipal engineer, the public works department, the school board, and the health department.[5] Recommendations from all these agencies are usually received by the planning commission or local governing body before the public hearing on the

---

33. New Jersey Stat.Ann. 40:55D–7.

34. Id. 40:55D–42. Cf. N.Y.—McKinney's Town Law § 274, held not to authorize monetary exactions in Riegert Apartments Corp. v. Planning Bd. of Clarkstown, 57 N.Y.2d 206, 455 N.Y.S.2d 558, 441 N.E.2d 1076 (1982).

35. Id. 40:55D–44.

§ 9.16

1. This "pre-application" review is often not expressly authorized by the enabling act. See generally, Green, Land Subdivision, in Principles and Practice of Urban Planning

443, 449–454 (W. Goodman & E. Freund eds. 1968).

2. E.g., West's Ann.Cal.Gov.Code § 66426 ("tentative map"); Mich.Comp.Laws Ann. § 560.105 ("preliminary plat"); New Jersey Stat.Ann. 40:55D–48 ("preliminary * * * subdivision approval").

3. See Green, supra note 1.

4. E.g., Mich.Comp.Laws Ann. § 560.111.

5. E.g., West's Ann.Cal.Gov.Code §§ 66453–66455.7; Mich.Comp.Laws Ann. §§ 560.113–560.119.

proposed subdivision.[6] Before approval is granted, there is often a good deal of discussion and negotiation between the subdivider and the local authorities involved in subdivision review, and the parties often agree on modifications of the subdivision design, and/or the physical improvements required to be installed before final plat approval will be granted.

As previously indicated, "tentative" or "preliminary" plat approval usually authorizes the subdivider to proceed with installation of required utility lines and street improvements. The subdivision control statutes almost always require the subdivider to post a bond or other security guaranteeing completion of the required improvements.[7] Some statutes also authorize alternatives to construction of improvements by the subdivider, such as construction by the local government on the basis of its usual procedures for local improvements, with the cost levied as a special assessment against the subdivision lots, or formation of a new special local improvement district with power to issue bonds, make the required improvements, and recover the cost by levying a special assessment against the subdivision lots.[8]

Local subdivision regulations often authorize a subdivision developer to obtain building permits after his "tentative" or "preliminary" plat is approved and he has posted the required security for installation of all required utility lines and street improvements.[9] Since most subdivision developers now market lots improved by construction of houses rather than unimproved building lots, subdividers usually prefer to build their houses first in order to avoid wear and tear on street paving, gutters, curbs, sidewalks, and the like. But a subdivider needs assurance that he will not be required to make costly modifications as a result of changes in either the zoning or the subdivision regulations applicable to his development before he proceeds with construction of houses and/or installation of required street improvements. In a number of states, the subdivision control enabling statutes expressly provide that, after "tentative" or "preliminary" approval, the subdivider shall be protected for a stated period from any substantial change in the subdivision or zoning regulations.[10]

At any time within the period for which the "tentative" or "preliminary" subdivision approval has been granted, a subdivider may submit his "final" subdivision plat for approval, provided that installation of the re-

6. The planning board hearing must, of course, satisfy both statutory and constitutional due process requirements as to notice and opportunity of interested parties to be heard. Thus in Mutton Hill Estates, Inc. v. Town of Oakland, 468 A.2d 989 (Me.1983), appeal after remand 488 A.2d 151 (1985), the board's action in denying subdivision approval was vacated because the planning board had invited opponents of the proposed subdivision to assist in preparation of the findings of fact necessary to support the board's decision. Neither the developer nor any representative of the developer was given notice of or attended the meetings in which the findings were prepared; the board's decision was later announced at an open meeting attended by the developer's representative. The court also held that the de-

veloper was unlikely ever to receive a fair and expeditious hearing from the planning board and remanded the case to the trial court to determine whether the proposed subdivision should be approved.

7. E.g., West's Ann.Cal.Gov.Code §§ 66499 through 66499.10; Mich.Comp.Laws Ann. § 560.182(1)(e); New Jersey Stat.Ann. 40:55D–53.

8. E.g., West's Ann.Cal.Gov.Code § 66499.5.

9. See Green, supra note 1.

10. E.g., Mich.Comp.Laws Ann. § 560.120 (2 years); New Jersey Stat.Ann. 40:55D–49 (3 years).

quired utility lines and street improvements has been completed. The subdivider is usually allowed to submit different parts of his tract for final approval at different times, so that he can initially build houses on only part of the tract and thus reduce the amount he must initially borrow to finance construction.[11] Some municipalities report that they actually require two "final" plats—an "engineering" plat which sets out details of the construction and location of subdivision utility lines and street improvements, and a plat "for record," which contains information primarily significant with respect to land titles such as precise lot lines, street boundaries, utility easement locations, and the like.[12] Local subdivision regulations usually provide for submission and approval of the "final" plat in substantially the same manner as the "tentative" or "preliminary" plat. The primary concern of the local authorities at the "final" plat stage is to be sure that the "final" plat (or plats) are in conformity with the "tentative" or "preliminary" plat and that all required improvements have been properly completed.[13] Some subdivision ordinances provide for approval of the "final" plat (or plats) by the local governing body even though the planning commission has authority to approve the "tentative" or "preliminary" plat.[14]

In those instances where a subdivider has not yet obtained building permits for all planned housing construction prior to receiving "final" plat approval, he needs assurance—which is provided by some current subdivision control statutes—that there will be no substantial change in the zoning or subdivision regulations applicable to his subdivision for a reasonable period of time. Many subdivision control enabling acts now so provide.[15] Even in the absence of a protective statutory provision, a substantial change of position by the subdivider in reliance on his "final" plat approval may estop the municipality from substantially changing the zoning or subdivision regulations applicable to the subdivision.[16] But it is generally hard to convince a court that the subdivider has substantially changed position unless he has actually started construction of houses before the regulations are changed.[17]

Some subdivision control enabling statutes authorize local governing bodies to classify as "minor" certain types of subdivisions—e.g., subdivisions that require creation of no new streets, do not involve a planned unit development, and do not require extension of any off-site improvements.[18] The review procedures for such "minor" subdivisions are substantially

11. E.g., West's Ann.Cal.Gov.Code § 66456; New Jersey Stat.Ann. 40:55D–49(b).

12. See Green, supra note 1.

13. E.g., New Jersey Stat.Ann. 40:55D–50. But see West's Ann.Cal.Gov.Code § 66464 as to agreements relating to improvements not completed when a final map is approved.

14. See, e.g., West's Ann.Cal.Gov.Code §§ 66452, 66457, 66458.

15. E.g., New Jersey Stat.Ann. 40:55D–52 (2 years, with possible 1-year extensions up to a maximum of 3 years); 53 Penn.Stat. § 10508(4) (3 years).

16. E.g., Ward v. City of New Rochelle, 20 Misc.2d 122, 197 N.Y.S.2d 64 (1959), affirmed

9 A.D.2d 911, 197 N.Y.S.2d 128 (1959), motion denied 7 N.Y.2d 1026, 200 N.Y.S.2d 68, 166 N.E.2d 859 (1960), affirmed 8 N.Y.2d 895, 204 N.Y.S.2d 144, 168 N.E.2d 821 (1960).

17. E.g., Elsinore Property Owners Association v. Morwand Homes, 286 App.Div. 1105, 146 N.Y.S.2d 78 (1955); Telimar Homes, Inc. v. Miller, 14 A.D.2d 586, 218 N.Y.S.2d 175 (1961), appeal denied 14 A.D.2d 701, 219 N.Y.S.2d 937 (1961); Garvin v. Baker, 59 So.2d 360 (Fla.1952); Blevens v. City of Manchester, 103 N.H. 284, 170 A.2d 121 (1961).

18. See New Jersey Stat.Ann. 4:55D–5.

simpler and more expeditious than those required for "major" subdivisions.[19]

In states where a statute authorizes local governments to require site plan review and approval, site plan review procedures generally resemble subdivision review procedures, although the substantive standards are not identical.[20] In states where local governments may require review and approval of both site plans and subdivision plans, there is a considerable overlap. In at least one state, fortunately, the statute expressly authorizes the local planning board "to review and approve or deny conditional uses or site plans simultaneously with review for subdivision approval without the developer being required to make further application to the planning board, or the planning board being required to hold further hearings.[21] The effect of preliminary and final site plan approval is the same, with respect to protection of a land developer, as the effect of preliminary and final approval of a subdivision."[22]

Once approved, a site plan is treated like an approved subdivision plat; compliance with the plan as approved is enforced by suspension of building permits and/or refusal to permit connection with public water and sewer systems.

§ 9.17   Subdivision Exactions and Other Development Charges

(a) Subdivision Exactions

Section 14 of the Standard City Planning Act authorized local governments to require subdividers to install the basic subdivision infra-structure—i.e., improved streets, water, sewer, and other utility mains and piping, and other facilities—at their own expense as a condition precedent to subdivision approval.[1] After World War II, as the American middle class began its migration to the suburbs, many suburban communities, in an effort to make new residential subdivisions "pay their way," enacted subdivision regulations imposing requirements that go far beyond those authorized by the Standard Act—e.g., requirements for dedication and/or improvement of off-

---

19. See, e.g., id. 40:55D–47.

20. See, e.g., id. 40:55D–41, authorizing "standards and requirements" relating to the following:

     a. Preservation of existing natural resources on the site;

     b. Safe and efficient vehicular and pedestrian circulation parking and loading;

     c. Screening, landscaping and location of structures;

     d. Exterior lighting needed for safety reasons in addition to any requirements for street lighting; and

     e. Conservation of energy and use of renewable energy sources.

New Jersey Stat.Ann. 40:55D–5 authorizes the local governing body to create a "minor" site plan classification when a new development "does not involve planned development, any new street or extension of any off-tract improvement." The approval procedure for "mi-

nor" site plans under id. 40:55D–46.1 are simpler than that for approval of other site plans under id. 40:55D–46 and 40:55D–50, which require both "preliminary" and "final" approval.

See also Wesley Investment Co. v. County of Alameda, 151 Cal.App.3d 672, 198 Cal.Rptr. 872 (1984), holding that a county may reject a proposed development through its site plan review procedure where the development contemplated a land use (a "7-11" convenience store) permitted by the county zoning ordinance but the county site plan ordinance authorized an administrative denial of that use.

21. See, New Jersey Stat.Ann. 40:55D–51.

22. See, e.g., id. 40:55D–49, 40:55D–52.

§ 9.17

1. SCPEA § 14 (1928). This section also authorizes provision in the regulations for "adequate and convenient open spaces for * * * recreation."

site land, for dedication of subdivision land for recreational or school use, and for cash payments into a park or school fund in lieu of land dedication.[2] Under state enabling acts identical with or similar to the Standard Act, these heavier exactions have often been held *ultra vires*,[3] although language only slightly more specific than the Standard Act language has sometimes been held to authorize park and school dedication requirements, or even "in lieu" charges.[4] In some cases, "in lieu" charges have been held invalid as unauthorized taxes.[5] But in recent years a number of states have adopted new enabling legislation which expressly authorizes subdivision exactions that go beyond those authorized by the Standard Act.[6]

2. Provisions for "in lieu" cash payments are desirable where a subdivision is too small to justify requiring the subdivider to donate the necessary land within the subdivision, or where the local park or school plans call for a particular new subdivision to be served by a park or school located outside that subdivision.

3. E.g., Briar West, Inc. v. City of Lincoln, 206 Neb. 172, 291 N.W.2d 730 (1980); Hylton Enterprises, Inc. v. Board of Supervisors, 220 Va. 435, 258 S.E.2d 577 (1979); Admiral Development Corp. v. City of Maitland, 267 So.2d 860 (Fla.App.1972); Rosen v. Village of Downers Grove, 19 Ill.2d 448, 167 N.E.2d 230 (1960); Arrowhead Development Co. v. Livingston County Road Commission, 413 Mich. 505, 322 N.W.2d 702 (1982) (off-site improvements); West Park Avenue, Inc. v. Ocean Township, 48 N.J. 122, 224 A.2d 1 (1966); Haugen v. Gleason, 226 Or. 99, 359 P.2d 108 (1961). Contra: Divan Builders, Inc. v. Planning Board of Wayne Township, 66 N.J. 582, 334 A.2d 30 (1975) (off-site improvements); Hylton Enterprises, Inc. v. Board of Supervisors of Prince William County, 220 Va. 435, 258 S.E.2d 577 (1979) (off-site improvement requirement was *ultra vires*).

See also Board of County Supervisors of Prince William County v. Sie–Gray Developers, Inc., 230 Va. 24, 334 S.E.2d 542 (1985), distinguishing *Hylton,* supra, and holding that a "voluntary agreement" to improve an off-site highway was enforceable against the developer. In *Sie–Gray* the developer did not challenge the off-site improvement requirement—unlike the developer in *Hylton*—but "voluntarily" offered to make the off-site improvements in order to avoid difficulty in obtaining subdivision approval. Two dissenting justices argued that the agreement was not really "voluntary" and should not be enforced because the developer's only options were either to accede to an admittedly illegal exaction or to undergo the expense of a court challenge to the off-site improvement requirement.

4. E.g., Jordan v. Menomonee Falls, 28 Wis.2d 608, 137 N.W.2d 442 (1965), appeal dismissed 385 U.S. 4, 87 S.Ct. 36, 17 L.Ed.2d 3 (1966); Jenad, Inc. v. Village of Scarsdale, 18 N.Y.2d 78, 271 N.Y.S.2d 955, 218 N.E.2d 673 (1966).

5. Haugen v. Gleason, supra note 3.

6. E.g., Ariz.Rev.Stat. § 9–463.01(D) to (F); West's Ann.Cal.Gov.Code §§ 66477, 66478; Colo.Rev.Stat.1973, 30–28–133(4)(a); New Jersey Stat.Ann. 40:55D–42; 24 Vermont Stat. Ann. § 4417.

It is, however, important that local governments follow the statutory procedural requirements. See, e.g., Arnett v. City of Mobile, 449 So.2d 1222 (Ala.1984), where the court struck down a requirement that subdividers reserve areas outside the subdivision for future streets because the city failed either to estimate the duration of the reservation or to appoint a board to fix the amount of compensation to be paid when the city acquired the reserved land, as required by Ala.Code §§ 11–52–50, –51.

Many of the recent subdivision control enabling acts specifically authorize local planning boards to require subdivision developers to construct or contribute to the cost of constructing off-site public facilities. E.g., the New Jersey Land Use Law, enacted in 1976, authorizes a municipality "to pay his pro rata share of the cost of providing only reasonable and necessary street improvements and water, sewerage and drainage facilities * * * located outside the property limits of the subdivision * * * but necessitated * * * by construction or improvements within such subdivision." N.J.Stat.Ann. § 40:55D–42. In N.J. Builders Ass'n v. Bernards Tp., 108 N.J. 223, 528 A.2d 555 (1987), the New Jersey Supreme Court held that "the plain meaning and obvious legislative intent" in using this language "was to limit municipal authority only to improvements the need for which arose as a *direct* consequence of the particular subdivision under review." (Emphasis added.) Subsequently, in Squires Gate, Inc. v. County of Monmouth, 247 N.J.Super. 1, 588 A.2d 824 (App. Div.1991), the intermediate court held that, although the county subdivision control enabling act did not contain the language from the Municipal Land Use Law, supra, the county enabling act should be held to contain "implied authority" to require a subdivision

In any case where a particular subdivision exaction is held to be authorized by the enabling act, it may be challenged on constitutional grounds—i.e., on the ground that it violates substantive due process and/or amounts to an uncompensated "taking" and/or on the ground that it denies equal protection of the laws. Subdividers' substantive due process and "taking" challenges have generally been rejected on either a "harm prevention" or an "equivalent benefit" rationale, or both.[7] Under the "harm prevention" rationale, subdivision exactions are a proper exercise of the police power because they prevent harms that would otherwise result from the subdivider's failure to provide an adequate system of improved streets, water mains, sanitary and storm sewers, and land for recreational and/or school use.[8] Under the "equivalent benefit" rationale, subdivision exactions provide the developer with a benefit roughly equivalent to the costs he must assume by increasing the value of the subdivision land.[9] The "equivalent benefit" rationale is often buttressed by the argument that street improvements, utility installations, and even neighborhood playgrounds result in sufficiently localized benefits to justify financing such public facilities by special assessments against the land which is benefited. Hence, it is argued, subdivision exactions that provide such localized benefits are really just an indirect and informal kind of special assessment.[10]

The courts have had little difficulty in sustaining subdivision exactions to provide public facilities that could have been financed by special assessment,[11] although such exactions have occasionally been struck down when, e.g., street improvements or utility main extensions would substantially benefit landowners other than the subdivider.[12] The courts have had more

---

developer to pay the cost of off-site bridge improvements "the need for which arose as a direct consequence of the particular subdivision under review."

7. Generally, see Reps & Smith, Control of Urban Land Subdivision, 14 Syracuse L.Rev. 405 (1963); Heyman & Gilhool, The Constitutionality of Imposing Increased Community Costs on New Suburban Residents Through Subdivision Exactions, 73 Yale L.J. 1119 (1964); Johnston, Constitutionality of Subdivision Control Exactions: The Quest for a Rationale, 52 Cornell L.Rev. 871 (1967); Ellickson, Suburban Growth Controls: An Economic and Legal Analysis, 86 Yale L.J. 385, 424–441, 450–489 (1977); Hagman, Landowner–Developer Provision of Communal Goods Through Benefit–Based and Harm–Avoidance "Payments" (BHAPS), 5 Zoning & Planning L.Reports 17–23, 25–32 (1982); D. Mandelker, Land Use Law §§ 9.11–9.14 (1982).

8. See Ayres v. City Council of City of Los Angeles, 34 Cal.2d 31, 207 P.2d 1 (1949); Associated Home Builders v. City of Walnut Creek, 4 Cal.3d 633, 94 Cal.Rptr. 630, 484 P.2d 606 (1971), appeal dismissed 404 U.S. 878, 92 S.Ct. 202, 30 L.Ed.2d 159 (1971); Petterson v. City of Naperville, 9 Ill.2d 233, 137 N.E.2d 371 (1956); Divan Builders, Inc. v. Planning Board of Wayne Township, supra note 3; Jordan v. Menominee Falls, supra note 4.

9. See Ayres v. City of Los Angeles, supra note 8; Divan Builders, Inc. v. Wayne Township, supra note 3; Jordan v. Village of Menominee Falls, supra note 4.

10. Reps & Smith, supra note 7; Johnston, supra note 7.

However, the argument suggested in the text was rejected in Village Square No. 1, Inc. v. Crow–Frederick Retail Limited Partnership, 77 Md.App. 552, 551 A.2d 471 (1989) (ordinance in question was not a scheme for "special benefit assessments" because another ordinance provided an exclusive mode for imposing such assessments); Mooney v. City of Laconia, 133 N.H. 30, 573 A.2d 447 (1990) ("school fee" was *ultra vires* because city did not follow its ordinance procedures for levying "special assessments").

11. Reps & Smith argue that this is the only proper basis for upholding subdivision exactions. The cases, however, seem to treat the "harm-based" and "benefit-based" (special assessments are one example) as equally valid alternative rationales.

12. E.g., Lake Intervale Homes, Inc. v. Parsippany–Troy Hills Township, 28 N.J. 423, 147 A.2d 28 (1958); Divan Builders, Inc. v. Planning Board of Wayne Township, supra note 3.

See also Howard County v. JJM, Inc., 301 Md. 256, 482 A.2d 908 (1984), invalidating a

difficulty, however, with subdivision exactions to provide land for parks and/or schools. By hypothesis, public parks and schools are open to the general public, and traditionally they have been financed out of general tax revenues. Indeed, it has sometimes been held that special assessments cannot be used to finance parks and schools.[13] But most courts now sustain subdivision exactions—both dedication and "in lieu" payment requirements—for parks and schools provided there is a rational police power nexus between the development of a particular subdivision and the exactions imposed on the subdivider,[14] although there are substantial differences from state to state as to what constitutes the requisite nexus.

Under the deferential judicial review standard adopted in California, subdivision exactions for parks will be sustained "on the basis of a general public need for recreational facilities caused by present and future subdivisions" and an express constitutional mandate for preservation of open space—viewed as a scarce resource in urban and suburban areas. When the leading California case was decided,[15] the statute provided that "[t]he land [dedicated], [in lieu] fees, or combination thereof are to be used only for the purpose of providing park or recreational facilities to serve the subdivision" and that "[t]he amount and location of land to be dedicated or the fees to be paid shall bear a reasonable relationship to the use of the park and recreational facilities by the future inhabitants of the subdivision."[16] But language in that case upholding subdivision exactions for parks clearly indicates that "the constitutionality of the exaction is not dependent upon exclusive use of the facilities by those who will occupy the subdivision."[17]

In several other states the rule is similar to California's: there is a "reasonable basis" for park and school exactions when it is shown that "a group of subdivisions approved over a period of years has been responsible for bringing into the community a considerable number of people," thus generating a "need" for new parks and schools, and that the new public facilities will substantially—though perhaps only indirectly—benefit the new subdivision's residents.[18]

county ordinance provision requiring developers to reserve a right of way within the proposed subdivision for a proposed state highway because the county failed to prove that the subdivision would generate a need for such a highway. The court thus adopted a very narrow "rational nexus" requirement for subdivision exactions. See infra note 14.

13. E.g., Heavens v. King County Rural Library District, 66 Wn.2d 558, 404 P.2d 453 (1965). Neighborhood playgrounds within or adjacent to a particular subdivision could clearly be financed by special assessments, however, since the benefit is quite localized.

14. E.g., Associated Home Builders v. City of Walnut Creek, supra note 8; Jordan v. Menominee Falls, supra note 4; Krughoff v. City of Naperville, 68 Ill.2d 352, 12 Ill.Dec. 185, 369 N.E.2d 892 (1977). But see, contra as to "in lieu" charges, Aunt Hack Ridge Estates, Inc. v. Planning Commission, 27 Conn.Sup. 74, 230 A.2d 45 (1967); Berg Development Co. v. Missouri City, 603 S.W.2d 273 (Tex.Civ.App.

1980); City of College Station v. Turtle Rock Corp., 680 S.W.2d 802 (Tex.1984).

15. Associated Home Builders v. City of Walnut Creek, supra note 8.

16. Former West's Ann.Cal.Bus. & Prof. Code § 11546(c), (e), which now constitutes (with some changes) West's Ann.Cal.Gov.Code § 66477(c), (e).

17. See Associated Home Builders v. City of Walnut Creek, 4 Cal.3d at 640 n. 5, 94 Cal.Rptr. at 635–636 n. 5, 484 P.2d at 612 n. 5.

18. See, e.g., Jordan v. Menominee Falls, supra note 4 (from which the language in the text is drawn); Home Builders of Kansas City v. Kansas City, 555 S.W.2d 832 (Mo.1977); Billings Properties, Inc. v. Yellowstone County, 144 Mont. 25, 394 P.2d 182 (1964); Collis v. City of Bloomington, 310 Minn. 5, 246 N.W.2d 19 (1976); Patenaude v. Town of Meredith, 118 N.H. 616, 392 A.2d 582 (1978); Jenad v. Village of Scarsdale, supra note 4; Call v. City of West Jordan, 614 P.2d 1257 (Utah 1980), appeal after remand 727 P.2d 180 (1986).

A few states may still adhere to the strict view, first enunciated in Illinois,[19] that the "need" for new public facilities must be "specifically and uniquely attributable" to the development of a particular residential subdivision and that the new facilities must directly and primarily benefit that subdivision. In the real world, however, only very large subdivisions could satisfy this test, and it seems to have been substantially relaxed even in Illinois.[20]

It has generally been assumed that subdivision developers do not bear the cost of subdivision exactions because either (1) the cost is passed along to the purchasers of new subdivision houses and lots,[21] or (2) the cost is borne, in the form of lower land prices, by the owners of undeveloped land.[22] Several courts have taken this into account in rejecting developers' challenges to subdivision exactions on substantive due process and "taking" grounds.[23] Developers clearly have no ground for a "taking" challenge if they do not, in fact, bear the cost of subdivision exactions. To the extent that subdivision exactions are alleged to be arbitrary or discriminatory, however, developers arguably should be allowed to challenge them on behalf of those who do ultimately bear the cost.

Subdivision exactions may raise troublesome "equal protection" issues to the extent that "old" and "new" residents of a community are subjected to different burdens, and because land development that proceeds without subdivision is by hypothesis not subject to subdivision exactions.[24] These issues have, in general, not been given adequate consideration by the courts.[25]

In Nollan v. California Coastal Commission,[26] the United States Supreme Court adopted the "harm prevention" rationale originally developed in subdivision exaction cases[27] in holding that exaction of a lateral beachfront easement as a condition of granting a permit to build a house on a beachfront lot was invalid both as a violation of substantive due process and as an uncompensated "taking" of private property for public use. The exaction was invalidated because the Court concluded that the exaction "utterly fails to further the end advanced as the justification for" the exaction—i.e., because there was no "rational nexus" between means and ends. But the Court recognized that such an exaction would be valid if there had been such a "rational nexus." Justice Scalia's majority opinion in *Nollan* also contains a rather confusing assertion that, although the "nexus"

---

19. See Pioneer Trust & Savings Bank v. Village of Mount Prospect, 22 Ill.2d 375, 176 N.E.2d 799 (1961).

20. See, e.g., Board of Education v. Surety Developers, 63 Ill.2d 193, 347 N.E.2d 149 (1975); Krughoff v. Naperville, supra note 14.

21. See Note, Subdivision Land Dedication: Objectives and Objections, 27 Stan.L.Rev. 419, 421–430 (1975).

22. See Adelstein & Edelson, Subdivision Exactions and Congestion Externalities, 5 J. Legal Studies 147 (1976); Hagman, supra note 7, at 26–27.

23. See, e.g., Associated Home Builders v. City of Walnut Creek, 4 Cal.3d at 642 n. 9,

644, 94 Cal.Rptr. at 637–638 n. 9, 639, 484 P.2d at 613 n. 9, 615; Jordan v. Menominee Falls, supra note 4; Aunt Hack Ridge Estates, Inc. v. Planning Commission, 160 Conn. 109, 273 A.2d 880 (1970).

24. See Heyman & Gilhool, supra note 7; Ellickson, ibid.

25. See discussion of discrimination issues in Associated Home Builders v. City of Walnut Creek, 4 Cal.3d at 642–643, 645, 94 Cal.Rptr. at 637–640, 484 P.2d at 613–616.

26. 483 U.S. 825, 107 S.Ct. 3141, 97 L.Ed.2d 677 (1987), discussed at greater length ante Section 2.

27. Id. at 838, 107 S.Ct. at 3148.

requirement in substantive due process and equal protection cases is whether "the State 'could rationally have decided' the measure adopted might achieve the State's objective," the test in "taking" cases is whether the measure adopted "substantially advances" a "legitimate state interest." [28] This is confusing in light of the use of the "substantially advances" test in deciding Euclid v. Ambler Realty Co.,[29] which was treated by the Court as a facially substantive due process challenge to the basic principles on which "zoning" are based.

(b) Other Development Charges: "Impact Fees" and "Impact Taxes"

The problem of making a land development that doesn't involve subdivision of the land pay for needs "generated" by the development can be solved in some cases by imposing dedication and land improvement requirements or "in lieu" charges as a condition of granting a building permit,[30] a variance,[31] a special exception or conditional use permit,[32] or a necessary rezoning to permit the proposed development.[33] Moreover, local governments can be authorized, as in New Jersey, to require a site plan review before unsubdivided land can be developed and to condition site plan approval in compliance with requirements similar to those imposed on subdivision developers.[34]

It is not clear whether any of the techniques discussed above can be used to finance the construction or expansion of centralized public facilities such as water and sewage treatment plants. In any case, many local governments have sought to finance such construction or expansion of facilities by imposing so-called "impact fees" or "impact taxes" on all land developers.[35]

---

28. 483 U.S. at 834 n. 3, 107 S.Ct. at 3147 n. 3.

29. 272 U.S. 365, at 395, 107 S.Ct. at 121 ("substantial relation to the public health, safety, morals, or general welfare").

30. See Rohn v. City of Visalia, 214 Cal. App.3d 1463, 263 Cal.Rptr. 319 (1989) (uncompensated dedication of 14% of plaintiff's land to correct the alignment of a boundary street at its intersection with another street at the corner of the land was made a condition of obtaining site plan approval and a building permit; but the condition was invalidated on the ground that "there was not a reasonable relationship between the condition imposed and the use of the property," since there was nothing in the record to indicate that the proposed change in the use of plaintiff's land would generate such increased vehicular traffic as to make the dedication necessary" and the dedication was clearly not "proportional to such increased vehicular traffic"); William J. Jones Insurance Trust v. City of Fort Smith, 731 F.Supp. 912 (W.D.Ark.1990) (city may not exact land for road widening as condition of granting a building permit for a convenience store, absent a showing that the proposed convenience store would increase traffic on abutting street; the required "rational nexus" was lacking). See also Hernando County v. Budget Inns, 555 So.2d 1319 (Fla.App.1990) (county's attempt to condition building permit on developer's promise to construct a frontage road in the future, although no frontage road

was presently needed, characterized by the court as an attempt to "bank" the developer's land to provide for future frontage road without compensating the developer, held to be an unconstitutional "taking"); Leroy Dev. Corp. v. Tahoe Regional Planning Agency, 733 F.Supp. 1399 (D.Nev.1990) (agreement requiring developer to provide water retention facilities and take other off-site flood mitigation measures was invalid because there was an inadequate "nexus" between ends and means).

31. See ante Section 9.7.

32. Southwick, Inc. v. City of Lacey, 58 Wn.App. 886, 795 P.2d 712 (1990) (conditions imposed on site plan approval and special use permit were valid where necessary to mitigate impact of proposed land development, and were not invalid as an unauthorized tax).

33. See, e.g., Scrutton v. County of Sacramento, 275 Cal.App.2d 412, 79 Cal.Rptr. 872 (1969).

34. See Rohn v. Visalia, supra note 30, and Southwick v. City of Lacey, supra note 32.

35. See Juergensmeyer & Blake, Impact Fees: An Answer to Local Governments' Capital Funding Dilemma, 14 Fla.St.U.L.Rev. 415 (1981); Hagman, supra note 7; D. Mandelker, Land Use Law § 9.14 (1982). California and Florida local governments seem to have pioneered the use of these development charges.

For a comprehensive treatment of "impact fees" and "impact taxes," see Am. Planning

These fees or taxes are usually levied when building permits are issued to a developer and are payable even if the land has not been subdivided or was subdivided before the advent of compulsory subdivision exactions. The fees collected from developers are placed in a fund to be used to finance new capital improvements and additions to existing facilities necessitated by the aggregate of new land development in the community.

Like subdivision exactions, "impact fees" and "impact taxes" were at first challenged as *ultra vires* because they were not specifically authorized by subdivision control enabling acts and, if regarded as taxes, were excise taxes which municipalities were generally not authorized to adopt.[36] As time went on, however, courts began to hold that "impact fees" could be sustained as "regulatory" measures authorized either by constitutional Home Rule provisions or by statutes containing broad general language delegating to municipalities the power to levy "user fees" of various kinds.[37] More recently, many states have enacted new legislation specifically authorizing the imposition of "impact fees" on developers to defray a proportionate share of the cost of providing a wide variety of off-site public services and facilities required by new residential, commercial, and industrial development.[38] Most of this legislation applies comprehensively to all kinds of off-site infrastructure, but some of the legislation authorizes imposition of "impact fees" for water and/or sewer facilities.[39] Most of this "impact fee"

Ass'n, Development Exactions (Planners Press 1987). See also Blaesser & Kentopp, Impact Fees: The "Second Generation," 38 Wash. U.J.Urb. & Contemp.L. 55 (1990), reprinted in 1991 Zoning and Planning Handbook 255.

36. Home Builders Ass'n v. Riddel, 109 Ariz. 404, 510 P.2d 376 (1973); Rancho Colorado, Inc. v. City of Broomfield, 196 Colo. 444, 586 P.2d 659 (1978); Lloyd E. Clarke, Inc. v. City of Bettendorf, 261 Iowa 1217, 158 N.W.2d 125 (1968); Hillis Homes, Inc. v. Snohomish County, 97 Wn.2d 804, 650 P.2d 193 (1982); Town of Longboat Key v. Lands End, Ltd., 433 So.2d 574 (Fla.App.1983).

37. E.g., Associated Home Builders v. City of Newark, 18 Cal.App.3d 107, 95 Cal.Rptr. 648 (1971); Westfield–Palos Verdes Co. v. City of Rancho Palos Verdes, 73 Cal.App.3d 486, 141 Cal.Rptr. 36 (1977); Cherry Hills Farms, Inc. v. City of Cherry Hills Village, 670 P.2d 779 (Colo.1983); Contractors and Builders Ass'n v. City of Dunedin, 329 So.2d 314 (Fla. 1976), on appeal after remand 358 So.2d 846 (Fla.App.1978), cert. denied 444 U.S. 867, 100 S.Ct. 140, 62 L.Ed.2d 91 (1979); Home Builders & Contractors Ass'n v. Board of Commissioners of Palm Beach County, 446 So.2d 140 (Fla.App.1983), review denied 451 So.2d 848 (Fla.1984); Hollywood, Inc. v. Broward County, 431 So.2d 606 (Fla.App.1983), review denied 440 So.2d 352 (Fla.1983).

38. For a thorough discussion of state "impact fee" statutes, see Morgan, State Impact Fee Legislation: Guidelines for Analysis, Part I, 42 Land Use Law and Zoning Digest, March 1990, p. 3; id. Part II, April 1990, p. 3. The

states where "impact fee" legislation has been enacted include Arizona, California, Illinois, Illinois, Maine, Nevada, New Jersey, Oregon, Tennessee, Texas, Vermont, Virginia, and Washington. For the statutory citations, see id. Part I, p. 3 nn. 2 through 13.

In Cranberry Tp. v. Builders Ass'n of Metropolitan Pittsburgh, 137 Pa.Cmwlth. 510, 587 A.2d 32 (1991), it was held that the Pennsylvania statute authorizing "impact fees" for highway improvements retroactively validated "impact fees" previously imposed, as against a claim that these fees were invalid because they were taxes rather than regulatory exactions.

In Lincoln Property Co. v. Cucamonga School District, 229 Cal.App.3d 394, 280 Cal. Rptr. 68 (1991), it was held that both constitutional and statutory provisions authorize California school districts to impose "school facilities fees" on residential land developers.

39. The Maine, Nevada, Oregon, and Texas statutes authorize imposition of "impact fees" to finance the full range of infrastructure facilities—water, sewer, road, and stormwater drainage. Others—e.g., the Illinois, Virginia, and Washington statutes—authorize "impact fees" only for a single type of facility. The Arizona and Illinois statutes confer on municipalities only the bare authority to adopt "impact fees." The Nevada, Oregon, Texas, and Vermont statutes, on the other hand, set out a comprehensive methodology to be used in calculating the amount of the "impact fees." Other statutes, including California's, are designed to impose limitations on various kinds

legislation was initiated by associations of land developers and builders seeking to prevent overreaching by local governments.[40] These developers' and builders' associations had apparently concluded that uniform statutory standards with respect to "impact fees" are desirable in order to assure fair and equitable treatment by local government officials.

As an alternative to "impact fee" legislation, under which the imposition of "impact fees" is considered to be designed to "regulate" land development, a number of states have enacted legislation authorizing municipalities to levy "excise taxes" on the business of land development.[41] Such legislation precludes *ultra vires* challenges to "impact taxes" levied by municipalities, provided the taxes are levied in accordance with the standards and procedures set out in the enabling legislation.[42]

"Impact fees" and "impact taxes" imposed pursuant to enabling legislation may, of course, be subject to successful challenge on constitutional grounds. In general, constitutional substantive due process, equal protection, and "taking" tests are applied to "impact fees" and "impact taxes" in the same way they are applied to the "subdivision exactions" discussed in this Section. Since the Supreme Court's decision in Nollan v. California Coastal Commission,[43] it is likely that state courts will begin to apply the *Nollan* "rational nexus" test when "impact fees" and "impact taxes" are challenged. This test requires a showing that imposition of the fee or tax "substantially advances" a "legitimate state interest" because the imposition of the fee or tax would otherwise amount to an uncompensated "taking for public use." [44]

The constitutional equal protection test may be more difficult to apply in "impact fee" and "impact tax" cases than in zoning cases because such a fee or tax is imposed in cases where new infrastructure facilities are to be used by both old and new users and the old and new fees or taxes are determined differently. Although the equal protection test generally recognized by the United States Supreme Court requires only "minimum rationality" when persons are placed in different classifications and consequently receive different treatment,[45] some state courts have imposed a stricter test for "impact fees." The test laid down in Banberry Dev. Corp. v. South Jordan City, for example,[46] is as follows:

> To determine the equitable share of the capital costs to be borne by newly developed properties, a municipality should determine the relative burdens previously borne and yet to be borne by those properties in comparison with the other properties in the municipality as a whole;

of "impact fees" authorized by other legislation.

40. Morgan, supra note 38, Part I, p. 4.

41. For a thorough discussion of state "impact tax" statutes, see Strauss & Leitner, 11 Zoning and Planning Law Report 9 (March 1988). States where "impact taxes" have been authorized, as a type of "excise tax," include Arizona, California, Kansas, Maine, Maryland, New York, Pennsylvania, Virginia, and perhaps West Virginia. Strauss & Leitner, supra, at 19.

42. See Strauss & Leitner, Financing Public Facilities with Development Excise Taxes: An Alternative to Exactions and Impact Fees, 11 Planning & Zoning Law Rep. 17 (1988).

43. 483 U.S. 825, 107 S.Ct. 3141, 97 L.Ed.2d 677 (1987).

44. 483 U.S. at 834 n. 3, 107 S.Ct. at 3147 n. 3.

45. See D. Mandelker, Land Use Law § 2.42 (2d ed. 1988).

46. 631 P.2d 899 (Utah 1981).

the fee in question should not exceed the amount sufficient to equalize the relative burdens on newly developed and other properties.

This test has, in substance, been incorporated in some of the recently enacted "impact fee" statutes.[47] But when a municipality imposes legislatively authorized "impact taxes," the sort of equalization required in *Banberry* would seem clearly to be unnecessary in view of the wide latitude in defining different classes of taxpayers which has been held to be permissible when tax laws are challenged under the equal protection clause.[48]

In recent years several municipalities have adopted so-called "linkage" programs which require developers of office and other commercial projects either to construct some "affordable housing" or to contribute to a fund to be used by the municipality to construct an equivalent amount of "affordable housing."[49] The rationale for these "linkage" programs is that office and commercial development creates new jobs that attract new employees and creates or exacerbates a shortage of "affordable housing" within the municipality and the region of which it is a part. Since most developers, in practice, choose to contribute to the "affordable housing" fund rather than to build such housing, "linkage" programs really result in imposition of a new form of "impact fee."

The earliest "linkage" programs were adopted in large cities such as Boston and San Francisco which suffered an acute shortage of "affordable housing." More recently, several smaller municipalities in suburban areas of New Jersey have required both commercial land developers and residential developers who choose not to build any "affordable housing" to pay "development fees" into municipal trust funds to enable these municipalities to build "affordable housing." All these "linkage" programs are subject to challenge on the grounds that they are either *ultra vires,* unconstitutional, or both. The San Francisco "linkage" program was based on the discretionary power of the city planning commission to grant or deny development permits, but it is far from clear that it was intended to provide a basis for

47. Morgan, State Impact Fee Legislation: Guidelines for Analysis, Part I, 42 Land Use Law & Zoning Digest, March 1990, p. 7, citing the Vermont statute as an example. The *Banberry* standard is also adopted in Bachrach et al., A Standard Development Impact Fee Enabling Statute, in A. Nelson, ed., Development Impact Fees 135 (1981); Juergensmeyer & Nichola, A Model Impact Fee Authorization Statute, id. at 156. The *Banberry* standard is derived from Ellickson, Suburban Growth Controls: An Economic and Legal Analysis, 86 Yale L.J. 385, 45–89 (1977) (arguing that "if a municipality mixes special and general revenues in financing a service, the portion financed by general revenues should presumptively be distributed equally per dwelling unit").

48. Morgan, supra note 47, at p. 7 ("The *Banberry* court's cost-accounting approach to development fees is of dubious constitutional significance in states other than Utah. Certainly there is no general constitutional principle of law, such as the guarantee of equal protection, requiring regulatory fees, user fees, utility rates and local and state taxes to be equalized among all potential beneficiaries."). See also D. Mandelker, Land Use Law § 9.18 at n. 109 ("Courts have upheld impact fees based on the purchase price of dwellings, differentials between the cost of the old and new segments of the public facility system, and benefits received by developers subject to the fee"), citing cases from Colorado, New Jersey, and Oregon.

49. See Kayden & Pollard, Linkage Ordinances and Traditional Exactions Analysis: The Connection Between Office Development and Housing, 50 Law & Contemp.Prob. 127 (1987); Alterman, Evaluating Linkage and Beyond: Letting the Windfall Recapture Genie Out of the Exactions Bottle, 34 Wash.U.J.Urban and Contemp.Law 3 (1988); Newman & Feola, Housing Incentives: A National Perspective, 21 Urban Law 307 (1989).

the city's "linkage" program.[50] Commentators have suggested that San Francisco would do better to rely on its Home Rule power and the required low-income housing element of its comprehensive plan.[51] When the Massachusetts court suggested the need for enabling legislation in connection with Boston's "linkage" program,[52] the state legislature proceeded to enact legislation specifically authorizing the Boston program as it then existed.[53] In New Jersey, the Supreme Court [54] held that the imposition of "development fees" was authorized as a means by which municipalities could satisfy their *Mount Laurel* II and Fair Housing Act "fair share" obligation.

The constitutional challenges to "linkage" programs may, of course, be based on substantive due process, equal protection, or "taking" grounds. Substantive due process requires that such programs satisfy the "rational nexus" test—i.e., it must appear that the developers who are subject to these programs create or contribute to the "affordable housing" problem these programs are intended to remedy. So far, there is little judicial authority with respect to the constitutional issues. The New Jersey Supreme Court held that the "linkage" programs it was considering did not violate due process or equal standards on their face because they were reasonable exercises of statutory zoning and police powers.[55] The California courts have sustained "exactions" similar to those required under the San Francisco "linkage" program applicable to commercial land developers.[56] But the Washington Supreme Court struck down a Seattle city ordinance that required owners of "affordable housing" who demolish it to convert the property to non-residential use to obtain a housing demolition license, which would be granted only if the owner gave current tenants relocation assis-

50. Share & Diamond, San Francisco's Office–Housing Production Program, 35 Land Use L. and Zoning Dig., No. 10, at 4 (1983).

51. Ibid.

52. Bonan v. City of Boston, 398 Mass. 315, 496 N.E.2d 640 (1986).

53. Mass.Gen.Laws Ann. 665, §§ 15–20.

54. Holmdel Builders Ass'n v. Township of Holmdel, 121 N.J. 550, 583 A.2d 277 (1990) ("development fees" are the functional equivalent of "mandatory set-asides" authorized in *Mount Laurel* II; provision of "affordable housing" is one of the purposes of zoning incorporated by reference into New Jersey's Fair Housing Law, which is to be construed in para materia with New Jersey's Municipal Land Use Law; but effectuation of municipal authority to impose "development fees" must await publication of rules by Council on Affordable Housing that will provide standards and guidelines for imposition of "development fees"; such fees were "regulatory exactions," not "taxes").

55. Holmdel Builders Ass'n v. Township of Holmdel, supra note 55 (the proper substantive due process test is the relaxed "reasonable relationship" test, not the "strong, almost but-for, causal nexus between off-site public facilities and private development traditionally required in order to justify exactions from" subdivision developers; it is reasonable to re-

quire commercial land developers to pay the "development fee" and to give residential developers a choice of actually building "affordable housing" or paying the "development fee").

56. See Terminal Plaza Corp. v. City & County of San Francisco, 177 Cal.App.3d 892, 223 Cal.Rptr. 379 (1986) (the court dismissed a "taking" challenge to an ordinance that imposed similar "exactions" on owners of residential hotels who wish to demolish an existing building, because all hotel owners retained the right to use or sell their properties, and it was shown that the plaintiff could not earn a reasonable return on his investments or that the ordinance had reduced the value of his property; but the court expressed concern "that the ordinance places a disproportionate burden of providing low cost housing upon residential hotel owners, rather than fairly dispersing the cost of conferring such a social benefit upon society as a whole"); Commercial Builders of Northern California v. City of Sacramento, 941 F.2d 872 (9th Cir.1991), cert. denied ___ U.S. ___, 112 S.Ct. 1997, 118 L.Ed.2d 593 (1992) (no unconstitutional "taking" as result of imposition of an "affordable housing" fee on commercial developers because a study by the City showed a substantial connection between commercial land development and an influx of low-income workers).

tance and either replaced a specific percentage of the housing to be demolished with other "affordable housing" or contributed to an "affordable housing" replacement fund.[57] In the Seattle case the "nexus" between the demolition of existing housing and the need for replacement of that housing was even clearer than it is when "impact fees" are imposed on commercial land developers.[58] But the Washington court held that the "affordable housing" requirements were unconstitutional because "the City may not constitutionally pass on the social cost of the development of the downtown * * * area to current owners of low income housing. The problem must be shared by the entire city, and those who plan to develop their property from low income housing to other uses cannot be penalized by being required to provide more housing."[59]

§ 9.18 Growth Management Programs

Suburban growth management became an issue in the 1960s because the pace of residential development often threatened to outrun the capacity of local governments to provide the needed new infrastructure of arterial roads, schools, water and sewage treatment plans, and parks. Before suburban communities began to exact "impact fees" or "impact taxes,"[1] these centralized public facilities had to be provided out of general tax revenues which in many cases did not grow as rapidly as the demand for new facilities. Hence many suburban communities adopted various land use control techniques to try to slow, and to manage efficiently, the rush to the suburbs.

a. Low Density Residential Zoning

Beginning in the 1950s some suburban communities started the practice of zoning most of their outlying undeveloped acreage exclusively for single family dwellings at very low densities, and older suburban communities that were already "overzoned" for high or medium density residential development "downzoned" large areas to permit only low density single family dwellings. The purpose, in either case, was to direct growth to the undeveloped areas closest to the existing built-up portions of the community, to assure that residential development in outlying areas would proceed slowly, and to assure that the demand for and cost of new public facilities would be minimized. As we have already seen the initial zoning of large portions of suburban communities for single family dwellings at low densities (i.e., with large minimum lot size requirements) was generally upheld when challenged by landowners and developers in the 1950s and 1960s.[2] And the courts also have sustained extensive "downzonings" to lower densities, provided that they are consistent with or pursuant to a comprehensive and carefully worked-out growth management plan.[3]

57. San Telmo Associates v. City of Seattle, 108 Wn.2d 20, 735 P.2d 673 (1987).

58. Compare *San Telmo,* supra note 57, with Terminal Plaza Corp. v. City & County of San Francisco, supra note 56.

59. *San Telmo,* supra note 57, 108 Wn.2d at 25, 735 P.2d at 675.

§ 9.18

1. See ante Section 9.17.

2. See ante Section 9.5 for discussion of large-lot zoning.

3. E.g., Carty v. City of Ojai, 77 Cal.App.3d 329, 143 Cal.Rptr. 506 (1978); Norbeck Village Joint Venture v. Montgomery County Council, 254 Md. 59, 254 A.2d 700 (1969).

b. Moratoria on Suburban Growth

In suburban communities where uncontrolled growth had already over-taxed public facilities such as sewage treatment plants, water supply systems, and schools, local governments in the late 1960s and early 1970s often resorted to temporary moratoria on subdivision approvals, building permits, or utility hook-ups. These moratoria have sometimes been struck down, but have usually been sustained if—and only if—the court is persuaded that (1) there is a genuine emergency to justify the moratorium—e.g., a health hazard resulting from inadequacy of the existing sewage treatment plant to handle additional waste; (2) the local government has a plan for coping with the emergency—e.g., a plan to expand the existing sewage treatment plant—and is actually implementing the plan; and (3) the moratorium does not violate constitutional guarantees of equal protection.[4]

c. Full–Fledged Growth Management Programs

Some local governments have adopted rather elaborate growth management programs.[5] These programs may or may not set an absolute limit on population growth by fixing in advance the community's maximum population when all its land area is fully developed. These programs usually specify the areas in which new development will be allowed to occur and indicate the sequence in which these areas will be permitted to develop. Many such programs establish an "urban growth boundary" beyond which urban development will not be permitted at all, unless and until the local government extends the boundary. Where the local government unit exercising the power to control land use is a county or a regional authority, the program may drastically limit the growth of existing municipalities and provide for dispersal of new development in outlying areas.

---

4. Moratoria of various kinds have been sustained in many cases—e.g., Sun Ridge Development, Inc. v. City of Cheyenne, 787 P.2d 583 (Wyo.1990) (construction moratorium to enforce drainage regulations); Gilbert v. State of California, 218 Cal.App.3d 234, 266 Cal. Rptr. 891 (1990) (moratorium on water service construction during period of water shortage); Kaplan v. Clear Lake City Water Auth., 794 F.2d 1059 (5th Cir.1986) (water and sewer connections); Ocean Acres Ltd. Partnership v. Dare County Bd. of Health, 707 F.2d 103 (4th Cir.1983) (septic tanks); Smoke Rise, Inc. v. Washington Suburban Sanitary Com'n, 400 F.Supp. 1369 (D.Md.1975); Belle Harbor Realty Corp. v. Kerr, 35 N.Y.2d 507, 364 N.Y.S.2d 160, 323 N.E.2d 697 (1974) (moratorium on building until inadequacy of sewerage was corrected). Perhaps the most striking case in which a moratorium was upheld is Associated Home Builders of Greater Eastbay, Inc. v. City of Livermore, 18 Cal.3d 582, 135 Cal.Rptr. 41, 557 P.2d 473 (1976), where the court sustained "an initiative ordinance, enacted by the voters of the city, prohibiting issuance of further residential building permits until local educational, sewage disposal, and water supply facilities complied with specific standards."

Cases in which moratoria were invalidated include, e.g., Westwood Forest Estates, Inc. v.

Village of South Nyack, 23 N.Y.2d 424, 297 N.Y.S.2d 129, 244 N.E.2d 700 (1969) (moratorium on construction of multi-family dwellings; the decision seems inconsistent with the decision in *Belle Harbor,* supra); Pritchett v. Nathan Rodgers Const. & Realty Corp., 379 So.2d 545 (Ala.1979) (invalid because sewer tap-ins were denied on an arbitrary, case-by-case basis); Dekalb County v. Townsend Associates, Inc., 243 Ga. 80, 252 S.E.2d 498 (1979) (necessity for sewer moratorium not proved).

Generally, see D. Mandelker, Land Use Law §§ 6.5 through 6.10 (2d ed. 1988).

5. See, generally, Mandelker §§ 10.1, 10.2 (1982); D. Godschalk, D. Brower, L. Bennett & B. Vestal, Constitutional Issues of Growth Management 8–10 (1977).

Local governments also occasionally attempt to control regional growth by limiting utility extensions outside municipal limits, with varying results. See, e.g., Dateline Builders, Inc. v. City of Santa Rosa, 146 Cal. App.3d 520, 194 Cal.Rptr. 258 (1983) (valid); Robinson v. City of Boulder, 190 Colo. 357, 547 P.2d 228 (1976) (invalid); Delmarva Enterprises, Inc. v. Mayor and Council of City of Dover, 282 A.2d 601 (Del.1971) (invalid).

Most suburban growth control programs link the approval of new development with the availability of essential public facilities ("infra-structure") and prohibit new development not served by adequate facilities. But the extension of certain kinds of public facilities such as public water supply may be subject to cross-cutting statutory or caselaw rules under which municipal utility departments may have a duty to extend services to growing suburban and exurban areas. The imposition of such a duty may, of course, undercut growth management programs that limit public utility extensions in order to control new development.[6]

Full-fledged growth management programs have been challenged and upheld in two leading cases, Golden v. Town of Ramapo [7] and Construction Industry Association v. City of Petaluma.[8] In *Ramapo,* the New York Court of Appeals sustained an elaborate program implemented by an amendment to the town's zoning ordinance, as against challenge on the grounds that the program was *ultra vires,* that it resulted in a "taking" of private property without "just compensation," and that it violated substantive due process because it had an "exclusionary" effect. In *Petaluma,* on the other hand, a United States Court of Appeals sustained an elaborate growth control program utilizing an annual quota of building permits,[9] against attack on the ground that it violated substantive due process, infringed the ill-defined constitutional "right to travel," and interfered unduly with interstate commerce.

The Ramapo growth management program was keyed to an ambitious capital improvement program, and was designed to assure that land development would go hand-in-hand with extension of essential public services and that development would proceed in an orderly and efficient manner outward from the existing developed areas.[10] To implement its growth management program, Ramapo adopted an amendment to its zoning ordinance which required all new residential development (except for individual single-family houses) to proceed on the basis of a special permit from the governing body. Permits were to be granted only if a developer had acquired a specified number of points. Points were awarded on the basis of proximity of a proposed development to each of five specified public facilities, up to a stated maximum for each of these facilities. Until a special permit was obtained, subdivision approval could not be obtained. Variances were authorized in some cases where the developer had acquired almost the number of points generally required, and developers could acquire points by themselves providing some of the specified facilities. Landowners could also obtain reduc-

6. See, e.g., Robinson v. City of Boulder, 190 Colo. 357, 547 P.2d 228 (1976); Reid Development Corp. v. Parsippany–Troy Hills Township, 31 N.J.Super. 459, 107 A.2d 20 (App.Div. 1954); Corcoran v. Village of Bennington, 128 Vt. 482, 266 A.2d 457 (1970). Cf. Westminster, Colorado, Growth Control cases discussed in 34 Land Use Law & Zoning Digest, March 1982, at pp. 15–16. See also Note, Control of Timing and Location of Government and Utility Extensions, 26 Stan.L.Rev. 945 (1974).

7. 30 N.Y.2d 359, 334 N.Y.S.2d 138, 285 N.E.2d 291 (1972), appeal dismissed 409 U.S. 1003, 93 S.Ct. 436, 34 L.Ed.2d 294 (1972).

8. 522 F.2d 897 (9th Cir.1975), certiorari denied 424 U.S. 934, 96 S.Ct. 1148, 47 L.Ed.2d 342 (1976).

9. Although there was no express statutory authorization for a "quota system," the Petaluma program was not attacked as *ultra vires,* perhaps because Petaluma as a home rule city enjoyed a very broad delegation of police power under its charter.

10. The Ramapo ordinance is set out in full in 24 Zoning Dig. 68 (1972). See also Emanuel, Ramapo's Managed Growth Program, 4 Planner's Notebook, No. 5, at p. 5 (Am.Inst. of Planners 1074).

tions in property tax assessments on land where development was not permitted for a substantial period under the growth management amendment. And the growth management plan itself provided that all of the undeveloped land in Ramapo should be available for development within the eighteen-year period adopted for completion of the town's capital facilities program.

The New York court first rejected an argument that the Ramapo growth management ordinance was *ultra vires,* holding that the New York zoning enabling legislation included, "by way of necessary implication, the authority to direct the growth of population for the purposes indicated," [11] and that delaying approval of residential subdivisions pending accumulation of the required number of points was justified under the New York subdivision control law.[12] Moreover, the court held that delaying land development, even as long as eighteen years in some cases, did not amount to a *de facto* "taking" when the plaintiffs challenged the Ramapo ordinance as "facially" invalid,[13] although the court noted that the constitutionality of the ordinance as applied to individual properties might be challenged in a later proceeding.[14] Finally, the court rejected the "exclusionary" zoning challenge.[15]

The *Ramapo* case has been both praised [16] and criticized.[17] Critics have argued that the Ramapo growth management program, in effect, perpetuated an underlying low-density zoning pattern which is clearly "exclusionary"; that much land in Ramapo might, in fact, be kept undeveloped for more than the projected eighteen years because of delays in making the capital improvements necessary to make outlying areas eligible for development; and that individual communities should not be permitted to promote their own "general welfare," narrowly defined, at the expense of the broader "general welfare" of the region or state. In light of the subsequent condemnation of exclusionary zoning in the *Berenson* case,[18] it seems clear that, in the future the New York courts will look more carefully at allegations that growth management programs like Ramapo's are really a device to exclude low- and moderate-income households. And Ramapo itself decided in March, 1983, to

---

11. 30 N.Y.2d at 371, 334 N.Y.S.2d at 146, 285 N.E.2d at 297.

12. 30 N.Y.2d at 374, 334 N.Y.S.2d at 148–149, 285 N.E.2d at 298.

13. 30 N.Y.2d at 380, 334 N.Y.S.2d at 153–154, 285 N.E.2d at 304.

14. 30 N.Y.2d at 382, 334 N.Y.S.2d at 155–156, 285 N.E.2d at 304.

15. The Court said, "far from being exclusionary, the present [zoning] amendments merely seek, by the implementation of sequential development and time growth, to provide a balanced community dedicated to the efficient utilization of land" on the basis of a "comprehensive plan" designed "to maximize population density consistent with orderly growth." But, as indicated in the text following note 17, the underlying zoning regulations, which were not altered by the growth management plan, provided for development

at average densities that were very low. Compare Associated Home Builders v. City of Livermore, 18 Cal.3d 582, 135 Cal.Rptr. 41, 557 P.2d 473 (1976), where the court observed, in upholding a moratorium on issuance of building permits, that the Livermore ordinance "impartially bans all residential construction, expensive or inexpensive" and thus avoided "any claim that the ordinance discriminates on a basis of race or wealth."

16. E.g., Freilich, Comment, 24 Zoning Dig. 72 (1972).

17. E.g., H. Franklin, Controlling Urban Growth—But for Whom? (Potomac Inst. 1973); Scott, Comment, 24 Zoning Dig. 75 (1972); Bosselman, Can the Town of Ramapo Pass a Law to Bind the Rights of the Whole World?, 1 Fla.St.U.L.Rev. 234 (1973).

18. Berenson v. Town of New Castle, 38 N.Y.2d 102, 378 N.Y.S.2d 672, 341 N.E.2d 236 (1975).

drop its famous point system because it proved to be impossible to provide public facilities on schedule.[19]

In *Petaluma*,[20] the courts had to consider a local government growth management program which was based on an explicit annual quota of building permits for residential development. Like Ramapo,[21] Petaluma had experienced explosive growth during the 1960s. Much of Petaluma's growth took the form of single-family residential development in the eastern part of the city, which contributed to a shortfall in moderately priced multi-family dwellings in this area. The growth management program adopted in 1972 limited residential growth in the 1972–77 period to 500 dwelling units per year but exempted housing projects with four units or less. To allocate the 500 building permits available each year, the program set up a "point system" modelled on the Ramapo point system but somewhat more elaborate. Thus the Petaluma point system, unlike the Ramapo system, awarded points for good environmental and architectural design of projects, for provision of recreational facilities, and for provision of low- and moderate-income housing in compliance with the city's housing policy, which allocated eight to twelve percent of the annual quota to such housing.

Among the stated objectives of the Petaluma growth management system were the prevention of "urban sprawl," creation of an urban growth boundary and a circumferential "greenbelt," and correction of the imbalances between the growth of the eastern and western parts of the city and between new single-family and multi-family residential development.

The United States District Court invalidated the Petaluma growth management system on the ground that, by substantially interfering with the growth which Petaluma would have experienced as a result of market forces, the program violated the constitutional "right to travel"—an intensely undefined right not expressed anywhere in the United States Constitution.[22] But the Court of Appeals reversed. Although the Court of Appeals accepted the District Court's conclusion that the Petaluma quota system would keep the supply of housing in Petaluma below anticipated market demand, with a consequent decline in regional housing quality and loss of population mobility, the Court of Appeals held that none of the plaintiffs had standing to raise the "right-to-travel" issue.[23] The court then rejected the plaintiffs' substantive due process and interference with interstate commerce arguments.

19. See 49 Planning, June 1983, p. 8.

20. Construction Industry Association v. City of Petaluma, 522 F.2d 897 (9th Cir.1975), certiorari denied 424 U.S. 934, 96 S.Ct. 1148, 47 L.Ed.2d 342 (1976).

21. For more detail on the Petaluma program, see McGivern, Putting a Speed Limit on Growth, 38 Planning 263 (1972).

22. Construction Industry Association v. City of Petaluma, 375 F.Supp. 574 (N.D.Cal. 1974), reversed 522 F.2d 897 (9th Cir.1975), cert. denied 424 U.S. 934, 96 S.Ct. 1148, 47 L.Ed.2d 342 (1976). The trial court adopted the "growth center" theory developed by economic consultants to the plaintiffs. See Gruen, The Economics of Petaluma: Uncon-stitutional Regional Socio–Economic Impacts, in II Management and Control 173. In Associated Home Builders v. City of Livermore, supra note 15, the California Supreme Court expressly held that "the indirect burden upon the right to travel imposed by the Livermore ordinance does not call for strict judicial scrutiny" but should "be measured by the more liberal standards that have traditionally tested the validity of land use restrictions under the municipal police power." 18 Cal.2d at 603–604, 135 Cal.Rptr. at 52–53, 557 P.2d at 485.

23. 522 F.2d at 904.

The Court of Appeals took the traditional deferential approach to the *Petaluma* plaintiffs' substantive due process argument, which was based on the alleged exclusionary effect of the growth management program and its failure to further any "legitimate governmental interest." The court pointed out that all kinds of land use controls have some exclusionary effect,[24] and that the Petaluma program's low- and moderate-income housing policy made the program "inclusionary" rather than "exclusionary" with respect to lower income households.[25] In any case, the court said, the exclusionary effect of the program could be justified because it bore a "rational relationship to a *legitimate state interest*"—i.e., "the preservation of Petaluma's small town character and the avoidance of the social and environmental problems caused by an uncontrolled growth rate."[26] The court relied heavily on the Supreme Court's decision in *Belle Terre*[27] and its own prior decision in Ybarra v. Town of Los Altos Hills.[28]

Perhaps the most significant passage in the *Petaluma* opinion is the response of the Court of Appeals to the argument that the Petaluma program violated substantive due process because it did not promote the "general welfare of the region or entire state":

> We agree with appellees that unlike the situation in the past most municipalities today are neither isolated nor wholly independent from neighboring municipalities and that, consequently, unilateral land use decisions by one local entity affect the needs and resources of an entire region. * * * It does not necessarily follow, however, that the *due process* rights of builders and landowners are violated merely because a local entity exercises in its own self-interest the police power lawfully delegated to it by the state. * * * If the present system of delegated zoning power does not effectively serve the state interest in furthering the general welfare of the region or entire state, it is the state legislature's and not the federal courts' role to intervene and adjust the system. * * * [T]he federal court is not a super zoning board and should not be called on to mark the point at which legitimate local interests in promoting the welfare of the community are outweighed by legitimate regional interests.[29]

Growth management has been out of style during the economic recession of the early 1980s. If the economy revives, however, it may once again move to center stage.[30] If it does, it will face a new obstacle in

---

24. Id. at 906.

25. Id. at 908.

26. Id. at 906.

27. Belle Terre v. Boraas, 416 U.S. 1, 94 S.Ct. 1536, 39 L.Ed.2d 797 (1974). See ante Section 9.4.

28. 503 F.2d 250 (9th Cir.1974) (one acre lot minimums and exclusive single-family zoning upheld). The Court said:

Both the Belle Terre ordinance and the Los Altos Hill regulation had the purpose and effect of permanently restricting growth; nonetheless, the court in each case upheld the particular law before it on the ground that the regulation served a legitimate governmental interest falling within the concept of the pub-

lic welfare: the preservation of quiet family neighborhoods (Belle Terre) and the preservation of a rural environment (Los Altos Hills).

29. 522 F.2d at 908.

30. A growth management program was recently upheld in Giuliano v. Edgartown, 531 F.Supp. 1076 (D.Mass.1982). But a residential growth management plan was struck down in Stoney-Brook Development Corp. v. Town of Fremont, 124 N.H. 583, 474 A.2d 561 (1984) (ordinance failed to comply with statute requiring careful study of local and regional development needs before adoption of municipal plan). For additional discussion of growth management programs, see Blumstein, A Prolegomenon to Growth Management and Exclu-

California: the statutory presumption that a local ordinance "directly" restricting either building permits or buildable lots has "an impact on the supply of residential lots available in the municipality and surrounding area" so as to impose on the local government the burden of justifying such restrictions.[31]

§ 9.19   Land Use Control for Aesthetic Purposes

It is clear that aesthetic considerations are significant in connection with much traditional zoning—e.g., zoning that imposes large minimum lot-size requirements.[1] But land use controls expressly based on aesthetic considerations have been more difficult for the courts to deal with.[2] The earliest cases involved the regulation or total prohibition of advertising signs in urban areas. At first, the courts generally invalidated such regulatory measures on the ground that aesthetic considerations were not within the police power and, therefore, regulation for aesthetic purposes violated substantive due process.[3] Later, however, urban sign controls were sustained on the basis of asserted non-aesthetic considerations such as safety and morals.[4] Still later, courts began to hold that urban sign controls could be sustained where aesthetic considerations were one, but not the only, factor justifying such controls. Other factors commonly invoked were traffic safety and protection of property values.[5] Ultimately, at least a few courts accepted aesthetic considerations standing alone as sufficient justification for urban advertising sign controls.[6] But, in the real world, aesthetic considerations never "stand alone," and the validity of comprehensive billboard-banning ordinances is now subject to doubt on the basis of First Amendment "free speech" considerations.[7]

sionary Zoning Issues, 43 L. & Contemp.Prob. 5 (1979); Brower & Pannabecker, Growth Management Update: An Assessment and Status Report, 19 Nat. Resources J. 16 (1979); Ellickson, Suburban Growth Controls: An Economic and Social Analysis, 86 Yale L.J. 385 (1977); Roberts, An Appropriate Economic Model of Judicial Review of Suburban Growth Control, 55 Ind.L.J. 441 (1980).

31. West's Ann.Cal. Evidence Code § 669.5. This rule was stated by way of dictum in Associated Home Builders v. City of Livermore, supra note 15.

§ 9.19

1. See ante Section 9.5. In Pearson v. City of Grand Blanc, 756 F.Supp. 314 (E.D.Mich. 1991), affirmed 961 F.Supp. 1211 (6th Cir. 1992), it was held that aesthetic considerations may properly be taken into account in denying an application to rezone from a residential to a commercial classification.

2. See, generally, D. Mandelker, Land Use Law §§ 11.1–11.13 (1982); Costonis, Law and Aesthetics: A Critique and a Reformulation of the Dilemmas, 80 Mich.L.Rev. 361 (1982).

3. E.g., City of Passaic v. Paterson Bill Posting, Etc. Co., 72 N.J.L. 285, 62 A. 267 (Err. & App.1905).

4. E.g., St. Louis Gunning Advertisement Co. v. City of St. Louis, 235 Mo. 99, 137 S.W. 929 (1911), appeal dismissed 231 U.S. 761, 34 S.Ct. 325, 58 L.Ed. 470 (1913).

5. E.g., United Advertising Corp. v. Borough of Metuchen, 42 N.J. 1, 198 A.2d 447 (1964).

6. E.g., Metromedia, Inc. v. San Diego, 26 Cal.3d 848, 164 Cal.Rptr. 510, 610 P.2d 407 (1981), reversed on other grounds 453 U.S. 490, 101 S.Ct. 2882, 69 L.Ed.2d 800 (1981); City of Lake Wales v. Lamar Advertising Association of Lakeland, 414 So.2d 1030 (Fla. 1982). See also State v. Jones, 305 N.C. 520, 290 S.E.2d 675 (1982) (junkyard regulation).

7. In *Metromedia*, supra note 6, the United States Supreme Court invalidated a city-wide ban on "off premises" billboards contained in a comprehensive sign control ordinance on First Amendment grounds. In addition to the usual exemption for "on premises" signs, the ordinance also contained exemptions for governmental signs, religious signs, time and temperature signs, temporary political signs, and the like. Unfortunately, there was no majority opinion in *Metromedia*, and many important issues are therefore left unanswered. The San Diego city council sought to salvage its sign ordinance by repealing all the

Since World War II, many urban and suburban communities have adopted architectural design regulations for new residential structures.[8] These regulations, which may be separately enacted or enacted as part of the local zoning ordinance, usually create a design review board with power to approve or reject the design of any proposed residential structure—especially, any proposed single family dwelling. The architectural design regulations generally include standards governing the exterior features of the residential structures covered by the regulations, and often include either an "anti-look-alike" provision—to prevent developers from building large numbers of almost identical houses—or a "design compatibility" provision—to prevent construction of new houses that are too dissimilar to the existing houses in the neighborhood. And sometimes the regulations include both "anti-look-alike" and "design compatibility" standards!

Architectural design regulations have only rarely been the subject of appellate court decisions. All of the cases came from residential suburbs, and most of them were decided before the courts generally had accepted aesthetic considerations, standing alone, as a proper basis for exercise of the zoning power. In a few cases architectural design regulations were held invalid on the ground that promotion of aesthetic values was not a proper zoning purpose. In other cases, the courts struck down design review requirements on the ground that they improperly delegated the zoning power. Most of the more recent cases, however, uphold architectural design regulations which require new residential structures to be approved by a

---

provisions dealing with noncommercial billboards—which would have satisfied the objections of the United States Supreme Court plurality—but the California Supreme Court then struck down the entire ordinance, as revised, on the ground that the provisions relating to commercial and noncommercial billboards were not severable. Metromedia, Inc. v. City of San Diego, 32 Cal.3d 180, 185 Cal.Rptr. 260, 649 P.2d 902 (1982).

At least two state court cases subsequent to *Metromedia* invalidated comprehensive sign ordinances like the San Diego ordinance. At least two other state court cases, however, sustained sign ordinances prohibiting only commercial billboards. See City of Lakewood v. Colfax Unlimited Association, Inc., 634 P.2d 52 (Colo.1981) (invalid); Norton Outdoor Advertising, Inc. v. Village of Arlington Heights, 69 Ohio St.2d 539, 433 N.E.2d 198 (1982) (invalid). Cf. Maurice Callahan & Sons, Inc. v. Outdoor Advertising Board, 12 Mass.App.Ct. 536, 427 N.E.2d 25 (1981) (valid); Singer Supermarkets, Inc. v. Zoning Board of Adjustment, 183 N.J.Super. 285, 443 A.2d 1082 (App. Div.1982) (valid).

The scope of the plurality opinion in *Metromedia,* supra note 6, was modified in City Council of City of Los Angeles v. Taxpayers for Vincent, 466 U.S. 789, 104 S.Ct. 2118, 80 L.Ed.2d 772 (1984), on remand 738 F.2d 353 (9th Cir.1984), where the Supreme Court sustained an ordinance prohibiting the posting of public property of any signs, including political campaign posters. For a recent case invalidating an ordinance prohibiting any change in the message carried by a nonconforming sign, solely on the basis of its content, as a violation of the sign owner's First Amendment rights, see Kevin Gray–East Coast Auto Body v. Village of Nyack, 171 A.D.2d 924, 566 N.Y.S.2d 795 (1991). See also National Advertising Co. v. Town of Babylon, 900 F.2d 551 (2d Cir.1990), cert. denied ___ U.S. ___, 111 S.Ct. 146, 112 L.Ed.2d 112 (1990) (an ordinance that prohibits all signs except those advertising on-site business is unconstitutional because it favors commercial over non-commercial speech); National Advertising Co. v. Town of Niagara, 942 F.2d 145 (2d Cir.1991) (ordinance provision that allows only on-site commercial advertising signs is invalid, and the entire ordinance must be invalidated because, under state law, the different provisions of the ordinance are not severable); Adams Outdoor Advertising of Atlanta, Inc. v. Fulton County, 738 F.Supp. 1431 (N.D.Ga.1990) (failure of ordinance to state explicitly what governmental interest was sought to be advanced made ordinance invalid on First Amendment free speech grounds); Tahoe Regional Planning Agency v. King, 233 Cal.App. 1365, 285 Cal. Rptr. 335 (1991) (ordinance banning all off-site non-commercial signs except temporary political signs was facially invalid as a violation of First Amendment free speech rights).

8. Generally, see D. Mandelker, Land Use Law §§ 11.12, 11.13 (1982).

design review board. All of these more recent cases relied on a protection of property values rationale.

In two of the leading cases, State ex rel. Saveland Park Holding Corp. v. Wieland [9] and Reid v. Architectural Board of Review,[10] the courts sustained ordinances requiring that the design of new houses should be sufficiently compatible with existing houses in the immediate neighborhood so as not to cause substantial depreciation in property values in the neighborhood. And in State ex rel. Stoyanoff v. Berkeley [11] the court sustained design control ordinance that contained both "anti-look-alike" and "design compatibility" standards. All three of these cases relied largely on a protection of property rights rather than a pure "aesthetic" rationale.

The protection of property values rationale may, of course, prove inadequate in light of the facts in a particular case. In Hankins v. Borough of Rockleigh,[12] for example, the New Jersey intermediate appeals court found the design requirements invalid "in light of the actual physical development of the community." Specifically, a prohibition of flat roofs was unreasonable because there were several flat-roofed buildings and buildings with flat-roofed extensions in the vicinity of the proposed new flat-roofed house.

It would seem that reliance on the protection of property values rationale is no longer necessary in states which have adopted the purely aesthetic rationale of the more recent billboard exclusion cases,[13] although in fact the property values rationale will be applicable in most cases. But "free speech" notions may yet provide a basis for constitutional challenge to architectural design regulations, since architectural expression may well be held to be within the protection of the First Amendment as a form of commercial speech.[14] If so, it is reasonably clear that architectural design review does more than merely regulate the "time, place, and manner" of architectural expression. It may—and often does—totally exclude a variety of architectural styles, and this might be found invalid as a content-based prohibition of commercial speech if the courts ultimately refuse to accept either aesthetic considerations alone or in combination with the protection of property values as a sufficiently important governmental interest to justify the prohibition.[15]

§ 9.20 Historic District and Landmark Controls

Architectural design regulations are intended to control the exterior appearance of new structures. Historical preservation regulations are intended to preserve the exterior appearance of existing buildings in "historic

9. 269 Wis. 262, 69 N.W.2d 217 (1955), certiorari denied 350 U.S. 841, 76 S.Ct. 81, 100 L.Ed. 750 (1955).

10. 119 Ohio App. 67, 192 N.E.2d 74 (1963).

11. 458 S.W.2d 305 (Mo.1970).

See also Novi v. City of Pacifica, 169 Cal. App.3d 678, 215 Cal.Rptr. 439 (1985) (ordinance requiring "variety in architectural design" is valid under "general welfare" standard and is not void for vagueness).

12. 55 N.J.Super. 132, 150 A.2d 63 (App. Div.1959).

13. See supra in text at note 6.

14. See Kolis, Architectural Expression: Police Power and the First Amendment, 16 Urb.L.Ann. 273 (1978); Costonis, supra note 2, at 447–458.

15. Ibid.

districts" and, in some instances, the exterior appearance of individual "historic structures." [1] The purpose is often—perhaps usually—at least partly "aesthetic"; but the appearance of "historic" buildings and districts may embody "historic" values that are not necessarily aesthetically attractive. Indeed, Professor John Costonis has recently advanced the view that preservation of "historic districts" and "historic structures"—like "aesthetic" regulation, generally—must be justified (if at all) on the ground that it may aid in preserving "[c]ultural stability and individual, group, and community identity." [2]

The historic preservation movement started with the designation of showplace areas such as Beacon Hill in Boston and the French Quarter in New Orleans as "historic districts." Today, "historic districts" have been created in almost all parts of the United States under powers delegated to local governments by state enabling legislation. The enabling statutes authorize local governments to enact historic district ordinances and to create local commissions to administer such ordinances. Usually the local government makes an inventory of historic areas and adopts an historic preservation plan as a basis for designating historic districts. Once an area is designated as an historic district, the demolition and exterior alteration of any building in the district—whether an individual building is itself of historical value—are prohibited without the approval of the historic district commission. Most historic district ordinances also prohibit new construction or repairs of existing buildings without commission approval. Approval will be granted, pursuant to standards set out in the ordinance, only if the proposed changes in existing buildings or new construction are appropriate in light of the character of the historic district.

Historic landmark regulations are generally similar to historic district regulations except for the fact that an "historic landmark" is ordinarily a single structure which is not part of an "historic district." Historic landmark preservation legislation is less common than historic district legislation, however. In some states, the statutory authority for landmark preservation is contained in the historic district legislation. Historic landmark preservation statutes provide for adoption of local landmark preservation ordinances and creation of local commissions to implement the ordinances. Like historic district ordinances, historic landmark ordinances require approval by the local landmark commission before a landmark structure can be demolished or substantially changed in exterior appearance, and before any new construction can take place on the landmark site. In addition, owners of landmark structures are often required by the landmark ordinance to keep their structures in good repair. However, to avoid "taking" claims, landmark statutes and ordinances often provide for the granting of waivers or variances when the owner demonstrates that he cannot earn a reasonable

§ 9.20

1. Generally, see D. Mandelker, Land Use Law §§ 11.14–11.25 (1982).

In Sameric Corp. of Chestnut Street, Inc. v. City of Philadelphia, 125 Pa.Cmwlth. 520, 558 A.2d 155 (1989), it was held that an historic district commission may constitutionally des-ignate the *interior* of a privately owned building—in this case, an "intact Art Deco movie palace"—as an historic landmark.

2. Costonis, Law and Aesthetics: A Critique and a Reformulation of the Dilemmas, 80 Mich.L.Rev. 361, 418 (1982).

return on his investment unless some alteration of the landmark structure or site is permitted.

Both historic district ordinances and landmark preservation ordinances have been challenged on the ground that they improperly delegate authority to the administrative agency (commission) without adequate standards to control its exercise of discretion.

In A–S–P Associates v. City of Raleigh,[3] the North Carolina court sustained the standards provided for review of exterior changes in buildings in the historic district, noting that delegation problems were minimized by appointing as members of the historic district commission persons with both experience and interest in architectural matters. The court expressly held that the basic standard—"incongruity"—was adequate. However, in Texas Antiquities Committee v. Dallas County Community College District,[4] it was held that a statute authorizing a state-level committee to designate "buildings of historical interest" did not provide sufficient standards. The court rejected the committee's argument that the presence of experts on the committee should eliminate the delegation problem.

Both historic district and landmark preservation regulations have been challenged on substantive due process and "taking" grounds in a number of cases. These challenges have been unsuccessful in a great majority of the cases. Some of the early cases, while not fully embracing the "aesthetic" rationale, gave it considerable weight as a basis for regulation. Other cases have emphasized more purely "historical" values, as in the A–S–P case,[5] where the court sustained the historic district designation of the "only intact nineteenth century neighborhood remaining in Raleigh * * * composed predominantly of Victorian houses." The A–S–P court also sustained the denial of a certificate of appropriateness for construction of a new office building in the Raleigh historic district, on the ground that this was necessary to prevent the intrusion of an architecturally incompatible structure in an area which had a unifying architectural theme. The court further noted that landowners were not prohibited from putting up new buildings in the historic district but were "only required to construct them in a manner that will not result in a structure incongruous with the historic aspects of the Historic District."[6] And the court expressly held that the property owner's inability to develop land in the historic district for its most profitable use did not constitute a *de facto* "taking."[7]

---

3. 298 N.C. 207, 258 S.E.2d 444 (1979).

4. 554 S.W.2d 924 (Tex.1977).

5. Supra note 3.

6. 298 N.C. at 218, 258 S.E.2d at 451.

See also Bellevue Shopping Center Associates v. Chase, 574 A.2d 760 (R.I.1990) (historic district commission may disapprove a plan for a new shopping center building on the basis of a finding that the proposed building would seriously impair the historic value of nearby structures).

7. Ibid. Figarsky v. Historic District Com'n, 171 Conn. 198, 368 A.2d 163 (1976), reached the same conclusion in a case where the owners of a house on the edge of the historic district wished to demolish it and construct a new one. The court, in dealing with the "taking" argument, said: "The plaintiffs had the burden of proving that the historic district commission acted illegally, arbitrarily, in a confiscatory manner or in abuse of discretion. This the plaintiffs failed to do. The plaintiffs went no further than to present evidence that their house was unoccupied and in need of extensive repairs. There is no evidence offered that the house, if repaired, would not be of some value, or that the proximity of the McDonald's hamburger stand rendered the property of no value as a part of the historic district."

Rebman v. City of Springfield [8] went even further than the A–S–P case, rejecting a "taking" claim in a case where the four-block historic district was created simply to preserve the noncommercial surroundings of an important historic building—Abraham Lincoln's house in Springfield, Illinois. The court said, "[I]t is clear that the use of the [plaintiff's] property not in conformity with the existing [historic district] zoning would be detrimental to the Lincoln Home area and the planning concept of the community." [9] The court also said that the creation of the historic district had enhanced the value of the plaintiff's property rather than depreciating it.

In Penn Central Transportation Co. v. City of New York,[10] the United States Supreme Court upheld, as against a "taking" challenge, the action of the New York City Landmarks Preservation Commission in refusing to approve an elaborate Penn Central proposal to construct a multistory office building behind and above the existing Grand Central Terminal, which had been given landmark status, because this would be destructive of the Terminal's historic and aesthetic features as a prime example of neoclassic Beaux Arts design. The plaintiff conceded that "New York City's objective of preserving structures and areas with special historic, architectural, or cultural significance is an entirely permissible governmental goal" and that "the restrictions imposed on its parcel are appropriate means of securing the purposes of the New York City law," so that only the "taking" issue was before the court.

Penn Central had practically precluded itself from challenging the specific application of the New York City Landmark Law to the Grand Central Terminal site by conceding that the Terminal site "must, in its present state, be regarded as capable of earning a reasonable return," and that the transferable development rights available to Penn Central by virtue of the site's designation as a landmark "are valuable, even if not as valuable as the rights to construct above the Terminal." Moreover, Penn Central had not sought approval for the construction of a smaller structure, so the court was not prepared to assume that Penn Central would be denied all use of the airspace above the Terminal—especially since "nothing the Commission has said or done suggests an intention to prohibit *any* construction above the Terminal." Having made these concessions, Penn Central was really limited to arguing that, in principle, all landmark preservation ordinances must necessarily amount to a *de facto* "taking" or violate substantive due process.

Penn Central argued, more specifically, (1) that a "taking" occurs whenever a landowner is precluded from using some of the air space within his land's "zoning envelope"; [11] (2) that any designation of a structure as a landmark is "inevitably arbitrary or at least subjective because it is basically a matter of taste,"; [12] (3) that landmark regulations are "inherently incapable of producing the fair and equitable distribution of benefits and burdens of governmental action which is characteristic of zoning laws and historic

---

8. 111 Ill.App.2d 430, 250 N.E.2d 282 (1969).

9. 111 Ill.App.2d at 412, 250 N.E.2d at 288.

10. 438 U.S. 104, 98 S.Ct. 2646, 57 L.Ed.2d 631 (1978) rehearing denied 439 U.S. 883, 99 S.Ct. 226, 58 L.Ed.2d 198 (1978).

11. 438 U.S. at 130, 98 S.Ct. at 2662.

12. 438 U.S. at 132, 98 S.Ct. at 2663.

district legislation"; [13] and (4) that the government acts "in an enterprise capacity" when it designates a structure as a landmark and thus appropriates private property "for some strictly governmental purpose." [14]

The majority in *Penn Central* rejected all these arguments. As to the first argument, the court said that "taking" jurisprudence "does not divide a single parcel [of land] into discrete segments and attempt to determine whether rights in a particular segment have been entirely abrogated," but rather focuses "on the nature and extent of the interference with rights in the parcel as a whole, here, the city tax block designated as the 'landmark site.' " [15] This holding is consistent with the decisions sustaining building setback and height restrictions,[16] and also with the analysis in the Brandeis dissent in Pennsylvania Coal Co. v. Mahon,[17] but seems inconsistent with the Holmes majority opinion in *Mahon*.[18]

The Court answered the second argument by pointing out that landmark site owners always have a right to judicial review of all landmark commission decisions and that "there is no basis whatsoever for a conclusion that courts will have any greater difficulty identifying arbitrary or discriminatory action in the context of landmark regulation than in the context of classic zoning or indeed in any other context." [19] With respect to the third argument, the Court said that even traditional zoning regulations do not apportion benefits and burdens equally among all landowners and asserted that since landowners as a class derive some benefit—through improvement of the quality of life in the city as a whole—from the preservation of historic landmarks, Penn Central was *not* "solely burdened and unbenefited" as it claimed.[20] And the Court responded to the fourth argument by stating that the government acts in a regulatory, not an "enterprise," capacity when it adopts and implements landmark preservation regulations.[21]

Although *Penn Central* left a number of questions unanswered, it clearly established the validity, in principle, of landmark regulations as against challenge under the Fourteenth Amendment. Moreover, it can be inferred that the court will not find a "taking" where a property owner can earn a "reasonable return" on his investment subject to the regulations of which he complains. And the court clearly indicated that, in considering whether a "reasonable return" can be earned, transferable development rights may be taken into account—at least where it is clear that they have substantial value.[22] We shall look more closely at the use of transferable development rights to mitigate "taking" claims in Section 22.

13. 438 U.S. at 133, 98 S.Ct. at 2664. The plaintiff here was arguing that designation of isolated landmarks for preservation could not achieve the "average reciprocity of advantage" cited in earlier cases as a basis for upholding police power regulations. See, e.g., the Brandeis dissent in Pennsylvania Coal Co. v. Mahon, 260 U.S. 393, 415, 43 S.Ct. 158, 161, 67 L.Ed. 322 (1922), and the Rehnquist dissent in *Penn Central*, 438 U.S. at 140, 98 S.Ct. at 2671.

14. 438 U.S. at 135, 98 S.Ct. at 2665.

15. 438 at U.S. at 130, 98 S.Ct. at 2662.

16. E.g., Gorieb v. Fox, 274 U.S. 603, 47 S.Ct. 675, 71 L.Ed. 1228 (1927); Welch v. Swa-

sey, 214 U.S. 91, 29 S.Ct. 567, 53 L.Ed. 923 (1909).

17. Supra note 12.

18. The Holmes opinion considered only the pillars of coal required to be left on the ground by the Pennsylvania statute.

19. 438 U.S. at 133, 98 S.Ct. at 2663.

20. 438 U.S. at 134, 98 S.Ct. at 2664.

21. 438 U.S. at 135, 98 S.Ct. at 2665.

22. 438 U.S. at 137, 98 S.Ct. at 2666. The New York Court of Appeals placed even more reliance on the value of Penn Central's transferable development rights as "reasonable

Other cases have considered the difficult issues arising when the owner of a landmark structure or a building in a historic district desires to demolish the structure and put up a more profitable building on the site. In Maher v. City of New Orleans,[23] the Fifth Circuit Court of Appeals rejected the owner's "taking" claim in such a case on the ground that the owner had failed to show that all reasonable uses of its property were precluded unless demolition was allowed. But in Lafayette Park Baptist Church v. Scott,[24] it was held that a historic district ordinance "must be interpreted to authorize demolition when the condition of the structure is such that the economics of restoration preclude the landowner from making any reasonable economic use of the property." [25] Other courts have applied the *Lafayette* holding to landmark structures not located in historic districts. A leading New York case, Lutheran Church in America v. City of New York,[26] overturned, as a "taking," the Landmark Preservation Commission's refusal to allow demolition of a landmark structure used as an office building, on a showing that the building had become inadequate for its office use. But *Lutheran Church* has been heavily criticized, and seems to have been substantially qualified by Society for Ethical Culture v. Spatt.[27] In *Spatt,* the court did not discuss the "enterprise" theory of "taking" [28] which was a partial basis for the decision in *Lutheran Church,* and held that a "taking" did not result from the mere fact that the landmark designation "stands as an effective bar against putting the property to its most lucrative use." [29]

The most important recent "landmark" cases have involved both "taking" and "free exercise of religion" issues. In St. Bartholomew's Church v. City of New York,[30] the Church challenged the New York Landmarks Commission's refusal to give the Church a permit to demolish its seven-story "community house" and erect a high-rise office tower in its place both on Fifth and Fourteenth Amendment and on First Amendment grounds. The federal district court granted summary judgment for the City on the Church's First Amendment claims, finding no merit in the Church's claim that the Landmarks Law was invalid on its face as a violation of the First Amendment's free exercise and establishment clauses.[31] After trial, the district court also denied the Church's claims that, "as applied," the Commission's refusal to permit demolition of the "community house" amounted to a "taking" and also violated the Church's First Amendment rights.[32] The district court held that the same test was applicable to both the "taking" and the First Amendment claims—the test being whether the Church could "no

compensation." See Penn Central Transportation Co. v. City of New York, 42 N.Y.2d 324, 335, 397 N.Y.S.2d 914, 920–921, 366 N.E.2d 1271, 1278 (1977).

23. 516 F.2d 1051 (5th Cir.1975), certiorari denied 426 U.S. 905, 96 S.Ct. 2225, 48 L.Ed.2d 830 (1976).

The Connecticut Supreme Court reach the same result on the same grounds in Figarsky v. Historic District Com'n, supra note 7.

24. 553 S.W.2d 856 (Mo.App.1977).

25. Id. at 862.

26. 35 N.Y.2d 121, 359 N.Y.S.2d 7, 316 N.E.2d 305 (1974).

27. 51 N.Y.2d 449, 434 N.Y.S.2d 932, 415 N.E.2d 922 (1980).

28. This theory is advanced in Sax, Takings and the Police Power, 74 Yale L.J. 36 (1964).

29. 51 N.Y.2d at 456, 434 N.Y.S.2d at 936, 415 N.E.2d at 926.

30. 728 F.Supp. 958 (S.D.N.Y.1989), affirmed 914 F.2d 348 (2d Cir.1990), cert. denied ___ U.S. ___, 111 S.Ct. 1103, 113 L.Ed.2d 214 (1991).

31. 728 F.Supp. at 963.

32. Id. at 974–975.

longer carry out its religious mission in its existing facilities" [33]—and concluded that the Church failed to carry its burden of proof under this test.[34] On appeal, the Second Circuit affirmed,[35] but used a somewhat different analysis. The Second Circuit's "taking" test was "[whether] the landmark designation would prevent or seriously interfere with the carrying out of the charitable purpose of the institution" [36]—identical in substance with the test applied by the district court—and concluded that the Landmarks Law was "a facially neutral regulation of general applicability within the meaning of Supreme Court decisions" [37] and thus did not violate the "free exercise of religion" clause, absent a showing of discriminatory motive, coercion with respect to religious practice, or deprivation of the Church's ability to carry out its religious mission in its existing facilities.[38]

The United States Supreme Court denied the petition for certiorari filed by St. Bartholemew's Church,[39] but on the same day granted certiorari [40] in a case [41] where the Washington Supreme Court had held that a Seattle "landmark" ordinance violated a church's First Amendment "free exercise" rights. Shortly thereafter, the United States Supreme Court summarily disposed of the case [42] by vacating the judgment and remanding the case to the Washington Supreme Court for further consideration in light of Employment Division v. Smith,[43] where the United States Supreme Court had held that government may constitutionally restrict certain activities associated with the practice of religion, pursuant to its general regulatory power, by a neutral, generally applicable law that happens to bear on religiously motivated actions.

§ 9.21 Environmental Protection

A good deal of the "open space" zoning discussed in earlier sections of this chapter is designed to protect the natural environment as well as to control suburban growth. Massive rezonings to an "open space" classification in Palo Alto, California in the early 1970s were carried out largely to protect the "lower Foothills" area on the outskirts of Palo Alto. As we have previously seen, these "open space" rezonings gave rise to a series of "taking" challenges.[1] San Diego's action in designating as "open space" a

---

33. Id. at 966–967.

34. Id. at 974–975.

35. 914 F.2d 348 (2d Cir.1990), cert. denied ___ U.S. ___, 111 S.Ct. 1103, 113 L.Ed.2d 214 (1991).

36. Id. at 356.

37. Id. at 355–56.

38. Id. at 354, relying on Employment Division v. Smith, 494 U.S. 872, 110 S.Ct. 1595, 108 L.Ed.2d 876 (1990), where the court said, "The critical distinction is thus between a neutral, generally applicable law that happens to bear on religiously motivated action, and a regulation that restricts certain conduct because it is religiously oriented."

39. Supra note 30.

40. First Covenant Church of Seattle, Wash. v. Seattle, 114 Wn.2d 392, 787 P.2d 1352 (1990), cert. granted and judgment vacat-ed ___ U.S. ___, 111 S.Ct. 1097, 113 L.Ed.2d 208 (1991).

41. Supra note 40.

42. ___ U.S. ___, 111 S.Ct. 1097, 113 L.Ed.2d 208 (1991).

43. See supra note 38. For comment on *First Covenant Church,* see McConnell, Free Exercise Revisionism and the *Smith* Decision, 57 U.Chi.L.Rev. 1109 (1990); Gordon, Free Exercise on the Mountaintop, 79 Calif.L.Rev. 91 (1991); Marshall, In Defense of *Smith* and Free Exercise Revisionism, 58 U.Chi.L.Rev. 308 (1991).

§ 9.21

1. See Arastra Limited Partnership v. City of Palo Alto, 401 F.Supp. 962 (N.D.Cal.1975), vacated 417 F.Supp. 1125 (1976); Dahl v. City of Palo Alto, 372 F.Supp. 647 (N.D.Cal.1974);

substantial tract located in a tidal marsh—apparently for the purpose of preserving it in its natural state—gave rise to the famous dissent in San Diego Gas & Electric Co. v. City of San Diego [2] in which four justices said that compensation is constitutionally mandated when—and if—a land use regulation is found to be a *de facto* "taking."

The *San Diego Gas & Electric* case involved what has generally come to be called "wetlands"—transitional marshy areas lying between dry land and bodies of water such as oceans, tidal estuaries, rivers, and lakes. Such "wetlands" help to preserve water quality by slowing water flow and allowing sediment and waste to settle, and they control water quantity by storing water during dry periods and arresting run-off during periods of heavy precipitation. In addition, "wetlands" provide a habitat for a diversity of plants and animals and a breeding ground for many commercially important animals such as fish and shellfish.

During the past two decades many states on the Atlantic, Pacific, and Gulf coasts have enacted statutes specifically designed to protect coastal wetlands,[3] and several states in the midwest and elsewhere have enacted statutes designed to protect inland wetlands.[4] Typically, these statutes authorize a designated state agency to map wetland areas and to regulate their use and development. Generally such statutes require that a permit be obtained for any substantial new development in a wetland area, or for dredging and filling, which are preliminary steps in most wetlands development.[5] The statutes usually contain quite restrictive standards for evaluation of permit applications and set out procedures for obtaining permits (including appeal procedures) and penalties for violation of the statute.

In some states, local government regulation of wetlands is also specifically authorized,[6] and even where it is not specifically authorized, it has been held that authority may be implied from the language of traditional zoning enabling statutes derived from the Standard Act.[7] On the other hand, state environmental protection legislation does not unconstitutionally infringe on

Eldridge v. City of Palo Alto, 57 Cal.App.3d 613, 129 Cal.Rptr. 575 (1976); Beyer v. City of Palo Alto, ibid. (companion case to *Eldridge*).

2. 450 U.S. 621, 636–638, 101 S.Ct. 1287, 1296, 67 L.Ed.2d 551 (1981). For a discussion of the California cases, see Cunningham, Inverse Condemnation as a Remedy for "Regulatory Takings," 8 Hastings Const. L.Q. 517 (1981).

3. E.g., Conn.Gen.Stat.Ann. § 22a–28 et seq.; 7 Del.Code § 6601 et seq.; Georgia Code, § 43–2601 et seq.; 38 Maine Rev.Stat.Ann. § 471 et seq.; Mass.Gen.Laws Ann. c. 130, § 105; New Hamp.Rev.Stat.Ann. 483–A:1 et seq.; New Jersey Stat.Ann. 13:9A–1 et seq.; Rhode Island Gen.Laws 1956, § 2–10–14.

4. E.g., Wis.Stat.Ann. 59.971, 144.26.

5. The Massachusetts statute, supra note 3, is an exception; it authorizes the state agency to adopt protective orders "regulating,

restricting or prohibiting dredging, filling, removing or otherwise altering, or polluting, coastal wetlands." While the statute does not specify how the protective order is to be implemented, it does provide that a "plan" of the lands affected as well as the order shall be recorded in the local land title registry. In practice, orders filed under the act specify uses allowed as of right, such as hunting and fishing; uses allowed only subject to conditions, such as roadways and utility lines; and uses for which a permit must be obtained, such as excavations for boat channels and beaches. See F. Bosselman & D. Callies, The Quiet Revolution in Land Use Control 205–34 (1971) for a discussion of the administration of the Massachusetts statute.

6. E.g., the Wisconsin statute, supra note 2.

7. E.g., Morland Development Co., Inc. v. City of Tulsa, 596 P.2d 1255 (Okl.1979).

local home rule powers.[8]   Indeed, in some cases the state legislation may be found to pre-empt the environmental protection field.[9]

Challenges by land developers to state and local wetlands protection statutes and ordinances have generally been based on the contention that the restriction of use and development results in a *de facto* "taking" of private property without "just compensation."   In several early cases, the "taking" challenge was successful in state courts.   In Morris County Land Improvement Co. v. Township of Parsippany–Troy Hills,[10] the New Jersey court held a local wetland ordinance unconstitutional both because the purpose of the ordinance was to acquire a public benefit by preserving the wetland as a flood retention basin and because the effect was to deprive the landowner of any reasonable use of the land.   In State v. Johnson,[11] the Maine court also held a wetlands protection statute unconstitutional as applied to the facts of the case, on the ground that the landowners' "compensation by sharing in the benefits which this restriction [on filling a wetland area] is intended to secure is so disproportionate to their deprivation of reasonable use that such exercise of the State's police power is unreasonable." [12]

More recently, both the New Jersey and the Maine courts seem to have changed their views on the constitutionality of wetlands protection programs which make substantial private use or development impossible.[13]   And in other states where the issue has been raised, such programs have generally been sustained.[14]   In Just v. Marinette County,[15] the Wisconsin court sustained a wetlands zoning ordinance enacted pursuant to a state wetlands protection statute against attack on the ground that it resulted in a *de facto* "taking."   Since the landowner had not applied for a special permit to fill the wetland area in question, as required by the ordinance, the court could presumably have avoided the constitutional issue, but it met the issue head on.   Although the court cited *Mahon* for the proposition that when a regulation goes too far it must be recognized as a *de facto* "taking" without compensation, and further conceded that a regulation primarily designed to produce a public benefit also amounts to a "taking," it distinguished wetlands regulations on the following theory:

8.   E.g., CEEED v. Coastal Zone Conservation Commission, 43 Cal.App.3d 306, 118 Cal. Rptr. 315 (1974).

9.   E.g., Lauricella v. Planning & Zoning Board, 32 Conn.Sup. 104, 342 A.2d 374 (1974). Contra: Golden v. Board of Selectmen, 358 Mass. 519, 265 N.E.2d 573 (1970).

10.   40 N.J. 539, 193 A.2d 232 (1963).

11.   265 A.2d 711 (Me.1970).

12.   Id. at 716.

13.   See New Jersey Builders Association v. Department of Environmental Protection, 169 N.J.Super. 76, 404 A.2d 320 (App.Div.1979), cert. denied 81 N.J. 402, 408 A.2d 796 (1979); Sands Point Harbor, Inc. v. Sullivan, 136 N.J.Super. 436, 346 A.2d 612 (App.Div.1975); In re Spring Valley Development, 300 A.2d 736 (Me.1973).

14.   E.g., Manor Development Corp. v. Conservation Commission, 180 Conn. 692, 433

A.2d 999 (1980); Graham v. Estuary Properties, Inc., 399 So.2d 1374 (Fla.1981), cert. denied 454 U.S. 1083, 102 S.Ct. 640, 70 L.Ed.2d 618 (1981); Santini v. Lyons, 448 A.2d 124 (R.I.1982); Moskow v. Commissioner of Department of Environmental Management, 384 Mass. 530, 427 N.E.2d 750 (1981); Sibson v. State, 115 N.H. 124, 336 A.2d 239 (1975); Chokecherry Hills Estates, Inc. v. Deuel County, 294 N.W.2d 654 (S.D.1980); Just v. Marinette County, 56 Wis.2d 7, 201 N.W.2d 761 (1972).   See also Candlestick Properties, Inc. v. San Francisco Bay Conservation and Development Commission, 11 Cal.App.3d 557, 89 Cal.Rptr. 897 (1970); Potomac Sand & Gravel Co. v. Governor of Maryland, 266 Md. 358, 293 A.2d 241 (1972), certiorari denied 409 U.S. 1040, 93 S.Ct. 525, 34 L.Ed.2d 490 (1972).

15.   Supra note 14.

[W]e have a restriction on the use of a citizens' property, not to secure a benefit for the public, but to prevent harm from the change in the natural character of the citizens' property. * * * What makes this case different * * * is the interrelationship of the wetlands, the swamps and the natural environment of shorelands to the purity of the water and to such natural resources as navigation, fishing, and scenic beauty. * * * The changing of wetlands and swamps to the damage of the natural relationship is not a reasonable use of that land which is protected from police regulation.[16]

The Wisconsin Court thus treated development of wetlands as a kind of "noxious use," so that severe restriction or even prohibition of development could be viewed as "harm prevention" rather than "creation of a benefit." Ultimately, despite a quotation from the Holmes opinion in *Mahon,* the rationale of the case is derived from *Mugler* [17] and the Brandeis dissent in *Mahon* [18] as modified by Professor Sax in his second "taking" article,[19] which argues that courts should not find a "taking" when the police power is used to protect the public interest in "common" natural resources such as wetlands. This rationale is reinforced by an extension to "shoreland" areas of the Wisconsin "public trust" doctrine traditionally applicable to navigable waters.[20]

Just was expressly relied upon in several more recent cases such as Graham v. Estuary Properties, Inc.,[21] where the Florida Court sustained the denial of a permit for a major residential and commercial development in a coastal wetland area on the ground that the proposed development would destroy a large stand of mangroves, which in turn would have an adverse impact on water quality in the adjacent coastal bay. The court said,[22]

> In this case, the permit was denied because of the determination that the proposed development would pollute the surrounding bays, i.e., cause a public harm. It is true that the public benefits in that the bay will remain clean, but that is a benefit in the form of maintaining the status quo. Estuary is not being required to change its development plan so that public waterways will be improved. That would be the creation of a public benefit beyond the scope of the state's police power.

16.   56 Wis. at 16, 201 N.W.2d at 767.

17.   Mugler v. State of Kansas, 123 U.S. 623, 8 S.Ct. 273, 31 L.Ed. 205 (1887).

18.   Pennsylvania Coal Co. v. Mahon, 260 U.S. 393, 417, 43 S.Ct. 158, 161, 67 L.Ed. 322 (1922).

19.   Sax, Takings, Private Property and Public Rights, 81 Yale L.J. 149 (1971) (to protect the public interest in wetlands as a "common" resource, the police power may be used to prevent private development even though this imposes a severe economic loss on the landowner).

20.   "The state of Wisconsin under the trust doctrine has a duty to eradicate the present pollution and to prevent further pollution in its navigable waters." 56 Wis.2d at 16, 201 N.W.2d at 768.

21.   399 So.2d 1374 (Fla.1981), certiorari denied sub nom. Taylor v. Green, 454 U.S. 1083, 102 S.Ct. 640, 70 L.Ed.2d 618 (1981). Although the New Hampshire court did not cite *Just* in Claridge v. New Hampshire Wetlands Board, 125 N.H. 745, 485 A.2d 287 (1984), where the court sustained very restrictive wetland regulations, the rationale in *Claridge* is substantially identical with the *Just* rationale. See also Lee County v. Morales, 557 So.2d 652 (Fla.App.1990), review denied 564 So.2d 1086 (Fla.1990) (downzoning of commercially zoned lots on a barrier island was not invalid on substantive due process or "taking" grounds where commercial development would endanger "the unique environmental, archeological, historical, and recreational resources of the island").

22.   399 So.2d at 1382.

In Graham v. Estuary Properties, Inc.,[23] the Florida court pointed out that refusal of a development permit would not frustrate the plaintiff's reasonable "investment-backed expectations of the use of the property" since the plaintiff only had a "subjective expectation that the land could be developed in the manner it now proposes." [24] The idea that severe restrictions on land use should not be held to amount to a *de facto* "taking" unless they frustrate "reasonable investment-backed expectations" is derived from *Penn Central* [25] and Kaiser Aetna v. United States,[26] although neither case is cited in *Graham*. *Penn Central* also provides support for severely restrictive wetlands regulations by its suggestion that a sufficient "reciprocity of advantage" may be found even where a regulation imposes a burden on the landowner much greater than the benefit he receives as a result of the regulation.[27]

The analysis employed in the more recent state court environmental protection cases will now have to be modified in light of Lucas v. South Carolina Coastal Commission, decided by the United States Supreme Court at the end of the 1991–92 Term.[28] In *Lucas* the Court adopted a new categorical rule requiring payment of compensation when land use regulations deprive land of *all* "economically beneficial use," subject to an exception where the State can identify pre-existing "background principles of nuisance and property law" prohibiting the uses proscribed by the regulations.[29] This means, said the Court, that in order to avoid the compensation requirement the regulations "must do no more than duplicate the result that could have been achieved by adjacent landowners * * * under the State's law of private nuisance, or by the State under its complementary power to abate nuisances that affect the public generally, or otherwise." [30] Although the new compensability rules laid down by the Court in *Lucas* will be applicable in only a few "regulatory taking" cases,[31] environmental regulations are more likely than other types of regulation to come within the scope

23. Supra note 21.

24. In Claridge v. New Hampshire Wetlands Board, supra note 21, the court also relied on the same argument, pointing out that when the plaintiffs bought their land it was already subject to State wetlands regulations and "had some knowledge that they would need approval" from the local wetlands commission.

25. Penn Central Transportation Co. v. City of New York, 438 U.S. 104, 127, 98 S.Ct. 2646, 2661, 57 L.Ed.2d 631 (1978), rehearing denied 439 U.S. 883, 99 S.Ct. 226, 58 L.Ed.2d 198 (1978).

26. 444 U.S. 164, 175, 100 S.Ct. 383, 390, 62 L.Ed.2d 332 (1979).

27. 438 U.S. at 134, 98 S.Ct. at 2664. The Court did not use the traditional term, "average reciprocity of advantage," but said that the owners of the Grand Central Terminal are benefited "both economically" and through improvement of "the quality of life in the city as a whole" by preservation of landmark structures such as the Terminal. Cf. Justice Rehnquist's dissent, 438 U.S. at 139, 98 S.Ct. at 2667.

28. ___ U.S. ___, 112 S.Ct. 2886, 120 L.Ed.2d 798 (1992). The case is discussed ante in Section 9.2 in text between notecall 77 and notecall 109. The Court's opinion was written by Justice Scalia, who was joined by Chief Justice Rehnquist and Justices O'Connor, Thomas, and White. Justice Kennedy concurred in the Court's judgment remanding the case to the South Carolina courts for further deliberations, but disagreed with the Court's rationale. Justices Blackmun and Stevens dissented with respect to both the Court's disposition of the case and the Court's rationale. Justice Souter did not vote, but filed a "statement" indicating that he thought the case should be dismissed on the ground that certiorari was improvidently granted.

29. See ante Section 9.2 in text between notecalls 93 and 97.

30. See ante Section 9.2 note 96.

31. In his dissent, Justice Blackmun described such regulations as "the most narrow subset of government regulations." See ante Section 9.2 in text at notecall 109.

of the new *Lucas* rules because environmental regulations can more often be argued to have deprived land of *all* "economically beneficial use."

One of the most significant state-level environmental protection programs presently under way is New Jersey's "Pinelands Plan," a "regional zoning master plan to protect the million-acre Pine Barrens ('Pinelands') from piecemeal development." [32] The area covered by the plan, mostly in private ownership, is larger than Rhode Island. Its varied topography is dominated by sandy-soiled forests of dwarf pine and scrub oak, but it includes a great deal of land used for the production of blueberries, cranberries, and, to a lesser extent, field crops. The most significant feature of the Pinelands from an ecological viewpoint, however, is that it overlies the Cohansey Aquifer—an enormous and unique freshwater resource located in the middle of the Boston–New York–Washington megalopolis. The Pinelands Plan is designed in large part to protect and preserve this freshwater resource. The details of the master zoning plan are too complex to set out here, but it should be noted that the plan relies largely on the transfer of development rights from the most severely restricted areas to other areas in order to meet the inevitable attempts to invalidate the plan on the ground that it results in massive *de facto* "takings" without just compensation. [33] In the next section we will consider the use of transferable development rights (TDRs) for this purpose.

§ 9.22 Transfer of Development Rights

The planned unit development (PUD), at least in its simplest form, is a density transfer technique. "Transfer of development rights" (TDR) is another density transfer technique, devised to achieve different purposes. [1] TDR was originally conceived as a technique to avoid the "taking" problems arising in landmark preservation programs. [2] With respect to its use for that purpose, Professor Mandelker has observed that, [3]

> A TDR program for landmark preservation is quite simple. Landmark owners in downtown and other commercial areas wish to demolish their [landmark] buildings and erect high-rise structures because the landmark is usually undersized for it site. The landmark does not fully use the allowable building densities. A TDR program transfers the unused density at the landmark site to a transfer site, which may be nearby or in another area of the community [designated as a "receiving district"]. Under one variant, the owner of the transfer site pays the owner of the landmark for the unused development rights at the landmark site. This payment provides the compensation necessary to

32. See Greenbaum, New Jersey's Pinelands Plan and the "Taking" Question, 7 Colum.J. of Envtl.L. 227 (1982).

33. See id. at 238.

§ 9.22

1. Generally, see J. Costinis, J. Berger & S. Scott, Regulation vs. Compensation in Land Use Control: Recommended Accommodation, A Critique, and an Interpretation (1977); F. James & D. Gale, Zoning for Sale: A Critical Analysis of Transferable Development Rights

Programs (Urban Inst.1977); The Transfer of Development Rights: A New Technique of Land Use Regulation (J. Rose ed. 1975).

2. See Note, Development Rights Transfer in New York City, 82 Yale L.J. 338 (1972). See also Penn Central Transportation Co. v. City of New York, 438 U.S. 104, 98 S.Ct. 2646, 57 L.Ed.2d 631 (1978), rehearing denied 439 U.S. 883, 99 S.Ct. 226, 58 L.Ed.2d 198 (1978).

3. D. Mandelker, Land Use Law § 11.26 (1982).

avoid a taking objection. Under another variant, the municipality creates an agency with the authority to acquire development rights. The agency later sells these rights to landowners at transfer sites.

A TDR program which relies on direct transfer of development rights from the landmark site to a transfer site has been in effect in New York for many years, and has been used to preserve both historic landmark structures and to preserve urban open space.[4] A TDR program designed to backstop landmark preservation regulations and utilizing a municipal agency with authority to buy and sell transferable development rights was proposed for Chicago,[5] but was not adopted.[6] A TDR program designed to protect specific ecologically sensitive areas in Puerto Rico has not been adopted,[7] but a similar TDR program has recently been adopted in New Jersey.[8] Proposals to authorize the large-scale use of TDRs in connection with growth management programs were introduced in both Maryland [9] and New Jersey,[10] but were not enacted. A number of local governments, however, have adopted TDR programs without the benefit of enabling legislation—e.g., Eden, New York (agricultural land preservation),[11] Montgomery County, Maryland (same),[12] St. George, Vermont (growth management),[13] and Collier County, Florida (protection of ecologically sensitive wetlands areas).[14]

Major attacks on the TDR program in New York City were mounted by the plaintiffs in Fred F. French Investing Co., Inc. v. City of New York [15] and Penn Central Transportation Co. v. City of New York.[16] In the *French* case,

4. See Note, supra note 2; Marcus, Air Rights Transfers in New York City, 36 L. & Contemp. Prob. 372 (1972); Marcus, Mandatory Development Rights Transfer and the Taking Clause: The Case of Manhattan's Tudor City Parks, 24 Buffalo L.Rev. 77 (1975). Denver, New Orleans, Portland, and Seattle also use the TDR device for landmark preservation. See 6 Zoning and Planning Law Report 134 (1983).

5. See Costonis, The Chicago Plan: Incentive Zoning and Preservation of Urban Landmarks, 85 Harv.L.Rev. 574 (1972); F. James & D. Gale, supra note 1, at 12–19.

6. See Chicago Plan Rule Out, Planning, July 1974, p. 8.

7. Costonis & Devoy, The Puerto Rico Plan: Environmental Protection Through Development Rights Transfer, in The Transfer of Development Rights: A New Technique of Land Use Regulation (J. Rose ed. 1975) at 200.

8. See Greenbaum, New Jersey's Pinelands Plan and the "Taking" Question, 7 Colum.J. of Envtl.L. 227, 238–249 (1982).

9. See Rose, A Proposal for the Separation and Marketability of Development Rights as a Technique to Preserve Open Space, 51 J. of Urb.L. 460, 474 (1974); Chavoosian, Norman & Nieswand, Transfer of Development Rights: A New Concept in Land Use Management (Mimeo, Leaflet No. 492, Cooperative Extension Service, Cook College, Rutgers University, 1973).

10. N.J. Assembly Bill 3192, 1975 Sess. See Chavoosian, Norman & Nieswand, supra note 9; F. James & D. Gale, supra note 1, at 200.

11. See Emanuel, Rural Eden Uses TDR as Tool to Save Agricultural Land, Practicing Planner, March 1977, at 15.

12. See Planning, July/August 1983, p. 7.

13. See Vermont Town Holds TDR as Tool to Control Future Development, 2 Land Use Planning Reports, July 1974, at 10–14; Wilson Precedent–Setting Swap in Vermont, in The Transfer of Development Rights: A New Technique of Land Use Control (J. Rose ed. 1975).

14. See Collier County Study Recommendations for TDR to Limit Development in Selected Areas, 2 Land Use Planning Reports, August 1974, at 7–8; Collier County, Special Regulations for (ST) Areas of Environmental Sensitivity, Zoning Ordinance § 9 (1974); F. Schnidman, Transferable Development Rights (TDR), in Windfalls for Wipeouts (D. Hagman & D. Miszynski ed. 1978), at 547.

15. 39 N.Y.2d 587, 385 N.Y.S.2d 5, 350 N.E.2d 381 (1976), appeal dismissed 429 U.S. 990, 97 S.Ct. 515, 50 L.Ed.2d 602 (1976).

16. 42 N.Y.2d 324, 397 N.Y.S.2d 914, 366 N.E.2d 1271 (1977), affirmed 438 U.S. 104, 98 S.Ct. 2646, 57 L.Ed.2d 631 (1978).

the New York court struck down an ordinance which sought to preserve urban open space by reclassifying the two Tudor City private parks as parks open to the public. The court held that the prohibition against private building development, coupled with the provision for public use, made the ordinance invalid under the due process clauses of the United States and New York constitutions. The court also held that the constitutional defect was not eliminated by a provision in the ordinance authorizing transfer of the development rights formerly attached to the private park sites to an area in midtown Manhattan where limited density increases were available, with additional increases possible after a public hearing and municipal approval. The court first noted that the development rights "are a potentially valuable and even a transferable commodity," but then went on to conclude that, in the concrete case before it, the development rights, when severed from the plaintiff's property, had only an extremely speculative value.

> By compelling the owner to enter an unpredictable real estate market to find a suitable receiving lot for the rights, or a purchaser who would then share the same interest in using additional development rights, the amendment renders uncertain and thus severely impairs the value of the development rights before they are severed. * * * Even though the development rights have not been nullified, their severance has rendered their value so uncertain and contingent as to deprive the property owner of their practical usefulness, except under rare and perhaps coincidental circumstances.[17]

In the *Penn Central* case, however, the New York court sustained the refusal of the New York Landmarks Preservation Commission to allow construction of a high-rise office building behind and above the existing Grand Central Terminal Building, and, in the course of its opinion, stated that the ability of Penn Central to transfer its unused development rights from the Terminal site to numerous other sites in midtown Manhattan provided significant compensation for the loss of the right to develop the air space above the Terminal Building.[18] When the United States Supreme Court reviewed *Penn Central,* it affirmed the judgment of the New York Court of Appeals in an opinion which contained the following language:

> Although appellants and others have argued that New York City's transferable development rights program is far from ideal, the New York courts here supportably found that, at least in the case of the Terminal, the rights afforded are valuable. While these rights may well not have constituted "just compensation" if a "taking" had occurred, the rights nevertheless undoubtedly mitigate whatever financial burdens the law has imposed on appellants and, for that reason, are to be taken into account in considering the impact of regulation.[19]

17. 39 N.Y.2d at 598, 385 N.Y.S.2d at 11–12, 350 N.E.2d at 388.

18. 42 N.Y.2d at 335, 397 N.Y.S.2d at 920–921, 366 N.E.2d at 1278. For Judge Breitel's explanation of his somewhat contradictory holdings in *Fred F. French Inv. Co.* and in *Penn Central,* see Breitel, A Judicial View of Transferable Development Rights, 30 Land Use & Zoning Dig., No. 2 (1978), at 5. Professor Costonis does not think the two cases can

be distinguished. See Costonis, The Disparity Issue: A Context for the Grand Central Terminal Decision, 91 Harv.L.Rev. 402, 419–420 (1977).

19. 438 U.S. at 137, 98 S.Ct. at 2666. See Marcus, The Grand Slam Grand Central Terminal Decision: A Euclid for Landmarks, Favorable Notice for TDR and a Resolution of the Regulatory Taking Impasse, 7 Ecology L.Q. 731 (1978). Accord: Dufour v. Montgom-

The literature on the TDR concept is voluminous. As the quoted excerpt from the *Fred F. French Inv. Co.* opinion indicates, criticism has focused on the inability of development rights transfer either to provide "just compensation" in cash as required by constitutional eminent domain clauses [20] or to mitigate the harshness of onerous regulations sufficiently to avoid judicial declarations of invalidity on substantive due process grounds [21] where the local TDR program does not provide for governmental purchase of the development rights. More generally, critics have argued that the "downzoning" of receiving sites in order to provide a market for development rights raises serious constitutional (substantive due process and "taking") and statutory (*ultra vires*) issues,[22] and that the relaxation of bulk and density zoning restrictions at the receiving sites to which development rights are transferred also raises serious constitutional and statutory issues because of the danger that public services will be overloaded, neighborhood amenities such as light and air will be reduced, and the urban landscape will be distorted.[23]

Quite recently, two courts have indicated that transfer of development rights may, under some circumstances, preclude a holding that very low-density zoning amounts to a "taking" or a deprivation of property without due process of law. In American Savings & Loan Association v. County of Marin,[24] the appellate court remanded the case to the trial court to determine whether the plaintiff's development plan for two contiguous tracts—where one tract was in a low-density coastal zone and the other in a zone allowing more intensive development—permitted the profitable development of the parcel as a whole, thus foreclosing a "taking" claim by virtue of the "entire parcel" rule enunciated in *Penn Central.* In Aptos Seascape Corp. v. County of Santa Cruz,[25] the appellate court directed the trial court to dismiss the plaintiff's "taking" claim on condition that the county grant the plaintiff compensatory densities or other TDR remedies in exchange for denying the plaintiff the right to develop ecologically sensitive beach land.

It seems likely that the next significant TDR test case will arise out of the proposed large-scale use of the TDR concept as part of the New Jersey "Pinelands" plan.[26] For the owner of a severely restricted "transferor-parcel," TDRs represent a right supplemental to the remaining beneficial use allowed on his land. If he owns or later purchases land in a qualifying "transferee-district," his TDRs will allow him greater bulk or density than the applicable zoning would normally permit. Whether or not the owner of

ery County Council, 35 Land Use Law & Zoning Digest, June 1983, p. 19 (Cir.Ct., Montgomery County, Md., Law No. 56964, 1983); City of Hollywood v. Hollywood, Inc., 432 So.2d 1332 (Fla.App.1983).

20. This problem is recognized by Costonis. Although he asserts that the United States Supreme Court has never passed on a claim that something other than cash may constitute "just compensation," he concedes that state courts have often held that only cash can constitute "just compensation." Costonis, "Fair" Compensation and the Accommodation Power: Antidote for the Taking Impasse in Land Use Controversies, 75 Colum.L.Rev. 1021 (1975).

21. See quotation in text ante at note 16. See also Note, The Unconstitutionality of Transferable Development Rights, 84 Yale L.J. 1101, 1110 (1975).

22. See Note, supra note 21, at 1112 n. 56.

23. See Note, Development Rights Transfer and Landmark Preservation: Providing a Sense of Orientation, 9 Urb.L.Ann. 131, 154 (1975).

24. 653 F.2d 364 (9th Cir.1981).

25. 138 Cal.App.3d 484, 188 Cal.Rptr. 191 (1982), appeal dismissed 464 U.S. 805, 104 S.Ct. 53, 78 L.Ed.2d 73 (1983).

26. See Greenbaum, supra note 8.

a "transferor-parcel" owns or buys land in a "transferee-district," he may sell his TDRs to any third party for use in the "transferee-district." [27]

27. Id. at 238. See also id. at 240–248.

Chapter 10

CONTRACTS FOR THE SALE OF LAND

Table of Sections

---

§ 10.1 Sales Contracts and the Statute of Frauds

Nearly every real estate transfer by sale is preceded by a sales contract. Such contracts may have various names, such as "earnest money agreement," "offer and acceptance," or "deposit receipt," depending on local tradition and the nature of the transaction. Most commonly the buyer submits an offer of purchase to the seller, and the seller's acceptance transmutes the offer into a contract. The offer is usually accompanied by an earnest money deposit, although such a deposit is not essential to the validity of the offer or the resulting contract.

There is, of course, no legal requirement that a contract precede a conveyance, and occasionally sales occur with no prior contractual relationship. Gifts of real estate rarely involve contracts, since by definition no consideration is to be paid by the recipient. But in sale-type transactions the contract is highly useful, since it allows each party to obtain various items of information and make various arrangements with the assurance that the other party is obligated to complete the transaction. For example, the buyer can confidently apply for the necessary financing to complete the purchase, arrange to sell other real estate, and obtain moving services from a van company. He or she can also investigate such matters as the title, zoning and other land use controls affecting the property, the physical condition of any improvements, and the land's boundaries, topography, and other features. The contract "ties up" the land, making the time and money

649

spent in these endeavors justifiable. The seller may have similar arrangements to make. Of course, if the parties wish to have the right to be excused from performance of the contract if they are dissatisfied with the results of their investigations, they will need to so provide in the contract, and this is very frequently done.

It may seem peculiar to include a chapter on contract law in a book about real property. Real estate sales contracts are subject to most of the same legal rules which govern other contracts. Offer, acceptance, and consideration are still essential, and the concepts of misconduct or mistake, illegality, and the like also apply.[1] But numerous special rules govern land sale contracts, especially in the areas of formation, conditions, and remedies. Many of these rules grew out of the special solicitude which the English equity courts showed for land sellers and purchasers; even today, equitable remedies play an important role in land contract litigation, and equitable concepts sometimes control results even in cases in which no equitable remedy is sought. This chapter is concerned with the special contractual rules and principles (often termed the law of "vendor and purchaser") which apply to real estate contracts, and with the relationship of the seller and purchaser up to the time legal title is transferred.

In principle, it should be possible to state with some precision just what matters must be agreed to by the parties in order to have a valid real estate sales contract. Unfortunately, there is little basis in the decided cases for determining what those elements are. The reason, peculiarly, is the existence and importance of the statute of frauds. The statute requires a writing for the enforceability of a contract, and a large number of cases deal with the elements which the writing must contain. It is usually impossible to determine whether a court is enumerating the essential ingredients of the agreement itself (under the common law of contracts) or the necessary elements of the writing (as a matter of judicial interpretation of the statute of frauds.)[2] Hence, as a practical matter the two sets of elements are indistinguishable, and they will be treated as such here. This situation is a bit inelegant, but it has the advantage of simplicity.

One further preliminary point is important. Real estate sales contracts are often employed as financing devices. For example, the purchaser may go into possession under a contract which requires a small initial down payment and regular periodic payments, say monthly for twenty years. He is to receive a deed only when the final installment is paid. Interest is usually computed and paid on the unpaid balance of the purchase price in the same fashion as is common on mortgage loans. This type of contract, often called an installment contract or a "contract for deed", is obviously the functional and economic equivalent of a purchase-money mortgage, although its legal consequences may be somewhat different.[3] The point is that it is not the sort of contract with which we are concerned here.

---

§ 10.1

1. See, e.g., Calamari & Perillo, Contracts (3d ed. 1987).

2. See Corbin, Contracts § 449 (1950).

3. See, e.g., Nelson & Whitman, Real Estate Finance Law §§ 3.26–3.37 (1985) for a detailed consideration of real estate installment contracts.

Instead, our focus is on what might be termed the "marketing contract"[4]—one whose function is to obligate the parties to engage in an immediate transfer of title, with financing (if any) provided either by the seller or by a third party lender under other documents. Such contracts are usually expected to be performed within a fairly short term—say, a matter of a few months—and they usually do not authorize the buyer to take possession until legal title has passed by delivery of a deed. Thus, the seller is not financing the buyer's occupancy of the property and the contract is not a substitute for mortgage financing. Most of the issues we will consider here are also applicable in some degree to installment or other financing contracts, but they raise many additional problems which are outside the scope of this book.

The Statute of Frauds. The notion that land sale contracts should be evidenced by a writing is an ancient one. Even before the enactment in 1677 of the English Statute of Frauds, Stat. 29 Car. II, c. 3, the courts of equity generally required a writing before granting specific performance of a real estate contract.[5] But the statute solidified and broadened the requirement. Its purpose, of course, was to prevent fraud—in particular, the situation in which one might claim to have entered into a land sale contract which was fictitious or which differed in its terms than those averred. It sought to make difficult the task of those who might lie about the contract or attempt to produce forged written evidence of its existence or terms.

Whether the statute has produced the desired results is not so easy to say. The nature of a writing requirement is to protect the sophisticated, sometimes at the expense of the naive. There is obviously some number of contracts, otherwise fully valid and relied upon, which are unenforceable simply because the party wishing to enforce them did not realize the necessity of procuring a writing from the other. Does this disadvantage of the statute outweigh its plain advantage of making the prospective defrauder's task more onerous? Perhaps not in the current age, when surely nearly everyone recognizes that the law of real estate contracts demands a writing. But the question may be a close one, and it is well worth mature consideration whether the statute facilitates as much fraud as it prevents.[6]

As it applied to real estate contracts, the text of the English statute was concise:

> * * * no action shall be brought * * * upon any contract or sale of lands, tenements or hereditaments or any interest in or concerning them * * * unless the agreement upon which such action shall be brought or some memorandum or note thereof shall be in writing, and signed by the party to be charged therewith, or some other person thereunto by him lawfully authorized.[7]

4. The term seems to have been coined by Professor John Hetland; see J. Hetland, California Real Estate Secured Transactions § 3.42 (Calif.Cont.Ed. of the Bar 1970).

5. See Kepner, Part Performance in Relation to Parol Contracts, 35 Minn.L.Rev. 1 (1950).

6. Arguments against the overall efficacy of the statute are collected in 2 Corbin, Con-

tracts § 275 notes 9–10 (1950). See also Braunstein, Remedy, Reason, and the Statute of Frauds: A Critical Economic Analysis, 1989 Utah L.Rev. 383, suggesting that the statute is unnecessary and sometimes a hindrance to efficient contract enforcement.

7. Stat. 29 Car. II, c. 3, § 4 (1677).

Other clauses of the statute applied to conveyances of title to land (a matter discussed later in this book) and to matters not uniquely related to real estate, such as contracts not to be performed within a year and agreements in consideration of marriage. On its face, the statute's effect seems simple, but virtually every word has been the subject of extensive judicial construction, often with results one would never surmise from a mere reading of the text itself. Hence, a study of the statute really becomes a study of the jurisprudence of its interpretation as represented by a massive body of decisions.

Every American state has a statute of frauds. Many are virtually verbatim copies of the English statute above, while others contain only minor variations. Moreover, even apparently significant modifications of the traditional language have had, for the most part, little or no effect on the opinions of the courts. A good illustration is found in the phrase "no action shall be brought" at the beginning of the statute. Perhaps ten or so states have chosen instead to provide that a contract lacking the necessary writing is "void," a term which certainly sounds much more far-reaching than the original language. But the decisions in these states usually reach the same results as would be expected in the "no action" jurisdictions on similar facts.[8]

What, then, is the meaning of the phrase? Plainly it means that a plaintiff cannot maintain a successful action to enforce the contract, either at law for damages or in equity for specific performance,[9] if the required writing was not made. Equally plainly, the contract is not "void" in any absolute sense. On the contrary, it has considerable legal significance. This is perhaps most obvious from the fact that the defendant in the enforcement action has, in effect, a power to validate the contract and thereby to make it fully enforceable merely by signing an appropriate writing; surely this power could not exist if the contract itself were deemed never to have existed.

The contract is significant in other ways as well despite the absence of a writing. For example, if both parties fully perform, the resulting legal relationships are precisely the same as those which would have existed if the statute had been fully complied with.[10] Neither party can thereafter rescind

---

8. See 3 Am.L.Prop. § 11.3 (1952).

9. In theory the statute applies equally to enforcement in law or equity, although the courts have been somewhat more inclined to circumvent its technical requirements in equitable actions; see Kepner, Part Performance in Relation to Parol Contracts for the Sale of Land, 35 Minn.L.Rev. 1 (1951); § 10.2, infra. Professor Costigan argued that the statute was not intended to preclude enforcement in equity, but his view did not prevail; see Costigan, Has There Been Judicial Legislation in the Interpretation of the Statute of Frauds?, 14 Ill.L.Rev. 1 (1919). The Pennsylvania cases speak of oral contracts being enforceable by way of "damages," but the term is used only to signify restitution of the party's out-of-pocket expenses, and not compensation for loss of bargain. See, e.g., Josephs v. Pizza Hut of

America, Inc., 733 F.Supp. 222 (W.D.Pa.1989), affirmed 899 F.2d 1217 (3d Cir.1990); Polka v. May, 383 Pa. 80, 118 A.2d 154 (1955); Weir v. Rahon, 279 Pa.Super. 508, 421 A.2d 315 (1980). See text at note 12 infra.

Only the contractual provisions dealing with the transfer of land are unenforceable; see Rongotes v. Pridemore, 88 N.C.App. 363, 363 S.E.2d 221 (1988) (statute of frauds does not prevent enforcement of an oral agreement pertaining to disposition of the proceeds of the sale where conveyance is already complete and unchallenged).

10. See McMahon v. Poisson, 99 N.H. 182, 107 A.2d 378 (1954); 2 Corbin, Contracts § 285 (1950). Full performance by only one party is sometimes held to permit enforcement by that party; see Bell v. Hill Brothers

or recover what he had before by claiming that the contract is a nullity. As we will see below, even partial performance by a party may make the contract enforceable, at least in equity, under certain circumstances, although the rules here are more complex and less certain than those which pertain to full performance.[11] Further, there is no doubt that a party to an unwritten contract can get rescission for fraud, and a purchaser under an oral contract who defaults may be able to recover in an action for restitution the funds paid, and perhaps other out-of-pocket expenses in reliance on the contract, insofar as they exceed the seller's actual damages.[12] The contract is valid as against third parties despite the absence of a writing, and one who attempts to interfere with it tortiously may be liable for doing so.[13] In all of these senses the contract subsists even though the statute of frauds bars its enforcement by one or both of the parties.

Writings Which Satisfy the Statute. It is often loosely said that the statute requires the contract to be written, but that is plainly not the case; a written contract is only one way to meet the statute's demands. A written offer, accepted in writing, is equally acceptable. Indeed, either an offer or an acceptance alone in writing should do if it contains the necessary elements, including an appropriate signature.[14] More surprisingly, a writing which forms no part of the contract itself may also suffice as a "memorandum", as the statute uses the term. A letter to a third party[15], a check[16], a note, or a set of escrow instructions[17] may do quite well. Even a deed or will prepared pursuant to the oral contract has been held sufficient.[18] It is not

Construction Co., Inc., 419 So.2d 575 (Miss. 1982); Wiggins v. Barrett & Associates, Inc., 295 Or. 679, 669 P.2d 1132 (1983).

11. See § 10.2, infra.

12. See, e.g., Rich v. Gulliver, 564 So.2d 578 (Fla.App.1990); L.Q. Development, Oreg. v. Mallory, 98 Or.App. 121, 778 P.2d 972 (1989), review denied 308 Or. 500, 784 P.2d 441 (1989) (despite conclusion by court that contract was "null and void," vendor could still be liable under restitution theory); Golden v. Golden, 273 Or. 506, 541 P.2d 1397 (1975); Stuesser v. Ebel, 19 Wis.2d 591, 120 N.W.2d 679 (1963), noted 1964 Wis.L.Rev. 167; Thompson v. Hunstad, 53 Wn.2d 87, 330 P.2d 1007 (1958); Pennsylvania cases cited in n. 9, supra. See Comment, Need for Uniformity in Statute of Frauds and Suggested Remedy: Recoupment in Real Estate Transactions, 49 Marq.L.Rev. 419 (1963), containing an exhaustive review of the various states' statutes of frauds.

13. Daugherty v. Kessler, 264 Md. 281, 286 A.2d 95 (1972).

14. Kaplan v. Lippman, 75 N.Y.2d 320, 552 N.Y.S.2d 903, 552 N.E.2d 151 (1990) (where option to purchase, which is an irrevocable offer, satisfies the statute, it is immaterial that acceptance is oral); Hessenthaler v. Farzin, 388 Pa.Super. 37, 564 A.2d 990 (1989) (mailgram of acceptance is sufficient); Tymon v. Linoki, 16 N.Y.2d 293, 266 N.Y.S.2d 357, 213 N.E.2d 661 (1965); Warner v. W & O, Inc., 263 N.C. 37, 138 S.E.2d 782 (1964); Annot., 30

A.L.R.2d 972 (1953). But see Anderson v. Garrison, 402 P.2d 873 (Okl.1965), requiring both offer and acceptance to be in writing; see Annot., 1 A.L.R.2d 841 (1948).

15. D'Angelo v. Schultz, 306 Or. 504, 760 P.2d 866 (1988), appeal after remand 110 Or. App. 445, 823 P.2d 997 (1992), review denied 313 Or. 209, 830 P.2d 595 (1992) (delivery of the writing not essential to satisfaction of statute); Smith v. McClam, 289 S.C. 452, 346 S.E.2d 720 (1986) (letter may satisfy statute even if not delivered to other contracting party). Boswell v. Rio De Oro Uranium Mines, Inc., 68 N.M. 457, 362 P.2d 991 (1961).

16. A.B.C. Auto Parts, Inc. v. Moran, 359 Mass. 327, 268 N.E.2d 844 (1971). See Annot., 9 A.L.R.4th 1009 (1981).

17. Leiter v. Eltinge, 246 Cal.App.2d 306, 54 Cal.Rptr. 703 (1966); T.D. Dennis Builder, Inc. v. Goff, 101 Ariz. 211, 418 P.2d 367 (1966).

18. Carolina Builders Corp. v. Howard-Veasey Homes, Inc., 72 N.C.App. 224, 324 S.E.2d 626 (1985), review denied 313 N.C. 597, 330 S.E.2d 606 (1985); Southern States Development Co., Inc. v. Robinson, 494 S.W.2d 777 (Tenn.App.1972) (undelivered deed); cf. Baker v. Glander, 32 Mich.App. 305, 188 N.W.2d 263 (1971) (deed insufficient); In re Beeruk's Estate, 429 Pa. 415, 241 A.2d 755 (1968) (will); cf. Hicks v. Hicks, 13 N.C.App. 347, 185 S.E.2d 430 (1971) (will insufficient where it did not indicate existence of agreement to devise.) Often a will or deed will not contain a suffi-

necessary that the writing have been intended to satisfy the statute, if it does so in fact.[19] Indeed, some courts will disregard the lack of writing if the defendant admits the existence of the contract in pleadings, deposition, or sworn testimony at trial; the cases are divided on this matter.[20] It is not even necessary that the writing be introduced as evidence; if it has been destroyed or is otherwise unavailable, its contents may be proved by parol or other evidence.[21]

Moreover, the necessary writing may be composed of more than one piece of paper. As we will see below, certain minimum elements must be present, but they need not all be contained in the same writing. Many courts are quite liberal in permitting two or more documents to be employed together to provide the necessary elements. This approach is likely to be

cient statement that a contract exists, and will fail to satisfy the statute for this reason. See generally 2 Corbin, Contracts § 509 (1950). Some cases refuse to consider a deed which is undelivered or a will whose testator is still living as satisfying the statute, but this result is illogical; the instrument may meet the memorandum requirements of the statute whether it is legally operative as a conveyance or not.

Other unusual modes of satisfying the memorandum requirement include Richardson v. Schaub, 796 P.2d 1304 (Wyo.1990) (property report filed with the United States Department of Housing and Urban Development); Timberlake v. Heflin, 180 W.Va. 644, 379 S.E.2d 149 (1989) (former wife's divorce complaint). Of course, the writing must contemplate the contract in question; see, e.g., Roskwitalski v. Reiss, 338 Pa.Super. 85, 487 A.2d 864 (1985), appeal denied 514 Pa. 619, 521 A.2d 933 (1987) (where listing agreement was found to be nothing more than invitation to bid, purchaser's signature on sales agreement form was insufficient to create binding contract).

19. See Fleckenstein v. Faccio, 619 P.2d 1016 (Alaska 1980); 4 Williston, Contracts § 579 (3d ed. 1961); 3 Am.L.Prop. § 11.5 note 3 (Supp.1977), citing numerous cases. The writing will not usually be deemed inadequate merely because the parties intended to enter into a more complete or formal contract later; see, e.g. Goren v. Royal Investments Inc., 25 Mass.App.Ct. 137, 516 N.E.2d 173 (1987), review denied 401 Mass. 1104, 519 N.E.2d 595 (1988); McLean v. Kessler, 103 Misc.2d 553, 426 N.Y.S.2d 704 (N.Y.Civ.Ct.1980); Leach v. Crucible Center Co., 388 F.2d 176 (1st Cir. 1968). But if the parties believe that they are merely in the negotiating stage, and have not yet reached an agreement, a writing reflecting their negotiations will not bind them; see Engle v. Lipcross Inc., 153 A.D.2d 603, 544 N.Y.S.2d 638 (1989); Smith v. Boyd, 553 A.2d 131 (R.I.1989); Leeds v. First Allied Connecticut Corp., 521 A.2d 1095 (Del.Ch.1986); Freeman v. Greenbriar Homes, Inc., 715 S.W.2d 394 (Tex.App.1986); Ford v. Blinn, 50 Or.App.

515, 623 P.2d 1110 (1981), review denied 290 Or. 853 (1981); King v. Wenger, 219 Kan. 668, 549 P.2d 986 (1976). Thus, both a "meeting of the minds" and a sufficient writing must be shown.

20. Compare Darby v. Johnson, 477 So.2d 322 (Ala.1985) (to enforce contract on basis of defendant's admission would promote perjury) with Hayes v. Hartelius, 215 Mont. 391, 697 P.2d 1349 (1985) (admission of contract is satisfactory basis for enforcing it); Robert Harmon & Bore, Inc. v. Jenkins, 282 S.C. 189, 318 S.E.2d 371 (App.1984) (same); Troyer v. Troyer, 231 Va. 90, 341 S.E.2d 182 (1986) (seller's deposition admitting the contract is a sufficient memorandum).

See Smith v. Boyd, 553 A.2d 131 (R.I.1989) (admission under oath of all elements of contract established enforceable contract); Gramatan Home Investors Corp. v. Whittemore, 147 Vt. 648, 518 A.2d 32 (1986) (statute waived as a defense where party resisting the contract failed to object to parol evidence offered to prove the existence of the agreement); Anchorage Hynning & Co. v. Moringiello, 697 F.2d 356 (D.C.Cir.1983) (statute waived by defendant's admission of contract's existence during discovery). But see Chomicky v. Buttolph, 147 Vt. 128, 513 A.2d 1174 (1986) (admission of existence of oral contract was insufficient to support enforcement of such contract); Isaac v. A & B Loan Co., 201 Cal. App.3d 307, 247 Cal.Rptr. 104 (1988) (statute of frauds not waived by admission in testimony in action which is not against other party to the alleged contract). See also Hickey v. Green, 14 Mass.App.Ct. 671, 442 N.E.2d 37 (1982), review denied 388 Mass. 1102, 445 N.E.2d 156 (1983), which reads Restatement (Second) Contracts § 129, comment d (1981) as endorsing enforcement of the contract if the defendant fails to deny its existence. See Martin v. Scholl, 678 P.2d 274 (Utah 1983) (where defendant admits contract, the requirement of "unequivocal referability" under the part performance doctrine is eliminated).

21. Reed v. Hess, 239 Kan. 46, 716 P.2d 555 (1986).

successful only if there is sufficient oral evidence tying the documents together and showing that they relate to the same transaction, but this is frequently not difficult to prove.[22]

The Writing's Content. What are the minimum elements which the writing must contain? The statute itself gives no clue except for its mention of the signature, and the other requirements mentioned below are entirely the product of case adjudication. The decisions are not easy to harmonize, although there is a basic core of requirements which are quite uniformly agreed upon. Some of the cases stop there, while others mention further matters whose absence is fatal, making generalization difficult. It is reasonably clear that not every term orally agreed upon by the parties must be included in the writing, although some cases go so far in demanding detail as almost to make this the rule.[23]

The essential matters required in virtually all jurisdictions include identification of the parties and of the land, some words indicating an intention to sell or buy, and a signature.[24] Each of these items warrants some discussion here. The parties are usually identified by their names, of course, but there seems no reason in principle to object to other forms of identification, such as "parents of John Jones" or the like. The cases appear to follow a rather odd distinction to the effect that a reference to a party as "owner" or "proprietor" is sufficient but a reference to "seller" or "vendor" is not, presumably because ownership can be determined from the public records while one's status as a seller depends on the enforceability of the very contract which the memorandum is supposed to reflect.[25]

The writing must identify the land to be sold. It is clear that this does not necessitate a formal legal description by metes and bounds or by reference to a recorded map or subdivision plat.[26] The courts are fairly

22. Cushman v. Smith, 528 So.2d 962 (Fla. 1988); McDonald's Corp. v. Butler Co., 158 Ill.App.3d 902, 110 Ill.Dec. 735, 511 N.E.2d 912 (1987), appeal denied 117 Ill.2d 545, 115 Ill.Dec. 401, 517 N.E.2d 1087 (1987); Pee Dee Oil Co. v. Quality Oil Co., 80 N.C.App. 219, 341 S.E.2d 113 (1986), review denied 317 N.C. 706, 347 S.E.2d 438 (1986); Butler v. Lovoll, 96 Nev. 931, 620 P.2d 1251 (1980); Ward v. Mattuschek, 134 Mont. 307, 330 P.2d 971 (1958); 4 Williston, Contracts §§ 580–584 (1961). The predominant view is that the documents need not refer internally to one another, provided that sufficient external evidence links them to one another and to the transaction in question; See Sackett v. Wilson, 258 Ga. 612, 373 S.E.2d 10 (1988); Dobbs v. Vornado, Inc., 576 F.Supp. 1072 (E.D.N.Y.1983); Gregerson v. Jensen, 617 P.2d 369 (Utah 1980), appeal after remand 669 P.2d 396 (1983); Karl v. JeBien, 231 Cal.App.2d 769, 42 Cal.Rptr. 461 (1965); Williston, supra, § 583. But some courts require internal references in the signed document to the unsigned ones; Scott v. Castle, 104 Idaho 719, 662 P.2d 1163 (1983); Hemingway v. Gruener, 106 Idaho 422, 679 P.2d 1140 (1984); Green v. Interstate United Management Service Corp., 748 F.2d 827 (3d Cir.1984)

(Pa. law); Hoffman v. S V Co., Inc., 102 Idaho 187, 628 P.2d 218 (1981); Young v. McQuerrey, 54 Hawaii 433, 508 P.2d 1051 (1973); Abboud v. CIR Cal Stables, 190 Neb. 396, 208 N.W.2d 682 (1973).

23. See, e.g., Troj v. Chesebro, 30 Conn. Sup. 30, 296 A.2d 685 (1972); Note, 24 Baylor L.Rev. 406 (1972).

24. Eliason v. Watts, 615 P.2d 427 (Utah 1980); Application of Sing Chong Co., Limited, 1 Hawaii App. 236, 617 P.2d 578 (1980); Williamson v. United Farm Agency of Alabama, Inc., 401 So.2d 759 (Ala.1981); Higbie v. Johnson, 626 P.2d 1147 (Colo.App.1980). See Dixon v. Hill, 456 So.2d 313 (Ala.Civ.App.1984) (under Alabama statute, when land is sold at auction, memorandum may be prepared by auctioneer and parties' signatures are unnecessary).

25. See 4 Williston, Contracts § 577 notes 11–14 (3d ed. 1961).

26. A few courts are much more demanding, actually insisting on a full and formal legal description; see, e.g., Martin v. Seigel, 35 Wn.2d 223, 212 P.2d 107 (1949), noted 27 Wash.L.Rev. 166 (1952). For recent cases, see 73 A.L.R.4th 135.

lenient, often accepting a street address, for example, if it is unambiguous. But it is difficult to reconcile the cases entirely. If a street address does not include the city and state, some cases hold it insufficient[27] while others deem it acceptable if the vendor owns only one parcel of land bearing that address or if the context of the negotiations makes it clear which land was the subject of the agreement[28]; this is surely the more reasonable approach.

If the written description of the land is ambiguous, the courts will usually admit extrinsic evidence as to the precise boundaries of the parcel to be conveyed.[29] A distinction is usually drawn between evidence which merely clarifies a written description and evidence which supplies a description not found in the writing.[30] Obviously this sort of legal formulation is subject to considerable manipulation by the courts, and cases which reject descriptions as inadequate may sometimes reflect a court's unstated reluctance, on other grounds, to enforce the contract. In the main, however, it is fair to say that descriptions which would be far too loose to give adequate guidance to a surveyor on the ground are often deemed adequate for purposes of the statute of frauds when supplemented by further evidence of negotiations and intent.[31]

Beyond the identification of the parties and the land, the signature, and some words indicating a sale, there is little agreement on the essential content of the memorandum. Much controversy has occurred over the price term. It seems fairly clear that if the parties did not agree on a price, no

27. See Jones v. Riley, 471 S.W.2d 650 (Tex.Civ.App.1971), refused n.r.e.; Hertel v. Woodard, 183 Or. 99, 191 P.2d 400 (1948).

28. Maccioni v. Guzman, 145 A.D.2d 415, 535 N.Y.S.2d 96 (1988) (address and tax numbers of property were sufficient where subject property was only property owned by vendor at that address); Garner v. Redeaux, 678 S.W.2d 124 (Tex.Civ.App.1984) (parol evidence admitted to show circumstances before and after agreement, and thus to supply county and state); Seabaugh v. Sailer, 679 S.W.2d 924 (Mo.App.1984) ("my farm" is sufficient description, where vendor owned only one farm); Guel v. Bullock, 127 Ill.App.3d 36, 82 Ill.Dec. 264, 468 N.E.2d 811 (1984) (street address without city or state is sufficient, where vendor owned property at such address in only one city); Taefi v. Stevens, 53 N.C.App. 579, 281 S.E.2d 435 (1981); Reed v. Alvey, 610 P.2d 1374 (Utah 1980); Klymyshyn v. Szarek, 29 Mich.App. 638, 185 N.W.2d 820 (1971); Corrado v. Montuori, 49 R.I. 78, 139 A. 791 (1928).

29. See generally 3 Am.L.Prop. § 11.5 (1952); Schachle v. Rayburn, 667 P.2d 165 (Alaska 1983); United States Employees of Lane County Credit Union v. Royal, 44 Or. App. 275, 605 P.2d 754 (1980); Fleckenstein v. Faccio, 619 P.2d 1016 (Alaska 1980); Stulsaft v. Mercer Tube & Manufacturing Co., 288 N.Y. 255, 43 N.E.2d 31 (1942), appeal denied 263 App.Div. 942, 33 N.Y.S.2d 814 (1942). But see Lubel v. J.H. Uptmore & Associates, 680 S.W.2d 518 (Tex.Civ.App.1984) (description insufficient, where attached map showed parcel with no beginning point).

30. See Calvary Temple Assembly of God v. Lossman, 200 Ill.App.3d 102, 146 Ill.Dec. 122, 557 N.E.2d 1309 (1990), appeal denied 135 Ill.2d 554, 151 Ill.Dec. 380, 564 N.E.2d 835 (1990) (writing "alone" was insufficient, as description of property; parol evidence not allowed to obtain sufficiency); Brooks v. Hackney, 100 N.C.App. 562, 397 S.E.2d 361 (1990) reversed on other grounds 329 N.C. 166, 404 S.E.2d 854 (1991) (unresolvable ambiguity in land description; contract unenforceable); Bennett v. Fuller, 67 N.C.App. 466, 313 S.E.2d 597 (1984) (where vendors did not own and did not intend to convey the entire land parcel described in the contract, court refused to enforce it); Fourteen West Realty, Inc. v. Wesson, 167 Ga.App. 539, 307 S.E.2d 28 (1983) (description as "part of Lot 197" was unenforceable). Plantation Land Co. v. Bradshaw, 232 Ga. 435, 207 S.E.2d 49 (1974); Wadsworth v. Moe, 53 Wis.2d 620, 193 N.W.2d 645 (1972). See generally Annots., 30 A.L.R.3d 935 (1970); 46 A.L.R.2d 894 (1956). A subsequent survey is no substitute for an adequate description in the writing; McCumbers v. Trans–Columbia, Inc., 172 Ga.App. 275, 322 S.E.2d 516 (1984); Ecolite Mfg. Co. v. R.A. Hanson Co., 43 Wn. App. 267, 716 P.2d 937 (1986); McMichael Realty & Insurance Agency, Inc. v. Tysinger, 155 Ga.App. 131, 270 S.E.2d 88 (1980).

31. See Boyd v. Mercantile–Safe Deposit & Trust Co., 28 Md.App. 18, 344 A.2d 148 (1975); Bliss v. Rhodes, 66 Ill.App.3d 895, 23 Ill.Dec. 718, 384 N.E.2d 512 (1978).

mention of the fact need be made in the writing and the court will assume that a reasonable price was to be paid.[32] But if a price was agreed to, the cases are badly divided as to whether the writing must include it.[33]

There is considerable confusion among the courts as to the necessity of further elements in the memorandum. The only general statements which can be made are virtually useless; as the Second Restatement of Contracts puts it:

> The "essential terms of unperformed promises" must be stated; "details or particulars" need not. What is essential depends on the agreement and its context and also on the subsequent conduct of the parties, including the dispute which arises and the remedy sought.[34]

One area of particular confusion involves the financing of the sale. If the buyer is to pay all cash or obtain financing from external sources, there is generally no necessity for those arrangements to be mentioned in the writing.[35] However, if the seller is to finance the purchase, as by taking back a note and mortgage for part of the price, many courts are much more strict in demanding that the detailed terms (interest rate, maturity, type of security instrument, frequency and amount of payments, etc.) be mentioned.[36] This approach seems justified, since there can be serious unfair-

---

32. United States v. 308.56 Acres of Land, 520 F.2d 660 (8th Cir.1975); 3 Am.L.Prop. § 11.5 note 25 (1952).

33. A few states' statutes insist on a memorandum "expressing the consideration", while a few others provide that no such expression is necessary; see Restatement (Second) of Contracts § 131, Reporter's Note, Comment a (1981). But Professor Corbin has pointed out that the "consideration" and the price are two quite different things, since in a bilateral contract the consideration given by the buyer is literally the promise to pay the price and not the price itself; see 2 Corbin, Contracts § 501 (1950). Recent cases seem to display an increasing tendency to regard the price as an essential term of the writing; see, e.g., D'Agostino v. Bank of Ravenswood, 205 Ill.App.3d 898, 150 Ill.Dec. 759, 563 N.E.2d 886 (1990), appeal denied 137 Ill.2d 664, 156 Ill.Dec. 560, 571 N.E.2d 147 (1991) (contract unenforceable where writing indicated no agreement had been reached between parties as to price); Cobble Hill Nursing Home, Inc. v. Henry and Warren Corp., 74 N.Y.2d 475, 548 N.Y.S.2d 920, 548 N.E.2d 203 (1989) (to be sufficient, price term need only be capable of determination at time of agreement without need for new expressions between parties); Brawley v. Brawley, 87 N.C.App. 545, 361 S.E.2d 759 (1987), review denied 321 N.C. 471, 364 N.E.2d 918 (1988) (exact price need not be stated but there must be a sufficiently definite method for determining the price in the contract); Estate of Younge v. Huysmans, 127 N.H. 461, 506 A.2d 282 (N.H.1985) (memorandum must identify parties, describe the land, and state the price); Malone Construction Co., Inc. v. Westbrook, 127 Ga.App. 709, 194 S.E.2d

619 (1972); Miller v. Bloomberg, 26 Ill.App.3d 18, 324 N.E.2d 207 (1975); cf. Tzitzon Realty Co., Inc. v. Mustonen, 352 Mass. 648, 227 N.E.2d 493 (1967).

34. Restatement (Second) of Contracts § 131 Comment g (1981); see Burgess v. Arita, 5 Hawaii App. 581, 704 P.2d 930 (1985); Tamir v. Greenberg, 119 A.D.2d 665, 501 N.Y.S.2d 103 (1986), appeal denied 68 N.Y.2d 607, 506 N.Y.S.2d 1032, 498 N.E.2d 434 (1986) (condition that vendor obtain cancellation of previous sales contract was so essential that its omission from the writing made the contract unenforceable).

35. Compare Cone v. Abood, 238 So.2d 169 (Fla.App.1970), cert. denied 240 So.2d 813 (Fla. 1970), in which the contract was enforced although the writing merely said "subject to long term loan", with Fox v. Sails at Laguna Club Development Corp., 403 So.2d 456 (Fla. App.1981), refusing specific performance because the contract made no statement about the method of payment of the price. See Busching v. Griffin, 465 So.2d 1037 (Miss. 1985), appeal after remand 542 So.2d 860 (1989) (price is essential term of writing, but will be presumed cash where no terms of payment are set out).

36. Burns v. Pugmire, 194 Ga.App. 898, 392 S.E.2d 62 (1990); Ashkenazi v. Kelly, 157 A.D.2d 578, 550 N.Y.S.2d 322 (1990); Trotter v. Allen, 285 Ala. 521, 234 So.2d 287 (1970); Montanaro v. Pandolfini, 148 Conn. 153, 168 A.2d 550 (1961); Monaco v. Levy, 12 A.D.2d 790, 209 N.Y.S.2d 555 (1961); 3 Am.L.Prop. § 11.5 n. 31 (Supp.1977). Cf. Booras v. Uyeda, 295 Or. 181, 666 P.2d 791 (1983) (financing

ness in imposing financing terms to which the seller did not agree. Moreover, courts are much more likely to insist on specificity in the financing terms when specific performance rather than damages is sought.[37]

There are, of course, numerous other terms to which parties often agree in oral contracts: the time of performance, provisions as to relinquishment of possession, the quality of the title to be conveyed, the risk of loss during the contract's executory period, and so on.[38] The courts typically take the view that these and similar matters are sufficiently minor or nonessential that their absence from the writing is not fatal,[39] although one finds occasional cases to the contrary.

The Signature. The English version of the statute, followed by most American jurisdictions, requires the writing to be signed by "the party to be charged or his agent." [40] The party referred to is the person resisting the

terms not stated with enough specificity to grant specific performance, but since purchaser could have prepaid financing without penalty, he may tender cash and have specific performance); Maccaro v. Andrick Dev. Corp., 280 S.C. 96, 311 S.E.2d 91 (App.1984) (where contract required vendor to take back purchase money mortgage but did not state whether it would contain due-on-sale clause, purchasers could refuse to accept such a clause); Wilson v. Holyfield, 227 Va. 184, 313 S.E.2d 396 (1984) (contract was enforceable, despite fact that provisions for financing by vendor did not provide for mortgage or other security and did not refer to any right of prepayment by purchaser); Beller & Gould v. Lisenby, 246 Ga. 15, 268 S.E.2d 611 (1980), appeal after remand 248 Ga. 353, 283 S.E.2d 237 (1981) (court will infer annual payments are intended where frequency not mentioned.) See generally Note, 24 Baylor L.Rev. 406 (1972); 6A Powell, Real Property, ¶ 925 notes 52–53 (1980).

37. See Genest v. John Glenn Corp., 298 Or. 723, 696 P.2d 1058 (1985); § 10.5 infra at note 16.

38. An excellent discussion of real estate contract drafting and the wide variety of clauses which should be considered is found in M. Friedman, Contracts and Conveyances of Real Property (5th ed. 1991).

39. See Kane v. McDermott, 191 Ill.App.3d 212, 138 Ill.Dec. 541, 547 N.E.2d 708 (1989) (terms relating to apportionment of taxes, closing date, and type of deed to be conveyed were not essential to enforcement); Busching v. Griffin, 465 So.2d 1037 (Miss.1985), appeal after remand 542 So.2d 860 (1989) (where type of deed is not mentioned, court will presume warranty deed was intended). The time of performance, for example, is rarely considered an essential ingredient of the contract; see, e.g., Safier v. Kassler, 124 A.D.2d 944, 508 N.Y.S.2d 352 (1986); Crittenden v. Crane, 107 Idaho 213, 687 P.2d 996 (App.1984); Nixon and Nixon, Inc. v. John New & Associates, 641

P.2d 144 (Utah 1982); Birnhak v. Vaccaro, 47 A.D.2d 915, 367 N.Y.S.2d 792 (1975); Billy Williams Builders & Developers, Inc. v. Hillerich, 446 S.W.2d 280 (Ky.1969). But see Kemp Const. v. Landmark Bancshares Corp., 784 S.W.2d 306 (Mo.App.1990) (complexity of the transaction required that closing date, default events, payment terms, insurance, etc. should be included).

The gradually increasing liberality with which the courts have tended to view the essentials of the memorandum is reflected in the version of the statute incorporated in the Uniform Land Transactions Act (ULTA), adopted by the National Conference of Commissioners on Uniform State Laws in 1975. ULTA § 2–201 requires only a writing, signed by the party against whom enforcement is sought, which identifies the land with "reasonable certainty", "states the price or a method of fixing the price", and "is sufficiently definite to indicate with reasonable certainty that a contract to convey has been made by the parties." See also § 2–202, which makes a contract enforceable even though the parties have not included in "the agreement" (presumably meaning the writing) a term dealing with one or more aspects of the contract.

40. Some of the statutes also require the agent's authority to be written; see, e.g., N.Y.—McKinney's Gen.Obl.Law § 5–703(2). See generally 4 Williston, Contracts § 587 (3d ed. 1960); Charles J. Arndt, Inc. v. City of Birmingham, 547 So.2d 397 (Ala.1989); Williams v. Singleton, 723 P.2d 421 (Utah 1986); Kennedy v. Justus, 64 N.M. 131, 325 P.2d 716 (1958). Contra, see Halstead v. Murray, 130 N.H. 560, 547 A.2d 202 (1988). Compare Barnum v. Frickey, 115 A.D.2d 977, 497 N.Y.S.2d 543 (1985) (corporation president's authority not required to be in writing, where he signs for the corporation) with Bhutta Realty Corp. v. Sangetti, 165 A.D.2d 852, 560 N.Y.S.2d 315 (1990) (signature by individual without indicating corporate capacity and absent any mention of corporate owner of prop-

contract; ordinarily it is the defendant in the litigation, but it may be the plaintiff if the contract is asserted as the basis for a counterclaim. Of course, at the time the writing is made it is generally impossible to predict which of the parties will be "charged", so good practice dictates signing by both. Perhaps half a dozen statutes substitute "the vendor" or a similar term for "the party to be charged." [41] Such provisions seem anomalous, since they appear to permit an unscrupulous seller to make up the necessary writing, sue the purchaser, and force the writing upon him or her. In reality, however, the courts are most unlikely to countenance such a result; it is usually held under such language that the purchaser-defendant must at least have seen and assented to the writing or it will not be binding upon him.[42]

The nature of the signature requirement is such that contracts are not always mutually enforceable. If the writing has been signed by only one party to the agreement, only that party is bound by it, and the other may escape its enforcement. Such a result may seem odd, but it follows from the basic policy of compelling performance only from those whose assent to the contract takes the form of a written signature, and it is by no means novel in the law of contracts.[43] The statute's point is that the *plaintiff's* assent to the bargain need not appear in the form of a written signature, but may be proved by oral testimony.[44] Observe that a signed writing is no substitute for the basic elements of the law of contracts; offer, acceptance, and consideration must still be proved whether the writing discloses them or not (although it commonly will do so.)

The courts are remarkably liberal with respect to the nature of the signature. Its form is not of critical importance. It may be in ink, pencil, or rubber stamp, and may even be typed or printed. It may be the signatory's full name, initials, an arbitrary mark, or "any symbol made or adopted with an intention, actual or apparent, to authenticate the writing as that of the signer." [45] The location of the signature on the page is ordinarily irrelevant,

erty was insufficient to meet signature requirement).

41. See, e.g., Ariz.Rev.Stat. § 33–301. A few cases have reached the same result by judicial construction of the "party to be charged" language, but they seem plainly wrong; see 4 Williston, Contracts § 586 note 8 (3d ed. 1960).

42. Schwinn v. Griffith, 303 N.W.2d 258 (Minn.1981), noted 8 Wm.Mitch.L.Rev. 991 (1982) (where statute requires only vendor's signature, a plaintiff-vendor must prove that the purchaser accepted delivery of the contract); 300 West End Avenue Corp. v. Warner, 250 N.Y. 221, 165 N.E. 271 (1928); National Bank v. Louisville Trust Co., 67 F.2d 97 (6th Cir.1933), certiorari denied 291 U.S. 665, 54 S.Ct. 440, 78 L.Ed. 1056 (1934). The New York Statute was subsequently amended to require signing by the "party to be charged."

43. See Restatement (Second) of Contracts § 135 (1981); 2 Corbin, Contracts § 282 (1950).

44. Lilling v. Slauenwhite, 145 A.D.2d 471, 535 N.Y.S.2d 428 (1988) (memorandum signed

only by purchaser not enforceable against seller, the party charged in the suit); Jolly v. Kent Realty, Inc., 151 Ariz. 506, 729 P.2d 310 (1986) (contract enforceable against vendor who signed writing despite absence of purchaser's signature); Cottom v. Kennedy, 140 Ill.App.3d 290, 94 Ill.Dec. 683, 488 N.E.2d 682 (1986); McCoy v. Alsup, 94 N.M. 255, 609 P.2d 337 (App.1980); First National Bank of St. Johnsbury v. Laperle, 117 Vt. 144, 86 A.2d 635 (1952); Annot., 30 A.L.R.2d 972 (1953).

45. Restatement (Second) of Contracts § 134 (1981); Durham v. Harbin, 530 So.2d 208 (Ala.1988) (writing including only vendor's typewritten notation and letterhead is insufficient to bind him, absent showing that vendor intended to authenticate the agreement by such inscriptions); Hansen v. Hill, 215 Neb. 573, 340 N.W.2d 8 (1983) (telegram sent by party is sufficient signature); Yaggy v. B.V.D. Co., 7 N.C.App. 590, 173 S.E.2d 496 (1970) (same); Dubrowin v. Schremp, 248 Md. 166, 235 A.2d 722 (1967), appeal after remand 257 Md. 623, 263 A.2d 827 (1970) (exchange of letters).

although a few statutes require the document to be "subscribed"—a term sometimes construed to mean signed at the end.[46]

Rescission and Modification. If the parties become dissatisfied with their agreement, they may decide either to rescind it or to modify its terms in some way. If such actions are accomplished without a writing, even though the original contract was supported by a memorandum satisfying the statute, what is their effect? The usual statement is that an oral rescission is effective, while an oral modification is not and leaves the original contract in force.[47] The first part of the statement is pretty clearly correct; the theoretical explanation is that the statute applies to contracts for the sale of land but not to contracts which rescind other contracts.[48]

The situation with respect to oral modifications is more complex. A modification obviously results in the formation of a new contract whose terms consist partly of the old contract and partly of the agreement which modifies it. The test is whether this new contract would fall within the statute of frauds if it were the only contract the parties had made. With the great majority of real estate sales contracts the answer is plainly affirmative, and the conclusion reached is that the new contract cannot be enforced.[49] What, then, is the parties' relationship? The standard answer is that the original contract (assuming it was supported by an adequate writing) is still in effect.[50]

---

46. See, e.g., Commercial Credit Corp. v. Marden, 155 Or. 29, 62 P.2d 573 (1936); Annot. 112 A.L.R. 937 (1938). It is doubtful that "subscribed" need be taken so literally, and some decisions treat the term as the equivalent of "signed"; see 2 Corbin, Contracts § 521 (1950); Butler v. Lovoll, 96 Nev. 931, 620 P.2d 1251 (1980); Radke v. Brenon, 271 Minn. 35, 134 N.W.2d 887 (1965).

47. See 4 Williston, Contracts §§ 592–93 (3d ed. 1960); Restatement (Second) of Contracts §§ 148–49 (1981).

48. Frank v. Motwani, 513 So.2d 1170 (La. 1987); Smith v. Mohan, 723 S.W.2d 94 (Mo. App.1987); Hastings v. Matlock, 171 Cal. App.3d 826, 217 Cal.Rptr. 856 (1985) (oral agreement settling lawsuit is effective to rescind contract). Johnson v. Brown, 71 N.C.App. 660, 323 S.E.2d 389 (1984); Sabot v. Rykowsky, 363 N.W.2d 550 (N.D.1985); Executive Towers v. Leonard, 7 Ariz.App. 331, 439 P.2d 303 (1968); Niernberg v. Feld, 131 Colo. 508, 283 P.2d 640 (1955), noted 28 Rocky Mt. L.Rev. 268 (1956); 2 Corbin, Contracts § 302 (1950); 42 A.L.R.3d 242 (1972). But see Allen v. Kingdon, 723 P.2d 394 (Utah 1986) (denying oral rescission of executory land sales contract absent part performance or detrimental reliance on such rescission). There are contrary decisions, sometimes based on the highly artificial notion that under the doctrine of equitable conversion the purchaser has "equitable title" during the executory period of the contract, and that a rescission conveys this interest back to the vendor and hence must be in writing under the provisions of the statute dealing with conveyances. See Reyes v.

Smith, 288 S.W.2d 822 (Tex.Civ.App.1956), refused n.r.e.; Annot., 38 A.L.R. 294 (1925).

49. Davis v. Patel, 32 Ark.App. 1, 794 S.W.2d 158 (1990); Player v. Chandler, 299 S.C. 101, 382 S.E.2d 891 (1989); Dickinson, Inc. v. Balcor Income Properties, 12 Kan. App.2d 395, 745 P.2d 1120 (1987) (requiring "substantial" modifications to be in writing); Clifford v. River Bend Plantation, Inc., 312 N.C. 460, 323 S.E.2d 23 (1984); Norris, Beggs & Simpson v. Eastgate Theatres, Inc., 261 Or. 56, 491 P.2d 1018 (1971); Restatement (Second) of Contracts § 149 (1981); 2 Corbin, Contracts § 304 (1950). If the modification deals with a term so incidental or nonessential that it would not have been required to be mentioned in the original writing, there is a good deal of authority that the contract as orally modified should be enforced. See, e.g., Stegman v. Chavers, 704 S.W.2d 793 (Tex.App. 1985) (change in who earnest money would be delivered to was incidental); Childress v. C.W. Myers Trading Post, Inc., 247 N.C. 150, 100 S.E.2d 391 (1957). In substance, these cases hold that the original memorandum is a sufficient writing to support the modified contract as well. But other cases hold that any modification, however minor, requires a written memorandum; see 4 Williston, Contracts § 594 (3d ed. 1960). See also Scott v. Castle, 104 Idaho 719, 662 P.2d 1163 (1983) (oral modifications enforced).

50. Restatement (Second) of Contracts § 149(2) (1981); Note, 24 Baylor L.Rev. 406 (1972); Note, 44 Iowa L.Rev. 693 (1959). But even this result may not follow if the court

In practice, however, oral modifications are very frequently given effect by the courts under principles of estoppel. Most oral modifications can fairly be described as reducing the difficulty of one party's performance or of eliminating or making less onerous a condition upon which a party's duties depend. In either case, the modification amounts to a waiver which, if detrimentally relied upon by the party whom it benefits, will be treated as estopping the other party from enforcing the contract's original terms.[51] Perhaps the most common illustration involves the time of performance. Even if the parties have agreed on a specific date for settlement and the passage of legal title, and even if they have agreed that this time is "of the essence," an oral statement by one that the other may have additional time will very often be given effect.[52] In such a case, the reliance may consist simply of delaying beyond the originally agreed time before performing. The party who agreed to accept late performance may reconsider and revoke the waiver by notifying the other party soon enough that the revocation causes no significant hardship;[53] but if the notice is given too late to meet this test, the waiver will be binding despite its oral character.

Where an estoppel results from a waiver, it makes little difference whether the waiver is intended mainly for the benefit of the waiving party or his opponent, nor does it matter who instigated the modification. Indeed, it is quite possible for the courts to infer a waiver from the course of a party's conduct even if no words of waiver are spoken. This occurs most frequently in contracts which call for a series of installment payments. If the vendor adopts a pattern of accepting late payments without objection, the courts will often find a waiver of the right to strict performance, and the vendor can assert legal remedies for the delinquencies only after first giving

can characterize the modification as a rescission followed by a new oral contract; under this view the rescission alone would be effective, and the parties would have no contractual relationship at all. See Burnford v. Blanning, 33 Colo.App. 444, 525 P.2d 494 (1974), reversed 189 Colo. 292, 540 P.2d 337 (1975). The Restatement, supra, takes the view that the rescission and new agreement are normally indivisible, but that in some cases the parties might intend the rescission to be effective even if the new contract is not, and that such intent should be given effect. There is obviously room for manipulation by the courts here.

51. The classic statement is Judge Cardozo's concurring opinion in Imperator Realty Co. v. Tull, 228 N.Y. 447, 127 N.E. 263 (1920), in which the parties to a real estate exchange orally agreed that a cash bond would be acceptable in lieu of clearing, as required by the original contract, certain city ordinance violations. When one party, relying on the modification, failed to clear the violations, the other refused to perform; the court held him liable in damages, in effect enforcing the modification. Cardozo's opinion suggests that the defendant could have withdrawn the modification, even "at the very hour of the closing," if he had been willing to grant reasonable additional time for the other to perform. See also

Richey v. Olson, 709 P.2d 963 (Colo.App.1985) (purchasers sought zoning variance and refrained from suing vendors in reliance on oral modification which imposed a moratorium on payments due); Delves v. Kingdom Voice Publications, Inc., 464 So.2d 1327 (Fla.App.1985) (purchaser took possession, put utilities in his name, and advertised the property for resale in reliance on oral extension of time); Wolff v. McCrossan, 296 Minn. 141, 210 N.W.2d 41 (1973) (time and terms of payment modified); Werner v. Timm, 4 Ill.App.3d 573, 281 N.E.2d 395 (1972) (vendors agreed to pay full year's taxes rather than pro-rata amount); Restatement (Second) of Contracts § 150 (1981); 4 Williston, Contracts § 595 (3d ed. 1961).

52. McGuire v. Norris, 180 Ga.App. 383, 349 S.E.2d 261 (1986); Joiner v. Elrod, 716 S.W.2d 606 (Tex.App.1986); Bower v. Davis & Symonds Lumber Co., 119 N.H. 605, 406 A.2d 119 (1979); Young v. Pottinger, 340 So.2d 518 (Fla.App.1976); Kimm v. Andrews, 270 Md. 601, 313 A.2d 466 (1974); Urton & Co. v. Poznik, 181 Colo. 15, 506 P.2d 741 (1973); Kammert Brothers Enterprises, Inc. v. Tanque Verde Plaza Co., 4 Ariz.App. 349, 420 P.2d 592 (1966), transferred to 102 Ariz. 301, 428 P.2d 678 (1967).

53. See Imperator Realty Co. v. Tull, supra note 51.

the purchaser a clear notice that strictly timely performance is now required, and allowing a reasonable time for the purchaser to come into compliance with the schedule in the written contract.[54]

While the great majority of estoppel cases involve waivers of time deadlines, waivers of other conditions or of various aspects of contract performance are also possible.[55] The effect of such waivers is clearly not the same as a true modification of the contract, since the waiving party is permitted to revoke the waiver and reinstate the original contract terms if this can be done before the other party has detrimentally relied.[56] Cases of waivers of time are unique in this respect, since the very fact of the passage of the originally-agreed time establishes the detrimental reliance and makes a revocation of the waiver unconscionable and hence impermissible.

In addition to waiver and estoppel, oral modifications of written contracts may be upheld by the courts on other theories, such as part performance, discussed in the next section as exceptions to the statute's operation.

§ 10.2 Part Performance

Like any rule that exalts formality over intention, the statute of frauds sometimes leaves courts feeling acutely uncomfortable. Two factors frequently combine to produce this discomfort. The first is a sense that, despite the absence of a suitable writing, the parties really did enter into the sort of contract the plaintiff alleges, so that the court's refusal to enforce the agreement will frustrate his or her reasonable, if poorly documented, expectations. The second is the court's observation that, due to actions taken or investments made by the plaintiff in reliance on the contract, serious and unrecompensed harm may result from its unenforceability.

It is not surprising that the desire to avoid the evident injustice created by these factors has manifested itself in the cases, mainly through the development of the doctrine of part performance. What is surprising is the ease with which courts apply this doctrine, overtly contradicting the literal terms of the statute to enforce contracts where no written memorandum has been made. Part performance is simply a judicially-created exception to a legislative rule * * * an idea which at first seems shocking.[1] Yet the doctrine has existed for so long, and is so well established in so many jurisdictions, that it is far too late to complain that the statute itself

---

54. Phair v. Walker, 48 Or.App. 641, 617 P.2d 616 (1980); Krentz v. Johnson, 36 Ill. App.3d 142, 343 N.E.2d 165 (1976), appeal after remand 59 Ill.App.3d 791, 17 Ill.Dec. 177, 376 N.E.2d 70 (1978). See G. Nelson & D. Whitman, Real Estate Finance Law § 3.29 (2d ed. 1985); Santini, Real Estate Finance—Installment Contract Sales: Avoiding the Harshness of Forfeiture, 15 Land & Water L.Rev. 771 (1980). The cases typically involve a long-term installment contract under which the buyer goes into possession while making regular payments, but the theory applies with equal force to a short-term marketing contract. Cf. Goldstein v. Hanna, 97 Nev. 559, 635 P.2d 290 (1981) (agent promised extension of time to exercise option; principal's silence constituted an estoppel.)

55. See 2 Corbin, Contracts § 310 (1950).

56. See Restatement (Second) of Contracts § 150 Comment c (1981); Imperator Realty v. Tull, supra note 51.

§ 10.2

1. A few states expressly recognize the part performance doctrine in statute; see, e.g., Idaho Code § 9–504; Official Code Ga.Ann. § 20–402; (Mich.Stat.Ann. § 26.910; Mont. Code Ann. § 70–20–101; see Orlando v. Prewett, 218 Mont. 5, 705 P.2d 593 (1985), refusing to apply the part performance doctrine to a contract to make a will. See also Ala.Code § 8–9–2 (requiring partial payment plus possession), applied in Swain v. Terry, 454 So.2d 948 (Ala.1984).

mentions no such exception. Note, however, that part performance is a substitute for the absent writing, and not for the contract itself, which must still be proved. Courts often require an exceptionally high standard of proof of the contract's terms, such as "clear and convincing" or the like.[2]

The doctrine of part performance is a misnomer, for the term seems to suggest that performance by a party of some duties under the contract will substitute for the absent memorandum. The reality is somewhat different; the acts which must be shown are not necessarily required by the contract at all. The three main types of acts acceptable to courts which recognize the doctrine are (1) payment of all or part (sometimes, a "substantial" part)[3] of the purchase price; (2) taking of possession (a few courts require "open and notorious possession"[4]) of the property; and (3) the making of substantial improvements on the land.[5] Note that in all three cases the acts in question are those of the purchaser. Only the first, payment of the price, can fairly be regarded as performance by the buyer of a contractual obligation; indeed, payment may well be the buyer's only obligation. Possession and improvements may occur pursuant to the contract in the sense that they would not have taken place if no contract existed, but they can hardly be viewed as performances under it; the vendor typically has little or no interest in whether the purchaser takes possession or improves the property.

The three types of acts mentioned above must appear in various combinations, depending on the jurisdiction, in order to qualify as "part performance." One, two, or all three may be required. Few courts will accept partial payment by itself,[6] but some will treat the taking of possession[7] or

---

2. See Peterson v. Petersen, 355 N.W.2d 26 (Iowa 1984); Darsaklis v. Schildt, 218 Neb. 605, 358 N.W.2d 186 (1984) ("clear, satisfactory, and unequivocal"); Houston v. McClure, 456 So.2d 788 (Ala.1984) ("clear, definite, and unequivocal in all its terms").

3. A very small payment may be insufficient. See Boesiger v. Freer, 85 Idaho 551, 381 P.2d 802 (1963).

4. See, e.g., Beverly Enterprises, Inc. v. Fredonia Haven, Inc., 825 F.2d 374 (11th Cir. 1987) ("possession must be clear and definite" so that it would reasonably appear to an outsider that the alleged contract existed); Rebel Van Lines v. City of Compton, 663 F.Supp. 786 (C.D.Cal.1987) (storage of material on subject land insufficient to meet "open and notorious possession" as required by California law); Butler v. McGee, 373 P.2d 595 (Wyo.1962); Watson v. Druid Hills Co., 355 S.W.2d 65 (Tex.Civ.App.1962), refused n.r.e.

5. Not all improvements will satisfy the demands of part performance. See Bradshaw v. Ewing, 297 S.C. 242, 376 S.E.2d 264 (1989) (improvements directed by a third party are irrelevant to this requirement; improvements by the party to the alleged contract must be permanent or substantially increase the value of the land); Rebel Van Lines v. City of Compton, 663 F.Supp. 786 (C.D.Cal.1987) (improvements required by a local zoning ordinance are merely performance of pre-existing legal

duty and are insufficient to meet requirement); Winters v. Alanco, Inc., 435 So.2d 326 (Fla.App.1983) ("valuable and permanent improvements" required; mere maintenance of property is insufficient).

6. Iowa Code Ann. § 622.33 recognizes partial payment or the taking of possession by the purchaser standing alone as sufficient; see Peterson v. Petersen, 355 N.W.2d 26 (Iowa 1984). See also Greene v. Scott, 3 Conn.App. 34, 484 A.2d 474 (1984), apparently recognizing payment alone as part performance; Jaye v. Tobin, 42 Mich.App. 756, 202 N.W.2d 712, 716 (1972) enforcement granted on the basis of payment alone, over strong objection in dissenting opinion); But see Bradshaw v. Ewing, 297 S.C. 242, 376 S.E.2d 264 (1989) (payment of part of purchase price insufficient); Jones v. Seven Hills Farm, Inc., 1991 WL 224159 (unpublished, full text in Westlaw) (same).

7. See, e.g., Saints in Christ Temple of Holy Ghost v. Fowler, 448 So.2d 1158 (Fla. App.1984); Harrison v. Oates, 234 Ark. 259, 351 S.W.2d 431 (1961). Chaffee and Re, Cases and Materials on Equity 609 (4th ed. 1958), lists 14 states as accepting possession alone. It is commonly held that possession which merely continues from some preexisting arrangement (e.g., a tenant who buys the leased property and remains in possession) is not sufficient. See, e.g., United States v. 29.16 Acres of Land, 496 F.Supp. 924 (E.D.Pa.1980).

the making of substantial improvements [8] as sufficient standing alone. More commonly, a combination of payment plus one of the other factors must be shown,[9] and a few jurisdictions require all three.[10] Four states—Kentucky, Mississippi, North Carolina, and Tennessee—do not recognize the part performance doctrine at all.[11]

If the part performance doctrine is satisfied, the result is that the contract will be enforced in equity (normally by means of a decree of specific performance) notwithstanding the lack of a written memorandum. The courts often say that part performance "takes the contract out of the statute of frauds," but such terminology is a bit misleading; technically, the only contracts which are "out of" the statute are those not covered by its terms in the first place because, for example, they do not involve agreements to buy and sell realty. It is more accurate to characterize the part performance doctrine simply as an exception to the statute. It is not easy to explain why the exception should operate only in equity and not at law, although this is usually said to be the case.[12] The reason is more historical than logical, and

See also Goldman v. Citicorp Savings of Florida, 552 So.2d 1124 (Fla.App.1989) (possession is indispensible element of part performance).

8. Strandberg v. Lawrence, 216 N.Y.S.2d 973 (1961). Pure improvement cases are rather unusual, since the improver generally goes into possession as well. There is a large body of cases finding possession plus improvements sufficient. See Montoya v. New Mexico Human Services Dept., 108 N.M. 263, 771 P.2d 196 (1989); Hostetter v. Hoover, 378 Pa.Super. 1, 547 A.2d 1247 (1988), appeal denied 523 Pa. 642, 565 A.2d 1167 (1989); Hoffman v. SV Co., 102 Idaho 187, 628 P.2d 218 (1981); 2 Corbin, Contracts § 433 (1950).

9. Cases recognizing part payment plus possession include Beverly Enterprises, Inc. v. Fredonia Haven, Inc., 825 F.2d 374 (11th Cir. 1987); Gibson v. Hrysikos, 293 S.C. 8, 358 S.E.2d 173 (App.1987); Walker v. Sandlin, 474 So.2d 1055 (Ala.1985); Forsberg v. Day, 127 Ariz. 308, 620 P.2d 223 (App.1980) (part payment plus possession); Wiggins v. White, 157 Ga.App. 49, 276 S.E.2d 104 (1981) (same); Caron v. Teagle, 345 So.2d 1331 (Ala.1977), appeal after remand 408 So.2d 494 (1981) (same). The first Restatement of Contracts took the view that possession plus either improvements or part payment would be sufficient; Restatement, Contracts § 197. See also Gibson v. Hrysikos, 293 S.C. 8, 358 S.E.2d 173 (App. 1987) (rental payments, possession and other acts indicative of a leasehold agreement are sufficient); Bradshaw v. Ewing, 297 S.C. 242, 376 S.E.2d 264 (1989) (all three elements should be analyzed, but payment deserves least weight); 20 Suffolk U.L.Rev. 400 (1986) (Rhode Island survey; possession plus improvements required); Powers v. Hastings, 93 Wn.2d 709, 612 P.2d 371 (1980) (any two of the three elements sufficient).

10. Carley v. Carley, 705 S.W.2d 371 (Tex. App.1986) (all three requirements met); Mo-

raitis v. Galluzzo, 487 So.2d 1151 (Fla.App. 1986), appeal after remand 511 So.2d 427 (1987), review denied 519 So.2d 987 (Fla.1988); Xanadu of Cocoa Beach, Inc. v. Zetley, 822 F.2d 982 (11th Cir.1987), cert. denied 484 U.S. 1043, 108 S.Ct. 777, 98 L.Ed.2d 863 (1988) (part payment, possession and valuable improvements with consent or acquisition of seller required); Coleman v. Dillman, 624 P.2d 713 (Utah 1981). See also Young v. Moore, 663 P.2d 78 (Utah 1983) (part performance not "confined to a fixed, inflexible formula."

11. See Chaffee and Re, note 7 supra; Williams v. Mason, 556 So.2d 1045 (Miss.1990) (contract not enforced despite proof that it existed and compliance with it by promisee for 20 years). Kentucky does recognize full performance by one party as an exception to the statute of frauds; see Denney v. Teel, 688 P.2d 803 (Okl.1984) (Ky. law). Even in those states not recognizing part performance as such, a sufficient representation by the reneging party may convince a court to enforce the contract under an estoppel theory. See, e.g., D & S Coal Co. v. USX Corp., 678 F.Supp. 1318 (E.D.Tenn.1988) (Tennessee law); Baliles v. City Service Co., 578 S.W.2d 621 (Tenn.1979) (vendor encouraged purchaser to build house on the property); Note, 10 Mem.St.U.L.Rev. 107 (1979).

12. See Phillips v. Britton, 162 Ill.App.3d 774, 114 Ill.Dec. 537, 516 N.E.2d 692 (1987); Lance J. Marchiafava, Inc. v. Haft, 777 F.2d 942 (4th Cir.1985) (Virginia law); Robert Harmon & Bore, Inc. v. Jenkins, 282 S.C. 189, 318 S.E.2d 371 (App.1984); Mauala v. Milford Management Corp., 559 F.Supp. 1000 (S.D.N.Y.1983) (N.Y. law); Winters v. Alanco, Inc., 435 So.2d 326 (Fla.App.1983); Trollope v. Koerner, 106 Ariz. 10, 470 P.2d 91 (1970); 2 Corbin, Contracts § 422 (1950); Annot., 59 A.L.R. 1305 (1929).

is related to the greater flexibility traditionally exercised by courts of equity, and perhaps to the notion, now discredited in its overt form, that the statute of frauds was not intended to apply to equitable proceedings in the first place.[13] In terms of modern policy, there appears to be no reason to deny the legal remedy of damages once part performance is shown,[14] but few cases can be found which grant it.[15]

Two main rationales for the doctrine of part performance are asserted by the courts; they correspond to the two reasons for judicial uneasiness with the statute of frauds mentioned at the beginning of this section. The first might be termed the evidentiary theory. Courts which follow it regard the statute's function as evidentiary in nature. The writing, if made, shows that a contract existed, but it is not the only satisfactory evidence. These courts treat acts of part performance as a substitute for the written evidence, and deem them to justify enforcement of the contract, at least in equity. Because they are concerned with the potential unreliability of such unwritten evidence, they often say that the part performance must be "unequivocally referable" to the contract—that is, that the acts cannot be explainable on any other ground.[16]

---

13. See Costigan, Interpretation of the Statute of Frauds, 14 Ill.L.Rev. 1 (1919); cf. Pound, Progress of the Law, 33 Harv.L.Rev. 936 (1920).

14. See, e.g., Wolfe v. Wallingford Bank & Trust Co., 122 Conn. 507, 191 A. 88 (1937), granting damages, discussed with approval in 2 Corbin, Contracts § 422 note 21 (1950).

15. Among them are Miller v. McCamish, 78 Wn.2d 821, 479 P.2d 919 (1971); White v. McKnight, 146 S.C. 59, 143 S.E. 552, 59 A.L.R. 1297 (1928). By contrast, the Restatement (Second) of Contracts limits its version of part performance (expanded in other respects) to decrees of specific performance; Restatement (Second) of Contracts § 129 (1981). The Uniform Land Transactions Act, on the other hand, is not so limited; see ULTA § 2–201(b) and Comment 3. It is fairly common for the courts to award damages in an equitable proceeding based on part performance if the land has passed to a bona fide purchaser and hence cannot be subjected to a decree of specific performance, or if specific performance is unavailable or impractical for other reasons; see, e.g., Danciger Oil & Refining Co. v. Burroughs, 75 F.2d 855 (10th Cir.1935), certiorari denied 295 U.S. 758, 55 S.Ct. 915, 79 L.Ed. 1700 (1935).

16. The classic case is Burns v. McCormick, 233 N.Y. 230, 135 N.E. 273 (1922). More recent holdings to the same effect include Wolske Brothers, Inc. v. Hudspeth Sawmill Co., 116 Idaho 714, 779 P.2d 28 (1989); Martin v. Scholl, 678 P.2d 274 (Utah 1983); Matthews v. Matthews, 215 Neb. 744, 341 N.W.2d 584 (1983); Buettner v. Nostdahl, 204 N.W.2d 187 (N.D.1973); Butler v. McGee, 373 P.2d 595 (Wyo.1962). See Merchants National Bank v. Steiner, 404 So.2d 14 (Ala.1981) ("indisputably related to the contract"). Many

jurisdictions use somewhat weaker language, as that the acts of part performance must be "clear and convincing evidence" of a contract. See Smith v. Smith, 466 So.2d 922 (Ala.1985) (possession must be such that an outsider "would naturally and reasonably infer that some contract existed relating to the land of the same general nature as the contract alleged."); Greene v. Scott, 3 Conn.App. 34, 484 A.2d 474 (1984) ("acts are of such a character that they can be reasonably and naturally accounted for in no other way" than by a contract of sale); Gegg v. Kiefer, 655 S.W.2d 834 (Mo.App.1983) (acts "were done in reliance on the contract" and failure to enforce it would result in a "grossly unjust or deepseated wrong"); Dunham v. Dunham, 204 Conn. 303, 528 A.2d 1123 (1987) (requiring conduct that is simply "referable to and consistent with" the alleged agreement).

The "unequivocal referability" element often is found lacking, with the result that the contract is not enforced. See Hall v. Hall, 222 Cal.App.3d 578, 271 Cal.Rptr. 773 (1990) (oral prenuptial agreement not "taken out" of statute since the acts urged as part performance could be explained as performance of husbandly or wifely duties); Mann v. White Marsh Properties, Inc., 321 Md. 111, 581 A.2d 819 (1990) (buyer searched title, took steps to assure zoning compliance, and made plans for a percolation test; acts were equally consistent with preliminary negotiations as with existence of contract); MH Investment Co. v. Transamerica Title Ins. Co., 162 Ariz. 569, 785 P.2d 89 (1989) (closing of escrow account was not unequivocally referable to existence of contract); Conklin v. Karban Rock, Inc., 94 Or.App. 593, 767 P.2d 444 (1989), review denied 307 Or. 719, 773 P.2d 774 (1989) (hiring attorney to obtain land use permit to quarry

Under this theory, little or no attention is paid to the harshness to the plaintiff of refusal to enforce the contract. The emphasis is on whether the acts are adequate evidence that a contract existed. Unfortunately, the "unequivocal referability" test is far too stringent to be practical. It is almost inconceivable that a case can arise in which no other explanation than a contract of sale can be given for a party's payment, possession, and improvements to real estate. For example, the acts might as well be motivated by a landlord-tenant relationship as by a sale in most cases.[17] Since the test is impractical, many courts simply do not apply it literally, and they often assert that the acts are explainable only by a contract when an objective observer could easily think of other explanations.[18] Hence the test is imprecise in operation and subject to considerable manipulation. Realistically, the question asked by most courts following the evidentiary theory is a fairly lenient one: if the acts are not *unequivocally* referable, do they nonetheless point with reasonable clarity to the presence of a contract?

The other main theoretical explanation for the part performance doctrine is much like estoppel, although courts sometimes show a wondrous ability to write entire opinions adopting it without using that term. Like estoppel in other contexts, it proceeds from the view that when a plaintiff has reasonably relied to his or her substantial detriment on the defendant's representations (here, that there is a binding contract), the defendant ought not to be permitted to disaffirm those representations even if some technical requirement for their enforcement (here, a writing) is unmet.[19] This ap-

---

additional land, held not unequivocally referable to an oral agreement to increase acreage covered by the leasehold); Lilling v. Slauenwhite, 145 A.D.2d 471, 535 N.Y.S.2d 428 (1988) (hiring engineer and obtaining building permit was not unequivocally referable to a contract).

17. See, e.g., Lebowitz v. Mingus, 100 A.D.2d 816, 474 N.Y.S.2d 748 (1984) (substantial improvements made by tenant could easily be explained by landlord-tenant relationship and tenant's desire to improve surroundings in which she lived); Wilson v. La Van, 22 N.Y.2d 131, 291 N.Y.S.2d 344, 238 N.E.2d 738 (1968). The New York view is perhaps the most rigid in the nation on this point; it makes a tenant's efforts to show part performance exceedingly difficult. See also Coleman v. Dillman, 624 P.2d 713 (Utah 1981); Merchants National Bank v. Steiner, 404 So.2d 14 (Ala.1981). But see Tzitzon Realty Co. v. Mustonen, 352 Mass. 648, 227 N.E.2d 493 (1967).

18. See, e.g., Shaughnessy v. Eidsmo, 222 Minn. 141, 23 N.W.2d 362 (1946). The formal test purports to consider *possible* rather than *actual* explanations of the acts of the putative purchaser, but many cases seem to turn on whether there is any real evidence of an alternate explanation; if there is none, the courts are much more willing to find that the acts are "unequivocally referable" to a sale contract.

19. Note that estoppel here is employed as a substitute for a writing, and hence is distin-

guishable from the "promissory estoppel" of Restatement (Second) of Contracts § 90, which serves as a substitute for consideration. Of course, the same acts might suffice for both purposes. The version of estoppel which the courts apply in part performance cases is often a narrow one, recognizing only three types of detrimental reliance—payment, taking of possession, and making of improvements. Both the Restatement (Second) of Contracts § 129 (1981) and the ULTA, at § 2–201(b)(4), adopt a broader approach to part performance which does not specify the particular acts of reliance that will trigger the doctrine. This broadening is eminently reasonable, but some courts have been reluctant to find part performance where the plaintiff's acts were other than the "standard" three. See Annot., Promissory Estoppel as Basis for Avoidance of Statute of Frauds, 56 A.L.R.3d 1037 (1974). Compare Weale v. Massachusetts General Housing Corp., 117 N.H. 428, 374 A.2d 925 (1977) (buyer's expenditure of $3000 for survey and plan of land not sufficient part performance) and Walker v. Ireton, 221 Kan. 314, 559 P.2d 340 (1977) (purchaser sold his other farm in reliance on oral contract; insufficient for part performance) with Rutt v. Roche, 138 Conn. 605, 87 A.2d 805 (1952) (seller evicted his tenants, obtained a new mortgage loan in reliance on oral contract of sale; part performance found) and Hickey v. Green, 14 Mass. App.Ct. 671, 442 N.E.2d 37 (1982), review denied 388 Mass. 1102, 445 N.E.2d 156 (1983) (purchasers contracted to sell their other

proach is sometimes termed the "fraud" theory, with the courts observing that they should not allow the use of the statute of frauds to perpetrate a fraud.[20] But the word fraud is an unfortunate misnomer here, for fraud usually connotes a representation made by one who presently intends not to fulfill it, while under part performance it is quite irrelevant whether the defendant intended to disaffirm the oral contract at the time it was formed. Almost equally misleading is the tendency of the court to say that this theory depends on a showing that the plaintiff would suffer "irreparable injury" if the contract were not enforced.[21] Such a statement is too strong, for no rigorous inquiry is generally made into the reparability of the injury. Still, it correctly suggests that here the courts are concerned with the magnitude of the harm which unenforceability would inflict on the plaintiff, and that a slight or modest hardship will not suffice.[22]

In principle, a court following the evidentiary theory of part performance would be unconcerned with the gravity of the hardship to the plaintiff, while a jurisdiction which adopted the estoppel approach would have little interest in whether the acts were "unequivocally referable" to a contract.[23] In practice, however, it is not unusual for courts to discuss both

house; sufficient for part performance); Capital Mortg. Holding v. Hahn, 101 Nev. 314, 705 P.2d 126 (1985) (purchaser refrained from participation in foreclosure sale on property on which it held junior deed of trust, in reliance on senior deed of trust holder's oral promise to convey to purchaser after foreclosure; court enforced promise on estoppel basis); Gillespie v. Dunlap, 125 Wis.2d 461, 373 N.W.2d 61 (App.1985), review denied 126 Wis.2d 520, 378 N.W.2d 293 (1985) (purchaser took possession, repaired property, and built up a successful business in it; estoppel found); Poinciana Properties, Ltd. v. Englander Triangle, Inc., 437 So.2d 214 (Fla.App.1983), review denied 447 So.2d 887 (Fla.1984) (tenant ordered specialized inventory and abandoned efforts to find another location); Interdonato v. Interdonato, 521 A.2d 1124 (D.C.App.1987) (oral agreement to dismiss a lawsuit in exchange for land, enforced under part performance doctrine). In general, the recent cases display an increasing tendency to view part performance as merely a species of estoppel, and to broaden the types of reliance behavior which will justify contract enforcement. A number of interesting cases are collected in 2 Corbin, Contracts § 440 nn. 44–50 (Supp.1971). See also Mauala v. Milford Management Corp., 559 F.Supp. 1000 (S.D.N.Y.1983).

20. See Darby v. Johnson, 477 So.2d 322 (Ala.1985) (court will enforce oral contract despite insufficient part performance, in the form of payment and possession, if there is actual fraud in the sense of defendant's intent from the outset not to perform the contract); Fannin v. Cratty, 331 Pa.Super. 326, 480 A.2d 1056 (1984) (innocent party may recover loss of bargain damages on oral contract if actual fraud is shown); Shaughnessy v. Eidsmo, 222 Minn. 141, 23 N.W.2d 362 (1946).

21. Id.; see Winters v. Alanco, Inc., 435 So.2d 326 (Fla.App.1983) (specific performance not granted where plaintiff's acts are "capable of adequate pecuniary measurement and compensation"); 3 Am.L.Prop. § 11.10 (1952).

22. See, e.g., Gegg v. Kiefer, 655 S.W.2d 834 (Mo.App.1983) (failure to enforce contract must cause a "grossly unjust and deep-seated wrong"). Some cases, especially in Massachusetts, emphasize the question whether the plaintiff could be adequately compensated by money, i.e., by restitution; if that is possible, no decree of specific performance is available. See, e.g., Hazleton v. Lewis, 267 Mass. 533, 166 N.E. 876 (1929). The size of the plaintiff's expenditures on improvements is commonly a decisive factor in such cases.

23. Another difference in principle might be expected to flow from the theory selected by the court. Since the traditional acts of part performance are by definition those of the purchaser, one might expect only purchasers to be permitted to take advantage of them in jurisdictions which follow the estoppel approach; in states which use the evidentiary theory, on the other hand, either party would logically be allowed to assert part performance, since once the evidence of the contract's existence is accepted, all parties should have a right of enforcement. This distinction is indeed followed in some cases. Compare Pearson v. Gardner, 202 Mich. 360, 168 N.W. 485 (1918) (evidentiary theory; vendor may assert) with Palumbo v. James, 266 Mass. 1, 164 N.E. 466 (1929) (estoppel theory; vendor may not assert). But it is perhaps equally common for courts to permit the vendor to employ the doctrine without any serious discussion of the theory being used; see, e.g., Hayes v. Hartelius, 215 Mont. 391, 697 P.2d

theories or implement both tests in the same opinion [24] or to switch between them in successive opinions.[25] Indeed, it is hard to discern any underlying theory at all in some of the cases. Moreover, judicial attitudes toward part performance vary widely from intense fondness to equally intense hostility. On the whole, the topic is not a neat one, but that is not surprising in light of the difficult competing choices it forces on the courts.

§ 10.3   Remedies for Contract Breach—Damages

Since parties often fail to fully perform their obligations under contracts of sale, it is important to understand the range of remedies available to the nonbreaching party. They are discussed in this and the succeeding sections. The main remedy at law is, of course, damages, and the most-used equitable remedy is specific performance. Restitution may be available as an alternative equitable remedy. Each of these remedies is generally available to both vendors and purchasers. Likewise, either party may assert a lien on the land, either as an aid to recovery of the price owed (for the vendor) or restitution of payments made (for the purchaser). The vendor may also have a self-help "remedy" which has no analogue favoring the purchaser: "forfeiture" or retention of payments received, without any corresponding obligation to convey the land.

We do not deal with all possible remedies here. The material in this chapter discusses only remedies for contract breach. Such other legal wrongs as fraud, mistake, concealment, and the like are beyond our scope.[1] Moreover, once the contract has been performed by the vendor's delivery of the deed, breaches by the vendor of contract terms relating to the property's title generally cannot be the subject of an action on the contract, and the purchaser's suit must instead be based on the deed's covenants of title, if any; this topic is discussed later in this book.[2]

Finally, we exclude remedies for breach of long-term installment contracts, which are in reality security instruments and are analogous to mortgages. In such cases, the courts sometimes borrow from the short-term marketing-type contract concepts discussed here, but they are best treated separately.[3] Even with these exclusions, the discussion of remedies in this

---

1349 (1985) (vendor may assert part performance, where he gave up possession of property to purchasers and withheld it from market for four years); Wiggins v. White, 157 Ga.App. 49, 276 S.E.2d 104 (1981).

24. See, e.g., In re Guardianship of Huesman, 354 N.W.2d 860 (Minn.App.1984), appeal after remand 381 N.W.2d 73 (1986); Martin v. Scholl, 678 P.2d 274 (Utah 1983); H. Pearce Real Estate Co., Inc. v. Kaiser, 176 Conn. 442, 408 A.2d 230 (1979). No criticism of a combined approach is intended, for there may be considerable sense in demanding both strong referability to a contract and a showing of serious harm to the plaintiff.

25. See, e.g., the Minnesota development described in Shaughnessy v. Eidsmo, 222 Minn. 141, 23 N.W.2d 362 (1946).

§ 10.3

1. See, e.g., Prosser, Torts § 110 (1971). The same matter might give rise to both breach of contract and fraud liability. See, e.g., Terry v. Panek, 631 P.2d 896 (Utah 1981) (false representation in contract that property had two wells.)

2. The contract provisions as to title are said to be "merged into the deed." See § 10.12 at notes 53–63, infra.

3. G. Nelson & D. Whitman, Real Estate Finance Law §§ 3.25–3.32 (2d ed. 1985); Lee, Remedies for Breach of the Installment Land Contract, 19 U.Miami L.Rev. 550 (1965).

section is relatively brief. For a treatment in greater depth, the reader is referred to Professor Dobbs' excellent treatise on remedies.[4]

Damages. The standard measure of general or "loss-of-bargain" damages for a total breach is the difference between the agreed contract price and the market value of the land on the date of breach.[5] Thus, if the parties contracted for a $100,000 price and the land's value had risen to $120,000 when the breach occurred, the purchaser could recover $20,000 if the vendor breached, while the vendor could recover no general damages if the purchaser breached. Conversely, if the value of the land had declined to $80,000, the vendor could recover $20,000 and the purchaser nothing. In a rough sense, general damages represent the non-breaching party's lost profit on the transaction. The measure is somewhat artificial, since no account is taken of further market fluctuations which might occur after the breach, which is typically deemed to occur on the date set for delivery of the deed in an "earnest money" type contract.[6] Thus in the first illustration above, the purchaser may ultimately have to pay $130,000 for a comparable piece of real estate, but his or her damages will still be limited to $20,000.

However, further transactions after the breach are not necessarily irrelevant. If the vendor, following the purchaser's breach, soon resells the property in an arms-length transaction, the courts will often treat the resale price as strong evidence of the value at the date of breach.[7] Indeed, some

---

4. D. Dobbs, Remedies §§ 12.7–.15 (1973).

5. The cases are legion. See, e.g., BSL Development Corp. v. Broad Cove, Inc., 178 A.D.2d 394, 577 N.Y.S.2d 98 (1991) (breach by vendor); Macal v. Stinson, 468 N.W.2d 34 (Iowa 1991) (breach by purchaser); Hickey v. Griggs, 106 N.M. 27, 738 P.2d 899 (1987) (breach by vendor); Harris v. Shell Development Corp., Nevada, Inc., 95 Nev. 348, 594 P.2d 731 (1979) (breach by purchaser); Sorenson v. Connelly, 36 Colo.App. 168, 536 P.2d 328 (1975) (breach by purchaser); Port Investment Co. v. Anderson, 23 Mich.App. 103, 178 N.W.2d 157 (1970) (breach by vendor). See ULTA § 2–505 (seller's damages); ULTA § 2–510 (buyer's damages).

6. See 5A Corbin, Contracts § 1098 (1964); Vines v. Orchard Hills, Inc., 181 Conn. 501, 435 A.2d 1022 (1980); Royer v. Carter, 37 Cal.2d 544, 233 P.2d 539 (1951); Wolf v. Cohen, 379 F.2d 477 (D.C.Cir.1967). Sometimes a later date, such as the date of trial, is used on the ground that the contract provided for no specific closing date (see Sullivan v. Esterle, 268 S.W.2d 919 (Ky.1954)) or that the plaintiff originally sought specific performance and did not give up that claim in favor of damages until trial (see Cameron v. Benson, 295 Or. 98, 664 P.2d 412 (1983); Dunning v. Alfred H. Mayer Co., 483 S.W.2d 423 (Mo.App. 1972)). If a party commits an anticipatory breach prior to the agreed closing date, the earlier date of breach will be used to fix damages; see Pearce v. Hubbard, 223 Ala. 231, 135 So. 179 (1931). The use of the closing date has been criticized on the ground that it may leave an innocent seller with the risk of

declining land value between the date of breach and the date of a later disposition of the land; see Askari v. R & R Land Co., 179 Cal.App.3d 1101, 225 Cal.Rptr. 285 (1986), holding that if the purchaser breaches and the land thereafter declines in value, and the vendor is prevented from remarketing it during the period of decline by the purchaser's having clouded the title or refusing to relinquish possession, the vendor can recover damages in the amount of the decline; Note, 26 Okla. L.Rev. 277 (1973). But this risk is mitigated by the courts' common reliance on the ultimate resale price as evidence of value; see cases cited in the following footnote.

7. Cedar Point Apartments, Ltd. v. Cedar Point Inv. Corp., 756 F.2d 629 (8th Cir.1985) (purchasers may use resale price obtained by breaching vendor six months later as evidence of market value on date of breach, but may not add as an element of damage the higher mortgage interest the resale buyer paid); Lanum v. Shellans, 523 F.Supp. 326 (W.D.Va. 1981); Aboud v. Adams, 84 N.M. 683, 507 P.2d 430 (1973); Duffin v. Patrick, 216 Kan. 81, 530 P.2d 1230 (1975); Costello v. Johnson, 265 Minn. 204, 121 N.W.2d 70 (1963). See also Bennett v. Price, 692 P.2d 1138 (Colo.App. 1984) (evidence of *listing* prices of similar properties is insufficient to support claim for damages); Teachout v. Wilson, 376 N.W.2d 460 (Minn.App.1985) (sale 2½ years after breach is insufficient evidence of value at time of breach); Benya v. Gamble, 282 S.C. 624, 321 S.E.2d 57 (App.1984), cert. dismissed 329 S.E.2d 768 (1985) (resale price 18 months later

cases go so far as to treat the two figures as identical.[8] No analogous argument can be made by an innocent purchaser whose vendor has breached, since it is literally impossible for the purchaser to buy an exactly identical piece of land. But if the purchaser has in fact already arranged an advantageous resale of the property by the time the vendor breaches, the resale price may well be considered strong evidence of value.[9] On the other hand, proof that the purchaser's lost value is less than would be indicated by the market value at breach (for example, because she or he had contracted to resell at a below-market price or intended to hold the property for a long term, and the market subsequently declined in fact) will convince at least a minority of courts to award the purchaser less than full benefit-of-bargain damages. This result is based on the notion that damages should merely compensate for the plaintiff's actual loss. Such a view has been severely criticized.[10]

In one situation—that of the vendor who has acted in good faith but cannot convey satisfactory title [11]—the courts divide sharply as to whether the purchaser can recover loss-of-bargain damages. Nearly half of the cases limit the purchaser on these facts to a restitutionary type of remedy—return of earnest money or other payments made with interest, plus such incidental damages as abstract, title examination, and loan application costs.[12] Under

may be introduced as prima facie evidence of market value at time of breach, in trial court's discretion).

Evidence of subsequent exchanges for other realty may be inadmissible on the issue of value, since the value of the land taken in trade is fixed only by the agreement of the parties to the exchange; Jackson v. Raisor, 248 S.W.2d 905 (Ky.1952). See generally Annot., 85 A.L.R.2d 116 (1962). But see Iowa–Mo Enterprises, Inc. v. Avren, 639 F.2d 443 (8th Cir.1981).

8. See, e.g., Middelthon v. Crowder, 563 So.2d 94 (Fla.App.1990); Coppola Enterprises, Inc. v. Alfone, 531 So.2d 334 (Fla.1988) (damages measured by vendor's actual profit on resale, irrespective of vendor's good or bad faith); Cohen v. Kranz, 15 A.D.2d 938, 226 N.Y.S.2d 509 (1962), affirmed 12 N.Y.2d 242, 238 N.Y.S.2d 928, 189 N.E.2d 473 (1963). In American Mechanical Corp. v. Union Machine Co., 21 Mass.App. 97, 485 N.E.2d 680 (1985), the purchaser breached and the land was immediately sold under a mortgage foreclosure. The court awarded the vendor damages equal to the difference between the contract price and the (lower) foreclosure proceeds; even though it conceded that the foreclosure probably did not bring fair value, it found that the vendor could not reasonably have avoided the loss. See also Spurgeon v. Drumheller, 174 Cal.App.3d 659, 220 Cal.Rptr. 195 (1985) (if vendor in fact resells property before trial for more than contract price, he cannot recover loss of bargain damages); Askari v. R & R Land Co., 179 Cal.App.3d 1101, 225 Cal.Rptr. 285 (1986) (if value of land rises after breach and before trial, vendor must offset this in-

crease against damages claimed from breaching purchaser).

9. See George E. Shepard, Jr., Inc. v. Kim, Inc., 52 N.C.App. 700, 279 S.E.2d 858 (1981), review denied 304 N.C. 392, 285 N.E.2d 831 (1981).

10. Simon & Novack, Limiting the Buyer's Market Damages to Lost Profits: A Challenge to the Enforceability of Market Contracts, 92 Harv.L.Rev. 1395 (1979). It is well established that the purchaser cannot recover more than loss-of-bargain damages by showing that he or she had an unusually advantageous resale opportunity, unless this fact was within the contemplation of the vendor when the contract was made. See Wolf v. Cohen, 379 F.2d 477 (D.C.Cir.1967); Annot., 11 A.L.R.3d 719 (1967). But see Foster v. Bartolomeo 581 N.E.2d 1033, 31 Mass.App.Ct. 592 (1991) (where land was being purchased for subdivision and development, measure of damages suffered by purchaser was lost development profits, rather than loss of bargain).

11. Ordinarily "satisfactory" means marketable title, but the parties may fix the quality of title the purchaser must accept by contract language. See § 10.12, infra. The definition of "good faith" is open to debate. The Kentucky court, for example, held that no good faith existed where the vendor knew that an interest in the land was held by a third party, even though he reasonably expected that party to cooperate in signing a deed; Raisor v. Jackson, 311 Ky. 803, 225 S.W.2d 657 (1950).

12. E.g., Walch v. Crandall, 164 Mich.App. 181, 416 N.W.2d 375 (1987); Wolofsky v. Behr-

this view, the vendor will be liable for loss of bargain only if acting in bad faith, as by intentionally impairing his or her own title, knowingly contracting to convey a better title than he or she had,[13] or refusing to cure a readily curable title defect. In effect, this approach makes the contract's provisions regarding title into conditions rather than covenants.[14] No satisfactory justification for limiting a good-faith vendor's liability in this fashion can be stated. The rule originated in the 1776 English case of Flureau v. Thornhill,[15] and may have stemmed from the notion that English land titles of that day were so uncertain that it was unreasonable to subject a vendor to substantial liability for the title's failure. Such an explanation should have little credibility in modern America, where a vendor generally knows the state of the title or can ascertain it with little expense or difficulty.

The rule limiting the purchaser's recovery to restitution of payments plus expenses is sometimes explained on the ground that to award loss-of-bargain damages would be inconsistent with the measure of recovery under title covenants in deeds, which is generally limited to the consideration paid. But contracts and deed covenants are fundamentally different;[16] the contract purchaser has usually not yet had an opportunity to make his or her own independent examination of title, while the deed grantee has done so. Moreover, the risk to the vendor of a major increase in market value (and hence of loss-of-bargain damages) is not very great in a short-term executory contract of sale, but would be far larger (and arguably quite unmanageable) in a deed covenant for title which might be the basis of a suit many years

man, 454 So.2d 614 (Fla.App.1984); Long v. Brown, 593 S.W.2d 371 (Tex.Civ.App.1979); Horton v. O'Rourke, 321 So.2d 612 (Fla.App. 1975) (purchaser can recover cost of improvements made to realty); Kramer v. Mobley, 309 Ky. 143, 216 S.W.2d 930 (1949); Seidlek v. Bradley, 293 Pa. 379, 142 A. 914, 68 A.L.R. 134 (1928). Some formulations of the rule extend it to non-title-related breaches by a good faith vendor; see Charles County Broadcasting Co., Inc. v. Meares, 270 Md. 321, 311 A.2d 27 (1973). Statutes adopting the rule are found in Montana, South Dakota, and Oklahoma. West's Ann.Cal.Civ.Code § 3306 was amended in 1983 to permit the purchaser to recover loss of bargain damages whether the vendor's breach was in good or bad faith. See Hartley, New Remedies for Seller's Breach of a Contract to Convey Real Property, 2 Cal. Real Prop.J. 22 (Fall 1984). See also Burgess v. Arita, 5 Hawaii App. 581, 704 P.2d 930 (1985) granting loss of bargain damages irrespective of the vendor's good faith. ULTA § 2–510(b) generally limits the buyer to restitution of funds paid plus incidental damages if the seller did not know of the title defect when entering into the contract. However, if the defect can be cured by application of the purchase price and the seller refused to cure it, the buyer can get benefit-of-bargain damages. Even in a jurisdiction that does not restrict the purchaser's recover of loss-of-bargain damages, the parties may do so by their agreement. The New York courts have held that this sort of clause is effective only if the vendor has acted in good faith; see Progressive Solar Concepts, Inc. v. Gabes, 161 A.D.2d 752, 556 N.Y.S.2d 105 (1990).

13. Mokar Properties Corp. v. Hall, 6 A.D.2d 536, 179 N.Y.S.2d 814 (1958); Carson v. Isabel Apartments, Inc., 20 Wn.App. 293, 579 P.2d 1027 (1978).

A few courts have recognized a further situation in which the purchaser's remedy is limited to restitution: the case in which the purchaser knows full well when entering into the contract that the vendor's title is defective and does not expect the vendor to cure it. See Madison v. Marlatt, 619 P.2d 708 (Wyo.1980); Kessler v. Rae, 40 A.D.2d 708, 336 N.Y.S.2d 680 (1972). Perhaps on these facts the purchaser's knowledge makes the vendor's behavior tantamount to good faith.

14. See § 10.12, infra, for a discussion of title covenants in sales contracts.

15. 2 W.Bl. 1078, 96 Eng.Rep. 635 (C.P. 1776). Lord Westbury is quoted as having said that title deeds of that day were "difficult to read, disgusting to touch, and impossible to understand." See Donovan v. Bachstadt, 91 N.J. 434, 453 A.2d 160 (1982); Oakley, Pecuniary Compensation for Failure to Complete a Contract for the Sale of Land, 39 Camb.L.J. 58, 69 (1980).

16. See D. Dobbs, Remedies § 12.8 at 836 (1973).

after the deed was delivered.[17] It may be rational to limit the vendor's liability for title defects in the case of a long-term installment sale contract,[18] but such a limitation makes no sense in a short-term earnest-money contract. Hence many courts, probably a majority, refuse to insulate even a good-faith vendor from loss-of-bargain liability.[19] When this more expansive measure of damages is applied the purchaser is, of course, also entitled to a return of any amounts paid as earnest money under the contract.[20]

In addition to "general" loss-of-bargain damages, two categories of "special" damage may be recovered by the non-breaching party to the contract.[21] The first might be termed expenses made in reliance on the contract, and the second is lost profits which the plaintiff would have earned in other transactions if the contract had been performed. Both of these categories are subject to the foreseeability [22] rule of Hadley v. Baxendale,[23] and thus can be the basis of recovery only if they were within the contemplation of the parties when the contract was made.

Expenditures in reliance on the contract are of various types. Some may be in the course of actual performance of the contract, such as the vendor's eviction of an existing tenant [24] or refurbishment of the premises so they will meet the contract's specifications.[25] Others are simply the ordinary expenses of sale, such as brokers' commissions, title search and examination fees, surveys, document drafting expenses, appraisals, and the like.[26] The foreseeability requirement is obviously no major barrier to recovery here, since the items in question are usually customary and common, and may even have been mentioned in the contract. Finally, there may be expenses which are not in pursuance of the contract's performance at all,

---

17. On the measure of damages for breach of deed covenants of title, see § 11.13, infra. Note that the return-of-purchase-price ceiling on the grantor's liability under a deed covenant does not depend on his or her good faith.

18. But see Missouri Slope Livestock Auction, Inc. v. Wachter, 107 N.W.2d 349 (N.D. 1961) in which the court (strongly guided by statute) refused to limit the vendor's liability even under a long-term installment contract.

19. Donovan v. Bachstadt, 91 N.J. 434, 453 A.2d 160 (1982); Forbes v. Wells Beach Casino, Inc., 409 A.2d 646 (Me.1979); Widebeck v. Sullivan, 327 Mass. 429, 99 N.E.2d 165 (1951); Hartzell v. Crumb, 90 Mo. 629, 3 S.W. 59 (1886). See Comment, 26 Okla.L.Rev. 277 (1973); 3 Am.L.Prop. § 11.67; Annot., 48 A.L.R. 12 (1927); Annot., 68 A.L.R. 137 (1930). There is no discernible trend toward or away from the rule limiting the vendor's liability.

20. See § 10.7 infra at notes 15–17.

21. A third category, damages for delay in performance, is treated at § 10.9, infra.

22. Restatement (Second) of Contracts § 351 (1981).

23. 9 Exch. 341, 156 Eng.Rep. 145 (1854). Cases refusing, on the basis of lack of foreseeability, to allow various elements of consequential damages to non-breaching purchasers, include Danburg v. Keil, 235 Va. 71, 365

S.E.2d 754 (1988) (expenditures made by purchaser in renovating and altering the premises prior to the closing, which never occurred as a result of vendor's breach); Lotito v. Mazzeo, 132 A.D.2d 650, 518 N.Y.S.2d 22 (1987) (increase in mortgage interest rates occurring after vendors' breach); Wall v. Pate, 104 N.M. 1, 715 P.2d 449 (1986) (loss of opportunity to assume an exceptionally low-interest mortgage on the premises).

24. McKinley v. Lagae, 207 Cal.App.2d 284, 24 Cal.Rptr. 454 (1962).

25. Aliferis v. Boudreau, 1 Mass.App.Ct. 845, 301 N.E.2d 688 (1973); 5A Corbin, Contracts § 1031 (1951).

26. Missouri Slope Livestock Auction, Inc. v. Wachter, 107 N.W.2d 349 (N.D.1961) (purchaser can recover title examination expense); Harris v. Shell Development Corp., Nevada, Inc., 95 Nev. 348, 594 P.2d 731 (1979) (vendor can recover for appraisal and other miscellaneous expenses.) It seems clear that the relevant expenses are those actually incurred on the first (abortive) sale, not those which might be incurred on resale; see Royer v. Carter, 37 Cal.2d 544, 233 P.2d 539 (1951). Courts sometimes use the latter figure, but properly speaking, it is only a proxy for the former. The better practice is to use the actual expenses of the first sale.

but are nonetheless made in reliance on it, such as travel [27] or commuting costs,[28] preparations for moving onto or off of the land,[29] expenses of arranging financing, and so on. Here foreseeability may be a serious question, turning on the defendant's knowledge or reasonable expectations about the plaintiff's preparations.[30] Further, courts may refuse to grant damages for expenditures incurred after the breach, on the ground that they were avoidable.[31] Courts may also refuse to allow full recovery for expenditures which have residual value to the plaintiff despite the breach, such as those of the vendor which can be applied to reduce the costs of resale.[32] For example, a seller who pays to have an abstract brought up to date in preparation for the aborted sale may be able to use that abstract to facilitate a subsequent sale.[33]

One other argument may persuade a court to deny recovery of expenses. The non-breaching party who is awarded loss-of-bargain damages or specific performance has in effect been given the same economic benefit which would have resulted from performance of the contract; hence the court may deny recovery for that party's incidental expenses on the ground that he or she would not have expected reimbursement for them if actual performance had

---

27. Fountain v. Mojo, 687 P.2d 496 (Colo. App.1984); Meyer v. Furgat, 133 Vt. 265, 336 A.2d 169 (1975).

28. Jensen v. Dalton, 9 Cal.App.3d 654, 88 Cal.Rptr. 426 (1970).

29. Missouri Slope Livestock Auction, Inc. v. Wachter, note 26 supra; Bush v. Cathey, 598 S.W.2d 777 (Tenn.App.1979).

30. See, e.g., Ranch Homes, Inc. v. Greater Park City Corp., 592 P.2d 620 (Utah 1979) (purchaser may not recover for expense of incorporating, corporate legal services, or fees to officers for management, architectural, or engineering services.) When the purchaser breaches, many cases permit recovery of the vendor's interest, taxes, insurance, and other carrying costs which accrue for a reasonable time after breach while he attempts to resell; see Van Moorlehem v. Brown Realty Co., 747 F.2d 992 (10th Cir.1984) (allowing recovery of property taxes until vendor resumed residency of house, but disapproving prejudgment interest and mortgage interest she paid, on the ground that since she had possession, interest would constitute a double recovery); Turner v. Benson, 672 S.W.2d 752 (Tenn.1984) (allowing vendors to recover for insurance, utilities, and repairs to property while attempting to remarket it after purchaser's breach); Askari v. R & R Land Co., 179 Cal. App.3d 1101, 225 Cal.Rptr. 285 (1986) (same, but vendor must offset his claim by any increase in property's value prior to trial); Taefi v. Stevens, 53 N.C.App. 579, 281 S.E.2d 435 (1981); Higbie v. Johnson, 626 P.2d 1147 (Colo. App.1980). But see Buschman v. Clark, 583 So.2d 799 (Fla.App.1991) (disapproving vendor's recovery of mortgage payments, insurance, and association dues for period following purchaser's breach); Macal v. Stinson, 468 N.W.2d 34 (Iowa 1991) (disapproving vendor's recovery of interest on loan they had to obtain when purchasers breached contract of sale); Quigley v. Jones, 255 Ga. 33, 334 S.E.2d 664 (1985) (disapproving vendor's recovery for taxes, insurance, utilities, repairs, or loss of use of sales proceeds during time he attempted to remarket property); Zipper v. Affordable Homes, Inc., 461 So.2d 988 (Fla.App.1984), review dismissed 469 So.2d 748 (Fla.1985) (disapproving prejudgment interest to vendor). See Annot., 17 A.L.R.2d 1300 (1951). ULTA § 2–514 permits recovery of expenses "incident to the contract" without a showing of foreseeability; this includes title and inspection expenses, but it is not so clear as to moving, travel, or financing costs.

31. Restatement (Second) of Contracts § 1350 (1981). Plainly this argument ought not to apply to the sorts of carrying costs incurred by the vendor who is attempting to remarket the property, as described in note 30, supra; these costs are generally unavoidable.

32. See Aliferis v. Boudreau, 1 Mass.App. Ct. 845, 301 N.E.2d 688 (1973) (vendor can recover for costs of renovating and equipping beauty school, less fair resale value of equipment).

33. If the court uses the actual expenses of resale as a proxy for the damages on the breached contract, this factor is taken into account automatically; see note 26 supra. No law requires the vendor to resell; if he or she does not, the expenditures will have little or no value, and the vendor should recover their full cost. A purchaser's incidental expenditures will seldom have any residual value after the vendor breaches, since they generally relate to the specific parcel of land which was the subject of the breached contract.

occurred.[34] By contrast, if the plaintiff is the purchaser and the rule of Flureau v. Thornhill limits recovery to a restitution of the payments made, the result is more analogous to rescission than to performance; the foregoing argument does not apply, the purchaser is out-of-pocket the expenses and can recover them.[35]

The actual results with respect to claims for expenses of sale, over and above loss-of-bargain damages, seem to be extraordinarily variable and inconsistent. For example, one can easily find cases both allowing [36] and denying [37] the vendor's claim for the real estate broker's commission. But the inconsistencies may be apparent rather than real, and may turn on what the court means by "market value" in the standard loss-of-bargain formula. For example, suppose V contracts to sell land to P for $100,000. V spends $10,000 on brokerage commissions, abstracts, and other fees, none of which will be refunded to V by the broker, title company, etc., despite P's breach of the contract, and none of which will have any value in facilitating a subsequent resale. Assume the land's value has declined by $5,000, so its gross market value is $95,000. If this figure is used to compute V's loss-of-bargain damages, V will get only $5,000 of recovery. V will presumably place the land back on the market, sell it for $95,000, and pay a new commission and other expenses on the resale of about $10,000. Plainly V has been undercompensated in damages unless the court also awards V the unrecoverable expenses of the first sale.[38] On the other hand, if V's loss-of-bargain damages are computed on the basis of the land's net market value at the time of breach, or $85,000, the resulting damage figure of $15,000 will fully compensate V without any further award for incidental expenses. The cases seldom mention whether the market value "found" by the court is gross or net of expenses, but the point is crucial in judging whether additional expenses of sale should be awarded. A few cases recognize this definition problem explicitly,[39] but all ought to do so.

In many cases, the purchaser under a land sale contract will have in mind some further use or disposition of the land. If that use would have produced profits over and above the land's fair market value, the buyer may be able to recover those profits, in addition to loss-of-bargain damages and expenses, from the breaching vendor. But he or she will have several hurdles to overcome. The first, if the vendor's breach was due to a good-faith lack of title, is the doctrine of Flureau v. Thornhill, discussed above. If the purchaser would be denied loss-of-bargain damages on this ground, loss

---

34. Soffe v. Ridd, 659 P.2d 1082 (Utah 1983); Higbie v. Johnson, 626 P.2d 1147, 1151 (Colo.App.1980); Mahoney v. Tingley, 10 Wn. App. 814, 520 P.2d 628 (1974), reversed 85 Wn.2d 95, 529 P.2d 1068 (1975). See D. Dobbs, Remedies § 12.8 note 73 (1973); C. McCormick, Damages § 186 notes 144–45 (1935); Restatement of Contracts § 333, comment a (1933).

35. See note 12, supra.

36. Gordon v. Pfab, 246 N.W.2d 283, 289 (Iowa 1976); Warner v. Wilkey, 2 Mass.App. Ct. 798, 307 N.E.2d 847 (1974); Popwell v. Abel, 226 So.2d 418 (Fla.App.1969); Jensen v.

Dalton, 9 Cal.App.3d 654, 88 Cal.Rptr. 426 (1970). See Corbin, Contracts § 1034 (Supp. 1980).

37. Mahoney v. Tingley, note 34 supra.

38. See note 26 supra.

39. Stephenson v. Butts, 187 Pa.Super. 55, 142 A.2d 319 (1958); Royer v. Carter, 37 Cal.2d 544, 233 P.2d 539 (1951), in which the court seemed to feel bound by statute (West's Ann.Cal.Civ.C. § 3307) to measure the vendor's loss-of-bargain damages based on "gross" market value, and hence properly awarded additional damages for his expenses.

of profits will be denied *a fortiori*.[40]   Second, the profit opportunity which the purchaser lost must have been "foreseeable" or "within the contemplation of the parties" under Hadley v. Baxendale.   This point is often hotly controverted, and the cases produce varying results, depending on the facts.[41] The final barrier is the requirement that the lost profits be proved with reasonable (although not total) certainty, and here again many purchasers' claims founder.[42]   In general, the courts quite naturally tend to view claims of lost profits somewhat cynically, as representing only the extravagant hopes of the plaintiff rather than realistic opportunities.   But if the proof is strong, recovery is possible.

The discussion above has centered on the problem of the total breach. However, partial breaches are also common.   A vendor, for example, may be unable to convey all of the land promised; the title may be subject to some outstanding claim or interest (such as a right of surface entry in favor of the owner of a mineral estate) which is at variance with the seller's duty under the contract; or the property may have physical defects which violate the contract.   In such cases the purchaser would have the right (if the breach is material) to avoid the contract and claim damages for a total breach. However, the purchaser may regard the land as essentially satisfactory notwithstanding the shortage or defect, and hence may wish to proceed with the transaction, at the same time claiming damages (or, what amounts to the same thing, an abatement of the price) to compensate for the partial breach.[43]

The courts are divided as to the proper measure of such damages or abatement, with the division following the same basic lines as the *Flureau* controversy discussed above.   About half of the cases measure the damages by the price of the land as fixed in the contract,[44] while the remainder

40. Surprisingly, this point has not often been explicitly decided in the cases. Cf. Rea v. Ford Motor Co., 355 F.Supp. 842, 852 (W.D.Pa.1973), vacated 497 F.2d 577 (3d Cir. 1974), certiorari denied 419 U.S. 868, 95 S.Ct. 126, 42 L.Ed.2d 106 (1974), on remand 406 F.Supp. 271 (W.D.Pa.1975), vacated 560 F.2d 554 (3d Cir.1977), certiorari denied 434 U.S. 923, 98 S.Ct. 401, 54 L.Ed.2d 281 (1977).

41. Finding foreseeability: Republic National Life Insurance Co. v. Red Lion Homes, Inc., 704 F.2d 484 (10th Cir.1983); C. & C. Blaschka, Inc. v. Frazer, 32 A.D.2d 774, 302 N.Y.S.2d 443 (1969), affirmed 30 N.Y.2d 645, 331 N.Y.S.2d 669, 282 N.E.2d 623 (1972); Caughey v. Ames, 315 Mich. 643, 24 N.W.2d 521 (1946). Finding no foreseeability: Susi v. Simonds, 147 Me. 189, 85 A.2d 178 (1951); Merritt v. Adams County Land & Investment Co., 29 N.D. 496, 151 N.W. 11 (1915). See generally Annot., 11 A.L.R.3d 719 (1967). ULTA § 2–514 adopts the foreseeability rule for consequential damages; Ehly v. Cady, 212 Mont. 82, 687 P.2d 687 (1984) (breaching vendor held liable for purchaser's loss of investment tax credit under federal income tax law, which loss was reasonably foreseeable). See also Community Dev. Service, Inc. v. Replacement Parts Mfg., Inc., 679 S.W.2d 721 (Tex.App.

1984) awarding lost profits to a *vendor* which was selling large numbers of lots as a real estate dealer.

42. See, e.g., Gilmore v. Cohen, 95 Ariz. 34, 386 P.2d 81, 11 A.L.R.3d 714 (1963). The problem is particularly acute in the case of a new business with no record of profitability; see Guard v. P & R Enterprises, Inc., 631 P.2d 1068 (Alaska 1981). See Note, The Requirement of Certainty in the Proof of Lost Profits, 64 Harv.L.Rev. 317 (1950).

43. Specific performance with abatement will generally be ordered against the vendor in these situations; see Moser v. Thorp Sales Corp., 334 N.W.2d 715 (Iowa 1983); Greene v. Jones, 377 So.2d 947 (Ala.1979); Ga.Code Ann. § 44–5–35, construed in McIntyre v. Varner, 156 Ga.App. 529, 275 S.E.2d 90 (1980). A court may decline to order specific performance if the defect or shortage is so great, and hence the abatement so large, that it virtually eats up the contract price, thus radically altering the parties' original agreement. See Merritz v. Circelli, 361 Pa. 239, 64 A.2d 796 (1949). See also § 10.5, infra, at note 11.

44. Kleiner v. Randall, 72 Or.App. 465, 696 P.2d 556 (1985), opinion clarified 74 Or.App. 27, 701 P.2d 458 (1985); Kuhlman v. Grim-

measure them by the land's market value at the date of breach.[45] To illustrate, suppose the contract provides for the sale of 10 acres at a price of $5,000 per acre. A subsequent survey discloses that the tract contains only 9 acres. At the date of settlement the land's value has risen to $6,000 per acre. Under the former rule mentioned, the purchaser's damages are $5,000, the pro-rata contract price of the shortage. The latter rule bases recovery on the value of the land, and would result in a damage award of $6,000, in effect giving the purchaser the benefit of the bargain. The analogy to the *Flureau* controversy is obvious. If the contract provides for the sale of the land "in gross" (by stating only a total price rather than a price per acre or other area measure), the courts are more reluctant to award damages for shortages of area, but they will generally do so if the deficiency is great or the vendor has affirmatively misrepresented the area to be conveyed; again, the measure may be based on either market value or contract price.[46] Other elements of damage are also conceivable; one purchaser was awarded $3,000 to cover the expense of redesigning a construction project to fit within the remaining land.[47]

Deficiencies which constitute contract breaches are not necessarily shortages in area. The vendor may tender the property in a damaged or defective condition, or may remove from it some fixtures or improvements of value. It may be encumbered with title defects that depreciate its value. In these cases, the courts often adopt damage measurements similar to the benefit-of-bargain approach discussed above: an abatement based on the diminished market value of the property,[48] or (where feasible) damages equal to the cost of remedying or correcting the defect.[49] It is less common in

minger, 213 Neb. 64, 327 N.W.2d 104 (1982); Hardin v. Hill, 149 Mont. 68, 423 P.2d 309 (1967); Queen v. Sisk, 238 N.C. 389, 78 S.E.2d 152 (1953). See also Cantor v. Hotchkiss, 465 So.2d 614 (Fla.App.1985) (where vendor was ordered to convey *more* land than contract provided, in order to cure an encroachment, purchasers were required to *increase* purchase price pro rata).

45. Weinstein v. Sprecher, 2 Wn.App. 325, 467 P.2d 890 (1970); Emery v. Medal Building Corp., 164 Colo. 515, 436 P.2d 661 (1968); Fant v. Howell, 547 S.W.2d 261 (Tex.1977).

46. See Parcel v. Myers, 214 Mont. 225, 697 P.2d 92 (1985) (no abatement where sale was in gross); Snow's Auto Supply, Inc. v. Dormaier, 108 Idaho 73, 696 P.2d 924 (App. 1985) (even if sale is in gross, purchaser is entitled to relief if vendor made fraudulent misrepresentation); Hodecker v. Butler, 64 Or.App. 167, 667 P.2d 540 (1983); Hardin v. Hill, supra note 44; Flygare v. Brundage, 76 Wyo. 350, 302 P.2d 759 (1956). Cf. Branton v. Jones, 222 Va. 305, 281 S.E.2d 799 (1981) (no abatement in sale in gross despite great acreage discrepancy.)

47. Pareira v. Wehner, 133 Vt. 74, 330 A.2d 84 (1974).

48. See, e.g., Cooper v. Burson 521 So.2d 745 (La.App.1988); Nugent v. Beckham, 37 N.C.App. 557, 246 S.E.2d 541 (1978) (abatement for title defects based on diminution in

market value.) A few jurisdictions will grant specific performance with abatement only for title defects or land shortages, and not for physical defects; see Ide v. Joe Miller & Co., 703 P.2d 590 (Colo.App.1984) (where well had much lower capacity than contract required, but contract price was already lower than market value, court refused to order abatement; purchasers given election to purchase "as is" at contract price, or to rescind); Merritz v. Circelli, 361 Pa. 239, 64 A.2d 796 (1949).

49. Cases basing damages for physical defects on the reduction they cause in market value include Tennant v. Lawton, 26 Wn.App. 701, 615 P.2d 1305 (1980); Billy Williams Builders & Developers, Inc. v. Hillerich, 446 S.W.2d 280 (Ky.1969); Briggs v. Woodfin, 388 So.2d 1221 (Ala.Civ.App.1980). Cf. Sallinger v. Mayer, 304 So.2d 730 (La.App.1974) (damages based on cost of repairs.) Some cases indicate that the cost-of-repair measure should be employed if the defects can be readily remedied without destruction of any part of the building, and the market value measure if correction of the defects would involve substantial demolition; see Coley v. Eudy, 51 N.C.App. 310, 276 S.E.2d 462 (1981). See generally Annot., Measure of Damages Where Vendor, After Execution of Contract of Sale but before Conveyance of Property, Removes Part of Property Contracted For, 97 A.L.R.3d 1220 (1980). If the defect is one of title, and

these situations to measure damages by a pro-rata reduction in the price, since there is usually no obvious way of allocating the price among various features of the improvements or title; hence, the purchaser is more likely to be awarded the full benefit of his or her bargain.[50]

§ 10.4   Remedies for Contract Breach—Liquidated Damages

Without question the most controversial issue involving realty contract damages is the validity and scope of the vendor's asserted right to retain, as liquidated damages, money which the breaching purchaser has paid toward the price. In nearly every transaction the purchaser will hand some "earnest money" to the seller or the broker at the time the contract is entered into. In some areas of the country the amount is customarily ten percent of the full price, while in other places it is commonly much less; the exact amount is subject to negotiation between the parties. Sometimes further payments are made by the buyer prior to settlement. If the buyer subsequently defaults, the seller very often takes the position that all such payments are forfeited as damages for the breach, while the purchaser claims the funds under the general principles of restitution discussed later in this chapter.

Such attempted forfeitures raise a variety of legal questions. The most obvious is simply whether the seller can keep the money if it exceeds the seller's actual damages as measured by the general principles discussed in the preceding section. It is of critical importance here to distinguish between long-term installment contracts which serve to secure a purchase-money debt and short-term marketing or "earnest money" contracts. Only the latter are dealt with here; cases involving the former are legion, but the principles involved are different because of their close analogy to mortgage law.[1]

The seller's right to forfeiture of earnest money is often mentioned in a contract clause, and its wording may be of great significance, but numerous states permit a forfeiture even in the absence of any clause.[2] The right is usually explained on the grounds (1) that the seller could always seek specific performance and hence is only retaining a portion of the entire price which a court of equity would award him, or (2) that the buyer, being in breach, has no standing to assert any rights under the contract.[3] There is

---

can be cured by a liquidated sum, the typical practice is to give the purchaser an abatement of the price in an amount necessary to clear the title; see, e.g., Streater v. White, 26 Wn. App. 430, 613 P.2d 187 (1980).

50. See D. Dobbs, Remedies § 12.8, at 839 (1973).

§ 10.4

1. See G. Nelson & D. Whitman, Real Estate Finance Law § 3.28 (2d ed. 1985), for an extended discussion of forfeitures in installment contracts; see also § 10.7 note 17, infra.

2. The classic case is Lawrence v. Miller, 86 N.Y. 131 (1881). See Birdwell v. Ferrell, 746 S.W.2d 338 (Tex.App.1988) (no retention of deposit will be permitted, where deposit was given to an escrow agent, not to the vendor, and no clause provided for retention); Northern Ill. Const. Co. v. Zale, 136 Ill.App.3d 822, 91 Ill.Dec. 527, 483 N.E.2d 1013 (1985) (court would ordinarily treat earnest money as liquidated damages, but will not do so where contract specifically provides that it is to be returned to purchaser).

3. See, e.g., Bruce Builders, Inc. v. Goodwin, 317 So.2d 868 (Fla.App.1975); Wasserman v. Steinman, 304 Pa. 150, 155 A. 302 (1931). See M. Friedman, Contracts and Conveyances of Real Property § 12.1(c) (3d ed. 1975). Friedman argues that the vendor is well-advised not to include a liquidated damages clause, and can thus avoid the risk that a court will construe it as limiting other remedies the vendor might later wish to pursue. See also S. Goldberg, Sales of Real Property

little logic in these statements; at the point at which the forfeiture occurs, there is no judicial finding that specific performance is available to the vendor, who in any event usually does not seek it. A seller who in fact sought specific performance would have to tender a conveyance of the land, while the seller who seeks a forfeiture has no intention of doing so. Moreover, courts generally do not make the validity of forfeiture turn on whether the vendor still has the property or has resold it;[4] yet the vendor obviously could not have specific performance if he or she had parted with the title. Finally, the buyer who seeks a refund of earnest money is arguably not relying on contract rights, but is merely asking relief from the seller's unjust enrichment. For all these reasons it is very doubtful that courts should impute an automatic right of forfeiture in every realty sale contract, and some refuse to do so.[5]

But even if a specific clause is included in the contract, the major question remains: will a court enforce the forfeiture of the buyer's money? The issue is typically phrased in terms of whether the retention represents a valid liquidation of damages or an invalid penalty. Most modern cases purport to follow the First Restatement[6] and hold that forfeiture is permissible only if (1) the seller's actual damages are difficult or impossible to measure and (2) the amount of the liquidated sum to be retained appeared, when the contract was entered into, to be a reasonable estimate of the actual damages. These requirements obviously suffer a bit from internal inconsistency, since if the damages were so hard to measure, almost any estimate of them might be considered reasonable. In practice, the "difficult to measure" standard has been largely assumed or ignored, and most of the cases have focused on the reasonableness of the figure.[7] A minority of decisions rejects

494 (1971). A numerical count of the cases bears out this advice, but it is questionable whether practitioners ought to rely on a rule of such doubtful fairness and analytic soundness. See Annot., 4 A.L.R.4th 993, 1025ff (1981).

4. See Pruett v. La Salceda, Inc., 45 Ill. App.3d 243, 3 Ill.Dec. 917, 359 N.E.2d 776 (1977); Gaynes v. Allen, 116 N.H. 469, 362 A.2d 197 (1976); Oliver v. Lawson, 92 N.J.Super. 331, 223 A.2d 355 (App.Div.1966), cert. denied 48 N.J. 574, 227 A.2d 133 (1967); Great United Realty Co. v. Lewis, 203 Md. 442, 101 A.2d 881 (1954).

5. See Kutzin v. Pirnie, 124 N.J. 500, 591 A.2d 932 (1991) (overruling prior common law rule, and holding that no retention of deposit would be permitted in absence of clause so providing); Frank v. Jansen, 303 Minn. 86, 226 N.W.2d 739 (1975).

6. Restatement of Contracts § 339 (1933). The second Restatement continues to use both of the tests mentioned, but places the emphasis on reasonableness "in light of the anticipated or actual harm * * * and the difficulties of proof of loss." Restatement (Second) of Contracts § 356 (1981). Comment b indicates that the greater the difficulty of proof of loss, the greater the latitude which should be al-

lowed in the setting of liquidated damages. See Shallow Brook Associates v. Dube, 135 N.H. 40, 599 A.2d 132 (1991); Preferred Sav. Bank, Inc. v. Elkholy, 303 S.C. 95, 399 S.E.2d 19 (1990); Crowley v. McCoy, 234 Neb. 88, 449 N.W.2d 221 (1989); Illingworth v. Bushong, 297 Or. 675, 688 P.2d 379 (1984); Marcam Mortg. Corp. v. Black, 686 P.2d 575 (Wyo. 1984); Clarkson, Miller & Muris, Liquidated Damages v. Penalties: Sense or Nonsense?, 1978 Wisc.L.Rev. 351.

7. A third factor sometimes mentioned is the intention of the parties to provide for liquidated damages rather than a penalty whose purpose is to compel performance. Yet it is clear that the label the parties placed on the clause is not controlling. In practice, little attention is usually paid to intention. See generally J. Calamari & J. Perillo, Contracts § 14–31 (2d ed. 1977). But see Hanson Dev. Co. v. East Great Plains Shopping Center, Inc., 195 Conn. 60, 485 A.2d 1296 (1985), in which both majority and dissenting opinions purport to analyze the intent question; Benya v. Gamble, 282 S.C. 624, 321 S.E.2d 57 (S.C.1984), cert. dismissed 329 S.E.2d 768 (1985) (reasonableness in light of damages which were either anticipated or were actually suffered was a jury question).

forfeiture entirely and permits the buyer to recover so much of the deposit as exceeds the vendor's actual damages.[8]

The traditional view called for testing the reasonableness of the liquidated damages clause as of the time the contract was formed. Courts have often felt uncomfortable with this approach in cases in which the property's market value has risen sharply after contracting and before breach, so that the seller has little actual damages or none at all; an estimate of damages which was reasonable when made may sometimes turn out to be a gross exaggeration. More recent cases display a willingness to take this factor into account, and to refuse enforcement of the forfeiture if it would result in a large windfall to the vendor in fact.[9] Note that the very fact that issues of reasonableness of amount, difficulty of estimation, and the like are pertinent and litigable in itself destroys much of the supposed advantage of liquidated damages clauses—their extra-judicial operation. With respect to the question of how great a gap the courts will tolerate between actual damages and the liquidated amount, the cases are much too variable to generalize, but unusually large earnest money deposits are commonly recoverable by purchasers.[10] The ironic result is that the vendor who was piggish may end up

---

8. See, e.g., Wilkins v. Birnbaum, 278 A.2d 829 (Del.1971). See also Walker v. Graham, 706 P.2d 278 (Wyo.1985), seeming to take the position that damages for breach of a real estate sale contract are per se not difficult to measure (under the first Restatement test), so that forfeiture of the purchaser's deposit is never appropriate; Reid v. Auxier, 690 P.2d 1057 (Okl.App.1984) (same, although contract recited that it would be "impractical and extremely difficult" to determine actual damages).

9. See Stabenau v. Cairelli, 22 Conn.App. 578, 577 A.2d 1130 (1990); Schrenko v. Regnante, 27 Mass.App.Ct. 282, 537 N.E.2d 1261 (1989), review denied 405 Mass. 1203, 542 N.E.2d 601 (1989); Lind Bldg. Corp. v. Pacific Bellevue Developments, 55 Wn.App. 70, 776 P.2d 977 (1989), review denied 113 Wn.2d 1021, 781 P.2d 1322 (1989); United Savings & Loan Association v. Reeder Development Corp., 57 Cal.App.3d 282, 129 Cal.Rptr. 113 (1976); Hutchinson v. Tompkins, 259 So.2d 129 (Fla.1972) (reasonableness is judged as of time contract made, unless the sum is inequitable at the time of breach.) The Restatement (Second) of Contracts § 356 (1981) seems to give equal weight to both anticipated and actual reasonableness. ULTA § 2–516 follows substantially the same formula. See Pima Sav. & Loan Ass'n v. Rampello, 168 Ariz. 297, 812 P.2d 1115 (App.1991) (forfeiture of 6% of price is reasonable on its face); Shapiro v. Grinspoon 541 N.E.2d 359, 27 Mass.App.Ct. 596 (1989) (upholding a retention of $.5 million, where it amounted to only 3.3% of the price and the parties were sophisticated and represented by counsel); Hong v. Somerset Associates, 161 Cal.App.3d 111, 207 Cal.Rptr. 597 (1984) (upholding a forfeiture of $25,000 on the sale of an apartment building for $1,325,000 as reasonable at the time of the

contract, and noting that, while the 3% presumption in the statute was inapplicable, the amount involved here was less than 3%).

The California cases give considerable emphasis to the mutuality of the process by which the liquidated damages were fixed, sometimes holding a clause invalid because it had not been the subject of negotiation by both parties; see United Savings & Loan Association v. Reeder, supra. The California case law development was short-circuited as to owner-occupied residential property in 1978 by the passage of West's Ann.Cal.Civ.Code § 1675, which presumes the validity of liquidated damages up to 3 percent of the purchase price, and presumes invalidity if an amount exceeding 3 percent is paid; both presumptions may be rebutted by proof of unreasonableness in the first situation and reasonableness in the second. Reasonableness is assessed by considering circumstances at the time the contract was made as well as any subsequent transactions which occur within 6 months of the buyer's breach. The statute does not call for any consideration of intention, mutual negotiation, or difficulty of proof of actual damages.

See also West's Rev.C.Wash.Ann. § 64.04, conclusively sustaining forfeiture of earnest money in real estate sale contracts if the amount forfeited does not exceed 5% of the purchase price and the contract expressly makes forfeiture the vendor's sole remedy.

10. See Annot., 4 A.L.R.4th 993 (1981); Annot., 6 A.L.R.2d 1401, at § 9–10 (1949). In Community Dev. Service, Inc. v. Replacement Parts Mfg., Inc., 679 S.W.2d 721 (Tex.App. 1984), the contract provided that retention of the earnest money was the vendor's sole remedy. The court concluded that this was not a

with only actual damages, and only after being put to the trouble of proving them in court.

The other principal issue raised by liquidated damages clauses is the degree to which they preclude the vendor's assertion of other remedies, especially actual damages and specific performance. One might expect the recovery of actual damages to be foreclosed almost automatically; after all, the evident purpose of the clause is to fix the vendor's damages recovery at the agreed amount. Indeed, many cases do take this view,[11] although it sometimes gives rise to the bizarre spectre of the seller's attempting to convince a court that the clause, obviously inserted for his or her own benefit, is invalid so that a larger sum can be recovered in actual damages![12] Surprisingly, numerous cases permit the seller to disregard the liquidated damages clause and seek actual damages if the wording plainly makes retention of the deposit optional with the seller.[13] Such an approach lets the seller have his or her cake and eat it, too, gaining a windfall if the deposit exceeds the damages, while preserving an action against the buyer if the deposit is inadequate to cover the damages. This collection of rights has been too much for some courts to swallow.[14] In jurisdictions where it works,

reasonable attempt to measure actual damages, since retention could be triggered by very minor defaults of the purchasers. Hence the court held the clause unenforceable, permitting the vendor to recover actual damages far in excess of the earnest money. See also Johnson v. Smith, Scott & Associates, Inc., 77 N.C.App. 386, 335 S.E.2d 205 (1985) (forfeiture of $2500 deposit on sale for $146,000 is not disproportionate to actual damages, and is enforceable). Some cases rather illogically focus on the size of the deposit in relation to the total price, a ratio which may have little to do with the vendor's prospective or actual damages; see Lefemine v. Baron, 556 So.2d 1160 (Fla.App.1990) (retention of 10% of price, while substantial, was not unconscionable, and was upheld); McNorton v. Pan American Bank, 387 So.2d 393 (Fla.App.1980), review denied 392 So.2d 1377 (Fla.1981) (retention of 50% of price shocking, and not permitted; contract was for sale of a mortgage); Vines v. Orchard Hills, Inc., 181 Conn. 501, 435 A.2d 1022 (1980) (retention by vendor of a deposit up to 10% of price is presumptively valid, but purchaser may rebut presumption by showing actual damages of vendor are smaller than deposit.)

11. Mahoney v. Tingley, 85 Wn.2d 95, 529 P.2d 1068 (1975); City of Kinston v. Suddreth, 266 N.C. 618, 146 S.E.2d 660 (1966).

12. See Universal Builders, Inc. v. Moon Motor Lodge, Inc., 430 Pa. 550, 244 A.2d 10 (1968) (construction contract); City of Kinston v. Suddreth, supra (vendor's argument rejected).

13. Bannon v. Knauss, 282 S.C. 589, 320 S.E.2d 470 (App.1984) (vendor may recover actual damages, although contract provided that breaching purchaser "shall forfeit the

earnest money deposit."); Noble v. Ogborn, 43 Wn.App. 387, 717 P.2d 285 (1986) (vendor may recover actual damages, where under contract he had "the election to retain the earnest money as liquidated damages, or to institute suit to enforce any right Seller has"); Campbell v. Salman, 384 So.2d 1331 (Fla.App.1980); Sorce v. Rinehart, 69 Wis.2d 631, 230 N.W.2d 645 (1975); cf. Harris v. Dawson, 479 Pa. 463, 388 A.2d 748 (1978), noted at 52 Temp.L.Rev. 829 (1979) (clause construed to make retention of $100 deposit the sole remedy at law, precluding recovery of actual damages). ULTA § 2–515(6) makes the liquidated damages clause the sole remedy at law or equity unless other remedies are specifically reserved. See also Cedrone v. Unity Sav. Ass'n, 609 F.Supp. 250 (E.D.Pa.1985) (contract provided that if title was defective, purchaser could rescind and recover his title expenses; held: this remedy was not clearly made exclusive, so purchaser may also recover loss-of-bargain damages).

14. See Hanson Dev. Co. v. East Great Plains Shopping Center, Inc., 195 Conn. 60, 485 A.2d 1296 (1985); Jarro Building Industries Corp. v. Schwartz, 54 Misc.2d 13, 281 N.Y.S.2d 420 (Sup.Ct.1967). The matter was well put by Mr. Justice Van Brunt, dissenting in Caeser v. Rubinson, 71 App.Div. 180, 185, 75 N.Y.S. 544, 547 (1902), reversed 174 N.Y. 492, 67 N.E. 58 (1903): "I am unable to comprehend how the amount fixed in an agreement can, by its terms, be both liquidated and unliquidated." See also Ropiza v. Reyes, 583 So.2d 400 (Fla.App.1991) (clause providing vendor the options of deposit retention, actual damages, and specific performance is unenforceable as a matter of law).

a large premium is placed on careful drafting to make it clear that retention of the deposit is an optional and not an exclusive remedy.

If liquidated and actual damages seem obviously inconsistent, the same is not true of liquidated damages and specific performance. In general, the courts have no difficulty awarding specific performance (if the other necessary elements are present) despite the presence of a liquidated damages clause.[15] In contrast to the question of actual damages discussed above, the opposite presumption applies here; specific performance is denied only if the clause makes it very clear that liquidated damages was intended to be the sole remedy.[16] One particular mode of wording can be fatal to specific performance. If the clause treats the purchase and the payment of the liquidated sum by the buyer as alternative performances, rather than treating the sum as damages for failure to perform, the effect is to give the purchaser the option of selecting payment or completion of the sale; under such a reading, it is obviously improper for a court to order completion if the purchaser has selected payment instead.[17] Real estate sales contracts are seldom written this way, and such a construction is one which a drafter for the vendor should certainly try to exclude.

15. Specific performance allowed: Bell v. Alsip, 435 So.2d 840 (Fla.App.1983), review dismissed 441 So.2d 631 (Fla.1983) (contract specifically reserved all remedies of both parties); Laseter v. Brown, 251 Ga. 179, 304 S.E.2d 72 (1983); Miller v. United States Naval Institute, 47 Md.App. 426, 423 A.2d 283 (1980); Rubinstein v. Rubinstein, 23 N.Y.2d 293, 296 N.Y.S.2d 354, 244 N.E.2d 49 (1968); Moritz v. Broadfoot, 35 Wis.2d 343, 151 N.W.2d 142 (1967); Stewart v. Griffith, 217 U.S. 323, 30 S.Ct. 528, 54 L.Ed. 782 (1910).

16. Specific performance denied: Seabaugh v. Keele, 775 S.W.2d 205 (Mo.App.1989) (vendors' actions demonstrated that they considered liquidated damages their only remedy); Gulf City Body & Trailer Works, Inc. v. Phoenix Properties Trust, Inc., 531 So.2d 870 (Ala.1988) (contract made forfeiture vendor's sole remedy); Hatcher v. Panama City Nursing Center, Inc., 461 So.2d 288 (Fla.App.1985) (contract provided that if "Purchaser's actual damages exceed $10,000, Purchaser is limited to the amount of $10,000 and shall apply such amount in satisfaction of Purchaser's claim"); Martin v. Dillon, 56 Or.App. 734, 642 P.2d 1209 (1982), review denied 293 Or. 340, 648 P.2d 853 (1982); Coney v. Commercial National Realty Co., 88 Ill.App.3d 1026, 44 Ill.Dec. 89, 410 N.E.2d 1181 (1980) (clause providing for forfeiture "in full of all claims against Purchaser"); Dillard Homes, Inc. v. Carroll, 152 So.2d 738 (Fla.App.1963).

Several recent Florida cases dealt with condominium purchase agreements which purported to limit the purchaser's sole remedy for vendor breach to a return of earnest money. The courts have rejected this language as "antithetical to fair dealing in the market-place" and have awarded purchasers both loss of bargain damages, see Blue Lakes Apartments, Ltd. v. George Gowing, Inc., 464 So.2d 705 (Fla.App.1985); Clone, Inc. v. Orr, 476 So.2d 1300 (Fla.App.1985); and specific performance, see Ocean Dunes of Hutchinson Island Dev. Corp. v. Colangelo, 463 So.2d 437 (Fla. App.1985). They have also refused to enforce the vendor's claim for forfeiture of deposit under such a clause; see IDEVCO v. Hobaugh, 571 So.2d 488 (Fla.App.1990). Cf, Simpson Dev. Corp. v. Herrmann, 155 Vt. 332, 583 A.2d 90 (1990) (similar clause upheld for vendor, where issue had not been properly preserved on appeal); Mancini–Ciolo, Inc. v. Scaramellino, 118 A.D.2d 761, 500 N.Y.S.2d 276 (1986) (such clause valid unless vendor acts in bad faith).

See also Ryan Mortg. Investors v. Fleming–Wood, 650 S.W.2d 928 (Tex.App.1983), in which the contract gave the purchaser an option to terminate if vendor could not convey title; "otherwise buyer shall be conclusively deemed to have accepted seller's title." The court construed this language as not excluding loss-of-bargain damages to the purchaser. See Ellis and Abramowitz, Contracts as Commodities: Issues and Approaches in Regard to Commercial Real Estate "Earnest Money" and "Option" Contracts—A Texas Lawyer's Perspective, 16 St. Mary's L.J. 541 (1985).

17. See Pace v. Garcia, 631 F.Supp. 1417 (W.D.Tex.1986) (Texas law); Thomason v. Thomas, 641 S.W.2d 685 (Tex.App.1982); 5A Corbin, Contracts § 1213 (1952); D. Dobbs, Remedies 824–25 (1973); Macneil, Power of Contract and Agreed Remedies, 47 Cornell L.Q. 495, 515 (1962).

Courts often enforce forfeiture-of-deposit clauses only grudgingly. Since they are obviously designed to protect the vendor, they are construed against him or her in cases of ambiguity.[18] Moreover, some jurisdictions impose rather severe time limits and election-of-remedies concepts on vendors. For example, the Utah courts require the seller to make an immediate refund of the deposit if he or she wishes to seek damages or specific performance; if the seller retains it for an appreciable period, it becomes the only remedy.[19] In the District of Columbia, a similar rule requires the seller to make an affirmative election to forfeit the deposit, without waiting to see whether liquidated or actual damages would be greater before doing so.[20] Yet despite these and comparable limitations in other states, the concept of forfeiture of the deposit retains surprising vitality, probably due to its ability to reduce litigation in the general run of cases. The deposit is in fact typically modest in amount and represents fair compensation to the vendor for the trouble, delay, and irritation associated with putting the property back on the market, even if the loss-of-bargain damages are minimal.

§ 10.5 Remedies for Contract Breach—Specific Performance

Both the vendor and purchaser are generally able to obtain a decree of specific performance compelling the other party to complete the contract. The traditional bromide tells us that specific performance should be ordered only when the remedy at law is inadequate.[1] When the purchaser seeks specific performance, this test is automatically deemed satisfied; each parcel of land is unique, and no other parcel can possibly be an exact substitute for the one the purchaser bargained to buy.[2] Hence, damages are inadequate per se. This notion is generally accepted as a truism, and the courts impose no duty on the purchaser to prove the unique qualities of the land for which

---

18. See, e.g., Giomona Corp. v. Dawson, 568 S.W.2d 954 (Mo.App.1978).

19. Dowding v. Land Funding Limited, 555 P.2d 957 (Utah 1976); Close v. Blumenthal, 11 Utah 2d 51, 354 P.2d 856 (1960).

20. Sampson v. McAdoo, 47 Md.App. 602, 425 A.2d 1 (1981) (D.C. law); Sheffield v. Paul T. Stone, Inc., 98 F.2d 250 (D.C.Cir.1938). Cf. Erwin v. Scholfield, 416 So.2d 478 (Fla.App. 1982), rejecting the argument that a complaint by the vendor praying for actual damages or specific performance was an election of remedies, and allowing the vendor's amended complaint for liquidated damages.

§ 10.5

1. Restatement (Second) of Contracts § 359 (1981); Kronman, Specific Performance, 45 U.Chi.L.Rev. 351 (1978); 5A Corbin, Contracts § 1136–39 (1964). The requirement of uniqueness is vigorously criticized in Schwartz, The Case for Specific Performance, 89 Yale L.J. 271 (1979).

2. Vincent v. Vits, 208 Ill.App.3d 1, 152 Ill.Dec. 941, 566 N.E.2d 818 (1991); Schumacher v. Ihrke, 469 N.W.2d 329 (Minn.App.1991);

Gleason v. Gleason, 64 Ohio App.3d 667, 582 N.E.2d 657 (1991); Friendship Manor, Inc. v. Greiman, 244 N.J.Super. 104, 581 A.2d 893 (1990), cert. denied 126 N.J. 321, 598 A.2d 881 (1991); Ludwig v. William K. Warren Foundation, 809 P.2d 660 (Okl.1990); GRW Enterprises, Inc. v. Davis, 797 S.W.2d 606 (Tenn.App. 1990); Shelton v. Keller, 24 Ark.App. 68, 748 S.W.2d 153 (1988); Carpenter v. Folkerts, 29 Wn.App. 73, 627 P.2d 559 (1981); Tabor v. Ragle, 526 S.W.2d 670 (Tex.Civ.App.1975), refused n.r.e.; ULTA § 2–511. See West's Ann.Cal.Civil Code § 3387, as amended in 1984 to provide that damages are conclusively inadequate to compensate a purchaser of a single-family dwelling who intends to occupy it, but in other cases of vendor breach are merely presumed inadequate.

Cf. Van Wagner Advertising Corp. v. S & M Enterprises, 67 N.Y.2d 186, 501 N.Y.S.2d 628, 492 N.E.2d 756 (1986) (specific performance of a contract to lease real estate to a tenant will not be awarded as a matter of course, despite physical uniqueness of the property); Straisa Realty Corp. v. Woodbury Associates, 154 A.D.2d 453, 546 N.Y.S.2d 19 (1989) (same).

he or she contracted.[3]

It is not so easy to apply this reasoning when the vendor seeks specific performance. After all, if the contract were performed, the vendor would receive only money—hardly a unique commodity. Yet the courts routinely award sellers specific performance.[4] One explanation, now thoroughly discredited, is that some principle of contract law requires mutuality of remedy, so that each party's remedies should be a mirror image of the other's. There is in fact no such operative principle, and situations in which the parties' remedies differ sharply are common.[5] Mutuality of remedy is probably a misguided extension of the quite proper notion of mutuality of obligation, which holds that each party is bound to a bilateral contract only if the other is also obligated. But mutuality of obligation offers no explanation for the practice of awarding specific performance to sellers.

The other main effort to justify specific performance for vendors has greater credibility. It emphasizes the practical inadequacy of damages as a seller's remedy. The Restatement (Second) of Contracts puts it as follows:

"* * * because the value of land is to some extent speculative, it may be difficult for [the seller] to prove with reasonable certainty the difference between the contract price and the market price of the land. Even if he can make this proof, the land may not be immediately convertible into money and he may be deprived of funds with which he could have made other investments. Furthermore, before the seller gets a judgment, the existence of the contract, even if broken by the buyer, operates as a clog on saleability, so that it may be difficult to find a purchaser at a fair price."[6]

While these assertions are sometimes true, they are certainly not correct in all cases. The land may well be highly liquid and readily saleable, and its value readily determinable by expert appraisal testimony. Specific perfor-

3. Treasure Valley Bank v. Long, 92 Or. App. 598, 759 P.2d 1108 (1988); O'Halloran v. Oechslie, 402 A.2d 67 (Me.1979); Restatement (Second) of Contracts § 374 comment e. But see Perron v. Hale, 108 Idaho 578, 701 P.2d 198 (1985), implying that the court might require proof of actual uniqueness even from a purchaser.

4. See, e.g., Deans v. Layton, 89 N.C.App. 358, 366 S.E.2d 560 (1988), review denied 322 N.C. 834, 371 S.E.2d 276 (1988); Lane v. Associated Housing Developers, 767 S.W.2d 640 (Tenn.App.1988); Thompson v. Kromhout, 413 N.W.2d 884 (Minn.App.1987); Barker v. Francis, 741 P.2d 548 (Utah App.1987); Abatti v. Eldridge, 103 Cal.App.3d 484, 163 Cal.Rptr. 82 (1980); Golden v. Frazier, 244 Ga. 685, 261 S.E.2d 703 (1979). Cf. ULTA § 2–506, which gives the seller specific performance only if the property cannot be resold by him or her at a reasonable price with reasonable effort. The ULTA, incidentally, speaks in terms of an "action for the price" rather than specific performance, but the two are substantially identical. The Pennsylvania courts permit either of these types of actions (the former at law and the latter in equity), but recognize

that they are virtually identical in result; Trachtenburg v. Sibarco Stations, Inc., 477 Pa. 517, 384 A.2d 1209 (1978).

5. For example, a written contract signed by only one of the parties may be enforced against only that party under the statute of frauds. On the demise of the doctrine of mutuality of remedy, see Restatement of Contracts § 372(1) and comment a (1933); 11 Williston, Contracts § 1433 (3d ed. 1968); Bleecher v. Conte, 29 Cal.3d 345, 173 Cal.Rptr. 278, 626 P.2d 1051 (1981) (purchaser may obtain specific performance although vendor has waived it); Jonmil, Inc. v. McMerty, 265 N.W.2d 257 (N.D.1978); Fleischer v. James Drug Stores, 1 N.J. 138, 62 A.2d 383 (1948). See Saliterman v. Bigos, 352 N.W.2d 494 (Minn.App.1984) (rejecting requirement of mutuality of remedy).

6. Restatement (Second) of Contracts § 360, Comment e (1981). See also Tombari v. Griepp, 55 Wn.2d 771, 350 P.2d 452 (1960); Comment, 48 Temp.L.Q. 847 (1975). Further arguments for the inadequacy of damages in real estate contracts are made in Kronman, Specific Performance, 45 U.Chi.L.Rev. 351, 355–64 (1978).

mance at the seller's behest ought to depend on a showing of actual, and not merely conceivable, difficulties of the type the Restatement describes; such is the rule with respect to non-realty contracts.[7] A few recent cases have begun to take this view. The most notable is Centex Homes Corporation v. Boag,[8] in which the developer of a 3600–unit luxury condominium housing project sought specific performance against a breaching purchaser of one of the apartment units. The Chancery Division of the New Jersey Superior Court relegated the seller to money damages,[9] emphasizing the absence of any unique qualities in a condominium unit in such a large project containing many virtually identical units. The lack of uniqueness *per se* seems somewhat irrelevant where it is the vendor who seeks specific performance. More to the point is the fact that the vendor's large pool of units and its extensive sales experience with them would probably make its proof of damages very straightforward and accurate. Hence, damages are an entirely satisfactory remedy and specific performance is unnecessary. Such a conclusion might as easily be reached in many other cases, not necessarily limited to those involving condominiums or other large developments with many similar parcels.[10] The Centex court's emphasis on lack of uniqueness suggests a more unorthodox question: should *purchasers* of real estate automatically be permitted to treat damages as inadequate, particularly in situations in which many substantially similar properties are readily obtainable? Thus far no American court has seen fit to depart from the traditional view on this point.

While lack of real uniqueness will not usually deprive the plaintiff of specific performance, other factors may. Obviously no remedy in specie can be ordered if the vendor no longer has the land, but has transferred it to a bona fide purchaser, or if for other reasons the vendor has no title.[11]

---

7. See Restatement (Second) of Contracts §§ 359–60 (1981). This is essentially the approach taken by ULTA § 2–506.

8. 128 N.J.Super. 385, 320 A.2d 194 (Ch. Div.1974), noted 48 Temp.L.Q. 847 (1975); 43 U.Cin.L.Rev. 935 (1974). See Pruitt v. Graziano, 215 N.J.Super. 330, 521 A.2d 1313 (1987) and Giannini v. First Nat. Bank, 136 Ill. App.3d 971, 91 Ill.Dec. 438, 483 N.E.2d 924 (1985), awarding condominium unit *purchasers* specific performance despite the vendor's assertion that it had many similar units on the market, rendering the real estate non-unique.

9. Since the contract contained a liquidated damages clause which the court construed as limiting damages to the amount paid at the time of the breach, the vendor was permitted to retain the $525 earnest money deposit but denied any further recovery.

10. The Idaho Supreme Court reached a similar conclusion in Suchan v. Rutherford, 90 Idaho 288, 410 P.2d 434 (1966), but it was also influenced by the fact that the sales contract contemplated the execution, at closing, of an 18–year installment contract; the court was reluctant to attempt enforcement in specie of such a contract which, it thought, might subsequently appear inequitable or involve further defaults. See also Manning v. Bleifus, 166 W.Va. 131, 272 S.E.2d 821 (1980) (dictum). More recently the Idaho courts have adopted a policy which permits one resisting specific performance to adduce evidence which rebuts the general presumption that land is unique; see Wood v. Simonson, 108 Idaho 699, 701 P.2d 319 (App.1985); Perron v. Hale, 108 Idaho 578, 701 P.2d 198 (1985).

11. Canton v. Monaco Partnership, 156 Ariz. 468, 753 P.2d 158 (1987); Smith v. Hooker/Barnes, Inc., 253 Ga. 514, 322 S.E.2d 268 (1984); Krantz v. Donner, 285 So.2d 699 (Fla. App.1973); Carson v. Isabel Apartments, Inc., 20 Wn.App. 293, 579 P.2d 1027 (1978); Henry S. Miller Co. v. Stephens, 587 S.W.2d 491 (Tex.Civ.App.1979), refused n.r.e. But see Giannini v. First Nat. Bank, 136 Ill.App.3d 971, 91 Ill.Dec. 438, 483 N.E.2d 924 (1985), granting specific performance of sale of a condominium unit despite the fact that the vendor had not yet converted the building into a condominium. See 6A Powell, Real Property ¶ 925(2) (1980).

If the vendor's title or interest is only partially deficient, the purchaser can generally get specific performance with abatement of the price; see § 10.3 supra at note 43. See

Similarly, if the plaintiff is in material breach or has failed to fulfill other conditions imposed by the terms of the contract, she or he cannot recover.[12] As we have already seen, a liquidated damages clause may be construed to exclude other remedies such as specific performance;[13] likewise, a clause in the contract may expressly deny specific performance.[14] A few courts have rejected specific performance as a remedy for purchasers who were buying only for immediate resale, on the grounds that their damages were readily computable and that the land's unique qualities were irrelevant to them except as reflected in their prospective profits.[15] Finally, many courts require a higher degree of specificity for enforcement of contracts at equity than in law; hence, damages may be available even though the contract's language is too vague to warrant specific performance.[16]

Stoltz v. Grimm, 100 Nev. 529, 689 P.2d 927 (1984); Coates v. Hale, 429 So.2d 761 (Fla.App. 1983); Langley v. Moore, 64 N.C.App. 520, 307 S.E.2d 817 (1983).

If the vendor has transferred title to one with notice of the contract, specific performance will lie against the title-holder; Hallmark Builders, Inc. v. Hickory Lakes of Brandon, Inc., 458 So.2d 45 (Fla.App.1984); Dean Operations, Inc. v. Pink Hill Associates, 678 S.W.2d 897 (Mo.App.1984); Glynn v. Marquette, 152 Cal.App.3d 277, 199 Cal.Rptr. 306 (1984). Cf. E.G. Realty, Inc. v. Nova–Park New York, Inc., 176 A.D.2d 680, 575 N.Y.S.2d 481 (1991) (denying specific performance against a purchaser from the vendor where granting relief would be inequitable).

In Dean v. Sneed, 392 So.2d 1169 (Ala.1981), the vendor placed his property back on the market after the purchaser breached; however, he was unsuccessful in reselling it, and brought an action for specific performance. The court held his resale efforts amounted to a waiver or abandonment of his right to specific performance.

12. See, e.g., Frumento v. Mezzanotte, 192 Conn. 606, 473 A.2d 1193 (1984) (purchaser who lacks sufficient funds to complete purchase on settlement date may not later obtain specific performance); Blackmore v. Honnas, 141 Ariz. 354, 687 P.2d 362 (App.1984) (purchaser who abandoned contract by taking no action for 6½ months after vendors' breach cannot obtain specific performance); Henderson v. Winkler, 454 So.2d 1358 (Ala. 1984) (after mutual rescission, purchaser may not obtain specific performance); Cohen v. Rasner, 97 Nev. 118, 624 P.2d 1006 (1981); Annot., 55 A.L.R.3d 10 (1974). Cf. Baugh v. Johnson, 6 Ark.App. 308, 641 S.W.2d 730 (1982) (vendor can get specific performance despite minor deficiency in land area.)

13. See the discussion at § 10.4 notes 15–17, supra and accompanying text; Kohrs v. Barth, 212 Ill.App.3d 468, 156 Ill.Dec. 551, 570 N.E.2d 1273 (1991); Seabaugh v. Keele, 775 S.W.2d 205 (Mo.App.1989); Gulf City Body & Trailer Works, Inc. v. Phoenix Properties Trust, Inc., 531 So.2d 870 (Ala.1988); In re Columbus Plaza, Inc., 79 B.R. 710 (Bkrtcy. S.D.Ohio 1987). But see Logue v. Seven–Hot Springs Corp., 926 F.2d 722 (8th Cir.1991) (liquidated damages not intended to be vendor's exclusive remedy); Saliterman v. Bigos, 352 N.W.2d 494 (Minn.App.1984) (even though contract limits *vendor's* remedy to rescission, *purchaser* may obtain specific performance; mutuality of remedy is not required).

14. S.E.S. Importers, Inc. v. Pappalardo, 53 N.Y.2d 455, 442 N.Y.S.2d 453, 425 N.E.2d 841 (1981); Bleecher v. Conte, 29 Cal.3d 345, 173 Cal.Rptr. 278, 626 P.2d 1051 (1981); Sun Bank of Miami v. Lester, 404 So.2d 141 (Fla.App. 1981), review denied 412 So.2d 467 (Fla.1982).

15. Watkins v. Paul, 95 Idaho 499, 511 P.2d 781 (1973); Schmid v. Whitten, 114 S.C. 245, 103 S.E. 553 (1920). But see Chan v. Smider, 31 Wn.App. 730, 644 P.2d 727 (1982) (purchaser may obtain specific performance even though he is purchasing property as an investment); Justus v. Clelland, 133 Ariz. 381, 651 P.2d 1206 (App.1982).

16. Honolulu Waterfront Ltd. Partnership v. Aloha Tower Development Corp., 692 F.Supp. 1230 (D.Hawaii 1988), affirmed 891 F.2d 295 (9th Cir.1989); Kane v. McDermott, 191 Ill.App.3d 212, 138 Ill.Dec. 541, 547 N.E.2d 708 (1989); Lindsley v. Anderson, 383 N.W.2d 530 (Iowa 1986); Genest v. John Glenn Corp., 298 Or. 723, 696 P.2d 1058 (1985); Eichhorst v. Mandalay Shores Cooperative Housing Ass'n, 477 So.2d 25 (Fla.App. 1985), review denied 486 So.2d 597 (Fla.1986) (no specific performance, where contract failed to state how a large existing mortgage would be satisfied); Smoliak v. Myhr, 361 N.W.2d 153 (Minn.App.1985) (land description too uncertain to give specific performance); Carr v. Redford, 678 S.W.2d 3 (Mo.App.1984) (same); McEachren v. Sherwood & Roberts, Inc., 36 Wn.App. 576, 675 P.2d 1266 (1984) (damages award proper, although contract was unclear as to rights to hay on farm); Anderson v. Overland Park Credit Union, 231 Kan. 97, 643 P.2d 120 (1982); Seal v. Polehn, 284 Or. 259, 586 P.2d 345 (1978), appeal after remand 52 Or.App. 389, 628 P.2d 746 (1981),

Perhaps the most important and least predictable barrier to specific performance is the notion that the remedy is inherently discretionary and should not be ordered where it would lead to an unjust result. Obviously this concept includes such matters as the plaintiff's fraud, deception, undue influence, concealment of material facts, or the like, even if the misbehavior is not so serious as to deny remedies at law or to make the plaintiff liable for damages; equity is more vigilant than law.[17] It also encompasses cases involving no misbehavior *per se* in which specific enforcement would produce hardship to the defendant or to third parties.[18] The most variable results are found when the hardship is simply an unfair price—too great if the vendor is the plaintiff, or too small if the purchaser is seeking enforcement. The answer here depends on numerous factors, some of which may be unarticulated: the size of the mismatch between price and value, the relative sophistication and bargaining power of the parties, and the adequacy of other remedies.[19]

review denied 291 Or. 368, 634 P.2d 1346 (1981); Dozier v. Matthews, 136 Ga.App. 375, 221 S.E.2d 236 (1975); Dassance v. Nienhuis, 57 Mich.App. 422, 225 N.W.2d 789 (1975); Rego v. Decker, 482 P.2d 834, 837 (Alaska 1971); Note, 5 U.C.L.A.–Alaska L.Rev. 112 (1975). If the contract requires the vendor to subordinate his purchase-money mortgage to a future construction loan, specific performance may be denied if the latter loan is not fully described in the contract; see Farrell v. Phillips, 414 So.2d 1119 (Fla.App.1982); G. Nelson & D. Whitman, Real Estate Finance Law § 12.9 (2d ed. 1985). But see Marder's Nurseries, Inc. v. Hopping, 171 A.D.2d 63, 573 N.Y.S.2d 990 (1991) (contract specifically enforceable despite its lack of statement of interest rate on purchase-money mortgage, where purchaser had the option of paying all cash); White Hen Pantry, Inc. v. Cha, 214 Ill.App.3d 627, 158 Ill.Dec. 310, 574 N.E.2d 104 (1991) (contract specifically enforceable despite lack of reference to type of deed, apportionment of taxes, closing date, and other minor matters).

17. Estate of Younge v. Huysmans, 127 N.H. 461, 506 A.2d 282 (1985) (specific performance denied due to purchaser's laches in seeking it); Cimina v. Bronich, 349 Pa.Super. 399, 503 A.2d 427 (1985) (specific performance of tenant's option to purchase denied, due to tenant's failure to pay taxes as required by lease); In re Estate of Mihm, 345 Pa.Super. 1, 497 A.2d 612 (1985) (specific performance denied, where purchasers breached a confidential relationship with vendor); Barnard & Son, Inc. v. Akins, 109 Idaho 466, 708 P.2d 871 (1985) (purchaser denied specific performance where both parties breached contract); Kauffmann v. Baker, 392 So.2d 13 (Fla.App.1980) (specific performance denied where both parties conspired to inflate the price and deceive the lender); Bliss v. Rhodes, 66 Ill.App.3d 895, 23 Ill.Dec. 718, 384 N.E.2d 512 (1978); Sienkiewicz v. Smith, 30 Wn.App. 235, 633 P.2d 905 (1981), reversed 97 Wn.2d 711, 649 P.2d 112 (1982) (specific performance denied where the

result of enforcement would have been creation of an illegal subdivision). But see Oneida City School Dist. v. Seiden & Sons, Inc., 177 A.D.2d 828, 576 N.Y.S.2d 442 (1991) (vendor awarded specific performance despite its knowledge that the purchaser would not be able to get zoning approval for its intended use of the land).

18. See Bailey v. Musumeci, 134 N.H. 280, 591 A.2d 1316 (1991) (specific performance refused against purchaser who acted under a unilateral mistake); Anderson v. Onsager, 155 Wis.2d 504, 455 N.W.2d 885 (1990); Dawdy v. Sample, 178 Ill.App.3d 118, 127 Ill.Dec. 299, 532 N.E.2d 1128 (1989), appeal denied 125 Ill.2d 564, 130 Ill.Dec. 479, 537 N.E.2d 808 (1989); Eastern Motor Inns, Inc. v. Ricci, 565 A.2d 1265 (R.I.1989); Thompson v. Kromhout, 413 N.W.2d 884 (Minn.App.1987); Nann v. Pignatelli, 3 Conn.App. 74, 485 A.2d 922 (1984), cert. denied 196 Conn. 805, 492 A.2d 1240 (1985) (specific performance denied where plaintiff purchaser insisted on having a 25–foot right-of-way to the land, but such was not required by the contract); Gordon v. Mazur, 308 N.Y. 861, 126 N.E.2d 304 (1955); Hilton v. Nelsen, 283 N.W.2d 877 (Minn.1979); 6A Powell, Real Property ¶ 925(3) (1980); Maggs, Remedies for Breach of Contract Under Article Two of the U.L.T.A., 11 Ga.L.Rev. 275 (1977).

19. Numerous cases deny specific performance where the price is grossly unfair; see, e.g., Wagner v. Estate of Rummel, 391 Pa.Super. 555, 571 A.2d 1055 (1990), appeal denied 527 Pa. 588, 588 A.2d 510 (1991) (chancellor should consider unfairness, where testimony indicated land was worth 100 times contract price); Jensen v. Southwestern States Management Co., 6 Kan.App.2d 437, 629 P.2d 752 (1981); Hodge v. Shea, 252 S.C. 601, 168 S.E.2d 82 (1969); Chalmers v. Raras, 200 Cal. App.2d 682, 19 Cal.Rptr. 531 (1962); Official Code Ga.Ann. § 37–805. Cf. Giannini v. First

Finally, note that specific performance does not always provide a full remedy for the plaintiff's harm, since the decree is almost invariably delayed beyond the date fixed by the contract. Hence, incidental damages may be awarded along with the order compelling performance.[20] An excellent example is Godwin v. Lindbert,[21] in which the purchaser obtained an order of specific performance but found that as a result of rising interest rates, the financing of the purchase would be much more costly than anticipated when the contract was formed. The court agreed and awarded damages to reflect the higher cost of mortgage funds. A similar argument can be made by a purchaser whose possession of the property is delayed during the prosecution of a specific performance action, and who seeks to recover the fair rental value of the property from the date agreed for performance until the actual

Nat. Bank, 136 Ill.App.3d 971, 91 Ill.Dec. 438, 483 N.E.2d 924 (1985), holding "there is no hardship in compelling the seller to do what he agreed to do when he thought it was to his advantage;" Resource Management Co. v. Weston Ranch and Livestock Co., 706 P.2d 1028 (Utah 1985), upholding specific performance of a contract to convey certain oil and gas royalty rights, although the value of those rights subsequently rose sharply in value; Seabaugh v. Sailer, 679 S.W.2d 924 (Mo.App. 1984) (specific performance upheld at $300 per acre, although two appraisers testified land was worth $1300 to $1400 per acre); Dean v. Gregg, 34 Wn.App. 684, 663 P.2d 502 (1983) (specific performance ordered despite financial hardship on vendor); Owens v. Church, 675 S.W.2d 178 (Tenn.App.1984) (fairness is judged at time of contracting); Bliss v. Rhodes, 66 Ill.App.3d 895, 23 Ill.Dec. 718, 384 N.E.2d 512 (1978) (unfair price alone insufficient to deny specific performance). See also Robert Lawrence Associates, Inc. v. Del Vecchio, 178 Conn. 1, 420 A.2d 1142 (1979) (specific performance ordered where price was fair when contract formed, although much lower than market value at time of performance due to purchaser's obtaining of rezoning); El Paso Natural Gas Co. v. Western Building Associates, 675 F.2d 1135 (10th Cir.1982); County of Lincoln v. Fischer, 216 Or. 421, 339 P.2d 1084 (1959); 11 A.L.R.2d 390 (1950). Denial of specific performance due to unfairness of price is strongly criticized by Schwartz, supra note 1, at 299–301.

20. See Restatement (Second) of Contracts § 358, Comment c (1981); Annot., 11 A.L.R. 4th 891 (1981); III Lounge, Inc. v. Gaines, 227 Neb. 585, 419 N.W.2d 143 (1988) (where vendor has possession during period of delay, he is liable for taxes, repairs, utilities and insurance accruing during that time); Cooperstein v. Patrician Estates, 117 A.D.2d 774, 499 N.Y.S.2d 423 (1986) (purchaser granted specific performance of contract to convey, plus damages due to vendor's failure to complete construction of house on the land); Woliansky v. Miller, 146 Ariz. 170, 704 P.2d 811 (App. 1985), appeal after remand 154 Ariz. 32, 739 P.2d 1349 (1987) (purchaser granted specific

performance plus damages due to deterioration in improvements between contract closing date and actual conveyance, nearly 5 years); Bravo v. Buelow, 168 Cal.App.3d 208, 214 Cal.Rptr. 65 (1985) (purchaser granted specific performance plus damages due to increase in cost of constructing house on the land). Cf. Stoltz v. Grimm, 100 Nev. 529, 689 P.2d 927 (1984) (incidental damages refused, since they did not result directly from vendor's default).

21. 101 Mich.App. 754, 300 N.W.2d 514 (1980); see also Housing Authority of Monterey County v. Monterey Senior Citizen Park, 164 Cal.App.3d 348, 210 Cal.Rptr. 497 (1985); Amick v. Hagler, 286 S.C. 481, 334 S.E.2d 525 (App.1985) (order assessing damages for purchaser's loss of advantageous financing was proper, but order that, in the alternative, vendor provide mortgage financing equivalent to that which had been originally obtained by purchaser was error); Fullerton v. McGowan, 6 Conn.App. 624, 507 A.2d 473 (1986); Appollo v. Reynolds, 364 N.W.2d 422 (Minn.App.1985) (closing delayed by vendor, but finally occurred; purchasers entitled to damages resulting from higher mortgage loan interest); Reis v. Sparks, 547 F.2d 236 (4th Cir.1976); Hutton v. Gliksberg, 128 Cal.App.3d 240, 180 Cal. Rptr. 141 (1982); Stratton v. Tejani, 139 Cal. App.3d 204, 187 Cal.Rptr. 231 (1982); Regan v. Lanze, 47 A.D.2d 378, 366 N.Y.S.2d 512 (1975), reversed 40 N.Y.2d 475, 387 N.Y.S.2d 79, 354 N.E.2d 818 (1976); Walker v. Benton, 407 So.2d 305 (Fla.App.1981); Turley v. Ball Associates Limited, 641 P.2d 286 (Colo.App.1981); Donovan v. Bachstadt, 91 N.J. 434, 453 A.2d 160 (1982) (damages, not specific performance, awarded), lower decision noted 12 Seaton Hall L.Rev. 916 (1982). But see Wall v. Pate, 104 N.M. 1, 715 P.2d 449 (1986) (where vendor breaches and no sale occurs, purchaser may not recover damages for loss of opportunity to assume advantageous mortgage); Smith v. Stout, 40 Wn.App. 646, 700 P.2d 343 (1985) (same). See generally Garland, Purchaser's Interest Rate Increase: Caveat Venditor, 27 N.Y.L.Sch.L.Rev. 745 (1982).

performance.[22] However, in most cases the purchaser has also been spared the necessity of investing cash in the property during the same period— except for perhaps an earnest money deposit. Thus the savings in interest on the funds tends to offset the rental-value damages, often leaving the purchaser with little or no net damages.[23]

§ 10.6 Remedies for Contract Breach—Vendor's Lien

Courts of equity generally recognize an implied lien, much like a mortgage on the land, in favor of the vendor for the amount of the unpaid purchase price.[1] Prior to the transfer of legal title by deed, the purchaser

22. But see Marshall v. Bare, 107 Idaho App. 201, 687 P.2d 591 (1984) (vendor may not recover rental value where purchaser goes into possession prior to passage of title).

23. Dillingham Commercial Co., Inc. v. Spears, 641 P.2d 1 (Alaska 1982); Meyer v. Benko, 55 Cal.App.3d 937, 127 Cal.Rptr. 846 (1976); Rekhi v. Olason, 28 Wn.App. 751, 626 P.2d 513 (1981); Walker v. Benton, supra n. 21. A similar analysis can be applied when the vendor seeks specific performance; the vendor has typically lost the interest which could have been earned on the purchase price, but at the same time has had the use or rental value of the property from the agreed closing date. See Paris v. Allbaugh, 41 Wn.App. 717, 704 P.2d 660 (1985) (where specific performance is ordered against vendor in default, he is entitled to interest on the price only to the extent that it is offset against rents and profits from the property during the period of delay); Shelter Corp. v. Bozin, 468 So.2d 1094 (Fla.App.1985) (same). Cf. Chan v. Smider, 31 Wn.App. 730, 644 P.2d 727 (1982) (in order for purchaser to limit defaulting vendor's interest claim as above, purchaser must not claim rents per se, but must waive rents and seek "remission of interest."); Miller v. Estate of Dawson, 14 Ark.App. 167, 686 S.W.2d 443 (1985) (where purchaser had possession during period of delay, he may retain rents and profits earned but must pay interest to the vendor on the unpaid balance of the purchase price from the date agreed for closing to the date of actual performance); Higbie v. Johnson, 626 P.2d 1147 (Colo.App.1980), in which the purchaser held possession (despite his breach of contract) during the relevant period; the vendor was awarded the full amount of interest foregone on the price. Occasionally decisions give the plaintiff a full recovery without deduction for the "savings" he or she has experienced, on the ground that the defendant could readily have avoided this result merely by performing as agreed. Such holdings seem designed more to penalize the defendant than to compensate the plaintiff fairly. See Matter of Hallmark Builders, Inc., 54 B.R. 292 (Bkrtcy.M.D.Fla.1985), granting a builder-vendor specific performance plus damages equal to the added construction loan interest it paid due to purchasers' delay; Reis v. Sparks, 547

F.2d 236 (4th Cir.1976). In Suter v. Arrowhead Investment Co., Limited, 387 So.2d 815 (Ala.1980), the plaintiff-vendor was permitted to recover both the rental value of the property and the interest the vendor was paying on his mortgage during the same period. The two recoveries are obviously duplicative, but may be explained on the ground that the vendor had no realistic way of renting the property immediately upon the purchaser's breach, which was entirely unexpected.

§ 10.6

1. See McGoodwin v. McGoodwin, 671 S.W.2d 880 (Tex.1984); Rader v. Dawes, 651 S.W.2d 629 (Mo.App.1983); Easterling v. Ferris, 651 P.2d 677 (Okl.1982). A number of states recognize the lien in statute; see, e.g., Idaho Code § 45–801, discussed in Estates of Somers v. Clearwater Power Co., 107 Idaho 29, 684 P.2d 1006 (1984) (judgment lien against vendor does not attach to vendor's lien); Mont.Code Ann. § 71–3–1301; Ohio Rev.Code § 5301.26; 42 Okla.Stat.1981, § 26; South Dakota Compiled Laws 44–6–1. The lien is confined to the purchase price of the land; the price of personal goods or sums owing on other debts cannot be included; Inwood North Homeowners' Ass'n v. Harris, 707 S.W.2d 127 (Tex.App.1986), judgment reversed on other grounds 736 S.W.2d 632 (Tex.1987) (vendor's lien does not include amount owing on assessments by owners association in subdivision); Lessard v. Lessard Acres, Inc., 349 So.2d 293 (La.1977); Grace Development Co., Inc. v. Houston, 306 Minn. 334, 237 N.W.2d 73 (1975). But see Krone v. McCann, 219 Mont. 353, 711 P.2d 1367 (1986) (vendor's lien may include attorneys' fees, where contract so provides).

In one unusual case, a *purchaser* was held to have a vendor's lien. See Washburn v. Central Premix Concrete Co., 98 Wn.2d 311, 654 P.2d 700 (1982): the purchaser's offer to buy the property was never accepted, but he paid a substantial deposit and took possession of the land. Later he moved out under circumstances that the court construed as a mutual oral rescission, but the vendor returned only a part of his deposit. The court held that the rescission was analogous to a resale of the

has an equitable title to the property under the doctrine of equitable conversion.[2] The vendor's lien exists on this equitable interest,[3] although as a practical matter it usually has little significance, since the vendor who has not conveyed legal title at the time the purchaser defaults will ordinarily seek either damages or specific performance, or even more commonly will attempt to terminate purchaser's rights under the contract and forfeit the payments made to date.[4] Thus, efforts to foreclose formally on the vendor's lien are rare when the default has occurred before "settlement."[5]

After legal title has been transferred to the purchaser, the vendor's (perhaps more aptly, "grantor's") lien is imposed on that interest and is of much greater practical importance, since retention of title is no longer an option open to the seller. Even here, however, the assertion of the vendor's lien is not very common. One reason is that in many transactions the contract provides for full payment of the price in cash at settlement. Even when payment is deferred, most vendors obtain and enforce the more specific type of security represented by a recorded purchase-money mortgage or deed of trust. In such cases the vendor's lien seems irrelevant, and neither the parties nor their lawyers are likely even to remember that it exists.[6]

The vendor's lien is an invention of the equity courts. As an "implied" lien it does not depend on any specific language in the sale contract, although it certainly may be mentioned therein and in some jurisdictions it is customary to do so.[7] It is commonly foreclosed by the same sort of judicial

---

land to the vendor, and allowed the purchaser a "vendor's lien" to aid recovery of his remaining deposit.

The vendor's lien was held personal to the vendor and nonassignable in Tri–State Nat. Bank v. Saffren, 726 P.2d 1081 (Wyo.1986).

2. The concept of equitable conversion is discussed at § 10.13, infra.

3. See Huffman v. Foreman, 163 Ind.App. 263, 323 N.E.2d 651 (1975); Butler v. Wilkinson, 740 P.2d 1244 (Utah 1987); D. Dobbs, Remedies 866 (1972). The ULTA recognizes the vendor's lien, but appears to restrict it to cases in which legal title has been transferred; ULTA § 2–508(a). Professor Pomeroy argued that the term "vendor's lien" was a misnomer. He urged that while prior to the passage of legal title the vendor had the rights mentioned in the text, they in no sense constituted a lien. After title was conveyed, he conceded that a lien existed, but preferred to term it the "grantor's lien". J. Pomeroy, Equity Jurisprudence §§ 1249, 1260 (Symonds ed. 1941). This usage, however, has not generally been followed by the courts.

4. Indeed, this right is sometimes itself termed a vendor's lien; see Stagg v. Van Sant, 390 So.2d 620 (Ala.1980); Dobbs, supra note 3.

5. But see Sebastian v. Floyd, 585 S.W.2d 381 (Ky.1979), in which the court held that forfeiture was unavailable to the vendor and relegated him to an action to foreclose the lien by judicial sale.

6. One may well have a vendor's lien without realizing it, much less mentioning it in the contract of sale or other documents; see Maroney v. Boyle, 141 N.Y. 462, 36 N.E. 511, 38 Am.St.Rep. 821 (1894). The lien is not necessarily irrelevant when the vendor has taken a purchase-money mortgage. In Goidl v. North American Mortgage Investors, 564 S.W.2d 493 (Tex.Civ.App.1978), the vendor took both a deed of trust and an express vendor's lien. By written agreement he subordinated the priority of the deed of trust to another deed of trust in favor of a third-party lender, but he made no reference to the vendor's lien in the subordination clause. The court held that the lien was not necessarily subordinated (although it admitted that it would make little commercial sense to subordinate the deed of trust and not the vendor's lien) and remanded the case for findings on the question of whether subordination of the lien was intended. See also Rader v. Dawes, 651 S.W.2d 629 (Mo.App.1983).

7. See, e.g., Arkansas State Highway Commission v. First Pyramid Life Insurance Co., 265 Ark. 417, 579 S.W.2d 587 (1979); R & P Enterprises v. LaGuarta, Gavrel & Kirk, Inc., 596 S.W.2d 517 (Tex.1980). Professor Pomeroy pointed out that where the lien is reserved by express language, especially in a recorded deed, it becomes a more powerful tool for the vendor in several respects. Courts are much less likely to find a waiver through the taking of other security; the recordation will give notice of the lien to all subsequent takers, precluding their assertion of BFP status; and

action in equity by which mortgages are foreclosed.[8] The term "foreclosed" is quite appropriate, since if the purchaser fails to pay the remaining balance of the price before foreclosure is decreed the purchaser's opportunity to acquire the land is permanently lost. Foreclosure may be by judicially-supervised sale, typically conducted by the sheriff, with the highest bidder taking the land.[9] The proceeds are paid first to the vendor in the amount of the unpaid portion of the contract price; any surplus proceeds are distributed to the contract vendee or to others who claim through or under him or her.[10] If the proceeds are insufficient to cover the remaining sale price, many jurisdictions will give the vendor a personal judgment for the deficiency.[11]

An alternative to foreclosure by judicial sale is strict foreclosure, a procedure under which the court gives the purchaser a specific time period within which to pay the remaining price.[12] If the purchaser fails to do so, the court decrees that full title is in the vendor, and the purchaser's rights are cancelled. In cases in which no legal title by deed has yet been conveyed, the result of strict foreclosure is not materially different than if the vendor had simply retained title and obtained a court decree forfeiting the purchaser's rights. There is ordinarily no possibility of the purchaser's recovering any of the payments made on the contract, a fact which obviously leads to potential injustice to the purchaser whenever strict foreclosure is ordered. In many jurisdictions statutes or court decisions prohibit the strict foreclosure of ordinary mortgages, and instead require foreclosure by sale.[13] Whether similar rules will or should be applied to the foreclosure of vendor's liens is often hard to tell, although a similar risk of unfairness is present.[14]

there is no doubt (as there sometimes is with respect to a purely implied lien) of its assignability by the vendor to another. See J. Pomeroy, Equity Jurisprudence §§ 1257–59 (Symonds ed. 1941).

8. See Quintana v. Anthony, 109 Idaho 977, 712 P.2d 678 (App.1985) (vendor's lien is not technically a mortgage, but courts of equity enforcing such liens should generally follow mortgage law concepts of debtor protection, including Idaho's "one-action" or "security first" rule, its fair value limitation on deficiency judgments, and its statutory post-foreclosure redemption; Sewer v. Martin, 511 F.2d 1134 (3d Cir.1975); 3 Am.L.Prop. § 11.74 (1952).

9. See Annot., 77 A.L.R. 270 (1932). In some states if the vendor obtains a decree for specific performance and the purchaser refuses to pay the price, the court can order the property sold at a public sale and the proceeds applied against the purchase obligation. In effect, this procedure converts specific performance into a judicial foreclosure of the vendor's lien. See Clements v. Leonard, 70 So.2d 840 (Fla.1954).

10. On judicial foreclosure of mortgages, see generally, G. Nelson & D. Whitman, Real Estate Finance Law § 7.16 (2d ed. 1985).

11. See Quintana v. Anthony, 109 Idaho 977, 712 P.2d 678 (App.1985); Carman v. Gibbs, 220 Neb. 603, 371 N.W.2d 283 (1985) (deficiency judgment is equally available after foreclosure of mortgage or vendor's lien); Ricard v. Equitable Life Assur. Soc., 462 So.2d 592 (Fla.App.1985) (vendor is entitled to a deficiency judgment in absence of some equitable reason for denying it; deficiency granted despite the facts that vendor was successful bidder at foreclosure sale with a bid of only 60% of selling price of property's equity, and that purchaser had made $200,000 in improvements); R & P Enterprises v. LaGuarta, Gavrel & Kirk, Inc., 596 S.W.2d 517 (Tex.1980); Clements v. Leonard, 70 So.2d 840 (Fla.1954). A jurisdiction which by statute limits or prohibits deficiency judgments after mortgage foreclosures is likely to take a similar position with respect to deficiency judgments following vendor's lien foreclosures; see Nevin v. Salk, 45 Cal.App.3d 331, 119 Cal.Rptr. 370 (1975).

12. See Zumstein v. Stockton, 199 Or. 633, 264 P.2d 455 (1953); 3 Am.L.Prop. § 11.75. On strict foreclosure of mortgages, see generally, G. Nelson & D. Whitman, Real Estate Finance Law § 7.9 (2d ed. 1985).

13. G. Nelson & D. Whitman, id.

14. In Sebastian v. Floyd, 585 S.W.2d 381 (Ky.1979), the court held that the vendor's lien was analogous to a mortgage and hence must be foreclosed as one—by judicial sale rather than strict foreclosure or forfeiture.

Since forfeiture of earnest money deposits is so widely accepted in American courts,[15] it is hard to see any reason for denying strict foreclosure of vendors' liens unless the result would be inequitable on the facts of the case.

Ordinarily the vendor's lien is asserted only when the vendor has not taken back some specific type of security interest in the land by way of mortgage or deed of trust. Indeed, many cases treat the taking of a purchase-money mortgage as inherently inconsistent with the equitable lien, and hence as waiving it, unless it is expressly reserved.[16] But if an express reservation is made in the documents, a purchase-money mortgage and a vendor's lien can exist side by side. The lien could have significant consequences if, for example, the vendor subordinated the mortgage to other claims on the land but did not mention the lien when doing so.[17]

In general, the lien remains on the property even if the purchaser makes a further transfer. But if (as very often happens) the original purchaser makes a resale to a bona fide purchaser for value, the new subpurchaser takes free of the lien.[18] This result is usually explained on the ground that the lien is equitable in origin, and that equity will not impose the lien on an innocent party; as it is often put, the legal interest acquired by a BFP will prevail over a prior equity.[19] Even if the lien were conceived as growing out of the contract, one would usually reach the same result by

It is arguable that strict foreclosure never disadvantages the purchaser, since if the land had substantial value in excess of the balance owing on the contract the purchaser would resell or refinance it and pay the debt; see Dieffenbach v. Attorney General of Vermont, 604 F.2d 187 (2d Cir.1979). But this view disregards the expenses of sale or refinancing, as well as the very real possibility that these actions may be entirely impractical in periods of monetary stringency or high interest rates. Many courts will refuse strict foreclosure in any case in which the value of the land is sufficient to represent substantial equity in the purchaser; see, e.g., Riffey v. Schulke, 193 Neb. 317, 227 N.W.2d 4 (1975); Marquardt v. Fisher, 135 Or. 256, 295 P. 499, 77 A.L.R. 265 (1931). Such an approach roughly parallels the minority doctrine which refuses to permit forfeiture of the purchaser's interest in the contract when it would be unconscionable to do so. See text at § 10.4 notes 6–10, supra.

15. See text at § 10.4 notes 6–7, supra.

16. Back v. Union Life Insurance Co., 5 Ark.App. 176, 634 S.W.2d 150 (1982); Oliver v. Mercaldi, 103 So.2d 665, 67 A.L.R.2d 1089 (Fla.App.1958); Finlayson v. Waller, 64 Idaho 618, 134 P.2d 1069 (1943). This result follows from statute in Ohio; see Ohio Rev.Code § 5301.26; Summer & Co. v. DCR Corp., 47 Ohio St.2d 254, 351 N.E.2d 485 (1976). But a mere promise to give a specific security instrument is not a waiver if the instrument is never given in fact; see In re Hercules Machine Co., 51 B.R. 530 (Bkrtcy.E.D.Tenn.1985); Hinkel v. Crowson, 83 Cal.App. 87, 256 P. 479 (1927); Annot., 119 A.L.R. 1180 (1939). In Oklahoma a statute apparently restricts the

vendor's lien to cases in which the debt is otherwise unsecured; 42 Okla.Stat. 1981, § 26. But see Whelan v. Midland Mortgage Co., 591 P.2d 287 (Okl.1978). See also In re Midwestern Companies, Inc., 49 B.R. 98 (Bkrtcy.W.D.Mo.1985) (Missouri law); Graves v. Joyce, 590 So.2d 1261 (La.App.1991) (vendor's lien and purchase-money mortgage may coexist); Rader v. Dawes, 651 S.W.2d 629 (Mo. App.1983) (express security does not necessarily waive vendor's lien; depends on intention).

17. Goidl v. North American Mortgage Investors, 564 S.W.2d 493 (Tex.Civ.App.1978); Rader v. Dawes, note 16 supra.

18. Stanovsky v. Group Enterprise & Const. Co., 714 S.W.2d 836 (Mo.App.1986); Anjo Restaurant Corp. v. Sunrise Hotel Corp., 98 Misc.2d 597, 414 N.Y.S.2d 265 (1979); Manz v. Johnson, 531 S.W.2d 934 (Tex.Civ.App. 1976); Sewer v. Martin, 511 F.2d 1134 (3d Cir.1975); Huffman v. Foreman, 163 Ind.App. 263, 323 N.E.2d 651 (1975). Typically judgment creditors are not treated as bona fide purchasers, since they do not give consideration contemporaneously with their acquisition of an interest in the land. But at least one state by statute protects even them from vendor's liens of which they have no notice; Ohio Rev.Code § 5301.26.

19. See 2 Pomeroy, Equity Jurisprudence §§ 413, 1253 (Symonds ed. 1941). The prevailing view is that the lien is implied in law and not derived from the contract; Weaver v. Blake, 300 N.W.2d 52 (S.D.1980); Old First National Bank & Trust Co. v. Scheuman, 214 Ind. 652, 13 N.E.2d 551, 119 A.L.R. 1165 (1938).

the operation of the recording acts; if the contract is unrecorded (as is usually the case with short-term earnest money agreements), the lien would be void as against subsequent BFP's (who record first, if the jurisdiction has a notice-race recording statute.)[20] The choice between these two rationales could be highly important, however, in a notice-race state if the BFP failed to record his or her conveyance. Most of the cases merely state the BFP's protected position without bothering to explain its theoretical basis.

Since the question whether the subsequent purchaser has notice of the lien is a crucial one, it is necessary to consider what will give notice. If the subpurchaser knows or has reason to know that the full purchase price on the prior contract is still unpaid, that is surely enough.[21] On the other hand, it is very doubtful whether mere knowledge that a prior contract existed will deny BFP status; after all, a very large proportion of land transfers are preceded by sales contracts. But if the contract or deed recites that part of the price will be paid after settlement, and if it is recorded or the subpurchaser has other notice of it, he or she should be bound by the lien.[22]

Vendors can waive their liens, and courts often find such waivers by examining their behavior.[23] Since a waiver can be inferred from any act which suggests an intent not to rely on the lien, the waiver cases are somewhat unpredictable and suggest that considerable judicial manipulation may be occurring to reach conclusions which are in reality supported by general considerations of fairness or other unstated reasons.[24]

§ 10.7 Remedies for Contract Breach—Restitution

Restitution suggests the returning, by a party to a contract, of the performance he or she has received from the other party.[1] It makes sense only if for some reason the contract will not be performed in accordance with

---

20. See the discussion of recording acts at § 11.9, infra, at notes 8–9.

21. See, e.g., Edwards–Town, Inc. v. Dimin, 9 Cal.App.3d 87, 87 Cal.Rptr. 726 (1970) (subpurchaser had notice from actual reading of prior contract); Rader v. Dawes, 651 S.W.2d 629 (Mo.App.1983) (mortgage lender had knowledge that vendors had not been paid in full).

22. If a deed in the chain of title recites the fact that payment of the price is deferred, it will give notice of the lien to the subpurchaser whether it is recorded or not, since one is presumed to have examined one's chain of title. Lindsey v. Thornton, 234 Ala. 109, 173 So. 500 (1937); C.D. Shamburger Lumber Co. v. Holbert, 34 S.W.2d 614 (Tex.Civ.App.1931). If the vendor's deed recites the existence of the lien and is recorded, it is all the more clear that the subpurchaser cannot be a BFP; Cooksey v. Sinder, 682 S.W.2d 252 (Tex.1984); In re Hercules Machine Co., 51 B.R. 530 (Bkrtcy.E.D.Tenn.1985).

ULTA § 2–508 deals explicitly with the issue by providing for the recordation of a "notice of lien" by the vendor; it does not, however, indicate what effect should be given to the recordation of the contract itself.

23. Courts often say that they are reluctant to find waivers except on very clear evidence; see Colquette v. Forbes, 680 S.W.2d 536 (Tex.App.1984); Edwards–Town, Inc. v. Dimin, 9 Cal.App.3d 87, 87 Cal.Rptr. 726 (1970). Nevertheless, waivers are sometimes found; see Pelican Homestead and Savings Association v. Royal Scott Apartments Partnership, 541 So.2d 943 (La.App.1989), writ denied 543 So.2d 9 (La.1989) (act of sale recited receipt of full cash price and granted "full acquittance and discharge therefor"); Lincoln National Life Insurance Company v. Overmyer, 530 N.E.2d 784 (Ind.App.1988) (grantors intentionally conveyed property free and clear in order to permit purchasers to obtain first mortgage from bank; vendor's lien was waived as to real estate, but would attach to any surplus remaining after mortgage foreclosure by bank).

24. See, e.g., Russo v. Cedrone, 118 R.I. 549, 375 A.2d 906 (1977) (waiver inferred from vendor's delay in asserting lien and his assignment of his interest before assertion of the lien); D. Dobbs, Remedies 869–70 (1972).

§ 10.7

1. See 5 Corbin, Contracts § 1102 (1964).

its original terms. While it is quite possible for a party to make restitution voluntarily, our concern here is with judicially-ordered restitution as a remedy for contract breach. It can be a much more attractive remedy than damages to a party who has made an unfavorable bargain. For example, a vendor whose land is worth $100,000 but who foolishly agrees to sell it for $80,000 might be delighted to have restitution if the purchaser commits a breach.

The terms restitution and rescission are frequently used together, sometimes as if they were synonymous. This usage is potentially confusing, and it is helpful to distinguish the two words.[2] Restitution refers to a judicial order compelling the defendant to return to the plaintiff the value of the performance the defendant has received, thus returning the plaintiff to his or her position before the contract was formed.[3] Rescission has at least two meanings, similar but distinct. One meaning is a mutual agreement between the parties to a contract to cancel it and excuse one another from performance, at the same time making restitution to each other of the values of performances made to date.[4] In this sense, rescission is not a remedy at all, but merely an agreed relationship between the parties. The term rescission is also used to describe cases in which a single party unilaterally treats his or her duty of performance under the contract as excused and ended.[5] Such a person will often demand restitution from the other party; hence, unilateral rescission and a claim for restitution frequently go hand in hand. This sort of rescission may be grounded on one or more of a number of legal doctrines, such as mutual mistake,[6] misrepresentation,[7]

2. To escape this confusion the Restatement (Second) of Contracts carefully avoids the use of the term rescission in its discussion of restitutionary remedies; see, e.g., Restatement (Second) of Contracts § 370ff (1981).

3. See Lee v. Thunder Dev., Inc., 77 Or. App. 7, 711 P.2d 978 (1985); 5 Corbin, Contracts § 1112 (1964).

4. See Bazurto v. Burgess, 136 Ariz. 397, 666 P.2d 497 (App.1983) (if parties to mutual rescission do not expressly reserve their claims to damages, such claims are impliedly waived); Esecson v. Bushnell, 663 P.2d 258 (Colo.App.1983) (mutual rescission may be inferred from parties' conduct, if sufficiently clear); Henderson v. Winkler, 454 So.2d 1358 (Ala.1984) (after a mutual agreement to rescind, neither party may obtain damages or specific performance); Preheim v. Ortman, 331 N.W.2d 62 (S.D.1983); J. Calamari & J. Perillo, Contracts 757–60 (1977); 5A Corbin, Contracts § 1236 (1964). The Uniform Commercial Code uses the term rescission exclusively in this sense; see U.C.C. § 2–209 comment 3.

5. See Juarez v. Hamner, 674 S.W.2d 856 (Tex.App.1984). Professor Corbin argued that the use of the term rescission in this context was improper and undesirable, although he conceded that it was well-ingrained in the language of the courts; he preferred to say that the party was legally permitted to abandon the contract. 5 Corbin, Contracts

§§ 1104–05 (1964). The two uses of the term rescission are discussed in Brannock v. Fletcher, 271 N.C. 65, 155 S.E.2d 532 (1967).

6. See, e.g., Grahn v. Gregory, 800 P.2d 320 (Utah App.1990) (rescission granted for mutual mistake); Lundeen v. Lappi, 361 N.W.2d 913 (Minn.App.1985) (same); Cummings v. Dusenbury, 129 Ill.App.3d 338, 84 Ill.Dec. 615, 472 N.E.2d 575 (1984) (rescission granted for unilateral mistake); Berry v. Romain, 194 Mont. 400, 632 P.2d 1127 (1981). Unilateral mistake is not usually enough; see, e.g., C.B. & T. Co. v. Hefner, 98 N.M. 594, 651 P.2d 1029 (App.1982), cert. denied 98 N.M. 590, 651 P.2d 636 (1982). See Note, 29 Wayne L.Rev. 1433 (1983), commenting on Miller v. Varilek, 117 Mich.App. 165, 323 N.W.2d 637 (1982), remanded for reconsideration 417 Mich. 998, 334 N.W.2d 376 (1983), on remand 129 Mich. App. 703, 342 N.W.2d 94 (1983).

7. See, Mulle v. Scheiler, 484 So.2d 47 (Fla. App.1986), review denied 492 So.2d 1334 (Fla. 1986) (where purchasers were defrauded, they may have restitution of the price paid even though changes in the property make it impossible to restore it to vendors in exactly the form conveyed); Gray v. Baker, 485 So.2d 306 (Miss.1986) (vendor may rescind, if purchaser conceals his intention to resell land to a subpurchaser who he knows is obnoxious to vendor, and to whom vendor would have been unwilling to sell directly); MacCurrach v.

duress,[8] undue influence, non-occurrence of a condition, impracticability, or frustration.[9] Since our present concern is with rescission based on the opposing party's breach of contract, the other grounds mentioned will not be discussed further here.[10]

There are important practical differences between mutual and unilateral rescission. When the former occurs, there is usually no need for judicial intervention if the parties' intent is clear. Unilateral rescission, on the other hand, often gives rise to litigation; the aggrieved party may find it necessary to resort to the court for a determination that a good ground for rescission exists. Here the terminology becomes increasingly confused, with some courts saying that they are confirming the rescission that has already occurred, while others state that they are "rescinding" or "granting a rescission" of the contract.[11]

Whether one conceives of unilateral rescission as an act of the aggrieved party or of the court, it is typically unsatisfactory in the plaintiff's eyes without a further granting of restitution, damages, or both. For example, if the purchaser under a land sale contract declares it rescinded because the vendor refuses to convey title as agreed, the purchaser may well seek not only a recovery of earnest money and other payments made but also a judgment for loss-of-bargain damages. It is obvious that there is no inherent inconsistency in these two claims; indeed, both must be met to make the purchaser whole. However, the theory (or at least the dicta) of many cases seems to treat them as mutually exclusive, on the view that restitution is available only if the contract has been rescinded, and that if such has occurred, damages (which must be based on the contract's continuing existence) are unobtainable. This theory demands that the plaintiff elect between affirming the contract and seeking damages, on the one hand, and rescinding the contract and seeking restitution on the other.[12]

Anderson, 678 S.W.2d 459 (Mo.App.1984); e.g., Ballard v. Carroll, 2 Ark.App. 283, 621 S.W.2d 484 (1981).

8. See, e.g., Wolf v. Marlton Corp., 57 N.J.Super. 278, 154 A.2d 625 (1959).

9. Restatement (Second) of Contracts § 377 (1981).

10. See Breuer–Harrison, Inc. v. Combe, 799 P.2d 716 (Utah App.1990); Cooper v. Peoples Bank, 725 P.2d 78 (Colo.App.1986); Metcalfe v. Talarski, 213 Conn. 145, 567 A.2d 1148 (1989). Sometimes a breach which justifies unilateral rescission is termed, quite inappropriately, a "failure of consideration"; see Ragen v. Weston, 191 Mont. 546, 625 P.2d 557 (1981), applying Mont.Code Ann. 28–2–1711; Royal v. Parado, 462 So.2d 849 (Fla.App.1985) (rescission not available for mere "failure of consideration", but only for fraud, accident, or mistake).

11. Countless examples could be given. See Dewey v. Arnold, 159 Ariz. 65, 764 P.2d 1124 (App.1988) (rescission occurs by party's action, notwithstanding later assistance by the courts). The confusion is often illustrated by inconsistent phrases in the same judicial opinion; see, e.g., Berry v. Romain, 194 Mont. 400, 632 P.2d 1127 (1981) ("A party to a contract may rescind * * *"; "The trial court was urged to rescind * * *"). See also Halvorson v. Birkland, 84 S.D. 328, 171 N.W.2d 77 (1969).

12. See, e.g., Patel v. Patel, 706 S.W.2d 3 (Ky.App.1986) (fraud by vendor); Carter v. Matthews, 288 Ark. 37, 701 S.W.2d 374 (1986) (purchaser may have damages as well as restitution in cases of fraud, but is limited to restitution in cases of mutual mistake); Ger v. Kammann, 504 F.Supp. 446 (D.Del.1980); Nemec v. Rollo, 114 Ariz. 589, 562 P.2d 1087 (1977); Hurwitz v. David K. Richards Co., 20 Utah 2d 232, 436 P.2d 794 (1968); Simmons v. Sorrentino, 2 Conn.Cir. 558, 203 A.2d 156 (1964), certiorari denied 151 Conn. 744, 201 A.2d 670 (1964); Bridgmon v. Walker, 218 Or. 130, 344 P.2d 233 (1959). See D. Dobbs, Remedies §§ 1.5, 12.9 (1973); 5 Corbin, Contracts § 1105 (1964); Annot, 40 A.L.R. 4th 627 (1985).

Some cases have resolved the plaintiff's dilemma on the facts above simply by redefining damages to include the return of the plaintiff's payments [13]—a rather artificial solution to an artificial problem. Today many courts would recognize that neither an express declaration of rescission nor an election of remedies is necessary. They would permit the damage and restitution claims to coexist so long as their combination did not produce a duplicative or unfair recovery. [14]

In general, one who seeks restitution must also give restitution. Even a party in breach is entitled to a return of that which has been given when compelled to return that which has been received. [15] Of course, the breaching party usually will owe loss-of-bargain or other damages; hence, his or her recovery in restitution will be reduced by that amount. The Restatement (Second) of Contracts aptly illustrates this concept: A enters into a contract to sell land to B for $100,000. B pays $30,000 toward the price, but then refuses to make further payments. A resells the land to another buyer for $95,000. B is entitled to restitution, despite the breach, but B's restitutionary recovery will be reduced by the damages for which B is liable. Here the damages are $5,000 (assuming the resale price is the equivalent of fair market value), so B can recover only $25,000 in restitution. [16] It is also quite possible, depending on the contract language and judicial attitudes, that B's payments or some portion of them can be treated by A as liquidated damages under principles we have discussed earlier, thus permitting A to retain most or all of the $30,000 rather than giving restitution of the $25,000 figure based on actual damages. [17]

13. There is no serious doubt that the purchaser can in fact recover both payments made and loss-of-bargain damages, subject to the Flureau v. Thornhill limitation; see Mazzochetti v. Cassarino, 49 A.D.2d 695, 370 N.Y.S.2d 765 (1975); Horner v. Holt, 187 Va. 715, 47 S.E.2d 365 (1948); § 10.3, supra. ULTA § 2–509(a)(1) agrees.

14. See Smeekens v. Bertrand, 262 Ind. 50, 311 N.E.2d 431 (1974); Shoreham Developers, Inc. v. Randolph Hills, Inc., 269 Md. 291, 305 A.2d 465 (1973); Jennings v. Lee, 105 Ariz. 167, 461 P.2d 161 (1969); D. Dobbs, Remedies 633–35 (1973). The ULTA rejects entirely the notion of election of remedies, and makes recovery on cumulative remedies depend entirely on the facts of the individual case; ULTA § 2–509, Comment 1.

15. Restatement (Second) of Contracts § 374 (1981). See Ben Lomond, Inc. v. Allen, 758 P.2d 92 (Alaska 1988) (defaulting buyer entitled to restitution of value of lot she transferred to builder, less damages incurred by builder); Blair v. Boulger, 358 N.W.2d 522 (N.D.1984), appeal dismissed, certiorari denied 471 U.S. 1095, 105 S.Ct. 2314, 85 L.Ed.2d 834 (1985) (vendor may not have rescission of contract unless she offers to make restitution of everything of value she has received from purchaser); see North Dak.Cent.Code § 9–09–04; Lancellotti v. Thomas, 341 Pa.Super. 1, 491 A.2d 117 (1985) (sale of business).

See Gegan, In Defense of Restitution: A Comment on Mather, Restitution As a Remedy for Breach of Contract: The Case of the Partially Performing Seller, 57 So.Cal.L.Rev. 723 (1984).

16. Id., Comment a, Illustration 1.

17. See text at § 10.4 notes 2–10, supra. See the excellent discussion in Vines v. Orchard Hills, Inc., 181 Conn. 501, 435 A.2d 1022 (1980). The question has arisen frequently in installment sales of land in which the purchaser goes into possession, makes payments, and then defaults. The classic work is Corbin, The Right of a Defaulting Vendee to the Restitution of Installments Paid, 40 Yale L.J. 1013 (1931). While some courts continue to uphold forfeiture clauses which permit the vendor to treat the amount paid as liquidated damages, there is a discernible trend toward requiring the vendor to make restitution of the payments received insofar as they exceed the vendor's actual damages. Such damages may be measured by the traditional loss-of-bargain formula or by the loss of rental value due to the purchaser's possession of the land. See Honey v. Henry's Franchise Leasing Corp., 64 Cal.2d 801, 52 Cal.Rptr. 18, 415 P.2d 833 (1966); Johnson v. Carman, 572 P.2d 371 (Utah 1977); Brannock v. Fletcher, 271 N.C. 65, 155 S.E.2d 532 (1967); Chace v. Johnson, 98 Fla. 118, 123 So. 519 (1929); Annot., 4 A.L.R.4th 993 (1981). Whether restitution is

Damages caused by one's own breach are not the only possible offset against one's restitutionary recovery. If the breaching purchaser has made improvements on the land, the restitution owed to the vendor may be reduced by their value. Similarly, if the vendor has held the purchaser's earnest money or other payments for an appreciable period, the interest that was or might have been earned on the funds may offset the vendor's recovery in restitution. On the other side, a purchaser who has benefitted from possession of the property during the contract's executory period may have his or her restitutionary recovery reduced by the rental value of that possession.[18] These offsets are highly discretionary; some courts seem to disregard them entirely, and others deal with them in only a rough or approximate manner. For example, the rental value of the purchaser's possession and the interest value of the payments held by the vendor may be deemed by the court to be equivalent, and hence to cancel one another, without any serious effort to analyze them.[19] Given the amounts involved and the cost and complexity of expert testimony and proof on such points, this sort of judicial looseness may be quite appropriate when the time between contract formation and breach is short. When long times elapse, however, neglect or approximation of these amounts (which in reality represent the time value of money) can produce bizarre and unfair results.[20]

Restitution is an appropriate remedy for breach only if the breach is "vital" or "total." [21] These terms are not so absolute as they seem; they are

ordered in these cases sometimes depends on the "wilfullness" of the default or other rather intangible considerations. But see Freedman v. Rector, 37 Cal.2d 16, 230 P.2d 629, 31 A.L.R.2d 1 (1951), ordering restitution for a wilfully defaulting purchaser. See generally G. Nelson & D. Whitman, Real Estate Finance Law § 3.29 (2d ed. 1985).

18. MCC Investments v. Crystal Properties, 451 N.W.2d 243 (Minn.App.1990) (vendor entitled to actual rent received, rather than reasonable rental value); Metcalfe v. Talarski, 213 Conn. 145, 567 A.2d 1148 (1989) (same); Kracl v. Loseke, 236 Neb. 290, 461 N.W.2d 67 (1990); Barnard & Son, Inc. v. Akins, 109 Idaho 466, 708 P.2d 871 (1985); Heifner v. Hendricks, 13 Ark.App. 217, 682 S.W.2d 459 (1985); Busch v. Nervik, 38 Wn.App. 541, 687 P.2d 872 (1984) (vendor ordered to return purchase price plus interest and value of improvements made by purchasers, less reasonable rental value for period of purchasers' possession). The rental value is normally computed only for the time the purchaser has actual possession; if the purchaser makes an appropriate offer to return the property and abandons it, he or she is not responsible for any further rental value, even if the purchaser does not immediately resume possession. Miller v. Sears, 636 P.2d 1183 (Alaska 1981); Limoli v. Accettullo, 358 Mass. 381, 265 N.E.2d 92 (1970); Restatement of Restitution § 67, Comment a (1937).

19. See Lane v. Unger, 599 F.Supp. 63 (E.D.Mo.1984), affirmed in part and reversed

in part without opinion 786 F.2d 1171 (8th Cir.1986) (vendors are entitled to compensation for purchasers' 8 months use of the property, and may retain purchasers' down payment for this purpose); Willcox Clinic, Ltd. v. Evans Products Co., 136 Ariz. 400, 666 P.2d 500 (App.1983) (restitution to purchaser of payments made must be reduced by any claim paid to purchaser by its title insurer); D. Dobbs, Remedies 846 (1973). Compare treatment of incidental damages in an action for specific performance, § 10.5 notes 20–23 supra.

20. See Kim v. Conway & Forty, Inc., 772 S.W.2d 723 (Mo.App.1989) (rescinding purchasers awarded prejudgment interest from date of vendor's breach); Brunner v. LaCasse, 234 Mont. 368, 763 P.2d 662 (1988), appeal after remand 241 Mont. 102, 785 P.2d 210 (1990) (same); Restatement of Restitution § 156, Comment a (1937), approving interest on the purchaser's payment from the date made. An illustration of the importance of considering the time value of money in a restitution action is found in G. Nelson & D. Whitman, Real Estate Finance Law § 3.29 n. 48 (2d ed. 1985).

21. See Folkers v. Southwest Leasing, 431 N.W.2d 177 (Iowa App.1988) (rescission available as a matter of right if damages cannot be ascertained with reasonable certainty); Beefy Trail, Inc. v. Beefy King International, Inc., 267 So.2d 853 (Fla.App.1972); Plitt v. McMillan, 244 Md. 450, 223 A.2d 772 (1966); 5 Corbin, Contracts § 1104 (1964).

intended to indicate simply that the breach must be a serious and important one, not minor or trivial.[22]   The test is whether the breach is sufficiently material to excuse the aggrieved party from any further duty of performance.[23]   Where the defendant makes an anticipatory repudiation of the contract, there is no doubt that the breach is sufficiently vital.[24]   In other cases, the availability of restitution may depend on the quantitative degree of breach, the breaching party's willfulness or bad faith, the length of time the breach continues, and other factors.[25]

Several doctrines impose further limitations on the availability of restitution.   Suppose the vendor has fully performed the contract, so that the purchaser is obligated to pay the full purchase price.   If the purchaser at that point commits a material breach or repudiation, the vendor may seek restitution.   In general, such a vendor has a choice of demanding a return of the land itself or of its value.[26]   But if the vendor seeks the money value of the land, the maximum recovery will be the agreed contract price.   In effect, the parties' agreement fixes this value for the property, and the vendor cannot be heard to say that a higher amount should be set.[27]   This rule is a salutary one, for there is little justification for consuming judicial time and energy in determining the value of land the parties have already evaluated to their satisfaction.[28]

If the vendor elects to seek a return of the land in specie, or if the purchaser's demand for restitution makes it necessary to give the vendor restitution as well, other problems arise.   Some cases dogmatically assert that, once a deed transferring title has been delivered and accepted, cancellation of the deed and restitution of the land in specie cannot be ordered at the behest of either party.[29]   Where it is the purchaser who seeks restitution, and where the breach consists of a defect in the title conveyed, these cases are merely illustrative of the general notion that once a purchaser has accepted a deed, the purchaser's remedies under the contract for title-related

---

22. See, e.g., Smith v. Continental Bank, 130 Ariz. 320, 636 P.2d 98 (1981) (no rescission for construction defects which could be remedied for $2,235 in a house sold for $33,000); Kohenn v. Plantation Baking Co., Inc., 32 Ill. App.3d 231, 336 N.E.2d 491 (1975) (no rescission for minor defects in industrial plant building.)

23. To say that the breach is material is equivalent to saying that substantial performance has not been rendered when due. Since each party's substantial performance is a constructive condition of the other party's duty to perform, a material breach excuses the other's performance.   The aggrieved party is therefore permitted to rescind and to seek restitution and/or damages.   See Dunham v. Belinky, 248 Ga. 479, 284 S.E.2d 397 (1981); J. Calamari & J. Perillo, Contracts § 11–22 (1977); Restatement (Second) of Contracts § 237 (1981).

24. An anticipatory repudiation is nearly always deemed a "total" breach; see 5 Corbin, Contracts § 1104 note 6; ULTA § 2–404; Juarez v. Hamner, 674 S.W.2d 856 (Tex.App.1984)

(one of two co-owners signed a written statement refusing to convey).

25. Restatement (Second) of Contracts § 241 (1981).

26. See Restatement (Second) of Contracts § 371–72 (1981).

27. Restatement (Second) of Contracts § 373, Comment b (1981).

28. This is not to say that further recovery is unavailable to the plaintiff, who may be able to show numerous forms of incidental or consequential damage.   As the text above suggests, restitution should not be treated as excluding such further damages.   See 5 Corbin, Contracts § 1113 (Kaufman Supp.1980).

29. See Suburban Properties, Inc. v. Hanson, 234 Or. 356, 382 P.2d 90 (1963); McMillan v. American Suburban Corp., 136 Tenn. 53, 188 S.W. 615 (1916); cf. Early v. Street, 192 Tenn. 463, 241 S.W.2d 531 (1951).   These cases generally preclude restitution only when breach of contract, rather than some other ground such as misrepresentation, is asserted.

breaches are "merged" into the deed—a matter discussed in a later section.[30] But the cases denying restitution are broader than this.[31]

The courts' reluctance to set aside or cancel deeds is understandable, for to do so may cause serious title problems or result in unfair loss to a purchaser who has spent money in moving costs or improvements. But many courts today would probably be more flexible, and would order specific restitution if no bona fide third party had relied on the conveyance,[32] the time elapsed since the conveyance was relatively brief,[33] the breach was a serious one,[34] and the plaintiff's alternate remedies seemed inadequate or uncertain.[35]

§ 10.8   Remedies for Contract Breach—Vendee's Lien

In general restitution is available to both vendors and purchasers under the principles discussed in the preceding section. Where the purchaser demands restitution,[1] courts generally recognize an equitable lien on the property in favor of the purchaser as an aid to his or her recovery.[2] The lien is based on the assumption that the vendor holds the legal title, either

---

30. See, e.g., Jolley v. Idaho Securities, Inc., 90 Idaho 373, 414 P.2d 879 (1966); Annots., 50 A.L.R. 180 (1927); 65 A.L.R. 1142 (1930); § 10.12, infra.

31. See, e.g., Carter v. Barclay, 476 S.W.2d 909 (Tex.Civ.App.1972), relying on the "merger" concept to deny restitution of the land in specie. The grantor sought restitution because the grantee's bank had refused payment of his check for the purchase price; merger seems a particularly inappropriate explanation of such a decision.

32. See Restatement (Second) of Contracts § 372 Illustration 4, (1981). If the purchaser wishes to seek (and must therefore make) restitution, he or she may find it necessary to secure the release of the interests acquired by any subsequent takers, such as mortgagees; see ULTA § 2–402, Comment 3.

33. The ULTA specifically grants the purchaser the right to "revoke his acceptance" for a substantial breach by the seller, despite the fact that he has already accepted title. The revocation must occur within a reasonable time after discovery of the breach, and in all events within two years after taking title or possession. ULTA § 2–402.

34. See Easterling v. Ferris, 651 P.2d 677 (Okl.1982).

35. See Benassi v. Harris, 147 Conn. 451, 162 A.2d 521 (1960). Where the breaching purchaser is paying by means of a promise of support or care of the vendor or by other services rather than money, it is often held that the vendor can get restitution and cancellation of the deed because of his difficulty of proving damages; see, e.g., Huntley v. Dubois, 129 Vt. 389, 278 A.2d 750 (1971); Myers v. Diehl, 365 P.2d 717 (Okl.1961). See generally 12 Williston, Contracts § 1456 (3d ed. 1970); D. Dobbs, Remedies 857–59 (1973).

§ 10.8

1. The lien is available in aid of restitution to the purchaser both in cases in which he or she elects restitution as a remedy and those in which it is forced upon him under the doctrine of Flureau v. Thornhill, § 10.3 note 15, supra. Even if the Flureau doctrine controls, the purchaser may be entitled to a further judgment for out-of-pocket expenses. The vendee's lien discussed here, however, is generally limited to the payments made to the vendor; it is sometimes extended to other expenditures made in reliance on the contract, but clearly does not include recovery of benefit-of-bargain damages. See Warner v. Peterson, 234 Mont. 319, 762 P.2d 872 (1988); Annot., 43 A.L.R.2d 1384 (1954).

2. Sparks v. Charles Wayne Group, 568 So.2d 512 (Fla.App.1990); Stanovsky v. Group Enterprise & Const. Co., 714 S.W.2d 836 (Mo. App.1986); Gribble v. Stearman & Kaplan, Inc., 249 Md. 289, 239 A.2d 573 (1968); Wayne Building & Loan Co. v. Yarborough, 11 Ohio St.2d 195, 228 N.E.2d 841 (1967); Cole v. Haynes, 216 Miss. 485, 62 So.2d 779 (1953); Elterman v. Hyman, 192 N.Y. 113, 84 N.E. 937, 127 Am.St.Rep. 862 (1908). ULTA § 2–512 recognizes the vendee's lien, but only for money paid toward the price and not for consequential or incidental damages. See Stahl v. Roulhac, 50 Md.App. 382, 438 A.2d 1366 (1982) (where mortgagee has notice of contract, vendee's lien has priority over mortgage but only for amount paid under contract as originally signed, and not for amounts paid under contract modification or for other incidental expenses, such as those incurred in obtaining financing). Some cases award the lien only if the vendee is not guilty of any breach of the contract; see, e.g., Tuttle v. Ehrehart, 102 Fla. 1129, 137 So. 245 (1931).

because it has never been conveyed or because the vendor has committed some act which justifies the purchaser's rescission.[3] The vendee's lien, like the vendor's lien discussed in Section 10.6, is a creation of equity and need not grow out of any specific language in the contract.[4] Foreclosure is by judicial action.

The lien is usually of serious value to the purchaser only if it has a priority higher than those of competing interests, such as mortgages or mechanics liens on the land or the rights of subsequent purchasers from the vendor. If there are no competing interests, the vendee hardly needs the lien, for he or she can simply get a personal judgment against the vendor and satisfy it by execution on the real estate. If such competing interests are created prior to the entering of the contract of sale, and if they are properly recorded or the vendee has other notice of them, the vendee's lien will be inferior.[5] On the other hand, the lien will have priority over interests created after the sales contract is signed unless the holders of those interests establish that they took in good faith, for value, and without notice of the contract.[6] Even this priority may be lost if the contract of sale itself contains language subordinating the purchaser's rights to those of persons acquiring later interests. Such language is commonly used in pre-construction earnest money agreements on condominium units or subdivision houses

3. In Davis v. William Rosenzweig Realty Operating Co., 192 N.Y. 128, 84 N.E. 943, 127 Am.St.Rep. 890 (1908), the New York Court of Appeals refused to recognize the vendee's lien where the vendee sought to rescind the contract for fraud, reasoning that the lien depended on the continued existence of the contract. This distinction was abrogated by the legislature in 1947 in N.Y.—McKinney's Civ. Prac.Law & Rules 3002(f), which recognizes the lien even if the contract is rescinded. Other jurisdictions also recognize the lien when rescission is sought; see, e.g., Reed v. Sixth Judicial District Court, 75 Nev. 338, 341 P.2d 100 (1959); Mihranian, Inc. v. Padula, 70 N.J. 252, 359 A.2d 473 (1976). Under the ULTA, a buyer has a right under some circumstances to revoke the sale because of the seller's substantial breach, even if the buyer has already accepted the real estate; ULTA § 2–402. A buyer who does so would be entitled to assert a vendee's lien, much as in cases of rescission.

4. See Elterman v. Hyman, 192 N.Y. 113, 84 N.E. 937, 127 Am.St.Rep. 862 (1908).

5. State Savings & Loan Association v. Kauaian Development Co., 50 Hawaii 540, 445 P.2d 109 (1968).

6. Hembree v. Mid–America Federal S. & L. Ass'n, 64 Ohio App.3d 144, 580 N.E.2d 1103 (1989); Stahl v. Roulhac, 50 Md.App. 382, 438 A.2d 1366 (1982); In re Pearl, 40 B.R. 860 (Bkrtcy.D.N.J.1984) (bankrupt debtor-in-possession and his or her receiver, acting under the "strong-arm" power of a trustee in bankruptcy to act as a judgment creditor of the bankrupt, will prevail over a vendee's lien based on a prior unrecorded contract of sale

from the bankrupt vendor; contrary result would follow if contract had been recorded, or had been unwritten and hence incapable of recordation); Hillblom v. Ivancsits, 76 Ill. App.3d 306, 32 Ill.Dec. 172, 395 N.E.2d 119 (1979); Palmer v. Crews Lumber Co., Inc., 510 P.2d 269, 82 A.L.R.3d 1030 (Okl.1973); In re Mayfair Construction Co., 170 F.Supp. 657 (D.N.J.1959). See generally Annot., 82 A.L.R.3d 1040 (1978). The notice which disqualifies the subsequent taker may be actual, or it may be constructive notice from the recorded contract; see Lockie v. Cooperative Land Co., 207 Cal. 624, 279 P. 428 (1928). The notice need not include information as to the vendee's identity or the amount of the lien; knowledge that a prior contract of sale existed is sufficient to place the later taker on inquiry notice; Palmer v. Crews Lumber Co., supra. But see Nelson v. Great Northwest Federal Sav. & Loan Ass'n, 37 Wn.App. 316, 679 P.2d 953 (1984), where the court refused to recognize either the purchaser's right to specific performance or a vendee's lien, as against a subsequent deed of trust holder which apparently had knowledge of the purchaser's contract. The result seems obviously wrong, and probably stems from the court's mistaken construction of the Washington view of equitable conversion; see Cascade Security Bank v. Butler, 88 Wn.2d 777, 567 P.2d 631 (1977).

ULTA § 2–512 provides for the recordation of a notice of lien by the vendee if he does not wish to record the contract or it is not in recordable form. It is doubtful that such a unilateral notice could properly be recorded in many jurisdictions at present.

in order to protect a lender who plans to make a subsequent construction loan mortgage.[7]

§ 10.9   Time of Performance

Timing is often of great importance in a real estate sale. If performance is delayed beyond the date to which the parties agreed, either buyer or seller may incur significant and unexpected inconvenience and expense. On the other hand, sales transactions are often complex, with each party involved in a variety of detailed and sometimes unpredictable arrangements; hence, delays are common. Since one party's desire for promptness often conflicts with the other's need to extend the time for performance, litigation frequently results.

There is no rule requiring the parties to agree in the contract about the timing of their performances,[1] and if they do not do so the courts will simply infer that performance within a reasonable time was intended.[2] But in the great majority of cases the parties do agree, at least concerning the time of "settlement" or "closing," which ordinarily means the date on which legal title is to be transferred by deed.[3] More commonly the parties will neglect to specify the time limits on various conditions which must be met, such as

---

7. In Arundel Fed. Sav. & Loan Ass'n v. Lawrence, 65 Md.App. 158, 499 A.2d 1298 (1985), the purchase contract provided that "the buyers understand and consent to the seller placing a construction mortgage on the property." This language was held sufficient to subordinate the vendee's lien to the construction mortgage, despite the court's observation that subordinations will "not be lightly implied." The court thought the language must have had some purpose, and could think of none except subordination. See also State Savings & Loan Association v. Kauaian Development Co., 50 Hawaii 540, 445 P.2d 109 (1968). See, e.g., Olympic Towers Purchase Agreement, reprinted in 1A P. Rohan & M. Reskin, Condominium Law & Practice, ¶ 118.17 (appendix 1976). The problem is discussed in G. Nelson & D. Whitman, Real Estate Finance Law § 12.9 (2d ed. 1985), questioning the enforceability of a vague, general subordination clause in a contract signed by an unsophisticated vendee.

The subordination concept can cut both ways. In State Savings & Loan Association v. Kauaian Development Co., 62 Hawaii 188, 613 P.2d 1315 (1980), the above-cited case was reconsidered by the court. The construction loan mortgage recited that it was "subject to" the condominium declaration, and from that language the court inferred that the mortgage was intended to be subordinate to all of the vendees' equitable liens, whether their contracts were entered into before or after the mortgage was made and recorded.

§ 10.9

1. Even if an agreement is reached as to the time of performance, most jurisdictions will construe their statutes of frauds as not requiring that the time be included in the written memorandum; see § 10.1 note 36, supra.

2. See, e.g., Hicks v. Bridges, 580 So.2d 743 (Miss.1991); Ochoa v. Crossen, 106 Or.App. 246, 806 P.2d 195 (1991); Angle v. Marco Builders, Inc., 128 Ariz. 396, 626 P.2d 126 (1981); Yale Development Co. v. Aurora Pizza Hut, Inc., 95 Ill.App.3d 523, 51 Ill.Dec. 409, 420 N.E.2d 823 (1981). If the contract states no time, either party may send the other a notice fixing a reasonable time for performance, and thereby place a time limit on his or her own liability; see Schneider v. Warner, 69 Wis.2d 194, 230 N.W.2d 728 (1975); ULTA § 2–302(a). See also Read v. GHDC, Inc., 254 Ga. 706, 334 S.E.2d 165 (1985) (contract construed as requiring performance within a reasonable time, and thus not to violate the 21–year perpetuities period); Ryland Group, Inc. v. Wills, 229 Va. 459, 331 S.E.2d 399 (1985) (same).

3. In some areas of the nation it is fairly common, if the vendor agrees to finance the purchase by means of an installment sale contract, to initialize the transaction with an earnest money agreement which calls for execution of the installment contract at the time of "closing." While legal title will not pass at this "closing", it is functionally analogous to the more common sort of transaction described in the text, and would presumably be treated similarly for present purposes.

the purchaser's obtaining of a mortgage loan commitment; again, a reasonable time will be allowed by the courts.

If a party does not perform within the agreed time, what legal consequences follow? Perhaps surprisingly, the results are often rather trivial. Unless time has been made "of the essence," it is usually said that failure of timely performance will be considered a breach of contract only at law, and that in equity no breach will be deemed to occur until the performance becomes unreasonably late. In other words, time is always of the essence at law (unless the parties expressly agree otherwise), but it is not of the essence in equity unless made so by the contract or surrounding circumstances.[4]

These statements are unsatisfactory as they stand and need further analysis, for the precise position of a late-performing party where time is not "of the essence" is more complex. First, it is clear that the late party has committed a breach, albeit nonmaterial, and is liable at law for damages.[5] These may be expanded to include loss-of-bargain damages if the delinquent party never performs, but if his or her performance is ultimately given within a reasonable time, the damages owed will be limited to harms resulting from the delay *per se*. Thus, a tardy seller might be liable for lost rents or profits which the buyer was forced to forego, and conceivably for higher interest on the buyer's mortgage loan if rates have risen during the delay,[6] while a late buyer might be compelled to reimburse the seller for interest and taxes paid during the delay.[7] But a delay in closing often results in savings as well as costs to the aggrieved party, and the courts will usually offset these savings against the damages, a process which may reduce the net recovery very materially.[8] As a result, recoveries may well be small or nominal.

---

4. For typical statements, see Hamilton v. Bradford, 502 F.Supp. 822 (S.D.Miss.1980); Kaiman Realty, Inc. v. Carmichael, 2 Hawaii App. 499, 634 P.2d 603 (1981), amended 650 P.2d 609 (Hawaii App.1982); 3 Am.L.Prop. § 11.45 (1952). Courts usually accept without question contractual language that time is essential, but occasionally a court will conclude that the parties didn't really mean it, or that it does not apply to some particular performance under the contract. See Royal Dev. & Management Corp. v. Guardian 50/50 Fund V, Ltd., 583 So.2d 403 (Fla.App.1991); cases cited at note 21, infra.

5. See, e.g., Richardson v. Van Dolah, 429 F.2d 912 (9th Cir.1970); 6 Williston, Contracts § 846 (3d ed. 1957); Restatement (Second) of Contracts § 242, Illustrations 4 & 5 (1981).

6. See Donovan v. Bachstadt, 91 N.J. 434, 453 A.2d 160 (1982). For cases awarding loss-of-financing damages as an adjunct to specific performance, see § 10.5, supra, at note 21.

7. These damages are essentially the same as are sometimes awarded incidentally to a grant of specific performance; see § 10.5, notes 20–23, supra.

8. For example, the buyer may lose rents or other revenues from the property, but may also save the taxes, utilities, maintenance ex-

penses, and mortgage loan interest which would have begun to accrue as of the agreed closing date, as well as the investment earnings on the cash down payment in excess of earnest money. See § 10.5 notes 20–23 supra; cf. § 10.3 note 30, supra. The Restatement indicates that for a breach which prevents the buyer's use of property for some period of time, " * * * the loss in value to the injured party is based on the profits that he would have made during that period." Restatement (Second) of Contracts § 348 Comment b (1981). "Profits" here presumably means net profits. The Restatement suggests alternative measures based on interest value or rental value if profits cannot be proved with reasonable certainty, but it is unclear as to whether the sorts of "savings" mentioned above would be deducted from this recovery; see id. at § 348 Comment b; § 352. Clearly such offsets are appropriate. See Walker v. Benton, 407 So.2d 305 (Fla.App.1981); Northwest Television Club, Inc. v. Gross Seattle, Inc., 96 Wn.2d 973, 634 P.2d 837 (1981), opinion changed 96 Wn.2d 973, 640 P.2d 710 (1982); Regan v. Lanze, 47 A.D.2d 378, 366 N.Y.S.2d 512 (1975), reversed 40 N.Y.2d 475, 387 N.Y.S.2d 79, 354 N.E.2d 818 (1976); Ellis v. Mihelis, 60 Cal.2d 206, 32 Cal.Rptr. 415, 384 P.2d 7 (1963); M. Friedman, Contracts and Conveyances of Real Property § 9.1 (3d ed. 1975).

A second aspect of the late-performing party's position, where time is not of the essence, is the ability to enforce the contract by a decree of specific performance if the delinquent party tenders performance, though late, within a reasonable time.[9] One party's tardiness (unless it is unreasonable) does not excuse the other party from performance. The delay in performance is a nonmaterial breach, one which is not deemed sufficiently "total" to permit the aggrieved party to rescind or abandon the contract.[10] In other words, strict performance on time is a covenant, but it is not a condition of the other party's duty to perform. The underlying policy viewpoint here is simply that moderate delays are common in real estate sales, and are rarely so harmful to the aggrieved party as to justify abrogation of the contract.

Suppose time is not of the essence and one party is late in performing (though not unreasonably so), but the other then repudiates the contract entirely. The first can plainly get specific performance as discussed above, but if he or she prefers damages for total breach instead there seems no reason to deny them. There is little authority on the point, but the few cases dealing with the issue award the late party damages,[11] and they are likely to be followed.[12] To do so runs counter to the axiom that time is always of the essence at law; on this point, the axiom is simply overbroad and inaccurate.

If time is made of the essence, much of the foregoing discussion is reversed. If late performance is tendered and voluntarily accepted, and the contract completed, the late party is still liable for damages for the delay as above. But strict performance on time, or at least the tender of such performance, is now treated as a condition, failure of which will be deemed a total breach and will fully discharge the other party. Thus one who is late cannot enforce the contract judicially, in law or equity, unless the other party is willing to waive the right to timely performance.[13] Some cases are

---

9. Colony Park Associates v. Gall, 154 Vt. 1, 572 A.2d 891 (1990); Forrest v. Forrest, 241 N.J.Super. 239, 574 A.2d 1004 (1990); Frenzen v. Taylor, 232 Neb. 41, 439 N.W.2d 473 (1989); Tarlo v. Robinson, 118 A.D.2d 561, 499 N.Y.S.2d 174 (1986) (delay of about 30 days from amended closing date, caused by purchaser's previously-scheduled trip to England, was reasonable); Blaustein v. Weiss, 409 So.2d 103 (Fla.App.1982); Leavitt v. Fowler, 118 N.H. 541, 391 A.2d 876 (1978); Stork v. Felper, 85 Wis.2d 406, 270 N.W.2d 586 (1978); Wood v. Wood, 216 Va. 922, 224 S.E.2d 159 (1976); Schoen v. Grossman, 33 Misc.2d 490, 230 N.Y.S.2d 771 (1962), affirmed 17 A.D.2d 778, 232 N.Y.S.2d 871 (1962), appeal denied 12 N.Y.2d 646, 238 N.Y.S.2d 1026, 188 N.E.2d 529 (1963). The ULTA agrees in substance; ULTA § 2–302(b).

10. See American Somax Ventures v. Touma, 547 So.2d 1266 (Fla.App.1989); Restatement (Second) of Contracts § 242(c) and Illustrations 4 & 5 (1981).

11. Tanenbaum v. Sears, Roebuck & Co., 265 Pa.Super. 78, 401 A.2d 809 (1979); Davis v. Lacy, 121 F.Supp. 246 (E.D.Ky.1954). See 5A Corbin, Contracts § 1177 (1960).

12. The ULTA seems to agree, since it provides that unless time is essential, " * * * the failure of one of the parties to tender his performance at the specified time does not discharge the other party from his duties under the contract * * * "; ULTA § 2–302(b). Presumably this means there is no discharge either at law or in equity. The Restatement (Second) of Contracts § 242, Illustrations 4 & 5 (1981) expressly approves the late party's recovery for total breach both in law and equity.

13. Department of Community Affairs v. Atrium Palace Syndicate, 247 N.J.Super. 511, 589 A.2d 1046 (1991), cert. denied 126 N.J. 338, 598 A.2d 895 (1991); Schneider v. Dumbarton Developers, Inc., 767 F.2d 1007 (D.C.Cir.1985); Fogarty v. Saathoff, 128 Cal. App.3d 780, 180 Cal.Rptr. 484 (1982); Holmby, Inc. v. Dino, 98 Nev. 358, 647 P.2d 392 (1982); Grace v. Nappa, 46 N.Y.2d 560, 415 N.Y.S.2d 793, 389 N.E.2d 107 (1979); Griffeth v. Zumbrennen, 577 P.2d 129 (Utah 1978); Schildt v. Cokinos, 263 Md. 261, 282 A.2d 499 (1971).

exceptionally rigid on this point; in Doctorman v. Schroeder,[14] the New Jersey Court of Errors and Appeals refused specific performance where the buyers were only thirty minutes late. Other cases are somewhat more lenient, particularly if it is the purchaser who is late and he or she stands to forfeit a large earnest money deposit.[15] But it is clear that substantial tardiness will result in loss of the right to enforce the contract.

If the time set for closing arrives and neither party tenders performance, what is their legal posture? If time is not of essence, neither is in material breach and the closing is automatically extended until one sets a new date and notifies the other. The notice must be given a reasonable time prior to the date it fixes.[16] If time is of the essence, the problem is more complex, and a court might either follow the automatic extension approach above [17] or treat both parties as discharged on the ground that a condition to each's right of performance has failed.[18] Their intent, as gleaned from their actions and surrounding circumstances, may be a helpful guide.[19]

What facts will make time of the essence? Most commonly the determination follows from language in the contract itself. A mere statement that performance shall occur on a given date is plainly not enough, but the phrase "time is of the essence of this contract" or words of similar import are usually sufficient.[20] However, such language can be seen as ambiguous where the contract calls for (and gives dates or time periods for) numerous

14. 92 N.J.Eq. 676, 114 A. 810 (1921). See also F.J. Miceli v. Dierberg, 773 S.W.2d 154 (Mo.App.1989), denying enforcement to a purchaser who was 3½ hours late, and who did not inform the vendor of the delay; Kulanski v. Celia Homes, Inc., 7 A.D.2d 1006, 184 N.Y.S.2d 234 (1959), in which the court denied enforcement to a vendor who tendered one day late, even though the date scheduled for closing was a legal holiday.

15. PR Pension Fund v. Nakada, 809 P.2d 1139 (Haw.App.1991); Williams Plumbing Co. v. Sinsley, 53 Cal.App.3d 1027, 126 Cal.Rptr. 345 (1975); Lance v. Martinez–Arango, 251 So.2d 707 (Fla.App.1971); Rymland v. Berger, 242 Md. 260, 219 A.2d 7 (1966). There is some tendency for courts to resort to a reinterpretation of time-of-the-essence doctrine to avoid forfeitures of purchasers' payments, a problem which could better be dealt with directly; see § 10.4, supra.

16. Fletcher v. Jones, 314 N.C. 389, 333 S.E.2d 731 (1985) (a tender seven weeks after opposing party indicated readiness to close sale was reasonable); Johnson v. Morris, 645 P.2d 51 (Utah 1982); Limpus v. Armstrong, 3 Mass.App.Ct. 19, 322 N.E.2d 187 (1975); Luna v. Atchafalaya Realty, Inc., 325 So.2d 835 (La. App.1976); 3 Am.L.Prop. § 11.44 (1952); ULTA § 2–302(e)(2).

17. Life Sav. & Loan Ass'n of America v. Bryant, 125 Ill.App.3d 1012, 81 Ill.Dec. 577, 467 N.E.2d 277 (1984); Dullanty v. Comstock Development Corp., 25 Wn.App. 168, 605 P.2d 802 (1980).

18. Goldston v. AMI Investments, Inc., 98 Nev. 567, 655 P.2d 521 (1982); Devine v. Williams Brothers, Inc., 4 Mass.App.Ct. 816, 348 N.E.2d 445 (1976); Guillory Corp. v. Dussin Investment Corp., 272 Or. 267, 536 P.2d 501 (1975); Associated Developers Co. v. Infanger, 85 Idaho 158, 376 P.2d 496 (1962); Triton Realty Co. v. Frieman, 210 Md. 252, 123 A.2d 290 (1956). See 6 Corbin, Contracts § 1258 (1962).

19. See Matter of Mastapeter, 56 B.R. 413 (Bkrtcy.D.N.J.1985) (where both parties act as if contract is still in full force despite passing of closing date, they have waived time-of-essence clause and purchaser may obtain specific performance); Smith v. Crissey, 478 So.2d 1181 (Fla.App.1985) (similar case; intent is question of fact, precluding summary judgment). See also 3A Corbin, Contracts § 663 (Kaufman Supp.1980, at 476–77).

20. Compare Shumaker v. Lear, 235 Pa.Super. 509, 345 A.2d 249 (1975) (provision that contract would be "null and void" if time provision was not met made time of the essence) with Kakalik v. Bernardo, 184 Conn. 386, 439 A.2d 1016 (1981) (contract "null and void" if financing condition not met by specified date; held not of essence) and Walker v. Weaver, 23 N.C.App. 654, 209 S.E.2d 537 (1974) (provision that sale "to be definitely closed within a period of 30 days" did not make time of the essence.) See also Dominion Investments v. Yasechko, 767 F.Supp. 1460 (N.D.Ind.1991); Palin v. Sasano, __ Hawaii App. __, 694 P.2d 390 (Haw.App.1985) (case withdrawn).

performances or conditions in addition to the closing itself. Are all of these times of the essence?[21] It is far better practice to state explicitly which times mentioned in the contract are considered essential.

Even if the contract does not make time essential, the surrounding circumstances may convince a court that the parties intended it to be such. Typical evidence in this respect might include the fact that one party was very concerned about a prompt settlement, and the other knew of this concern;[22] that land values were changing rapidly;[23] or that the property involved was a wasting asset, such as a producing mine or oil well or a short-term leasehold.[24]

The drafters of the ULTA were dissatisfied with the usual "time is of the essence" phrase in another respect; they felt it was unclear and uncommunicative to many lay people. The ULTA therefore requires, if the contract is to make time of the essence, that it explicitly provide " * * * that failure to perform at the time specified discharges the duties of the other party." [25] Such language is certainly a better statement of the legal result than is provided by the usual phraseology, but it can hardly be considered "plain

21. See Tantillo v. Janus, 87 Ill.App.3d 231, 42 Ill.Dec. 291, 408 N.E.2d 1000 (1980) (court assumed clause applied to all times mentioned); cf. Blum v. Kenyon, 29 Mass.App. Ct. 417, 560 N.E.2d 742 (1990) (essentiality of time for exercise of option does not make time of closing of contract essential); CDC Nassau Associates v. Fatoullah, 163 A.D.2d 227, 558 N.Y.S.2d 946 (1990), appeal denied 77 N.Y.2d 802, 566 N.Y.S.2d 587, 567 N.E.2d 981 (1991) (same); Bicknell v. Barnes, 255 Ark. 697, 501 S.W.2d 761 (1973) (clause may not apply to all times mentioned.) In Kossler v. Palm Springs Developments, Limited, 101 Cal.App.3d 88, 161 Cal.Rptr. 423 (1980), appeal after remand 139 Cal.App.3d 893, 189 Cal.Rptr. 253 (1983), the court concluded that the general "time of the essence" clause applied to the three days given to the seller to accept the buyer's offer, and to the seven days after acceptance within which an escrow was to be opened. But it felt the clause could not have been intended to apply to the closing, since the property was a house under construction, the completion date could not be known, and the parties did not intend to close until the house was completed. Cf. Cox v. Funk, 42 N.C.App. 32, 255 S.E.2d 600 (1979) (time in financing condition was essential, although contract contained no time-of-essence clause); Siegel v. Banker, 486 A.2d 1163 (D.C.App.1984) (same). See also Kalina v. Eckert, 345 Pa.Super. 220, 497 A.2d 1384 (1985) (financing condition made time essential; purchasers were permitted to enforce contract when they obtained oral assurance from lender within required time that loan would be made, although formal loan commitment was not made until 2 days after expiration of required time); Schultz v. Topakyan, 193 N.J.Super. 550, 475 A.2d 91 (1984) (if purchasers obtain required financing commitment within period allowed by financing clause, they have a reasonable time after expiration of the period to notify vendor).

22. See, e.g., Builders Sand, Inc. v. Turtur, 678 S.W.2d 115 (Tex.App.1984); Kipahulu Investment Co. v. Seltzer Partnership, 4 Hawaii App. 625, 675 P.2d 778 (1983), cert. denied 67 Hawaii 685, 744 P.2d 781 (1984). Cf. Henry v. Sharma, 154 Cal.App.3d 665, 201 Cal.Rptr. 478 (1984) (one party's need for prompt closing does not make time essential, where other party is unaware of the need). See also In re King, 41 B.R. 797 (Bkrtcy.M.D.Pa.1984) (where purchasers request extension of time to close, but sellers refuse, the parties have made time essential); Chicago Title Ins. Co. v. Renaissance Homes, Ltd., 139 Ariz. 494, 679 P.2d 517 (1983) (even though time is not stated to be essential, an extension of time granted to the purchaser of state land under a competitive bidding statute is unlawful and makes the contract void).

23. Local 112, I.B.E.W. Bldg. Ass'n v. Tomlinson Dari–Mart, Inc., 30 Wn.App. 139, 632 P.2d 911 (1981); Blocker v. Lowry, 285 Ala. 448, 233 So.2d 233 (1970); Thlocco Oil Co. v. Bay State Oil & Gas Co., 207 Okl. 83, 247 P.2d 740 (1952); Kersch v. Taber, 67 Cal.App.2d 499, 154 P.2d 934 (1945).

24. Herber v. Sanders, 336 S.W.2d 783 (Tex.Civ.App.1960).

25. ULTA § 2–302(b)(2) and Comment 2. The Act expressly provides that "time is of the essence" is not a sufficient statement; id. at § 2–302(c). The Restatement (Second) of Contracts § 242(c) (1981) finds acceptable any language which indicates "that performance or an offer to perform by that date is important." Comment d says "time is of the essence" does not necessarily have this effect, but will be considered with other circumstances.

language" likely to be understood by consumers.[26]

Even if the contract contains no language making time essential, either party can make it such by notice to the other. The notice can make the originally-agreed date strictly binding if it is given within a reasonable time prior to that date; otherwise, the notice can set a new and later date on which strict performance must be made, again assuming a reasonable time is allowed between the notice and the date it fixes.[27] This looks suspiciously like a power to make a unilateral modification of the contract, but it is a power that is very widely recognized. Once the notice has been given, it binds both parties and neither can revert to the former situation, in which time was not essential, without the other's consent.[28]

Even when no agreement makes time essential, the surrounding circumstances may do so if they suggest that the parties considered the exact time of performance to be of importance.[29] Such circumstances might include a rapidly fluctuating market or a rapidly wasting asset, or various arrangements being made by one party with the other's knowledge which depend upon performance strictly on time.[30]

---

26. See generally Browne, Development of the FNMA/FHLMC Plain Language Mortgage Documents—Some Useful Techniques, 14 Real Prop.Prob. & Tr.J. 696 (1979); Squires, A Comprehensible Due-on-Sale Clause, 27 Prac.Lawyer 67 (No. 3, April 1981).

27. Knight v. McClean, 171 A.D.2d 648, 566 N.Y.S.2d 952 (1991) (16 days notice unreasonable); Mohen v. Mooney, 162 A.D.2d 664, 557 N.Y.S.2d 108 (19 days reasonable); Goldring v. Sletko Realty, Inc., 129 Misc.2d 756, 494 N.Y.S.2d 56 (1985) (eight days' notice unreasonable); Merry v. A.W. Perry, Inc., 18 Mass.App.Ct. 628, 469 N.E.2d 73 (1984), review denied 393 Mass. 1104, 471 N.E.2d 1354 (1984) (vendor's letter to purchaser made time essential, although it did not set a specific closing date, but merely requested a statement that purchaser would "be ready to perform shortly"); Fowler v. Ross, 142 Cal.App.3d 472, 191 Cal.Rptr. 183 (1983) (where time was not initially essential as to financing condition, vendor's extension of 50 days to obtain financing was reasonable and made time essential); Drazin v. American Oil Co., 395 A.2d 32 (D.C.App.1978); Rhodes v. Astro–Pac, Inc., 51 A.D.2d 656, 378 N.Y.S.2d 195 (1976), affirmed 41 N.Y.2d 919, 394 N.Y.S.2d 623, 363 N.E.2d 347 (1977); Shullo Construction Co. v. Miller, 2 Ohio App.2d 177, 207 N.E.2d 393 (1965); Schmidt v. Reed, 132 N.Y. 108, 30 N.E. 373 (1892), criticized in Walsh, Equity 361–377 (1930). For an extreme case, see Tedco Development Corp. v. Overland Hills, Inc., 200 Neb. 748, 266 N.W.2d 56 (1978), criticized in Thomas, Specific Performance of Land Purchases, 12 Creighton L.Rev. 295 (1978).

The ULTA follows the same rule, at least if the contract fixes a particular time for performance, although it requires the more explicit sort of language quoted in the text at note 22, supra; ULTA § 2–302(d); Comment 2 argues

that the rule is " * * * a reasonable recognition of the frequent need for certainty as to the right to refuse to perform because of the other party's breach." See also Moore v. Lovelace, 413 So.2d 1100 (Ala.1982) (parties' agreement to extend closing date, coupled with one party's refusal to agree to further extensions, made time essential.)

A similar approach is generally employed by the courts if the contract sets no date for performance; an appropriate notice can both fix a reasonable date and make it "of the essence." See Schneider v. Warner, 69 Wis.2d 194, 230 N.W.2d 728 (1975). Here the ULTA differs; it permits a party to fix a date unilaterally, but not to make it essential. ULTA § 2–302 Comment 2. See Annot., Necessity and Reasonableness of Vendor's Notice to Vendee of Requisite Time of Performance of Real Estate Sales Contract After Prior Waiver or Extension of Original Time of Performance, 32 A.L.R. 4th 8 (1984).

28. Jahnke v. Palomar Financial Corp., 22 Ariz.App. 369, 527 P.2d 771 (1974); Wyatt v. Bergen, 98 N.J.Eq. 502, 130 A. 595 (1924), affirmed 98 N.J.Eq. 738, 130 A. 597 (1925).

29. See Barker v. Francis, 741 P.2d 548 (Utah App.1987); Restatement (Second) of Contracts § 242(c) (1981) (" * * * the circumstances * * * indicate that performance * * * by that day is important.")

30. Menke v. Foote, 199 Neb. 800, 261 N.W.2d 635 (1978); Blocker v. Lowry, 285 Ala. 448, 233 So.2d 233 (1970); Mercury Gas & Oil Corp. v. Rincon Oil & Gas Corp., 79 N.M. 537, 445 P.2d 958 (1968); Lockhart–Hutchens v. Bergstrom, 434 S.W.2d 453 (Tex.Civ.App. 1968), refused n.r.e.; Neumann v. Gorak, 243 Wis. 503, 11 N.W.2d 155 (1943); Johnson v. Schuchardt, 333 Mo. 781, 63 S.W.2d 17, 89

The cases suggest that courts are often hostile to strict application of time clauses in contracts. They frequently find waivers of the essentiality of time, both from written or oral statements of waiver[31] and from the surrounding circumstances. The statute of frauds is typically held no barrier to such waivers.[32] Silence or failure to demand strict performance may be construed as a waiver, particularly where the opposing party is under the reasonable impression that timely performance will not be insisted upon.[33] Acceptance without objection of late performance of part of the other party's obligations may be taken to waive late performance of the remainder.[34] Once a waiver has been made, the waiving party can reinstate the essentiality of time only by notifying the other party of the intention to do so and stating a reasonable time for the latter to come into compliance.[35] For these reasons, a clause making time essential often turns out to be much less effective than one would expect.

The concept of reasonableness adds to the uncertainty of judicial enforcement of time clauses. We have seen that in several situations a court may be called upon to determine what is a reasonable time;[36] perhaps the most common is the case in which time is not of the essence and one party is not ready to close the sale on the agreed date. It is obvious that such determinations are scarcely predictable in advance of litigation. What is a reasonable time depends on the parties' expectations, the nature of the transaction, and the surrounding circumstances.[37] In the ordinary case at

A.L.R. 914 (1933); Edgerton v. Peckham, 11 Paige 352 (N.Y.1844). Cf. Kasten Construction Co. v. Maple Ridge Construction Co., 245 Md. 373, 226 A.2d 341 (1967).

31. See, e.g., Cedar Point Apartments, Limited v. Cedar Point Investment Corp., 693 F.2d 748 (8th Cir.1982), cert. denied 461 U.S. 914, 103 S.Ct. 1893, 77 L.Ed.2d 283 (1983); Kossler v. Palm Springs Developments, Limited, 101 Cal.App.3d 88, 161 Cal.Rptr. 423 (1980), appeal after remand 139 Cal.App.3d 894, 189 Cal.Rptr. 253 (1983); Kohenn v. Plantation Baking Co., Inc., 32 Ill.App.3d 231, 336 N.E.2d 491 (1975); Loper v. O'Rourke, 86 Misc.2d 441, 382 N.Y.S.2d 663 (1976). See generally 3A Corbin, Contracts §§ 716, 754 (1960); 3 Am.L.Prop. § 11.46 (1952); 6A Powell, Real Property ¶ 925(2) (1981).

32. See § 10.1, supra, at notes 48–50.

33. Stevens v. Cliffs at Princeville Associates, 67 Hawaii 236, 684 P.2d 965 (1984) (despite time-of-essence language in financing condition, vendors did not object to purchasers' delay in seeking financing, and thus waived clause by their conduct); Goldstein v. Hanna, 97 Nev. 559, 635 P.2d 290 (1981) (vendor's agent advised purchaser that time would be extended; vendor bound by waiver, since he did nothing to correct purchaser's impression); Reed v. Eller, 33 Wn.App. 820, 664 P.2d 515 (1983); Tantillo v. Janus, 87 Ill.App.3d 231, 42 Ill.Dec. 291, 408 N.E.2d 1000 (1980); Bolton v. Barber, 233 Ga. 646, 212 S.E.2d 766 (1975); County of Lincoln v. Fischer, 216 Or. 421, 339 P.2d 1084 (1959). But silence is not always deemed a waiver; see Schulze v. Kwik–Chek Realty Co., 212 Va. 111, 181 S.E.2d 629 (1971).

34. Leiter v. Eltinge, 246 Cal.App.2d 306, 54 Cal.Rptr. 703 (1966); Restatement (Second) of Contracts § 247 and Illustration 2 (1981). Most of the cases involve installment sales contracts requiring a series of regular payments by the purchaser. If a pattern of acceptance of late payments by the vendor is established, a finding of waiver will frequently follow; see G. Nelson & D. Whitman, Real Estate Finance Law 93–95 (2d ed. 1985); see Legg v. Allen, 72 Or.App. 351, 696 P.2d 9 (1985). Law § 3.29 (2d ed. 1985). But see Jones v. Clark, 418 P.2d 792 (Wyo.1966).

35. In re Simpson, 7 B.R. 41 (Bkrtcy. D.Ariz.1980); Church of God in Christ, Inc. v. Congregation Kehillath Jacob, 370 Mass. 828, 353 N.E.2d 669 (1976); Kammert Brothers Enterprises, Inc. v. Tanque Verde Plaza Co., 102 Ariz. 301, 428 P.2d 678 (1967); Clifton Park Affiliates, Inc. v. Howard, 36 A.D.2d 984, 320 N.Y.S.2d 981 (1971); Ashworth v. Hankins, 248 Ark. 567, 452 S.W.2d 838 (1970). If the waiver itself was verbal, it may have included the necessary statement as to when strict performance would be required; if it did not, or if it was by conduct rather than words, an appropriate notice must be given.

36. See text at notes 2, 9, 16, 27 and 35 supra.

37. Safeway System, Inc. v. Manuel Brothers, Inc., 102 R.I. 136, 228 A.2d 851 (1967).

least, a few weeks will be considered a reasonable delay,[38] but special facts may extend the time much more. The Illinois Court of Appeals, drawing on its knowledge of the slowness of zoning procedures, found a delay of seventeen months reasonable where the contract provided for closing after a rezoning of the property had been obtained.[39] On the whole, the price for this sort of judicial flexibility and discretion is a lack of certainty which, in turn, probably encourages the settlement of many disputes concerning the timing of the parties' obligations.

§ 10.10   Concurrent Conditions and Tender

The word "condition", in its technical sense, refers to contract language, or a contractual provision supplied by the court, that makes a party's duty of performance depend on some event that must occur or some fact that must be true. If the condition has not been met, no performance is due and a court will not order performance or hold the party liable for its absence.[1] Real estate sales contracts often contain numerous conditions. Some may be events entirely outside the control of the parties: "I am obligated to sell you this land only if the governmental price support system for tobacco is terminated" or "I will buy your house only if Mount St. Helens does not erupt before the closing." Other conditions may involve intimately the behavior of the parties themselves: "I am obligated to buy this land only if I am able to sell my farm in Iowa by June 1."

Where a condition depends on the actions or efforts of a party to the contract, it is common to include in the contract a promise by that party that he or she will try (or use "good faith", "reasonable efforts", or the like) to accomplish it. For example, the contract in the preceding illustration might include a promise by the purchaser to attempt in good faith to sell the Iowa farm. Even if no such promise is spelled out, courts may read it into the contract.[2] In its absence there is a serious risk that a court might find

---

38. Johnson v. Gregg, 807 S.W.2d 680 (Mo. App.1991) (25 months unreasonable); FDIC v. Slinger, 913 F.2d 7 (1st Cir.1990) (3½ years reasonable, where lis pendens that made closing impossible was not removed for 3 years); Henry v. Sharma, 154 Cal.App.3d 665, 201 Cal.Rptr. 478 (1984); Fletcher v. Jones, 314 N.C. 389, 333 S.E.2d 731 (1985) (seven weeks reasonable); Johnson v. Smith, Scott & Associates, Inc., 77 N.C.App. 386, 335 S.E.2d 205 (1985) (two weeks reasonable); Safeway System, Inc. v. Manuel Bros., supra note 37 (6 days reasonable); Freeman v. Boyce, 66 Hawaii 327, 661 P.2d 702 (1983) (4 months reasonable); Ronne v. Ronne, 568 P.2d 1021 (Alaska 1977) (one month reasonable); Schlee v. Bryant, 247 Md. 689, 234 A.2d 457 (1967) (2 days reasonable); cf. Rogers v. Cardinal Realty, Inc., 115 N.H. 285, 339 A.2d 23 (1975) (10 months unreasonable).

39. Yale Development Co. v. Aurora Pizza Hut, Inc., 95 Ill.App.3d 523, 51 Ill.Dec. 409, 420 N.E.2d 823 (1981); see also Kaiser v. Crouch, 504 P.2d 429 (Okl.1972) (120 days reasonable where contract required purchasers to build a house on the property); Hicks v. Bridges, 580 So.2d 743 (Miss.1991) (specific performance granted despite 11 month delay); Hochard v. Deiter, 219 Kan. 738, 549 P.2d 970 (1976) (specific performance granted despite 3½ years delay). But see E. Shepherdstown Developers, Inc. v. J. Russell Fritts, Inc., 183 W.Va. 691, 398 S.E.2d 517 (1990), holding 40 months an unreasonable delay despite the fact that the closing was conditioned on planning commission approval of the buyer's construction project.

§ 10.10

1. See Restatement (Second) of Contracts § 224ff (1981); 3A Corbin, Contracts §§ 626–27 (1960); J. Calamari & J. Perillo, Contracts § 11–1 (1977).

2. See Restatement (Second) of Contracts § 225 Comment d, § 226 Comment c (1981). If the court finds the condition from the parties' words or conduct it is an "express" or "implied in fact" condition; if the court supplies it in the interest of fairness and justice, but without purporting to find it in the parties' agreement, it is an "implied in law" or

that the party whose duty depends on the condition has, in effect, the power to turn the duty on or off at will. Such a power renders the obligation illusory, and may lead a court to deny enforcement of the contract entirely.[3] For present purposes, however, the point is simply that contract language may at the same time comprise both a promise or covenant, obligating a party to take certain actions, and a condition to one of the parties' performance of other duties.[4] Thus a vendor may provide, "I promise to obtain a report from a licensed pest inspector on the house, and you are obligated to buy only if it shows no infestation by termites."

Many conditions in sales contract, such as those in the illustrations above, are conditions precedent, in the sense that some further duty of performance will become due only after they are satisfied.[5] Consider, however, the essential core of such a contract: the buyer's promise to pay the purchase price and the seller's promise to convey the land: "V agrees to deed Blackacre to P on June 1 for $50,000 cash." These words obviously represent covenants by each party; because they contemplate a simultaneous exchange of performances, they will also be construed as concurrent conditions.[6] Thus, the substantial performance, or at least the tender of such performance, by each party is treated as a constructive[7] condition of the other party's duty to perform. If V does not tender a deed, P has no duty to pay the price; if P does not tender the price, V has no duty to deliver a deed.[8] If both parties fail to tender, neither is in breach.

"constructive" condition. The distinction is often a flimsy one, and the text of the Restatement eschews these terms; id. and § 226, Reporter's Note to Comment c. See Emmert v. O'Brien, 72 Or.App. 752, 697 P.2d 222 (1985) (where contract contained condition that zoning use permit would be obtained, vendor had implied obligation to refrain from frustrating its occurrence, and possibly an affirmative obligation to use reasonable efforts to bring it about); Moreland Dev. Co. v. Gladstone Holmes, Inc., 135 Cal.App.3d 973, 186 Cal. Rptr. 6 (1982) (condition that purchaser's board of directors approve contract did not make obligation illusory, as directors had duty of good faith). Of course, the duty to exercise good faith efforts to satisfy the condition may be spelled out in the contract; see, e.g. Mann v. Addicott Hills Corp., 238 Va. 262, 384 S.E.2d 81 (1989).

3. See, e.g., Gerruth Realty Co. v. Pire, 17 Wis.2d 89, 115 N.W.2d 557 (1962); 1 Corbin, Contracts § 149 (1960). See also Nalley v. Harris, 176 Ga.App. 553, 336 S.E.2d 822 (1985) (where purchaser's obligation is conditioned upon "satisfaction" of third party structural inspector, contract is not illusory); Trenta v. Gay, 191 N.J.Super. 617, 468 A.2d 737 (1983) (attorney review clause permits party's attorney to reject contract for any reason, and does not require him or her to explain reason to other party); Omni Group, Inc. v. Seattle–First National Bank, 32 Wn.App. 22, 645 P.2d 727 (1982) (condition that buyer be "satisfied" with feasibility report on property was not illusory; contract was enforceable).

4. See First National Bank of DeKalb County v. National Bank of Georgia, 249 Ga. 216, 290 S.E.2d 55 (1982); Restatement (Second) of Contracts § 225 Comment d; § 227 Comment d (1981); J. Calamari & J. Perillo, Contracts §§ 11–8, 11–9 (1977).

5. See the discussion at § 10.11, infra.

6. Bell v. Elder, 782 P.2d 545 (Utah App. 1989); Esplendido Apartments v. Olsson, 144 Ariz. 355, 697 P.2d 1105 (App.1984); Fletcher v. Jones, 314 N.C. 389, 333 S.E.2d 731 (1985); Kossler v. Palm Springs Developments, Limited, 101 Cal.App.3d 88, 161 Cal.Rptr. 423 (1980); 3 Am.L.Prop. § 11.44 (1952); 3A Corbin, Contracts § 663 (1960); Restatement (Second) of Contracts § 238 (1981); ULTA § 2–301 ("concurrent obligations").

7. The condition is "constructive" simply because in the usual contract no language specifies that a condition exists; the language is, in effect, supplied by the court. See note 2, supra.

8. See Carpenter v. Parsons, 186 Ga.App. 3, 366 S.E.2d 367 (1988); Shaw v. Ferguson, 767 P.2d 1358 (Okl.App.1986). The discussion in the text refers to cash sales. If the contract calls for the price to be paid in installments, with conveyance of title upon payment of the last installment—a common arrangement— the tender of all installments except the last is obviously a condition precedent to the vendor's duty to convey; Hensley v. Williams, 726 P.2d 90 (Wyo.1986); Church of God in Christ, Inc. v. Congregation Kehillath Jacob, 370

This notion may seem too elementary to be worth stating; to the modern mind it would seem absurd to compel V to hand over a deed if he has not gotten his money, or vice versa. But the doctrine of constructive concurrent conditions was not always accepted by the courts [9] and it has important modern consequences. The most significant is the requirement of tender: one may not treat the other party as in breach of the promises of the contract which contemplate simultaneous performance—payment of the price and transfer of the title—until one has performed or tendered one's own performance.[10] In general, the tendered performance need only be substantial and not perfect;[11] as we saw in the preceding section, for example, a tender later than the agreed date is sufficient if it is not unreasonably late.[12] But the parties may contract for a strict rather than a substantial performance, as illustrated by the "time of the essence" clause discussed in the preceding section.[13] And if the performance is only substantial rather than full, the other party (although obligated to perform) is entitled to damages or, in the case of the purchaser, an abatement of the price, to reflect the deficiency.[14]

A party who fails to tender is denied damages,[15]

Mass. 828, 353 N.E.2d 669 (1976). And the vendor may sue for the unpaid installments without tendering a deed. But payment of the last installment and conveyance of the title are usually treated as concurrent conditions. Sharbono v. Darden, 220 Mont. 320, 715 P.2d 433 (1986); Ideal Family and Youth Ranch v. Whetstine, 655 P.2d 429 (Colo.App. 1982); Burke Aviation Corp. v. Alton Jennings Co., 377 P.2d 578 (Okl.1962); 3A Corbin, Contracts § 664 (1960); 3 Am.L.Prop. § 11.44 (1952).

See also Braught v. Granas, 73 Or.App. 488, 698 P.2d 1012 (1985), in which the court (apparently erroneously) termed the performances of buyer and seller under an installment contract "independent." The vendors brought an action for damages, and the purchasers defended on the ground that the vendors had defaulted in payments on a preexisting installment contract on the same land, thus impairing their title. The court held that it was the purchasers' default in payments which had caused the vendors' default; hence, the title defect did not excuse the purchaser's breach.

Contracts often contain numerous promises in addition to those to convey the land and pay the purchase price. If these other performances are not intended to be exchanged simultaneously, they are not usually treated as concurrent conditions. For example, in Fogarty v. Saathoff, 128 Cal.App.3d 780, 180 Cal.Rptr. 484 (1982), the seller's promises to furnish a title insurance policy and a termite clearance were conditions precedent to the buyer's duty to pay the price. But the seller's obtaining of a mortgage loan commitment within a specified time was deemed a condition precedent both to the seller's obligations mentioned above and to the duty of the par-

ties to close. Since the loan commitment was not obtained, the seller properly cancelled the contract and the purchaser was denied specific performance.

9. See e.g., Pordage v. Cole, 1 Wms. Saund. 319 (Kings Bench 1669), discussed in 3A Corbin, Contracts § 662 (1960).

10. McGee v. V.T. Pierret Realty & Construction Co., Inc., 407 So.2d 1288 (La.App. 1981); Cobb v. Cougle, 351 A.2d 110 (Me.1976); Ace Realty, Inc. v. Looney, 531 P.2d 1377 (Okl.1974); Huszar v. Certified Realty Co., 266 Or. 614, 512 P.2d 982 (1973); 3A Corbin, Contracts § 663 (1960).

11. See Schneider v. Dumbarton Developers, Inc., 767 F.2d 1007 (D.C.Cir.1985) (a tender of performance by one who adds conditions not included in the original contract is not substantial performance); Hausam v. Wodrich, 574 P.2d 805 (Alaska 1978); Prager's, Inc. v. Bullitt Co., 1 Wn.App. 575, 463 P.2d 217 (1969); J. Calamari & J. Perillo, Contracts 410–12 (1977); ULTA § 2–301 comment 2, pointing out that the concept of substantial performance is similar to the concept of marketable title; see § 10.12, infra. But see Wilson v. Klein, 715 S.W.2d 814 (Tex.App. 1986) (an offer by a purchaser of a sum less than that which is due is not a valid tender, even if the purchaser believes the sum is correct).

12. See § 10.9, supra, at note 9.

13. Id. at note 13.

14. Kossler v. Palm Springs Developments, Limited, 101 Cal.App.3d 88, 161 Cal.Rptr. 423 (1980); § 10.9, supra, at note 5.

15. Ching–Ming Chen v. Advantage Co., 713 S.W.2d 79 (Tenn.App.1986); Daybreak

restitution,[16] and often specific performance.[17] Professor Corbin pointed out that specific performance may well be granted despite the plaintiff's failure to tender, since the tender is implicit in the filing of the action itself, and since the court can make its decree conditional on the plaintiff's actual delivery into court of the necessary documents or funds.[18] In theory this is correct, but as a practical matter the action often will be filed so long after the agreed closing date that the passage of time will prevent the ostensible tender from complying with the contract.[19]

What is a tender? The term conjures a picture of a vendor with a deed in outstretched hand or a purchaser holding out a cashier's check. Such actions may once have been required and are certainly acceptable, but the modern notion of tender is more relaxed. What is required is a clear offer to perform, coupled with the present ability to do so.[20] Increasingly the courts have dropped the use of the term "tender" in recent years, employing instead such phrases as "ready, willing, and able to perform" which denote a more lenient attitude.[21] But these cases do not eliminate the need to communicate the offer of performance to the other party; it is not enough to be secretly willing and able.[22] The offer may be conditioned on the opposing

Const. Specialties, Inc. v. Saghatoleslami, 712 P.2d 1028 (Colo.App.1985); Hellrung v. Hoechst, 384 S.W.2d 561 (Mo.1964); 3A Corbin, Contracts § 663 (1960).

16. Pelletier v. Dwyer, 334 A.2d 867 (Me. 1975); Cohen v. Kranz, 12 N.Y.2d 242, 238 N.Y.S.2d 928, 189 N.E.2d 473 (1963).

17. Johnson v. Morris, 645 P.2d 51 (Utah 1982); Nix v. Clary, 640 P.2d 246 (Colo.App. 1981); Green, Inc. v. Smith, 40 Ohio App.2d 30, 317 N.E.2d 227 (1974); Glave v. Brandlein, 196 So.2d 780 (Fla.App.1967).

18. 3A Corbin, Contracts § 663, at 179–180; § 1175 at 298–99 (1960). See Fleenor v. Church, 681 P.2d 1351 (Alaska 1984); Goldston v. AMI Investments, Inc., 98 Nev. 567, 655 P.2d 521 (1982).

19. See § 10.9, supra. This is particularly true if time was of the essence, but even if it was not, an unreasonable time will often have elapsed. See also Crow v. Bertram, 725 S.W.2d 634 (Mo.App.1987) (purchaser's long delay in tendering constituted abandonment of the contract, depriving him of right to specific performance). But see Wilhorn Builders, Inc. v. Cortaro Management Co., 82 Ariz. 48, 308 P.2d 251 (1957), permitting the vendor to tender after filing an action to enforce the contract; Restatement (Second) of Contracts § 238 Comment c and Illustration 5 (1981).

20. Restatement (Second) of Contracts § 238 requires that the party must, "with manifested present ability to do so, offer performance of his part of the simultaneous exchange." It declines to employ the word "tender." ULTA § 2–301 retains use of the term. See Brooks v. Shipp, 481 So.2d 655 (La.App. 1985); Suss v. Schammel, 375 N.W.2d 252 (Iowa 1985).

21. Kottis v. Cerilli, 526 A.2d 506 (R.I. 1987); Harrison v. Baker, 402 So.2d 1270 (Fla. App.1981); Chandler v. Independent School District No. 12, 625 P.2d 620 (Okl.1981); Pond v. Lindell, 194 Mont. 240, 632 P.2d 1107 (1981); Rokowsky v. Gordon, 501 F.Supp. 1114 (D.Mass.1980) ("ready to perform"); Pelletier v. Dwyer, 334 A.2d 867 (Me.1975); Green, Inc. v. Smith, 40 Ohio App.2d 30, 317 N.E.2d 227 (1974) ("ready, willing, able, and eager.") See also Hutton v. Gliksberg, 128 Cal.App.3d 240, 180 Cal.Rptr. 141 (1982) (letter from mortgage lender to escrow officer, committing to make loan, was sufficient tender by purchaser; actual cash deposit into escrow not customary and not required.) But see Kuderer v. United States, 739 F.Supp. 1422 (D.Or.1990) (a draft drawn on an unincorporated business trust is not the equivalent of cash, and is not a proper tender); Carr v. Enoch Smith Co., 781 P.2d 1292 (Utah App.1989) (a letter expressing an intent to pay is not a proper tender); Naumburg v. Pattison, 103 N.M. 649, 711 P.2d 1387 (1985) (an offer to "shortly pay the outstanding balance" is not a proper tender).

22. See, e.g., Nix v. Clary, 640 P.2d 246 (Colo.App.1981) (" * * * must give unequivocal notice of an unconditional commitment to be bound by the contract.") The communication may be to the other party's attorney or some other appropriate agent; see Parks Enterprises, Inc. v. New Century Realty, Inc., 652 P.2d 918 (Utah 1982) (title company held not to be vendor's agent); Cobb v. Cougle, 351 A.2d 110 (Me.1976); Trapuzzano v. Lorish, 467 Pa. 27, 354 A.2d 534 (1976). See also Heatherly v. Rosenberg, 372 So.2d 766 (La.App.1979), writ denied 375 So.2d 957 (La.1979).

party's tender of his or her own due performance [23], but if it is accompanied by further conditions, it is not a valid tender.[24]

Under some circumstances tender is excused and a party who does not tender nonetheless has full remedies. This is so if the opposing party has repudiated the contract [25] or if other circumstances make plain his or her unwillingness to perform.[26] Moreover, one need not tender if the other side's performance has become impossible. For example, a purchaser is excused from tender if the vendor has sold the property to another,[27] or if the title is subject to such defects that the vendor cannot reasonably expect to cure them by the time he or she must close.[28]

§ 10.11   Precedent Conditions

As the preceding section suggests, a condition may be precedent to a

23. See Pond v. Lindell, 194 Mont. 240, 632 P.2d 1107 (1981) (purchasers placed $9,600 contract balance in escrow with instructions that it be released only upon issuance of title policy showing vendor's merchantable title; held a good tender); Restatement (Second) of Contracts § 238 Comment b (1981).

24. Mayer v. Boston Metropolitan Airport, Inc., 355 Mass. 344, 244 N.E.2d 568 (1969).

25. Jitner v. Gersch Dev. Co., 101 Or.App. 220, 789 P.2d 704 (1990); McClure v. Gower, 259 Ga. 678, 385 S.E.2d 271 (1989); Pee Dee Oil Co. v. Quality Oil Co., 80 N.C.App. 219, 341 S.E.2d 113 (1986), review denied 317 N.C. 706, 347 S.E.2d 438 (1986); Norton v. Herron, 677 P.2d 877 (Alaska 1984); McDermott v. Burpo, 663 S.W.2d 256 (Mo.App.1983); Woliansky v. Miller, 135 Ariz. 444, 661 P.2d 1145 (App. 1983), appeal after remand 146 Ariz. 170, 704 P.2d 811 (1985), appeal after remand 154 Ariz. 32, 739 P.2d 1349 (1987); Goldston v. AMI Investors, Inc., 98 Nev. 567, 655 P.2d 521 (1982); First Federal Savings & Loan Association v. Pardue, 545 F.Supp. 433 (N.D.Tex. 1982), affirmed 703 F.2d 555 (5th Cir.1983); Hogan v. Leary, 115 N.H. 88, 333 A.2d 724 (1975); Howard v. Thomas, 270 Or. 6, 526 P.2d 552 (1974); Igo Co. v. Parks, 252 Minn. 158, 89 N.W.2d 625 (1958). But see Young v. Koehl, 417 So.2d 24 (La.App.1982), requiring a tender despite the other party's repudiation of the contract.

26. See Tower v. Halderman, 162 Ariz. 243, 782 P.2d 719 (1989); Meunier v. Liang, 521 So.2d 475 (La.App.1988); Lee v. Thunder Development, Inc., 77 Or.App. 7, 711 P.2d 978 (1985); Goldring v. Sletko Realty, Inc., 129 Misc.2d 756, 494 N.Y.S.2d 56 (1985); Hubler v. Oshman, 700 S.W.2d 694 (Tex.App.1985) (where vendor is unavailable to accept tender despite purchaser's best efforts to tender, purchaser can enforce contract without making a tender); Baker v. McCue–Moyle Dev. Co., 695 S.W.2d 906 (Mo.App.1984); McDermott v. Burpo, 663 S.W.2d 256 (Mo.App.1983); Fleenor v. Church, 681 P.2d 1351 (Alaska 1984) (while vendor's conduct did not clearly indicate his

unwillingness to perform, it made purchaser's tender sufficiently difficult that a delay in tendering was justified); Bacchetta v. Conforti, 107 A.D.2d 616, 484 N.Y.S.2d 1 (1985), affirmed without opinion 65 N.Y.2d 627, 491 N.Y.S.2d 157, 480 N.E.2d 746 (1985) (where vendor's counsel refused to give an instruction as to where funds should be wired by purchaser from her California bank, purchaser was not required to make any further tender); Chandler v. Independent School District No. 12, 625 P.2d 620 (Okl.1981); Good v. Tri–Cep, Inc., 248 Ga. 684, 285 S.E.2d 527 (1982); Jahnke v. Palomar Financial Corp., 22 Ariz. App. 369, 527 P.2d 771 (1974).

A party's words or actions indicating unwillingness to perform the contract are sometimes said to amount to a waiver of the other party's duty to tender; see, e.g., Concepts, Inc. v. Innovative Property Management, Inc., 180 Ga.App. 903, 350 S.E.2d 805 (1986); Strout Realty, Inc. v. Benson, 699 S.W.2d 795 (Mo. App.1985).

27. Robert Lawrence Associates, Inc. v. Del Vecchio, 178 Conn. 1, 420 A.2d 1142 (1979).

28. Spagat v. Schak, 130 Ill.App.3d 130, 85 Ill.Dec. 389, 473 N.E.2d 988 (1985); Langston v. Huffacker, 36 Wn.App. 779, 678 P.2d 1265 (1984) (purchaser may have specific performance despite his failure to deposit purchase price into escrow by closing date, where such failure was due to vendor's failure to clear her title by that date, and where purchaser was ready, willing and able to close); Bradley v. Apel, 531 S.W.2d 678 (Tex.Civ.App.1975); Cohen v. Kranz, 12 N.Y.2d 242, 238 N.Y.S.2d 928, 189 N.E.2d 473 (1963). But see Esplendido Apartments v. Olsson, 144 Ariz. 355, 697 P.2d 1105 (App.1984) (vendor's title defects were no excuse for purchaser's failure to tender, where purchaser was unaware of defects); Willener v. Sweeting, 107 Wn.2d 388, 730 P.2d 45 (1986) (same); Eaton Corp. v. Easton Associates, Inc., 728 F.2d 285 (6th Cir.1984) (in an *option* contract, purchaser must tender even if vendor's title is defective, in order to exercise option and gain right to specific performance).

party's duty to perform rather than concurrent.[1] If a condition precedent does not occur, no duty of performance arises, and if the party who is protected by the condition fails to perform he or she is not in breach of the contract.[2] Both vendors and purchasers frequently insert a variety of conditions in sales contracts so that they will not be bound to proceed with the sale if various investigations or arrangements prove disappointing. A seller may not wish to go forward if the buyer's credit references are unsatisfactory[3] or if the seller is unable to acquire certain other real estate. The purchaser may condition the duty to buy on the completion of certain improvements on the land, the production of suitable investigative reports on structural quality or pest infestation, or the availability of local governmental approvals such as rezonings, building permits, or sewer connections. As we will see in the next section, the courts will infer a covenant by the vendor to provide a title of acceptable quality, and will also treat the existence of such a title as a condition precedent to the buyer's duty to purchase.[4]

Without doubt the most common condition found in sales contracts is one based on the availability of new mortgage financing to enable the buyer to purchase. Such clauses have been in use for many decades, yet continue to be very widely litigated. During the 1970s and 1980s, as a consequence of relatively high and volatile interest rates, increasing numbers of real estate sales were financed by the purchaser's assumption of or taking subject to a preexisting mortgage, typically carrying an interest rate lower than current rates. This technique raises the need for a different kind of financing condition since the lender's approval is commonly needed, under a "due-on-sale" clause in the mortgage,[5] in order for the transaction to proceed. The

§ 10.11

1. § 10.10, supra, at note 4. See generally Bowman, Escrow Agreements: How Enforceable Are They?, 34 L.A.Bar.Bull. 41 (No. 2, 1958), for an able discussion of common conditions precedent. Courts sometimes find conditions from contract language that is far from clear. See, e.g., Binford v. Shicker, 553 N.E.2d 845 (Ind.App.1990) (contract stated buyers agreed to apply for mortgage loan to purchase property; court held that this promise was also a condition, discharging buyers when they were unable to obtain loan).

2. See Arthur Rutenberg Corp. v. Pasin, 506 So.2d 33 (Fla.App.1987) (purchaser who is unable to obtain financing as provided in contract condition is entitled to refund of "nonrefundable" deposit).

In principle, a condition can be subsequent rather than precedent or concurrent. A condition subsequent is one which, if it occurs, will discharge a contractual duty that has already arisen. Such conditions are quite rare in contracts generally and are almost never found in real estate sales contracts. Hence, they will receive no further attention here. See 3A Corbin, Contracts § 628 (1960); J. Calamari & J. Perillo, Contracts § 11–5 (1977). The Second Restatement does not employ the term "condition subsequent" at all, but instead treats such an occurrence under

its provisions on discharge of contractual duties; see Restatement (Second) of Contracts § 224 Comment e, § 230 (1981). It also states a preference for interpreting conditions as precedent rather than as discharging duties which have already matured; id, at § 227(3). The Missouri cases seem consistently to term conditions "subsequent" when all other courts would call them "precedent"; see Maynard v. Bazazzadegan, 732 S.W.2d 950 (Mo.App.1987).

3. See also Norton v. Herron, 677 P.2d 877 (Alaska 1984) (contract's statement that down payment was to come from sale of purchaser's Montana property did not make such sale a condition precedent). The seller would ordinarily be concerned with the buyer's credit only if the seller were financing all or part of the price by way of a purchase-money mortgage or an installment sale contract. Such transactions are common.

4. See § 10.12 infra.

5. See generally G. Nelson & D. Whitman, Real Estate Finance Law §§ 5.21–5.26 (2d ed. 1985). See Maxwell, The Due-on-Sale Clause: Restraints on Alienation and Adhesion Theory in California, 28 U.C.L.A.L.Rev. 197 (1981); § 341 of the Garn–St. Germain Depository Institutions Act of 1982, 12 U.S.C.A. § 1701j–3, generally making due-on-sale clauses en-

parties are well-advised to make such approval a condition of the duty to close the sale;[6] surprisingly, the point is often overlooked.[7]

As we have already seen,[8] a condition which is entirely under the control of the party whose performance depends on it has the effect of letting him out of the contract at will. In such a contract there is no mutuality of obligation, and hence neither party can enforce the contract.[9] The courts dislike this result, and very often avoid it by construing the contract in a manner which denies the party in question unfettered discretion as to whether the condition will be met. Most often this is accomplished by reading the condition as containing an implicit covenant to use "good faith", "reasonable efforts", or the like to make the condition occur.[10] Thus the

forceable as a matter of preemptive federal law. See also Investors Savings & Loan Association v. Ganz, 174 N.J.Super. 356, 416 A.2d 918 (1980), upholding a clause which permitted the lender to demand repayment of the loan if the borrower moved out of the house.

6. See Zavradinos v. Lund, 741 S.W.2d 863 (Mo.App.1987); Wendy's of Montana v. Larsen, 196 Mont. 525, 640 P.2d 464 (1982) (sale conditioned on consent of vendor under prior contract which was to be assumed; consent was not obtained and the sale was not completed, but the court nonetheless allowed retention by seller of buyer's earnest money); McDaniel v. Kudlik, 598 S.W.2d 350 (Tex.Civ. App.1980).

7. See Wallstreet Properties, Inc. v. Gassner, 53 Or.App. 650, 632 P.2d 1310 (1981). If there is no condition, and the lender's refusal to consent to the sale makes it impossible to proceed under the original contractual terms, a court asked to order specific performance for the vendor is faced with a difficult problem. Compare Barry M. Dechtman, Inc. v. Sidpaul Corp., 178 N.J.Super. 444, 429 A.2d 411 (1981), reversed 89 N.J. 547, 446 A.2d 518 (1982) (contract too uncertain to be enforced), with Schrader v. Benton, 2 Hawaii App. 564, 635 P.2d 562 (1981) (contract enforced with court restructuring the transaction). See also Nelson v. Cannon, 126 Ariz. 381, 616 P.2d 56 (App.1980) (contract provided for buyer to assume existing first mortgage and obtain new second mortgage; first mortgagee refused to consent to second mortgage, but buyer waived it and paid cash down to balance on first mortgage; held, buyer could specifically enforce the contract in this manner.)

A real estate broker has been held negligent in advising a purchaser that a mortgage loan condition was not necessary in a contract of sale; see Gerard v. Peterson, 448 N.W.2d 699 (Iowa App.1989). It is quite conceivable that a broker who failed to advise the inclusion of a contract clause conditioning a purchaser's loan assumption on approval by the existing lender would also be considered negligent. But see Minton v. Spivey, 505 So.2d 476 (Fla. App.1987), review denied 513 So.2d 1063 (Fla. 1987), awarding a commission to a broker

when the buyer refused to complete the purchase, ostensibly on the ground that the mortgage to be "wrapped around" contained a due-on-sale clause. The court found there was no evidence that the lender would have exercised the clause.

8. § 10.10, supra, at notes 2–3.

9. Resource Management Co. v. Weston Ranch & Livestock Co., 706 P.2d 1028 (Utah 1985); Long Investment Co. v. O'Donnel, 3 Wis.2d 291, 88 N.W.2d 674 (1958); Restatement (Second) of Contracts § 226 Illustration 4 (1981); J. Calamari & J. Perillo, Contracts § 4–17 (1977); 1 Corbin, Contracts § 149 (1960). Courts frequently attempt to construe contract provisions so as to narrow the unfettered discretion of the party who appears to have control of the condition, thereby making that party's obligation meaningful and enforcing the contract. See, e.g., Hunt v. Shamblin, 179 W.Va. 663, 371 S.E.2d 591 (1988).

10. See, e.g., Wooten v. DeMean, 788 S.W.2d 522 (Mo.App.1990) ("reasonable efforts"); Price v. Bartkowiak, 715 F.Supp. 76 (S.D.N.Y.1989) (New York law) ("genuine effort; must act in good faith); Educational Placement Services, Inc. v. Watts, 789 S.W.2d 902 (Tenn.App.1989) ("reasonable effort); Phillipe v. Thomas, 3 Conn.App. 471, 489 A.2d 1056 (1985) (both objective reasonableness and subjective good faith are required); Wiggins v. Shewmake, 374 N.W.2d 111 (S.D.1985) ("best efforts"); Smithloff v. Benson, 173 Ga.App. 870, 328 S.E.2d 759 (1985) ("good faith and fair dealing"); Endres v. Warriner, 307 N.W.2d 146 (S.D.1981); Temkin, Too Much Good Faith in Real Estate Purchase Agreements? Give Me an Option, 34 Kan.L.Rev. 43 (1985). But not all conditions require the efforts or participation of a party to the contract. See, e.g., Laz–Karp Realty, Inc. v. Gilbert, 777 F.Supp. 1085 (D.R.I.1990) (where condemnation and conveyance to vendor of a portion of property by city was a condition precedent, purchaser had no duty to become involved in or facilitate condemnation).

The Restatement (Second) treats this result as an example of the more general duty of

language of the condition is treated as a covenant as well. A party who has failed to make the good faith effort required is liable for breach of that covenant, even though the duty to perform the main body of the contract has not arisen. The breach is typically treated as a material or total one, much as if the defaulting party had refused to complete the sale itself.[11] On the other hand, if the condition is unfulfilled despite the exertion of good faith efforts, the party protected by the condition is excused from further performance and can get restitution of any payments made to date.[12]

good faith which it imposes on all contracting parties; id. at § 226 Comment d, § 205. Compare the similar treatment often given to clauses requiring the "satisfaction" of a party with certain facts; a good faith element is generally imposed by the courts. See, e.g., Beverly Way Associates v. Barham, 226 Cal. App.3d 49, 276 Cal.Rptr. 240 (1990); Greer Properties, Inc. v. LaSalle Nat. Bank, 689 F.Supp. 831 (N.D.Ill.1988) (vendor had right to withdraw from contract if it determined "in its own best business judgment" that cost of environmental cleanup was excessive, provided vendor's judgment was exercised in good faith); Hanscom v. Gregorie, 562 A.2d 1232 (Me.1989) (condition permitted purchaser to terminate contract if inspector found "substantial" defects; the condition depended on the inspector's judgment, and since it was exercised honestly, purchaser's termination was proper); Ledford v. Wheeler, 620 P.2d 903 (Okl.App.1979); Western Hills, Oregon, Limited v. Pfau, 265 Or. 137, 508 P.2d 201 (1973); Kadner v. Shields, 20 Cal.App.3d 251, 97 Cal. Rptr. 742 (1971) (buyer contracted to assume existing mortgage if he approved it; he then disapproved it because of its acceleration and prepayment clauses, but subsequently bought another house and gave a mortgage on similar terms. The court held he had failed to act as a reasonably prudent person, and found him in breach of the first contract. Cf. text at notes 22–24, infra.)

11. In the typical case, the purchaser is seeking restitution of earnest money deposit, and the claim is rejected due to his or her lack of good faith; see, e.g., Price v. Bartkowiak, 729 F.Supp. 14 (S.D.N.Y.1989) (purchasers acted in bad faith, where they rejected a loan commitment that met the terms of the condition and continued to search for better terms); Schollian v. Ullo, 558 So.2d 776 (La.App.1990), writ denied 564 So.2d 325 (La.1990) (purchasers did not make application for mortgage loan until date it was to have been approved, according to contract; their tardiness was held to constitute bad faith); Hendel v. Scheuer, 150 A.D.2d 431, 541 N.Y.S.2d 40 (1989); Cobbs v. Fred Burgos Const. Co., 477 So.2d 335 (Ala.1985) (purchaser did not act in good faith, where he withdrew loan application after being unable to reach agreement with lender about financing of changes he desired in stock plans for house); Bushmiller v. Schiller, 35 Md.App. 1, 368 A.2d 1044

(1977); Brack v. Brownlee, 246 Ga. 818, 273 S.E.2d 390 (1980); Anaheim Co. v. Holcombe, 246 Or. 541, 426 P.2d 743 (1967). Cf. Lindenbaum v. Royco Property Corp., 165 A.D.2d 254, 567 N.Y.S.2d 218 (1991) (purchasers were not in bad faith, despite their failure to sell their previous house as required by new lender's loan commitment); Nicholls v. Pitoukkas, 491 N.E.2d 574 (Ind.App.1986) (failure to apply for mortgage loan, as required by contract, was not a breach, where purchasers were manifestly unqualified for loan and it would not have been granted in any event); Burnett v. Brito, 478 So.2d 845 (Fla.App.1985) (same). See also Carmichael v. Lambert Const. Co., 487 So.2d 1367 (Ala.App.1986) (where purchaser's employer transfers him to another state after he signs contract of purchase, he is excused from further efforts to obtain a loan, and is entitled to restitution of his earnest money; good faith does not require that he give up his job or purchase a home he cannot occupy).

An alternative explanation sometimes used by the courts is that the buyer's lack of good faith serves as a waiver of the condition, eliminating it and imposing a duty to complete the contract; failure to do so is then a breach. See, e.g., Schottland v. Lucas, 396 So.2d 72 (Ala.1981). See also Highland Inns Corp. v. American Landmark Corp., 650 S.W.2d 667 (Mo.App.1983), in which the court imposed on the purchaser an implied covenant, not merely to attempt to obtain, but to obtain in fact, the required financing.

12. Weaver v. Hilzen, 147 A.D.2d 634, 538 N.Y.S.2d 40 (1989); Storen v. Meadors, 295 S.C. 438, 369 S.E.2d 651 (1988); Ide v. Joe Miller & Co., 703 P.2d 590 (Colo.App.1984) (provision in contract relating to well capacity was condition precedent, giving purchasers choice of rescission or waiver of the condition and purchase at the contract price); Teachout v. Wilson, 376 N.W.2d 460 (Minn.App.1985) (contract was not avoided by bank's refusal to make loan after review of gas station's financial records, where bank's reason was purchaser's inadequate collateral and request for 100% loan rather than any inadequacy disclosed by financial records); Brown v. Matton, 406 So.2d 1269 (Fla.App.1981); Mobil Oil Corp. v. V.S.H. Realty, Inc., 408 So.2d 585 (Fla.App.1981); Management, Inc. v. Master-

Most of the cases employing this judicial technique involve conditions of financing; it is nearly always held that the buyer (who is, after all, the only party who can apply for mortgage financing) has a duty to make good faith efforts to arrange it.[13]   A similar approach is often used with other types of conditions, such as the sale of the buyer's other house [14] or the approval by a lender of a loan assumption.[15]   Often a question arises as to whether the party with the duty to use good faith efforts has tried hard enough.   For example, in a contract involving a condition of financing, is it sufficient for the buyer to apply for a loan with only a single lending institution?   Results in such cases vary,[16] with appellate courts often presuming to decide the question themselves despite its factual aspects.

sons, Inc., 189 Mont. 435, 616 P.2d 356 (1980); Brack v. Brownlee, supra note 11.

See also Daybreak Const. Specialties, Inc. v. Saghatoleslami, 712 P.2d 1028 (Colo.App. 1985), in which the purchasers of an uncompleted condominium unit sought damages from the developer. The majority of the court conceded the developer's breach, but refused to award damages because the purchasers had never filed a loan application, and thus were themselves in breach. The dissent argued that applying for a loan would have been a useless act in light of the unfinished condition of the condominium, and hence that damages should be awarded.

13.   Brack v. Brownlee, supra note 11; Century 21 Acadia Realty & Development Co., Inc. v. Brough, 393 So.2d 287 (La.App.1980); Manning v. Bleifus, 166 W.Va. 131, 272 S.E.2d 821 (1980); Bushmiller v. Schiller, 35 Md.App. 1, 368 A.2d 1044 (1977); Betnar v. Rose, 259 Ark. 820, 536 S.W.2d 719 (1976); Highlands Plaza, Inc. v. Viking Investment Corp., 2 Wn. App. 192, 467 P.2d 378 (1970); Lach v. Cahill, 138 Conn. 418, 85 A.2d 481 (1951). See J. Calamari & J. Perillo, Contracts § 11–9 (1977); Restatement (Second) of Contracts § 225 Illustration 8 (1981); Aiken, "Subject to Financing" Clauses in Interim Contracts for Sale of Realty, 43 Marq.L.Rev. 265 (1960). See also Fourteen West Realty, Inc. v. Screws, 147 Ga. App. 362, 248 S.E.2d 722 (1978), distinguishing prior Georgia authority and holding that a duty of good faith arose from contract language making the transaction conditional upon buyer's "ability" to obtain the requisite financing. The duty extends to good faith in actions taken after the loan application has been made which might jeopardize it; see Bruyere v. Jade Realty Corp., 117 N.H. 564, 375 A.2d 600 (1977) (buyers divorced, causing lender to withdraw loan commitment); Schottland v. Lucas, 396 So.2d 72 (Ala.1981) (buyer attempted to frustrate his own loan application).

On financing conditions generally, see Annot., 81 A.L.R.2d 1338 (1962). See also Annot., Vendor's Action Against Vendee's Prospective Lender for Misrepresentation Respecting or Failure to Complete Loan Commitment, 30 A.L.R.4th 474 (1984).

14.   Cox v. Funk, 42 N.C.App. 32, 255 S.E.2d 600 (1979). See also Friend v. McGarry, 141 Misc.2d 479, 533 N.Y.S.2d 357 (1988) (implied covenant of good faith and fair dealing required purchaser to use good faith efforts to sell his old house even where sale contract was not explicitly conditioned on such sale, where new loan commitment required sale of the house).

15.   Farahzad v. Monometrics Corp., 119 A.D.2d 721, 501 N.Y.S.2d 136 (1986); Dawson v. Malloy, 428 So.2d 297 (Fla.App.1983), review denied 436 So.2d 99 (Fla.1983); McDaniel v. Kudlik, 598 S.W.2d 350 (Tex.Civ.App.1980).

16.   Grossman v. Melinda Lowell, P.A., 703 F.Supp. 282 (S.D.N.Y.1989) (contract required "best efforts," which means more than mere good faith; three phone calls and one written application not sufficient); Hoelscher v. Schenewerk, 804 S.W.2d 828 (Mo.App.1991) (one application insufficient, where contract clause called for three); Gast v. Miller, 44 Ohio Misc.2d 15, 541 N.E.2d 497 (1988) (one application sufficient); Stevens v. Cliffs at Princeville Associates, 67 Hawaii 236, 684 P.2d 965 (1984) (one application sufficient, where neither party knew of any other institution which would have approved the loan); Weger v. Silveria, 460 So.2d 49 (La.App.1984) (one application sufficient); Holst v. Guynn, 696 P.2d 632 (Wyo.1985) (where condition calls for VA loan, purchaser is not required to seek conventional loan after rejection by VA; purchaser's notification of lender that he had become unemployed was not an act of bad faith); Nalley v. Harris, 176 Ga.App. 553, 336 S.E.2d 822 (1985) (three oral inquiries sufficient; borrower had no duty to submit written applications); Bushmiller v. Schiller, 35 Md. App. 1, 368 A.2d 1044 (1977) (one application insufficient); Liuzza v. Panzer, 333 So.2d 689 (La.App.1976) (same); Century 21 Acadia Realty & Development, Inc. v. Brough, 393 So.2d 287 (La.App.1980) (one application sufficient.) See also Neiss v. Franze, 101 Misc.2d 871, 422 N.Y.S.2d 345 (1979) (two applications sufficient); Johnson v. Werner, 63 A.D.2d 422, 407 N.Y.S.2d 28 (1978) (sufficiency of efforts is question for trier of fact.) See Annot., 78 A.L.R.3d 880 (1977).

Clauses expressing financing conditions are often remarkably vague; it is not unusual to see "Contract subject to financing" or "Contingent on buyer obtaining loan." [17]   At the other extreme, clauses sometimes spell out the minimum amount, maximum interest rate, minimum term, type of institutional lender, type of loan (FHA, VA, privately-insured or conventional), and even set out the number of applications which must be made. [18] Vague clauses are an invitation to litigate.   If the court finds the language too indefinite, the entire contract will usually be treated as a nullity which neither party can enforce. [19]   The buyer may argue that the contract gives him or her the power to fill in the missing terms, but such a power would quite arguably make the obligation to buy illusory, and the contract would be unenforceable for that reason. [20]

Most courts, however, are quite willing to supply the missing terms in a financing condition by referring to reasonable expectations and practices in the locality.   Even clauses which include no details about the loan at all are frequently upheld. [21]   There can be no sound objection to this practice, for if the purchaser has not taken the trouble to spell out the protection in detail, it is eminently sensible for the court to give only "reasonable" protection, while to deny enforcement altogether is an unnecessary frustration of the parties' agreement.

Recent changes in the financial markets have made the drafting of a comprehensive condition-of-financing clause quite challenging.   Interest

17. See Raushenbush, Problems and Practices with Financing Conditions in Real Estate Contracts, 1963 Wis.L.Rev. 566. Suppose a lender gives a loan commitment, but later revokes it through no fault of the purchaser. Does the condition require merely that a commitment be issued, or that the loan be available at closing? See Rosen v. Empire Valve & Fitting, Inc., 381 Pa.Super. 348, 553 A.2d 1004 (1989) (holding that condition was not satisfied where commitment was revoked); Northeast Custom Homes, Inc. v. Howell, 230 N.J.Super. 296, 553 A.2d 387 (1988) (same).

18. For an exceptionally thorough clause, see Feldman v. Oman Associates, Inc., 20 Ill. App.3d 436, 314 N.E.2d 338 (1974). For an equally lengthy but very poorly drafted clause which the court held violated the New Jersey "Plain Language" Act, see Wheatly v. Myung Sook Suh, 217 N.J.Super. 233, 525 A.2d 340 (App.Div.1987).

19. The courts of Wisconsin, New York, and Maryland have been notably stringent in rejecting conditions as too indefinite. See, e.g., Imas Gruner & Associates, Limited v. Stringer, 48 Md.App. 364, 427 A.2d 1038 (1981) (contract is unenforceable unless amount, interest rate, and term are specified); Nodolf v. Nelson, 103 Wis.2d 656, 309 N.W.2d 397 (1981); Perkins v. Gosewehr, 98 Wis.2d 158, 295 N.W.2d 789 (1980) (amount of loan is insufficient description, with court mentioning numerous other factors as desirable additions); Gerruth Realty Co. v. Pire, 17 Wis.2d 89, 115 N.W.2d 557 (1962) (at a minimum, the amount of the loan must be stated); Neiss v.

Franze, 101 Misc.2d 871, 422 N.Y.S.2d 345 (1979) (amount, interest rate, and term must be specified.) See also Peterson v. Wirum, 625 P.2d 866 (Alaska 1981) (condition not limited to loan from a specific lender, despite mention of that lender in the contract clause.)

Unduly vague language is often found in conditions dealing with matters other than financing as well. See, e.g., Hitt v. Lord, 194 Ga.App. 655, 391 S.E.2d 681 (1990) (contract condition that closing was subject to rezoning, but which was silent as to whose duty it was to have the property rezoned, was too vague to enforce).

20. See Gerruth Realty Co. v. Pire, supra note 19.

21. See Gildea v. Kapenis, 402 N.W.2d 457 (Iowa App.1987) ("subject to buyer obtaining suitable financing interest rate no greater than 12¾%" was sufficient description of financing); Wiggins v. Shewmake, 374 N.W.2d 111 (S.D.1985) ("13% conventional loan" was sufficient); Manning v. Bleifus, 166 W.Va. 131, 272 S.E.2d 821 (1980); O'Halloran v. Oechslie, 402 A.2d 67 (Me.1979); Gaynes v. Allen, 116 N.H. 469, 362 A.2d 197 (1976); Smith v. Vernon, 6 Ill.App.3d 434, 286 N.E.2d 99 (1972); Restatement (Second) of Contracts § 204 (1981). The ULTA would appear to be in general agreement; ULTA § 2–202 provides that a contract does not fail for indefiniteness even though the parties have not included a term dealing with one or more aspects of the contract. But see cases cited at note 19, supra.

rates have fluctuated in an unprecedented manner. A wide array of new mortgage loan formats has become available, characterized by adjustable interest rates, graduated payment schedules, or balances indexed to inflation statistics.[22] Borrowers are also faced with a broad range of possible mortgage clauses dealing with such matters as prepayment fees, late charges, and provisions for acceleration upon future sale of the property.[23] Few printed form contracts of sale contain financing clauses which deal with all of these financing issues, and even fewer lay parties or real estate brokers are likely to insert language covering them. Good practice undoubtedly would require mention of these factors in the contract, but most courts would not insist on it as a prerequisite to judicial enforcement. Instead the cases tend to regard any reasonable mortgage terms as satisfying the condition, even if they include fairly burdensome provisions of the type mentioned above.[24]

Even if a condition is too indefinite to be enforced, the actual behavior of the parties may supply sufficient additional information to warrant enforcement. For example, if the buyer proceeds to apply for and obtain a

22. See generally G. Nelson & D. Whitman, Real Estate Finance Law § 11.4 (2d ed. 1985); Thomas, Alternative Residential Mortgages for Tomorrow, 26 Prac.Law. 55 (Sept. 1980); Hyer & Kearl, Legal Impediments to Mortgage Innovation, 6 Real Est.L.J. 211 (1978). In Zepfler v. Neandross, 497 So.2d 901 (Fla.App.1986), the financing condition called for an interest rate "not to exceed 13.5%," but did not specify whether a fixed-rate or adjustable-rate loan was intended. The buyers obtained a commitment for an adjustable rate loan at 13% with a 2.5% cap on future rate increases. The court held that this commitment did not satisfy the condition, and permitted the buyers to rescind and recover their earnest money.

23. See G. Nelson, et al., note 22, at §§ 5.21–23, 6.1–.3, 6.6.

24. The condition was silent on the particular loan provision in question, but was held to have been satisfied by a loan containing the provision, in the following cases: Gaynes v. Allen, 116 N.H. 469, 362 A.2d 197 (1976) (prepayment penalty and variable interest rate); Yasuna v. National Capital Corp., 273 Md. 617, 331 A.2d 49 (1975) (action for commission by mortgage loan broker; condominium construction loan procured, but required progress fees, 50 percent presale of units, and other "common and predictable" features of construction loans); Smith v. Vernon, 6 Ill. App.3d 434, 286 N.E.2d 99 (1972) (loan-to-value ratio lower than borrower had anticipated); Fry v. George Elkins Co., 162 Cal.App.2d 256, 327 P.2d 905 (1958) (prepayment penalty). But see Woodland Realty, Inc. v. Winzenried, 82 Wis.2d 218, 262 N.W.2d 106 (1978), noted 62 Marq.L.Rev. 123 (1978) (loan gave lender right to increase interest rate; condition, which was silent on the point, held not satisfied).

The language of the condition of financing may also impose unexpected burdens on the vendor. In Walsh v. Kelly, 49 N.Y.2d 959, 428 N.Y.S.2d 883, 406 N.E.2d 741 (1980), the sale was conditioned upon the purchaser's obtaining an FHA mortgage. The loan was obtained, but the vendor refused to pay the "discount points" charged by the lender. The court held that, in light of the wide prevalence of the charging of such points and the fact that FHA regulations prohibited payment of the charges by the buyer, the vendor had implicitly promised to pay them. Again, the better practice is to deal with the question by specific language in the contract.

Where a loan commitment is obtained, but it contains conditions that were not mentioned in the financing clause of the contract of sale, it is usually held that the commitment does not satisfy the contract. A typical example is a condition that the purchaser sell an existing house to qualify for the new mortgage loan. See, e.g., Kressel, Rothlein & Roth v. Gallagher, 155 A.D.2d 587, 547 N.Y.S.2d 653 (1989) (buyers not required to accept loan commitment conditioned on their selling their existing house); Farrell v. Janik, 225 N.J.Super. 282, 542 A.2d 59 (1988) (buyers not required to accept loan commitment conditioned on their selling their existing house at a fixed minimum price); Educational Placement Service, Inc. v. Watts, 789 S.W.2d 902 (Tenn.App.1989) (corporate buyer not required to accept loan commitment that required personal guarantee of corporation's president); Jones v. Seiwert, 164 Ill.App.3d 954, 115 Ill.Dec. 869, 518 N.E.2d 394 (1987) (loan commitment was conditioned upon repairs being made to the property; duty to make repairs held to be on vendors, so that when they failed to do so, the financing condition was unmet and purchasers were entitled to return of earnest money).

mortgage loan commitment on terms which are reasonable and satisfactory to him or her, that action should be sufficient to give the requisite content to an otherwise vague financing condition.[25]

A financing condition which is sufficiently detailed to be enforced may still produce questions of interpretation.[26] One common problem arises when the buyer cannot obtain institutional financing on qualifying terms; the seller, to avoid losing the sale, may then offer to provide the financing by taking back a purchase-money mortgage, or may attempt to arrange financing through private sources such as friends or relatives. If the buyer demurs to such an offer, the court may have to determine whether the clause contemplates only institutional financing.[27] If the terms of the private mortgage offer meet the specifications of the condition, the case should turn on whether some other legitimate objective of the condition would be frustrated by forcing the buyer to accept a non-institutional loan.[28]

25. See Highlands Plaza, Inc. v. Viking Investment Corp., 2 Wn.App. 192, 467 P.2d 378 (1970); 1 Corbin, Contracts § 101 (1960). But see Thomas v. Harris, 127 Ga.App. 361, 193 S.E.2d 260 (1972), holding that lack of mutuality may be cured by subsequent performance, but that indefiniteness cannot; Nodolf v. Nelson, 103 Wis.2d 656, 309 N.W.2d 397 (1981). An alternative approach to saving a contract with an indefinite condition is the waiver of the condition by the party it protects; see cases cited at note 30, infra.

26. Thus, a condition which does not specify the time within which the buyer must obtain financing will be construed to allow a reasonable time; see Bradford v. Alvey & Sons, 621 P.2d 1240 (Utah 1980); see § 10.9, supra. See also Clarke v. Hartley, 7 Ohio App.3d 147, 454 N.E.2d 1322 (1982) (where financing condition called for VA loan, buyers were not obliged to sell their other home, as required by VA, in order to satisfy duty of good faith in seeking loan); Meaux v. Adams, 456 So.2d 670 (La.App.1984) (purchaser is not required to notify vendor immediately that loan application has been rejected, absent contract clause so requiring).

27. These cases often depend on the precise language of the condition. Cases holding that the condition contemplated only institutional financing, and that the purchaser had no duty to proceed with vendor financing, include Gardner v. Padro, 164 Ill.App.3d 449, 115 Ill.Dec. 445, 517 N.E.2d 1131 (1987); Macho Assets, Inc. v. Spring Corp., 128 A.D.2d 680, 513 N.Y.S.2d 180 (1987), appeal denied 69 N.Y.2d 609, 516 N.Y.S.2d 1025, 509 N.E.2d 360 (1987); Biersbach v. Landin, Ltd., 454 So.2d 779 (Fla.App.1984); Woods v. Austin, 347 So.2d 897 (La.App.1977); Glassman v. Gerstein, 10 A.D.2d 875, 200 N.Y.S.2d 690 (1960); Marino v. Nolan, 24 A.D.2d 1005, 266 N.Y.S.2d 65 (1965), affirmed mem. 18 N.Y.2d 627, 272 N.Y.S.2d 776, 219 N.E.2d 291 (1966); Makris v. Nolan, 115 N.H. 135, 335 A.2d 655 (1975); Merritt v. Davis, 265 So.2d 69 (Fla.

App.1972). Cf. Kovarik v. Vesely, 3 Wis.2d 573, 89 N.W.2d 279 (1958) (specific bank mentioned in the condition, but held not to be a material factor; vendor's offered financing held to satisfy the condition). See also Peterson v. Wirum, 625 P.2d 866 (Alaska 1981). Restatement (Second) of Contracts § 226 Illustration 6 (1981) indicates that where the condition mentions a specific lender, it is not satisfied by an offer of an equivalent loan from the vendor. See Harrington v. Norris B. Strickland & Associates, Inc., 161 Ga.App. 518, 289 S.E.2d 17 (1982); Smalley v. Layne, 428 So.2d 298 (Fla.App.1983).

28. In the *Merritt* and *Marino* cases, supra note 27, the courts emphasized the advantage to the purchaser of obtaining the results of the institutional lender's appraisal as a check on whether the property was overpriced—an advantage which would be lost if the buyer were forced to accept purchase-money mortgage financing from the vendor. If there is evidence that this was an important objective of the buyer, the courts are justified in letting the buyer reject non-institutional financing.

A carefully structured condition of financing can provide the buyer a very effective hedge against overpricing. Suppose it is well known that lenders in the community will not make uninsured conventional loans in excess of 80% of the property's appraised value. If the condition requires a conventional institutional loan of 80% of the contract price, an underappraisal by the institution will result in failure of the condition and will give the buyer the right to escape the entire transaction. A similar technique can be used with FHA or VA loans. The court upheld the purchaser's right to rescind and recover his earnest money on similar facts in Thaly v. Namer, 496 So.2d 1211 (La.App.1986). Of course, a more direct approach for the purchaser is simply to condition the obligation to buy on the property's appraising for at least the contract price; see, e.g., Connor v. Cal–Az Properties, Inc., 137 Ariz. 53, 668 P.2d 896 (App.1983), upholding such a condition.

If it becomes difficult or impossible to fulfill a condition, a contracting party may purport to waive the condition and seek enforcement of the contract despite its failure. If the condition was inserted for the sole benefit of the waiving party, the waiver will be effective. However, if the condition was intended to benefit the other party, or both of them, enforcement will be denied.[29] The difficulty arises in deciding for whose benefit the condition was inserted. Financing conditions are nearly always viewed as benefiting only the buyer, so that he or she can waive them unilaterally.[30] This seems

29. See generally 3A Corbin, Contracts § 752ff (1960). Cases holding such waivers effective include Harper v. Gibson, 284 S.C. 274, 325 S.E.2d 586 (1985); Bossi v. Whalen, 19 Mass.App.Ct. 966, 473 N.E.2d 1167 (1985); Defreitas v. Holley, 93 A.D.2d 852, 461 N.Y.S.2d 351 (1983) (condition relating to termite infestation was exclusively for buyer's protection, and could be waived by buyer); Jay Vee Realty Corp. v. Jaymar Acres, Inc., 436 So.2d 1053 (Fla.App.1983) (condition that government agency issue plat approval could be waived by buyer). Contrary cases, finding the condition for mutual benefit and denying a party a unilateral right of waiver, include Oak Bee Corp. v. N.E. Blankman & Co., Inc., 551 N.Y.S.2d 559 (1990), appeal denied 76 N.Y.2d 713, 563 N.Y.S.2d 769, 565 N.E.2d 518 (1990); Poquott Dev. Corp. v. Johnson, 104 A.D.2d 442, 478 N.Y.S.2d 960 (1984) (conditions relating to subdivision of land sold were for benefit of both parties, where vendor was to retain some of the resulting lots); CHG International, Inc. v. Robin Lee, Inc., 35 Wn. App. 512, 667 P.2d 1127 (1983) (time of essence clause was for benefit of both parties; could not be unilaterally waived). Note that a party who renders performance that was conditioned upon some event, without waiting for that event to have occurred, may be held to have waived the condition; see, e.g., Field v. Perry, 564 So.2d 504 (Fla.App.1990), review denied 576 So.2d 290 (Fla.1991).

A similar but less common occurrence is the elimination of a condition by estoppel. As Professor Corbin points out, the distinction between waiver and estoppel is that only the waiving party's action is necessary to a waiver, while an estoppel involves the detrimental reliance of the other party on the first's representations. See, e.g., Gorzelsky v. Leckey, 402 Pa.Super. 246, 586 A.2d 952 (1991), appeal denied 528 Pa. 630, 598 A.2d 284 (1991) (where vendor was tardy in submitting subdivision plan to local government for approval, vendor cannot rely on lack of timely approval to discharge his duty to perform the contract); Dziadiw v. 352 State Street Corp., 107 A.D.2d 1003, 484 N.Y.S.2d 727 (1985) (where purchaser has, by his own action, prevented fulfillment of financing condition, he cannot rely on it as defense to specific performance); Alliance Financial Services, Inc. v. Cummings, 526 So.2d 324 (La.App.1988) (same); In re Sombrero Reef Club, Inc., 15 B.R. 177 (Bkrtcy.

S.D.Fla.1981) (buyer estopped to rely on unfulfilled financing condition where he made false statements that he had obtained the necessary financing and seller, delaying in reliance on these statements, lost opportunity to make other sales of the property.)

30. Xhelili v. Larstanna, 150 A.D.2d 560, 541 N.Y.S.2d 132 (1989); Friedman v. Chopra, 220 N.J.Super. 546, 533 A.2d 48 (1987), cert. denied 110 N.J. 164, 540 A.2d 165 (1988) (purchaser is free to accept a mortgage loan for a lower amount than specified in condition clause); Koets, Inc. v. Benveniste, 169 Ga.App. 352, 312 S.E.2d 846 (1983), affirmed 252 Ga. 520, 314 S.E.2d 912 (1984); McDermott v. Burpo, 663 S.W.2d 256 (Mo.App.1983); Blue Lakes Apartments, Ltd. v. George Gowing, Inc., 464 So.2d 705 (Fla.App.1985) (purchaser is free to obtain alternate financing from a lender other than the one recommended by the seller, or to buy for cash); Appollo v. Reynolds, 364 N.W.2d 422 (Minn.App.1985) (condition that FHA discount points not exceed five was for vendors' protection, and was waived by their continued insistence that purchasers complete the contract); Lieberman v. Pettinato, 126 Misc.2d 215, 481 N.Y.S.2d 608 (1984), affirmed 120 A.D.2d 646, 502 N.Y.S.2d 242 (1986) (financing condition was for buyer's benefit and could be waived by him, but provision requiring notice to sellers was for their benefit, permitting them to cancel contract where timely notice of buyer's intention to waive financing was not given to them); Loda v. H.K. Sargeant & Associates, Inc., 188 Conn. 69, 448 A.2d 812 (1982); Renouf v. Martini, 577 S.W.2d 803 (Tex.Civ.App.1979); Lipscomb v. Chadbourne, 378 So.2d 147 (La.App.1979); Koedding v. Slaughter, 481 F.Supp. 1233 (E.D.Mo.1979), affirmed 634 F.2d 1095 (8th Cir.). But see Dale Mortg. Bankers Corp. v. 877 Stewart Avenue Associates, 133 A.D.2d 65, 518 N.Y.S.2d 411 (1987), appeal denied 70 N.Y.2d 612, 523 N.Y.S.2d 496, 518 N.E.2d 7 (1987) (contract stated that either party could cancel if financing was not obtained; thus, condition benefitted both parties); Hanson v. Moeller, 376 N.W.2d 220 (Minn.App.1985) (financing condition was for benefit of both parties, and could not be waived by purchaser).

If the contract provides that failure of the condition makes the contract "null and void", a court may hold that it cannot be waived; see

generally correct, although an exception should be recognized where the seller is also taking back a subordinated purchase-money mortgage and is therefore vitally concerned that the buyer deal with a reputable primary lender on terms which will not endanger the buyer's ability to pay the debt.[31]

With other types of conditions, it is not always easy to identify the beneficiary. Where the condition is based on approvals of rezonings, building permits, sewer connections, or the like by a local government agency, and where the obvious purpose is to protect the buyer's right to construct certain improvements on the land, unilateral waiver by the buyer is usually allowed.[32] Here again, however, the seller may have an interest in fulfillment of the condition if he or she is taking back a secured purchase-money obligation, since the land's value as security may well be dependent on issuance of the approvals.[33] One may imagine other equally compelling arguments for the seller;[34] it is simply a question of fact whether he or she

Ormond Realty v. Ninnis, 341 Pa.Super. 101, 491 A.2d 169 (1985); Keller v. Reich, 646 S.W.2d 141 (Mo.App.1983) (where condition required that title defects be cured within 60 days or contract would be "null and void," buyers had power to waive the condition, but only by giving notice to vendors within the 60-day period; upon their failure to do so, they could not later obtain specific performance); Berger v. McBride & Son Builders, Inc., 447 S.W.2d 18 (Mo.App.1969); Davies, Some Thoughts on the Drafting of Conditions in Contracts for the Sale of Land, 15 Alberta L.Rev. 422 (1977); cf. McCain v. Cox, 531 F.Supp. 771 (N.D.Miss.1982), affirmed 692 F.2d 755 (5th Cir.1982) ("null and void" means voidable at the election of the non-defaulting party). If the clause is too indefinite to be enforced, see notes 17–20 supra and accompanying text, it is strongly arguable that the purchaser can solve the problem by waiving the clause; see Cook v. Eilers, 586 S.W.2d 42 (Mo.App.1979); Krause v. Holand, 33 Wis.2d 211, 147 N.W.2d 333 (1967).

31. See Fleischer v. McCarver, 691 S.W.2d 930 (Mo.App.1985), in which the vendors were taking a note and deed of trust on other property as part of the purchase price. They objected to the primary institutional financing obtained by the purchaser on the ground that its interest rate was higher than provided in the financing clause of the contract, and it required the purchaser to maintain a large deposit in the lender's bank. Both of these features, in the vendors' view, made their position more risky. The court held the financing condition was for their benefit as well as the purchasers, and refused to permit the purchasers to waive it unilaterally. But see Highlands Plaza, Inc. v. Viking Investment Corp., 2 Wn.App. 192, 467 P.2d 378 (1970).

32. W.W.W. Associates, Inc. v. Giancontieri, 152 A.D.2d 333, 548 N.Y.S.2d 580 (1989) (termination of certain litigation involving vendors); Berryhill v. Hatt, 428 N.W.2d 647 (Iowa 1988) (availability of adjacent property

to purchaser); Regional Gravel Products, Inc. v. Stanton, 135 A.D.2d 1079, 524 N.Y.S.2d 114 (1987), appeal dismissed 71 N.Y.2d 949, 528 N.Y.2d 827, 524 N.E.2d 147 (1988) (land use approvals); Schreiber v. Karpow, 290 Or. 817, 626 P.2d 891 (1981) (septic tank and building permits); Prestige House, Inc. v. Merrill, 51 Or.App. 67, 624 P.2d 188 (1981) (building permits); Eliason v. Watts, 615 P.2d 427 (Utah 1980) (septic tank permit; held not to benefit seller although he owned nearby land); Turk v. D. Katz & Sons, Inc., 254 Pa.Super. 177, 385 A.2d 583 (1978) (rezoning); Godfrey Co. v. Crawford, 23 Wis.2d 44, 126 N.W.2d 495 (1964) (rezoning); Richardson v. Snipes, 46 Tenn. App. 494, 330 S.W.2d 381 (1959) (rezoning). Cf. Epstein Hebrew Academy v. Wondell, 327 S.W.2d 926 (Mo.1959), involving an option to buy land which contained a condition of rezoning. The court found that the condition could not have been inserted for the buyer's protection, since if the buyer were dissatisfied with the zoning (or anything else) it could merely decline to exercise the option. Hence, it concluded that the condition must have been for the vendor's benefit—without explaining why the vendor would be concerned about rezoning—and refused to let the purchaser waive the condition.

On rezoning conditions generally, see Annot., 76 A.L.R.2d 1195 (1961).

33. Cf. Prestige House, Inc. v. Merrill, supra note 32, in which the vendor was providing financing for the sale, but never indicated that it was concerned about the issuance of the building permits from a security viewpoint. The argument in the text was considered but rejected in Major v. Price, 196 Va. 526, 84 S.E.2d 445 (1954).

34. For example, the rezoning of the land being sold might enhance the value of nearby land retained by the vendor. See LaGrave v. Jones, 336 So.2d 1330 (Ala.1976), accepting a similar argument in principle but rejecting it on the facts for lack of convincing evidence.

has a genuine interest in the realization of the condition.[35]

§ 10.12 Title Quality

A title is not a piece of paper; rather, it is an abstract concept which represents the legal system's conclusions as to how the interests in a parcel of realty are arranged and who owns them. As we have already seen, interests in land can be divided along numerous dimensions, including both time and space,[1] and among numerous persons.[2] Nearly all of these interests are capable of being transferred individually, but in most real estate sales the buyer intends to get them all—that is, he or she wants a possessory fee simple absolute.

A lay person might suppose that whether this is the sort of title contracted for, and whether the vendor can in fact convey it in conformity to the contract, are rather simple questions; after all, the vendor either does or does not own the land. Unfortunately, the American system of proof of title does not lend itself well to such straightforward thinking. The principal reason is that there is generally no mechanism for discovering with absolute certitude the state of the title to land.[3] The recording system, contrary to popular conception, does not provide a title searcher with a statement as to who has the title; rather, it serves merely as a depository or library for copies of documents which have been recorded by parties to prior transactions affecting the land.[4] The searcher is invited to sift through these papers and decide the condition of the title by reconstructing its history. There is no guarantee that all relevant instruments are present, that those which are present are authentic and valid, or that the title is free of claims based on such doctrines as adverse possession which give rise to no documentation at all.[5]

But even if one sets aside these deficiencies of the recording system, one rarely finds perfect titles in the records. All too commonly prior conveyances, especially those from many decades ago, are marred by inconsistent and confusing legal descriptions, missing signatures, erratic spellings of names, absent notarial acknowledgements, and the like. One encounters unsatisfied mortgages made so long ago that they are probably (but not certainly) barred by the statute of limitations; grants of easements whose location on the land is given only in vague or general terms; and spouses who probably had marital rights which they did not relinquish when the property was sold. The list of possible defects is much longer than we have suggested here, but the point should be clear: without a knowledge of extrinsic facts now lost and unrecoverable, a searcher can often make only an educated guess about the condition of title. Title is a matter of judgment, and a searcher's judgment is seldom uncontrovertible.

---

35. Hing Bo Gum v. Nakamura, 57 Hawaii 39, 549 P.2d 471 (1976).

§ 10.12

1. See Ch. 3, supra.

2. See Ch. 5, supra.

3. The exception is the "Torrens" or title registration system, available in eleven states but little used in most of them. Even in this system there are serious inadequacies in the averment made to the public; see § 11.15, infra.

4. The recording system is discussed in § 11.9–11.11, infra.

5. These deficiencies of the recording system are discussed at § 11.9, infra at notes 21–48.

For these reasons the concept of marketability of title has developed. In a sense, marketability is defined circularly: a marketable title is one which a court will force upon an unwilling contract purchaser.[6] But more broadly, the concept reflects a compromise with the view that buyers want, and sellers should convey, perfect titles. Since perfect titles are rare and hard to identify, the law instead holds the vendor to a lesser standard. It infers in every realty sale contract, unless a contrary intent appears, a covenant that the title transferred will be free of all reasonable risks of attack—in other words, that it will be marketable.[7] The key is reasonableness. The title need not be perfect, but if it is sufficiently doubtful or risky that a reasonable buyer (or a buyer's reasonable counsel) would object to it, the vendor has not fulfilled his or her contractual duty.[8] In a sense, it is the reasonable reaction of the marketplace for land which decides the question.

Both a covenant and a condition are involved here. The law reads into the contract a promise by the vendor to convey marketable title. The concept of marketable title is similar to that of substantial performance,[9]

---

6. See, e.g., Lake Forest, Inc. v. Bon Marche Homes, Inc., 410 So.2d 362 (La.App. 1982). The statement in the text, while suggesting that equity will not order a purchaser to perform a contract and take an unmarketable title, should not be taken to imply that a different standard applies at law; in fact, the standard at law and in equity are identical.

The marketable title concept may even have criminal law consequences. See Fraidin v. State, 85 Md.App. 231, 583 A.2d 1065 (1991), cert. denied 322 Md. 614, 589 A.2d 57 (1991), in which a foreclosure trustee was convicted of theft by deception. He had conducted a sale at which he stated the land's title was clear, when he knew that it was encumbered by a mortgage, and had subsequently attempted to conceal the mortgage for three months thereafter.

7. See generally 3 Am.L.Prop. § 11.47 (1952); 6A Powell, Real Property ¶ 925[2] (1981); ULTA § 2–304(b)(1); Annot., Marketable Title, 57 A.L.R. 1253 (1928). The concept originated in England in Marlow v. Smith, 2 P.Will. 198 (1723). Prior to that time, a purchaser could escape the contract only by proving that the title was in fact defective. This is clearly no longer the case; see, e.g., Stover v. Whiting, 157 Mich.App. 462, 403 N.W.2d 575 (1987) (" * * * it is not necessary that the title actually be bad in order to render it unmarketable"). See also Stapylton v. Scott, 16 Vesey 272 (Ch.1809); O. Browder, R. Cunningham, J. Julin & A. Smith, Basic Property Law 1047 (1979).

8. Hundreds of cases state this test of reasonableness in similar terms. See, e.g., Regan v. Lanze, 40 N.Y.2d 475, 481–482, 387 N.Y.S.2d 79, 83, 354 N.E.2d 818, 822 (1976):

"A marketable title * * * is one which can be readily sold or mortgaged to a person of reasonable prudence, the test of the marketability of a title being whether there is

an objection thereto such as would interfere with a sale or with the market value of the property. The law assures to a buyer a title free from reasonable doubt, but not from every doubt, and the mere possibility or suspicion of a defect, which according to ordinary experience has no probable basis, does not demonstrate an unmarketable title. If 'the only defect in the title' is 'a very remote and improbable contingency,' a 'slender possibility only,' a conveyance will be decreed."

See also Sanders v. Coastal Capital Ventures, Inc., 296 S.C. 132, 370 S.E.2d 903 (1988), cert. denied 298 S.C. 204, 379 S.E.2d 133 (1989); Vazquez v. Davis, 466 So.2d 671 (La.App.1985), writ denied 468 So.2d 574 (La.1985) ("readily sold or mortgaged in the ordinary course of business by reasonable persons familiar with the facts and questions involved"); Liberty Lake Sewer Dist. v. Liberty Lake Utilities Co., 37 Wn.App. 809, 683 P.2d 1117 (1984) ("It need not be perfect in the sense it is free of every conceivable technical criticism, but only from those possibilities of a defect which would give rise to a reasonable question of its validity"); In re Garfinkle, 672 F.2d 1340 (11th Cir.1982); Brown v. Kelly & Picerne, Inc., 518 F.Supp. 730 (D.Mass.1981), affirmed 676 F.2d 682 (1st Cir.1982); Darby v. Keeran, 211 Kan. 133, 505 P.2d 710 (1973); Ehlers, What Constitutes Marketable Title in Oregon, 33 Ore.L.Rev. 77 (1953).

See United States v. Mansion House Center, North Redevelopment Co., 607 F.Supp. 392 (E.D.Mo.1985) (where contract requires title to be marketable "in the opinion of" a party, that party's decision as to marketability need not be legally correct but must be made in good faith).

9. See ULTA § 2–301 Comment 3.

and a failure to tender marketable title is thus deemed a material breach; this breach, in turn, constitutes the nonoccurrence of a constructive condition.[10] Hence, the buyer is both discharged from further performance and given remedies for breach, including specific performance with abatement,[11] rescission and restitution,[12] reimbursement for out-of-pocket expenses, and possibly loss-of-bargain damages. This last remedy is subject to the limitation of Flureau v. Thornhill, discussed earlier.[13]

All of this assumes that the contract itself either makes no mention of the quality of title or merely repeats the general legal mandate that the title must be marketable. In their agreement the parties are free to vary this standard by express language, and may make it either more or less rigorous.[14] They might, for example, provide that the vendor will convey "whatever title I have, but with no promise that I have any;" or on the other hand, "I promise to convey a perfect title, subject to no risks or objections whatever." This sort of phraseology is not very common, but would probably be construed at face value by the courts. Less forceful statements, however, are often construed as not departing from marketability at all.[15] It

10. See § 10.10, supra, at notes 1–2. A contract may, however, be construed to excuse performance by both parties without further liability if the vendor is unable to perfect title. See, e.g., CHG International, Inc. v. Robin Lee, Inc., 35 Wn.App. 512, 667 P.2d 1127 (1983), in which the parties understood when the contract was signed that the vendor's title was imperfect. When the vendor was unable to acquire the outstanding interest by the closing date (time being essential), both parties were discharged and the purchaser could not later waive the time provision and obtain specific performance.

11. See, e.g., Satterly v. Plaisted, 52 A.D.2d 1074, 384 N.Y.S.2d 334 (1976), affirmed 42 N.Y.2d 933, 397 N.Y.S.2d 1008, 366 N.E.2d 1362 (1977); Lawton v. Byck, 217 Ga. 676, 124 S.E.2d 369 (1962); 6A Powell, Real Property ¶ 925 (1981), at notes 47–48; cf. Barnes v. Sind, 341 F.2d 676 (4th Cir.1965), rehearing denied 347 F.2d 324 (1965), certiorari denied 382 U.S. 891, 86 S.Ct. 183, 15 L.Ed.2d 149 (1965) (no abatement allowed under Maryland law.) See generally Note, 24 Okla.L.Rev. 495 (1971).

12. This is doubtless the most common remedy sought. See, e.g., In re Cantin, 114 B.R. 339 (Bkrtcy.D.Mass.1990); Regency Highland Associates v. Sherwood, 388 So.2d 271 (Fla.App.1980), review denied 397 So.2d 778 (Fla.1981); § 10.7, supra. But see Man Ngok Tam v. Hoi Hong K. Luk, 154 Wis.2d 282, 453 N.W.2d 158 (App.1990), review denied 454 N.W.2d 806 (1990), refusing to grant rescission where the vendor breached the covenant of marketable title by conveying subject to a mortgage, but then discharged the mortgage before the purchaser was harmed by it.

13. See § 10.3, supra, at notes 11–19. In general, the condition that title must be marketable is viewed as protecting only the pur-

chaser, and the vendor cannot use his or her lack of title as a discharge of his own duties. But if the contract provides that it shall become "null and void" or "terminate" if title is unmarketable, the vendor may well assert the clause to avoid liability in a purchaser's action for damages or specific performance with abatement. To do so, however, the vendor will probably be required to show good faith. See Wolofsky v. Waldron, 526 So.2d 945 (Fla. App.1988); Trabucco v. Nelson, 8 Mass.App. Ct. 641, 396 N.E.2d 466 (1979) (vendor in good faith; specific performance denied). Cf. Space Center, Inc. v. 451 Corp., 298 N.W.2d 443 (Minn.1980) (failure to cure title defect was vendor's fault, so vendor may not rely on "null and void" language.) See generally Annot., 13 A.L.R.4th 927 (1982).

14. Alcan Aluminum Corp. v. Carlsberg Financial Corp., 689 F.2d 815 (9th Cir.1982); Ayers v. Hodges, 517 S.W.2d 589 (Tex.Civ.App. 1974).

15. See, e.g., Shannon v. Mathers, 271 Or. 148, 531 P.2d 705 (1975) (contract made obligation to buy conditional upon purchasers' approval of title report; held, they can reject title only if it is unmarketable); Bull v. Weisbrod, 185 Iowa 318, 170 N.W. 536 (1919) (vendor agreed to sell all his right, title, and interest, but to convey by warranty deed; held, title must be marketable). On the other hand, such seemingly strong language as "good title" or even "indisputable title" is commonly held to require only a marketable title; see 3 Am.L.Prop. § 11.47 notes 7–10 (1952); ULTA § 2–304(c). But some courts may too readily find language disclaiming marketability of title; see Mid–State Homes v. Moore, 515 So.2d 716 (Ala.Civ.App.1987) (contract stated, "Sellers covenant to convey to the Buyers all rights, title and interest of the Seller;" held, title need not be marketable).

is almost as if the marketability standard is a magnet, drawing the courts toward it unless the parties make their contrary wishes exceptionally clear.

In modern cases the most frequent contractual variant of marketable title is "insurable title": a title which a "reputable title company would approve and insure," or the like.[16] Such language usually imposes a more lenient standard than marketable title, since title insurers are often willing to disregard minor or remote defects which might nonetheless make a title technically unmarketable.[17] As a consequence of careless drafting, it is often debatable whether the parties intended to substitute insurability for marketability as a standard, or whether they intended to require that the vendor meet both standards; the latter is the preferred construction unless the language plainly adopts insurability as the sole test.[18] Another problem with the insurability standard arises because of the fact that title insurance policies always contain printed lists of "general exceptions"—matters which the company does not insure against, and for which it may not even search. Policies and companies vary, and some employ much broader lists of general exceptions or exclusions than others.[19] Suppose a particular title defect is within the standard exceptions used by some but not all local title companies in some but not all types of policies; does the title comply with the contract or not?[20] Careful drafting is essential to avoid this sort of dispute.

---

16. The language is taken from Laba v. Carey, 29 N.Y.2d 302, 327 N.Y.S.2d 613, 277 N.E.2d 641 (1971). Note that the title policy itself may (or may not) insure that the title is marketable; see Annot., Defects Affecting Marketability of Title Within Meaning of Title Insurance Policy, 18 A.L.R.4th 1311 (1982).

17. See, e.g., Kipahulu Investment Co. v. Seltzer Partnership, 4 Hawaii App. 625, 675 P.2d 778 (1983), cert. denied 67 Hawaii 685, 744 P.2d 781 (1984) (contract called for both marketable and insurable title; actual title satisfied the title insurer, but was still unmarketable). Holmby, Inc. v. Dino, 98 Nev. 358, 647 P.2d 392 (1982). On the operations of title insurers generally, see § 11.14, infra.

18. Hudson–Port Ewen Associates, L.P. v. Kuo, 165 A.D.2d 301, 566 N.Y.S.2d 774 (1991), affirmed 78 N.Y.2d 944, 573 N.Y.S.2d 637, 578 N.E.2d 435 (1991) (where contract provided title would be insurable and also in fee simple free of encumbrances, purchaser was entitled to insist that both standards be satisfied); Brown v. Yacht Club of Coeur D'Alene, Ltd., 111 Idaho 195, 722 P.2d 1062 (App.1986) (contract required title to be both marketable and insurable; these standards are distinct and both must be met); Regency Highland Associates v. Sherwood, 388 So.2d 271 (Fla.App. 1980), review denied 397 So.2d 778 (Fla.1981); Kopp v. Barnes, 10 A.D.2d 532, 204 N.Y.S.2d 860 (1960); New York Investors, Inc. v. Manhattan Beach Bathing Parks Corp., 229 App. Div. 593, 243 N.Y.S. 548 (1930), affirmed 256 N.Y. 162, 176 N.E. 6 (1931), reargument denied 256 N.Y. 640, 177 N.E. 174 (1931); La Course v. Kiesel, 366 Pa. 385, 77 A.2d 877 (1951); Hebb v. Severson, 32 Wn.2d 159, 201

P.2d 156 (1948); cf. Creative Living, Inc. v. Steinhauser, 78 Misc.2d 29, 355 N.Y.S.2d 897 (1974), affirmed without opinion 47 A.D.2d 598, 365 N.Y.S.2d 987 (1975), appeal denied 36 N.Y.2d 643, 368 N.Y.S.2d 1026, 329 N.E.2d 677 (1975) (insurer is sole judge of title's acceptability). See S. Goldberg, Sales of Real Property 420 (1971); Comment, Title Insurance and Marketable Title, 31 Ford.L.Rev. 559 (1963).

19. See § 11.14, infra, at notes 17–20. Among the common exclusions are claims in eminent domain and matters of governmental regulation. Some policies have much longer lists, including rights of parties in possession, encroachments, unrecorded easements and liens, and reserved rights under federal or state patents. See G. Nelson & D. Whitman, Real Estate Transfer, Finance, and Development (4th ed. 1992) at ch. 2, for reproductions of illustrative policies.

20. See Laba v. Carey, 29 N.Y.2d 302, 327 N.Y.S.2d 613, 277 N.E.2d 641 (1971): " * * * the title company's approval must be unequivocal unless the exceptions are those contemplated by the contract." Other contract language in that case provided that title would be subject to existing restrictive covenants, so the court held that the title was insurable notwithstanding exceptions in the insurance policy for such covenants. See also Kopp v. Barnes, 10 A.D.2d 532, 204 N.Y.S.2d 860 (1960). In many cases, however, there is no such explicit contract language to guide interpretation of the insurability clause. Yet without some guidance, the insurability clause can become a nullity; one court observed that virtually any title could be considered insur-

A purchaser cannot object to the taking of a title which is subject only to defects mentioned and agreed to in the contract itself. Hence, if the parties are familiar with the title, or if a current title report or abstract is at hand, they can list the specific encumbrances which are acceptable to the buyer; this is an excellent practice. However, printed form contracts often contain broad clauses, such as "title will be subject to easements and restrictions of record." The buyer may have no idea at the time the contract is signed what easements or restrictions exist, and may be surprised and disappointed when a subsequent search discloses very burdensome or inconvenient matters, but the clause will probably be upheld.[21] Obviously purchasers should avoid general contract clauses of this kind. They are, fortunately, typically construed quite narrowly against the vendor; for example, "subject to restrictions" generally does not require the buyer to take the property if there are existing *violations* of restrictive covenants.[22]

Another factor which might be thought to vary the standard of title quality is the type of deed to be used for conveyance, a matter usually dealt with in the contract itself. Deeds generally may contain extensive covenants of title (a "full warranty" deed), more limited covenants (a "special warranty" deed), or no covenants at all (a "quitclaim deed".) There is no intrinsic link between the deed and the quality of the title it passes; a quitclaim deed can convey a perfect title, while a warranty deed may transmit a title which is severely defective. The distinction lies only in the nature of the seller's liability under the deed if defects exist.[23] Yet because quitclaim deeds are commonly used where the seller's title is doubtful, one might argue that a contract calling for a quitclaim deed should not be construed to promise marketable title. The New York Court of Appeals, however, reached a contrary result in Wallach v. Riverside Bank,[24] holding that the type of deed called for was irrelevant so long as the contract contemplated sale of the land itself rather than merely some limited interest

---

able if the company added enough exceptions or the insured were willing to pay a high enough premium; see Hebb v. Severson, supra note 18. See generally S. Goldberg, Sales of Real Property 420 (1971).

Guidance in construing the insurability clause may be derived from other sources. In Van Arsdale v. Dimil Land Co., 325 So.2d 471 (Fla.App.1975), title was to be insurable "in the usual form." A statute reserved three-fourths of the oil and gas deposits under the land (and most other undeveloped land in the state). The title company's listing of this reservation as an exception to its policy coverage was held not to make the title uninsurable. Cf. Presidential Gardens/Duke Street Ltd. Partnership v. Salisbury Slye, Ltd., 802 F.2d 106 (4th Cir.1986) (where prior adverse deed was a legal nullity, title was insurable despite title company's insistence on showing the deed as a exception to coverage of the policy).

21. See McCain v. Cox, 531 F.Supp. 771 (N.D.Miss.1982), affirmed 692 F.2d 755 (5th Cir.1982); Kirkwall Corp. v. Sessa, 48 N.Y.2d 709, 422 N.Y.S.2d 368, 397 N.E.2d 1172 (1979).

22. See Lohmeyer v. Bower, 170 Kan. 442, 227 P.2d 102 (1951); Hebb v. Severson, supra note 18. But see Camp v. Commonwealth Land Title Ins. Co., 787 F.2d 1258 (8th Cir. 1986) (breach in existing restrictive covenant is not a title defect; title is marketable).

23. See § 11.13, infra, for a discussion of deed warranties.

24. 206 N.Y. 434, 100 N.E. 50 (1912). See also Hirlinger v. Hirlinger, 267 S.W.2d 46 (Mo.App.1954) (contract called for executor's deed which contained no warranties, but title must still be marketable.) Similarly, a contract clause calling for marketable title does not require the vendor to convey by warranty deed; see Department of Public Works and Buildings v. Halls, 35 Ill.2d 283, 220 N.E.2d 167 (1966); Tymon v. Linoki, 16 N.Y.2d 293, 266 N.Y.S.2d 357, 213 N.E.2d 661 (1965); Boekelheide v. Snyder, 71 S.D. 470, 26 N.W.2d 74 (1947). But see ULTA § 2–304(b)(2), re-

in it. This is the view of the Uniform Land Transactions Act [25] and would probably be followed by most courts today.[26]

What sorts of defects can make a title unmarketable? The list is long, with manifold variations. It can conveniently be divided into three types of imperfections: (1) those attributable to some flaw in the vendor's chain of ownership, so that vendor might never have had fee title at all; (2) those resulting from encumbrances—rights of others in the land, even though they do not negate the vendor's fee title; and (3) events which have deprived the vendor of title, such as the adverse possession of another or governmental action in eminent domain.[27] We will not attempt here to list and provide authority for every possible kind of defect which renders title unmarketable; the cases tend to turn on factual variations which raise few questions of theoretical importance, and rather complete lists are found in other works.[28] But the next few paragraphs will illustrate some of the more controversial issues of marketable title.

Chain of title problems which can affect marketability include conveyances known by the purchaser to be forged, undelivered, procured by fraud or duress, or executed by a minor. A title traced through a judicial or other legal proceeding is unmarketable if it was conducted without jurisdiction or without compliance with statute. A fiduciary's deed will not convey a marketable title if he or she acted beyond authority or in violation of duty. Perhaps the most interesting chain of title issue is raised by the vendor who claims title by adverse possession. If the contract requires a title "of record," adverse possession alone obviously fails to qualify,[29] but if it does not the courts have difficulty deciding whether the title is marketable. Such a title may be perfectly good, of course, but its validity depends on the existence of extrinsic facts: Was the possession open and notorious, continuous, hostile, and so on?[30] Unless the vendor or a predecessor in title has already established these issues in litigation with the record owner, they might be raised in a later action brought against the purchaser. Such a risk of litigation might well be thought unreasonably burdensome, and hence deemed to make the vendor's title unmarketable. The question is likely to turn on the court's assessment of the practical probability that an attack will

---

quiring the vendor to convey by warranty deed unless the contract provides otherwise.

25. ULTA § 2–304(d). However, if the contract provides for a quitclaim deed, the buyer is limited to a restitutionary remedy in the event title is unmarketable, and may not get loss-of-bargain damages or (presumably) specific performance with abatement.

26. The buyer may, of course, agree to convey less than a marketable title if the contract makes this intention clear; see ULTA § 2–304(d); text at note 14, supra.

27. A similar taxonomy was followed by R.G. Patton in 3 Am.L.Prop. § 11.49 (1952).

28. Lengthy citations can be found in 3 Am.L.Prop. § 11.49 (1952); 6A Powell, Real Property ¶ 925(2) (1980); M. Friedman, Contracts and Conveyances of Real Property, ch. 4 (1975); S. Goldberg, Sales of Real Property 355–69 (1971).

29. Babo v. Bookbinder Financial Corp., 27 Ariz.App. 73, 551 P.2d 63 (1976) (dictum). The reason is that the adverse possessor has no document to record. An exception exists in a few states which by statute permit one who has acquired title by adverse possession, and has then relinquished possession, to file for record a sworn statement of the claim. See, e.g., 68 Penn.Stat. §§ 81–88. A similar result follows where the contract requires the vendor to show marketable title by an abstract, since there will usually be no document in the abstract reflecting the adverse possession. See Tri–State Hotel Co. v. Sphinx Investment Co., Inc., 212 Kan. 234, 510 P.2d 1223 (1973); Hillebrenner v. Odom, 237 Ark. 720, 375 S.W.2d 664 (1964). See Annot., 46 A.L.R.2d 544 (1956).

30. The elements of adverse possession are discussed at § 11.7, infra.

be made or will succeed, and unless that risk is very low,[31] the title is unmarketable until the vendor establishes the necessary facts in a forum that will bind the record owner.[32]

A broader question is whether the title must be fully deducible from the public records to be marketable, assuming that the contract itself is silent on the point.[33] The cases are fairly evenly divided, but perhaps the majority have not required that every link in the chain be of record; missing transfers can, for example, be explained by affidavits or other evidence, provided that the result is not to impose unreasonable risks on the purchaser.[34]

Even if a vendor's chain of title to land is complete and unobjectionable, the title itself may still be unmarketable as a result of encumbrances on it in

31. A recent formulation states that an adverse possession title will be marketable if the court finds "(1) that the outstanding claimants could not succeed were they in fact to assert a claim, and (2) that there is no real likelihood that any claim will ever be asserted."; Conklin v. Davi, 76 N.J. 468, 388 A.2d 598 (1978). Compare Simis v. McElroy, 160 N.Y. 156, 54 N.E. 674, 73 Am.St.Rep. 673 (1899) ("the proof must * * * exclude to a moral certainty any right or claim * * * " by the record owner), with Rehoboth Heights Development Co. v. Marshall, 15 Del.Ch. 314, 137 A. 83 (1927) (doubt of the validity of vendor's title " * * * appears to rest on mere speculation, conjecture, and imagination.") See also Barter v. Palmerton Area School Dist., 399 Pa.Super. 16, 581 A.2d 652 (1990) (lengthy adverse possession may give rise to a marketable title); Kipahulu Investment Co. v. Seltzer Partnership, 4 Hawaii App. 625, 675 P.2d 778 (1983), cert. denied 67 Hawaii 685, 744 P.2d 781 (1984) (title based on adverse possession was unmarketable, where there was no proof that adverse possessor had given its cotenants notice as required to begin running of statutory period); Mrs. E.B. Smith Realty Co. v. Hubbard, 130 Ga.App. 672, 204 S.E.2d 366 (1974) (serious risk of litigation of adverse possession title; purchaser can rescind.) A few cases are more strict, and hold adverse possession titles unmarketable per se until a quiet title or other appropriate action eliminates the record owner's rights; see Holland v. Lavigne, 88 R.I. 376, 148 A.2d 522 (1959); McLaughlin v. Brown, 126 S.W. 292 (Tex.Civ. App.1910). On the other hand, a few cases appear to treat adverse possession titles as marketable per se with little discussion of the risk they present. But these cases typically involve possession periods much longer than the statute of limitations. See, e.g., Smith v. Windsor Manor Co., 352 Pa. 449, 43 A.2d 6 (1945). See generally Annot., 46 A.L.R.2d 544 (1956).

32. The court in which the vendor and purchaser litigate the marketability of the title cannot bind the record owner or cut off his or her rights unless the latter is a party to

the action, not a common situation. Hence, the vendor must ordinarily pursue a separate action against the record owner if the court determines that the vendor's adverse possession title is too risky to force upon the purchaser. Cf. Bartos v. Czerwinski, 323 Mich. 87, 34 N.W.2d 566 (1948); Lynbrook Gardens v. Ullman, 291 N.Y. 472, 53 N.E.2d 353 (1943), certiorari denied 322 U.S. 742, 64 S.Ct. 1144, 88 L.Ed. 1575 (1944). If the action brought by the vendor is a general one to quiet the title, and service is only by publication, it may be subject to collateral attack, but most courts would probably hold that it nonetheless makes the vendor's title marketable. See Note, Enhancing the Marketability of Land: The Suit to Quiet Title, 68 Yale L.J. 1245 (1959).

33. The contract, of course, can provide for a "marketable record title", and can thereby foreclose the issue. See, e.g., Lucas v. Independent School District No. 284, 433 N.W.2d 94 (Minn.1988); Gaines v. Dillard, 545 S.W.2d 845 (Tex.Civ.App.1976), refused n.r.e. (title by accretion does not meet contract's requirement of title shown by abstract); Hurley v. Werly, 203 So.2d 530 (Fla.App.1967).

34. See Annot., 57 A.L.R. 1253, 1324 (1928); 3 Am.L.Prop. § 11.48 notes 16–23 (1952); Brown v. Kelly & Picerne, Inc., 518 F.Supp. 730 (D.Mass.1981), affirmed 676 F.2d 682 (1st Cir.1982) (a merchantable title must be of record); Chavez v. Gomez, 77 N.M. 341, 423 P.2d 31 (1967) (same); Douglass v. Ransom, 205 Wis. 439, 237 N.W. 260 (1931). But see In re Governor's Island, 45 B.R. 247 (Bkrtcy.E.D.N.C.1984) (a 60-year chain of recorded conveyances is not necessary for a title to be marketable); Meeks v. Romen Petroleum, Inc., 452 So.2d 1191 (La.App.1984), writ denied 457 So.2d 13 (La.1984) (title need not be entirely of record to be marketable). See also McCarthy v. Timberland Resources, Inc., 219 Mont. 278, 712 P.2d 1292 (1985) (where proffered deed does not contain land description complying with state recording requirements, it is deemed not to pass a marketable title, even though it describes land correctly).

favor of other parties.[35]   A wide variety of encumbrances may be found, including leases, covenants, mineral reservations, mortgages, easements, party wall agreements, marital rights, contracts, options, and various types of liens.   Any such encumbrances will make title unmarketable unless the buyer contracted to accept them or they are so minor or so unlikely to be asserted as to be *de minimis*.[36]   A question often arises as to whether the purchaser must accept a title subject to an encumbrance that was readily visible when the contract was signed, was in fact known to the purchaser, or is beneficial to the land.   On each of these points the courts are divided, and cases can be found favoring the vendor where one, two, or all three of the factors mentioned are present.[37]   The theoretical justification for compelling

35. Occasionally a court will apply some doctrine other than marketable title to permit a buyer to rescind a purchase contract for a defective title. See, e.g., Ger v. Kammann, 504 F.Supp. 446 (D.Del.1980) (neither party knew of sewer easement running under house; purchaser can rescind for mutual mistake); Dover Pool & Racquet Club, Inc. v. Brooking, 366 Mass. 629, 322 N.E.2d 168 (1975) (zoning ordinance prohibited purchaser's intended use; held, mutual mistake.)

36. See, e.g., G/GM Real Estate Corp. v. Susse Chalet Motor Lodge, Inc., 61 Ohio St.3d 375, 575 N.E.2d 141 (1991) (lapsed memorandum of lease in public records was trivial defect; title was marketable); Caselli v. Messina, 148 Misc.2d 671, 567 N.Y.S.2d 972 (1990) (buyer must accept title despite existence of an unviolated restrictive covenant, where contract stated buyers would take subject to covenants that did not render title unmarketable; a dubious result); Lovell v. Jimal Holding Corp., 127 A.D.2d 747, 512 N.Y.S.2d 138 (1987) (prior mortgage, barred by the statute of limitations, does not impair marketability); Camp v. Commonwealth Land Title Ins. Co., 787 F.2d 1258 (8th Cir.1986) (breach in existing restrictive covenant was not a title defect; title was marketable); Medallion Homes, Inc. v. Thermar Investments, Inc., 698 S.W.2d 400 (Tex.App.1985) (void assignment of interest recorded by former owner of land without authority to do so was sufficiently minor matter that it did not impair marketability of title); TXO Production Corp. v. Page Farms, Inc., 287 Ark. 304, 698 S.W.2d 791 (1985) (conflicting prior deed, which contained land description void on its face, did not impair marketability of title); Donaghy v. Roudebush, 614 F.Supp. 585 (D.N.J.1985) (prior liens of record did not impair marketability, where they had been foreclosed by court order and could not now be asserted); Belrose v. Baker, 121 N.H. 48, 426 A.2d 454 (1981) (intrusion of easement was very minor; title held marketable.) Cf. Staley v. Stephens, 404 N.E.2d 633 (Ind.App. 1980) (house violated set-back line in restrictive covenants by 0.6 to 1.6 feet; title unmarketable); Egeter v. West and North Properties, 92 Or.App. 118, 758 P.2d 361 (1988) (easement to drive cattle made title to residential

land unmarketable, although easement would be used only infrequently); Coons v. Carstensen, 15 Mass.App.Ct. 431, 446 N.E.2d 114 (1983) (conservation restrictive covenant rendered title unmarketable).

Several recent cases have considered and rejected the argument that the presence of hazardous waste on land, in violation of state or federal environmental statutes, constitutes a failure of marketable title. See, e.g., Mill Creek Apartments v. Chicago Title Ins. Co., 231 Cal.App.3d 1654, 283 Cal.Rptr. 231 (1991); In re McMahon, 94 B.R. 255 (Bkrtcy. D.R.I. 1988); Chicago Title Ins. Co. v. Kumar, 24 Mass.App.Ct. 53, 506 N.E.2d 154, 156–57 (1987). However, if a lien has actually been imposed on the property for payment of clean-up costs, title is obviously unmarketable.

37. Cases requiring the buyer to accept the encumbrance include Whitman v. Larson, 172 A.D.2d 968, 568 N.Y.S.2d 485 (1991) (purchaser must accept land subject to visible easements of an open and notorious nature); Egeter v. West & North Properties, 92 Or.App. 118, 758 P.2d 361 (1988) (same, but unimproved public road easement was not sufficiently notorious to charge buyers with notice of it); Alcan Aluminum Corp. v. Carlsberg Financial Corp., 689 F.2d 815 (9th Cir.1982) (power line easement open, notorious, and visible); Alumni Association of University of North Dakota v. Hart Agency, Inc., 283 N.W.2d 119 (N.D.1979) (buyer knew of existing lease); Ludke v. Egan, 87 Wis.2d 221, 274 N.W.2d 641 (1979) (buyer knew of easement); Thompson v. Shaw Real Estate, Inc., 210 Va. 714, 173 S.E.2d 812 (1970) (electric line easement does not make title unmarketable if known or visible and of reasonable width, although contract provided there would be no easements); Taxman v. McMahan, 21 Wis.2d 215, 124 N.W.2d 68 (1963) (party wall known or visible); Wood v. Evanitzsky, 168 Pa.Super. 484, 79 A.2d 213 (1951), judgment reversed 369 Pa. 123, 85 A.2d 24 (1951) (buyer knew of public road); Ford v. White, 179 Or. 490, 172 P.2d 822 (1946) (visible power line easement). Contrary cases include Waters v. North Carolina Phosphate Corp., 310 N.C. 438, 312

the buyer to take the land is that he or she must have recognized and planned for the encumbrance. Hence, the purchaser is treated as if it had been specifically agreed to in the contract. This result is nearly always followed where the encumbrance is an easement for a visible public road or street along one edge of the property.[38]

There are several situations in which the courts find title to be unmarketable even though the alleged "encumbrance" does not literally affect title at all. For example, land which has no public access, or to which access is severely limited, may be treated as having unmarketable title until the vendor provides a suitable easement or a public way is created.[39] Encroachments of significant dimensions are regarded as making title unmarketable, whether they involve an improvement on the subject property which encroaches on a neighboring parcel[40] or vice versa.[41] This result follows whether or not the statute of limitations or prescriptive period has run on the trespass. Ordinances affecting land *use* present another interesting problem. Obviously title and use are quite distinct concepts, and it is very generally held that the presence, or even the violation, of subdivision, housing, or building codes does not constitute an encumbrance on title.[42]

S.E.2d 428 (1984) (purchasers not required to take subject to a recorded, obvious power line easement which did not benefit the property); Gossels v. Belluschi, 4 Mass.App.Ct. 810, 348 N.E.2d 115 (1976); Ziskind v. Bruce Lee Corp., 224 Pa.Super. 518, 307 A.2d 377 (1973); Atlas Realty of East Meadow, Inc. v. Ostrofsky, 56 Misc.2d 787, 289 N.Y.S.2d 784 (1967); Siegel v. Shaw, 337 Mass. 170, 148 N.E.2d 393 (1958).

A similar line of reasoning may be adopted by courts with reference to other types of title "defects." See, e.g., Hall v. Fitzgerald, 671 P.2d 224 (Utah 1983) (where purchaser under installment contract knows that vendor is acquiring the land under a prior installment contract, the "equitable title" of the vendor is a sufficient form of marketable title).

38. Tabet Lumber Co. v. Golightly, 80 N.M. 442, 457 P.2d 374 (1969) (public highway); Eaton v. Trautwein, 288 Ky. 97, 155 S.W.2d 474 (1941) (sidewalk); Annot., 64 A.L.R. 1477 (1929).

39. Wilfong v. W.A. Schickedanz Agency, Inc., 85 Ill.App.3d 333, 40 Ill.Dec. 625, 406 N.E.2d 828 (1980); Regan v. Lanze, 40 N.Y.2d 475, 387 N.Y.S.2d 79, 354 N.E.2d 818 (1976). But see Sinks v. Karleskint, 130 Ill.App.3d 527, 85 Ill.Dec. 807, 474 N.E.2d 767 (1985) (title was marketable despite lack of legally assured access, where purchasers had notice of problem at the inception of the contract); Bob Daniels and Sons v. Weaver, 106 Idaho 535, 681 P.2d 1010 (App.1984) (similar). A limitation on access which is inconvenient but not total is not regarded as a title defect; Kirkwall Corp. v. Sessa, 39 A.D.2d 185, 333 N.Y.S.2d 108 (1972), appeal after remand 60 A.D.2d 563, 400 N.Y.S.2d 349 (1977), reversed 48 N.Y.2d 709, 422 N.Y.S.2d 368, 397 N.E.2d 1172 (1979).

40. DeJong v. Mandelbaum, 122 A.D.2d 772, 505 N.Y.S.2d 659 (1986) (encroachment on adjacent land does not render title unmarketable if adjacent owner has given an easement legalizing the encroachment); Zatzkis v. Fuselier, 398 So.2d 1284 (La.App.1981), writ denied 405 So.2d 533 (La.1981); Sydelman v. Marici, 56 A.D.2d 866, 392 N.Y.S.2d 333 (1977); Zale Corp. v. E.I. DuPont de Nemours & Co., 494 S.W.2d 229 (Tex.Civ.App.1973); Klavens v. Siegel, 256 Md. 476, 260 A.2d 637 (1970). Cf. Mertens v. Berendsen, 213 Cal. 111, 1 P.2d 440 (1931) (encroachment varying from seven-eighths of an inch to two inches is so minor that title is still marketable.)

41. Mid–State Homes, Inc. v. Brown, 47 Ala.App. 468, 256 So.2d 894 (1971). See generally Annot., 47 A.L.R.2d 331 (1956); 3 Am. L.Prop. § 11.49 notes 93–97 (1952).

42. Seth v. Wilson, 62 Or.App. 814, 662 P.2d 745 (1983) (subdivision ordinance); McCrae v. Giteles, 253 So.2d 260 (Fla.App. 1971) (housing code); Hocking v. Title Insurance & Trust Co., 37 Cal.2d 644, 234 P.2d 625 (1951) (subdivision ordinance violation); Cox v. Supreme Savings & Loan Association, 126 Ill.App.2d 293, 262 N.E.2d 74 (1970) (building code violation); Gnash v. Saari, 44 Wn.2d 312, 267 P.2d 674 (1954) (same); Berger v. Weinstein, 63 Pa.Super. 153 (1916) (same). See Note, 1958 Wis.L.Rev. 128. Cf. Brunke v. Pharo, 3 Wis.2d 628, 89 N.W.2d 221 (1958), noted 1958 Wis.L.Rev. 640 (housing code violations breach deed covenant against encumbrances if enforcement action is under way.)

Contra, see Voorheesville Rod & Gun Club, Inc. v. E.W. Tompkins Co., 158 A.D.2d 789, 551 N.Y.S.2d 382 (1990), appeal dismissed 76 N.Y.2d 888, 561 N.Y.S.2d 550, 562 N.E.2d 875 (1990) (failure of vendor to subdivide land into

Zoning is treated differently, perhaps on the ground that it is easier for the vendor to become aware of violations of zoning ordinances, and thus that he or she should be responsible for them. The zoning ordinance itself is not deemed an encumbrance, but an existing violation is generally treated as making title unmarketable.[43] If the zoning will seriously frustrate the buyer's planned use of the property, even an unviolated ordinance will often justify avoidance of the contract, albeit on grounds other than unmarketability of title. Such grounds include misrepresentation, excessive hardship, breach of express warranty,[44] and mutual or unilateral mistake.[45]

At what point in time must the vendor's title be marketable or otherwise in compliance with the contract? The question sometimes arises when the land is subject to mortgages or liens which the vendor plans to discharge out of the proceeds of the sale. So long as the sale price is sufficient to accomplish this, and reasonable precautions have been taken to prevent release of the purchaser's funds until it is clear that good title will be transferred, the buyer has no ground to object; the closing will make the title marketable.[46] A more serious timing question arises if the defect is not merely a lien which can be paid off, but some encumbrance which may be difficult to cure or even a complete absence of title. The traditional view is that the vendor need not have marketable title until the closing,[47] but some

legal lots rendered title unmarketable); Shinn v. Thrust IV, Inc., 56 Wn.App. 827, 786 P.2d 285 (1990), review denied 114 Wn. 1023, 792 P.2d 535 (1990) (replatting of subdivision by vendor caused potential violation of earlier restrictive covenants, and thus rendered title unmarketable). See generally Freyfogle, Real Estate Sales and the New Implied Warranty of Lawful Use, 71 Cornell L.Rev. 1 (1985), advocating adoption by the courts of an implied warranty protecting purchasers against both public and private restrictions that make use of the property illegal.

43. Radovanov v. Land Title Co. of America, 189 Ill.App.3d 433, 136 Ill.Dec. 827, 545 N.E.2d 351 (1989); Venisek v. Draski, 35 Wis.2d 38, 150 N.W.2d 347 (1967); Lohmeyer v. Bower, 170 Kan. 442, 227 P.2d 102 (1951); Moyer v. De Vincentis Construction Co., 107 Pa.Super. 588, 164 A. 111 (1933). New York has consistently refused to follow this view; see, e.g., Wind v. Healy, 147 N.Y.S.2d 562 (Sup.1955). See Note, 1958 Wis.L.Rev. 128; Dunham, Effect on Title of Violation of Building Covenants and Zoning Ordinances, 27 Rocky Mt.L.Rev. 255 (1955); 6A Powell, Real Property ¶ 925[4][b] (1981); Annot., 39 A.L.R.3d 362, 370 (1971). Note that the question of zoning changes during the executory period of the contract is discussed in § 10.13, infra, at note 33.

44. See Scharf v. Tiegerman, 166 A.D.2d 697, 561 N.Y.S.2d 271 (1990); Sachs v. Swartz, 233 Ga. 99, 209 S.E.2d 642 (1974).

45. Schultz v. County of Contra Costa, 157 Cal.App.3d 242, 203 Cal.Rptr. 760 (1984); Dover Pool & Racquet Club, Inc. v. Brooking, 366 Mass. 629, 322 N.E.2d 168 (1975); Gardner

Homes, Inc. v. Gaither, 31 N.C.App. 118, 228 S.E.2d 525 (1976), review denied 291 N.C. 323, 230 S.E.2d 675 (1976). See generally Annot., 39 A.L.R.3d 362 (1971). See also the discussion of zoning and equitable conversion, § 10.13 infra, at note 33.

46. See Bailey v. First Mortg. Corp. of Boca Raton, 478 So.2d 502 (Fla.App.1985) ("encumbrances and leases not provided for contractually and not earmarked to be satisfied by the proceeds of the sale constitute defects"); George v. Nevett, 462 So.2d 728 (Ala.1984) (where vendor fails to make provision for discharge of prior lien out of settlement proceeds, vendor is liable in damages for fraud); In re Criswell, 52 B.R. 184 (Bankr.E.D.Va.1985) (purchasers' attorney negligently failed to ensure that prior encumbrance was paid off at settlement; his knowledge of the encumbrance is imputed to purchasers, making their claim against vendor dischargeable in bankruptcy); Holmby, Inc. v. Dino, 98 Nev. 358, 647 P.2d 392 (1982); Jensen v. Bledsoe, 100 Idaho 84, 593 P.2d 988 (1979); Lone Star Development Co. v. Miller, 564 F.2d 921 (10th Cir.1977); 3 Am.L.Prop. 133 (1952); Annot., 53 A.L.R.3d 678 (1973). Cf. Rankin v. McFerrin, 626 P.2d 720 (Colo.App.1980) (title not marketable if balance on outstanding liens exceeds sale price.) The buyer is entitled to reasonable assurances that the discharge of the encumbrances will occur; see Kaiser v. Wright, 629 P.2d 581 (Colo.1981); First National Bank of Nevada v. Ron Rudin Realty Co., 97 Nev. 20, 623 P.2d 558 (1981).

47. Rusch v. Kauker, 479 N.W.2d 496 (S.D. 1991); English v. Sanchez, 110 N.M. 343, 796 P.2d 236 (1990); Seligman v. First Nat. Invest-

recent cases have given the purchaser a right of immediate rescission if it appears very unlikely that the vendor can cure the title problems.[48] The question is particularly acute in long term installment contracts which might place the buyer in the position of paying for many years with no assurance of ever getting a good title.

The law imposes no duty to examine the title on either party, but as a practical matter the buyer is expected to do so, since he or she will otherwise have no basis for rejecting it as unmarketable. Of course, the contract may obligate the seller to pay some of the buyer's search expenses, as by furnishing a preliminary title report from a title insurer or providing to the buyer a current abstract.[49] This is a common practice in the western and midwestern United States, but not on the East Coast.[50] The buyer who discovers defects that make the title objectionable must notify the seller of them with specificity and allow the seller a reasonable time to cure them; only if the vendor fails to do so may the buyer avoid the contract.[51] The

ments, Inc., 184 Ill.App.3d 1053, 540 N.E.2d 1057 (1989); Hosch v. Brown, 258 Ga. 7, 364 S.E.2d 833 (1988), on remand 186 Ga.App. 446, 367 S.E.2d 888 (1988); Meeks v. Romen Petroleum, Inc., 452 So.2d 1191 (La.App.1984), writ denied 457 So.2d 13 (La.1984); Brinson v. Luley, 448 So.2d 583 (Fla.App.1984); Wright v. Bryan, 226 Va. 557, 311 S.E.2d 776 (1984); Neves v. Wright, 638 P.2d 1195 (Utah 1981); Yale Development Co. v. Andermann, 37 Ill. App.3d 33, 344 N.E.2d 701 (1976); Luette v. Bank of Italy, 42 F.2d 9 (9th Cir.1930), certiorari denied 282 U.S. 884, 51 S.Ct. 87, 75 L.Ed. 779 (1930); 3 Am.L.Prop. § 11.15 (1952), ULTA § 2–304(b)(1) requires the vendor to have marketable title "at the time for conveyance," but also obligates the vendor to provide documentation of his title "a reasonable time before the conveyance." The case law plainly does not impose this latter duty.

The timing of the title's marketability is subject to the parties' agreement; see Carter v. Rich, 111 Idaho 684, 726 P.2d 1135 (1986) (title must be marketable when last installment is paid, unless parties contract for marketability at an earlier date, such as date of contracting); Ideal Family and Youth Ranch v. Whetstine, 655 P.2d 429 (Colo.App.1982) (where contract required vendor to deposit deed in escrow at time installment contract was signed, vendor had obligation to have marketable title at that time).

48. Risse v. Thompson, 471 N.W.2d 853 (Iowa 1991) (a title defect existing prior to buyer's making last installment payment is not a breach if the defect can be removed); Breuer–Harrison, Inc. v. Combe, 799 P.2d 716 (Utah App.1990) (if long-term contract vendor's title is subject to an irremediable easement, vendor is considered in anticipatory breach of contract); Mid–State Homes, Inc. v. Moore, 460 So.2d 172 (Ala.Civ.App.1984) (failure of vendor's title may give purchaser under installment contract a right to rescind and recover payments, but gives her no right to

remain in possession without making further payments); Eychaner v. Springer, 34 Colo. App. 412, 527 P.2d 903 (1974); Gustafson v. Gervais, 291 Minn. 60, 189 N.W.2d 186 (1971); Leavitt v. Blohm, 11 Utah 2d 220, 357 P.2d 190 (1960).

The buyer who has legitimate doubts about the vendor's title is entitled to demand reasonable assurances that they will be resolved, and to treat the vendor as in breach if such assurances are not forthcoming; see Shaffer v. Earl Thacker Co., 3 Hawaii App. 81, 641 P.2d 983 (1982), appeal after remand 6 Hawaii 188, 716 P.2d 163 (1986); Restatement (Second) of Contracts § 251, Illustrations 3, 5 (1981). See also Stark v. Borner, 226 Mont. 356, 735 P.2d 314 (1987), appeal after remand 234 Mont. 254, 762 P.2d 857 (1988) (vendor cannot enforce a forfeiture provision of an installment contract while the vendor is unable to tender marketable title); Smith v. Hawkins, 84 Or.App. 336, 733 P.2d 929 (1987) (similar).

49. See ULTA § 2–304(e), which requires the seller to furnish title evidence to the buyer unless the parties agree otherwise. In most jurisdictions the seller has no affirmative duty actually to disclose title defects to the purchaser. But Massachusetts so requires by statute, if the matter is an "encumbrance" and the seller has knowledge of it; see Mass. Gen.Laws Ann. c. 184, § 21; Security Title and Guaranty Co. v. Mid–Cape Realty, Inc., 723 F.2d 150 (1st Cir.1983), holding this statute inapplicable where the title defect in question is not merely an encumbrance but a total failure of title.

50. See generally Payne, Ancillary Costs in the Purchase of Homes, 35 Mo.L.Rev. 455 (1970); Annot., 52 A.L.R. 1460 (1928).

51. Gentile v. Kim, 101 A.D.2d 939, 475 N.Y.S.2d 631 (1984) (where purchasers gave notice of title defect 30 days prior to settlement date, a reasonable time had been al-

time to cure may well extend the agreed closing date, and this will probably follow even if time was made of the essence.[52]

If the purchaser accepts a deed, a doctrine known as merger[53] limits any claims based on title matters to those which can be brought under the deed's title covenants; the contract's covenants of title, whether express or implied, are said to be "merged into the deed" and can no longer be the basis of legal

lowed and purchasers were entitled to recover down payment); Houston v. Whitworth, 444 So.2d 1095 (Fla.App.1984) (ten days not a reasonable allowance of time to cure title defect); Laird v. Lacey, 263 Ark. 570, 566 S.W.2d 145 (1978); Huddleston v. Fergeson, 564 S.W.2d 448 (Tex.Civ.App.1978); Ace Realty, Inc. v. Looney, 531 P.2d 1377 (Okl.1974); Padgett v. Bryant, 121 Ga.App. 807, 175 S.E.2d 884 (1970); Cohen v. Kranz, 12 N.Y.2d 242, 238 N.Y.S.2d 928, 189 N.E.2d 473 (1963); Easton v. Montgomery, 90 Cal. 307, 27 P. 280 (1891). See also ULTA § 2–305. The notice must be specific and demand a cure of the defects; see Real Estate World, Inc. v. Southeastern Land Fund, Inc., 137 Ga.App. 771, 224 S.E.2d 747 (1976), affirmed in part, reversed in part 237 Ga. 227, 227 S.E.2d 340 (1976). The buyer can place the seller in breach without such notification or time allowance where the defect is plainly incurable; see Bertrand v. Jones, 58 N.J.Super. 273, 156 A.2d 161 (1959), cert. denied 31 N.J. 553, 158 A.2d 452 (1960) (public sewer easement); Siegel v. Shaw, 337 Mass. 170, 148 N.E.2d 393 (1958) (public sewer easement); Oppenheimer v. Knepper Realty Co., 50 Misc. 186, 98 N.Y.S. 204 (1906) (party wall).

The contract itself may, of course, fix a time within which title defects must be cured. See, e.g., Bailey v. First Mortg. Corp. of Boca Raton, 478 So.2d 502 (Fla.App.1985) (contract allowed 120 days for cure, but sellers disavowed contract prior to expiration of that period; buyers need not wait until end of 120 days to claim restitution of earnest money); Keller v. Reich, 646 S.W.2d 141 (Mo.App. 1983), described at § 10.11 note 30, supra.

52. Modern authority on this point is scant, and is often obscured by inadequate fact statements in the reported cases. See O'Hara Group Denver, Limited v. Marcor Housing Systems, Inc., 197 Colo. 530, 595 P.2d 679 (1979) (time probably of the essence); compare Sugden, Vendors 408 (1873 ed.). Trainer v. Lammers, 161 Minn. 336, 201 N.W. 540 (1925), has been cited for the contrary position; see Annot., 57 A.L.R. at 1520 (1928). The case contains dictum that the vendor must have good title at the agreed closing date and no later if time is of the essence, but in fact it involved an attempt by the purchaser to close prior to the agreed date, and without giving appropriate notice of his objection to the title defect; the court held the purchaser's actions to be wrongful and denied his attempt to rescind. Another case which has been cited for the proposition that no additional time

will be allowed to cure title defects if time is essential is Kinsley Milling Co. v. Wait, 112 Kan. 809, 213 P. 160 (1923). But there the title defect was the existence of an unvacated street easement, which the court treated as essentially incurable and thus not subject to the rule allowing a reasonable time for cure; see note 51, supra.

As a matter of policy, if the buyer waits until just prior to closing to notify the seller of the title defects, a reasonable extension of time ought to be available for cure even if this means postponing an essential closing date. It is, after all, the buyer's lassitude in notifying the vendor of the nature of the defects which has caused the problem. Thus, the buyer has little ground for complaint about the postponement. The ULTA follows and refines this approach; it allows an extension beyond the essential closing date only if the buyer fails to notify the seller of title defects within ten days after receipt of the title evidence. See ULTA § 2–305(b). Compare the closely analogous situation of the buyer who enters into an oral modification making the vendor's performance easier, and who then disavows the modification on the eve of the closing, relying on the statute of frauds. The buyer cannot hold the seller in breach of the original contract without allowing an additional time for performance, even if time was of the essence. See Imperator Realty Co. v. Tull, 228 N.Y. 447, 127 N.E. 263 (1920), discussed at § 10.1, supra.

The contract itself may define the period within which the vendor may cure any objections to title, and such a provision will be enforced; see Ort v. Horn, 1 Ohio App.2d 420, 205 N.E.2d 30 (1964).

Note that the extension of the closing date to permit a reasonable time to cure is available only for title defects; if any other sort of performance by the vendor is not complete and time is of the essence, the vendor will be in breach. See, e.g., Grace v. Nappa, 46 N.Y.2d 560, 415 N.Y.S.2d 793, 389 N.E.2d 107 (1979) (vendor promised to provide a mortgagee's estoppel statement at closing, but failed to do so; time was of the essence, and the vendor was in breach.)

53. Professor Corbin suggested that merger is a poor description of this process, which is in reality similar to an accord and satisfaction; 6 Corbin, Contracts § 1319 (1962), followed in Pryor v. Aviola, 301 A.2d 306 (Del.Super.1973).

action.[54] This doctrine is not a popular one with modern courts, since it can readily defeat meritorious claims. There was once considerable authority that it applied to all contractual covenants,[55] but it has been persistently narrowed and limited, mainly by holdings that it is inapplicable to matters which are "collateral" to or not ordinarily mentioned in the deed.[56] Hence, it is now largely limited to title provisions of the contract.[57] For example, covenants relating to the physical condition of the property, improvements to be built, and the like are not subject to merger.[58]

54. See, e.g., Colorado Land & Resources, Inc. v. Credithrift of America, Inc., 778 P.2d 320 (Colo.App.1989); Russell v. Mullis, 479 So.2d 727 (Ala.1985) (if the contractual provisions are incorporated into the deed, they survive to confer an independent cause of action); Bennett v. Behring Corp., 466 F.Supp. 689, 701–702 (S.D.Fla.1979); Knudson v. Weeks, 394 F.Supp. 963 (W.D.Okl.1975). The best recent collection of cases is M. Friedman, Contracts and Conveyances of Real Property § 7.2 (5th ed. 1991). On deed covenants, see generally § 11.13, infra.

55. See 3 Am.L.Prop. § 11.65 (1952).

56. See, e.g., Hammerquist v. Warburton, 458 N.W.2d 773 (S.D.1990) (covenant regarding use of land does not merge); Colorado Land & Resources, Inc. v. Credithrift of America, Inc., 778 P.2d 320 (Colo.App.1989) (merger applies only to title, possession, quantity or emblements of the land); Durden v. Century 21 Compass Points, Inc., 541 So.2d 1264 (Fla. App.1989), review denied 548 So.2d 663 (Fla. 1989) (warranties and indemnities of personal representative of vendor do not merge into deed); G.G.A., Inc. v. Leventis, 773 P.2d 841 (Utah App.1989) (purchaser's right of first refusal not extinguished by merger); Reeves v. McClain, 56 Wn.App. 301, 783 P.2d 606 (1989) (covenant to furnish title insurance is collateral and not merged into deed); Sullivan v. Cheshire, 190 Ga.App. 763, 380 S.E.2d 294 (1989) (covenant regarding condition of ponds on the premises is collateral and does not merge); American National Self Storage, Inc. v. Lopez–Aguiar, 521 So.2d 303 (Fla.App.1988), review denied 528 So.2d 1182 (Fla.1988) (covenant to extend utilities to site does not merge); Knight v. McCain, 531 So.2d 590 (Miss.1988) (containing a thorough review of the cases nationwide); Barela v. Locer, 103 N.M. 395, 708 P.2d 307 (1985) (right of first refusal in vendor, created in contract of sale, did not merge into deed); Matter of Wauka, Inc., 39 B.R. 734 (Bkrtcy.N.D.Ga.1984) (same); Peterson v. Peterson, 431 So.2d 672 (Fla.App.1983) (agreement to convey life estate, but that it would terminate if grantee ceased to reside on the property, was "collateral" and did not merge with deed); McGovern Builders, Inc. v. Davis, 12 Ohio App.3d 153, 468 N.E.2d 90 (1983) (purchaser's obligation to pay remaining price on contract was not merged into deed); Davis v. Weg, 104 A.D.2d 617, 479 N.Y.S.2d 553 (1984) (contract clause regarding compliance with local ordinances was not merged into deed, where it included "survival" language); Yaksich v. Relocation Realty Service Corp., 89 Misc.2d 410, 391 N.Y.S.2d 822 (1977); Chicago Title & Trust Co. v. Wabash–Randolph Corp., 384 Ill. 78, 51 N.E.2d 132 (1943).

57. See Annot., 38 A.L.R.2d 1310 (1954) (obligations of vendor rarely merged into the deed unless they relate to title); Annot., 52 A.L.R.2d 647 (1957) (obligations of purchaser, including assumption of mortgages, construction of improvements, and payment of additional money, seldom deemed merged into the deed.) Judge Seldin said it well in Burwell v. Jackson, 9 N.Y. 535 (1854), quoted in Wallach v. Riverside Bank, 206 N.Y. 434, 100 N.E. 50 (1912): " * * * there is an implied warranty on the part of the vendor that he has a good title which continues until merged in the deed of conveyance." It is doubtful than any more should ever have been made of the merger doctrine than this. See Secor v. Knight, 716 P.2d 790 (Utah 1986) (vendor's obligation to clear title of recorded covenants is merged into deed, even though such covenants were recorded after contract was entered into; there was no fraud by vendors, but real estate broker breached duty by failing to advise purchasers of covenants); Wilson v. Landstrom, 281 S.C. 260, 315 S.E.2d 130 (1984) (where vendor accepts a "second" mortgage at time of settlement, she is deemed to have amended the sale contract to provide for such a mortgage).

58. Clackamas County Service Dist. v. American Guaranty Life Ins. Co., 77 Or.App. 88, 711 P.2d 980 (1985) (contractual provisions dealing with provision of sewage treatment were not merged into deed); Williams v. Runion, 173 Ga.App. 54, 325 S.E.2d 441 (1984) (builder's warranty of quality of house not merged into deed); Hudgins v. Bacon, 171 Ga.App. 856, 321 S.E.2d 359 (1984) (same); Borden v. Litchford, 619 S.W.2d 715 (Ky.App. 1981); Hairston Enterprises, Inc. v. Lee, 162 Ga.App. 475, 291 S.E.2d 404 (1982); Campbell v. Rawls, 381 So.2d 744 (Fla.App.1980); Rouse v. Brooks, 66 Ill.App.3d 107, 22 Ill.Dec. 858, 383 N.E.2d 666 (1978) (express warranties of quality not merged); Yaksich v. Relocation Realty Service Corp., supra note 56 (requirement that septic tank be inspected and ap-

Merger is subject to judicial manipulation in several ways. It is said to be inapplicable to cases of fraud or mistake.[59] Thus, a buyer of the "Brooklyn Bridge" has a remedy on the contract even if only a quitclaim deed was delivered. Merger may also be rejected on a showing of the parties' contrary intent, which may be inferred from contract language or the parties' behavior and circumstances.[60]

Despite its weakening in recent years, merger is still an unruly horse. It is generally confined to title matters, but exactly what a court will deem related to title is hard to predict.[61] The Uniform Land Transactions Act rejects the merger doctrine entirely unless the parties agree in the contract that acceptance of a deed will terminate the purchaser's contractual claims.[62] A more moderate judicial approach would limit the application of merger to cases in which the proof affirmatively showed the intent of the parties to discard claims based on the contract and to rely exclusively on the deed.[63] Such cases are probably rare.

proved, not merged); Annot., 25 A.L.R.3d 383, 432 (1969) (warranties of quality not merged). But see Gordon v. Bartlett, 452 So.2d 1077 (Fla.App.1984) (contractual provision for attorneys fees merged into deed).

59. Newton v. Brown, 222 Neb. 605, 386 N.W.2d 424 (1986) (no merger where deed was prepared under mutual mistake); Schultz v. Contra Costa County, 157 Cal.App.3d 242, 203 Cal.Rptr. 760 (1984) (no merger where purchaser bought at tax sale under unilateral mistake that lot was buildable under local zoning ordinance); Southpointe Development, Inc. v. Cruikshank, 484 So.2d 1361 (Fla.App. 1986), review denied 492 So.2d 1330 (Fla.1986) (no merger where portion of property was erroneously omitted from deed); Hi Tor Industrial Park, Inc. v. Chemical Bank, 114 A.D.2d 838, 494 N.Y.S.2d 751 (1985) (purchaser's claim for fraud is not barred by merger clause in contract unless it refers specifically to the matter alleged to have been misrepresented); Schlange–Schoeningen v. Parrish, 767 F.2d 788 (11th Cir.1985) (same); Haley v. Oaks Apartments, Ltd., 173 Ga.App. 44, 325 S.E.2d 602 (1984) (fraud claim not barred by merger doctrine, in light of contract clause that representations in question would survive closing); Jensen v. Miller, 280 Or. 225, 570 P.2d 375 (1977); Bicknell v. Barnes, 255 Ark. 697, 501 S.W.2d 761 (1973).

60. Reed v. Hassell, 340 A.2d 157 (Del.Super.1975); Webb v. Graham, 212 Kan. 364, 510 P.2d 1195 (1973); Vaughey v. Thompson, 95 Ariz. 139, 387 P.2d 1019 (1963). It is clear that a stipulation against merger in the contract will be sustained; see Gray v. Lynch Contractors, Inc., 156 Ga.App. 473, 274 S.E.2d 614 (1980); Randolph Hills, Inc. v. Shoreham Developers, Inc., 266 Md. 182, 292 A.2d 662 (1972). From the purchaser's viewpoint, such a clause is nearly always desirable. Of course, the parties may also provide expressly

for merger, and their agreement will be given effect; see Jones v. Dearman, 508 So.2d 707 (Ala.1987).

Merger may be so evidently unfair that a court may go to rather astonishing lengths to "find" evidence that it was not intended by the parties; see, e.g., Mayer v. Sumergrade, 111 Ohio App. 237, 167 N.E.2d 516 (1960).

61. See, e.g., Olper v. Wynne, 402 So.2d 1309 (Fla.App.1981) (contract clause guaranteeing access to land not merged into deed); Bakken v. Price, 613 P.2d 1222 (Wyo.1980) (contract covenant to provide a title insurance policy held to be merged into deed; a vigorous dissent); Miles v. Mackle Brothers, 73 Wis.2d 84, 242 N.W.2d 247 (1976) (contract covenant that vendor would pay future taxes, held merged into deed which contained clause stating that title was subject to the lien of current taxes).

Whether a discrepancy in land description between contract and deed actuates the merger doctrine has been controversial; compare Dennett v. Mt. Harvard Development Co., 43 Colo.App. 422, 604 P.2d 699 (1979) with Weiland v. Bernstein, 12 A.D.2d 945, 210 N.Y.S.2d 916 (1961); see also Tillotsen v. Frazer, 199 Mont. 342, 649 P.2d 744 (1982) (merger operated, where purchasers did not complain until twelve years after accepting deed.)

62. See ULTA § 1–309, abolishing merger; ULTA § 2–402, permitting the purchaser to revoke the contract in some circumstances even after accepting a deed. For a case in which the contract expressly called for merger, see Ballard v. Walsh, 353 Mass. 767, 233 N.E.2d 926 (1968).

63. See the heavy emphasis on intent in Szabo v. Superior Court, 84 Cal.App.3d 839, 148 Cal.Rptr. 837 (1978); cases cited at note 60, supra.

§ 10.13 The Executory Period and Equitable Conversion

During the period between formation and performance of a land sale contract, a variety of events may occur which raise questions about the contract's significance. Some of them have their principal effect on only one of the parties: the death of a party, a judgment obtained against him or her, or the like. Such events may trigger the operation of legal rules, such as an intestate succession statute or a judgment lien act, which depend on *characterization* of the party's interest as real or personal property. In most American jurisdictions, this characterization is based on the theory of equitable conversion, which holds that once the parties have entered into a contract that equity would specifically enforce, the buyer's interest in the contract is converted into real estate and the seller's interest into personal property. This result is said to follow from the view that equity regards as having been done that which ought to be done, and which equity would order done—namely, the conveyance of the title to the buyer and payment of the price to the seller.[1]

Other events during the executory period of the contract may bring the parties into conflict with one another, usually because they involve a loss in value of the property itself. Some such events cause physical damage: fire, windstorm, flood, frost damage to crops, and so on. Other risks flow from changes in the land's legal status: an amendment to a zoning ordinance, the imposition of new housing code requirements, or a taking by eminent domain, for example. Here the question is *allocation of the risk* between vendor and purchaser. Typically the buyer surveys the loss and decides that he or she no longer wants the property, or is willing to take it only with an abatement of the purchase price. Can the vendor enforce the contract on its original terms, notwithstanding the loss? Again, most American courts turn to the doctrine of equitable conversion and conclude that since the realty is already owned by the purchaser "in equity", the purchaser also has the risk of loss and must pay the full purchase price.

§ 10.13

1. The doctrine's modern form originated with Lord Eldon's opinion in Seaton v. Slade, 7 Ves.Jun. 265 (1802); see Davis, The Origin of the Doctrine of Equitable Conversion by Contract, 25 Ky.L.Rev. 58 (1936). See generally 3 Am.L.Prop. §§ 11.22–.35 (1952); 3A Corbin, Contracts § 667 (1960); Simpson, Legislative Changes in the Law of Equitable Conversion by Contract: I, 44 Yale L.J. 559 (1935).

Equitable conversion is often employed by the courts as an adjunct to the resolution of ordinary priority and recording issues. See, e.g., In re Estate of Clark, 447 N.W.2d 549 (Iowa App.1989) (under equitable conversion, purchasers' interest is not impaired by vendor's deed to a third party during contract's executory period); Lincoln Park Federal Sav. & Loan Ass'n v. DRG, Inc., 175 Ill.App.3d 176, 124 Ill.Dec. 790, 529 N.E.2d 771 (1988) (contract purchasers have an equitable title that is protected by recording act from a prior unrecorded mortgage); Himmighoefer v. Medallion Industries, Inc., 302 Md. 270, 487 A.2d 282

(1985) (under equitable conversion, vendors may not effectively encumber purchasers' interest by suffering imposition of a mechanics lien); Life Sav. & Loan Ass'n v. Bryant, 125 Ill.App.3d 1012, 81 Ill.Dec. 577, 467 N.E.2d 277 (1984) (under equitable conversion, purchasers under installment contract have an interest in the land with priority over a subsequent mortgage executed by the vendor); De-Boer v. Oakbrook Home Ass'n, Inc., 218 Neb. 813, 359 N.W.2d 768 (1984) (under equitable conversion, vendors may not effectively encumber purchasers' interest by executing a restrictive covenant after contract has been entered into).

See also Texas American Bank/Levelland v. Resendez, 706 S.W.2d 343 (Tex.App.1986) (under equitable conversion, purchasers under unrecorded installment contract have priority over judgment lien docketed against vendor after contract was signed; the equitable interest is not subject to the recording act, and in any event, judgment lien creditors are not protected by the recording act).

In both its characterization and risk aspects, equitable conversion might strike the objective observer as a grand *non-sequitur*. To say that equity will specifically enforce the contract certainly does not compel one to disregard reality and view the contract as already performed. Yet enforceability of the contract in equity is commonly treated as a talisman, employed to decide cases for which it has no practical relevance at all. The decisions often seem adamant in their unwillingness to discuss the underlying policy issues; equitable conversion almost becomes a substitute for thinking about the real questions in the case.[2] As Professor Dobbs has written, it is an example of a "moral principle * * * carried to the limit of its logic, rather than to the limit of its morality."[3]

Characterization of the Parties' Property Interests. The most common characterization issue arises because of the death of a contracting party. Consider first the vendor's death. If equitable conversion has occurred, the vendor's interest is considered personal property. True, the "bare" legal title descends to the vendor's heirs or devisees,[4] but they hold it subject to an obligation (sometimes termed a "trust"[5]) to convey to the purchaser under the contract. The proceeds of the sale will go to the decedent's personal representative (the administrator or executor), and after the usual expenses, taxes, and debts are paid, will be turned over to the legatees or next-of-kin. Thus, the heirs or devisees receive nothing when they give up the legal title.[6]

In most states this set of rules is unimportant when the vendor dies intestate, since the heirs and the next-of-kin are typically the same persons taking the same shares in the property; whether it is seen as realty or personalty is irrelevant. But when the decedent dies testate, and the will identifies different persons as devisees of the land and legatees of personalty, equitable conversion assumes great importance. The principles outlined above are usually followed in cases in which the will was made before the contract. The courts tend to see the contract as the equivalent of an outright conveyance of title; if such a conveyance occurred, it would leave the decedent's estate bereft of the land in question.[7] The devisees would be disappointed, but could hardly complain, since the result would presumably

---

2. Consider Bleckley v. Langston, 112 Ga. App. 63, 143 S.E.2d 671 (1965), in which the court followed equitable conversion despite its own conclusion that a contrary rule would be "* * * more expedient, and more in accord with practical common sense and business practices."

3. D. Dobbs, Remedies 40 (1973).

4. A review of terminology may be helpful here. "Heirs" are the persons who take the decedent's real estate under the relevant statute if he or she dies intestate. If the decedent dies testate as to real estate, it passes to the "devisees" under the will. Personal property passes to "next-of-kin" if the decedent is intestate, or to "legatees" if disposed of by the will.

5. Griggs Land Co. v. Smith, 46 Wash. 185, 89 P. 477 (1907).

6. Hays v. Coe, 88 Md.App. 491, 595 A.2d 484 (1991), cert. granted 325 Md. 329, 600 A.2d 850 (1992); Matter of Hill's Estate, 222 Kan. 231, 564 P.2d 462 (1977); Lindsey's Estate v. Taylor, 13 Ill.App.3d 717, 300 N.E.2d 572

(1973); Konecny v. Von Gunten, 151 Colo. 376, 379 P.2d 158 (1963); Shay v. Penrose, 25 Ill.2d 447, 185 N.E.2d 218 (1962). Cf. Estate of Atkinson, 19 Wis.2d 272, 120 N.W.2d 109 (1963), discussed in Church, Equitable Conversion in Wisconsin, 1970 Wis.L.Rev. 404, 410–14. See generally Hermann, The Doctrine of Equitable Conversion: I, Conversion by Contract, 12 DePaul L.Rev. 1, 27–35 (1962). If the conversion was in effect at the time of death, the fact that the contract is subsequently rescinded or terminated is irrelevant; the legatees get the land itself. See Clapp v. Tower, 11 N.D. 556, 93 N.W. 862 (1903).

7. The loss of the heirs or devisees is similar to that resulting from ademption—the disposition by the decedent before death of property which the will purports to convey; see Righter v. First Reformed Church of Boonton, 17 N.J.Super. 407, 86 A.2d 305 (1952). See generally Atkinson, Wills § 134 (2d ed. 1953).

be consistent with the decedent's wishes. The same logic applies to the decedent's sale by contract. However, if the will is made after the contract is formed, and yet it specifically identifies and devises the land, it is much harder to believe that the decedent did not wish to have the devisees receive the land's value. Some cases have awarded the purchase price to them, rejecting the logic of equitable conversion in favor of a construction which seems to follow the grantor's intent.[8] Even when the will predates the contract, it is by no means obvious that the decedent intended to disfavor the devisees and favor the legatees when he or she contracted to sell the land, and a few states have enacted statutes which give the devisees not only the naked legal title but also the right to enforce the contract in equity and get the purchase money.[9]

If it is the purchaser who dies, the result is a mirror image of the principles discussed above. The purchaser's interest descends as realty to the heirs or devisees, while the purchase price must be paid by the personal representative out of the personalty assets of the estate, and thus reduces the amount passing to the legatees or next-of-kin.[10] The land passes free and clear of the indebtedness. This result is an application of the doctrine of exoneration, which is more familiarly employed to require the personal representative to satisfy mortgages on the decedent's realty at no expense to the heirs or devisees.[11] Whether the decedent would have wanted this to occur is often doubtful, and England and a few American states have eliminated or weakened the doctrine of exoneration, but in most it still operates.[12]

On the whole, following equitable conversion probably does little harm in the context of devolution upon the death of the vendor or purchaser. Certainly the decedent's intent is the most desirable guide to such cases,[13] but all too often that intent is opaque. So long as equitable conversion does

---

8. Father Flanagan's Boys' Home v. Graybill, 178 Neb. 79, 132 N.W.2d 304 (1964). The same conclusion may be reached even under a general devise of "all my lands" or the like, if the decedent in fact had no land other than that under contract of sale, so that equitable conversion would render the devise meaningless; see Covey v. Dinsmoor, 226 Ill. 438, 80 N.E. 998 (1907). Cf. In re McDonough's Estate, 113 Ill.App.2d 437, 251 N.E.2d 405 (1969), in which the decedent owned other land as well, so that the general devise still had some effect notwithstanding the operation of equitable conversion.

9. See, e.g., Rowe v. Newman, 290 Ala. 289, 276 So.2d 412 (1972), construing Ala.Code § 13, tit. 61. See also Funk v. Funk, 563 N.E.2d 127 (Ind.App.1990), in which the contract was entered into by the vendor's attorney in fact while the vendor was in a coma. The court concluded that there was insufficient evidence that the vendor intended to deprive his devisees under his previously-executed will of the benefit of the land, and refused to apply equitable conversion.

10. This result follows with both general and specific devises; see Timberlake v. Heflin, 180 W.Va. 644, 379 S.E.2d 149 (1989); First

Camden National Bank v. Broadbent, 66 N.J.Super. 199, 168 A.2d 677 (1961); In re Reid's Estate, 26 Cal.App.2d 362, 79 P.2d 451 (1938); Cutler v. Meeker, 71 Neb. 732, 99 N.W. 514 (1904); Palmer v. Morrison, 104 N.Y. 132, 10 N.E. 144 (1887).

11. See generally Johnson, Executor or Heir: Who Pays the Mortgage?, 113 Trusts & Estates 244 (1974); Atkinson, Wills § 137 (2d ed. 1953); 3 Am.L.Prop. §§ 11.27, 14.25 (1952); Note, 40 Harv.L.Rev. 630 (1927).

12. See, e.g., Vernon's Ann. Missouri Stat. § 474.450 (exoneration only when property encumbered after will executed, and even then only when no contrary intent appears); Goodfellow v. Newton, 320 Mass. 405, 69 N.E.2d 569 (1946). See 3 Am.L.Prop. § 11.27 (1952). The English abrogation of the doctrine of exoneration is found in 17 & 18 Vict., c. 113 (1854), and 40 & 41 Vict., c. 34 (1877), with the latter applying specifically to unpaid purchase money.

13. See Church, Equitable Conversion in Wisconsin, 1970 Wis.L.Rev. 404.

not distract the courts from their primary task of assessing intent where possible, it is a reasonably satisfactory method of determining the property's course.

A second issue which equitable conversion is often called upon to resolve is the amenability of the contracting parties' interests to the claims of judgment creditors. In most states a judgment becomes, by statute, a lien on the defendant's real property in the county where it is docketed. If the judgment is against a vendor who has already contracted to sell certain land, the vendor may argue that under equitable conversion his or her interest is no longer real property, and hence that the lien does not attach. This view is supported by the argument that the vendor's position is similar to that of an ordinary mortgagee who holds an interest in the land only as security for payment of the remainder of the purchase price. The cases are nearly evenly divided, with a slight majority rejecting equitable conversion and recognizing the lien.[14] Where this result is reached, there is some indication in the cases that once notified of the lien, the purchaser must make any further payments on the contract to the judgment creditor rather than the vendor.[15] The purchaser does not, however, have any obligation to examine the vendor's title and discover newly filed judgments before making each contract payment; the burden of doing so would be unreasonable, and the purchaser is protected in making payments to the vendor until receiving actual notice.[16] Provided he or she pays the appropriate person, the purchaser's essential right to enforce the contract is otherwise unaffected by the judgment against the vendor.[17]

14. Recognizing lien: Bedortha v. Sunridge Land Co., 312 Or. 307, 822 P.2d 694 (1991); Monroe v. Lincoln City Employees Credit Union, 203 Neb. 702, 279 N.W.2d 866 (1979); First Security Bank v. Rogers, 91 Idaho 654, 429 P.2d 386 (1967); Walker v. Fairbanks Investment Co., 268 F.2d 48 (9th Cir.1959) (Alaska law); West Virginia Pulp & Paper Co. v. Cooper, 87 W.Va. 781, 106 S.E. 55 (1921). Not recognizing lien: Cannefax v. Clement, 818 P.2d 546 (Utah 1991); Bank of Hawaii v. Horwoth, 71 Haw. 204, 787 P.2d 674 (1990); Marks v. City of Tucumcari, 93 N.M. 4, 595 P.2d 1199 (1979); Mueller v. Novelty Dye Works, 273 Wis. 501, 78 N.W.2d 881 (1956); Stecker v. Snyder, 118 Colo. 153, 193 P.2d 881 (1948) (no lien where contract lacked a forfeiture clause); Jones v. Howard, 142 Mo. 117, 43 S.W. 635, 64 Am.St.Rep. 546 (1897). See generally Lacy, Creditors of Land Contract Vendors, 24 Case W.Res.L.Rev. 645 (1973); 3 Am. L.Prop. § 11.29 note 20 (1952). Note that the denial of a judgment lien is not necessarily a disaster for the creditor, who can seek garnishment of the debt owed to the vendor by the purchaser; see, e.g., Rural Acceptance Corp. v. Pierce, 157 Ind.App. 90, 298 N.E.2d 499 (1973). Some courts might reject this approach because the debt is conditional upon marketability of the vendor's title, but all would probably recognize a creditor's bill in equity to collect the payments owed by the purchaser. See Lacy, supra, at 665–81.

15. Heider v. Deitz, 234 Or. 105, 380 P.2d 619 (1963). This gives the creditor an immediate right to the future payments without the need to go through an execution sale, a result which is very hard to justify; it may put the purchaser to a difficult choice in determining to whom the payments are legally owed. It seems preferable to require the creditor to employ a sale, garnishment, or equitable process to implement his or her claim to the payments. See Lacy, supra note 14, at 658–65.

16. Burke v. Johnson, 37 Kan. 337, 15 P. 204 (1887); Filley v. Duncan, 1 Neb. 134 (1871); cf. Wehn v. Fall, 55 Neb. 547, 76 N.W. 13 (1898) (no constructive notice if purchaser has gone into possession.) See Church, supra note 13, at 418 note 66. Cf. Lang v. Klinger, 34 Cal.App.3d 987, 110 Cal.Rptr. 532 (1973), in which the court rejected equitable conversion and imposed upon the innocent purchaser's interest the lien arising from a judgment against the vendor, apparently on the ground that the title insurer would have to pay the loss.

17. Hogan v. Weeks, 178 A.D.2d 968, 579 N.Y.S.2d 777 (1991); Clarence M. Bull, Inc. v. Goldman, 30 Md.App. 665, 353 A.2d 661 (1976); Wenzel v. Roberts, 236 Wis. 315, 294 N.W. 871 (1940). This is usually so even if the contract is unrecorded and the vendor's creditor has no other notice of it, since the record-

A creditor who obtains a judgment against the purchaser, on the other hand, will argue for equitable conversion since it would characterize the purchaser's interest as real estate and thus subject it to the judgment lien statute. While the results in the decided cases often turn on precise statutory language (most notably whether the statute stipulates that equitable interests are lienable), conversion is usually followed in this context.[18] If the vendor terminates the contract because of the purchaser's default, the creditor's rights will also be cut off,[19] but the creditor can assert whatever theories would have been available to the purchaser to reinstate or enforce the contract.[20]

Beyond the matters of devolution on death and rights of creditors, equitable conversion has been used to resolve numerous other characterization questions, including the meaning of "owner" or some similar term under various contracts[21] and statutes.[22] The construction of state inheri-

ing acts do not protect judgment creditors; they are thought not to be "for value." See Rural Acceptance Corp. v. Pierce, 157 Ind. App. 90, 298 N.E.2d 499 (1973); West Federal Savings & Loan Association v. Interstate Investment, Inc., 57 Wis.2d 690, 205 N.W.2d 361 (1973); Cumming v. First National Bank of Sigourney, 199 Iowa 667, 202 N.W. 556 (1925); § 11.10, infra, at notes 13–18. The result might differ, however, if a judgment sale of the vendor's interest to a bona fide purchaser were held while the contract was still executory; see 3 Am.L.Prop. § 11.29 notes 29–34 (1952). Moreover, if the purchaser is in possession of the land, that possession will usually constitute constructive notice to the judgment creditor, obviating the latter's BFP claim; see Cook v. City of Indianapolis, 559 N.E.2d 1201 (Ind.App.1990).

18. Hannah v. Martinson, 232 Mont. 469, 758 P.2d 276 (1988); Butler v. Wilkinson, 740 P.2d 1244 (Utah 1987); Fulton v. Duro, 107 Idaho 240, 687 P.2d 1367 (1984), affirmed 108 Idaho 392, 700 P.2d 14 (1985); Farmers State Bank v. Slaubaugh, 366 N.W.2d 804 (N.D. 1985); Bank of Santa Fe v. Garcia, 102 N.M. 588, 698 P.2d 458 (1985), certiorari denied 102 N.M. 613, 698 P.2d 886 (1985) (lien attaches to entire purchasers' estate and improvements, not merely purchasers' "equity" as of date lien is docketed); Action Realty Co. v. Miller, 191 Neb. 381, 215 N.W.2d 629 (1974); Fridley v. Munson, 46 S.D. 532, 194 N.W. 840 (1923); Gorham v. Farson, 119 Ill. 425, 10 N.E. 1 (1887). See also Cascade Security Bank v. Butler, 88 Wn.2d 777, 567 P.2d 631 (1977), holding the purchaser's interest lienable but without expressly adopting the theory of equitable conversion. For a thorough analysis of Washington law, see Hume, Real Estate Contracts and the Doctrine of Equitable Conversion in Washington: Dispelling the *Ashford* Cloud, 7 U. Puget Sound L.Rev. 233 (1984). Cases rejecting equitable conversion and holding the purchaser's interest not subject to the judgment lien include Matter of Estate of Ventling, 771 P.2d 388 (Wyo.1989); Stanley v.

Velma A. Barnes Real Estate, Inc., 571 P.2d 871 (Okl.App.1977) (purchaser has no lienable interest until purchase is price paid in full.) See 3 Am.L.Prop. § 11.29 notes 1–15 (1952); Annot., 1 A.L.R.2d 727 (1948).

19. See Welling v. Mount Si Bowl, Inc., 79 Wn.2d 485, 487 P.2d 620 (1971).

20. Jahnke v. Palomar Financial Corp., 22 Ariz.App. 369, 527 P.2d 771 (1974); Cf. Warren v. Rodgers, 82 N.M. 78, 475 P.2d 775 (1970). A similar result is reached in the case of an assignment or mortgage of the purchaser's interest; see Murray First Thrift & Loan Co. v. Stevenson, 534 P.2d 909 (Utah 1975); Fincher v. Miles Homes of Missouri, Inc., 549 S.W.2d 848 (Mo.1977), noted 43 Mo.L.Rev. 371 (1978).

21. See, e.g., Stapley v. American Bathtub Liners, Inc., 162 Ariz. 564, 785 P.2d 84 (App. 1989) (purchaser who takes possession during executory period with consent of vendor owes no rent); Cote v. A.J. Bayless Markets, Inc., 128 Ariz. 438, 626 P.2d 602 (App.1981) (purchaser is successor in interest of original landlord, and can maintain action against tenant for breach of lease covenants); Withers v. Board of County Commissioners, 96 N.M. 71, 628 P.2d 316 (App.1981), writ quashed 96 N.M. 116, 628 P.2d 686 (1981) (purchaser is "owner" for purposes of invitation to bid on county land which gave special rights to adjacent owners); Campbell v. Miller, 562 S.W.2d 827 (Tenn.App.1977) (purchaser has capacity to enter into contract for removal of dirt and rock from the land).

22. See, e.g., Dominion Bank v. Wilson, 867 F.2d 203 (4th Cir.1989) (option to purchase land, once exercised, was real property and not subject to a personal property security agreement under UCC Art. 9); Matter of Jones, 768 F.2d 923 (7th Cir.1985) (vendor's interest was personalty, and hence not exempt from claims of creditors under Indiana homestead exemption statute); First Nat. Bank v.

tance or estate tax statutes which operate on real property has also been determined by reference to equitable conversion in a number of cases.[23] The doctrine has sometimes been applied in deciding whether a sale contract by the co-owners works a severance of a joint tenancy or a tenancy by the entireties, although this seems a singularly inappropriate use of equitable conversion.[24]

Risk of Loss. Equitable conversion treats the purchaser as the owner of the land during the contract's executory period. Hence, the purchaser is obliged to complete the contract and pay the remaining price even if some

McGinnis, 819 P.2d 1080 (Colo.App.1991) (contract purchaser had a sufficient interest to maintain a quiet title action); Schmeusser v. Schmeusser, 559 A.2d 1294 (Del.1989), appeal after remand 593 A.2d 590 (1991) (by virtue of equitable conversion, husband's entering into contract to sell his land constituted fraud in divorce action); Stangland v. Brock, 109 Wn.2d 675, 747 P.2d 464 (1987) (vendor's interest in land under contract did not pass as "real property" under vendor's will); Chelan County v. Wilson, 49 Wn.App. 628, 744 P.2d 1106 (1987) (contract of sale of portion of vendor's land transferred equitable interest, thereby violating subdivision ordinance); In re Booth, 43 B.R. 197 (Bkrtcy.D.Vt.1984) (Bankruptcy Code); Jacobs v. Great Pacific Century Corp., 197 N.J.Super. 378, 484 A.2d 1312 (1984), affirmed 204 N.J.Super. 605, 499 A.2d 1023 (1985) (equitable conversion not applied to give vendor right to interest earned on cooperative apartment purchasers' earnest money deposits, where to do so would contravene policy behind New York and New Jersey statutes requiring escrowing of such deposits); Currington v. Johnson, 685 P.2d 73 (Alaska 1984) (where tenants had exercised option to purchase property, equitable title passed to them, making unlawful detainer an inappropriate form of action for determination of their rights); Title Insurance & Trust Co. v. Chicago Title Insurance Co., 97 Nev. 523, 634 P.2d 1216 (1981) (purchaser is "successor in interest" under statute requiring notice for deed of trust foreclosure); Dillon v. Afbic Development Corp., 597 F.2d 556 (5th Cir.1979) (vendor is not liable for discriminatory acts of purchaser which violate Fair Housing Act); Committee of Protesting Citizens v. Val Vue Sewer District, 14 Wn.App. 838, 545 P.2d 42 (1976) (purchaser is "owner" for purposes of citizen approval of creation of special district); Byrne v. Kanig, 231 Pa.Super. 531, 332 A.2d 472 (1974) (purchaser obligated to pay lien of sewer assessment); Society Linnea v. Wilbois, 253 Iowa 953, 113 N.W.2d 603 (1962) (purchaser is "owner" for purposes of mechanics lien statute), discussed in 7 Williston, Contracts § 930 (3d ed. 1963); Buck v. McNab, 139 So.2d 734 (Fla.App.1962), cert. denied 146 So.2d 374 (Fla.1962) (purchaser can get specific performance of contract from deceased vendor's successors, despite his failure to file a timely claim against vendor's estate.)

Equitable conversion does not necessarily exculpate the vendor from the usual responsibilities of real estate ownership. See, e.g., Rodeck v. United States, 697 F.Supp. 1508 (D.Minn.1988), holding that a vendor's interest in an executory land contract was still real estate, notwithstanding equitable conversion, for purposes of the notice provisions of the Federal Tax Lien Act; McKone v. Guertzgen, 811 P.2d 728 (Wyo.1991), holding both vendor and purchaser liable for cost of removing abandoned underground gasoline storage tanks; City of Webster Groves v. Erickson, 763 S.W.2d 278 (Mo.App.1988), cert. denied 493 U.S. 814, 110 S.Ct. 62, 107 L.Ed.2d 29 (1989) (vendor is liable for public nuisance ordinance violation); Passnault v. Board of Administrative Appeals, 309 Md. 466, 525 A.2d 222 (1987), holding a vendor responsible for building code violations.

23. In re Highberger's Estate, 468 Pa. 120, 360 A.2d 580 (1976); In re Ryan's Estate, 102 N.W.2d 9 (N.D.1960); In re Briebach's Estate, 132 Mont. 437, 318 P.2d 223 (1957). But see Matter of Houghton's Estate, 147 N.J.Super. 477, 371 A.2d 735 (1977), affirmed 75 N.J. 462, 383 A.2d 713 (1978) (state agency regulation adopting equitable conversion held invalid); Connell v. Crosby, 210 Ill. 380, 71 N.E. 350 (1904) (equitable conversion inappropriate for resolution of tax cases).

24. See Yannopoulos v. Sophos, 243 Pa.Super. 454, 365 A.2d 1312 (1976); Gustin v. Stegall, 347 A.2d 917 (D.C.App.1975), certiorari denied 425 U.S. 974, 96 S.Ct. 2174, 48 L.Ed.2d 798 (1976), rehearing denied 429 U.S. 875, 97 S.Ct. 199, 50 L.Ed.2d 159 (1976); In re Estate of Fischer, 22 Wis.2d 637, 126 N.W.2d 596 (1964); Tingle v. Hornsby, 111 So.2d 274 (Fla. App.1959). A severance is ordinarily thought to occur when the co-owners no longer have unity of time, title, interest, or possession; see § 5.4, supra. If all co-owners execute the contract as vendors, the unities among them are obviously not disturbed and no severance should be deemed to occur unless there is other evidence that they wish to terminate the right of survivorship. The characterization of their interest as realty or personalty is irrelevant. See In re Estelle's Estate, 122 Ariz. 109, 593 P.2d 663 (1979); Yannopoulos v. Sophos, supra (concurring opinion).

unforeseen event, not the fault of the vendor, causes a major loss in value before the closing. This is the majority view.[25] Yet it is subject to strong criticism on both theoretical and practical grounds. As Dean Stone observed long ago, the doctrine is theoretically objectionable because it is circular: Since the contract is specifically enforceable in equity, the buyer is treated as the owner; and since the buyer is deemed the owner, equity will impose the loss on the buyer and compel him or her to complete the contract.[26]

Equitable conversion as a risk-allocation tool for short-term earnest money contracts is equally questionable in practical terms, at least in cases of physical damage occurring while the vendor is in possession. First, it rarely comports with lay parties' expectations; they generally assume the risk is on the vendor.[27] Second, the vendor is far more likely than the purchaser to carry insurance against the loss, since the vendor has usually owned the land for some time, while the buyer thinks of his or her ownership as not yet having begun. Third, until the purchaser takes possession the vendor is in the better position to take whatever precautions might prevent the occurrence of the loss.[28] For these reasons, equitable conversion's broad imposition of risk on the buyer has been resoundingly condemned by nearly all academic writers who have considered it.[29] In practice it causes much less trouble than one might expect, mainly because of the prevalence of casualty insurance and the fact that the parties have the power to make their own agreement in contradiction of equitable conversion's rule.[30] Nearly all printed form sale contracts do so, usually imposing the risk on the vendor. Thus, equitable conversion is primarily a trap for amateur conveyancers.

Losses due to changes in the property's legal status are often imposed on the purchaser under equitable conversion. The property's value may fall,

25. See, e.g., Ridenour v. France, 442 N.E.2d 716 (Ind.App.1982); Northwest Kansas Area Vocational–Technical School v. Wolf, 6 Kan.App.2d 817, 635 P.2d 1268 (1981); Duhon v. Dugas, 407 So.2d 1334 (La.App.1981) (under Louisiana statute); Ambrose v. Harrison Mutual Insurance Association, 206 N.W.2d 683 (Iowa 1973); Bleckley v. Langston, 112 Ga. App. 63, 143 S.E.2d 671 (1965); Ross v. Bumstead, 65 Ariz. 61, 173 P.2d 765 (1946). See generally 3A Corbin, Contracts § 667 (1962); 7 Williston, Contracts § 928 (3d ed. 1963); Fineberg, Risk of Loss in Executory Contracts for the Sale of Real Property, 14 Colum.J.L. & Soc.Prob. 453 (1979); Note, 22 Drake L.Rev. 626 (1973); Hirshler & Fleischer, Risk of Loss in Executory Contracts for the Purchase of Lands, 34 Va.L.Rev. 965 (1948); Annot., 27 A.L.R.2d 444 (1953).

26. Stone, Equitable Conversion by Contract, 13 Colum.L.Rev. 369, 386 (1913), quoted at length in Skelly Oil Co. v. Ashmore, 365 S.W.2d 582 (Mo.1963).

27. The writers know of no systematic study of this point, but one of them has surveyed his first-year law students for many years; a large majority of them invariably

express the view that the vendor probably has the risk.

28. See the discussion in Appleton Electric Co. v. Rogers, 200 Wis. 331, 228 N.W. 505 (1930); Church, Equitable Conversion in Wisconsin, 1970 Wis.L.Rev. 404, 421–22.

29. See articles cited in notes 25, 26, & 28, supra.

30. See Bellucci v. Moore, 585 So.2d 490 (Fla.App.1991) (clause permitting purchaser to rescind if damage to property exceeded 3% of sale price); Winterchase Townhomes, Inc. v. Koether, 193 Ga.App. 161, 387 S.E.2d 361 (1989), cert. vacated 260 Ga. 152, 392 S.E.2d 533 (1990) (clause permitting purchaser to rescind contract or purchase and receive insurance proceeds in the event of damage to property); Smith v. Mohan, 723 S.W.2d 94 (Mo. App.1987) (clause permitting purchaser to rescind contract if property was damaged and not restored by vendor within 30 days); Rector v. Alcorn, 241 N.W.2d 196 (Iowa 1976); Coolidge & Sickler v. Regn, 7 N.J. 93, 80 A.2d 554 (1951). See generally J. Pomeroy, Equity Jurisprudence § 1159ff (5th ed. 1941).

for example, due to a rezoning or loss of benefits under a zoning ordinance,[31] a change in a building code,[32] or an eminent domain action.[33] In these cases the arguments against equitable conversion in the previous paragraph lose much of their force. One cannot insure against a zoning change or a condemnation suit, and there may be little one can do to prevent the loss that ensues. It is also much more debatable whether the usual expectation of the parties would favor the purchaser.[34]

A number of jurisdictions have modified or rejected equitable conversion as an allocator of risk. A few place the risk on the purchaser only if he or she has taken possession of the property.[35] There is considerable sense to this; the purchaser in possession probably expects to have responsibility for the property, and is normally in a good position to insure and protect against loss. Several other courts have rejected equitable conversion entirely and placed the loss on the vendor irrespective of possession.[36] Both of these

31. Mohave County v. Mohave–Kingman Estates, Inc., 120 Ariz. 417, 586 P.2d 978 (1978); J.C. Penney Co. v. Koff, 345 So.2d 732 (Fla.App.1977); DiDonato v. Reliance Standard Life Insurance Co., 433 Pa. 221, 249 A.2d 327 (1969). See also Goldfarb v. Dietz, 8 Wn. App. 464, 506 P.2d 1322 (1973) (risk on purchaser under court's construction of contract language, not equitable conversion.) Cf. Clay v. Landreth, 187 Va. 169, 45 S.E.2d 875 (1948), refusing to enforce the contract where the zoning change made the property unusable for the purchaser's intended purpose; La Rosa Del Monte Express, Inc. v. G.S.W. Enterprises Corp., 483 So.2d 472 (Fla.App.1986), review denied 492 So.2d 1332 (Fla.1986) (lease may be rescinded for total failure of consideration, where zoning ordinance prevents use for which property was leased). See generally Annot., 39 A.L.R.3d 362 (1971). Note that if the zoning is changed so as to make the existing use of the property a violation of the ordinance, the title is probably unmarketable under the principles discussed in § 10.12, supra, and the purchaser will usually have a power to avoid the contract.

32. Cox v. Supreme Savings & Loan Association, 126 Ill.App.2d 293, 262 N.E.2d 74 (1970).

33. Hauben v. Harmon, 605 F.2d 920 (5th Cir.1979) (applying Florida law); Arko Enterprises, Inc. v. Wood, 185 So.2d 734 (Fla.App. 1966); Annot., 27 A.L.R.3d 572 (1969). If the event which causes the loss also imposes an encumbrance on the vendor's title, the contract's title covenants may well give the purchaser a right of rescission; see, e.g., Byrne v. Kanig, 231 Pa.Super. 531, 332 A.2d 472 (1974) (imposition by city of lien for sewer improvement assessment.) Note that an eminent domain action may possibly produce a windfall—that is, an award in excess of the contract price—and that the purchaser will be entitled to it under equitable conversion. See Alhambra Redevelopment Agency v. Transamerica Financial Services, 212 Cal.App.3d 1370, 261 Cal.Rptr. 248 (1989); County of San

Diego v. Miller, 13 Cal.3d 684, 119 Cal.Rptr. 491, 532 P.2d 139 (1975), allowing such an award to a purchaser holding only an unexercised option.

34. The vendor was denied specific performance after a rezoning diminished the property's value for the purchaser's intended use in Clay v. Landreth, 187 Va. 169, 45 S.E.2d 875, 175 A.L.R. 1047 (1948); Anderson v. Steinway & Sons, 178 App.Div. 507, 165 N.Y.S. 608 (1917), affirmed 221 N.Y. 639, 117 N.E. 575 (1917). The rationale of both decisions was that specific enforcement would be inequitable in light of the loss it would impose on the buyer. Yet the court in Clay v. Landreth implied that the vendor might still get damages for the purchaser's refusal to perform, a suggestion which makes little sense if, as the court argued, the parties did not intend for the buyer to take land which he could not use as planned. Cf. Kend v. Crestwood Realty Co., 210 Wis. 239, 246 N.W. 311 (1933), in which the court refused to grant the purchasers cancellation and rescission of the contract on similar facts, but implied that neither would it give the vendor specific performance.

35. Smith v. Warth, 483 S.W.2d 834 (Tex. Civ.App.1972) (risk on party having "beneficial interest", which the court apparently deemed indicated by possession); Potwin v. Tucker, 128 Vt. 142, 259 A.2d 781 (1969); Briz–Ler Corp. v. Weiner, 39 Del.Ch. 578, 171 A.2d 65 (1961); Appleton Electric Co. v. Rogers, 200 Wis. 331, 228 N.W. 505 (1930) (rendered obsolete by passage of the Uniform Vendor and Purchaser Risk Act, discussed infra). See 3A Corbin, Contracts § 669 (1960).

36. Skelly Oil Co. v. Ashmore, 365 S.W.2d 582 (Mo.1963), noted at 1964 Wash.U.L.Q. 128; Lampesis v. Travelers Insurance Co., 101 N.H. 323, 143 A.2d 104 (1958); Anderson v. Yaworski, 120 Conn. 390, 181 A. 205 (1935); Ashford v. Reese, 132 Wash. 649, 233 P. 29 (1925); Libman v. Levenson, 236 Mass. 221, 128 N.E. 13 (1920). See also Tate v. Wood, 169 W.Va.

categories of decisions generally distinguish between "substantial" or "material" losses and those which are not so severe. If the vendor has the risk and the loss is substantial, the vendor cannot enforce the contract at all, and must return the buyer's payments. If the loss is insubstantial, the vendor may have specific performance, but must allow an abatement against the price to account for the damage.[37] This approach causes at least two difficulties. First, it is not necessarily easy to determine whether a given loss is "substantial;" the term is not self-defining, and litigation may be necessary.[38] Second, it is often unclear whether, in the case of a substantial loss, the *purchaser* may insist upon specific performance with abatement if the vendor wishes to treat the contract as terminated. If one thinks of the continued and unimpaired existence of the improvements on the land as an implied condition precedent to the duty to complete the contract, the question is whether the condition is for the benefit of both parties or only the buyer.[39] In the usual case the answer should rather obviously be the latter.[40] Under this view, the buyer can waive the condition and enforce the contract.

There have been two major statutory attempts to resolve the question of risk of loss. The first, the Uniform Vendor and Purchaser Risk Act (UVPRA), was drafted by Professor Williston and promulgated by the Commissioners on Uniform State Laws in 1935; it has been adopted in ten states.[41] The second is Section 2–406 of the Uniform Land Transactions Act (ULTA), adopted by the Commissioners in 1975 but not yet enacted by any legislature. Both take the same basic approach, leaving the risk of loss on the vendor until possession or legal title is transferred to the purchaser.

584, 289 S.E.2d 432 (1982), suggesting in dictum that the destruction of the improvements on land might "void the contract" on grounds of impossibility of performance. The foregoing cases do not discuss the significance of possession; some of the jurisdictions cited might shift the risk to a purchaser in possession, placing themselves with the states mentioned in note 35, supra. See generally 3A Corbin, Contracts § 668 (1960).

37. See, e.g., Hawkes v. Kehoe, 193 Mass. 419, 79 N.E. 766 (1907).

38. Perhaps the most intriguing case is Skelly Oil Co. v. Ashmore, supra note 36, in which the purchaser had planned to demolish the building which was destroyed by fire before the closing. The court found the loss material, but the dissent argued that the fire had actually saved the buyer money.

39. See § 10.11, supra, at notes 30–35. The condition might be thought for the benefit of both parties if the vendor were taking a purchase money mortgage or for other reasons had a continuing interest in the presence of the improvements on the land.

40. See Skelly Oil Co. v. Ashmore, supra note 36, granting the purchaser specific performance with abatement for a material loss; Bornemann v. Richards, 245 La. 851, 161 So.2d 741 (1964) (same result under La. statute); Phinizy v. Guernsey, 111 Ga. 346, 36 S.E. 796, (1900). See also Laurin v. DeCarolis Construction Co., 372 Mass. 688, 363 N.E.2d 675 (1977) (willful destruction by vendor, but court implied same result would follow an innocent loss). Compare the dictum in Libman v. Levenson, 236 Mass. 221, 128 N.E. 13, 22 (1920) (when a substantial loss occurs, " * * * the contract is no longer binding upon either party") with Anderson v. Yaworski, 120 Conn. 390, 181 A. 205 (1935) (" * * * the vendee may treat it as discharged.") See generally 3 Am. L.Prop. § 11.30 (1952). There seems to be no serious doubt that the purchaser can have specific performance if he or she is willing to pay the full price without abatement; see Stapper v. Rusch, 127 Tex. 151, 92 S.W.2d 431 (1936).

41. The UVPRA is the law in California, Hawaii, Illinois, Michigan, New York (with significant changes), North Carolina, Oklahoma, Oregon, South Dakota, and Wisconsin. See generally Pusateri, Risk of Loss After Contract to Sell Real Property: Adoption of Uniform Vendor and Purchaser Risk Act in Illinois, 52 Ill.B.J. 464 (1964); Lacy, The Uniform Vendor and Purchaser Risk Act and the Need for a Law–Revision Commission in Oregon, 36 Or.L.Rev. 106 (1957). See Unger v. Nunda Township Rural Fire Protection Dist., 135 Ill.App.3d 758, 90 Ill.Dec. 416, 482 N.E.2d 123 (1985) (purchaser with legal right of possession, who had been removing trees from it, had sufficient possession to have risk of loss under UVPRA).

They deny the vendor the right to enforce the contract and compel him to return the buyer's deposit if a material loss occurs while he has the risk. Yet both acts leave the law in an uncertain state on several points. They appear to apply only to physical damage [42] and to takings in eminent domain; whether they would influence a court in a case of loss by zoning amendment or other change of legal status is unclear. Both employ the concept of materiality of loss [43] without attempting to define it in dollar or percentage terms. For example, it is by no means obvious whether a $1000 fire in a single-family home would qualify. The UVPRA is also deficient in failing to indicate whether, after a material loss, the purchaser may none-theless specifically enforce the contract with abatement of the price,[44] and whether, if the loss is non-material and the contract is enforced against the purchaser, the latter is entitled to a price abatement for the damage.[45] The ULTA answers both of these questions affirmatively.[46] The inadequacies of both of these model acts suggest that neither is an adequate substitute for a competently-drafted contract clause which deals explicitly with all of the matters discussed above.[47]

The legal rules governing risk of loss are complicated when the loss is covered by a casualty insurance policy. If there is only one policy and it insures the party on whom the law or the contract imposes the risk of loss, the problems are minimal.[48] But all too often the logic of equitable conver-sion puts the risk on the buyer when the seller is the only party insured. If the seller recovers the full price for the land and also collects from his insurer, he or she seems to receive an unwarranted stroke of good fortune. The seller may argue that there is no reason to give the buyer any benefit

---

42. UVPRA speaks of the "subject matter" being "destroyed"; ULTA speaks of "casualty loss."

43. UVPRA is triggered if a "material part" is destroyed; ULTA operates if there is a "substantial failure of the real estate to conform to the contract." See National Factors, Inc. v. Winslow, 52 Misc.2d 194, 274 N.Y.S.2d 400 (1966) (loss of $10,000 on $180,-000 property was not material, where purchaser had planned to rebuild on the site.)

44. The New York cases permit the purchaser to enforce with abatement under the UVPRA despite the statute's silence on the point; Jewell v. Rowe, 119 A.D.2d 634, 500 N.Y.S.2d 787 (1986) (purchaser may have rescission or specific performance with abatement); Lucenti v. Cayuga Apartments, Inc., 59 A.D.2d 438, 400 N.Y.S.2d 194 (1977), appeal after remand 66 A.D.2d 928, 410 N.Y.S.2d 928 (1978), appeal dismissed 46 N.Y.2d 997, 416 N.Y.S.2d 242, 389 N.E.2d 837 (1979): Burack v. Tollig, 10 N.Y.2d 879, 223 N.Y.S.2d 505, 179 N.E.2d 509 (1961); contra, see Dixon v. Salvation Army, 142 Cal.App.3d 463, 191 Cal.Rptr. 111 (1983).

45. The New York version of UVPRA, unlike the official version, explicitly provides for abatement on these facts; see N.Y.—McKinney's Gen.Obl.Law § 5–1311, applied in National Factors, Inc. v. Winslow, 52 Misc.2d 194, 274 N.Y.S.2d 400 (1966).

46. ULTA § 2–406(1), (2).

47. See M. Friedman, Contracts and Conveyances of Real Property 382 (3d ed. 1975). Ordinarily the parties can vary existing law at their pleasure by appropriate contract language. See Caulfield v. Improved Risk Mutuals, Inc., 66 N.Y.2d 793, 497 N.Y.S.2d 903, 488 N.E.2d 833 (1985) (contract clause controls over UVPRA). But see Tinker v. McLellan, 165 Cal.App.2d 291, 331 P.2d 464 (1958), in which the buyers had taken possession prior to closing. A contract clause imposed the risk of loss on the vendor, but when a flood damaged the property after the buyers had unjustifiably delayed closing, the court held them estopped to assert the contract language and put the risk on them under the UVPRA.

48. The principal difficulty is simply that the insurance may be inadequate in amount. Many casualty policies contain "co-insurance clauses." A typical clause provides that if the policy's face amount is not at least 80% of the property's replacement cost, the insurer's liability for any loss is limited to the fraction of the loss which the policy amount bears to 80% of the property's replacement cost. For example, suppose the replacement cost of the improvements is $100,000 and the policy amount $60,000. If a $1000 loss occurs, the insurer will pay only 60/80, or $750.

from the insurance, which is, after all a personal contract of indemnity between insurer and insured.[49] But the seller's windfall has been too much for most modern courts to swallow, and the cases generally permit the seller to enforce the contract only if he or she is willing to abate the price to the extent of the insurance recovery.[50] This result, which is often explained as the imposition of a constructive trust on the insurance funds in favor of the purchaser, greatly mitigates the original unfairness of equitable conversion.[51]

Occasionally a case arises in which the positions of the parties are reversed: the purchaser has insurance, but the risk is on the vendor. Here again is an opportunity for a windfall, this time to the purchaser. Can the purchaser collect the insurance proceeds and at the same time escape the

49. Such an argument has succeeded in a few courts; see Long v. Keller, 104 Cal.App.3d 312, 163 Cal.Rptr. 532 (1980) (purchaser was in possession; had risk under UVPRA); Whitley v. Irwin, 250 Ark. 543, 465 S.W.2d 906 (1971); Twin City Fire Insurance Co. v. Walter B. Hannah, Inc., 444 S.W.2d 131 (Ky.1969) (construing statute); Brownell v. Board of Education, 239 N.Y. 369, 146 N.E. 630, 37 A.L.R. 13, 19 (1925). These cases generally follow Rayner v. Preston, 18 Ch. Div. 1 (1881). Note also the possibility that the insurer will attempt to deny the vendor's claim on the ground that he or she has no loss, and therefore nothing to indemnify, if the risk is on the buyer. This argument has usually been rejected; see Kintzel v. Wheatland Mutual Insurance Association, 203 N.W.2d 799 (Iowa 1973); cases cited note 52, infra.

50. See, e.g., Hendricks v. M.C.I., Inc., 152 Wis.2d 363, 448 N.W.2d 289 (1989); Alabama Farm Bureau Mut. Ins. Co. v. Meyers, 516 So.2d 661 (Ala.Civ.App.1987); New Hampshire Ins. Co. v. Vetter, 326 N.W.2d 723 (S.D.1982); Berlier v. George, 94 N.M. 134, 607 P.2d 1152 (1980); Cheatwood v. De Los Santos, 561 S.W.2d 273 (Tex.Civ.App.1978), refused n.r.e.; Fellmer v. Gruber, 261 N.W.2d 173 (Iowa 1978); Wilson v. Fireman's Insurance Co., 403 Mich. 339, 269 N.W.2d 170 (1978) (vendor insured, but premiums paid by purchaser); Chapline v. North American Acceptance Corp., 25 Ariz.App. 465, 544 P.2d 682 (1976); Rawlins v. Cook, 294 Ala. 733, 321 So.2d 208 (1975); Gilles v. Sprout, 293 Minn. 53, 196 N.W.2d 612 (1972); Briz–Ler Corp. v. Weiner, 39 Del. Ch. 578, 171 A.2d 65 (1961); Oakes v. Wingfield, 95 Ga.App. 871, 99 S.E.2d 241 (1956); Vogel v. Northern Assurance Co., 219 F.2d 409 (3d Cir.1955); Dubin Paper Co. v. Insurance Co. of North America, 361 Pa. 68, 63 A.2d 85 (1949). See also Petrie v. LeVan, 799 S.W.2d 632 (Mo.App.1990), in which the vendor had both the risk and the insurance, but the parties were unaware of the storm damage to the property when they closed, with the vendor receiving both the full price and, later, recovery on the insurance policy. The court found unjust enrichment and or-

dered the vendor to pay the insurance proceeds to the purchaser.

Even the New York Court of Appeals, which has generally denied the purchaser the benefit of the vendor's insurance, granted that privilege to a purchaser who had paid the insurance premiums; Raplee v. Piper, 3 N.Y.2d 179, 164 N.Y.S.2d 732, 143 N.E.2d 919, 64 A.L.R.2d 1397 (1957). Several of the foregoing cases indicate that the abatement in favor of the purchaser should be reduced by the amount of premiums paid by the vendor while the purchaser had the risk of loss. See generally Davis v. Skinner, 474 So.2d 1136 (Ala.Civ. App.1985). Annot., 64 A.L.R.2d 1402 (1959). Cf. McGuire v. Wilson, 372 So.2d 1297 (Ala. 1979), an action by the vendor's insurer against the purchaser for negligence on a subrogation theory; the court held the vendor did not hold the insurance proceeds as a trustee for the purchaser, and thus sustained the insurer's subrogation claim.

Note that the parties can resolve the question of entitlement to the insurance proceeds by language in the contract of sale; see, e.g., Smith v. Buege, 182 W.Va. 204, 387 S.E.2d 109 (1989), in which the court upheld a clause giving the vendor's insurance proceeds to the purchaser, as against an argument by the insurer that the clause constituted an unconsented and therefore improper assignment of the policy.

51. Perhaps surprisingly, the ULTA does not address the question of disposition of the proceeds of the seller's insurance where the purchaser has the risk of loss. It does, however, allow the purchaser credit for the proceeds as an alternate measure of abatement of price if the risk is on the seller; ULTA § 2–406(b)(1), (2). See text at note 46, supra. The tentative draft of the UVPRA, prepared by Professor Williston, gave the purchaser a clear right to enforce the contract with abatement of price in the amount of insurance proceeds received by the seller, but this language was not included in the Commissioners' official version; see O. Browder, et al., Basic Property Law 1089 (3d ed. 1979).

contract or buy the land at an abated price? To do so the purchaser must meet several objections. First, if he or she refuses to complete the contract (plainly a permissible course of action on these facts), the insurer may argue that no loss at all has occurred, and hence that no claim can be made on the insurance policy.[52] This argument has considerable force. Even if the purchaser proceeds with the contract and buys with an abatement of price, the insurer can take much the same position. Moreover, if the insurer pays the claim, the vendor may argue that the insurance was intended for his or her benefit as well, despite the fact that the policy did not name the vendor as an insured; this argument is likely to succeed only if the contract stipulated that the purchaser would carry insurance.[53] The vendor may then insist that the abatement of price owing to the loss be reduced by the insurance proceeds, or if the purchaser defaults on the contract the vendor may seek to recover the insurance proceeds.

Time of Conversion. Both the characterization and risk cases seem to assume that it is easy to tell when equitable conversion has occurred. But that is not always so. It is clear enough that there must be a fully formed contract of sale; an unexercised option, for example, is not enough.[54] Moreover, the contract must be enforceable in equity. Hence, an oral contract which has not been the subject of part performance [55] or a contract which is so unjust as to be unenforceable [56] will not work a conversion. If the seller's title is defective, no conversion occurs, at least for purposes of shifting away the risk of loss, until the defects are cured.[57] Note that conversion does not

52. Sanford v. Breidenbach, 111 Ohio App. 474, 173 N.E.2d 702 (1960); Phillips v. Bacon, 245 Ga. 814, 267 S.E.2d 249 (1980). For an analogous case in which the insurance company successfully defended a suit by its insured vendor on the ground that the purchaser had paid him the full price, and thus that he had no loss, see Westfall v. American States Insurance Co., 43 Ohio App.2d 176, 334 N.E.2d 523 (1974); see also Paramount Fire Insurance Co. v. Aetna Casualty & Surety Co., 163 Tex. 250, 353 S.W.2d 841 (1962), noted 17 Sw.L.J. 334 (1963), which may be explainable on the ground that the purchaser was in possession when the loss occurred. Contra, and probably the majority view, see Wolf v. Home Insurance Co., 100 N.J.Super. 27, 241 A.2d 28 (1968), affirmed 103 N.J.Super. 357, 247 A.2d 345 (1968); Vogel v. Northern Assurance Co., 219 F.2d 409 (3d Cir.1955). See generally Fineberg, Risk of Loss in Executory Contracts for the Sale of Real Property, 14 Colum.J.L. & Soc.Prob. 453, 478–82 (1979).

53. See Kintzel v. Wheatland Mutual Insurance Association, 203 N.W.2d 799 (Iowa 1973) (vendor identified as such on the face of policy insuring purchaser); Kindred v. Boalbey, 73 Ill.App.3d 37, 29 Ill.Dec. 77, 391 N.E.2d 236 (1979); Nevada Refining Co. v. Newton, 88 Nev. 333, 497 P.2d 887 (1972); Marbach v. Gnadl, 73 Ill.App.2d 303, 219 N.E.2d 572 (1966). Cf. Phillips v. Bacon, supra note 52 (no contract clause; purchaser's insurer not liable to vendor.) See generally Couch, Insurance § 29–103 (1960).

54. See Tate v. Wood, 169 W.Va. 584, 289 S.E.2d 432 (1982); County of San Diego v. Miller, 13 Cal.3d 684, 119 Cal.Rptr. 491, 532 P.2d 139 (1975); Eddington v. Turner, 27 Del. Ch. 411, 38 A.2d 738, 155 A.L.R. 562 (1944); In re Bisbee's Estate, 177 Wis. 77, 187 N.W. 653 (1922). See 3 Am.L.Prop. § 11.23 (1952); Annot., 172 A.L.R. 438 (1948).

55. Guzman v. Acuna, 653 S.W.2d 315 (Tex.App.1983) (part of contract was so illegible as to be unenforceable; no equitable conversion occurred). See § 10.2, supra.

56. See § 10.5, supra, at notes 17–19; 3 Am.L.Prop. § 11.24 (1952). See also Metz v. United States, 933 F.2d 802 (10th Cir.1991), cert. denied ___ U.S. ___, 112 S.Ct. 416, 116 L.Ed.2d 436 (1991) (under Kansas law, a contract to devise property by will is not specifically enforceable, and hence gives rise to no equitable conversion).

57. Sharbono v. Darden, 220 Mont. 320, 715 P.2d 433 (1986). But see Life Sav. & Loan Ass'n v. Bryant, 125 Ill.App.3d 1012, 81 Ill. Dec. 577, 467 N.E.2d 277 (1984) (conversion occurred when contract was signed, despite vendor's lack of title; but case involved purchaser's priority as against vendor's mortgagee, not risk of loss); Northwest Kansas Area Vocational–Technical School v. Wolf, 6 Kan. App.2d 817, 635 P.2d 1268 (1981); Phillips v. Bacon, 245 Ga. 814, 267 S.E.2d 249 (1980); Amundson v. Severson, 41 S.D. 377, 170 N.W. 633 (1919).

depend on actual enforcement of the contract; if it is enforceable at the critical time (the loss, death of a party, etc.), the fact that it is later rescinded or abandoned is immaterial.[58]

If none of the barriers mentioned above is present, conversion is generally assumed to occur the moment the contract of sale is signed.[59] But occasionally a court has seized on the presence of unfulfilled conditions in the contract as a basis for denying that there has been a conversion,[60] and dictum is fairly common to the effect that the contract must be "unconditional" to effect a conversion.[61] The basis of this language is presumably that equity will not enforce the contract until the conditions have been met, but this reasoning is too broad. If the condition in question is also a covenant—that is, if a party has promised to fulfill it—the parties properly consider themselves bound by the contract, and equity will enforce it.[62] Certainly such common conditions as the mutual tender of the deed and the price or the completion of promised repairs by the vendor should not defeat equitable conversion. Only if the condition is dependent on the actions of a third party, as in conditions of financing or rezoning, can one logically deny that conversion has occurred until the third party has acted.[63] Unfortunately, there is little helpful discussion of this distinction in the cases.[64]

§ 10.14   Options and Preemptive Rights

A real estate option consists of two concepts linked together: first, an offer to sell property on certain defined terms; and second, a contractual undertaking to leave that offer open for a period of time. Ordinarily an offeror may revoke an offer to sell at will before it has been accepted, but in an option the optionor suspends the power to revoke by contracting not to do

---

58. Frietze v. Frietze, 78 N.M. 676, 437 P.2d 137 (1968); Clapp v. Tower, 11 N.D. 556, 93 N.W. 862 (1903).

59. See Shay v. Penrose, 25 Ill.2d 447, 185 N.E.2d 218 (1962).

60. The best-known example is Sanford v. Breidenbach, 111 Ohio App. 474, 173 N.E.2d 702 (1960). See also Jacobs v. Great Pacific Century Corp., 197 N.J.Super. 378, 484 A.2d 1312 (1984), affirmed 204 N.J.Super. 605, 499 A.2d 1023 (1985) (dictum); Frankiewicz v. Konwinski, 246 Mich. 473, 224 N.W. 368 (1929); Rodisch v. Moore, 266 Ill. 106, 107 N.E. 108 (1914). See Re, Equity and Equitable Remedies 585 (1975); Annot., 27 A.L.R.2d 444, 453 (1953).

61. See, e.g., Hall v. Pioneer Crop Care, Inc., 212 Kan. 554, 512 P.2d 491 (1973); Byrne v. Kanig, 231 Pa.Super. 531, 332 A.2d 472 (1974).

62. See § 10.11, supra.

63. See Lincoln Park Federal Sav. & Loan Ass'n v. DRG, Inc., 175 Ill.App.3d 176, 124 Ill.Dec. 790, 529 N.E.2d 771 (1988) (conversion occurs when enforceable contract is entered into, even though price has not been paid). Cf. United Bank of Bismarck v. Trout, 480 N.W.2d 742 (N.D.1992) (where purchaser did

not pay earnest money, no enforceable contract was formed and no equitable conversion occurred). Compare In re Governor Mifflin Joint School Authority Petition, 401 Pa. 387, 164 A.2d 221 (1960) (unfulfilled condition of rezoning; no equitable conversion), and Simmons v. Krall, 201 Ga.App. 893, 412 S.E.2d 559 (1991) (unfulfilled condition that vendor cover land and sow grass; no equitable conversion) with Filsam Corp. v. Dyer, 422 F.Supp. 1126 (E.D.Pa.1976) (unfulfilled condition that vendor make repairs; conversion has occurred.) There is some suggestion in the cases that, where the condition is for the benefit of only one party, that party may take advantage of equitable conversion for risk-of-loss purposes while the other may not. See Northern Texas Realty & Construction Co. v. Lary, 136 S.W. 843 (Tex.Civ.App.1911), error refused. Cf. Re, Equity and Equitable Remedies 585 (1975), suggesting that, for purposes of devolution upon death, if only one party could enforce the contract there is no equitable conversion on either side.

64. See, however, the good discussions in Matter of Estate of Clark, 447 N.W.2d 549 (Iowa App.1989) and Filsam Corp. v. Dyer, note 63 supra.

so.[1] If consideration is paid for the option, the promise to hold the offer of sale irrevocable is specifically enforceable.[2] If and when the offer is accepted, the option is said to be exercised.

As a practical matter, an optionor must take the property off the market for the period of the option, or must at least warn interested potential buyers that any transaction with them is subject to being preempted by the exercise of the option. Since this means that the optionor may be forced to forego acceptance of other, more attractive offers, the optionor ordinarily demands a significant price for the option itself.

In many situations the option is an attractive and convenient technique for acquiring land, especially for future development. For example, a subdivision builder may identify a tract of land which seems suitable for development, but only after many conditions are satisfied. Rezoning may be needed, approval of the subdivision by the local planning commission may be necessary, soil tests must be made, surveys must be obtained, and the builder must arrange land acquisition and construction financing. In theory the land seller and the builder could enter into a "firm" contract in which each of these matters was recited in detail as a condition precedent to the builder's obligation to proceed with the sale. As more and more conditions were added that give the purchaser a potential "out," the contract would approach in practical effect an option (except that it would probably provide for return of the earnest money if the conditions were not met). But the drafting of such conditions is complex and their subsequent interpretation is open to dispute. An option is a more efficient approach. It is a much simpler document, and it permits the builder to become fully satisfied with all of the matters mentioned, as well as any others that arise in the course of investigation, with no obligation to purchase the land unless all of these concerns are met.[3]

In the context just described, an option typically stands alone. But leases frequently include options as well, either to extend the lease term, to purchase the premises, or both. If the lease is terminated prematurely because of the tenant's default, controversy often arises as to the continued viability of the option. The cases are divided on the issue.[4]

An option is not a contract of sale, since it does not impose any duty on the purchaser to buy the property. However, some purported contracts are in fact options. If the contract provides that, in the event of the purchaser's breach, the vendor's sole remedy is the retention of the earnest money or

---

§ 10.14

1. Sutton Place Dev. Co. v. Bank of Commerce, 149 Ill.App.3d 513, 103 Ill.Dec. 122, 501 N.E.2d 143 (1986), appeal denied 114 Ill.2d 558, 108 Ill.Dec. 426, 508 N.E.2d 737 (1987).

2. See In re Wilhoit, 69 B.R. 365 (Bkrtcy. M.D.Fla.1987) (consideration must actually be paid, and not merely recited); Property Assistance Corp. v. Roberts, 768 P.2d 976 (Utah App.1989); Crowley v. Bass, 445 So.2d 902 (Ala.1984); Hott v. Pearcy/Christon, Inc., 663 S.W.2d 851 (Tex.App.1983); Keaster v. Bozik, 191 Mont. 293, 623 P.2d 1376 (1981) (nominal consideration is sufficient to sustain option); Restatement (Second) of Contracts § 25 (1981);

Brown, Real Estate Purchase Options, 12 Nova L.Rev. 147 (1987). Cf. Normile v. Miller, 313 N.C. 98, 326 S.E.2d 11 (1985) (absent a promise to hold the offer open, it is not an option and is revoked by the offeror's sale to another party).

3. See Temkin, Too Much Good Faith in Real Estate Purchase Agreements? Give Me an Option, 34 Kan.L.Rev. 43 (1985).

4. See § 6.66, supra; Ebrecht v. Ponchatoula Farm Bureau Ass'n, 498 So.2d 55 (La. App.1986), writ denied 501 So.2d 233 (La.1987) (right of first refusal in lease is limited to the term of the lease).

some other sum as liquidated damages,[5] the practical effect is to render the contract nothing more than an option.[6]

The drafting of options is a more exacting process than the parties sometimes realize. There is a temptation to think of the option as a short, simple document that merely describes the land and the parties and sets forth the method of exercising the option and the selling price.[7] However, the option, if exercised, will become a binding contract of sale. Hence it should contain provisions dealing with every matter that would be included in a well-drawn contract, and must at a minimum contain the elements essential to satisfy the statute of frauds,[8] for while the option itself may not be within the coverage of the statute, the contract that results from its exercise surely will be.[9] It is also important that the precise manner of exercise of the option be spelled out; countless disputes have occurred over this matter.

The optionee generally pays cash for the option itself. In the simplest case there is only a single payment at the time the option is entered into.

5. Ordinarily the mere presence of a liquidated damages clause does not preclude the vendor from claiming non-damage remedies, such as specific performance. However, an express preclusion of such remedies will be given effect. See § 10.4 n. 16, supra.

6. See, e.g., Cutter Dev. Corp. v. Peluso, 212 Conn. 107, 561 A.2d 926 (1989) (concurring opinion); Dodek v. CF 16 Corp., 537 A.2d 1086 (D.C.App.1988); Pace v. Garcia, 631 F.Supp. 1417 (W.D.Tex.1986) (Texas law); Broady v. Mitchell, 572 S.W.2d 36 (Tex.Civ.App.1978); Green Manor Corp. v. Tomares, 266 Md. 472, 295 A.2d 212 (1972). In some contexts the distinction between an option and a contract limiting the vendor to liquidated damages may be significant. See Pollard v. City of Bozeman, 228 Mont. 176, 741 P.2d 776 (1987) (if document is a contract, purchaser is responsible for property taxes); Interactive Properties Corp. v. Blue Cross & Blue Shield of Greater New York, 114 Misc.2d 255, 450 N.Y.S.2d 1001 (1982) (if document is a contract, real estate broker has earned a commission); State v. Bakers Basin Realty Co., 138 N.J.Super. 33, 350 A.2d 236 (1975), affirmed 74 N.J. 103, 376 A.2d 1189 (1977) (if document is a contract, purchaser has standing to claim a portion of eminent domain award).

The courts are seriously divided as to whether an optionee's interest is compensable in eminent domain; see County of San Diego v. Miller, 13 Cal.3d 684, 119 Cal.Rptr. 491, 532 P.2d 139 (1975); Spokane School Dist. No. 81 v. Parzybok, 96 Wn.2d 95, 633 P.2d 1324 (1981); Annot., 85 A.L.R.2d 588 (1962).

7. Compare Busching v. Griffin, 542 So.2d 860 (Miss.1989) (option failed to mention the type of deed, the quality of the title, taxes, or the method by which the purchase price would be paid, but court nonetheless found option enforceable) with Christmas v. Turkin, 148 Ariz. 602, 716 P.2d 59 (1986) (option failed to state manner in which purchase price would be paid; held too indefinite to be enforced).

8. Compare Fried v. Barad, 175 Ill.App.3d 382, 125 Ill.Dec. 175, 530 N.E.2d 93 (1988), appeal denied 124 Ill.2d 556, 129 Ill.Dec. 150, 535 A.2d 915 (1989) (option enforced, although it stated that price would be paid "on such terms as [optionor] is willing to accept") with Christmas v. Turkin, 148 Ariz. 602, 716 P.2d 59 (1986) (option held unenforceable, where it provided that the balance of the price would be paid as the parties might later negotiate). See also Castrucci v. Young, 33 Ohio Misc.2d 41, 515 N.E.2d 658 (1986) (where option does not state method of payment of the price, court will enforce it if the optionee tenders cash.)

The option itself is not a contract of sale of land, and hence is outside the statute; see W.M., R.W., and T.R. Bowler v. TMG Partnership, 357 N.W.2d 109 (Minn.1984); Old Nat. Bank of Washington v. Arneson, 54 Wn.App. 717, 776 P.2d 145 (1989), review denied 113 Wn.2d 1019, 781 P.2d 1321 (1989). Cf. Scutti Enterprises, Inc. v. Wackerman Guchone Custom Builders, Inc., 153 A.D.2d 83, 548 N.Y.S.2d 967 (1989), appeal denied 75 N.Y.2d 709, 555 N.Y.S.2d 692, 554 N.E.2d 1280 (1990) (option to repurchase, reserved in deed, is within statute of frauds). In all events, when the option is exercised a contract for the sale of land is formed and the statute must be satisfied. As to the elements required by the statute of frauds, see § 10.1 nn. 21–26, supra. Note that there is no requirement that the option must be exercised in writing, provided that other writings exist to satisfy the statute; Kaplan v. Lippman, 75 N.Y.2d 320, 552 N.Y.S.2d 903, 552 N.E.2d 151 (1990).

9. Old Quarry Ass'n v. Hickey, 659 F.Supp. 1064 (D.Conn.1986).

Other, more complex, arrangements are possible, under which the optionee pays additional amounts at prescribed intervals in order to extend the option's life.

The sale price is a particularly critical feature of an option, and may be handled in one of several ways. Many options are for a stated price. Alternatively, the option may describe a method of arriving at the price, as by an appraisal to be conducted [10] or by the application of an external index such as the Consumer Price Index to an initially stated amount.[11] In no event should the price be left to future agreement of the parties. The consideration paid for the option itself may or may not be credited against the price if the option is exercised. Likewise, if the option is contained in a lease, a provision may be included crediting the rental payments against the selling price.[12]

Time is considered essential in the exercise of an option even if it is not stated to be such, so that the optionee who is even slightly tardy loses the power to exercise.[13] The courts are also quite rigorous in enforcing the option's terms with respect to the place and manner of exercise; substantial performance is not enough.[14] Thus it is well for the drafter to specify these matters with great precision.

10. Wells v. Gootrad, 112 Idaho 912, 736 P.2d 1366 (App.1987) (where parties did not follow option's procedure for obtaining appraisal, court had authority to appoint appraiser); Castrucci v. Young, 33 Ohio Misc.2d 41, 515 N.E.2d 658 (1986) (option to purchase for "reasonable market value" was enforceable, since the value was readily ascertainable); TCC Enterprises v. Estate of Erny, 149 Ariz. 257, 717 P.2d 936 (App.1986) (where option is contained in a lease, the appraised value is to be measured subject to the lease); Contos v. Lipsky, 433 So.2d 1242 (Fla.App. 1983) (same).

11. If the option itself fails to establish the price or a mechanism for determining it, the court may fix the price as the current market value; Kaufman v. Lassiter, 520 So.2d 692 (Fla.App.1988), appeal after remand 563 So.2d 209 (1990).

12. See Conner v. Alvarez, 285 S.C. 97, 328 S.E.2d 334 (1985).

13. Finkle v. Gulf & Western Mfg. Co., 744 F.2d 1015 (3d Cir.1984); Rice v. Wood, 91 N.C.App. 262, 371 S.E.2d 500 (1988); TST, Ltd. v. Houston, 256 Ga. 679, 353 S.E.2d 26 (1987); Lewis v. Chase, 23 Mass.App. 673, 505 N.E.2d 211 (1987), review denied 399 Mass. 1105, 507 N.E.2d 105 (1987); Edwards v. Rouse, 290 S.C. 449, 351 S.E.2d 174 (1986); Trueman–Aspen Co. v. North Mill Inv. Corp., 728 P.2d 343 (Colo.App.1986); In re Schnur Enterprises, Inc., 42 B.R. 202 (Bkrtcy.W.D.Pa.1984); Howard Cole & Co. v. Williams, 157 Fla. 851, 27 So.2d 352 (1946); Ritchie v. Cordray, 10 Ohio App.3d 213, 461 N.E.2d 325 (1983) (time is essential, but may be waived by optionor); Annot., 87 A.L.R.3d 805 (1978); Annot., 72 A.L.R.2d 1127 (1960). New York is the only jurisdiction consistently indicating a willingness to give the optionee relief from tardy exercise where the optionor has not been prejudiced and the optionee would otherwise suffer a loss out of proportion to his or her fault; see Tritt v. Huffman & Boyle Co., 121 A.D.2d 531, 503 N.Y.S.2d 842 (1986), appeal denied 68 N.Y.2d 611, 510 N.Y.S.2d 1025, 502 N.E.2d 1007 (1986); Grunberg v. George Associates, 104 A.D.2d 745, 480 N.Y.S.2d 217 (1984); Board of Higher Education v. Bass and D'Alessandro Enterprises, Inc., 85 A.D.2d 543, 445 N.Y.S.2d 6 (1981).

In most jurisdictions the "mailbox rule" followed in contract acceptance cases is not applicable to an option; unless the parties specifically agree to exercise by deposit in the mails, actual receipt of the notice of exercise within the allotted time is necessary. See Santiago v. United States, 642 F.Supp. 267 (D.P.R.1986); Musgrove v. Long, 248 Ga. 902, 287 S.E.2d 23 (1982). Cf. Bruss v. Klein, 210 Ill.App.3d 72, 154 Ill.Dec. 683, 568 N.E.2d 904 (1991) (parties agreed to exercise by deposit in mail); Smith v. Hevro Realty Corp., 199 Conn. 330, 507 A.2d 980 (1986) (same); Getty Refining & Marketing Co. v. Zwiebel, 604 F.Supp. 774 (D.Conn.1985) (same).

14. Stratman v. Dietrich, 765 P.2d 603 (Colo.App.1988); Manning v. Bergeron, 430 So.2d 108 (La.App.1983), writ denied 437 So.2d 1154 (La.1983); Master Builders, Inc. v. Cabbell, 95 N.M. 371, 622 P.2d 276 (1980), cert. denied 95 N.M. 426, 622 P.2d 1046 (1981). Cf. Nielson v. Droubay, 652 P.2d 1293 (Utah 1982) (substantial performance was sufficient, where optionor had waived strict performance). Where the option does not state the method of exercise, it can be exercised by tender of the

When an optionor transfers optioned property, the option remains effective against the land if the transferee has actual or constructive notice of it.[15] In most jurisdictions the recording acts apply to options, so that recordation will provide constructive notice.[16] This result is perhaps surprising, since under the doctrine of equitable conversion, an unexercised option is not yet, for most purposes, an interest in real property;[17] but applicability of the recording acts is obviously of immense practical utility.

The Right of First Refusal or Preemptive Right. A right of first refusal (also termed a preemptive right) is a conditional option; it can be exercised only if the seller first decides to accept some other person's offer to buy the property. The holder of the preemptive right then has the option to purchase the property, typically at the same price and on the same terms as the third party's offer. Under a less common arrangement, the holder may have the right to buy at a fixed price or at some percentage of the third party's offering price.[18] Where the holder must match a third party's offer, the holder obviously has a right to be informed clearly of the terms of that offer.[19]

Rights of first refusal are problematic in many ways. Where the price is fixed by the third party's offer, the implicit assumption is that the third party will wish to buy exactly the land subject to the right. But difficult problems of construction arise if the third party's offer is to purchase a larger parcel that includes the subject property,[20] or to purchase only a part of the subject property. Similarly, if the third party's offer is an exchange of land rather than money, or is somehow unique in financing or other terms, and consequently is hard or impossible for the holder of the right to match, is the right lost?[21] Is the right triggered by a foreclosure

purchase price; Tristram's Group, Inc. v. Morrow, 22 Mass.App.Ct. 980, 496 N.E.2d 176 (1986); Petition of Hilltop Development, 342 N.W.2d 344 (Minn.1984). If the optionor anticipatorily repudiates the option, the optionee need not perform the futile act of exercising it in order to recover damages for breach; Bitzes v. Sunset Oaks, Inc., 649 P.2d 66 (Utah 1982).

15. Spokane School Dist. No. 81 v. Parzybok, 96 Wn.2d 95, 633 P.2d 1324 (1981); Dunlap v. Fort Mohave Farms, Inc., 89 Ariz. 387, 363 P.2d 194 (1961). See generally Annot., 17 A.L.R.2d 331 (1951). A transfer of the land does not relieve the optionor of liability for performance of the option, and if the transferee refuses to perform, the optionor may be liable in damages; Martinesi v. Tidmore, 158 Ariz. 53, 760 P.2d 1102 (App.1988).

16. See § 11.9 n. 40, infra.

17. See Bauserman v. Digiulian, 224 Va. 414, 297 S.E.2d 671 (1982); Eddington v. Turner, 27 Del.Ch. 411, 38 A.2d 738 (1944). See generally § 10.13 supra.

18. If the method of determining the price is stated ambiguously, the court may conclude that the right is unenforceable; see Doyle v. McNulty, 478 A.2d 577 (R.I.1984).

19. Hancock v. Dusenberry, 110 Idaho 147, 715 P.2d 360 (App.1986).

20. Landa v. Century 21 Simmons & Co., 237 Va. 374, 377 S.E.2d 416 (1989) (right to purchase is triggered by a third party offer to buy a larger parcel); Hinson v. Roberts, 256 Ga. 396, 349 S.E.2d 454 (1986) (same; holder of right is entitled to disclosure of the terms of third-party offer in order to calculate amount to be allocated to the subject land); Crow–Spieker No. 23 v. Helms Const. & Dev. Co., 103 Nev. 1, 731 P.2d 348 (1987) (right to purchase is not triggered by a third party offer to buy a larger parcel, provided the sale is not "engineered" to avoid the right; the right continues to be held in an unripened or suspended state until an offer for the subject land alone is received); Chapman v. Mutual Life Ins. Co., 800 P.2d 1147 (Wyo.1990) (same). Cf. Sawyer v. Firestone, 513 A.2d 36 (R.I.1986) (preemptive right to purchase is not triggered by a proposed sale of a larger parcel to a third party, but the holder of the right can enjoin the sale). See Annot., 34 A.L.R.4th 1217 (1984).

21. See Hewatt v. Leppert, 259 Ga. 112, 376 S.E.2d 883 (1989) (giving an option to purchase to a third party does not trigger a right of first refusal, but nonetheless breaches it, since it takes the property off the market); Vincent v. Doebert, 183 Ill.App.3d 1081, 132 Ill.Dec. 293, 539 N.E.2d 856 (1989) (third par-

sale, [22] or by a gift [23] or a testamentary transfer [24] to a third party?   What about a long-term lease to a third party? [25]   If the holder of the right declines to exercise it when a third-party offer is made, but that offer does not result in a sale, is the right still exercisable when the owner subsequently wishes to sell to a different third party? [26]   Careful drafting (something rarely found in rights of first refusal) is necessary to resolve these questions.

If the owner of property subject to a right of first refusal sells to a third party who has notice of the right, without giving the holder of the right appropriate notice and an opportunity to exercise the right, it will typically survive the sale and continue to be exercisable against the third party.[27] The owner may also be held liable for damages for breaching the right of first refusal, and if a sufficient degree of culpability is shown, punitive

ty's offer was accompanied by a guaranty by a guarantor with a net worth of $10 million; while holder of the right of first refusal could not match this precisely, his offer was sufficiently close to be enforceable); Ellis v. Chevron, U.S.A., Inc., 201 Cal.App.3d 132, 246 Cal. Rptr. 863 (1988) (third party offered to lease the subject property and additional land, and to build a large retail store on both parcels; holder of right declined to match the offer to acquire the additional property or to build the building; owner had no duty to accept holder's offer); Hasty v. Health Services Centers, Inc., 258 Ga. 625, 373 S.E.2d 356 (1988) (right of first refusal was triggered by owner's giving of an option to purchase to a third party, where right spoke of a sale resulting from "an offer to purchase * * * or otherwise"); McCulloch v. M & C Beauty Colleges, Inc., 194 Cal. App.3d 1338, 240 Cal.Rptr. 189 (1987) (where third party offers better security for deferred portion of purchase price than is offered by the holder of the right, the holder is entitled to purchase if a reasonable person would consider his offer the equivalent of the third party's); Mucci v. Brockton Bocce Club, Inc., 19 Mass.App.Ct. 155, 472 N.E.2d 966 (1985), review denied 394 Mass. 1102, 475 N.E.2d 401 (1985) (right of first refusal was triggered by a third party offer that was conditioned on the offeror's obtaining of financing and of liquor and victualler's licenses); Northwest Television Club, Inc. v. Gross Seattle, Inc., 96 Wn.2d 973, 634 P.2d 837 (1981) (right of first refusal was triggered by third parties' offer that was conditioned upon third parties' sale of their own house; holder of right was permitted to exercise it by an offer conditioned on sale of the holder's house).

The problem is well described in C. Robert Nattress & Associates v. CIDCO, 184 Cal. App.3d 55, 229 Cal.Rptr. 33, 43 (1986):

If the literal matching of terms were required, a triggering offeror could by offering some unique consideration such as existing trust deed notes, a bag of diamonds or a

herd of Arabian horses, effectively defeat the lessee's right of first refusal.   How would the holder of the right of first refusal in such a case make an offer to exercise the right of first refusal on the same terms and conditions as in the triggering offer?

The court concluded that only a reasonable economic equivalence, and not a precise matching of terms, was required.   But see Matson v. Emory, 36 Wn.App. 681, 676 P.2d 1029 (1984), concluding that the holder of the right must match the third party offer quite precisely, provided that the owner is acting in good faith in demanding such a match.

22. Hornsby v. Holt, 257 Ga. 341, 359 S.E.2d 646 (1987) (right of first refusal is triggered by a foreclosure by trustee under power of sale).

23. Mericle v. Wolf, 386 Pa.Super. 82, 562 A.2d 364 (1989) (right was not triggered by a transfer by gift to a charity).

24. Smith v. Estate of La Tray, 161 A.D.2d 1178, 555 N.Y.S.2d 968 (1990) (testamentary transfer does not trigger right of first refusal); Brooks v. Terteling, 107 Idaho 262, 688 P.2d 1167 (1984) (same).

25. Wilson v. Whinery, 37 Wn.App. 24, 678 P.2d 354 (1984) (long-term lease to third party triggers right of first refusal).   See also Rollins v. Stokes, 123 Cal.App.3d 701, 176 Cal. Rptr. 835, 840 (1981) (granting of option to purchase to a third party triggers right of first refusal).

26. See Meridian Bowling Lanes, Inc. v. Meridian Athletic Ass'n, Inc., 105 Idaho 509, 670 P.2d 1294 (1983).

27. This assumes, of course, that the third party purchaser has notice of the right, and hence is not a bona fide purchaser under the applicable recording act.   Hornsby v. Holt, 257 Ga. 341, 359 S.E.2d 646 (1987) (where right of first refusal is recorded, purchaser of property has constructive notice of it and takes subject to its exercise); Versai Manage-

damages may be assessed.[28]

Perpetuities and Restraints on Alienation. The application of the rule against perpetuities has raised persistent problems with options and rights of first refusal.[29] Cases that apply the rule generally assume or argue that an option is similar to a springing executory interest, and hence is void unless it may be exercised no later than 21 years after some life in being at its creation. Whether the rule should be applied to options at all is open to very serious doubt on both theoretical and practical grounds. An option is merely an irrevocable offer to sell, and until exercised creates no present or future interest in the land.[30] Moreover, even options for very long terms do not appear to raise very serious problems of practical inalienability of land titles. Land subject to an option may be "off the market" in the sense that the owner is not actively attempting to sell it, but it is not, strictly speaking, inalienable, since a conveyance executed by both the optionor and the optionee will pass a good title. The necessity of the buyer's negotiating with both and getting both to sign may be somewhat burdensome, but hardly more so than, for example, obtaining the signatures of two tenants in common.

As a tool to control excessively lengthy options and rights of first refusal, the rule against perpetuities is blunt indeed. As Professor Leach pointed out many years ago, any competent drafter can easily create an option that will satisfy the rule and yet will last more than a hundred years.[31] Thus it serves mainly as a trap for the unwary. And finally, when the rule is violated, the option is void in its entirety, rather than merely being limited in duration—surely a Draconian remedy and one that few business people would expect or elect. Plainly the rule against perpetuities, which was designed to prevent family property settlements from tying up titles for undue periods, is ill-adapted to options and preemptive rights; if they need to be restricted in time, a better method can surely be found.

Nevertheless, courts frequently apply the rule to options [32] and rights of first refusal.[33] If the term of the option is fixed at less than twenty-one

ment, Inc. v. Monticello Forest Products Corp., 479 So.2d 477 (La.App.1985) (same).

28. Arlington State Bank v. Colvin, 545 N.E.2d 572 (Ind.App.1989) (punitive damages based on proof of malice, fraud, gross negligence, or oppressive conduct).

29. On the operation of the rule, see generally §§ 3.17–.18 supra.

30. Some courts have taken this view; see Gartley v. Ricketts, 107 N.M. 451, 760 P.2d 143 (1988); Robroy Land Co. v. Prather, 95 Wn.2d 66, 622 P.2d 367 (1980); Mercer v. Lemmens, 230 Cal.App.2d 167, 40 Cal.Rptr. 803 (1964); Warren v. City of Leesburg, 203 So.2d 522, 526 (Fla.App.1967); Weitzman v. Weitzmann, 87 Ind.App. 236, 161 N.E. 385 (1928); Keogh v. Peck, 316 Ill. 318, 147 N.E. 266, 38 A.L.R. 1151 (1925). See also Dominion Bank v. Wilson, 867 F.2d 203 (4th Cir.1989) (once option has been exercised, purchaser's interest is real property under doctrine of equitable conversion, and cannot be encumbered as personal property).

31. Leach, Perpetuities in Perspective: Ending the Rule's Reign of Terror, 65 Harv. L.Rev. 721, 737–38 (1952).

32. Kershner v. Hurlburt, 277 S.W.2d 619 (Mo.1955); Note, Options and the Rule Against Perpetuities, 13 U.Fla.L.Rev. 214 (1960); 6 American Law of Property § 26.66 (A.J. Casner ed. 1952); Restatement of Property §§ 393–94, 413 (1944); Annot., 66 A.L.R.3d 1294 (1975).

33. Rights of first refusal are frequently created with no time limits on their exercise, and have sometimes been held to violate the rule against perpetuities; see Morrison v. Piper, 160 A.D.2d 1066, 553 N.Y.S.2d 548 (1990) (right of first refusal for lifetimes of the parties and of their donees or legatees exceeded the perpetuities period and was void); Lake of the Woods Ass'n, Inc. v. McHugh, 238 Va. 1, 380 S.E.2d 872 (1989); Ferrero Const. Co. v. Dennis Rourke Corp., 311 Md. 560, 536 A.2d 1137 (1988); Coxe v. Wyatt, 83 N.C.App. 131, 349 S.E.2d 75 (1986), review denied 319 N.C.

years, either alone or in combination with some life in being, there is no difficulty.[34] But if the option's exercise may occur in the indefinite future, or is tied to a future event whose timing is uncertain (and which can conceivably occur outside the lifetime of the parties [35] and more than twenty-one years after the creation of the option,[36]) some courts have taken the view that the rule against perpetuities is violated, and thus that the option is void.[37] Other courts, taking a more practical approach to the issue, hold

103, 353 S.E.2d 107 (1987); Annot., 40 A.L.R.3d 920 (1971). Ferrero Const. Co., supra, contains a thorough listing of the cases.

For the contrary and probably more prevalent view, that rights of first refusal do not fall within the rule against perpetuities if the purchase price is based on a current third-party offer or other measure of market value, see Weber v. Texas Co., 83 F.2d 807 (5th Cir.1936), cert. denied 299 U.S. 561, 57 S.Ct. 23, 81 L.Ed. 413 (1936); Cambridge Co. v. East Slope Investment Corp., 700 P.2d 537 (Colo. 1985); Shiver v. Benton, 251 Ga. 284, 304 S.E.2d 903 (1983), appeal after remand 254 Ga. 107, 326 S.E.2d 756 (1985); Meridian Bowling Lanes, Inc. v. Meridian Athletic Ass'n, Inc., 105 Idaho 509, 670 P.2d 1294 (1983); Perritt Co. v. Mitchell, 663 S.W.2d 696 (Tex.App. 1983); Hartnett v. Jones, 629 P.2d 1357 (Wyo. 1981); Ritchey v. Villa Nueva Condominium Ass'n, 81 Cal.App.3d 688, 146 Cal.Rptr. 695 (1978); Watergate Corp. v. Reagan, 321 So.2d 133 (Fla.App.1975).

34. Matter of Estate of Crowl, 737 P.2d 911 (Okl.1987) (option exercisable immediately upon optionor's death was valid); Old Quarry Ass'n v. Hickey, 659 F.Supp. 1064, 1071 (D.Conn.1986) (right of first refusal exercisable during optionee's lifetime and for 15 years thereafter was valid).

35. An alternative approach to saving the option, available only when the optionee is a natural person, is to hold that the right to exercise is personal to the optionee and can only be exercised during his or her life. See Silvicraft, Inc. v. Southeast Timber Co., 34 Ark.App. 17, 805 S.W.2d 84 (1991); Nichols v. Lake Toxaway Co., 98 N.C.App. 313, 390 S.E.2d 770 (1990), review denied 327 N.C. 141, 394 S.E.2d 178 (1990); Morrison v. Piper, 77 N.Y.2d 165, 565 N.Y.S.2d 444, 566 N.E.2d 643 (1990), appeal after remand 171 A.D.2d 958, 567 N.Y.S.2d 903 (1991) (right of first refusal); Bloomer v. Phillips, 164 A.D.2d 52, 562 N.Y.S.2d 840 (1990); McDonald v. Moore, 57 Wn.App. 778, 790 P.2d 213 (1990), review denied 115 Wn.2d 1013, 797 P.2d 513 (1990); Nickels v. Cohn, 764 S.W.2d 124 (Mo.App. 1989); Mazzeo v. Kartman, 234 N.J.Super. 223, 560 A.2d 733 (1989); Layne v. Henderson, 232 Va. 332, 351 S.E.2d 18 (1986) (option to be exercised within the life of the survivor of three brothers); Barnhart v. McKinney, 235 Kan. 511, 682 P.2d 112 (1984) (notwithstanding that option stated it bound the parties' heirs and assigns).

36. The time period is usually fixed; see Certified Corp. v. GTE Products Corp., 392 Mass. 821, 467 N.E.2d 1336 (1984) (25–year fixed-term option violated rule against perpetuities). Alternatively, the option's exercise may be tied to some future event of uncertain occurrence. Cases holding such options violative of the rule against perpetuities include Central Delaware County Authority v. Greyhound Corp., 527 Pa. 47, 588 A.2d 485 (1991) (option to be exercised upon cessation of public use of the property by county); D.T.P. v. Red Bridge Properties, Inc., 576 A.2d 1377 (R.I.1990) (option to be exercised within 60 days after successful resolution of pending litigation involving the property); Otter Creek Dev. Co. v. Friesenhahn, 295 Ark. 318, 748 S.W.2d 344 (1988), rehearing denied 295 Ark. 318, 750 S.W.2d 411 (1988) (option to be exercised within 90 days of availability of a building permit); Barnhart v. McKinney, 235 Kan. 511, 682 P.2d 112 (1984) (option to be exercised within 120 days after city's acquisition of land for new highway); Peele v. Wilson County Board of Education, 56 N.C.App. 555, 289 S.E.2d 890 (1982), review denied 306 N.C. 386, 294 S.E.2d 210 (1982) (right of first refusal to be exercised if property ceased to be used for school purposes).

The rule against perpetuities has also been applied, with inexorable logic, to firm contracts of sale; see Dorado Ltd. Partnership v. Broadneck Dev. Corp., 317 Md. 148, 562 A.2d 757 (1989) (contract of sale, with closing to be held 90 days after seller delivered evidence of sewer allocations to buyer, was void under rule against perpetuities); Ryland Group, Inc. v. Wills, 229 Va. 459, 331 S.E.2d 399 (1985) (closing under contract to be held within 30 days after development of lot did not violate rule against perpetuities; court construed contract to require closing within a reasonable time, which would be far less than 21 years). Cf. Stewart v. Tuli, 82 Md.App. 726, 573 A.2d 109 (1990) (where contract provided for closing after vendor cleared title, which event was to occur within a reasonable time, such time was less than 21 years and contract did not violate rule against perpetuities); Rodin v. Merritt, 48 N.C.App. 64, 268 S.E.2d 539 (1980), review denied 301 N.C. 402, 274 S.E.2d 226 (1980) (same).

37. See Otter Creek Development Co. v. Friesenhahn, supra note 36.

that the parties must be understood to have contracted with a reasonable time in mind, and that such a time is surely less than 21 years; thus the option or right of first refusal is sustained.[38] Moreover, an option contained in a long-term lease, to purchase or to extend the lease and exercisable only within the lease's term, is almost universally upheld no matter how long the term; the courts reason that the option actually increases the probability of the property's development and marketability, since it may induce the tenant to make improvements that would otherwise be foregone because the tenant could not be sure of retaining them when the lease ended.[39]

An alternative and far more flexible basis for attacking an option is the doctrine of restraints on alienation.[40] Options are typically judged under a standard of reasonableness, and an option that is exercisable for an indefi-

---

38. Mazzeo v. Kartman, 234 N.J.Super. 223, 560 A.2d 733 (1989); Scutti Enterprises, Inc. v. Wackerman Guchone Custom Builders, Inc., 153 A.D.2d 83, 548 N.Y.S.2d 967 (1989), appeal denied 75 N.Y.2d 709, 555 N.Y.S.2d 692, 554 N.E.2d 1280 (1990) (option exercisable only after local government granted subdivision approval; this event was held to be within the "administrative contingency" savings clause of the New York perpetuities statute); Snyder v. Bowen, 359 Pa.Super. 47, 518 A.2d 558 (1986) (exercise of option after a delay of 13 years was within a reasonable time, and was valid); Young v. Cass, 255 Ga. 508, 340 S.E.2d 185 (1986) (option exercisable within 90 days following notification of optionee that tenants on the premises had died; construed to mean that such notification had to occur within a reasonable time of the tenants' death, and hence less than 21 years); Byke Const. Co. v. Miller, 140 Ariz. 57, 680 P.2d 193 (App.1984) (where option states no time limit, it must be exercised within a reasonable time); Eastern Shopping Centers, Inc. v. Trenholm Motels, Inc., 33 A.D.2d 930, 306 N.Y.S.2d 354 (1970) (where option states no time limit, it must be exercised within a reasonable time). But see Dorado Limited Partnership v. Broadneck Dev. Corp., 317 Md. 148, 562 A.2d 757 (1989), refusing to conclude that county's grant of sewer permits was intended to occur within a reasonable time.

Courts also sometimes "save" rights of first refusal that are not time-limited by construing them to be exercisable only within a reasonable time, which is less than 21 years; see Continental Cablevision of New England Inc. v. United Broadcasting Co., 873 F.2d 717 (4th Cir.1989), appeal after remand 932 F.2d 333 (1991); Brauer v. Hobbs, 151 Mich.App. 769, 391 N.W.2d 482 (1986); Shiver v. Benton, 251 Ga. 284, 304 S.E.2d 903 (1983), appeal after remand 254 Ga. 107, 326 S.E.2d 756 (1985).

Some jurisdictions have modified the common-law rule against perpetuities, taking a "wait and see" or "second look" approach under which an option or right of first refusal is upheld if is *in fact* exercised within the perpetuities period. See Great Bay School &

Training Center v. Simplex Wire & Cable Co., 131 N.H. 682, 559 A.2d 1329 (1989); Hansen v. Stroecker, 699 P.2d 871 (Alaska 1985) (option exercised within 9 years, validity upheld); JLJ Associates, Inc. v. Persiani, 41 Conn.Sup. 79, 550 A.2d 650 (1988) (same). Cf. Lake of the Woods Ass'n v. McHugh, 238 Va. 1, 380 S.E.2d 872 (1989) ("wait and see" statute could not be applied retroactively to right of first refusal created before adoption of the statute); Kentucky–West Virginia Gas Co. v. Martin, 744 S.W.2d 745 (Ky.App.1987) ("wait and see" statute did not save right of first refusal, where it was exercised 45 years after its creation).

A further but disingenuous method of upholding a sale contract or deed reserving a right of first refusal in the grantor is to assert that it is analogous to right of entry following a fee simple on condition subsequent, rather than an executory interest, and hence is an interest outside the scope of the rule against perpetuities; see Robertson v. Murphy, 510 So.2d 180 (Ala.1987).

39. See § 6.66 supra; Texaco Refining and Marketing, Inc. v. Samowitz, 213 Conn. 676, 570 A.2d 170 (1990); Polemi v. Wells, 759 P.2d 796 (Colo.App.1988); Housing Authority of Monterey County v. Monterey Senior Citizen Park, 164 Cal.App.3d 348, 210 Cal.Rptr. 497 (1985); Crossroads Shopping Center v. Montgomery Ward & Co., 646 P.2d 330, 332 (Colo. 1981); Producers Oil Company v. Gore, 610 P.2d 772 (Okl.1980) (right of first refusal limited to term of the lease); Wing, Inc. v. Arnold, 107 So.2d 765 (Fla.App.1958).

40. See Metropolitan Transportation Authority v. Bruken Realty Corp., 67 N.Y.2d 156, 501 N.Y.S.2d 306, 492 N.E.2d 379 (1986) (preemptive rights "are best regulated by the rule against unreasonable restraints on alienation * * * rather than by the inflexible rule against remote vesting").

nite period of time,[41] or that includes no provision for adjustment of the price to reflect market value changes, may well be held unreasonable and void.[42] On the other hand, an option or right of first refusal is nearly always upheld if the price is based on current market value, or on the price offered by a third party.[43] The cases often mix together rule against perpetuities and restraint on alienation concepts, or treat the latter as merely a branch of the former.

In reality options and rights of first refusal, even if they produce a sale at a price far below market value, do not violate either of these concepts. As noted above, the title to the land is both clear and marketable, provided that both the optionor and optionee can be persuaded to join in the conveyance. Is there, then, any sound basis for objecting to the enforcement of long-term options and rights of first refusal that do not adjust the price to market level? Two such objections may be made: first, that the option may turn out to be a very bad deal for the optionor, and second, that because the price is depressed, the optionor may have very little incentive to improve or even to maintain the condition of the property.

The "bad deal" argument should carry very little weight. The whole point of many options is to allow the optionee to lock in the price against the possibility of future market increases. In effect, the optionee is purchasing from the optionor insurance against the risk of such increases. The optionor, of course, is free to demand as high an insurance premium as he or she wishes for absorbing this risk, and is ordinarily as capable of estimating it in advance as is the optionee. That the optionor may eventually be forced to sell the property for less than its current value is surely no reason to object to enforcement of the option.[44]

The fact that an option at a price that does not track market values over time may discourage further investment in the property by the optionor,[45] on the other hand, does have significant public policy implications. Such a property may, for example, be left out of an important and desirable real

---

41. Girard v. Myers, 39 Wn.App. 577, 694 P.2d 678 (1985) (right of first refusal was a void restraint on alienation, where there was no time limit on its exercise and no procedures for exercise were stated). Cf. O'Berry v. Gray, 510 So.2d 1135 (Fla.App.1987), review denied 518 So.2d 1275 (Fla.1987) (option exercisable for a period of 60 days after optionee or optionor's death was not an unreasonable restraint on alienation). See also Ala.Code 1975, § 35–4–76(a), limiting the duration of an option to two years if it is not limited by its terms.

42. DeWolf v. Usher Cove Corp., 721 F.Supp. 1518 (D.R.I.1989) (three-year right of first refusal, with repurchase price fixed as original purchase price plus 10% per year; court revised the repurchase price to be land's fair market value at the time of exercise); Brine v. Fertitta, 537 So.2d 113 (Fla.App. 1988); Trecker v. Langel, 298 N.W.2d 289 (Iowa 1980) (30–year fixed-price right of first refusal); Girard v. Myers, 39 Wn.App. 577,

694 P.2d 678 (1985) (right of first refusal providing for a price 11% below a third party offer, and containing no time limit on holder of right's response to such an offer); Iglehart v. Phillips, 383 So.2d 610 (Fla.1980). Compare Nickels v. Cohn, 764 S.W.2d 124 (Mo.App. 1989), upholding a right of first refusal at a price based on the owner's original acquisition cost plus the cost of improvements he made while holding the property.

43. See Smith v. Mitchell, 301 N.C. 58, 269 S.E.2d 608 (1980).

44. This argument is well made in Powertest Corp. v. Evans, 665 F.Supp. 134 (D.Conn. 1986). See also Matter of Frederick's Estate, 599 P.2d 550 (Wyo.1979).

45. No such effect results from an option or preemptive right with a price approximating current market value, a point well made by Judge Cole's dissent in Ferrero Construction Co. v. Dennis Rourke Corp., 311 Md. 560, 536 A.2d 1137, 1147–1149 (1988).

estate development; indeed, it may become a slum.[46] While tying up the land may be tolerable in the short term (and indeed, is to some degree the inevitable result of every fixed-price option), it is surely arguable that some time constraint should be placed on it.

A few jurisdictions have accomplished this by statute,[47] but in the absence of legislation a court could well follow the principle articulated in North Bay Council, Inc. v. Grinnell.[48] There the court purported to apply the rule against perpetuities to a preemptive right with no stated time limit, but instead of holding the right void, the court simply limited its duration to the lifetime of the holder plus 21 years. Whether this is necessary with a preemptive right to buy at a current market price, as was involved in the cited case, is debatable. But the concept could very well be applied to fixed-price options with terms beyond the perpetuities period. Of course, it is highly artificial to pretend that this has anything to do with the rule against perpetuities; it would be more candid for a court simply to announce that, as a matter of public policy, it would refuse to recognize any term beyond the optionee's life plus 21 years for an option or right of first refusal that did not provide for a sale price approximating current market value.[49] Indeed, since the optionee's life span has little to do with the public policy involved, a fixed limit of 21 years "borrowed" from the rule against perpetuities would be quite appropriate and far preferable to an outright voiding of the option.

Assignment of Options and Preemptive Rights. Ordinary options are routinely considered assignable by their holders, and are in fact frequently assigned. An objection to assignability would be countenanced only if the option itself prohibited assignment, or the circumstances indicated that the optionor had relied on some special qualities of the optionee.[50] An option contained in a lease is typically presumed not to be assignable apart from the leasehold, although the parties can contract for a different result.[51] If the leasehold itself is assigned, the option is generally deemed to run with it to the assignee.[52]

---

46. Ironically, a fixed-price option to purchase granted to a lessee under a lease has precisely the opposite result: that is, it gives the lessee a strong incentive to make improvements to the premises, since the lessee knows that their value will redound entirely to his or her benefit. Such options should always be upheld. See Iglehart v. Phillips, 383 So.2d 610, 615 (Fla.1980).

47. See West's Fla.Stat.Ann. § 689.-22(3)(a)(7), limiting options in gross to 40 years from the date of their creation; Ala.Code § 35–4–76(a), limiting options (except for repurchase options and those contained in leases) to 20 years.

48. 123 N.H. 321, 461 A.2d 114 (1983).

49. An interesting alternative form of remedy was suggested by the court in Iglehart v. Phillips, 383 So.2d 610, 615 (Fla.1980). The court found that the grantors' right of first refusal, based on the original selling price plus the cost of improvements, was unenforceable. It allowed the grantors to rescind the

transaction, on the view that the option to repurchase was a material part of the consideration for which they bargained in the sale. However, it also gave the grantees a lien on the property to assist them in recovering their original investment as adjusted to reflect the inflation in the value of the dollar from the date of the original sale to the date of the rescission.

50. Melrose Enterprises, Inc. v. Pawtucket Form Const. Co., 550 A.2d 300 (R.I.1988); Stuart v. Ennis, 482 So.2d 1168 (Ala.1985) (option between close personal friends was not assignable). But see Shower v. Fischer, 47 Wn.App. 720, 737 P.2d 291 (1987) (option is presumed nontransferrable).

51. Gilbert v. Van Kleeck, 284 A.D. 611, 132 N.Y.S.2d 580 (1954); Bewick v. Mecham, 26 Cal.2d 92, 156 P.2d 757 (1945).

52. See § 6.66 supra.

The assignability of preemptive rights to purchase is much more in doubt. A preemptive right is commonly granted because the optionee has an interest in other nearby land which would be augmented in value if the land in question were purchased. Under these circumstances, a court may suppose that an assignment of the preemptive right to someone who holds no interest in the nearby land would be contrary to the original parties' intent.[53]

53. HSL Linda Gardens Properties, Ltd. v. Seymour, 163 Ariz. 396, 788 P.2d 129 (1990) (where two tenants in common give each other preemptive rights, either may enforce the right, so long as he owns his interest, against the successors of the other); Old Nat. Bank of Washington v. Arneson, 54 Wn.App. 717, 776 P.2d 145 (1989), review denied 113 Wn.2d 1019, 781 P.2d 1321 (1989) (right of first refusal is presumed nontransferrable, but may be assigned if parties so intended).

Chapter 11

CONVEYANCES AND TITLES

Table of Sections

§ 11.1　Deeds

The American legal system recognizes a variety of methods of transferring interests in land, but the deed is unquestionably the most common. Other transfer devices include wills, intestate succession, adverse possession and prescription [1], dedication [2], legislative acts of transfer [3], and various court decrees such as removal of clouds on title and judgments in eminent domain. In nearly all sales of real property, the deed is the instrument used to effect the ultimate transfer of legal title.[4] Hence it is of vast practical importance.

Historical Background of the Modern Deed. In early English history, conveyances of possessory freehold interests in land did not depend on

---

§ 11.1

1. Technically, adverse possession and prescription do not result in a transfer, but rather a new right or title arising in the adverse user. See § 11.7, infra. But the practical effect is similar to a transfer.

2. See § 11.6, infra.

3. These include both acts which grant government land to private parties, see 2 R. Patton & C. Patton, Land Titles § 290 (1957), and acts which acquire private land for public use, see 2 Nichols, Eminent Domain § 3.1(1) (3d ed. 1973).

4. It is possible for the parties to contract that title will be passed by will; see, e.g., Larkins v. Howard, 252 Ala. 9, 39 So.2d 224, 7 A.L.R.2d 541 (1949), holding that a devisee was a bona fide purchaser for purposes of the recording act. But such transactions are rare, mainly because of the inherent uncertainty as to when the testator will die and legal title will pass.

759

written instruments. Instead, a method known as feoffment with livery of seisin was employed.[5] The parties met on, or in sight of, the land in the presence of witnesses.[6] The feoffor announced orally the transfer of the land to the feoffee, and handed over a twig or clump of earth to symbolize the conveyance. It was sometimes customary to prepare a written "charter of feoffment" memorializing the livery of seisin, but this was not considered essential and was merely evidence of the transfer, not an instrument of transfer itself.[7]

By contrast, interests other than possessory freeholds, such as leaseholds, easements, and future interests, were not conveyed by livery but by means of a grant. The grant was originally an oral conveyance, but at a very early date it became obligatory to make it by a written deed—that is, an instrument under seal. Thus, the grant was the first direct ancestor of the modern deed.[8] Since the grant was not seen as conveying seisin, it was not necessary for the delivery of the deed to take place on the land itself.

Livery of seisin was often inconvenient, since it required the parties to travel to the location of the land. The common law conveyancers soon developed a technique for transferring a possessory fee simple while circumventing this disadvantage. The conveyor would first grant a lease to the conveyee with a duration of, say, one year, leaving the conveyor with a reversion. As soon as the conveyee had entered upon the land, the conveyor would transfer the reversion to the conveyee by means of a second grant, termed a "release." The two interests would merge, giving the grantee a fee simple absolute. Since the first interest was not a freehold and the second was a future interest, livery was not necessary to transfer either of them.[9]

With the enactment of the Statute of Uses in 1536,[10] several new types of conveyances which avoided the need for livery of seisin came into use. The statute, in substance, converted equitable interests in land into legal interests. While most of the affected equitable interests arose in the form of "uses", or explicit arrangements under which one person held title for the benefit of another, the statute also applied to the sort of equitable interest, the ancestor of the doctrine of equitable conversion discussed in the previous

---

5. The seisin, which was intangible but was treated virtually as a tangible object, represented in a rather mystical sense the right of possession of the land. See generally Payne, The English Theory of Conveyancing Prior to the Land Registration Acts, 7 Ala. L.Rev. 227 (1955); Thorne, Livery of Seisin, 52 L.Q.Rev. 345 (1936); Holdsworth, An Historical Introduction to the Land Law 113 (1927); 2 Pollock & Maitland, History of English Law 182 (1895).

6. The purpose of the witnesses was to create a general public awareness of the transfer so that jurors would remember it if it were later challenged. In the Teutonic law, which followed the same general method of conveyance, it was customary to assemble a group of small boys from the neighborhood, compel them to watch the livery of seisin, and then to give each a sharp clout on the head so that the occasion would be impressed on his memory. See J. Lawler & G. Lawler, A Short Historical Introduction to the Law of Real Property 41–42 (1940).

7. Professor Powell points out that the charters were made after the fact, and hence described the livery in the past tense. Some modern deeds continue to follow this usage with such terminology as "I have this day granted and conveyed * * * " 6A Powell, Real Property ¶ 880 (1980).

8. Payne, supra note 5, at 243–44.

9. See 6A Powell, Real Property ¶ 880 (1980).

10. 27 Hen. VIII, Ch. 10 (1536). See generally § 3.11, supra; 3 Am.L.Prop. § 12.12 (1952).

chapter [11], which arose in the purchaser under a land sale contract—provided the contract recited the payment of consideration. Thus a document which employed contract-like language, reciting that the vendor "has bargained and sold" the land to the purchaser, was treated under the statute as recognizing that the vendor's legal title was held merely as a trustee, and hence as immediately vesting that title in the purchaser. It became known as a "bargain and sale deed", and was required to be in writing only if it conveyed a freehold. No entry on the land was necessary.[12] A similar process of reasoning was applied to the "covenant to stand seized", a promise by which a person owning land agreed to hold it for the use of another to whom he or she was related by blood or marriage. The familial relationship was enough to supply the needed consideration, and the courts applied the Statute of Uses to "execute" the use and place legal title in the hands of the relative. No writing was necessary.[13]

Parliament recognized the potential of the Statute of Uses for facilitating secret conveyances, and thus defeating the crown's collection of the feudal incidents at which the Statute was aimed. Hence it enacted the Statute of Enrollments [14], which required the public registration of all conveyances of freeholds by bargain and sale deeds. But the land owners and their lawyers found that they could avoid enrollment by employing the lease and release; since the lease component was not a freehold and the release could be made by grant rather than bargain and sale, both parts were outside the Statute of Enrollments. Moreover, the lease could now be made by bargain and sale, avoiding even the need for the lessee to enter on the land.[15] The lease and release enjoyed a vast expansion of popularity as a result.

Thus, up to the time of the enactment of the Statute of Frauds in 1676 [16], some types of conveyances, including "bargains and sales" of freeholds and grants were required to be by written deed, while others, including livery of seisin and covenants to stand seised, were not.[17] Writings were by then very usual even for transactions in which they were not legally essential. The Statute of Frauds, in substance, insisted that every conveyance of an interest in land except short-term leases be written. This requirement has been carried over into every American jurisdiction [18], and is of great modern importance.

As we will see below, the American approach to conveyancing has been

<hr>

11. See the discussion of equitable conversion, § 10.13 supra.

12. Sargent v. Coolidge, 399 A.2d 1333 (Me. 1979), appeal after remand 433 A.2d 748 (1981); 1 R. Patton & C. Patton, Land Titles § 3 (1957).

13. 3 Am.L.Prop. § 12.12 (1952). The covenant to stand seized was recognized by the New Hampshire Supreme Court in French v. French, 3 N.H. 234 (1825).

14. 27 Hen. VIII, Ch. 16 (1536); see id.

15. Lutwitch v. Minton, Cro.Jac. 604, 79 Eng.Repr. 516 (1620), holding that when a

leasehold was created by bargain and sale deed, the tenant was deemed immediately in possession without any necessity for entry on the land. See T. Bergin & P. Haskell, Preface to Estates in Land and Future Interests 108 (1966); Payne, supra note 5, at 261.

16. 29 Car. II, Ch. 3 (1676).

17. See Goodwin, Before the Statute of Frauds, Must An Agreement to Stand Seised Have Been in Writing?, 7 Harv.L.Rev. 464 (1894).

18. See 6A Powell, Real Property ¶ 881 (1980).

far less technical than the English.[19]   American courts have shown little interest in classifying deeds as bargain-and-sale, lease and release, or the like, and they generally try diligently to give effect to the grantor's intention irrespective of the choice of conveying language.   Yet the early English history remains pervasive, manifesting itself in the language commonly employed in printed deed forms and in the requirement of delivery.   Modern quitclaim deeds often use the term "release" and warranty deeds in many states still have the grantor "bargain and sell" the land.   A few states still follow the common law in requiring private seals for the validity of deeds.[20] A number of statutes have been enacted authorizing the use of a particular phrase, such as "grants" or "bargains and sells" and imputing certain warranties of title when the statutory phrase is used.[21]   The recitation of consideration, plainly unnecessary in modern times [22], remains customary as a holdover from the days of the Statute of Uses and the bargain and sale deed.   In sum, the common law's technicality is no longer with us, but much of its phraseology remains.

Elements of a Deed.   What must a deed contain?   The list of essential elements is strikingly similar to that which governs contracts for the sale of land.[23]   It includes identification of the parties, description of the land, some words indicating a present intent to convey, and the grantor's signature.[24] The signature alone is not generally considered a sufficient identification of the grantor.[25]   However, the identification of the parties need not appear in any particular clause [26] and need not be precisely accurate.[27]   Several states have statutes which regulate the naming of the parties to a deed, sometimes requiring full names, both prior and present names, addresses, or marital status.[28]   In the absence of such a statute the courts tend to be very liberal

19. See generally 3 Am.L.Prop. § 12.13 (1952). The English, too, have become much less technical. The Real Property Act of 1845, 8 & 9 Vict. Ch. 106, § 2, made a simple deed of grant sufficient to convey any interest, whether possessory or not.

20. See, e.g., Williams v. North Carolina State Board of Education, 284 N.C. 588, 201 S.E.2d 889 (1974).

21. The statutes are collected in 6A Powell, Real Property ¶ 885 (1980).

22. In most states, neither actual consideration nor its recitation is necessary to validity of the deed; see note 44, infra.

23. See § 10.1, supra, at notes 22–29.

24. Greer v. Kooiker, 312 Minn. 499, 253 N.W.2d 133 (1977). See generally 3 Am. L.Prop. § 12.38 (1952); R. Patton & C. Patton, Land Titles §§ 331–65 (1957). See Rekis v. Lake Minnewaska Mountain Houses, Inc., 170 A.D.2d 124, 573 N.Y.S.2d 331 (1991), appeal dismissed 79 N.Y.2d 851, 580 N.Y.S.2d 201, 588 N.E.2d 99 (1992) (deed with no description of property is void, but if description is later filled in, grantor may be estopped to challenge its validity, as against a subsequent bona fide purchaser). See generally 3 Am.L.Prop.

§ 12.38 (1952); R. Patton & C. Patton, Land Titles §§ 331–65 (1957).

25. See, e.g., Christian v. Johnson, 556 S.W.2d 172 (Ky.App.1977) (deed by corporation is void where signed by president who is identified as such on signature line, but where corporation is not otherwise identified). There is little to commend such a rigid approach. Compare Milstid v. Pennington, 268 F.2d 384 (5th Cir.1959) (deed was signed by both husband and wife, but granting clause named wife twice and omitted husband; held, deed conveyed husband's interest.) See generally 2 R. Patton & C. Patton, Land Titles § 333 (1957).

26. St. Michael and Archangel Russian Orthodox Greek Catholic Church v. Uhniat, 451 Pa. 176, 301 A.2d 655 (1973).

27. Shulansky v. Michaels, 14 Ariz.App. 402, 484 P.2d 14 (1971); Barton v. Baptist General Convention, 477 P.2d 679 (Okl.1970). The name given in the deed may be an alias or an assumed name; see Marky Investments, Inc. v. Arnezeder, 15 Wis.2d 74, 112 N.W.2d 211 (1961); Gallagher v. Girote, 23 Ill.2d 170, 177 N.E.2d 103 (1961).

28. See generally 6A Powell, Real Property ¶ 886 (1980).

in accepting identifying language.[29]

An interesting problem arises if a deed is delivered with the grantee's name left blank, but the grantor expects or even authorizes the person to whom delivery is made to fill in his own name or that of someone he chooses. Plainly the deed is void until a grantee's name is actually inserted.[30] But once this is done the majority of the cases sustain the deed, often implying authority from the grantor's acquiescence even if none was given explicitly.[31] One might expect the authority to expire if the grantor died before the name was written in, but even that sequence of events has been held to result in a valid deed on the ground that the grantee's agency was "coupled with an interest" and thus was irrevocable.[32]

A deed to a nonexistent grantee is said to be void. Examples include a deed to a deceased grantee, to the heirs of a living grantee, or to a corporation which has not yet been formed or has been dissolved.[33] Yet the courts are generally quite willing to reform such deeds if by doing so they can carry out the grantor's intent.[34]

29. For numerous cases upholding deeds in which the grantee's name was not given, but in which the grantee was described as someone's child, heir, trustee, or the like, see 2 R. Patton & C. Patton, Land Titles § 336 note 46 (1957). See also 3 Am.L.Prop. § 12.40 (1952). See Garraway v. Yonce, 549 So.2d 1341 (Miss. 1989) (deed named trustees of school district and their successors as grantees; held, identity was sufficiently ascertainable and deed was valid).

30. Myers v. Francis, 548 So.2d 833 (Fla. App.1989); Karlen v. Karlen, 89 S.D. 523, 235 N.W.2d 269 (1975).

31. Mehus v. Thompson, 266 N.W.2d 920 (N.D.1978); Gajewski v. Bratcher, 221 N.W.2d 614 (N.D.1974), appeal after remand 240 N.W.2d 871 (1976); Hanson v. Beehive Security Co., 14 Utah 2d 157, 380 P.2d 66 (1963). The deed is void where there is a clear absence of authorization from the grantor; see Robinson v. Bascom, 85 N.M. 453, 513 P.2d 190 (App.1973); West v. Witschner, 482 S.W.2d 733 (Mo.1972); Application of County Collector, 1 Ill.App.3d 707, 274 N.E.2d 164 (1971). See generally 2 R. Patton & C. Patton, Land Titles § 336 (1957); 4 Tiffany, Real Property § 969 (1939), discussing the problem raised by statutes which require the authority of the grantor's agent to be in writing. The case for upholding the deed is particularly compelling when the property has passed to a bona fide purchaser who has relied on the completed deed, thereby giving rise to an estoppel against the grantor; see 3 Am.L.Prop. § 12.41 (1952). But see Green v. MacAdam, 175 Cal.App.2d 481, 346 P.2d 474 (1959), where the grantee's action was completely unauthorized and the court upheld the grantor as against the claim of a BFP.

32. Kindred v. Crosby, 251 Iowa 198, 100 N.W.2d 20 (1959); Womack v. Stegner, 293 S.W.2d 124 (Tex.Civ.App.1956), refused n.r.e. These cases also refer to the deliveree of the deed as having "equitable title," but this apparently means nothing more than that a court of equity would sustain the deed, giving a decree of reformation if necessary.

33. Oregon v. Bureau of Land Management, 876 F.2d 1419 (9th Cir.1989) (deed listing fictitious name as grantee is void); Piedmont and Western Investment Corp. v. Carnes–Miller Gear Co., 96 N.C.App. 105, 384 S.E.2d 687 (1989), review denied 326 N.C. 49, 389 S.E.2d 93 (1990) (deed conveyed to dissolved corporation is void and is not retroactively validated upon grantee's reincorporation); Sharp v. Riekhof, 747 P.2d 1044 (Utah 1987) (a trust, as distinct from a trustee, cannot hold property, and a deed conveying property to a trust is void). See Annot., 148 A.L.R. 252 (1944). In the case of a conveyance of a future interest, it is sufficient if the takers will be ascertainable when the interest becomes possessory.

34. See, United States v. Stubbs, 776 F.2d 1472 (10th Cir.1985) (deed to estate of deceased person was valid, where grantor intended that result); e.g., John Davis & Co. v. Cedar Glen No. Four, Inc., 75 Wn.2d 214, 450 P.2d 166 (1969) (corporation not organized when deed delivered, but takes title when subsequently organized); Haile v. Holtzclaw, 414 S.W.2d 916 (Tex.1967) (deed to "the W.B. Haile Estate" sustained as conveyance to heirs of the decedent); Wilson v. Dearing, Inc., 415 S.W.2d 475 (Tex.Civ.App.1967) (deed to deceased grantee may be treated as to his heirs or assigns to carry out grantor's intent). See generally 3 Am.L.Prop. § 12.40 (1952); Annot., 148 A.L.R. 252, 257 (1944).

Some words indicating an intent to make a present transfer of the title must be included in the deed. This requirement is not construed technically, and nearly any appropriate words, such as "give," "transfer," "deed over," or the like will suffice.[35] Difficulty is encountered only with such words as "I will to * * *"[36], which suggest an intent that the conveyance operate at death rather than immediately, or with words which merely covenant or warrant the title rather than purporting to transfer it.[37] The title of the document is not controlling, and if it contains words of grant and the other necessary elements it will be treated as a deed whether it is labelled as one or not.[38]

The remaining essential elements of the deed are the land description and the grantor's signature. Descriptions are of such importance that they are discussed separately in the next section.[39] The signature requirement is liberally construed, and need not necessarily be met by the grantor's writing his or her name. Virtually any mark or writing which is intended to serve as the grantor's approval of the instrument will do[40], and if the grantor is present he may have an agent do the actual writing if desired.[41]

The traditional deed contained several formal parts.[42] The "premises" included the parties' names, the recitation of consideration, a description of the land, and the granting clause. The "habendum" clause, so called because in the medieval period it began with the Latin phrase "habendum et tenendum" ("to have and to hold") followed, and limited the estate being granted if, for example, only a life tenancy were being conveyed. A "reddendum" clause might then follow if the grantor wished to make a reservation of some part of the interest conveyed. The deed would conclude with the warranties of title, a formal reference to the execution and date, and the signature lines. A certificate of acknowledgement by a notary public would be added and in some states, lines for the signatures of attesting witnesses.

35. Saltzman v. Ahern, 306 So.2d 537 (Fla. App.1975); Bonkowski v. Commissioner, 458 F.2d 709 (7th Cir.1972), certiorari denied 409 U.S. 874, 93 S.Ct. 121, 34 L.Ed.2d 127 (1972). See also Harris v. Strawbridge, 330 S.W.2d 911 (Tex.Civ.App.1959), refused n.r.e., upholding a deed whose only words of conveyance were "to have and to hold;" Veltmann v. Damon, 696 S.W.2d 241 (Tex.App.1985) (same), affirmed in part and reversed in part 701 S.W.2d 247 (Tex.1985).

36. Caldwell v. Caldwell, 140 Ga. 736, 79 S.E. 853 (1913).

37. See, e.g., Lilly v. Earl, 463 So.2d 143 (Ala.1984) (where deed omitted words of grant, although it contained warranty of title, and where grantees named in granting clause were not same as those in habendum clause, deed was void); Raley v. Raley, 121 Miss. 555, 83 So. 740 (1920); Hummelman v. Mounts, 87 Ind. 178 (1882).

38. See Petersen v. Schafer, 42 Wn.App. 281, 709 P.2d 813 (1985) (joint venture agreement which contained words of present conveyance was, in effect, a deed); Berry v. Berry, 32 Ill.App.3d 711, 336 N.E.2d 239 (1975); Hinchliffe v. Fischer, 198 Kan. 365, 424 P.2d 581 (1967) ("private annuity contract" deemed a deed).

39. See § 11.2, infra.

40. See Runge v. Moore, 196 N.W.2d 87 (N.D.1972); J.D. Loizeaux Lumber Co. v. Davis, 41 N.J.Super. 231, 124 A.2d 593 (1956), cert. denied 22 N.J. 269, 125 A.2d 753 (1956).

41. Hildebrandt v. Hildebrandt, 9 Kan. App.2d 614, 683 P.2d 1288 (1984) (if agent has previously been given power of attorney, she may sign the grantor's name and bind him whether or not he is present and without stating in the deed that she is acting as an agent); Haffa v. Haffa, 115 Ill.App.2d 467, 253 N.E.2d 507 (1969).

42. See 3 Am.L.Prop. § 12.39 (1952); 4 Tiffany, Real Property § 966 (1939).

Today it is clear that none of this formality is necessary[43], although printed forms of deeds commonly follow it. Only the basic elements discussed in the preceding paragraphs are essential. For example, in most states no consideration need be recited or paid.[44] No habendum nor reddendum is required, although of course the grantor must say so if he wishes to limit the estate or to make a reservation. Except in a few states no seal is necessary.[45] A certificate of acknowledgement by a notary or other officer is required for recordation in nearly all states[46], and attestation by one or more witnesses is also needed for recording in several jurisdictions[47], but except in a few states neither item is essential to the deed's validity as between the parties themselves.[48]

Construction of Deeds. When the language of a deed is ambiguous or confusing, judicial construction may be necessary to determine the parties' intent.[49] Of course, there are countless types of possible ambiguities which may be introduced by thoughtless drafting, but some common patterns

43. See Harris v. Strawbridge, 330 S.W.2d 911 (Tex.Civ.App.1959), refused n.r.e.

44. Sintz v. Stone, 562 So.2d 228 (Ala. 1990), appeal after remand 572 So.2d 1270 (1990); Barlow Society v. Commercial Security Bank, 723 P.2d 398 (Utah 1986); Jackson v. Reed, 438 So.2d 750 (Ala.1983); Rose v. Dunn, 284 Ark. 42, 679 S.W.2d 180 (1984); Cuzick v. Lesly, 16 Ark.App. 237, 700 S.W.2d 63 (1985) (no consideration necessary in absence of fraud, duress, or undue influence); Chase Federal Sav. & Loan Ass'n v. Schreiber, 479 So.2d 90 (Fla.1985) (rejecting the doctrine, derived from the Statute of Uses, that valuable consideration, consanguinity, or marital relation is necessary to a valid deed), certiorari denied 476 U.S. 1160, 106 S.Ct. 2282, 90 L.Ed.2d 723; Easterling v. Ferris, 651 P.2d 677 (Okl.1982); Cave v. Cave, 593 S.W.2d 592 (Mo.App.1979); Huffman v. Foreman, 163 Ind.App. 263, 323 N.E.2d 651 (1975); LaDam v. Squires, 127 Vt. 95, 241 A.2d 58 (1968); see 4 Tiffany, Real Property § 984 (3d ed. 1939). In the period immediately following the Statute of Uses (1536), recitation of consideration was necessary to the validity of a bargain and sale deed, see text at notes 11–12, supra, and also rebutted the presumption of a resulting use or trust in favor of the grantor; see J. Cribbet & C. Johnson, Property 293 (4th ed. 1978). It is no longer necessary for either purpose, although the recitation may raise in a few states a rebuttable presumption that consideration was paid in fact, and this in turn may be helpful in a grantee's attempt to rely on the recording acts as a bona fide purchaser. See J.C. Vereen & Sons, Inc. v. City of Miami, 397 So.2d 979 (Fla.App.1981); Farrar v. Young, 158 W.Va. 977, 216 S.E.2d 575 (1975); § 11.10, infra; note 22 supra; 3 Am.L.Prop. § 12.43 (1952). See also Stephens v. Stephens, 280 Ala. 312, 193 So.2d 755 (1966). Note, however, the distinction between requiring consideration (which most jurisdictions do not) and setting aside a deed for "failure of consider-

ation." The latter situation arises most frequently when a deed is given in return for a promise of support, usually of an elderly grantor, until death. If the promise is not performed, a court may set aside the deed if no rights of innocent third parties would be impaired. See, e.g., Fritz v. Fritz, 377 N.W.2d 20 (Minn.App.1985); Baker v. Pattee, 684 P.2d 632 (Utah 1984).

45. See note 20, supra.

46. See 2 R. Patton & C. Patton, Land Titles § 354 (1957); McElwain v. Wells, 174 W.Va. 61, 322 S.E.2d 482 (1984) (acknowledgement required for recording of deed, but not for validity); Abraham v. Mihalich, 330 Pa.Super. 378, 479 A.2d 601 (1984) (same). But see Saunders v. Callaway, 42 Wn.App. 29, 708 P.2d 652 (1985) (acknowledgement is necessary to validity of deed or of lease exceeding one year).

47. 3 Am.L.Prop. § 12.59 note 4 (1952) lists 18 states as requiring at least one witness. See, e.g., In re Ryan, 851 F.2d 502 (1st Cir. 1988) (two witnesses required for valid recordation); Leasing Enterprises, Inc. v. Livingston, 294 S.C. 204, 363 S.E.2d 410 (App.1987) (same); Earp & Schriver, Inc. v. Earp, 466 So.2d 1225 (Fla.App.1985) (witnesses required, but deed lacking witnesses is not void, and under curative statute, becomes fully valid five years after recording); Sweat v. Yates, 463 So.2d 306 (Fla.App.1984) (witnesses need not sign in presence of grantor or each other, nor sign prior to delivery).

48. See Hout v. Hout, 20 Ohio St. 119 (1870); Lewis v. Herrera, 10 Ariz. 74, 85 P. 245 (1906), affirmed 208 U.S. 309, 28 S.Ct. 412, 52 L.Ed. 506 (1906).

49. If the deed is unambiguous, neither construction nor the consideration of extrinsic evidence is said to be necessary. See, e.g., O'Brien v. Village Land Co., 794 P.2d 246 (Colo.1990); Cole v. Minor, 518 So.2d 61 (Ala. 1987); Ouellette v. Butler, 125 N.H. 184, 480 A.2d 76 (1984).

emerge from the cases and will be discussed here. We must first deal with a preliminary question: should a court consider "extrinsic" evidence—that is, facts which do not appear on the face of the document—in construing a deed? Relevant facts might include the parties' statements at the time the deed was given, the nature of the land and surrounding circumstances, and the prior or subsequent behavior of the parties. An old bromide states that if the ambiguity is "patent", or apparent on the face of the deed, no extrinsic evidence may be considered, while if the confusion is "latent," or discernible only in the light of outside facts, further extrinsic proof can be introduced to explain the deed.[50] This quite irrational distinction has now been very widely abandoned, and most courts freely admit testimony which will help resolve the ambiguity without bothering to classify it as latent or patent.[51] There is also some tendency to resolve ambiguities against the deed's drafter.[52]

One common ambiguity arises from the use of language which seems to suggest that only an easement rather than a possessory estate is being granted or reserved.[53] For example, a deed reference to a "right of way" for road or railway purposes is usually construed as conveying only an easement, since most rights of way are indeed easements.[54] On the other hand a "strip of land for a right of way" is more likely to be deemed to convey

50. See Bradshaw v. McElroy, 62 N.C.App. 515, 302 S.E.2d 908 (1983); MacKay v. Breault, 121 N.H. 135, 427 A.2d 1099 (1981); Walters v. Tucker, 281 S.W.2d 843 (Mo.1955); Bybee v. Hageman, 66 Ill. 519 (1873); McBane, The Rule Against Disturbing Plain Meaning of Writings, 31 Cal.L.Rev. 145 (1943); Annot., 68 A.L.R. 12 (1930).

51. See Bledsoe v. Hill, 747 P.2d 10 (Colo. App.1987); Ouellette v. Butler, 125 N.H. 184, 480 A.2d 76 (1984); Weaver v. Ellis, 127 Ill. App.3d 725, 82 Ill.Dec. 717, 469 N.E.2d 251 (1984); First Hartford Corp. v. Kennebec Water Dist., 490 A.2d 1209 (Me.1985); Matzell v. Distaola, 105 A.D.2d 500, 481 N.Y.S.2d 453 (1984), appeal denied 64 N.Y.2d 608, 489 N.Y.S.2d 1025, 478 N.E.2d 209 (1985); Knadler v. Adams, 661 P.2d 1052 (Wyo.1983); United States v. Zorger, 407 F.Supp. 25 (W.D.Pa.1976), affirmed 546 F.2d 421 (3d Cir. 1976); First National Bank of Oregon v. Townsend, 27 Or.App. 103, 555 P.2d 477 (1976); Garcia v. Garcia, 86 N.M. 503, 525 P.2d 863 (1974); Darman v. Dunderdale, 362 Mass. 633, 289 N.E.2d 847 (1972); 3 Am. L.Prop. § 12.91 (1952). If the court is unable to determine the intent even with the aid of extrinsic evidence, the deed may simply be held void for ambiguity. See Myers v. Francis, 548 So.2d 833 (Fla.App.1989) ("hopelessly confused" deed is totally void); Minor v. Neely, 247 Ga. 253, 275 S.E.2d 333 (1981); Schade v. Stewart, 205 Cal. 658, 272 P. 567 (1928).

52. See, e.g., United States v. 9.41 Acres in Sebastian County, Ark., 725 F.Supp. 421 (W.D.Ark.1989); Sally–Mike Properties v. Yokum, 175 W.Va. 296, 332 S.E.2d 597 (1985); United States v. Stearns Co., 595 F.Supp. 808

(E.D.Ky.1984), affirmed 816 F.2d 279 (6th Cir. 1987), cert. denied 484 U.S. 953, 108 S.Ct. 344, 98 L.Ed.2d 370 (1987).

53. The issue may be important because of the discovery of oil or other valuable subsurface rights, or because an easement can be lost by abandonment while a possessory estate cannot. The cases often describe the question as "easement versus fee simple," but this is inaccurate since the term "fee simple" indicates the duration of the interest rather than denoting it as possessory or as an easement. Easements can be (and usually are) of perpetual duration and therefore held in "fee simple." See generally § 8.1, supra.

54. Robert Jackson Real Estate Co. v. James, 755 S.W.2d 343 (Mo.App.1988) (reservation of a "private road" created only an easement); International Paper Co. v. Hufham, 81 N.C.App. 606, 345 S.E.2d 231 (1986), review denied 318 N.C. 506, 349 S.E.2d 860 (1986) (words "right and privilege to enter * * * and use" conveyed only an easement; railroad's subsequent deed to adjoining landowners conveyed nothing since railroad's interest terminated with its abandonment of use as a railway); Roeder Co. v. Burlington Northern, Inc., 105 Wn.2d 567, 716 P.2d 855 (1986) (deed "for all railroad and other right of way purposes" conveyed easement, not possessory estate); Chournos v. D'Agnillo, 642 P.2d 710 (Utah 1982); Andersen v. Edwards, 625 P.2d 282 (Alaska 1981); Pearson v. Chambers, 18 N.C.App. 403, 197 S.E.2d 42, 89 A.L.R.3d 762 (1973); but see Cleary Petroleum Corp. v. Harrison, 621 P.2d 528 (Okl.1980). See Annot., 6 A.L.R.3d 973 (1966).

possessory title, with the language identifying the use to be made of the strip treated as merely precatory and nonbinding.[55] The cases are not particularly consistent, and the wise drafter will make clear what sort of interest is intended.

Another familiar constructional problem arises from the use of reservations and exceptions in deeds. In theory, a reservation gives the grantor a new interest in the land which did not exist before the delivery of the deed, such as a life estate or a new easement across the land conveyed. An exception, by comparison, denotes the retention by the grantor of some previously existing interest in or portion of the land granted, as "I hereby grant all of Lot 6 except the north 50 feet thereof."[56] There is little practical difference between the two terms and nearly all modern cases regard them as interchangeable, with no penalty attaching to an incorrect usage.[57] A more serious problem is the rule that neither a reservation nor an exception can be made in favor of a person other than the grantor; thus, "I hereby reserve an easement in favor of my next-door neighbor" is ineffective. The supposed difficulty is the absence of any granting language running to the third party.[58] But this conclusion stems from an unduly technical construction of the words "reserve" or "except," and several recent cases have rejected it and recognized that the third party receives the interest in question.[59]

55. Safeco Title Ins. Co. v. Citizens & Southern Nat. Bank, 190 Ga.App. 809, 380 S.E.2d 477 (1989) (deed granting "a strip of land * * * in fee simple" gave a possessory estate, not merely an easement); Farmers Reservoir and Irrigation v. Sun Production Co., 721 P.2d 1198 (Colo.App.1986); Little Miami, Inc. v. Wisecup, 13 Ohio App.3d 239, 468 N.E.2d 935 (1984) (deed of land "on which to construct a Rail Road and for no other purpose" conveyed an estate in fee simple, not merely an easement); Midland Valley Railroad Co. v. Arrow Industrial Manufacturing Co., 297 P.2d 410 (Okl.1956); but see Harvest Queen Mill & Elevator Co. v. Sanders, 189 Kan. 536, 370 P.2d 419 (1962); Bernards v. Link, 199 Or. 579, 248 P.2d 341 (1952), adhered to 200 Or. 205, 263 P.2d 794 (1953).

56. See Lincoln Savings and Loan Ass'n v. Colorado, 768 P.2d 733 (Colo.App.1988) (grant of property "less" the area containing a particular easement is an "exception"); Hartman v. Potter, 596 P.2d 653, 656–657 (Utah 1979); Piper v. Mowris, 466 Pa. 89, 351 A.2d 635 (1976); Comment, 36 Calif.L.Rev. 470 (1948); Bigelow & Madden, Exception and Reservation of Easements, 38 Harv.L.Rev. 180 (1924); 2 R. Patton & C. Patton, Land Titles § 344 (1957); Annot., 34 A.L.R. 698 (1930).

57. Russell v. Garver, 55 Wash.App. 175, 777 P.2d 12 (1989) (parties' intent controls, irrespective of their use of "reservation" or "exception"); Sally–Mike Properties v. Yokum, 175 W.Va. 296, 332 S.E.2d 597 (1985); Lutz v. McLain, 538 P.2d 472 (Colo.App.1975); Mott v. Stanlake, 63 Mich.App. 440, 234 N.W.2d 667 (1975); Hurd v. Byrnes, 264 Or. 591, 506 P.2d 686 (1973); Adkins v. Arsht, 50

F.Supp. 761 (E.D.Ill.1943). Cf. Earle v. International Paper Co., 429 So.2d 989 (Ala.1983), distinguishing exceptions from reservations for purposes of the rule against perpetuities.

58. Estate of Thomson v. Wade, 69 N.Y. 570, 516 N.Y.S.2d 614, 509 N.E.2d 309 (1987); Pitman v. Sweeney, 34 Wn.App. 321, 661 P.2d 153 (1983); Cayce v. Carter Oil Co., 618 F.2d 669 (10th Cir.1980); Tallarico v. Brett, 137 Vt. 52, 400 A.2d 959 (1979); Canter v. Lindsey, 575 S.W.2d 331 (Tex.Civ.App.1978), refused n.r.e.; Bauer v. Bauer, 180 Neb. 177, 141 N.W.2d 837 (1966); Leidig v. Hoopes, 288 P.2d 402 (Okl.1955). Cf. Johnson v. Republic Steel Corp., 262 F.2d 108 (1958), holding the words "excepted and conveyed" to be a sufficient grant to a third party. The older cases frequently found valid an exception or reservation to the grantor's spouse, reasoning that the spouse's dower, curtesy, homestead, or other marital rights somehow validated the conveyance. See Glasgow v. Glasgow, 221 S.C. 322, 70 S.E.2d 432 (1952); Saunders v. Saunders, 373 Ill. 302, 26 N.E.2d 126, 129 A.L.R. 306 (1940); Boyer v. Murphy, 202 Cal. 23, 259 P. 38 (1927).

59. Simpson v. Kistler Inv. Co., 713 P.2d 751 (Wyo.1986); Katkish v. Pearce, 490 A.2d 626 (D.C.App.1985) (deed conveying fee title "subject to" an easement to clearly identified third parties is effective to give them easement); Jakobson v. Chestnut Hill Properties, Inc., 106 Misc.2d 918, 436 N.Y.S.2d 806 (1981) (same); Mott v. Stanlake, 63 Mich.App. 440, 234 N.W.2d 667 (1975); Willard v. First Church of Christ, Scientist, Pacifica, 7 Cal.3d

A final constructional issue derives from the common law rule that no subsequent language in a deed would be permitted to derogate from the estate conveyed in the granting clause.[60] This "repugnancy" rule (so-called because words repugnant to the granting clause are disregarded) has been increasingly discredited, and most modern cases either reject it entirely [61] or give only a rather mild priority to the granting clause.[62] The touchstone today is the intent of the parties as discerned from the "four corners" of the document and appropriate extrinsic evidence.

Defects in Deeds. Two types of deed defects may be considered. The first is an error, usually inadvertent, which causes the deed to reflect inaccurately the intention of at least one of the parties [63], even though there is nothing amiss in its essential formalities. Here reformation of the deed in equity is available to the aggrieved plaintiff if the defendant was also under a mistake or was guilty of fraud or other inequitable conduct [64]; even the

473, 102 Cal.Rptr. 739, 498 P.2d 987 (1972), noted 61 Calif.L.Rev. 548 (1973); Garza v. Grayson, 255 Or. 413, 467 P.2d 960 (1970); Townsend v. Cable, 378 S.W.2d 806 (Ky.1964). See Comment, Reservation of a Property Interest in a Deed in Favor of the Grantor's Spouse Is Effective When That Is the Grantor's Intent, 60 N.D.L.Rev. 317 (1984), commenting on Malloy v. Boettcher, 334 N.W.2d 8 (N.D.1983); Lasater, Reservations in Favor of Strangers to the Title: California Abandons the Common Law Rule, 24 Hast.L.J. 469 (1973); Harris, Reservations in Favor of Strangers to the Title, 6 Okla.L.Rev. 127 (1953). Rather nonsensically, the *Willard* case, supra, upholds a reservation to a third party but states in dicta that a contrary result would follow with an exception! Id. at note 35. A few states have reversed the common law rule by statute; see 6A Powell, Real Property ¶ 887[5] (1980).

60. See In re Fleck's Estate, 261 Iowa 434, 154 N.W.2d 865 (1967); Herd, Deed Construction and the "Repugnant to the Grant" Doctrine, 21 Tex.Tech.L.Rev. 635 (1990); Annot., 84 A.L.R. 1054 (1930); 6A Powell, Real Property ¶ 893 (1980); 4 Tiffany, Real Property § 980 (1939).

61. Turner v. Lassiter, 484 So.2d 378 (Ala. 1985); Heyen v. Hartnett, 235 Kan. 117, 679 P.2d 1152 (1984); Smith v. Graham, 705 S.W.2d 705 (Tex.App.1985); Robinson v. King, 68 N.C.App. 86, 314 S.E.2d 768 (1984), review denied 311 N.C. 762, 321 S.E.2d 144 (1984) (recounting the checkered history of the "repugnancy" rule in North Carolina). Nevling v. Natoli, 290 Pa.Super. 174, 434 A.2d 187 (1981); Copello v. Hart, 293 So.2d 734 (Fla. App.1974); Holland v. Holland, 509 S.W.2d 91 (Mo.1974); Colonial Investment Co. v. MacKenzie, 8 Wn.App. 264, 505 P.2d 834 (1973); Watson v. Raley, 250 Md. 266, 242 A.2d 488 (1968); Selman v. Bristow, 402 S.W.2d 520 (Tex.Civ.App.1966), refused n.r.e., 406 S.W.2d 896 (Tex.1966); Grayson v. Holloway, 203

Tenn. 464, 313 S.W.2d 555 (1958). But see Hornets Nest Girl Scout Council v. Cannon Foundation, Inc., 79 N.C.App. 187, 339 S.E.2d 26 (1986), applying the "repugnancy" rule despite acknowledgement that it has been criticized as harsh, technical, and tending to frustrate the grantor's intent.

62. Elliott v. Cox, 100 N.C.App. 536, 397 S.E.2d 319 (1990); Knell v. Price, 318 Md. 501, 569 A.2d 636 (1990); Kerr–McGee Corp. v. Henderson, 763 P.2d 92 (Okl.1988); Goodson v. Capehart, 232 Va. 232, 349 S.E.2d 130 (1986); Saxon v. Johnson, 393 So.2d 1007 (Ala. Civ.App.1980), writ denied 393 So.2d 1012 (Ala.1981); First National Bank of Oregon v. Townsend, 27 Or.App. 103, 555 P.2d 477 (1976); Bean v. Bean, 253 S.C. 340, 170 S.E.2d 654 (1969). See Healy, Conflict Between the Granting and Habendum Clauses, 11 N.Y.U.Intra.L.Rev. 201 (1965).

63. Either grantor or grantee may seek reformation. It is usually said that the mistake must be one of fact and not of law; see Paradise Hills Church, Inc. v. International Church, 467 F.Supp. 357 (D.Ariz.1979); Lea v. Byrd, 242 Ark. 673, 415 S.W.2d 336 (1967); but see Grossman Furniture Co. v. Pierre, 119 N.J.Super. 411, 291 A.2d 858 (1972).

64. See Andres v. Claassen, 238 Kan. 732, 714 P.2d 963 (1986) (where grantee added language expanding description of land before grantor signed deed, but did not call it to grantor's attention, deed was properly reformed to coincide with grantor's intent; Cordova v. Gosar, 719 P.2d 625 (Wyo.1986); Ellison v. Watson, 53 Or.App. 923, 633 P.2d 840 (1981), review denied 292 Or. 109, 642 P.2d 310 (1981); Cleary Petroleum Corp. v. Harrison, 621 P.2d 528 (Okl.1980); 6A Powell, Real Property ¶ 894 (1980); 4 Tiffany, Real Property § 985 (3d ed. 1939). If the defendant was not at fault nor under a mistake, no reformation will be ordered; McKee v. Douglas, 362 S.W.2d 870 (Tex.Civ.App.1962), refused n.r.e.

defendant's silence in the face of knowledge of the error is enough.[65] The proof to support reformation must be "clear and convincing,"[66] and the equitable nature of the action precludes reformation against a bona fide purchaser who has relied on the face of the deed.[67]

The second type of defect is one which affects the essential formalities of the deed's execution and delivery or which casts doubt on the grantor's capacity. In cases of this type the grantor or his successors typically rely on the defect in an effort to have the deed cancelled or set aside. A variety of such defects is possible, and the courts generally label the deed as "void" or "voidable," depending on which particular defect exists. These labels are somewhat misleading, since they seem to suggest that a void deed is automatically nugatory, while a voidable deed will be set aside only upon the grantor's request. In fact they have no such meaning; in either case a court will cancel the deed at the grantor's instance if the grantee has made no further conveyance. The distinction between void and voidable deeds arises only if the grantee has retransferred the land to a bona fide purchaser for value.[68] If the defect is regarded as making the deed void, even a BFP will have no title, but if the deed is merely voidable the title will be unassailable in the hands of a BFP.[69]

The defect which most clearly will make a deed void, and thus defeat even a BFP, is forgery—for example, a false signature or an attempt to enlarge the scope of a deed by an addition, alteration, or deletion after it is signed.[70] The ground for this rule is surely not that the BFP could have

65. See Paradise Hills Church, Inc. v. International Church, supra note 63; Demetris v. Demetris, 125 Cal.App.2d 440, 270 P.2d 891 (1954).

66. Bourne v. Lajoie, 149 Vt. 45, 540 A.2d 359 (1987); Gasaway v. Reiter, 736 P.2d 749 (Wyo.1987); Praggastis v. Sandner, 40 Or.App. 477, 595 P.2d 520 (1979); LeMehaute v. LeMehaute, 585 S.W.2d 276 (Mo.App.1979); Lazenby v. F.P. Asher, Jr. & Sons, Inc., 266 Md. 679, 296 A.2d 699 (1972); Galyen v. Gillenwater, 247 Ark. 701, 447 S.W.2d 137 (1969).

67. In re R & J Construction Co., 43 B.R. 29 (Bkrtcy.E.D.Mo.1984); United States v. La-Rosa, 765 F.2d 693 (7th Cir.1985) (subsequent purchaser was on notice of mutual mistake in deed because boundary markers on the land did not correspond with description in deed; reformation ordered); Touchstone v. Peterson, 443 So.2d 1219 (Ala.1983) (subsequent purchaser was on notice of grantor's right of reformation due to grantor's continued possession of land, and was not BFP; reformation ordered); Jones v. Carrier, 473 A.2d 867 (Me. 1984) (no reformation against BFP, or in favor of one not an original party to deed). But see Bailey v. Ewing, 105 Idaho 636, 671 P.2d 1099 (App.1983) (reformation may be ordered against a bona fide purchaser if he is fully and fairly compensated for the loss).

68. In one situation the term "voidable" generally does indicate that the deed may be set aside, even against a BFP, by the grantor's disaffirmance; that is the case of a minor grantor who seeks to set aside the deed after reaching majority. A few states term a minor's deed "void," meaning that not even a disaffirmance is necessary. See note 79 infra.

If the grantor remains in possession, his presence on the land will usually impart inquiry notice to any subsequent purchaser, precluding BFP status. See Stevens v. American Savings Institution, Inc., 289 Or. 349, 613 P.2d 1057 (1980); Houston v. Mentolos, 318 So.2d 427 (Fla.App.1975).

69. See, e.g., Bennion Insurance Co. v. 1st OK Corp., 571 P.2d 1339 (Utah 1977).

In recent years there has been in the Midwest a rash of recordings of bogus "land patents" purporting to represent transfers of original title from the federal government. These documents have typically been filed by farmers who thought they might somehow stave off mortgage foreclosure. They have mainly succeeded in arousing the ire of the courts. See, e.g., Wisconsin v. Glick, 782 F.2d 670 (7th Cir.1986). Yet the Iowa Supreme Court has held that county recorders have no authority to reject such bogus instruments; see Proctor v. Garrett, 378 N.W.2d 298 (Iowa 1985) (recorder has no discretion to reject a proffered filing of a "common law lien" which is a legal nullity); § 11.9, infra at note 2.

70. Southeast Bank, N.A. v. Sapp, 554 So.2d 1193 (Fla.App.1989), review denied 564

prevented the loss by using greater care; in many cases a forgery is entirely undetectable by untrained persons.[71] Rather, the rule is based on the innocence and lack of complicity of the grantor, who is favored by the law simply because he or she is entirely blameless.[72]

Fraud in the execution is usually treated like forgery, making the deed absolutely void.[73] It exists when the grantor is tricked into signing a deed in the mistaken belief that it is some other document, as when the grantee slips the deed in among other papers the grantor is signing.[74] The conclusion that the deed is void is particularly probable if the grantor is elderly, illiterate, ill, confused, or has particular reason to trust the grantee.[75] By comparison, if a deed's signing is induced by the grantee's fraudulent representations, such as a bad check or a false financial statement, but the grantor understands the nature of the deed, the document is usually regarded as only voidable rather than void.[76] The distinction again is placed on the ground of the grantor's culpability; with fraud in the execution the grantor is regarded as blameless while with fraud in the inducement, the courts feel

So.2d 1087 (Fla.1990); Lewis v. Barnett, 694 S.W.2d 743 (Mo.App.1985); Bennerson v. Small, 842 F.2d 710 (3d Cir.1988), cert. denied 488 U.S. 845, 109 S.Ct. 121, 102 L.Ed.2d 94 (1988); Lange v. Wyoming National Bank, 706 P.2d 659 (Wyo.1985), appeal after remand 741 P.2d 109 (1987) (where grantee altered deed, it was in effect a forgery and void, and mortgage given to bank by grantee was also void despite bank's good faith and giving of value); First National Bank in Albuquerque v. Enriquez, 96 N.M. 714, 634 P.2d 1266 (1981); Rasmussen v. Olsen, 583 P.2d 50 (Utah 1978) (grantee obliterated reservation clause in deed; held, the interest granted is not enlarged thereby, even in favor of a BFP); Cumberland Capital Corp., Inc. v. Robinette, 57 Ala.App. 697, 331 So.2d 709 (1976); Arizona Central Credit Union v. Holden, 6 Ariz.App. 310, 432 P.2d 276 (1967); Reed v. Fain, 145 So.2d 858 (Fla.1961). If the grantor's name is signed by another who is acting as his agent or with his approval, it is not a forgery and the deed is good; see Haffa v. Haffa, 115 Ill.App.2d 467, 253 N.E.2d 507 (1969); note 41, supra. Note that a grantee under a forged deed may nonetheless get title by adverse possession by remaining in possession long enough under appropriate conditions; see Bergesen v. Clauss, 15 Ill.App.2d 337, 155 N.E.2d 20 (1958); § 11.7, infra.

71. Consider, for example, the battle of expert witnesses over the authenticity of the signature on the widely-publicized "Mormon will" attributed to Howard Hughes; see Rhoden v. First National Bank of Nevada, 96 Nev. 654, 615 P.2d 244 (1980).

72. See Harding v. Ja Laur Corp., 20 Md. App. 209, 315 A.2d 132 (1974). Of course the BFP is blameless too, but the courts will not disturb the status quo of the putative grantor's ownership where both parties are innocent.

73. Upson v. Goodland State Bank & Trust Co., 823 P.2d 704 (Colo.1992); Cumberland Capital Corp. v. Robinette, 57 Ala.App. 697, 331 So.2d 709 (1976); Nixon v. Nixon, 260 N.C. 251, 132 S.E.2d 590 (1963); Annot., 11 A.L.R.3d 1074 (1967). This sort of fraud is also known as "fraud in the factum." See also Reed v. Thomas, 355 So.2d 277 (La.App. 1978), writ denied 357 So.2d 1153 (La.1978) (grantor and her heirs were barred by prescription from seeking to set aside deed obtained by fraud in the execution, where they had known of the fraud for 35 years.) If "extrinsic" fraud is practiced on the court in a proceeding leading to a judicial sale, the sheriff's deed or other conveyance is void even against a BFP; see Groves v. Witherspoon, 379 F.Supp. 52 (E.D.Tenn.1974).

74. See Bennion Insurance Co. v. 1st OK Corp., 571 P.2d 1339 (Utah 1977).

75. Houston v. Mentelos, 318 So.2d 427 (Fla.App.1975) (limited to cases of fraud in the execution by McCoy v. Love, infra note 77); Hoffer v. Crawford, 65 N.W.2d 625 (N.D.1954).

76. Hill v. Watts, 801 S.W.2d 176 (Tex.App. 1990); Malcom v. Wilson, 534 So.2d 241 (Ala. 1988); Dines v. Ultimo, 532 So.2d 1131 (Fla. App.1988); Blaise v. Ratliff, 672 S.W.2d 683 (Mo.App.1984); Fallon v. Triangle Management, 169 Cal.App.3d 1103, 215 Cal.Rptr. 748 (1985); Ingram v. Horn, 294 Ala. 353, 317 So.2d 485 (1975), appeal after remand 361 So.2d 999 (1977); Bicknell v. Jones, 203 Kan. 196, 453 P.2d 127 (1969); Pure Oil Co. v. Swindall, 58 S.W.2d 7 (Tex.Com.App.1933); cases cited in notes 70–72, supra. See also Nobles v. Marcus, 533 S.W.2d 923 (Tex.1976) (grantor signed as corporate officer, but lacked authority from corporation; defect amounted to fraud, deed was voidable); Watson Realty Corp. v. Quinn, 452 So.2d 568 (Fla.1984) (proof of fraud need be only by preponderance of evidence).

he or she could and should have been more careful. This rationale is an overgeneralization, since the degree of blame varies with a wide spectrum of additional facts. The cases are not wholly consistent in following this distinction or in their classification of the two kinds of fraud.[77]

One other common defect, lack of delivery, is generally held to make the deed void; it is discussed in a subsequent section.[78] A deed executed by a minor is said to be "voidable," but most of the cases permit the grantor to disaffirm it even as against a BFP by acting within a reasonable time after reaching majority.[79] Virtually all other defects result in only a finding of voidability and not outright voidness.[80] They include insanity or lack of capacity [81], duress [82], undue influence [83], mistake [84] and breach of fiduciary

77. If the grantor realizes that the document is a deed, but is duped as to its coverage or details, it is generally held merely voidable; see McCoy v. Love, 382 So.2d 647 (Fla.1979) (grantee prepared deed, informed elderly illiterate grantor that it conveyed much less land than it in fact described; held, fraud in the inducement; deed voidable); Grube v. Bessenger, 259 Mich. 57, 242 N.W. 837 (1932) (grantor's husband told her he would fill in description of his land, but filled in her land instead; deed voidable). But if the grantor is tricked into believing the deed is some other sort of document, it is usually held void; see 11 A.L.R.3d 1074 (1967). But see Guice v. Burrage, 156 F.2d 304 (5th Cir.1946) (illiterate grantors were told the deed was a mineral lease; held voidable).

78. See § 11.3, infra.

79. See Searcy v. Hunter, 81 Tex. 644, 17 S.W. 372 (1891); Annot., 16 A.L.R.2d 1420, 1421 note 1 (1951); 2 R. Patton & C. Patton, Land Titles § 334 (1957); Burby, Real Property § 119 (3d ed. 1965). See note 66, supra, and accompanying text respecting the use of the term "voidable." The cases regard the minor as innocent per se, and thus protect him or her even against a BFP. The underlying policy is of dubious merit. A few states follow an even more extreme rule, holding a minor's deed absolutely void even without his or her disaffirmance; see Sparks v. Sparks, 101 Cal. App.2d 129, 225 P.2d 238 (1950), based on West's Ann.Cal.Civ. Code § 33.

A minor who has misrepresented his or her age, is considered by some jurisdictions estopped to disaffirm the deed; see Lewis v. Van Cleve, 302 Ill. 413, 134 N.E. 804 (1922); Annot., 29 A.L.R.3d 1270 (1970).

80. First Fiduciary Corp. v. Blanco, 276 N.W.2d 30 (Minn.1979). Many possible defects not mentioned in the text may be conceived. See, e.g., Mason v. Pitt, 21 Mo. 391 (1855) (property sold without compliance with platting law; BFP protected). As to the validity of deeds executed without compliance with platting and subdivision ordinances, see generally Annot., 77 A.L.R.3d 1058 (1977).

81. Emanuel v. Emanuel, 78 N.C.App. 799, 338 S.E.2d 620 (1986) (deed made by grantor who is *non compos mentis* is voidable, not void); Simon v. Marlow, 515 F.Supp. 947 (W.D.Va.1981); Levine v. O'Malley, 33 A.D.2d 874, 307 N.Y.S.2d 919 (1969); Mock v. Stricklin, 315 P.2d 247 (Okl.1957). But see Sooner Federal Sav. & Loan Ass'n v. Smoot, 735 P.2d 555 (Okl.1987) (if grantor lacks ability to understand transactions, deed is void rather than voidable); Shepard v. First American Mortg. Co., 289 S.C. 516, 347 S.E.2d 118 (App. 1986) (where immediate grantee knew of grantor's incapacity, deed is void even against subsequent BFP). A contrary rule, treating the deed as void, is usually followed if the grantor has been placed under a guardianship, since a title examination will disclose the proceedings and hence the grantor's incapacity; see 2 C. Patton & R. Patton, Land Titles § 334 (1957). Judicial opinions sometimes state that a deed from an incompetent is void, but almost invariably the statements are dictum since no BFP was involved; see, e.g., Runge v. Moore, 196 N.W.2d 87 (N.D.1972); McCutcheon v. Brownfield, 2 Wn.App. 348, 467 P.2d 868 (1970). Incapacity exists if the grantor does not understand the nature of the conveyance or his property or, in a deed of gift, if he or she does not know the natural objects of his or her bounty; see Davis v. Pitti, 472 S.W.2d 382 (Mo.1971); Eyler v. Spencer, 244 Md. 454, 223 A.2d 757 (1966).

82. Goodwin v. City of Dallas, 496 S.W.2d 722 (Tex.Civ.App.1973); Campbell v. Genshlea, 180 Cal. 213, 180 P. 336 (1919).

83. First Interstate Bank v. First Wyoming Bank, 762 P.2d 379 (Wyo.1988); United Companies Financial Corp. v. Wyers, 518 So.2d 700 (Ala.1987); Fritz v. Mazurek, 156 Conn. 555, 244 A.2d 368 (1968); Cox v. Schnerr, 172 Cal. 371, 156 P. 509 (1916). See 4 Tiffany, Real Property § 988 (3d ed. 1939). See also Stewart v. Dickerson, 455 So.2d 809 (Ala.1984), appeal after remand 473 So.2d 1078 (Ala.Civ. App.1985), applying Ala.Code 1975, § 8-9-12, which permits a grantor to disaffirm (except as against a BFP) a deed given in consideration of a promise to support the grantor for life.

84. See Tilbury v. Osmundson, 143 Colo. 12, 352 P.2d 102 (1960). Cancellation of the

duty.[85] For a discussion of the substantive legal rules governing these defects the reader is referred to other sources.[86]

§ 11.2 Land Descriptions

Both contracts of sale and deeds, to be valid, must describe or otherwise identify the land affected. The Statute of Frauds insists on a written identification; physical markers on the earth's surface or such other sources as maps or surveyor's notes are not enough unless they are identified or referred to in the instrument.[1] The doctrines of practical location of boundaries, discussed later, may result in modification of a boundary without a writing, and a court may reform a writing which does not comport with the parties' intent,[2] but in general a written description is essential.

Methods of Describing Land. A land description is a statement defining a series of boundary lines on the earth's surface which delineate a two-dimensional geometric figure. The parcel of land thus described is limited horizontally on the surface by this geometric figure and extends vertically from the earth's center to the "sky," [3] unless by its terms it is more limited.[4]

deed is ordinarily the appropriate remedy if the grantor was mistaken about the fact that the document was a deed, see Felonenko v. Siomka, 55 Or.App. 331, 637 P.2d 1338 (1981), while reformation is proper if the mistake related to the precise contents of the deed; see 3 Am.L.Prop. § 12.86 at notes 26–31 (1952); text at notes 63–67, supra.

85. See Daughton v. Parson, 423 N.W.2d 894 (Iowa App.1988); Loftis v. Eck, 288 S.C. 154, 341 S.E.2d 641 (App.1986); 4 Scott, Trusts § 285 (3d ed. 1967).

86. See T. Atkinson, Wills §§ 54–61 (2d ed. 1953); 1 Corbin, Contracts §§ 6–7, 228 (1963); 5 Scott, Trusts §§ 467–68, 472 (3d ed. 1967).

§ 11.2

1. Rekis v. Lake Minnewaska Mountain Houses, Inc., 170 A.D.2d 124, 573 N.Y.S.2d 331 (1991), appeal dismissed 79 N.Y.2d 851, 580 N.Y.2d 201, 588 N.E.2d 99 (1992). The description may, of course, incorporate or refer to other sources of information outside the document itself; see Brasher v. Tanner, 256 Ga. 812, 353 S.E.2d 478 (1987); Stauth v. Brown, 241 Kan. 1, 734 P.2d 1063 (1987) (reference to plat is sufficient, even though plat is not recorded). But see Sparks v. Douglas County, 39 Wn.App. 714, 695 P.2d 588 (1985) (reference to "line of said road as surveyed" was insufficient description, where no such survey had ever been made). See generally Annot, 73 A.L.R.4th 135 (1989). See the excellent discussion in O. Browder, et al., Basic Property Law 760–772 (5th ed. 1989). The cases are divided as to whether the description may be added by the grantee after the deed is delivered; see Annot., 11 A.L.R.2d 1372 (1950).

2. Torrao v. Cox, 26 Mass.App.Ct. 247, 525 N.E.2d 1349 (1988). See § 11.8, infra (bound-

aries by practical location); Palmer, Reformation and the Statute of Frauds, 65 Mich.L.Rev. 421 (1967).

3. The Latin phrase was "cujus est solum ejus est usque ad coelum." It is not taken literally in modern cases. As to subsurface rights, see Edwards v. Sims, 232 Ky. 791, 24 S.W.2d 619 (1929), holding that a surface owner also owns the portions of a valuable cave which run under his land. But see Boehringer v. Montalto, 142 Misc. 560, 254 N.Y.S. 276 (1931), holding a sewer easement at a depth of 150 feet was not an encumbrance on the title of the surface owner since he could not reasonably make use of the soil at that depth.

Aircraft overflights have raised difficult questions about the upper extent of land ownership. Such flights at a reasonable altitude are clearly privileged. The Restatement (Second) of Torts § 159 (1965) regards an overflight as a trespass only if it interferes substantially with the landowner's use and enjoyment and enters the "immediate reaches" of the land. 500 feet is presumptively not "immediate," and 50 feet presumptively is, with distances between 50 and 500 feet presenting a question of fact. The Restatement relies heavily on United States v. Causby, 328 U.S. 256, 66 S.Ct. 1062, 90 L.Ed. 1206 (1946), and Griggs v. Allegheny County, 369 U.S. 84, 82 S.Ct. 531, 7 L.Ed.2d 585 (1962), rehearing denied 369 U.S. 857, 82 S.Ct. 931, 8 L.Ed.2d 16 (1962). See also Thornburg v. Port of Portland, 233 Or. 178, 376 P.2d 100 (1962); Harvey, Landowners' Rights in the Air Age: The Airport Dilemma, 56 Mich.L.Rev. 1313 (1958); Note, 16 Vand.L.Rev. 430 (1963).

4. A "land" parcel may also be explicitly limited in the third dimension, consisting of

A wide variety of methods of specifying boundary lines is possible. Some of these methods involve an "official" determination of the location and extent of parcels of land, physically marked by monuments on the land and shown on a map maintained in a government office. Two systems for doing this, the Government Survey System and the subdivision plat, are discussed below.[5] The written description of a parcel in these systems may consist simply of a reference to an appropriate parcel number on the official map.[6]

But there are many areas of the nation not covered by either of these systems, and even where they are available the parties may wish to carve out and transfer only a portion of an official parcel. In such cases the parties must describe the land conveyed without governmental assistance or review. They do so by writing a "metes and bounds" description which begins at some geographic "point of beginning" and specifies or "calls" each boundary line in turn, until the last line described returns to the point of beginning. These descriptions are often lengthy, cumbersome, and rife with potential for error; they must be used with the greatest care.[7]

The earliest "metes and bounds" descriptions relied heavily on natural monuments. In older deeds, references such as "beginning at the great white oak tree," "along Mill Creek 50 chains," or the like were very common. The lack of permanence of these monuments sometimes created severe problems for later buyers and their counsel; if the tree were removed or the creek changed course, it might be virtually impossible to locate the boundaries.[8] Artificial or manmade monuments, such as roads, bridges, fences, stakes, and posts are more widely used today, but are subject to the same objection to some degree. Yet some use of monuments is essential, since present technology does not permit sufficiently precise location of points on the earth by means of astronomical measurement of latitude and longitude. It is also common for a metes and bounds description to refer to the boundaries of adjoining land, as in "west 20 chains, more or less, to the land of Mary Jones." The adjoining land may be thought of as an artificial monument.

Many modern metes and bounds descriptions make no reference to either natural or artificial monuments except to establish a point of begin-

---

specific regions above or below the surface, such as mining rights between given depths or air rights between given heights or altitudes. But even this sort of parcel must be defined by the sort of two-dimensional figure in the horizontal plane discussed in the text as well.

5. See text at notes 10–13, infra.

6. Sometimes careless or hurried drafters use a much more convenient, but less accurate parcel designator, the street address. It does not really locate the land's boundaries, but some courts will uphold it and use extrinsic evidence to identify the boundaries. See City of St. Louis v. Parcel 107 of Land, 702 S.W.2d 123 (Mo.App.1985) (where lot number was omitted from deed, but street address was given and indicated which lot number was intended, description was sufficient); Park West Village, Inc. v. Avise, 714 P.2d 1137 (Utah 1986) (street address was sufficient de-

scription in land option). But see Martin v. Seigel, 35 Wn.2d 223, 212 P.2d 107 (1949) (street address insufficient).

7. This does not imply that the Government Survey System or officially-approved subdivision plats are always perfect. See, e.g., Van Deven v. Harvey, 9 Wis.2d 124, 100 N.W.2d 587 (1960), involving serious discrepancies in a plat. Moreover, even an error-free description can give rise to severe title problems; see Howard v. Kunto, 3 Wn.App. 393, 477 P.2d 210 (1970), in which each of a series of neighboring lot owners had occupied (and in some cases built houses upon) the lot next door to the one he owned!

8. A description which raises these problems is reprinted and commented upon in Cunningham, Making Land Surveys and Preparing Descriptions to Meet Legal Requirements, 19 Mo.L.Rev. 234 (1954).

ning. Instead, they employ successive calls of courses and distances, with the first call starting at the point of beginning and the last call returning to it. A course is a statement of direction, and is usually expressed as some number of degrees, minutes, and seconds east and west of due north or south. By convention, north or south is first specified, and the numbers and words which follow indicate how far the course differs from due north or south. Thus a course in a northeasterly direction would be stated as "North 45 degrees East," while a course directly west could be written either as "North 90 degrees West" or "South 90 degrees West." [9] If a particular boundary is not a straight line, it can be described as an arc or a series of arcs by specifying the center and the radius of each.

In each call a distance must be stated together with the course. Thus, a complete call might read "North 37 degrees 40' 35" East 29.55 feet." Most descriptions in American deeds give the distance in feet, rods, or chains. Table 1 provides the information necessary to convert distances from any of the common units to other units.

Table 1

Units	Inches	Links	Feet	Yards	Rods	Chains	Miles	Meters
1 inch	1	0.126 263	0.083 333 3	0.027 777 8	0.005 050	0.001 262	0.000 015 783	0.025 400.05
1 link	7.92	1	0.66	0.22	0.04	0.01	0.000 125	0.201 168 4
1 foot	12	1.515 152	1	0.333 333	0.060 606	0.015 151	0.000 189 394	0.304 800 6
1 yard	36	4.545.45	3	1	0.181 818	0.045 454	0.000 568 182	0.914 401 8
1 rod	198	25	16.5	5.5	1	0.25	0.003 125	5.029 210
1 chain	792	100	66	22	4	1	0.0125	20.116 84
1 mile	63 360	8 000	5 280	1 760	320	80	1	1 609.347 2
1 meter	39.37	4.970 960	3.280 833	1.093 611 1	0.198 838	0.049 710	0.000 621 370	1

Two systems provide for governmental recognition of "official" land parcels. The first, the Government Survey System, was devised by Thomas Jefferson and adopted by the Continental Congress in 1785. Most of the land added to the United States since that time has been surveyed under the system, with Texas being the notable exception. Thus, it is generally available throughout the country except along the Atlantic seaboard and in Kentucky, Tennessee, and West Virginia. The system is based on the establishment of sets of Principal Meridians and intersecting Base Lines; there are 36 such sets in the contiguous 48 states. [10] The Principal Meridians run north-south and the Base Lines run east-west. Spaced out parallel to each Base Line at intervals of approximately six miles and running east-west are additional lines dividing the land into "Townships." Similarly, spaced parallel to each Principal Meridian at six-mile intervals are north-south lines which divide the land into "Ranges." Thus, one may describe a parcel of land in the form of a square about six miles on a side by stating both a Township number and a Range number. These numbers are counted from the intersection of the Principal Meridian and the Base Line, as in "Township 2 North, Range 6 West, Cimmaron Base and Meridian." Often such a description will be abbreviated to "T 2 N, R 6 W, C.B. & M."

The six-mile square defined in this way is, rather confusingly, also called a "Township." The term thus refers to both the north-south divisions along

---

9. See Brown, Boundary Control and Legal Principles 5–9 (1957).

10. See generally R. Patton & C. Patton, Land Titles § 116 (1957). A map locating and identifying the Principal Meridians and Base Lines is found in U.S. Department of the Inte-

rior, Restoration of Lost or Obliterated Corners & Subdivision of Sections: A Guide for Surveyors (1974), reprinted in G. Nelson & D. Whitman, Real Estate Transfer, Finance and Development (4th ed. 1992).

the Principal Meridian and to the square land areas which they help to identify. Note that these townships are not political or governmental subdivisions, but merely land descriptions. Each township is divided into thirty-six "sections" about one mile square.[11] The sections are numbered consecutively, starting with Section 1 in the northeast corner of the township and running back and forth to Section 36 in the southeast corner. A section, being an approximate square mile, contains about 640 acres. The corners of the sections and townships are marked with monuments on the ground.[12]

Each section may be further divided into halves, quarters, and so on, so that one might own "the North half of the Southwest quarter of Section 21." If this parcel were in the township described in the example above, its full description would be abbreviated as "N ½ of SW ¼, Sec. 21, T 2 N, R 6 W, C.B. & M." A half of a quarter section, as described here, would contain about 80 acres.

The other principal system of officially recognized land descriptions, available in every state, is the plat. A plat is a map, usually showing a number of new lots, which meets certain standards of format and accuracy. In many localities a plat is a legal prerequisite to every subdivision of land. It must be approved by some agency of city or county government, such as a planning commission or city council, and is filed for permanent record with the county recorder or other recording office. The plat differs from the Government Survey System in important ways. It is not prepared by government employees, but rather by the landowner or an engineer or surveyor hired by the owner. The parcels it creates are not generally of identical shape or uniform size, but are laid out by the developer to make them attractive in the market. However, the subdivider does not have carte blanche, for governmental approval of the plat may be conditioned upon compliance with a "subdivision ordinance" imposing requirements regarding lot size, street width and curvature, monumentation of lots on the ground, and the like.[13]

The plat must of necessity contain one or more references to known monuments external to the subdivision itself, so that it can be located in relation to its environment. Once it has been approved and recorded, it can form the basis for legal descriptions of its individual lots. Such descriptions are usually brief and convenient, as in "Lot 3, Block D, Ridgefield Acres Subdivision as shown in Plat Book B, page 23, Official Records of Orange County, California." No detailed recitation of the boundaries of the lot is needed, since they are shown on the plat. Nearly all modern residential

---

11. The dimensions given in the text are approximate, mainly because the curvature of the earth requires that all north-south lines (such as the Principal Meridians and their fellows) must converge toward the North Pole; hence they are not precisely parallel, and the resulting townships are not precisely square. See A. Axelrod, C. Berger & Q. Johnstone, Land Transfer and Finance 435 (1978).

12. The government survey system is far from perfect; the surveyors made numerous errors. See, e.g., Rivers v. Lozeau, 539 So.2d 1147 (Fla.App.1989), review denied 545 So.2d 1368 (Fla.1989) (the true location of a government section is where the original surveyor established it, regardless of whether subsequent surveys show it as erroneous); Helehan v. O.M. Ueland, 223 Mont. 228, 725 P.2d 1192 (1986) (same).

13. See §§ 9.15–.16 supra; D. Hagman & J. Juergensmeyer, Urban Planning & Land Development Control Law § 7.1ff (2d ed. 1986); Melli, Subdivision Control in Wisconsin, 1953 Wis.L.Rev. 389; 2 R. Patton & C. Patton, Land Titles § 120 (1957).

subdivisions are platted, and plats are commonly employed for land which has been assembled for commercial projects, such as shopping centers, as well.[14]

Beyond the Government Survey and plat systems, other governmentally-approved land description systems are available in some localities. These include "official maps" prepared by city or county engineers or surveyors, records of survey maps prepared and filed for record by individual surveyors, maps prepared by highway departments or other public agencies, and maps produced by property tax assessors.[15] These maps vary in accuracy, and it may or may not be considered good practice to use them as the basis for a land description. Tax maps, for example, are mainly concerned with identifying each parcel in general terms, and not with fixing accurate boundaries.

The metes and bounds, Government Survey, and plat systems are not mutually exclusive. A plat, for example, may be created within a given section of land in the Government Survey system and located by reference to a section corner. An owner may employ a metes and bounds description to carve out and convey a portion of a platted lot or a part of a section in the Government Survey system. Indeed, both the plat and Government Survey systems often provide convenient references to points of beginning of metes and bounds descriptions.

Other descriptive techniques may also be used. One which is both common and dangerous is to specify a quantitative part of a larger parcel which is already described, such as "the West 50 feet of Lot 13." This is satisfactory if Lot 13 is precisely rectangular and its boundaries run exactly north-south and east-west, but if this is not so the description is ambiguous. Is the 50 feet measured along the northerly boundary or the southerly boundary (which may not be parallel to each other); is it measured at right angles to the westerly boundary; or is it measured due east from the westernmost point of the lot?[16] Fractional parts of larger parcels can also be troublesome, as in "the West half of Lot 13." Should the new boundary run exactly north-south or should it be parallel to the existing westerly boundary? Most courts would probably hold the latter.[17] Other forms of quantity or fractional description may be so unclear as to force a court to declare the conveyance void for vagueness: for example, a statement of acreage, unaccompanied by any indication of the shape of the land.[18] If a

14. Urban Land Institute, Shopping Center Development Handbook 31–39 (1985).

15. A California view of these additional systems is found in Ogden, California Real Property Law 424–45, reprinted in G. Lefcoe, Land Development Law 570–71 (1966).

16. See Walters v. Tucker, 281 S.W.2d 843 (Mo.1955) (perpendicular to westerly boundary, so as to produce a strip of 50-foot width).

17. See 2 R. Patton & C. Patton, Land Titles § 146 notes 98–99 (1957).

18. Haines v. Mensen, 233 Neb. 543, 446 N.W.2d 716 (1989) ("part of" a quarter-quarter section was insufficient); Gorbics v. Close, 722 S.W.2d 672 (Tenn.App.1986) (description in will of "one acre in northwest corner" of tract was insufficient); Neil v. Jones, 497 So.2d 797

(Miss.1986) ("30 acres" in a specified quarter-quarter section was insufficient); Overby v. Cavanaugh, 434 So.2d 1365 (Miss.1983) (deed describing "18½ A Mid E side" of a certain parcel was void, since the acreage could be in any number of possible shapes). But see Kauka Farms, Inc. v. Scott, 256 Ga. 642, 352 S.E.2d 373 (1987) (20 acres "surrounding" an existing home was sufficient to describe a circle centered on the home); Stephenson v. Rowe, 315 N.C. 330, 338 S.E.2d 301 (1986) (30 acres "surrounding" an existing home; court allowed devisee to make reasonable choice of land, with home near center); Sally–Mike Properties v. Yokum, 175 W.Va. 296, 332 S.E.2d 597 (1985) ("one fourth acre * * * to include all of the burial ground now on said" land was sufficient description in view of pre-

conveyance uses a fractional description (e.g., "one-fourth of my farm"), but contains no clue as to which geographic portion of the land is intended, it may be construed as an undivided tenancy in common.[19]

A final type of description is one which depends entirely on extrinsic knowledge of the grantor's land ownership. One form is the "omnibus" or "Mother Hubbard" clause: "I hereby grant all of my land in Adams County," or the like. Another is the "after-acquired property" clause sometimes found in mortgages: "This mortgage shall bind all of the land which I may acquire in Adams County until the debt secured hereby is repaid." As between the original parties to the instrument, these sorts of descriptions are generally upheld.[20] But they are very difficult for a subsequent title examiner to find, since one obviously cannot tell by looking at the recorder's index entry for such a document whether it affects the land one is now searching. Hence, instruments using descriptions of this kind may be treated as unrecorded for purposes of the recording acts.[21]

Monuments. Monuments having significant width raise interesting problems. For example, public streets and highways are usually easements in favor of some public agency, with the so-called "underlying fee" remaining in private ownership. Where this is so, the usual rule of construction is that a conveyance describing land with a call "to Main Street" will actually convey title to the center of the street, subject to the street easement.[22] The

---

sumption of square shape and existence of graves which would serve as reference points). See also Brooks v. Hackney, 329 N.C. 166, 404 S.E.2d 854 (1991) (where description was ambiguous, but purchaser had possessed and used land for eight years, purchaser was estopped to assert description's inadequacy). See Asotin County Port District v. Clarkston Community Corp., 2 Wn.App. 1007, 472 P.2d 554 (1970); Grand Lodge of Georgia, IOOF v. City of Thomasville, 226 Ga. 4, 172 S.E.2d 612 (1970) ("running south about 8 acres to a stake"); Weston v. Dantagnan, 184 So.2d 388 (Miss.1966); Harris v. Woodard, 130 N.C. 580, 41 S.E. 790 (1902). But see Bybee v. Hageman, 66 Ill. 519 (1873), upholding "one acre and a half in the northwest corner of section five." The court noted that Illinois was a Government Survey state and that square parcels were very common, and concluded that a square shape was intended. See also Miracle Construction Co. v. Miller, 251 Minn. 320, 87 N.W.2d 665 (1958), admitting extrinsic evidence to locate a parcel described only as "house, out-buildings, and approx. 3½ acres surrounding same"; Moss v. Moss, 57 Ala. App. 688, 331 So.2d 702 (1976) (acreage is presumed square, but presumption will not be applied where geometry of the larger parcel is inconsistent with it.)

19. Aspen–Western Corp. v. Board of County Commissioners, 650 P.2d 1326 (Colo.App. 1982) (withdrawn); Mounce v. Coleman, 133 Ariz. 251, 650 P.2d 1233 (App.1982) (20 acres out of 160–acre parcel gives fractional interest); Morehead v. Hall, 126 N.C. 213, 35 S.E. 428 (1900). But see Ellett v. Liedtke, 668

S.W.2d 880 (Tex.App.1984), noted 37 Baylor L.Rev. 1059 (1985) (conveyance of "one-half of an undivided interest" was void, since there was no method of determining the size of the undivided interest).

20. Whitehead v. Johnston, 467 So.2d 240 (Ala.1985), noted at 37 Ala.L.Rev. 699 (1986); Partnership Properties Co. v. Sun Oil Co., 552 So.2d 246 (Fla.App.1989) (specific description of parcel controls over "Mother Hubbard" clause); Roeder Co. v. Burlington Northern, Inc., 105 Wn.2d 567, 716 P.2d 855 (1986); Amos v. Coffey, 228 Va. 88, 320 S.E.2d 335 (1984); Luthi v. Evans, 223 Kan. 622, 576 P.2d 1064 (1978); Valvoline Oil Co. v. Krauss, 335 So.2d 64 (La.App.1976); Aure v. Mackoff, 93 N.W.2d 807 (N.D.1958); Hickson Lumber Co. v. Gay Lumber Co., 150 N.C. 282, 63 S.E. 1045 (1909); Pettigrew v. Dobbelaar, 63 Cal. 396 (1883); 2 R. Patton & C. Patton, Land Titles § 123 (1957).

21. Luthi v. Evans, supra note 19 (holding no constructive notice imparted by recording). See G. Nelson & D. Whitman, Real Estate Finance Law § 9.3 (2d ed. 1985) at 687; 3 Glenn, Mortgages § 418 (1943). See the discussion of the chain of title concept, § 11.11 infra, at notes 6–17. Observe that the problem (unlike most chain of title problems) is particularly acute if a tract index system is used.

22. See Town of Moorcroft v. Lang, 779 P.2d 1180 (Wyo.1989); Holida v. Chicago & Northwestern Transp. Co., 398 N.W.2d 742 (S.D.1986); Boucher v. Boyer, 301 Md. 679,

policy ground for the rule is obvious; if the street easement is someday vacated, it makes little sense to hold that some former owner or developer can begin use a strip of land 20 or 30 feet wide. The rule is sometimes applied, although not as consistently, even if the instrument describes the boundary as running along one side or edge of the street.[23] A very clear expression of intention is necessary for the grantor to except the street from the document's coverage.[24] A similar rule is applied to railroad and other rights of way, and to rivers or streams, provided, of course, that the title to the bed is in fact in private ownership and held by the grantor.[25]

Rivers and streams which serve as boundaries pose additional problems because they can and do change course. When such changes are slow and imperceptible, the law's policy is to treat the legal boundary as changing with the stream itself, whether the boundary is the stream's border, its center, or some other line in it. In this way, the upland owner's adjacency to the stream is preserved.[26] Where the stream's edge is the boundary, if accretion (a gradual buildup of alluvial soil on the bank) or reliction (a gradual recession of water from the bank) occurs, the additional area becomes the property of the abutting littoral landowner.[27] Similarly, if slow

484 A.2d 630 (1984); McConiga v. Riches, 40 Wn.App. 532, 700 P.2d 331 (1985) (rule in text applied to private road); Safwenberg v. Marquez, 50 Cal.App.3d 301, 123 Cal.Rptr. 405 (1975); Smith v. Hadad, 366 Mass. 106, 314 N.E.2d 435 (1974); Cities Service Corp. v. Dunlap, 100 F.2d 294 (5th Cir.1935), rehearing denied 101 F.2d 314 (1939), reversed 308 U.S. 208, 60 S.Ct. 201, 84 L.Ed. 196 (1939); 2 R. Patton & C. Patton, Land Titles § 143 (1957); Annot., 49 A.L.R.2d 982 (1956). Cf. City of Albany v. State of New York, 28 N.Y.2d 352, 321 N.Y.S.2d 877, 270 N.E.2d 705 (1971), refusing to apply the presumption where the conveyance itself was made by a municipal government. There is considerable authority that the presumption should not apply if the easement has already been vacated or abandoned by the time the conveyance is made; see Torrey v. Pearce, 92 Ariz. 12, 373 P.2d 9 (1962), noted 5 Ariz.L.Rev. 143 (1963); Morrissey v. Achziger, 147 Colo. 510, 364 P.2d 187 (1961); but see Fahey v. City of Bend, 252 Or. 267, 449 P.2d 438 (1969). See 2 R. Patton & C. Patton, Land Titles § 143 note 65 (1957). The same principle is applied when the property is described by reference to a recorded map or plat showing the street; see Baker v. Ramirez, 190 Cal.App.3d 1123, 235 Cal.Rptr. 857 (1987).

23. See Greenberg v. L.I. Snodgrass Co., 161 Ohio St. 351, 119 N.E.2d 292 (1954); cf. 3 Am.L.Prop. § 12.112 note 17 (1952).

24. See Bowers v. Atchison, Topeka, & Santa Fe Railway Co., 119 Kan. 202, 237 P. 913, 42 A.L.R. 228 (1925).

25. United States v. Goodrich Farms Partnership, 753 F.Supp. 879 (D.Colo.1991), affirmed 947 F.2d 906 (10th Cir.1991) (deed conveys to center of nonnavigable stream); Padilla v. City of Santa Fe, 107 N.M. 107, 753 P.2d 353 (App.1988) (call to a range of mountains is

construed to extend to the ridge line or comb of mountains); Roeder Co. v. Burlington Northern, Inc., 105 Wn.2d 567, 716 P.2d 855 (1986) (railroad easement); Williams v. Baughman, 477 So.2d 734 (La.App.1985), writ denied 479 So.2d 921 (La.1985) (stream); Guarnera v. Florida, 436 So.2d 313 (Fla.App.1983) (drainage and utility easement); State v. Hardee, 259 S.C. 535, 193 S.E.2d 497 (1972); Annot., 78 A.L.R.3d 604 (1977). The rationale here is that ownership of the stream bed is of little practical value in light of the rights of the various riparian owners to the water itself, and hence the grantor is unlikely to have intended to reserve the bed. Again, as with roadways, the presumption may be rebutted by a description which expressly runs to or along the bank of the stream; see Knutson v. Reichel, 10 Wn.App. 293, 518 P.2d 233, 78 A.L.R.3d 598 (1973). As to private ownership of river and stream beds generally, see 2 R. Patton & C. Patton, Land Titles §§ 130–32 (1957).

26. There is a strong presumption that a riparian or littoral owner does not intend to separate the land from access to the water; see, e.g., Haynes v. Carbonell, 532 So.2d 746 (Fla.App.1988). See Board of Trustees of Internal Improvement Trust Fund v. Medeira Beach Nominee, Inc., 272 So.2d 209 (Fla.App. 1973), for a further discussion of the policies underlying the rules mentioned in the text. See also Lundquist, Artificial Additions to the Riparian Land: Extending the Doctrine of Accretion, 14 Ariz.L.Rev. 315 (1972).

27. Bruce v. Garges, 259 Ga. 268, 379 S.E.2d 783 (1989) (where land is enlarged by accretion, rights of easement-holders to water access are also extended); Bonifay v. Dickson, 459 So.2d 1089 (Fla.App.1984) (same); Stid-

erosion results in the wearing away of soil on the stream's bank, the littoral owner loses title to the affected area.[28] If the parcel's boundary is the center of the stream or some other line rather than its edge, the result of accretion, reliction, or erosion is simply to shift the line, but the practical consequences are much the same; the littoral owner gains or loses useable land. It is generally immaterial whether the change is natural or is the result of some construction project, although one owner is not allowed to acquire another's land by causing accretion to occur.[29]

If a stream suddenly shifts course, or soil is added to or removed from its bank very rapidly rather than gradually, the process is known as avulsion and the boundaries of the littoral owners are not affected. The stream's original thread, bank, or other previous boundary line remains such despite the change of course.[30] This distinction between quick and slow changes obviously requires resolution of close questions of fact in particular cases.[31] It does not appear to be relevant whether the change was natural or man-

ham v. City of Whitefish, 229 Mont. 170, 746 P.2d 591 (1987) (where abutting littoral owners gained land by reliction of lake, their boundaries should be extended in an equitable manner to give each a proportionate share of the lakefront); United States v. Pappas, 814 F.2d 1342 (9th Cir.1987) (similar result with respect to river frontage); Puyallup Indian Tribe v. Port of Tacoma, 717 F.2d 1251 (9th Cir.1983), cert. denied 465 U.S. 1049, 104 S.Ct. 1324, 79 L.Ed.2d 720 (1984), rehearing denied 466 U.S. 954, 104 S.Ct. 2162, 80 L.Ed.2d 547 (1984); Lethin v. United States, 583 F.Supp. 863 (D.Or.1984); Bonelli Cattle Co. v. Arizona, 414 U.S. 313, 94 S.Ct. 517, 38 L.Ed.2d 526 (1973), noted 35 La.L.Rev. 178 (1974) and 53 N.C.L.Rev. 185 (1974); Smith v. Bruce, 241 Ga. 133, 244 S.E.2d 559 (1978), appeal after remand 243 Ga. 278, 253 S.E.2d 709 (1979); Matson v. State, 12 Wn.App. 635, 531 P.2d 836 (1975). See Note, Accretion and Severed Mineral Estates, 53 U.Chi.L.Rev. 232 (1985); Dunlavey, Defining Accretion, Avulsion, and Reliction, Title News, Nov. 1981, at 16; 2 R. Patton & C. Patton, Land Titles §§ 300–04 (1957).

A similar concept may be applied to a deed which employs a "meander line" of a body of water as a boundary. See Thomas v. Nelson, 35 Wn.App. 868, 670 P.2d 682 (1983) (normally, a reference to the "meander line" gives grantee title to the actual water's edge, even though this may result in additions of land through accretion; but this result may be reversed by proof that the parties intended the *surveyed* meander line to serve as the boundary irrespective of later accretions).

28. 101 Ranch v. United States, 714 F.Supp. 1005 (D.N.D.1988), affirmed 905 F.2d 180 (8th Cir.1990) (where submergence of land occurs on a navigable lake or stream, the result is the passage of title to the United States); Wyatt v. Griffin, 242 Ark. 562, 414 S.W.2d 377 (1967); Borough of Wildwood Crest v. Masciarella, 92 N.J.Super. 53, 222 A.2d 138

(1966), affirmed 51 N.J. 352, 240 A.2d 665 (1968). If the process of erosion goes on long enough, an owner can lose his entire land, and the next adjoining owner will then become a littoral owner. If this occurs and the bank subsequently begins to accrete, the courts are divided as to whether the new littoral owner remains such even if the soil added is in the same physical location as the lost land of the original littoral owner. Compare Winkle v. Mitera, 195 Neb. 821, 241 N.W.2d 329 (1976) and Kruse v. Grokap, Inc., 349 So.2d 788 (Fla. App.1977) (title to accreted land belongs to new owner), with United States v. 1,629.6 Acres of Land, More or Less, in Sussex County, Delaware, 503 F.2d 764 (3d Cir.1974) and Mikel v. Kerr, 499 F.2d 1178 (10th Cir.1974) (title to accreted land restored to former owner).

29. State Department of Natural Resources v. Pankratz, 538 P.2d 984 (Alaska 1975); H.K. Porter Co., Inc. v. Board of Supervisors, 324 So.2d 746 (Miss.1975); Borough of Wildwood Crest v. Masciarella, supra note 27; Littlefield v. Nelson, 246 F.2d 956 (10th Cir. 1957). See Lundquist, Artificial Additions to Riparian Land: Extending the Doctrine of Accretion, 14 Ariz.L.Rev. 315 (1972); Smith, Right of Riparian Owner to Artificial Accretion, 25 Miss.L.J. 174 (1954); Annots., 134 A.L.R. 467 (1941); 63 A.L.R.3d 249 (1975); 3 Am.L.Prop. § 15.29 note 8 (1952).

30. Osterloh v. Idaho, 105 Idaho 50, 665 P.2d 1060 (1983); Longabaugh v. Johnson, 163 Ind.App. 108, 321 N.E.2d 865 (1975); Garrett v. State, 118 N.J.Super. 594, 289 A.2d 542 (1972); City of Long Beach v. Mansell, 3 Cal.3d 462, 91 Cal.Rptr. 23, 476 P.2d 423 (1970).

31. See Anderson–Tully Co. v. Franklin, 307 F.Supp. 539 (D.Miss.1969) (avulsion must be so rapid as to be distinctly perceptible or measurably visible at the time of its progress);

made [32], but the character of the river or stream itself may be important; if the stream is one which frequently undergoes fairly major changes in course, it is more likely that such changes will be considered accretive rather than avulsive.[33]

Resolving Discrepancies. Since metes and bounds descriptions are often long and complicated, it is easy for a drafter or copyist to make an error in them. Sometimes the mistake and the needed correction are obvious, but if they are not the courts often resort to a list of priorities which have been developed over the years to resolve inconsistencies in descriptions. They are based on common-sense assumptions about the relative probability of error in various types of descriptive statements. While they are not carved in stone and are sometimes disregarded in light of extrinsic evidence of a contrary intent [34], they are nonetheless useful. The following are the priorities, listed in descending order with the highest and most reliable first:

1. natural monuments

2. artificial monuments and marked or surveyed lines

3. adjacent tracts or boundaries

4. courses or directions

5. distances

6. area or quantity.[35]

The operation of the priorities may be illustrated by a deed describing a boundary as "105 feet to the Southeast corner of the Cassady Tract," when in fact the distance to the Cassady Tract is 150 feet. Since a call to an

Sieck v. Godsey, 254 Iowa 624, 118 N.W.2d 555 (1962).

32. See cases and sources cited in note 28, supra. The California cases generally treat all man-made changes as avulsive and as not modifying existing boundaries; see City of Long Beach v. Mansell, supra note 29. Dicta to this effect can be found in occasional cases from other jurisdictions; see, e.g., Trustees of Internal Improvement Fund v. Sutton, 206 So.2d 272 (Fla.App.1968), requiring "natural and actual continuity of accretion" to the land of the riparian owner.

33. See Sieck v. Godsey, supra note 28; Beck, The Wandering Missouri River, A Study in Accretion Law, 43 N.D.L.Rev. 429 (1967).

34. See Cities Service Oil Co. v. Dunlap, 115 F.2d 720 (5th Cir.1940), rehearing denied 117 F.2d 31 (1941), certiorari denied 313 U.S. 566, 61 S.Ct. 940, 85 L.Ed. 1525 (1941).

35. See, e.g., DD & L, Inc. v. Burgess, 51 Wn.App. 329, 753 P.2d 561 (1988); Providence Properties, Inc. v. United Virginia Bank, 219 Va. 735, 251 S.E.2d 474 (1979); Pritchard v. Rebori, 135 Tenn. 328, 186 S.W. 121 (1916); 2 R. Patton & C. Patton, Land Titles §§ 148–155 (1957); McCarver, Legal Principles for Determining Boundary Lines, J.Mo.Bar, April–May 1987, at 147. There are hundreds of cases

illustrating these principles. See, e.g., Harmon v. Ingram, 572 So.2d 411 (Ala.1990) (natural monuments control over artificial monuments, which in turn control over courses and distances); Sun Valley Shamrock Resources, Inc. v. Travelers Leasing Corp., 118 Idaho 116, 794 P.2d 1389, 1392 (1990) (call to an adjacent road, if permanent in nature and established with reasonable certainty, controls over courses and distances); Withington v. Derrick, 153 Vt. 598, 572 A.2d 912 (1990) (attached map or plat controls over written description); Bouligny v. Delatte, 550 So.2d 929 (La.App. 1989) (same); Spainhour v. B. Aubrey Huffman & Associates, Ltd., 237 Va. 340, 377 S.E.2d 615 (1989) (recorded distance prevails over acreage). But see Pencil v. Buchart, 380 Pa.Super. 205, 551 A.2d 302 (1988) (acreage mentioned in original deeds from common grantor controls over monuments set by surveyor 100 years later); Morris v. Monroe, 165 Ga.App. 788, 302 S.E.2d 704 (1983) (artificial monument controls over course and distance); Tresemer v. Albuquerque Public School District, 95 N.M. 143, 619 P.2d 819 (1980) (natural monument controls over artificial monument); Hoban v. Cable, 102 Mich. 206, 60 N.W. 466 (1894) (artificial monument controls over course and distance); Hall v. Eaton, 139 Mass. 217, 29 N.E. 660 (1885) (course controls over distance). See Comment, Boundary Law:

adjacent tract controls over a call of distance, the court will treat the distance as 150 feet.[36]

§ 11.3 Delivery and Acceptance

A deed is effective only when it is delivered, and an undelivered deed passes no title.[1] Ordinarily delivery involves a physical transfer of possession of the deed from the grantor to grantee, but this is not essential.[2] Delivery is a question of the grantor's intent, and evidence of intent that the deed be presently operative will suffice even if the grantor retains the deed itself and has done no other overt act indicating delivery.[3] Moreover, a manual handing over of the deed to the grantee is not necessarily a delivery if it is not accompanied by the requisite intent, although it generally raises a strong presumption of delivery, while nondelivery is presumed if the grantor retains possession.[4]

Delivery is seldom an issue in arms-length sales of real estate, since the parties' intention to make an immediate transfer is usually perfectly clear. The problems generally arise in gratuitous intra-family transfers. Here the grantor's intent, perhaps cloudy and imperfectly formed, is often to make a disposition of the property which will take effect only at death, but which will avoid the formality, publicity, and expense of probate of a will. To accomplish this, the grantor executes a deed but does not make an immediate manual delivery to the grantee; indeed, the grantee is often told nothing

The Rule of Monument Control in Washington, 7 U.P.S.L.Rev. 355 (1983).

36. Quality Plastics, Inc. v. Moore, 131 Ariz. 238, 640 P.2d 169 (1981).

§ 11.3

1. Jorgensen v. Crow, 466 N.W.2d 120 (N.D.1991); Winegar v. Froerer Corp., 813 P.2d 104 (Utah 1991). See generally 3 Am. L.Prop. § 12.64 (1952); 6A Powell, Real Property ¶ 891 (1980).

2. Abraham v. Mihalich, 330 Pa.Super. 378, 479 A.2d 601 (1984); Jones v. Innkeepers, Inc., 12 Ark.App. 364, 676 S.W.2d 761 (1984); B–T Limited v. Blakeman, 705 P.2d 307 (Wyo. 1985). As Lord Coke's famous dictum put it, "As a deed may be delivered to the party without words, so may a deed be delivered by words without any act of delivery;" 1 Co.Litt. 36A. See Boohaker v. Brashier, 428 So.2d 627 (Ala.1983); Gonzales v. Gonzales, 267 Cal. App.2d 428, 73 Cal.Rptr. 83 (1968).

3. See, e.g., In re Van Houten, 56 B.R. 891 (Bkrtcy.W.D.Mich.1986) (trust beneficiary's letter to trustee bank, telling it to transfer property from the trust to certain grantees, was sufficient evidence of intent to deliver deed); McDuffie v. First Nat. Bank of Tuskaloosa, 450 So.2d 451 (Ala.1984); In re Estate of Lloyd, 676 S.W.2d 889 (Mo.App.1984); Ferrell v. Stinson, 233 Iowa 1331, 11 N.W.2d 701 (1943), noted 29 Iowa L.Rev. 500 (1944), in which even the intent was quite debatable. If the grantor is ill or incapacitated, nods or

gestures can constitute a delivery; see Arwe v. White, 117 N.H. 1025, 381 A.2d 737 (1977). See generally Annot., 87 A.L.R.2d 787 (1963); Note, The Issue of Delivery Raised by "Dispositive" Conveyances, 18 Drake L.Rev. 67 (1968).

4. See Sofsky v. Rosenberg, 76 N.Y.2d 927, 563 N.Y.S.2d 52, 564 N.E.2d 662 (1990) (grantee's possession of deed gives rise to presumption of delivery despite grantor's retention of income from land and failure to record deed for 23 years after delivery); Hans v. Hans, 482 So.2d 1117 (Miss.1986) (deed in possession of grantor's widow; presumption of nondelivery is raised); May v. McCormick, 704 P.2d 709 (Wyo.1985) (deed in possession of grantee; presumption of delivery is raised). For example, the grantor may hand the deed to the grantee to inspect it, but without intending a present transfer. See, e.g., Walter v. Grover, 540 A.2d 120 (Me.1988) (deed handed to grantee for safekeeping; no delivery); Shroyer v. Shroyer, 425 S.W.2d 214 (Mo.1968); Hotaling v. Hotaling, 193 Cal. 368, 224 P. 455, 56 A.L.R. 734 (1924). But if the grantee proceeds wrongfully to convey title to a bona fide purchaser, a court may hold the grantor estopped to deny that a delivery occurred, notwithstanding lack of intent; see Webb v. Stewart, 255 Or. 523, 469 P.2d 609 (1970); text at notes 33–34 infra. On the presumption of delivery (perhaps better termed an "inference," shifting the burden of going forward with evidence) resulting from the grantee's possession of the deed, see 20th

of the arrangement. The deed may be retained by the grantor in his or her home or office, or it may be placed in a safety deposit box which is held in the grantor's name, the grantee's name, or held jointly by both of them.[5] These acts may be accompanied by a variety of more or less explicit statements of intent. Typically the grantee obtains the deed after the grantor's death, and then engages in a title dispute with the grantor's heirs or residuary devisees who claim that the deed was never delivered. From a planning viewpoint this is a very sorry affair and constitutes a virtual invitation to litigation.

The essential problem is that the grantor has attempted to use the deed as a will. An intent that the instrument take effect at the maker's death is perfectly appropriate to a will, but it will not do for a deed at all; what is required for delivery of a deed is intent that some interest be transferred *immediately*. Much of the controversy would be swept away if the requisite formalities for deeds and wills were the same. It would then make little difference, in terms of ultimate validity, whether or not the grantor intended an immediate transfer, for the courts could enforce the deed as a will.[6] But the formalities do differ rather drastically. In particular, deeds require no attestation by witnesses in most states, while wills require attestation of a particular and rigorous kind.[7] Hence an instrument which fails as a deed for lack of delivery can seldom be treated as a valid will even if the grantor's intent would be carried out by doing so.

Courts sometimes overcome these difficulties by finding the requisite intent to make an immediate transfer in the face of such seemingly contrary facts as the grantor's continued possession of both the deed and the land, particularly if the grantee or some other person has been told about the deed.[8] It is difficult to generalize, since the cases tend to turn on the grantor's precise words and actions, and perhaps on the court's view of the grantee's worthiness as against competing claimants.[9] For example, placing the deed in a jointly-held safety deposit box may or may not be a sufficient

---

Century Plumbing Co. v. Sfregola, 126 Cal. App.3d 851, 179 Cal.Rptr. 144 (1981).

5. Another possibility is the "death escrow," created by handing the deed to a third party to deliver upon the grantor's death; it is discussed in § 11.4, infra.

6. This would not solve all problems, for there might still be a dispute between the "grantee" under the putative deed and the devisees under a subsequent formal will's residuary clause, with the latter arguing that the will revoked the former deed if it is regarded as a will. In addition, a document which is in form of a deed but in substance a will would have to be probated and would be subject to related rules and procedures. But see Noble v. Fickes, 230 Ill. 594, 82 N.E. 950 (1907), in which the court denied probate of a deed on the ground that the testamentary intent must appear on the face of the document and not from extrinsic evidence. It is hardly conceivable that such reasoning would be followed today.

7. As to deeds, see § 11.1, supra, at note 47. As to wills, see Atkinson, Wills §§ 65–74 (2d ed. 1953).

8. See, e.g., Ferrell v. Stinson, 233 Iowa 1331, 11 N.W.2d 701 (1943). In theory, continued possession of the land by the grantor is not necessarily inconsistent with delivery; see Richardson v. Kelley Land & Cattle Co., 504 F.2d 30 (8th Cir.1974); Hartley v. Stibor, 96 Idaho 157, 525 P.2d 352 (1974); Hackett v. Hackett, 429 P.2d 753 (Okl.1967). But if the deed purports to convey a possessory fee simple and there is no reservation of a lease or life estate to the grantor, it is difficult to imagine that the grantor actually intends a present transfer; see Den–Gar Enterprises v. Romero, 94 N.M. 425, 611 P.2d 1119 (App. 1980), cert. denied 94 N.M. 628, 614 P.2d 545 (1980); Avery v. Lillie, 260 Iowa 10, 148 N.W.2d 474 (1967).

9. See, e.g., the court's comments about the grantor's fondness for the grantees in Ferrell v. Stinson, supra note 8; Chillemi v. Chillemi, 197 Md. 257, 78 A.2d 750 (1951), in which the

delivery.[10] Recording of the deed, although not common in these cases, may be influential, for there is a presumption that a deed recorded by the grantor has been delivered.[11] Where the grantor remains in possession of the property, receives income from it, pays taxes on it, or the like, the courts sometimes find that the "immediate" transfer was subject to a retained life estate in the grantor despite the fact that neither the document nor the grantor said anything about such a life estate.[12] There is, of course, an air of artificiality about all discussion of the grantor's intent, since the grantor is usually dead and cannot testify.[13]

The traditional view is that a delivery to a grantee cannot pass title conditionally; if the grantor delivers the deed to the grantee but states that no title shall pass unless or until some future event occurs, the condition is not legally binding. As it is sometimes put, the grantee cannot be his or her own escrow holder.[14] But the courts divide as to where this leaves the deed itself. Where the condition is simply the grantor's death, the deed is usually

court severely disapproved of the grantee wife's profligate behavior.

10. Lenhart v. Desmond, 705 P.2d 338 (Wyo.1985) (despite deposit of deed in jointly held safe deposit box, court accepted the (still living) grantor's testimony that he did not intend a present transfer); Bennion v. Hansen, 699 P.2d 757 (Utah 1985) (insufficient evidence that placing of deed in safe deposit box was accompanied by intent to deliver); Kresser v. Peterson, 675 P.2d 1193 (Utah 1984) (evidence of intent to deliver, when grantor placed deed in jointly held safe deposit box, was sufficient). Finding a delivery through a deposit in a jointly-held safety deposit box, see McMahon v. Dorsey, 353 Mich. 623, 91 N.W.2d 893 (1958). Finding no delivery despite deposit in a jointly-held box, see Wiggill v. Cheney, 597 P.2d 1351 (Utah 1979) (grantor's intent was apparently testamentary); Hayes v. May, 36 A.D.2d 549, 318 N.Y.S.2d 759 (1971) (no clear evidence of intent; joint custody of deed "inconsistent with the claim of a complete delivery"); Moseley v. Zieg, 180 Neb. 810, 146 N.W.2d 72 (1966), adhered to 181 Neb. 691, 150 N.W.2d 736 (1967).

11. See Gross v. Gross, 239 Mont. 480, 781 P.2d 284 (1989); Myers v. Key Bank, 68 N.Y.2d 744, 497 N.E.2d 694 (1986); Brown v. Board of County Com'rs, 720 P.2d 579 (Colo. App.1985); Kresser v. Peterson, 675 P.2d 1193 (Utah 1984); Hans v. Hans, 482 So.2d 1117 (Miss.1986); Estate of Whitt v. Commissioner, 751 F.2d 1548 (11th Cir.1985), cert. denied 474 U.S. 1005, 106 S.Ct. 523, 88 L.Ed.2d 456 (1985). See also Poulsen v. Poulsen, 672 P.2d 97 (Utah 1983) (no presumption of delivery, where acknowledgement by notary was defective, thus making recording improper). Bulifant v. Slosjarik, 221 Va. 983, 277 S.E.2d 151 (1981); Pollock v. Brown, 569 S.W.2d 724 (Mo.1978); Fike v. Harshbarger, 20 Md.App. 661, 317 A.2d 859 (1974), affirmed 273 Md. 586, 332 A.2d 27

(1975); Whitworth v. Whitworth, 233 Ga. 53, 210 S.E.2d 9 (1974); Controlled Receivables, Inc. v. Harman, 17 Utah 2d 420, 413 P.2d 807 (1966) (presumption is "strong and controlling" in absence of clear and convincing contrary evidence); Halleck v. Halleck, 216 Or. 23, 337 P.2d 330 (1959). The presumption (which, like that arising from possession, see note 4 supra, is better described as an inference which shifts the burden of going forward with evidence) is rebuttable; see Odom v. Forbes, 500 So.2d 997 (Miss.1987); Lenhart v. Desmond, 705 P.2d 338 (Wyo.1985) (presumption rebutted); Martinez v. Martinez, 101 N.M. 88, 678 P.2d 1163 (1984) (presumption rebutted); Baker v. Pattee, 684 P.2d 632 (Utah 1984) (presumption not rebutted); Havens v. Schoen, 108 Mich.App. 758, 310 N.W.2d 870 (1981); Wynne v. Pino, 78 N.M. 520, 433 P.2d 499 (1967); Ellison v. Garber, 39 Tenn.App. 668, 287 S.W.2d 564 (1955). In Massachusetts the presumption is conclusive, a rule which is greatly advantageous to title examiners; see Mass.Gen.L.Ann., c. 183, § 5.

Lack of recording raises no presumption of nondelivery; see Cantrell v. Henry, 696 S.W.2d 12 (Tenn.App.1985).

12. See, e.g., Agrelius v. Mohesky, 208 Kan. 790, 494 P.2d 1095 (1972); Berigan v. Berrigan, 413 Ill. 204, 108 N.E.2d 438 (1952).

13. Lenhart v. Desmond, 705 P.2d 338 (Wyo.1985) (grantor's testimony accepted). If the grantor is alive and is the plaintiff, his testimony as to his own intent may or may not be persuasive; compare Havens v. Schoen, supra note 11 (grantor's testimony accepted), with Controlled Receivables, Inc. v. Harman, 17 Utah 2d 420, 413 P.2d 807 (1966) (grantor's testimony rejected.)

14. A true escrow—a delivery to an independent third party to be delivered to the grantee on certain conditions—is entirely permissible; see § 11.4, infra.

held void because the underlying intent is testamentary.[15] This result makes little sense in light of the fact, discussed in the next section, that a delivery to a third person for delivery upon the grantor's death is usually held to vest an immediate future interest in the grantee! In both situations the condition must usually be proved by parol evidence.

Other types of conditions, unrelated to the grantor's death, are more troublesome. The majority of the cases probably hold that the deed is valid and the condition is disregarded,[16] despite the inconsistency of this approach with the basic axiom that delivery must convey title unconditionally. A growing minority view enforces the condition and gives the grantee title only if it has been fulfilled.[17] There is little to commend the majority approach. It has the advantage of protecting subsequent bona fide purchasers from the grantee, but it is most unlikely that any court following the minority view would apply it against a BFP.[18]

The rule against conditional delivery does not make it impossible for a grantor to defer the grantee's possession until a future date or to make it conditional upon a future event. This objective can be accomplished simply by drafting the deed so as to convey a future interest, such as a springing executory interest contingent on the event's occurrence. The concept of delivery is not offended in the slightest by doing so. The key, however, is to express the condition in the deed itself rather than merely to make it

---

15. See Raim v. Stancel, 339 N.W.2d 621 (Iowa App.1983) (condition that grantee care for grantor until his death; deed held void); First National Bank v. Bloom, 264 N.W.2d 208 (N.D.1978); Broomfield v. Broomfield, 242 Ark. 355, 413 S.W.2d 657 (1967); Mueller v. Marshall, 166 Cal.App.2d 367, 333 P.2d 260 (1958); Juel v. Doll, 51 Wn.2d 435, 319 P.2d 543 (1957); Coles v. Belford, 289 Mo. 97, 232 S.W. 728 (1921). A few cases are contrary; see Takacs v. Takacs, 317 Mich. 72, 26 N.W.2d 712 (1947), holding the deed valid and the condition ineffective; Ritchie v. Davis, 26 Wis.2d 636, 133 N.W.2d 312 (1965), apparently taking the same view.

16. State ex rel. Pai v. Thom, 58 Hawaii 8, 563 P.2d 982 (1977) (condition that purchaser pay the agreed price); Bolyea v. First Presbyterian Church, 196 N.W.2d 149 (N.D.1972); Paoli v. Anderson, 208 So.2d 167 (Miss.1968) (condition that grantee survive grantor); Ivancovich v. Sullivan, 149 Cal.App.2d 160, 307 P.2d 989 (1957); Sweeney v. Sweeney, 126 Conn. 391, 11 A.2d 806 (1940) (condition that grantee survive grantor); Wipfler v. Wipfler, 153 Mich. 18, 116 N.W. 544 (1908) (condition that grantor fail to return from a dangerous journey); West's Ann.Cal.Civ.Code § 1056. The rule originated in Whyddon's Case, Cro. Eliz. 520, 78 Eng.Repr. 769 (1596). See generally Turner, Conditional Delivery of a Deed to the Grantee, 44 Ky.L.Rev. 218 (1956); Gavit, The Conditional Delivery of Deeds, 30 Colum.L.Rev. 1145 (1930); 3 Am.L.Prop. § 12.66 (1952). See also Powderly v. Aetna Casualty

& Surety Co., 72 Misc.2d 251, 338 N.Y.S.2d 555 (1972), holding that while a delivery cannot make title pass upon the happening of future conditions, it is permissible to hand the deed to the grantee but condition the delivery itself on some event, such as the recording of certain documents or the results of a title examination. The distinction seems insubstantial.

17. See Martinez v. Martinez, 101 N.M. 88, 678 P.2d 1163 (1984), upholding a delivery conditioned on the purchaser paying the remainder of the contract price. But this case can be explained as well on the ground that the grantors handed the deed to the grantees with instructions that it was to be placed in escrow with a bank; hence, no immediate delivery, conditional or otherwise, to the grantees was intended. See also United States v. 222.0 Acres of Land, 306 F.Supp. 138 (D.Md.1969), adhered to 324 F.Supp. 1170 (1971); Parrillo v. Siravo, 101 R.I. 524, 225 A.2d 515 (1967); Kitchens v. Kitchens, 142 So.2d 343 (Fla.App.1962); Chillemi v. Chillemi, 197 Md. 257, 78 A.2d 750 (1951), noted 31 B.U.L.Rev. 437 (1951); 12 Md.L.Rev. 248 (1951).

18. See Kitchens v. Kitchens, supra note 17. Note that the law of delivery theoretically has little solicitude for BFP's; an undelivered deed is simply void, no matter into whose hands the putative title may later pass. See text at notes 33–34, infra; compare the discussion of void and voidable deeds in § 11.1, supra, at note 68–86.

accompany the delivery. The most common illustration is the reservation in the deed of a life estate in the grantor. The delivery is perfectly satisfactory, since an interest in the land (in this case a future interest) is *presently* transferred by the deed.[19]

A more challenging issue is posed if the grantor reserves not only a life estate but also a power to revoke the future interest or to dispose of the property in fee simple. This combination of continued possession and the power of revocation seem to put the grantor in a position practically identical to that of a testator under a will. There is, of course, the technical distinction that the deed presently conveys an interest, subject to later divestment, while a will conveys nothing at all until death. Numerous cases, probably a majority, uphold the arrangement on this quite unsatisfying ground.[20] Perhaps the courts have been influenced by the ease with which a grantor may accomplish the same thing through the alternative means of a revocable inter vivos trust, which has the ambulatory characteristics of a will without its formality.[21] If this is so, logic suggests carrying the analogy further and forsaking the line of authority which now strikes down deeds intended to take effect at the grantor's death, at least if the intention is expressed in writing or otherwise proved by suitably convincing evidence.[22]

Delivery may be made to the grantee's agent rather than to the grantee personally.[23] In practice the difficulty is determining whose agent the recipient is. The question is one of fact, and can become exceedingly perplexing where the parties and the agent are members of the same family, or where the agent is the attorney of one or both parties.[24] If there are several grantees, as cotenants or as holders of present and future interests,

19. See, e.g., Russell v. Walz, 458 N.E.2d 1172 (Ind.App.1984); Parramore v. Parramore, 371 So.2d 123 (Fla.App.1978); Branton v. Martin, 243 S.C. 90, 132 S.E.2d 285 (1963); Thomas v. Williams, 105 Minn. 88, 117 N.W. 155 (1908); 3 Am.L.Prop. § 12.65 (1952).

20. See, e.g., Harris v. Neely, 257 Ga. 361, 359 S.E.2d 885 (1987); St. Louis County National Bank v. Fielder, 364 Mo. 207, 260 S.W.2d 483 (1953); Meairs v. Kruckenberg, 171 Kan. 450, 233 P.2d 472, 31 A.L.R.2d 525 (1951); Tennant v. John Tennant Memorial Home, 167 Cal. 570, 140 P. 242 (1914). Contra, see Peebles v. Rodgers, 211 Miss. 8, 50 So.2d 632 (1951); Butler v. Sherwood, 196 App.Div. 603, 188 N.Y.S. 242 (1921), affirmed 233 N.Y. 655, 135 N.E. 957 (1922). See generally Garvey, Revocable Gifts of Legal Interests In Land, 54 Ky.L.Rev. 19 (1965).

21. See generally J. Dukeminier & S. Johanson, Family Wealth Transactions 448–461 (2d ed. 1978); Atkinson, Wills § 42 (2d ed. 1953). Other types of non-will transfers at death which are both revocable and relatively informal include life insurance and government bond beneficiary designations and joint bank accounts.

22. This appears to be precisely the step taken in Estate of O'Brien, 109 Wn.2d 913,

749 P.2d 154 (1988). The court conceded that the grantor's intent was not to pass title until her death, but nonetheless upheld the delivery. There was a vigorous dissent.

23. United States v. Capobianco, 652 F.Supp. 325 (E.D.Pa.1987) (handing deed to third party is not a delivery unless party is instructed to deliver it to grantee); Fike v. Harshbarger, 20 Md.App. 661, 317 A.2d 859 (1974), affirmed 273 Md. 586, 332 A.2d 27 (1975); Whitworth v. Whitworth, 233 Ga. 53, 210 S.E.2d 9 (1974) (parent deemed agent of child grantee).

24. See, e.g., Chapman v. Chapman, 473 So.2d 467 (Miss.1985) (where deed was retained by grantor husband's attorney, there was no delivery to co-grantee wife); Stout v. Clayton, 674 S.W.2d 821 (Tex.App.1984) (deed retained by attorney employed by one of the grantees; court upheld jury finding of delivery); Gilmer v. Anderson, 34 Mich.App. 6, 190 N.W.2d 708 (1971) (handing deed to grantor's attorney not a delivery; he was exclusively grantor's agent); Capozzella v. Capozzella, 213 Va. 820, 196 S.E.2d 67 (1973) (procurement of deed by attorney for husband was a sufficient delivery to wife); Bull v. Fenich, 34 Wn.App. 435, 661 P.2d 1012 (1983).

delivery to only one of them is sufficient.[25]

Once a deed has been delivered, what happens to it is largely irrelevant. Its loss or destruction will not take away the grantee's title.[26] If the grantee redelivers it to the grantor, no retransfer of title takes place.[27] If someone alters the deed, the act has no legal significance.[28] Deeds are usually retained by their grantees following delivery, but they have only evidentiary value and even that is relatively unimportant if the deed is recorded.

Delivery is not complete without the grantee's acceptance of the deed,[29] but the concept of acceptance is a highly artificial one. Acceptance is presumed if the conveyance would be beneficial to the grantee,[30] and some cases hold it is not even necessary to show that the grantee knew of the deed or its delivery.[31] As a practical matter the role of the doctrine of acceptance is mainly to allow the grantee to disclaim the conveyance if it is not wanted.[32]

In theory, failure of either delivery or acceptance makes the deed void, and not even a subsequent bona fide purchaser could take title through such a deed. This rule is a harsh one, for there is obviously no way a title examiner who inspects a deed on record can tell whether it was delivered or not. The presumption of delivery which flows from recording is obviously helpful here, but in most states it can be rebutted.[33] If the grantor has voluntarily permitted the deed to leave his or her hands or has been

25. See Perkins v. Kerby, 308 So.2d 914 (Miss.1975); Kresser v. Peterson, 675 P.2d 1193 (Utah 1984); Controlled Receivables, Inc. v. Harman, 17 Utah 2d 420, 413 P.2d 807 (1966).

26. Miami Holding Corp. v. Matthews, 311 So.2d 802 (Fla.App.1975), cert. denied 325 So.2d 8 (Fla.1975); Capozzella v. Capozzella, supra note 24; Newell v. Edwards, 7 N.C.App. 650, 173 S.E.2d 504 (1970).

27. Payne v. Carver, 534 So.2d 566 (Ala. 1988); In re Estate of Bright, 215 N.W.2d 253 (Iowa 1974); Gonzales v. Gonzales, 267 Cal. App.2d 428, 73 Cal.Rptr. 83 (1968); Kramer v. Dorsch, 173 Neb. 869, 115 N.W.2d 457 (1962). See also Buckley v. Chevron, U.S.A., Inc., 149 Misc.2d 476, 565 N.Y.S.2d 419 (1991) (delivery is not impaired by grantee's handing deed to his attorney after receiving it). See also the remarkable English case, Sen v. Headley, [1991] Ch. 425, [1991] 2 All E.R. 636, holding in apparent disregard of the Statute of Frauds that a delivery of the *prior* title deeds was an effective conveyance of land as a gift *causa mortis*.

28. Perry v. Perry, 234 Ark. 1066, 356 S.W.2d 419 (1962); Hansen v. Walker, 175 Kan. 121, 259 P.2d 242 (1953).

29. Salmon v. Thompson, 391 So.2d 984 (Miss.1980); Kirkman v. Faulkner, 524 P.2d 648 (Colo.App.1974); Fritz v. Fritz, 479 S.W.2d 198 (Mo.App.1972). See Annot., 74 A.L.R.2d 992 (1960); 6A Powell, Real Property ¶ 892 (1980); 3 Am.L.Prop. § 12.70 (1952). Cf. Halleck v. Halleck, 216 Or. 23, 337 P.2d 330

(1959), adopting the English rule that acceptance is unnecessary.

30. In re Van Houten, 56 B.R. 891 (Bkrtcy. W.D.Mich.1986); Williams v. Herring, 15 N.C.App. 642, 190 S.E.2d 696 (1973), appeal after remand 20 N.C.App. 183, 201 S.E.2d 209 (1973); Winick v. Winick, 26 A.D.2d 663, 272 N.Y.S.2d 869 (1966), appeal denied 19 N.Y.2d 581, 279 N.Y.S.2d 1026, 226 N.E.2d 707 (1967). Cf. CUNA Mortgage v. Aafedt, 459 N.W.2d 801 (N.D.1990) (acceptance of deed in lieu of foreclosure by mortgagee not presumed, despite its recordation by grantor, where acceptance would have caused mortgagee to lose benefits of HUD mortgage insurance); Messer v. Laurel Hill Associates, 93 N.C.App. 439, 378 S.E.2d 220 (1989), appeal after remand 102 N.C.App. 307, 401 S.E.2d 843 (1991) (acceptance not presumed when deed contained covenant obligating grantee to pave a street); County of Worth v. Jorgenson, 253 N.W.2d 575 (Iowa 1977) (no presumption of acceptance where property was a "white elephant.")

31. See Williams v. Herring, supra note 30; but see the contrary view expressed in Blankenship v. Myers, 97 Idaho 356, 544 P.2d 314 (1975); Caron v. Wadas, 1 Mass.App.Ct. 651, 305 N.E.2d 853 (1974).

32. See, e.g., Underwood v. Gillespie, 594 S.W.2d 372 (Mo.App.1980) (grantee's tearing up of deed was sufficient evidence of nonacceptance); Hood v. Hood, 384 A.2d 706 (Me. 1978) (grantee expressly rejected conveyance.)

33. See cases cited at note 11, supra.

negligent in allowing the grantee to obtain or record it, a court will probably be eager to hold the grantor estopped to deny delivery as against a subsequent bona fide purchaser.[34] And the purchaser may get notice of the grantor's claim from the latter's continued possession. But there remains a residual risk to later purchasers that delivery will be found not to have occurred and that the grantor will be found to have engaged in no behavior on which to predicate notice or an estoppel.

§ 11.4   Escrows

Technically speaking, an escrow is an instrument deposited[1] by its maker with some custodian with instructions that it be delivered to another party on the occurrence of one or more future conditions. In most cases the instrument is a deed deposited by the grantor.[2] In a colloquial sense, the escrow is the entire arrangement under which such a deed is deposited and then delivered. Thus, one speaks of "opening an escrow," and the deed is said to be "in escrow." Recording or delivery of the deed is referred to as the "close of escrow." Since the escrow is a particular means of delivering a deed, it is logically related to the general discussion of delivery in the preceding section.

There are two principal types of escrows, and both raise interesting legal issues. One is the commercial or sales escrow,[3] handled by a lending institution, attorney, title insurance company, or professional "escrow company" and widely employed, especially in the western United States and in many urban areas elsewhere, to "settle" or "close" all types of real estate sales. The other is the "death escrow," in which a grantor deposits a deed with a custodian (usually a friend or relative) accompanied by instructions to deliver it to the grantee upon the grantor's death; in substance, it is a substitute for a will, and raises delivery problems similar to those discussed in the preceding section. The treatment here will focus first on the sales escrow, and will then compare with it the death escrow.

Sales Escrows. The use of an escrow agent or "escrowee" to consummate a real estate sale has several advantages.[4] The escrowee can compute

---

34. Webb v. Stewart, 255 Or. 523, 469 P.2d 609 (1970); Tutt v. Smith, 201 Iowa 107, 204 N.W. 294, 48 A.L.R. 394 (1925), discussed in W. Burby, Real Property 297 (3d ed. 1965). See 3 Am.L.Prop. § 12.68 note 17 (1952).

§ 11.4

1. In an escrow it appears that the delivery to the custodian must be of physical possession of the document, and that mere intent to deliver will not suffice. See 4 Tiffany, Real Property § 1049 (1939); Rundell, Delivery and Acceptance of Deeds in Wisconsin, 1 Wis. L.Rev. 65 (1921), at notes 41–43. This rule is unlike that for delivery directly to the grantee discussed in § 11.3, supra, at notes 2–3.

2. The escrow concept originally applied only to deeds, but is now employed with other sorts of instruments as well; see Norwich Lumber Co. v. Yatroussis, 5 Conn.Cir. 95, 243 A.2d 311 (1967). In California, for example, a liquor license must be transferred by escrow;

West's Ann.Cal.Bus. & Prof.Code § 24074. Money may also be the subject of an escrow; see Edward Rose Sales Co. v. Shafer, 41 Mich. App. 105, 199 N.W.2d 655 (1972). In most sales escrows, the payment of the purchase money into escrow is one of the conditions to the delivery of the deed. The discussion in the text, however, is concerned exclusively with escrows for delivery of deeds.

3. See Comment, The Independent Escrow Agent: The Law and the Licensee, 38 So.Cal. L.Rev. 289 (1965); Sooy, Escrow and Closing the Sale, in California Real Property Sales Transactions Ch. 11 (1981). When a non-professional escrowee is employed, the arrangement is often attacked on the ground that he or she is not an escrowee at all, but merely the agent of one of the parties.

4. See generally, Mann, Escrows—Their Use and Value, 1949 U.Ill.L.F. 398. This article, the most thorough treatment available on

the various charges and credits to each party and handle the mailing of checks, recording of documents, and other administrative aspects of the transfer. The parties may hand the escrowee their papers and funds at any convenient time, and need not meet together for a formal closing. This is particularly helpful in transactions involving numerous parties. In some areas of the nation, escrow companies work hand-in-hand with title insurers. The insurer will check the public records at the end of the business day prior to the closing of the escrow, and will report to the escrowee if no instruments have been recorded which might impair the title being transferred. The escrowee can then close the escrow and record the deed and other documents at the beginning of the next business day, virtually eliminating the possibility that closing could occur without knowledge of some adverse recorded instrument.[5]

A further advantage of the escrow is the legal rule that, when the stated conditions are satisfied and the custodian delivers the deed to the grantee, the delivery "relates back" to the date the deed was handed to the custodian, at least for some purposes.[6] Thus, the closing can occur and the deed can be validly delivered by the escrowee even if the grantor dies or becomes incapacitated after placing the deed in escrow.[7] This is an extremely useful feature of escrows, and can save vast time and effort which might otherwise be expended in having guardians appointed, locating heirs or devisees, persuading them to execute deeds, and so on. It is particularly desirable

the subject, is reproduced in part in J. Cribbet, Principles of the Law of Property 172–88 (2d ed. 1974). See also Walker & Eshee, The Safeguards and Dilemmas of Escrows, 16 Real Est.L.J. 45 (1987); Young, Escrow Agreements: Bridges Over Troubled Closings, 58 Wis.Bar.Bull. 9 (Sept. 1985).

5. See Ferguson v. Caspar, 359 A.2d 17, 21, note 9 (D.C.App.1976). An alternative approach is reported to be used in Cook County, Illinois, where title searches cannot be made up to the current date because of backlogs in the recorder's office. The escrowee records the deed as soon as the purchase money is deposited, and then searches the title to the date of recording. If an adverse conveyance is discovered, the escrowee records a quit-claim deed, previously executed by the purchaser for this purpose, to return title to the grantor. See Mann, supra note 4, at 404–05.

6. Hartman v. Wood, 436 N.W.2d 854 (S.D. 1989). See generally Annot., 117 A.L.R. 69 (1938); Jackson v. Jackson, 67 Or. 44, 135 P. 201 (1913). The "relation back" feature will prevail as against the grantor's death or insanity, against spousal rights which accrue at death, and against the rights of subsequent takers from the grantor who are not bona fide purchasers for value; see DeBoer v. Oakbrook Home Ass'n, Inc., 218 Neb. 813, 359 N.W.2d 768 (1984) (after deed is deposited in escrow, grantor may not further encumber property by covenants); First National Bank & Trust Co. v. Scott, 109 N.J.Eq. 244, 156 A. 836 (1931); Chaffin v. Harpham, 166 Ark. 578, 266 S.W.2d 685 (1924). Cf. Ellison Associates v. Eastwood

Management Corp., 63 B.R. 756 (S.D.N.Y.1983) (relation back inapplicable between original parties to escrow); Caulfield v. Improved Risk Mutuals, Inc., 107 A.D.2d 1013, 486 N.Y.S.2d 531 (1985), reversed 66 N.Y.2d 793, 497 N.Y.S.2d 903, 488 N.E.2d 833 (1985) (no relation back for purposes of risk of loss by fire); Doxey–Layton Co. v. Clark, 548 P.2d 902 (Utah 1976) (no relation back for purposes of running of statute of limitations on action to reform the deed); Albiani v. Loudd, 4 Mass. App.Ct. 165, 344 N.E.2d 188 (1976) (no relation back to defeat transfer, where grantee corporation did not exist when conveyance was placed in escrow.) The doctrine is flexible, and is unlikely to be applied to such issues as rights to rents and profits or liability for taxes as between the grantor and grantee. See Dixon v. O'Connor, 180 Neb. 427, 143 N.W.2d 364 (1966); Mohr v. Joslin, 162 Iowa 34, 142 N.W. 981 (1913). These issues are usually resolved by reference to the parties' expressed or inferred intent, and the courts are often influenced by which party had the right to possession during the executory period of the contract. See Annot., supra, at 81–82.

7. Fuqua v. Fuqua, 528 S.W.2d 896 (Tex. Civ.App.1975), refused n.r.e.; Donnelly v. Robinson, 406 S.W.2d 595 (Mo.1966); Davis v. Stegall, 246 Miss. 593, 151 So.2d 813 (1963); Masquart v. Dick, 210 Or. 459, 310 P.2d 742 (1957); Clodfelter v. Van Fossan, 394 Ill. 29, 67 N.E.2d 182 (1946); Morris v. Clark, 100 Utah 252, 112 P.2d 153 (1941), certiorari denied 314 U.S. 584, 62 S.Ct. 361, 86 L.Ed. 472 (1941).

from the purchaser's viewpoint to employ an escrow if the sale is by long-term installment contract, since the risk of the grantor's death or incapacity before completion of the contract is a substantial one.[8]

Two requirements must be met for the doctrine of relation back to operate. The first is that there must be an enforceable contract of sale between the grantor and grantee,[9] and the second is that the grantor must have reserved no legal power to recall the deed from the custodian.[10] The genesis of both of these requirements is in the ancient law of delivery of deeds, and in particular the notion that a delivery must place the deed beyond the grantor's control. It makes some sense to demand that the grantor have no power to retrieve the deed, since such a power strongly suggests that the grantor has not yet formed a firm intention to deliver it. But the insistence on an enforceable contract of sale has been strongly criticized [11] and seems to serve little purpose, especially in light of the courts' willingness to admit oral testimony of intent when considering the validity of a direct delivery from grantor to grantee and the fact that no contract is needed in such cases.[12] In sale transactions there is ordinarily a contract, but if it is not embodied in a writing sufficient to satisfy the statute of frauds,[13] the relation back of the escrow may be defeated.[14] There is no legal requirement that the escrow instructions themselves be written,[15] although all professional escrowees demand a writing for obvious practical reasons. If the instructions are written they will often contain all of the elements required to solve the statute of frauds problem even if the contract of sale is oral.[16] There is some authority that even the deed itself may be a sufficient

8. The escrow arrangement has a further advantage if the installment contract sale is subject to (or "wraps around") a prior mortgage or other lien which is not discharged when the contract is signed, but the payments on which are to be made by the vendor. The escrowee can be instructed to collect the contract purchaser's payments each month and to disburse the appropriate amount to the holders of the prior lien. This obviates the risk that the contract vendor will fail to make the payments on the prior encumbrances and will abscond with the funds. On wrap-around encumbrances, see generally Note, 10 Pac.L.J. 932 (1979); Note, 1972 Duke L.J. 785; G. Nelson & D. Whitman, Real Estate Transfer, Finance, and Development 1102–1112 (3d ed. 1987).

9. See Penick v. May, 240 So.2d 461 (Miss. 1970); Merry v. County Board of Education, 264 Ala. 411, 87 So.2d 821 (1956), noted 9 Ala.L.Rev. 130 (1956); Johnson v. Wallden, 342 Ill. 201, 173 N.E. 790 (1930); Jozefowicz v. Leickem, 174 Wis. 475, 182 N.W. 729 (1921); Fitch v. Bunch, 30 Cal. 208 (1866). A California Court of Appeals recognized an unexercised option as a sufficient contract in Caras v. Parker, 149 Cal.App.2d 621, 309 P.2d 104 (1957). A few cases do not require an underlying contract; see, e.g., Calbreath v. Borchert, 248 Iowa 491, 81 N.W.2d 433 (1957). Note that the contract requirement is inapplicable to death escrows; see text at note 28, infra.

10. Brandt v. Schucha, 250 Iowa 679, 96 N.W.2d 179 (1959); Malcolm v. Tate, 125 Or. 419, 267 P. 527 (1928); Kenney v. Parks, 125 Cal. 146, 57 P. 772 (1899); Loubat v. Kipp & Young, 9 Fla. 60 (1860). Whether the right of recall or control is actually exercised by the grantor is irrelevant for this purpose.

11. See, e.g., 4 Tiffany, Real Property § 1052 (1939); Ballentine, Delivery in Escrow, 29 Yale L.J. 831 (1920); Aigler, Is a Contract Necessary to Create an Effective Escrow? 16 Mich.L.Rev. 569 (1918); Tiffany, Conditional Delivery of Deeds, 14 Colum.L.Rev. 389 (1914).

12. See § 11.3, supra, at notes 8–13.

13. See § 10.1, supra.

14. West Federal Savings & Loan Association v. Interstate Investment, Inc., 57 Wis.2d 690, 205 N.W.2d 361 (1973).

15. Bentz v. Wallowa Title Co., 93 Or.App. 27, 761 P.2d 10 (1988); Lewis v. Shawnee State Bank, 226 Kan. 41, 596 P.2d 116 (1979); Kennedy v. District–Realty Title Insurance Corp., 306 A.2d 655 (D.C.App.1973); Young v. Bishop, 88 Ariz. 140, 353 P.2d 1017 (1960); Osby v. Reynolds, 260 Ill. 576, 103 N.E. 556 (1913).

16. T.D. Dennis Builder, Inc. v. Goff, 101 Ariz.2d 211, 418 P.2d 367 (1966); Wood Building Corp. v. Griffitts, 164 Cal.App.2d 559, 330 P.2d 847 (1958).

writing.[17]

If the requirements of the preceding paragraph are not met, and there is consequently no "true" escrow, two conclusions follow. First, the grantor has a legal power to recall the deed at any time before the escrowee actually delivers it.[18] Second, if the grantor remains alive and competent and does not recall the deed, the conditions set out in the escrow instructions are met, and the escrowee delivers the deed to the grantee, there will be no relation back.[19] Such a delivery is itself perfectly good, however, as of the time it occurs.[20]

In the "true" escrow, a dispute sometimes arises as to when the second delivery occurs. The cases are not entirely consistent, but there is considerable authority that the deed is deemed delivered out of escrow when all conditions have occurred,[21] even if manual delivery or recording is delayed.[22] This view coincides with the general theory that delivery is a matter of the grantor's intent; the escrow instructions presumably reflect the desire that title should pass as soon as all conditions have been met.

It is fundamental to the escrow concept that title cannot pass until all conditions have been fulfilled.[23] Suppose, however, the grantee bribes or connives with the escrowee to get hold of the deed even though some condition, such as full payment of the purchase price, remains unmet. As between grantor and grantee, all courts would agree that no title has passed.[24] But the problem is more difficult if the grantee records the deed and then sells the land to a bona fide purchaser for value. In some cases the grantor's continued possession will give the purchaser notice that something is amiss, but if that is not so the purchaser may have no clue that the delivery out of escrow was wrongful; indeed, it may not even be apparent to the grantee that an escrow was involved in the prior transfer. Rather surprisingly, most of the decisions hold that title is still in the grantor as against the bona fide purchaser.[25] This result, which has been severely

17. Southern States Development Co., Inc. v. Robinson, 494 S.W.2d 777 (Tenn.App.1972); but see Baker v. Glander, 32 Mich.App. 305, 188 N.W.2d 263 (1971); Main v. Pratt, 276 Ill. 218, 114 N.E. 576 (1916). In many cases the deed will not contain all of the necessary contractual elements; see § 10.1, supra, at note 19.

18. See Chaffin v. Harpham, 166 Ark. 578, 266 S.W. 685 (1924); Jozefowicz v. Leickem, 174 Wis. 475, 182 N.W. 729 (1921). This right of recall presumably exists whether the grantor expressed it when depositing the deed in escrow or not.

19. See cases cited at note 9, supra.

20. Campbell v. Thomas, 42 Wis. 437 (1877).

21. See Boatmen's Nat. Bank v. Dandy, 804 S.W.2d 783 (Mo.App.1990); Sturgill v. Industrial Painting Corp., 82 Nev. 61, 410 P.2d 759 (1966); Holman v. Toten, 54 Cal.App.2d 309, 128 P.2d 808 (1942); Park Avenue Methodist Episcopal Church v. Park Avenue Colored Methodist Episcopal Church, 244 Ill.App. 148 (1927); Val Verde Hotel Co. v. Ross, 30

N.M. 270, 231 P. 702 (1924). The variety of theories which may be employed is discussed in Roberts v. Osburn, 3 Kan.App.2d 90, 589 P.2d 985 (1979). See also Andover Land Co. v. Hoffman, 264 Cal.App.2d 87, 70 Cal.Rptr. 38 (1968) (when all conditions are met, purchaser has "equitable title.")

22. Recording will almost surely be treated as the equivalent of manual delivery by the escrowee; see § 11.3, supra, at note 11.

23. See Ferguson v. Caspar, 359 A.2d 17 (D.C.App.1976); Dixon v. O'Connor, 180 Neb. 427, 143 N.W.2d 364 (1966).

24. See, e.g., Allen v. Allen Title Co., 77 N.M. 796, 427 P.2d 673 (1967).

25. See Watts v. Archer, 252 Iowa 592, 107 N.W.2d 549 (1961); Clevenger v. Moore, 126 Okl. 246, 259 P. 219, 54 A.L.R. 1237 (1927); Everts v. Agnes, 6 Wis. 453 (1858). See 3 Am.L.Prop. § 12.68 note 19 (1952); Roberts, Wrongful Delivery of Deeds in Escrow, 17 Ky.L.Rev. 31 (1928); Annots., 48 A.L.R. 405 (1927), 54 A.L.R. 1246 (1928). The BFP will prevail if the deed was obtained from the

criticized by scholars,[26] is certainly objectionable if the escrowee was at fault in any degree; the grantor should in fairness bear responsibility for selecting and employing the escrowee as an agent, as opposed to the subsequent purchaser who had no dealings with the escrowee at all. Even in states following the majority rule, the grantor may be estopped to deny the delivery if he or she was negligent in selecting the escrowee or failed to assert title within a reasonable time after learning of the purchaser's claim.[27]

Death Escrows. Many of the concepts discussed above in connection with sales escrows are equally applicable to cases in which the grantor hands a deed to a custodian for delivery upon the grantor's death. There are, however, some important differences. Most death escrows are gratuitous, and there is no underlying contract. But no contract is required for a valid death escrow; all that is necessary is that the grantor place the deed beyond his or her control, reserving no power over it once it has been deposited.[28] Moreover, to defeat the escrow a power to recall the deed must be fairly explicit; it is not enough that the custodian testifies he or she would have returned the deed to the grantor upon request.[29]

The rule that enforces death escrows without underlying contracts seems to be based, not altogether logically, on the fact that the only condition in a death escrow, the death of the grantor, is *certain* to occur; thus, it is in a sense not a condition at all. From this premise the courts reason that no further legal element (other than the absence of a power of recall) is necessary to commit the grantor irrevocably to the transaction, and thus to constitute a delivery.[30] This reasoning may help to explain why some (although not all) courts have refused to enforce death escrows involving a more elaborate condition, such as the survival of the grantor by the grantee.[31] Such courts seem to view the possibility that the condition will

escrowee by fraud rather than by his knowing participation in the grantee's scheme; see Clevenger v. Moore, supra. The Florida Supreme Court held the contrary in Houston v. Adams, 85 Fla. 291, 95 So. 859 (1923), but that holding is limited to fraud in the execution by McCoy v. Love, 382 So.2d 647 (Fla.1979).

26. See Mann, supra note 4, at 417–18, quoting 4 Thompson, Real Property §§ 3954–55 (1924).

27. In a subsequent appeal of Clevenger v. Moore, supra note 25, the court found that the grantor had indeed estopped herself to attack the BFP's title by her own failure to assert her claim expeditiously; 126 Okl. at 361, 298 P. at 299.

28. See, e.g., Herron v. Underwood, 152 Ill.App.3d 144, 503 N.E.2d 1111 (1987), appeal denied 115 Ill.2d 541, 110 Ill.Dec. 456, 511 N.E.2d 428 (1987); Daugherty v. DeWees, 172 W.Va. 553, 309 S.E.2d 52 (1983); Blackmer v. Blackmer, 165 Mont. 69, 525 P.2d 559 (1974); Cain v. Morrison, 212 Kan. 791, 512 P.2d 474 (1973); Bailey v. Williams, 326 S.W.2d 115 (Mo.1959); Ritchie v. Davis, 26 Wis.2d 636, 133 N.W.2d 312 (1965); Smith v. Fay, 228

Iowa 868, 293 N.W. 497 (1940); Johnson v. Johnson, 24 R.I. 571, 54 A. 378 (1903).

Since nonprofessionals are commonly employed in death escrows, they are frequently attacked on the ground that the escrowee is merely the grantor's agent, and not an escrowee at all. In most jurisdictions this is a question of fact, but the Georgia courts appear to have entirely rejected the validity of death escrows, reasoning that the agent's authority must expire upon the principal's death; see Stinson v. Gray, 232 Ga. 542, 207 S.E.2d 506 (1974); Cooper v. Littleton, 197 Ga. 381, 29 S.E.2d 606 (1944).

29. See Herron v. Underwood, supra note 28; Chandler v. Chandler, 409 So.2d 780 (Ala. 1981); Brown v. Hutch, 156 So.2d 683 (Fla. App.1963), cert. denied 162 So.2d 665 (Fla. 1964). On the other hand, the testimony of the grantor herself that she intended to have continuing control over the deed may be quite persuasive; see Cain v. Morrison, supra note 28.

30. See cases cited in note 28, supra.

31. See Raim v. Stancel, 339 N.W.2d 621 (Iowa App.1983) (oral condition that grantee

fail as giving the grantor a fatal measure of additional control. From a policy standpoint, this distinction has no more to commend it than the contract requirement in sales escrows; it is hard to see any good reason to deny enforcement to a death escrow which includes further conditions.[32]

The notion that the condition in a simple death escrow is certain to occur has another potentially important consequence. It leads most courts to treat the delivery *to the custodian* as immediately passing title to the grantee. The interest thus conveyed is deemed a future interest to become possessory on the grantor's death—presumably a springing executory interest, although most cases do not bother to identify it—with the grantor retaining what is often termed a life estate, although it is technically a fee simple subject to an executory limitation.[33] Such a conveyance is, of course, entirely valid.[34] This result commonly follows despite the fact that none of the parties has said anything whatever about a future interest. Such a construction seems bizarre but it has a certain logic, for death is indeed inevitable and by hypothesis no act of the grantor's can retrieve the deed prior to his death. The relation back doctrine which governs sales escrows is wholly inapplicable under this view of death escrows, for the first delivery is legally the only delivery![35] The holding that the grantee immediately receives a future interest, rather than having a mere expectancy until the grantor's death, may have significant consequences in terms of such doctrines as waste, liability of third parties for damage to the land, gift and inheritance taxes, and the grantee's ability to make conveyances while the grantor is still alive; but these issues are seldom discussed in the cases.[36]

Duties of Escrowees. The escrowee is an agent of both parties until the close of the escrow,[37] and thereafter, the grantor's agent with respect to the

care for grantor until his death renders delivery after grantor's death invalid); Atchison v. Atchison, 198 Okl. 98, 175 P.2d 309 (1946); Stanforth v. Bailey, 344 Ill. 38, 175 N.E. 784 (1931). Cases upholding death escrows which incorporated additional conditions include Videon v. Cowart, 241 So.2d 434 (Fla.App.1970), cert. denied 245 So.2d 88 (Fla.1971) (condition that grantee ask for the deed); Smith v. Fay, supra note 28 (condition that grantee survive grantor.)

32. See 2 Walsh, Real Property § 214 notes 7, 17 (1947), discussed in 3 Am.L.Prop. 321 (1952); 4 Tiffany, Real Property § 1054 notes 76–78 (1939).

33. Pipes v. Sevier, 694 S.W.2d 918 (Mo. App.1985). See cases cited note 28, supra; Mann, supra note 4, at 420–22. But see Herron v. Underwood, 152 Ill.App.3d 144, 105 Ill.Dec. 105, 503 N.E.2d 1111 (1987) (in death escrow, no title passes until grantor's death). In a few states, statutes explicitly describe the grantor's retained interest as a "life estate." On springing executory interests, see § 3.12 supra.

34. See, e.g., Callaghan v. Reed, 44 Or.App. 489, 605 P.2d 1382 (1980); § 11.3 supra, at note 19.

35. Masquart v. Dick, 210 Or. 459, 310 P.2d 742 (1957).

36. See the discussion of rights of non-BFP transferees from the grantor after he has given the deed to the custodian in 4 Tiffany, Real Property § 1054 note 66 (1939).

37. Bob Daniels and Sons v. Weaver, 106 Idaho 535, 681 P.2d 1010 (App.1984) (neither party can make the escrowee his unilateral agent; escrowee must act only upon mutual instructions of both parties). But a party may unilaterally and effectively amend the instructions to change the method of disbursement of his own funds from the escrow; see Contemporary Investments, Inc. v. Safeco Title Ins. Co., 145 Cal.App.3d 999, 193 Cal.Rptr. 822 (1983) (seller may amend instructions to provide for payment of real estate commission to him rather than directly to real estate broker, in absence of escrowee's knowledge of any assignment of the funds to the broker). Compare Maganas v. Northroup, 135 Ariz. 573, 663 P.2d 565 (1983), in which the brokers' rights to disbursement of their commissions from the escrow were clearly spelled out in the escrow instructions; the court exonerated the escrowee from liability for complying with an amendment which was signed by one of the brokers, acting as agent for the others, but which deprived one of them of payment of part of his commission from the escrow.

See also Patel v. Gannaway, 726 F.2d 382 (8th Cir.1984), in which the court cautioned

purchase money and the grantee's agent with respect to the deed.[38] The agent's fundamental duty is to comply strictly with the escrow instructions,[39] and not to do anything contrary to them which might damage either of the parties.[40] He or she is held to a duty of reasonable care and skill,[41] which cannot be relieved by language in the contract with the parties.[42] The cases often describe the escrowee as a fiduciary, but this must be understood as limited to the context of the escrow instructions received;[43] the agent is not required to give the parties legal or financial advice or to correct errors in documents drawn by the parties or their advisors.[44] The cases reflect no

lawyers about the ethical risks of serving as an escrowee while at the same time representing one of the parties as an attorney; Collins v. Norton, 136 Ga.App. 105, 220 S.E.2d 279 (1975); Leiter v. Eltinge, 246 Cal.App.2d 306, 54 Cal.Rptr. 703 (1966).

The agency is limited to acts authorized by the agent's instructions, and does not extend to other matters, such as interpreting the parties' contract or giving consents or waivers in their behalf; see Barr v. Pratt, 105 Or.App. 220, 804 P.2d 496 (1991). Cf. In re Ellison Associate, 63 B.R. 756 (S.D.N.Y.1983) (under New York law, escrowee is trustee, not agent, of both parties).

38. Ferguson v. Caspar, 359 A.2d 17 (D.C.App.1976); Edward Rose Sales Co. v. Shafer, 41 Mich.App. 105, 199 N.W.2d 655 (1972). Thus, if the agent decamps with the funds before the closing, the loss is the buyer's, but if afterward, the seller's; see Lawyers Title Insurance Corp. v. Edmar Construction Co., Inc., 294 A.2d 865 (D.C.App.1972); Pagan v. Spencer, 104 Cal.App.2d 588, 232 P.2d 323 (1951). The notary who conducts closings in Louisiana is in a similar position; see Roth v. B & L Enterprises, Inc., 420 So.2d 1094 (La. 1982).

39. George A. Fuller Co. v. Alexander & Reed, 760 F.Supp. 381 (S.D.N.Y.1991); Kirk Corp. v. First American Title Co., 220 Cal. App.3d 785, 270 Cal.Rptr. 24 (1990); H.B.I. Corp. v. Jimenez, 803 S.W.2d 100 (Mo.App. 1990); Lacy v. Ticor Title Ins. Co., 794 S.W.2d 781 (Tex.App.1990); First Montana Title Co. v. North Point Square Ass'n, 240 Mont. 33, 782 P.2d 376 (1989); Fretz v. First American Title Ins. Co., 161 Ariz. 174, 777 P.2d 672 (App. 1989); Toro Petroleum Corp. v. Newell, 33 Ill.App.3d 223, 338 N.E.2d 491 (1974); National Bank of Washington v. Equity Investors, 81 Wn.2d 886, 506 P.2d 20 (1973), appeal after remand 83 Wn.2d 435, 518 P.2d 1072 (1974).

40. See, e.g., Miller v. Craig, 27 Ariz.App. 789, 558 P.2d 984 (1976), in which, prior to closing, the buyer obtained a judgment against the sellers rescinding the sale and awarding her recovery of her $5,000 earnest money. The escrowee refunded the money, but on appeal the judgment was reversed and the funds awarded to the sellers; Miller v. Crouse, 19 Ariz.App. 268, 506 P.2d 659 (1973). The sellers then brought an action for $5,000

against the escrowee; they prevailed on the ground that he breached his duty by not retaining the funds until the time for appeal in the prior suit had expired.

41. See, e.g., Zimmerman v. First American Title Ins., 790 S.W.2d 690 (Tex.App.1990) ("a high degree of care"); Reeves v. McClain, 56 Wn.App. 301, 783 P.2d 606 (1989); Perkins v. Clinton State Bank, 593 F.2d 327 (8th Cir. 1979); Buffington v. Title Insurance Co. of Minnesota, 26 Ariz.App. 97, 546 P.2d 366 (1976) ("scrupulous honesty, skill and diligence"); Woodworth v. Redwood Empire Savings & Loan Association, 22 Cal.App.3d 347, 99 Cal.Rptr. 373 (1971) ("ordinary skill and diligence"); Andersen v. Northwest Bonded Escrows, Inc., 4 Wn.App. 754, 484 P.2d 488 (1971) ("care, skill, diligence, and knowledge"); Wade v. Lake County Title Co., 6 Cal.App.3d 824, 86 Cal.Rptr. 182 (1970). See also Hannon v. Western Title Ins. Co., 211 Cal.App.3d 1122, 260 Cal.Rptr. 21 (1989) (no duty to deposit funds in interest-bearing account pending disbursement).

42. Selby v. Burtch, 193 Cal.App.3d 147, 238 Cal.Rptr. 212 (1987); Akin v. Business Title Corp., 264 Cal.App.2d 153, 70 Cal.Rptr. 287 (1968).

43. Giddens Const. Co., Inc. v. Fickling & Walker Company, 188 Ga.App. 558, 373 S.E.2d 792 (1988), judgment reversed 258 Ga. 891, 376 S.E.2d 655 (1989), on remand 191 Ga.App. 255, 382 S.E.2d 436 (1989); Toro Petroleum Corp. v. Newell, supra note 39; National Bank of Washington v. Equity Investors, supra note 39.

44. Patel v. Gannaway, 726 F.2d 382 (8th Cir.1984) (where buyer is aware of existing liens on the property and the inadequacy of the title insurance commitment, and insists on going forward, escrowee is not liable for subsequent losses caused by foreclosure of the liens); Schaefer v. Manufacturers Bank, 104 Cal.App.3d 70, 163 Cal.Rptr. 402 (1980); Axley v. Transamerica Title Insurance Co., 88 Cal. App.3d 1, 151 Cal.Rptr. 570 (1978); Cocke v. Transamerica Title Insurance Co., 16 Ariz. App. 556, 494 P.2d 756 (1972); National Bank of Washington v. Equity Investors, supra note 38. See Templeton, Escrow Obligations and Liabilities, Title News, Mar.–Apr. 1986, at 9,

clear rule as to the escrowee's duty to divulge to the parties information about the transaction which may be important to them.[45]

An escrowee who breaches his or her duties is liable in damages for the loss thus caused.[46] Consequential damages may be included,[47] as may punitive damages if the escrowee's default was reckless or willful.[48]

§ 11.5 Estoppel by Deed

A deed may be executed and delivered by a person who has no title to the described land, or who has a lesser interest than the deed purports to convey. Such a grantor may be subject to liability for breach of covenants relating to title in an earlier contract of sale [1] or in the deed itself.[2] But our concern in this section is not with the grantor's liability in damages. Instead, we consider what legal results follow if the grantor later acquires part or all of the very title the previous deed described.[3]

The law's response to this situation is to deny to the grantor the right, as against the grantee and his or her successors, to assert the title thus

for a wry description of some of the dilemmas of serving as an escrowee. An escrowee who undertakes to prepare documents or give advice that amounts to the practice of law may be held to the professional standards of the legal profession; see Bowers v. Transamerica Title Ins. Co., 100 Wn.2d 581, 675 P.2d 193 (1983). Compare Pope v. Savings Bank of Puget Sound, 850 F.2d 1345 (9th Cir.1988) (no attorney liability, where escrowee did not undertake practice of law).

45. Styrk v. Michie, 61 Wn.App. 463, 810 P.2d 1366 (1991), review denied 818 P.2d 1098 (1991) (duty to inform seller that the loan-to-value ratio for her subordinated purchase-money mortgage exceeded the amount agreed to by the parties); Kitchen Krafters, Inc. v. Eastside Bank, 242 Mont. 155, 789 P.2d 567 (1990) (duty to inform contract purchaser that prepayment had been sent directly to vendor, rather than applied on preexisting mortgage). Compare Cano v. Lovato, 105 N.M. 522, 734 P.2d 762 (App.1986), cert. denied 104 N.M. 246, 719 P.2d 1267 (1986) (duty to inform buyer about title defects) with Roscoe v. U.S. Life Title Ins. Co., 105 N.M. 589, 734 P.2d 1272 (1987) (no duty to inform buyer about balloon payment clause in mortgage he assumed). Compare also Contini v. Western Title Insurance Co., 40 Cal.App.3d 536, 115 Cal. Rptr. 257 (1974) with Lee v. Title Insurance & Trust Co., 264 Cal.App.2d 160, 70 Cal.Rptr. 378 (1968). See also Garton v. Title Insurance & Trust Co., 106 Cal.App.3d 365, 165 Cal.Rptr. 449 (1980); United Homes, Inc. v. Moss, 154 So.2d 351 (Fla.App.1963). There is authority that the escrow agent has a duty to disclose to one party fraud the other party intends to commit. See Manley v. Ticor Title Ins. Co. of Cal., 168 Ariz. 568, 816 P.2d 225 (1991). See Jacobsen, California Escrow Agents: A Duty to Disclose Known Fraud?, 17 Pac.L.J. 309 (1985).

46. Banville v. Schmidt, 37 Cal.App.3d 92, 112 Cal.Rptr. 126 (1974); Ruth v. Lytton Savings & Loan Association, 266 Cal.App.2d 831, 72 Cal.Rptr. 521 (1968).

47. Wade v. Lake County Title Co., supra note 41.

48. Sanders v. Park Towne, Limited, 2 Kan.App.2d 313, 578 P.2d 1131 (1978); Toro Petroleum Corp. v. Newell, supra note 39; Giddens Const. Co., Inc. v. Fickling & Walker Company, supra note 43; Eastern Atlantic Transp. and Mechanical Engineering, Inc. v. Dingman, 727 S.W.2d 418 (Mo.App.1987). Cf. Edwards v. Stewart Title & Trust, 156 Ariz. 531, 753 P.2d 1187 (App.1988) (no punitive damages awarded, where escrowee's conduct was not outrageous).

§ 11.5

1. On covenants of title in contracts, see generally § 10.12, supra. In many cases the doctrine of merger will preclude the grantee's assertion of any claim based on the contract's covenants once he or she has accepted the deed; see § 10.12, supra, at notes 53–63.

2. See § 11.13, infra.

3. The discussion in the the text deals with deeds, but it is clear that the same principles apply to mortgages, leases, or other conveyances which purport to transfer an interest in land. See, e.g., Hardigan v. Kimball, 553 A.2d 1265 (Me.1989) (contract of sale); McLaughlin v. Lambourn, 359 N.W.2d 370 (N.D.1985) (contract for deed); Alabama Home Mortg. Co. v. Harris, 582 So.2d 1080 (Ala.1991) (mortgage); Rosewood Resources, Inc. v. Jonesboro State Bank, 535 So.2d 1083 (La.App.1988) (mortgage); Pearll v. Williams, 146 Ariz. 203, 704 P.2d 1348 (App.1985) (mortgage); Perego v. Seltzer, 260 Cal.App.2d 825, 67 Cal.Rptr. 636 (1968) (mortgage); Aure v. Mackoff, 93 N.W.2d 807 (N.D.1958) (assignment of oil and gas royalty).

acquired. The theory is one of estoppel: if the grantor, by language in the deed, represents to the grantee that title of a certain quality is being conveyed, the grantor is estopped to deny later that such title has passed to the grantee.[4] This theory is sensible only if the deed does in fact make a representation about the quality of the title it conveys; not all deeds do so. Older cases often distinguished between warranty and quitclaim deeds on this score. But that approach can be misleading, for language of warranty may really represent nothing (e.g., "I hereby warrant whatever title I may have at this time, if any,") while a quitclaim deed may assert that title of a certain quality is being conveyed (e.g., "I hereby set over and quitclaim a fee simple absolute.")[5] The modern trend is simply to look for language in the deed which fairly constitutes an assertion about the title's quality; if it is found, estoppel by deed will operate. The ordinary warranty deed will nearly always be sufficient, and most quitclaims will not.[6]

In its bare form, this doctrine of estoppel would merely permit the grantee to sue the grantor and compel the delivery of a new conveyance. But most modern courts take the doctrine a step further, and treat the title as passing automatically to the grantee as soon as the grantor gets it.[7] This

4. See generally 3 Am.L.Prop. §§ 15.19–15.24 (1952); 1 R. Patton & C. Patton, Land Titles §§ 215–220 (2d ed. 1957); 6A Powell, Real Property ¶ 927 (1980); Note, Estoppel by Deed, 37 Baylor L.Rev. 1059 (1985). In general, it makes no difference by what route or method the grantor subsequently acquires the title. But acquisition from the grantee himself is an exception, and no estoppel against the grantor will arise in such a case, since there is no inconsistency with the purport of the original deed; see, e.g., Sorenson v. Wright, 268 N.W.2d 203 (Iowa 1978); Turner v. Miller, 276 So.2d 690 (Miss.1973); 4 Tiffany, Real Property § 1233 (1939).

5. See, e.g., White v. Ford, 124 N.H. 452, 471 A.2d 1176 (1984) (quitclaim deed in which statute implies certain limited covenants of title triggers estoppel by deed); Stevens v. Stevens, 10 Wn.App. 493, 519 P.2d 269 (1974) (quitclaim deed, but contained express conveyance of after-acquired title); Hagensick v. Castor, 53 Neb. 495, 73 N.W. 932 (1898) (no warranty, but representation sufficient for an estoppel); Sabine Production Co. v. Guaranty Bank & Trust Co., 432 So.2d 1047 (La.App. 1983), writ denied 484 So.2d 570 (La.1983). For the traditional view that a quitclaim does not trigger an estoppel, see Barlow Soc. v. Commercial Security Bank, 723 P.2d 398 (Utah 1986); Idaho ex rel. Moore v. Scroggie, 109 Idaho 32, 704 P.2d 364 (1985); Van Pelt v. Estate of Clarke, 476 So.2d 746 (Fla.App.1985).

Some states have statutes expressly applying the doctrine to any deed " * * * purport-ing to convey an estate in fee simple absolute * * * "; see notes 29–31, infra, and accompanying text. See also Miss.Code 1972, § 89–1–39, specifically applying the doctrine to quit-claim deeds; see Turner v. Miller, 276 So.2d 690 (Miss.1973). But see McLaurin v. Royalties, Inc., 231 Miss. 240, 95 So.2d 105 (1957),

refusing to apply the statute where the quit-claim deed expressly purported to convey only the grantor's present interest. See also Perkins v. Kerby, 308 So.2d 914 (Miss.1975): grantor must describe "a precise or definite legal estate or right by a solemn assurance that he will not be permitted to deny." This seems a bit of an overstatement.

6. See Walliker v. Escott, 608 P.2d 1272 (Wyo.1980) (despite statutory declaration that a quitclaim deed will not pass after-acquired title, such a deed will do so where it purports to transfer "a definite, specific interest" * * * in this case, a fractional share of the mineral rights). See also Sabine Production Co. v. Guaranty Bank & Trust Co., 432 So.2d 1047 (La.App.1983), writ denied 438 So.2d 570 (La. 1983) (operation of estoppel by deed is based on the presence in the deed of an assertion that title is in fact being transferred); Harkins & Co. v. Lewis, 535 So.2d 104 (Ala.1988) (after-acquired title did not pass, where the prior deed was not intended to include the interest later acquired); Sorenson v. Wright, 268 N.W.2d 203 (Iowa 1978); Dixieland Realty Co. v. Wysor, 272 N.C. 172, 158 S.E.2d 7 (1967); Smith v. Berberich, 168 Neb. 142, 95 N.W.2d 325 (1959). See generally Annots., 58 A.L.R. 345 (1929); 144 A.L.R. 554 (1943). It is not necessary that all covenants of title be present in the deed to create an estoppel; generally any one of them is sufficient. See 1 R. Patton & C. Patton, Land Titles § 216 note 98 (1957).

7. See, e.g., Campbell v. Butler, 770 P.2d 7 (Okl.1988); Southern Missouri Sav. & Loan v. Thomas, 754 S.W.2d 937 (Mo.App.1988); Schwenn v. Kaye, 155 Cal.App.3d 949, 202 Cal.Rptr. 374 (1984); Turner v. Lassiter, 484 So.2d 378 (Ala.1985); McNeal v. Bonnel, 412

simplifies title examinations, since a searcher who discovers a situation raising an estoppel by deed can simply assume that the grantee got the title without being concerned with whether any judicial action was taken to obtain it.   Under this view it is sometimes picturesquely said that the belated title obtained by the grantor "feeds the estoppel." [8]

Estoppel ordinarily presupposes reasonable reliance by the innocent party on the other's representations; the one who relies must be ignorant of the true facts.[9]   The cases are divided as to whether this rule applies to estoppel by deed.[10]   But even if the original grantee must believe the deed is good, it makes no sense to demand good faith reliance on the part of those who take in later succession from the grantee.   In most cases they will search the title and may well discover that the grantor gave a deed before obtaining title.   If they are penalized for that knowledge, the main value of estoppel by deed to title examiners is lost.   Plainly title should inure to such remote grantees whether they have become aware of their need for the inurement or not.   This point seems to be assumed without discussion in the cases.

The notion of automatic inurement is obviously very convenient in some situations, but it also raises several important questions.   One is whether it is an exclusive remedy.   Suppose the grantee, upon discovering that the grantor had no title, brings an action based on the deed's title covenants. Can the grantor, by acquiring the title and permitting it to inure to the grantee, cure the breach of covenant and defeat the suit?   The modern cases are fairly uniform in holding that the grantee has a choice of accepting the title or pursuing the action for damages, since the inurement doctrine is intended for the grantee's benefit.[11]

The inurement theory may also influence the resolution of the claims of competing grantees.   If the grantor, after acquiring the belated title, purports to deed it to a second grantee, which of the two grantees will have the title?   If the second pays no value or has notice of the claim of the first, plainly the first will prevail.[12]   But if the second is an innocent purchaser for

S.W.2d 167 (Mo.1967); Robben v. Obering, 279 F.2d 381 (7th Cir.1960); Aure v. Mackoff, 93 N.W.2d 807 (N.D.1958); Guy v. Poss, 212 Ga. 724, 95 S.E.2d 682 (1956). See generally 3 Am.L.Prop. § 15.21 (1952). Sometimes automatic inurement of after-acquired title is explained on the basis of theories other than estoppel. For example, the grantor's conveyance may be treated as the equivalent of a contract to convey, which the courts will specifically enforce when he acquires title. See G. Osborne, Mortgages § 37 (2d ed. 1970), for a discussion of this and other, more obscure theories in the context of mortgages.

8.   Perkins v. Coleman, 90 Ky. 611, 14 S.W. 640 (1890).

9.   See, e.g., United States v. Ruby Co., 588 F.2d 697 (9th Cir.1978), certiorari denied 442 U.S. 917, 99 S.Ct. 2838, 61 L.Ed.2d 284 (1979).

10.   Ignorance of true facts required: Shell Oil Co. v. Trailer & Truck Repair Co., 828 F.2d 205 (3d Cir.1987) (N.J. law); McLaughlin v. Lambourn, 359 N.W.2d 370 (N.D.1985); Per-

kins v. Kerby, 308 So.2d 914 (Miss.1975); Viele v. Van Steenberg, 31 Fed. 249 (8th Cir. 1887).   Estoppel applied even though true facts appeared on the face of the deed; Ayer v. Philadelphia & Boston Face Brick Co., 159 Mass. 84, 34 N.E. 177 (1893). See W. Burby, Real Property 320 (3d ed. 1965).

11.   Resser v. Carney, 52 Minn. 397, 54 N.W. 89 (1893); 3 Am.L.Prop. § 15.23 (1952).

12.   Duke v. Hopper, 486 S.W.2d 744 (Tenn. App.1972) (first deed binding on grantor's heirs); Dillard v. Brannan, 217 Ga. 179, 121 S.E.2d 768 (1961) (second grantee not alleged to be a BFP; first grantee prevails); Lucas v. Cowan, 357 P.2d 976 (Okl.1960) (first deed binding on second grantee with notice); Scott v. Cohen, 115 F.2d 704 (5th Cir.1940), certiorari denied 312 U.S. 703, 61 S.Ct. 806, 85 L.Ed. 1136 (1941) (same); Donohue v. Vosper, 189 Mich. 78, 155 N.W. 407 (1915), affirmed 243 U.S. 59, 37 S.Ct. 350, 61 L.Ed. 592 (1917) (same).

value, the cases divide.[13] Some courts emphasize the notion of automatic inurement and recognize title in the original grantee on the ground that it passed to the grantee the instant the grantor acquired it; thus, the grantor had nothing to pass by a second deed.[14] Other cases, probably more numerous, focus on the estoppel concept and give priority to the bona fide purchaser, reasoning that only the grantor and not the innocent second grantee is estopped.[15]

But this debate is largely irrelevant unless the recording acts are taken into account. The first deed is recordable, and if the grantee does not in fact record it, it will be void as against subsequent good faith purchasers for value who do record.[16] But if the first deed is recorded, its grantee will argue that the recording acts cannot divest the interest it grants, and further that no later grantee can be a good faith purchaser, since the recordation of the first deed will give constructive notice. The second grantee's response is that the first deed cannot be deemed *properly* recorded, since it is outside the "chain of title." In a jurisdiction in which title searches are based on indexes of grantors' and grantees' names, this is a fairly persuasive argument. Once the searcher has constructed a chain of conveyances backward in time from the present, using the grantee index, he or she will then employ the grantor index to discover whether any prior owner made a conveyance which was adverse to the chain.[17] The first deed in the illustration above is such a conveyance. The difficulty is that it was recorded prior to the time the grantor obtained the land. Searchers ordinarily look for adverse conveyances under each prior owner's name only *during* the time that owner appears to have held title.[18] To search earlier

13. See 4 H. Tiffany, Real Property § 1234 notes 56–57 (1939); W. Burby, Real Property § 128 (2d ed. 1965); Lawler, Estoppel to Assert an After–Acquired Title in Pennsylvania, 3 U.Pitt.L.Rev. 165, 176–77 (1937).

14. See Annot., 25 A.L.R. 83 (1923); 4 H. Tiffany, supra note 13, at note 56. Clear holdings are sparse, and cases cited for rejecting the subsequent BFP's claim often do not make it clear whether he was in fact a BFP; see, e.g., Letson v. Roach, 5 Kan.App. 57, 47 P. 321 (1896), affirmed 58 Kan. 817, 50 P. 1101 (1897).

15. Builders Sash & Door Co. v. Joyner, 182 N.C. 518, 109 S.E. 259 (1921); Gallagher v. Stern, 250 Pa. 292, 95 A. 518 (1915); See Annot., supra note 14.

16. Life Sav. & Loan Ass'n v. Bryant, 125 Ill.App.3d 1012, 81 Ill.Dec. 577, 467 N.E.2d 277 (1984) (where second grantee had notice of first conveyance, and hence was not a BFP, estoppel worked to give title to first grantee, whose claim was not divested by operation of the recording act). In a pure "notice" jurisdiction, the second grantee who lacks notice need not even record. See generally § 11.9, infra, at notes 9–10.

If the second interest is not created by deed, but is a judgment lien, the matter is more complex. In a number of states the recording acts do not protect judgment creditors, usually on the ground that they have not paid contemporaneous value; see § 11.10, infra, at notes 10–17. But such a creditor might still be regarded on equitable grounds as having priority over the grantee under the deed. The result is likely to turn on the specific language of the judgment lien statute. A smattering of cases is collected in Swenson, Statutory Estoppel by Deed, 1950 Wash.U.L.Q. 361, 375–76; 4 Tiffany, Real Property § 1234 notes 64–67 (1939).

17. On title search procedures, see § 11.11, infra, at notes 2–3.

18. See Philbrick, Limits of Record Search and Therefore of Notice, Part I, 93 U.Pa. L.Rev. 125, 177–186 (1944). As one author described it:

Do conveyancers do this [search each owner's name back to the beginning of the records]? They do not. The cost of such examination would exceed the value of the land. Perhaps they hope that by ignoring the specter of estoppel by deed, they can prevent it from materializing.

R. Swain, 1949 Supplement to Crocker's Notes on Common Forms, Sixth (Conveyancers') Edition 95–96 (1949), quoted in Harr & Liebman, Property and Law 527 (1977).

years is not impossible, but it is a great deal of additional effort since in theory such a conveyance could have been recorded many decades earlier, and to be entirely safe one would have to search under each prior owner's name back in time to the beginning of the records.

The majority of courts, especially in recent years, have held that because the first deed is recorded so early, a searcher has no duty to find it. From this premise they reason that it gives no constructive notice to later purchasers, who therefore prevail over the first deed [19] either (1) because of the general principle favoring BFP's discussed above,[20] or (2) because the first deed must be treated as if it were unrecorded, so that subsequent BFP's may regard it as void under the normal operation of the recording acts.[21] The cases often do not bother to distinguish these two rationales, and the distinction is usually of little importance.[22]

The "chain of title" reasoning reflected in these holdings is sensible only if searches are performed in a grantor-grantee index system. If the public records are maintained on a tract index basis, the early-recorded deed presents no inconvenience for searchers, for it will appear (albeit out of chain-of-title order) on the same page of the index book which lists all other instruments affecting the parcel in question. Hence, it will give constructive notice to later purchasers.[23] Perhaps the most interesting question is raised in areas of the nation where the official records employ only name indexes but where searches are ordinarily performed by private title or abstract companies in their own private "plants" equipped (as they almost invariably are) with tract indexes.[24] There is no reason in good policy to apply "chain of title" thinking in such a context; if the searching firm in fact has the early-recorded deed in its records, and could have found it in the ordinary course of its tract-index search, then the firm (and arguably the purchaser as

19. Far West Sav. & Loan Ass'n v. McLaughlin, 201 Cal.App.3d 67, 246 Cal.Rptr. 872 (1988); Schuman v. Roger Baker & Associates, Inc., 70 N.C.App. 313, 319 S.E.2d 308 (1984); Security Pacific Finance Corp. v. Taylor, 193 N.J.Super. 434, 474 A.2d 1096 (1984); Sabo v. Horath, 559 P.2d 1038 (Alaska 1976); Richardson v. Atlantic Coast Lumber Corp., 93 S.C. 254, 75 S.E. 371 (1912); Breen v. Morehead, 104 Tex. 254, 136 S.W. 1047 (1911); Wheeler v. Young, 76 Conn. 44, 55 A. 670 (1903). Contra, see Lucas v. Cowan, 357 P.2d 976 (Okl.1960), in which the court may have been influenced by the use in Oklahoma of abstracts based on tract indexes, see text at note 25, infra; Ayer v. Philadelphia & Boston Face Brick Co., 159 Mass. 84, 34 N.E. 177 (1893); Tefft v. Munson, 57 N.Y. 97 (1875). See Johanson, Estoppel by Deed and the Recording System: The "Ayer Rule" Re-examined, 43 B.U.L.Rev. 441 (1963) (collecting the cases on both sides at notes 83 and 91); Cross, The Record "Chain of Title" Hypocrisy, 57 Colum.L.Rev. 787, 793 (1957). For a discussion of other "chain of title" problems, see § 11.11, infra, at notes 6–15.

20. See text at note 15, supra.

21. Perhaps the clearest decision to this effect is Sabo v. Horath, supra note 19, holding that the first deed cannot be deemed "duly recorded." See also Schuman v. Roger Baker & Associates, Inc., supra note 19; Southeastern Sav. & Loan Ass'n v. Rentenbach Constructors, Inc., 114 B.R. 441 (E.D.N.C.1989) (deed has "same effect on notice as no registration").

22. The distinction could be important if the second grantee is a BFP but fails to record in a notice-race jurisdiction, and thus is disqualified from the protection of the recording act.

23. Balch v. Arnold, 9 Wyo. 17, 59 P. 434 (1899).

24. See Whitman, Optimizing Land Title Assurance Systems, 42 Geo.Wash.L.Rev. 40, 58 (1973); Erskine Florida Properties, Inc. v. First American Title Ins. Co., 557 So.2d 859 (Fla.1989) (title company was negligent in failing to search in official tract index); Cipriano v. Tocco, 772 F.Supp. 344 (E.D.Mich.1991) (indexing only in tract index was sufficient to give constructive notice, although statute required indexing in grantor-grantee index as well).

well) should be held to have notice of it.[25]

About twenty states have statutes relating to estoppel by deed.[26] They vary widely in content, but many of them contain language adopting the automatic inurement theory. Since most of these statutes say nothing about the rights of subsequent bona fide purchasers from the grantor,[27] some courts have construed them as mechanically favoring the estoppel grantee against such purchasers, and thus as rejecting the "chain of title" reasoning discussed above.[28] Such a construction seems both unwarranted and undesirable.

The statutes vary the law in other ways as well. Some of them explicitly recognize that a deed with no warranties will raise an estoppel, provided that it purports to convey some particular quantum of title.[29] Some provide that only a purported conveyance of a fee simple absolute will estop the grantor, while others recognize an estoppel from the purported conveyance of any interest in the land.[30] Some exclude from the effects of the estoppel a spouse who signs the deed only to waive a dower, curtesy, homestead, or other similar claim.[31] In most cases in which the facts would raise an estoppel under court-made principles but not under the narrower statute, the courts have felt free to treat the statute as not preempting the field.[32]

25. There is no discussion of this point in the published decisions, but at least one court has implicitly rejected the argument in the text. In Ryczkowski v. Chelsea Title & Guaranty Co., 85 Nev. 37, 449 P.2d 261 (1969) and Snow v. Pioneer Title Insurance Co., 84 Nev. 480, 444 P.2d 125 (1968), the court relieved title insurance companies of liability for their failure to find early-recorded deeds. It reasoned that under the chain-of-title theory such deeds must be deemed unrecorded, and thus within the scope of the exemption in the title policies in question for matters "not shown by the public records." Neither opinion describes the search procedures used by the title companies, but it is rather likely that both employed company-owned tract indexes, and that the deeds in question were missed as a consequence of simple negligence by the companies' searchers. If this is correct the cases are an appalling misapplication of the chain-of-title theory, and can hardly be considered indicative of the probable future course of the law on this point.

26. The development and content of the statutes is thoroughly examined in Swenson, Statutory Estoppel by Deed, 1950 Wash.U.L.Q. 361.

27. One exception is Virginia Code 1950, § 55–105, which provides that a subsequent purchaser is "not affected" by a deed recorded before its grantor has acquired legal or record title. This language is apparently intended to adopt the chain of title reasoning.

28. Compare Bernardy v. Colonial & United States Mortgage Co., 17 S.D. 637, 98 N.W. 166 (1904) (estoppel grantee prevails), with Ford v. Unity Church Society, 120 Mo. 498, 25 S.W. 394 (1893) (subsequent BFP prevails). See Swenson, supra note 26, at 372–75.

29. See, e.g. Colo.Rev.Stat.1973, § 38–30–104 Ill.Rev.Stat.1977, ch. 30, § 6; Miss.Code 1972, § 89–1–39. The same result is generally reached under court-made law; see cases cited at note 5, supra. See also Stevens v. Stevens, supra note 5, construing West's Rev.Code Wash.Ann. 64.04.070 as permitting after-acquired title to pass under a quitclaim which specifically stated that such title would pass. Cf. South Dakota Codified Laws 43–25–8 (after-acquired title does not pass under statutory form of quit-claim deed.)

30. Ark.Stat. § 50–404 (applies to any estate); Iowa Code Ann. § 557.4. Cf. West's Ann.Cal.Civ.Code § 1106 (fee simple only); Kan.Stat.Ann. 67–207 (indefeasible fee simple absolute only).

31. See Iowa Code Ann. § 557.4. Cf. Virginia Code 1950, § 55–52 (if spouse joins in estoppel deed, it will bar dower or curtesy claim to after-acquired title).

32. Robben v. Obering, 279 F.2d 381 (7th Cir.1960); Barberi v. Rothchild, 7 Cal.2d 537, 61 P.2d 760 (1936). But see Schultz v. Cities Service Oil Co., 149 Kan. 148, 86 P.2d 533 (1939), refusing to go beyond the statute and apply the doctrine of inurement to a mineral deed.

§ 11.6 Dedication

A dedication is a transfer of an interest in land from a private owner to the public generally or to a public body, such as a municipal corporation.[1] Such a transfer might, of course, be made by deed,[2] and many dedications are effected in this manner. But dedications are flexible and may be made in a variety of ways, including acts of an owner which could by no means constitute valid deeds under the statute of frauds.

Offers of Dedication. A valid dedication requires both an offer to dedicate by the owner and an acceptance by the public. The offer must comprise some words or acts on the part of the owner evincing an intent to turn the property over to the public. A clear oral statement will suffice, for compliance with the statute of frauds is unnecessary.[3] If a writing is used, it need not be executed with any particular formality.[4] Words written on a document used for some other purpose, such as a map of the land, will often do,[5] as when sales of lots are made by reference to a map which shows streets or other public areas.[6] Many states have formal statutory procedures under which the submission to and approval of a subdivision plat by a local government acts as an offer and acceptance of dedication of any public areas, such as streets and parks, shown on the plat.[7] But these procedures

---

§ 11.6

1. There is authority in some jurisdictions recognizing dedications to churches or other religious bodies, but the point of these cases seems to be simply to uphold a gift to an organization which is not yet in existence. See, e.g., Atkinson v. Bell, 18 Tex. 474 (1857); Boyce v. Kalbaugh, 47 Md. 334 (1877); Beatty v. Kurtz, 27 U.S. (2 Pet.) 566, 7 L.Ed. 521 (1829). See Tigner, Dedication—Part I, 15 Baylor L.Rev. 179, 179–80 (1963); 4 Tiffany, Real Property § 1098 (1939). This objective may be desirable enough, but it is doubtful whether extending the doctrine of dedication in this way is necessary to achieve it, and modern cases seldom do so.

2. In its earliest meaning, a dedication was a conveyance to the general public, and not to a particular governmental agency. Hence, it could have no specific grantee, and could not be accomplished by deed; see Lander v. Village of South Orange, 58 N.J. 509, 279 A.2d 633 (1971); 4 Tiffany, Real Property § 1099 (1937). But this usage is now obsolete, and dedications to municipal corporations and other agencies, including those made by express deeds, are generally recognized. See, e.g., Banks v. Wilhoite, 508 S.W.2d 580 (Ky.1974); Bolinger v. City of Bozeman, 158 Mont. 507, 493 P.2d 1062 (1972).

3. Cherokee Valley Farms, Inc. v. Summerville Elementary School District, 30 Cal. App.3d 579, 106 Cal.Rptr. 467 (1973); Greenco Corp. v. City of Virginia Beach, 214 Va. 201, 198 S.E.2d 496 (1973).

4. Cooper v. City of Great Bend, 200 Kan. 590, 438 P.2d 102 (1968). See generally 3 Am.L.Prop. § 12.133 (1952).

5. See Doyle v. Lowrey, 698 S.W.2d 56 (Mo. App.1985) (word "reserved" written on portion of street width, as shown on recorded plat, was sufficient to dedicate street easement to public); Ross v. Hall County Board of Commissioners, 235 Ga. 309, 219 S.E.2d 380 (1975); Moore v. Queener, 62 Tenn.App. 490, 464 S.W.2d 296 (1970); Allied American Investment Co. v. Pettit, 65 Ariz. 283, 179 P.2d 437 (1947). Cf. Muzzy v. Wilson, 259 Or. 512, 487 P.2d 875 (1971), in which the term "alley" was held insufficient evidence of intent to dedicate.

6. Rudisill v. Icenhour, 92 N.C.App. 741, 375 S.E.2d 682 (1989); Village of Climax Springs v. Camp, 681 S.W.2d 529 (Mo.App. 1984); Bonifay v. Dickson, 459 So.2d 1089 (Fla.App.1984); Carolina Land Co., Inc. v. Bland, 265 S.C. 98, 217 S.E.2d 16 (1975); Ocean Island Inn, Inc. v. City of Virginia Beach, 216 Va. 474, 220 S.E.2d 247 (1975); Andrews v. Country Club Hills, Inc., 18 N.C.App. 6, 195 S.E.2d 584 (1973); O'Quinn v. Burks, 231 So.2d 660 (La.App.1970). Cf. Manuel v. Fontenot, 457 So.2d 258 (La.App.1984) (where plat was recorded, not for purposes of selling lots, but merely to assist in description of parcel being donated to nonprofit school, road shown on plat was not dedicated to public).

7. See, e.g., Laughlin v. Morauer, 849 F.2d 122 (4th Cir.1988) (Virginia law); Donald v. City of Vancouver, 43 Wn.App. 880, 719 P.2d 966 (1986); Harshbarger v. County of Jerome, 107 Idaho 805, 693 P.2d 451 (1984); Ruby Drilling Co. v. Billingsly, 660 P.2d 377 (Wyo. 1983); Morris v. Parish of Jefferson, 487 So.2d 647 (La.App.1986) (substantial compliance

generally do not eliminate the possibility of a common law dedication as well.[8]

A common law dedication may be accomplished without any statement, written or spoken, for one who invites or merely permits the public to use his or her land for a long period may be held to have made an offer of implied dedication.[9] Some courts rationalize implied dedications on the theory that the owner, having admitted the public to use of the land over a long time, is estopped to deny permanent public access.[10] Traditionally, proof of the owner's intent to dedicate has been an essential element in an implied dedication,[11] but in recent years a few courts have virtually eliminated the need for actual intent. In these jurisdictions an implied dedication may result despite the owner's stout protestations of objection to the public use, if it actually occurred nonetheless. The best-known illustration is Gion v. City of Santa Cruz,[12] in which the general public had used a privately-

with statutory dedication procedure is sufficient); McClendon v. Shelby County, 484 So.2d 459 (Ala.Civ.App.1985), cert. denied 484 So.2d 465 (Ala.1986) (once dedication by recording of plat has occurred, parties purchasing surrounding land have constructive notice of the dedication); Kan.Stat.Ann. 12–406, applied in City of Council Grove v. Ossmann, 219 Kan. 120, 546 P.2d 1399 (1976); State ex rel. Herman v. Cardon, 112 Ariz. 548, 544 P.2d 657 (1976); Idaho Code §§ 50–1309ff, applied in Boise City By and Through Amyx v. Fails, 94 Idaho 840, 499 P.2d 326 (1972). But see Cavin v. Ostwalt, 76 N.C.App. 309, 332 S.E.2d 509 (1985) (under statute, N.C.Gen.Stat. 153A–333, approval of plat by county does not constitute acceptance of dedicated streets shown thereon); Stambaugh v. Township of Reed, 86 Pa. Cmwlth. 316, 484 A.2d 853 (1984), affirmed 98 Pa.Cmwlth. 306, 510 A.2d 1289 (1986); Lewis v. DeKalb County, 251 Ga. 100, 303 S.E.2d 112 (1983). A plat which does not indicate clearly that the streets are to become public may be insufficient as a statutory dedication; see Reiman v. Kale, 83 Ill.App.3d 773, 38 Ill.Dec. 671, 403 N.E.2d 1275 (1980).

8. McConiga v. Riches, 40 Wn.App. 532, 700 P.2d 331 (1985); City of Covington v. Glockner, 486 So.2d 837 (La.App.1986), writ denied 488 So.2d 693 (La.1986); State Department of Highways v. Town of Silverthorne, 707 P.2d 1017 (Colo.App.1985), dismissed 736 P.2d 411 (Colo.1987). One exception is Mass. Gen.Laws Ann. c. 84, § 4 et seq., applied in Uliasz v. Gillette, 357 Mass. 96, 256 N.E.2d 290 (1970).

9. Templeman v. Resmondo, 507 So.2d 494 (Ala.1987); Moreland v. Henson, 256 Ga. 685, 353 S.E.2d 181 (1987); Smith v. Sponheim, 399 N.W.2d 899 (S.D.1987); Las Vegas Pecan & Cattle Co. v. Zavala County, 682 S.W.2d 254 (Tex.1984); Rogers v. Sain, 679 S.W.2d 450 (Tenn.App.1984) (extended use by public shows intent to dedicate); Horton v. Wayne County, 243 Ga. 789, 256 S.E.2d 775 (1979); City of Daytona Beach v. Tona–Rama, Inc.,

271 So.2d 765 (Fla.App.1972), decision quashed 294 So.2d 73 (Fla.1974). The period must be "long", but no specific time is prescribed; it may be shorter than the statute of limitations for adverse possession or prescription. See Cole v. Dych, 535 S.W.2d 315 (Tenn.1976).

10. See CRW, Inc. v. Twin Lakes Property Owners Ass'n, Inc., 521 So.2d 939 (Ala.1988); Agnew v. Haskell, 71 Or.App. 357, 692 P.2d 650 (1984); Swift v. Kniffen, 706 P.2d 296 (Alaska 1985) (recognizing estoppel theory but refusing to apply it in absence of an oral grant by owner and detrimental reliance by public). A classic statement of this theory is McCormick v. Baltimore, 45 Md. 512 (1877).

11. See City of Fort Payne v. Fort Payne Athletic Association, Inc., 567 So.2d 1260 (Ala. 1990); Stone v. International Paper Co., 293 S.C. 138, 359 S.E.2d 83 (App.1987); Star Island Associates v. City of St. Petersburg Beach, 433 So.2d 998 (Fla.App.1983); McConiga v. Riches, 40 Wn.App. 532, 700 P.2d 331 (1985); State Department of Highways v. Town of Silverthorne, 707 P.2d 1017 (Colo.App.1985); Jarvis v. Powers, 80 N.C.App. 355, 343 S.E.2d 195 (1986); City of Alexandria v. Kara Baptist Academy, Inc., 680 S.W.2d 416 (Mo.App.1984) (mere presence of word "public" on area of recorded plat was insufficient to show intent to dedicate it); Greenco Corp. v. City of Virginia Beach, 214 Va. 201, 198 S.E.2d 496 (1973); Zimmerman v. Newport, 416 P.2d 622 (Okl. 1966); Gooding v. Sulphur Springs Country Club, 422 S.W.2d 522 (Tex.Civ.App.1967).

12. 2 Cal.3d 29, 84 Cal.Rptr. 162, 465 P.2d 50 (1970), noted in 18 U.C.L.A.L.Rev. 795 (1971); 44 So.Cal.L.Rev. 1092 (1971); 4 Loyala L.A.L.Rev. 438 (1971). See also Lincoln Parish Police Jury v. Davis, 559 So.2d 935 (La. App.1990) (relaxing the intent requirement); City of Los Angeles v. Venice Peninsula Properties, 205 Cal.App.3d 1522, 253 Cal.Rptr. 331 (1988) (distinguishing Gion on the ground that the lagoon in question was neither a "beach or shoreline" nor a public road, and that there

owned beach for many years despite the owners' half-hearted and ineffectual efforts to stop the use. The California Supreme Court held that a dedication had occurred, with intent to dedicate being inferred as a matter of law from public use for the prescriptive period and the inadequacy of the owners' attempts to halt it. The "intent" thus found is obviously highly artificial.[13] The decision seems to recognize a sort of dedication by prescription, similar to an ordinary prescriptive easement [14] except that the adverse use is by the public generally rather than by any identifiable person or group.[15] Moreover, the *Gion* court presumed, from the long public use, the hostility required for prescription.[16] From the viewpoint of the local government, this approach combines the most advantageous features of prescription and "standard" implied dedication, eliminating the need to prove explicitly either intent or hostility. The *Gion* decision has been controversial, and many courts continue to insist that the public body satisfy in full the elements of dedication or prescription, rather than combining the two.[17]

An effective dedication can be made only by the owner of the land; one cannot transfer more rights than one has. If a possessory estate in fee simple is to be dedicated, it is necessary for the holders of all private interests, such as mortgagees, lessees, easement holders, and the like to join.[18] However, if only an easement is dedicated, the joinder of those whose rights are not inconsistent with the easement is unnecessary. For example,

was no evidence of public use which even approximated the extent of the public use in *Gion*); Seaway Co. v. Attorney General, 375 S.W.2d 923 (Tex.Civ.App.1964), refused n.r.e. The reasoning of the *Gion* case was rejected in Department of Natural Resources v. Mayor & Council of Ocean City, 274 Md. 1, 332 A.2d 630 (1975), and Automotive Products Corp. v. Provo City Corp., 28 Utah 2d 358, 502 P.2d 568 (1972). See generally Note, 48 N.Y.U.L.Rev. 369 (1973).

13. After *Gion* was decided, the California legislature amended West's Ann.Cal.Civ.Code § 813 to permit an owner to record a notice giving the public permission to use his or her land and thereby conclusively rebutting prescription; it also enacted Civil Code § 1009 to prohibit all dedications arising out of public use (whether or not a notice under § 813 has been recorded) unless the owner makes an express written offer of dedication.

14. See generally § 8.7, supra; Thomas v. City of Rainsville, 502 So.2d 346 (Ala.1987).

15. See Department of Natural Resources v. Mayor and Council of Ocean City, 274 Md. 1, 332 A.2d 630 (1975). It remains unclear whether, under the reasoning of the *Gion* case, an owner can protect his rights from both dedication and prescription by posting signs which grant the public permission to enter but purport to make that permission revocable; this technique is often employed, particularly by owners of urban office buildings which are set back from the public sidewalk. See Note, supra note 10, at 374. It is also unclear whether the California Supreme Court would have recognized a dedication if

public use had been for less than the prescriptive period (which is only a brief 5 years in California and was easily satisfied in *Gion.*)

16. Most cases take the opposite tack, presuming permission rather than hostility from the public use in the absence of any specific evidence; see e.g., Ford v. Alabama By-Products Corp., 392 So.2d 217 (Ala.1980); Daytona Beach v. Tona–Rama, Inc., 294 So.2d 73 (Fla. 1974). But there is some authority favoring the *Gion* court's position; see Daytona Beach v. Tona–Rama, Inc., supra, at 9 (Boyd, J., dissenting).

17. State ex rel. Haman v. Fox, 100 Idaho 140, 594 P.2d 1093 (1979); Daytona Beach v. Tona–Rama, Inc., supra note 16; Department of Natural Resources v. Cropper, 274 Md. 25, 332 A.2d 644 (1975); Department of Natural Resources v. Mayor and Council of Ocean City, supra note 15. Both theories were held to be satisfied in Seaway Co. v. Attorney General, 375 S.W.2d 923 (Tex.Civ.App.1964), refused n.r.e. Cf. Nature Conservancy v. Machipongo Club, Inc., 419 F.Supp. 390 (E.D.Va.1976), affirmed in part, reversed in part on other grounds 571 F.2d 1294 (4th Cir.1978), in which the court concluded that there was no meaningful distinction between implied dedication and prescription. See generally 6A Powell, Real Property ¶ 926[2] (1980).

18. Lane Title & Trust Co. v. Brannan, 103 Ariz. 272, 440 P.2d 105 (1968) (mortgagee must join); Lexington–Fayette County Planning & Zoning Commission v. Levas, 504 S.W.2d 685 (Ky.1973) (tenant cannot dedicate without landlord's joinder).

a public easement may be dedicated along the route of a preexisting nonexclusive private easement without creating any conflict between the two.[19]

A dedicator need not necessarily transfer all that he or she has, and controversy sometimes develops as to precisely what rights have been dedicated.[20] The donor can, of course, explicitly specify the interest being dedicated;[21] if this is not done, the courts are likely to examine the nature of the expected public use and infer from it the probable intent of the parties. Thus, roads and streets are commonly deemed to be easements[22] while park and school sites are somewhat more likely to be considered possessory estates in the absence of evidence of a contrary intent.[23] Some states regard dedications under statutory procedures, even of roads and streets, to give the public possessory estates in fee simple, while common law dedications are thought to convey only easements.[24]

Whatever the interest conveyed, the donor may impose restrictions on the use of the dedicated land, either by way of covenants running with the land or more commonly by the granting of a defeasible interest which leaves a reversionary right in the grantor, to become possessory if the restrictions are ever violated.[25] For example, land dedicated as a school site may be

19. See Jennings v. High Farms Corp., 28 A.D.2d 693, 281 N.Y.S.2d 110 (1967). If the public easement involves construction of improvements which would interfere with the private easement, the private easement-holder will have an action for removal of the improvements or for compensation; see Sargent v. Brunner Housing Corp., 31 A.D.2d 823, 297 N.Y.S.2d 879 (1969), affirmed 27 N.Y.2d 513, 312 N.Y.S.2d 993, 261 N.E.2d 105 (1970).

20. Jacobs v. Lyon Township, 181 Mich. App. 386, 448 N.W. 861 (1989) judgment vacated, case remanded for further findings of fact, 434 Mich. 922, 455 N.W.2d 715 (1990) (dedication of public streets which terminate at the edge of navigable water inherently implies a right to public access to water). For example, whether an easement or a possessory estate was dedicated will usually determine whether the public or the donor is entitled to minerals in the ground; see Annot., 62 A.L.R.2d 1311 (1958). But see City of Evanston v. Robinson, 702 P.2d 1283 (Wyo.1985) (statutory street dedication, although in "fee simple," did not convey underlying mineral rights to city).

21. See, e.g., Park County Rod and Gun Club v. Department of Highways, 163 Mont. 372, 517 P.2d 352 (1973); Rainier Avenue Corp. v. City of Seattle, 80 Wn.2d 362, 494 P.2d 996 (1972), certiorari denied 409 U.S. 983, 93 S.Ct. 321, 34 L.Ed.2d 247 (1972); City of Bartlesville v. Ambler, 499 P.2d 433 (Okl. 1971), construing wording on plat to dedicate only an easement.

22. Village of Kalkaska v. Shell Oil Co., 433 Mich. 348, 446 N.W.2d 91 (1989); Town of Moorcroft v. Lang, 761 P.2d 96 (Wyo.1988) (dedication of streets does not carry mineral rights); Jones v. Deeter, 152 Cal.App.3d 798,

199 Cal.Rptr. 825 (1984); Southwestern Bell Telephone Co. v. State Corp. Commission, 233 Kan. 375, 664 P.2d 798 (1983); Morad v. Brown, 549 P.2d 312 (Wyo.1976); Board of County Commissioners v. Cottingim, 448 P.2d 1014 (Okl.1969). See 3 Am.L.Prop. § 12.132 notes 10–12 (1952). A contrary result is often reached if the dedication is under a statutory procedure; see cases cited in note 19, infra. Note that if only an easement is dedicated, the donor continues to hold the so-called "underlying fee" or servient estate, and may use it for in any way which does not interfere with the public easement; see, e.g., City of Daytona Beach v. Tona–Rama, 294 So.2d 73 (Fla.1974).

23. See Gion v. City of Santa Cruz, supra note 12, at n. 3; Washington Boulevard Beach Co. v. City of Los Angeles, 38 Cal.App.2d 135, 100 P.2d 828 (1940). But see Rainier Avenue Corp. v. City of Seattle, supra note 21, presuming a dedication for a park gives only an easement.

24. See, e.g., Becnel v. Citrus Lands of Louisiana, Inc., 429 So.2d 459 (La.App.1983); Bonifay v. Dickson, 459 So.2d 1089 (Fla.App.1984); Horsham Township v. Weiner, 435 Pa. 35, 255 A.2d 126 (1969); Gunn v. Delhi Township, 8 Mich.App. 278, 154 N.W.2d 598 (1967); Moeur v. City of Tempe, 3 Ariz.App. 196, 412 P.2d 878 (1966); Village of Folsom v. Alford, 204 So.2d 100 (La.App.1967).

25. Historic Licking Riverside Civic Ass'n v. City of Covington, 774 S.W.2d 436 (Ky. 1989); Coral Gables v. Old Cutler Bay Homeowners Corp., 529 So.2d 1188 (Fla.App.1988); Donald v. City of Vancouver, 43 Wn.App. 880, 719 P.2d 966 (1986) (restriction in form of fee simple defeasible); Wheeler v. Monroe, 86

explicitly restricted to use for school purposes. The public body is bound by such restrictions unless it employs its power of eminent domain to enlarge its rights, in which event payment of compensation may well be necessary.[26] Moreover, courts and statutes often infer and enforce a use restriction merely from the fact that a particular use was mentioned or contemplated at the time of the dedication.[27]

Acceptance. A dedication, like an ordinary conveyance by deed, must be accepted to be complete. But dedications impose practical burdens of maintenance and supervision on local governments which they may not wish to assume. For this reason, acceptance is not presumed as it is for deeds between private parties;[28] instead, affirmative proof of acceptance is necessary.[29] The acceptance may take any one of several forms. A formal resolution of the local government's legislative body or some similar action will certainly suffice.[30] Much less formal behavior can also constitute an acceptance: taking over of maintenance or construction of improvements,[31]

N.M. 296, 523 P.2d 540 (1974), appeal dismissed 419 U.S. 1014, 95 S.Ct. 487, 42 L.Ed.2d 288 (1974); Stephenson v. County of Monroe, 43 A.D.2d 897, 351 N.Y.S.2d 232 (1974); Leverton v. Laird, 190 N.W.2d 427 (Iowa 1971); State Highway Department v. Alexander, 222 Ga. 354, 149 S.E.2d 788 (1966); In re Application of Mareck, 257 Minn. 222, 100 N.W.2d 758 (1960). In McKernon v. City of Reno, 76 Nev. 452, 357 P.2d 597 (1960), the court refused to read into the dedication a reversionary interest in favor of the donor where none had been explicitly reserved.

26. See, e.g., State of Louisiana v. Richardson, 453 So.2d 572 (La.App.1984); Burns v. Board of Supervisors, 226 Va. 506, 312 S.E.2d 731 (1984) (under state statute, dedication of streets in subdivision inherently transfers easements for water and sewer lines under streets to public as well; but public body has no title to such actual lines as have been installed by dedicator, and may acquire them only by purchase or condemnation); Ink v. City of Canton, 4 Ohio St.2d 51, 212 N.E.2d 574 (1965); Comment, The Effect of Condemnation Proceedings by Eminent Domain upon a Possibility of Reverter or Power of Termination, 19 Vill.L.Rev. 137 (1973); Annot., 60 A.L.R.3d 581 (1974).

27. See, e.g., Ackerman v. Steisel, 104 A.D.2d 940, 480 N.Y.S.2d 556 (1984), affirmed 66 N.Y.2d 833, 498 N.Y.S.2d 364, 489 N.E.2d 251 (1985) (parking of sanitation trucks on land dedicated for park use was impermissible); Lord v. City of Wilmington, 332 A.2d 414 (Del.Ch.1975), affirmed 378 A.2d 635 (Del. 1977); Stephenson v. County of Monroe, 43 A.D.2d 897, 351 N.Y.S.2d 232 (1974); Gallagher v. City of Omaha, 189 Neb. 598, 204 N.W.2d 157 (1973); Archbold v. McLaughlin, 181 F.Supp. 175 (D.D.C.1960). But see Mainer v. Canal Authority, 467 So.2d 989 (Fla.1985) (absent fraud or bad faith, public body may use land for any purpose after it has been acquired by condemnation, settlement, or do-

nation); Wheeler v. Monroe, 86 N.M. 296, 523 P.2d 540 (1974), appeal dismissed 419 U.S. 1014, 95 S.Ct. 487, 42 L.Ed.2d 288 (1974), refusing to infer any such restrictions in a statutory dedication. See generally 6A Powell, Real Property ¶ 926[3] (1980), at notes 73–79.

28. See § 11.3, supra, at notes 29–32. Of course, acceptance of a deed is a perfectly satisfactory method of accepting the dedication of the land it conveys; see Rolleston v. Sea Island Properties, Inc., 254 Ga. 183, 327 S.E.2d 489 (1985), cert. denied 474 U.S. 823, 106 S.Ct. 77, 88 L.Ed.2d 63 (1985).

29. Dotson v. Payne, 71 N.C.App. 691, 323 S.E.2d 362 (1984); Chandler v. Independent School District, 625 P.2d 620 (Okl.1981); Orange County v. Chandler–Sherman Corp., 54 Cal.App.3d 561, 126 Cal.Rptr. 765 (1976); Jackson v. Byrn, 216 Tenn. 537, 393 S.W.2d 137 (1965).

30. See, e.g., Worley Highway District v. Yacht Club, 116 Idaho 219, 775 P.2d 111 (1989); Delta County Board of Commissioners v. Sherill, 757 P.2d 1085 (Colo.App.1987); Vachon v. Town of Lisbon, 295 A.2d 255 (Me. 1972) (lease by town to school district was effective acceptance by town.)

31. Baugus v. Wessinger, 303 S.C. 412, 401 S.E.2d 169 (1991); Bryant v. Kern & Co., Inc., 196 Ga.App. 165, 395 S.E.2d 620 (1990); Concerned Citizens v. Holden Beach Enterprises, Inc., 95 N.C.App. 38, 381 S.E.2d 810 (1989); Ledlow v. City of Pell City, 497 So.2d 86 (Ala. 1986) (20 years usually required); Smith v. Sponheim, 399 N.W.2d 899 (S.D.1987); City of Canon City v. Cingoranelli, 740 P.2d 546 (Colo. App.1987). Several states have statutes providing that public use or maintenance for some period of years will make a roadway public; see Hillelson v. Grover, 105 A.D.2d 484, 480 N.Y.S.2d 779 (1984) (10 years use and maintenance); Wilson v. Seminole Coal, Inc., 175 W.Va. 518, 336 S.E.2d 30 (1985) (10 years

cessation of property taxation,[32] or any other acts indicating the government's assumption of control over the land. If the dedication is made under a statutory procedure, approval of the donor's plat is generally considered a sufficient acceptance of areas marked on the plat for public use.[33] Finally, long and substantial public use of land offered for dedication will constitute an acceptance even in the absence of any action by the local government.[34]

Some sort of acceptance must occur within a "reasonable" time after the offer of dedication is made, but very long time periods have often been approved.[35] The donor may withdraw the offer of dedication at any time prior to acceptance, and withdrawal may be inferred from acts of the donor which are inconsistent with the dedication, such as selling the subject land or fencing it to keep the public out.[36] However, a sale of land by reference to

use and maintenance); Guzzardo v. Campo, 486 So.2d 912 (La.App.1986), writ denied 488 So.2d 1026 (La.1986) (3 years maintenance); Sun Plaza West Dev. Corp. v. City of Holmes Beach, 465 So.2d 542 (Fla.App.1985) (4 years maintenance, even if completed many years prior to the present action, is sufficient to establish dedication). See also Bonifay v. Dickson, 459 So.2d 1089 (Fla.App.1984) (4–year Florida statute, which limits acceptance to the width of roadway which has actually been maintained by the public body, is not exclusive, and acceptance of a common law dedication by public use may encompass a wider strip than actually maintained); Kratina v. Board of Commissioners, 219 Kan. 499, 548 P.2d 1232 (1976); State v. Birch, 115 N.J.Super. 457, 280 A.2d 210 (1971); Incorporated Town of Mountain View v. Lackey, 225 Ark. 1, 278 S.W.2d 653 (1955); City of Grand Forks v. Flom, 79 N.D. 289, 56 N.W.2d 324 (1952).

32. LaSalle National Bank v. City of Chicago, 19 Ill.App.3d 883, 312 N.E.2d 322 (1974); United States v. 329.22 Acres of Land, 307 F.Supp. 34 (M.D.Fla.1968), affirmed 418 F.2d 551 (5th Cir.1969).

33. Moeur v. City of Tempe, 3 Ariz.App. 196, 412 P.2d 878 (1966); see Annot., 11 A.L.R.2d 524, 574 (1950). Cf. Thompson v. Town of Portland, 159 Conn. 107, 266 A.2d 893 (1970) (approval by planning commission was insufficient acceptance, where statute required an "official layout" of streets by the town.)

34. Laughlin v. Morauer, 849 F.2d 122 (4th Cir.1988) (70 years public use); Hays v. Vanek, 217 Cal.App.3d 271, 266 Cal.Rptr. 856 (1989) Moreland v. Henson, 256 Ga. 685, 353 S.E.2d 181 (1987) Hughes v. Town of Mexico Beach, 455 So.2d 566 (Fla.App.1984) (acceptance by public use of some streets in platted subdivision constitutes acceptance of all streets shown, absent proof of a more limited acceptance); State ex rel. v. Metropolitan Government of Nashville and Davidson County, 679 S.W.2d 946 (Tenn.1984); Kirkland v. Gross, 286 S.C. 193, 332 S.E.2d 546 (1985)

(public use for 20 years required); Haley v. City of Rapid City, 269 N.W.2d 398 (S.D.1978); Viscardi v. Pajestka, 576 S.W.2d 16 (Tex.1978); Stevenson v. Cosgrove, 38 Ill.App.3d 672, 347 N.E.2d 857 (1976); City of Hollywood v. Zinkil, 283 So.2d 581 (Fla.App.1973), quashed in part and remanded 321 So.2d 65 (Fla.1975), appeal after remand 403 So.2d 528 (Fla.App.1981); Moseley v. Searcy, 363 S.W.2d 561 (Mo.1962). Limited or sporadic public may not suffice; see, e.g., Vestavia Hills Board of Education v. Utz, 530 So.2d 1378 (Ala.1988); Luchetti v. Bandler, 108 N.M. 682, 777 P.2d 1326 (App. 1989), cert. denied 108 N.M. 681, 777 P.2d 1325 (1989).

35. See, e.g., Stozenski v. Borough of Forty Fort, 456 Pa. 5, 317 A.2d 602 (1974) (21 years by statute); Osborne v. Town of North Wilkesboro, 280 N.C. 696, 187 S.E.2d 102 (1972) (15 years by statute); Town of Glenarden v. Lewis, 261 Md. 1, 273 A.2d 140 (1971) (48 years); Ackerman v. Spring Lake Township, 12 Mich. App. 498, 163 N.W.2d 230 (1968) (26 years). But see Estojak v. Mazsa, 522 Pa. 353, 562 A.2d 271 (1989) (21 years delay excessive; dedication failed); Potis v. Coon, 344 Pa.Super. 443, 496 A.2d 1188 (1985) (acceptance must occur within 21 years by statute); Wells v. Miller, 42 Wn.App. 94, 708 P.2d 1223 (1985) (opening for public use must occur within five years by statute); Meder v. City of Milford, 190 Conn. 72, 458 A.2d 1158 (1983) (69 years too long.)

36. See Vivian v. Roscommon County Board of Road Commissioners, 433 Mich. 511, 446 N.W.2d 161 (1989) (landowner's erection of fence blocking road site acts to withdraw offer of dedication); Cavin v. Ostwalt, 76 N.C.App. 309, 332 S.E.2d 509 (1985); Ocean Island Inn, Inc. v. City of Virginia Beach, 216 Va. 474, 220 S.E.2d 247 (1975); Mauck v. Bailey, 247 Md. 434, 231 A.2d 685 (1967); 6A Powell, Real Property ¶ 926 [2] (1980), at note 59. But see Village of Climax Springs v. Camp, 681 S.W.2d 529 (Mo.App.1984) (a quitclaim deed by the dedicator to another party, prior to acceptance of the dedication, is insufficient to act as a withdrawal of the dedica-

a plat showing public streets is generally held to create private easements for access in favor of the lot owners as well as to constitute a public dedication.[37] The donor's later withdrawal of the dedication cannot affect these private rights, which can only be given up by the lot owners themselves.[38] The same principle applies if, after dedication, the local government vacates the dedicated land; the private easements remain in effect unless released by their owners.[39]

Relinquishment of Dedicated Land. After a dedication has been accepted, the donor cannot take the land back unilaterally; however, the local government may give up its rights by a formal resolution vacating the property,[40] or by abandonment. Mere nonuse, even for a very long time, will not constitute an abandonment unless it is accompanied by some further evidence that the local government no longer intends to assert rights in the land.[41] When public land is vacated or abandoned, a dispute often arises as to who is entitled to it. If the public's interest was only an easement, the land is simply freed of the servitude and the owners of the servient estate (usually those who own the abutting lots) now have unencumbered possession.[42] But if the public interest was a possessory fee simple, the cases are divided as between the original donor and the owners of the abutting land. The donor will usually prevail if he or she expressly reserved a reversionary

tion). See generally Annot., 36 A.L.R.4th 625 (1985).

37. Price v. Walker, 95 N.C.App. 712, 383 S.E.2d 686 (1989); Foreal Homes, Inc. v. Incorporated Village of Muttontown, 128 A.D.2d 585, 512 N.Y.S.2d 849 (1987); Bonifay v. Dickson, 459 So.2d 1089 (Fla.App.1984) (private easement for access to beach across land dedicated as a public easement); State ex rel. Riddle v. Department of Highways, 154 W.Va. 722, 179 S.E.2d 10 (1971); Stanfield v. Brewton, 228 Ga. 92, 184 S.E.2d 352 (1971); United States v. Certain Land in County of Worcester, 311 F.Supp. 1039 (D.Md.1970); Dykes v. City of Houston, 406 S.W.2d 176 (Tex.1966); Highland Sewer and Water Authority v. Engelbach, 208 Pa.Super. 1, 220 A.2d 390 (1966); Koff v. Frank, 22 Misc.2d 551, 194 N.Y.S.2d 753 (1959). On the scope of the implied easement, see § 8.6 supra.

38. Rudisill v. Icenhour, 92 N.C.App. 741, 375 S.E.2d 682 (1989); Riek v. Binnie, 352 Pa.Super. 246, 507 A.2d 865 (1986); Bond v. Dunmire, 129 Ill.App.3d 796, 84 Ill.Dec. 862, 473 N.E.2d 78 (1984); Carolina Land Co., Inc. v. Bland, 265 S.C. 98, 217 S.E.2d 16 (1975); Feldman v. Monroe Township Board, 51 Mich. App. 752, 216 N.W.2d 628 (1974). See 3 Am. L.Prop. § 12.134 note 12 (1952).

39. McPhillips v. Brodbeck, 289 Ala. 148, 266 So.2d 592 (1972); Potter v. Citation Coal Corp., 445 S.W.2d 128 (Ky.1969); Highway Holding Co. v. Yara Engineering Corp., 22 N.J. 119, 123 A.2d 511 (1956).

40. See, e.g., Etzler v. Mondale, 266 Minn. 353, 123 N.W.2d 603 (1963). In some jurisdictions a court order approving the vacation is necessary; see Bangle v. Green, 34 Mich.App. 287, 191 N.W.2d 160 (1971).

41. Cruz v. City of Coral Gables, 560 So.2d 1196 (Fla.App.1990); Worley Highway District v. Yacht Club, 116 Idaho 219, 775 P.2d 111 (1989); Raftopoulos v. Farrow, 691 P.2d 1160 (Colo.App.1984) (no abandonment implied from nonuse, nondevelopment, failure to include land on official county highway map, or statement by county commissioner that county had no interest in land); D.C. Transit Systems, Inc. v. State Roads Commission, 259 Md. 675, 270 A.2d 793 (1970), appeal after remand 265 Md. 622, 290 A.2d 807 (1972); Calhoun County v. Wilson, 425 S.W.2d 846 (Tex.Civ. App.1968), refused n.r.e.; Moore v. Kuljis, 207 So.2d 604 (Miss.1967). Cf. Walton v. City of Clermont, 109 So.2d 403 (Fla.App.1959), cert. denied 115 So.2d 5 (Fla.1959) (city's failure to object to planting of trees in public street was not an abandonment.) See also Red Rock Petroleum Co. v. City of Choctaw, 689 P.2d 1286 (Okl.App.1984), in which the court upheld the statutory authority of the Oklahoma courts to determine whether a dedicated street has been vacated, as against the argument that this judicial power unconstitutionally encroached on the municipality's powers.

42. Iowa State Highway Commission v. Dubuque Sand & Gravel Co., 258 N.W.2d 153 (Iowa 1977); State ex rel. State Highway Commission v. Johns, 507 S.W.2d 75 (Mo.App. 1974); Potter v. Citation Coal Co., supra note 39; Burkart v. City of Fort Lauderdale, 156 So.2d 752 (Fla.App.1963), quashed 168 So.2d 65 (Fla.1964); Chickasha Cotton Oil Co. v. Town of Maysville, 249 F.2d 542 (10th Cir. 1957). Note, however, that existing private easements in favor of other surrounding owners may continue to exist despite the vacation by the public; see notes 37, 39, supra.

interest.[43] If this was not done, the courts often find a way to award the land to the abutting owners.[44] This result is sometimes hard to explain in theoretical terms, but it generally represents sounder policy, particularly in the case of a long, thin strip of land created by the vacation of a street.

Compelled Dedications. Perhaps the most controversial aspect of dedications is the extent to which local governments can force developers to donate land for various public purposes by conditioning the granting of building permits or other development approvals on such dedications. Generally developers have little objection to dedicating streets and storm and sanitary sewers to the public, since maintenance of these facilities would be a financial burden on the lot owners if they remained private. But many local governments also demand dedications of land for school and park purposes, and cash fees in lieu of land, ostensibly covering the cost of current or projected expansion of water and sewerage treatment facilities, have also become common. These demands are costly, and are often resisted by developers. In general, the courts have approved such compulsory dedications only if the facilities thus provided have some reasonable nexus with the expected burdens on public services imposed by the new residents of the development. Judicial formulations of this test vary widely,[45] and statutes may also play a role.[46] More extended discussion is found in another section of this book.[47]

§ 11.7   Adverse Possession

Adverse possession is a strange and wonderful system, whereby the occupation of another's land gains the occupier title[1]—but only if the

43. Trustees of Howard College v. McNabb, 288 Ala. 564, 263 So.2d 664 (1972); Peninsular Point, Inc. v. South Georgia Dairy Co–Op., 251 So.2d 690 (Fla.App.1971); Grant v. Koenig, 67 Misc.2d 1028, 325 N.Y.S.2d 428 (1971), affirmed 39 A.D.2d 1000, 333 N.Y.S.2d 591 (1972).

44. Christian v. Purdy, 60 Wn.App. 798, 808 P.2d 164 (1991); Tidewater Area Charities, Inc. v. Harbour Gate Owners Association, Inc., 240 Va. 221, 396 S.E.2d 661 (1990); Glass v. Carnes, 260 Ga. 627, 398 S.E.2d 7 (1990); Central Metairie Civic Ass'n, Inc. v. Jefferson Parish Council, 484 So.2d 706 (La.App.1986), writ denied 486 So.2d 751 (La.1986); Umpqua Sav. & Loan Ass'n v. Security Bank, 71 Or. App. 555, 693 P.2d 57 (1984) (under city ordinance vacating dedicated street, title passed to abutting lot owners; bank's deed of trust on one such lot, which included "all rights" in the lot, covered the additional land acquired by virtue of the street vacation). Statutory wording often leads courts to this conclusion; see, e.g., Peterson v. City of Reno, 84 Nev. 60, 436 P.2d 417 (1968); Piper v. Reder, 44 Ill. App.2d 431, 195 N.E.2d 224 (1963); City of Dayton v. Woodgeard, 116 Ohio App. 248, 187 N.E.2d 921 (1962) (fee in vacated street "accretes" to abutting lot owners under statute). Absent a statute, the same result might be reached by construing the original donor/developer's deeds of the lots as implicitly convey-

ing the right to abutting dedicated streets if they are ever vacated.

45. Compare Krughoff v. City of Naperville, 68 Ill.2d 352, 12 Ill.Dec. 185, 369 N.E.2d 892 (1977), with Associated Home Builders of Greater East Bay, Inc. v. City of Walnut Creek, 4 Cal.3d 633, 94 Cal.Rptr. 630, 484 P.2d 606 (1971), appeal dismissed 404 U.S. 878, 92 S.Ct. 202, 30 L.Ed.2d 159 (1971). See Annot., 43 A.L.R.3d 862 (1972).

46. See, e.g., West's Rev.Code Wash.Ann. 35.21.710, 82.02.020, limiting local governments to a 0.25% excise tax in lieu of all other fees, but still permitting certain dedications of land; West's Ann.Cal.Gov't Code § 65995, construed in Shapell Industries, Inc. v. Governing Bd. of Milpitas Unified School Dist., 1 Cal. App.4th 218, 1 Cal.Rptr.2d 818 (1991).

47. See § 9.14, supra.

§ 11.7

1. Though the adverse possessor gains legal title, it is not likely to be "marketable" title for a purchaser. This is because, first, the title is subject to litigation and, second, conveyancers generally have the notion that title must be marketable of record. See Rehoboth Heights Development Co. v. Marshall, 15 Del.Ch. 314, 137 A. 83 (1927) (adverse possession title sure enough to be marketable); Sim-

occupation is indeed wrongful. To gain title the wrongful occupant must be in "adverse possession" for at least the statutory period of limitation on the owner's action to recover possession. So, there are two aspects, the statutory period and the doctrine of adverse possession, which is a judicial gloss on the statute. In most cases if an owner has a possessory action, the defendant's possession will be "adverse," but there can be exceptions.[2] Title gained is usually in fee simple absolute, but in cases when the fee is divided between a present possessory and future estates, the adverse possessor will get only the possessory title—that is, title replacing that of the one who had a possessory action running.[3] Adverse possession title is not derived from the former owner but begins a new chain of title. Thus, adverse possession provides a rare instance in which original title may arise in a mature society.

Few adverse possession cases deal with the statute of limitations itself. Title cannot be gained if the owner is one against whom the statute will not run. For this reason, title cannot be gained to land owned by the United States, the states, and, at least as to land held for public use, by local governments.[4] Statutes of limitation contain various tolling conditions, such as for owners who are insane, infants, imprisoned, absent from the state, or in military service when the cause of action first accrues.[5] Tolling provisions may more or less delay the statute's running and so delay acquisition of title.[6]

Nearly all the many adverse possession decisions deal with the definition and application of the judicial doctrine of adverse possession. A typical formulation, abstracted from the opinions to be cited, is that possession, to be adverse, must be: (1) actual, (2) open and notorious, (3) hostile, (4) exclusive, and (5) continuous. Sometimes courts add a couple of other troublesome elements, probably subsets of "hostile," called (6) claim of right or of title and (7) good faith. Statutes, often special ones that shorten the normal limitation period, sometimes require "color of title" or payment of taxes,

---

is v. McElroy, 160 N.Y. 156, 54 N.E. 674 (1899) (not marketable). The only certain way to make the title marketable is to establish a paper record by a favorable court decision. See § 10.12, infra.

2. For instance, a holdover tenant or tenant at sufferance may be dispossessed, but his possession is not considered adverse. And, because, as we will see, adverse possession must be "open and notorious," it would seem possible for the owner to have a possessory action against one whose occupancy was underground or otherwise hidden and thus not adverse.

3. Heath v. Turner, 309 N.C. 483, 308 S.E.2d 244 (1983); Cessna v. Carroll, 178 Kan. 650, 290 P.2d 803 (1955) (dictum); Fitzgerald v. Fitzgerald, 194 Va. 925, 76 S.E.2d 204 (1953); Annot., 58 A.L.R.2d 299, 302–05 (1958); Restatement of Property, § 222, Comment f (1944). In some cases, however, life tenants have been allowed to possess adversely to reversioners or remaindermen after the life ten-

ancy has been terminated by repudiation, renunciation, or the like. Annot., supra.

4. See exhaustive Annot., 55 A.L.R.2d 554 (1957). But see Mackinac Island Dev. Co. v. Burton Abstract and Title Co., 132 Mich.App. 504, 349 N.W.2d 191 (1984) (where the adverse possessor's hostility and the notoriety of its possession were strongly proved by the fact that, during possession it negotiated a sale of an easement over the land to the state, acquisition of title from the state, under specific statute, was permitted). Of course, a state government may *acquire* title by adverse possession; see Tanner v. Brasher, 254 Ga. 41, 326 S.E.2d 218 (1985).

5. See, e.g., Ill.—S.H.A. ch. 83, ¶ 9; New Jersey Stats.Ann. 2A:14–21; West's Rev.Code Wash.Ann. 4.16.080, 4.16.090.

6. See, e.g., Rehoboth Heights Development Co. v. Marshall, 15 Del.Ch. 314, 137 A. 83 (1927).

perhaps combined with good faith.[7] The balance of this section will be organized under the elements just listed.

With an important exception to be noted, adverse possession must be "actual." This certainly requires some degree of physical occupation; how much is the subject of many, many cases. Because the question is one of mixed fact and law, we simply have to reconcile ourselves to a wide range of judicial results. Of course the clearest case is one who fences a parcel, has substantial structures on it, and maintains visible marks of use all over it. Fences or walls are not essential, though courts are sensitive to some marks that show the boundaries of possession, such as partial fence lines, mowed grass, cultivation lines, trees or shrubs, paved areas, or other objects or improvements so located as to suggest bounds.[8] Possessory acts must be substantial and must leave some physical evidence, not only to be actual but also to meet the overlapping requirement that they be "open and notorious." If a court concludes the acts are too insubstantial or temporary, there is no actual possession.[9] Seasonal or sporadic use of unenclosed land gives rise to many difficult questions of actual possession, as well as of open and notorious and continuous possession. Most such cases involve grazing animals, cutting timber, or harvesting natural crops. Some decisions seem to adopt a rule that these activities cannot be sufficient for adverse possession of unenclosed land, but others make the issue turn on whether the acts were normal and appropriate use of land so situated.[10] Enclosure of the land, perhaps even use of it up to some natural physical boundary, introduces an important factor favorable to the possessor.[11] Adverse possession on the

7. Drennen Land & Timber Co. v. Angell, 475 So.2d 1166 (Ala.1985); Slemmons v. Massie, 102 N.M. 33, 690 P.2d 1027 (1984) (a mortgage does not constitute color of title as required by statute). Payment of taxes is unnecessary under such a statute if the adverse possessor is exempt from taxation; see United States v. Stubbs, 776 F.2d 1472 (10th Cir.1985). See Parsons v. Anderson, 690 P.2d 535 (Utah 1984) (adverse possessor must pay taxes under statute *before* true owner pays them). See also Annot., Presumptions and Evidence Respecting Identification of Land on which Property Taxes Were Paid to Establish Adverse Possession, 36 A.L.R.4th 843 (1985).

8. E.g., Ewing's Lessee v. Burnet, 36 U.S. (11 Pet.) 41, 9 L.Ed. 624 (1837) (jury question; unfenced); Morrison v. Boyd, 475 So.2d 509 (Ala.1985); Peters v. Juneau–Douglas Girl Scout Council, 519 P.2d 826 (Alaska 1974); Bryan v. Reifschneider, 181 Neb. 787, 150 N.W.2d 900 (1967); Krona v. Brett, 72 Wn.2d 535, 433 P.2d 858 (1967).

9. Compare Monroe v. Rawlings, 331 Mich. 49, 49 N.W.2d 55 (1951) (sufficient acts); and Kenney v. Bridges, 123 Mont. 95, 208 P.2d 475 (1949) (sufficient acts); with Van Valkenburgh v. Lutz, 304 N.Y. 95, 106 N.E.2d 28 (1952) reargument denied 304 N.Y. 590, 107 N.E.2d 82 (1952) (acts not sufficient); Harris v. Walden, 314 N.C. 284, 333 S.E.2d 254 (1985).

10. Compare Crowley v. Whitesell, 702 S.W.2d 127 (Mo.App.1985) (fencing "wild"

land, selling some timber, running cattle on it, and clearing brush were sufficient acts to constitute adverse possession); Alaska National Bank v. Linck, 559 P.2d 1049 (Alaska 1977); Peters v. Juneau–Douglas Girl Scout Council, 519 P.2d 826 (Alaska 1974); Monroe v. Rawlings, 331 Mich. 49, 49 N.W.2d 55 (1951); and Kenney v. Bridges, 123 Mont. 95, 208 P.2d 475 (1949) (above allowing adverse possession); with Hyland v. Kirkman, 204 N.J.Super. 345, 498 A.2d 1278 (1985) (historical and archeological exploration, making measurements, occasional cutting of trees, and posting of "no trespassing" signs, were not sufficient to constitute adverse possession); McDonnold v. Weinacht, 465 S.W.2d 136 (Tex.1971); and Murray v. Bousquet, 154 Wash. 42, 280 P. 935 (1929) (not allowing adverse possession). See generally the thorough Annot., 48 A.L.R.3d 818 (1973).

11. Whittemore v. Amator, 148 Ariz. 173, 713 P.2d 1231 (1986) (fence helpful in establishing extent of adverse possession); Brumagim v. Bradshaw, 39 Cal. 24 (1870) (natural boundary); Miceli v. Foley, 575 A.2d 1249 (Md.App.1990) ("visible boundary," a fence, marked extent of adverse possession); Springer v. Durette, 217 Or. 196, 342 P.2d 132 (1959) (natural boundary); McDonnold v. Weinacht, 465 S.W.2d 136 (Tex.1971) (dictum, fencing); Northwoods Development Corp. v. Klement, 24 Wis.2d 387, 129 N.W.2d 121 (1964) (fencing). But see Murray v. Bousquet, 154 Wash. 42, 280 P. 935 (1929) (fencing not sufficient).

surface of the earth is normally possession of the underlying earth, but this is generally not so as to underground minerals that, by severance, are owned by someone other than the surface owner.[12] The best test of actual possession, increasingly recognized in the courts, is, were the acts of possession such as would be normal for an owner to make of land situated such as this in all the circumstances? [13]

An important exception to the requirement of actual possession is the doctrine of "constructive possession." One who is in actual adverse possession of part of a parcel of land and who holds a "colorable" document of title to the entire parcel is, with qualifications to be noted, regarded as being in adverse possession of the whole parcel.[14] Colorable title, or "color of title," is often defined as a document that appears to give title but, for some reason not apparent on its face, does not.[15] Typical examples are sheriffs' deeds for tax or other public sales that are void for some reason such as improper sale procedures.[16] Obviously the adverse possessor may not claim constructive possession over areas not described in the colorable instrument.[17] There also must be some limit to how large a parcel may be constructively possessed; presumably it would have to be reasonable in size to the area actually possessed.[18] Some decisions have imposed a requirement that the possessor have a good faith belief that the instrument is valid, which is also required by a number of special adverse possession statutes.[19]

"Open and notorious" possession usually means possession that gives visible evidence to one on the surface of the possessed land. The purpose of this element is to afford the owner opportunity for notice. He need not actually have seen the evidence but is charged with seeing what reasonable

12. Spurlock v. Santa Fe Pacific Railroad Co., 143 Ariz. 469, 694 P.2d 299 (App.1984), certiorari denied 472 U.S. 1032, 105 S.Ct. 3513, 87 L.Ed.2d 642 (1985); Failoni v. Chicago & North Western Railway Co., 30 Ill.2d 258, 195 N.E.2d 619 (1964). This result has been reversed by statute in Georgia see Official Code Georgia Ann. § 44–5–168, discussed in Milner v. Bivens, 255 Ga. 49, 335 S.E.2d 288 (1985) (if severed mineral interest is not being worked by its owner, the surface owner may acquire it by adverse possession); Stoebuck, Adverse Possession of Severable Minerals, 68 W.Va.L.Rev. 274 (1966).

13. See Ewing's Lessee v. Burnet, 36 U.S. (11 Pet.) 41, 9 L.Ed. 624 (1837); Alaska National Bank v. Linck, 559 P.2d 1049 (Alaska 1977); Monroe v. Rawlings, 331 Mich. 49, 49 N.W.2d 55 (1951); Krona v. Brett, 72 Wn.2d 535, 433 P.2d 858 (1967).

14. Lott v. Muldoon Road Baptist Church, Inc., 466 P.2d 815 (Alaska 1970); Monroe v. Rawlings, 331 Mich. 49, 49 N.W.2d 55 (1951); Cobb v. Spurlin, 73 N.C.App. 560, 327 S.E.2d 244 (1985); Taylor v. Brattain, 76 N.C.App. 574, 334 S.E.2d 242 (1985), modified and affirmed 317 N.C. 146, 343 S.E.2d 536 (1986). See also New York–Kentucky Oil & Gas Co. v. Miller, 187 Ky. 742, 220 S.W. 535 (1920).

15. Lott v. Muldoon Road Baptist Church, Inc., 466 P.2d 815 (Alaska 1970); Monroe v. Rawlings, 331 Mich. 49, 49 N.W.2d 55 (1951); 3 Am.L.Prop. § 15.11 (1952); Annot., 38 A.L.R.2d 986, 991 (1954).

16. E.g., New York–Kentucky Oil & Gas Co. v. Miller, 187 Ky. 742, 220 S.W. 535 (1920) (private deeds); Monroe v. Rawlings, 331 Mich. 49, 49 N.W.2d 55 (1951) (tax deed); Annot., 71 A.L.R.2d 404 (1960) (judgment or decree); Annot., 38 A.L.R.2d 986 (1954) (tax deed). Lott v. Muldoon Road Baptist Church, Inc., 466 P.2d 815 (Alaska 1970), holds that a trust deed trustee's reconveyance deed was colorable title to an adverse possessor who had given the trust deed.

17. Bryan v. Reifschneider, 181 Neb. 787, 150 N.W.2d 900 (1967); Jackson ex dem. Gilliland v. Woodruff, 1 Cow. 276 (N.Y.1823).

18. Jackson ex dem. Gilliland v. Woodruff, preceding note (dictum).

19. 3 American Law of Property, supra note 14; Annot., 71 A.L.R.2d 404, 408 (1960); Annot., 38 A.L.R.2d 986, 1032–87 (1954) (statutes reviewed). See Lott v. Muldoon Road Baptist Church, Inc., 466 P.2d 815 (Alaska 1970).

inspection would disclose.[20] Possession that is "actual" is very likely to be open and notorious unless it is hidden in some unusual way. When possession is of a cave, with no entrance apparent from the disseisee's land, it is not open and notorious.[21] One might also imagine a strange case in which possessory acts were carried out only under cover of darkness. The nature of the acts on the ground usually determines if they are notorious, but in some instances courts have given weight also to the possessor's reputation as owner or his having public records evidencing ownership.[22]

"Hostility" is the very marrow of adverse possession; it has even redundantly been called adversity. To say that possession is hostile should mean nothing more than that it is without permission of the one legally empowered to give possession, usually the owner.[23] Any kind of permissive use, as by a tenant, licensee, contract purchaser in possession, or easement holder is rightful, not hostile. The better view is that unexplained possession is presumed hostile, so that it is up to the one who wishes to do so to establish that it is rightful. Permission is usually by the owner's express act, but there are some cases in which it is proper to infer permission, as when an owner might customarily allow others to make light use of vacant land.[24] Anytime an adverse possessor and owner have discussed the adverse possession, permissive agreement may have occurred. However, the owner's mere knowledge of the possession, his demands upon the possessor, or, by the better view, even the latter's offer to compromise do not destroy hostility.[25]

20. See Alaska National Bank v. Linck, 559 P.2d 1049 (Alaska 1977); Kenney v. Bridges, 123 Mont. 95, 208 P.2d 475 (1949).

21. Marengo Cave Co. v. Ross, 212 Ind. 624, 10 N.E.2d 917 (1937). See also the fantastic case of Edwards v. Sims, 232 Ky. 791, 24 S.W.2d 619 (1929).

22. Alaska National Bank v. Linck, 559 P.2d 1049 (Alaska 1977) (paying taxes); Kenney v. Bridges, 123 Mont. 95, 208 P.2d 475 (1949) (colorable recorded deed, paying taxes).

23. Nevells v. Carter, 122 Me. 81, 119 A. 62 (1922); Ottavia v. Sevarese, 338 Mass. 330, 155 N.E.2d 432 (1959); Mellenthin v. Brantman, 211 Minn. 336, 1 N.W.2d 141 (1941) (recommended reading); Krona v. Brett, 72 Wn.2d 535, 433 P.2d 858 (1967); Lanham v. Marley, 475 N.E.2d 700 (Ind.App.1985); 3 Am.L.Prop. supra note 14, at § 15.4.

24. Van Valkenburgh v. Lutz, 304 N.Y. 95, 106 N.E.2d 28 (1952), reargument denied 304 N.Y. 590, 107 N.E.2d 82 (1952) might be explained as a case of implied, neighborly permission, though the court does not speak so. Implied permission may explain some of the "squatter" cases, too. See, e.g., Northern Pacific Railway v. Devine, 53 Wash. 241, 101 P. 841 (1909). If the possession is initially permissive, it can become hostile only by virtue of "a distinct and open disavowal of the title of the owner, brought home to the owner"; Miller v. Stovall, 717 P.2d 798 (Wyo.1986). A similar rule is applied when one claims adverse possession title from his cotenant, since

the possession of both parties was initially rightful and therefore "permissive;" see, e.g., Center Line Enterprises, Inc. v. Washington, 465 So.2d 1129 (Ala.1985) (" * * * there must be a repudiation of the rights of cotenants and a claim of exclusive ownership brought home to their knowledge * * * [by] positive information of the facts, however informally communicated or acquired.") See also Seignious v. Metropolitan Atlanta Rapid Transit Authority, 252 Ga. 69, 311 S.E.2d 808 (1984) (a grantor is normally estopped from claiming adverse possession title as against his grantee, but such is possible where the grantor gives unequivocal notice that he is claiming the property adversely); Joy v. Hull, 687 S.W.2d 282 (Mo.App.1985) (similar); Berg v. Fairman, 107 Idaho 441, 690 P.2d 896 (1984) (occupation of land by blood relative of owner is presumed permissive, and "some unequivocal act indicating the occupier's intent to claim adversely must be shown").

25. Some decisions take the position that if the possessor, in offering a compromise, admits the owner's title, going beyond merely an offer to compromise a doubtful claim, this destroys hostility. Mann v. LaSalle Nat. Bank, 205 Ill.App.3d 304, 150 Ill.Dec. 230, 562 N.E.2d 1033 (1990), appeal denied 136 Ill.2d 545, 153 Ill.Dec. 375, 567 N.E.2d 333 (1991); Morgan v. Wertz, 104 S.W.2d 63 (Tex.Civ.App. 1937). The correct view is that the possessor's knowledge or offer has nothing to do with hostility. Warren v. Bowdran, 156 Mass. 280, 31 N.E. 300 (1892); Patterson v. Reigle, 4 Pa. 201 (1846).

This brings us to the most difficult, thoroughly maddening, question in all adverse possession, ·whether an adverse possessor's subjective state of mind, imprecisely often called "intent," can destroy hostility. It is the view here, along with that of most decisions and of nearly all scholars, that what the possessor believes or intends should have nothing to do with it.[26] Yet in many decisions a variety of states of mind, too many to explore more than leading examples here, have purportedly defeated adverse possession. An extreme view is that an adverse possessor must have "a bona fide claim * * * that he has got a right as owner."[27] The most persistent problem is whether the possessor's so-called "mistake," i.e., an absence of knowledge that he does not own, is fatal. In most jurisdictions this will not defeat hostility; in a few it will, at least in mistaken-boundary cases.[28] If, in addition, the possessor admits (probably during clever cross-examination) he intended to claim only to wherever the true boundary was, then more jurisdictions have denied hostility.[29] Presumably, then, a possessor who said he knew he was occupying his neighbor's land and intended to get it if he could would be better off. Requirement of a particular state of mind reduces the capacity of adverse possession to quiet titles in mistaken-boundary cases.

Notions about state of mind and intent apparently came into adverse possession law through use of the phrases "claim of right" or "claim of title."[30] Perhaps these phrases would cause no harm if they could be strictly limited to mean that the adverse possessor's use and possession must be of a character an owner would make. But because the phrases cause much trouble, it would be better if they, and the notions they have spawned, were forgotten.

Some question has existed whether permissive or other rightful possession may, without a break in physical possession, become adverse. Most of the cases involve lessees who enter permissively or co-tenants whose entry is rightful under the principle that a co-tenant is entitled to full possession.

26. See Peters v. Juneau–Douglas Girl Scout Council, 519 P.2d 826 (Alaska 1974); Ottavia v. Savarese, 338 Mass. 330, 155 N.E.2d 432 (1959); Mellenthin v. Brantman, 211 Minn. 336, 1 N.W.2d 141 (1941); Norgard v. Busher, 220 Or. 297, 349 P.2d 490 (1960); City of Rock Springs v. Sturm, 39 Wyo. 494, 273 P. 908 (1929); 3 Am.L.Prop. supra note 14, at § 15.4; Annot., 80 A.L.R.2d 1171, 1183 (1961). The *Norgard* decision cites a string of leading secondary authorities on the point.

27. Jasperson v. Scharnikow, 150 Fed. 571, 572 (9th Cir.1907); Phillips v. Parker, 483 So.2d 972 (La.1986) (good faith required). See also Harsha v. Anastos, 693 P.2d 760 (Wyo. 1985) (adverse possession title will be denied if claimant lacks clean hands). After many years of confusion, the Washington law was clarified to eliminate all requirements as to subjective belief or intent in Chaplin v. Sanders, 100 Wn.2d 853, 676 P.2d 431 (1984).

See Helmholtz, Adverse Possession and Subjective Intent, 61 Wash.U.L.Q. 331 (1983), suggesting that even though most courts formally reject good faith as a requirement for adverse possession, they frequently manipulate the other elements of the doctrine in order to rule against bad faith claimants. See also Merrill, Property Rules, Liability Rules, and Adverse Possession, 79 Nw.U.L.Rev. 1122 (1985), commenting on this thesis; Bucknall, Two Roads Diverged: Recent Decisions on Possessory Title, 22 Osgood Hall L.J. 375 (1984), discussing intent requirements under Ontario law.

28. Connelly v. Buckingham, 136 Mich. App. 462, 357 N.W.2d 70 (1984); Mellenthin v. Brantman, 211 Minn. 336, 1 N.W.2d 141 (1941) (will not); Predham v. Holfester, 32 N.J.Super. 419, 108 A.2d 458 (1954) (will); Krona v. Brett, 72 Wn.2d 535, 433 P.2d 858 (1967) (will not); City of Rock Springs v. Sturm, 39 Wyo. 494, 273 P. 908 (1929) (will not); Annot., 80 A.L.R.2d 1171, 1173–74 (1961).

29. E.g. Price v. Whisnant, 236 N.C. 381, 72 S.E.2d 851 (1952); Brown v. Hubbard, 42 Wn.2d 867, 259 P.2d 391 (1953); Annot., 80 A.L.R.2d 1171, 1174–81 (1961).

30. Carpenter v. Coles, 75 Minn. 9, 77 N.W. 424 (1898).

The answer is that such continuing possession may become adverse to the landlord or other co-tenants if the elements of adverse possession are present and especially if the element of hostility is supplied by an "ouster," which means the possessor's repudiation of the original rightful possession. A clear case would be the lessee or co-tenant who expressly notified his landlord or co-tenants that he denied their interests and was holding possession in his own right alone.[31] For an ouster, claim of right and intent are appropriate elements. Many courts require that the disseisee be aware of the words or act of ouster. But the ouster need not be, and in most cases is not, by express claim but by circumstances showing clearly that the possessor now claims in repudiation of the disseisee's rights. Courts give weight to colorable title documents; the possessor's purporting to give conveyances, leases, and mortgages; his paying taxes; long-continued possession; intensive use of the land; community reputation; and so forth.[32] Naturally courts are reluctant to find an ouster if the evidence of it is incomplete or ambiguous or if the disseised owner may have given permission,[33] but in practice it is not rare.

That adverse possession must be "exclusive" means that it must not be shared with the disseised owner.[34] Two or more persons may be co-adverse possessors; if they acquire title, it will be as tenants in common.[35] One may be in adverse possession through another whom he has put in possession as a tenant.[36] Some decisions have undercut the meaning of exclusivity by holding that, in cases of attempted oral conveyances, the owner, continuing in possession, becomes a tenant (adverse to himself) of the grantee, who becomes an adverse possessor.[37] Of course an adverse possessor may be in exclusive possession of part of a parcel of land and the owner in possession of another part; that is usually so in mistaken boundary cases.

The final element, that adverse possession must be "continuous," means that it must continue without significant interruption for a solid block of time at least as long as the period of limitation. What is a significant interruption depends upon the nature of the land. Brief and ordinary

---

31. Johnson v. James, 237 Ark. 900, 377 S.W.2d 44 (1964) (dictum); Adams v. Johnson, 271 Minn. 439, 136 N.W.2d 78 (1965) (dictum); 3 Am.L.Prop. supra note 14, at §§ 15.6, 15.7; Annot., 82 A.L.R.2d 5, 21–25, 104–06 (1962) (302–page annotation).

32. See Johnson v. James, 237 Ark. 900, 377 S.W.2d 44 (1964); Adams v. Johnson, 271 Minn. 439, 136 N.W.2d 78 (1965); Annot., 82 A.L.R.2d 5, 64–217 (1962). But see Olwell v. Clark, 658 P.2d 585 (Utah 1982) (one co-tenant's payment of taxes for about 40 years was not ouster of other co-tenants).

33. See Estate of Wells v. Estate of Smith, 576 A.2d 707 (D.C.App.1990) (court reluctant to find ouster by holdover tenant); Denton v. Denton, 627 S.W.2d 124 (Tenn.App.1981) (one co-tenant's purchase of tax title is for benefit of all co-tenants and is not adverse to them unless they are aware of the co-tenancy); Mercer v. Wayman, 9 Ill.2d 441, 137 N.E.2d 815 (1956); Smith v. Tremaine, 221 Or. 33, 350 P.2d 180 (1960).

34. Dzuris v. Kucharik, 164 Colo. 278, 434 P.2d 414 (1967); Russell v. Gullett, 285 Or. 63, 589 P.2d 729 (1979); Moore v. Johnson, 471 So.2d 1250 (Ala.1985). If two competing persons possess the land adversely, neither will get title, but if an adverse possessor allows others to use the land under his permission, exclusivity is not defeated; see Ortmeyer v. Bruemmer, 680 S.W.2d 384 (Mo.App.1984).

35. Preston v. Smith, 41 Tenn.App. 222, 293 S.W.2d 51 (1955) (husband and wife acquired title as tenants in common, not by entirety); 4 H. Tiffany, Real Property § 1141 (1975).

36. Nevells v. Carter, 122 Me. 81, 119 A. 62 (1922); 4 H. Tiffany, supra note 35, at § 1146.

37. Nevells v. Carter, 122 Me. 81, 119 A. 62 (1922); Russell v. Gullett, 285 Or. 63, 589 P.2d 729 (1979). See generally, Annot., 43 A.L.R.2d 6 (1955).

absences, while the possessor goes to town, is gone overnight, or is away working or on vacation, for instance, would surely not break any adverse possession. With land that is, by its nature, suitable and normally used for seasonal pursuits, then seasonal use may be continuous enough.[38] Again, the test should be whether the adverse possessor used the land as a true owner would. Courts seem sensitive to breaks caused by the owner's intermittent possession; such breaks of a few days or weeks every now and then are likely to defeat both exclusivity and continuity of possession.[39]

An interesting question within the subject of continuity is "tacking," the adding together of periods of possession that are continuous but by different persons. This is allowed, provided there is a sufficient nexus, often called "privity," between successors. This nexus is provided if the earlier possessor gives the next one a colorable title document that describes the area possessed or if the next one is his heir.[40] To ask how it is an adverse possessor, who has not yet title, can pass anything by the methods to transfer title, is to conjure up musty questions about whether possession is the source of title or is itself vestigal title. The answers are too wonderful (not to say too lengthy) to work out here; suffice it to say the adverse possessor may tack by such methods. And tacking may occur, without any formal or even express transfer, simply by the earlier possessor's turning over possession to his successor. This may occur when an adversely possessed strip is turned over in connection with the conveyance of adjoining land the possessor owns or by a pointing out of boundaries or by other acts or words that evince a turning over.[41] Courts seem to have more problems with an informal turning over than with a documentary transfer. The informal transfer is easier to justify in theory, though, because a possessory "title" should be transferable by a transfer of possession.

Is the "strange and wonderful" doctrine of adverse possession justified? Some decisions smack of a desire to punish the landowner who is not diligent or to award the possessor who is. Diligence is a quality society might promote, though hardly at the expense of the owner's title. But other broader reasons exist: that after a long time uncertain boundaries be stabilized; that persons who have taken interests in the land or dealt with the adverse possessor in reliance upon his apparent ownership be protected; and that those who will keep land productive by using it be given permanence. Adverse possession is best explained as a doctrine of repose. Perhaps, too, the mystical connection between possession and title is worth

---

38. Alaska National Bank v. Linck, 559 P.2d 1049 (Alaska 1977) (vacant land, seasonal use); Howard v. Kunto, 3 Wn.App. 393, 477 P.2d 210 (1970) (summer home).

39. Dzuris v. Kucharik, 164 Colo. 278, 434 P.2d 414 (1967); Miceli v. Foley, 83 Md.App. 541, 575 A.2d 1249 (1990) (entry to make survey did not break continuity); Mendonca v. Cities Service Oil Co., 354 Mass. 323, 237 N.E.2d 16 (1968); Williams v. Mobil Oil Exploration and Producing Southeast, Inc., 457 So.2d 962 (Ala.1984) (acts of entry which are rare and widely separated in time do not constitute adverse possession); Ortmeyer v. Bruemmer, 680 S.W.2d 384 (Mo.App.1984) ("temporary absences without an intent to

abandon will not break continuity but intermittent and sporadic occupancy will").

40. Moore v. Johnson, 471 So.2d 1250 (Ala. 1985); Sawyer v. Kendall, 64 Mass. (10 Cush.) 241 (1852) (dictum); Bryan v. Reifschneider, 181 Neb. 787, 150 N.W.2d 900 (1967) (dictum); Belotti v. Bickhardt, 228 N.Y. 296, 127 N.E. 239 (1920) (dictum); Sinclair Refining Co. v. Romohr, 95 Ohio App. 93, 117 N.E.2d 489 (1953); Annot., 43 A.L.R.2d 1061 (1955).

41. Bryan v. Reifschneider, 181 Neb. 787, 150 N.W.2d 900 (1967); Brand v. Prince, 35 N.Y.2d 634, 364 N.Y.S.2d 826, 324 N.E.2d 314 (1974); Belotti v. Bickhardt, 228 N.Y. 296, 127 N.E. 239 (1920); Howard v. Kunto, 3 Wn.App. 393, 477 P.2d 210 (1970).

something. Title by possession, along with prescription, is an old subject in English law; it had its counterparts in Roman law.[42] If we had no doctrine of adverse possession, we should have to invent something very like it.

§ 11.8 Practical Location of Boundaries

It often happens that an owner is uncertain as to the precise location on the ground of the parcel's boundaries. This uncertainty may result from an ambiguous or confusing description in the deed or other documents,[1] but it is not always easy to locate boundaries even if the written description is clear. A survey may be obtained, but it can be very costly, especially if the parcel is large, its terrain is uneven, or it is overgrown with vegetation. In some states it is possible to bring an equitable or statutory proceeding for judicial determination of the boundaries,[2] but that course is likely to be even more expensive. To avoid these costs, abutting owners frequently enter into informal relationships which fix the boundaries between them. In general the law tends to uphold these determinations, even though they often have the effect of placing a boundary somewhere other than at its "true" location as a surveyor would fix it by following the written description.

At least four fairly distinct doctrines fit this general discussion: (1) boundaries by agreement; (2) boundaries by acquiescence; (3) estoppel; and (4) boundary determinations by a common grantor. Each of these doctrines is a type of "practical location" of boundaries[3] and is discussed in this section. Any discussion of them is hampered by the inconsistency, overlap, and uncertainty which characterizes their treatment in the courts. They are, however, doctrinally distinct from the concept of adverse possession, covered in the preceding section, which also operates to adjust boundary locations in many cases.

None of the doctrines discussed here require a writing satisfying the statute of frauds,[4] yet all of them have the effect of reducing the size of one owner's parcel while enlarging another's—a process any lay person would surely describe as a transfer of land. The courts do *not* consider a transfer to take place; instead, they hold that boundary in question has simply been redefined or reconstrued by the parties' actions.[5] This highly artificial

---

42. Taylor ex dem. Atkyns v. Horde, 1 Burr. 60, 97 Eng.Rep. 190 (K.B.1757); Stokes v. Berry, 2 Salk. 421, 91 Eng.Rep. 366 (K.B. 1699); Britton 250–51 (Nichols transl. 1901); Buckland, A Manual of Roman Private Law §§ 47–49 (1925); Walsh, Title by Adverse Possession, 16 N.Y.U.L.Q.Rev. 532 (1939).

§ 11.8

1. On construction of ambiguous descriptions, see § 11.2, supra, at notes 33–34.

2. See, e.g., Shirk v. Schmunk, 192 Neb. 25, 218 N.W.2d 433 (1974) applying Neb.Rev.Stat. § 34–301; Curtis Fishing & Hunting Club, Inc., v. Johnson, 214 Va. 388, 200 S.E.2d 542 (1973), applying what is now Virginia Code § 8.01–179. See generally 2 Tiffany, Real Property § 652 (3d ed. 1939).

3. See Browder, The Practical Location of Boundaries, 56 Mich.L.Rev. 487 (1958); Lamm v. McTighe, 72 Wn.2d 587, 434 P.2d 565 (1967).

4. A few courts have rejected one or more of the doctrines mentioned because they operate without compliance with the statute of frauds. See, e.g., Andrews v. Andrews, 252 N.C. 97, 113 S.E.2d 47 (1960), refusing to enforce oral boundary line agreements.

5. E.g., Trappett v. Davis, 102 Idaho 527, 633 P.2d 592 (1981); DeWitt v. Lutes, 581 S.W.2d 941 (Mo.App.1979); Hoyer v. Edwards, 182 Ark. 624, 32 S.W.2d 812 (1930); 1 R. Patton & C. Patton, Land Titles § 159 note 42 (2d ed. 1957); 2 Tiffany, Real Property § 653 note 79 (3d ed. 1939). The concept that a boundary agreement is not a transfer can be traced back to an agreement between William Penn and Lord Baltimore resolving a dispute over the boundary between Pennsylvania and Maryland; see Penn v. Lord Baltimore, 1 Ves. Sr. 444, 27 Eng.Repr. 1132 (1750); Browder, supra note 3, at note 43.

viewpoint has a practical advantage: it avoids the need for a writing, and in effect rewrites the documents of title by operation of law to reflect the change the parties have wrought.[6] Thus, if the distance call in the deed is "500 feet," it may henceforth be treated as if it read "517 feet" or "483 feet," and every future deed of the land which copies or incorporates the original description will also be so read.[7]

Two underlying policies justify this seemingly bizarre disregard for the statute of frauds and the literal meaning of the written word. One is repose: the notion that the law ought not to tinker with the well-settled and long-held understanding of the people involved, even if it does not comport with their documents.[8] The other is estoppel: if one reasonably relies on another's representations (even those arising from conduct rather than words), the law should not allow the representations to be withdrawn or denied.[9] These two ideas, repose and estoppel, mixed together in varying proportions and recognized at varying levels of consciousness, form the policy underpinnings of the cases we now consider.

Agreement. To establish a boundary by agreement, it must first be shown either that the parties were uncertain or unaware of the correct location, or that a dispute as to the true location existed between them.[10] Some courts recognize only uncertainty or only dispute, while others, probably the majority, recognize both. If the basis of the agreement is uncertainty, it is usually said that both owners must be uncertain,[11] while if the agreement is based on a dispute it appears to be no objection that one party is both certain and correct. The insistence of the courts on uncertainty or a dispute is deeply embedded, and springs from a conviction that if the parties *know* that their agreement will shift the boundary, they are doing nothing

---

6. Browder, supra note 3, at 497–98. As one court put it, "the new boundary effectively attaches to the respective deeds and, in legal effect, becomes the true dividing line between the parties." Duncan v. Peterson, 3 Cal.App.3d 607, 83 Cal.Rptr. 744 (1970). Mineral rights underlying the strip also become the property of the new owner; Sachs v. Board of Trustees, 89 N.M. 712, 557 P.2d 209 (1976), appeal after remand 92 N.M. 605, 592 P.2d 961 (1978).

7. As to the binding effect on future owners, see text at notes 57–59, infra.

8. See Sachs v. Board of Trustees, 89 N.M. 712, 557 P.2d 209 (1976), appeal after remand 92 N.M. 605, 592 P.2d 961 (1978); Finley v. Yuba County Water District, 99 Cal.App.3d 691, 160 Cal.Rptr. 423 (1979); Baldwin v. Brown, 16 N.Y. 359 (1857); Browder, supra note 3, at 511.

9. See Sceirine v. Densmore, 87 Nev. 9, 479 P.2d 779 (1971); Buza v. Wojtalewicz, 48 Wis.2d 557, 180 N.W.2d 556 (1970); Browder, supra note 3, at 498. In many situations to be discussed infra the estoppel appears in a rather diluted form, and little is required in the way of detrimental reliance; Wisconsin takes the reliance element more seriously than most courts. See also the California decisions

which permit "substantial loss" to substitute for a holding for the statute of limitations period in boundary line agreement cases; note, 9 Loy.L.A.L.Rev. 637, 654–57 (1976).

10. Fogerty v. State, 187 Cal.App.3d 224, 231 Cal.Rptr. 810 (1986), cert. denied 484 U.S. 821, 108 S.Ct. 81, 98 L.Ed.2d 43 (1987); Miller v. Stovall, 717 P.2d 798 (Wyo.1986); Thompson v. Jamison, 699 S.W.2d 687 (Tex.App.1985) (uncertainty required); Sanlando Springs Animal Hospital, Inc. v. Douglass, 455 So.2d 596 (Fla.App.1984) (dispute or uncertainty required); Fritzler v. Dumler, 209 Kan. 16, 495 P.2d 1027 (1972); Downing v. Boehringer, 82 Idaho 52, 349 P.2d 306 (1960); McRae Land & Timber Co. v. Ziegler, 65 So.2d 876 (Fla.1953). See generally Annot., 69 A.L.R. 1430 (1930); Annot., 113 A.L.R. 421 (1938).

11. Kendall v. Lowther, 356 N.W.2d 181 (Iowa 1984); Martin v. Lopes, 28 Cal.2d 618, 170 P.2d 881 (1946). The uncertainty need not originate in or be apparent from the deeds, and the owners need not have had a survey made or gone to any other efforts to resolve the uncertainty; Mello v. Weaver, 36 Cal.2d 456, 224 P.2d 691 (1950); Ekberg v. Bates, 121 Utah 123, 239 P.2d 205 (1951). But see Skinner v. Francisco, 404 Ill. 356, 88 N.E.2d 867 (1949).

less than conveying land from one to another, and hence must employ a writing to satisfy the statute of frauds.[12] A related rule, widely but not universally followed, holds the agreement unenforceable if the parties mistakenly thought they were actually identifying the true boundary rather than merely selecting a line (which they understood might or might not be the true boundary) as a way of settling their uncertainty or compromising their dispute.[13] The point is to bind the parties only if they recognized the risk they were taking by entering into the agreement.[14] Unfortunately, these rules concerning uncertainty, dispute, and mistake leave enormous latitude for judicial discretion and manipulation, and as Professor Browder put it, "reduce the predictability of decision on the effect of such agreements almost to zero."[15]

A second fundamental requirement is the agreement itself. Since no particular formality is necessary, agreements can be found from a wide variety of types of communication. Yet it is common for a court to reject the proffered boundary because no agreement has been adequately proved.[16]

Agreement

The final element in establishment of a boundary by agreement is the taking (and relinquishing) of possession by the parties to the agreed line.[17] Possession serves an evidentiary purpose here, and is roughly analogous to the part performance doctrine in land sale contracts.[18] There is considerable confusion as to how long the possession must continue in order to finalize the boundary change. Some cases, probably a majority, seem to require no particular period,[19] while others demand a "long" period[20] or one equal to

Possession

12. Madsen v. Clegg, 639 P.2d 726 (Utah 1981); United States v. Williams, 441 F.2d 637, 648–649 (5th Cir.1971); Thompson v. Bain, 28 Wn.2d 590, 183 P.2d 785 (1947); 2 Tiffany, Real Property § 653 note 80 (3d ed. 1939).

13. Blaisdell v. Nelsen, 66 Or.App. 511, 674 P.2d 1208 (1984); Sceirine v. Densmore, 89 Nev. 9, 479 P.2d 779 (1971); Duval County Ranch Co. v. Foster, 318 S.W.2d 25 (Tex.Civ. App.1958), refused n.r.e.; Ginther v. Duginger, 6 Ill.2d 474, 129 N.E.2d 147 (1955); 2 Tiffany, Real Property § 653 note 83 (3d ed. 1939); Browder, supra note 3, at 498–504. The "mistake rule" was rejected in Martin v. Lopes, 28 Cal.2d 618, 170 P.2d 881 (1946); Zachery v. McWilliams, 28 Cal.App.3d 57, 104 Cal.Rptr. 293 (1972) (discussing conflicts in the California cases); Schlender v. Maretoli, 140 Kan. 533, 37 P.2d 993 (1934); Harne v. Smith, 79 Tex. 310, 15 S.W. 240 (1891).

14. See Short v. Mauldin, 227 Ark. 96, 296 S.W.2d 197 (1956).

15. Browder, supra note 3, at 504.

16. E.g., Berry v. Sbragia, 76 Cal.App.3d 876, 143 Cal.Rptr. 318 (1978); Huggans v. Weer, 189 Mont. 334, 615 P.2d 922 (1980); Martin v. Hinnen, 3 Kan.App.2d 106, 590 P.2d 589 (1979). Absent an express agreement, a court may find an implied one if the elements of a boundary by acquiescence are present; see text at notes 25–26, infra.

17. See Humphrey v. Futter, 169 Cal. App.3d 333, 215 Cal.Rptr. 178 (1985), questioning whether California law requires actual occupation to the agreed line. Browder, supra note 3, at 493–94. The actual possession required may be quite minimal if the terrain is rough and difficult; see Aborigine Lumber Co. v. Hyman, 245 Cal.App.2d 938, 54 Cal.Rptr. 371 (1966).

18. See § 10.2 supra at notes 14–16.

19. Wells v. Williamson, 118 Idaho 37, 794 P.2d 626 (1990); Campbell v. Noel, 490 So.2d 1014 (Fla.App.1986) (5 years occupancy to line, although shorter than adverse possession period, was sufficient); Piotrowski v. Parks, 39 Wn.App. 37, 691 P.2d 591 (1984) (parties must merely take such possession as will give notice of the boundary's location to their successors in interest); Jones v. Seward, 265 Ark. 225, 578 S.W.2d 16 (1979), appeal after remand 274 Ark. 339, 625 S.W.2d 443 (1981); Cothran v. Burk, 234 Ga. 460, 216 S.E.2d 319 (1975); McGee v. Eriksen, 51 Mich.App. 551, 215 N.W.2d 571 (1974). In many cases long possession to the agreed line had occurred in fact, and it is difficult to tell whether the court believes a shorter period would have produced a different result.

20. See, e.g., Seddon v. Edmondson, 411 So.2d 995 (Fla.App.1982) ("occupation * * * for a period of time sufficient to show a settled recognition of the line as the permanent boundary."); Lake for Use and Benefit of Ben-

the statute of limitations for adverse possession.[21] A few courts also require the parties to mark their new boundary on the ground with a fence or monuments,[22] and at least one jurisdiction has accepted such markings as a substitute for actual possession.[23]

Acquiescence. Even if there is no explicit agreement between abutting owners, their long recognition and acceptance of a particular line as their boundary may make it so.[24] Many courts treat boundaries by acquiescence as a species of agreed boundaries, with the lengthy acquiescence "constituting" or creating a "conclusive presumption" of an agreement [25] even though there is no evidence whatever of any agreement in fact.[26] Other courts regard agreement and acquiescence as separate but parallel doctrines.[27] Because of the affinity of the two theories, courts often do not clearly distinguish the elements of each. For example, the cases are seriously split as to whether a boundary by acquiescence must originate from uncertainty or dispute as to the true location.[28]

ton v. Crosser, 202 Okl. 582, 216 P.2d 583 (1950).

21. Bearden v. Ellison, 560 So.2d 1042 (Ala.1990) (10 years required); Herrmann v. Woodell, 107 Idaho 916, 693 P.2d 1118 (App. 1985); Humphrey v. Futter, 169 Cal.App.3d 333, 215 Cal.Rptr. 178 (1985) (acceptance of the line must continue for the adverse possession period, or until there has been such reliance that alteration of the boundary would result in substantial loss); Townsend v. Koukol, 148 Mont. 1, 416 P.2d 532 (1966). See also Wisconsin and Minnesota cases cited at note 31, infra. Cf. Paurley v. Harris, 75 Idaho 112, 268 P.2d 351 (1954), abandoning a rule requiring the full limitations period. The Utah and California courts have virtually merged the doctrines of agreed boundaries and boundaries by acquiescence, and hence routinely require possession for the limitations period in order to validate a boundary agreement; see notes 25, 31, infra.

22. Piotrowski v. Parks, 39 Wn.App. 37, 691 P.2d 591 (1984); Johnston v. Monahan, 2 Wn.App. 452, 469 P.2d 930 (1970); Osberg v. Murphy, 88 S.D. 485, 221 N.W.2d 4 (1974). A physical marker or set of monuments might be very significant in giving notice to subsequent purchasers of the land, see text at notes 57–58, infra, but it is hard to see why it should be essential as between the parties to the agreement.

23. Cothran v. Burk, 234 Ga. 460, 216 S.E.2d 319 (1975).

24. The acquiescence in the line as a boundary must be by both parties, not just one; see Heriot v. Lewis, 35 Wn.App. 496, 668 P.2d 589 (1983). See generally 2 Tiffany, Real Property, § 654 (3d ed. 1939); Browder, supra note 3, at 504–19.

25. See, e.g., Stone v. Rhodes, 107 N.M. 96, 752 P.2d 1112 (App.1988); Herrmann v. Woodell, 107 Idaho 916, 693 P.2d 1118 (1985); Montgomery v. Sellers, 48 Or.App. 719, 618

P.2d 5 (1980); Raborn v. Buffalo, 260 Ark. 531, 542 S.W.2d 507 (1976); Paquin v. Guiorguiev, 117 R.I. 239, 366 A.2d 169 (1976); Motzkus v. Carroll, 7 Utah 2d 237, 322 P.2d 391 (1958). Utah and California have merged the two theories in a series of confusing and ambiguous cases, so that it is virtually impossible to judge whether an agreement, a long acquiescence, or both are required. See Madsen v. Clegg, 639 P.2d 726 (Utah 1981); Hobson v. Panguitch Lake Corp., 530 P.2d 792 (Utah 1975); Comment, Boundaries by Agreement and Acquiescence in Utah, 1975 Utah L.Rev. 221; Armitage v. Decker, 218 Cal.App.3d 887, 267 Cal.Rptr. 399 (1990); Joaquin v. Shiloh Orchards, 84 Cal.App.3d 192, 148 Cal.Rptr. 495 (1978); Comment, Agreed Boundaries and Boundaries by Acquiescence: The Need for a Straight Line From the Courts, 9 Loy. L.A.L.Rev. 637 (1976).

26. See Broadhead v. Hawley, 109 Idaho 952, 712 P.2d 653 (App.1985) (neither actual dispute nor agreement is required for boundary by acquiescence). It is generally unclear whether these courts would refuse to find a boundary by acquiescence if they were presented with direct evidence that no agreement had ever been made. The Utah court seems to have done so in Madsen v. Clegg, supra note 25, but Utah's boundary cases are unusually murky and contradictory. See Browder, supra note 3, at 507.

27. E.g., Seddon v. Edmondson, 411 So.2d 995 (Fla.App.1982).

28. Requiring doubt or dispute: Clair W. & Gladys Judd Family Ltd. Partnership v. Hutchings, 797 P.2d 1088 (Utah 1990) (overlap in deed descriptions establishes uncertainty); Stevenson v. Prairie Power Co-op., Inc., 794 P.2d 641 (Idaho App.1989); Mark IX, Inc. v. Surette, 492 So.2d 745 (Fla.App.1986); Henderson v. March, 100 Nev. 604, 691 P.2d 424 (1984); Chappell v. Bonds, 677 P.2d 955

It is clear that the period of acquiescence must be lengthy; some courts, probably the majority, have "borrowed" the period of the adverse possession statute (typically 5 to 20 years) and apply it here,[29] while others require only a reasonably long time.[30] A few follow more complex or ambiguous rules with respect to time,[31] or have special statutes governing the period of acquiescence.[32]

The nature of "acquiescence" is also controversial. For example, if one owner puts up a fence and the other simply makes no objection, has the latter acquiesced? Most of the cases hold that silence is enough,[33] but a few require some overt words or actions which indicate acceptance or at least recognition of the fence as a boundary.[34] Certain other elements are more clearly required by the decisions. The asserted boundary must be marked

(Colo.App.1983); Seddon v. Edmondson, supra; Corson v. Williford, 44 Or.App. 145, 605 P.2d 1194 (1980); Beduhn v. Kolar, 56 Wis.2d 471, 202 N.W.2d 272 (1972). Not requiring doubt or dispute: Camp v. Liberatore, 1 Ark. 300, 615 S.W.2d 401 (App.1981); Tresemer v. Albuquerque Public School District, 95 N.M. 143, 619 P.2d 819 (1980); Corrigan v. Miller, 96 Mich.App. 205, 292 N.W.2d 181 (1980). See also McDonald v. O'Steen, 429 So.2d 407 (Fla. App.1983) inferring the necessary doubt or uncertainty from the placement and duration of a fence. See 2 Tiffany, Real Property, § 654 notes 93–94 (3d ed. 1939). In Halladay v. Cluff, 685 P.2d 500 (Utah 1984), the Utah Supreme Court adopted a much more restrictive requirement of "objective uncertainty," in the sense of actual difficulty in locating the boundary, rather than mere lack of knowledge or difference of opinion. This change proved unsatisfactory, and the same court abandoned it six years later in Staker v. Ainsworth, 785 P.2d 417 (Utah 1990).

29. LeeJoice v. Harris, 404 N.W.2d 4 (Minn.App.1987) (15 years); Sanlando Springs Animal Hospital, Inc. v. Douglass, 455 So.2d 596 (Fla.App.1984) (Wyo.1983) (10 years); Allred v. Reed, 362 N.W.2d 374 (Minn.App. 1985) (15 years); Seddon v. Edmondson, supra note 27; Muench v. Oxley, 90 Wn.2d 637, 584 P.2d 939 (1978); Inn Le'Daerda, Inc. v. Davis, 241 Pa.Super. 150, 360 A.2d 209 (1976); Odegaard v. Craig, 171 N.W.2d 133 (N.D.1969); Barr's Estate v. Guay, 127 Vt. 374, 250 A.2d 512 (1969).

30. Parsons v. Anderson, 690 P.2d 535 (Utah 1984) (absent unusual circumstances, 20 years required; 15 years in instant case was too short); Stith v. Williams, 227 Kan. 32, 605 P.2d 86 (1980); Tresemer v. Albuquerque Public School District, 95 N.M. 143, 619 P.2d 819 (1980); Dodds v. Lagan, 595 P.2d 452 (Okl. App.1979). Idaho abandoned strict adherence to the statute of limitations in Paurley v. Harris, supra note 21.

31. See, e.g., McGee v. Eriksen, 51 Mich. App. 551, 215 N.W.2d 571 (1974) (period must exceed statute of limitations unless line is a product of a "bona fide controversy."); Amato

v. Haraden, 280 Minn. 399, 159 N.W.2d 907 (1968) (long period, "usually" time prescribed in statute of limitations); Hobson v. Panguitch Lake Corp., 530 P.2d 792 (Utah 1975) (usually at least 20 years required, although statute of limitations is only 7 years); Beasley v. Konczal, 87 Wis.2d 233, 275 N.W.2d 634 (1979) (period must exceed statute of limitations unless line is marked by a fence erected in settlement of a dispute); Minson Co. v. Aviation Finance, 38 Cal.App.3d 489, 113 Cal. Rptr. 223 (1974) (limitations period applies, but shorter time is sufficient if to deny the new boundary would result in substantial loss); see Comment, 9 Loy.L.A.L.Rev. 637, 654–57 (1976). The Minnesota and Wisconsin cases cited may be read simply as imposing a more lenient time rule in cases of agreed boundaries than in boundaries by acquiescence.

32. Colo.Rev.Stat.1973, 38–44–109 (20 years); Official Code Georgia Ann. § 44–4–6 (7 years); Iowa Code Ann. § 650.6 (10 years); see Sille v. Shaffer, 297 N.W.2d 379 (Iowa 1980).

33. Stevenson v. Prairie Power Co-op., Inc., 794 P.2d 641 (Idaho App.1989); Production Credit Association v. Terra Vallee, Inc., 303 N.W.2d 79 (N.D.1981); Price v. Mauch, 1 Ark. 348, 616 S.W.2d 738 (App.1981); Platt v. Martinez, 90 N.M. 323, 563 P.2d 586 (1977); Ivener v. Cowan, 175 N.W.2d 121 (Iowa 1970); Amato v. Haraden, 280 Minn. 399, 159 N.W.2d 907 (1968). It is clear that where one owner objects overtly to the other's claimed boundary, there is no acquiescence; see Waters v. Spell, 190 Ga.App. 790, 380 S.E.2d 55 (1989); Brown v. McDaniel, 261 Iowa 730, 156 N.W.2d 349 (1968).

34. See, e.g., Kiker v. Anderson, 226 Ga. 121, 172 S.E.2d 835 (1970) ("acts and declarations of adjoining landowners"); Wojahn v. Johnson, 297 N.W.2d 298 (Minn.1980) ("passive consent" not enough).

physically on the ground,[35] usually by a fence or other barrier, which must be put in place with the intention of marking a boundary and not for some other purpose, such as containing livestock[36] or complying with a city ordinance.[37] Its presence must be known to both adjoining owners,[38] and they must take possession to the marked line.[39]

There is no necessity that the adjoining parcels be held by the same owners for the entire period of acquiescence. If either tract is transferred and the acquiescence continues, the time periods of the successive owners will be tacked together.[40] Since the deed given by the owner whose land is enlarged by the new boundary is unlikely to describe the added strip explicitly, one might argue that there is no privity between the grantor and grantee. But the argument is irrelevant, for here (unlike adverse possession) privity is unnecessary to the tacking of ownerships.[41]

Estoppel. The doctrines of agreement and acquiescence discussed above are based in part on rather loose notions of estoppel.[42] But when an estoppel can be made out with greater specificity, the owner who claims land beyond his or her paper boundary may prevail without meeting such requirements as an agreement, a marking on the ground, or the long passage of time. A boundary by estoppel arises when one owner erroneously represents to the other that the boundary between them is located along a certain line; the second, in reliance on the representations, builds improvements which encroach on the true boundary or takes other detrimental actions. The party who made the representations is then estopped to deny them, and the boundary is in effect shifted accordingly.[43]

---

35. Knutson v. Jensen, 440 N.W.2d 260 (N.D.1989); Sille v. Shaffer, 297 N.W.2d 379 (Iowa 1980); Hales v. Frakes, 600 P.2d 556 (Utah 1979); Dodds v. Lagan, 595 P.2d 452 (Okl.App.1979); Vella v. Ratto, 17 Cal.App.3d 737, 95 Cal.Rptr. 72 (1971).

36. Roderick v. Durfey, 746 P.2d 1186 (Utah 1987); Stone v. Turner, 106 N.M. 82, 738 P.2d 1327 (App.1987); Croft v. Sanders, 238 S.C. 507, 323 S.E.2d 791 (1984); Dodds v. Lagan, 595 P.2d 452 (Okl.App.1979); Aley v. Hacienda Farms, Inc., 584 S.W.2d 126 (Mo. App.1979); Ferrari v. Meeks, 181 N.W.2d 201 (Iowa 1970). A fence which has been nailed to existing trees is unlikely to have been erected as a boundary marker; Hoskins v. Cook, 239 Ark. 285, 388 S.W.2d 914 (1965). See generally Annot., 7 A.L.R.4th 53, 92 (1981).

37. Dooley's Hardware Mart v. Trigg, 270 Cal.App.2d 337, 75 Cal.Rptr. 745 (1969).

38. Sille v. Shaffer, supra note 35; Dodds v. Lagan, supra note 36; Parr v. Worley, 93 N.M. 229, 599 P.2d 382 (1979); Fuoco v. Williams, 18 Utah 2d 282, 421 P.2d 944 (1966); Hakanson v. Manders, 158 Neb. 392, 63 N.W.2d 436 (1954). In Platt v. Martinez, 90 N.M. 323, 563 P.2d 586 (1977), the fence was obscured by the terrain and heavy brush from the view of the owner on whose land it encroached; hence no boundary by acquiescence was established. See also Griffin v. Werdell,

182 Iowa 969, 164 N.W. 760 (1917) (encroachment below surface of ground not visible; no boundary established).

39. Wood v. Myrup, 681 P.2d 1255 (Utah 1984); Aley v. Hacienda Farms, Inc., supra note 36; Sachs v. Board of Trustees, 89 N.M. 712, 557 P.2d 209 (1976), appeal after remand 92 N.M. 605, 592 P.2d 961 (1978); Paquin v. Guiorguiev, 117 R.I. 239, 366 A.2d 169 (1976); Landrum v. Taylor, 217 Kan. 113, 535 P.2d 406 (1975); Hartley v. Ruybal, 160 Colo. 80, 414 P.2d 114 (1966). The extent of required acts of possession depends on the nature of the property and the uses to which it is suited, and may be quite limited; see Little v. Gray, 137 Vt. 569, 409 A.2d 574 (1979).

40. Cornelison v. Flanagan, 198 Okl. 593, 180 P.2d 823 (1947); Renwick v. Noggle, 247 Mich. 150, 225 N.W. 535 (1929).

41. Siegel v. Renkiewicz' Estate, 373 Mich. 421, 129 N.W.2d 876 (1964). Cf. § 11.7 supra at notes 40–41.

42. See text at note 9, supra.

43. See Burkey v. Baker, 6 Wn.App. 243, 492 P.2d 563 (1971); Browder, supra note 3, at 519–25; 2 Tiffany, Real Property § 656 (3d ed. 1939). Cf. Desruisseau v. Isley, 27 Ariz.App. 257, 553 P.2d 1242 (1976), rejecting the doctrine of estoppel in boundary disputes.

The cases are divided as to the knowledge which the person making the representation must possess. Most indicate that the representer must know that the true boundary is not where he or she says it is,[44] and a few take the rather extreme position that the representer must have intended to deceive the other owner, or must at least have been grossly negligent in making the representations.[45] But a substantial minority of cases disregard lack of knowledge and estop the representer anyway.[46] There must, of course, be a representation made,[47] although a surprising number of cases find it from an owner's silence in the face of knowledge that the neighbor is building an encroaching structure.[48] But if the party being encroached upon issues a warning or protest, estoppel is obviously defeated.[49]

An owner who claims estoppel must have relied reasonably on the other's representations. If the claimant's actions were induced by other factors,[50] or if the claimant knew the true location of the boundary,[51] there is no basis for estoppel. The reliance must lead to a substantial and costly change of position; the most common is the construction of improvements,[52] but a prospective buyer who purchases land in reliance on an erroneous statement of the boundary by an adjoining owner may also assert estoppel.[53] There is no requirement that the reliance continue for any particular period of time.[54]

Common Grantor. It is plain that a line established or marked by a common grantor may form the basis for a boundary by agreement or acquiescence between two abutting owners. However, a separate legal doctrine may make such a line their boundary even though the elements of agreement or acquiescence are not present. This doctrine operates only if the common grantor marks the line on the ground and sells both parcels by

---

44. LeeJoice v. Harris, 404 N.W.2d 4 (Minn.App.1987); Wojahn v. Johnson, 297 N.W.2d 298 (Minn.1980); Summers v. Holder, 254 Or. 180, 458 P.2d 429 (1969); United States v. Wilcox, 258 F.Supp. 944 (N.D.Iowa 1966). Where both parties acted under a mistake as to the true location, one court ordered the land conveyed to the encroaching party upon his payment of its reasonable value; see Faulkner v. Lloyd, 253 S.W.2d 972 (Ky.1952).

45. Production Credit Association v. Terra Vallee, Inc., 303 N.W.2d 79 (N.D.1981); Dodds v. Lagan, 595 P.2d 452 (Okl.App.1979); Rautenberg v. Munnis, 108 N.H. 20, 226 A.2d 770 (1967), appeal after remand 109 N.H. 25, 241 A.2d 375 (1968). Contra, see Douglass v. Rowland, 540 S.W.2d 252 (Tenn.App.1976); Roman v. Ries, 259 Cal.App.2d 65, 66 Cal.Rptr. 120 (1968). See generally 2 Tiffany, Real Property § 656 note 11 (3d ed. 1939).

46. Burkey v. Baker, 6 Wn.App. 243, 492 P.2d 563 (1971); see Browder, supra note 3, at 521 note 147.

47. Keel v. Covey, 206 Okl. 128, 241 P.2d 954 (1952).

48. Wojahn v. Johnson, supra note 44; Amato v. Haraden, 280 Minn. 399, 159 N.W.2d 907 (1968); Hansen v. Pratt, 240 Ark. 746, 402 S.W.2d 108 (1966); Kennedy v. Oleson, 251 Iowa 418, 100 N.W.2d 894 (1960).

49. Dart v. Thompson, 261 Iowa 237, 154 N.W.2d 82 (1967); Dye v. Ebersole, 218 Ark. 97, 234 S.W.2d 376 (1950).

50. Thomas v. Harlan, 27 Wn.2d 512, 178 P.2d 965, 170 A.L.R. 1138 (1947); Aransas Properties, Inc. v. Brashear, 410 S.W.2d 934 (Tex.Civ.App.1967).

51. See State v. Hall, 244 Mont. 161, 797 P.2d 183 (1990). One opinion suggests the claimant will be disqualified if he had the means of learning the truth (as by obtaining a survey), but this is an extreme position; Gilbertson v. Charlson, 301 N.W.2d 144 (N.D. 1981).

52. Dunn v. Fletcher, 266 Ala. 273, 96 So.2d 257 (1957); cf. Dart v. Thompson, supra note 49 (trenches & footings not sufficient expenditure); Downing v. Boehringer, 82 Idaho 52, 349 P.2d 306 (1960) (small irrigation ditch not sufficient expenditure).

53. Clark v. Moru, 19 Wis.2d 503, 120 N.W.2d 888 (1963); Frericks v. Sorensen, 113 Cal.App.2d 759, 248 P.2d 949 (1952); 2 Tiffany, Real Property § 656 note 10 (3d ed. 1939).

54. Mahrenholz v. Alff, 253 Iowa 446, 112 N.W.2d 847 (1962); Browder, supra note 3, at 523 note 161.

reference to it. Moreover, the deeds employed must not use metes and bounds descriptions, but must mention only lot numbers; otherwise, the deed descriptions and not the marked line will control.[55]

Subsequent Purchasers. All four of the modes of practical location discussed above act to shift boundaries so that they do not coincide with the literal language of the relevant deeds. Once this shift has occurred, the cases generally assume that it is binding on all future owners of both parcels involved.[56] One who buys the enlarged parcel is unlikely to complain about this assumption, but a subsequent purchaser of the diminished parcel may be shocked to discover that he or she does not own as much land as the deed described. A purchaser who has no notice of the change of boundary will be protected according to some decisions[57] while others refuse to do so.[58] But purchasers without notice are very rare, since the presence of a fence or other physical marker, or the visible extent of the existing owners' possession, will usually give the purchaser actual or constructive notice of the boundary's changed location.[59]

Adverse Possession Distinguished. Adverse possession often operates to adjust boundaries with much the same effects as does practical location. But adverse possession has its own set of required elements, discussed in the preceding section; they differ from the elements of practical location in several important ways. The most obvious is hostility: an adverse possessor's claim will be defeated if he or she acted with the true owner's permission, and in some states the possessor must also know that the land being encroached upon does not belong to him or her.[60] No such hostility is necessary for a boundary by practical location.[61] Indeed, agreement or permission is presumed or inferred in the case of a boundary by acquiescence[62] and is literally present in the other three modes of practical location.

A second distinction involves notice. In all forms of practical location, including acquiescence, the owner encroached upon must have actual knowledge of the encroachment.[63] On the other hand, adverse possession must be merely "open and notorious," and whether the true owner gets actual

---

55. Winans v. Ross, 35 Wn.App. 238, 666 P.2d 908 (1983); Miller v. Stovall, 717 P.2d 798 (Wyo.1986); Phillippe v. Horns, 188 Neb. 304, 196 N.W.2d 382 (1972); Daley v. Gruber, 361 Mich. 358, 104 N.W.2d 807 (1960), following Maes v. Olmsted, 247 Mich. 180, 225 N.W. 583 (1929); Thiel v. Damrau, 268 Wis. 76, 66 N.W.2d 747 (1954); Roetzel v. Rusch, 172 Okl. 465, 45 P.2d 518 (1935). The seminal case is Herse v. Questa, 100 App.Div. 59, 91 N.Y.S. 778 (1904).

56. Goff v. Lever, 566 So.2d 1274 (Miss. 1990); O'Neil v. Buchanan, 136 Vt. 331, 388 A.2d 431 (1978); Garrett v. United States, 407 F.2d 146 (8th Cir.1969); Trautman v. Ahlert, 147 N.W.2d 407 (N.D.1966). See 2 Tiffany, Real Property § 653 note 87 (3d ed. 1939). The written descriptions in future deeds are deemed revised to reflect the change; see note 7, supra.

57. Duff v. Seubert, 110 Idaho 865, 719 P.2d 1125 (1985); United States v. Williams,

441 F.2d 637 (5th Cir.1971); Proctor v. Libby, 110 Me. 39, 85 A. 298 (1912).

58. See Browder, supra note 3, at 530 note 188.

59. Schultz v. Plate, 48 Wn.App. 312, 739 P.2d 95 (1987); Duff v. Seubert, 110 Idaho 865, 719 P.2d 1125 (1985); Piotrowski v. Parks, 39 Wn.App. 37, 691 P.2d 591 (1984); Sanlando Springs Animal Hospital, Inc. v. Douglass, 455 So.2d 596 (Fla.App.1984).

60. See § 11.7, infra, at notes 23–28.

61. One decision argues that the doctrine of boundary by acquiescence was developed by the courts precisely to alleviate the difficulty of proving hostility in adverse possession; Buza v. Wojtalewicz, 48 Wis.2d 557, 180 N.W.2d 556 (1970). See also Morton v. Hall, 239 Ark. 1094, 396 S.W.2d 830 (1965).

62. See text at note 25 supra.

63. See text at note 38 supra.

knowledge of it is generally irrelevant.[64] The time periods required for a successful boundary shift may also be different. While adverse possession always requires occupancy for the full period of the statute of limitations, the cases are divided as to whether boundaries by acquiescence [65] or agreement [66] do so, and boundaries fixed by a common grantor or by estoppel require no specific time period at all.

Despite these distinctions, it is entirely conceivable that the same factual evidence may give rise to a boundary change either by adverse possession or by acquiescence if all of the elements of both are present. The only apparently irreconcilable inconsistency between them is that of hostility versus permission, and if the party who is encroached upon is simply silent, either conclusion might easily be reached.[67]

§ 11.9   The Recording System—Introduction

Ownership of land can exist only because it is recognized and enforced by the legal institutions of the state. Hence, it is not surprising that virtually all modern governments have developed and operate systems which permit interested persons to discover who owns any given parcel. In most countries, these systems are designed and organized in a way which allows the government to make affirmative statements to the inquirer about the condition of the title; thus, one who requests the information might be told by a governmental official that "This land is owned by A, subject to a one-year lease to B, an easement held by C, and a mortgage to the D Bank." Copies of the documents which created the lease, easement, and mortgage may also be given to the searcher for his or her scrutiny.

In America, each state is responsible for the records of title to land within its borders, usually on a county-by-county basis; the Federal Government operates no general title records system. Eleven states have systems like the paradigm described above which makes affirmative statements respecting the title. These so-called title *registration* or "Torrens" systems are described in a later section. But every state maintains a *recording* system, far more widely used, which functions on very different principles. The recording system comprises the only publicly-maintained set of title records in most states, and it is the predominant system even in states which also operate a registration system.[1] Recording systems are complex and have many inadequacies, but their use is so widespread that an understanding of them is essential to real estate law practice.

---

64. See, e.g., Hakanson v. Manders, 158 Neb. 392, 63 N.W.2d 436 (1954), comparing the two theories; § 11.7, infra, at notes 20–22.

65. See text at notes 19–21 supra.

66. See text at notes 29–32 supra.

67. See, e.g., Rosen v. Ihler, 267 Wis. 220, 64 N.W.2d 845 (1954), certiorari denied 348 U.S. 972, 75 S.Ct. 533, 99 L.Ed. 757.

§ 11.9

1. See Garro, Recording of Real Estate Transactions in Latin America: A Comparison with the Recording System in the United States, 1984 Ariz.J.Int.L. 90. Note carefully the distinction between the terms "registration," referring to a Torrens-type system that makes affirmative statements about titles, discussed in § 11.15 infra, and "recording," referring to the predominant American system described in this section. Unfortunately, this terminology is not always followed; for example, in a few states conventional recording is called "registration" and the official whose duty is to maintain the recording system is called the "register of deeds" or some similar term. See, e.g., North Carolina Gen.Stat. § 47–17.1.

In fundamental concept, the recording system is much like a library of title-related documents. These documents include all of the instruments which have been employed in prior legal transactions affecting the land, and which someone has taken the trouble to "record," or add to the library's collection. The searcher is expected to visit the library, use an official index system to identify and read the documents which relate to the land in question, and then to decide, by the application of his or her knowledge of real estate law and practice, who owns the land and to what encumbrances it is subject. This system is frugal in its expenditure of public funds and personnel. The government employees' only tasks are to receive, copy, index, and return the documents and to maintain the collection. The more demanding work of searching, analyzing, and reaching of legal conclusions from the instruments is left to the private users. The government makes no averment as to the state of the title. In this way the recording system differs markedly from "registration" systems of the kind described in the first paragraph of this section.[2]

Unfortunately, the recording system is seriously deficient with respect to the reliability of the information it yields to searchers. The unreliability stems from several sources, summarized here and discussed in greater length below: (1.) The recorded documents may appear to be valid and enforceable, yet may turn out to be fatally defective for reasons which cannot be detected by reading them.[3] (2.) Land titles may be affected by a variety of events and claims which are outside the coverage of the recording system, and thus are binding despite the fact that nothing appears in the public records concerning them.[4] (3.) A full search of the records requires tracing the chain of title instruments back to a grant from a sovereign; yet in many cases such a search would be prohibitively time-consuming and difficult, and searchers commonly limit their searches to, say, 40 to 60 years. Hence there is a residual risk that earlier, unexamined documents could adversely affect the title. (4.) Finally, there is the possibility that the searcher may make a clerical error in the search (the process of assembling the relevant instruments) or a mistake in the examination (the process of reading and analyzing the instruments found in the search), and consequently reach an incorrect conclusion as to the state of the title.[5]

2. See Whitman, Optimizing Land Title Records Systems, 42 Geo.Wash.L.Rev. 40, 63 (1973). Registration systems also incorporate provisions for indemnifying those injured by errors in the system to a much greater extent than do recording systems; see id. For a good discussion of the recorder's "archivist" role, see Woodward v. Bowers, 630 F.Supp. 1205 (M.D.Pa.1986) (recorder's action in accepting for filing a deed containing a racially restrictive covenant did not violate federal civil rights legislation). See also Proctor v. Garrett, 378 N.W.2d 298 (Iowa 1985) (recorder has no discretion to reject a proffered filing of a "common law lien" which is a legal nullity).

3. See text at notes 44–48, infra.

4. See Stroup, The Unreliable Record Title, 60 N.D.L.Rev. 203 (1984); text at notes 22–40, infra.

5. An error may also be made by the public employees who operate the system. If negligence is proved, they are liable; see, e.g., Baccari v. DeSanti, 70 A.D.2d 198, 431 N.Y.S.2d 829 (1979); Ralston Purina Co. v. Cone, 344 So.2d 95 (La.App.1977); Maddox v. Astro Investments, 45 Ohio App.2d 203, 343 N.E.2d 133, 74 O.O.2d 312 (1975). In most states recording officials are required by law to be bonded, but the bond is often for a limited amount, usually considerably less than the value of the average parcel of real estate. Recovery against the local government itself may be barred by sovereign immunity, and courts will obviously be reluctant to levy large personal judgments against public officials in their individual capacities. For all of these reasons, negligence suits against recorders often result in inadequate recovery. See Badger v. Benfield, 78 N.C.App. 427, 337

These inadequacies in the recording system have led to the development by private industry of two devices which supplement the public records: abstracts and title insurance. An abstract is a commercially-prepared set of copies or summaries of all of the documents in the public records affecting a particular parcel of land. One who obtains an abstract can "examine" the title without the need to visit the courthouse, and the risk of missing a relevant document is on the abstract company, not the examiner. Title insurance goes further; the insurance company or its agents perform both the search and the examination, and issue a policy promising to indemnify the insured if the title turns out to be defective except in the specific ways noted in the policy itself. Neither abstracts nor title insurance are perfect solutions to the problems of the recording system, but they are helpful and are widely used. They are discussed in detail in a later section.[6]

Recording and Priorities. If the owner of land purports to make two competing or inconsistent conveyances, their priority is ordinarily determined by the chronological order of their delivery. To illustrate, suppose O, who owns land, delivers a deed to A. The next day O delivers another deed of the same land to B. A will have the title to the land and B will have nothing except a possible claim against O for fraud or on any covenants of title in the O–B deed.[7] The same principles apply if O delivers leases, grants of easements, or any other sorts of conveyances. For example, if O gives mortgages to both A and B, the first mortgage in time will have priority, and the second in time will be junior to it.

The recording system has the rather extraordinary ability to reverse, in some situations, the results described above. The recording acts give O and his or her successors a power, under certain circumstances, to give B a conveyance which has priority over A's. If both conveyances are deeds, this means that B will have the land and A will have nothing. For this surprising result to occur, two factors must be present. First, A must have failed to record the first deed; a conveyance which is properly recorded can never be divested by the operation of the recording acts.[8] Second, B's behavior must be such as to qualify for the protection of the act. On this point there is a good deal of variation among the states, but their statutes

---

S.E.2d 596 (1985), review denied 316 N.C. 374, 342 S.E.2d 890 (1986) (even though instrument was not indexed in timely fashion, the recorder is not liable where the injured party knew of the failure to index, and hence caused his own loss).

6. See § 11.14, infra.

7. See Berger, An Analysis of the Doctrine that "First in Time is First in Right," 64 Neb.L.Rev. 349, 364–65 (1985); § 11.13, infra, on covenants of title.

8. The first-recorded instrument will be immune from attack under the recording act, even though its competitor instrument is filed very soon thereafter; see Daughters v. Preston, 131 Ill.App.3d 723, 86 Ill.Dec. 944, 476 N.E.2d 445 (1985) (first deed filed at 9:23 am; prevails over subsequent deed filed at 10:38 am); Goldstein v. Gold, 106 A.D.2d 100, 483 N.Y.S.2d 375 (1984), affirmed 66 N.Y.2d 624, 495 N.Y.S.2d 32, 485 N.E.2d 239 (1985). But

see In re Berkley Multi–Units, Inc., 91 B.R. 150 (Bkrtcy.M.D.Fla.1988), refusing to give priority to a mortgage that was recorded one minute before competing mortgages; "no reasonable definition of 'constructive notice' would contemplate a literal one minute's difference in recordation time as notice of a prior recorded mortgage." There are situations in which a conveyance is recorded at a time or in a manner which make it very difficult or impossible for a searcher to locate; some courts treat such conveyances as unrecorded even though they have literally been recorded. See § 11.11, infra, at notes 6–18. If the document has been presented to the recording office, but the public officials have failed to index it properly, the cases divide as to whether it has been "recorded." See § 11.11, infra, at notes 4–5.

can be divided into three general groups.[9] About half of the statutes protect B if he or she is a bona fide purchaser for value; they are usually called "notice" statutes, although the term is somewhat misleading since both lack of notice and payment of value are usually essential to B's protection. Whether B records is irrelevant under this approach. Roughly the other half of the statutes impose the same bona fide purchaser qualification, but add to it the further requirement that B record before A's deed is recorded. Since this conjures a mental picture, wholly fictitious, of A and B racing one another to the courthouse, this second group of statutes is usually called "notice-race." A third type of statute pays no attention to B's BFP status, but simply defeats A if B records first. Only three states, Delaware, Louisiana and North Carolina, have acts applying this pure "race" approach to the general run of conveyances, although a few others employ it for mortgages or other special types of conveyances.

In general, no one is obliged to record anything,[10] and there is no direct penalty if a conveyance goes unrecorded. As between the original parties, an instrument is fully binding whether it is recorded or not. But the recording acts provide a strong incentive for every grantee to record, for one who fails to do so is taking the risk that his or her grantor will make a subsequent conveyance that will diminish or destroy the efficacy of the prior transfer. This principle is well recognized by people in the real estate and lending business, and the vast majority of conveyances today are immediately and properly recorded. Hence, litigation concerning the recording system's operation is not very common.

The discussion above oversimplifies the categorization of recording acts somewhat. A good deal can be learned by examining their language in more detail. Perhaps the most common form runs along these lines:

> Every conveyance not recorded is void as against any subsequent purchaser or mortgagee in good faith and for valuable consideration * * * whose conveyance is first duly recorded.[11]

9. See generally the discussions in Mattis, Recording Acts: Anachronistic Reliance, 25 Real Prop.Prob. & Tr.J. 17 (1990); Sweat, Race, Race–Notice and Notice Statutes: The American Recording System, Probate & Property (1989) (listing 21 pure notice jurisdictions, 26 race-notice jurisdictions and 3 pure race jurisdictions); Baird & Jackson, Information, Uncertainty, and the Transfer of Property, 13 J. Legal Studies 299 (1984); 6A Powell, Real Property ¶ 905 (1981); 4 Am.L.Prop. § 17.5 (1952). The Uniform Simplification of Land Transfers Act adopts a notice-race approach; see USLTA § 3–202. See also Note, Recording Statutes: Their Operation and Effect, 17 Washb.L.J. 615 (1978); Johnson, Purpose and Scope of Recording Acts, 47 Iowa L.Rev. 231 (1962).

10. Blakely v. Kelstrup, 218 Mont. 304, 708 P.2d 253 (1985) (unrecorded deed is valid as between the parties to it); Landmark v. Schaefbauer, 41 B.R. 766 (Bkrtcy.D.Minn.1984) (similar); In re Hartman Paving, Inc., 745 F.2d 307 (4th Cir.1984) (improperly acknowledged deed of trust is valid as between the

parties to it). One rather peculiar exception is Ariz.Rev.Stat. § 33–411.01 (supp.1981), which requires the transferor to record within 60 days of the transfer, and in lieu of doing so makes him or her liable to indemnify the transferee in any action in which the latter's interest is at issue. Another is Md.Real Prop. Code § 3–101 (1981), which requires recording for validity of a transfer of legal title, even as between the immediate parties to the instrument. See also Patterson v. Wachovia Bank & Trust Co., N.A., 68 N.C.App. 609, 315 S.E.2d 781 (1984) (under N.C.Gen.Stat. § 47–26, a deed of gift is void as between the parties if not recorded within two years).

11. See, e.g., N.Y.—McKinney's Real Prop. Law § 291; Utah Code Ann.1953, 57–3–3; West's Rev.Code of Wash.Ann. 65.08.070. A slightly different form, in which the protected parties are described in an "exception" clause, is represented by West's Ann.Cal.Civ.Code § 1007:

Every grant * * * is conclusive against the grantor, also against everyone subsequently

This statute is of the "notice-race" type, since the subsequent purchaser, to prevail, must both be a BFP and record first. It could easily be modified to make it a pure "notice" type by deleting the last phrase quoted, " * * * whose conveyance is first duly recorded." Many "notice" statutes follow this form.[12] An alternative form of "notice" statute, found in many states, is as follows:

> No instrument affecting real estate is of any validity against subsequent purchasers for a valuable consideration, without notice, unless filed in the office of the recorder.[13]

The wording of the "race" type statutes is also instructive. The North Carolina [14] and Louisiana [15] statutes are similar, and can be paraphrased as follows:

> No conveyance shall be valid, as against [N.C.: purchasers for valuable consideration] [La.: third parties] until it is recorded.

Under both versions above, having notice of the prior conveyance will not disqualify a subsequent purchaser who records first.[16] But under the North Carolina version, in order to prevail the subsequent purchaser must have paid value for the land,[17] while there seems to be no "value" requirement in Louisiana.[18]

claiming under him, except a purchaser or incumbrancer who in good faith and for a valuable consideration acquires a title or lien by an instrument that is first duly recorded.

12. See Ark.Stat. § 16–115.

13. See Ala.Code 1975, § 35–4–90; Ariz. Rev.Stat. § 33–412; Iowa Code Ann. § 558.41. Classification of statutes as "notice" or "notice-race" can sometimes be difficult. The Colorado statute was formerly the subject of considerable confusion on this score; see Frees–Krey, Inc. v. Page, 42 Colo.App. 8, 591 P.2d 1339 (1978), reversed on other grounds 617 P.2d 1188 (Colo.1980); Eastwood v. Shedd, 166 Colo. 136, 442 P.2d 423 (1968). It was amended in 1984 to state "this is a race-notice recording statute;" West's Colo.Rev.Stat.Ann. § 38–35–109. See Note, The Colorado Recording Act: Race–Notice or Pure Notice?, 51 Den. L.J. 115 (1974); Cottonwood Hill, Inc., v. Ansay, 782 P.2d 1207 (Colo.App.1989).

See also Leasing Enterprises, Inc. v. Livingston, 294 S.C. 204, 363 S.E.2d 410 (1987) (amendment in 1958 changed S.C. statute from "notice" to "race-notice"); Utah Farm Production Credit Ass'n v. Wasatch Bank, 734 P.2d 904 (Utah 1986) (statute is "notice-race" despite prior case suggesting it was pure "race").

14. N.C.Gen.Stat. § 47–18.

15. LSA–R.S. § 9:2721.

16. See Schuman v. Roger Baker & Associates Inc., 70 N.C.App. 313, 319 S.E.2d 308

(1984); Hill v. Pinelawn Memorial Park, Inc., 304 N.C. 159, 282 S.E.2d 779 (1981); Phillips v. Parker, 483 So.2d 972 (La.1986); Bolding v. Eason Oil Co., 248 La. 269, 178 So.2d 246 (1965). Sometimes the temptation to discuss notice in "race" jurisdictions seems irresistible. In Hair v. Hales, 95 N.C.App. 431, 382 S.E.2d 796 (1989), a set of restrictive covenants had been recorded only one minute prior to the deed of the innocent purchasers, who had no actual notice of it. The court held the purchasers also had no constructive notice, and therefore were free of its provisions. The result is inconsistent both with the pure "race" language of the statute and with its philosophy that notice is immaterial.

17. Chrysler Credit Corp. v. Burton, 599 F.Supp. 1313 (M.D.N.C.1984); Hill v. Pinelawn Memorial Park, Inc., supra n. 16.

18. The Louisiana cases consistently refer to the act's protection to "third parties," with no reference to whether such parties have paid value. See Redman, The Louisiana Law of Recordation: Some Principles and Some Problems, 34 Tul.L.Rev. 491 (1965). Cf. American Legion Chappepeela Post No. 255 v. Morel, 577 So.2d 346 (La.App.1991), writ denied 580 So.2d 924 (La.1991), apparently recognizing a "value" requirement. The case appears to be an aberration and has no basis in the statute, but may be explainable on the ground that the parties to the subsequent deed were father and son, and the court was using the "value" element as a way of forcing the grantee son into his father's shoes.

Delaware's statute,[19] while worded differently, presumably has the same effect as Louisiana's in permitting the subsequent purchaser who records first to prevail without paying value. Slightly simplified, it reads:

A deed shall have priority from the time that it is recorded.

There is thus far no indication that the Delaware courts will read a "value" requirement into the statute.[20]

Interests and Conveyances Outside the Acts. From the description of recording acts above one might imagine that all types of interests, created in all possible ways, are within the coverage of the acts. However, this is not the case. As we will see, several types of interests in land are excluded from the acts by statutory or constitutional provisions. Other interests are excluded if they are created or transferred in certain specific ways. The priority of interests which are outside the scope of the acts is determined by common-law rules, and the usual rule is that first in time is first in right, whether recorded or not.[21] The result is that the records are less reliable than they might be; one cannot be fully confident of the results of one's search, for some interests in the land may be legally recognized despite the fact that the records make no reference at all to them.

The most commonly-encountered exclusion from the operation of the recording acts is the short-term lease. Nearly all of the statutes protect leases of one to three years' duration without the necessity of recording them,[22] perhaps in recognition of the fact that they are not customarily recorded and that the tenant's possession will usually (though not always) give subsequent purchasers notice of the lease.

Unfiled mechanics' and materials suppliers liens are usually excluded from the acts for some period after they arise. The lien acts typically provide that if a notice of lien is recorded within, say, 60 to 120 days after the right to payment arises, the lien's priority relates back to the date the work was commenced. Hence a purchaser may be bound by the lien despite the fact that a record search during this "relation back" period would have

19. 25 Del.Code § 153. The equivalent section for mortgages, containing virtually identical language, is 25 Del.Code § 2106. The statute was amended in 1968 to make it pure "race," but it was not construed by the Delaware courts until the 1980s; see N & W Dev. Co. v. Carey, 1983 WL 17997 (Del.Ch.1983, not reported in A.2d).

20. See Cravero v. Holleger, 566 A.2d 8 (Del.Ch.1989), describing the statute as "pure race;" First Mortg. Co. v. Federal Leasing Corp., 456 A.2d 794 (Del.1982) reaching the same result with respect to the mortgage recording statute. Cf. Eastwood v. Shedd, 166 Colo. 136, 442 P.2d 423 (1968), in which the court refused to read a "value" requirement into the Colorado statute.

21. An exception exists with respect to the set of interests created in equity by way of resulting and constructive trusts, rights to reform or set aside conveyances, and the like. Such rights are not ordinarily reflected in recorded documents, and they may indeed take priority over persons whose claims are recorded. However, a rule of equity nearly always subordinates them to the rights of subsequent bona fide purchasers for value; see, e.g., § 11.1 supra at notes 66–84 (rights to set aside deeds); 4 A. Scott, Trusts § 408 (3d ed. 1967) (resulting trusts), § 474 (constructive trusts); Hocking v. Hocking, 137 Ill.App.3d 159, 91 Ill.Dec. 847, 484 N.E.2d 406 (1985) (resulting trust); Osin v. Johnson, 243 F.2d 653 (D.C.Cir.1957). The net result of this rule of equity is much like that of a notice-type recording act.

22. See In re Fry Brothers, 52 B.R. 169 (Bkrtcy.S.D.Ohio 1985) (under Ohio law, lease exceeding 3 years is within recording act); Reeves v. Alabama Land Locators, Inc., 514 So.2d 917 (Ala.1987) (20 year lease is within recording act); 4 Am.L.Prop. § 17.8 note 10 (1952).

revealed nothing.[23]

Spousal rights arising from common-law dower and curtesy and from similar statutory schemes are valid without recording, and indeed do not give rise to any recordable document. It is common to recite the grantor's marital status in a deed, but in general a false recitation is not binding against an undisclosed spouse.[24] Since it is virtually impossible for a grantee to know with certainty that a grantor is unmarried, some decisions have refused to enforce such spousal rights as against bona fide purchasers.[25]

Finally, conveyances made by [26] or to [27] the Federal government cannot be defeated by state recording acts. The reason lies in the Supremacy Clause of the U.S. Constitution, which makes Federal law preemptive of state law. In general, Federal agencies voluntarily record conveyances of land they acquire, but in the absence of a specific congressional act requiring recordation [28] they incur no legal risk if they fail to do so.

In addition to the types of interests discussed above which are outside the recording acts, there are numerous other claims which will prevail without recording because of the specific manner in which they are created. In some cases these claims can be discovered, at least in theory, by searching in places other than the recording office. For example, wills and transfers by intestate succession need not be recorded,[29] but can ordinarily be found in the records of the appropriate probate court. Takings by eminent domain are sometimes held not subject to the recording acts, but some record of

---

23. See generally G. Nelson & D. Whitman, Real Estate Finance Law § 12.4 (2d ed. 1985). In some jurisdictions the lien relates back only if the work of the lienor is "visible," thus providing some limited degree of protection to bona fide purchasers; see Kloster–Madsen, Inc. v. Tafi's, Inc., 303 Minn. 59, 226 N.W.2d 603 (1975). See also Himmighoefer v. Medallion Industries, Inc., 302 Md. 270, 487 A.2d 282 (1985) (where mechanics lien was filed after builder entered into contract of sale, doctrine of equitable conversion permitted purchaser to acquire title free of lien). Compare Country Lumber, Inc. v. Newington Builders Finish Co., 4 Conn.App. 589, 495 A.2d 1121 (1985) (judgment lien against vendor prevails over purchasers' interest under prior recorded contract of sale; this case seems grossly wrong).

24. The recital creates, at most, a presumption of its truthfulness which can be rebutted; see Uniform Simplification of Land Transfers Act (USLTA) § 2–305(a)(8).

25. See Petta v. Host, 1 Ill.2d 293, 115 N.E.2d 881 (1953). USLTA continues to follow the traditional rule favoring the undisclosed spouse as against even a bona fide purchaser; USLTA § 3–202(a)(3). But see State v. Pettis, 149 Wis.2d 207, 441 N.W.2d 247 (App.1989), review denied 439 N.W.2d 144 (1989), based on Wisconsin statute which extinguishes claims based on homestead rights if an otherwise valid conveyance has been re-

corded for five years and if the conveyance fails to indicate marital status.

26. Thus one who takes land by a Federal patent need not record it to be protected from subsequent BFP's from the government; United States v. Schurz, 102 U.S. (12 Otto) 378, 26 L.Ed. 167 (1880); Rankin v. Miller, 43 Iowa 11 (1876).

27. See United States v. Snyder, 149 U.S. 210, 13 S.Ct. 846, 37 L.Ed. 705 (1893) (federal tax lien); Norman Lumber Co. v. United States, 223 F.2d 868 (4th Cir.1955), certiorari denied 350 U.S. 902, 76 S.Ct. 181, 100 L.Ed. 792 (1955) (federal eminent domain taking). See generally 8 Thompson, Real Property § 4295 (1963). This limitation on the power of the states is explicitly recognized in the USLTA's recording act language; see USLTA § 3–202(a)(6). Note that the government is bound by constructive notice of instruments which are recorded in the state recording system; see Yaist v. United States, 656 F.2d 616 (Ct.Cl.1981).

28. See, e.g., the Federal Tax Lien Act, 26 U.S.C.A. § 6323, which requires the Internal Revenue Service to record notices of liens it claims; see also United States v. Union Central Life Insurance Co., 368 U.S. 291, 82 S.Ct. 349, 7 L.Ed.2d 294 (1961); Haye v. United States, 461 F.Supp. 1168 (N.D.Cal.1978); Plumb, Federal Tax Liens, ch. 2, § 2 (1972).

29. See 4 Am.L.Prop. § 17.8 (1952), at notes 21–28.

them is usually maintained by the government agency doing the taking.[30] The assets of a bankrupt are transferred to the trustee in bankruptcy by virtue of federal statute, and no indication of the transfer need appear in the local real estate records, although the docket of the bankruptcy court will reflect the action. A purchaser who has no knowledge of the bankruptcy can claim title as against the trustee only by paying the "present fair equivalent value," a higher standard than the recording acts normally impose.[31] A purchaser who pays less has only a lien on the property to aid in recovery of the payment.

Note that the ability of a searcher to locate documents which are maintained outside the recording system may be more theoretical than real. In the case of eminent domain, for example, there may be dozens of state and local agencies with the power, and it is hardly practical for a searcher to check with them all as part of the ordinary title search process. It is similarly not feasible for a purchaser to check the records of all bankruptcy courts. In many jurisdictions a variety of agencies, including welfare, taxing, utility, and corporation departments, can acquire liens on real estate in the course of their operations. Where they maintain their own records rather than filing their claims of liens in the recording system, title searches are made more complex and much more subject to possible error.[32]

Other claims are outside the recording acts because they are created by a process which does not involve a document; hence there is literally

30. See, e.g., State ex rel. State Highway Commission v. Meeker, 75 Wyo. 210, 294 P.2d 603 (1956); Norman Lumber Co. v. United States, 223 F.2d 868 (4th Cir.1955), certiorari denied 350 U.S. 902, 76 S.Ct. 181, 100 L.Ed. 792 (1955). But see Alabama v. Abbott, 476 So.2d 1224 (Ala.1985) (order of condemnation in favor of state is a conveyance subject to recording act; if unrecorded, a subsequent BFP will prevail over it).

31. See 11 U.S.C.A. § 549. The purchaser is protected only if the land is located in a different county than the bankruptcy court; purchasers are expected to check the federal court docket in the county where the land is situated. The cited section also authorizes the trustee to record a copy of the petition in the relevant county's land records; if this is done, no subsequent purchaser is protected. With respect to the amount of value which a purchaser must pay to receive protection, compare § 11.10, infra, at notes 3–5 on the more lenient requirements of the recording acts.

32. This fragmentation of sources of title records is a severe problem in some jurisdictions. One compilation for Cleveland, Ohio listed 76 types of records in 16 different public offices which might contain land title data, and hence which should be checked in a thorough title search; Johnstone & Hopson, Lawyers and Their Work 274–75 (1967).

It is widely held that public records in a wide variety of governmental offices give constructive notice to title searchers. See, e.g.,

Pelfresne v. Village of Williams Bay, 917 F.2d 1017 (7th Cir.1990), appeal after remand 965 F.2d 538 (7th Cir.1992) (under Wisconsin law, judgment docket card gives constructive notice, but actual judgment order does not); South Creek Associates v. Bixby & Associates, 781 P.2d 1027 (Colo.1989) (municipal government's adoption of planned unit development zoning gives constructive notice of easement referred to in the plan); Federal Intermediate Credit Bank v. O/S Sablefish, 111 Wn.2d 219, 758 P.2d 494 (1988) (judgment gives constructive notice by virtue of its docketing, whether recorded in real estate records or not); Aldridge v. Aldridge, 527 So.2d 96 (Miss.1988) (lis pendens records give constructive notice); Cano v. Lovato, 105 N.M. 522, 734 P.2d 762 (App.1986) (same); Von Elbrecht v. Jacobs, 286 S.C. 240, 332 S.E.2d 568 (1985) (property tax lien gives constructive notice); Kinney v. Vallentyne, 15 Cal.3d 475, 124 Cal.Rptr. 897, 541 P.2d 537 (1975) (judgment liens); Hahn v. Alaska Title Guaranty Co., 557 P.2d 143 (Alaska 1976) (notice of federal land order appearing in Federal Register). But see Ellingsen v. Franklin County, 117 Wn.2d 24, 810 P.2d 910 (1991) (road easement recorded with county engineer but not in real estate records gave no constructive notice); Illinois National Bank v. Chegin, 35 Ill.2d 375, 220 N.E.2d 226 (1966), in which the court refused to impute constructive notice of a statutory lien where the statute made no provision for recording it and it was not recorded in fact; Dunn v. Stack, 418 So.2d 345 (Fla.App.1982) (lease in records of probate court gave no constructive notice.)

nothing to record. Illustrations include acquisition of title by adverse possession,[33] creation of easements by prescription, implication, and necessity,[34] some forms of dedication,[35] and adjustments of boundaries by the various techniques of practical location.[36] In most cases these modes of creating interests are incomplete until the claimant takes possession or makes use of the land, so one might suppose that a searcher could discover the claim by a physical inspection of the land. But this is by no means always the case, for the possession or use may have both begun and been completed long before the title search in question is made, so that the claimant's interest is fully protected even though no further trace of it appears on the ground.[37]

Occasionally controversy develops as to whether a particular instrument is entitled to be recorded. The statutes usually speak in terms of "conveyances of interests in real estate" or similar language. There is no question that any document conveying a legal, as opposed to an equitable, interest is recordable, provided it includes the notarial acknowledgment usually required by statute.[38] Moreover, contracts of sale and other papers creating equitable interests are now very widely considered recordable.[39] Option

33. See § 11.7, supra.

34. See §§ 8.4–8.5, 8.7, supra; McKeon v. Brammer, 238 Iowa 1113, 29 N.W.2d 518, 174 A.L.R. 1229 (1947). But see Bush v. Duff, 754 P.2d 159 (Wyo.1988) (unrecorded easement of necessity gives no constructive notice to foreclosing mortgagee, and foreclosure destroys easement even though its owner is not a party to the foreclosure); Tiller v. Hinton, 19 Ohio St.3d 66, 482 N.E.2d 946 (1985) (BFP takes free of unrecorded implied easement); Gill Grain Co. v. Poos, 707 S.W.2d 434 (Mo.App. 1986) (same). See Eichengrunn, The Problem of Hidden Easements and the Subsequent Purchaser Without Notice, 40 Okla.L.Rev. 34 (1987).

35. Dedications may result from oral statements and accompanying actions, with no writing involved; see § 11.6 supra, at note 3. Cf. Board of County Commissioners v. White, 547 P.2d 1195 (Wyo.1976), refusing to recognize a prescriptive dedication of a public road because the statutory procedures, including recordation of a certificate declaring the existence of the road, were not met; Nohowel v. Hall, 218 Md. 160, 146 A.2d 187 (1958), protecting a subsequent bona fide purchaser against a prior unrecorded common law dedication.

36. See § 11.8, supra.

37. See Mugaas v. Smith, 33 Wn.2d 429, 206 P.2d 332, 9 A.L.R.2d 846 (1949) (adverse possession completed prior to title search; no visible evidence of adverse claim); Otero v. Pacheco, 94 N.M. 524, 612 P.2d 1335 (App. 1980), cert. denied 94 N.M. 674, 615 P.2d 991 (1980) (purchasers held to have constructive notice of implied easement from "visibility" of a buried sewer line.)

38. If an instrument is not acknowledged, it is usually deemed unrecorded even though the recording officials actually accepted it and placed it in the records. See Summa Investing Corp. v. McClure, 569 So.2d 500 (Fla.App. 1990); Nordman v. Rau, 86 Kan. 19, 119 P. 351 (1911); Maxwell, The Hidden Defect in Acknowledgment and Title Security, 2 U.C.L.A.L.Rev. 83 (1954). Moreover, such an instrument is typically held to give no constructive notice to searchers; see note 42 infra.

39. See, e.g., Buras v. Shell Oil Co., 666 F.Supp. 919 (S.D.Miss.1987); Leman v. Quinn, 107 A.D.2d 452, 565 N.Y.S.2d 541 (1991); Kingsley v. Makay, 253 Md. 24, 251 A.2d 585 (1969); Glauner v. Malone, 316 F.2d 291 (3d Cir.1963) (V.I. law); 6A Powell, Real Property ¶ 904(4) (1981); Annot., 26 A.L.R. 1546 (1923). Note that many types of equitable interests can be created without a writing, and these are usually held to be outside the recording system; in general, however, the equitable doctrine of bona fide purchaser will operate, much like the recording acts, to protect later buyers without notice of the equitable interest. See note 21, supra; Barrish v. Flitter, 715 F.Supp. 692 (E.D.Pa.1989); Doane Agricultural Service, Inc. v. Neelyville Grain Co., Inc., 516 S.W.2d 788 (Mo.App.1974) (BFP is protected from prior equitable lien). Cf. Lewisville State Bank v. Blanton, 520 S.W.2d 607 (Tex.Civ.App.1975), reversed 525 S.W.2d 696 (Tex.1975), refusing to apply the bona fide purchaser doctrine to protect a subsequent judgment creditor as against the prior holder of a non-documentary (and hence unrecorded) equitable lien; Osin v. Johnson, 243 F.2d 653 (D.C.Cir.1957) (same, unless judgment creditor proves he or she relied on the records.) Cases of the latter sort usually turn on a general

agreements are somewhat more problematic, since it can be argued that they create no interest in real estate, but only a right to accept an offer and form a contract. Yet treating them as granting interests in land has obvious practical advantages, and most modern decisions regard them as recordable.[40]

A grantor who does not want his or her conveyance recorded may try to achieve this objective by refusing to appear before a notary for the necessary acknowledgment. This is a common practice when a long-term installment contract is executed, since the vendor may anticipate that in the event of a default, it will be easier to terminate the contract and resell the land if the record title is not clouded by the contract.[41] The purchaser, in turn, may attempt to get on record anyway, either by persuading the recorder to accept the instrument despite the absence of an acknowledgment or by executing, acknowledging, and recording some new document, perhaps termed a "notice of interest," which recites the existence of the previous contract. Such a paper is not a conveyance and may well be held legally unrecordable. Whichever technique is used, it is probable that the courts will hold the recorded instrument to give no constructive notice to future purchasers.[42] But as a practical matter, the purchaser will still have largely achieved the objective, for the instrument will give actual notice to those who in fact search the records and discover it, and thus will preclude them from using the recording acts to defeat it.[43]

refusal to accord BFP status to judgment creditors; see Annot., 87 A.L.R. 1505 (1933); see § 11.10, infra, at notes 14–16.

40. Versai Management, Inc. v. Monticello Forest Products Corp., 479 La.App. 477 (La. App.1985); Matter of Berge, 39 B.R. 960 (Bkrtcy.W.D.Wis.1984); Daniel v. Kensington Homes, Inc., 232 Md. 1, 192 A.2d 114 (1963); Strong v. Clark, 56 Wn.2d 230, 352 P.2d 183 (1960); Connolly v. Des Moines & Central Iowa Railway Co., 246 Iowa 874, 68 N.W.2d 320 (1955). The USLTA imposes no limits whatever on the sorts of documents which can be recorded, taking the view that " * * * the decision as to what to record is a private rather than a public one." USLTA § 2–301, Comment 1.

41. See G. Nelson & D. Whitman, Real Estate Finance Law § 3.30 (2d ed. 1985).

42. See Spady v. Graves, 307 Or. 483, 770 P.2d 53 (1989) (court order issued without jurisdiction gives no constructive notice); Department of Banking and Finance v. Davis, 227 Neb. 172, 416 N.W.2d 566 (1987); In re Big River Grain, Inc., 718 F.2d 968 (9th Cir.1983) (defectively acknowledged instrument gives no constructive notice, but acknowledgment statute should be construed liberally; where notary used individual rather than corporate form, but body of deed contained the additional facts which should have appeared in corporate acknowledgment, the deed was properly recordable); Matter of New Concept Realty & Dev., Inc., 753 F.2d 804 (9th Cir.1985) (similar); Low v. Sanger, 478 P.2d 60 (Wyo.1970) (instrument recorded without acknowledgment gives no

constructive notice); Kilgore v. Buice, 229 Ga. 445, 192 S.E.2d 256 (1972) (same); Coggins v. Mimms, 373 So.2d 964 (Fla.App.1979) (purchaser's recordation of "notice of contract" is improper and gives no constructive notice); Brown v. Johnson, 98 Cal.App.3d 844, 159 Cal.Rptr. 675 (1979) ("notice of vendor's lien" is not a recordable document; gives no constructive notice.) See generally Annots., 3 A.L.R.2d 577 (1949), 59 A.L.R.2d 1299 (1958).

But see In re Casbeer, 793 F.2d 1436 (5th Cir.1986) (instrument gives constructive notice even though acknowledgement contains latent defect, under Texas law); Mills v. Damson Oil Corp., certification to Mississippi Supreme Court, 437 So.2d 1005, 1006 (Miss.1983), further discussion by 5th Circuit Court of Appeals, 720 F.2d 874 (5th Cir.1983) (same result under Mississippi law); Hildebrandt v. Hildebrandt, 9 Kan.App.2d 614, 683 P.2d 1288 (1984) (same); Big Four Petroleum Co. v. Puirk, 755 P.2d 632 (Okl.1988) (executor's lease was properly recorded and gave constructive notice, even though not confirmed by probate court as required by law; In re Wonderfair Stores, Inc., 511 F.2d 1206 (9th Cir. 1975) (deed recorded with latent defect in acknowledgment does give constructive notice.)

43. See Metropolitan Nat. Bank v. United States, 901 F.2d 1297 (5th Cir.1990) (defectively acknowledged deed of trust gave no constructive notice, but might have given actual notice if subsequent lienor had in fact searched the records; but there was no evidence that lienor had done so); Annot., 3 A.L.R.2d 577, 589 (1949).

The discussion above suggests that title searches may give an incomplete and unreliable picture because the law recognizes and protects numerous types of instruments and interests that are unrecorded. A further source of unreliability arises from the fact that the instruments in the records may not be legally efficacious. A recorded deed, for example, may be a forgery,[44] procured by fraud in the execution,[45] executed by a minor,[46] or never delivered.[47] Any one of these defects will make the deed void, and the fact that it is recorded in no sense enhances its validity. Such defects are virtually impossible for a title searcher to detect, yet they can have a devastating effect on title.[48] In sum, even a complete and careful title search may produce seriously incomplete or legally erroneous results and may subject the buyer of land to risks of major dimensions.[49]

§ 11.10 The Recording System—Bona Fide Purchaser Status

Payment of Value. Nearly all of the recording acts protect subsequent conveyees only if they are bona fide purchasers. This status has two elements: paying value and taking in good faith with no notice of the prior conveyance. We first consider the value requirement. Obviously donees do not qualify, nor do heirs or devisees [1] except in the very unusual cases in which they have bargained and paid for their reward.[2] There is considerable disagreement as to how much a grantee must pay. A few cases seem to accept any amount, however nominal,[3] but most require an amount which is substantial in relation to the property's value, and not grossly inadequate.[4] There is general agreement, on the other hand, that the full market value

---

44. See Lloyd v. Chicago Title Ins. Co., 576 So.2d 310 (Fla.App.1990); Benson v. Diehl, 228 Mont. 199, 745 P.2d 315 (1987); § 11.1, supra, at note 70. USLTA § 3–202(a)(5)(i) retains this rule.

45. Id. at note 71. USLTA § 3–202(a)(5)(iii) retains this rule.

46. Id. at note 77. USLTA § 3–202(a)(5)(ii) apparently retains this rule.

47. § 11.3, supra, at notes 15–16; Stone v. French, 37 Kan. 145, 14 P. 530 (1887). USLTA § 2–202 reverses this rule and upholds the innocent third party who relied on the putative delivery, but permits the victimized grantor to record an affidavit that there was no delivery, and thus to prevent BFP rights from arising. See also Mass.Gen.Laws Ann. c. 183, § 5, making recording conclusive evidence of delivery.

48. A variety of other defects, such as fraud in the inducement and most types of incapacity, make the instrument voidable rather than void, and thus will not defeat a bona fide purchaser; see § 11.1, supra, at notes 76, 80–85. Yet if they exist they put the purchaser to the risk of proving his or her BFP status, perhaps in expensive litigation.

49. See Andersen, Conveyancing Reform: A Great Place to Start, 25 Real Prop.Prob. & Tr.J. 333 (1990); Stroup, The Unreliable Record Title, 60 N.D.L.Rev. 203 (1984); Fiflis, Land Transfer Improvement: The Basic Facts and Two Hypotheses for Reform, 38 U.Colo.

L.Rev. 431, 453–54 (1966); Straw, Off–Record Risks for Bona Fide Purchasers of Interests in Real Property, 72 Dick.L.Rev. 35 (1967).

§ 11.10

1. Jordan v. Copeland, 545 So.2d 27 (Ala. 1989); Gregg v. Link, 774 S.W.2d 174 (Tenn. App.1988); Gullett v. Burton, 176 W.Va. 447, 345 S.E.2d 323 (1986); Bagwell v. Henson, 124 Ga.App. 92, 183 S.E.2d 485 (1971) (donee); Fritz v. Mazurek, 156 Conn. 555, 244 A.2d 368 (1968) (donee); Dennen v. Searle, 149 Conn. 126, 176 A.2d 561 (1961) (devisee).

2. See Horton v. Kyburz, 53 Cal.2d 59, 346 P.2d 399 (1959), permitting the devisee to prevail, as a BFP, over a prior constructive trust.

3. See, e.g., Walters v. Calderon, 25 Cal. App.3d 863, 102 Cal.Rptr. 89 (1972), finding nominal consideration sufficient to confer BFP status as against a prior constructive trust.

4. Anderson v. Anderson, 435 N.W.2d 687 (N.D.1989) (recitation of $10 and other good and valuable consideration was nominal, and insufficient to establish BFP status); Phillips v. Latham, 523 S.W.2d 19 (Tex.Civ.App.1975), refused n.r.e., appeal after remand 551 S.W.2d 103 (Tex.Civ.App.1977), refused n.r.e.; United States v. West, 299 F.Supp. 661 (D.Del.1969); Alexander v. O'Neil, 77 Ariz. 91, 267 P.2d 730 (1954); Worthy v. Caddell, 76 N.C. 82, 86 (1877).

need not be paid.[5] The payment need not be in the form of money, but can be represented by goods or services instead.[6] Love and affection or familial relationship are usually held insufficient.[7]

The grantee who gives a promise to pay, as distinct from an actual payment, is not considered to have given value;[8] nor is the giving of a mortgage or other lien to secure a future payment.[9] However, an exception is made for a negotiable instrument given by the grantee which is in fact negotiated to a holder in due course.[10] The reason for different treatment is based on the severe limitations which the law imposes upon the maker's defenses on the note in the latter case, so that the grantee is very likely to be legally compelled to pay it even if the title to the land turns out to be defective.[11] Observe also that the payment need not be an irrevocable transfer; it is universally agreed that a lender who takes a mortgage on land has given value despite the fact that the "value" advanced is expected to be repaid.[12]

There is much more controversy over the status of judgment creditors. In most states a judgment becomes a lien on the defendant's land in the county where the judgment is docketed. If the defendant appears to have record title, but in fact has made an unrecorded conveyance prior to the entry of the judgment, will the subsequent plaintiff's lien prevail over the non-recording grantee? A substantial minority of the acts contain language explicitly protecting the creditors,[13] but absent such language the usual

---

5. Cheatham v. Gregory, 227 Va. 1, 313 S.E.2d 368 (1984) ($400 paid for 2.5 acres in 1973 was "value;" recording acts do not require fair and adequate consideration); Asher v. Rader, 411 S.W.2d 477 (Ky.1967). See generally 4 Am.L.Prop. § 17.10 notes 8–9 (1952).

6. Lundgren v. Lundgren, 245 Cal.App.2d 582, 54 Cal.Rptr. 30 (1966).

7. Baker National Bank v. Lestar, 153 Mont. 45, 453 P.2d 774 (1969); Dennen v. Searle, supra note 1. But see Strong v. Whybark, 204 Mo. 341, 102 S.W. 968 (1907). A promise of marriage may be valuable consideration; see Berge v. Fredericks, 95 Nev. 183, 591 P.2d 246 (1979).

8. Lattin v. Gray, 75 Nev. 128, 335 P.2d 778 (1959); Bell v. Pierschbacher, 245 Iowa 436, 62 N.W.2d 784 (1954). USLTA § 1–201(31)(iv) following UCC § 1–201(44)(d), takes the opposite approach; it provides that one pays value if he or she gives "any consideration sufficient to support a simple contract."

9. South Carolina Tax Commission v. Belk, 266 S.C. 539, 225 S.E.2d 177 (1976); Chevron Oil Co. v. Clark, 291 F.Supp. 552 (S.D.Miss. 1968), reversed in part 432 F.2d 280 (5th Cir. 1970); Alden v. Trubee, 44 Conn. 455 (1877). See 4 Am.L.Prop. § 17.10 note 10 (1952).

10. Dunn v. Stack, 418 So.2d 345 (Fla.App. 1982); Donalson v. Thomason, 137 Ga. 848, 74 S.E. 762 (1912); Davis v. Ward, 109 Cal. 186, 41 P. 1010 (1895). In Middlemas v. Wright, 493 S.W.2d 282 (Tex.Civ.App.1973), the grantee's personal check (a negotiable instrument)

was regarded as valuable consideration despite the fact that it was never presented for payment.

11. The holder in due course is subject only to so-called "real defenses," which include infancy, incapacity, duress, fraud in the execution, and discharge in insolvency proceedings. See U.C.C. § 3–305(2).

12. Some of the acts include "mortgagees" or "creditors" as protected parties, but even if there is no such reference, mortgagees who make contemporaneous loans are invariably protected. See Nev.Rev.Stat. 111.320; Wyo. Stat. § 34–1–101; Valley National Bank v. Avco Development Co., 14 Ariz.App. 56, 480 P.2d 671 (1971); Del Carlo v. Sonoma County, 245 Cal.App.2d 36, 53 Cal.Rptr. 771 (1966); Smith v. Good, 119 S.W.2d 593 (Tex.Civ.App. 1938), error refused; Manufacturers' Trust Co. v. People's Holding Co., 110 Fla. 451, 149 So. 5 (1933).

13. See, e.g., Department of Revenue v. Price–Williams, 545 So.2d 7 (Ala.1989), appeal after remand 594 So.2d 48 (1992); Mooring v. Brown, 763 F.2d 386 (10th Cir.1985) (under Colorado law, judgment lienor is protected by recording act from date a transcript of judgment is recorded); Prudent Projects v. Travelers Ins. Co., 3 Conn.App. 429, 489 A.2d 396 (1985); Rowe v. Schultz, 131 Ariz. 536, 642 P.2d 881 (1982); West's Ann.Cal.Civ.Code § 1214; 21 Pa.Stat. § 351; District of Columbia Code 1981, § 45–801, construed in Osin v. Johnson, 243 F.2d 653 (D.C.Cir.1957) (approv-

answer is no.[14] Often this conclusion is based on the literal language of the pertinent judgment lien statute, which typically imposes the lien on "the defendant's real property"—not the record property, the courts frequently hold, but the actual property as depleted by unrecorded conveyances.[15] An alternative basis for the same result is that the creditor is simply not a "purchaser" in the sense used by the recording statute.[16]

In reality, these cases require reconciliation of an ambiguity in the interaction of the recording act and the judgment lien act, although the decisions do not always explicitly recognize that fact. From a policy view-point, it is hard to envision a sound basis for denying protection to the judgment creditor, who has usually gone to the trouble and expense of filing and prosecuting a lawsuit in reliance on the state of the record title. For the law to inform such a person, at the conclusion of this perilous course, that the judgment is uncollectible despite the record's indication to the contrary, is a cruel trick. The winner in such a case is the prior grantee (often another creditor of the defendant) who was too careless or devious to record. Such a result is pernicious, but is widely reached. If the creditor completes the collection process by foreclosing the lien or holding an execution sale, the buyer at that sale is uniformly held protected by the recording act.[17] This usually follows even if the creditor purchases at his or her own sale.[18]

ing priority for a judgment creditor as against prior unrecorded conveyances, but doing so as against a prior unrecorded constructive trust only if the creditor could show actual reliance on the record title); Vernon's Ann.Tex.Civ. Stat. art. 6627, construed in Aldridge v. North East Independent School District, 428 S.W.2d 447 (Tex.Civ.App.1968), error refused; Gulf Oil Corp. v. Beck, 293 Ala. 158, 300 So.2d 822 (1974). See generally 4 Am.L.Prop. § 11.29 note 1 (1952). If the prior conveyance is a contract of sale rather than a deed or mortgage, the cases are divided as to whether, under the doctrine of equitable conversion, the vendee will have priority over the judgment creditor; see § 10.13, supra, at notes 14–15; Lacy, Creditors of Land Contract Vendors, 24 Case W.Res.L.Rev. 645 (1973).

14. FDIC v. Malin, 802 F.2d 12 (2d Cir. 1986) (N.Y. law); Dime Sav. Bank v. Roberts, 167 A.D.2d 674, 563 N.Y.S.2d 253 (1990), appeal dismissed 77 N.Y.2d 939, 569 N.Y.S.2d 612, 572 N.E.2d 53 (1991); Siegel Mobile Home Group, Inc. v. Bowen, 114 Idaho 531, 757 P.2d 1250 (Idaho App.1988); Texas American Bank/Levellan v. Resendez, 706 S.W.2d 343 (Tex.App.1986); Geller v. Meek, 496 N.E.2d 103 (Ind.App.1986); Buell Cabinet Co., Inc. v. Sudduth, 608 F.2d 431 (10th Cir.1979); Clarence M. Bull, Inc. v. Goldman, 30 Md.App. 665, 353 A.2d 661 (1976). See Annot., 4 A.L.R. 434 (1914). Nearly all of the statutes which protect only "bona fide purchasers" have been construed not to include judgment creditors in that term; those which protect "all persons except the parties to the conveyance" or the like have received a more mixed reception in the courts when the rights of subsequent judg-

ment creditors are at stake. For illustrations of the two types, see § 10.9 at notes 11 & 14, supra. See generally Note, Status of Judgment Creditors Under the Recording Acts, 32 N.Dame L.Rev. 471 (1957). South Carolina follows an unusual rule under which the judgment creditor is protected only if the debt or claim arose prior to the delivery of the unrecorded conveyance, even though the judgment is docketed afterward; see Prudential Insurance Co. v. Wadford, 232 S.C. 476, 102 S.E.2d 889 (1958).

15. Wilson v. Willamette Industries, Inc., 280 Or. 45, 569 P.2d 609 (1977); Kartchner v. State Tax Commission, 4 Utah 2d 382, 294 P.2d 790 (1956); Oklahoma State Bank v. Burnett, 65 Okl. 74, 162 P. 1124, 4 A.L.R. 430 (1917); Holden v. Garrett, 23 Kan. 98 (1879) (judgments are liens on "actual and not apparent ownership.")

16. See Davis v. Johnson, 241 Ga. 436, 246 S.E.2d 297 (1978); Wilson v. Willamette Industries, Inc., supra note 15.

17. Keefe v. Cropper, 196 Iowa 1179, 194 N.W. 305 (1923); Sternberger & Willard v. Ragland, 57 Ohio St. 148, 48 N.E. 811 (1897); Note, 24 Minn.L.Rev. 807 (1940).

18. Hansen v. G & G Trucking Co., 236 Cal.App.2d 481, 46 Cal.Rptr. 186 (1965). Even if the creditor merely bids the amount of the judgment debt, so that no money changes hands, he or she has in substance paid value by giving up the claim on the judgment in return for the land. See 4 Am.L.Prop. § 17.30 note 9 (1952).

A common problem is raised by the creditor who takes a mortgage or other interest in land as further security for a pre-existing debt. For example, a bank may make an unsecured loan and later ask the debtor to give it a mortgage as security. Unless the bank somehow changes its position detrimentally in return for the mortgage, as by granting an extension of time for repayment, agreeing to forbear bringing suit, or giving some other concession such as a reduction in interest rate, it will by the large majority of cases be deemed not to have given value under the recording acts.[19] Hence, the bank's mortgage will be subordinate to any prior unrecorded conveyances the debtor has made. A similar result follows with respect to mechanics lien claimants; since they originally perform their work without taking any interest in the land, and since they give no further value in return for the lien, an earlier conveyance, even though unrecorded, will have priority.[20]

The rule, then, is that the "value" must be paid contemporaneously with or subsequent to the conveyance to be protected; otherwise the conveyee is not "out" anything in reliance on the records. But consider the case of the creditor who has previously made an unsecured loan, and who later takes a deed of the land in full or partial satisfaction of the debt. The creditor's position here is superficially similar to one who takes a mortgage to secure an antecedent debt, as discussed in the previous paragraph. Yet there is a vast difference, for here the creditor has detrimentally changed legal position by treating the debt as satisfied, typically by cancelling the debtor's promissory note and thereby giving up all further claim against the debtor. Surprisingly, a number of courts have misunderstood this distinction, and have found no value to have been paid.[21] This is plainly incorrect; the creditor should be protected, and the more recent decisions adopt this view.[22]

Taking Without Notice. The second aspect of bona fide purchaser status is lack of notice of the prior unrecorded conveyance. Thus it is necessary to consider what sorts of notice might be imputed to a purchaser of real estate. Three main types of notice are discussed in the cases: (1) actual knowledge, gained from whatever source; (2) constructive notice of facts which would be apparent upon a visual inspection of the property and an interrogation of

---

19. Manufacturers & Traders Trust Co. v. First National Bank, 113 So.2d 869 (Fla.App. 1959); Salem v. Salem, 245 Iowa 62, 60 N.W.2d 772 (1953); Gabel v. Drewrys Limited, U.S.A., Inc., 68 So.2d 372 (Fla.1953); Brown v. Mifflin, 220 Ark. 166, 246 S.W.2d 567 (1952); Tripler v. MacDonald Lumber Co., 173 Cal. 144, 159 P. 591 (1916); Annot., 39 A.L.R.2d 1088 (1955). The USLTA takes the contrary position, treating a pre-existing claim as value for recording act purposes; USLTA § 1–201(31), following UCC § 1–201(44).

20. See Stout v. Lye, 103 U.S. (3 Otto) 66, 26 L.Ed. 428 (1880). Contra, see Shade v. Wheatcraft Industries, Inc., 248 Kan. 531, 809 P.2d 538 (1991) (mortgage loses priority to mechanics lien that attaches after mortgage is given but before it is recorded, if lien claimant has no actual knowledge of mortgage). In many cases, the "relation back" feature of mechanics liens provides the lien claimant with a better priority than he or she would gain through the recording acts; see, G. Nelson & D. Whitman, Real Estate Finance Law § 12.4 (2d ed. 1985).

21. See 4 Am.L.Prop. § 17.10 note 29 (1952), citing numerous cases refusing to treat the creditor as a BFP.

22. Fox v. Templeton, 229 Va. 380, 329 S.E.2d 6 (1985); Wight v. Chandler, 264 F.2d 249 (10th Cir.1959); Orphanoudakis v. Orphanoudakis, 199 Va. 142, 98 S.E.2d 676 (1957); Reserve Petroleum Co. v. Hutcheson, 254 S.W.2d 802 (Tex.Civ.App.1952), refused n.r.e.

those in possession of it;[23] and (3) constructive notice of information found in the public records.

Overlying all of these is the doctrine of "inquiry notice", which holds that one who has information from any source suggesting the existence of a prior conveyance must make a reasonable investigation of it; a purchaser who fails to do so will be held to the knowledge that such an investigation would have disclosed.[24] In such cases, an inquiry of one's own grantor is prima facie insufficient, for that is the very person who has the strongest incentive to conceal the prior conveyance.[25] Incidentally, the term "constructive notice," as used in the recording act cases, refers generically to any notice which is imputed by legal rules. Thus, notice growing out of the fact of an adverse claimant's possession, from the public records, or from the doctrine of inquiry notice is "constructive" if the purchaser does not in fact make the necessary search or investigation; the law simply imputes the knowledge to the purchaser anyway.[26]

23. In several states, including Massachusetts and Missouri, the recording acts refer to "actual notice." See Mass.Gen.Laws Ann. c. 183, § 4; Vernon's Ann.Mo.Stat. § 442.400. The Missouri cases treat notice as a question of fact, and do not automatically deem the purchaser to have notice of the rights of a party in possession; but such possession is evidence of actual notice, and if the later purchaser has actual notice of the possessor's presence, he or she is required to make a reasonable inquiry; see Drey v. Doyle, 99 Mo. 459, 12 S.W. 287 (1889); Note, 16 Mo.L.Rev. 142 (1951). The Massachusetts courts are more lenient toward the later purchaser, and do not even require an inquiry of a known possessor; see Toupin v. Peabody, 162 Mass. 473, 39 N.E. 280 (1895).

The Ohio statute refers simply to "knowledge," and it is unclear to what extent the Ohio courts will recognize constructive notice; see Emrick v. Multicon Builders, Inc., 57 Ohio St.3d 107, 566 N.E.2d 1189 (1991).

A few other states use the phrase "actual notice" or similar terminology, but in fact recognize constructive notice of more or less the conventional type described in the text. See, e.g., Ark.Stat. § 16–115, construed to include inquiry notice in Bowen v. Perryman, 256 Ark. 174, 506 S.W.2d 543 (1974); Kan. Stat.Ann. § 58–2223 (1976), construed to include constructive notice in Lane v. Courange, 187 Kan. 645, 359 P.2d 1115 (1961) (and see Note, 17 Washburn L.J. 615, 620 (1977)); New Mexico Stat.Ann.1978, § 14–9–3, construed to include constructive notice in Taylor v. Hanchett Oil Co., 37 N.M. 606, 27 P.2d 59 (1933). See 4 Am.L.Prop. § 17.12 note 3 (1952).

24. See Guthrie v. National Advertising Co., Ind.App. 556 N.E.2d 337 (1990); Miller v. Hennen, 438 N.W.2d 366 (Minn.1989); Williston Co-op. Credit Union v. Fossum, 427 N.W.2d 804 (N.D.1988), appeal after remand 459 N.W.2d 548 (1990); Miebach v. Colasurdo,

102 Wn.2d 170, 685 P.2d 1074 (1984); Earth Builders, Inc. v. North Dakota, 325 N.W.2d 258 (N.D.1982); First Alabama Bank v. Brooker, 418 So.2d 851 (Ala.1982); Burlington Northern, Inc. v. Hall, 322 N.W.2d 233 (N.D. 1982); Modrok v. Marshall, 523 P.2d 172 (Alaska 1974); Jaramillo v. McLoy, 263 F.Supp. 870 (D.Colo.1967). Massachusetts, in reliance on the "actual notice" language of its recording act, supra, has virtually eliminated the doctrine of inquiry notice; see Mister Donut of America, Inc. v. Kemp, 368 Mass. 220, 330 N.E.2d 810 (1975); Richardson v. Lee Realty Corp., 364 Mass. 632, 307 N.E.2d 570 (1974); In re Dlott, 43 B.R. 789 (Bkrtcy. D.Mass.1983). Precisely the contrary conclusion was reached on this same language in the Utah act; see Johnson v. Bell, 666 P.2d 308 (Utah.1983) ("actual notice" includes facts which would lead a prudent person to make inquiry and thereby gain actual knowledge of the state of title); Diversified Equities, Inc. v. American Sav. & Loan Ass'n, 739 P.2d 1133, 1137 n. 5 (Utah App.1987) ("a duty to inquire is not a duty to disbelieve, aggressively investigate, and set straight.") See also Amoskeag Bank v. Chagnon, 133 N.H. 11, 572 A.2d 1153 (1990), advancing the unusual rule that purchasers have a duty to make further inquiry upon finding a defectively recorded mortgage in the records, while attaching creditors do not have such a duty.

25. See Berge v. Fredericks, 95 Nev. 183, 591 P.2d 246 (1979).

26. See 5 Tiffany, Real Property § 1284 (3d ed. 1939), arguing that inquiry notice is a species of actual, rather than constructive notice. The distinction is not of any great importance, and the cases are not entirely consistent, but it seems more sensible to regard all legally-imputed notice, including inquiry notice, as "constructive."

Actual notice may come from a variety of sources. For example, the grantor may inform the purchaser of a preexisting encumbrance, such as a lease or easement.[27] A conveyee under the prior instrument or others in the locality may also do so.[28] The purchaser may have learned of the conveyance in the course of business dealings or personal relationships.[29] It may be discovered during a visit to the property or an examination of the public records. Actual notice of facts which suggest the existence of third parties' interests in the land may form the basis for a duty to make a further reasonable investigation under the doctrine of "inquiry notice," but the purchaser need not pursue rumors or ambiguous statements.[30]

A purchaser who buys property in the possession of someone other than the grantor will be held to constructive notice of the rights which an inquiry of the possessor would have disclosed.[31] Moreover, the inquiry must be a rather direct one; a mere casual conversation with the possessor may not be enough.[32] If the possessor is also a former record owner, about half the cases

27. Guthrie v. National Advertising Co., 556 N.E.2d 337 (Ind.App.1990); Massey v. Wynne, 302 Ark. 589, 791 S.W.2d 368 (1990); McDonald v. McGowan, 402 So.2d 1197 (Fla. App.1981); Hunt Trust Estate v. Kiker, 269 N.W.2d 377 (N.D.1978).

28. First Alabama Bank v. Key, 394 So.2d 67 (Ala.Civ.App.1981). Cf. Levine v. Bradley Real Estate Trust, 457 N.W.2d 237 (Minn.App. 1990) (where easement claimant stated that an easement might be signed, but did not state that it actually existed, the statement did not give notice of the easement).

29. First Alabama Bank v. Brooker, 418 So.2d 851 (Ala.1982); Chisholm v. Mid–Town Oil Co., 57 Tenn.App. 434, 419 S.W.2d 194 (1966). Cf. Durden v. Hilton Head Bank & Trust Co. N.A., 198 Ga.App. 232, 401 S.E.2d 539 (1990) (purchaser not held to knowledge of prior deed, even though his attorney had prepared it some months earlier for another client).

30. Berger v. Polizzotto, 148 A.D.2d 651, 539 N.Y.S.2d 401 (1989), appeal denied 74 N.Y.2d 612, 546 N.Y.S.2d 556, 545 N.E.2d 870 (1989) (knowledge that prior deal had "broken up" was not sufficient to put purchaser to further inquiry); Friendship Manor, Inc. v. Greiman, 244 N.J.Super. 104, 581 A.2d 893 (1990), certification denied 126 N.J. 321, 598 A.2d 881 (1991) (knowledge that prior owner had made fraudulent conveyances placed subsequent grantee on duty to make further inquiry); First Alabama Bank v. Brooker, 418 So.2d 851 (Ala.1982); Strong v. Strong, 128 Tex. 470, 98 S.W.2d 346 (1936); Williams v. Smith, 128 Ga. 306, 57 S.E. 801 (1907). See also Corey v. United Savings Bank, Mutual, 52 Or.App. 263, 628 P.2d 739 (1981), review denied 291 Or. 368, 634 P.2d 1346 (1981) (painted arrows on shopping center parking lot insufficient to put buyer on inquiry notice of easement in favor of adjoining land.)

31. In re Probasco, 839 F.2d 1352 (9th Cir. 1988) (California law); In re Taylor, 43 B.R. 524 (Bkrtcy.N.D.Ala.1984); Willett v. Centerre Bank, 792 S.W.2d 916 (Mo.App.1990); Williston Co-op. Credit Union v. Fossum, 459 N.W.2d 548 (N.D.1990); Peoples Nat. Bank v. Birney's Enterprises, Inc., 54 Wn.App. 668, 775 P.2d 466 (1989); Citizens Bank v. Hodges, 107 N.M. 329, 757 P.2d 799 (1988), cert. denied 107 N.M. 74, 752 P.2d 789 (1988); Peruzzi Bros., Inc. v. Contee, 72 Md.App. 118, 527 A.2d 821 (1987); Grandnorthern, Inc. v. West Mall Partnership, 359 N.W.2d 41 (Minn.App.1984); Hooker v. Dunster, 74 Or.App. 636, 704 P.2d 515 (1985); Bailey v. Banther, 173 W.Va. 220, 314 S.E.2d 176 (1983); Claremont Terrace Homeowners' Ass'n v. United States, 146 Cal. App.3d 398, 194 Cal.Rptr. 216 (1983); Grand Island Hotel Corp. v. Second Island Development Co., 191 Neb. 98, 214 N.W.2d 253 (1974). See McCannon v. Marston, 679 F.2d 13 (3d Cir.1982) (Pennsylvania law), applying the rule in favor of an unrecorded purchaser in possession of a condominium unit in a large project, notwithstanding the burden which a later purchaser of the entire building or a block of units would meet in inquiring of a large number of such unit possessors. USLTA § 3–202 follows the rule.

32. See, e.g., Webb v. Stewart, 255 Or. 523, 469 P.2d 609 (1970), in which the plaintiff, a prior record owner, remained in possession. The purchaser's agent remarked to him, "Well, it looks like you've sold your house." Plaintiff confirmed that he had done so, but was permitted by the court to show that no proper delivery of the deed had ever occurred. The agent's inquiry was held insufficient. See also Willis v. Stager, 257 Or. 608, 481 P.2d 78 (1971).

On the other hand, there is no need to inquire of the possessor about the rights of other persons to whom the possessor might have made conveyances; see Mellon National

excuse the purchaser from making an inquiry, at least if the possessor has been there only for a relatively short time since the conveyance; the holdover's presence is supposedly explainable by the notion that the present owner has merely allowed the predecessor to remain on the land temporarily.[33] But since there are so many possible alternate explanations for the former owner's continued possession, the more sensible rule is to require an inquiry in all cases.[34]

It seems simple to expect the purchaser to inquire of the possessor, but in practice several tricky problems arise. They stem mainly from the rule that no inquiry is necessary if the seller personally is in possession, since such possession is consistent with the record title and an inquiry would presumably be redundant.[35] Suppose there are two or more people in possession, and one of them is the record owner. Is a prospective purchaser bound to inquire of the other possessors, or can it simply be assumed that they are licensees of the record owner who will have to vacate the property when the sale is completed? The latter inference is a particularly natural one when all of the possessors are members of the same family; if a mother and father contract to sell their house, it hardly seems necessary to make an inquiry of their children! The bulk of the cases agree, holding that no inquiry need be made of those who possess along with the record owner;[36] but one finds occasional contrary decisions.[37] Some cases only eliminate the need to inquire of other possessors if the record owner appears to be "in control" and the others "subordinate;"[38] but this seems a slender thread on which to hang a purchaser's title.

A similar problem is raised by the possession of a tenant of the record owner. If the lease is recorded or the purchaser is given a copy of it, he or she might assume that there is no need for a further inquiry of the tenant. Such an assumption can be fatal, for the great majority of the cases hold the purchaser to inquiry notice of any option to purchase, lease extension, or other rights of the tenant even if they were negotiated after the original lease was signed and do not appear in it.[39] Thus, one cannot safely fail to

Mortgage Co. v. Jones, 54 Ohio App.2d 45, 374 N.E.2d 666 (1977).

33. Vann v. Whitlock, 692 P.2d 68 (Okl. App.1984); First Savings & Loan Association v. Avila, 538 S.W.2d 846 (Tex.Civ.App.1976), refused n.r.e.; Raub v. General Income Sponsors of Iowa, Inc., 176 N.W.2d 216 (Iowa 1970); Iseli v. Clapp, 254 Md. 664, 255 A.2d 315 (1969); Annot., 105 A.L.R. 845 (1936); 4 Am. L.Prop. § 17.14 (1952).

34. See Perimeter Development Corp. v. Haynes, 234 Ga. 437, 216 S.E.2d 581 (1975); Webb v. Stewart, supra note 32; 5 Tiffany, Real Property § 1292 (3d ed. 1939).

35. Kane v. Huntley Financial, 146 Cal. App.3d 1092, 194 Cal.Rtpr. 880 (1983); Valley National Bank v. Avco Development Co., 14 Ariz.App. 56, 480 P.2d 671 (1971). See 4 Am. L.Prop. § 17.14 (1952).

36. See Kane v. Huntley Financial, supra note 35; Yancey v. Harris, 234 Ga. 320, 216 S.E.2d 83 (1975) (dictum); In re Mavromatis' Estate, 70 Misc.2d 55, 333 N.Y.S.2d 191 (1972);

Triangle Supply Co. v. Fletcher, 408 S.W.2d 765 (Tex.Civ.App.1966), refused n.r.e.; Diamond v. Wasserman, 14 Misc.2d 781, 178 N.Y.S.2d 91 (1958), reversed 8 A.D.2d 623, 185 N.Y.S.2d 411 (1959); Strong v. Strong, 128 Tex. 470, 98 S.W.2d 346 (1936). See 4 Am. L.Prop. § 17.13 (1952).

37. J.C. Else Coal Co. v. Miller and Banker, 45 Ill.App.2d 475, 196 N.E.2d 233 (1964).

38. See 5 Tiffany, Real Property § 1290 (3d ed. 1939).

39. Grosskopf Oil, Inc. v. Winter, 156 Wis.2d 575, 457 N.W.2d 514 (1990), review denied 461 N.W.2d 445 (1990); In re Fry Brothers, 52 B.R. 169 (Bkrtcy.S.D.Ohio 1985); Vitale v. Pinto, 118 A.D.2d 774, 500 N.Y.S.2d 283 (1986); Cohen v. Thomas & Son Transfer Line, Inc., 196 Colo. 386, 586 P.2d 39 (1978); Zale Corp. v. Decorama, Inc., 470 S.W.2d 406 (Tex.Civ.App.1971), refused n.r.e.; Martinique Realty Corp. v. Hull, 64 N.J.Super. 599, 166 A.2d 803 (1960). See Annots., 37 A.L.R.2d

inquire of the tenant even though her or his possession is "consistent with the record." A careful purchaser will insist that all tenants execute "estoppel statements" which set out the status of their leases in detail with the understanding that the purchaser is relying on them.

What sort of possession will place a purchaser on inquiry notice? The courts commonly say it must be visible, open, exclusive, and unambiguous.[40] Yet one can find cases imputing notice from very limited and ambiguous acts of possession. In Miller v. Green [41] a landlord sold farm land to his tenant. The tenant, who failed to record, did not reside on the land, and his only acts there were to plow two of a total of 63 acres and to have his father haul a number of loads of manure onto the land. The Wisconsin Supreme Court thought this sufficient to give notice to a subsequent purchaser who was in fact entirely unaware of this limited activity. A more sensible case is Wineberg v. Moore,[42] in which the prior purchaser of the property, which consisted of 880 acres of timber land with a residential cabin, did not reside there. However, there were personal possessions of his in the cabin, and he had posted several "no trespassing" signs which gave his name and address. The court found these acts sufficient to give notice to a later purchaser, although it conceded that they did not "present the strongest case possible."

Even if there is no human occupancy of the land at all, structures on it may be enough to give notice. The signs in Wineberg v. Moore furnish one illustration. Similarly, a prospective purchaser who observes a driveway running across the subject property to a neighboring house should inquire of

1112 (1953); 74 A.L.R. 350 (1931); 4 Am. L.Prop. § 17.12 note 12. There is a small minority view; see Gates Rubber Co. v. Ulman, 214 Cal.App.3d 356, 262 Cal.Rptr. 630 (1989); Stumph v. Church, 740 P.2d 820 (Utah App.1987); Scott v. Woolard, 12 Wn.App. 109, 529 P.2d 30 (1974). See also Howard D. Johnson Co. v. Parkside Development Corp., 169 Ind.App. 379, 348 N.E.2d 656 (1976), refusing to impute notice where the tenant had covenant rights on the lessor's retained land, not the land under lease.

· In a similar vein, the possession of a tenant will give notice of the landlord's interest even if it is not of record, at least if an inquiry of the tenant would have disclosed it in fact; see In re Fletcher Oil Co., 124 B.R. 501 (Bkrtcy. E.D.Mich.1990) (Michigan law); In re Forbrook Construction Co., 474 F.Supp. 876 (D.Minn.1979); Hansen v. G & G Trucking Co., 236 Cal.App.2d 481, 46 Cal.Rptr. 186 (1965). See also In re Investment Sales Diversified, Inc., 38 B.R. 446 (Bkrtcy.D.Minn.1984), and 49 B.R. 837 (Bkrtcy.D.Minn.1985), imposing a duty to make an inquiry not only of the tenant or vendee in possession, but also of his or her landlord or vendor and possibly other parties further back in that chain of title.

Under pure "race" statutes, such as those of Louisiana and North Carolina, a subsequent purchaser need not lack notice to prevail. Nevertheless, the recordation of an instrument in the chain of title does impart constructive

notice of its existence, and that notice may be legally significant in areas outside the context of the recording act; see, e.g., Chrysler Credit Corp. v. Burton, 599 F.Supp. 1313 (M.D.N.C. 1984) (recorded instrument may give notice so as to withdraw a subsequent purchaser's protection under the fraudulent conveyance act); Knutson v. Christeson, 684 S.W.2d 549 (Mo. App.1984) (same).

40. Lamb v. Lamb, 569 N.E.2d 992 (Ind. App.1991) (clearing of underbrush does not impart constructive notice of contract purchaser's claim); Burnex Oil Co. v. Floyd, 106 Ill.App.2d 16, 245 N.E.2d 539 (1969), appeal after remand 4 Ill.App.3d 627, 281 N.E.2d 705 (1971); Bump v. Dahl, 26 Wis.2d 607, 133 N.W.2d 295 (1965), rehearing denied 26 Wis.2d 607, 134 N.W.2d 665 (1965); Ames v. Brooks, 179 Kan. 590, 297 P.2d 195 (1956).

41. 264 Wis. 159, 58 N.W.2d 704 (1953). Compare Bradford v. Kimbrough, 485 So.2d 1114 (Ala.1986), in which the jury found that farming and bulldozing operations by prior claimant were insufficient to impart constructive notice, with White v. Boggs, 455 So.2d 820 (Ala.1984), in which maintaining a grove of trees on the land and using it as a driveway were found sufficient.

42. 194 F.Supp. 12 (N.D.Cal.1961); see also Chaffin v. Solomon, 255 Or. 141, 465 P.2d 217 (1970).

the neighbor about a possible easement.[43] A structure on adjacent land which encroaches on the subject property also gives notice of the adjoining owner's rights.[44] But many types of improvements, unlike those just mentioned, furnish no clue as to the identity of the person who erected them, and thus provide no starting point for an inquiry; this is generally so of buildings, growing crops, and the like. Cases can be found which impute constructive notice on such facts,[45] but they are analytically unsound.[46]

The third principal source of notice is that given by the records themselves. At first blush this statement seems irrelevant; if the earlier conveyance is recorded, there is no way a subsequent purchaser can take priority over it, whether he or she has notice of it or not. But the idea that the records give constructive notice is nonetheless important, for a recorded document in the chain of title to the land may describe or make reference to another, unrecorded one, and thus give notice of the latter.[47] This is a

43. Gill Grain Co. v. Poos, 707 S.W.2d 434 (Mo.App.1986) (prescriptive easement for "field road" was sufficiently discoverable by visual inspection that purchaser had constructive notice of it); Dana Point Condominium Ass'n, Inc. v. Keystone Service Co., 141 Ill. App.3d 916, 491 N.E.2d 63 (1986) (signs and stickers on walls of laundry rooms in condominium buildings, identifying tenant which leased rooms and kept coin-operated machines there, were sufficient to place condominium unit purchasers on notice of lease); Xar Corp. v. Di Donato, 76 A.D.2d 972, 429 N.Y.S.2d 59 (1980) (existence of advertising sign on property gives constructive notice of signowner's unrecorded easement rights); Otero v. Pacheco, 94 N.M. 524, 612 P.2d 1335 (App.1980), cert. denied 94 N.M. 674, 615 P.2d 991 (1980); Fenley Farms, Inc. v. Clark, 404 N.E.2d 1164 (Ind.App.1980); Salt Lake, Garfield & Western Railway Co. v. Allied Materials Co., 4 Utah 2d 218, 291 P.2d 883 (1955) (railway tracks, poles); Maule Industries, Inc. v. Sheffield Steel Products, Inc., 105 So.2d 798 (Fla.App. 1958), certiorari denied 111 So.2d 41 (Fla.1959) (railroad track gives notice, not only of easement, but also of associated covenant rights.)

44. Nikas v. United Construction Co., 34 Tenn.App. 435, 239 S.W.2d 41 (1950) (encroachment by party wall).

45. See Vandehey Development Co. v. Suarez, 108 Or.App. 154, 814 P.2d 1094 (1991), review denied 312 Or. 235, 819 P.2d 731 (1991) (prior grantees camped on land from time to time, improved roof of building on it, cut the grass, and placed lawn furniture on it; constructive notice found); Harker v. Cowie, 42 S.D. 159, 173 N.W. 722 (1919) (growing crops); Carnes v. Whitfield, 352 Ill. 384, 185 N.E. 819 (1933).

46. See Bearden v. John Hancock Mut. Life Ins. Co., 708 F.Supp. 1196 (D.Kan.1987) (growing crops give no notice of existence of lease on land); W.I.L.D. W.A.T.E.R.S., Ltd. v. Martinez, 152 A.D.2d 799, 543 N.Y.S.2d 579 (1989) (vacant building with sign indicating a

long-gone business was insufficient to put purchaser on inquiry); Stibor v. Farrell, 177 Neb. 437, 129 N.W.2d 449 (1964); 4 Am.L.Prop. § 17.15 (1952). In Burnex Oil Co. v. Floyd, 106 Ill.App.2d 16, 245 N.E.2d 539 (1969), appeal after remand 4 Ill.App.3d 627, 281 N.E.2d 705 (1971) the presence of Phillips Petroleum Co.'s brand name on the pumps of a service station was held insufficient to give constructive notice of Phillips' lease. See also Anderson v. Barron, 208 Ga. 785, 69 S.E.2d 874 (1952), in which the court found no constructive notice from the owner's infrequent visits to the land, posting of no-trespassing signs, occasional cutting and removal of timber, and payment of taxes.

47. Updike v. First Federal Sav. & Loan Ass'n, 93 B.R. 795 (Bkrtcy.M.D.Ga.1988); Camino Real Enterprises, Inc. v. Ortega, 107 N.M. 387, 758 P.2d 801 (1988); South Creek Associates v. Bixby & Associates, Inc., 753 P.2d 785 (Colo.App.1987), affirmed 781 P.2d 1027 (Colo.1989); Harper v. Paradise, 233 Ga. 194, 210 S.E.2d 710 (1974); Sedillo Title Guaranty, Inc. v. Wagner, 80 N.M. 429, 457 P.2d 361 (1969); Turner v. McIntosh, 379 S.W.2d 470 (Ky.1964); Jefferson County v. Mosley, 284 Ala. 593, 226 So.2d 652 (1969); Guerin v. Sunburst Oil & Gas Co., 68 Mont. 365, 218 P. 949 (1923). Cf. Anderson v. Graham Investment Co., 263 N.W.2d 382 (Minn.1978) (constructive notice of one recorded adverse conveyance made by grantor does not give notice of other unrecorded adverse conveyances.) The scope of the "chain of title" is discussed in § 11.11 infra.

If the instrument containing the reference is itself not entitled to be recorded or is defectively acknowledged, most cases hold that it gives no constructive notice of its contents. See § 11.9 note 42, supra, and accompanying text.

One might assume that the principle of notice from the contents of recorded documents has no application in pure "race" jurisdic-

perfectly reasonable notion if the reference is clear and complete, but in many cases it is not, and the courts have had considerable difficulty in dealing with broad and ambiguous references. Suppose a prior deed recites that title is conveyed "subject to an easement in favor of Mary Jones." Unfortunately the easement's location is not given, its scope is not indicated, and a title searcher may have no idea which Mary Jones is involved or where she may be found. If a court imputes inquiry notice on such facts, the investigative burden it imposes can be a very heavy one. The test should be whether a reasonable inquiry has been made.[48] If the reference is quite indefinite, it may provide no starting point for an investigation at all, and hence it may be reasonable to make none. In a few states statutes have been enacted to limit the searcher's duty of inquiry to cases in which the prior conveyance referred to is itself recorded.[49]

The concept of constructive notice from public records operates to expand the scope of title searches, for many types of records besides those in the recorder's office are often deemed to give notice. Property tax, special assessment, and court records are commonly included, as are various sorts of liens or claims of local government agencies.[50] The common law doctrine of lis pendens has a similar effect. It holds that the commencement of any judicial action which may affect a land title, and in which the land is specifically described, acts as constructive notice of the action's pendency, so that a purchaser who buys thereafter will be bound by the court's decree as fully as the original parties.[51] In some states statutes provide for recorda-

tions, in which notice is supposedly irrelevant to the operation of the recording act. However, the North Carolina courts have held that if the chain of title contains a deed which not only recites the existence of an unrecorded encumbrance, but describes it fully and conveys the property "subject to" or in subordination of it, it will be binding on subsequent purchasers. This result is said not to comprise an exception to the pure race theory, but to follow from the concept of estoppel. See Terry v. Brothers Investment Co., 77 N.C.App. 1, 334 S.E.2d 469 (1985).

Recorded instruments impart constructive notice only to those who are expected to search the records—normally, those who are acquiring interests in the land. For example, a building contractor who is employed to construct improvements on land will not be held to have constructive notice of the existence of easements or other encumbrances from their presence in the public records. Statler Mfg., Inc. v. Brown, 691 S.W.2d 445 (Mo.App.1985).

48. See United States v. Smith, 803 F.2d 647 (11th Cir.1986) (prior-recorded document, while containing erroneous description, was sufficient to impose duty of inquiry on later taker); Miller v. Alexander, 13 Kan.App.2d 543, 775 P.2d 198 (1989) (similar); Bourne v. Lay & Co., 264 N.C. 33, 140 S.E.2d 769 (1965); Tramontozzi v. D'Amicis, 344 Mass. 514, 183 N.E.2d 295 (1962); Grammer v. New Mexico Credit Corp., 62 N.M. 243, 308 P.2d 573 (1957). But see Camp Clearwater, Inc. v. Plock, 52 N.J.Super. 583, 146 A.2d 527 (1958), affirmed

59 N.J.Super. 1, 157 A.2d 15 (1959), in which the court imputed notice from a very general reference to prior grants of rights to use a lake. See also Fertitta v. Bay Shore Development Corp., 252 Md. 393, 250 A.2d 69 (1969).

49. See Colo.Rev.Stat.1973, § 38–35–108, construed in Swofford v. Colorado National Bank, 628 P.2d 184 (Colo.App.1981); Mass. Gen.Laws Ann. c. 184, § 25; New Jersey Stat. Ann. 46:22–2, (reservations and exceptions by reference to prior conveyances); N.Y.— McKinney's Real Property Law § 291–e, on the basis of which the court held a title marketable despite an indefinite reference to a prior contract of sale in L.C. Stroh & Sons, Inc. v. Batavia Homes & Development Corp., 17 A.D.2d 385, 234 N.Y.S.2d 401 (1962).

The Uniform Simplification of Land Transfers Act takes an additional step, providing that a reference to another instrument gives no notice unless the latter is recorded and the reference includes its "record location", such as a book and page number in the official records; see USLTA § 3–207. See generally L. Simes and C. Taylor, The Improvement of Conveyancing by Legislation 101–06 (1960).

50. See § 11.9 note 32, supra.

51. See Chrysler Corp. v. Fedders Corp., 670 F.2d 1316 (3d Cir.1982), explaining the background of common law and statutory lis pendens, and holding the New Jersey lis pendens statute constitutional; Partlow v. Clark, 295 Or. 778, 671 P.2d 103 (1983) (any court

tion of notices of lis pendens in the land records system, but most of these statutes are not exclusive and leave some room for the operation of the doctrine even when no notice is recorded.[52] The result is that a searcher must check the relevant court dockets as a part of every title examination.

There are a number of cases holding that one who takes by quitclaim deed cannot be a bona fide purchaser. The theory seems to be that a grantor who refuses to give any covenants of title in effect admits, or at least creates a strong suspicion, that the title is defective.[53] The clear majority of modern cases reject this rule,[54] and for good reason. There are many factors other than a questionable title which may cause sellers to use quitclaims; indeed, in some areas of the nation they are the typical mode of transfer. Moreover, the fact that a quitclaim deed is employed provides no specific information about earlier title defects which the purchaser can investigate. Hence, to say that it is constructive notice begs the question: notice of what, precisely? There is no sound basis for denying the protection of the recording acts to purchasers who take by quitclaim.

decree affecting land gives constructive notice as if it were recorded in the county's deed records); Jones v. Jones, 249 Miss. 322, 161 So.2d 640 (1964); Jarrett v. Holland, 213 N.C. 428, 196 S.E. 314 (1938); Rardin v. Rardin & Brewer, 85 W.Va. 145, 102 S.E. 295, 10 A.L.R. 300 (1919); G. Nelson & D. Whitman, Real Estate Finance Law § 7.13 (2d ed. 1985); White, Lis Pendens in the District of Columbia: A Need for Codification, 36 Cath.U.L.Rev. 703 (1987); Janzen, Texas Statutory Notice of Lis Pendens: A Deprivation of Property Interest Without Due Process, 19 St. Mary's L.J. 377 (1987); Notes, 47 Harv.L.Rev. 1023 (1934); 25 Cal.L.Rev. 480 (1937).

52. See Whitehurst v. Abbott, 225 N.C. 1, 33 S.E.2d 129 (1945); Note, 20 Iowa L.Rev. 476 (1934); West's Ann.Cal.Code Civ.Proc. § 409. A few statutes require recordation of a notice in the land records in all cases; see West's Fla.Stat.Ann. § 48.23; Mich.Comp.Laws Ann. § 600.2701; Virginia Code 1950, §§ 8.01–268, 8.01–269. See Da Silva v. Musso, 76 N.Y.2d 436, 560 N.Y.S.2d 109, 559 N.E.2d 1268 (1990) (where notice of lis pendens is cancelled despite continuation of litigation, a subsequent purchaser is not bound by the outcome of the litigation despite having actual knowledge of it); Howard, McRoberts & Murray v. Starry, 382 N.W.2d 293 (Minn.App.1986) (recorded lis pendens imparts constructive notice despite typographical error in legal description); Rolling "R" Construction, Inc. v. Dodd, 477 So.2d 330 (Ala.1985) (statutory provision for recording notice of lis pendens supersedes common law doctrine, and no constructive notice arises in absence of recordation); First Nat. Bank v. Dent, 683 P.2d 722 (Alaska 1984) (once a mechanics' lien has been recorded, subsequent purchasers have constructive notice of any suit filed to enforce it, even though no notice of lis pendens as to the suit has been recorded); Williams v. Bartlett, 189 Conn. 471, 457 A.2d 290 (1983), appeal dismissed 464 U.S.

801, 104 S.Ct. 46, 78 L.Ed.2d 67 (1983), upholding the constitutionality of the 1981 Connecticut lis pendens statute.

53. See Coons v. Baird, 148 Ind.App. 250, 265 N.E.2d 727 (1970); Hall v. Tucker, 414 S.W.2d 766 (Tex.Civ.App.1967), refused n.r.e.; Pierson v. Bill, 133 Fla. 81, 182 So. 631 (1938); Morris v. Wicks, 81 Kan. 790, 106 P. 1048 (1910). A few of the decisions deny BFP status when there is a quitclaim anywhere in the chain of title, but most of those which consider a quitclaim significant do so only if the present grantee takes directly by quitclaim. There is also considerable debate as to exactly what language will take the deed out of the quitclaim classification. See 4 Am.L.Prop. § 17.16 (1952); 5 Tiffany, Real Property § 1227 (3d ed. 1939).

There is a little authority for a similar rule which would deny BFP status to one who purchases for a grossly inadequate price; see Jordan v. Warnke, 205 Cal.App.2d 621, 23 Cal.Rptr. 300 (1962); Asisten v. Underwood, 183 Cal.App.2d 304, 7 Cal.Rptr. 84 (1960). This problem is better handled as an issue of payment of value than of lack of notice; see text at notes 3–5, supra.

54. Miller v. Hennen, 438 N.W.2d 366 (Minn.1989); Palamarg Realty Co. v. Rehac, 80 N.J. 446, 404 A.2d 21 (1979); Sabo v. Horvath, 559 P.2d 1038 (Alaska 1976); Williams v. McCann, 385 P.2d 788 (Okl.1963); Pulley v. Luttrell, 13 Ill.2d 355, 148 N.E.2d 731 (1958); Strong v. Whybark, 204 Mo. 341, 102 S.W. 968 (1907); Moelle v. Sherwood, 148 U.S. 21, 13 S.Ct. 426, 37 L.Ed. 350 (1893). See Note, 28 Ore.L.Rev. 258 (1949); Annot., 162 A.L.R. 556 (1946). A few states have adopted the majority rule by statute; see, e.g., Minn.Stat.Ann. § 507.34. USLTA § 3–203(c) specifically permits one who takes a quitclaim to be a purchaser for value, and § 1–201(31)(iv) defines "value" to include any consideration sufficient to support a simple contract.

The courts have sometimes found additional reasons to deny BFP status to purchasers. It is widely held that one has notice of matters recited in the documents in one's own chain of title even if they are not recorded; the basis of this rule is simply that purchasers can reasonably be expected to, and ordinarily do, examine their own muniments of title.[55] A more extreme and debatable position is represented by several cases which hold that a subsequent purchaser gets no protection from the recording acts if there are earlier links in his or her own chain of title that are unrecorded.[56] Under a notice-race statute, this position can be supported (although rather weakly) by arguing that to "record first", one must record not only one's own deed but also those of one's predecessors in title.[57] In a sense, it is both illogical and impractical to treat a purchaser whose predecessor is unrecorded as lacking bona fide purchaser status; after all, the presence of unrecorded links in one's title chain gives one no indication that there are also prior adverse conveyances and provides no starting point for an inquiry into such conveyances. On the other hand, the rule stated provides a strong incentive to make the public records complete.[58] Perhaps the most extreme illustration of this sort of reasoning is found in Messersmith v. Smith,[59] in which a

55. Burlington Northern, Inc. v. Hall, 322 N.W.2d 233 (N.D.1982); Hughes v. North Carolina State Highway Commission, 275 N.C. 121, 165 S.E.2d 321 (1969); Green v. Maddox, 97 Ark. 397, 134 S.W. 931 (1911); Gilbough v. Runge, 99 Tex. 539, 91 S.W. 566 (1906). See 5 Tiffany, Real Property § 1293 notes 63–64 (3d ed. 1939). The rule is an extension on the notion that a purchaser is on constructive notice of all recitations in documents which appear in the public records in the chain of title; see text at notes 47–49, supra. See also In re TMH Corp., 62 B.R. 932 (Bkrtcy.S.D.N.Y. 1986) (if the original lease is not exhibited to assignee of lease, assignee has duty to inquire of lessor; such inquiry would have revealed lessor's security interest in leasehold, and hence assignee has constructive notice of that interest).

56. Zimmer v. Sundell, 237 Wis. 270, 296 N.W. 589 (1941), noted 1942 Wis.L.Rev. 127; Annot., 133 A.L.R. 886 (1941); Miller v. Hennen, 438 N.W.2d 366 (Minn.1989). Walker v. Wilson, 469 So.2d 580 (Ala.1985) appears to follow this view, although the opinion is too garbled to be certain. For the purchaser to lose protection, the unrecorded deed must be in the portion of the title chain which is between the purchaser and the most recent grantor who is common to the present purchaser and the adverse claimant.

57. 4 Am.L.Prop. § 17.10 note 31. Cf. Quinn v. Johnson, 117 Minn. 378, 135 N.W. 1000 (1912), in which the court seems to place emphasis on the notice-race nature of the statute; but there the purchasers in fact recorded the previously-unrecorded deed in their chain at the same time they recorded their own deed, and the court found them fully qualified for protection under the act.

58. See Note, 1942 Wis.L.Rev. 127. The *Zimmer* rule, see note 56 supra, makes good sense only if the purchaser whose chain contains the gap is competing with a subsequent (rather than a prior) purchaser. To illustrate, assume that O owns land and makes three successive deeds of it. O first conveys to A, who fails to record. Next, O conveys to B, who also fails to record; B, in turn, conveys to C, a BFP who records. Finally, O conveys to D, a BFP who records. Graphically, the situation is as follows:

HTE5548

It is C whose position is placed in jeopardy by the *Zimmer* rule. In a contest between C and D, it is reasonable to treat C as unrecorded, for a searcher in D's position in a name index system cannot find C's deed by any practical means. The B–C deed is "wild", and virtually all cases allow D to prevail over C; see § 11.11, infra, at notes 6–8. On the other hand, if the contest is between C and A, there seems no justification at all for denying C the protection of the recording system. The fact that the O–B deed is unrecorded surely does not suggest that C is not relying on the recording acts to give protection from persons like A; nor does it give C a clue as to the existence of the O–A deed. Ironically, *Zimmer* itself is analogous to the latter situation and therefore seems unjustifiable on its facts.

59. 60 N.W.2d 276 (N.D.1953). In *Messersmith*, as in *Zimmer*, the adverse claimant was prior, not subsequent, to the holder under the defectively-recorded chain. Thus, standard chain-of-title reasoning is in no sense served by the decision; Cf. § 11.11, infra, at notes 6–8.

recorded deed in the purchaser's chain of title had been acknowledged by its grantor over the telephone rather than by personal appearance. The court held that since this acknowledgement was improper, the deed should be deemed unrecorded. This deprived the purchaser of BFP status and subordinated him to the rights of a claimant under an earlier, unrecorded, and entirely unrelated adverse deed made by a predecessor in title. The case is doubly objectionable, since the purchaser had neither a way of detecting the faulty acknowledgement nor, even if he had known of it, of determining from it that there was a prior unrecorded adverse deed.[60]

Once a bona fide purchaser has perfected title by operation of the recording acts, he or she can pass that perfected status along to a chain of future grantees even if they do not qualify as BFPs.[61] This "shelter" principle means that even one who has actual knowledge of an adverse conveyance can have, in an indirect sense, the protection of the recording acts. If this principle were not followed, the results could be disastrous. Imagine a case in which, after a BFP bought land, information about a prior adverse conveyance was widely disseminated in the press. The BFP would own the land in theory, but as a practical matter it would be unmarketable because so few other BFP's would exist to purchase it. Thus the shelter principle is essential to protect the BFP's market. It is not applied to a former non-BFP owner who reacquires the land after it has passed through the hands of a BFP, for to do so would permit the former owner to "cleanse" the title unjustly.[62]

Timing of Notice. The discussion above assumes that the purchaser either has or does not have notice of a prior adverse conveyance. But buying land is a process which may occur over a span of time; the buyer pays the price (perhaps in installments), receives a deed, and records it. If he or she receives notice at some point in this process, will it vitiate the protection of the recording acts? It seems clearly established that at a minimum the buyer, to be protected, must make payment before receiving notice.[63] Some cases go farther and insist on receipt of a conveyance as

---

60. Moreover, the decision does not serve the objective, mentioned above, of giving the purchaser an incentive to make the records more complete; he had no way of knowing that they were "incomplete," and indeed they were only in the most narrow and technical sense. See generally Maxwell, The Hidden Defect in Acknowledgment and Title Security, 2 U.C.L.A.L.Rev. 83 (1954). USLTA § 2–301(b) entirely does away with the requirement for an acknowledgment.

61. Corey v. United Savings Bank, Mutual, 52 Or.App. 263, 628 P.2d 739 (1981), review denied 291 Or. 368, 634 P.2d 1346 (1981); Hendricks v. Lake, 12 Wn.App. 15, 528 P.2d 491 (1974); Application of County Treasurer, 30 Ill.App.3d 235, 332 N.E.2d 557 (1975), appeal after remand 66 Ill.App.3d 437, 23 Ill. Dec. 197, 383 N.E.2d 1224 (1978); W.W. Planning, Inc. v. Clark, 10 Ariz.App. 86, 456 P.2d 406 (1969); Aldrich v. Wilson, 265 Minn. 150, 120 N.W.2d 849 (1963). See generally 1 R. Patton & C. Patton, Land Titles § 15 (1957).

62. Chergosky v. Crosstown Bell, Inc., 463 N.W.2d 522 (Minn.1990); Walker v. Wilson, 469 So.2d 580 (Ala.1985); Murray v. Johnson, 222 Ga. 788, 152 S.E.2d 739 (1966); Southern Life Insurance Co. v. Pollard Appliance Co., 247 Miss. 211, 150 So.2d 416 (1963); Rose v. Knapp, 153 Cal.App.2d 379, 314 P.2d 812 (1957); Hatcher v. Hall, 292 S.W.2d 619 (Mo. App.1956).

63. See Sams v. McCaskill, 282 S.C. 481, 319 S.E.2d 344 (App.1984); Doane Agricultural Service, Inc. v. Neelyville Grain Co., Inc., 516 S.W.2d 788 (Mo.App.1974); Black River Associates, Inc. v. Koehler, 126 Vt. 394, 233 A.2d 175 (1967); Annot., 109 A.L.R. 163 (1937). Sometimes no payment occurs until after the purchaser takes and records the deed. Such a purchaser may be protected as against constructive (though not actual) notice if the adverse conveyance is recorded after the purchaser records but before he or she pays. Without this protection the buyer who searches the title once when taking and re-

well,[64] and a few notice-race jurisdictions even require that it be recorded before notice is received.[65] The better view is to require only payment, since it is at that point that the buyer incurs an irrevocable detriment and thereby earns the act's protection. The buyer who gains notice prior to payment can simply assert the adverse conveyance as a defense to the contract of sale and refuse to pay.[66]

The problem is more complex when the land is being purchased on a long-term installment contract. Suppose the owner deeds the land to John, who fails to record, and then purports to sell it to Mary on an installment contract calling for payments of $1,000 per year for 20 years. Assume that Mary examines title when the contract is signed, but discovers no title defects. She then makes a down payment, records the contract, and takes possession. After she has made regular installment payments for ten years, John, who holds the prior adverse conveyance, records it. Does she have constructive notice from this recording? To so hold would in effect compel her to re-examine the records before making each payment—an "intolerable burden."[67] The great majority of the cases would continue her protection unless she received actual notice.[68]

But actual notice is quite possible; John may visit Mary, exhibit his conveyance, and insist that he owns the land. If this occurs, she would plainly be foolish to make any further payments to her (presumably crooked) grantor.[69] Equally plainly, she ought to be protected to the extent of the

cording his or her deed would have to search it again before making payment. The cases are in disagreement; compare Lowden v. Wilson, 233 Ill. 340, 84 N.E. 245 (1908) with Kentucky River Coal Corp. v. Sumner, 195 Ky. 119, 241 S.W. 820 (1922) and Lown v. Nichols Plumbing and Heating, Inc., 634 P.2d 554, 560 (Alaska 1981) (see especially Rabinowitz, C.J., dissenting.)

64. Mills v. Damson Oil Corp., 686 F.2d 1096 (5th Cir.1982), rehearing denied 691 F.2d 715 (1982) (Mississippi law); South Carolina Tax Commission v. Belk, 266 S.C. 539, 225 S.E.2d 177 (1976). This is evidently the approach of USLTA § 3–202(a)(3), which protects the purchaser only if he had no knowledge of the adverse claim "at the time his interest was created."

65. See 1 R. Patton & C. Patton, Land Titles § 10 notes 24–25, § 13 notes 77–82 (2d ed. 1957). This view can be reached as a construction of the "who records first" language in the typical notice-race statute, which arguably implies that recording is an integral part of the behavior which must be completed while lacking notice. It is unlikely that any pure "notice" jurisdiction would take this view; see, e.g., Hemingway v. Shatney, 152 Vt. 600, 568 A.2d 394 (1989), rejecting it under a "notice" statute. See Professor Powell's dissent from this position in Note, 14 Calif.L.Rev. 482 (1926); 4 Am.L.Prop. § 17.11 notes 46–49 (1952). Of course, if the purchaser receives the sort of constructive notice which results from the recordation of the prior adverse conveyance, he will lose if he has not recorded

first in a notice-race state; but that follows directly from the "who records first" language, and is not really a function of notice at all.

66. See 5 Tiffany, Real Property § 1304 (3d ed. 1939); Goldstein v. Gold, 106 A.D.2d 100, 483 N.Y.S.2d 375 (1984), affirmed 66 N.Y.2d 624, 495 N.Y.S.2d 32, 485 N.E.2d 239 (1985).

67. The phrase is from J. Cribbet, Property 287 note 67 (2d ed. 1975). See also Lown v. Nichols Plumbing and Heating, Inc., 634 P.2d 554 (Alaska 1981) (Rabinowitz, C.J., dissenting: "unduly burdensome".) Note, however, that the purchaser may still have to examine the title before the first payment is made, even if he or she previously received a conveyance and examined the title at that time; see note 63, supra.

68. Henson v. Wagner, 642 S.W.2d 357 (Mo.App.1982); Giorgi v. Pioneer Title Insurance Co., 85 Nev. 319, 454 P.2d 104 (1969); Dame v. Mileski, 80 Wyo. 156, 340 P.2d 205 (1959); Lowden v. Wilson, 233 Ill. 340, 84 N.E. 245 (1908). The principal contrary case, widely criticized, is Alexander v. Andrews, 135 W.Va. 403, 64 S.E.2d 487 (1951).

69. See Black River Associates, Inc. v. Koehler, 126 Vt. 394, 233 A.2d 175 (1967). The New York recording statute, unusual in this respect, protects the purchaser for payments made both before and after notice if he or she was in good faith at the time of contracting; see N.Y.—McKinney's Real Prop.

payments she has already made while in good faith, and the cases uniformly do so. There are at least three methods that courts have developed to achieve this *pro tanto* protection.[70] The most common is to award the land to the prior claimant, but to give the contract purchaser a right to recover the payments she has made with interest, usually with a lien on the land to assist in that recovery.[71] A second approach is to give the contract purchaser a fractional interest as a tenant in common based on the portion of the total price which she has paid prior to receiving notice; the adverse claimant would hold the remaining fractional share.[72] The third method is to permit the contract buyer to complete the purchase simply by paying the remaining installments to the adverse claimant.[73] Only this method gives the purchaser the full benefit of her bargain, certainly a desirable objective in light of her innocence. Courts exercise considerable latitude in the cases, taking into account the relative equities of the parties and the value of the property. If the contract purchaser has made improvements on the land, she will generally be compensated for them.[74]

§ 11.11　The Recording System—Indexes, Search Methods, and Chain of Title

The previous discussion has indicated that a purchaser of land has constructive notice of matters in the public records only if they are in the chain of title. Indeed, instruments which are recorded but are outside the chain of title may be treated as if they were not recorded at all. The term "chain of title" is a shorthand way of describing the collection of documents which one can find by the use of the ordinary techniques of title search.

Law § 294, subd. 3; La Marche v. Rosenblum, 82 Misc.2d 1046, 371 N.Y.S.2d 843 (1975), affirmed 50 A.D.2d 636, 374 N.Y.S.2d 443 (1975).

70. See generally Durst v. Daugherty, 81 Tex. 650, 17 S.W. 388 (1891); Annot., 109 A.L.R. 163 (1937). For many years Washington took the view that a contract purchaser received no protection from the recording acts until making the final payment on the contract; see McVean v. Coe, 12 Wn.App. 738, 532 P.2d 629 (1975). But the Washington position was reversed by legislation in 1984. See West's Rev.Code Wash.Ann. 65.08.060, which now makes clear that a contract of sale is a "conveyance" covered by the recording act; Tomlinson v. Clarke, 60 Wn.App. 344, 803 P.2d 828 (1991) (statute is retroactive, covering conveyances made before its enactment). See also Perry v. O'Donnell, 749 F.2d 1346 (9th Cir.1984), holding that the old Washington view does not represent California law, and that a California contract purchaser is entitled to *pro tanto* protection under the recording act.

A lessee is protected in the same general way as a contract purchaser—that is, only to the extent of rental payments made prior to receipt of notice. See Egbert v. Duck, 239 Iowa 646, 32 N.W.2d 404 (1948). This means that a long-term lease may be terminated

prematurely, with great hardship to the lessee. See Johnson, Purpose and Scope of Recording Statutes, 47 Iowa L.Rev. 231, 235 (1962).

71. In a similar context, see Hocking v. Hocking, 137 Ill.App.3d 159, 91 Ill.Dec. 847, 484 N.E.2d 406 (1985) (installment contract purchaser held entitled to reimbursement of portion of the price he paid before gaining notice that the land was subject to a resulting trust); Scult v. Bergen Valley Builders, Inc., 76 N.J.Super. 124, 183 A.2d 865 (1962), affirmed 82 N.J.Super. 378, 197 A.2d 704 (1964); Westpark, Inc. v. Seaton Land Co., 225 Md. 433, 171 A.2d 736 (1961); Seguin v. Maloney–Chambers Lumber Co., 198 Or. 272, 253 P.2d 252 (1953), rehearing denied 198 Or. 272, 256 P.2d 514 (1953); Davis v. Ward, 109 Cal. 186, 41 P. 1010 (1895).

72. It is hard to find any modern authority which actually applies this approach. It is supported in dictum in Durst v. Daugherty, supra note 70.

73. Sparks v. Taylor, 99 Tex. 411, 90 S.W. 485 (1906); Green v. Green, 41 Kan. 472, 21 P. 586 (1889).

74. See Henry v. Phillips, 163 Cal. 135, 124 P. 837 (1912) (dictum); 5 Tiffany, Real Property § 1305 note 44 (3d ed. 1939).

Hence, it can be understood only through comprehension of the way the records are indexed and searched.

Since the typical recorder's office may contain thousands of volumes and millions of documents, some form of index is essential so that searchers can locate instruments that affect the land whose title is being searched. Thus the office contains two types of volumes: index books and books which hold the actual copies of the legal instruments. The latter are sometimes called "deed books," even though they include other types of documents, such as leases, mortgages, and releases in addition to deeds.

There are two dominant methods of indexing. The oldest and most common is based on the names of the parties to each instrument. Under this "name index" system, two separate alphabetical indexes are maintained: one by the names of the grantors or other persons against whom the document operates, and the other by the names of the grantees or other persons in whose favor it operates. A separate set of these indexes is typically constructed each year, and they may be consolidated periodically into index books covering, say, 5–year or 10–year time spans. A few counties employ computers to produce and regularly update a consolidated set of grantor and grantee indexes for the entire time covered by the records.

An alternative and far superior approach to indexing is the tract or parcel index, but it is available in only a handful of states.[1] Here a separate page or set of pages in the index books is devoted to each tract of land, such as a quarter-quarter section, a specific block in a subdivision, or even an individual parcel of land. This page reflects the history of the tract's title from the time of the original conveyance from the sovereign.

In both name and tract index systems, the index books do not contain copies of the actual documents. Instead, they merely give the names of the parties, the recording date, the book and page number of the deed book in which the full copy of each instrument is to be found, and sometimes a brief legal description of the land affected. The searcher must jot down the book and page number and must then pull down and open the relevant deed book to read the instrument itself.

In a name index system the search procedure is generally as follows.[2] The searcher begins by looking for the name of the putative present owner

---

§ 11.11

1. States having tract indexes in all counties include Nebraska, North Dakota, Oklahoma, South Dakota, Utah, and Wyoming. States which permit tract indexing on a county option basis include Kansas, Ohio, Wisconsin and Minnesota. New York City has a "block index" system. See generally Note, The Tract and Grantor–Grantee Indices, 47 Iowa L.Rev. 481 (1962). The USLTA mandates a tract index; see § 6–207; it also requires those who present instruments for recordation to supply "information fixing the location sufficiently to enable the recording officer to determine where in the geographic index the document is to be indexed;" § 2–302(a)(4). This requirement should reduce significantly the costs of operating a tract index

system. See Maggs, Land Records of the Uniform Simplification of Land Transfers Act, 1981 So.Ill.U.L.J. 491, 500–01.

2. See generally Behringer & Altergott, Searching Title and Clearing Away What You Find, 4 Prac.Real Est.Law. 11 (No. 6, Nov. 1988); Berryhill, Title Examination in Virginia, 17 U.Rich.L.Rev. 229 (1983); Johnson, Title Examination in Massachusetts, reproduced as chapter 39, J. Casner & B. Leach, Cases & Text on Property (2d ed. 1969). In most jurisdictions, the doctrine of "idem sonans" requires the searcher to examine not only documents indexed under the precise name of the apparent owner, but also those indexed under similar-sounding names. See First Financial Bank, F.S.B. v. Johnson, 477

in the grantee index, working backward from the present date. When it is found, the searcher notes the name of the corresponding grantor of that instrument, and then seeks his or her name in the grantee index. This process is repeated until the searcher has worked backward in time through a chain of successive conveyances extending back to the sovereign.[3] The second phase of the search is to look up the name of each of the prior owners, as discovered by the foregoing process, in the grantor index to determine whether any of them made an "adverse" conveyance—that is, one to a person outside the chain of title. In the third phase, the searcher must pull down the relevant deed books and read carefully each instrument which has been identified from both the grantee and grantor indexes, to determine that it is in regular order, is properly executed, and purports to transfer the land in question. Finally, the searcher must check whatever public records are maintained separately from the indexes to the deed books, such as court dockets and probate indexes, tax and assessment records, and the like.

A search in a jurisdiction using a tract index is much simpler, since all instruments affecting a given parcel will be indexed on a single page or a set of consecutive pages in the index book. It is easy to construct the chain of title and to identify potentially adverse conveyances merely by running one's eye down the appropriate column. Of course, the instruments themselves must still be read and the other public records checked.

Whether a name or a tract index is used, the accuracy of the index is obviously crucial; an instrument which is copied into the deed books, but is unindexed or erroneously indexed as a result of carelessness by the recording personnel, is as impossible to find as a needle in a haystack. Should such a document be considered as "recorded" in litigation between its grantee and a later grantee from a common grantor who seeks the protection of the recording act? The cases are divided, and often turn on the specific language of the act. The majority regard mere copying of the instrument into the deed book as a sufficient recording to protect its proponent,[4] but the modern trend is to treat misindexed instruments as unrecorded.[5] Both the

So.2d 1267 (La.App.1985), rejecting this doctrine in Louisiana.

3. In some jurisdictions this phase of the search is greatly simplified by the widespread custom of including in each deed a clause referring to the book and page number of preceding deed in the chain. This is sometimes termed a "being" clause, since it may appear immediately after the legal description and read " * * * being that same land conveyed by A to B by deed recorded in Book ——, page ——, Official Records of Jones County." This clause makes it unnecessary to search the grantee index for the next previous link in the chain. For a discussion of an ingenious extension of this idea to make searches even easier, see Payne, The Alabama Law Institute's Land Title Acts Project, Part I, 24 Ala. L.Rev. 175; Part II, 24 Ala.L.Rev. 647 (1972).

Note that in some jurisdictions it is common to extend the search back only some fixed number of years, such as 40 or 60, rather than all the way to a conveyance from the sover-

eign. See Whitman, Transferring North Carolina Real Estate, Part I: How the Present System Functions, 49 N.C.L.Rev. 413, 425–26 (1971).

4. See, e.g., United States v. Lomas Mortgage, USA, Inc., 742 F.Supp. 936 (W.D.Va. 1990) (Virginia law); Hildebrandt v. Hildebrandt, 9 Kan.App.2d 614, 683 P.2d 1288 (1984); Haner v. Bruce, 146 Vt. 262, 499 A.2d 792 (1985); Maddox v. Astro Investments, 45 Ohio App.2d 203, 343 N.E.2d 133 (1975); Jones v. Folks, 149 Va. 140, 140 S.E. 126 (1927); Annot., 63 A.L.R. 1057 (1929); Cross, The "Record Chain of Title" Hypocrisy, 57 Colum.L.Rev. 787, 790 Note 15 (1957); 4 Am. L.Prop. § 17.31 (1952).

5. See Hochstein v. Romero, 219 Cal. App.3d 447, 268 Cal.Rptr. 202 (1990); Howard Savings Bank v. Brunson, 244 N.J.Super. 571, 582 A.2d 1305 (1990); Skidmore, Owings & Merrill v. Pathway Financial, 173 Ill.App.3d 512, 123 Ill.Dec. 395, 527 N.E.2d 1033 (1988); Frank v. Storer, 66 Md.App. 459, 504 A.2d

earlier and later grantees are innocent in this situation, but the former could at least have discovered the error by returning to the recorder's office a few days after the recording to check the indexing. The latter, on the other hand, had no basis for a suspicion that the earlier document even existed, and could not possibly have corrected the indexing error. The losing party may, of course, have an action against the recorder or the bonding company.

Chain of Title Problems. Because of the way titles are searched in name-index records systems, certain types of adverse conveyances are difficult or impossible to find even though they are extant in the deed books and are accurately indexed. There are four generic types of such problems, discussed below.[6] The courts have tended to protect searchers in these cases by treating the conveyances in question as if they were unrecorded and as giving no constructive notice.[7] The treatment here focuses on name-index systems, since most of these difficulties do not arise in the less-common tract-index systems. The illustrations below are based on an assumed chain of title from the sovereign to A, B, and C in succession, and an adverse conveyance by one of them, unknown to the searcher, to X.

The first problem is the "wild" deed. Assume that B, a former owner who is in the chain of title and is readily identifiable by a searcher, made an unknown and unrecorded deed, adverse to the chain of title, to X. Further assume that X then deeded to Y, and that deed was regularly recorded. A searcher may check the grantor index under B's name but will find nothing, since the B–X deed is unrecorded. The X–Y deed is recorded, but it is

---

1163 (1986), certiorari granted 306 Md. 369, 509 A.2d 133 (1986) (unindexed instrument imparts no constructive notice, at least where party benefitting from the instrument has control of it and knows it has not been indexed); Badger v. Benfield, 78 N.C.App. 427, 337 S.E.2d 596 (1985), review denied 316 N.C. 374, 342 S.E.2d 890 (1986) (unindexed instrument is treated as unrecorded); Thomas v. Thomas, 286 S.C. 294, 333 S.E.2d 76 (App. 1985) (same); Liberty Loan Corp. of Darlington, S.C. v. Mumford, 283 S.C. 134, 322 S.E.2d 17 (App.1984), certiorari granted 284 S.C. 367, 326 S.E.2d 657 (1985), certiorari dismissed 287 S.C. 254, 335 S.E.2d 805 (1985) (where mortgage by person named Mumford was indexed under "Mul" rather than "Mum," indexing was improper and document was not effectively recorded); Hanson v. Zoller, 187 N.W.2d 47 (N.D.1971); Mortensen v. Lingo, 13 Alaska 419, 99 F.Supp. 585 (1951); Prouty v. Marshall, 225 Pa. 570, 74 A. 550 (1909). See also Pruitt v. Ferguson, 224 Va. 507, 297 S.E.2d 714 (1982) (BFP protected, where name of party was misspelled on transcript of deed hand-copied into records in 1877).

Variations in the way a person is identified in the indexes do not necessarily constitute mis-indexing. In Still v. Security Federal Sav. & Loan Ass'n, 71 B.R. 252 (Bkrtcy.E.D.Tenn. 1986), the indexes showed a deed to Josephine Hill, and a deed of trust one minute later from

"William A. Hill, et ux." The court found that a competent searcher would have realized that "et ux," an abbreviation for et uxor ("and wife"), referred to Mrs. Hill, and thus that the deed of trust was properly recorded and indexed. See also Cipriano v. Tocco, 772 F.Supp. 344 (E.D.Mich.1991) (indexing in tract index was sufficient to give constructive notice, although statute required indexing in grantor-grantee index as well).

6. The classic discussion is Cross, The Record Chain of Title Hypocrisy, 57 Colum.L.Rev. 787 (1957). In addition to the chain of title problems discussed in the text of this section, see the treatment of the "omnibus" legal description, § 11.2 supra at notes 18–19, which raises a similar problem.

7. The opinions are often sloppy on this matter, concluding merely that the instrument gives no constructive notice. But to protect the subsequent searcher and his client, it is necessary both to treat it as giving no constructive notice and to deem it unrecorded; obviously, if it is regarded as "recorded," no subsequent conveyee can prevail against it under the recording acts. A good example of a more careful statement is found in Sabo v. Horvath, 559 P.2d 1038 (Alaska 1976): "The Horvaths' deed, recorded outside the chain of title, does not give constructive notice to the Sabos and is not 'duly recorded' under the Alaskan Recording Act."

impossible for the searcher to discover from the index books, since neither X's nor Y's name is known to the searcher. It can be found only by browsing through all of the deed books themselves, a task which might take several years! The cases uniformly treat the X–Y deed, contrary to literal fact, as if it were unrecorded and as imparting no constructive notice.[8] If they did not do so, the result would be an unconscionable burden on title examiners and a severe flaw in the system's basic operation. Observe that in a tract index system the wild deed is perfectly easy for the searcher to find, since it is indexed on the same page or pages as all other instruments affecting the parcel in question; hence it is considered to be properly recorded, and there is no need for any special rule governing it.[9]

A second chain-of-title problem is raised by the conveyance which is recorded too late. Again, assume B is a former owner in the regular chain of title who makes an adverse conveyance to X. X fails to record at that time. B thereafter conveys to C in the chain of title. C records C's deed, but is not a BFP, perhaps because C does not pay value or has knowledge of the adverse conveyance to X. (This assumption is necessary, since if C were a BFP the "shelter" principle discussed earlier would protect any later grantee from C.[10]) Some time after C records, X finally records the old deed from B. The problem is this: if C now contracts to sell the land to D, is D's title searcher expected to find the B–X deed? If so, the searcher must search in the grantor index for adverse conveyances by B, not only during the period B owned the land, but on up to the present date as well—thus taking account of the fact that someone like X might have recorded a deed long after receiving it. It is not impossible for a searcher to do this, but it adds very considerably to the time and expense of the search. The cases are fairly evenly divided, with somewhat more than half requiring the more extensive search effort and treating X's later-recorded deed as properly recorded; the minority deem it unrecorded.[11] The problem does not arise in a tract-index

8. Nile Valley Federal Sav. & Loan Ass'n v. Security Title Guarantee Corp., 813 P.2d 849 (Colo.App.1991); Far West Sav. & Loan Ass'n v. McLaughlin, 201 Cal.App.3d 67, 246 Cal.Rptr. 872 (1988); Palmer v. Forrest, Mackey & Associates, Inc., 251 Ga. 304, 304 S.E.2d 704 (1983); Hillblom v. Ivancsits, 76 Ill.App.3d 306, 32 Ill.Dec. 172, 395 N.E.2d 119 (1979); Capper v. Poulsen, 321 Ill. 480, 152 N.E. 587 (1926); Board of Education of Minneapolis v. Hughes, 118 Minn. 404, 136 N.W. 1095 (1912); Abbott v. Parker, 103 Ark. 425, 147 S.W. 70 (1912). See 4 Am.L.Prop. § 17.17 (1952); 1 R. Patton & C. Patton, Land Titles § 69 notes 71–74 (2d ed. 1957).

9. Miller v. Hennen, 438 N.W.2d 366 (Minn.1989); Utah Farm Production Credit Ass'n v. Wasatch Bank, 734 P.2d 904 (Utah 1986); Andy Associates, Inc. v. Bankers Trust Co., 49 N.Y.2d 13, 424 N.Y.S.2d 139, 399 N.E.2d 1160 (1979) (under New York City block index). It can be argued that the tract index system, with its greater power to disclose out-of-chain documents, is actually disadvantageous in the sense that it brings to light "wild" and other types of instruments dis-

cussed in the text which impair the marketability of titles, and which would be cut off by chain-of-title reasoning in a name index system. See L. Simes, Handbook for More Efficient Conveyancing 93–94 (1961).

10. See § 11.10, supra, at notes 61–62.

11. Perry v. O'Donnell, 749 F.2d 1346 (9th Cir.1984); Rolling "R" Construction, Inc. v. Dodd, 477 So.2d 330 (Ala.1985). See also Swanson v. Grassedonio, 647 S.W.2d 716 (Tex. App.1982), in which the late-recorded instrument was a "correction" of a prior recorded instrument and had the effect of limiting the prior instrument's effect; it was held to be outside the chain of title. Treating the late-recorded deed as unrecorded and as imparting no constructive notice, see Residents of Green Springs Valley Subdivision v. Town of Newburgh, 168 Ind.App. 621, 344 N.E.2d 312 (1976) (question of fact whether late-recorded conveyance is outside chain of title); Jefferson County v. Mosley, 284 Ala. 593, 226 So.2d 652 (1969); Kiser v. Clinchfield Coal Corp., 200 Va. 517, 106 S.E.2d 601 (1959), appeal dismissed 361 U.S. 8, 80 S.Ct. 57, 4 L.Ed.2d 49 (1959); Morse v. Curtis, 140 Mass. 112, 2 N.E.

system, since the B–X deed is easy to spot on the index page even though it is recorded out of time sequence.

The third problem is raised by the deed which is recorded too early. Imagine that B purports to deed the land to X before B has any title, and X immediately records the deed. Later B acquires the title from A. The doctrine of estoppel by deed is usually held to pass title to X instantly on these facts, at least if the B–X deed contained warranties or represented that title was being conveyed.[12] But if B later purports to convey to C, the question is raised whether C's title searcher can be expected to find the B–X deed. This is not impossible, but to do so the searcher must examine the grantor index under B's name not only during the time B owned the land, but for a lengthy and burdensome prior period as well [13], in order to account for the possibility that B made an adverse conveyance before acquiring title. Most of the recent cases have excused the searcher from this obligation, holding that the B–X deed must be regarded as unrecorded.[14] As before, the problem does not exist in a tract-index system.[15]

The final chain-of-title problem involves a common owner of two or more parcels who includes, in a conveyance of one parcel, language purporting to encumber the title to one or more other parcels retained. To illustrate, assume that A owns adjacent parcels 1 and 2, and sells parcel 1 to X including in the deed a covenant promising to restrict parcel 2 to single-family residential use. Later A sells parcel 2 to B without mentioning the restriction. Is B bound by it?

Consider the difficulty which B will face in discovering that the A–X deed exists and affects parcel 2. In many states which use name indexes, the index books include a "brief description" column which indicates in summary form what land is affected by each indexed document. Some statutes mandate that this column be included in the index books, while in other states it is maintained by the recorder voluntarily as a convenience to searchers. If the column exists, it is by no means certain that the recording office personnel will fill it in correctly in the present situation, marking entry for the A–X deed as affecting both parcel 1 and parcel 2. They will

929 (1885). See In re Dlott, 43 B.R. 789 (Bkrtcy.D.Mass.1983), asserting that modern title searchers in Massachusetts normally run each owner's name in the grantor index down to the date of the search, rather than merely for the period of his or her apparent ownership, and questioning the continuing vitality of Morse v. Curtis. Treating the late-recorded deed as properly recorded, see Spaulding v. H.E. Fletcher Co., 124 Vt. 318, 205 A.2d 556 (1964); Woods v. Garnett, 72 Miss. 78, 16 So. 390 (1894); Cross, supra note 6, at notes 25–26. Angle v. Slayton, 102 N.M. 521, 697 P.2d 940 (1985) (late-recorded deed is properly recorded and gives constructive notice).

12. See § 11.5, supra.

13. To be safe, the searcher would need to look under B's name in the grantor index books for about 80 years prior to the B–C deed, since this would be a reasonable estimate of B's maximum "conveyancing life." Some states follow a doctrine of lineal warran-

ty which would bind a descendant to a warranty deed made by his or her ancestor, so that one could not safely stop even at 80 years! See Johnson, Title Examination in Massachusetts, reproduced as chapter 39, J. Casner & B. Leach, Cases & Text on Property (2d ed. 1969), at 903. Johnson reports that despite the searcher's rather clear legal duty to examine for early-recorded deeds in Massachusetts, most searchers in fact do not do so.

14. Southeastern Sav. & Loan Ass'n v. Rentenbach Constructors, Inc., 114 B.R. 441 (E.D.N.C.1989), affirmed 907 F.2d 1139 (4th Cir.1990) (early-recorded deed is treated as unrecorded); Schuman v. Roger Baker & Associates, Inc., 70 N.C.App. 313, 319 S.E.2d 308 (1984) (same); Security Pacific Finance Corp. v. Taylor, 193 N.J.Super. 434, 474 A.2d 1096 (1984) (same). See § 11.5, supra, at notes 17–21.

15. See Balch v. Arnold, 9 Wyo. 17, 59 P. 434 (1899).

probably do so only if the deed's impact on parcel 2 is very obvious or they read it very carefully; neither of these is likely.

Arguably, a searcher is entitled to rely on the "brief description" column only if it is legally mandated; failing that, the searcher's only alternative is to read every conveyance by A in the county during the time A owned parcel 2, no matter what land the "brief description" entry for each of them mentions, and to see whether any of them affect parcel 2. Such a task can be monumental if B is an active real estate dealer or subdivider who has sold hundreds of land parcels.

Unlike the other chain of title problems, this one does not necessarily disappear in a tract index system. The question simply becomes whether the recording personnel are sophisticated enough to recognize that the A–X deed affects both parcels 1 and 2, and thus should be indexed under both tracts. Moreover, the problem is not limited to restrictive covenants; it can arise any time a deed of one parcel contains language imposing any encumbrance—an easement, a lease, or a lien, for example—on another parcel. In name-index jurisdictions the cases are about evenly divided as to whether the "buried" language creating the encumbrance is regarded as properly recorded; [16] they usually contain little or no analysis of the role of the "brief description" column in the searcher's task. In a state with official tract indexes, there is a stronger argument for protecting the searcher, since tract indexes are inherently predicated on the notion that the recorder's staff can and should discover what land is affected by every document they index.[17]

16. Protecting the searcher, see Witter v. Taggart, 78 N.Y.2d 234, 573 N.Y.S.2d 146, 577 N.E.2d 338 (1991) (purchaser "is not chargeable with constructive notice of conveyances recorded outside of that purchaser's direct chain of title where, as in Suffolk County, the grantor-grantee system of indexing is used"); Basore v. Johnson, 689 S.W.2d 103 (Mo.App. 1985); Dunlap Investors Limited v. Hogan, 133 Ariz. 130, 650 P.2d 432 (1982) (grantor's retained land was burdened by an easement reserved in the recorded deed but not even explicitly described therein); Garden of Memories, Inc. v. Forest Lawn Memorial Park Association, 109 N.J.Super. 523, 264 A.2d 82 (1970), certification denied 56 N.J. 476, 267 A.2d 58 (1970); Glorieux v. Lighthipe, 88 N.J.L. 199, 96 A. 94 (1915).

Finding the encumbrance validly recorded, see Szakaly v. Smith, 544 N.E.2d 490 (Ind. 1989); Hi–Lo Oil Co. v. McCollum, 38 Ohio App.3d 12, 526 N.E.2d 90 (1987); Stegall v. Robinson, 81 N.C.App. 617, 344 S.E.2d 803 (1986), review denied, stay denied 317 N.C. 714, 347 S.E.2d 456 (1986); Bishop v. Reuff, 619 S.W.2d 718 (Ky.App.1981); Piper v. Mowris, 466 Pa. 89, 351 A.2d 635 (1976); Guillette v. Daly Dry Wall, Inc., 367 Mass. 355, 325 N.E.2d 572 (1975); Finley v. Glenn, 303 Pa. 131, 154 A. 299 (1931).

In Genovese Drug Stores, Inc. v. Connecticut Packing Co., 732 F.2d 286 (2d Cir.1984), two physically distinct portions of a shopping center were owned by two landlords who had entered into a recorded Joint Development Agreement that each of them must consent to leases made by the other. One of them then leased to a drug store tenant and included in that lease a covenant against the placing in the center of any "Foto–Mat" type store. Later the other landlord entered into a lease with Foto–Mat. The drug store sought an injunction against operation of the Foto–Mat store. While a memorandum of the drug store lease was recorded, the court held it was not in the chain of title of the property leased to Foto–Mat; this is an undeniably correct conclusion, since the drug store's landlord had no title to the Foto–Mat property at all. The court also held, more debatably, that the Joint Development Agreement, while recorded in the relevant chain of title, was not sufficient to give Foto–Mat constructive notice that the drug store's landlord had covenanted away its power to consent to the Foto–Mat lease.

17. In a tract-index system, then, the question is essentially one of official misindexing; see text at notes 4–5 supra. By contrast, the court in the *Guillette* case, supra note 16, specifically rejected the searcher's defense of reliance on the "brief legal description" entry, observing that such entries were not required by law in Massachusetts.

On the whole, the chain of title problems illustrate quite effectively the deficiencies of the recording system, especially in its use of name indexes. In many areas of the western, midwestern, and southwestern United States few title searches are conducted in the public records. Instead, title insurance and abstract companies have created sets of private records, called "title plants," in which they do their searches. Since the plants are invariably arranged on a tract-index basis, most of the chain-of-title problems discussed above are of no practical importance in these areas of the nation. It would make little sense for a court to adopt the sorts of rules described above for the protection of name-index searchers in a case in which the actual search was made in a private tract index which contained and properly indexed the out-of-chain documents. Since the whole chain-of-title concept is a judicially-created exception to the literal language of the recording acts, made in recognition of the practical difficulty of finding out-of-chain documents through use of the official indexes, there seems to be no reason to extend it to situations where that difficulty does not exist.[18]

§ 11.12 Curative and Marketable Title Acts

Under the conventional recording system, a purchaser of land must obtain an historical search of the records back to a conveyance from the sovereign in order to be certain that the record title is good. This sort of complete search is expensive and time-consuming. Moreover, in most cases it has little practical value, since most titles which are good "of record" for the past several decades are good in fact, and nothing recorded in more remote times casts any serious doubt on them. Nevertheless, one cannot be certain that no old documents create title defects until one has looked at them; the searcher who limits his or her search to a shorter period than the entire chain of title is taking a distinct and significant risk.

At least four types of legislation have been enacted in various states which reduce this risk. The oldest and most widespread is the statute of limitations in an action to recover possession of land,—the basis of the doctrine of adverse possession.[1] There is no doubt that adverse possession has cured millions of title defects; indeed, that is probably the main justification for the doctrine. But the title examiner who relies on adverse possession as a substitute for a full historical search is merely exchanging one significant risk for another. The problem is that adverse possession depends on a long list of facts which usually do not appear of record, which the searcher probably does not know are true, and which even if true may be hard to prove in court. Have the owners in the record chain of title been in possession which was actual, open, hostile, exclusive, and continuous for the statutory period? Has the statute's running been tolled by the infancy,

---

18. See § 11.5, supra, at notes 24–26. None of the decisions from states where private-plant searches predominate have given this issue any discussion. For example, the court seems to have applied chain-of-title reasoning despite evidence that the title insurer had actual knowledge of the out-of-chain encumbrance in Dunlap Investors Limited v. Hogan, supra note 16. See also Far West Sav. & Loan Ass'n v. McLaughlin, 201 Cal.App.3d 67, 246 Cal.Rptr. 872 (1988), in which the court

applied standard chain of title reasoning to a "wild deed" transaction in southern California, where virtually every title search is performed by title companies in tract-indexed private plants. The same is probably true of Snow v. Pioneer Title Ins. Co., 84 Nev. 480, 444 P.2d 125 (1968).

§ 11.12

1. See generally § 11.7 supra.

imprisonment, or insanity of the holder of paramount title?[2] Is that paramount title held by a governmental body against which the statute will not run?[3] Is it a future interest, against which the limitations period does not commence until it becomes possessory?[4] To learn the answers to these questions is generally far more effort than a full historical search of the records! Yet without clear answers, a searcher who relies on adverse possession is simply foolish.[5]

Another type of legislation, the curative act, dates back to colonial times in some states and has become quite widespread. Curative acts attempt to make prior conveyances, typically those more than two or three years old, valid and recordable despite some minor defect they may contain.[6] Among the kinds of defects often dealt with are improper executions, acknowledgments, recordings, exercises of powers of attorney and appointment, parties, and judicial proceedings. Of course, there are plenty of other types of defects which may arise in conveyances and which the acts do not affect; they are no panacea.[7] Not all states have curative statutes, and some have acts of very limited scope. From the viewpoint of a title searcher, the acts have little impact on the need for a full historical search. They merely permit an examiner to have greater confidence in the validity of conveyances found in the title chain which might otherwise be considered ineffective or dubious. The result is to make a somewhat greater proportion of titles marketable.

The next step in the development of legislation to improve the title search process has been the enactment of special statutes which bar certain specific types of very old but apparently valid claims to land. The most common types of such claims are "ancient" mortgages[8] and some varieties of future interests, such as rights of entry and possibilities of reverter.[9] The

---

2. See § 11.7, supra, at note 5; P. Basye, Clearing Land Titles § 54 (1970).

3. See § 11.7, supra, at note 4; Basye, supra note 2, at § 53.

4. Gilley v. Daniel, 378 So.2d 716 (Ala. 1979); Wilson v. McDaniel, 247 Ark. 1036, 449 S.W.2d 944 (1970), appeal after remand 250 Ark. 316, 465 S.W.2d 100 (1971); 2A Powell, Real Property ¶ 301 (1979); 19 A.L.R.2d 729 (1951). An exception exists where the adverse possession begins before the time the title is split into present and future interests; see Restatement of Property § 226; Hubbard v. Swofford Brothers Dry Goods Co., 209 Mo. 495, 108 S.W. 15 (1907). See generally Basye, supra note 2, at § 55.

5. See Basye, supra note 2, at § 52.

6. The best and most comprehensive treatment is Basye, supra note 2, at § 201ff. A Model Curative Act is presented and discussed in L. Simes & C. Taylor, The Improvement of Conveyancing by Legislation 17–27 (1960).

7. Crotts Andrews v. All Heirs & Devisees of Bellis, 297 Ark. 3, 759 S.W.2d 532 (1988) (curative statute did not validate a certificate of acknowledgment which was not signed by a notary).

8. See Basye, supra note 2, at § 76. One might imagine that the running of the statute of limitations on the underlying note or other indebtedness would be a sufficient protection against the enforceability of the mortgage, but in most states the mortgage can be foreclosed even if the debt is barred; Phinney v. Levine, 116 N.H. 379, 359 A.2d 636 (1976); Basye, supra note 2, at § 72; G. Nelson & D. Whitman, Real Estate Finance Law § 6.9 (2d ed. 1985).

9. See Simes & Taylor, supra note 6, at 201–17. The Indiana Dormant Mineral Interest Act, West's Ann.Ind.Code 32–5–11, adopted in 1971, extinguishes mineral interests that are "unused" for 20 years unless a notice of claim is filed. The constitutionality of the act was upheld in Short v. Texaco, Inc., 273 Ind. 518, 406 N.E.2d 625 (1980), affirmed 454 U.S. 516, 102 S.Ct. 781, 70 L.Ed.2d 738 (1982). "Use" under the act can be either actual or attempted production of minerals, payment of rents or royalties, or payment of taxes. See McCoy v. Richards, 581 F.Supp. 143 (S.D.Ind. 1983), affirmed 771 F.2d 1108 (7th Cir.1985), holding that a deed conveying a portion of an existing severed mineral interest was not a "use" of that interest, and that the recording of the deed in the deed book at the recorder's

interest being cut off must be quite old, commonly thirty to fifty years. In the case of mortgages the period is typically measured from the due date of the debt if stated in the mortgage, and otherwise from its execution date. Provision is usually made for the recording of a notice periodically as a means of keeping the old claim alive if its owner desires. The constitutionality of the statutes barring old future interests has been attacked frequently on the ground that they constitute takings of property without due process of law, but most of the decisions have upheld them.[10]

These statutes, like the curative acts, help make some titles marketable, but they do not eliminate the need for a full historical search of the records, for there are too many other possible types of defects which they do not affect. A more ambitious attempt to shorten search periods is represented by the "marketable record title" acts.[11] These acts, which exist in 18 states,[12] simply make void most types of claims to land if they are not reflected in the records between the date of the "root of title" and a date some stated number of years later. The root of title is defined as the most recent deed or other title transaction recorded in an unbroken chain of title at least some specified number of years in the past—typically 20 to 40 years.[13] For example, if the statute specified 30 years and a search were

office did not satisfy the act's requirement for filing a notice of claim, which was required to be recorded in a separate Dormant Mineral Interest Record.

10. Cline v. Johnson County Board of Education, 548 S.W.2d 507 (Ky.1977); Presbytery of Southeast Iowa v. Harris, 226 N.W.2d 232 (Iowa 1975), certiorari denied 423 U.S. 830, 96 S.Ct. 50, 46 L.Ed.2d 48 (1975); Hiddleston v. Nebraska Jewish Education Society, 186 Neb. 786, 186 N.W.2d 904 (1971); Town of Brookline v. Carey, 355 Mass. 424, 245 N.E.2d 446 (1969); Trustees of Schools of Township No. 1 v. Batdorf, 6 Ill.2d 486, 130 N.E.2d 111 (1955). Contra, see Board of Education of Central School District No. 1 v. Miles, 15 N.Y.2d 364, 259 N.Y.S.2d 129, 207 N.E.2d 181 (1965), noted 51 Corn.L.Q. 402 (1966); Biltmore Village v. Royal Biltmore Village, 71 So.2d 727 (Fla. 1954).

11. See generally Basye, supra note 2, at §§ 171–198; Simes & Taylor, supra note 6, at 295; Halligan, Marketable Title and Stale Records: Clearing Exceptions and Closing Deals, 59 Wis.Bar.Bull. 23 (No. 5, May 1986); Comment, The Nebraska Marketable Title Act: Another Tool in the Bag, 63 Neb.L.Rev. 124 (1983); Barrett, Marketable Title Acts—Panacea or Pandemonium, 53 Corn.L.Rev. 45 (1967); Swenson, Marketable Title Acts, 6 Utah L.Rev. 472 (1959). The constitutionality of the Acts has been uniformly upheld, despite the fact that they provide for no notice to the holders of old interests being cut off. See Bennett v. Whitehouse, 690 F.Supp. 955 (W.D.Okl.1988); Wichelman v. Messner, 250 Minn. 88, 83 N.W.2d 800 (1957); Pindar, Marketability of Titles—Effect of Texaco, Inc. v. Short, 34 Mercer L.Rev. 1005 (1983); Aigler, Constitutionality of Marketable Title Acts, 50

Mich.L.Rev. 185 (1951); Aigler, A Supplement to "Constitutionality of Marketable Title Acts" 1951–1957, 56 Mich.L.Rev. 225 (1957).

12. States with marketable title statutes (with year of enactment) are Connecticut (1967), Florida (1963), Illinois (1941), Indiana (1941), Iowa (1919), Kansas (1973), Michigan (1945), Minnesota (1943), Nebraska (1947), North Carolina (1973), North Dakota (1951), Ohio (1961), Oklahoma (1961), South Dakota (1947), Utah (1963), Vermont (1969), Wisconsin (1941), and Wyoming (1975). The Uniform Simplification of Land Transfers Act (USLTA) also contains a marketable title act as Art. 3, Part 3. See Curtis, Simplifying Land Transfers: The Recordation and Marketable Title Provisions of the Uniform Simplification of Land Transfers Act, 62 Or.L.Rev. 363 (1983).

13. The most common period in existing acts is 40 years; USLTA § 3–301(4) adopts a 30-year period. Several decisions hold that the root of title must purport to convey some specific interest in the land; hence, a quitclaim deed would not ordinarily do. See Wilson v. Kelley, 226 So.2d 123 (Fla.App.1969); Smith v. Berberich, 168 Neb. 142, 95 N.W.2d 325 (1959); Schmid, The Utah Marketable Record Title Act—A Review and Update, 7 Utah Bar J. 17, 24–25 (1979). The fact that a deed in the chain prior to the root of title is a complete forgery does not prevent the operation of the acts; see Marshall v. Hollywood, Inc., 236 So.2d 114 (Fla.1970), certiorari denied 400 U.S. 964, 91 S.Ct. 366, 27 L.Ed.2d 384 (1970); Harrell v. Wester, 853 F.2d 828 (11th Cir.1988) (deed taken in violation of fiduciary duty can be a root of title). USLTA goes farther, providing that even the root of title itself may be a "nullity"; USLTA § 3–301(4);

being made in 1985, a deed recorded in 1960 could not be the root of title, but one recorded in 1950 could be. If there were no exceptions to the coverage of the acts, it would be entirely unnecessary to search earlier than the root of title, since nothing found there could affect the present title.

Marketable title acts are in a sense both more and less powerful than the specialized statutes dealing with ancient reversionary interests described earlier. The latter cut off all such interests which are sufficiently old unless some formal notice of them is recorded in the more recent records. Marketable title acts, on the other hand, will not affect ancient rights if a specific reference to them is made in any document recorded in the chain of title within the appropriate time period following the root. But marketable title acts are far more potent, in that they terminate not merely reversionary future interests but also most other types of pre-root claims [14] unless they are preserved by one of the methods described in the next paragraph. Hence forgeries, gaps in the chain of title, and technical defects in conveyances are simply irrelevant if they are prior to the root of title. Even interests not based on recordable documents, such as adverse possession titles and prescriptive easements, are barred if they were perfected before the root.

There are several ways in which pre-root interests can be preserved as against the operation of a marketable title act. One mentioned above is a specific timely reference to such an interest in a post-root document in the chain of title.[15] Another is the timely re-recording of a pre-root instrument which creates or refers to the interest, or of a notice (specifically authorized by most of the acts) of a claim arising under a pre-root instrument.[16] The recording during the post-root period of a conveyance of the adverse interest has much the same effect. Note, however, that under all of these provisions, the instrument or notice must be recorded within the statutory time (for example, 40 years) after the root of title. Finally, a person who is occupying

see also City of Miami v. St. Joe Paper Co., 364 So.2d 439 (Fla.1978), appeal dismissed 441 U.S. 939, 99 S.Ct. 2153, 60 L.Ed.2d 1040 (1979); Allen v. St. Petersburg Bank & Trust Co., 383 So.2d 1171 (Fla.App.1980). However, if the root contains defects which are obvious on its face or if it specifically refers to some prior adverse claim, the searcher will take subject to these matters; see ITT Rayonier, Inc. v. Wadsworth, 346 So.2d 1004 (Fla.1977); Reid v. Bradshaw, 302 So.2d 180 (Fla.App.1974). See the discussion of the "wild" or forged deed as a root of title in Hyland v. Kirkman, 204 N.J.Super. 345, 498 A.2d 1278, 1289 (1985); South Florida Water Management Dist. v. Muroff, 508 So.2d 510 (Fla.App.1987) (clause in deed reserving mineral estate in grantor can constitute a root of title to the mineral estate). See also Marchant v. Park City, 788 P.2d 520 (Utah 1990) (a conveyance of personal property—a house—without real property does not establish a root of title to the real property).

14. See Rush v. Sterner, 143 Mich.App. 672, 373 N.W.2d 183 (1985) (interests originat-

ing by way of exception or reservation are cut off by the Act).

15. See Kirkman v. Wilson, 98 N.C.App. 242, 390 S.E.2d 698 (1990) (a reference, in any muniment of title during the 30–year period following the root, to the will which created the claimants' future interests, would be sufficient to preserve them against termination by the Act); Blakely v. Capitan, 34 Ohio App.3d 46, 516 N.E.2d 248 (1986) (a court decree and a certificate of transfer from a decedent's estate during the 40–year period, both of which mentioned the restrictive covenants in question, were sufficient to preserve them against termination by the Act); Heifner v. Bradford, 4 Ohio St.3d 49, 446 N.E.2d 440 (1983) (conveyance by will within 40–year period is sufficient to preserve claim).

16. See, e.g., Strong v. Detroit & Mackinac Ry. Co., 167 Mich.App. 562, 423 N.W.2d 266 (1988) (railroad easement preserved by filing of notice). Cf. Cunningham v. Haley, 501 So.2d 649 (Fla.App.1986) (restrictive covenants cut off by act, where no notice was filed within the statutory period).

the land may, under some of the acts, have possession treated as the equivalent of notice of his or her claim.[17]

A person need not be a bona fide purchaser to be protected from pre-root claims by a marketable title act, and under most of the acts need not take possession of the land.[18] A few acts limit their protection to persons who acquire fee simple interests,[19] but under most of the statutes any sort of interest or claim is protected.

The usefulness of marketable title acts is impaired by the fact that they contain a number of exceptions—lists of various types of pre-root claims which the acts do not eliminate. At least one exception, for interests of the United States government, is inevitable, since it is plain that state law cannot divest federal land interests without the government's consent. Exceptions for rights of parties in possession [20] and for observable easements and use restrictions are common, and may be justified on the ground that any reasonably thorough title examination will include an inspection of the property, which indeed is necessary under ordinary recording act principles.

But almost as common, and much more disruptive, are exceptions for a variety of "special interest" claims which have been lobbied into the statutes of many states; they include public easements and rights of way, mineral interests, water rights, utility easements, railroad easements, and the like.[21] The exceptions usually apply whether the claim is physically observable or not. The holders of these claims—utility and mining companies and city and county governments, for example—wish to avoid the burden of rerecording their rights periodically, and sometimes argue that their records are so incomplete or complex that rerecording would be impractical. Yet the exceptions tend to defeat the very purpose of the marketable title acts: to limit the title search period. A searcher must go back beyond the root of

---

17. Under the USLTA version, it is necessary only that the possession exist at the time the title search is made, assuming a reasonable inquiry would have revealed it; USLTA § 3–306(2). Under the Model Act, on the other hand, the possession must have continued by the record owner continuously for more than 40 years with no transactions on record affecting her interest; Model Act § 4(b), reprinted in Simes & Taylor, supra note 6, at 8. See State v. Cox Corp., 29 Utah 2d 127, 506 P.2d 54 (1973).

18. See Merritt v. Merritt, 146 Vt. 246, 500 A.2d 534 (1985), in which the court appears to have required BFP status for one to claim the protection of the Vermont marketable title act. However, the prior claim against which protection was sought was simply an *unrecorded post-root deed,* and hence would properly have been avoided by the court under the normal operation of the recording acts, but only, of course, as against a BFP. Thus, the case illustrates that the presence of a marketable title act does not eliminate the usual BFP requirement of the recording act.

19. See the construction of the Minnesota act in Wichelman v. Messner, 250 Minn. 88, 83 N.W.2d 800 (1957). Some of the statutes require the root of title itself to be a purported

conveyance of fee simple title; see, e.g., Town of Belle Prairie v. Kliber, 448 N.W.2d 375 (Minn.App.1989).

20. See Sackett v. Storm, 480 N.W.2d 377 (Minn.App.1992); Zimmerman v. Cindle, 48 Ohio App.3d 164, 548 N.E.2d 1315 (1988) (possession must be "clearly observable"); City of Jacksonville v. Horn, 496 So.2d 204 (Fla.App. 1986); Rush v. Sterner, 143 Mich.App. 672, 373 N.W.2d 183 (1985); Heath v. Turner, 309 N.C. 483, 308 S.E.2d 244 (1983); Sickler v. Pope, 326 N.W.2d 86 (N.D.1982) (possession of surface estate does not preserve claim to severed mineral estate).

21. The Florida Supreme Court has held state sovereignty lands exempt from the Florida Marketable Title Act, although the basis for this result is not easy to discern in the language of the act itself; see Coastal Petroleum Co. v. American Cyanamid Co., 492 So.2d 339 (Fla.1986), cert. denied 479 U.S. 1065, 107 S.Ct. 950, 93 L.Ed.2d 999 (1987). See Powell, Unfinished Business—Protecting Public Rights to State Lands From Being Lost Under Florida's Marketable Record Title Act, 13 Fla. St.U.L.Rev. 599 (1985).

title at least carefully enough to determine whether any of the pre-root documents involve interests the acts recognize as exceptions. If there are many exceptions, this effort is tantamount to performing a full historical search.[22]

Perhaps the most intriguing problem with marketable title acts arises because of the possibility that two conflicting chains of title can exist simultaneously. This can occur because an owner delivers two deeds of the same property to two grantees; because a forger with no title starts a new paper chain with a "wild" deed; or, perhaps most commonly, because an owner delivers two deeds which inadvertently contain overlapping land descriptions. To illustrate, assume a marketable title act with a 40–year period. O owns land in fee simple, and in 1910 delivers a deed to A. A in turn deeds the land to B in 1920. Then, in 1930, X (a forger) purports to deed the same land to Y. A diagram may help:

$$O \xrightarrow{\text{1910}} A \xrightarrow{\text{1920}} B$$

$$X \xrightarrow{\text{1930}} Y$$

[C7686]

In 1980, who owns the land? The answer is Y, based on the typical statutory language which provides that one's title is subject to any "interest arising out of a title transaction recorded after the root of title."[23] The 1930 deed to Y is a root of title, and from the viewpoint of Y or anyone who might buy from Y, there is no document recorded after that root of title which reflects the existence of any conflicting interest. One might argue that the A–B deed in 1920 is also a root of title, and indeed it is. However, the title which the act confirms in B through that root is subject to Y's interest under the language of the act quoted above, since the X–Y deed was recorded in 1930, later than the 1920 A–B root of title. In summary, B's title is subject to Y's but Y's is not subject to B's; hence, Y prevails.[24]

---

22. See Note, Property Law—North Carolina's Marketable Title Act—Will the Exceptions Swallow the Rule?, 52 N.C.L.Rev. 211 (1973). Even Simes and Taylor conceded that their Model Act, which had very few exceptions, would not "usher in an era of forty year abstracts of title", but they argued that the task of the title examiner would "definitely be lightened." Simes & Taylor, supra note 6, at 5.

23. The quoted language is from USLTA § 3–303(3); see also Model Act § 2(d), reprinted in Simes & Taylor, supra note 6, at 7. The idea that claims are preserved by the recording of more recent instruments conveying or referring to them can be troublesome. In Kittrell v. Clark, 363 So.2d 373 (Fla.App.1978), certiorari denied 383 So.2d 909 (Fla.1980), the more recent instrument was a will which was probated. Neither the will nor the probate inventory gave any legal description of the land, but the court nonetheless found it suffi-

cient to preserve the devisee's claim; there was a vigorous dissent from the Florida Supreme Court's denial of certiorari.

24. The result reached in the text is supported by Whaley v. Wotring, 225 So.2d 177 (Fla.App.1969). Compare Exchange National Bank v. Lawndale National Bank, 41 Ill.2d 316, 243 N.E.2d 193 (1968), in which the Illinois Supreme Court held that the act was not intended to be applied where there were two competing chains of title, or to confirm a chain from a root of title which was "wild" or forged. There seems no warrant in the statutory language for this conclusion, and the drafters of the Model Act plainly disagreed with it; see Simes & Taylor, supra note 6, at 13–14. See also City of Miami v. St. Joe Paper Co., 364 So.2d 439 (Fla.1978), appeal dismissed 441 U.S. 939, 99 S.Ct. 2153, 60 L.Ed.2d 1040 (1979), explicitly holding that a wild deed can be a root of title. See Hyland v. Kirkman, cited in note 13 supra.

Note that the result would be different if B had conveyed to C in, say, 1935, so that the chains of title were as follows:

$$0 \xrightarrow{\ 1910\ } A \xrightarrow{\ 1920\ } B \xrightarrow{\ 1935\ } C$$

$$X \xrightarrow{\ 1930\ } Y$$

[C7687]

The B–C deed is a root of title (since it is more than 40 years old) and C's claim would be superior to that of Y, which arose prior to 1935. Indeed, the result would also be reversed if B had conveyed to C, not in 1935, but in, say, 1960. Such a conveyance is too recent to be a root of title, but it will still act to preserve C's claim under the language quoted in the preceding paragraph. On these facts, the marketable title act would make both C's claim and Y's claim "subject to" one another. In effect, the act would not resolve the conflict between the two, and general principles of deeds, recording and priorities would be called upon to do so. Since the X–Y deed was a forgery (and out of the chain of title of C as well), C should prevail.[25]

Finally, assume that the conveyance from B to C was made and recorded, not in 1935 or 1960, but in 1975. It is obviously too recent to be a root of title. Moreover, it will not be effective to preserve C's claim from the competing X–Y title chain. The reason is that in 1970, 40 years after the X–Y deed was recorded, the act confirmed the title in Y. A conveyance in a competing chain recorded later than 1970 will not revive that previously extinguished interest.[26]

All of the early marketable title statutes were adopted in states which employed either official or unofficial (abstract company) parcel indexes. The problem of two conflicting chains of title is trivial in a parcel index system, since an examination of the relevant index page or pages will immediately reveal both chains. In recent years states such as North Carolina, Connecticut, and Vermont, where official name indexes are widely used by searchers, have enacted marketable title legislation. In such a state, consider the facts raised in the latter diagram above, with B conveying to C in either 1935 or 1960. A searcher who examines Y's title will conclude that the act makes it good, having no reason to suspect the existence of the competing A–B–C chain; a searcher examining C's title will similarly discover no clue that the X–Y deed exists. In this setting the legal rules discussed in the preceding paragraphs, particularly when they give viability to a chain of title originating in a forged deed, are intolerable, since they operate to defeat purchasers who have reasonably relied on the records.[27]

---

25. See Minnich v. Guernsey Sav. & Loan Ass'n, 36 Ohio App.3d 54, 521 N.E.2d 489 (1987), finding that the Act did not resolve the competing chains, and resorting to construction of an 1883 deed to do so; Heath v. Turner, 309 N.C. 483, 308 S.E.2d 244 (1983); Holland v. Hattaway, 438 So.2d 456 (Fla.App. 1983).

26. See statutory citations at note 16, supra; Simes & Taylor, supra note 6, at 13–14.

27. See Webster, The Quest for Clear Land Titles—Making Land Title Searches Shorter and Surer in North Carolina via Marketable Title Legislation, 44 N.C.L.Rev. 89, 108–110 (1965).

Several methods of resolving this dilemma have been employed. Under a few of the acts, only grantees who take possession are protected.[28] They will doubtless discover the existence of a competing chain if claimants under it are already in possession. Another possibility is simply to add language excepting from the act's operation the rights of all parties in possession.[29] But the drafters of the Model Act rejected these approaches on the ground that they were only partial solutions, since they did not deal with vacant land, and since they required reference to facts outside the record.[30] USLTA excepts the rights of persons in possession, and also incorporates a provision, borrowed from Florida, preserving the rights of anyone whose name is carried on the real property tax rolls within three years of the time marketability is determined; thus, inspecting the land and checking the tax records will nearly always disclose any competing chain.[31]

§ 11.13　Covenants of Title in Deeds

The law does not generally read into a deed a representation or promise that it conveys any title, or title of any particular quality. Often the grantor will wish to exclude any such promise quite expressly, and hence will employ the term "quitclaim" or similar language to indicate that no covenants as to title are being made.[1] However, it is customary in most areas of the nation for the grantor in an ordinary sale transaction to include covenants regarding the title. A deed containing such covenants is conventionally termed a "warranty deed," although this term is somewhat misleading since a technical covenant of warranty is only one of the six types of common covenants found in deeds.

Deed covenants of title are not a highly effective means of title assurance. They depend on the covenantor's continued solvency and availability for suit, and recovery under them is seriously limited by the doctrines discussed in this section. Most grantees rely on additional modes of title assurance, such as examination of public records under the recording system and the purchase of title insurance. Yet deed covenants remain important, and continue to form the basis of suits, both by disappointed grantees and by

28. North Dakota Cent.Code 47–19.1–01.

29. See USLTA § 3–306(2); Webster, supra note 27, at 109.

30. See Simes & Taylor, supra note 6, at 353. The drafters did, however, include a provision preserving the rights of a record owner who has been in continuous possession for 40 years or more down to the date marketability is being determined. Model Act § 4(b), reprinted in Simes & Taylor, supra note 6, at 8.

31. USLTA § 3–306(3); see West's Fla. Stat.Ann. § 712.03(6). A related problem arises from the fact that a claimant can preserve his or her interest by recording a notice of the claim periodically; see, e.g., USLTA § 3–305; Model Act § 4(a). If there is no tract index, such a notice may be "wild" in relation to the record chain of title and impossible to find. This problem can be resolved by requiring a separate tract index for such no-

tices, see, e.g., Iowa Code Ann. § 614.18, or by requiring the claimant to record the notice under the name of the person who has record title at the time the notice is recorded; see Simes & Taylor, supra note 6, at 358.

§ 11.13

1. Quitclaim deeds are commonly used when there is a serious doubt as to whether the grantor has any title at all, when the conveyance is gratuitous, or when the grantor is a person of little financial substance so that a claim on a title covenant could not be collected. A quitclaim deed will, of course, convey whatever interest the grantor has in the described land, whether or not the grantor is even aware of owning the interest; see Reid v. Southeastern Materials, 396 So.2d 667 (Ala. 1981).

their title insurers, with the latter acting under their right of subrogation after indemnifying insured grantees for their losses.

Deed covenants for title are conceptually similar to the implied (and sometimes express) covenant of marketable title found in realty sales contracts. Yet there are several major differences. One is the doctrine of merger, which disallows any recovery on the contract covenants of title once the grantee accepts a deed, so that the deed's covenants (if any) take up just when the contract's leave off.[2] Another difference lies in the standards of acceptable title. The concept of marketable title which applies to contracts requires substantial but not perfect performance;[3] thus a title is objectionable only if it poses significant risks, while a title which is good in fact may be deemed unmarketable if it presents a risk of litigation which the court feels a purchaser should not be forced to accept.[4] No such notions apply to deed covenants for title. They are deemed violated only if the title is actually bad or defective, not merely risky or in doubt.[5] From the purchaser's perspective, the contract approach is usually more attractive and flexible, but the merger doctrine means that the contract claim must be asserted before the deed is delivered.

A third distinction between contract and deed covenants relates to the available remedies. Under the contract, the purchaser may get specific performance with abatement for the title defect, rescission and restitution, or damages.[6] In about half the states damages may include the loss of bargain, and in the other half are limited to restitution plus out-of-pocket expenses.[7] A claim based on deed covenants, other than the covenant of further assurances, can give rise only to damages, and recovery is nearly always limited to the amount the grantor received for the property, plus interest and in some cases attorneys' fees.[8] Specific performance is technically denied except for further assurances; however, if the grantor has subsequently acquired the title which the deed covenants promised, the doctrine of estoppel by deed will vest it in the grantee automatically unless the latter rejects it in preference to damages.[9]

American law generally recognizes six distinct types of title covenants in deeds. In many areas it is customary to spell them out in detail on the face of the deed, but some states have statutes which impose certain of the covenants whenever specific words, such as "grant," "convey and warrant,"

---

2. See West 90th Owners Corp. v. Schlechter, 165 A.D.2d 46, 565 N.Y.S.2d 9 (1991), appeal dismissed 77 N.Y.2d 939, 569 N.Y.S.2d 612, 572 N.E.2d 53 (1991); Simpson v. Johnson, 100 Idaho 357, 597 P.2d 600 (1979); § 10.-12, supra, at notes 53–63. The Uniform Land Transactions Act rejects the merger doctrine entirely; ULTA § 1–309.

3. See ULTA § 2–301 comment 3.

4. See § 10.12, supra, at notes 6–8.

5. Roper v. Elkhorn at Sun Valley, 100 Idaho 790, 605 P.2d 968 (1980) (a claimed easement by a third party is not a breach of deed covenants if it turns out to be unfounded); Boulware v. Mayfield, 317 So.2d 470 (Fla. App.1975) (unsatisfied mortgage of record does not breach deed covenants, if it has in fact

been paid); Fong v. Batton, 214 So.2d 649 (Fla.App.1968) (gap in record chain of title does not breach deed covenants). But see Fechtner v. Lake County Savings & Loan Association, 66 Ill.2d 128, 5 Ill.Dec. 252, 361 N.E.2d 575 (1977), containing dictum that a grantee under a covenant of warranty should be in "much the same position" as a purchaser under a contract covenant of marketable title; Frimberger v. Anzellotti, 25 Conn.App. 401, 594 A.2d 1029 (1991).

6. See § 10.12 supra at notes 11–13.

7. See § 10.3 supra at notes 11–19. The limitation applies only if the vendor contracted in good faith.

8. See text at notes 54–62, infra.

9. See § 11.5, supra, at note 11.

or the like are used in a deed.[10] A grantor may also use express words to limit the coverage of the covenants. For example, it is common in some areas for grantors to give a full set of covenants, but to limit their application to title defects caused or created by the grantor personally, and not those created by his or her predecessors in title.[11] Such a deed is sometimes loosely termed a "special warranty deed." It is also common to list in the deed, as exceptions to the covenants, any specific encumbrances that the grantee has agreed to accept.[12] Examples might include a mortgage which the grantee is assuming, a recorded declaration of use restrictions, or an existing easement for utility lines.[13] Such a listing is very desirable, for it avoids any subsequent dispute as to whether such matters were intended to be within the coverage of the covenants.

The six traditional title covenants [14] may be used separately or together in any combination the parties agree upon. The first three are known as "present" covenants, and the latter three as "future" covenants, for reasons explained below. The basic coverage of each covenant is as follows.

Seisin. The medieval notion of seisin connoted possession, and a few jurisdictions today simply treat this covenant as promising that the grantor is in possession of the land, whether that possession is legal or wrongful.[15] In most states, however, the covenant of seisin is in substance a promise that the grantor owns the estate in the land which the deed purports to convey.[16]

---

10. See, e.g., West's Ann.Cal.Civ.Code § 1113 ("grant"); Ore.Rev.Stat. 93.850 ("conveys and warrants"); Vernon's Ann.Tex.Civ. Stat. art. 1297 ("grant" or "convey"); Utah Code Ann.1953, 57–1–12 ("conveys and warrants"); West's Rev.Code Wash.Ann. 64.04.030 ("conveys and warrants"); id. at 64.04.040 ("bargains, sells, and conveys"); Winn v. Mannhalter, 708 P.2d 444 (Alaska 1985) (in absence of words "conveys and warrants" no covenants of title are implied in conveyance of real estate); Annot., Right of Purchaser at Execution Sale, Upon Failure of Title, to Reimbursement or Restitution from Judgment Creditor, 33 A.L.R.4th 1206. ULTA § 2–306 imputes in every deed, unless there is an expression to the contrary, title warranties of right to convey, against encumbrances, of quiet enjoyment, and to defend the title; there are no implied covenants of seisin or further assurances. By ULTA § 2–304, every land sale contract is presumed to call for a deed containing these covenants unless the contrary is agreed.

11. See Tanglewood Land Co., Inc. v. Wood, 40 N.C.App. 133, 252 S.E.2d 546 (1979).

12. See Leach v. Gunnarson, 290 Or. 31, 619 P.2d 263 (1980).

13. The exceptions may also be stated in more general terms, such as " * * * subject to any and all easements appearing of record." See Pruitt v. Meadows, 393 So.2d 986 (Ala. 1981). This is a less desirable practice, since it does not call clearly to the attention of the parties the specific encumbrances which exist.

14. See Levin, Warranties of Title—A Modest Proposal, 29 Vill.L.Rev. 649 (1984), recommending legislation to eliminate distinctions between the two classes of covenants, present and future, described in the text.

15. See, e.g., Baughman v. Hower, 56 Ohio App. 162, 10 N.E.2d 176 (1937); 6A R. Powell, Real Property ¶ 896 note 9 (1980); 4 Tiffany, Real Property § 1000 (3d ed. 1939). Some decisions treat the covenant as promising both possession and title; see Bernklau v. Stevens, 150 Colo. 187, 371 P.2d 765 (1962). The presence of an adverse possessor on the land breaches the covenant of seisin, even if the possessor has not yet acquired title; Double L. Properties, Inc. v. Crandall, 51 Wn.App. 149, 751 P.2d 1208 (1988). Cf. Utah Stat.Ann. § 57–1–1.

16. Ives v. Real–Venture, Inc., 97 N.C.App. 391, 388 S.E.2d 573 (1990), review denied 327 N.C. 139, 394 N.E.2d 174 (1990) (a deed purports to convey both surface and mineral estates to the land described unless its terms limit the conveyance; grantor who delivers an unrestricted deed, but who lacks title to mineral estate, has breached covenant of seisin); Riddle v. Nelson, 84 N.C.App. 656, 353 S.E.2d 866 (1987) (grantee is entitled, under covenant of seisin, to the precise land described in the deed and not merely an equivalent amount of land); Knudson v. Weeks, 394 F.Supp. 963 (W.D.Okl.1975); Copello v. Hart, 293 So.2d 734 (Fla.App.1974); Thompson v. Thomas, 499 S.W.2d 901 (Tenn.App.1973).

It is usually held that the existence of an outstanding encumbrance, such as an easement or mortgage, is not a breach.[17]

Right to Convey. In most cases, the covenants of seisin and right to convey are virtually synonymous,[18] but there can be differences, at least theoretically. For example, a grantor who owned land subject to a valid restraint on alienation might satisfy the covenant of seisin but not the right to convey.[19] It is also possible for one to have a right to convey but lack seisin, as in the case of a grantor acting under a power of appointment or serving as attorney in fact for the owner; in theory such a conveyance might breach the covenant of seisin, although damages would be only nominal.[20]

Against Encumbrances. An encumbrance is some outstanding right or interest in a third party which does not totally negate the title which the deed purports to convey.[21] Typical encumbrances include mortgages, liens, easements, leases, and restrictive covenants.[22] In general, the principles which define encumbrances in the context of the marketable title concept, discussed earlier,[23] apply equally to deed covenants against encumbrances. One problem which arises frequently is the encumbrance which is not expressly excepted in the deed, but which is either plain and obvious or is well-known to the grantee. The cases are badly divided;[24] some of them distinguish between the grantee's knowledge in fact (which is no defense to a claimed breach) and the open visibility of the encumbrance (which is a defense).[25] Public street or sidewalk rights of way, if visible, are nearly

---

17. See 3 Am.L.Prop. § 12.127 notes 22–26 (1952); Powell, supra, at ¶ 896 notes 5–8; cf. Thompson v. Thomas, 499 S.W.2d 901 (Tenn. App.1973), noted in 4 Memphis St.L.Rev. 650 (1974) (public easement for flooding violates covenant of seisin).

18. Knudson v. Weeks, 394 F.Supp. 963 (W.D.Okl.1975).

19. In theory, seisin and right to convey are also distinct in the case of land occupied by an adverse possessor, who has (wrongful) seisin, but no right to convey.

20. But see Avery v. McHugh, 423 S.W.2d 17 (Mo.App.1967), finding no breach of the covenant of seisin where the grantor had no title but acted under authority of a valid trust agreement.

21. See Fahmie v. Wulster, 81 N.J. 391, 408 A.2d 789 (1979); Aczas v. Stuart Heights, Inc., 154 Conn. 54, 221 A.2d 589 (1966).

22. Cameron v. Martin Marietta Corp., 729 F.Supp. 1529 (E.D.N.C.1990) (illegal contamination by hazardous chemicals was not an encumbrance); U.S. v. Allied Chemical Corp., 587 F.Supp. 1205 (N.D.Cal.1984) (same). Encroachments from or onto the subject property are usually considered encumbrances; see Bryant v. Moritz, 97 Or.App. 481, 776 P.2d 1299 (1989), review denied 308 Or. 465, 781 P.2d 1214 (1989); In re Meehan's Estate, 30 Wis.2d 428, 141 N.W.2d 218 (1966). But see Commonwealth Land Title Ins. Co. v. Stephenson, 101 N.C.App. 379, 399 S.E.2d 380 (1991) (mislocated septic tank system, which en-

croached on neighboring property, held not an encumbrance).

23. See § 10.12, supra, at notes 35–45.

24. Grantee's knowledge of encumbrance is a defense: Ludke v. Egan, 87 Wis.2d 221, 274 N.W.2d 641 (1979); Marathon Builders, Inc. v. Polinger, 263 Md. 410, 283 A.2d 617 (1971) (dictum). Grantee's knowledge is no defense; grantor liable: Fidelity Nat. Title Ins. Co. v. Miller, 215 Cal.App.3d 1163, 264 Cal.Rptr. 17 (1989) (grantor was in breach of covenant against encumbrances even though he had informed grantee of existence of the encumbrance); Etheridge v. Fried, 183 Ga. App. 842, 360 S.E.2d 409 (1987) (grantor was in breach of covenant even though grantee had constructive notice of a prior recorded deed which defeated grantor's title to portion of land conveyed); Gill Grain Co. v. Poos, 707 S.W.2d 434 (Mo.App.1986) (similar); In re Sale of Land Situate in Wayne Township, 50 Pa. Cmwlth. 533, 413 A.2d 1162 (1980); Ziskind v. Bruce Lee Corp., 224 Pa.Super. 518, 307 A.2d 377 (1973); Gerdes v. Shew, 4 N.C.App. 144, 166 S.E.2d 519 (1969); Jones v. Grow Investment & Mortgage Co., 11 Utah 2d 326, 358 P.2d 909 (1961). It is obvious that knowledge of the encumbrance should be no defense where the parties agreed or clearly contemplated that the grantor would remove it; see, e.g., Dillard v. Earnhart, 457 S.W.2d 666 (Mo. 1970).

25. Leach v. Gunnarson, 290 Or. 31, 619 P.2d 263 (1980). Cf. Gill Grain Co. v. Poos,

always held not to violate the covenant.[26]

Another common point of controversy is the existence of violations of building, housing or similar municipal codes. Technically, such matters do not affect title at all, and the great bulk of the cases hold that they do not breach the covenant against encumbrances.[27] One widely cited case recognizes an exception if the violation has already become the subject of enforcement proceedings by local government officials at the time the covenant is given.[28] A similar issue is raised by existing violations of zoning ordinances. They are often held to make titles unmarketable in the context of executory contracts,[29] and there is some authority for extending this notion to deed covenants against encumbrances.[30] Another related question arises if the property being conveyed has been included in a local improvement district for, say, street paving or sewer line installation. If the district has already imposed assessments secured by liens on the properties it covers, these are plainly encumbrances. However, there is no breach of the covenant against encumbrances if the district merely plans or expects to impose such liens in the future.[31]

Warranty and Quiet Enjoyment. These two covenants are usually considered identical in their coverage.[32] While not technically promising that the grantee is receiving good and unencumbered title, they have much the same practical effect, for they obligate the grantor to indemnify the grantee

707 S.W.2d 434 (Mo.App.1986) (visible appearance of prescriptive easement is no defense to action on covenant of title); Northrip v. Conner, 107 N.M. 139, 754 P.2d 516 (1988) (unrecorded easement, visible on the ground, violated covenant against encumbrances, where deed excepted from the covenant only "easements of record").

26. See McKnight v. Cagle, 76 N.C.App. 59, 331 S.E.2d 707 (1985), cert. denied 314 N.C. 541, 335 S.E.2d 20 (1985); Hawks v. Brindle, 51 N.C.App. 19, 275 S.E.2d 277 (1981); Tabet Lumber Co. v. Golightly, 80 N.M. 442, 457 P.2d 374 (1969); Old Falls, Inc. v. Johnson, 88 N.J.Super. 441, 212 A.2d 674 (1965). But see Campagna v. Parker, 116 Idaho 734, 779 P.2d 409 (1989) (public road easement breached covenants of title, where it did not provide the sole access to the property and did not enhance its value); Commissioner, Department of Highways v. Rice, 411 S.W.2d 471 (Ky.1966).

27. Seth v. Wilson, 62 Or.App. 814, 662 P.2d 745 (1983) (ordinance prohibiting subdivision of land); Fahmie v. Wulster, 81 N.J. 391, 408 A.2d 789 (1979) (regulation of stream culvert size); Domer v. Sleeper, 533 P.2d 9 (Alaska 1975) (fire code); McCrae v. Giteles, 253 So.2d 260 (Fla.App.1971) (housing code); Stone v. Sexsmith, 28 Wn.2d 947, 184 P.2d 567 (1947) (electrical code).

28. Brunke v. Pharo, 3 Wis.2d 628, 89 N.W.2d 221 (1958), noted 1958 Wis.L.Rev. 640; see Note, 1958 Wis.L.Rev. 128.

29. See § 10.12, supra, at notes 42–43; Annot., 39 A.L.R.3d 362 (1971); Oatis v. Delcuze, 226 La. 751, 77 So.2d 28 (1954).

30. Wilcox v. Pioneer Homes, Inc., 41 N.C.App. 140, 254 S.E.2d 214 (1979); but see Barnett v. Decatur, 261 Ga. 205, 403 S.E.2d 46 (1991), on remand 199 Ga.App. 893, 407 S.E.2d 139 (1991) (no breach of covenants of title, although lot was sold illegally in violation of zoning ordinance); Frimberger v. Anzellotti, 25 Conn.App. 401, 594 A.2d 1029 (1991) (illegal filling of wetlands without permit was not a breach of covenants of title); Marathon Builders, Inc. v. Polinger, 263 Md. 410, 283 A.2d 617 (1971), finding no violation of the covenant against encumbrances despite the fact that the zoning prohibited all use of the property; there was, however, no existing violation.

31. Brewer v. Peatross, 595 P.2d 866 (Utah 1979); Wells v. DuRoss, 54 Ohio App.2d 50, 374 N.E.2d 662 (1977). But see First American Federal Sav. & Loan Ass'n v. Royall, 77 N.C.App. 131, 334 S.E.2d 792 (1985) (where city required installation of new water line by grantee and would not issue a certificate of occupancy without it, the grantor was in breach of the covenant against encumbrances, since the city had authority to impose a special assessment lien to cover cost of water line).

32. See Brown v. Lober, 75 Ill.2d 547, 27 Ill.Dec. 780, 389 N.E.2d 1188 (1979); Spiegel v. Seaman, 160 N.J.Super. 471, 390 A.2d 639 (1978); Fritts v. Gerukos, 273 N.C. 116, 159 S.E.2d 536 (1968); 6A Powell, Real Property ¶ 900 (1980); 3 Am.L.Prop. § 12.129 (1952).

for any loss resulting from an "eviction" or disturbance of the grantee due either to an absence of title to all or part of the land, or to an outstanding encumbrance.[33] They include an obligation on the grantor's part to defend against any legal attack on the grantee's title or possession.[34]

Further Assurances. This is a promise by the grantor to execute any additional documents that may be needed in the future to perfect the title which the original deed purported to convey. It is the only one of the six standard covenants that can be enforced by specific performance as well as damages.[35] In most cases a grantor's after-acquired title will inure to the grantee automatically [36] and no further instrument is needed, so this covenant is not asserted very frequently.

Timing of Breach. The three "present" covenants (seisin, right to convey, and against encumbrances) are so called because they are breached, if at all, the moment the deed is delivered and accepted; the grantor either has or does not have seisin and the right to convey, and encumbrances either do or do not exist.[37] The statute of limitations begins to run against the grantee at that time,[38] and thus may bar any claim before the grantee even discovers that the title is defective. Moreover, the present covenants are usually held not to "run with the land" and hence do not benefit remote grantees who trace their title through the covenantee.[39] This view is a relic

33. See Booker T. Washington Const. & Design Co. v. Huntington Urban Renewal Authority, 181 W.Va. 409, 383 S.E.2d 41 (1989); Fechtner v. Lake County Savings & Loan Association, 66 Ill.2d 128, 5 Ill.Dec. 252, 361 N.E.2d 575 (1977). But see Northeast Petroleum Corp. v. Vermont, 143 Vt. 339, 466 A.2d 1164 (1983) (existence of recorded judgment lien breaches covenant of warranty).

34. Dillon v. Morgan, 362 So.2d 1130 (La. App.1978); Hull v. Federal Land Bank, 134 Vt. 201, 353 A.2d 577 (1976); Foley v. Smith, 14 Wn.App. 285, 539 P.2d 874 (1975). The grantor is also precluded by the covenants from personally attacking the grantee's title; see Lewicki v. Marszalkowski, 455 A.2d 307 (R.I.1983) (grantor may not claim by adverse possession the land she has conveyed by deed with covenant of warranty). But see Sharpton v. Lofton, 721 S.W.2d 770 (Mo.App.1986) (grantor's action to set deed aside is not precluded by covenant of warranty in deed).

35. See Spiegel v. Seaman, 160 N.J.Super. 471, 390 A.2d 639 (1978); 4 Tiffany, Real Property § 1015 (3d ed. 1939). The other covenants can give rise only to an action for damages; see Forrest v. Hanson, 424 S.W.2d 899 (Tex.1968).

36. See generally § 11.5, supra.

37. Double L. Properties, Inc. v. Crandall, 51 Wn.App. 149, 751 P.2d 1208 (1988); Brown v. Lober, 75 Ill.2d 547, 27 Ill.Dec. 780, 389 N.E.2d 1188 (1979); Philbin Investments, Inc. v. Orb Enterprises, Limited, 35 N.C.App. 622, 242 S.E.2d 176 (1978), certiorari denied 295 N.C. 90, 244 S.E.2d 260 (1978); A.C. Drinkwater Jr., Farms, Inc. v. Ellot H. Raffety Farms, Inc., 495 S.W.2d 450 (Mo.App.1973); Thomp-

son v. Thomas, 499 S.W.2d 901 (Tenn.App. 1973); Marathon Builders, Inc. v. Polinger, 263 Md. 410, 283 A.2d 617 (1971). No eviction is necessary to constitute a breach of the present covenants; see Creason v. Peterson, 24 Utah 2d 305, 470 P.2d 403 (1970). However, in the absence of an eviction, the grantee's damages may be only nominal; see text at note 63, infra.

38. Cecil Lawter Real Estate School, Inc. v. Town & Country Shopping Center Co., 143 Ariz. 527, 694 P.2d 815 (App.1984); Brown v. Lober, supra; Cape Co. v. Wiebe, 196 Neb. 204, 241 N.W.2d 830 (1976); Bernklau v. Stevens, 150 Colo. 187, 371 P.2d 765, 95 A.L.R.2d 905 (1962). ULTA § 2–521 applies the same rule to its six-year statute of limitations. But see Christiansen v. Utah–Idaho Sugar Co., 590 P.2d 1251 (Utah 1979), adopting the unusual rule that the cause of action on a covenant against encumbrances does not accrue until the grantee has notice of the breach. See generally Annot., 95 A.L.R.2d 913 (1965). See also Turner v. Eubanks. 26 Ark.App. 22, 759 S.W.2d 37 (1988) (even though statute of limitations has run on covenants, a claim for breach can be employed by the grantee as an offset to unrelated claims by the grantor).

39. Colonial Capital Corp. v. Smith, 367 So.2d 490 (Ala.Civ.App.1979); Bridges v. Heimburger, 360 So.2d 929 (Miss.1978); Babb v. Weemer, 225 Cal.App.2d 546, 37 Cal.Rptr. 533 (1964); Smith v. Peoples Bank & Trust Co., 254 N.C. 588, 119 S.E.2d 623 (1961); Sandler v. New Jersey Realty Title Insurance Co., 36 N.J. 471, 178 A.2d 1 (1962); Mitchell v. Warner, 5 Conn. 497 (1825). One court has even

of the common-law notion that a cause of action was not assignable. Since the present covenants are breached when made, the grantee has only a cause of action and not a continuing covenant. Causes of action generally are now freely assignable, and there seems to be no sound objection to treating the grantee's subsequent deed as implying an assignment, thus permitting remote grantees to sue on present covenants. This is a reasonable construction of the parties' probable intent, but only a few courts have been willing to take this step.[40]

The treatment of the three "future" covenants (warranty, quiet enjoyment, and further assurances) is quite different. They are breached only when the covenantee is actually disturbed by one with paramount title, an event termed an "eviction"[41] even though it does not necessarily signify actual loss of possession. The statute of limitations commences only from the date of the eviction,[42] so there is little risk of the grantee's being barred without awareness of the claim. And since no cause of action accrues until an eviction occurs, the unbreached covenant is held to run with the land and to benefit remote grantees.[43] For all of these reasons, future covenants are often much more advantageous to covenantees than are present covenants.

Since the future covenants are breached only by an eviction, the grantee who is not disturbed in any way has no action.[44] On the other hand, a serious physical interference with the grantee's possession by the holder of

held that the covenant against encumbrances cannot be the subject of an *express* assignment; Commonwealth Land Title Ins. Co. v. Stephenson, 101 N.C.App. 379, 399 S.E.2d 380 (1991). ULTA § 2–312 provides that all title covenants will run with the land unless there is a contrary agreement; so does Colo.Rev. Stat.1973, 118–1–21. See generally Comment, Covenants of Title Running with the Land in California, 49 Cal.L.Rev. 931 (1961); Comment, 7 U.Miami L.Rev. 378 (1953).

40. Schofield v. Iowa Homestead Co., 32 Iowa 317 (1871). See 3 Am.L.Prop. § 12.127 note 11 (1952).

41. Wells v. Tennant, 180 W.Va. 166, 375 S.E.2d 798 (1988); Colonial Capital Corp. v. Smith, 367 So.2d 490 (Ala.Civ.App.1979); Brown v. Lober, 75 Ill.2d 547, 27 Ill.Dec. 780, 389 N.E.2d 1188 (1979); Bridges v. Heimburger, 360 So.2d 929 (Miss.1978).

42. Self v. Petty, 469 So.2d 568 (Ala.1985); Brown v. Lober, supra.

43. Bridges v. Heimburger, 360 So.2d 929 (Miss.1978); Marathon Builders, Inc. v. Polinger, 263 Md. 410, 283 A.2d 617 (1971); Linville v. Nance Development Co., 180 Kan. 379, 304 P.2d 453 (1956). See generally 3 Am. L.Prop. § 12.131 (1952). If the grantor had no title whatever, it might be argued that there is no "land" with which the covenant can run. If this argument succeeded it would produce the bizarre result of withdrawing the protection of the covenant from the remote grantee who needed it most, but it is usually rejected

on the ground that a delivery of possession, actual or constructive, establishes the necessary succession, see Solberg v. Robinson, 34 S.D. 55, 147 N.W. 87 (1914), or on the basis that the covenantor is estopped to deny that he passed some estate, see Wead v. Larkin, 54 Ill. 489 (1870). It is clear that there must be "privity" between the original covenantee and remote plaintiffs, and that an adverse possessor who can trace no chain of deeds back to the covenantor cannot recover on the covenant; see Deason v. Findley, 145 Ala. 407, 40 So. 220 (1906). See generally 4 Tiffany, Real Property § 1022 notes 84–86 (1939).

44. Elliott v. Elliott, 252 Ark. 966, 482 S.W.2d 123 (1972) (mere filing of suit against grantee is not an eviction); Veterans' Land Board v. Akers, 408 S.W.2d 795 (Tex.Civ.App. 1966), refused n.r.e. (land office's issuance of prospecting permit to third party is not an eviction). See also Brewster v. Hines, 155 W.Va. 302, 185 S.E.2d 513 (1971) and Rabon v. Turner, 115 So.2d 243 (La.App.1959) (dictum that an entire failure of grantor's title would be an eviction without more.) An exception exists if the paramount title is in the government; no further eviction is necessary. See Thompson v. Dildy, 227 Ark. 648, 300 S.W.2d 270 (1957); Cover v. McAden, 183 N.C. 641, 112 S.E. 817 (1922); Efta v. Swanson, 115 Minn. 373, 132 N.W. 335 (1911). If the grantee already owns the interest which the grantor does not convey, it is impossible for the grantee to suffer an eviction; see Gibson v. Turner, 156 Tex. 289, 294 S.W.2d 781 (1956).

paramount title will obviously suffice;[45] so will a court decree ordering the grantee off the land or decreeing that he or she has no title.[46] An eviction may be "constructive," operating without a physical disturbance.[47] Thus, if the grantee voluntarily surrenders possession to one who has paramount title[48] or buys that title from its holder,[49] an eviction has occurred. And if a grantor pays damages on a deed covenant to a grantee, the former has been constructively evicted for purposes of an action against an earlier grantor on the covenant of warranty in a prior deed.[50]

Note, however, that there is no eviction in any case unless the interference is by one who *in fact* has a title superior to the grantee's; it is not enough that the grantee believes that a third party has legal grounds for the eviction.[51] For this reason, it is usually wise for the grantee to notify the grantor of any litigation with a party claiming paramount title and to invite the grantor to defend it. Unless the grantor has an opportunity to intervene and participate in the lawsuit, he or she will not be bound by *res judicata* and may later make an independent attack, in an action against the grantor on the covenant, on the validity of the asserted paramount title.[52] Rather ironically, a grantee who is successful in resisting the claim of a third party has obviously not been evicted and can recover nothing on the deed covenants, even though the grantee may have a significant outlay for costs and attorneys' fees.[53]

Damages. Perhaps the broadest principle governing the recovery of damages on deed covenants is that the covenantor cannot be made to pay more than the price received for the land.[54] This rule, which applies no

45. McCleary v. Bratton, 307 S.W.2d 722 (Mo.App.1957). If the holder of paramount title is already in possession when the deed containing the covenant is delivered, an eviction occurs upon delivery; see Hull v. Federal Land Bank, 134 Vt. 201, 353 A.2d 577 (1976); Haas v. Gahlinger, 248 S.W.2d 349 (Ky.1952).

46. Foley v. Smith, 14 Wn.App. 285, 539 P.2d 874 (1975); Schneider v. Lipscomb County National Farm Loan Association, 146 Tex. 66, 202 S.W.2d 832 (1947).

47. See generally Annot., 172 A.L.R. 18 (1948); Booker T. Washington Const. & Design Co. v. Huntington Urban Renewal Auth., 181 W.Va. 409, 383 S.E.2d 41 (1989) (when grantee who holds under warranty deed is sued by a prospective contract purchaser because the grantee's title is unmarketable, the grantee has suffered an eviction and the warranty is breached).

48. Brewster v. Hines, 155 W.Va. 302, 185 S.E.2d 513 (1971), noted at 74 W.Va.L.Rev. 415 (1972).

49. Greenwood v. Robbins, 108 N.J.Eq. 122, 154 A. 333 (1931); Morgan v. Haley, 107 Va. 331, 58 S.E. 564 (1907).

50. Kramer v. Carter, 136 Mass. 504 (1884).

51. See Roper v. Elkhorn at Sun Valley, 100 Idaho 790, 605 P.2d 968 (1980); Green v. Ayres, 272 Or. 117, 535 P.2d 762 (1975); Brew-ster v. Hines, 155 W.Va. 302, 185 S.E.2d 513 (1971).

52. Holzworth v. Roth, 78 S.D. 287, 101 N.W.2d 393 (1960); May v. Loeb, 57 Ga.App. 788, 196 S.E. 268 (1938), affirmed 186 Ga. 742, 198 S.E. 785 (1938). See generally 3 Am. L.Prop. § 12.131 notes 19–27 (1952).

53. McDonald v. Delhi Sav. Bank, 440 N.W.2d 839 (Iowa 1989); Chaney v. Haeder, 90 Or.App. 321, 752 P.2d 854 (1988); Elliott v. Elliott, 252 Ark. 966, 482 S.W.2d 123 (1972); Jarrett v. Scofield, 200 Md. 641, 92 A.2d 370 (1952). There is some thought in the cases that the grantee who litigates the title successfully might recover costs and attorneys' fees if the grantor has "thrust him into litigation" with the third party; see First Fiduciary Corp. v. Blanco, 276 N.W.2d 30 (Minn.1979).

54. See Woods v. Schmitt, 439 N.W.2d 855 (Iowa 1989); MGIC Financial Corp. v. H.A. Briggs Co., 24 Wn.App. 1, 600 P.2d 573 (1979); Teems v. City of Forest Park, 137 Ga.App. 733, 225 S.E.2d 87 (1976); Tucker v. Walker, 246 Ark. 177, 437 S.W.2d 788 (1969); Ledbetter v. Howard, 395 S.W.2d 951 (Tex.Civ.App.1965); Davis v. Smith, 5 Ga. 274 (1848); Annots., 100 A.L.R. 1194 (1937); 61 A.L.R. 127 (1929). Thus a grantee who discharged a paramount mortgage by paying more than the original price he paid for the land was limited, in an action on a covenant against encumbrances, to

matter which covenants are involved, is obviously harsh in some applications. If the land's value has risen sharply or if it was originally worth more than the grantee paid for it, the recovery on the covenant may pay only a small fraction of the actual loss, particularly if there is a total failure of title. The same is true if the grantee has built valuable buildings on the land, although the loss of an improver who acted in good faith will usually be mitigated by statutes or judicial doctrines relating to mistaken improvements.[55] The limitation of damages to the price received by the covenantor has been criticized,[56] and a few New England states have adopted a contrary rule allowing recovery of the value as of the time of eviction.[57] But that approach opens the grantor to liability for an amount which may be many times the price received and which may extend, especially under the "future" covenants, for many decades into the future. Given the wide availability of title insurance as an alternative form of protection for the grantee which can, in theory, be increased in dollar coverage whenever he or she desires, it is very doubtful that the law should place such a vast and uncertain potential burden on the grantor in the absence of fraud or a very clear promise to undertake it.[58]

A further limitation is usually applied if there is only a partial breach of the covenants of title. Suppose there is a shortage in the land owned by the grantor, so that the deed conveys only 80 percent (in terms of value, not necessarily acreage) of the land it describes. If the price paid for the whole was $100,000, but it would be worth much more at the time of the eviction or the trial, most cases nevertheless limit the grantee's recovery to the pro-rata share of the original price, or $20,000.[59] Whether this sort of constraint on damages is necessary to fair treatment of the grantor is very much open to doubt.

recovery of the latter amount; Forrer v. Sather, 595 P.2d 1306 (Utah 1979). Note that consequential damages, such as lost profits on a prospective resale of the property, are not recoverable; Clark v. Cypress Shores Development Co., 516 So.2d 622 (Ala.1987); Bridges v. Heimburger, 360 So.2d 929 (Miss.1978). Such damages may, however, be recovered upon a showing that the grantor committed fraud; see First Nat. Bank v. Halo Investments, 394 N.W.2d 158 (Minn.App.1986).

55. Lockhart v. Phenix City Investment Co., 549 So.2d 48 (Ala.1989). The holder of the paramount title is usually given an option to sell the land to the mistaken improver at its unimproved value, or to purchase the improvements at an amount equal to the value they add to the property. See, e.g., Madrid v. Spears, 250 F.2d 51 (10th Cir.1957); State Mutual Insurance Co. v. McJenkin Insurance & Realty Co., 86 Ga.App. 442, 71 S.E.2d 670 (1952); Brunt v. McLaurin, 178 Miss. 86, 172 So. 309 (1937); D. Dobbs, Remedies § 12.8 note 72 (1973).

56. See Groetzinger, Breach of the Warranty Covenants in Deeds and the Allowable Measure of Damages, 17 N.H.Bar J. 1 (1975);

Hymes v. Esty, 133 N.Y. 342, 31 N.E. 105 (1892).

57. Connecticut, Maine, Massachusetts, and Vermont do not limit recovery to the amount the covenantor received; see Annot., 61 A.L.R. 10, 31–32 (1929) for extensive quotations from the cases. See also Bridwell v. Gruner, 212 Ark. 992, 209 S.W.2d 441 (1948), which is ambiguous but may be a departure from the majority rule.

58. See Gray v. Paxton, 662 P.2d 1105 (Colo.App.1983); D. Dobbs, Remedies § 12.8 at 837 (1973). ULTA § 2–513 retains the majority rule.

59. McClure v. Turner, 165 Ga.App. 380, 301 S.E.2d 304 (1983); Hillsboro Cove, Inc. v. Archibald, 322 So.2d 585 (Fla.App.1975); Grey v. Konrad, 133 Vt. 195, 332 A.2d 797 (1975); French v. Bank of Southwest National Association, 422 S.W.2d 1 (Tex.Civ.App.1967), refused n.r.e.; Epstein v. Van Gilder, 13 Pa.D. & C.2d 761, 27 Leh.L.J. 498 (1958); Ragsdale v. Langford, 358 S.W.2d 936 (Tex.Civ.App.1962), refused n.r.e. Cf. Gonzales v. Garcia, 89 N.M. 337, 552 P.2d 468 (1976) (grantor can recover full value of the deficiency.) See Annot., 94 A.L.R.3d 1091 (1979).

Where the breach is not a deficiency in land area, but instead the property is subject to an encumbrance such as an easement or restrictive covenant that has not been removed by the grantee, the cases allow recovery for the diminution in value of the land, subject to the absolute limitation that damages may not exceed the total price received. But by analogy to the area-deficiency cases, the reduction in value is generally measured as of the date of the sale rather than the time of eviction.[60] If the grantee actually purchases the outstanding encumbrance at a reasonable price, the amount thus spent is the measure of damages,[61] although again capped by the total price. Note that if the property's market value is significantly higher than the price paid, the latter can be a much more attractive strategy, since the grantee's recovery is not subject to any limitation based on a pro-rata portion of the original price paid. Finally, if the encumbrance in question is one which can be removed for a liquidated amount, such as a mortgage or a mechanics lien, that amount is the measure of damages.[62]

Damage claims raise several other interesting issues. The "present" covenants are breached when the deed is delivered, if at all, but that does not mean substantial damages can be collected immediately. The grantee must show actual harm, which practically amounts to requiring an eviction; otherwise one can have only nominal damages.[63] Yet if the grantee waits for an eviction before suing on the covenants, there is a considerable risk that any substantial recovery will be barred by the statute of limitations. Another problem arises if the deed containing the covenants was a gift, with no dollar consideration received by the covenantor. Some authority permits recovery on the covenant, with the upper limit fixed by the land's value at the time of the conveyance.[64] Finally, note that if the grantee recovers

60. See, e.g., Gill Grain Co. v. Poos, 707 S.W.2d 434 (Mo.App.1986); Yonkers City Post No. 1666, Veterans of Foreign Wars of the United States, Inc. v. Josanth Realty Corp., 67 N.Y.2d 1029, 503 N.Y.S.2d 321, 494 N.E.2d 452 (1986), on remand 143 A.D.2d 267, 532 N.Y.S.2d 169 (1988); Ellison v. F. Murray Parker Builders, Inc., 573 S.W.2d 161 (Tenn.App. 1978); East Montpelier Development Corp. v. Barre Trust Co., 127 Vt. 491, 253 A.2d 131 (1969); Reed v. Rustin, 375 Mich. 531, 134 N.W.2d 767 (1965); Evans v. Faught, 231 Cal. App.2d 698, 42 Cal.Rptr. 133 (1965). See also In re Meehan's Estate, 30 Wis.2d 428, 141 N.W.2d 218 (1966). For earlier cases, see Annot., 61 A.L.R. 10, 90 note 71 (1929). In a state like Connecticut, which generally follows the minority rule measuring damages at the time of eviction, see note 57, supra, the reduction in market value resulting from an easement would also be measured as of the eviction; but the only modern case found dealing with the question is ambiguous as to the date of measurement of damages. See Aczas v. Stuart Heights, Inc., 154 Conn. 54, 221 A.2d 589 (1966).

61. Bryant v. Moritz, 97 Or.App. 481, 776 P.2d 1299 (1989); review denied 308 Or. 465, 781 P.2d 1214 (1989); Skipper v. McMillan, 349 So.2d 808 (Fla.App.1977); Downtown

Parking Co. v. Vorbeck, 524 P.2d 629 (Colo. App.1974); Creason v. Peterson, 24 Utah 2d 305, 470 P.2d 403 (1970).

62. Again, the recovery is limited to the price the covenantor received. See Ticor Title Ins. Co. v. Graham, 576 N.E.2d 1332 (Ind.App. 1991); Forrer v. Sather, 595 P.2d 1306 (Utah 1979); Evans v. Faught, 231 Cal.App.2d 698, 42 Cal.Rptr. 133 (1965); Wolff v. Commercial Standard Insurance Co., 345 S.W.2d 565 (Tex. Civ.App.1961), refused n.r.e.

63. Fong v. Batton, 214 So.2d 649 (Fla.App. 1968); Dillard v. Earnhart, 457 S.W.2d 666 (Mo.1970); Fisk v. Powell, 349 Mich. 604, 84 N.W.2d 736 (1957); In re Meehan's Estate, 30 Wis.2d 428, 141 N.W.2d 218 (1966); Pacific Bond & Mortgage Co. v. Rohn, 101 Utah 335, 121 P.2d 635 (1942); 6A Powell, Real Property ¶ 896 note 15 (1980); Annot., 61 A.L.R. 10, 76 note 27 (1929). But see Fechtner v. Lake County Savings & Loan Association, 66 Ill.2d 128, 5 Ill.Dec. 252, 361 N.E.2d 575 (1977), approving recovery of substantial damages for judgment liens on the land although the plaintiff/grantee had not discharged them and they had not been foreclosed.

64. Smith v. Smith, 243 Ga. 56, 252 S.E.2d 484 (1979); Annot., 61 A.L.R. 10, 150 note 89 (1929). But see Ragsdale v. Ragsdale, 172

damages equal to the full price paid for the land, the grantee will be obliged to reconvey to the grantor upon request any interest which was in fact received by the original deed; otherwise, it is reasoned that the grantee would be unjustly enriched.[65]

Since the "future" covenants run with the land and can be asserted by remote grantees, the question arises whether the upper limit of damages is the price the covenantee paid for the land or the amount the covenantor received. The two figures may well be different. Suppose A sells land to B with a covenant of warranty for $10,000. Later B sells the same land to C for $15,000. If C brings an action against A on the covenant, there is wide agreement that C's recovery will be limited to the $10,000 A received.[66] However, if B sells to C for only $5,000, the cases are seriously divided as to whether C can recover the full $10,000 A received or only the $5,000 C paid.[67] The argument for the latter figure is based on the notion that C should not recover more than actual damages, but inflation or improvements built by C may well make C's damages exceed the price paid. It is hard to see how A can reasonably complain about reimbursing C's actual damages up to the amount A received.

In addition to the measures of damages discussed above, two other factors often form a basis for damage claims: interest and litigation costs, including attorneys' fees. Both are widely recognized as proper.[68] However, there is a good deal of confusion about the basis and measurement of interest. One common approach allows interest only for the period, if any, that the plaintiff has been denied actual possession or use of the property as a result of the title defect.[69] This same idea is embodied in decisions which

S.W.2d 381 (Tex.Civ.App.1943), affirmed 142 Tex. 476, 179 S.W.2d 291 (1944), allowing no recovery where no price was paid. If the transaction was an exchange rather than a sale, there may be no explicit dollar price stated; the value of the land which the covenantee gave up will be the upper limit of the recovery. See Maxwell v. Redd, 209 Kan. 264, 496 P.2d 1320 (1972); 61 A.L.R. 10, 150 (1928).

65. Fong v. Batton, 214 So.2d 649 (Fla.App. 1968); 4 Tiffany, Real Property § 1016 notes 38–40 (3d ed. 1939). In some jurisdictions it is customary for the court to order or decree a reconveyance as a condition of entering judgment in damages for the covenantee; see, e.g., Wood v. Setliff, 232 Ark. 233, 335 S.W.2d 305 (1960). The same principle applies when there is a total failure of title to a physical portion of the land; that portion must be reconveyed; id.

66. Smith v. Smith, 243 Ga. 56, 252 S.E.2d 484 (1979); Bridges v. Heimburger, 360 So.2d 929 (Miss.1978). ULTA § 2–513(2) agrees. However, if C has only a partial loss of value, say, one-half, the cases allow him to measure his damages as of the date of the deed to himself, rather than the earlier deed given by A; thus he could recover $7,500, since that

would not exceed the total consideration received by A. See ULTA § 2–513 comment 2.

67. Compare Brooks v. Black, 68 Miss. 161, 8 So. 332 (1890) (remote grantor liable for amount received) with Taylor v. Wallace, 20 Colo. 211, 37 P. 963 (1894) (recovery limited to amount grantee paid). Modern authority on the point is very scant. See Annot., 61 A.L.R. 10, 120–24 (1929); J. Cribbet, Real Property 276–77 (2d ed. 1975).

68. See, e.g., Foley v. Smith, 14 Wn.App. 285, 539 P.2d 874 (1975). But see Maxwell v. Redd, 209 Kan. 264, 496 P.2d 1320 (1972), where the court refused to allow interest because the transaction had been an exchange of land rather than a sale, and the parties had never agreed to any specific price or value for the parcels exchanged.

69. See Yonkers City Post No. 1666, Veterans of Foreign Wars of the United States, Inc. v. Josanth Realty Corp., 104 A.D.2d 980, 481 N.Y.S.2d 95 (1984), reversed on other grounds 67 N.Y.2d 1029, 503 N.Y.S.2d 321, 494 N.E.2d 452 (1986), on remand 143 A.D.2d 267, 532 N.Y.S.2d 169 (1988); Hillsboro Cove, Inc. v. Archibald, 322 So.2d 585 (Fla.App.1975); Forrest v. Hanson, 424 S.W.2d 899 (Tex.1968).

allow interest only from the date of the grantee's eviction.[70] Another view holds that even if the plaintiff has had possession for the entire time since taking the deed, he or she may be liable as a trespasser to the holder of paramount title for so-called mesne profits, and hence should get interest for the full period as an approximate way of compensating for that liability.[71] Arguably this idea breaks down if the grantee purchases the paramount title, since he or she obviously cannot then be sued for mesne profits; but it might be assumed that the price paid for the outstanding interest must have included a factor representing the mesne profits the true owner could otherwise have collected.[72]

Perhaps surprisingly, the majority of cases allow the grantee to recover the court costs and attorneys' fees expended in litigating the title with a third party who turns out to hold a paramount interest.[73] It does not matter whether the grantee was the plaintiff or the defendant in that action, so long as the grantee prosecuted it in good faith and the fees are reasonable.[74] Indeed, attorneys' fees for negotiating to acquire the outstanding title without litigation can be recovered.[75] At one time it was generally held that a grantee could not get attorneys' fees without first giving the grantor notice of the litigation and requesting him or her to represent the grantee,[76] but most of the recent cases do not impose this requirement. Note carefully that only attorneys' fees in the action against the third party can be recovered; fees in the action against the grantor on the title covenants themselves are not collectable.[77]

§ 11.14   Title Insurance

As the preceding sections have shown, the recording system is quite imperfect in its ability to warn prospective purchasers of land that title defects are present. The risk of such defects can be reduced by curative

See generally Annot., 61 A.L.R. 10, 174–82 (1929).

70. See, e.g., Tucker v. Walker, 246 Ark. 177, 437 S.W.2d 788 (1969).

71. Davis v. Smith, 5 Ga. 274 (1848). Some cases consider the actual liability of the grantee for mesne profits. If, for example, the grantee is insulated by the statute of limitations from such liability for a portion of the time he or she has been in possession, interest is computed only for the remaining time. See Smith v. Nussbaum, 71 S.W.2d 82 (Mo.App. 1934); Hilliker v. Rueger, 228 N.Y. 11, 126 N.E. 266 (1920); Curtis v. Brannon, 98 Tenn. 153, 38 S.W. 1073 (1897).

72. See Harding v. Larkin, 41 Ill. 413 (1866).

73. The fees must be both actual and reasonable; see Liddycoat v. Ulbricht, 276 Or. 723, 556 P.2d 99 (1976); Morgan v. Haley, 107 Va. 331, 58 S.E. 564 (1907), discussing but rejecting the majority view; cases cited at note 77, infra. See 4 Tiffany, Real Property § 1020 (3d ed. 1939). Cf. Elliott v. Elliott, 252 Ark. 966, 482 S.W.2d 123 (1972) (under Texas

law, no recovery for attorneys' fee in absence of agreement to pay them.)

74. Nelson v. Growers Ford Tractor Co., 282 So.2d 664 (Fla.App.1973); Louisville Public–Warehouse Co. v. James, 139 Ky. 434, 56 S.W. 19 (1900); Annot., 61 A.L.R. 10, 167 note 28 (1929).

75. Creason v. Peterson, 24 Utah 2d 305, 470 P.2d 403 (1970).

76. See Bloom v. Hendricks, 111 N.M. 250, 804 P.2d 1069 (1991); Mellor v. Chamberlin, 100 Wn.2d 643, 673 P.2d 610 (1983); Smith v. Nussbaum, 71 S.W.2d 82 (Mo.App.1934); 61 A.L.R. 10, 162 note 16 (1929). Even if notice is not a prerequisite to recovery of attorneys' fees, it is still a wise precaution, since it will bind the covenantor to a judicial determination that the third party in fact has paramount title; see text at note 52, infra.

77. Mellor v. Chamberlin, supra note 76. Forrer v. Sather, 595 P.2d 1306 (Utah 1979); Bridges v. Heimburger, 360 So.2d 929 (Miss. 1978); Skipper v. McMillan, 349 So.2d 808 (Fla.App.1977). But see Flynn v. Allison, 97 Idaho 618, 549 P.2d 1065 (1976).

statutes and marketable title acts, but it is still great enough to be a serious concern. Title insurance has arisen as a way of compensating for this risk.

A title insurance policy is a contract of indemnity. It states the name of the person or persons in whom the title is vested, and it lists all significant encumbrances or other title defects which the insurer knows are present, usually through a title search, and for which it therefore assumes no liability. If it later develops that the title was differently vested or was subject to other defects or encumbrances on the date of the policy, the insurer is obligated to indemnify the insured for any losses caused by the discrepancy.[1]

There are two general kinds of title insurance policies, insuring respectively mortgage lenders and owners. Lenders' policies are more widely used, and many lenders insist upon them (at the borrower's expense) in every mortgage loan. Nearly all secondary market purchasers of mortgages also require lender's title insurance, a fact which largely explains the explosive growth of the title industry since World War II. Owners' policies are nearly universally written on real estate sales in the western United States, where it is customary for the seller to pay for an owner's policy for the buyer. They are less common in the midwest and east, where buyers are expected to pay for their own title insurance.[2]

Title insurance differs from most other insurance lines in important ways. It is paid for by a single premium, and the coverage under an owner's policy lasts indefinitely so long as the owner or his or her heirs, devisees, or corporate successors continue to hold the land.[3] It covers the condition of

§ 11.14

1. See generally Pedowitz, Title Insurance and You: What Every Lawyer Should Know! 3 (1979), an excellent source book of title insurance commentary and forms published by the American Bar Association Section of Real Property, Probate and Trust Law. Other basic sources include Burke, Law of Title Insurance (1986); Pedowitz, Title Insurance: The Lawyer's Expanding Role (1985); Smith and Lubell, Real Estate Financing: Protecting the Lender with Title Insurance, 5 Real Estate Rev. 14 (No. 1, 1975); Payne, Title Insurance and the Unauthorized Practice of Law Controversy, 53 Minn.L.Rev. 423 (1969); Johnstone, Title Insurance, 66 Yale L.J. 492 (1957); Johnson, The Nature of Title Insurance, 33 J. of Insurance & Risk 393 (1966); Cribbet, The Lawyer and Title Insurance, 1 Real Prop.Prob. & Trust J. 355 (1966).

Some title insurance policies (but not all) insure not only against defects of title, but also that title is marketable; see Annot., Defects Affecting Marketability of Title Within Meaning of Title Insurance Policy, 18 A.L.R.4th 1311 (1982).

The public regulation of the title insurance industry is beyond the scope of the present discussion. See generally Note, The Title Insurance Industry and Government Regulation, 53 Va.L.Rev. 1523 (1967); Roberts, Title Insur-

ance: State Regulation and the Public Perspective, 39 Ind.L.J. 4 (1963). Iowa law prohibits domestic title insurance, although there is a great deal of such insurance written on Iowa titles by out-of-state companies; see Cook, Iowa's Prohibition of Title Insurance—Leadership or Folly?, 33 Drake L.Rev. 684 (1984); Chicago Title Insurance Co. v. Huff, 256 N.W.2d 17 (Iowa 1977), upholding Iowa's statutory prohibition.

2. See generally B. Burke, American Conveyancing Patterns (1978); U.S. Department of Housing and Urban Development & Veterans Administration, Report on Mortgage Settlement Costs (1972); Payne, Ancillary Costs in the Purchase of Homes, 35 Missouri L.Rev. 455 (1970).

3. Note that while future inter vivos transferees of the insured are not directly covered by the policy, the original insured continues to be protected if he or she conveys the land away and is later sued on a title covenant in the conveyance; see ALTA Owners Form B–1970, Conditions 1(a), 2; Stewart Title Guaranty Co. v. Lunt Land Corp., 162 Tex. 435, 347 S.W.2d 584 (1961). The American Land Title Association (ALTA), the title industry's trade and lobbying organization, issues standard forms which are widely used by title insurers. Form B–1970 will be referred to in a number of the following footnotes; it is reproduced in

the title only as of the policy's date, and defects arising afterward cannot be the basis of a claim.[4] It indemnifies only for losses which result from title matters; other problems, such as physical defects or government regulations which inhibit the use of the property, do not bring the policy into play.[5]

Unlike other insurance carriers, whose level of risk is largely a function of the characteristics and behavior of the persons and property they insure, title insurers have considerable control of the risk they undertake. By a careful examination of the record title (and in some cases a physical inspection of the land) before issuance of each policy, the company can identify most types of defects and encumbrances which might pose unacceptable risks, and can list them in the policy as exceptions to coverage. In some areas of the nation, the companies employ staff members to do searches, usually in their own private "title plants" which duplicate the public records but are organized on the basis of parcel indexes. In other areas the companies use "approved attorneys" who make their examinations from commercial abstracts or directly from the public records and are paid by their private clients, but whose findings are reported to the title insurance company and form the basis for issuance of its policies.[6] Where company staff performs the search, the premium charged is usually an "all-inclusive rate" which covers both the search and insurance functions. A preliminary report or "binder" is generally sent to the proposed insureds prior to the closing of the transaction; it lists the significant encumbrances and defects the search has disclosed, and constitutes the company's commitment to issue a policy with no further exceptions.

It might be considered foolish for a title company to issue policies without procuring a careful search of the records first, since such a practice will obviously lead to larger claims in the long run. But is a search legally required?[7] Most binders and policies contain no explicit statement that a

G. Nelson & D. Whitman, Real Estate Transfer, Finance & Development 216 (2d ed. 1981). Form A–1970 is similar to B–1970, but does not insure against unmarketability of title. A "plain language" ALTA form is reprinted in G. Nelson & D. Whitman, Real Estate Transfer, Finance & Development 248 (4th ed. 1992).

A lender's policy protects not only the original mortgagee, but also secondary market assignees of the note and mortgage and any government agency insuring or guaranteeing the loan; it continues in effect if the insured buys the property at a foreclosure sale or takes a deed in lieu of foreclosure. See ALTA Loan Form 1970, Conditions 1(a), 2(a).

4. See, e.g., Safeco Title Insurance Co. v. Moskopoulos, 116 Cal.App.3d 658, 172 Cal. Rptr. 248 (1981); National Mortgage Corp. v. American Title Insurance Co., 299 N.C. 369, 261 S.E.2d 844 (1980).

5. Nishiyama v. Safeco Title Insurance Co., 85 Cal.App.3d Supp. 1, 149 Cal.Rptr. 355 (1978) (illegal subdivision); Title and Trust Co. of Florida v. Barrows, 381 So.2d 1088 (Fla. App.1979), cert. denied 383 So.2d 1190 (Fla.

1980) (access obstructed by water at high tide); Mafetone v. Forest Manor Homes, Inc., 34 A.D.2d 566, 310 N.Y.S.2d 17 (1970) (street grade did not permit physical access to subject property); Hocking v. Title Insurance & Trust Co., 37 Cal.2d 644, 234 P.2d 625 (1951) (building permit unavailable because subdivider had failed to post bond for street paving.)

6. See Title Research Corp. v. Rausch, 450 So.2d 933 (La.1984), upholding the right of a commercial title company to microfilm local public land records in order to create a private title plant; First American Title Ins. Co. v. First Title Service Co., note 8 infra; Brohman, Has Title Insurance Changed the Attorney's Role in Real Estate Transactions?, 60 Fla.B.J. 47 (Feb.1986); Annot., Title Insurance Company's Rights in Title Information, 38 A.L.R.4th 968 (1985). On methods of title search by title insurers, see Whitman, Optimizing Land Title Assurance Systems, 42 G.Wash.L.Rev. 40 (1973).

7. See Comment, Title Insurance: The Duty to Search, 71 Yale L.J. 1161 (1962). In a few states, statutes specifically mandate that a search be made; see, e.g., Ariz.Rev.Stat. § 20–1567; Colo.Rev.Stat.1973, 10–11–106;

search has been made, although prospective insureds obviously treat the binder as a report of a search, and hence as a summary of the title defects disclosed by it. Several recent cases have held that there is an implied duty to make a reasonable search and, equally important, to disclose its results to the customer. They tend to treat the title insurer much like an abstracter,[8] liable on the basis of negligence if a search is not done and reported with ordinary care and skill.[9] In essence these cases give the insured a right to be fully informed of title defects the insurer finds in the public records, even if they are within the scope of one of the general exclusions from policy coverage discussed below or if the title insurer believes they present such minor risks that it is unnecessary to list them as exceptions in the policy.[10]

West's Fla.Stat.Ann. § 627.7845; North Carolina Gen.Stat. § 58–132; see Comment, infra note 10, at note 119. These statutes make no reference to any duty to disclose search results to the insured; however, such a duty might be inferred. See also Erskine Florida Properties, Inc. v. First American Title Ins. Co. of St. Lucie County, Inc., 557 So.2d 859 (Fla.1989) (title company acting as abstractor has duty to search all relevant public records).

8. See, e.g., First American Title Ins. Co. v. First Title Service Co., 457 So.2d 467 (Fla. 1984), on remand 458 So.2d 822 (Fla.App.1984) (abstract company supplying abstract to developer held liable to developer's customers, and hence liable upon subrogation theory to the customers' title insurer, for negligence in preparation of abstract); Williams v. Polgar, 391 Mich. 6, 215 N.W.2d 149 (1974), recognizing an action against an abstracter in tort for negligence, although arising out of his or her contractual duty to compile the abstract with reasonable care and skill. The liability of an attorney who makes a personal search of the records is similar; see, e.g., Gleason v. Title Guarantee Co., 300 F.2d 813 (5th Cir.1952), rehearing denied 317 F.2d 56 (1963). See Theberge, Attorney Negligence in Real Estate Title Examination and Will Drafting: Elimination of the Privity Requirement as a Bar to Recovery by Foreseeable Third Parties, 17 N.Eng.L.Rev. 955 (1982); Annot., Negligence in Preparing Abstract of Title as Ground of Liability to One Other than Person Ordering Abstract, 50 A.L.R.4th 314 (1986).

9. See Cottonwood Enterprises v. McAlpin, 111 N.M. 793, 810 P.2d 812 (1991); Moore v. Title Ins. Co. of Minnesota, 148 Ariz. 408, 714 P.2d 1303 (App.1985); Garton v. Title Insurance & Trust Co., 106 Cal.App.3d 365, 165 Cal.Rptr. 449 (1980); L. Smirlock Realty Corp. v. Title Guarantee Co., 52 N.Y.2d 179, 437 N.Y.S.2d 57, 418 N.E.2d 650 (1981), appeal after remand 97 A.D.2d 208, 469 N.Y.S.2d 415 (1983) (dictum); Shotwell v. Transamerica Title Insurance Co., 16 Wn.App. 627, 558 P.2d 1359 (1976), affirmed on other grounds 91 Wn.2d 161, 588 P.2d 208 (1978); McLaughlin v. Attorneys' Title Guaranty Fund, Inc., 61 Ill.App.3d 911, 18 Ill.Dec. 891, 378 N.E.2d 355 (1978); Contini v. Western Title Insurance Co., 40 Cal.App.3d 536, 115 Cal.Rptr. 257 (1974). A duty to search can be readily inferred from ALTA Owners Policy Form B–1970 Condition 14, which states "The Premium Specified in Schedule A is the Entire Charge for Title Search, Title Examination and Title Insurance."

Finding title insurer had no duty to examine title and no liability in tort, see Culp Const. Co. v. Buildmart Mall, 795 P.2d 650 (Utah 1990); Walker Rogge, Inc. v. Chelsea Title & Guar. Co., 116 N.J. 517, 562 A.2d 208 (1989), appeal after remand 254 N.J.Super. 380, 603 A.2d 557 (1992) (no tort liability unless insurer expressly agreed to search title or to provide an abstract); Brown's Tie & Lumber Co. v. Chicago Title Co., 115 Idaho 56, 764 P.2d 423 (1988); Houston Title Co. v. Ojeda de Toca, 733 S.W.2d 325 (Tex.App.1987), reversed on other grounds 748 S.W.2d 449 (Tex.1988).

The California legislature reversed the holding of the *Garton* case, supra in 1981; West's Ann.Cal.Civ.Code § 12340.11 provides that a preliminary title report is not an abstract, and does not impose an abstractor's liability on a title company. See Southland Title Corp. v. Superior Court, 231 Cal.App.3d 530, 282 Cal. Rptr. 425 (1991). The statute was held inapplicable to preliminary reports issued before its enactment in White v. Western Title Ins. Co., 40 Cal.3d 870, 221 Cal.Rptr. 509, 710 P.2d 309 (1985), noted 14 West.St.L.Rev. 173, 191 (1986). Since the statute applies only to preliminary reports, it still appears possible in California to assert a tort claim against a title company that has issued a policy.

See Breuer–Harrison, Inc. v. Combe, 799 P.2d 716 (Utah App.1990) (title company has no liability to vendor of land, who was not insured under the policy); Note, Does the Title Insurer Qua Title Insurer Owe a Duty to Any but its Insured?, 7 Okl.City L.Rev. 293 (1982).

10. See Heyd v. Chicago Title Ins. Co., 218 Neb. 296, 354 N.W.2d 154 (1984) (title insurer held liable as an abstractor for negligently failing to discover and report that the in-

While these decisions represent a rather clear trend, there may still be jurisdictions which, if presented with the question, would find no duty at all to search.

An insured might attempt to use tort rather than contract principles in an action against a title insurer for several other reasons. Most policies contain clauses requiring the insured to report all claims within a very short period—typically 60 or 90 days—after the insured discovers the loss; a tort theory might permit the insured to evade this time limit.[11] A few courts have permitted measures of damage under tort theories which would be difficult or impossible to sustain under contract law, such as lost business profits caused by delayed construction due to a title defect.[12] In a rather celebrated case, a California Court of Appeal awarded $200,000 in tort damages for the insureds' mental distress; the title insurer had failed to find and report an easement, and then refused for three years to pay for the loss or eliminate the easement![13] Typical title policies contain language which restricts all claims "to the provisions and conditions and stipulations of this policy,"[14] but it is doubtful that this sort of exculpatory clause will be permitted by the courts to bar tort recovery.[15]

Most title policies contain a number of more-or-less standard exclusions for matters which are not insured against. They include laws and governmental ordinances[16] and exercises of eminent domain rights unless appearing in the public records. It is nearly universal to exclude title matters created or agreed to by the insured,[17] and matters which the insured knows

sured's house encroached on a public street, despite policy language excluding coverage of matters which an accurate survey would have shown). See generally Comment, Washington Title Insurers' Duty to Search and Disclose, 4 U.P.S.L.Rev. 212 (1980), quoting numerous authorities to the effect that title insurance customers reasonably expect to be fully informed of the results of the company's search.

11. See, e.g., ALTA Owners Policy B–1970 Condition 4.

12. Use of a tort theory may also allow punitive damages; see Lawyers Title Ins. Corp. v. Vella, 570 So.2d 578 (Ala.1990). See Red Lobster Inns of America, Inc. v. Lawyers Title Insurance Corp., 492 F.Supp. 933 (E.D.Ark.1980), affirmed 656 F.2d 381 (8th Cir. 1981).

13. Jarchow v. Transamerica Title Insurance Co., 48 Cal.App.3d 917, 122 Cal.Rptr. 470 (1975), noted 8 Sw.U.L.Rev. 203 (1976); 1976 B.Y.U.L.Rev. 895. The policy limit in the case was only $75,000. Ordinarily, lost profits are not recoverable under a title insurance policy; see Lawyers Title Ins. Co. v. Synergism One Corp., 572 So.2d 517 (Fla.App.1990), review denied 583 So.2d 1037 (Fla.1991). See also Southland Title Corp. v. Superior Court, 231 Cal.App.3d 530, 282 Cal.Rptr. 425 (1991), where the tort liability claim simply represented the insured's attempt to get a recovery larger than the policy limit.

14. See, e.g., ALTA Owners Policy B–1970 Condition 12.

15. See Comment, supra note 10, at 231. But see Harrison v. Commonwealth Land Title Insurance Co., 97 Cal.App.3d 973, 159 Cal. Rptr. 209 (1979), in which the court refused to allow tort recovery for negligence in the title company's production of a "lot book guarantee" which had a stated maximum liability of $100; the company had missed a deed of trust on the property, but the court concluded that the customer could not reasonably have relied on the guarantee in light of the stated limitation.

16. These are probably not technically title matters, and thus would not be covered in any event; see note 5, supra.

17. See Schuman v. Investors Title Ins. Co., 78 N.C.App. 783, 338 S.E.2d 611 (1986), review denied 316 N.C. 554, 344 S.E.2d 9 (1986) (where lender agreed to subordinate the lien of its deed of trust to another deed of trust, it could not maintain a claim on its title insurance policy for damages resulting from its loss of priority, even though the policy described its deed of trust as a first lien); Keown v. West Jersey Title & Guaranty Co., 161 N.J.Super. 19, 390 A.2d 715 (1978), certification denied 78 N.J. 405, 396 A.2d 592 (1978); Annot., 87 A.L.R.3d 515 (1978). To actuate this language, the insured must have actual knowledge of the defect, and it must not be a matter readily discernible from the public records; see L. Smirlock Realty Corp. v. Title

about at the date of the policy or the date the insured acquires his or her interest, and of which the insurer has not been notified.[18] Less widespread, but quite common, are boiler-plate exceptions for various types of title claims if they are not shown by the public records; these often include rights of persons in possession, property taxes and assessments, matters which a survey would disclose, public rights-of-way, easements, water and mining rights, and mechanics liens.[19] Policy coverages vary considerably, and owners' policies are usually weaker than lenders' policies; some contracts contain so many exceptions and exclusions that there is very little protection against off-record risks.[20]

The insurer has three related duties under a title insurance policy; to indemnify the loss by payment of damages, to cure the title defects if feasible, and to defend the insured in the event of a judicial attack on the title.[21] Damages are calculated in much the same manner as for breach of

Guarantee Co., 52 N.Y.2d 179, 437 N.Y.S.2d 57, 418 N.E.2d 650 (1981), appeal after remand 97 A.D.2d 208, 469 N.Y.S.2d 415 (1983).

18. See Lawyers Title Ins. Corp. v. First Federal Sav. Bank & Trust, 744 F.Supp. 778 (E.D.Mich.1990); Southern Title Insurance Co. v. Crow, 278 So.2d 294 (Fla.App.1973), cert. denied 284 So.2d 221 (Fla.1973) (knowledge of original insured mortgagee not imputed to assignee of mortgage); Annot., 75 A.L.R.3d 600 (1977). A similar duty exists under common law principles even if not spelled out in the contract; see Collins v. Pioneer Title Insurance Co., 629 F.2d 429 (6th Cir.1980).

19. There are plenty of constructional problems with these exceptions; see, e.g., Transamerica Title Ins. Co. v. Northwest Bldg. Corp., 54 Wn.App. 289, 773 P.2d 431 (1989), review denied 113 Wn.2d 1008, 779 P.2d 727 (1989); Walker Rogge, Inc. v. Chelsea Title & Guar. Co., 116 N.J. 517, 562 A.2d 208 (1989) (exception for survey matters); Lynburn Enterprises, Inc. v. Lawyers Title Ins. Corp., 191 Ga.App. 710, 382 S.E.2d 599 (1989) (exception for survey matters); Lawyers Title Ins. Corp. v. D.S.C. of Newark Enterprises, Inc., 544 So.2d 1070 (Fla.App.1989); Carefree Villages, Inc. v. Keating Properties, Inc., 489 So.2d 99 (Fla.App.1986) (exception for parties in possession); McDaniel v. Lawyers' Title Guaranty Fund, 327 So.2d 852 (Fla.App.1976) (existence of electrical transmission lines and towers may evidence "possession" of the property by the electric utility company); Annot., 98 A.L.R. 537 (1964). See also Pedowitz, Title Insurance: Non–Coverage of Hazardous Waste Super–Liens, 13 Probate & Property 46 (Spring 1985).

20. The Florida legislature in 1985 adopted an unusual set of limitations on the power of title insurers to exclude certain matters from policy coverage. See West's Fla.Stat.Ann. § 627.7842. If a current survey is supplied, the company may exclude only the survey matters shown on it; if the seller provides an affidavit that no other party is in possession or claims possession, the company may not exclude rights of parties in possession; and if the seller provides an affidavit that no improvements have been made without payment within the past 90 days, the company may not exclude coverage of mechanics' liens.

A number of companies have developed new owners' policy endorsement forms in recent years for single-family homes. They insure that off-record survey matters, rights of possessors, easements, and the like will not interfere with ordinary residential use of the property; this is a compromise between full coverage and no coverage for such matters. Many companies will waive the usual exceptions or issue endorsements overriding them, and some companies will also issue affirmative coverage of such matters as zoning, usury, and truth-in-lending compliance, if an additional fee is paid and the company is furnished with added information which satisfies it that the risk is acceptable; see Beasley, Special Forms of Coverage, in Pedowitz, supra note 1, at 19.

21. Title matters outside the coverage of the policy are also outside the insured's duty to defend; see Bidart v. American Title Ins. Co., 103 Nev. 175, 734 P.2d 732 (1987). If the insurer refuses to defend the title, attorneys' fees expended by the insured in doing so are recoverable under the policy, but attorneys' fees in a suit by the insured against the insurer are not recoverable absent the insurer's bad faith; see Eureka Investment Corp. v. Chicago Title Ins. Co., 743 F.2d 932 (D.C.Cir.1984). See also Lake Havasu Community Hospital, Inc. v. Arizona Title Ins. Co., 141 Ariz. 363, 687 P.2d 371 (App.1984) (attorney employed by title insurer to represent insured in title litigation violated ethical standards by improperly communicating confidential information, obtained from insured, to insurer; insurer thereby became liable for full policy amount). See generally Taub, Rights and Remedies under a Title Policy, in Pedowitz, supra note 1, at 69.

title covenants in deeds, although the insured need not show an eviction.[22] If there is no loss to the insured, nothing can be recovered on the policy.[23] For a complete failure of title, the insured under an owner's policy can recover the value of the land so long as it does not exceed the policy limit.[24] If an encumbrance exists which can be paid off by a liquidated sum, that amount is the recovery on the policy.[25] For other types of encumbrances, such as easements or restrictive covenants, the measure of recovery is the difference in value of the land with and without the encumbrance, provided the policy limit is not exceeded.[26] Under a lender's policy, the insurer can always discharge its duty fully by paying the mortgagee the loan balance with accrued interest and costs and taking an assignment of the note and

22. See § 11.13, supra, at notes 54–67; Securities Service, Inc. v. Transamerica Title Insurance Co., 20 Wn.App. 664, 583 P.2d 1217 (1978); Southern Title Guaranty Co. v. Prendergast, 494 S.W.2d 154 (Tex.1973).

23. Youngblood v. Lawyers Title Ins. Corp., 923 F.2d 161 (11th Cir.1991) (where insured owner resold land in question, giving no warranty of title against easements, insured suffered no loss from existence of subsequently discovered easement, and hence had no claim on title policy); Fidelity Nat. Title Ins. Co. v. Kidd, 99 N.C.App. 737, 394 S.E.2d 225 (1990) (where insured was not obligated to pay for land to the extent its title was defective, insured suffered no loss from title failure); Far West Fed. Bank v. Transamerica Title Ins. Co., 99 Or.App. 340, 781 P.2d 1259 (1989), review denied 309 Or. 441, 789 P.2d 5 (1990) (where person with paramount title agreed not to execute on judgment, insured had no loss); Cohen v. Security Title and Guaranty Co., 212 Conn. 436, 562 A.2d 510 (1989) (where deed conveyed more land than title policy described, insured suffered no loss); Grunberger v. Iseson, 75 A.D.2d 329, 429 N.Y.S.2d 209 (1980) (mortgage was insured as having third priority, but in fact had fourth priority; second mortgage was foreclosed and produced no surplus, so insured mortgagee would have been wiped out regardless of priority; no loss due to title defect); First Commerce Realty Investors v. Peninsular Title Insurance Co., 355 So.2d 510 (Fla.App.1978) (no loss on mortgage policy, where property's value exceeded both the mortgage amount and the policy limit, despite the title defect); Sattler v. Philadelphia Title Insurance Co., 192 Pa.Super. 337, 162 A.2d 22 (1960) (no loss since asserted judgment lien was invalid); Taub, supra note 21, at 76 notes 58–59. Note that even if an asserted title defect turns out not to exist, the insurer may still be liable if it breaches its duty to defend; see notes 28–32 infra and accompanying text.

24. See Aja v. Appleton, 86 Nev. 639, 472 P.2d 524 (1970); Annot., 60 A.L.R.2d 977 (1958).

25. Arizona Title Insurance & Trust Co. v. Smith, 21 Ariz.App. 371, 519 P.2d 860 (1974); Caravan Products Co. v. Ritchie, 55 N.J. 71, 259 A.2d 223 (1969); Stewart Title Guaranty Co. v. Lunt Land Corp., 162 Tex. 435, 347 S.W.2d 584 (1961). Some owners' policies contain a "proportionate payment" clause which is intended to induce customers to buy coverage equal to the land's full value. If this is not done, and there is a claim based on less than a total failure of title, the clause provides for payment of only a fraction of the actual loss; the fraction is the ratio of the policy limit to the total value of the land. See Stone v. Lawyers Title Insurance Corp., 537 S.W.2d 55 (Tex.Civ.App.1976), affirmed in part, reversed in part 554 S.W.2d 183 (Tex.1977); Southern Title Guaranty Co. v. Prendergast, 494 S.W.2d 154 (Tex.1973).

Virtually all policies provide that any payment of a claimed loss for less than the full policy amount acts to reduce the remaining coverage to the extent of the payment; see, e.g., ALTA Owner's Policy B–1970, Condition 8. However, payments for litigation and other related expenses do not have a corresponding effect.

26. Stewart Title Guarantee Company v. Cheatham, 764 S.W.2d 315 (Tex.App.1988); Fohn v. Title Insurance Corp. of St. Louis, 529 S.W.2d 1 (Mo.1975); Sullivan v. Transamerica Title Insurance Co., 35 Colo.App. 312, 532 P.2d 356 (1975); Southwest Title Insurance Co. v. Plemons, 554 S.W.2d 734 (Tex.Civ.App.1977), refused n.r.e. There is a persistent debate as to whether the values in question are determined as of the policy date or the date the title defect is discovered; compare Overholtzer v. Northern Counties Title Insurance Co., 116 Cal.App.2d 113, 253 P.2d 116 (1953) (date of discovery) and Title Insurance Co. v. Industrial Bank of Richmond, 156 Va. 322, 157 S.E. 710 (1931) with Southern Title Guaranty Co. v. Prendergast, 494 S.W.2d 154 (Tex.1973) (date of policy, where policy expressly so provided) and Beaullieu v. Atlanta Title & Trust Co., 60 Ga.App. 400, 4 S.E.2d 78 (1939) (date of purchase).

mortgage.[27]

The insurer's duties to attempt to cure title defects and to defend the title are closely allied. Most policies mention only the latter,[28] but the cases rather uniformly recognize an obligation to make a good faith effort to bring the title into compliance with the policy as well, provided this can be done by an expenditure within the policy limits.[29] The duty to defend likewise includes a good faith element, and the insurer cannot escape its obligations by asserting that the attack on the title is ill-founded or unsuccessful.[30] If the insurer refuses to defend when called upon by the insured, it will be liable for the insured's costs and reasonable attorney's fees expended in the defense of the title.[31] On the other hand, the insured is usually denied

27. See ALTA Loan Policy 1970, Conditions 5, 6(a)(iii), 8(a); Paramount Properties Co. v. Transamerica Title Insurance Co., 1 Cal.3d 562, 83 Cal.Rptr. 394, 463 P.2d 746 (1970). Even without this language, an insurer who paid a mortgagee's claim for the full loan balance would be subrogated to the mortgagee's rights under general insurance principles. For this reason, an owner-mortgagor who fails to obtain an owner's policy is taking a double risk; not only does he get no protection from the lender's policy, but he may find himself being sued by the title insurer, as subrogee or assignee of the lender, on the note or the covenants of title in the mortgage. This may occur even though the owner paid the title insurance premium for the lender's policy!

A title insurer's liability on a mortgagee's policy depends not merely on the existence of a title defect, but on the mortgagee's sustaining an actual loss on its loan. See Falmough Nat. Bank v. Ticor Title Ins. Co., 920 F.2d 1058 (1st Cir.1990); Gibraltar Savings v. Commonwealth Land Title Ins. Co., 905 F.2d 1203 (8th Cir.1990); Blackhawk P.C.A. v. Chicago Title Ins. Co., 144 Wis.2d 68, 423 N.W.2d 521 (1988); Southwest Title Ins. Co. v. Northland Bldg. Corp., 552 S.W.2d 425 (Tex.1977).

When a title insurer pays a claim on either an owner's or a lender's policy, it is subrogated to the rights of its insured, and hence may make a claim on the covenants of title that appeared in the insured's deed or mortgage. See, e.g., Title Insurance Company of Minnesota v. Costain Arizona, Inc., 791 P.2d 1086, 164 Ariz. 203 (App.1990). It is unclear whether the title insurer's own negligence in examining the title will act to deprive it of the right of subrogation; compare Leamer Abstracting Co. v. Rosengartner, 210 Neb. 719, 317 N.W.2d 57 (1982) and Meridian Title Ins. Co. v. Lilly Homes, Inc., 735 F.Supp. 182 (E.D.Va.1990) (negligence bars subrogation claim) with In re Hagle, 89 B.R. 952 (Bkrtcy.M.D.Fla.1988) and Fidelity Nat. Title Ins. Co. v. Miller, 215 Cal. App.3d 1163, 264 Cal.Rptr. 17 (1989) (negligence does not bar subrogation claim).

28. See ALTA Owners Policy B–1970, Condition 3(a); Davis v. Stewart Title Guaranty Co., 726 S.W.2d 839 (Mo.App.1987); Lambert v. Commonwealth Land Title Ins. Co., 53 Cal.3d 1072, 282 Cal.Rptr. 445, 811 P.2d 737 (1991).

29. See Jarchow v. Transamerica Title Insurance Co., supra note 13; Southern Title Guaranty Co. v. Prendergast, supra note 26; Lawyers Title Insurance Corp. v. McKee, 354 S.W.2d 401 (Tex.Civ.App.1962); Burks v. Louisville Title Insurance Co., 95 Ohio App. 509, 121 N.E.2d 94 (1953). Cf. Securities Service, Inc. v. Transamerica Title Insurance Co., 20 Wn.App. 664, 583 P.2d 1217 (1978) (no duty to clear title by expenditures in excess of policy limits). The duty to clear the title arises only when there is some objective evidence that a title defect exists; Jarchow, supra note 13, at note 18. The extent of the duty may depend on the precise language of the policy, although the Jarchow decision, supra, argues that the company's duties are based not solely on the policy but also on "the reasonable expectations of the public and the insured as to the type of service which the insurance entity holds itself out as ready to offer."

30. Jesko v. American–First Title & Trust Co., 603 F.2d 815 (10th Cir.1979); Jarchow v. Transamerica Title Insurance Co., supra note 13. See Hosack & O'Connor, Handling Bad Faith Claims Against Title Insurers, 5 Cal. Law. 31 (Jun.1985).

31. National Heat & Power Corp. v. City Title Insurance Co., 57 A.D.2d 611, 394 N.Y.S.2d 29 (1977), appeal denied 42 N.Y.2d 811, 399 N.Y.S.2d 1027, 369 N.E.2d 1193 (1977); Foremost Construction Co. v. Killam, 399 S.W.2d 593 (Mo.App.1966); Paramount Properties Co. v. Transamerica Title Insurance Co., 1 Cal.3d 562, 83 Cal.Rptr. 394, 463 P.2d 746 (1970). If the coverage of the policy is uncertain or disputed, the insurer must defend if the claim is potentially or arguably covered by the policy; see Ticor Title Ins. Co. of California v. American Resources, Ltd., 859 F.2d 772 (9th Cir.1988) (Hawaii law); Israelsky v. Title Insurance Company of Minnesota, 212 Cal.App.3d 611, 261 Cal.Rptr. 72 (1989). Where the insured's title must be defended

recovery of attorney's fees expended in an action against the title insurer itself.[32]

§ 11.15 Title Registration

The conventional recording system makes no averments to the public about the state of the title to any parcel of land. Instead, it simply invites searchers to inspect the copies of instruments which it contains and to draw their own conclusions as to title.[1] However, an alternative method of maintaining land records in which government assumes a far larger role, termed the Torrens or title registration system, is available in eleven states and in Guam and Puerto Rico.[2] It is named for Richard Robert Torrens, who became the first premier of the state of South Australia in the 1850's. He was experienced in the English system for registration of title to merchant ships, and devised a system of land title registration based on similar concepts; it began operation in 1858. Torrens' ideas became popular in many countries of the British Commonwealth and Europe, and were the inspiration for statutes enacted in about twenty American states, beginning with Illinois in 1895.[3]

Despite this fairly widespread legal adoption, the Torrens system has been implemented in America with significant numbers of land parcels in

against multiple claims, some of which are potentially covered by the policy and some of which are not, the courts will apportion the insurer's contribution to the defense accordingly; Enron Corp. v. Lawyers Title Ins. Corp., 940 F.2d 307 (8th Cir.1991).

In some cases the insured may prefer not to request the insurer to defend, but may elect to provide his or her own defense instead; if this occurs, the insurer is not liable for the costs of defense. See Buquo v. Title Guaranty & Trust Co., 20 Tenn.App. 479, 100 S.W.2d 997 (1936). The duty to defend has been held to extend to defense of self-help behavior rather than legal action on the part of an adverse claimant; see McMinn v. Damurjian, 105 N.J.Super. 132, 251 A.2d 310 (1969).

Note that if the insurer refuses to defend, its liability for costs of defense of the title probably does not count toward the policy limit, but is considered a separate category limited only by reasonableness. This follows from the policy's promise that the company will provide a defense "at its own cost" (ALTA Owner's Policy B–1970, Condition 3(a)), and also from the concept of tort liability for breach of a duty of good faith, see Jarchow v. Transamerica Title Insurance Co., supra note 13.

32. Espinoza v. Safeco Title Insurance Co., 598 P.2d 346 (Utah 1979); Securities Service, Inc. v. Transamerica Title Insurance Co., supra note 29; Jesko v. American–First Title & Trust Co., supra note 30. But see Tumwater State Bank v. Commonwealth Land Title Ins. Co., 51 Wn.App. 166, 752 P.2d 930 (1988).

§ 11.15

1. See § 11.9, supra, at note 2.

2. Colo.Rev.Stat.1973, 38–36–101 et seq.; Official Code Georgia Ann. tit. 60; Haw.Rev. Stat. Ch. 501; Ill.—S.H.A. ch. 30, ¶ 45–90; Mass.Gen.Laws Ann. c. 185; Minn.Stat.Ann. § 508.01 et seq.; N.Y.—McKinney's Real Prop.Law art. 12; North Carolina Gen.Stat. c. 43; Ohio Rev.Code § 5309; Va.Code 1950, § 55–112; West's Rev.Code Wash.Ann. 65.12.

See generally Comment, The Torrens System of Title Registration: A New Proposal for Effective Implementation, 29 U.C.L.A.L.Rev. 661 (1982); Lane & Edson, P.C., Improving Land Title Registration Systems (1979) (report prepared for U.S. Dep't of Housing and Urban Development); B. Shick & I. Plotkin, Torrens in the United States (1978); T. Mapp, Torrens' Elusive Title (Alberta L.Rev.Book Series No. 1, 1978); R. Powell, Registration of Title to Land in the State of New York (1938); Patton, The Torrens System of Land Title Registration, 19 Minn.L.Rev. 519 (1935).

3. The major incentive for the Illinois statute's passage was the destruction of the Cook county official land records in the Chicago fire of 1871. The original act was held unconstitutional because it provided for administrative rather than judicial determination of title in People v. Chase, 165 Ill. 527, 46 N.E. 454 (1897). A new version was immediately passed and remains in effect as Ill.Rev.Stat. ch. 30. The Land Commission of the Trust Territory of the Pacific Islands has jurisdiction to register land titles within the territory; see Pangelinan v. Tudela, 733 F.2d 1341 (9th Cir.1984).

only a few locales. Its use is voluntary, not legally mandated; it is up to each owner whether or not to register his or her land, or to permit it to continue under the recording system instead. Important activity under the system occurs today only in Hawaii, Cook County (Chicago) Illinois, Hennepin County (Minneapolis) and Ramsey County (St. Paul) Minnesota, and selected areas of Ohio and Massachusetts. Ten states have repealed their statutes, and only two of them, California and Illinois, had much land registered.[4] A casual observer might conclude that Torrens is an idea whose time has come—and gone. Yet academic writers continue to advance the thesis that Torrens, at least in some revised form, has intrinsic superiority over the recording/title insurance system which is far more widely used today.[5]

The essence of the system is the certificate of title—a document issued by an official of state or local government which states the identity of the owners of the title, which may be numerous if there are cotenants or present and future interests. It also lists as "memorials" all encumbrances (easements, liens, mortgages, leases, covenants, and the like) to which that title is subject. With certain exceptions discussed below, the certificate's statement as to the vesting of the title is, in theory, conclusive;[6] that is, it is legally

---

4. In the former edition of Professor Powell's treatise, he estimated that some 10,000 titles were registered in four Southern California counties prior to 1937, and related the story of a single claim of $48,000 which entirely wiped out the assurance fund of the California system in that year. See Gill v. Johnson, 21 Cal.App.2d 649, 69 P.2d 1016 (1937); R. Powell, Real Property ¶ 921 note 40 (1968).

The Illinois system, the most recent casualty of the repeal movement, was abrogated by the 1990 legislature. New registrations were prohibited effective January 1, 1992, but adverse instruments affecting already-registered land could be accepted until January 1, 1997. The statute provided for the *recordation* of all existing certificates of registration, either upon the transfer of the land, or in all events in 1997. See Ill.—S.H.A. ch. 30, § 1201 et seq.

5. See Comment, supra note 2; Lobel, A Proposal for a Title Registration System for Realty, 11 U.Rich.L.Rev. 501 (1977); Whitman, Optimizing Land Title Assurance Systems, 42 Geo.Wash.L.Rev. 40 (1973); Cribbet, Conveyancing Reform, 35 N.Y.U.L.Rev. 1291, 1303 (1960); Heinrich, The Case for Land Registration, 6 Mercer L.Rev. 320 (1955); A. Cameron, The Torrens System 18 (1915). The only notable recent attack on the Torrens concept is that of Shick & Plotkin, supra note 2; but the authors are consultants to the title insurance industry, a dedicated foe of Torrens. Hence, their objectivity is questionable. Moreover, they make no effort to suggest improvements which could make the system more efficient and functional.

6. The degree of conclusiveness is actually somewhat variable; see Petition of Mill City Heating & Air Conditioning Co. v. Nelson, 351

N.W.2d 362 (Minn.1984) (a mechanics' lienor is entitled to rely on the certificate of title to registered land, and need not give the usual pre-lien notice to a party who has an unregistered contract to buy the land, unless the lienor has actual knowledge of the contract or the purchaser is in possession). Compare Tetrault v. Bruscoe, 398 Mass. 454, 497 N.E.2d 275 (1986) (all easements not shown as memorials are cut off by registration) with Henmi Apartments, Inc. v. Sawyer, 3 Hawaii App. 555, 655 P.2d 881 (1982) (a valid implied easement can arise over land registered under the Torrens system).

Technically, the American statutes usually provide that the certificate is conclusive only in its statement of the identity of the fee title owner. The memorials, on the other hand, are not guarantees of the validity of the encumbrances they list; they are more in the nature of cautionary notes to the effect that the fee title seems to be subject to the matters identified. If an encumbrance is erroneously dropped off the certificate by the registrar it ceases to exist, and the system's indemnity fund is liable to its owner. But if an encumbrance which is shown on the certificate turns out to be invalid for other reasons, the fund is not liable.

Many of the American systems also make provision for the issuance of mortgagees' certificates. They, too, are conclusive as to the validity of the mortgages they show, but not necessarily as to priority—a critical feature from the mortgagee's viewpoint. Some of the British Commonwealth systems provide for registration of other non-fee interests, such as leaseholds.

impossible for it to be incorrect. Of course, the responsible officials may make an error, vesting title in the wrong person or failing to include a valid encumbrance as a memorial. But the certificate is still legally binding; one who is the victim of such a mistake loses his or her interest in the land, and has recourse only by way of a claim for monetary compensation against the indemnity fund which the system operates for that purpose.

The official certificate is retained by the registrar, although in most of the systems a duplicate copy is issued to the owner as well. If encumbrances are added or removed, appropriate notations are made on the official certificate. If an owner transfers his or her land, the deed (and the owner's duplicate, if applicable) are brought to the registry and a new certificate is issued in the name of the new owner. Thus in principle the certificate is always up-to-date and always reliable. No historical search of the title is ever necessary or relevant. A title examiner who represents a prospective purchaser of the land need only inspect the current certificate and read and evaluate the documents referred to in the current memorials.[7] The title examination process is vastly simplified and duplication of searches as successive transfers of the same land occur is eliminated.

The public employees of the Torrens registry must make, on a day-to-day basis, decisions as to how the state of the title to each parcel changes. For example, assume one of the memorials on a certificate of title represents a lien on the land. If a release of the lien is presented at the registry and deemed to be authentic by the appropriate judicial or administrative official, the lien itself will be marked cancelled on the certificate; moreover, the next time a certificate for that parcel is issued (for example, when the fee title is next transferred), the lien will be omitted entirely. Overall, much of the work of data retrieval and evaluation which is done by private attorneys or title insurers in the recording system is handled by public servants in the Torrens system.[8]

The principal barrier to the large-scale success of Torrens systems in the United States has been the cost and difficulty of initial registration. None of the American statutes makes registration compulsory. An owner who wishes to register land must file a petition in an *in rem* judicial or quasijudicial proceeding much like a quiet title action. An official title examiner or, under some systems, an approved private attorney investigates the title and reports to the court. Notice is given by mail, posting, and publication to all persons having any interest in the land. In some systems, such as that of Massachusetts, an official survey is made of the land parcel. A hearing is scheduled, and if there is no persuasive contrary evidence, the owner's petition is granted and a certificate of registration is issued, bringing the land within the system. This procedure is time-consuming, probably taking at least six to eight months, and may cost $550 to $750 or more in attorney's fees and official costs.[9]

7. The registrar maintains files or books containing the originals or copies of all documents referred to in the memorials so that an examiner can review them. These files or books are usually indexed by tract or parcel, permitting easy location. The Torrens system obviously lends itself to computer production of certificates and indexing of files.

8. See Whitman, supra note 5, at 63.

9. These estimates are given by Shick & Plotkin, supra note 2, at 89, for the Twin Cities area, which probably has the best-functioning Torrens system in the nation. The

Except in special cases, the registering owner does not get much direct return for this investment. The costs of future title examinations may be lower as a result of registration,[10] but those will be expenses of future owners and may not be reflected in the market price of the property when it is resold. Unless a judicial proceeding is needed to clear up clouds on the property's title anyway, it is difficult to convince a landowner that the expenditure of time and money is worthwhile.[11] For this reason, there are relatively few new registrations even in areas of the nation in which the system is well-known and well-regarded.[12]

In principle, a Torrens certificate offers an owner a far more impregnable form of assurance of title than a search in the conventional recording system, even if the latter is augmented by title insurance. However, existing American Torrens systems are characterized by numerous features which make their protection of the certificate-holder less than ideal. All of the statutes contain lists of exceptions—types of interests which can exist in the land even though they are unmentioned in the certificate. These lists are much like those found in marketable title acts [13] and title insurance policy exceptions,[14] and exist for much the same reasons. The "overriding interests" typically include such matters as claims of the United States,[15]

---

same authors estimate time of one year to 18 months, and costs of $1,500 to $2,100 in Massachusetts, where the official examiner's fee is much higher than in Minnesota and where a survey is a required part of every initial registration; id. at 115. They estimate the time and cost in Cook County, Illinois to be similar to those of the Twin Cities; id. at 135. All of these estimates assume an uncontested proceeding, as is usually the case. Attorneys' fees in a contested registration could be much higher.

See Wilkinson v. Weyerhaeuser Corp., 67 N.C.App. 154, 312 S.E.2d 531 (1984), review denied 311 N.C. 310, 317 S.E.2d 909 (1984) (in contested proceeding for registration of title, parties opposing registration are entitled to jury trial on issues of fact raised by them); Matter of Campbell's Estate, 66 Hawaii 354, 662 P.2d 206 (1983) (land court has no authority to register a consolidation or resubdivision of land parcels without receiving the prior approval of local government officials who are responsible for administration of the relevant subdivision ordinance).

10. Shick and Plotkin argue that these future savings may be small or non-existent; id. at 65. However, this is in part attributable to the hostility with which the title insurance industry views Torrens and its consequent maintenance of pricing policies which do not reflect the actual cost savings which flow from avoidance of historical searches. To some extent attorneys who examine titles reflect the same bias; see id. at 68–69. One study of the Cook County, Illinois system estimated that the average cost savings per parcel was about $100 in 1967 prices, and that the present value of aggregate savings from a total conversion to Torrens in Cook County would be

$76 million in 1976 prices. Janczyk, An Economic Analysis of the Land Title Systems for Transferring Real Property, 6 J. Legal Studies 213 (1977).

11. Some additional owners might be willing to stand the cost of initial registration in order to forestall adverse possessors, since adverse possession will not run against Torrens land under the American statutes. And some developers of subdivisions might find registration of their original acreage to be an efficient way of reducing the title-related closing costs of the lots they create.

12. For example, in Hennepin County, Minnesota, with something over one-third of the parcels registered under the Torrens system, and with deeds being recorded at the rate of about 25,000 to 30,000 per year, applications for new registrations were typically between 100 and 200 per year during the mid–1970's. Shick & Plotkin, supra note 2, at 87–88.

13. See § 11.12, supra, at note 15.

14. See § 11.14, supra, at note 19.

15. In general, the United States government cannot be compelled to participate in the registration process against its will. See Johnson, Rights Arising Under Federal Law Versus the Torrens System, 9 Miami L.Q. 258 (1955). The government's cooperation has been quite limited. For example, Federal law gives priority to a federal tax lien only from the time the notice of lien is filed by the IRS "in one office within the county * * * as designated by the laws of such state"; 26 U.S.C.A. § 6323(f)(1). But the statute has been held not to mandate registration as a memorial on a certificate of title if the land

rights of parties in possession under short-term leases, property tax and special assessment liens, mechanics liens, and public rights-of-way.[16]

Other factors also militate against the Torrens certificate's conclusiveness and reliability. One is the possibility that, at the time of initial registration, some person whose rights in the land would have been disclosed by a careful search was missed or ignored and was given no notice of the proceeding. The order registering the land is, of course, subject to any appeal filed by a party to the proceeding within the usual brief period. But a claimant who was reasonably discoverable but received no notice may also have the power to attack the registration collaterally, perhaps years afterward, on the ground that the court lacked jurisdiction and that it would be unconstitutional to impose its judgment on him or her.[17] Most of the existing statutes place time limits, typically several years in length, on collateral attacks, but it is doubtful that they will control an attack based on constitutional grounds.[18] No case yet decided seems to present this problem where the registered land has passed to a good faith purchaser. A similar problem exists if some third party claims that the original decree was procured by fraud. It is unlikely that a court would set aside a registration on this ground if the property had passed to a good faith purchaser for value, but there is some risk of this result.[19]

has been Torrenized; see United States v. Rasmuson, 253 F.2d 944 (8th Cir.1958). The real objection of the IRS to Torrens memorialization is that it requires the inclusion of a legal description of the land in the notice of lien, a step the IRS sees as excessively burdensome; see United States v. Union Central Life Insurance Co., 368 U.S. 291, 82 S.Ct. 349, 7 L.Ed.2d 294 (1961).

16. See, e.g., Henmi Apartments, Inc. v. Sawyer, 3 Hawaii App. 555, 655 P.2d 881 (1982) (implied easement may arise against land registered under the Torrens system). These exceptions are discussed fully in Lane & Edson, supra note 2, at V–21 to V–30. The courts have occasionally found or inferred other exceptions; see, e.g., State v. Bishop, 46 A.D.2d 654, 359 N.Y.S.2d 817 (1974), holding that registered title to coastal land is subject to diminution due to movement of the mean high-water mark by erosion.

17. Francisco v. Look, 537 F.2d 379 (9th Cir.1976); Konantz v. Stein, 283 Minn. 33, 167 N.W.2d 1 (1969); Couey v. Talalah Estates Corp., 183 Ga. 442, 188 S.E. 822 (1936); Sheaff v. Spindler, 339 Ill. 540, 171 N.E. 632 (1930). See also Petition of Furness, 62 Cal.App. 753, 218 P. 61 (1923) (decree covered more land than was described in the petition; third party claimant may attack decree collaterally as to excess land.) In each of these cases the party whose title was attacked was the original registrant, not a bona fide purchaser from the registrant.

In Estate of Koester v. Hale, 297 Minn. 387, 211 N.W.2d 778 (1973), the court employed a provision of the statute to "correct" a certificate which had erroneously included more land than the registrant owned; the abutting plaintiff had received no notice of the registration. The defendants, however, had not relied on or paid for the additional land, and hence seem not to have been considered by the court as good faith purchasers. See Note, Konantz, Koester, McCrossan, and Title to Torrens Property, 4 Wm.Mitch.L.Rev. 59 (1978).

Not every interested party is necessarily entitled to notice. Under the Minnesota statute, no notice need be given to adverse possessors on the land who have not yet acquired legal title, nor is notice given to neighboring landowners unless the registrant wishes to have the registration establish the boundaries of the land, an optional feature. See Marsh v. Carlson, 390 N.W.2d 897 (Minn.App.1986).

Note that due process does not require actual personal notice to every claimant, but only notice reasonably calculated to inform those who can be identified by reasonable effort; see Mennonite Board of Missions v. Adams, 462 U.S. 791, 103 S.Ct. 2706, 77 L.Ed.2d 180 (1983); Mullane v. Central Hanover Bank & Trust Co., 339 U.S. 306, 70 S.Ct. 652, 94 L.Ed. 865 (1950); American Land Co. v. Zeiss, 219 U.S. 47, 31 S.Ct. 200, 55 L.Ed. 82 (1911); Title and Document Restoration Co. v. Kerrigan, 150 Cal. 289, 88 P. 356 (1906).

18. See Couey v. Talalah Estates Corp., supra note 17; Sheaff v. Spindler, supra note 17.

19. R.G. Patton argued that there was no ultimate danger to a good faith purchaser for value from a collateral attack based on fraud in registration; see 4 Am.L.Prop. § 17.47 (1952). The cases seem to bear this out; sev-

Subsequent transfers which involve fraud or forgery are also problematic. It is generally conceded that, if the registrar is duped by the wrong-doer and actually issues a new certificate, it will be conclusive in favor of a subsequent good faith purchaser for value, and the party whose interest has been cut off will be left only with a claim against the indemnity fund.[20] But bona fide purchaser status can be elusive. For example, in Hoffman v. Schroeder[21] a forger executed a mortgage to a lending institution and the registrar issued a mortgagee's duplicate certificate to the lender. The court found that the lender was not in good faith because its employee, a notary public who took the forger's acknowledgement on the documents, did not demand identification of the forger as notaries are normally expected to do. The mortgage was held invalid despite the issuance of the certificate.[22]

To the extent that the Torrens system adopts the concepts of actual and constructive notice which apply in the traditional recording system,[23] the certificate itself is made less reliable. Yet the courts have been reluctant to abandon these concepts. It is fairly clear that a purchaser who has actual knowledge of some adverse claim to the land will take subject to it, even though the certificate fails to memorialize it.[24] Some of the statutes incorporate the notion of constructive notice by making the certificate subject to the rights of certain categories of persons in possession. Where there is no clear statutory statement, the cases are divided as to whether possession will give

eral decisions recognize collateral attacks and set aside registrations for fraud, but emphasize that no rights of good faith purchasers had intervened. See McDonnell v. Quirk, 22 Mass.App.Ct. 126, 491 N.E.2d 646 (1986) (fraud in registration of title may not be asserted against a BFP who has relied upon the registration); Petition of Brainerd National Bank, 383 N.W.2d 284 (Minn.1986) (court will not set aside a Torrens title decree on grounds of excusable neglect of counsel for a party whose interest was cut off by the decree); Kozdras v. Land/Vest Properties, Inc., 382 Mass. 34, 413 N.E.2d 1105 (1980); Village of Savage v. Allen, 255 Minn. 73, 95 N.W.2d 418 (1959); Baart v. Martin, 99 Minn. 197, 108 N.W. 945 (1906); Note, Forgeries and Land Registration, 101 Law Q.Rev. 79 (1985).

20. Eliason v. Wilborn, 281 U.S. 457, 50 S.Ct. 382, 74 L.Ed. 962 (1930); Fialkowski v. Fialkowski, 1 W.W.R. 216 (Alta.1911). Note that forgeries are rare, since the registry will not issue a new certificate in the ordinary course of business unless the old owner's duplicate is presented for cancellation. In addition, the registries in some states maintain files of signature cards against which purported conveyances are checked.

21. 38 Ill.App.2d 20, 186 N.E.2d 381 (1962). The lender lost its mortgage on the land, but was given a claim against the assurance fund.

22. The opinion seems to offer as an alternative holding the rather shocking notion that the lender was not protected by the Torrens Act because it was "not a registered owner in the sense that it did not obtain its registration as a result of a transfer from the true regis-

tered owner, but from one who impersonated her." In substance, the Illinois court followed the English decisions, represented by Gibbs v. Messer, [1891] A.C. 248, which had held that the direct recipient of a defective transfer under the registration system is not protected from the defects in question, even if he or she is a bona fide purchaser. Under this view, only later BFP transferees who are not parties to the defective transaction are protected. See Mapp, supra note 2, at 131. It is difficult to read the Illinois Torrens Act as supporting the court's holding on this point, and it does not seem to serve sound policy in cases in which the immediate transferee has no reason to suspect that the transaction is defective. The Privy Council took the opposite approach in Frazer v. Walker, [1967] 1 A.C. 569, which held a registered mortgage good in the mortgagee's hands even though it was forged. The Queen's Bench of Saskatchewan reached a similar conclusion in Hermanson v. Martin, [1982] 6 W.W.R. 312. This issue has been widely debated in the British Commonwealth Torrens systems, but has been given little attention in the American cases.

23. See § 11.10, supra, at notes 23–52.

24. C.S. McCrossan, Inc. v. Builders Finance Co., 304 Minn. 538, 232 N.W.2d 15 (1975); Butler v. Haley Greystone Corp., 347 Mass. 478, 198 N.E.2d 635 (1964); Killam v. March, 316 Mass. 646, 55 N.E.2d 945 (1944); Annot., 42 A.L.R.2d 1387 (1955). But see Knaefler v. Mack, 680 F.2d 671 (9th Cir.1982) (under Hawaii law, certificate is conclusive even if holder has actual knowledge of adverse claim).

constructive notice to a Torrens purchaser who has no actual knowledge; the majority of decisions refuse to do so.[25] To some extent the cases turn on the language of the specific statute, and on whether the adverse claim existed before initial registration of the land or was created later.[26]

On the whole, it is doubtful that Torrens has a bright future in America. In several respects it is theoretically superior to the recording system, but the latter is strongly supported by a network of title insurers and attorneys whose livelihood would be jeopardized by any radical change. The criticisms of Torrens are valid enough: slow and expensive original registration, indemnity funds of doubtful adequacy, and gaps in the conclusiveness of the certificate. In areas having few registered parcels consumers, lenders, and brokers find the system unfamiliar, confusing, irritating, and error-prone. In addition, title insurers are fond of pointing out that the Torrens system makes no provision for payment of the litigation expenses of one whose land interests are erroneously terminated by the system or who must make a claim on the assurance fund.[27] Finally, the Torrens systems typically ensure that mortgages shown on the certificate are *valid*, but do not ensure their *priority*—a fatal oversight from a lender's point of view.

But it is probable that all of these difficulties could be cured if any state legislature had the will to undertake the task.[28] One of the most attractive proposals, advocated by several writers,[29] is the introduction of a procedure for registering "possessory titles"—that is, registration on only a "day forward" basis with no attempt, or only a very inexpensive effort, to identify and memorialize preexisting claims. Each parcel would be registered on a mandatory basis when it was next transferred. This approach, which is widely used in England,[30] has the effect of placing land within the system gradually and cheaply. Over a period of years, unidentified claims can then be cut off by a statute similar to marketable title legislation, eventually making the certificate conclusive. A form of possessory title registration is now operating successfully in Hennepin County, Minnesota.[31] Such a stat-

---

25. Compare Wells v. Lizama, 396 F.2d 877 (9th Cir.1968), In re Juran, 178 Minn. 55, 226 N.W. 201 (1929), and Abrahamson v. Sundman, 174 Minn. 22, 218 N.W. 246 (1928) (no constructive notice) with Follette v. Pacific Light and Power Corp., 189 Cal. 193, 208 P. 295 (1922) (constructive notice imputed, where possession existed before original registration). See also Francisco v. Look, 537 F.2d 379 (9th Cir.1976), which seems to rely on both actual and constructive notice.

26. See Konantz v. Stein, 283 Minn. 33, 167 N.W.2d 1 (1969), drawing this distinction. If the claim predated the original registration and was reasonably discoverable, the claimant may have a constitutional right to attack the registration collaterally; see note 17, supra, and accompanying text.

Note that some types of adverse claims, specifically those founded on adverse possession or prescription, are not permitted to come into existence once the title has been registered; see Konantz v. Stein, supra.

27. Moreover, most of the existing Torrens systems require claimants to exhaust their remedies against other parties (e.g., forgers) before presenting claims to the assurance

fund. See Lane & Edson, supra note 2, at V–47. Compare the duties of title insurers, discussed at § 11.14, supra, at notes 28–32. Given the frequency with which title insurers seem to refuse to defend their insureds and to resist payment of claims, this may be a less significant difference between title insurance and Torrens than it first appears; but the basic criticism is correct.

28. The report of Lane & Edson, supra note 2, represents an excellent effort to draft a modern Torrens statute which addresses these deficiencies. Cf. McCormack, Torrens and Recording: Land Title Assurance in the Computer Age, 18 Wm.Mitch.L.Rev. 61 (1992), arguing that as convention recording systems are computerized, they approach the advantages of Torrens systems without the corresponding disadvantages.

29. See Comment, supra note 2; Lane & Edson, supra note 2; Whitman, supra note 5.

30. See Fiflis, English Registered Conveyancing: A Study in Effective Land Transfer, 59 Nw.U.L.Rev. 468 (1964).

31. Minn.Stat.Ann. ch. 508A, available in Hennepin County effective July 1, 1990. The registration in Minnesota, unlike that in Eng-

ute was drafted in Colorado under the support of a federal grant and would have operated on a test basis in a single county.   But the vehement opposition of the title insurance industry defeated the bill in 1980 and 1981, and it is unlikely to be revived.   The opponents of Torrens clearly have no interest in seeing it improved.

land, is optional with the landowner and not automatic. Five years after registration, the possessory title certificate can be converted into a regular Torrens certificate. See Note, Possessory Title Registration: An Improvement of the Torrens System, 11 Wm.Mitch. L.Rev. 825 (1985); Sclar, Minnesota Simplifies Land Registration, 11 Real Est.L.J. 258 (1983).

*

Appendix

PROPERTY LAW RESEARCH
ON WESTLAW®

Analysis

Section 1. Introduction

Cunningham, Stoebuck & Whitman's *Law of Property* provides a strong base for analyzing even the most complex property law problem. Whether your research requires examination of case law, statutes, administrative materials, commentary or texts, West books and WESTLAW are excellent sources of research materials.

In the area of property law, WESTLAW expands your library by giving you access to documents issued by state courts as well as the *Restatement of the Law of Property,* texts and periodicals such as *The Law of Distressed Real Estate* (Clark Boardman), *Hofstra Property Law Journal,* and the *Land and Water Law Review.* To assist you in keeping up-to-date on decisions affecting property law, WESTLAW provides a topical highlights database for property issues. With WESTLAW, unparalleled resources are at your fingertips.

Additional Resources

If you have not used WESTLAW or have questions not addressed in this appendix, see the *WESTLAW Reference Manual* or call the West Reference Attorneys at 1–800–688–6363. The West Reference Attorneys are trained, licensed attorneys, available throughout the workday and on weekends to answer your WESTLAW or West book research questions.

Section 2.   Property Law Databases

Each database on WESTLAW is assigned an abbreviation called an identifier, which you use to access the database. You can find identifiers for all databases in the WESTLAW Directory and in the *WESTLAW Database List.* When you need to know more detailed information about a database, use the Scope command. Scope displays coverage, unique commands and related databases for each database and service.

The chart below lists WESTLAW databases that contain information on property law. Because new information is continually being added to WESTLAW, you should check the WESTLAW Directory for any new database information.

Description	Database Identifier	Coverage (see Scope for more specific information)
STATE DATABASES		
Case Law		
Case law from all 50 states	MRP–CS	Varies by state
Individual State Cases *	XXRP–CS	Varies by state
SPECIALIZED MATERIALS		
Restatement of the Law—Property	REST–PROP	Current
Tax Management Portfolios—Real Estate Series	TM–RE	Varies
Tax Management Real Estate Journal	TM–REJ	1987
WESTLAW Topical Highlights— Real Property	WTH–RP	Current data

TEXTS & PERIODICALS

Description	Database Identifier	Coverage (see Scope for more specific information)
Law Reviews, Texts and Bar Journals	RP–TP	Varies by title
Practising Law Institute Real Estate Law and Practice Course Handbook Series	PLI–REAL	From 9/84
The Journal of Real Estate Taxation	WGL–JRETAX	1985
Real Estate Law Report	WGL–RELR	From 6/91
All Law Reviews, Texts, Bar Journals and CLE	TP–ALL	Varies
Texts and Treatises	TEXTS	Varies

PUBLIC RECORDS DATABASES

Description	Database Identifier	Coverage
Prentice Hall Public Records—California Notice of Default Data	PH–CADLFT	Varies

* XX is a state's two-letter postal abbreviation.

Section 3. Menu–Driven WESTLAW: EZ ACCESS®

EZ ACCESS is West Publishing Company's menu-driven research system. It is ideal for new or infrequent WESTLAW users because it requires no experience or training on WESTLAW.

To access EZ ACCESS, type **ez**. Whenever you are unsure of the next step, or if the choice you want is not listed, simply type **ez;** additional choices will be displayed. Once you retrieve documents with EZ ACCESS, use standard WESTLAW commands to browse your documents. For more information on browsing documents, see the *WESTLAW Reference Manual* or the *WESTLAW User Guide.*

Section 4. Retrieving a Document with a Citation: Find and Jump

4.1 Find

Find is a WESTLAW service that allows you to retrieve a document by entering its citation. Find allows you to retrieve documents from anywhere in WESTLAW without accessing or changing databases or losing your search result. Find is available for many documents including case law (federal and state), state statutes, the *United States Code Annotated*®, the *Code of Federal Regulations,* the *Federal Register,* federal rules, and state and federal public laws.

To use Find, type **fi** followed by the document citation. Below is a list of examples.

To Find This Document	Type
Young v. Iowa Department of Transportation, 1992 WL 296123 (Iowa)	**fi 1992 wl 296123**
United States v. 19.7 Acres of Land, 692 P.2d 809 (Wash.1984)	**fi 692 p2d 809**
Michigan Compiled Laws Annotated § 554.134	**fi mi st 554.134**

To Find This Document	Type
26 *U.S.C.A.* § 168	**fi 26 usca 168**
57 *Federal Register* 40496	**fi 57 fr 40496**
36 *Code of Federal Regulations*	**fi 36 cfr 51.5**
§ 51.5 *	
United States Public Law 103–3 *	**fi us pl 103–3**

* To retrieve historical versions of the C.F.R. or public laws using a citation, access the appropriate database and search for your terms in the citation field.

4.2 Jump

Retrieving Cited References: While viewing a case online, use Jump to automatically retrieve a cited case or section of the *United States Code Annotated.* Use your mouse to select the > or ► symbol displayed before the citation, or press the **Tab** key until the cursor reaches the desired location, then press **Enter.** The cited document will be displayed.

Between Headnotes and Text: In West-reported cases, you can also use Jump to move between the headnotes and the corresponding text in an opinion. Simply select the Jump marker (> or ►) next to a headnote number to move to the corresponding text in an opinion. From an opinion, select the Jump marker (> or ►) at the beginning of a segment of the text to return to the corresponding headnote. If a segment of text relates to several headnotes, Jump will return you to the first headnote in the string. For example, if the text relates to headnotes [3] [4] [5], Jump will return you to headnote 3.

Headnote to Key Number Service: You can jump directly from a headnote in a West-reported case to the Key Number service. The Key Number service provides you with the complete topic and key number outline used by West's editors to classify headnotes to specific topic and key numbers. To jump from a headnote to the Key Number service, select a Jump marker at the beginning of any line of the classification hierarchy of a headnote. You will go directly to the point in the Key Number service where the line you selected is displayed. WESTLAW displays your selection in context so that you can determine additional key numbers that may be related to your research project.

Within the Key Number Service: You can jump from one level of the Key Number service to another. Just select the Jump marker preceding the line for which you would like to see the next level.

Section 5. Natural Language Searching: WIN™ (WESTLAW is Natural™)

Overview: Using Natural Language searching (WIN), you can retrieve documents on WESTLAW by simply describing your issue in plain English. If you are a relatively new user, Natural Language searching makes it easier to retrieve cases on point. If you are an experienced user, Natural Language increases your research proficiency by giving you a valuable alternative search method.

When you enter a Natural Language description, WESTLAW automatically identifies legal phrases, removes common words and generates variations of terms in your description. WESTLAW then searches for the legal phrases and other concepts in your description. Based on the frequency with which each concept occurs in the database and in each document, WESTLAW retrieves the 20 documents that most closely match your description, beginning with the document most likely to match.

5.1 Natural Language Searching

To use Natural Language searching, access the database containing documents relevant to your issue. If your current search method is Terms and Connectors, type **nat** at the Enter Query screen to change to the Natural Language search method. The Enter Description screen will be displayed. Then enter your Natural Language description:

when is denial of a zoning variance undue hardship

5.2 Concept Ranking

WESTLAW displays the 20 documents that most closely match your description, beginning with the document most likely to match. To change the maximum number of documents retrieved with a Natural Language search, access the Options Directory by typing **opt**. Follow the on-screen instructions to designate the number (from 1 to 100) of documents retrieved.

5.3 Browsing a Natural Language Search Result

Best Command: To display the portion of the document you are viewing that most closely matches your description, type **best**. WESTLAW will display the page containing the highest rated portion.

Standard Browsing Commands: You can also browse your Natural Language search result using standard WESTLAW browsing commands, such as citations list (L), Locate (Loc), page mode (P) and term mode (T). When you browse your Natural Language search result in term mode, the five portions of each document that most closely match your description are displayed.

5.4 Modifying Your Natural Language Search

Restrictions: You can add restrictions, such as court, date, added date, attorney and judge, to a Natural Language search. Note: Restrictions available may vary depending on the database you have selected.

To add restrictions before you run your description, type **res** at the Enter Description screen. Enter your restriction on the displayed Restrictions screen. Then press **Enter** to return to the Enter Description screen and type your description.

To add restrictions after you have run your description, type **q** to display the Edit Description screen. Then type **res,** erase any description that remains, and press **Enter.** Enter the restriction you would like to add in the appropriate space. To move from one restriction to the next, press the **Tab** key.

Legal Phrases: WESTLAW automatically identifies many legal phrases or terms of art in your Natural Language description and puts them in quotation marks for you. To identify additional phrases yourself, place quotation marks around the terms you want to identify as a phrase when you type your description.

Suppose you are performing legal research to determine when damages may be awarded for a temporary taking. To identify the phrase *temporary taking,* place the phrase in quotation marks when you type your description:

when may damages be awarded for a "temporary taking"

Alternative Terms: To add alternative terms from the online thesaurus after you have run a description, type **q** to display the Edit Description screen. Then type **thes**, erase any of the original description that remains, and press **Enter.** WESTLAW will display a screen showing the concepts in your original description that have related concepts. To view a list of related concepts for a concept listed, type the concept number. To add one or more of these concepts to your description as alternative terms, type their corresponding numbers.

To add your own alternative terms to your description, add the alternative terms following the concepts to which they relate. Enclose the alternative term in parentheses ( ). For example, using the description from § 5.1,

**when is denial (refusal rejection) of a zoning variance
(deviation) undue (unnecessary unusual) hardship**

Section 6. Terms and Connectors Query Formulation

Overview: With standard Terms and Connectors searching, you enter a *query,* which consists of key terms from your research issue and connectors specifying the relationship between these terms.

Terms and Connectors searching is useful when you want to retrieve a document for which you do have specific information, such as the title or the citation. Terms and Connectors searching is also useful when you want to retrieve documents relating to a specific issue. To change from Natural Language searching to Terms and Connectors searching, type **tc** at the Enter Description screen.

6.1 Terms

Plurals and Possessives: Plurals are automatically retrieved when you enter the singular form of a term. This is true for both regular and irregular plurals (e.g., *child* retrieves *children*). If you enter the plural form of a term, you will not retrieve the singular form.

If you enter the non-possessive form of a term, WESTLAW automatically retrieves the possessive form as well. However, if you enter the possessive form, only the possessive form is retrieved.

Automatic Equivalencies: Some terms have alternative forms or equivalencies; for example, *5* and *five* are equivalent terms. WESTLAW automatically retrieves equivalent terms. The *WESTLAW Reference Manual* contains a list of equivalent terms.

Compound Words and Acronyms: When a compound word is one of your search terms, use a hyphen to retrieve all forms of the word. For example, the term **long-term** retrieves *long-term, long term* and *longterm.*

When using an acronym as a search term, place a period after each of the letters in the acronym to retrieve any of its forms. For example, the term **f.m.v.** (fair market value) retrieves *fmv, f.m.v., f m v* and *f. m. v.*

Root Expander and Universal Character: When you use the Terms and Connectors search method, placing a root expander (!) at the end of a root term generates ALL other terms with that root. For example, adding the ! symbol to the root *restrict* in the query

restrict! /s covenant

instructs WESTLAW to retrieve such words as *restrict, restrictive, restricting* and *restriction.* The universal character (*) stands for one character and can be inserted in the middle or at the end of a term. For example, the term

compensat * * *

will retrieve *compensating* or *compensation.* But adding only two asterisks to the root *jur* in the term

jur * *

instructs WESTLAW to retrieve all forms of the root with up to two additional characters. Terms like *jury* or *juror* are retrieved by this query. However, terms with more than two letters following the root, such as *jurisdiction,* are not retrieved. Plurals are always retrieved, even if more than two letters follow the root.

Phrase Searching: To search for a phrase on WESTLAW, place it within quotation marks. For example, to search for references to the Rule Against Perpetuities as it relates to trusts, type **"rule against perpetuities" /p trust.** When you are using the Terms and Connectors search method, you should use phrase searching only when you are certain that the phrase will not appear in any other form.

6.2 Alternative Terms

After selecting the terms for your query, consider which alternative terms are necessary. For example, if you are searching for the term *contract,* you might also want to search for the term *agreement.* You should consider both synonyms and antonyms as alternative terms.

6.3 Connectors

After selecting terms and alternative terms for your query, use connectors to specify the relationship that should exist between search terms in your retrieved documents. The connectors you can use are described below:

Use:	To retrieve documents containing:	Example:
& (and)	terms in the same document	**lessee & damages**
or (space)	either term or both terms	**payment rent*****
/p	both terms in the same paragraph	**lessee /p damages**
/s	both terms in the same sentence	**owner /s lease**
+ s	first term preceding the second within the same sentence	**pretermitted + s heir**
/n	terms within "n" terms of each other (where "n" is a number)	**delay /3 rental**

| + n | first term preceding the second by "n" words (where "n" is a number) | **inter-vivos + 2 trust** |

| **Use:** | **To exclude documents with:** | **Example:** |
| % (but not) | terms following the % symbol | **quiet /3 title % to(298)** |

6.4 Restricting Your Search by Field

Overview: Documents in each WESTLAW database consist of several segments, or fields. One field may contain the citation, another the title, another the synopsis, and so forth. Not all databases contain the same fields. Also, depending on the database, fields of the same name may contain different types of information.

To retrieve only those documents containing your search terms in a specified field, restrict your search by field. To view the fields and field content for a specific database, see Scope or type **f** while in the database. Note that in some databases, not every field is available for every document.

To restrict your search to a specific field, type the field name or abbreviation followed by your search terms enclosed in parentheses. For example, to retrieve a case entitled *Franz v. Real Estate Marketing, Inc.,* restrict your search to the title field:

ti(franz & "real estate marketing")

The fields discussed below are available in WESTLAW databases you might use for property law research.

Digest and Synopsis Fields: The digest (di) and synopsis (sy) fields, provided in case law databases by West Publishing Company's editors, summarize the main points of a case. Restricting your search to these fields limits your result to cases in which your terms are related to a major issue in the case.

Consider restricting your search to one or both of these fields if

- you are searching for common terms or terms with more than one meaning, and you need to narrow your search; or

- you cannot narrow your search by moving to a smaller database.

For example, to retrieve cases that discuss whether storage of hazardous waste constitutes a nuisance, access the Multistate Real Property Cases database (MRP–CS) and type the following query:

sy,di(hazard! /s waste material /p nuisance)

Headnote Field: The headnote field (he) is a part of the digest field, but does not contain the topic number, hierarchical classification information, key number or title. The headnote field contains only the one-sentence summary of the point of law and any supporting statutory citations given by the author of the opinion. A headnote field restriction is useful when you are searching for specific statutory sections or rule numbers. For example, to retrieve headnotes that cite 42 U.S.C.A. § 1437a, type the following query:

he(42 + 5 1437a)

Topic Field: The topic field (to) is also a part of the digest field. It contains the West digest topic name and number, the key number, and the

hierarchical classification information. You should restrict search terms to
the topic field in a case law database if

- a digest field search retrieves too many documents; or
- you want to retrieve cases with digest paragraphs classified under
  more than one topic.

An example of the first type of topic field search is the following: The topic
Deeds is topic number 120. To retrieve Michigan cases that discuss the
circumstances under which a court will consider parol or extrinsic evidence
in construing a deed, access the Michigan Real Property cases database
(MIRP–CS) and type a query like the following:

to(120)   /p   parol extrinsic

The second type of topic field search allows you to retrieve West headnotes
classified under more than one topic and key number. Search for the topic
name in the topic field; for example, to search for any state cases that
discuss the effect of divorce on tenancy in common, access the Multistate
Real Property Cases database (MRP–CS) and type a query like the following:

to("tenancy in common")   /p   divorce dissolution

For a complete list of West digest topics and their corresponding topic
numbers, access the Key Number service; type **key.**

> Be aware that slip opinions and cases from looseleaf services do
> not contain the digest, headnote or topic fields.

Prelim and Caption Fields: When searching in a database containing
statutes or regulations, restrict your search to the prelim (pr) and caption
(ca) fields to retrieve documents in which your terms are important enough
to appear in a section name or heading. For example, to retrieve California
statutes discussing discrimination in housing, access the California Statutes
Annotated database (CA–ST–ANN) and type the following query:

pr,ca(discriminat!   /p   housing)

6.5   Restricting Your Search by Date

You can instruct WESTLAW to retrieve documents *decided or issued*
before, after, or on a specified date, as well as within a range of dates. The
following are examples of queries that contain date restrictions:

da(bef 1991   &   aft 1986)   &   historic +2 district
da(1990)   &   historic +2 district
da(4/26/90)   &   historic +2 district

You can also instruct WESTLAW to retrieve documents *added to a database*
on or after a specified date, as well as within a range of dates. The following
are examples of queries that contain added date restrictions:

ad(aft 1–1–89)   &   historic +2 district
ad(aft 2–1–91   &   bef 3–1–91)   &   historic +2 district

Section 7.   Verifying Your Research with Citators

Overview: WESTLAW contains four citator services that assist you in
checking the validity of cases you intend to rely on. These four citator

services—Insta–Cite®, Shepard's® Citations, Shepard's PreView™ and Quick-*Cite*™—help you perform many valuable research tasks, saving you hours of manual research. Sections 7.1 through 7.4 provide further information on these services.

WESTLAW also contains Shepard's Citations for federal statutes and Shepard's Citations for state statutes are being added on a state by state basis.

For citations not covered by the citator services, including persuasive secondary authority such as restatements, treatises and law review articles, use a technique called WESTLAW as a citator to retrieve cases that cite your authority (see Section 7.5).

7.1 Insta–Cite®

Insta–Cite is West Publishing Company's case history and citation verification service. It is the most current case history service available. Use Insta–Cite to see if your case is still good law. Insta–Cite provides the following types of information about a citation:

Direct History. In addition to reversals and affirmances, Insta–Cite gives you the complete reported history of a litigated matter including any related cases. Insta–Cite provides the federal direct history of a case from 1754 and the state direct history from 1879. Related references (cases related to the litigation) are provided from 1983 to date.

Negative Indirect History. Insta–Cite lists subsequent cases that may have a substantial negative impact on your case, including cases overruling your case or calling it into question. Cases affected by decisions from 1972 to date will be displayed on Insta–Cite. To retrieve negative indirect history prior to 1972, use Shepard's Citations (discussed in Section 7.2).

Secondary Source References. Insta–Cite also provides references to secondary sources that cite your case. These secondary sources currently include the legal encyclopedia *Corpus Juris Secundum* ®.

Parallel Citations. Insta–Cite provides parallel citations for cases, including citations to *U.S. Law Week,* and many looseleaf reporters.

Citation Verification. Insta–Cite confirms that you have the correct volume and page number for a case, as well as the correct spelling of proper names. Citation verification information is available from 1754 for federal cases and from 1879 for state cases.

7.2 Shepard's® Citations

For case law, Shepard's provides a comprehensive list of cases and publications that have cited a particular case. Shepard's also includes explanatory analysis to indicate how the citing cases have treated the case, e.g., "followed," "explained."

Shepard's Citations for statutes provides a comprehensive list of cases citing a particular statute, as well as information on subsequent legislative action.

The federal court rule divisions for each of the statute citators currently available on WESTLAW provide a comprehensive list of cases citing a particular federal court rule. Federal court rule publications include:

Supreme Court Rules	Federal Rules of Criminal Procedure
Federal Rules of Evidence	Federal Rules of Civil Procedure
Bankruptcy Rules	Federal Rules of Appellate Procedure

7.3 Shepard's PreView™

Shepard's PreView gives you a preview of citing references from West's® National Reporter System® that will appear in Shepard's Citations. Depending on the citation, Shepard's PreView provides citing information days, weeks or even months before the same information appears in Shepard's online. Use Shepard's PreView to update your Shepard's results.

7.4 Quick*Cite*™

Quick*Cite* is a citator service that enables you to automatically retrieve the most recent citing cases on WESTLAW, including slip opinions.

There is a four- to six-week gap between a citing case's availability on WESTLAW and its listing in Shepard's PreView. This gap occurs because cases go through an editorial process at West Publishing Company before they are added to Shepard's PreView. To retrieve the most recent citing cases, therefore, you need to search case law databases on WESTLAW for references to your case.

Quick*Cite* formulates a query using the title, the case citation(s) and an added date restriction. Quick*Cite* then accesses the appropriate database, either ALLSTATES or ALLFEDS, and runs the query for you. Quick*Cite* also allows you to tailor the query to your specific research needs; you can choose a different date range or select another database.

Quick*Cite* is designed to retrieve documents that cite cases. To retrieve citing references to other documents, such as statutes and law review articles, use WESTLAW as a citator (see below).

7.5 Using WESTLAW as a Citator

Using WESTLAW as a citator, you can search for documents citing a specific statute, regulation, rule, agency decision or other authority. To retrieve documents citing Cal.Gov.Code § 1950.5, for example, access the California Real Property Cases database (CARP–CS), select Terms and Connectors as your search method, and search for the citation alone:

1950.5

If the citation is not a unique term, add descriptive terms. For example, to retrieve cases citing Cal.Pub.Util. § 21669, discussing airport noise abatement, access the California Real Property Cases database (CARP–CS) and type a query like the following:

21669 /p noise

7.6 Selected Citator Commands

The following are some of the commands that can be used in the citator services. For a complete list, see the *WESTLAW User Guide* or the *WESTLAW Reference Manual.*

Command:	*Definition:*
ic xxx or **ic**	Retrieves an Insta–Cite result when followed by a case citation (where xxx is the citation), or when entered from a displayed case, Shepard's result or Shepard's PreView result.
sh xxx or **sh**	Retrieves a Shepard's result when followed by a case or statute citation (where xxx is the citation), or when entered from a displayed case, Insta–Cite result or Shepard's PreView result.
sp xxx or **sp**	Retrieves a Shepard's PreView result when followed by a case citation (where xxx is the citation), or when entered from a displayed case or statute, Insta–Cite result or Shepard's result.
qc xxx or **qc**	Retrieves a Quick*Cite* result when followed by a case citation (where xxx is the citation), or when entered from a displayed case, Insta–Cite result, Shepard's result or Shepard's PreView result.
sc	Retrieves the scope of coverage for a specific service when viewing a result from that service.
sc xx	Retrieves the scope of coverage (where xx is the citator service), e.g., **sc ic**.
sh sc xxx	Retrieves the scope of coverage for a specific publication in Shepard's, where xxx is the publication abbreviation (e.g., **sh sc f.r.d.**).
xx pubs	Retrieves a list of publications available with the citator and their abbreviations (where xx is the citator).
xx cmds	Retrieves a list of commands (where xx is the command for Insta–Cite, Shepard's or Shepard's PreView).
sh analysis	Retrieves a list of Shepard's analysis codes, e.g., *extended, revised,* etc.
sh courts	Retrieves a list of courts and their abbreviations.
loc	Automatically restricts an Insta–Cite, Shepard's or Shepard's PreView result to selected categories.
loc auto	Restricts all subsequent Insta–Cite, Shepard's or Shepard's results to selected categories.
xloc	Cancels a Locate request.
xloc auto	Cancels a Locate Auto request.

Section 8.   Research Examples

8.1   Retrieving Law Review Articles

A colleague refers you to a law review article by Michael H. Schill, *An Economic Analysis of Mortgagor Protection Laws,* 77 Va.L.Rev. 489 (1991). How can you retrieve the article on WESTLAW?

Solution

• If you know the citation, access the Virginia Law Review database (VALR). Using the Terms and Connectors search method, search for terms from the citation in the citation field (ci):

ci(77 +5   489)

• If you know the title of the article, but not which journal it appears in, access the Real Property—Law Reviews, Texts and Bar Journals database (RP–TP). Using the Terms and Connectors search method, search for key terms in the title field (ti):

ti(economic   /s   mortgagor)

8.2 Retrieving Statutes

You need to retrieve any Arizona statutes concerning actions to quiet title.

Solution

• Access the Arizona Statutes—Annotated database (AZ–ST–ANN). Search for your terms in the prelim (pr) and caption (ca) fields:

pr,ca("quiet title")

• When you know the citation for a specific section of a state statute, use Find to retrieve the statute. (Note: For more information on Find, see Section 4 of this appendix.) For example, to retrieve Ariz.Rev.Stat.Ann. § 12–1102, discussing complaints in quiet title actions, type

fi az st s 12–1102

• To look at surrounding statutory sections, use the Documents in Sequence command. To retrieve the section preceding § 12–1102, type **d–**. To retrieve the section immediately following § 12–1102, type **d+**.

• To see if a statute has been amended or repealed, use the Update service. Simply type **update** while viewing the statute to display any session law available on WESTLAW that amends or repeals the statute.

Because slip copy versions of laws are added to WESTLAW before they contain full editorial enhancements, they are not retrieved with Update. To retrieve slip copy versions of laws, access the United States Public Laws database by typing **db us-pl** (or access the appropriate state legislative service database by typing **db xx-legis**, where **xx** is the state's two-letter postal abbreviation) and then type **ci(slip)** and descriptive terms, e.g., **ci(slip) &** [**term**]. Slip copy documents are replaced by the editorially enhanced versions within a few working days. Update also does not retrieve legislation that enacts a new statute or covers a topic that will not be incorporated into the statutes. To retrieve this legislation, access US–PL (or access the appropriate state legislative service database) and enter a query containing terms that describe the new legislation.

8.3 Retrieving Treatise Materials

Your client is a tenant who needs to know if she can withhold rent because her landlord has not made much needed repairs in her apartment. Where can you retrieve background information on this issue?

Solution

- The Restatement of the Law—Property database (REST–PROP) contains the full text of the nine volume treatise adopted and promulgated by the American Law Institute (ALI). Type **db rest-prop** to access the database; then enter a Natural Language description like the following:

may a tenant withhold rent when the landlord fails to make repairs

8.4 Retrieving Continuing Legal Education Materials

You have been retained by a real estate developer to draft a shopping center lease. You want to review articles that can give you practical pointers on what you should include in the document.

Solution

- The PLI–REAL database contains selected documents from the Real Estate Law and Practice Course Handbook series of continuing legal education materials published by the Practising Law Institute (PLI). Type **db pli-real** to access the database, type **tc** to change your search method to Terms and Connectors, and search for key terms in the title field (ti):

ti("shopping center" /3 lease)

8.5 Using Citator Services

One of the cases discussed in the Restatement of the Law—Property is *Schneiker v. Gordon,* 732 P.2d 603 (Colo.1987). You wish to see if this case is still good law and if other cases have cited this case.

Solution

- Use Insta–Cite to retrieve the case history and negative indirect history of *Schneiker.* While viewing the case, type **ic.**
- You want to Shepardize® *Schneiker.* Type **sh.**

  Limit your Shepard's result to decisions containing a reference to a specific headnote, such as headnote four. Type **loc 4.**
- Check Shepard's PreView for more current cases citing *Schneiker.* Type **sp.**
- Check Quick*Cite* for the most current cases citing *Schneiker.* Type **qc** and follow the online instructions.

8.6 Retrieving Multistate Property Cases

You are writing a brief on behalf of your client, a municipality. As part of your research you wish to quickly review cases from a variety of jurisdictions that discuss the zoning of adult bookstores and related businesses.

Solution

- The Multistate Real Property Cases database (MRP–CS) contains decisions selected for relevance to the topic of real property from the state courts of all 50 states and the District of Columbia. Type **db mrp-cs** to access the database and restrict your search to the digest field (di) and to the synopsis field (sy):

sy,di(zon! /s adult /s bookstore business)

• To retrieve cases decided after 1990, add a date restriction to your search.

sy,di(zon! /s adult /s bookstore business) & da(aft 1990)

8.7 Following Recent Developments

As the new associate in the firm, you are expected to keep up on and summarize recent legal developments in the area of real property law. How can you do this efficiently?

Solution

• One of the easiest ways to stay abreast of recent developments in real property law is by accessing the WESTLAW Topical Highlights—Real Property database (WTH–RP). The WTH–RP database summarizes recent legal developments, including court decisions, legislation and materials released by administrative agencies.

  To access the database, type **db wth-rp.** You will automatically retrieve a list of documents added to the database in the last two weeks.

• To read a summary of a document listed, type its corresponding number.

• You can also search this database by typing **s** to display the Enter Query screen. At the Enter Query screen, type your query. For example, to retrieve references discussing eminent domain, type a query like the following:

"eminent domain"

Table of Cases

A

Aaron v. Havens—§ 6.47, n. 9, 10, 13, 14, 29.
Abatti v. Eldridge—§ 10.5, n. 4.
Abbey v. Wheeler—§ 5.8, n. 20, 32.
Abbiss v. Burney—§ 3.10, n. 5; § 3.18, n. 8.
Abbott v. Bob's U–Drive—§ 8.15, n. 10, 21, 30.
Abbott v. Holway—§ 2.8, n. 21; § 4.4, n. 14.
Abbott v. Parker—§ 11.11, n. 8.
Abbott v. Wagner—§ 4.11, n. 9.
Abbott House v. Village of Tarrytown—§ 9.4, n. 14.
Abboud v. Cir Cal Stables—§ 10.1, n. 22.
A. B. C. Auto Parts, Inc. v. Moran—§ 10.1, n. 16.
Abel v. Girard Trust Co.—§ 2.4, n. 12.
Abo Petroleum Corp. v. Amstutz—§ 3.10, n. 17.
Aborigine Lumber Co. v. Hyman—§ 11.8, n. 17.
Aboud v. Adams—§ 10.3, n. 7.
Abraham v. Abraham—§ 5.15, n. 7.
Abraham v. Mihalich—§ 11.1, n. 46; § 11.3, n. 2.
Abrahams v. Abrahams—§ 3.23, n. 3.
Abrahamson v. Sundman—§ 11.15, n. 25.
Abram v. Litman—§ 6.42, n. 36.
Academy Spires, Inc. v. Brown—§ 6.38, n. 41; § 6.42; § 6.42, n. 10, 15; § 6.43, n. 20; § 6.79, n. 7.
Accounting of Estate of Isganaitis—§ 3.17, n. 2; § 3.21, n. 11.
A. C. Drinkwater, Jr., Farms, Inc. v. Ellot H. Raffety Farms, Inc.—§ 11.13, n. 37.
Ace Realty, Inc. v. Looney—§ 10.10, n. 10; § 10.12, n. 51.
Ackerman v. Little—§ 6.59, n. 17, 18.
Ackerman v. Spring Lake Tp.—§ 11.6, n. 35.
Ackerman v. Steisel—§ 11.6, n. 27.
Action Realty Co., Inc. v. Miller—§ 10.13, n. 18.
Acton v. Blundell—§ 7.4; § 7.4, n. 2.
Aczas v. Stuart Heights, Inc.—§ 11.13, n. 21, 60.
Adams v. Church—§ 5.6, n. 4.
Adams v. Cullen—§ 8.4, n. 2, 7.
Adams v. Dugan—§ 3.25, n. 5.
Adams v. Eagle—§ 2.12, n. 9.
Adams v. Johnson—§ 11.7, n. 31, 32.
Adams v. Lay—§ 6.13, n. 12.
Adams' Estate, In re—§ 6.82, n. 13.
Adams Outdoor Advertising of Atlanta, Inc. v. Fulton County, Ga.—§ 9.19, n. 7.
A. D. Juilliard & Co. v. American Woolen Co.—§ 6.69, n. 2, 3.

Adkins v. Arsht—§ 11.1, n. 57.
Admiral Development Corp. v. City of Maitland—§ 9.17, n. 3.
Adrian v. Rabinowitz—§ 6.21, n. 3.
Agins v. City of Tiburon, 100 S.Ct. 2138—§ 9.2, n. 34; § 9.2A; § 9.2A, n. 30.
Agins v. City of Tiburon, 598 P.2d 25—§ 9.2, n. 60, 66; § 9.2A, n. 6, 40.
Agnew v. Haskell—§ 11.6, n. 10.
Agrelius v. Mohesky—§ 11.3, n. 12.
Ailes v. Decatur County Area Planning Com'n—§ 9.6, n. 9.
Aja v. Appleton—§ 11.14, n. 24.
Akin v. Business Title Corp.—§ 11.4, n. 42.
Akron, City of v. Chapman—§ 9.6, n. 9.
Alabama v. Albert—§ 11.9, n. 30.
Alabama Farm Bureau Mut. Ins. Co. v. Meyers—§ 10.13, n. 50.
Alabama Home Mortg. Co., Inc. v. Harris—§ 11.5, n. 3.
Alamo Land & Cattle Co., Inc. v. Arizona—§ 6.35, n. 5.
Alaska Nat. Bank v. Linck—§ 11.7, n. 10, 13, 20, 22, 38.
Alban v. R. K. Co.—§ 8.3, n. 7; § 8.9, n. 2, 18.
Albany, City of v. State of New York—§ 11.2, n. 22.
Albers v. County of Los Angeles—§ 9.1, n. 17.
Albert v. Orwige—§ 8.13, n. 3.
Albiani v. Loudd—§ 11.4, n. 6.
Albright v. Albright—§ 5.8, n. 19; § 5.9, n. 6.
Albro v. Allen—§ 5.4, n. 2; § 5.11, n. 7.
Alcan Aluminum Corp. v. Carlsberg Financial Corp.—§ 10.12, n. 14, 37.
Alden v. Trubee—§ 11.10, n. 9.
Aldrich v. Wilson—§ 11.10, n. 61.
Aldridge v. Aldridge—§ 11.9, n. 32.
Aldridge v. North East Independent School Dist.—§ 11.10, n. 13.
Alexander v. Andrews—§ 11.10, n. 68.
Alexander v. Boyer—§ 5.4, n. 13.
Alexander v. O'Neil—§ 11.10, n. 4.
Alexander's Dept. Stores of N. J., Inc. v. Arnold Constable Corp.—§ 8.17, n. 3.
Alexandria, City of v. Kara Baptist Academy, Inc.—§ 11.6, n. 11.
Aley v. Hacienda Farms, Inc.—§ 11.8, n. 36.
Alhambra Redevelopment Agency v. Transamerica Financial Services—§ 10.13, n. 33.
Aliferis v. Boudreau—§ 10.3, n. 25, 32.
Allan's Will Trusts, Re—§ 3.20, n. 6.
Allen v. Allen—§ 5.9, n. 6.
Allen v. Allen Title Co.—§ 11.4, n. 24.
Allen v. Housing Authority of Chester County—§ 6.38, n. 40; § 6.43, n. 16.
Allen v. Kingdon—§ 10.1, n. 48.

B

Buchan v. Buchan—§ 3.13, n. 2, 3.
Buchanan v. Banta—§ 6.78, n. 6.
Bucholz v. City of Omaha—§ 9.9, n. 34.
Buck v. Del City Apartments, Inc.—§ 6.6, n. 2, 6.
Buck v. McNab—§ 10.13, n. 22.
Buckles–Irvine Coal Co. v. Kennedy Coal Corporation—§ 8.8, n. 9.
Buckley v. Chevron, U.S.A., Inc.—§ 11.3, n. 27.
Buckley v. Mooney—§ 8.23, n. 1; § 8.32, n. 8, 9, 16.
Buckner v. Hawkins—§ 2.2, n. 9.
Buckout v. Swift—§ 1.4, n. 11.
Buell Cabinet Co., Inc. v. Sudduth—§ 11.10, n. 14.
Buettner v. Nostdahl—§ 10.2, n. 16.
Buffalo Seminary v. McCarthy—§ 3.18, n. 19.
Buffington v. Title Ins. Co. of Minnesota—§ 11.4, n. 41.
Buford v. Dahlke—§ 5.4, n. 15.
Builders Sand, Inc. v. Turtur—§ 10.9, n. 22.
Builders Sash & Door Co. v. Joyner—§ 11.5, n. 15.
Builders Service Corp., Inc. v. Planning & Zoning Com'n of Town of East Hampton—§ 9.5, n. 10.
Bulifant v. Slosjarik—§ 11.3, n. 11.
Bull v. Fenich—§ 11.3, n. 24.
Bull v. Prichard—§ 3.18, n. 9.
Bull v. Weisbrod—§ 10.12, n. 15.
Bully Hill Copper Min. & Smilting Co. v. Bruson—§ 8.5, n. 8.
Bump v. Dahl—§ 11.10, n. 40.
Bundy v. United States Trust Co. of New York—§ 3.19, n. 12.
Bunker Hill Tp. v. Goodnoe—§ 9.4, n. 25.
Bunting v. Hromas—§ 2.9, n. 4.
Buquo v. Title Guaranty & Trust Co.—§ 11.14, n. 31.
Burack v. I. Burack, Inc.—§ 5.7, n. 3.
Burack v. Tollig—§ 10.13, n. 44.
Buras v. Shell Oil Co.—§ 11.9, n. 39.
Burchell's Estate, In re—§ 3.15, n. 26, 34.
Burford v. Sun Oil Co.—§ 9.2A; § 9.2A, n. 52.
Burgess v. Arita—§ 10.1, n. 34; § 10.3, n. 12.
Burk v. Burk—§ 5.8, n. 12.
Burkart v. City of Fort Lauderdale—§ 11.6, n. 42.
Burke v. Johnson—§ 10.13, n. 16.
Burke Aviation Corp. v. Alton Jennings Co.—§ 10.10, n. 8.
Burkey v. Baker—§ 11.8, n. 43, 46.
Burks v. Louisville Title Ins. Co.—§ 11.14, n. 29.
Burling v. Leiter—§ 8.4, n. 12.
Burlington County Nat. Bank of Medford v. Braddock—§ 2.12, n. 25.
Burlington Northern, Inc. v. Hall—§ 11.10, n. 24, 55.
Burnett v. Brito—§ 10.11, n. 11.
Burnett v. Quell—§ 4.3, n. 20.
Burnett v. Snoddy—§ 3.23, n. 4.
Burnex Oil Co. v. Floyd—§ 11.10, n. 40, 46.
Burnford v. Blanning—§ 10.1, n. 50.
Burnham v. Baltimore Gas & Elec. Co.—§ 3.16, n. 28; § 5.7, n. 10.
Burns v. Board of Sup'rs of Stafford County—§ 11.6, n. 26.

Burns v. City of New York—§ 6.64, n. 1.
Burns v. Dufresne—§ 6.71, n. 2.
Burns v. Hale—§ 4.5, n. 3.
Burns v. McCormick—§ 10.2, n. 16.
Burns v. Nolette—§ 5.2, n. 3, 37.
Burns v. Pugmire—§ 10.1, n. 36.
Burns Trading Co. v. Welborn—§ 6.59, n. 8.
Burr v. Tierney—§ 2.7, n. 17.
Burrell v. City of Kankakee—§ 9.2, n. 128.
Burriss v. Burriss—§ 2.10, n. 15.
Burrows v. City of Keene—§ 9.2A, n. 21, 48.
Burt v. Edmonds—§ 5.5, n. 9.
Burton v. Boren—§ 3.15, n. 25.
Burton v. Chesapeake Box & Lumber Corporation—§ 6.61, n. 6, 7; § 8.15, n. 4, 5.
Burwell v. Jackson—§ 10.12, n. 57.
Busbee v. Haley—§ 4.11, n. 8.
Busby v. Thompson—§ 2.15, n. 9.
Busch v. Nervik—§ 10.7, n. 18.
Busching v. Griffin, 542 So.2d 860—§ 10.14, n. 7.
Busching v. Griffin, 465 So.2d 1037—§ 10.1, n. 35, 39.
Buschman v. Clark—§ 10.3, n. 30.
Buschmeyer v. Eikermann—§ 5.12, n. 20.
Bush v. Cathey—§ 10.3, n. 29.
Bush v. Duff—§ 11.9, n. 34.
Bushmiller v. Schiller—§ 10.11, n. 11, 13, 16.
Buss v. Gruis—§ 6.74, n. 2.
Butler v. Bruno—§ 7.6, n. 3, 4, 8, 12, 17, 18, 21.
Butler v. Butler—§ 5.11, n. 7.
Butler v. Haley Greystone Corp.—§ 11.15, n. 24.
Butler v. Lovoll—§ 10.1, n. 22, 46.
Butler v. McGee—§ 10.2, n. 4, 16.
Butler v. Prudden—§ 2.12, n. 25.
Butler v. Sherwood—§ 11.3, n. 20.
Butler v. Wilkinson—§ 10.6, n. 3; § 10.13, n. 18.
Buttars v. Buttars—§ 2.7, n. 20.
Butz v. Butz—§ 6.17, n. 5, 8.
Butz v. Economou—§ 9.2, n. 120.
Buza v. Wojtalewicz—§ 11.8, n. 9, 61.
Buzenac, Petition of—§ 5.3, n. 24.
Bybee v. Hageman—§ 11.1, n. 50; § 11.2, n. 18.
Byke Const. Co., Inc. v. Miller—§ 3.18, n. 19; § 3.20, n. 13; § 10.14, n. 38.
Byrd v. Allen—§ 3.24, n. 16.
Byrd v. Peterson—§ 6.70, n. 12.
Byrne v. Kanig—§ 10.13, n. 22, 33, 61.

C

Cadell v. Palmer—§ 3.19, n. 2.
Caesar v. Rubinson—§ 10.4, n. 14.
Caffey v. Parris—§ 8.6, n. 9.
Cagle v. Schaefer—§ 4.10, n. 9.
Cain v. Belden—§ 3.24, n. 16.
Cain v. Morrison—§ 11.4, n. 28.
Cairo & Fulton R. Co. v. Turner—§ 9.1, n. 1.
Caito v. Ferri—§ 6.63, n. 10, 11.
Caito v. United California Bank—§ 5.2, n. 30.
C & A Land Co. v. Rudolf Inv. Corp.—§ 6.78, n. 8.
Calbreath v. Borchert—§ 11.4, n. 9.

E

Edward Rose Sales Co. v. Shafer—§ 11.4, n. 2, 38.

Edwards v. Bradley—§ 2.12, n. 21, 37; § 2.15, n. 3; § 3.7, n. 16.

Edwards v. Habib—§ 6.55; § 6.55, n. 11; § 6.81; § 6.81, n. 1.

Edwards v. Hammond—§ 3.13, n. 8.

Edwards v. Lee's Adm'r—§ 5.8, n. 9.

Edwards v. Rouse—§ 10.14, n. 13.

Edwards v. Sims—§ 2.1, n. 2; § 7.1, n. 8; § 11.2, n. 3; § 11.7, n. 21.

Edwards v. Stewart Title & Trust of Phoenix, Inc.—§ 11.4, n. 48.

Edwards v. Tobin—§ 6.63, n. 6.

Edwards–Town, Inc. v. Dimin—§ 10.6, n. 21, 23.

Efta v. Swanson—§ 11.13, n. 44.

Egbert v. Duck—§ 11.10, n. 70.

Egerton v. Massey—§ 3.10, n. 4; § 3.13, n. 11.

Egeter v. West and North Properties—§ 10.12, n. 36, 37.

E.G. Realty, Inc. v. Nova–Park New York, Inc.—§ 10.5, n. 11.

Ehle, In re—§ 3.25, n. 4.

Ehly v. Cady—§ 10.3, n. 41.

Eichhorst v. Mandalay Shores Co-op. Housing Ass'n, Inc.—§ 10.5, n. 16.

Eidelbach v. Davis—§ 8.6, n. 9.

E. I. DuPont de Nemours and Co. v. Zale Corporation—§ 6.13, n. 13, 16.

884 West End Ave. Corporation v. Pearlman—§ 6.54, n. 3.

Ekberg v. Bates—§ 11.8, n. 11.

El Di, Inc. v. Town of Bethany Beach—§ 8.20, n. 6.

Eldridge v. City of Palo Alto—§ 9.5, n. 23; § 9.21, n. 1.

Eliason v. Watts—§ 10.1, n. 24; § 10.11, n. 32.

Eliason v. Wilborn—§ 11.15, n. 20.

Elida, Inc. v. Harmor Realty Corp.—§ 6.26, n. 7.

Elkhorn City Land Co. v. Elkhorn City—§ 4.5, n. 11.

Elko v. Elko—§ 5.5, n. 19.

Eller v. Eller—§ 5.11, n. 12.

Ellett v. Liedtke—§ 11.2, n. 19.

Ellingsen v. Franklin County—§ 11.9, n. 32.

Elliott v. Cox—§ 11.1, n. 62.

Elliott v. Elliott—§ 11.13, n. 44, 53, 73.

Elliott v. Joseph—§ 6.35, n. 8.

Ellis v. Campbell—§ 5.11, n. 5.

Ellis v. Chevron, U.S.A., Inc.—§ 10.14, n. 21.

Ellis v. McDermott—§ 6.30, n. 1.

Ellis v. Mihelis—§ 10.9, n. 8.

Ellis v. Snyder—§ 5.9, n. 14.

Ellison v. F. Murray Parker Builders, Inc.—§ 11.13, n. 60.

Ellison v. Garber—§ 11.3, n. 11.

Ellison v. Watson—§ 11.1, n. 64.

Ellison Associates v. Eastwood Management Corp.—§ 11.4, n. 6, 37.

Ellwest Stereo Theaters Inc. of Texas v. Byrd—§ 9.4, n. 40.

Elmora & West End Bldg. & Loan Ass'n v. Dancy—§ 4.6, n. 4.

Elmore v. Austin—§ 3.4, n. 6; § 3.23, n. 4.

Elmore v. Elmore—§ 5.7, n. 6.

Elocin, Inc., Appeal of—§ 9.12, n. 39.

El Paso Natural Gas Co. v. Western Bldg. Associates—§ 10.5, n. 19.

Elsasser v. Elsasser—§ 3.16, n. 13.

Elsinore Property Owners Assn. v. Morwand Homes—§ 9.16, n. 17.

Elterman v. Hyman—§ 10.8, n. 2, 4.

Emanuel v. Emanuel—§ 11.1, n. 81.

Emery v. Medal Bldg. Corp.—§ 10.3, n. 45.

Emmert v. O'Brien—§ 10.10, n. 2.

Emmons v. Sanders—§ 5.5, n. 10.

Employment Div., Dept. of Human Resources of Oregon v. Smith—§ 9.20; § 9.20, n. 38.

Emrick v. Bethlehem Tp.—§ 2.5, n. 17; § 3.4, n. 2.

Emrick v. Multicon Builders, Inc.—§ 11.10, n. 23.

Enders v. Wesley W. Hubbard & Sons, Inc.—§ 6.71, n. 8.

Enderson v. Kelehan—§ 7.6, n. 17, 18.

Endres v. Warriner—§ 10.11, n. 10.

Energy Transportation Systems, Inc. v. Kansas City Southern Ry. Co.—§ 8.9, n. 17.

Engle v. Lipcross Inc.—§ 10.1, n. 19.

Engle v. Terrell—§ 5.9, n. 16.

Englewood, City of v. Apostolic Christian Church—§ 9.4, n. 43.

English v. Sanchez—§ 10.12, n. 47.

Enron Corp. v. Lawyers Title Ins. Corp.—§ 11.14, n. 31.

Enslein v. Enslein—§ 6.50, n. 1, 6, 8.

Entertainment Concepts, Inc., III v. Maciejewski—§ 9.4, n. 41.

Entrepreneur, Ltd. v. Yasuna—§ 6.27, n. 6; § 6.77, n. 3; § 6.78, n. 12.

Epperson, Matter of Estate of—§ 2.14, n. 12.

Epstein v. Van Gilder—§ 11.13, n. 59.

Epstein Hebrew Academy v. Wondell—§ 10.11, n. 32.

Erickson v. Erickson—§ 5.2, n. 40; § 5.3, n. 18.

Erskine Florida Properties v. First American Title Ins. Co. of St. Lucie County, Inc.—§ 11.5, n. 24; § 11.14, n. 7.

Erving v. Jas. H. Goodman & Co. Bank—§ 6.83, n. 1.

Erwin v. Felter—§ 5.3, n. 40.

Erwin v. Scholfield—§ 10.4, n. 20.

Escalera v. New York City Housing Authority—§ 6.81, n. 7.

Esecson v. Bushnell—§ 10.7, n. 4.

E. Shepherdstown Developers, Inc. v. J. Russell Fritts, Inc.—§ 10.9, n. 39.

Espinoza v. Safeco Title Ins. Co.—§ 11.14, n. 32.

Esplendido Apartments v. Olsson—§ 10.10, n. 6, 28.

Esposito v. South Carolina Coastal Council—§ 9.2, n. 74.

Estancias Dallas Corporation v. Schultz—§ 7.2, n. 3, 9, 25.

Estate of (see name of party)

Estelle's Estate, In re—§ 10.13, n. 24.

Estfan v. Hawks—§ 6.66, n. 3.

Estojak v. Mazsa—§ 11.6, n. 35.

ETCO Corp. v. Hauer—§ 6.63, n. 5.

Etheridge v. Fried—§ 11.13, n. 24.

Etzler v. Mondale—§ 11.6, n. 40.

Euclid, Ohio, Village of v. Ambler Realty Co.—§ 7.2, n. 8; § 9.2; § 9.2, n. 1, 23, 60; § 9.3; § 9.3, n. 9; § 9.4; § 9.4, n. 1, 17; § 9.17.
Eureka Inv. Corp., N.V. v. Chicago Title Ins. Co.—§ 11.14, n. 21.
Evans v. Adams—§ 4.11, n. 4.
Evans v. Covington—§ 5.8, n. 2.
Evans v. Faught—§ 11.13, n. 60, 62.
Evans v. Foss—§ 8.32, n. 14.
Evans v. Merriweather—§ 7.4, n. 3, 5, 9.
Evanston, City of v. Robinson—§ 11.6, n. 20.
Evco Corp. v. Ross—§ 6.86, n. 1.
Everett Factories & Terminal Corporation v. Oldetyme Distillers Corporation—§ 6.70, n. 6; § 8.24, n. 3; § 8.28, n. 3.
Evershed v. Berry—§ 6.17, n. 1.
Everts v. Agnes—§ 11.4, n. 25.
Eves v. Zoning Bd. of Adjustment of Lower Gwynedd Tp.—§ 9.9, n. 30.
Ewald v. Corbett—§ 5.8, n. 8.
Ewing v. Caldwell—§ 5.6, n. 12.
Ewing's Lessee v. Burnet—§ 11.7, n. 8, 13.
Exchange Nat. Bank of Chicago v. Lawndale Nat. Bank of Chicago—§ 11.12, n. 24.
Executive Towers v. Leonard—§ 10.1, n. 48.
Exham v. Beamish—§ 3.20, n. 11.
Ex parte (see name of party)
Exton Quarries, Inc. v. Zoning Bd. of Adjustment of West Whiteland Tp.—§ 9.4, n. 23.
Exxon Corp. v. Pollman—§ 6.66, n. 1.
Exxon, Inc. v. City of Frederick—§ 9.8, n. 27.
Eychaner v. Springer—§ 10.12, n. 48.
Eyler v. Spencer—§ 11.1, n. 81.

F

Fahey v. City of Bend—§ 11.2, n. 22.
Fahmie v. Wulster—§ 11.13, n. 21, 27.
Fahnestock's Estate, In re—§ 2.12, n. 26.
Fahrenwald v. LaBonte—§ 6.71, n. 17.
Failoni v. Chicago and North Western Railway Co.—§ 11.7, n. 12.
Fair v. Fair—§ 5.12, n. 25.
Fair v. Negley—§ 6.42, n. 40.
Fairchild v. Fairchild—§ 5.8, n. 6.
Fallon v. Davidson—§ 5.8, n. 6.
Fallon v. Triangle Management—§ 11.1, n. 76.
Falls City v. Missouri Pac. R. Co.—§ 2.2, n. 12.
Falmouth Nat. Bank v. Ticor Title Ins. Co.—§ 11.14, n. 27.
Fannin v. Cratty—§ 10.2, n. 20, 21.
Fant v. Howell—§ 10.3, n. 45.
Farahzad v. Monometrics Corp.—§ 10.11, n. 15.
Farley v. Stacey—§ 2.13, n. 32; § 5.12, n. 25.
Farmers & Bankers Life Ins. Co. v. St. Regis Paper Co.—§ 6.54, n. 1.
Farmers Inv. Co. v. Bettwy—§ 7.5, n. 7, 8.
Farmers' Mutual Fire & Lightning Ins. Co. of Andrew County v. Crowley—§ 2.16, n. 2.
Farmers Reservoir & Irr. Co. v. Sun Production Co.—§ 11.1, n. 55.
Farmers State Bank v. Slaubaugh—§ 10.13, n. 18.
Farnes v. Lane—§ 8.1, n. 7; § 8.9, n. 5.
Faroldi v. Nungesser—§ 6.13, n. 1, 3.
Farrar v. Young—§ 11.1, n. 44.

Farrell v. Janik—§ 10.11, n. 24.
Farrell v. Phillips—§ 10.5, n. 16.
Far West Federal Bank, S.B. v. Transamerica Title Ins. Co.—§ 11.14, n. 23.
Far West Sav. and Loan Ass'n v. McLaughlin—§ 11.5, n. 19; § 11.11, n. 8, 18.
Fasano v. Board of County Com'rs of Washington County—§ 9.9; § 9.9, n. 20; § 9.10; § 9.10, n. 3.
Fassitt v. Seip—§ 5.9, n. 1.
Father Flanagan's Boys' Home v. Graybill—§ 10.13, n. 8.
Faulkner v. Lloyd—§ 11.8, n. 44.
Fay v. Smiley—§ 5.5, n. 14.
Fayette County Board of Education v. Bryan—§ 3.23, n. 3.
Fechtner v. Lake County Sav. and Loan Ass'n—§ 11.13, n. 5, 33, 63.
Federal Deposit Ins. Co. v. Malin—§ 11.10, n. 14.
Federal Deposit Ins. Corp. v. Slinger—§ 10.9, n. 38.
Federal Intermediate Credit Bank of Spokane v. O/S Sablefish—§ 11.9, n. 32.
Federal Land Bank of Baltimore v. Walker—§ 3.16, n. 30.
Feeney's Estate, In re—§ 3.18, n. 8.
Fees–Krey, Inc. v. Page—§ 11.9, n. 13.
Feiges v. Racine Dry Goods Co.—§ 6.79, n. 9.
Fekkes v. Hughes—§ 5.3, n. 36.
Feld v. Merriam—§ 6.47; § 6.47, n. 6, 8, 10, 11, 19, 31.
Feldman v. Monroe Tp. Bd.—§ 11.6, n. 38.
Feldman v. Oman Associates, Inc.—§ 10.11, n. 18.
Fellmer v. Gruber—§ 10.13, n. 50.
Felonenko v. Siomka—§ 11.1, n. 84.
Female Orphan Society v. Young Men's Christian Ass'n—§ 2.2, n. 8.
Fenley Farms, Inc. v. Clark—§ 11.10, n. 43.
Fenton v. Wendell—§ 5.12, n. 22.
Ferguson v. Caspar—§ 11.4, n. 5, 23, 38.
Ferguson v. Etter—§ 6.83, n. 1.
Ferguson v. Quinn—§ 4.3, n. 12.
Ferguson v. Rochford—§ 4.4, n. 13.
Ferrari v. Meeks—§ 11.8, n. 36.
Ferrell v. Stinson—§ 11.3, n. 3, 8.
Ferrero Const. Co. v. Dennis Rourke Corp.—§ 2.2, n. 17; § 3.18, n. 23; § 10.14, n. 33, 45.
Ferrigno v. O'Connell—§ 6.67, n. 2.
Ferris v. Montgomery Land & Imp. Co.—§ 5.12, n. 2, 25.
Fertitta v. Bay Shore Development Corp.—§ 11.10, n. 48.
Festing v. Allen—§ 3.10, n. 2; § 3.13, n. 2, 3.
Fetting Mfg. Jewelry Co. v. Waltz—§ 6.20, n. 16.
Fewell v. Fewell—§ 4.11, n. 4.
F. Groos & Co. v. Chittim—§ 6.72, n. 2.
F. H. Stoltze Land Co. v. Westberg—§ 6.14, n. 1; § 6.17, n. 1.
Fialkowski v. Fialkowski—§ 11.15, n. 20.
Fidelity & Columbia Trust Co. v. Williams—§ 3.15, n. 17, 25.
Fidelity Federal Sav. and Loan Ass'n v. de la Cuesta—§ 2.2, n. 15.
Fidelity Nat. Title Ins. Co. v. Miller—§ 11.13, n. 24; § 11.14, n. 27.

Green Manor Corp. v. Tomares—§ **10.14, n. 6.**

Green Point Sav. Bank v. Board of Zoning Appeals of Town of Hempstead—§ **9.8, n. 13.**

Greenstein v. Conradi—§ **6.33, n. 20.**

Greenwich Trust Co. v. Shively—§ **3.20, n. 6.**

Greenwood v. Robbins—§ **11.13, n. 49.**

Greer v. Kooiker—§ **11.1, n. 24.**

Greer v. Parker—§ **3.24, n. 1.**

Greer Properties, Inc. v. LaSalle Nat. Bank— § **10.11, n. 10.**

Gregerson v. Jensen—§ **10.1, n. 22.**

Gregg v. Link—§ **11.10, n. 1.**

Greil Bros. Co. v. Mabson—§ **6.28, n. 1.**

Greiner v. Klein—§ **5.13, n. 22.**

Grey v. Konrad—§ **11.13, n. 59.**

Gribble v. Stearman & Kaplan, Inc.—§ **10.8, n. 2.**

Griffeth v. Zumbrennen—§ **10.9, n. 13.**

Griffin v. Ayers—§ **5.8, n. 25.**

Griffin v. Griffin—§ **5.8, n. 21.**

Griffin v. Werdell—§ **11.8, n. 38.**

Griggs v. Allegheny County, Pa.—§ **2.1, n. 5;** § **9.1, n. 14;** § **11.2, n. 3.**

Griggs Land Co. v. Smith—§ **10.13, n. 5.**

Grimm v. Grimm—§ **4.3, n. 1;** § **6.23, n. 9.**

Grogan v. Grogan—§ **5.12, n. 11.**

Gromelski v. Bruno—§ **6.13, n. 20.**

Gross v. Fox—§ **6.57, n. 8;** § **6.58, n. 4.**

Gross v. Gross—§ **11.3, n. 11.**

Gross v. Peskin—§ **6.85, n. 2.**

Grosskopf Oil, Inc. v. Winter—§ **11.10, n. 39.**

Grossman v. Hill—§ **2.2, n. 12;** § **2.15, n. 5.**

Grossman v. Melinda Lowell, Attorney at Law, P.A.—§ **10.11, n. 16.**

Grossman Furniture Co. v. Pierre—§ **11.1, n. 63.**

Grosz v. City of Miami Beach, Florida—§ **9.4, n. 46.**

Groves v. Witherspoon—§ **11.1, n. 73.**

Grube v. Bessenger—§ **11.1, n. 77.**

Grubel v. MacLaughlin—§ **9.4, n. 30.**

Gruman v. Investors Diversified Services— § **6.71, n. 1, 14.**

Grunberg v. George Associates—§ **10.14, n. 13.**

Grunberger v. Iseson—§ **11.14, n. 23.**

Grunebaum, Matter of Will of—§ **3.21, n. 11.**

GRW Enterprises, Inc. v. Davis—§ **10.5, n. 2.**

G.S.T. v. City of Avon Lake—§ **9.2A, n. 15.**

Guaranty Trust Co. of New York v. New York & Queens County Ry.—§ **8.24, n. 8.**

Guard v. P & R Enterprises, Inc.—§ **10.3, n. 42.**

Guardianship of (see name of party)

Guarnera v. Florida—§ **11.2, n. 25.**

Guel v. Bullock—§ **10.1, n. 28.**

Guerin v. Sunburst Oil & Gas Co.—§ **11.10, n. 47.**

Guffey, State ex rel. Ludlow v.—§ **9.8, n. 13.**

Guice v. Burrage—§ **11.1, n. 77.**

Guilford v. Gardner—§ **2.15, n. 1.**

Guillette v. Daly Dry Wall, Inc.—§ **11.11, n. 16.**

Guilliams v. Koonsman—§ **3.13, n. 6.**

Guillory Corp. v. Dussin Inv. Co.—§ **10.9, n. 18.**

Gulf City Body & Trailer Works, Inc. v. Phoenix Properties Trust, Inc.—§ **10.4, n. 16;** § **10.5, n. 13.**

Gulf Oil Corp. v. Beck—§ **11.10, n. 13.**

Gulf Reston, Inc. v. Rogers—§ **6.47;** § **6.47, n. 7, 11, 17, 18, 32.**

Gullett v. Burton—§ **11.10, n. 1.**

Gundersen v. Village of Bingham Farms— § **9.4, n. 4.**

Gunn v. Delhi Tp., Ingham County—§ **11.6, n. 24.**

Gunn v. Scovil—§ **6.50, n. 6.**

Gunnison v. Evans—§ **2.12, n. 6.**

Gurunian v. Grossman—§ **6.63, n. 8.**

Gustafson v. Gervais—§ **10.12, n. 48.**

Gustin v. Stegall—§ **10.13, n. 24.**

Guthrie v. National Advertising Co.—§ **11.10, n. 24, 27.**

Guy v. Poss—§ **11.5, n. 7.**

Guzman v. Acuna—§ **10.13, n. 55.**

Guzzardo v. Campo—§ **11.6, n. 31.**

H

Haas v. Gahlinger—§ **11.13, n. 45.**

Haas v. Haas—§ **5.8, n. 23.**

Haase v. Zobkiw—§ **8.4, n. 6.**

Hacker v. Nitschke—§ **6.36, n. 13.**

Hackett v. Hackett—§ **11.3, n. 8.**

Hadacheck v. Sebastian—§ **9.2;** § **9.2, n. 14;** § **9.6, n. 8.**

Hadley v. Baxendale—§ **6.42, n. 22;** § **10.3;** § **10.3, n. 23.**

Haffa v. Haffa—§ **11.1, n. 41, 70.**

Hagan v. Sabal Palms, Inc.—§ **8.28, n. 7.**

Hagensick v. Castor—§ **11.5, n. 5.**

Hagle, In re—§ **11.14, n. 27.**

Hahn v. Alaska Title Guaranty Co.—§ **11.9, n. 32.**

Hahn v. Hahn—§ **5.9, n. 3.**

Haile v. Holtzclaw—§ **11.1, n. 34.**

Haines v. Mensen—§ **11.2, n. 18.**

Hair v. Caldwell—§ **2.12, n. 32.**

Hair v. Farrell—§ **2.11, n. 16.**

Hair v. Hales—§ **11.9, n. 16.**

Hairston Enterprises, Inc. v. Lee—§ **10.12, n. 58.**

Hakanson v. Manders—§ **11.8, n. 38, 64.**

Halamka v. Halamka—§ **5.13, n. 11.**

Hale v. Elkhorn Coal Corporation—§ **2.7, n. 17.**

Hales v. Frakes—§ **11.8, n. 35.**

Haley v. City of Rapid City—§ **11.6, n. 34.**

Haley v. Oaks Apartments, Ltd.—§ **10.12, n. 59.**

Hall v. Douglas—§ **5.12, n. 9;** § **5.13, n. 18.**

Hall v. Eaton—§ **11.2, n. 35.**

Hall v. Fitzgerald—§ **10.12, n. 37.**

Hall v. Garson—§ **6.57, n. 8;** § **6.58, n. 4.**

Hall v. Hall, 271 Cal.Rptr. 773—§ **10.2, n. 16.**

Hall v. Hall, 216 N.W. 798—§ **4.6, n. 11.**

Hall v. Hamilton—§ **5.4, n. 1;** § **5.11, n. 7.**

Hall v. Leonard—§ **3.12, n. 6.**

Hall v. Korth—§ **9.11, n. 21.**

Hall v. Major—§ **6.21, n. 3.**

Hall v. McBride—§ **2.14, n. 13.**

Hall v. Pioneer Crop Care, Inc.—§ **10.13, n. 61.**

O

P

S

T

W

Index

†